TEACHER'S EDITION

Carlene Baurichter
Bangor High School, Wisconsin

José Gregory
Marist School, Georgia

Jonathan Kinman
Independence High School, North Carolina

Bill Polasky
Stillman Valley High School, Illinois

Kyle VanderWall
Grandville High School, Michigan

Fabric of a Nation

A BRIEF HISTORY WITH SKILLS AND SOURCES

FOR THE AP® COURSE

Jason Stacy
Southern Illinois University Edwardsville, Illinois

Matthew J. Ellington
Ruben S. Ayala High School, California

bedford, freeman & worth
high school publishers

Boston | New York

AP® is a trademark registered by the College Board, which is not affiliated with, and does not endorse, this product.

For Bedford/St. Martin's

Senior Vice President, Humanities & Social Science and BFW High School: Charles Linsmeier
Senior Program Director for High School: Ann Heath
Executive Program Manager, HS Humanities: Nathan Odell
Executive Marketing Manager, HS: Janie Pierce-Bratcher
Senior Developmental Editor: Caitlin Kaufman
Associate Editor: Corrina Santos
Assistant Editor: Carla Duval
Executive Content Project Manager: Gregory Erb
Senior Workflow Project Manager: Lisa McDowell
Production Supervisor: Robin Besofsky
Lead Media Project Manager: Jodi Isman
Senior Media Editor: Kimberly Morté
Editorial Services: Lumina Datamatics, Inc.
Composition: Lumina Datamatics, Inc.
Cartographer: Mapping Specialists, Ltd.
Text Permissions Editor: Michael McCarty
Photo Permissions Editor: Christine Buese
Photo Researcher: Carolyn Arcabascio
Director of Design, Content Management: Diana Blume
Text Design: Lumina Datamatics, Inc.
Cover Design: William Boardman
Cover Image: The Promise. Paulette Aileen Suder Peters. 1986, Elkhorn, Nebraska, Gift of the artist. International Quilt Study Center & Museum, University of Nebraska–Lincoln, 2005.011.0001
Printing and Binding: LSC Communications

Copyright © 2020 by Bedford/St. Martin's

All rights reserved. No part of this book may be reproduced, stored in a retrieval system, or transmitted in any form or by any means, electronic, mechanical, photocopying, recording, or otherwise, except as may be permitted by law or expressly permitted in writing by the Publisher.
Manufactured in the United States of America.

1 2 3 4 5 6   24 23 22 21 20

For information, write: Bedford/St. Martin's, 75 Arlington Street, Boston, MA 02116

ISBN 978-1-319-17817-8 (Student Edition)
ISBN 978-1-319-18268-7 (Teacher's Edition)

Acknowledgments
Text acknowledgments and copyrights appear at the back of the book on page C-1, which constitutes an extension of the copyright page. Art acknowledgments and copyrights appear on the same page as the art selections they cover.

About the Teacher's Edition Authors

Carlene Baurichter
Bangor High School
Wisconsin

Carlene has taught social studies for six years. She has taught AP* U.S. History since her first year as an educator and has also taught AP* U.S. Government and Politics. For the past three years, she has been a content author for the AP* study website, Albert.io. In 2017, Carlene was accepted as one of nearly 35 teachers nationwide to take part in the White House History Teacher Institute in Washington D.C. She coordinates National History Day in her district every year and was one of 100 teachers nationwide to receive a scholarship from the program to take part in their Legacies of WWI course.

José Gregory
Marist School
Georgia

José has taught social studies for over sixteen years, including AP* U.S. History, starting at a traditional public school in Miami and then at a magnet school for the performing arts in Atlanta. He currently teaches at an independent Catholic school and serves as a Table Leader for the AP* U.S. History reading. As an AP* consultant for the College Board, he presents on topics in AP* U.S. History at a variety of state and national conferences, including AP* Summer Institutes and one-day workshops.

Jonathan Kinman
Independence High School
North Carolina

Jon has taught AP* U.S. History (along with AP* European History, AP* Human Geography, and AP* Psychology) within the diverse urban school system in Charlotte-Mecklenburg Schools since the 1999–2000 school year. He has served as an AP* U.S. History Reader and serves in the AP* U.S. History online mentoring program. Jon has hosted many workshops and mentoring sessions within the AP* U.S. History community.

Bill Polasky

Stillman Valley High School
Illinois

Bill has taught history for twenty-seven years. In 2018, he was a finalist for Illinois Teacher of the Year and was honored as an Illinois Top Ten Teacher of the Year for 2018–2019. He is a twice-over National Board for Professional Teaching Standards (NBPTS) Certified Master Teacher, and a 2019 nominee for the Gilder Lehrman Illinois History Teacher of the Year. Bill is active within the College Board community, serving as a Reader or Table Leader at the AP® U.S. History Reading for over twenty years, and as an item writer for ETS for the AP® U.S. History Exam. As a National Consultant to the College Board, he has served or currently serves as the faculty consultant/presenter for numerous one-day training sessions and AP® U.S. History Summer Institutes throughout the country, providing training for hundreds of teachers over the past twenty years. He is a co-author of the *Bedford AP® U.S. History Survival Guide* (2014), the author of the *Teacher's Manual for Documenting United States History: Themes, Concepts, and Skills for the AP® Course* (2015), and has served as a contributing author on numerous AP® U.S. History textbook ancillary and support materials.

Kyle VanderWall

Grandville High School
Michigan

Kyle has taught history for eighteen years at Grandville High School in Grandville, MI. For sixteen of those years, he has taught AP® U.S. History. Over that span, the program has grown significantly. The AP® U.S. History course at Grandville is designed for sophomores and has no prerequisites for admission. During the last ten years, Kyle has led numerous workshops around the country to help improve historical pedagogy. His instructional design and work focuses on increasing students' self-efficacy of historical inquiry. For the past ten years, he has participated in the AP® Reading as both a Reader and Table Leader scoring the Long-Essay and Document-Based Questions.

A Guided Tour of *Fabric of a Nation*

Welcome to *Fabric of a Nation*, the first book for APUSH that fully integrates content, skills, sources, and exam prep. As current and former AP® U.S. History teachers ourselves, we set out to make a book that was built from the ground up to meet the needs of AP® U.S. History teachers, and hopefully solve some of the problems we tend to encounter. In this brief introduction, we'd like to walk you through some of the features of the book itself, so that you can fully understand not just what this book is, but why we built it this way — and maybe answer some questions that you have along the way.

— Jason Stacy and Matthew Ellington, Authors of *Fabric of a Nation*

Book Structure

Why a brief book?

First, a brief historical narrative that adheres solely to the Themes and Key Concepts of the Course Framework addresses a major issue that arises with books that go beyond the framework: students are unable to prioritize within such vast narratives, and are never able to form a sense of what is important to remember and think critically about — this makes developing the skills for the course an uphill battle.

Second, a brief narrative also reflects the reality of how teachers must pace this course throughout the school year — there is a lot of historical narrative ground to cover, and essentially only about 90 instructional days in which to do so (see below for more on how we arrived at this number).

Finally, a brief narrative allows for the inclusion of skills-focused instruction specifically tailored to the AP® United States History Practices and Skills. This book fully integrates instruction on the specific skills and practices of the AP® course into a brief narrative.

Why a modular approach?

This is the first book created specifically for the AP® U.S. History course that completely adheres to the periodization of the AP® U.S. History Course Framework. To achieve this, the textbook has a modular structure, supporting students as they learn content and skills through active reading and writing. This structure lends itself best to addressing the periodization, Key Concepts, and Themes of the course.

The traditional textbook structure — of long chapters bookended by introductory and review material — does not lend itself well to how AP® U.S. History teachers need to pace the course throughout a full school year and does not allow for enough emphasis to be placed on the skills of the course. A modular approach, by contrast, presents each module as a discrete unit of study that integrates narrative, primary sources, pedagogy, and practice. This also makes it easy to see how Themes, Key Concepts, and skills are interrelated.

What does a modular approach look like?

Fabric of a Nation updates the traditional textbook by dividing the Key Concepts of the nine AP® U.S. History time periods into eighty-six modules, each of which requires no more than one or two days of classroom instruction — this leaves room for teachers to spend days on exam preparation, assessment, and additional skills practice.

In addition to mirroring the nine AP® U.S. History periods at a unit level, the number of modules within each period of the book also reflects the percentage of class time the Course Framework recommends spending on each period:

Period	Number of Modules
1 (5%)	4
2 (10%)	10
3 (12%)	10
4 (10%)	9
5 (13%)	11
6 (13%)	11
7 (17%)	14
8 (15%)	13
9 (5%)	4

How is the instruction on the AP® U.S. History Skills and Practices integrated into the narrative of the book?

This is a book wherein pedagogy, documents, skills practice, and text all play an equal and central role — as they do in the AP® classroom. This unified structure offers a powerful active-thinking process calling on students to "do" history, connecting all of the parts of a good AP® U.S. History class like links of a chain. By integrating sources and lessons on historical thinking that suit the narrative, then asking students to process sources in ways that call for direct application of historical reasoning skills and disciplinary practices, the book provides "just-in-time" guidance that models the interplay of skills required for college-level thinking and on the AP® exam. Through this process, students both "read" and "do" history before moving on to the next key concept and skill. This book involves students in historical thinking and writing activities through an innovative approach that incorporates sources to teach and practice AP® reasoning skills as central processes of learning U.S. history.

This structure maintains the flow of the text so that students can be tasked to work and think through a module on their own, and also supports students using the text for self-study since the text and various exercises are interlinked. The placement of these sources and pedagogy about thinking and writing offer just-in-time opportunities for primary source analysis, historical reasoning, exam prep, and writing practice. This integration of "read/do" before moving onto the next part of the historical narrative also reflects the active reading process that is key to applying the historical thinking skills required by the course.

How is the instruction on AP® Skills and Practices scaffolded throughout the book?

In order for students to have enough time to practice and fully master the kind of writing they need to do on the essay portion of the AP® exam, they need to encounter and do at least some practice with all of the course practices and skills by the end of Period 3.

This book scaffolds its pedagogical features to reflect that necessary emphasis on skills at the beginning of the year:

- The first third of the book (Periods 1–3) focuses on introducing the AP® U.S. History practices and skills.

- The second third of the book (Periods 4–6) deepens and refines students' ability to apply those practices and skills.

- The final third of the book (Periods 7–9) is geared toward making sure students have full command of the AP® practices and skills and are ready for the exam. Thus, it focuses heavily on practice that requires use of the full set of practices and skills.

Is this book intended to be a lock-step curriculum?

No, it's not a lock-step curriculum. There are many, many places in this book where teachers can choose to omit, add, or take a different path. But we did want to create a book that could be treated as a curriculum, for those who need or want that level of structure. We've provided very detailed guides to doing just that in the blue pages (planning pages before each Period) of this Teacher's Edition.

How exactly does this book scaffold the introduction of the skills and practices of the course?

In the four modules of Period 1 (Module 1-1 to Module 1-4) we introduce reasoning skills, working with sources, and writing skills at the lower levels of the scaffold. The skills and practices instruction in this period also stages the introduction of the question types with Period 1 for SAQ. In simple terms, the scaffold here is: *Identify and Describe*. Period 2 moves up one level of the scaffold in all areas and focuses primarily on LEQ with only an introduction to DBQ in the last two modules. In simple terms the scaffold here for the skills is: *Explain*. Period 3 finishes the scaffold. In simple terms the scaffold here for the skills is: *Evaluate*.

Book Features

Skills Practice Features

This book contains three types of AP® Skills practice features, each of which is woven throughout the narrative:

Primary Sources

Both written and visual, these sources appear at relevant points in the narrative so that students are able to connect historical events with historical voices. This feature begins with a short paragraph that contextualizes the source by relating its author, occasion, and purpose to the larger historical narrative. Each feature culminates in 2-5 questions designed to guide students in reading, understanding, interpreting, and evaluating the source(s). Most of these work with a single primary source, but as the book progresses students will encounter features that contain 2-4 primary source documents.

Secondary Sources

Integrated into the historical narrative in the same way as the primary sources, this feature pairs two secondary sources to give students practice interpreting and analyzing writing by historians. In addition to preparing students to answer the short-answer questions (SAQs) on the AP® exam, this feature also helps them see how to interpret the historical narrative to create a historical argument.

AP® Writing Historically Activities

These activities give students a chance to practice all of the different types of writing tasks required by the AP® exam.

Skills Instruction Features

There are three major types of skill-building features that offer guided, scaffolded instruction that builds to practice later in the book. These three categories and titles reflect what the text teaches, and have staying power because they speak to what history teachers ask students to do:

AP® Thinking Historically

The pedagogy behind this feature addresses the execution of patterns of thought and reasoning that are key to success in the AP® U.S. History course.

These patterns of thought are:

- Causation
- Comparison
- Continuity and Change
- Contextualization

This feature is not only integrated into module narratives, but the habits of mind it teaches are also demonstrated in module narratives, and then applied through the instruction provided in the Analyzing Sources and Writing Historically features and practiced via the Primary Sources, Secondary Sources, and Writing Activities features.

AP® Analyzing Sources

The pedagogy behind this feature addresses how to interpret both written and visual primary (and secondary) sources for direct — that is, simple — use as evidence. As the book progresses, this feature shifts toward how to interpret each type of source more analytically for deeper understanding — Historical Situation, Intended Audience, Purpose, and Point of View. These are guided, step-by-step instructions on "doing" history that develop students' grasp of the historical thinking skills and practices of the course but stop short of taking students through how to do the work of long-form writing.

The skills taught by this feature are applied through the instruction provided in the Writing Historically feature and practiced via the Primary Sources, Secondary Sources, and Writing Activities features.

AP® Writing Historically

The pedagogy behind this feature addresses how to write effectively for the AP® U.S. History course. These provide step-by-step walkthroughs of various writing skills to help students eventually master the essays that are on the AP® exam.

The writing taught in these writing workshops includes:

- making a historical argument (*ACE*)
- breaking down a prompt
- writing a thesis
- developing arguments to demonstrate complex understandings

This feature is also integrated throughout the modules in the early teaching stages, but at the end of the module they are linked to particular short-answer question (SAQ), long-essay question (LEQ), and document-based question (DBQ) prompts.

How to Use This Teacher's Edition

Welcome to the Teacher's Edition for *Fabric of a Nation: A Brief History with Skills and Sources for the AP® Course*. This invaluable resource for both experienced and new AP® U.S. History instructors was written by seasoned AP® instructors and College Board consultants to help you get the most out of this book and its supplements. Here you'll find thoughtful advice on planning and teaching a successful AP® U.S. History course. By using this Teacher's Edition and the accompanying Teacher's Resource Materials, you will have at your fingertips everything you need to be effective and efficient in your AP® U.S. History instruction.

Plan and Prepare

As you prepare your lessons, look to each period's BLUE PAGES for help with relevant resources, pacing guides, suggested assignments, as well as alignment information. Need to move quickly through a period? The Essential Activity is the least you should do to cover period content.

Expert Advice and Creative Ideas at Your Fingertips

This Teacher's Edition includes helpful advice in the margins — right when you need it — to give you ideas for teaching skills, themes, differentiating instruction, connecting to resources, and more.

Teaching Idea notes provide advice on working with sources, generating class discussions, checking for understanding, and more. Also find online, video, and literary suggestions in these notes.

TEACHING IDEA
Incorporating Websites

Use the National Museum of the Amer Indian website and visit their section for education, which contains lessons and resources to use in the classroom (americanindian.si.edu). Two lessons y may want to use with students are:

- We Have a Story to Tell: Native Peop of the Chesapeake Region
- Pacific Northwest History and Cultur Why Do the Foods We Eat Matter?

These lessons help students see h studying American Indian tribes is rele to the present day and perhaps even t own lives. Highlighting their legacies and how these tribes are still around today will help bring history alive for students.

TEACHING IDEA
Check for Understanding

Students need to understand that despite the widespread popular appeal for the ideals of suburbanization, the suburbs remained racially divided. Consider the following activity to begin a lesson on this development. Have students brainstorm at least three reasons why suburbs were racially divided and have them select the most significant reason. Next, have students meet with two other students who selected a different reason and have students share responses.

EXPLORING AP® THEMES
Geography and the Environment

Students tend to develop a better und standing of history if they see why it m be relevant and significant to their lives Since this module focuses on geograp and the environment, have them briefl discuss how the natural and man-ma environments where they live and whe their school is located have shaped th development. Doing so will help stude see how this may also be true for the v ous American Indian tribes, hence res in diverse societies.

EXPLORING AP® THEMES
Social Structures

Before students read the excerpt from *The Feminine Mystique*, consider having them complete the following exercise, which can be used as an intro to the document analysis. No historical events happen in a vacuum, and the women's rights movement is no exception. Have students provide at least two historical reasons why the civil rights movement influenced the women's rights movement. Next, have them write 2 or 3 sentences explaining their reasoning.

▲ **Differentiation**

If students are struggling to provide evidence, have students work in pairs to first create a Venn diagram that compares the civil rights movement to the women's rights movement. This should help students to see the influences.

Exploring AP® Themes notes suggest ways to help students draw thematic connections throughout the course.

Differentiation notes suggest ways of adapting instruction for advanced and lower-level learners.

BUILDING AP® SKILLS
Argumentation

Writing is a recursive skill and therefore needs to be explicitly modeled and scaffolded throughout the year. Weighing historical evidence is a difficult concept for many students. The most effective arguments acknowledge multiple perspectives and weigh the evidence. To practice this skill, consider providing students with three categories that help explain the development of slavery in the British North American colonies: cash crops, race, and the Atlantic World to select one category. Their task is to write a three-to-four sentence statement that recognizes the importance of two categories while weighing their selected topic as the most important. Here is an example: "Although the growth of slavery can be attributed to the dependence on cash crops and the devel-

Building AP® Skills notes discuss how to teach and practice AP® historical thinking skills and reasoning processes.

BUILDING AP® SKILLS
Claims and Evidence in Sources

The historical thinking skills articulated by the College Board are organized in a scaffolded manner and therefore teachers should consider the skill hierarchy to inform their instruction. For example, have students identify and highlight two major claims made by Samuel de Champlain. This is the first skill for students to master in claims and evidence in sources and is an appropriate task for students early in the school year. One challenge students face is understanding how to privilege specific evidence in a document. To help students overcome this challenge, ask them to highlight shorter phrases of 8-10 words. Shortening their selections will help them become readers that are more discreet in their selections.

APPLY THE TIP

Assign students to complete a T-chart on the goals and accomplishments of La Follette and Progressives and the Populists in the West. Create these charts on poster paper, then place them around the room and allow students time for a gallery walk to compare their products.

APPLY THE TIP

To better understand why resource-rich areas of North America developed differently from those with more limited natural resources, have students research "three-sister farming." Students should discover that tribes that lived in more fertile soil, normally those with access to rivers, and with better climate, were able to partake in this type of agriculture. Doing so allowed them to have richer diets that could sustain larger populations. A useful source for this research would be Catherine Boekmann's "The Three Sisters: Corn, Beans, and Squash" available on The Older Farmer's Almanac website (almanac.com).

Apply the Tip notes suggest activities for extending the AP® Tips in the Student Edition.

TRM

The **TRM** icon indicates extension material—such as handouts, maps, and model answers—that is available in the Teacher's Resource Materials online and on the Teacher's Resource Flash Drive.

TRM Suggested Responses to Questions

TRM Module 1.1 AP® Analyzing Sources Handout

How to Use This Teacher's Edition

Reach Students Anywhere

Find these and more resources online in our unique multimedia products.

LaunchPad is a digital platform that offers the Student Edition, Teacher's Edition, and Teacher's Resource Materials all in a convenient place. With curated learning modules, premium student tools, and an integrated gradebook, LaunchPad is your one-stop shop for your online or blended course.

LaunchPad comes equipped with LearningCurve, an adaptive and automatically graded learning tool that guides students to mastery of the course content.

Your Complete Quizzing Solution, contains hundreds of helpful content review questions and nine complete simulated AP® Exams. The ExamView® Test Generator lets you quickly create paper, Internet, and LAN-based tests. Not only can you create and format a test in minutes, but the platform is fully customizable, allowing you to enter your own questions, edit existing questions, set time limits, incorporate multimedia, and scramble answers and change the order of questions to prevent plagiarism. Detailed results reports feed into a gradebook.

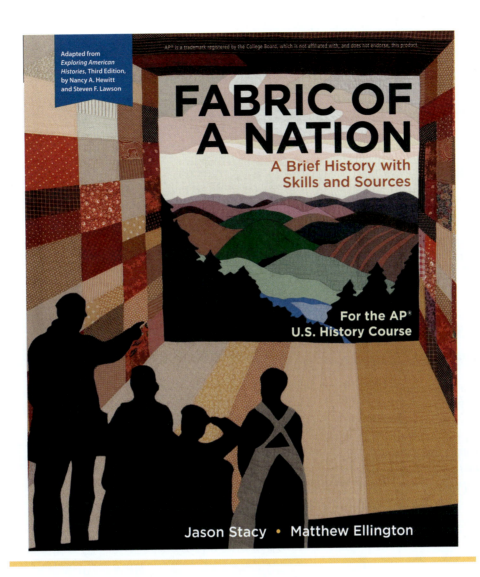

About the Cover Image

The Promise, Paulette Aileen Suder Peters, 1986

The Promise was a finalist in the Great American Quilt Contest hosted by the Museum of American Folk Art in New York City in 1986, which commemorated the centennial of the Statue of Liberty.

Peters's quilt represents the symbolism of the Statue of Liberty by embodying the hopeful spirit of new immigrants gazing across the American landscape. Peters used several techniques to focus the eye of the viewer toward the landscape, including both the pointed hand of one of the silhouettes, as well as the vertical quilting lines of the pier on which the immigrant family stands, pointing to the future.

Fabric of a Nation

A BRIEF HISTORY WITH SKILLS AND SOURCES

FOR THE AP® U.S. HISTORY COURSE

Jason Stacy
Southern Illinois University, Edwardsville

Matthew Ellington
Ruben S. Ayala High School, Chino Hills, California

Adapted from
Exploring American Histories,
Third Edition
by
Nancy A. Hewitt and Steven F. Lawson

bedford, freeman & worth
high school publishers
Boston | New York

AP® is a trademark registered by the College Board, which is not affiliated with, and does not endorse, this product.

For Bedford/St. Martin's

Vice President, Editorial, Macmillan Learning Humanities: Leasa Burton
Senior Program Director for History: Michael Rosenberg
Senior Executive Program Manager for History: William J. Lombardo
Senior Program Director, High School: Ann Heath
Executive Program Manager, HS Humanities: Nathan Odell
Director of Content Development, Humanities: Jane Knetzger
Senior Developmental Editor: Caitlin Kaufman
Associate Editor: Corrina Santos
Assistant Editor: Carla Duval
Senior Marketing Manager, HS: Janie Pierce-Bratcher
Marketing Coordinator: Tiffani Tang
Executive Content Project Manager: Gregory Erb
Senior Workflow Project Manager: Lisa McDowell
Production Supervisor: Robin Besofsky
Lead Media Project Manager: Jodi Isman
Senior Media Editor: Kimberly Morté
Editorial Services: Lumina Datamatics, Inc.
Composition: Lumina Datamatics, Inc.
Cartographer: Mapping Specialists, Ltd.
Text Permissions Editor: Michael McCarty
Photo Permissions Editor: Christine Buese
Photo Researcher: Carolyn Arcabascio, Lumina Datamatics, Inc.
Director of Design, Content Management: Diana Blume
Text Design: Lumina Datamatics, Inc.
Cover Design: William Boardman
Cover Image: The Promise. Paulette Aileen Suder Peters. 1986, Elkhorn, Nebraska, Gift of the artist. International Quilt Study Center & Museum, University of Nebraska–Lincoln, 2005.011.0001
Printing and Binding: LSC Communications

Copyright © 2020 by Bedford/St. Martin's

All rights reserved. No part of this book may be reproduced, stored in a retrieval system, or transmitted in any form or by any means, electronic, mechanical, photocopying, recording, or otherwise, except as may be permitted by law or expressly permitted in writing by the Publisher.
Manufactured in the United States of America.

1   2   3   4   5   6   24   23   22   21   20   19

For information, write: Bedford/St. Martin's, 75 Arlington Street, Boston, MA 02116

ISBN 978-1-319-17817-8 (Student Edition)
ISBN 978-1-319-18268-7 (Teacher's Edition)

Acknowledgments
Text acknowledgments and copyrights appear at the back of the book on page C-1, which constitute an extension of the copyright page. Art acknowledgments and copyrights appear on the same page as the art selections they cover.

Brief Contents

Fabric of a Nation: **What's Inside** xxxii

PERIOD 1: 1491–1607

Europeans Make Claims in the Americas 2

Module 1-1 Diverse American Indian Societies 4

Module 1-2 Portugal and Spain Expand Their Reach 17

Module 1-3 The Columbian Exchange 24

Module 1-4 Spanish Colonial Society 30

PERIOD 2: 1607–1754

Colonial America amid Global Change 40

Module 2-1 European Challengers to Spanish North America 43

Module 2-2 Early British Colonies in Maryland, Virginia, and North Carolina 54

Module 2-3 Religious Dissent and Colonial Conflicts in New England 70

Module 2-4 The British West Indies and South Atlantic Colonies 83

Module 2-5 The Middle Colonies 90

Module 2-6 The Eighteenth-Century Atlantic Economy 98

Module 2-7 Slavery Takes Hold in the South 107

Module 2-8 Imperial Contests in Trade and War 118

Module 2-9 Religious and Political Awakenings 130

PERIOD 3: 1754–1800

A Revolutionary Era 146

Module 3-1 International Conflicts Cause Colonial Tensions 149

Module 3-2 Resistance to Britain Intensifies 160

Module 3-3 The American Revolution Begins 173

Module 3-4 Winning the War for Independence 185

Module 3-5 Governing in Revolutionary Times, 1776–1787 195

Module 3-6 Reframing the American Government 207

Module 3-7 Legacies of the American Revolution 217

Module 3-8 George Washington Unites a Nation 230

Module 3-9 Political Parties in Years of Crisis 237

PERIOD 4: 1800–1848

Democracy, Industrialization, and Reform   254

Module 4-1 Political and Economic Transformations   257

Module 4-2 Defending and Redefining the Nation   272

Module 4-3 Transportation and Market Revolutions Change America   287

Module 4-4 The Second American Party System   300

Module 4-5 Conflicts of the Jacksonian Era   309

Module 4-6 Slavery and Southern Society   319

Module 4-7 Social Reform Movements   330

Module 4-8 Abolitionism and Sectionalism   343

PERIOD 5: 1844–1877

Expansion, Division, and Civil War   354

Module 5-1 Manifest Destiny   357

Module 5-2 Compromise and Conflict   367

Module 5-3 From Sectional Crisis to Southern Secession   377

Module 5-4 Disunion and War   389

Module 5-5 Victory for the North   403

Module 5-6 Reconstruction Begins   411

Module 5-7 Reform and Resistance   427

Module 5-8 Reconstruction Undone   434

PERIOD 6: 1865–1898

A Gilded Age   446

Module 6-1 Westward Expansion and American Indian Resistance   449

Module 6-2 Industry in the West   460

Module 6-3 The New South   473

Module 6-4 America Industrializes   482

Module 6-5 Working People Organize   490

Module 6-6 A New Wave of Immigrants   501

Module 6-7 Becoming an Urban Nation   511

Module 6-8 Society and Culture in the Gilded Age   524

Module 6-9 Gilded Age Ideologies   532

Module 6-10 Politics and Protest   537

PERIOD 7: 1890–1945

New Imperialism and Global Conflicts   552

Module 7-1 Progressivism and Social Reform   555

Module 7-2 Progressive Political Reforms   570

Module 7-3 The Awakening of Imperialism   586

Module 7-4 Foreign Policy and World War I   598

Module 7-5 The Effects of World War I at Home   610

Module 7-6 The Transitional 1920s   620

Module 7-7 Economic Instability and Depression   637

Module 7-8 The New Deal   646

Module 7-9 America Enters World War II   662

Module 7-10 Life on the Homefront   670

Module 7-11 Victory in World War II   681

PERIOD 8: 1945–1980

Cold War America   696

Module 8-1 The Early Cold War, 1945–1953   699

Module 8-2 The Second Red Scare   710

Module 8-3 Peacetime Transition and the Boom Years   716

Module 8-4 Cultural Shifts in 1950s America   722

Module 8-5 Civil Rights in an Era of Conformity   729

Module 8-6 The Cold War Expands at Home and Abroad, 1953–1961   739

Module 8-7 The Vietnam War   748

Module 8-8 The Fight for Civil Rights, 1961–1979   755

Module 8-9 Liberalism and Its Challengers, 1960–1973   766

Module 8-10 American Politics in Transition, 1968–1980   777

Module 8-11 The Persistence of Liberalism and the Rise of the New Right   791

PERIOD 9: 1980–THE PRESENT

Challenges in a Globalized World   802

Module 9-1 The Triumph of Conservatism   804

Module 9-2 The End of the Cold War   817

Module 9-3 Toward the Twenty-First Century   826

Module 9-4 The Global War on Terror and Political Conflict at Home   833

Practice AP® Exam   PE-1

Glossary/Glosario   GL-1

Credits   C-1

Index   I-1

Contents

Fabric of a Nation: What's Inside   xxxii

PERIOD 1: 1491–1607
Europeans Make Claims in the Americas   2

Module 1-1
Diverse American Indian Societies   4
- **AP® THINKING HISTORICALLY** Active Reading and Effective Note Taking   6

The Aztecs, the Maya, and the Incas   7
- **AP® THINKING HISTORICALLY** Analyzing Sources   8
  - **Source:** Anonymous Mixtec artisan, *Necklace with Gold Frog Ornaments* (photograph), Aztec empire, 15th–16th century   9

Native Cultures to the North   10
- **AP® ANALYZING SOURCES** Pueblo "Cliff Palace" at Mesa Verde, Colorado (photograph)   11
- **AP® THINKING HISTORICALLY** Applying Comparison   14
- **AP® WRITING HISTORICALLY** Breaking Down Short-Answer Question Prompts   15

Module 1-2
Portugal and Spain Expand Their Reach   17

Portugal and Spain Pursue Long-Distance Trade   18

Europeans Cross the Atlantic   19
- **AP® WRITING HISTORICALLY** Responding to a Short-Answer Question Using ACE   21

Module 1-3
The Columbian Exchange   24

The Columbian Exchange Transforms Four Continents   24

European Encounters with West Africa   27
- **AP® ANALYZING SOURCES** Mvemba A Nzinga, *Letter to John III, King of Portugal*, 1526   27
- **AP® WRITING HISTORICALLY** Using Categories to Respond to a Short-Answer Question   28

Module 1-4
Spanish Colonial Society   30

Spanish Incursions in the Americas   31
- **AP® ANALYZING SOURCES** Anonymous artists, *Hernán Cortés Assisted by the Tlaxcalan People of Mexico* (mural), 1560   32

Spain Establishes Colonial Rule   33

Spain Debates the Human Costs of Colonization   34
- **AP® ANALYZING SOURCES** Bartolomé de Las Casas, *Brief Account of the Destruction of the Indies*, 1542 & Juan Ginés de Sepúlveda, *Concerning the Just Causes of the War against the Indians*, 1547   35

Spain's Global Empire Declines   36
- **AP® WRITING HISTORICALLY** Responding to a Short-Answer Question   37

PERIOD 1 REVIEW 1491–1607   39
AP® EXAM PRACTICE Through 1607   39-a

PERIOD 2: 1607–1754
Colonial America amid Global Change   40

Module 2-1
European Challengers to Spanish North America   43

The French Expand into North America   44
- **AP® ANALYZING SOURCES** Samuel de Champlain, *Voyages of Samuel de Champlain: 1567–1635*   44

The Dutch Expand into North America 46

AP® THINKING HISTORICALLY Using Comparison and Causation in Historical Arguments 47

Spain's Fragile North American Empire 49

AP® ANALYZING SOURCES King Philip IV of Spain, *Letter to Don Luis Valdés*, 1647 49

AP® WRITING HISTORICALLY Crafting a Thesis Statement Based on Comparison 51

Module 2-2
Early British Colonies in Maryland, Virginia, and North Carolina 54

Economic Causes of English Colonization 54

AP® ANALYZING SOURCES Thomas More, *Utopia; or, the Best State of a Commonwealth*, 1516 55

The English Establish Jamestown 56

AP® ANALYZING SOURCES Powhatan, *Deerskin Cloak* (photograph), c. 1608 56

Tobacco Fuels Growth in Virginia 58

AP® ANALYZING SOURCES John Rolfe, *Letter on Jamestown Settlement*, 1618 58

AP® ANALYZING SOURCES Matthaeus Merian, *Native Attack on Jamestown* (engraving), 1622 59

AP® ANALYZING SOURCES John Martin, *The manner how to bring the Indians into subjugation*, 1622 60

The Second Chesapeake Colony: Maryland 61

Tobacco Economies, Class Rebellion, and the Emergence of Slavery 62

AP® ANALYZING SOURCES Virginia House of Burgesses, *Selected Statutes Passed*, 1662–1669 63

AP® ANALYZING SOURCES Nathaniel Bacon, *Declaration against Governor William Berkeley*, 1676 64

AP® THINKING HISTORICALLY Connecting Distant Causes to Immediate Causes 65

Daily Life in the Colonies 66

AP® WRITING HISTORICALLY Writing Topic Sentences for an Essay 68

Module 2-3
Religious Dissent and Colonial Conflicts in New England 70

The Protestant Reformation 71

Pilgrims Arrive in Massachusetts 72

AP® ANALYZING SOURCES *The Mayflower Compact*, 1620 72

Puritans Form Communities in New England 73

AP® ANALYZING SOURCES John Winthrop, *A Model of Christian Charity*, 1630 73

Challenges Arise in the New England Colonies 75

Conflicts in England Echo in the Colonies 77

AP® ANALYZING SOURCES John Locke, *Second Treatise on Civil Government*, 1690 77

Puritan Religious Anxieties Lead to Colonial Conflict 78

AP® WRITING HISTORICALLY Crafting a Thesis Statement Based on Continuity and Change 80

Module 2-4
The British West Indies and South Atlantic Colonies 83

The English Compete for the West Indies 84

AP® ANALYZING SOURCES Richard Ligon, *Map of Barbados*, 1657 84

The British West Indies Influence South Carolina 85

AP® ANALYZING SOURCES *South Carolina Slave Code*, 1640 85

Daily Life in Eighteenth-Century South Carolina 86

AP® WRITING HISTORICALLY Writing a Full Essay 88

Module 2-5
The Middle Colonies 90

Colonies Develop in New York and New Jersey 91

AP® ANALYZING SOURCES *Letter from a Gentleman of the City of New York to Another. Concerning the Troubles which happened in that Province in the time of the late Happy REVOLUTION*, 1689 91

Penn's Goal of a Peaceable Kingdom 92

AP® ANALYZING SOURCES William Penn, *The Frame of the Government of the Province of Pennsylvania*, 1682 93

Expansion and Conflict in Pennsylvania 94

AP® WRITING HISTORICALLY Presenting Context in a Historical Argument 95

Module 2-6
The Eighteenth-Century Atlantic Economy 98

Colonial Traders Join Global Networks 98

Imperial Policies Focus on Profits 100

AP® ANALYZING SOURCES British Parliament, *Navigation Act*, 1660 100

Mercantilism Changes Colonial Societies 101

AP® WRITING HISTORICALLY Responding to a Short-Answer Question with Secondary Sources 103

> **Source:** Richard Bushman, *The Refinement of America: Persons, Houses, Cities*, 1993 103
>
> **Source:** T. H. Breen, *The Marketplace of the Revolution: How Consumer Politics Shaped American Independence*, 2005 103
>
> **Source:** E. A. J. Johnson, "Some Evidence of Mercantilism in Massachusetts Bay," *The New England Quarterly*, 1928 106
>
> **Source:** Ellen Newell, "Putting the 'Political' Back in Political Economy (This Is Not Your Parents' Mercantilism)," *The William and Mary Quarterly*, 2012 106

Module 2-7

Slavery Takes Hold in the South 107

The Human Cost of the Atlantic Slave Trade 107

AP® ANALYZING SOURCES King Charles II, *Royal African Company Charter*, 1672 109

The Rise of Slavery Reshapes Southern Colonial Society 109

Africans Resist Enslavement 111

AP® ANALYZING SOURCES George Cato, *Account of the Stono Rebellion, 1739* (recording), 1937 111

AP® WRITING HISTORICALLY Responding to a Document-Based Question with Three Primary Sources 112

> **Document 1** Virginia House of Burgesses, *Selected Statutes Passed 1662–1667* 113
>
> **Document 2** Joseph Ball, *Instructions on Managing Enslaved Workers*, 1743 114
>
> **Document 3** *Instructions given by Richard Corbin, Esq., to his agent for the management of his plantations*, Virginia, 1759 115

Module 2-8

Imperial Contests in Trade and War 118

AP® ANALYZING SOURCES Experience Mayhew and Thomas Prince, *Indian Converts: or, Some Account of the Lives and Dying Speeches of a Considerable Number of the Christianized Indians of Martha's Vineyard, in New-England*, 1727 119

American Indians Resist European Intrusion 119

European Rivalry and American Indian Alliances 120

AP® ANALYZING SOURCES Thomas Oliver, *Letter to Queen Anne*, 1708 121

AP® ANALYZING SOURCES *Treaty of Utrecht*, 1713 122

Imperial Conflicts on the Southern Frontier 122

AP® WRITING HISTORICALLY Responding to a Document-Based Question with Five Primary Sources 123

> **Document 1** William Nahaton, *Petition to Free an Indian Slave*, 1675 124
>
> **Document 2** Benjamin Church, *A Visit with Awashonks, Sachem of the Sakonnet*, 1675 124
>
> **Document 3** John Easton, *A Relation of the Indian War*, 1675 125
>
> **Document 4** Edward Randolph, *Assessment of the Causes of King Philip's War*, 1675 126
>
> **Document 5** Mary Rowlandson, *Narrative of the Captivity and Restoration of Mrs. Mary Rowlandson*, 1682 126

Module 2-9

Religious and Political Awakenings 130

Colonial Family Life and the Limits of Patriarchal Order 131

The Great Awakening Takes Root 131

AP® ANALYZING SOURCES Benjamin Franklin, *Poor Richard's Almanack*, 1739 132

Dissent and Resistance Rise 134

AP® WRITING HISTORICALLY Responding to a Document-Based Question 136

> **Document 1** George Whitefield, *Marks of a True Conversion*, 1739 137
>
> **Document 2** Nathan Cole, *On George Whitefield Coming to Connecticut*, 1740 138
>
> **Document 3** Benjamin Franklin, *On George Whitefield, the Great Revivalist*, 1739 138
>
> **Document 4** Jonathan Edwards: *Sinners in the Hands of an Angry God*, 1741 139
>
> **Document 5** John Collet, *George Whitefield Preaching at a Revival* (painting), 1760 140
>
> **Document 6** Anonymous, *George Whitefield* (engraving), London Newspaper, 1763 140

PERIOD 2 REVIEW 1607–1754 144

AP® EXAM PRACTICE Through 1754 145-a

PERIOD 3: 1754–1800

A Revolutionary Era 146

Module 3-1
International Conflicts Cause Colonial Tensions 149

The Seven Years' War Begins 150
- **AP® ANALYZING SOURCES** Benjamin Franklin, "Join or Die" (political cartoon and editorial), *Pennsylvania Gazette*, 1754 151

The Costs of Victory 152
- **AP® ANALYZING SOURCES** Anonymous, *Impressment by the British* (engraving), c. mid-1700s 152
- **AP® ANALYZING SOURCES** *North America before and after the Seven Years' War* (maps) 154

Unresolved Issues in the Colonies 155
- **AP® ANALYZING SOURCES** William Trent, *Diary Entry*, July 27, 1763 156
- **AP® THINKING HISTORICALLY** Evaluating Causes 157
- **AP® WRITING HISTORICALLY** Short-Answer Question Practice 159
  - **Source:** Gordon Wood, *The Radicalism of the American Revolution*, 1993 159
  - **Source:** Jon Butler, *Becoming America: The Revolution Before 1776*, 2000 159

Module 3-2
Resistance to Britain Intensifies 160

Intensifying Conflict and Resistance, 1763–1766 161

The Colonies Forge New Ties 161
- **AP® ANALYZING SOURCES** Patrick Henry, *Virginia Resolves*, 1765 163
- **AP® ANALYZING SOURCES** *London Merchants' Petition to Repeal the Stamp Act*, 1766 165

Ongoing Tension, 1767–1773 165
- **AP® ANALYZING SOURCES** Anonymous, "A Lady's Adieu to her TEA-TABLE" (poem), *Massachusetts Gazette*, February, 1770 166
- **AP® ANALYZING SOURCES** *Witness Testimony in the Trial of the British Soldiers of the Nineteenth Regiment of Foot*, Boston, 1770 167

Widening Resistance, 1773–1774 168
- **AP® ANALYZING SOURCES** "Account of the Boston Tea Party," *Massachusetts Gazette*, 1773 169
- **AP® WRITING HISTORICALLY** Evaluating Continuity and Change in an Essay 170

Module 3-3
The American Revolution Begins 173

The Continental Congress Convenes 174

Armed Conflict Erupts 174
- **AP® ANALYZING SOURCES** "Memory of a British Officer Stationed at Lexington and Concord," *Atlantic Monthly*, 1775 175
- **AP® ANALYZING SOURCES** Thomas Paine, *Common Sense*, 1776 & Charles Inglis, *The true interest of America impartially stated, in certain [strictures] on a pamphlet [entitled] Common sense*, 1776 177

The Colonies Declare Independence 178
- **AP® ANALYZING SOURCES** Thomas Jefferson, *Declaration of Independence*, 1776 179

Choosing Sides 180
- **AP® ANALYZING SOURCES** Oneida Leaders, *Message to Massachusetts Provincial Congress*, 1775 181
- **AP® ANALYZING SOURCES** Christine Barnes, wife of an absent loyalist farmer, *Letter*, April 1775 182
- **AP® ANALYZING SOURCES** Phillis Wheatley, "On Being Brought from Africa to America" (poem), 1770 183
- **AP® WRITING HISTORICALLY** Establishing Context in an Essay Introduction 184

Module 3-4
Winning the War for Independence 185

Critical Years of Warfare, 1776–1777 185

Women Contribute to the Revolution 186
- **AP® ANALYZING SOURCES** Esther De Berdt Reed, *The Sentiments of an American Woman*, 1780 187

France Allies with the Patriots 188
- **AP® ANALYZING SOURCES** *Treaty of Alliance between the United States and France*, 1778 189

Patriots Achieve Victory 191

- AP® ANALYZING SOURCES *Treaty of Paris*, 1783 193
- AP® WRITING HISTORICALLY Evaluating Effects in an Essay 193

Module 3-5
Governing in Revolutionary Times, 1776–1787 195

States Form Their Own Governments, 1776–1786 195

A Revolutionary National Government, 1777–1781 196

- AP® ANALYZING SOURCES *Articles of Confederation*, 1781 197

New Economic Challenges, 1780–1783 198

Conflicts Over Western Lands, 1778–1787 198

- AP® ANALYZING SOURCES *Northwest Ordinance*, 1787 201

Indebted Farmers Fuel Political Crises, 1783–1787 202

- AP® ANALYZING SOURCES *Correspondence between Daniel Shays and Benjamin Lincoln*, Massachusetts, 1787 203
- AP® WRITING HISTORICALLY Making Evaluative Comparisons in an Essay 203

Module 3-6
Reframing the American Government 207

Making a Constitution 207

Americans Debate Ratification 209

- AP® ANALYZING SOURCES Alexander Hamilton, *Federalist Argument at the New York State Convention*, June 1788 209
- AP® WRITING HISTORICALLY Evaluating Continuity and Change in a Document-Based Essay 211
  - Document 1 Patrick Henry, *Virginia Resolves*, 1765 212
  - Document 2 Thomas Paine, *Common Sense*, 1776 212
  - Document 3 Delegates to the Pennsylvania Constitutional Convention, *The Address and Reasons of Dissent of the Minority of the Convention of Pennsylvania to Their Constituents*, 1787 213
  - Document 4 James Madison, *Federalist No. 10*, 1787 213
  - Document 5 John Williams, backcountry farmer, *Argument at the New York State Ratification Convention*, 1788 214
  - Document 6 *The Massachusetts Centinel*, "The Federal Pillars" (political cartoon and poem), August 1788 214

Module 3-7
Legacies of the American Revolution 217

Veteran Farmers Struggle in a Post-War Economy 217

Revolutionary Women Seek Wider Roles 218

- AP® ANALYZING SOURCES Judith Sargent Murray, "On the Equality of the Sexes," *Massachusetts Magazine*, 1790 219

Developing a Distinct American Culture 220

The Racial Limits of an American Culture 221

Slavery's Ongoing Legacy 222

- AP® ANALYZING SOURCES *Petition of Enslaved African Americans to the Massachusetts Legislature*, 1777 & Thomas Cole, Peter Bassnett Matthewes, and Matthew Webb, *Petition to the South Carolina Senate*, 1791 223
- AP® WRITING HISTORICALLY Making Evaluative Comparisons in a Document-Based Essay 225
  - Document 1 *Petition of Enslaved African Americans to the Massachusetts Legislature*, 1777 226
  - Document 2 Colonel Daniel Brodhead, *Letter to General George Washington*, 1779 226
  - Document 3 Boston King, *Memoirs of Boston King*, 1796 226
  - Document 4 *Northwest Ordinance*, 1787 227
  - Document 5 *United States Constitution, Article I*, 1787 227
  - Document 6 *Pennsylvania Act for the Gradual Abolition of Slavery*, 1780 227
  - Document 7 *Treaty of Greenville, Article 9*, 1795 228

Module 3-8
George Washington Unites a Nation 230

Organizing the Federal Government 230

- AP® ANALYZING SOURCES James Madison, *Speech Proposing the Bill of Rights*, 1789 231

Hamilton Forges a Financial Plan 232

- AP® ANALYZING SOURCES Alexander Hamilton, *Report on the Subject of Manufactures*, 1791 233

A New Capital for a New Nation 233

- AP® ANALYZING SOURCES Benjamin Banneker, *Letter to Thomas Jefferson*, 1791 234
- AP® WRITING HISTORICALLY Short-Answer Question Practice 236

Module 3-9
Political Parties in Years of Crisis   237

Foreign Trade and Foreign Wars   237

The Whiskey Rebellion   239

Further Conflicts on the Frontier   240
- **AP® ANALYZING SOURCES** *Pinckney Treaty, Article IV*, 1795   241

A Two-Party System Forms   241
- **AP® ANALYZING SOURCES** Anonymous, *The Providential Detection*, (anti-Jefferson political cartoon), 1797   242
- **AP® ANALYZING SOURCES** *Sedition Act*, 1798   244
- **AP® ANALYZING SOURCES** *Kentucky Resolution*, 1799   244

The Election of 1800   245

AP® WRITING HISTORICALLY Evaluating Causation in a Document-Based Essay   246
- **Document 1** Benjamin Franklin Bache, *Remarks Occasioned by the Late Conduct of Mr. Washington*, 1797   247
- **Document 2** George Washington, *Farewell Address*, 1797   247
- **Document 3** John Adams, *Speech to Congress*, 1797   247
- **Document 4** Anonymous, *The Providential Detection*, (anti-Jefferson political cartoon), 1797   248
- **Document 5** *Sedition Act*, 1798   248
- **Document 6** *Kentucky Resolution*, 1799   249
- **Document 7** Thomas Jefferson, *Inaugural Address*, 1801   249

PERIOD 3 REVIEW 1754–1800   251

AP® EXAM PRACTICE Through 1800   253-a

PERIOD 4: 1800–1848
Democracy, Industrialization, and Reform   254

Module 4-1
Political and Economic Transformations   257

A New Administration Faces Challenges   258

Acquiring the Louisiana Territory   258
- **AP® ANALYZING SOURCES** William Clark, *Journal Entry*, October 12, 1804   259

The Supreme Court Extends Its Reach   261

Democratic-Republicans Expand Federal Powers   261

The U.S. Population Grows and Migrates   262

Technology Reshapes Agriculture and Industry   265
- **AP® ANALYZING SOURCES** Eli Whitney, *Petition for Renewal of Patent on Cotton Gin*, 1812   265

Transforming Domestic Production   266

Technology, Cotton, and Enslavement   267
- **AP® ANALYZING SOURCES** Harriet Jacobs, *Incidents in the Life of a Slave Girl*, 1861   269
- **AP® ANALYZING SOURCES** Thomas Jefferson, *Letter to Rufus King*, July 1802 **&** Leonora Sansay, *Letter to Aaron Burr*, November 1802   270
- **AP® WRITING HISTORICALLY** Short-Answer Question Practice   271

Module 4-2
Defending and Redefining the Nation   272

Tensions at Sea and on the Frontier   273
- **AP® ANALYZING SOURCES** Chief Tecumseh, *Address to Governor William Henry Harrison*, 1810   274

War Erupts with Britain   274

Governments Fuel Economic Growth   277

Americans Expand the Nation's Borders   279
- **AP® ANALYZING SOURCES** *Monroe Doctrine*, 1823   279

Regional Economic Development   280

The Panic of 1819   281

Slavery in Missouri   282
- **AP® ANALYZING SOURCES** Senator Rufus King (New York), *Speech to Congress on the Admission of Missouri to the United States*, 1819 **&** Senator Freeman Walker (Georgia), *Speech to Congress on the Admission of Missouri to the United States*, 1820   282
- **AP® WRITING HISTORICALLY** Responding to a Long-Essay Question   284

Module 4-3

Transportation and Market Revolutions Change America 287

Creating an Urban Landscape 288

The Lure of Urban Life 289

The Roots of Urban Disorder 290

The New Middle Class 291

> **AP® ANALYZING SOURCES** 1850 U.S. Census of the Isaac and Amy Post Household (table) 292

Factory Towns and Women Workers 293

> **AP® ANALYZING SOURCES** Harriet H. Robinson, *Loom and Spindle or Life among the Early Mill Girls*, 1898 294

The Decline of Craft Work 294

The Panic of 1837 295

> **AP® WRITING HISTORICALLY** Responding to a Document-Based Question 296
>
> > **Document 1** Basil Hall, *Travels in North America, in the year 1827 and 1828* 297
> >
> > **Document 2** Joseph Davis, *The Azariah Caverly Family* (painting), 1836 297
> >
> > **Document 3** Harriet Martineau, *Society in America*, 1837 298
> >
> > **Document 4** *Address of the Workingmen's Party of Charlestown, Massachusetts*, 1840 298
> >
> > **Document 5** *American Whig Review*, 1845 298
> >
> > **Document 6** *The Cultivator*, March 1846 298
> >
> > **Document 7** Horace Bushnell, *The Age of Homespun*, 1851 299

Module 4-4

The Second American Party System 300

Voting Rights Expand 300

Racial Restrictions and Antiblack Violence 302

Political Realignments 303

The Presidential Election of 1828 304

> **AP® ANALYZING SOURCES** *Proceedings of the Anti-Jackson Convention in Richmond*, 1828 & *New Jersey Pro-Jackson Convention*, 1828 305

A Democratic Spirit? 306

> **AP® ANALYZING SOURCES** Alexis de Tocqueville, *Letter to Louis de Kergorlay*, 1831 307
>
> **AP® WRITING HISTORICALLY** Short-Answer Question Practice 307
>
> > **Source:** Alexander Keyssar, *Broadening the Franchise*, 2000 307
> >
> > **Source:** James Oliver Horton and Lois E. Horton, *The Limits of Democratic Expansion*, 1997 308

Module 4-5

Conflicts of the Jacksonian Era 309

Confrontations over Tariffs and the Bank 309

> **AP® ANALYZING SOURCES** John C. Calhoun, *Address to the Southern States*, 1831 310

The Battle for Texas 311

> **AP® ANALYZING SOURCES** *Texas Declaration of Independence*, 1836 312

American Indians Resist Removal 313

> **AP® ANALYZING SOURCES** *Indian Removal Act*, 1830 313

Van Buren and the Panic of 1837 317

The Whigs Win the White House 317

> **AP® WRITING HISTORICALLY** Short-Answer Question Practice 318
>
> > **Source:** David F. Ericson, *The Nullification Crisis, American Republicanism, and the Force Bill Debate*, 1995 318
> >
> > **Source:** Jane H. Pease and William H. Pease, *The Economics and Politics of Charleston's Nullification Crisis*, 1981 318

Module 4-6

Slavery and Southern Society 319

A Plantation Society Develops in the South 320

Urban Life in the Slaveholding South 320

The Consequences of Slavery's Expansion 321

Enslaved Labor Fuels the Southern Economy 322

> **AP® ANALYZING SOURCES** Advertisement of a South Carolina Slave Dealer, 1835 322
>
> **AP® ANALYZING SOURCES** Solomon Northup, *Twelve Years a Slave*, 1853 323

Developing an African American Culture 324

Resistance and Rebellion 325

White Southerners Who Were Not Slaveholders 327

Planters Seek to Unify White Southerners 327

> **AP® ANALYZING SOURCES** John C. Calhoun, *Slavery a Positive Good*, 1837 328
>
> **AP® WRITING HISTORICALLY** Short-Answer Question Practice 329
>
> > **Source:** *Enslaved Population, 1820 and 1860* (maps) 329

Module 4-7
Social Reform Movements   330

Building a National Culture   330

The Roots of the Second Great Awakening   332
- **AP® ANALYZING SOURCES** Charles G. Finney, *An Influential Woman Converts*, 1830   332
- **AP® ANALYZING SOURCES** Lyman Beecher, *The Evils Of Intemperance*, 1827   333

New Visions of Faith and Reform   334

Transcendentalism   335

Varieties of Reform   336

The Problem of Poverty   337
- **AP® ANALYZING SOURCES** Matthew Carey, *Appeal to the Wealthy of the Land*, 1833 & Emily G. Kempshall, *Letter to the Rochester Female Charitable Society*, 1838   337

The Temperance Movement   339

Utopian Communities   340
- **AP® WRITING HISTORICALLY** Responding to a Long-Essay Question   340

Module 4-8
Abolitionism and Sectionalism   343

The Beginnings of the Antislavery Movement   343
- **AP® ANALYZING SOURCES** David Walker, *Walker's Appeal to the Coloured Citizens of the World*, 1830   344
- **AP® ANALYZING SOURCES** Elizabeth Emery and Mary P. Abbott, *Letter to* The Liberator, 1836   345

Abolition Gains Ground and Enemies   345
- **AP® ANALYZING SOURCES** Frederick Douglass, *Narrative of the Life of Frederick Douglass, an American Slave, Written by Himself*, 1845   346

Abolitionism and Women's Rights   347
- **AP® ANALYZING SOURCES** Elizabeth Cady Stanton, *Declaration of Sentiments*, 1848   348

The Rise of Antislavery Parties   349
- **AP® WRITING HISTORICALLY** Responding to a Long-Essay Question   349

PERIOD 4 REVIEW 1800–1848   352

AP® EXAM PRACTICE Through 1848   353-a

PERIOD 5: 1844–1877
Expansion, Division, and Civil War   354

Module 5-1
Manifest Destiny   357

Traveling the Overland Trails   357
- **AP® ANALYZING SOURCES** Elizabeth Smith Geer, *Oregon Trail Diary*, 1847   358

The Politics of Expansion: Oregon and Texas   359

Pursuing War with Mexico   360
- **AP® ANALYZING SOURCES** President James K. Polk, *War Message*, 1846 & Abraham Lincoln, *Spot Resolutions*, 1847   361

The Gold Rush   363

A Crowded Land   364
- **AP® WRITING HISTORICALLY** Short-Answer Question Practice   366
  - **Source:** Nathaniel Currier, *An available candidate. The one qualification for a Whig president* (political cartoon), 1848   366

Module 5-2
Compromise and Conflict   367

Debates over Slavery Intensify   368

California and the Compromise of 1850   368
- **AP® ANALYZING SOURCES** John C. Calhoun, *The Clay Compromise Measures*, 1850   369

The Fugitive Slave Act Inspires Northern Protest   370
- **AP® ANALYZING SOURCES** William C. Nell, *Meeting of Colored Citizens of Boston*, 1850 & President Millard Fillmore, *Proclamation 56 Calling on Citizens to Assist in the Recapture of a Fugitive Slave*, 1851   372

Further Expansion under President Pierce   373
- **AP® ANALYZING SOURCES** *New York Daily Times*, "Commodore Perry at the Loo Choo Isles," 1853   374
- **AP® WRITING HISTORICALLY** Responding to a Long-Essay Question   374

Contents

Module 5-3

From Sectional Crisis to Southern Secession   377

Popularizing the Antislavery Movement   378

The Kansas-Nebraska Act Stirs Dissent   378

AP® ANALYZING SOURCES American (Know-Nothing) Party Platform, 1856 & Republican Campaign Song, 1856   380

The *Dred Scott* Decision   382

AP® ANALYZING SOURCES Abraham Lincoln, *Speech at Edwardsville, Illinois*, 1858   383

From Crisis to Secession   384

AP® ANALYZING SOURCES Jefferson Davis, *Inaugural Address*, 1861   385

AP® WRITING HISTORICALLY Short-Answer Question Practice   387

> **Source:** Michael P. Johnson, *Toward a Patriarchal Republic: The Secession of Georgia*, 1977   387
> **Source:** J. Mills Thornton, *Politics and Power in a Slave Society: Alabama, 1800–1860*, 1978   387

Module 5-4

Disunion and War   389

The South Embraces Secession   389

Both Sides Prepare for War   390

AP® ANALYZING SOURCES Robert Toombs, *Speech to the Georgia General Assembly*, 1860   392

Military and Political Conflicts, 1861–1863   392

Union Politicians and Emancipation   395

AP® ANALYZING SOURCES President Abraham Lincoln, *Letter to Horace Greeley*, 1862   395

AP® ANALYZING SOURCES The *Charleston Mercury*, "President Lincoln and His Scheme of Emancipation," 1862   397

The Front and the Homefront   397

AP® WRITING HISTORICALLY Long-Essay Question Practice   402

Module 5-5

Victory for the North   403

Key Victories for the Union   403

African Americans Contribute to Victory   405

The Final Battles of a Total War   406

AP® ANALYZING SOURCES Ulysses S. Grant, *The Personal Memoirs of Ulysses S. Grant*, 1885   407

AP® WRITING HISTORICALLY Short-Answer Question Practice   409

> **Source:** Chandra Manning, *The Fight Against Slavery*, 2007   409
> **Source:** Gary Gallagher, *The Fight to Save the Union*, 2011   410

Module 5-6

Reconstruction Begins   411

African Americans Embrace Freedom   412

AP® ANALYZING SOURCES Henry Bram, *To the President of these United States*, 1865   413

AP® ANALYZING SOURCES Colonel Eliphalet Whittlesey, *Report on the Freedmen's Bureau*, 1865   415

Lincoln and Johnson's Reconstruction Plans   417

AP® ANALYZING SOURCES *Mississippi Black Code*, 1865   419

Congressional Reconstruction and Resistance   420

The Struggle for Universal Suffrage   423

AP® ANALYZING SOURCES Elizabeth Cady Stanton, *Speech to the Equal Rights Association*, 1869   424

AP® WRITING HISTORICALLY Using Context to Craft an Essay Conclusion   424

Module 5-7

Reform and Resistance   427

Early Reconstruction in the South   427

AP® ANALYZING SOURCES Thomas Nast, *This Is a White Man's Government* (political cartoon), 1874   428

AP® ANALYZING SOURCES *Sharecropper Contract*, 1882   430

White Resistance   431

AP® ANALYZING SOURCES *Independent Monitor*, "A Prospective Scene in the 'City of Oaks,' 4th of March, 1869" (political cartoon)   432

AP® WRITING HISTORICALLY Short-Answer Question Practice   433

> **Source:** Eric Foner, *Reconstruction: America's Unfinished Revolution, 1863–1877*, 1998   433
> **Source:** Elliott West, "Reconstructing Race," *Western Historical Quarterly* 34, Spring 2003   433

Module 5-8

Reconstruction Undone   434

The Retreat from Reconstruction   434

AP® ANALYZING SOURCES James Garfield, *Speech Delivered at Warren, Ohio*, 1872   435

The Presidential Compromise of 1876 436

AP® ANALYZING SOURCES President Rutherford B. Hayes, *Inaugural Address*, 1877 437

The Legacies of Reconstruction 438

AP® WRITING HISTORICALLY Responding to a Document-Based Question 439

> **Document 1** Abraham Lincoln, *Speech at Edwardsville, Illinois*, 1858 440
>
> **Document 2** *A Declaration of the Immediate Causes which Induce and Justify the Secession of the State of Mississippi from the Federal Union*, 1861 440
>
> **Document 3** *New York Herald*, "What to Do with the Slaves When Emancipated," 1862 440
>
> **Document 4**: *Civil Rights* Act, 1866 441
>
> **Document 5** Elizabeth Cady Stanton and Susan B. Anthony, *Equal Rights Association: Stanton-Anthony Resolutions*, 1869 441
>
> **Document 6** Senator Hiram Revels (Mississippi), *On Readmission of Georgia to the Union*, 1870 441
>
> **Document 7** Thomas Nast, *This Is a White Man's Government* (political cartoon), 1874 442

PERIOD 5 REVIEW 1844–1877 444

AP® EXAM PRACTICE Through 1877 445-a

PERIOD 6: 1865–1898

A Gilded Age 446

Module 6-1

Westward Expansion and American Indian Resistance 449

The Great Plains 449

Federal Policy and Foreign Investment 450

American Indian Civilizations 452

> **AP® ANALYZING SOURCES** Anonymous Shoshone artisan, *Buffalo Hunting*, c. 1875 454

Conflict Escalates in the West 454

Reforming American Indian Policy 457

> **AP® ANALYZING SOURCES** Zitkala-Ša, *The School Days of an Indian Girl*, 1921 458

American Indian Assimilation and Resistance 459

> **AP® WRITING HISTORICALLY** Short-Answer Question Practice 459

Module 6-2

Industry in the West 460

The Mining and Lumber Booms 461

The Life of a Cowboy 463

> **AP® ANALYZING SOURCES** *Buffalo Bill's Wild West and Congress of Rough Riders of the World* (poster), 1893 **&** George C. Duffield, *Driving Cattle from Texas to Iowa*, 1866 464

The Rise of Commercial Ranching and Farming 465

> **AP® ANALYZING SOURCES** Ida Lindgren, *Letter*, August 25, 1874 466

Homesteaders Farm the Great Plains 467

Mormons, Californios, and the Chinese Go West 469

> **AP® ANALYZING SOURCES** *Chinese Exclusion Act*, 1882 471
>
> **AP® WRITING HISTORICALLY** Short-Answer Question Practice 472
>
> > **Source:** Frederick Jackson Turner, *The Frontier in American History*, 1920 472
> >
> > **Source:** Patricia Nelson Limerick, *The Legacy of Conquest: The Unbroken Path of the American West*, 1987 472

Module 6-3

The New South 473

Building a New South 473

> **AP® ANALYZING SOURCES** Henry Grady, *The New South*, 1886 474

Black America and Jim Crow 476

> **AP® WRITING HISTORICALLY** Putting It All Together: Developing Historical Complexity in an Essay 477

Module 6-4

America Industrializes 482

The New Industrial Economy 482

Innovations and Inventions 483

Industrial Consolidation 485

> **AP® ANALYZING SOURCES** *U.S. Workforce by Industry in 1870 and 1900* (graphs) 486

The Growth of Corporations 487

> **AP® ANALYZING SOURCES** Horace Taylor, *What a Funny Little Government* (political cartoon), 1900 487

AP® WRITING HISTORICALLY Short-Answer Question Practice 489

> **Source:** Matthew Josephson, *The Robber Barons*, 1934 489
> **Source:** Daniel Yergin, *The Prize: The Epic Quest for Oil, Money & Power*, 2012 489

Module 6-5

Working People Organize 490

The Industrialization of Labor 490

AP® ANALYZING SOURCES John Morrison, *Testimony of a Machinist before the Senate Committee on the Relations between Labor and Capital*, 1883 491

AP® ANALYZING SOURCES Bernhard Gillam, "Hopelessly Bound to the Stake" (political cartoon), *Puck* magazine, 1883 493

Organizing Unions 494

Labor Clashes Escalate 496

AP® ANALYZING SOURCES United States Supreme Court, *In re Debs*, 1895 499

AP® WRITING HISTORICALLY Short-Answer Question Practice 500

> **Source:** Friedrich Grätz, "The Tournament of To-Day — A Set-to Between Labor and Monopoly" (political cartoon), *Puck* magazine, 1883 500

Module 6-6

A New Wave of Immigrants 501

Immigrants Arrive from Many Lands 502

AP® ANALYZING SOURCES F. Victor Gillam, "The Immigrant. Is He an Acquisition or a Detriment?" (political cartoon), *Judge*, 1903 502

Creating Immigrant Communities 503

Hostility toward Recent Immigrants 505

AP® ANALYZING SOURCES Saum Song Bo, *A Chinese View of the Statue of Liberty*, 1885 & United States Supreme Court, *Yick Wo v. Hopkins*, 1886 505

AP® ANALYZING SOURCES Secret Oath of the American Protective League, 1893 507

AP® WRITING HISTORICALLY Responding to a Long-Essay Question 509

Module 6-7

Becoming an Urban Nation 511

The New Industrial City 512

Black Migration to Northern Cities 513

Cities Expand Upward and Outward 514

AP® ANALYZING SOURCES Intersection of State Street and Madison Street, Chicago (photograph), 1900 515

How the Other Half Lived 515

AP® ANALYZING SOURCES Jacob Riis, "'Knee Pants' at forty-five cents a dozen — A Ludlow Street Sweater's Shop" (photograph), *How the Other Half Lives*, 1890 516

Political Machines and City Bosses 517

AP® ANALYZING SOURCES Jane Addams, *Why the Ward Boss Rules*, 1898 518

Urban Reformers 519

AP® WRITING HISTORICALLY Document-Based Question Practice 520

> **Document 1** Charles Loring Brace, *The Dangerous Classes of New York and Twenty Years Among Them*, 1872 520
> **Document 2** James Bryce, *The American Commonwealth*, Vol. 1, 1888 520
> **Document 3** F. J. Kingsbury, "The Tendency of Men to Live in Cities," *Journal of Social Science*, No. 33, 1895 520
> **Document 4** George Waring, *Street-cleaning and the Disposal of a City's Wastes*, 1897 521
> **Document 5** Geo. P. Hall & Son, *Curve at the Brooklyn Terminal, New York & Brooklyn Bridge* (photograph), 1898 521
> **Document 6** Royal Melendy, *The Saloon in Chicago*, 1900 522
> **Document 7** Theodore Dreiser, *Sister Carrie*, 1900 522

Module 6-8

Society and Culture in the Gilded Age 524

Wealthy and Middle-Class Leisure Pursuits 524

Changing Gender Roles 525

AP® ANALYZING SOURCES *The Delineator*, a women's magazine (illustration), 1900 & Theodore Roosevelt, *Professionalism in Sports*, 1890 527

Working-Class Leisure in Industrial America 528

AP® WRITING HISTORICALLY Long-Essay Question Practice 530

Module 6-9

Gilded Age Ideologies 532

Doctrines of Success 532

Challenges to Laissez-Faire 534

AP® ANALYZING SOURCES Andrew Carnegie, *The Gospel of Wealth*, 1889 & "A Workingman's Prayer," *The Coming Nation*, 1894 534

AP® WRITING HISTORICALLY Short-Answer Question Practice 535

> **Source:** Thomas Nast, "Uncle Sam" (political cartoon), *The President's Message*, 1887 535

Module 6-10
Politics and Protest 537

Weak Presidencies and an Inefficient Congress 538

The Business of Politics 539

Farmers Unite 540

> AP® ANALYZING SOURCES Mary Elizabeth Lease, *Monopoly Is the Master*, 1890 541
>
> AP® ANALYZING SOURCES Bernhard Gillam, "Party of Patches: Grand Balloon Ascension — Cincinnati, May 20th, 1891" (political cartoon), *Judge*, 1891 543

Populists and Depression Politics 543

> AP® ANALYZING SOURCES John Altgeld, *Letter to George Pullman*, August 21, 1894 544

Political Realignment in the Election of 1896 545

Decline of the Populists 547

> AP® WRITING HISTORICALLY Short-Answer Question Practice 548
>
> **Source:** Richard Hofstadter, *The Age of Reform: From Bryan to F.D.R.*, 1955 548
> **Source:** Charles Postel, *The Populist Vision*, 2007 548

PERIOD 6 REVIEW 1865–1898 550

AP® EXAM PRACTICE Through 1898 551-a

PERIOD 7: 1890–1945
New Imperialism and Global Conflicts 552

Module 7-1
Progressivism and Social Reform 555

The Roots of Progressivism 556

> AP® ANALYZING SOURCES Lincoln Steffens, *The Shame of the Cities*, 1904 556

Female Progressives and the Poor 557

> AP® ANALYZING SOURCES United States Supreme Court, *Muller v. Oregon*, 1908 & Louisa Dana Haring, "Unjust to Working Woman," *Woman's Tribune*, 1908 558

Fighting for Women's Suffrage 559

> AP® ANALYZING SOURCES National American Woman Suffrage Association, "Where Women Vote — Wyoming," *Woman Suffrage: History, Arguments, Results*, 1917 561

Progressivism and the Fight for Racial Equality 562

> AP® ANALYZING SOURCES Booker T. Washington, *The Atlanta Exposition Address*, 1895 & Ida B. Wells, "The Negro Problem from the Negro Point of View," *World Today*, 1904 563

Morality, Prohibition, and Social Control 565

> AP® ANALYZING SOURCES Frances Willard, *Address before the Second Biennial Convention of the World's Woman's Christian Temperance Union*, 1893 566
>
> AP® ANALYZING SOURCES Margaret Sanger, *First Speech from a Debate On Birth Control*, 1920 568
>
> AP® WRITING HISTORICALLY Short-Answer Question Practice 569
>
> **Source:** C. Vann Woodward, *Origins of the New South, 1877–1913*, 1971 569
> **Source:** Glenda Elizabeth Gilmore, *Gender and Jim Crow: Women and the Politics of White Supremacy in North Carolina: 1896–1920*, 1996 569

Module 7-2
Progressive Political Reforms 570

New Immigrants and New Challenges 570

> AP® ANALYZING SOURCES "The Calamity," *New York Times*, 1911 572

Municipal and State Reform 572

Conservation and Preservation of the Environment 574

Theodore Roosevelt and the Square Deal 576

> AP® ANALYZING SOURCES Upton Sinclair, *The Jungle*, 1906 577

The Retreat from Progressivism 578

> AP® ANALYZING SOURCES Woodrow Wilson, *The New Freedom: A Call For the Emancipation of the Generous Energies of a People*, 1913 579

Woodrow Wilson and the New Freedom Agenda 580

The Progressive Legacy 582

> AP® WRITING HISTORICALLY Document-Based Question Practice 583
>
> **Document 1** Booker T. Washington, *The Atlanta Exposition Address*, 1895 583
> **Document 2** W. E. B. Du Bois, *The Talented Tenth*, 1903 583
> **Document 3** Ida B. Wells, "The Negro Problem from the Negro Point of View," *World Today*, 1904 583
> **Document 4** Committee on the Negro "Call" for a National Conference, *Founding Document of the National Association for the Advancement of Colored People (NAACP)*, 1909 584
> **Document 5** *The Crisis*, September 1912 584
> **Document 6** *Congressional Anti-Lynching Bill*, 1918 585
> **Document 7** NAACP, *The Shame of America* (full-page advertisement in the *New York Times*), 1922 585

Module 7-3

The Awakening of Imperialism 586

The Economics of Expansion 587

Cultural Justifications for Imperialism 587

> **AP® ANALYZING SOURCES** Rudyard Kipling, "The White Man's Burden" (poem), 1899 588

The War with Spain 589

> **AP® ANALYZING SOURCES** Assistant Secretary of State William Rufus Day, *Diplomatic Cable to Stewart L. Woodford* (U.S. Minister to Spain), 1898 590
>
> **AP® ANALYZING SOURCES** Albert Beveridge, *The March of the Flag*, 1898 592

The Philippine War 592

> **AP® ANALYZING SOURCES** President William McKinley, *Remarks to a Methodist Delegation*, 1899 593
>
> **AP® ANALYZING SOURCES** Platform of the American Anti-Imperialist League, *The Commons*, 1899 594

Extending U.S. Imperialism, 1899–1913 595

Opening the Door in China 596

> **AP® WRITING HISTORICALLY** Long-Essay Question Practice 597

Module 7-4

Foreign Policy and World War I 598

Wilson and American Foreign Policy, 1912–1917 598

Making the World Safe for Democracy 601

> **AP® ANALYZING SOURCES** Woodrow Wilson, *Remarks to the Senate*, 1917 601

Fighting the War at Home 603

> **AP® ANALYZING SOURCES** Eugene V. Debs, *Antiwar Speech in Canton, Ohio*, 1918 605

Waging Peace after World War I 606

> **AP® ANALYZING SOURCES** Woodrow Wilson, *Address at Pueblo, Colorado*, 1919 607
>
> **AP® WRITING HISTORICALLY** Short-Answer Question Practice 608
>
>> **Source:** Arthur S. Link, *Woodrow Wilson and the Progressive Era, 1910–1917*, 1963 608
>>
>> **Source:** John Whiteclay Chambers II, *The Tyranny of Change: America in the Progressive Era, 1890–1920*, 2000 609

Module 7-5

The Effects of World War I at Home 610

Postwar Social Turmoil 610

> **AP® ANALYZING SOURCES** A. Mitchell Palmer, "The Case against the Reds," *Forum*, 1920 611

Innovation and Consumerism 613

> **AP® ANALYZING SOURCES** *Model T Fords Coming Off the Assembly Line* (photograph), 1900 615

Urban Growth and Perilous Prosperity 617

> **AP® WRITING HISTORICALLY** Long-Essay Question Practice 619

Module 7-6

The Transitional 1920s 620

Culture Wars and Challenges to Social Conventions 621

> **AP® ANALYZING SOURCES** F. Scott Fitzgerald, *The Great Gatsby*, 1925 622

The Harlem Renaissance and Black Nationalism 623

> **AP® ANALYZING SOURCES** A. Philip Randolph and Chandler Owen, *The New Negro — What Is He?*, 1919 623
>
> **AP® ANALYZING SOURCES** Zora Neale Hurston, *How It Feels to Be Colored Me*, 1928 624
>
> **AP® ANALYZING SOURCES** Claude McKay, "If We Must Die" (poem), 1919 626

Prohibition, Fundamentalism, and Modern American Life 626

> **AP® ANALYZING SOURCES** Clarence Darrow and William Jennings Bryan, *Transcript from* The State of Tennessee v. John Thomas Scopes, 1925 627

Immigration Restriction 628

The Resurrection of the Ku Klux Klan 630

> **AP® ANALYZING SOURCES** Gerald W. Johnson, "The Ku Kluxer," *American Mercury*, 1924 **&** *Women of the Ku Klux Klan*, 1927 631

Politics and the Fading of Prosperity 632

> **AP® WRITING HISTORICALLY** Document-Based Question Practice 634
>
>> **Document 1** Marcus Garvey, *Address to the Second United Negro Improvement Association (UNIA) Convention*, 1921 634
>>
>> **Document 2** Sinclair Lewis, *Babbit*, 1922 634
>>
>> **Document 3** *Blood and Sand* (film advertisement), 1922 634
>>
>> **Document 4** *Edythe Turnham and Her Knights of Syncopation* (photograph), Seattle, Washington, 1925 635
>>
>> **Document 5** Clarence Darrow and William Jennings Bryan, *Transcript from* The State of Tennessee v. John Thomas Scopes Trial, 1925 635
>>
>> **Document 6** *Women of the Ku Klux Klan*, 1927 636
>>
>> **Document 7** *The Brox Sisters Listening to the Radio* (photograph), c. 1925 636

Module 7-7
Economic Instability and Depression   637

Financial Crash   637

Hoovervilles and Dust Storms   639
- **AP® ANALYZING SOURCES** Ann Marie Low, *Dust Bowl Diary*, 1934   640

Challenges for Minorities   640
- **AP® ANALYZING SOURCES** John Vachon, *Picket Line* (photograph), Chicago, 1941   641

Financial Strain and Organized Protest   643
- **AP® ANALYZING SOURCES** Mrs. W. T. Gammel, *Letter to Governor Harvey Parnell*, 1931   644
- **AP® WRITING HISTORICALLY** Long-Essay Question Practice   645

Module 7-8
The New Deal   646

Steps Toward Relief   646
- **AP® ANALYZING SOURCES** President Franklin Roosevelt, *Message to Congress on Making the Civilian Conservation Corps a Permanent Agency*, 1937   650

New Deal Critics   651
- **AP® ANALYZING SOURCES** Huey Long, *Every Man a King*, 1934   652

The New Deal Moves to the Left   653
- **AP® ANALYZING SOURCES** Charles Fusco, *Interview on the New Deal*, 1938   655

Organized Labor Strikes Back   656

A Half Deal for Minorities   657
- **AP® ANALYZING SOURCES** John P. Davis, "A Black Inventory of the New Deal," *The Crisis*, 1935   658

Decline of the New Deal   659
- **AP® ANALYZING SOURCES** Clifford K. Berryman, "Old Reliable" (political cartoon), 1938   660
- **AP® WRITING HISTORICALLY** Short-Answer Question Practice   660
  - **Source:** William E. Leuchtenburg, *Franklin D. Roosevelt and the New Deal, 1932–1940*, 1963   660
  - **Source:** Barton J. Bernstein, "The New Deal: The Conservative Achievements of Liberal Reform," *Towards a New Past: Dissenting Essays in American History*, 1969   661

Module 7-9
America Enters World War II   662

The Road toward War   662
- **AP® ANALYZING SOURCES** *Kellogg-Briand Pact*, 1928   663

The Challenge to Isolationism   664
- **AP® ANALYZING SOURCES** Charles Lindbergh, *Who Are the War Agitators?*, September, 1941   666

The United States Enters the War   666
- **AP® ANALYZING SOURCES** Monica Sone, *Memories of the Pearl Harbor Attack on December 7, 1941*, 1953   668
- **AP® WRITING HISTORICALLY** Short-Answer Question Practice   669
  - **Source:** Winsor McCay, *Let Sam Do It* (political cartoon), 1931   669

Module 7-10
Life on the Homefront   670

Managing the Home-Front Economy   670
- **AP® ANALYZING SOURCES** Carl Murphy, *An Open Letter Home*, 1943   672
- **AP® ANALYZING SOURCES** President Franklin Roosevelt, *State of the Union Address*, 1944   673

New Opportunities for Women   674
- **AP® ANALYZING SOURCES** Office of War Information, *Rosie the Riveter* (poster), 1943   675

Fighting for Equality at Home   675
- **AP® ANALYZING SOURCES** Lawrence E. Davies, "Zoot Suits Become Issue on Coast," *New York Times*, 1943   677

The Ordeal of Japanese Americans   678
- **AP® ANALYZING SOURCES** Russell Lee, *Japanese American Child on the Way to Internment* (photograph), 1942   678
- **AP® ANALYZING SOURCES** Charles Kikuchi, *Internment Diary*, 1942   680
- **AP® WRITING HISTORICALLY** Long-Essay Question Practice   680

Module 7-11
Victory in World War II   681

Global War Erupts   682

War in the Pacific   683

Contents

Ending the War 685

AP® ANALYZING SOURCES Father Johannes Siemes, *Eyewitness Account of the Hiroshima Bombing*, 1945 686

Evidence of the Holocaust 687

The Impact of World War II 689

AP® WRITING HISTORICALLY Short-Answer Question Practice 690

Source: David S. Wyman, *The Abandonment of the Jews: America and the Holocaust, 1941–1945*, 1984 690

Source: Richard Breitman and Allan J. Lichtman, *FDR and the Jews*, 2013 690

PERIOD 7 REVIEW 1890–1945 692

AP® EXAM PRACTICE Through 1945 695-a

PERIOD 8: 1945–1980

Cold War America 696

Module 8-1

The Early Cold War, 1945–1953 699

Mutual Misunderstandings 700

AP® ANALYZING SOURCES Henry Wallace, *The Way to Peace*, 1946 701

The Truman Doctrine, the Marshall Plan, and Economic Containment 702

Military Containment 703

The Korean War 706

AP® ANALYZING SOURCES John N. Wheeler, *Letter Home from Korean War*, 1950 707

AP® WRITING HISTORICALLY Short-Answer Question Practice 708

Source: William Appleman Williams, *The Tragedy of American Diplomacy*, 1959 708

Source: John Lewis Gaddis, *The United States and the Origins of the Cold War*, 1972 709

Module 8-2

The Second Red Scare 710

Loyalty and the Second Red Scare 710

AP® ANALYZING SOURCES Motion Picture Association of America, *Press Release*, December 3, 1947 711

AP® ANALYZING SOURCES Paul Robeson, *Statement on the Un-American Activities Committee*, 1949 712

McCarthyism 714

AP® WRITING HISTORICALLY Short-Answer Question Practice 715

Source: Herblock, "Fire" (political cartoon), *The Washington Post*, June 1949 715

Module 8-3

Peacetime Transition and the Boom Years 716

Economic and Political Challenges, 1945–1948 716

AP® ANALYZING SOURCES Representative Homer D. Angell, *Speech Supporting the Taft-Hartley Bill*, April 1947 718

The Boom Years 718

Changes in Living Patterns 720

AP® ANALYZING SOURCES *Restrictive Housing Covenant in King County, Washington*, April 1929 721

AP® WRITING HISTORICALLY Long-Essay Question Practice 721

Module 8-4

Cultural Shifts in 1950s America 722

The Rise of Television and a New Teenage Culture 722

AP® ANALYZING SOURCES Senate Subcommittee to Investigate Juvenile Delinquency, *Interim Report on Comic Books and Juvenile Delinquence*, 1955 724

Social Changes of the 1950s 725

AP® ANALYZING SOURCES Betty Friedan, *The Feminine Mystique*, 1963 726

AP® WRITING HISTORICALLY Long-Essay Question Practice 728

Module 8-5

Civil Rights in an Era of Conformity 729

The Rise of the Southern Civil Rights Movement 729

School Segregation and the Montgomery Bus Boycott 730

AP® ANALYZING SOURCES North Carolina State Legislature, *Jim Crow Public Transportation Laws in Effect in 1954* 731

Combatting White Resistance to Desegregation   733

AP® ANALYZING SOURCES *The Southern Manifesto*, 1956   733

AP® ANALYZING SOURCES Ella Baker, "Bigger Than a Hamburger," *Southern Patriot*, June 1960   735

The Civil Rights Movement and Minority Struggles in the West   736

AP® WRITING HISTORICALLY Short-Answer Question Practice   737

> **Source:** Jacquelyn Dowd Hall, "The Long Civil Rights Movement and the Political Uses of the Past," *Journal of American History*, 2005   737
>
> **Source:** Steven F. Lawson, "Long Origins of the Short Civil Rights Movement, 1954–1968," in *Freedom Rights: New Perspectives on the Civil Rights Movement*, 2011   738

Module 8-6

The Cold War Expands at Home and Abroad, 1953–1961   739

Nuclear Weapons and Containment   740

Interventions in the Middle East, Latin America, and Africa   741

AP® ANALYZING SOURCES President Dwight D. Eisenhower, *Farewell Address*, 1961   743

Modern Republicanism and the Election of 1960   743

Kennedy, the Cold War, and Cuba   745

AP® ANALYZING SOURCES President John F. Kennedy, *Address before the American Society of Newspaper Editors*, April 20, 1961   746

AP® WRITING HISTORICALLY Short-Answer Question Practice   747

> **Source:** Edward Valtman, "This hurts me more than it hurts you!" (political cartoon), *Hartford Times*, October 1962   747

Module 8-7

The Vietnam War   748

Early Intervention in Vietnam, 1954–1963   748

Johnson Escalates the War in Vietnam   749

AP® ANALYZING SOURCES *Gulf of Tonkin Resolution*, 1964   750

AP® ANALYZING SOURCES Philip Caputo, *A Rumor of War*, 1977   751

Nixon and the Failure of Vietnamization   752

AP® WRITING HISTORICALLY Short-Answer Question Practice   754

Module 8-8

The Fight for Civil Rights, 1961–1979   755

Freedom Rides   756

Kennedy Supports Civil Rights   756

AP® ANALYZING SOURCES Martin Luther King Jr., *Letter from Birmingham Jail*, April 1963   757

Freedom Summer and Voting Rights   758

AP® ANALYZING SOURCES *Prospectus for the Mississippi Freedom Summer*, 1964   759

From Civil Rights to Black Power   760

Racial Struggles Continue   761

AP® WRITING HISTORICALLY Document-Based Question Practice   763

> **Document 1** *Brown v. Board of Education of Topeka*, 1954   763
>
> **Document 2** Martin Luther King Jr., *Speech at Holt Street Baptist Church*, December 5, 1955   763
>
> **Document 3** *Sit-in at a Woolworth's Lunch Counter* (photograph), Jackson, Mississippi, May 28, 1963   764
>
> **Document 4** Malcom X, *Speech to Mississippi Youth*, December, 1964   764
>
> **Document 5** Huey Newton and Bobby Seale, *Black Panther Party Platform and Program*, October 1966   764
>
> **Document 6** *Chicago Student Non-Violent Coordinating Committee Leaflet*, 1967   765
>
> **Document 7** *Kerner Commission Report*, 1968   765

Module 8-9

Liberalism and Its Challengers, 1960–1973   766

Federal Efforts toward Social Reform, 1960–1968   767

AP® ANALYZING SOURCES Michael Harrington, *The Other America*, 1962   768

The New Left and the Counterculture   769

Liberation Movements   771

AP® ANALYZING SOURCES Dolores Huerta, *Statement before U.S. Senate Subcommittee on Migratory Labor*, 1969   773

The Revival of Conservatism   775

AP® WRITING HISTORICALLY Long-Essay Question Practice   776

Module 8-10

American Politics in Transition, 1968–1980   777

The Election of 1968   778

AP® ANALYZING SOURCES Richard M. Nixon, *Address Accepting the Presidential Nomination at the Republican National Convention*, August 8, 1968   778

Pragmatic Conservatism   779

The Cold War Thaws   780

The Nixon Landslide and Watergate Scandal, 1972–1974   781

Jimmy Carter and the Limits of Affluence   782

The Perils of Détente   784

AP® ANALYZING SOURCES Warren Christopher, *Presidential Review Memorandum on Human Rights*, May 20, 1977   785

Challenges in the Middle East   786

AP® WRITING HISTORICALLY Document-Based Question Practice   787

- **Document 1** "Vietnam: The Public's Need to Know," *The Washington Post*, June 17, 1971   787
- **Document 2** Anonymous, *Letter to Florida Governor Reubin Askew*, 1972   787
- **Document 3** *Confidence and Concern: Citizens View American Government*, 1973   788
- **Document 4** *Articles of Impeachment Adopted by the House of Representatives Committee on the Judiciary*, July 27, 1974   788
- **Document 5** President Carter, *Address to the Nation on Energy and National Goals* (also known as "The Malaise Speech"), July 15, 1979   789
- **Document 6** *U.S. Embassy Workers Being Held Hostage in Tehran, Iran* (photograph), November 4, 1979   789
- **Document 7** *United States Unemployment Rate and Inflation Rate (the "Misery Index")* (graph), 1970–1980   790

Module 8-11

The Persistence of Liberalism and the Rise of the New Right   791

The Women's Movement   792

AP® ANALYZING SOURCES Gloria Steinem, *Testimony before the Senate Judiciary Committee Hearing on the Equal Rights Amendment*, May 6, 1970 **&** *The Phyllis Schlafly Report 5, no. 7*, February 1972   792

Environmentalism   794

AP® ANALYZING SOURCES Michael McCloskey, *Ecotactics: The Sierra Club Handbook for Environmental Activists*, 1970   794

New Forms of Conservatism   795

AP® WRITING HISTORICALLY Short-Answer Question Practice   797

- **Source:** Dan T. Carter, *From George Wallace to Newt Gingrich: Race in the Conservative Counterrevolution, 1963–1994*, 1996   797
- **Source:** Daniel Williams, *God's Own Party: The Making of the Christian Right*, 2010   797

PERIOD 8 REVIEW 1945–1980   798

AP® EXAM PRACTICE Through 1980   801-a

PERIOD 9: 1980–THE PRESENT

Challenges in a Globalized World   802

Module 9-1

The Triumph of Conservatism   804

Reagan and Reaganomics   804

AP® ANALYZING SOURCES Reginald Stuart, "Michigan Requests Federal Loan to Bolster Unemployment Fund," *New York Times*, 1980   805

AP® ANALYZING SOURCES Presidential Campaign for Ronald Reagan, *Morning in America* (televised commercial), 1984   807

Social Conservatism   808

Reagan and the Cold War, 1981–1988   809

AP® ANALYZING SOURCES Ronald Reagan, *Tear Down This Wall* (speech at the Berlin Wall), 1987   810

Human Rights and the Fight against Communism   811

Fighting International Terrorism   812

AP® ANALYZING SOURCES Ronald Reagan, *Address to the Nation on the Iran Arms Contra Aid Controversy*, 1987   814

The Nuclear Freeze Movement   814

AP® ANALYZING SOURCES Ronald Reagan, *Address at the University of Virginia*, 1988   816

AP® WRITING HISTORICALLY Long-Essay Question Practice   816

Module 9-2

The End of the Cold War 817

"Kinder and Gentler" Conservatism 817

The Breakup of the Soviet Union 819

> AP® ANALYZING SOURCES Francis Fukuyama, *The End of History?*, 1989 819

Globalization and the New World Order 821

Managing Conflict after the Cold War 823

> AP® WRITING HISTORICALLY Short-Answer Question Practice 825
>
> | Source: Jeff Hook, *If at first . . .* (political cartoon), 1990 825

Module 9-3

Toward the Twenty-First Century 826

Clinton's Domestic and Economic Policy 827

> AP® ANALYZING SOURCES President Bill Clinton, *Address to Congress on Health Care Reform*, 1993 827

The Computer Revolution 829

The Changing American Population 830

> AP® ANALYZING SOURCES Jennifer Medina, "New Suburban Dream Born of Asia and Southern California," *New York Times*, 2013 831
>
> AP® WRITING HISTORICALLY Short-Answer Question Practice 832
>
> | Source: St. Louis Federal Reserve, *U.S. Productivity in the 1990s* (graph) 832

Module 9-4

The Global War on Terror and Political Conflict at Home 833

Bush and Compassionate Conservatism 834

> AP® ANALYZING SOURCES George W. Bush, *Presidential Nomination Acceptance Speech*, 2000 834
>
> AP® ANALYZING SOURCES Sanctuary Building of the First Baptist Church in Dallas, Texas, 2014 835

International and Domestic Challenges 836

> AP® ANALYZING SOURCES Office of the President, *Proposal to Create the Department of Homeland Security*, 2002 & President George W. Bush, *News Conference on Iraq*, 2003 837

The Great Recession 840

Obama and Domestic Politics 841

> AP® ANALYZING SOURCES President Barack Obama, *Address to Congress on Health Care*, 2009 842
>
> AP® ANALYZING SOURCES Frederick C. Harris, *The Price of the Ticket: Barack Obama and the Rise and Decline of Black Politics*, 2012 844

Obama and the World 844

> AP® ANALYZING SOURCES President Barack Obama, *Remarks by the President on the Middle East and North Africa*, 2011 846
>
> AP® ANALYZING SOURCES Edward Snowden, *Interview for The Guardian*, July 18, 2014 847

The 2016 Election 848

The Trump Presidency 849

> AP® ANALYZING SOURCES Sam Schlinkert, "Facebook Is Invading Your Phone," *Daily Beast*, 2013 850

A Century of Anxiety and Hope 851

> AP® WRITING HISTORICALLY Short-Answer Question Practice 852
>
> | Source: John D'Emilio and Estelle Freedman, *Intimate Matters: A History of Sexuality in America*, 1998 852
> | Source: Matthew D. Lassiter, *The Silent Majority: Suburban Politics in the Sunbelt South*, 2006 853

PERIOD 9 REVIEW 1980–the Present 854

AP® EXAM PRACTICE Through the Present 856-a

Practice AP® Exam PE-1

Glossary/Glosario GL-1

Credits C-1

Index I-1

About the Authors

Jason Stacy

JASON STACY is Professor of U.S. History and Social Science Pedagogy at Southern Illinois University Edwardsville. Before joining the history department at SIU-Edwardsville, Stacy taught AP® U.S. History for eight years at Adlai E. Stevenson High School in Lincolnshire, Illinois. Stacy has served as an AP® U.S. History Reader, Table Leader, Exam Leader, Consultant, Senior Auditor, and question author for the AP® U.S. History exam. Author and editor of multiple books on Walt Whitman, his research has appeared in *Social Education*, the *Walt Whitman Quarterly Review*, and *American Educational History*. Stacy is also a contributing editor for the *Walt Whitman Archive*, where he edits Whitman's journalism. In 2014, Stacy served as president of the Illinois Council for the Social Studies.

Matthew Ellington

MATTHEW ELLINGTON has taught AP® U.S. History at Ruben S. Ayala High School in Chino Hills, CA for the last twenty years, where he has also served as Instructional Coach, Induction Mentor for new teachers, and Social Science Department Chairperson. Ellington has been an active AP® U.S. History workshop consultant for the College Board since 2001 and has regularly participated in the AP® U.S. Reading since 2000. He has also served as a College Board AP® Mentor and as a member on the College Board's Consultant Advisory Panel. Ellington was a contributor to *America's History for the AP® Course,* Ninth Edition, co-author of *The Survival Guide for AP® U.S. History,* and featured in *Teaching Ideas for AP® History: A Video Resource.*

To Our Fellow Teachers

We created *Fabric of a Nation* to meet the needs of AP® U.S. History students in our classrooms and yours. As veteran AP® U.S. History teachers, exam readers, and workshop consultants, we have experienced firsthand the challenges in teaching this course, especially as the curriculum framework and preparation levels of our students have changed over the years.

Fabric of a Nation unites historical knowledge, thinking and reasoning skills, and scaffolded pedagogy to maximize student success in the class and on the AP® U.S. History exam. Unlike college textbooks that have been repackaged with some AP® add-ons, we wrote *Fabric of a Nation* specifically for AP® students. The narrative is shorter and the pedagogy focuses on essential content and skills appropriate for all high school AP® students.

Fabric of a Nation provides an accessible and brief historical narrative that brings the College Board's curriculum framework to life. It's tightly focused on the content of the course, grounded in modern scholarship, and written to meet the diverse backgrounds of today's AP® U.S. History students.

We've incorporated primary sources, representing a diverse range of voices and types of documents, seamlessly into the narrative, with analysis and comparison questions to broaden students' historical understanding and critical thinking skills.

Fabric of a Nation's nine periods are aligned with the College Board's nine units, with each divided into simple lesson modules that can be taught in one to two days, similar to the pacing found in the College Board's unit guides.

We've scaffolded the pedagogical instruction to provide students with step-by-step directions and practice for how to think historically, analyze documents, and write short-answer, document-based, and long-essay questions. Using sample responses, graphic organizers, and a graduated approach, each module builds and reinforces the knowledge and skills students need to understand history and be successful on the AP® Exam.

Finally, *Fabric of a Nation* also includes AP®-style practice questions at the end of every period, stimulus-based multiple-choice, short-answer, document-based, and long-essay questions, all created by experienced item writers to closely mimic the questions students will encounter on the exam.

Fabric of a Nation is the only textbook on the market made specifically for today's AP® U.S. History classroom by AP® U.S. History teachers. We're confident your students will benefit from it.

JASON STACY

MATTHEW ELLINGTON

Fabric of a Nation: What's Inside

A United Approach to AP® U.S. History

Weaving together content, skills, sources, and exam practice

In 2014, the College Board rolled out the new AP® U.S. History course, which centered less on memorizing content and more on developing skills. Since then, very little has changed in the world of AP® U.S. History textbooks — content is still king. Until now. *Fabric of a Nation* is the first book to truly embrace this dramatic shift in the AP® course and in how history is taught.

A Brief Book

You only have so much time in a school year. In order to focus on skills development, you need more *focused* content. *Fabric of a Nation* delivers a brief, approachable historical narrative that covers all of the essential content of the AP® course, with plenty of interesting anecdotes and a crisp writing style to keep students engaged.

Straightforward Modular Organization

Fabric of a Nation has an easy-to-use modular organization that pulls together content, sources, skills and AP® Exam practice into brief 1- to 2-day lessons. Modules help solve the problem of when to introduce which skills, how to blend sources with content, and how to pace the course throughout the year. Everything you and your students need is there.

Scaffolded Instructional Design

Inspired by the authors' classroom experience and sound pedagogical principles, the instruction in *Fabric of a Nation* scaffolds learning throughout the course of the book.

- Periods 1–3: Focused Instruction. The first three periods of the textbook provide step-by-step support as your students learn to think critically about historical developments and processes and put that thinking to work in their writing.

- Periods 4–6: Guided Practice. In the second portion of the book, the instruction moves to guided writing practice as students deepen their understanding and apply new writing skills.

- Period 7–9: Independent Practice. Finally, the book shifts to independent practice in the run-up to the exam. In this portion of the book, the features assess students' command of their newly developed skills, preparedness for the exam, and ability to produce college-level writing.

Module Introductions Guide Learning

Learning Targets

Reflecting the essential content of the AP® U.S. History curriculum framework, Learning Targets offer a preview of the historical developments covered in the module and set expectations for student skill development.

Thematic Focus

Each module has a special focus on at least one of the eight AP® U.S. History course themes, so you can be sure that your students develop an understanding of how the module content fits into the big picture of history.

Historical Reasoning Focus

Drawn from the historical reasoning processes and thinking skills outlined in the AP® U.S. History framework, these brief module introductions help students approach the module's narrative the way a historian would.

Module 2-1

European Challengers to Spanish North America

LEARNING TARGETS

By the end of this module, you should be able to:
- Explain the European and North American context that shaped colonization of North America between 1607 and 1754.
- Explain how European colonies developed in various ways between 1607 and 1754.
- Explain how relations between Europeans and American Indians changed between 1607 and 1754.

THEMATIC FOCUS

Migration and Settlement
America in the World

Throughout the seventeenth and early eighteenth centuries, the English, French, and Dutch established colonies that challenged Spanish control in North America.

HISTORICAL REASONING FOCUS

Comparison
Causation

As you learned in Module 1-1, historians think comparatively to identify, describe, and analyze the similarities and differences between two or more historical events, individuals, groups, regions, developments, or concepts. Considering how these different aspects of history relate to each other is a critical step toward gaining a fuller understanding of the past. While comparison is a fundamental historical reasoning tool, it's also important to remember that it is just one aspect of historical analysis. One way historians strengthen comparative understanding is by examining the causes of the historical developments they compare. This is because meaningful historical comparisons don't just record observations — they uncover reasons that help explain similarities and differences. Making this connection to underlying causes is an important part of historical analysis.

TASK ▶ As you read this module, think about the similarities and differences in the interactions between European colonizers and American Indians prior to 1754. Make sure that, wherever you make these comparisons, you also ask the important question of *why*. If you see a similarity between two European colonies, for instance, ask yourself what factors help explain it. If, let's say, you locate a difference between the lives of women in two European colonies, ask yourself what caused it.

Module Task

Designed to promote active reading and prompt critical thinking about key AP® U.S. History developments, each module-opening task frames how to apply the historical reasoning processes and thinking skills to the content.

Fabric of a Nation: What's Inside

Instructional Features Woven Throughout

Skill-building is best done in-context. That's why *Fabric of a Nation* weaves features throughout the text that help students engage with important historical developments and encounter relevant primary and secondary sources.

AP® Analyzing Sources

These boxes, placed at relevant points in the narrative, provide students with opportunities to analyze the sourcing, situation, and arguments of both written and visual primary sources.

AP® ANALYZING SOURCES

Source: Samuel de Champlain, *Voyages of Samuel de Champlain: 1567–1635*

"Near the spot which had thus been selected for a future settlement [in Quebec], Champlain discovered a deposit of excellent clay, and, by way of experiment, had a quantity of it manufactured into bricks, of which he made a wall on the brink of the river. . . . In the mean time, Champlain had been followed to his rendezvous by a herd of adventurers from the maritime towns of France, who, stimulated by the freedom of the trade, had flocked after him in numbers all out of proportion to the amount of furs which they could hope to obtain from the wandering bands of savages that might chance to visit the St. Lawrence [River]. The river was lined with . . . [Frenchmen] anxiously watching the coming of the savages, all impatient and eager to secure as large a share as possible of the uncertain and mea-

AP® ANALYZING SOURCES

Ashmolean Museum, University of Oxford, UK/Bridgeman Images

Source: Powhatan, Chief of Algonquian-speaking Powhatan Confederation, *Deerskin Cloak*, c. 1608

About the source: Chief Powhatan wore this deerskin cloak for tribal ceremonies. The objects in this cloak are made of shells, which were considered items of value by the Powhatan people. The circles could represent regions under Powhatan's control, the animals most likely represent deer, and the individual in the center represents Chief Powhatan.

Questions for Analysis

1. Describe the arrangement of the images and materials that make up this cloak.
2. Explain what the arrangement of the images and materials that make up this cloak reveals about the Powhatan and the Algonquian-speaking peoples.
3. Explain the role Powhatan politics played in fostering conflict with European colonists.

AP® THINKING HISTORICALLY — Connecting Distant Causes to Immediate Causes

So far, this module has explored how the English, from the time of Jamestown's founding in 1607, developed tobacco exporting colonies in present-day Maryland, Virginia, and North Carolina. These tobacco economies generated great wealth over the next century and a half. Here, we'll walk through how to organize your reflections on both the immediate and distant causes that allowed these tobacco economies to flourish in the seventeenth and early eighteenth centuries.

Step 1 List and categorize your historical knowledge.

A good place to start is by taking a few minutes to jot down all possible causes of the growth of tobacco economies in Virginia, Maryland, and North Carolina that you can think of. Remember to draw on your knowledge of Period 1 as well. A solid strategy to generate ideas is to ask yourself causation questions divided into some broad categories: politics, economy, society/culture, interactions with the environment, and technology.

Next, think about whether each of the causes you listed is more immediate or distant from its effect (in this case, the creation of wealthy tobacco economies in the Chesapeake and northern

Profit motives led to the tobacco economies in Virginia, Maryland, and North Carolina **[distant cause]**. These profit motives stemmed from the English monarchy's competition with Spain **[distant cause]**. Spain grew rich and powerful from American colonies, and the English crown sought similar gains by chartering the Virginia Company as a profit-seeking joint-stock corporation **[distant cause]**. John Rolfe's discovery that Caribbean tobacco grew well in the Chesapeake caused tobacco to become the primary cash crop in the Chesapeake **[immediate cause]**. Tobacco as a profitable crop resulted from Rolfe's discovery, but the English crown's long-standing goal of making colonies profitable in North America was also an important cause **[explanation of immediate and distant causes]**.

Notice these statements move from distant to immediate causes, starting with the English desire to find profit in North America as the Spanish had in Central and South America, moving to the specific source of English profit (tobacco), and ending with an explanation of the immediate and distant causes of the English tobacco economy in the seventeenth century.

Taking these steps to think about the forces behind immediate causes shaping developments will help you deepen your historical analysis. By showing causation as a chain of linked events, you gain practice in strategies for clarifying and supporting historical arguments.

ACTIVITY

Use the steps provided in this box to explain the immediate and distant environmental factors that led the English to adopt a cash crop system in Virginia by the mid-seventeenth century.

AP® Thinking Historically

These features appear at useful points in the narrative to help students develop the historical thinking skills and reasoning processes that are key to success in the AP® U.S. History course. They cover topics such as distinguishing between distant and immediate causes, using comparison and causation in arguments, and more. These mini-workshops build essential thinking skills that are the foundation of college-level historical writing.

Fabric of a Nation: What's Inside

AP® WRITING HISTORICALLY — Crafting a Thesis Statement Based on Continuity and Change

In Module 2-1, we discussed how to write an effective thesis statement based on the historical reasoning processes of comparison and causation. Here, we will show one way to approach answering an essay prompt that focuses on continuity and change.

Remember, historians draw conclusions about extended periods of time by examining the ways that some things stayed the same across a timespan even as other things changed. When you write any essay, you need to write a thesis statement that conveys a clear argument, followed by body paragraphs that interpret historical facts to prove the claims your thesis makes. Prompts that deal with continuity and change typically require you to focus on how much things changed or remained the same over the course of an era, or between two eras. In other words, how much change occurred? How much remained stable?

Step 1 Break down the prompt.

First, notice that this prompt asks you to explain the continuities and changes in New England colonial society between 1620 and 1700. This means that to answer it you must make an argument that addresses things that remained relatively the same during this period as well as things that changed. Your answer should explain *why* these continuities and changes took place.

Step 2 List and categorize your relevant historical knowledge.

Now, let's take a few moments to gather ideas for continuities and changes that you can use in your answer. We suggest creating a chart like the example provided here, which breaks the topic of the prompt down into at least three sub-topics to focus a historical argument. In this example, we've chosen sub-topics a little more specific than the ones we've used in previous AP® Writing Historically exercises (economics, politics, technology, etc.). Keep in mind that your sub-topics

New England colonial society in the period from 1620 to 1700 showed continuity in its ongoing conflicts with American Indians, which were caused by growth of the colonial population, but also experienced changes in the reasons for population growth — initially caused by those who dissented from Puritanism and left England and later caused by growth of the population through natural increase.

Notice that this thesis incorporates both the reasons for continuities *and* changes in New England between 1620 and 1700. It also includes a statement that alerts the reader to your "turn," where the thesis moves from continuities to changes: "but also experienced changes in the reasons for population growth" is the cue that we're changing directions.

ACTIVITY
Follow steps 1-3 to create your own thesis for the following essay prompt:

Explain the continuities and changes in social conflicts in New England between 1620 and 1700.

AP® Writing Historically

Appearing at the end of each module, these essential sections provide scaffolded, step-by-step instruction that walks students through how to approach each of the writing tasks on the AP® Exam: Short-Answer Questions, Long-Essay Questions, and Document-Based Questions.

An Emphasis on Visual Analysis

From stimulus-based multiple-choice questions to SAQs and DBQs, visual primary and secondary sources have become a major part of the AP® U.S. History Exam, and a major challenge for students. To support students and build visual analysis skills, *Fabric of a Nation* provides an analytical question with every image in the book, asking students to draw on their historical knowledge to analyze and respond.

◀ **Mrs. Elizabeth Freake and Baby Mary (1674)** This portrait shows Elizabeth Freake, the wife of merchant John Freake, and their eighth child, Mary. Here Elizabeth and her daughter capture Puritan simplicity in their white head coverings and aprons, but also display their family's wealth and John Freake's commercial ties through their silk gowns and embroidered cloth. **What does this painting reveal about Puritan values and society?**

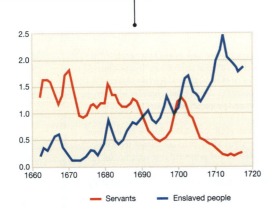

◀ **Indentured Servants and Enslaved People in Six Maryland Counties (1662–1717)** This chart illustrates a dramatic shift in the Chesapeake labor force between 1662 and 1717. Although based on a study of estate inventories from six Maryland counties, what does the trend shown here suggest about the nature and conditions of labor on Chesapeake farms?

XXXV

Integrated AP® Exam Practice

Fabric of a Nation gives students ample opportunity to practice their new AP® skills via AP® Exam Practice sections that appear at the end of every period and a full-length practice AP® Exam at the back of the book. In addition to the eighty AP® Thinking Historically and AP® Writing Historically activities, there are 195 Multiple-Choice Questions, 40 Short-Answer Questions, 9 Document-Based Questions, and 27 Long-Essay Questions in the AP® Exam Practice sections.

AP® EXAM PRACTICE THROUGH 1754

Multiple-Choice Questions

Choose the correct answer for each question.

Questions 1–2 refer to the following excerpt.

> **Source:** Bernal Díaz del Castillo, *The Conquest of New Spain*, 1632
>
> "I must now speak of the skilled workmen whom Montezuma employed in all the crafts they practiced, beginning with the jewelers and workers in silver and gold . . . which excited the admiration of our great silversmiths at home. . . . There were other skilled craftsmen who worked with precious stones . . . and very fine painters and carvers.
>
> But why waste so many words on the goods in their great market? If I describe everything in detail I shall never be done. . . . Having examined and considered all that we had seen, we turned back to the great market and the swarm of buying and selling. The mere murmur of their voices talking was loud enough to be heard more than three miles away. Some of our soldiers who had been in many parts of the world, in Constantinople, in Rome, and all over Italy, said that they had never seen a market so well laid out, so orderly, and so full of people."

1. The scene described in the excerpt is an example of which of the following developments in the 1600s?
   a. A debate among European religious and political leaders about how non-Europeans should be treated
   b. The Columbian Exchange facilitating the European shift from feudalism to capitalism
   c. The mutual misunderstandings between Europeans and Native Americans as each group sought to make sense of the other
   d. The development of a caste system by the Spanish that defined the status of the diverse population in their empire

2. The events described in the passage most directly foreshadowed which of the following developments?
   a. Spanish attempts to convert Native populations to Christianity
   b. Native peoples seeking to maintain their economic prosperity through diplomatic negotiations and military resistance
   c. The Europeans' and American Indians' adoptions of useful aspects of each other's culture
   d. Spanish efforts to extract wealth from the New World

Questions 3–5 refer to the following excerpt.

> **Source:** Nathaniel Bacon, *Declaration*, 1676
>
> "We cannot in our hearts find one single spot of Rebellion of Treason or that we have in any manner aimed at subverting the settled Government. . . . We appeal to the Country itself . . . of what nature their Oppressions have been . . . let us trace the men in Authority and Favor [here] . . . let us observe the sudden rise of their Estates composed with the Quality in which they first entered this country . . . let us [also] consider whether any Public work for our safety and defense or for the Advancement of and propagation of [our] trade . . . is here . . . in [any] way adequate to our vast charge. . . .
>
> Another main article of our guilt is our open and manifest aversion of all . . . Indians, this we are informed is a Rebellion . . . we do declare and can prove that they have been for these Many years enemies to the King and Country . . . but yet have by persons in authority [here] been defended and protected even against His Majesties loyal Subjects. . . .
>
> [M]ay all the world know that we do unanimously desire to represent our sad and heavy grievances to his most sacred Majesty . . . where we do well know that our Causes will be impartially heard and Equal justice administered to all men."

Fabric of a Nation: What's Inside

Unmatched Student and Instructor Support

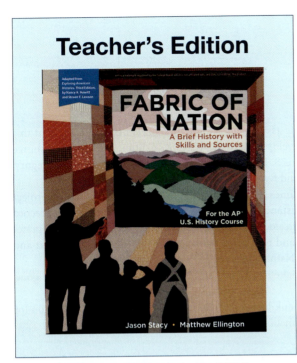

TEACHER'S EDITION ISBN: 978-1-319-18268-7

The wrap-around Teacher's Edition for *Fabric of a Nation* is an invaluable resource for both experienced and new AP® U.S. History instructors. Written by seasoned AP® instructors and workshop presenters, the Teacher's Edition includes thoughtful instruction for planning, pacing, differentiating, and enlivening your AP® U.S. History course in alignment with the College Board's requirements. The Teacher's Resource Materials accompany the Teacher's Edition and contain materials to effectively plan the course, including a detailed suggested pacing guide, handouts, lecture presentation slides, and lesson plans.

LaunchPad

Fabric of a Nation is available in our fully interactive LaunchPad digital platform. With LaunchPad, students can read, highlight, and take notes on any device, online or offline. You have the ability to assign every question from the book as well as supplemental quizzes and activities, and students' results automatically sync to your gradebook. LaunchPad also houses the Teacher's Resource Materials, test bank, adaptive quizzing, and more.

LearningCurve

LearningCurve, LaunchPad's adaptive quizzing engine, formatively assesses and improves students' command of the AP® U.S. History course content. Through their responses, the program determines any areas of weakness and offers additional questions and links to e-book content to strengthen understanding and build content mastery.

ExamView® Assessment Suite includes nine AP®-style practice exams (one per period) as well as a rich selection of comprehension questions on the historical narrative perfect for quizzes. The ExamView® Test Generator lets you quickly create paper, Internet, and LAN-based tests. Tests can be created in minutes, and the platform is fully customizable, allowing you to enter your own questions, edit existing questions, set time limits, and incorporate multimedia. To discourage plagiarism and cheating, the test bank can scramble answers and change the order of questions. Detailed results reports feed into a gradebook.

Acknowledgments

We are fortunate to have had the assistance of some incredible people throughout this project, especially with the development of the Teacher's Edition and teacher resource materials. Our thanks to AP® U.S. History teachers Carlene Baurichter, Jose Gregory, Nicki Griffin, Jon Kinman, Bill Polasky, and Kyle Vanderwall.

We especially would like to thank James Sabathne for his early contributions to this project and Shannan Mason for her research assistance and ability to turn around quality work in record time. We would also like to thank the dedicated team at Bedford, Freeman, & Worth. We are grateful for Carla Duval's attention to detail and to Caitlin Kaufman for her indefatigable spirit and exceptional editing skills. Thanks also to Nathan Odell, who first proposed this project to us.

Jason Stacy also wishes to thank Michelle, Abigail, and Margaret Stacy, who make all good things possible for him.

Matthew Ellington also wishes to thank Jacqueline, Audrey, Daniel, and David Ellington for their consistent love and encouragement in all life's adventures.

Reviewers of *Fabric of a Nation*

These reviewers participated in many ways in shaping the content of the textbook. They reviewed modules; gave advice on content, AP® course alignment, pedagogy, and more; and participated in an early survey about the book and the AP® course that it serves.

Carlene Baurichter, *Bangor High School, Wisconsin*

Becky Berry, *Morgantown High School, West Virginia*

Jose Gregory, *Marist School, Georgia*

Robin Grenz, *Hagerty High School, Florida*

Constance Hines, *Wiregrass Ranch High School, Florida*

Pete Joseph, *RHAM High School, Connecticut*

Jon Kinman, *Charlotte Mecklenburg Schools, North Carolina*

Steve Klawiter, *Lafayette High School, Missouri*

Joan O'Brien, *The MacDuffie School, Massachusetts*

Barbara Ramsey, *Asheville, North Carolina*

Rhonda Rush, *Homewood High School, Alabama*

Matt Tassinari, *Palmdale High School, California*

Bob Topping, *Palmetto Ridge High School, Florida*

Alan Vitale, *Northwest School of the Arts, North Carolina*

James Zucker, *Loyola High School, California*

We also thank the nearly 200 teachers of AP® U.S. History who participated in an initial survey to help the authors and editors to craft this textbook program for the AP® course.

Reviewers of *Exploring American Histories*

Fabric of a Nation was adapted from *Exploring American Histories*, Third Edition, and a number of instructors helped to guide its development. Over the years this book has had the privilege of being reviewed by hundreds of scholars. We appreciate the time and thoughts the following reviewers of *Exploring American Histories* put into their feedback for the third edition in particular, which helped authors Nancy A. Hewitt and Steven F. Lawson refine the textbook and ensure that the content is useful to both instructors and students.

Rob Alderson, *Perimeter College at Georgia State University*

Chad Gregory, *Tri-County Technical College*

Larry Grubbs, *Georgia State University*

Don Knox, *Wayland Baptist University*

Leslie Leighton, *Georgia State University*

Amani Marshall, *Georgia State University*

Ricky Moser, *Kilgore College*

David Soll, *University of Wisconsin, Eau Claire*

Ramon Veloso, *Palomar College*

Fabric of a Nation

A BRIEF HISTORY WITH SKILLS AND SOURCES

FOR THE AP® U.S. HISTORY COURSE

PERIOD 1: 1491–1607

Europeans Make Claims in the Americas

AP® Overview for Period 1

The dynamism of Period 1 is rooted in transformations that occurred in the Western Hemisphere and Eastern Hemisphere as a result of the convergence of societies after 1491. Yet this period also charges students with understanding American Indian societies prior to European contact. These distinct and vibrant communities were as complex as they were varied. The Columbian Exchange, Spanish colonization, the enslavement of American Indians and Africans, as well as the attendant results of these developments are key understandings for students to focus on. The biological, environmental, and political changes wrought by these processes are fundamental to students' ability to see the interconnected nature of historical inquiry.

Period 1 consists of four modules that contain abbreviated historical narratives and foundational skill development. Even though Period 1 accounts for no more than 6% of the material assessed on the AP® Exam, it contains crucial elements of historical knowledge needed to understand Period 2. Additionally, material from Period 1 can be included in both a Short-Answer Question (SAQ) and a Long-Essay Question (LEQ). Period 1 invites teachers to see the importance of the historical trends while introducing students to historical thinking skills.

Module 1-1: Diverse American Indian Societies focuses on the strength and cultural distinctiveness of American Indian societies prior to European contact. Comparison is a complimentary skill because of the variance among American Indian beliefs, systems, and traditions students will learn. Students and teachers should leverage the AP® theme geography and the environment to better understand the factors that shaped American Indian societies. The skill development and thematic focus situate students to experience success early in the year. Module 1 takes into account the foundational skills of note taking and primary source analysis and how concentrating on those can lead to positive ripple effects as the year progresses.

Module 1-2: Portugal and Spain Expand Their Reach highlights European exploration and colonization of the Americas. Students will learn about the intellectual, technological, and ideological rationale for European imperial powers settling in the New World. Moreover, these same factors are evaluated as Spain and Portugal looked to seize labor and resources in Africa. Students should think about the AP® theme America in the world and how a fledgling Atlantic world was emerging as a result of imperial conquest. To glean this historical development is to comprehend the gravity of an interconnected Atlantic world and the subsequent colonization among other European powers in years to come. Naturally, the reasoning process of causation is used to help students make meaning of colonization.

Module 1-3: The Columbian Exchange discusses complex transformations that impacted the development of the Atlantic world. This biological and economic exchange would devastate indigenous persons in the New World while enriching and expanding populations in the Old World. Students should find a natural connection to the focus on the AP® theme geography and the environment, as well as the historical thinking skill causation. Even though many students will focus on the interactions among American Indian tribes and European explorers and colonists, including the decimation of American Indian tribes by war and disease, they should not lose sight of the forays into Africa by European powers. This should be emphasized because understanding this development will help students explain the emergence of the Atlantic world. The scaffolded approach of the Short-Answer Question at the conclusion of this module complements the abbreviated historical narrative presented in this module.

Module 1-4: Spanish Colonial Society focuses on the religious motivations of the Spanish and how the Spanish attempted to conquer the Americas and alter the social structures of American Indian societies. The focus on continuities and changes over time will help students categorize the labor and religious policies that accompany Spanish colonization. For as colonization continued, the Spanish reaped economic profit at the expense of indigenous persons and the forced migration of African laborers. The Spanish established colonies in the Americas, grew wealthy, and developed a caste system that strictly defined classes in Spanish society, placing American Indians and Africans at the bottom of the hierarchy. This module builds off the previous module by again focusing on students' ability to answer a Short-Answer Question.

Pacing Guide
Course Pacing for Period 1

Module #	Lesson Title	Instructional Period*	AP® Theme	AP® Topic	AP® Reasoning Process/Skill	Homework
1-1	N/A	N/A	Geography and the Environment	1.1	Comparison / Historical Thinking Skills 1, 2, 3, 4, 5	**Reading and Source Analysis:** 1-1
	Diverse American Indian Societies	1	Geography and the Environment	1.2	Comparison / Historical Thinking Skills 1, 2, 3, 5	**Activities:** AP® Thinking Historically: Active Reading and Effective Note Taking AP® Thinking Historically: Analyzing Sources
	Workshops: AP® Thinking Historically: Active Reading and Effective Note Taking AP® Thinking Historically: Analyzing Sources	1	Geography and the Environment	1.2	Comparison / Historical Thinking Skills 1, 2, 3, 5	**Activities:** AP® Thinking Historically: Applying Comparison AP® Writing Historically: Breaking Down Short-Answer Question Prompts
	Workshops: AP® Thinking Historically: Applying Comparison AP® Writing Historically: Breaking Down Short-Answer Question Prompts	1	Geography and the Environment	1.2	Comparison / Historical Thinking Skills 1, 5	**Reading and Source Analysis:** 1-2
1-2	Portugal and Spain Expand Their Reach	1	America in the World	1.3	Causation / Historical Thinking Skills 1, 2, 3, 5	**Activity:** AP® Writing Historically: Responding to a Short-Answer Question Using ACE
	Workshop: AP® Writing Historically: Responding to a Short-Answer Question Using ACE	1	America in the World	1.3	Causation / Historical Thinking Skills 1, 2, 3	**Reading and Source Analysis:** 1-3 **Activity:** AP® Writing Historically: Using Categories to Respond to a Short-Answer Question
1-3	The Columbian Exchange **Review:** AP® Writing Historically: Using Categories to Respond to a Short-Answer Question	1	Geography and the Environment	1.4 1.6	Causation / Historical Thinking Skills 1, 2, 3, 5	**Reading and Source Analysis:** 1-4 **Activity:** AP® Writing Historically: Responding to a Short-Answer Question
1-4	Spanish and Colonial Society **Review:** AP® Writing Historically: Responding to a Short-Answer Question	1	Social Structures	1.5	Continuity and Change / Historical Thinking Skills 1, 2, 3, 5	Prepare for Assessment
Formative Assessment	AP® Exam Practice Through 1607 • 18 MCQs • 4 SAQs	0-1	All AP® U.S. History Course Themes	1.7 Personal Progress Check • 15 MCQs • 2 SAQs • 1 LEQ	All AP® History Reasoning Processes/ Skills	
Summative Assessment	Unit 1 Test Bank • 55 MCQs • 4 SAQs • 1 DBQ • 4 LEQs	0-1	All AP® U.S. History Course Themes		All AP® History Reasoning Processes/ Skills	
Assessment		1		1.7		

*Based on a standard 50-minute class period.

PERIOD 1 Europeans Make Claims in the Americas

Period 1 Resources

The following resources can be found in the Resources section of the book's digital platform, by clicking on the link buttons in the Teacher's Edition e-book, or by opening the Teacher's Resource Materials.

- **TRM** Period 1 Overview Video
- **TRM** AP® Concepts and Skills Video
- **TRM** Period 1 Lecture Presentation Slides
- **TRM** Period 1 Workshop Rubrics
- **TRM** Period 1 Suggested Responses to Questions
- **TRM** Period 1 Guided Reading Worksheets

Module 1-1

- **TRM** Handout 1.1 – I-D-E-A
- **TRM** Module 1.1 AP® Thinking Historically Handout 1
- **TRM** Handout 1.2 – Comparing Pre-Columbian Civilization
- **TRM** Map 1A – The Americas
- **TRM** Handout 1.3 – HIPP Template
- **TRM** Module 1.1 AP® Thinking Historically Handout 2
- **TRM** Module 1.1 AP® Analyzing Sources Handout
- **TRM** Handout 1.4 – Comparing Northern Native Civilizations
- **TRM** Map 1B – North America
- **TRM** Module 1.1 AP® Thinking Historically Handout 3

Module 1-2

- **TRM** Map 1C – The World
- **TRM** Handout 1.5 – Comparing Spanish and Portuguese Exploration

Module 1-3

- **TRM** Handout 1.6 – Feudalism vs. Capitalism
- **TRM** Module 1.3 AP® Analyzing Sources Handout
- **TRM** Map 1D – Africa

Module 1-4

- **TRM** Module 1.4 AP® Analyzing Sources Handout 1
- **TRM** Module 1.4 AP® Analyzing Sources Handout 2
- **TRM** Handout 1.7 – Causes and Effects of Spanish Exploration

Period 1 Essential Activity

In many ways, the history of the Atlantic world from 1491 to 1607 is defined by the Columbian Exchange. The societal upheavals caused by this event can be understood by comparing life in Europe and the Americas before and after the Columbian Exchange. Historians often refer to transformational events such as this as turning points. The following activity helps students imagine how contact between European colonizers and American Indians transformed both societies. One way you can prepare students for success is to remind them that American Indian societies prior to European contact were not inert populations; instead, they were dynamic societies marked by a wide variance in lifestyles.

Divide the class into groups of three or four students. Next, have students create a T-chart marked with the columns "Before" and "After," in reference to the Columbian Exchange. In the "Before" column, have students describe the lifestyles, worldviews, or views of the environment for American Indians and the Europeans before contact. To distill students' focus, consider having them select three-to-four distinct American Indian tribes in different regions of North and South America. Likewise, have students concentrate on either Spain or Portugal when thinking about European nations prior to contact. In the "After" column, have students describe a change to the entry they wrote in the "Before" column. One outcome will be for students to use the Columbian Exchange as a turning point in history. A related outcome will be for students to work on the skill of selecting and explaining historical evidence.

Period 1 Alignment to the Fall 2019 AP® United States History Course Framework*

Relationship to College Board Units
Period 1 in this book covers Topics 1.1–1.4 in Unit 1 of the College Board course framework. Students will be ready to take the Personal Progress Check for Unit 1 once they have completed this period.

Course Themes
Period 1 develops these course themes outlined in the course framework:

- **Geography and the Environment (GEO):** Geographic and environmental factors shaped the development of Native American societies, fostering diversity while the Columbian Exchange of crops, animals, diseases, and more between Old World and New World fundamentally altered both Native American and European societies.
- **America in the World (WOR):** Relying on technological innovations and driven by a desire for trade and economic competition, European countries began to fund voyages of exploration and conquest opening a New World for Europeans. Interactions between Columbus and Native American societies in the Caribbean established patterns for future relations.
- **Social Structures (SOC):** Spanish conquistadors used local allies and technological superiority to overpower the Aztecs and other powerful American Indian societies in Central and South America. As Spain built a large empire in the New World, it relied on the *encomienda* system to force American Indians to labor on Spanish plantations and introduced a caste system, which crated a social hierarchy based on race.

Course Skills
Period 1 helps students to develop the following AP® Historical Thinking Skills identified in the course framework.

- **Skill 1: Developments and Processes** (Modules 1-1, 1-2, 1-3, 1-4)
- **Skill 2: Sourcing and Situation** (Modules 1-1, 1-2, 1-3, 1-4)
- **Skill 3: Claims and Evidence in Sources** (Modules 1-1, 1-2, 1-3, 1-4)
- **Skill 4: Contextualization** (Module 1-1)
- **Skill 5: Making Connections** (Modules 1-1, 1-2, 1-3, 1-4)

Period 1 helps students to develop the following AP® History Reasoning Processes identified in the course framework.

- **Reasoning Process 1: Comparison** (Module 1-1)
- **Reasoning Process 2: Causation** (Modules 1-2, 1-3)
- **Reasoning Process 3: Continuity and Change** (Module 1-4)

Learning Objectives and Historical Developments

Module	AP® Topics	Learning Objectives	Historical Developments and Key Concepts
1-1	1.1, 1.2	Unit 1: Learning Objective A Unit 1: Learning Objective B	KC-1.1.I.A, KC-1.1.I.B, KC-1.1.I.C, KC-1.1.I.D
1-2	1.3	Unit 1: Learning Objective C	KC-1.2.I.A
1-3	1.4, 1.6	Unit 1: Learning Objective D Unit 1: Learning Objective F	KC-1.2.I.B, KC-1.2.I.C, KC-1.2.II.A, KC-1.2.III.A, KC-1.2.III.B, KC-1.2.III.C
1-4	1.5	Unit 2: Learning Objective E	KC-1.2.II.B, KC-1.2.II.C, KC-1.2.II.D

TRM A detailed alignment that can be sorted by Course Framework Unit, Topic, Learning Objective, Historical Development/Key Concept, or textbook period, is available in the Teacher's Resource Materials and via the book's online platform.

*Should changes be made to the Course Framework in the future, an updated alignment will be placed on our catalog page at bfwpub.com/fabric1e.

TEACHING IDEA

AP® Central

A great resource to help you teach this period is to read the information in the AP® U.S. History study guide for 1491–1607, available from the AP® United States History Classroom Resources section of AP® Central (apcentral.collegeboard.org).

PERIOD 1: 1491–1607

Europeans Make Claims in the Americas

▲
The Codex Mendoza, c. 1540 These images are taken from the *Codex Mendoza*, a collection of histories of American Indian leaders in Central America and a catalog of tribute they paid to the Spanish Crown. The illustrations shown here are of ceremonial outfits and shields acquired by the Spanish as tribute.

PERIOD 1

Over 25,000 years ago, Asian peoples started migrating to the Americas by land and sea. Major migrations occurred 12,000–14,000 years ago. Over time these peoples developed an astonishing array of cultures and societies, from small hunting-and-gathering bands to complex empires. By the fourteenth and fifteenth centuries of the common era, extensive commercial and political networks existed among the Mississippians, the Aztecs, and the Incas, although only the latter two continued to thrive by the late 1400s.

In southern Europe, too, during the fifteenth century, economic, cultural, and political advances fueled interest in long-distance trade and exploration. Italy and Portugal led these efforts, and their complete control of trade routes across the Mediterranean and around Africa to Asia led Spain to look west in hopes of gaining access to China and the Indies. In doing so, the Spanish unexpectedly came into contact with the Americas.

When Spanish explorers happened upon Caribbean islands and the nearby mainland, they created contacts between European and American populations whose lives would be dramatically transformed in a matter of decades. While native residents of the Americas were sometimes eager to trade with the newcomers and to form alliances against their traditional enemies, they fought against those they considered invaders. Yet some of the most significant invaders — plants, pigs, and especially germs — were impossible to defend against. Even Europeans whose primary goal was conversion to Christianity brought diseases that devastated local populations, and plants and animals that transformed their landscape, diet, and traditional ways of life.

From the 1490s to the 1590s, the most dramatic and devastating changes for native peoples occurred in Mexico, the West Indies, Central America, and parts of South America. But events there also foreshadowed what would happen throughout the Americas. As Spanish conquistadors and European competitors explored, they carried sufficient germs, seeds, and animals to transform native societies even before Europeans established permanent settlements in North America. As American Indian populations died out in some regions and fended off conquest in others, the Spanish and Portuguese turned increasingly to the trade in enslaved Africans to provide the labor to produce enormously profitable items like sugar, coffee, and tobacco.

PERIOD 1 PREVIEW

Module	AP® Thematic Focus
1-1: Diverse American Indian Societies	**Geography and the Environment** Geographic and environmental factors shaped the development of American Indian societies, fostering diversity. The implementation of intensive agriculture and the cultivation of crops such as maize led to the formation of large and complex American Indian societies in Central America and the Andes Mountain region. Societies in other regions were often smaller, resulting in a diverse fabric of indigenous cultures.
1-2: Portugal and Spain Expand Their Reach	**America in the World** Relying on technological innovations and driven by a desire for trade and economic competition, European countries began to fund voyages of exploration and conquest. Portugal secured trading posts in Africa as well as profitable ocean trade routes to the Middle East and Asia. Spain financed Christopher Columbus's voyages to the Americas, opening the door to a New World for Europeans. Interactions between Columbus and American Indian societies in the Caribbean established patterns for future relations.
1-3: The Colombian Exchange	**Geography and the Environment** The Columbian Exchange — of crops, animals, diseases, and more — shaped the development of both American Indian and European societies. Crops transplanted from the Americas led to the growth of Europe's population, and the mineral wealth from the New World contributed to the transition from feudalism to capitalism in Europe. Yet for indigenous peoples in the Americas, the primary effect of the Columbian Exchange was the introduction of European diseases, which decimated the native population. The creation of an "Atlantic World" linking Europe, the Americas, and Africa in an economic system that relied on the forced labor of American Indians and Africans also sped up as Britain, France, and the Netherlands began to colonize.
1-4: Spanish Colonial Society	**Social Structures** Spanish conquistadors used local allies and technological superiority to overpower the Aztecs and other powerful American Indian societies in Central and South America. As Spain built a large empire in the New World, it relied on the *encomienda* system to force American Indians to labor on Spanish plantations and introduced a caste system, which created a social hierarchy based on race. Over time, the harsh treatment of American Indians fostered debate within Spanish society and contributed to establishment of the mission system.

TEACHING IDEA

AP® Central

Read the information on the 2008 Curriculum Module of "White-Native American Contact in Early American History," available from the AP® United States History Classroom Resources section of AP® Central (apcentral.collegeboard.org).

PERIOD 1 Europeans Make Claims in the Americas

TRM Suggested Responses to Questions

TEACHING IDEA

Bell Ringer

Write the following questions on the board:
1. Why start Period 1 with the year 1491?
2. How does this impact the narrative of the module?

Then ask students to write down their answers and have them share responses after a couple of minutes. Discuss their answers and emphasize that 1491 represents the year before Christopher Columbus's arrival in the New World. Hence, this first module focuses on the diverse American Indian societies before the arrival of Europeans. Also point out the end-point for this period, 1607, which represents the founding of the first permanent English colony in what would become the United States — Jamestown, Virginia.

BUILDING AP® SKILLS

Developments and Processes

Constructed response questions on the AP® exam use certain "task verbs," such as *describe*, *explain*, and *analyze*. You might point out to students that they will see these tasks frequently as they progress through the course. The acronym I-D-E-A is a great way to introduce these concepts to students and then help them create "student-friendly" definitions of these verbs.

TRM Find **Handout 1.1 – I-D-E-A** in the Teacher's Resource Materials.

Module 1-1

Diverse American Indian Societies

LEARNING TARGETS
By the end of this module, you should be able to:
- Describe the diverse societies that populated the Americas prior to European exploration.
- Explain causes of internal migration and patterns of settlement in the Western Hemisphere before 1600.
- Explain how geographic and environmental factors, as well as competition over natural resources, shaped American Indian communities prior to 1600.

THEMATIC FOCUS
Geography and the Environment

Geographic and environmental factors shaped the development of American Indian societies, fostering diversity. The implementation of intensive agriculture and the cultivation of crops such as maize led to the formation of large and complex American Indian societies in Central America and the Andes Mountain region. Societies in other regions were often smaller, resulting in a diverse fabric of indigenous cultures.

HISTORICAL REASONING FOCUS
Comparison

In everyday life, we often compare two or more things to understand each one better. For example, if you want to understand the weather today, it often helps to compare it to yesterday's weather. Likewise, if you want to understand what everyday life is like for people in rural communities, it's helpful to have a sense of what daily life is like for the average city dweller. Historians apply this same principle to their work, too: They use comparison to illuminate the similarities and differences between two or more historical events, individuals, groups, regions, developments, or concepts.

TASK ▶ As you read this module, practice thinking comparatively about the relationships between and among the peoples, events, and concepts you encounter. Keep in mind that historical comparison is most effective when it takes into account both similarities *and* differences between two or more things. Your goal for this module is to consider things in relation to each other. As you read, keep track of what important aspects they share in common as well as where they diverge.

The first people in the Americas almost certainly arrived as migrants from northeast Asia. Although the timing of these migrations remains in doubt, they likely began at least 25,000 years ago. It is also difficult to estimate the population of the Americas before contact with Europeans — estimates of its peak range from 37 million to 100 million, the vast majority of whom lived within a few hundred miles of the equator. Only around 4 to 7 million people lived in what would become the present-day United States. By the fifteenth century, like other regions of the world, the Americas were home to diverse societies, ranging from coastal fishing villages to nomadic hunter-gatherers to settled horticulturalists to large city-centered empires.

The complex societies that emerged in the Americas were made possible by an agricultural revolution that began about 10,000 years ago when these societies established crop systems, domesticated animals, and developed tools. Between 8000 and 2000 B.C.E., some communities in the Americas established agricultural systems that encouraged more stable settlements and spurred population growth. **Horticulture** — a form of agriculture in which people work small plots of land with simple tools — became highly developed in the area of present-day Mexico. There, men and women developed improved strains of maize (corn). They also cultivated protein-rich beans,

horticulture A form of agriculture in which people work small plots of land with simple tools.

4

BUILDING AP® SKILLS

Comparison

Since the historical reasoning focus of this module is comparison, you may want to take a moment to make sure students understand what that is. One way to do this is to work on a definition for this term together as a class. For guidance, refer to the College Board's Course and Exam Description ("CED"), which defines these terms, to ensure appropriate alignment. First, have students brainstorm what comes to mind when they consider what "comparison" means. Second, they should check with a dictionary to inform what their definition should be for this reasoning process. Lastly, write or display on the board how the CED defines comparison so that the class can work on creating a final definition that is aligned with that of the College Board.

Diverse American Indian Societies

Period 1: 1491–1607

MAP 1.1 The Settling of the Americas Beginning about 25,000 B.C.E., Asian peoples likely migrated to America across a land bridge after expanding glaciers lowered sea levels. Others probably followed the coastline in boats. As the glaciers retreated, ice-free corridors allowed migration into present-day Wisconsin, New Mexico, Florida, Central America, and Chile. **In what ways did climate shape early native migrations?**

squash, tomatoes, potatoes, and manioc (a root vegetable) — this combination of crops not only offered an especially nutritious diet but also kept the soil fertile. Moreover, high yields produced surplus food that was stored or traded to neighboring communities.

By 500 C.E., complex societies rooted in intensive agriculture began to thrive in the equatorial region, and by 1500 C.E. the spread of maize cultivation northward into the present-day American Southwest and beyond fostered economic developments that necessitated irrigation and led to the diversification of native societies. While these impressive civilizations arose on swamplands, grasslands, and in the mountains, small bands of hunters and gatherers also continued to thrive in deserts and forests.

> **AP® TIP**
> Explain the impact of maize cultivation on various native peoples from South America, Central America, and North America.

TEACHING IDEA
Analyzing Art and Images

Visual literacy is important on the AP® exam. This is the case because the multiple-choice questions and document-based questions always contain some type of visual, including maps, political cartoons, quantitative data (i.e., graphs and charts), and photographs. Spend some time with students discussing what else besides climate may account for the migration routes identified on Map 1.1. Possible answers students may share or you may want to point out include: *natural resources and physical features of the regions.*

TEACHING IDEA
Incorporating Websites

Visit the Smithsonian's National Museum of the American Indian website to view exhibitions and collections, and to conduct research on pre-Columbian civilizations (americanindian.si.edu). This site also contains film and media and a section for educators that can provide visuals for concepts covered in the classroom. Specifically, check out the digitized collections found by visiting the gallery home page and locating the Native American and Indigenous History and Culture link (collections.si.edu/search/gallery.htm). You may browse by topic and/or images.

EXPLORING AP® THEMES
Geography and the Environment

Students tend to develop a better understanding of history if they see why it may be relevant and significant to their lives. Since this module focuses on geography and the environment, have them briefly discuss how the natural and man-made environments where they live and where their school is located have shaped their development. Doing so will help students see how this may also be true for the various American Indian tribes, hence resulting in diverse societies.

TRM Suggested Responses to Questions

TRM Module 1.1 AP® Thinking Historically Handout 1

TEACHING IDEA

Active Reading Strategies

Reading comprehension is an essential skill for students to perform well on the AP® exam. Consequently, you may want them to use strategies to be "active" readers and take effective notes that demonstrate understanding of the material. In addition to the activity outlined on this page, you can have students explore one or more of the following approaches to active reading:

- **Dual-column notes:** Students take dual-column notes after dividing their notebook paper in half. On the left, they write their notes as they read. Then, on the right, they supplement material as presented in class. Doing so will give students a more comprehensive understanding of the content.

- **Visuals:** Students create images of the most important content found in what they are reading (i.e., plants, pigs, and germs from the excerpt on this page). Students could either draw these in the margins of their notes or use index cards to turn them into visual memory clues. For those who may prefer, they can find and print images from the Internet.

Period 1: 1491–1607

MODULE 1-1 Diverse American Indian Societies

AP® THINKING HISTORICALLY — Active Reading and Effective Note Taking

In order to fully understand, analyze, and interpret history — including everything from historical documents and artifacts to retellings of events to definitions of key historical concepts — it is essential to read actively. Although this may sound difficult and time-consuming, all that's required for active reading is to think about the meaning of what you read while you read it. Sometimes, we are able to allow a piece of writing, usually fiction, to carry us away, and it's even possible to forget that you are reading at all. As the words fill your imagination, it can feel a bit like you are watching a movie or television show. Unlike fiction, history requires that you think about the text as you read it and write down your observations.

If it is possible to do so, writing annotations in the margins of the text is a fast and efficient form of active reading. If you cannot write in your text, using sticky notes, writing in a notebook, or recording your notes on a digital device will also work.

The following steps walk through one way to approach active reading.

Step 1 Select a manageable section to read, and focus on interpreting it quickly.

Usually, a manageable amount is roughly a paragraph. Let's break down one of the paragraphs you already read, in the introduction to Period 1, and see how you might take notes on it:

> When Spanish explorers happened upon Caribbean islands and the nearby mainland, they created contacts between European and American populations whose lives would be dramatically transformed in a matter of decades. While native residents of the Americas were sometimes eager to trade with the newcomers and to form alliances against their traditional enemies, they fought against those they considered invaders. Yet some of the most significant invaders — plants, pigs, and especially germs — were impossible to defend against. Even Europeans whose primary goal was conversion to Christianity brought diseases that devastated local populations, and plants and animals that transformed their landscape, diet, and traditional ways of life.

Step 2 Decide which aspects of the section are important to remember, and write down the relevant information in your own words.

Usually a paragraph presents a claim the author is trying to prove by using evidence to support it. Both the central claim and the evidence are important to remember.

Let's take another look at the first sentence in step 1. Notice how it establishes a moment in time with the word "when." While the sentence doesn't pinpoint a specific date, the word "when" tells you that this is an event in which the subject of the sentence (in this case, the "Spanish") does something of historical significance ("created contacts between Europeans and American populations"). Once you've worked this out, it's time to write your brief version of it in a note — as an annotation in the margins next to the text source, on a sticky note placed over the paragraph, or in a notebook. If you take notes in the form of an outline, this sentence would be a bullet point under which the rest of the paragraph would appear as sub-categories. It may help to think of each of these sub-categories as evidence that helps establish the historical significance of the paragraph's topic.

Now, let's take a closer look at the next sentence in the paragraph. This sentence tells you something about the "contacts" of the first sentence. The fact that this sentence begins with "while" signals that it establishes a contrast. When you see the word "while" at the beginning of a sentence, be prepared for it to "turn," usually after a comma, and present a concept that contrasts with the first half of the sentence. In this case, the contrast is between the eagerness of the "residents of the Americas" to "trade" and "form alliances against . . . enemies" and their resistance to "those they considered invaders." So, in this subcategory, the contacts between the Spanish and the people of the Caribbean islands were complex, involving both an eagerness to trade or form alliances and a willingness to resist perceived invaders.

Finally, let's turn to the last two sentences in the paragraph. The word "yet" in this context tells you that even though the previous sentence was true, there are other important factors that haven't been discussed. In this case, these factors are the "most significant invaders" — unexpected ones like plants, pigs, and germs — that ultimately "transformed" life in the Caribbean islands. If you were taking notes on this sentence, these should also be a sub-category to "invaders," since they are examples of specific kinds of invaders brought about by this contact.

TEACHING IDEA

AP® Thinking Historically Workshop

Because students will take notes for the entire academic year in AP® U.S. History, it is essential to give students a framework that is manageable and renewable. The following activity seeks to build off the skills and strategies on active reading and note taking. Start by handing out note cards with the following labels: Europeans Make Claims in the Americas; Diverse American Indian Societies; The Aztecs, the Maya, and the Incas; and Native Cultures to the North. Each of these are a heading or subheading in the module.

Pass out two additional blank note cards. Ask students the following questions:

1. What is the purpose of module headings and subheadings?
2. How might you use those to help you frame your notes?
3. What are some other ways to frame your notes, aside from headings and subheadings?

Students may need assistance with question three. Therefore, pass out the two additional note cards and ask students to write "establishing historical context" on one card and "essential historical content" on the other. At this point, students have headings, subheadings, historical situation, and historical content. Now ask students to arrange the cards in the order they think will help them stay organized while taking notes. Using the book in conjunction with the historical thinking skills they are learning will help students stay organized while practicing a framework that can be replicated.

MODULE 1-1 Diverse American Indian Societies

An outline of the entire paragraph could look something like this:

- Spanish created contacts between Europeans and Native Americans
  - Native Americans eager to trade/form alliances
  - also fought against those they considered invaders
    - most significant invaders
      - plants, pigs, and germs
      - transformed landscape, diet, and ways of life

If you are annotating in your book, you might write the first bullet point in the margin to provide a handy guide to the paragraph's topic. Then, you can underline the subcategories in the paragraph itself.

ACTIVITY

As you read the rest of Module 1-1, create a set of notes in outline form, following the strategies laid out in steps 1 and 2. Remember, the purpose of taking notes is to make a personalized record of the important ideas and the specific evidence used to prove them.

The Aztecs, the Maya, and the Incas

Three significant civilizations had emerged in the Americas by the early sixteenth century: Aztec and Mayan societies, both in the equatorial region, and the Incan society along the Pacific coast in present-day Peru. Technologically advanced, with particularly sophisticated knowledge of mathematics and astronomy, all three societies capitalized on vast mineral wealth to build large urban centers, formed highly ritualized religions, and developed complex political systems. Since they carried out most of their commerce over land or along rivers and coastlines, they did not build large boats. They also lacked horses, which had disappeared from the region thousands of years earlier. Still, the Aztecs, Maya, and Incas established grand cities and civilizations.

Around 1325 C.E., the **Aztecs**, who called themselves Mexica, built their capital, **Tenochtitlán**, on the site of present-day Mexico City. As seminomadic warriors who had invaded and then settled in the region, the Aztecs drew on local residents' knowledge of irrigation and cultivation and adopted their written language. Aztec commoners, who tilled communally owned lands, were ruled over by priests and nobles. The nobles formed a warrior class and owned vast estates on which they employed both serfs and enslaved people captured from non-Aztec communities in the region. Priests promised fertility — for the land and its people — but demanded human sacrifices, including thousands of men and women from captured tribes.

To sustain their society, Aztecs increased agriculture by expanding and intensifying use of a technological innovation known as *chinampas*. Chinampas, basically artificial islands, took advantage of well-watered swampy and lake areas by constructing man-made frames into which lake mud and plants were layered to create plots of good soil. In this way, Aztecs adapted to watery environments, increasing production of maize, beans, and squash. Aztecs also extended their trade networks, offering pottery, cloth, and leather goods in exchange for textiles and obsidian to make sharp-edged tools and weapons. As will be shown by Malintzin's story (see Module 1-3), enslaved people made up an important component of this trade.

The **Maya**, another grand civilization, slowly settled the vast region south of Tenochtitlán and spread up into the Yucatán peninsula between roughly 900 B.C.E. and 300 C.E. They established large cities that were home to skilled artisans and developed elaborate systems for irrigation and water storage. Farmers worked the fields and labored to build huge stone temples and palaces for rulers who claimed to be descended from the gods. Learned men developed mathematical calculations, astronomical systems, hieroglyphic writing, and a calendar.

Yet the Maya civilization began to decline around 800 C.E. An economic crisis, likely the result of drought and worsened by heavy taxation, probably drove peasant families into the interior. Many towns and religious sites were abandoned. Despite these difficulties, some communities survived the crisis and reemerged as thriving city-states over the course of several centuries. By the early sixteenth century, they were trading with the Aztecs.

The **Incas** developed an equally impressive civilization in the Andes Mountains along the Pacific coast. The Incan empire, like the Aztec empire, was built on the accomplishments of earlier

Aztecs Spanish term for the Mexica, an indigenous people who built an empire in present-day Mexico in the centuries before the arrival of the Spaniards.

AP® TIP
Analyze the ways in which the worldviews of the Maya, Incan, and Aztec societies diverged from those of Europeans.

Maya People who established large cities on the Yucatán peninsula with strong irrigation and agricultural techniques. The Maya civilization was strongest between 300 and 800 C.E.

Incas Andean people who built an empire in the centuries before the arrival of the Spaniards amid the fertile land of the Andes Mountains along the Pacific coast. Reaching the height of their power in the fifteenth century, the Incas controlled some sixteen million people.

BUILDING AP® SKILLS
Comparison

To help students understand similarities and differences between the three main pre-Columbian civilizations in the Americas, ask students to complete the following chart on the Aztecs, Maya, and Incas. By knowing the location, time periods, and main accomplishments of these civilizations, students will be better prepared to conduct the review on the next page. A reproducible version of this chart is available in the Teacher's Resource Materials.

▲ **Differentiation**

This activity can be extended by having students conduct additional research beyond what is presented in this module. Advanced students would benefit and so would other learners who may be interested in going more in-depth about these main civilizations. After the extended learning is completed, students can complete a Venn diagram on the three main civilizations and identify their main similarities and differences as requested by the review.

TRM Find **Handout 1.2 – Comparing Pre-Columbian Civilizations** in the Teacher's Resource Materials.

EXPLORING AP® THEMES
Geography and the Environment

Give students a map of the Americas and have them label where the three main civilizations were located: the Aztecs in Mexico, Maya in Mesoamerica, and Incas in South America. Encourage students to be specific by giving them more guidance on what region within each of the three areas the civilizations were located. For example, the Aztecs must be placed in the central to southern region of Mexico, the Maya in the Yucatan Peninsula and Central America, and the Incas along the Andes Mountains in the western part of the continent along the Pacific coast. Additionally, have students research the climate and main crops in each respective region. Conclude this activity with a class discussion on how geography impacted the development of these civilizations. A reproducible version of this map is available in the Teacher's Resource Materials.

TRM Map 1A – The Americas

BUILDING AP® SKILLS
Claims and Evidence in Sources

This is a good place to have students begin to work on identifying how historians and journalists use specific and relevant evidence to support a claim and provide reasoning (how or why) that ties back to their thesis to develop their argument. This extremely important skill of analyzing claims and evidence in sources will help students throughout the course and on the AP® exam as they interpret secondary sources and eventually work on making, supporting, and developing their own historically defensible claims in essays. Introduce this skill by providing students with an excerpt from Charles C. Mann's book, *1491: New Revelations of the Americas Before Columbus*, focusing specifically on the text in Chapter 8. Then, instruct them to use three different color highlighters to identify his claim/thesis, historical evidence used to support his claim/thesis, and the "linkage statements" that provide his reasoning and ties back to his claim/thesis.

societies. At the height of their power, in the fifteenth century, the Incas controlled some sixteen million people spread over 350,000 square miles. They constructed an expansive system of roads and garrisons to ensure the flow of food, trade goods, and soldiers from their capital at Cuzco through the surrounding mountains and valleys.

The key to Incan success was their cultivation of fertile mountain valleys. Cuzco, some eleven thousand feet above sea level, lay in the center of the Incan empire. Its residents cultivated potatoes and other crops on terraces watered by an elaborate irrigation system. Miners dug gold and silver from the mountains, and artisans crafted the metals into jewelry and decorative items. Thousands of laborers constructed elaborate palaces and temples. And like the Aztec priests, Incan priests sacrificed humans to the gods to stave off natural disasters and military defeat.

REVIEW

- What similarities do you see between the Aztec, Incan, and Mayan civilizations?
- What differences do you note between these three peoples?

AP® THINKING HISTORICALLY — Analyzing Sources

Although it might be tempting to think of history as a fixed set of events set squarely in the rearview mirror of civilization, the reality of how history is made is much more complex. Just as there are many ways to tell a story, there are many ways to look at history. It may help to think of it this way: Let's say you're at your annual family reunion, and everyone is gathered around the dinner table, reminiscing about what happened at the reunion last year. Multiple people are talking, perhaps even interrupting each other. Some people may be talking quietly to the person sitting next to them; others might be calling out to someone across the table. There's probably a general consensus about some aspects of last year's event — everyone can agree, for instance, when and where it was, and who was there. But when it comes to remembering details, each family member likely has something unique to contribute, and while these stories can work together to create a unified narrative (Aunt Phyllis remembers your side of the family was late, and your brother chimes in that it was because your flight was delayed), they can also illuminate several different, often dissonant, perspectives. You draw on all of these individual voices and opinions and use them to form your own ideas about what happened, and why.

Likewise, historians construct history out of rich primary source materials that have survived from the past. These sources come in a variety of formats, including texts, material artifacts, architecture, and images. Historians examine these sources, sometimes considering them individually, but usually in combination with others. Analyzing many primary sources from a particular time period, even if they conflict with each other, allows historians to draw broad conclusions about that time period, and thereby construct a historical narrative that says something useful about the past to readers in the present. Interpreting sources in this way is a historian's most fundamental task — in other words, how we think about these sources shapes our understanding of history. Because of this, analyzing primary sources is a crucial way to uncover meaning from the past.

The AP® exam will also ask you to analyze and interpret primary sources in nearly every **section of the test. The multiple-choice section** contains several sources, each accompanied by two to five questions. One of the four Short-Answer Questions will require you to analyze a primary source in your response. Finally, the Document-Based Question, or DBQ, is an essay prompt that asks you to examine seven primary sources and write an essay using your analysis of them to support a historical argument.

One strategy for reading sources effectively on the AP® exam is to start by reading the prompts or questions before reading the primary source or sources. Knowing what questions you'll have to answer can help you tailor your reading to the task.

Next, you should look for information about the source. Historians begin to form their interpretation of a primary source based on what they are able to identify about its basic qualities. Complete information about a source is not always available, but historians work with what is known. You can do the same by asking yourself some key questions:

- **Historical situation:** What kind of source is it — a physical artifact, a piece of writing, an image, or something else? When was the source made? What events and/or circumstances shaped its creation?

TEACHING IDEA

AP® Central

Make use of the College Board's resource Artifact & Analysis in the Related Articles and Teaching Resources, available from the Classroom Resources section of AP® Central (apcentral.collegeboard.org).

TRM Suggested Responses to Questions

TRM Module 1.1 AP® Thinking Historically Handout 2

BUILDING AP® SKILLS
Sourcing and Situation

Analyzing sources for their content (or main idea) and relevance to a question being asked (i.e., document-based questions that will be discussed in later modules) is fundamental to doing well in the course and on the AP® exam. Additionally, such documents must also be analyzed for sourcing (or "extended analysis"): their Historical situation, Intended audience, Purpose, or Point of view and their historical significance. To that end, use the acronym HIPP to remember the four possible ways of doing sourcing or "extended analysis" of documents. It is also important to note that students must go beyond mere identification of sourcing or "extended analysis" and explain their historical significance. As a classroom activity, you can give students a document from or referring to this time and have them analyze it for both content (or main idea) and sourcing (or "extended analysis") using the corresponding handout. Possible documents to consider are the "Portrait of Hendrick" from the Library of Congress' website (loc.gov) or "Theire sitting at meate" available from the Encyclopedia Virginia's website (encyclopediavirginia.org).

TRM Find **Handout 1.3 – HIPP Template** in the Teacher's Resource Materials.

TEACHING IDEA

AP® Thinking Historically Workshop

Although students need to begin working on developing the skill of analyzing sources through historical situation, intended audience, author's purpose, or point of view, these are higher-order skills that will take many students some time to master. Therefore, think of ways in which students understand reading across the curriculum, because this will allow them to use skills they are comfortable with as they develop additional skills. Many students are familiar with the concepts of claim, evidence, and reasoning.

Once students begin reading the document, ask them to identify these concepts in the document. After students have identified the claim, ask them to connect the claim to author's purpose. Consider asking students how the evidence in the document informs the historical context. Finally, ask students to connect the historical reasoning to either author's purpose or point of view. In this way, you are bridging skills they know with skills they are working to master.

- **Intended audience:** Who was this source created for, and how do you know?
- **Purpose:** Why was the source created? How do you know?
- **Point of view:** Who created the source? How do various aspects of the creator's identity — such as their gender, social class, race, ethnicity, livelihood, or religion — affect your reading of the source?

On the AP® exam, a "source" line either above or below the document will provide at least some of this information, but you may have to hunt within the source itself for other details as well as rely on your own historical knowledge. Regardless of what information is provided up front, you should still take the time to think about each of these factors. Drawing your own conclusions about historical situation, intended audience, purpose, and point of view is an excellent stepping stone to historical interpretation and analysis.

Step 1 Carefully read the source.

This is the most vital step. This means actually reading written sources, but for visual texts, your "reading" will be a close examination of the object itself. As you read a source, identify the most telling parts of the whole. Consider the key questions about historical situation, intended audience, purpose, and point of view to determine these key parts. Who created the source and why? What kind of source is it? When was it made and what events shaped its creation? You may not be able to answer all of these questions, but even answering some of them will help you better understand the historical significance of your source.

Step 2 Annotate the source.

If possible, mark these key parts by circling, underlining, or bracketing them. If you cannot write on your source, taking notes on a separate piece of paper is also helpful. Use the questions on historical situation, intended audience, purpose, and point of view as your guide. Annotate the parts you have marked by putting the ideas they convey into your own words and asking questions about details that confuse or interest you. How thoroughly you annotate depends on the task you are asked to complete. If you're reading a source for a multiple-choice question, for instance, you will probably only circle a few key words and underline a few important phrases, and your own notes on the source may be short phrases or even a single word. If you are reading a source in order to respond to a prompt, your annotation may be more thorough.

Let's take a look at how we might read and annotate a primary source that is a historical artifact. This means your "reading" of this source must be a close look at its details. Begin by reading the source line for the image. Here, it tells you that the maker of the artifact is unknown, that the objects in the images form a gold necklace of small, interlocking frogs, which have been

Source: Anonymous Mixtec artisan, *Necklace with Gold Frog Ornaments*, Aztec empire, 15th–16th century

About the source: Mixtec and Aztec peoples associated frogs with rain and fertility.

(Continued)

EXPLORING AP® THEMES

Geography and the Environment

Now that students have a better understanding of the three main civilizations in the Americas, have them research as part of a homework assignment how the physical features of their habitats impacted each society. For example, students should find that the high altitudes of the Andes Mountains made the cultivation of certain crops extremely difficult and forced them to carve agricultural terraces in flatter areas. Meanwhile, the Maya and Aztecs, both located at lower elevations and with access to many bodies of water, had an easier time growing crops like maize and beans and found it easier to trade with one another. Similarly, we find more temples and larger complexes built in Mexico and Mesoamerica than in the Andes because of the challenges presented by the higher elevations.

TEACHING IDEA

Challenging Misconceptions

One of the main misconceptions students tend to have about American Indians is that they comprised a monolithic group. In reality, American Indians tended to identify themselves primarily along their respective tribal lines. Consequently, they did not belong to a single "American Indian nation." Discuss with students how this lack of unity and tradition of independence would affect their eventual interactions with European colonizers and then Americans.

TEACHING IDEA

Incorporating Websites

Use the Gilder Lehrman Institute of American History website and visit their online journal History Now, which contains essays by scholars on major topics in American history (gilderlehrman.org). For Period 1, *The Americas to 1620* by Christopher L. Miller, is the featured essay. This webpage also includes a visual timeline with the main events and historical developments of the pre-Columbian civilizations. Have students scroll through the interactive timeline to read the short narratives and watch the multiple videos describing the lives of American Indians.

TEACHING IDEA

AP® Central

Make use of the College Board's resource Critical Interpretation of Images in the Related Articles and Teaching Resources, available from the Classroom Resources section of AP® Central (apcentral.collegeboard.org).

TEACHING IDEA

Visual Literacy

Students may sometimes struggle with interpreting visual images and can often be superficial in their analysis. Students may only be able to describe what they see in a visual without understanding or explaining the meaning and historical significance of certain symbols. In the Necklace with Gold Frog Ornaments image on page 9, students may simply state that the identified tribes wore jewelry without delving deeper into what else they can deduce from the image. The information about the source and the meaning of the frogs may not come with the source line on the AP® exam. Therefore, you may want to practice this skill with students. Work through analyzing a different artifact from the Maya and/or Incas (e.g., calendar or a structure from Machu Picchu) with your students as a classroom activity. Possible artifacts may be found in the Smithsonian Institution's gallery by locating the Native American and Indigenous History and Culture link (collections.si.edu/search/gallery.htm). As you help students go from describing what they see in an image to explaining what the image means, they may have to "read between the lines" and make reasonable inferences. Some questions for students to consider: *What do you see? Are there any symbols you can identify and know their meaning? Do you recognize any information on the source line? Does it remind you of any other visuals previously seen in class? Can you put it in context?*

TEACHING IDEA

Analyzing Art and Images

When considering artifacts, be sure to have students draw conclusions that are supported by historical evidence. This will help them explain exactly how the artifact fits into the broader historical period.

TEACHING IDEA

Analyzing Art and Images

Point out to students that they can make more than one historical claim about the same artifact. The important thing is not the number of claims, but that relevant historical evidence supports each one.

---

arranged to show you how it might have been worn, that it was produced under the Aztec empire, and that it was created during the fifteenth or sixteenth century (the 1400s or 1500s).

This source also includes an additional "About the source" line. These are sometimes included to provide you with additional information to help you interpret the source. In this case, the "About the source" line tells you that the religious beliefs held by Mixtec and Aztec peoples placed special significance in frogs. You can see that details of the golden frogs are uniform and relatively well-detailed. This tells you that the maker of this necklace not only had access to precious materials (gold), but was highly skilled in metallurgy, a specialized craft that likely took years to learn. From this information, you can also make the educated guess, or *inference*, that the maker of this necklace had adequate time to make a detailed and valuable object.

Each module of this book includes sources that provide opportunities for you to practice historical analysis. These sources serve as paths for you to gain meaning from the past, and working with them is an essential part of the process of building your skills.

ACTIVITY

Throughout this book, you will encounter AP® Analyzing Sources boxes that will ask you to carefully examine and answer questions designed to foster critical thinking about a variety of historical sources. The following three questions ask about the frog necklace we introduced in step 2. For each question, we have provided a partial sample response. Add at least one additional response of your own to each of these questions.

1. Identify a feature of the Aztec economy, technology, culture, environment, or society revealed by this artifact.
   - Technology: The image of the frog ornaments from an Aztec necklace shows that Aztec society was an advanced civilization supporting craft specialization of artists because the detail and quality work in gold is more than what amateurs or non-specialists in less developed economies produced.
   - Environment: The large amount of gold used in making the Aztec frog ornaments for a single necklace suggests that the Aztec empire was rich and controlled, or had access to, large amounts of precious metals, including gold.
   - Your turn!

2. Identify an Aztec priority revealed by this artifact.
   - The Aztecs depended upon producing a surplus of food through agriculture so they prioritized fertility. Since frogs likely symbolized fertility and gold was valuable to the Aztecs, craftsmen likely made this object to be worn by leaders to express their elite position in the social hierarchy.
   - Your turn!

3. Describe an Aztec adaptation to the environment reflected in this artifact.
   - Aztecs adapted to a swampy environment surrounding their capital by creating innovative floating gardens called chinampas.
   - Chinampas allowed the Aztecs to undertake large-scale agriculture to feed their population.
   - Your turn!

Native Cultures to the North

To the north of these grand civilizations, smaller societies also thrived. In present-day Arizona and New Mexico, the Hohokam established communities around 500 C.E. and developed extensive irrigation systems. In present-day Utah and Colorado, ancient **Pueblo** villages supported settled populations by farming maize, which had spread to the region after domestication in Central America, as well as beans and squash. As time went on, the Pueblo people gathered themselves into small urban centers built from adobe bricks made from clay and water and used advanced irrigation techniques to survive the arid climate of the Southwest. By around 750 C.E., they were building adobe and masonry homes cut into cliffs. Although they eventually migrated south and constructed large buildings that included administrative offices, religious centers, and craft shops, the Pueblo peoples returned to their cliff dwellings in the 1100s for protection from invaders. There, persistent drought eventually caused them to disperse into smaller settled groups.

Pueblo American Indian peoples who lived in present-day New Mexico and Arizona and built permanent multi-story adobe dwellings.

BUILDING AP® SKILLS

Comparison

To help students understand similarities and differences between some of the main pre-Columbian civilizations in what would become known as the United States, ask students to complete a chart on the main geographical regions. By knowing the locations, environments, and main accomplishments of these civilizations, students will be better prepared to conduct the review on page 13.

TRM Find **Handout 1.4 – Comparing Northern Native Civilizations** in the Teacher's Resource Materials.

AP® ANALYZING SOURCES

Source: Pueblo "Cliff Palace" at Mesa Verde, Colorado

About the source: This Pueblo "cliff palace" was built around 1200 C.E. and inhabited for around 100 years. Residents grew corn, beans, and squash, traded goods, and competed with neighboring towns.

Questions for Analysis

1. Identify a Pueblo adaptation to the environment apparent in this image.
2. Describe the interactions of the Pueblo who lived in this structure with other nearby peoples, based on the evidence in this photograph.
3. Explain what this image reveals about the Pueblo people. Consider things like the economy, technology, environment, politics, and society in your response.

Farther north, on plains that stretched from present-day Colorado into Canada, hunting societies developed around the herds of bison that roamed there. A weighted spear-throwing device, called an *atlatl*, allowed hunters to capture smaller game, while nets, hooks, and snares allowed them to catch birds, fish, and small animals. Societies in the Great Plains as well as the Great Basin (between the Rockies and the Sierra Nevada) generally remained small and widely scattered. Given the arid conditions in these regions, communities needed a large expanse of territory to ensure their survival as they followed migrating animals or seasonal plant sources. Here the adoption of the bow and arrow, in about 500 C.E., proved the most significant technological development.

Other American Indian societies, like the Mandan, settled along rivers in the heart of the continent (present-day North and South Dakota). The rich soil along the banks fostered farming, while forests and plains attracted diverse animals for hunting. Around 1250 C.E., however, an extended drought forced these settlements to contract, and competition for resources increased among Mandan villages and with other groups in the region.

Hunting-gathering societies also emerged along the Pacific coast, where the abundance of fish, small game, and plant life provided the resources to develop permanent settlements. Although the Chumash Indians remained hunters and foragers, they settled in permanent villages near present-day Santa Barbara, California, where they harvested resources from the land and the ocean. Women gathered acorns and pine nuts, while men fished, using enormous ocean-going canoes called *tomol*, and hunted. The Chumash, whose villages sometimes supported up to a thousand inhabitants without farming, participated in regional exchange networks up and down the coast.

The American Indians of the Pacific Northwest were composed of diverse peoples of different languages and cultures who lived in resource-rich regions near the Pacific Ocean. Ocean resources supported these hunters and gatherers as they gave up nomadic life and settled down into a village life. They depended upon the sea and rivers for rich salmon harvests, and elk from the forests. They worshipped maritime and woodland deities, who were portrayed in detailed totem poles carved from the cedars of the dense forests of the region. American Indians in the Pacific Northwest also built ocean-going canoes from cedar and often hauled in thousands of pounds of fish in a single harvest. The Chinook peoples in the Pacific Northwest used the cedars to build extensive plank houses, some hundreds of feet long, in which lived extended kinship groups with up to seventy family members under a single roof.

> **AP® TIP**
> Consider the ways in which — and reasons why — American Indian societies in resource-rich areas of North America differed from areas with more limited natural resources.

TRM Suggested Responses to Questions

TRM Module 1.1 AP® Analyzing Sources Handout

EXPLORING AP® THEMES

Geography and the Environment

Display a map of North America. Have the entire class work together to identify three important American Indian tribes in each of the main regions. Then, give students a list of the main types of dwellings (teepees, longhouses, adobe homes, cliff dwellings, and igloos) used by various tribes and have students place them in the correct regions. Have students explain how the dwellings reflect adaptations to the environment.

BUILDING AP® SKILLS

Comparison

Have students work on a Venn diagram that identifies some of the main similarities and differences between two of the tribes from North America in different regions. Information should be grouped into three categories: political, economic, and social.

TEACHING IDEA

Check for Understanding

Have students create a T-chart to compare the impact of maize cultivation on the Pueblo and Aztec. Be sure that they consider both similarities and differences to show understanding of historical complexity.

APPLY THE TIP

To better understand why resource-rich areas of North America developed differently from those with more limited natural resources, have students research "three-sister farming." Students should discover that tribes that lived in more fertile soil, normally those with access to rivers, and with better climate, were able to partake in this type of agriculture. Doing so allowed them to have richer diets that could sustain larger populations. A useful source for this research would be Catherine Boekmann's "The Three Sisters: Corn, Beans, and Squash" available on The Older Farmer's Almanac website (almanac.com).

EXPLORING AP® THEMES

Geography and the Environment

Give students an outline map of North America and ask them to plot the location of one (1) American Indian tribe in each region using the list from the Course Framework. Since the thematic focus for this module is geography and the environment, have students label the main characteristics that shaped the diverse societies, including the climate and natural resources available to build dwellings in each region. Model an example such as the Pueblo or Anasazi people and how they lived in an arid region that required the construction of irrigation systems and adobe and cliff dwellings. A reproducible version of this map is available in the Teacher's Resource Materials.

TRM Map 1B – North America

TEACHING IDEA

Incorporating Websites

Use the Stanford History Education Group website and visit their section titled "Reading Like a Historian," which contains online history lessons including coverage of the Incan Empire, Emperor Atahualpa, and Aztec Emperor Moctezuma (sheg.stanford.edu). Additionally, utilize the section called "Beyond the Bubble," which has history assessments that focus on Inca Fortification, Tupac Amaru II, and Portrait of an Iroquois Leader. Visit these resources to read their descriptions and then decide which to use in class with students. Since this book is specifically for U.S. History instead of World History, you may want to focus on the assessment based on the Portrait of an Iroquois Leader.

Period 1: 1491–1607

MODULE 1-1 Diverse American Indian Societies

> **AP® TIP**
> Make a list of the characteristics that led to the development of mixed agriculture and hunting societies in Eastern North America.

The Ute peoples foraged and hunted nomadically in the Great Basin region, which stretched over an enormous desert in what is now southwestern Colorado and southeastern Utah. They held few possessions, and lived in small egalitarian kinship bands. The bands survived in the desolate desert by hunting and gathering. In the most barren areas, they survived on fish found in the few rivers in the area, small animals, and plant foods including seeds from grasses and piñon nuts. Ute family bands traded with each other, as well as with other regional tribes, including Pueblo peoples, over an extensive network throughout the American Southwest.

In the northeast regions of North America, the Iroquois people lived in villages of up to several hundred inhabitants and cultivated maize as well as vegetables like squash and beans. Since the Iroquois lived in semi-sedentary villages, they built large long houses out of the rich forests of the Northeast, often living communally in extended groups that spanned multiple generations and families. Women exercised considerable power within village life, since they passed descent and inheritance through the maternal lines in a matrilineal kinship system, and women selected male village leaders. The Iroquois also depended upon deer hunting and fishing, which proved abundant throughout the region. Iroquois culture revolved around a warrior ethos that valued individual honor in battle, where ritual humiliation of an opponent was often more important than killing an opponent.

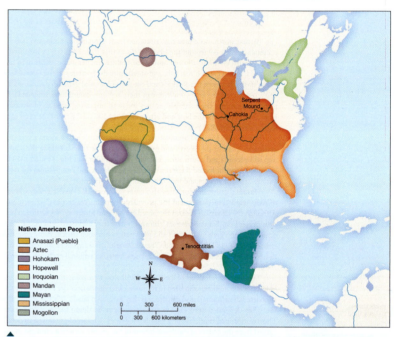

MAP 1.2 American Indian Peoples, c. 500–1500 c.e. Some American Indians, like the Mississippians, developed extensive trade networks over land or along rivers and coastlines. Others, such as the Aztec, developed extensive agricultural economies based on Mayan precedents and practiced trade. Other groups, like the Pueblo, battled over scarce resources. **How did geographic location shape these differences?**

▲ **Serpent Mound Memorial** Mississippians constructed this mound, located in Locust Grove, Ohio, between 950 and 1200 C.E. Worshippers of the sun, the Mississippians aligned the head of the serpent with the sunset of the summer solstice (June 20 or 21). Artifacts found at this site indicate the Mississippians extended Hopewell trade networks. **Based on this information, what can you conclude about the Mississippian economy during this period?**

Even larger societies with more elaborate social, religious, and political systems developed near the Mississippi River. A group that came to be called the Hopewell people established a thriving culture in the early centuries C.E. The river and its surrounding lands provided fertile fields and easy access to distant communities. Centered in present-day southern Ohio and western Illinois, the Hopewell constructed towns of four to six thousand people. Artifacts from their burial sites reflect extensive trading networks that stretched from the Missouri River to Lake Superior, and from the Rocky Mountains to the Appalachian region and Florida.

Beginning around 500 C.E., the Hopewell culture gave birth to larger and more complex societies that flourished in the Mississippi River valley and to the south and east. As bows and arrows spread into the region, people hunted more game in the thick forests. But Mississippian groups also learned to cultivate corn. The development of corn as a staple crop allowed the population to expand dramatically, and more complex political and religious systems developed in which elite rulers gained greater control over the labor of farmers and hunters. Mississippian peoples created massive earthworks sculpted in the shape of serpents, birds, and other creatures. Some earthen sculptures stood higher than 70 feet and stretched longer than 1,300 feet. Mississippians also constructed huge temple mounds that could cover nearly 16 acres.

By about 1100 C.E., the Cahokia people established the largest Mississippian settlement, which may have housed ten to thirty thousand inhabitants (Map 1.2). Powerful chieftains extended their trade networks from the Great Lakes to the Gulf of Mexico, conquered smaller villages, and created a centralized government. But in the 1200s, environmental factors affected the Cahokian people, too. Deforestation, drought, and perhaps disease as well as overhunting diminished their strength, and many settlements dispersed. After 1400, increased warfare and political turmoil joined with environmental changes to cause Mississippian culture as a whole to decline.

AP® TIP
Create a list of characteristics that illustrates the development of increasingly complex societies in North America before 1500 C.E.

REVIEW

How did the societies of North America differ from those of the equatorial region and the Andes Mountain region?

BUILDING AP® SKILLS

Comparison

Comparison is one of the main reasoning processes tested on the AP® exam. Since the review activity on this page focuses on differences, do another activity that emphasizes similarities. First, divide the class into groups and give them categories for comparison (i.e., geography/environment, political, social, and economic, etc.) between the diverse societies of North America and the Aztecs, Maya, and Incas farther south. Conduct a class discussion to address any misunderstandings.

TEACHING IDEA

Incorporating Websites

Use the National Museum of the American Indian website and visit their section for education, which contains lessons and resources to use in the classroom (americanindian.si.edu). Two lessons you may want to use with students are:

■ We Have a Story to Tell: Native Peoples of the Chesapeake Region

■ Pacific Northwest History and Cultures: Why Do the Foods We Eat Matter?

These lessons help students see how studying American Indian tribes is relevant to the present day and perhaps even their own lives. Highlighting their legacies and how these tribes are still around today will help bring history alive for students.

TEACHING IDEA

Check for Understanding

Help students monitor their progression in the course and mastery of the material covered. Ask them to self-reflect on the main things learned thus far and write their own "Top 5" list of key takeaways. Then, conduct a class discussion after writing their answers on the board. The objective is to reach consensus as to what the top takeaways should be up to this point. Clarify any misunderstandings demonstrated by their answers.

TRM Suggested Responses to Questions

TRM Module 1.1 AP® Thinking Historically Handout 3

BUILDING AP® SKILLS
Comparison

The comparison activity on this page focuses on the American Southwest and Northeast regions with the Pueblo and Iroquois tribes. As an alternate activity, have students do the same type of comparing and contrasting with two of the following: Great Plains, Great Basin, American Southwest, Mississippi River Valley, Northwest, and present-day California.

Period 1: 1491–1607

MODULE 1-1 Diverse American Indian Societies

AP® THINKING HISTORICALLY — Applying Comparison

Now that you have read this module, it's time to reflect on what you learned about diverse American Indian societies prior to the sixteenth century and consider how to approach thinking comparatively about their histories. In this example, we'll discuss how to apply the historical reasoning skill of comparison to the Pueblo and the Iroquois.

Step 1 Make a list identifying characteristics of each group.

As you think, it may help to ask yourself what you know about each group's
- politics
- economy
- society
- interactions with the environment

A graphic organizer containing two lists that highlight the main attributes of the Pueblo and Iroquois societies might look like this:

	Pueblo	Iroquois
Politics	Experienced conflicts with invaders.	Women exercised considerable power, maternal lines of inheritance. Women selected leaders. Warrior ethos.
Economy	Farmed beans and squash, using irrigation.	Depended upon hunting/fishing as well as agriculture.
Society	Built homes in cliffs, settled.	Lived in villages, semi-sedentary.
Interactions with the Environment	Dry environment. Built homes in cliffs or adobe. Irrigation necessary to practice agriculture.	Lived in forests, built long houses from wood. Acquired food from game as well as small-scale agriculture.

Step 2 Compare your two lists.

Compare your two lists by looking for ways the two groups share similarity, as well as by keeping an eye out for where they differ. The following example shows how you might organize the similarities and differences between the Pueblo and the Iroquois:

Similarities	Differences
Both the Pueblo and Iroquois built houses from their environment.	The Pueblo used clay bricks or cliff dwellings for housing. The Iroquois used wood to build long houses.
Both the Pueblo and Iroquois practiced agriculture.	The Pueblo used irrigation to farm in their arid environment. The Iroquois, living in a more temperate zone, did not need extensive irrigation systems.
Both the Pueblo and the Iroquois lived in towns.	Pueblo towns were sedentary, whereas the Iroquois were semi-sedentary, and moved their villages as access to game and fertile land necessitated.

ACTIVITY

Follow steps 1 and 2 to explore similarities and differences between the Pueblo and Iroquois peoples' political systems, economies, societies, and interactions with the environment. You can use the information from the examples we walked through in steps 1 and 2 to generate ideas and organize your thoughts, and you can bring in other observations you had while reading this module.

TEACHING IDEA
AP® Thinking Historically Workshop

If students are struggling to understand all of the elements in this Applying Comparison activity consider narrowing their focus with this workshop. Begin by dividing students into groups of four. Within those groups subdivide students into groups of two, labeled A and B. Assign Group A Pueblo, politics, and interactions with the environment, and assign Group B Iroquois, politics, and interactions with the environment. After each group has identified the assigned characteristics delineated in step 1, have them combine Group A and B to reestablish their original group of four students. Now they are ready to move on to step 2 in the activity. Because each has narrowed their focus and become experts on one group, they can help each other establish similarities and differences.

MODULE 1-1 Diverse American Indian Societies

AP® WRITING HISTORICALLY: Breaking Down Short-Answer Question Prompts

All of the writing you do on the AP® exam, and most of the writing you do in this course, will be in response to different types of writing prompts. These prompts give you a basic guide for what to include in your answer by telling you to write about specific topics, time periods, places, and groups of people. In other words, you're always going to be writing about some combination of *who*, *what*, *when*, and *where*.

On the AP® U.S. History exam, you will be asked to choose to answer three out of four total Short-Answer Question (or SAQ) prompts. These questions are much more open-ended and multilayered than those in the multiple-choice section of the exam. The tasks that Short-Answer Questions ask you to complete are actually more like mini essay questions. While this means that you need to answer these questions in complete sentences, your response should be one short paragraph rather than a multi-paragraph essay.

Another unique aspect of Short-Answer Questions is that they have three parts, each of which is given its own letter label. Each part sets a limit on your response by asking you to complete one distinct task. The following Short-Answer Question asks you to reflect on what you have learned in Module 1-1:

Answer (a), (b), and (c). Confine your response to the period before 1600.

   a. Briefly describe ONE specific historical similarity in adaptation to the environment made by two American Indian groups.
   b. Briefly describe ONE specific historical difference in adaptation to the environment made by two American Indian groups.
   c. Briefly describe ONE specific historical difference in the economies of two American Indian groups.

After quickly reading this question, you're probably wondering where to begin. It asks you to do a lot of things in a short paragraph — and, since the AP® exam is timed, you're likely working with a short timeframe, too. Let's walk through one pre-writing strategy for breaking down a Short-Answer Question: annotating the prompt. This process is an excellent way to figure out what your response needs to include — and exclude. In order to succeed on the exam, not only do you have to understand what a prompt is asking you to do, you also have to know what falls outside of the task at hand. Reading the question closely and annotating it to distill each of the tasks you must complete will help you avoid writing something off topic. Responses that fail to adequately address all parts of the question will not earn full credit.

Step 1 Read the instructions.

First, consider the part of the question that comes before the three parts of the prompt:

Answer (a), (b), and (c). Confine your response to the period before 1600.

These instructions place limits that apply to all parts of the prompt. In this case, the question is telling you that everything you write will have to discuss the period before 1600. So, you should note "before 1600" as the *time*. You may also find it helpful to write "before 1600" before or after each part of the prompt so that it's fresh in your memory.

Step 2 Read and annotate each part of the question.

Next, read part (a) carefully and label the limits of the *topic*, *task*, and *place*.

- The *topic* is how American Indian groups adapted to the environment.
- The *task* is to identify exactly one specific historical similarity.
- The *place* is America.

Continue to annotate for topic, task, and place for parts (b) and (c). A complete annotation of the question will look something like this:

Answer (a), (b), and (c). Confine your response to the period [before 1600.] ← TIME

TASK 1a —
PLACE —
   a. Briefly describe ONE specific historical similarity in adaptation to the environment made by two American Indian groups. ← before 1600   — TOPIC 1

TASK 1b —
   b. Briefly describe ONE specific historical difference in adaptation to the environment made by two American Indian groups. ← before 1600

TASK 2 —
TOPIC 2 —
   c. Briefly describe ONE specific historical difference in the economies of two American Indian groups. ← before 1600

(Continued)

TRM Suggested Responses to Questions

TEACHING IDEA

AP® Thinking Historically Workshop

If your students are not yet ready to try the activity on their own, try the following workshop. Begin by dividing students into groups of three. Instruct students to move through the activity together so each member is on pace with the others. For each part (a, b, and c) have students write individual answers and then compare responses. Students are allowed to use one example, combine answers, or rework an entirely new answer constructed by the group. The goal is for students to see more examples, receive help from each other, and become more confident about their understanding of how to write a quality response to a Short-Answer Question.

Period 1: 1491–1607

MODULE 1-1 Diverse American Indian Societies

What do all of these annotations tell you about the answer you need to write? Your response to part (a) will describe both two American Indian groups *and* an adaptation to the environment they share before 1600. For part (b), you will also describe two American Indian groups — which do not have to be the same two groups you named in part (a) — *and* name a difference in their adaptation to the environment before 1600. Likewise, part (c) calls for you to select two American Indian groups and describe differences in their economies prior to 1600.

Step 3 Respond to the prompt and support your answer with at least two historical facts.

You may be wondering what it means to "describe" the historical similarities and differences specified by this Short-Answer Question. While each part of this prompt does call for you to state historical facts, a "describe" task signals that you need to include details to illustrate those facts. Think of it this way: When you simply state what something is — a chair, a desk, a book — you're not painting a picture of what it looks like. But when you describe something — a black leather office chair with wheels, an old metal desk that's been painted white, an AP® U.S. history textbook with a quilt on the cover — you're pointing out several characteristics and prominent features.

Thus, a prompt that asks you to describe something is asking for a plural response, which means you need to provide at least two facts in your answer. An effective response to the Short-Answer Question we annotated in step 2 may look something like this:

> Both the Pueblo and the Iroquois lived in environments that allowed for agriculture, so both grew their own crops to help feed their people. However, the Pueblo lived in an arid environment, so they used irrigation systems, whereas the Iroquois lived in a temperate zone with fertile soil and regular rainfall, and therefore grew crops without extensive use of irrigation systems. Also, since the Iroquois lived in a temperate environment, they practiced hunting to supplement their food supply, relying on game such as deer and fish.

This answer does everything parts (a), (b), and (c) ask for — it offers

- one similarity between how two American Indian groups (the Pueblo and Iroquois) adapted to their environment: use of agriculture. ("Both the Pueblo and the Iroquois lived in environments that allowed for agriculture, so both grew their own crops to help feed their people.")
- one difference between how two American Indian groups (the Pueblo and Iroquois) adapted to their environment: The Pueblo used irrigation systems, while the Iroquois depended on the natural environment. ("However, the Pueblo lived in an arid environment, so they used irrigation systems, whereas the Iroquois lived in a temperate zone with fertile soil and regular rainfall, and therefore grew crops without extensive use of irrigation systems.")
- one difference between the Pueblo and Iroquois economies that contains two examples illustrating that difference: The Iroquois supplemented their diet by practicing hunting as well as agriculture. ("Also, since the Iroquois lived in a temperate environment, they practiced hunting to supplement their food supply, relying on game such as deer and fish.")

ACTIVITY

Now you try it. Read and break down the three parts of the following Short-Answer Question by annotating for time, place, task, and topic. Then, write a one-paragraph response that fully addresses the prompt.

Answer (a), (b), and (c). Confine your response to the period before 1600.

a. Briefly describe ONE specific historical similarity in the economies of two American Indian groups.
b. Briefly describe ANOTHER specific historical similarity in the economies of two American Indian groups.
c. Briefly describe ONE specific historical difference in the societies of two American Indian groups.

TEACHING IDEA

Strategy for Short-Answer Questions

Sometimes students approach SAQs as if they were "short essays," which they are not. Consequently, they may try to write more than is necessary or allowed on the AP® exam. SAQs are limited to a single box for each of the questions and anything written outside of it is not supposed to count. To help students become accustomed to this space limitation, provide them with 4" x 6" index cards so they do not end up writing more than two or three sentences per part.

▲ Differentiation

The SAQ in the Writing Historically section can be modified to address the needs of both struggling and advanced learners. The first prompt in part (a), for example, can be changed from "describe" to "identify." That would allow students to perform a lower-level thinking skill before advancing to description. Similarly, for more advanced learners, the third prompt in part (c), can be changed from "describe" to "explain." Use 4" x 6" index cards to keep their writing to two or three sentences.

BUILDING AP® SKILLS

Contextualization

Contextualization is one of the main skills tested on the AP® exam. At this point, have students conduct a class discussion on what occurred in this first model that "sets the stage" or "lays a foundation" for what they will see down the road with the arrival of the Europeans. Specifically, ask students to write a timed 10-minute paragraph on contextualization. When they have completed their paragraphs, ask them to share their answers with a partner and note any use of different examples. For successful completion of this activity, provide students with the College Board's definition for contextualization and have them make connections to Period 1 title, "Europeans Make Claims in the Americas." How did the material learned in Module 1-1 "set the stage" or "lay a foundation" for Europeans to make claims in the Americas? Answers will vary.

EXPLORING AP® THEMES

Geography and the Environment

As students transition to the next module, have them make a thematic connection. Discuss how the topography of what is the present-day United States may have facilitated interactions between the arriving Europeans and the American Indian tribes discussed in this module. Additionally, brainstorm how the lack of a single and united "American Indian nation" (unlike the Aztec or Incan Empires) and the tradition of tribal independence may have allowed for European colonization as will be discussed in the upcoming modules.

TEACHING IDEA

Check for Understanding

Students may wonder exactly how to "identify" and "describe," two tasks that they'll see frequently in SAQs. Both ask students to state historical facts, but an "identify" task tends to point them to a singular answer, while a "describe" task usually signals that they need to add details to the historical facts they "identify." Have students think of it this way: when they identify something — a desk or a book — they're usually singling out one thing. But when they're describing something — a metal desk that's been painted white or an AP® U.S. History textbook with a quilt on the cover — they're pointing out several characteristics and prominent features.

Module 1-2

Portugal and Spain Expand Their Reach

LEARNING TARGETS
By the end of this module, you should be able to:
- Explain how European economic and military competition led to exploration and colonization of the New World.
- Explain how maritime technology contributed to European exploration and colonization.
- Explain how new transoceanic methods to conduct trade shaped European exploration and colonization.

THEMATIC FOCUS
America in the World

Relying on technological innovations and driven by a desire for trade and economic competition, European countries began to fund voyages of exploration and conquest. Portugal secured trading posts in Africa as well as profitable ocean trade routes to the Middle East and Asia. Spain financed Christopher Columbus's voyages to the Americas, opening the door to a New World for Europeans. Interactions between Columbus and American Indian societies in the Caribbean established patterns for future relations.

HISTORICAL REASONING FOCUS
Causation

One reason people frequently look to the past is to understand the consequences of their decisions. This is because historical events have causes, and knowing what causes something often allows you to understand it better. For instance, staying up late to binge-watch your favorite TV show on a Sunday night will cause you to lose out on necessary sleep, and you will know why you're tired when your alarm for school goes off on Monday morning.

When historians seek to uncover why an event occurred, they use the historical pattern of thought called causation to establish why that development happened. Causation is more complicated, however, than one event leading into the next. For instance, the brief introduction that opens this module describes European exploration as the result of three causes: the value of Asian goods, blocked overland trade routes, and desires of monarchs to amass wealth. Important historical events result from — and are caused by — more than one factor. The three causes we describe at the beginning of this module are only a small slice of the story about what ushered in an era of European exploration.

TASK ▶ As you read the rest of this module, take special note of the many additional causes that combined to lead Columbus and the Spanish to begin European colonization of the Americas.

Rising birthrates and productivity in early fifteenth-century Europe, aided by an improved climate and new approaches to farming that increased Europe's food supply overall, fueled a resurgence of trade with other parts of the world. The profits from agriculture and commerce allowed the wealthy and powerful to begin investing in the arts and luxury goods. Indeed, a cultural **Renaissance** (from the French word for "rebirth") flourished, first in the Italian city-states, and then spread throughout much of the rest of Europe. This cultural rebirth went hand in hand with political unification as more powerful rulers extended their control over smaller city-states and principalities, forming nation-states led by monarchs. All of these factors combined to stabilize a continent that, only a few generations earlier, had been devastated by the plague. As trade thrived and European elites prospered, the wealthy developed tastes for fine Asian manufactured goods, as well as spices from India and China.

During this time, Portuguese and Spanish monarchs initiated efforts to explore the world, hoping to find new ways to gain access to valuable Asian goods. Powerful Italian city-states and merchants controlled the most important routes through the Mediterranean, while Muslims

Renaissance The cultural and intellectual flowering that began in fifteenth-century Italy and then spread north throughout the late fifteenth and sixteenth centuries. During this time, European rulers pushed for greater political unification of their states.

17

BUILDING AP® SKILLS
Causation

In framing class discussion and activities, remember that students' past classes and their knowledge or skill base might need to be refreshed or taught anew. Early in the course students might not be able to address some of the College Board's skills — much knowledge and understanding is needed to truly address "change over time." Likewise, students might not have a solid base to write a full DBQ or LEQ yet. The pedagogy comes early in this text because the course is not yet heavy in content. The historical skill "causation" requires students to assess the patterns of historical events and look for those results. Build upon the skills outlined by the College Board to ensure student success. To help students build the skill of causation, have them track events or ideas that caused or encouraged European exploration as they read this entire module. Students should annotate the module as they read.

PERIOD 1

TRM Suggested Responses to Questions

BUILDING AP® SKILLS
Causation

The plague or "Black Death" is thought to have been spread by infected rats and fleas resulting in 80–200 million deaths throughout Europe between 1347 and 1351. The lasting impacts on the social structures within Europe were still being felt until the middle of the 1400s when European countries and populations rebounded. European monarchs looked to regain power and to build wealth through exploration and conquest.

Have students read excerpts and accounts of the Black Death by going to EyeWitness to History and searching for "The Black Death, 1348" (eyewitnesstohistory.com). Students should seek the causes and effects of the plague on Europe and its society. In looking for this causation of mass cultural changes within European society (challenges to the religion, rulers, and social order), students will gain understanding into the toll of mass death upon a society. In modules to come (such as Module 1-3) students will see the impact of mass death on American Indians and their societies due to contact with Europeans and their diseases.

Discuss the impact a plague or mass death has on a society. Connect the discussion to modern outbreaks such as Ebola, avian flu, measles, etc. and their possible impacts on societies.

EXPLORING AP® THEMES
Social Structures

Under the system of feudalism most of European society was, in some ways, forced to look up to someone with a higher status. This led to clear class distinctions and limited the hope of social movement. Discuss the basic premise of feudal society within Europe. Note how all authority stopped at and with the pope.

The basic understanding of this social system will help in content in future modules. Students can create a feudal pyramid of power with pope and king at the peak of power and serfs at the bottom.

▲ Differentiation

Have students research the life of a common laborer or serf in medieval Europe — this will help give more insight into the class structure of feudal Europe. Why would Europeans during the late 1400s risk their health and even their lives to "explore" new, distant places? What could they gain? Answers will vary.

Portugal and Spain Expand Their Reach 17

Period 1: 1491–1607

MODULE 1-2 Portugal and Spain Expand Their Reach

EXPLORING AP® THEMES
Geography and the Environment

Have students create an early Age of Exploration/Explorers' Map using a blank world map. Ask students to mark the specific routes explorers took and shade map areas to represent which European country funded each exploration. Examples of explorers to include: Leif Erikson, Marco Polo, Bartolomeu Dias, Vasco de Gama, Ferdinand Magellan, Francisco Pizarro, Christopher Columbus, Vasco Nunez de Balboa, Hernando Cortes, Juan Ponce de Leon, etc. A reproducible version of this map is available in the Teacher's Resource Materials.

TRM Map 1C – The World

BUILDING AP® SKILLS
Causation

Have a mini-debate or class discussion utilizing the impacts of the newly independent Spain's role in stimulating or impacting exploration of new territories. Was this exploration inevitable? Challenge students to defend the question of whether the exploration by Europeans led to positive or negative changes in the long term. If students state the exploration was/wasn't positive — for whom was it positive/negative? Show students how to cite support with facts as opposed to opinions.

---

missionaries People who travel to foreign lands with the goal of converting those they meet and interact with to a new religion.

controlled more minor pathways, as well as the overland routes further east to India and China. Effectively blocked from access to existing eastward routes, and craving opportunity for greater wealth by conducting trade themselves, Portugal (and later, Spain) sought trade routes to Asia that could bypass those controlled by their Italian and Muslim rivals. These efforts were aided by explorers, **missionaries**, and merchants who traveled to Morocco, Turkey, India, and other distant lands. They brought back trade goods and knowledge of astronomy, shipbuilding, mapmaking, and navigation that allowed the Portuguese and Spanish to venture farther south along the Atlantic coast of Africa, and, eventually, west into the uncharted Atlantic Ocean.

REVIEW
What historical factors during the fifteenth century caused Europeans to establish trade with other continents?

Portugal and Spain Pursue Long-Distance Trade

caravel A small and swift sailing ship invented by the Portuguese during the fifteenth century.

astrolabe A tool invented by Greek astronomers and sailors for navigation or astrological problems.

Cut off from the Mediterranean by Italian city-states and Muslim rulers in North Africa, the Kingdom of Portugal looked toward the Atlantic. Although a tiny nation, Portugal benefited from the leadership of its young prince, Henry, who launched explorations of the African coast in the 1420s, hoping to find a passage to India via the Atlantic Ocean. Prince Henry — known as Henry the Navigator — gathered information from astronomers, geographers, mapmakers, and craftsmen in the Arab world and recruited Italian cartographers and navigators along with Portuguese scholars, sailors, and captains. He then launched efforts aimed at exploration, observation, shipbuilding, and long-distance trade that revolutionized Europe and shaped developments in Africa and the Americas.

Under Henry, the Portuguese developed ships known as **caravels** — vessels with narrow hulls and triangular sails that were especially effective for navigating the coast of West Africa. Innovative Portuguese **mariners** encouraged by Prince Henry created state-of-the-art maritime charts, maps, and astronomical tables. They improved navigational instruments including the mariner's **astrolabe** and advanced ship designs, which featured the triangular lateen sail, originally an Arab invention, and a stern-post rudder, both of which improved maneuverability. The Portuguese mastered the complex wind and sea currents along the African coast. Soon Portugal was trading in gold, ivory, and enslaved people from West Africa.

In 1482 Portugal built Elmina Castle, a trading post and fort on the African Gold Coast, in present-day Ghana. Further expeditions were launched from the castle; five years later, a fleet led by Bartolomeu Dias rounded the Cape of Good Hope, on the southernmost tip of Africa. This feat demonstrated the possibility of sailing directly from the Atlantic to the Indian Ocean. Vasco da Gama followed this route to India in 1497, returning to Portugal in 1499, his ships laden with valuable cinnamon and pepper.

By the early sixteenth century, Portuguese traders started participating in Indian Ocean trade bringing Asian goods to Europe. They established fortified trading posts at key locations on the Indian Ocean and extended their expeditions to Indonesia, China, and Japan. Within a decade, the Portuguese had become the European leaders in international trade.

Meanwhile its neighbor, a newly independent Spain, was also eager to explore the wider world. A vibrant and religiously tolerant culture had existed in Muslim Spain from the eighth to the tenth century, but that was followed by a long period of persecution of Christians. When Christians began reconquering Spain after 1200, Muslims and Jews alike became targets. Then in 1469, the marriage of Isabella of Castile and Ferdinand II of Aragon sealed the unification of Christian Spain. By 1492 their combined forces expelled the last Muslim conquerors from the Iberian peninsula. Promoting Catholicism to create a more unified national identity, Isabella and Ferdinand launched an **Inquisition** against supposed heretics and executed or expelled some 200,000 Jews as well. After the reconquest and the Inquisition, Catholic Spain used its wealth and military power to expand its reach by forging its own trade networks with North Africa, India, and other Asian lands. The legacy of the reconquest of the Spanish Peninsula and the Inquisition added an intense desire to spread Catholicism to Spain's motivations for exploration.

Inquisition A religious judicial institution designed to find and eliminate beliefs that did not align with official Catholic practices. The Spanish Inquisition was first established in 1478.

With expanding populations and greater agricultural productivity, Portugal and Spain developed more efficient systems of taxation, built larger military forces, and adapted gunpowder to new kinds of weapons. The surge in population provided the men to labor on merchant vessels, staff forts, and protect trade routes. More people began to settle in cities, which grew into important commercial centers.

AP® TIP
Be sure you can explain how religious motivations contributed to the exploration and settlement of the Americas.

APPLY THE TIP

Divide the class into small groups and have students briefly brainstorm what Europe received from Africa, then brainstorm what Europe received from the Americas. Have students then list what Africa and the Americas received from Europe. This will lend itself to a compare and contrast for all three locations. Answers from students will vary, but early in their contact Europeans tended to use Africa as ports and trading outposts.

Enslavement of African peoples soon followed first contacts, but early slavery in Africa was based on the trade of goods. European contact within the Americas tended to create permanent settlements, and the enslavement of American Indians was almost simultaneous with first contacts. The themes of settlement and slavery will play prominent roles in the coming modules.

Europeans Cross the Atlantic

Period 1: 1491–1607

MAP 1.3 **Fifteenth-Century Trade Routes in Africa and the Mediterranean** While overland trade routes had long connected West Africa with the Mediterranean, by the 1430s, the Portuguese had opened a new trade route down the west coast of Africa, and, eventually, around the Cape of Good Hope at the southern tip of the continent, which allowed the Portuguese access to the Indian Ocean. **What economic, political, and geographic factors made it possible for Portugal to open a new trade route along the west coast of Africa?**

TEACHING IDEA

Connecting the Dots

After students have reviewed Map 1.3, have students discuss the importance of trade routes coming into Europe. Make sure to highlight the overland route and where the routes originated. Students should be able to explain how clear trade routes were coming from deep within the African continent. The established trade routes will be fundamental in later discussions dealing with slavery and the slave trade. In discussing slavery, mention the historical role and types of slavery throughout world history. Make connections to today by mentioning sweatshops, wage-slavery, and human trafficking as well as their roles in modern society.

BUILDING AP® SKILLS

Making Connections

Show the class a route map of China's "New Silk Road Project" that includes both the land corridors and the maritime corridors (thenewsilkroadproject.com). Have students list similarities and differences between this modern map and Map 1.3.

Once students have compiled their lists, discuss the similarities and differences between the two maps. Highlight the importance of Africa and Asia in terms of world trade during the fifteenth century and within modern times. Students should be able to recognize the similarities and differences in the physical routes.

TEACHING IDEA

Incorporating Videos

Show clips from "National Geographic's America Before Columbus" (available on YouTube). Have students view the clip showing reasons for Spanish exploration up through Columbus and his first interactions with American Indians (0:38:00-0:46:25). Discuss the misconceptions and cultural misunderstandings from both the Europeans and American Indians.

REVIEW

- In what ways were the motivations for Spanish and Portuguese overseas exploration similar?
- In what ways did these motivations differ?

Europeans Cross the Atlantic

The first Europeans to see lands in the western Atlantic were Norsemen. In the late tenth century, Scandinavian seafarers led by Erik the Red reached Greenland. Sailing still farther west, Erik's son, Leif Erikson, led a party that discovered an area in North America that they called Vinland, near the Gulf of St. Lawrence. The Norse established a small settlement there around 1000 C.E., and people from Greenland continued to visit Vinland for centuries. By 1450, however, the Greenland settlements had disappeared.

Nearly a half century after Norse settlers abandoned Greenland, a Genoese navigator named Christopher Columbus visited the Spanish court of Ferdinand and Isabella and proposed an

TEACHING IDEA

Incorporating Primary Sources

The wood carvings, pictures, and accounts from early European explorers exemplified the misconceptions among the Europeans and American Indians. Create a gallery walk for students in which they view some of the earliest wood carvings and pictures created by European explorers. The following art pieces may be used in this activity:

- Johann Froschauer's 1505 engraving of the first known depiction of cannibalism in the New World. Find the piece at the History Collection's website and search for The Lost Colony of Roanoke (historycollection.co). The image will appear in Section 4.

- Theodor de Bry's engravings from 1593 depicting American Indians have been collected by the University of Houston and can be accessed by searching for "Theodor de Bry's America" (digital.lib.uh.edu). The overall collection has many carvings and images to highlight the Spanish accounts of American Indians.

As students view images, help them look for contextual clues as to the messages and bias in how the American Indians are portrayed.

TEACHING IDEA

Geography Instruction

Using Map 1.4, have students review the three major American Indian empires that occupied the areas Europeans were exploring at this time. Ask students to compare and contrast the Incan, Aztec, and Mayan empires to Spain's empire. Then, students should create two Venn diagrams, one for the three American Indian empires and one contrasting the Spanish empire with all three of the American Indian empires. Students will note that all four were ruled by kings and had strong central governments and rich histories. By contrast, the religions and range of each empire varied vastly.

Period 1: 1491–1607

MODULE 1-2 Portugal and Spain Expand Their Reach

exploration of the Indies. Portuguese explorers used this name for the region that included present-day South Asia and Southeast Asia and surrounding islands. Because Italian city-states controlled the Mediterranean and Portugal dominated the routes around Africa, Spain sought a third path to the rich Eastern trade. Columbus claimed he could find it by sailing west across the Atlantic to Japan, China, or present-day India.

Columbus's 1492 proposal was timely. Having just expelled the last Muslims and Jews from Granada and imposed Catholic practices on a now-unified nation, the Spanish monarchs sought to expand their empire. After winning Queen Isabella's support, the Genoese captain headed off in three small ships with ninety men. They stopped briefly at the Canary Islands and then headed due west on September 6, 1492.

In making his calculations, Columbus made a number of errors that led him to believe that it was possible to sail from Spain to Asia in about a month. The miscalculations nearly led to mutiny, but disaster was averted when a lookout finally spotted a small island on October 12. Columbus named the island San Salvador and made contact with local residents, whom he named Indians in the belief that he had found the East Indies islands near Japan or China. Columbus was impressed with their warm welcome and considered the gold jewelry they wore as a sign of great riches in the region.

Although native inhabitants and Columbus's men did not speak a common language, the American inhabitants aided the Spanish in exploring the area, likely in hopes of encouraging trade. The crew then sailed on to an island they named Hispaniola. Leaving a small number of men behind, Columbus sailed back to Spain with samples of gold jewelry, captured and enslaved American Indians, and tales of more wonders to come.

Columbus and his crew were welcomed as heroes when they returned to Spain in March of 1493. The success of these voyages encouraged adventurous Spaniards to travel throughout the Caribbean, South America, and regions immediately to the north in search of trade routes to Asia,

> **AP® TIP**
> Make sure you can explain how contact between Europe, Africa, and the Americas shaped social, cultural, and political changes in Europe.

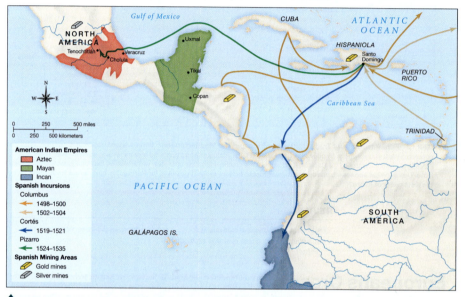

MAP 1.4 Spanish Incursions into American Empires Columbus first landed on the island he called San Salvador, and later sailed to an island he named Hispaniola. On a second voyage, he explored the coast of Central America and Cuba. Later "conquistadors" conquered farther inland, eventually overturning the Aztec and Incan empires. **Based on your knowledge of Columbus, what might explain his routes in these two voyages? In what ways did Cortés and Pizarro build upon Columbus's first routes?**

BUILDING AP® SKILLS

Claims and Evidence in Sources

Utilizing Christopher Columbus's journals, have students read his accounts and make a creative representation of their findings. This can be done by creating a highlights video of some of his observations, a newspaper, a mini journal, etc. Excerpts of Columbus's journal can be found at Fordham University's Internet History Sourcebooks Project by searching for "Christopher Columbus" (sourcebooks.fordham.edu).

Students could look specifically for places where his observations contradict themselves.

There are many examples where Columbus discusses caring for the American Indians and views them as friendly, peaceful peoples only to report a few lines later how American Indians were then harmed by his crew by his orders. How reliable are Columbus's accounts? What role would bias play in his accounts? Demonstrate to students how there is a need to objectively evaluate eye witness accounts and look for undue bias and mistruths, which will help them cultivate important AP® skills.

gold, silver, or other riches in the Americas. It also inspired the first expeditions by the Portuguese in South America, and later the French and English in North America.

Sponsored by the Catholic Spanish monarchy, Columbus's discovery of islands seemingly unclaimed by any known or recognized power led the pope to confer Spanish sovereignty over all lands already claimed or to be claimed approximately 500 miles west of the Cape Verde Islands, off the coast of west Africa. A protest by Catholic Portugal led to a treaty finalized in 1506 that moved the line 270 leagues farther west, granting Portugal control of territory that became Brazil and Spain control of the rest of what became known as South America. Thus, in the eyes of the Spanish and Portuguese monarchies and the Roman Catholic pope, Iberians ruled the Americas. Although it became clear within a decade that Columbus had not in fact discovered a route to the Indies, it took much longer for Europeans to understand the revolutionary nature of the process he had unleashed: a global system of exchange that came to be known as the Columbian Exchange (see Module 1-3).

> **AP® TIP**
> Compare the effects of competition between European nations on the development of their respective colonies in the Americas.

REVIEW

- How did religious, economic, and political factors shape Portuguese and Spanish claims on the land in Central and South America?

AP® WRITING HISTORICALLY — Responding to a Short-Answer Question Using ACE

When you try to convince someone that your opinion on an issue is important, you typically use evidence to persuade them. For instance, let's say your school district is considering starting the school day an hour earlier, and you are not in favor of this change. Saying that you don't want to start school earlier because you like to sleep in wouldn't be persuasive, but presenting statistics that link a later start time to improved academic performance is much more convincing.

Historians also use evidence to support their claims. However, not all evidence is equally strong, and no evidence can stand alone without commentary connecting it to a claim. The following steps discuss one way to make sure you provide effective support for your own interpretations of history.

For Short-Answer Questions in particular, *ACE* is a powerful mnemonic device for remembering all of the components of an effective answer. This three-part writing technique is also a great way to structure a short historical argument in a timed environment. So, what does *ACE* stand for?

- Answer
- Cite
- Explain

Let's take a look at how you can use *ACE* to respond to a Short-Answer Question:

Answer parts (a), (b), and (c).
  a. Briefly explain how ONE economic factor led to European exploration in the fifteenth century.
  b. Briefly explain how ONE specific technology that aided European exploration in the fifteenth century.
  c. Briefly explain how ANOTHER specific technology aided European exploration in the fifteenth century.

In the following steps, we will walk through how to use *ACE* to respond to part (a).

Step 1 State an answer to the prompt that makes a historically defensible claim.

You begin a historical argument by stating an *answer* to the prompt — the A in *ACE*. This is not as simple as it sounds. It's important to make sure that your answer isn't merely restating the prompt — it needs to make a claim in response to the prompt. In other words, you need to take a position that you are prepared to defend with evidence. The following answer is weak:

> In the fifteenth century there were many economic factors that led to European exploration.

(Continued)

TEACHING IDEA

Building Vocabulary

Students hear, and teachers use, the word "economic" many times during a class period. Ensure your students understand what "economic" means by asking them to define the term. Answers will vary but make sure your students understand that the term involves more than just a government's role in financial policy; economics is also at the local and individual levels and involves any exchange of goods and services.

TRM Suggested Responses to Questions

TEACHING IDEA

Think/Pair/Share

Have students answer an assigned SAQ question from the text's question set or from the *Fabric of a Nation* test bank and list possible evidence to support their answer. Place students in groups or pairs and have them create a mini-poster listing their answers and evidence. Have the class conduct a quick gallery walk — where classmates add additional examples or evidence to other groups' posters. When groups rotate back to their original poster they will have more information to enhance and *ACE* their answer. Having students rotate through 3-4 different questions will help them brainstorm as well as gain new ideas on their original question.

▲ Differentiation

Have students work in groups or pairs. Select an assortment of higher/lower level questions for students to address from the Period 1 text or from the *Fabric of a Nation* test bank. The more factual or information-based questions tend to cause less difficulty for students. Follow-up by discussing the "how"/"why" type questions, which are more complex and require greater levels of understanding. Students tend to cite basic information listed directly in a passage. Encourage students to slow down and fully support their answers with specific evidence from the text along with additional outside information.

BUILDING AP® SKILLS

Claims and Evidence in Sources

Have students read "King Ferdinand's letter to the Taino-Arawak Indians" (document is in the public domain and accessible online by searching for it by title). Have a class discussion and highlight how King Ferdinand "claimed" the Taino-Arawak American Indians, their land, and even their souls as "his." Students should understand how there was little to no regard for the American Indian's culture or resources. Have students brainstorm possible impacts on Europeans' actions toward American Indians resulting from this power they "claimed" over the American Indians.

Related activity: Have students write a letter back to King Ferdinand citing the treatment they faced under Columbus.

BUILDING AP® SKILLS
Argumentation

Students tend to simply recite or re-list details directly from the question or sources as opposed to fully addressing the stated questions. Ensure your students are addressing and answering the specific question being asked of them. To build students' skills, have them annotate questions before they answer them. Students should practice the process of question annotation by underlining the specific topic of each question and the specific action students are being asked to address in their answer.

Example: "To what extent did improved life expectancy lead to Portuguese expansion of trade into Asia?"

Student annotation skills should help them *ACE*:

1. Address improved life expectancy.
2. Cite Portugal.
3. Explain how it led to growth in trade with Asia.

TEACHING IDEA
Think/Pair/Share

Expand on the question from page 21, "Briefly explain how ONE economic factor led to European exploration in the fifteenth century." Have students work in pairs to debate which economic factor they can most strongly tie to European exploration and then work together to create an *ACE* for part (a).

TEACHING IDEA
AP® Thinking Historically Workshop

As students work on using the *ACE* strategy, often the first two components (Answer and Cite) are the easiest to complete. To ensure students understand the explanation part of *ACE*, provide students with a response that effectively uses *A* and *C* from *ACE*, but falls short on the *E*. Their job is to edit the response to illustrate the explanation needed to answer the prompt. This activity can be used as an exit card at the end of the activity.

Notice how this answer just restates the question. The claim it makes (that "there were many economic factors that led to European exploration") cannot be supported with evidence, because no specific factors have been named. A good answer offers new information in its claim, thus bringing focus to your historical argument. For example:

> Starting in the fifteenth century, Europeans developed new trade routes.

This sentence provides a specific claim: that Europeans' development of "new trade routes" was an economic factor that led to exploration.

Step 2 Cite evidence to support your claim.

This brings us to *C*, for *cite*. After presenting your idea in the form of a claim, you need to cite — that is, back up — your claim with evidence that proves it. Your historical examples can be people, acts of government, ideologies, movements of the past, and more. Be sure to use historical terms, phrases, and labels to clearly communicate the connection between your historical argument and the evidence you're providing. The more specific this aspect of your evidence is, the better — this is a place to name drop and add detail. Take a look at the following two examples, both of which cite evidence to prove the claim we came up with in step 1:

> Starting in the fifteenth century, Europeans developed new trade routes **[answer]**. The Portuguese led the way in exploration under Henry the Navigator **[cite]**.

The citation of evidence in this sentence is weak — in fact, it's simply a claim. There is no proof here that the Portuguese did, in fact "[lead] the way in exploration." Instead, consider this stronger example of citing evidence:

> Starting in the fifteenth century, Europeans developed new trade routes **[answer]**. Europeans developed these trade routes to acquire scarce and highly profitable luxury goods from Asia, such as spices **[cite]**.

This stronger response cites specific information to back up the claim that "Europeans developed new trade routes." Notice how this citation builds upon the answer by connecting "new trade routes" to "profitable luxury goods . . . such as spices."

Step 3 Explain how your evidence proves your claim.

The last step in *ACE* is vital: You need to *explain* how the evidence you cited proves your answer is a valid one. If your answer and citation of evidence are telling your reader what your historical argument is, then the explanation of your evidence addresses the question of, "So what?" No historical argument is complete unless you have told your reader — whether a teacher, a classmate, or an AP® exam grader — exactly how your evidence supports your claim.

Let's take a look at two example explanations that build on the answer and citation in steps 1 and 2:

> Starting in the fifteenth century, Europeans developed new trade routes **[answer]**. Europeans developed these trade routes to acquire scarce and highly profitable luxury goods from Asia, such as spices **[cite]**. The Portuguese king, Henry the Navigator, wanted these spices **[explain]**.

Although at first glance it might seem like the writer has provided an explanation for how the cited evidence supports the claim that "Europeans developed new trade routes," this example is ultimately not very strong. It's unclear why obtaining "scarce and highly profitable luxury goods" appealed to Henry the Navigator. The following response to part (a) is stronger:

> Starting in the fifteenth century, Europeans developed new trade routes **[answer]**. Europeans developed these trade routes to acquire scarce and highly profitable luxury goods from Asia, such as spices **[cite]**. European monarchs, including Henry the Navigator, hoped to sell these luxury goods in Europe to generate wealth for their kingdoms **[explain]**.

Notice how this response answers the question by noting an economic factor (new trade routes), citing a specific example of what Europeans sought on these new trade routes (luxury goods such as spices), and explaining why the example of luxury goods supports the answer (they generated wealth for European kingdoms).

TEACHING IDEA
Building Vocabulary

To help students build their creativity and expand their range of answers when addressing SAQs, play an elimination activity. Ask students to brainstorm evidence related to a specific topic (i.e., reasons for European exploration, fifteenth-century new technology or innovations, etc.). Once students have compiled a list of evidence related to the assigned topic, the class then calls out the terms written on their list of evidence that supports the claim. The class eliminates any duplicate "evidence" from their lists as duplicate terms are called out. This quick activity forces students to brainstorm ideas and evidence when compiling possible support to an assigned question's topic. Students will ultimately need to decide what is valid/invalid support that is relevant to the SAQ questions. Students that give evidence that seems too far "off-topic" should explain their answers; this will encourage students to defend their thinking skills and challenge the class as a whole. This quick activity will help build skills and provide an insight into students' understanding of evidence and how it relates to the assigned questions.

Now that we've walked through how to answer part (a), let's put it all together. Carefully read the example of how a response to prompt (b) follows *ACE*:

Henry the Navigator encouraged innovations in seafaring **[answer]**. The caravel, a new kind of vessel, was an important example of these innovations **[cite]**. The caravel was a small and maneuverable ship that was capable of traveling long distances **[explain]**.

ACTIVITY

1. **Respond to part (c):**
   c. Briefly explain how ANOTHER specific technology aided European exploration in the fifteenth century.
   You may wish to use the astrolabe as an example of a specific technology.

2. Use *ACE* to respond to the following Short-Answer Question.
   Answer parts (a), (b), and (c).
   a. Briefly explain ONE specific historical development that led to European exploration in the fifteenth century.
   b. Briefly explain ANOTHER specific historical development that led to European exploration in the fifteenth century.
   c. Briefly explain ONE result of European exploration in the fifteenth century.

BUILDING AP® SKILLS

Making Connections

Have students create a Venn diagram between Spanish and Portuguese exploration.

- Similarities might include: both countries were seeking trade routes to Asia, both countries were Catholic, both countries established colonies, both countries were changed by their contact with other cultures, the basic motivation of Gold/God/Glory to justify their expansion.

- Differences might include: the basic route the two countries took, the eventual use of enslaved people, the range of resources brought back to their home country.

TRM Find **Handout 1.5 – Comparing Spanish and Portuguese Exploration** in the Teacher's Resource Materials.

TEACHING IDEA

Teachable Moment

Another useful tip when trying to ensure that students' answers cite specific details is to have them try to use evidence that requires capitalizing — proper names of events, people, developments, etc. usually provide strong evidence.

TRM Suggested Responses to Questions

TEACHING IDEA

Class Discussion

The learning targets in each module are packed full of individual details that, once connected, help students understand the complex concepts embedded in American history. As a class, discuss each learning target. Either display the learning targets on a screen or write them on a whiteboard. Call students' attention to the verb, such as "explain," at the beginning of each learning target. This tells the students what they need to do. Next, focus on what needs to be explained in each learning target: for instance, "how patterns of trade . . . changed and developed . . ." Dissecting each learning target in this way helps make sure that students are clear on what they should be able to do by the end of the module.

Module 1-3

The Columbian Exchange

LEARNING TARGETS

By the end of this module, you should be able to:

- Explain how patterns of trade, including technology, foodstuffs, and livestock, changed and developed during the Columbian Exchange, and the ways Europeans and American Indians negotiated this change.
- Explain how cultural interaction, cooperation, competition, and conflict between European empires, between American Indian nations, and between Europeans and American Indians influenced political, economic, and social developments in North America.
- Explain how differing American Indian and European labor systems developed in North America and explain their effects on the lives of the people of North America, Europe, and Africa.

THEMATIC FOCUS

Geography and the Environment

The Columbian Exchange — of crops, animals, diseases, and more — shaped the development of both American Indian and European societies. Crops transplanted from the Americas led to the growth of Europe's population, and the mineral wealth from the New World contributed to the transition from feudalism to capitalism in Europe. Yet for indigenous peoples in the Americas, the primary effect of the Columbian Exchange was the introduction of European diseases, which decimated the native population. The creation of an "Atlantic World" linking Europe, the Americas, and Africa in an economic system that relied on the forced labor of American Indians and Africans also sped up as Britain, France, and the Netherlands began to colonize.

HISTORICAL REASONING FOCUS

Causation

Historians use the historical pattern of thought called causation in explaining the relationship between an event and its effects. Put simply, this way of looking at history seeks to illustrate how one event leads to the next. It might be helpful to think of an effect as the outcome of a cause.

There are two major ways to use causation to consider the interplay of causes and effects. As you remember, when historians look to understand why a development occurred, they sometimes examine a cause, or multiple causes, that culminate in an effect. At other times, historians start with a major development and examine resulting effects. Historians taking this second approach are interested in how consequences can help us make predictions and guide better decision-making in the future.

The effects described in the opening to this module — the beginnings of numerous ongoing exchanges, changes to environments on four continents, and the creation of the Atlantic World — are only the beginning of the story of the outcomes of European exploration.

TASK ▶ As you read Module 1-3, be sure to keep track of the many additional effects that followed from Columbus's journey and the Spanish colonization of the Americas.

The Columbian Exchange Transforms Four Continents

Atlantic World The interactions between the peoples from the lands bordering the Atlantic Ocean (Africa, the Americas, and Western Europe) beginning in the late fifteenth century.

Ongoing contact between Europe and the Americas, initiated by Columbus, started the process called the *Columbian Exchange*. This exchange — at times accidental and at other times purposeful — traded diseases, plants, animals, peoples, ideas, and resources between Africa, Europe, and the Americas. The numerous major and long-lasting effects this process unleashed transformed the economies and environments of all four continents. The lands bordering the Atlantic — Africa, the Americas, and Western Europe — were knit together by these exchanges into an "**Atlantic World**," especially as the French, Dutch, and English followed the lead of the Portuguese and Spanish and began to establish their own colonies in the New World.

EXPLORING AP® THEMES

Geography and the Environment

Encourage students to list connections to the AP® theme geography and the environment while reading this module. At the end of the module, discuss how the Columbian Exchange shaped the development of the Atlantic World.

The Columbian Exchange Transforms Four Continents

AP® TIP
Consider how widespread epidemics aided Spanish conquest of the Americas.

The Spaniards were aided in their conquest of the Americas as much by germs as by guns or horses. Because native peoples in the Western Hemisphere had had almost no contact with the rest of the world for millennia, they lacked immunity to most germs carried by Europeans. This meant that Europeans' presence on their continents initiated demographic disasters, which native peoples called the Great Dying. These diseases, coupled with warfare, first eradicated the Arawak and Taino on Hispaniola, wiping out some 300,000 people. In the Incan empire, the population plummeted from about 9 million in 1530 to less than half a million by 1630. Among the Aztecs, the Maya, and their neighbors, the population collapsed from some 40 million people around 1500 to about 3 million a century and a half later. European germs spread northward as well, leading to catastrophic epidemics among the Pueblo peoples of the Southwest and the Mississippian cultures of the Southeast. Initially, the devastating decline in Indian populations ensured the victory of Spain and other European powers over American populations.

Columbian Exchange The biological exchange between the Americas and the rest of the world between 1492 and the end of the sixteenth century. Although its initial impact was strongest in the Americas and Europe, it was soon felt globally.

In the **Columbian Exchange**, America provided Europeans with high-yielding, nutrient-rich foods like maize, tomatoes, and potatoes, as well as new indulgences like tobacco and cacao. In exchange, Europe and Africa sent rice, wheat, rye, oats, soybeans, lemons, and oranges to the Western Hemisphere (Map 1.5). These grain crops transformed the American landscape, particularly in North America, where wheat eventually became a major food source. As a part of the Columbian Exchange, Europeans also brought animals unknown in the Americas, including cattle, horses, chickens, pigs, and honeybees. Cattle and pigs, in particular, changed native diets, while horses inspired new methods of farming, transportation, and warfare throughout the Americas.

The conquered Incan and Aztec empires also provided vast quantities of gold and silver to Spain, making it the treasure-house of Europe and ensuring its dominance on the continent for several decades. Elite Europeans exploited the labor of poor Europeans, American Indians, and Africans in these colonial societies to extract these precious resources, and also enhanced their wealth through the cultivation of **staple crops** such as sugar. Sugar was first developed in the East Indies, but became a source of enormous profits once it took root in the Portuguese colony of Brazil. Moreover, when mixed with cacao, sugar created an addictive drink known as chocolate. Africans' partial immunity to malaria and yellow fever made them attractive to Europeans seeking enslaved labor to produce valuable exports of sugar and tobacco on Caribbean islands after the native population was decimated.

The continued desire of European nations to acquire colonies in the Americas was a direct result of witnessing the enormous wealth garnered by Spanish conquests. Between 1500 and 1650, Spanish ships carried home more than 180 tons of gold and 16,000 tons of silver from Mexico and Bolivia. About one-fifth of this amount, and indeed one-fifth of all other exports from Spanish colonies, was taken by the Spanish crown for taxes. The rest was dispersed among wealthy supporters of the expeditions, the families of **conquistadors** or *encomenderos*, or soldiers and sailors who returned from America.

Indeed, the great wealth of the Americas transformed economies throughout Europe, and profits from colonialism and slavery played an important role in this transformation. Starting just after 1500, Western Europe experienced a globally unprecedented period of sustained growth resulting from

◀ **An Aztec with Smallpox** Smallpox followed the Spanish conquest, killing thousands of native peoples. This illustration by the Spanish missionary Bernardino de Sahagún shows a woman with smallpox aided by a native healer. **In what ways does this image represent a European perspective on native disease?**

TEACHING IDEA

Incorporating Secondary Sources

Search for Alfred W. Crosby's essay, "The Columbian Exchange," on the Gilder Lehrman Institute of American History website (gilderlehrman.org). Have students read the essay, highlighting causes in one color and effects in another color, or have them write a list of causes and effects on a separate page as they read. Discuss the causes and effects of the Columbian Exchange as a class, as well as the long-term effects that they may have had on our lives today.

▲ Differentiation

For students who benefit from a visualization of concepts, search for the "Interactive Map: Columbian Exchange" on the Gilder Lehrman website (gilderlehrman.org). Give students time to navigate the interactive map, exploring and reading about how people, animals, plants, and microbes moved between Europe, Africa, and the Americas via the Columbian Exchange. Have students write down at least one cause and effect per category (people, animals, plants, microbes).

BUILDING AP® SKILLS
Comparison

Increased wealth amassed by Europeans via trading resources that were acquired in the Americas helped spur Europe's shift from feudalism to capitalism. To help students understand feudalism, watch the first minute or so of Citizens Project's video, "What was Feudalism? | 4 Minute History" (available on YouTube). After learning a bit about feudalism from the video, discuss its definition with the class and ask students to identify issues that existed in the feudal system. Next, watch the Simple Politics video, "What is Capitalism?" (available on YouTube). Discuss the definition of capitalism. Then have students complete a Venn diagram to compare and contrast feudalism with capitalism. It is important to understand the differences between these economic systems, as the shift from feudalism to capitalism had a great impact on European civilization and its colonization of the Americas.

TRM Find **Handout 1.6 – Feudalism vs. Capitalism** in the Teacher's Resource Materials.

EXPLORING AP® THEMES
Social Structures

Pose this question to the class: "In what ways did the Columbian Exchange cause a shift from feudalism to capitalism?" Have students use their knowledge of feudalism and capitalism to explain how amassing wealth in the Americas could cause fundamental shifts in the social structures of European nations. If able, students could also explain to what extent the Columbian Exchange changed European society.

Period 1: 1491–1607

MODULE 1-3 The Columbian Exchange

▲ **MAP 1.5 The Columbian Exchange, Sixteenth Century** When Europeans made contact with Africa and the Americas, they initiated an exchange of plants, animals, and germs that transformed the food, labor, and mortality of all four continents. **What positive and negative ramifications of the Columbian Exchange on the Atlantic World are shown on this map?**

feudalism A social and economic system organized by a hierarchy of hereditary classes. Lower social orders owed loyalty to the social classes above them and, in return, received protection or land.

capitalism An economic system based on private ownership of property and the open exchange of goods between property holders.

aristocratic Members of the highest class of society, typically nobility who inherited their ranks and titles.

capturing the land resources of the Americas. This influx of wealth from the Columbian Exchange accelerated the end of **feudalism**, a European social and economic system in which peasants lived and worked on a noble lord's land in exchange for military protection, and helped trigger the rise of a new order: **capitalism**.

At the same time, American riches generated in the Columbian Exchange increasingly flowed beyond Spain's borders. The Netherlands was a key beneficiary of this wealth, becoming a center for Spanish shipbuilding and trade. Still, the Dutch were never completely under Spanish control, and they traded gold, silver, and other items to France, England, and other European nations. Goods also followed older routes across the Mediterranean to the Ottoman empire, where traders could make huge profits on exotic items from the Americas. Thus, while some Europeans suffered under Spanish power, others benefited from the riches brought to the continent. By the late sixteenth century, the desire for a greater share of those riches revitalized imperial dreams among the French and English as well as the Dutch. Rulers of European nations of the Atlantic World began to fund expeditions to North America.

The Spanish limited the bulk of the benefits of the Columbian Exchange to **aristocratic** families and merchants. Enriched European nobles spent their wealth mainly on luxury goods imported from the Americas, Asia, or other European nations. Very little of this wealth was invested in improving conditions at home. Indeed, the rapid infusion of gold and silver fueled inflation, making it harder for ordinary people to afford the necessities of life.

REVIEW

- What were the short-term consequences of Columbus's voyages in both Europe and the Americas?
- How did the Columbian Exchange transform both the Americas and Europe?

TEACHING IDEA
Incorporating Videos

Assign students to watch Episode 23 "The Columbian Exchange" from the Crash Course US History series (available on YouTube). The video is broken up into four categories, so have students make a chart to keep track of each one. Once the video is over, discuss the causes and effects of the Columbian Exchange as a class.

Period 1: 1491–1607

European Encounters with West Africa

Enslaved Africans were among the most lucrative "goods" traded by European merchants. Slavery had been practiced in Europe, the Americas, Africa, and other parts of the world for centuries. But in most times and places, enslaved people were captives of war or individuals sold in payment for deaths or injuries to conquering enemies. Under such circumstances, enslaved people generally retained some legal rights, and bondage was rarely permanent and almost never inheritable. With the advent of large-scale European participation in the African slave trade, however, the system of bondage began to change, transforming Europe and Africa and, in turn, the Americas.

In the fifteenth century, Europeans were most familiar with North Africa, a region deeply influenced by Islam and characterized by large kingdoms, well-developed cities, and an extensive network of trading centers. In northeast Africa, including Egypt, city-states flourished, with ties to India, the Middle East, and China. In northwest Africa, Timbuktu linked North Africa to empires south of the Sahara as well as to Europe. Here enslaved Africans labored for wealthier Africans in a system of bound labor long familiar to Europeans.

By the mid-sixteenth century, European nations established competing forts along the African coast from the Gold Coast and Senegambia in the north to the Bight of Biafra and West Central Africa farther south. The men and women shipped from these forts to Europe generally came from communities that had been raided or conquered by more powerful groups. African empires able to trade captives at the coast for European goods, most notably guns, gained power, which they used to expand and capture more humans for trade.

Enslaved Africans from the interior of West Africa arrived at the coast exhausted, hungry, dirty, and with few clothes. They worshipped gods unfamiliar to Europeans, and their cultural customs and social practices seemed, to them, strange and primitive. Over time, it was the image of the enslaved West Africans that came to dominate European visions of the entire continent.

AP® ANALYZING SOURCES

Source: Mvemba A Nzinga (also known as Afonso I), King of the Kongo, *Letter to John III, King of Portugal*, 1526

"Sir, in our Kingdoms there is another great inconvenience which is of little service to God, and this is that many of our people, keenly desirous as they are of the wares and things of your Kingdoms, which are brought here by your people, and in order to satisfy their voracious appetite, seize many of our people, freed and exempt men, and very often it happens that they kidnap even noblemen and the sons of noblemen, and our relatives, and take them to be sold to the white men who are in our Kingdoms; and for this purpose they have concealed them; and others are brought during the night so that they might not be recognized.

And as soon as they are taken by the white men they are immediately ironed and branded with fire, and when they are carried to be embarked, if they are caught by our guards' men the whites allege that they have bought them but they cannot say from whom, so that it is our duty to do justice and to restore to the freemen their freedom, but it cannot be done if your subjects feel offended, as they claim to be.

And to avoid such a great evil we passed a law so that any white man living in our Kingdoms and wanting to purchase goods in any way should first inform three of our noblemen and officials of our court whom we rely upon in this matter. . . . But if the white men do not comply with it they will lose the aforementioned goods. And if we do them this favor and concession it is for the part Your Highness has in it, since we know that it is in your service too that these goods are taken from our Kingdom, otherwise we should not consent to this. . . ."

Questions for Analysis
1. Identify one conflict that Nzinga mentions in his letter.
2. Describe how Nzinga proposes to resolve this conflict.
3. Explain the effects of the Columbian Exchange in Africa that are evident in this letter.

TEACHING IDEA

Geography Instruction

Have students label a map of Africa to increase understanding of the locations specified on this page. Locations should include:

- Kingdom of Egypt
- Timbuktu
- Sahara Desert
- Gold Coast
- Senegambia
- Bight of Biafra

A reproducible version of this map is available in the Teacher's Resource Materials.

TRM Map 1D – Africa

TRM Suggested Responses to Questions

TRM Module 1.3 AP® Analyzing Sources Handout

TEACHING IDEA

Incorporating Secondary Sources

Narratives of American history tend to focus on Africans as being enslaved, and American Indians as dying of disease before being conquered. Though this is an accurate portrayal of the experiences of many Africans and American Indians, there is more to the story. Many American Indians were also enslaved and forced to work for European conquerors. Have students read "Indian Slavery in the Americas" by Alan Gallay, which can be found on the Gilder Lehrman website (gilderlehrman.org). After reading, discuss how the system of slavery changed over time, as well as what caused Europeans to shift from enslaving American Indians to enslaving Africans.

TEACHING IDEA

Incorporating Primary Sources

Using the source written by Mvemba A Nzinga, discuss the learning target, "Explain how differing American Indian and European labor systems developed in North America and explain their effects on the lives of the people of North America, Europe, and Africa." Focus specifically on how Africans were affected by the system of slavery.

Period 1: 1491–1607

MODULE 1-3 The Columbian Exchange

As traders from Portugal, Spain, Holland, and England brought back more stories and more enslaved Africans, these negative portraits took deeper hold. Woodcuts and prints circulated in Europe showing half-naked Africans who were portrayed more like apes than humans. Biblical stories also seemingly reinforced notions of Africans as naturally inferior to Europeans. In the Bible, Ham had sinned against his father, Noah. Noah then cursed Ham's son Canaan to a life of slavery. Increasingly, European Christians considered Africans the "sons of Ham," infidels who deserved a life of bondage. This self-serving idea was used to justify the enslavement of black men, women, and children.

These images of West Africa failed to reflect the diverse peoples who lived there and the diverse societies that developed in the area's tropical rain forests, plains, and savannas. As the slave and gun trades expanded in the sixteenth and seventeenth centuries, they destabilized large areas of western and central Africa, with smaller societies decimated by raids and even larger kingdoms damaged by the extensive commerce in human beings.

Ultimately, men, women, and children were captured by Africans as well as Portuguese, Spanish, Dutch, and English traders. Still, Europeans did not yet institute a system of perpetual slavery, in which enslavement was transmitted from one generation to the next. Instead, Africans formed another class of bound labor, alongside peasants, indentured servants, criminals, and apprentices. Crucially, distinctions among bound laborers on the basis of race did not exist. Wealthy Englishmen, for instance, viewed both African and Irish laborers as ignorant and unruly heathens, though the Irish never experienced wholesale enslavement and exportation to foreign lands in the same fashion as enslaved Africans. However, as Europeans began to conquer and colonize the Americas and demands for labor increased dramatically, ideas about race and slavery changed significantly.

In this way, the Atlantic World fused cultures through the contacts and migrations of people, both forced and free, from Europe and Africa to create new societies and social systems.

REVIEW

- How and why did Europeans expand their connections with Africa and the Middle East in the fifteenth century?
- How did early European encounters with West Africans influence Europeans' ideas about African peoples and reshape existing systems of slavery?

AP® WRITING HISTORICALLY — Using Categories to Respond to a Short-Answer Question

Often, Short-Answer Questions on the AP® exam will ask you to focus your analysis on a specific topic category. You likely remember some common categories introduced in the AP® Thinking Historically box in Module 1-1 (p. 14). The following list of categories builds on it:

- politics
- economy
- society/culture (including demographics, religion, ideology)
- interactions with the environment
- technology

Even if you do not have a specific task to complete, asking yourself questions about these topic categories is still a useful study and pre-writing strategy. Categorizing what you have learned will help you break the bigger picture of your historical knowledge into smaller, and more memorable, lists.

Let's take a look at an AP®-style Short-Answer Question that asks you to think about causation. These kinds of prompts offer excellent opportunities to use the category strategy because they often provide you with the exact topic(s) you will need to focus on.

Answer (a), (b), and (c). Confine your response to the period before 1607.
a. Briefly describe ONE specific economic effect of the Columbian Exchange in the Western Hemisphere.
b. Briefly describe ONE specific economic effect of the Columbian Exchange in Europe.
c. Briefly describe ONE specific social effect of the Columbian Exchange on the Western Hemisphere.

Step 1 Break down the prompt, then reflect on your historical knowledge of causes relevant to the topic.

One of the first things you probably noticed about this question is that parts (a), (b), and (c) all ask about effects. This is how you know you're dealing with a causation prompt, even if the word "cause" never appears. Effects don't pop up out of nowhere — they are always linked to causes.

28

EXPLORING AP® THEMES
Social Structures

Discuss how changes in the slave trade (from enslavement to serve a sentence or pay a debt to perpetual slavery) impacted social structures in the Americas. Consider short-term impacts as well as long-term impacts. Students might delve into their prior knowledge about the system of slavery in the United States to help explain the long-term impacts on the structure of society.

TRM Suggested Responses to Questions

TEACHING IDEA
AP® Thinking Historically Workshop

This workshop is designed as a bell ringer in advance of the writing historically activity. Provide students with the following terms: economic, staple crops, *encomienda*, Columbian Exchange, conquistadors, and enslaved labor. Ask students to funnel the history (that is, work from broadest to most specific) using each term. A completed product should look something like this: Economic, Columbian Exchange, conquistadors, *encomienda*, enslaved labor, and staple crops. Ask students why the use of the last four terms provides a better answer to part (a) in the practice question. This helps establish a framework for the use of categories to develop more specific answers.

MODULE 1-3 The Columbian Exchange

Since this question asks about what you have just learned in this module, a great place to start is simply to reflect on what you have read about the Columbian Exchange, keeping causes and effects of historical events and developments in mind. At this point, if you aren't too pressed for time, it may be helpful simply to brainstorm as many effects as you can think of, regardless of the analysis category they fall under. What were the political effects? Social and cultural? Economic? Technological? Environmental?

If you are writing in a timed environment and are comfortable with your knowledge of the question topic, you should look for what categories the prompt has specified before you begin to brainstorm. In this case, the prompt asks you to discuss economic and social effects.

Step 2 Create a list of effects, broken out by categories for analysis.

Create a list of effects that fall under each category. This will help you organize your thoughts and give you a blueprint for your written response to the question. The following example shows one way you might organize such a list:

Categories	Effects of the Columbian Exchange
Economics	Europeans used the forced labor of American Indians and Africans to obtain resources like gold and silver, as well as foodstuffs like sugar, maize, and chocolate. These resources were then sold in Europe.
	These new resources were part of the Columbian Exchange and generated great wealth for European nations.
Society	The Columbian Exchange also brought diseases like smallpox, which decimated American Indian populations. The high mortality caused by these diseases made it easier for the Spanish and Portuguese to conquer and control American Indian lands in the Western Hemisphere.

Notice how this list provides explanations for each of the three parts of the prompt in the example answer that follows:

a. Briefly identify ONE specific economic effect of the Columbian Exchange in the Western Hemisphere.

During the Columbian Exchange, Europeans used the forced labor of American Indians to obtain resources, and also enhanced their wealth **[answer]** through the cultivation of staple crops such as sugar **[cite]**, which economically affected the Western Hemisphere by making American Indians subservient to European pursuit of profit **[explain]**.

b. Briefly describe ONE specific economic effect of the Columbian Exchange in Europe.

During the Columbian Exchange, new resources from the Western Hemisphere were introduced to European markets **[answer]**, including silver and gold, as well as food such as maize and luxuries like chocolate for Europeans **[cite]**. The influx of wealth into Spain was distributed unevenly and created a surge of inflation in the country **[explain]**.

c. Briefly describe ONE specific social effect of the Columbian Exchange on the Western Hemisphere.

The Columbian Exchange also brought diseases like smallpox **[answer]**, which decimated American Indian populations **[cite]**. The high mortality caused by these diseases made it easier for the Spanish and Portuguese to conquer and control American Indian lands in the Western Hemisphere **[explain]**.

ACTIVITY

Write a full response to the following Short-Answer Question. Be sure to start by breaking down the question, pre-writing using the analytic categories named in the prompt, and make your argument by using the Answer-Cite-Explain (*ACE*) strategy. For a review of *ACE*, see page 21.

Answer (a), (b), and (c). Confine your response to the period before 1607.
   a. Briefly explain ONE specific economic effect of the Columbian Exchange on West Africa.
   b. Briefly explain ONE specific social effect of the Columbian Exchange on West Africa.
   c. Briefly explain ONE specific political effect of the Columbian Exchange on West Africa.

BUILDING AP® SKILLS

Argumentation

When discussing economic, political, or social changes, students should avoid using general terms like economy, politics, or society. Encourage students to be more specific in their explanations. For example, if a question is asking about economic changes due to the Columbian Exchange, students should specifically mention topics such as the rise of capitalism in Europe due to increased wealth and resources. If a question is asking about changes in social structure, students should mention how the Columbian Exchange was one factor leading to the decline of the feudal system in Europe, instead of saying that it simply changed society.

TRM Suggested Responses to Questions

TEACHING IDEA

Incorporating Videos

Assign students to watch Episode 1, "The Black Legend, Native Americans, and Spaniards" from the Crash Course US History series (available on YouTube). This short 11-minute episode is very helpful to introduce students to the content that the course instructor will engage with in greater complexity and detail.

Module 1-4

Spanish Colonial Society

LEARNING TARGETS

By the end of this module, you should be able to:

- Explain how religious ideas and racial, ethnic, gender, class, and regional identities affected European and American Indian societies in North America before the seventeenth century.

THEMATIC FOCUS

Social Structures

Spanish conquistadors used local allies and technological superiority to overpower the Aztecs and other powerful American Indian societies in Central and South America. As Spain built a large empire in the New World, it relied on the *encomienda* system to force American Indians to labor on Spanish plantations and introduced a caste system, which created a social hierarchy based on race. Over time, the harsh treatment of American Indians fostered debate within Spanish society and contributed to establishment of the mission system.

HISTORICAL REASONING FOCUS

Continuity and Change

You've probably heard the saying, "The more things change, the more they stay the same." Although it's one of those common phrases, like "Such is life" or "Better late than never," it can also be a good way to look at the historical pattern of thought called continuity and change. When historians take this approach to history, they draw conclusions about extended periods of time by examining the ways that some things stayed the same across a timespan even as other things changed.

Examining continuity and change is also a useful way to highlight significant shifts and developments over a period of time. While noting changes throughout history is important, so too is focusing on significant commonalities across time to show the continuities. Important continuities can unify our understanding of movements, ideas, concepts, and societies across decades, or a century, or even more.

When you consider continuities and changes throughout the AP® U.S. History course, it's important to remember to think comparatively, because, at its core, this historical practice is really the comparison of the beginning and end of a given time period. This comparison asks: Between the starting point and ending point of a time period, how much did things change, and how much did they stay the same?

TASK ▶ As you read this module, challenge yourself to think comparatively by noting changes and continuities in Spanish colonization from 1492 to 1607. Annotating brief descriptions of important continuities and changes is a solid strategy to help you organize your thoughts on what you will learn.

AP® TIP

Make sure you can explain how and why the *encomienda* system benefitted the Spanish in the New World.

Columbus made a total of four voyages to the Caribbean to claim land for Spain, and even tried to build a permanent Spanish settler colony that he could rule as governor. In his quest to create an orderly settlement, he tried to convince those who accompanied him from Spain to build houses, plant crops, and cut logs for forts, but they, too, had come for gold. When the American Indians stopped trading willingly, Spaniards used force to demand riches, coercing as much gold as possible from the indigenous peoples in the Caribbean.

On his final voyage, Columbus introduced a system of *encomienda* in the Caribbean, by which leading men, the *encomenderos*, received land and the unpaid labor from all American Indians residing on it. The *encomienda* system spread widely and persisted as Spanish *conquistadors* made new efforts to locate gold and increase their wealth through whatever means they deemed necessary.

Spanish Incursions in the Americas

By the time of Columbus's death in 1506, the islands he had discovered were dissolving into chaos as traders and adventurers fought with American Indians and one another over the spoils of conquest. Once Spanish explorers subdued tribes like the Arawak and Taino in the Caribbean, they headed toward the mainland. They justified the brutal subjugation of American people and lands through European concepts of law and religion. In one such case, King Ferdinand and Queen Isabella of Spain issued a legal document called the *requerimiento* as the basis for Spanish interaction with American Indians in 1513. Conquistadors began to spread its message to groups such as the Maya, Tlaxcalan, and Aztecs: The Pope had granted Spanish monarchs the authority to claim lands and protect priests preaching the faith in the Americas — and if anyone resisted, they forfeited the protection of the crown and could be "justly" enslaved or killed.

In 1519, as the Spanish invaded the mainland, an American Indian girl named Malintzin was thrust into the center of this chaotic and violent world. Ultimately, she witnessed events that transformed not only her world but also the world at large. Malintzin, whose birth name is lost to history, lived in the rural area between the expanding kingdom of the Mexica and the declining Mayan states of the Yucatán peninsula. Raised in a noble household, Malintzin was fluent in Nahuatl, the language of the Mexica. In 1515 or 1516, when she was between the ages of eight and twelve, she was either taken by or given to Mexica merchants, perhaps as a peace offering to stave off military attacks. She then entered a well-established slave trade, consisting mostly of women and girls, who were sent eastward to work in the expanding cotton fields or the households of slaveholders. During her captivity there, Malintzin learned the Mayan language. Although she could not have known it at the time, her circumstances would again change dramatically in just a few years' time.

In 1517 the Maya drove Spanish adventurers from the banks of local rivers and were able to maintain control of their lands. But when the Spaniards returned in 1519, they defeated the Maya in battle. As a result, the Maya offered the Spaniards food, gold, and twenty enslaved women, including Malintzin. The Spanish leader, Hernán Cortés, baptized the enslaved women and assigned each of them Christian names, although the women did not consent to this ritual. Cortés then divided the women among his senior officers, giving Malintzin, named Doña Marina by Cortés, to the highest-ranking noble in his group.

Already fluent in Nahuatl and Mayan, Malintzin soon learned Spanish. Within a matter of months, she became the Spaniards' chief translator. When Diego de Velásquez, the Spanish governor of Cuba, granted Cortés the right to explore and trade along the coast of South America, Malintzin had no choice but to go with him. Although Velásquez gave Cortés no direct authority to attack native peoples in the region or claim land for himself, the conquistador saw this expedition as an opportunity to amass great wealth. With Malintzin acting as a translator, Cortés forged alliances with local rulers willing to join in an attack against the Mexica (whom the Spaniards called Aztecs). From the perspective of local communities such as the Tlaxcalan, Cortés's presence offered an opportunity to strike back against the brutal Aztec regime.

As Cortés moved into territories ruled by the Aztecs, his success depended on his ability to understand Aztec ways of thinking and

> **AP® TIP**
> Consider the ways that native peoples sought to defend and maintain their independence and culture in the face of European intrusion.

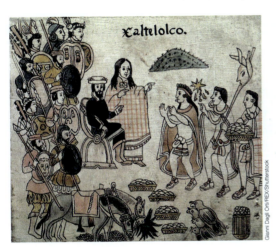

◀ **Hernán Cortés and Malintzin Meet Montezuma at Tenochtitlán, 1519**
This image depicts Cortés and Malintzin meeting Montezuma in November 1519. It is a reproduction of an image created by Tlaxcalan artists and represents an American Indian perspective on these events. **Identify Cortés, Malintzin, and Montezuma. What can you infer about the artists' attitude toward Cortés and Malintzin based on this image?**

TEACHING IDEA

Building Vocabulary

Point out the word "conquistador" to students, and its direct meaning ("conqueror"). This is an important place to begin developing student awareness of the concept that words and labels have both meaning and power. Note that this label was self-proclaimed; it was not a name given or originating from the American Indians. Ask students what "conquistador" meant to the Spanish based on their interactions with American Indians. Discuss with students any implications that arise from this word.

TEACHING IDEA

Incorporating Videos

Have students watch excerpts from "Engineering an Empire: The Aztecs," from the History Channel (available on YouTube). This production combines a study of indigenous Aztec religion, culture, and technology with an accounting of the consequences of their contact and conflict with Cortes.

TRM Suggested Responses to Questions

TRM Module 1.4 AP® Analyzing Sources Handout 1

MODULE 1-4 Spanish Colonial Society

◀ **The Aztec City of Tenochtitlán** German geographers drew this map of Tenochtitlán in 1524 based on Aztec sources. At its peak, the city was populated by 100,000 people and contained a marketplace, schools, the emperor's palace, and a ball-game court. The Aztecs viewed Tenochtitlán as the intersection of the secular and divine worlds. **What does this map reveal about life in Tenochtitlán?**

to convince subjugated groups to fight against their despotic rulers. Malintzin thus accompanied Cortés at every step, making diplomacy possible between the Spanish and leaders of native peoples subjugated by the Aztec empire.

Despite their assumption of cultural superiority, many Spaniards who accompanied Cortés were astonished by Aztec cities, canals, and temples, which rivaled those in Europe. Seeing these architectural wonders may have given some soldiers pause about trying to conquer the kingdom. But when the Aztec chief, Montezuma, presented Cortés with large quantities of precious objects including gold-encrusted jewelry as a peace offering, he unwittingly confirmed that the Aztecs had the vast wealth that the Spanish had come for.

When Cortés and his men marched to Tenochtitlán in 1519, Montezuma was indecisive in his response. After an early effort to ambush the Spaniards failed, the Aztec leader allowed Cortés to march his men into the capital city, where they took Montezuma hostage. In response, Aztec warriors attacked the Spaniards, but Cortés and his men managed to fight their way out of Tenochtitlán. They suffered heavy losses and might have been crushed by their Aztec foes but for the alliances forged with native groups in the surrounding area. Given protection by American Indian allies, the Spanish regrouped. The remaining Spanish soldiers and their allies returned to batter the Aztecs with a combination of cannons, steel weapons, horses, and trained dogs that yielded a final victory.

AP® ANALYZING SOURCES

Source: Anonymous artists, *Hernán Cortés Assisted by the Tlaxcalan People of Mexico*, 1560

About the source: This image is from the manuscript *Lienzo de Tlaxcala* and shows a mural painted for Tlaxcalan nobles.

Questions for Analysis

1. Identify the groups portrayed in this image.
2. Identify who is depicted as the winner of this conflict.
3. Describe an apparent continuity between the pre-Columbian and post-Columbian Tlaxcalan culture revealed by this image.
4. Describe at least two apparent changes between pre-Columbian and post-Columbian Tlaxcalan culture revealed by this image.

AP® TIP

Consider the early success of Spanish conquistadors. What role did the Colombian Exchange play in their efforts?

It is important to note that the germs the Spanish soldiers carried with them played a large role in allowing them to sustain their subjugation of the Aztecs. Smallpox swept through Tenochtitlán in 1521, killing thousands and leaving Montezuma's army dramatically weakened. This human catastrophe as much as military resources and strategies allowed Cortés to conquer the capital that year. He then claimed the entire region as New Spain, and assigned soldiers to construct the Spanish capital of Mexico City at Tenochtitlán. Moreover, he asserted Spanish authority over the native groups including those that had allied with him.

As news of Cortés's victory spread, and as *encomenderos* grew incredibly wealthy from the silver, gold, and other resources extracted from the American lands through the forced labor of American Indians and shipped across the Atlantic, other Spanish conquistadors sought glory in the Americas as well. Most important, in 1524 Francisco Pizarro conquered the vast Incan empire in present-day Peru. Once again, the Spaniards were helped by the spread of European diseases and non-Incan native peoples who had been ruled by the Incas. This victory ensured Spanish access to vast supplies of silver in Potosí (in present-day Bolivia) and the surrounding mountains. While the Spanish used enslaved American Indians at Potosí, their larger conquests also ensured the spread of enslaved African labor from Caribbean plantations to mainland agriculture and mining ventures. By 1535, Spain controlled the most densely populated regions of South America, which also contained the greatest mineral wealth.

REVIEW

What factors shaped Spanish colonial society in the Western Hemisphere?

Spain Establishes Colonial Rule

The Spanish monarchs, Ferdinand and Isabella, sought to incorporate the Americas into their empire as an engine that generated wealth for the crown. To do this, they took for themselves the *quinto real* ("royal fifth") — that is, 20 percent of wealth produced in Spanish colonies. To secure this wealth they divided colonial lands into viceroyalties, appointing governors called viceroys to ensure order. Moreover, they sent numerous political and military representatives, also royally appointed, to help govern locally. By the late sixteenth century, Spanish supremacy in the Americas and the wealth acquired there transformed the European economy.

In Spain, these economic transformations enriched nobles with access to wealth drained from the Americas, but produced hard times for peasants. The influx of silver, for instance, caused inflation that raised prices and impoverished peasants. Threatened by poverty and starvation, peasants joined King Philip II's (r. 1556–1598) military campaigns as soldiers and sailors. The king, a devout Catholic, claimed to be doing God's work as Spain conquered Italy and Portugal, including the latter's colonies in Africa, and tightened its grip on the Netherlands, which had been acquired by Spain through marriage in the early sixteenth century.

Throughout the sixteenth century Spain's colonial projects also established a new social order in the regions they ruled. The colonies brought Spanish, American Indians, and Africans into frequent contact, and colonial societies included people mixing in various ways. In feudal fashion, the Spanish Crown demanded more tax, **tribute**, and labor from those ranked lower in social class. Through the mechanisms of a variety of labor systems, people of American Indian and African ancestry owed work or tribute to Spanish colonial elites. To account for who owed how much, the Spanish wrote guidelines for taxation founded in ethnicity, but taking influences from other factors, for example education, to define classes in colonial society. From these defined expectations a system emerged, which later hardened and formalized into the **Spanish caste system**.

Spanish caste system A system developed by the Spanish in the sixteenth century that defined the status of diverse populations based on a racial hierarchy that privileged Europeans.

This system categorized people by the degrees of their racial ancestry into a social hierarchy, which ultimately shaped the future of societies throughout the Western Hemisphere. An individual's place indicated how much labor or tax they owed. In theory, one's racial ancestry determined one's caste, but given mixing of diverse people of the Atlantic World both ancestry and skin color blurred. In practice, it also considered qualities such as education and wealth. For example, a darker skinned educated landowner might be perceived as of higher class than a lighter skinned landless craftsman. Passing into a higher caste meant lower taxes, or escaping forced labor in addition to other social benefits. The caste system in descending order of rank included: those born in Spain

---

EXPLORING AP® THEMES

Geography and the Environment

Engage students in a discussion about historical contingency, centering around the impact that disease, specifically smallpox, had upon the Aztec capabilities and abilities to wage war against the Spanish. Point out that initially, the Spanish themselves did not even know that they had carried mass illness to the American Indians, so this was not premeditated and deliberate on their part. That being said, strategically speaking, disease worked out very much to the Spanish empire's advantage as it went about establishing New Spain. Have students consider what alternate scenarios may have unfolded in the New World had unintentional biological warfare *not* been a factor as the European and American worlds came in contact with one another.

TEACHING IDEA

Incorporating Secondary Sources

Assign students to read Chapter 9, "The Columbian Exchange," from John Richards's *The Unending Frontier*, and in groups have them create a timeline of the central events of exploration and colonial development. To further develop their skills for Short-Answer Questions, have each student, individually or in groups, engage in one of the three following tasks: identify and explain three things in the piece that stayed the same over time, identify and explain three things in the piece that changed over time, or identify and explain three eras or phases to Spanish colonial development that emerged over time.

▲ Differentiation

By placing students in groups or pairs for the previous activity, students can benefit by skill and ability level pairings as determined by the instructor. Additionally, by further dividing the task into thirds for the SAQ formulation practice, students can then engage in a jigsaw-model activity. In this model of instruction, students are tasked with completing a separate individual component or segment of the whole exercise. Then students with different segments are assembled into groups by the instructor, and contribute their assigned segment to an overall group process akin to assembling the pieces of a jigsaw puzzle. The use of this model of instruction allows for more sharing and distribution of the workload and content-acquisition to take place in class in a large number of combinations, offering the potential to get every student involved and making contributions.

TEACHING IDEA

Connecting the Dots

Point out to students that one of the reasons that the Spaniards could engage in exploration, exploitation, and colonization upon such a large scale was that, from the very beginning, their colonies were state-run ventures, with all of the concomitant resources of the state able to be brought to bear in the advancement of the process. As such, from a financial, personnel, institutional, and military standpoint, Spanish colonies were able to engage in a process of nation-building that was wide and deep with very long-term commitments. As a harbinger of things to come, and also as a nice set-up for some future comparing-and-contrasting, make sure to plant the seed with students that not all European colonizers will initially follow this model, which may lead to some very different initial colonial results for the other European powers.

---

called *peninsulares*, people born of Spanish parents in the colonies called *criollos*, and those sharing Spanish and American Indian parentage called *mestizos*. The Spanish ranked *mulattos*, of mixed Spanish and African parentage, below mestizos, but placed Africans, however, above indigenous American Indians they called *indios*. The Spanish considered the indios child-like wards of Spanish elites in need of parenting to enforce civilized behavior. Similarly, the Spanish enforced a lower status on Africans through laws prohibiting them from many government positions, and the priesthood.

REVIEW

What purpose did the Spanish caste system serve?

Spain Debates the Human Costs of Colonization

Despite the obvious material benefits, the Spaniards were not blind to the enormous human costs of colonization, and the conquest of the Americas inspired heated debates within Spain that raised critical questions about Spanish responsibilities to God and humanity. Catholic leaders believed that the conversion of native peoples to Christianity was critical to Spanish success in the Americas. However, most royal officials and colonial agents viewed the extraction of precious metals as far more important. They argued that cheap labor was essential to creating wealth. Yet the brutal conditions of enslaved labor led to the death of huge numbers of American Indians, and it was understandably difficult for those who survived to see any benefit in converting to the very religion the Spanish used to justify such brutal mistreatment.

Engraving of the Black Legend, 1598 In the late 1500s, Theodor de Bry and his sons created a series of engravings of interactions between Spanish soldiers and American Indians based on reports from explorers and missionaries. **How does this image express de Bry's attitude toward Spanish interactions with American Indians?**

By 1550, news of the widespread torture and enslavement of American Indians convinced the Spanish King Charles I (r. 1519–1556), who was also Emperor Charles V of the Holy Roman Empire, to gather a group of theologians, jurists, and philosophers at Valladolid to discuss the moral and legal implications of conquest. Bartolomé de Las Casas took a leading role in defending the rights of American Indians. A former conquistador, Las Casas had spent many years preaching to them in America. He asked, "And so what man of sound mind will approve a war against men who are harmless, ignorant, gentle, temperate, unarmed, and destitute of every human defense?" Las Casas reasoned that even if Spain defeated the American Indians, the souls of those killed would be lost to God, while among the survivors "hatred and loathing of the Christian religion" would prevail. He even suggested replacing the labor of enslaved American Indians with that of enslaved Africans, apparently less concerned with the souls of black people.

AP® ANALYZING SOURCES

Source: Bartolomé de Las Casas, Catholic Dominican priest, *Brief Account of the Destruction of the Indies*, 1542

"They are by nature the most humble, patient, and peaceable, holding no grudges, free from embroilments, neither excitable nor quarrelsome. . . . They are also poor people, for they not only possess little but have no desire to possess worldly goods. For this reason they are not arrogant, embittered, or greedy. . . . They are very clean in their persons, with alert, intelligent minds, docile and open to doctrine, very apt to receive our holy Catholic faith, to be endowed with virtuous customs, and to behave in a godly fashion. And once they begin to hear the tidings of the Faith, they are so insistent on knowing more and on taking the sacraments of the Church . . . that, truly, the missionaries who are here need to be endowed by God with great patience in order to cope with such eagerness. . . .

Yet into this sheepfold, into this land of meek outcasts there came some Spaniards who immediately behaved like ravening wild beasts, wolves, tigers, or lions that had been starved for many days. . . ."

Source: Juan Ginés de Sepúlveda, Catholic priest and theologian, *Concerning the Just Causes of the War against the Indians*, 1547

"[T]he Spanish have a perfect right to rule these barbarians of the New World and the adjacent islands, who in prudence, skill, virtues, and humanity are as inferior to the Spanish as children to adults, or women to men, for there exists between the two as great a difference as between savage and cruel races and the most merciful, between the most intemperate and the moderate and temperate and, I might even say, between apes and men. . . .

Compare, then, these gifts of prudence, talent, magnanimity, temperance, humanity, and religion with those possessed by these half-men . . . , in whom you will barely find the vestiges of humanity, who not only do not possess any learning at all, but are not even literate or in possession of any monument to their history except for some obscure and vague reminiscences of several things put down in various paintings; nor do they have written laws, but barbarian institutions and customs. Well, then, if we are dealing with virtue, what temperance or mercy can you expect from men who are committed to all types of intemperance and base frivolity, and eat human flesh? . . . [B]efore the arrival of the Christians . . . they waged continual and ferocious war upon one another with such fierceness that they did not consider a victory at all worthwhile unless they sated their monstrous hunger with the flesh of their enemies. . . ."

Questions for Analysis

1. Identify a specific similarity between Las Casas's and Sepúlveda's descriptions of the native people in the Western Hemisphere.
2. Identify a specific difference between Las Casas's and Sepúlveda's descriptions of the native people in the Western Hemisphere.
3. Describe a specific historical difference in the way Las Casas and Sepúlveda believed native people should be treated by the Spanish.

Period 1: 1491–1607

MODULE 1-4 Spanish Colonial Society

Juan Ginés de Sepúlveda, a Catholic theologian positioned in the royal court, attacked Las Casas's arguments. Although he had never set foot in America, he read reports of cannibalism and other violations of "natural law" among native peoples. He argued that since the American Indians were savages, the civilized Spaniards were obligated to "destroy barbarism and educate these people to a more humane and virtuous life." If they refused such help, Spanish rule "can be imposed upon them by force of arms." Although Sepúlveda spoke for the majority at Valladolid, Las Casas and his supporters continued to press their case as Spain expanded its reach into North America.

REVIEW

- What consequences did Spain's acquisition of an American empire have in Europe?

Spain's Global Empire Declines

mission system System established by the Spanish in 1573 in which missionaries, rather than soldiers, directed all new settlements in the Americas.

AP® TIP
Be sure you can explain the role religion played in Spanish colonization of the Americas changed over time.

As religious conflicts escalated in Europe between Catholics and Protestants, the Spaniards in America continued to push north from Florida and Mexico in hopes of expanding their empire. The nature of Spanish expansion, however, changed. In 1573, Spanish authorities decided that missionaries, rather than soldiers, should direct all new settlements in what is known as the **mission system**.

Franciscan priests began founding missions on the margins of Pueblo villages north of Mexico. They named the area Nuevo México (New Mexico), and many learned American Indian languages. Over the following decades, as many as twenty thousand Pueblos officially converted to Catholicism, although many still retained traditional beliefs and practices. Missionaries made a considerable effort to eradicate such beliefs and practices, including destroying Pueblo religious artifacts and flogging ceremonial leaders, but to little avail. Often years after their 'conversion' to Catholicism Spanish authorities discovered Pueblo Indians performing their traditional religious rituals in secret.

At the same time as they sought religious conversion, the Franciscans tried to force the Pueblo people to adopt European social and economic customs. They insisted that men rather than women farm the land and that the Pueblos speak, cook, and dress like the Spaniards. Yet the missionaries largely ignored Spanish laws intended to protect American Indians from coerced labor, demanding that the Pueblos build churches, provide the missions with food, and carry their goods to market. Wealthy landowners who followed the missionaries into New Mexico also demanded tribute in the form of goods and labor. Tribute payments that the Spanish enforced, violently, impoverished the Pueblo and diminished emergency stores of grains, leading to starvation during the fairly frequent droughts. The Spanish attempts to extract wealth ruined Pueblo societies' longstanding and delicate ecologically balanced agriculture suited to the arid climate.

In 1598 Juan de Oñate, a member of a wealthy mining family, established a trading post and fort in the upper Rio Grande valley. The 500 soldiers who accompanied him seized corn and clothing from Pueblo villages and murdered or raped those who resisted. Indians at the Acoma pueblo rebelled, killing 11 Spanish soldiers. The Spanish retaliated, slaughtering 500 men and 300 women and children. Fearing reprisals from outraged Pueblo Indians, most Spanish settlers withdrew from the region.

In 1610 the Spanish returned, founded Santa Fe, and established a network of missions and estates owned by *encomenderos*. This time the Pueblo people largely accepted the new situation. In part, they feared military reprisals if they challenged Spanish authorities. But they were also facing drought, disease, and raids by hostile Apaches and Navajos. The Pueblos hoped to gain protection from Spanish soldiers and priests. Yet their faith in the Franciscans' spiritual power soon began to fade when conditions did not improve. Although Spain maintained a firm hold on Florida and its colonies in the West Indies, it had to exert ever greater efforts to suppress growing resistance among the Pueblo people. Thus as other European powers expanded their reach into North America, the Spaniards were left with few resources to protect their eastern frontier.

REVIEW

- In what ways did Spanish policy change toward native peoples after 1573?
- What effects did these changes have on the Pueblo people?

TEACHING IDEA

Check for Understanding

As a module-concluding activity, direct students to individually complete a cause and effect graphic organizer on Spanish exploration. These graphic organizers can then be used to facilitate a gallery walk, where students can evaluate each product and subject it to peer review and modification.

TRM Find **Handout 1.7 – Causes and Effects of Spanish Exploration** in the Teacher's Resource Materials.

AP® WRITING HISTORICALLY: Responding to a Short-Answer Question

On the AP® exam, Short-Answer Questions may ask you to make an argument about continuity and change — that is, which aspects of specific historical patterns, events, and developments are consistent across a span of time, and which ones evolved and morphed over time.

Let's walk through how you can use your historical knowledge to answer a continuity and change-focused Short-Answer Question on the period before 1607. The following prompt is one you might encounter on the exam:

Answer (a), (b), and (c).
- a. Briefly describe ONE specific continuity in Spanish policy toward native peoples between 1492 and 1607.
- b. Briefly describe ONE specific change in Spanish policy toward native peoples between 1492 and 1607.
- c. Briefly explain ONE specific reason for the change in Spanish policy toward native peoples between 1492 and 1607.

Step 1: Break down the prompt and review your historical knowledge of continuities and changes relevant to the topic.

This prompt asks you to think about continuities and changes over more than a century of Spanish incursions into the Americas. That's longer than a human lifespan, and it may be tough to know where to begin. In this particular case, a good place to start is by reviewing everything you have learned about Spanish colonization — which just so happens to be what you learned about in Period 1. Focus your review by breaking it out into questions about continuities and about changes, making a list of the answers to them as you go over your historical knowledge. Remember, some good categories to consider whenever you catalog what changed and what remained the same include:

- politics
- economy
- society/culture
- interactions with the environment
- technology

Step 2: Choose a specific category for analysis and divide the time period specified by the prompt.

The next thing to do is choose a category for analysis. It's important to keep in mind that, on the exam, you will not have time to consider all of the categories in step 1 — and even if you're not confined by a timed environment, it's still wise to keep the scope of your analysis manageable in order to write a focused answer. In this case, a category that stands out is society. This is because the interactions between native peoples and the Spanish customs changed from being driven primarily by military conquest to a system of religious missions primarily concerned with converting native peoples to Catholicism.

Now that you've chosen a category for analysis that stands out, you should begin to think about how to address the long time frame specified by the question. Strong continuity and change responses often choose an event to divide the period into two parts. Splitting your analysis in this way gives you a way to compare and contrast the continuities and changes you have observed with evidence from throughout the time period.

This is where your review in step 1 of what you have learned will come in handy — you will likely already have thought of more than one major event or development that fits the bill. In this case, we'll take the shift to the missionary system in 1573 for all new settlements as our dividing event.

Step 3: Create a graphic organizer that connects continuities and changes to supporting evidence.

Now that we have decided upon the timespan to use for the earlier and later parts of the period and chosen at least one category to focus our analysis of continuities and changes, the next step is to develop a graphic organizer that will map out that analysis by bringing in supporting evidence.

To prove an example of continuity, you should cite evidence from both earlier and later parts of a given period of time. In this case, we need to show ongoing characteristics of Spanish colonization, and using evidence from both before and after 1573 will make a compelling case.

(Continued)

TRM Suggested Responses to Questions

TEACHING IDEA

AP® Thinking Historically Review

This workshop is designed to be a bell ringer to get students thinking about how to approach the Short-Answer Question on Spanish colonization. Begin the class by dividing students into groups of three or four. Provide each group with a map of the Western Hemisphere and ask students to locate and label at least three American Indian groups. Next, ask students to define how the American Indian groups they identified were affected by Spanish colonization. Even though the question focuses on Spanish policy, focusing on American Indians can lead students to a more complete understanding of what the Short-Answer Question is asking.

Likewise, to prove a claim that something changed, you should use examples from both earlier and later parts of a given time period. Here, this means collecting evidence that shows significant shifts in the characteristics of colonization both before and after 1573.

Your graphic organizer can take a number of different forms — including lists, tables, outlines, or mind maps — based on whatever helps you see the connection between continuities and changes and your evidence. Your organizer should also leave space for you to provide evidence for your claims. These pieces of evidence are specific historical facts that support your claims for both before and after your dividing event — in this case, the shift to missionary control of new Spanish colonies after 1573. The following example uses a table to organize an argument about Spanish colonization:

Continuities in Spanish Colonization

Claims of Continuity	Evidence in Earlier Period, 1492–1573	Evidence in Later Period, 1574–1607
Society: Starting in 1492, the Spanish forced American Indians to adopt Spanish customs, including Catholicism.	The Reconquista in Spain, and the Inquisition afterward, inspired the Spanish to pursue a policy of forced conversion of American Indians after 1492.	The attempts to forcibly convert American Indians to Spanish customs and Catholicism continued in the sixteenth century as the Spanish conquered larger areas of the Western Hemisphere. For example, Spanish missionaries' efforts to convert the Pueblo in present-day New Mexico after 1573 included destroying their religious symbols and physically punishing their religious leaders.

Changes in Spanish Colonization

Claims of Change	Evidence in Earlier Period, 1492–1573	Evidence in Later Period, 1574–1607
Society: After 1573, the Spanish used missionaries to convert American Indians to Catholicism and to force them to adopt Spanish culture.	In 1513, Ferdinand and Isabella instituted the requerimiento, an official document that established Spanish policy toward American Indians. The Spanish read this document to the American Indians they encountered in the New World, using it as a legal justification for Spanish conquest.	After 1573, the Spanish used Franciscan priests to convert American Indians to Catholicism, thereby using religion as a way to change American Indian culture to suit Spanish needs.

ACTIVITY

Practice thinking and writing historically by applying what you learned in Period 1 in your response to the following Short-Answer Question. Start by breaking down the prompt, and make your argument by using the *ACE* strategy.

Answer (a), (b), and (c).
  a. Briefly describe ONE change in the lives of American Indians resulting from Spanish colonization in the period 1492 to 1607.
  b. Briefly describe ANOTHER change in the lives of American Indians resulting from Spanish colonization in the period 1492 to 1607.
  c. Briefly describe ONE continuity in the lives of American Indians during Spanish colonization in the period 1492 to 1607.

PERIOD 1 REVIEW 1491–1607

KEY CONCEPTS AND EVENTS

aristocratic, 26
astrolabe, 18
Atlantic World, 24
Aztecs, 7
capitalism, 26
caravel, 18
Columbian Exchange, 25
conquistadors, 25
encomienda, 30
feudalism, 26
Franciscan, 36
horticulture, 4
Incas, 7
Inquisition, 18
mariners, 18
Maya, 7
missionaries, 18
mission system, 36
Pueblo, 10
Renaissance, 17
requerimiento, 31
Spanish caste system, 33
staple crops, 25
Tenochtitlán, 7
tribute, 33

KEY PEOPLE

Christopher Columbus, 19
Hernán Cortés, 31
Ferdinand II of Aragon, 18
Isabella of Castile, 18
King Charles I, 35
Malintzin (Doña Marina), 31
Montezuma, 32
Francisco Pizarro, 33

CHRONOLOGY

c. 27,000 B.C.E	First peoples migrate from Asia to the Americas
c. 8000–2000 B.C.E	Agriculture develops near equator and in the Andes Mountains
c. 500	Maize cultivation spreads north to present-day United States
	Rise of settlements and complex societies (including the Pueblo and the Mississippians) in present-day United States
c. 700–1100	Maize continues to spread throughout present-day United States
c. 1000	Norse reach North America
c. 1100	Peak of Mississippian Cahokia population
1200s	Droughts and competition contract some native societies, including the Cahokia and Mandan
1325	Aztec capital of Tenochtitlán built
1420s	Portugal explores coastal West Africa
1482	Portugal builds trading posts in West Africa
1492	Columbus's first voyage
	Columbian Exchange begins
1500	Portugal claims Brazil as a colony
c. 1500–1630	Epidemics ravage New World natives
1502	First enslaved Africans brought to New World
1503	*Encomienda* system established
1513	*Requerimiento* statute established
1519	Attack on Tenochtitlán led by Cortés
1524	Francisco Pizarro conquers Incan empire
c. 1550	Sugar production begins in Brazil
1573	Mission system established in Spanish colonies
1598	Spanish massacre of Pueblo Indians

AP® EXAM PRACTICE THROUGH 1607

TRM Suggested Responses to Questions

Answers to Multiple-Choice Questions

1. c
2. a
3. d
4. b
5. d
6. d
7. c
8. a
9. d
10. a
11. d
12. a
13. a
14. c
15. b
16. a
17. b
18. b

Multiple-Choice Questions

Choose the correct answer for each question.

Questions 1–4 refer to the following map.

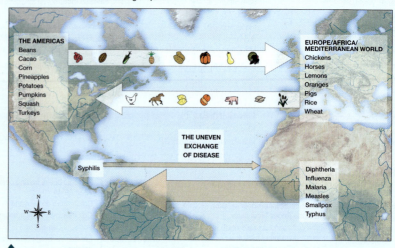

▲ The Columbian Exchange

1. Which of the following was an economic effect on Europeans as a result of the Columbian Exchange?
   a. The Columbian Exchange brought diseases to Western Europe, causing a decline in the European population.
   b. The Columbian Exchange brought new foodstuffs to Western Europe, leading to a declining workforce.
   c. The Columbian Exchange introduced new consumable goods to Europe, which stimulated new means to profit.
   d. The Columbian Exchange introduced new raw materials into Europe, stimulating the need for an enslaved workforce.

2. Which of the following was an economic effect on American Indian peoples as a result of the Columbian Exchange?
   a. American Indians were forced into a labor system that benefitted Europeans.
   b. American Indians utilized new foodstuffs to grow their populations.
   c. American Indian populations declined because new diseases damaged their crops.
   d. American Indians discovered new markets for their precious metals.

3. Prior to European contact, North American Indians were
   a. dominated by the Plains Indians, who possessed horses.
   b. dominated by the eastern woodland tribes, who possessed firearms.
   c. dependent on imports of foodstuffs from Mexican tribes for survival.
   d. distinct societies with different economies and lifestyles.

4. As the Spanish explored North America prior to 1600, they discovered
   a. a Northwest Passage (an all-water route) to Asia.
   b. massive storehouses of precious metals among American Indian tribes.
   c. little of interest to keep them pushing north to Canada.
   d. evidence that Europeans had significant contact with American Indians prior to 1492.

Questions 5–7 refer to the following image.

The New World as Paradise, engraving by Theodor de Bry, 1588

5. This image portrays European perceptions of the New World in all of the following ways EXCEPT:
   a. American Indians lived in harmony with nature.
   b. American Indians were uncivilized compared to Europeans.
   c. The New World represented a land of plenty with abundant resources.
   d. The New World contained dangers like disease and wild beasts.

6. By 1588, Spanish development of the Americas flourished mostly because
   a. American Indian populations eagerly embraced the *encomienda* system.
   b. the Spanish collaborated with American Indians to the advantage of both.
   c. American Indians willingly converted to Catholicism.
   d. the Spanish used American Indian labor to extract precious materials for export to Europe.

7. The engraving was most likely intended to
   a. convince American Indians to defend their political sovereignty.
   b. justify the poor treatment of American Indians by Europeans.
   c. stimulate European interest in the settlement and development of the New World.
   d. illustrate American Indian religious traditions to Europeans.

Period 1: 1491–1607

Questions 8–10 refer to the following excerpt.

Source: Howard Zinn, *A People's History of the United States: 1492–Present*, 1980

"Widely dispersed over the great land mass of the Americas, [American Indians] numbered 15 or 20 million people by the time Columbus came, perhaps 5 million in North America. Responding to the different environments of soil and climate, they developed hundreds of different tribal cultures, perhaps two thousand different languages. They perfected the art of agriculture, and figured out how to grow maize (corn), which cannot grow by itself and must be planted, cultivated, fertilized, harvested, husked, shelled. They ingeniously developed a variety of other vegetables and fruits, as well as peanuts and chocolate and tobacco and rubber."

8. The passage best supports which of the following historical developments prior to 1492?
   a. Prior to the arrival of Europeans, American Indians had developed advanced agricultural techniques.
   b. American Indian migration stemmed from a search for new sources of economic competition.
   c. American Indians shared a common set of cultural traits, including a communion with nature.
   d. Most American Indians supported themselves by hunting and gathering.

9. The passage would be most useful as a source of information about which of the following?
   a. The role of the African slave trade in the development of plantation-based agriculture
   b. Improvements in maritime technologies that fueled the Columbian Exchange
   c. Economic, cultural, and racial justifications for the subjugation of Americans Indians
   d. Exchanges of goods between Europe and the Americas that stimulated the growth of European capitalism

10. Which of the following pieces of evidence could be used to support Zinn's depiction of American Indian culture during the late fifteenth and early sixteenth centuries?
    a. Written accounts by Europeans of early transatlantic voyages to the Americas
    b. Written evidence by American Indians of permanent, indigenous villages in the American Northeast
    c. European testimony of cooperative farming between American Indians and European colonists
    d. Religious debates about whether American Indians could be converted to Christianity

Questions 11–13 refer to the following excerpt.

Source: Bartolomé de Las Casas, *A Short Account of the Destruction of the Indies*, 1542

"The reason the Christians have murdered on such a vast scale and killed anyone and everyone in their way is purely and simply greed. They have set out to line their pockets with gold and to amass private fortunes as quickly as possible so that they can then assume a status quite at odds with that into which they were born. Their insatiable greed and overweening ambition know no bounds."

11. The excerpt from Las Casas can be used most directly to prove which of the following developments in the period 1491 to 1607?
    a. Many Europeans adopted aspects of American Indian culture and tradition.
    b. European settlers often misunderstood American Indian cultures and traditions.
    c. American Indians often sought diplomatic solutions to conflict.
    d. Europeans disagreed about how American Indians should be treated.

12. Which of the following contributed most directly to the developments described by Las Casas?
    a. Advances in European maritime technologies
    b. European encroachment on American Indians' land
    c. Widespread epidemics
    d. The importation of enslaved labor

13. What motivations led the Spanish to the "greed" that Las Casas describes?
    a. Massive resources of precious metals found in native lands
    b. Coordinated American Indian resistance
    c. The Spanish desire to convert native peoples to Catholicism
    d. The need by the Spanish to replace native laborers with Europeans

AP® Exam Practice: Through 1607

Period 1: 1491–1607

Questions 14–16 refer to the following map.

American Indian Economies, Late Fifteenth Century

14. This map best supports which conclusion about American Indian economies before European contact?
   a. American Indian economies were less advanced than those in Europe.
   b. American Indians lived a more "natural" lifestyle than Europeans.
   c. American Indian economies were diverse and adapted to local resources.
   d. American Indians exhibited a greater respect for natural resources than Europeans.

15. In which region of the map were American Indians the most mobile?
   a. The American Southwest
   b. The Great Basin and western plains
   c. California and the Northwest
   d. The Northeast and the Atlantic seaboard

16. Prior to European contact, American Indians in the Southwest had already developed which of the following?
   a. A culture highly dependent on maize
   b. An economy based on livestock
   c. An economy dependent entirely on hunting
   d. The *encomienda* system

Period 1: 1491–1607

Questions 17–18 refer to the following excerpt.

Source: Hernán Cortés, *Letter to King Charles I of Spain*, 1520

"In these chapels are the images or idols, although, as I have before said, many of them are also found on the outside; the principal ones, in which the people have greatest faith and confidence, I precipitated from their pedestals, and cast them down the steps of the temple, purifying the chapels in which they had stood, as they were all polluted with human blood, shed in the sacrifices.

In the place of these I put images of Our Lady and the Saints, which excited not a little feeling in Moctezuma and the inhabitants, who at first remonstrated [protested], declaring that if my proceedings were known throughout the country, the people would rise against me; for they believed that their idols bestowed on them all temporal good, and if they permitted them to be ill-treated, they would be angry and withhold their gifts, and by this means the people would be deprived of the fruits of the earth and perish with famine.

I answered, through the interpreters, that they were deceived in expecting any favors from idols, the work of their own hands, formed of unclean things; and they must learn there was but one God, the universal Lord of all, who had created the heavens and the earth, and all things else, and had made them and us; that he was without beginning and immortal, and they were bound to adore and believe him, and no other creature or thing. I said every thing I could to divert them from their idolatries, and draw them to a knowledge of God our Lord."

17. Which option best characterizes a cause of Cortés's actions in the temple of Tenochtitlán?
    a. The Spanish were motivated by economic gain in the Western Hemisphere.
    b. The Spanish considered conversion to Catholicism a prime motivation to their conquest of the Western Hemisphere.
    c. The Spanish were wary of American Indian religious practices and believed destruction of native temples would frighten the Aztecs into submission.
    d. The Spanish believed that the destruction of Aztec temples would lead to the destruction of Aztec crops and aid their conquest.

18. Which of the following is the best inference a historian could make from the passage?
    a. The Spanish believed that Aztec economic success was due to pagan rituals.
    b. The Aztecs believed that their economic success depended upon the worship of their gods.
    c. The Spanish believed that the powerful Aztec gods were a threat to Spanish beliefs.
    d. The Aztecs believed Cortés's action would prove their gods weaker than the Catholic god.

Short-Answer Questions

Read each question carefully and write a short response. Use complete sentences.

1. Using the following excerpts, answer (a), (b), and (c).

Source: John R. Richards, *The Unending Frontier*, 2006

"The Columbian connection had a devastating effect on the indigenous human societies of the Americas.... New disease vectors suddenly introduced into the vulnerable populations of the New World began a sequence of horrific pandemics. Rapidly spreading infectious disease devastated indigenous peoples of the New World. It thinned their numbers, destroyed their institutions, and broke their resistance to Spanish aggression.... Demographic recovery after major pandemics was hindered by reduced fertility, stillbirths, and other physical effects, as well as by cultural depression, hopelessness, and malaise resulting from Spanish colonial domination."

Source: Nancy Qian and Nathan Nunn, *The Columbian Exchange*, 2010

"The New World provided soils that were very suitable for the cultivation of a variety of Old World products.... The increased supply lowered the prices of these products significantly, making them affordable to the general population for the first time in history. The production of these products also resulted in large inflows of profits back to Europe, which some have argued fueled the Industrial Revolution and the rise of Europe. The Old World gained access to new crops that were widely adopted.... The improvement in agricultural productivity ... had significant effects on historic population growth and urbanization."

TRM Suggested Responses to Questions

AP® Exam Practice: Through 1607

Period 1: 1491–1607

a. Briefly explain ONE major difference between Richards's and Nunn and Qian's interpretations of the results of the Columbian Exchange.
b. Briefly explain how ONE specific historical event or development from the period 1492 to 1607 not explicitly mentioned in the excerpts could be used to support Richards's argument.
c. Briefly explain how ONE specific historical event or development from the period 1492 to 1607 not explicitly mentioned in the excerpts could be used to support Nunn and Qian's argument.

2. Using the following map, answer (a), (b), and (c).

Spanish Explorations in North America, 1528–1542

a. Briefly explain ONE important cause of the explorations depicted in the map.
b. Briefly explain ONE important effect of the explorations depicted in the map on Spanish settlements in North America.
c. Briefly explain ONE important effect of the explorations depicted in the map on American Indian settlements in North America.

3. Answer (a), (b), and (c).
a. Briefly explain ONE important technological change that led to the growth of Spanish colonies in the Americas prior to 1607.
b. Briefly explain ONE important economic change that led to the development of Spanish colonies in the Americas prior to 1607.
c. Briefly explain the impact of ONE of the changes that you described in (a) or (b) on the Spanish colonies in the Americas prior to 1607.

4. Answer (a), (b), and (c)
a. Briefly explain ONE important similarity between Spanish views of the natural environment and American Indians' views of the natural environment.
b. Briefly explain ONE important difference between Spanish views of the natural environment and American Indians' views of the natural environment.
c. Briefly explain ONE important outcome of the difference you identified in part (b).

PERIOD 2: 1607–1754
Colonial America amid Global Change

AP® Overview for Period 2

Period 2 is replete with subjects fundamental to students' foundational knowledge of historical developments that molded colonial America. Indeed, far from a static period, European colonization in the seventeenth and eighteenth centuries ushered in transformational changes that affected American Indians, European imperialists, as well as free and enslaved Africans. Imperial wars in the West Indies, South America, and North America disrupted trade routes and exacerbated tensions among European powers. Concomitant to these developments was the continuous commodification of human beings through the enslavement of Africans. Even though colonization by Europeans is the dominant topic in this period, American Indians, enslaved Africans, free Africans, and white indentured servants were never inert through these processes.

The learning modules for Period 2 build out this historical framework through a concise narrative of major events. Intertwined in the narrative is primary source instruction as well as scaffolded skill development germane to the expectations of the AP® U.S. History course and exam. Even though Period 2 represents no more than 8% of the material for the AP® test, teachers should see this as an opportunity to concentrate on skill-building, as well as teach subjects that can both humanize history and give students a contextual understanding of the processes that led to the formation of the United States.

Module 2-1: European Challengers to Spanish North America should ground students in an understanding of how the Spanish Empire colonized the New World. This module focuses on how the French and Dutch sought to colonize the New World amid Spain's dominance in North America. Much of the focus in this module is developing the reasoning processes of comparison and causation. Although the title brings European powers to the forefront, concerted effort is made throughout the module to build ways of understanding how American Indians reacted to colonization efforts. Teachers should sequence the skills in this module, as each writing exercise builds momentum toward being able to write a cogent thesis.

Module 2-2: Early British Colonies in Maryland, Virginia, and North Carolina situates the reasoning process of causation as the focus so that teachers can emphasize what factors led to settlement in each British North American colony. Teachers should emphasize the regional patterns of settlement in the colonies, as the division of modules in Period 2 mirrors those trends. The establishment of cash crop colonies is an important process students need to understand so they can make connections to conflicts with American Indians and among other colonists. Furthermore, the enslavement of Africans is explored and should be front and center when students think about the causes of British colonization. Writing topic sentences is an introductory way of thinking about making a historical interpretation or developing an argument in an essay.

Module 2-3: Religious Dissent and Colonial Conflicts in New England focuses on continuity and change as well as causation. Using these reasoning processes encourages students to see New England colonists as a complex, distinctive group of religious reformers, with a self-promulgated mission of spreading their beliefs. Yet, they were also a people deeply interested and entrenched in the economic self-interest of the developing Atlantic world. Colonization in New England was fraught with conflict with American Indians, the English government, and even among Puritan dissenters. The module ends with students continuing to develop their writing skills by focusing on how to write a thesis statement that accounts for the continuities and changes within New England.

Module 2-4: The British West Indies and South Atlantic Colonies will present students with one of the most disturbing patterns of colonization, as the effort to commodify human beings by enslaving Africans becomes central to settlement patterns in the West Indies and South Carolina. The historical reasoning focuses on causation, which will aid students' efforts to understand not only settlement patterns but also the broader processes associated with the Atlantic world. This module has rich primary sources that will amplify this development for students. Nearly halfway through the modules of Period 2, this module ends with students pulling skill development from each of the first four modules as they write a long essay.

Module 2-5: The Middle Colonies will readily prompt teachers to utilize the historical thinking skill of contextualization to instruct the processes that influenced settlement in the Middle Colonies. Because students have studied each of the other regions of British colonization in North America, they should be ready to examine the broader events or developments that shaped colonization patterns in the Middle Colonies. Teachers should highlight the treatment of American Indians, the use of enslaved laborers, demographics, and religion to assist students in the process of drawing comparisons. Being mindful of these differences better enables students to complete the last exercise in this module, which focuses on presenting the context of a historical argument.

Module 2-6: The Eighteenth-Century Atlantic Economy is the start of the final four modules of Period 2 focusing on the development of the colonies within the wider Atlantic world. Central to this understanding are the imperial economic policies used by the British to sustain profit from the colonies in North America. In particular, mercantilism is a concept with historical ripple effects. Put another way, if students can glean the expansive effects of the mercantile system, they will be better equipped to make connections later in Periods 2 and 3. Causation is the reasoning process of this module and thus connects well to how the content unfolds in the module. The concluding activity mirrors the expectation of understanding the differences in historical interpretations.

Module 2-7: Slavery Takes Hold in the South focuses on the events and processes that led colonists in the southern colonies to establish a racially distinctive slave system, whereby enslaved Africans came to define labor in the South. The process of enslavement will be evident throughout the module, but teachers should be mindful of having students recognize how enslaved persons resisted their enslavement or negotiated the terms of their labor. All of this means teachers can naturally infuse the reasoning process of causation in their instruction. The scaffolding of the DBQ is thorough, and teachers should allocate instructional time to guide students through this process.

Module 2-8: Imperial Contests in Trade and War brings students to the end of the chronological look at this process in Period 2. No fewer than seven wars are mentioned during this module; however, students should bear in mind the import of understanding broad events that led to these wars and which are most significant. Because this module focuses on the reasoning process of comparison, the module is situated well to inform students of the similarities, differences, and varying levels of importance among these conflicts. The final component of this module builds off the activity at the end of Module 2-7. Instead of using three documents, students now try to incorporate five documents in a historical analysis.

Module 2-9: Religious and Political Awakenings focuses on the social, cultural, and religious changes in the eighteenth century. The reasoning process is causation, which encourages teachers to help students build deeper understandings of the relationships among multiple historical events. The two most prominent events in this module, the Enlightenment and Great Awakening, are highlighted throughout. Since this should be the case, students should also note the extent to which the module illustrates both global and regional influences of these events. In this way, the module is built to highlight the causes and effects of these movements. The scaffolded instruction throughout the modules in Period 2 helps prepare students to answer the DBQ question in Module 2-9.

(Continued)

Pacing Guide

Course Pacing for Period 2

Module #	Lesson Title	Instructional Period*	AP® Theme	AP® Topic	AP® Reasoning Process/Skill	Homework
2-1	N/A	N/A	Migration and Settlement America in the World	2.1 2.2	Comparison / Historical Thinking Skills 1, 2, 3, 5	**Reading and Source Analysis:** 2-1
	The French Expand into North America	1	Migration and Settlement America in the World	2.2	Comparison Causation / Historical Thinking Skills 1, 2, 3, 5	**Activities:** AP® Thinking Historically: Using Comparison and Causation in Historical Arguments AP® Writing Historically: Crafting a Thesis Statement Based on Comparison
	Workshops: AP® Thinking Historically: Using Comparison and Causation in Historical Arguments AP® Writing Historically: Crafting a Thesis Statement Based on Comparison	1	Migration and Settlement America in the World	2.2	Comparison / Historical Thinking Skills 1, 2, 3, 4, 5	**Reading and Source Analysis:** 2-2
2-2	Early British Colonies in Maryland, Virginia, and North Carolina	1	Geography and the Environment America in the World Migration and Settlement	2.2	Causation / Historical Thinking Skills 1, 2, 3, 5	**Activities:** AP® Thinking Historically: Connecting Distant Causes to Immediate Causes AP® Writing Historically: Writing Topic Sentences for an Essay
	Workshops: AP® Thinking Historically: Connecting Distant Causes to Immediate Causes AP® Writing Historically: Writing Topic Sentences for an Essay	1	Geography and the Environment America in the World Migration and Settlement	2.2	Causation / Historical Thinking Skills 1, 2, 3, 4, 5, 6	**Reading and Source Analysis:** 2-3
2-3	Religious Dissent and Colonial Conflicts in New England	1	Geography and the Environment Migration and Settlement American and Regional Culture Social Structures	2.3	Continuity and Change / Historical Thinking Skills 1, 2, 3, 5	**Activities:** AP® Writing Historically: Crafting a Thesis Statement Based on Continuity and Change
	Workshop: AP® Writing Historically: Crafting a Thesis Statement Based on Continuity and Change	1	Geography and the Environment Migration and Settlement American and Regional Culture Social Structures	2.3	Continuity and Change / Historical Thinking Skills 1, 3, 5	**Reading and Source Analysis:** 2-4
2-4	The British West Indies and South Atlantic Colonies	1	Work, Exchange, and Technology Geography and the Environment Migration and Settlement	2.3	Causation / Historical Thinking Skills 1, 2, 3, 5	**Activities:** AP® Writing Historically: Writing a Full Essay
	Workshop: AP® Writing Historically: Writing a Full Essay	1	Work, Exchange, and Technology Geography and the Environment Migration and Settlement	2.3	Causation / Historical Thinking Skills 1, 2, 3, 5, 6	**Reading and Source Analysis:** 2-5

(Continued)

Module #	Lesson Title	Instructional Period*	AP® Theme	AP® Topic	AP® Reasoning Process/Skill	Homework
2-5	The Middle Colonies	1	Geography and the Environment Migration and Settlement America in the World American and Regional Culture	2.3	Contextualization / Historical Thinking Skills 1, 2, 3, 4, 5	**Activity**: AP® Writing Historically: Presenting Context in a Historical Argument
	Workshop: AP® Writing Historically: Presenting Context in a Historical Argument	1	Geography and the Environment Migration and Settlement America in the World American and Regional Culture	2.3	Contextualization / Historical Thinking Skills 1, 2, 3, 4, 5, 6	**Reading and Source Analysis:** 2-6 **Activity:** AP® Writing Historically: Responding to a Short-Answer Question with Secondary Sources
2-6	The Eighteenth-Century Atlantic Economy **Review:** AP® Writing Historically: Responding to a Short-Answer Question with Secondary Sources	1	Work, Exchange, and Technology	2.4 2.5	Causation / Historical Thinking Skills 1, 2, 3, 5	**Reading and Source Analysis:** 2-7
2-7	Slavery Takes Hold in the South	1	Work, Exchange, and Technology American and Regional Culture Social Structures	2.6	Causation / Historical Thinking Skills 1, 2, 3, 5	**Activity:** AP® Writing Historically: Responding to a Document-Based Question with Three Primary Sources
	Workshop: AP® Writing Historically: Responding to a Document-Based Question with Three Primary Sources	1	Work, Exchange, and Technology American and Regional Culture Social Structures	2.6	Causation / Historical Thinking Skills 1, 2, 3, 4, 5, 6	**Reading and Source Analysis:** 2-8 **Activity:** AP® Writing Historically: Responding to a Document-Based Question with Five Primary Sources
2-8	Imperial Contests in Trade and War **Review:** AP® Writing Historically: Responding to a Document-Based Question with Five Primary Sources	1	America in the World	2.7	Comparison / Historical Thinking Skills 1, 2, 3, 5	**Reading and Source Analysis:** 2-9 **Activity:** AP® Writing Historically: Responding to a Document-Based Question
2-9	Religious and Political Awakenings **Review:** AP® Writing Historically: Responding to a Document-Based Question	1	American and Regional Culture Social Structures	2.7 2.8	Causation / Historical Thinking Skills 1, 2, 3, 5	Prepare for Assessment
Formative Assessment	AP® Exam Practice • 18 MCQs • 4 SAQs	0-1	All AP® U.S. History Course Themes	2.8 Personal Progress Check • 15 MCQs • 2 SAQs • 1 LEQ	All AP® History Reasoning Processes/Skills	
Summative Assessment	Unit 1 Test Bank • 55 MCQs • 4 SAQs • 1 DBQ • 4 LEQs	0-1	All AP® U.S. History Course Themes		All AP® History Reasoning Processes/Skills	

*Based on a standard 50-minute class period.

PERIOD 2 Colonial America amid Global Change

Period 2 Resources

The following resources can be found in the Resources section of the book's digital platform, by clicking on the link buttons in the Teacher's Edition e-book, or by opening the Teacher's Resource Materials.

- **TRM** Period 2 Overview Video
- **TRM** AP® Concepts and Skills Video
- **TRM** Period 2 Lecture Presentation Slides
- **TRM** Period 2 Workshop Rubrics
- **TRM** Period 2 Suggested Responses to Questions
- **TRM** Period 2 Guided Reading Worksheets

Module 2-1
- **TRM** Handout 2.1 – European Nations Settlement Patterns
- **TRM** Module 2.1 AP® Analyzing Sources Handout 1
- **TRM** Module 2.1 AP® Thinking Historically Handout
- **TRM** Module 2.1 AP® Analyzing Sources Handout 2
- **TRM** Handout 2.2 – Historical Thinking Word Bank

Module 2-2
- **TRM** Module 2.2 AP® Analyzing Sources Handout 1
- **TRM** Module 2.2 AP® Analyzing Sources Handout 2
- **TRM** Module 2.2 AP® Analyzing Sources Handout 3
- **TRM** Module 2.2 AP® Analyzing Sources Handout 4
- **TRM** Module 2.2 AP® Analyzing Sources Handout 5
- **TRM** Module 2.2 AP® Analyzing Sources Handout 6
- **TRM** Module 2.2 AP® Analyzing Sources Handout 7
- **TRM** Module 2.2 AP® Thinking Historically Handout
- **TRM** Handout 2.3 – Organizational Framework

Module 2-3
- **TRM** Module 2.3 AP® Analyzing Sources Handout 1
- **TRM** Module 2.3 AP® Analyzing Sources Handout 2
- **TRM** Module 2.3 AP® Analyzing Sources Handout 3
- **TRM** Handout 2.4 – New England: Geography and the Environment

Module 2-4
- **TRM** Module 2.4 AP® Analyzing Sources Handout 1
- **TRM** Handout 2.5 – Thomas Walduck's Acrostic
- **TRM** Module 2.4 AP® Analyzing Sources Handout 2

Module 2-5
- **TRM** Map 2A – The Thirteen Colonies
- **TRM** Module 2.5 AP® Analyzing Sources Handout 1
- **TRM** Module 2.5 AP® Analyzing Sources Handout 2

Module 2-6
- **TRM** Module 2.6 AP® Analyzing Sources Handout
- **TRM** Handout 2.6 – English Colonies Established in North America, 1607–1750

Module 2-7
- **TRM** Module 2.7 AP® Analyzing Sources Handout 1
- **TRM** Module 2.7 AP® Analyzing Sources Handout 2
- **TRM** Handout 2.7 – Note Cards for Paragraph Analysis

Module 2-8
- **TRM** Module 2.8 AP® Analyzing Sources Handout 1
- **TRM** Handout 2.8 – Comparing Causes and Outcomes of Resistance
- **TRM** Module 2.8 AP® Analyzing Sources Handout 2
- **TRM** Module 2.8 AP® Analyzing Sources Handout 3

Module 2-9
- **TRM** Handout 2.9 – Spheres of Influence in the Colonial Period
- **TRM** Module 2.9 AP® Analyzing Sources Handout

Period 2 Essential Activity

An overarching theme of Colonial America from 1607 to 1754 is how established societies remade their cultural, economic, and political systems because of transformational demographics in the Atlantic world. To facilitate a more comprehensive understanding of this historical development, teachers should consider the following activity to help students explore the contours of the Atlantic world. Organize students into four groups with the following labels: British North American Colonies, England, Ivory/Gold/Slave Coasts, and West Indies.

Next subdivide students to work in groups of three to four. Then, have students look at Map 2.6 on page 99. Students will have three tasks in their groups, and teachers can have students create a chart on butcher-block paper with three spaces to write their responses: Demographic Transformations; Cultural, Economic, or Political Changes; and Interdependence of Atlantic World.

The first task is to identify the demographic groups in their region and explain how those populations transformed during the colonial period in the Atlantic world. Encourage students to make discrete selections in this process. For example, a group assigned to the West Indies may decide to focus on Barbados. Likewise, a group assigned to the British North American colonies may determine their answer will focus on the Chesapeake region. Next, students will write a two or three sentence explanation of how those demographic changes acted as the impetus for cultural, economic, or political changes in their region. The last task is for students to write a two or three sentence explanation for how the changes in their assigned region were interdependent with at least two other regions.

Period 2 Alignment to the Fall 2019 AP® United States History Course Framework*

Relationship to the College Board Units

Period 2 in this book covers Topics 2.1–2.8 in Unit 2 of the College Board course framework. Students will be ready to take the Personal Progress Check for Unit 2 once they have completed this period.

Course Themes

Period 2 develops these course themes outlined in the course framework:

- **Migration and Settlement (MIG):** Throughout the seventeenth and early eighteenth centuries, the English, French, and Dutch established colonies that challenged Spanish control in North America.
- **America in the World (WOR):** Starting in the seventeenth century, British North American colonists were pulled into a series of conflicts with other European colonists and their Native American allies as European nations increasingly sought control over the Western Hemisphere.
- **Geography and the Environment (GEO):** English colonies in North America developed economies shaped by their geography and environment. Colonies in New England and the mid-Atlantic built mixed economies based on trade, commerce, and farming while colonies in the Chesapeake, Lower South, and Caribbean relied on cash crop agriculture.
- **American and Regional Cultures (ARC):** Distance from Great Britain and inspiration from religious movements and new political ideologies contributed to a growing sense of distinctness from England, even as fragmentation within the colonies increased.
- **Work, Exchange, and Technology (WXT):** During the eighteenth century, the Atlantic economy became increasingly complex, leading to increased attempts by European powers to systematize trade policies advantageous to home countries. These trade policies shaped the lives of colonial subjects in North America.
- **Social Structures (SOC):** Slavery shaped the economy and society of British North America. While slavery was more prevalent in the Southern colonies, its existence in the middle and northern colonies proved significant as well.

Course Skills

Period 2 helps students to develop the following AP® Historical Thinking Skills identified in the course framework.

- **Skill 1: Developments and Processes** (Modules 2-1, 2-2, 2-3, 2-4, 2-5, 2-6, 2-7, 2-8, 2-9)
- **Skill 2: Sourcing and Situation** (Modules 2-1, 2-2, 2-3, 2-4, 2-5, 2-6, 2-7, 2-8, 2-9)
- **Skill 3: Claims and Evidence in Sources** (Modules 2-1, 2-2, 2-3, 2-4, 2-5, 2-6, 2-7, 2-8, 2-9)
- **Skill 4: Contextualization** (Modules 2-1, 2-2, 2-5, 2-7)
- **Skill 5: Making Connections** (Modules 2-1, 2-2, 2-3, 2-4, 2-5, 2-6, 2-7, 2-8, 2-9)
- **Skill 6: Argumentation** (Modules 2-2, 2-4, 2-5, 2-7, 2-9)

Period 2 helps students to develop the following AP® History Reasoning Processes identified in the course framework.

- **Reasoning Process 1: Comparison** (Modules 2-1, 2-8)
- **Reasoning Process 2: Causation** (Modules 2-1, 2-2, 2-4, 2-6, 2-7, 2-9)
- **Reasoning Process 3: Continuity and Change** (Module 2-3)

Learning Objectives and Historical Developments

Module	Topics	Learning Objectives	Historical Developments and Key Concepts
2-1	2.1, 2.2	Unit 2: Learning Objective A Unit 2: Learning Objective B	KC-2.1.I.A, KC-2.I.B
2-2	2.2	Unit 2: Learning Objective B	KC-2.1.I.C, KC-2.1.II.A, KC-2.1.II.E
2-3	2.3	Unit 2: Learning Objective C	KC-2.1.II.B, KC-2.1.II.E
2-4	2.3	Unit 2: Learning Objective C	KC-2.1.II.C
2-5	2.3	Unit 2: Learning Objective C	KC-2.1.II.D
2-6	2.4, 2.5	Unit 2: Learning Objective D Unit 2: Learning Objective E	KC-2.1.III.A, KC-2.1.III.B, KC-2.2.I.C, KC-2.1.III.C, KC-2.1.III.E, KC-2.1.III.F
2-7	2.6	Unit 2: Learning Objective F	KC-2.2.II.A, KC-2.2.II.B
2-8	2.7	Unit 2: Learning Objective G	KC-2.2.II.C
2-9	2.7, 2.8	Unit 2: Learning Objective H Unit 2: Learning Objective I Unit 2: Learning Objective J	KC-2.2.I, A, KC-2.2.I.B, KC-2.1.III.D, KC-2.2.I.D

TRM A detailed alignment that can be sorted by Course Framework Unit, Topic, Learning Objective, Historical Development/Key Concept, or textbook period, is available in the Teacher's Resource Materials and via the book's online platform.

*Should changes be made to the Course Framework in the future, an updated alignment will be placed on our catalog page at bfwpub.com/fabric1e.

TEACHING IDEA

AP® Central

A great resource to help you teach this period is to read the information in the AP® U.S. History study guide for 1607–1754, available from the AP® United States History Classroom Resources section of AP® Central (apcentral.collegeboard.org).

PERIOD 2: 1607–1754

Colonial America amid Global Change

▲ **British Colonial Banner, 1745** This cotton banner was carried by the British at the siege of the French at Louisbourg (1745), Nova Scotia, during King George's War, also known as the War of Austrian Succession (1744–1748). King George's War was one of many colonial wars fought between the British and the French for control over North America during the eighteenth century. While the British soldiers and New England colonists who carried out the siege captured Louisbourg, the fort was later returned to the French as part of the Treaty of Aix-la-Chapelle, which ended the war in 1748.

England and France began to challenge Spanish dominance of the Western Hemisphere in the early seventeenth century. As these three kingdoms struggled with one another militarily, economically, and socially, each also consolidated power on the North American continent.

These nations engaged in shifting patterns of cooperation and competition with native populations in ways that reflected their cultural, social, religious, and economic interests. The French steadily established trade networks with native peoples in Canada, while the Spanish in the Southwest sought to convert American Indians to Catholicism while at the same time exploiting their labor. The English colony at Jamestown tried to replicate the success of the Spanish, hoping to find easy profits in gold and silver mines, but the climate and geography of Virginia were radically different from the Central American regions that the Spanish had begun to exploit nearly a hundred years before. Thus, the early Jamestown settlers built a colony that differed from the ordered and authoritarian *encomienda* system of the Spanish, where native peoples worked under close Spanish supervision. Instead, a labor system in which English-born indentured servants agreed to a set time of labor in return for passage to the English colony provided much of the labor in the colony during the early seventeenth century. However, this arrangement gave way to a racial caste system in which enslaved Africans made up the bulk of the labor force on large cash-crop plantations by the turn of the eighteenth century. In the western backcountry regions of Virginia, the majority of the population was made up of independent farmers, many of whom were former servants themselves. These backcountry settlers negotiated — and often violated — a shifting borderland of conflict and trade with American Indians.

As the seventeenth century progressed, growing European settlements in the New World led to the development of a transatlantic world in which Europeans, American Indians, and Africans traded, competed, interacted, and exploited each other along networks that stretched from the foothills of the Appalachian Mountains to the cities of London, Paris, and Madrid to the villages of West Africa and back to the islands of the Caribbean.

Great Britain's colonies in North America formed an integral part of this transatlantic world. Beginning in the early 1650s, Britain pursued economic policies designed to monopolize trade with its colonies and protect British economic interests, and the strategy proved successful. Starting in the late seventeenth century, the British fought a series of colonial wars with other European powers, most often the French, to establish English cultural, ideological, and economic dominance in the North Atlantic and the North American interior. While these wars were costly on many levels, repeated victories cemented Great Britain's dominance of the North American Atlantic seaboard from the late 1600s and well into the 1700s. Despite the consolidation of British power in North America, colonists used European models to shape a distinctly British North American culture. For example, the Enlightenment, a European intellectual movement that embraced science and reason as the hallmarks of human progress, gained popularity among elites. Likewise, the Great Awakening, a wave of renewed religious enthusiasm, swept North America during the 1740s with a spiritual intensity that touched all classes and challenged England's tradition of strict class differentiation.

Colonial society also underwent immense shifts as these religious and political awakenings transformed colonists' sense of their relation to both spiritual and secular authorities. Over time, the colonial elite had developed a strong belief in the rights of the colonies to control their own destinies. As this belief grew more popular, local communities began to take steps to defend those rights, and many colonial assemblies grew accustomed to control over local government.

Yet even as aspects of a distinctly American identity began to emerge, the diversity and divisions among colonists increased as class, racial, religious, and regional differences multiplied across the colonies. Immigrants from Germany, Ireland, and Scotland created their own communities; economic inequality deepened in cities; conflicts between American Indians and settlers intensified along the frontier; and growing reliance on the labor of enslaved Africans reshaped economic and social relations in British North America, particularly in the southern colonies.

TEACHING IDEA

Incorporating Podcasts

Teaching Tolerance's website has an excellent podcast for teachers on how to teach "hard history" — covering America's history of enslavement that is a vital topic for students to understand, but can be difficult for teachers to discuss. Search for "Teaching Hard History Podcast" at tolerance.org.

TEACHING IDEA

Graphic Organizer

As students read about Period 2, have them create a chart to compare the economic, social, and imperial policies, as well as relations with American Indian groups, for the Spanish, French, Dutch, and British.

PERIOD 2 PREVIEW

Module	AP® Thematic Focus
2-1: European Challengers to Spanish North America	**Migration and Settlement ▪ America in the World** Throughout the seventeenth and early eighteenth centuries, the English, French, and Dutch established colonies that challenged Spanish control in North America.
2-2: Early British Colonies in Maryland, Virginia, and North Carolina	**Geography and the Environment** The earliest English colonies sought profit through agriculture and the cash crop tobacco, which became a valuable commodity in the Atlantic world.
2-3: Religious Dissent and Colonial Conflicts in New England	**Geography and the Environment ▪ Migration and Settlement ▪ American and Regional Culture** The first English settlers in New England, mostly Puritans, established an economy of agriculture and commerce within a society of independent family farms and small towns. Distance from Great Britain led to self-governing towns that contained elements of democratic practice. These democratic elements included participatory town meetings, and elected colonial legislatures.
2-4: The British West Indies and South Atlantic Colonies	**Work, Exchange, and Technology ▪ Geography and the Environment ▪ Migration and Settlement** Throughout the late seventeenth and early eighteenth centuries, the colonies of the southern Atlantic coast and the British West Indies developed plantation societies that depended on the labor of enslaved Africans to harvest crops such as rice and sugar for export.
2-5: The Middle Colonies	**Geography and the Environment ▪ Migration and Settlement ▪ America in the World ▪ American and Regional Culture** Starting in the 1660s, the English began to colonize the mid-Atlantic region in North America and build economies based on trade and societies built generally on religious and ethnic tolerance.
2-6: The Eighteenth-Century Atlantic Economy	**Work, Exchange, and Technology** During the eighteenth century, the Atlantic economy became increasingly complex, leading to increasing attempts by European powers to systematize trade policies advantageous to home countries. These trade policies shaped the lives of colonial subjects in North America.
2-7: Slavery Takes Hold in the South	**Work, Exchange, and Technology ▪ American and Regional Culture ▪ Social Structures** Slavery shaped the economy and society of British North America. While slavery was more prevalent in the southern colonies, its existence in the middle and northern colonies proved significant as well. Enslaved Africans and African Americans found overt and covert ways to rebel against slavery and maintain their families and distinct culture.
2-8: Imperial Contests in Trade and War	**America in the World** Starting in the seventeenth century, British North American colonists were pulled into a series of conflicts with other European colonists and their Native American allies as European nations increasingly sought control over the Western Hemisphere.
2-9: Religious and Political Awakenings	**American and Regional Culture ▪ Social Structures** Inspired by religious movements and new political ideologies, British North Americans developed a sense of distinctness from England while, at the same time, experiencing fragmentation within the colonies themselves.

Module 2-1

European Challengers to Spanish North America

LEARNING TARGETS

By the end of this module, you should be able to:

- Explain the European and North American context that shaped colonization of North America between 1607 and 1754.
- Explain how European colonies developed in various ways between 1607 and 1754.
- Explain how relations between Europeans and American Indians changed between 1607 and 1754.

THEMATIC FOCUS

Migration and Settlement

America in the World

Throughout the seventeenth and early eighteenth centuries, the English, French, and Dutch established colonies that challenged Spanish control in North America.

HISTORICAL REASONING FOCUS

Comparison

Causation

As you learned in Module 1-1, historians think comparatively to identify, describe, and analyze the similarities and differences between two or more historical events, individuals, groups, regions, developments, or concepts. Considering how these different aspects of history relate to each other is a critical step toward gaining a fuller understanding of the past. While comparison is a fundamental historical reasoning tool, it's also important to remember that it is just one aspect of historical analysis. One way historians strengthen comparative understanding is by examining the causes of the historical developments they compare. This is because meaningful historical comparisons don't just record observations — they uncover reasons that help explain similarities and differences. Making this connection to underlying causes is an important part of historical analysis.

TASK ▶ As you read this module, think about the similarities and differences in the interactions between European colonizers and American Indians prior to 1754. Make sure that, wherever you make these comparisons, you also ask the important question of *why*. If you see a similarity between two European colonies, for instance, ask yourself what factors help explain it. If, let's say, you locate a difference between the lives of women in two European colonies, ask yourself what caused it.

TRM Suggested Responses to Questions

In the late sixteenth century, French, Dutch, and English investors became increasingly interested in establishing colonies in North America. But until Catholic Spain's grip on the Atlantic world was broken, other nations could not hope to compete for an American empire. Throughout the seventeenth century, the French, Dutch, and English established colonies in the Western Hemisphere, which led to conflict with both the Spanish and American Indians.

Period 2: 1607–1754

MODULE 2-1 European Challengers to Spanish North America

The French Expand into North America

Although French rulers shared Spain's Catholic faith, the two nations were rivals, and the defeat of its Armada by English naval forces in 1588 weakened Spain enough to provide the rest of Europe with greater access to North America. Once in North America, the French adopted attitudes and policies that differed significantly from those of Spain. This was due in part to their greater interest in trade than in conquest. The French had fished the North Atlantic since the mid-sixteenth century, and in the 1580s they built stations along the Newfoundland coast for drying codfish. French traders then established relations with local American Indians, exchanging iron kettles and other European goods for valuable beaver skins.

By the early seventeenth century, France's King Henry IV (r. 1589–1610) sought to profit more directly from the resources in North America, focusing on developing the increasingly lucrative trade in American fish and furs. In 1608, Samuel de Champlain founded Quebec, the first permanent French settlement in North America. Accompanied by several dozen men armed with guns, Champlain joined a Huron raid on the Iroquois, who resided south of the Great Lakes. By ensuring a Huron victory, the French made the Huron people a powerful ally — but the battle also fueled lasting bitterness among the Iroquois.

Trade relations flourished between the French and their American Indian allies during the seventeenth century. Fur traders, who journeyed throughout the St. Lawrence River Valley in eastern Canada with the aid of the Huron, were critical to sustaining the French presence and warding off intrusion by the English — especially because relatively few French men and even fewer French women settled in North America during this period. French government policies discouraged mass migration, and peasants were also concerned by reports of short growing seasons and severe winters in Canada. Also, while French policy urged Catholic priests and nuns to migrate to the new world, Protestants, known as **Huguenots**, were barred from doing the same. Thus, into the 1630s, what few permanent French settlements existed in North America were mostly populated by fishermen, fur traders, and Catholic missionaries.

In their ongoing search for new sources of furs, the French established a fortified trading post at Montreal in 1643, and over the next three decades they continued to push farther west into the Great Lakes. But in doing so, the French carried European diseases into new areas, ignited warfare

---

TEACHING IDEA

Check for Understanding

Students should know when making historical comparisons, it is often more difficult to explain similarities. Therefore, consider assigning students the task of identifying and listing as many characteristics as they can of colonization for the French in Module 2-1. In this way, students are relieved of the pressure to *explain* similarities and instead can be tasked with simply *identifying* the similarities. Creating lists of characteristics allows students to identify similarities at the conclusion of the module, which better prepares them to make the difficult transition of explaining the similarities they identified.

TRM Suggested Responses to Questions

TRM Module 2.1 AP® Analyzing Sources Handout 1

EXPLORING AP® THEMES

Geography and the Environment

The theme of geography and the environment couples well with causation because both geographical location and environmental characteristics were significant causes of migration patterns. Throughout Module 2-1, students should account for how each European nation encountered and reacted to the unique geography of their respective settlements. Have students create a chart such as the one shown here for each European nation and explain how the geographical location and environment were factors in migration patterns.

French
Geographical Locations: Great Lakes, Mississippi River Valley, St. Lawrence River
Environment: Interior lands away from large coastal settlements of the British, waterways, less populated areas, variety of climates
Explanation: French migration patterns were shaped by the natural environment and geographical location because they were often located on the interior of North America along waterways, which were less densely populated.

TRM Find **Handout 2.1 – European Nations Settlement Patterns** in the Teacher's Resource Materials.

AP® ANALYZING SOURCES

Source: Samuel de Champlain, *Voyages of Samuel de Champlain: 1567–1635*

"Near the spot which had thus been selected for a future settlement [in Quebec], Champlain discovered a deposit of excellent clay, and, by way of experiment, had a quantity of it manufactured into bricks, of which he made a wall on the brink of the river. . . . In the mean time, Champlain had been followed to his rendezvous by a herd of adventurers from the maritime towns of France, who, stimulated by the freedom of the trade, had flocked after him in numbers all out of proportion to the amount of furs which they could hope to obtain from the wandering bands of savages that might chance to visit the St. Lawrence [River]. The river was lined with . . . [Frenchmen] anxiously watching the coming of the savages, all impatient and eager to secure as large a share as possible of the uncertain and meager booty for which they had crossed the Atlantic. Fifteen or twenty [ships] were moored along the shore, all seeking the best opportunity for the display of the worthless trinkets for which they had [greedily] hoped to obtain a valuable cargo of furs."

Questions for Analysis
1. Identify a similarity in the motives of Champlain and his fellow Frenchmen.
2. Describe the motives of the Frenchmen who joined Champlain on his journey.
3. Explain a cause of a similarity in the motives of Champlain and his fellow Frenchmen.

BUILDING AP® SKILLS

Claims and Evidence in Sources

The historical thinking skills articulated by the College Board are organized in a scaffolded manner and therefore teachers should consider the skill hierarchy to inform their instruction. For example, have students identify and highlight two major claims made by Samuel de Champlain. This is the first skill for students to master in claims and evidence in sources and is an appropriate task for students early in the school year. One challenge students face is understanding how to privilege specific evidence in a document. To help students overcome this challenge, ask them to highlight shorter phrases of 8-10 words. Shortening their selections will help them become readers that are more discreet in their selections.

The French Expand into North America

Ambush of the Villasur Expedition, (c. 1720) An unknown artist painted this battle scene on buffalo hide. In 1720, Spanish soldiers and Pueblo warriors tried to expel the French from the lower Mississippi Valley. Instead, French soldiers and their American Indian allies ambushed the expedition and killed forty-five men. **What conclusions can you draw about the future of conflict in North America from this image?**

among more native groups, and stretched their always small population of settlers ever thinner. Some Frenchmen took American Indian wives, who provided them with both domestic labor and kinship ties to powerful trading partners. Despite Catholic criticism of these marriages, they enhanced French traders' success and fostered alliances among the Ojibwe and Dakota nations to the west. These alliances, in turn, created a middle ground in which economic and cultural exchanges led to a remarkable degree of mutual adaptation. French traders benefited from American Indian women's skills in preparing beaver skins for market as well as from American Indian canoes, while natives adopted iron cooking pots and European cloth.

In 1682, French adventurers and their American Indian allies, led by René-Robert Cavelier, journeyed from the Great Lakes down the Mississippi River in search of a southern outlet for furs. The party traveled to the Gulf of Mexico and claimed all the land drained by the river's tributaries for France, naming it Louisiana in honor of King Louis XIV (r. 1643–1715). The new territory of Louisiana promised great wealth, but its development stalled when initial attempts to establish a colony failed.

After repeated attempts at **colonization** in the early eighteenth century, French settlers solidified their grasp along Louisiana's Gulf coast by establishing forts at Biloxi and Mobile bays, where they traded with local Choctaw Indians. Recruiting settlers from Canada and France, the small outposts survived despite conflicts among settlers, pressure from the English and the Spanish, a wave of epidemics, and a lack of supplies from France. Still, Louisiana counted only three hundred French settlers by 1715.

Continuing to promote commercial relations with diverse American Indian nations, the French also built a string of missions and forts along the upper Mississippi and Illinois Rivers during the early eighteenth century. French outposts in the Mississippi River valley became multicultural communities of diverse American Indian groups, French fur traders, and Catholic Jesuit missionaries. These small settlements in the continent's interior allowed France to challenge both English and Spanish claims to North America. In addition, extensive trade with a range of American Indian nations ensured that French power was far greater than the small number of French settlers suggests.

colonization The process of settling and controlling an already inhabited area for the economic benefit of the settlers, or colonizers.

REVIEW

- What were the goals of the French in North America?
- What steps did they take to accomplish these goals?

TEACHING IDEA

Building Vocabulary

Colonization is a major concept for Module 2-1, and students should spend time thinking about ways to connect colonization to the many factors of varying European settlement patterns. One way teachers can encourage this is to provide categories of analysis germane to colonization such as religion, economy, and culture. Have students select what they interpret to be the most important factor(s) of colonization for each European nation. Students are explicitly identifying the causes of colonization while implicitly comparing European motivations.

Example:

- French – Economy
- Dutch – Economy
- Spain – Religion

Period 2: 1607–1754

MODULE 2-1 European Challengers to Spanish North America

TEACHING IDEA

Incorporating Secondary Sources

Teachers looking to expand either their knowledge or that of their students on information relevant to Module 2-1 should consider reading historian Alan Taylor's book, *American Colonies*. In particular, Chapter 5 of Part I addresses the intricate details of the Iroquois and the influence their geographical position had on interactions with European colonizers. For instance, part of Chapter 5 is specific to the Dutch colonial patterns and the impact on American Indians.

EXPLORING AP® THEMES

Geography and the Environment

When students encounter non-text-based documents they often struggle to illustrate their knowledge of the document and its broader connections to historical developments. Map 2.1 offers students the opportunity to work on this skill in several ways. For instance, teachers should encourage students to avoid repeating what is provided in the source and instead give descriptions that explore patterns, trends, or inferences. Create groups of four students and assign each group the same European empire. Using the same European empire will allow students to have a better conversation as they compare responses. Once you have selected the European empire, ask students to write a one-to-two sentence description that captures patterns, trends, or inferences about settlement patterns depicted in the map.

TEACHING IDEA

Class Discussion

Remember this module focuses on the interactions between European colonizers *and* American Indians. To emphasize the role American Indians played in this complex process, have students form groups of three to four and assign American Indian tribes specifically mentioned in this module such as the Iroquois, Huron, Algonquians, and Mohawks. Each group has to decide whether the American Indians' geographical location or economic interests were the primary factor in determining their relations with European colonizers. Remind students both options are legitimate answers; however, their task is to privilege one factor and defend their selection. Students will write one-to-two sentence responses that substantiate their selection.

The **Dutch Expand** into North America

Calvinism Developed in Switzerland by John Calvin, a version of Protestantism in which civil judges and reformed ministers ruled over a Christian society.

Like the French, the Dutch sought North American colonies. As Spain's shipbuilding center, the Netherlands benefited from the wealth pouring in from Spain's American empire, and an affluent merchant class emerged. But the Dutch also embraced **Calvinism**, a form of Protestantism, and sought to separate themselves from Catholic Spain. In 1581 the Netherlands declared its independence from King Philip II (r. 1556–1598), and their ships aided England in defeating the Armada in 1588. Although Spain refused to recognize their independence for several decades, by 1600 the Netherlands was both a Protestant haven and the trading hub of Europe, controlling trade routes to much of Asia and parts of Africa.

In 1609 the Dutch established a fur-trading center on the Hudson River in present-day New York. From the beginning, their goals were primarily economic, and the Protestant Dutch made no pretense of bringing religion to American Indians in the region. The small number of

▲ **MAP 2.1 European Empires in North America (1715–1750)** European nations competed with one another and with numerous American Indian nations for control of vast areas of North America. Although wars continually reshaped areas under European and American Indian control, this map shows the general outlines of the empires claimed by each European nation, the key forts established to maintain those claims, and the major American Indian nations in each area. **Based on this map, what regions are most likely to experience the greatest conflict? What leads you to this conclusion?**

The Dutch Expand into North America

AP® TIP

Be sure to make note of ways that the relations between American Indians and Europeans of all nations in the New World illustrate continuity over time.

Dutch traders who settled there developed especially friendly relations with the powerful Mohawk nation, and in 1614 their trading post was relocated to Fort Orange, near present-day Albany.

In 1624, to fend off French and English raids on ships sent downriver from Fort Orange, the Dutch established New Amsterdam on Manhattan Island, which they purchased from the Lenape tribe. New Amsterdam was the centerpiece of the larger New Netherland colony and attracted a diverse community of traders, fishermen, and farmers. As the colony grew, it developed a representative government and became known for its religious toleration.

The European settlers of New Netherlands may have tolerated one another, but the same could not be said for settlers and local American Indians. Wealthy Dutch settlers secured land in New Netherland in exchange for the import of approximately fifty families who were expected to work for the landowner. Tensions increased as Dutch colonists carved out farms north of New Amsterdam where large communities of Algonquian-speaking American Indians lived. In 1639 conflict escalated when the Dutch demanded an annual tribute in wampum beads or grain. Local Algonquians resisted, raiding farms on the frontier and killing at least two colonists. In 1643 the Dutch launched a surprise attack on an American Indian encampment on Manhattan Island, murdering eighty people, mostly women and children. Outraged Algonquians burned and looted homes north of the city, killed livestock, and murdered settlers in response. For two decades, sporadic warfare continued, but eventually the Algonquians were defeated.

Iroquois Confederacy
A group of allied American Indian nations that included the Mohawk, Oneida, Onondaga, Cayuga, Seneca, and later the Tuscarora. The Confederacy was largely dissolved by the final decade of the 1700s.

At the same time, the Dutch eagerly traded for furs with Mohawk Indians along the upper Hudson River. The Mohawks, rivals to Algonquians, were a powerful tribe that had the backing of the even more powerful **Iroquois Confederacy**. Their ties to American Indian nations farther west allowed them to provide beaver skins to Dutch traders long after beavers had been over-hunted in the Hudson valley. From this trade the Mohawk and Iroquois allies sought guns. They hoped to secure captives from other American Indian tribes to restore their population, which was decimated by disease. Moreover, they hoped to fend off economic competition from rival tribes. Still, the Mohawk people did not deceive themselves. As one treaty proposition declared in 1659, "The Dutch say we are brothers and that we are joined together with chains, but that lasts only so long as we have beavers."

> "The Dutch say we are brothers and that we are joined together with chains, but that lasts only so long as we have beavers."
> — Mohawk treaty proposition, 1659

Meanwhile reports of atrocities in the conflicts between the Dutch and Algonquians circulated in the Netherlands, damaging New Amsterdam's reputation and slowing migration dramatically. A series of wars between 1652 and 1674 with their former ally England further weakened Dutch power in America. In 1664, England sent a naval convoy to take New Amsterdam. More focused on the profitable Asian trade and colonial projects in Southeast Asia, the Dutch surrendered it to the English.

REVIEW

- How did the economic relationship between the Dutch and the American Indians compare to that of the French?

AP® THINKING HISTORICALLY | Using Comparison and Causation in Historical Arguments

In this U.S. History course, and on the AP® Exam, you will sometimes be asked to make historical arguments about events or ideas that cross multiple time periods or compare different societies or peoples. A strong comparison argument should involve an explanation of the causes of differences and similarities. Therefore, causation often plays a crucial role in supporting a comparison. Here, we'll walk through how to connect the two historical reasoning skills to begin to develop an argument about early European colonization of the New World.

Step 1 List and categorize your relevant historical knowledge.

A good place to start a historical comparison is by simply considering what you learned about the early era of Spanish colonization in Period 1 alongside your knowledge of the characteristics

(Continued)

APPLY THE TIP

Students often struggle more with identifying continuities than changes. Therefore, early in the year teachers should expect students to identify and explain changes while modifying their expectations for students' ability to demonstrate understanding of continuities of a historical situation. To help foster a better grasp of continuities, consider modeling this AP® Tip by providing a word bank of continuities and have students select one and explain it in two or three sentences.

TEACHING IDEA

Check for Understanding

To help demystify the skill of comparison, have students list and define the causes of colonization for the French and the Dutch. After they have completed this task, students should weigh the most significant similarity and difference. In doing this, they are developing the ability to compare and distinguish between different pieces of historical evidence.

TRM Suggested Responses to Questions

TRM Module 2.1 AP® Thinking Historically Handout

TEACHING IDEA

Check for Understanding

Similar to the task for French colonization at the beginning of Module 2-1, consider assigning students the task of identifying and listing as many characteristics as possible of colonization for the Dutch in Module 2-1. In this way, students are relieved of the pressure to explain similarities and differences and instead are tasked with simply identifying the similarities and differences. Developing this throughout the module better prepares students to make the difficult transition of explaining the similarities and differences they identified.

EXPLORING AP® THEMES

Geography and the Environment

Earlier in Module 2-1, students focused on the role geography and the environment played in settlement patterns for the French and Dutch empires. Now that students have completed their charts, have them develop a comparison about the impact geography and the environment between the Dutch and French had on settlement patterns. Focusing on only two European nations at a time will make this an easier task.

	Similarities	Differences
Geography	Along rivers	Seacoast (Dutch)
Environment	Densely populated	More diverse resources

TEACHING IDEA

Check for Understanding

Dutch settlement before 1664 created a polyglot population interested in capitalizing on trade with American Indians such as the Mohawks and Iroquois Confederacy. Concomitant to this interest, the Dutch also developed a permanent settlement in New Amsterdam. Point out to students that comparisons can be drawn between European powers and *within* European settlements, as well. The Dutch provide a useful example. Have students compare the relations with American Indians near Fort Orange with relations near New Amsterdam.

BUILDING AP® SKILLS

Comparison

Before writing about the causes of comparisons, have students complete a Venn diagram to help ensure they understand the similarities and differences they will be writing about. This will not only help ensure accuracy, but it will also develop students' confidence in their ability to approach a difficult writing task.

TEACHING IDEA

Class Discussion

Gallery walks can be an inviting, collaborative, and active process to help students imagine a range of possibilities for answering questions about historical events. Think of a gallery walk as a space in your classroom where you display completed student work. As in an art gallery, students peruse at their leisure. This can also help scaffold the instruction further because all students participate in this space. Before outlining the characteristics and causes of similarities and differences, have students distill their focus more. For instance, students could select one similarity and one difference about colonization between only two European powers. In this way, you are limiting their approach and focusing their energies on the topics they are confident about. Next, provide a bank of terms such as the one shown below and have students evaluate one cause of the similarity and difference they identified.

Religion	Geographic Location	Environment	Economic System	Migration

After students have completed their evaluation of one cause of a similarity and difference in European colonization, have students post their answers on butcher block paper and conduct a gallery walk in the class where they look at their peers' responses.

Period 2: 1607–1754

MODULE 2-1 European Challengers to Spanish North America

of seventeenth-century French, Dutch, and Spanish colonies discussed in this module. In this way, you are already comparing both two different eras (the sixteenth and seventeenth centuries) and multiple peoples (the French, Dutch, and Spanish). If you are unsure how to approach this kind of comparative thinking, it may help to ask yourself questions about the features of each of these nation's colonies. It's also helpful to break these features into different major categories for analysis. The following categories, which were introduced in Period 1, are a good place to start:

- politics
- economy
- society/culture
- interactions with the environment
- technology

As you think about each of these categories, make note of anywhere two or more of the colonies show similarities and/or differences. Keep in mind that categories often overlap and that this is just a strategy to begin your prewriting. One way to approach this process is by creating a table like the one that follows. In it, we have taken one category — economy — and modeled how you might jot down descriptions of a similarity and a difference between two or more colonies before connecting them to causes.

Economic Similarities and Differences

Colony	Characteristics	Causes of Characteristics
French	Traded with American Indians (similar to Dutch)	Colonies sparsely populated by Europeans and aimed primarily at establishing trade relations with American Indians
Spanish	Established the encomienda system to control American Indian labor	Spanish monarchs used forced American Indian labor for mining and agriculture
Dutch	Sought fur trade with American Indians (similar to French)	Colonies sparsely populated by Europeans and aimed primarily at establishing trade relations with American Indians

Remember, this process is just one way to use causation to establish reasons for each historical development you note. Any system that allows you to quickly categorize similarities and differences along with their causes is one you should continue to develop as you approach writing in this course.

Step 2 Summarize your thoughts in a short paragraph.

Gather your thoughts by writing one sentence comparing and/or contrasting at least two, if not all three, colonies for each of the categories we explored in step 1 (politics, economy, society/culture, interactions with the environment, and technology).

Be sure to include all three nations, and remember that comparison should always take differences into account. Then, support your comparisons by adding one to three sentences that explain the causes of the similarity or the causes of the difference. The purpose of writing these sentences down isn't to craft and support a well-developed argument. For now, you should merely focus on clearly expressing your knowledge of how historical events relate to each other and explaining the causes for those similarities and differences. For example, a summary comparing the economies of each nation's colonies might look like this:

> By the time the French and Dutch began colonization in North America, the Spanish had established the encomienda system of forced labor for American Indian communities in Central and South America. This system required that American Indians perform manual labor on behalf of the Spanish, including farming and mining for precious metals in some regions. Because the encomienda system grew out of the Spanish need for forced labor, it depended upon a relatively large population of occupying Spanish forces, colonists, and religious authorities who sought to convert American Indians to Catholicism. The French and the Dutch, on the other hand, established sparsely populated colonies in the early seventeenth century, at least a generation after the Spanish, and concentrated primarily on establishing trade networks with American Indians for goods such as furs.

TEACHING IDEA

AP® Thinking Historically Workshop

Consider narrowing students' focus during a brainstorm session that helps prepare them for the workshop. Assign groups one of the three European nations and have them develop two comparisons with one of the other European nations. So, if students were assigned the French, they could choose to compare with either the Spanish or Dutch. Students then exchange answers with a group who made comparisons with the same grouping of nations. In this way, students are developing a thorough brainstorm over two of the three nations involved in the workshop, which will help prepare them to be successful. This also helps teachers identify which nations students are confident in and which they will need to spend more time on during the workshop.

Although this short paragraph is very general and straightforward, it is a strong example of how to connect comparison to causation in that it brings together the Spanish desire to transform native societies for Spanish benefit and the relatively large Spanish colonial population required to oversee the *encomienda* system. Likewise, this paragraph establishes that the late arrival of the Dutch and French, and their desire to create trade networks with American Indians rather than a forced labor system, resulted in their colonies' sparse populations.

ACTIVITY

Write a short, one- to three-sentence summary that compares *and* explains the causes of similarities and differences between the French, Dutch, and Spanish colonies in North America for at least two of the following categories:

- politics
- society/culture
- interactions with the environment
- technology

Spain's Fragile North American Empire

In the early decades of the sixteenth century, Spain continued to push north from Mexico in an attempt to expand its empire. As the French, Dutch, and English challenged Spain for North American colonies throughout the seventeenth century, the Spanish were spread dangerously thin on the northern reaches of their American holdings. Even as they tried to maintain a firm hold on Florida and the West Indies, staving off growing resistance from the Pueblo people forced more Spanish attention to *Nuevo México*. Thus, as other European powers expanded their reach into North America, the Spaniards were left with few resources to protect their northern and eastern frontiers.

Spain's use of the mission system, directed by Franciscan priests, to extend its control into *Nuevo México* provoked resistance from Pueblos (see Module 1.4). Following Pueblo resistance, which led to both the Acoma massacre and the flight of Spanish settlers, the Spanish crown developed a new plan for the region. In 1610 the Spanish returned with a larger military force, founded Santa Fe, and established a new network of missions and estates owned by *encomenderos*.

As the Spanish renewed their efforts to colonize *Nuevo México*, the Pueblo people largely accepted the situation. In part, they feared military reprisals if they challenged Spanish authorities. Moreover, they had been weakened by disease and untimely drought and were struggling to fend off raids by hostile Apache and Navajo tribes. In accepting Spanish rule, the Pueblos hoped to gain protection by Spanish soldiers and priests.

However, the Pueblo people did not see their living conditions improve, and tensions between the Spanish and the Pueblo nation continued to simmer. Throughout the mid-seventeenth century, Spanish forces failed to protect the Pueblo Indians against new and devastating raids by Apache and Navajo warriors, and Catholic prayers proved unable to stop Pueblo deaths in a 1671 epidemic. Finally, relations worsened when another drought in the 1670s led to famine among many Pueblo Indians.

AP® ANALYZING SOURCES

Source: King Philip IV of Spain, *Letter to Don Luis Valdés*, 1647

"To my governor and captain-general of the province of Nueva Vizcaya: It has been learned in my royal Council of the Indies that that province adjoins the barbarous nations . . . who are now at war, though they are usually at peace; that while they were so at peace, there went among them to trade certain [magistrates] and religious instructors who carried off and sold their children to

(Continued)

TEACHING IDEA

Categorization

For students struggling to compare the French, Dutch, and Spanish colonies across two categories, consider assigning them one of the following tasks:

1. Compare two European empires within one of the following categories:
   - Politics
   - Society/culture
   - Interactions with the environment
   - Technology

2. Assign students either similarities *or* differences between two or more of the European empires and have them compare at least two of the following categories:
   - Politics
   - Society/culture
   - Interactions with the environment
   - Technology

TRM Suggested Responses to Questions

TRM Module 2.1 AP® Analyzing Sources Handout 2

EXPLORING AP® THEMES

America in the World

Students need to be continually aware that Module 2-1 invites them to evaluate the interactions between American Indians and European colonizers. American Indians were historical actors in this development and often resisted European colonizers' demands. To further develop this awareness, have students select two American Indian tribes who resisted the authority of a European empire. Next, have them write a two to three sentence response explaining the how and why for resistance.

TEACHING IDEA

Incorporating Websites

When students study the various ways in which European nations attempted to colonize and subjugate American Indians, they should also examine European voices critical of this worldview. One prominent voice students should consider is that of Bartolome de Las Casas. The Gilder Lehrman Institute of American History hosts a site specifically designed to assist AP® U.S. History teachers and students (ap.gilderlehrman.org). Teachers can locate the Las Casas document on this site and can use this document for primary source analysis development or as a bell ringer to begin class.

TEACHING IDEA

Incorporating Secondary Sources

The history of enslaved American Indians is not a well-known narrative. Therefore, after students read the primary source by Bartolome de Las Casas, teachers should think about assigning an essay about enslaved American Indians by history professor Alan Gallay found on Gilder Lehrman's AP® U.S. History website (ap.gilderlehrman.org). Not only does this brief essay pair well with the Las Casas document, it also extends learning for students on a difficult topic to teach.

Period 2: 1607–1754

MODULE 2-1 European Challengers to Spanish North America

TEACHING IDEA

Active Reading Strategies

Before having students identify a cause of the developments that led Philip to send a letter to Don Luis Valdés, have students go through a primary source analysis. As students read the document, have them use one highlighter color to highlight any historical vocab they do not understand. After conducting a class conversation about the terms they highlighted, consider having students use a different highlighter color to illustrate their understanding of King Philip's major claims in the document. After they have accomplished these tasks they will be more confident in their understanding of the document and will be better able to answer the accompanying questions.

TEACHING IDEA

Check for Understanding

Students struggling to describe a similarity in the letters of Alfonso and Philip might first try to identify a similarity in the documents. After students have read both documents, have them identify — and they can do this by underlining passages in the documents — a significant similarity. After the class has identified the similarities, have a class discussion about the similarities they located and why they consider those to be of note. Now students are ready to answer the Questions for Comparison.

---

serve in the mines and elsewhere, disposing of them as slaves or giving them as presents, which amounts to the same thing. As a result they became disquieted, and the governor, Don Luis de Valdés, began to punish them immoderately and without regard for the public faith, for, after calling them to attend religious instruction, he seized and shot some of them. Thereupon they revolted, took up their arms and arrows, and made some raids; they broke into my treasury, and it has cost me over 50,000 pesos to pacify them, although they are not entirely quieted yet. It is very fitting to my service and to their peace to command strictly that the barbarous Indians shall not be made slaves nor sent as presents to anyone, nor made to serve anywhere against their will when they are at peace and are not taken in open war."

Questions for Analysis
1. Identify a cause of the developments that led Philip to send this letter.
2. Explain Philip's purpose in sending this letter.

Questions for Comparison Mvemba A Nzinga (also known as Alfonso I), King of the Kongo, *Letter to John III, King of Portugal*, 1526 (p. 27)
1. Describe a similarity in the letters of Alfonso and Philip.
2. Explain a reason for a difference in the letters of Alfonso and Philip.

When some Pueblo Indians openly returned to their traditional priests, Spanish officials hanged three Pueblo leaders for idolatry as well as whipped and incarcerated forty-three others. Among those punished was Popé, who planned a broad-based revolt upon his release. On August 10, 1680, seventeen thousand Pueblo Indians initiated a coordinated assault on numerous Spanish missions and forts in what came to be known as the **Pueblo revolt**. They destroyed buildings and farms, burned crops and houses, and demolished Catholic churches. In response, the Spanish retreated to Mexico without launching any significant immediate counterattack. However, they returned in the 1690s and reconquered parts of *Nuevo México*, aided by growing internal conflict among the Pueblos and raids by the Apache. In 1696, the Pueblo resistance was finally crushed, and new lands were opened for Spanish settlement. At the same time, Franciscan missionaries improved relations with the Pueblos by allowing them to retain more indigenous practices.

Despite the Spanish reconquest, the Pueblo revolt limited Spanish expansion in the long run by strengthening other indigenous peoples in the region. In the aftermath of the revolt, some Pueblo refugees moved north and taught the Navajo how to grow corn, raise sheep, and ride horses. Through trading with the Navajo and raiding Spanish settlements during the early eighteenth century, the Ute, Shoshone, and Comanche peoples also gained access to horses. By the 1730s, the Comanche launched mounted bison hunts, and raids on other American Indian nations. They traded with the Spanish for more horses and guns, bringing American Indian captives for Spanish enslavement. Thus the Pueblos provided other indigenous nations with the means to support larger populations, wider commercial networks, and more warriors, allowing them to continue to contest Spanish rule.

Pueblo revolt 1680 uprising of Pueblo Indians against Spanish forces in New Mexico that led to the Spaniards' temporary retreat from the area. The uprising was sparked by mistreatment and the suppression of Pueblo culture and religion.

◀ **San Esteban del Rey Mission** Opened in 1644, this Spanish mission in present-day New Mexico taught Christianity and Hispanic customs for the Acoma (Pueblo) people. Spanish missionaries prohibited traditional Pueblo practices such as performing dances and wearing masks. The mission was one of the few to survive Pueblo revolts in the late seventeenth century. **In what ways is the San Esteban del Rey Mission representative of the Spanish relationship with the Pueblo people?**

Spain's Fragile North American Empire

Period 2: 1607–1754

AP® TIP
Compare the Pueblo revolt to the conflicts between the Dutch and Algonquians, and the French and Huron. What continuities do you notice in imperial relations with American Indians during the seventeenth century?

In response to early eighteenth-century French settlements in the lower Mississippi valley, Spain also sought to reinforce its claims to Texas, named for the Tejas Indians, along the northeastern frontier of its North American empire. Here, Spain established missions and forts along the route from San Juan Batista to the border of present-day Louisiana. Although small and scattered, these outposts were meant to ensure Spain's claim to Texas. But the presence of large and powerful American Indian nations, including the Caddo and the Apache, forced the small number of Spanish residents to accept many native customs in order to maintain their presence in the region.

REVIEW
- How did the French and Dutch colonies in North America differ from the Spanish colonies to the south?

AP® WRITING HISTORICALLY: Crafting a Thesis Statement Based on Comparison

As you progress through this course, you will have many chances to practice using different historical thinking skills and reasoning processes both to convey your historical knowledge and to make a compelling argument. Let's take a look at an essay prompt that asks you to compare the causes of historical developments that you read about in this module:

> Compare French and Spanish colonial relations with American Indians, explaining the reasons for similarities and differences in interactions during the period between 1492 and 1754.

Step 1: Break down the prompt.
This prompt is asking you to respond by making an argument. You'll need to use the historical reasoning process of comparison. How do we know this? The prompt contains a couple of key words and phrases. First, it asks you to "compare" French and Spanish colonial relations with American Indians. Second, the prompt asks you to "explain the reasons for similarities and differences" — in other words, your explanation must explain why these similarities and differences occured. This will ensure your response is a full-fledged argument and not just a description of what you know about history.

Step 2: List and categorize your relevant historical knowledge.
Let's take a look at how you might use this historical reasoning process to craft a thesis that responds to this prompt. You can pre-write by simply writing down the features of each colonial power. One way to do this is to make a chart that characterizes Spanish and French interactions with American Indians. For each characterization, note a piece of evidence that supports your assertion. Don't worry about noting any similarities or differences yet; for right now you should only concentrate on organizing your observations about each colonial power. We suggest you identify at least three features and a matching piece of evidence for each, but locate and characterize as many as you can support in the time you are given. As you brainstorm, try to include as many "proper nouns" (people, events, court cases, laws, wars, inventions, and so on) as you can. Your chart may look something like this:

Colonial Power	Interactions with American Indians	Citations of Evidence
Spanish	1. Early cooperation 2. Later forced labor 3. Forced religious conversion	1. Malintzin's aid to Cortés 2. *Encomienda* system 3. Mission system
French	1. Early cooperation 2. Native enslavement rare 3. Less drive to convert	1. French alliance with Hurons 2. French established trade networks with American Indians rather than systems of enslavement to extract natural resources. 3. Thinly populated French settlements

(Continued)

TRM Suggested Responses to Questions

TEACHING IDEA

Check for Understanding

If students need further assistance in decoding the Long-Essay Question on this page, try giving them a formula they can replicate for subsequent questions such as the one shown here: Historical Thinking Skill Task(s) | Historical Topics | Time Period

- **Historical Thinking Skill Task(s):** Compare similarities and differences, and consider reasons for each. Identifying these skills informs students they are attempting to use both comparison and causation.

- **Historical Topics:** French and Spanish relations with American Indians. For students to successfully answer any AP® question, they need to decode what the prompt is asking for. So even though students have studied French, Spanish, and Dutch relations with American Indians in this module, this question requires students to focus on only the French and Spanish.

- **Time Period:** 1492–1754. AP® questions provide chronological associations for students and in this case, students should try to understand the bookend time periods. In other words, most students will associate 1492 with Columbus's voyage and 1754 with the beginning of the French and Indian War, as they will learn in Module 2-8. Knowing this informs their outline for the historical developments and processes they can include in their response.

TEACHING IDEA

Connecting the Dots

The Long-Essay Question in Module 2-1 provides students a wide breadth of time to consider framing their response, 1492–1754. Students should do their best to illustrate change over time, regardless of the selected historical thinking skill for the essay. Before you have students complete the brainstorming chart provided, consider having students select three examples that illustrate change over time in chronological order. Remind students the focus is not to name discrete dates, but rather to demonstrate an understanding of change over time. This will ensure the focal points of the essay are well organized.

▲ Differentiation

Have students substantiate their understanding of the selected events by writing one sentence that links each event. If they selected Columbus's voyage in 1492 with Bartolome de Las Casas's critique in 1552 it will look something like this: *When the Spanish first began exploring the New World in the late-fifteenth-century economic profit was the main goal; however, during the early-sixteenth-century some religious leaders expressed dismay over how indigenous persons were being treated by imperial authorities*. This helps prepare students to take the next step in the writing process, which is to explore specific evidence to substantiate historical claims.

BUILDING AP® SKILLS
Argumentation

Timed writing presents unique challenges to students. One significant challenge is training students to transition from one idea to the next in their essays. If students are struggling to demonstrate transitions, consider having them write one sentence that introduces historical evidence. After they complete this task, ask them to select a transition and write a transition statement that explains the evidence they selected. Incorporating a two-step process can make the task of transitioning seem less intimidating, especially early in the school year. Following these steps ensures students are practicing how to explain the relationships that exist between pieces of evidence as they learn how to explain historical evidence.

Here is an example: Both the French and the Spanish sent missionaries to the New World to spread Christianity to indigenous persons. However, the Spanish employed more coercive tactics to convert American Indians, while the French remained more peaceful in their attempts.

BUILDING AP® SKILLS
Argumentation

If students are struggling to compose a thesis that addresses similarities, differences, and the causes of those comparisons, consider breaking the thesis writing process down further. For instance, instead of requiring students to compose a thesis that addresses all parts of the question, think about creating groups of three in your class so each student writes one part of the thesis. One student is responsible for writing the similarity, one student addresses the difference, and one student writes about the causes of the comparisons made in the thesis. The activity will work best when the students discuss each section and help one another compose each part. In this way, students are still learning the required parts of the thesis.

Once you have characterized each nation's interactions with American Indians, you can compare them. We suggest creating a new chart, like the one that follows, to note the similarities and the differences in French and Spanish colonists' interactions with American Indians.

Similarity or Difference	Explanation
Similarity: The Spanish and French both relied on cooperation from American Indian allies to expand their empires, as shown by Malintzin's aid to Cortes, and by the French alliance with Hurons against the Iroquois in the early seventeenth century.	The reason both relied on their allies was that the French, like the Spanish before them, came in numbers too few to conquer the populations of the lands they colonized.
Difference: The Spanish enslaved large numbers of American Indians, as seen in the *encomienda* and the mission system, while the French established direct rule over few Great Lakes region American Indians, enslaving far fewer in thinly populated French settlements.	The reasons for differences in the treatment of and relationship to American Indians was due to the large amounts of gold and silver found in Spanish colonies, which motivated them to make earlier and more extensive efforts to enslave American Indians to provide manpower for the mines; by contrast, there was a relative lack of such resources in French-occupied lands during this era.

As this chart demonstrates, you should write statements that not only draw direct comparisons when addressing similarities but also incorporate evidence.

When you make a claim about a difference between French and Spanish colonies, you should present an idea about one colony supported by evidence, insert a transition noting the contrasting relationship, and then present the idea and evidence about the other colony. Transition words such as "but," "although," "whereas," or "however" are all good ways to signal and emphasize a contrasting relationship.

After noting each similarity and difference, add explanations of the reasons for these similarities and differences. These explanations only need to be a phrase or a sentence. The important thing is to make sure that you've given some thought to how you will apply causation to support your argument.

Step 3 Write a thesis statement.

Now that you have taken a few moments to plan a response that fully addresses all aspects of the prompt, it's time to use these claims to craft a thesis statement that will introduce your argument and begin your essay. In this case, your thesis should clearly convey two things: an overview of your interpretation of the similarities *and* differences in Spanish and French interactions with American Indians in North America prior to 1754, and what you assert are the reasons for those similarities and differences.

A weak thesis will look something like this:

> While both the Spanish and the French colonized North America and the American Indians there, the Spanish were cruel to the American Indians, whereas the French were generally more accepting of their cultural practices.

While it's true that this thesis contains an assertion about similarities and differences between the French and the Spanish in their interactions with American Indians, it depends upon vague claims about the "cruel" Spanish and the "accepting" French that will be difficult to defend in an essay. Also note that this thesis does not attempt to explain the reasons for the similarities and differences it names.

A stronger thesis will look something like this:

> Spanish and French colonies showed similarity in their interactions with American Indians in that both formed mutually beneficial alliances with some local tribes during the early periods of conquest; however, the French, who depended primarily on trade with native peoples, employed forced labor far less than the Spanish, who sought precious metals and agricultural products in the regions they colonized, and therefore forced native peoples to produce these goods.

TEACHING IDEA
AP® Writing Historically Workshop

After students have completed their thesis statements, organize the students in groups of four or five. Each student shares their thesis statement and the group highlights the following:

- Similarities
- Differences
- Spanish
- French
- Relations with American Indians
- Causes

Each group highlights the elements they can find and then turn in their best example. In a class of 25–30, this gives the teacher five or six examples to go over with the class before assigning the activity to complete the module. In this way, teachers are giving feedback and providing further feedback before students attempt the thesis on their own.

Spain's Fragile North American Empire

Period 2: 1607–1754

Here, the thesis provides a detailed argument that completely answers the prompt by noting that both the Spanish and the French formed early alliances with American Indians, but also establishes that the differences between the Spanish and the French relations with native peoples were based on their different laboring needs. While the French depended primarily on trade, the Spanish established colonies based on the extraction of precious metals and agricultural production, which required a controlled labor force.

ACTIVITY

Carefully read the following prompt, then follow steps 1-3 to pre-write. Make sure to draw a link between comparison and causation. Finally, use the information from your pre-writing to craft a thesis statement.

Compare French and the Dutch colonial relations with American Indians, explaining the reasons for similarities and differences in interactions during the period between 1608 and 1754.

TEACHING IDEA

Building Vocabulary

Whenever students write thesis statements, they should employ vernacular connected to the historical thinking skills embedded in the question. Early in the year, students might struggle with how to intuitively integrate these words and phrases in their theses. Consider providing a word bank categorized by skill so students can incorporate these into their responses.

Causation:		
Direct cause	Indirect cause	This led to
Contributed to	In response to	Directly enabled
Resulted from	Long-term result	Short-term cause
Contingent upon	Resulted in	As a result

Comparison:		
Similar to	Different from	On the one hand
On the other hand	However	Striking similarity
Disagreed on	An important distinction	An important difference
This contrasts with	Even though	Although

These phrases can be used to start or end sentences and also can provide useful transitions as students illustrated similarities and differences in a thesis statement.

TRM Find **Handout 2.2 – Historical Thinking Word Bank** in the Teacher's Resource Materials.

TRM Suggested Responses to Questions

Module 2-2

Early British Colonies in Maryland, Virginia, and North Carolina

LEARNING TARGETS

By the end of this module, you should be able to:

- Explain how environmental factors affected the development of the Chesapeake and North Carolina colonies between 1607 and 1754.
- Explain the similarities and differences between the social development of the Chesapeake and North Carolina colonies between 1607 and 1754.

THEMATIC FOCUS

Geography and Environment

The earliest English colonies sought profit through agriculture and the cash crop tobacco, which became a valuable commodity in the Atlantic world.

HISTORICAL REASONING FOCUS

Causation

Module 1-2 introduced ways historians use causation to establish why an event occurs, as well as how a strong analysis takes multiple causes into account. Another way historians look at causation is by looking past immediate causes to uncover distant causes that still play important roles in a given historical development. By discussing causes — and the causes of those causes — historians enrich their analyses. For example, the profitability of the fur trade was an immediate cause of the economic relationship between the French and the American Indians during the seventeenth century. But what brought the French to North America in the first place? One clear reason was King Henry IV's desire for profit — and this is therefore a distant cause of that economic relationship.

TASK ▶ As you will read in this module, the rapid expansion of tobacco plantations and English settlement fostered conflicts with American Indian nations and also fueled tensions among settlers themselves. While reading, note the immediate causes of these conflicts — battles over land as the English expanded their tobacco plantations — and their connection to more distant causes, especially the motive behind the founding of the tobacco colonies: profit.

The English, like the French and the Dutch, entered the race for an American empire well after the Spanish. England did not have a permanent settlement in the Americas until the founding of Jamestown at the mouth of Chesapeake Bay in 1607. Founded and developed by profit seekers, English colonists succeeded in building a tobacco economy in that area.

Economic Causes of English Colonization

Changes in the English economy, which occurred throughout western Europe as a result of the Columbian exchange, shaped British efforts to compete with Spain for North America during the early seventeenth century. As the sixteenth century came to a close, **inflation** posed a major challenge for the ruling class and to the economic stability of England. Costly wars with France, the conquest of Ireland, and, most significantly, the influx of Spanish silver all contributed to the crippling increase in prices that in turn diminished nobles' traditional sources of wealth.

Much of the nobility responded to these challenges by seeking new sources of wealth in the Atlantic economy.

To develop an export economy, sixteenth-century English elites began to defy the traditional feudal order by enclosing lands. **Enclosure movements** essentially claimed that only noble title-holders had the right to use land, and evicted English commoners, who had until that point lived and farmed there. These changes, in turn, led to social conflict. Evictions of commoners, combined with increasingly high rents as land to live on became more scarce, created a homeless population that struggled to feed themselves. Already lacking access to land, English peasants also faced higher food prices due to the economic pressure from Spanish silver. Making matters worse, enclosure decreased the production of grain crops, creating food shortages and famine. Commoners resisted these trends through a series of revolts in the sixteenth century in which they fought to regain access to common lands by destroying enclosures. The English nobility, however, had the upper hand. They successfully suppressed each revolt, and the trend of enclosure only intensified during the seventeenth and eighteenth centuries.

Understanding the causes and effects of the enclosure movement provides two important insights into English colonization during the seventeenth century. First, it reflected the monarchy's and the nobility's efforts to seek new sources of wealth. English colonial outposts, starting with Jamestown in 1607, were fundamentally profit-seeking from the very beginning. Second, the enclosure movement created a large landless population available for colonial settlement. English elites took advantage of this situation by arresting many landless, unemployed people and convicting them as criminal vagrants and vagabonds. Convicts were then sold into **indentured servitude**, a form of bound labor. Contracts of indenture allowed the purchase of a laborer for a set number of years, typically seven. Fearing arrest, many commoners chose to avoid imprisonment by indenturing themselves. In the first half of the seventeenth century, the vast majority of British colonial workers in North America were indentured servants.

indentured servitude Servants contracted to work for a set period of time without pay. Many early migrants to the English colonies indentured themselves in exchange for the price of passage to North America.

AP® ANALYZING SOURCES

Source: Thomas More, *Utopia; or, the Best State of a Commonwealth*, 1516

"[Y]our sheep, which are naturally mild, and easily kept in order, may be said now to devour men . . . ; for wherever it is found that the sheep of any soil yield a softer and richer wool than ordinary, there the nobility and gentry, and even those holy men, the abbots! not contented with old rents which their farms yielded, do no good to the public, [but] resolve to do it hurt instead of good. They stop the course of agriculture, . . . and inclose the grounds that they may lodge their sheep in them. . . . [T]he owners as well as tenants . . . are turned out of their possessions by trick or by main force, or, being wearied out by ill usage, they are forced to sell them: by which means those miserable people, both men and women, . . . with their poor, but numerous families . . . are all forced to change their seats, not knowing whither to go. . . . [W]hat is left for them to do, but to steal, and so be hanged, . . . or to go about and beg?"

Questions for Analysis
1. Identify the injustices More cites in this excerpt.
2. Describe the historical trends or events that shaped the developments described by More.
3. Explain how the developments described by More shaped early English colonization of North America.

REVIEW
- What were some of the causes of English colonization of North America?

BUILDING AP® SKILLS

Argumentation

When students formulate theses, they should avoid framing their interpretation with overly broad categories such as social, political, and economic. It is equally true that theses with too-specific terms can limit a stated argument. The beginning of Module 2-2 offers students a balance of economic rationale that is neither too specific nor broad. Consider providing students with the following categories: imperial competition, inflation, and colonial outposts. Next, have students develop a response using these terms to both define England's economic rationale for colonization and weigh the relative significance of each category. Working on this skill early in the module heightens their awareness of causation.

TRM Suggested Responses to Questions

TRM Module 2.2 AP® Analyzing Sources Handout 2

TEACHING IDEA

Connecting the Dots

If students struggle to connect the questions for analysis from the Thomas More document, consider having them condense their focus. For instance, instead of having students explain how the influences of More's description shaped later colonization movements, have students make an immediate connection to the issue of enclosure. This will not only focus their analysis, it will also encourage them to read the document for a discrete connection. If you want to make it a class activity, have students work in groups of three or four students and pass out different highlighter colors to each person. Once they have read the document, ask each student to highlight one brief excerpt from the document that connects to the enclosure. After they share results, students will select the best example to share with the entire class.

TEACHING IDEA

Check for Understanding

This module starts with an explanation about long-term, intermediate, and short-term causation to help frame the activities. To develop this understanding give students the following list of terms and have them place the words in order from long-term to most immediate cause of English colonization.

Imperial wars	Columbian Exchange	Inflation	Enclosure movements
Colonial outposts	Population surplus	Indentured servitude	

Period 2: 1607–1754

MODULE 2-2   Early British Colonies in Maryland, Virginia, and North Carolina

The English Establish Jamestown

APPLY THE TIP

The previous model examined the settlement patterns of the Dutch and French; in particular, the module provided ways to find similarities in their respective approaches to developing trade with American Indians. Students can use prior knowledge to identify differences in how the French and Dutch differed from the English concerning trade agreements with American Indians. Consider having students write one sentence that identifies a similarity between the Dutch and French economic ventures with local tribes of American Indians. In the subsequent sentence, have students identify a difference with English goals of trade. Taking the time to develop two sentences, which focus on identifying the comparison, can make this assignment more approachable.

TRM Suggested Responses to Questions

TRM Module 2.2 AP® Analyzing Sources Handout 2

TEACHING IDEA

Incorporating Primary Sources

One of the best sites for primary sources is the Library of Congress (loc.gov). For the early periods of AP® U.S. History, the wealth of resources provided can be especially helpful for teachers to bridge seventeenth-century history to a twenty-first-century audience. For instance, reading a conversation between Chief Powhatan and John Smith (according to the memory of John Smith) can be an excellent activity for the beginning of class as students prepare to delve into the subject. The document can be found by going to the Library of Congress website and searching for "John Smith and Powhatan Exchange Views, 1608." The document allows students a window into a very remote and distant past, invites a critical analysis of the varying world views of the Powhatans and English, and allows students to ask fundamental questions about the intentions of the English settlers in the earliest stages of settlement.

joint-stock companies Companies in which large numbers of investors own stock. They were able to quickly raise large amounts of money and shared risk and reward equally among investors.

AP® TIP
Compare the settlement of Jamestown to the early settlements established by the Dutch and French in North America.

Powhatan Confederacy Large and powerful confederation of Algonquian-speaking American Indians in Virginia. The Jamestown settlers had a complicated and often combative relationship with the leaders of the Powhatan Confederacy.

England's success in colonizing North America depended in part on a new economic model in which investors purchased shares in **joint-stock companies** that could raise large amounts of money quickly. If the venture succeeded, investors shared the profits. If they failed, no investor suffered the whole loss. In 1606 a group of London merchants formed the Virginia Company, and King James I (r. 1603–1625) granted them the right to settle a vast area of North America that stretched from present-day New York to North Carolina. Among the leaders of the group of 104 colonists who set out for the New World under the banner of the Virginia Company was a man named John Smith. Born in 1580, Smith left England as a young man "to learne the life of a Souldier." After fighting and traveling throughout Europe, the Mediterranean, and North Africa for several years, Captain Smith returned to England around 1605, joining the Virginia Company when it was formed a year later.

Arriving on the coast of North America in the Chesapeake Bay in April 1607, 104 colonists established Jamestown, named in honor of the king. Although the Virginia Company claimed the land for themselves and their country, the area was already controlled by a powerful American Indian leader, Chief Powhatan (proper name Wahunsonacock). He presided over the confederation of some 14,000 Algonquian-speaking peoples from twenty-five to thirty tribes, which surrounded the small Jamestown settlement. Indeed, the English chose the site of this settlement mainly for its easy defense, made possible by the **Powhatan Confederacy**, which was far more powerful than the English settlers. For the first two years the settlers depended on them to survive.

Although bothered by the swampy, mosquito-infested environment of Jamestown and struggling for survival, the colonists were still able to divide their energies between searching for gold and silver and building a military encampment. Despite the Englishmen's aggressive stance in building this military fort, Powhatan assisted the new settlers in hopes they could provide him with English cloth, iron hatchets, and even guns. His capture and eventual release of John Smith in 1607 suggests his interest in developing trade relations with the newcomers even as he sought to subordinate them.

AP® ANALYZING SOURCES

Source: Powhatan, Chief of Algonquian-speaking Powhatan Confederation, *Deerskin Cloak*, c. 1608

About the source: Chief Powhatan wore this deerskin cloak for tribal ceremonies. The objects in this cloak are made of shells, which were considered items of value by the Powhatan people. The circles could represent regions under Powhatan's control, the animals most likely represent deer, and the individual in the center represents Chief Powhatan.

Questions for Analysis

1. Describe the arrangement of the images and materials that make up this cloak.
2. Explain what the arrangement of the images and materials that make up this cloak reveals about the Powhatan and the Algonquian-speaking peoples.
3. Explain the role Powhatan politics played in fostering conflict with European colonists.

BUILDING AP® SKILLS

Sourcing and Situation

Students are expected to know how to account for the historical situation of a primary source. However, many students do not know how to identify the source's place among broader historical developments. This document is from 1608. Consider providing an abbreviated timeline such as the following to have students label relevant historical events.

1607	1608	1609	1610
Jamestown Settled	Document	John Smith Captured	End of "Starving Time"

After students have associated events to the dates provided, have them write one sentence that describes the trend of English settlement in the period provided, 1607–1610. This particular statement will likely identify the English position as weak compared to that of Powhatan. Sometimes sentence starters can be a useful way of scaffolding this assignment. Sentence starter: Even though the English settled a permanent colony in Jamestown in 1607, [*students fill in remainder of sentence*].

MODULE 2-2   Early British Colonies in Maryland, Virginia, and North Carolina

The English Establish Jamestown

Fort James at Jamestown, Virginia, 1607 This image, created by Jamestown colonist John Hull, portrays the earliest iteration of the settlement. What does this image reveal about how the English perceived their colony in relation to the land, sea, and people they encountered?

AP® TIP
Be sure to note how British conflicts with the Powhatan were related to land, resources, and political boundaries.

"Goodman Jackson pitied me . . . [a]nd . . . much marvelled that you would send me a servant to the Company; he said I had been better knocked on the head."

Richard Frethorne, indentured servant at Jamestown, letter to his parents in England, 1623

When Powhatan Indians captured Smith and two other Virginia Company men in 1607, all but Smith were executed. Chief Powhatan then performed what was likely an adoption ceremony to bring Smith into his family and under his rule. The ceremony would have involved him sending out one of his daughters — in this case, Pocahontas, who was about twelve years old — to indicate that the captive was spared. In Chief Powhatan's culture, the capture, ceremony, and release of an English leader established his dominance over Smith and the English. But Virginia Company leaders like Captain Smith considered Powhatan and his warriors a threat rather than an asset. When unable to feed themselves that first year, Jamestown residents raided Powhatan villages for corn and other food, making Powhatan increasingly distrustful of the colonists.

On top of these rising tensions, a severe drought between 1606 and 1612 limited the Powhatan Indians' surpluses of food, and they became less willing to trade it to the English as a result. For their part, the English settlers' fear of their Powhatan neighbors led them to resist an exchange the Powhatan likely would have accepted: guns for food. The food shortage in Jamestown was worsened by a number of other things as well: Some colonists refused to do manual labor; an injury forced John Smith to return to England in late 1609, thus severing the strongest link between the colony and Powhatan; nearby water was tainted by salt from the ocean; and diseases that festered in the low-lying area of Jamestown had killed more than half of the original settlers.

Meanwhile, the Virginia Company devised a new plan to stave off the collapse of its colony. It started selling seven-year joint-stock options to raise funds and recruited new settlers to produce staple crops, glassware, or other items for export. Interested individuals who could not afford to invest cash could sign an indenture for service in Virginia. After seven years, these indentured servants would gain their freedom and receive a hundred acres of land. In June 1609, a new contingent of colonists attracted by this plan — five hundred men and a hundred women — sailed for Jamestown.

The new arrivals, however, had not brought enough supplies to sustain the colony through the winter. Chief Powhatan did offer some aid, but American Indians, too, suffered from shortages in the winter of 1609–1610. A "starving time" settled on Jamestown. Some settlers resorted to cannibalism. By the spring of 1610, seven of every eight settlers who had arrived in Jamestown since 1607 were dead.

That June, the sixty survivors decided to abandon the settlement and sail for home, but they changed their minds when they met three English ships in the harbor that were loaded with supplies and three hundred more settlers. Emboldened by fresh supplies and an enlarged population, Jamestown's new leaders adopted a more aggressive military strategy, attacking native villages, burning crops, killing many American Indians, and taking others captive. They believed that such brutality would convince neighboring tribes to obey English demands for food and labor.

REVIEW

What factors shaped early English encounters with American Indians in Virginia?

BUILDING AP® SKILLS

Developments and Processes

The following group activity is designed to encourage students to think about the relative significance of the various factors of English relations with the Powhatans in the early years of settlement. Divide the class into groups of three or four students. Assign each group the following causes of English/Powhatan disputes: capture of John Smith, drought from 1606 to 1612, rise of indentured servants, English raids on Powhatan villages. Have each group rank the events from least to most important as it relates to why relations between the two groups fractured in the early years of settlement.

TEACHING IDEA

Incorporating Secondary Sources

"Historic Jamestowne" hosts a site devoted to telling the story of the settlement of Jamestown (historicjamestowne.org). One of the features of the site is an in-depth look at the tragic events surrounding the "starving time" of 1609–1610.

TEACHING IDEA

Incorporating Secondary Sources

Smithsonian magazine offers a revisionist look at what led to the early demise of settlers in Jamestown. While recognizing the role of incompetence, the article shears away at interpretations too dependent on this one variable. Instead of privileging incompetence, the article focuses on the role other factors such as the drought played in the struggle to maintain a viable colony. Find the article by going to the Smithsonian magazine's website and searching for "Rethinking Jamestown" (smithsonianmag.com).

TEACHING IDEA

Incorporating Secondary Sources

Chapter 5 of Ira Berlin's seminal book on the development of slavery, *Many Thousands Gone: The First Two Centuries of Slavery in North America*, provides an in-depth look at how tobacco fueled a slave system, an economic system, and a mentality toward Virginia's role in the Atlantic world. This reading can be used to supplement students' understanding of the long-term consequences of the profitability of tobacco in the Chesapeake.

TRM Suggested Responses to Questions

TRM Module 2.2 AP® Analyzing Sources Handout 3

BUILDING AP® SKILLS

Claims and Evidence in Sources

Sometimes students struggle to make connections between pieces of historical evidence provided in documents. Consider providing students with the historical terms you want them to analyze in a document, such as *tobacco* and *profit*. Once they identify the terms in the document ask them a direct question such as: In what ways did the profitability of tobacco change the economic possibilities of those persons living in Jamestown? Students can answer in one sentence and thus have identified and described evidence from a document.

EXPLORING AP® THEMES

Work, Exchange, and Technology

As tobacco became more profitable, relations between English settlers and American Indians deteriorated. However, the Powhatan Confederacy did not want the interactions between the two groups to spiral into conflict. Consider having students account for the causes of the reactions of the Powhatans and English to the development of a tobacco economy. Put another way, have students name one reason why the Powhatans wanted to make peace and the English settlers did not.

Period 2: 1607–1754

MODULE 2-2 Early British Colonies in Maryland, Virginia, and North Carolina

Tobacco Fuels Growth in Virginia

cash crop A crop produced for profit rather than for subsistence.

It was not military aggression, however, but the discovery of a viable **cash crop** that saved the colony. Orinoco tobacco, grown in the West Indies and South America, had sold well in England and in other European markets addicted since the sixteenth-century Columbian exchange. Virginia colonist John Rolfe began to experiment with its growth in 1612, just as the drought lifted. Production of the leaf soared as eager investors poured seeds, supplies, and labor into Jamestown. Exports multiplied rapidly, from 2,000 pounds in 1615 to 40,000 pounds five years later and an incredible 1.5 million pounds by 1629.

AP® ANALYZING SOURCES

Source: John Rolfe, *Letter on Jamestown Settlement*, 1618

"[A]n industrious man not other ways employed, may well tend four acres of corn, and 1,000 plants of tobacco, and where they say an acre will yield but three or four barrels, we have ordinarily four or five, but of new ground six, seven, and eight, and a barrel of peas and beans, which we esteem as good as two of corn, . . . so that one man may provide corn for five [people], and apparel for two [people] by the profit of his tobacco . . . had we but carpenters to build and make carts and ploughs, and skillful men that know how to use them, and train up our cattle to draw them, . . . yet our want of experience brings but little to perfection but planting tobacco, and yet of that many are so covetous to have much, they make little good. . . ."

Questions for Analysis
1. Describe the appeal of planting tobacco, according to Rolfe.
2. Describe the challenges faced by colonists in Virginia, according to Rolfe.

Questions for Comparison: Samuel de Champlain, *Voyages of Samuel de Champlain: 1567–1635* (p. 44)
1. Explain the similarity in the causes of French and English colonization illustrated by de Champlain and Rolfe.
2. Explain how these documents reveal the differences in the economic activities of French colonists in Quebec and British colonists in Virginia.

headright system Created in Virginia in 1618, it rewarded those who imported indentured laborers and settlers with fifty acres of land.

AP® TIP
Pay close attention to how living conditions in the British colonies promoted self-sufficiency and independence among the colonists.

Tobacco cultivation only made tensions between the English and the American Indians rise. As production increased and prices declined, farmers could increase their profits only by obtaining more land and more laborers. That is why the Virginia Company was willing to offer land to indentured laborers who spent seven years clearing new fields and creating new plantations. In 1618 the Virginia Company developed a **headright system** (later used in many colonies) that rewarded those who imported laborers — at first indentured servants, and later enslaved Africans — with land. Wealthy Englishmen normally earned fifty acres of land for each laborer they imported to Virginia. Yet in most cases, the land the Virginia Company offered these would-be colonists was already settled by members of the Powhatan Confederacy. Thus, the rapid increase in tobacco cultivation intensified competition and hostility between English colonists and American Indians.

In 1614, Chief Powhatan tried one last time to create an alliance between his confederacy and the English settlers. Perhaps, encouraged by the return of rain in 1612, he believed that increased productivity would ensure better trade relations with the English. In 1614 he agreed to allow his daughter Pocahontas to marry John Rolfe. Pocahontas converted to Christianity and traveled to England with Rolfe and their infant son in 1617. While there, she fell ill and died, and Rolfe returned to Virginia just as relations with the Powhatan Confederacy began to change.

Powhatan died in 1618, and his younger brother Opechancanough became chief. During this time, the Virginia Company, even using its new headright system, struggled to import enough indentured servants to do the work required in Virginia to keep its cash-crop economy, based on tobacco cultivation, afloat. Too few English workers were willing to brave the risks to meet the

APPLY THE TIP

While it is true that self-sufficiency and independence were values promoted by settlers in seventeenth-century Virginia, it is equally true that these same members valued racial arguments that rationalized the process of colonization. Have your students account for one way in which the colonists used racial justifications to subjugate American Indians.

Tobacco Fuels Growth in Virginia

Period 2: 1607–1754

◀ **Pocahontas (1616)** Simon van de Passe created this portrait of Pocahontas during her visit to England in 1616. The engraving was commissioned by the Virginia Company to promote settlement in Jamestown. While van de Passe clothes her in English aristocratic style, he retains her dark complexion and direct gaze. **What does this portrayal of Pocahontas reveal about how the English viewed American Indians? What does it reveal about English colonization in North America?**

company's demands for labor. Even landless and poor English commoners feared the prospects of death from starvation, disease, or the Powhatan to volunteer.

Faced with unmet demand for more laborers, one Virginia Company solution was the purchase and transport of convicts from English prisons to Virginia as indentured servants. Another was to petition the crown for the right to establish a local governing body. The hope was that this would aid recruiting efforts by fostering the idea that the Company honored the traditional rights of Englishmen in the colony. In 1619, King James granted Virginia the **House of Burgesses**. Its members could make laws and levy taxes, although the English governor or the company council in London held **veto** power. Lastly, the company set out to recruit more female settlers in order to increase the colony's population. These strategies worked: Later that year, more young women and men arrived as indentured servants. Also in 1619, an English ship brought twenty Africans, first taken from present-day Angola by the Portuguese, to Jamestown. These Africans were the first to be enslaved in colonial Virginia.

House of Burgesses Local governing body in Virginia established by the English crown in 1619.

veto The right to block a decision made by a governing body.

AP® ANALYZING SOURCES

Source: Matthaeus Merian, *Native Attack on Jamestown*, 1622

About the source: This image portrays Opechancanough's attack on a Virginian settlement, and a simultaneous attack on Jamestown is pictured in the background. After Opechancanough's raids, the Virginia colony was placed under a governor appointed by the king.

Questions for Analysis

1. Describe the upper left quadrant, the upper right quadrant, the lower left quadrant, and the lower right quadrant of this picture. Write a sentence that describes each.
2. Describe what is happening in the background and foreground of this picture.
3. Explain what van de Passe intended his audience to think happened before the attack.
4. Explain how van de Passe's decisions about what to place in each quadrant, as well as in the background versus the foreground, reflect European views of American Indians and North American colonization.

TEACHING IDEA

Analyzing Art and Images

The portrait of Pocahontas provides students with the opportunity to work to analyze a document with both text and visual cues. Students need to move beyond the recognition that this document focuses on Pocahontas in Virginia to an analysis of the importance of her dress and the inscription at the bottom of the document. Seventeenth-century English is tough to decode sometimes; therefore, have students write down only the words they understand in the inscription. After they finish this task, have a class conversation about the inferences they can make between the words they decoded and her portrait.

TRM Suggested Responses to Questions

TRM Module 2.2 AP® Analyzing Sources Handout 4

TEACHING IDEA

Building Vocabulary

To help students understand the meaning of demographic changes in Virginia, start by providing a definition of demographics. Here is a definition from Merriam-Webster: "demographics: the statistical characteristics of human populations (such as age or income) used especially to identify markets." Next, ask students to make predictions between Virginia's demographics before 1650 with cultural attitudes with American Indians.

TEACHING IDEA

Incorporating Websites

As examples of evolving scholarship in the subject of U.S. history, you may wish to provide your class with these additional readings:

- "The Language of Enslavement" by Lucy Ferriss. Available on The Chronicle of Higher Education's website (chronicle.com).
- "How We Think about the Term 'Enslaved' Matters" by Nell Irvin Painter. Available on The Guardian's website (theguardian.com).
- "The Fallacy of 1619: Rethinking the History of Africans in Early America" by Michael Guasco. Available on the African American Intellectual History Society's website (aaihs.org). For interested students, have them also read excerpts of Guasco's book, *Slaves and Englishmen: Human Bondage in the Early Modern Atlantic World*.
- "The 1619 Project" initiative of The New York Times (nytimes.com).

TEACHING IDEA

Analyzing Art and Images

Consider having students work on sourcing the document depicting an attack on the Jamestown settlement. To help students along in this process, have students describe what they see in the picture regarding American Indian motivations at the time or the English government's reaction to the attacks. In doing this, you are helping students understand how to identify the situation in a historical document.

TEACHING IDEA

Incorporating Secondary Sources

The National Park Service has a webpage dedicated to John Smith's map of Virginia from 1612. There students can see the full picture, as well as learn more about the map and the context in which it was produced. Go to the National Park Service website and search for "Smith Maps" (nps.gov).

TEACHING IDEA

Check for Understanding

Module 2-2 details several battles between the English and Powhatans. While it is important to understand the nature of those conflicts, it is also important for students to identify trends, change over time, and continuities. Consider allowing students to select trends, change over time, or continuities to write a two-to-three sentence explanation for how English settlers interacted with the Powhatans from 1607 to 1622.

TRM Suggested Responses to Questions

TRM Module 2.2 AP® Analyzing Sources Handout 5

Period 2: 1607–1754 MODULE 2-2 Early British Colonies in Maryland, Virginia, and North Carolina

◀ **Map of Virginia (1612)** John Smith published a remarkably accurate map of Virginia in 1612. It included major geographical features and the names of some 200 American Indian towns. Smith placed a sketch of a Susquehannock warrior in the upper right-hand corner; at his feet, Smith noted that the Susquehannock were "a Gyant-like people." **How does this map express the hopes and fears of early English colonists in Virginia?**

Church of England National church established by King Henry VIII after he split with the Catholic Church in 1534.

Although the English colony still hugged the Atlantic coast, its expansion increased conflict with native inhabitants. In March 1622, after repeated English incursions on land cleared and farmed by American Indians, Chief Opechancanough and his allies launched a surprise attack that killed nearly a third of the colonists. In retaliation, Englishmen renewed their assaults on native villages, killing inhabitants, burning cornfields, and selling captive American Indians into slavery.

The English proclaimed victory over the American Indians in 1623, but hostilities continued. In 1624, in the midst of the crisis, King James annulled the Virginia Company charter and took control of the colony, seeking a greater share both of control and of the growing profits of the Chesapeake. For Virginia, he appointed the governor and a small advisory council, required that legislation passed by the House of Burgesses in Jamestown be ratified by the **Privy Council** in London, and demanded that property owners pay taxes to support the **Church of England**. These regulations became the model for royal colonies throughout North America.

Still, royal proclamations could not halt American Indian opposition. In 1644 Opechancanough launched a second uprising against the English, killing hundreds of colonists. After two years of bitter warfare, however, he was finally captured and then killed. With the English population now too large to eradicate, the native peoples in the Chesapeake finally submitted to English authority in 1646.

AP® ANALYZING SOURCES

Source: John Martin, Jamestown councilman, *The manner how to bring the Indians into subjugation*, 1622

"The manner how to bring in the Indians into subjugation[1] without making an utter [extinction] of them together with the reasons.

First, by disabling the main body of the enemy from having . . . [all necessities]. As namely corn and all manner of [food] of any worth.

This is to be acted two manner of ways.—First by keeping them from setting corn at home and fishing. Secondly by keeping them from their accustomed trading for corn.

For the first it is performed by having some 200 soldiers on foot, continually [harassing] and burning all their Towns in winter, and spoiling their wares. . . .

For the second there must [be] provided some 10 ships, that in May, June, July and August may scour the bay and keep the rivers yet are belonging to [Opechancanough].

By this arises two happy ends.—First the assured taking of great purchases in skins and prisoners. Secondly in keeping them from trading for corn on the Eastern shore and from the southward from whence they have five times more than they set themselves."

[1] Under control of the English.

BUILDING AP® SKILLS

Claims and Evidence in Sources

Vocabulary, academic and historical, can trip students up as they read through primary sources. Highlight the following words before having students read the document by John Martin: *subjugation*, *accustomed*, *whence*, and *scour*. Understanding these terms gives students more confidence as they approach a difficult document.

MODULE 2-2 Early British Colonies in Maryland, Virginia, and North Carolina

This course being taken they have no means, but must yield to obedience, or fly to bordering neighbors who neither will receive them nor indeed are able, for they have but ground cleared for their own use."

Questions for Analysis
1. Identify the specific strategies Martin proposes to subjugate American Indians near Jamestown.
2. Describe the benefits that Martin believes his plan will bring to British colonists.
3. Explain what this document reveals about seventeenth-century English views of American Indians.

REVIEW

- How did the Virginia colony change between 1607 and the mid-1600s?
- What caused these changes?

The Second Chesapeake Colony: Maryland

By the 1630s, despite ongoing conflicts with American Indians, Virginia was well on its way to bringing England commercial success. In 1632, King Charles I (r. 1625–1649) established the colony of Maryland. Taken together, Maryland and Virginia formed the Chesapeake region of the English empire during the seventeenth century. In the expanding tobacco economies that developed in the region, the most successful planters used indentured servants for labor, including some Africans as well as thousands of English and Irish immigrants. Between 1640 and 1670, some 40,000 to 50,000 of these migrants settled in Virginia and neighboring Maryland.

In founding Maryland, King Charles I granted most of the territory north of Chesapeake Bay to English nobleman Cecilius Calvert and appointed him Lord Baltimore, giving him and his descendants the power to govern the new colony. Calvert's family, unlike most English people, remained Catholic after the Church of England was founded in 1534. Because of the persecution he and fellow Catholics had endured in the century since, he planned to create Maryland as a refuge of (relative) religious toleration, where Catholics and Protestants could worship in peace. Appointing his brother as governor, he carefully prepared for the first settlement by recruiting artisans and farmers (mainly Protestant) as well as wealthy merchants and aristocrats (mostly Catholic) to settle the colony. Although conflict continued to fester between members of the small set of Catholic elite and the Protestant majority, Governor Calvert convinced the Maryland assembly to pass the **Act of Religious Toleration** in 1649, granting religious freedom to all Christians.

The history of religious toleration in Maryland and its status as a haven for Catholics roughly mirrored the political and religious landscape back in England during the mid-seventeenth century. In 1642, disagreement over

Act of Religious Toleration 1649 act passed by the Maryland Assembly granting religious freedom to all Christians.

▲ **MAP 2.2 The Growth of English Settlement in the Chesapeake (c. 1650)**
With the success of tobacco, English plantations and forts spread along the James River and north to St. Mary's. By 1650 most Chesapeake tribes had been vanquished or forced to move north and west. The fall line, which marked the limit of navigable waterways, kept English settlements close to the Atlantic coast but also ensured easy shipment of goods. **What geographic factors determined the location of the English settlements on this map?**

BUILDING AP® SKILLS

Contextualization

At this point, students have already studied the rationale for colonization among the French, Spanish, Dutch, and English. Teachers should consider incorporating time to practice the skill of contextualization. To scaffold the skill, think about providing a framework from which students can practice how to write contextualization, as opposed to having them brainstorm and then work on the writing mechanics. To accomplish this simply give students the characteristics of contextualization, which means they have a broader process relevant to the time with a couple supporting details to substantiate their understanding. It could look something like this:

Broad concept: European colonization | Supporting details: Economic benefits in North America for the English + land + tobacco.

In this way, students are taking the answers provided and writing the rest of the answer. Here is an example: *English settlement patterns in North America were a part of a broader effort among European colonization efforts aimed at securing resources. For instance, the English were interested in developing an economically successful colony to support the wealth of the mother country. The discovery of tobacco in 1619 aided this effort and meant English settlers would have to continue to take land from American Indians. While European empires may have varied in the means used to advance their economies, each country sought resources not available in their home country.*

EXPLORING AP® THEMES

America in the World

The map provided illustrates the trend of English settlements in Virginia. To work on both comparison and the use of maps, consider providing your students with a map detailing the places where American Indians lived. The comparison allows teachers to facilitate discussions about movement, settlement, competition for resources, and change over time.

EXPLORING AP® THEMES

Migration and Settlement

Students have read and written about the role of religion in European colonization. Consider taking time to divide your students into groups of three or four to have a class discussion. You can give each group a European country (Dutch, Spanish, French, and English) and ask that they come up with a group response of a few sentences describing the extent to which religion influenced settlement patterns.

BUILDING AP® SKILLS

Claims and Evidence in Sources

Since it is early in the year, consider working on the skill of identifying claims in a text-based source as it is a critical skill for students to understand. To further students' comprehension of how different colonies handled the issue of liberty, especially religious freedom, consider providing students with excerpted copies of two important primary sources from Massachusetts and Maryland — the Massachusetts Body of Liberties (1641) and the Maryland Toleration Act (1649). An online transcript of the Massachusetts Body of Liberties is available by searching on the Commonwealth of Massachusetts website (mass.gov). The Maryland Toleration Act is available through The Avalon project (avalon.law.yale.edu). Have students identify claims about religious freedom and compare how each region delineated religious freedom.

TEACHING IDEA

Check for Understanding

After students have read the information about the tobacco economies in the seventeenth century, consider having students work on categorizing and explaining migration patterns. For instance, you can distill students' focus by giving them a category of analysis such as economics. After giving students this category, have them compare and contrast the economic motivations of settlers from the West Indies with those from England.

TEACHING IDEA

Incorporating Websites

The wealth amassed by sugar production in the West Indies and tobacco in the Chesapeake furthered the international slave trade throughout the seventeenth century. The Slave Voyages website enables teachers to examine the effects of forced migration upon enslaved persons (slavevoyages.com). There is even a video reconstruction of a slave ship, which enables students to glean a better understanding of the conditions enslaved persons endured.

AP® TIP
Make sure you can explain not only the reasons for religious toleration in Maryland, but also describe its long-term effects on the development of other British colonies.

whether a king could rule without consent of his Parliament erupted in violence, and the **English Civil War** began. King Charles I was executed in 1649, and a parliamentary leader named Oliver Cromwell came to power as the war drew to its close in 1651, when Charles I's son, Charles II, was exiled from England. Cromwell, who cemented his position of power as Lord Protector of the Commonwealth of England in 1653, was less accepting of Catholics than the king had been. Thus, the Act of Toleration was repealed in 1654, only five years after its initial passage. With aid from Maryland's Protestant colonists, new colonial governors appointed by Cromwell's Parliament then passed a new law prohibiting the open practice of Catholicism. However, the tide began to turn against Cromwell's rule as the decade wore on, and Calvert negotiated a return to his position as governor of Maryland. In 1657 the Act of Toleration was again passed by the colonial assembly.

Over the course of the next sixty years, however, the Act would be contested multiple times, and Catholics were eventually barred from voting in 1718. Despite the many challenges to its legitimacy, it set an important standard of religious freedom on the North American continent.

REVIEW

- How did religious conflict in Europe shape Maryland's shifting policies on religious tolerance?

Tobacco Economies, Class Rebellion, and the Emergence of Slavery

When the English monarchy was restored to Charles II (r. 1660–1685) in 1660, he established eight English noblemen as the leaders of a Carolina colony. The economy of the northern region, in present-day North Carolina, came to rely on plantations focused primarily upon producing tobacco. Thus, the new colony functioned in much the same way as the Chesapeake colonies. Although the political leaders of Carolina hoped to recreate a system of feudal manors in North America, they faced a labor shortage, however, as few migrants wished to brave the risks merely to remain peasants working the lands of different lords. The farmers and laborers that *did* emigrate to northern Carolina would eventually rise up and force the ruling class to offer land at reasonable prices and a semblance of self-government.

Before 1650, neither the Chesapeake colonies nor northern Carolina had yet developed a legal code of slavery, but from that point on, this began to change. Improved economic conditions in England meant fewer people were willing to gamble on a better life in North America, and as fewer people were arrested for crimes and vagrancy, the population of convicts that could be bought from English prisons dwindled. To compensate for the shortage of white indentured servants, landowners in the Chesapeake and northern Carolina colonies increasingly came to rely on the labor of enslaved Africans in order to continue to produce the tobacco that generated wealth and fueled colonial growth. Thus, even though the number of enslaved African laborers remained small until late in the century, colonial leaders already began to take steps to increase their control over the African population. In 1660, the House of Burgesses passed an act that allowed black laborers to be enslaved, and, in 1662, defined slavery as an inherited status passed from mothers to children. In 1664, Maryland followed suit. In 1695, the Carolina colony, not yet divided into North and South Carolina, adopted a formal **slave code** that was based on Virginia's laws.

While enslaved Africans became, in time, a crucial component of the tobacco labor force, indentured servants still continued to make up the majority of bound workers in Virginia, Maryland, and northern Carolina for most of the seventeenth century. Enslaved Africans labored under harsh conditions, and punishment for even minor infractions could be severe. Plantation owners beat, whipped, and branded enslaved people for a variety of behaviors. During this time, some white indentured servants made common cause with black laborers, both indentured servants and enslaved, who worked side by side with them on tobacco plantations. They ran away together, stole goods from slaveholders, and planned uprisings and rebellions. Contracted white laborers, however, had a far greater chance of gaining their freedom even before slavery was fully entrenched in colonial law.

AP® TIP
Be sure you can explain the factors that led colonies in the Chesapeake and Carolinas to justify slavery and create increasingly harsh slave codes during the 1600s.

slave code Laws restricting enslaved peoples' rights, largely due to slaveholders' fears of rebellion.

Tobacco Economies, Class Rebellion, and the Emergence of Slavery

Period 2: 1607–1754

AP® ANALYZING SOURCES

Source: Virginia House of Burgesses, *Selected Statutes Passed 1662–1669*

1662
"Whereas some doubts have arisen whether children got by any Englishman upon a Negro woman should be slave or free, be it therefore enacted and declared by this present Grand Assembly, that all children born in this country shall be held bond or free only according to the condition of the mother . . ."

1667
"Whereas some doubts have risen whether children that are slaves by birth, and by the charity and piety of their owners made partakers of the blessed sacrament of baptism, should by virtue of their baptism be made free, it is enacted and declared by this Grand Assembly, and the authority thereof, that the conferring of baptism does not alter the condition of the person as to his bondage or freedom. . . ."

September, 1668
"Whereas it has been questioned whether servants running away may be punished with corporal punishment by their master or magistrate, since the act already made gives the master satisfaction by prolonging their time by service, it is declared and enacted by this Assembly that moderate corporal punishment inflicted by master or magistrate upon a runaway servant shall not [deprive] the master of the satisfaction allowed by the law, the one being as necessary to reclaim them from persisting in that idle course as the other is just to repair the damages sustained by the master."

October, 1669
"Whereas the only law in force for the punishment of [disobedient] servants resisting their master, mistress, or overseer cannot be inflicted upon Negroes, nor the obstinacy of many of them be suppressed by other than violent means, be it enacted and declared by this Grand Assembly if any slave resists his master (or other by his master's order correcting him) and by the extremity of the correction should chance to die, that his death shall not be accounted a felony, but the master (or that other person appointed by the master to punish him) be acquitted from molestation, since it cannot be presumed that premeditated malice (which alone makes murder a felony) should induce any man to destroy his own estate."

Questions for Analysis
1. Identify the main point of each law in this document.
2. Describe how the laws treat violence by slaveholders toward enslaved Africans differently from efforts of enslaved Africans to resist slaveholders.
3. Explain the factors that led the Virginia House of Burgesses to pass slave codes in the 1660s.

AP® TIP
Trace the causes for the increasing racial divide between enslaved Africans and poor white settlers.

By the 1660s and 1670s, the population of former servants who had become free formed a growing and increasingly unhappy class. Most were struggling economically, working as common laborers or tenants on large estates. Those who managed to move west and claim land on the frontier were confronted by hostile American Indians such as the Susquehannock nation. Virginia governor Sir William Berkeley, who levied taxes to support nine forts on the frontier, had little patience with the complaints of these colonists. The labor demands of wealthy tobacco planters needed to be met, and frontier settlers' call for an aggressive American Indian policy would hurt the profitable deerskin trade with the Algonquian.

In late 1675, conflict erupted when frontier settlers, many former indentured servants, attacked American Indians in the region. Rather than attacking only the Susquehannock nation, the settlers also assaulted communities allied with the English. When a large force of local Virginia militiamen surrounded a Susquehannock village, they ignored pleas for peace and murdered five chiefs. Susquehannock warriors retaliated with raids on frontier farms. Despite the outbreak of open warfare, Governor Berkeley still refused to send troops, so disgruntled farmers turned to

---

TRM Suggested Responses to Questions

TRM Module 2.2 AP® Analyzing Sources Handout 6

BUILDING AP® SKILLS
Claims and Evidence in Sources

Primary sources connected to legal history can be dense documents for students to read. Therefore, try removing some of the more likely distracting vocabulary in the document to encourage a better read among students. In this particular document, you could select and define the following: baptism, corporal punishment, obstinacy, premeditated malice.

TEACHING IDEA
Incorporating Websites

To better understand the context and nature of slave codes in the British North American colonies, consider providing a sample of slave codes from Barbados. Samples can be found on the website for The Gilder Lehrman Center for the Study of Slavery, Resistance, and Abolition (glc.yale.edu).

BUILDING AP® SKILLS
Making Connections

Promoting lively, open dialogue in an AP® U.S. History classroom is an essential ingredient for any successful course. Sometimes it is useful to provide students with a statement with options for interpretation. Consider giving students the following statement: "Governor Berkeley's interest in maintaining peaceful relations with American Indians was based on his desire to profit from the immense fur trade. Neither he nor the governing class in Virginia developed economic conditions conducive to social mobility." Students choose to either support, oppose, or modify the statement. Once they have selected one of the three, students should form groups and write a collective response to the interpretation.

Period 2: 1607–1754

MODULE 2-2 Early British Colonies in Maryland, Virginia, and North Carolina

BUILDING AP® SKILLS

Claims and Evidence in Sources

Students often struggle to make sense of quantitative documents. Their goal should be to illustrate the big picture or trend illustrated in the document. Sentence starters can be a useful way to help students learn this important skill. For instance, consider providing one of the following:

■ The trend of a surge of enslaved persons toward the end of the seventeenth century can be attributed to _____.

■ The overall decline in the use of indentured servants toward the end of the seventeenth century was likely caused by _____.

TRM Suggested Responses to Questions

TRM Module 2.2 AP® Analyzing Sources Handout 7

TEACHING IDEA

Check for Understanding

Bacon's Rebellion is often used as a turning point in the development of slavery as a race-based, chattel system in the British North American colonies. Turning points in history ask students to evaluate what happened immediately before and immediately after a historical event. The goal is to measure the extent to which the development in question was a catalyst for change. Consider asking your students to write three or four sentences determining whether or not Bacon's Rebellion was a turning point in the development of slavery as a race-based, chattel system.

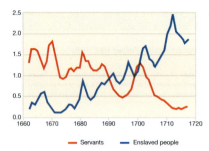

◀ **Indentured Servants and Enslaved People in Six Maryland Counties (1662–1717)** This chart illustrates a dramatic shift in the Chesapeake labor force between 1662 and 1717. **Although based on a study of estate inventories from six Maryland counties, what does the trend shown here suggest about the nature and conditions of labor on Chesapeake farms?**

Based on Gloria L. Main, *Tobacco Colony: Life in Early Maryland, 1650–1720* (Princeton: Princeton University Press, 1982), 26.

Bacon's Rebellion 1676 uprising in Virginia led by Nathaniel Bacon. Bacon and his followers, many of whom were former indentured servants, were upset by the Virginia governor's unwillingness to send troops to intervene in conflicts between settlers and American Indians and by the lack of representation of western settlers in the House of Burgesses.

Nathaniel Bacon. Bacon came from a wealthy family and was related to Berkeley by marriage, but that did not stop him from defying the governor's authority and calling up an army to attack American Indians across the colony. **Bacon's Rebellion** had begun.

Frontier farmers formed an important part of Bacon's coalition, but affluent planters who had been left out of Berkeley's inner circle also joined Bacon in hopes of gaining access to power and profits, as did bound laborers, black and white, who assumed that anyone who opposed the governor was on their side. Bacon's gathering forces included free, indentured, and enslaved black people rebelling for greater freedoms and opportunities.

In the summer of 1676, Governor Berkeley declared Bacon guilty of treason. Rather than waiting to be captured, Bacon led his army toward Jamestown. Berkeley then arranged a hastily called election to undercut the rebellion. Even though Berkeley had rescinded the right of men without property to vote, Bacon's supporters won control of the House of Burgesses, and Bacon won new adherents. These included "news wives," lower-class women who spread information (and rumors) about oppressive conditions to aid the rebels. As Bacon and his followers marched across Virginia, his men plundered the plantations of Berkeley and his supporters. In September they reached Jamestown after the governor and his administration fled across Chesapeake Bay. The rebels burned the capital to the ground, victory seemingly theirs.

AP® ANALYZING SOURCES

Source: Nathaniel Bacon, *Declaration against Governor William Berkeley*, 1676

"FIRST. For having upon specious pretences of public works raised great unjust taxes upon the Commonalty for the advancement of private favorites and other sinister ends, but no visible effects in any measure adequate. For not having during this long time of his government, in any measure advanced this hopeful Colony, either by fortifications, towns or trade.

2. For having abused and rendered contemptible the Magistrates of Justice, by advancing to places of judicature scandalous and ignorant favorites.

3. For having wronged his Majesty's prerogative and interest by assuming monopoly of the beaver trade, and for having in that unjust gain betrayed and sold his Majesty's Country and the lives of his loyal subjects to the barbarous heathen.

4. For having protected, favored, and emboldened the Indians against his Majesty's loyal subjects; never contriving, requiring, or appointing any due or proper means of satisfaction for their many invasions, robberies, and murders committed upon us.

5. For having, when the army of English was just upon the track of those Indians, who now in all places burn, spoil, murder, and when we might with ease have destroyed them who then were in open hostility, for then having expressly countermanded and sent back our army, by passing his word for the peaceable demeanor of the said Indians, who immediately prosecuted their evil intentions, committing horrid murders and robberies in all places, being protected by the said engagement and word past of him the said Sir William Berkeley; having ruined and laid desolate a great part of his Majesty's Country, and have

TEACHING IDEA

Connecting the Dots

1676 was a pivotal year in the British North American colonies for many reasons, not the least of which related to conflict with American Indians. To illustrate similarities and differences well, consider providing students access to the lecture "The Name of the War: King Philip's War and the Origins of American Identity" by historian Jill Lepore, found on the Gilder Lehrman site for AP® U.S. History (ap.gilderlehrman.org), which helps explain the context of King Philip's (Metacom) War.

now drawn themselves into such obscure and remote places, and are by their success so emboldened and confirmed, by their confederacy so strengthened, that the cries of blood are in all places, and the terror and consternation of the people so great, are now become, not only a difficult, but a very formidable enemy, who might at first with ease have been destroyed."

Questions for Analysis
1. Identify who Bacon and his followers believed caused the complaints listed in this document.
2. Describe the causes of conflict Bacon attributed to local American Indians.
3. Explain why Bacon appealed to both the king and his fellow countrymen in his charges against the governor.
4. Explain how this document reveals the changes in relations between the English and American Indians brought about by expanding the Virginia settlement.

Only a month later, however, Bacon died of dysentery, and the movement he formed unraveled. Governor Berkeley, using reinforcements brought by the English navy, quickly reclaimed power. He hanged twenty-three rebel leaders and incited his followers to plunder the estates of planters who had supported Bacon. But he could not undo the damage to American Indian relations on the Virginia frontier. Bacon's army had killed or enslaved hundreds of once-friendly American Indians and left behind a tragic, bitter legacy.

An even more important consequence of the rebellion was that wealthy planters and investors realized the depth of frustration among poor whites who were willing to make common cause with their black counterparts. Having regained power, the planter elite worked to crush any such interracial alliance. Virginia legislators began to improve the conditions and rights of poor white settlers while imposing new restrictions on black people. At nearly the same time, in an effort to meet the growing demand for labor in the West Indies and the Chesapeake, King Charles II chartered the Royal African Company in 1672 to carry enslaved Africans to North America. Thus, the march toward full-blown racial slavery in the English colonies was well underway.

> **AP® TIP**
> Analyze the long-term effects of slavery on the development of social classes and political power in the colonies.

REVIEW
- How did Nathaniel Bacon justify his rebellion?
- What were the results of his rebellion?

AP® THINKING HISTORICALLY | Connecting Distant Causes to Immediate Causes

So far, this module has explored how the English, from the time of Jamestown's founding in 1607, developed tobacco exporting colonies in present-day Maryland, Virginia, and North Carolina. These tobacco economies generated great wealth over the next century and a half. Here, we'll walk through how to organize your reflections on both the immediate and distant causes that allowed these tobacco economies to flourish in the seventeenth and early eighteenth centuries.

Step 1 List and categorize your historical knowledge.

A good place to start is by taking a few minutes to jot down all possible causes of the growth of tobacco economies in Virginia, Maryland, and North Carolina that you can think of. Remember to draw on your knowledge of Period 1 as well. A solid strategy to generate ideas is to ask yourself causation questions divided into some broad categories: politics, economy, society/culture, interactions with the environment, and technology.

Next, think about whether each of the causes you listed is more immediate or distant from its effect (in this case, the creation of wealthy tobacco economies in the Chesapeake and northern

(Continued)

TEACHING IDEA

Incorporating Websites

Teachers looking to incorporate the use of shorter secondary source essays should consider using the Gilder Lehrman site for AP® U.S. History (ap.gilderlehrman.org). Go to the essays from Period 2 and locate the essay by Ira Berlin, "The Origins of Slavery," about the beginning of slavery in the British North American colonies. Students should find the essay to be both useful and readable.

APPLY THE TIP

The continued development of slavery is a relevant topic through Period 5 of the Course Framework. To develop the central focus of this AP® Tip, consider focusing on the short-term consequences of slavery's development in Periods 2, 3, and 4. Understanding the immediate effects in each period allows students to understand change over time. Have students write down five significant consequences for slavery's development in Period 2 at the end of Module 2-2.

TRM Suggested Responses to Questions

TRM Module 2.2 AP® Thinking Historically Handout

BUILDING AP® SKILLS

Argumentation

Writing is a recursive skill and therefore needs to be explicitly modeled and scaffolded throughout the year. Weighing historical evidence is a difficult concept for many students. The most effective arguments acknowledge multiple perspectives and weigh the evidence. To practice this skill, consider providing students with three categories that help explain the development of slavery in the British North American colonies: cash crops, race, and the Atlantic World. Divide students into groups and allow each to select one category. Their task is to write a three-to-four sentence statement that recognizes the importance of two categories while weighing their selected topic as the most important. Here is an example: "Although the growth of slavery can be attributed to the dependence on cash crops and the development of a trade network in the Atlantic world, the most significant factor was the race-based chattel system that developed for economic gain."

TEACHING IDEA

Building Vocabulary

Although students were introduced to the concept of using vernacular germane to a historical thinking skill in Module 2-1, it is a good idea to return to and develop this skill throughout your course. As students are creating their causation statements, consider giving them a word bank to assist the successful completion of step 2. (This word bank varies slightly from Module 2-1.)

Causation:		
Direct cause	Indirect cause	This led to
Immediate effect	In response to	An important outcome
Resulted from	Long-term result	Short-term cause
Contingent upon	The source of	The basis of

TRM Find **Handout 2.3 – Organizational Framework** in the Teacher's Resource Materials.

TEACHING IDEA

AP® Writing Historically Workshop

If students are struggling to conceptualize their causation statements, consider starting with a graphic organizer to help clarify the expectations for the assignment. Create a pyramid with "Distant Effects" at the bottom tier, "Immediate Effects" in the middle tier, and "Summary" at the smallest, topmost tier. This will illustrate how students should strive to get more specific as they approach immediate effects and their summary of those.

Carolina colonies). Annotate each cause by labeling it as immediate or distant. Your list of annotated causes may look something like this:

Effect	Distant Causes	Immediate Causes
Profit from tobacco (economy)	English desire to compete with Spain	Tobacco grown in Jamestown for profit
Control by joint-stock company (politics)	English crown poorer than Spain's	English investors pooled resources to share risk and profit
Fertile soil, no gold (interaction with environment)	English sought quick profit from environmental exploitation	No gold, but fertile soil in Virginia led to growing cash crop for European markets

Step 2 Write at least three causation statements linking distant to immediate causes.

Now extend your brainstorm by asking yourself what factors led to the immediate causes in particular. This may lead you to add new distant causes to your list, or you may find that distant causes you have already listed match up to your immediate causes.

To help organize your thoughts about the links between the distant and immediate causes you have listed, it's a good idea to write at least three causation statements that explicitly connect them. It is important that you do not merely state what each cause is — you must explain the relationship between the distant and immediate causes. In other words, you need to give at least one reason why a given distant cause led to an immediate cause, generating a chain of causation that shows why tobacco economies emerged. The following example statements have distant and immediate causes labeled.

> Profit motives led to the tobacco economies in Virginia, Maryland, and North Carolina **[distant cause]**. These profit motives stemmed from the English monarchy's competition with Spain **[distant cause]**. Spain grew rich and powerful from American colonies, and the English crown sought similar gains by chartering the Virginia Company as a profit-seeking joint-stock corporation **[distant cause]**. John Rolfe's discovery that Caribbean tobacco grew well in the Chesapeake caused tobacco to become the primary cash crop in the Chesapeake **[immediate cause]**. Tobacco as a profitable crop resulted from Rolfe's discovery, but the English crown's long-standing goal of making colonies profitable in North America was also an important cause **[explanation of immediate and distant causes]**.

Notice these statements move from distant to immediate causes, starting with the English desire to find profit in North America as the Spanish had in Central and South America, moving to the specific source of English profit (tobacco), and ending with an explanation of the immediate and distant causes of the English tobacco economy in the seventeenth century.

Taking these steps to think about the forces behind immediate causes shaping developments will help you deepen your historical analysis. By showing causation as a chain of linked events, you gain practice in strategies for clarifying and supporting historical arguments.

ACTIVITY

Use the steps provided in this box to explain the immediate and distant environmental factors that led the English to adopt a cash crop system in Virginia by the mid-seventeenth century.

Daily Life in the Colonies

In the first decades of settlement in the Chesapeake, the scarcity of women and workers ensured that many white women improved their economic and legal status. Maintaining a farm required the work of both women and men, which made marriage an economic as well as a social and religious institution. Where women were in especially short supply and mortality was high, young women who arrived as indentured servants and completed their term might marry older men of property. If their husbands died first, widows often took control of

Daily Life in the Colonies

Period 2: 1607–1754

AP® TIP
As you read this section, make sure to identify patterns of continuity and of change in colonial women's roles during the first half of the eighteenth century.

the estate and passed on the property to their children. By the late seventeenth century, however, as the sex ratio in the Chesapeake evened out, women lost the opportunity to marry "above their class" and widows lost control of family estates. Even though women still performed vital labor, the spread of indentured servitude and slavery lessened the recognition of their contributions. As a result, most white women in the colonies were assigned primarily domestic roles during this time period. They also found their legal and economic rights restricted in ways that mirrored those of their female counterparts in Great Britain.

The divisions between rich and poor, created and sustained by the Chesapeake and northern Carolina colonies' economic reliance on the cash crop of tobacco, became much more pronounced in the early decades of the eighteenth century. Tobacco was the most valuable product in the region, and the largest tobacco plantation owners lived in relative luxury. They developed trading contacts in seaport cities on the Atlantic coast and in the Caribbean and imported luxury goods from Europe. They also began training some enslaved people as domestic workers to relieve white women of the strain of household labor.

Small farmers could also purchase and maintain land based on the profits from tobacco. In 1750, two-thirds of white families farmed their own land in Virginia, a larger percentage than in northern colonies. An even higher percentage did so in North Carolina. Yet small farmers in the tobacco colonies became increasingly dependent on large landowners, who controlled markets, politics, and the courts. Many artisans in North Carolina, Virginia, and Maryland, too, depended on wealthy planters for their livelihood. Artisans worked directly for planters, or for the shipping companies and merchants that relied on plantation orders. And the growing number of tenant farmers in this region relied completely on large landowners for their sustenance.

However, some people in these colonies fared far worse during the mid-eighteenth century. One-fifth of all white people owned little more than the clothes on their backs. At the same time, free black people found their opportunities for landownership and economic independence increasingly curtailed, while those who were enslaved had little hope of gaining their freedom and held almost no property of their own.

In the first half of the eighteenth century, the colonial population of Virginia, Maryland, and North Carolina also surged. Some of the growth occurred from natural increase, but immigration of Germans and Scots-Irish to lands in the western parts of these colonies accounted for a significant portion. By the 1740s, German families created pockets of self-contained communities

MAP 2.3 Ethnic and Racial Diversity in British North America, 1750 In 1700 the English dominated most regions, while the Dutch controlled towns and estates in the Hudson River valley. By 1750, however, growing numbers of Africans and African Americans, Germans, Scots-Irish immigrants, and smaller communities of other ethnic groups predominated in various regions. **What accounts for the presence of these diverse populations in British North America?**

TEACHING IDEA

Geography Instruction

Students should be taught to see both explicit information from a map and implicit trends. To foster the skill of inference, consider assigning groups of students the following pairs of ethnic groups: Germans and Scots-Irish | Africans and English. Have students develop a rationale about their relative proximity to one another using at least one historical development, process, or phenomenon to explain their claim.

TEACHING IDEA

Connecting the Dots

As students study the continued movement westward in the seventeenth century, consider incorporating an assignment that focuses their attention on the effect this movement had on American Indians. You can provide for them a list of conflicts and have them identify the ethnic group and tribe in conflict. This will not only make them aware of the continuous nature of the conflicts, but also the regionalization of this issue.

Potential conflicts to choose from: First Powhatan War, Second Powhatan War, Pequot War, Metacom's War, Bacon's Rebellion.

▲ **Differentiation**

Consider pairing an advanced student with a lower-level student and having them prepare a short presentation on one of the conflicts listed.

MODULE 2-2 Early British Colonies in Maryland, Virginia, and North Carolina

Enslaved People Working on a Tobacco Plantation (c. 1750) This wood engraving, created by nineteenth-century English author and engraver Frederick W. Fairholt, was based on a mid-eighteenth-century drawing. Fairholt depicts enslaved people packing tobacco leaves in hogsheads and rolling them to waiting ships while whites oversee their work. **How do the items Fairholt included in this image compare with John Smith's map from over a century before (p. 60)? What might explain the differences you see?**

BUILDING AP® SKILLS

Claims and Evidence in Sources

In non-text-based documents, it is essential for students to examine the document in a holistic manner. This is not a natural process for many students. To help develop this skill, assign the evaluation of the document in five parts such as the following: background, foreground, left, right, and words. Evaluating the document in these phases builds a more complete understanding of the document's contents and purpose.

above the fall line in the back-country of North Carolina and the Chesapeake colonies. They worshipped in German churches, read German newspapers, and preserved German traditions. Likewise, Scots-Irish immigrants established their own churches and communities in the areas where they settled.

REVIEW

- Describe the economic and ethnic diversity in the Chesapeake colonies during the middle of the eighteenth century.

TRM Suggested Responses to Questions

AP® WRITING HISTORICALLY — Writing Topic Sentences for an Essay

In Module 2-1, we discussed how to create a thesis statement that responds to an essay prompt. Here, we will take you one step further and walk through how to write topic sentences of body paragraphs that fully support your thesis. By linking the topic sentences of each of your body paragraphs to the thesis of your essay, you show your readers that you have given thought to how the claims you make, and the evidence you provide to support them, can show that your thesis is valid.

While the prompt in Module 2-1 asked you to complete a comparative analysis that takes causation into account, the prompt we are going to discuss here focuses solely on causation. Being able to distinguish and explain the links between immediate and distant causes is a useful skill for prompts like this one:

> Explain the causes of the development of tobacco economies in the Chesapeake between 1607 and 1754.

Step 1 Break down the prompt, then list and categorize your relevant historical knowledge.

When you make an argument in response to a causation prompt, we recommend taking a few minutes to pre-write about the immediate and distant causes of the effect outlined in the prompt. Following the steps outlined in the AP® Thinking Historically box on pages 47–49 is one way to organize your thoughts in preparation for writing your thesis statement.

TEACHING IDEA

Incorporating Websites

The historian John Lewis Gaddis has a useful commentary on the skill of causation that can be found on Period 8 of Gilder Lehrman's AP® U.S. History website (ap.gilderlehrman.org). Even though the lecture is based on the Cold War, the first 4 ½ minutes deal exclusively with the skill of causation and avoid any commentary on content. Students may find it helpful to see a historian explain the nuances of causation.

Step 2: Craft a thesis statement that fully responds to the prompt.

The following example shows a strong thesis that would follow from using those pre-writing strategies to think about the causes of tobacco economies in the Chesapeake:

> Tobacco economies developed in the Chesapeake due to the influences of profit motives, the environmental factors of soil and climate, and as a result of a robust Atlantic world economy in which goods and labor were traded across three continents.

You may have already noticed that this thesis contains three major claims about three distinct topics for analysis:

- Claim 1 topic: The influence of profit motives
- Claim 2 topic: The environmental factors
- Claim 3 topic: The Atlantic economy

You can think of three as the magic number for writing essays: A three-part thesis not only creates a robust response to the prompt, it also helps you outline your essay by providing your reader with a clear preview of the historical argument you plan to make.

The topics in our example thesis are particularly strong because they directly relate to the causes of the development of tobacco economies in the Chesapeake between 1607 and 1754. Moreover, the claims about these topics offer a wealth of historical information to help convince your reader that your thesis is true. For example, you already know that John Smith, on behalf of the Virginia Company, sought settlement in Virginia to bring profit to the company's investors. Also, you know that, while gold proved elusive in Virginia, tobacco grew readily and established a growing market in Europe. Each of these topics will be one of your body paragraphs, and your topic sentence of each of these paragraphs will introduce one of these topics.

Step 3: Use your thesis claims to write topic sentences for each body paragraph of your essay.

From here, the next step is to create topic sentences for the body of your essay. Each of these body paragraphs should start with a clear topic sentence that presents a part of your thesis. Remember to write a sentence that reflects your thesis by asserting a claim. It may help to think of topic sentences as a way to inform your reader which part of your thesis — and therefore which part of your answer to the prompt — that particular paragraph will argue. A good rule of thumb is that a strong topic sentence can stand alone as one way to answer the prompt. The following example shows topic sentences proving each of the three claims in our example thesis.

1. Profit motives led to the tobacco economies in Virginia, Maryland, and North Carolina.
2. Environmental factors such as soil and climate helped cause the development of tobacco economies in Virginia, Maryland, and North Carolina.
3. The Atlantic world trading economy, with extensive trading of goods and labor, fostered the creation of tobacco economies in the Chesapeake and North Carolina.

All of these topic sentences present an answer to the prompt in the form of a claim that you can argue. From there, you can structure the rest of your body paragraph around providing evidence that supports your topic sentence claim.

ACTIVITY

Carefully read the following essay prompt:

> Explain the causes of the development of slavery in Virginia, Maryland, and North Carolina between 1607 and 1754.

1. Pre-write in response to this prompt by listing causes (both immediate and distant) and writing at least three statements that link the two.
2. Write a three-part thesis that fully responds to this prompt.
3. Write three topic sentences in support of your thesis. Be sure that each topic sentence directly addresses one of the three causes outlined in your thesis.

BUILDING AP® SKILLS

Making Connections

Because this question spans all of Period 2 in the AP® U.S. History Course Framework, consider having students work on developing a thesis that spans multiple parts of the question. To achieve this, have students brainstorm as many turning point events as they can from the period in question, 1607–1754. Next, have them select two or three turning points that are immediately relevant to the question. If students have developed a thorough list, they should see examples that span the time period. Having breadth to the response allows students to illustrate change over time.

TEACHING IDEA

Connecting the Dots

Part of the usefulness in developing thesis statements that offer an interpretation to a historical development is rooted in students' ability to shepherd an argument throughout their response. Every Long-Essay Question gives students topics to help establish a line of reasoning. For this question, students need to focus on the terms *development* and *tobacco economies*. As students write their topic sentences they should be mindful of the extent to which their topic sentences explore each of those concepts. Give students two highlighter colors and have them highlight each term separately in their topic sentence to ensure their inclusion of the terms.

TEACHING IDEA

AP® Writing Historically Workshop

If students need extra time to develop topic sentences, consider condensing this activity by providing students with a completed thesis. You might decide as a teacher to write three different thesis statements and use those so students do not have to spend time writing the thesis. After providing groups of three or four students with an exemplary thesis, ask students to select one of the categories of analysis in the thesis and develop a topic sentence. This gets students to step 3 in the activity; again, this could be used if a group was struggling to conceptualize the design of a strong topic sentence.

TRM Suggested Responses to Questions

TEACHING IDEA

Connecting the Dots

There are subtle and distinct differences between the groups of New England settlers labeled Pilgrims and Puritans. It may be helpful to frontload the definitions before students read this section of Module 2-3. This will be an especially useful exercise given this module focuses on continuities and changes over time within New England. Comparing the timing, views of the Anglican Church, leaders, and number of migrants are good categories to begin a basic understanding of the differences and similarities between Pilgrims and Puritans.

Module 2-3

Religious Dissent and Colonial Conflicts in New England

LEARNING TARGETS

By the end of this module, you should be able to:

- Explain how the environment and geography of New England affected colonial development between 1607 and 1754.
- Explain how the relationship between New England settlers and American Indians evolved from 1607 to 1754.
- Explain how and why social conflicts emerged within the New England colonies as their populations grew and territory expanded.

THEMATIC FOCUS

Geography and the Environment
Migration and Settlement
American and Regional Culture
Social Structures

The first English settlers in New England, mostly Puritans, established an economy of agriculture and commerce within a society of independent family farms and small towns. Distance from Great Britain led to self-governing towns that contained elements of democratic practice. These democratic elements included participatory town meetings and elected colonial legislatures, but religious debates also led to conflicts with dissenters in the colony.

HISTORICAL REASONING FOCUS

Causation

Continuity and Change

In Module 1-4, you began to learn about how historians examine extended periods of time by identifying and describing patterns of continuity and change over time. Just as historians deepen their comparative analyses when they consider how causation factors into historical developments (see Module 2-1, p. 43), they also deepen understanding of continuity and change over time by incorporating explanations of causation. This is because uncovering the cause of a particular change or continuity fosters a fuller understanding of why these changes and continuities occur. Going beyond merely describing continuities and changes is also one way to examine why some aspects of a topic changed even as factors caused other aspects to persist unchanged across a timespan.

In this module, you will learn about how the arrival of the Pilgrims, who came seeking to separate from the Anglican Church, brought changes to North America. We will discuss the immediate cause of their journey (they sought religious refuge) as well as the reasons for the changes they brought.

TASK ▶ As you read this module, think about continuities and changes over time in New England colonial society from 1620 to 1754. Be sure to go beyond merely noting continuities and changes in order to consider why those developments unfolded as they did.

The **Protestant Reformation**, from its beginning in 1517, transformed the religious and political landscape of Europe throughout the sixteenth century. The formation of new, Protestant denominations such as the Church of England during this time shattered the dominance of the Catholic Church and profoundly altered personal beliefs and royal alliances throughout Europe. The resulting conflicts had long-lasting effects that shaped the following century as well. In Great Britain, for instance, critics of the Church of England formed a number of congregations in the early seventeenth century, and some sought refuge in Virginia. In the 1610s, to raise capital, the Virginia Company began offering legal charters to groups of private investors, who were promised their own tract of land in the Virginia colony with minimal company

Pilgrims Also known as Separatists, a group of English religious dissenters who established a settlement at Plymouth, Massachusetts, in 1620. Unlike more mainstream Protestants, the Pilgrims aimed to cut all connections with the Church of England.

oversight. One such charter was purchased by a group of English **Pilgrims** (also known as Separatists) who wanted to form a separate church and community in a land untainted by other faiths. Setting sail on the *Mayflower* from England in September 1620, they never made it to Virginia. Blown off course by a storm, they landed far up the coast, north of the Dutch in New Amsterdam. Because a religious community wholly separate from the Anglican Church was more important to the Pilgrims than its specific location, they decided to remain on the Massachusetts coast, establishing a permanent settlement at Plymouth.

The Protestant Reformation

The Catholic Church, in partnership with monarchs and the nobility, had long served as the dominant religion of Western Europe, but by the early sixteenth century, critiques of its practices began to multiply. Many saw the Catholic Church as corrupt and driven by the Pope's involvement in conflicts among European monarchs. These views appeared in popular songs and printed images as well as in writings by **theologians** such as Martin Luther, giving rise to what would become known as the Protestant Reformation. Luther, a professor of theology in Germany, believed that faith alone led to salvation, which could be granted only by God. He challenged the Catholic Church's widespread practice of selling **indulgences**, which were documents that absolved the buyer of sin. The church profited enormously from these sales, but they suggested that God's grace could be purchased. In 1517 Luther wrote an extended argument against indulgences and sent it to the local bishop. Although intended for clerics and academics, his writings soon gained a wider audience.

Luther's followers, who protested Catholic practices, became known as Protestants. His teachings circulated widely through sermons and printed texts, and his claim that ordinary people should read and reflect on the Scriptures appealed to the emerging literate middle class. Luther's attacks on indulgences and corruption attracted those who resented the church's wealth and priests' lack of attention to their flocks.

The Protestant Reformation quickly spread through central and northern Europe. Protestants challenged Catholic policies and practices but did not form a single church of their own. Instead, a number of theologians started distinct denominations in various regions of Europe. In Switzerland, John Calvin developed a version of Protestantism in which civil magistrates and reformed ministers ruled over a Christian society. Calvin argued that God had decided at the beginning of time who was saved and who was damned. Calvin's idea, known as **predestination**, energized Protestants who understood salvation as a gift from an all-knowing God in which the "works" of sinful humans played no part. Protestant challenges and Catholic attempts to maintain authority led to intense conflicts. National competition for wealth and colonies in North America among the Spanish, French, Dutch, and English was complicated in the context of the Protestant Reformation. Spanish and French Catholicism shaped their colonial efforts, as did Protestantism in the Netherlands and England.

predestination Religious belief that God has pre-determined who is worthy of salvation, and thus it could not be earned through good works or penance.

Protestantism grew in England under sponsorship of the monarchy in the 1530s. When the pope refused to annul the marriage of King Henry VIII (r. 1509–1547) and Catherine of Aragon, Henry denounced papal authority and established the Church of England, also known as the Anglican Church, with himself at its head as "defender of the faith." Despite the king's conversion to Protestantism, the Church of England retained many Catholic practices, which is why groups such as the Pilgrims and, later, the **Puritans**—who would go on to colonize New England during the seventeenth century—also attracted followers.

Puritans Radical English Protestants who hoped to reform the Church of England. The first Puritan settlers in the Americas arrived in Massachusetts in 1630.

The Protestant Reformation ultimately helped shape the alliances that shattered Spain's American monopoly. As head of the Church of England, Queen Elizabeth I (r. 1558–1603) — daughter of Henry VIII — sought closer political and commercial ties with fellow Protestant nations like the Netherlands, sending military aid in support of its efforts to free itself from Spanish rule. She also agreed to raids on Spanish ships. English thefts of Spanish silver funneled wealth to England and the crown. King Philip II of Spain (r. 1556–1598) retaliated by sending a massive Armada to spearhead an invasion of England in 1588. However, the English, aided by Dutch ships, defeated the Spanish — an event that helped ensure other nations could compete for riches and colonies in North America.

AP® TIP
Be sure you can explain how the Protestant Reformation created a justification for challenging traditional authorities.

REVIEW

- Which religious beliefs and practices continued in Europe after the Protestant Reformation?
- How did religious beliefs and practices change in Europe as a result of the Protestant Reformation?

TEACHING IDEA

Incorporating Secondary Sources

The initial meeting of Pilgrims and their American Indian counterparts is a subject replete with misunderstanding. To buttress students' awareness of the issues of historical myths surrounding this meeting, consider assigning the article, "Native Intelligence," by Charles C. Mann. This article can be found searching the title on the Smithsonian magazine's website (smithsonianmag.com). The article discusses the initial meeting, how it has been captured in books, the first Thanksgiving, and what students are to make of this monumental moment in history.

BUILDING AP® SKILLS

Developments and Processes

Religious developments in Europe are central to the imperial struggle for colonies. The Protestant Reformation led to many changes within England and Europe. Understanding this development allows students to explain the multiple effects of a specific historical development. If students are not familiar with the Protestant Reformation, or are confused by the names and movements, it may be helpful to work on defining the major historical figures and identifying the changes wrought by their beliefs. For instance, have students define the religious views of Martin Luther, John Calvin, and King Henry VIII. After they have successfully defined each person, invite students to identify one significant religious change as a result of their belief.

EXPLORING AP® THEMES

Migration and Settlement

To allow students to connect the context of settlement patterns in New England with religious developments in England, consider assigning students a timeline activity. To complete the activity, assign students three significant religious developments in Europe between 1517 and 1620. The activity is designed to develop their understanding of events in Europe so they remain mindful of the effects religious changes in Europe had on the colonization of the British North American colonies.

1517   1620

Period 2: 1607–1754

MODULE 2-3 Religious Dissent and Colonial Conflicts in New England

Pilgrims Arrive in Massachusetts

Mayflower Compact Written agreement created by the Pilgrims upon their arrival in Plymouth. It was the first written constitution adopted in North America.

The Pilgrim Separatists who booked passage on the *Mayflower* in 1620 migrated as organized households, each headed by an elder male church member and accompanied by their families and servants. Landing off course at Cape Cod in present-day Massachusetts, the male heads of households, led by William Bradford, signed a pact to form a "civill body politick" that followed the Separatist model of a self-governing religious congregation. They considered their agreement necessary because they settled in a region where they had no legal authority. They wrote and signed the first written constitution adopted in North America, the **Mayflower Compact**, before leaving the ship.

AP® ANALYZING SOURCES

Source: *The Mayflower Compact,* 1620

"We whose names are underwritten, the loyal subjects of our dread sovereign lord, King James, by the grace of God, of Great Britain, France, and Ireland King, Defender of the Faith, etc., having undertaken, for the glory of God, and advancement of the Christian faith, and honor of our king and country, a voyage to plant the first colony in the northern parts of Virginia, do by these presents solemnly and mutually, in the presence of God and one of another, *covenant and combine ourselves together into a civil body politic,* for our better ordering and preservation, and furtherance of the ends aforesaid; and by virtue hereof, to enact, constitute, and frame such *just and equal laws,* ordinances, Acts, *constitutions,* and offices, from time to time, as shall be thought most *meet and convenient for the general good of the colony; unto which we promise all due submission and obedience.* In witness whereof we have hereunder subscribed our names, at Cape Cod, the 11th day of November, in the year of the reign of our sovereign lord, King James, of England, France, and Ireland the eighteenth, and of Scotland the fifty-fourth, Anno Domini, 1620."

Questions for Analysis
1. Identify the signers' justification for forming this government.
2. Explain how the signers of the Mayflower Compact established a degree of independence from the crown.
3. Explain how the signers of the Mayflower Compact declared allegiance to the crown.

AP® TIP
As you read about the relations between American Indians and Plymouth settlers, compare them with those between American Indians and the settlers of Jamestown.

After several forays along the coast, the Pilgrims eventually located an uninhabited village surrounded by cornfields, where they established Plymouth. Uncertain of native intentions, the Pilgrims were unsettled by sightings of American Indians. They did not realize that a smallpox epidemic in the area only two years earlier had killed nearly 90 percent of the local Wampanoag population. Indeed, fevers and other diseases proved far more deadly to the Pilgrim settlers than did the Wampanoag. By the spring of 1621, only half of the 102 English colonists from the *Mayflower* remained alive.

Desperate to find food, the survivors were stunned when two English-speaking American Indians—Samoset and Squanto—appeared at Plymouth that March. Both had been captured as young boys by English explorers, and they now negotiated a fragile peace between the Pilgrims and Chief Massasoit of the Wampanoag tribe. Although concerned by the power of English guns, Massasoit hoped to create an alliance that would assist him against his traditional native enemies, including the Massachusetts tribe. With Wampanoag assistance, the surviving Pilgrims soon regained their health.

In the summer of 1621, reinforcements arrived from England, and the next year the Pilgrims received a royal charter granting Separatists rights to Plymouth and a degree of self-government. Although some Pilgrims hoped to convert the American Indians, other leaders favored a more aggressive, military stance. In their eyes, the Massachusetts Indians posed an especially serious threat. In 1623, Captain Myles Standish kidnapped and killed the Massachusetts chief and his younger brother. Pilgrims led by Standish and allied Wampanoags then attacked a Massachusetts village. Standish's strategy, though controversial, ensured that Chief Massasoit of the Wampanoags

---

TRM Suggested Responses to Questions

TRM Module 2.3 AP® Analyzing Sources Handout 1

BUILDING AP® SKILLS

Claims and Evidence in Sources

To further the goals of the questions related to the Mayflower Compact, consider having students highlight the document before answering the questions. Provide two highlighter colors for each student: one used to highlight the challenges to the crown described in the document and the other for loyalties expressed to the crown. Identifying specific elements of the document will enable students to answer the questions.

TEACHING IDEA

Analyzing Art and Images

Jean Leon Gerome Ferris's painting, "The First Thanksgiving" (1671), is one of the more famous depictions of what the gathering was like for settlers and American Indians. Encourage students to challenge ideas found in the painting such as the dress worn by American Indians. Find this painting on the Library of Congress website by searching for the title (loc.gov).

achieved dominance in the region. Successful in war and diplomacy, the Pilgrims gradually expanded their colony during the 1620s.

REVIEW

- How did the Pilgrims maintain specific aspects of English society in Plymouth?
- How did the society the Pilgrims developed in Plymouth differ from specific aspects of English society?

Puritans Form Communities in New England

The Puritans, a new group of English dissenters who hoped to purify the Church of England rather than separate from it, arrived in North America a decade later, in 1630, with plans to develop their own colony. Puritans believed that their country's church and government had grown corrupt and the English people were therefore being punished by an all-powerful God. Events during the early seventeenth century often seemed to support this theory. The English population had boomed but harvests failed, leading to famine, crime, unemployment, and inflation. At the same time the growing enclosure movement, in which landlords fenced in fields and hired a few laborers and tenants to replace a large number of peasant farmers, had increased the number of landless vagrants. Then, the English cloth industry nearly collapsed under the weight of competition from abroad. In the Puritans' view, all of these problems were divine punishments for the nation's sins.

The Puritans envisioned New England as a safe haven from God's wrath. Under Puritan lawyer John Winthrop's leadership, a group of affluent Puritans obtained a royal charter for the Massachusetts Bay Company in 1623. New England was, however, more than just a place of safety to the Puritans. Unlike the Pilgrims, they believed that England and the Anglican Church could be redeemed. By prospering spiritually and materially in America, they hoped to establish a model "City upon a Hill" that would then inspire reform among residents of the mother country.

AP® TIP
Analyze how the differences between the original Pilgrims and the Puritans shaped the development of social structures, political systems, and economic goals of the New England colonies.

AP® ANALYZING SOURCES

Source: John Winthrop, *A Model of Christian Charity*, 1630

"Now the only way to . . . provide for our posterity . . . is to follow the counsel of Micah, to do justly, to love mercy, to walk humbly with our God. For this end, we must be knit together, in this work, as one man. . . . We must be willing to abridge ourselves of our superfluities, for the supply of others' necessities. We must uphold a familiar commerce together in all meekness, gentleness, patience and liberality. We must delight in each other; make others' conditions our own; rejoice together, mourn together, labor and suffer together, always having before our eyes our commission and community in the work, as members of the same body. . . . We shall find that the God of Israel is among us, when ten of us shall be able to resist a thousand of our enemies; when he shall make us a praise and glory that men shall say of succeeding plantations, 'The Lord make it like that of New England.' For we must consider that we shall be as a city upon a hill. The eyes of all people are upon us. So that if we shall deal falsely with our God in this work we have undertaken, and so cause him to withdraw his present help from us, we shall be made a story and a by-word through the world. We shall open the mouths of enemies to speak evil of the ways of God, and all professors for God's sake. We shall shame the faces of many of God's worthy servants, and cause their prayers to be turned into curses upon us till we be consumed out of the good land whither we are agoing. . . ."

Questions for Analysis
1. Describe the kind of society Winthrop envisions in this document.
2. Explain how this document reveals the ways in which seventeenth-century New England society continued English traditions.
3. Explain how this document reveals the ways in which seventeenth-century New England society broke from English traditions.
4. Explain how this document illustrates Puritan beliefs.

TEACHING IDEA

Check for Understanding

Now that students have read information germane to the settlement patterns of Pilgrims and Puritans, consider taking time to do an activity designed to check for understanding. It can be as simple as providing a historical timeframe, 1620–1640, and having students outline the continuities and changes within New England. This provides a great breadth of possible answers and allows students the opportunity to select information they are comfortable explaining.

TRM Suggested Responses to Questions

TRM Module 2.3 AP® Analyzing Sources Handout 2

TEACHING IDEA

Incorporating Primary Sources

Throughout the year, be sure to take time to help develop students' understanding of language used in a primary source. For instance, in the John Winthrop document, it may help students to have the following words defined before reading the document: *posterity*, *abridge*, and *superfluities*. Next, have students highlight the parts of the document where John Winthrop represents the belief Puritans had of an active God. This belief informed their view of themselves, their environment, and American Indians.

BUILDING AP® SKILLS

Developments and Processes

A fundamental skill for students to master is the ability to identify and explain historical developments and processes. Because this module focuses on continuities and changes, consider assigning the following activity. In this activity, students have two tasks. The first is to identify both American Indian and Pilgrim strategies for living within close proximity to one another in the period 1620–1630. Following this, have groups identify the extent to which the arrival of the Massachusetts Bay Colony settlers could be deemed a turning point in settlement patterns and attitudes toward the neighboring American Indian tribes in the period 1630–1640.

TEACHING IDEA

Incorporating Secondary Sources

Recent scholarship has challenged the traditional view of New England's role in the Atlantic world economy. Instead of viewing New England as a reserved community of small farmers, fishermen, and shipbuilders, scholars such as Wendy Warren have acknowledged that view while also illustrating how integral New England was to the development of the international slave trade in the seventeenth century. Consider assigning students Chapter 2 of Warren's book, *New England Bound*, to buttress students' understanding of the economic developments in New England.

TEACHING IDEA

Incorporating Secondary Sources

Although Gary B. Nash's groundbreaking study, *Red, White, and Black — The Peoples of Early North America*, was published in 1974 it remains an important work in the historical analysis of this time. Chapter 4 details the challenges and successes of New England settlement patterns. Moreover, it infuses the lives of American Indians and the effects of both the Pequot War and Metacom's War. Assign the reading to students and discuss the concepts in class.

About one-third of all English Puritans chose to leave their homeland for North America, and a large proportion of those chose to sail with their entire families. They were better supplied, more prosperous, and more numerous than either their Pilgrim or Jamestown predecessors. The settlers, arriving on seventeen ships, included the households of ministers, merchants, craftsmen, farmers, and — significantly — their servants, many of whom served on contracts of indenture. Moreover, they settled in a cold climate that reduced the spread of disease. These demographic and geographic factors also helped ensure the rapid growth of the colony.

The first Puritan settlers arrived on the coast north of Plymouth in 1630 and named their community Boston, after the port city in England from which they had departed. Established in the midst of growing conflicts leading to the English Civil War and growing fears of royally sanctioned persecution of Puritans, the Massachusetts Bay Company relocated its capital and records to New England. Through this process, the Puritans converted their commercial charter into the founding document of a self-governing colony. They also instituted a new political practice, in which adult male church members participated in the election of a governor, deputy governor, and legislature. Although the Puritans suffered a difficult first winter in New England, they quickly recovered and soon cultivated sufficient crops to feed themselves and a steady stream of new migrants. During the 1630s, the time of the **Puritan Migration**, at least eighteen thousand people made their way to North America. Even without a cash crop like tobacco or sugar, the Puritan colony flourished.

Two factors aided Puritans in quickly forming and developing new communities throughout New England. Cleared agricultural lands, farmed very recently by American Indians, had been made more available by the effects of Columbian Exchange diseases, which severely reduced the native farming populations. Also, Puritan ideology idealized small, close-knit village communities as a means to achieve a religiously moral society. These small communities of faithful neighbors, led by male church members, could watch over each other's salvation. Male church members acted as patriarchs of their households, responsible to each other, and the dependents of the community — both family and servant.

Opposed to the lavish rituals and hierarchy of the Church of England and believing that few Anglicans truly felt the grace of God, Puritans set out to establish a simpler form of worship in New England that focused on their inner lives and on the purity of their church and community. They followed the teachings of John Calvin, believing in an all-knowing God whose true word was presented in the Bible. The biblically sanctioned church was a congregation formed by a group of believers who made a covenant with God. Only a small minority of people, known as Saints, were granted God's grace.

Whether one was a Saint and thereby saved was predetermined by and known only to God. Still, some Puritans believed that the chosen were likely to lead a saintly life. Visible signs included individuals' passionate response to the preaching of God's Word, their sense of doubt and despair over their own soul, that wonderful sense of reassurance that came with God's "saving grace," and blessed fortune manifested in land ownership and higher economic statuses of "visible saints." Puritans believed God's hand in the world appeared in nature as well. Comets and eclipses were considered "remarkable providences." They also celebrated as a sign of God's favor a smallpox epidemic that killed several thousand Massachusetts Indians in 1633–1634, and military victories over American Indians such as the massacre at a fort near Mystic River in 1637.

These shared religious beliefs helped forge a unified community where faith guided civil as well as spiritual decisions. Soon after the colony was established Puritan ministers were discouraged from holding political office, although political leaders were devout Puritans who were expected to promote a godly society. These leaders determined who got land, how much, and where; they also served as judge and jury for those accused of crimes or sins. Their leadership was largely considered successful — even if colonists differed over who should get the most fertile strip of land, they agreed on basic principles.

Puritans assigned wives and daughters solely domestic roles with rare exceptions. By the eighteenth century Puritan women, and indeed almost all women throughout the colonies, found their legal and economic rights restricted to those accorded their female counterparts in Great Britain. In a process of **Anglicization**, in which English social and legal traditions came to dominate colonial cultural and political institutions, colonial courts adopted English

Puritan Migration The mass migration of Puritans from Europe to New England during the 1620s and 1630s.

AP® TIP
Be sure to make note of the role Puritan religious beliefs played in the development of a distinct American culture.

Anglicization Adoption of English customs and traditions. This shaped colonial culture and politics in eighteenth-century North America.

BUILDING AP® SKILLS

Making Connections

Understanding and describing continuities can be a more challenging task than identifying and describing changes. Anglicization is a concept that affords teachers the opportunity to develop students' comprehension of how to make connections centered on continuities across time. This process begins at this part of Module 2-3 but can continue through Module 2-9. Teachers should select major historical developments such as settlement of the British North American colonies, the development of mercantilism, and the French and Indian War.

Challenges Arise in the New England Colonies

common law Law established from custom and the standards set by previous judicial rulings.

patriarchal family Model of the family in which fathers have absolute authority over wives, children, and servants. Most colonial Americans accepted the patriarchal model of the family, at least as an ideal.

> **AP® TIP**
> Compare the effects of government policies, economic systems, and culture on the development of patriarchy in the Chesapeake and in New England during this era.

common law. According to English common law, a wife's status was defined as *femme covert*, which meant that she was legally covered over by (or hidden behind) her husband. The husband controlled his wife's labor, the house in which she lived, the property she brought into the marriage, and any wages she earned. He was also the legal guardian of their children, and through the instrument of a will he could continue to control the household after his death. The **patriarchal family** — a model in which fathers held absolute authority over wives, children, and servants — came to be seen in Puritan colonies and throughout British North America as a crucial bulwark against disorder. Families with wealth were especially eager to control the behavior of their sons and daughters as the parents sought to build social, commercial, and political alliances.

By the 1640s, the settlers had turned their colony into a thriving commercial center. During the English Civil War (1642–1651), New England settlements spread as a result of both natural increase and migration. English communities stretched from Connecticut through Massachusetts and Rhode Island and into Maine and what became New Hampshire. They shipped codfish, lumber, grain, pork, and cheese to England in exchange for manufactured goods and to the West Indies for rum and molasses. This trade, along with the healthy climate, relatively egalitarian distribution of property amongst male church members, and more equal ratio of women to men, ensured a stable and prosperous colony. Meanwhile, the English king and Parliament, embroiled in war, paid little attention to events in North America, allowing these New England colonies to develop with little oversight.

REVIEW

- How did the Puritans maintain specific aspects of Pilgrim society in Massachusetts Bay?
- In what ways did the Puritans change society in Massachusetts Bay?

Challenges Arise in the New England Colonies

English men and women settled New England in the 1620s and 1630s seeking religious sanctuary, and to support communities unified by common faith. Yet they, too, like the colony at Jamestown, suffered divisions in their ranks. Almost from the beginning, certain Puritans challenged some of the community's fundamental beliefs and, in the process, the community itself. Dissenters such as Roger Williams and Anne Hutchinson even led groups of discontented Puritans to establish new communities.

In the early 1630s, Roger Williams, a Salem minister, criticized Puritan leaders for not being sufficiently pure in their rejection of the Church of England and the English monarchy. He preached that not all the Puritan leaders were Saints and that some were bound for damnation. By 1635 Williams was forced out of Salem and moved south with his followers to found Providence in the area that became Rhode Island. Believing that there were very few Saints in the world, Williams and his followers accepted that one must live among those who were not saved. Thus, unlike Massachusetts Bay, Providence welcomed Quakers, Baptists, and Jews to the community, and Williams's followers insisted on a strict separation of church and state. Williams also forged alliances with the Narragansetts, the most powerful American Indian nation in the region.

Remarkably, Anne Hutchinson, a wife and mother, led another such dissenting group. Born in Lincolnshire in 1591, Anne was well educated when she married William Hutchinson, a merchant, in 1612. The Hutchinsons and their children began attending Puritan sermons and by 1630 embraced the new faith. Four years later, they followed the Reverend John Cotton to Massachusetts Bay.

The Reverend Cotton soon urged Anne Hutchinson to use her exceptional knowledge of the Bible to hold prayer meetings in her home on Sundays for pregnant and nursing women who could

---

TEACHING IDEA

Connecting the Dots

An important, and often overlooked, part of comparing colonies in New England with the Chesapeake is the impact of demographic changes. To help students connect the dots with this important distinction, consider assigning students the following graphic organizer to help conceptualize the importance of demographics in early settlement patterns.

New England Demographics	Chesapeake Demographics
Family Characteristics	Family Characteristics
Effects on Settlement Patterns	Effects on Settlement Patterns

▲ **Differentiation**

Split the class in half and have one half fill in the "New England Demographics" column and the other half the "Chesapeake Demographics" column. Once students have finished, pair two students from separate groups to discuss their findings.

TEACHING IDEA

Incorporating Websites

The Gilder Lehrman website for APUSH students has some helpful and brief secondary source essays (ap.gilderlehrman.org). One of the topics explored in Period 2 on the site is dissent in New England. This essay, "The Puritans and Dissent: The Case of Roger Williams and Anne Hutchinson" by historian Francis J. Bremer, can be a powerful resource for students.

TEACHING IDEA

Incorporating Primary Sources

Like most historical controversies, the trial of Anne Hutchinson did not exist in a vacuum. The effects of this story would be felt years after the trial. Teaching American History possesses a useful repository of primary sources that can support students' learning through primary sources (teachingamericanhistory.org). Search for "Letter to the General Court and Testimony, Mary Dyer" for the details concerning the case of Mary Dyer in 1659 and 1660, which can buttress any lesson on Anne Hutchinson.

BUILDING AP® SKILLS

Comparison

Choosing strategic moments to concentrate on comparison not only builds understanding but also confidence in students' ability to navigate this difficult skill. This part of Module 2-3 is a good moment to have students compare the ways Spanish and English imperial powers interacted with American Indians. Consider having students identify at least two similarities and two differences between these two nations. The final step is to allow students to select one similarity and one difference and describe their selection. Identifying and describing are related but distinct skills that take time to process.

TEACHING IDEA

Incorporating Videos

Teachers looking to expand their knowledge of Metacom's War (King Philip's War) can use a lecture by historian Jill Lepore on Gilder Lehrman's APUSH site, Period 2 (ap.gilderlehrman.org). The lecture discusses the context, events, and memory of the war. Teachers can also turn to Lepore's book, *The Name of War: King Philip's War and the Origins of American Identity*, to advance their understanding of this seminal moment in New England history.

TEACHING IDEA

Check for Understanding

Students can use interactions between American Indians and British settlers to illustrate both continuities and changes in colonial New England. In this way, students are using the topic of American Indians to see the continuities and changes. For a quick check for understanding, simply provide the graphic below and have students fill in their answer. This is also an ideal activity for a think-pair-share as a bell ringer for class. (Answers provided in italics.)

American Indians

Changes: *Justification for multiple wars such as Pequot and King Philip's War*

Continuities: *Westward movement as the impetus for conflict*

---

not attend regular services. Hutchinson, like Cotton, preached that individuals must rely solely on God's grace rather than a saintly life or good works to ensure salvation.

Hutchinson began challenging Puritan ministers who opposed this position, charging that they posed a threat to their congregations. She soon attracted a loyal and growing following that included men as well as women. A year after Williams's departure in 1637, Puritan leaders denounced Hutchinson's views and condemned her meetings. After she refused to recant, she was accused of sedition, or trying to overthrow the government by challenging colonial leaders, and put on trial. Hutchinson mounted a vigorous defense. An eloquent speaker, Hutchinson ultimately claimed that her authority to challenge the Puritan leadership came from "an immediate revelation" from God, "the voice of his own spirit to my soul." Unmoved, the Puritan judges convicted her of heresy and banished her from Massachusetts Bay.

Hutchinson was seen as a threat not only because of her religious beliefs but also because she was a woman. The Reverend Hugh Peter, for example, reprimanded her at trial: "You have stept out of your place, you have rather bine a Husband than a Wife and a preacher than a Hearer; and a Magistrate than a Subject." Many considered her challenge to Puritan authority especially serious because she also challenged traditional gender hierarchies. After being banished from Massachusetts Bay, Hutchinson, her family, and dozens of her followers joined Williams's Rhode Island colony. The likelihood of later radical women experiencing the success of Hutchinson diminished as the colonies developed larger populations and more elaborate formal institutions of politics, law, and culture.

As Anne Hutchinson and Roger Williams confronted religious leaders, Puritans and Pilgrims faced serious threats from their American Indian neighbors as well. The Pequot nation, which was among the most powerful tribes in New England, had been allies of the English for several years. Yet some Puritans feared that the Pequots, who opposed the colonists' continued expansion, "would cause all the Indians in the country to join to root out all the English." Also, unlike the Spanish, who believed native peoples could be converted to Christianity, many Puritans believed that Native Americans were irredeemable in the eyes of God and destined to damnation. Using the death of two Englishmen in 1636 to justify a military expedition against the Pequots, the colonists went on the attack. The Narragansetts, whom Roger Williams had befriended, allied with the English in the **Pequot War** (1636–1638). After months of bloody conflict, the English and their American Indian allies launched a brutal attack on a Pequot fort in May 1637 that left some four hundred men, women, and children dead. This massacre by the Puritans all but decimated the Pequots, and the American Indian population in the area never recovered. In New England, at most 16,000 native people remained by 1670, a loss of about 80 percent over fifty years. Meanwhile the English population had reached more than 50,000, with settlers claiming ever more land.

Relations between the New England colonists and American Indians grew even worse in 1671, when the English demanded that the Wampanoag Indians, who had been their allies since the 1620s, surrender their guns and be ruled by English law. Instead, many Wampanoags hid their weapons and, over the next several years, raided frontier farms and killed several settlers. English authorities responded by hanging three Wampanoag men. By 1675 the Wampanoag chief Metacom, called King Philip by the English, came to believe that Europeans had to be forced out of New England if American Indians were going to survive. As conflict escalated between the English and the Wampanoags, Metacom gained the support of other tribes, and together formed a coalition that attacked white settlements in what was known as **Metacom's War**. In these attacks, they burned fields, killed male settlers, and took women and children captive. The war came to an end when Mohawk allies of the English ambushed and killed Metacom in 1676. The remaining tribes allied with Metacom, short on weapons, moved north and gradually intermarried with tribes allied with the French.

Pequot War 1636–1637 conflict between New England settlers, their Narragansett allies, and the Pequots. The English saw the Pequots as both a threat and an obstacle to further English expansion.

Metacom's War 1675–1676 conflict between New England settlers and the region's American Indians. The settlers were the eventual victors, but fighting was fierce and casualties on both sides were high.

REVIEW

- How did conflicts in the Puritan colonies, both internally and with American Indians, reflect Puritan society in particular, and the English colonists in general?

Conflicts in England Echo in the Colonies

As Puritans formed new lives in North America, those who remained in England became embroiled in armed conflict against their fellow countrymen. Differences over issues of religion, taxation, and royal authority had strained relations between Parliament and the crown for decades, as James I (r. 1603–1625) and his son Charles I (r. 1625–1649) sought to consolidate their own power at Parliament's expense, demanding conformity to the Anglican Church of England. By 1642 the relationship between Parliament and King Charles I broke down completely, and the country descended into a civil war that lasted until 1651. During this time, the Puritan migration to New England virtually halted.

Oliver Cromwell, a Puritan, emerged as the leader of the Protestant parliamentary forces against the crown, and, after several years of fighting, claimed victory. Charles I was executed in 1649, Parliament established a Republican commonwealth, and bishops and elaborate rituals were banished from the Church of England. Cromwell ruled England as a military dictator until his death in 1658 — when rival groups of nobles, Anglicans, English commercial elites, and English people overthrew Puritan rule and invited Charles I's son, Charles II (r. 1660–1685), to return from exile on the continent, and restored the monarchy and the Church of England.

Shortly after he was restored to the English throne, Charles II came to terms with expanded Puritan settlements in New England. He formalized his rule in this region by granting the requests of Connecticut and Rhode Island for royal charters, accepting their authority to rule in local matters. Because the charters could be changed only with the agreement of both parties, Connecticut and Rhode Island maintained this local autonomy throughout the colonial period. Before the end of his reign, the English could claim dominance — in population, trade, and politics — over the other European powers vying for empires along the northern Atlantic coast.

However, Charles's death in 1685 marked an abrupt shift in crown-colony relations. Charles's successor, King James II (r. 1685–1688), instituted a more authoritarian regime both at home and abroad. In 1686 he consolidated the colonies in the Northeast into the **Dominion of New England** and established tighter controls. Within the Dominion of New England, James II's officials banned town meetings, challenged land titles granted under the original colonial charters, and imposed new taxes. Fortunately for the colonists, the Catholic James II alienated his subjects in England as well as in the colonies, inspiring a bloodless coup in 1688, the so-called **Glorious Revolution**. His Protestant daughter, Mary II (r. 1689–1694) and her husband, William of Orange (r. 1689–1702), then ascended the throne, introducing more democratic systems of governance in England and the colonies. Soon after, John Locke, a physician and philosopher, published the widely circulated *Two Treatises of Government* supporting the initiatives of William and Mary by insisting that government depended on the consent of the governed.

Dominion of New England
The consolidation of Northeastern colonies by King James II in 1686 to establish greater control over them, resulting in the banning of town meetings, new taxes, and other unpopular policies. The Dominion was dissolved during the Glorious Revolution.

AP® ANALYZING SOURCES

Source: John Locke, English political philosopher, *Second Treatise on Civil Government*, 1690

"If man in the state of nature be so free, as has been said; if he be absolute lord of his own person and possessions, equal to the greatest, and subject to no body, why will he part with his freedom? Why will he give up this empire, and subject himself to the dominion and control of any other power? To which 'tis obvious to answer, that though in the state of nature he hath such a right, yet the enjoyment of it is very uncertain, and constantly exposed to the invasion of others; for all being kings as much as he, every man his equal, and the greater part no strict observers of equity and justice; the enjoyment of the property he has in this state is very unsafe, very unsecure. This makes him willing to quit this condition, which however free, is full of fears and continual dangers: And 'tis not without reason, that he seeks out, and is willing to join in society with others who are already united, or have a mind to unite

(Continued)

TEACHING IDEA

Class Discussion

Lead students in a discussion to compare the ideas about government expressed by John Locke to the ideas expressed by John Winthrop in "A Model of Christian Charity" on page 73.

BUILDING AP® SKILLS

Sourcing and Situation

Students should be taught to think about the connections between the source title and information provided by the source. An easy first step is to ask students to identify the context surrounding the document. For this example, have students brainstorm one major event, development, or process before, during, or after 1690 *in Europe* germane to the document and one major event, development, or process before, during, or after 1690 *in New England* connected to the document. Next, have students select one of their answers and write a one-sentence response about the historical situation in which John Locke wrote this document.

EXPLORING AP® THEMES

Work, Exchange, and Technology

This is an optimal moment to work on building out an understanding of select AP® themes associated with the course, as these relate to topics within and across time. For this particular task, students will be defining three major concepts: transatlantic trade, labor systems, and interrelatedness. At the beginning of the exercise, require students to define each term and/or process as a stand-alone term. Think of this as a note card definition. Next, students will incorporate the use of *all three terms* to compare and contrast the Chesapeake societies with settlements in New England. This will likely take more than two or three societies.

TRM Suggested Responses to Questions

TRM Module 2.3 AP® Analyzing Sources Handout 3

BUILDING AP® SKILLS

Contextualization

After covering a significant amount of information, it is a good idea to think about practicing contextualization as a way to bring closure or transition to another concept. Because students are reading about major developments in England that caused significant changes in the North American colonies, working on the skill of contextualization makes sense. To start, have students select one of the following key topics: transatlantic trade, labor systems, or American Indians. Next, students need to write a one-to-two sentence claim about its usefulness in explaining the context of significant changes within the British North American colonies. Students' last step is to select at least two terms to substantiate their claim. In this way, students are working on explaining broader processes to historical developments.

TEACHING IDEA

Check for Understanding

Remember the goal of this module is for students to understand the continuities and changes to colonial society in New England. To encourage students to make distinctions between pieces of evidence, consider assigning them accessible choices to illustrate important changes. For example, provide students with four legitimate choices and have them select the one issue they feel best represents the most significant changes in New England.

TEACHING IDEA

Incorporating Secondary Sources

Eminent historian of seventeenth-century New England, Edmund S. Morgan did much to advance our understanding of the reality of who the Puritans were, how they lived, and what they came to represent. An accessible read for students, *The Genuine Article*, focuses on several early American history topics, with special attention to the role of New England. Part One of the book is entirely devoted to New England history and might be more accessible than some of his other major works on Puritans. Teachers can select one of the short chapters to support their instruction.

---

for the mutual preservation of their lives, liberties and estates, which I call by the general name, property.

The great and chief end, therefore, of men's uniting into commonwealths, and putting themselves under government, is the preservation of their property. . . ."

Questions for Analysis

1. Identify the reasons Locke provides for the existence of a government.
2. Describe the historical developments that contribute to the ideas Locke expresses in this document.
3. Explain how Locke's ideas could be used to undermine royal authority.

Eager to restore political order and create a commercially profitable empire, William and Mary established the new colony of Massachusetts with a charter in 1692 (which included Plymouth, Massachusetts Bay, and Maine) and restored town meetings and an elected assembly. The 1692 charter granted the English crown the right to appoint a royal governor and officials to enforce customs regulations. It ensured religious freedom to members of the Church of England and allowed all male property owners (not just Puritans) to be elected to the assembly. In Maryland, too, the crown imposed a royal governor and replaced the Catholic Church with the Church of England as the established religion. And in New York, wealthy English merchants won the backing of the newly appointed royal governor, who instituted a representative assembly for the colony, and supported a merchant-dominated ruling assembly for New York City. Thus, taken as a whole, William and Mary's policies instituted a partnership between England and colonial elites by allowing colonists to retain long-standing local governmental institutions but also asserting royal authority to appoint governors and ensure the influence of the Church of England.

In the early eighteenth century, England's North American colonies took the form that they would retain until the revolution in 1776. In 1702, East and West Jersey united into the colony of New Jersey. Delaware separated from Pennsylvania in 1704. By 1710 North Carolina became fully independent of South Carolina. Finally, in 1732, the colony of Georgia was chartered as a buffer between Spanish Florida and the plantations of South Carolina.

REVIEW

How did conflict in England shape the North American English colonies during the late seventeenth and early eighteenth century?

Puritan Religious Anxieties Lead to Colonial Conflict

King William's War 1689–1697 war that began as a conflict over competing French and English interests on the European continent but soon spread to the American frontier. Both sides pulled American Indian allies into the war.

In the late seventeenth century, Puritan ministers were divided over the issue of increasing mercantile wealth and powers of Boston commercial elites. Some ministers denounced the materialism and accompanying irreligious behaviors. Other Puritan ministers created new theology that tried to meld the old and new. The Glorious Revolution in England (1688) offered Puritan ministers hope of regaining their customary authority. The outbreak of **King William's War** in 1689, however, quickly ended any notion of an easy return to peace and prosperity. Instead, continued conflicts, burdensome local taxes to pay for colonial defense against the French and their American Indian allies, and additional fears of American Indian attacks on rural settlements heightened the sense that Satan was at work in the region. Soon, accusations of witchcraft joined outcries against other forms of ungodly behavior. Even though the war ended with neither the French nor the English gaining substantial territory, the conflict left New Englanders with some lingering anxiety about their relations with the French, American Indians, and even the English government.

TEACHING IDEA

Check for Understanding

This is a turning point activity meant to spark a conversation about students' understanding of the extent to which the Glorious Revolution was a turning point for colonists in the British North American colonies. Using a graphic organizer, such as the example below, can help students brainstorm their thoughts. To explore a turning point, students need to think about the event itself (Glorious Revolution), what transpired before and after the event, and how that influenced the extent to which it was a turning point.

Before	Glorious Revolution	After

Belief in witchcraft had been widespread in Europe and England for centuries. It was part of a general belief in supernatural causes for events that could not otherwise be explained — severe storms, a suspicious fire, a rash of deaths among livestock. When a community began to suspect witchcraft, they often pointed to individuals who challenged cultural norms.

Women who were difficult to get along with, eccentric, poor, or simply too independent, most especially those widows inheriting and controlling land, were easy to imagine as cavorting with evil spirits and invisible demons. Some 160 individuals, mostly women, were accused of witchcraft in Massachusetts and Connecticut between 1647 and 1692. Puritans had executed fifteen witches, who had been prosecuted and convicted according to the laws of the time, prior to 1692 and the Salem accusations. At Salem they again targeted potentially powerful females as shown by the accusations, 80 percent of which Puritans aimed at women. Convictions of witches at Salem led to more executions. Puritans pressed one witch to death under the weight of stones, and offered the spectacle of public hanging for the other nineteen convicted witches. Many of the accused were poor, childless, or disgruntled women, but widows who inherited property also came under suspicion, especially if they fought for control against distant male relatives and neighbors. Considering Puritan theology of predestination and potentially visible sainthood, female inheritance posed a powerful force, which might have undermined Puritan patriarchal authority of religion and society.

Shortages of land in established Puritan communities intensified social conflicts. In New England, the land available for farming shrank as the population soared. By 1700, a New England wife who married at age twenty and survived to forty-five bore an average of eight children, most of whom lived to adulthood. In the original Puritan colonies, the population rose from 100,000 in 1700 to 400,000 in 1750, and many parents were unable to provide their children with sufficient land for profitable farms. A shortage of land led many New England men to seek their fortune farther west, leaving young women with few eligible bachelors to choose from. Marriage prospects were affected as well by battles over inheritance. Still, for most Puritan women daily rounds of labor shaped their lives more powerfully than legal statutes or inheritance rights. The result was increased migration to the frontier, where families were more dependent on their own labor and a small circle of neighbors. And even this option was not accessible to all. Before 1700, servants who survived their indenture had a good chance of securing land, but by the mid-eighteenth century only two of every ten were likely to become landowners.

Husbands and wives depended on each other to support their family. An ideology of marriage as a partnership took practical form in communities across the colonies, including New England. By the early eighteenth century, many colonial writers promoted the idea of marriage as a partnership, even if the wife remained the junior partner through common law and the concept of *femme covert*.

In Puritan towns, and also commercial cities such as Boston and Salem, the wives of artisans often learned aspects of their husband's craft and assisted their husbands in a variety of ways. Given the overlap between living spaces and workplaces in the eighteenth century, extended households of artisan women often cared for apprentices, journeymen, and laborers as well as their own children. Husbands meanwhile labored alongside their subordinates and represented their families' interests to the larger community. Both spouses were expected to provide

> **AP® TIP**
> Analyze the relationship between the Salem witch trials and the development of a patriarchal system in the New England colonies.

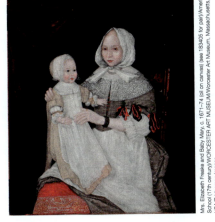

◀ **Mrs. Elizabeth Freake and Baby Mary (1674)** This portrait shows Elizabeth Freake, the wife of merchant John Freake, and their eighth child, Mary. Here Elizabeth and her daughter capture Puritan simplicity in their white head coverings and aprons, but also display their family's wealth and John Freake's commercial ties through their silk gowns and embroidered cloth. **What does this painting reveal about Puritan values and society?**

TEACHING IDEA

Incorporating Videos

Historian Mary Beth Norton offers an insightful analysis of the realities and myths of the witchcraft hysteria in late seventeenth-century New England. This lecture can be found on Gilder Lehrman's APUSH website on Period 2 and is titled, "In the Devil's Snare" (ap.gilderlehrman.org).

EXPLORING AP® THEMES

Geography and the Environment

To further develop an awareness of the AP® themes and especially the role geography and the environment played in the settlement patterns of New England, consider assigning students the following activity. This could be used as a bell ringer at the start of class or as a brief formative assessment at the end of class to assess students' understanding.

AP® Theme: Geography and the Environment	
Characteristic of Geography:	Subsequent Effect:
Characteristic of Environment:	Subsequent Effect:

Students begin by identifying a specific characteristic for both geography and the environment. Their next step is to describe a direct effect of the distinctive quality they identified. The goal is for students to see the role of geography and the environment in New England settlement patterns.

TRM Find **Handout 2.4 – New England: Geography and the Environment** in the Teacher's Resource Materials models of godliness and to encourage prayer and regular church attendance among household members.

The way of life of rural Puritans shared vast similarities to the ways most land-owning, but not plantation-owning, farming families lived in all the colonies. On farms, where the majority of Puritans lived, women and men played crucial if distinct roles. In general, wives and daughters labored inside the home as well as in the surrounding yard with its kitchen garden, milk house, chicken coop, dairy, or washhouse. Husbands and sons worked the fields, kept the livestock, and managed the orchards. Some families in all the colonies supplemented their own family labor with that of indentured servants, hired field hands, or, even in New England, a small number of enslaved Africans or African Americans. Most families exchanged surplus crops and manufactured goods such as cloth or sausage with neighbors. Some sold at market, creating an economic network of small producers.

Indeed, in the late seventeenth and early eighteenth centuries, many farm families in long-settled areas participated in a **household mode of production**. Men lent each other tools and draft animals and shared grazing land, while women gathered to spin, sew, and quilt. Individuals with special skills like midwifery or blacksmithing assisted neighbors, adding farm produce or credit to the family ledger. One woman's cheese might be bartered for another woman's jam. A family that owned the necessary equipment might brew barley and malt into beer, while a neighbor with a loom would turn yarn into cloth. The system of exchange, managed largely through barter, allowed individual households to function even as they became more specialized in what they produced. Whatever cash was obtained could be used to buy sugar, tea, and other imported goods.

New England colonial mothers, like rural mothers in other non-exporting farming communities, combined childbearing and child rearing with a great deal of other work. While some affluent families could afford wet nurses and nannies, most women fended for themselves or hired temporary help for particular tasks. Puritan mothers in New England with babies on the hip and children under foot hauled water, fed chickens, collected eggs, picked vegetables, prepared meals, spun thread, and manufactured soap and candles. In this way they shared common experiences with the rural women of every other British North American colony.

> **AP® TIP**
> Compare the development of social classes in seventeenth- and eighteenth-century New England with the development of social classes in the Chesapeake and Carolina.

REVIEW

- How did Puritan society change between 1630 and 1700?
- What aspects of Puritan society remained the same between 1630 and 1700?

AP® WRITING HISTORICALLY — Crafting a Thesis Statement Based on Continuity and Change

In Module 2-1, we discussed how to write an effective thesis statement based on the historical reasoning processes of comparison and causation. Here, we will show one way to approach answering an essay prompt that focuses on continuity and change.

Remember, historians draw conclusions about extended periods of time by examining the ways that some things stayed the same across a timespan even as other things changed. When you write any essay, you need to write a thesis statement that conveys a clear argument, followed by body paragraphs that interpret historical facts to prove the claims your thesis makes. Prompts that deal with continuity and change typically require you to focus on how much things changed or remained the same over the course of an era, or between two eras. In other words, how much change occurred? How much remained stable?

Take a moment to read the following prompt carefully before we walk through a step-by-step process for writing a strong thesis that fully responds to the question.

> Explain the reasons for continuities and changes in New England colonial society during the period from 1620 to 1700.

TRM Suggested Responses to Questions

BUILDING AP® SKILLS

Argumentation

One challenge for students as they write thesis statements is to develop the ability to weigh their categories of analysis. Put another way, they are to acknowledge claims, while privileging other claims. When students craft their thesis, be sure to encourage them to weigh the categories of analysis.

TEACHING IDEA

AP® Writing Historically Workshop

To further students' understanding of decoding a prompt and developing a thesis that addresses all parts of the prompt, consider assigning the elements of the question to small groups so students understand each element before writing the thesis. This question involves the use of the following categories:

- Continuities
- Changes
- New England Colonial Society
- 1620–1754

Assign one category to each group of three or four students and have them develop an explanation for the class to consider. Once all groups have presented, students are better equipped to grapple with the elements of the question.

Step 1 | Break down the prompt.

First, notice that this prompt asks you to explain the continuities and changes in New England colonial society between 1620 and 1700. This means that to answer it you must make an argument that addresses things that remained relatively the same during this period as well as things that changed. Your answer should explain *why* these continuities and changes took place.

Step 2 | List and categorize your relevant historical knowledge.

Now, let's take a few moments to gather ideas for continuities and changes that you can use in your answer. We suggest creating a chart like the example provided here, which breaks the topic of the prompt down into at least three sub-topics to focus a historical argument. In this example, we've chosen sub-topics a little more specific than the ones we've used in previous AP® Writing Historically exercises (economics, politics, technology, etc). Keep in mind that your sub-topics can (and should!) be a direct product of the specific time and place the prompt asks you to write about. Since what you have recently read about New England settlers' conflicts with American Indians and population growth during the seventeenth and early eighteenth centuries are all relevant to the essay prompt, we have chosen these for our sub-topics.

As you gather evidence, remember to choose at least one piece from early in the given time period and one piece from later in the time period to support your claim of either continuity or change for each sub-topic. Once you have outlined your pieces of evidence, you should be able to clearly see whether they lend themselves more to a claim of continuity or change. It's helpful to make a note for yourself, as we've done in our example chart. Make sure that your chart contains both continuities *and* changes before moving on.

To complete the chart, add a final column that addresses the reasons for each continuity or change — remember, you're being asked to *explain the reasons for* these developments and patterns.

Essay Topic: New England Colonial Society from 1620 to 1700

Sub-Topic	Evidence: Early New England Society	Evidence: Later New England Society	Claim: Change or Continuity	Reasons for Change / Continuity
Conflict with American Indians	Standish and Pilgrims against Massachusetts Indians in 1623; Pequot War, circa 1636–1638	Metacom's War, 1676	Continuity	Success of New England society led to expansion in both periods, causing conflicts with American Indians throughout the time period.
Population Growth	Early growth primarily from migration (example: Pilgrims in 1620s); Great Puritan Migration of 1630s	Later growth more from natural increase (large farm families, and spread of settlement to Connecticut and part of Maine that became New Hampshire)	Change	Events in England caused early influxes of migrants fleeing religious persecution, but later developments in England, such as the Glorious Revolution, led to fewer reasons for dissenters to leave.

You now have the blueprint for a thesis statement and a basic outline for an entire essay. A thesis that fully addresses a prompt about continuity and change will need to include at least one claim of continuity and one claim of change. The sub-topics from our pre-writing will come in handy for explaining the reasons for each claim of continuity or change.

At this point, you should take a moment to summarize your thoughts on paper by writing out one claim that asserts a continuity in one of your sub-topics. This statement should be directly comparative — that is, make sure to combine a reference to earlier and later aspects of the time period given in the prompt. A statement claiming continuity built from our example chart might look something like this:

> Between 1620 and 1700, the New England colonies continued to experience conflict with American Indians, starting with the initial conflicts between Myles Standish and the Massachusetts Indians in the 1620s, the Pequot War in the 1630s, and Metacom's War in the 1670s **[claim of continuity]**.

(Continued)

BUILDING AP® SKILLS

Making Connections

Throughout this section on writing historically, students have been encouraged to think across the time period to illustrate change over time. To help students reflect on their ability to demonstrate knowledge over a broad time period, consider giving them a timeline to place their sub-topics on. In this way, students are ensuring they are seeing the totality of the question.

1620 — 1754

TEACHING IDEA

Check for Understanding

As students list and categorize their evidence, be sure to encourage them not to create categories that are too restrictive, such as the use of proper nouns that are too specific. This type of categorization lends itself to a narrow view of a broad topic, which can be problematic in a timed-essay setting.

TEACHING IDEA

Check for Understanding

When writing about continuities and changes, remind students they are likely to develop more categories of analysis dealing with changes. Imbalance in this way is acceptable. The main factor to remember for students is the inclusion of continuities and not the balance between changes and continuities. Consider giving students two highlighter colors — one to highlight the change and one to highlight the continuity in their thesis.

Before moving on to address changes, follow up your comparative claim with an explanation of the reasons why there was continuity in this sub-topic of New England society:

> This continuing conflict with American Indians was caused by the expansion of English settlements as their population continued to grow and depend upon independent farms and new settlements **[reason for continuity]**.

Repeat this process with a claim about change drawn from one of your sub-topics. Again, the statement you write should be directly comparative. To mark a change that contrasts the earlier part of the time period against the later part, you may find it helpful to use a transition word such as *but*, *although*, *whereas*, or *however*. As you did with your continuity claim, follow up with an explanation of the causes of the change in this sub-topic of New England society. Here's one example of a change statement that addresses causation:

> Between 1620 and 1700, the reasons for population growth in the New England colonies changed from migration from England to natural reproduction **[claim of continuity]**. Internal conflict in England during the 1640s slowed Puritan migration to New England, however, the success of the New England colonies and their high birth rate contributed to the natural increase of the population of these colonies, despite the slowing of immigration **[reason for continuity]**.

Step 3 Write a thesis statement.

Now you're ready to write a thesis statement that incorporates both of these claims. Again, it's important to make sure that your thesis presents historical claims about both changes and continuities as well as explains the reasons for both change and continuity. Let's take a look at a thesis that effectively responds to our example prompt:

> New England colonial society in the period from 1620 to 1700 showed continuity in its ongoing conflicts with American Indians, which were caused by growth of the colonial population, but also experienced changes in the reasons for population growth — initially caused by those who dissented from Puritanism and left England and later caused by growth of the population through natural increase.

Notice that this thesis incorporates both the reasons for continuities *and* changes in New England between 1620 and 1700. It also includes a statement that alerts the reader to your "turn," where the thesis moves from continuities to changes: "but also experienced changes in the reasons for population growth" is the cue that we're changing directions.

ACTIVITY

Follow steps 1-3 to create your own thesis for the following essay prompt:

> Explain the continuities and changes in social conflicts in New England between 1620 and 1700.

Module 2-4

The British West Indies and South Atlantic Colonies

LEARNING TARGETS
By the end of this module, you should be able to:
- Explain how plantation economies based on staple crops developed along the southern Atlantic coast and in the British West Indies.
- Explain the reasons for the development of slavery as labor model in the colonies of the southern Atlantic coast and the British West Indies.
- Explain how slavery shaped daily life in the Carolinas.

THEMATIC FOCUS
Work, Exchange, and Technology
Geography and the Environment
Migration and Settlement

Throughout the late seventeenth and early eighteenth centuries, the colonies of the southern Atlantic coast and the British West Indies developed plantation societies that depended on the labor of enslaved Africans to harvest crops such as rice and sugar for export.

HISTORICAL REASONING FOCUS
Causation

Module 1-3 (p. 24) discussed the ways historians understand events by studying and interpreting their effects. When historians examine events and developments through the lens of causation, they study the interplay of both causes and effects in order to come to a better understanding of their significance. This analysis can be deepened by explaining not only how one event led to other events, but also discussing reasons why later events were affected. This approach to studying history treats it as a chain reaction — we can understand the relationships between historical developments as links in that chain.

For an example of how you might examine the ripple effects caused by historical developments, pay close attention to the beginning of this module, which notes how the financial success of early English plantation economies led to the founding of new colonies in North America. In 1609, the English established a small settlement on the Caribbean island of Bermuda. Later, rice and sugar plantations in Barbados encouraged the English to set up new plantation economies in North Carolina and South Carolina — because they hoped to generate even more wealth in a similar fashion. The combined effects of the wealth generated by North American plantation colonies and the intensification of English and Spanish imperial contests for the Americas then led to further expansion, including the founding of a Georgia colony.

TASK ▶ As you read this module, keep a close eye on the causes of historical developments and think about the reasons for their effects. Consider the larger significance of these effects — what do they mean in the grand scheme of history? How can they help explain why history unfolded as it did? Asking yourself these questions will help you sharpen your understanding of this period in American history.

TRM Suggested Responses to Questions

TEACHING IDEA

Incorporating Secondary Sources

Traditionally taught as a continuous pattern of Europeans enslaving Africans and transporting them to the Americas, the development of slavery in the British West Indies and North American colonies sometimes possesses an abstract quality for students. Incorporating historians' research can infuse nuance into this extremely complex historical development. Stephanie Smallwood's *Saltwater Slavery: A Middle Passage from Africa to American Diaspora* reimagines this process as she seeks to reconstruct this forced migration pattern from the enslaved persons' perspective. Chapter 6, in particular, is relevant to the topics in Module 2-4 and could be used as assigned reading.

In the seventeenth century, English investors, in partnership with the crown, sought opportunities for profitable exports by establishing plantation economies in the Caribbean, then known as the West Indies, and on lands south of Virginia. Because of the financial success of these efforts on islands in the West Indies, in 1660 the crown founded the Carolina colony. Much later, as a result of imperial rivalry with Spain for North American lands, the crown founded the Georgia colony in 1732 to secure the vast wealth generated in southern cash-crop colonies (Maryland, Virginia, North Carolina, and South Carolina).

APPLY THE TIP

When students think of settling in the Americas, most associate the colonies in British North America; however, no less important were the colonies in the West Indies. Consider having students identify at least three islands in the West Indies controlled by the British that had a significant effect on colonization patterns.

TRM Suggested Responses to Questions

TRM Module 2.4 AP® Analyzing Sources Handout 1

BUILDING AP® SKILLS
Causation

As stated in the module, causation means to think about both the causes and effects of historical developments. For instance, as students are considering why slavery developed in the way it did, they should also be cognizant of immediate effects. To assess students' understanding of this process, consider asking students to *identify* immediate causes for the use of tobacco and sugar as cash crops in the British West Indies. After students have successfully identified causes, have them *explain* the effects tobacco and sugar plantations had on the development of chattel slavery in the British West Indies.

TEACHING IDEA
Incorporating Primary Sources

Non-text documents present unique challenges for students. Given the lack of descriptions, students have to infer much about the document's relevance to a given topic. The source title is always the first stopping point for any document analysis because it situates the source in a specific context. For instance, this document is after Barbados transitioned from tobacco to sugar and moved to a race-based chattel labor system. Many students will not intuitively arrive at this conclusion. To help them along in this process consider providing two time periods with two questions. The time periods could be 1620–1640 and 1640–1660. Next, ask students to identify the primary crop(s) and source(s) of labor in each time period. Discussing possible answers to these questions allows students to have a better discussion about the import of the document.

Period 2: 1607–1754

MODULE 2-4 The British West Indies and South Atlantic Colonies

The English Compete for the West Indies

Hoping to mimic Spanish successes with tobacco in the Caribbean, English investors turned their sights to the islands in the early seventeenth century. In the 1620s, the English developed more permanent settlements on the Caribbean islands of St. Christopher, Barbados, and Nevis, which came to be known as the British West Indies during that era.

Barbados, with its highly profitable tobacco plantations, quickly emerged as the most attractive of the West Indies colonies. English migrants settled there in growing numbers, bringing in white indentured servants, many of whom were Irish and Scottish, to raise livestock in the early years, although cultivating tobacco and cotton soon took priority. English tobacco plantations throughout the West Indies quickly became the economic engine of English colonization and expansive **imperialism**. This economic expansion in turn led to demands for new forms of labor to ensure profitable returns on investment. Investors sent large numbers of the indentured servants across the Atlantic, and growing numbers of Africans were forced onto ships for sale in the Americas.

In the 1630s, falling tobacco prices resulted in economic stagnation on Barbados. By that time, however, a few forward-looking planters were already considering another avenue to wealth: sugarcane. English and European consumers absorbed as much sugar as the market could provide, but producing sugar was difficult, expensive, and labor intensive. In addition, the sugar that was sent from America needed further refinement in Europe before being sold to consumers. The Dutch had built the best refineries in Europe, but their small West Indies colonies could not supply sufficient raw sugar. By 1640 they formed a partnership with English planters, offering them the knowledge and financing to cultivate sugar on British-controlled Barbados, which was then refined in the Netherlands. That decision reshaped the economic and political landscape of North America and intensified competition for both land and labor. Thus, as the English developed an economy based on sugar in the West Indies, they also developed a harsh system of slavery.

imperialism A policy of expanding the border and increasing the global power of a nation, typically via military force.

AP® TIP
The causes of British expansion in the Americas, and its effects on England, North America, and Africa, are key topics for the AP® U.S. History Exam

AP® ANALYZING SOURCES

Source: Richard Ligon, *Map of Barbados*, 1657

About the source: Most of the writing on the map (particularly the small labels along the coastline) delineates individual plantation holdings by British sugar planters. Near the center of the island are these words: "The ten thousand acres of land which belong to the merchants of London."

Questions for Analysis
1. Describe at least three types of details that Ligon illustrated in this map.
2. Explain how the goals of the English colonists in Barbados influenced the details included in this map.
3. Explain how English goals for Barbados shaped the society that developed in the colony.

EXPLORING AP® THEMES
Work, Exchange, and Technology

Throughout the West Indies, geography and environment played a significant role in how each island developed. The map of Barbados offers clues to this by what information is not explicit on the document. This activity can be done in conjunction with the previous note about incorporating primary sources. Have students look up the definition to leeward and windward. Next, ask students to note on which side of the island they see more developments and ships. Finally, students should write a two-to-three sentence explanation of why the leeward side of the island developed more rapidly than the windward.

TEACHING IDEA
Incorporating Websites

Earlier in Module 2-2, the website Slave Voyages was mentioned as a resource to be utilized to examine the process of forced migration (slavevoyages.org). This resource is again immediately relevant because of the wealth of information and resources specifically connected to the growth of slavery in the West Indies. Teachers can utilize maps, videos, and example lesson plans.

Period 2: 1607–1754

The British West Indies Influence South Carolina

Sugar Manufacturing in the West Indies
This seventeenth-century engraving depicts the use of enslaved labor in the production of sugar in the West Indies. The Dutch, English, and French used enslaved labor to plant sugarcane and then cut, press, and boil it to produce molasses. The molasses was turned into rum and refined sugar, both highly profitable exports. **What activities are portrayed in this image? In what ways were the sugar and tobacco economies of the Western Hemisphere similar?**

By 1660 Barbados had become the first English colony with a black majority population. Twenty years later, there were seventeen enslaved people for every white indentured servant on Barbados. The growth of slavery on the island depended almost wholly on imports from Africa, since enslaved people in Barbados died faster than they could reproduce themselves. As an effect of high death rates, brutal working conditions, and massive imports, Barbados systematized its slave code, defining enslaved Africans as chattel — that is, as mere property more akin to livestock than to human beings. The booming sugar industry spurred the development of plantation slavery, and in turn gave rise to the slave codes that legally enforced slavery in the British West Indies.

REVIEW

How did the seventeenth-century Atlantic economy influence that of the West Indies?

The British West Indies Influence South Carolina

AP® TIP
Compare the motivations for settlement in the Carolinas with those in the Chesapeake and New England colonies.

In return for help in securing his rule after returning from exile and taking back the throne in 1660, and in hopes of creating financially rewarding colonies, Charles II granted the extensive lands that became the states of North and South Carolina to eight English nobles. In what is now South Carolina, English planters with West Indies connections quickly came to shape and dominate seventeenth-century society. They created a mainland version of Barbados by introducing enslaved Africans as laborers and carving out plantations. Early South Carolina plantations produced the labor-intensive cash crop of rice, which was then exported to the British West Indies, where it was used to feed enslaved Africans working in the tobacco, and later sugar, plantations.

AP® ANALYZING SOURCES

Source: *South Carolina Slave Code*, 1640

"And be it enacted, . . . That all negroes and Indians, (free Indians in amity with this government, and negroes, mulattoes and mestizos, who are now free, excepted) mullattoes or mestizos who now are, or shall hereafter be, in this Province, and all their issue and offspring, born or to be born, shall be, and they are hereby declared to be, and remain forever hereafter, absolute slaves, and shall follow the condition of the mother, and shall be deemed, held, taken, reputed and adjudged in law, to be chattels personal, in the hands of their owners and possessors, and their executors, administrators and assigns, to all intents, constructions and purposes whatsoever. . . ."

(Continued)

BUILDING AP® SKILLS

Making Connections

Throughout each module in the period 1607–1754, students should be aware of how the Atlantic world developed. The following can be a quick bell ringer activity at the beginning of the class or an exit card activity at the conclusion of class. Consider asking students to define an Atlantic economy by incorporating each of the following terms: West Indies, British North American colonies, Africa, and Great Britain. Answers will take multiple sentences and should be seen by students as a task driven to make connections and not as an assignment to develop an argument.

TRM Suggested Responses to Questions

TRM Module 2.4 AP® Analyzing Sources Handout 2

TEACHING IDEA

Incorporating Secondary Sources

Familiarizing students with the brutal nature of sugar plantations is one way to humanize the history they are studying. Historians Richard S. Dunn and Alan Taylor offer two different descriptions of the process of manufacturing sugar on islands in the West Indies. For a more elaborate description see Richard S. Dunn's *Sugar and Slaves: The Rise of the Planter Class in the English West Indies, 1624–1713*, Chapter 6, pages 188–201. To offer students a more concise version, see Alan Taylor's *American Colonies: The Settling of North America*, Chapter 10, pages 208–211.

▲ Differentiation

Although not a prerequisite, this activity pairs especially well with the use of either secondary source in the note about sugar plantations from the perspective of historians Richard S. Dunn and Alan Taylor.

Use the engraving on this page in concert with either secondary source. Have students compare the engraving with the description by the historian and answer two questions: What is in the engraving and the description? What is missing in the engraving that was included in the description?

TEACHING IDEA

Incorporating Primary Sources

In 1710 Thomas Walduck wrote a famous acrostic about Barbados. Provide students with the text found in the Teacher's Resource Materials. After students read and annotate the text, ask groups of students to agree, modify, or disagree with the meaning of the piece.

TRM Find **Handout 2.5 – Thomas Walduck's Acrostic** in the Teacher's Resource Materials.

BUILDING AP® SKILLS

Claims and Evidence in Sources

Before answering the questions for analysis, begin by asking students to describe one specific historical link between slavery in Barbados and slavery in South Carolina. By starting with a more holistic approach to the development described in the document, students are better equipped to answer the questions and illustrate meaningful connections.

BUILDING AP® SKILLS

Making Connections

Tracing the demographic shifts concomitant to the development of slavery as a labor system is a necessary connection for students to understand. To help further their understanding, simply provide a defensible conclusion and ask them to explain the reasons for this historical development. So it might look something like this:

Demographic shifts and patterns attendant to the development of slavery were seen across multiple slave societies. For instance, relative to the population as a whole, as the percentage of enslaved persons increased, the percentage of free white persons decreased. Explain how the concept of demographic shifts relates to the development of restrictive slave codes in South Carolina.

Period 2: 1607–1754

MODULE 2-4 The British West Indies and South Atlantic Colonies

> [B]e it further enacted by the authority aforesaid, That no person whatsoever shall permit or suffer any slave under his or their care or management, and who lives or is employed in Charlestown, or any other town in this Province, to go out of the limits of the said town, or any such slave who lives in the country, to go out of the plantation to which such slave belongs . . . without a letter . . . which . . . shall be signed by the master or other person having the care or charge of such slave. . . .
>
> [E]very slave who shall be found out of Charlestown, or any other town . . . or out of the plantation to which such slave belongs . . . if such slave lives in this country, without such letter . . . , or without a white person in his company, shall be punished with whipping on the bare back, not exceeding twenty lashes. . . .
>
> [A]nd be it further enacted by the authority aforesaid, That if any slave who shall be out of the house or plantation where such slave shall live, or shall be usually employed, or without some white person in company with such slave, shall refuse to submit to or undergo the examination of any white person, it shall be lawful for any such white person to pursue, apprehend, and moderately correct such slave; and if any such slave shall assault and strike such white person, such slave may be lawfully killed."

Questions for Analysis

1. Identify the restrictions placed on enslaved people by the Slave Code.
2. Describe the developments that led the South Carolina legislature to pass the Slave Code.
3. Describe the negative effects of the Slave Code on the society of South Carolina.
4. Explain how the Slave Code makes slavery a permanent condition for enslaved peoples.
5. Explain the reasons for the negative effects of the Slave Code on South Carolina society.

AP® TIP
Compare the land-owning classes in South Carolina, the Chesapeake, and the New England colonies.

The city of Charleston was one of the main ports receiving enslaved Africans in the early 1700s. The same trade in human cargo that brought misery to millions of Africans generated huge profits for traders, investors, and plantation owners and helped turn America's seaport cities, like Charleston, into centers of culture and consumption. The enslaved labor needed to produce sugar and rice in South Carolina was controlled by a small, but enormously wealthy class of landholders who oversaw the politics and economy of the colony. The necessity for a large labor force also created a population of enslaved Africans that by the early eighteenth century outnumbered white settlers in the colony.

REVIEW

- How did the economy of the West Indies affect the economy that developed in South Carolina during the late 1600s?
- In what ways was the economy of South Carolina distinct from that of the Chesapeake colonies during this time period?

Daily Life in Eighteenth-Century South Carolina

In South Carolina, immigrants could acquire land more easily than in older colonies such as New England, but their chances for economic autonomy were increasingly influenced by the spread of slavery. As hundreds and then thousands of Africans were imported into South Carolina in the 1720s and 1730s, economic and political power became more entrenched in the hands of planters and merchants. Increasingly, they controlled the markets, wrote the laws, and set the terms by which white as well as black families lived. Farms along inland waterways and on the frontier were crucial in providing food and other items for urban residents and for planters with large labor forces. But farm families depended on commercial and planter elites to market their goods and help defend their communities against hostile American Indians or Spaniards.

86

BUILDING AP® SKILLS

Causation

The following activity can be used as a bell ringer at the beginning of class. Causation is the focus of this module and students should be tracing causes and effects throughout the module to both understand historical developments and answer the Long-Essay Question at the conclusion of Module 2-4. To assess their understanding of immigration to the planter class consider asking students to identify *one specific* cause for European immigrants' continued reliance on the planter class.

MODULE 2-4 The British West Indies and South Atlantic Colonies

Daily Life in Eighteenth-Century South Carolina

Period 2: 1607–1754

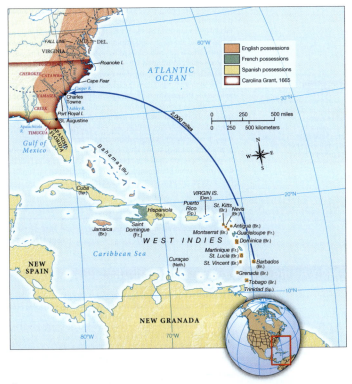

▲ **MAP 2.4 West Indies and Carolina in the Seventeenth Century** Beginning in the 1630s, sugar cultivation transformed West Indies colonies. The British consumed sugar in large quantities, ensuring the economic success of Barbados and its neighbors and a vast increase in the enslaved population. In the 1660s, Barbados planters obtained a charter for Carolina and sent many early settlers — white planters and merchants as well as enslaved laborers — to this mainland colony. **Given where Barbados is located, what potential commercial rivalries could it cause between European powers during the seventeenth century?**

> **AP® TIP**
> Analyze the extent of opportunity for land ownership in South Carolina, the Chesapeake, and New England during the early 1700s.

subsistence farmers Farmers who grow crops for their own needs rather than for profit.

During this time, more than two-thirds of white families in South Carolina owned no enslaved labor and farmed their own lands. Yet small farmers became increasingly dependent on large landowners, who controlled markets, political authority, and the courts. As in the Chesapeake and North Carolina colonies, artisans in South Carolina depended on wealthy planters for their livelihood. Artisans worked either for plantation owners directly, or for the shipping companies and merchants that relied on plantation orders.

In 1745, some forty thousand Scots who had supported the Catholic monarchs in England prior to the Glorious Revolution were shipped to the Carolinas after a failed rebellion. They were mostly Presbyterian Protestants, although there was also a significant minority of Catholics who had fought for independence from Great Britain. They swelled the existing ranks of **subsistence farmers** in the South Carolina backcountry. These farmers purchased few goods manufactured by artisans, relying instead on home production. To complicate matters, these tenant farmers relied almost entirely on large landowners for access to land to earn their sustenance, whether by farming or hunting.

EXPLORING AP® THEMES

Work, Exchange, and Technology

The development of a transatlantic world is a specific concept delineated in the Course Framework. To assess students' understanding of this process, consider asking students first to identify how Spain, France, and England all played a role in this historical development. Next, ask students to explain how the West Indies contributed to the changing nature of the transatlantic world in the seventeenth century.

TEACHING IDEA

Geography Instruction

The West Indies are divided up into the Bahamas, the Greater Antilles, and the Lesser Antilles. To help students understand how this influenced the history they are studying consider first defining these areas.

- Bahamas: Chain of islands off the immediate east coast of Spanish Florida
- Greater Antilles: Four large islands of Cuba, Hispaniola, Jamaica, and Puerto Rico
- Lesser Antilles: Chain of islands east of Puerto Rico to South America

Next, ask students to compare the imperial control visible in these groups. How might the imperial control within and across the groupings influence imperial relations in the seventeenth century?

TEACHING IDEA

Building Vocabulary

Throughout this module, students are making meaning of race-based chattel slavery and socioeconomic hierarchy. Focus on the causes for the development of a socioeconomic hierarchy in South Carolina. Consider asking students to identify at least two causes for this historical process.

Like other poor people in the colonies, some in South Carolina fared far worse than the few plantation owners who controlled its economy and politics. One-fifth of all white southerners owned little more than the clothes on their backs in the mid-eighteenth century. The few free black people found almost no opportunities for land ownership and economic independence, and the majority who were enslaved faced fully developed slave codes, based on those in Barbados, at the very outset of colonization. Thus, like their counterparts in North Carolina and the Chesapeake, they had little hope of gaining their freedom.

Economic changes driving expansion of existing and the development of new plantation systems in the British American colonies did produce positive effects for some colonists. Large landholders able to secure bound labor generated massive wealth that could be passed down to their families. The mechanization of cloth production in England during the eighteenth century also demanded vast amounts of labor and raw materials from both the English countryside and the colonies. It ensured, for example, the enormous profitability of indigo that was cultivated on southern plantations and used to dye English textiles in the mid-to-late eighteenth century. Thus, cash-crop indigo, tobacco, rice, and sugar plantations, each with profits built through the bound labor of hundreds of enslaved black people, benefited white plantation families, who passed their profits and land to their children, creating a class of inherited wealth.

> **AP® TIP**
> Be sure you can explain the effects of land ownership and slavery on the development of the social structures in South Carolina during the first half of the eighteenth century.

REVIEW

- What factors contributed to the rise of slavery in South Carolina?
- How did the economy of inherited wealth contribute to the expansion of slavery?

AP® WRITING HISTORICALLY — Writing a Full Essay

In Modules 2-1 through 2-3, you practiced how to think about, write a thesis for, and write topic sentences in support of a historical argument in response to an essay prompt. Now it's time to put all of that practice together into a full essay.

So far, these essay prompts have asked you to consider continuity and changes over time, explain causes, and draw comparisons; here we will focus on a prompt that deals primarily with *effects*. Although this may seem like a totally new historical reasoning process, it isn't. You may find it helpful to think of causation as a coin with two sides: on the one side, causes, and on the other, effects. Let's take a look at a prompt that focuses on a time and place in history you have just finished reading about:

> Explain the effects of economics in shaping the development of the societies of South Carolina and the English Caribbean in the period from 1660 to 1754.

Step 1 Break down the prompt and pre-write your response.

As with any other prompt, you should start by thinking broadly about what you know about the topic — in this case, about the societies in South Carolina and the British West Indies between 1660 and 1754. Don't forget that you are also being asked to make an argument that analyzes a specific aspect of those societies: the economics that shaped their development. You can apply any of the pre-writing strategies from previous modules to organize your thoughts.

Step 2 Write a thesis statement.

Next, generate a working thesis that fully answers the prompt. As you do so, you can use your pre-writing to guide your argument. Your essay should be a representation of both your content knowledge and historical reasoning skills. To make sure you are showcasing both, choose thesis claims — in this case, about economic effects — that you can defend with evidence. The following is an example of a strong thesis:

> The profitability of sugar as a cash crop for the English Caribbean colonies and the Carolinas shaped these societies by creating a large, enslaved population, a small upper class of wealthy landholders, and a class of poor whites who were forced to the margins of colonial society.

TEACHING IDEA

Building Vocabulary

Primary sources from the sixteenth and seventeenth century can be very challenging for students. To help students move beyond the obvious historical connections such as the selling of enslaved persons from the advertisement, consider asking them to define the relationship of "Windward" and "Rice Coast" to the growth of slavery in South Carolina.

TRM Suggested Responses to Questions

EXPLORING AP® THEMES

Social Structures

Historians have written about and debated the extent to which enslaved people possessed agency to alter their status as laborers. This activity is not meant to gauge the level of success but rather the frequency of resistance. Most historians acknowledge the fact that enslaved persons continuously resisted the terms of their status. Ask students to identify and explain at least one way in which enslaved people resisted the system of forced migration and enslavement.

BUILDING AP® SKILLS

Argumentation

Before having students engage with the Writing Historically activity, check to make sure students understand "effects of economics" from the Long-Essay Question. You can either brainstorm possible ways of categorizing this concept or you can provide a couple such as labor systems and Atlantic world to students to see if they can explain why those are relevant to the prompt.

TEACHING IDEA

Check for Understanding

Part of a strong thesis is adherence to the elements of the prompt. For instance, the sample thesis includes both effects and information on economics. Have students circle terms dealing with economics (profitability and cash crop) and underline terms relevant to effects (shaped, created, who were forced).

Step 3 Use your thesis claims to write topic sentences for each body paragraph, then use evidence to build a paragraph to support each topic sentence.

Now that you have a thesis, it's time to plan your essay. Just as you practiced in Module 2-2, one way to do this is to write all of the topic sentences for your body paragraphs up front. Once you have written your topic sentences, it's time to assemble your evidence. Historians use historical facts, analyzed in light of their arguments, to prove the topic sentences of their body paragraphs, which in turn, form their theses.

Let's say one of your topic sentences is:

> After the fall of tobacco prices in the 1630s, planters in Barbados turned to the production of sugar cane, which European consumers consumed in vast quantities.

This topic sentence helps you answer the prompt by establishing both an economic cause ("the profitability of sugar") and an effect ("large, enslaved labor force"). Now you're ready to prove this with historical evidence. Remember to use *ACE* here. The claim in the topic sentence of the paragraph is your answer. You now need to *cite* the evidence you pulled together in your pre-writing in order to support that claim. And finally, the most important part of the paragraph is the *explanation* of how your evidence supports your claim. Connecting your evidence to your claim in the body paragraph of an essay often requires a more detailed explanation than responses to Short-Answer Questions, as you can see in the following example:

> The production of sugar in the English Caribbean and the Carolinas required a large labor force, which led them to become oppressive slavery-based economies **[claim with evidence of cause]**. By the 1660s, enslaved Africans, who had already been a part of the transatlantic economy for over a generation, provided a convenient labor force for sugar production in Barbados **[evidence of effect]**. Charleston, in the Carolinas, served as a port of entry for many of these enslaved Africans, and the colony itself began to produce sugar, and later rice, as an easily consumable good for enslaved populations in the English colonies **[evidence of effect]**. By the late seventeenth century, slavery shaped English societies in the Caribbean and the Carolinas, where enslaved Africans outnumbered white colonists, and legal systems were formed to make slavery permanent in order to sustain the colonies' profitability **[explanation of effect]**.

ACTIVITY

Using your knowledge of history from Modules 2-1 through 2-4, answer the following essay prompt.

> Explain how physical environments shaped the development of English North American colonies in New England, the Chesapeake, and the Carolinas in the period from 1607 to 1754.

You may wish to use the following outline to guide your response:

I. Thesis statement presenting three claims
II. Claim 1 body paragraph
   A. Topic sentence presenting claim 1
   B. Cite evidence of claim 1
   C. Explain how evidence supports claim 1
III. Claim 2 body paragraph
   A. Topic sentence presenting claim 2
   B. Cite evidence of claim 2
   C. Explain how evidence supports claim 2
IV. Claim 3 body paragraph
   A. Topic sentence presenting claim 3
   B. Cite evidence of claim 3
   C. Explain how evidence supports claim 3

TEACHING IDEA

Connecting the Dots

If students are struggling with writing topic sentences have them graphically highlight the category of analysis in the exemplar topic sentence. Next, have students see where that is located in the thesis. This might help students visualize what a topic sentence is and the function it serves.

TEACHING IDEA

Check for Understanding

The use of evidence in any Long-Essay Question is more valuable than the volume of evidence stated. To emphasize this point, consider setting a limit of two pieces of evidence per paragraph — their goal being to develop the connections between the pieces of evidence as well as their separate connection to the question.

TEACHING IDEA

AP® Writing Historically Workshop

To make sure students understand the design or construction of an essay, provide groups of four or five students with five pieces of different colored paper. Students are tasked with defining what items would be found in the first two paragraphs of an essay. That is, the opening paragraph and first body paragraph. This should be done without their textbooks so they are not simply copying the book. Teachers are looking to see if students can identify contextualization, thesis, topic sentence, evidence, and explanation of evidence. Once students have correctly identified each section, consider having students put the papers in the order they should be presented in the essay. Sounds simple, but students routinely struggle with how to organize essays and this organization exercise can ground their understanding before writing the full essay.

TRM Suggested Responses to Questions

TEACHING IDEA

Geography Instruction

As students study the colonization of the British North American colonies they are presented with different groupings of colonies such as New England, Chesapeake, Middle Colonies, and southern colonies. It is a crucial prerequisite that students know the colonies within each of the aforementioned groupings. Consider beginning this module by having students identify which colonies are included in the Middle Colonies. As an add-on activity, you could have students color-code each grouping on a black and white map of the original thirteen British North American colonies. A reproducible version of this map is available in the Teacher's Resource Materials.

TRM Map 2A – The Thirteen Colonies

BUILDING AP® SKILLS

Contextualization

Because this module focuses on the skill of contextualization, consider discussing with students the *characteristics* of what it means to provide the context of historical developments and processes. When historians establish the context of a particular event, they center the explanation on an overarching concept, big-picture event, or broader process. To make this concept relevant, historians must substantiate this broad event with specific details. In this way, the historian provides a broader picture with specific details. To simplify this with students simply tell them contextualization's characteristics of a broader event with substantive, relevant details.

Module 2-5

The Middle Colonies

LEARNING **TARGETS**

By the end of this module, you should be able to:
- Explain how environmental factors affected the development of the Middle Colonies.
- Explain the reasons different settlers immigrated to the Middle Colonies.
- Explain the various factors that led to economic and social diversity in the Middle Colonies.

THEMATIC **FOCUS**

Geography and the Environment
Migration and Settlement
America in the World
American and Regional Culture

Starting in the 1660s, the English began to colonize the mid-Atlantic region in North America. The economies they developed were based on trade, and the societies they formed were built on relative religious and ethnic tolerance.

HISTORICAL REASONING **FOCUS**

Contextualization

You've probably heard the saying, "Context is everything" at least once before. Context is what helps you fully understand the world around you and the people in it. Let's think about a simple example of why context matters and how it shapes our perceptions. Let's say it's freezing outside and snowing — you put on a heavy jacket and gloves before heading out the door, and everyone you see outside is dressed similarly. Given the context of the weather, your outfit makes sense — but deciding to wear that same outfit in Hawaii in August would no doubt raise a few eyebrows. Or, take a more immediately relevant example: You are reading this book about U.S. history, and how much attention you pay to it probably makes sense within the context of how well you want to do on the AP® U.S. History Exam. The context that you want to get a high score therefore leads you to read more carefully.

This concept of contextualization also helps guide historians in examining and interpreting the past. Context shapes and influences events; you can think of it as providing reasons for what happens. The bigger and more important those reasons, the more relevant to the event that context is. For instance, the context of the Atlantic economy shaped the decisions made by British colonists in New England, the Chesapeake, and the Carolinas. All three regions, though very different in their own ways, created economies that "fit" within the context of the Atlantic trade system.

TASK ▶ As you read this module, pay special attention to the contexts that shaped the development of the Middle Colonies — and challenge yourself to think about how those contexts differed from those that influenced the societies that arose in New England, the Chesapeake region, and the South Atlantic colonies.

T he most important developments of the Middle Colonies occurred in the context of the restoration of the English monarchy in 1660, when English kings began granting North American land to men loyal to the crown. These land grants served both as rewards for the nobles who had secured the monarchy for Charles II, and also as part of a larger quest to build a North American empire that would produce vast wealth for the monarchy and English nation-state. During his reign, Charles II appointed English gentlemen as the proprietors of a string of colonies stretching from Carolina to New York.

The Middle Colonies grew in the coastal lands the British seized from the Netherlands in the 1660s, sandwiched between Maryland and the Puritan New England colonies. The English monarchy, first under the rule of Charles II and later under his brother King James II (r. 1685–1688), aggressively conquered, chartered, populated, and developed the Middle Colonies in less than twenty years, setting in place patterns that persisted long after the Glorious Revolution halted James's reign in 1688.

Colonies Develop in New York and New Jersey

Colonies Develop in New York and New Jersey

Leisler's Rebellion 1689 class revolt in New York led by merchant Jacob Leisler. Urban artisans and landless renters rebelled against new taxes and centralized rule.

After the English wrested control of New Amsterdam from the Dutch in 1664, they renamed it New York, appointing King Charles's brother James, whose title at the time was the Duke of York, to rule it. Later in 1664, the Duke of York divided the territory and granted a colony to Sir George Carteret, which eventually became the Middle Colony of New Jersey. English rule for the next twenty-four years imposed little change on the less than ten-thousand Dutch colonists in the Hudson River valley.

The Glorious Revolution, which deposed James II in 1688, also resulted in a class revolt in New York called **Leisler's Rebellion**. When news arrived of the Glorious Revolution in 1689, a German-born merchant named Jacob Leisler led a faction that rallied against the centralized rule and taxes that had been levied under James II, overthrowing the royal authorities appointed to run New York by the deposed king. Once in power, Leisler favored middling and lower-class colonists with government positions, and often sided with tenants in disputes against their landlords. Leisler's time in power was, however, short-lived. As royally appointed representatives of King William and Mary arrived to govern New York in 1691, they sided with the elites who had opposed Leisler. He was put on trial and executed later that year for leading a revolt against royal authority. The legacy of his rebellion, however, would live on. Class issues surrounding access to land would remain a critical issue in the Middle Colonies, and social unrest would persist into the 1740s, when protests echoing issues central to Leisler's Rebellion erupted on estates in New Jersey and along the Hudson River in New York.

> **AP® TIP**
> Compare Leisler's Rebellion and Bacon's Rebellion (Module 2-2). How were the causes, events, and outcomes similar and how did they differ? What are the reasons for these similarities and differences?

AP® ANALYZING SOURCES

Source: Letter from a Gentleman of the City of New York to Another. Concerning the Troubles which happened in that Province in the time of the late Happy REVOLUTION, 1689

"[A]gainst Expectation it soon happened, that on the last day of said Month of May, Capt. Leisler having a Vessel with some Wines in the Road, for which he refused to pay the Duty, did in a Seditious manner stir up the meanest sort of the Inhabitants (affirming, That King James being fled the Kingdom, all manner of Government was fallen in this Province) to rise in Arms, and forcibly possess themselves of the Fort and Stores . . . where a party of Armed Men came from the Fort, and forced the Lieut. Governor to deliver them the Keys; and seized also in his Chamber a Chest with Seven Hundred Seventy Three Pounds, Twelve Shillings, in Money of the Government. . . .

About a week after, Reports came from Boston, That their Royal Highnesses, the Prince and Princess of Orange were proclaimed King and Queen of England. . . . Capt. Leisler . . . did proclaim the same, though very disorderly, after which he went with his Accomplices to the Fort . . . and drank the Health and Prosperity of King William and Queen Mary with great Expressions of Joy.

Two days after, a printed Proclamation was procured by some of the Council, . . . appointed to collect the Revenue until Orders should arrive from England. . . . But as soon as those Gentlemen entered upon the Office, Capt. Leisler with a party of his Men in Arms, and Drink, fell upon them at the Custom-House, and with Naked Swords beat them thence, endeavoring to Massacre some of them, which were Rescued by Providence. Whereupon said Leisler beat an Alarm, crying about the City, 'Treason, Treason.' . . .

The said Capt. Leisler, finding almost every man of Sense, Reputation, or Estate in the place to oppose and discourage his Irregularities, caused frequent false Alarms to be made, and sent several parties of his armed Men out of the Fort, drag'd into nasty [Jails]. . . Gentlemen, and others, . . . without any Process, or allowing them to Bail. . . .

In this manner he the said Leisler, with his Accomplices, did force, pillage, rob and steal from their Majesties good Subjects within this Province, almost to their utter Ruin, vast Sums of Money, and other Effects. . . ."

Questions for Analysis
1. Identify the actions Leisler took after receiving word of the overthrow of James II, according to this letter.
2. Describe the author's attitude toward Leisler's Rebellion.
3. Explain how this document illustrates the reasons for Leisler's Rebellion.

EXPLORING AP® THEMES
American and Regional Culture

Colonization of British North America was a varied and complex process. One specific way in which the patterns of colonization differed was the role of religion. Consider asking students what role religious institutions played in mitigating internal rebellions in other colonies such as New England. This buttresses an understanding of how religion was a central factor in the development of colonial societies.

TRM Suggested Responses to Questions

TRM Module 2.5 AP® Analyzing Sources Handout 1

BUILDING AP® SKILLS
Sourcing and Situation

This document is a useful source to teach students the importance of tone and how it influences the purpose or point of view of an author. Consider having students underline any words or phrases they connect with tone. Examples from the document include the following: he refused, Seditious manner, rise in Arms, forcibly possess, very disorderly. Next, ask students to make a connection between the tone and the author's purpose or point of view about Leisler's Rebellion.

BUILDING AP® SKILLS
Claims and Evidence in Sources

To further explore how documents influence our understanding of the past, consider asking students to compare and contrast the book's definition of Leisler's Rebellion with that of the source provided in the textbook. How many details found in the document are referenced in the book's description? Leaving bias aside as something present in all historical documents, what specific conditions might account for the way the "Gentleman of the City of New York" recalls the rebellion?

MODULE 2-5 The Middle Colonies

Period 2: 1607–1754

▸ **Wealth Inequality in Northern Cities, 1690–1775** During the eighteenth century, the wealth of merchants rose much faster than that of artisans and laborers. **Over this period, how did the wealth of the top 10 percent of this population change in relation to the next wealthiest 30 percent and the poorest 60 percent?**

Data from Gary B. Nash, *The Urban Crucible: Social Change, Political Consciousness, and the Origins of the American Revolution* (Cambridge, MA: Harvard University Press, 1979).

BUILDING AP® SKILLS

Claims and Evidence in Sources

When students are presented with quantitative documents they should look for a way to illustrate historical trends or patterns from the source. Provide the following three steps to help students accomplish this task (possible answers provided in italics):

1. What is the big picture historical concept in this chart? (*wealth in northern urban areas*)
2. What result is evident in the chart? (*wealthy controlled more*)
3. What is the time period? (*establishment of colonies to American Revolution*)

Next, have students develop the answers into a one-to-two sentence explanation. A possible answer could be: *The chart illustrates the stratification of wealth that occurred from the establishment of colonies up until the American Revolution. This trend illustrates how the wealthy controlled more colonial assets over time.*

TEACHING IDEA

Building Vocabulary

An important and distinctive characteristic of the Middle Colonies was the polyglot nature of the populations, especially in urban areas. Consider having students identify a list of the different racial and ethnic groups in New York from 1607 to 1740.

TEACHING IDEA

Challenging Misconceptions

For many students, slavery is regional — to the southern colonies — and has less of an impact in northern colonies and cities over time. This is a misconception. Students need to be aware that although southern colonies, and later states, embraced and strengthened their hold over a chattel slavery system, northern colonies were complicit in the early years of slavery's development. Perhaps no city was more intricately linked to this process than New York City. Consider having students write an explanation that compares the lives of the enslaved in New York City and Charleston in the period before 1763.

In the 1690s, Dutch landholding families and wealthy English merchants in New York gained the backing of the newly appointed royal governor, who instituted representative assemblies through elections dominated by elite landlords. New York City already had a relatively diverse population, including small numbers of Jewish merchant families who had migrated when it was known as New Netherlands, and it evolved as a center of commerce in the Atlantic economy. The colony would exert extensive economic, cultural, and social influence throughout the eighteenth century.

The emergence of an elite class of merchants in New York revealed growing colonial inequality. Wealthy urban merchants and professionals lived alongside a middle class of artisans and shopkeepers, as well as a growing underclass comprised of unskilled laborers, widows, orphans, the elderly, the disabled, and the unemployed. The colony of New York was also a society with an enslaved population. Black people accounted for about 14 percent of its inhabitants by the late 1770s. By the 1710s, New York City hosted the second largest slave market in the mainland colonies. While some enslaved people who passed through this market worked on agricultural estates in the Hudson River valley and New Jersey, even more labored as dockworkers, seamen, blacksmiths, and household servants in New York City. These enslaved laborers sometimes lived in slaveholders' homes, but more often they resided together in separate, impoverished communities. Symbolizing their lack of acceptance by the white population, black people, both free and enslaved, were regularly taken outside the city limits for burial.

AP® TIP
Compare the social classes that developed in New York with those that developed in the Chesapeake and New England. What evidence can you cite to explain the causes of those similarities and differences?

REVIEW

How did international conflicts shape the colony of New York during the seventeenth and eighteenth centuries?

Penn's Goal of a Peaceable Kingdom

In 1681, King Charles II granted the lands that would become the colonies of Delaware and Pennsylvania to William Penn, a convert to a pacifist Protestant sect known as the Society of Friends, or Quakers. Quakers were considered radical and were severely persecuted in England, and so Penn founded Pennsylvania as a Quaker religious haven in North America. As governor of the colony, Penn moved to Philadelphia in 1682, and, unlike other English colonial proprietors, personally governed it.

William Penn provided a more inclusive model of colonial rule. He established friendly relations with the local Lenni-Lenape Indians and drew up a Frame of Government in 1682 that recognized religious freedom for all Christians and allowed all property-owning men to vote and hold office. Under Penn's leadership, Philadelphia grew into a bustling port city, while the rest of Pennsylvania attracted thousands of middle-class farm families, most of them Quakers, as well as artisans and merchants. During this time, Africans and African Americans formed only a small percentage of Pennsylvania's population, despite the notable concentration of enslaved black dockworkers, porters, and seaman in Philadelphia in the late seventeenth century.

Penn's Goal of a Peaceable Kingdom

AP® ANALYZING SOURCES

Source: William Penn, *The Frame of the Government of the Province of Pennsylvania*, 1682

"I know what is said by the several admirers of monarchy, aristocracy and democracy, which are the rule of one, a few, and many, and are the three common ideas of government, when men discourse on that subject. But I choose to solve the controversy with this small distinction, and it belongs to all three: any government is free to the people under it (whatever be the frame) where the laws rule, and the people are a party to those laws, and more than this [anything else] is tyranny, oligarchy, or confusion. . . .

[W]hen all is said, there is hardly one frame of government in the world so ill designed by its first founders, that, in good hands, would not do well enough; and story tells us, the best, in ill ones, can do nothing that is great or good; witness the Jewish and Roman states. Governments, like clocks, go from the motion men give them; and as governments are made and moved by men, so by them they are ruined too. Wherefore governments rather depend upon men, than men upon governments. Let men be good, and the government cannot be bad; if it be ill, they will cure it. But if men be bad, let the government be never so good, they will endeavor to warp and spoil it to their turn."

Questions for Analysis
1. Identify the attributes of a good government according to Penn.
2. Identify the kinds of government Penn draws on to make his case.
3. Describe the requirements that men who would create a good government must meet.
4. Explain the context influencing Penn's claim that, "Let men be good, and the government cannot be bad; if it be ill, they will cure it."

In its first four decades, the population of Pennsylvania boomed as immigrants were drawn by Penn's tolerant policies. These colonists demanded more land and pushed westward to find unclaimed territory, or lands for sale. At the beginning of the eighteenth century, German and Scots-Irish immigrants joined Anglo-American settlers in rural areas of New Jersey, Pennsylvania, and Delaware. Many immigrants to Pennsylvania settled in areas that were dotted with Iroquois, Algonquian, and Siouan towns. Perhaps inheriting Penn's peaceable vision, or maybe due to a lack of coordinated colonial military effort to dislodge American Indians, Pennsylvanian colonists mostly negotiated with them to purchase farmland.

At the same time, groups of Delaware and Shawnee Indians, who had been pushed out of New Jersey and the Ohio Valley by pressure from settlers, also moved into

MAP 2.5 Frontier Settlements and American Indian Towns in Pennsylvania, 1700–1740 German and Scots-Irish immigrants to Pennsylvania mingled with American Indian settlements in the early eighteenth century as Delaware and Shawnee groups were pushed west from New Jersey. In the 1720s and 1730s, however, European migration escalated dramatically in the fertile river valleys. In response, once-independent American Indian tribes joined the Delaware and Shawnee nations to strengthen their position against the influx of colonists. **What environmental factors contributed to the location of the European settlements on this map?**

TRM Suggested Responses to Questions

TRM Module 2.5 AP® Analyzing Sources Handout 2

BUILDING AP® SKILLS
Contextualization

At this point in the module, students are prepared to practice the skill of contextualization. Consider providing students with a broad process and accompany that with a question that allows them to distill their focus so they can develop the facts to substantiate the big picture. For instance, *increased migration* is a broad event connected to this module. Ask students the following: How did an increasingly diverse immigrant population affect relations with American Indians? In this way, you have provided students with a pathway to illustrate the characteristics of contextualization delineated at the beginning of this module.

BUILDING AP® SKILLS
Comparison

If you are looking to develop students' understanding of how to compare colonies, consider having students compare the treatment of American Indians in Pennsylvania and the Massachusetts Bay Colony. Students should expect to find some similarities and very distinct differences.

EXPLORING AP® THEMES
Geography and the Environment

Map 2.5 can be used to teach basic geography skills. Consider asking students to connect migration patterns over the first half of the eighteenth century (1700–1750) with the import of waterways. Also, be sure to ask students to make a connection between American Indian settlements in the first half of the eighteenth century (1700–1750) with the import of waterways.

MODULE 2-5 The Middle Colonies

> " Let men be good, and the government cannot be bad; if it be ill, they will cure it. "
>
> — William Penn, 1682

Pennsylvania. They negotiated with colonists, the colonial government, and other American Indian tribes to establish new farming communities for themselves. All along the Pennsylvania frontier, the lines between American Indian and European immigrant settlements blurred. Many communities prospered in the region, with white settlers exchanging European and colonial goods for access to American Indian-controlled orchards, waterways, and lands.

Of the migrants attracted to Penn's colony in the early eighteenth century, Benjamin Franklin was the most notable. Franklin was apprenticed to his brother, a printer, an occupation that matched his interest in books, reading, and politics. At age sixteen, Benjamin published (anonymously) his first essays in his brother's paper, the *New England Courant*. Two years later, a family dispute led Benjamin to try his luck in New York and then Philadelphia. His fortunes were fragile, but he combined hard work with a quick wit, good luck, and political connections, which together led to success. In 1729 Franklin purchased the *Pennsylvania Gazette* and became the colony's official printer.

REVIEW

How did colonists' motivations for settlement in New York, New Jersey, and Pennsylvania during the late 1600s differ?

Expansion and Conflict in Pennsylvania

redemptioners Immigrants who borrowed money from shipping agents to cover the costs of transport to America, loans that were repaid, or "redeemed," by colonial employers. Redemptioners worked for their "redeemers" for a set number of years.

AP® TIP
Be sure you can explain the causes of and reactions to increased immigration to the Pennsylvania colony between 1700 and 1750.

After William Penn died in 1718, his sons and closest advisers struggled to gain control over the colony. A surge of new laborers came to the British North American colonies in the 1720s, and many settled in the Middle Colonies. The population of the Middle Colonies swelled from 50,000 in 1700 to 250,000 in 1750. The increase was due in part to wheat prices. Hoping to take advantage of this boon, Anglo-Americans, Germans, Scots-Irish, and other non-English groups settled western Pennsylvania and New York's Mohawk River valley, hoping to labor on or purchase grain farms in the Middle Colonies. Shipping agents offered many people seeking passage to America loans for their passage that were repaid when the immigrants found a colonial employer who would redeem (that is, repay) the agents. In turn, these **redemptioners**, who often traveled with families, labored for that employer for a set number of years, much like indentured servants. The redemption system was popular in the Middle Colonies, especially among German immigrants who hoped to establish farms on the Pennsylvania frontier. While many succeeded, their circumstances could be extremely difficult.

In prosperous parts of the Middle Colonies, many landless laborers abandoned rural life and searched for urban opportunities during the first half of the eighteenth century. They moved to Philadelphia or other towns and cities in the region, seeking jobs as dockworkers, street vendors, or servants, or as apprentices in one of the skilled trades. But the surplus of redemptioners, and other immigrant laborers too poor to purchase land, meant there were far fewer jobs than job-seekers.

Aside from German emigrants, in the 1720s and 1730s Scots-Irish settlers also flooded into Pennsylvania, fleeing bad harvests and high rents back home. During this time, conflicts erupted regularly between the earlier British Quaker colonists and newer immigrant settlers, as well as between the various recent immigrant groups. Scots-Irish and German colonists took each other to court, sued land surveyors, and even burned down cabins built by their immigrant foes. Some English Quakers viewed the actions of these newcomers as threats to their society. The new immigrants also overwhelmed native communities that had welcomed earlier settlers. American Indians were increasingly pushed to the margins as growing numbers of European settlers encroached on frontier territories. In 1728 James Logan, William Penn's longtime secretary, complained that the "[Germans] crowd in upon us and the Irish yet faster." For Logan, these difficulties were worsened by what he considered the "idle," "worthless," and "indigent" habits of Scots-Irish and other recent arrivals.

Anglo-Americans hardly set high standards themselves, especially when negotiating with American Indians. Even in Pennsylvania, where William Penn had previously established a reputation for (relatively) fair dealing, the desire for American Indian land led to dishonesty and trickery. Conflicts among American Indian nations also aided colonial leaders in prying territory from

---

TEACHING IDEA

Building Vocabulary

Historians often use labels such as rural, urban, suburban, or hinterland to describe places. Students, however, may be less familiar with these terms and therefore will struggle to decode them when reading. Consider pausing at this point in the reading and checking to see if students can define both urban and rural. Next, have students identify different occupations in each of these areas.

- **Urban:** Relates to densely populated city centers with more diverse economic opportunities. Occupations: artisans, dock workers, apprentices.

- **Rural:** Relates to more dispersed population centers along the frontier of colonies. Occupations: Indentured servant, subsistence farmer, planter elite.

APPLY THE TIP

Backcountry unrest and coastal elite conflict is a recurring phenomenon throughout seventeenth- and eighteenth-century colonial history. Consider building out this concept by having students pick one ethnic group in the backcountry, delineate their grievances, and explain their reactions to their respective colonial government. In this way, students are developing an understanding of inter-colonial conflict, which is an essential part of this time in history.

TEACHING IDEA

Check for Understanding

One way to assess students' understanding of the causes of colonization in the Middle Colonies is to have them take a stance on a historical question. For instance, consider having students decide whether the need for land or relations with American Indians defined migration patterns more in eighteenth-century Pennsylvania. Divide the class in half and have students debate their stance with supporting evidence.

Walking Purchase 1737 treaty that allowed Pennsylvania to expand its boundaries at the expense of the Delaware Indians. The treaty, likely a forgery, allowed the British to add territory that could be walked off in a day and a half.

AP® TIP

Compare the relations between colonists and American Indians in Pennsylvania to those in both the Chesapeake and in Massachusetts Bay.

them. Hoping to assert their authority over the independent-minded Delaware Indians, Iroquois chiefs insisted that they held rights to much of the Pennsylvania territory and therefore must be the ones to negotiate with colonial officials. Those colonial authorities, however, produced a questionable treaty supposedly drafted by Penn in 1686 that allowed them to claim large portions of the contested territory. James Logan "discovered" a copy of this treaty, which allowed the English to control an area that could be walked off in a day and a half. Seeking to maintain control of at least some territory, the Iroquois finally agreed to this **Walking Purchase**. The Delaware tribe, far smaller, was then pressured into letting Pennsylvania officials walk off the boundaries. Through this and other deceptions colonists dispossessed the Iroquois and Delaware of vast lands in Pennsylvania during the first half of the eighteenth century.

However, some religiously minded immigrants worked to improve relations with American Indians in Pennsylvania, at least temporarily. The tone had been set by William Penn's Quakers, who generally accepted American Indian land claims and tried to pursue honest and fair negotiations. German Moravians, who settled in eastern Pennsylvania in the 1740s, developed good relations with area tribes. On Pennsylvania's western frontier, Scots-Irish Presbyterians established alliances with Delaware and Shawnee groups. These alliances, however, were rooted less in religious principles than in the hope of profiting from the fur trade as these tribes sought new commercial partners when their French allies became too demanding.

REVIEW

- What were the results of William Penn's interactions with American Indians?

AP® WRITING HISTORICALLY | **Presenting Context in a Historical Argument**

Contextualizing a topic is key to making an effective historical argument. Choosing the right context for your thesis will help focus your reader's attention and open the door to your main argument. This is why, regardless of the details of a given prompt, or what type of essay prompt you encounter, you should always start your essay by presenting context in direct response to the prompt. Remember, context is an influence that shapes a given situation. Starting off with a meaningful context helps to set up the parameters of your response by illustrating how important background influences helped shape the topic at hand. In other words, it sets the scene for the argument you're about to make. The following essay prompt asks you to draw on what you have learned in this module:

> Explain the effects of two developments in England on the New York colony in the period from 1650 to 1700.

You are probably wondering how presenting a contextualization statement will help you craft an effective historical argument about effects. Here, we'll walk through how to craft an effective one, and show how it strengthens a response to this prompt.

Step 1 Break down the prompt and pre-write your response.

The first thing you should do is what you've been doing so far in response to essay questions: break down the prompt and pre-write to organize your thoughts on its topic — in this case, the effects of two developments in England on the New York colony between 1650 and 1700, along with the causes that underpin them. One development during this period could be the restoration of the monarchy in 1660, which led King Charles II to pursue the conquest of New Amsterdam. Another could be the overthrow of James II in the Glorious Revolution, which was a factor that spurred Leisler's Rebellion in 1689.

(Continued)

TEACHING IDEA

Check for Understanding

Even though this module focuses on contextualization, students should be mindful of other skills as they read. For instance, consider pausing to devote some time to check for how well students are grasping change over time. You could give them a time period (1682–1737) and ask that they address a major historical change such as relations with American Indians in Pennsylvania to develop a one or two sentence explanation illustrating the change.

▲ Differentiation

This activity could easily be expanded into a research paper for students who need more of a challenge. Allow students to select the major historical change during a specific time that they believe had the most impact. Students should research primary and secondary sources to back up their claims.

TRM Suggested Responses to Questions

TEACHING IDEA

Check for Understanding

If students are struggling to begin the Writing Historically activity, consider reminding them of the characteristics of contextualization: a broader historical process plus details that substantiate their understanding of the connection between the broad process they selected and the prompt.

TEACHING IDEA

AP® Writing Historically Workshop

Because students are allowed to make comparisons with different regions to establish contextualization, consider providing students with the following options: New England, Chesapeake, and southern colonies from 1630–1700. Students can select the region they know best and develop contextualization by showing how the development of one of these regions influenced events in New York. This way, you are providing the correct broad process and students get to focus their energies on explaining how their selection is relevant.

TEACHING IDEA

Class Discussion

Create a T-chart for this next activity, which helps explain the use of both immediate context and preceding context. Next, ask students to identify which row relates to the broader historical processes.

Immediate Context, Evidence for Immediate Context, or Influence of Immediate Context on the Topic | Preceding Context, Evidence for Preceding Context, and Influence of Preceding Context on the Topic.

After they identify the answer (Evidence for Immediate Context and Evidence for Preceding Context), ask them to explain why their answer is correct. They should use language from the Writing Historically exercise if they struggle to explain their selection. For example, both use a broader event or process such as the Glorious Revolution and the English Civil War.

BUILDING AP® SKILLS

Contextualization

Part of the characteristic of contextualization is the use of specific details to substantiate the broader event or process relevant to the prompt. Using the chart provided, which explains the use of both immediate context and preceding context, ask students to identify which row relates to specific details to substantiate the broader event or process.

Immediate Context, Evidence for Immediate Context, or Influence of Immediate Context on the Topic | Preceding Context, Evidence for Preceding Context, and Influence of Preceding Context on the Topic.

After they identify the answer (Influence of Immediate Context on the Topic and Influence of Preceding Context on the Topic), ask them to explain why their answer is correct. They should use language from the Writing Historically exercise if they struggle to explain their selection. For example, both specific ideas are relevant to the broader process.

TEACHING IDEA

Check for Understanding

If students struggle to see where or how the exemplar connects the contextualization to the prompt, ask students to identify where they think the author is connecting the ideas to the question.

Period 2: 1607–1754

MODULE 2-5 The Middle Colonies

Step 2 Set the context.

From there, quickly scan your pre-writing for events and developments that form an *immediate context* that helps explain the surrounding background of the topic at hand. For instance, developments in England also affected colonies other than New York during this same time period. Recall James II's unpopular Dominion of New England and how it was overturned after the Glorious Revolution in 1688. You should keep in mind that sometimes your pre-writing observations will not easily lend themselves to picking out details of context from within the prompt's time range (in this case, 1650–1700). When this happens, you should look for a *preceding context* — that is, an event or development from a time period immediately before the one named in the prompt.

Next, you should think about how to prove that the context you've chosen exists — and how you'll explain why its influence on the topic of the prompt is important. One way to quickly do this is to create a table. The following examples show both an immediate context and a preceding context.

Immediate Context	
Immediate Context:	Turmoil in England in the late 1600s affected its policies toward its colonies in British North America.
Evidence for Immediate Context:	James II sought to strengthen his rule in England and its colonies. For example, he created the Dominion of New England in 1686 to better control the New England colonies, but his overthrow in the Glorious Revolution in 1688 led to the end of the Dominion in the old Puritan colonies in 1689.
Influence of Immediate Context on the Topic:	English policies during this period sought to determine who would control England and the empire, and in turn, conflicts over these policies determined who had power in the various colonies.

Preceding Context	
Preceding Context:	Well before the founding of New York, domestic English policies affected British colonies in North America.
Evidence for Preceding Context:	For example, persecution of Catholics in England during the 1630s led to the founding of Maryland and the English Civil War of the 1640s led to a slowing of immigration to New England.
Influence of Preceding Context on the Topic:	In this way, English policies affected the British North American colonies well before 1650.

Step 3 Connect the context to your thesis.

Now it's time to write your contextualization statement. A full contextualization statement should be at least three sentences long. Remember, you're not just stating the context — you are also proving its existence by citing historical evidence *and* offering an explanation of its influence on the topic of the prompt. In other words, you're not only asserting its relevance but describing *how* relevant it is. Here is an example of an immediate context statement for this prompt:

> Turmoil in England between 1650 and 1700 affected many British colonies in North America. James II sought to strengthen his rule in England and its colonies. For example, he created the Dominion of New England in 1686 to better control the New England colonies, but it came to an end in 1689, after his overthrow in the Glorious Revolution. English policies during this period sought to determine who would control England and the empire, and in turn, conflicts over these policies determined who had power in the various colonies.

Here is an example of a preceding context statement for this prompt:

> Well before the founding of New York in 1664, domestic English policies affected British colonies in North America. For example, persecution of Catholics in England during the 1630s led to the founding of Maryland, and the English Civil War of the 1640s caused English immigration to New England to slow. In this way, English policies affected the British North American colonies well before 1650.

You may be wondering where either of these context statements fit into your essay as a whole. Since context helps set the stage for the topic, the best strategy is usually to present it early on in your response. You may find it helpful to think of it as a setup for your thesis statement — it's a bridge between the larger topic of the prompt and the argument you are about to make in response to it. The contextualization statements we just wrote, for instance, could lead into the following thesis statement:

> Throughout the mid-to-late seventeenth century two internal English developments — the restoration of the monarchy in 1660 and the Glorious Revolution in 1688 — determined who controlled the colony of New York.

Notice how each of the contextualization statements sets up the claim that two domestic English developments determined who controlled New York colony: first the restoration of Charles II, and then the overthrow of James II during the Glorious Revolution. In your essay, evidence from your pre-writing, such as the establishment of the colony in 1664 and Leisler's Rebellion after the Glorious Revolution, will help prove these claims.

ACTIVITY

Carefully read and respond to the following essay prompt.

> Explain the effects of religion on the Pennsylvania colony in the period 1682 to 1754.

As you begin to think about your essay, consider what you learned up through this module to break down the prompt and pre-write. In writing your introductory paragraph, be sure to begin with an immediate or preceding context that leads into a thesis statement that presents multiple claims. From there, write body paragraph topic sentences that will guide your response, keeping in mind that each topic sentence should present a claim that is part of your thesis. Finally, complete your essay, proving each of your claims by explaining how the historical evidence you've chosen to include proves your argument. Here is a brief outline to help you plan your essay:

I. Introductory paragraph
   A. Immediate/preceding context statement
      1. Cite evidence of immediate/preceding context
      2. Explain influence of immediate/preceding context
   B. Thesis statement presenting three claims

II. Claim 1 body paragraph
   A. Topic sentence presenting claim 1
   B. Cite evidence of claim 1
   C. Cite additional evidence of claim 1
   D. Explain how evidence supports claim 1

III. Claim 2 body paragraph
   A. Topic sentence presenting claim 2
   B. Cite evidence of claim 2
   C. Cite additional evidence of claim 2
   D. Explain how evidence supports claim 2

IV. Claim 3 body paragraph
   A. Topic sentence presenting claim 3
   B. Cite evidence of claim 3
   C. Cite additional evidence of claim 3
   D. Explain how evidence supports claim 3

> **TRM** Suggested Responses to Questions

TEACHING IDEA

Building Vocabulary

Economic history can be challenging for students because they lack familiarity with terminology. For instance, in the colonial period the use of the phrase "commercial networks" is often used to describe the economy of the Atlantic world. This term is connected to South Atlantic system, transatlantic system, mercantilism, and the development of the Atlantic world. At the beginning of Module 2-6 consider having students write a definition of "commercial networks."

▲ Differentiation

To take this activity a step further, have students work in groups and exchange definitions so students can see the breadth of possibility for properly defining this concept.

Module 2-6

The Eighteenth-Century Atlantic Economy

LEARNING TARGETS

By the end of this module, you should be able to:

- Explain the causes and effects of the transatlantic trade system on the North American colonial economy during the seventeenth and eighteenth centuries.
- Explain the causes and effects of the transatlantic trade system on North American colonial society during the seventeenth and eighteenth centuries.
- Explain the effects of British mercantilist policies on its North American colonies.

THEMATIC FOCUS

Work, Exchange, and Technology

During the eighteenth century, the Atlantic economy became increasingly complex, leading to deepening attempts by European powers to systematize trade policies advantageous to home countries. These trade policies shaped the lives of colonial subjects in North America.

HISTORICAL REASONING FOCUS

Causation

TASK ▶ As you read this module, think about the effects of the economic and political developments you encounter, and be sure to consider the reasons why they occurred. In other words, why did a particular development lead to the results that followed? Think about the ways important effects led, in turn, to subsequent effects.

During the eighteenth century, the combined forces of global trade and international warfare altered the political and economic calculations of imperial powers. This was especially true for British North America, where colonists settled as families and created towns that provided key markets for Britain's commercial expansion. Over the course of the century, British colonists became increasingly avid consumers of products from around the world. Meanwhile the king and Parliament sought greater control over these far-flung commercial networks.

Colonial Traders Join Global Networks

In the late seventeenth and early eighteenth centuries, trade became truly global. Not only did goods from China, India, the Middle East, Africa, and North America gain currency in England and the rest of Europe, but the tastes of European consumers also helped shape goods produced in other parts of the world. For instance, by the early eighteenth century the Chinese manufactured porcelain teapots and bowls specifically for the English market. Similarly, European tastes shaped the trade in cloth, tea, tobacco, and sugar. The exploitation of enslaved African laborers also contributed significantly to this global commerce. They were considered a crucial item of trade in their own right, and their labor in the Americas ensured steady supplies of sugar, rice, tobacco, and indigo for the world market.

By the early eighteenth century, both the volume and the diversity of goods multiplied. Silk, calico, porcelain, olive oil, wine, and other items were carried from the East to Europe and the

Colonial Traders Join Global Networks

Period 2: 1607–1754

▲ **MAP 2.6 North Atlantic Trade in the Eighteenth Century** North Atlantic trade provided various parts of the British empire with raw materials, manufactured goods, and labor. Ultimately, people and goods were exchanged among four key points: the West Indies, mainland North America, West Africa, and Great Britain. **Describe the effects of the North Atlantic trade on two of the regions shown on this map.**

BUILDING AP® SKILLS

Claims and Evidence in Sources

To help students see the global connections of the commercial networks that developed in the seventeenth and eighteenth centuries, consider providing students with Map 2.6 and asking them to identify where in the world some of the most contentious battles for supremacy in trade might take place (*West Indies*). After they identify the area in question, have students write a one-to-two sentence explanation with substantive details.

American colonies. The colonies filled returning ships with cod, mackerel, shingles, pine boards, barrel staves, rum, sugar, rice, and tobacco. A healthy trade also grew up within North America as New England fishermen, New York and Charleston merchants, and Caribbean planters met one another's needs. Salted cod and mackerel flowed to the Caribbean, and rum, molasses, and enslaved people flowed back to the mainland. This commerce required ships, barrels, docks, warehouses, and wharves, all of which ensured a lively trade in naval stores such as lumber, tar, pitch, rope, and rosin.

A flow of information was critical to the flow of goods and credit. During this time, coffeehouses flourished in port cities around the Atlantic, providing access to the latest news. Merchants, ship captains, and traders met in person to discuss new ventures and to learn of recent developments. British and American periodicals reported on parliamentary legislation, commodity prices in India and Great Britain, the state of trading houses in China, the outbreak of disease in foreign ports, and stock ventures in London. Still, these markets were volatile. Speculative bubbles expanded all too often and burst, bankrupting thousands of overextended investors.

REVIEW

• How did the transatlantic trade network create a common British Atlantic culture?

BUILDING AP® SKILLS

Claims and Evidence in Sources

Similar to the use of quantitative primary sources, maps can be leveraged to explain historical patterns. For instance, Map 2.6 illustrates the transatlantic economy in the eighteenth century. Rather than having students memorize familiar routes, consider assigning students a project meant to assess their ability to illustrate trends. If students are unsure of how to begin this process, you can provide them with concepts they could use to explain the trends from the map. Manufacturing, raw materials, and enslaved labor are a few that students can start with as they work on illustrating trends. Once they select trends they are comfortable with, have each student write a one-to-three sentence response illustrating the economic patterns from the map.

TEACHING IDEA

Check for Understanding

As students study economic patterns, they must continue to draw connections to other paradigms such as cultural history. These can often be done in tandem. For instance, consider assigning students the following graphic organizer to help them make historical connections between economic and cultural history.

Economic Patterns	Transatlantic Trade	Cultural Effects
Enslaved labor	→	Forced migration
Abundant natural resources	→	Demographic shifts

Period 2: 1607–1754

MODULE 2-6 The Eighteenth-Century Atlantic Economy

Imperial Policies Focus on Profits

mercantilism Economic system centered on maintaining a favorable balance of trade for the home country, with more gold and silver flowing into that country than flowed out. Seventeenth- and eighteenth-century British colonial policy was heavily shaped by mercantilism.

European rulers worked to ensure that this international trade and their colonial possessions benefited their own treasuries. Spain's restrictions on trade and royal monopolies were attempts to protect its domestic manufacturing and traditional arrangements of aristocratic power. Using this model, Spain extracted vast quantities of gold and silver from the Americas initially, but when those natural resources were exhausted, these strategies were not able to maintain the Spanish empire's prosperity and stability. By the mid-seventeenth century, it was clear that a different approach to generating colonial wealth was necessary. Eventually, both the French king Louis XIV and his English rivals embraced a system known as **mercantilism**, which centered on the maintenance of a favorable balance of trade, with more gold and silver flowing into the home country than flowed out. France honed the system. Beginning in the 1660s, Louis XIV taxed foreign imports while removing all barriers to trade within French territories. Colonies provided valuable raw materials that could be used to produce manufactured items for sale to foreign nations and to colonists.

AP ANALYZING SOURCES

Source: British Parliament, *Navigation Act,* 1660

"Be it enacted, etc., that no commodity of the growth, production, or manufacture of Europe, shall be imported into any land, island, plantation, colony, territory, or place, to his Majesty belonging, or which shall hereafter belong unto or be in possession of his Majesty, his heirs and successors, in Asia, Africa, or America . . . , but which shall be bona fide[1], and without fraud, laden and shipped in England, Wales, or the town of Berwick-upon-Tweed, and in English-built shipping . . . ; and whereof the master and three fourths of the mariners, at least, are English, and which shall be carried directly thence to the said lands, islands, plantations, colonies, territories, or places; and from no other place or places whatsoever; any law, statute, or usage to the contrary notwithstanding; under the penalty of the loss of all such commodities of the growth, production, or manufacture of Europe, as shall be imported into any of them, from any other place whatsoever, by land or water; and if by water, of the ship or vessel, also, in which they were imported, with all her guns, tackle, furniture, ammunition, and apparel; one third part to his Majesty, his heirs and successors; one third part to the governor of such land, island, plantation, colony, territory, or place into which such goods were imported, if the said ship, vessel, or goods, be there seized, or informed against and sued for; or, otherwise, that third part, also, to his Majesty, his heirs and successors; and the other third part to him or them who shall seize, inform, or sue for the same in any of his Majesty's courts in such of the said lands, islands, colonies, plantations, territories, or places where the offence was committed, or in any court of record in England. . . ."

[1] Made in good faith.

Questions for Analysis
1. Identify three rules that regulated exports to the colonies.
2. Describe the penalties for merchants who broke these rules.
3. Explain the reasons governing authorities in England could have used to justify the Navigation Acts.

Navigation Acts Acts passed by Parliament in the 1650s and 1660s that prohibited smuggling, established guidelines for legal commerce, and set duties on trade items.

While France's mercantile system was limited by the size of its empire, England benefited more fully from such policies. The English crown had access to a far wider array of natural resources from which to manufacture goods and a larger market for these products. In 1651, under Oliver Cromwell, Parliament passed the first Navigation Act, which King Charles II renewed in 1660 after the restoration. Over the next three decades, Parliament passed a series of **Navigation Acts** that required merchants to conduct trade with English colonies in English-owned ships. In addition, certain items imported from foreign ports had to be carried in English ships or in ships with predominantly English crews. Finally, a list of "enumerated articles" — including tobacco, cotton, sugar,

---

TEACHING IDEA

AP Central

Make use of the College Board's resource *America on the World Stage: Essays from the American Organization of Historians and AP*, available from the Classroom Resources section of AP Central (apcentral.collegeboard.org). At this time, have students read and annotate the article "America, the Atlantic, and Global Consumer Demand, 1500–1800." Whole-class discussion to follow.

TRM Suggested Responses to Questions

TRM Module 2.6 AP Analyzing Sources Handout

EXPLORING AP THEMES

Work, Exchange, and Technology

One of the challenges of teaching late-seventeenth and early-eighteenth-century history is getting students to understand the chronology of the era. As an example, if quizzed, how many students would be able to identify the colonies that were established and producing goods for England by 1660? Probably not very many would. Therefore, consider using the chart provided in the Teacher's Resource Materials that delineates both the type of colony and the year of establishment. This will no doubt help students as they encounter subsequent Navigation Laws and ultimately as they read about Great Britain's lax control over trade in the British North American colonies before 1754.

TRM Find **Handout 2.6 – English Colonies Established in North America, 1607–1750** in the Teacher's Resource Materials

BUILDING AP SKILLS

Sourcing and Situation

Students should always begin a primary source analysis with the source title. For instance, this source title provides important clues about the significance of the information from the document. The year 1660 is one of those clues. Encourage students to pause and brainstorm at least two goods British colonies were developing and therefore needed to be controlled by England's mercantile system. (*Sugar, tobacco, lumber, shipbuilding*)

BUILDING AP SKILLS

Making Connections

Mercantilism is a required term for students to know in order to understand the economic developments in the colonial period. This is also a nuanced term with many defining prongs for students to examine. For instance, each of the following influenced the nature of mercantilism for Great Britain: access to natural resources, exporting substantial sums of goods, control of wealth (hard money), taxation policies, colonial landholdings, a manufacturing sector, and navigation laws. Consider assigning groups of three or four students one of the influential terms listed above and have them write a definition explaining how their term influenced mercantile policies of Great Britain. After the groups are finished with their terms, ask students how they would take in more of the possible answers to buttress their definition of mercantilism.

Mercantilism Changes Colonial Societies

◀ *A View of Charleston, South Carolina, c. 1760s* This eighteenth-century oil painting by English artist Thomas Mellish offers a view of Charleston harbor c. 1760s. A ship flying an English flag sails in the foreground. The other ships and small boats along with the substantial buildings surrounding the harbor reflect Charleston's status as one of the main commercial centers of the North American colonies. **Based on this painting, how did the English view colonial cities?**

and indigo — had to be shipped from the colonies to England before being re-exported to foreign ports. Thus the crown benefited directly and indirectly from nearly all commerce conducted by its colonies. But colonies, too, often benefited, as when Parliament helped subsidize the development of indigo in South Carolina.

AP® TIP
Be sure you can explain why North American colonists resented the mercantile policies adopted by the British government during this time period.

In 1663 Parliament expanded its imperial reach through additional Navigation Acts, which required that goods sent from Europe to English colonies also pass through British ports. And a decade later, ship captains had to pay a duty or post bond before carrying enumerated articles between colonial ports. These acts ensured not only greater British control over shipping but also additional revenue for the crown as captains paid duties in West Indies, mainland North American, and British ports. Beginning in 1673, England sent customs officials to the colonies to enforce the various parliamentary acts. By 1680, London, Bristol, and Liverpool all thrived as barrels of sugar and tobacco and stacks of deer and beaver skins were unloaded and bolts of dyed cloth and cases of metal tools and guns were put on board for the return voyage. As mechanization and manufacturing expanded in England, Parliament sought to keep the profits at home by quashing nascent industries in the colonies. It thus prohibited the sale of products such as American-made textiles (1699), hats (1732), and iron goods (1750). In addition, Parliament worked to restrict trade among the North American colonies, especially between those on the mainland and in the West Indies.

REVIEW

In what ways was mercantilism both a continuation of and a change in British policies toward its North American colonies?

Mercantilism Changes Colonial Societies

Despite the increasing regulation, American colonists could own British ships and transport goods produced in the colonies. Indeed, by the mid-eighteenth century, North American merchants oversaw 75 percent of the trade in manufactures sent from Bristol and London to the colonies and 95 percent of the trade with the West Indies. Ironically, then, a system established to benefit Great Britain ended up creating a mercantile elite in its North American colonies. Most of those merchants traded in goods, but some traded in human cargo.

The Atlantic slave trade generated enormous wealth for colonial elites like merchants, investors, and plantation owners. These funds helped turn America's seaport cities into thriving urban centers. North American seaports such as Charleston, with their elegant homes, fine shops, and lively social seasons, captured the most dynamic aspects of colonial life. Just as important, communities that were once largely rural — like Salem, Massachusetts and Wilmington, Delaware — grew into thriving commercial centers in the late seventeenth century. Although cities like New York, Boston, Philadelphia, Baltimore, and Charleston contained less than 10 percent of the colonial population, they served as focal points of economic, political, social, and cultural activity during the eighteenth century.

Affluent urban families created a **consumer revolution** in North America. Changing patterns of consumption challenged traditional definitions of status. Less tied to birth and family pedigree,

consumer revolution A process through which status in the colonies became more closely linked to financial success and a refined lifestyle rather than birth and family pedigree during the seventeenth and eighteenth centuries. The consumer revolution was spurred by industrialization and increased global trade.

BUILDING AP® SKILLS

Making Connections

Mercantilism was a far-reaching economic scheme meant to control and prop up the wealth of the mother country (Great Britain). Students need to remember that laborers also affected the growth of the British economy. Consider organizing groups of three or four students and assign each group one of the following regions/countries: Africa, West Indies, North American colonies, and England. Have each group write an explanation of how each region used enslaved labor to prop up England's wealth in the mercantile system.

APPLY THE TIP

While it is true that many colonists resented the controlling nature of mercantile policies from Great Britain, it is equally true that many colonists embraced the system because it led to vast amounts of wealth within the colonies. To challenge students who are showing an early mastery of skill and content, consider asking them to explain how colonists embraced and resented mercantile policies.

TEACHING IDEA

Analyzing Art and Images

This oil painting can be used as an effective bell ringer at the beginning of class. For instance, consider asking students two questions related to the purpose of the painting.

1. How does the artist portray the purpose of port cities such as Charleston?
2. How does the artist portray the balance of power between England and British North American colonies such as South Carolina?

This would be a great introduction to a class period dealing with mercantilism and the reactions to the system from the English and the British North American colonists.

EXPLORING AP® THEMES

Geography and the Environment

Consider using Map 2.6 on page 99 for the following activity. This activity encourages students to think both visually and through writing about how the Navigation Laws worked. Have students locate both the West Indies and the British North American colonies. Next, have them write an explanation describing how the Navigation Laws would have applied to each region — bearing in mind they need to emphasize what part of trade Great Britain would have been most interested in profiting from and controlling.

TEACHING IDEA

Check for Understanding

In Module 2-3, Anglicization was presented as an idea with many cultural and political ties to how colonists saw themselves in the colonial period. Challenge students to take this understanding to another level by connecting Anglicization to the socio-economic development of colonists during this period. This can be done in two steps. In step one ask students to revisit their knowledge of the cultural and political part of Anglicization from Module 2-3. In step two ask students to write how Anglicization began as a cultural and political idea and continued to develop into an economic idea, as well.

EXPLORING AP® THEMES

American and Regional Culture

The economic trends of the colonial period affected many groups in distinctly different ways. For instance, mercantile policies affected those in port cities in ways that rural colonists would not have understood as well. To further students' understanding of this concept consider assigning students three groups of colonists: rural farmers, urban merchants, and new migrants. For each group, students need to explain at least one economic effect of Britain's mercantile policies. Focusing on economics is just one way to explore this particular theme. Religion and demographic changes can also be used to explore this theme.

Period 2: 1607–1754

MODULE 2-6 The Eighteenth-Century Atlantic Economy

◀ **Industrious Americans in Boston, 1770** This English engraving appeared as a broadsheet in London. It depicts American colonists engaged in agricultural and artisanal labors on the outskirts of Boston. **Compare this image to the painting of the Charleston port on p. 101. What similarities and differences do you notice? What accounts for both?**

AP® TIP
Understanding the ways that slavery supported the affluent classes in all of the colonial regions provides an important foundation for the AP® course.

status in the colonies became more closely linked to financial success and a refined lifestyle. Successful British men of humble origins and even those of Dutch, Scottish, French, and Jewish heritage might join the British-dominated colonial gentry.

While some certainly worried about the concentration of wealth in too few hands, most colonial elites in the early eighteenth century happily displayed their profits. Leading merchants in Boston, Salem, New York, and Philadelphia emulated British styles and built fine homes that had separate rooms for sleeping, eating, and entertaining guests. Mercantile elites also redesigned the urban landscape, donating money for brick churches and stately town halls. They constructed new roads, wharves, and warehouses to facilitate trade, and they invested in bowling greens and public gardens.

The spread of international commerce created a lively cultural life and great affluence in colonial cities. The colonial elite replicated British fashions, including elaborate tea rituals. In Boston, the wives of merchants served fine teas imported from East Asia in cups and saucers from China while decorated bowls held sugar from the West Indies. However, the emergence of a colonial aristocracy existed within view of growing inequality. Increasing income gaps and differences in property ownership accelerated in the eighteenth century. The frequent wars of the late seventeenth and early eighteenth centuries contributed to these economic and social divisions by boosting the profits of merchants, shipbuilders, and artisans. They temporarily improved the wages of seamen as well. But in their aftermath, rising prices, falling wages, and a lack of jobs led to the concentration of wealth in fewer hands.

Economic trends and migration to the British North American colonies produced growing numbers of young people seeking land and employment. Thus many free laborers migrated from town to town and from country to city seeking work. They hoped to find farmers who needed extra hands for planting and harvesting, ship captains and contractors who would hire them to load or unload cargo or assist in the construction of homes and churches, or wealthy families who needed cooks, laundresses, or nursemaids.

Seasonal and temporary demands for labor created a mass of transient workers described as "the strolling poor." Many New England towns developed systems to "warn out" those who were not official residents. Modeled after the British system, warning-out was meant to ensure that strangers did not become public dependents. Still, being warned did not mean immediate removal. Sometimes transients were simply warned that they were not eligible for poor relief. At other times, constables returned them to an earlier place of residence. In many ways, warning-out served as an early registration system, allowing authorities to encourage the flow of labor, keep residents under surveillance, and protect the town's financial resources. But it rarely aided those in need of work.

Residents who were eligible for public assistance might be given food and clothing or boarded with a local family. Many towns began appointing Overseers of the Poor to deal with the growing problem of poverty. By 1750 every seaport city had constructed an almshouse that sheltered residents without other means of support. In 1723, the Bridewell prison was added to Boston Almshouse, built in 1696. Then, in 1739, a workhouse was opened on the same site to employ the "able-bodied" poor in hopes that profits from it would help fund the almshouse and prison. Still, these efforts at relief fell far short of the need, especially in hard economic times.

Meanwhile, in the rural countryside, where the vast majority of colonial Americans lived, families remained the central unit of economic organization. Yet even farms were affected by the transatlantic circulation of goods and people. In areas along the Atlantic coast, rural families were drawn into commercial networks in a variety of ways. Towns and cities needed large supplies of

102

TEACHING IDEA

Incorporating Primary Sources

As you teach economic history, be sure to consider the inclusion of primary sources to support instructional practices and enhance students' understanding of the economic trends they have been reading. For instance, after reading the warning of Gottlieb Mittelberger available in the Teacher's Resource Materials, how would students incorporate the perspective he gives in the excerpt? Put another way, amidst the economic growth of the colonial period, what problems did some migrants see in their attempt to profit in the British North American colonies?

TRM Find **Handout 2.7 – Gottlieb Mittelberger's Warning** in the Teacher's Resource Materials vegetables, meat, butter, barley, wheat, and yarn. Farm families sold these goods to residents and bought sugar, tea, and other imported items that diversified their diet. Few rural families purchased ornamental or luxury items, but cloth or cheese bought in town saved hours of labor at home.

REVIEW

- What cultural changes did British North Americans experience in the early 1700s?

AP® WRITING HISTORICALLY
Responding to a Short-Answer Question with Secondary Sources

The AP® U.S. History Exam has three different types of Short-Answer Questions:

- secondary source interpretation questions, which require you to understand the claims that two historians make about a specific time period, and how evidence from specific events or developments during that time period can be used to support one historian's claims;
- primary source interpretation questions, which give you a source — typically an image — and ask you to draw connections between that source and larger historical developments;
- and finally, questions without primary or secondary sources that require you to use your knowledge of a time period, which you encountered in Period 1.

You may be able to guess what a *secondary source* is from the name alone: It's a second-hand account of a historical event or development created after the fact by someone who was not there. Books and scholarly articles about history, written by historians, are the most common form of secondary source you will be asked to read and write about in this course. In fact, these types of Short-Answer Questions will always provide you with two short secondary sources that discuss the same topic. Most often, you will be asked to compare their arguments in some meaningful way and cite a piece of evidence to support one or both of their claims.

Let's take a look at a typical Short-Answer Question on a pair of secondary sources:

Using the following excerpts, answer (a), (b), and (c).

Source: Richard Bushman, *The Refinement of America: Persons, Houses, Cities*, 1993

"Small tokens of gentility[1] can be found scattered through all of American society in the eighteenth century, like pottery shards in an excavated house lot. Estate inventories of many middling people show a teacup, a silver spoon, knives and forks, and a book or two among the household possessions. Over the course of the century, probably a majority of the population adopted some of the amenities associated with genteel living. But it would be an error to conclude that by [1776] most Americans were genteel. Gentility flecked lives without coloring them. Gentility was the proper style of the gentry alone in the eighteenth century...."

[1] Refinement.

Source: T. H. Breen, *The Marketplace of the Revolution: How Consumer Politics Shaped American Independence*, 2005

"Within a few decades during the middle of the eighteenth century, imported goods transformed monochrome spaces into Technicolor.... Imported goods reflected cosmopolitan tastes and manners, so that an American who managed to purchase a porcelain teacup or a modest pewter bowl could fancy that he or she partook of a polite society centered in faraway places such as London or Bath. These wonderful objects arouse suspicion today that however much local ministers may have once railed against the corrupting influence of luxury, they did not really discourage the members of their congregations from buying goods that yielded so much personal satisfaction."

(Continued)

103

TRM Suggested Responses to Questions

BUILDING AP® SKILLS
Claims and Evidence in Sources

To help students develop an awareness of the design of this style of Short-Answer Question, consider facilitating a discussion about the extent to which historians disagree on historical topics. For instance, ask students in what circumstances historians might reach conclusions that are subtle in their differences. Next, ask students when they can imagine historians reaching conclusions that offer stark contrasts. Understanding the range of possibilities helps prepare students for the task of reading and interpreting secondary sources.

BUILDING AP® SKILLS
Sourcing and Situation

Another quality conversation to have with students about this section of the Short-Answer Question is about the style of historical writing they are encountering in these brief excerpts. For instance, students are used to reading a textbook and mining it for information. When they read articles or books by historians, they are looking for an interpretation of information they should already know. Ask probing questions so students can see these important differences. What qualities do they notice about textbook reading that differ from reading brief excerpts from historians? Where in the excerpt does the interpretation become evident? Does the author use transitions to emphasize a particular point? Does the title of the book lend any clues to the stated interpretation?

TEACHING IDEA
AP® Writing Historically Review

Historical and academic vocabulary can sometimes confuse students who are attempting to unpack the meaning of a particular source. To help students understand the accompanying sources, provide students with a list of the following words: gentility, refinement, middling, genteel, gentry, and monochrome. Have students form six groups and assign each group one of the terms. Once they have defined the word, students travel to all the other groups, one at a time, until they have completed definitions for each term. Now students are ready to read the excerpts. You can follow up on their reading of the excerpts with a conversation about the importance of continually developing their vocabulary, as opposed to skipping over words they are unsure of in sources.

Period 2: 1607–1754   MODULE 2-6 The Eighteenth-Century Atlantic Economy

a. Briefly describe ONE major difference between Bushman's and Breen's historical interpretations of the impact of consumer goods on colonial society.
b. Briefly explain how ONE specific historical event or development from the period 1650 to 1754 that is not explicitly mentioned in the excerpts could be used to support Bushman's argument.
c. Briefly explain how ONE specific historical event or development from the period 1650 to 1754 that is not explicitly mentioned in the excerpts could be used to support Breen's argument.

In this particular question, part (a) calls for you to think historically using comparison. Parts (b) and (c) assess your content knowledge, and your skill in using evidence to support an argument. In the following steps, we'll walk through how to approach each one.

Step 1 Read both excerpts and summarize their viewpoints.

Read each secondary source carefully, and take a moment to clarify the general topic or development that both historians are writing about. It may be helpful to annotate the prompt or jot it down so that you can keep it in mind as you think about each source individually. For example, notice that both historians discuss the existence of consumable goods, even luxuries, in the homes of average colonial Americans. Note also that both historians talk about relatively small objects like eating utensils, bowls, tea cups, etc.

Now that you have focused on the general topic under discussion by both historians, jot down a quick summary of what each one has to say about that subject. Remember, although there will be differences in the historians' interpretations, the historians will also have points in common as well. Rarely will two sources express polar opposite views of a given historical development. Your summary of each historian's claims, like the example that follows, should thus address both commonalities and differences:

> Richard Bushman argues that small luxury goods ("tokens of gentility") were found in the homes of most Americans. T. H. Breen also argues that items of gentility were found in the homes of average British colonists **[points in common]**.
>
> Bushman claims it would be a mistake to assume that most Americans were "genteel." Breen argues that these items allowed average British colonists to imagine themselves as part of a broader genteel culture, and therefore were a more important part of their identity than Bushman claims **[points of difference]**.

Notice that part (a) asks you for the major difference between their interpretations. In this case, Bushman and Breen agree about the existence of a few luxury items in American homes, but there are also subtle differences in their arguments. Whereas Bushman claims that it is a mistake to assume the few luxury items in colonial homes made Americans genteel, Breen implies that these few items allowed colonists to connect with faraway gentility in Europe, thereby making these items an important part of average colonists' identity.

Step 2 Use *ACE* to answer each part of the prompt.

The next step is to apply the *ACE* strategy (answer, cite, explain) you learned in Period 1 to part (a):

> Briefly describe ONE major difference between Bushman's and Breen's historical interpretations of the impact of consumer goods on colonial society.

Start by writing a claim that states a difference between Bushman's and Breen's interpretations. You may find it helpful to use words such as *but, although, whereas, while, on the other hand,* or *however,* in order to transition from your claim about one historian's interpretation to the other. These transition words will help highlight the contrasting relationship between the two historians' ideas. The following example shows a strong claim in response to this part of the Short-Answer Question:

> Bushman argues that these items had little effect on the everyday lives of average British colonists, who understood that "gentility" was reserved for the upper classes **[Bushman's claim]**. Breen, on the other hand, argues that these items allowed average British colonists to imagine themselves as part of a broader genteel culture, and therefore were a more important part of their identity than Bushman claims **[Breen's claim]**.

However, it is not enough to merely state a claim about the difference between the two historians' interpretations. You must prove to your reader that your claim is valid, and to do this,

---

TEACHING IDEA

Class Discussion

If students are struggling with step 1, which asks them to read the sources and summarize the viewpoints presented by the historians, remind students of the need to write their answers in their own words. Imagine a threshold of using the historians' words and the students' words — students should err on the side of including their own language. While it is acceptable to use ideas from the sources, simply paraphrasing the source is not in keeping with the task. To further this idea, ask students what action verb they read in the question (*describe*). Also, ask them to identify the historical thinking skill associated with the question (*difference — comparison*). If students follow the guidelines in step 1 and describe the difference in their own words, they will be on the right path. This will likely take two or three sentences.

TEACHING IDEA

Check for Understanding

As students learn about using the *ACE* strategy to answer, cite, and explain their response, encourage them also to think concretely about the historical reasoning processes and historical thinking skills in the question. Recall that students will be assessed on their ability to utilize the following reasoning processes on the Free Response section of the AP® exam. They are as follows:

- Continuity and Change
- Comparison
- Causation

Ask students to highlight the tasks for each stem. If they can identify a historical thinking skill or reasoning process, consider asking them to underline that part of the question. Coupling this mindset with the *ACE* strategy ensures students have properly decoded the question.

you will need to cite evidence from both passages. Lastly, you should explain how the evidence you chose from the two interpretations proves your claim. The example answer that follows provides a particularly effective explanation for this part of the prompt. Note how it addresses causation by offering reasons for the differences in Breen and Bushman's interpretations:

> Bushman argues that luxury items had little effect on the everyday lives of average British colonists, while Breen argues that these items allowed many colonists to imagine themselves as part of a broader genteel culture **[answer contrasting the central claims of each historian]**. Bushman views the presence of teacups, silver spoons, knives, and forks as mere "tokens of gentility," whereas Breen believes they allowed colonists to participate in a "polite society centered in faraway places such as London" **[citation quoting evidence from excerpts]**. Therefore, while Bushman claims it is a mistake to assume most colonists were "genteel" based on such artifacts, Breen argues that because these items allowed many colonists to imagine themselves as part of a broader genteel culture, they were therefore a more important part of their identity than Bushman argues **[explanation linking answer and evidence to part (a)]**.

Now you're ready to move on to part (b) of the question:

> Briefly explain how ONE specific historical event or development from the period 1650 to 1754 that is not explicitly mentioned in the excerpts could be used to support Bushman's argument.

Start by brainstorming evidence from your knowledge of history that you can use to support Bushman's argument. Select the best historical example you think of to showcase that knowledge. One strategy for doing this is to consider the context that shaped the topic under discussion by both historians. For example, for this part of the question, we can think of a few pieces of evidence that come from this module:

- The majority of colonists were agriculturalists and relatively poor compared to elites in the colonies.
- Most goods that were consumed in average colonial homes, like clothing, were manufactured at home.
- Throughout the eighteenth century, colonial elites increasingly held a larger portion of the colonies' wealth.

As you did with part (a), apply *ACE* to part (b). Make a claim that *answers* the prompt — that is, present a historical event or development that supports Bushman's interpretation. Then, using your knowledge of history, *cite* evidence demonstrating your claim. Lastly, *explain* how the evidence you chose to include proves your claim. The following example is a strong answer to part (b):

> Bushman's argument can be supported by noting the few luxury goods average colonists owned **[answer]**. While luxury goods increasingly became accessible to some colonists after 1650, for the majority of British Americans the everyday goods they used, like clothing, were overwhelmingly made at home **[citation]**. This shows that for most Americans, a genteel lifestyle was still very far from their everyday lives **[explanation]**.

Notice how this response supports Bushman's argument that while some items of gentility found their way into the homes of colonial Americans, the bulk of their consumable goods were made at home. This piece of historical evidence best supports Bushman's contention that even though average colonists might have had a few luxury items, the items that they literally lived in (their clothes) were still homespun and far from genteel.

From here, you can repeat the steps you took to answer part (b) in order to respond to part (c):

> Briefly explain how ONE specific historical event or development from the period 1650 to 1754 that is not explicitly mentioned in the excerpts could be used to support Breen's argument.

The following example is a strong answer to part (c):

> Breen's argument can be supported by noting the rise of mercantilist policies to require colonists to purchase finished goods through English ports **[answer]**. The Navigation Acts, based on the economic policy of mercantilism, shows that the English were increasingly interested in profiting

(Continued)

TEACHING IDEA

Building Vocabulary

When answering Short-Answer Question prompts that ask for specific historical events or developments, it is helpful to be as specific as possible. Students should think about the incorporation of proper nouns that ground their response in historical information. You can use the exemplary responses to emphasize this point. Ask students to read over the responses and see if they can add any historical terms to the answer given. For instance, mercantilism could be included in the third answer because that system enabled colonial elites to hold more wealth over time. Put another way, this activity is best suited for students who demonstrate an understanding of the task and are looking to challenge themselves further.

TEACHING IDEA

Class Discussion

The use of exemplars with dialogue is a proven way to increase students' understanding of how to answer questions. Consider using the exemplar answer for parts b and c. You can retype the answer so it does not contain references to where *ACE* is incorporated in the response. After you allow students to identify the separate parts of *ACE*, reveal the answers to them and debrief their responses. Also, consider having students underline where the exemplar employs historical reasoning and/or reasoning skills in the response.

TEACHING IDEA

Group Activity

The closing activity is a great way to assess whether or not students gleaned the necessary information about how to write responses for Short-Answer Questions. Given this is early in the year, consider having students work in groups of three or four students. Each student in the group writes responses for (a), (b), and (c). After they are finished, have the group debrief answers and select the best (a), best (b), and best (c) in the group. It could be that three different students make up the composite answer; could be that two students make up the composite. The number of students represented in the final answer is not important; instead, what does matter is their ability to select the best answer for each part. After students have finished, consider conducting a gallery walk where each group gets to read the other composite responses.

▲ Differentiation

More advanced students can write the responses individually, but still share responses in a gallery walk.

---

from the sale of luxury goods to the colonies **[citation]**. This imperial policy proves that the consumption of luxury goods was increasingly widespread in the seventeenth century, and supports Breen's contention that the genteel lifestyle, in varying degrees, increasingly shaped the lives of British colonists **[explanation]**.

Notice that this answer supports Breen's interpretation by pointing out that one of the goals of mercantilism was to profit from a market for England's manufactured goods in the colonies, thereby showing that the market for finished goods, like teacups and utensils, was growing through the eighteenth century.

You will find opportunities to practice this type of Short-Answer Question in each Period of this textbook. As you practice, remember to systematically *ACE* each of the three parts.

ACTIVITY

Carefully read the following pair of secondary sources and answer the accompanying Short-Answer Question.

Using the following excerpts, answer (a), (b), and (c).

Source: E. A. J. Johnson, "Some Evidence of Mercantilism in Massachusetts Bay," *The New England Quarterly*, 1928

"By 1763 the American colonies were reconciled to the English mercantilist policy. . . . Mercantilism as a theory of statecraft...was dominant in Europe during the entire colonial period. . . . Mercantilism had for its primary purpose the creation of a strong state. . . . Governments extended their control over commerce and industry on the theory that the economic activity of the individual should be subordinated to the welfare of the nation. The state must become a self-sufficient unit, independent from other competing nations."

Source: Ellen Newell, "Putting the 'Political' Back in Political Economy (This Is Not Your Parents' Mercantilism)," *The William and Mary Quarterly*, 2012

"The nature of wealth and the role of colonies formed only part of the debates that raged over trade, markets, money, consumption, . . . morality, and the proper role of government in commerce. Free-trade ideas circulated as early as the late sixteenth century and gained traction in the early seventeenth century. . . . [T]he Navigation Acts, although devastating to some colonial economies in the short term, opened a huge English free-trade zone . . . which benefited the northern colonies enormously. . . . [T]hey were free to trade directly with non-English nations — that is, until the 1760s, when authorities expanded the enumerated list to include many heretofore-unregulated exports and imports."

a. Briefly describe ONE major difference between Johnson's and Newell's historical interpretations of British mercantilist policy.
b. Briefly explain how ONE specific historical event or development from the period 1607 to 1754 that is not explicitly mentioned in the excerpts could be used to support Johnson's argument.
c. Briefly explain how ONE specific historical event or development from the period 1607 to 1754 that is not explicitly mentioned in the excerpts could be used to support Newell's argument.

Module 2-7

Slavery Takes Hold in the South

LEARNING TARGETS

By the end of this module, you should be able to:

- Explain how the surplus of land, the European demand for colonial goods, and the lack of indentured servants contributed to the rise of the Atlantic slave trade in the British colonies.
- Explain how the rise of slavery supported the economic system of the southern colonies.
- Explain how racial laws supported the slavery-based economy in the southern colonies.
- Explain how enslaved Africans and African Americans developed ways to undermine the system of slavery and maintain their family structures, gender roles, and cultures.

THEMATIC FOCUS

Work, Exchange, and Technology
American and Regional Culture
Social Structures

Slavery shaped the economy and society of British North America. While it was more prevalent in the southern colonies, its existence in the middle and northern colonies proved significant as well. Enslaved Africans and African Americans found overt and covert ways to rebel against slavery and maintain their families and distinct cultures.

HISTORICAL REASONING FOCUS
Causation

The historical events and developments you will explore in this module lend themselves particularly well to an analysis of causation. For instance, enslaved African resistance to slavery led to repressive slave codes in many British colonies.

TASK ▶ As you read this module, prepare to explain causation by writing down your observations about major historical developments and the chain reaction effect of their causes. Don't forget to consider the contexts shaping all of these important events, since a contextualization statement sets the stage for a strong essay thesis. One way to help keep all of this at the forefront of your mind as you read is to periodically ask yourself why developments occurred. The overarching question you should keep in mind as you read this module is: Why did some English colonies develop economies that relied on enslaved labor?

TRM Suggested Responses to Questions

TEACHING IDEA

Building Vocabulary

Historian Ira Berlin's contributions to our understanding of the differences between a "society with slaves" and a "slave society" has allowed students of history to better conceptualize the development of slavery in the eighteenth century. This paradigm is a useful way to study how colonies such as Georgia and South Carolina quickly moved toward a slave society. Moreover, students will be better equipped to make historical connections between the process of creating a racial slave system in the West Indies and in South Carolina. Consider beginning the class by asking students to identify societies with slaves and slave societies.

BUILDING AP® SKILLS

Claims and Evidence in Sources

Olaudah Equiano experienced the tragedies of enslavement and forced migration that students will read about in Module 2-7. Not only was he sold into slavery, but he also traveled the world and recorded memories of his experiences in *The Interesting Narrative of the Life of Olaudah Equiano*. This seminal primary source is worthy of time in class and helps students better understand the process of enslavement. A copy of an excerpted version can be found on the Gilder Lehrman website for Period 2 (ap.gilderlehrman.org). Consider reading this excerpt in class and ask students to record observations about how this excerpt explains the horrors of the Middle Passage.

The Human Cost of the Atlantic Slave Trade

As part of an expansion of England's role in the Atlantic slave trade, Parliament chartered the Royal African Company to bring enslaved Africans to British colonies in 1660. Between 1700 and 1808, some 3 million captive Africans were carried on British and Anglo-American ships, about 40 percent of the total of those sold in the Americas in this period. Half a million Africans died on the voyage across the Atlantic. Huge numbers also died in Africa, while being marched to the coast or held in forts waiting to be forced aboard ships. Yet despite this astounding death rate, the slave trade yielded enormous profits and had far-reaching consequences: The Africans whom British traders bought and sold transformed labor systems in the colonies, fueled international trade, and enriched merchants, planters, and their families and communities.

European traders worked closely with African merchants to gain their human cargo, trading muskets, metalware, and linen for men, women, and children. Originally many of those sold into slavery were war captives. African groups securing trade with Europeans rose in wealth and power, building empires and defeating rivals to conquer vast interior lands. Many Africans who traded in enslaved labor feared the consequences if their rivals secured the lucrative trade with Europeans

TEACHING IDEA

Incorporating Websites

To deepen student understanding of the transatlantic slave trade, you may wish to incorporate the following in your class:

- "The Atlantic Slave Trade in Two Minutes" by Andrew Kahn and Jamelle Boule. Available on Slate's website (slate.com).
- "The 1808 Slave Trade Abolition Deadline" lesson by Heather Dahl. Available on Slave Voyages' website under resources (slavevoyages.org).
- "Finding Historical Evidence" lesson by Brian Hamilton. Available on Slave Voyages' website under resources (slavevoyages.org).
- "Database Scavenger Hunt" lesson by Brian Hamilton. Available on Slave Voyages' website under resources (slavevoyages.org).
- "Researching the Transatlantic Slave Trade" lesson by Christine Kadonsky and David Eltis. Available on Slave Voyages' website under resources (slavevoyages.org).

TEACHING IDEA

AP® Central

Make use of the College Board's resource *America on the World Stage: Essays from the American Organization of Historians and AP®*, available from the Classroom Resources section of AP® Central (apcentral.collegeboard.org). At this time, have students read and annotate the article "The Origins of American Slavery." Whole-class discussion to follow.

Period 2: 1607–1754

MODULE 2-7 Slavery Takes Hold in the South

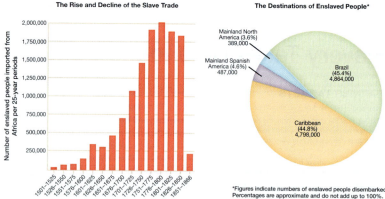

The Slave Trade in Numbers, 1501–1866 Extraordinary numbers of enslaved Africans were shipped to other parts of the world from the sixteenth to the nineteenth century. The slave trade transformed mainland North America, Brazil, and the West Indies. **What broad conclusions about the transatlantic slave trade can you draw from this data?**

Source: Estimates Database. 2009. Voyages: Trans-Atlantic Slave Trade Database, http://www.slavevoyages.org/tast/assessment/estimates.faces. Accessed June 15, 2010.

Middle Passage The brutal second leg of the forced journey of enslaved Africans from Africa to the Americas. Historians estimate that millions of enslaved Africans died before they arrived in the Americas.

for their guns. Over time, African traders moved farther inland to fill the demand, devastating large areas of Africa, particularly the Congo-Angola region in the southwest, which supplied some 40 percent of all enslaved people who crossed the Atlantic.

The trip across the Atlantic, known as the **Middle Passage**, was a brutal and often deadly experience for enslaved Africans. Exhausted and undernourished by the time they boarded the large oceangoing vessels, the captives were placed in dark and crowded holds. Most had been poked and prodded by slave traders, and some had been branded to ensure that a trader received the exact individuals he had purchased. Once in the hold, they might wait for weeks before the ship finally set sail. By that time, the foul-smelling and crowded hold became a nightmare of disease and despair. There was never sufficient food or fresh water for the captives, and women especially were subject to sexual abuse by crew members. Many captives could not communicate with each other since they spoke different languages.

Those who survived the voyage were most likely to find themselves in the slave markets of Barbados or Jamaica, where they were put on display for potential buyers. Once purchased, enslaved people went through a period known as seasoning as they regained their strength, became accustomed to their new environment, learned commands in a new language, and became experts at the labor they would be forced to perform. Some did not survive seasoning, falling prey to

Illustration of a Slave Trader's Ship This image, which was created during the eighteenth century, portrays people being captured in Africa alongside a ship transporting them to enslavement in the Western Hemisphere. **What is the perspective on slavery portrayed in this image?**

BUILDING AP® SKILLS
Causation

The bar graph explaining the significant growth of the slave trade during the colonial years is a great resource to use in a group assignment. Moreover, the graph can also be used as a way to teach students to find patterns in quantitative documents. To help students process how to think about causation in this module, provide groups of students with one main cause for the growth illustrated in the bar graph: cash crops. Next, give specific cash crops to groups such as sugar, rice, tobacco, and indigo. In groups, students are to identify where this cash crop was most prominently grown in the Atlantic world and how it connects to the causes of the development of slavery.

TEACHING IDEA
Connecting the Dots

To further the ability of students to find patterns or trends in quantitative documents, consider using the pie chart illustrating the destinations of enslaved persons. Remind students to avoid repeating data from the document. The statement, "The West Indies was a main destination for enslaved persons as 45% were sold there," does not illustrate that the student knows much about why the West Indies accounted for such a high percentage. A better response sounds something like this: "Plantations outside of North America such as those found in the West Indies accounted for a large percentage of enslaved persons due to the extreme wealth created by sugar plantations." This statement tells us the student understands the larger context to the document. Consider giving groups of three or four students a writing assignment of two or three sentences. Students must illustrate a broader trend from the pie chart. After groups are finished, they can share responses to see how each group interpreted the information. Teachers can select the most comprehensive answer to share with the class.

TEACHING IDEA
Incorporating Videos

One of the more powerful resources on the website Slave Voyages is a video that uses blueprints for a slave ship to illustrate the interior of what the ship looked like to the enslaved persons aboard. Teachers should visit the Slave Voyages website, select the heading "Trans-Atlantic," and then select slave ship in 3D video (slavevoyages.org). Less than five minutes long, the video is an excellent resource to use as a bell ringer for the beginning of class.

BUILDING AP® SKILLS
Making Connections

Throughout the eighteenth century enslaved persons from Africa were likely to be sold either in the West Indies or Brazil. For British North American colonies, Jamaica and Barbados were the two primary islands where slavery grew quickly. Consider asking students to identify at least two direct causes for this historical development. (*Sugar plantations, wealth of planters in the West Indies was greater than in North American colonies such as Virginia.*)

TEACHING IDEA
Incorporating Websites

While news in the eighteenth century did not necessarily travel quickly, it nevertheless was shared among readers in the Atlantic world. Colonies did not exist in a vacuum and were instead keenly aware of developments elsewhere. Consider going to The Gilder Lehrman website, selecting Period 2, and using a document reporting news of a revolt among the enslaved in the West Indies in 1733, printed in New York (ap.gilderlehrman.org). This not only helps explain the details of the revolt, but it also reinforces the interconnectedness of the Atlantic world.

malnutrition and disease or committing suicide. Others adapted to the new circumstances and adopted enough European or British ways to survive even as they sought means to resist the shocking and oppressive conditions.

AP® ANALYZING SOURCES

Source: King Charles II, *Royal African Company Charter*, 1672

"The Royal African [Company's] Limits for Trade granted them by His [Majesty's] Charter....

In the River Gambia, upon James Island, the [Company] have built a Fort, where seventy men, at least, are kept. And there is a Factory from whence Elephants' Teeth, Bees-wax, and Cowhides are exported in very considerable quantities. The River Gambia is very large, and runs up very high (much higher than any discovery hath bin made) and it is supposed the Gold comes most from places, at the head of this River....

The Slaves they [purchased] are sent, for a Supply of Servants, to all His [Majesty's] American Plantations which cannot subsist without them. The Gold and Elephants' Teeth, and other Commodities, which are procured in Africa, are all brought into England. The Gold is always coined in His [Majesty's] Mint. And the Elephants Teeth, and all other goods, which the Company receives, either from Africa or the Plantations, in returne for their Negros, are always sold publicly...."

Questions for Analysis

1. Identify the goods the Royal African Company acquired along the coast of West Africa.
2. Describe a cause stated in this Charter for the founding of the Royal African Company.
3. Explain how this document reveals the developments that led to the founding of the Royal African Company.

REVIEW

How did the transatlantic slave trade affect the societies of both British North America and West Africa?

The Rise of Slavery Reshapes Southern Colonial Society

> **AP® TIP**
> Analyze the causes and effects of the southern colonies' transition into slave societies during the late seventeenth and early eighteenth centuries.

Societies that featured cash-crop plantation economies reliant in part on enslaved labor during the mid-seventeenth century transformed into societies shaped by slavery itself during the late seventeenth and early eighteenth centuries. Southern Carolina was, from the start, heavily influenced by the economies of the British West Indies, and developed from its founding as a slave society. Enslaved labor allowed plantation owners to expand cultivation of cash crops like tobacco, rice, and indigo, which promised high profits for planters as well as merchants. These developments made southern elites more dependent on the global market, and limited opportunities for poorer white people and all black people, both free and enslaved. They also ensured that American Indians and many white colonists were pushed farther west as planters sought more land for their ventures.

In the 1660s, Virginia legislators followed a model established in Barbados by passing laws legalizing human bondage and encoding a slave society (see Module 2-2). A series of laws passed by the House of Burgesses during this time transformed the colony into a society almost completely reliant on a system of chattel slavery in which enslavement was defined as a distinct status based on racial identity and passed on through future generations. As time went on, these laws became harsher: One granted slaveholders the right to kill enslaved people who defied their authority. In 1680 it was declared illegal for "any negro or other slave to carry or arme himself with any club, staffe, gunn, sword, or any other weapon of defence or offence." Nor could enslaved people leave slaveholders' premises without a certificate of permission.

APPLY THE TIP

The transition from a "society with slaves" to a "slave society" was a distinct economic and social decision made by southern colonies in the late-seventeenth and early-eighteenth centuries. Students need to understand the difference between the two descriptions to fully glean the impact of cash crops and the Atlantic economy. Give students one cause, such as cash crops, and ask them to use cash crops as a means of explaining why southern colonies made this transition to a "slave society."

TEACHING IDEA

Incorporating Websites

Gilder Lehrman has a video recording of historian Philip D. Morgan delivering a lecture titled "The Atlantic Slave Trade" (ap.gilderlehrman.org). Viewed in part, or whole, this resource gives students a deeper view into the world of the enslaved.

EXPLORING AP® THEMES

Work, Exchange, and Technology

To gain a sense of how well students gleaned the differences between a slave society and a society with enslaved persons, consider the following assignment. Divide students into groups of three or four and assign the following regions to groups: New England, Middle Colonies, Chesapeake, and southern colonies. For each region, students must label it as either a slave society or a society with enslaved persons and then give evidence to substantiate their claim. This can be used as an exit card at the conclusion of class.

BUILDING AP® SKILLS

Making Connections

In this module, students are presented with the idea of a "gang labor" system of slavery. Present the idea of a "task system" of slavery to students whereby enslaved persons were given a discrete list of tasks to perform during the workday and when it was complete, their work was done for the day. Ask students to compare and contrast these two systems. Consider providing starter questions for them such as: *Why would some slaveholders choose a gang labor system? Why would other slaveholders select a task system? How would both systems affect the enslaved?*

---

slave laws A series of laws that defined slavery as a distinct status based on racial identity and which passed that status on through future generations.

AP® TIP
Make sure you can explain the impact of slave laws on the social structure and regional culture of the southern colonies.

The enactment of these **slave laws** was driven largely by the desires for profits through a more massive and controlled labor force, which the population of neither enslaved American Indians nor indentured servants was large enough to fill.

Increasingly harsh laws in Virginia, Maryland, and North Carolina rose alongside the tobacco economy, and likewise the numbers of imported enslaved Africans. By 1668, one-third of all Africans and African Americans in Virginia and Maryland were still free, but the numbers dwindled year by year. Once the Royal African Company started supplying the Chesapeake with enslaved people directly from Africa in the 1680s, the pace of change quickened. By 1750, 150,000 black people resided in the Chesapeake, and only about 5 percent remained free.

Enslaved women, like men, performed heavy field work, and few bore more than one or two children. When these conditions, along with brutal work regimens, sparked resistance by the enslaved, fearful whites imposed even stricter regulations, further distinguishing between white indentured servants and enslaved black people.

While slavery in the Carolinas was influenced by developments in the Chesapeake, it was shaped even more directly by practices in the British West Indies. During the late seventeenth century, many wealthy families from Barbados, Antigua, and other sugar islands also established plantations in the Carolinas. At first, they brought enslaved people from the West Indies to oversee cattle and pigs and assist in the slaughter of livestock and curing of meat for shipment back to the West Indies. Some enslaved laborers grew rice, using techniques learned in West Africa, to supplement their diet. Slaveholders soon realized that rice might prove very profitable. Although not widely eaten in Europe, it could provide cheap and nutritious food for sailors, orphans, convicts, and peasants. Thus, relying initially on enslaved Africans' knowledge, planters began cultivating rice for export.

As rice cultivation expanded, slavery in the southern Carolinas turned more brutal, just as slavery in Virginia had. Harsher and harsher slave codes were enacted to ensure control of the growing labor force. No longer could enslaved people carry guns, join militias, meet in groups, or travel without a pass. As planters imported more enslaved people directly from Africa, sex ratios, already male dominated, became even more heavily skewed. Colonial authorities initiated military patrols by whites to enforce laws and labor practices. Some plantations along the Carolina coast turned into camps where thousands of enslaved people worked under harsh conditions of the "**gang labor**" system.

By 1720 black people outnumbered white people in the Carolinas, and fears of slave rebellions inspired South Carolina officials to, again, impose even harsher laws and more brutal enforcement measures. When indigo was introduced as a cash crop in the 1740s, the demand for enslaved labor increased further. Although far fewer enslaved people—about 40,000—resided in South Carolina than in the Chesapeake, they already constituted more than 60 percent of the colony's total population by 1750.

During the mid-eighteenth century, Africans and African Americans formed only a small percentage of the northern population: just 5 percent of the combined populations of the Middle Colonies and New England. Some enslaved black people worked on agricultural estates in the Hudson River valley and New Jersey, even more labored as household servants, dockworkers, seamen, and blacksmiths in New York City alongside British colonists and European immigrants.

Fertility rates among enslaved Africans and African Americans were much lower than those among whites in the early eighteenth century, and fewer infants survived to adulthood. It was not until the 1740s that the majority of enslaved people were born in the colonies rather than imported, as some southern slaveholders began to realize that encouraging reproduction gave them economic benefits. Still, enslaved women, most of whom worked in the fields, gained only minimal relief from their labors during pregnancy.

REVIEW

- How did economic trends shape slave laws in the southern colonies?

Africans Resist Enslavement

Enslaved laborers in British North America resisted their subjugation in a variety of ways. They secretly tried to retain customs, belief systems, languages, and naming practices from their homelands. They also secretly broke tools, burned down buildings, ruined stored seeds with moisture, stole livestock and food, faked illness, and some even poisoned slaveholders. They openly resisted, too, challenging slaveholders and overseers by refusing to work, or running away. Some fought back physically in the face of punishment for disrupting whites' authority. A few planned revolts.

The consequences for resisting were severe, from whipping, mutilation, and branding to summary execution. Southern white people, living amid large numbers of black people, were most deeply concerned about resistance and rebellion. As more enslaved people were imported directly from Africa, both the fear and the reality of rebellion increased.

In New York City in 1712, several dozen enslaved Africans and American Indians set fire to a building. When white people rushed to the scene, the insurgents attacked them with clubs, pistols, axes, and staves, killing eight and injuring many more. The rebels were soon defeated by the militia, however. Authorities executed eighteen insurgents, burning several at the stake as a warning to others, while six of those imprisoned committed suicide. In 1741 a series of suspicious fires in the city led to accusations against a white couple who owned an alehouse where black people gathered to drink. To protect herself from prosecution, an Irish indentured servant testified that she had overheard discussions of an elaborate plot involving black and white conspirators. Frightened of any hint that the poor might band together regardless of race, authorities immediately arrested suspects and eventually executed thirty-four people, including four white people. They also banished seventy-two black people from the city.

The most serious slave revolt, however, erupted in South Carolina, where a group of enslaved Africans led the **Stono Rebellion** in 1739. On Sunday, September 9, a group of enslaved men who had recently arrived stole weapons from a country store and killed the owners. They then marched south, along the Stono River, beating drums and recruiting others to join them. Torching plantations and killing whites along the route, they had gathered more than fifty insurgents when armed whites overtook them. In the ensuing battle, dozens of rebels died. The militia, along with American Indians hired to assist them, killed another twenty over the next two days and then captured a group of forty, who were executed without trial.

AP® TIP
Be sure you can explain why black people and poor white people had "common cause" to rebel against colonial elites during the early eighteenth century.

Stono Rebellion 1739 uprising by enslaved Africans and African Americans in South Carolina. In its aftermath, white fear of slave revolts intensified.

AP® ANALYZING SOURCES

Source: George Cato, great-great-grandson of Stono Rebellion leader Cato, *Account of the Stono Rebellion, 1739* (recording), 1937

"How it all start? Dat what I ask but nobody ever tell me how 100 slaves between de Combahee and Edisto rivers come to meet in de woods not far from de Stono River on September 9, 1739. And how they elect a leader, my kinsman, Cato, and late dat day march to Stono town, break in a warehouse, kill two white men in charge, and take all de guns and ammunition they wants. But they do it. Wid dis start, they turn south and march on.

They work fast, coverin' 15 miles, passin' many fine plantations, and in every single case, stop, and break in de house and kill men, women, and children. Then they take what they want, 'cludin' arms, clothes, liquor and food.

Governor Bull and some planters . . . ride fast and spread de alarm and it wasn't long 'til de militiamen was on de trail in pursuit of de slave army. When found, many of de slaves was singin' and dancin' and Cap. Cato and some of de other leaders was cussin' at them sumpin awful. From dat day to dis, no Cato has tasted whiskey, 'less he go 'gainst his daddy's warnin'. Dis war last less than two days but it sho' was pow'ful hot while it last.

I reckons it was hot, 'cause in less than two days, 21 white men, women, and chillun, and 44 Negroes, was slain. My granddaddy say dat in de woods and at Stono, where de war start, dere was more than 100 Negroes in line. When de militia come in sight of them at Combahee swamp, de drinkin' dancin' Negroes scatter in de brush and only 44 stand deir ground."

(Continued)

TEACHING IDEA

Building Vocabulary

The following activity is meant to be a bell ringer at the beginning of the hour. As students study how enslaved persons resisted their station and by extension slaveholders, it is important to distinguish between resistance and rebellion. Consider beginning the hour by having students define the terms resistance and rebellion. Next, ask students to extend their definitions to include the subject of slavery. Finally, have students predict which form of protest was more successful and why.

TEACHING IDEA

Incorporating Secondary Sources

Historian Jill Lepore's book, *New York Burning: Liberty, Slavery, and Conspiracy in Eighteenth-Century Manhattan*, captures the conspiracy of the 1741 fires in New York City. For teachers looking to extend their understanding of the depth of fear over slave rebellions, this book presents a riveting account of the events before, during, and after 1741. For students, Chapter 2 connects especially well to the reading in Module 2-7 as Lepore draws out the details of the fire, the context of the conspiracy, and the immediate reactions New Yorkers had in 1741.

TRM Suggested Responses to Questions

TRM Module 2.7 AP® Analyzing Sources Handout 2

BUILDING AP® SKILLS

Sourcing and Situation

Teachers looking to explore how the 1741 conspiracy illustrated how fearful people were over slave rebellions, and how justice was lost in the process, should consult an excerpted copy of Judge Daniel Horsmanden's 1744 publication, *A Journal of the proceedings in the detection of the conspiracy*. Gilder Lehrman's site has an excerpted copy of the document and gives an overall context to the publication of Horsmanden's account (ap.gilderlehrman.org). It also details the pervasive fear that gripped New York in 1741.

TEACHING IDEA

Incorporating Primary Sources

To further the work on causation have students start the document analysis by examining the source title. After reading through the source title they should think about why a colony such as South Carolina would be ripe for rebellion. Have students list specific aspects about the condition of slavery in South Carolina that would have motivated enslaved persons to rebel.

TEACHING IDEA

Check for Understanding

Before students attempt the pre-write strategy, ask students to define the different ways to conceptualize two important elements of the question: slavery and wealthy landowners. "Wealthy landowners" will no doubt be more of a linear definition; however, "slavery" is a term students can bring to bear in several different ways. For instance, ask students what different conditions of slavery existed in the southern colonies and how that informs this particular question.

TRM Suggested Responses to Questions

Period 2: 1607–1754

MODULE 2-7 Slavery Takes Hold in the South

Commander Cato speak for de crowd. He say: "We don't lak slavery. We start to [join] de Spanish in Florida. We surrender but we not whipped yet and we 'is not converted.'" De other 43 say: "Amen." They was taken, unarmed, and hanged by de militia. . . . He die but he die for doin' de right, as he see it."

Questions for Analysis

1. Identify three actions that the Stono rebels undertook as part of their rebellion.
2. Explain the goals of the Stono Rebellion, using the actions of the Stono rebels described in this document as evidence.
3. Explain how this document reveals the causes that led to the Stono Rebellion.

This revolt echoed widely in a colony where black people outnumbered white people nearly two to one, direct importation from Africa was at an all-time high, and Spanish authorities in Florida promised freedom to enslaved people who had fled. In 1738 the Spanish governor formed a black militia company, and he allowed thirty-eight fugitive families to settle north of St. Augustine and build Fort Mose for their protection. When warfare erupted between Spain and Britain over commercial rivalries in 1739, the enslaved people who participated in the Stono Rebellion may have seen their chance to gain freedom as a group. But as with other rebellions, this one failed, and the price of failure was death.

REVIEW

- How did enslaved Africans and African Americans use the economic interests of slaveholders to rebel against their enslavement?

AP® WRITING HISTORICALLY — Responding to a Document-Based Question with Three Primary Sources

Often, historians draw on primary sources to support their arguments. This is because primary sources reveal many things about the time period they're from. They aren't just evidence of what happened; they can also provide windows to look at why and how things happened.

Throughout this course, you will encounter essay prompts that also provide primary sources for you to analyze as part of your response. These are typically known as Document-Based Questions. While these kinds of prompts may look unfamiliar at first, the process for answering them is actually just a combination of skills you've already learned and practiced in your writing.

Here, we will show you how to expand a primary source analysis to three documents instead of just one or two. We will also walk through some strategies for using primary sources to support a fully developed thesis statement. First, however, let's consider the following prompt, which deals with what you have learned in this module:

Explain the effects of slavery on wealthy landowners and enslaved people in the southern British colonies between 1650 and 1750.

Step 1 Break down the prompt and pre-write as you would for any essay prompt.

Before you review the documents provided, you should treat this prompt like you would approach any essay prompt: Consider the topics and task of the prompt. One key element of supporting document-based essays is your ability to use evidence not mentioned in the documents to help prove your argument. If you brainstorm some potential evidence related to the prompt *before* you analyze the documents, you will have evidence that you can use in your arguments along with

---

TEACHING IDEA

AP® Writing Historically Workshop

Part of a student's job when they encounter any Free Response Question is to unpack the meaning of the question, the elements to answer, and the historical time frame in which they are writing. For this activity, focus students on the time frame. Provide groups of four or five students a blank timeline of the years 1650 to 1750. Ask students to develop three ideas relevant to the effects of slavery on wealthy landowners and three ideas about the effects of slavery upon enslaved people. The six answers they come up with should be plotted along the timeline to demonstrate an understanding of a broad sweep across the period. Weaker responses may only be able to address part of the period. So, while students are writing about a time in history and not a history of a time, they nevertheless need to balance the evidence in their response to illustrate change over time.

the evidence you find in the documents. The following chart shows one way to pre-write for our example prompt:

Group	Cause of Slave Economy	Social Effects of Slave Economy
Wealthy landholders	Acquired large plantations and enslaved workers to grow cash crops (tobacco, rice, and, later, indigo).	Established an upper class (the gentry) that feared both slave uprisings (Stono Rebellion) and free Africans in colony. Slaveholders organized society to ensure their profit.
Enslaved Africans	Forced importation to North America to work large, cash-crop plantations.	Lived under harsh conditions. Rebelled covertly (destruction of property) and overtly (Stono Rebellion).

Step 2 Read and annotate the documents, keeping your initial ideas for claims in mind.

Now you're ready to consider how the documents that accompany the prompt will help you support the claims from your pre-write. As you read each document, you should note the key sections or phrases you find that can support your claims. However, you should also be aware that reading the documents might actually lead you to revise and refine your claims or come up with entirely new ones. This awareness will prevent you from "hunting and pecking" solely for information that supports your pre-existing ideas. Often a close look at documents requires historians to revise their beliefs about a time period and topic. This is the essence of good historical scholarship.

As you read each document, you should annotate sections that will help you support the ideas you jotted down. When you annotate, you may find it helpful to ask yourself the following questions:

- What is the document about? What historical situation does it describe or reference?
- Who is the author and what is his or her position in society? What biases or perspectives might someone in this position bring to the topic at hand?
- Who was the intended audience for this document?
- What was the author's purpose in writing this document?
- What point of view does the author of this document express?
- How does this document relate back to the prompt? In this case, try to link each document to the effects of slavery on the wealthy landowners and enslaved people in the southern British colonies between 1650 and 1750.
- Does this document remind you of any other historical developments? Jot down any relevant evidence from your own background knowledge that comes to mind.

We have annotated each document to show how you might do this for the claims we worked out in step 1.

DOCUMENT 1

Source: Virginia House of Burgesses, *Selected Statutes Passed 1662–1667*

1662

Slave codes created a clear separation between white and black people, making intermarriage illegal, and making slavery permanent.

"Whereas some doubts have arisen whether children got by any Englishman upon a Negro woman should be slave or free, be it therefore enacted and declared by this present Grand Assembly, that all children born in this country shall be held bond or free only according to the condition of the mother; and that if any Christian shall commit fornication with a Negro man or woman, he or she so offending shall pay double the fines imposed by the former act."

This reminds us that enslaved women were often subject to the sexual exploitation by slaveholders. This law makes clear that the children of enslaved women were also enslaved even if their fathers were free white men.

(Continued)

EXPLORING AP® THEMES
Social Structures

Encourage students to develop nuanced understandings of Free Response Questions by training them to see the layers within questions. As an example, there is no monolith to the idea of enslaved Africans; to be sure, Africans were enslaved, but as students have read they have gleaned information that explains how many different types of conditions existed. When students are outlining they should be mindful of this fact. Ask students to identify how many different ways they could define "enslaved Africans" and then have them explain their contentions.

BUILDING AP® SKILLS
Sourcing and Situation

As students read the primary sources in this condensed DBQ, ask students what they are looking for in the source title. Items such as author, place, year, and context in which it was written should come up. These questions, along with those listed on page 114, ensure students have a thorough read of each source.

BUILDING AP® SKILLS
Claims and Evidence in Sources

Although the list of questions in step 2 is a thorough list for students to consider, it may be too much for students to handle early in the year. Think about condensing this list down to two or three questions such as the following:

- What is the document about?
- How does the document relate back to the prompt?
- Does the document remind you of any other historical developments?

If students can answer two or three of these questions successfully they are off to a good start. If they are struggling to answer the questions, your remediation is easier to track.

TEACHING IDEA
Check for Understanding

The exemplar annotations are excellent teaching tools to use with students. Select focus points to instruct early in this process such as the abbreviated extractions from the document. Put another way, when students notice what has been circled or underlined, they will notice these are discrete decisions. Students should mirror this practice. Encourage a class discussion about how students avoid the habit of over-highlighting a document, in other words, how to avoid highlighting nearly the entire document.

TEACHING IDEA

Check for Understanding

To build the skill of not over-highlighting, consider assigning students Document 1 and give them guidelines for their annotations. Have them highlight no more than 5–8 words at a time — no hard rule on the number of words — just give them a range to shoot for. In that way, they are focusing on condensing their read to only the essential parts of the document. This practice lends itself to a more discreet analysis of the document.

BUILDING AP® SKILLS

Argumentation

Bearing in mind this question centers on the reasoning process of causation, students should be aware their analyses of documents should trace back to this line of reasoning. Therefore, have students connect their annotations to an explanation of how this relates to causation. This can be as simple as a one-sentence response indicating the relationship between their annotation and the skill.

1667

"Whereas some doubts have risen whether children that are slaves by birth, and by the charity and piety of their owners made partakers of the blessed sacrament of baptism, should by virtue of their baptism be made free, it is enacted and declared by this Grand Assembly, and the authority thereof, that the conferring of baptism does not alter the condition of the person as to his bondage or freedom; that diverse masters, freed from this doubt may more carefully endeavor the propagation of Christianity by permitting children, through slaves, or those of greater growth if capable, to be admitted to that sacrament."

Conversion to Christianity does not change an enslaved person's status. We did not consider this when we generated evidence in step 1. It shows the extent to which slavery shaped the society of the southern colonies: Its preservation was more important than Christian faith. In this case, economics trumped religion.

DOCUMENT 2

Source: Joseph Ball, *Instructions on Managing Enslaved Workers*, 1743

"I will have what Goods I send to Virginia to the use of my Plantation there, kept in my House at Morattico.

If I should not send Goods enough, you must Supply the rest out of the stores there with my Tobacco.

The Coarse Cotton . . . was assign'd for blankets for my Negroes: there must be four yards a half to each Blanket. They that have [now] two blankets already; that is one tolerable one, and one pretty good one, must have what is wanting to make it up, 4½ yards in a blanket. And Everyone of the workers must have a Good Suite of the Welsh Plain [wool] made as it should be. Not [too] Scanty, nor bobtail'd. And Each of the Children must have a Coat of Worser Cotton . . . and two shirts or shifts of [coarse linen] and the Workers must Each of them have Summer Shirts of the brown Rolls. And All the workers must have Good strong Shoes, & stockings; and they that go after the [livestock], or Much in the Wet, must have two pair of Shoes . . . and all must be done in Good time; and not for Winter to be half over before they get their summer Clothes; as the Common Virginia fashion is.

If any of the Negroes should be sick, let them [lie] by a Good fire; and have fresh Meat & [broth]; and blood, and [purge] them, as you shall think proper. . . . I would have no Doctor unless in very violent Cases: they Generally do more harm than Good. . . .

Let not the overseers abuse my People. Nor let them abuse their overseer.

Let the Breeding Wenches have Baby Clothes, for [which] you may tear up old sheets, or any other old Linen . . . (I shall Send things proper hereafter) and let them have Good Midwives; and what is necessary. Register all the Negro Children that shall be born and after keep an account of their ages among my Papers."

Used cheap, but strong, fabric to clothe the people he enslaved—thus keeping costs low. This supports one of our initial claims: "Slaveholders organized society to ensure their profit."

Recommends against calling a doctor. Fears that doctors do more "harm" to enslaved people. Possibly concerned about cost and/or protecting an investment?

Africans Resist Enslavement

DOCUMENT 3

Source: *Instructions given by Richard Corbin, Esq., to his agent for the management of his plantations*, Virginia, 1759

> "As it will be Necessary to . . . Suggest to you my Thoughts upon the business you have undertaken, I shall endeavor to be particular and Circumstanial. . . .
>
> Observe a prudent and a Watchful Conduct over the Overseers that they attend their business with diligence; keep the Negroes in good order and enforce obedience by the Example of their own Industry, [which] is a more effectual method in every respect . . . than Hurry and Severity; the ways of Industry are constant and regular, not to be in a hurry at one time and do nothing at another, but to be always Usefully and Steadily employed. . . .
>
> Take an Exact account of all the Negroes & [animals] at each Plantation and send to me; & [though] once a year may be sufficient to take this acct, yet it will be advisable to see them once a Month at least, as such an Inspection will fix more closely the overseers attention to these points.
>
> As complaints have been made by the Negroes in respect to their provision of corn, I must desire you to put that matter under such a Regulation, as your own Prudence will dictate. . . . The allowance to be sure is Plentiful and they ought to have their Belly full but care must be taken with this Plenty that no [waste] is Committed. . . .
>
> [Large casks of tobacco] should always be provided the 1st Week in Sept; every morning of that month is fit for Striking & Stripping; every morning therefore of this month, they should Strike as much [tobacco] as they can strip whilst the Dew is upon the Ground and what they Strip in the morning must be Stem'd in the Evening; this method constantly practiced, the Tobacco will be prised before Christmas. . . ."

Annotations (margin):

- This supports two of our claims: White slaveholders "established an upper class (the gentry) that feared . . . slave uprisings" and "slaveholders organized society to ensure their profit." Corbin appears to direct his reader to make sure overseers do not overwork enslaved people here. This may be advice to prevent rebellion, and it may also be to ensure the longevity of an enslaved person's work life.
- Here Corbin links enslaved Africans and African Americans with livestock, providing us with a useful piece of evidence to support our claim that enslaved individuals were considered property rather than people.
- Here Corbin tries to balance his desire to prevent slave rebellions with his wish to maintain low costs, thereby ensuring profit.

Step 3 Connect evidence from the documents with your claims to generate a thesis statement.

Now that you've annotated the documents, you should consider how each supports the claims you wrote down before you began your reading. This is also where you can use your annotations from reading the documents to refine, expand, and introduce new ideas to the table you started in step 1. Make sure to note where and how the documents support your claims — in this case, for the social effects of the slave economy. An effective expanded chart may look like this one:

Affected Group	Cause of Slave Economy	Social Effects of Slave Economy	Document Evidence
Wealthy landholders	Acquired large plantations and enslaved people to grow cash crops (tobacco, rice, and, later, indigo).	Established an upper class (the gentry) that controlled colonial politics. Feared both slave uprisings (Stono Rebellion) and free Africans in colony. Created slave codes to regulate enslaved population.	Slave codes created a clear separation between white and black people, making intermarriage illegal (Document 1). They also made slavery permanent by forbidding slaveholders from freeing enslaved people through baptism, and ensuring that any children of an enslaved woman were also enslaved (Document 1).
		Fed and clothed enslaved population cheaply, to ensure profits.	Slaveholder Joseph Ball used cheap, but strong, fabric to clothe enslaved laborers (Document 2).
		Kept enslaved people constantly working in harsh conditions to prevent rebellion.	Slaveholder Richard Corbin instructed his overseers to keep enslaved people working "Usefully and Steadily" (Document 3).

(Continued)

TEACHING IDEA

Check for Understanding

Annotation will help students here. Have students annotate all of Document 3 to check for an understanding of how well they critically read the document. After students are finished annotating the document, reveal the exemplar to discuss how their annotations are similar or different. Pay special attention to their comments about abbreviated sections of the document and their ability to connect their annotations to causation.

TEACHING IDEA

Check for Understanding

Have students think-pair-share this activity. Place students into groups and have them compare how they organized both their evidence and the documents. The goal is not for students to see a correct or incorrect organizational pattern; instead, the primary objective is to see how many different ways a DBQ can be successfully organized. Above all, encourage students to make informed interpretations.

Period 2: 1607–1754

MODULE 2-7 Slavery Takes Hold in the South

Affected Group	Cause of Slave Economy	Social Effects of Slave Economy	Document Evidence
Enslaved people	Forced importation to North America to work large, cash-crop plantations.	Lived under harsh conditions, encouraged to suppress family ties and culture. Rebelled covertly (destruction of property) and overtly (open rebellion, Stono).	Slave codes imply that as the enslaved population grew, intermarriage between white and black people, as well as baptism, was increasingly used as an excuse to free the enslaved. Children of enslaved women and slaveholders remained enslaved (Document 1). Slaveholder Joseph Ball implies that economic concerns were more important than his enslaved workers' health or comfort by carefully limiting their clothing and blankets, perhaps because of the cost (Document 2). Slaveholder Richard Corbin advises that overseers "keep the Negroes in good order and enforce obedience" so as to prevent laziness and rebellion (Documents 3).

When you write a full essay in response to a Document-Based Question, you will need to write a thesis and make a plan to organize your essay. For now, however, let's just focus on how to use documents to support a claim in writing. These skills are especially important for writing body paragraphs of essays, but they're also important for using evidence from the documents to support your claims in any written argument.

Step 4 **Use evidence from both the documents and your historical knowledge to support your argument.**

Here, we will take some time to practice writing paragraphs that state and support a claim. In this case, you will need to incorporate a claim regarding social effects of the southern economy, evidence from your own knowledge of history that supports that claim, *and* evidence from the documents that also supports your claim.

This may sound like a lot of work, and while it may seem difficult at first, the more you practice the easier it will become. When you effectively support an argument, weaving the sources in with your historical evidence is seamless. One way historians use a source as evidence is to showcase specific parts of it, quoting short segments that are especially compelling for their arguments. It may help to think of a quotation as a kind of argument booster — if it's not adding some weight to your claim, you're not quoting the right piece of evidence from your source. You should also remember, when quoting a source, that you need to indicate where it came from — whether by stating the last name of the author or by including the document number in parentheses. The following examples each show a paragraph that supports a claim about the wealthy landowners from the chart in step 3. Claims, evidence, and explanations of evidence are all labeled, and we have annotated these paragraphs to help you understand how they effectively support each claim.

Slaveholders feared slave rebellions and a growing population of free black people, which led slaveholders to create oppressive systems of control **[topic sentence claim]**. Often, enslaved people rebelled against these harsh conditions, as in the Stono Rebellion, where a short but bloody slave revolt inspired fear of future uprisings in South Carolina and throughout the South **[evidence from historical knowledge]**. *For example*, slaveholder Richard Corbin advised that overseers "keep the Negroes in good order and enforce obedience" so as to prevent laziness and rebellion (Doc. 3) **[evidence from documents]**. Here, Corbin *shows* his fear of rebellion and his interest in keeping enslaved people docile **[explanation of evidence]**.

"For example..." cues the reader to look for evidence in a sentence.

When a sentence tells a reader what something "shows," this is a cue that evidence is being explained as to how it supports a claim.

TEACHING IDEA

Group Activity

Place students in groups of three or four and hand out note cards with the following labels:

- Topic sentence
- Historical evidence
- Evidence from documents
- Explanation of evidence

Next, give them a copy of the exemplar body paragraph 1 without the labels and have students write what sentences they think pair up with the labels. So they are looking for one sentence for each labeled note card. This will help show students the extent to which they understand the different purposes of each sentence.

TRM Find **Handout 2.7 – Note Cards for Paragraph Analysis** in the Teacher's Resource Materials

Africans Resist Enslavement

Period 2: 1607–1754

Margin annotations	Main text
"Also" here tells the reader that you are about to provide another piece of evidence.	Slaveholders also created harsh slave codes that narrowed enslaved people's avenues to freedom by ensuring that the children of enslaved women remained enslaved and curtailed the rights of free black people by making intermarriage with white people illegal (Doc. 1) **[evidence from documents]**. This suppressed the growth of the population of free black people—not only was slavery a permanent and inheritable status, but the options free black people had for marriage were severely limited **[explanation of evidence]**. These codes also forbade baptism as a justification for freedom (Doc. 1) **[evidence from documents]**, thereby closing yet another avenue to freedom for enslaved Africans and African Americans **[explanation of evidence]**.

(Margin notes continued:)
- "This" refers to "slave codes" and the verb "suppressed" alerts the reader to the beginning of an explanation of how the evidence supports a claim.
- "Also" tells the reader that this is another piece of evidence to prove the second supporting statement.
- "Thereby" tells the reader that the second half of this sentence explains the significance of the evidence regarding the second supporting statement regarding "enslaved African Americans." Here is another cue that evidence follows.
- "Additionally" here tells the reader that a second piece of evidence is about to follow.
- And this cues the reader that an explanation follows.

Southern society was also shaped by the economic need to keep labor costs low to generate maximum profit **[topic sentence claim]**. Concern for enslaved people's health and comfort was secondary for slaveholders, since they depended upon profit from sugar, indigo, and rice crops, which enslaved Africans and African Americans were forced to cultivate **[evidence from historical knowledge]**. For example, slaveholder Joseph Ball's economic concerns were more important than the health or comfort of the people he kept enslaved, as seen by the cheap clothing he used to outfit them (Doc. 2) **[evidence from documents]**. Additionally, in Document 2, Ball recommended against calling a doctor for enslaved people who were sick or injured **[evidence from documents]**. This could suggest that Ball's interests, like those of many plantation owners, were primarily in the profit generated by enslaved labor rather than the health of those he enslaved **[explanation of evidence]**.

Notice how these paragraphs don't just drop in quotes from sources, nor do they simply list the documents in order. Instead, each paragraph presents the documents in a way that best serves each paragraph's claims, and each paragraph repeats the *ACE* strategy throughout: first by stating a claim, and then following this claim with evidence, which you found in your original brainstorm of the prompt and in annotating the documents. Also, note how the writer immediately follows each piece of evidence with an explanation of how it supports the claim in the paragraph's topic sentence.

ACTIVITY

Generate a new claim about the social effects of slave economies on enslaved people and write a paragraph that uses at least one of the three documents *and* your own historical knowledge as evidence to support your claim. Make sure that your paragraph includes explanations of why your evidence supports your claim. You may wish to use the table in step 3 and the annotations to the documents in step 2 to help you construct your paragraph. You may also wish to add your own annotations to the documents and expand the table to include your own thoughts. An outline to help guide your writing follows.

I. Body paragraph
   A. Topic sentence presenting claim
   B. Supporting statement citing evidence of claim (from historical knowledge)
   C. Citation of additional evidence of claim (from a document)
   D. Explanation of how evidence cited supports claim

TEACHING IDEA

Group Activity

To build off the Teaching Idea from page 116, have students write a body paragraph and label each sentence with the same labels:

- Topic sentence/claim
- Historical evidence
- Evidence from documents
- Explanation of evidence

Strong body paragraphs will include each type of sentence. Students in this activity are assessing their ability to mimic the qualities of the exemplar.

TRM Suggested Responses to Questions

BUILDING AP® SKILLS
Comparison

The goal of this module is to compare European colonizers and their interactions with various American Indians. However, to familiarize students with the reasoning process of comparison consider having them compare different English colonizers and their relations with American Indians. Students will find there are some similarities and differences, and this exercise may help students become more comfortable with comparing European interactions. This could be done as a bell ringer at the beginning of the class period that covers information from Module 2-8 because much of the information was covered in previous modules.

Module 2-8

Imperial Contests in Trade and War

LEARNING TARGETS
By the end of this module, you should be able to:
- Explain how economic competition led to conflict between European colonial powers.
- Explain how economic competition led to conflicts and alliances between European colonial powers and American Indians.
- Explain how American Indians resisted European expansion in North America.

THEMATIC FOCUS
America in the World

Starting in the seventeenth century, British North American colonists were pulled into a series of conflicts with other European colonists and their American Indian allies as European nations increasingly sought control over the Western Hemisphere.

HISTORICAL REASONING FOCUS
Comparison

TASK ▶ As you read Module 2-8, focus your historical thinking by considering comparison in particular. Note similarities and differences in the ways European colonizers interacted with American Indians prior to 1754. Each time you note similarities or differences, think critically about both the reasons for those parallels between different societies as well as why they diverge.

Throughout the early and mid-seventeenth century, English, Dutch, and French colonists profited from trade relations and military alliances with American Indian nations. Nonetheless, European demands for land fueled repeated conflicts with tribes. Already devastated by European-borne diseases, their very survival was at stake.

English colonists most often followed the example that the Spanish set before them, taking American Indian land by force. Most English colonists rebuffed American Indian efforts at trade in favor of theft and conflict from the very start — examples of this include some colonists in the Virginia Company at Jamestown and the atrocities committed by Myles Standish in New England during the first half of the seventeenth century. Such aggressive policies created a frontier of exclusion in which American Indians were not welcome in English communities. Continued intrusions on American Indians' lands led to the **Anglo-Powhatan Wars** in 1620s Virginia, and the Pequot War with New England Puritans in the 1630s (see Module 2-3). These wars, combined with the devastation of diseases brought to North America by the English, killed American Indians in every colonial region and opened up lands to be colonized by the English through the 1640s.

By contrast, colonization by the Dutch in New Amsterdam, and the French in the Great Lakes, succeeded primarily through trade with American Indians. These commercial alliances led to fewer violent conflicts in the first half of the seventeenth century. However, both of these nations sent far fewer colonists to North America, and as a result were significantly less motivated to invade American Indian land than the English. A few English colonists followed a similarly more

Anglo-Powhatan Wars Series of conflicts in the 1620s between the Powhatan Confederacy and English settlers in Virginia and Maryland.

118

TEACHING IDEA

Class Discussion

To generate ideas at the beginning of this module, consider encouraging students to think broadly about how they will compare European colonizers. You can accomplish this by asking groups of three or four students to brainstorm broad categories of analysis that could be used to compare how European colonizers interacted with American Indians. Think of this as analogous to thesis categories. Thesis categories provide a direction for the historical analysis. If students are struggling to develop categories, you can provide one or more of the following: land, trade, religion.

American Indians Resist European Intrusion

AP® TIP
Be sure you can explain the causes for the differences in colonial relations with American Indians across different European nations.

peaceable route. For example, in New England Roger Williams purchased the lands for his Rhode Island colony from local tribes. A small number of Puritans led by missionary John Eliot attempted to establish "praying towns," communities in which Puritan missionaries taught American Indians how to read the Bible, and a few students attended Harvard College. Most "praying Indians," however, continued to embrace traditional rituals and beliefs alongside Christian practices. The efforts produced few total converts, and the lack of acceptance of American Indians within Puritan society at large persisted.

AP® ANALYZING SOURCES

Source: Experience Mayhew and Thomas Prince, *Indian Converts: or, Some Account of the Lives and Dying Speeches of a Considerable Number of the Christianized Indians of Martha's Vineyard, in New-England*, 1727

> "She said she remembered the discourse which I formerly had with her, and said she had been thereby encouraged to seek after God, and she manifested a desire that I would further instruct her.
>
> I then put many questions to her for the trial of her understanding, and found she well understood the principles of the Christian faith; as the doctrine of original sin, the guilt which it brought on all mankind, and the depravation of the humane nature by it, by which man is now naturally inclined to that which is evil only, and that continually. She owned, that from this corrupt fountain all those actual sins do flow, which mankind commit, and said, her own sins had been very many and great.
>
> I found also that she had a distinct understanding of the doctrine of redemption by Jesus Christ. I put several questions to her concerning his person, offices, and the righteousness he fulfilled in his obedience and sufferings for sinners; all which she answered well, and declared her belief of his resurrection from the dead, and ascension into Heaven, &c.
>
> I likewise found she understood the doctrine of regeneration, and the absolute necessity of it, in order to the eternal salvation of sinners. She owned that, without holiness of heart and life, none could have any saving benefit by Jesus Christ, or ever enter into the kingdom of God."

Questions for Analysis
1. Identify the evidence Mayhew and Prince provide for their claim to have converted this native woman to Christianity.
2. Explain the reasons that may have led Mayhew and Prince to present this conversion in this light.
3. Explain the reasons for the differences between Spanish and English interactions with American Indians.

American Indians Resist European Intrusion

The European conflicts in North America put incredible pressure on American Indian peoples to choose sides. Although it was increasingly difficult for native peoples in colonized areas to remain autonomous, American Indian nations were not simply pawns of European powers. Some actively sought European allies against their native enemies, and nearly all desired European trade goods like cloth, guns, and horses. Moreover, struggles among English, French, and Spanish forces both reinforced conflicts among American Indian peoples that existed before European settlement and created new ones.

Colonial conflicts with American Indians started almost immediately in New England, and continued with the Pequot War of 1636 to 1638. War broke out again in the 1670s, this time with the Wampanoag Indians, in Metacom's War (see Module 2-3). There was no easy victory, however, and the war dragged on, becoming increasingly brutal on both sides. Some 1,000 English settlers

---

TRM Suggested Responses to Questions

TRM Module 2.8 AP® Analyzing Sources Handout 1

BUILDING AP® SKILLS
Comparison

To check for understanding about how well students comprehend what comparison looks like in writing, consider the following assignment that can be completed as an exit ticket. The introduction to Module 2-8 utilizes words and phrases historians would employ while writing a comparative analysis of a historical process. Have students read the first three paragraphs of Module 2-8 and make note of the words and phrases they notice that are useful to comparison. Possible answers include: *Most English colonists, Continued, By contrast,* and *similarly*.

TEACHING IDEA
Connecting the Dots

Before students answer the questions for this document, ask them to make a comparison between how "praying towns" and "praying Indians" were seen before and during Metacom's War. Students should also examine the same question using this document from 1727. What similarities and differences do students note about the goals of colonists?

BUILDING AP® SKILLS
Argumentation

To develop an understanding of European interactions with American Indians consider the following assignment. In many respects, Metacom's War was a dramatic conflict both for the damage of the war and for the aftermath. To assess understanding of this event, ask students the extent to which this conflict could be deemed a turning point in relations between American Indians and the British. Turning points are moments in history where the narrative is altered in some significant way. Students can support the idea that King Philip's War immensely changed relations, they can deny this was a turning point, and they can also acknowledge both sides of the argument. The point is to encourage students to develop historical interpretations.

BUILDING AP® SKILLS

Making Connections

On page 118 there is a teaching note dedicated to having students develop categories of analysis. To further the use of categories to compare relations between Europeans and American Indians, consider the following activity. Give students three categories of analysis: religion, land, and trade. Next, ask students to give an analysis of why and how each was an important variable in the relationship between American Indians and European colonizers. The last step is to have students pick the most important variable (religion, land, or trade) and defend their selection in two or three sentences.

TEACHING IDEA

Connecting the Dots

In addition to reading with an eye for comparison in this module, students should also be aware of the causes of the similarities and differences. As an example, throughout this module the need for land, the trading of guns and furs, and slave trading are integral parts of the divergent relationships between American Indians and the several European colonizers. Consider providing students with the following terms: land, guns, fur, and slave trading. Next, ask students to select two or three terms and write a sentence explaining how these relate to the causes of differences in the interactions between American Indians and European colonizers.

EXPLORING AP® THEMES

America in the World

Throughout colonization, American Indians resisted, accommodated, and levered the actions of Europeans. For this activity, focus students on how American Indians resisted colonization. Have students select two examples of resistance and compare both the *causes* and *outcomes* of resistance. You can have students exchange answers with similar selections to encourage a broad view of the activity.

TRM Find **Handout 2.8 – Comparing Causes and Outcomes of Resistance** in the Teacher's Resource Materials.

---

were killed and dozens were taken captive during the war. Metacom's forces attacked Plymouth and Providence and marched within twenty miles of Boston. The English, for their part, allied with predominately Iroquois-speaking tribes and attacked Wampanoag villages, killing hundreds of American Indians and selling hundreds more into slavery in the West Indies, including Metacom's wife and son. Food shortages and disease combined with battlefield injuries to kill as many as 4,500 men, women, and children. About a quarter of the remaining American Indian population of New England died between 1675 and 1676.

As the carnage of Metacom's war spilled into New York, Iroquois leaders and colonists met at Albany in 1677 in hopes of salvaging their lucrative fur trade. There they formed an alliance, the **Covenant Chain**, to prevent future conflict. In the following decades, furs and land continued to define the complex relations between American Indians and Europeans across the northern regions of North America.

The trade in guns was especially significant in escalating conflicts among tribes during the late seventeenth century. By that period the English were willing to trade guns for American Indian captives sold as enslaved labor. American Indians had always taken captives in war, but some of those captives had been adopted into the victorious nation. This changed as the English in Carolina began exchanging guns for captives, shipping most to Caribbean plantations. As slave trading spread, more peaceful tribes were forced to acquire guns for self-protection, further escalating raiding by American Indian foes and enslavement. These raids also had the effect of forcing many American Indian nations off traditional lands.

These dynamics eventually led to two major early-eighteenth-century conflicts in the Carolinas: the **Tuscarora War** (1711–1715), in which British, Dutch, and German colonists banded together against the Tuscarora Indians, and the **Yamasee War** (1715–1717), won by the English against a coalition of several American Indian tribes. Although the English victories had high costs, in terms of both lives and money, they opened up the interior of North America for expanded English settlement, ensuring the growth of the plantation system. In the aftermath of both wars, the Creek emerged as a powerful new confederation, the Cherokee became the major trading partner of the British, and the Yamasee nation was seriously weakened. Moreover, as the British gained a Cherokee alliance their Creek and the Caddo enemies reacted by strengthening their alliance with the French. American Indians, however, still continued raids into the Carolinas into the 1720s and 1730s.

Tuscarora War War launched by Tuscarora Indians from 1711 to 1715 against European settlers in North Carolina and their allies from the Yamasee, Catawba, and Cherokee nations. The Tuscaroras lost their lands when they signed the peace treaty and many then joined the Iroquois Confederacy to the north.

Yamasee War A pan-American Indian war from 1715 to 1717 led by the Yamasee who intended, but failed, to oust the British from South Carolina.

REVIEW

How were English and French interactions with American Indians during this era similar, and in what ways did they differ?

European Rivalry and American Indian Alliances

Developments in North America in the late seventeenth and early eighteenth centuries were driven as much by events in Europe as by those in the colonies. From 1689 until 1713, Europe was in an almost constant state of war, with continental conflicts spilling over into colonial possessions in North America. The result was increased tensions between colonists of different nationalities, American Indians and colonists, and colonists and their home countries.

France was at the center of much of the European warfare of the period, as Louis XIV hoped to expand France's borders and gain supremacy in Europe. To this end, he built a powerful professional army under state authority. Between 1689 and 1697, France and England fought their first sustained war in North America, King William's War (see Module 2-3). The war began over conflicting French and English interests on the European continent, but it soon spread to the American frontier when English and Iroquois forces attacked French and Huron settlements around Montreal and northern New York.

AP® TIP
Trace how European wars not only shaped conflicts in the colonies, but also began to shift colonial attitudes toward the British government.

European Rivalry and American Indian Alliances

Period 2: 1607–1754

Queen Anne's War 1702–1713 war over control of Spain and its colonies; also known as the War of the Spanish Succession. Although the Treaty of Utrecht that ended the war in 1713 was intended to bring peace by establishing a balance of power, imperial conflict continued to escalate.

Although neither side had gained significant territory when peace was declared in 1697, the war had important consequences. Many colonists serving in the English army died of battle wounds, smallpox, and inadequate rations. Those who survived resented their treatment and the unnecessary deaths of so many comrades. The Iroquois fared even worse. Their fur trade was devastated, and hundreds of Mohawks and Oneidas were forced to flee from France's American Indian allies along the eastern Great Lakes.

A second protracted conflict, known as the War of the Spanish Succession, or **Queen Anne's War** (1702–1713), had even more devastating effects on North America. The conflict erupted in Europe when the Spanish monarch died without an heir, launching a contest for the Spanish kingdom and its colonies. France and Spain squared off against England, the Netherlands, Austria, and Prussia. In North America, however, England alone faced France and Spain, with each nation hoping to gain additional territory. Both sides recruited American Indian allies.

AP® ANALYZING SOURCES

Source: Thomas Oliver, writing on behalf of the colonial government of Massachusetts, *Letter to Queen Anne*, 1708

"And they are Animated & Encouraged to such Barbarity's by the french setting the heads of your . . . [Majesty's] Subjects, at a price upon bringing in their Scalps, and they kill many in cold blood. . . . They have the advantage of Retiring for shelter, to the Obscured Recesses of a Vast rude Wilderness, full of Woods, Lakes, Rivers, ponds, Swamps, Rocks and Mountains, whereto they make an Easy and quick Passage, by means of their . . . Canoes of great Swiftness and light of Carriage. . . . [T]heir skill and dexterity for the making and Using of them is very extraordinary, which renders our Tiresome marches after them Ineffectual. These Rebels have no fixt Settlements, but are Ambulatory, & make frequent removes . . . , having no other Houses, but Tents or hutts made of Barque or Kinds of Trees, Matts &c. which they soon provide in all places where they come, So that it is Impracticable to pursue or follow them with any Body of Regular Troops, they are supported and Encouraged by the french, who make them yearly Presents . . . of Clothing, Armes and Ammunition, Besides the Supply they Afford them for the Beaver and Furrs, which they take in hunting, and Constantly keep their Priests & Emissaries among them, to steady them in their Interests, and the bigotries . . . [which] they have Instilled into them. The French also oft times join them in their Marches on our Frontiers. . . . [T]he most probable Method of doing Execution upon them & Reduceing them, is by men of their own Colour, way & manner of living. And if yor Majesty shall be Graciously pleased to Command the Service of the Mohawks, and other Nations of the Western Indians that are in friendship and Covenant with your . . . [Majesty's] Several Governments, against these Eastern Indian Rebels, for which they Express themselves to stand ready, and to whom they are a Terrour. They would with the Blessing of God in Short time [destroy] or Reclaim them, and prevent the Incursions made upon us from Canada or the East. . . ."

Questions for Analysis
1. Identify Oliver's proposed solution to American Indian raids in Massachusetts.
2. Describe the tactics employed by American Indians and their French allies in this excerpt.
3. Explain how this document reveals the connection between mercantilism and conflicts in the Americas during the late 1600s and early 1700s.

After more than a decade of savage fighting, Queen Anne's War ended in 1713 with the **Treaty of Utrecht**, which aimed to secure a lasting peace by balancing the interests of the great powers in Europe and their colonial possessions. While England benefited the most in North America the treaty was not able to keep conflict from continuing. Indeed, Spain, France, and Britain all strengthened fortifications along their North American borders.

TRM Suggested Responses to Questions

TRM Module 2.8 AP® Analyzing Sources Handout 2

BUILDING AP® SKILLS
Sourcing and Situation

After students have read the document and before they answer the questions for analysis, consider asking students to compare the author's view of the French with the author's view of American Indians allied with France. The more informal assessments you can give students during the module, the better.

BUILDING AP® SKILLS
Developments and Processes

During this module, students have been reminded of and exposed to many conflicts between American Indians and Europeans. Sometimes when students encounter so much information at once they can get overwhelmed and the content becomes difficult to deconstruct. Consider giving students blocks of time in history to help foster their understanding of change over time. So it can look something like this:

- 1620–1660
- 1660–1700
- 1700–1740

Within each time, list any relevant information about the conflicts, agreements, and times of peace between American Indians and European colonizers. Next have students write a one-to-two sentence explanation about how relations changed, or maintained continuity, over time.

▲ **Differentiation**

Divide students into groups and assign each group a time period to research the conflicts, agreements, and times of peace between American Indians and European colonizers. Have each group present their findings to the class, then lead a discussion to help students connect the findings of each period.

MODULE 2-8 Imperial Contests in Trade and War

TRM Suggested Responses to Questions

TRM Module 2.8 AP® Analyzing Sources Handout 3

TEACHING IDEA

Building Vocabulary

The Treaty of Utrecht is an excellent document that allows students to conduct a close read on vernacular specific to the time. For instance, the term "subject" is used multiple times in multiple ways. Consider having students compare how the term relates to the British, French, and American Indians. This close read fosters the ability to have a better discussion about what the document says about relations at the end of Queen Anne's War.

EXPLORING AP® THEMES

Geography and the Environment

Before teaching about the southern frontier conflicts, consider having students look again at Map 2.1 on page 46. Ask students to identify at least two reasons the geographical location of Georgia was problematic in European relations. Possible answers include: *proximity to Spanish, proximity to rival American Indians, western frontier.*

Period 2: 1607–1754

AP® ANALYZING SOURCES

Source: *Treaty of Utrecht*, 1713

"The subjects of France inhabiting Canada, and others, shall hereafter give no hinderance or molestation to the five nations or cantons of Indians, subject to the domination of Great Britain, nor to the other natives of America, who are friends to the same. In like manner, the subjects of Great Britain shall behave themselves peaceably towards the Americans who are subjects or friends to France; and on both sides they shall enjoy full liberty of going and coming on account of trade. As also the natives of those countries shall, with the same liberty, resort, as they please, to the British and French colonies, for promoting trade on one side and the other, without any molestation or hinderance, either on the part of the British subjects or of the French. But it is to be exactly and distinctly settled by [government officials], who are, and who ought to be accounted the subjects and friends of Britain or of France."

Questions for Analysis
1. Identify at least four North American groups involved in Queen Anne's War.
2. Describe the causes of the conflict addressed in this section of the treaty.
3. Explain the reasons underlying the causes of conflict in Queen Anne's War.

REVIEW
- How were King William's War and Queen Anne's War similar, and in what ways did they differ?

Imperial Conflicts on the Southern Frontier

King George's War 1739–1748 war between France, Spain, and England fought in North America. King George's War secured Georgia for the English, though Louisbourg was ceded to the French in return.

AP® TIP

Analyzing the reasons why colonists questioned British rule in response to the imperial wars of the early and mid-eighteenth century is key to understanding the historical developments of the late eighteenth century.

From 1739 to 1748, England and Spain fought yet another war — **King George's War** — in North America. It started with Spanish anger at the founding of the English colony of Georgia by King George II (r. 1727–1760) in 1732. Tensions between the two nations grew, and in August 1739, finally erupted into violence. The Spanish navy captured an English ship captain who was trading illegally in the Spanish West Indies and punished him by cutting off one of his ears. In response, Great Britain attacked the Spanish colony of St. Augustine (in present-day Florida) and Cartagena (in present-day Colombia). Spain sent troops into Georgia, but the colonial militia pushed back the attack. This American war became part of a more general European conflict (the War of Austrian Succession). Once again France and Spain joined forces. By the time the war ended in 1748, the British had ensured the future of Georgia and reaffirmed their military superiority.

The British victory cost the lives of many colonial settlers and soldiers, however, and some colonists began to wonder whether their interests and those of the crown were truly the same. King William's War (1689–1697), Queen Anne's War (1702–1713), and King George's War (1739–1748) had all failed to settle the contest for supremacy in North America. Europeans and their American Indian allies resumed fighting a mere six years later in a new conflict: the French and Indian War (1754–1763), also known in Europe as the Seven Years' War (since it started two years later there). Early in the war, a young British officer from the colony of Virginia named George Washington led troops against the French in the Ohio River valley. Yet another in the series of imperial contests for North America, this war too had high costs in lives and treasure. Moreover, it intensified some colonists' questioning of British colonial rule. Unlike King William's War, Queen Anne's War, and King George's War, the Seven Years' War decisively changed the balance of power in North America, setting the stage for outright conflict between British colonists and the British government.

REVIEW
- What were two of the common causes of Britain's colonial wars between 1689 and 1754?
- What were two common effects of those wars?

Period 2: 1607–1754

Imperial Conflicts on the Southern Frontier

AP® WRITING HISTORICALLY
Responding to a Document-Based Question with Five Primary Sources

In Module 2-7, you began to develop your skills in reading and analyzing primary sources in response to a Document-Based Question. While you worked with three sources in that module, here we will walk through how to work with five sources in response to a prompt, as well as how to bring in evidence not found in the documents themselves. Consider the following prompt:

> Explain the similarities and differences in the motives of the English and American Indians for fighting Metacom's War.

Step 1 Break down the prompt and pre-write as you would for any essay prompt.

Jot down a few ideas drawn from your own knowledge of history, as if you were preparing to answer a prompt that was not accompanied by primary source documents. Keep in mind that the prompt is asking you to discuss both similarities *and* differences. The following table shows some ideas that might immediately come to mind as you begin to brainstorm:

The English	American Indians
• Metacom's War primarily took place in New England.	• Metacom's people called the Wampanoag.
• By 1670s, New Englanders felt increasingly threatened by American Indians with guns and sought to take them away.	• New England generally at peace with Wampanoag since 1630s (Pequot War).
• New Englanders continually expanded into American Indian territories as population grew.	• Wampanoag rejected New Englanders' attempt to disarm them.
• Confiscation of guns and territorial expansion caused American Indian raids on New England frontier villages.	• Wampanoag feared New Englanders' encroachment on their land.
• Religiously motivated New Englanders considered Native Americans inferior to Christians.	• Raids on New England villages led to reprisals, escalating the conflict.
• New Englanders believed expansion was God's will and civilized an untamed wilderness.	

This initial brainstorming activity allows you to see some similarities and some differences in the motives both the New Englanders and the Wampanoag had to fight Metacom's War. Some of this information might serve as the evidence not found in the documents that you will need to bring in to your arguments. Before moving on, you may find it helpful to take a few moments to arrange this information in terms of similarity and difference to help focus your reading of the documents. The following table illustrates one way you can approach this part of the pre-writing process:

Similarities	Differences
• Both had been at peace with each other since the Pequot War of the 1630s.	• New Englanders were expanding because of a growing population.
• Both were competing for the same land.	• Wampanoag territory was encroached upon by New Englanders.
• Both perceived the other as a threat.	• New Englanders tried to confiscate Wampanoag guns to ensure safety of settlers.
• Both engaged in retaliatory attacks immediately preceding and during the war, which escalated the conflict.	• Wampanoag, after forty years of peace with New Englanders, perceived confiscation of guns to be a threat.
	• New Englanders considered their colony to be God's "City Upon a Hill," and were therefore righteously motivated to "civilize" what they considered the wilderness.
	• Wampanoag did not see the war in terms of a religious crusade, but as a defensive measure against the growing power of New England.

Now that you've written down a few ideas, it is a good idea to generate a couple of preliminary claims. Reviewing the information we just brainstormed, you could make the following two:

Claim 1 (similarity): Both the Wampanoag and New Englanders were competing over the same land.

Claim 2 (difference): The New Englanders increasingly sought to protect settlers in land they believed their right to settle. The Wampanoag sought to defend their traditional territories from English encroachment.

(Continued)

TRM Suggested Responses to Questions

TEACHING IDEA

Building Vocabulary

As students examine the language in the Document-Based Question, ask students what "the extent of similarity" means to them. Encourage students to think about weighing the significance of their categories of analysis. Also, when the question says "the extent of similarity" it is trying to see whether students know they can illustrate both similarities and differences. Therefore, students could acknowledge similarities while privileging differences. This is evidence of a student who possesses some understanding of nuance early in the school year.

TEACHING IDEA

Check for Understanding

Developing historical evidence to a prompt is a process with great variance. We will use this Document-Based Question as an example. Some students will see this question as one that privileges similarities while acknowledging differences. Others will emphasize differences. Both are acceptable because they are staying within the confines of the question. The important aspect is not balanced between similarities and differences; instead, the crucial factor is whether or not students are acknowledging both.

TEACHING IDEA

AP® Writing Historically Review

The following can be used as a bell ringer to begin class and help students brainstorm about possible interpretations of this DBQ. Assign each student one of two roles: one group will be assigned motives of the English and the other motives of American Indians for fighting Metacom's War. Working individually, they are given three minutes to develop one claim for the rationale to fight, given their assigned perspective. Students then have three minutes to meet with as many other students who were assigned the same role to collect as many perspectives on the question as they can. Next, students select their best rationale. Their final move is to spend two minutes sharing responses with students who were assigned the opposite role. In less than ten minutes students will have brainstormed a basic list of claims before you begin the writing activity.

Period 2: 1607–1754

MODULE 2-8 Imperial Contests in Trade and War

Step 2 Read and annotate the documents, keeping your initial ideas for claims in mind.

While you read the documents, keep your pre-writing from step 1 in mind. Be sure to annotate the following documents for evidence that points to the motivations of both the New Englanders and the Wampanoag. When you see an example that matches or adds to your list of similarities and differences, quickly make note of it. We have provided a few annotations to the documents to help guide your reading, but you can and should add your own.

When you annotate, remember to ask yourself the following questions:

- What is the document about? What historical situation does it describe or reference?
- Who is the author and what is his or her position in society? What biases or perspectives might someone in this position bring to the topic at hand?
- Who was the intended audience for this document?
- What was the author's purpose in writing this document?
- What point of view does the author of this document express?
- How does this document relate back to the prompt?
- Does this document remind you of any other historical developments?

BUILDING AP® SKILLS

Claims and Evidence in Sources

In addition to the close reading strategies used in this module, encourage students to see another aspect of the document: the big picture. Often students spend too much time combing through the fine details presented in the document and they fail to grasp the overall meaning of the document. Students should ask themselves what the big picture is in each document and what that means to their interpretation. Consider asking students to identify both the big picture and how it relates to their argument before they annotate the document.

DOCUMENT 1

Source: William Nahaton, *Petition to Free an Indian Slave*, 1675

Here, Nahaton requests the release of a Wampanoag woman who has been sold into slavery. She is related to him (he uses the word "kin"). This establishes that the English enslaved American Indians around the time of Metacom's War. Did the Wampanoag take English captives too? If so, that is a **similarity** for motivation for continued conflict.

"To the honored counsel now siting at boston to the humble petition of william [n]ahaton hee humbly sheweth.

I have [seen] a woman taken by the mohegins and now brought to boston which woman although she did belong to [King] phillip his Company yet shee is [kin] to me and all so to john hunter as severall of the indians of punkapoag do know[.] my humble and right request there fore to the Renowned Counsel is that if it may stand with there pleasure and with out furtur inconvenience her Life may be spared and her Liberty granted under such conditions as the honored Counsel see most fit: shee being a woman whatever her mind hath been it is very probable she hath not dun much mischefe and if the honored counsel shall plese so grant me that favor I shall understand to leve her at punkapoag[.] . . . I shall obtaine so much favor from the honored counsel which will further oblige him who is your honored to command william [n]ahaton."

DOCUMENT 2

Source: Benjamin Church, *A Visit with Awashonks, Sachem of the Sakonnet*, 1675

"The next Spring advancing, while Mr. Church was diligently settling his new Farm, stocking, leasing, and disposing of his Affairs . . . ; and hoping that his good success would be inviting unto other good Men to become his Neighbours; Behold! The rumor of a War between the English and the Natives gave check to his projects. People began to be very jealous of the Indians, and indeed they had no small reason to suspect that they had form'd a design of War upon the English. . . ."

Church mentions some English grievances in the new settlements: New Englanders "began to be very jealous" of the Wampanoag in the newly settled regions and had "reason to suspect" they meant to make war on the English. Our pre-writing assumed that the English were the aggressors and the Wampanoag were on the defensive. However, this points to another possible **similarity**: Both New Englanders and the Wampanoag saw each other as threats.

Imperial Conflicts on the Southern Frontier

Period 2: 1607–1754

Another new piece of info: The Wampanoag had begun to seek alliances with local American Indians. This supports the claim that the Wampanoag feared English aggression and also gives the English a reason to seek allies.

Among the rest he sent Six Men to Awashonks Squaw-Sachem of the Sakonnet Indians . . . : Awashonks so far listened unto them as to call her Subjects together, to make a great Dance, which is the custom of that Nation when they advise about Momentous Affairs. . . . [S]he . . . calls her Nobles round her, orders Mr. Church to be invited into her presence. Complements being past, and each one taking Seats. She told him, King Philip had sent Six Men of his . . . to draw her into a confederacy with him in a War with the English. . . .

Then Mr. Church turn'd to Awashonks, and told her, if Philip were resolv'd to make War, her best way would be to . . . shelter her self under the Protection of the English. . . .

*Aha! Both sought native allies. This is an important **similarity** we did not note prior to reading. Keep this information in mind for a new claim.*

Then he told Awashonks he thought it might be most advisable for her to send to the Governour of Plymouth, and shelter her self, and People under his Protection. She lik'd his advice, and desired him to go on her behalf to the Plymouth Government, which he consented to: And at parting advised her what ever she did, not to desert the English Interest, [and] joyn with her Neighbours in a Rebellion which would certainly prove fatal to her. . . . She thank'd him for his advice, and sent two of her Men to guard him to his House. . . ."

DOCUMENT 3

Source: John Easton, *A Relation of the Indian War*, 1675

*More new info: Easton notes that the Wampanoag claimed the English had broken treaties with them, and tried to weaken Wampanoag society by encouraging drunkenness. This could be a **difference** in motivations, since the English considered their expansion an improvement of the "wilderness." This connects to Doc. 4, where the author describes English views of their new settlements.*

"Another Grievance was, when their King sold Land, the English would say, it was more than they agreed to, and a Writing must be prove against all them, and some of their Kings had [done wrong] to sell so much. He left his [people] none, and some being given to Drunknes the English made them drunk and then cheated them in Bargains, but now their Kings were forewarned not for to part with Land, for nothing in Comparison to the Value thereof. Now [some of] the English had owned for King or Queen, they would disinherit, and make another King that would give or sell them these Lands; that now they had no Hopes left to keep any Land. Another Grievance, the English [cattle] and Horses still increased; that when they removed 30 Miles from where English had any thing to do, they could not keep their Corn from being spoiled, they never being used to fence, and thought when the English bought Land of them they would have kept their [cattle] upon their owne Land. Another Grievance, the English were so eager to sell the Indians [liquor], that most of the Indians spent all in Drunknes, and then ravened upon the sober Indians, and they did believe often did hurt the English [cattle], and their King could not prevent it."

*Here are more native grievances against the English and another important **difference**. The livestock New Englanders brought to their new settlements wandered into Wampanoag fields and destroyed their crops.*

*Here is another **difference** in motivations: According to this document, Wampanoag attacks on English livestock were caused by the alcohol provided by the English! It is important to remember that this is told from the Wampanoag perspective, but it nonetheless could be a motivation.*

(Continued)

TEACHING IDEA

Class Discussion

Many students will see good annotations and think they need to develop three or four ideas per document. While it is good training to have students annotate each document thoroughly, remind students they should select the best annotation to illustrate their interpretation. Have a class discussion about which part of the document students are going to use so students can hear all of the different possibilities.

TEACHING IDEA

Incorporating Secondary Sources

Sam Wineburg's book, *Historical Thinking and Other Unnatural Acts: Charting the Future of Teaching the Past*, is a book meant for teachers who aspire to inculcate processes of historical thinking for their students. The book challenges teachers to think about instructional practices and the incorporation of primary sources. Although the entire book is useful for teachers, Part III of the book is especially relevant to the challenges of teaching the DBQ.

TEACHING IDEA

Check for Understanding

To assess how well students understand relating the content of a document to a category of analysis, consider the following assignment. Provide students with three categories of analysis: land, religion, and trade. Next, have students select one document they are confident in using and ask them to connect their annotation to the category of analysis. Accomplishing this is an essential part of developing an argument for the Document-Based Question.

BUILDING AP® SKILLS

Sourcing and Situation

Sam Wineburg's book, *Historical Thinking and Other Unnatural Acts: Charting the Future of Teaching the Past*, contains content relevant to how students interact with primary sources. In Part II of the book, there is a section devoted to how students read primary sources about Abraham Lincoln. This section in particular is useful for teachers to read in advance of Module 2-8. Beyond accounting for reasons why students struggle with primary sources, the section also explores ways students and teachers can improve their use of documents.

Period 2: 1607–1754

MODULE 2-8 Imperial Contests in Trade and War

DOCUMENT 4

*This is another important **difference** in motivations. While the Wampanoag saw the English as destroying their crops and society, the English saw themselves as, in this case, building roads that were "beneficial." This connects to Doc. 3, which describes how the Wampanoag perceived New England settlements.*

Source: Edward Randolph, *Assessment of the Causes of King Philip's War*, 1675

"He was especially anxious about road building, paying attention to utility as well as to that which was beneficial to grace and beauty. For the roads were carried straight through the country without wavering, and were paved with quarried stone, and made solid with masses of tightly packed sand. Hollows were filled up and bridges were built across whatever wintry streams or ravines cut the roads. And both sides were an equal and parallel height with the result that the road for its entire course had a level and beautiful appearance. Besides these things, he measured the whole road mile by mile and set up stone columns as distance indicators. He also placed other stones on either side of the road at lesser intervals so that it would be easier for those who had horses to mount them from the stones without requiring a groom to help."

DOCUMENT 5

*An English woman who has been captured and enslaved by the Wampanoag is evidence of a **similarity** in motivations for fighting Metacom's War. Both retaliated by taking captives. This connects to Document 1.*

New Englanders perceived Wampanoag lands as "wilderness" and uncivilized, but the Wampanoag saw the land they cultivated as destroyed by New Englanders rather than improved. This connects to Documents 3 and 4, which also discuss different perceptions of English settlement.

Source: Mary Rowlandson, *Narrative of the Captivity and Restoration of Mrs. Mary Rowlandson*, 1682

"The first week of my being among [the Wampanoag] . . . I was at this time knitting a pair of white cotton stockins for my mistriss and had not yet wrought upon a Sabbath day; when the Sabbath came they bade me go to work; I told them it was the Sabbath-day, and desired them to let me rest, and told them I would do as much more tomorrow; to which they answered me, they would break my face. And here I cannot but take notice of the strange providence of God in preserving the heathen: They were many hundreds, old and young, some sick, and some lame, many had [infants] at their backs, the greatest number at this time with us, were *Squaws*, and they travelled with all they had, bag and baggage, and yet they got over this River aforesaid; and on *Munday* they set their *Wigwams* on fire, and away they went: On that very day came the English Army after them to this River, and saw the smoak of their *Wigwams*, and yet this River put a stop to them. God did not give them courage or activity to go over after us; we were not ready for so great a mercy as victory and deliverance; if we had been, God would have found out a way for the *English* to have passed this River, as well as for the *Indians* with their *Squaws* and *Children*, and all their Luggage. . . .

On *Munday* (as I said) they set their Wigwams on fire, and went away. It was a cold morning, and before us there was a great Brook with ice on it; some waded through it, up to the knees & higher, but others went till they came to a Beaver dam, and I amongst them, where through the good providence of God, I did not wet my foot. I went along that day mourning and lamenting, leaving farther my own Country, and travelling into the vast and howling *Wilderness*. . . . We came that day to a great Swamp, by the side of which we took up our lodging that night. When I came to the brow of the hill, that looked toward the Swamp, I thought we had been come to a great *Indian* Town (though there were none but our own

Imperial Conflicts on the Southern Frontier

Period 2: 1607–1754

Rowlandson is afraid of Wampanoag power, yet still believes God will protect her. This is a **difference** between the Wampanoag and the New Englanders: Puritans believed their expanding settlements were divinely sanctioned.

Company). The *Indians* were as thick as the trees: it seemed as if there had been a thousand Hatchets going at once: if one looked before one, there was nothing but Indians, and behind one, nothing but Indians, and so on either hand, I my self in the midst, *and no Christian soul near me, and yet how hath the Lord preserved me in safety! Oh the experience that I have had of the goodness of God, to me and mine!*"

Step 3 Connect evidence from the documents to your claims to set the context and craft a thesis statement.

We can now incorporate information from our original list of similarities and differences between English and American Indian motivations for Metacom's War with the information we found in the documents. The following example shows how you might expand on the table from step 1:

Similarities	Differences
• Both were competing for the same land (outside information). • Both sought allies in other American Indian tribes (Doc. 2). • Both engaged in retaliatory attacks immediately preceding and during the war. The Wampanoag attacked Plymouth and Providence. New Englanders killed Metacom's wife and son and starved the Wampanoag (historical knowledge). • Both took captives during the conflict — William Nahaton's "kin" and Mary Rowlandson (Docs. 1 and 5).	• New Englanders expanded into Wampanoag territory because of a growing population (historical knowledge). • New Englanders tried to confiscate Wampanoag guns to ensure safety of settlers (historical knowledge). • New Englanders considered their colony to be God's "City Upon a Hill," and were therefore righteously motivated to "civilize" what they considered the "wilderness" (outside information and Docs. 4 and 5). • The Wampanoag, after forty years of peace with New Englanders, perceived confiscation of guns to be a threat (historical knowledge). • The Wampanoag considered the English a destructive force on their lands, causing destruction of their fields and spreading drunkenness through their society (Doc. 3). • Wampanoag did not see the war in terms of a religious crusade, but as a defensive measure against the aggressive power of New England (Doc. 3).

Now that you have two preliminary claims and have outlined both outside information and documentary information to support them, you're ready to write your thesis. For this prompt, your thesis must include an argument for at least one similarity and one difference. It must also present at least one reason for a similarity and one reason for a difference. The following thesis is weak:

> Both the English and the American Indians wanted the same land, but they fought for it in different ways.

You probably noticed that this thesis does not really discuss different motivations. Instead, it points out a simple similarity in a very general way (they "both wanted the same land"), and then introduces a difference that does not answer the question (they "fought" for the land "in different ways"). Here's how you might improve the original thesis:

> Though both the Wampanoag and New Englanders fought over the same land and perceived each other as threats during Metacom's War in the 1670s, which often led them to fight the war in similar ways. New Englanders were primarily motivated to protect settlers in newly settled land they believe their right to settle, while the Wampanoag were motivated largely to defend their traditional territories and society from English encroachment.

This is a stronger thesis because it speaks to motivations for both similarities and differences. It notes that both Wampanoag and New Englanders competed for the same land and perceived

(Continued)

TEACHING IDEA

Categorizing Evidence

After students complete step 3, consider having them select one of the categories they may have used in the module such as land, religion, or trade. Next, have students categorize their evidence and the documents to the category. This ensures they have a focus for how they want to explain the evidence they are using.

EXPLORING AP® THEMES

America in the World

Although an older book, Gary B. Nash's *Red, White, and Black: The Peoples of Early North America* is still a useful read for teachers and students interested in understanding the broader contours of colonial history. Chapter 6 in particular is useful for students studying American Indian resistance to European encroachment. Included in this essay is an elaborate discussion of King Philip's (Metacom's) War. The incorporation of this chapter can help students think about this theme early in the course.

each other as threats — both motivations for similarities. This thesis also addresses motivations for differences by asserting that New Englanders perceived themselves as protecting their settlers and saw settlement as their right, while the Wampanoag, on the other hand, tried to defend their traditional territories and society from English invasion.

You probably also noticed that the key words "though" and "while" in this thesis each direct the reader to the items that you consider "similarities" and "differences." The word "though" gathers the similar motivations of the New Englanders and Wampanoag into the first part of the thesis and sets the reader up for the differences. The word "while" separates the different motivations. These two claims will be the basis for the essay's body paragraphs.

Now that you have your thesis and the evidence that you will use to support the claims in your thesis, you are ready to write your introduction. Remember that your introduction should begin with some context to help situate your reader within the time period and topic of your essay. The contextualization statement should explain either the immediate context (events or developments that happened at the same time as your topic) or preceding context (events or developments that happened right before your topic). Then, you should explain how the context relates to your topic. This leads to your thesis. Since the New Englanders had engaged in wars with American Indians before Metacom's War, a preceding context statement will work best in this case:

> Since the English first arrived in North America, they competed with American Indians for land **[preceding context statement]**. During the Pequot War of the 1630s, New Englanders fought a bloody conflict with local tribes as their colony expanded and their population grew. While the outcome of this conflict was devastating to the Pequot peoples, it resulted in several decades of relative peace in New England between the English settlers and American Indians **[support for context statement]**. Though both the Wampanoag and New Englanders fought over the same land and perceived each other as threats during Metacom's War in the 1670s, which often led them to fight the war in similar ways, New Englanders were primarily motivated to protect settlers in newly settled land they believe their right to settle, while the Wampanoag were motivated largely to defend their traditional territories and society from English encroachment **[thesis statement]**.

Step 4 Use evidence from both the documents and your historical knowledge to support your argument.

Now you are ready to write your first body paragraph, which will prove your claim that "both the Wampanoag and New Englanders fought over the same land and perceived each other as threats during Metacom's War in the 1670s, which often led them to fight the war in similar ways." A weak body paragraph might look like this:

> Both New Englanders and the Wampanoag fought over territory during Metacom's War. Both of them sought alliances with different American Indian tribes as seen in Document 2. They also both attacked each other's communities during the conflict. Moreover, they both took captives during the conflict, as seen in Documents 1 and 5.

This paragraph is relatively simplistic. It merely states similarities without many details — there are no direct quotations from the documents, for instance — and it includes no explanation as to why this information supports its claim.

A stronger version of this body paragraph will prove a claim by citing specific evidence (both in the documents and through outside evidence not found in the documents) and clearly explain how each piece of evidence provides support. Also, notice that we have added "supporting" statements that provide more precise validation for each claim and set up the sentences that include evidence. And, as we did in Module 2-7 (p. 107), we have annotated this paragraph to help you understand how it effectively supports the topic sentence claim.

Words like "One," "Another," "Likewise," and "Finally," cue your reader that you have begun a supporting statement.

Phrases like "For example..." tell your reader that you are about to provide specific historical evidence for your supporting statement.

> Both the Wampanoag and New Englanders fought over the same land and perceived each other as threats immediately before and during Metacom's War, which motivated each to fight the war in some similar ways **[claim]**. One similarity is that both sought American Indian allies in their cause **[first supporting statement]**. For example, each tried to form an alliance with the Awashonk people (Document 2)

TEACHING IDEA

Check for Understanding

Before going over the exemplar, have students identify what they see as the claim, supporting statement, and evidence from the documents in the first paragraph of the exemplar. Distinguishing between these sentences helps prepare students to mimic the skill at the end of the module.

Imperial Conflicts on the Southern Frontier — Period 2: 1607–1754

> Phrases like "The attempt... shows..." and words like "prove" let your reader know that you are about to explain how your evidence proves your claim.

[evidence from documents]. The attempt to find American Indian allies shows a similar motivation to fight the war in similar ways by the English and the Wampanoag [explanation of evidence]. Another similarity is that both the Wampanoag and the English took captives as a way to acquire free labor and to terrorize the other side [second supporting statement]. For example, William Nahaton, an American Indian, related the tale of a relative captured by English American Indian allies, the Mohegan, who then sold her into slavery in Boston (Document 1) [evidence from documents]. Likewise, Mary Rowlandson was captured by the Wampanoag and forced to work for them as an enslaved laborer. They also threatened her with violence if she did not work for them (Document 5) [evidence from documents]. Both the capture of Nahaton's relative by the English and Mary Rowlandson by the Wampanoag show that each side was motivated to fight the other through the capturing of members of each other's communities [explanation of evidence]. Finally, throughout the war, both performed retaliatory attacks on each other as a way to break each other's will to fight [third supporting statement]. For example, the Wampanoag attacked the New England towns of Plymouth, Massachusetts and Providence, Rhode Island during the war [evidence from historical knowledge]. In retaliation, the English murdered Metacom's wife and child as part of their war against the Wampanoag people. [evidence from historical knowledge]. The attacks on New England towns by the Wampanoag and the murder of Metacom's wife and son prove that both sides were propelled to commit retaliatory attacks on each other during the war [explanation of evidence].

ACTIVITY

Generate a new claim about differences between the English and the American Indians' motives for fighting Metacom's War and write a body paragraph to support your claim. Use at least two of the documents *and* your own historical knowledge as evidence to support your claim. Make sure that your paragraph includes explanations for why your evidence supports your claim.

You can use the table in step 3 and the annotations to the documents in step 2 to help you construct your paragraph. You may also wish to add your own annotations to the documents and expand the table to include your own thoughts. An outline to help guide your writing follows.

I. Body paragraph
   A. Topic sentence presenting claim
   B. Supporting statement citing evidence of claim (from historical knowledge)
   C. Citation of additional evidence of claim (from a document)
   D. Explanation of how evidence cited supports claim

Note: You can use more than two pieces of evidence to support your claim. Just be sure that you explain how each piece of evidence connects to that claim.

TEACHING IDEA

Check for Understanding

To emphasize the skill of comparison and help prepare students to complete the activity at the end of the module, consider having students identify all of the words or phrases that employ the reasoning process of comparison. Being cognizant of this skill prepares students to be mindful of including these words and phrases when they write. Incorporating these words and phrases is part of answering the question in a more nuanced fashion. Possible words include: *Similarity, Likewise, Both, Each side, Both performed*.

TRM Suggested Responses to Questions

TEACHING IDEA

Building Vocabulary

For some students, this may be the first course they encounter college-level vocabulary, both historical vocab and academic vocab. Although many teachers would expect students to know the definition of patriarchy and hierarchy, many students have simply not encountered terms such as these. Therefore, at the outset consider going over a few difficult terms that relate to the narrative at the beginning of this module.

- Hierarchy
- Patriarchy
- Matriarchy

Module 2-9

Religious and Political Awakenings

LEARNING TARGETS

By the end of this module, you should be able to:

- Explain how economic ties between the colonies affected the development of British North American colonial society.
- Explain the impact of transatlantic print culture on the development of British North American colonial society.
- Explain the impact of Protestant evangelicalism on the development of British North American colonial society.
- Explain how the Great Awakening and the spread of Enlightenment ideals enhanced the religious and ideological diversity of British North America.
- Explain how traditions of self-government, Enlightenment ideas, religious diversity, and colonial conceptions of British imperial corruption fueled resistance to British imperial power.

THEMATIC FOCUS

American and Regional Culture
Social Structures

Inspired by religious movements and new political ideologies, British North Americans developed a sense of distinctness from England while, at the same time, experiencing fragmentation within the colonies themselves.

HISTORICAL REASONING FOCUS

Causation

TASK ▶ As you read this module, pay careful attention to historical developments, including simultaneous historical events, that help explain the era discussed in this module. Remember also to consider how context shapes the most important events you read about, and to periodically ask yourself why important developments occurred. The overarching question you should keep in mind as you read this module is: What aspects of the Enlightenment and Great Awakening led to fragmentation in colonial society, and why?

During the early eighteenth century, challenges to the culture of traditional patriarchy and religion in the colonies sparked a religious response. Young people experienced increased independence from their parents, and colonial people in general had greater mobility, moving more frequently in the dynamic economy. Additionally, towns and cities developed clearer hierarchies by class and status, which at times protected wealthier individuals from punishment for misdeeds and undermined social confidence in the patriarchal order. The practices of traditional religion faced challenges as well: Generally reduced religious enthusiasm during the later seventeenth century led some to believe that new approaches to religion were needed in order to correct society's ills. The combined contexts of a more open, less patriarchal society, and the failure of traditional religion to inspire devout Christian followers unleashed powerful religious forces — later called the Great Awakening — that swept through the colonies in the early eighteenth century.

Colonial Family Life and the Limits of Patriarchal Order

By the early eighteenth century, many colonial writers promoted the idea of marriage as a partnership, even if the wife remained the junior partner. This concept took practical form in communities across the colonies. In towns, the wives of artisans often learned aspects of their husband's craft. Given the overlap between homes and workplaces in the eighteenth century, women often cared for apprentices, journeymen, and laborers as well as their own children. Husbands meanwhile labored alongside their subordinates and represented their families' interests to the larger community. Both spouses were expected to provide models of godliness and to encourage prayer and regular church attendance among household members.

On farms, where the vast majority of colonists lived, women and men played crucial if distinct roles. In general, wives and daughters labored inside the home as well as in the surrounding yard. Husbands and sons worked the fields, kept the livestock, and managed the orchards. Many families supplemented their own labor with that of servants, enslaved people, or hired field hands. And surplus crops and manufactured goods such as cloth or sausage were exchanged with neighbors or sold at market, creating an economic network of small producers.

Colonial mothers combined childbearing and child rearing with a great deal of other work. While some affluent families could afford wet nurses and nannies, most women fended for themselves or hired temporary help for particular tasks. Infants were the most vulnerable to disease, and childbirth was also a dangerous ordeal for colonial women. In 1700 roughly one out of thirty births ended in the mother's death. Women who bore six to eight children thus faced death on a regular basis. When a mother died while her children were still young, her husband was likely to remarry soon afterward in order to maintain the family and his livelihood. Even though fathers held legal guardianship over their children, there was little doubt that childcare was women's work.

While most families accepted the idea of female subordination in return for patriarchal protection, there were signs of change in the early eighteenth century. Ads for runaway spouses, servants, and enslaved people; reports of domestic violence; poems about bossy wives; petitions for divorce; and legal suits charging rape, seduction, or breach of contract make clear that ideals of patriarchal authority did not always match the reality. A variety of evidence points to increasing tensions around issues of control—by husbands over wives, fathers over children, and men over women.

Divorce was as rare in the colonies as it was in England. In New England, colonial law allowed for divorce, but few were granted and almost none to women before 1750. In other colonies, divorce could be obtained only by an act of the colonial assembly and was therefore confined to the wealthy and powerful. A quicker and cheaper means of ending an unsatisfactory marriage was to abandon one's spouse. Colonial divorce petitions citing desertion and newspaper ads for runaway spouses suggest that husbands fled in at least two-thirds of such cases. In the rare instances when women did obtain a divorce, they had to bring multiple charges against their husbands. Domestic violence, adultery, or abandonment alone were not enough to secure a divorce. Indeed, ministers and relatives were likely to counsel abused wives to change their behavior or suffer in silence.

> **AP® TIP**
> Make sure to note the pattern of continuity in how patriarchy affected the lives of women in colonial society as the eighteenth century progressed.

REVIEW

What were the effects of social changes in colonial society during the early eighteenth century?

The Great Awakening Takes Root

Enlightenment European cultural movement spanning the late seventeenth century to the end of the eighteenth century emphasizing rational and scientific thinking over traditional religion and superstition.

By the eighteenth century, the **Enlightenment**, a European cultural movement that emphasized rational and scientific thinking over traditional religion and superstition, had taken root in the colonies, particularly among elites. The development of a lively transatlantic print culture spread the ideas of Enlightenment thinkers like the English philosopher John Locke, the German intellectual Immanuel Kant, and the French writer Voltaire. These thinkers argued that through reason humans could discover the laws that governed the universe and thereby improve society. Benjamin Franklin, a leading printer in Philadelphia, was one of the foremost advocates of Enlightenment ideas in the colonies. His experiments with electricity reflected his faith in rational thought, and his publication of *Poor Richard's Almanack* spread such ideas throughout the colonies in the 1720s and 1730s.

Period 2: 1607–1754

MODULE 2-9 Religious and Political Awakenings

TRM Suggested Responses to Questions

TRM Module 2.9 AP® Analyzing Sources Handout

TEACHING IDEA

Incorporating Websites

Students may be very unfamiliar with the tone and style found in *Poor Richard's Almanack*; therefore, consider giving them some brief background notes to what Benjamin Franklin was producing when he wrote this publication. The Benjamin Franklin Historical Society has an entire section devoted to providing background and substance on the meanings of the *Almanack* (benjaminfranklin-history.org).

TEACHING IDEA

Check for Understanding

The goal of this module is to see how the Enlightenment and Great Awakening caused fissures in colonial society. Devote some time for students to think conceptually about each event. For instance, consider assigning groups of students one of the following categories of analysis: religion, social, political. Next, ask students to define how the Enlightenment connects to each category. The goal is for students to make more discrete interpretations about the effects of the Enlightenment.

AP® ANALYZING SOURCES

Source: Benjamin Franklin, *Poor Richard's Almanack*, 1739

"Kind Reader,
Encouraged by thy former Generosity, I once more present thee with an Almanack, which is the 7th of my Publication. While thou art putting Pence in my Pocket, and furnishing my Cottage with necessaries, Poor Dick is not unmindful to do something for thy Benefit. . . .

Ignorant Men wonder how we Astrologers foretell the Weather so exactly, unless we deal with the old black Devil. Alas! . . . For Instance; The Stargazer peeps at the Heavens thro' a long Glass: . . . He spies perhaps VIRGO (or the Virgin;) she turns her Head round as it were to see if any body observ'd her; then crouching down gently, with her Hands on her Knees, she looks wistfully for a while right forward. He judges rightly what she's about: And having calculated the Distance and allow'd Time for its Falling, finds that next Spring we shall have a fine April shower. . . . O the wonderful Knowledge to be found in the Stars! Even the smallest Things are written there, if you had but Skill to read. . . .

Besides the usual Things expected in an Almanack, I hope the profess'd Teachers of Mankind will excuse my scattering here and there some instructive Hints in Matters of Morality and Religion. And be not thou disturbed, O grave and sober Reader, if among the many serious Sentences in my Book, thou findest me trifling now and then, and talking idly. In all the Dishes I have hitherto cook'd for thee, there is solid Meat enough for thy Money. There are Scraps from the Table of Wisdom, that will if well digested, yield strong Nourishment to thy Mind. . . .

When I first begun to publish, the Printer made a fair Agreement with me for my Copies, by Virtue of which he runs away with the greatest Part of the Profit.—However, much good may't do him; I do not grudge it him; he is a Man I have a great Regard for, and I wish his Profit ten times greater than it is. For I am, dear Reader, his, as well as thy

Affectionate Friend,
R. SAUNDERS."

Questions for Analysis

1. Describe Franklin's tone, citing examples from the text to support your characterization.
2. Explain the causes of the popularity of *Poor Richard's Almanack*.
3. Explain how this excerpt from *Poor Richard's Almanack* undermines a traditional source of social authority.

AP® TIP

Analyze the differences between the ideas of the Enlightenment and more traditional views about social structures in the colonies and in Europe. How did these ideas shape political and religious developments in the colonies?

Opposed to the religious concept of **original sin**, Enlightenment thinkers generally believed that human beings were born neither necessarily good nor evil, but instead open to the world around them and were innately capable of understanding the logic behind natural laws and the construction of governments that protected their individual rights as human beings. From this stemmed a general belief that governments were created for the benefit of people, rather than as a means of keeping them under control. John Locke led the way in the late seventeenth century, with his argument that human beings created government to bring people out of a state of nature, where individuals had to protect their own rights, into a civilized state where government represented the people's interest and instituted laws for the general good. The French "philosophe" Baron de Montesquieu refined this idea in the mid-eighteenth century by arguing that good government was divided into executive, legislative, and judicial branches that prevented any one individual or group of individuals from acquiring too much power to the detriment of the people. Likewise, another French philosopher, Voltaire, advocated for free speech based on his belief that truth and justice were born of rational discourse rather than the dictates of all-powerful monarchs or priests wielding divine power.

The Enlightenment provided colonists with a worldview with more room for acceptance of religious diversity than had previously existed. Enlightenment ideas also undermined what many likely saw as the religious vitality of the colonies. While many Enlightenment thinkers believed in

The Great Awakening Takes Root

a Christian God, they rejected the revelations and rituals that defined traditional church practices and challenged the claims of many ministers that God was directly engaged in the daily workings of the world.

There were, however, opposing forces. Many Protestant ministers, possibly afraid that material concerns increasingly overshadowed spiritual devotion or that growing religious diversity was undermining the power of the church, lamented the state of faith in eighteenth-century America. Ministers eager to address this crisis of faith — known as **New Light clergy** — worked together to reenergize the faithful and were initially welcomed, or at least tolerated, by more traditional **Old Light clergy**.

Some New Lights took inspiration from German **Pietist** ideas decrying the power of established churches and urged individuals to follow their hearts rather than their heads in spiritual matters. Pietist ideas influenced John Wesley, the founder of **Methodism** and a professor of theology at Oxford University, where he taught some of its central ideas to his students, including George Whitefield. Like the Pietists, Whitefield considered the North American colonies a perfect place to restore intensity and emotion to religious worship.

Ministers in the British North American colonies also questioned the status of religion, challenging the religiosity of urban churches that embodied class distinctions, with wealthier members paying high rents to seat their families in the front pews. Farmers and shopkeepers rented the cheaper pews in the middle of the church, while the poorest sat on free benches at the very back or in the gallery. One such clergyman was Jonathan Edwards, a Congregational minister in New England. A brilliant scholar who studied natural philosophy and science as well as theology, Edwards viewed the natural world as powerful evidence of God's design. He came to view the idea that God elected some individuals for salvation and others for damnation as a source of mystical joy. His sermons of 1733 to 1735 joined Enlightenment ideas with religious fervor, and they initiated a revival that reached hundreds of parishioners.

At around the same time, the English clergyman George Whitefield was perfectly situated to extend the series of revivals in North America that scholars later called the **Great Awakening**. Gifted with a powerful voice, he understood that the expanding networks of communication and travel — developed to promote commerce — could also be used to promote religion. Advertising in newspapers and broadsides and traveling by ship, coach, and horseback, Whitefield made seven trips to the North American colonies beginning in 1738 as part of a fifteen-month preaching tour that reached tens of thousands of colonists, from Georgia to New England to the Pennsylvania backcountry, and inspired other ministers in the colonies.

Like Edwards, he asked individuals to invest less in material goods and more in spiritual devotion. If they admitted their depraved and sinful state and truly repented, God would hear their prayers. Whitefield's preaching style was larger than life: He shouted and raged, and gestured dramatically, drawing huge crowds everywhere he went. He attracted 20,000 people to individual events, at a time when the entire city of Boston counted just 17,000 residents. New Light ministers carried on Whitefield's work throughout the 1740s, honing their methods and appeal. Less concerned with what church their followers belonged to than with their core beliefs, New Lights denounced sophisticated and educated clergy, and used spontaneous speeches and outdoor venues to attract crowds, and invited colonists from all walks of life to build a common Christian

New Light clergy Colonial clergy who called for religious revivals and emphasized the emotional aspects of spiritual commitment. The New Lights were leaders in the Great Awakening.

Old Light clergy Colonial clergy from established churches who supported the religious status quo in the early eighteenth century.

Great Awakening Series of religious revivals in colonial America that began in 1720 and lasted to about 1750.

MAP 2.7 Religious Diversity in 1750 The appeal of Whitefield and other New Light ministers led to increased religious diversity by 1750. Baptist churches multiplied in New England, where Congregationalists long held sway while Presbyterian and Lutheran churches spread across the South where Anglicanism was the established church. Non-evangelical houses of worship, such as Quaker meeting houses and Jewish synagogues, also gradually increased in number. **Explain two historical trends before 1750 that caused the religious diversity shown on this map.**

EXPLORING AP® THEMES

American and Regional Culture

Some students may not be familiar with the terms related to the Great Awakening such as New Light, Old Light, Pietist, and Methodist. Consider helping students develop broader understandings by having them define each term on its own. Next, ask students to select one term and relate it to the causes or consequences of the Great Awakening.

TEACHING IDEA

Analyzing Art and Images

George Whitefield was one of the most prominent and successful New Light preachers of the Great Awakening. To help understand the broad appeal he had in the American colonies, consider using the painting of George Whitefield preaching by John Collett (see p. 140). If students are not familiar with what to look for, consider dividing the painting into quadrants. In this way, students are focused on one part of the painting at a time, which may lend itself to a better grasp of the details.

TEACHING IDEA

Incorporating Primary Sources

Benjamin Franklin was in many ways the most ubiquitous person of the mid-to-late-eighteenth-century. His presence in Philadelphia during the Great Awakening is but one of many moments that substantiate this view. Have students read Franklin's thoughts on the effectiveness of George Whitefield, which can be found on page 138. Ask students to highlight two or three specific statements or observations Franklin notes about Whitefield's effectiveness.

BUILDING AP® SKILLS
Causation

One of the more obvious splinters in American society during the Great Awakening was the divide between the Old Light and New Light techniques. Have students use a category of analysis such as class, race, or institutions to center their response to the following question: What was one major cause of the growing divide between New Light and Old Light techniques during the Great Awakening?

EXPLORING AP® THEMES
American and Regional Culture

Because this section focuses on both the Enlightenment and Great Awakening, consider assessing students' ability to use both of these events to evaluate the context of the mid-late eighteenth-century colonial society. For this exercise, give students the choice to defend the view that the Enlightenment and Great Awakening were either complementary movements or competing movements. Expect a wide array of answers. Students need to see how historical questions can lead people to very different conclusions. The important thing to remember is to stay rooted in factual evidence. This will help further students' understanding of the continuities and changes in a fledgling American culture.

Period 2: 1607–1754

MODULE 2-9 Religious and Political Awakenings

> **AP® TIP**
> As you consider the Great Awakening, evaluate the ways in which the divisions it generated reflected existing divisions in the social structures of the colonies.

community. Some became traveling preachers, preferring to carry their message throughout the colonies than to be limited to a single church.

New Light clergy brought young people to religion by the thousands. In addition, thousands of colonists who were already church members were "born again," recommitting themselves to their faith. Poor women and men who felt little connection to preaching when they sat on the back benches eagerly joined the crowds at outdoor revivals, where they could stand as close to the pulpit as a rich merchant.

REVIEW

• How did the ideologies that shaped both the Great Awakening and the Enlightenment undermine imperial authority in the British North American colonies?

Dissent and Resistance Rise

> **AP® TIP**
> Pay particular attention to the role social class played in shaping responses to both the Enlightenment and the Great Awakening.

> " [The people of Boston] should drink rat poison rather than listen to corrupt, unconverted clergy. "
> — James Davenport, 1742

Initially, the Great Awakening drew support from large numbers of ministers from traditional churches because it increased religious enthusiasm and church attendance. The early embrace by Old Light clergy diminished, however, as revivals spread farther afield, as critiques of educated clergy became more pointed, and as worshippers left established congregations for new churches. As the Great Awakening peaked in the early 1740s, ministers and other colonial leaders increasingly feared that revivalists provided lower-class whites, free black people, women, and even the enslaved with compelling critiques of those in power. A backlash developed among more settled ministers and their congregations.

In the North, too, Old Light ministers and local officials began to question New Light techniques and influences. One New Light preacher, James Davenport, attracted huge crowds when he preached in Boston in the early 1740s — thousands of colonists were drawn to Boston Common day after day to hear him speak. Boston officials finally called a grand jury into session to silence him.

Even some New Light ministers considered Davenport extreme. Yet revivals continued throughout the 1740s, though they lessened in intensity over time as churches and parishioners settled back into a more ordered religious life. Moreover, the central ideas of revivalist preaching — criticism of educated clergy, itinerancy, and extemporaneous preaching — worked against the movement's chances of becoming a more permanent institution. The Great Awakening continued to echo across the colonies for at least another generation, but its influence was felt more often in attitudes and practices rather than in institutions.

In various ways, revivalists also highlighted the democratic tendencies in the Bible, particularly in the New Testament. Even as they proclaimed God's wrath against sinners, they also preached that a lack of wealth and power did not diminish a person in God's eyes. And the style of passionate and popular preaching they brought to the colonies would shape American politics as well as religion for centuries to come. New Light clergy allowed colonists to view their resistance to traditional authorities as part of their effort to create a better and more just world. For example, colonists soon mobilized to resist what they saw as tyrannical actions by the wealthy colonial officials and others in authority. Thus, the effects of eighteenth-century religious awakenings rippled out from churches and revivals to influence social and political relations.

At the same time, the environment of the colonies contributed to changes in their attitudes toward colonial authorities. The settlements of the seventeenth century could be regulated with a small number of officials. With eighteenth century geographical expansion, population growth, and commercial development, colonial authorities — whether appointed by the crown or selected by local residents — found themselves confronted with a more complex, and more contentious, situation. In New England, most colonies developed participatory town meetings, which elected members to their colonial legislatures. In the South, wealthy planters exercised greater authority locally and colony wide, but they still embraced ideals of self-governance and political liberty.

Throughout the British American colonies, officials were usually educated men who held property and had family ties to other colonial elites. Although ultimate political authority — or sovereignty — rested with the king and Parliament, many decisions were made by local officials because English officials were often too distant to have a hand in daily colonial life. Not surprisingly, those with wealth and power continued to win office.

Still, evidence from throughout the colonial period indicates that deference to authority was not always enough to maintain order. Roger Williams and Anne Hutchinson, Bacon's Rebellion, the Stono Rebellion, the Salem witchcraft trials, and both New York class rebellions, one led by Jacob Leisler in 1689 and the other a series of tenant revolts in the 1740s, all demonstrate the frequency and range of colonial conflict and protest. These episodes of dissent and protest were widely scattered across time and place. But as the ideas circulated by New Light clergy and Enlightenment thinkers converged with changing political relations, resistance to established authority became more frequent and more collective.

Protests against colonial elites multiplied after the 1730s. A lack of access to reasonably priced food, especially bread, inspired regular protests in the eighteenth century. During the 1730s, the price of bread — a critical staple in colonial diets — rose despite falling wheat prices and a recession in seaport cities. Bread rioters attacked grain warehouses, bakeries, and shops, demanding more bread at lower prices. In New England, such uprisings were often led by women, who were responsible for putting bread on the table. When grievances involved domestic or consumer issues, women felt they had the right to make their voices heard, a right reinforced by New Light clergy's insistence on their moral obligations to society.

Public markets were another site where struggles over food led to collective protests. In 1737, for instance, Boston officials decided to construct a public market and charge fees to farmers who sold their goods there. Adopting a rational approach to voice their concerns, residents petitioned city officials. When their reasoned appeals had no effect, however, protestors demolished the market building and stalls in the middle of the night. Local authorities could find no witnesses to the crime.

In seaport cities, a frequent source of conflict was the **impressment** of colonial men who were seized and forcibly drafted into service in the Royal Navy. Impressment grew increasingly common as King William's War was followed by Queen Anne's, only to be followed by King George's War. The challenge to impressment, which was viewed as a sign of the corrupt practices of imperial authorities, energized diverse groups of colonists. Sailors, dockworkers, and men drinking at taverns along the shore feared being pressed into military service, while colonial officials worried about labor shortages. Those officials petitioned the British government to stop impressment, but working men who faced the navy's high mortality rates, bad food, rampant disease, and harsh discipline also took action on their own behalf. Asserting their growing sense of political liberty, they fought back against both colonial and British authorities. In 1747 in Boston, a general impressment during King George's War led to three days of rioting. An observer noted that "Negros, servants, and hundreds of seamen seized a naval lieutenant, assaulted a sheriff, and put his deputy in stocks, surrounded the governor's house, and stormed the Town House (city hall)." Such riots did not end the system of impressment, but they showed that many colonists now refused to be deprived of what they considered their natural rights.

In the mid-eighteenth century, colonists protested with increasing force against many aspects of colonial life that they found unsatisfying. The issues repeatedly raised, the political responses that failed to fully address them, and resultant further protest show a pattern of dissent and discontent with deep roots. Beginning in the 1730s, conflicts among the elite led astute political leaders in cities like New York and Philadelphia to seek support from a wider constituency, channeling the "popular" will for their own ends. In 1731, for instance, a new royal charter confirmed New York City's existence as a "corporation" and stipulated the rights of freemen (residents who could vote in local elections after paying a small fee) and freeholders (individuals, whether residents or not, who held property worth £40 and could vote on that basis). A large number of artisans, shopkeepers, and laborers had the financial means to vote, and shopkeepers and master craftsmen now sat alongside wealthier men on the Common Council. Yet most laboring men did not participate actively in elections until 1733, when local elites led by Lewis Morris aimed to mobilize the mass of voters against royal officials, like New York Governor William Cosby, who had been appointed in London.

Morris, a wealthy man and a judge, joined other colonial elites in accusations that the royal officials recently appointed to govern New York were tied to ministerial corruption in England. When Morris, as chief justice of the provincial court, ruled against Governor Cosby in a lawsuit, Cosby retaliated by suspending Morris from office. In the aftermath, Morris and his supporters — the Morrisites — took his case to the people, who were in the midst of a serious economic depression.

---

impressment The forced enlistment of civilians into the army or navy. The impressment of residents of colonial seaports into the British navy was a major source of complaint in the eighteenth century.

AP® TIP
Be sure you can explain the ways in which the goals and interests of colonists diverged from those of the British government during the eighteenth century.

BUILDING AP® SKILLS
Making Connections

Dissent is an important topic throughout American history and the colonial period is no exception. To allow students a breadth of possible responses, consider having students define how each of the following played a role in dissent in colonial history.

- Enslaved persons
- Backcountry settlers
- Religious movements
- Political movements

After students have defined each, instruct students to select the one group of dissenters they believe had the widest appeal in colonial history. Students will then write a response defining and defending their interpretation. This is a great chance to encourage a diversity of responses.

APPLY THE TIP

The goals and interests of colonists diverging from the British is a crucial understanding for students. Yet, students also need to develop an appreciation for the difference between redress of grievances and a rebellion. Have students develop a one-to-three sentence response citing a historical example of seeking redress of grievances without a complete rebellion. This will allow students to illustrate a more comprehensive understanding of continuity and change.

BUILDING AP® SKILLS
Argumentation

As students consider causation during this module, reinforce the skill by allowing students multiple opportunities to demonstrate growth. For example, provide students with a prompt that can be supported, modified, or refuted. This assesses their ability to create an informed interpretation. The prompt can be something such as this statement: By the 1740s colonists were transformed by the Enlightenment and were thus illustrating a collective political consciousness.

TEACHING IDEA
Incorporating Secondary Sources

Jill Lepore's book, *New York Burning: Liberty Slavery, and Conspiracy in Eighteenth-Century Manhattan*, provides excellent context using the example of the trial of John Peter Zenger. Details in the preface and throughout the book provide a historical context to the trial, dissent, and political power in the eighteenth century.

TEACHING IDEA

Understanding Dissent

The trial of John Peter Zenger is an accessible and exciting story students are sure to engage in during Module 2-9. The Historical Society of the New York Courts has an excellent resource center devoted to helping students understand the trial and the effects of dissent in eighteenth-century New York (nycourts.gov). Search for *Crown v. John Peter Zenger* to find it.

EXPLORING AP® THEMES

American and National Identity

As students work their way through the various examples of dissent in colonial society they need to be reminded of the difference between influence, context, and causation. The examples of dissent in this module perhaps influenced revolutionary thought and rhetoric but were far removed from being considered causes of the revolutionary movement of the late-eighteenth-century. To help students understand this concept have them select one example of political dissent and give an explanation about how it influenced revolutionary thought, but was not a cause of the American Revolutionary War.

TRM Suggested Responses to Questions

Period 2: 1607–1754

MODULE 2-9 Religious and Political Awakenings

Morrisites launched an opposition newspaper, published by a man named John Peter Zenger, to mobilize artisans, shopkeepers, and laborers around an agenda to stimulate the economy and elect men supportive of workers to the city's common council.

In his *New-York Weekly Journal*, Zenger leaped into a political fray, accusing Governor Cosby and his cronies of corruption, incompetence, election fraud, and tyranny. Zenger's vicious attacks led to his indictment for **seditious** libel and his imprisonment in November 1734. At the time, **libel** related only to whether published material undermined government authority, not whether it was true or false. But Zenger's lead attorney, Andrew Hamilton of Philadelphia, argued that truth must be recognized as a defense against charges of libel. Appealing to a jury of Zenger's peers, Hamilton proclaimed, "It is not the cause of a poor printer, nor of New York alone, which you are now trying. . . . It is the best cause. It is the cause of liberty." In response, jurors ignored the law as written and acquitted Zenger.

Although the decision in the Zenger case did not lead to a change in British libel laws, it did signal the willingness of colonial juries to side with fellow colonists against the king and Parliament in at least some situations. Zenger's journalistic challenge to ruling power, and the ability of the political movement he championed to inspire ordinary freemen to participate in elections, foreshadowed political developments near the end of the eighteenth century.

For the time being, however, even as freemen gained a greater voice in urban politics and newspapers readily attacked corrupt officials whose actions posed threats to the rightful liberties of the British colonists, challenges to the powerful could only succeed when the elite were divided. Moreover, the rewards freemen gained sometimes served merely to reinforce class divisions. Many city workers, for instance, had benefited when Morris used his influence to ensure the building of the city's first permanent almshouse in 1736 — a project that employed large numbers of artisans and laborers during an economic rut. Once built, however, the almshouse became a symbol of the growing gap between rich and poor. Its existence was also used by future politicians to justify eliminating other forms of relief, ultimately leaving the poor in worse shape than before.

seditious Behavior or language aimed at starting a rebellion against a government.

libel A false written statement designed to damage the reputation of its subject.

> **AP® TIP**
> Understanding the causes and effects of the Zenger case is key to analyzing how colonial ideas regarding the rights of citizens and the perceived corruption of British government developed during the 1700s.

REVIEW

- How did politics and religion bring colonists together across economic lines in the first half of the eighteenth century?
- How did religion and politics highlight and reinforce class divisions during this era?

AP® WRITING HISTORICALLY — Responding to a Document-Based Question

In Modules 2-7 and 2-8, you practiced writing essay paragraphs that weave together your knowledge of history and multiple primary sources to support a historical argument. Now, we will walk you through some strategies for writing a full essay in response to a Document-Based Question accompanied by six primary source documents, all of which relate in some way to the topic of the prompt:

> Explain the causes and effects of the Great Awakening in the period between 1630 and 1760.

Step 1 Break down the prompt and pre-write as you would for any essay prompt.

Remember, the first part of any Document-Based Question is the prompt itself. As you have probably already noticed, these prompts often ask you to make a historical claim about a specific time period, or even a relatively narrow span of time. As always, carefully read the prompt and identify the requirements and limits for your response. In this case, the prompt asks for an explanation of causes and effects of the Great Awakening, and everything you use to construct and support your argument should fall between 1630 and 1760.

Before you read the primary sources that accompany a Document-Based Question, remember that it can be helpful to take a moment and quickly jot down the historical knowledge that you would use to answer this prompt if it did not provide any primary sources

136

TEACHING IDEA

Connecting the Dots

As students unpack the Document-Based Question have them brainstorm at least two events which preceded the Great Awakening that could be considered an influence on the beliefs connected to the Great Awakening.

MODULE 2-9 Religious and Political Awakenings

to analyze. Search your memory for historical terms, including people, events, acts, and developments you would want to use as evidence to prove the relevance of your knowledge to the topic at hand. Doing this will get you into the right mindset to read the sources — you will already be searching for perspectives (that is, evidence) to support your interpretation of history, and the details you note before beginning to read will help you remember historical situations that influenced, but aren't directly referenced in, the documents themselves. For example, prewriting for this prompt may lead you to the following claim:

> Economic inequality increased in the colonies during the late seventeenth and early eighteenth centuries. This economic inequality was worsened by religious leaders, who were typically considered members of the upper class. This class division within religious denominations was one of the causes of the religious changes of the Great Awakening and its appeal among the common people.

What are some other causes of the Great Awakening between 1630 and 1760? You may wish to take a moment to write them down before moving to step 2.

Step 2 Read and annotate the documents, keeping your initial ideas for claims in mind.

Now that you've written down a few ideas that will help focus your reading, you should turn to the documents. Remember, if reading the documents jogs your memory about more relevant historical information or gives you additional ideas for historical claims to make in your essay, add them to your pre-writing notes.

Annotate the documents as you read them. Because the prompt asks us about causes of the Great Awakening, you should be on the lookout for statements that can help you prove your claims about those causes. We have provided a few annotations to the first two documents to help guide your reading for the first two sources, but you can and should add your own in addition to annotating the remaining four.

When you annotate, remember to ask yourself the following questions:

- What is the document about? What historical situation does it describe or reference?
- Who is the author and what is his or her position in society? What biases or perspectives might someone in this position bring to the topic at hand?
- Who was the intended audience for this document?
- What was the author's purpose in writing this document?
- What point of view does the author of this document express?
- How does this document relate back to the prompt?
- Does this document remind you of any other historical developments?

DOCUMENT 1

Noting that the world is troublesome appeals to the poor.

Unlike the wealthy and educated, Whitefield's listeners could be insecure about their ability to use "fine" words. This hints that he speaks to those who see ministers as members of the colonial elite.

Source: George Whitefield, *Marks of a True Conversion*, 1739

"Are ye converted, and become like little children? . . . Doth the devil trouble you? Doth the world trouble you? Go tell your Father of it, go directly and complain to God. Perhaps you may say, I cannot utter fine words, but do any of you expect fine words from your children? If they come crying, and can speak but half words, do not your hearts yearn over them? And has not God unspeakably more pity to you? If ye can only make signs to him; 'As a father pitieth his children, so will the Lord pity them that fear him.' I pray you therefore be bold with your Father, saying, 'Abba, Father! Satan troubles me, the world troubles me . . . heavenly Father, plead my cause!' The Lord will then speak for you some way or other."

He encourages his listeners to see God, rather than secular authorities or "Old Light" ministers, as their authority. It appears here that Whitefield is appealing directly to common listeners and aiming his critique at more educated ministers and elites.

(Continued)

TEACHING IDEA

Check for Understanding

To help students understand the context of the Great Awakening, have them circle the category of analysis for the historical context of the question — *class division within religious denominations*. Challenge students to come up with their own category of analysis they could envision using to establish context.

BUILDING AP® SKILLS

Claims and Evidence in Sources

In addition to the questions listed for step 2, remind students to be looking for cause and effect as they read through the documents. As students become familiar with this concept of attaching elements of the question to their outline, their understanding of the question will grow and they will feel more confident in answering the prompt.

TEACHING IDEA

AP® Writing Historically Review

Perceptive students will notice the documents begin over one hundred years after the beginning of the time period in the question. Therefore, students can focus the pre-1739 information on contextualization, as well as developing categories of analysis for the causes of the Great Awakening. Too often, students let the documents control their response, and this DBQ is a good reminder for students to respond to the documents while also incorporating their own knowledge. A quick bell ringer to work on the causes of the Great Awakening can help students be better prepared for this activity. Consider assigning groups of students the following periods: 1630–1676, 1676–1700, and 1700–1730. In each period, students will brainstorm major religious events to start developing a sense of what categories of analysis would work well for this question.

Period 2: 1607–1754   MODULE 2-9   Religious and Political Awakenings

TEACHING IDEA

Check for Understanding

George Whitefield is referenced in five of the six documents for this Document-Based Question. This is an excellent opportunity to look for outside evidence that can substantiate students' claims about this question.

BUILDING AP® SKILLS

Developments and Processes

Social history can be an intimidating topic for students to study because it is often couched in broader historical developments. The Great Awakening is no exception. Even though the Great Awakening was a tremendously influential movement, it happened in concert with the Enlightenment and imperial battles over colonies. To help students understand the basics of the movement and the connections across the colonial period, consider using Episode 5, "The Seven Years War and the Great Awakening" from the Crash Course US History series (available on YouTube). The last two minutes in particular are useful to understanding the Great Awakening.

ACTIVE READING TIP

Because Whitefield is from England, he brings an outsider's perspective to colonial society. This document shows he made appeals that were relevant to middle and lower class listeners. It will come in handy when you need evidence that growing economic divisions within the colonies helped cause the Great Awakening.

DOCUMENT 2

Source: Nathan Cole, *On George Whitefield Coming to Connecticut*, 1740

Many colonists were hungry for messages like Whitefield's. His appeal was broad and reached the common people. Does Cole seem open to this message? Is he sympathetic to Whitefield's appeal to the common people?

More evidence of interest in Whitefield's message among average people. Cole is clearly astounded by the reaction to Whitefield.

Whitefield's message is "clothed with authority," as opposed to secular and religious elites. This hints that he is sympathetic to Whitefield's message.

Whitefield encouraged a direct relationship with God, as opposed to seeing religious authorities as intermediaries, and Cole evidently agrees.

". . . I heard no man speak a word all the way three mile but every one pressing forward in great haste and when we got down to the old meeting house there was a great multitude; it was said to be 3 or 4000 of people assembled together. We got off from our horses and shook off the dust and the ministers were then coming to the meeting house. I turned and looked toward the great river and saw the ferry boats running swift forward and backward bringing over loads of people; the oars rowed nimble and quick. Every thing men horses and boats all seemed to be struggling for life; the land and the banks over the river looked black with people and horses all along the 12 miles. I see no man at work in his field but all seemed to be gone—when I saw Mr. Whitefield come upon the [platform] he looked almost angelical, a young slim slender youth before some thousands of people and with a bold undaunted countenance, and my hearing how God was with him every where as he came along it solemnized my mind and put me in a trembling fear before he began to preach; for he looked as if he was clothed with authority from the great God, and a sweet solemn solemnity sat upon his brow. And my hearing him preach gave me a heart wound; by God's blessing my old foundation was broken up and I saw that my righteousness would not save me; then I was convinced of the doctrine of Election and went right to quarreling with God about it because all that I could do would not save me; and he had decreed from Eternity who should be saved and who not."

ACTIVE READING TIP

This document shows that Whitefield threatened the traditional religious authority. This will be useful for proving that religious elites in the colonies no longer had a strong hold on the religious sensibilities of average colonists, and that this weak hold opened average colonists to Whitefield's new message.

DOCUMENT 3

Source: Benjamin Franklin, *On George Whitefield, the Great Revivalist*, 1739

"In 1739 arriv'd among us from England the Rev. Mr. Whitefield, who had made himself remarkable there as an itinerant Preacher. . . . The Multitudes of all Sects and Denominations that attended his Sermons were enormous and it was [a] matter of Speculation to me who was one of the Number, to observe the extraordinary Influence of his Oratory on his Hearers, and how much they admir'd and respected him, notwithstanding his common Abuse of them, by assuring them they were naturally half Beasts and half Devils. It was wonderful to see the

Change soon made in the Manners of our Inhabitants; from being thoughtless or indifferent about Religion, it seem'd as if all the World were growing Religious. . . .

He us'd indeed sometimes to pray for my Conversion, but never had the Satisfaction of believing that his Prayers were heard. . . .

He had a loud and clear Voice, and articulated his Words and Sentences so perfectly that he might be heard and understood at a great Distance, especially as his [listeners], however numerous, observ'd the most exact Silence. He preach'd one Evening from the Top of the Court House Steps, which are in the middle of Market Street, and on the West Side of Second Street which crosses it at right angles. Both Streets were fill'd with his Hearers to a considerable distance. Being among the hindmost in Market Street, I had the Curiosity to learn how far he could be heard, by retiring backwards down the Street towards the River; and I found his Voice distinct till I came near Front Street. . . . Imagining then a Semicircle, of which my Distance should be the Radius, and that it were fill'd with [listeners], . . . I computed that he might well be heard by more than Thirty Thousand. . . .

His delivery . . . was so improv'd by frequent Repetitions that every Accent, every Emphasis, every Modulation of Voice, was so perfectly well turn'd and well plac'd, that without being interested in the Subject, one could not help being pleas'd with the Discourse, a Pleasure of much the same kind with that receiv'd from an excellent Piece of Music. This is an Advantage itinerant Preachers have over those who are stationary: as the latter cannot well improve their Delivery of a Sermon by so many Rehearsals."

ACTIVE READING TIP
Benjamin Franklin was a wealthy man by the time he heard Whitefield preach. Though he is sympathetic to Whitefield's sermon, he sets himself outside of the scene, as an observer watching the reaction of the common people.

DOCUMENT 4

Source: Jonathan Edwards, *Sinners in the Hands of an Angry God*, 1741

"So that thus it is that natural men are held in the hand of God over the pit of hell; they have deserved the fiery pit, and are already sentenced to it; and God is dreadfully provoked, his anger is as great towards them as to those that are actually suffering the executions of the fierceness of his wrath in hell, and they have done nothing in the least to appease or abate that anger, neither is God in the least bound by any promise to hold them up one moment: the devil is waiting for them, hell is gaping for them, the flames gather and flash about them, and would fain lay hold on them, and swallow them up; the fire pent up in their own hearts is struggling to break out; and they have no interest in any Mediator, there are no means within reach that can be any security to them. . . . That world of misery, that lake of burning brimstone, is extended abroad under you. . . .

The God that holds you over the pit of hell, much as one holds a spider, or some loathsome insect, over the fire, abhors you, and is dreadfully provoked: his wrath towards you burns like fire; he looks upon you as worthy of nothing else, but to be cast into the fire; he is of purer eyes than to bear to have you in his sight; you are ten thousand times more abominable in his eyes, than the most hateful venomous serpent is in ours. . . . And there is no other reason to be given, why you have not dropped into hell since you arose in the morning, but that God's hand has held you up. There is no other reason to be given why you have not gone to hell, since you have sat here in the house of God, provoking his pure eyes by your sinful wicked manner of attending his solemn worship. Yea, there is nothing else that is to be given as a reason why you do not this very moment drop down into hell."

ACTIVE READING TIP
Jonathan Edwards is a traditional Puritan minister, but he uses emotional preaching and vivid images to inspire his listeners to repent. Notice that he does not use abstract reasoning in his sermon, but instead, appeals to listeners' fears and emotions with images of hell.

(Continued)

TEACHING IDEA

Check for Understanding

As students annotate documents, remind them to look for the big picture of each document. In other words, what is the document really addressing and how does it relate to the question? To put this idea into practice, consider having students annotate for one way in which the document relates to the causes or consequences of the Great Awakening.

BUILDING AP® SKILLS

Claims and Evidence in Sources

Remind students there are many rooms in the house of dissent. Therefore, students should avoid thinking of all religious reformers as radical New Lights. Document 4 provides students with the opportunity to see this perspective. Have students look for evidence in the document that substantiates the view of Jonathan Edwards as a reformer with a more traditional and less radical voice.

TEACHING IDEA

Analyzing Art and Images

Students should be able to draw on prior knowledge to help evaluate the meaning of this document. Remember one trick is to reduce the painting to quadrants and look at one square at a time. Students should be able to come up with one historical takeaway about the painting's relevance to either the causes or consequences of the Great Awakening.

TEACHING IDEA

Analyzing Art and Images

Think of Document 6 in the same way as the previous note. For example, you can repeat the use of quadrants in this engraving and look for big historical takeaways. This engraving is especially useful for effects. Ask students to demonstrate this understanding by writing one sentence about the effects of the Great Awakening portrayed in the engraving.

DOCUMENT 5 Source: John Collet, *George Whitefield Preaching at a Revival*, 1760

ACTIVE READING TIP
Notice the many kinds of listeners in this image, and notice their reactions. Though some pray on their knees, some listen quietly, and one toasts Whitefield with a mug of beer, in each case the listeners show respect for Whitefield. Notice, also, how each is dressed differently. What do these different forms of dress tell us about the social classes of his listeners?

DOCUMENT 6 Source: Anonymous engraver, *George Whitefield*, London newspaper, 1763

ACTIVE READING TIP
While in this image Whitefield is also surrounded by listeners, some of them appear positively devilish. Notice that two of them, one an angel and one a devil, pull at Whitefield's ears. Also notice that the audience is disorganized and distracted while listening to Whitefield. Compare this to Document 5. Also, notice that this image was published in a London newspaper. What are the biases in this image? Who might hold these biases? Why might they hold these biases?

Step 3 Connect evidence from the documents to your claims to set the context and craft a thesis statement.

After reading and annotating the sources, use your annotations to connect the main point of each source to both immediate and distant causes of the Great Awakening. One good way to organize your thoughts is to summarize the useful points of a document next to some of the historical information you jotted down after you read the prompt. Here's an example of how you might revise the claim you jotted down before reading the documents to include what you now know about the sources:

> British North Americans had become increasingly wealthy during the late seventeenth and early eighteenth centuries, but the wealth was not shared equally. This made appeals to a return of religiosity among ministers like Edwards and Whitefield particularly appealing to colonists of middling means, who had not experienced the rise in wealth to the same extent as their economic superiors.

Beneath that claim, you should now summarize the documents you plan to use to support it in your own words. The following is an example of a summary of Document 1:

> Whitefield spoke to listeners who had experienced trouble in the world and didn't have the "fine" words to speak to God in their appeal to Him. Whitefield demanded that his listeners overcome their insecurity and be "bold" in their prayers to their Father.

Here is an example of how you might summarize Document 2:

> Listeners to Whitefield, like Cole, noted that thousands of regular people attended his sermons. In fact, Nathan Cole claimed that the fields were empty of workers when Whitefield came to speak. For Cole, Whitefield spoke with an authority unlike the traditional religious elite. He promoted a direct relationship with God, thereby encouraging Cole and others like him to circumvent religious authority in their religious life.

Using your own thoughts to describe the documents is the most important part of this step. Notice how this strategy leads you to only selectively quote from the documents. In the first summary, only key words like "fine" and "bold" are quoted, rather than entire sentences. In the second summary, Cole's words are paraphrased rather than quoted. Both summaries directly relate to our initial claim from step 2.

Repeat this process by using your annotation and interpretation of the documents to refine three or four claims you made prior to reading them. Then, connect information in the documents to your claims by summarizing them in your own words. Try to use all six of the documents to support these claims. This means that, on average, each claim you make should be supported by two different documents.

Now that you have connected information from the documents to your claims, it's time to write a thesis that combines at least three of your claims. Don't forget to introduce the context of your response before you write your thesis statement. This context statement, which alerts the reader to events or trends that shape your thesis, should ideally be supported with an example to make it concrete. Remember, your thesis needs to include at least one cause and one effect, as in the following example:

> During the early eighteenth century, the economics of mercantilism started to create greater wealth inequality in the colonies **[context statement]**. While merchants in cities like New York and Philadelphia and planters in Virginia and South Carolina grew rich, not all colonists enjoyed such profits. Even among wealthier colonists, mercantilism led to greater resentment toward the British as the unequal system of trade ultimately benefited England at the expense of its colonies **[context support]**. The Great Awakening was caused by increasing class divisions in colonial society **[thesis claim 1—cause]** and though members of all social classes were affected by the sermons of ministers like George Whitefield and Jonathan Edwards, the appeal was especially strong among the common people **[thesis claim 2—effect]**, which meant that the Great Awakening posed a threat to traditional ministers in the colonies and divided many churches into "Old Light" and "New Light" congregations **thesis claim 3—effect]**.

Notice how this thesis includes all of the claims that you could make in the body paragraphs of your essay. The first claim, which would be your first body paragraph, speaks to causes, while the second and third claims, which would correspond to your second and third body paragraphs, speak to effects.

(Continued)

BUILDING AP® SKILLS

Making Connections

Before having students complete step 3, consider forming groups to complete the following activity. This activity is designed to have students write, evaluate, and select exemplary summary statements. Start the activity by having students write one document summary. Groups select the best response and then group members edit the exemplar. Once edited, group members transfer their exemplar to butcher block paper. A gallery walk is an excellent way to end this activity. In a gallery walk, students peruse the gallery of responses, which are posted around the room, and take notes about the strength of each response.

TEACHING IDEA

Check for Understanding

Provide students with a clean copy of this paragraph. Next, have students label sentences they see as explaining causes and effects. They should see separate sentences, some addressing causation, and others addressing effects. This check for understanding will help prepare students to have a better conversation about the exemplar.

TEACHING IDEA

Group Activity

Take one completed row of the exemplars (Claim, Supporting Statement, Historical Evidence, and Document Evidence) and give students separate copies of each. Have students label each independently. This will assess whether or not students understand the purposes and design of each sentence.

BUILDING AP® SKILLS

Claims and Evidence in Sources

Modeling historical writing can be a useful exercise for all students, regardless of skill development early in the year. Sometimes this can be accomplished by examining how historians write about topics. Teachers can consult Patricia U. Bonomi's book, *Under the Cope of Heaven: Religion, Society, and Politics in Colonial America*. There are sections devoted to the origins of the movement and the distinction between Old Lights and New Lights. Choosing specific paragraphs that enhance an understanding of how to make a claim and substantiate it with historical evidence can help make the process of writing from documents seem more manageable.

MODULE 2-9 Religious and Political Awakenings

Period 2: 1607–1754

Step 4 Use evidence from both the documents and your historical knowledge to support your argument.

Use your knowledge from all of the modules in Period 2 and any other developments you have studied in class to find a piece of historical evidence about the colonies or the Great Awakening that supports each of your claims about causes. The following table shows how you might prepare to write body paragraphs for the thesis from step 3:

Claim	Supporting Statement	Historical Evidence	Document Evidence
The Great Awakening was caused by rising wealth inequality among British North Americans during the late seventeenth and early eighteenth centuries.	This inequality made appeals to a return of religiosity among ministers like Edwards and Whitefield particularly appealing to colonists of middling means, who had not experienced the rise in wealth to the same extent as their economic superiors.	Affluent urban families created a consumer revolution in North America (Module 2-6). Protests like Leisler's Rebellion against colonial elites multiplied after the 1680s (Module 2-5).	Whitefield spoke to listeners who had experienced trouble in the world and didn't have the "fine" words to speak to God in their appeal to Him. Whitefield demanded that his listeners overcome their insecurity and be "bold" in their prayers to their Father (Doc. 1). Listeners to Whitefield noted that thousands of regular people attended his sermons. In fact, Nathan Cole noted that the fields were empty of workers when Whitefield came to speak. For Cole, Whitefield spoke with an authority unlike the traditional religious elite. He promoted a direct relationship with God, thereby encouraging Cole and others like him to circumvent authorities in their religious life (Doc. 2).
Members of all social classes were affected by the sermons of ministers like George Whitefield and Jonathan Edwards. The appeal was especially strong among the common people.	Whitefield's and Edwards's sermons were appealing to all social classes in the colonies.	Benjamin Franklin, a wealthy member of the colonial elite, was impressed by the effect of Whitefield's sermon on listeners (Module 2-5).	John Collett's contemporary painting shows listeners from both upper and lower classes listening respectfully to Whitefield's sermon. Each attendee reacts in different ways (quiet listening, kneeled praying, toasting), but nonetheless appears respectful of Whitefield's sermon (Doc. 5).
The Great Awakening posed a threat to traditional ministers in the colonies and divided many churches into "Old Light" and "New Light" congregations.	Whitefield and Edwards broke down traditional class divisions, since their universal appeal questioned colonial hierarchies and paved the way for greater egalitarianism.	Many churches in the colonies divided into "New Light" and "Old Light" congregations, which split over the ability of lay people to have a direct connection to the divine (Module 2-9 and Doc. 3).	Many "Old Light" congregations were threatened by the Great Awakening and perceived ministers like Whitefield to be a threat, as seen by an engraving in a London newspaper, which portrayed Whitefield as influenced by the devil (Doc. 6).

Now, for each of your claims, you have the makings of a body paragraph that will prove your thesis. For example:

The Great Awakening was caused by rising wealth inequality among British North Americans during the late seventeenth and early eighteenth centuries **[topic sentence claim]**. This inequality made appeals to a return of religiosity by ministers like Edwards and Whitefield particularly appealing to colonists of middling means, who had not experienced the rise in wealth to the same extent as their economic superiors and had rebelled against rising inequality in uprisings like Leisler's Rebellion **[supporting statement from historical knowledge]**. Whitefield spoke to listeners who had experienced trouble in the world and didn't have the "fine" words to speak to God in their appeal to Him (Doc. 1) **[evidence from documents]**. Whitefield demanded that his listeners overcome their insecurity and be "bold" in their prayers to their Father (Doc. 1) **[evidence from documents]**. Listeners to Whitefield noted that thousands of regular people attended his sermons (Doc. 2) **[evidence from documents]**. In fact, Nathan Cole claimed that the fields were empty of workers when Whitefield came to speak (Doc. 2) **[evidence from documents]**. For Cole, Whitefield spoke with an authority unlike the traditional religious elite and promoted a direct relationship with God, thereby encouraging Cole and others like him to circumvent authorities in their religious life **[explanation of evidence]**.

Notice that this body paragraph includes your first claim and a supporting statement that bolsters the claim with more specific information. Also notice that this supporting statement includes a piece of outside information, Leisler's Rebellion, to give evidence of past rebellions against colonial elites. Then, the paragraph uses evidence from the documents to prove its claim, and ends with an explanation of this evidence to show how it supports the paragraph's claim.

ACTIVITY

Complete the following outline and use it to write a full essay in response to the Document-Based Question in this box. We have included the example paragraph from step 4 as one of the body paragraphs in the outline, but you do not have to use it in your essay. Establish a new immediate or preceding context to start your introductory paragraph and lead into the thesis statement provided.

I. Introductory paragraph
  A. Immediate/preceding contextualization statement
    1. Cite evidence of immediate/preceding context
    2. Explain influence of immediate/preceding context
  B. Thesis statement presenting three claims: *The Great Awakening was caused by increasing class divisions in colonial society and though members of all social classes were affected by the sermons of ministers like George Whitefield and Jonathan Edwards, the appeal was especially strong among the common people, which meant that the Great Awakening posed a threat to traditional ministers in the colonies and divided many churches into "Old Light" and "New Light" congregations.*

II. Claim 1 body paragraph
  A. Topic sentence presenting claim 1: *The Great Awakening was caused by rising wealth inequality among British North Americans during the late seventeenth and early eighteenth centuries.*
  B. Supporting statement citing evidence of claim 1 (from historical knowledge): *This inequality made appeals to a return of religiosity by ministers like Edwards and Whitefield particularly appealing to colonists of middling means, who had not experienced the rise in wealth to the same extent as their economic superiors and had rebelled against rising inequality in uprisings like Leisler's Rebellion.*
  C. Cite additional evidence of claim 1 (from a document): *Whitefield spoke to listeners who had experienced trouble in the world and didn't have the "fine" words to speak to God in their appeal to Him (Doc. 1). Whitefield demanded that his listeners overcome their insecurity and be "bold" in their prayers to their Father (Doc. 1).*
  D. Cite additional evidence of claim 1 (from another document): *Listeners to Whitefield noted that thousands of regular people attended his sermons (Document 2). In fact, Nathan Cole claimed that the fields were empty of workers when Whitefield came to speak (Doc. 2).*
  E. Explain how evidence supports claim 1: *For Cole, Whitefield spoke with an authority unlike the traditional religious elite and promoted a direct relationship with God, thereby encouraging Cole and others like him to circumvent authorities in their religious life.*

III. Claim 2 body paragraph
  A. Topic sentence presenting claim 2: *Members of all social classes were affected by the sermons of ministers like George Whitefield and Jonathan Edwards, though the appeal was especially strong among the common people.*
  B. Supporting statement citing evidence of claim 2 (from historical knowledge)
  C. Cite additional evidence of claim 2 (from a document)
  D. Cite additional evidence of claim 2 (from another document)
  E. Explain how evidence supports claim 2

IV. Claim 3 body paragraph
  A. Topic sentence presenting claim 3: *The Great Awakening posed a threat to traditional ministers in the colonies and divided many churches into "Old Light" and "New Light" congregations.*
  B. Supporting statement citing evidence of claim 3 (from historical knowledge)
  C. Cite additional evidence of claim 3 (from a document)
  D. Cite additional evidence of claim 3 (from another document)
  E. Explain how evidence supports claim 3

TEACHING IDEA

Connecting the Dots

Have students complete this activity at home and bring their finished copies with the sentences labeled as they are in the activity. Students should note which sentences are the topic, supporting evidence, and evidence from documents. This activity encourages mindfulness about what students are writing.

EXPLORING AP® THEMES

American and Regional Culture

Nuanced historical writing often acknowledges the importance of some events while privileging other events. In a basic way, this is the start of developing interpretations. To end this module, give students two events: the Enlightenment and the Great Awakening. Ask students which event had a greater effect on the changes within American culture before 1754. Students will practice acknowledging the importance of one event while privileging the other.

PERIOD 2 REVIEW 1607–1754

KEY CONCEPTS AND EVENTS

Act of Religious Toleration, *61*
Anglicization, *74*
Anglo-Powhatan Wars, *118*
Bacon's Rebellion, *64*
Calvinism, *46*
cash crop, *58*
Church of England, *60*
colonization, *45*
common law, *75*
consumer revolution, *101*
Covenant Chain, *120*
Dominion of New England, *77*
enclosure movements, *55*
English Civil War, *62*
Enlightenment, *131*
gang labor, *110*
Glorious Revolution, *77*
Great Awakening, *133*
headright system, *58*
household mode of production, *80*
House of Burgesses, *59*
Huguenots, *44*

imperialism, *84*
impressment, *135*
indentured servitude, *55*
indulgences, *71*
inflation, *54*
Iroquois Confederacy, *47*
joint-stock companies, *56*
King George's War, *122*
King William's War, *78*
Leisler's Rebellion, *91*
libel, *136*
Mayflower Compact, *72*
Metacom's War, *76*
Methodism, *133*
Middle Passage, *108*
mercantilism, *100*
Navigation Acts, *100*
New Light clergy, *133*
Old Light clergy, *133*
original sin, *132*
patriarchal family, *75*
Pequot War, *76*

Pietist, *133*
Pilgrims, *71*
Powhatan Confederacy, *56*
predestination, *71*
Privy Council, *60*
Protestant Reformation, *70*
Pueblo revolt, *50*
Puritan Migration, *74*
Puritans, *71*
Queen Anne's War, *121*
redemptioners, *94*
seditious, *136*
slave code, *62*
slave laws, *110*
Stono Rebellion, *111*
subsistence farmers, *87*
theologians, *71*
Treaty of Utrecht, *121*
Tuscarora War, *120*
veto, *59*
Walking Purchase, *95*
Yamasee War, *120*

KEY PEOPLE

Nathaniel Bacon, *64*
Sir William Berkeley, *63*
Cecilius Calvert, *61*
John Calvin, *71*
René-Robert Cavelier, *45*
Samuel de Champlain, *44*
William Cosby, *135*
Oliver Cromwell, *62*
James Davenport, *134*
Jonathan Edwards, *133*
Benjamin Franklin, *94*
Andrew Hamilton, *136*
Anne Hutchinson, *75*
Immanuel Kant, *131*

King Charles I, *61*
King Charles II, *62*
King Henry IV, *44*
King Henry VIII, *71*
King James I, *56*
King James II, *77*
John Locke, *77*
Martin Luther, *71*
Mary II, *77*
Chief Massasoit, *72*
Baron de Montesquieu, *132*
Lewis Morris, *135*
Chief Opechancanough, *58*
William Penn, *92*

Pocahontas, *57*
Popé, *50*
Chief Powhatan, *56*
Queen Elizabeth I, *71*
John Rolfe, *58*
John Smith, *56*
John Wesley, *133*
George Whitefield, *133*
William of Orange, *77*
Roger Williams, *75*
John Winthrop, *73*
Voltaire, *131*
John Peter Zenger, *136*

PERIOD 2 REVIEW 1607–1754

CHRONOLOGY

Date	Event
1580s	French establish fur trade with American Indians
1607	The English found Jamestown colony
1608	Samuel de Champlain founds first permanent French settlement in North America
1609	Dutch establish fur trading outpost on the Hudson River
By 1612	Tobacco becomes main cash crop in Virginia
1619	House of Burgesses created in Virginia
	First enslaved Africans brought to Virginia colony
1620	Mayflower Compact establishes Plymouth Colony
1620s	British West Indies established
1620s–30s	Anglo-Powhatan and Pequot Wars lead to expansion of English settlements
1623	Massachusetts Bay Company established
c. 1630	Virginia colony becomes commercially successful
1630s	Puritan colonies spread quickly on American Indian lands
1635	Dissenters establish Providence, Rhode Island
1637	Massacre of Pequots by Puritan colonists
1642–51	English Civil War leads to colonial population surge
1647–92	Salem witch paranoia
1651	Parliament passes first Navigation Acts
1660	Barbados reaches majority black population
1660s	Slave laws passed by Virginia House of Burgesses
1660s–70s	Economic inequality in the colonies rises, frustrating a growing common class
1672	Royal African Company brings enslaved Africans to North America
1675	Bacon's Rebellion
1675–78	Metacom's War (also known as King Philip's War)
1680	Pueblo Revolt
	Royal African Company formed
c. 1680	British economy surges due to mercantilism
1682	French claim all land drained by Mississippi River tributaries and name the colony Louisiana
	William Penn establishes Quaker haven in Philadelphia
1686	American Indian land seized with fraudulent treaties by Penn
1688	Leisler's Rebellion
1689–97	King William's War
1689–1713	Europe in constant state of war, conflict spills into colonies
c. 1700–1808	Approximately 3 million enslaved Africans cross Middle Passage
c. 1700	Charleston becomes leading importer of enslaved Africans
c. 1700s	Disparity in land ownership leads to wealth inequality
	Popular publications spread Enlightenment ideas throughout British colonies
c. 1700–50	Colonial population rise leads to conflict with American Indians
c. 1700–60s	Rice and indigo become cash crops
1720s–30s	Planters and merchants make economic and political gains
1730s	Economic recession triggers protests against elites
1730s–40s	Great Awakening
1739	Stono Rebellion
1739–48	War between England and Spain reaches into North America
1740s	Number of enslaved African Americans born in colonies outnumbers imports of enslaved Africans
1742	Great Awakening peaks
1747	Impressment leads to riots in Boston
1754–63	French and Indian War (also known as Seven Years' War)

TRM Suggested Responses to Questions

Answers to Multiple-Choice Questions

1. b
2. d
3. c
4. a
5. c
6. c
7. b
8. c
9. d
10. b
11. a
12. c
13. a
14. b
15. b
16. d
17. b
18. c

AP® EXAM PRACTICE THROUGH 1754

Multiple-Choice Questions

Choose the correct answer for each question.

Questions 1–2 refer to the following excerpt.

> **Source:** Bernal Díaz del Castillo, *The Conquest of New Spain*, 1632
>
> "I must now speak of the skilled workmen whom Montezuma employed in all the crafts they practiced, beginning with the jewelers and workers in silver and gold . . . which excited the admiration of our great silversmiths at home. . . . There were other skilled craftsmen who worked with precious stones . . . and very fine painters and carvers.
>
> But why waste so many words on the goods in their great market? If I describe everything in detail I shall never be done. . . . Having examined and considered all that we had seen, we turned back to the great market and the swarm of buying and selling. The mere murmur of their voices talking was loud enough to be heard more than three miles away. Some of our soldiers who had been in many parts of the world, in Constantinople, in Rome, and all over Italy, said that they had never seen a market so well laid out, so orderly, and so full of people."

1. The scene described in the excerpt is an example of which of the following developments in the 1600s?
   a. A debate among European religious and political leaders about how non-Europeans should be treated
   b. The Columbian Exchange facilitating the European shift from feudalism to capitalism
   c. The mutual misunderstandings between Europeans and Native Americans as each group sought to make sense of the other
   d. The development of a caste system by the Spanish that defined the status of the diverse population in their empire

2. The events described in the passage most directly foreshadowed which of the following developments?
   a. Spanish attempts to convert Native populations to Christianity
   b. Native peoples seeking to maintain their economic prosperity through diplomatic negotiations and military resistance
   c. The Europeans' and American Indians' adoptions of useful aspects of each other's culture
   d. Spanish efforts to extract wealth from the New World

Questions 3–5 refer to the following excerpt.

> **Source:** Nathaniel Bacon, *Declaration*, 1676
>
> "We cannot in our hearts find one single spot of Rebellion of Treason or that we have in any manner aimed at subverting the settled Government. . . . We appeal to the Country itself . . . of what nature their Oppressions have been . . . let us trace the men in Authority and Favor [here] . . . let us observe the sudden rise of their Estates composed with the Quality in which they first entered this country . . . let us [also] consider whether any Public work for our safety and defense or for the Advancement of and propagation of [our] trade . . . is here . . . in [any] way adequate to our vast charge. . . .
>
> Another main article of our guilt is our open and manifest aversion of all . . . Indians, this we are informed is a Rebellion . . . we do declare and can prove that they have been for these Many years enemies to the King and Country . . . but yet have by persons in authority [here] been defended and protected even against His Majesties loyal Subjects. . . .
>
> [M]ay all the world know that we do unanimously desire to represent our sad and heavy grievances to his most sacred Majesty . . . where we do well know that our Causes will be impartially heard and Equal justice administered to all men."

145-a

AP® Exam Practice: Through 1754

3. The excerpt is best understood in the context of
   a. the gradual Anglicization of the British colonies over time.
   b. the first Great Awakening and the spread of Enlightenment ideas.
   c. the diverging goals and interests of European leaders and colonists.
   d. the development of plantation economies in the British West Indies.

4. Who of the following was most likely to have supported the perspective expressed in Bacon's *Declaration*?
   a. Male indentured servants
   b. Plantation-owning colonial politicians
   c. Colonial representative assemblies
   d. Fur-trading American Indians

5. Which of the following was an important consequence of the historical processes discussed in the excerpt?
   a. A decrease in British conflicts with American Indians over land, resources, and political boundaries
   b. An increasing attempt of the British government to incorporate North American colonies into a coherent imperial structure in pursuit of mercantilist aims
   c. Expanded use of enslaved labor in the plantation systems of the Chesapeake
   d. The development of autonomous political communities influenced by the spread of Protestant evangelism

Questions 6–9 refer to the following excerpt.

Source: William Penn, *Frame of Government of Pennsylvania*, 1682

"I know what is said by the several admirers of monarchy, aristocracy, and democracy, which are the rule of one, a few, and many, and are the three common ideas of government, when men discourse on the subject. But I choose to solve the controversy with this small distinction, and it belongs to all three: Any government is free to the people under it (whatever be the frame) where the laws rule, and the people are a party to those laws, and more than this is tyranny, oligarchy, or confusion."

6. The ideas expressed by William Penn in the excerpt most directly reflect the influence of
   a. transatlantic print culture.
   b. the First Great Awakening.
   c. European Enlightenment ideas.
   d. British mercantilist policies.

7. The ideas expressed in the excerpt contributed most to which of the following developments in colonial Pennsylvania?
   a. The abolition of slavery
   b. The influx of large numbers of European immigrants in the early 1700s
   c. British government efforts to exert more direct control over the colony
   d. Widespread violence between Pennsylvania colonists and American Indians

8. A defining characteristic of Pennsylvania and the other Middle Colonies was their
   a. plantation economies based on exporting staple crops such as tobacco and rice.
   b. relatively homogeneous population of self-sufficient family farmers.
   c. high degree of cultural and ethnic diversity.
   d. lack of organized religion and low levels of church attendance.

9. The approach toward governing described in the excerpt was most similar to which of the following?
   a. The local governments created in the Spanish and French colonies
   b. The establishment of colonial legislatures such as the Virginia House of Burgesses
   c. The constitutional monarchy created in England after the Glorious Revolution
   d. The use of town hall meetings in colonial New England

Questions 10–12 refer to the following graph.

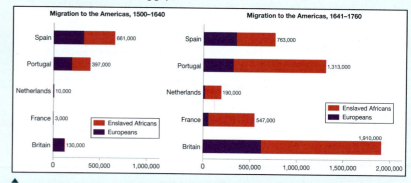

Transatlantic Migration

Source of Data: Stanley L. Engerman and Kenneth L. Sokoloff, "Factor Endowments, Institutions, and Differential Paths of Growth Among New World Economies: A View from Economic Historians of the United States," in *How Latin America Fell Behind: Economic Histories of Brazil and Mexico, 1800–1914*, ed. Stephen Haber (Palo Alto, CA: Stanford University Press, 1997), 264.

10. The population trend reflected on these graphs for the colonies of France and the Netherlands most directly resulted from which government policies?
    a. Seeking to subjugate and enslave American Indians
    b. Allowing intermarriage and fostering trade alliances with American Indians
    c. Prompting agriculture and settlement on land taken from American Indians
    d. Defining caste systems and regulating the labor and taxes paid to the state

11. After 1640, the migration trends to British colonies depicted on these graphs led to which of the following?
    a. Increased British colonial conflicts with American Indians over land, resources, and political boundaries
    b. Greater colonial resistance to Anglicization and intercolonial commercial ties
    c. Diminished colonial rivalry between Britain and France
    d. Reduced cultural pluralism and intercolonial intellectual exchange

12. The long-term effects of the migration trends portrayed on these graphs are most directly explained by
    a. mutual misunderstandings between Europeans and American Indians.
    b. participation by all British colonies to varying degrees in the transatlantic slave trade.
    c. the decline in the *encomienda* system in the Spanish colonies.
    d. French, Dutch, and Spanish colonies' alliance with, and arming of, American Indian groups.

AP® Exam Practice: Through 1754

Period 2: 1607–1754

Questions 13–16 refer to the following excerpt.

> **Source:** Benjamin Franklin, "Father Abraham's Speech" from *Poor Richard's Almanack*, 1757
>
> "If you would be wealthy . . . *think of Saving as well as Getting*: the Indies *have not made* Spain *rich, because her* Outgoes are greater than her Incomes. Away then with you expensive Follies, and you will not have so much Cause to complain of hard Times, [and] heavy Taxes. . . . 'Tis easier to suppress the first Desire, than to satisfy all that follow it . . . think what you do when you run in Debt; *You give another Power over your Liberty*. . .
>
> This Doctrine, my Friends, is *Reason* and *Wisdom*; but after all, do not depend too much upon your own *Industry*, and *Frugality*, and *Prudence*, though excellent Things, for they all may be blasted without the Blessing of Heaven; and therefore ask that Blessing humbly, and be not uncharitable to those that at present seem to want it, but comfort and help them."

13. Which of the following developments led most directly to the publication of *Poor Richard's Almanack*?
    a. The rise of Protestant evangelism in the mid-eighteenth century
    b. The cultural exchanges generated by transatlantic print culture
    c. The experiences and experiments in colonial self-government
    d. Romantic beliefs in human perfectibility spreading in reaction to the Enlightenment

14. Which of the following persons or groups would have been least likely to agree with the point of view of the excerpt?
    a. A Baptist minister
    b. Members of the colonial commercial elite
    c. An Enlightenment scholar
    d. An indentured servant

15. Franklin's statement that "the Indies *have not made* Spain *rich, because her* Outgoes are greater than her Incomes" is a criticism of which of the following developments?
    a. The *encomienda* system
    b. European mercantilism
    c. Indentured servitude
    d. The Enlightenment

16. Franklin's warning about debt and freedom most directly supports which of the following developments?
    a. That many colonists were enslaved because of debt
    b. That many colonists were able to go into debt to acquire their freedom
    c. That many colonists saved their money for consumable goods
    d. That many colonists became indebted to purchase consumable goods

Period 2: 1607–1754

Questions 17–18 refer to the following image.

▲ John Winthrop IV, Harvard Professor of Mathematics and Natural Philosophy, 1773

17. What does John Winthrop IV's position at Harvard suggest about changes in eighteenth-century New England society?
    a. Religion continued to be of prime importance to New England elites.
    b. The ideals of the Enlightenment increasingly shaped New England elites.
    c. Most New England colonists could not afford higher education.
    d. Most New England colonists had concerns about the direction of elite society.

18. Which of the following statements best characterizes the portrayal of John Winthrop IV in this image?
    a. As a descendent of a minister
    b. As a model of religious values
    c. As a man of science and ideas
    d. As a common man

AP® Exam Practice: Through 1754

Period 2: 1607–1754

Short-Answer Questions

Read each question carefully and write a short response. Use complete sentences.

1. Using the following two excerpts, answer (a), (b), and (c).

   Source: Sally Schwartz, *A Mixed Multitude: The Struggle for Toleration in Colonial Pennsylvania*, 1987

   "The extremely heterogeneous population confronted Pennsylvania with a unique set of problems that could have impeded the creation of a stable society. Nevertheless, despite the inevitable tensions, exacerbated by waves of new immigration, war, and religious conflict, colonial Pennsylvanians managed to develop new ideals of pluralism and tolerance on which they built their province. . . . William Penn set forth a new ideological basis for pluralism and tolerance that transformed the tentative pattern of relative harmony and toleration into one of official policy. . . . [H]e drafted a series of constitutions that guaranteed religious freedom and promoted his colony not only in the British Isles but on the Continent as well."

   Source: Peter Silver, *Our Savage Neighbors: How Indian War Transformed Early America*, 2008

   "Pennsylvania, New Jersey, Delaware, northern Maryland, and parts of New York — colonies that together made the eighteenth century mid-Atlantic perhaps the most racially, ethnically, and religiously mixed place in the world . . . were unintended byproducts of a force that is now alien: early modern settler colonialism, in which huge numbers of Europeans and Africans were drawn across the ocean, in freedom and in bondage, and replanted in new landscapes. . . . With few exceptions, living together made the different sorts of people living there feel frightened of one another's intentions. Forced proximity brought many groups to a fresh appreciation for their own distinctive ways, ways they thought of as 'traditional' and fought to recover amid the disturbing novelties that came with diversity. Most strove both to make the other peoples around them act more like themselves and keep, if they could, from coming to resemble their neighbors, making for a jittery, culturally competitive society."

   a. Briefly explain ONE major difference between Schwartz's and Silver's historical interpretations about the influence of demography in shaping colonial society between 1650 and 1754.

   b. Briefly explain how ONE specific historical event, development, or circumstance from the period 1650 to 1754 that is not explicitly mentioned in the excerpts could be used to support Schwartz's argument.

   c. Briefly explain how ONE specific historical event, development, or circumstance from the period 1650 to 1754 that is not explicitly mentioned in the excerpts could be used to support Silver's argument.

TRM Suggested Responses to Questions

Period 2: 1607–1754

AP® Exam Practice: Through 1754

2. Using the graph that follows, answer (a), (b), and (c).

Enslaved Africans Imported to British North America, 1671–1750
Source of data: http://www.slavevoyages.org/assessment/estimates

a. Briefly explain ONE specific historical factor that accounts for the change illustrated in the graph.
b. Briefly explain ONE specific historical event or development resulting from the change illustrated in the graph.
c. Briefly explain ONE specific historical response of enslaved people to the conditions they experienced in the colonies prior to 1750.

3. Answer (a), (b), and (c).
a. Briefly explain ONE specific historical similarity between New England and the Middle Colonies in the period from 1660 to 1750.
b. Briefly explain ONE specific historical difference between New England and the Middle Colonies in the period from 1660 to 1750.
c. Briefly explain ONE specific historical cause that accounts for the difference you indicated in (b).

4. Answer (a), (b), and (c).
a. Briefly explain why ONE of the following choices was the largest factor influencing American colonists to reject their identity as subjects of the British Empire.
   - The ideas of the Enlightenment
   - The end of the Seven Years' War
   - The first Great Awakening
b. Provide ONE specific historical example to support your argument in (a).
c. Provide specific evidence why ONE of the other options was a less important factor influencing colonists to reject their identity as subjects of the British empire.

Document-Based Question

Question 1 is based on the accompanying documents. The documents have been edited for the purpose of this exercise. *Suggested reading period: 15 minutes. Suggested writing time: 45 minutes.*

1. Evaluate the extent of change in the labor systems of the British North American colonies between 1600 and 1750.

DOCUMENT 1

Source: The General Court of Massachusetts, *An Act of Assessment on Spinning*, 1655

"This Court . . . Does therefore Order . . . That all hands not necessarily employed on other occasions, as Women, Girls and Boys, shall and hereby are enjoined to Spin according to their skill and ability; and that the Select men in every Town do consider the condition and capacity of every family, and accordingly do assess them at one or more Spinners; And because Several Families are necessarily employed the greatest part of their time in other business, yet if opportunities were attended, some time might be spared, at least be some of them for this work. . . ."

DOCUMENT 2

Source: Gabriel Thomas, *An Historical Description [of Pennsylvania]*, 1698

"I must say, even the present encouragements are very great and inviting for poor people (both men and women) of all kinds, can here get three times the wages for their Labor they can in England or Wales.

I shall instance in a few. . . . The first was a blacksmith (my next neighbor) who himself and one Negro man he had, got fifty shillings in one day, by working up a hundred pound weight of iron. . . . And for carpenters, both house and ship, bricklayers, masons, either of these tradesmen will get between five and six shillings every day constantly. As to journeymen shoemakers, they have two shillings per pair both for men and women's shoes; and journeymen tailors have 12 shillings per week. . . .

The maidservant's wages is commonly between six and ten pounds per annum, with very good accommodation. And for the women who get their livelihood by their own industry, their Labor is very dear. . . .

[T]he chief reason why wages of servants of all sorts is much higher here than there, arises from the great fertility and produce of the place; if these large stipends were refused them, they would quickly set up for themselves. . . .

First, their land costs them little or nothing in comparison [to] the farmers in England. . . . In the second place, they have constantly good price for their corn, by reason of the great and quick [trade] into Barbados and other Islands; through which means silver is become more plentiful than here in England. . . . Thirdly they pay no tithes and their Taxes are inconsiderable. . . ."

DOCUMENT 3

Source: *Estimated Number of White and Black Headrights to Virginia*

Years	White Headrights	Black Headrights
1650–1659	18,836	317
1660–1669	18,369	609
1670–1679	13,867	411
1680–1689	10,401	619
1690–1699	9,379	1,847

DOCUMENT 4

Source: Robert Beverley, *The History and Present State of Virginia*, 1705

"Slaves are the Negroes . . . following the condition of the Mother, . . . They are called Slaves, in respect of the time of their Servitude, because it is for Life.

Servants, are those which serve for only a few years, according to the time of the Indenture, or the Custom of the Country. . . .

The Male-Servants, and Slaves of both Sexes, are employed together in Tilling and Manuring the Ground, in Sowing and Planting Tobacco, Corn, etc. Some Distinction indeed is made between them in the Clothes, and Food; but the Work of both, is no other than what the Overseers, the Freemen, and the Planters themselves do.

Sufficient Distinction is also made between the Female-Servants and Slaves; for a White Woman is rarely or never put to work in the [fields], if she be good for anything else. . . .

The work of their Servants and Slaves, is no other than what every common Freeman does. Neither is any freeman required to do more in a day than his Overseer. And I can assure you with a great deal of Truth, that generally their Slaves are not worked near so hard, nor so many Hours in a day, as the [Farmers], and Day-Laborers in *England*. An Overseer is a Man, that having served his time, has acquired the Skill and Character of an experienced Planter, and is therefore entrusted with the Direction of the Servants and Slaves."

DOCUMENT 5

Source: An Indentured Contract of Apprenticeship between William Matthews and Thomas Windover, 1718

"I, William Mathews . . . of the city of New York . . . does voluntarily and of his own free will . . . put himself as an apprentice [shoemaker] to Thomas Windover. . . .

[William Mathews] will live and . . . serve from August 15, 1718, until the full term of seven years be completed and ended. . . . [He] shall faithfully serve his master, shall faithfully keep his secrets, and gladly obey his lawful commands everywhere. . . . He shall not waste his said master's goods nor lend them unlawfully to any. He shall not . . . contract matrimony within the [seven years].

At cards, dice, or any other unlawful game, he shall not play. . . with his own goods or the goods of others. Without a license from his master he shall neither buy nor sell during the said term. He shall not absent himself day or night from his master's service without his leave, not haunt alehouses, but in all things he shall behave himself as a faithful apprentice toward his master. . . .

The master . . . shall, by the best means or methods, teach or cause the apprentice to be taught the art or mystery of a [shoemaker]. He shall find and provide unto the said apprentice sufficient meat, drink, apparel, lodging, and washing fit for an apprentice. During the said term, every night in winter he shall give the apprentice one quarter of schooling. At the expiration of the said term he shall provide him with a sufficient new suit of apparel, four shirts, and two necklets."

DOCUMENT 6

Source: South Carolina Assembly, *An Act for the Better Ordering and Governing of Negroes and Other Slaves in This Province*, 1740

"I. *And be it enacted* . . . That all Negroes and Indians . . . mullatoes or mestizos who now are, or shall hereafter be, in this Province, and all their issue and offspring, born or to be born, shall be, and they are hereby declared to be, and remain forever hereafter, absolute slaves. . . .

II. . . . *Be it further enacted* . . . That no person whatsoever shall permit or suffer any slave under his or their care or management . . . to go out of the plantation . . . without a letter. . . .

XXX. *And be it further enacted* . . . That no slave who shall dwell, reside, inhabit, or be usually employed in Charlestown, shall presume to buy, sell, deal, traffic, barter, exchange or use commerce for any goods, wares, provisions, grain, [foodstuffs], or commodities, of any sort or kind whatsoever. . . .

XLIII. . . . *Be it therefore enacted* . . . That no men slaves exceeding seven in number, shall herein be permitted to travel together in any high road in this Province, without some white person with them; and it shall and may be lawful for any [white] person or persons . . . to apprehend all and every such slaves, and shall and may whip them, not exceeding twenty lashes on the bare back.

LVI. And whereas, several Negroes did lately rise in rebellion, and did commit many barbarous murders at Stono and in other parts adjacent thereto; and whereas, in suppressing the said rebels, several of them were killed and others taken alive and executed. . . . Be it enacted . . . That all and every act . . . committed, and executed, in and about suppressing and putting all . . . the said . . . Negroes to death, is and are hereby declared lawful, to all intents and purposes whatsoever. . . ."

Period 2: 1607–1754

AP® Exam Practice: Through 1754

DOCUMENT 7

Source: Benjamin Franklin, *Observations Concerning the Increasing of Mankind, Peopling of Countries, &c*, observations on the population of Pennsylvania, 1751

"Land being thus plenty in America, and so cheap as that a laboring Man, that understands [agriculture], can in a short Time save Money enough to purchase a Piece of new Land sufficient for a Plantation, whereon he may subsist a family; such are not afraid to marry. . . .

Labor will never be cheap here, where no man continues long a laborer for others, but gets a plantation of his own; no man continues long a journeyman to a trade, but goes among those new settlers, and sets up for himself, etc. Hence labor is no cheaper now in Pennsylvania than it was thirty years ago, though so many thousand laboring people have been imported. . . .

The labor of slaves can never be so cheap here as the labor of workingmen is in Britain. . . . Why then will Americans purchase slaves? Because slaves may be kept as long as a man pleases, or has occasion for their labor; while hired men are continually leaving their masters (often in the midst of business) and setting up for themselves."

Long-Essay Questions

Please choose one of the following three questions to answer. *Suggested writing time: 40 minutes.*

2. Evaluate the extent of difference between the influence of religion in the colonialism of the British and that of the Spanish in North America between 1492 and 1700.
3. Evaluate the extent to which British mercantilist policies shaped the economic development of the New England colonies between 1660 and 1754.
4. Evaluate the extent to which the chattel slave system shaped the economic development of the Chesapeake colonies between 1660 and 1754.

TRM Suggested Responses to Questions

PERIOD 3: 1754–1800
A Revolutionary Era

AP® Overview for Period 3

Following the French and Indian War, American colonists maintained the natural right to be an equal member of the English imperial system. This belief in Anglicization would experience significant fissures as Americans drifted in fits and starts toward an identity of their own as they sought redress of grievances from the British. A protracted political struggle between Great Britain and the American colonies gave way to momentum for independence as Americans defined and redefined an American identity. Period 3 begins with this epic story and traces subsequent decisions the fledgling American nation made concerning governmental institutions, political parties, enslaved persons, women, American Indian lands, economic systems, federalism, and westward expansion. Though this period is teeming with important ideas, as well as important content, such as liberty vs. order, the resentment of distant authority vs. local control, and the varying beliefs in republicanism, students must also see beyond the political events. The issues of African Americans, African laborers, women, and American Indians attendant to the revolutionary period are crucial parts of this narrative and provide students a full accounting of the period 1754–1800.

The Period 3 learning modules are the last in the first third in the organization of this book. This means students still experience the intense scaffolding of skills and content the first three periods offer, which prepares them for Periods 4–6, which starts to shear away some of the scaffolding. Period 3 accounts for 10–17% of the material assessed on the AP® exam. Period 3 can be the focus of a Short-Answer Question, Long-Essay Question, Document-Based Essay Question, and Multiple-Choice Questions.

Module 3-1: International Conflicts Cause Colonial Tensions describes the French and Indian War, which serves as the fulcrum of analysis as students evaluate the causes and effects of this imperial struggle over land in North America. Attendant to this event is the changing nature of the relationship between Great Britain and its North American colonies. The thematic focus of America in the world and politics and power help students imagine how to frame their analysis. Causation is a natural accompaniment to the events in this module and students should consider long-term, intermediate-term, and short-term causes and effects of the altered relationship between Great Britain and the North American colonists. The reasoning process of causation is thoroughly built out at the end of the narrative and judicious planning helps teachers leave time for the thinking historically activity.

Module 3-2: Resistance to Britain Intensifies focuses on a complicated development marked by the movement from a continued belief in Anglicization to a redress of grievances to a formal break from Great Britain. Amidst these changes were dynamic expressions of natural rights that slowly manifested in the development of a unique American identity. Patient students will leave with a deeper comprehension of how contingencies shaped the causes of the American Revolution. The reasoning process of continuity and change helps remind students of the wide variance in reaction to British imperial authority during this turbulent time. The thematic focus of politics and power and American and national identity brings political history alongside social history as students work through the interdependent forces of political resistance and social change.

Module 3-3: The American Revolution Begins is less a study covering events of the war for independence, but more an evaluation of the disparate decisions people made as American patriots plunged into war with Great Britain. The political, intellectual, and economic causes of the war are evaluated throughout, with special attention paid to how divided American society became over fundamental issues related to natural rights. This module extends the analysis beyond the patriots to include an analysis of how the war affected African Americans and loyalists. The reasoning process of contextualization is implicit in the narrative and explicitly taught at the conclusion of this module. The thematic focus of politics and power and American and regional culture emphasizes cultural forces shaped political responses.

Module 3-4: Winning the War for Independence privileges not only the strategy, battles, and personalities of the Revolutionary War, but also the roles of women and the foreign alliance with France in the victory over the British. The thematic focus of America in the world and social structures reinforces the approach of this module. Throughout the analysis of the war, crucial turning-point battles and decisions are highlighted to enable students to narrow their focus. The reasoning process of causation encourages students to make thoughtful determinations about which causes to emphasize.

Module 3-5: Governing in Revolutionary Times, 1776–1787 depicts the "Critical Period" — a time in which the new nation used the Articles of Confederation as the basis of a national government. While the articles fostered unity during the war, they revealed different ideologies about the proper meshing of state and federal authority. Reconciling the need for state autonomy with the necessity of a national government able to answer prevalent questions such as western territory are essential questions to ponder throughout this module. Students should be aware of both the successes and the weaknesses of the Articles of Confederation and should also focus on what the revolution meant for American Indians. The thematic approach of politics and power furthers students' focus on the political developments in this module. The reasoning process of comparison encourages students to make comparisons within this module and with topics from Module 3-4, as well.

Module 3-6: Reframing the American Government
contains a brief narrative of events relevant to the making of a national constitution that frames the content of this module. A lively evaluation of the context, creation, debates, and subsequent ratification of the Constitution invites students to examine the continuities and changes to the diverging sense of an American identity. Students should also be aware of the inherent contradictions of how the framers espoused beliefs in republicanism despite also allowing for processes that increased enslavement for African Americans and African laborers. The design for this module intentionally leaves time and space for teachers to have students work on the Document-Based Question at the end of this module. Politics and power and American and regional culture are the thematic focal points and while the former is a natural pairing, teachers should help students see how cultural attitudes were shaped by the political forces of this time.

Module 3-7: Legacies of the American Revolution
is a discussion framed largely by political history, but it is also useful and necessary to move beyond political history in order to understand the breadth of the revolution. The political class of the late eighteenth century was somewhat static and students receive a much more intellectually honest understanding of the revolution when they engage in historical inquiry that seeks to comprehend how social classes, ethnic groups, and gender roles changed and stayed the same in this period. This module privileges thematic focus areas of American and national identity and social structures as a way to foster understanding of these historical developments. The reasoning process of causation and comparison allow students to conceptualize these developments across time and within the developments of this time period.

Module 3-8: George Washington Unites a Nation
describes the efforts of George Washington and his administration to bring order to government out of the tumult of the 1770s and 1780s. The success of the government was not only driven by its new structure and function, as laid out by the Constitution, but also by how the people in government were able to find solid footing as they set political precedents. Treasury Secretary Alexander Hamilton's financial plan was chief among the efforts to stabilize the new nation's economy. Students should note that all of the functional changes in government happened at the same time the new nation was deciding, and later building, the new capital of the nation. The reasoning process of causation draws students in to see the immediate causes and effects of decisions made by the Federalists as the nascent nation came into existence. Politics and power is the central thematic focus of this module, which will help students see both unity and division within Washington's cabinet and across the new nation.

Module 3-9: Political Parties in Years of Crisis
focuses on the sectional divisions and developing factions lingering beneath the surface of the republic despite success under the leadership of George Washington. Although the impetus for partisanship was the varied definitions of republicanism, the French Revolution and subsequent Quasi-War with France proved to be events that unearthed brewing partisan divisions. Students should see the development of political parties as an organic process that stemmed from different beliefs about the best way to implement a republican style of government. The reasoning process of causation will help ground students in thinking about the factors that influenced this development. The thematic focus of politics and power, America in the world, and American and regional culture all help situate the internal and external sources of partisan disputes in the late eighteenth century.

Pacing Guide
Course Pacing for Period 3

Module #	Lesson Title	Instructional Period*	AP® Theme	AP® Topic	AP® Reasoning Process/Skill	Homework
3-1	N/A	N/A	Politics and Power / America in the World	3.1 / 3.2	Causation / Historical Thinking Skills 1, 2, 3, 5	**Reading and Source Analysis:** 3-1
	International Conflicts Cause Colonial Tensions	1	Politics and Power / America in the World	3.2 / 3.12	Causation / Historical Thinking Skills 1, 2, 3, 5	**Activities:** AP® Thinking Historically: Evaluating Causes AP® Writing Historically: Short-Answer Question Practice
	Review: AP® Writing Historically: Short-Answer Question Practice **Workshop:** AP® Thinking Historically: Evaluating Causes	1	Politics and Power / America in the World	3.2 / 3.12	Causation / Historical Thinking Skills 1, 2, 3, 5	**Reading and Source Analysis:** 3-2

(Continued)

Module #	Lesson Title	Instructional Period*	AP® Theme	AP® Topic	AP® Reasoning Process/Skill	Homework
3-2	Resistance to Britain Intensifies	1	American and National Identity; Politics and Power	3.3	Continuity and Change / Historical Thinking Skills 1, 2, 3, 5, 6	**Activity:** AP® Writing Historically: Evaluating Continuity and Change in an Essay
	Workshop: AP® Writing Historically: Evaluating Continuity and Change in an Essay	1	American and National Identity; Politics and Power	3.3	Continuity and Change / Historical Thinking Skills 1, 2, 3, 4, 5	**Reading and Source Analysis:** 3-3
3-3	The American Revolution Begins	1	American and Regional Culture; Politics and Power	3.4	Causation / Historical Thinking Skills 1, 2, 3, 4, 5	**Reading and Source Analysis:** 3-4 **Activity:** AP® Writing Historically: Establishing Context in an Essay Introduction
3-4	Winning the War for Independence **Review:** AP® Writing Historically: Establishing Context in an Essay Introduction	1	America in the World; Social Structures	3.5	Causation / Historical Thinking Skills 1, 2, 3, 5	**Activity:** AP® Writing Historically: Evaluating Effects in an Essay
	Workshop: AP® Writing Historically: Evaluating Effects in an Essay	1	America in the World; Social Structures	3.5	Causation / Historical Thinking Skills 1, 2, 3, 5	**Reading and Source Analysis:** 3-5
3-5	Governing in Revolutionary Times, 1776–1787	1	Politics and Power	3.6	Comparison / Historical Thinking Skills 1, 2, 3, 5, 6	**Activity:** AP® Writing Historically: Making Evaluative Comparisons in an Essay
	Workshop: AP® Writing Historically: Making Evaluative Comparisons in an Essay	1	Politics and Power	3.6	Comparison / Historical Thinking Skills 1, 2, 3, 5	**Reading and Source Analysis:** 3-6
3-6	Reframing the American Government	1	Politics and Power; American and Regional Culture	3.7 3.8	Continuity and Change / Historical Thinking Skills 1, 2, 3, 5, 6	**Activity:** AP® Writing Historically: Evaluating Continuity and Change in a Document-Based Essay
	Workshop: AP® Writing Historically: Evaluating Continuity and Change in a Document-Based Essay	1	Politics and Power; American and Regional Culture	3.8	Continuity and Change / Historical Thinking Skills 1, 2, 3, 4, 5	**Reading and Source Analysis:** 3-7
3-7	Legacies of the American Revolution	1	American and National Identity	3.9	Comparison and Causation / Historical Thinking Skills 1, 2, 3, 5, 6	**Activity:** AP® Writing Historically: Making Evaluative Comparisons in a Document-Based Essay
	Workshop: AP® Writing Historically: Making Evaluative Comparisons in a Document-Based Essay	1	American and National Identity	3.9	Comparison and Causation / Historical Thinking Skills 1, 2, 3, 4, 5	**Reading and Source Analysis:** 3-8 **Activity:** AP® Writing Historically: Short-Answer Practice

(Continued)

Module #	Lesson Title	Instructional Period*	AP® Theme	AP® Topic	AP® Reasoning Process/Skill	Homework
3-8	George Washington Unites a Nation **Review:** AP® Writing Historically: Short-Answer Question Practice	1	Politics and Power	3.10 3.11	Causation / Historical Thinking Skills 1, 2, 3, 4, 5, 6	**Reading and Source Analysis:** 3-9
3-9	Political Parties in Years of Crisis	1	Politics and Power America in the World American and Regional Culture	3.11	Causation / Historical Thinking Skills 1, 2, 3, 5	**Activity:** AP® Writing Historically: Evaluating Causation in a Document-Based Essay
	Workshop: AP® Writing Historically: Evaluating Causation in a Document-Based Essay	1	Politics and Power America in the World American and Regional Culture	3.13	Causation / Historical Thinking Skills 1, 2, 3, 4, 5	Prepare for Assessment
Formative Assessment	AP® Exam Practice • 18 MCQs • 4 SAQs	0-1	All AP® U.S. History Course Themes	3.13 Personal Progress Check • 15 MCQs • 2 SAQs • 1 LEQ	All AP® History Reasoning Processes / Skills	
Summative Assessment	Unit 1 Test Bank • 55 MCQs • 4 SAQs • 1 DBQ • 4 LEQs	0-1	All AP® U.S. History Course Themes		All AP® History Reasoning Processes / Skills	

*Based on a standard 50-minute class period.

Period 3 Resources

The following resources can be found in the Resources section of the book's digital platform, by clicking on the link buttons in the Teacher's Edition e-book, or by opening the Teacher's Resource Materials.

- **TRM** Period 3 Overview Video
- **TRM** AP® Concepts and Skills Video
- **TRM** Period 3 Lecture Presentation Slides
- **TRM** Period 3 Workshop Rubrics
- **TRM** Period 3 Suggested Responses to Questions
- **TRM** Period 3 Guided Reading Worksheets

Module 3-1

- **TRM** Handout 3.1 – Causes and Effects of the French and Indian War
- **TRM** Module 3.1 AP® Analyzing Sources Handout 1
- **TRM** Map 3A – Eastern United States
- **TRM** Module 3.1 AP® Analyzing Sources Handout 2
- **TRM** Module 3.1 AP® Analyzing Sources Handout 3
- **TRM** Handout 3.2 – Dueling Dates, 1754 & 1763
- **TRM** Module 3.1 AP® Analyzing Sources Handout 4
- **TRM** Module 3.1 AP® Thinking Historically Handout

Module 3-2

- **TRM** Module 3.2 AP® Analyzing Sources Handout 1
- **TRM** Module 3.2 AP® Analyzing Sources Handout 2
- **TRM** Module 3.2 AP® Analyzing Sources Handout 3
- **TRM** Module 3.2 AP® Analyzing Sources Handout 4
- **TRM** Module 3.2 AP® Analyzing Sources Handout 5

Module 3-3

- **TRM** Module 3.3 AP® Analyzing Sources Handout 1
- **TRM** Handout 3.3 – Advantages and Challenges of the American Revolution
- **TRM** Module 3.3 AP® Analyzing Sources Handout 2
- **TRM** Module 3.3 AP® Analyzing Sources Handout 3
- **TRM** Module 3.3 AP® Analyzing Sources Handout 4
- **TRM** Handout 3.4 – Patriots vs. Loyalists: Traits & Characteristics
- **TRM** Module 3.3 AP® Analyzing Sources Handout 5
- **TRM** Module 3.3 AP® Analyzing Sources Handout 6

Module 3-4

- **TRM** Module 3.4 AP® Analyzing Sources Handout 1

- **TRM** Module 3.4 AP® Analyzing Sources Handout 2
- **TRM** Handout 3.5 – Competing Strategies for Victory in the Revolutionary War
- **TRM** Module 3.4 AP® Analyzing Sources Handout 3

Module 3-5
- **TRM** Module 3.5 AP® Analyzing Sources Handout 1
- **TRM** Handout 3.6 – Strengths and Weaknesses of the Articles of Confederation
- **TRM** Module 3.5 AP® Analyzing Sources Handout 2
- **TRM** Module 3.5 AP® Analyzing Sources Handout 3

Module 3-6
- **TRM** Handout 3.7 – Federalist vs. Antifederalist: Competing Philosophies
- **TRM** Module 3.6 AP® Analyzing Sources Handout

Module 3-7
- **TRM** Module 3.7 AP® Analyzing Sources Handout 1
- **TRM** Module 3.7 AP® Analyzing Sources Handout 2
- **TRM** Handout 3.8 – Secondary Source Critique

Module 3-8
- **TRM** Handout 3.9 – Bill of Rights Debate
- **TRM** Module 3.8 AP® Analyzing Sources Handout 1
- **TRM** Module 3.8 AP® Analyzing Sources Handout 2
- **TRM** Module 3.8 AP® Analyzing Sources Handout 3

Module 3-9
- **TRM** Handout 3.10 – Pros and Cons of War or Neutrality
- **TRM** Module 3.9 AP® Analyzing Sources Handout 1
- **TRM** Module 3.9 AP® Analyzing Sources Handout 2
- **TRM** Module 3.9 AP® Analyzing Sources Handout 3
- **TRM** Module 3.9 AP® Analyzing Sources Handout 4

Period 3 Essential Activity

One of the livelier debates among the revolutionary generation was determining the origins of the American Revolution. To people such as John Adams, the revolution began before the war and for others, such as Benjamin Rush, the revolution began as governmental systems were established. The continuities and changes to ideas of governmental systems, functions, political parties, and American foreign policy invite a dynamic study. This activity seeks to take one aspect of Period 3 — the structures and functions of government — and build understanding that forces students to think across the time period.

Articles of Confederation → Structure
→ Function

Constitution of 1787 → Structure
→ Function

The first part of this activity attempts to have students account for both the structures of the federal government and the functions of the federal government under the Articles of Confederation and the U.S. Constitution of 1787, which means students will not reference the Bill of Rights. When students think about structures, encourage them to concentrate on the design of the government. An example would be a unicameral and bicameral legislature. For functions, this is when students should think about specific powers given to the different branches of government such as the ability to raise an army. Students can brainstorm on butcher-block paper so they have ample room for outlining their answers.

Function → Political Systems
→ Economic Systems
→ Foreign Policy

The last part of this activity is geared toward having students delineate how the functions of the Constitution of 1787 led to changes in political systems, economic systems, and foreign policy. Students should use their brainstorm from part one of the activity to select functions which will help explain the changes in this chart. Upon completion, students will have chartered an explanation about how the structures and functions of governmental systems changed throughout Period 3.

Period 3 Alignment to the Fall 2019 AP® United States History Course Framework*

Relationship to the College Board Units
Period 3 in this book covers Topics 3.1–3.13 in Unit 3 of the College Board course framework. Students will be ready to take the Personal Progress Check for Unit 3 once they have completed this period.

Course Themes
Period 3 develops these course themes outlined in the course framework:

- **America in the World (WOR):** In response to British efforts to exert greater control and increase tax revenues, the thirteen colonies rebelled against Great Britain and with French assistance fought a successful war for independence. In the

1790s, the United States grappled with foreign policy challenges resulting from the French Revolution and the harassment of U.S. shipping by both the British and French navies.

- **American and National Identity (NAT):** The American Revolution and the emigration of thousands of loyalists led to the creation of a society separate from Great Britain.
- **Social Structures (SOC):** The events and ideas that underpinned the American Revolution challenged traditional gender and ethnic structures during the conflict and raised questions about the status of women and African Americans afterwards.
- **Politics and Power (POL):** In the mid-1780s, Americans replaced the Articles of Confederation with a new Constitution to strengthen the federal government while attempting to maintain rights gained in the Revolution. During the 1790s, debates over how to interpret the Constitution and the proper role of the federal government in economic and international policy led to the emergence of two competing political factions — Federalists and Democratic-Republicans.
- **American and Regional Cultures (ARC):** New forms of national culture developed in the United States alongside regional variations. American writers, artists, and intellectuals expressed themselves in ways that reflected these varied cultures.
- **Migration and Settlement (MIG):** Westward migration during the mid-1700s led to the creation of new communities and fostered ethnic tensions as well as regional conflicts. American Indians grappled with the impacts of migration and settlement as they adjusted alliances and sought to maintain access to resources and control of land.

Course Skills

Period 3 helps students to develop the following AP® Historical Thinking Skills identified in the course framework.

- **Skill 1: Developments and Processes** (Modules 3-1, 3-2, 3-3, 3-4, 3-5, 3-6, 3-7, 3-8, 3-9)
- **Skill 2: Sourcing and Situation** (Modules 3-1, 3-2, 3-3, 3-4, 3-5, 3-6, 3-7, 3-8, 3-9)
- **Skill 3: Claims and Evidence in Sources** (Modules 3-1, 3-2, 3-3, 3-4, 3-5, 3-6, 3-7, 3-8, 3-9)
- **Skill 4: Contextualization** (Modules 3-2, 3-3, 3-7, 3-8, 3-9)
- **Skill 5: Making Connections** (Modules 3-1, 3-2, 3-3, 3-4, 3-5, 3-6, 3-7, 3-8, 3-9)
- **Skill 6: Argumentation** (Modules 3-2, 3-5, 3-6, 3-7, 3-8)

Period 3 helps students to develop the following AP® History Reasoning Processes identified in the course framework.

- **Reasoning Process 1: Comparison** (Modules 3-5, 3-7)
- **Reasoning Process 2: Causation** (Modules 3-1, 3-3, 3-4, 3-7, 3-8, 3-9)
- **Reasoning Process 3: Continuity and Change** (Modules 3-2, 3-6)

Learning Objectives and Historical Developments

Module	Topics	Learning Objectives	Historical Developments and Key Concepts
3-1	3.1, 3.2, 3.12	Unit 3: Learning Objective A Unit 3: Learning Objective B Unit 3: Learning Objective N Unit 3: Learning Objective O	KC-3.1.I.A, KC-3.1.I.B, KC-3.1.I.C, KC-3.3.I.A, KC-3.3.I.B, KC-3.2.III.C
3-2	3.3	Unit 3: Learning Objective C	KC-3.1.II.A, KC-3.1.II.B, KC-3.1.II.C, KC-3.1.II.D
3-3	3.4	Unit 3: Learning Objective D	KC-3.2.I.A, KC-3.2.I.B
3-4	3.5	Unit 3: Learning Objective E	KC-3.1.II.E
3-5	3.6	Unit 3: Learning Objective F Unit 3: Learning Objective G	KC-3.2.I.C, KC-3.2.I.D, KC-3.2.I.E
3-6	3.7, 3.8	Unit 3: Learning Objective H Unit 3: Learning Objective I	KC-3.2.II.A, KC-3.2.II.B, KC-3.3.I.C, KC-3.2.II.C.i, KC-3.2.II.D, KC-3.2.II.E
3-7	3.9	Unit 3: Learning Objective J	KC-3.2.II.C.ii
3-8	3.10, 3.11	Unit 3: Learning Objective K Unit 3: Learning Objective L Unit 3: Learning Objective M	KC-3.3.II.A, KC-3.3.II.B, KC-3.3.I.D, KC-3.3.I.E, KC-3.2.III.A, KC-3.2.III.ii
3-9	3.11, 3.13	Unit 3: Learning Objective M Unit 3: Learning Objective P	KC-3.2.III.B, KC-3.3.II.C, KC-3.2.III.D

TRM A detailed alignment that can be sorted by Course Framework Unit, Topic, Learning Objective, Historical Development/Key Concept, or textbook period, is available in the Teacher's Resource Materials and via the book's online platform.

*Should changes be made to the Course Framework in the future, an updated alignment will be placed on our catalog page at bfwpub.com/fabric1e.

TEACHING IDEA

AP® Central

A great resource to help you teach this period is to read the information in the AP® U.S. History study guide for 1754–1800, available from the AP® United States History Classroom Resources section of AP® Central (apcentral.collegeboard.org).

PERIOD 3: 1754–1800

A Revolutionary Era

▲ **Pewters' Banner, 1788** This painted silk banner was carried by the Society of Pewterers of the City of New York at a parade to celebrate the ratification of the U.S. Constitution in 1788. Pewter is a tin alloy used to make inexpensive utensils and kitchenware. Skilled artisans used images like this banner to make clear that their work was woven into the fabric of the new republic.

Following King William's War (1689–1697), Queen Anne's War (1702–1713), and King George's War (1744–1748), the Seven Years' War (1756–1763) — which began in 1754 in North America and was known as the French and Indian War — was Britain's largest victory in the ongoing imperial contest for North America. Expelling the French from North America came at a high price, however. This latest war had left Britain in massive debt, and the new policies the crown created to raise money to pay it off were unpopular with North American colonists.

British Parliament's efforts to impose greater control over its North American colonies sparked a strong reaction. Impressment and quartering, the Proclamation of 1763, and the Sugar Act in 1764 were just some of the policies that drew protest from colonists. These protests became more effective as colonists developed organizations and systems of communication that allowed them to spread their ideas far and wide. This also helped unite colonists across classes, as many British laws — such as those that placed limits on westward expansion — were unpopular with everyone.

Although many colonists were displeased with British policies by 1774, many others still supported them. Indeed, the majority of colonists did not participate in any protest activities. For the most part, the aim of those who did protest continued to be resistance to particular acts, not independence from Britain — that is, colonists sought greater liberty within the empire.

Colonists and colonies moved reluctantly from resistance to revolution. When faced with threats from British troops, a sufficient number of colonists took up arms and made war a reality. This surge of violent conflict finally gave the advantage to those few radical political leaders urging independence.

The patriots' eventual victory over Great Britain won independence, but the new country faced many difficult problems in its aftermath. The nation owed a huge debt to private citizens and state and foreign governments, and difficult economic times followed. Continental soldiers had not been paid, and they demanded to be given what they were owed so that they could return home and reestablish their former lives. This was just one of many economic issues that devastated many war veterans and their families during the remainder of the eighteenth century.

These problems affected American Indians and African Americans as well as whites. Warfare between settlers and American Indians west of the Appalachian Mountains, from the Ohio River valley to Georgia, continued for decades. At the same time, slaveholders seeking more fertile fields also expanded into the trans-Appalachian region.

In the 1780s and 1790s, the United States faced numerous obstacles to securing its place as a nation. Financial hardship, massive debts, conflicts with American Indians, and European diplomacy had to be addressed by a federal government that, under the Articles of Confederation, was relatively weak. By 1787 concerns about national security, fueled by frontier conflicts that sometimes erupted into outright rebellion, persuaded some political leaders to embrace a new governmental structure. While it required numerous compromises among groups with competing ideas and interests, the Constitution was drafted and, after fierce debates, narrowly accepted.

George Washington thus took office as the first American president at the head of a more powerful federal government. His administration sought to enhance American power at home and abroad. Secretary of the Treasury Alexander Hamilton proposed a series of measures to stabilize the American economy, pay off Revolutionary War debts, and promote trade and industry. However, these Federalist policies drew opposition from leaders like Thomas Jefferson and James Madison, whose positions aligned with many ordinary farmers and frontiersmen.

By 1796, Jefferson and Madison had formed a separate political party, the Democratic-Republicans, and in 1800 they gained control of Congress and won the presidency for their candidate, Thomas Jefferson. Power thus transitioned peacefully from one political party to another, a promising sign for the future of the young United States.

PERIOD 3 PREVIEW

Module	AP® Thematic Focus
3-1: International Conflicts Cause Colonial Tensions	**Politics and Power ▪ America in the World** By 1764, the British had fought a number of colonial wars with European powers over control of North America. The Seven Years' War proved to be the costliest and most consequential of these wars. British victory left Great Britain in control of much of North America, but also deeply in debt. The policies Great Britain introduced in the aftermath of the war raised tensions with British colonists.
3-2: Resistance to Britain Intensifies	**American and National Identity ▪ Politics and Power** In the aftermath of the Seven Years' War, British North Americans increasingly believed that British colonial policies benefited England at their expense. In reaction to colonial rebellion, British officials tried a number of different responses, including compromising and exercising greater control over the colonies. All of these strategies had limited success.
3-3: The American Revolution Begins	**Politics and Power ▪ American and Regional Culture** By 1774, many British colonialists began to see themselves as members of a society separate from Great Britain. In response to the Coercive Acts, British colonists increasingly tried to exert political power against the British government. After a series of armed conflicts and the publication of Thomas Paine's *Common Sense*, the Second Continental Congress declared the thirteen colonies independent from Great Britain, forcing many colonists to choose a side.
3-4: Winning the War for Independence	**America in the World ▪ Social Structures** The events and ideas that underpinned the American Revolution challenged traditional ethnic and gender structures during the conflict. During the American Revolution the former British colonies defined themselves as an independent nation and sought allies in their conflict with Great Britain.
3-5: Governing in Revolutionary Times, 1776–1787	**Politics and Power** In the aftermath of the American Revolution, Americans debated the proper role of a national government and faced internal conflicts that challenged the ideals of the American Revolution itself.
3-6: Reframing the American Government	**Politics and Power ▪ American and Regional Culture** By the mid-1780s, it became increasingly clear that the Articles of Confederation government could not maintain control over the new republic. During this period, Americans debated how best to strengthen the federal government without undermining the rights gained in the Revolution. During the debates over the new constitution, various regional interests vied for influence over the new federal government.
3-7: Legacies of the American Revolution	**American and National Identity ▪ Social Structures** The ideals of the American Revolution raised questions about the status of women and African Americans. They also gave rise to a movement to educate young Americans for future republican citizenship. During this time, new forms of national culture developed in the United States alongside continued regional variations. A distinctly American culture began to emerge as the work of writers, artists, and intellectuals reflected new national and regional cultures.
3-8: George Washington Unites a Nation	**Politics and Power** During George Washington's first term, the new federal government aimed to strengthen federal authority through new economic policies and the establishment of a new capital. These policies led to divisions within Washington's cabinet based on regional interests and differing interpretations of the new Constitution.
3-9: Political Parties in Years of Crisis	**Politics and Power ▪ America in the World ▪ American and Regional Culture ▪ Migration and Settlement** During the 1790s, Americans debated the proper role of the federal government, including how it should shape economic and international policy. These debates ultimately led to two competing political factions — Federalists and Democratic-Republicans — as well as regional divisions. The French Revolution, along with the wars between France and Great Britain, further divided Americans along partisan and regional lines during this time period. Westward migration during the mid-1700s led to the creation of new communities and fostered ethnic tensions as well as regional conflicts. American Indians grappled with the impacts of migration and settlement as they adjusted alliances and sought to maintain access to resources and control of land.

Module 3-1

International Conflicts Cause Colonial Tensions

LEARNING TARGETS
By the end of this module, you should be able to:
- Explain the developments that led to the Seven Years' War (also known as the French and Indian War).
- Explain how the aftermath of the Seven Years' War raised tensions between British government and colonial society.

THEMATIC FOCUS
Politics and Power
America in the World

By 1764, the British had fought a number of colonial wars with European powers over control of North America. The Seven Years' War proved to be the costliest and most consequential of these wars. British victory left Great Britain in control of much of North America, but also deeply in debt. The policies Great Britain introduced in the aftermath of the war raised tensions with British colonists.

HISTORICAL REASONING FOCUS
Causation

Identifying causes and effects throughout history is a valuable skill, but true historical analysis moves beyond mere observation. Throughout this course, and on the AP® Exam, you will be asked to explain the extent to which certain causes led to certain effects. In other words, you will need to evaluate what you know and take a position on the level of importance of a given cause in relation to an effect. Defending that position with historical evidence forms the backbone of a strong historical argument.

Often, the importance of a cause is related to its distance in time and place from its effect — as you've probably guessed, less important causes are typically farther away, and more important causes are usually closer. Some powerful events, however, generate effects decades and continents away from their origins. For example, the Protestant Reformation began in Europe during the early sixteenth century, but it shaped English colonization of North America throughout the seventeenth and eighteenth centuries.

TASK ▶ As you read the rest of this module, take special note of the many events and developments that increased tension between Britain and its colonies between the 1750s and 1770s. Prepare to evaluate the role that each cause played in creating conflict. Which ones played a greater role? Which ones were less important? As you answer these questions for yourself, think about how you could support an argument asserting which causes were most influential.

The war that erupted in the Ohio River valley in 1754 caused an enormous shift in political and economic relations in colonial North America. What began as a small-scale regional conflict expanded into a brutal and lengthy war with battles around the world. Known as the French and Indian War in North America and the Seven Years' War in Great Britain and Europe, where battles first broke out in 1756, the extended conflict led to a dramatic expansion of British territory in North America and to increasing demands from American colonists for more control over their own lives. In the long run, British imperial wars led to growing discord between England and its colonies. American colonists grew increasingly tired of spending their lives and money on

---

TRM Suggested Responses to Questions

TEACHING IDEA

Class Discussion

As you begin this module, write the following statement on the board or display it from your projector: "Wars don't always solve old problems; sometimes they create new ones." Guide the class in a discussion of what this concept might mean in terms of current conflicts involving the United States such as in the Middle East after September 11, 2001. Use the class conclusions then as a bridging exercise for letting students know what they may discover as the imperial struggles for control of North America in the mid-eighteenth century unfold and conclude.

TEACHING IDEA

Connecting the Dots

To help students understand the short-term and long-term causes of mid-eighteenth century conflict in North America, place students in groups and ask them to fill out a cause and effect chart on the topic of the French and Indian War. Instruct the students to come up with three causes for the conflict, and to indicate each cause's attendant effects. Have them then assign a rank order of importance to their three causes and three effects, and justify their rank orders. If desired, this product can then further be used as a thesis-building exercise in response to the instruction, "Evaluate the relative importance of the various short- and/or long-term causes of the French and Indian War."

TRM Find **Handout 3.1 – Causes and Effects of the French and Indian War** in the Teacher's Resource Materials.

Period 3: 1754–1800

MODULE 3-1 International Conflicts Cause Colonial Tensions

TEACHING IDEA

Incorporating Videos

Have students view excerpts of Episode 1 of the PBS documentary, "The War That Made America: Part 1, A Country Between" (available on YouTube). This segment depicts Washington's unintentional triggering of the French and Indian War, American Indian tribal priorities and motivations, and Braddock's defeat and its larger consequences for expanding the war.

TEACHING IDEA

Connecting the Dots

Point out to students that the Albany Plan of Union was rejected not only by Britain but by the colonies themselves. Ask students to place themselves in the position of the British empire and the colonies, respectively, and see if they can explain why this was the case. The reasoning for the imperial position is rather straightforward: The British Empire had no reason to want to see the colonies militarize independently of the crown. Although that is clear enough, the more interesting and telling fact is the colonial rejection of the plan — meaning that the colonies did not trust one another and felt no sense of common unity at this stage. Once this latter point has been made, assign students in small groups to create a thesis as to why the colonists reacted to the plan as they did, and to hypothesize on what would have to change or take place to create a shift in colonial attitudes.

The Seven Years' War Begins

Seven Years' War (French and Indian War) 1754–1763 global conflict between European nations, primarily Britain and France, that began in North America in 1754 and erupted in Europe in 1756. France ultimately ceded all of its North American territories to England and Spain, but the enormous cost of the war also damaged the British economy.

Albany Plan of Union 1754 plan put together by Benjamin Franklin to create a more centralized colonial government that would establish policies regarding defense, trade, and territorial expansion, as well as aim to facilitate better relations between colonists and American Indians. The plan was never implemented.

seemingly endless conflicts with origins across the Atlantic Ocean. During King William's War (1689–1697), Queen Anne's War (1702–1713), and King George's War (1739–1748), North America was just one theater in a larger global conflict — and the same proved true of the Seven Years' War.

One of the young colonial officers who would lead troops during the **Seven Years' War** was George Washington. Born in 1732 to a prosperous farm family in eastern Virginia, Washington had a comfortable upbringing. By the time he was twenty years old, he had invested in western properties as well as inherited the large estate at Mount Vernon, Virginia. He then set about expanding its boundaries and its enslaved workforce. Washington was soon appointed Lieutenant Colonel in the Virginia militia, and in the fall of 1753 Virginia's governor sent him to warn the French against encroaching on British territory in the Ohio River valley. The French commander rebuffed Washington and, within six months, gained control of a British post near present-day Pittsburgh, Pennsylvania, and named it Fort Duquesne. With help from American Indians hostile to the French, Washington's surprise attack on Fort Duquesne in May 1754 led the governors of Virginia and North Carolina to provide the newly promoted Colonel Washington with more troops. The French then responded with a much larger force that compelled Washington to surrender just two months later, in July 1754.

Even before Washington and his troops were defeated, the British attempted to protect the colonies against threats from the French and American Indians. To limit such threats, the British tried to form an alliance with the powerful Iroquois Confederacy, composed of six northeastern tribes. Thus the British invited an official delegation from the Iroquois to a meeting in the summer of 1754 in Albany, New York, with representatives from several colonies. Benjamin Franklin used the meeting to introduce an **Albany Plan of Union** that would establish a council of representatives from the various colonial assemblies to debate issues of frontier defense, trade, and territorial expansion and to recommend terms agreeable to both colonists and American Indians. Their deliberations were to be overseen by a president-general appointed and supported by the British crown. Despite the British government's goal of improving relations with the Iroquois, Franklin's plan excluded American Indian representatives from participation.

This meeting created new bonds among a small circle of colonial leaders, but it failed to establish a firmer alliance with the Iroquois or resolve problems of colonial governance. British officials opposed Franklin's plan, fearing it would undermine the authority of the royal government. It was rejected outright by the individual colonies, unwilling to give up any of their independence in military, trade, and political matters. Meanwhile, Iroquois delegates, angered by Franklin's plan, left the Congress and broke off talks with the British.

For most American Indian nations, contests among European nations for land and power offered them the best chance of survival in the eighteenth century, and the Seven Years' War was no exception. They had leverage as long as various European imperial powers needed their trade items, military support, and political alliances — but this leverage would vanish if one European nation controlled most of North America.

Still, American Indians adopted different strategies during the Seven Years' War. The Delaware, Huron, Miami, and Shawnee nations,

◀ **Colonel George Washington** This 1772 oil painting by Charles Willson Peale portrays George Washington as a colonel in the Virginia militia. Washington commanded this militia during the Seven Years' War following the death of General Braddock. After the war, Washington prospered as a planter and land speculator. **How does this portrayal of Washington reflect the expansion of British power in North America?**

Oil on canvas, 1772, by Charles Wilson Peale/Granger

TEACHING IDEA

Incorporating Primary Sources

"The French and Indian War," a History Now lesson from the Gilder Lehrman Institute of American History (gilderlehrman.org), provides students with the opportunity to evaluate different primary sources representing the points of view and priorities of the colonists, the British empire, and the American Indian tribes.

The Seven Years' War Begins

AP® ANALYZING SOURCES

Source: Benjamin Franklin, "Join or Die" (political cartoon and editorial), *Pennsylvania Gazette*, 1754

"The Confidence of the French in this Undertaking seems well-grounded on the present disunited State of the British Colonies, and the extreme Difficulty of bringing so many different Governments and Assemblies to agree in any speedy and effectual Measures for our common Defence and Security; while our Enemies have the very great Advantage of being under one Direction, with one Council, and one Purse. Hence, and from the great Distance of Britain, they presume that they may with Impunity violate the most solemn Treaties subsisting between the two Crowns, kill, seize and imprison our Traders, and confiscate their Effects at Pleasure (as they have done for several Years past) murder and scalp our Farmers, with their Wives and Children, and take an easy Possession of such Parts of the British Territory as they find most convenient for them. . . ."

Questions for Analysis
1. Describe the symbolism in Franklin's image.
2. Explain the advantages of the French over British North Americans.
3. Explain Franklin's argument, using both the image and the text to support your response.

AP® TIP
Analyze the ways in which European conflicts affected American Indian groups in North America during the mid-1700s.

for example, allied themselves with the French, hoping that a French victory would stop the far more numerous British colonists from invading their settlements in the Ohio River valley. Nations of the Iroquois Confederacy, on the other hand, tried to play one power against the other, hoping to win concessions from the British in return for their military support. The Creek, Choctaw, and Cherokee also tried to prolong the existing standoff between different European powers by bargaining alternately with the British in Georgia and the Carolinas, the French in Louisiana, and the Spaniards in Florida. Faced with invasion of their lands, some American Indian tribes, like the Abenaki in northern New England, launched attacks on colonial settlements. They also seized British ships amid the chaos of war, seeking to enrich themselves and establish themselves as a power in the Atlantic Ocean.

The British government soon decided to send additional troops to defend its American colonies against attacks from American Indians and intrusions from the French. General Edward Braddock and two regiments arrived in 1755 to expel the French from Fort Duquesne. At the same time, colonial militia units were sent to battle the French and their American Indian allies along the New York and New England frontiers. Colonel Washington joined Braddock as his personal aide-de-camp. Within months, however, Braddock's forces were ambushed, bludgeoned by French and

TRM Suggested Responses to Questions

TRM Module 3.1 AP® Analyzing Sources Handout 1

EXPLORING AP® THEMES

Migration and Settlement

Provide students with a blank map of the eastern half of the North American landmass (from the Atlantic to the Mississippi). Using the Internet, instruct the students to find and plot the locations of various American Indian tribes on this handout. After students complete this exercise, give them a clear transparency sheet. Have them trace the continent, the British and French colonial boundaries in North America, and the locations of the principal cities as they stood in 1754. Then, have students overlay the transparency onto their tribal map. Ask students to explain how the relationship between the two maps could explain tribal strategies in dealing with the two European powers. A reproducible version of this map is available in the Teacher's Resource materials.

TRM Map 3A – Eastern United States

EXPLORING AP® THEMES

Geography and Environment

Students should understand that Franklin's entreaties to the colonies to "Join or Die" in his 1754 cartoon failed to garner serious support. The colonies were not inclined to incorporate themselves into a united federation at this point. The reasons for that involved issues of identity and politics. However, the reasons for this failure to unite also involved factors of regional culture, and geography/environment. Have students research and compile information that accounts for the failure in colonial acceptance of the Albany Plan of Union in the four categories of identity, politics, culture, and geography/environment. Upon completion of this phase, have students engage in a Four Corners exercise, whereby they move to the pre-designated corner of the room corresponding to which of the four factors they individually believe played the greatest role in influencing colonial rejection of the Albany Plan of Union.

▲ Differentiation

Divide the class into four groups. Have each group research one of the four categories of identity, politics, culture, and geography/environment. Allow each group to give a presentation arguing why their topic played the greatest role in influencing colonial rejection of the Albany Plan of Union.

Period 3: 1754–1800

MODULE 3-1 International Conflicts Cause Colonial Tensions

TEACHING IDEA

Additional Practice

a) Explain why ONE of the following factors was the most significant factor contributing to British victory in the French and Indian War.

- American Indian alliances
- Colonial cooperation
- British military might

b) Provide ONE specific example to support your explanation in part (a).

c) Provide historical evidence or example why ONE of the other options is less convincing as having a significant effect on British victory in the French and Indian War.

TRM Suggested Responses to Questions

TRM Module 3.1 AP® Analyzing Sources Handout 2

BUILDING AP® SKILLS

Making Connections

Assign students to define the term, "guerrilla warfare." Have students compile a list of factors as to the challenges a guerrilla campaign represents to a conventional military force. Students then will rank their factors in order of importance, and justify their rankings. Lastly, have students research to discover which other wars in American history involved a guerrilla campaign, and establish the attendant similarities and differences in a T-chart format for the respective series of conflicts.

AP® TIP

Be sure you can explain why stronger relationships developed between the French and American Indians than did between the English and American Indians in colonial North America.

American Indian forces, and Braddock was killed. Other British forces did little better during the next three years. Despite having far fewer colonists in North America than the British, the French had established extensive trade networks and alliances with powerful American Indian nations that helped outweigh their military disadvantages. Alternating **guerrilla** tactics with conventional warfare, the French and allied American Indian nations captured several important forts, built a new one on Lake Champlain, and moved troops deep into British territory. The ineffectiveness of the British and colonial armies also encouraged tribes along the New England and Appalachian frontiers to reclaim land from colonists. Bloody raids devastated many outlying settlements, leading to the death and capture of hundreds of Britain's colonial subjects.

As the British faced defeat after defeat in North America, European nations began to contest imperial claims elsewhere in the world. In 1756 France and Great Britain officially declared war against each other. Eventually Austria, Russia, Sweden, most of the German states, and Spain allied with France, while Portugal and Prussia sided with Great Britain. As the winter of 1757 approached, French victory appeared all but certain.

REVIEW

How did British interests shape colonial involvement in the Seven Years' War?

The Costs of Victory

As the Seven Years' War grew into a global military conflict, Britain implemented increasingly unpopular policies to meet its demands. For instance, the English desperately needed sailors to fight for Britain as naval warfare erupted in the Mediterranean Sea and the Atlantic and Indian Oceans, and battles raged not only in North America and Europe, but in far-flung places such as the West Indies, India, and the Philippines. Britain's solution to its shortage of sailors was brutal: The Royal Navy forced young colonial men living in port cities into military service via impressment (see Module 2-9). Seamen and dockworkers had good reason to fight off impressment agents. Men in the Royal Navy faced low wages, bad food, harsh punishment, rampant disease, and high mortality. The efforts to capture new "recruits" often met violent resistance from merchants and common folk alike, especially in the North American colonies where several hundred men might be impressed at one time. In such circumstances, whole communities joined in the battle. American employers and politicians who opposed impressment learned that they gained important advantages in directing the anger of colonists away from themselves and toward British policies. Even after the war's conclusion, impressment riots occurred in places such as Boston and New York City.

AP® ANALYZING SOURCES

Source: Anonymous, *Impressment by the British*, c. mid-1700s

Questions for Analysis

1. Identify who is portrayed in the image.
2. Describe how each of these individuals are portrayed.
3. Describe the likely intended audience for this engraving.
4. Explain how the artist conveys a specific point of view on impressment.

The Costs of Victory

Period 3: 1754–1800

MAP 3.1 The Seven Years' War, 1754–1763 Clashes between colonial militia units and allied French and American Indian forces erupted in North America in 1754. The conflict helped launch a wider war that engulfed Europe as well as the West Indies and India. In the aftermath of this first global war, Britain gained control of present-day Canada and India, but France retained its West Indies colonies. **Based on this map, what territorial disputes were most significant in North America during the Seven Years' War?**

TEACHING IDEA

Incorporating Videos

Have students watch excerpts of the PBS documentary, "The War That Made America: Part 4, Unintended Consequences" (available on YouTube). This segment includes the global aspects of the Seven Years' War, tensions between colonial assemblies and British governors and generals, the Battle of Quebec, and the British imperial administrative challenges of managing a newly enlarged post-war North American empire.

TEACHING IDEA

Geography Instruction

Use Map 3.1 to point out to students that the Seven Years' War truly was the "first world war." Ask students what this would mean in terms of the differences in both priorities and war aims for the colonists and the British empire as a whole, and assign students to write a one-sentence proof of understanding.

Throughout the war, British military officers also quartered their troops in colonial homes, as there were not enough public buildings to seize and harsh winters made camping in tents intolerable. Thus, colonial towns and cities were required to house and support the British military in lavish mansions for the officers and modest homes for the troops — and any who objected were threatened with violence. This, too, united colonists across social classes in protest.

Despite growing unrest due to British wartime policies, the tide of the Seven Years' War began to turn in their favor by the summer of 1758. As Prussian troops held the line on the European front, Britain poured more soldiers and arms into its North American campaign. With the aid of colonial troops, British forces recaptured the fort at Louisburg on Cape Breton Island, a key to France's defense of Canada. Then British troops, with Washington's aid, once again seized Fort Duquesne and renamed it Fort Pitt. Other British forces took control of Fort Frontenac along the St. Lawrence River as well as Forts Ticonderoga and Crown Point on Lake Champlain. French efforts in North America suffered as Prussia defeated France and its allies in Europe and Britain gained key victories in India. The British won Quebec and control of Canada, albeit at the cost of many lives, by 1759.

TEACHING IDEA

Differing Views

The concepts of perspective, perception, and self-interest become increasingly important in this module and the next one. To help generate an appreciation for them among your students, place students into one of several groups (imperial rulers, colonists, American Indians, enslaved Africans, the rich, the poor, the landed, the landless, men, women, etc.) and explain to them that they are to place themselves into the mindset and worldview of that group for this lesson. Then pose this question to the class: "Of all the various groups in North America, who is being exploited by whom, and who is doing the exploiting of whom?" After allowing time for the groups to determine their respective views on this question, moderate a dialogue wherein each group is allowed to pose questions to one another and air any grievances they may have. This exercise is useful for pointing out to students how colonial priorities and concerns (localist) were just beginning to grind against the priorities and concerns of the vastly larger global imperial networks (internationalist) in which they were mere cogs, while at the same time the colonies themselves were rife with internal divisions and contradictions. As a component of the Course Theme of either social structures or America in the world, such ideas are quite testable on the AP® exam with regards to Period 3.

Period 3: 1754–1800

MODULE 3-1 International Conflicts Cause Colonial Tensions

Despite these key victories, the war dragged on in North America, Europe, India, and the West Indies for three more years. Finally, King George III (r. 1760–1820) grew concerned enough with the expense of imperial conflict to open peace negotiations with France in 1762. He agreed to give up a number of conquered territories in order to finalize the **Peace of Paris** in 1763. Spain ceded Florida to Great Britain to regain control of its Cuban and Philippine colonies. While France was expelled from North America, it rewarded Spanish support by granting Spain Louisiana and all French lands west of the Mississippi River. The British empire reigned supreme, however, as it established its control over India, North America east of the Mississippi, all of Canada, and a number of Caribbean islands. Although the Peace of Paris had successfully negotiated international relationships, many internal conflicts in the British Empire were still unresolved.

Peace of Paris 1763 peace treaty ending the Seven Years' War (French and Indian War). Under its terms, Britain gained control of North America east of the Mississippi River and of present-day Canada.

TEACHING IDEA

Connecting the Dots

Once the French and Indian War concluded, discontent began to fulminate within the colonies, directed at their heretofore protector, Great Britain. Ask students to explain why in coalition warfare, friction almost inevitably arises between the member factions of the winning coalition in the postwar period. Have students explain the deeply paradoxical nature of this historical trend.

TRM Suggested Responses to Questions

TRM Module 3.1 AP® Analyzing Sources Handout 3

BUILDING AP® SKILLS

Comparison

Assign students in pairs to complete a "Dueling Dates" activity. For this activity, 1754 and 1763 are juxtaposed as a couplet of "Dueling Dates." Students will prove or justify that each of these dates constitutes a turning point in the history of the United States. They must give cause (involving evidence) for why each date could legitimately be called a turning point in American history. Then, choose one from each pair to defend the date as a better indication of a watershed year than the other.

TRM Find **Handout 3.2 – Dueling Dates, 1754 & 1763** in the Teacher's Resource Materials.

AP® ANALYZING SOURCES

Source: North America before and after the Seven Years' War

Questions for Analysis
1. Identify the changes in territorial holdings shown on these two maps.
2. Describe why some territorial holdings increased while others decreased.
3. Explain how the changing territorial holdings could influence European colonists' relationships with American Indians.

REVIEW

- What were some of the early signs of conflict between Great Britain and British North Americans?
- What gains did Great Britain make in the aftermath of the Seven Years' War?

Unresolved Issues in the Colonies

The war that erupted between 1754 and 1763 reshaped European empires and transformed patterns of global trade. Yet the Peace of Paris did not resolve many of the problems that had plagued the colonies before the war, and it created new ones as well. British victory encouraged thousands of colonists to move farther west, into lands once controlled by France and currently occupied by American Indian nations, worsening already strained relations. To make matters worse, British traders often either deceived American Indians outright or ignored American Indian trading practices such as gift giving and restrictions against trading with enemies.

The harsh realities of the British regime led some American Indians to seek a return to ways of life that preceded the arrival of white men. A visionary named Neolin preached that American Indians had been corrupted by contact with Europeans and urged them to purify themselves by returning to their ancient traditions, abandoning white ways, and reclaiming their lands. Neolin was a prophet, not a warrior, but his message inspired others, including an Ottawa leader named Pontiac.

When news arrived in early 1763 that France was about to cede all of its North American lands to Britain and Spain, Pontiac convened a council of more than four hundred Ottawa, Potawatomi, and Huron leaders near Fort Detroit. Drawing on Neolin's vision, he proclaimed, "It is important my brothers, that we should exterminate from our land [Britain], whose only object is our death. You must all be sensible," he continued, "that we can no longer supply our wants the way we were accustomed to do with our Fathers the French." Pontiac then mobilized support to drive out the British. In May 1763, Pontiac's forces laid siege to Detroit and soon gained the support of eighteen American Indian nations. They then attacked Fort Pitt and other British frontier outposts as well as white settlements along the Virginia and Pennsylvania frontier.

American Indian diplomacy fell short of gaining French support for renewed conflict, and Pontiac and his followers failed to push the British back. Hoping to avoid further costly frontier clashes and to improve trade relations with American Indians, the British crown issued a proclamation in October 1763 forbidding colonial settlement west of a line running down the Appalachian Mountains to create a buffer between American Indians and colonists.

MAP 3.2 British Conflicts with American Indians, 1758–1763 The entrance of British troops into former French territory in the Ohio River valley during and following the Seven Years' War fueled conflicts with American Indian nations. Colonists in Pennsylvania and the Carolinas also battled with American Indians, including tribes who had formerly been neutral, or even allies. In 1763, at the war's conclusion, Parliament established the Proclamation Line to limit westward expansion and thereby diminish such hostilities. **To what extent did the Proclamation Line of 1763 reveal differing priorities between British officials and North American colonists?**

BUILDING AP® SKILLS
Argumentation

As a pre-writing exercise, have the students use the "Twenty-Five Word Drill" and/or the "Fifty-Word Drill" to address the following question: "Explain the continuities and changes in the relationship between Europeans and American Indians as a result of the Seven Years' War, elaborating upon what stayed the same and what became different during the period 1750 to 1765." In addressing this prompt, students are required to write a response that is, depending upon the given class time constraint or teaching objective, no more than 25 or 50 words total (give or take). The product of the former exercise winds up as a concise statement of thesis, while the latter becomes more of an elaborate conclusive statement on the question. Again depending upon the desired outcome, the teacher may utilize this exercise in any of the following ways:

- in timed and untimed settings
- in groups and individually
- as a class activity and as homework
- as the basis for discussion
- as the lead-in to writing a full-length response and as a stand-alone item

Period 3: 1754–1800

MODULE 3-1 International Conflicts Cause Colonial Tensions

APPLY THE TIP

Ask students to work with a partner to create a thesis statement in response to the AP® Tip. When completed, combine the student pairs into quads, and have them share and critique their theses, modify them if necessary, and move one of the two forward, to compare and compete against the other quad groups in the room. Go through several rounds until a class winner is established. Then assign students to write the full essay either in class or as a homework assignment.

TRM Suggested Responses to Questions

TRM Module 3-1 AP® Analyzing Sources Handout 3

TEACHING IDEA

Incorporating Videos

Assign students to watch Episode 5 "The Seven Years War and Great Awakening" from the Crash Course US History series (available on YouTube). Use this 10-minute episode as a concise content review for students of the major issues and events of Module 3–1 as part of preparation for either assessment or reinforcement antecedent to moving forward into the next module.

Proclamation Line of 1763 Act of Parliament that restricted colonial settlement west of the Appalachian Mountains. The Proclamation Line sparked protests from rich and poor colonists alike.

AP® TIP

Analyze the impact the Proclamation of 1763 had on the class unity that had begun to develop during the Seven Years' War.

The **Proclamation Line of 1763** denied colonists the right to settle west of the Appalachian Mountains. Imposed by the British government following the Peace of Paris, the Proclamation Line frustrated colonists who sought the economic benefits won by a long and bloody war. Small farmers, backcountry settlers, and squatters who had hoped to improve their lot by acquiring rich farmlands were told to stay put. Meanwhile Washington and other wealthy **speculators** purchased additional western lands, certain that the Proclamation was merely "a temporary expedient to quiet the Minds of the Indians."

The Peace of Paris ignored the claims of American Indian tribes to territories they occupied, even as it left unresolved disputes between the colonies over lands in the Ohio River valley and elsewhere along British North America's new frontiers. Moreover, it raised tensions between colonists and England. Victory had come at an incredible cost: Over the course of the war, the national debt of Great Britain more than doubled. At the same time, as the North American colonies grew and conflicts with American Indians along their frontiers intensified in response to that growth, the costs of running these colonies increased fivefold. With an empire that now stretched around the globe, the British crown and Parliament needed more funds than ever to pay off war debts, administer their far-flung territories, and keep sufficient currency in circulation for expanding international trade. As you will read in later Modules, the methods they undertook to raise these funds served only to provoke growing resistance from American colonists.

AP® ANALYZING SOURCES

Source: William Trent, *Diary Entry*, July 27, 1763

"Fifty-seven Indians all on horseback were seen from the fort, going down the road and some on foot. Soon after some were seen returning, some appeared . . . cutting some wheat with their knives and a scythe[.] [W]e imagine they are hungry. . . .

[A]s soon as they came over, Captain Ecuyer's . . . speech was delivered . . . , letting them know that we took this place from the French, that this was our home and we would defend it to the last, that we were able to defend it against all the Indians in the woods, that we had ammunition and provisions for three years (I wish we had for three months), that we paid no regard to the Ottawas and Chippawas, that we knew that if they were not already attacked, that they would be in a short time in their own country which would find enough for them to do.

That they had pretended to be our friends, at the same time they murdered our traders in their towns and took their goods, that they stole our horses and cows from here, and killed some of our people, and every three or four days we hear the death halloo[1], which we know must be some of their people who have been down the country and murdered some of the country people. That if they intended to be friends with us to go home to their towns and sit quietly till they heard from us. . . .

The Yellow Bird, a Shawnee chief, asked for the four rifle guns we had taken from the four Indians the 25th[.] [T]hey were answered, if it appeared that their nation had done us no harm, and that they continued to behave well, when we were convinced of it that they should either have their guns or pay for them. He was very much enraged. . . . White Eyes and Wingenum seemed to be very much irritated and would not shake hands with our people at parting."

[1] A war cry.

Questions for Analysis

1. Identify the main conflicts Trent describes in this excerpt.
2. Explain how this diary entry reveals Trent's attitude toward American Indians.
3. Explain the context for the events Trent describes in this excerpt.

REVIEW

- How did the British justify the Proclamation Line of 1763?
- How did British North Americans react to the Proclamation Line?

EXPLORING AP® THEMES

American and National Identity

Divide the classroom in half. Then take each half and organize students into pairs. Provide students with the following statement: "The creation of a distinctly American identity began with the end of the Seven Years' War." Task one half of the class pairs with supporting that statement, and task the other half with rejecting it. Student pairs may research to articulate and support their argument. When research and support are complete, recombine the class into pairs with a student from each side on the question. Students are to make their case to one another. After this phase, conduct a whole class vote to determine the extent of student agreement/disagreement with the topic statement.

MODULE 3-1 International Conflicts Cause Colonial Tensions

Unresolved Issues in the Colonies
Period 3: 1754–1800

AP® THINKING HISTORICALLY — Evaluating Causes

When historians analyze causation, they move beyond merely describing and explaining causes and effects in order to evaluate their significance — especially in relation to other historical developments. This means that simply noting that numerous factors combine to create major events is a good first step on the path to historical analysis, but it doesn't quite go far enough. You must decide how significant those causes are in the grand scheme of history, and in order to accomplish this you must look at how they relate to each other. Historians commonly argue that certain causes are more responsible for a given historical development than others. In doing so, they often argue against the importance of other causes, working to convince their audience that certain historical evidence helps establish that some causes of a given development are, in fact, less significant.

In this course, and on the exam, you will often be asked to consider causation in much the same way that a historian would: by taking — and defending — a position about the relative importance of several causes of an event. Let's take a look at an example of an essay question that deals with some of the historical developments you have learned so far:

> Evaluate the extent to which international historical developments led to conflict in British North America between 1750 and 1770.

Step 1 — Break down the prompt.
In this module, you read about how international wars caused rising tensions in the American colonies between the 1750 and 1770, and since the time range of the prompt stretches back into Period 2, you will also need to bring your historical knowledge from that era to bear in your response. At first glance, it may be difficult to know where to start. This is why, for now, we're not going to do any writing. Instead, we will take you through one approach to brainstorming causes and making judgments about how significant they are to the topic of the prompt.

Step 2 — Write down a list of causes.
Use Period 2, Module 3-1, and content drawn from your classwork to make a list of the factors that led to rising tensions in the North American colonies. The following list of causes shows some that may have sprung to mind as you read the prompt:

- British rivalry with the French over control of North America
- The Albany Plan of Union
- Conflict and alliances with American Indians before, during, and after the French and Indian War
- The Treaty of Paris of 1763
- Proclamation Line of 1763

Step 3 — Determine and explain the importance of each cause.
Once you've generated a list of causes, you should start to think about how important each one is. A continuum is a useful tool for considering the relationship between and among concepts and events. It is a little bit like a timeline, except it requires you to rate the importance of a given concept or event on a scale. Doing this will help you clarify your thoughts about how important a given development really is to the topic at hand — in this case, the international developments or events that led to rising tensions in Britain's North American colonies. Here is a continuum of importance for causes offering some options for how to express positions along it:

(Continued)

TRM Suggested Responses to Questions

TRM Module 3.1 AP® Thinking Historically Handout

TEACHING IDEA

Six Degrees of Separation

Have the students complete a "Six Degrees of Separation" activity. For this exercise, students are given two events spanning time but related by their theme. They must select four events in chronological order that link the first event in the series with the last. They will write the name of each selected event and create an argument to support each of the events they selected (explain to them that they must answer the question, "Why does it belong as a link in your chain of events?" for each link). Students must emphasize both cause and effect and/or demonstrate continuity or change over time in their linking. This can be done either as a formative assessment in class, or as a homework assignment involving student research of their textbooks, activities/lessons, lecture notes, and knowledge of the time period. The lesson may also be undertaken by students individually or in small groups. The prompt for this particular activity is as follows:

> "Six Degrees of Separation: From Washington's attack on Fort Duquesne in 1754 to the signing of the Peace of Paris in 1763."

BUILDING AP® SKILLS

Argumentation

This would be a good time to engage in a thesis-building exercise. Place students into groups of three, and provide them with the following prompt: "Evaluate the extent to which the French and Indian War changed the relationship between Great Britain and the American colonies." Instruct the students to create a thesis and plan of attack for this question. When this is complete, place the products on the board or butcher paper. Have the class vote on which thesis they believe is the strongest. Once the class has established a winning thesis, instruct students that they will be writing a response to the prompt using the winning thesis/plan of attack from this exercise as their shared common introduction during the next class meeting.

Period 3: 1754–1800   **MODULE 3-1**   International Conflicts Cause Colonial Tensions

EXPLORING AP® THEMES

American and Regional Culture

Have students create a three-way Venn diagram indicating the grievances that the North (including the Middle Colonies), the South, and the West had against Great Britain by 1763.

TEACHING IDEA

AP® Thinking Historically Workshop

Developing continuums is an excellent way of having students visualize how to determine the most important causes to use for an interpretation. If students are struggling to decide which causes are the most important, consider the following workshop idea. Divide the class into groups of four and have students brainstorm a list of at least five causes for international historical developments relevant to the years 1750–1770. Here is a sample list if students are struggling: French and Indian War, Albany Plan of Union, Proclamation of 1763, Mercantile economy, colonization, migration, Pontiac's Rebellion, French/Huron alliance, Iroquois alliances, Treaty of Paris.

After the groups have determined a list, subdivide each group into two groups of two students. Next, have students label the terms they developed as long-term, intermediate term, or short-term causes. Then, ask students to determine their top two short-term causes. To end the exercise, have the original groups of four reconvene and share answers.

Step 4 Make a chart to explain how you rated the events in your continuum.

Next, place your causes into a chart, adding a column to explain why you ranked a cause as higher or lower in importance. In order to get the most out of this exercise, your chart should include at least five different causes — and there should be at least three different levels of importance represented. The following table shows one way to use the idea of a continuum to evaluate the relative importance of each cause you listed in step 2. Two causes have been completed for you.

Causes	Relative Importance	Explanation of Importance
British rivalry with the French over control of North America	Major cause	The ongoing rivalry between European powers, both in Europe and in North America, led to conflict in the colonies. George Washington's claim of western land was met with French resistance, which began the Seven Years' War.
The Albany Plan of Union	Minor cause	The British resistance to the Albany Plan of Union played a much lesser role in causing conflict in the colony, as the colonies themselves were divided over whether to accept the proposal and ultimately rejected unity.
Conflict and alliances with American Indians before, during, and after the French and Indian War		
The Treaty of Paris of 1763		
Proclamation Line of 1763		

ACTIVITY

Complete the chart in step 4 by evaluating the importance of the three remaining causes.

For a challenge, go back to your completed chart, alter the level of importance for one of the causes, and write one to three sentences explaining why you think the change should be made.

Unresolved Issues in the Colonies

Period 3: 1754–1800

AP® WRITING HISTORICALLY — Short-Answer Question Practice

ACTIVITY

Read the following question carefully and write a short response. Use complete sentences.

Using the following excerpts, answer (a), (b), and (c).

Source: Gordon Wood, *The Radicalism of the American Revolution*, 1993

"In our enthusiasm to contrast the 'traditional' society of the mother country with the 'modernity' of the colonies, we have often overlooked how dominantly British and traditional the colonists' culture was; indeed, in some respects colonial society was more traditional than that of the mother country. Most colonial leaders in the mid-eighteenth century thought of themselves not as Americans but as Britons. They read much the same literature, the same law books, the same history, as their brethren at home, and they drew most of their conceptions of society and their values from their reading. Whatever sense of unity the disparate colonies of North America had came from their common tie to the British crown and from their membership in the British empire. Most colonists knew more about events in London than they did about occurrences in neighboring colonies. They were provincials living on the edges of a pan-British world, and all the more British for that."

Source: Jon Butler, *Becoming America: The Revolution Before 1776*, 2000

"The transformation of the [British mainland] colonies between 1680 and 1770 exhibited the settlers' increasing fascination with power and authority, a determination to make the world anew in yet untested images. Men and women of all kinds pressed on to control their own destiny, sometimes collectively, sometimes individually as America's population, economy, secular life, and religion became more complex and variegated. Colonists created a far more independent economy than their 'colonial' status might have suggested was desirable or possible. Most European settlers extended and enlivened traditional religious expression in the New World. . . . Provincial politics gave European settlers persuasive control over colonial affairs. . . .

Modernity could also support and even create new problems that would afflict America. . . . Most spectacularly, the slaveholding that overwhelmed Spanish America and the British Caribbean by the 1650s, was perfected in the British mainland colonies after 1680. . . .

The result was America in its aspirations, its character, its flaws, and its achievements — a surprising America that seventeenth-century migrants never imagined."

a. Briefly describe ONE major difference between Wood's and Butler's historical interpretations of colonial identity in the mid eighteenth century.
b. Briefly explain how ONE specific historical event or development between 1680 and 1763 that is not explicitly mentioned in the excerpts could be used to support Wood's argument.
c. Briefly explain how ONE specific historical event or development between the period 1680 and 1763 that is not explicitly mentioned in the excerpts could be used to support Butler's argument.

TRM Suggested Responses to Questions

TEACHING IDEA

AP® Writing Historically Review

Because it is still early in the academic year, consider truncating this Short-Answer Question by providing students with an example of the main argument of each historian so students can work on the writing skills associated with the question. For instance, after reading the excerpt by Gordon Wood, remind students that his main argument is about the dependency, and in many ways, the aspirations many colonials had in considering themselves Englishmen and carrying on lives that mirrored these dreams. For as much as they were colonists, as Wood contends, they were also more aware of events and policies from Great Britain than their fellow colonists. Jon Butler, on the other hand, asserts how distinctively independent the colonists were in the years leading to the American Revolution. Indeed, their understanding of global events shaped colonials' expansive view of the world. Now that students have the examples of the interpretations they can concentrate on what the question is asking of them in parts (a), (b), and (c).

TRM Suggested Responses to Questions

TEACHING IDEA

Understanding Political Changes

As you begin this module, a really useful exercise in analogic thinking to share with your students concerning the increasingly acrimonious relationship between Britain and the colonies at this time would be the parent–child metaphor. As adolescents, this is a metaphor that generates an almost instant understanding. The colonies increasingly felt in this period that they had come of age, and all of the resentments or frustrations that your students may feel toward parental authority clashing with their desires was mirrored in what the colonies felt and perceived in their relationship with the British empire during this period.

BUILDING AP® SKILLS

Sourcing and Situation

Have students read excerpts from John Locke's *Second Treatise on Government*, which can be found in condensed chapter form at Liberty Online's website (libertyonline.hypermall.com). Of particular value would be chapters 1, 2, 7, 9, 12, and 19, or any combination thereof. Consider how colonists at this time would have interpreted Locke's arguments and how they would have utilized them to justify their own beliefs and actions during this module. Students could read separate excerpts and then jigsaw together their conclusions, or be asked to summarize each of the chapter's main points as a group activity (a refresher of the jigsaw model can be found on page 33).

Module 3-2

Resistance to Britain Intensifies

LEARNING TARGETS

By the end of this module, you should be able to:
- Explain how British imperial policies after the Seven Years' War led to tensions with British North American colonists.
- Explain the ways in which Americans revised their ideas about government and individual liberty in reaction to British policies after the Seven Years' War.

THEMATIC FOCUS

Politics and Power
American and National Identity

In the aftermath of the Seven Years' War, British North Americans increasingly believed that British colonial policies benefited England at their expense. In reaction to colonial rebellion, British officials tried a number of different responses, including compromising and exercising greater control over the colonies. All of these strategies had limited success.

HISTORICAL REASONING FOCUS

Continuity and Change

In Periods 1 and 2, you practiced identifying and proving continuities and changes in patterns of development throughout history, and now it's time to add another layer to your historical analysis. Many essay prompts in this course and on the AP® Exam will ask you to explain whether a particular era is characterized best by its continuities or changes. Professional historians perform this kind of analysis by evaluating evidence, weighing continuities against changes, and drawing conclusions about which are most and least significant.

TASK ▶ Just as you did in Module 3-1, you will need to evaluate what you know and use it to craft a historical argument — this time, on the significance of continuities versus changes. As you read the rest of this module, consider the time period from the end of the Glorious Revolution to the 1770s (which you will learn about in this module). As a start, identify continuities and changes in relations between Britain and the thirteen original North American colonies across this span. Prepare to evaluate these continuities and changes by asking yourself some questions: How important is each development in the grand scheme of things? Which historical trends best characterize shorter periods within this span of time, and which ones best characterize the timespan as a whole? Is the entire period best understood by looking to its continuities or to its changes? As you answer these questions for yourself, think about how you could use them to support a historical argument.

B etween the end of the Glorious Revolution in 1689 and the beginning of the French and Indian War in 1754, British officials and their colonial subjects coexisted in relative harmony. Economic growth led Britain to ignore much of the smuggling and domestic manufacturing that took place in the colonies, since these activities did not disrupt Britain's mercantile policies. Similarly, although the king and Parliament held ultimate **political sovereignty**, or final authority, over the American colonies, it was easier to allow some local control over political decisions, given the communication challenges created by distance. This pattern of **salutary (benign) neglect** led some American colonists to view themselves as more independent of British control than the crown and Parliament believed them to be. Many colonists came to see free trade (or smuggling, from the British perspective), domestic manufacturing, and local self-governance as rights rather than privileges.

Thus when British officials decided to assert greater control, many colonists protested. Between 1764 and 1774, as British Parliament sought to extend its political and economic control over the American colonies, colonists periodically resisted. With each instance of resistance,

salutary neglect British colonial policy from around 1700 to 1760 that relaxed supervision of internal colonial affairs as long as the North American colonies produced sufficient raw materials and revenue. Also known as benign neglect.

160

TEACHING IDEA

Building Vocabulary

Share with students the importance not just of understanding what the term "salutary neglect" meant in the context of colonial growth, but also the importance for them as AP® students to be able to academically empower themselves by being able to use this term fluently and seamlessly within their historical conversations and written work. This can be accomplished by both modeling and encouraging student use of this vocabulary intermixed into the regular vernacular of their discussions. For instance, rather than saying, "the colonies were left alone a lot," encourage students to speak in terms of "salutary neglect impacted the colonies a great deal," or something to that effect. Explicitly recognize and praise such student efforts.

Parliament demanded further submission to royal authority. With each demand for submission, colonists responded with greater assertions of their rights. Still, no one imagined that a revolution was in the making.

Intensifying Conflict and Resistance, 1763–1766

To King George III and to Parliament, asserting control over the colonies was both right and necessary. In 1763 King George appointed George Grenville to lead the British government. Faced with an economic depression in England, he believed that regaining political and economic control in the colonies could help resolve this financial crisis.

Eighteenth-century wars, especially the Seven Years' War, cost a fortune. British subjects in England paid taxes to help offset the nation's debts, even though few of them benefited as directly from the British victory in 1763 as did their counterparts in North America. The colonies would cost the British treasury more if the crown could not control colonists' movement into American Indian territories, limit smuggling and domestic manufacturing, and house British troops in the colonies cheaply.

To reassert control, Grenville's Parliament launched a three-pronged program. First, it sought stricter enforcement of existing laws, such as the seventeenth-century Navigation Acts (see Module 2-6), which prohibited trade with English rivals, established guidelines for legal commerce, and set duties (taxes) on trade items. Second, Parliament extended wartime policies into peacetime. For example, the **Quartering Act** of 1765 ensured that British troops would remain in the colonies to carry out imperial policies, including enforcing impressment and cracking down on smuggling. Colonial governments were expected to support them by allowing them to use vacant buildings and providing them with food and supplies. Predictably, tensions between colonists and British officials rose, as wealthier local leaders joined forces with ordinary colonists in protest. This was one of the first steps in a conflict that would escalate over the next ten years.

The third part of Grenville's colonial program was the most important. It called for the passage of new laws to raise funds and reestablish authority. The first revenue act passed by Parliament was the American Duties Act of 1764, known as the **Sugar Act**. It imposed import duties on coffee, wines, and other luxury items. The act actually reduced the import tax on foreign molasses, which was regularly smuggled into the colonies from the West Indies, but insisted that the duty be collected. The crackdown on smuggling increased the power of customs officers and established the first vice-admiralty courts in North America to ensure that the Sugar Act raised money for the crown. That same year, Parliament passed the **Currency Act**, which prohibited colonial assemblies from printing paper money or bills of credit. Taken together, these provisions meant that colonists would pay more money into the British treasury even as the supply of money (and illegal goods) diminished in the colonies.

Some colonial leaders protested the Sugar Act through speeches, pamphlets, and petitions, and Massachusetts established a **committee of correspondence** to circulate concerns to leaders in other colonies. Although dissent remained largely disorganized and ineffective, the passage of the Sugar and Currency Acts caused anxiety among many colonists, which was heightened by the passage of the Quartering Act the next year.

Quartering Act 1765 act ensuring British troops would remain stationed in the colonies after the end of the Seven Years' War.

Sugar Act 1764 act of Parliament imposing an import tax on sugar, coffee, wines, and other luxury items. It sparked colonial protests that would escalate over time as new revenue measures were enacted.

Currency Act 1764 act of Parliament preventing colonial assemblies from printing paper money or bills of credit, curtailing the ability of local colonial economies to expand.

committee of correspondence Type of committee first established in Massachusetts to circulate concerns and reports of protest and other events to leaders in other colonies in the aftermath of the Sugar Act.

REVIEW

How did British colonial officials attempt to raise funds in the aftermath of the Seven Years' War?

The Colonies Forge New Ties

The ties forged between poorer and wealthier colonists over issues of westward expansion, impressment, new taxes, and quartering grew stronger in the 1760s, but they tended to be localized in seaport cities or in specific areas of the frontier. Creating bonds across the colonies required considerably more effort in a period when communication and transportation beyond local areas were limited. Means had to be found to disseminate information and create a sense of common purpose if the colonists

---

BUILDING AP® SKILLS

Comparison

Ask students in groups to compare the points of view and priorities of English and colonial governments on the kind of relationship the colonies should have to the mother country. The constant theme that should arise is that the British priority is centered upon expense, finance, and money, while the colonial priority is centered upon access or denial of rights. This results in differing proportions of grievance and misunderstanding between the two camps that will only increase over time.

▲ Differentiation

Organize students into groups of two or three, and assign groups to the point of view of either the British or the colonists. Have groups create either visual art or a political cartoon that represents the priority or point of view of their assigned group.

were going to persuade Parliament to take their complaints seriously. One important model for such intercolonial communication was the Great Awakening (see Module 2-10).

Even though the Great Awakening had spent its religious passion in most parts of North America by the 1760s, the techniques of mass communication and critiques of excessive wealth and corruption it initiated provided emotional and practical ways of forging ties among widely dispersed colonists. Many evangelical preachers had condemned the lavish lifestyles of colonial elites and the spiritual corruption of local officials. Now in the context of conflicts with Great Britain, colonial leaders used such rhetoric to paint Parliament and British officials as corrupt aristocrats with little faith and less compassion. Political protestors also adopted the tactics and style of New Light sermons, and these mass gatherings offered public spectacles designed to inspire unified action against British imperial policies.

Even as colonial resistance to new British policies mounted, Grenville decided to impose a stamp tax on the colonies similar to that long used in England, announcing his plans in 1764. The stamp tax required that a revenue stamp be affixed to all transactions involving paper items, from newspapers and contracts to playing cards and diplomas. In the spring of 1765, a full year after Grenville's announcement, Parliament enacted the **Stamp Act**. The tax was to be collected by colonists appointed for the purpose, and the money was to be spent within the colonies at the direction of Parliament for "defending, protecting, and securing the colonies." To the British government, the Stamp Act seemed completely fair. After all, Englishmen paid on average 26 shillings in tax annually, while Bostonians averaged just 1 shilling. Moreover, Parliament believed the act was purposely written to benefit the American colonies.

The colonists saw it in a more threatening light. The Stamp Act differed from earlier parliamentary laws in three important ways. First, by the time it passed, the colonies were experiencing rising unemployment, falling wages, and a downturn in trade made worse by the Sugar and Currency Acts passed the previous year. Second, critics viewed the Stamp Act as an attempt to control the *internal* affairs of the colonies. It was not an indirect tax on trade, paid by importers and exporters as part of the long-established global mercantilist system, but a direct tax on daily business. Third, such a direct interference with economic affairs in the colonies unleashed concerns of both local officials and ordinary residents that Parliament was taxing colonists who had no representation in its debates and decisions. The question of representation became a mainstay of colonial protests. Whereas the British accepted the notion of "**virtual representation**," by which members of Parliament gave voice to the views of particular classes and interests, the North American colonies had developed a system of representation based on locality. According to colonial leaders, only members of Parliament elected by colonists could truly represent their interests.

In New York City, Boston, and other cities, merchants, traders, and artisans formed groups — such as the **Sons of Liberty**, **Daughters of Liberty**, and **Vox Populi** — dedicated to the repeal of the Stamp Act. Even before it was implemented, angry mobs throughout the colonies attacked stamp distributors. Some were beaten, others tarred and feathered, and all were forced to take an oath never to sell stamps again.

Colonists lodged more formal protests with the British government as well. The Virginia House of Burgesses, led by Patrick Henry, passed five resolutions, known as the **Virginia Resolves**, denouncing taxation without representation. Colonial newspapers reprinted them, and orators performing to eager audiences in Massachusetts and elsewhere recited them from memory. The Massachusetts House also created a circular letter — a written protest circulated to the other colonial assemblies — calling for a congress to be held in New York City in October 1765 to consider the threat posed by the Stamp Act.

These protests revealed the growing power of the written word, printed images, political rhetoric, and public spectacle in spreading new ideas among colonists. Broadsides, political cartoons, handbills, newspapers, and pamphlets circulated widely, reinforcing discussions and proclamations at taverns, rallies, demonstrations, and more formal political assemblies. As the protests turned violent in Boston, Sons of Liberty leaders like Samuel Adams gave intense and emotional political speeches, in the style of the itinerant preachers of the Great Awakening, to inspire mass demonstrations.

Activists also used more visual tactics to convey their ideas to the public. At dawn on August 14, 1765, the Boston Sons of Liberty hung an **effigy** of stamp distributor Andrew Oliver on a tree and

---

Stamp Act 1765 act of Parliament that imposed a duty on all transactions involving paper items. The Stamp Act prompted widespread, coordinated protests and was eventually repealed.

virtual representation British claim that direct representation of colonists was unnecessary because Parliament virtually represented the interests of the colonies.

AP® TIP
Analyze how popular action against the British fostered an increasing sense of unity among colonists during the 1760s.

EXPLORING AP® THEMES

Politics and Power

Assign students to research the concept of virtual representation, and search for connections, parallels, and differences between the concept in the British-colonial relationship and political relationship between the United States and Washington D.C. or Puerto Rico.

TEACHING IDEA

Connecting the Dots

This is a good place to call the students' attention to the symbiotic relationship that developed over time between the Sons of Liberty and the Committees of Correspondence. The latter represented the elite of the colonial population, and many future leaders of the revolution were involved with it. The former represented a much more grassroots and working-class element of colonial society.

The Committees focused upon political ideas and legal argument, while the Sons of Liberty focused upon action and intimidation, much of which was violent. Ultimately these two groups needed each other, as they gradually evolved into the leadership and the rank-and-file muscle of the American Revolution, respectively.

AP® ANALYZING SOURCES

Source: Patrick Henry, *Virginia Resolves*, 1765

"*Whereas*, the honorable House of Commons in England have of late drawn into question how far the General Assembly of this colony hath power to enact laws for laying of taxes and imposing duties, payable by the people of this, his majesty's most ancient colony: for settling and ascertaining the same to all future times, the House of Burgesses of this present General Assembly have come to the following resolves: . . .

[R]*esolved*, That the first adventurers and settlers of this, his majesty's colony and dominion, brought with them and transmitted to their posterity, and all other his majesty's subjects, since inhabiting in this, his majesty's colony, all the privileges, franchises, and immunities that have at any time been held, enjoyed, and possessed, by the people of Great Britain. . . .

[R]*esolved*, That his majesty's liege people of this most ancient colony have uninterruptedly enjoyed the right of being thus governed by their own Assembly in the article of their taxes and internal police, and that the same hath never been forfeited, or any other way given up, but hath been constantly recognized by the kings and people of Great Britain. . . .

[R]*esolved*, therefore, That the General Assembly of this colony have the only and sole exclusive right and power to lay taxes and impositions upon the inhabitants of this colony; and that every attempt to vest such power in any person or persons whatsoever, other than the General Assembly aforesaid, has a manifest tendency to destroy British as well as American freedom."

Questions for Analysis

1. Identify the problem Henry outlines in the Virginia Resolves.
2. Describe the solution Henry proposes in the Virginia Resolves.
3. Identify an intended audience of the Virginia Resolves in British politics, and explain the way a section of it is directed to this audience.

TRM Suggested Responses to Questions

TRM Module 3.2 AP® Analyzing Sources Handout 1

BUILDING AP® SKILLS

Argumentation

Place students into groups of three or four and present the students with the Long-Essay prompt, "Evaluate the extent to which the concept of salutary neglect either helped or hindered colonial efforts at self-determination in the eighteenth century." Have students engage in a thesis and contextualization-building exercise known as 4-1-1, whereby they must create an introductory paragraph consisting of four sentences of contextualization, one sentence for a thesis, and one sentence for a plan of attack in their paper.

▲ **Differentiation**

For an additional challenge, have students write their introductory paragraphs on butcher paper or the chalkboard/whiteboard. Allow students time to do a gallery walk of all products, then hold a class vote to determine which opening paragraph they believe to be the strongest. After tallying the vote, assign students individually to write the full essay based upon the introductory selection that was the winner of their voting exercise. This assignment could either be in class the same day, the next day, or for homework.

---

called for his resignation. A mock funeral procession, joined by farmers, artisans, apprentices, and the poor, marched to Boston Common. In this public spectacle the crowd, led by shoemaker and Seven Years' War veteran Ebenezer Mackintosh, carried the fake corpse to the Boston stamp office and then destroyed the building.

Regardless of the specific strategy they adopted, colonial protesters carefully chose their targets: stamp agents, sheriffs, judges, and colonial officials. Even when violence erupted, it remained focused, with most crowds destroying stamps and stamp offices first and then turning to the private property of tax collectors or politically connected Stamp Act supporters. Such actions also revealed growing autonomy on the part of middling- and working-class colonists, who attacked men of wealth and power and sometimes chose men from the ranks of artisans rather than the wealthy as their leaders. However, colonial elites still considered themselves the leaders of the anti-stamp tax movement, and they refused to support actions they considered too radical. By and large, they preferred attempts to inspire others through the power of their written political arguments and public speeches.

It was these more affluent protesters who dominated the **Stamp Act Congress** that met in New York City in October 1765, where twenty-seven delegates from nine colonies petitioned Parliament to repeal the Stamp Act. Taxation without representation, they argued, was **tyranny**. Delegates then urged colonists to boycott British goods and refuse to pay the stamp tax. Yet they still proclaimed their loyalty to king and country. Even as delegates at the Stamp Act Congress declared themselves loyal, albeit dissatisfied, British subjects, they participated in the process of developing a common identity in the American colonies.

> "There ought to be no New England man; no New Yorker, known on the continent, but all of us Americans."
>
> — Christopher Gadsden, delegate to Stamp Act Congress, 1765

BUILDING AP® SKILLS

Comparison

Ask students to create a pro/con list about the advantages and disadvantages of remaining within the British empire. Have them then discuss the merits of each side. Answers may vary, but some possible responses are included in italics:

- Pros: *Benefits of a guaranteed trading partner, the defense of the Royal Navy for colonial goods in trans-Atlantic trade, the defense of the British Army against American Indian conflicts, access to a major market for colonial exports, the continued legacy of life under the most liberal political regime in Europe, that of a parliamentary constitutional monarchy.*
- Cons: *An arbitrary and continuous abridgement of their rights and liberties, the economically stifling policies of mercantilism, the inability to gain the best prices for their own goods, their being forced to pay prices for finished goods above market price due to British trade monopolies, the fact that Britain's economic and political interest always came first.*

TEACHING IDEA

Connecting the Dots

Have students revisit the question introduced on page 149, that "Wars don't always solve old problems; sometimes they create new ones." Task students with creating a web map of the problems that arose out of the French and Indian War, as well as another web map of the problems it solved. In this activity, students begin with the central statement in the middle of a piece of paper, and then draw offshoots that are positives to the top of the page, and offshoots that are negatives to the bottom of the page. If any problems or solutions can be interlinked, they are connected by a line with a brief explanation.

TEACHING IDEA

Additional Practice

Show students the two maps on page 154, North America in 1754 and North America in 1763. Then have them address the following SAQ prompt:

a) Briefly explain ONE reason for the difference in the two maps.

b) Briefly explain how ONE piece of evidence that demonstrates that the change depicted between the two maps would create difficulties between Great Britain and the American colonies.

c) Briefly explain how ANOTHER piece of evidence demonstrates that the change depicted between the two maps would create difficulties between Great Britain and the American colonies.

◀ **A Patriot Merchant's Mansion**
Jeremiah Lee, the wealthiest merchant in Massachusetts, moved his family into a newly built Marblehead mansion in 1768. It was decorated with hand-carved moldings, furniture made by colonial craftsmen, and hand-painted wallpaper from England. Despite his strong ties to British commercial circles, he was an ardent patriot and friend of Samuel Adams and used his wealth to promote the colonists' cause. **What accounts for colonial merchants' resistance to British trade policy in the mid-to-late 1700s?**

> " Those who are taxed without their own consent, given by themselves, or their representatives, are slaves. We are taxed without our own consent given by ourselves, or our representatives. We are therefore — I speak it with grief — I speak it with indignation — we are slaves. "
>
> John Dickinson, Pennsylvania attorney and Quaker, 1767

Declaratory Act 1766 act announcing Parliament's authority to pass any law "to bind the colonies and peoples of North America" closer to Britain.

Thus the battle against the Stamp Act continued to unfold across the colonies with riots, beatings, and resignations reported from Newport, Rhode Island, to New Brunswick, New Jersey, to Charleston, South Carolina. On November 1, 1765, when the Stamp Act officially took effect, not a single stamp agent remained in his post in the colonies.

Eventually the British Parliament responded to colonial protests and even more to rising complaints from English merchants and traders whose business had been damaged by the colonists' boycott. Parliament repealed the Stamp Act in March and the Sugar Act in April of 1766, and King George III granted his approval. Celebrating their victories, American colonists paid little attention to Parliament's simultaneous passage of the **Declaratory Act**, which announced Parliament's authority to pass any law "to bind the colonies and peoples of North America" closer to Britain. No new tax or policy was established; Parliament simply wanted to proclaim Great Britain's political supremacy in the aftermath of the successful Stamp Act protests.

From the colonists' perspective, the crisis triggered by the Stamp Act demonstrated the limits of parliamentary control. Colonists had organized effectively and forced Parliament to repeal the hated legislation. Individual leaders, like Patrick Henry of Virginia and Samuel Adams of Massachusetts, became more widely known through their fiery speech styles and their success in appealing to the masses. The protests that raged across the colonies — and attracted support from a wide range of colonists — demonstrated the growing influence of ordinary citizens, and the effectiveness of their attacks on stamp agents and the homes of British officials.

For all the success of the Stamp Act protests, however, American colonists still could not imagine in 1765 that protest would ever lead to open revolt against British rule. Disagreements over who should hold political power over the colonies would continue for the next decade. More well-to-do colonists were concerned that a revolution against British authority might fuel a dual revolution in which small farmers, tenants, servants, enslaved people, and laborers would rise up against the political and economic elites in the colonies. Even most middle- and working-class protesters believed that the best solution to the colonies' problems was to gain greater economic and political rights within the British empire, not to break from it.

BUILDING AP® SKILLS

Causation

Have students create a "ladder of escalation," in which each "rung" represents a British action, including the British rationale or motive for said action, and the next rung represents a colonial reaction to British action, complete with colonial motive or rationale. Start with the Proclamation of 1763 as the bottom rung, and have the Declaration of Independence in 1776 as the top rung.

▲ **Differentiation**

Arrange students in groups that are deliberately mixed by ability, and have them discuss and craft a thesis paragraph using the ladder of escalation created that addresses the following question: "What steps could have been taken by either side to prevent the American Revolution?"

AP® ANALYZING SOURCES

Source: *London Merchants' Petition to Repeal the Stamp Act*, 1766

"And that, in consequence of the trade between the colonies and the mother country, as established and permitted for many years, and of the experience which the petitioners have had of the readiness of the Americans to make their just remittances to the utmost of their real ability, they have been induced to make and venture such large exportations of British manufactures, as to leave the colonies indebted to the merchants of Great Britain in the sum of several millions sterling; at that at this time the colonists, when pressed for payment, appeal to past experience, in proof of their willingness; but declare it is not in their power, at present, to make good their engagements, alleging, that the taxes and restrictions laid upon them, and the extension of the jurisdiction of vice admiralty courts established by some late acts of parliament, particularly . . . by an act passed in the fifth year of his present Majesty, for granting and applying certain stamp duties, and other duties, in the British colonies and plantations in America, with several regulations and restraints, which, if founded in acts of parliament for defined purposes, are represented to have been extended in such a manner as to disturb legal commerce and harass the fair trader, have so far interrupted the usual and former most fruitful branches of their commerce, restrained the sale of their produce, thrown the state of the several provinces into confusion, and brought on so great a number of actual bankruptcies, that the former opportunities and means of remittances and payments are utterly lost and taken from them; and that the petitioners are, by these unhappy events, reduced to the necessity of applying to the House, in order to secure themselves and their families from impending ruin; to prevent a multitude of manufacturers from becoming a burthen to the community, or else seeking their bread in other countries, to the irretrievable loss of this kingdom; and to preserve the strength of this nation entire."

Questions for Analysis

1. Identify the reasons why these London merchants opposed the Stamp Act.
2. Explain how this document challenges the British government's view of the Stamp Act as fair.
3. Evaluate the extent to which the concerns expressed by the London merchants in this excerpt shaped Parliament's decision to repeal the Stamp Act.

REVIEW

What were the colonists' primary grievances with Great Britain after 1765?

Ongoing Tension, 1767–1773

Townshend Acts 1767 acts of Parliament that instituted an import tax on a range of items including glass, lead, paint, paper, and tea. They prompted a boycott of British goods and contributed to violence between British soldiers and colonists.

After the passage of the Declaratory Act in 1766, relative harmony prevailed in the colonies for about a year. Then, in June 1767, Charles Townshend rose to power as the new chancellor of the exchequer in England. He persuaded Parliament to return to the taxation model of the Sugar Act of 1764. The **Townshend Acts**, like the Sugar Act, established an import tax on a range of items sent to the colonies, including glass, lead, paint, paper, and tea.

This time, even an indirect tax led to immediate highly organized protests and calls for a boycott of taxed items. In 1767 and 1768, John Dickinson, a prominent Pennsylvania attorney and Quaker, published a series of letters attacking the Townshend Acts. He presented himself as an ordinary colonist by using the pen name "A Farmer." Arguing that any duty on goods was a tax, he insisted, "Those who are taxed without their own consent, given by themselves, or their representatives, are slaves. We are taxed without our own consent given by ourselves, or our representatives. We are therefore — I speak it with grief — I speak it with indignation — we are slaves." Clearly, colonists thought boycott necessary and effective to demonstrate and secure their rights as British subjects.

In February 1768, Samuel Adams wrote a circular letter reminding colonists of the importance of the boycott, and the Massachusetts Assembly made sure it reached other colonial assemblies. In response, Parliament posted two more British army regiments in Boston and New York City to enforce the law. Angry colonists did not retreat when confronted by this show of military force. Instead, a group of outspoken colonial leaders demanded that colonists expand the boycotts by refusing to import goods of any kind from Britain.

TRM Suggested Responses to Questions

TRM Module 3.2 AP® Analyzing Sources Handout 2

TEACHING IDEA

Connecting the Dots

Compare the arguments in *London Merchants' Petition to Repeal the Stamp Act* to those made by the Virginia House of Burgesses in *Virginia Resolves* on page 163.

TEACHING IDEA

Incorporating Videos

Have students watch the first 30 minutes of the PBS documentary, "Liberty! Episode 1: The Reluctant Revolutionaries" (available on YouTube). This excerpt begins during the 1750s and stops with the repeal of the Stamp Act/passage of the Declaratory Act.

BUILDING AP® SKILLS

Claims and Evidence

Assign students John Dickinson's "Letters from a Pennsylvania Farmer," which can be found online in a condensed form on America in Class's website (americainclass.org). Have them annotate, identify the author's central argument, and discuss their observations in small groups. Ultimately, have each student group craft a conclusive statement, which is one sentence (it may be complex) created by the group to capture the most central and important ideas of the reading. Instruct student groups that this statement is to be their "takeaway" from the excerpt.

TRM Suggested Responses to Questions

TRM Module 3.2 AP® Analyzing Sources Handout 3

TEACHING IDEA

Challenging Misconceptions

Explain to the students that the boycott against English merchandise in the 1760s never could have succeeded without the involvement of women. As such, women and the support of women was vital to the growing movement that was increasingly frustrated with imperial rule over North America. Have students research and share other economically directed protest policies in U.S. history in which women played a prominent role.

AP® ANALYZING SOURCES

Source: Anonymous, "A Lady's Adieu to her TEA-TABLE" (poem), *Massachusetts Gazette*, February, 1770.

"Farewell the teaboard with its gaudy equipage
Of cups and saucers, creambucket, sugar tongs,
The pretty-tea-chest, also lately stored
With Hyson, Congo and best double-fine.[1]
Full many a joyous moment have I sat by ye
Hearing the girls tattle, the old maids talk scandal,
And the spruce coxcomb[2] laugh at—maybe—nothing.
Though now detestable
Because I am taught (and I believe it true)
Its use will fasten slavish chains upon my country
To reign triumphant in America."

[1] "Hysen," "Congo," and "double-fine" refer to types and grades of tea.
[2] A vain man.

Questions for Analysis

1. Identify an action recommended by the speaker of this poem.
2. Describe how the speaker justifies her economic boycott with at least one moral claim.
3. Explain the context surrounding the publication of this poem.

This widespread boycott depended especially on the support of women, who were often in charge of the day-to-day purchase of household items. Women were expected to boycott a wide array of British goods. To provide substitutes for boycotted goods they produced homespun shirts and dresses and brewed herbal teas to replace British products. Despite the hardships, many embraced the boycott. Among other efforts, some women organized spinning bees in which dozens of participants produced yards of homespun cloth. Textiles woven from homespun came to symbolize female commitment to the cause of liberty, and the wearing of such homespun publicly announced that commitment.

Refusing to drink tea offered another way for women to protest parliamentary taxation. In February 1770, more than "300 Mistresses of Families, in which number the Ladies of the Highest Rank and Influence," signed a petition in Boston, pledging to stop drinking tea. Dozens of women from less prosperous families signed their own boycott agreement.

Angry over Parliament's taxation policies, Boston men also considered the soldiers, who moonlighted for extra pay, as economic competitors. Throughout the winter of 1769–1770, boys and young men

Library of Congress, LC-USZ62-12711

The Edenton Proclamation, 1774 In Edenton, North Carolina, a group of women published a proclamation in 1774 stating their allegiance to the cause of liberty by refusing to serve or drink British tea. Their public statement received much attention in the American and the British press. This political cartoon, which satirizes the women who signed the declaration, appeared in several London newspapers. **How does this cartoon mock rebellion among the colonial elite?**

harassed the growing number of British soldiers stationed in the city. On the evening of March 5, 1770, young men began throwing snowballs at the lone soldier guarding the Boston Customs House. An angry crowd began to form, now joined by a group of sailors led by Crispus Attucks, a freedman of mixed African and American Indian ancestry. The guard called for help, and Captain Thomas Preston arrived at the scene with seven British soldiers. He appealed to the "gentlemen" present to leave. Instead, the taunts of the crowd continued, and snowballs, stones, and other projectiles flew in greater numbers. Then a gun fired, and soon more shooting erupted. Eleven men in the crowd were hit, and four were "killed on the Spot," including Attucks.

Despite confusion about who, if anyone, gave the order to fire, colonists expressed outrage at the shooting of ordinary men on the streets of Boston. Samuel Adams and other Sons of Liberty recognized the incredible potential for anti-British propaganda. Adams organized a mass funeral for those killed, and thousands watched the caskets being paraded through the city. Newspaper editors and broadsides printed by the Sons of Liberty labeled the shooting a "massacre." But when the accused soldiers were tried in Boston for the so-called **Boston Massacre**, the jury acquitted six of the eight of any crime. Still, ordinary colonists as well as colonial leaders were growing more convinced that British rule had become tyrannical and that such tyranny must be opposed.

Boston Massacre 1770 clash between colonial protesters and British soldiers in Boston that led to the death of five colonists. The bloody conflict was used to promote the patriot cause.

AP® ANALYZING SOURCES

Source: *Witness Testimony in the Trial of the British Soldiers of the Nineteenth Regiment of Foot, Boston, 1770*

"Q. Do you know any of the prisoners at the bar?

A. I particularly saw that tall man (pointing to Warren, one of the prisoners). Next day after the firing in King street, I saw more of them whom I cannot particularly swear to now.

Q. Did you see the soldiers before the justices on examination?

A. Yes.

Q. Did you then observe you had seen any of them the night before in King street?

A. I was well persuaded next day in my own mind, that I saw that tall one; but a few days after, I saw another man belonging to the same regiment, so very like him, that I doubt whether I am not mistaken with regard to him.

Q. Were there any other of the party you knew?

A. I am well satisfied I saw the corporal there.

Q. Did you see White there?

A. I do not remember.

Q. What was the situation of the corporal?

A. He was the corner man at the left of the party.

Q. Did you see either of the persons, you think you know, discharge their guns?

A. Yes; the man I take to be the tall man, discharged his piece as it was upon a level.

Q. Did you see the corporal discharge his gun?

A. I did not.

Q. Where did you stand?

A. I was behind them in the circle.

(Continued)

TEACHING IDEA

Incorporating Primary Sources

Have students study Paul Revere's 1770 engraving, "Bloody Massacre Perpetrated in King Street in Boston" in small groups using the HIPP template (a refresher of HIPP and the HIPP template can be found on page 8). This engraving can be found at Gilder Lehrman's website (gilderlehrman.org). This is very useful for engaging students in a discussion of point of view and perception, and the fact that the study and recording of history is an inherently interpretive act, and has often been performed by those with specific motives or agendas. What is not recorded or preserved for the record can be as important as what is recorded and preserved for the record. This would be a good place to compare Revere's interpretation of events to John Smith's interpretation of events from Jamestown in Period 2.

TRM Suggested Responses to Questions

TRM Module 3.2 AP® Analyzing Sources Handout 4

TEACHING IDEA

Incorporating Secondary Sources

Assign students to read Edward J. Balleisen's review of T.H. Breen's *The Marketplace of Revolution: How Consumer Politics Shaped American Independence*, which is available on JSTOR (jstor.org). Have them identify the author's thesis or central argument, in preparation for a whole-class discussion.

APPLY THE TIP

Divide students into three large groups, labeled "philosophical," "political," and "economic." Task each group with determining how their category related to continuing colonial resistance to a tax on tea. Upon completion of this stage of the activity, recombine the class into groups of three students, with each category represented in each group. Have students share out, jigsaw-style, and then rank the categories as to their importance in continuing colonial resistance, along with a rationale for their rank. These can then be shared as an entire class.

TEACHING IDEA

Analyzing Art and Images

Assign students the 1774 illustrated primary source, "The Bostonians Paying the Excise Man," which can be found on the Library of Congress website (loc.gov). Take the HIPP template and divide the class into four groups: one each for historical context, intended audience, purpose, and point of view, and have each group complete the exercise for their assigned element (a refresher of HIPP and the HIPP template can be found on page 8). Upon completion, recombine the groups with individuals from each element jigsaw-fashion and have students share and teach their findings (a refresher of the jigsaw model can be found on page 33).

> Q. What part of the circle did the tall man stand in?
> A. He stood next but one to the corporal. The tall man, whoever he was, was the man I saw discharge his piece.
> Q. Was any thing thrown at the soldiers?
> A. Yes, there were many things thrown, what they were I cannot say.
> Q. How did the soldiers stand?
> A. They stood with their pieces before them to defend themselves; and as soon as they had placed themselves, a party, about twelve in number, with sticks in their hands, who stood in the middle of the street, gave three cheers, and immediately surrounded the soldiers, and struck upon their guns with their sticks, and passed along the front of the soldiers, towards Royal Exchange lane, striking the soldiers' guns as they passed; numbers were continually coming down the street."

Questions for Analysis

1. Identify one detail in this testimony that might differ from an anti-British observer's testimony.
2. Describe the context surrounding the testimony of this witness.
3. Explain how this testimony conveys sympathy for the British soldiers.

AP® TIP
Analyze how political, economic, and philosophical developments ensured that a tax on tea led to continued conflicts between the colonies and Great Britain.

To ensure that colonists throughout North America learned about the Boston Massacre, once again committees of correspondence formed to spread the news — including an engraving by Bostonian Paul Revere that suggested the soldiers shot at a peaceful and notably respectable looking crowd with few lower class participants. These committees became important pipelines for sending information about plans and protests across the colonies.

Parliament was already considering the repeal of the Townshend duties, and in the aftermath of the shootings, public pressure increased to do so. Merchants in England and North America insisted that parliamentary policies had resulted in economic losses on both sides of the Atlantic. In response, Parliament repealed all of the Townshend duties except the import tax on tea, which it kept in place to demonstrate its political authority to tax the colonies.

REVIEW

What factors contributed to rising tensions between Britain and its North American colonies between 1764 and 1770?

Widening Resistance, 1773–1774

Tea Act 1773 act of Parliament, also known as the tea tax, that aimed to reduce the financial debts of Britain and the British East India Company by providing the company with a tea monopoly in the British American colonies. This resulted in colonial protests.

For a brief period after the Boston Massacre, and the repeal of the Townshend duties, the **Tea Act** of 1773 (tea tax) was collected. Tea tax funds ensured that British officials in the colonies were less dependent on local assemblies for financial support to carry out their duties, and general prosperity seemed to lessen the antagonism between colonists and royal authorities. This lull in hostility ended in May 1773 when Parliament passed a new act that granted the financially struggling East India Company a monopoly on shipping and selling tea in the colonies. This eliminated the role of colonial merchants, who often dealt in smuggled Dutch tea. Thus, although the act did not add any new tax or raise the price of tea, it did fuel a new round of protests as merchants were pushed into joining with radicals to assert their rights.

Committees of correspondence quickly organized another colony-wide boycott. In some cities, like Charleston, South Carolina, tea was unloaded from East India Company ships but never sold. In others, like New York, the ships were turned back at the port. In Boston, ships loaded with tea sat anchored in the harbor. On the night of December 16, 1773, the Sons of Liberty organized

Widening Resistance, 1773–1774

Period 3: 1754–1800

AP® ANALYZING SOURCES

Source: "Account of the Boston Tea Party," *Massachusetts Gazette*, 1773

"Just before the dissolution of the meeting [discussing the new Tea Act], . . . a number of brave and resolute men, dressed in the Indian manner, approached near the door of the assembly, gave the war-whoop, which rang through the house, and was answered by some in the galleries, but silence was commanded, and a peaceable deportment enjoined until the dissolution. The Indians, as they were then called, repaired to the wharf, where the ships lay that had the tea on board, and were followed by hundreds of people, to see the event of the transactions of those who made so grotesque an appearance. The Indians immediately repaired on board Captain Hall's ship, where they hoisted out the chests of tea, and when on deck stove the chests and emptied the tea overboard. Having cleared this ship, they proceeded to Captain Bruce's, and then to Captain Coffin's brig. They applied themselves so dexterously to the destruction of this commodity, that in the space of three hours they broke up three hundred and forty-two chests, which was the whole number in these vessels, and discharged the contents into the dock. When the tide rose it floated the broken chests and the tea insomuch that the surface of the water was filled therewith a considerable way from the south part of the town to Dorchester Neck, and lodged on the shores. There was the greatest care taken to prevent the tea from being purloined by the populace; one or two being detected in endeavoring to pocket a small quantity were stripped of their acquisitions and very roughly handled. . . ."

Questions for Analysis
1. Describe the events of the Boston Tea Party, according to this document.
2. Explain the causes that led colonists to dress as American Indians during the Boston Tea Party.
3. Evaluate the extent of continuity in colonists' responses to British policies between 1765 and 1774.

TRM Suggested Responses to Questions

TRM Module 3.2 AP® Analyzing Sources Handout 5

TEACHING IDEA

Incorporating Videos

Have students watch the final 30 minutes of the PBS documentary, "Liberty! Episode 1: The Reluctant Revolutionaries" (available on YouTube). This excerpt continues from the repeal of the Stamp Act/passage of the Declaratory Act to the closing of the port of Boston via the Coercive Acts.

TEACHING IDEA

AP® Central

Have students write full responses to the 2019 AP® U.S. History released exam Long-Essay Question number 2 on self-government and British imperial authority, which is available on the College Board's The Exam section under "2019: Free-Response Questions" (apcentral.collegeboard.org).

▲ Differentiation

Provide students with the rubric for the 2019 released exam LEQ administered. Instruct students to take their completed LEQs and share them in groups of three for peer review utilizing the rubric.

Boston Tea Party Rally against British tax policy organized by the Sons of Liberty on December 16, 1773, consisting of about fifty men disguised as American Indians who boarded British ships and dumped about forty-five tons of tea into the Boston Harbor.

Coercive Acts 1774 acts of Parliament passed in response to the Boston Tea Party. The acts closed the port of Boston until residents paid for the damaged property and moved Massachusetts court cases against royal officials back to England in a bid to weaken colonial authority.

Quebec Act 1774 act of Parliament extending the boundary of Quebec to areas of the Ohio River valley that American colonists wanted to settle. This act also set up a colonial government without a local representative assembly in Quebec.

what came to be known as the **Boston Tea Party**. After a massive rally against British policy, a group of about fifty men disguised as American Indians boarded the British ships and dumped forty-five tons of tea into the sea.

Although hundreds of spectators knew who had boarded the ship, witnesses refused to provide names or other information to British investigators. The Boston Tea Party was a direct challenge to British authority and resulted in large-scale destruction of valuable property.

Parliament responded immediately with a show of force. The **Coercive Acts**, passed in 1774, were intended to punish Massachusetts and to discourage similar protests in other colonies. These acts closed the port of Boston until residents paid for the tea, moved Massachusetts court cases against royal officials back to England, and revoked the colony's charter in order to strengthen the authority of royal officials and weaken that of the colonial assembly. The British government also approved a new Quartering Act, which forced Boston residents to accommodate more soldiers in their own homes or build more barracks, and passed the **Quebec Act**, which extended the boundary of Quebec to areas of the Ohio River valley that American colonists wanted to settle as well as set up a colonial government without a local representative assembly. Colonists viewed all of these acts as part of a larger pattern in British policy, one they believed aimed to strip them of their rights and liberties. Taken together, this legislation, which colonists called the **Intolerable Acts**, spurred a militant reaction.

Committees of correspondence spread news of the fate of Boston and of Massachusetts. Colonial leaders, who increasingly identified themselves as patriots, soon formed committees of safety — armed groups of colonists who gathered weapons and munitions and vowed to protect themselves against British encroachments on their rights and institutions. Other colonies sent

---

BUILDING AP® SKILLS

Comparison

Engage students in a "Dueling Dates" exercise. Write "1763 vs. 1776" on the chalkboard/whiteboard. Instruct students to come up with reasons why each year could be considered to be a turning point in U.S. history, and then to determine which year represents the greater turning point. Have the class stand up and move to opposite sides of the room based upon which date they feel has the greater significance. Question both sides of the room on their choice, compelling them to defend it.

support, both political and material, to Massachusetts and instituted a boycott of British goods. All ranks of people throughout the colonies joined the boycott.

By passing the Coercive Acts, Parliament had hoped to dampen the long-smoldering conflict with the colonies. Instead, it flared even brighter, with radical leaders committing themselves to the use of violence, moderate merchants and shopkeepers making common cause with radicals, and ordinary women and men embracing a boycott of all British goods.

REVIEW

- What attempts did British officials make to prevent colonial rebellion?
- Why did these attempts to prevent rebellion fail?

AP® WRITING HISTORICALLY — Evaluating Continuity and Change in an Essay

In Module 3-1, we discussed how historians craft complex historical arguments by evaluating the relative importance of several different causes of historical developments. This approach to thinking and writing about the past is one way that historians provide unique commentaries on the meaning of history rather than merely summarizing a series of events.

As you may already have guessed, this approach is one you can also apply to thinking and writing about continuity and change. Let's take a look at an essay prompt that asks you to think about the extent of continuity and change during a particular time period:

> Evaluate the extent of change in relations between Britain and its North American colonies in the period from 1675 to 1774.

Step 1 Break down the prompt.

Phrases like "the extent of" or "the extent to which" are an easy way to tell that a prompt is asking you to rate the importance of whatever concepts, developments, or events you choose to include in your response. In prompts that ask about continuity or change, you're being asked to use your knowledge *and* best judgment to characterize the time period in question.

Another way to think of it is to reword the prompt. Any time a prompt asks about "the extent of" something, it's essentially asking you "how much?" For instance, our example prompt could just as easily read, "How much change was there in the relations between Britain and its North American colonies in the period from 1675 to 1774?" This may help you see more clearly that this prompt isn't posing a simple yes/no question — it's asking you to take an argumentative position. And, as with all essays, you will need to defend that position with historical evidence.

Before moving on, take a moment to remember that any prompt that mentions just one element of continuity and change without mentioning the other is still asking you to consider both. Historians almost never discuss any topic in terms of complete change or complete continuity. Instead, they locate some significant qualities of continuity, and also note important elements of change.

Step 2 List and categorize your historical knowledge.

Take a moment to think about the history of relations between Britain and the colonies between 1675 and 1775. Gather ideas for continuities and changes you may decide to use in your answer. Write a list of continuities and a list of changes. Use Period 2, Modules 3-1 to 3-2, and content drawn from your classwork.

Next, think about your list of continuities and changes. Is the time period mostly characterized by continuity or by change? Which were most important, and why? To help you clarify your thoughts, try visualizing items from your list as sitting along a continuum. Remember, thinking along a continuum of change also entails thinking about continuity. The absence of change in a time period means the era was one featuring continuity. Thus, any aspect of British relations with colonies that barely changed is actually great evidence for continuity.

TRM Suggested Responses to Questions

TEACHING IDEA

Six Degrees of Separation

Have the students complete a "Six Degrees of Separation" activity. The prompt for this activity is: "From the beginning of the French and Indian War to the signing of the Declaration of Independence."

For the purpose of this exercise, students are given two events spanning time, but related by their theme. They must select four events in chronological order that link the first event in the series with the last. They will write the name of each selected event, and create an argument to support each of the events they selected (explain to them that they must answer the question, "Why does it belong as a link in your chain of events?" for each link). As part of this process, students will choose what overarching theme is the basis for their linkages. Students must emphasize both cause and effect and/or demonstrate continuity or change over time in the linking. This can be done either as a formative assessment in class, or as a homework assignment involving student research of their textbooks, activities/lessons, lecture notes, and knowledge of the time period.

▲ Differentiation

The lesson may also be undertaken by students individually or in small groups, depending upon the situation and instructional context of the teacher and course. Additionally, a more advanced use of this exercise could have students be tasked in different groups to follow a specific theme from Period 3 through their activity. Assigned themes could include American and national identity, politics and power, and America in the world.

EXPLORING AP® THEMES

American and National Identity

As part of the process of engaging students with the sample prompt on continuity and change, have students discuss in small groups how concepts of American and national identity could have played a role in the changing of relations between the British empire and its North American colonies. Students may use both their class notes and the textbook itself to assist them in gathering information to draw their conclusions.

To organize your thoughts, you can use the pre-writing strategies you learned in Period 2 to create a chart that considers relevant aspects of the five major analysis categories (politics, economy, society, technology, and interactions with the environment), and breaking your evidence into earlier and later parts of the time range given by the prompt. Next, add two columns to your chart: one to evaluate the extent of continuity or change, and one to craft a sentence that uses the evidence to support that evaluation. This final piece of the organizer is called an evaluative claim. The following graphic organizer shows one way to pre-write a response to our example prompt:

Sub-Topic	Evidence: Early Period	Evidence: Later Period	Evaluative Claim: Continuity/Change	Explanation of Evaluative Claims
Society	Anglicization; use of English Common Law	Use of English political ideas in newspapers; appeals for natural rights as 'rights of Englishmen'	Great Continuity	Despite some variation, the culture of the colonies and colonial leaders self-identified as English throughout the period of 1675 to 1775. Even as conflicts worsened, the colonists favored better treatment as English subjects with few calls for independence before 1775.
Politics — dispossession of American Indian lands	British military support for taking and/or holding lands seized from American Indians; King George's War & Queen Anne's War	Proclamation of 1763	Major Change	In the period before 1763, the English North American colonies and the British military collaborated to seize new lands from American Indians. After the Seven Years' War, British policy shifted against colonial expansion, checking colonial westward movement with the Proclamation of 1763. The change resulted, in part, from British goals to replace the French in the fur trade by improving relations with American Indian nations.
Economics	British de facto policy of "salutary neglect"	British revenue raising measures in the form on taxes and stricter enforcement.	Major Change	Before the Seven Years' War, the British only loosely enforced mercantilist policies. After the war, the British strengthened enforcement through legislation like the Sugar Act and new taxes on internal colonial commerce like the Stamp Act.

Step 3 Write a thesis statement that brings together all of your evaluative claims.

You may have noticed that the graphic organizer in step 2 includes claims about both continuity and change. This is a crucial part of pre-writing for a continuity and change essay. Arguments that present only one side of the continuity/change continuum do not convey your full understanding of a historical topic. When you craft your thesis statement, you will also usually want to avoid making claims from an extreme end of the continuum — these are typically difficult to support with evidence and thus make it hard for you to capture the variety of factors that contribute to historical patterns of continuity and change.

With this in mind, use your graphic organizer from step 2 to write a thesis statement answering the prompt. A strong thesis provides a direct answer — in this case, about the relative amount of change in relations between Britain and its North American colonies — and typically expresses at least three claims. Remember, a solid thesis will include claims of both continuity and change. Here is an example of a strong thesis:

> While relations between Britain and its North American colonies showed some continuity between 1675 and 1774 — in the dominance of English culture and the attractiveness of English concepts of 'rights' across the entire time period — the costly victory in the Seven Years' War spurred some major shifts in British imperial policies toward its colonies during this time, evidenced by both the seizure of American Indian nations' lands and new attempts to collect taxes from the colonies to enrich the British crown. Ultimately, the changes overwhelmed longer term continuities and resulted escalating conflict between Britain and its North American colonies.

(Continued)

TEACHING IDEA

AP® Central

Have students in groups break down the documents of the 2017 AP® U.S. History exam DBQ on pre-Revolution identity and unity, which is available on the College Board's AP® United States History Past Exam Questions section under "2017: Free-Response Questions" (apcentral.collegeboard.org). Students may be tasked with writing a response to this question for homework or the following day in class.

TEACHING IDEA

AP® Writing Historically Workshop

The following activity is designed to occur after students have written a thesis statement. This workshop is especially useful for students struggling with the concept of defending both continuities and changes through their essay. Consider dividing students into groups of four and assigning each group either continuity or change. In this way, students are distilling their focus to one end of the skill. During the activity portion of the workshop, students will write exclusively about continuity or change. After students have written a sample body paragraph, based on the directions in the activity, have students conduct a gallery walk so they can envision using continuities or changes in their essays.

Period 3: 1754–1800

MODULE 3-2 Resistance to Britain Intensifies

ACTIVITY

Write three paragraphs that support the thesis provided in step 3. Each paragraph should defend one of the claims in the thesis. You may use the graphic organizer in step 2 as well as the following outline to guide your writing.

I. **Evaluative claim of continuity or change 1:** Relations between Britain and its North American colonies showed some continuity between 1675 and 1774 in the dominance of English culture and the attractiveness of English concepts of 'rights' across the entire time period.
   A. **Topic sentence presenting claim 1:** This sentence should reiterate the claim about the extent of continuity regarding society from the thesis.
   B. **Cite evidence of claim 1 from earlier period of time frame:** This sentence should provide evidence from before 1763 to support claim 1.
   C. **Cite additional evidence of claim 1 from later period of time frame:** This sentence should provide evidence from after 1763 to support claim 1.
   D. **Explain how evidence supports claim 1:** These sentences should explain why you believe the evidence from the earlier period and the later period represent the extent of continuity from before 1763 and after 1763. Be sure that your explanation does not include information past the end date of the prompt, 1774.

II. **Evaluative claim of continuity or change 2:** The costly victory in the Seven Years' War spurred some major shifts in British imperial policies toward its colonies during this time, evidenced by the seizure of American Indian nations' lands.
   A. **Topic sentence presenting claim 2:** This sentence should reiterate the claim about the extent of change regarding politics from the thesis.
   B. **Cite evidence of claim 2 from earlier period of time frame:** This sentence should provide evidence from before 1763 to support claim 2.
   C. **Cite additional evidence of claim 2 from later period of time frame:** This sentence should provide evidence from after 1763 to support claim 2.
   D. **Explain how evidence supports claim 2:** These sentences should explain why you believe the evidence from the earlier period and the later period represent the extent of change from before 1763 and after 1763. Be sure that your explanation does not include information past the end date of the prompt, 1774.

III. **Evaluative claim of continuity or change 3:** The costly victory in the Seven Years' War spurred some major shifts in British imperial policies toward its colonies during this time, evidenced by new attempts to collect taxes from the colonies to enrich the British crown.
   A. **Topic sentence presenting claim 3:** This sentence should reiterate the claim about the extent of change regarding economics from the thesis.
   B. **Cite evidence of claim 3 from earlier period of time frame:** This sentence should provide evidence from before 1763 to support claim 3.
   C. **Cite additional evidence of claim 3 from later period of time frame:** This sentence should provide evidence from after 1763 to support claim 3.
   D. **Explain how evidence supports claim 3:** These sentences should explain why you believe the evidence from the earlier period and the later period represent the extent of change from before 1763 and after 1763. Be sure that your explanation does not include information past the end date of the prompt, 1774.

TEACHING IDEA

Incorporating Videos

Assign students to watch Episode 6 "Taxes & Smuggling—Prelude to Revolution" from the Crash Course US History series as a general content overview (available on YouTube).

Module 3-3

The American Revolution Begins

LEARNING TARGETS
By the end of this module, you should be able to:
- Explain the factors that ultimately led the thirteen colonies to move beyond protests and boycotts to declaring independence from Great Britain.
- Explain why some British North American colonists supported independence while others opposed it.
- Explain the effects of divided public opinion during the early American Revolution.

THEMATIC FOCUS
Politics and Power
American and Regional Culture

By 1774, many British colonists began to see themselves as members of a society separate from Great Britain. In response to the Coercive Acts, British colonists increasingly tried to exert political power against the British government. After a series of armed conflicts and the publication of Thomas Paine's *Common Sense*, the Second Continental Congress declared the thirteen colonies independent from Great Britain, forcing many colonists to choose a side.

HISTORICAL REASONING FOCUS
Contextualization

As you recall, when historians contextualize, they write about the ways in which particular historical events connect to broader regional or global processes. In contextualizing they explain the way or ways a development exerted a shaping influence on a historical topic. They also explain the significance of contexts.

Module 3-3 provides some important context for understanding the role the Continental Congress played in the founding of the United States of America. The men who participated were white, relatively wealthy, and — at least in the eyes of many of their contemporaries — radical activists. Although the Continental Congress aimed to represent the best interests of their fellow Americans, it was not a perfect arrangement. Many participants were slaveholders, although some were abolitionists. No women or people of color were included in its ranks. Nonetheless, these men reached important milestones in American history. Not only did the Continental Congress declare independence from Great Britain at the start of the American Revolution, it also constructed a national government once the war was won. This government has continued to form the backbone of American laws and politics since its inception.

What aspects of the context surrounding the formation of the Continental Congress were most significant? As with any question dealing with contextualization, the answer depends on your perspective. If you consider the effects of the American Revolution on women, for instance, the most significant factor may be that men held the recognized political power, both during wartime and in its aftermath. If you think about the reasons why the movement for independence gained enough traction to erupt into a war in the first place, you might use your knowledge from Modules 3-1 and 3-2 to point to the inter-colonial connections cemented by events during and after the Seven Years' War. Or, you might even go further back in history, and look at how the Great Awakening both transformed methods of communication and shaped distinctly American values that fundamentally clashed with the concept of monarchy.

TASK ▶ As you read Module 3-3, try and place the events you learn about within the larger context of the American Revolution. Think about how, depending upon different perspectives and factors, a particular aspect of context may rise, or fall, in relative significance.

TRM Suggested Responses to Questions

TEACHING IDEA

Challenging Misconceptions

As you begin this module, an important concept to get across to the students is that when it comes to military history or warfare, the exam (and by extension the AP® U.S. History Course) places heavier emphasis upon "causes and consequences" than upon "bullets and bombs." Students should be trained to expect to be evaluated on such elements, more so than on specific battles and combat. This is often a shift from what students intuitively expect military history to be about in their course of study, and it is useful for the instructor to proactively address this common student misconception.

BUILDING AP® SKILLS

Causation

A useful formative initial module exercise to engage in with students at this point is a "How did we get here?" activity, whereby students in small groups are given a single event (e.g., Boston Tea Party, etc.) and have to explain its significance in the context of the beginning of the American Revolution. Then, student groups must migrate in the room and mingle with other student groups, to find which group's events or contexts led their particular assigned event, and which event or context their group's assigned event served as a catalyst for.

In the wake of the passage of the Intolerable Acts in 1774, committees of correspondence spread news of the fate of Boston and of Massachusetts. Colonial leaders, who increasingly identified themselves as **patriots**, soon formed committees of safety—armed groups of colonists who gathered weapons and vowed to protect themselves against British assaults on their rights and institutions. Other colonies sent support, both political and material, to Massachusetts and instituted a boycott of British goods. As with previous boycotts, all ranks of people throughout the colonies joined in.

patriots American colonists who favored the movement for independence during the 1770s.

TEACHING IDEA

Connecting the Dots

Have students review the Albany Plan of Union, which the colonies rejected, and then juxtapose that against the First Continental Congress, in which the colonies voluntarily came together. Have students investigate and answer the critical question of what is different now that accounts for the different outcomes in different periods by substantially the same actors. This can reinforce the notion that in history, "everything happens for a reason," and the goal for students should be to sleuth out these "reasons."

TEACHING IDEA

Differing Views

Have student groups research the specific philosophical and policy positions of both the Committees of Correspondence and the First Continental Congress. Assign one half of the groups to the Committees of Correspondence and one half of the groups to the First Continental Congress. When this segment is completed by all the groups, then match each Committee of Correspondence group with a First Continental Congress group. Have the groups compare their findings, and then collectively answer the following question, "What else could the colonials have done to avoid war, yet also achieve their desired outcomes?"

TEACHING IDEA

Incorporating Videos

Have the students view the first 30 minutes of the PBS documentary, "Rebels and Redcoats Episode 1: The Shot Heard Around the World" (available on YouTube).

That spring, a group of patriots meeting in Virginia called for colonies to send representatives to a Continental Congress to meet later that year to discuss relations between the North American Colonies and Great Britain.

The Continental Congress Convenes

Continental Congress Congress convened in Philadelphia in 1774 in response to the Coercive Acts. The delegates hoped to reestablish the freedoms colonists had previously enjoyed.

AP® TIP
Analyze how Enlightenment ideas influenced the arguments colonial elites made at the Continental Congress in 1774.

When the **Continental Congress** convened in Philadelphia in September 1774, fifty-six delegates represented every colony but Georgia. Many of these men — and they were all men — had met before. Some had worked together in the Stamp Act Congress in 1765; others had joined forces in the intervening years on committees of correspondence or in petitions to Parliament.

Although the delegates held a wide range of views on the subject of colonial relations with Britain — some radical, others moderate, a few conservative — they were able to agree that the colonies must resist further parliamentary violations of their liberties. They talked not of independence but rather of reestablishing the freedoms that colonists had enjoyed in an earlier period. Washington voiced the sentiments of many. Although opposed to the idea of independence, he echoed John Locke by refusing to submit "to the loss of those valuable rights and privileges, which are essential to the happiness of every free State, and without which life, liberty, and property are rendered totally insecure."

To demonstrate their unified resistance to the Coercive Acts, delegates called on colonists to continue the boycott of British goods and to end all colonial exports to Great Britain. Committees were established in all of the colonies to plan and carry out these actions. Delegates also insisted that Americans were "entitled to a free and exclusive power of legislation in their several provincial legislatures." By 1774 a growing number of colonists supported these measures and the ideas on which they were based.

The delegates at the Continental Congress showed no interest in challenging race and class relations within the colonies themselves. Nonetheless, it was a significant event because the congress drew power away from individual colonies and local organizations and instead placed emphasis on colony-wide plans and actions. To some extent, the delegates shifted leadership of the protests away from more radical artisans, like Ebenezer Mackintosh, and put planning in the hands of men of wealth and standing. Moreover, even as they denounced Parliament, many representatives felt a special loyalty to the king and wanted him to step in and repair the damage done to British–colonial relations.

Continental Army Army created by the Second Continental Congress after the battles of Lexington and Concord began the Revolutionary War in 1775.

The Continental Congress adjourned in October 1774 with plans to reconvene in May 1775. During the intervening months, patriots honed their arguments for resisting British tyranny, and committees of correspondence continued to circulate the latest news. While some patriots called for nonviolent resistance, the eruption of armed clashes between British soldiers and local farmers created a strong push for independence. It also led the Continental Congress to establish the **Continental Army** in June 1775. A year later, in July 1776, the congress declared independence.

REVIEW

- How did the Continental Congress represent continuities with traditional British politics?
- In what ways did its tactics differ?

Armed Conflict Erupts

As debates over liberty intensified under the Intolerable Acts, patriots along the Atlantic coast expanded their efforts. The Sons of Liberty and other patriot groups spread propaganda against the British, gathered and stored weapons, and organized and trained local militia companies. In addition to boycotting British goods, female patriots manufactured bandages and bullets. Some northern colonists freed enslaved African Americans who agreed to enlist in the militia. Others kept close watch on the movements of British troops.

On April 18, 1775, Boston patriots observed British movement in the harbor. British soldiers were headed to Lexington, intending to confiscate guns and ammunition hidden there and in neighboring Concord and perhaps to arrest patriot leaders. To warn his fellow patriots, Paul Revere raced to Lexington on horseback but was stopped on the road to Concord by the British. By that time, however, a network of riders was spreading the alarm to Concord.

Armed Conflict Erupts

Period 3: 1754–1800

AP® ANALYZING SOURCES

Source: "Memory of a British Officer Stationed at Lexington and Concord," *Atlantic Monthly*, 1775

"We set out upon our return; before the whole had quitted the Town we were fired on from Houses and behind Trees, and before we had gone ½ a mile we were fired on from all sides, but mostly from the Rear, where People had hid themselves in houses till we had passed, and then fired; the Country was an amazing strong one, full of Hills, Woods, stone Walls, &c., which the Rebels did not fail to take advantage of, for they were all lined with People who kept an incessant fire upon us, as we did too upon them, but not with the same advantage, for they were so concealed there was hardly any seeing them: in this way we marched between 9 and 10 miles, their numbers increasing from all parts, while ours was reducing by deaths, wounds, and fatigue; and we were totally surrounded with such an incessant fire as it's impossible to conceive; our ammunition was likewise near expended. . . ."

Questions for Analysis
1. Identify an intended audience for this document, and explain the way a section of the passage is directed to this audience.
2. Describe the key details that the British officer recalls in this account.
3. Explain the context that shaped the colonial tactics described here.

TRM Suggested Responses to Questions

TRM Module 3.3 AP® Analyzing Sources Handout 1

EXPLORING AP® THEMES

America in the World

Have students create a double T-chart, indicating the British advantages and challenges in the Revolutionary War, and the American advantages and challenges in the Revolutionary War. Lead the students to note that each belligerent's relative strengths and weaknesses are mirror images of one another. Upon completion, have the students engage in a group discussion about which side faced the greater impediments to victory, all the while keeping students in check from racing to the foregone conclusion of American victory that is seen with the benefit of hindsight. This is an excellent time to engage students with the concept of contingency, whereby students should appreciate that the outcomes that transpired did not necessarily have to be, and were certainly not inevitable.

TRM Find **Handout 3.3 – Advantages and Challenges of the American Revolution** in the Teacher's Resource Materials.

APPLY THE TIP

Assign students in pairs to determine their top three historical developments that shaped the debate over declaring independence. Have students post these around the room and conduct a gallery walk. Then have students vote upon which three historical developments they believe as a class to be most significant.

---

minutemen Militia groups trained to prepare quickly for local defense in case of British attack.

Early in the morning of April 19, the first shots rang out on the village green of Lexington. After a brief exchange between British soldiers and local militiamen—known as **minutemen** for the speed with which they assembled—eight colonists lay dead. The British troops then marched on Concord, where they burned colonial supplies. However, patriots in nearby towns were ready and waiting. Borrowing guerrilla tactics from American Indians, colonists hid behind trees, walls, and barns to batter the British as they marched back to Boston, killing 73 and wounding 200.

Word of the conflict traveled quickly. Outraged Bostonians attacked British troops and forced them to retreat to ships in the harbor. The victory was short lived, however, and the British soon regained control of Boston. But colonial forces entrenched themselves on hills just north of the city. Then, in May, militias from Connecticut and Massachusetts captured the British garrison at Fort Ticonderoga, New York. The battle for North America had begun.

Second Continental Congress Assembly of colonial representatives that served as a national government during the American Revolution. Despite limited formal powers, the Continental Congress coordinated the war effort and conducted negotiations with outside powers.

When the **Second Continental Congress** convened in Philadelphia on May 10, 1775, the most critical question for some delegates, like Pennsylvania patriot John Dickinson, was how to ensure time for discussion and negotiation. Armed conflict had erupted, but should, or must, revolution follow? Other delegates, including Patrick Henry, insisted that independence was the only appropriate response to armed attacks on colonial residents.

Just over a month later, on June 16, British forces under General Sir William Howe attacked patriot fortifications on Breed's Hill and Bunker Hill, north of Boston. The British won the **Battle of Bunker Hill** when patriots ran out of ammunition. But the redcoats—so called because of their bright red uniforms—suffered twice as many casualties as the patriots. The victory allowed the British to maintain control of Boston for nine more months, but the heavy losses emboldened patriot militiamen.

AP® TIP
Evaluate the relative significance of historical developments that shaped the debate over declaring independence.

The Battle of Bunker Hill convinced the Continental Congress to establish an army to defend the colonies. They appointed forty-three-year-old George Washington as commander in chief, and he headed to Massachusetts to take command of militia companies already engaged in battle. Since the congress had not yet proclaimed itself a national government, Washington depended largely on the willingness of local militias to accept his command and of individual colonies to supply soldiers, arms, and ammunition. Throughout the summer of 1775, Washington wrote numerous letters to patriot political leaders detailing the army's urgent need for men and supplies. He also sought to remove incompetent officers and improve order among the troops, who spent too much time drinking and socializing.

BUILDING AP® SKILLS

Argumentation

For the AP® Tip above, after students have completed their rankings and rationales, instruct students to engage in a thesis and contextualization-building exercise known as 4-1-1, whereby they must create an introductory paragraph consisting of four sentences of contextualization, one sentence for a thesis, and one sentence for a plan of attack in their paper.

TEACHING IDEA

Incorporating Secondary Sources

Assign students to read the *Annual Editions* articles, "Winter of Discontent," by Norman Gleb, about the crisis of the Continental Army during the winter at Valley Forge, and "Hamilton Takes Command," by William Sterne Randall, concerning the rise to prominence and Washington's attention of Alexander Hamilton. Both articles can be found from the *Smithsonian Magazine*'s website (smithsonianmag.com).

▲ Differentiation

For the aforementioned pair of *Annual Editions* articles, assign academically stronger students to fully annotate one article or the other, and then do a mini teach-in session in which the students who annotated lead small-group discussions with their classmates who were assigned the article to read only, generating greater understanding for the class in a student-led, student-driven model of collaboration and instruction. Once each assigned article group has completed their discussion, the groups could be jigsawed together to allow for even more student engagement and leadership in the learning process.

TEACHING IDEA

Understanding Social Changes

This would be a good place to point out to students that the Revolution was a struggle for equality with some very specific parameters or limitations with regards to issues of race and class. Having an all-class discussion, updating an earlier theme of "Who is exploiting whom?" with regards to Lord Dunmore's Proclamation (available on the Gilder Lehrman website, gilderlehrman.org) and its attendant effects in the colonies (on African Americans, whites, indentured servants, enslaved people, freedmen, the British authorities, and colonial elites), would go a long way toward allowing students to understand the complex nature of personal relationships and political freedom in the colonies during the war.

▲
The Battle of Bunker Hill On June 16, 1775, 2,500 British infantry sought to dislodge 1,500 patriot volunteers from Breeds Hill, 600 yards below Charlestown's strategic Bunker Hill. Although the British managed to expel the patriots during a third assault, more than a thousand British soldiers were wounded or killed. **How do the details from this image and the historical situation of the battle reveal the future difficulties the British would encounter during the war?**

As he worked to build a disciplined army, Washington developed his military strategy with two immediate goals in mind: driving the British out of Boston and securing the colonies from attack by British forces and their American Indian allies in New York and Canada. He had mixed success. Although American troops captured Montreal in November 1775, the cold weather and the spread of smallpox decimated the reinforcements sent to aid the campaign, and the Continental Army ultimately failed to dislodge the British from Quebec. Despite the fiasco in Canada, the patriots also achieved important victories during the winter of 1775–1776. In March 1776, Washington surprised the British with a bombardment that drove them from Boston and forced them to retreat to Nova Scotia.

When the British retreated from Boston, the war had already spread into Virginia. In spring 1775, local militias forced Lord Dunmore, Virginia's royal governor, to take refuge on British ships in Norfolk harbor. Dunmore encouraged white servants and enslaved black people to join him there, and hundreds of black men fought with British troops when the governor led his army back into Virginia in November 1775. Dunmore reclaimed the governor's mansion and issued an official proclamation that declared "all [indentured] Servants, Negroes or others (appertaining to Rebels)" to be free if they were "able and willing to bear Arms" for the British.

Dunmore's Proclamation, offering freedom to enslaved people who fought for the crown, heightened concerns among patriot leaders about the consequences of declaring independence. They feared movements rejecting British authority might also reinforce other challenges to the social hierarchies that granted them elite status and rule. During the 1760s, Baptist preachers had rejected class and racial distinctions, and even in the South, they invited poor white people and enslaved black people to their services. By 1775, 15 percent of whites in Virginia and hundreds of African Americans had joined Baptist churches. In England itself, a group of radicals drew on

Dunmore's Proclamation
1775 proclamation issued by the British commander Lord Dunmore that offered freedom to all enslaved African Americans who joined the British army. The proclamation heightened concerns among some patriots about the consequences of independence.

Armed Conflict Erupts

> "A government of our own is our natural right. . . . 'Tis time to part [with England]."
> —Thomas Paine, 1776

anti-authoritarian ideas developed during the English Civil War (1642–1651) to criticize British rule over its expanding empire. Through pamphlets and newspapers, their ideas circulated widely in the colonies. In addition, Enlightenment thinkers generally emphasized individual talent over inherited privilege.

Thus, many delegates at the Continental Congress, which included large-scale planters, successful merchants, and professional men, still hesitated to act. They held out hope for a negotiated settlement that would increase the colonies' political liberty without disrupting social and economic hierarchies. The king and Parliament, however, refused to compromise in any way with colonies they considered in rebellion. Instead, in December 1775, the king prohibited any negotiation or trade with the colonies, increasing the leverage of radicals who argued independence was a necessity. The January 1776 publication of *Common Sense*, by Thomas Paine, bolstered their case. A recent transplant to the colonies, Paine had been a government employee in England, where he was repeatedly hired and dismissed from various jobs, before Benjamin Franklin persuaded him to try his luck in America, where he came to work for *Pennsylvania Magazine* in late 1774. In *Common Sense*, Paine wielded both biblical references and Enlightenment ideas to provide a rationale for independence and an emotional plea for creating a new democratic republic that would ensure liberty and equality for all Americans. He urged colonists to separate from England. It was an instant success, impressing everyone from patriot leaders to ordinary farmers and artisans, who debated his ideas at taverns and coffeehouses.

By the spring of 1776, a growing number of patriots believed that independence was necessary. Colonies began to take control of their legislatures and instruct their delegates to the Continental Congress to support independence. Meanwhile, the congress requested economic and military assistance from France. And in May, the congress advised colonies that had not yet done so to establish independent governments. Still, many colonists opposed the idea of breaking free from Britain—among them, Charles Inglis, the rector at Trinity Church in New York City, who insisted that "limited monarchy is the form of government which is most favorable to liberty."

AP® ANALYZING SOURCES

Source: Thomas Paine, *Common Sense*, 1776

"But there is another and greater distinction, for which no truly natural or religious reason can be assigned, and that is, the distinction of men into KINGS and SUBJECTS. Male and female are the distinctions of nature, good and bad, the distinction of heaven; but how a race of men came into the world so exalted above the rest, and distinguished like some new species, is worth enquiring into, and whether they are the means of happiness or of misery to mankind.

In the early ages of the world, according to the scripture chronology, there were no kings; the consequence of which was, there were no wars: it is the pride of kings which throws mankind into confusion. Holland without a king hath enjoyed more peace for this last century than any of the monarchical governments in Europe. . . .

Government by kings was first introduced into the world by the Heathens, from whom the children of Israel copied the custom. It was the most prosperous invention the Devil ever set on foot for the promotion of idolatry. The Heathens paid divine honors to their deceased kings, and the Christian world hath improved on the plan, by doing the same to their living ones. How impious is the title of sacred majesty applied to a worm who in the midst of his splendor is crumbling into dust!"

Questions for Analysis
1. Identify the subject of this excerpt from *Common Sense*.
2. Describe Paine's main argument in this excerpt.
3. Explain how Paine appeals to his audience in this excerpt.

(Continued)

TEACHING IDEA

Incorporating Primary Sources

Assign students to read excerpts of *Common Sense* beyond what is provided in the AP® Analyzing Sources (available through online search). Engage the students in a full-class discussion of the piece. This would also be a good time to point out that *Common Sense* is mentioned by name in the curriculum framework for AP® U.S. History, so it is specifically a document of enough importance and significance to warrant its inclusion on the annual AP® examination as an item of assessment. As such, it deserves close and careful study.

TRM Suggested Responses to Questions

TRM Module 3.3 AP® Analyzing Sources Handout 2

EXPLORING AP® THEMES

Politics and Power

Utilize brief excerpts of Rousseau's *Social Contract*, along with excerpts of Locke's *Two Treatises of Government*, to have the class identify specific excerpts of *Common Sense* that bear either of their influences in the eyes of the students, and make them give their rationales/reasons why. All three documents are readily available online.

TEACHING IDEA

Incorporating Primary Sources

Point out to students that the Declaration of Independence was very deliberately written as an informational, educational, and persuasive document. The fact that much of the repetitive sentence structure of the list of grievances would not score highly if it were an assignment in a high school English class only further underscores this point. The repetitive nature of the narrative of grievances has the effect of building a case over time, and that is the point of much of Jefferson's exercise here as its primary author. Not all modules are as primary source-heavy as this one, but there is no getting around the truth that students must know the main arguments of the Declaration of Independence both as it related to its own time and also in terms of how its rhetoric and ideals would be adopted and co-opted by later generations of Americans in later struggles for social or political equality. Assign students in groups of three to read the Declaration in its entirety in small groups point by point, each student taking turns being the reader. After the reader has read one sentence or point, the other two members of the group must make one comment each about what was read. Then the group rotates roles as they move on to the next sentence or point. Follow this up by assigning students to answer the questions in the text on the Declaration excerpt on page 179.

TEACHING IDEA

Incorporating Videos

Have students watch excerpts of the musical *1776*, specifically portions involving exchanges between Benjamin Franklin, Richard Henry Lee, Edward Rutledge, John Adams, and John Dickinson over the pros and cons and political wrangling regarding the idea of colonial separation and the creation of the Declaration of Independence. This is approximately the first 60 minutes of the film, which can be found on Daily Motion's website by searching for "1776 – Broadway Musical" (dailymotion.com). Despite its age and fictional aspects, this musical still has the potential to focus the attention of students on the important notion (historically speaking) that not all colonials of the time believed that revolution and separation was a universally good thing. This is not always a truth that students fully internalize; living in this present, it often seems to students that not only was the Revolution bound to happen but that the colonists were all in it together and its success was thoroughly foregone. Judicious use of excerpts of this picture, previewed by the instructor with an eye toward specific points to be called into view, can resonate powerfully with students.

BUILDING AP® SKILLS

Comparison

Have students write down a response to the following: "Between the British rulers and their colonial subjects, which side was most unwilling to accommodate the wishes of the other, and why do you think so? Who had the most to lose by accommodation, and who had the most to gain?" Ask students to compare their responses with someone of the opposing viewpoint.

Source: Charles Inglis, Anglican minister of Trinity Church in New York City, *The true interest of America impartially stated, in certain [strictures] on a pamphlet [entitled] Common sense*, 1776

"I find no Common Sense in this pamphlet but much uncommon phrenzy. It is an outrageous insult on the common sense of Americans; an insidious attempt to person their minds and seduce them from their loyalty and truest interest. The principles of government laid down in it, are not only false, but too absurd to have ever entered the head of a crazy politician before. . . .

It is probable that this pamphlet like others will soon sink in oblivion—that the destructive plan it holds out will speedily be forgotten, and vanish like the baseless fabric of a vision; yet while any honest man is in danger of being seduced by it . . . I think it a duty which I owe to God, to my King and Country, to counteract in this manner, the poison it contains. . . .

[I]t will be proper to bestow a few minutes in examining what is here alledged concerning monarchy in general; against which this republican marshals a formidable host of arguments. The reader will remember, that monarchy may be either absolute; or mixed and combined with the other simple forms of government. Our author makes no distinction between these; and although all he says, and a thousand times more that might be said, were true with respect to the former; yet all this would not militate in the least against the mild and tempered monarchy of Great-Britain."

Questions for Analysis
1. Identify Inglis's intended audience.
2. Describe Inglis's response to *Common Sense*.
3. Explain how Inglis appeals to his audience in this excerpt.

Questions for Comparison
1. Identify the main differences between Paine's and Inglis's arguments.
2. Describe the biases that each author brings to his argument.
3. Explain who in the colonies would find each argument most appealing, and why.

REVIEW
Why did the Second Continental Congress ultimately decide to declare independence in July 1776?

The Colonies Declare Independence

As colonists argued back and forth, Richard Henry Lee of Virginia introduced a motion to the Continental Congress in early June 1776 resolving that "these United Colonies are, and of right ought to be, Free and Independent States." A heated debate followed in which Lee and John Adams argued passionately for independence. Eventually, even more cautious delegates, like Robert Livingston of New York, were convinced. Livingston concluded that "they should yield to the torrent if they hoped to direct it." He then joined Adams, Thomas Jefferson, Benjamin Franklin, and Roger Sherman on a committee to draft a formal statement justifying independence.

The thirty-three-year-old Jefferson took the lead in preparing the declaration, building on ideas expressed by Paine, Adams, and Lee. He also drew on language used in dozens of "declarations" written by town meetings, county officials, and colonial assemblies, particularly the Virginia Declaration of Rights drafted by George Mason in May 1776. Several of these documents insisted on religious freedom, since the power of faith strengthened the view of many Americans that they were uniquely blessed with liberty. Another principle central to these documents was the contract

Period 3: 1754–1800

theory of government, proposed by the seventeenth-century British philosopher John Locke. Locke argued that sovereignty resided in the people, who submitted voluntarily to laws and authorities in exchange for protection of their life, liberty, and property. The people could therefore reconstitute or overthrow a government that abused its powers. Jefferson summarized this argument and then listed the abuses and crimes perpetrated by King George III against the colonies, which justified patriots' decision to break their contract with British authorities.

Once prepared, the **Declaration of Independence** was debated and revised. In the final version, all references to slavery were removed. But delegates agreed to list among the abuses suffered by the colonies the fact that the king "excited domestic insurrections amongst us," referring to the threat posed by Dunmore's Proclamation. On July 2, 1776, delegates from twelve colonies approved the Declaration, with only New York abstaining. Independence was publicly proclaimed on July 4 when the Declaration was published as a broadside to be circulated throughout the colonies.

Probably no more than half of American colonists actively supported the patriots. Perhaps a fifth actively supported the British. The rest tried to stay neutral or were largely indifferent unless the war came to their doorstep. Both patriots and loyalists included men and women from all classes and races and from both rural and urban areas.

Declaration of Independence
Document declaring the independence of the colonies from Great Britain. Drafted by Thomas Jefferson and then debated and revised by the Continental Congress, the Declaration was made public on July 4, 1776.

AP® ANALYZING SOURCES

Source: Thomas Jefferson, *Declaration of Independence*, 1776

"When, in the course of human events, it becomes necessary for one people to dissolve the political bands which have connected them with another, and to assume, among the powers of the Earth, the separate and equal station to which the laws of nature and of nature's God entitle them, a decent respect to the opinions of mankind requires that they should declare the causes which impel them to the separation.

We hold these truths to be self-evident; that all men are created equal; that they are endowed, by their Creator, with certain unalienable rights; that among these are life, liberty, and the pursuit of happiness.—That to secure these rights, governments are instituted among men, deriving their just powers from the consent of the governed; that whenever any form of government becomes destructive of these ends, it is the right of the people to alter or to abolish it, and to institute new government, laying its foundation on such principles, and organizing its powers in such form, as to them shall seem most likely to effect their safety and happiness. Prudence, indeed, will dictate, that governments long established, should not be changed for light and transient causes; and accordingly all experience hath shewn, that mankind are more disposed to suffer, while evils are sufferable, than to right themselves by abolishing the forms to which they are accustomed. But when a long train of abuses and usurpations, pursuing invariably the same object, evinces a design to reduce them under absolute despotism, it is their right, it is their duty, to throw off such government, and to provide new guards for their future security. . . ."

Questions for Analysis
1. Identify the origin of the authority to rule, according to Jefferson.
2. Describe the responsibilities of people with regard to government, according to Jefferson.
3. Explain the relationship that this document illustrates between government and human beings' inalienable rights.

REVIEW

- What arguments did colonists make in support of independence?
- What arguments did colonists make for remaining in the British empire?

TEACHING IDEA

AP® Central

Assign students to read the article, "The Declaration of Independence in World Context." This can be found as part of the series *America on the World Stage: Essays from the American Organization of Historians and AP®* available in the Related Articles and Teaching Resources section of the Classroom Resources for AP® U.S. History on AP® Central (apcentral.collegeboard.org).

TRM Suggested Responses to Questions

TRM Module 3.3 AP® Analyzing Sources Handout 3

TEACHING IDEA

Building Vocabulary

It is important that the students fully internalize the meaning and appropriate usage of the history terms "social contract" and "natural law." These two ideals are critical to the understanding of the founding period's concept of government, and to employ these terms accurately in written work is to "speak the language of the historian." Have students call out aspects of these terms that you write on the board. Then, as a class, clean up the suggestions and come up with a solid definition for each.

TEACHING IDEA

Building Vocabulary

Introducing students to the concept of realpolitik would be very useful at this point. The idea that all nations operate upon a foreign policy set of objectives ruthlessly devoted to their national self-interest is what makes the French alliance — shunning an absolute monarch and supporting an aspirational democratic republic — understandable. Another way to connect this idea to students is to write "The enemy of my enemy is my friend" on the board, and ask them to discuss what that means.

TEACHING IDEA

Class Discussion

Pose the following question for students in a large or small group setting: "Was the American Revolution about home rule, or about who was to rule at home?" As students engage with the question and one another, guide them to consider the question in terms of class, ethnicity, and American Indian relations. Culminate the activity by having students engage in a thesis-building exercise to respond to the prompt.

Period 3: 1754–1800

MODULE 3-3 The American Revolution Begins

Choosing Sides

AP® TIP
Analyze the economic, political, and philosophical reasons why colonists decided to join the war.

Once independence was declared, there was far more pressure to choose sides. The stance of political and military leaders and soldiers was clear. But to win against Great Britain required the support of a large portion of the civilian population as well. As battle lines shifted back and forth across New England, the Middle Atlantic region, and the South, civilians caught up in the fighting were faced with difficult decisions.

Men who took up arms against the British before independence was declared and the women who supported them clearly demonstrated their commitment to the patriot cause. In some colonies, patriots organized local committees, courts, and assemblies to assume governance should British officials lose their authority. At the same time, white servants and enslaved black people in Virginia who fled to British ships or marched with Lord Dunmore made their loyalties known as well.

Both Britain and the colonists sought American Indian allies. The Continental Congress, recognizing the importance of American Indians to the outcome of any colonial war, appointed commissioners from the "United Colonies" to meet with representatives of the Iroquois Confederacy in August 1775. Early in the war, many American Indian nations proclaimed their neutrality, but neither the colonists nor the British respected such declarations, each pressuring native peoples to join their efforts. Colonial troops killed the Shawnee chief Cornstalk under a flag of truce in 1777, leading that nation to ally, finally, with the British—as did the majority of American Indians during the conflict, viewing Americans' pursuit of their lands as a threat.

Their help enabled British success early in the conflict. In May 1775, Colonel Guy Johnson, the British superintendent for American Indian affairs, left Albany, New York and sought refuge in Canada. He was accompanied by 120 British loyalists and 90 Mohawk warriors led by their mission-educated chief, Joseph Brant (Thayendanegea). While Brant's group

▲
African Americans in New York City Amid the Upheavals of 1776 On July 9, the day New York's Provincial Congress approved the Declaration of Independence, a rowdy crowd of soldiers and civilians toppled a statue of King George III. However, an etching of the event presents it as the work of African Americans, with most whites simply observing. **What does this portrayal suggest about the artist's sympathies?**

Choosing Sides

Colonel Guy Johnson and Karonghyontye (Captain David Hill), 1776
Benjamin West painted this portrait of Colonel Johnson, British superintendent of Indian affairs, with the Mohawk chief Karonghyontye. Johnson directed joint Mohawk and British attacks against patriots during the Revolution. His red coat and musket are combined with moccasins, a wampum belt, and an American Indian blanket while Karonghyontye holds a peace pipe, representing the Mohawk-British alliance before and during the war. **What does this painting reveal about the relations between American Indians and the British during the American Revolution?**

of Mohawk warriors were already committed to the British, some Oneida Indians, influenced by missionaries and patriot sympathizers, wanted to support the colonies. Others, however, urged neutrality, including Oneida's chief warriors, who declared that the English and patriots were *"two brothers of one blood."* As the war continued, British forces and their American Indian allies fought bitter battles against patriot militias and Continental forces all along the frontier. Each side destroyed property, ruined crops, and killed civilians. In the summer and fall of 1778, American Indian and American civilians suffered through a series of brutal attacks in Wyoming, Pennsylvania; Onoquaga, New York; and Cherry Valley, New York. Patriots and American Indians also battled along the Virginia frontier after pioneer and militia leader Daniel Boone established a fort there in 1775. In the South, 6,000 patriot troops laid waste to Cherokee villages in the Appalachian Mountains in retaliation for the killing of white intruders along the Watauga River.

AP® ANALYZING SOURCES

Source: Oneida Leaders, *Message to Massachusetts Provincial Congress*, 1775

"Now we more immediately address you, our brother, the Governour and the Chiefs of New-England.

Brothers! We have heard of the unhappy differences and great contention betwixt you and old England. We wonder greatly, and are troubled in our minds.

Brothers! Possess your minds in peace respecting us Indians. We cannot intermeddle in this dispute between two brothers. The quarrel seems to be unnatural; you are two brothers of one blood. We are unwilling to join on either side in such a contest, for we bear an equal affection to both of you, Old and New-England. Should the great King of England apply to us for our aid, we shall deny him. If the Colonies apply, we will refuse. The present situation of you two brothers is new and strange to us. We Indians cannot find nor recollect in the traditions of our ancestors the like case or a similar instance.

Brothers! For these reasons possess your minds in peace, and take no umbrage that we Indians refuse joining in the contest; we are for peace.

Brothers! We have now declared our minds; please write to us that we may know yours.

We, the sachems, warriors, and female governesses of Oneida, send our love to you, brother Governour, and all the other chiefs in New-England.

Signed by,
William Sunoghsis, Viklasha Watshaleagh, William Kanaghquassea, Peter Thayehcase, Germine Tegayavher, Nickhes Ahsechose, Thomas Yoghtanawca, Adam Ohonwano."

Questions for Analysis
1. Identify the goals expressed in this message.
2. Explain the relevant context shaping this message.
3. Evaluate the extent of change in relations between American Indian nations and the British between 1765 and 1775 revealed by this message.

BUILDING AP® SKILLS

Making Connections

As students cover this material, have them link the outcomes of white–American Indian relations depicted on this page with colonial motivations in the Seven Years' War, and colonial reactions to the Proclamation of 1763. Have students construct a connective web-map or graphic organizer that ties each of these events together.

TRM Suggested Responses to Questions

TRM Module 3.3 AP® Analyzing Sources Handout 4

Period 3: 1754–1800

MODULE 3-3 The American Revolution Begins

EXPLORING AP® THEMES

American and Regional Culture

Have students develop a T-chart that lays out the primary characteristics of loyalists and patriots. After students have completed their chart, ask them the following questions:

- How might geographic settlement play a role in determining one's primary affiliation?
- What might have been the effect on political affiliation had wealth been more equally distributed in the American South?

TRM Find **Handout 3.4 – Patriots vs. Loyalists: Traits & Characteristics** in the Teacher's Resource Materials.

TRM Suggested Responses to Questions

TRM Module 3.3 AP® Analyzing Sources Handout 5

loyalists Colonial supporters of the British during the American Revolution.

AP® TIP
Be sure you can explain the reasons why women's actions were critical to the success of the American Revolution.

Meanwhile, many colonists who remained loyal to the king found safe haven in cities like New York, Newport, and Charleston, which remained under British control throughout much of the war. Although the British army welcomed **loyalists**, those who made their loyalist sympathies clear still risked a good deal. When British troops were forced out of cities or towns they had temporarily occupied, many loyalists faced harsh reprisals. Patriots had no qualms about invading the homes of loyalists, punishing women and children, and destroying or confiscating property.

Although many loyalists were members of the economic and political elite, others came from ordinary backgrounds. Tenants, small farmers, and enslaved people joined the loyalist cause in defiance of the patriot elite, which included landlords and wealthy plantation owners. Many poorer loyalists lived in the Hudson valley, their sympathy for the British heightened by the patriot commitments of the powerful men who controlled the region's local politics. When the fighting moved south, many backcountry farmers in North Carolina also supported the British, who challenged the domination of patriot leaders among the colony's eastern elite.

Colonists who sought to remain neutral during the war faced hostility. Some 80,000 Quakers, Mennonites, Amish, Shakers, and Moravians considered war immoral and refused to bear arms, hire substitutes, or pay taxes to new state governments. Both sides treated the pacifists poorly: British authorities harassed Quakers in the areas they controlled, and patriots routinely fined and imprisoned Quakers for refusing to support the revolution. In June 1778, Pennsylvania authorities jailed nine Mennonite farmers who refused to take an oath of allegiance to the revolutionary government and then sold their property, leaving their wives and children destitute. Meanwhile, Quaker meetings regularly disciplined members who offered aid to either side. Betsy Ross was among those disowned Quakers when her husband joined the patriot forces, and she sewed flags for the Continental troops.

Some female patriots accompanied their husbands, fiancés, or partners as camp followers, cooking, washing clothes, nursing, and providing other services for soldiers. Most patriot women remained at home, however, and demonstrated their commitment by raising funds, gathering

AP® ANALYZING SOURCES

Source: Christine Barnes, wife of an absent loyalist farmer, *Letter*, April 1775

"[T]he greatest terror I was ever thrown into was on Sunday last. A man came up to the gate and loaded his musket, and before I could determine which way to run he entered the house and demanded a dinner. I sent him the best I had upon the table. He was not contented, but insisted upon bringing in his gun and dining with me; this terrified the young folks, and they ran out of the house. I went in and endeavored to pacify him by every method in my power, but I found it was to no purpose. He still continued to abuse me, and said that when he had eat his dinner he should want a horse and if I did not let him have one he would blow my brains out. He pretended to have an order from the General for one of my horses, but did not produce it. His language was so dreadful and his looks so frightful that I could not remain in the house, but fled to the store and locked myself in. He followed me and declared he would break the door open. Some people very luckily passing to meeting prevented his doing any mischief and staid by me until he was out of sight, but I did not recover from my fright for several days. The sound of drum or the sight of a gun put me into such a tremor that I could not command myself. I have met with but little molestation since this affair, which I attribute to the protection sent me by Col. Putnam and Col. Whitcomb. . . ."

Questions for Analysis
1. Describe how Barnes characterizes the invader of her home.
2. Describe the role Barnes plays in her household during her husband's absence.
3. Explain the results of the unpleasant encounter Barnes describes.

Choosing Sides

Period 3: 1754–1800

MAP 3.3 Choosing Sides in the American Revolution This map portrays the conflicted loyalties of British North Americans during the American Revolution. **What commonalities do you see between loyalist strongholds? What accounts for these commonalities?**

information, and/or sending clothes, bedding, and other goods to soldiers at the front. The Continental Army suffered desperate shortages of supplies from the beginning of the war. Patriot leaders urged northern women to increase cloth production, while calling on southern women to harvest crops for hungry troops. The response was overwhelming. Women in Hartford, Connecticut produced 1,000 coats and vests and 1,600 shirts in 1776 alone. Across the colonies, women collected clothing door-to-door and opened their homes to sick and wounded soldiers.

A small number of African Americans also sided with the patriots. In Boston, a formerly enslaved woman named Phillis Wheatley believed in the movement for independence. Born in Gambia around 1753, she was sold into slavery and brought to Boston in 1761, where she was bought by the Wheatley family. Although they were slaveholders, the Wheatleys were nevertheless considered progressive: Phillis received a thorough education that included subjects such as Greek and Latin. Freed in 1773, Phillis penned a collection of poetry in 1776 and sent a copy to General Washington, who was himself a slaveholder. In her book, she urged readers to recognize black people as children of God.

AP® ANALYZING SOURCES

Source: Phillis Wheatley, "On Being Brought from Africa to America" (poem), 1770

> " 'Twas mercy brought me from my *Pagan* land,
> Taught my benighted[1] soul to understand
> That there's a God, that there's a *Saviour* too;
> Once I redemption neither sought nor knew.
> Some view our sable[2] race with scornful eye,
> "Their colour is a diabolic dye."
> Remember, *Christians*, negroes, black as *Cain*,
> May be refin'd, and join th' angelic train."

[1] Pitiful and ignorant.
[2] Black.

Questions for Analysis
1. Identify the role of God in this poem.
2. Explain how the speaker of this poem conveys her attitude toward her captivity.
3. Explain how Wheatley's poem asserts African Americans' desire for independence during this time period.

REVIEW
- What motivations led different groups of people to ally with each side in the American Revolution?

TEACHING IDEA

Incorporating Primary Sources

To further explore the works of Phillis Wheatley, consider having students read the following poems and letters by her:

- "To S.M., a Young Painter, on Seeing His Works" (1773 poem)
- "To the University of Cambridge, in New-England" (1773 poem)
- "To His Excellency General Washington" (1776 letter with poem enclosed). Students could also read George Washington's response.

TRM Suggested Responses to Questions

TRM Module 3.3 AP® Analyzing Sources Handout 6

TEACHING IDEA

Incorporating Secondary Sources

To provide a fuller context for teaching Phillis Wheatley and her work, consider directing students to some of these sources:

- June Jordan's poem, "The Difficult Miracle of Black Poetry: Or Something Like a Sonnet for Phillis Wheatley" available on the Poetry Foundation's website (poetryfoundation.org).
- Henry Louis Gates Jr.'s "Jefferson Lecture" available on the National Endowment for the Humanities' website by searching for author and using the Award/Honor filter (neh.gov).
- Eve L. Ewing's poem, "1773" available on The New York Times feature on "A New Literary Timeline of African-American History" (nytimes.com).
- Alice Walker's essay, "In Search of Our Mothers' Gardens" from her collection by the same name.
- Kevin Young's poem, "Homage to Phillis Wheatley" available on the *Paris Review*'s website (theparisreview.org).

TRM Suggested Responses to Questions

TEACHING IDEA

AP® Writing Historically Review

One way students can establish contextualization is by focusing on a different historical category than the one used in the prompt. For example, this question focuses on economics, therefore students can use any one of the following categories of analysis: political, social, religious, global, regional, or environmental. Regardless of the selection students make, it is important that they demonstrate how their example influenced the topic of the question. Students can accomplish this by connecting two or three facts that relate to their broad topic. So a sketch of an example could look similar to this: Regional expansion + Pontiac's Rebellion + Proclamation of 1763. Once students have a rough outline, they can construct three or four sentences that explain the broader context of the question.

Period 3: 1754–1800

MODULE 3-3 The American Revolution Begins

AP® WRITING HISTORICALLY — Establishing Context in an Essay Introduction

As you learned in Period 2, contextualizing your historical arguments is a key piece of writing history. In fact, a statement that draws a clear connection between the significance of context to the argument you make in your thesis is a requirement for both of the essays on the AP® Exam.

As you complete the following activity, aim to keep your contextualization of your thesis between three to four sentences long. Your thesis statement should be one or two sentences.

ACTIVITY

Carefully read the following essay prompt. Then, write an introductory paragraph that provides the context to your response, *briefly* explains that context, and leads into a thesis that answers the question.

> Evaluate the extent to which British economic policies between 1763 and 1776 led to the Declaration of Independence on July 4, 1776.

Module 3-4

Winning the War for Independence

LEARNING TARGETS

By the end of this module, you should be able to:

- Explain what factors led the Continental Army to win the Revolutionary War.
- Explain the changes in American society that resulted from the American Revolution.
- Explain how the American Revolution affected other nations.

THEMATIC FOCUS

America in the World
Social Structures

The events and ideas that underpinned the American Revolution challenged traditional ethnic and gender structures during the conflict. During the American Revolution the former British colonies defined themselves as an independent nation and sought allies in their conflict with Great Britain.

HISTORICAL REASONING FOCUS

Causation

TASK ▶ As you read this module, take special note of the many events that contributed to the Continental Army's eventual victory in the American Revolution. As you do, prepare to evaluate the importance of the effects of these events. Which ones played a greater role? Which ones were less important? As you answer these questions for yourself, think about how you could support an argument asserting which causes had the most influential effects.

TRM Suggested Responses to Questions

TEACHING IDEA

Incorporating Videos

Assign students to watch Episode 7 "Who Won the American Revolution" from the Crash Course US History series as a general content overview before introducing this module (available on YouTube).

TEACHING IDEA

Incorporating Primary Sources

Assign students to read various excerpts of Joseph Plumb Martin's memoir of his time in the Continental Army, *A Narrative of a Revolutionary Soldier: Some of the Adventures, Dangers and Sufferings of Joseph Plumb Martin*, which is available on Wikisource (en.wikisource.org). Have students discuss and record their impressions of Martin's service, as well as evaluate the usefulness and limitations of Martin's source as a historical account.

▲ **Differentiation**

Consider assigning interested students to compare Martin's depictions of soldierly life with more contemporary depictions of the life of the colonial soldier, in motion pictures such as *The Patriot*. Ask them to evaluate and articulate the similarities and the differences.

After July 4, 1776, battles between British and colonial troops intensified, but it was not until December that the patriots would celebrate another major military victory. Over the course of the eighteenth century, Great Britain had developed the world's most powerful military force, including a huge navy. Moreover, by declaring independence, the colonists had lost their main trading partner — finding ways to sustain their economy while funding a war was a tough challenge. To succeed, the patriots needed support from men and women on the home front as well as the battlefront and assistance from Europeans experienced in fighting the British.

Critical Years of Warfare, 1776–1777

The Continental Army did not gain a single military victory between July and December 1776. In the summer of 1776, General Washington tried to lead his army out of Boston to confront British troops set to invade New York City, but many soldiers deserted — they believed New Yorkers should defend New York. Ultimately, Washington arrived in New York with 19,000 men, many of whom were poorly armed and poorly trained and some of whom were coerced into service by local committees of safety.

Meanwhile, British ships sailed into New York harbor or anchored off the coast of Long Island. General William Howe, hoping to overwhelm the colonists, ordered 10,000 troops to march into the city in the weeks immediately after the Declaration of Independence was signed. Still, the Continental Congress rejected Howe's offer of peace and a royal pardon. Howe then prepared to take New York City by force and thereafter isolate New York and New England from the other colonies. On August 27, 1776, British forces killed or wounded over 1,500 patriots in a fierce battle on Long Island.

By November, the British had captured Fort Lee in New Jersey and made headway north of New York City. Meanwhile Washington led his weary troops into Pennsylvania as the Continental

BUILDING AP® SKILLS

Comparison

Assign students to research and explain the difference between the British military tactics of the age, described as "conventional" warfare, and the colonial tactics of the era described as "unconventional" warfare. Then have students research and discuss the similarities and differences in the meanings of these two terms as applied to combat in the present day.

TEACHING IDEA

Connecting the Dots

This is a good place to impress upon students the extent to which the British doctrine in the Revolutionary War of seizing and holding the cities and urban areas was a great mistake. Since the colonies were predominantly an agrarian society, the great balance of the population resided in the countryside, where the Continental Army moved freely. Furthermore, as a primarily pre-industrial society, holding the urban areas did not have the anticipated and desired effect of bringing the colonial economy and war effort to a standstill.

Congress, fearing a British attack on Philadelphia, fled to Baltimore. Although General Howe might have ended the war there and then through an aggressive campaign, he wanted to wear down the Continental Army and force the colonies to sue for peace. Washington did not have the troops or arms to launch a major assault, but he hoped the British would accept American independence once they saw how difficult it would be to defeat the colonies. So the war continued.

Fortunately for Washington, Howe followed the European tradition of suspending battle during the winter months. This allowed the patriots to regroup, repair weapons and wagons, and recruit soldiers. Camped in eastern Pennsylvania, Washington learned that Hessian troops (Germans paid to fight for the British) had been sent to occupy the city of Trenton, New Jersey, just across the Delaware River. On Christmas Eve, Washington's troops crossed the river to attack Trenton in an icy rain, and quickly won. They then marched on Princeton and emerged victorious once more on January 3, 1777. The British army soon retreated back to New York City.

By mid-January 1777, the tide began to turn in favor of the Continental Army, but victory was far from certain. British forces remained strong, and Washington's troops were devastated by smallpox throughout the remainder of winter. His army numbered fewer than 5,000 men when General Howe resumed battle in the spring, planning to capture Philadelphia to force a patriot surrender. Washington's force was too small to defeat Howe's army, but delayed his advance by guerrilla attacks. En route, Howe learned that he was expected to reinforce General John Burgoyne's soldiers, who were advancing south from Canada. Instead he continued inching toward Philadelphia. Meanwhile Burgoyne and his 7,200 troops regained control of Fort Ticonderoga on July 7.

Howe managed to capture Philadelphia in September 1777. But in so doing, he had withheld his troops from reinforcing General Burgoyne, who was pressing southward. In mid-September Burgoyne faced a brutal onslaught from patriot forces at Freeman's Farm, outside Saratoga, New York. The patriots defeated the British, with the British suffering twice the casualties of the Continentals. In early October, Burgoyne lost a second battle for the strategic site. The defeat proved decisive. Ten days later, he surrendered his remaining army of 5,800 men to General Gates at Saratoga.

The **Battle of Saratoga** gave an important victory to the Continental Army, and stunned the British. It undercut the significance of Howe's victory at Philadelphia and indicated the general's misunderstanding of the nature of the war he was fighting. Meanwhile the patriot victory energized Washington and his troops as they dug in at **Valley Forge** for a long winter. It also gave Benjamin Franklin, the Continental Congress envoy to Paris, greater leverage for convincing French officials to support American independence.

> **AP® TIP**
> Analyze the impact the patriot victory in the Battle of Saratoga had on the domestic war effort as well as on patriot relations with European nations.

Battle of Saratoga Key Revolutionary War battle fought at Saratoga, New York. The patriot victory there in October 1777 provided hope that the colonists could triumph and increased the chances that the French would formally join the patriot side.

REVIEW

- How did the patriot forces fare in 1776?
- How and why did the tide of war turn in 1777?

Women Contribute to the Revolution

Whether black or white, enslaved or free, women and children faced hardship and uncertainty as a result of the war. Even those who did not directly engage enemy troops took on enormous burdens: Farm wives plowed and planted and carried on their domestic duties, while in cities, women worked ceaselessly to find sufficient food, wood, candles, and cloth to care for themselves and their children. As the war intensified, Continental and British forces slaughtered cattle and hogs for food, stole corn and other crops or burned them to keep the enemy from obtaining supplies, looted houses and shops, and kidnapped or liberated enslaved people and servants.

In these desperate circumstances, many women asserted themselves in order to survive. When merchants hoarded goods to make greater profits when prices rose, housewives raided stores and warehouses and took the supplies they needed. Others learned as much as they could about finances, submitting reports to local officials when their family properties were damaged or looted. Growing numbers of women banded together to assist one another, help more impoverished families, and supply troops with badly needed clothes, food, bandages, and bullets — as did the wives of patriot leaders, who formed voluntary associations, like the Ladies Association of Philadelphia, to provide critical resources for the army.

While most women worked tirelessly on the home front, some cast their fate with the army as camp followers, who provided critical services to the military and suffered, as the troops did, from scarce supplies and harsh weather. Families living in regions surrounding battlefields were especially vulnerable to the shifting fortunes of war, but some women made the most of it, serving as spies and couriers for British or Continental forces. Lydia Darragh, a wealthy Philadelphian, eavesdropped on conversations among the British officers who occupied her house and carried detailed reports to Washington hidden in the folds of her dress. Others, like Nancy Hart Morgan of Georgia, took more direct action. Morgan lulled half a dozen British soldiers into a sense of security at dinner, hid their guns, and shot two before neighbors came to hang the rest.

Some patriot women took up arms on the battlefield. A few, such as Margaret Corbin, accompanied their husbands to the front lines. When her husband was killed in battle in 1776, Corbin took his place loading and firing cannons. In addition, a small number of women, like

AP® ANALYZING SOURCES

Source: Esther De Berdt Reed, *The Sentiments of an American Woman*, 1780

"We know that at a distance from the theatre of war, if we enjoy any tranquility, it is the fruit of your watchings, your labours, your dangers. If I live happy in the midst of my family; if my husband cultivates his field, and reaps his harvest in peace; if, surrounded with my children, I myself nourish the youngest, and press it to my bosom, without being affraid of seeing myself separated from it, by a ferocious enemy; if the house in which we dwell; if our barns, our orchards are safe at the present time from the hands of those incendiaries, it is to you that we owe it. And shall we hesitate to evidence to you our gratitude? Shall we hesitate to wear a cloathing more simple; hair dressed less elegant, while at the price of this small privation, we shall deserve your benedictions. Who, amongst us, will not renounce with the highest pleasure, those vain ornaments, when she shall consider that the valiant defenders of America will be able to draw some advantage from the money which she may have laid out in these; that they will be better defended from the rigours of the seasons, that after their painful toils, they will receive some extraordinary and unexpected relief; that these presents will perhaps be valued by them at a greater price, when they will have it in their power to say: This is the offering of the Ladies. The time is arrived to display the same sentiments which animated us at the beginning of the Revolution, when we renounced the use of teas, however agreeable to our taste, rather than receive them from our persecutors; when we made it appear to them that we placed former necessaries in the rank of superfluities, when our liberty was interested; when our republican and laborious hands spun the flax, prepared the linen intended for the use of our soldiers; when exiles and fugitives we supported with courage all the evils which are the concomitants of war. Let us not lose a moment; let us be engaged to offer the homage of our gratitude at the altar of military valour, and you, our brave deliverers, while mercenary slaves combat to cause you to share with them, the irons with which they are loaded, receive with a free hand our offering, the purest which can be presented to your virtue,

BY AN AMERICAN WOMAN"

Questions for Analysis

1. Identify the sacrifices Reed claims women have made for the Revolution.
2. Describe the ideal patriot wife, according to Reed.
3. Explain the historical situation that shaped Reed's argument.

TEACHING IDEA

Incorporating Secondary Sources

Assign students to read "Daughters of Liberty: The Women Who Fought in the Revolution" available online at Saber and Scroll (saberandscroll.weebly.com). Have students annotate the piece, and engage in a whole-class discussion on the material regarding the role of women in the Revolution. This can be a lead-in to answering the questions and discussing the piece by Ester De Berdt Reed.

TRM Suggested Responses to Questions

TRM Module 3.4 AP® Analyzing Sources Handout 1

Deborah Sampson, disguised themselves as men and enlisted as soldiers. A former indentured servant who had become a teacher since her term of service ended in 1778, Sampson disguised herself as a man and enlisted in the Continental Army. Under the name Robert Shurtliff, Sampson marched, fought, and lived with her Massachusetts regiment for a year. Her ability to carry off the deception was helped by the era's standards of hygiene: Soldiers rarely undressed fully to bathe, and most slept in their uniforms.

As in all wars, women faced fear and hardship during the American Revolution, but also embraced new opportunities in the public sphere. Women contributed significantly to the patriot cause, but they also faced serious challenges — and although many were glad of women's political and practical contributions to the war effort, patriot leaders failed to treat them as equal partners in the revolution.

REVIEW

How did the American Revolution affect the status of women in the colonies?

France Allies with the Patriots

Despite significant Continental victories in the fall of 1777, the following winter proved especially difficult. The quarters at Valley Forge were marked by bitter cold, poor food, inadequate clothing, and scarce supplies. A French volunteer arrived to see "a few militia men, poorly clad, and for the most part without shoes; many of them badly armed." Many recent recruits were also poorly trained. The Continental Army continued to be plagued by problems of recruitment, discipline, wages, and supplies. Critical assistance from foreign volunteers arrived with Baron Friedrich von Steuben, a Prussian officer recruited by Benjamin Franklin, the Marquis de Lafayette of France, Johann Baron de Kalb of Bavaria, and Thaddeus Kosciusko and Casimir Pulaski, both of Poland. Despite these contributions and the strong leadership of Washington and his officers, the Continental Congress considered an alliance with France critical to patriot success. In December 1776, the congress sent Benjamin Franklin to Paris to serve as its unofficial liaison. Franklin was enormously successful, securing supplies and becoming a favorite among the French aristocracy and ordinary citizens alike. France's long rivalry with Britain made it a likely ally, and the French government had secretly provided funds to the patriots early in the war.

The French initially resisted a formal compact with the upstart patriots. Only after the patriot victory at Saratoga in October 1777 did the French king agree to an alliance. In February 1778, Franklin secured an agreement that approved trading rights between the United States and all French possessions. France then recognized the United States as an independent nation, relinquished French territorial claims on mainland North America, and sent troops to reinforce the Continental Army. In return, the United States promised to defend French holdings in the Caribbean. A year later, Spain allied itself with France to protect its own North American holdings.

Portrait of the Marquis de La Fayette with an Aide-de-Camp during the American War of Independence (oil on campus), French School, (18th century)/Musee de la Ville de Paris, Musee Carnavalet, Paris, France/Archives Charmet/Bridgeman Images

◀ **The Marquis de La Fayette with an Aide-de-Camp**
This eighteenth-century portrait of the Marquis de Lafayette was painted by a Frenchman during the Revolution. It shows him with his aide-de-camp, probably from the French West Indies. Lafayette joined the Continental Army in September 1777, led patriot forces in numerous battles, camped at Valley Forge, and trapped British forces under General Cornwallis at the decisive Siege of Yorktown. **In what ways does this image portray the American Revolution as a conflict with international effects?**

TEACHING IDEA

Analyzing Art and Images

Assign students to access the Library of Congress website to view numerous versions of the image, "Molly Pitcher at the Battle of Monmouth, June 1778" (loc.gov). Have students discuss the significance of the images' portrayal of the role of women in the revolution, as well as the audience, purpose, and point of view of the images, in line with HIPP training that students have previously encountered (a refresher of HIPP can be found on page 8).

EXPLORING AP® THEMES

America in the World

This is a good place to revisit the previously introduced concept of realpolitik with students. Emphasize that regardless of their degree of zeal for their cause, the Revolutionary colonists faced virtually no prospects for success without financial and military assistance from outside European powers. Further emphasize that from the French and Spanish points of view, assistance provided to the colonists represented a marriage of convenience to further their foreign policy aims.

AP® ANALYZING SOURCES

Source: *Treaty of Alliance between the United States and France*, 1778

"The most Christian king and the United States of North-America, . . . having resolved . . . to join their councils and efforts against the enterprizes of their common enemy, . . . have, after the most mature deliberation, concluded and determined on the following articles:

Art. 1. If war should break out between France and Great-Britain, during the continuance of the present war between the United States and England, his majesty and the said United States, shall make it a common cause, and aid each other mutually with their good offices, their counsels and their forces, . . . as becomes good and faithful allies.

Art. 2. The essential and direct end of the present defensive alliance, is, to maintain effectually the liberty, sovereignty and independence, absolute and unlimited, of the said United States, as well in matters of government as of commerce.

Art. 3. The two contracting parties shall, each on its own part, and in the manner it may judge most proper, make all the efforts in its power against their common enemy, in order to attain the end proposed."

Questions for Analysis
1. Describe the causes motivating the French to ally with the United States.
2. Explain the effects that France's recognition of the United States government had on other nations.
3. Evaluate the relative importance of political, economic, and military motivations behind a French alliance with the United States.

TRM Suggested Responses to Questions

TRM Module 3.4 AP® Analyzing Sources Handout 2

TEACHING IDEA

Six Degrees of Separation

Have students in groups create a chain of historical causation in response to the following six degrees prompt: "From the Treaty of Paris of 1763 to the signing of the Franco-American Treaty of Alliance in 1778."

TEACHING IDEA

Differing Views

Assign students to read one of two articles from the JSTOR archive, either Lawrence Kaplan, "Toward Isolationism: The Jeffersonian Republicans and the Franco-American Alliance of 1778" or Marie-Jeanne Rossignol, "Early Isolationism Revisited: Neutrality and Beyond in the 1790s" (jstor.org).

Then, pair up students assigned each article, and have them explain their assigned author's thesis and main points. After each has done so, have the pair take a position as to which author makes the more compelling argument. Tabulate these conclusions for the entire class as the basis for an overall class discussion on the two monographs.

AP® TIP
Take note of both the intended and the unintended results of the developing alliance between France and the Continental Congress.

British leaders responded by declaring war on France. Yet doing so ensured that military conflicts would spread well beyond North America and military expenditures would skyrocket. French forces attacked British outposts in Gibraltar, the Bay of Bengal, Senegal in West Africa, and Grenada in the West Indies. At the same time, the French supplied the United States with military officers, weapons, funds, and critical naval support. Faced with this new alliance, Britain's Prime Minister Lord North (1771–1782) decided to concentrate British forces in New York City. For the remainder of the war, New York City provided the sole British stronghold in the North, serving as a supply center and prisoner-of-war camp.

The French alliance did create one unintended problem for the Continental Army. When Americans heard that France was sending troops, fewer men volunteered for military service. As the war dragged on, fewer and fewer men volunteered to fight. Bonuses paid to enlistees produced ever-declining results. Local officials had the authority to draft men into the army or to accept substitutes for draftees. In the late 1770s, some draftees forced enslaved men to take their place; others hired landless laborers, the handicapped, or the mentally unfit as substitutes.

As the war spread south and west in 1778–1779, Continental forces were stretched thin, and enlistments faltered further. Soldiers faced injuries, disease, and shortages of food and ammunition. They also risked capture by the British, one of the worst fates to befall a Continental. Considered traitors by the British, most captives were held on ships in New York harbor. They faced filthy accommodations, a horrid stench, inadequate water, and widespread disease and abuse. Altogether, between 8,000 and 11,500 patriots died in British prisons in New York — more than died in battle.

The Continental Congress faced enormous financial problems. With no authority to impose taxes on American citizens, the congress resorted to borrowing money from wealthy patriots, accepting loans from France and the Netherlands, and printing money of its own — some $200 million by 1780. However, money printed by the states was used far more widely than were Continental dollars. "Continentals" depreciated so quickly that by late 1780 it took one hundred

TEACHING IDEA

Making Connections

Some of the consistent domestic economic byproducts of warfare in any society are increased inflation and taxation. For Americans of the Revolutionary Era, this was no exception. Point this out to students, and have them engage in investigative inquiry to determine some of the reasons why this was the case.

APPLY THE TIP

Pair up students and have them create a list of the economic problems that plagued the new government and the new nation. Then, have the paired groups join up into groups of six and have students share their lists. Next, have them determine which problem or problems are the gravest, and also attempt to create solutions to some of the problems via role-play or simulation, that they will then share with the whole class.

▲ **MAP 3.4 The War in the North, 1775–1778** After early battles in Massachusetts, patriots invaded Canada but failed to capture Quebec. The British army captured New York City in 1776 and Philadelphia in 1777, but New Jersey remained a battle zone through 1778. Meanwhile General Burgoyne secured Canada for Britain and then headed south, but his forces were defeated by patriots at the crucial Battle of Saratoga. **Why did the British focus on capturing port cities during the early battles of the American Revolution? What were the effects of this strategy?**

> **AP® TIP**
> Analyze how economic problems affected the development of government during the American Revolution.

continentals to buy one silver dollar's worth of goods. Mired in a chaotic wartime economy, by 1779 the cost of goods skyrocketed. Housewives, sailors, and artisans in Philadelphia and other cities attacked merchants who were hoarding goods, forcing officials to distribute food to the poor. The congress finally improved its financial standing slightly by using a $6 million loan from France to back certificates issued to wealthy patriots. Meanwhile states raised money through taxes to provide funds for government operations, backing for its paper money, and other expenses. Most residents found such taxes incredibly burdensome given wartime inflation, and even the most patriotic began to protest increased taxation. Thus the financial status of the new nation remained precarious.

REVIEW

In what ways did the American Revolution become an international conflict by 1780?

Patriots Achieve Victory

From 1778 to 1781, the battlefront in the Revolution moved south, as the King George III believed that southern colonists' sympathies were more loyalist than patriot. British troops captured Savannah, Georgia in 1778 and soon extended their control over the entire state. In May 1780, General Charles Cornwallis reclaimed Charleston, South Carolina. He then evicted patriots from the city, purged them from the state government, gained military control of the state, and imposed loyalty oaths on all Carolinians able to fight. To aid his efforts, local loyalists organized militias to battle patriots in the interior. Banastre Tarleton led one especially vicious company of loyalists in slaughtering civilians and murdering many patriots who surrendered. In retaliation, patriot planter Thomas Sumter organized 800 men who showed a similar disregard for regular army procedures, raiding largely defenseless loyalist settlements.

By 1780 British chances for victory seemed more hopeful. Cornwallis was in control of Georgia and South Carolina, and local loyalists were eager to gain control of the southern countryside. Meanwhile Continental soldiers in the North mutinied in early 1780 over enlistment terms and pay. Patriot morale was low, funds were scarce, and civilians were growing weary of the war.

Yet somehow the patriots prevailed. A combination of luck, strong leadership, and French support turned the tide. In October 1780, when Continental hopes looked especially bleak, a group of 800 patriots routed loyalist troops and keeping Cornwallis from advancing into North Carolina. Continental forces supplemented by local patriot militias then checked Cornwallis in South Carolina. British troops suffered enormous losses, and Continentals had a chance to regroup.

In August 1781, frustrated at the large amount of local support patriots carried in the South, Cornwallis hunkered down in Yorktown on the Virginia coast and waited for reinforcements from New York. In response, Washington coordinated strategy with French allies to cut off Cornwallis's escape. Comte de Rochambeau, a French nobleman, marched 5,000 troops south from Rhode Island to Virginia as General Lafayette led his troops south along Virginia's eastern shore. At the same time, French naval ships headed north from the West Indies. One French naval unit cut off a British fleet trying to resupply Cornwallis by sea while another joined up with Americans to bombard Cornwallis's forces. By mid-October, British supplies had run out, and it was clear that reinforcements would not be forthcoming. On October 19, 1781, at the **Battle of Yorktown**, Cornwallis and the British army admitted defeat.

The Continental Army had managed the impossible. It had defeated the British army and won the colonies' independence. Yet even with the surrender after the Battle of Yorktown, the war continued here and there. Peace negotiations in Paris dragged on as French, Spanish, British, and American representatives sought to settle a host of issues. Meanwhile, British forces challenged Continental troops in and around New York City. Patriot representatives in Paris — Benjamin Franklin, John Adams, and John Jay — continued to negotiate peace terms, but the French foreign minister opposed the Americans' republican principles. Given the importance of the French to the American victory, the Continental Congress had instructed its delegates to defer to French wishes. This blocked the American representatives from signing a separate peace with the British. Eventually U.S. delegates finalized a treaty that secured substantial benefits for the young nation. Its terms granted the United States control of all lands south of Canada and north of Louisiana and Florida stretching to the Mississippi River. In addition, the treaty recognized the United States to be "free Sovereign and independent states." Spain signed a separate treaty with Great Britain in which it regained control of Florida. Despite their role in the war, none of the American Indian nations that occupied the lands under negotiation were consulted. On September 2, 1783, delegates

Battle of Yorktown Decisive battle in which the surrender of British forces on October 19, 1781, at Yorktown, Virginia, effectively sealed the patriot victory in the American Revolution.

TEACHING IDEA

Incorporating Videos

Have Students watch the PBS documentary, "Liberty! The American Revolution – Episode 5" (available on YouTube).

EXPLORING AP® THEMES

American and National Identity

An important point to make with students here is how the ignoring of American Indians in Great Power treaty negotiations was to be a constant in American diplomatic history. This can be used as a springboard into classroom discussion concerning colonial views of who was and was not considered an American for the purposes of citizenship and rights.

TEACHING IDEA

Geography Instruction

After studying the map on this page, engage the students in a discussion to explain the tactical and strategic reasons why drawing the British forces into the interior was so important to American success in the southern campaigns of the Revolution.

TRM Find **Handout 3.5 – Competing Strategies for Victory in the Revolutionary War** in the Teacher's Resource Materials.

TEACHING IDEA

Check for Understanding

Assign students to do online research to compile a specific itemization of the terms and conditions established by the Treaty of Paris of 1783. Once they have done so, have them in pairs answer the following question for each of the terms and conditions: "What will this mean for the new nation?"

▲ **MAP 3.5 The War in the West and the South, 1777–1782** Between 1780 and 1781, major battles between Continental and British troops took place in Virginia and the Carolinas, and the British general Cornwallis finally surrendered at Yorktown, Virginia in October 1781. But patriot forces also battled British troops and their American Indian allies from 1777 to 1782 in the Ohio River valley, the lower Mississippi River, and the Gulf coast. **How do the battles shown on this map differ from those in the northeast?**

Treaty (Peace) of Paris
1783 treaty that formally ended the American Revolution.

of the United States and Britain signed the **Treaty (Peace) of Paris**, formally ending the American Revolution.

Americans had managed to defeat one of the most powerful military forces in the world. That victory resulted from the convergence of many circumstances. Certainly Americans benefited from fighting on their own soil. Their knowledge of the land and its resources as well as earlier experiences fighting against American Indians and the French helped prepare them for battles against the British.

Just as important, British troops and officers were far removed from centers of decision making and supplies. Even supplies housed in Canada could not be easily transported the relatively short distance into New York. British commanders were often hesitant to make decisions independently, but awaiting instructions from England proved costly on several occasions, especially since strategists in London often had little sense of conditions in America.

Both sides depended on outsiders for assistance, but here, too, Americans gained the advantage. The British army relied heavily on German mercenaries, American Indian allies, and freedpeople to bolster its regular troops. In victory, such "foreign" forces were relatively reliable, but in defeat, many of them chose to look out for their own interests. The patriots meanwhile marched with French and Spanish armies well prepared to challenge British troops and motivated to gain advantages for France and Spain if Britain was defeated.

TEACHING IDEA

Building Vocabulary

Explain the distinction to students between the terms "strategy" and "tactics." The former represents the overall plan to achieve victory, while the latter constitutes the day to day specific steps and means to implement and fulfill the strategy. With these definitions laid out, have student groups choose a graphic organizer template to employ to depict the strategy and tactics of the Continental Army in the Revolutionary War.

Perhaps most important, a British victory was nearly impossible without conquering new American states one by one. Mobilized by Enlightenment ideals articulated in the Declaration of Independence, a large percentage of colonists now supported the patriot cause. British troops would have to contend not only with Continental soldiers but also with an aroused citizenry fighting for independence.

AP® ANALYZING SOURCES

Source: *Treaty of Paris*, 1783

"**Article I**
His Brittanic Majesty acknowledges the said United States . . . to be free, sovereign and independent States; that he treats with them as such; and for himself, his heirs and successors, relinquishes all claims to the gouvernment, propriety and territorial rights of the same, and every part thereof. . . .

Article V
It is agreed that Congress shall earnestly recommend it to the legislatures of the respective states, to provide for the restitution of all estates, rights and properties, which have been confiscated, belonging to real British subjects, and also of the estates, rights and properties of persons resident in districts in the possession of his Majesty's arms, and who have not borne arms against the said United States. And that persons of any other description shall have free liberty to go to any part or parts of any of the thirteen United States, and therein to remain twelve months, unmolested in their endeavours to obtain the restitution of such of their estates, rights and properties, as may have been confiscated; and that Congress shall also earnestly recommend to the several states a reconsideration and revision of all acts or laws regarding the premises, so as to render the said laws or acts perfectly consistent, not only with justice and equity, but with that spirit of conciliation, which on the return of the blessings of peace should universally prevail."

Questions for Analysis

1. Identify one intended audience of the Treaty of Paris, and explain how this passage appeals to that audience.
2. Identify another intended audience of the Treaty of Paris, and explain how this passage appeals to that audience.
3. Describe the key provisions in these articles of the treaty.
4. Evaluate the extent to which ideals of the American Revolution shaped the Treaty of Paris.

REVIEW

What major factors allowed the Americans to win the American Revolution?

AP® WRITING HISTORICALLY — Evaluating Effects in an Essay

As you recall from Module 3-1, historians deepen analyses of causes and effects by evaluating their significance, particularly in relation to other historical developments. In doing so, historians decide how significant certain causes and effects are in the grand scheme of history — which means that they commonly argue certain causes and effects are more responsible for a given development than others. Remember, historical evidence is a crucial aspect of historical arguments. It helps establish that some causes and effects of a given development have the level of significance an argument assigns to them.

In this course, and on the exam, you will often be asked to consider causation the way a historian would: by taking — and defending — a position about the relative importance of particular

(Continued)

TRM Suggested Responses to Questions

TRM Module 3.4 AP® Analyzing Sources Handout 3

TEACHING IDEA

Incorporating Videos

Assign students to watch Adam Norris's "APUSH Review: Video #12: Events Leading To The American Revolution" (available on YouTube). Use this 8-minute episode as a concise content review for students of the major issues and events of the conflict of the American Revolution itself as part of preparation for either assessment or reinforcement antecedent to moving forward into the next module.

TRM Suggested Responses to Questions

Period 3: 1754–1800

MODULE 3-4 Winning the War for Independence

patterns or developments. Although we focused solely on how to evaluate causes in Module 3-1, it's important to remember that causation is like a coin, with causes on one side and effects on the other. Here, we'll walk you through how an essay prompt might ask you to make an argument about the relative importance of effects of a specific historical development:

> Evaluate the relative significance of the United States' alliance with France during the American Revolution.

Step 1 Break down the prompt.
In this module, you read about how the Continental Army emerged victorious from the American Revolution. The time period specified by the prompt lets you know that you can and should draw on what you learned in previous modules to construct your answer. Remember that you may want to consider and discuss other factors besides the alliance between the U.S. and France as you plan your argument about how important that alliance was.

Step 2 List and categorize your historical knowledge.
Use Module 3-1 through 3-4, along with any relevant knowledge drawn from your classwork, to make a list of the events that contributed to American victory and can be directly tied to the alliance with France.

Just as in Module 3-1, creating a continuum to map the relationships between and among concepts and events will help you make important judgment calls about how significant a given development really is to the topic at hand — in this case, patriot victory in the American Revolution. Next, place your effects into a chart, adding a column to explain why you ranked each as higher or lower in significance. The following model shows the first row of a table that you could make in response to the prompt:

Effects of French Alliance	Relative Significance	Explanation of Significance
The assistance of the French Navy	Greater Effect	A highly significant effect of the French alliance was the assistance of the French Navy. The French Navy kept the English Navy busy preventing easy resupply and movement of troops, and played a key role in trapping Cornwallis at Yorktown leading to the British surrender.

ACTIVITY
Complete the chart in step 2 by identifying, evaluating the significance of, and explaining at least two additional effects of the French alliance with the Americans. Make sure that more than one level of significance is represented in your finished chart.
Then, write an introductory paragraph for the example prompt at the beginning of this box. Be sure that your paragraph includes a contextualization statement that leads to a thesis statement. Your thesis should draw on your pre-writing and include three claims of causes and effects of the French alliance with the Americans. You may use the following outline to help organize your paragraph.

I. Introductory paragraph
   A. Immediate/preceding contextualization statement
      1. Cite evidence of immediate/preceding context
      2. Explain influence of immediate/preceding context
   B. Thesis statement presenting three evaluative claims about the United States' alliance with France during the American Revolution, situated along a continuum of relative significance. For example: "While the French alliance was significant because ... and ... other factors like ... were relatively less significance to the Patriot cause."

BUILDING AP® SKILLS
Contextualization

Place students into groups of 3 or 4 and instruct them to establish a back-story addressing the review question on page 193. Have them engage in the contextualization-building exercise known as 4-1-1, whereby they must create an introductory paragraph consisting of four sentences of contextualization, one sentence for a thesis, and one sentence for a plan of attack in their paper.

▲ **Differentiation**

For an additional challenge, break up and recombine the students into groups where they are each with new and different partners from the first exercise. Allow students time to do peer review and critique of each other's opening paragraphs, and then have each group craft a newer, stronger product based upon their reviewing and sharing. Lastly, assign each group to provide specific evidence that could be used within the main body of a paper to support their argument. This assignment could either be in class the same day, the next day, or for homework.

TEACHING IDEA

AP® Writing Historically Workshop

The goal of this workshop activity is to help students prepare to complete the activity on this page. Provide students with the following list of important effects of the French-American alliance: trade agreements, improved morale, agreement to fight the duration of the war, no territorial gains by French government. Now that students have a list of appropriate information, have them select the two examples they know best. Now they are ready to order the information from greatest to least important for their body paragraph.

Module 3-5

Governing in Revolutionary Times, 1776–1787

LEARNING TARGETS
By the end of this module, you should be able to:
- Explain how colonial governments changed during the American Revolution.
- Explain the different ideas about the appropriate structure of government that patriots held during this period.

THEMATIC FOCUS
Politics and Power

In the aftermath of the American Revolution, Americans debated the proper role of a national government and faced internal conflicts that challenged the ideals of the American Revolution itself.

HISTORICAL REASONING FOCUS
Comparison

TASK ▶ As you read the rest of Module 3-5, think comparatively by noting similarities and differences in the new governments that formed between the outset of the American Revolution, in 1776, and the early years of the United States, from 1783 to 1787. As you do, ask yourself some questions: Are these governments best characterized by their similarities to each other, or by their differences? How important are each of these similarities and differences in the context of the ideology of the American Revolution? Think about how you can use the answers to these questions to support a historical argument.

Amid the constant upheavals of war, patriot leaders established new governments. At the national level, responsibilities ranged from coordinating and funding military operations to developing diplomatic relations with foreign countries and American Indian nations. At the state level, they wrote and **ratified** constitutions, enforced laws, and attempted to raise men, funds, and material support for the military efforts both local and continental. Whether state or national, new governments tried to assure their followers that they were not simply replacing old forms of oppression with new ones.

States Form Their Own Governments, 1776–1786

Without a formal central government, state governments played crucial roles throughout the American Revolution. Even before the Continental Congress declared American independence, some colonies had forced royal officials to flee and established new state governments. Some states abided by the regulations in their colonial charters or by English common law. Others created new governments based on a written constitution.

These constitutions reflected the context of opposition to centralized power fueled by the struggle against British tyranny. In Pennsylvania, patriots developed one of the most democratic constitutions. They replaced the governor with an executive council. The legislature consisted of a single house elected by popular vote. Legislators could only serve for four in any seven years to discourage the formation of a political aristocracy. Although Pennsylvania's constitution was among the most radical, all states limited centralized power in some way.

TRM Suggested Responses to Questions

BUILDING AP® SKILLS
Continuity and Change

Have students combine themselves into groups of 3 or 4, and instruct them to create a timeline entitled "Colonial/American incidents of resentment of distant authority, 1607–1787," using Periods 2 and 3 of their textbook as a resource. This exercise should help students to visually process the notion that colonial recalcitrance in the face of external pressures was an idea of long-standing. Furthermore, it will be illuminating for students to discover that the word "distant" is a relative term, and that elements of colonial/American society could and did feel the intrusion of the state from leadership both imperial and national.

▲ **Differentiation**

After the timeline is complete, create new teacher-combined student groups in pairs whereby advanced students are paired with struggling students to prepare a short biopic on two of the timeline incidents. The specific incidents will be teacher-assigned to each student pair. Upon completion of this task, have student pairs fold into quads to teach and share, and then from there into groups of eight to further teach and share. This will benefit students of all levels as they can both grow into the process, and then take on roles to share their knowledge with others who had different topics, ultimately concluding in a large-scale overall product of thorough chronological organization and factual detail.

TEACHING IDEA

Differing Views

Write, "the United <u>States</u>" on the board, underlining the word "States." Then next to it, write, "the <u>United</u> States," underlining the word "United." Ask students to explain if they see any difference in meaning or distinction between the two phrases, and elaborate upon what those differences and distinctions are. Discuss with students the potential challenges and pitfalls of each quoted perspective for the new nation as it takes its place as an independent nation-state in a world of empires and monarchies.

TEACHING IDEA

Additional Practice

Have students in small groups address the following LEQ prompt: "Evaluate the extent to which the Declaration of Independence's assertion that 'All men are created equal' was manifested in the daily lives of the American people in the period 1776–1787." Have students create the essay components of context and thesis for this prompt, and then share those out, leading to a full class discussion on the concept.

TEACHING IDEA

Connecting the Dots

Discuss with students that the Revolution created a momentum for freedom that the founders could not anticipate or fully control. When the conflict began, few could have foreseen the contradictions that the conflict would expose with regards to organized religion, slavery, voting rights, gender rights, and American Indians.

EXPLORING AP® THEMES

Politics and Power

Discuss with students how the widespread diffusion of a variety of religious practices and faiths at this time almost naturally would lead to no one denomination wanting to trust any of the others with the levers of governmental power and authority. As such, the only practical solution over time came to be having religion officially separated from state power. This becomes the pragmatic origin point of the separation of church and state, whereby each denomination surrenders any specific claim to secular powers, as a form of "mutually agreed unilateral disarmament."

AP® TIP

Analyze how social structures and specific historical developments in each colony shaped the state governments that developed during the American Revolution.

As a check against tyranny, most states adopted Virginia's model, including a bill of rights in their constitutions that ensured citizens' rights and freedoms: freedom of the press, freedom of elections, the right to speedy trials by one's peers, the right to humane punishments, and the right to form militias. Some states also insisted on people's freedom of speech and assembly, the right to petition and to bear arms, and equal protection of the laws. Almost all prohibited titles of nobility and any symbols of inherited aristocracy, such as family crests and shields.

The New Jersey constitution of 1776 gave all free inhabitants who met the property qualifications the right to vote in elections, thus allowing some propertied single and widowed women and free black people to vote — until New Jersey passed a law specifically limiting the franchise to men in 1807. Most new state constitutions, however, allowed only white men with property to vote. Nearly all granted significant power to the legislative branch, where white men of property dominated.

During the Revolution few legislatures moved in any way to eliminate the most oppressive institution, slavery. The exception was Vermont. Already containing only a few enslaved people, it abolished slavery in its 1777 constitution. The new Pennsylvania state legislature also passed a gradual abolition law in 1780 — under it, all African American children born enslaved could claim freedom at the age of twenty-eight.

The creation of new state constitutions also generally marked the end of the line for direct government sponsorship of churches. In many states, freedom of religion became a guaranteed right. In other states, legislatures made laws in the 1780s that reduced or eliminated government funds for religion. Anglican churches had long benefited from British support by taxing residents to support their ministries during the Revolution. These taxes in effect privileged one form of Christianity over other faiths, and were ended as a result of new guarantees of free worship.

But more than wartime tactics, what prompted the biggest change in how the states approached religious practices was the fact that white Americans no longer generally shared the Anglican faith. Churches that had dominated the various colonies now faced greater competition, especially in frontier areas, where offshoots like the Baptists and Methodists gained thousands of converts. The Society of Friends, or Quakers, and the Presbyterians also gained new followers during the latter half of the eighteenth century, while Catholics and Jews experienced greater tolerance than in the colonial era as a result of a growing ethos of religious freedom that uncoupled religious practice from secular government. This ensured that no single religious voice or perspective dominated the new nation. Instead, all Christians competed for members, money, and political influence. After the Revolution, in 1786, the Virginia Assembly approved the **Statute of Religious Freedom**, which made church attendance and support voluntary. Many other states followed Virginia's lead.

Statute of Religious Freedom
1786 Virginia Assembly statute that ensured the separation of church and state and largely guaranteed freedom of religion. Many other states followed Virginia's lead.

REVIEW

- What similarities did the new state governments share between 1776 and 1786?
- What accounted for the differences between these governments?

A Revolutionary National Government, 1777–1781

For most of the American Revolution, the Continental Congress acted in place of a national government while the delegates worked to devise a more permanent structure. In 1777, they drafted the Articles of Confederation, which created a central government with limited powers. They submitted them to the states for approval, and while eight of the thirteen ratified the plan by mid-1778, some states delayed while the delegates worked to resolve conflicting land claims in the trans-Appalachian west. Nearly three more years passed before the last state, Maryland, approved the Articles.

TEACHING IDEA

Connecting the Dots

This would be a useful point to walk through the sequence of American governing bodies for students, to assure their understanding of them. Write on the board or display on the projector the following heading: "The Sequence of American Government, 1776–1787." Then list underneath that heading, one at a time and with a brief discussion of each, the following entities:

- First Continental Congress, 1774–1775
- Second Continental Congress, 1775–1777
- Articles of Confederation, 1777–1787
- Constitution, 1787–present

Students need to be able to distinguish between the temporal, ad-hoc nature of the first two entities and the more formalized nature of the last two. To that point, it may be useful to share with students the idea that the Articles government may best be referred to as "U.S. Government, version 1.0," and the constitutional government as, "U.S. Government, version 2.0."

A Revolutionary National Government, 1777–1781

Period 3: 1754–1800

Many patriot leaders made it clear that independence would mean further expansion and had little regard for American Indians, much of whose land had already been claimed when the states were still colonies. States like Connecticut, Georgia, New York, Massachusetts, and Virginia hoped to use western lands to reward soldiers and expand their settlements. States without such claims, like Maryland, argued that if such lands were "wrested from the common enemy by the blood and treasure of the thirteen States," they should be considered "common property, subject to be parceled out by Congress into free and independent governments." In 1780 New York State finally ceded its western claims to the Continental Congress, and others followed suit.

With land disputes settled, Maryland ratified the **Articles of Confederation** in March 1781. A new national government was finally formed, unifying the rebellious states just as it appeared they would gain their independence. Still, the Continental Congress's guarantee that western lands would be "disposed of for the common benefit of the United States" ensured continued conflicts with American Indians as the Confederation government took charge.

Articles of Confederation
Plan for national government proposed by the Continental Congress of 1777 and ratified in March 1781. The Articles of Confederation gave the national government limited powers, reflecting widespread fear of centralized authority, and were replaced by the Constitution in 1789.

AP® ANALYZING SOURCES

Source: Articles of Confederation, 1781

"ART. 2. Each state retains its sovereignty, freedom, and independence, and every power, jurisdiction, and right which is not by this Confederation expressly delegated to the United States in Congress assembled.

ART. 3. The said states hereby severally enter into a firm league of friendship with each other for their common defence, the security of their liberties, and their mutual and general welfare; binding themselves to assist each other against all force offered to or attacks made upon them on account of religion, sovereignty, trade, or any other pretence whatever. . . .

ART. 9. . . . The United States in Congress assembled shall never engage in a war nor grant letters of marque[1] or reprisal in time of peace, nor enter into any treaties or alliances, nor coin money nor regulate the value thereof, nor ascertain the sums and expenses necessary for the defence and welfare of the United States, or any of them; nor emit bills, nor borrow money on the credit of the United States, nor appropriate money, nor agree upon the number of vessels of war to be built or purchased, or the number of land or sea forces to be raised, nor appoint a commander-in-chief of the army or navy, unless nine states assent to the same; nor shall a question on any other point, except for adjourning from day to day, be determined, unless by the votes of a majority of the United States in Congress assembled. . . .

ART. 13. Every state shall abide by the determinations of the United States in Congress assembled on all questions which by this Confederation are submitted to them. And the Articles of this Confederation shall be inviolably observed by every state, and the Union shall be perpetual; nor shall any alteration at any time hereafter be made in any of them; unless such alteration be agreed to in a Congress of the United States, and be afterwards confirmed by the legislatures of every state."

[1]An authorization to commit piracy.

Questions for Analysis

1. Identify the powers these articles give the new national government.
2. Identify the powers these articles give state governments.
3. Explain how the Articles of Confederation were designed to prevent laws like the acts of the 1760s and 1770s that so angered the colonists.

REVIEW

How did the Articles of Confederation government's policies on western expansion compare to those of the British crown prior to the American Revolution?

TRM Suggested Responses to Questions

TRM Module 3.5 AP® Analyzing Sources Handout 1

TEACHING IDEA

Discussing Political Changes

Provide students with a basic list of facts about the structure of the Articles of Confederation government, the challenges it faced, and the policies it enacted. Then have students create a chart whereby they itemize each fact from the list as a "strength" or "weakness." Next, have students further categorize the strengths or weaknesses as either "legal," "political," "economic, "diplomatic," or "organizational." Have students discuss and elaborate upon the patterns that emerge.

TRM Find **Handout 3.6 – Strengths and Weaknesses of the Articles of Confederation** in the Teacher's Resource Materials.

EXPLORING AP® THEMES

American and National Identity

Have students discuss in groups of six to eight the following questions:

- "Based upon your study of American history thus far, at this point, who was 'An American'?"

- "What does this say about the founders? What does this say about us generally?"

- "What challenges does this create for or explain about our own time?"

Instructors may wish to initially provide some exemplary groups of people for students to consider as a line of departure, such as women, enslaved Africans, American Indians, property owners, etc.

BUILDING AP® SKILLS

Argumentation

This would be a good time to engage in a thesis-building exercise. Place students into groups of three, and instruct them to craft a thesis and plan of attack in response to the review question on this page. When this is complete, place the products on the board or on butcher paper. Have the class vote on which thesis they believe is the best one. Once the class has established a winning thesis, instruct students that they will be writing or outlining (teacher's discretion) a response to the prompt using the winning thesis/plan of attack from this exercise as their shared common introduction during the next class meeting.

Period 3: 1754–1800

MODULE 3-5   Governing in Revolutionary Times, 1776–1787

TEACHING IDEA

Connecting the Dots

It is important here to discuss with students that the United States' economic woes as a new republic had deep roots from the nation's previous life as a set of imperial colonies. Under the British policy of mercantilism, the natural economic growth and development that would have taken place as they grew was artificially stunted to keep them both dependent upon Britain and operating to the maximal benefit of British self-interest over their own. As such, the fledgling United States had an economy that was much more fragile and dependent upon the whims and policies of outside powers and commerce than was desired.

APPLY THE TIP

Place students into pairs and have them create a list of obstacles and challenges the new government faced. Then pair up the pairs of students into quads, and have them share their respective products, and then come up with an overall rank order for their collective challenges. This can then be used as material for a thesis-writing exercise by the instructor if so desired.

TEACHING IDEA

Understanding Political Changes

Make sure that students understand that much of the legal justification the British empire used for keeping troops on the western frontier and giving aid and comfort to American Indian tribes there, in violation of the Treaty of Paris of 1783, was due to the United States' violations of the same treaty with regards to the lack of fair treatment and compensation of loyalist colonists after the war. This became the pretext for many of the British policies and actions in the upper Great Lakes region, which reflected what the British empire wanted to do all along: to hamstring the new United States early and often.

New Economic Challenges, 1780–1783

The United States faced serious financial instability in its formative years. As the American Revolution ground to an end, issues of military pay sparked conflict and threatened the new nation. Some Continental soldiers continued to fight, but others focused on the long-festering issue of overdue wages. Uprisings by ordinary soldiers were common but successfully suppressed by Washington, who maintained a uniquely well-fed and loyal unit for such purposes. When the Continental Congress decided in June 1783 to discharge the remaining troops without providing back pay, a near mutiny erupted in Pennsylvania, where nearly three hundred soldiers marched on the congress in Philadelphia. Washington sent troops to put down the mutiny, but bloodshed was avoided when the Pennsylvania soldiers agreed to accept half pay and certificates for the remainder. Despite this compromise, the issue of back pay would continue to plague the nation.

Complaints from Continental officers about payment, however, posed a greater problem. In 1780 officers extracted a promise from the Continental Congress for half pay for life but had received no pay at all in the last years of the war. Officers encamped at Newburgh, New York, awaiting a peace treaty, petitioned the confederation government in December 1782 for back pay for themselves and their soldiers, again with no success. By March 1783, most soldiers had returned home without pay, but some five hundred officers remained at Newburgh. Quietly encouraged by political supporters, dissident officers circulated veiled threats of a military takeover. However, on March 15, the officers were confronted by General George Washington. In an emotional speech, he urged them to respect civilian control of the government. Congressional leaders promised the officers full pay for five years. However, lacking sufficient funds, they could provide only "commutation certificates," promising future payment.

Many confederation leaders, such as Alexander Hamilton, were sympathetic to the officers' plight and hoped to use pressure from this formidable group to enhance the powers of the congress. Hamilton had been pressing state governments to grant the confederation congress a new duty of 5 percent on imported goods in order to provide the federal government with an independent source of revenue. The threat posed by an uprising of Continental Army officers proved useful in his efforts to convince states like New York to agree to his plan.

Despite such efforts at creating revenue, the economy declined further as post-war American diplomacy failed to open up international trade. In 1783 the British Parliament denied the United States the right to trade with the British West Indies. The following year, Spain, seeking leverage against the United States in disputes over western territories, prohibited American ships from accessing the port of New Orleans. Spain and Great Britain also threatened U.S. sovereignty by conspiring with American citizens on the frontier, promising them protection from American Indians. To arrange that protection they offered American Indians lucrative trade, including guns. At the same time, British troops remained in forts on America's western frontier and urged American Indians to harass settlers there. Off the coast of North Africa, Barbary pirates attacked U.S. merchant ships. These international obstacles to United States trade after the Revolution slowed the economic growth necessary to stabilize the new nation.

Almost immediately after achieving independence, financial distress among small farmers and tensions with American Indians on the western frontier intensified concerns that the confederation government was not up to ensuring order and prosperity for its citizens. While some patriots demanded a new political compact to strengthen the national government, others feared reproducing British tyranny.

> **AP® TIP**
>
> Analyze the various challenges facing the new republic after victory in the American Revolution. As you continue to read Period 3, evaluate the relative significance of these obstacles to creating a stable government.

REVIEW

What financial challenges did the new national government face during the American Revolution?

Conflicts Over Western Lands, 1778–1787

The Continental Congress struggled to settle western land claims, and patriots had an uphill climb to build alliances with additional American Indian nations. The two issues were intertwined, and both were difficult to resolve. Most American Indian nations had long-standing complaints against colonists who intruded on their lands, and many patriot leaders made it clear that independence would mean further expansion. Regardless of American Indian rights, new states claimed western lands, and after a 1777 proposal under the Articles of Confederation to use lands in the

TEACHING IDEA

Incorporating Primary Sources

The Gilder Lehrman website provides students with a series of documents regarding the Newburgh Conspiracy from several points of view (ap.gilderlehrman.org). Assign students in groups to read and break down three to five documents to determine their historical situation, intended audience, purpose, and point of view, in line with the HIPP format of document analysis (a refresher of HIPP can be found on page 8). Student products can then be shared out in a jigsaw fashion so students can evaluate and ascertain the nature of the Newburgh crisis and the issues at stake (a refresher of the jigsaw model can be found on page 33).

MODULE 3-5   Governing in Revolutionary Times, 1776–1787

trans-Appalachian west for the benefit of the new nation passed in the Continental Congress, American Indian nations saw little hope that their territories would be respected. Throughout the rest of the American Revolution, conflicts between patriots and American Indians allied with Britain only intensified.

In the Ohio and Mississippi River valleys, the British recruited Sioux, Chippewa, and Sauk warriors to attack Spanish forces along the Mississippi, and armed Ottawa, Fox, and Miami warriors to assault white Americans migrating into the Ohio River valley. British forces also moved deeper into this region, establishing a post on the Wabash River. In response, the United States and its new, mostly European, allies struck back in 1778. Although Detroit remained in British hands, British-allied American Indian forces were defeated at St. Louis, giving the patriots greater

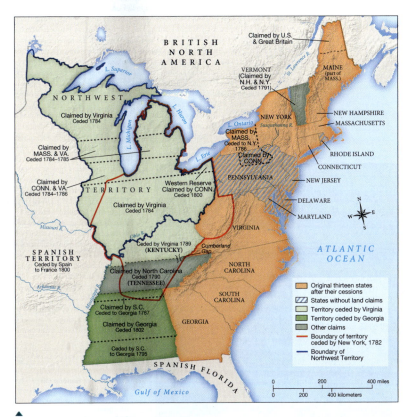

▲ **MAP 3.6 Cessions of Western Land, 1782–1802** Beginning under the Articles of Confederation, political leaders sought to resolve competing state claims to western territory based on colonial charters. The confederation congress and, after ratification of the Constitution, the U.S. Congress gradually persuaded states to cede their claims and create a "national domain," part of which was then organized as the Northwest Territory. **Using this map, determine how regional cultures along the Atlantic seaboard could be reflected in these newly ceded territories.**

TEACHING IDEA

Geography and Political Change

Impress upon students that the greatest achievement of the Articles government was its ability to successfully get all of the states to surrender their western land claims to the national government. For in so doing, it took away a major source of regional tension and competition that could easily have culminated in the states fighting among themselves. Point out to students that in general, this is precisely what the great European powers expected was going to happen; to their view, history had consistently proven that federated republics were an impossibility in the long term, and that upon the collapse of the Confederation system, the Great Powers would be able to swoop in and pick up what pieces there were to be had. Students should understand that this was the prevailing mode of thinking about the United States in the capitals of Europe, which also explains why they were in no hurry to help this government succeed through any initial cooperation with it.

TEACHING IDEA

Geography Instruction

Have students study Map 3.6. Ask them to use additional sources to identify where the location of New Orleans would be on that map. Then have them determine why any European power that controlled the city could make economic life extremely difficult for American citizens, and also conclude why gaining possession of New Orleans would ultimately be of great importance to the United States.

TEACHING IDEA

Incorporating Secondary Sources

Assign students to read and annotate Gregory Evans Dowd's essay, "There Was No Winning Strategy for the Indians," from his book *Spirited Resistance: The North American Indian Struggle for Unity, 1745–1815.* Class roundtable discussion to follow.

BUILDING AP® SKILLS

Continuity and Change

This is a good point to remind students that from the colonial perspective, the central reason for the Seven Years' War was to gain access to this very land region that, as citizens of the United States, these same former colonists were now accessing, exploiting, and developing. This represents a central continuity in the thinking and priorities of white Europeans in North America that is fully consistent in both the colonial and post-colonial periods. That continuity was that, for the most part, there was no place for American Indians in this narrative.

---

control in the Ohio River valley. In 1779, patriot General John Sullivan led a campaign to wipe out British allies in central New York by destroying Mohawk, Seneca, Cayuga, and Onondaga villages. It successfully ended attacks by Britain's Iroquois allies and disrupted British lines of supply extending south from Canada. However, over the next two years, Iroquois warriors and British troops would continually retaliate by attacking white settlements in central and eastern New York, killing or capturing dozens of American colonists.

Battles between American Indian nations and American settlers did not end with the American Revolution. Warfare between settlers and American Indians west of the Appalachian Mountains, from the Ohio River valley to Georgia, continued for decades. Despite the continued presence of British and Spanish troops in the Ohio River valley, the United States hoped to convince American Indian nations that it controlled the territory. During the Revolution Americans had moved west, occupying American Indian lands. After the war, vast numbers of squatters, mainly white men and women, continued to live on land to which they had no legal claim. In the fall of 1784, George Washington traveled west to survey nearly thirty thousand acres of territory he had been granted as a reward for leading the Continental Army. He found much of it occupied by squatters who refused to acknowledge his ownership. Such flaunting of property rights deepened Washington's concerns about the weaknesses of the confederation government.

The confederation congress was less concerned about individual property rights, however, and more occupied with the ongoing refusal of some states to give up the American Indian lands they claimed to federal control. Between 1783 and 1785, the congress finally persuaded the two last states with the largest claims, Virginia and Massachusetts, to relinquish all the remainder of their territories north of the Ohio River.

American Indians did not just stand by and watch as white Americans argued over who had the rights to their lands. As eastern American Indians were increasingly pushed into the Ohio River valley, they crowded onto lands already claimed by other nations. Initially, these migrations increased conflict among nations, but eventually some leaders used this forced intimacy to launch united tribal movements against further American theft of their land. In 1784 some two hundred American Indian leaders from the Iroquois, Shawnee, Creek, Cherokee, and other nations gathered in St. Louis, where they complained to the Spanish governor that the Americans were "extending themselves like a plague of locusts." Nevertheless, the United States continued to push its boundaries. In October 1784, U.S. commissioners met with Iroquois delegates at Fort Stanwix, New York, and demanded they surrender land in western New York and the Ohio River valley. When the Seneca chief Cornplanter and other leaders refused, the commissioners insisted that "you are a subdued people" and must submit. An exchange of gifts and captives taken during the Revolution finally ensured the deal.

◀ **Cornplanter, Seneca Chief** Cornplanter, son of a white father and Seneca mother, fought alongside the British during the Revolution. Afterward, however, he argued that American Indians must adapt to American control. He helped negotiate three treaties that ceded large tracts of American Indian land to the U.S. government, arousing opposition from more militant leaders. **What elements of this portrait portray the influence of European culture on Cornplanter?**

AP® ANALYZING SOURCES

Source: *Northwest Ordinance*, 1787

"Sec. 13. And for extending the fundamental principles of civil and religious liberty, which form the basis whereon these republics, their laws, and constitutions are erected; to fix and establish those principles as the basis of all laws, constitutions, and governments, which for ever hereafter shall be formed in the said territory; to provide, also, for the establishment of States, and permanent government therein, and for . . . [their] admission to a share in the federal councils on an equal footing with the original States, at as early periods as may be consistent with the general interest: . . . .

Article III. Religion, morality, and knowledge, being necessary to good government, and the happiness of mankind, schools and the means of education shall forever be encouraged. The utmost good faith shall always be observed towards the Indians; their lands and property shall never be taken from them without their consent; and in their property, rights, and liberty, they shall never be invaded or disturbed, unless in just and lawful wars authorized by Congress; but laws founded in justice and humanity shall, from time to time, be made, for preventing wrongs being done to them, and for preserving peace and friendship with them. . . .

Article VI. There shall be neither slavery nor involuntary servitude in the said territory, otherwise than in the punishment of crimes, whereof the party shall have been duly convicted: Provided, always, That any person escaping into the same, from whom labor or service is lawfully claimed in any one of the original States, such fugitive may be lawfully reclaimed, and conveyed to the person claiming his or her labor or service as aforesaid."

Questions for Analysis

1. Describe the key provisions included in this excerpt from the Northwest Ordinance of 1787.
2. Explain how this excerpt illustrates the effects of the American Revolution on American Indians.
3. Explain how this excerpt illustrates the effects of the American Revolution on enslaved Africans and African Americans in the United States.
4. Explain how the effects of the American Revolution on American Indians compare to its effects on enslaved Africans and African Americans.

TRM Suggested Responses to Questions

TRM Module 3.5 AP® Analyzing Sources Handout 2

TEACHING IDEA

Connecting the Dots

Point out to students that the pattern of United States–American Indian formal diplomatic relations for the next 100 years will be a constant, consistent repetition of the cycle that is being established here. That cycle runs as follows: American Indians and the U.S. government sign a treaty that establishes specific boundaries and respective territories for both claimants; whites violate the stipulations of this agreement, and settle in lands designated as American Indian territories by the agreement; violence ensues; American Indians are blamed for the violence and the U.S. military is deployed to pacify the area; new agreements are reached, which extend the areas of white settlement farther west than they were in the previous agreements. This became essentially standard operating procedure for the next century, and students should be prepared to see this as a harbinger of things to come in future modules.

BUILDING AP® SKILLS

Sourcing and Situation

Assign students to access the online Newberry Library Digital Collection, "American Indians in an Age of Empire and Revolution, 1750–1783" (dcc.nerberry.org). Have students either individually or in pairs explore the source documents and answer the questions that follow. This can be done in a document-by-document guided lesson, where the instructor stops the class after each document and elaborates upon its significance and meaning, or as an overall lesson whereby students read and respond to the online material in its entirety, and after that, the instructor engages with the material and student conclusions.

American Indian leaders not at the meeting disavowed the **Treaty of Fort Stanwix**. But the confederation government insisted it was legal, and New York State began surveying and selling the land. With a similar mix of negotiation and coercion, U.S. commissioners signed treaties at Fort McIntosh, Pennsylvania (1785), and Fort Finney, Ohio (1786), claiming lands held by the Wyandot, Delaware, Shawnee, and others.

To regulate this vast territory, Thomas Jefferson drafted the **Northwest Ordinance** in 1785. It provided that the territory be surveyed and divided into adjoining townships. He hoped to carve nine small states out of the region to enhance the representation of western farmers and thus ensure the continued dominance of their views in the national government. The congress revised his proposal, however, stipulating that only three to five states be created and thereby limiting the future clout of western settlers in the federal government.

The population of the territory grew rapidly, with speculators buying up huge tracts of land and selling smaller parcels to eager settlers. In response, congressional leaders modified the Northwest Ordinance in 1787, clarifying the process by which territories could become states. The congress appointed territorial officials and guaranteed residents the basic rights of U.S. citizens. After a territory's population reached 5,000, residents could choose an assembly, but the territorial governor retained the power to veto legislation. When a would-be state reached a population of 60,000, it could apply for admission to the United States. Thus the congress established an orderly system by which territories became states in the Union.

The 1787 ordinance addressed concerns about American Indians and the question of slavery in the territories. It encouraged fair treatment of American Indian nations but did not include any means of enforcing such treatment and failed to resolve the status of American Indian nations' land claims.

Northwest Ordinances 1785 act of the confederation congress that provided for the survey, sale, and eventual division into states of the Northwest Territory. A 1787 act then clarified the process by which territories could become states.

AP® TIP
Be sure you can explain how the Northwest Ordinance reflected developing ideas about the powers of government in the new republic.

EXPLORING AP® THEMES

Migration and Settlement

This is a good point to discuss with students that most European migration in the United States took place in an east-to-west direction that resulted in parallel tracks of society replicating itself. Consequently, the slavery-and-plantation-based agrarian crop monoculture of the Tidewater region spread itself across North America south of the Ohio River, while the small subsistence-based family farm and non-slavery-based economic diversity of New England resettled itself into lands north of the Ohio River. To this end, the Northwest Ordinance's provisions regarding slavery can be seen to tie into larger historical forces that were in play. Had migration patterns in the United States been more along the lines of southeast-to-northwest and northeast-to-southwest, the social structures of frontier regions would have turned out quite differently.

It abolished slavery throughout the Northwest Territory but mandated the return of fugitives from slavery to prevent a flood of fugitives and satisfy the interests of slaveholding politicians.

The 1787 legislation did not address territory south of the Ohio River. Slaveholders, seeking more fertile fields, had brought tens of thousands of enslaved black people into Kentucky, Tennessee, and the Mississippi Territory. Moreover, as Americans streamed westward south of the Ohio River they confronted Creek, Choctaw, and Chickasaw tribes, well supplied with weapons by Spanish traders, as well as armed Cherokee who had sided with the British during the Revolution. Conflicts there were largely ignored by the national government for the next quarter century.

REVIEW

- What dilemmas did the Northwest Ordinances seek to resolve?
- How did the Northwest Ordinance of 1787 represent a continuation of pre-American Revolution policy, and how did it represent a change?

Indebted Farmers Fuel Political Crises, 1783–1787

Farmers enlisted and fought in the American Revolution, hoping to expand their political rights and roles in the new nation. Such efforts initially seemed to bear fruit. Most state constitutions written during the Revolution specifically allowed men with little (or even no) property, such as small-scale farmers, to vote and hold office. One such farmer was Daniel Shays. One of six children born to Irish parents in Hopkinton, Massachusetts, Shays received little formal education. In 1772, at age twenty-five, he married, had a child, and settled into farming. By June of 1775, he was among the patriots defending Bunker Hill. After distinguishing himself in the Continental Army, Shays purchased a farm in 1780 and hoped to return to a normal life. Instead, economic turmoil rocked the region as it did the nation in the years following the revolution.

Many farmers had fallen into debt while fighting for independence. They returned to an economic recession and increased taxes as state governments labored to repay wealthy creditors and fund their portion of the federal budget. Thus the economic interests of small farmers and workers diverged sharply from those of wealthy merchants and large landowners. As conflicts between debtors and creditors escalated between 1783 and 1787, state governments came down firmly on the side of the wealthy. But indebted farmers did not give up. They continued their revolutionary efforts by voting, petitioning, and protesting to gain more favorable policies. In western Massachusetts, where many farmer-veterans faced eviction, Shays kept his farm and represented his town at county conventions that petitioned the state government for economic relief. However, the legislature largely ignored the farmers' concerns.

For the time being, national political elites worried far more about international threats to prosperity and the independence of the new nation. The continued efforts of Great Britain and Spain to undercut U.S. sovereignty and ongoing struggles with American Indian nations posed especially serious dangers. George Washington, James Madison, Alexander Hamilton, and others questioned whether the Articles of Confederation held enough power to deal with international threats to the new nation. When James Madison and Alexander Hamilton attended the 1786 convention in Annapolis to address problems related to interstate commerce, they discovered that their concerns about the weakness of the confederation were shared by many large landowners, planters, and merchants. Despite these elite concerns, state political leaders resisted reductions in the powers they had been granted under the Articles of Confederation.

Meanwhile, when farmers' efforts to petition government failed, tense conflicts ensued. Debt-ridden farmers in New Hampshire marched on the state capital in September 1786, demanding reform. But they were confronted by cavalry units, who quickly seized and imprisoned their leaders.

The internal discord in congress also inspired radicals to more coordinated action. In 1786, angered by the state's failure to act, armed groups of farmers attacked courthouses throughout western Massachusetts. Although a reluctant leader, Daniel Shays headed the largest band of more than a thousand farmer-veteran-soldiers. In January 1787, this group headed at the federal arsenal at Springfield, Massachusetts, to seize guns and ammunition. Shays's rebels, however, were routed by state militia and pursued by Massachusetts Governor James Bowdoin's army. Many rebel leaders were

---

TEACHING IDEA

Incorporating Videos

Have students watch excerpts of the PBS documentary, "Liberty! The American Revolution: Episode 6" (available on YouTube). This video deals with the problems and challenges that made the Articles government essentially unworkable.

TEACHING IDEA

AP® Central

Have students engage in a pre-writing exercise using the 1985 College Board AP® U.S. History DBQ whereby students had to evaluate the validity of the statement concerning the Articles of Confederation. This is available on the College Board's past exam questions resource "AP® United States History Document-Based Questions 1973–1999" (apcentral.collegeboard.org). As this prompt does not conform to the current AP® DBQ model, writing a full response to it may be of limited utility. However, the use of the documents for student practice in sourcing, making connections, and discovering claims and evidence in sources is of great value. Students may utilize the HIPP template as document analysis practice, and students may also use the 4-1-1 model of contextualization and thesis construction to develop their skills in argumentation (a refresher of HIPP and the HIPP template can be found on page 8; a refresher of the 4-1-1 model can be found on page 163).

EXPLORING AP® THEMES

Politics and Power

Write on the board the metaphor, "The Articles of Confederation was essentially a 'rope of sand.'" Although this famous metaphor was created by Daniel Webster in the 1830s during the debates over the validity of nullification, it is specifically useful to apply it to the time and place of the Articles' existence as the central American government. In light of what they have done and read thus far in the module, ask students to explain what they think that claim means. Then have them explore the idea of why it would make sense that, after what they perceived as tyrannical rule by an overpowering government, Americans themselves would initially swing the pendulum far in the other direction, and craft a government that was intentionally and deliberately constrained and weak. Have students explore the concept of why too little government could turn out, in its own way, to be as problematic as too much government.

Indebted Farmers Fuel Political Crises, 1783–1787

Period 3: 1754–1800

Shays's Rebellion 1786 rebellion by western Massachusetts farmers caused primarily by economic hardships in the aftermath of the American Revolution.

captured; others, including Shays, escaped to Vermont and New York. Four were convicted and two were hanged before Bowdoin granted amnesty to the others in hopes of avoiding further conflict.

This uprising, known as **Shays's Rebellion**, alarmed many state and national leaders who feared such insurgencies might emerge elsewhere. On December 26, 1786, Washington wrote to a fellow politician to express his concerns about the rebellion: "If the powers [of the central government] are inadequate, amend or alter them; but do not let us sink into the lowest states of humiliation and contempt." Hamilton agreed, claiming that Shays's Rebellion "marked almost the last stage of national humiliation." Congress thus decided to convene a convention in Philadelphia in 1787 to revise and thereby strengthen the Articles of Confederation.

AP® ANALYZING SOURCES

Source: *Correspondence between Daniel Shays and Benjamin Lincoln*, Massachusetts, 1787

"January 30th, 1787.

To General Lincoln, commanding the government troops at Hadley. . . .

We are sensible of the embarrassments the people are under; but that virtue which truly characterizes the citizens of a republican government, hath hitherto marked our paths with a degree of innocence. . . . At the same time, the people are willing to lay down their arms, on the condition of a general pardon, and return to their respective homes, as they are unwilling to stain the land, which we in the late war purchased at so dear a rate, with the blood of our brethren and neighbours. Therefore, we pray that hostilities may cease . . . until our united prayers may be presented to the General Court, and we receive an answer, as a person is gone for that purpose. . . .

daniel shays, captain."

"January 31st, 1787

Gentlemen,

Your request is totally inadmissible, as no powers are delegated to me which would justify a delay of my operations. Hostilities I have not commenced.

I have again to warn the people in arms against the government, immediately to disband, as they would avoid the ill consequences which may ensue, should they be inattentive to this caution.

b. lincoln."

Questions for Analysis

1. Identify the causes of Shays's Rebellion, as outlined in these letters.
2. Identify Shays's demands.
3. Identify Lincoln's warning to Shays.
4. Explain how the ideals of the American Revolution shaped the context of Shays's Rebellion.

REVIEW

- What economic struggles did farmers face in the aftermath of the American Revolution?
- How did political leaders contribute to these struggles?

AP® WRITING HISTORICALLY | Making Evaluative Comparisons in an Essay

So far, you have practiced how to craft evaluative claims in response to essay prompts that ask you to consider causation as well as continuity and change. In this course, you will also come across writing tasks that ask you to make evaluative comparisons. This means you must judge

(Continued)

TRM Suggested Responses to Questions

TRM Module 3.5 AP® Analyzing Sources Handout 3

BUILDING AP® SKILLS
Comparison

Have students engage in a Dueling Dates Turning Points activity, whereby they are given two dates, either 1776 vs. 1787, or 1783 vs. 1787. Students in groups have to write a claim statement explaining why each date could be considered a watershed moment in American history, and then prove why, in their view, one of the dates represents the greater/more important turning point of their assigned pairing. This is excellent preparation for Short-Answer Question prompts, and students can be asked to write one on their assigned pairing as a culminating activity.

TRM Suggested Responses to Questions

EXPLORING AP® THEMES
Politics and Power

Have students use their textbook to compare and contrast Bacon's Rebellion to Shays's Rebellion in terms of what the central issues and grievances were, as well as the class cleavages that both crises illuminated. Then, engage students in a discussion based around the following questions: Before the outbreak of each crisis, what were the characteristics of the dominant and non-dominant political groups? Who benefitted from and who was hurt by maintaining the status quo and why/how? What were the benefits that would have accrued to whom if the sought-after changes of each crisis had been implemented? What does this tell us about the political and social power structures of seventeenth- and eighteenth-century America?

TEACHING IDEA
Six Degrees of Separation

Have students engage in a Six Degrees of Separation activity in small groups, based upon the following prompt: "From the signing of the Declaration of Independence to the meeting of the Constitutional Convention." Groups may then, as a potential differentiation piece, post their products on butcher paper or the chalkboard for a student gallery walk of products.

Period 3: 1754–1800

MODULE 3-5 Governing in Revolutionary Times, 1776–1787

whether two events, developments, ideologies, processes, or groups are best characterized by their similarities or differences. As with other historical reasoning processes, in order to make evaluative comparisons you must weigh similarities against differences, and draw conclusions about which is more significant. Here, we will take you step-by-step through one way to approach this type of writing task. Read the following prompt:

> Evaluate the extent of similarity between the new state governments formed in the United States during the period from 1776 to 1786.

Step 1 Break down the prompt.

Remember, phrases like "the extent of" or "the extent to which" tell you that you are being asked to evaluate the importance of whatever concepts, developments, or events you choose to include in your response. In other words, you aren't being asked a question with a simple yes or no answer. You must make an argument, supported by historical evidence, that asserts *how much* similarity or difference exists between two concepts, historical developments, or groups during a time period it specifies. Our example prompt is essentially asking, "How much similarity existed between the new state governments formed in the United States between 1776 and 1786?"

Before moving to the next step, take a moment to remember that any prompt that mentions similarities without mentioning differences — or vice versa — is still asking you to consider both. This is because historians don't tend to present topics in terms of complete similarity or complete difference. While comparative historical arguments typically assert that either similarity or difference is more prominent, the most effective arguments are qualified — that is, they establish that elements of both are present.

Step 2 List and categorize your historical knowledge.

Think about the history of new governments formed in the United States between 1776 and 1786. Write lists of similarities and differences. Remember, you don't have to stick to just the content in this module. You can, and should, use content drawn from your classwork, outside reading, and other parts of this textbook.

Next, create a graphic organizer to map out your claims and evidence about similarities and differences, along with their relative importance. Think about your list of similarities and differences. Were the American governments during the decade specified by the prompt mostly characterized by their similarities, or did their differences stand out more? Which similarities and differences were most important, and why? As with other evaluative writing tasks, it may help to imagine that the items from your list in step 2 sit along a continuum. And, as with continuity and change, a continuum of comparison should also include contrasts. In other words, a lack of similarity naturally points to an element of difference, and vice versa. The following continuum may help you better visualize this relationship:

You should start your graphic organizer in much the same way you would approach thinking about continuity and change — by considering relevant aspects of the five major analysis categories (politics, economy, society, technology, and interactions with the environment). In this case, there is no need to break your evidence into earlier and later parts of the time range given by the prompt, which is very short. Next, add two columns to your chart: one to evaluate the extent of similarity or difference, and one to craft an evaluative claim from the supporting evidence in your chart. Your completed chart may look something like this:

TEACHING IDEA

Building Vocabulary

One of the most important things the instructor must do is make sure the students understand exactly what it is that any AP® writing question is asking them to do. As such, it is essential that the instructor takes the student through a tutorial of the verbs of a question, as well as the meanings of other language within the prompt. In this specific instance, the instructor must be sure that the students understand what the verb "evaluate" actually means. This verb represents their marching orders, and in this case, definitionally speaking, it is asking them to "weigh, determine, or judge." Furthermore, the next two words, "the extent," signal to the students that this is a question of degree, on a continuum. Framed in simpler terms, this is a "how much" question. It is critical that students have it impressed upon them that therefore logic dictates, irrespective of any "to what extent" question's content, that their thesis addressing such a prompt can only fall into one of three avenues of approach: to a large amount, a minimal amount, or a somewhat mixed degree — with preponderance leaning moderately on one side or the other (the latter representing the most complex and nuanced response/position). This sort of tutorial is essential in helping your students understand what it is they are being asked to do, which will consequently make fully answering the question a far more accessible proposition.

Indebted Farmers Fuel Political Crises, 1783–1787

Period 3: 1754–1800

New State Governments 1776-1786	Evaluation of Similarity or Difference	Claim for Supporting Evidence
Republican government (no nobility or monarch)	Very similar	New state governments reflected the context of opposition to centralized power fueled by the struggle against British tyranny. All new state governments rejected the British constitutional model, which included a hereditary aristocracy and king/queen.
Civil rights (speech, trial, etc.)	Moderately different	As a check against tyranny most states, adopting Virginia's model, included in their constitutions a bill of rights that ensured citizens freedom of the press, freedom of elections, speedy trials by one's peers, humane punishments, and the right to form militias. Some states also insisted on people's freedom of speech and assembly, the right to petition and to bear arms, and equal protection of the laws. However, many states restricted full African American and women's citizenship, placing them under the control of white males.
Voting rights	Very different	In Pennsylvania, patriots developed one of the most democratic constitutions. They replaced the governor with an executive council. The legislature consisted of a single house elected by popular vote. Legislators could only serve for four in any seven years to discourage the formation of a political aristocracy. The New Jersey constitution of 1776 enfranchised all free inhabitants who met the property qualifications. New Jersey thereby allowed some propertied single and widowed women and free black people to vote. States in the South, like Virginia and South Carolina, restricted African American and women's voting rights.
Freedom of religion	Somewhat similar	Government support of churches ended in most states with the establishment of the United States. Many new state constitutions granted freedom of religion. In other states legislatures made laws in the 1780s reducing or eliminating government funds for religion. Anglican churches had long benefited from British support and taxed residents to support their ministry during the Revolution. But in 1786, the Virginia Assembly approved the Statute of Religious Freedom, which made church attendance and support voluntary. Many other states followed Virginia's lead and removed government support for established churches.

When you make a claim that addresses a difference, using transition words such as *but*, *although*, *whereas*, or *however* help highlight the contrast. When you write a claim that presents a similarity, using transition words and phrases such as *similarly*, *likewise*, or *in like manner* is an easy way to make sure you have emphasized your point.

Step 3 Write a thesis statement that brings together all of your evaluative claims.

Be sure that your thesis indicates an extent of similarity. It should also make at least one claim for similarity and one for difference. Ideally, your thesis statement will have either more similarities or more differences. Favoring one over the other makes sure you take an argumentative position on one side of the continuum. Here is an example of a strong thesis:

> Starting in 1776, rebellious colonial elites created new state governments that showed moderate difference in the extent of participatory democracy they offered citizens, but were ultimately vastly similar in that almost all established representative republics, banned titles of aristocracy, and eliminated state support for religion.

Notice how this thesis makes claims about "moderate" difference and "vast" similarity. The phrase "moderate difference" in the first claim of the thesis tells the reader where the sub-topic of

(Continued)

TEACHING IDEA

AP® Writing Historically Workshop

This activity seeks to build in a comparison between groups of two students over how to incorporate the skill of comparison in an essay. Start by dividing students into groups of four and assigning each group either similarity or difference. Next, have the group select the best thesis from step 3 to work with. Students will then form subgroups of two, and using the same evidence, write a comparison paragraph. In this way, the group will have two separate takes on how to incorporate this skill into an analytical body paragraph. Have students use the outline provided in the activity on page 206 to determine which is the best response.

Period 3: 1754–1800

MODULE 3-5 Governing in Revolutionary Times, 1776–1787

participatory democracy falls on the continuum of similarity and difference. Likewise, the phrase "vastly similar" conveys that in the case of the other thesis claims (on the topics of representative government, aristocratic titles, and state support of religion) the similarities far outweighed the differences.

ACTIVITY

Write an essay that supports the thesis provided in step 3. For a challenge, you may wish to construct your own thesis statement. Remember, your introductory paragraph should begin with a contextualization statement that leads into the thesis. Each body paragraph should defend one of the claims in that thesis. You may use the graphic organizer in step 2 as well as following outline to guide your writing.

I. Introductory paragraph
   A. Immediate/preceding contextualization statement
      1. Cite evidence of immediate/preceding context
      2. Explain influence of immediate/preceding context
   B. **Thesis statement presenting three evaluative claims of comparison, situated along a continuum of relative importance:** Starting in 1776, rebellious colonial elites wrote new state governments that showed moderate difference in the extent of participatory democracy they offered citizens, but were ultimately vastly similar in that almost all established representative republics, banned titles of aristocracy, and eliminated state support for religion.
II. **Evaluative claim of comparison 1:** Colonial elites wrote new state governments that showed moderate difference in the extent of participatory democracy they offered citizens.
   A. Topic sentence presenting claim 1
   B. Cite evidence of claim 1
   C. Explain how evidence supports claim 1
III. **Evaluative claim of comparison 2:** Rebellious colonial elites wrote new state governments that showed vast similarity in establishing representative republics that banned titles of aristocracy.
   A. Topic sentence presenting claim 2
   B. Cite evidence of claim 2
   C. Explain how evidence supports claim 2
IV. **Evaluative claim of comparison 3:** Rebellious colonial elites wrote new state governments that showed vast similarity in eliminating state support for religion.
   A. Topic sentence presenting claim 3
   B. Cite evidence of claim 3
   C. Explain how evidence supports claim 3

TEACHING IDEA

Incorporating Videos

Assign students to watch Episode 8 "The Constitution, the Articles, and Federalism" from the Crash Course US History series (available on YouTube). Use this 13-minute episode as a concise content review for students of the major issues and events of Module 3-5 as part of preparation for either assessment or reinforcement antecedent to moving forward into the next module.

Module 3-6

Reframing the American Government

LEARNING TARGETS

By the end of this module, you should be able to:

- Explain how Americans tried to create governments based on the ideas of the American Revolution after 1783.
- Explain the ways in which the structure of government both changed and remained the same in the face of new challenges during this period.

THEMATIC FOCUS

Politics and Power

American and Regional Culture

By the mid-1780s, it became increasingly clear that the Articles of Confederation government could not maintain control over the new republic. During this period, Americans debated how best to strengthen the federal government without undermining the rights gained in the Revolution. During the debates over the new constitution, various regional interests competed for influence over the new federal government.

HISTORICAL REASONING FOCUS

Continuity and Change

TASK ▶ As you read this module, consider what continuities remained during this period of debates regarding the proper role of the national government, and consider the changes wrought by the newly proposed constitution and the debates that revolved around its ratification.

> "173 despots would surely be as oppressive as one.... An elective despotism was not the government we fought for."
>
> Thomas Jefferson, *Notes on the State of Virginia*, 1785

In the decade following the Revolution, Americans of all stripes engaged in heated disagreements over the best means to unify and stabilize the United States. Many, especially those in positions of economic and political influence, had come to question the strength of the government under the Articles of Confederation — even if they hardly agreed on where to go from there. As financial distress among patriotic small farmers and tensions with American Indians on the western frontier continued to escalate, the worry that revising the Articles would lead to the very tyranny that tens of thousands of patriots had just fought a war to escape began to be outweighed by the necessity of changes to steady the course for the new nation.

Making a Constitution

Constitutional Convention
Meeting to draft the United States Constitution in Philadelphia from May to September of 1787. This document established the framework for a strong federal government with executive, legislative, and judicial branches.

The fifty-five delegates who met at the **Constitutional Convention** in Philadelphia in May 1787 were white, educated men of property, mainly lawyers, merchants, and planters. Only eight had signed the Declaration of Independence eleven years earlier. The elite status of the delegates and the absence of many leading patriots raised concern among those who saw the convention as a threat to the rights of states and of citizens. Not wanting to alarm the public, delegates agreed to meet in secret until they had hammered out a new framework of government.

On May 25, the convention opened, and delegates quickly turned to the key question: Revise the Articles of Confederation or draft an entirely new document? The majority of men came to Philadelphia with the intention of strengthening the existing government by amending the Articles, including James Monroe of Virginia. However, a core group who sought a more powerful central government — including James Madison — had met before the convention and drafted a plan to replace the Articles. This Virginia Plan proposed a strong centralized state, including a bicameral (two-house) legislature in which representation was to be based on population. Members of the two houses would select the national executive and the national judiciary, and would settle disputes

---

TRM Suggested Responses to Questions

TEACHING IDEA

Incorporating Videos

As this module begins, this is an ideal point to introduce the Annenberg Trust short film from The Constitution Project, *Creating a Constitution*. This 24-minute piece gives a good rundown on the issues that demonstrated a need for an improved governmental model other than the Articles of Confederation, as well as a synopsis of the critical issues at the convention itself (annenbergclassroom.org).

TEACHING IDEA

Connecting the Dots

Have students combine themselves into pairs, and have them quickly review the specific and general weaknesses of the Articles of Confederation (see note on page 197). Discuss their findings, and compile an overall list from class contributions on the board or projector. Then, place student pairs into groups of four, and have students research the Constitution to identify and explain what specific clauses or powers of the new Constitution were designed to fix the weaknesses of the Articles government.

▲ Differentiation

Student groups from the above-described lesson could be tasked with creating an illustration or product that represents the concern about the Articles' weaknesses and the proposed remedies within the Constitution to counter that weakness. This is a unique way to have learners engage in a physical or tactile or visual process, which can help to provide connections for a wide range of students. This can also be assigned with an economical use of time in mind, so as not to evolve into a large-scale project that gets the AP® course off-schedule.

APPLY THE TIP

This activity can be accomplished by placing students into two groups: one group titled, "Governing rules and laws that stayed the same pre- and post-Constitution," and the other titled, "Governing rules and laws that changed post-Constitution." Each group is to compile its respective information and then partner up with a member of the opposite group and teach/discuss their findings.

Virginia Plan Plan put forth at the beginning of the 1787 Constitutional Convention that introduced the ideas of a strong central government, a bicameral legislature, and a system of representation based on population.

New Jersey Plan A proposal to the 1787 Constitutional Convention that highlighted the needs of small states by creating one legislative house in the federal government and granting each state equal representation in it.

three-fifths compromise Compromise between northern and southern delegates to the 1787 Constitutional Convention to count enslaved persons as three-fifths of a free person in deciding the proportion of representation in the House of Representatives and taxation by the federal government.

> **AP® TIP**
> Evaluate the degree of continuity in how colonial elites exercised political power prior to the American Revolution and in the new republic.

> **AP® TIP**
> Evaluate the extent to which the provisions of the Constitution represented a change from the laws governing the colonies between 1607 and 1776.

electoral college A group comprised of electors who vote in the formal election of the president and vice president after the general election votes are tallied. The electoral college was a compromise between determining the president via a direct popular vote or via congressional vote.

---

between states. Although most delegates opposed the **Virginia Plan**, it launched discussions in which strengthening the central government was assumed to be the goal.

Discussions of the Virginia Plan raised an issue that nearly paralyzed the convention: the question of representation. Heated debates pitted large states against small states. In mid-June, William Patterson introduced the **New Jersey Plan**, which highlighted the needs of smaller states. In this plan, Congress would consist of only one house, with each state having equal representation.

The convention finally appointed a special committee to solve the problem of representation in order for all delegates to agree to a new Constitution to replace the Articles. This committee helped the convention reach a compromise in which representation in the House would be determined by population — counted every ten years in a national census — while in the Senate each state, regardless of size, would have equal representation. While the Senate had more authority than the House in many areas, only the House could introduce funding bills. Members of the House of Representatives were to be elected by voters in each state; members of the Senate would be appointed by state legislatures.

Included within this compromise was one of the few direct considerations of slavery at the Philadelphia convention. With little apparent debate, the committee decided that representation in the House of Representatives was to be based on a record of the entire free population and three-fifths of "all other persons" — that is, enslaved African Americans. If delegates had moral scruples about this **three-fifths compromise**, most found them outweighed by the urgency of settling the troublesome question of representation.

Still, slavery was on the minds of delegates. In the same week that the Philadelphia convention accepted the institution of slavery as shown by the three-fifths compromise, the confederation congress in New York City outlawed slavery in the Northwest Territory. News of that decision likely inspired representatives from Georgia and South Carolina to insist that the Constitution protect the slave trade. Delegates in Philadelphia agreed that the importation of enslaved people would not be interfered with for at least twenty years. Another provision demonstrating federal support for slavery guaranteed the return of fugitives from slavery to slaveholders. At the same time, northern delegates insisted that the three-fifths formula be used in assessing taxation as well as representation, ensuring that the states with enslaved people paid for the increased size of their congressional delegations with increased taxes.

Two other issues provoked considerable debate in the following weeks. All delegates supported federalism, a system in which states and the central government shared power, but they disagreed over the balance of power between them. They also disagreed over the degree of popular participation in selecting national leaders.

The new Constitution increased the powers of the central government significantly. For instance, Congress would now have the right to raise revenue by levying and collecting taxes and tariffs and coining money; raise armies; regulate interstate commerce; settle disputes between the states; establish uniform rules for the **naturalization** of immigrants; and make treaties with foreign nations and American Indians. But Congress could veto state laws only when those laws challenged "the supreme law of the land," and states retained all rights that were not specifically granted to the federal government.

One of the important powers retained by the states was the right to determine who was eligible to vote, but the Constitution regulated the influence eligible voters would have in national elections. Members of the House of Representatives were to be elected directly by popular vote for two-year terms. Senators — two from each state — were to be selected by state legislatures for a term of six years. Selection of the president was even further removed from voters. The president would be selected by an **electoral college**, and state legislatures would decide how to choose its members. Finally, the federal judicial system was to be wholly removed from popular influence. Justices on the Supreme Court were to be appointed by the president and approved by the Senate. Once approved, they served for life to protect their judgments from the pressure of popular opinion. In addition, the Constitution created a separation of powers between these three branches — congressional, executive, and judicial — that limited the authority of each.

With the final debates concluded, delegates agreed that approval by nine states, rather than all thirteen, would make the Constitution the law of the land. Some delegates sought formal reassurance that the powers granted the federal government would not be abused and urged inclusion of a bill of rights, like the Virginia Declaration of Rights. But weary men eager to finish their business voted down the proposal. On September 17, 1787, the Constitution was approved and sent to the states for ratification.

REVIEW

How did the various proposals at the Constitutional Convention reflect regional interests?

Americans Debate Ratification

Federalists Supporters of ratification of the Constitution, many of whom came from urban and commercial backgrounds.

Antifederalists Opponents of ratification of the Constitution. They were generally from more rural and less wealthy backgrounds than the Federalists.

The confederation congress sent the Constitution to state legislatures and asked them to call conventions to consider ratification. These conventions could not modify the document, but only accept or reject it. Thousands of copies of the Constitution also circulated in newspapers and as broadsides. Pamphleteers, civic leaders, and ministers proclaimed their opinions publicly while ordinary citizens in homes, shops, and taverns debated the wisdom of establishing a stronger central government.

Fairly quickly, two sides emerged. The **Federalists**, who supported ratification, came mainly from urban and commercial backgrounds and lived in towns, cities, or large staple crop producing plantations along the Atlantic coast. They viewed a stronger central government as essential to the economic and political stability of the nation. Their opponents were generally more rural, less wealthy, and more likely to live in interior or frontier regions. Labeled **Antifederalists**, they opposed increasing the powers of the central government.

AP® ANALYZING SOURCES

Source: Alexander Hamilton, *Federalist Argument at the New York State Convention*, June 1788

"I will not agree with gentlemen who trifle with the weaknesses of our country; and suppose, that they are enumerated to answer a party purpose, and to terrify with ideal dangers. No; I believe these weaknesses to be real, and pregnant with destruction. Yet, however weak our country may be, I hope we never shall sacrifice our liberties. . . .

Sir, it appears to me extraordinary, that, while gentlemen in one breath acknowledge that the old confederation requires many material amendments, they should in the next deny, that its defects have been the cause of our political weakness, and the consequent calamities of our country. . . . [T]he states have almost uniformly weighed the requisitions by their own local interests; and have only executed them so far as answered their particular conveniency or advantage. Hence there have ever been thirteen different bodies to judge of the measures of Congress, and the operations of government have been distracted by their taking different courses. . . .

Shall we take the old Confederation, as the basis of a new system? . . . certainly not. Will any man who entertains a wish for the safety of his country, trust the sword and the purse with a single Assembly organized on principles so defective—so rotten? Though we might give to such a government certain powers with safety, yet to give them the full and unlimited powers of taxation and the national forces would be to establish a despotism; the definition of which is, a government in which all power is concentrated in a single body. . . . These considerations show clearly, that a government totally different must be instituted. . . . [T]he convention . . . therefore formed two branches, and divided the powers, that each might be a check upon the other. . . .

Sir, the natural situation of this country seems to divide its interests into different classes. . . . It became necessary, therefore, to compromise; or the Convention must have dissolved without effecting any thing. . . .

(Continued)

BUILDING AP® SKILLS

Comparison

Assign students to create a T-chart indicating the differing beliefs and characteristics of Federalists and Antifederalists. Engage the class in a discussion as to why or how these differences might explain where the two groups stood on key policy positions of their day.

TRM Find **Handout 3.7 – Federalist vs. Antifederalist: Competing Philosophies** in the Teacher's Resource Materials.

TRM **Suggested Responses to Questions**

TRM **Module 3.6 AP® Analyzing Sources Handout**

BUILDING AP® SKILLS

Making Connections

Provide students with a map of the thirteen original states. Have them draw arrows from each state itemizing their positions on slavery and proportional vs. equal representation. Then have students discuss the patterns they see in terms of regional interests. This exercise can then be used as a gateway into assigning students to craft an essay response to the review question on this page.

EXPLORING AP® THEMES

American and National Identity

Provide students with a series of quotations from Alexander Hamilton and Thomas Jefferson, which can readily be found on Wikiquote (wikiquote.org). Have students translate or summarize the quotes into language they understand in terms of what each founding father is saying. Next, provide students with a list of the major controversial issues of the period (establishment of the U.S. Bank, alliance with France, etc.) and have students predict/explain how they think each founder would have regarded the issue.

TEACHING IDEA

Incorporating Primary Sources

This module is replete with the foundational documents of the Republic, and this should be an opportunity in the AP® U.S. History Course to develop many of them as learning tools early and often. The exemplar described below could be applied with any number of founding documents.

Assign students to read and annotate Federalist #10 (or #51, or Brutus, etc.), and then lead an all-class discussion to make sure students fully understand Madison's concept of faction and the merits of a strong government to counter and steer faction's influences. Have students write a summary of their conclusions and takeaways from the assignment and class discussion following a pattern called "Fifty-Word Drill," in which students must craft their concluding response in 50 words (instructor may allow some discretion in the word limit, but not by much; the goal is for students to have to be comprehensive, yet concise).

"The first thing objected to is that clause which allows a representation for three fifths of the negroes. . . . It is the unfortunate situation of the Southern States to have a great part of their population, as well as property, in blacks. The regulation complained of was one result of the spirit of accommodation, which governed the Convention; and without this indulgence, no union could possibly have been formed. But, Sir, considering some peculiar advantages which we derive from them, it is entirely just that they should be gratified. The Southern States possess certain staples, tobacco, rice, indigo, &c. which must be capital objects in treaties of commerce with foreign nations; and the advantages which they necessarily procure in these treaties, will be felt throughout all the States. . . . [Moreover] representation and taxation go together, and one uniform rule ought to apply to both. Would it be just to compute these slaves in the assessment of taxes; and discard them from the estimate in the apportionment of representatives?"

Questions for Analysis

1. Identify the claims that Hamilton makes in this excerpt.
2. Explain how Hamilton supports the claims he makes in this excerpt.
3. Evaluate the extent to which the ideals of the American Revolution shaped the dissent offered by some delegates to the Constitutional Convention.

The Federalist Papers
85 essays by Federalists Alexander Hamilton, James Madison, and John Jay. Published in newspapers throughout the U.S., *The Federalist Papers* promoted the ratification of the Constitution.

AP® TIP
Evaluate the extent to which the division between Federalists and Antifederalists reflected ongoing class and regional divisions in North America.

The pro-Constitution position was presented in a series of editorials that appeared in New York newspapers in 1787 to 1788 and published collectively as *The Federalist Papers*. The authors James Madison, John Jay, and Alexander Hamilton articulated broad principles embraced by most supporters of the Constitution. Most notably, in *Federalist No. 10*, Madison countered the common wisdom that small governmental structures were most effective in representing the interests of their citizens and avoiding the development of political parties. He argued that in large units groups with competing interests had to collaborate and compromise, providing the surest check on the "tyranny of the majority."

Alexander Hamilton, a young New York politician, played a particularly important role in the Federalist effort, authoring 51 of the 85 total *Federalist Papers*. Born in poverty in the British West Indies and orphaned at eleven, he was apprenticed to a firm of merchants that sent him to the American colonies. There Hamilton was attracted to the activities of radical patriots and joined the Continental Army in 1776, where Washington noticed his abilities and kept him close by to manage the war as his chief of staff from 1777 to 1781. After the war, Hamilton established himself as a lawyer and financier in New York City, eventually winning election to the New York State legislature in 1786, where he focused on improving the state's finances. Although Hamilton played only a small role in the Constitutional Convention of 1787, he worked tirelessly with his fellow *Federalist Papers* authors for ratification of the Constitution.

Still, Antifederalists worried that a large and powerful central government could lead to tyranny. Small farmers claimed that a strong congress filled with merchants, lawyers, and planters was likely to place the interests of creditors above those of ordinary (and indebted) Americans. Even some wealthy patriots, like Mercy Otis Warren of Boston, feared that the Constitution would empower a few individuals who cared little for the "true interests of the people." And the absence of a bill of rights concerned many Americans.

Federalists worked in each state to overcome criticism of the Constitution by persuasive arguments and the promise of a bill of rights once the Constitution was ratified. They gained strength from the quick ratification of the Constitution by Delaware, Pennsylvania, New Jersey, Georgia, and Connecticut by January 1788. Federalists also gained the support of influential newspapers based in eastern cities and tied to commercial interests. Still, the contest in many states was heated. In Massachusetts, Antifederalists, including leaders of Shays's Rebellion (see Module 3-5), gained the majority among convention delegates. Federalists worked hard to overcome the objections of their opponents, even drafting a preliminary bill of rights. On February 6, Massachusetts delegates voted 187 to 168 in favor of ratification. Maryland and South Carolina followed in April and May. A month later, New Hampshire Federalists won a close vote, making it the ninth state to ratify the Constitution.

However, two of the most populous and powerful states—New York and Virginia—had not yet ratified. Passionate debates erupted in both ratifying conventions, and Federalists decided it was better

> "The *rights* of mankind are simple. They require no learning to unfold them. They are better *felt*, than explained. Hence in matters that relate to liberty, the mechanic and the philosopher, the farmer and the scholar, are all upon a footing. But the case is widely different with respect to *government*. It is a complicated science, and requires abilities and knowledge of a variety of other subjects, to understand it."
>
> Benjamin Rush, editorial in the *Pennsylvania Gazette*, 1787

BUILDING AP® SKILLS

Comparison

Assign students to create a Venn diagram comparing the beliefs of the Federalists and Antifederalists. After completing this exercise, pose the following question to the class: "Between the Federalists and Antifederalists, who had or made the better argument?" Engage in a whole-class discussion to follow.

TEACHING IDEA

Incorporating Secondary Sources

Assign students to read staggered excerpted chapters of Herbert J. Storing's *What the Anti-Federalists Were For: The Political Thought of the Opponents of the Constitution*. Chapters may be assigned to students in groups of three, with one student given chapters 1, 4, and 7, the second student given chapters 2, 5, and 8, and the third student given chapters 3, 6, and 9. The next day, have students present a summary of their conclusions of each chapter to their peers, to create a skeletal outline and summation of Storing's overall work and thesis.

▲ **Differentiation**

If desired, this assignment can be reduced by assigning just one chapter to each student in the class and having them jigsaw together their conclusions in class the following day (a refresher of the jigsaw model can be found on page 33).

Americans Debate Ratification

Votes of State-Ratifying Conventions This table shows the votes in the various state conventions for ratifying the new constitution. **Choose three of the state convention vote tallies and explain what might account for each tally.**

State	Date	For	Against
Delaware	December 1787	30	0
Pennsylvania	December 1787	46	23
New Jersey	December 1787	38	0
Georgia	January 1788	26	0
Connecticut	January 1788	128	40
Massachusetts	February 1788	187	168
Maryland	April 1788	63	11
South Carolina	May 1788	149	73
New Hampshire	June 1788	57	47
Virginia	June 1788	89	79
New York	July 1788	30	27
North Carolina	November 1788	194	77
Rhode Island	May 1790	34	32

to wait until these states acted before declaring victory. After promising that a bill of rights would be added quickly, Virginia Federalists finally won ratification by a few votes. A month later, New York approved the Constitution by a narrow margin. The divided nature of the votes, and the fact that two states (North Carolina and Rhode Island) had still not ratified, meant that the new government would have to prove itself quickly.

Most political leaders hoped that the partisanship of the ratification battle would fade away with the Constitution approved. The electoral college's unanimous decision to name George Washington the first president and John Adams as vice president helped calm the political turmoil. The two took office in April 1789, launching the new government.

REVIEW

Why were the Federalists able to win ratification of the Constitution?

AP® WRITING HISTORICALLY — Evaluating Continuity and Change in a Document-Based Essay

You're ready to apply your skills in evaluating continuity and change to a Document-Based Question. The following prompt asks you to bring together your knowledge from Modules 3-5 and 3-6 with a close, active reading of six relevant documents:

Evaluate the extent to which arguments over powers granted to the United States government changed between 1765 and 1789.

Step 1 Break down the prompt.

As with previous essays, be sure to *ACE* this question and create a list of information you already know about the prompt. Remember, it may be helpful to treat this prompt as if no documents were provided. For example, what are some arguments about the continuity of the powers of a distant government from before and after the Constitutional Convention of 1787? And what are some new arguments during the same period that mark a change?

It will also be helpful to recall that the way the prompt is worded provides important clues about what your response must do — when you are asked to "evaluate the extent" of something, it means you need to evaluate the importance of historical developments in relation to the topic of the prompt.

Step 2 Read and annotate the documents.

Now consider the six documents that accompany the prompt, some of which will be familiar to you from previous modules. To what extent does each document reflect some of the arguments for continuity you noted in step 1? To what extent does it reflect arguments for change? Remember to ask yourself the following questions as you read each document:

- What is the document about? What historical situation does it describe or reference?
- Who was the intended audience for this document?
- What was the author's purpose in writing this document?
- What point of view does the author of this document express?
- How does this document relate back to the prompt? In this case, try to link each document to a specific effect of the market revolution on society as you annotate.
- Does this document remind you of any other historical developments? Jot down any relevant evidence from your own background knowledge that comes to mind.

(Continued)

TEACHING IDEA

Incorporating Videos

Assign students to watch Adam Norris's "APUSH Review: Video #15: The Constitutional Convention, Compromises, and the Federalist Papers" (available on YouTube). Use this 7-minute episode as a concise content review for students of the Federalist–Antifederalist split and constitutional ratification itself as part of preparation for either summative assessment or reinforcement antecedent to moving forward into the next module.

TRM Suggested Responses to Questions

BUILDING AP® SKILLS

Argumentation

As students engage with the Writing Historically prompt on this page, this a good place to return to the foundational first principles of addressing an AP® prompt. Specifically, this means begin by searching for and decoding/translating the verb of the prompt, the "action word," into meaningful directives for the students. In this instance, the verb is "explain." Discuss with students that "explain" in this instance means to "lay out," or "display/demonstrate," more than it means to merely "tell." And again, the qualifying clause "the extent to which" in plain English is best translated as, "how much." This simple deconstruction allows students to quickly grasp that their position on any question of extent boils down to one of three avenues: substantial, minimal, or somewhat mixed/in-between, with a percentage of preponderance leaning incrementally toward one side or the other.

EXPLORING AP® THEMES

Politics and Power

Provide the students with the Bill of Rights. Assign them in small groups to determine which right is protected by each amendment, and then also to explain how prior experiences with government, either under the Articles or under imperial crown law, influenced the creation or design of each amendment.

TEACHING IDEA

AP® Writing Historically Workshop

Although the best responses to the Document-Based Question display an understanding of the documents and the question, remember it is early in the school year and having students organize a response around the documents is a good way to have them work on categorizing evidence. Think of this in three steps. First, you can ask students to decide whether the document is evidence of change or continuity. Next, have them derive a thesis category by determining which categories can be made with the evidence provided. Finally, have students create an order for their responses as this will help provide a better flow for their essays.

DOCUMENT 1

Source: Patrick Henry, *Virginia Resolves*, 1765

"*Whereas*, the honorable House of Commons in England have of late drawn into question how far the General Assembly of this colony hath power to enact laws for laying of taxes and imposing duties, payable by the people of this, his majesty's most ancient colony: for settling and ascertaining the same to all future times, the House of Burgesses of this present General Assembly have come to the following resolves:—

. . . *Resolved*, That the first adventurers and settlers of this, his majesty's colony and dominion, brought with them and transmitted to their posterity, and all other his majesty's subjects, since inhabiting in this, his majesty's colony, all the privileges, franchises, and immunities that have at any time been held, enjoyed, and possessed, by the people of Great Britain. . . .

. . . *Resolved*, That his majesty's liege people of this most ancient colony have uninterruptedly enjoyed the right of being thus governed by their own Assembly in the article of their taxes and internal police, and that the same hath never been forfeited, or any other way given up, but hath been constantly recognized by the kings and people of Great Britain.

. . . *Resolved*, therefore, That the General Assembly of this colony have the only and sole exclusive right and power to lay taxes and impositions upon the inhabitants of this colony; and that every attempt to vest such power in any person or persons whatsoever, other than the General Assembly aforesaid, has a manifest tendency to destroy British as well as American freedom."

DOCUMENT 2

Source: Thomas Paine, *Common Sense*, 1776

"But there is another and greater distinction, for which no truly natural or religious reason can be assigned, and that is, the distinction of men into KINGS and SUBJECTS. Male and female are the distinctions of nature, good and bad, the distinction of heaven; but how a race of men came into the world so exalted above the rest, and distinguished like some new species, is worth enquiring into, and whether they are the means of happiness or of misery to mankind.

In the early ages of the world, according to the scripture chronology, there were no kings; the consequence of which was, there were no wars: it is the pride of kings which throws mankind into confusion. Holland without a king hath enjoyed more peace for this last century than any of the monarchical governments in Europe. . . .

Government by kings was first introduced into the world by the Heathens, from whom the children of Israel copied the custom. It was the most prosperous invention the Devil ever set on foot for the promotion of idolatry. The Heathens paid divine honors to their deceased kings, and the Christian world hath improved on the plan, by doing the same to their living ones. How impious is the title of sacred majesty applied to a worm who in the midst of his splendor is crumbling into dust!"

DOCUMENT 3

Source: Delegates to the Pennsylvania Constitutional Convention, *The Address and Reasons of Dissent of the Minority of the Convention of Pennsylvania to Their Constituents*, 1787

"We dissent, first, because . . . a very extensive territory cannot be governed on the principles of freedom. . . .

We dissent, secondly, because the powers vested in congress by this constitution must necessarily annihilate and absorb the legislative, executive, and judicial powers of the several states; and produce, from their ruins, one consolidated government, which from the nature of things, will be an iron-handed despotism, as nothing short of the supremacy of despotic sway could connect and govern these United States under one government. . . .

The powers of congress, under the new constitution, are complete and unlimited over the purse and the sword; and are perfectly independent of, and supreme over, the state governments, whose intervention in these great points, is entirely destroyed. By virtue of their power of taxation, congress may command the whole, or any part of the properties of the people. They may impose what imposts upon commerce—they may impose what land-taxes and taxes, excises, duties on all the instruments, and duties on every fine article that they may judge proper. In short, every species of taxation whether of an external or internal nature, is comprised in section the 8th, of article the first [of the Constitution], . . . 'the congress shall have power to lay and collect taxes, duties, imposts, and excises, to pay the debts, and provide for the common defence and general welfare of the united states.'"

DOCUMENT 4

Source: James Madison, *Federalist No. 10*, 1787

"The latent causes of faction are thus [planted] in the nature of man; and we see them everywhere brought into different degrees of activity, according to the different circumstances of civil society. . . . So strong is this propensity of mankind, to fall into mutual animosities, that where no substantial occasion presents itself, the most frivolous and fanciful distinctions have been sufficient to kindle their unfriendly passions, and excite their most violent conflicts. But the most common and durable source of factions, has been the various and unequal distribution of property. . . . The regulation of these various and interfering interests forms the principal task of modern legislation, and involves the spirit of party and faction in the necessary and ordinary operations of the government. . . .

By what means is this object attainable? . . . Either the existence of the same passion or interest in a majority, at the same time, must be prevented; or the majority, having such coexistent passion or interest, must be rendered, by their number and local situation, unable to concert and carry into effect schemes of oppression. . . .

Hence, it clearly appears, that the same advantage, which a republic has over a democracy, in controlling the effects of faction, is enjoyed by a large over a small republic—is enjoyed by the union over the states composing it. Does this advantage consist in the substitution of representatives, whose enlightened views and virtuous sentiments render them superior to local prejudices, and to schemes of injustice? It will not be denied, that the representation of the union will be most likely to possess these requisite endowments. Does it consist in the greater security afforded by a greater variety of parties, against the event of any one party being able to outnumber and oppress the rest? In an equal degree does the increased variety of parties, comprised within the union, increase this security. Does it . . . consist in the greater obstacles opposed to the concert and accomplishment of the secret wishes of an unjust and interested majority? Here, again, the extent of the union gives it the most palpable advantage."

(Continued)

DOCUMENT 5

Source: John Williams, backcountry farmer, *Argument at the New York State Ratification Convention*, 1788

"I believe that this country has never before seen such a critical period in political affairs. . . . Indeed, Sir, it appears to me, that many of our present distresses flow from a source very different from the defects in the Confederation. Unhappily for us, immediately after our extrication from a cruel and unnatural war, luxury and dissipation overran the country, banishing all that economy, frugality, and industry, which had been exhibited during the war. . . . Let us, then, abandon all those foreign commodities which have hitherto deluged our country; which have loaded us with debt, and which, if continued, will forever involve us in difficulties. How many thousands are daily wearing the manufactures of Europe, when by a little industry and frugality, they might wear those of their own country! . . . [T]he best government ever devised, without economy and frugality will leave us in a situation no better than the present. . . .

[L]et us examine whether [the Constitution] be calculated to preserve the invaluable blessings of liberty, and secure the inestimable rights of mankind. . . . [I]f it be found to contain principles that will lead to the subversion of liberty, . . . let us insist upon the necessary alterations and amendments. . . .

In forming a constitution for a free country like this, the greatest care should be taken to define its powers, and guard against an abuse of authority. The Constitution should be so formed as not to swallow up the State governments: the general government ought to be confined to certain national objects; and the States should retain such powers, as concern their own internal police. . . ."

DOCUMENT 6

Source: *The Massachusetts Centinel*, "The Federal Pillars," August 1788

About the source: The text above the illustration reads, "*On the erection of the Eleventh Pillar of the great National DOME, we beg leave most sincerely to felicitate* "OUR DEAR COUNTRY." The pillars, from left to right, are labeled as follows: Delaware, Pennsylvania, New Jersey, Georgia, Connecticut, Massachusetts, Maryland, South Carolina, New Hampshire, Virginia, New York, North Carolina (rising toward New York), Rhode Island (leaning and cracked), The text between the New York and North Carolina columns reads, "Rise it will," and the text to the right of the Rhode Island column reads, *"The foundation good — it may yet be* SAVED.*"* The illustration is accompanied by the following poem:

The FEDERAL EDIFICE.

ELEVEN Stars, in quick succession rise —
ELEVEN COLUMNS strike our wond'ring eyes,
Soon o'er the *whole*, shall swell the beauteous DOME,
COLUMBIA's boast — and FREEDOM's hallow'd home.
 Here shall the ARTS in glorious splendor shine!
And AGRICULTURE give her stores divine!
COMMERCE refin'd, dispense us more than gold,
And this new world, teach WISDOM to the old —
RELIGION here shall fix her blest abode,
Array'd in *mildness*, like its parent GOD!
JUSTICE and LAW, shall endless PEACE maintain,
And the "SATURNIAN AGE,"[1] *return again.*

[1] An era of strong government.

Step 3 Pre-write to organize your thoughts, and then write a thesis statement that brings together all of your evaluative claims.

After you have finished pre-writing to organize your thoughts, write a thesis statement answering the prompt. Remember, a strong thesis provides a direct answer — in this case, about the relative amount of change in arguments over what powers the U.S. government should have between 1765 and 1789. It should also make at least three claims, with claims for continuity and for change both included.

While three claims are the minimum for an effective historical argument, and you may wish to stick to this structure for essays you write in timed situations, you should not always feel confined to the three-claim, five-paragraph arrangement. There is no magic formula for writing a good essay — if you have something more to say and have strong evidence to back it up, it deserves to go on the page.

ACTIVITY

You are now ready to plan and write a full essay in response to the Document-Based Question at the beginning of this box. Follow steps 1 through 3 to pre-write and craft a thesis statement that responds to the prompt.

Be sure to use at least five of the six documents provided to support your historical argument, and to bring in evidence from outside the documents. Remember, you must explain *how* all of your evidence supports your claims — this is the most important part of an effective historical argument. For a challenge, try adding a fourth claim to your thesis or using all six documents to support your argument.

You may use the following outline to guide your response:

I. Introductory paragraph
   A. Immediate/preceding contextualization statement
      1. Cite evidence of immediate/preceding context
      2. Explain influence of immediate/preceding context
   B. Thesis statement presenting three to four evaluative claims that are situated along a continuum of relative importance

(Continued)

II. Claim 1 body paragraph
   A. Topic sentence presenting evaluative claim of change or continuity 1
   B. Supporting statement citing evidence of claim 1 (from historical knowledge)
   C. Cite additional evidence of claim 1 (from a document)
   D. Cite additional evidence of claim 1 (from another document)
   E. Explain how evidence supports claim 1
III. Claim 2 body paragraph
   A. Topic sentence presenting evaluative claim of change or continuity 2
   B. Supporting statement citing evidence of claim 2 (from historical knowledge)
   C. Cite additional evidence of claim 2 (from a document)
   D. Cite additional evidence of claim 2 (from another document)
   E. Explain how evidence supports claim 2
IV. Claim 3 body paragraph
   A. Topic sentence presenting evaluative claim of change or continuity 3
   B. Supporting statement citing evidence of claim 3 (from historical knowledge)
   C. Cite additional evidence of claim 3 (from a document)
   D. Cite additional evidence of claim 3 (from another document)
   E. Explain how evidence supports claim 3
V. (Optional) Claim 4 body paragraph
   A. Topic sentence presenting evaluative claim of change or continuity 4
   B. Supporting statement citing evidence of claim 4 (from historical knowledge)
   C. Cite additional evidence of claim 4 (from a document)
   D. Cite additional evidence of claim 4 (from another document)
   E. Explain how evidence supports claim 4

Module 3-7

Legacies of the American Revolution

LEARNING TARGETS
By the end of this module, you should be able to:
- Explain how American culture both changed and remained the same during the second half of the eighteenth century.
- Explain how regional attitudes about slavery both changed and remained the same during the second half of the eighteenth century.
- Explain the ways in which the American Revolution transformed American society during the second half of the eighteenth century.

THEMATIC FOCUS
American and National Identity
Social Structures

The ideals of the American Revolution raised questions about the status of women and African Americans. They also gave rise to a movement to educate young Americans for future republican citizenship. During this time, new forms of national culture developed in the United States alongside continued regional variations. A distinctly American culture began to emerge as the work of writers, artists, and intellectuals reflected new national and regional cultures.

HISTORICAL REASONING FOCUS
Comparison and Causation

TASK ▶ While reading this module, compare the effects of the changes in American society on the poor, women, American Indians, and African Americans in the aftermath of the American Revolution.

The ideals of the Declaration of Independence forced many Americans to negotiate the inequalities at home. Throughout the last twenty years of the eighteenth century, Americans whose voices were previously oppressed sought to define themselves within the new egalitarian rhetoric. However, others were ambivalent about expanding the ideal of equality to embrace all Americans.

The victory over Great Britain won independence but left the United States confronting difficult problems. When the Treaty of Paris was finally signed in 1783, thousands of British troops and their loyalist supporters left the colonies for Canada, the West Indies, or England. Church leaders enjoyed government support in the colonial period, but now had to compete for members and funds. Most soldiers simply wanted to return home and reestablish their former lives. But the government's inability to pay back wages and the huge debt the nation owed to private citizens and state and foreign governments hinted at difficult economic times ahead. Poor and middling veterans and small farmers suffered economically in the postwar period, but they were not alone. Women faced challenges as they sought to enhance their role in the nation. African Americans, too, whose hopes for freedom had been raised by the Revolution, continued to fight for full-fledged citizenship and an end to slavery.

Veteran Farmers Struggle in a Post-War Economy

Many Revolutionary War veterans, most often would-be farmers, found the adjustment to post-war life difficult. Many men waited more than twenty years to receive any compensation for fighting in the American Revolution. In the meantime they struggled to reestablish or establish farms and businesses and pay off debts accrued while engaged in the war for independence.

TRM Suggested Responses to Questions

EXPLORING AP® THEMES
American and Regional Culture

At the start of this module, an important reality to have students take into consideration is the overwhelming degree to which American society and culture were rural and agrarian in orientation and worldview. Most Americans were born, lived, and died within a 20-mile radius, which made for an extremely localized and parochial view of the world. The emphasis upon westward movement and settlement often misses this vital point to understanding the typical American's known world in this period.

TEACHING IDEA
Building Vocabulary

An important word to elaborate upon at this point is "egalitarian." This word has major prominence in this period, as the concept of deference, which is the inherent acquiescence and respect that was due to one's social superiors in the hierarchical universe that was imperial–colonial America (and another equally important piece of historical vocabulary), declined dramatically during this period. Have students discuss and explore how or why the rhetoric of revolution and equality would inevitably lead to this new ethos of egalitarianism at the expense of deference.

TEACHING IDEA

Incorporating Secondary Sources

Assign students to read and annotate one of two works by Mary Beth Norton, either the short monograph, "Women and the Revolution" (available through online search by title) or Chapter 6, "We Commenced Perfect Statesmen," from her book *Liberty's Daughters*. Whole-class discussion to follow.

▲ **Differentiation**

Assign more advanced students to read the chapter-length book excerpt, and less advanced students to read the short monograph. Then, conduct two separate roundtables simultaneously in class. However, to integrate the learning and practice sound inclusion, place the students into pairs, with one student from each assigned reading, and instruct them to share and teach their findings and conclusions to their paired partner.

TEACHING IDEA

Building Vocabulary

Republican motherhood is the most important gender term for students to master from the Revolutionary period. Point out to students that although this ideal called for an elevated worth in the roles of women, as the raisers of the next generation of American (male) leaders, the concept does not particularly alter women's roles in society; in effect, this is simply a matter of a greater significance being attached to a preexisting role of domestic nurturer that was embraced by society as the appropriate "place" for women.

Period 3: 1754–1800

MODULE 3-7 Legacies of the American Revolution

Disputes over western lands were deeply intertwined with the economic difficulties that plagued the new nation. Victory in the Revolution was followed by years of economic depression and growing debt. While the war fueled the demand for domestic goods and ensured high employment, both the demand and the jobs declined in peacetime. International trade was also slow to recover from a decade of disruption. Meanwhile the nation owed a huge war debt. Individuals, the states, and the federal government all viewed western lands as a solution to their problems. Farm families could start over on "unclaimed" land; states could distribute land instead of cash to veterans or creditors; and congress could sell land to fund its debts. Yet there was never enough land to meet these conflicting needs, nor did the United States, given American Indian nations' land claims and occupation of the trans-Appalachian west, hold secure title to the territory.

Some national leaders, including Hamilton, focused on other ways of repaying the war debt. Fearing that wealthy creditors would lose faith in a nation that could not repay its debts, they urged states to grant the federal government a percentage of import duties as a way to increase its revenue. But states had their own problems. Legislators in Massachusetts and other states passed hard-money laws that required debts to be repaid in gold or silver rather than in paper currency. Affluent creditors favored these measures to ensure repayment in full. But small farmers, including Revolutionary War veterans, who had borrowed paper money during the war, now had to repay those loans in hard currency as the money supply shrank. Taxes, too, were rising as states sought to cover the interest on wartime bonds held by wealthy investors.

> **AP® TIP**
> Make sure you can explain the economic effects the American Revolution had on different social classes in the United States.

REVIEW

What challenges did veterans face after the American Revolution?

Revolutionary Women Seek Wider Roles

Women's diverse contributions to the American Revolution played vital roles in securing the patriot victory. While their influence was praised in the post-Revolutionary era, state laws rarely expanded their rights. All states limited women's economic independence, although a few did allow married women to enter into business. Many states legalized divorce, but in practice it was still available only to the wealthy and well connected. Meanwhile states excluded women from juries, legal training, and, with one exception, voting rights.

Abigail Adams had written her husband John in 1776, "[I]f perticuliar care and attention is not paid to the Laidies we are determined to foment a Rebelion." While she and other elite women sought a more public voice, only New Jersey granted women — widowed or single and property

◀ **Judith Sargent Stevens, later Murray, c. 1772** Born into a wealthy Massachusetts family, Judith Sargent was allowed to study alongside her brother until she married John Stevens at age 18. In the 1770s, she wrote well received essays on social and political topics and later promoted women's education and independence. Widowed at 35, she soon married Universalist minister John Murray and continued to publish into her sixties. **How does the artist of this portrait display the confidence of Judith Sargent Stevens? How does the artist maintain popular perceptions of women during the period?**

John Singleton Copley (1738–1815), Portrait of Mrs. John Stevens (Judith Sargent, later Mrs. John Murray), 1770–1772. Oil on canvas, 50 × 40 in. Daniel J. Terra Art Acquisition Endowment Fund, 2000.6. Terra Foundation for American Art, Chicago/Art Resource, NY

218

TEACHING IDEA

Incorporating Primary Sources

Assign students to read excerpts of Benjamin Rush's essay, "Thoughts Upon Female Education," and summarize its central points. This essay is available on The Albert M. Greenfield Digital Center for the History of Women's Education (greenfield.brynmawr.edu). Then, have students read selected excerpts of *Abigail Adams: Letters*, edited by Edith Gelles, from the *Library of America* series, concerning female equality. Have students compare and contrast the two with regards to their views on the roles of women in society. This can be done through a graphic organizer as a physical product, an inside-circle–outside-circle class discussion with the room divided into groups defending the beliefs of one author or the other, or through whole-class discussion with the instructor guiding and moderating the dialogue.

Revolutionary Women Seek Wider Roles

AP® TIP

As you continue to read about women's roles in American history, keep in mind how the restriction of their right to vote affected historical developments related to politics and power.

republican motherhood
Concept proposed by some American political leaders in the 1790s, which supported women's education so that they could in turn instruct their sons in principles of republican government.

owning — the right to vote, a right that the state rescinded less than three decades later. The vast majority of women could only hope to shape political decisions by influencing their male relatives and friends.

Many leaders of the early republic viewed wives and mothers as necessary to the development of a strong nation, leading to a push for women's education. In 1787 Benjamin Rush, in his *Essay on Female Education*, developed a notion of **republican motherhood**. He claimed that women could best shape political ideas and relations by "instructing their sons in principles of liberty and government." To prepare young women for this role, Rush suggested educating them in literature, music, composition, geography, history, and bookkeeping.

Judith Sargent Murray offered a more radical approach to women's education, arguing that "girls should be enabled to procure for themselves the necessaries of life; independence should be placed within their grasp." A few American women in the late eighteenth century did receive broad educations, and some ran successful businesses; wrote plays, poems, and histories; and established urban salons where women and men discussed the issues of the day. Notably, Quaker women testified against slavery in the 1780s, writing statements on the topic in separate women's meetings. Almost no other religious groups, however, offered women such spiritual autonomy.

AP® ANALYZING SOURCES

Source: Judith Sargent Murray, "On the Equality of the Sexes," *Massachusetts Magazine*, 1790

"Are we [women] deficient in reason? . . . [I]f an opportunity of acquiring knowledge hath been denied us, the inferiority of our sex cannot fairly be deduced from thence. . . . May we not trace its source in the difference of education, and continued advantages? Will it be said that the judgment of a male of two years old, is more sage than that of a female's of the same age? . . . But from that period what partiality! . . . As their years increase, the sister must be wholly domesticated, while the brother is led by the hand through all the flowery paths of science. . . . Now, was she permitted the same instructors as her brother, . . . for the employment of a rational mind an ample field would be opened. In astronomy she might catch a glimpse of the immensity of the Deity, and thence she would form amazing conceptions of the august and supreme Intelligence. In geography she would admire Jehovah in the midst of his benevolence; thus adapting this globe to the various wants and amusements of its inhabitants. In natural philosophy she would adore the infinite majesty of heaven, clothed in condescension; and as she traversed the reptile world, she would hail the goodness of a creating God. . . . Will it be urged that those acquirements would supersede our domestick duties. I answer that every requisite in female economy is easily attained; and, with truth I can add, that when once attained, they require no further mental attention. Nay, while we are pursuing the needle, or the superintendency of the family, I repeat, that our minds are at full liberty for reflection; that imagination may exert itself in full vigor; and that if a just foundation is early laid, our ideas will then be worthy of rational beings. . . . [I]s it reasonable, that a candidate for immortality . . . be allowed no other ideas, than those which are suggested by the mechanism of a pudding, or the sewing the seams of a garment?"

Questions for Analysis
1. Identify the reason why women are perceived as "deficient" in reason, according to Murray.
2. Describe the changes Murray demands in this excerpt.
3. Explain what Murray believes will be the result of these changes.

Questions for Comparison Esther De Berdt Reed, *The Sentiments of an American Woman*, 1780 (p. 187)
1. Describe how Murray's characterization of women differs from Reed's.
2. Evaluate the extent to which the legacy of the American Revolution accounts for the differences in each woman's account.

TRM Suggested Responses to Questions

TRM Module 3.7 AP® Analyzing Sources Handout 1

BUILDING AP® SKILLS

Claims and Evidence in Sources

Assign students to read Chapter 6, "The Question of Female Citizenship: Court Records from the New Nation," in *Going to the Source, Volume 1: To 1877: The Bedford Reader in American History*, and respond to the analytical questions and graphic organizers. This activity compels students to interpret primary source records, addressing their respective strengths and shortcomings as a means to grapple with the larger historical question of the role of women and their identity as women in the new republic.

EXPLORING AP® THEMES

Social Structures

This would be a good place to enrich student exploration and understanding of the changing roles of women during this time by assigning students to read and answer the source questions for Judith Sargent Murray (p. 219) and Samuel Jennings (p. 221). As part of this assignment, instruct students to compare and contrast the portrayal of women in both works and to analyze the works in terms of HIPP (which is essential to DBQ training and preparation for students), as well as answer the "Questions for Analysis" (a refresher of HIPP can be found on page 8).

▲ Differentiation

Task student groups of varying ability levels to utilize the above-mentioned exercise as material in preparation to construct thesis statements on the continuities and changes in the presentation of sex and gender roles. Have students perform this task within specific time constraints. Student-group products can then be shared for critique and improvement with the whole class.

TEACHING IDEA

Discussing Cultural Changes

It is important to discuss with students the need that post-Revolutionary Americans felt to break from Britain not just in nation-state terms, but also in cultural ones. Americans of the early republic felt a keen desire to establish their own identity as something separate and unique from Britain. As an exemplar of this that can enhance student understanding of the concept, explain to students here that this is the point in American history where the consumption of coffee began in earnest, as a deliberate and conscious turn away from the British cultural custom of consuming tea. It is with a whole series of small gestures such as this that the creation of a unique national identity is carved out by a people, no matter who they are. The fledgling United States was no exception.

BUILDING AP® SKILLS

Sourcing and Situation

Assign students to visit the Library of Congress website (loc.gov) to view the artwork of Revolutionary artists such as John Trumbull, Charles Wilson Peale, John Singleton Copley, Benjamin West, and Gilbert Stuart, and read excerpts from the introduction and conclusion of *Of Arms and Artists: The American Revolution Through Painters' Eyes*, by Paul Staiti. Discuss with students how the history of memory is influenced, if not created, in many ways by the artwork of a particular era, all the while with the creation of that memory being the central objects of the works themselves.

▲ **Differentiation**

For students interested in art and political expression, assign them to read "What We Talk About When We Talk About Confederate Monuments," by Sarah E. Gardener, available on the Origins: Current Events in Historical Perspective website (origins.osu.edu). They can then create a brief independent-study style class presentation on the similarities and differences in style, historical interpretation, social purpose, and cultural intent of the artwork created in both the post-Revolutionary and post-Civil War periods and what they say about how any societies remember events.

Period 3: 1754–1800

MODULE 3-7 Legacies of the American Revolution

> **AP® TIP**
> Compare the opportunities for women during the late eighteenth century with the roles New England women occupied — at home, in public, or at church — between 1620 and 1750.

In 1789 Massachusetts became the first state to institute free elementary education for all children, and female academies also multiplied in this period. While schooling for affluent girls was often focused on preparing them for domesticity, the daughters of artisans and farmers learned practical skills so they could assist in the family enterprise. Gains for these women fell short of the revolutionary political rights granted to voting citizens, but nevertheless this expanded education built a foundation upon which later generations of women pushed for equal rights.

African American and American Indian women lived under even more severe constraints than white women. Most black women lived enslaved to white slaveholders, and those who were free could usually find jobs only as domestic servants or agricultural workers. Among American Indian nations, years of warfare enhanced men's role as warriors and diplomats while reducing matrilineal traditions and women's political influence. U.S. government officials and Protestant missionaries encouraged American Indians to embrace gender roles that mirrored those of Anglo-American culture, further diminishing women's roles. American Indian women forced to move west also lost authority tied to their traditional control of land, crops, and households.

REVIEW

- To what extent was the status of white women in late-eighteenth-century America generally similar to that of poor white men?
- To what extent did the American Revolution provide new opportunities for women?

Developing a Distinct American Culture

The widespread desire to define and promote a specifically American culture began as soon as the Revolution ended. In 1783 Noah Webster, a schoolmaster, declared that "America must be as independent in *literature as in Politics*, as famous for *arts* as for *arms*." Before the Revolution, public education for children was widely available in New England and the Middle Atlantic region. In the South, only those whose parents could afford private schooling — perhaps 25 percent of the boys and 10 percent of the girls — received any formal instruction. Few young people enrolled in high school in any part of the colonies. Following the Revolution, state and national leaders proposed ambitious plans for public education, and in 1789 Massachusetts became the first state to demand that each town provide free schools for local children, though attendance policies were decided by the towns.

The American colonies boasted nine colleges that provided higher education for young men, including Harvard, Yale, King's College (Columbia), Queen's College (Rutgers), and the College of William and Mary. After independence, many Americans worried that these institutions were tainted by British and aristocratic influences. They pushed for the founding of new colleges based on republican ideals.

Artists, too, devoted considerable attention to historical themes, though in the late eighteenth century, they tended more to Enlightenment perspectives. Charles Willson Peale painted Revolutionary generals while serving in the Continental Army and became best known for his portraits of George Washington. Samuel Jennings offered a more radical perspective on the nation's character by incorporating women and African Americans into works like *Liberty Displaying the Arts and Sciences* (1792), but highlighted the importance of learning and rationality. So, too, did William Bartram, the son of a botanist. He journeyed through the southeastern United States and Florida, and published beautiful, and scientifically accurate, engravings of plants and animals in his *Travels* (1791). His less expensive engravings circulated more widely than more expensive paintings. Bartram's inexpensive and popular engravings highlighted national symbols like flags, eagles, and Lady Liberty.

In 1780, the Massachusetts legislature established the American Academy of Arts and Sciences to promote American literature and science. Six years later, Philadelphia's American Philosophical Society created the first national prize for scientific endeavor. Philadelphia was also home to the

BUILDING AP® SKILLS

Argumentation

Assign students to create a thesis and plan of attack with contextualization utilizing the 4-1-1 model of introductory paragraph construction for one of the two review questions on this page (a refresher of the 4-1-1 model can be found on page 163). Assign alternating questions to the class. Then, the next day, pair up students so that each student is with a partner that addressed the opposite prompt. Allow students to peer-review and critique each other's work.

Samuel Jennings, *Liberty Displaying the Arts and Sciences*, 1792 Samuel Jennings painted this image for the newly established Library Company of Philadelphia, many of whose directors were Quakers who opposed slavery. The directors requested that he include Lady Liberty with her cap on the end of a pole. **How does this image characterize the ideals of the American Revolution?**

nation's first medical college, founded at the University of Pennsylvania. As in the arts, American scientists built on developments in continental Europe and Britain but prided themselves on contributing their own expertise.

REVIEW

How did changes in education during the late 1700s reflect the ideas and principles of the American Revolution?

The Racial Limits of an American Culture

White Americans in the early republic often used native names and symbols as they set about creating a distinct national identity. Some working-class Americans followed in the tradition of the Boston Tea Party, dressing as American Indians to protest economic and political tyranny (see Module 3-9). But more affluent white people also embraced American Indian names and symbols. Tammany societies, which promoted patriotism and republicanism in the late eighteenth century, were named after a mythical Delaware chief called Tammend. They attracted large numbers of lawyers, merchants, and skilled artisans.

Poets, too, focused on American Indians. In his 1787 poem "Indian Burying Ground," for instance, Philip Freneau offered a sentimental portrait that highlighted the lost heritage of a nearly

TEACHING IDEA

Additional Practice

Assign students in pairs to respond to one of the following Short-Answer Question prompts:

Option 1:
a) Explain ONE way in which education advanced democracy in the early republic.
b) Explain ONE way in which education did NOT advance democracy in the early republic.
c) Provide ONE piece of evidence that demonstrates how education did or did not advance democracy in the early republic.

Option 2:
a) Explain ONE way in which artistic creation advanced democracy in the early republic.
b) Explain ONE way in which artistic creation did NOT advance democracy in the early republic.
c) Provide ONE piece of evidence that demonstrates how artistic creation did or did not advance democracy in the early republic.

Upon conclusion of the writing time, have the pairs fold into quads, with two members from each question. Have the quad share their responses, for both peer-teaching of content and peer-review of product.

Period 3: 1754–1800

MODULE 3-7   Legacies of the American Revolution

> **TEACHING IDEA**
>
> **Challenging Misconceptions**
>
> Introduce students to the concept of the "Noble-Savage Paradox," in which white Americans both romanticized a fictional, monolithic American Indian culture and society as in some ways a pure and uncorrupted vision of human relations, and simultaneously demonized the same cultures and societies as primitive, backward, and barbaric. Point out that Jefferson in particular held that there was currency in both of these views. Have students discuss what this curious parallel split in perceptions of the American Indian and his or her way of life says about Anglo-American relationships to indigenous cultures and American (Native and European settler) concepts of identity.

extinct native culture in New England. The theme of lost cultures and heroic (if still "savage") American Indians became even more pronounced in American poetry in the following decades. Such sentimental portraits were less popular along the nation's frontier, where American Indians continued to fight for their lands and rights. Cultural representations most often emphasized American Indians' supposed savagery and deceit.

Whether their depictions were realistic, sentimental, or derogatory, American Indians were almost always presented to the American public through the eyes of whites. Cultural leaders among American Indians gained little recognition from U.S. society, working mainly within their own nations either to maintain traditional languages and customs or to introduce their people to European-American ideas and beliefs they found useful.

Most white Americans believed that American Indians were untamed and uncivilized, but not innately different from Europeans. As U.S. frontiers expanded, white Americans considered ways to "civilize" American Indians and incorporate them into the nation. The improved educational opportunities available to white Americans generally excluded American Indians, and government officials left the schooling of American Indians to religious groups. Several denominations sent missionaries, ministers, and teachers to the Seneca, Cherokee, and other tribes, and a few American Indian students themselves went on to American colleges to be trained as ministers or teachers for their own people. Outside of missionaries, few whites bothered to learn American Indian languages. And even these attempts to bring American Indians into early republican society still failed to recognize the legitimacy of American Indian cultures. Moreover, however well-intentioned educators were, these sentiments never outweighed most white Americans' desire simply to colonize American Indian land.

> **AP® TIP**
>
> Compare Americans' treatment of American Indians during the early years of the republic with that of European colonists prior to the American Revolution.

REVIEW

- Describe white Americans' attitudes toward American Indian cultures during the late eighteenth century.

> **TEACHING IDEA**
>
> **Connecting the Dots**
>
> This would be a good point to revisit and reinforce the concept that for colonies of Spanish and French origin, this relationship regarding education, religious conversion, and cultural integration was far different. Under the English, and later, the United States model of white–American Indian relations, the most desirable outcome from the white settler point of view was for the American Indians to simply go away. This stood in marked contrast to the experiences of white and American Indians in the colonies with more pronounced French or Spanish heritage.

Slavery's Ongoing Legacy

Although the earliest state constitutions offered revolutionary change in many respects, few of them addressed the issue of slavery. As you read in Module 3-5, only Vermont (which technically remained outside of the United States until 1791) abolished slavery in its 1777 constitution, and legislators in Pennsylvania provided for a very gradual abolition.

In southern states like Virginia, the Carolinas, and Georgia, however, life for enslaved people grew increasingly harsh during the war. Because British forces promised freedom to black people who fought with them, slaveholders and patriot armies in the South took extreme measures attempting to keep enslaved African Americans from reaching British lines. When the British retreated, some generals, like Lord Dunmore and Sir Henry Clinton, took black volunteers with them. Others left behind thousands to fend for themselves.

Nonetheless, the ideals of the American Revolution dealt a blow to human bondage in the northern states. For many black people, Revolutionary ideals required the end of slavery. In Massachusetts, two enslaved people sued for their freedom in county courts in 1780–1781. Quock Walker, who had been promised his emancipation by a former slaveholder, sued his current slaveholder to gain his freedom. About the same time, an enslaved woman, Mum Bett, who was the widow of a Revolutionary soldier, initiated a similar case, which she won. When Walker won his case as well, his former slaveholder appealed the local court's decision, and the Massachusetts Supreme Court cited Mum Bett's case in its ruling that slavery conflicted with the state constitution.

Northern free black communities grew rapidly during the war, especially in seaport cities. In the South, too, thousands of enslaved people gained freedom, either by joining the British army

AP® ANALYZING SOURCES

Source: Petition of Enslaved African Americans to the Massachusetts Legislature, 1777

"The petition of a great number of blacks detained in a state of slavery in the bowels of a free and Christian country. . . . Your petitioners apprehend that they have in common with all other men a natural and unalienable right to that freedom which the Great Parent of the Universe has bestowed equally on all mankind and which they have never forfeited by any compact or agreement whatever, but . . . were unjustly dragged by the hand of cruel power . . . to be sold like beasts of burden and like them condemned to slavery for life. . . . [Y]our petitioners . . . express their astonishment that it has never been considered that every principle from which America has acted in the course of their unhappy difficulties with Great Britain pleads stronger than a thousand arguments in favor of your petitioners. They therefore humbly beseech your honors . . . to cause an act of the legislature to be passed whereby they may be restored to the enjoyments of that which is the natural right of all men. . . ."

Questions for Analysis
1. Identify the grievances presented in this petition.
2. Describe the context that shaped this petition.
3. Evaluate the extent to which the sentiments expressed in this document reflect the ideas of the American Revolution.

Source: Thomas Cole, Peter Bassnett Matthewes, and Matthew Webb, free African Americans, *Petition to the South Carolina Senate*, 1791

"That in the enumeration of free citizens by the Constitution of the United States for the purpose of representation of the Southern states in Congress your [petitioners] have been considered under that description as part of the citizens of this state.

Although by the . . . 1740 . . . Negro Act, now in force, your [petitioners] are deprived of the rights and privileges of citizens by not having it in their power to give testimony on oath in prosecutions on behalf of the state; from which cause many culprits have escaped the punishment due to their atrocious crimes, nor can they give their testimony in recovering debts due to them, or in establishing agreements made by them . . . except in cases where persons of color are concerned, whereby they are subject to great losses and repeated injuries without any means of redress.

That by . . . said Act, they are debarred of the rights of free citizens by being subject to a trial without the benefit of a jury. . . .

Your [petitioners] show that they have at all times since the independence of the United States contributed and do now contribute to the support of the government by cheerfully paying their taxes proportionable to their property with others who have been during such period, and now are, in full enjoyment of the rights and immunities of citizens, inhabitants of a free independent state."

Questions for Analysis
1. Identify the grievances presented in this petition.
2. Describe the solutions Cole, Matthewes, and Webb seek.
3. Explain how the effects of the American Revolution led to this petition.

Questions for Comparison
1. Describe the similarities the two documents share.
2. Describe how the two documents differ.
3. Evaluate the extent to which specific historical developments and contextual factors shaped those differences.

TRM Suggested Responses to Questions

TRM Module 3.7 AP® Analyzing Sources Handout 2

EXPLORING AP® THEMES

American and Regional Culture

Assign students to read both sources and respond to their accompanying questions. Then, the next day in class, place the students into groups of three or four and assign each group one of the following roles: Judith Sargent Murray (see page 219), Thomas Jefferson, John Adams, a Quaker farmer in western Pennsylvania, and a Baptist minister in Charleston, South Carolina. Task each group with determining the position or thoughts of their individual with regards to the two documents on this page. Also, assign them to formulate one question that they would like to ask one of the other groups and why. Allow students to ask those questions, and give the other groups time to formulate a response.

EXPLORING AP® THEMES

American and National Identity

At this point in the module, a definite consistent thread or theme concerning the processes of identity formation in the early republic should be emerging for students. Engage students in a discussion of how the concept of the "other" was central to the development of early United States culture and society. It is important to have students consider how aspects of cultural formation predicated upon NOT being something (British, indigenous, African, etc.) played as significant a role in this cultural and social formation as did the aspirational bonds of what citizens of the United States wanted their society and culture to be.

TEACHING IDEA

Incorporating Secondary Sources

Assign students to read Chapter 9, "The Slow Death of Slavery in the North," from Ira Berlin's *Many Thousands Gone*. Have students identify Berlin's thesis, and be prepared to defend or critique his main points. The next day, divide the class into groups of three to five students for this purpose, and moderate their discussions and interactions by the instructor floating from group to group.

TRM Find **Handout 3.8 – Secondary Source Critique** in the Teacher's Resource Materials.

APPLY THE TIP

In order to analyze how the growth of slavery (and the support it received from the U.S. government) shaped society and culture in the new republic, divide the students into eight groups of two or three students and assign each group to address this concept in just one of the following categories: economics, gender, class structure, rule of law, northern states, southern states, western states, religion. When this phase is complete, reshuffle the class into two or three groups of eight students, with each category represented, and have students engage in a jigsaw process whereby each student shares with his/her new larger group what he/she has learned. Follow this up with a thesis-building exercise that addresses the prompt of the AP® Tip.

AP® TIP
Be sure you can explain how African Americans challenged traditional authority in the new United States.

or by fleeing in the midst of battlefield chaos. As many as one-quarter of those enslaved in South Carolina had emancipated themselves by the end of the Revolution.

The evacuation of the British at the end of the war also led to the exodus of thousands of African Americans who had fought against the patriots. Before leaving America, British officials granted certificates of manumission (freedom) to more than 1,300 men, 900 women, and 700 children. Most of these freed black people settled in Nova Scotia, where they received small pieces of land from the British, but they generally lacked the resources to make these homesteads profitable. Despite these obstacles, some created a small Afro-Canadian community in Nova Scotia. Others starving in 'Nova Scarcity' migrated internationally to areas considered more hospitable, such as Sierra Leone along the western coast of Africa.

Some Protestant churches were also challenged from within by free black people who sought a greater role in how churches were run. In 1794 Richard Allen, who had been born into slavery, founded the first African American church in the United States: the African Methodist Episcopal Church (AME) in Philadelphia. Initially, this church remained within the larger white Protestant fold, but by the early 1800s, Allen's church served as the basis for the first independent black denomination.

It was no accident that the first independent black church was founded in Philadelphia, which attracted large numbers of free black people after the state adopted a gradual emancipation law in 1780. At the same time, the limits on emancipation in the South nurtured the growth of free black communities in the North. Many African Americans migrated to seaport cities like Philadelphia, New York, and New Bedford where they focused on finding jobs, supporting families, and securing the freedom of enslaved relatives. Others, like Richard Allen, sought to establish churches, schools, and voluntary societies and claim a political voice.

Some northern states, such as New Jersey, granted property-owning black people the right to vote. Others, such as Pennsylvania, did not specifically exclude them. Although the northern states with the largest enslaved populations — New York and New Jersey — did not pass gradual abolition laws until 1799 and 1804, the free black population increased throughout the region.

Southern states, by contrast, at first maintained their laws protecting slavery in the years immediately following the Revolution, although some major changes did occur. A few slaveholders took revolutionary ideals to heart and emancipated the people they had enslaved following the war. Others granted emancipation in their wills. In addition, several states prohibited the importation of enslaved people from Africa during or immediately following the Revolution. They all stopped far short, however, of ending slavery.

At the same time, however, the enslaved population of the United States continued to grow rapidly. Southern legislators soon made it difficult for slaveholders to free enslaved people and for free black people to remain in the region. Slaveholders migrated into the newly claimed lands in the trans-Appalachian west, bringing tens of thousands of enslaved African Americans with them. The growth of the enslaved population in the South and West thus resulted just as much from the American Revolution as did the halting first steps northern states took to end slavery in the north.

Some white people aided black people in their struggles for freedom. Quakers, the only religious group to oppose slavery in the colonial period, became more outspoken. By the 1790s, nearly all Quakers had freed the people they had enslaved and withdrawn from the slave trade. Anthony Benezet, a writer and educator, worked tirelessly for the abolition of slavery. In 1770 he founded, and thereafter directed, the Negro School of Philadelphia, which was one of several such schools founded by the Quakers.

AP® TIP
Analyze how the growth of slavery, and the support it received from the U.S. government, shaped society and culture in the new republic.

Because the new nation had failed to end slavery, its role in America's national culture made it more difficult for white people to imagine African Americans as anything more than lowly laborers, despite free black people who clearly demonstrated otherwise. Thus, most white people in America either believed or assumed black people were inferior — and that no amount of education could change that. In the North, states did not generally incorporate black children into their plans for public education. Moreover, most southern planters had little desire to teach enslaved people to read and write. African Americans in cities with large free black populations often took matters into their own hands and funded schools. Reverend Allen opened a Sunday school for children in 1795 at his church, and other free black

TEACHING IDEA

Incorporating Primary Sources

The Stanford History Education Group's "Reading Like a Historian" online platform contains the lesson, "Slavery in the Constitution," which can be accessed by visiting the website (sheg.stanford.edu) and searching for the term "slavery." This resource provides students with the opportunity to investigate and analyze a series of primary sources to determine the various positions of the founders on slavery, as well as address the apparent contradiction between the Declaration's claim that "All men are created equal," and the Constitution's original legal enshrinement of chattel slavery.

people formed literary and debating societies during this era. Still, only a small percentage of African Americans received an education equivalent to that available to white people in the early republic.

In the emergent new national culture, sympathetic depictions of Africans and African Americans by white artists and authors appeared infrequently. Most were produced in the North and were intended for the rare patrons who opposed slavery. These portrayals were, however, far from flattering: They exaggerated black peoples' perceived physical and intellectual differences from whites, to imply inferiority. Whether their depictions were intended to be "realistic," sentimental, or derogatory, Africans and African Americans, like American Indians, were almost unfailingly rendered through the eyes of white people.

Aware of the limited opportunities available in the United States, some African Americans considered the benefits of moving elsewhere. In the late 1780s, the Newport African Union Society in Rhode Island developed a plan to establish a community for black Americans in Africa. Many white people, too, viewed the settlement of black Americans in Africa as the only way to solve the nation's growing racial dilemma.

REVIEW

- To what extent was the status of African Americans in early America similar to women and poor white people?
- In what ways was it different?

AP® WRITING HISTORICALLY — Making Evaluative Comparisons in a Document-Based Essay

Just as you worked with documents to evaluate continuity and change in Module 3-6, here, you will practice making evaluative comparisons in an essay that incorporates primary source documents as support for a historical argument. The following Document-Based Question asks you to combine your knowledge from this module and your background knowledge with a close, active reading of seven accompanying documents:

> Evaluate the extent of similarity in the status and lifestyles of American Indians and African Americans in the period from 1763 to 1800.

Step 1 Break down the prompt.

As with previous essays, be sure to ACE this question and create a list of information you already know about the prompt. Remember, it may be helpful to treat this prompt as if no documents were provided.

Remember, the wording of the prompt provides important clues about what your response must do. When you are asked to "evaluate the extent" of something, you are essentially being asked, "How much?" It means you need to evaluate the importance of the historical developments you bring into your response.

Step 2 Read and annotate the documents.

Now consider the seven documents that accompany the prompt. As you read each source, remember to ask yourself the following questions:

- What is the document about? What historical situation does it describe or reference?
- Who was the intended audience for this document?
- What was the author's purpose in writing this document?
- What point of view does the author of this document express?
- How does this document relate back to the prompt? In this case, try to link each document to a specific effect of the market revolution on society as you annotate.
- Does this document remind you of any other historical developments? Jot down any relevant evidence from your own background knowledge that comes to mind.

(Continued)

TRM Suggested Responses to Questions

BUILDING AP® SKILLS

Argumentation

As in previous modules, students' understanding the nature of the question they are confronted with at a very basic level is of paramount importance. As students engage with the Writing Historically prompt, this a good place yet again to reinforce the foundational first principles of addressing an AP® prompt. Specifically, this means begin by searching for and decoding/translating the verb of the prompt, the "action word," into meaningful directives for the students. In this instance, the verb is "explain." Discuss with students that "explain" in this instance means to "lay out," or "display/demonstrate," more than it means to merely "tell." Additionally, the qualifying clause, "the extent of the similarity in," in plain English is best translated as, "how much is going to be the same." This provides the instructor with the place again to show students that simple prompt deconstruction on their part will set them up to position their response to this question (and any others like it, irrespective of content) as adhering to one of only three avenues: substantial similarity, minimal similarity, or somewhat mixed similarity, with a percentage of preponderance in similarity leaning incrementally toward one particular facet or another. From here, students can then begin to construct a well-grounded argument.

Period 3: 1754–1800   **MODULE 3-7** Legacies of the American Revolution

TEACHING IDEA

AP® Writing Historically Workshop

Because this question asks students to address two elements, consider having students work through the following activity to ensure they answer the prompt fully. First, have students individually define what the question means by status and lifestyle. Next, have students conduct a think-pair-share to compare their understandings of the terms. After students are acclimated to the historical relevance of the terms, have them group each document to either status or lifestyle. After students have completed these steps, they will be more prepared to move on to the activity on page 228.

Finally, keep in mind how you can use each document to support the historical argument you are planning to make. How can you use each to compare the effect of the American Revolution on American Indians and African Americans during the late eighteenth century?

DOCUMENT 1

Source: Petition of Enslaved African Americans to the Massachusetts Legislature, 1777

"To The Honorable Council and House of Representatives for the State of Massachusetts Bay in General Court assembled, January 13, 1777

The petition of a great number of blacks detained in a state of slavery in the bowels of a free and Christian country. . . . Your petitioners apprehend that they have in common with all other men a natural and unalienable right to that freedom which the Great Parent of the Universe has bestowed equally on all mankind and which they have never forfeited by any compact or agreement whatever, but . . . were unjustly dragged by the hand of cruel power . . . and in defiance of all the tender feelings of humanity brought here . . . to be sold like beasts of burden and like them condemned to slavery for life. . . . In imitation of the laudable example of the good people of these states your petitioners . . . cannot but express their astonishment that it has never been considered that every principle from which America has acted in the course of their unhappy difficulties with Great Britain pleads stronger than a thousand arguments in favor of your petitioners. They therefore humbly beseech your honors . . . to cause an act of the legislature to be passed whereby they may be restored to the enjoyments of that which is the natural right of all men. . . ."

DOCUMENT 2

Source: Colonel Daniel Brodhead, *Letter to General George Washington*, 1779

"I had only six hundred & five Rank & File, including volunteers & Militia; with those I marched to the upper town on the River, called the Yahrungwago, I met with no opposition from the enemy after killing six or seven, & wounding a number out of a party of warriors consisting of Forty, that were coming against the settlements—this was done in a few minutes by the advanced Guard—composed of fifteen Light Infantry & eight Delaware Indians, without any loss on our side, except three men very slightly wounded—we destroyed in the whole, one hundred & sixty-five Cabins, 130 of which were deserted on the approach of the troops; & the most of them were new & large enough for accommodation of three or four Indian families. . . .

I congratulate you on your success against the Indians and the more savage tories, & am quite happy in the reflection that our efforts promise a lasting tranquility to the Frontiers we have covered. Something still remains to be done to the westward, which I expect leave to execute, & then I conceive the wolves of the forest will have sufficient cause to howl as they will be quite destitute of food. . . ."

DOCUMENT 3

Source: Boston King, *Memoirs of Boston King*, 1796

"About this time, peace was restored between America and Great Britain which diffused universal joy among all parties except us, who had escaped slavery and taken refuge in the English army; for a report prevailed at New-York that all the slaves, in number two thousand, were to be delivered up to their masters, altho' some of them had been three or four years among the English. This dreadful rumour filled us with inexpressible anguish and terror, especially when we saw our old masters coming from Virginia, North-Carolina and other parts and seizing upon slaves in the streets of New-York, or even dragging them out of their beds. Many of the slaves had very cruel masters, so that the thought of returning home with them embittered life to us. For some days we lost our appetite for food, and sleep departed from our eyes. The English had compassion upon us in the day of our distress, and issued out a Proclamation importing 'That all slaves should be free who had taken refuge in the British lines and claimed the sanction and privileges of the Proclamations respecting the security and protection of Negroes.' In consequence of this, each of us received a certificate from the commanding officer at New-York, which dispelled our fears and filled us with joy and gratitude."

DOCUMENT 4

Source: *Northwest Ordinance,* 1787

"Sec. 13. And for extending the fundamental principles of civil and religious liberty, which form the basis whereon these republics, their laws, and constitutions are erected; to fix and establish those principles as the basis of all laws, constitutions, and governments, which for ever hereafter shall be formed in the said territory; to provide, also, for the establishment of States, and permanent government therein, and for . . . [their] admission to a share in the federal councils on an equal footing with the original States, at as early periods as may be consistent with the general interest: . . . .

Article III. Religion, morality, and knowledge, being necessary to good government, and the happiness of mankind, schools and the means of education shall forever be encouraged. The utmost good faith shall always be observed towards the Indians; their lands and property shall never be taken from them without their consent; and in their property, rights, and liberty, they shall never be invaded or disturbed, unless in just and lawful wars authorized by Congress; but laws founded in justice and humanity shall, from time to time, be made, for preventing wrongs being done to them, and for preserving peace and friendship with them. . . .

Article VI. There shall be neither slavery nor involuntary servitude in the said territory, otherwise than in the punishment of crimes, whereof the party shall have been duly convicted: Provided, always, That any person escaping into the same, from whom labor or service is lawfully claimed in any one of the original States, such fugitive may be lawfully reclaimed, and conveyed to the person claiming his or her labor or service as aforesaid."

DOCUMENT 5

Source: *United States Constitution, Article I,* 1787

"[Section 2:] Representatives and direct Taxes shall be apportioned among the several States which may be included within this Union, according to their respective Numbers, which shall be determined by adding to the whole Number of free Persons, including those bound to Service for a Term of Years, and excluding Indians not taxed, three fifths of all other Persons. . . .

[Section 9:] The Migration or Importation of such Persons as any of the States now existing shall think proper to admit, shall not be prohibited by the Congress prior to the Year one thousand eight hundred and eight, but a Tax or duty may be imposed on such Importation, not exceeding ten dollars for each Person."

DOCUMENT 6

Source: *Pennsylvania Act for the Gradual Abolition of Slavery,* 1780

"And whereas the condition of those persons who have heretofore been denominated negro and mulatto slaves, has been attended with circumstances which not only deprived them of the common blessings that they were by nature entitled to, but has cast them into the

(Continued)

deepest afflictions by an unnatural separation and sale of husband and wife from each other, and from their children, an injury the greatness of which can only be conceived by supposing that we were in the same unhappy case. In justice, therefore, to persons so unhappily circumstanced, and who, having no prospect before them whereon they may rest their sorrows and their hopes, have no reasonable inducement to render that service to society which they otherwise might, and also in grateful commemoration of our own happy deliverance from that state of unconditional submission to which we were doomed by the tyranny of Britain:

Be it enacted and it is hereby enacted by the Representatives of the Freemen of the Commonwealth of Pennsylvania in General Assembly met, and by the authority of the same, That all persons, as well negroes and mulattoes as others who shall be born within this state, from and after the passing of this act, shall not be deemed and considered as servants for life or slaves; and that all servitude for life or slavery of children in consequence of the slavery of their mothers, in the case of all children born within this state from and after the passing of this act as aforesaid, shall be and hereby is utterly taken away, extinguished and forever abolished."

DOCUMENT 7

Source: *Treaty of Greenville, Article 9*, 1795

"Should any Indian tribes meditate a war against the United States or either of them, and the same shall come to the knowledge of the before-mentioned tribes, or either of them, they do hereby engage to give immediate notice thereof to the general or officer commanding the troops of the United States, at the nearest post. And should any tribe, with hostile intentions against the United States, or either of them, attempt to pass through their country, they will endeavour to prevent the same, and in like manner give information of such attempt, to the general or officer commanding, as soon as possible, that all causes of mistrust and suspicion may be avoided between them and the United States. In like manner the United States shall give notice to the said Indian tribes of any harm that may be meditated against them, or either of them, that shall come to their knowledge; and do all in their power to hinder and prevent the same, that the friendship between them may be uninterrupted."

ACTIVITY

Plan and write an essay in response to the Document-Based Question at the beginning of this box. Be sure to start by writing a contextualization statement that leads to a thesis with at least three claims. In the body of your essay, use at least six of the seven documents to support your historical argument, and include additional evidence from your own historical knowledge. Remember, you must explain *how* all of your evidence supports your claims — this is the most important part of an effective historical argument. For a challenge, try adding a fourth claim to your thesis.

You may use the following outline to guide your response:

I. Introductory paragraph
   A. Immediate/preceding contextualization statement
      1. Cite evidence of immediate/preceding context
      2. Explain influence of immediate/preceding context
   B. Thesis statement presenting three to four evaluative claims of comparison that are situated along a continuum of relative importance
II. Claim 1 body paragraph
   A. Topic sentence presenting an evaluative claim of comparison 1
   B. Supporting statement citing evidence of claim 1 (from historical knowledge)
   C. Cite additional evidence of claim 1 (from a document)
   D. Cite additional evidence of claim 1 (from another document)
   E. Explain how evidence supports claim 1

III. Claim 2 body paragraph
   A. Topic sentence presenting evaluative claim of comparison 2
   B. Supporting statement citing evidence of claim 2 (from historical knowledge)
   C. Cite additional evidence of claim 2 (from a document)
   D. Cite additional evidence of claim 2 (from another document)
   E. Explain how evidence supports claim 2
IV. Claim 3 body paragraph
   A. Topic sentence presenting evaluative claim of comparison 3
   B. Supporting statement citing evidence of claim 3 (from historical knowledge)
   C. Cite additional evidence of claim 3 (from a document)
   D. Cite additional evidence of claim 3 (from another document)
   E. Explain how evidence supports claim 3
V. (Optional) Claim 4 body paragraph
   A. Topic sentence presenting evaluative claim of comparison 4
   B. Supporting statement citing evidence of claim 4 (from historical knowledge)
   C. Cite additional evidence of claim 4 (from a document)
   D. Cite additional evidence of claim 4 (from another document)
   E. Explain how evidence supports claim 4

TRM Suggested Responses to Questions

Module 3-8

George Washington Unites a Nation

LEARNING TARGETS

By the end of this module, you should be able to:
- Explain how the Washington administration enacted economic policies to stabilize the federal government.
- Explain how different interpretations of the Constitution caused conflict between Americans during Washington's first administration.

THEMATIC FOCUS
Politics and Power

During George Washington's first term, the new federal government aimed to strengthen federal authority through new economic policies and the establishment of a new capital. These policies led to divisions within Washington's cabinet based on both regional interests and differing interpretations of the new Constitution.

HISTORICAL REASONING FOCUS
Causation

TASK ▶ While reading this module, consider the causes of Washington's policies and their intended effects. Also consider the unintended consequences, especially in terms of differing interpretations of the new Constitution.

TEACHING IDEA

Incorporating Videos

To lay the groundwork for the Washington presidency, have the class watch the "History Channel – The Presidents 1789-1825 Washington to Monroe" excerpt on George Washington (available on YouTube; Washington clip is 00:00:18 – 00:21:40). This 20-minute overview of his administration is a useful way to create context for the module to come, in an economy of time.

Most political leaders hoped that the partisanship of the ratification battle (see Module 3-6) would fade away with the Constitution approved. The electoral college's unanimous decision to name George Washington the first president and John Adams vice president helped calm the political turmoil. The two took office in April 1789, launching the new government.

Several issues arose after George Washington's inauguration as president. The government needed to be organized and staffed. Looming issues of state and national war debt demanded urgent attention and led some to call for a system for levying, collecting, and distributing funds. Diplomatic relations with foreign powers and American Indian nations needed to be reestablished. Many state ratifying conventions demanded a bill of rights for the newly adopted Constitution, which had not yet been drafted. Finally, both those in favor of and those who had fought against the Constitution had to be convinced that this new government would respond more capably to the varied needs of its citizens.

Organizing the Federal Government

To bring order to his administration, President George Washington quickly established four departments — State, War, Treasury, and Justice — by appointing respected leaders to fill the posts. Washington named Thomas Jefferson secretary of state; Henry Knox, secretary of war; Alexander Hamilton, secretary of the treasury; and Edmund Randolph, attorney general at the head of the Department of Justice.

Congress, meanwhile, worked to establish a judicial system. The Constitution called for a Supreme Court but provided no specific guidelines. The Judiciary Act of 1789 established a Supreme Court composed of six justices along with thirteen district courts and three circuit courts to hear

---

TEACHING IDEA

Building Vocabulary

Discuss with your students the meaning of the word, "precedent," specifically as it applies to Washington's situation. Students need to note that as chief executive, Washington was very much "building the ship as he was sailing it," and even more importantly, he was fully cognizant of this reality for the entirety of his two terms of office. The fact that he was daily establishing procedures and methods and perceptions for the presidency and the government at-large was never lost upon him and was at the forefront of his mind for nearly every action he took as president. This added a special layer to his decision-making processes that students should consider as they study the man and his administration.

Organizing the Federal Government

▲ **Federal Hall** This drawing shows Federal Hall, located on Wall Street in New York City. The building housed the Stamp Act Congress in 1765 and the confederation congress from 1785 to 1788. In 1789 it became the seat of Congress under the new Constitution (the capital was later moved to Philadelphia in December 1790), and the site of President Washington's first inauguration. **How does this image represent the egalitarian ideals of the American Revolution? How does it also differentiate Federal Hall as more significant than the other buildings in the image?**

Bill of Rights The first ten amendments to the Constitution. These ten amendments helped reassure Americans who feared that the federal government established under the Constitution would infringe on the rights of individuals and states.

cases appealed from the states. Congress also quickly produced a bill of rights. Representative James Madison gathered more than two hundred resolutions passed by state ratifying conventions and honed them down to twelve amendments, which Congress approved and submitted to the states for ratification. In 1791 ten of the amendments were ratified, and these became the **Bill of Rights**. It guaranteed the rights of individuals and states in the face of a powerful central government, including freedom of speech, the press, religion, and the right to petition.

AP® ANALYZING SOURCES

Source: James Madison, *Speech Proposing the Bill of Rights*, 1789

"It appears to me that this house is bound by every motive of prudence, not to let the first session pass over without proposing to the state legislatures some things to be incorporated into the constitution, as will render it as acceptable to the whole people of the United States, as it has been found acceptable to a majority of them. I wish, among other reasons why something should be done, that those who have been friendly to the adoption of this constitution, may have the opportunity of proving to those who were opposed to it, that they were as sincerely devoted to liberty and a republican government, as those who charged them with wishing the adoption of this constitution in order to lay the foundation of an aristocracy or despotism. It will be a desirable thing to extinguish from the bosom of every member of the community any

(Continued)

BUILDING AP® SKILLS

Argumentation

Write the following question on the board/projector: "The Bill of Rights was an unnecessary and redundant addition to the Constitution." Divide students into groups of six. In each group, task three students with supporting the claim, and three students with refuting the claim. Instruct student triads to share their reasoning with their opposite counterparts of their group of six, and then have the group of six record their arguments and assertions in a T-chart format.

▲ Differentiation

Whole groups from the activity above can then be tasked with crafting a thesis statement, including contextualization in the 4-1-1 model, to address the prompt (a refresher of the 4-1-1 model can be found on page 163). This will allow students of varying ability levels to both contribute to the process and learn better how to develop argument by learning and sharing with their peers.

TRM Find **Handout 3.9 – Bill of Rights Debate** in the Teacher's Resource Materials.

TRM **Suggested Responses to Questions**

TRM **Module 3.8 AP® Analyzing Sources Handout 1**

TEACHING IDEA

Incorporating Secondary Sources

Assign students to read Gordon Wood's "Origins of the Bill of Rights," available through Google search from the American Antiquarian Society. Require students to both identify Wood's thesis and create a summative conclusive statement on their takeaways on his work. Have students share these out in small-group format, with students rotating among several of their peers.

Period 3: 1754–1800
MODULE 3-8 George Washington Unites a Nation

apprehensions, that there are those among his countrymen who wish to deprive them of the liberty for which they valiantly fought and honorably bled. And if there are amendments desired, of such a nature as will not injure the constitution, and they can be ingrafted so as to give satisfaction to the doubting part of our fellow citizens; the friends of the federal government will evince that spirit of deference and concession for which they have hitherto been distinguished."

Questions for Analysis

1. Describe Madison's justification for the Bill of Rights.
2. Explain the political context that shaped this speech.
3. Evaluate the extent to which Madison's argument draws from the ideals expressed in the Declaration of Independence.

REVIEW

- How did Washington's administration reflect Federalist goals and principles?
- In what ways did the Bill of Rights achieve the goals of the Antifederalists?

Hamilton Forges a Financial Plan

Hamilton played a leading role in advocating and establishing the new national government, particularly by seeking to stabilize and strengthen the national economy. The new government's leaders recognized that without a stable economy, even the best political structure could falter. Thus Hamilton's appointment as secretary of the treasury was especially significant. In formulating his economic policy, Hamilton's main goal was to establish the nation's credit. Paying down the debt and establishing a national bank would strengthen the United States in the eyes of the world and tie wealthy Americans more firmly to the federal government.

Hamilton advocated funding the national debt at face value and taking on the remaining state debts as part of the national debt. To pay for this policy, he planned to raise revenue through government bonds and new taxes. Hamilton also called for the establishment of a central bank to carry out the financial operations of the United States. In three major reports to Congress — on public credit and a national bank in 1790 and on manufactures in 1791 — he laid out a system of state-assisted economic development.

Hamilton's proposal to repay at face value the millions of dollars in securities issued by the United States under the Articles of Confederation generated political controversy. Thousands of soldiers, farmers, and shopkeepers had been paid with these securities during the war; but needing money in its aftermath, most sold them to speculators for a fraction of their value. These speculators would make enormous profits if the securities were paid off at face value. One of the policy's most ardent critics, Patrick Henry, claimed that Hamilton's policy was intended "to erect, and concentrate, and perpetuate a large monied interest" that would prove "fatal to the existence of American liberty." Despite such passionate opponents, Hamilton gained the support of Washington and other key national leaders.

The federal government's assumption of the remaining state war debts also faced fierce opposition, especially from southern states like Virginia that had already paid off their debt. Hamilton again won his case, though this time only by agreeing to reimburse states that had repaid their debts. To secure the necessary votes, Hamilton and his supporters agreed to move the nation's capital from Philadelphia to a more central location along the Potomac River. Jefferson hoped the move, by shifting the capital away from a commercial center, would reduce the growing influences of merchants and monied interests in the new nation's politics.

Funding the national debt, assuming the remaining state debts, and redeeming state debts already paid would cost $75.6 million (about $1.5 billion today). But Hamilton believed maintaining some debt was useful. He thus proposed establishing a Bank of the United States, funded by $10 million in stock to be sold to private stockholders and the national government. The bank would serve as a storage place for federal revenues, and would grant loans and sell bills of credit to merchants and investors, thereby creating a permanent national debt. This, he argued, would bind investors to the United States, turning the national debt into a "national blessing."

TEACHING IDEA

Building Vocabulary

Point out to students that a rather common euphemism for the "necessary and proper clause" of the constitution is "the elastic clause," because of the ability of the central government to stretch its powers, like elastic, when this interpretation is applied in practice. Use of this terminology is fully acceptable in academic conversation and AP® written work.

Period 3: 1754–1800

A New Capital for a New Nation

AP® TIP

Comparing the arguments put forward by Alexander Hamilton and Thomas Jefferson for and against the constitutionality of creating a national bank is key to understanding the emerging political differences in the 1790s.

Not everyone agreed. Jefferson and Madison argued vehemently against the Bank of the United States, noting that there was no constitutional sanction for a federal bank. Hamilton fought back, arguing that Congress had the right to make "all Laws which shall be necessary and proper" for carrying out the provisions of the Constitution. Once again, he prevailed. Congress chartered the bank for a period of twenty years, and Washington signed the legislation into law.

The final piece of Hamilton's plan focused on raising revenue. Congress quickly agreed to pass tariffs on a range of imported goods, which generated some $4 million to $5 million annually. Some congressmen viewed these tariffs as a way to protect new industries in the United States, from furniture to shoes. Excise taxes placed on a variety of consumer goods, most notably whiskey, generated another $1 million each year.

Hamilton's financial policies, supported by Washington, proved enormously successful in stabilizing the American economy, repaying outstanding debts, and tying men of wealth to the new government. The federal bank effectively collected and distributed the nation's resources. Commerce flourished, revenues rose, and confidence revived among foreign and domestic investors. And while the United States remained an agricultural nation, Hamilton's 1791 "Report on the Subject of Manufactures" foreshadowed the growing significance of industry, which gradually lessened U.S. dependence on European nations.

AP® ANALYZING SOURCES

Source: Alexander Hamilton, *Report on the Subject of Manufactures*, 1791

"It ought readily to be conceded, that the cultivation of the earth . . . has intrinsically a strong claim to pre-eminence over every other kind of industry.

But, that it has a title to any thing like an exclusive predilection, in any country, ought to be admitted with great caution. That it is even more productive than every other branch of Industry requires more evidence, than has yet been given in support of the position. That its real interests, precious and important as without the help of exaggeration, they truly are, will be advanced, rather than injured by the due encouragement of manufactures, may, it is believed, be satisfactorily demonstrated. And it is also believed that the expediency of such encouragement in a general view may be shewn to be recommended by the most cogent and persuasive motives of national policy."

Questions for Analysis

1. Identify the significance of agriculture and manufacturing, according to Hamilton.
2. Describe the comparison Hamilton makes between agriculture and manufacturing.
3. Explain the purpose of Hamilton's report, as well as how it relates to his overall financial plan for the nation.

REVIEW

- How did Hamilton's policies stabilize the national economy?
- Why did these policies draw political opposition?

A New Capital for a New Nation

The construction of Washington City, the new capital, provided an opportunity to highlight the nation's distinctive culture and identity. But here, again, slavery emerged as a crucial part of that identity. Jefferson's plan, accepted by Washington and Hamilton, situated the capital between Virginia and Maryland, an area where more than 300,000 enslaved workers lived. To construct the capital, between 1792 and 1809, the government hired hundreds of enslaved men and a few

APPLY THE TIP

Assign students to read the primary source passages, "Hamilton's Opinion as to the Constitutionality of the Bank of the United States: 1791" and Jefferson's "Opinion on the Constitutionality of a National Bank: 1791," from The Avalon Project (avalon.law.yale.edu). Have students in small groups create two illustrations or products to represent the argument or central philosophy underpinning each of the two sources in the excerpt.

TRM Suggested Responses to Questions

TRM Module 3.8 AP® Analyzing Sources Handout 2

TEACHING IDEA

Check for Understanding

Assign students to read John Steele Gordon's "Alexander Hamilton: The Founding Wizard," from American Heritage's website (americanheritage.com). Follow up by playing a YouTube excerpt of music lyrics from *Hamilton: An American Musical*, "Cabinet Battle #1 (clean version)."

TEACHING IDEA

Incorporating Secondary Sources

Assign students to read "Capitalism and the Rise of the Republican Opposition," by Joyce Appleby, available through online search from Study the Past's website. Brief small-group (5-7 students per group) discussion to follow, culminating in a small-group thesis-building activity addressing the following prompt: "Explain the extent to which general economic forces, rather than specific governmental policies, created political divisions in the United States between 1783 and 1796."

▲ **Differentiation**

Upon completion of the thesis-building exercise, there are several directions you could lead your class. Students could be tasked with writing a full essay based upon their thesis. Students could post their theses around the room, have a gallery walk, and vote on the strongest one. They could then be assigned to write a response to the prompt based upon that winning thesis, either for homework or in the next class. Students could be placed into groups to pre-write or outline a full essay based upon either their own theses or the class-selected one. Instructors should apply any and all of these strategies as the conditions of their classroom context dictate.

women, paying slaveholders $5 per month for each individual's labor. Enslaved men cleared trees and stumps, built roads, dug trenches, baked bricks, and cut and laid sandstone while enslaved women cooked, did laundry, and nursed the sick and injured. A small number performed skilled labor as carpenters or assistants to stonemasons and surveyors. Some four hundred enslaved laborers worked on the Capitol building alone, more than half the workforce.

Free black people also participated in the development of Washington. Many worked alongside enslaved laborers, but a few held important positions. Benjamin Banneker, for example, a self-taught clock maker, astronomer, and surveyor, was hired as an assistant to the surveyor Major Andrew Ellicott. In 1791 Banneker helped to plot the 100-square-mile site on which the capital was to be built.

African Americans often worked alongside Irish immigrants, whose wages were kept in check by the availability of enslaved labor. Most workers, regardless of race, faced poor housing, sparse meals, malarial fevers, and limited medical care. Despite these obstacles, in less than a decade, a system of roads was laid out and cleared, the Executive Mansion was built, and the north wing of the Capitol was completed.

AP® ANALYZING SOURCES

Source: Benjamin Banneker, *Letter to Thomas Jefferson*, 1791

"I am fully sensible of the greatness of that freedom which I take with you on the present occasion; a liberty which seemed to me scarcely allowable, when I reflected on that distinguished, and dignifyed station in which you Stand. . . . Sir I freely and Chearfully acknowledge, that I am of the African race. . . . Sir, Suffer me to recall to your mind that time in which the Arms and tyranny of the British Crown were exerted with every powerful effort in order to reduce you to a State of Servitude, look back I intreat you on the variety of dangers to which you were exposed, reflect on that time in which every human aid appeared unavailable. . . . This Sir, was a time in which you clearly saw into the injustice of a State of Slavery, and in which you had just apprehensions of the horrors of its condition, it was now Sir, that your abhorrence thereof was so excited, that you publickly held forth this true and invaluable doctrine, which is worthy to be recorded and remember'd in all Succeeding ages. 'We hold these truths to be Self evident, that all men are created equal, and that they are endowed by their creator with certain unalienable rights, that among these are life, liberty, and the pursuit of happyness.' . . . [A]s Job proposed to his friends 'Put your Souls in their Souls stead,' thus shall your hearts be enlarged with kindness and benevolence toward them, and thus shall you need neither the direction of myself or others in what manner to proceed herein. . . .

And now, Sir, altho my Sympathy and affection for my brethren hath caused my enlargement thus far, I ardently hope that your candour and generosity will plead with you in my behalf, when I make known to you, that it was not originally my design; but that having taken up my pen in order to direct to you as a present, a copy of an Almanack which I have calculated for the Succeeding year. . . . And altho I had almost declined to make my calculation for the ensuing year, in consequence of that time which I had allotted therefor being taking up at the Federal Territory by the request of Mr. Andrew Ellicott, yet finding myself under Several engagements to printers of this state to whom I had communicated my design, on my return to my place of residence, I industriously apply'd myself thereto, which I hope I have accomplished with correctness and accuracy, a copy of which I have taken the liberty to direct to you. . . ."

Questions for Analysis

1. Identify the comparison Banneker makes between the colonies under British rule and enslaved African Americans.
2. Explain the purpose of Banneker's comparison.
3. Explain how this letter reflects the historical situation in which it was written.

TRM Suggested Responses to Questions

TRM Module 3.8 AP® Analyzing Sources Handout 2

TEACHING IDEA

Incorporating Primary Sources

Have students read the following five sources from the textbook: Benjamin Banneker on this page, both sources on page 223, Esther DeBerdt Reed on page 187, and Phyllis Wheatley on page 183. Assign students to explain the commonalities in the points of view of all five sources with regards to natural rights. Discuss with students the intersection of race and gender with regards to the contradictions inherent in the eighteenth-century American conception of liberty. Have them complete a Venn diagram on the challenges and priorities of adherents of racial and gender reform in the early republic.

TRM Find **Handout 3.10 – Early Republic Racial and Gender Reform** in the Teacher's Resource Materials.

More prosperous immigrants and foreign professionals were also involved in creating the U.S. capital. Irish-born James Hoban designed the Executive Mansion. Pierre Charles L'Enfant, a French engineer, developed the plan for the city's streets. William Thornton, a West Indian physician turned architect, drew the blueprints for the Capitol building, the construction of which was directed by Englishman Benjamin Latrobe. Perhaps what was most "American" about the new capital was the diverse nationalities and races of those who designed and built it.

Washington's founders envisioned the city as a beacon to the world, proclaiming the advantages of the nation's republican principles. But its location on a slow-moving river and its clay soil left the area hot, humid, and dusty in the summer and muddy and damp in the winter and spring. When federal government officially moved to Washington in June 1800, they considered themselves on the frontiers of civilization. The tree stumps that remained on the mile-long road from the Capitol to the Executive Mansion made it nearly impossible to navigate in a carriage. On rainy days, when roads proved impassable, officials walked or rode horses to work. Many early residents painted Washington in harsh tones. New Hampshire congressional representative Ebenezer Matroon wrote a friend, "If I wished to punish a culprit, I would send him to do penance in this place . . . this swamp — this lonesome dreary swamp, secluded from every delightful or pleasing thing."

Despite its critics, Washington was the seat of federal power and thus played an important role in the social and political worlds of American elites. From January through March, the height of the social season, the wives of congressmen, judges, and other officials created a lively schedule of teas, parties, and balls in the capital city. When Thomas Jefferson became president, he opened the White House to visitors on a regular basis. Yet for all his republican principles, when Jefferson moved into the executive mansion, he brought several enslaved people with him.

> "If I wished to punish a culprit, I would send him to do penance in this place . . . this swamp — this lonesome dreary swamp, secluded from every delightful or pleasing thing."
>
> Ebenezer Matroon, New Hampshire congressman, 1800

▲ **The United States Capitol** This watercolor by William Russell Birch presents a view of the Capitol in Washington, D.C., before it was badly burned by the British during the War of 1812. Birch had emigrated from England in 1794 and lived in Philadelphia. As this painting suggests, neither the Capitol nor the city was as yet a vibrant center of republican achievements. **Compare this image to Federal Hall (p. 231). What similarities and differences are apparent in each? What accounts for these similarities and the differences?**

TEACHING IDEA

Connecting the Dots

Engage the class in an activity of association by disassociation called "Odd One Out." Start by writing the following terms on the board/projector:

- Hamilton's Report on the Subject of Manufactures
- The Bill of Rights
- The presidential cabinet
- Washington City
- The national debt

Then place students in small groups and ask them, "Which one is the Odd One Out and why? How do the remaining terms relate?" Give students approximately 7–10 minutes to complete this part, then share out student answers and discuss their conclusions and reasoning as a whole-class activity. There is no specific correct answer; the goal is to get students thinking in categorical habits of mind and defending their rationales.

BUILDING AP® SKILLS

Comparison

As a summative assessment, assign students to respond to the following LEQ prompt: "Compare the economic priorities and philosophies of Alexander Hamilton to those of Thomas Jefferson."

MODULE 3-8 George Washington Unites a Nation

In decades to come, Washington City would become Washington, D.C., a city with broad boulevards decorated with beautiful monuments to the American political experiment. And the executive mansion would become the White House, a proud symbol of republican government. Yet Washington was always characterized by wide disparities in wealth, status, and power, which were especially visible when enslaved people labored in the executive mansion's kitchen, laundry, and yard.

REVIEW

What roles did different groups of people have in constructing the new nation's capital city?

AP® WRITING HISTORICALLY — Short-Answer Question Practice

ACTIVITY

Read the following question carefully and write a short response. Use complete sentences.

Answer (a), (b), and (c), confining your response to the period 1754 to 1800.
a. Briefly describe ONE specific economic policy of the Washington administration.
b. Briefly explain how ONE specific historical event or development led to the economic policy described in (a).
c. Briefly explain how ONE specific historical event or development resulted from the policy described in (a).

TRM Suggested Responses to Questions

BUILDING AP® SKILLS

Argumentation

As a general strategy, the *ACE* method explained by the authors on page 21 for LEQ purposes, as in, "Answer the question, Cite your evidence, and Explain its meaning," is also very useful for Short-Answer Questions. For each of the three tasks of an SAQ, use this model. In so doing, the three tasks of an SAQ are then addressed in nine discrete steps. If this method is followed, the depth of student responses to the three directed tasks of the SAQ should be such that it increases the likelihood of every SAQ point being earned with a comfortable margin.

TEACHING IDEA

AP® Writing Historically Review

Short-Answer Questions are a straightforward way of assessing students' historical knowledge about a subject. This activity seeks to broaden students' understanding of what good responses will include. Divide students into groups of three or four and have each student write full answers for parts (a), (b), and (c). Next, have students select the best answers to (a), (b), and (c) within their group. The selections become the group answer, and students will cut and paste those answers to a blank piece of paper. Have students score the responses and turn in the group answers. This activity gives the teacher an opportunity to see if students recognize good writing. Additionally, teachers will also see how well students understand whether responses are worthy of scoring points.

Module 3-9

Political Parties in Years of Crisis

LEARNING **TARGETS**

By the end of this module, you should be able to:
- Explain the impact of the French Revolution on American politics.
- Explain the factors that led to the emergence of a two-party system.
- Explain why the Democratic-Republicans triumphed in the 1800 election, resulting in the first transfer of power between political parties under the Constitution.

THEMATIC **FOCUS**

Politics and Power
America in the World
American and Regional Culture
Migration and Settlement

During the 1790s, Americans debated the proper role of the federal government, including how it should shape economic and international policy. These debates ultimately led to two competing political factions — Federalists and Democratic-Republicans — as well as regional divisions. The French Revolution, along with the wars between France and Great Britain, further divided Americans along partisan and regional lines during this time period. Westward migration during the mid-1700s led to the creation of new communities and fostered ethnic tensions as well as regional conflicts. American Indians grappled with the impacts of migration and settlement as they adjusted alliances and sought to maintain access to resources and control of land.

HISTORICAL REASONING **FOCUS**

Causation

TASK ▶ As you read this module, consider the causes of the rise of the two earliest political factions in the United States: the Federalists and Democratic-Republicans. What effects did this rise in partisanship have on American politics during the last decade of the eighteenth century?

TEACHING IDEA

Incorporating Videos

Assign students to watch Episode 9 "Where US Politics Came From" from the Crash Course US History series (available on YouTube). Use this 13-minute episode as a concise formative content introduction for students of the initial major issues and events of Module 3-9 as part of preparation for either assessment or reinforcement.

BUILDING AP® SKILLS

Comparison

Assign students in pairs to create a T-chart comparing and contrasting the characteristics and beliefs of the Federalists and Anti-federalists. Share these as a whole-group exercise, to assure that all students have compiled the essential information concerning the two political groups.

▲ **Differentiation**

For the above exercise, student groups could instead be assigned to create a "cereal box" product for one or both of the emerging political groups. This has the potential to engage students of multiple ability levels and is a more involved, tactile, and kinesthetic approach to accomplish the same task as the basic T-chart. Templates and exemplars for creation of this type of product may be found at SampleTemplates' website by searching for "Cereal Box Book Reports" (sampletemplates.com).

By 1792 Hamilton had succeeded in implementing most of his plan for U.S. economic development (see Module 3-8). Yet as Washington began his second term in the spring of 1793, signs of strain appeared throughout the nation. America faced new challenges to foreign trade and diplomacy. Migration to the frontier increased, which intensified conflicts between American Indians and white settlers and increased hostilities between the United States and Great Britain. Yellow fever swept through Philadelphia and other cities, causing fear and disrupting political and economic life. Finally, the excise tax on whiskey fueled armed protests among frontier farmers. This cluster of crises split the Federalists into warring factions during Washington's second term, giving rise to the first form of the two-party system in American politics. By the time the election of 1796 took place, Federalist party candidates faced opposition from members of a new party, the Democratic-Republicans.

Foreign Trade and Foreign Wars

Jefferson and Madison led the opposition to Hamilton's policies during the 1780s and 90s. They drew notable support from farmers who envisioned the country's future rooted in agriculture, not the commerce and industry supported by Hamilton and his allies. Jefferson agreed with the Scottish economist Adam Smith that an international division of labor could best provide for the world's people. Americans

EXPLORING AP® THEMES

Politics and Power

This is an important place at which to revisit earlier class conversations on James Madison's Federalist #10, with specific regards to the concept of "faction." Point out to students that virtually all of Madison's concerns about factions and their capacity for creating disunity and tension within the republic will be on full display as this module unfolds.

TEACHING IDEA

Incorporating Secondary Sources

Assign students to read and annotate Albert H. Bowman's "Jefferson, Hamilton, and American Foreign Policy" available on JSTOR (jstor.org). Whole-class discussion to follow in the next class meeting.

▲ Differentiation

Follow up the roundtable discussion of the above article by playing a YouTube excerpt of music lyrics from *Hamilton: An American Musical*, "Cabinet Battle #2 (clean version)." Conclude by assigning students in small groups to create a visual illustration or representation of the differences between the two factions' approach to foreign relations.

EXPLORING AP® THEMES

America and the World

Point out to students that Washington's Neutrality Proclamation is a classic example of realpolitik in action. Although the self-preservationist motivations to avoid a major European continental land war for the United States are clear enough, make sure that students also understand the legal reasoning that Washington utilized to come to his decision. First of all, the Franco-American alliance was strictly defensive, and the Neutrality Proclamation did not violate the United States' defensive alliance with France, as the Jeffersonians were claiming. As such, it did not apply to offensive wars, and in this instance, it was France that had declared war upon other European powers in 1793, rather than the reverse being the case. Additionally, the Washington administration could claim the treaty had been signed with the French government, not the French people. As such, when the French royal government fell, i.e., the king was deposed and the Republic of France proclaimed, the United States could claim to be released from any such treaty obligation, as the signatory government was no longer in existence.

▲
Americans Trade with China This painting by a Chinese artist c. 1800 shows the Hongs at Canton, where ships from foreign countries arrived to unload and load goods. The foreign ships were limited to this small area outside Canton's city walls. There each nation established a trading post identified by its national flag and overseen by a Chinese merchant. **How does this image of a Chinese port represent Hamilton's vision for American trade?**

Neutrality Proclamation 1793 proclamation declaring U.S. neutrality in any conflicts between other nations, including France and Great Britain. Britain largely ignored U.S. neutrality and seized American merchant vessels heading for France.

could supply Europe with food and raw materials in exchange for manufactured goods. Jefferson felt his views were confirmed when wars in Europe, including a revolution in France, disrupted European agriculture in the 1790s and thus increased demands for the goods produced by American farms and plantations.

Although trade with Europe remained the most important source of goods and wealth for the United States, some merchants expanded into other parts of the globe. In the mid-1780s, the first American ships reached China, where they traded ginseng root and sea otter pelts for silk, tea, and chinaware. Still, events in Europe exerted far greater influences on the United States at the time than those in the Pacific world.

The **French Revolution** (1789–1799) was especially significant for U.S. politics. The ideals of freedom of speech, assembly, and religion declared in the American Declaration of Independence resonated with French men and women who opposed the tyrannical rule of King Louis XVI (r. 1774–1792). The resulting uprising disrupted French agriculture, increasing demand for American wheat, while the efforts of French revolutionaries to institute an egalitarian republic gained support from many Americans. The followers of Jefferson and Madison formed Republican societies, and members adopted the French term *citizen* when addressing each other. At the same time, the importance of workers and farmers among France's revolutionary forces reinforced critiques of the "monied power" that drove the Federalist policies promoted by Hamilton and Washington.

In late 1792, as French revolutionary leaders began executing thousands of their opponents in the Reign of Terror, wealthy Federalists grew more anxious. The beheading of King Louis XVI horrified them, as did the revolution's condemnation of Christianity. When France declared war against Prussia, Austria, and finally Great Britain, merchants worried about the impact on trade. In response, President Washington proclaimed U.S. neutrality in April 1793, prohibiting Americans from providing support or war materials to any belligerent nations — including France and Great Britain.

While the **Neutrality Proclamation** limited the shipment of certain items to Europe, Americans simultaneously increased trade with colonies in the British and French West Indies.

Indeed, U.S. ships captured much of the lucrative sugar trade. Britain, however, ignored U.S. neutrality. The Royal Navy stopped U.S. ships carrying French sugar and seized more than 250 vessels. At the same time, farmers in the Chesapeake and Middle Atlantic regions filled the growing demand for wheat in Europe, causing their profits to climb.

Yet these benefits did not bring about a political reconciliation. Although Jefferson condemned the French Reign of Terror, he protested the Neutrality Proclamation by resigning his cabinet post. Tensions escalated when the French envoy to the United States, Edmond Genêt, sought to enlist Americans in the European war. Republican clubs poured out to hear him speak and donated generously to the French cause. The British took more aggressive action supplying American Indians in the Ohio River valley with guns and encouraged them to raid U.S. settlements.

More concerned with the potential harm of Britain's meddling in the American West, President Washington sent John Jay to England to resolve concerns over trade with the British West Indies, compensation for seized American ships, the continued British occupation of frontier forts, and southerners' ongoing demands for reimbursement of enslaved people evacuated by the British during the Revolution. Jay returned from England in 1794 with a treaty, but it was widely criticized in Congress and the popular press. While securing limited U.S. trading rights in the West Indies, it failed to address British reimbursement for captured cargoes or enslaved people and granted Britain eighteen months to leave frontier forts. It also demanded that U.S. planters repay British firms for debts accrued during the Revolution. While the **Jay Treaty** was eventually ratified, it remained a source of political dispute.

Jay Treaty 1796 treaty that required British forces to withdraw from U.S. soil, required American repayment of debts to British firms, and limited U.S. trade with the British West Indies.

REVIEW

• How did Washington's foreign policies cause political debates in the United States?

The Whiskey Rebellion

Despite these foreign crises, it was the effect of Hamilton's policies on the American frontier that crystallized opposing factions into distinctly opposed parties. In the early 1790s, Republican societies from Maine to Georgia demanded the removal of British and Spanish troops from frontier areas, while frontier farmers lashed out at enforcement of the so-called whiskey tax. Many farmers on the frontier grew corn and turned it into whiskey to make it easier to transport and more profitable to sell. The whiskey tax hurt these farmers, hundreds of whom petitioned the federal government for relief.

Western Pennsylvania farmers were particularly angry and rallied in 1792 and 1793 to protest the tax and those who enforced it. Adopting tactics from Stamp Act protests and Shays's Rebellion, farmers blocked roads, burned sheriffs in effigy, marched on courthouses, and assaulted tax

"An Exciseman," c. 1791 This early cartoon depicts an excise agent, carrying two casks of whiskey to "Squire Vultures," with whom he intends to divide his take. He is pursued by two farmers opposed to the whiskey tax, who yell, "let us tar and feather the rascal." The exciseman is eventually hung over a barrel of whiskey, which is set on fire and explodes. **Explain the context of this image.**

TEACHING IDEA
Differing Views

Assign students to create a triple T-chart on the pros and cons of war with Great Britain, war with France, and war with neither power. Share and discuss the student conclusions as a whole-class activity.

TRM Find **Handout 3.10 – Pros and Cons of War or Neutrality** in the Teacher's Resource Materials.

BUILDING AP® SKILLS
Continuity and Change

Assign students to research their notes and text and compile information to compare the Whiskey Rebellion to one other rebellion from 1607 to 1800. Share out the class products for general discussion.

EXPLORING AP® THEMES
Social Structures

Discussion of the Whiskey Rebellion is a good place to point out to students that the rural–urban divide in terms of culture and economics, which is still with us today, is a long-standing part of the American social fabric. Both sides have a long history of not understanding one another and talking and acting past one another in a way that has historically bred stereotypes and resentment. Point out to students that they will be seeing this tension periodically in future periods, such as the populism of Jacksonian democracy, the People's Party of the late nineteenth century, and the phenomenon of Trumpism in contemporaneous times.

EXPLORING AP® THEMES

Politics and Power

Task students with contrasting the outcome of Shays's Rebellion with that of the Whiskey Rebellion in terms of the power of the state. The importance of this difference and the central reason for it — having an executive branch of government — cannot be stressed enough, and is something that tends to show up on the AP® examination in several different formats. Point out to students that for Americans of the time who viewed limited government as a positive good, i.e., adherents to the old Articles of Confederation, the power of the state as evidenced here would be seen as an undesirable overstepping and trampling upon individual liberties. This is a useful conversation to have with students, who often tend to presume that the Constitution was greeted by all as a universally good thing.

BUILDING AP® SKILLS

Continuity and Change

Revisit earlier important discussions of the pattern of American Indian–white relations first explored in Module 3-5, noting that whether the governing bodies were Great Britain or the United States, the consistent pattern underlying the process of westward expansion remained the same. American Indians and the British or American government sign a treaty that establishes specific boundaries and respective territories for both claimants; whites violate the stipulations of this agreement, and settle in lands designated as American Indian territories by the agreement; violence ensues; American Indians are blamed for the violence and the U.S. military is deployed to pacify the area; new agreements are reached, which extend the areas of white settlement further west than they were in the previous agreements. Remind students of the consistency of this pattern repeating itself throughout American Indian relations with Anglo-Americans in North America.

Whiskey Rebellion Uprising by western Pennsylvania farmers who led protests against the excise tax on whiskey in the early 1790s.

AP® TIP

Compare the Whiskey Rebellion to Bacon's Rebellion (Module 2-2), colonial responses to the Proclamation of 1763 (Module 3-1), and Shays's Rebellion (Module 3-5).

---

collectors. Government operations in Philadelphia were largely paralyzed by a yellow fever epidemic from August to November 1793, but the lack of response only fueled the rebels' anger. By 1794 all-out rebellion had erupted.

Washington, Hamilton, and their Federalist supporters worried that the rebellion could spread and might encourage greater efforts from American Indians to fight against intrusions on their lands. Since Spanish and British soldiers were eager to stir trouble along the frontier, the **Whiskey Rebellion** might spark their intervention as well. Federalists also suspected that pro-French immigrants from Scotland and Ireland helped fuel the insurgency.

Unlike 1786, however, when the federal government had little power to intervene in Shays's Rebellion, the Constitution offered more powerful federal options. Washington federalized militias from four states, calling up nearly thirteen thousand soldiers to put down the uprising. The army that marched into western Pennsylvania in September 1794 vastly outnumbered and easily suppressed the "whiskey rebels." Having gained victory, the federal government prosecuted only two of the leaders, who although convicted were later pardoned by Washington.

Washington proved that the Constitution provided the necessary powers to put down internal threats. Yet in doing so, the administration horrified many Americans who condemned the force used against the farmers as excessive. Jefferson and Madison gave voice to popular outrage from within the government. The Revolutionary generation had managed to compromise on many issues, from representation and slavery to the balance between federal and state authority. But now Hamilton's economic policies had led to a frontier uprising, and Washington had used a federal army to destroy popular dissent.

REVIEW

- How did the Constitution allow the federal government to respond differently to the Whiskey Rebellion than it did to Shays's Rebellion under the Articles of Confederation?

Further Conflicts on the Frontier

In one area, political elites leading the new nation shared a common concern: the continued threats to U.S. sovereignty by American Indian, British, and Spanish forces. Ratification of the Constitution of the United States changed little in relations between American Indians and the new nation. In 1790 Congress had passed the **Indian Trade and Intercourse Act** to regulate relations on the frontier and to ensure fair and equitable dealings. White Americans, however, widely ignored the act. Migration to the frontier increased, which, yet again, intensified conflicts between American Indians and white settlers and increased hostilities between the United States and Great Britain. The British continued supplying American Indians in the Ohio River valley with guns and encouraging them to raid U.S. settlements.

The government's failure to halt the flood of settlers into the Ohio and Mississippi River valleys proved costly. In 1790 Little Turtle, a war chief of the Miami nation, gathered a large force of Shawnee, Delaware, Ottawa, Chippewa, Sauk, Fox, and other American Indians. This alliance of tribes successfully attacked federal troops in the Ohio River valley that fall. A year later, the allied American Indian warriors defeated a large United States force. The stunning defeat shocked Americans. In the meantime, Spanish authorities negotiated with Creeks and Cherokees, encouraging and arming their attacks on U.S. settlements on the southern frontier.

At the same time, the events of the Whiskey Rebellion added to the chaos and fear for the viability of the new nation. Washington decided to deal with American Indians in the Northwest Territory first, sending 2,000 men under the command of General Anthony Wayne into the Ohio frontier. In August 1794, Wayne's forces attacked 1,500 to 2,000 American Indians gathered at a British fort. In the **Battle of Fallen Timbers**, American Indian allies, led by Little Turtle, suffered a devastating defeat. As a result, a year later, the warring American Indians in the Northwest Territory signed the **Treaty of Greenville**, granting the United States vast tracts of land.

Treaty of Greenville 1795 treaty signed following the Battle of Fallen Timbers. The treaty forced American Indians in the Northwest Territory to cede vast tracts of land to the U.S.

Amid this turmoil, in November 1794, John Jay signed his controversial treaty with Great Britain. With Britain agreeing to withdraw its forces from the U.S. frontier by 1796, the treaty may have helped persuade American Indian nations to accept U.S. peace terms at Greenville. Nonetheless, the Jay Treaty's requirement that Americans make "full and complete compensation" to British firms for Revolutionary War debts without the British compensating U.S. merchants or slaveholders for their losses nearly led Congress to reject it. In June 1795, however, the Senate finally approved the treaty without a vote to spare.

Before Jay's controversial treaty took effect, Spain agreed to negotiate an end to hostilities on the southern frontier of the United States. Envoy Thomas Pinckney negotiated the more popular **Pinckney Treaty**, which was supported by many Federalists — particularly from the west and south — who had opposed the Jay Treaty. Ratified in 1796, it recognized the thirty-first parallel as the boundary between U.S. and Spanish territory in the South and opened the Mississippi River and the port of New Orleans to U.S. shipping.

Pinckney Treaty 1796 treaty that defined the boundary between U.S. and Spanish territory n the South and opened the Mississippi River and New Orleans to U.S. shipping.

AP® ANALYZING SOURCES

Source: *Pinckney Treaty, Article IV*, 1795

"It is . . . agreed that the western boundary of the United States which separates them from the Spanish colony of Louisiana, is in the middle of the channel or bed of the river Mississippi, from the northern boundary of the said states to the completion of the thirty-first degree of latitude north of the equator. And his Catholic Majesty has likewise agreed that the navigation of the said river, in its whole breadth from its source to the ocean, shall be free only to his subjects and the citizens of the United States, unless he should extend this privilege to the subjects of other powers by special convention."

Questions for Analysis
1. Identify the western boundary of the United States set by this article in the treaty.
2. Explain why the boundary provided significant economic opportunities for United States citizens.
3. Explain how the Pinckney Treaty signaled a shift in America's international relations, particularly with Great Britain and Spain.

REVIEW
- What led to armed conflicts between the U.S. government and American Indians in the 1790s?
- What resulted from those conflicts?

A Two-Party System Forms

Democractic-Republicans Political party that emerged out of opposition to Federalist policies in the 1790s. The Democratic-Republicans chose Thomas Jefferson as their presidential candidate in 1796, 1800, and 1804.

In September 1796, when President Washington decided not to run again, he offered a Farewell Address in which he warned against the "spirit of party." "It agitates the community with ill-founded jealousies and false alarms," he claimed, and "kindles the animosity of one part against another." By then, Hamilton's economic policies, Washington's assault on the whiskey rebels, and Jay's Treaty led Jefferson, Madison, and other disenchanted politicians to form a distinct political party. They called themselves **Democratic-Republicans** and supported Jefferson for president. The election of 1796 was the first to be contested by candidates identified with opposing parties. Federalists supported John Adams for president and Thomas Pinckney for vice president. The Democratic-Republicans chose Thomas Jefferson and Aaron Burr of New York to represent their interests. The electoral college, hoping to bring the warring sides together, chose Federalist John Adams as president and

---

TRM Suggested Responses to Questions

TRM Module 3.9 AP® Analyzing Sources Handout 1

TEACHING IDEA

Class Discussion

Place the class into groups of four. Assign each group to itemize Jay's Treaty and Pinckney's Treaty in terms of the following four categories: provisions, benefits, limitations, and reception. Once this process is complete, merge the groups of four into groups of eight, and have these groups discuss their results and conclusions with an eye toward comparison and contrast. These treaties can be found on the Library of Congress website by searching by title (loc.gov).

▲ Differentiation

Assign students to read specific clauses of the treaties. Then, have students jigsaw their findings together to get them to understand the provisions, benefits, limitations, and reception (a refresher of the jigsaw model can be found on page 33).

TEACHING IDEA

Incorporating Primary Sources

Assign students to read and annotate Washington's Farewell Address, with the major point of emphasis being the two key elements of his address: his disapproval of political parties, and his disapproval of foreign entanglements. Point out to students that this document and this president are both mentioned explicitly by name within the AP® U.S. History Curriculum Framework, and as such, are fully assessable on the National Exam. Therefore, students' familiarity with both of them is essential.

BUILDING AP® SKILLS

Making Connections

Point out to students that the outcome of the election of 1796 proves that the founders were not clairvoyant, and did not anticipate political parties. This turned out to be one of their biggest errors when it came to crafting the nation-state governed by the Constitution and it led to a host of almost immediate practical problems in governance, as the leader of one political faction would find his chief political rival as his vice president. As such, there was no way that the Twelfth Amendment could not have come into existence; the realities of basic governance required it. This will be useful when analyzing the political cartoon on page 242.

Period 3: 1754–1800

MODULE 3-9 Political Parties in Years of Crisis

TEACHING IDEA

Incorporating Videos

Assign students to watch Adam Norris's "APUSH Review: Video #16: The Presidencies of Washington & Adams, And The 1st Party System" (available on YouTube). Use this 8-minute episode as a concise formative content introduction for students of the final major issues and events of Module 3-9 as part of preparation for either summative assessment or content reinforcement.

TRM Suggested Responses to Questions

TRM Module 3.9 AP® Analyzing Sources Handout 2

◂ MAP 3.7 **The Election of 1796** In the presidential election of 1796, the nation split regionally between supporters of Adams's Federalists and Jefferson's Democratic-Republicans. **What economic factors account for the regional divisions between Federalists and Democratic-Republicans?**

Thomas Jefferson as vice president. The two disagreed fundamentally on a wide range of issues, and events soon heightened these divisions. The effects of an administration divided against itself were nearly disastrous, and opposing interests became more thoroughly entrenched.

Adams and Jefferson had disagreed on almost every major policy issue during Washington's administration. Not surprisingly, the new president rarely took advice from his vice president. At the same time, Adams retained most of Washington's appointees, who often sought advice from Hamilton, undercutting Adams's authority. Worse still, the new president had poor political instincts and faced numerous challenges.

AP® ANALYZING SOURCES

Source: Anonymous, *The Providential Detection*, 1797

About the source: In this image, the American eagle takes the Constitution away from Jefferson before he can burn it on the "Altar to Gallic [French] Despotism." Fueling the flames are the works of Thomas Paine and French philosophers, whom Federalists saw as threats to order. In Jefferson's right hand is a letter from Jefferson to the Italian Philip Mazzei, also a supporter of the French Revolution. The letter supposedly criticized George Washington.

Questions for Analysis

1. Identify the figure in the lower right corner of the image.
2. Describe the way the image portrays 'Providence'.
3. Explain why the cartoonist might pair 'Providence' and the figure in the lower right corner of the image.
4. Explain the significance of the eagle.
5. Explain the message the artist conveys about Thomas Jefferson.

242

TEACHING IDEA

Connecting the Dots

Engage the class in an activity of association by disassociation called "Odd One Out." Write the following terms on the board/projector:

- Washington's Proclamation of Neutrality
- The Battle of Fallen Timbers
- Pinckney's Treaty
- The Bank of the United States
- The Whiskey Rebellion
- The Democratic-Republican Party

Then place students in small groups and ask them, "Which one is the Odd One Out and why? How do the remaining terms relate?" Give students approximately 7–10 minutes to complete this part, then share out student answers and discuss their conclusions and reasoning as a whole-class activity. There is no specific correct answer; the goal is to get students thinking in categorical habits of mind and defending their rationales.

A Two-Party System Forms

AP® TIP

Evaluate the relative significance of the crises that occurred during John Adams's administration.

At first, foreign disputes actually enhanced the authority of the Adams administration. The Federalists remained pro-British, and French seizures of U.S. ships threatened to provoke war. In 1798 Adams tried to negotiate compensation for the losses suffered by merchants. When an American delegation arrived in Paris, however, three French agents demanded a bribe to initiate talks.

Adams made public secret correspondence from the French agents, whose names were listed only as X, Y, and Z. Americans, including Democratic-Republicans, expressed outrage at this French insult to U.S. integrity, which became known as the **XYZ affair**. Congress quickly approved an embargo act that prohibited trade with France and permitted privateering against French ships. For the next two years, the United States fought an undeclared war with France.

Alien and Sedition Acts 1798 security acts passed by the Federalist-controlled Congress. The Alien Act allowed the president to imprison or deport noncitizens; the Sedition Act placed significant restrictions on political speech.

Naturalization Act 1798 act passed by the Federalist-controlled Congress that raised the residency requirement for citizenship from five to fourteen years to delay the naturalization of immigrants who largely voted Democratic-Republican.

Despite praise for his handling of the XYZ affair, Adams feared dissent from opponents at home and abroad. Consequently, the Federalist majority in Congress passed a series of security acts in 1798 referred to collectively as the **Alien and Sedition Acts**. The Alien Act allowed the president to order the imprisonment or deportation of noncitizens and was directed primarily at Irish and Scottish dissenters who criticized the government's pro-British policies. The Sedition Act outlawed "false, scandalous, or malicious statements against President or Congress." In the following months, nearly two dozen Democratic-Republican editors and legislators were arrested for sedition, and some were fined and imprisoned. Finally, the Federalist majority in Congress also approved the **Naturalization Act**, which raised the residency requirement for citizenship from five to fourteen years in an attempt to delay immigrants, who tended to support Democratic-Republicans, from voting by postponing their citizenship.

▲ **Matthew Lyon and Roger Griswold** This cartoon reflects the real-life conflict between Federalists and Democratic-Republicans throughout American politics in the 1790s. The caption reads: "He in a trice struck Lyon thrice / Upon his head, enrag'd sir, / Who seiz'd the tongs to ease his wrongs, / And Griswold thus engag'd, sir." **What factors not addressed in the U.S. Constitution caused this kind of conflict?**

APPLY THE TIP

Divide the class into groups of three. Assign each group one of the following categories: political, legal, or diplomatic. Then have students identify and elaborate upon which crises of the Adams administration they believe fit into their category and why. Then, recombine the groups into triads, with one member of each category represented, and have them share their findings. Finally, have this triad construct a contextualization and thesis introductory paragraph based upon the 4-1-1 model of argument construction (a refresher of the 4-1-1 model can be found on page 163).

TEACHING IDEA

Incorporating Primary Sources

Assign students to read excerpts of the Alien and Sedition Acts and the Naturalization Act, with brief annotation. The next day, place students in groups of five to eight to have them discuss and ascertain the meaning and significance in what they processed the previous night. Conclude the exercise with a thesis-building activity wherein students craft introductory paragraphs in response to the following prompt: "To what extent did the Alien and Sedition Acts and Naturalization Act cause more problems than they solved?"

TRM Suggested Responses to Questions

TRM Module 3.9 AP® Analyzing Sources Handout 3

TEACHING IDEA

Connecting the Dots

Point out to students that opponents of the Constitution in general and the elastic clause in particular, and especially Americans who considered themselves Antifederalists, saw in the passage of the Alien and Sedition Acts the manifestation of all of their worst fears about a central government that was legally able to define the limits of its powers. To a large degree, these Antifederalistic individuals and groups pointed to the new laws with a sense of, "See? We told you so." This is an important conversation to have with students in terms of the generally agreed-upon appropriate powers of the United States government at any one time as being highly situational, and always being akin to something like the unending swinging of a pendulum, moving far in one direction at one time, only to shift or correct and move in the opposite direction over time.

TRM Suggested Responses to Questions

TRM Module 3.9 AP® Analyzing Sources Handout 2

AP® ANALYZING SOURCES

Source: *Sedition Act,* 1798

"SECTION 2. *And be it further enacted,* That if any person shall write, print, utter, or publish, or shall cause or procure to be written, printed, uttered, or published, or shall knowingly and willingly assist or aid in writing, printing, uttering, or publishing any false, scandalous and malicious writing or writings against the government of the United States, with intent to defame the said government, or either house of the said Congress, or the said President, or to bring them or either of them into disrepute; or to excite against them, or either, or any of them, the hatred of the good people of the United States, or to stir up sedition within the United States, or to excite any unlawful combinations therein, for opposing or resisting any law of the United States, or any act of the President of the United States, and one in pursuance of any such law, or of the powers in him vested by the Constitution of the United States, or to resist, oppose or defeat any such law or act, or to aid, encourage or abet any hostile designs of any foreign nation against the United States, their people or government, then such person, being thereof convicted before any court of the United States having jurisdiction thereof, shall be punished by a fine not exceeding ten thousand dollars, and by imprisonment not exceeding two years."

Questions for Analysis
1. Identify the dangers expressed by the authors of this document.
2. Describe the political debates in the U.S. during the 1790s that shaped this legislation.
3. Explain what conflict this legislation aimed to resolve.

Questions for Comparison   James Madison, *Federalist No. 10,* 1787 (p. 213)
1. Evaluate the extent to which the Sedition Act contradicts the claims James Madison makes in *Federalist No. 10.*
2. Evaluate the extent to which historical changes since the 1780s made these contradictions possible.

Virginia and Kentucky Resolutions Resolutions passed by legislatures in Virginia and Kentucky that declared the Alien and Sedition Acts (1798) "void and of no force" in their states.

Democratic-Republicans were understandably infuriated by the Alien and Sedition Acts. They considered the attack on immigrants an attempt to limit the votes of farmers, artisans, and frontiersmen, who formed the core of their supporters. The Sedition Act threatened Democratic-Republican critics of Federalist policies and the First Amendment's guarantee of free speech. Jefferson and Madison encouraged states to pass resolutions that would counter this violation of the Bill of Rights. Using language drafted by the two Democratic-Republican leaders, legislators passed the **Virginia and Kentucky Resolutions**, which declared the Alien and Sedition Acts "void and of no force." They protested against the "alarming infractions of the Constitution," particularly the freedom of speech that "has been justly deemed, the only effectual guardian of every other right." Virginia even claimed that states had a right to nullify any powers exercised by the federal government that were not explicitly granted to it.

AP® ANALYZING SOURCES

Source: *Kentucky Resolution,* 1799

"*Resolved,* . . . That the several states who formed [the Constitution], being sovereign and independent, have the unquestionable right to judge of its infraction, and *that a nullification by those sovereignties, of all unauthorized acts done under color of that instrument,*

244

TEACHING IDEA

Building Vocabulary

The introduction of the term "nullification," along with the concept of a compact theory of government, at this point sets the stage for the major political and legal arguments about governance for the next sixty years of the course. Even more of this doctrine will come with the pushback against the civil rights movement in the twentieth century and sanctuary cities in the twenty-first. Mastery of these terms and the governing philosophies behind them are essential to any student argument on the divisive political issues that are to come, so students should be prepared to explore what the doctrines of nullification and compact theory entail, for both local governance and national union.

▲ Differentiation

Students could be tasked with reading excerpts of the Kentucky Resolution and debating its merits as a response to the Alien and Sedition Acts and Naturalization Act. The instructor could then pose the following questions: "What makes for an effective law?" "What makes for a good law?" "What makes for a just law?"

is the rightful remedy: That this Commonwealth does, upon the most deliberate reconsideration, declare that the said Alien and Sedition Laws are, in their opinion, palpable violations of the said Constitution; and, however cheerfully it may be disposed to surrender its opinion to a majority of its sister states in matters of ordinary or doubtful policy, yet, in momentous regulations like the present, which so vitally wound the best rights of the citizen, it would consider a silent acquiesecence as highly criminal: That although this Commonwealth, as a party to the Federal Compact, will bow to the laws of the Union, yet it does at the same time declare that it will not now, nor ever hereafter, cease to oppose in a constitutional manner, every attempt, from what quarter soever offered, to violate that compact. . . ."

Questions for Analysis
1. Identify the proper role of government, according to this document.
2. Explain how the Kentucky Resolution sought to prevent an over-powerful federal government.
3. Explain how the Kentucky Resolution sought to balance federal and state power.

Although the Alien and Sedition Acts curbed public expressions of dissent in the short run, they reinforced popular concerns about the power wielded by the Federalists. Combined with the ongoing war with France, continuing disputes over taxes, and relentless partisan denunciations in the press, these acts set the stage for the presidential election of 1800.

REVIEW
- How did the Adams administration justify the Alien and Sedition Acts?
- How did the Democratic-Republicans challenge this justification?

The Election of 1800

By 1800 Adams had negotiated a peaceful settlement of U.S. conflicts with France, considering it one of the greatest achievements of his administration. However, other Federalists, including Hamilton, disagreed and continued to seek open warfare and an all-out victory. Thus the Federalists faced the election of 1800 deeply divided. Democratic-Republicans meanwhile united behind Jefferson and portrayed the Federalists as the "new British" tyrants.

For the first time, congressional caucuses selected candidates for each party. The Federalists agreed on Adams and Charles Cotesworth Pinckney of South Carolina. The Democratic-Republicans again chose Jefferson and Burr as their candidates. The campaign was marked by bitter accusations.

In the first highly contested presidential election, the different methods states used to record voters' preferences gained more attention. Only five states determined members of the electoral college by popular vote. In the rest, state legislatures appointed electors. Created at a time when political parties were considered harmful to good government, the electoral college was not prepared for the situation it faced in January 1801. Federalist and Democratic-Republican caucuses nominated one candidate for president and one for vice president on party tickets. As a result, Jefferson and Burr received exactly the same number of electoral college votes, requiring the House of Representatives to break the tie. There Burr sought to gain the presidency with the help of Federalist representatives ardently opposed to Jefferson. But Alexander Hamilton stepped in and warned against Burr's leadership. This helped Jefferson emerge victorious, but it also inflamed animosity

> **AP® TIP**
> Understanding the role of the electoral college and political parties played in the election of 1800 is key to evaluating the extent of their influence on the development of American political systems.

BUILDING AP® SKILLS

Comparison

Instruct students in small groups to read the Kentucky Resolution on pages 244–245, and Madison's *Speech Proposing the Bill of Rights* on page 231. Task students with comparing and contrasting not only similarities and differences in the main ideas of each but also the respective historical situations that led to the creation of each document. With that completed, pose the following question to students: "To what extent do you find these two documents to be philosophically similar or dissimilar, and why?" Students could further be tasked with writing a thesis to address this question in their small groups.

TEACHING IDEA

Incorporating Videos

Show students the 8-minute excerpt of "History Channel – The Presidents 1789–1825 Washington to Monroe" on John Adams (available on YouTube; Adams's clip is 00:12:40 – 00:21:27) for a succinct overview of his administration and the challenges, successes, and limitations it encountered.

TEACHING IDEA

Six Degrees of Separation

Have students engage in a Six Degrees of Separation activity in small groups, based upon the following prompt: "From the battles of Lexington & Concord to the election of 1800." Groups may then, as a potential differentiation piece, post their products on butcher paper or the chalkboard for a student gallery walk of products.

BUILDING AP® SKILLS

Argumentation

Assign the class in small groups to craft a 4-1-1 contextualization and thesis for the following LEQ prompt: "Explain the continuities and changes in the sense of American identity between 1776 and 1800." (A refresher of the 4-1-1 model can be found on page 163.) Then, assign the students to write individual responses based upon the introductory paragraph they created, either in-class or as a homework assignment.

Period 3: 1754–1800

MODULE 3-9 Political Parties in Years of Crisis

TEACHING IDEA

Incorporating Videos

Show students "The Duel," from PBS's *The American Experience* series, which discusses the Burr–Hamilton conflict in the context of the formation of American political parties. This video is available on Vimeo (vimeo.com).

EXPLORING AP® THEMES

Politics and Power

Discuss with students the significance of the "Revolution of 1800," pointing out that the concept of those in governing power surrendering that power entirely was an utterly foreign concept to the autocratic, monarchial world of the eighteenth century. Those in power usually lost that power through death, revolution, or external conquest. This context, and the contemporary French Revolution, is what gave the Federalists such anxiety and fears of what may befall them in the post-Federalist era when their opponents controlled the machinery of the state.

TRM Suggested Responses to Questions

TEACHING IDEA

Incorporating Secondary Sources

Assign students to read and annotate Garry Wills's "Liberté, Egalité, Animosité," available on the American Heritage website (americanheritage.com). This could be done before the previous note, as a contextualizing exercise to lead into further discussion, or as a stand-alone annotation summative exercise post-discussion from the previous note.

Presidential Candidate	Electoral Vote
Thomas Jefferson (Republican)	73
Aaron Burr (Republican)	73
John Adams (Federalist)	65
C.C. Pinckney (Federalist)	64
John Jay (Federalist)	1

◀ **MAP 3.8 The Election of 1800** The presidential election represented the first peaceful transference of political power from one faction to another in American history. While the results of the election tended to divide along regional lines, the political conflict between Federalists and Democratic-Republicans led to greater support among many Americans for Jefferson's Democratic-Republicans. **What political changes since 1796 are reflected in this map? What continuities do you see?**

between Burr and Hamilton that eventually led Burr to kill Hamilton in a duel in 1804.

President Jefferson labeled his election a revolution achieved not "by the sword" but by "the suffrage of the people." The election of 1800 was hardly a popular revolution, given the restrictions on suffrage and the methods of selecting the electoral college. Still, between 1796 and 1800, partisan factions had been transformed into opposing parties, and the United States had managed a peaceful transition from one party to another.

REVIEW

- What main issues divided the Federalists and the Democratic-Republicans?
- What do the Alien and Sedition Acts and the election of 1800 reveal about the political partisanship in America during the late 1700s?

AP® WRITING HISTORICALLY — Evaluating Causation in a Document-Based Essay

In Modules 3-6 and 3-7, we walked through how to craft and support evaluative claims in response to Document-Based Questions dealing with continuity and change and with comparison. Now it's time to try your hand at a Document-Based Question that asks about causation. The following prompt asks you to combine your knowledge from this module and your background knowledge with a close, active reading of seven accompanying documents:

> Evaluate the extent to which the ideals of the American Revolution shaped political conflict between 1797 and 1801.

Step 1 Break down the prompt.

As with previous essays, be sure to *ACE* this question and create a list of information you already know about the prompt. Remember, it may be helpful to approach this prompt as if no documents were provided.

Remember, when you are asked to "evaluate the extent" of something, it means you need to make an argument that tackles how important each of the historical developments you choose to write about is in relation to the topic of the prompt.

Step 2 Read and annotate the documents.

Now carefully read and consider the seven documents that accompany this prompt. As you read, remember to ask yourself the following questions:

- What is the document about? What historical situation does it describe or reference?
- Who was the intended audience for this document?

- What was the author's purpose in writing this document?
- What point of view does the author of this document express?
- How does this document relate back to the prompt? In this case, try to link each document to a specific effect of the market revolution on society as you annotate.
- Does this document remind you of any other historical developments? Jot down any relevant evidence from your own background knowledge that comes to mind.

Finally, keep in mind how you can use each document to support the historical argument you are planning to make. How can these primary sources serve as evidence in your essay?

DOCUMENT 1

Source: Benjamin Franklin Bache, *Remarks Occasioned by the Late Conduct of Mr. Washington*, 1797

"One of the usurpations which at one period was meditated by [the Federalists] was that of rearing up again the fragments of the British throne in America, and placing upon it Mr. George Washington. This personage indeed began to assume the tone of a king in his public speeches, precisely when Louis XVI was obliged to cease the practice; and the pomp gratified the Americans, as a symbol of national importance, which might familiarize foreign powers to their new position, and thus produce various practical benefits. The American chief however had principally in view upon this occasion to obtain consequence in his favour. He accordingly ended, as we shall find, in making government subordinate to his passions. Men of extensive reputation at length refusing to serve with him, he was surrounded himself with ministers and other agents before little known; some of whom, in return for an accommodating temper, appear to be making a property of their employer. Certain to find in American an enemy to such proceedings, Mr. Washington and his immediate followers have renounced their connections of gratitude to France, to form connections of intrigue with England. They think that it depends upon foreigners, *what shall be the politics of the American people*; and that the temper of the royalty and aristocracy of England are each more fruited to their views, than that of democracy of France."

DOCUMENT 2

Source: George Washington, *Farewell Address*, 1797

"All obstructions to the execution of the laws, all combinations and associations, under whatever plausible character, with the real design to direct, control, counteract, or awe the regular deliberation and action of the constituted authorities, are destructive of this fundamental principle, and of fatal tendency. They serve to organize faction, to give it an artificial and extraordinary force; to put, in the place of the delegated will of the nation the will of a party, often a small but artful and enterprising minority of the community; and, according to the alternate triumphs of different parties, to make the public administration the mirror of the ill-concerted and incongruous projects of faction, rather than the organ of consistent and wholesome plans digested by common counsels and modified by mutual interests."

DOCUMENT 3

Source: John Adams, *Speech to Congress*, 1797

"[French disrespect of American diplomats] evinces a disposition to separate the people of the United States from the government, to persuade them that they have different affections, principles, and interests from those of their fellow citizens whom they themselves have chosen to manage their common concerns, and thus to produce divisions fatal to our peace. Such attempts ought to be repelled with a decision which shall convince France and the world that we are not a degraded people, humiliated under a colonial spirit of fear and sense of inferiority, fitted to be the miserable instruments of foreign influence, and regardless of national honor, character, and interest."

(Continued)

DOCUMENT 4

Source: Anonymous, *The Providential Detection*, 1797

About the source: In this image, the American eagle takes the Constitution away from Jefferson before he can burn it on the "Altar to Gallic [French] Despotism." Fueling the flames are the works of Thomas Paine and French philosophers, whom Federalists saw as threats to order. In Jefferson's right hand is a letter from Jefferson to the Italian Philip Mazzei, also a supporter of the French Revolution. The letter supposedly criticized George Washington.

DOCUMENT 5

Source: *Sedition Act*, 1798

"SECTION 2. *And be it further enacted*, That if any person shall write, print, utter, or publish, or shall cause or procure to be written, printed, uttered, or published, or shall knowingly and willingly assist or aid in writing, printing, uttering, or publishing any false, scandalous and malicious writing or writings against the government of the United States, with intent to defame the said government, or either house of the said Congress, or the said President, or to bring them or either of them into disrepute; or to excite against them, or either, or any of them, the hatred of the good people of the United States, or to stir up sedition within the United States, or to excite any unlawful combinations therein, for opposing or resisting any law of the United States, or any act of the President of the United States, and one in pursuance of any such law, or of the powers in him vested by the Constitution of the United States, or to resist, oppose or defeat any such law or act, or to aid, encourage or abet any hostile designs of any foreign nation against the United States, their people or government, then such person, being thereof convicted before any court of the United States having jurisdiction thereof, shall be punished by a fine not exceeding ten thousand dollars, and by imprisonment not exceeding two years."

DOCUMENT 6

Source: *Kentucky Resolution,* 1799

"*Resolved,...* That the several states who formed [the Constitution], being sovereign and independent, have the unquestionable right to judge of its infraction, and *that a nullification by those sovereignties, of all unauthorized acts done under color of that instrument, is the rightful remedy*: That this Commonwealth does, upon the most deliberate reconsideration, declare that the said Alien and Sedition Laws are, in their opinion, palpable violations of the said Constitution; and, however cheerfully it may be disposed to surrender its opinion to a majority of its sister states in matters of ordinary or doubtful policy, yet, in momentous regulations like the present, which so vitally wound the best rights of the citizen, it would consider a silent acquiesecence as highly criminal: That although this Commonwealth, as a party to the Federal Compact, will bow to the laws of the Union, yet it does at the same time declare that it will not now, nor ever hereafter, cease to oppose in a constitutional manner, every attempt, from what quarter soever offered, to violate that compact...."

DOCUMENT 7

Source: Thomas Jefferson, *Inaugural Address*, 1801

"During the throes and convulsions of the ancient world, during the agonizing spasms of infuriated man, seeking through blood and slaughter his long-lost liberty, it was not wonderful that the agitation of the billows should reach even this distant and peaceful shore; that this should be more felt and feared by some and less by others, and should divide opinions as to measures of safety. But every difference of opinion is not a difference of principle. We have called by different names brethren of the same principle. We are all Republicans, we are all Federalists. If there be any among us who would wish to dissolve this Union or to change its republican form, let them stand undisturbed as monuments of the safety with which error of opinion may be tolerated where reason is left free to combat it. I know, indeed, that some honest men fear that a republican government can not be strong, that this Government is not strong enough; but would the honest patriot, in the full tide of successful experiment, abandon a government which has so far kept us free and firm on the theoretic and visionary fear that this Government, the world's best hope, may by possibility want energy to preserve itself? I trust not."

ACTIVITY

Plan and write an essay in response to the Document-Based Question at the beginning of this box. Your thesis should include at least three evaluative claims about causes and effects. To help your reader determine which claims are causes and which are effects in your thesis, you may find it helpful to use some of the following phrases to connect them:

"[cause]..., and as a consequence...[effect]"

"[cause]..., and subsequently...[effect]"

"[cause]..., and therefore...[effect]"

"[cause]..., and as a result...[effect]"

In the body of your essay, be sure to use at least six of the seven documents provided to support your historical argument. Your essay should also include evidence from your own historical knowledge. Remember, you must explain *how* all of your evidence supports your thesis claims — this is the most important part of an effective historical argument. For a challenge, try adding a fourth claim to your thesis.

You may use the following outline to guide your response:

I. Introductory paragraph
   A. Immediate/preceding contextualization statement
      1. Cite evidence of immediate/preceding context
      2. Explain influence of immediate/preceding context
   B. Thesis statement presenting three to four evaluative claims, situated along a continuum of relative importance, linking causes to effects

(Continued)

TEACHING IDEA

AP® Writing Historically Workshop

This workshop seeks to carve out extended time for two essential elements in a Document-Based Question: a defensible claim and document organization. Have students share which categories of analysis they would use to connect ideals of the American Revolution to political conflict. This is a crucial step in establishing a line of reasoning. Next, have students categorize the documents by matching each document with a category of analysis. These essential steps prepare students to write their response for the activity on this page.

II. Claim 1 body paragraph
   A. Topic sentence presenting an evaluative claim of causation 1
   B. Supporting statement citing evidence of claim 1 (from historical knowledge)
   C. Cite additional evidence of claim 1 (from a document)
   D. Cite additional evidence of claim 1 (from another document)
   E. Explain how evidence supports claim 1
III. Claim 2 body paragraph
   A. Topic sentence presenting evaluative claim of causation 2
   B. Supporting statement citing evidence of claim 2 (from historical knowledge)
   C. Cite additional evidence of claim 2 (from a document)
   D. Cite additional evidence of claim 2 (from another document)
   E. Explain how evidence supports claim 2
IV. Claim 3 body paragraph
   A. Topic sentence presenting evaluative claim of causation 3
   B. Supporting statement citing evidence of claim 3 (from historical knowledge)
   C. Cite additional evidence of claim 3 (from a document)
   D. Cite additional evidence of claim 3 (from another document)
   E. Explain how evidence supports claim 3
V. (Optional) Claim 4 body paragraph
   A. Topic sentence presenting evaluative claim of causation 4
   B. Supporting statement citing evidence of claim 4 (from historical knowledge)
   C. Cite additional evidence of claim 4 (from a document)
   D. Cite additional evidence of claim 4 (from another document)
   E. Explain how evidence supports claim 4

PERIOD 3 REVIEW 1754–1800

KEY CONCEPTS AND EVENTS

Albany Plan of Union, 150
Alien and Sedition Acts, 243
Antifederalists, 209
Articles of Confederation, 197
Battle of Bunker Hill, 175
Battle of Fallen Timbers, 240
Battle of Saratoga, 186
Battle of Yorktown, 191
Bill of Rights, 231
Boston Massacre, 167
Boston Tea Party, 169
Coercive Acts, 169
committee of correspondence, 161
Continental Army, 174
Continental Congress, 174
Constitutional Convention, 207
Currency Act, 161
Daughters of Liberty, 162
Declaration of Independence, 179
Declaratory Act, 164
Democractic-Republicans, 241
Dunmore's Proclamation, 176
effigy, 162
electoral college, 208
The Federalist Papers, 210
Federalists, 209
French Revolution, 238
guerilla, 152
Indian Trade and Intercourse Act, 240
Intolerable Acts, 169
Jay Treaty, 239
loyalists, 182
minutemen, 175
naturalization, 208
Naturalization Act, 243
Neutrality Proclamation, 238
New Jersey Plan, 208
Northwest Ordinances, 201
patriots, 173
Peace of Paris, 154
Pinckney Treaty, 241
political sovereignty, 160
Proclamation Line of 1763, 156
Quartering Act, 161
Quebec Act, 169
ratified, 195
republican motherhood, 219
salutary (benign) neglect, 160
Second Continental Congress, 175
Seven Years' War (French and Indian War), 150
Shays's Rebellion, 203
Sons of Liberty, 162
speculators, 156
Stamp Act, 162
Stamp Act Congress, 163
Statute of Religious Freedom, 196
Sugar Act, 161
Tea Act, 168
three-fifths compromise, 208
Townshend Acts, 165
Treaty of Fort Stanwix, 201
Treaty of Greenville, 240
Treaty (Peace) of Paris, 192
tyranny, 163
Valley Forge, 186
Virginia and Kentucky Resolutions, 244
Virginia Plan, 208
Virginia Resolves, 162
virtual representation, 162
Vox Populi, 162
Whiskey Rebellion, 240
XYZ Affair, 243

KEY PEOPLE

Abigail Adams, 218
John Adams, 178
Samuel Adams, 162
Richard Allen, 224
Crispus Attucks, 167
Benjamin Banneker, 234
William Bartram, 220
Mum Bett, 222
Daniel Boone, 181
Edward Braddock, 151
Joseph Brant (Thayendanegea), 180
John Burgoyne, 186
Charles Cornwallis, 191
John Dickinson, 165
Lord Dunmore, 176
Philip Freneau, 221
Edmond Genêt, 239
King George III, 154
George Grenville, 161
Alexander Hamilton, 147
Patrick Henry, 162
Sir William Howe, 175
John Jay, 191
Thomas Jefferson, 147
Samuel Jennings, 220
Guy Johnson, 180
Johann Baron de Kalb, 188
Henry Knox, 230
Thaddeus Kosciusko, 188
Marquis de Lafayette, 188
Richard Henry Lee, 178
Little Turtle, 240
King Louis XVI, 238
Ebenezer Mackintosh, 163
James Madison, 147
George Mason, 178
James Monroe, 207
Judith Sargent Murray, 218
Neolin, 155
Lord North, 189
Andrew Oliver, 162
Thomas Paine, 177
Charles Willson Peale, 220
Charles Cotesworth Pinckney, 245
Thomas Pinckney, 241

(Continued)

PERIOD 3 REVIEW 1754–1800

Pontiac, *155*
Casimir Pulaski, *188*
Edmund Randolph, *230*
Paul Revere, *168*
Comte de Rochambeau, *191*
Betsy Ross, *183*
Benjamin Rush, *219*
Deborah Sampson, *188*
Daniel Shays, *202*
Adam Smith, *237*
Baron Friedrich von Steuben, *188*
Thomas Sumter, *191*
Banastre Tarleton, *191*
Charles Townshend, *165*
Mercy Otis Warren, *210*
George Washington, *150*
Anthony Wayne, *240*
Noah Webster, *220*
Phillis Wheatley, *183*

CHRONOLOGY

1700–60	Salutary (benign) neglect spurs independent thought in colonies
1754	Washington attacks Fort Duquesne
	Introduction of Albany Plan of the Union
1754–63	Seven Years' War reshapes political and trade boundaries
1760	British alienation of American Indian groups amplifies tensions
1763	Peace of Paris
	Proclamation of 1763 antagonizes colonists
1764–65	Stamp Act gives rise to colonial opposition until repeal in 1766
1765	Expansion of Quartering Act encourages united colonial resistance
1767	Townshend Acts result in colonial protests
1770	Colonial boycotts of British goods multiply
	Boston Massacre
1772	Massachusetts Committee of Correspondence created
1773	Boston Tea Party
1774	Parliament passes the Intolerable Acts to punish colonies for protesting
	First Continental Congress convenes
1775	British forces attack at Lexington and Concord
	Second Continental Congress convenes
	Costly British victory at Battle of Bunker Hill
1776	Thomas Paine publishes *Common Sense*
	General Washington forces British retreat from Boston
	Thomas Jefferson and other members of Continental Congress draft Declaration of Independence
	General Howe's troops occupy New York City
	Benjamin Franklin serves as unofficial liaison in Paris
1777	Continental Army victory at Battle of Saratoga secures French alliance
	Articles of Confederation drafted
	Slavery abolished in Vermont
1778–79	American Revolution spreads south and west
1780	British sustain heavy battle losses
1780s	Quaker men and women fight for abolition of slavery
1781	Continental victory at Battle of Yorktown leads to peace negotiations
	Last state ratifies Articles of Confederation
1783	Treaty of Paris officially ends the American Revolution
	Congress discharges army
	British deny U.S. West Indies trade access
	Noah Webster advocates for universal education
1785	Northwest Ordinance of 1785
1786–87	Shays's Rebellion spurs revision of Articles of Confederation
1787	Northwest Ordinance of 1787
	Constitutional Convention meets to reform Articles of Confederation
	Virginia Plan and New Jersey Plan introduced
	Three-fifths compromise added to Constitution
1787–88	Publication of *The Federalist Papers*
1787–90	Ratification of the Constitution
1789	Massachusetts creates free public schools
	Judiciary Act of 1789 passed
1789–91	Ratification of Bill of Rights
1790	Indian Trade and Intercourse Act passed
1790s	Free African American literary and debate societies emerge
1791	Hamilton releases "Report on the Subject of Manufactures"

PERIOD 3 REVIEW 1754–1800

1792	American farmers protest taxes
1792–1809	Construction of Washington, D.C. largely through the labor of enslaved people
1793	Washington issues Neutrality Proclamation, prohibiting America from providing support or war materials to warring nations
1794	Whiskey Rebellion
	First independent African American church founded by Richard Allen
1795	Jay Treaty ratified
	Treaty of Greenville marks large land gains for U.S.
1796	Democratic-Republican party emerges
	Pinckney Treaty opens Mississippi River to U.S.
1797	XYZ Affair
1798	Alien and Sedition Acts restrict expressions of dissent
c. 1800	Slaveholders press slavery westward
1800	Federal government relocates to Washington, D.C.
1801	House of Representatives vote breaks Jefferson-Adams tie in presidential election

TRM Suggested Responses to Questions

Answers to Multiple-Choice Questions

1. d
2. b
3. c
4. d
5. a
6. b
7. c
8. a
9. b
10. d
11. a
12. c
13. c
14. b
15. b

AP® EXAM PRACTICE THROUGH 1800

Multiple-Choice Questions

Choose the correct answer for each question.

Questions 1–3 refer to the following graph.

▲ British Military Spending and Net Tax Income, 1700–1790

1. Which of the following most directly contributed to the trends seen in the graph between 1740 and 1765?
   a. Inability of the British navy to secure trade on the high seas
   b. Failure of the British government to recognize colonial dissatisfaction with imperial policy
   c. Decreased British imperial interest in governing its North American colonies
   d. Intensifying rivalries in North America between European powers seeking to expand

2. The graph would be most useful as a source of information about which of the following?
   a. European and American Indian alliances during the Seven Years' War
   b. British attempts to consolidate control over its American colonies
   c. American colonists' increasing demands for self-rule
   d. British efforts to collect taxes without direct colonial consent

3. Which of the following pieces of evidence would best support the graph's depiction of economic changes during this era?
   a. Ship logs recording the goods carried between the colonies and the Caribbean
   b. Political pamphlets calling for increased resistance to British imperial policies
   c. Parliamentary records detailing the cost of stationing troops in the colonies
   d. The diary of an American merchant describing the collection of customs duties

Questions 4–6 refer to the following engraving.

Protesting the Stamp Act in Portsmouth, New Hampshire, 1760s

4. The activities of the colonists in the 1760s depicted in the engraving could best be used as evidence to support which of the following arguments?
   a. Colonial elites feared the dangers of self-rule and popular sovereignty.
   b. Commoners sought to preserve policies favoring Protestantism in the colonies.
   c. Colonists of all classes protested Britain's pro-expansion policies.
   d. British efforts to raise revenue from the colonies sparked major resistance.

5. Political protests of the 1760s, such as the one depicted in the engraving, flourished for all of the following reasons except
   a. Parliament's adoption of a policy of salutary neglect after the Seven Years' War.
   b. organized resistance by colonial leaders such as Benjamin Franklin to British imperial policy.
   c. the spread of a transatlantic print literature across the colonies.
   d. British efforts to restrict colonists' westward expansion into unsecured areas.

6. In response to events in the 1760s, American colonists most commonly
   a. embraced ideas of hereditary privilege.
   b. argued for natural rights and republicanism.
   c. demanded abolition of slavery.
   d. departed from ideas popularized by the Enlightenment.

Period 3: 1754–1800

Questions 7–8 refer to the following excerpt.

> **Source:** Edmund Morgan, *The Birth of the Republic: 1763–1789*, 1992
>
> "This widespread ownership of property is perhaps the most important single fact about the Americans of the Revolutionary period. It meant that they were not divided so widely between rich and poor as the people of the Old World. Most of the men and women who settled the colonies had come with expectations of a better life for themselves and their children, and most had achieved it . . . [T]here was as yet no professed belief in social equality . . . in every colony there were aristocrats . . . , [but] there were no peasants for them to lord it over — except always the slaves."

7. Which of the following most likely resulted in the period from 1754 to 1776 from the trend described in the excerpt?
   a. The colonies began to unite after perceived constraints on their political and economic activities.
   b. Colonists provided financial and material support for the Revolution despite economic hardships.
   c. The American Revolution was energized by laborers, and women, as well as elites and intellectuals.
   d. The patriots succeeded in overthrowing Britain because of their overwhelming financial advantages.

8. The passage would be most useful as a source of information about which of the following?
   a. The impact of Enlightenment ideas on colonial society
   b. Radical agitators and extralegal violence
   c. Changing notions of family and gender roles
   d. Growing sectionalism and regional specialization

Questions 9–10 refer to the following excerpt.

> **Source:** Thomas Paine, "The American Crisis," December 19, 1776
>
> "These are the times that try men's souls. The summer soldier and the sunshine patriot will, in this crisis, shrink from the service of their country; but he that stands it now, deserves the love and thanks of man and woman. Tyranny, like hell, is not easily conquered; yet we have this consolation with us, that the harder the conflict, the more glorious the triumph. What we obtain too cheap, we esteem too lightly: it is dearness only that gives every thing its value. Heaven knows how to put a proper price upon its goods; and it would be strange indeed if so celestial an article as freedom should not be highly rated. Britain, with an army to enforce her tyranny, has declared that she has a right (not only to tax) but to 'bind us in all cases whatsoever,' and if being bound in that manner, is not slavery, then is there not such a thing as slavery upon earth. Even the expression is impious; for so unlimited a power can belong only to God."

9. Which of the following best explains the challenge faced by patriots as described in the excerpt?
   a. Debates between the states over the fate of slavery
   b. Early military struggles against the British army
   c. Criticisms levied in Parliament by those opposed to the colonial war
   d. The Enlightenment ideal of freedom as the highest of all virtues

10. The sentiments expressed in the excerpt are most similar to sentiments expressed by which of the following groups?
    a. Women advocating a greater role in American society
    b. Frontier settlers in favor of seizing American Indian lands
    c. Protestant evangelists during the First Great Awakening
    d. Antifederalists opposed to ratification of the Constitution

Questions 11–12 refer to the following excerpt.

> **Source:** *Alien Act*, 1798
>
> "Be it enacted by the Senate and House of Representatives of the United States of America in Congress assembled, That whenever there shall be a declared war between the United States and any foreign nation or government, or any invasion or predatory incursion shall be perpetrated, attempted, or threatened against the territory of the United States, by any foreign nation or government, and the President of the United States shall make public proclamation of the event, all natives, citizens, denizens, or subjects of the hostile nation or government, being males of the age of fourteen years and upwards, who shall be within the United States, and not actually naturalized, shall be liable to be apprehended, restrained, secured and removed, as alien enemies."

AP® Exam Practice: Through 1800

Period 3: 1754–1800

11. Which of the following contributed most directly to the conflicts addressed in the passage?
    a. Political tensions between Federalists and Democratic-Republicans
    b. Westward expansion and the development of frontier culture
    c. State alliances with American Indian tribes on the eastern seaboard
    d. War with Great Britain

12. The passage of the legislation in this excerpt most directly resulted in which of the following?
    a. Supreme Court decisions that enhanced the power of the federal government at the expense of the states
    b. A long-term decline in foreign immigration to the United States
    c. Control of the federal government shifting to the Democratic-Republican Party
    d. Expansion of slavery in the United States

Questions 13–15 refer to the following map.

▸ Status of Slavery in the United States Following the American Revolution

13. The map could be best used to support a characterization of the dominant national attitude regarding slavery in the United States in the 1780s as
    a. abolitionist seeking emancipation.
    b. free-soil opposing the westward expansion of slavery.
    c. sectional resulting from early federal and state government policies.
    d. perfectionist avoiding compromise in favor of principle.

14. In the years immediately following the Revolutionary War, the regional differences depicted in the map posed the greatest threat to
    a. maintaining existing systems of labor.
    b. creating a sense of national identity and unity.
    c. promoting peaceful relations with neighboring countries.
    d. solving the nation's financial crisis.

15. Which of the following most directly contributed to the status of the Indiana and Ohio Territories as shown in the map?
    a. Federal treaty obligations with American Indian tribes
    b. Compromises at the Constitutional Convention
    c. The end of the Seven Years' War
    d. Passage of the Northwest Ordinance

TRM Suggested Responses to Questions

Period 3: 1754–1800

AP® Exam Practice: Through 1800

Short-Answer Questions

Read each question carefully and write a short response. Use complete sentences.

1. Using the following excerpts, answer (a), (b), and (c).

   Source: T. H. Breen, "Ideology and Nationalism on the Eve of the American Revolution," 1997

   "[In England,] ordinary people — laboring men and women as well as members of a self-confident middling group — who bellowed out the words to the newly composed "Rule Britannia" and who responded positively to the emotional appeal of "God Save the King" gave voice to the common aspirations of a militantly Protestant culture. Or, stated negatively, they proclaimed their utter contempt for Catholicism and their rejection of everything associated with contemporary France. . . .

   For most English people, the expression of national identity seems to be been quite genuine. Indeed, by noisy participation in patriotic rituals, the middling and working classes thrust themselves into a public sphere of national politics. . . .

   Within an empire strained by the heightened nationalist sentiment of the metropolitan center [of London], natural rights acquired unusual persuasive force [for the American colonists]. Threatened from the outside by a self-confident military power, one that seemed intent on marginalizing the colonists within the empire, Americans countered with the universalist vocabulary of natural rights, in other words, with a language of political resistance that stressed a bundle of God-given rights. . . ."

   Source: Gary B. Nash, *The Unknown American Revolution*, 2005

   "Many of the figures we will encounter were from the middle and lower ranks of American society, and many of them did not have pale complexions. From these ranks, few heroes have emerged to enter the national pantheon. For the most part, they remain anonymous. Partly this is because they faded in and out of the picture, rarely achieving the tenure and status of men such as John Adams and John Hancock of Boston, Robert Morris and Benjamin Franklin of Philadelphia, Alexander Hamilton and John Jay of New York, or Thomas Jefferson, Patrick Henry, and George Washington of Virginia, all of whom remained on the scene from the Revolution's beginning to the very end. But, although they never rose to the top of society, where they could trumpet their own achievements and claim their place in the pages of history, many other men and women counted greatly at the time. . . . The shortness of their lives also explains the anonymity of ordinary people. It is safer to conduct a revolution from the legislative chamber than fight for it on the battlefield, healthier to be free than enslaved, and one is more likely to reach old age with money than with crumbs."

   a) Briefly describe ONE major difference between Breen's and Nash's historical interpretations of the Revolution.

   b) Briefly explain how ONE specific historical event or development between 1754 to 1800 that is not explicitly mentioned in the excerpts could be used to support Breen's argument.

   c) Briefly explain how ONE specific historical event or development from the period 1754 to 1800 that is not explicitly mentioned in the excerpts could be used to support Nash's argument.

AP® Exam Practice

AP® Exam Practice: Through 1800

Period 3: 1754–1800

2. Using the following graph, answer (a), (b), and (c).

Massachusetts Paper Dollars Worth $100 of Gold, January 1777–April 1780

a. Briefly explain ONE specific historical factor that caused the change illustrated in the graph.
b. Briefly explain ONE significant historical event or development resulting from the change illustrated in the graph.
c. Briefly explain ANOTHER significant historical event or development resulting from the change illustrated in the graph.

3. Answer (a), (b), and (c).
   a) Briefly explain ONE specific historical cause of British participation in the Seven Years' War (1754–1763).
   b) Briefly explain ONE specific historical event or development that resulted from British participation in the Seven Years' War (1754–1763).
   c) Briefly explain how ONE specific British imperial policy resulting from the Seven Years' War (1754–1763) changed relations between Britain and its North American colonies.

4. Answer (a), (b), and (c).
   a) Briefly explain ONE specific historical argument used to oppose ratifying the Constitution in the 1780s.
   b) Briefly explain ONE specific historical argument used to support ratifying the Constitution in the 1780s.
   c) Briefly explain how ONE specific historical event or development represents an accomplishment of the national government under the Constitution between 1787 and 1820.

Document-Based Question

Question 1 is based on the accompanying documents. The documents have been edited for the purpose of this exercise. *Suggested reading period: 15 minutes. Suggested writing time: 45 minutes.*

1. Evaluate the extent to which revolutionary ideals changed American society in the period 1776 to 1800.

DOCUMENT 1 **Source:** *The Declaration of Independence*, 1776

"When in the Course of human events, it becomes necessary for one people to dissolve the political bands which have connected them with another, and to assume among the powers of the earth, the separate and equal station to which the Laws of Nature and of Nature's God entitle them, a decent respect to the opinions of mankind requires that they should declare the causes which impel them to the separation.

We hold these truths to be self-evident, that all men are created equal, that they are endowed by their Creator with certain unalienable Rights, that among these are Life, Liberty and the pursuit of Happiness.—That to secure these rights, Governments are instituted among Men, deriving their just powers from the consent of the governed,—That whenever any Form of Government becomes destructive of these ends, it is the Right of the People to alter or to abolish it, and to institute new Government, laying its foundation on such principles and organizing its powers in such form, as to them shall seem most likely to effect their Safety and Happiness."

TRM Suggested Responses to Questions

Period 3: 1754–1800

AP® Exam Practice: Through 1800

DOCUMENT 2   **Source:** *The New Jersey State Constitution*, 1776

"That all inhabitants of this Colony, of full age, who are worth fifty pounds proclamation money, clear estate in the same, and have resided within the county in which they claim a vote for twelve months immediately preceding the election, shall be entitled to vote for Representatives in Council and Assembly; and also for all other public officers, that shall be elected by the people of the county at large."

DOCUMENT 3   **Source:** *Letter from Henry Knox to George Washington*, 1786

"This dreadful situation has alarmed every man of principle and property in New England. . . . Our government must be braced, changed, or altered to secure our lives and property. We imagined that the mildness of our government and the virtue of the people were so correspondent, that we were not as other nations requiring brutal force to support the laws—But we find that we are men, actual men, possessing all the turbulent passions belonging to that animal and that we must have a government proper and adequate for him—The people of Massachusetts for instance, are far advanced in this doctrine, and the men of reflection, and principle, are determined to endeavor to establish a government which shall have the power to protect them in their lawful pursuits, and which will be efficient in all cases of internal commotions or foreign invasions. . . ."

DOCUMENT 4   **Source:** *The Northwest Ordinance*, 1787

"Art. 3. Religion, morality, and knowledge, being necessary to good government and the happiness of mankind, schools and the means of education shall forever be encouraged. . . .

Art. 6. There shall be neither slavery nor involuntary servitude in the said territory, otherwise than in the punishment of crimes whereof the party shall have been duly convicted: *Provided, always,* That any person escaping into the same, from whom labor or service is lawfully claimed in any one of the original States, such fugitive may be lawfully reclaimed and conveyed to the person claiming his or her labor or service as aforesaid."

DOCUMENT 5   **Source:** *Fugitive Slave Law*, 1793

"For the better security of the peace and friendship now entered into by the contracting parties, against all infractions of the same, by the citizens of either party, to the prejudice of the other, neither party shall proceed to the infliction of punishments on the citizens of the other, otherwise than by securing the offender, or offenders, by imprisonment, or any other competent means, till a fair and impartial trial can be had by judges or juries of both parties, as near as can be, to the laws, customs, and usage's of the contracting parties, and natural justice. . . . And it is further agreed between the parties aforesaid, that neither shall entertain, or give countenance to, the enemies of the other, or protect, in their respective states, criminal fugitives, servants, or slaves, but the same to apprehend and secure, and deliver to the state or states, to which such enemies, criminals, servants, or slaves, respectively below."

DOCUMENT 6

Source: *Keep Within Compass*, c. 1795

About the source: The text at the top reads: "How blest the Maid whose bosom no headstrong passion knows, Her days in Joy she Passes, her nights in soft repose." The text at the bottom reads: "Virtuous Woman is a Crown to her Husband." The text running in a circle around the central image reads: "Keep within compass and you shall be sure to avoid many troubles which others endure."

DOCUMENT 7

Source: *Years States Eliminated Established Churches*

Connecticut	1818
Delaware	never had established church
Georgia	1789
Maryland	1776
Massachusetts	1780
New Hampshire	1790
New Jersey	1776
New York	1777
North Carolina	1776
Pennsylvania	never had established church
Rhode Island	never had established church
South Carolina	1790
Virginia	1786

Long-Essay Questions

Please choose one of the following three questions to answer. *Suggested writing time: 40 minutes.*

2. Evaluate the extent to which the Seven Years' War (1754–1763) fostered change in the relationship between England and the North American colonies in the period 1754 to 1774.
3. Evaluate the extent to which immigration and migration fostered change in American society in the period 1754 to 1800.
4. Evaluate the extent to which the American Revolution fostered change in the status of African Americans and women in the period 1775 to 1800.

TRM Suggested Responses to Questions

PERIOD 4: 1800–1848

Democracy, Industrialization, and Reform

AP® Overview for Period 4

Westward expansion, a growing population, increasingly distinctive regional identities, along with varying demographics and labor systems characterized the economic systems of early-nineteenth-century America. Technological innovations in transportation, manufacturing, and agriculture helped establish a national economy and there were significant changes to society and Americans' sense of national identity. To meet the challenges created by industrialization and westward expansion, and influenced by religious and intellectual movements, social reform advocates organized to broaden democratic systems and beliefs. Accompanying the economic changes was the development of a modern democracy with increased political participation. Despite this democratic spirit, the exponential increase in the use of enslaved laborers throughout the southern states continued in the early-nineteenth century. Period 4 is defined by the making and remaking of American culture, political systems, and economic structures.

In addition to acquiring content knowledge of essential topics and historical developments, this period also cultivates the AP® historical thinking skills and reasoning processes necessary for students to succeed in the course and on the AP® exam. This is the first period in the book where students will see less scaffolding of historical thinking skills associated with the writing in AP® U.S. History. Period 4 accounts for 10–17% of the AP® exam and can be the source of questions on the Short-Answer, Long-Essay, and Document-Based Questions.

Module 4-1: Political and Economic Transformations introduces the political debates, westward expansion, and technological innovations that transformed American society during the Jeffersonian Era. Although the era was dominated by Jefferson's Democratic-Republican Party, Federalist John Marshall stood as a bulwark of nationalist interpretations of the U.S. Constitution. Indeed, while the Democratic-Republicans and Federalists of the First Party System continued debating the construction of the U.S. Constitution and the appropriate exercise of power by the federal government, the American economy also underwent significant changes. The North became more industrialized and the nature of work fundamentally transformed in conjunction with an increasingly diverse population. In the South, however, agriculture continued to reign supreme as cotton became king, and planters continued the commodification of enslaved people. The thematic focus of politics and power and work, exchange, and technology pair well with the reasoning process of causation as students explore the reasons why the political and economic systems changed.

Module 4-2: Defending and Redefining the Nation discusses how as the early-nineteenth century was characterized by similar ideas about government from Democratic-Republicans, foreign policy events changed some previously held beliefs about economic and political systems. The War of 1812 served as a turning point for America's foreign policy, the role of the federal government in the economy, and relations with American Indians. The federal government now sought economic growth through Henry Clay's American System and a stronger foreign policy when it issued the Monroe Doctrine in 1823. Despite the surge of nationalism following the War of 1812, differences in regional economic development, the Panic of 1819, and the political issue of slavery as evidenced by the Missouri Compromise in 1820 increased sectionalism. This module also affords students with various opportunities to work on the reasoning process of comparison and causation. The thematic focus of politics and power and America in the world commands students' attention to how domestic events can affect foreign policy.

Module 4-3: Transportation and Market Revolutions Change America highlights that although the Market Revolution is about economic transformations at its core, the effects of this revolution spanned a wide breadth of society. This module is about the socioeconomic effects of the Market Revolution through the lens of women, immigrant groups, reformers, and urban residents. Students need to be aware that the United States went through changes because of both internal and external factors. Put another way, citizens within the United States affected numerous changes in lifestyles, reforms, and occupations. Women, in particular, experienced continuity in the societal pressure to embrace the cult of domesticity. Over time though, women would use separate spheres to change American society. Likewise, immigrant groups changed the culture, demographics, and economy. The thematic focus of social structures requires students to comprehend an expansive view of the Market Revolution and the reasoning process of comparison and causation works in concert with the selected content for this module. The brief narrative also affords time to devote to the Document-Based Question at the end.

Module 4-4: The Second American Party System expands on how unlike the revolutionary generation, the second generation embraced the two-party system as a positive development that furthered democratic reforms in the early-nineteenth century. This change was most notably the result of popular political figures such as Henry Clay, Andrew Jackson, and John C. Calhoun. However, students should bear in mind that democratic reforms had origins at the state and local level. Despite the democratic reforms, endemic violence against African Americans and the continued commodification of enslaved persons continued throughout the period of political reform. This module focuses on the critical state reforms that predate national political reforms. The thematic focus of politics and power squares students' analysis on the democratic changes so prevalent during this time.

Module 4-5: Conflicts of the Jacksonian Era delves into the political revolution inspired by Andrew Jackson and supported by many Jacksonian Democrats. The political consensus, so it seemed, embraced the idea of an energetic federal government in helping spur on economic growth and opportunity. Jacksonian Democrats challenged the role of the federal government in acting as an impetus for economic growth. Aside from economic challenges, this module also focuses on expansion westward and the attendant responses of the American government to the presence of American Indians. The continuation of expansion and political changes into the 1840s concludes this module. The thematic focus of politics and power and the reasoning process of causation allow students to evaluate the many factors that led to political change throughout the Jacksonian Era.

Module 4-6: Slavery and Southern Society elaborates on the economic decisions made after the American Revolution by Southerners to embrace a slave society, which had the effect of exponential growth in both the number of enslaved persons and the profitability of cotton as the chattel slave system moved westward in the nineteenth century. Slavery's expansion westward happened in concert with the rise in cotton and an increasingly static economic and social hierarchy developed as the planter elite class defended and protected this labor system. The planter elite used non-slave holding whites to defend this system, even though non-slave holding whites did not economically benefit from such an arrangement. Enslaved persons continuously sought ways to resist the institution of slavery as they melded cultural backgrounds, covertly and overtly battled overseers, and were the most dynamic factor in the development of an abolitionist movement. The thematic focus of geography and the environment, American and regional culture, and social structures frames the content of this module in a way that encourages students to use the reasoning processes of causation and continuity and change to conceptualize the broad factors that influenced the institution of slavery.

Module 4-7: Social Reform Movements provides the context and causes for the development of a burgeoning national culture in the nineteenth century. The most powerful impetus for reform was the broad appeal of the Second Great Awakening, which had powerful effects on the wealthy as well as middling classes from the frontier. The duality of reform is explained through the developments of social reform movements such as temperance and the expansion of nativism. Responsible for not only artistic and literary achievements that richly added to the national culture, the transcendentalists were also social and political reformers. The thematic focus of American and regional culture asks students to consider reform movements that had national appeal and reform movements that were regional. The reasoning process of causation is presented through a scaffolded approach to writing a long-essay question that explains how to write more nuanced responses.

Module 4-8: Abolitionism and Sectionalism covers expansion in the nineteenth century that unearthed new economic opportunities for individuals and varied greatly in different regions of the United States. As economic prospects increased for white citizens, the expansion of an enslaved labor force in the South was met with mixed reactions. Few white Northerners joined the effort to abolish slavery, as most acquiesced to southern demands or remained ambivalent to the ideology of the planter elite. Although white abolitionists were influential advocates in the abolitionist movement, by far the most strident advocates of abolitionism were enslaved and free African Americans. Women, in particular, played a crucial role in the abolitionist movement. Eventually, a divide in the abolitionist movement occurred over disagreements of the future of the women's rights movement. The thematic focus of American and regional culture connects well with the reasoning process of comparison because of the varying regional attitudes over expansion and abolitionism.

Pacing Guide
Course Pacing for Period 4

Module #	Lesson Title	Instructional Period*	AP® Theme	AP® Topic	AP® Reasoning Process/Skill	Homework
4-1	N/A	N/A	Work, Exchange, and Technology; Politics and Power	4.1, 4.2, 4.3	Causation / Historical Thinking Skills 1, 2, 3, 5	**Reading and Source Analysis:** 4-1
	Political and Economic Transformations	1	Work, Exchange, and Technology; Politics and Power	4.1, 4.2, 4.3	Causation / Historical Thinking Skills 1, 2, 3, 5	**Activity:** AP® Writing Historically: Short-Answer Question Practice; **Reading and Source Analysis:** 4-2
4-1, 4-2	**Review:** AP® Writing Historically: Short-Answer Question Practice; Defending and Redefining the Nation	1	Politics and Power; America in the World	4.1, 4.2, 4.3, 4.4	Comparison; Causation / Historical Thinking Skills 1, 2, 3, 5	**Activity:** AP® Writing Historically: Responding to a Long-Essay Question

(Continued)

Module #	Lesson Title	Instructional Period*	AP® Theme	AP® Topic	AP® Reasoning Process/Skill	Homework
4-2	**Workshop:** AP® Writing Historically: Responding to a Long-Essay Question	1	Politics and Power America in the World	4.3	Comparison Causation / Historical Thinking Skills 1, 2, 3, 4, 5, 6	**Reading and Source Analysis:** 4-3
4-3	Transportation and Market Revolutions Change America	1	Social Structures	4.5 4.6	Causation Comparison / Historical Thinking Skills 1, 2, 3, 5	**Activity:** AP® Writing Historically: Responding to a Document-Based Question
	Workshop: AP® Writing Historically: Responding to a Document-Based Question	1	Social Structures	4.6	Causation Comparison / Historical Thinking Skills 1, 2, 3, 4, 5, 6	**Reading and Source Analysis:** 4-4
4-4	The Second American Party System	1	Politics and Power	4.7 4.8 4.9 4.10	Continuity and Change / Historical Thinking Skills 1, 2, 3, 5	**Activity:** AP® Writing Historically: Short-Answer Question Practice **Reading and Source Analysis:** 4-5
4-4 4-5	**Review:** AP® Writing Historically: Short-Answer Question Practice Conflicts of the Jacksonian Era	1	Politics and Power	4.8 4.9	Causation / Historical Thinking Skills 1, 2, 3, 5	**Activity:** AP® Writing Historically: Short-Answer Question Practice **Reading and Source Analysis:** 4-6
4-5 4-6	**Review:** AP® Writing Historically: Short-Answer Question Practice Slavery and Southern Society	1	Geography and the Environment American and Regional Culture Social Structures	4.12	Causation Continuity and Change / Historical Thinking Skills 1, 2, 3, 5	**Activity:** AP® Writing Historically: Short-Answer Question Practice **Reading and Source Analysis:** 4-7
4-6 4-7	**Review:** AP® Writing Historically: Short-Answer Question Practice Social Reform Movements	1	American and Regional Culture	4.11	Causation / Historical Thinking Skills 1, 2, 3, 4, 5	**Activity:** AP® Writing Historically: Responding to a Long-Essay Question
4-7	**Workshop:** AP® Writing Historically: Responding to a Long-Essay Question	1	American and Regional Culture	4.11	Causation. Historical Thinking Skills 1, 2, 3, 4, 5, 6	**Reading and Source Analysis:** 4-8
4-8	Abolitionism and Sectionalism	1	American and Regional Culture	4.13	Comparison / Historical Thinking Skills 1, 2, 3, 5	**Activity:** AP® Writing Historically: Responding to a Long-Essay Question
	Workshop: AP® Writing Historically: Responding to a Long-Essay Question	1	American and Regional Culture	4.14	Comparison / Historical Thinking Skills 1, 2, 3, 4, 5, 6	Prepare for Assessments
Formative Assessment	AP® Exam Practice • 18 MCQs • 4 SAQs	0–1	All AP® U.S. History Course Themes	4.14 Personal Progress Check • 15 MCQs • 2 SAQs • 1 LEQ	All AP® History Reasoning Processes/Skills	
Summative Assessment	Unit 1 Test Bank • 55 MCQs • 4 SAQs • 1 DBQ • 4 LEQs	0–1	All AP® U.S. History Course Themes		All AP® History Reasoning Processes/Skills	

*Based on a standard 50-minute class period.

PERIOD 4 Democracy, Industrialization, and Reform

Period 4 Resources

The following resources can be found in the Resources section of the book's digital platform, by clicking on the link buttons in the Teacher's Edition e-book, or by opening the Teacher's Resource Materials.

- **TRM** Period 4 Overview Video
- **TRM** AP® Concepts and Skills Video
- **TRM** Period 4 Lecture Presentation Slides
- **TRM** Period 4 Workshop Rubrics
- **TRM** Period 4 Suggested Responses to Questions
- **TRM** Period 4 Guided Reading Worksheets

Module 4-1

- **TRM** Module 4.1 AP® Analyzing Sources Handout 1
- **TRM** Handout 4.1 – Analyzing Supreme Court Cases, 1803–1824
- **TRM** Map 4A – The United States, 1820s
- **TRM** Module 4.1 AP® Analyzing Sources Handout 2
- **TRM** Module 4.1 AP® Analyzing Sources Handout 3
- **TRM** Module 4.1 AP® Analyzing Sources Handout 4

Module 4-2

- **TRM** Module 4.2 AP® Analyzing Sources Handout 1
- **TRM** Handout 4.2 – Regional Reasoning for the War of 1812
- **TRM** Module 4.2 AP® Analyzing Sources Handout 2
- **TRM** Map 4B – The Pacific Rim
- **TRM** Handout 4.3 – Examining the Growing National Economy
- **TRM** Handout 4.4 – Influence of Regional Economy on Politics
- **TRM** Module 4.2 AP® Analyzing Sources Handout 3

Module 4-3

- **TRM** Module 4.3 AP® Analyzing Sources Handout 1
- **TRM** Module 4.3 AP® Analyzing Sources Handout 2

Module 4-4

- **TRM** Module 4.4 AP® Analyzing Sources Handout 1
- **TRM** Handout 4.5 – Interpreting Visuals
- **TRM** Module 4.4 AP® Analyzing Sources Handout 2

Module 4-5

- **TRM** Module 4.5 AP® Analyzing Sources Handout 1
- **TRM** Module 4.5 AP® Analyzing Sources Handout 2
- **TRM** Module 4.5 AP® Analyzing Sources Handout 3
- **TRM** Handout 4.6 – Causes and Effects of the Panic of 1837

Module 4-6

- **TRM** Module 4.6 AP® Analyzing Sources Handout 1
- **TRM** Module 4.6 AP® Analyzing Sources Handout 2
- **TRM** Module 4.6 AP® Analyzing Sources Handout 3

Module 4-7

- **TRM** Module 4.7 AP® Analyzing Sources Handout 1
- **TRM** Module 4.7 AP® Analyzing Sources Handout 2
- **TRM** Module 4.7 AP® Analyzing Sources Handout 3
- **TRM** Handout 4.7 – Antebellum Reform Movements

Module 4-8

- **TRM** Module 4.8 AP® Analyzing Sources Handout 1
- **TRM** Module 4.8 AP® Analyzing Sources Handout 2
- **TRM** Module 4.8 AP® Analyzing Sources Handout 3
- **TRM** Module 4.8 AP® Analyzing Sources Handout 4

Period 4 Essential Activity

The Market Revolution was brought on by a confluence of events and long-term developments that slowly transformed the American economy after the War of 1812 through the middle of the nineteenth century. Disparate factors such as immigration, expansion, transportation, technological innovation, banking reforms, government intervention, and the mechanization of the workforce often overlapped as causes of the economic transformation. This group activity seeks to have students think through the definition, causes, regional trends, and effects on individual groups of people.

For this activity, have students use the period 1800–1848. Students begin with a blank map of the United States, colored markers, and a piece of butcher-block paper. The first task is for students to define the Market Revolution by accounting for the factors that caused this economic transformation. Students record their definition on the butcher-block paper. Remind students this definition can be multiple sentences. The next task is to color code the following regions: Northeast, Upper South, Lower South, Northwest Territory, and western frontier. The map should be attached to the butcher-block paper so students can see how each group determined the boundaries of each region. The final task is for students to select at least two groups of people in each region and explain how the Market Revolution shaped their roles or opportunities. Well-rounded answers will use race, ethnicity, and gender in their responses.

The final product illustrates conceptual understandings as students connect the causes and geographical differences of the Market Revolution. Moreover, by the end of this activity students will also demonstrate specific understandings of how the Market Revolution affected specific groups of people.

Period 4 Alignment to the Fall 2019 AP® United States History Course Framework*

Relationship to the College Board Units

Period 4 in this book covers Topics 4.1–4.14 in Unit 4 of the College Board course framework. Students will be ready to take the Personal Progress Check for Unit 4 once they have completed this period.

Course Themes

Period 4 develops these course themes outlined in the course framework:

- **Work, Exchange, and Technology (WXT):** Technological developments, including the steam engine, mass production of interchangeable parts, and the cotton gin, propelled American manufacturing in the North, the spread of slavery in the South, and an improved transportation network throughout the nation. These technological advances, combined with the expansion of the federal government's power, spurred the industrialization of the American economy.
- **Politics and Power (POL):** The expansion of white male suffrage changed American politics as a new two-party system featuring the Democrats and Whigs replaced the first two-party system consisting of the Federalists and Democratic-Republicans. Westward settlement, conflicts with American Indians and European nations, and Supreme Court rulings contributed to the expansion of federal power even as citizens debated the role of the federal government in American society.
- **America in the World (WOR):** The United States used force and diplomacy to expand and solidify its control of North America by purchasing Louisiana from France, participating in the War of 1812 against Great Britain, and acquiring Florida from Spain. The U.S. also continued a policy of signing treaties with American Indians and using force against American Indians to gain access to new lands and resources.
- **Social Structures (SOC):** The market revolution boosted urbanization by drawing international and internal migrants to industrializing cities in the Northeast and Midwest and changed women's roles by placing a new emphasis on domesticity.
- **American and Regional Cultures (ARC):** A new national culture combining European and American elements took shape with the spread of public education and printed materials. The Second Great Awakening and transcendentalism sparked an array of social reform efforts, further transforming American culture. In the South, enslaved people began to develop a distinct African American culture even as they sought ways to resist their condition.
- **Geography and the Environment (GEO):** Industrialization and geographic differences led to increased regional economic specialization as factories were increasingly located in Northern and Midwestern cities while many rural Americans engaged in farming, logging, or mining. In the South, cotton planting expanded westward in response to growing demand from northern and British mills.

Course Skills

Period 4 helps students to develop the following AP® Historical Thinking Skills identified in the course framework.

- **Skill 1: Developments and Processes** (Modules 4.1, 4.2, 4.3, 4.4, 4.5, 4.6, 4.7, 4.8)
- **Skill 2: Sourcing and Situation** (Modules 4.1, 4.2, 4.3, 4.4, 4.5, 4.6, 4.7, 4.8)
- **Skill 3: Claims and Evidence in Sources** (Modules 4.1, 4.2, 4.3, 4.4, 4.5, 4.6, 4.7, 4.8)
- **Skill 4: Contextualization** (Modules 4.2, 4.3, 4.7, 4.8)
- **Skill 5: Making Connections** (Modules 4.1, 4.2, 4.3, 4.4, 4.5, 4.6, 4.7, 4.8)
- **Skill 6: Argumentation** (Modules 4.2, 4.3, 4.7, 4.8)

Period 4 helps students to develop the following AP® History Reasoning Processes identified in the course framework.

- **Reasoning Process 1: Comparison** (Modules 4.2, 4.3, 4.8)
- **Reasoning Process 2: Causation** (Modules 4.1, 4.2, 4.3, 4.5, 4.6, 4.7)
- **Reasoning Process 3: Continuity and Change** (Modules 4.4, 4.6)

Learning Objectives and Historical Developments

Module	Topics	Learning Objectives	Historical Developments and Key Concepts
4-1	4.1, 4.2, 4.3	Unit 4: Learning Objective A Unit 4: Learning Objective B	KC-4.1.I.A, KC-4.I.B, KC-4.3.I.A.i
4-2	4.3, 4.4	Unit 4: Learning Objective C Unit 4: Learning Objective D	KC-4.1.I.D, KC-4.2.III.D, KC-4.3.II.C, KC-4.3.I, KC-4.3.I.A.II
4-3	4.5, 4.6	Unit 4: Learning Objective E Unit 4: Learning Objective F	KC-4.2.I.A, KC-4.2.I.B, KC-4.2.I.C, KC-4.2.III.B, KC-4.2.III.A, KC-4.2.II.B, KC-4.2.II.A, KC-4.2.II.C
4-4	4.7	Unit 4: Learning Objective G	KC-4.1.I
4-5	4.8	Unit 4: Learning Objective H	KC-4.1.I.C, KC-4.3.I.B
4-6	4.12, 4.13	Unit 4: Learning Objective L Unit 4: Learning Objective M	KC-4.1.III.B.ii, KC-4.1.II.D, KC-4.3.II.B.ii, KC-4.2.III.C, KC-4.3.II.A
4-7	4.9, 4.10	Unit 4: Learning Objective I Unit 4: Learning Objective J	KC-4.1.II.B, KC-4.1.II.C, KC-4.1.II.A.i
4-8	4.11, 4.14	Unit 4: Learning Objective K	KC-4.1.II.A.ii, KC-4.1.III.A, KC-4.1.III.B.i, KC-4.3.II.B.i, KC-4.1.III.C

TRM A detailed alignment that can be sorted by Course Framework Unit, Topic, Learning Objective, Historical Development/Key Concept, or textbook period, is available in the Teacher's Resource Materials and via the book's online platform.

*Should changes be made to the Course Framework in the future, an updated alignment will be placed on our catalog page at bfwpub.com/fabric1e.

TEACHING IDEA

AP® Central

A great resource to help you teach this period is to read the information in the AP® U.S. History study guide for 1800–1848, available from the AP® United States History Classroom Resources section of AP® Central (apcentral.collegeboard.org).

PERIOD 4: 1800–1848

Democracy, Industrialization, and Reform

▲ **Spinning Cotton in a New England Mill, c. 1835** Industrialization created new and sometimes dangerous job opportunities for men, women, and children in factories that knit the economic production of the North and South together. In this photograph, self-acting mules, powered by a water wheel or steam engine through belt-and-shafting, spun cotton fibers into cloth as the machines automatically wound the yarn onto spindles. A child was employed to crawl under the threads and sweep up under the mule minded by the woman on the left.

Debates regarding the rightful powers of the federal government over the state government and of the state over the individual continued in the first half of the nineteenth century. In the early 1800s, Federalists and Democratic-Republicans argued over a range of issues including tariffs, foreign policy, and how to interpret the meaning of the Constitution. The steady expansion of voting rights for white men increased political participation and led to the creation of new parties, the Democrats and Whigs, which fought a series of closely contested elections in the 1830s and 1840s.

While American politics was being remade, innovations in technology and infrastructure transformed the growing economy of the United States. These changes allowed goods to be produced more efficiently and to be traded more easily between the various regions of the United States and between the nation and the world. The newly resulting regional specialization led to greater economic integration through trade but also to clearer economic and social differences between different regions. A "market revolution" affected where and how Americans worked and lived, reshaped regional and national identities, and influenced how citizens interacted with each other at home, in the marketplace, and at work.

Throughout the first half of the nineteenth century, U.S. policymakers sought to extend American power internally and abroad in hopes of expanding their markets and opportunities to exploit land and resources west of the Mississippi River. As westward expansion continued, the debate over the fate of enslaved Americans and whether slavery should be allowed in new territories and states became increasingly heated. Compromises over the expansion of slavery proved successful in the first half of the nineteenth century but became increasingly difficult toward the middle of the century.

Throughout this period, Americans debated the legacy of the American Revolution, whether the expansion of slavery was part of or harmful to that legacy, whether voting rights could be limited to landholders and to men, and whether federal policies threatened states' rights. By the end of this time period, Americans had resolved some of these debates, while others continued to cause tension in the United States.

PERIOD 4 PREVIEW

Module	AP® Thematic Focus
4-1: Political and Economic Transformations	**Work, Exchange, and Technology ▪ Politics and Power** With the election of 1800, Democratic-Republicans consolidated control of Congress and the presidency, while the Supreme Court remained under Federalist influence. Westward settlement and expansion, armed conflicts with American Indians, foreign policy challenges from England and France, and Supreme Court rulings all contributed to an expansion of the federal government's power during the early 1800s. Technological developments including the steam engine, mass production of interchangeable parts, and the cotton gin propelled American manufacturing in the North, the spread of slavery in the South, and an improved transportation network throughout the nation. These technological advances, combined with the expansion of the federal government's power, spurred the industrialization of the American economy.
4-2: Defending and Redefining the Nation	**Politics and Power ▪ America in the World** The United States' participation in the War of 1812 and conflicts with American Indian nations solidified U.S. control of its western lands at the same time as the Monroe Doctrine and efforts to promote foreign trade expanded America's global presence. Tensions and war with England, the emergence of distinct, regional economies, and disagreements over the expansion of slavery also led to growing political debates as regional interests often outweighed national concerns.
4-3: Transportation and Market Revolutions Change America	**Social Structures** The market revolution boosted urbanization by drawing international and rural migrants to industrializing cities in the Northeast and fast-growing towns in the Midwest. It also increased class distinctions as rising prosperity benefited the business elite and led to the growth of both the middle class and the working poor. Middle- and upper-class women's roles changed, with a growing societal emphasis on domesticity.
4-4: The Second American Party System	**Politics and Power** By the 1820s, states expanded voting rights to all white men by ending property requirements while simultaneously restricting voting rights for women, African Americans, and American Indians. As a more popularly oriented style of campaigning emerged, Jackson's presidential election victory in 1828 confirmed the staying power of the new Democratic Party and signaled the end of a political system dominated by eastern elites.
4-5: Conflicts of the Jacksonian Era	**Politics and Power** Debates about the use of federal power — including its ability to impose tariffs, the continued existence of the Bank of the United States, and American Indian policy — contributed to sectional crises over developments such as state nullification of federal tariffs, the forced relocation of thousands of American Indians, the Panic of 1837, and the formation of the Whig Party.
4-6: Slavery and Southern Society	**Geography and the Environment ▪ American and Regional Culture ▪ Social Structures** The expansion of cotton planting generated wealth for the planter elite, triggered the forced internal migration of enslaved people, and limited the growth of industry and cities in the South. Despite brutality and the prevalence of slave codes, a vibrant African American culture emerged on plantations and among free black people in the South. Enslaved laborers regularly resisted in various ways while many free black people worked to improve their status.
4-7: Social Reform Movements	**American and National Identity** A new national culture combining European and American elements took shape in the early 1800s with the spread of public education and printed materials. The Second Great Awakening and transcendentalism sparked an array of social reform efforts, further transforming American culture.
4-8: Abolitionism and Sectionalism	**American and Regional Culture** Antislavery movements in the North steadily grew from the 1820s until the Civil War (1860–1865) as reformers split over banning the expansion of slavery into new territories or abolishing slavery throughout the United States. A women's rights movement also emerged, fueled in part by the backlash many women experienced from their participation in abolitionist organizations.

Module 4-1

Political and Economic Transformations

LEARNING TARGETS

By the end of this module, you should be able to:
- Explain the causes and effects of political debates in the Jeffersonian Era.
- Explain how technology reshaped both the American economy and the lives of distinct groups of Americans.

THEMATIC FOCUS

Work, Exchange, and Technology
Politics and Power

With the election of 1800, Democratic-Republicans consolidated control of Congress and the presidency, while the Supreme Court remained under Federalist influence. Westward settlement and expansion, armed conflicts with American Indians, foreign policy challenges from England and France, and Supreme Court rulings all contributed to an expansion of the federal government's power during the early 1800s. Technological developments including the steam engine, mass production of interchangeable parts, and the cotton gin propelled American manufacturing in the North, the spread of slavery in the South, and an improved transportation network throughout the nation. These technological advances, combined with the expansion of the federal government's power, spurred the industrialization of the American economy.

HISTORICAL REASONING FOCUS

Causation

TASK ▶ As you read this module, consider the short- and long-term effects of the political changes that occurred under a Democratic-Republican-controlled White House and Congress during the early nineteenth century. At the same time, take note of both short- and long-term effects of major technological advancements on how Americans worked and lived between the late eighteenth century and the early nineteenth century.

Thomas Jefferson, like other Democratic-Republicans, envisioned the United States as a republic composed of small, independent farmers who had little need and less desire for expansive federal power. Despite Jefferson's early efforts to impose this vision on the government, developments in international affairs soon converged with Supreme Court rulings to expand federal power. But Jefferson, too, contributed to this expansion. Imagining the nation's extensive frontiers as a boon to its development, he purchased the Louisiana Territory from France in 1803. The purchase and development of this vast territory increased federal authority. It also raised new questions about the place of American Indians and African Americans in a republican society.

As the United States expanded geographically, technological ingenuity became a highly valued commodity. The spread of U.S. settlements into new territories necessitated improved forms of transportation and communication and increased demands for muskets and other weapons to protect the nation's frontier. The growing population also fueled improvements in agriculture and manufacturing to meet demands for clothing, food, and farm equipment. Continued conflicts with

---

TRM Suggested Responses to Questions

BUILDING AP® SKILLS

Causation

Causation is one of the main historical reasoning processes in the course and on the AP® exam and is the focus for this module. Therefore, the more students get to practice it the better. Provide students with the two main visions of America during the Jeffersonian Era, those of the Democratic-Republicans and of the Federalists. While the former envisioned an agrarian nation compromised of small independent farmers and a federal government with limited powers, the latter wanted an industrializing and more urban society that could eventually challenge Europe and a federal government with a lot of power so it could achieve these goals. For homework, students will have to research and identify the three main causes or reasons for each vision of the country.

TEACHING IDEA

Incorporating Websites

Visit the Stanford History Education Group site to obtain a lesson plan on Alexander Hamilton vs. Thomas Jefferson (sheg.stanford.edu). Specifically, this lesson focuses on the differences between two very different politicians who, although committed to republicanism, held very different visions for the fledgling nation. This is a useful lesson because students are required to understand these competing visions, and it also will help students with the reasoning process of comparison.

TEACHING IDEA

Class Discussion

As a bell ringer, before you begin teaching this period, have students look at the timeline in the Period 4 Review Chronology on page 353. Ask them to highlight the main political events and developments for the period using one color and then the economic ones using another color. Then, write a double-headed arrow on the board with a start date of 1800 and end date of 1848.

Conduct a class discussion on which political and economic answers they think might be most important and place one category on top and the other on the bottom of the arrow. Revisit this activity after teaching the entire period so students can compare (and contrast) their original answers with those at the end. Since the period timeline starts in 1791 and ends in 1850, it would be perfectly acceptable for students to use examples that do not technically fall within the provided date range on the arrow.

TEACHING IDEA

Incorporating Websites

Assign students to watch Episode 30 "Haitian Revolutions" from the Crash Course US History series (available on YouTube). Ask students to pay attention to the elements of radicalism and how this could have affected politics in the United States so they can correctly answer the review question. Lastly, have them make a comparison between Gabriel Prosser's rebellion in 1800 with the Haitian Revolution by explaining either one similarity or difference.

TEACHING IDEA

AP® Central

Use the Long-Essay Question from the 2004 AP® U.S. History exam, question 2, on the Revolution of 1800, which is available on the College Board's AP® U.S. History Past Exam Questions section under "2004: Form B" (apcentral.collegeboard.org). Brainstorm with students and discuss how they would tackle this question. The main objective of this activity is to help them build writing skills by focusing on the skill of argumentation. Specifically, work on how to make an argument by writing a thesis statement that fully answers the question, support that argument by identifying historical evidence, and develop the argument by providing reasoning.

▲ Differentiation

Consider having advanced learners individually address two other points on the AP® rubric — contextualization and "historical complexity." Conversely, any struggling learners should work in pairs and support each other. To conclude the activity, have students share out their answers and discuss strengths and weaknesses.

EXPLORING AP® THEMES

Work, Exchange, and Technology

This is one of the thematic focuses for this module. Accordingly, have students create a thematic outline that highlights, in chronological order, the main technological innovations that transformed the American economy during this period (1800–1848). Students should refer to the Period 4 Review Chronology on page 353. For additional guidance, give students the organizational categories of production, transportation, and communication so that they can keep their evidence organized.

Period 4: 1800–1848

MODULE 4-1 Political and Economic Transformations

Great Britain and France also highlighted the need to develop the nation's natural resources and technological capabilities. Yet even though American ingenuity was widely praised, the daily lives of most Americans changed only slowly. And for some, especially enslaved women and men, technological advances merely added to their burdens.

A New Administration Faces Challenges

In 1801 Democratic-Republicans worked quickly to implement their vision of limited federal power. Holding the majority in Congress, they repealed the whiskey tax and let the Alien and Sedition Acts expire. Jefferson significantly reduced government expenditures, and immediately set about slashing the national debt, cutting it nearly in half by the end of his second term. Democratic-Republicans also worked to curb the powers granted to the Bank of the United States and the federal court system.

Soon, however, international upheavals forced Jefferson to make fuller use of his presidential powers. The U.S. government had paid tribute to the **Barbary States** of North Africa during the 1790s to gain protection for American merchant ships. The new president opposed this practice and in 1801 refused to continue the payments. The Barbary pirates quickly resumed their attacks, and Jefferson sent the U.S. Navy and Marine Corps to retaliate. Although a combined American and Arab force did not achieve their objective of capturing Tripoli, the Ottoman viceroy agreed to negotiate a new agreement with the United States. Seeking to avoid all-out war, Congress accepted a treaty with the Barbary States that reduced the tribute payment.

Jefferson had also followed the developing crisis in the West Indies during the 1790s. In 1791 enslaved people on the sugar-rich island of Saint Domingue (later known as Haiti) launched a revolt against French rule. Inspired in part by the American Declaration of Independence, the **Haitian Revolution** escalated into a complicated conflict in which free people of color, white slaveholders, and enslaved people formed competing alliances with British and Spanish forces as well as with leaders of the French Revolution. Finally, in December 1799, Toussaint L'Ouverture, a military leader and freedperson, claimed the presidency of the new Republic of Haiti. But Napoleon Bonaparte seized power in France that same year and sent thousands of troops to reclaim the island. Toussaint was shipped off to France, where he died in prison. Many Haitians fled to the United States, but other Haitian rebels continued the fight.

In the United States, reactions to the revolution were mixed, but southern whites feared that it might incite rebellions among the enslaved. In 1800 Gabriel, an enslaved blacksmith in Richmond, Virginia, plotted such a rebellion. Inspired by both the American and Haitian revolutions, supporters rallied around the demand for "Death or Liberty." Although Gabriel's plan failed when informants betrayed him to authorities, news of the plot traveled across the South and terrified white residents. Their anxieties were heightened when, in November 1803, prolonged fighting, yellow fever, and the loss of sixty thousand soldiers forced Napoleon to admit defeat in Haiti. Haiti became the first independent black-led nation in the Americas.

Haitian Revolution Revolt against French rule by free and enslaved black people in the 1790s on the island of Saint Domingue. It led to the establishment of the Republic of Haiti, the first independent black-led nation in the Americas, in 1803.

REVIEW

• How did the Haitian Revolution affect politics in the United States?

Acquiring the Louisiana Territory

In France's defeat Jefferson saw an opportunity to gain navigation rights on the Mississippi River, which the French controlled. This was a matter of crucial concern to Americans living west of the Appalachian Mountains. Jefferson sent James Monroe to France to offer Napoleon $2 million to ensure Americans the right of navigation and deposit (i.e., offloading cargo from ships) on the Mississippi. To Jefferson's surprise, Napoleon offered instead to sell the entire Louisiana Territory for $15 million.

The president agonized over the constitutionality of this **Louisiana Purchase**. Since the Constitution contained no provisions for buying land from foreign nations, a strict interpretation would prohibit the purchase. In the end, though, the opportunity proved too tempting, and the president finally agreed to buy the Louisiana Territory. Jefferson justified his decision by arguing that the

Louisiana Purchase U.S. government's 1803 purchase from France of the vast territory stretching from the Mississippi River to the Rocky Mountains and from New Orleans to present-day Montana, doubling the size of the nation.

TEACHING IDEA

Class Discussion

During the Jeffersonian Era, America encountered a series of foreign challenges. These included:

1) The Barbary States interfering with American trade in the Mediterranean and requiring tribute.

2) England and France stopping merchant vessels in violation of American neutrality and impressing Americans.

3) Europeans and American Indians inhabiting areas along the frontier and preventing westward expansion.

Conduct a class discussion on which of these challenges represented the main threat to the United States, and have students explain the reasoning behind their answers.

AP® TIP
Analyze how the Louisiana Purchase affected political parties and regional development in the early nineteenth century.

territory would allow for the removal of more American Indians from east of the Mississippi River, end European influence in the region, and expand U.S. trade networks. Opponents viewed the purchase as benefiting mainly agrarian interests and suspected Jefferson of trying to offset Federalist power in the Northeast. Neither party seemed especially concerned about the French, Spanish, or native peoples living in the region. They came under U.S. control when the Senate approved the purchase in October 1803. And the purchase proved popular among ordinary Americans, most of whom focused on the opportunities it offered rather than the expansion of federal power it ensured.

At Jefferson's request, Congress had already appropriated funds for an expedition known as the **Corps of Discovery** to explore territory along the Missouri River. That expedition could now explore much of the Louisiana Territory. The president's personal secretary, Meriwether Lewis, headed the venture and invited fellow Virginian William Clark to serve as co-captain. The two set off with about forty-five men on May 14, 1804. For two years, they traveled thousands of miles up the Missouri River, through the northern plains, over the Rocky Mountains, and beyond the Louisiana Territory to the Pacific coast. Sacagawea and her husband joined them in April 1805 as they headed into the Rocky Mountains. Throughout the expedition, members meticulously recorded observations about local plants and animals as well as American Indian residents, providing valuable evidence for scientists and fascinating information for ordinary Americans.

Sacagawea was the only American Indian to travel as a permanent member of the expedition, but many other native women and men assisted the Corps when it journeyed near their villages. They provided food and lodging for the Corps, hauled baggage up steep mountain trails, and traded food, horses, and other items. The one African American on the expedition, an enslaved man named York, also helped negotiate trade with local American Indians. York, who realized his value as a trader, hunter, and scout, asked Clark for his freedom when the expedition ended in 1806. York did eventually become a free man, but it is not clear whether it was by Clark's choice or York's escape.

AP® ANALYZING SOURCES

Source: William Clark, *Journal Entry*, October 12, 1804

"After breakfast, we went on shore to the house of the chief of the second village named Lassel, where we found his chiefs and warriors. They made us a present of about seven bushels of corn, a pair of leggings, a twist of their tobacco, and the seeds of two different species of tobacco. The chief then delivered a speech expressive of his gratitude for the presents and the good counsels which we had given him; his intention of visiting [the president of the United States] but for fear of the Sioux; and requested us to take one of the Ricara chiefs up to the Mandans and negociate a peace between the two nations.... After we had answered and explained the magnitude and power of the United States, the three chiefs came with us to the boat. We gave them some sugar, a little salt, and a sun-glass. Two of them left us, and the chief of the third [village] ... accompanied us to the Mandans....

[The Ricara] express a disposition to keep at peace with all nations, but they are well armed with [muskets], and being much under the influence of the Sioux, who exchanged the goods which they got from the British for Ricara corn, their minds are sometimes poisoned and they cannot always be depended on."

Questions for Analysis
1. Describe Clark's characterization of the Ricara Indians.
2. Describe the attitude of the Ricara Indians toward American explorers and other American Indian nations, according to Clark.
3. Explain how this document illustrates the influence the Corps of Discovery had on relations between American Indian nations.

BUILDING AP® SKILLS

Causation

When students use the reasoning process of causation, they not only have to understand the difference between primary and secondary causes but also the difference between short- and long-term effects. Therefore, have students think about how the political debates of the Jeffersonian Era (e.g., how to interpret the U.S. Constitution as was the case with the Louisiana Purchase) could result in long-term effects during the Age of Jackson. Since that material has not been covered yet, ask them to keep that in mind as they read the remaining modules and take notes.

TRM Suggested Responses to Questions

TRM Module 4.1 AP® Analyzing Sources Handout 1

TEACHING IDEA

Incorporating Websites

Visit the Stanford History Education Group site to obtain a lesson plan on the Louisiana Purchase (sheg.standford.edu). Specifically, this lesson focuses on the criticism and opposition President Thomas Jefferson faced from Federalists.

BUILDING AP® SKILLS

Comparison

Divide the class in half and assign each student one of the two political party affiliations from the First Party System — Federalists and Democratic-Republicans. Then, have them research how each political party professed to interpret the U.S. Constitution (loose/broad vs. strict/narrow) and cite examples that were consistent and inconsistent with such characterizations. Help students focus on the similarities and differences since this activity strives to highlight the skill of comparison. Lastly, discuss whether their respective interpretations were constitutionally permissible or not. Have students explain their answers and provide evidence like the "necessary and proper" clause or implied powers to support their positions.

TEACHING IDEA

Research

In pairs, have students research the expedition of Meriwether Lewis and William Clarke (Corps of Discovery Expedition) and the role played by Sacagawea. Specifically, have students find out about the different types of indigenous cultures they encountered, the plants and animals unknown in the east, and the topography of the land (i.e., Northern Plains, Rocky Mountains, and the Pacific Northwest, etc.) that might lead others to eventually head west and allow for scientific and economic advancements.

TEACHING IDEA

Incorporating Websites

Visit the Stanford History Education Group site to obtain a lesson plan on the expedition conducted by Lewis and Clarke of the Louisiana Territory (sheg.stanford.edu). Specifically, this lesson focuses on the complex relationships between these explorers and the American Indian tribes they encountered along the way to the Pacific Northwest.

TEACHING IDEA

Incorporating Websites

Have students conduct a virtual visit to President Thomas Jefferson's Monticello (monticello.org). Afterward, have them read the background information on the purchase of the Louisiana Territory (available by searching for the topic). Then create a detailed timeline of the purchase as a class.

MAP 4.1 Lewis and Clark and Zebulon Pike Expeditions, 1804–1807 The expeditions led by Meriwether Lewis, William Clark, and Zebulon Pike illustrate the vast regions explored in just four years after the U.S. purchase of the Louisiana Territory. Journeying through and beyond the borders of that territory, the explorers gathered information about American Indian nations, plants, animals, and the natural terrain even as Comanche and Shoshone nations, with access to horses, transformed the region. **According to this map, what were the competing territorial claims to North America in the early 1800s?**

Other expeditions followed Lewis and Clark's venture. In 1806 Lieutenant Zebulon Pike led a group to explore the southern portion of the Louisiana Territory (Map 4.1). After traveling from St. Louis to the Rocky Mountains, the expedition entered Mexican territory. In early 1807, Pike and his men were captured by Mexican forces. They were returned to the United States at the Louisiana border that July. Pike had learned a great deal about lands that would eventually become part of the United States and about Mexican desires to overthrow Spanish rule, information that proved valuable over the next two decades.

Early in this series of expeditions, in November 1804, Jefferson easily won reelection as president. His popularity among farmers, already high, increased when Congress reduced the minimum allotment for federal land sales from 320 to 160 acres. This act allowed more farmers to purchase land on their own rather than via speculators. Yet, in spite of this continued popularity among his core of supporters, Jefferson's original vision of limiting federal power had already been undermined by his own actions — and those of the Supreme Court. That erosion would continue through Jefferson's second term.

REVIEW

- How did Jefferson reconcile his support for the Louisiana Purchase with his limited view of federal power?
- Why did Federalists oppose the Louisiana Purchase even though they believed the Constitution permitted it?

EXPLORING AP® THEMES

Politics and Power

The First Party System, comprised of Federalists and Democratic-Republicans, disagreed on various domestic and foreign policy issues and the appropriate role for the federal government in the American economy and society at large. Conduct a class discussion on which groups of Americans tended to support each respective political party. Students should identify, for example, that Federalists were most popular in the New England area, in cities, and among the more educated and affluent members of society. Conversely, Democratic-Republicans were normally supported by Americans in the South and emerging West, who tended to be farmers in rural areas with lower levels of education and money. Lastly, you can also help students make connections to the present day and the demographical generalizations that could be made about the two main political parties — the Democrats and Republicans.

The Supreme Court Extends Its Reach

In 1801, just before the Federalist-dominated Congress turned over power to the Democratic-Republicans, it passed a new **Judiciary Act**. The act created six additional circuit courts and sixteen new judgeships, which President Adams filled with Federalist "midnight appointments" before he left office. Jefferson accused the Federalists of having "retired into the judiciary" and worried that "from that battery all the works of Republicanism are to be beaten down and destroyed." Meanwhile John Marshall, chief justice of the United States (1801–1835), insisted that the powers of the Supreme Court must be equal to and balance those of the executive and legislative branches.

One of the first cases to test the Court's authority involved a dispute over President Adams's midnight appointments. Jefferson's secretary of state, James Madison, refused to deliver the appointment papers to several of the appointees, including William Marbury. Marbury and three others sued Madison to receive their commissions. In *Marbury v. Madison* (1803), the Supreme Court ruled that it was not empowered to force the executive branch to give Marbury his commission. But in his decision, Chief Justice Marshall declared that the Supreme Court did have the duty "to say what the law is." He thus asserted a fundamental constitutional power: that the Supreme Court had the authority to decide which federal laws were constitutional. The following year, the Court also claimed the right to rule on the constitutionality of state laws. In doing so, the justices rejected Democratic-Republicans' claim that state legislatures had the power to repudiate federal law. Instead, the Supreme Court declared that federal laws took precedence over state laws.

Over the next dozen years, the Supreme Court continued to assert Federalist principles. In 1810 it insisted that it was the proper and sole arena for determining matters of constitutional interpretation. Then in 1819, the highest court reinforced its loose interpretation of the Constitution's implied powers clause in *McCulloch v. Maryland*. This clause gave the federal government the right to "make all laws which shall be necessary and proper" for carrying out the explicit powers granted to it by the Constitution. Despite Democratic-Republicans' earlier opposition to a national bank, Congress chartered the Second Bank of the United States in 1816, and its branch banks issued notes that circulated widely in local communities. Legislators in Maryland, believing that branch banks had gained excessive power, approved a tax on their operations. Marshall's Court ruled that the establishment of the bank was "necessary and proper" for the functioning of the national government and rejected Maryland's right to tax the branch bank, claiming that "the power to tax involves the power to destroy."

By the 1820s the Supreme Court, under the forceful direction of John Marshall, had established the power of **judicial review**—the authority of the nation's highest court to rule on cases involving states as well as the nation. It also had strengthened property rights and reinforced the supremacy of national laws over state laws. From the Court's perspective, the judiciary was as important an institution in framing and preserving a national agenda as Congress or the president.

Marbury v. Madison 1803 Supreme Court decision that established the authority of the Supreme Court to rule on the constitutionality of federal laws.

AP® TIP
The significance of the Marshall Court's role in defining the power of judicial review is a "must know" for the AP® exam.

McCulloch v. Maryland 1819 Supreme Court decision that reinforced the federal government's ability to employ an expansive understanding of the implied powers clause of the Constitution.

judicial review The Supreme Court's ability to rule on cases at both the federal and state level.

REVIEW

How did the Supreme Court's rulings in the *Marbury* and *McCulloch* cases strengthen the power of federal government?

Democratic-Republicans Expand Federal Powers

Although Democratic-Republicans generally opposed Marshall's rulings, they, too, continued to expand federal power. Once again, international developments drove the Jefferson administration's political agenda. By 1805 the security of the United States was threatened by continued conflicts between France and Great Britain. Both sought alliances with the young nation, and both ignored U.S. claims of neutrality. Indeed, each nation sought to punish Americans for trading with the other. Britain's Royal Navy began stopping American ships carrying sugar and molasses from the French West Indies and, between 1802 and 1811, impressed more than eight thousand sailors from such ships, including many American citizens. France claimed a similar right to stop U.S. ships that continued to trade with Great Britain.

BUILDING AP® SKILLS

Developments and Processes

While Democratic-Republicans maintained control of the executive and legislative branches of government, the Federalists oversaw the judiciary. Using a blank version of the chart below, have students identify the historical significance of the two Supreme Court cases covered in this section that ultimately expanded the power of the federal government over states. Then have them research and do the same for the additional three cases that also helped establish supremacy of federal laws over the states. Have students complete the following chart, which is available in the Teacher's Resource Materials. Possible answers are included in italics.

Supreme Court Case	Historical Significance
Marbury v. Madison (1803)	*Established judicial review, making the Supreme Court the final arbiter of what is constitutional when it comes to federal laws.*
McCulloch v. Maryland (1819)	*Determined that a state cannot tax a federal entity and that the national bank was constitutional.*
Fletcher v. Peck (1810)	*Established judicial review for state laws.*
Cohens v. Virginia (1821)	*Established judicial review of state supreme court decisions.*
Gibbons v. Ogden (1824)	*Determined that the federal government, and not states, had the power to regulate interstate commerce.*

TRM Find **Handout 4.1 – Analyzing Supreme Court Cases, 1803–1824** in the Teacher's Resource Materials.

BUILDING AP® SKILLS

Developments and Processes

To enhance understanding of the Supreme Court cases discussed in this module, have students research Chief Justice John Marshall (1801–1835). Specifically, ask students to identify how he embodied Federalist ideas and placed the judiciary on equal footing with the executive and legislative branches and helped establish the supremacy of the federal government over the states. To help students get started, have them search for Chief Justice John Marshall on the Biography website (biography.com).

Period 4: 1800–1848

MODULE 4-1 Political and Economic Transformations

TEACHING IDEA

Geography Instruction

Give students a map in which they can identify the territorial growth that took place between 1800 and 1821. Specifically, this includes the admission of: 1) Ohio (1803); 2) Louisiana (1812); 3) Indiana (1816); 4) Mississippi (1817); 5) Illinois (1818); 6) Alabama (1819); 7) Maine (1820); and culminating with 8) Missouri (1821). Missouri is the end-point for this activity because of its significance, which will be highlighted in an upcoming module with one of the main compromises on the issue of slavery. A reproducible version of this map is available in the Teacher's Resource Materials.

TRM Map 4A – The United States, 1820s

TEACHING IDEA

Connecting the Dots

Democratic-Republicans, the political party led by Thomas Jefferson, were usually characterized as "strict constructionists" of the U.S. Constitution. Nonetheless, there are a couple of examples of Jefferson engaging in "loose" interpretation of the supreme law of the land and expanding the power of the federal government. Have students focus on the Louisiana Purchase (1803) and the Embargo Act (1807) and write 2 or 3 sentences explaining how and/or why these examples represent a broad or "loose" interpretation of the U.S. Constitution.

Embargo Act 1807 act that prohibited American ships from leaving their home ports until Britain and France repealed restrictions on U.S. trade. The act had a devastating impact on American commerce.

AP® TIP

Evaluate the extent to which foreign conflicts further encouraged regional divisions in the United States during the early nineteenth century.

Unable to convince foreign powers to recognize U.S. neutrality, Jefferson and Madison pushed for congressional passage of an embargo that they hoped would, like colonial boycotts, force Great Britain's hand. In 1807 Congress passed the **Embargo Act**, which prohibited U.S. ships from leaving their home ports until Britain and France repealed their restrictions on American trade. Although the act kept the United States out of war, it had a devastating impact on national commerce.

New England merchants immediately voiced their outrage, and some began sending goods to Europe via Canada. In response, Congress passed the Force Act, granting extraordinary powers to customs officials to end such smuggling. The economic pain caused by the rapid decline in trade spread well beyond the merchant class. Farmers and urban workers as well as southern **planters** directly suffered the embargo's effects. Exports nearly stopped, and sailors and dockworkers faced escalating unemployment. With the recession deepening, American concerns about the expansion of federal power reemerged. Congress and the president had not simply regulated international trade; they had brought it to a halt.

Still, despite the effects of the Embargo Act, many Americans viewed Jefferson favorably. He had devoted his adult life to the creation of the United States. He had purchased the Louisiana Territory, opening up vast lands to American exploration and development. This geographical boon encouraged inventors and artisans to pursue ideas that would help the early republic take full advantage of its resources and recover from its current economic plight. Some might have wondered, however, how a Democratic-Republican president had so significantly expanded the power of the federal government.

REVIEW

- What were the causes and consequences of the Embargo Act?

The U.S. Population Grows and Migrates

Although Democratic-Republicans initially hoped to limit the powers of the national government, the rapid growth of the United States pulled in the opposite direction. An increased population, combined with the exhaustion of farmland along the eastern seaboard, fueled migration to the West as well as the growth of cities. These developments heightened conflicts with American Indians and over slavery, but they also encouraged innovations in transportation and communication and improvements in agriculture and manufacturing.

As white Americans encroached more deeply on lands long settled by native peoples, American Indian tribes were forced ever westward. As early as 1800, groups like the Shoshone, who originally inhabited the Great Plains, had been forced into the Rocky Mountains by American Indians moving into the plains from the Mississippi and Ohio valleys (Map 4.2). Sacagawea must have realized that the expedition she accompanied would only increase pressure on the Shoshone and other nations as white migration escalated.

Although the vast majority of Americans continued to live in rural areas, a growing number moved to cities as eastern farmland lost its fertility and young people sought job opportunities in manufacturing, skilled trades, and service work. Cities were defined at the time as places with 8,000 or more inhabitants, but New York City and Philadelphia both counted more than 100,000 residents by 1810. In New York, immigrants, most of them Irish, made up about 10 percent of the population in 1820 and twice that percentage five years later. At the same time, the number of African Americans in New York City increased to more than 10,000. Cities began to emerge along the nation's frontier as well. After the Louisiana Purchase, New Orleans became a key commercial center while western migration fueled cities like Cincinnati. Even smaller frontier towns, like Rock Island, Illinois, served important functions for migrants traveling west. Trading posts appeared across the Mississippi valley, which eased the migration of thousands headed farther west. They served as sites of exchange between American Indians and white Americans and created the foundations for later cities.

EXPLORING AP® THEMES

Work, Exchange, and Technology

Since this module explicitly states the negative impacts of trade restrictions like the Embargo Act during Jefferson's administration, brainstorm with students the main positive impact it had on the economy. Students should point out that although these restrictions were bad for trade and commerce, they did help create and promote American manufacturing and industries, although this might have been an unintended consequence. This was particularly true, for example, in the textiles, lumber, and shipbuilding industries in New England and the Mid-Atlantic.

MAP 4.2 American Indian Land Cessions, 1790–1820 With the ratification of the Constitution, the federal government gained greater control over American Indian relations, including land cessions. At the same time, large numbers of white settlers poured into regions west of the Appalachian Mountains. The U.S. government gained most American Indian land by purchase or treaty, but these agreements were often the consequence of military victories by the U.S. Army. **What does the map's portrayal of American Indian land cessions reveal about the pace and direction of white settlement during this era?**

TEACHING IDEA

Geography Instruction

Map 4.2 identifies land cessions to the United States between 1790 and 1820, but not the main battles or treaties with American Indians. Have students research the Battle of Fallen Timbers in 1794, the Treaty of Greenville in 1795, Battle of Tippecanoe in 1811, and Battle of Horseshoe Bend in 1814.

Most Americans who headed west hoped to benefit from the increasingly liberal terms for land offered by the federal government. Small farmers sought sufficient acreage to feed their families and grow some crops for sale. They were eager to settle in western sections of the original thirteen states, in the Ohio River valley, or in newly opened territories along the Missouri and Kansas Rivers. In the South, these small farmers had to compete with slave-holding planters who headed west in the early nineteenth century. Migrants to the Mississippi valley also had to contend with a sizable population of Spanish and French residents, as well as Chickasaw and Creek Indians in the South and Shawnee, Chippewa, Sauk, and Fox communities farther north.

The development of roads and turnpikes hastened the movement of people and the transportation of goods. Frontier farmers wanted to get their produce to eastern markets quickly and cheaply. Before completion of the Lancaster Turnpike in Pennsylvania, it cost as much to carry wheat overland the sixty-two miles to Philadelphia as it did to ship it by sea from Philadelphia to London. Those who lived farther west faced even greater challenges. With the admission of Kentucky (1792), Tennessee (1796), and Ohio (1803) to the Union, demands for congressional support for building transportation routes grew louder. By 1819 five more states had been admitted along the Mississippi River, from Louisiana to Illinois.

> **AP® TIP**
> Be sure you can explain how migration within and expansion of the United States affected the federal legislation passed during the early nineteenth century.

BUILDING AP® SKILLS

Causation

Give students 10 minutes to identify and describe what caused/promoted westward expansion between 1800 and 1820. Possible answers include: *abundance of land out west while eastern farmlands had been exhausted, economic opportunities for a growing population, construction of roads that facilitated movement, land cessions by American Indians, etc.*

Period 4: 1800–1848

MODULE 4-1 Political and Economic Transformations

BUILDING AP® SKILLS

Claims and Evidence in Sources

Provide students with a copy of the article titled "Hamilton" by Ron Chernow. This secondary source from the Gilder Lehrman site discusses Alexander Hamilton, the nation's first secretary of the treasury who was known for his economic plan (gilderlehrman.org). Have students read the article to identify the author's claim or argument, historical evidence, and reasoning used to support it.

TEACHING IDEA

Class Discussion

Write the following question on the board: Who should pay for the construction of internal improvements like roads and canals? Provide students with three possible answers: private companies, states, or federal government. After brainstorming their answers in pairs, have students share responses and discuss as an entire class. Then, ask students to find what the secretary of the treasury at the time, Albert Gallatin, believed. Finally, have students compare his position with that of Alexander Hamilton's economic plan from Period 2.

◀ **Prices at George Davenport's Trading Post, Rock Island, Illinois, c. 1820**
What do the items listed for sale reveal about the daily lives of people living or traveling near the trading post?

Item	Price	Item	Price
Ax	$6.00	Large copper kettle	$30.00
Beaver trap	$8.00	Lead	$0.20 per pound
Black silk handkerchief	$2.00	Lead shot for guns	$1.00 per 5 pounds
Breechcloth	$3.00	Medium copper kettle	$10.00
Bridles	$2.00–$10.00	Muskrat spear	$2.00
Chain for staking down traps	$0.75 per 6 feet	Muskrat trap	$5.00
Combs	$1.00 per pair	Muslin or calico shirt	$3.00
File (for sharpening axes)	$2.00	Ordinary butcher knife	$0.50
Flannel	$1.00 per yard	Sheet iron kettle	$10.00
Flannel mantle	$3.00	Small copper kettle	$3.00
Gunflints	$1.00 per 15	Spurs	$6.00 per pair
Hand-size mirrors	$0.25	Tin kettle	$14.00
Heavy wool cloth	$10.00 per yard	Tomahawk	$1.50
Hoe	$2.00	Trade gun	$20.00–$25.00
Horn of gunpowder	$1.50	Wool blanket	$4.00
Horses	$35.00–$50.00	Wool mantle (short cloak or shawl)	$4.00

Source: Will Leinicke, Marion Lardner, and Ferrel Anderson, *Two Nations, One Land* (Rock Island, IL: Citizens to Preserve Black Hawk Park, 1981).

During Jefferson's administration, secretary of the treasury Albert Gallatin urged Congress to fund roads and canals to enhance the economic development of the nation. He advocated a "great turnpike road" along the Atlantic seaboard from Maine to Georgia as well as roads to connect the four main rivers that flowed from the Appalachians to the Atlantic Ocean. Although traditionally such projects were funded by the states, in 1815 Congress approved funds for a **National Road** from western Maryland through southwestern Pennsylvania to Wheeling, West Virginia. This so-called Cumberland Road was completed in 1818 and later extended into Ohio and Illinois.

National Road Road constructed using federal funds that ran from western Maryland through southwestern Pennsylvania to Wheeling, West Virginia; also called the Cumberland Road. Completed in 1818, it was part of a larger push to improve the nation's infrastructure.

Carrying people and goods by water was even faster and cheaper than transporting them over land, but rivers ran mainly north and south. In addition, although loads could be delivered quickly downstream, the return voyage was long and slow. While politicians advocated the construction of canals along east-west routes to link river systems, inventors and mechanics focused on building boats powered by steam to overcome the problems of sending goods upriver.

In 1804 Oliver Evans, a machinist in Philadelphia, invented a high-pressure steam engine attached to a dredge that cleaned the silt around the docks in Philadelphia harbor. He had insufficient funds, however, to pursue work on a steam-powered boat. Robert Fulton, a New Yorker, improved on Evans's efforts, using the low-pressure steam engine developed in England. In 1807

▲ **Robert Fulton's *Clermont*, c. 1813** This painting of the *Clermont* by an unknown artist was published as a lithograph in France c.1830, suggesting Europeans' interest in American innovations. As the illustration shows, early steamboats included paddle wheels and sails to guide their travels. Here the *Clermont* plies the Hudson River alongside sail boats as it passes a cluster of houses on the far shore. **What does this painting suggest about the state of technological development in the early 1800s?**

EXPLORING AP® THEMES

Work, Exchange, and Technology

Give students a map where they can draw the first three significant transportation projects that ultimately allowed for the emergence of a national infrastructure: 1) Lancaster Turnpike in Pennsylvania, 2) Cumberland Road or National Road, and 3) Erie Canal. Then, ask students to identify who paid for each project — private investors, federal government, and state of New York, respectively. This activity can also help students with the Short-Answer Question practice at the end of the module.

Fulton launched the first successful steamboat, the *Clermont*, which traveled up the Hudson River from New York City to Albany in only thirty-two hours. The powerful Mississippi River proved a greater challenge, but by combining Evans's high-pressure steam engine with a flat-bottom hull that avoided the river's sandbars, mechanics who worked along the frontier improved Fulton's design and launched the steamboat era in the West.

REVIEW

- Why did Americans move to cities and to the West during the early 1800s?

Technology Reshapes Agriculture and Industry

Advances in agricultural and industrial technology paralleled the development of roads and steamboats. Here, too, a single invention spurred others, inducing a **multiplier effect** that inspired additional dramatic changes. Two inventions—the cotton gin and the spinning machine—were especially notable in transforming southern agriculture and northern industry, transformations that were deeply intertwined.

American developments were also closely tied to the earlier rise of industry in Great Britain. By the 1770s, British manufacturers had built spinning mills in which steam-powered machines spun raw cotton into yarn. Eager to maintain their monopoly on industrial technology, the British made it illegal for engineers to emigrate. They could not stop everyone who worked in a cotton mill, however, from leaving. At age fourteen, Samuel Slater was hired as an apprentice in an English mill that used a yarn-spinning machine designed by Richard Arkwright. Slater was promoted to supervisor of the factory, but at age twenty-one he sought greater opportunities in America. While working in New York City, he learned that Moses Brown, a wealthy Rhode Island merchant, was eager to develop a machine like Arkwright's. Funded by Rhode Island investors and assisted by local craftsmen, Slater designed and built a spinning mill in Pawtucket.

The mill opened in December 1790 and began producing yarn, which was then woven into cloth in private shops and homes. By 1815 a series of cotton mills dotted the Pawtucket River. These factories offered workers, most of whom were the wives and children of farmers, a steady income, and they ensured employment for weavers in the countryside. They also increased the demand for cotton in New England just as British manufacturers sought new sources of the crop as well.

Ensuring a steady supply of cotton required another technological innovation, this one created by Eli Whitney. After graduating from Yale, Whitney agreed to serve as a private tutor for a planter family in South Carolina. On the ship carrying him south, Whitney met the widow Catherine Greene, who invited him to stay at her Mulberry Plantation near Savannah, Georgia. There local planters complained to him about the difficulty of making a profit on cotton. Long-staple cotton, grown in the Sea Islands, yielded enormous profits, but the soil in most of the South could sustain only the short-staple variety, which required hours of intensive labor to separate its sticky green seeds from the cotton fiber.

In 1793, in as little as ten days, Eli Whitney built a machine that could speed the process of deseeding short-staple cotton. Using mesh screens, rollers, and wire brushes, Whitney's **cotton gin** could clean as much cotton fiber in one hour as several workers could clean in a day. Recognizing the gin's value, Whitney received a U.S. patent, but because the machine was easy to duplicate, he never profited from his invention.

AP® TIP
Make sure that you are able to explain the relationship between cotton production in the South and industrial growth in the North during the first half of the nineteenth century.

cotton gin Machine invented by Eli Whitney in 1793 to deseed short-staple cotton. The cotton gin dramatically reduced the time and labor involved in deseeding, facilitating the expansion of cotton production in the South and West.

AP® ANALYZING SOURCES

Source: Eli Whitney, *Petition for Renewal of Patent on Cotton Gin*, 1812

"So alluring were the advantages developed by this invention that in a short time the whole attention of the planters of the middle and upper country of the Southern States was turned to planting green seed cotton. The means furnished by this discovery of cleaning that species of cotton were at once so cheap and expeditious and the prospects of advantage so alluring that it suddenly became the general crop of the country."

(Continued)

TEACHING IDEA

Incorporating Websites

Assign students to watch Episode 12 "The Market Revolution" from the Crash Course US History series (available on YouTube). Ask students to pay attention to the transformation of the American economy as the nation began to industrialize and establish a national market.

BUILDING AP® SKILLS

Comparison

Have students compare agricultural and industrial–technological innovations. They need to identify at least three innovations under each category and then describe how these technologies impacted the American economy. Some answers, such as the cotton gin and spinning machine, can be used in either column. Student answers may vary.

TRM Suggested Responses to Questions

TRM Module 4.1 AP® Analyzing Sources Handout 2

Period 4: 1800–1848

MODULE 4-1 Political and Economic Transformations

BUILDING AP® SKILLS

Claims and Evidence in Sources

Provide students with a copy of the article titled "The Early Republic" by Joseph Ellis. This secondary source from the Gilder Lehrman site discusses the first party system and the "Revolution of 1800" (gilderlehrman.org). Have students read the article to identify the author's claim or argument, historical evidence, and reasoning used to support it.

TEACHING IDEA

Understanding People Who Made a Difference

Have students research Samuel Slater, Moses Brown, Eli Whitney, and Francis Cabot Lowell and identify their main contributions to the factory system in the United States. After students share their findings, conduct a class discussion on who was most influential and why. Student answers will vary.

Little or no regard, however, was paid to the claims of your memorialist, and the infringements of his rights became almost as extensive as the cultivation of cotton. He was soon reduced to the disagreeable necessity of resorting to courts of justice for the protection of his property.

After . . . a laboured trial, it was discovered that the defendants had only *used*—and that as the law then stood they must both *make* and *use* the machine, or they could not be liable. The court decided that it was a fatal though inadvertent defect in the law, and gave judgment for the defendant.

It was not until the year 1800 that this defect in the law was amended. Immediately after the amendment of the law your memorialist commenced a number of suits; but so effectual were the means of procrastination and delay resorted to by the defendants that he was unable to obtain any decision on the merits of his claim until the year 1807—not until he had been eleven years in the law, and thirteen years of his patent term had expired. . . .

[B]efore the invention of your memorialist, the value of this species of cotton, after it was cleaned, was not equal to the expence of cleaning it—that since; the cultivation of this species has been a great source of wealth to the community & of riches to thousands of her citizens. . . ."

Questions for Analysis
1. Identify the claims Whitney makes about his cotton gin in this excerpt.
2. Explain why Whitney was unable to profit from his invention.
3. Explain the long-term impact of the cotton gin on the economy of the South.

Fortunately, Whitney had other ideas that proved more profitable. In June 1798, amid U.S. fears of a war with France, the U.S. government granted him an extraordinary contract to produce 4,000 rifles in eighteen months. Adapting the plan of Honoré Blanc, a French mechanic who devised a musket with interchangeable parts, Whitney demonstrated the potential for using machines to produce various parts of a musket, which could then be assembled in mass quantities. With Jefferson's enthusiastic support, the federal government extended Whitney's contract, and by 1809 his New Haven factory was turning out 7,500 guns annually. Whitney's factory became a model for the **American system of manufacturing**, in which water-powered machinery and the division of production into several small tasks allowed less skilled workers to produce mass quantities of a particular item. Moreover, the factories developed by Whitney and Slater became training grounds for younger mechanics and inventors who devised improvements in machinery or set out to solve new technological puzzles. Their efforts also transformed the lives of generations of workers—enslaved and free—who planted and picked the cotton, spun the yarn, wove the cloth, and sewed the clothes that cotton gins and spinning mills made possible.

American system of manufacturing Production system focused on water-powered machinery, division of labor, and the use of interchangeable parts. The introduction of the American system in the early nineteenth century greatly increased the productivity of American manufacturing.

REVIEW

How did Eli Whitney's cotton gin and factory production of interchangeable parts affect the early nineteenth-century American economy?

Transforming Domestic Production

Slater and Whitney were among the most influential American inventors, but both required the assistance and collaboration of other inventors, machinists, and artisans to implement their ideas. The achievement of these enterprising individuals was seen by many Americans as part of a larger spirit of inventiveness and technological ingenuity that characterized U.S. identity. Although many Americans built on foreign ideas and models, a cascade of inventions did appear in the United States between 1790 and 1820.

Cotton gins and steam engines, steamboats and interchangeable parts, gristmills and spinning mills, clocks and woodworking lathes—each of these items and processes was improved over time and led to myriad other inventions. For instance, in 1811 Francis Cabot invented a power loom

---

EXPLORING AP® THEMES

Geography and the Environment

Environmental factors play a significant role in the development of geographical regions. One of the main reasons why the factory system was concentrated in the North while the South primarily focused on growing raw materials like cotton to feed northern factories was the climate and soil. Since long-staple cotton was only primarily grown on the coast (i.e., Sea Islands) and most of the South was better suited to growing short-staple cotton, there was a need for an invention that could make the deseeding process more efficient and profitable. That invention came in the form of Eli Whitney's cotton gin. Ask students to write one-to-three sentences explaining the implications for slavery's expansion as a result of the cotton gin.

for weaving, a necessary step once spinning mills began producing more yarn than hand weavers could handle. Eventually clocks would be used to routinize the labor of workers in those mills so that they all arrived, ate lunch, and left at the same time.

Despite these rapid technological advances, the changes that occurred in the early nineteenth century were more evolutionary than revolutionary. Most political leaders and social commentators viewed gradual improvement as a blessing. For many Americans, the ideal situation consisted of either small mills scattered through the countryside or household enterprises that could supply neighbors with finer cloth, wool cards, sturdier chairs, or other items that improved household comfort and productivity.

The importance of domestic manufacturing increased after passage of the Embargo Act as imports of cloth and other items fell dramatically. Small factories, like those along the Pawtucket River, increased their output, and so did ordinary housewives. Blacksmiths, carpenters, and wheelwrights busily repaired and improved the spindles, looms, and other equipment that allowed family members to produce more and better cloth from wool, flax, and cotton. These developments allowed some Americans, especially in towns and cities, to achieve a middling status between poorer laborers and wealthier elites. In this middling sector of society, new ideas about companionate marriage, which emphasized mutual obligations, may have encouraged husbands and wives to work more closely in domestic enterprises. While husbands generally carried out the heavier or more skilled parts of home manufacturing, like weaving, wives spun yarn and sewed together sections of cloth into finished goods.

At the same time, daughters, neighbors, and servants remained critical to the production of household items. In early nineteenth-century Hallowell, Maine, Martha Ballard labored alongside her daughters and a niece, producing cloth and food for domestic consumption, while she supplemented her husband's income as a surveyor by working as a midwife. Yet older forms of mutuality also continued, with neighbors sharing tools and equipment and those with specialized skills assisting neighbors in exchange for items they needed. Perhaps young couples imagined themselves embarking on more egalitarian marriages than those of their parents, but most still needed wider networks of support.

In wealthy households north and south, servants and enslaved people took on a greater share of domestic labor in the late eighteenth and early nineteenth centuries. Most female servants in the North were young and unmarried. Some arrived with children in tow or became pregnant while on the job, a mark of the rising rate of out-of-wedlock births following the Revolution. Planters' wives in the South had fewer worries in this regard because if enslaved women became pregnant, their children added to the slaveholder's labor supply. Moreover, on larger plantations, slaveholders increasingly assigned a few enslaved women to spin, cook, wash clothes, make candles, and wait on table. Plantation mistresses might also hire the wives of small farmers and landless laborers to spin cotton into yarn, weave yarn into cloth, and sew clothing for members of the household, both enslaved and free. While mistresses in both regions still engaged in household production, they expanded their roles as domestic managers.

However, most Americans at the turn of the nineteenth century continued to live on family farms, to produce or trade locally to meet their needs, and to use techniques handed down for generations. Yet by 1820, their lives, like those of wealthier Americans, were transformed by the expanding economy. Gradually, more and more families would sew clothes with machine-spun thread made from cotton ginned in the American South, work their fields with newly invented cast-iron plows, and vary their diet by adding items shipped from other regions by steamboat.

> **AP® TIP**
> Understanding the economic changes during the early 1800s is key to analyzing how the lives of women and families throughout the U.S. changed during this era.

REVIEW

- How did technological advances in the early 1800s affect the lives of Americans?
- How did those effects differ for Americans of different races and social classes?

Technology, Cotton, and Enslavement

Some of the most dramatic technological changes occurred in agriculture, and none was more significant than the cotton gin, which led to the vast expansion of agricultural production and slavery in the South. This in turn fueled regional specialization, ensuring that residents in one area of the nation — the North, South, or West — depended on those in other areas. Southern planters relied on a growing demand for cotton from northern merchants and manufacturers. At the same

---

TEACHING IDEA

Connecting the Dots

Using the board or projector, have students create a timeline of the main inventions between 1790 and 1820 that transformed domestic production. For guidance, refer to the Period 4 Review Chronology timeline on page 353. Students could also look at the previous comparison activity on agricultural and industrial innovations for additional examples.

BUILDING AP® SKILLS

Causation

Ask students: What were the main causes of a "cotton kingdom" emerging in the Deep South? Possible answers include: 1) *Depleting nutrients from the soil in the East required westward movement*; 2) *The increased production and profitability of cotton, thanks to Eli Whitney's cotton gin*; and 3) *Growing textile manufacturing industry in the Northeast*.

Then ask students: How did this transform regional economies? Possible answers include: 1) *South focused on providing raw materials, primarily cotton*; 2) *Northeast provided most of the manufactured goods (e.g., textiles/cloth)*; and 3) *West focused on growing food (i.e., grain and livestock) to feed the nation, including factory workers in the Northeast*.

TEACHING IDEA

Class Discussion

Have students look up some of the main forms of resistance used by enslaved people. Then, ask them to evaluate their relative effectiveness and explain what made some better options than others. Possible answers include: *working slowly, breaking tools, pretending to be sick/injured, running away, or self-mutilation.*

BUILDING AP® SKILLS

Claims and Evidence in Sources

Provide students with a copy of the article titled "The New Nation, 1783–1815" by Alan Taylor. This secondary source from the Gilder Lehrman site discusses the early republic (gilderlehrman.org). Have students read the article to identify the author's claim or argument, historical evidence, and reasoning used to support it.

EXPLORING AP® THEMES

Work, Exchange, and Technology

Have students look at the Key Concepts, Events, and People in the Period 4 Review on page 352 and identify which terms should be organized under the theme work, exchange, and technology. Then, ask them to define each term and describe the historical significance: How and/or why does it matter?

MODULE 4-1 Political and Economic Transformations

Year	Production in Bales
1790	3,135
1795	16,719
1800	73,145
1805	146,290
1810	177,638
1815	208,986
1820	334,378
1825	532,915
1830	731,452

◀ **Growth of Cotton Production in the United States, 1790–1830** What technological advancements in the North and South led to the changes in U.S. cotton production shown in this table?

Source: Lewis Cecil Gray, *History of Agriculture in the Southern United States to 1860*, vol. 2 (Gloucester, MA: Peter Smith, 1958).

time, planters, merchants, manufacturers, and factory workers became more dependent on western farmers to produce grain and livestock to feed the nation.

As cotton gins spread across the South, cotton and slavery expanded into the interior of many southern states as well as into the lower Mississippi valley. While rice and sugar were also produced in the South, cotton quickly became the most important crop. In 1790 southern farms and plantations produced about 3,000 bales of cotton, each weighing about 300 pounds. By 1820, with the aid of the cotton gin, the South produced more than 330,000 bales annually. For southern black people, increased production meant increased burdens. Because seeds could be separated from raw cotton with much greater efficiency, farmers could plant vastly larger quantities of the crop. Although family members, neighbors, and hired hands performed this work on small farms with only a few or no enslaved people, wealthy planters, with perhaps a dozen enslaved laborers, took advantage of rising cotton prices in the early eighteenth century to purchase more enslaved labor.

The dramatic increase in the amount of cotton planted and harvested each year was paralleled by a jump in the size of the enslaved population. Thus, even as northern states began to abolish the institution, southern plantation owners significantly increased the number of enslaved people they held. In 1790 there were fewer than 700,000 enslaved people in the United States. By 1820 there were nearly 1.5 million. Despite this population increase, growing competition for field hands drove up the price of enslaved people, which roughly doubled between 1795 and 1805.

Although the international slave trade was banned in the United States in 1808, some planters smuggled in women and men from Africa and the Caribbean. Most planters, however, depended on enslaved women to bear more children, increasing the size of their labor force through natural reproduction. In addition, planters in the Deep South — from Georgia and the Carolinas west to Louisiana — began buying enslaved people from farmers in Maryland and Virginia, where cotton and slavery were less profitable. Expanding slave markets in New Orleans and Charleston marked the continued importance of this domestic or internal slave trade as cotton moved west.

In the early nineteenth century, most white southerners believed there was enough land to go around. And the rising price of cotton allowed small farmers to imagine they would someday be planters. Some southern American Indians also placed their hopes in cotton. Cherokee and Creek Indians cultivated the crop, even purchasing enslaved African Americans to increase production. Some villages now welcomed ministers to their communities, hoping that embracing white culture might allow them to retain their current lands. Yet other native residents foresaw the increased pressure for land that cotton cultivation produced and organized to defend themselves from whites' invasion. Regardless of the policies adopted by American Indians, cotton and slavery expanded rapidly into Cherokee- and Creek-controlled lands in the interior of Georgia and South Carolina. And the admission of the states of Louisiana, Mississippi, and Alabama between 1812 and 1819 marked the rapid spread of southern agriculture farther west.

Enslaved men and women played critical roles in the South's geographical expansion. Without their labor, neither cotton nor sugar could have become mainstays of the South's economy. The heavy work of carving out new plantations led most planters to select young enslaved men and women to move west, breaking apart families in the process. Some enslaved people resisted their removal and, if forced to go, used their role in the labor process to limit slaveholders' control by working slowly, breaking tools, and feigning illness or injury. Other enslaved women and men hid

Technology, Cotton, and Enslavement

AP® ANALYZING SOURCES

Source: Harriet Jacobs, *Incidents in the Life of a Slave Girl*, 1861

"But I now entered on my fifteenth year [1828]—a sad epoch in the life of a slave girl. My master began to whisper foul words in my ear. Young as I was, I could not remain ignorant of their import. I tried to treat them with indifference or contempt.... I turned from him with disgust and hatred. But he was my master. I was compelled to live under the same roof with him—where I saw a man forty years my senior daily violating the most sacred commandments of nature. He told me I was his property; that I must be subject to his will in all things. My soul revolted against the mean tyranny. But where could I turn for protection?... [T]here is no shadow of law to protect... from insult, from violence, or even from death; all these are inflicted by fiends who bear the shape of men. The mistress, who ought to protect the helpless victim, has no other feelings towards her but those of jealousy and rage....

Even the little child... before she is twelve years old... will become prematurely knowing in evil things. Soon she will learn to tremble when she hears her master's footfall. She will be compelled to realize that she is no longer a child. If God has bestowed beauty upon her, it will prove her greatest curse. That which commands admiration in the white woman only hastens the degradation of the female slave."

Questions for Analysis

1. Describe the perils faced by young enslaved women such as Harriet Jacobs.
2. Explain how this document reflects the ways in which slavery negatively affected Southern society.
3. Explain how the expansion of American slavery during the early nineteenth century contributed to the dynamic Jacobs describes in this document.

TRM Suggested Responses to Questions

TRM Module 4.1 AP® Analyzing Sources Handout 3

TEACHING IDEA

Incorporating Websites

To further students' understanding of Harriet Jacobs, have them access Lapham's Quarterly's virtual tour of "Incidents in the Life of Harriet Jacobs" (laphamsquarterly.org). This resource utilizes different locations in Jacobs's life to provide information, quotes, and images.

BUILDING AP® SKILLS

Comparison

Ask students to compare the lives of enslaved people who worked inside the plantation's main house as opposed to those who served as "field hands." Then, conduct a class discussion and clarify any misunderstandings. Students usually provide the obvious advantages of working inside the house such as not being exposed to the weather and elements outside like extremely hot temperatures during summer months. Therefore, they may need more guidance with the negative aspects of working inside the home. Possible answers may include: *abuse (physical, psychological, emotional, and sexual); isolation; tension with members of the house.*

---

out temporarily as a respite from brutal work regimes or harsh punishments. Still others fled to areas controlled by American Indians, hoping for better treatment, or to regions where slavery was no longer legal.

Yet given the power and resources wielded by whites, most enslaved people had to find ways to improve their lives within the system of bondage. The end of the international slave trade helped black people in this regard since planters had to depend more on natural reproduction to increase their labor supply. To ensure that enslaved people lived longer and healthier lives, planters were forced to provide better food, shelter, and clothing. Some enslaved people gained leverage to fish, hunt, or maintain small gardens to improve their diet. With the birth of more children, southern black people also developed more extensive kinship networks, which often allowed other family members to care for children if their parents were compelled to move west. Enslavement was still brutal, but enslaved people made small gains that improved their chances of survival.

To find release from the oppressive burdens of daily life, enslaved people not only joined the camp meetings and religious revivals that burned across the southern frontier in the late eighteenth and early nineteenth century but also established their own religious ceremonies. These were often held in the woods or swamps at night, away from the prying eyes of planters and overseers.

Evangelical religion, combined with revolutionary ideals promoted in the United States and Haiti, proved a potent mix, and planters rarely lost sight of the potential dangers this posed to the system of bondage. Outright rebellions occurred only rarely, yet the Haitian Revolution and Gabriel's conspiracy in Virginia reminded enslaved people and slaveholders alike that uprisings were possible. Clearly, the power of new American identities could not be separated from the dangers embedded in the nation's oppressive racial history.

> **AP® TIP**
> Be sure you can explain both the overt and covert ways in which enslaved people maintained community and identity.

APPLY THE TIP

While some enslaved people resisted the "peculiar institution" of slavery, others adapted to their harsh realities and found ways to survive this horrific system of exploitation. Have students focus on the roles played by two of the main institutions that allowed African Americans to survive such horrors: 1) Family (including "extended kinship networks"); and 2) Religion (especially the Methodist and Baptist churches). Lastly, also discuss how the non-importation of additional enslaved people since 1808 changed some of the behavior of slaveholders. For example, some slaveholders provided better food, shelter, clothing, etc., since it would be harder to replace enslaved people. On the other hand, this also resulted in some slaveholders' increased desire to encourage or even force reproduction and birth of new enslaved people.

TRM Suggested Responses to Questions

TRM Module 4.1 AP® Analyzing Sources Handout 3

TEACHING IDEA

Connecting the Dots

Even though many enslaved people resisted against the institution of slavery, there were very few actual rebellions during the first half of the nineteenth century. Have students research Gabriel Prosser, Denmark Vessey, and Nat Turner. Then ask them to make a connection to the previously studied Stono Rebellion, which was the only significant one during the colonial period. Conclude the activity by discussing with students why there were so few slave rebellions and of limited success in the United States.

EXPLORING AP® THEMES

American and Regional Culture

Use the National Museum of African American History and Culture website and visit their exhibition on slavery and freedom (nmaahc.si.edu). This exhibit includes valuable objects like Nat Turner's Bible and Harriet Tubman's shawl, which allow students to connect with the past and analyze artifacts that provide clues to African American history and culture. Specifically, have students identify and discuss the role played by religion in the fight against slavery and the acquisition of freedom. To conclude, show the video of the museum's founding director leading a tour of this exhibition to celebrate "Juneteenth," which marks Emancipation Day or what some consider the nation's second Independence Day.

Period 4: 1800–1848

MODULE 4-1 Political and Economic Transformations

AP® ANALYZING SOURCES

Source: Thomas Jefferson, *Letter to Rufus King*, U.S. Minister to Great Britain, July 1802

"The course of things in the neighboring islands of the West Indies appears to have given a considerable impulse to the minds of the slaves in different parts of the U.S. A great disposition to insurgency has manifested itself among them, which, in one instance, in the state of Virginia, broke out into actual insurrection. This was easily suppressed; but many of those concerned, (between 20 and 30, I believe) fell victims to the law. So extensive an execution could not but excite sensibility in the public mind, and beget a regret that the laws had not provided, for such cases, some alternative, combining more mildness with equal efficacy. The legislature of the state, at a subsequent meeting, took the subject into consideration, and have communicated to me . . . their wish that some place could be provided, out of the limits of the U.S., to which slaves guilty of insurgency might be transported; and they have particularly looked to Africa as offering the most desirable receptacle. We might for this purpose, enter into negotiations with the natives, on some part of the coast, to obtain a settlement and, by establishing an African company, combine with it commercial operations, which might . . . procure profit . . ."

Questions for Analysis

1. Describe Jefferson's proposal as expressed in his letter.
2. Explain how Jefferson's thoughts on slave uprisings in this excerpt reflect his perspective on slavery.

Source: Leonora Sansay, *Letter to Aaron Burr*, November 1802

"The arrival of General Rochambeau seems to have spread terror among the negroes [in Haiti]. I wish they were reduced to order so that I might see the so much vaunted habitations where I should repose beneath the shade of orange groves, walk on carpets of rose leaves and Frenchipone; be fanned to sleep by silent slaves. . . .
But the moment of enjoying these pleasures is, I fear, far distant. The negroes have felt during ten years the blessing of liberty, for a blessing it certainly is, however acquired, and they will not easily be deprived of it. They have fought and vanquished French troops, and their strength has increased . . . and the climate itself combats for them. . . .
Every evening several old Creoles . . . assemble at our house, and talk of their affairs. One of them . . . now lives in a miserable hut. . . . Yet he still hopes for better days, in which hope they all join him."

Questions for Analysis

1. Describe the changes Sansay depicts in Haiti during the prior decade.
2. Explain how Sansay's point of view influenced her account of the situation in Haiti.

Questions for Comparison

1. Explain how these documents reveal why the Virginia rebellion failed while the uprising in Haiti eventually succeeded.
2. Explain how the Virginia rebellion and Haitian Revolution influenced debates over the future of slavery in the United States.
3. Evaluate the extent of similarity between Jefferson's response to the Virginia rebellion and Sansay's response to the Haitian Revolution.

REVIEW

- What led to the spread of slavery in the South?
- How did enslaved people resist enslavement?

TEACHING IDEA

Building Vocabulary

Ask students to look up the definition and origin of the word "creole." Then conduct a brief discussion on the black and white dichotomy that has existed in the United States and how race can be seen as a social construct.

AP® WRITING HISTORICALLY — Short-Answer Question Practice

ACTIVITY

Read the following question carefully and write a short response. Use complete sentences.

Answer (a), (b), and (c).
a. Briefly explain ONE specific effect of a technological development on agriculture in the United States from the period 1790 to 1820.
b. Briefly explain ONE specific effect of a technological development on industry in the United States from the period 1790 to 1820.
c. Briefly explain ONE specific effect of a technological development on transportation in the United States from the period 1790 to 1820.

TRM Suggested Responses to Questions

TEACHING IDEA

Additional Practice

Below is a Short-Answer Question asking students to identify and explain the effects of technological development on agriculture, industry, and transportation. In answering this SAQ, remember to use the *ACE* strategy: Answer, Cite, and Explain for each part (a refresher of *ACE* can be found on page 21). Students should Answer by clearly stating a specific effect, Cite by providing an example or piece of evidence to support their answer, and Explain by articulating how the evidence supports their answer or by discussing the historical significance of the effect and evidence. Ideally, each part of the *ACE* strategy would be completed in a separate sentence resulting in a three-sentence response for each part (a, b, and c) and a nine-sentence overall response for an SAQ.

Answer (a), (b), and (c)

a) Briefly explain ONE specific effect of a technological development on agriculture in the United States from the period 1790 to 1820.

b) Briefly explain ONE specific effect of a technological development on industry in the United States from the period 1790 to 1820.

c) Briefly explain ONE specific effect of a technological development on transportation in the United States from the period 1790 to 1820.

If students are struggling to answer this SAQ, you should review the content from the module before proceeding. Of course, they will not have that option during the AP® U.S. History exam. In that case, they could brainstorm a list of major technological developments of the time. Consider how those developments could connect to agriculture, industry, or transportation. While not ideal, it's OK if students use the same development to answer two or even all three parts of the SAQ as long as they clearly explain how that development specifically impacted the stated area. They might also consider brainstorming backward by identifying changes in agriculture, industry, and transportation and then asking yourself what new technologies might have led to those changes.

TEACHING IDEA

AP® Writing Historically Review

To scaffold this writing activity, organize students into groups of four. Assign each student one of the following topics: technology, agriculture, industry, or transportation. Allow students 5-7 minutes to review and brainstorm information relevant to their topic. After students research their respective information, have groups share responses. Students should use the information gathered in the group activity to help them write their Short-Answer Question responses.

TRM Suggested Responses to Questions

TEACHING IDEA

Check for Understanding

You may find it helpful to remind students that comparison and causation are distinct yet closely related skills that historians often employ together when examining a topic. Comparison asks them to analyze similarities and differences while causation asks them to analyze what led to and resulted from events or developments. Students can keep both in mind as they read by comparing causes and effects and asking why similarities and differences occurred.

Module 4-2

Defending and Redefining the Nation

LEARNING TARGETS

By the end of this module, you should be able to:
- Explain the causes and effects of the War of 1812.
- Explain how and why regional political and economic differences increased during this period.
- Explain the short- and long-term effects of the Missouri Compromise and the Panic of 1819.

THEMATIC FOCUS

Politics and Power
America in the World

The United States' participation in the War of 1812 and conflicts with American Indian nations solidified U.S. control of its western lands at the same time as the Monroe Doctrine and efforts to promote foreign trade expanded America's global presence. Tensions and war with England, the emergence of distinct, regional economies, and disagreements over the expansion of slavery also led to growing political debates as regional interests often outweighed national concerns.

HISTORICAL REASONING FOCUS

Comparison
Causation

TASK ▶ As you read this module, consider how historical developments during the first two decades of the nineteenth century continued to strengthen the power of the federal government and contributed to growing regional differences.

In March 1809 Thomas Jefferson was succeeded by his friend and ally James Madison. Both men sought to end foreign interference in American affairs and to resolve conflicts between American Indians and white residents on the nation's frontier. By 1815 the United States had weathered a series of domestic and foreign crises. Even though Jefferson and Madison both believed in a national government with limited powers, they each found themselves expanding federal authority, especially in response to the tensions with England and the War of 1812. After the war, Democratic-Republicans in Congress sought to use federal authority to settle boundary disputes in the West, make investments in transportation, and reestablish a national bank. Federal power was again asserted to settle disputes with Britain and Spain over U.S. borders in the north and the south.

More secure borders and state and federal investments in transportation fueled overseas trade and the development of increasingly distinct regional economies. Regional economies ensured economic interdependence, but also political differences. For instance, when the nation's first severe recession hit in 1819, many southern planters and midwestern farmers blamed it on the banks. In reality, falling prices for cotton and wheat abroad as well as overextension of credit by U.S. banks contributed to the recession. Whatever the cause, the interdependence of regional economies ensured that everyone suffered. At the same time, these economies were built on distinct forms of labor, with the South becoming more dependent on slavery and the North less so. When Missouri, situated between the old Northwest Territory and expanding southern cotton lands, applied for statehood in 1819, these regional differences set off a furious national debate over the continued westward extension of slavery.

TEACHING IDEA

Understanding People Who Made a Difference

Have students research James Madison and focus on his contributions to the American nation during his presidency (1809–1817) and not the role he played during the constitutional period as the "Father of the Constitution." Specifically, tell students to highlight his reasoning for entering the War of 1812 to defend the nation from British policies (e.g., impressment) and ordering William Henry Harrison to attack Prophet Town and prevent American Indians from posing a threat along the frontier.

BUILDING AP® SKILLS

Causation

In small groups of three, have students discuss the following causes of the Recession (or Panic) of 1819 and decide which played a more significant role: 1) Speculation and the overextension of credit (loans given with insufficient collateral); or 2) Falling prices of agricultural products like cotton and wheat due to the decline in overseas demand after the end of the Napoleonic Wars.

Tensions at Sea and on the Frontier

Tensions at Sea and on the Frontier

Non-Intercourse Act Act passed by Congress in 1809 allowing Americans to trade with every nation except France and Britain. The act failed to stop the seizure of American ships or improve the economy.

When President Madison took office, Great Britain and France remained embroiled in the Napoleonic Wars in Europe and refused to modify their policies toward American shipping or to recognize U.S. neutrality. American ships were subject to seizure by both nations, and British authorities continued to impress "deserters" into the Royal Navy. Just before Madison's inauguration in March 1809, Congress replaced the Embargo Act with the **Non-Intercourse Act**, which restricted trade only with France and Britain and their colonies. Although the continued embargo against Britain encouraged U.S. manufacturing, and the act allowed trade with other European nations, many Americans still opposed Congress using its power to restrict their right to trade.

In the midst of these crises, Madison also faced difficulties in the Northwest Territory. In 1794 General Anthony Wayne had won a decisive victory against a multi-tribe coalition at the Battle of Fallen Timbers. But this victory inspired two forceful native leaders to create a pan-American Indian alliance in the Ohio River valley. The Shawnee prophet Tenskwatawa and his half-brother Tecumseh, a warrior, encouraged native peoples to resist white encroachments on their territory and to give up all aspects of white society and culture, including liquor and other popular trade goods. They imagined an American Indian nation that stretched from the Canadian border to the Gulf of Mexico.

Although powerful Creek and Choctaw nations in the lower Mississippi valley refused to join the alliance, American Indians in the upper Midwest rallied around the brothers. In 1808 Tenskwatawa and Tecumseh established Prophet Town along the Tippecanoe River in Indiana Territory. The next year, William Henry Harrison, the territorial governor, tricked several American Indian leaders into signing a treaty selling three million acres of land to the United States for only $7,600. An enraged Tecumseh dismissed the treaty, claiming the land belonged to all the American Indians together.

AP® TIP Make sure you can explain why American Indian leaders in the Ohio River Valley promoted separation from white society and culture.

▲ **Opposition to the Embargo Act** Although Congress repealed the Embargo Act in 1809, lawmakers still barred the United States from trading with Great Britain and France, both of which attacked American shipping in violation of U.S. neutrality. This political cartoon by Alexander Anderson criticizes the embargo, which proved costly to merchants, sailors, and dockworkers. Here a merchant carrying a barrel of goods curses the snapping turtle "Ograbme," which is *embargo* spelled backward. **Who during this time period would most agree with the perspective expressed in this image? Who would most disagree with it?**

TEACHING IDEA

Building Vocabulary

Have students define these vocabulary terms: *recession*, *panic*, *speculation*, *credit*, *collateral*, *bankruptcies*, *mortgages*, *foreclosures*, *supply*, and *demand*. They should use a dictionary (class copy or online version) or an economics textbook from your social studies department to complete this task.

TEACHING IDEA

Challenging Misconceptions

Back in Module 1-1, students covered the common misconception of American Indians lacking agency and being seen simply as the victims in history. While covering this module, have students research Tecumseh and Tenskwatawa. Specifically, have students focus on how these two brothers wanted to prevent further encroachment by whites into their ancestral lands in the Ohio River valley and called for the elimination of liquor and other goods that were destructive to their tribal ways and customs. Conclude the activity by asking students what stood in the way of creating a successful American Indian nation.

TEACHING IDEA

Class Discussion

Use the image to ask students the following: Who during this period would most agree with the perspective expressed in the image and who would most disagree with it? Challenge students to support their responses with historical evidence from the module. Class discussion to follow.

EXPLORING AP® THEMES

America in the World

Have students look at the Key Concepts, Events, and People in the Period 4 Review on page 352 and identify which terms should be organized under the theme America in the world. Then, ask them to define each term and describe the historical significance — how and/or why does it matter?

TRM Suggested Responses to Questions

TRM Module 4.2 AP® Analyzing Sources Handout 1

TEACHING IDEA

Class Discussion

Ask students to discuss why regional interests (New England, South, and West) resulted in different reactions to going to war with Great Britain in 1812.

TRM Find **Handout 4.2 – Regional Reasoning for the War of 1812** in the Teacher's Resource Materials.

Period 4: 1800–1848

MODULE 4-2 Defending and Redefining the Nation

AP® ANALYZING SOURCES

Source: Chief Tecumseh, *Address to Governor William Henry Harrison*, 1810

"*Brother.* Since the peace was made you have kill'd some of the Shawanese, Winebagoes, Delawares, and Miamies and you have taken our lands from us, and I do not see how we can remain at peace with you if you continue to do so. You have given goods to the Kickapoos for the sale of their lands . . . which has been the cause of many deaths among them. You have promised us assistance but I do not see that you have given us any.

You try to force the red people to do some injury. It is you that is pushing them on to do mischief. You endeavor to make distinctions, you wish to prevent the Indians to do as we wish them: to unite and let them consider their land as the common property of the whole.

You take tribes aside and advise them not to come into this [coalition] and untill our design is accomplished we do not wish to accept of your invitation to go and visit the President.

The reason I tell you this is you want by your distinctions of Indian tribes in allotting to each a particular track of land to make them to war with each other. You never see an Indian come and endeavour to make the white people do so. You are continually driving the red people when at last you will drive them into the great Lake where they can't eather stand or work."

Questions for Analysis

1. Identify the main elements of Tecumseh's complaint.
2. Describe how prior events created the context for Tecumseh's speech.
3. Explain how differing views of land ownership contributed to conflict between American Indian nations and the U.S. during the early nineteenth century.

In November 1811, fearing the growing power of the Shawnee leaders, President Madison ordered Harrison to attack Prophet Town. With more troops and superior weapons, the U.S. army defeated the allied American Indian forces and burned Prophet Town to the ground. The rout damaged Tenskwatawa's stature as a prophet, and he and his supporters fled to Canada, where skirmishes continued along the U.S.-Canadian border.

REVIEW

How did the federal government respond to the challenges posed by both Great Britain and American Indians between 1800 and 1812?

War Erupts with Britain

War of 1812 1812–1815 war between the United States and Great Britain. The war was one consequence of ongoing conflict between Great Britain and France, as each nation sought to forcibly restrict the United States' trade with the other.

Convinced that British officials in Canada fueled American Indian resistance, many Democratic-Republicans demanded an end to British intervention on the western frontier as well as British interference in transatlantic trade. Some called for the United States to declare war. Yet merchants in the Northeast, who hoped to renew trade with Great Britain and the British West Indies, feared the commercial disruptions that war entailed. Thus New England Federalists adamantly opposed a declaration of war.

For months, Madison avoided taking a clear stand on the issue. On June 1, 1812, however, with diplomatic efforts exhausted, Madison sent a secret message to Congress outlining U.S. grievances against Great Britain. Within weeks, Congress declared war although the vote counts in the House of Representatives and the Senate revealed sharp divisions on the matter.

Supporters of the **War of 1812** claimed that a victory over Great Britain would end threats to U.S. sovereignty and raise Americans' stature in Europe. However, the nation was ill prepared

---

BUILDING AP® SKILLS

Causation

As a class, discuss the following prompt: Evaluate the relative significance of the causes of the War of 1812 (a.k.a. "Mr. Madison's War"). Possible discussion points include: 1) British disruption of transatlantic trade and the policy of impressment (or forced military service); 2) British policy of arming American Indians along the western frontier and still maintaining forts in the interior of the continent; 3) Emergence of "war hawks" in the new states along the frontier who wanted to expand; 4) Desire to earn the world's respect by defending against the undermining of national sovereignty. Then reach consensus on how these causes should rank in order of importance.

TEACHING IDEA

Incorporating Websites

Visit the Stanford History Education Group site to obtain an assessment of the War of 1812 (sheg.stanford.edu). Specifically, this assessment focuses on the reasons for President James Madison obtaining a declaration of war against Great Britain. For homework, have students analyze President Madison's proclamation and then answer the two questions on the assessment, which should be considered formative. Lastly, in class, conduct a short discussion to ensure student understanding and provide clarifications.

War Erupts with Britain

Bank of the United States
National bank established in 1791. The bank was responsible for holding large portions of federal funds and distributing loans and currency.

AP® TIP
Evaluate the role of the War of 1812 in increasing the regional divisions of the early 1800s.

to launch a major offensive against such an imposing foe given cuts in federal spending, falling tax revenues, and diminished military resources. The U.S. navy, for example, established under President Adams, had been reduced to only six small gunboats by President Jefferson. Democratic-Republicans had also failed to recharter the **Bank of the United States** when it expired in 1811, so the nation lacked a vital source of credit. Nonetheless, many in Congress believed that Britain would be too engaged by the ongoing conflict with France to attack the United States.

Meanwhile U.S. commanders devised plans to attack Canada, but the U.S. army and navy proved no match for Great Britain and its American Indian allies. Instead, Tecumseh, who was appointed a brigadier general in the British army, helped capture Detroit. Joint British and American Indian forces also launched successful attacks on Fort Dearborn, Fort Mackinac, and other points along the U.S.-Canadian border.

Even as U.S. forces faced numerous defeats in the summer and fall of 1812, American voters reelected James Madison as president. While Madison won most western and southern states, where the war was most popular, he lost in New England and New York, where Federalist opponents held sway.

After a year of fighting, U.S. forces drove the British back into Canada (Map 4.3). A naval victory on Lake Erie led by Commodore Oliver Perry proved crucial to U.S. success. Soon after, Tecumseh was killed in battle and U.S. forces burned York (present-day Toronto). Yet just as U.S. prospects in the war improved, New England Federalists demanded retreat. The war devastated the New England maritime trade, causing economic distress throughout the region. In 1813, state legislatures in New England withdrew their support for any invasion of "foreign British soil," and Federalists in Congress sought to block war appropriations and the deployment of local militia units into the U.S. army.

But the New England Federalists were not powerful enough to change national policy, particularly after news arrived in March 1814 that Andrew Jackson and his Tennessee militiamen had defeated a force of Creek Indians, important British allies. Cherokee warriors, longtime foes of the Creek, joined the fight. At the **Battle of Horseshoe Bend**, in present-day Alabama, the combined U.S.-Cherokee forces slaughtered eight hundred Creek warriors. Although some Americans were appalled at the slaughter, in the resulting treaty the Creek nation lost two-thirds of its tribal domain to the U.S. and its Cherokee allies.

Despite successes like this, the United States was no closer to winning the war when the British defeated Napoleon in June 1814. Emboldened by that major victory, in August 1814 the British sailed up the Chesapeake directly for Washington City. As American troops retreated, Dolley Madison

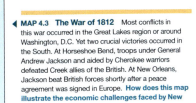

MAP 4.3 The War of 1812 Most conflicts in this war occurred in the Great Lakes region or around Washington, D.C. Yet two crucial victories occurred in the South. At Horseshoe Bend, troops under General Andrew Jackson and aided by Cherokee warriors defeated Creek allies of the British. At New Orleans, Jackson beat British forces shortly after a peace agreement was signed in Europe. **How does this map illustrate the economic challenges faced by New England during the War of 1812?**

TEACHING IDEA

Class Discussion

Ask students, why would American Indians (e.g., Creeks, Tecumseh, etc.) normally side with the English during conflicts with Americans and/or the United States? Possible answer: Americans were being more antagonistic toward the American Indians as they sought to expand into the interior of the continent. Cherokee sided with the United States, but that was an exception to the general rule and they would eventually be rewarded with the policy of removal in later years.

BUILDING AP® SKILLS

Claims and Evidence in Sources

Provide students with a copy of the article titled "Age of Jefferson and Madison" by Peter S. Onuf. This secondary source from the Gilder Lehrman site discusses some of the main historical events from the Jeffersonian Era (gilderlehrman.org). Have students read the article to identify the author's claim or argument, historical evidence, and reasoning used to support it.

EXPLORING AP® THEMES

America in the World

Ask students: Why can the United States be considered the world's "Ugly-Duckling" during the two first decades of the nineteenth century? Possible answers: The United States was not respected by Britain (impressment), France (interference with trade), American Indians (conflicts along the western frontier), Spain (conflicts along the Florida border), etc.

TEACHING IDEA

Class Discussion

One of the main effects of the War of 1812 was the death of the Federalist Party. After pointing this out to students, conduct a class discussion on the main reason for their disappearance — the Hartford Convention. Students must focus on what this political party called for that made them look unpatriotic since they were advancing regional interests instead of national concerns.

BUILDING AP® SKILLS

Causation

For homework, have students research and explain at least two examples of an emerging nationalism after the War of 1812. Examples can be events, developments, or people.

> **AP® TIP**
>
> Compare the Hartford Convention to the Virginia and Kentucky Resolutions (Module 3-9).

Hartford Convention 1814 convention of Federalists opposed to the War of 1812. Delegates to the convention considered a number of constitutional amendments, as well as the possibility of secession.

Treaty of Ghent Accord signed in December 1814 that ended the War of 1812 and returned to U.S. and Britain the lands each controlled before the war.

and Peter Jennings, an enslaved man, gathered up government papers and valuable belongings before fleeing the White House. The redcoats then burned and sacked Washington, destroying the White House and the Capitol in the process. U.S. troops quickly rallied, defeating the British in Maryland and expelling them from Washington and New York. But later in 1814 the British, seemingly undaunted, blockaded major ports and landed thousands of seasoned troops at New Orleans.

In the midst of the protracted conflict, the New England Federalists revived their efforts to end the war. They called a meeting at Hartford, Connecticut in December 1814 to "deliberate upon the alarming state of public affairs." Some participants at the **Hartford Convention** called for New England's secession from the United States. Most supported amendments to the U.S. Constitution that would constrain federal power by limiting presidents to a single term and ensuring they were elected from diverse states (ending Virginia's domination of the office). Other amendments would require a two-thirds majority in Congress to declare war or prohibit trade.

However, despite outward appearances, Great Britain was losing steam as well, its treasury and national mood depleted by a decade of warfare. At the end of 1814, representatives of the two countries met in Ghent, Belgium to negotiate a peace settlement. On Christmas Eve, the **Treaty of Ghent** was signed, returning to each nation the lands it controlled before the war.

▲ **The Battle of New Orleans** On January 8, 1815, General Andrew Jackson's troops launched grapeshot and canister bombs against British forces in New Orleans in this final battle of the War of 1812. Jackson's troops included American Indian allies, backcountry immigrants, and French-speaking black soldiers. This engraving by Francisco Scacki shows the slain British commander, Major General Sir Edward Pakenham, in the center foreground. **What details in this image indicate the decisive defeat of the British army? How might a British artist present this battle differently?**

News of the treaty had not yet reached North America in January 1815, when U.S. troops under General Andrew Jackson attacked and routed the British army at the **Battle of New Orleans**. The victory cheered Americans, who, unaware that peace had already been achieved, made Jackson a national hero. The victory also made the New England Federalists look foolish, and potentially subversive, in the eyes of many Americans. The party would never fully recover its reputation.

Although the War of 1812 achieved no formal territorial gains, it did represent an important defense of U.S. sovereignty and garnered international prestige for the young nation. In addition, American Indians on the western frontier lost a powerful ally when British representatives at Ghent failed to act as advocates for their allies. Thus, in practical terms, the U.S. government gained greater control over vast expanses of land in the Ohio and Mississippi River valleys.

REVIEW

- Why did Congress declare war on Great Britain in 1812?
- What changed as a result of the War of 1812, and what remained the same?

Governments Fuel Economic Growth

AP® TIP
Analyze how the federal government supported American industrial growth and western expansion during the early 1800s.

In 1800 Thomas Jefferson captured the presidency by advocating a reduction in federal powers and a renewed emphasis on the needs of small farmers and workingmen. Once in power, however, Jefferson and his Democratic-Republican supporters faced a series of economic and political developments that led many to embrace a loose interpretation of the U.S. Constitution and support federal efforts to aid economic growth.

Population growth and commercial expansion encouraged these federal efforts. In 1811 the first steamboat traveled down the Mississippi from the Ohio River to New Orleans; over the next decade, steamboat traffic expanded. This development helped western and southern residents but hurt trade on overland routes between northeastern seaports and the Ohio River valley. The federal government began construction of the Cumberland Road in 1811 to reestablish this regional connection by linking Maryland and Ohio. Congress passed additional bills to fund ambitious federal transportation projects, but President Madison vetoed much of this legislation, believing that it overstepped even a loose interpretation of the Constitution.

After the War of 1812, British merchants resumed the sale of textiles and manufactured goods to the American market. Eager to regain lost market share and thin large inventories built up over the years since passage of Jefferson's Embargo Act, British importers began selling their wares below market prices. In response, Congress passed the **Tariff of 1816**, the first tariff legislation with the goal of protecting American manufacturers rather than simply raising federal revenue. Unlike future tariffs during the era, the 1816 tariff received some southern support as a temporary measure to stem British efforts to undermine the American economy. Within a few years, Democratic-Republican representative Henry Clay of Kentucky sketched out a plan to promote U.S. economic growth and advance commercial ties throughout the nation. Ultimately called the **American System** (not to be confused with the American system of manufacturing in Module 4-1), it combined federally funded internal improvements, such as roads and canals, to aid farmers and merchants with federal tariffs to protect U.S. manufacturing. Western expansion fueled demand for these internal improvements. The non-American Indian population west of the Appalachian Mountains more than doubled between 1810 and 1820, from 1,080,000 to 2,234,000. Many veterans of the War of 1812 settled there after receiving 160-acre parcels of land in the region as payment for service. Congress admitted four new states to the Union in just four years: Indiana (1816), Mississippi (1817), Illinois (1818), and Alabama (1819).

Congress also negotiated with American Indian nations to secure trade routes farther west. In the 1810s, Americans began trading along an ancient trail from Missouri to Santa Fe, a town in northern Mexico. But the trail cut across territory claimed by the Osage Indians. In 1825 Congress approved a treaty with the Osage to guarantee right of way for U.S. merchants. The Santa Fe Trail soon became a critical route for commerce between the United States and Mexico.

American System Plan proposed by Henry Clay to promote the U.S. economy by combining federally funded internal improvements to aid farmers with federal tariffs to protect U.S. manufacturing and a national bank to oversee economic development; not to be confused with the American system of manufacturing (see Module 4-1).

TEACHING IDEA

Class Discussion

Divide the class into two groups. Have one group prepare arguments for and the other against passing a high tariff using the prompt "Resolved: The federal government, in 1816, should or should not pass a protective tariff." Clarify any student misunderstandings and make sure to point out that the British had flooded the American market with cheap goods after the War of 1812. For homework, have students review why Alexander Hamilton's proposed protection for American manufacturers was not adopted in the 1790s.

APPLY THE TIP

Have students visit the two following websites so they can develop a deeper understanding of the American System proposed by Henry Clay.

- Visit the History, Art & Archives website and search for "1824 'American System' Speech" (history.house.gov).

- Visit the United States Senate website and search for "Classic Senate Speeches" and find Henry Clay of Kentucky (senate.gov).

After visiting the sites, have students work on a timeline showing the evolution of a national infrastructure that allowed for economic growth. Lastly, discuss with students how the federal government fueled economic growth and westward expansion via the American System.

EXPLORING AP® THEMES

American and National Identity

The main effect of the War of 1812 was the increase in nationalism. Although the military conflict was a stalemate, many Americans saw it as a "victory" since the nation obtained greater control of the lands in the Ohio and Mississippi River valleys and the British abandoned their interests in maintaining alliances with American Indians. Have students read the lyrics to the *Star-Spangled Banner* written by Francis Scott Key, which officially became the national anthem in 1931. Then discuss with the entire class how the words represent a new sense of an American and national identity.

TEACHING IDEA

Incorporating Websites

Visit the Stanford History Education Group site to obtain an assessment on "Clay's American System" (sheg.standford.edu). This assessment focuses on many Americans' opposition to the proposal. For homework, have students analyze the two documents opposing the American System and answer the assessment questions, which should be considered formative. They should also read Henry Clay's speech before the U.S. Senate defending his proposal. Lastly, in class, conduct a short discussion on which argument students find most persuasive and why.

TEACHING IDEA

Incorporating Videos

Ask students to watch a video on the history of the creation of the Erie Canal, the main connector between East and West and most important internal improvement project of the time. This extraordinary engineering feat was completed in 1825 and some portions are still operational today. The video is available on the History Channel's website by going to Topics, Landmarks, and then Erie Canal (history.com).

BUILDING AP® SKILLS

Causation

Conduct a class discussion on how the Erie Canal connecting the Hudson River and Lake Erie impacted the various regions in the country. While the relationship between the Northeast and Midwest became stronger, the South became increasingly more isolated. Another main effect was the rise of New York City as it became the main seaport in the country.

East of the Appalachian Mountains, state governments funded most internal improvement projects. The most significant of these was New York's **Erie Canal**, a 363-mile waterway stretching from the Mohawk River to Buffalo that was completed in 1825. Self-taught men directed this extraordinary engineering feat by which thousands of workers carved a swath forty-feet wide and four feet deep through limestone cliffs, mountains, forests, and swamps. The canal, which rises 566 feet along its route, required the construction of 35 locks to lift and lower boats. The arduous and dangerous work was carried out mainly by Irish, Welsh, and German immigrants, many of whom settled along its route. Tolls on the Erie Canal quickly repaid the tremendous financial cost of its construction. Freight charges and shipping times plunged. And by linking western farmers to the Hudson River, the Erie Canal ensured that New York City became the nation's premier seaport (Map 4.4).

▲ **MAP 4.4 Roads and Canals to 1837** During the 1820s and 1830s, state and local governments as well as private companies built roads and canals to foster migration and commercial development. The Erie Canal, completed in 1825, was the most significant of these projects. Many other states, particularly in the Northeast and the old Northwest, sought to duplicate that canal's success over the following decade. **Compare the system of roads and canals in the Northeast, old Northwest, and South. What conclusions can you draw about each region based on this map?**

Period 4: 1800–1848

The Erie Canal's success inspired hundreds of similar projects in other states. Canals carried manufactured goods from New England and the Middle Atlantic states to rural households in the Ohio River valley. Western farmers, in turn, shipped agricultural products back east. Canals also linked smaller cities within Pennsylvania and Ohio, facilitating the rise of commercial and manufacturing centers like Harrisburg, Pittsburgh, and Cincinnati. Canals also allowed vast quantities of coal to be transported out of the Allegheny Mountains, fueling industrial development throughout the Northeast.

REVIEW

How were the National Road and Erie Canal both a result of economic change and a cause of further economic change?

Americans Expand the Nation's Borders

In 1816, in the midst of the nation's economic resurgence, James Monroe, a Democratic-Republican from Virginia, won an easy victory in the presidential election over Rufus King, a New York Federalist. To improve relations with Britain and resolve problems on the frontier, Monroe sent John Quincy Adams to London. He negotiated treaties that limited U.S. and British naval forces on the Great Lakes, set the U.S.-Canadian border at the forty-ninth parallel, and established joint British-U.S. occupation of the Oregon Territory. In 1817 and 1818, the Senate approved these treaties, which further restricted American Indian rights and power.

President Monroe harbored grave concerns about the nation's southern boundary as well. He sought to limit Spain's power in North America and stop Seminole Indians in Florida and Alabama from claiming lands the defeated Creeks ceded to the United States. Shifting from diplomacy to military force, in 1817 the president sent General Andrew Jackson to force the Seminoles back into central Florida. But he ordered Jackson to avoid direct conflict with Spanish forces for fear of igniting another war. However, in spring 1818, Jackson attacked two Spanish forts, hanged two Seminole chiefs, and executed two British citizens.

Jackson's attacks spurred outrage among Spanish and British officials and many members of Congress. The threat of conflict with Britain, Spain, and the Seminole prompted President Monroe to establish the nation's first peacetime army. In the end, the British chose to ignore the execution of citizens engaged in "unauthorized" activities, while Spain decided to sell the Florida Territory to the United States. Indeed, in the **Adams-Onís Treaty** (1819), negotiated by John Quincy Adams, Spain ceded all its lands east of the Mississippi to the United States. Success in acquiring Florida encouraged the administration to look for other opportunities to limit European influence in the Western Hemisphere. By 1822 Argentina, Chile, Peru, Colombia, and Mexico had all overthrown Spanish rule. That March, President Monroe recognized the independence of these southern neighbors, and Congress quickly established diplomatic relations with the new nations. The following year, President Monroe claimed that the Western Hemisphere was part of the U.S. sphere of influence. Although the United States did not have sufficient power to enforce what later became known as the **Monroe Doctrine**, it had declared its intention to challenge Europeans for authority in the Americas.

Monroe Doctrine Assertion by President James Monroe in 1823 that the Western Hemisphere was part of the U.S. sphere of influence. Although the United States lacked the power to back up this claim, it signaled an intention to challenge Europeans for authority in the Americas.

AP® TIP
Analyze the impact the Monroe Doctrine had on relations between the United States and other nations, both in the Americas and in Europe.

AP® ANALYZING SOURCES

Source: Monroe Doctrine, 1823

"[T]he American continents, by the free and independent condition which they have assumed and maintain, are henceforth not to be considered as subjects for future colonization by any European powers. . . .

In the wars of the European powers in matters relating to themselves we have never taken any part, nor does it comport with our policy so to do. It is only when our rights are

(Continued)

TEACHING IDEA

AP® Central

Ask students to answer question 3 of the Long-Essay Questions from the 2013 AP® U.S. History exam, which is available on the College Board's AP® U.S. History Past Exam Questions section under "2013: Free-Response Questions" by clicking Scoring Guidelines (apcentral.collegeboard.org). This question asks students about American foreign policy. After reading and grading their responses, select a "high," "medium," and "low" essay that could be used as classroom samples. Make sure to obtain students' permission first and remove their names from the typed version of their responses. Partially use the lower-scoring essays to highlight "missed opportunities" and areas of improvement. Then, conclude the activity with a top-scoring essay that received all or most of the points on the College Board rubric.

▲ Differentiation

All students would benefit from doing a rewrite of this essay after discussing the strengths and weaknesses of the samples. The main objective of this activity is to help students improve their writing skills and develop a better understanding of the format you want them to use that is likely to be rewarded on the AP® exam. For guidance, refer to the outline on page 286 under the "Writing Historically" section in this module.

TRM Suggested Responses to Questions

TRM Module 4.2 AP® Analyzing Sources Handout 2

TEACHING IDEA

Connecting the Dots

Since George Washington's *Farewell Address*, United States foreign policy was primarily one of neutrality and non-intervention until the 1820s. Ask students: How was the Monroe Doctrine (1823) a departure from this tradition of isolationism? The answer should cover how the United States was now interested in creating a sphere of influence and establishing hegemony over the Western Hemisphere.

EXPLORING AP® THEMES

America in the World

In the aftermath of the War of 1812, the United States had a newfound self-esteem and confidence that manifested itself in how it interacted with European nations. Have students identify and describe the main treaties entered into with Spain (*Adams-Onís* or *Purchase of Florida Treaty in 1819*) and Great Britain (*Webster-Ashburton Treaty*, etc.).

invaded or seriously menaced that we resent injuries or make preparation for our defence. With the movements in this hemisphere we are, of necessity, more immediately connected, and by causes which must be obvious to all enlightened and impartial observers. The political system of the allied powers is essentially different in this respect from that of America. This difference proceeds from that which exists in their respective Governments. And to the defence of our own, which has been achieved by the loss of so much blood and treasure, and matured by the wisdom of their most enlightened citizens, and under which we have enjoyed unexampled felicity, this whole nation is devoted. We owe it, therefore, to candor, and to the amicable relations existing between the United States and those powers, to declare that we should consider any attempt on their part to extend their system to any portion of this hemisphere as dangerous to our peace and safety. . . ."

Questions for Analysis

1. Identify the reasons why the Monroe Doctrine was issued, based on this excerpt.
2. Explain how the Monroe Doctrine represented a continuation of the expansion of federal power.
3. Evaluate the extent to which economic considerations shaped the creation of the Monroe Doctrine.
4. Evaluate the extent to which the Monroe Doctrine was a result of the War of 1812.

By the late 1820s, U.S. residents were moving to and trading with newly independent Mexican territories. Southern whites began settling on Mexican lands in east Texas, while traders traveled the Santa Fe Trail. Meanwhile New England manufacturers and merchants began sending goods via clipper ships to another Mexican territory, Alta California.

Some Americans looked even farther afield. In the early nineteenth century, U.S. ships carried otter pelts and other merchandise across the Pacific, returning with Chinese porcelains and silks. In the early 1800s, the Alta California and China trades converged, expanding the reach of U.S. merchants and the demand for U.S. manufactured goods. Some Americans then set their sights on Pacific islands, especially Hawaii and Samoa.

Expanded trade routes along with wartime disruptions of European imports fueled the expansion of U.S. manufacturing, which improved opportunities for entrepreneurs and workers. By 1813 the area around Providence, Rhode Island boasted seventy-six spinning mills. Two years later, Philadelphia claimed pride of place as the nation's top industrial city, turning out glass, chemicals, metalwork, and leather goods.

REVIEW

How did the United States use diplomacy and military force to expand its borders during the early nineteenth century?

Regional Economic Development

The roads, rivers, canals, and steamboats that connected a growing nation meant that people in one region could more easily exchange the goods they produced for those they needed. This development fostered the emergence of distinct, regional economies. In the South, for instance, vast American Indian land cessions and the acquisition of Florida ensured the expansion of cotton cultivation. At the same time, overcultivation in older regions of the Southeast forced many planters to relocate further west and south. In the process, they extended slavery into new lands to produce cash crops like sugar, rice, and most predominately cotton. Farmers often planted as much cotton as they could manage and used profits from these staple crops to buy grain and other food items from the West and manufactured shoes and cloth from the North.

TEACHING IDEA

Geography Instruction

Give students a map of the Pacific Rim so they can label the expanding trade networks at the time. Specifically, the lucrative trade in the Pacific included Northern California, China, and eventually Hawaii and Samoa. Have students identify the types of luxury goods like porcelain brought back from Asia that made that trade so alluring. A reproducible version of this map is available in the Teacher's Resource Materials.

TRM Map 4B – The Pacific Rim

Plantation homes in long-settled areas like Montpelier in the Virginia piedmont became more fashionable as they incorporated luxury goods imported from China and Europe. But, after decades of overcultivation, the soil in the Chesapeake region became depleted limiting the profits from tobacco and making a shift to cotton impossible. As agricultural production declined, some Virginia planters made money by selling enslaved people to planters farther south and west while others diversified their plantings by growing wheat and foodstuffs.

Many white Americans benefited from the expansion of southern agriculture west of the Appalachians. Southern farmers and planters who cultivated cotton made substantial profits in the 1810s. So did western farmers, who shipped vast quantities of agricultural produce to the South. Towns like Cincinnati, located across the Ohio River from Kentucky, sprang up as regional centers of commerce. Americans living in the Northeast increased their commercial connections with the South as well. Northern merchants became more deeply engaged in the southern cotton trade, opening warehouses in cities like Savannah and Charleston and sending agents into the countryside to bargain for cotton to be spun into thread in mills powered by water.

The southern cotton boom thus fueled northern industrial growth, the improvement of roads, the expansion of canals, and the building of larger and faster ships. Factory owners and merchants in New England could ship growing quantities of yarn, thread, and cloth along with shoes, tools, and leather goods to the South. Meanwhile, merchants in Philadelphia and Pittsburgh built ties to western farmers, exchanging manufactured goods for agricultural products. Over time America's regional economies became not only more distinctive but also increasingly interdependent.

REVIEW

• How did the economies of the North and South benefit from the westward expansion of southern agriculture?

The Panic of 1819

Panic of 1819 The nation's first severe recession. It lasted four years and resulted from irresponsible banking practices and the declining demand abroad for American goods, including cotton.

The **Panic of 1819** resulted primarily from irresponsible banking practices in the United States and was deepened by the declining overseas demand for American goods, especially cotton. Beginning in 1816, American banks, including the newly chartered **Second Bank of the United States**, loaned huge sums to settlers seeking land on the frontier and merchants and manufacturers expanding their businesses. Loans were often not backed by sufficient collateral because many banks assumed that continued economic growth would ensure repayment. Then, as agricultural production in Europe revived with the end of the Napoleonic Wars, the demand for American foodstuffs dropped sharply. Farm income plummeted by roughly one-third in the late 1810s.

In 1818 the directors of the Second Bank, fearing a continued expansion of the money supply, tightened the credit they provided to branch banks. This sudden effort to curtail credit led to economic panic. Some branch banks failed immediately. Others survived by calling in loans to companies and individuals, who in turn demanded repayment from those to whom they had extended credit. The chain of indebtedness pushed many people to the brink of economic ruin just as factory owners cut their workforce and merchants decreased orders for new goods. Individuals and businesses faced bankruptcy and foreclosure, and property values fell sharply.

Bankruptcies, foreclosures, unemployment, and poverty spread across the country. Cotton farmers were especially hard hit by declining exports and falling prices. Planters who had gone into debt to purchase land in Alabama and Mississippi were unable to pay their mortgages. Many western residents, who had invested all they had in new farms, lost their land or simply stopped paying their mortgages. This further strained state banks, some of which collapsed, leaving the national bank holding mortgages on vast amounts of western territory.

Many Americans viewed banks as the cause of the panic. Some states defied the Constitution and the Supreme Court by trying to tax Second Bank branches or printing state banknotes with no specie (gold or silver) to back them. Some Americans called for government relief, but there was no system to provide the kinds of assistance needed. When Congress debated how to reignite the nation's economy, regional differences quickly appeared. Northern manufacturers called for even higher tariffs to protect them from foreign competition, but southern planters argued that high

---

TEACHING IDEA

Connecting the Dots

Have students identify regional economic differences in a growing national economy that was becoming simultaneously more distinctive and interdependent. This also highlighted the need for a national economic policy, but the national bank was still controversial and many Americans were skeptical of federal authority and the appropriate role of the government in the economy.

TRM Find **Handout 4.3 – Examining the Growing National Economy** in the Teacher's Resource Materials.

EXPLORING AP® THEMES

American and National Identity

Have a class discussion on the following question: How could sectionalism develop and grow at the same time as nationalism? Possible answers include: 1) *Sectionalism — augmented as time went on and the divergent economic systems and related political issues (e.g., extension of slavery) heightened tensions between regions*; 2) *Nationalism — continued to increase in the aftermath of the War of 1812 and at a time of political unity during the "Era of Good Feelings."*

TEACHING IDEA

Check for Understanding

Ask students to think about the following question: How did economic divisions lead to political differences? Then, have them complete a chart that looks at the influence of economy on politics in the South, North, and West.

TRM Find **Handout 4.4 – Influence of Regional Economy on Politics** in the Teacher's Resource Materials.

Period 4: 1800–1848

MODULE 4-2 Defending and Redefining the Nation

TEACHING IDEA

Class Discussion

Ask students the following questions: What was the Tallmadge Amendment? Why does it serve as a good example of the growing sectionalism at the time? Possible answers include: *The Tallmadge Amendment was a document for northerners proposing Missouri could be admitted as a state if 1) it banned further importation of enslaved people; and 2) it passed a gradual emancipation law to emancipate enslaved people already in the territory. This proposal would be opposed by southern congressmen.*

Auction in Chatham Street, New York, 1820 Widespread unemployment between 1819 and 1823 resulted in evictions for thousands of families. Public auctions of the furniture, dishes, and other household goods of evicted families were held regularly in cities across the country. This depiction of an 1820 auction in New York's Chatham Square was painted by E. Didier in 1843, during the next major economic panic. **What details in this image convey the hardships created by the Panic of 1819?**

tariffs raised the price of manufactured goods while agricultural profits declined. Meanwhile, workingmen and small farmers feared that their economic needs were being ignored by politicians tied to bankers, planters, manufacturers, and merchants.

By 1823 the panic had largely dissipated, but the prolonged economic crisis shook national confidence, and citizens became more skeptical of federal authority and more suspicious of banks, particularly the Bank of the United States. From 1819 until the Civil War, one of the greatest limitations on national growth remained the cycle of economic expansion and contraction.

REVIEW

What were the causes and consequences of the Panic of 1819?

Slavery in Missouri

A second national crisis highlighted regional systems of labor. In February 1819 the Missouri Territory applied for statehood. New York congressman James Tallmadge Jr. proposed that Missouri be admitted only if it banned further importation of enslaved people and passed a gradual emancipation law. Southern congressmen blocked Tallmadge's proposals, but the northern majority in the House of Representatives then rejected Missouri's admission.

Southern politicians were outraged, claiming that since the Missouri Territory allowed slavery, so should the state of Missouri. With cotton production moving ever westward, southern congressmen wanted to ensure the availability of new lands. They also wanted to ensure the South's power in Congress. Because the northern population had grown more rapidly than that in the South, by 1819 northern politicians controlled the House of Representatives. The Senate, however, was evenly divided. If northerners could block the admission of slave states like Missouri while allowing the admission of free states, the balance of power in the Senate would tip in the North's favor.

AP® TIP
Analyze how Missouri's application to statehood as a slave state highlighted political as well as economic divisions among the regions of the United States.

TRM Suggested Responses to Questions

TRM Module 4.2 AP® Analyzing Sources Handout 3

AP® ANALYZING SOURCES

Source: Senator Rufus King (New York), *Speech to Congress on the Admission of Missouri to the United States*, 1819

"The question respecting slavery in the old thirteen States had been decided and settled before the adoption of the constitution, which grants no power to Congress to interfere with, or to change what had been previously settled—the slave States, therefore, are free to continue

---

TEACHING IDEA

Geography Instruction

Give students Map 4A of the United States as it looked in 1820 listed on page 263 in your Teacher's Resource Materials. Then have them highlight the southern boundary of Missouri at the 36°30′ line. Explain that this was going to become the line of demarcation separating free territories from those that still allowed enslavement. Next, have students identify the remaining lands in the Louisiana Territory. To conclude this activity, have students debate who should decide whether to allow enslavement in a territory applying for statehood. Should it be up to the state or federal government? What about letting the people in the territory decide for themselves? A reproducible version of this map is available in the Teacher's Resource Materials.

or to abolish slavery. Since the year 1808 Congress have possessed power to prohibit and have prohibited the further migration or importation of slaves into any of the old thirteen States, and at all times, under the constitution, have had power to prohibit such migration or importation into any of the new States or territories of the United States. The constitution contains no express provision respecting slavery in a new State that may be admitted into the Union; every regulation upon the subject belongs to the power whose consent is necessary to the formation and admission of new States into the Union. Congress may, therefore, make it a condition of the admission of a new State, that slavery shall be for ever prohibited within the same. . . ."

Questions for Analysis
1. Identify King's arguments about the power of Congress to regulate slavery in the new states.
2. Identify the evidence from the Constitution that King uses to support his argument.
3. Explain the connection between King's argument and the prevailing economic system in the North.

Source: Senator Freeman Walker (Georgia), *Speech to Congress on the Admission of Missouri to the United States*, 1820

"I cannot but remark, sir, to what lengths arguments might be carried, predicated upon the supposition of the existence of the power, on the part of congress, to impose conditions and restrictions.

If you have the authority to impose the one now sought to be imposed, may you not impose any other? If you have the right to inhibit the introduction of slaves into the new state, you have a right to inhibit the introduction of any other species of property. And you may go a step further, and prescribe the manner in which the soil shall be cultivated. In fine, there is no restriction or condition whatever, which may not, with equal propriety, be imposed."

Questions for Analysis
1. Identify Walker's arguments about the power of Congress to regulate slavery in the new states.
2. Explain the connection between Walker's argument and the prevailing economic system in the South.

Questions for Comparison
1. Identify King's and Walker's respective arguments about the power of Congress to regulate slavery in new states.
2. Explain the causes underlying the differences between King's and Walker's arguments.
3. Evaluate the extent to which the Missouri Compromise reconciled the debate over slavery in the territories.

For southern planters, the decision on Missouri defined the future of slavery. With foreign trade in enslaved people outlawed, planters relied on natural increase and trading enslaved people from older to newer areas of cultivation to meet the demand for labor. Moreover, free black people packed the congressional galleries in Washington to listen to congressmen debate Missouri statehood, leading supporters of slavery to worry that any signs of weakness would fuel resistance to slavery. Recent attacks on Georgia plantations by a coalition of formerly enslaved African Americans who had escaped bondage and Seminole Indians lent power to such fears.

In 1820 Representative Henry Clay of Kentucky forged a compromise that resolved the immediate issues and promised a long-term solution. Maine was to be admitted as a free state and Missouri as a slave state, thereby maintaining the balance between North and South in the U.S. Senate (Map 4.5). At the same time, Congress agreed that the southern border of Missouri — latitude 36°30' — was to serve as the boundary between slave and free states throughout the Louisiana Territory.

AP® TIP
Compare the concessions of the Missouri Compromise to the compromises reached at the Constitutional Convention in 1787 (Module 3-6).

BUILDING AP® SKILLS

Sourcing and Situation

One of the four possible types of sourcing or "extended analysis" students can do with documents on the AP® exam is point of view ("POV"). Since the two documents for the activity on page 283 provide opposing views, have students discuss how each person's identity informs what they say in the documents. After recognizing that one is a northerner and the other a southerner, get them to focus and explain why that would be significant. Refer to the proficiency statements from the College Board.

▲ **Differentiation**

When analyzing sources there are four things students can do that could be rewarded on the AP® exam — historical situation, intended audience, purpose, and/or point of view (which they are doing above), have students do the other sourcing or "extended analysis" for these documents. Doing so will provide students with a deeper understanding of the documents. Remember that students must go beyond identification and focus on the significance.

TEACHING IDEA

Digging Deeper: Henry Clay

Have students research why Henry Clay was known as "The Great Compromiser." Specifically, tell students to highlight his role in the Missouri Compromise, which was covered in this module. They should also find his involvement in future compromises (e.g., Compromise of 1850) dealing with the political issue of slavery as the nation moved toward Civil War.

BUILDING AP® SKILLS

Argumentation

When writing a response to an "extent" question, students should use a modifier/qualifier. Ask them to look at the rubric to complement the outline provided with the actual language like a thesis being "historically defensible" and providing a line of reasoning. Linkage statements (skill of supporting an argument) in the form of a concluding sentence would also be helpful. For historical evidence, students benefit from treating an LEQ as if it were a DBQ and thinking about documents from the period (1800–1820) dealing with the tension between the federal government and states. Lastly, have students attempt "historical complexity," for which there are multiple avenues they can take to try earning that point. Discuss these observations with students and clarify any misunderstandings.

EXPLORING AP® THEMES

Politics and Power

Ask students to connect the dots and make a thematic connection between the debates over the appropriate distribution of power between federal and state governments covered in this module with those in the past (Module 3-6). Specifically, students must draw parallels to the early republic and debates about the Articles of Confederation and how it should be replaced by the U.S. Constitution.

Period 4: 1800–1848

MODULE 4-2 Defending and Redefining the Nation

▲
MAP 4.5 The Missouri Compromise and Westward Expansion, 1820s The debate over the Missouri Compromise occurred as the United States began expanding farther westward. Within a few years of its adoption, the growth of U.S. settlements in eastern Texas and increased trade with a newly independent Mexico suggested the importance of drawing a clear boundary between slave and free states. **In what ways did the Missouri Compromise line decrease sectional tensions, and in what ways did it fuel them?**

Missouri Compromise 1820 act that established the southern border of Missouri as the boundary between slave and free states.

The **Missouri Compromise** ended the crisis for the moment. Still, the debates made clear how quickly a disagreement over slavery could escalate into clashes that threatened the survival of the nation.

REVIEW

- Why was the issue of slavery in Missouri so controversial?

AP® WRITING HISTORICALLY | **Responding to a Long-Essay Question**

The following long-essay prompt asks you to draw on what you have learned in Module 4-1 and Module 4-2.

> Evaluate the extent to which debates about the role of the federal government increased tensions between North and South in the period from 1800 to 1820.

Let's walk through one way to approach writing a response.

Step 1 Break down the prompt.

Remember, a phrase like "the extent to which" is a signal that you will need to rate the importance of whatever historical developments you choose to include in your response. In other words, this prompt is asking to you take a stance about *how much* the debates about the role of the federal government increased sectional tensions between 1800 and 1820.

TRM Suggested Responses to Questions

Step 2: List and categorize your historical knowledge.

Jot down any specific historical information you can remember that is relevant to the prompt. Remember to try to include as many "proper nouns" (people, events, court cases, laws, wars, inventions, and so on) as you can. You may wish to use the list and continuum strategies we worked with in Period 3 (p. 157) to pre-write for this prompt, but it is important to try different approaches to writing in order to find what works best for you.

Regardless of the approach you take during this step, you should keep ACE in mind as a basic rule of thumb when you pre-write: in addition to *answering* the prompt, you also need to *cite* historical evidence and — most importantly — *explain* why the evidence you chose supports your answer.

The following graphic organizer shows another way you can lay the foundation for the structure of your essay. The first column will help you answer the most basic aspect of the prompt: What were the debates about the role of the federal government between 1800 and 1820? The middle column will help you craft claims and gather supporting evidence about the role these debates played in increasing sectional tensions. Finally, the last column makes sure that you can explain the importance of the role each debate played.

Debates about Government (What was a debate over the role of the federal government during this time?)	Impact of the Debates (How did the debate increase sectional tensions?)	Extent of Impact (How much of an impact did that debate have on sectional tensions?)
How active should the federal government be in promoting economic growth? Examples: • Bank of the U.S. • National Road • Clay's American System	Many northerners supported active government efforts to expand economic growth, whereas southerners believed that most of the benefits would flow to northern industry while the costs would disproportionately hurt the South.	Significant—many northerners believed southerners were unwilling to place the greater good over regional interests, while many southerners feared a more active government might also take a more active role in regulating slavery.
	• Tariffs—Northern manufacturers favored high tariffs to protect industry from foreign competition, and southern farmers opposed tariffs as those decreased demand for cotton and raised prices on textiles.	• Tariffs—Tariff of 1816 was the first American protective tariff passed. Although it had some southern support, it was meant to be temporary and passed in part as a patriotic measure in the aftermath of the War of 1812.
	• Internal Improvements—Northern business interests supported federal construction of roads and canals as those expanded markets and increased access to raw materials. Southern farmers opposed federally funded improvements as those justified tariff revenues and contributed to a stronger federal government.	• Internal Improvements—President Madison's repeated vetoes of federally funded roads demonstrated Democratic-Republican and southern opposition to federal spending on infrastructure that would not directly benefit them.

After completing the organizer, ask yourself if other developments that were not nationally debated contributed directly or indirectly to increasing sectional tensions. For instance, what about technological innovations such as steamboats or the cotton gin? Since the prompt asks you to evaluate the extent to which debates led to tensions, a strong essay will address the extent to which other factors may have contributed to those tensions.

(Continued)

TEACHING IDEA

AP® Writing Historically Workshop

The question, "Evaluate the extent to which debates about the role of the federal government increased tensions between the North and South in the period from 1800 to 1820," by virtue of the wording, will lead many students to discuss only the ways in which tension increased. However, the beginning of the question, "the extent to which," implicitly offers students the opportunity to illustrate historical developments in which the North and South found consensus and did not see an increase in tension. For example, even though there was disagreement over the status of Missouri, westward expansion from 1800 until 1819 was generally met with nationalistic enthusiasm. Students' ability to recognize contradiction within a question is evidence of a more complex response. During step 2, after students have completed the outline from the graphic organizer in the textbook, ask students to account for historical developments that illustrate consensus or a decrease in tension.

Step 3 Set the context and craft a thesis.

Remember, your thesis should bring together at least three evaluative claims that respond to the prompt. You should lead into your thesis with a statement that contextualizes it. Your contextualization sets the stage for your argument by showing how your thesis connects to a larger historical development that occurred just before or early on in the time period specified by the essay prompt.

You might contextualize your thesis in this case by tying it to developments such as the debates between Hamilton and Jefferson over the Bank of the United States in the 1790s, Hamilton's financial plan, and Hamilton's and Jefferson's competing visions for the country. While your contextualization statement does not have to include all — or any — of those things, do not feel like you must limit yourself to a single aspect of the historical situation surrounding the argument you plan to make in your essay. Remember, context is the big picture, and your contextualization statement can point out multiple aspects of that big picture.

ACTIVITY

Use steps 1 through 3 to plan and write an essay in response to the Long-Essay Question at the beginning of this box. Your introduction must include a contextualization statement that leads into the thesis of your historical argument. Your thesis should include three or four evaluative claims based on your graphic organizer from step 2. Each of your body paragraphs should open with one of the claims in your thesis and include at least two pieces of evidence for that claim. Finally, be sure to explain *how* the evidence you've chosen to include in each body paragraph supports that particular claim — this is key to an effective historical argument.

You may use the following outline to guide your response:

I. Introductory paragraph
   A. Immediate/preceding contextualization statement
      1. Cite evidence of immediate/preceding context
      2. Explain influence of immediate/preceding context
   B. Thesis statement presenting three to four evaluative claims, situated along a continuum of relative importance, linking causes to effects

II. Claim 1 body paragraph
   A. Topic sentence presenting an evaluative claim of causation 1
   B. Supporting statement citing evidence of claim 1
   C. Cite additional evidence of claim 1
   D. Explain how evidence supports claim 1

III. Claim 2 body paragraph
   A. Topic sentence presenting an evaluative claim of causation 2
   B. Supporting statement citing evidence of claim 2
   C. Cite additional evidence of claim 2
   D. Explain how evidence supports claim 2

IV. Claim 3 body paragraph
   A. Topic sentence presenting an evaluative claim of causation 3
   B. Supporting statement citing evidence of claim 3
   C. Cite additional evidence of claim 3
   D. Explain how evidence supports claim 3

V. (Optional) Claim 4 body paragraph
   A. Topic sentence presenting an evaluative claim of causation 4
   B. Supporting statement citing evidence of claim 4
   C. Cite additional evidence of claim 4
   D. Explain how evidence supports claim 4

Module 4-3

Transportation and Market Revolutions Change America

TRM Suggested Responses to Questions

LEARNING TARGETS

By the end of this module, you should be able to:
- Explain the causes and effects of urbanization.
- Explain how the market revolution increased class divisions and changed women's roles.
- Explain how the market revolution impacted various regions and groups.

THEMATIC FOCUS

Social Structures

The market revolution boosted urbanization by drawing international and rural migrants to industrializing cities in the Northeast and fast-growing towns in the Midwest. It also increased class distinctions as rising prosperity benefited the business elite and led to the growth of both the middle class and the working poor. Middle- and upper-class women's roles changed, with a growing societal emphasis on domesticity.

HISTORICAL REASONING FOCUS

Comparison

Causation

The title of this module, in naming two "revolutions" that took place during the first half of the nineteenth century, suggests that these technological and economic developments brought profound and unexpected changes in the lives of Americans. Keeping causation and comparison in mind as you read will help you remember to not only compare the effects of these major changes, but examine how and why these effects differed.

TASK ▶ As you read this module, identify the major changes resulting from the market and transportation revolutions and compare the ways those changes affected different groups of people and different regions in the United States.

---

market revolution Innovations in agriculture, industry, communication, and transportation in the early 1800s that fueled increased efficiency and productivity and linked northern industry with western farms and southern plantations.

Commercial and industrial development, immigration from Europe, and migration from rural areas led to the rapid growth of cities in the northern United States from 1820 on. Such growth both built on and furthered the expansion of roads and canals, which were funded by federal and state governments in the 1810s and 1820s. By linking northern industries with western farms and southern plantations, these innovations in transportation fueled a **market revolution** as the manufacture of goods became better organized and innovations in industry, agriculture, and communication increased efficiency and productivity. These changes fostered urbanization, which, in turn, reinforced economic growth and innovation. However, it also created social upheaval. Cultural divisions intensified in urban areas where Catholics and Protestants, workers and the well-to-do, immigrants, African Americans, and native-born whites lived side by side. Class dynamics also changed with the development of a clear middle class of shopkeepers, professionals, and clerks.

Industrial enterprises in the Northeast transformed the nation's economy even though they employed less than 10 percent of the U.S. labor force. In the 1830s and 1840s, factories grew considerably in size, and some investors, especially in textiles, constructed factory towns. New England textile mills relied increasingly on the labor of girls and young women, while urban workshops hired children, young women and men, and older adults. Although men still dominated the

TEACHING IDEA

Building Vocabulary

Have students use the textbook as well as online resources to define the following vocabulary terms: urbanization, "market revolution," upper class, middle class, and lower class. Then conduct a brief discussion on the three social classes that existed at the time to ensure student understanding. Possible discussion points are included in italics.

- Upper Class: *comprised of the business elite in the North and planter aristocracy in the South*

- Middle Class: *mostly shopkeepers, professionals, businessmen, and clerks*

- Lower Class: *working poor (e.g., factory workers in the North and landless farmers in the South)*

BUILDING AP® SKILLS

Comparison

Write the following question on the board: What is the main difference between a "political" and an "economic" revolution? Then ask students to write down their answers and have them share out loud after a couple of minutes. Discuss their answers and emphasize that economic revolutions relate to sources of labor, markets, industries, and technological innovations (e.g., transportation and communication systems, etc.) and how these underwent profound expected and unexpected changes. Lastly, point out the title for the module—Transportation and Market Revolutions Change America.

skilled trades, making chairs, clocks, shoes, hats, and fine clothing, employment in these trades slowly declined as industrial jobs expanded. An economic panic in 1837 intensified this trend and increased tensions that made it more difficult for workers to organize across differences of skill, ethnicity, race, and sex.

Creating an Urban Landscape

> **AP® TIP**
> Analyze both the intended and unintended effects of the construction of the Erie Canal.

Across the North, urban populations boomed. As commercial centers, seaports like New York and Philadelphia were the most populous cities in the early nineteenth century. Between 1820 and 1850, the number of cities with 100,000 inhabitants increased from two to six; five were seaports. The sixth was the river port of Cincinnati, Ohio. Smaller boomtowns like Rochester, New York emerged along inland waterways as the completion of the Erie Canal in 1825 spurred agriculture and industry.

Development along the Erie Canal illustrates the ways that advances in transportation transformed the surrounding landscape and ecology. As soon as the first stretch was completed in 1819, its economic benefits became clear. As the 40-foot-wide canal was extended across central and western New York State, settlers rushed to establish farms, mills, and ports. They chopped down millions of trees to construct homes and businesses and to open land for cattle, sheep, wheat, and orchards. As bear and deer fled to still-forested areas, farmers shipped grain, cattle, and hogs to eastern markets or to emerging cities like Rochester. There flour millers and butchers turned wheat, cattle, and hogs into flour, beef, and pork, products that were now easier and cheaper to ship east and south.

As the population in western New York and along the Great Lakes increased, residents demanded more and more manufactured goods. This demand fueled the growth of factories, especially in New England. Cotton, lumber, and flour mills were constructed near waterfalls for power, transforming isolated villages into mill towns while endangering the natural habitats of fish and

▲ **"Erie-Canal, Lockport," c. 1850** This steel engraving, based on an 1839 painting, depicts one of five locks that lifted boats sixty feet over a limestone ridge near the western end of the canal. The remarkable engineering feat required 1200 laborers to blast the ridge, clear the rocks, and build the locks. The village of Lockport, which emerged at the site, grew rapidly after 1825. **How does this image portray the changes the Erie Canal brought to local towns?**

BUILDING AP® SKILLS

Causation

Since one historical reasoning focus of this module is causation and a learning target is to "explain the causes and effects of urbanization," emphasize an area that tends to be more challenging for students — explanation. Many students merely identify information and never progress to explaining. Consequently, provide students with some of the main causes of urbanization (e.g., commercial and industrial development in cities, internal migration from rural areas, and European immigration, etc.) to remove the identification component out of the way. Then, ask students to write 2 or 3 sentences explaining how and/or why these served as causes for urbanization. This aligns with the College Board's proficiency statements under the AP® historical thinking skills and reasoning processes.

TEACHING IDEA

Understanding the Transportation Revolution

This module is titled "Transportation and Market Revolutions Change America." Have students create a timeline, organizing in chronological order the following inventions in transportation: 1) Railroads; 2) Roads; 3) Clipper ships; 4) Canals. Then have them discuss how these innovations changed the American economy and society.

EXPLORING AP® THEMES

Social Structures

Have students look at the Key Concepts, Events, and People in the Period 4 Review on page 352 and identify which terms should be organized under the theme social structures. Then, ask them to define each term and describe the historical significance — how and/or why does it matter?

wildlife. As thousands of newcomers cleared more and more land in Ohio and Michigan, they expanded trade between areas fueled by the Erie Canal and the Great Lakes and older towns from New England to New York City. Moreover, Midwesterners could ship food south via the Ohio and Mississippi Rivers in exchange for southern cotton, rice, and sugar.

Business and political leaders in Philadelphia and Baltimore, seeing the economic benefits created by the Erie Canal, demanded state funding for canals linking them to the Midwest. Where state funding proved insufficient, they persuaded English bankers and merchants to invest in American canals as well as railroads, which were just beginning to compete with waterways as a method to transport people and goods.

REVIEW

What economic and environmental changes did the construction of the Erie Canal cause?

The Lure of Urban Life

As transportation improved and the economy expanded, cities across the North increased not only in size but also in diversity. During the 1820s, some 150,000 European immigrants entered the United States; during the 1830s, nearly 600,000; and during the 1840s, more than 1,700,000. This surge of immigrants included more Irish and German settlers than ever before as well as large numbers of Scandinavians. Many settled along the eastern seaboard. Others migrated west, including thousands of Irish immigrants who labored in difficult and dangerous conditions to build the Erie Canal. Many Irish workers eventually settled in local communities along the canal's route. Others added to the growth of frontier cities such as Cincinnati, St. Louis, and Chicago.

Late eighteenth-century Irish immigrants, many of whom were Protestants, were joined by hundreds of thousands more in the 1830s and 1840s, when Irish Catholics poured into the United States. The Irish countryside was then plagued by bad weather, a potato blight, and harsh economic policies imposed by the English government. From 1845 to 1846 a full-blown famine forced hundreds of thousands more Irish Catholic families to emigrate. Young Irish women, who could easily find work as domestics or seamstresses, emigrated in especially large numbers. Poor harvests, droughts, failed revolutions, and repressive landlords convinced large numbers of Germans, including Catholics, Lutherans, and Jews, and Scandinavians, to flee their homelands as well. By 1850 the Irish made up about 40 percent of immigrants to the United States, and Germans nearly a quarter.

> **AP® TIP**
> Be sure you can explain the factors that encouraged European immigration to the United States during the early nineteenth century.

These immigrants provided an expanding pool of cheap labor as well as skilled artisans who further fueled northern commerce and industry. Banks, mercantile houses, and dry-goods stores multiplied. Urban industrial enterprises included both traditional workshops and mechanized factories. Credit and insurance agencies emerged to aid entrepreneurs in their ventures. The increase in business also drove the demand for ships, commercial newspapers, warehouses, and other commercial necessities, which created a surge in jobs for many urban residents.

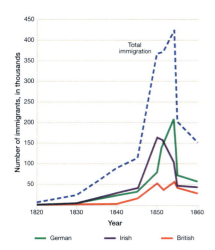

Immigration to the United States, 1820–1860 Famine, economic upheaval, and political persecution led masses of people from Ireland, Germany, and Britain to migrate to the United States from the 1820s through the 1850s. The vast majority settled in cities and factory towns in the North or on farms in the Midwest. An economic recession in the late 1850s finally slowed immigration, though only temporarily. **How did the changes in German and Irish immigration shown in this graph change urban life in nineteenth-century America?**

TEACHING IDEA

Understanding Quantitative Data

According to Chief Reader reports, one of the areas where students tend to struggle on the AP® exam is interpreting visual images, which they tend to take too literally. This is particularly true when interpreting quantitative data like graphs and charts. Therefore, you may want to practice this skill with students as much as possible. Using the graph on this page, have students attempt to put in context the information provided and categorize it into "push and pull" factors. The caption provides some evidence but students may also have prior knowledge (e.g., potato famine) or find supporting evidence in the text. As you help students go from describing what they see to explaining what it means, they may have to "read between the lines" and make inferences, but these inferences must be reasonable. It would benefit them to model a few examples to show this distinction.

APPLY THE TIP

To better understand why European immigration to the United States increased significantly after the 1830s, have students research the advancements of transatlantic voyages during the time. Students should discover that such voyages were now both shorter and less expensive. Additional topics they may research include the Irish Potato Famine (the Great Famine) and the German Revolutions of 1848/1849.

TEACHING IDEA

AP® Central

Use question 1 from the 2016 AP® U.S. History exam SAQ on immigration to the United States by decade, 1820–1859, to help students practice interpreting quantitative data. This question is available on the College Board's AP® United States History Past Exam Questions section under "2016: Free-Response Questions" (apcentral.collegeboard.org). In addition to interpreting the graph, students should identify and explain at least one cause and two effects of changes in immigration during the time period of the SAQ.

TEACHING IDEA

AP® Central

Even though the wording of the question does not align to the current exam, Long-Essay Question 3 from the 2007 Form B exam can serve as a useful content review for students. You could assign the entire question or have students work in groups on one element of the question. This question is available on the College Board's AP® U.S. History Past Exam Questions section under "2007: Form B" (apcentral.collegeboard.org).

▲ Differentiation

Consider having advanced learners do a comparison of all three immigrant groups identified in the question instead of having the option of choosing two as per the prompt. On the other hand, provide struggling learners with scaffolding by giving them categories that can serve as points of comparison for the two immigrant groups they select.

TEACHING IDEA

Class Discussion

Ask students to research what Americans did for entertainment in the major cities during the 1830s and 1840s. Specifically, have them consider theater, minstrel shows, and taverns/clubs. To conclude, have a quick debrief on what students learned about popular culture at the time. They should point out that there were regional, class, and racial/ethnic distinctions as opposed to having a standardized American form of leisure.

TEACHING IDEA

AP® Central

Even though the wording of the question does not align to the current exam, Long-Essay Question 3 from the 2009 Form B exam can serve as a useful content review for students. You could assign the entire question or have students work in groups on one element of the question. This question is available on the College Board's AP® U.S. History Past Exam Questions section under "2009: Form B" (apcentral.collegeboard.org).

EXPLORING AP® THEMES

Geography and the Environment

Environmental factors played a significant role in the development of geographical regions. For example, one of the main reasons why the factory system was concentrated in the Northeast was the topography of the land and bodies of water. Have students research what made that region ideal for factories. Then, discuss their answers and emphasize the importance of having fast rivers with waterfalls to generate power for the factories and mills. Lastly, point out that the abundance of natural harbors like Boston and New York City allowed for the development of these seaports to ship manufactured goods.

Businesses focused on leisure also flourished. In the 1830s theater became affordable to working-class families, who attended comedies, musical revues, and morality plays. They also joined middle- and upper-class audiences at productions of Shakespeare and contemporary dramas. Minstrel shows mocked self-important capitalists but also portrayed African Americans in crude caricatures. One of the most popular characters was Jim Crow, who appeared originally in an African American song. In the 1820s he was incorporated into a song-and-dance routine by Thomas Rice, a white performer who blacked his face with burnt cork.

The lures of urban life were especially attractive to the young. Single men and women and newly married couples flocked to cities. By 1850 half the residents of New York, Philadelphia, and other seaport cities were under sixteen years old. Young men sought work in factories, construction, and the maritime trades or in banks and commercial houses, while young women competed for jobs as seamstresses and domestic servants.

REVIEW

How did increased immigration to the United States during the first half of the nineteenth century change city life?

The Roots of Urban Disorder

While immigrant labor stimulated northern economic growth, immigrant families transformed the urban landscape. They crowded into houses and apartments and built ethnic institutions, including synagogues and convents — visible indicators of the growing diversity of northern cities. While most native-born Protestants applauded economic growth, cultural diversity aroused anxieties. Anti-Catholicism and antisemitism flourished in the 1830s and 1840s. Crude stereotypes portrayed Jews as manipulative moneylenders and Catholic nuns and priests as sexually depraved. Ethnic groups also battled stereotypes. Irishmen, for example, were often pictured as habitual drunkards.

Still, rising immigration did not deter rural Americans from seeking economic opportunities in the city. Native-born white men often set out on their own, but most white women settled in cities under the supervision of a husband, landlady, or employer. African Americans, too, sought greater opportunities in urban areas. In the 1830s, Philadelphia's vibrant African American community grew, as people were attracted by its churches, schools, and **mutual aid societies**. New Bedford, Massachusetts, a thriving whaling center, recruited black workers and thus attracted enslaved people who had fled the South as well.

Yet even as cities welcomed many migrants and immigrants, newcomers also faced dangers. Racial and ethnic minorities regularly faced discrimination and hostility. Physical battles erupted between immigrant and native-born residents, Protestant and Catholic gangs, and white and black workers. Criminal activity flourished as well, and disease spread quickly through densely populated neighborhoods. When innovations in transportation made it possible for more affluent residents to distance themselves from crowded inner cities, they moved to less congested neighborhoods on the urban periphery. Horse-drawn streetcar lines, first built in New York City in 1832, hastened this development.

By the 1840s, economic competition intensified, fueling violence among those driven to the margins. Native-born white employers and workers pushed Irish immigrants to the bottom of the economic ladder, where they competed with African Americans. Yet Irish workers insisted that their whiteness gave them a higher status than even the most skilled black laborers. When black **temperance** reformers organized a parade in Philadelphia in August 1842, white onlookers — mostly Irish laborers — attacked the marchers, and the conflict escalated into a riot.

Americans who lived in small towns and rural areas regularly read news of urban violence and vice. Improvements in printing created vastly more and cheaper newspapers, while the construction of the first telegraph in 1844 ensured that news could travel more quickly from town to town. Tabloids wooed readers with sensational stories of crime, sex, and scandal. Even more

temperance The movement to moderate and then ban the sale and consumption of alcohol that emerged in the early nineteenth century as part of the larger push for improving society.

respectable newspapers reported on urban mayhem, and religious periodicals warned parishioners against urban immorality. In response to both a real and a perceived increase in crime, cities replaced voluntary night watchmen with paid police forces.

REVIEW

What challenges did urban residents in the United States face during the first half of the nineteenth century?

The New Middle Class

Members of the emerging middle class, which developed first in the North, included ambitious businessmen, successful shopkeepers, doctors, and lawyers as well as teachers, journalists, ministers, and other salaried employees. At the top rungs, successful entrepreneurs and professionals adopted affluent lifestyles. At the lower rungs, a growing cohort of salaried clerks and managers hoped that their hard work, honesty, and thrift would be rewarded with upward mobility.

Education, religious affiliation, and sobriety were important indicators of middle-class status. A well-read man who attended a well-established church and drank in strict moderation was marked as belonging to this new rank. He was also expected to own a comfortable home, marry a pious woman, and raise well-behaved children. The rise of the middle class inspired a flood of advice books, ladies' magazines, religious periodicals, and novels advocating new ideals of womanhood. These publications emphasized the centrality of child rearing

▲ **Shoe Shopping from *Godey's Lady's Book*** In the 1830s and 1840s women's magazines appeared, to promote new ideals of middle-class womanhood and to guide them as consumers. This 1848 image of women shopping for shoes from *Godey's Lady's Book* encouraged female outings to elegant emporiums. The lavish engravings created by *Godey's* quickly made it the best-selling "ladies" magazine in the United States. **How does this image reflect the social and economic changes that took place during the mid-1800s?**

TEACHING IDEA

Check for Understanding

Help students continue to monitor their progress in the course and mastery of the material covered. Ask them to self-reflect on the main things learned thus far about how many Americans reacted to this first wave of immigration and how these immigrant groups adapted to their new environments. Then have them identify their "Top 3" list of key takeaways. Conduct a class discussion after students share out and you write their answers on the board. The objective is to reach consensus as to what the top takeaways should be up to this point. Clarify any misunderstandings demonstrated by their answers. Possible answers include: 1) *rise in nativism and xenophobia*; 2) *establishment of organizations like the "Know-Nothings" and the Order of the Star-Spangled Banner*; 3) *limiting economic opportunities for immigrants (e.g., "NINA" or "No Irish Need Apply")*; 4) *creation of ethnic neighborhoods and institutions (e.g., parochial schools, synagogues, and convents, etc.)*; and 5) *calls for assimilation hoping to prevent discrimination and hostility*.

TEACHING IDEA

Incorporating Websites

Visit the Stanford History Education Group site to obtain a lesson plan on Irish immigration during the Antebellum Era by searching for "Irish immigration" (sheg.stanford.edu). Specifically, this lesson focuses on the mistreatment and discrimination they encountered at the hands of nativist and xenophobic organizations like the Know-Nothing Party.

BUILDING AP® SKILLS

Causation

Urbanization resulted in multiple effects, including the creation of new problems and challenges for cities to address. Brainstorm with students what some of the main ones were and then discuss how they would rank them. Possible answers include: *overcrowding*, *crime/violence*, *vice and immorality*, *poor sanitation and diseases*, etc. Culminate the discussion with possible solutions to these problems (e.g., *reform movements*, *creation of police departments*, etc.)

Period 4: 1800–1848 MODULE 4-3 Transportation and Market Revolutions Change America

TRM Suggested Responses to Questions

TRM Module 4.3 AP® Analyzing Sources Handout 1

TEACHING IDEA

Understanding Social Changes

Not all American women bought into the notion of the "cult of domesticity," read magazines that reinforced traditional gender roles, or focused most of their lives on being mothers and consumers in the new market economy. Have students research ladies like Amelia Bloomer, who opposed this ideology and challenged societal expectations or the belief of separate spheres for men and women. Additionally, poor women could not afford to conform to these middle-class standards and some did not want to be defined or controlled by men and entered "Boston marriages." Conduct a class discussion after students share out their findings. Clarify any misunderstandings demonstrated by their answers.

TEACHING IDEA

AP® Central

Even though the wording of the question does not align to the current exam, the Document-Based Question from the 2006 exam can serve as a useful content review for students. You could assign the entire question or have students work in groups on one element of the question. This question is available on the College Board's AP® U.S. History Past Exam Questions section under "2006: Free-Response Questions" (apcentral.collegeboard.org).

AP® ANALYZING SOURCES

Source: 1850 U.S. Census of the Isaac and Amy Post Household

About the source: In 1850, for the first time, the federal census listed each member of the household by name as well as by age, sex, race (then labeled "Color"), and place of birth. Some census takers noted the relationship of each household member to the family head. This census taker did not, nor did he note Color. That information appears in brackets and came from other genealogical records.

Names of Residents in Household	Relation to Head of Household	Age/Sex/Color*	Occupation for Males over 15 Years	Place of Birth
Isaac Post	[Head]	50 / male / [white]	Druggist	New York
Amy Post	[wife]	45** / female / [white]		New York
Jacob K. Post	[son]	20/ male / [white]	Clerk	New York
Joseph Post	[son]	16 / male / [white]	Clerk	New York
Willet Post	[son]	3/ male / [white]		New York
Sarah Hallowell	[sister-in-law]	30/ female / [white]		New York
Ansel Bowen	[boarder]	28/ male / [white]	Teacher	New York
Elizabeth Bowen	[boarder]	28/ female / [white]		New York
Bridget Head	[servant]	23/ female / [white]		Ireland
Mary Ann Pitkin	[boarder]	10/ female / [black]		New York

Source: Seventh U.S. Federal Census, 1st Ward, Rochester, N.Y., 2 August 1850.
*The options for "Color" in the 1850 Census were "White, Black, and Mulatto." The bracketed information is from the 1855 N.Y. State Census and Rochester city directories.
**Amy Post was 47 in summer 1850, not 45.

Questions for Analysis

1. Identify the occupations of the men and the number of families represented in this household.
2. Describe the relationships among the women in this household and the work they likely performed.
3. Evaluate the extent to which the families represented in this household conformed to ideals of the middle-class American family during the mid-1800s.

cult of domesticity New ideals of womanhood that emerged alongside the middle class in the 1830s and 1840s that called for women to be confined to the domestic sphere and devote themselves to the care of children, the home, and hard-working husbands.

separate spheres Widespread belief in the late 1700s and early 1800s that men and women had separate roles and should occupy separate places in society. According to this belief, men should occupy the social public sphere, while women belonged in the domestic private sphere.

and homemaking to women's identities. This **cult of domesticity** ideally restricted wives to home and hearth, where they provided their husbands with respite from the cares and corruptions of the world.

In reality, however, entrance to the middle class required the efforts of wives as well as husbands. While upper middle-class men were expected to provide financial security, women helped cement social and economic bonds by entertaining the wives of business associates, serving in charitable and temperance societies, and organizing Sabbath schools. Families struggling to enter the middle class might take in boarders or extended family members to help secure their financial status. The adoption of new marital ideals of affection and companionship also made the boundaries between public and domestic life more fluid. In many middle-class families, husbands and wives both participated in church, civic, and reform activities, even if many did so through single-sex organizations. At the same time, husbands joined in domestic activities in the evening, presiding over dinner or reading to children.

The ideal of **separate spheres** of work and home had even less relevance to the millions of women who toiled on farms and factories or as domestic servants, providing goods and services

EXPLORING AP® THEMES

Social Structures

Students tend to develop a better understanding of history if they see why it may be relevant and significant to their lives. Establishing personal connections is a great tool for learning. Since this module focuses on social structures, have them briefly discuss how the role of women has changed and continued to be the same since the "cult of domesticity" was established in the mid-nineteenth century. Then ask if there is still a need for women to challenge traditional gender roles and fight for equality in twenty-first-century America.

AP® TIP

Consider the degree to which the cult of domesticity illustrated continuity with the eighteenth-century ideals of republican motherhood (Module 3-7).

for middle-class, and elite, families. In turn, those middle-class families played a crucial role in the growing market economy and the jobs it created. Wives and daughters were responsible for much of the family's consumption. They purchased cloth, rugs, chairs, clocks, and housewares, and, if wealthy enough, European crystal and Chinese porcelain figures. Middling housewives bought goods once made at home, such as butter and candles, and arranged music lessons and other educational opportunities for their children.

Although increasingly recognized for their ability to consume wisely, middle-class women also performed significant domestic labor. While many could afford servants, they often joined domestics and daughters in household tasks. Except for those in the upper middle class, most women still cut and sewed garments, cultivated gardens, canned fruits and vegetables, cooked at least some meals, and entertained guests. As houses expanded in size and clothes became fancier, domestic servants shouldered the most laborious and time-consuming chores, but many mothers and daughters still performed domestic labor as well. However, such work was increasingly invisible, focused inwardly on the family rather than outwardly as part of the market economy.

Middle-class men contributed to the consumer economy by creating and investing in industrial and commercial ventures. Moreover, in carrying out business and professional obligations, many enjoyed restaurants, the theater, or sporting events. Men attended plays and lectures with their wives and visited museums and circuses with their children. They also purchased hats, suits, mustache wax, and other symbols of middle-class masculinity.

REVIEW

- What values and beliefs did the new middle class embrace?
- What factors shaped the lives of mid-1800s middle class men and women, and how did their experiences differ?

Factory Towns and Women Workers

In the late 1820s investors and manufacturers joined forces to create factory towns in the New England countryside. The most famous mill town, Lowell, Massachusetts, was based on an earlier experiment in nearby Waltham. In the Waltham system, every step of the production process was mechanized; and planned communities included factories, boardinghouses, government offices, and churches. Agents for the Waltham system recruited the daughters of New England farm families as workers, assuring parents that they would be watched over by managers and foremen as well as landladies. The young women were required to attend church and observe curfews, and their labor was regulated by clocks and bells to ensure discipline and productivity.

Farm families needed more cash because of the growing market economy, and daughters in the mills could contribute to family finances and save money for the clothes and linens required for married life. Factory jobs also provided an alternative to marriage as young New England men moved west and left a surplus of women behind. Boardinghouses provided a relatively safe, all-female environment for the young mill workers, and sisters and neighbors often lived together. Despite nearly constant supervision, many rural women viewed factory work as an adventure. They could set aside a bit of money for themselves, attend lectures and concerts, meet new people, and acquire a wider view of the world.

During the 1830s, however, working conditions began to deteriorate. Factory owners cut wages, lengthened hours, and sped up machines. Boardinghouses became overcrowded, and company officials regulated both rents and expenses so that higher prices for lodging did not necessarily mean better food or furnishings. Factory workers launched numerous strikes in the 1830s against longer hours, wage cuts, and speedups in factory production. The solidarity required to sustain these strikes was forged in boardinghouses and at church socials as well as on the factory floor. At age twelve, Harriet Robinson led a walkout at the Lowell Mills in 1836. In her memoir, written in 1898, she noted, "As I looked back at the long line that followed me, I was more proud than I have ever been since at any success I have achieved."

TEACHING IDEA

Incorporating Secondary Sources

Provide students with a copy of the article titled "Women and the Early Industrial Revolution in the United States" by Thomas Dublin. This secondary source from the Gilder Lehrman site discusses the impact of the market revolution on women and the eventual deterioration of working conditions (gilderlehrman.org). Once students have finished reading the article, have them discuss their impressions in small groups.

TEACHING IDEA

AP® Central

Use question 2 from the 2017 AP® U.S. History exam DBQ on the market revolution and women, which is available on the College Board's AP® United States History Past Exam Questions section under "2017: Free-Response Questions" (apcentral.collegeboard.org). Since this LEQ is based on the historical thinking skill of "periodization," which is no longer targeted on the AP® exam, you may want to modify it. Specifically, turn it into a question based on the reasoning process of continuity and change.

TRM Suggested Responses to Questions

TRM Module 4.3 AP® Analyzing Sources Handout 2

TEACHING IDEA

Incorporating Primary Sources

Give students a copy of the "Boarding House Rules from the Handbook to Lowell, 1848" (available through online search). After reading this primary source, have a discussion on which rules students would find most restrictive and why.

TEACHING IDEA

Class Discussion

Write the following question on the board: Should child labor be prohibited by the government or should parents be allowed to make that decision? Then ask students to write down their answers, including their reasoning, and have them share out after a couple of minutes. Discuss their answers and point out that laws regulating children in the workplace were not passed until the twentieth century. The same questions could be asked for women or any other groups that should be afforded "protected status."

AP® ANALYZING SOURCES

Source: Harriet H. Robinson, *Loom and Spindle or Life among the Early Mill Girls*, 1898

"In 1831 Lowell was little more than a factory village. Several corporations were started, and the cotton-mills belonging to them were building. Help was in great demand; and stories were told all over the country of the new factory town, and the high wages that were offered to all classes of work-people,—stories that reached the ears of mechanics' and farmers' sons, and gave new life to lonely and dependent women in distant towns and farmhouses. . . .

Troops of young girls came by stages and baggage-wagons, men often being employed to go to other States and to Canada, to collect them at so much a head, and deliver them at the factories. . . .

I worked first in the spinning-room as a 'doffer.' The doffers were the very youngest girls, whose work was to doff, or take off, the full bobbins, and replace them with the empty ones. . . .

These mites had to be very swift in their movements, so as not to keep the spinning-frames stopped long, and they worked only about fifteen minutes in every hour. The rest of the time was their own, and when the overseer was kind they were allowed to read, knit, or go outside the mill-yard to play. . . .

The working-hours of all the girls extended from five o'clock in the morning until seven in the evening, with one-half hour for breakfast and dinner. Even the doffers were forced to be on duty nearly fourteen hours a day, and this was the greatest hardship in the lives of these children. For it was not until 1842 that the hours of labor for children under twelve years of age were limited to ten per day; but the 'ten-hour law' itself was not passed until long after some of these little doffers were old enough to appear before the legislative committee on the subject, and plead, by their presence, for a reduction of the hours of labor."

Questions for Analysis

1. Describe the effect the Lowell mills had on the surrounding community, according to Robinson.
2. Describe Robinson's attitude toward the experience of working in the mills.
3. Explain how the Lowell mills exploited female labor.

Despite mill workers' solidarity, it was difficult to overcome the economic power wielded by manufacturers. Working women's efforts at collective action were generally short lived, lasting only until a strike was settled. Then employees returned to their jobs until the next crisis hit. And as competition increasingly cut into profits, owners resisted mill workers' demands more vehemently. When the Panic of 1837 intensified fears of job loss, women's organizing activities were doomed until the economy recovered.

REVIEW

- What aspects of the Waltham-Lowell system did farm families and young women initially find attractive?
- How did the Waltham-Lowell system exploit the workers in its factories?

The Decline of Craft Work

deskilling The replacement of skilled labor with unskilled labor and machines.

While the construction of factory towns expanded economic opportunities for young women, the gradual decline of time-honored crafts narrowed the prospects for workingmen. Craft workshops gradually increased in size and hired fewer skilled workers and more men who performed single tasks, like attaching soles to shoes. Many tasks also became mechanized during the nineteenth century. The final product was less distinctive than an entire item crafted by a skilled artisan, but it was less expensive and available in mass quantities.

The shift from craft work to factory work threatened to undermine workingmen's skills, pay, and labor conditions. Masters began hiring foremen to regulate the workforce and installing bells and clocks to regulate the workday. As this process of **deskilling** transformed shoemaking, printing, tailoring, and other trades, laboring men fought to maintain their status.

EXPLORING AP® THEMES

Work, Exchange, and Technology

The market revolution fundamentally changed the type of work performed by many Americans, including a departure from the craftwork performed by artisans to single tasks that could be performed by unskilled workers and/or machines in the factory system. Have students evaluate both the positive and negative effects of "deskilling." Possible answers included in italics.

- **Positive:** *Deskilling allowed for mass production of goods, lowered prices of products, and afforded employment opportunities to women and children.*

- **Negative:** *Deskilling made workers easily replaceable, lowered pay, and decreased quality of work conditions.*

AP® TIP
Be sure you can explain how the changes in the lives of workers shaped the development of political parties in the 1800s.

unions Groups of workers seeking rights and benefits from their employers through their collective efforts.

Some workers formed mutual aid societies to provide assistance in times of illness, injury, or unemployment. Others participated in religious revivals or joined fraternal orders to find the camaraderie they once enjoyed at work. The expansion of voting rights in the 1820s offered another avenue for action. The first workingmen's political party was founded in Philadelphia in 1827, and working-class men in the North joined forces to support politicians sympathetic to their needs. Most workingmen's parties focused on practical proposals: government distribution of free land in the West, abolishing compulsory militia service and imprisonment for debt, public funding for education, and regulations on banks and corporations. Although the electoral success of these parties was modest, the major political parties of the 1830s — the Democrats and the Whigs — adopted many of their proposals.

Workingmen also formed **unions** to demand better wages and working conditions. In the 1820s and 1830s, skilled journeymen held mass meetings to protest employers' efforts to lengthen the workday, merge smaller workshops into larger factories, and cut wages. In New York City in 1834, labor activists formed a citywide federation, the General Trades Union, which provided support for striking workers. The National Trades Union was established later that year, with delegates representing more than twenty-five thousand workers across the North. These organizations aided skilled workers but refused admission to women and unskilled men.

It proved difficult to establish broader labor organizations, however. Most skilled workers considered unskilled workers as competitors, not allies. Many workingmen feared women workers would undercut their wages and so refused to organize alongside them. And anti-immigrant and racist beliefs among many native-born Protestant workers interfered with organizing across racial and ethnic lines. With the onset of the Panic of 1837, the common plight of workers became clearer. But the economic crisis made unified action nearly impossible as individuals sought to hold on to what little they had.

REVIEW
- How did workingmen respond to the decline of craft work, and what limited the success of their responses?
- What factors limited the success of workers' unions during the early 1800s?

The Panic of 1837

Panic of 1837 Severe economic recession that began shortly after Martin Van Buren's presidential inauguration. The Panic of 1837 started in the South and was rooted in the changing fortunes of American cotton in Great Britain.

AP® TIP
Analyze the impact of the Panic of 1837 on workers, immigrants, unions, and women.

The **Panic of 1837** began in the South but hit northern cotton merchants hard (see "Van Buren and the Panic of 1837" in Module 4-5). As a result, cotton shipments were sharply curtailed, textile factories drastically cut production, unemployment rose, and merchants and investors went broke. Those still employed saw their wages cut in half. In Rochester, the Posts temporarily moved in with family members and their oldest son left school to help save their pharmacy from foreclosure. Petty crime, prostitution, and violence also rose as men and women struggled to make ends meet.

In Lowell, hours increased and wages fell. Just as important, the process of deskilling intensified. Factory owners considered mechanization one way to improve their economic situation. A cascade of inventions, including power looms, steam boilers, and the steam press, transformed industrial occupations and led factory owners to invest more of their limited resources in machines. At the same time, the rising tide of immigrants provided a ready supply of relatively cheap labor. Artisans tried to maintain their traditional skills and status, but in many trades they were fighting a losing battle.

By the early 1840s, when the panic subsided, new technologies did spur new jobs. Factories demanded more workers to handle machines that ran at a faster pace. In printing, the steam press allowed publication of more newspapers and magazines, creating positions for editors, publishers, printers, engravers, reporters, and sales agents. Similarly, mechanical reapers sped the harvest of wheat and inspired changes in flour milling that required engineers to design machines and mechanics to build and repair them.

These changing circumstances fueled new labor organizations as well. Many of these unions comprised a particular trade or ethnic group, and almost all continued to address primarily the needs of skilled male workers. Textile operatives remained the one important group of organized female workers. In the 1840s, workingwomen joined with workingmen in New England to fight for a ten-hour day. Slowly, however, farmers' daughters left the mills as desperate Irish immigrants flooded in and accepted lower wages.

For most women in need, charitable organizations offered more support than unions. Organizations like Philadelphia's Female Association for the Relief of Women and Children in Reduced Circumstances provided a critical safety net for many poor families since public monies for such purposes were limited. Although most northern towns and cities now provided some

---

TEACHING IDEA

Class Discussion

Have students evaluate the relative significance of the following as causes for the limited success of labor unions (i.e., General Trades Union and National Trades Union, etc.) during the first half of the nineteenth century: 1) racial/ethnic prejudice; 2) growing power of the businesses; 3) exclusion of women; 4) cheap labor provided by immigrants; and 5) mechanization and deskilling of factory work. The existing social structures prevented many individuals from developing a class consciousness and organize as common laborers. Conduct a class discussion and clarify any student misunderstandings.

TEACHING IDEA

Understanding Economic Changes

One of President Andrew Jackson's most controversial political moves was killing the Second Bank of the United States. Shortly thereafter, the Panic of 1837 took place. For homework, have students research how the death of the national bank negatively impacted the American economy and what the new president, Martin Van Buren, did to put the economy back on track (*the independent treasury*). To what extent was his response a solution to the growing economic problems?

Period 4: 1800–1848

MODULE 4-3 Transportation and Market Revolutions Change America

form of public assistance, they never had sufficient resources to meet local needs in good times, much less the extraordinary demands posed by the panic.

REVIEW

What were the immediate and longer-term effects of the Panic of 1837 on the North?

TRM Suggested Responses to Questions

BUILDING AP® SKILLS

Argumentation

Remember that when writing a response to an "extent" question, students should use a modifier/qualifier. And if the prompt asks for students to evaluate the "relative significance," then they should rank the categories. In Document-Based Questions, it is also important that students know how to group documents into categories and do both "content" and sourcing or "extended analysis" so they can use them correctly. Ask students to look at the rubric to complement the outline provided with the actual language like a thesis being "historically defensible" and providing a line of reasoning. Linkage statements (skill of supporting an argument) in the form of a concluding sentence would also be helpful. For historical evidence, students benefit from using outside information and explaining its significance. Lastly, have students attempt "historical complexity," for which there are multiple avenues they can take to try earning that point. Discuss these observations with students and clarify any misunderstandings.

AP® WRITING HISTORICALLY — Responding to a Document-Based Question

The following Document-Based Question asks you to combine what you have learned in Period 4 thus far, your background knowledge, and a close reading of seven documents:

> Evaluate the extent to which the market revolution shaped American society in the period from 1800 to 1848.

In the steps that follow, we will walk through one way to approach this prompt.

Step 1 Break down the prompt, then organize and categorize your historical knowledge.

Be sure to note the topic of the prompt — the effects of the market revolution — and the time range it specifies: 1800–1848. This span includes historical developments from this module as well as from Modules 4-1 and 4-2, and you should be prepared to bring in evidence from all three to support your response.

The way the prompt is worded also provides important clues about what your response must do — as you will recall from your essay practice in Period 3, when you are asked to "evaluate the extent" of something, it means your essay needs to make an argument that tackles the importance of historical developments in relation to the topic of the prompt.

As with previous essays, once you *ACE* this question, you should briefly create a list of information you already know about the prompt. Remember, it may be helpful to approach this prompt as if no documents were provided.

The following graphic organizer presents one way to begin organizing your historical knowledge prior to moving onto the documents. The first row has been partially completed for you as an example, but the "Importance" has been left blank — that's because only you can determine how important a given effect is within the context of your essay's argument. Your evaluation of this example may also depend on the other effects you decide to explore in your pre-writing.

Effects	Evidence	Explanation of Significance	Importance
Women's roles in society changed	• Cult of domesticity • Separate spheres • Godey's Lady's Book	Women, particularly married middle- and upper-class women living in cities, were expected to focus on child-rearing and homemaking while refraining from the world of work and public affairs.	

Step 2 Read and annotate the documents.

As you read and annotate each of the seven documents that accompany the prompt, remember to ask yourself the following questions:

- What is the document about? What historical situation does it describe or reference?
- Who was the intended audience for this document?
- What was the author's purpose in writing this document?

TEACHING IDEA

AP® Writing Historically Workshop

Recall that students are responsible for including one piece of evidence in their response that is not provided in the documents. To help students conceptualize transferable ways of brainstorming throughout the year, consider the following activity. The goal is for students to "hit the gaps" in the documents. Put another way, Document-Based Questions always have gaps in between documents. In this question, the following three bookends of years could be used to brainstorm: 1800–1827, 1828–1836, and 1840–1845. Using these categories might condense students' focus as they brainstorm.

- What point of view does the author of this document express?
- How does this document relate back to the prompt?
- Does this document remind you of any other historical developments?

Finally, keep in mind how you can use each document to support the historical argument you are planning to make. How can these primary sources serve as evidence in your essay?

DOCUMENT 1

Source: Basil Hall, *Travels in North America, in the year 1827 and 1828*

"The chief source of the commercial and agricultural prosperity of Rochester is the Erie canal, as that village is made the emporium of the rich agricultural districts bordering on the Genesee river; and its capitalists both send out and import a vast quantity of wheat, flour, beef, and pork, pot and pearl ashes, whiskey, and so on. In return for these articles, Rochester supplies the adjacent country with all kinds of manufactured goods, which are carried up by the canal from New York. . . .

Much of all this prosperity may be traced to the cheapness of conveyance on the Erie Canal. . . .

[E]verything in this bustling place appeared to be in motion. The very streets seemed to be starting up of their own accord, ready-made, and looking as fresh and new, as if they had been turned out of the workmen's hands but an hour before, or that a great boxful of new houses had been sent by steam from New York, and tumbled out on the half-cleared land. The canal banks were at some places still un turfed; the lime seemed hardly dry in the masonry of the aqueduct, in the bridges, and in the numberless great saw-mills and manufactories. In many of these buildings the people were at work below stairs, while at top the carpenters were busy nailing on the planks of the roof."

DOCUMENT 2

Source: Joseph Davis, *The Azariah Caverly Family*, 1836

(Continued)

DOCUMENT 3

Source: Harriet Martineau, *Society in America*, 1837

"We saw to-day, the common sight of companies of slaves travelling westwards; and the very uncommon one of a party returning into South Carolina. When we overtook such a company proceeding westwards, and asked where they were going, the answer commonly given by the slaves was, 'Into Yellibama.' . . .

We saw several plantations while we were in this [Montgomery, Alabama] neighbourhood. Nothing can be richer than the soil of one to which we went, to take a lesson in cotton-growing. It will never want more than to have the cotton seed returned to it. We saw the plough, which is very shallow. Two throw up a ridge, which is wrought by hand into little mounds. After these are drilled, the seed is put in by hand. This plantation consists of nine hundred and fifty acres, and is flourishing in every way. . . .

The profits of cotton-growing, when I was in Alabama, were thirty-five per cent. One planter whom I knew had bought fifteen thousand dollars' worth of land within two years, which he could then have sold for sixty-five thousand dollars. He expected to make, that season, fifty or sixty thousand dollars of his growing crop. It is certainly the place to become rich in; but the state of society is fearful. . . . I describe this region as presenting an extreme case of the material advantages and moral evils of a new settlement, under the institution of slavery."

DOCUMENT 4

Source: *Address of the Workingmen's Party of Charlestown, Massachusetts*, 1840

"[W]e are the real producers. By our toil and sweat, our skill and industry, is produced all wealth of the community. . . . And yet what is our condition? We toil on from morning to night, from one year's end to another, increasing our exertions with each year, and with each day, and still we are the poor and dependent. Here, as everywhere else, they who pocket the proceeds of our labor, look upon us as the lower class, and term us the mob. . . .

[C]ompetition is less among manufacturers than it was. The principal manufacturers having adopted in regard to labor nearly uniform prices, changing the whole character of our laboring population by bringing them under control of corporate bodies. These corporations check individual enterprise, lessen competition between individual capitalists, bind the capitalists together in close affinity of interest, and enable them to exert a sovereign control over the prices of labor."

DOCUMENT 5

Source: *American Whig Review*, 1845

"We call our country a happy country; happy, indeed, in being the home of noble political institutions, the abode of freedom; but very far from being happy in possessing a cheerful, light-hearted, and joyous people. Our agricultural regions even are infected with the same anxious spirit of gain. If ever the curse of labor was upon the race, it is upon us; nor is it simply now 'by the sweat of thy brow thou shalt earn thy bread.' Labor for a livelihood is dignified. But we labor for bread, and labor for pride, and labor for pleasure. A man's life with us does consist of the abundance of the things which he possesseth. To get, and to have the reputation of possessing, is the ruling passion. To it are bent all the energies of nine-tenths of our population."

DOCUMENT 6

Source: *The Cultivator*, March 1846

"The undersigned respectfully offers his PATENT REAPER to the farmers of New-York, and the Western States generally . . . He can now warrant the raking of wheat from the machine to be accomplished with ease and completeness, by a man comfortably *seated upon* it. . . .

It has been extensively and most successfully in use in Virginia, . . . and during the last two years has been extensively introduced into most of the wheat growing States of the Union. . . .

The Reaper is warranted to cut from 15 to 20 acres a day—to save an average of a bushel of wheat to the acre that would be lost by ordinary cradling, to be durable, and not liable to get out of order, and the raking as stated above. Price $100, payable on delivery. . . .

C. H. McCormick"

DOCUMENT 7

Source: Horace Bushnell, *The Age of Homespun*, 1851

"[I]t has occurred to me that I may . . . [describe] this first century as the Homespun Age of our people. . . .

Another advance, and one that is equally remarkable, is indicated by the transition from a dress of homespun to a dress of factory cloths, produced by machinery and obtained by the exchanges of commerce, at home or abroad. This transition . . . is already so far made that the very terms, '*domestic manufacture*,' have quite lost their meaning; being applied to that which is neither domestic, as being made in the house, nor manu-facture, as being made by the hands.

This transition from mother and daughter power, to water and steam power . . . carry with it a complete revolution of domestic life and social manners. . . . If it carries away the old simplicity, it must also open higher possibilities of culture and social ornament."

ACTIVITY

Plan your response to the Document-Based Question at the beginning of this box by completing the graphic organizer in step 2 and annotating each of the documents. Then, use your pre-writing to craft an argumentative essay that cites both evidence from the documents and from your own historical knowledge.

Make sure to contextualize your argument in the opening paragraph before moving on to your thesis statement. Remember, your thesis should make three to four evaluative claims. Each of your body paragraphs should open with one of your thesis claims and contain supporting evidence from both your historical knowledge and the documents. Finally, remember to explain how all of the evidence you choose to include supports the topic sentence claim in each paragraph.

You may use the following outline to guide your response.

I. Introductory paragraph
   A. Immediate/preceding contextualization statement
      1. Cite evidence of immediate/preceding context
      2. Explain influence of immediate/preceding context
   B. Thesis statement presenting three to four evaluative claims, situated along a continuum of relative importance, linking causes to effects
II. Claim 1 body paragraph
   A. Topic sentence presenting an evaluative claim of causation 1
   B. Supporting statement citing evidence of claim 1 (from historical knowledge)
   C. Cite additional evidence of claim 1 (from a document)
   D. Cite additional evidence of claim 1 (from another document)
   E. Explain how evidence supports claim 1
III. Claim 2 body paragraph
   A. Topic sentence presenting evaluative claim of causation 2
   B. Supporting statement citing evidence of claim 2 (from historical knowledge)
   C. Cite additional evidence of claim 2 (from a document)
   D. Cite additional evidence of claim 2 (from another document)
   E. Explain how evidence supports claim 2
IV. Claim 3 body paragraph
   A. Topic sentence presenting evaluative claim of causation 3
   B. Supporting statement citing evidence of claim 3 (from historical knowledge)
   C. Cite additional evidence of claim 3 (from a document)
   D. Cite additional evidence of claim 3 (from another document)
   E. Explain how evidence supports claim 3
V. (Optional) Claim 4 body paragraph
   A. Topic sentence presenting evaluative claim of causation 4
   B. Supporting statement citing evidence of claim 4 (from historical knowledge)
   C. Cite additional evidence of claim 4 (from a document)
   D. Cite additional evidence of claim 4 (from another document)
   E. Explain how evidence supports claim 4

TRM Suggested Responses to Questions

TEACHING IDEA

Class Discussion

As you start Module 4-4, which focuses on the Second American Party System, draw a double arrow on the board or as a projection with a starting date of 1790 and an end of 1840. Then add three lines above to represent changes and three at the bottom for continuities. Lastly, as students read the module and/or you go over the material, have them identify significant political changes and continuities during this time. Possible answers are included in italics.

- Changes: 1) *Property qualifications were removed, leading to universal white male suffrage*; 2) *Some white women increased their political influence via male relatives*; 3) *Power shift from the eastern elite (e.g., Virginia tidewater region) to the backcountry or western frontier (e.g., Andrew Jackson, etc.)*; and 4) *Disfranchisement of African American males grew in northern states.*

- Continuities: 1) *Women could not vote*; 2) *African Americans could not vote in southern states*; 3) *American Indians could not vote (except in their own nations).*

This activity can serve as a bell ringer and will help students answer the review question on the next page.

Module 4-4

The Second American Party System

LEARNING **TARGETS**
By the end of this module, you should be able to:
- Explain the factors that led to the rise of a second two-party system of politics in the United States.
- Explain the continuities and changes in American politics from the first two-party system featuring the Federalists and Democratic-Republicans to the beginnings of a second two-party system featuring Democrats and National Republicans, later replaced by the Whigs.

THEMATIC **FOCUS**
Politics and Power

By the 1820s, states expanded voting rights to all white men by ending property requirements while simultaneously restricting voting rights for women, African Americans, and American Indians. As a more popularly oriented style of campaigning emerged, Jackson's presidential election victory in 1828 confirmed the staying power of the new Democratic Party and signaled the end of a political system dominated by eastern elites.

HISTORICAL REASONING **FOCUS**
Continuity and Change

Module 4-4 examines the emergence of America's second political party system — the Democrats and National Republicans, later replaced by the Whigs — during the 1820s and early 1830s. Comparing the developments these "new" parties brought to America's political landscape to those brought about by the first party system of Federalists and Democratic-Republicans in the 1790s and early 1800s is one way to better understand the degree of change that occurred during this period of American history.

TASK ▶ As you read this module, consider how much American party politics changed from the Jeffersonian era (1790s–1810s) to the Jacksonian era (1820s–1830s). Keep in mind that any time you think about change, you should also identify continuity. What aspects of America's politics and way of life remained the same between these two major presidential eras?

With the Panic of 1819 and the debates over Missouri shaking many Americans' faith in their economic and political leaders and the frontier moving ever westward, the nation was ripe for change. Workingmen, small farmers, and frontier settlers, who had long been locked out of the electoral system by property qualifications and eastern elites, demanded the right to vote. The resulting political movement ensured voting rights for nearly all white men during the 1820s. Yet African Americans lost political and civil rights in the same period, and American Indians fared poorly under the federal administrations brought to power by this expanded electorate. While some white women gained greater political influence as a result of the voting rights gained by fathers and husbands, they did not achieve independent political rights. Finally, as a wave of new voters entered the political fray, ongoing conflicts over slavery, tariffs, and the rights of American Indian nations transformed party alignments.

Voting Rights Expand

Between 1788 and 1820, the U.S. presidency was dominated by Virginia elites and after 1800 by Democratic-Republicans. With little serious political opposition at the national level, few people bothered to vote in presidential elections. Far more people engaged in political activities at the state and local levels. Many towns attracted large audiences to public celebrations on the Fourth of July and election days. Female participants sewed symbols of their partisan loyalties on their clothes and joined in parades and feasts organized by men.

TEACHING IDEA

Analyzing Art and Images

Show students a collection of famous paintings representing the expansion of voting rights and growing popularity and participation in mass politics during the 1820s and 1830s. Since this module includes a painting by John Lewis Krimmel, select some of the main works of George Caleb Bingham (e.g., *The County Election*, *Canvassing for a Vote*, *Country Politician*, *The Verdict of the People*, etc.). Divide students into small groups and have them research and interpret one of the paintings selected and then let each group share their findings with the rest of the class by conducting presentations.

Voting Rights Expand

Election Day in Philadelphia, 1815
This engraving, based on a painting by German immigrant John Lewis Krimmel, depicts an election-day celebration in Philadelphia in 1815. The image highlights the widespread popular participation of men, women, and children in political events even before the expansion of voting rights for white men in the 1820s. **What does the bustling scene and presence of American flags in this engraving suggest about popular sentiment toward elections?**

The Panic of 1819 stimulated even more political activity as laboring men, who were especially vulnerable to economic downturns, demanded the right to vote so they could hold politicians accountable. In New York State, Martin Van Buren, a rising star in the Democratic-Republican Party, led the fight to eliminate property qualifications for voting. At the state constitutional convention of 1821, the committee on suffrage argued that the only qualification for voting should be "the virtue and morality of the people." By the word *people*, Van Buren and the committee meant white men.

Despite opposition from powerful and wealthy men, by 1825 most states along the Atlantic seaboard had lowered or eliminated property qualifications on white male voters. Meanwhile states along the frontier that had joined the Union in the 1810s established universal white male suffrage from the beginning. And by 1824 three-quarters of the states (18 of 24) allowed voters, rather than state legislatures, to elect members of the electoral college.

Yet as white workingmen gained political rights in the 1820s, democracy did not spread to other groups. American Indian nations were considered sovereign entities, so American Indians voted in their own nations, not in U.S. elections. Women were excluded from voting because of their perceived dependence on men. And African American men faced increasing restrictions on their political rights. No southern legislature had ever granted black people the right to vote, and northern states began disfranchising them as well in the 1820s. In many cases, expanded voting rights for white men went hand in hand with new restrictions on black men. In New York State, for example, the constitution of 1821, which eliminated property qualifications for white men, raised property qualifications for African American voters.

When African American men protested their disfranchisement, some whites spoke out on their behalf. They claimed that denying rights to men who had in no way abused the privilege of voting set "an ominous and dangerous precedent." In response, opponents of black suffrage offered explicitly racist justifications. Some argued that black voting would lead to interracial socializing, even marriage. Others feared that black voters might hold the balance of power in close elections, forcing white civic leaders to accede to their demands. Gradually, racist arguments won the day, and by 1840, 93 percent of free black people in the North were excluded from voting.

AP® TIP
Analyze how giving the vote to white men who did not own property affected American politics during the early and mid-1800s.

REVIEW

- How and why did voting rights change for white men, women, and African Americans in the 1820s?

TEACHING IDEA

Class Discussion

Have students evaluate the relative importance of the following political issues during the 1820s and 1830s: 1) slavery; 2) tariffs; 3) rights of American Indians; and 4) power of federal government. Then, ask them to move to one of the four corners in the classroom after labeling each with one of these political issues. Next, allow each group to share out their "Top 3" reasons, including historical evidence, to support why that political issue is most important. After each group has shared out, allow students to switch groups if they were persuaded by someone else's argument.

▲ Differentiation

One way to modify this activity is by switching students to a group they did not select and asking them to defend that position. Doing so will allow them to work on identifying and eventually trying to support and defend a counter-argument. This is one of the ways students can potentially develop nuanced distinctions and think in a more sophisticated manner. The "historical complexity" point, which tends to be the most difficult to obtain on the DBQ and LEQ, would be practiced with this activity. Refer to the College Board rubrics for guidance.

BUILDING AP® SKILLS

Causation

In small groups of three, have students discuss the following causes of the rise of the Second American Party System and decide which played a more significant role: 1) opposition to Andrew Jackson; 2) death of the Federalists party; 3) disagreements over the appropriate role of the federal government and interpretations of the U.S. Constitution; 4) economic issues (e.g., tariffs and funding internal improvements); and 5) emergence of new political figures. After reaching consensus, have each group write a paragraph that summarizes their position.

EXPLORING AP® THEMES

Politics and Power

Have students look at the Key Concepts, Events, and People in the Period 4 Review on page 352 and identify which terms should be organized under the theme politics and power. Then, ask them to define each term and describe the historical significance — how and/or why does it matter?

TEACHING IDEA

Class Discussion

In pairs, have students review the following restrictions on African Americans:
1) could not become citizens through naturalization; 2) could not enroll in federal militias; 3) segregated in public schools, transportation, and accommodations; and 4) not allowed to settle in some states. Then, have students prepare for a class debate on which was most damaging to the African American community. Students must provide reasoning for supporting their position. To conclude, ask the entire class: Why were Democratic-Republicans so pro-restrictions?

TEACHING IDEA

AP® Central

Use question 2 from the 1999 AP® U.S. History exam LEQ on the Second American Party System as a bell ringer. Have students outline what specific relevant information could be used to answer this prompt. This is available on the College Board's Past Exam Questions resource "AP® United States History Document-Based Questions 1973–1999" (apcentral.collegeboard.org).

Period 4: 1800–1848

MODULE 4-4   The Second American Party System

Racial Restrictions and Antiblack Violence

Restrictions on voting followed other constraints on African American men and women. As early as 1790, Congress limited naturalization (the process of becoming a citizen) to white aliens, or immigrants. It also excluded them from enrolling in federal militias. In 1820 Congress authorized city officials in Washington, D.C. to adopt a separate legal code governing free and enslaved black people. This federal legislation encouraged states, in both the North and the South, to add their own restrictions, including the segregation of public schools, transportation, and accommodations. Some northern legislatures even denied African Americans the right to settle in their state.

In addition, black people faced mob and state-sanctioned violence across the country. In 1822 officials in Charleston, South Carolina accused Denmark Vesey, a free black, of following the revolutionary leader Toussaint L'Ouverture's lead and plotting a conspiracy to free the city's enslaved inhabitants. Vesey had helped to organize churches, mutual aid societies, and other black institutions. His accomplishments were considered threatening to the future of slavery by challenging assumptions about black inferiority. Vesey may have organized a plan to free enslaved people in the city, but it is also possible that white officials concocted the plot to terrorize African Americans. Despite scant evidence, Vesey and thirty-four of his alleged co-conspirators were found guilty and hanged. The African Methodist Episcopal Church where they supposedly planned the insurrection was demolished. Black people in the North also suffered from violent attacks by whites. For example, in 1829 white residents of Cincinnati attacked black neighborhoods, and more than half of the city's black residents fled. Many of them resettled in Ontario, Canada. They were soon joined by black Philadelphians who had been attacked by groups of white residents in 1832. Such attacks continued in northern cities throughout the 1830s.

◀ **Record of Thirty-five Men Executed for Conspiring to Revolt against Slaveholders**
This official record of executions related to an alleged 1822 conspiracy of several enslaved people lists the name of Denmark Vesey, the only free black man accused, fifth. The enslaved men are listed next to slaveholders' names, including the governor of South Carolina, twenty-one other men, and six women. There were no appeals of their convictions, and the hangings took place quickly. **In what ways does this record reflect the treatment of African Americans during this time period?**

REVIEW

- In what ways did African Americans have their rights restricted and safety threatened during the first half of the nineteenth century?

Political Realignments

Restrictions on black political and civil rights converged with the continued decline of the Federalists. Federalist majorities in New York State had approved the gradual abolition law of 1799. In 1821 New York Federalists advocated equal rights for black and white voters as long as property qualifications limited suffrage to respectable citizens. But Federalists were losing power, and the concerns of African Americans were low on the Democratic-Republican agenda.

Struggles within the Democratic-Republican Party now turned to a large extent on the limits of federal power. Many Democratic-Republicans had come to embrace a more expansive view of federal authority and a looser interpretation of the U.S. Constitution. Others argued forcefully for a return to limited federal power and a strict construction of the Constitution. At the same time, rising young politicians — like Martin Van Buren and Andrew Jackson — and newly enfranchised voters sought to seize control of the party from its longtime leaders.

The election of 1824 brought these conflicts to a head, splitting the Democratic-Republicans into rival factions that by 1828 coalesced into two distinct entities: the **Democrats** and the **National Republicans**. Unable to agree on a single presidential candidate in 1824, the Democratic-Republican congressional caucus fractured into four camps backing separate candidates: John Quincy Adams, Andrew Jackson, Henry Clay, and Secretary of the Treasury William Crawford.

As the race developed, Adams and Jackson emerged as the two strongest candidates. John Quincy Adams's stature rested on his diplomatic achievements and the reputation of his father, former president John Adams. He favored internal improvements and protective tariffs that would bolster northern industry and commerce. Jackson, on the other hand, relied largely on his fame as a war hero and American Indian fighter to inspire popular support. He advocated limited federal power.

As a candidate who appealed to ordinary voters, Jackson held a decided edge. Outgoing and boisterous, Jackson took his case to the people. Emphasizing his humble origins, he appealed to small farmers and northern workers. Just as important, Jackson gained the support of Van Buren, who also wanted to expand the political clout of the "common [white] man" and limit the reach of a central government that was becoming too powerful.

The four presidential candidates created a truly competitive race, and turnout at the polls increased significantly. Jackson won the popular vote by carrying Pennsylvania, New Jersey, the Carolinas, and much of the West and led in the electoral college with 99 electors. But with no candidate gaining an absolute majority in the electoral college, the Constitution called for the House of Representatives to choose the president from the three leading contenders — Jackson, Adams, and Crawford. Clay, who came in fourth, asked his supporters to back Adams, ensuring his election. Once in office, President Adams appointed Clay secretary of state. Jackson claimed that the two had engineered a **"corrupt bargain,"** but Adams and Clay, who shared many ideas, formed a logical alliance.

President Adams also ran into vigorous opposition in Congress, led by Van Buren. John C. Calhoun, who had been elected vice president, also opposed his policies. Van Buren argued against federal funding for internal improvements since New York State had financed the Erie Canal with its own monies. Calhoun, meanwhile, joined other southern politicians in opposing any expansion of federal power for fear it would then be used to restrict the spread of slavery.

The most serious battle in Congress, however, involved tariffs. The Tariff of 1816 had excluded most cheap English cotton cloth from the United States to aid New England manufacturing. In 1824 the tariff was extended to more expensive cotton and woolen cloth and to iron goods. During the presidential campaign, Adams and Clay appealed to northern voters by advocating even higher duties on these items. When Adams introduced tariff legislation that extended duties to raw materials like wool, hemp, and molasses, he gained support from both Jackson and Van Buren, who considered these tariffs beneficial to farmers on the frontier. Despite the opposition of Vice President Calhoun and congressmen from southeastern states, the **Tariff of 1828** was approved, raising duties on imports to an average of 62 percent.

Democrats and National Republicans Two parties that resulted from the split of the Democratic-Republicans in the early 1820s. Andrew Jackson emerged as the leader of the Democrats, while figures like Henry Clay and John Quincy Adams emerged as leaders of the National Republicans.

"corrupt bargain" Agreement between Henry Clay and John Quincy Adams in the 1824 presidential election that Clay would withdraw from the race in exchange for an appointment in Adams's cabinet.

Tariff of 1828 Tariff that extended duties to include raw materials such as wool, hemp, and molasses. It was passed despite strong opposition from southeastern states.

TEACHING IDEA

Building Vocabulary

Have students individually define the term "abomination." Then engage the class in a discussion on their definitions to reach a consensus. Next, ask students: Why was the Tariff of 1828 so offensive to many southerners? After discussing it, follow up by asking if these justified calls for nullification and contemplating secession.

EXPLORING AP® THEMES

Politics and Power

Students tend to face challenges in understanding splits within political parties and how supporters may change their beliefs over time. This was the case with the Democratic-Republicans under Thomas Jefferson when they eventually split into the Democrats (led by Andrew Jackson) and National-Republicans (led by John Quincy Adams), who would eventually become the Whigs (led by Henry Clay). Ask students to research the differences that emerged within the political party that resulted in the split. Possible answers included in italics.

- Democrats: *Wing of the party that still believed in limited federal power and strict interpretation of the U.S. Constitution.*

- National-Republicans: *Wing of the party that believed in stronger federal power (e.g., internal improvements and tariffs) and looser interpretation of the U.S. Constitution.*

TEACHING IDEA

Class Discussion

During the 1820s, General Andrew Jackson emerged as the new leader of the Democrats. When elected in 1828, he became known as the "President of the Common Man" and a "Champion of Democracy." Many also saw him as a "self-made" man and someone the masses could identify with even though he became a wealthy individual. Ask students: To what extent are these characterizations accurate? Give students time to brainstorm their answers before sharing out with the rest of the class. Lastly, tell them to visit the following website dedicated to his home — The Hermitage (thehermitage.com).

TEACHING IDEA

AP® Central

Use question 3 of the 2011 AP® U.S. History exam LEQ on political parties and national unity as a bell ringer. Have students work on developing thesis categories based on the question. This question is available on the College Board's AP® U.S. History Past Exam Questions section under "2011: Free-Response Questions" (apcentral.collegeboard.org).

The Tariff of 1828, however, was Adams's only notable legislative victory. His foreign policy was also stymied by a hostile Congress. Adams thus entered the 1828 election campaign with little to show in the way of domestic or foreign achievements, and Jackson and his supporters took full advantage of the president's political vulnerability.

REVIEW

- What factors led Jackson to call Adams's victory in the presidential election of 1824 "corrupt"?

The Presidential Election of 1828

The election of 1828 tested the power of the two major factions in the Democratic-Republican Party. President Adams followed the traditional approach of "standing" for office. He told supporters, "If my country wants my services, she must ask for them." Jackson and his supporters chose instead to "run" for office. They took their case directly to the voters, introducing innovative techniques to create enthusiasm among the electorate.

Van Buren managed the first truly national political campaign in U.S. history, seeking to re-create the original Democratic-Republican coalition among farmers, northern artisans, and southern planters while adding a sizable constituency of frontier voters. He was aided in the effort by Calhoun, who again ran for vice president and supported the Tennessee war hero despite their disagreement over tariffs. Jackson's supporters organized state nominating conventions rather than relying on the congressional caucus. They established local Jackson committees in critical states like Virginia and New York. They organized newspaper campaigns and developed a logo, the hickory leaf, based on the candidate's nickname, "Old Hickory."

Jackson traveled the country to build loyalty to himself as well as to his party. His Tennessee background, rise to great wealth, and reputation as an American Indian fighter ensured his popularity among southern and western voters. He also reassured southerners that he advocated "judicious" duties on imports, suggesting that he might try to lower the 1828 rates. At the same time, his support of the Tariff of 1828 and his military credentials created enthusiasm among northern workingmen and frontier farmers.

President Adams's supporters demeaned the "dissolute" and "rowdy" men who attended Jackson rallies. They also launched personal attacks on the candidate and on his wife, Rachel. They questioned the timing of her divorce from her first husband and remarriage to Jackson. A Cincinnati newspaper

1824 Election
- 13.1% (41 electoral votes) John Quincy Adams
- 30.5% (84 electoral votes) Andrew Jackson
- 13.2% (37 electoral votes) Henry Clay
- 43.1% (99 electoral votes) William H. Crawford

Percentage of the Popular Vote*

1828 Election
- 44% (83 electoral votes) John Quincy Adams
- 56% (178 electoral votes) Andrew Jackson

Percentage of the Popular Vote*

*Popular vote percentages are approximate.

▲ **The Elections of 1824 and 1828** Andrew Jackson lost the 1824 election to John Quincy Adams when the decision was thrown into the House of Representatives. In 1828 Jackson launched the first popular campaign for president, mobilizing working-class white men who were newly enfranchised. Three times as many men—more than one million voters—cast ballots in 1828 than in 1824, ensuring Jackson's election as president. **What changed and what remained the same between the 1824 and 1828 electoral results? What factors account for those changes and continuities?**

TEACHING IDEA

Connecting the Dots

In the election of 1828, the manner of conducting political campaigns drastically changed. Have students research how politics became more innovative after this first popular campaign for president. Possible answers include: *state nominating conventions instead of "king caucus" in Congress, personality and reputation became as important as position on issues, "Old Hickory" was more successful because he campaigned while John Quincy Adams "sat" for the race.*

TEACHING IDEA

Incorporating Secondary Sources

Provide students with a copy of the article titled "The Age of Jackson" by Ted Widmer. This secondary source from the Gilder Lehrman site discusses the main events, developments, and processes that characterized the era (gilderlehrman.org).

TEACHING IDEA

Understanding Quantitative Data

According to Chief Reader reports, one of the areas where students tend to struggle on the AP® exam is interpreting visual images, which they tend to take too literally. This is particularly true when interpreting quantitative data like graphs and charts. Therefore, you may want to practice this skill with students as much as possible. Using the pie charts on this page, have students reconcile the differences in numbers between popular vote and Electoral College votes. As you help students go from describing what they see to explaining what it means, they may have to "read between the lines" and make inferences, but these inferences must be reasonable. It would benefit them to model a few examples to show this distinction.

headline asked: "Ought a convicted adulteress and her paramour husband be placed in the highest offices of this free and Christian land?"

Adams distanced himself from his own campaign. He sought to demonstrate his statesman-like gentility by letting others speak for him. This strategy worked well when only men of wealth and property could vote. But with an enlarged electorate and an astonishing turnout of more than 50 percent of eligible voters, Adams's approach failed and Jackson became president.

The election of 1828 formalized a new party alignment. During the campaign Jackson and his supporters referred to themselves as "the Democracy" and forged a new national Democratic Party. In response Adams's supporters called themselves National Republicans. The competition between Democrats and National Republicans heightened interest in national politics among ordinary voters and ensured that the innovative techniques introduced by Jackson would be widely adopted in future campaigns.

AP® ANALYZING SOURCES

Source: *Proceedings of the Anti-Jackson Convention in Richmond*, 1828

"[W]e are unanimous, and unhesitating in the opinion, that Andrew Jackson is altogether unfit for the Presidency, and that his election would be eminently dangerous—... we must, in the most solemn manner, protest against a claim to civil rule, founded exclusively upon military renown,—and avow, that nothing has occurred in the history of our country, so much calculated to shake our confidence in the capacity of the people for self-government, as the efforts, which have been made, and are yet making, to elevate to the first office in the nation, the man, who, disobeying the orders of his superiors, trampling on the laws and constitution of his country, sacrificing the liberties and lives of men, has made his own arbitrary will, the rule of his conduct....

For civil government,—and in no station more emphatically, than in that of President of the United States,—a well governed temper is of admitted importance; Gen. Jackson's friends lament the impetuosity[1] of his, and all the work has evidence of its fiery misrule.

To maintain peace and harmony, in the delicate relations existing between the government of the Union and the various State governments, in our confederacy, requires a courtesy and forbearance in their intercourse, which no passions should disturb....

[Our claims] in accusing General Jackson of being unmindful of their [law and constitution]... will be acknowledged by impartial posterity, when they review the history of his Indian campaigns—and especially when they read the stories, of the cold blooded massacre, at the Horse-shoe [Bend]—and of the decoyed and slaughtered [Seminole] Indians at St. Mark's [in Florida]....

[W]e regard Gen. Jackson, as wholly disqualified for the Presidency, and look to the prospect of his election with forebodings."

[1] Recklessness.

Questions for Analysis
1. Identify the main criticisms leveled against Jackson in this excerpt.
2. Explain how the criticisms of Jackson in this excerpt play to the perceived strengths of his opponent in the 1828 election.

Source: *New Jersey Pro-Jackson Convention*, 1828

"[Andrew Jackson] is an American, and nothing but an American. Without the aid of family or patronage, his intrinsic merit alone, has placed him before the American people, as worthy of the highest honours of the country.... His entire devotion to his country's welfare; his stern integrity; his unbending republican simplicity; his enlarged and national views, commend themselves to the intelligence and affections of a free and generous people."

(Continued)

TRM Suggested Responses to Questions

TRM Module 4.4 AP® Analyzing Sources Handout 1

TEACHING IDEA

Creating Campaign Posters

The election of 1828 was notorious for the mudslinging campaign that took place between President John Quincy Adams and the Democrats' nominee, General Andrew Jackson. Divide the class into groups of three and have them create a political campaign poster for and one against the nomination of Andrew Jackson for president of the United States. Possible campaign angles included in italics.

- For Jackson: *military hero*, "*common man*," "*self-made man*," and "*champion of democracy*."

- Against Jackson: *immoral* (*bigamist with his wife Rachel*), "*American Indian killer*," and "*mobocracy*."

Students may also want to include some references to the incumbent, President John Quincy Adams, and refer to him as an "elitist" or an experienced "statesman" depending on their position.

EXPLORING AP® THEMES

Politics and Power

Write the following question on the board: Is the abuse of federal power more consistent with Federalist ideology or that of the Democrats? Then, provide students with a copy of the Alien and Sedition Acts under President John Adams and the political cartoon of "King Andrew" (available through online search). After reading and analyzing the political cartoon, conduct a discussion on the abuse of power. Is it something that occurs across political party lines and has more to do with who is in charge than with political ideology? Allow students to share their answers.

TEACHING IDEA

Incorporating Primary Sources

Provide students with a copy of the First Inaugural Address of Andrew Jackson. Visit the Yale Avalon Project site and look under 19th Century Documents to obtain the text (avalon.law.yale.edu). After everyone reads the address, conduct a class discussion on the main objectives expressed by the new president. Clarify any student misunderstandings.

BUILDING AP® SKILLS

Comparison

In this Analyzing Sources section, you may want to ask the students the additional question, "Briefly describe ONE major difference between the *Proceedings of the Anti-Jackson Convention in Richmond*, 1828 and the *New Jersey Pro-Jackson Convention*, 1828 characterization of Andrew Jackson."

APPLY THE TIP

Have students research the inauguration of President Andrew Jackson and the subsequent celebration at the White House and then have them draw connections to the theme American and national identity. Specifically, provide them with a copy of Robert Cruikshank's print, "President's Levee or All Creation Going to the White House" available from the Library of Congress (loc.gov). Then have them complete the following chart from the Teacher's Resource Materials to analyze the following VISUAL criteria: Visual, Interpretation, Symbols, Understanding, Analysis, Limitations. Afterward, conduct a class discussion on how Andrew Jackson's election ushered in a new era of populism and mass politics that transformed American society and the nation's identity.

TRM Find **Handout 4.5 – Interpreting Visuals** in the Teacher's Resource Materials.

Andrew Jackson was rocked in the cradle of the Revolution. His mind is deeply imbued with the spirit and principles, which, at that day, pervaded the community, and gave a tone to public feeling. While yet a boy, he stood forth in defense of his country's rights, and gave earnest of that lofty spirit of independence, which has ever since characterized the man, whether in the field, the senate chamber, or the retirement of domestic life. . . .

General Jackson has long been known to the American people, as a firm and incorruptible patriot; an honest and able politician, and a virtuous man, yet, a system of warfare has been opened upon him, at which candour and decency must blush and be ashamed. . . .

And why is it that such desperate efforts are made to tarnish the fame of General Jackson? It is because he is sustained by the people, and is advancing with sure and rapid strides in their affections. It is that ill-gotten power may be retained, until the line of safe precedents shall be better established. Those who are now in power, are aware, that they have been weighed and found wanting. Fear hath taken hold of them, and their hour is at hand. Hence it is that every means is resorted to, and truth and honesty sacrificed, to accomplish their unhallowed purpose."

Questions for Analysis

1. Identify the main points argued in favor of Jackson in this excerpt.
2. Describe how this excerpt characterizes opposition to Jackson's campaign.

Questions for Comparison

1. Explain how these sources reflect the new, popular campaign style introduced during the 1828 presidential election.
2. Evaluate the extent to which each document bases its argument on Jackson's personal character versus his actions in office or his political agenda.

REVIEW

How did the election of 1828 lead to the rise of a second party system?

A Democratic Spirit?

AP® TIP
Evaluate the degree to which the inauguration of Andrew Jackson illustrated a change in American national identity.

On March 4, 1829, crowds of ordinary citizens came to see Jackson's inauguration. Jackson's wife, Rachel, had died of heart failure shortly after his election, leaving her husband devastated. Now Jackson, dressed in a plain black suit, walked alone to the Capitol as vast throngs of supporters waved and cheered. A somber Jackson read a brief inaugural address, took the oath of office, and then rode his horse through the crowds to the White House.

The size and enthusiasm of the crowds soon shattered the decorum of the inauguration. Author Margaret Bayard Smith reported mobs "scrambling, fighting, [and] romping" through the White House reception. Jackson was nearly crushed to death by "rabble" eager to shake his hand. Tubs of punch laced with rum, brandy, and champagne were finally placed on the lawn to draw the crowds outdoors.

While Jackson and his supporters viewed the event as a symbol of a new democratic spirit, others were less optimistic. Bayard Smith and other conservative political leaders saw echoes of the French Revolution in the unruly behavior of the masses. Supreme Court justice Joseph Story, too, feared "the reign of King 'Mob.'"

Tensions between the president and the capital's traditional leaders intensified when Jackson appointed Tennessee senator John Eaton as secretary of war. Eaton had had an affair with a woman thought to be of questionable character and later married her. When Jackson announced his plans to appoint Eaton to his cabinet, congressional leaders urged him to reconsider. When the president appointed Eaton anyway, the wives of Washington's leading politicians snubbed Mrs. Eaton. This time Jackson was outmaneuvered in what became known as the **Petticoat Affair**, and Eaton was eventually forced from office.

A Democratic Spirit?

Period 4: 1800–1848

AP® ANALYZING SOURCES

Source: Alexis de Tocqueville, *Letter to Louis de Kergorlay*, 1831

"My American informants tell me that there was no aristocracy but, instead a class of great landowners leading a simple, rather intellectual life characterized by its air of good breeding, its manners, and a strong sense of family pride. . . .

The aristocratic bias that marked the republic's early years was replaced by a democratic thrust of irresistible force. . . . I've seen several members of these old families. . . . They regret the loss of everything aristocratic: patronage, family pride, high tone. . . .

What I see in America leaves me doubting that government by the multitude, even under the most favorable circumstances—and they exist here—is a good thing. There is general agreement that in the early days of the republic, statesmen and members of the two legislative houses were much more distinguished than they are today. They almost all belonged to that class of landowners I mentioned above. The populace no longer chooses with such a sure hand. It generally favors those who flatter its passions and descend to its level."

Questions for Analysis

1. Describe how de Tocqueville's letter characterizes American political democracy.
2. Explain how a specific historical development in the early 1800s changed American political democracy in the ways de Tocqueville describes in his letter.
3. Explain how the 1828 presidential election and events in Jackson's first term created a context for de Tocqueville's argument.

TRM Suggested Responses to Questions

TRM Module 4.4 AP® Analyzing Sources Handout 2

TEACHING IDEA

Incorporating Secondary Sources

Give students excerpts from Alexis de Tocqueville's *Democracy in America*. This book provides an analysis of the political and social structures of the era, including the inherent contradictions of Americans loving freedom while still embracing the institution of slavery and mistreating American Indians. Since this is such a large work divided in two volumes, focus on the Introduction, Chapter III: Social Condition of the Anglo-Americans, or Chapter XVIII: The Present and Probable Future Condition of the Three Races that Inhabit the Territory of the United States.

In the aftermath of Eaton's resignation, Jackson asked his entire cabinet to resign so he could begin anew. Afterward, however, his legislative agenda stalled in Congress, and National Republicans regained the momentum they had lost with Adams's defeat. The Petticoat Affair reinforced concerns that the president used his authority to reward his friends, as did his reliance on an informal group of advisers, known as the Kitchen Cabinet. While his administration opened up government posts to a wider range of individuals, ensuring more democratic access, Jackson often selected appointees based on personal ties. He believed that "to the victor goes the spoils," and the resulting **spoils system**—continued by future administrations—assigned federal posts as gifts for partisan loyalty rather than as jobs that required experience or expertise.

spoils system Patronage system introduced by Andrew Jackson in which federal offices were awarded on the basis of political loyalty. The system remained in place until the late nineteenth century.

REVIEW

In what ways did President Jackson break from traditional political norms during his first term in office?

AP® WRITING HISTORICALLY — Short-Answer Question Practice

ACTIVITY

Read the following question carefully and write a short response. Use complete sentences.

Using the following excerpts, answer (a), (b), and (c).

Source: Alexander Keyssar, *Broadening the Franchise*, 2000

"[T]he disfranchised were unable to precipitate change by themselves. When the right to vote was enlarged, it happened because some men who were already enfranchised . . . saw themselves as having a direct interest in enlarging the electorate. One such interest was military preparedness. . . . [A]fter the War of 1812, many middle-class citizens concluded

(Continued)

TRM Suggested Responses to Questions

TEACHING IDEA

Class Discussion

Write the following quote and question on the board: "To the victor goes the spoils!" Should loyal political friends and supporters be rewarded with government jobs? Then ask students if it might be a better option to hire the most qualified individuals for any given position and consider their levels of experience and expertise. Or is it more democratic to eliminate an entrenched privileged elite? After students share out their answers, discuss the pros and cons of the "spoils system."

TEACHING IDEA

AP® Writing Historically Review

When students encounter brief excerpts by historians, it is essential that they decode the basic argument. Sometimes, students misinterpret excerpts because of confusion over the words historians use. For example, in the first excerpt students might need help with the following words: precipitate, enfranchised, and solidarity. In the second excerpt, the following words might necessitate explanation: foiled, grassroots, and populist. Consider the long-term: You are helping build students' vocabulary now so they can define difficult words independently later in the year.

EXPLORING AP® THEMES

Politics and Power

Help students make a thematic connection between the expansion of suffrage to the "common white man" in the 1820s and 1830s and voting requirements in the present day. Discuss how expanding suffrage to certain groups may benefit those in charge.

TEACHING IDEA

AP® Central

Use question 3 of the 2014 AP® U.S. History exam LEQ on the Democrats and Whigs, which is available on the College Board's AP® U.S. History Past Exam Questions section under "2014: Free-Response Questions" (apcentral.collegeboard.org).

TEACHING IDEA

Check for Understanding

For students struggling with how to approach this SAQ practice, guide them through the following steps. In answering (a), have students look for an important way the two historians differ by considering the groups of people they discuss, the types of factors they emphasize (e.g., political, economic, social, geographic), their overall assessment of the changes, or another significant difference. If students struggle to identify and explain a difference, ask them to approach the task in (a) by summarizing and then contrasting the main point of each excerpt. Be sure students cite evidence in the form of a very short quote from or specific reference to each excerpt and explain how the evidence they cited illustrates the difference they highlighted. Continue to prompt students to use the *ACE* strategy in parts (b) and (c) as they provide a significant and relevant piece of historical information not mentioned in the excerpts, and use it to support that historian's interpretation (a refresher on *ACE* can be found on page 21). Students should strive for a fully developed, nine sentence response to this SAQ. Refer to the Writing Historically feature at the end of Module 2-6 for more guidance on how to answer an SAQ with secondary sources.

---

that extending the franchise to the 'lower orders' would enhance their own security and help to preserve their way of life, by assuring that such men would continue to serve in the army and the militias. . . .

In the South, the issue had an added twist: enfranchising all white Southerners was a means of making sure that poor whites would serve in militia patrols guarding against slave rebellions. . . . [And] it would contribute to white solidarity. . . . Economic self-interest also played a role in the expansion of the franchise. . . . As territories began to organize themselves into states, inhabitants of sparsely populated regions embraced white manhood suffrage, . . . believ[ing] that a broad franchise would encourage settlement and in so doing . . . stimulate economic development. . . ."

Source: James Oliver Horton and Lois E. Horton, *The Limits of Democratic Expansion*, 1997

"The expansion of the franchise for white men, however, was often accompanied by the restriction or elimination of the franchise for black men. . . . [T]hrough the early years of the nineteenth century . . . Federalists . . . foiled several attempts to institute racial restrictions. The War of 1812 was a turning point. . . . Discredited by their opposition to the war, Federalists lost control of state politics and were unable to stop Republicans . . . from limiting the black vote. . . . As the roster of eligible white voters expanded in every state, . . . a new political grassroots style brought General Andrew Jackson to the presidency in 1828. Political parties vied for the votes of common working people, and candidates portrayed themselves as ordinary men. . . . This 'age of the common man' was the age of the common white man, as black men . . . lost the franchise in many states. Party politics became a struggle between white men for the support and loyalty of other white men. Although the Jacksonians' political ideology was populist in that it attacked a somewhat vague 'privilege,' [it] incorporate[ed] a growing belief in white superiority and [a] distinctly racial orientation. . . ."

a. Briefly explain ONE major difference between Keyssar's and James Horton's and Lois Horton's interpretations of the changes in voting rights.
b. Briefly explain how ONE specific historical event or development from the period that is not explicitly mentioned in the excerpts could be used to support Keyssar's argument.
c. Briefly explain how ONE specific historical event or development that is not explicitly mentioned in the excerpts could be used to support James Horton's and Lois Horton's argument.

Module 4-5

Conflicts of the Jacksonian Era

LEARNING TARGETS

By the end of this module, you should be able to:
- Explain the causes and effects of major political controversies in the 1830s.
- Explain the causes and effects of the Panic of 1837.

THEMATIC FOCUS
Politics and Power

Debates about the use of federal power — including its ability to impose tariffs, the continued existence of the Bank of the United States, and American Indian policy — contributed to sectional crises over developments such as state nullification of federal tariffs, the forced relocation of thousands of American Indians, the Panic of 1837, and the formation of the Whig Party.

HISTORICAL REASONING FOCUS
Causation

TASK ▶ As you read this module, consider how battles over tariff rates, the re-chartering the Bank of the United States, and the land claims of American Indians all shaped the events leading into the 1830s. Be sure to take note of the ways in which the political and economic challenges in the 1830s changed American politics, affected the lives of American Indians, and deepened sectional divisions between the North and South.

TRM Suggested Responses to Questions

President Andrew Jackson hoped to make government more responsive to the needs of white workers and frontier farmers. But Jackson's notion of democracy did not extend to American Indians or African Americans. During his presidency, American Indian nations actively resisted his efforts to take more of their land, and African Americans continued to resist their enslavement. Of more immediate importance, once President Jackson had to take clear positions on tariffs and other controversial issues, he could not please all of his constituents. Jackson also confronted experienced adversaries like Henry Clay, Daniel Webster, and former president John Quincy Adams, who was elected to the House of Representatives from Massachusetts in 1830. President Jackson thus faced considerable difficulty in translating popular support into public policy.

Confrontations over Tariffs and the Bank

The Democratic Party that emerged in the late 1820s was built on an unstable foundation. The coalition that formed around Jackson included northern workers who benefited from high tariffs as well as southern farmers and planters who did not. It brought together western voters who sought federal support for internal improvements and strict constructionists who believed such expenditures were unconstitutional. In nearly every legislative battle, then, decisiveness aroused conflict. In 1830 Congress passed four internal improvement bills with strong support from National Republicans. Jackson vetoed each one, which pleased his southern constituency but not his frontier supporters.

Southern congressmen, however, were more interested in his stand on tariffs. The tariff of 1828 still enraged many southern planters and politicians, but most believed that once Jackson reached the White House, he would reverse course and reduce this **Tariff of Abominations**. Instead, he avoided the issue, and southern agriculture continued to suffer. Agricultural productivity in Virginia and other states of the Old South was declining from

Tariff of Abominations White southerners' name for the 1828 tariff act that benefited northern manufacturers and merchants at the expense of agriculture, especially southern plantations.

TEACHING IDEA

Class Discussion

As a bell ringer, start the class with a timeline of the main political controversies between 1830 and 1840: 1) tariffs (and nullification); 2) the Second Bank of the United States; 3) American Indians' rights and role in American society; and 4) the Panic of 1837. Students can refer to the timeline in the review section at the end of Period 4 for guidance. Also point out that during this entire time, both nationalism and sectionalism were growing simultaneously. To conclude, tell students to focus on the causes and effects of these major political controversies as the material is covered in class.

BUILDING AP® SKILLS

Making Connections

One of the main political battles in the 1830s was over the "Tariff of Abominations," which most southerners adamantly opposed. This eventually led South Carolina to argue for nullification, which eventually turned into a crisis by 1832. Have students connect back to material previously covered where nullification had come up. Specifically, students should connect to the Virginia Resolution (written by James Madison) and the Kentucky Resolution (written by Thomas Jefferson) that were based on the "compact theory." Conclude the activity by having a discussion on whether it should be up to the federal government and/or states to decide what is constitutional. Point out that the Federalists had flirted with the idea of nullification back in the Hartford Convention during the War of 1812.

TEACHING IDEA

AP® Central

Use question 3 of the 2003 AP® U.S. History exam LEQ on nullification as a bell ringer. Have students outline the specific historical evidence they would use to develop an answer. This question is available on the College Board's AP® U.S. History Past Exam Questions section under "2003: Form B" (apcentral.collegeboard.org).

TRM Suggested Responses to Questions

TRM Module 4.5 AP® Analyzing Sources Handout 1

TEACHING IDEA

Incorporating Primary Sources

Give students a copy of the Daniel Webster v. Robert Hayne's debate over tariffs and nullification, which can be found on Teaching American History's website (teachingamericanhistory.org). The Webster-Hayne debates that took place on the Senate floor in 1830 should be read for homework and then discussed during the following class. Specifically, ask students to examine the evidence used by each senator to support their claims.

Period 4: 1800–1848

MODULE 4-5 Conflicts of the Jacksonian Era

soil exhaustion, while prices for cotton and rice had not fully recovered after the Panic of 1819. At the same time, higher duties on manufactured items raised prices for southerners on many goods.

Even as Calhoun campaigned with Jackson in 1828, the South Carolinian developed a philosophical argument to negate the effects of high tariffs on his state. In *The South Carolina Exposition and Protest*, published anonymously in 1828, Calhoun argued that states should have the ultimate power to determine the constitutionality of laws passed by Congress. When Jackson, after taking office, realized that his vice president advocated **nullification** — the right of individual states to declare individual laws void within their borders — it further damaged their relationship, which was already frayed by the Petticoat Affair (see Module 4-4).

nullification The doctrine that individual states have the right to declare federal laws unconstitutional and, therefore, void within their borders. South Carolina attempted to invoke the doctrine of nullification in response to the tariff of 1832.

AP® ANALYZING SOURCES

Source: John C. Calhoun, *Address to the Southern States*, 1831

"The great and leading principle is, that the General Government emanated from the people of the several states, forming distinct political communities, and acting in their separate and sovereign capacity, and not from all the people forming one aggregate political community; that the Constitution of the United States is, in fact, a compact, to which each state is a Party, . . . and that the several states, or parties, have the right to judge of its infractions; . . . be it called what it may — State-right, veto, nullification, or by any other name — I conceive it to be the fundamental principle of our system, resting on facts as certain as our revolution itself, . . . and I firmly believe that on its recognition depend the stability and safety of our political institutions. . . .

Whenever separate and dissimilar interests have been separately represented in government; whenever the sovereign power has been divided in its exercise, the experience and wisdom of ages have devised but one mode by which such political organization can be preserved . . . to give each co-estate the right to judge of its powers, with a negative or veto on the acts of the others, in order to protect against encroachments the interests it particularly represents."

Questions for Analysis

1. Identify Calhoun's purpose in giving this address.
2. Describe the context surrounding Calhoun's address.
3. Evaluate the extent to which Calhoun's argument reflects the political debates and growing sectional tensions of the 1820s and 1830s.

When Congress debated the tariff issue in 1830, South Carolina senator Robert Hayne defended nullification. Claiming that the North intended to crush the South economically, he argued that only the right of states to nullify federal legislation could protect southern society. In response, Daniel Webster denounced nullification and the states' rights doctrine on which it was built. Jackson further antagonized southern political leaders by supporting Webster's position.

Matters worsened in 1832 when Congress confirmed the high duties set four years earlier. In response South Carolina held a special convention that approved an **Ordinance of Nullification**. It stated that duties on imports would not be collected in the state after February 1, 1833, and threatened secession if federal authorities tried to collect them.

Ordinance of Nullification 1832 law passed by South Carolina proclaiming several congressional tariff acts null and void within the state and threatening secession if the federal government attempted to enforce the tariffs.

The tariff crisis thus escalated in the fall of 1832 just as Jackson faced reelection. The tariff debates had angered many southerners, and Calhoun refused to run again as his vice president. Fortunately for Jackson, opponents in Congress had provided him with another issue that could unite his supporters and highlight his commitment to ordinary citizens: the renewal of the charter of the Bank of the United States.

Period 4: 1800–1848

AP® TIP
Analyze how Jackson administration policies affected both the power of the federal government and regional divisions in the U.S.

Clay and Webster persuaded Nicholas Biddle, head of the bank, to request an early recharter of the bank. Jackson's opponents in Congress knew they had the votes to pass a new charter in the summer of 1832, and they hoped Jackson would veto the bill and thereby split the Democratic Party just before the fall elections. The Second Bank was nothing short of a political mess. The bank had stabilized the economy during the 1820s by regularly demanding gold or silver payments from state-chartered banks. This kept those banks from issuing too much paper money and thereby prevented inflation and higher prices. This tight-money policy also kept banks from expanding too rapidly in the western states. Most financial elites applauded the bank's efforts, but its policies created hostility among the wider public. When state-chartered banks closed because of lack of gold or silver payments, ordinary Americans were often stuck with worthless paper money. Tight-money policies also made it more difficult for individuals to get credit to purchase land, homes, or farm equipment.

As the president's opponents had hoped, Congress approved the new charter, and Jackson vetoed it. Yet rather than dividing the Democrats, Jackson's veto gained enormous support from voters across the country. In justifying his action, the president cast the Second Bank as a "monster" that was "dangerous to the liberties of the people" — particularly farmers, mechanics, and laborers — while promoting "the advancement of the few." Finally, Jackson noted that since wealthy Britons owned substantial shares of the bank's stock, national pride demanded ending the Second Bank's reign over the U.S. economy. Jackson rode the enthusiasm for his bank veto to reelection over National Republican candidate Henry Clay. Within a year, the Second Bank was dead, deprived of government deposits by Jackson.

Soon after his reelection, however, the president faced a grave political crisis related to the tariff issue. Jackson now supported lower tariffs, but he was adamant in his opposition to nullification. In early 1833, he persuaded Congress to pass a **Force Bill**, which gave him authority to use the military to enforce national laws in South Carolina. At the same time, Jackson made clear that he would work with Congress to reduce tariffs. The resulting Tariff of 1833, negotiated by Henry Clay, gradually lowered import duties over the next decade allowing South Carolina to rescind its nullification ordinance without losing face. However, in a symbolic act of resistance, South Carolina nullified the Force Bill. Open conflict was avoided, but the question of nullification remained unresolved.

Force Bill 1833 bill passed by Congress in response to South Carolina's Ordinance of Nullification. It gave the president the authority to use military force to enforce national laws.

REVIEW
Why did issues involving tariff rates and the Bank of the United States cause political discord during the 1820s and 1830s?

The Battle for Texas

As southern agriculture expanded westward during the early nineteenth century, some whites looked toward Texas for fresh land. White southerners had begun moving into eastern Texas in the early nineteenth century, but the Adams-Onís Treaty of 1819 (see Module 4-2) guaranteed Spanish control of the territory. Then in 1821 Mexicans overthrew Spanish rule and claimed Texas as part of the new Republic of Mexico. But Mexicans faced serious competition from Comanche Indians, who controlled vast areas in northern Mexico and launched frequent raids into Texas.

Eager to increase settlement in the area and to create a buffer against the Comanche, the Mexican government granted U.S. migrants some of the best land in eastern Texas. It hoped these settlers would eventually spread into the interior, where Comanche raids had devastated Mexican communities. To entice more southerners, the Mexican government negotiated a special exemption for U.S. planters when it outlawed slavery in 1829. But rather than spreading into the interior, American migrants stayed east of the Colorado River, out of reach of Comanche raids and close to U.S. markets in Louisiana.

Moreover, U.S. settlers resisted assimilation into Mexican society. Instead, they continued to worship as Protestants, speak English, send their children to separate schools, and trade mainly with the United States. By 1835 the 27,000 white southerners and 3,000 enslaved people far outnumbered the 3,000 Mexicans living in eastern Texas.

TEACHING IDEA

Understanding the Bank War

Have students research the arguments for and against the re-charter of the Second Bank of the United States in the 1830s. They must identify who supported and opposed it and their reasoning. Possible answers included in italics.

- Support: *Nicholas Biddle*, *National Republicans — then Whigs* (e.g., *Henry Clay* and *Daniel Webster*), *businessmen and merchant class*.
  - Reasoning: *Supporters believed the Second Bank of the United States was necessary to have a strong and stable economy.*
- Opposition: *President Andrew Jackson*, *Democrats*, and *farmers*.
  - Reasoning: *Those in opposition mistrusted the institution that they believed benefitted eastern elites.*

▲ **Differentiation**

To supplement this activity, have students search for political cartoons depicting the "bank war" and identifying how President Andrew Jackson eventually killed this financial institution. For specific examples, look up in the Library of Congress (loc.gov): 1) General Jackson Slaying the Many Headed Monsters; 2) The Downfall of Mother Bank; 3) The Doctors Puzzled or the Desperate Case of Mother U.S. Bank; 4) Set to Between Old Hickory and Bully Nick; or 5) Symptoms of a Locked Jaw. Plain Sewing Done Here.

BUILDING AP® SKILLS

Developments and Processes

Have students research Stephen Austin and Sam Houston and focus on their contributions to settling the area and leading the Texas independence movement. Specifically, tell students to highlight the role each played in the history of the "Lone Star State" and the impact the independence movement had on the *Tejanos* (Mexican Americans in Texas), and how it became a political issue for the United States.

TEACHING IDEA

Incorporating Websites

Visit the Stanford History Education Group site to obtain a lesson plan on the Texas Revolution (sheg.stanford.edu). Specifically, this lesson focuses on the causes of this independence movement. Was the government of Mexico to blame, or the American settlers who refused to assimilate, or both? What role did the U.S. government play?

Forming a majority of the east Texas population and eager to expand their plantations and trade networks, growing numbers of U.S. settlers demanded independence. Then in 1836 Mexicans elected a strong nationalist leader, General Antonio López de Santa Anna, as president. He sought to calm **Tejanos** (Mexican Texans) angered by their vulnerability to Comanche attacks and to curb U.S. settlers seeking further concessions. However, when Santa Anna appointed a military commander to rule Texas, U.S. migrants organized a rebellion and, on March 2, declared their independence. Some elite Tejanos, long neglected by authorities in Mexico City, sided with the rebels. But the rebellion appeared to be short lived. On March 6, 1836, General Santa Anna crushed settlers defending the **Alamo** in San Antonio. Soon thereafter, he captured the U.S. settlement at Goliad.

Alamo Texas fort captured by General Santa Anna on March 6, 1836, from rebel defenders. Sensationalist accounts of the siege of the Alamo increased popular support in the United States for Texas independence.

AP® ANALYZING SOURCES

Source: *Texas Declaration of Independence,* 1836

"When a government has ceased to protect the lives, liberty and property of the people, from whom its legitimate powers are derived, and for the advancement of whose happiness it was instituted, and . . . becomes an instrument in the hands of evil rulers for their oppression.

When . . . the whole nature of their government has been forcibly changed, without their consent, from a restricted federative republic, composed of sovereign states, to a consolidated central military despotism, in which every interest is disregarded but that of the army and the priesthood, both the eternal enemies of civil liberty . . . and the usual instruments of tyrants. . . .

When . . . anarchy prevails, and civil society is dissolved into its original elements. In such a crisis, . . . the inherent and inalienable rights of the people to . . . take their political affairs into their own hands in extreme cases, enjoins it as a right towards themselves, and a sacred obligation to their posterity, to abolish such government, and create another in its stead, calculated to rescue them from impending dangers, and to secure their future welfare and happiness.

Nations, as well as individuals, are amenable for their acts to the public opinion of mankind. A statement of a part of our grievances is therefore submitted to an impartial world, in justification of the hazardous but unavoidable step now taken, of severing our political connection with the Mexican people, and assuming an independent attitude among the nations of the earth."

Questions for Analysis

1. Identify the main points of this excerpt from the Texas Declaration of Independence.
2. Describe the events that led Texans to declare their independence.
3. Evaluate the extent to which Texas's independence influenced U.S. politics and westward settlement during the mid-1800s.

Questions for Comparison   Thomas Jefferson, *Declaration of Independence,* 1776 (p. 179)

1. Evaluate the extent of similarity between the grievances listed in the Texas Declaration of Independence and the U.S. Declaration of Independence.
2. Evaluate the extent of difference between the relationship of England and the thirteen colonies with that of Mexico and the territory of Texas.
3. Evaluate the extent to which the Texas Declaration of Independence was modeled on the U.S. Declaration of Independence.

At this point, Santa Anna was convinced that the uprising was over. But the U.S. government, despite its claims of neutrality, aided the rebels with funds and army officers. American newspapers picked up the story of the Alamo and published personal accounts of the battle, describing the Mexican fighters as brutal butchers bent on saving Texas for the pope. These stories, though more fable than fact, increased popular support for the war at a time when many Americans were increasingly hostile to Catholic immigrants in the United States.

TRM Suggested Responses to Questions

TRM Module 4.5 AP® Analyzing Sources Handout 2

TEACHING IDEA

Incorporating Websites

Have students visit the website The Alamo: the Mission, the Battle, the Legend so they can "Remember the Alamo!" (thealamo.org). Additionally, students should investigate Davy Crockett to determine what is historically accurate as opposed to fable by exploring the following resources:

- NPR's author interview with Bob Thompson on his book, *Born on a Mountaintop: On the Road with Davy Crockett and the Ghosts of the Wild Frontier* (npr.org).
- Evan Andrews's article, "10 Things You May Not Know About Davy Crocket," which can be found on the History Channel's website (history.com).

EXPLORING AP® THEMES

Politics and Power

Make thematic connections to the revolutionary period. Specifically, have students research how the political theories of John Locke (i.e., natural rights) and Jean-Jacques Rousseau (i.e., social contract theory) influenced the Texas Declaration of Independence in 1836. Ask students to make a connection between anti-Catholic sentiments in Texas at that time and colonial America in the aftermath of the passage of the Quebec Act.

As hundreds of armed volunteers headed to Texas, General Sam Houston led rebel forces in a critical victory at San Jacinto in April 1836. While the Mexican government refused to recognize rebel claims, it did not try to regain the lost territory. Few of the U.S. volunteers arrived in time to participate in the fighting, but some settled in the newly liberated region. The Comanche nation quickly recognized the Republic of Texas and developed trade relations with residents to gain access to the vast U.S. market. Still, Santa Anna's failure to recognize Texas independence kept the U.S. government from granting the territory statehood for fear it would lead to war with Mexico.

President Jackson also worried that admitting a new slave state might split the national Democratic Party before the fall elections. To limit debate on the issue, Congress passed a **gag rule** in March 1836 that tabled all antislavery petitions without being read. Nevertheless, thousands of antislavery activists still flooded the House of Representatives with petitions opposing the annexation of Texas.

gag rule Rule passed by the House of Representatives in 1836 to postpone action on all antislavery petitions without hearing them read in an attempt to stifle debate over slavery. It was renewed annually until it was rescinded in 1844.

REVIEW

- What factors led to the Battle of Texas?

American Indians Resist Removal

AP® TIP

Compare the federal government policies during the early nineteenth century to government policies toward American Indians both during the colonial era and the late eighteenth century.

Under Jackson, the United States also faced continued challenges from American Indian nations. The acquisition of American Indian land was another long-standing issue that earned Jackson the support of white southerners and most frontier settlers. Yet not all Americans agreed with his effort to force American Indians off their lands. In the 1820s nations like the Cherokee gained the support of Protestant missionaries who hoped to "civilize" American Indians by converting them to Christianity and "American" ways. Congress had previously granted these groups federal funds to advance these goals. Jackson, however, was unsupportive of such efforts and sided with political leaders who sought to force eastern American Indians to accept homelands west of the Mississippi River.

In 1825, three years before Jackson was elected president, Creek Indians in Georgia and Alabama were forcibly removed to the Unorganized Territory (previously part of Arkansas Territory and later called Indian Territory) based on a fraudulent treaty. Jackson supported this policy. When he became president, politicians and settlers in Georgia, Florida, the Carolinas, and Illinois demanded federal assistance to force American Indian communities out of their states.

The largest American Indian nations vehemently protested their removal. The Cherokee, who had fought alongside Jackson at Horseshoe Bend, adopted a republican form of government in 1827 based on the U.S. Constitution. John Ross served as the president of the Cherokee constitutional convention and a year later was elected principal chief. He and the other chiefs then declared themselves a sovereign nation within the borders of the United States. The Georgia legislature rejected Cherokee claims of independence and argued that American Indians were simply guests of the state, a position that gained added significance when gold was discovered in Cherokee territory in 1829. Ross appealed to Jackson to recognize Cherokee sovereignty, but the president was offended by what he saw as a challenge to his authority. He urged Congress to pass the **Indian Removal Act** in 1830, by which the Cherokee and other American Indian nations would be forced to exchange their lands in the Southeast for a "clear title forever" on territory west of the Mississippi River. The majority of Cherokees refused to accept these terms.

Indian Removal Act 1830 act, supported by President Andrew Jackson, by which American Indian peoples in the East were forced to exchange their lands for territory west of the Mississippi River.

AP® ANALYZING SOURCES

Source: *Indian Removal Act*, 1830

"AN ACT to provide for an exchange of lands with the Indians residing in any of the States or Territories, and for their removal west of the river Mississippi.

Be it enacted, &c., That it shall and may be lawful for... any territory belonging to the United States, west of the river Mississippi, not included in any State or organized Territory... to be

(Continued)

TEACHING IDEA

Incorporating Websites

To better understand how the Cherokee used the judicial system to attempt to protect their rights, have students read and brief *Cherokee Nation v. the State of Georgia*, which can be found in its entirety on the Library of Congress website (loc.gov). Afterward, have them read Tyler Boulware's article, "Cherokee Indians" from the New Georgia Encyclopedia (georgiaencyclopedia.org) to develop a better understanding of this tribe.

BUILDING AP® SKILLS

Developments and Processes

Some American Indian tribes attempted to become more "civilized" or "Americanized" so they could be left alone. Have students identify some of the main ways groups like the Cherokee tried to become more like white Americans. Possible answers include: *converting to Christianity*; *adopting a republican form of government based on a constitution*; *creating a written language*; *embracing white gender roles*; *and even becoming slaveholders*.

TRM Suggested Responses to Questions

TRM Module 4.5 AP® Analyzing Sources Handout 3

TEACHING IDEA

Understanding People Who Made a Difference

Have students research Sequoyah and focus on his contributions to Cherokee society. Specifically, tell students to focus on his development of a syllabary and how doing so helped his community become more "civilized" in the eyes of mainstream Americans. Lastly, have students look up Elias Boudinot and the Cherokee Phoenix newspaper.

TEACHING IDEA

Understanding People Who Made a Difference

Have students research Black Hawk and Osceola and focus on their contributions to defend their respective American Indian tribes from the encroachment by white Americans.

APPLY THE TIP

To better understand how the Supreme Court of the United States attempted to help American Indian tribes resist violations against their sovereignty during the nineteenth century, have students read a summary of *Worcester v. Georgia* from Oyez's website (oyez.org). Afterward, have them read Tim Alan Garrison's article, "*Worcester v. Georgia* (1832)," from the New Georgia Encyclopedia (georgiaencyclopedia.org).

---

divided into a suitable number of districts, for the reception of such tribes or nations of Indians as may choose to exchange the lands where they now reside, and remove there . . .

Sec. 2. *And be it further enacted*, That it shall and may be lawful for the President to exchange any or all of such districts . . . with any tribe or nation of Indians . . . with which the United States have existing treaties, for the whole or any part or portion of the territory claimed and occupied by such tribe or nation . . . where the land claimed and occupied by the Indians, is owned by the United States, or the United States are bound to the State within which it lies to extinguish the Indian claim thereto.

Sec. 3. *And be it further enacted*, That . . . it shall and may be lawful for the President solemnly to assure the tribe or nation with which the exchange is made, that the United States will forever secure and guaranty to them, and their heirs or successors, the country so exchanged with them . . . *Provided always*, That such lands shall revert to the United States, if the Indians become extinct, or abandon the same. . . .

Sec. 8. *And be it further enacted*, That for the purpose of giving effect to the provisions of this act, the sum of five hundred thousand dollars is hereby appropriated. . . ."

Questions for Analysis

1. Identify the main provisions of this excerpt from the Indian Removal Act.
2. Explain the factors that led to passage of the Indian Removal Act.
3. Evaluate the extent to which the Indian Removal Act represented a continuity in U.S. government relations with American Indians.

AP® TIP
Be sure you can explain how various American Indian tribes resisted removal during the nineteenth century.

Second Seminole War 1835–1842 war between the Seminoles, including enslaved African Americans who had escaped captivity and had joined the tribe, and the U.S. government over whether the Seminoles would be forced to leave Florida and settle west of the Mississippi River. Despite substantial investments of men, money, and resources, it took seven years for the United States to achieve victory.

Cherokee Nation v. Georgia 1831 Supreme Court ruling that denied the Cherokee claim to be a separate independent nation, ruling that all American Indian nations were "domestic dependent nations" rather than fully sovereign governments.

As the dispute between the Cherokee nation and Georgia unfolded, Jackson made clear his intention to implement the Indian Removal Act. In 1832 he sent federal troops into western Illinois to force Sauk and Fox peoples to move farther west. Instead, whole villages, led by Chief Black Hawk, fled to the Wisconsin Territory. Black Hawk and a thousand warriors confronted U.S. troops at Bad Axe, but the Sauk and Fox warriors were decimated in a brutal daylong battle. The survivors were forced to move west. Meanwhile the Seminole Indians prepared to go to war to protect their territory. Between 1832 and 1835, federal authorities forcibly removed the majority of Florida Seminoles to Indian Territory, although a minority fought back. Jackson and his military commanders expected that this **Second Seminole War** would be short lived. However, they misjudged the Seminoles' strength; the power of their charismatic leader, Osceola; and the resistance of black fugitives living among the Seminoles.

The conflict continued long after Jackson left the presidency. During the seven-year guerrilla war, 1,600 U.S. troops died. U.S. military forces defeated the Seminoles in 1842 only by luring Osceola into an army camp with false promises of a peace settlement. Instead, officers took him captive, finally breaking the back of the resistance. Still, to end the conflict, the U.S. government had to allow enslaved African Americans who had escaped and were living among the Seminoles to accompany the tribe to Indian Territory.

Unlike the Seminole, members of the Cherokee nation challenged removal by peaceful means, believing that their prolonged efforts to coexist with white society would ensure their success. American Indian leaders like John Ross had urged Cherokees to embrace Christianity, white gender roles, and a republican form of government as the best means to ensure control of their communities. Large numbers had done so, but in 1829 and 1830, Georgia officials sought to impose new regulations on the Cherokee living within the state's borders. Tribal leaders took them to court, demanding recognition as a separate nation and using evidence of their Americanization to claim their rights. In 1831 **Cherokee Nation v. Georgia** reached the Supreme Court, which denied a central part of the Cherokee claim. It ruled that all American Indians were "domestic dependent nations" rather than fully sovereign governments. Yet the following year, in *Worcester v. Georgia*, the Court declared that the state of Georgia could not impose *state* laws on the Cherokee, for they had "territorial boundaries, within which their authority is exclusive," and that both their land and their rights were protected by the federal government.

EXPLORING AP® THEMES

Politics and Power

Although the Supreme Court of the United States (head of the judiciary branch) had decided that American Indians had some legally recognizable rights, it would be up to the executive branch (the president) to enforce the law. Instead of protecting the interests of American Indians, President Andrew Jackson said about *Worcester v. Georgia*: "John Marshall had made his decision; now let him enforce it!" After sharing this information with students, ask them to explain the power struggle between these two branches of government and how it eventually allowed for an American Indian policy that led to the forced relocation of thousands. What was President Jackson's reasoning for not enforcing the law?

President Jackson, who sought Cherokee removal, argued that only the tribe's removal west of the Mississippi River could ensure its "physical comfort," "political advancement," and "moral improvement." Most southern whites, seeking to mine gold and expand cotton production in Cherokee territory, agreed. But Protestant women and men in the North launched a massive petition campaign in 1830 supporting the Cherokees' right to their land. The Cherokee themselves prevented action through Jackson's second term.

In December 1835, however, U.S. officials convinced a small group of Cherokee men — without tribal sanction — to sign the **Treaty of New Echota**. It proposed the exchange of 100 million acres of Cherokee land in the Southeast for $68 million and 32 million acres in Indian Territory. Outraged Cherokee leaders like John Ross lobbied Congress to reject the treaty. But in May 1836, Congress approved the treaty by a single vote and set the date for final removal two years later (Map 4.6).

In 1838, the U.S. army forcibly removed Cherokees who had not yet resettled in Indian Territory. That June, General Winfield Scott, assisted by 7,000 U.S. soldiers, forced some 15,000 Cherokees into forts and military camps. American Indian families spent the next several months without sufficient food, water, sanitation, or medicine. In October, when the

Treaty of New Echota 1836 treaty in which a group of Cherokee men agreed to exchange their land in the Southeast for money and land in Indian Territory. Despite the fact that the treaty was obtained without tribal sanction, it was approved by the U.S. Congress.

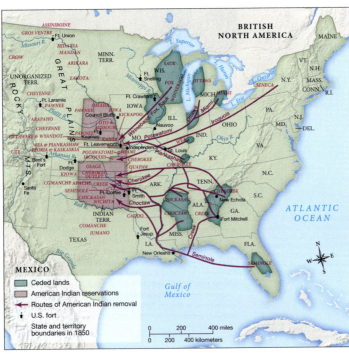

▲ **MAP 4.6 American Indian Removals and Relocations, 1820s–1840s** In the 1820s and 1830s, the federal government used a variety of tactics, including military force, to expel American Indian nations residing east of the Mississippi River. As these tribes resettled in the West, white migration along the Oregon and other trails began to increase. The result, by 1850, was the forced relocation of many western American Indian nations as well. **Compare this map with Map 4.2 (p. 263). What do these maps reveal about the impact of American expansionism on American Indians?**

TEACHING IDEA

Incorporating Secondary Sources

Give students excerpts from Helen Hunt Jackson's *A Century of Dishonor* (1881). This book provides a criticism of government policies toward American Indians and advocates for more equitable treatment of the nation's first peoples.

TEACHING IDEA

Differing Views

Historically, the American government entered various treaties with American Indian tribes that many would find legally dubious and would bring legal challenges. The Treaty of New Echota, for example, was questioned by Chief John Ross on behalf of the Cherokee Nation. Discuss with students how the different views of land ownership by white Americans and American Indians (individual vs. communal) and of governance were at the center of these disagreements.

TEACHING IDEA

Analyzing Art and Images

Provide the class with one of the most iconic paintings depicting the "Trail of Tears" by Robert Lindneux (readily available through online search). Give students time to analyze the visual and then do a comparison to the "Indian Emigrants" woodcut.

BUILDING AP® SKILLS

Claims and Evidence in Sources

Analyze the woodcut for limitations and bias. Ask students to answer: 1) What does the document not tell you?; 2) What other sources might offer alternative perspectives?; and 3) How does knowing this image appeared in a textbook affect its reliability?

Period 4: 1800–1848

MODULE 4-5 Conflicts of the Jacksonian Era

▲ **Cherokee Removal, 1838** This woodcut appeared in a U.S. geography textbook from about 1850. The title "Indian Emigrants" and the image of Cherokee disembarking from a steamboat falsely suggest that the emigration was voluntary and the means of travel relatively easy. The U.S. fort on the hill symbolizes the role of the federal government in forcing the Cherokee to move west of the Mississippi. **Based on the title of this image and its portrayal of the Cherokees, what was the purpose of this woodcut? Explain your reasoning.**

Trail of Tears The forced march of some 15,000 Cherokees from Georgia to areas west of the Mississippi River that were designated as Indian Territory, beginning in 1831. Inadequate planning, food, water, sanitation, and medicine led to the deaths of thousands of Cherokees.

Cherokees finally began the march west, torrential rains were followed by snow. Although the U.S. army planned for a trip of less than three months, the journey actually took five months. As supplies ran short, thousands of American Indians died. The remaining Cherokees completed this **Trail of Tears**, as it became known, in March 1839. But thousands more remained near starvation a year later.

Following the Trail of Tears, Seneca Indians petitioned the federal government to stop their removal from western New York. Federal agents had negotiated the Treaty of Buffalo Creek with several Iroquois leaders in 1838. But some Seneca chiefs claimed the negotiation was marred by bribery and fraud. With the aid of Quaker allies, the Seneca petitioned Congress and the president for redress. Perhaps reluctant to repeat the Cherokee and Seminole debacles, Congress approved a new treaty in 1842 that allowed the Seneca to retain two of their four reservations in western New York. The contest for American Indian lands continued well past Jackson's presidency, but the president's desire to force indigenous nations westward would ultimately prevail.

REVIEW

- How did American Indian nations challenge attempts to forcibly relocate them?
- Compare the experiences of the Seminole, Cherokee, and Seneca Indians as each group faced forcible relocation.

Van Buren and the Panic of 1837

Whig Party Political party formed in the 1830s to challenge the power of the Democratic Party. The Whigs attempted to forge a diverse coalition from around the country by promoting commercial interests and moral reforms.

Although Jackson proposed the Indian Removal Act, it was President Martin Van Buren who confronted ongoing challenges from American Indian nations. When Van Buren ran for president in 1836, the newly formed **Whig Party**, so named as a retort to Jackson's perceived "kinglike" conduct, hoped to defeat him by bringing together diverse supporters: evangelical Protestants who objected to Jackson's American Indian policy, financiers and commercial farmers who advocated internal improvements and protective tariffs, merchants and manufacturers who favored a national bank, and southerners who were antagonized by the president's heavy-handed use of federal authority. But the Whigs could not agree on a single candidate, and this lack of unity allowed Democrats to prevail. Although Van Buren won the popular vote by only a small margin (50.9 percent), he secured an easy majority in the electoral college.

Inaugurated on March 4, 1837, President Van Buren soon faced a major financial crisis. The Panic of 1837 started in the South and was rooted in the changing fortunes of American cotton in Great Britain. During the 1820s and 1830s, British banks lent large sums to states such as New York to fund internal improvements, which drove the market revolution but also fueled inflation. The British also invested heavily in cotton plantations, and southern planters used the funds to expand production and improve shipping facilities.

In late 1836, the Bank of England, faced with bad harvests at home and a declining demand for textiles, tightened credit to limit the flow of money out of the country. This forced British investors to call in their loans, which drove up interest rates in the United States just as cotton prices started to fall. Some large American cotton merchants were forced to declare bankruptcy. The banks where they held accounts, many in the South, then failed — ninety-eight of them in March and April 1837 alone.

The economic crisis hit the South hard. Cotton prices continued to fall, cut by nearly half in less than a year. Land values declined dramatically, port cities came to a standstill, and cotton communities on the southern frontier collapsed. Because regional economies were increasingly intertwined, the panic radiated throughout the United States. Northern brokers, shippers, and merchants were devastated by losses in the cotton trade, and northern banks were hit by unpaid debts incurred for canals and other internal improvements. In turn, entrepreneurs who borrowed money to expand their businesses defaulted in large numbers, and shopkeepers, artisans, factory workers, and farmers in the North and Midwest suffered unemployment and foreclosures.

In the North and West, many Americans blamed Jackson's war against the Bank of the United States for precipitating the panic, and Americans everywhere were outraged at Van Buren's refusal to intervene in the crisis. While it is unlikely that any federal policy could have resolved the nation's economic problems, the president's apparent disinterest in the plight of the people inspired harsh criticisms from ordinary citizens as well as political opponents. Worse, despite brief signs of recovery in 1838, the depression deepened in 1839 and continued for four more years.

REVIEW

What were the causes and consequences of the Panic of 1837?

The Whigs Win the White House

AP® TIP
Analyze how changes in voting rights affected the strategies and platforms adopted by American political parties during the mid-1800s.

Eager to exploit the weakness of Van Buren and the Democrats, the Whig Party organized its first national convention in fall 1840 and united behind military hero William Henry Harrison, the party's largest vote-getter in the previous election. Harrison was born to a wealthy planter family in Virginia, but he was portrayed as a self-made man who lived in a simple log cabin and drank hard cider. His running mate, John Tyler, another Virginia gentleman and a onetime Democrat, joined the Whigs because of his opposition to Jackson's stand on nullification. Whig leaders hoped he would attract southern votes. Taking their cue from the Democrats, the Whigs organized rallies, barbecues, parades, and mass meetings. They turned the tables on their foe by portraying Van Buren as an aristocrat and Harrison as a war hero and friend of the common man. Whigs celebrated American innovation and the entrepreneurial spirit, proclaimed farmers and skilled workers the backbone of the country, and insisted on their moral and religious superiority to Democrats. At the same time, eager to remind voters that Harrison had defeated Tenskwatawa at the Battle of Tippecanoe, the Whigs adopted the slogan "Tippecanoe and Tyler Too."

TEACHING IDEA

Connecting the Dots

Although President Jackson had many supporters, he also had a lot of enemies and opponents. Have students brainstorm and identify who were the main groups that opposed him. Possible answers include: *evangelical Protestants who opposed his American Indian policies*; *supporters of internal improvements (commercial farmers) and high tariffs (manufacturers/financiers)*; *supporters of a national bank (businessmen and merchants)*; and *southerners who opposed use of strong federal power (e.g., "force bill" during nullification crisis)*. This diverse coalition would eventually unite and help create and bring to power the Whig Party.

BUILDING AP® SKILLS

Causation

One of the main learning targets for this module is to explain the causes and effects of the Panic of 1837. Therefore, have students complete the following chart. Possible answers are italicized.

Causes	Effects
■ *The Death of the Second National Bank after President Andrew Jackson vetoed the re-charter bill in 1832.*	■ *Higher interest rates in the United States.*
■ *Tightening of credit by the Bank of England after bank failures made it call in loans abroad (i.e., in the United States).*	■ *Lower prices for southern cotton.*
	■ *Bankruptcies and bank failures.*
	■ *Land values declined dramatically.*
	■ *Unemployment and foreclosures.*

▲ Differentiation

Some students may struggle to identify the main causes of the Panic of 1837. If that is the case, then provide them with the two main causes and ask them to focus on the main effects. Conversely, for advanced learners, have them evaluate the relative significance or importance of both the causes and effects.

TRM Find **Handout 4.6 – Causes and Effects of the Panic of 1837** in the Teacher's Resource Materials.

TEACHING IDEA

Project Idea

The election of 1840 was known as the "Log Cabin and Hard Cider" campaign. Divide the class into groups of three and have them create a political campaign poster for the Whig nominee for president, William Henry Harrison, and one against the Democrat nominee, President Martin Van Buren. Some possible points for students to consider:

- William Henry Harrison: "self-made" man who lived in a log cabin and drank hard cider, war hero (Battle of Tippecanoe) and friend of the "common man," moral and religious "superiority" to Democrats.

- Martin Van Buren: out of touch aristocrat who did not get the economy back on track with his "independent treasury."

TRM Suggested Responses to Questions

TEACHING IDEA

AP® Central

Use the 2011 AP® U.S. History exam DBQ on political campaigns as a bell ringer. Have students use the documents to work on sourcing. This question is available on the College Board's AP® U.S. History Past Exam Questions section under "2011: Form B" (apcentral.collegeboard.org).

The Whigs also welcomed women into the campaign. By 1840 thousands of women had circulated petitions against Cherokee removal, organized temperance and antislavery societies, promoted religious revivals, and joined charitable associations. They embodied the kind of moral force that the Whig Party claimed to represent. In October 1840, Whig senator Daniel Webster spoke to a gathering of 1,200 women, calling on them to encourage their brothers and husbands to vote for Harrison.

The Whig strategy paid off handsomely on election day. Harrison won easily, and the Whigs gained a majority in Congress. Yet the election's promise was shattered when Harrison died of pneumonia a month after his inauguration. Whigs in Congress now had to deal with John Tyler, whose sentiments were largely southern and Democratic. Vetoing legislation to increase tariffs and recharter the Bank of the United States, Tyler infuriated Whigs who eventually kicked him out of the party. Tyler's actions allowed the Democratic Party to regroup and set the stage for close elections in 1844 and 1848.

REVIEW

- What tactics did Whigs use to win the election of 1840?
- How did these tactics reflect changes in campaigning since the election of 1824?

AP® WRITING HISTORICALLY — Short-Answer Question Practice

ACTIVITY

Read the following question carefully and write a short response. Use complete sentences.

Use the following excerpts to answer (a), (b), and (c).

Source: David F. Ericson, *The Nullification Crisis, American Republicanism, and the Force Bill Debate*, 1995

"On the surface, the nullification crisis revolved around the question of sovereignty: Which level of government has the last say on such matters as the tariff rates? Does the federal government, the state governments, or really neither (because the governmental system was set up in such a way that there is no locus of 'last say')? Here, of course, the participants in the crisis had recourse to the Constitution, and their conflict was defined by opposing constitutional philosophies. Another question, though, emerged beneath the sovereignty question during the course of the crisis: What is the nature of the American republic? Is it a federation of smaller, state republics, a national republic, or both, in roughly equal proportions? Answering this question seemed to be the only conclusive way of answering the sovereignty question, and, since the Constitution did not provide an answer, the participants had to appeal to some deeper political standard or theory to try to do so."

Source: Jane H. Pease and William H. Pease, *The Economics and Politics of Charleston's Nullification Crisis*, 1981

"Intensifying Charleston's nullification experience was anxiety over the city's stagnant economy in the 1820s. Between 1820 and 1830 her imports had diminished every year but one. In 1825 the international cotton market collapsed, and the dramatic growth in the city's cotton exports earlier in the decade leveled off. In the wake of that collapse, general economic depression followed. Unemployment and inflation plagued Charleston's inhabitants. Up-country legislators threatened to reduce the city's representation in a state government which already taxed city property and commercial income more heavily than agricultural land and produce. Charleston's appeals for aid to internal improvements went unheard in the rest of the state. Then, in 1828, her languishing economy seemed further threatened by the new federal tariff."

a. Briefly explain ONE major difference between Ericson's and Jane Pease's and William Pease's interpretations of the nullification crisis.
b. Briefly explain how ONE specific historical event or development from the period that is not explicitly mentioned in the excerpts could be used to support Ericson's argument.
c. Briefly explain how ONE specific historical event or development that is not explicitly mentioned in the excerpts could be used to support Jane Pease's and William Pease's argument.

EXPLORING AP® THEMES

Politics and Power

Make thematic connections between the ongoing power struggle between states and the federal government over who had the final say on the constitutionality of laws. As covered in Module 4-1, the Supreme Court of the United States had already determined that it had the power of judicial review as decided in *Marbury v. Madison*. Ask students to discuss how southerners continuing to assert the right of nullification could eventually tear the nation apart. Students should point out that if states could nullify tariffs they may also be able to invalidate federal restrictions on the institution of slavery.

TEACHING IDEA

AP® Writing Historically Review

Students are often able to capture the basic arguments in secondary sources by the end of the year. Therefore, to build on the skill of marshaling evidence to support a historical argument, provide the following categories of analysis, which are found in the excerpts: agricultural economy, Federalism, Nullification, and Jacksonian Democracy. Students' main task is to brainstorm all of the relevant historical evidence that connects to each category. After students complete their brainstorm, have them cross-reference their brainstorm with each excerpt. Through this process, students should be able to find one piece of historical evidence that can be used to support each source.

Module 4-6

Slavery and Southern Society

LEARNING TARGETS

By the end of this module, you should be able to:

- Explain how the geography of the South and the westward expansion of slavery impacted the development of the South.
- Explain how the lives of white and black people in the South changed and remained the same in the era before the Civil War.

THEMATIC FOCUS

Geography and the Environment
American and Regional Culture
Social Structures

The expansion of cotton planting generated wealth for the planter elite, triggered the forced internal migration of enslaved people, and limited the growth of industry and cities in the South. Despite brutality and the prevalence of slave codes, a vibrant African American culture emerged on plantations and among free black people in the South. Enslaved laborers regularly resisted in various ways while many free black people worked to improve their status.

HISTORICAL REASONING FOCUS

Causation
Continuity and Change

TASK ▶ As you read this module, consider how the South's continued reliance on a system of enslaved labor caused its economy and society to develop differently from those of the North. Be sure to take note of the social tensions that developed within the South as a result. Also consider how enslaved people resisted their bondage in covert and occasionally overt ways. How did enslaved and free black people in the South contribute to the development of a distinctly African American culture during the first half of the nineteenth century?

TRM Suggested Responses to Questions

PERIOD 4

The cotton gin, developed in the 1790s, ensured the growth of southern agriculture into the 1840s. As the cotton kingdom spread west, planters, those who owned the largest plantations, forged a distinctive culture around the institution of slavery. But this agricultural economy based on slavery limited the development of cities, technology, and educational institutions, leaving the South increasingly dependent on the North and West for many of its needs. In addition, westward expansion extended the trade in enslaved people within the South, shattering black families. Still, southern planters viewed themselves as national leaders, both the repository of traditional American values and the engine of economic progress.

Because enslaved labor formed the backbone of the southern economy, enslaved workers gained some leverage against slaveholders and overseers. But black people did not simply define themselves in relation to whites. They also developed relationships, identities, and cultural practices within their living quarters. Many also found small ways to resist their enslavement on an everyday basis. Others resisted more openly, and a small number organized rebellions against those holding them in bondage.

White slaveholders' fears of rebellion led to stricter regulations of black life, and actual uprisings temporarily reinforced white solidarity. Yet yeoman farmers, poor white people, and middle-class professionals all voiced some doubts about the ways in which slavery affected southern society. To ensure white unity, planters wielded their economic and political authority, highlighted bonds of kinship and religious fellowship, and promoted an ideology of white supremacy. Their efforts only intensified as northern states and other nations began outlawing slavery.

AP® TIP

Analyze the ways in which plantation owners maintained political control and economic power while ensuring that poor white southerners felt superior to people of other races, particularly African Americans.

TEACHING IDEA

Geography Instruction

Give students a map of the United States from the Antebellum Era. Then, ask them to label the main port/trading cities in the South. Specifically, they need to identify the location of Charleston, New Orleans, Baltimore, and Savannah. Lastly, have students research the main crops being exported from each respective city. Conclude this activity with a class discussion on why port cities had such an economic impact, particularly with regard to exporting agricultural products.

BUILDING AP® SKILLS

Change and Continuity

By now, students should be familiar with the double-headed arrow graphic organizer. Write one on the board with a start date of 1790 and end date of 1850 and conduct a class discussion on which were the "Top 3" changes and continuities in the South. One category goes on top and the other below the arrow.

- Possible changes: *movement from "Old South" to the "Deep South"; some industries developed; cotton replaced tobacco, rice, and sugar as the main crop.*

- Possible continuities: *region remained mostly rural and underdeveloped (few cities); still relied on labor from enslaved people; plantation system and cash crops continued to define southern society.*

TEACHING IDEA

Incorporating Websites

Visit the Boone Hall Plantation & Gardens' website (boonehallplantation.com) to explore Boone Hall Plantation in Charleston, South Carolina. This will allow students to develop a better idea of the layout of plantations that exercised so much political and economic power in southern society.

TEACHING IDEA

Incorporating Websites

Visit the Stanford History Education Group site to obtain an assessment on the former living conditions of enslaved people by searching for "slave quarters" (sheg.stanford.edu). Specifically, this lesson focuses on the sourcing of documents about these lodgings and their limitations.

TEACHING IDEA

Class Discussion

Divide the class in two and ask half of the students to research the main jobs performed by male enslaved people. Meanwhile, the other students research the same question for female enslaved workers. While conducting their respective research, ask students to think about other factors that may impact the division of labor that may not be associated with sex. Students should identify that age, physical condition, and skillset normally played a more significant role than sex. To conclude, conduct a class discussion for students to share their findings and to address any misunderstandings.

▲ **Differentiation**

For advanced learners, ask students to go beyond the division of labor for enslaved workers and to identify how this also created a social hierarchy. Ask them to identify which workers were most valuable and considered to be at the top while others were in the middle and lower tiers.

Period 4: 1800–1848

MODULE 4-6 Slavery and Southern Society

A Plantation Society Develops in the South

AP® TIP
Analyze how the development of a "southern aristocracy" shaped the political and economic landscape of the American South during the 1800s.

Plantation slavery existed throughout the Americas in the early nineteenth century. Extensive plantations worked by large numbers of enslaved people existed in the West Indies and South America. In the U.S. South, however, the unstable cotton market and a scarcity of fertile land kept most plantations relatively small before 1830. But over the next two decades, territorial expansion and the profits from cotton, rice, and sugar allowed successful southern planters to build grand houses and purchase a variety of luxury goods.

As plantations grew, a wealthy aristocracy sought to ensure productivity by employing harsh methods of discipline. For instance, although plantation owner James Henry Hammond imagined himself a progressive slaveholder, he used the whip often, hoping thereby to ensure that his estate generated sufficient profits to support a lavish lifestyle.

The wives of wealthy southern men, meanwhile, managed their own families and the enslaved household workers as well as the feeding, clothing, and medical care of the entire enslaved labor force. Plantation mistresses also organized social events, hosted relatives and friends for extended stays, and sometimes directed the plantation in their husband's absence.

Still, plantation mistresses were relieved of the most arduous labor by enslaved women, who cooked, cleaned, and washed for the family, cared for the children, and even nursed the babies. Wealthy white women benefited from the best education, the greatest access to music and literature, and the finest clothes and furnishings. Yet the pedestal on which plantation mistresses stood was shaky, built on a patriarchal system in which husbands and fathers held substantial power. For example, most wives tried to ignore the sexual relations that husbands initiated with enslaved women. A few, such as Catherine Hammond, the wife of a South Carolina politician named James Henry Hammond, did not. She moved to Charleston with her two youngest daughters when she discovered James's sexual abuse of an enslaved mother and daughter. Others, however, took out their anger and frustration on enslaved women already victimized by their husbands. Moreover, some mistresses were slaveholders themselves, gave them as gifts or bequests to family members and friends, and traded them on the open market.

Not all slaveholders were wealthy planters like the Hammonds, with an enslaved labor force of fifty or more people and extensive landholdings. Far more planters in the 1830s and 1840s held between twenty and fifty enslaved pepole, and an even larger number of farmers kept just three to six people in bondage. The largest group of white southerners were not slaveholders. As Hammond wrote a friend in 1847, "The planters here are essentially what the nobility are in other countries. They stand at the head of society & politics."

> " The planters here are essentially what the nobility are in other countries. They stand at the head of society & politics. "
>
> James Henry Hammond, wealthy slaveholder and politician, 1847

REVIEW

How would you characterize the lifestyle of plantation owners and their families during the mid-nineteenth century?

Urban Life in the Slaveholding South

The insistence on the supremacy of slaveholders had broad repercussions. The richest men in the South invested in slavery, land, and household goods, with little left to develop industry, technology, or urban institutions. The largest factory in the South, the Tredegar Iron Works in Richmond, Virginia, employed several hundred free and enslaved African Americans by 1850. Most southern industrialists, however, like South Carolina textile manufacturer William Gregg, employed poor white women and children. But neither Tredegar nor a scattering of textile mills fundamentally reshaped the region's economy, leaving it much less industrialized than the North's.

The South also fell behind in urban development. The main exception was port cities. Yet even in Baltimore, Charleston, and Savannah, commerce was often directed by northern agents, especially cotton brokers. In addition, nearly one-third of southern whites had no access to cash and instead bartered goods and services, further restricting the urban economy.

Southern cities did attract many free black people. The growing demand for cheap domestic labor in urban areas and planters' greater willingness to emancipate less valuable single enslaved women meant that free black women generally outnumbered men in southern cities. These women worked mainly as washerwomen, cooks, and general domestic laborers, while free black men typically became skilled artisans, dockworkers, or sailors. Free black people competed for these jobs with enslaved

---

EXPLORING AP® THEMES

Geography and the Environment

Environmental factors play a significant role in the development of geographical regions. Ask students: How did the southern environment and climate lead to a greater dependency on slavery? Since the South primarily focused on growing raw materials like tobacco, rice, sugar, indigo, and eventually cotton, most of the wealth was invested in land and labor instead of industries. Therefore, the plantation system developed in the region instead of growth taking place around a town or city as seen in the North. This lack of major urban centers also served to deter investments in transportation systems. The over-cultivation of land also led to westward expansion and the extension of slavery to the western regions.

▲ **Differentiation**

To help students develop a deeper understanding of the environmental impact caused by the cultivation of the first main cash crop during the colonial period, tobacco, have them research how it affects the land. Specifically, students should discover that tobacco tends to deplete nutrients from the soil and since colonists were not engaging in crop rotation, this increased the need and demand for additional western lands.

people and growing numbers of European immigrants who flocked to southern cities in the 1840s and 1850s. The presence of immigrants and free black people, as well as the reputation of ports as escape hatches for enslaved people fleeing the South, ensured that cities remained suspect in the South.

The scarcity of cities and industry in the South also curtailed the development of transportation. State governments invested little in roads, canals, and railroads. Most small farmers traded goods locally, and most planters used the South's extensive river system to ship goods to commercial hubs. Only Virginia and Maryland, with their proximity to the nation's capital, developed extensive road and rail networks.

REVIEW

- What major factors affected mid-nineteenth-century industrialization, urbanization, and transportation developments in the South? Explain your reasoning.

The Consequences of Slavery's Expansion

Outside the South, industry and agriculture increasingly benefited from technological innovation. Planters, however, continued to rely on intensive manual labor. Even reform-minded planters focused on fertilizer and crop rotation rather than machines to enhance productivity. The limited use of new technologies — such as iron plows or seed drills — resulted from a lack of investment capital and planters' refusal to purchase expensive equipment that they feared might be broken or purposely sabotaged by enslaved people. Instead, they relied on continually expanding the acreage under cultivation.

One result of these practices was that a declining percentage of white southerners came to control vast estates with large numbers of enslaved laborers. Between 1830 and 1850, the absolute number of both enslaved people and slaveholders grew. But slaveholders became a smaller proportion of all white southerners, dropping to under a third by 1850, because the white population grew faster than the number of slaveholders. At the same time, distinctions among wealthy planters, small slaveholders, and white people who were not slaveholders also increased.

The concern with productivity and profits and the concentration of more enslaved people on large plantations did have some limited benefits for black women and men. The end of the international slave trade in 1808 forced planters to rely more heavily on natural reproduction to increase their labor force. Thus many planters thought more carefully about how they treated those they

▲ **MAP 4.7 The Spread of Cotton Production, 1820–1860** While tobacco, rice, and sugar remained important crops in a few states, cotton became the South's and the nation's major export. The need to find more fertile fields led planters to migrate to Alabama, Mississippi, and Louisiana. As a result of cotton's success, the number of enslaved people increased dramatically, the internal slave trade expanded, and labor demands intensified. **How do the changes in cotton production shown on this map reflect the economic and social changes occurring simultaneously in the region?**

TEACHING IDEA

Connecting the Dots

Have students write a paragraph on how the banning of the international slave trade in 1808 led to some improved conditions for enslaved people. Specifically, since more enslaved people could no longer be brought into the United States (unless smuggled) and as such could not easily be replaced, American planters had to provide better food and treatment. On the other hand, this new legal prohibition also resulted in reliance on a domestic self-replicating workforce (often accomplished by rape and compulsory pregnancy against women who had no rights and no protections) and the frequent breaking of family bonds as family members were often sold "down river" from the "Old South" to the "Deep South." In conjunction with the over-cultivation of eastern lands, this led to the extension of slavery westward.

BUILDING AP® SKILLS

Comparison

Have students research how enslaved people were generally treated in other parts of the Americas, including the West Indies/Caribbean and Brazil. Students can start by referencing the information from the modules in Period 2. Then, ask students to complete a Venn diagram comparing and contrasting the institution of slavery. Make sure students can identify how the 1808 injunction against importing enslaved people helped as well as harmed the lives of slaves in the United States compared to their treatment elsewhere.

Period 4: 1800–1848

MODULE 4-6 Slavery and Southern Society

enslaved, who were increasingly viewed as "valuable property." It was no longer good business to work enslaved people to death or cripple them by severe punishments.

Nonetheless, slaveholders continued to whip and sexually exploit enslaved people and made paltry investments in their diet and health care. Most enslaved people lived in small houses with dirt floors and little furniture and clothing. They ate a diet high in calories, especially fats and carbohydrates, but with little meat, fish, fresh vegetables, or fruits. The high mortality rate among enslaved infants and children — more than twice that of white children to age five — reflected this limited care.

The spread of slavery into Mississippi, Louisiana, Alabama, Missouri, and eventually Texas affected both white and black families, though again not equally. The younger sons of wealthy planters were often forced to move to the frontier, and their families generally lived in rough quarters on isolated plantations. A woman traveler noted that the men "think only of making money, and their houses are hardly fit to live in." A planter's wife complained, "Mississippi and Alabama are a dreary waste." Such moves were far more difficult for enslaved people, however. Between 1830 and 1850, more than 440,000 enslaved people were forced to move from the Upper South to the Lower South (Map 4.7), often tearing them away from their families. On the southern frontier, they endured especially harsh conditions as they cleared and cultivated new lands.

By the 1830s, slave markets blossomed in key cities across the South. Solomon Northup (see the AP* Analyzing Sources box on p. 323) was held in one in Washington, D.C., where a woman named Eliza watched as her son Randall was "won" by a planter from Baton Rouge. She promised "to be the most faithful slave that ever lived" if he would also buy her and her daughter. The slave trader threatened the desperate mother with a hundred lashes, and her tears could not change the outcome. As slavery spread westward, such scenes were repeated thousands of times.

REVIEW

- How did the 1808 ban on the importation of enslaved people and the westward spread of slavery affect the lives of enslaved African Americans?

Enslaved Labor Fuels the Southern Economy

The labor of enslaved African Americans drove the nation's economy as well as the South's. In 1820 the South produced some 500,000 bales of cotton, much of it exported to England. By 1850 the region produced nearly 3 million bales, feeding textile mills in New England and abroad. A decade later, cotton accounted for nearly two-thirds of the U.S. export trade and added nearly $200 million a year to the American economy.

AP® ANALYZING SOURCES

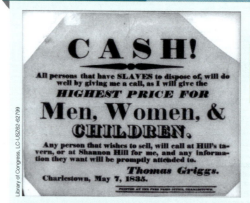

Source: *Advertisement of a South Carolina Slave Dealer*, 1835

Questions for Analysis

1. Identify the intended audience for this advertisement.
2. Describe the perspective toward enslaved people expressed in this image.
3. Explain how the slave trade shaped the South's economy and demographics during the mid-1800s.

Enslaved laborers, of course, saw little of this wealth. Enslaved carpenters, blacksmiths, and other skilled laborers were sometimes hired out and allowed to keep a small amount of the money they earned. They traveled to nearby households, compared their circumstances to those on other plantations, and sometimes made contact with free black people. Some of them also learned to read and write and had access to tools and knowledge denied to field hands. Still, they were constantly hounded by whites who demanded travel passes and deference, and they were often suspected of involvement in rebellions.

Enslaved household workers sometimes received old clothes and bedding or leftover food from slaveholders. Yet they were under the constant surveillance of whites, and women especially were vulnerable to sexual abuse. Moreover, the work they performed was physically demanding. James Curry, an enslaved man who escaped bondage, recalled that his mother, a cook in North Carolina, rose early each morning to milk cows, bake bread, and churn butter. She was responsible for meals for her fellow enslaved people and their slaveholders. In summer, she cooked her last meal around eight o'clock, after which she milked the cows again. Then she returned to her quarters, put her children to bed, and often fell asleep while mending clothes.

Once enslaved children reached the age of ten to twelve, they were put to work full-time, usually in the fields. Although field labor was defined by its relentless pace and drudgery, it also brought together large numbers of enslaved people for the entire day and thus helped forge bonds among laborers on the same plantation. Songs provided a rhythm for their work and offered them the chance to communicate their frustrations or hopes.

Field labor was generally organized by task or by gang. Under the task system, typical on rice plantations, enslaved people could return to their quarters once the day's task was completed. This left time for them to cultivate gardens, fish, or mend clothes. In the gang system, widely used on cotton plantations, men and women worked in groups under the supervision of a driver. Often working from sunup to sundown, they swept across fields hoeing, planting, or picking.

AP® ANALYZING SOURCES

Source: Solomon Northup, *Twelve Years a Slave*, 1853

"The hands are required to be in the cotton field as soon as it is light in the morning, and, with the exception of ten or fifteen minutes, which is given them at noon to swallow their allowance of cold bacon, they are not permitted to be a moment idle until it is too dark to see, and when the moon is full, they often times labor till the middle of the night. They do not dare to stop even at dinner time, nor return to the quarters, however late it be, until the order to halt is given by the driver.

The day's work over in the field, the baskets are . . . carried to the gin-house, where the cotton is weighed. No matter how fatigued and weary he may be—no matter how much he longs for sleep and rest—a slave never approaches the gin-house with his basket of cotton but with fear. If it falls short in weight—if he has not performed the full task appointed him, he knows that he must suffer. And if he has exceeded it by ten or twenty pounds, in all probability his master will measure the next day's task accordingly. . . . Most frequently they have too little, and therefore it is they are not anxious to leave the field. After weighing, follow the whippings; and then the baskets are carried to the cotton house, and their contents stored away like hay, all hands being sent in to tramp it down. . . .

This done, the labor of the day is not yet ended, by any means. Each one must then attend to his respective chores. One feeds the mules, another the swine—another cuts the wood, and so forth; besides, the packing is all done by candle light. Finally, at a late hour, they reach the quarters, sleepy and overcome with the long day's toil. Then a fire must be kindled in the cabin, the corn ground in the small hand-mill, and supper, and dinner for the next day in the field, prepared. All that is allowed them is corn and bacon, which is given out at the corncrib and smoke-house every Sunday morning. . . . That is all—no tea, coffee, sugar, and with the exception of a very scanty sprinkling now and then, no salt. . . .

(Continued)

BUILDING AP® SKILLS

Claims and Evidence in Sources

Provide students with a copy of the article titled "Slavery and Anti-Slavery" by David Brion Davis. This secondary source from the Gilder Lehrman site discusses the institution of slavery (gilderlehrman.org). Have students read the article to identify the author's claim or argument, historical evidence, and reasoning used to support it.

TRM Suggested Responses to Questions

TRM Module 4.6 AP® Analyzing Sources Handout 2

Period 4: 1800–1848

MODULE 4-6 Slavery and Southern Society

> The softest couches in the world are not to be found in the log mansion of the slave. The one whereon I reclined year after year, was a plank twelve inches wide and ten feet long. My pillow was a stick of wood. The bedding was a coarse blanket, and not a rag or shred beside. Moss might be used, were it not that it directly breeds a swarm of fleas. . . .
>
> An hour before day light the horn is blown. . . . Then the fears and labors of another day begin."

Questions for Analysis

1. Describe how Northup characterizes the daily challenges and fears faced by enslaved men on cotton plantations.
2. Describe the economic context that contributed to the working conditions Northup describes.
3. Explain how the publication of accounts such as Northup's affected the debate over slavery.

Questions for Comparison   Harriet Jacobs, *Incidents in the Life of a Slave Girl*, 1861 (p. 269)

1. Explain how Northup's and Jacobs's accounts highlight the differing experiences of enslaved men and women.
2. Evaluate the extent of similarity between the factors that contributed to Northup's and Jacobs's accounts.

REVIEW

- What factors shaped daily life for enslaved African Americans during the first half of the nineteenth century?

Developing an African American Culture

Amid hard work and harsh treatment, enslaved people created social bonds and a rich culture of their own. Thus African Americans continued for generations to employ African names, like Cuffee and Binah. Even if slaveholders gave them English names, they might use African names in the slave quarters to sustain family memories and community networks. Elements of West African and Caribbean languages, agricultural techniques, medical practices, forms of dress, folktales, songs and musical instruments, dances, and courtship rituals demonstrated the

◀ "A Slave Wedding," c. 1800
This rare water color painting of an African American wedding probably dates from the turn of the nineteenth century. The distance between the slave quarters and the plantation house suggests this may be a South Carolina scene. The enslaved women and men are dressed in their finest clothing and the musicians appear to be playing African-style instruments made from gourds. **How does this painting depict the blending of African and American cultures?**

TEACHING IDEA

Class Discussion

Ask students when and how African traditions evolved into an African American culture. Then, give them time to research some of the main cultural elements that emerged during the first half of the nineteenth century. For example, tell students to focus on music, dress, language, and rituals (e.g., "jumping the broom" for marriage). To conclude the discussion, play a traditional African American spiritual that provided strength and resolve to enslaved people. For resources visit the PBS article, "Singing in Slavery: Songs of Survival, Songs of Freedom," by Kenyetta D. Berry (pbs.org).

EXPLORING AP® THEMES

Social Structures

Since this theme focuses on the development of social organizations and their impact on society, have students research the two main institutions that have played instrumental roles in the African American community — family and church. Specifically, have students research the concept of "extended kinship networks" and the role of the Baptist and Methodist churches in the African American community. While some churches advocated for enslaved people to accept slavery as "God's will," others used the Bible to justify their calls for liberation.

continued importance of these cultures to African Americans. This hybrid culture was disseminated as enslaved people hauled cotton to market, forged families across plantation boundaries, or were sold farther south. It was also passed across generations through storytelling, music, rituals, and healthcare. Most enslaved women's births were attended by black midwives, and African American healers sought southern equivalents to herbal cures used in West Africa.

Religious practices offer an important example of this blended culture among enslaved people. Africans from Muslim communities often continued to pray to Allah even if they were also required to attend Protestant churches, while black Protestant preachers developed rituals that combined African and American elements. In the early nineteenth century, many enslaved people eagerly embraced the evangelical teachings offered by Baptist and Methodist preachers, which echoed some of the expressive spiritual forms in West Africa. On Sundays, those who listened in the morning to white ministers proclaim slavery as God's will might gather in the evening to hear their own preachers declare God's love and the possibilities of liberation, at least in the hereafter. Enslaved people often incorporated drums, dancing, or other West African elements into these worship services.

Although most black preachers were men, a few enslaved women gained a spiritual following. Many enslaved women embraced religion enthusiastically, hoping that Christian baptism might substitute for West African rituals that protected newborn babies. These women sometimes called on church authorities to intervene when white slaveholders, overseers, or even enslaved men abused them. They also considered the church one means of recognizing marriages between enslaved people that were not acknowledged legally.

REVIEW

How and why did enslaved people blend elements of African and American culture?

Resistance and Rebellion

Many slaveholders worried that black preachers and West African folktales inspired black people to resist enslavement. Fearing defiance, planters went to incredible lengths to control the people they held in bondage. Although they were largely successful in quelling open revolts, they were unable to eliminate more subtle forms of opposition, like slowing the pace of work, feigning illness, and damaging equipment. More overt forms of resistance — such as truancy and running away, which disrupted work and lowered profits — also proved impossible to stamp out.

The forms of everyday resistance enslaved people employed varied in part on their location and resources. Skilled artisans, mostly men, could do more substantial damage because they used more expensive tools, but they were less able to protect themselves through pleas of ignorance. Field laborers could often damage only hoes, but they could do so regularly without exciting suspicion. Enslaved household workers could burn dinners, scorch shirts, break china, and even poison slaveholders. Often considered the most loyal to slaveholders, they were also among the most feared because of their intimate contact with white families. Enslaved single men were the most likely to run away, planning their escape to get as far away as possible before their absence was noticed. Women who fled plantations were more likely to hide out for short periods in the local area. Eventually, isolation, hunger, or concern for children led most of these truants to return if slave patrols did not find them first.

Despite their rarity, efforts to organize slave uprisings, such as the one supposedly hatched by Denmark Vesey in 1822, continued to haunt southern whites. Rebellions in the West Indies, especially the one in Haiti, also echoed through the early nineteenth century. Then in 1831 an enslaved man named Nat Turner — who had previously seemed obedient — organized a revolt in rural Virginia that stunned whites across the South. Turner was a religious visionary who believed that God had given him a mission. On the night of August 21, he and his followers killed his enslavers, the Travis family, and then headed to nearby plantations in Southampton County. The insurrection led to the deaths of fifty-seven white men, women, and children and liberated more than fifty enslaved people. But on August 22, outraged white militiamen burst on the scene and

TEACHING IDEA

Incorporating Websites

Visit the Stanford History Education Group site to obtain a lesson plan on the leader of the largest antebellum slave rebellion, Nat Turner (sheg.standoford.edu). Specifically, this lesson focuses on sourcing and corroborating accounts about him.

BUILDING AP® SKILLS

Contextualization

Ask the class for the reasons why there were very few rebellions against the institution of slavery during the nineteenth century. Write on the board the three that have already been covered: Gabriel Prosser, Denmark Vessey, and Nat Turner. Possible answers include: 1) *limited options for enslaved people;* 2) *highly codified system restricting African Americans whether enslaved or free;* and 3) *even some poor whites supported the institution although they did not benefit from it.*

TEACHING IDEA

Class Discussion

Start this activity by asking students: How did supporters of slavery try to justify the unjustifiable? Then conduct a class discussion on the three main pro-slavery arguments: 1) Slavery was an economic "necessity" for the South; 2) The institution was a "positive good" for enslaved people; and 3) The Bible and God did not specifically prohibit slavery and the institution allowed planters to "civilize" and Christianize Africans. Discuss the logical fallacies of these arguments. To conclude, ask students how the rebellions studied in Module 4-1 inform their understanding of the "positive good" argument.

APPLY THE TIP

After having students identify from the reading the restrictions placed on enslaved and free African Americans, have them research the actual stricter slave codes. For example, Virginia and South Carolina were notorious for theirs, especially after Nat Turner's rebellion and the *Amistad* case. Students should also pay attention to how whites were restricted by some of these slave codes (e.g., could not teach an enslaved person how to read or write, etc.). For an overview of the history of slavery including the emergence of slave codes, have students visit the History Channel's website and search for "Slavery in America" (history.com). Lastly, you may also want students to make connections between these slave codes and the original example that most southern states followed — the Barbados Slave Codes.

Nat Turner's rebellion 1831 slave uprising in Virginia led by Nat Turner. Turner's rebellion generated panic among white southerners, leading to tighter control of African Americans and white southerners, leading to the passage of stricter slave codes in southern states.

abolitionists Members of the movement seeking to end the system of slavery.

AP® TIP
Evaluate the impact of Nat Turner's Rebellion and the Amistad case on the treatment of enslaved people in the South.

---

eventually captured the black rebels. Turner managed to hide out for two months but was eventually caught, tried, and hung. Virginia executed fifty-five other African Americans suspected of assisting Turner.

Nat Turner's rebellion instilled panic among white Virginians, who beat and killed some 200 black people with no connection to the uprising. White southerners worried they might be killed in their sleep by seemingly submissive enslaved people. News of the rebellion traveled through enslaved communities as well, inspiring both pride and anxiety. The execution of Turner and his followers reminded African Americans how far whites would go to protect the institution of slavery.

A mutiny on the Spanish slave ship *Amistad* in 1839 reinforced white southerners' fears of rebellion. When Africans being transported for sale in the West Indies seized control of the ship near Cuba, the U.S. navy captured the vessel and imprisoned the enslaved rebels. But international treaties outlawing the Atlantic slave trade and pressure applied by abolitionists led to a court case in which former president John Quincy Adams defended the right of the Africans to their freedom. The widely publicized case reached the U.S. Supreme Court in 1841, and the Court freed the rebels. While the ruling was cheered by **abolitionists**, who supported ending slavery, white southerners were shocked that the justices would liberate enslaved men.

Slave revolts led many southern states to impose harsher controls; however, Nat Turner's rebellion led some white Virginians to question slavery itself. In December 1831, the state assembly established a special committee to consider the crisis. Representatives from western counties, where slavery was never profitable, argued for gradual abolition laws and the colonization of the state's black population in Africa. Hundreds of women in the region sent petitions to the Virginia legislature supporting these positions.

While advocates of colonization gained significant support, eastern planters vehemently opposed abolition or colonization, and leading intellectuals argued for the benefits of slavery. Professor Thomas Dew, president of the College of William and Mary, insisted that slaveholders performed godly work in raising Africans and African Americans from the status of brute beast to civilized Christian. "Every one acquainted with southern slaves," he claimed, "knows that the slave rejoices in the elevation and prosperity of his master." In the fall of 1832 the Virginia legislature embraced Dew's proslavery argument, rejected gradual emancipation, and imposed new restrictions on enslaved and free black people.

From the 1820s to the 1840s, more stringent codes were passed across the South. Most southern legislatures prohibited slaveholders from manumitting the people they kept enslaved, made it illegal to teach enslaved people to read or write, placed new limits on independent black churches, abolished enslaved people's already limited access to courts, outlawed marriage between enslaved people, banned antislavery literature, defined rape as a crime only against white women, and outlawed assemblies of more than three black people without a white person present.

States also regulated the lives of free black people. Some prohibited them from residing within state borders, others required free African Americans to post large bonds to ensure good behavior, which could be claimed for perceived infractions by community authorities, and most forbade those who left the state from returning. The homes of free people could be raided at any time, and the children of free black women were subject to stringent apprenticeship laws that kept many in virtual slavery.

Such measures proved largely successful in controlling enslaved people and significantly worsened the lives of African Americans in the South. White people paid a much smaller price. Restricting education and mobility for black people often hindered schooling and transportation for poor whites as well. Moreover, characterizing the region's primary labor force as savage and lazy discouraged investment in industry and other forms of economic development. And the regulations increased tensions between poorer whites, who were often responsible for enforcement, and wealthy whites, who benefited most clearly from their imposition.

REVIEW

- What were the most common methods enslaved people used to rebel?
- What restrictions were placed on enslaved and free black people after Nat Turner's rebellion?

EXPLORING AP® THEMES

Social Structures

Visit the National Archives site for teachers to obtain a lesson plan on the case *U.S. v. Amistad* (docsteach.org). In their quest for freedom, a group of enslaved people organized themselves and took over a ship engaging in the international slave trade. This lesson focuses on the role of the federal court system and the ultimate decision made by the nation's highest court. To conclude, discuss with students how this case impacted the broader American society and influenced the growing antislavery movement in the country.

White Southerners Who Were Not Slaveholders

yeoman farmers Southern independent landowners who were not slaveholders. Although yeoman farmers had connections to the South's plantation economy, many realized that their interests were not always identical to those of the planter elite.

Yeomen farmers, independent owners of small plots who were generally not slaveholders, had a complex relationship with the South's plantation economy. Many were related to slaveholders, and they often depended on planters to ship their crops to market. Some made extra money by hiring themselves out to planters. Yet yeomen farmers also recognized that their economic interests and daily experiences often diverged from those of planters. This was particularly clear on slavery's frontier, where many yeomen farmers had to carve fields out of forests without the benefit of enslaved labor. They joined with friends and neighbors for barn raisings, corn shuckings, quilting bees, and other collective endeavors that combined labor with sociability. Church services and church socials also brought small farm families together.

While most yeomen farmers believed in slavery, they sometimes challenged planters' authority and assumptions. In the Virginia slavery debates, for example, small farmers from western districts advocated gradual abolition. As growing numbers gained the right to vote in the 1830s and 1840s, they voiced their concerns in county and state legislatures. They advocated more liberal policies toward debtors and demanded greater representation in state legislatures. They also protested planters' obstruction of common lands and waterways, such as building dams upriver that deprived farmers downriver of fishing rights. Yeomen farmers questioned certain ideals embraced by elites. Although plantation mistresses considered manual labor beneath them, the wives and daughters of many small farmers worked in the fields, hauled water, and chopped wood. Still, yeomen farmers' ability to diminish planter control was limited by the continued importance of cotton to the southern economy.

White southerners who owned no property at all had fewer means of challenging planters' power. These poor whites depended on hunting and fishing in frontier areas, performing day labor on farms and plantations, or working on docks or as servants in southern cities. Poor white people competed with free and enslaved black people for employment and often harbored resentments as a result.

AP® TIP
Evaluate the degree to which the power held and policies enacted by the plantation-owning aristocracy reflected continuity in American development since 1619.

Some poor whites remained in the same community for decades, establishing themselves on the margins of society. They attended church regularly, performed day labor for affluent families, and taught their children to defer to those higher on the social ladder. Other poor whites moved frequently and survived by combining legal and illegal ventures. They might perform day labor while also stealing food from local farmers. These men and women often had few ties to local communities and little religious training or education. Although poor white people unnerved southern elites by flouting the law and sometimes befriending poor black people, they could not mount any significant challenge to planter control.

The South's small but growing middle class distanced themselves from poorer whites in pursuit of stability and respectability. They worked as doctors, lawyers, teachers, and shopkeepers and often looked to the North for models to emulate. Many were educated in northern schools and developed ties with their commercial or professional counterparts in that region. They were avid readers of newspapers, religious tracts, and literary periodicals published in the North. And like middle-class northerners, southern businessmen often depended on their wives' social and financial skills to succeed.

Nonetheless, middle-class southern men shared many of the social attitudes and political priorities of slaveholders. They participated alongside planters in benevolent, literary, and temperance societies and agricultural reform organizations. Most middle-class southerners also adamantly supported slavery. In fact, some suggested that bound labor might be useful to industry. Despite the emergence of a small middle class, however, the gap between rich and poor continued to expand in the South.

REVIEW
- How did slavery shape the lives of white southerners who were not slaveholders?

Planters Seek to Unify White Southerners

Planters faced another challenge as nations in Europe and South America began to abolish slavery. Antislavery views, first widely expressed by Quakers, gained growing support among evangelical Protestants in Great Britain and the United States and among political radicals in Europe. Slave rebellions in Haiti and the British West Indies in the early nineteenth century intensified these efforts. In 1807 the British Parliament forbade the sale of enslaved people

---

TEACHING IDEA

Incorporating Videos

Have students watch selected clips from the 1997 movie *Amistad* about mutiny aboard a slave ship and the fight for freedom that went all the way to the Supreme Court of the United States. This movie also highlights the role played by former president John Quincy Adams.

APPLY THE TIP

To develop a better understanding of the power held in the South by the plantation-owning aristocracy and how this was a continuity since 1619, have students revisit the establishment of the House of Burgesses, which was created that same year. That first colonial assembly and experiment in self-government in Virginia limited representation to large landowners who were the most powerful during the colonial period.

TEACHING IDEA

Class Discussion

Ask students: Why would lower-class whites (e.g., yeomen farmers) and the small but emerging middle-class support the institution of slavery even though it did not directly benefit them? Possible answers include: *many saw enslaved people (and free African Americans) as economic competition*; *racial "superiority" complex regardless of class or education*.

Period 4: 1800–1848

MODULE 4-6 Slavery and Southern Society

within its empire and in 1834 emancipated all those who remained enslaved. France followed suit in 1848. As Spanish colonies such as Mexico and Nicaragua gained their independence in the 1820s and 1830s, they, too, eradicated the institution. Meanwhile gradual abolition laws in the northern United States slowly eliminated slavery there. Although slavery continued in Brazil and in Spanish colonies such as Cuba, and serfdom remained in Russia, international attitudes toward human bondage were shifting.

In response, planters wielded their political and economic power to forge tighter bonds among white southerners. According to the three-fifths compromise in the U.S. Constitution, areas with large enslaved populations gained more representatives in Congress than those without. The policy also applied to state elections, giving such areas disproportionate power in state politics. In addition, planters used their resources to provide credit for those in need, offer seasonal employment for poorer whites, transport crops to market for yeomen farmers, and help out in times of crisis. Few whites could afford to antagonize these affluent benefactors.

While planters continued to insist that the U.S. Constitution protected slavery and the right of states to enforce their own labor systems, they did not take white solidarity for granted. From the 1830s on, they relied on the ideology of **white supremacy** to cement the belief that all white people, regardless of class or education, were superior to all black people. Following on Thomas Dew, southern elites argued with growing intensity that the moral and intellectual failings of black people meant that slavery was not just a necessary evil but a positive good. At the same time, they insisted that black people harbored deep animosity toward whites, which could be controlled only by regulating every aspect of their lives. Combining racial fear and racial pride, planters forged bonds with poor and middle-class whites to guarantee their continued dominance. They continued to seek support from state and national legislators as well.

AP® ANALYZING SOURCES

Source: John C. Calhoun, *Slavery a Positive Good*, 1837

"I hold that in the present state of civilization, where two races of different origin, and distinguished by color, and other physical differences, as well as intellectual, are brought together, the relation now existing in the slave-holding States between the two, is, instead of an evil, a good—a positive good. . . . [T]here never has yet existed a wealthy and civilized society in which one portion of the community did not, in point of fact, live on the labor of the other. . . . [L]ook at the sick, and the old and infirm slave, on one hand, in the midst of his family and friends, under the kind superintending care of his master and mistress, and compare it with the forlorn and wretched condition of the pauper in the poor house. . . . I fearlessly assert that the existing relation between the two races in the South, against which these blind fanatics are waging war, forms the most solid and durable foundation on which to rear free and stable political institutions. It is useless to disguise the fact. There is and always has been in an advanced stage of wealth and civilization, a conflict between labor and capital. The condition of society in the South exempts us from the disorders and dangers resulting from this conflict; and which explains why it is that the political condition of the slave-holding States has been so much more stable and quiet than those of the North."

Questions for Analysis
1. Identify the moral and economic justifications for slavery that Calhoun uses in this speech.
2. Describe the political and social contexts surrounding Calhoun's speech.
3. Explain how Calhoun's argument reflects an ideology of white supremacy.

REVIEW
How were planters able to maintain southern support for slavery after it was ended in the North and in other countries?

BUILDING AP® SKILLS

Contextualization

Help students put the institution of slavery in context with what was happening around the world at the time. Antislavery movements were already taking place in Great Britain (1830s), Latin America (except for Brazil) (1820s), Mexico (1830s), and the British West Indies (1830s). Ask students to brainstorm how these movements influenced the United States abolitionist movement. They should also identify that slavery existed in Brazil, Cuba, and Puerto Rico (the last two being Spanish colonies) and would survive in these places even beyond abolition in the United States in 1865.

TRM Suggested Responses to Questions

TRM Module 4.6 AP® Analyzing Sources Handout 3

AP® WRITING HISTORICALLY — Short-Answer Question Practice

ACTIVITY

Read the following question carefully and write a short response. Use complete sentences.

Use the maps that follow to answer (a), (b), and (c).

Source: *Enslaved Population, 1820 and 1860*

Enslaved Population, 1820
• One dot equals 200 enslaved people

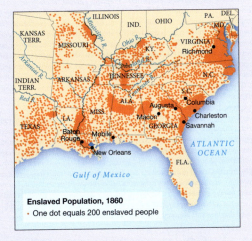

Enslaved Population, 1860
• One dot equals 200 enslaved people

a. Briefly explain how ONE specific historical event or development contributed to a change in the enslaved populations shown on the maps.
b. Briefly explain ONE specific effect of a change in the enslaved populations shown on the maps.
c. Briefly explain ANOTHER specific effect of a change in the enslaved populations shown on the maps.

TRM Suggested Responses to Questions

TEACHING IDEA

Check for Understanding

The prerequisite for answering this type of question is for students to identify a significant change between the two maps. A quick examination of the maps should reveal at least three changes: the westward and southern expansion of slavery, the overall increase of the enslaved population in the South, and the slight but noticeable increase of slavery in areas where it was already well established, such as the Virginia and South Carolina coasts and alongside the southern Mississippi River. Whichever change(s) students choose to write about, ask them to consider why it happened (one cause) and what impacts it had (two effects). Use the *ACE* strategy to create an approximately nine-sentence response to this SAQ that fully answers each part (a refresher on *ACE* can be found on page 21).

TEACHING IDEA

AP® Writing Historically Review

This question requires students to examine causes and effects of the increase in enslaved populations in the mid-nineteenth century. Consider the following group activity as a way of ensuring students are using accurate information in their responses. By doing this, you are now focusing on how well students write about the information in their responses and not whether the information provided is accurate. Divide students into groups of three or four and have each student individually brainstorm one cause and two effects of the information provided in the maps. After each student has outlined a response, have the groups share answers and select the best example for the one cause and two effects. In this way, students are comparing and selecting accurate evidence for their answers.

TRM Suggested Responses to Questions

Module 4-7

Social Reform Movements

LEARNING TARGETS
By the end of this module, you should be able to:
- Explain what factors contributed to the rise of a new national culture in the first half of the 1800s.
- Explain the causes of the Second Great Awakening.
- Explain how social reform efforts impacted American society in the first half of the 1800s.

THEMATIC FOCUS
American and National Identity

A new national culture combining European and American elements took shape in the early 1800s with the spread of public education and printed materials. The Second Great Awakening and transcendentalism sparked an array of social reform efforts, further transforming American culture.

HISTORICAL REASONING FOCUS
Causation

TASK ▶ While this module focuses mostly on the effects of cultural and religious developments, remember to take the causes of those developments into account as you read. In particular, consider how the emergence of a distinctly American culture, the religious revivals of the Second Great Awakening, the spread of transcendentalist ideas, and the growing popularity of social reform movements changed the lives of Americans throughout the United States.

TEACHING IDEA

Class Discussion

As a bell ringer, write the following questions on the board: Should public schools only teach academic subjects (e.g., history)? Or should they also focus on character education and citizenship? The answers depend on the learning objectives for such a system. After students share out their answers, get students to see the nexus between public education and the building of a national culture. By providing American children with a "common education," educators could not only teach the subject matter but also cultivate the values and republican ideas that set the nation apart from others. Conclude by asking students how else we could raise little boys to grow up and become the next George Washington and embody civic virtue? Do point out the limited opportunities for girls, racial minorities, and those from lower classes.

In his inaugural address in March 1801, President Thomas Jefferson argued that the vast distance between Europe and the United States was a blessing, allowing Americans to develop their own unique culture and institutions. For many Americans, education offered one means of ensuring a distinctive national identity. Public schools could train American children in republican values, while the wealthiest among them could attend private academies and colleges. Newspapers, sermons, books, magazines, and other printed works could also help forge a common identity among the nation's far-flung citizens. Even the presence of American Indians and African Americans contributed to art and literature that were uniquely American. Yet educational opportunities differed by race and class as well as by sex.

The development of a common American identity continued as men and women of all classes and races embraced the Protestant religious revival known as the Second Great Awakening to express deeply held beliefs and reclaim a sense of the nation's godly mission. Yet evangelical Protestantism was not the only religious tradition to thrive in this period. Catholic churches and Jewish synagogues multiplied with immigration, and in the North Quaker meetings and Unitarian congregations flourished as well. New religious groups also attracted thousands of followers while transcendentalists sought deeper engagements with nature as another path to spiritual renewal.

Both religious commitments and secular problems spurred social activism in the 1830s and 1840s. In cities, small towns, and rural communities, northerners founded organizations, launched campaigns, and established institutions to better the world around them. Yet even Americans who agreed that society needed to be reformed still often disagreed over priorities and solutions. Moreover, while some activists employed moral arguments to persuade Americans to follow their lead, others insisted that laws that imposed reform were the only effective means of change.

Building a National Culture

At the turn of the nineteenth century, many Americans sought to create a new and distinct culture to complement the country's newly established political independence. To promote his vision of a distinctly American literature, Noah Webster published the *American Spelling Book* (1810) and the *American Dictionary of the English Language* (1828). Webster's books were widely used in the nation's expanding network of schools and academies and led to more standardized spelling and pronunciation of commonly used words.

BUILDING AP® SKILLS

Making Connections

For homework, ask students to review how the War of 1812 contributed to the rise of a new national culture in the first half of the nineteenth century. They should identify that although the war itself was technically a "stalemate," it did build up American confidence and stimulated interest in creating institutions that would be distinct from those of Europe. Lastly, tell students to incorporate evidence from the reading in this module (e.g., Noah Webster's books).

Marmaduke Multiply's Merry Method of Making Minor Mathematics, c. 1815 After Noah Webster introduced his *American Spelling Book* in 1810, math instructors introduced books for young people like the one shown here. The book uses rhymes and colorful illustrations to teach students multiplication tables. **What does the publication of educational books such as this one suggest about the value Americans placed on public schooling during the early 1800s?**

Romantic era Early nineteenth-century artistic and intellectual movement that reflected a belief in human perfectibility and challenged Enlightenment ideas of rationality by insisting on the importance of human passion, the mysteries of nature, and the virtues of common folk.

At the same time, developments in Europe, particularly liberal social ideas and **Romantic era** beliefs in human perfectibility, shaped American art, literature, philosophy, and architecture in the early nineteenth century. European Romantics, like the English poet William Wordsworth, the German philosopher Immanuel Kant, and the French painter Eugène Delacroix, challenged Enlightenment ideas of rationality by insisting on the importance of human passion, the mysteries of nature, and the virtues of common folk.

American novelists in the early republic drew on these ideas as they sought to educate readers about virtue. Advances in printing and the manufacture of paper increased the circulation of novels, a literary genre developed in Britain and continental Europe at the turn of the eighteenth century. Improvements in girls' education then produced a growing audience for novels among women. American authors like Susanna Rowson placed ordinary women and men in moments of high drama that tested their moral character. Novelists also emphasized new marital ideals, by which husbands and wives became affectionate partners and companions in creating a home and family.

Washington Irving was one of the most well-known literary figures in the early republic. He wrote a series of popular folktales, including "The Legend of Sleepy Hollow" and "Rip Van Winkle," that were published in his *Sketchbook* in 1820. They drew on the Dutch culture of the Hudson valley region and often poked fun at more celebratory tales of early American history. In one serious essay, Irving challenged popular accounts of colonial wars that ignored courageous actions by American Indians while applauding white atrocities.

Still, books that glorified the nation's past were also enormously popular. Just as European Romantics emphasized individual, especially heroic, action, so too did America's earliest historical writers. Among the most influential were Mason Weems, author of the *Life of Washington* (1806), a celebratory if fanciful biography, and Mercy Otis Warren, who wrote a three-volume *History of the Revolution* (1805). The influence of American authors increased as residents in both urban and rural areas purchased growing numbers of books.

AP® TIP
Evaluate the degree to which mid-nineteenth century American culture continued to be influenced by ideas developed in Europe.

REVIEW

- How did Romanticism contribute to the development of a national identity?

TEACHING IDEA

Project Ideas

Following the image of *Marmaduke Multiply's Merry Method of Making Minor Mathematics*, have students create a short children's book on the American Revolution. Assign each student to create a single page with a colorful illustration depicting an event of historical significance (e.g., Boston Tea Party, etc.). Since this publication would target a young audience, only require one or two sentences per page. Students should include images associated with the theme of American and national identity, such as founding documents and our founding fathers.

TEACHING IDEA

Incorporating Primary Sources

Have students read a popular folktale from Washington Irving like "The Legend of Sleepy Hollow" or "Rip Van Winkle" in its entirety. These stories can be found on Project Gutenberg's website (gutenberg.org). Or you can provide students with excerpts from the *Life of Washington* (1806) by Mason Weems or the *History of the Revolution* by Mercy Otis Warren. Whatever you select, conclude the activity by having students write a paragraph on how the writing represents an emerging American identity.

EXPLORING AP® THEMES

American and Regional Culture

Have students look at the Key Concepts, Events, and People in the Period 4 Review on page 352 and identify which terms should be organized under the theme American and regional culture. Then, ask them to define each term and describe the historical significance — how and/or why does it matter?

Period 4: 1800–1848

MODULE 4-7 Social Reform Movements

The Roots of the Second Great Awakening

Second Great Awakening Evangelical revival movement that began in the South in the early nineteenth century and then spread to the North. The social and economic changes of the first half of the nineteenth century were a major spur to religious revivals, which in turn spurred social reform movements.

Amid the wave of scientific discoveries of the late eighteenth and early nineteenth centuries, religious leaders sought to renew American spirituality. However, like the first Great Awakening (see Module 2-9), the spiritual renewal of the **Second Great Awakening** was rooted less in established churches and educated ministers than in new religious organizations and popular preachers. Methodist and Baptist churches were especially vital to this development. In 1780, only fifty Methodist churches existed in the United States. By 1820, it was the largest denomination in the nation, followed closely by Baptists. Believing that everyone could gain salvation, the two denominations appealed to small farmers, workers, and the poor as well as to women and African Americans. In some cases, women and black people joined this popular ministry, and a few attracted followings independent of any church. Jemima Wilkinson, a white woman who called herself "the Publick Universal Friend," developed a gender-neutral persona. Proclaiming herself the "Spirit of Light," she preached throughout the Northeast.

In rural and frontier areas, Baptists, Methodists, and Presbyterians organized camp meetings, where a dozen or more preachers, many without formal training, tapped into deep wells of spirituality. The first camp meeting, held in Cane Ridge, Kentucky in 1801, attracted some 10,000 men and women. White and black people, enslaved and free, attended these meetings and were encouraged to dance, shout, sing, and pray. For the next two decades, camp meetings continued to attract large crowds across the South and West.

Although diverse religious traditions flourished in the United States, evangelical Protestantism proved the most powerful in the 1820s and 1830s, spreading northward from its southern and western roots. Evangelical churches hosted revivals, celebrated conversions, and organized prayer and missionary societies. The Second Great Awakening transformed Protestant churches and the social fabric of northern life.

boomtown Areas that rapidly developed following the swift arrival of capital, typically from mining enterprises or the railroad, in the west.

Ministers like Charles Grandison Finney adopted techniques first wielded by southern Methodists and Baptists: plain speaking, powerful images, and mass meetings. But Finney molded these techniques for a more affluent audience and held his "camp meetings" in established churches. By the late 1820s, **boomtown** growth along the Erie Canal aroused deep concerns among religious leaders about the rising tide of sin. In response, the Reverend Finney arrived in Rochester in September 1830. He began preaching in local Presbyterian churches, leading crowded prayer meetings that lasted late into the night. Individual worshippers walked to special benches designated for anxious sinners, who were prayed over in public. Female parishioners played crucial roles, encouraging their husbands, sons, friends, and neighbors to submit to God.

AP® TIP
Analyze the ways in which the Second Great Awakening enhanced ideals associated with American values as well as challenged the power of the South's aristocracy, including the system of slavery.

Thousands of Rochester residents joined in the evangelical experience as Finney's powerful message engulfed other denominations. The significance of these revivals went far beyond an increase in church membership. Finney converted "the great mass of the most influential people" in the city: merchants, lawyers, doctors, master craftsmen, and shopkeepers. Equally important, he proclaimed that if Christians were "united all over the world," the return of Jesus Christ "might be brought about in three months." Preachers in Rochester and the surrounding towns took up his call, and converts committed themselves to preparing the world for Christ's arrival.

AP® ANALYZING SOURCES

Source: Charles G. Finney, *An Influential Woman Converts*, 1830

"The wife of a prominent lawyer . . . was one of the first converts. She was a woman of high standing, a lady of culture and extensive influence. . . .
Mrs. M. had been a [happy], worldly woman, and very fond of society. She afterward told me that when I first came there, she greatly regretted it, and feared [that] . . . a revival would greatly interfere with the pleasures and amusements that she had promised herself that winter."

TEACHING IDEA

AP® Central

Use the 2002 AP® U.S. History exam DBQ on the emergence of nationalism and sectionalism after the War of 1812 and during the "Era of Good Feelings" as a bell ringer. This question is available on the College Board's AP® U.S. History Past Exam Questions section under "2002: Form B" (apcentral.collegeboard.org). Have students write a thesis for the question. Next, students should pick one category of their thesis and then categorize two or three documents. Then, have students write a body paragraph using the documents and work on linking document analysis to their thesis.

BUILDING AP® SKILLS

Contextualization

Have students identify and explain why religious revivals primarily took place along the frontier and in an area like the "burned-over" district in New York State around the Erie Canal. Additionally, have them explain why many converts tended to be women, the poor, and African Americans. Possible answers: 1) *The need for stability in emerging and growing places (e.g., boomtowns)*; 2) *Religion tends to provide a sense of place and community*; 3) *Religion can also provide hope (e.g., possibility of liberation for enslaved people and social mobility for the poor) and an acceptable forum for women to have a voice and play a greater role in society.*

TRM Suggested Responses to Questions

TRM Module 4.7 AP® Analyzing Sources Handout 1

"On conversing with her I found that the Spirit of the Lord was indeed dealing with her. . . . She was bowed down with great conviction of sin. . . . I pressed her earnestly to renounce sin, and the world, and self, and everything for Christ. . . . [W]e knelt down to pray; and my mind being full of the subject of the pride of her heart . . . I very soon introduced the text: 'Except ye be converted and become as little children, ye shall in no wise enter into the kingdom of heaven.' . . . [A]lmost immediately I heard Mrs M. . . . repeating that text:

'Except ye be converted and become as little children—as little children—Except ye be converted and become as little children.' I observed that her mind was taken with that, and the Spirit of God was pressing it upon her heart. I therefore continued to pray, holding that subject before her mind. . . .

[H]er heart broke down, her sensibility gushed forth, and before we rose . . . , she was indeed a little child. . . ."

Questions for Analysis
1. Describe Finney's depiction of Mrs. M.
2. Describe the context surrounding Finney's revival efforts.
3. Explain why Finney targeted wealthy and influential individuals such as Mrs. M. for conversion.

Developments in Rochester were replicated in cities across the North. Presbyterian, Congregational, and Episcopalian churches overflowed with middle-class and wealthy Americans, while Baptists and Methodists ministered to more laboring women and men. Black Baptists and Methodists evangelized in their own communities, combining powerful preaching with rousing spirituals. In Philadelphia, African Americans built fifteen churches between 1799 and 1830. A few black women joined men in evangelizing to their fellow African Americans.

Tens of thousands of black and white converts embraced evangelicals' message of moral outreach. No reform movement gained greater impetus from the revivals than temperance, whose advocates sought to moderate and then ban the sale and consumption of alcohol. In the 1820s Americans fifteen years and older consumed six to seven gallons of distilled alcohol per person per year (about double the amount consumed today). Middle-class evangelicals, who once accepted moderate drinking as healthful, now insisted on eliminating alcohol consumption altogether.

AP® ANALYZING SOURCES

Source: Lyman Beecher, *The Evils Of Intemperance*, 1827

"When we behold an individual cut off in youth or in middle age, or witness the [fading] energies, improvidence, and unfaithfulness of a neighbor, it is but a single instance, and we become accustomed to it; but such instances are multiplying in our land in every direction, and are to be found in every department of labor, and the amount of earnings prevented or squandered is incalculable: to all which must be added the accumulating and frightful expense incurred for the support of those and their families whom intemperance has made paupers. In every city and town the poor-tax, created chiefly by intemperance, is augmenting. The receptacles for the poor are becoming too strait for their accommodation. We must pull them down and build greater to provide accommodations for the votaries of inebriation; for the frequency of going upon the town has taken away the reluctance of pride, and destroyed the motives to providence which the fear of poverty and suffering once supplied. The prospect of a destitute old-age, or of a suffering family, no longer troubles the vicious portion of our community. They drink up their daily earnings, and bless God for the poor-house, and begin to look upon it as, of right, the drunkard's home, and contrive to arrive thither as early as idleness and excess will give them a passport to this sinecure of vice. Thus is the insatiable destroyer of industry

(Continued)

TEACHING IDEA

Understanding People Who Made a Difference

Since Charles Grandison Finney is already covered in the module, have students research Peter Cartwright and focus on the contributions he made during the Second Great Awakening along the frontier and the Midwest. Have students highlight the role he played in the history of the Methodist Church in the country.

TEACHING IDEA

Analyzing Art and Images

To supplement the textual documents used under the "Analyzing Sources" from Charles G. Finney and Lyman Beecher, have students analyze a visual about the temperance crusade and/or the role of women. You may want students to look at the "Drunkard's Progress," which can easily be found online.

TRM Suggested Responses to Questions

TRM Module 4.7 AP® Analyzing Sources Handout 2

EXPLORING AP® THEMES

American and Regional Culture

Have students make a thematic connection between the Second Great Awakening and the First. Specifically, have students compare and contrast the causes for each religious revival. While both resulted from a reaction/backlash to a decline in religious piety, the first happened as a reaction to the Enlightenment and the second during the context of the Romantic Era and beliefs in human perfectibility. Also worth noting is the difference between the religious men who led each movement. The first was led by educated ministers and established churches and the second by more popular and emotional preachers from the new emerging religious sects. Lastly, the first led to challenging authority while the second tried making democratic ideals a reality.

marching through the land, rearing poor-houses, and augmenting taxation: night and day, with sleepless activity, squandering property, cutting the sinews of industry, undermining vigor, engendering disease, paralyzing intellect, impairing moral principle, cutting short the date of life, and rolling up a national debt, invisible, but real and terrific as the debt of England; continually transferring larger and larger bodies of men from the class of contributors to the national income to the class of worthless consumers."

Questions for Analysis

1. Describe Beecher's portrayal of the effects of alcohol.
2. Explain how Beecher's argument fits within the broader context of the Second Great Awakening.
3. Evaluate the extent to which Beecher's argument is primarily based on social, economic, or moral claims.

REVIEW

- How did the Second Great Awakening change American society during the mid-nineteenth century?

New Visions of Faith and Reform

AP® TIP
Evaluate the degree to which the development of religious sects in the United States reflected the growing diversity of its inhabitants.

Although enthusiasm for temperance and other reforms faded during the Panic of 1837 and many churches lost members, the Second Great Awakening continued in its aftermath. But now evangelical ministers competed for souls with a variety of other religious groups, many of which supported good works and social reform. The Society of Friends, the first religious group to refuse fellowship to slaveholders, expanded throughout the early nineteenth century, but largely in the North and Midwest. Having divided in 1827 and again in 1848, the Society of Friends continued to grow. So, too, did its influence in reform movements as activists like Amy Post carried Quaker testimonies against alcohol, war, and slavery into the wider society. Unitarians also combined religious worship with social reform. They differed from other Christians by believing in a single unified higher spirit rather than the Trinity of the Father, the Son, and the Holy Spirit. Emerging mainly in New England in the early nineteenth century, Unitarian societies slowly spread west and south in the 1830s. Opposed to evangelical revivalism and dedicated to a rational approach to understanding the divine, Unitarians attracted prominent literary figures such as James Russell Lowell and Harvard luminaries like William Ellery Channing.

Other churches grew as a result of immigration. Dozens of Catholic churches were established to meet the needs of Irish and some German immigrants. With the rapid increase in Catholic churches, Irish priests multiplied in the 1840s and 1850s, and women's religious orders became increasingly Irish as well. At the same time, synagogues, Hebrew schools, and Hebrew aid societies signaled the growing presence of Jewish immigrants, chiefly from Germany, in the United States. These religious groups were less active in social reform and more focused on assisting their own congregants in securing a foothold in their new home.

Entirely new religious groups also flourished in the 1840s. One of the most important was the Church of Jesus Christ of Latter-Day Saints, or Mormons, founded by Joseph Smith. Smith began to receive visions from God at age fifteen and was directed to dig up gold plates inscribed with instructions for redeeming the Lost Tribes of Israel. *The Book of Mormon* (1830), supposedly based on these inscriptions, served, along with the Bible, as the scriptural foundation of the Church of Jesus Christ of Latter-Day Saints, which Smith led as the Prophet.

Smith founded not only a church but a theocracy (a community governed by religious leaders). In the mid-1830s Mormons established a settlement at Nauvoo, Illinois and recruited followers—black and white—from the eastern United States and England. When Smith voiced antislavery views, some local residents expressed outrage. But it was his claim to revelations sanctioning polygamy that led local authorities to arrest him and his brother. When a mob then lynched the Smith brothers,

---

TEACHING IDEA

Incorporating Websites

One of the main religious groups that emerged at the time and is still around today is the Mormons, or the Church of Jesus Christ of Latter-Day Saints. Have students visit their official website (churchofjesuschrist.org) and that of the historically Mormon university, Brigham Young University, "BYU" (byu.edu). While on these sites, have students identify information associated with social reforms and doing good works in the present day.

TEACHING IDEA

Connecting the Dots

As religion became even more diverse in the United States during the Second Great Awakening, the various sects/denominations became heavily involved in reform efforts and mutual aid groups that transformed American society and culture. Divide the class into five groups and assign a religious affiliation for them to research. Specifically, have students research Quakers (or "Society of Friends"), Unitarians, Catholics, Jewish people, or Millerites (now Seventh Day Adventists) and identify what they were involved in to fix the problems that existed in the nation at the time.

Brigham Young, a successful missionary, took over as Prophet. In 1846 he led 12,000 followers west, 5,000 of whom settled near the Great Salt Lake, in what would soon become the Utah Territory. Isolated from anti-Mormon mobs, Young established a thriving theocracy. In this settlement, leaders practiced polygamy and denied black members the right to become priests.

New religious groups also formed by separating from established denominations. William Miller, a prosperous farmer and Baptist preacher, claimed that the Bible proved that the Second Coming of Jesus Christ would occur in 1843. Thousands of Americans joined the Millerites. When various dates for Christ's Second Coming passed without incident, however, Millerites developed competing interpretations for the failure and divided into distinct groups. The most influential group formed the Seventh-Day Adventist Church in the 1840s.

REVIEW

- What religious changes took place in America during the 1830s and 1840s?

Transcendentalism

transcendentalism Movement founded in the 1830s that proposed that individuals look inside themselves and to nature for spiritual and moral guidance rather than to formal religion.

Another important movement for spiritual renewal was rooted in the transcendent power of nature. The founder of this **transcendentalist** school of thought was Ralph Waldo Emerson. Raised a Unitarian, Emerson began challenging the church's ideas. His 1836 essay entitled "Nature" expounded his newfound belief in a Universal Being. This Being existed as an ideal reality beyond the material world and was accessible through nature. Emerson's natural world was distinctly American and suggested that moral perfection could be achieved in the United States. Emerson expressed his ideas in widely read essays and books and in popular lectures.

▲ **Thomas Cole, View of the Round-Top in the Catskills Mountains, 1827** Thomas Cole was born in England in 1801, migrated to America in 1818, and lived for many years in Catskill, New York with his wife and children until his death in 1848. Many of his paintings captured a romantic view of nature that combined a hint of wildness with the beauty of mountain mists and sunlit rivers shown here. **How does the portrayal of nature in this painting reflect transcendentalist ideas of the time?**

BUILDING AP® SKILLS

Making Connections

Give students excerpts of Henry David Thoreau's essay titled "Civil Disobedience," which can be found on Project Gutenberg's website (gutenberg.org). Then conduct a discussion on how this transcendentalist writing influenced social reformers and transformed American culture. Next, help students make connections to future leaders like Mohandas Gandhi in India and Dr. Martin Luther King Jr. in the United States during the twentieth century.

▲ **Differentiation**

If your students do not have prior knowledge about these individuals, ask them to do research first so connections can be made about their use of peaceful, non-violent protesting.

TEACHING IDEA

Incorporating Primary Sources

Give students excerpts of Ralph Waldo Emerson's essay titled "Nature" and Henry David Thoreau's "Walden," which can both be found on Project Gutenberg's website (gutenberg.org). Then conduct a discussion on how these transcendentalist writings influenced social reformers and transformed American culture. This activity may also be a great opportunity to do some interdisciplinary planning and collaboration with the language arts department.

EXPLORING AP® THEMES

Analyzing Art and Images

Have students research the Hudson River School and some of its main artists, including Thomas Cole and George Catlin. A good resource for them is the Met Museum's website (metmuseum.org). Ask them to write a paragraph answering the following questions: Why paint romanticized landscapes? Possible answers: *In addition to the value being placed on nature at the time, these images represented an abundance of land that made America special. It certainly also made it distinct from Europe.*

TEACHING IDEA

Incorporating Secondary Sources

Provide students with a copy of the article titled "The Age of Reform" by Ronald G. Walters. This secondary source from the Gilder Lehrman site discusses the main social reforms that characterized the Antebellum Era (gilderlehrman.org). After they read it for homework, have a class discussion to share their observations and correct any misunderstandings.

APPLY THE TIP

Allow students to make connections between the role played by white middle-class women in the social reforms of the Antebellum Era and the early years after the American Revolution and the role of "republican motherhood." After conducting a class discussion, point out that they will see something similar during the Progressive Era (late nineteenth century and beginning of the twentieth century). To make it relevant to their own lives and the present day, ask students to draw connections as well to the activism revolving around social issues and what happens at schools today. Do they see any patterns? Does there tend to be a strong representation of middle-class parents, especially mothers, being involved? If so, what accounts for it? Possible answers will vary, but students should identify that these individuals tend to have the time and money, both very valuable resources, to get involved in social issues.

Emerson's hometown of Concord, Massachusetts served as a haven for writers, poets, intellectuals, and reformers who were drawn to transcendentalism. In 1840 Margaret Fuller, a close friend of Emerson, became the first editor of *The Dial*, a journal dedicated to transcendental thought. In 1844 she moved to New York City, where Horace Greeley hired her as a critic at the *New York Tribune*. She soon published a book, *Woman in the Nineteenth Century* (1845), which combined transcendental ideas with arguments for women's rights.

Henry David Thoreau also followed the transcendentalist path. He grew up in Concord and read "Nature" while a student at Harvard in the mid-1830s. In July 1845 Thoreau moved to a cabin near Walden Pond and launched an experiment in simple living. A year later he was imprisoned overnight for refusing to pay his taxes as a protest against slavery and the Mexican-American War. In the anonymous *Civil Disobedience* (1846), Thoreau argued that individuals of conscience had the right to resist government policies they believed to be immoral. Five years later, he published *Walden*, which highlighted the interplay among a simple lifestyle, natural harmony, and social justice.

Like Emerson, many American artists embraced the power of nature. Led by Thomas Cole, members of the **Hudson River School** painted romanticized landscapes from New York's Catskill and Adirondack Mountains. Some northern artists also traveled to the West, painting the region's grand vistas. Pennsylvanian George Catlin portrayed the dramatic scenery of western mountains, gorges, and waterfalls and also painted moving portraits of Plains Indians.

REVIEW

- In what ways were the transcendentalist movement and Second Great Awakening similar, and in what ways did they differ?

Varieties of Reform

AP® TIP
Compare the role of women in social reform movements of the 1800s to that of women during the American Revolution.

Middle-class Protestants formed the core of many reform movements in the mid-nineteenth-century North. They had more time and money to devote to social reform than did their working-class counterparts and were less tied to traditional ways than their wealthy neighbors. Nonetheless, workers and farmers, African Americans and immigrants, Catholics and Jews also participated in efforts to improve society.

Reformers used different techniques to pursue their goals. Since women could not vote, for example, they were excluded from direct political participation. Instead, they established charitable associations, distributed food and medicine, constructed asylums, circulated petitions, organized boycotts, arranged meetings and lectures, and published newspapers and pamphlets. Other groups with limited political rights — African Americans and immigrants, for instance — embraced similar modes of action and also formed mutual aid societies. Native-born white men wielded these forms of activism and, in addition, organized political campaigns and lobbied legislators. The reform techniques chosen were also affected by the goals of a particular movement. Moral suasion worked best with families, churches, and local communities, while legislation was more likely to succeed if the goal involved transforming people's behavior across a whole state or region.

Reformers often used a variety of tactics to support a single cause, and many changed their approach over time. For instance, reformers who sought to eradicate prostitution in the 1830s prayed in front of urban brothels and attempted to rescue "fallen" women. They soon launched *The Advocate of Moral Reform*, a monthly journal filled with morality tales, advice to mothers, and lists of men who visited brothels. In small towns, moral reformers sought to alert young women and men to the dangers of city life. By the 1840s, urban reformers opened Homes for Virtuous and Friendless Females to provide safe havens for vulnerable women. And across the country, moral reformers began petitioning state legislators to make punishments for men who hired prostitutes as harsh as those for prostitutes themselves.

REVIEW

- What strategies did reformers employ during the mid-1800s?

The Problem of Poverty

Poverty had existed since the colonial era, but the Panic of 1837 aroused greater public concern. Leaders of both government and private charitable endeavors increasingly linked relief to the moral character of those in need. Affluent Americans had long debated whether the poor would learn habits of industry and thrift if they were simply given aid without working for it. The debate was deeply gendered. Women and children were considered the worthiest recipients of aid, and middle- and upper-class women the appropriate dispensers of charity. Successful men, meanwhile, often linked poverty to weakness and considered giving pennies to a beggar an unmanly act that indulged the worst traits of the poor.

While towns and cities had long relegated the poorest residents to almshouses or workhouses, charitable societies in the early nineteenth century sought to change the conditions that produced poverty. As the poor increased with urban growth, northern charitable ladies began visiting poor neighborhoods, offering blankets, clothing, food, and medicine to needy residents. But the problem seemed intractable, and many charitable organizations began building orphan asylums, hospitals, and homes for working women to provide deserving but vulnerable individuals with resources to improve their life chances.

The "undeserving" poor faced grimmer choices. They generally received assistance only through the workhouse or the local jail. By the 1830s images of rowdy men who drank or gambled away what little they earned, prostitutes who tempted respectable men into vice, and immigrants who preferred idle poverty to virtuous labor became stereotypical figures in debates over the causes of and responses to poverty.

At the same time, young poor women — at least if they were white and Protestant — were increasingly portrayed as the victims of immoral men or unfortunate circumstance. In fictional tales, naive girls were seduced and abandoned by manipulative men. One of the first mass-produced books in the United States, Nathaniel Hawthorne's *The Scarlet Letter* (1850), was set in Puritan New England but addressed contemporary concerns about the seduction of innocents. It illustrated the social ostracism and poverty suffered by a woman who bore a child out of wedlock.

Other fictional tales placed the blame for fallen women on foreigners, especially Catholics. Such works drew vivid portraits of young nuns ravished by priests and then thrown out pregnant and penniless. These stories heightened anti-Catholic sentiment, which periodically boiled over into attacks on Catholic homes, schools, churches, and convents.

AP® ANALYZING SOURCES

Source: Matthew Carey, *Appeal to the Wealthy of the Land*, 1833

"Let us now turn to the appalling case of seamstresses, . . . [who are] Beset . . . by poverty and wretchedness, with scanty and poor fare, miserable lodgings, clothing inferior in quality . . . , without the most distant hope of amelioration of condition. . . .

IT is frequently asked — what remedy can be found for the enormous and cruel oppression experienced by females employed as seamstresses . . . I venture, to suggest a few [reforms].

1. Public opinion, a powerful instrument, ought to be brought to bear on the subject. All honourable members of society, male and female, ought to unite in denouncing those who 'grind the faces of the poor.' . . .
2. Let the employments of females be multiplied as much as possible . . . especially in shop-keeping in retail stores. . . .
6. Let schools be opened for instructing poor women in cooking. . . .
8. Ladies who can afford it, ought to give out their sewing and washing, and pay fair prices. . . .

(Continued)

TEACHING IDEA

Class Discussion

Write the following questions on the board: Are the poor worthy of receiving help? Should the government play a role in providing assistance? Should it be strictly up to private organizations and charities to help? Allow students to work in pairs so they can brainstorm ideas and prepare for a class debate on these issues. Ask them who they think is "most deserving" of receiving assistance or help and to explain their answers. As you guide the discussion by serving as a moderator, think of follow-up questions you may want to ask. Lastly, ask the entire class if there is an obligation for the wealthy or those who are better off to help the most vulnerable and needy in our society.

TRM Suggested Responses to Questions

TRM Module 4.7 AP® Analyzing Sources Handout 3

TEACHING IDEA

Incorporating Primary Sources

Give students excerpts of *The Scarlet Letter* by Nathaniel Hawthorne. Then conduct a discussion on how it portrayed a woman as the victim of an immoral man and/or of unfortunate circumstances. Ask students what this writing says about American culture at the time and how it could have influenced social reformers. This activity may also be a great opportunity to do some interdisciplinary planning and collaboration with the language arts department.

EXPLORING AP® THEMES

American and National Identity

Historically, some Americans have blamed the problems of poverty and crime on immigrants. During the mid-nineteenth century, this was especially true for the Irish who tended to be less educated and mostly Catholic. Have students research "No Irish Need Apply" (NINA), the Order of the Star-Spangled Banner or "Know Nothings," and stereotypes of the Irish and alcohol consumption. After students share their findings, have them brainstorm possible solutions to address these problems and the concerns of those who were nativist and xenophobic. Lastly, try to make connections to the present day and the immigration debates taking place in the country.

Period 4: 1800–1848

MODULE 4-7 Social Reform Movements

TEACHING IDEA

Class Discussion

Obtain a copy of the community service requirement for students to graduate from your school. If your school does not have one, then find one from a neighboring school by visiting their website. Then have a classroom discussion on whether your high school should have such a requirement. After students share their answers, try to draw parallels between the need for addressing the problem of poverty in the Antebellum Era and today.

BUILDING AP® SKILLS

Sourcing and Situation

When assigning the "Analyzing Sources" activity on this page, you may want to ask students to go beyond identification and explain the significance of their answers. For example, in addition to identifying the "intended audience" for Matthew Carey's *Appeal to the Wealthy of the Land*, have students explain why the group being targeted may influence/impact what the document says. This would be consistent with the proficiency statements from the College Board.

---

9. In the towns in the interior of the state, and in those in western states, there is generally a want of females as domestics, seamstresses, etc. . . . [The rich should] provide for sending some of the superabundant poor females of our cities to those places."

Questions for Analysis
1. Identify Carey's intended audience.
2. Explain the purpose of Carey's appeal.

Source: Emily G. Kempshall, *Letter to the Rochester Female Charitable Society,* 1838

"[T]he Board . . . have asked my reasons for withdrawing my . . . [membership]. . . . I look upon the <u>funds</u> of your society, however judiciously distributed, among the destitute sick of our city, as being wholly inadequate to meet their necessities. . . . I dare not draw a single Dollar, to relieve one poor family, lest in doing this I rob another <u>poorer</u> family, perhaps of what they must have. . . . I know [also] . . . that whole Districts are appointed to females as visitors of the [Society] where no decent female should go, to look after and try to assist, their vile and degraded inhabitants. . . .

And now were I addressing the . . . Common Council of this City I would say, 'Give the ladies power to point, in their visits of mercy, to a work House, where idle drunken fathers and mothers <u>must</u> go and <u>work</u>.'. . . [T]his being granted . . . the objection to becoming a visitor . . . will be lessened at once. . . .

[H]as not the day gone by, when your Flag of Charity may wave over its Lake, River, Canal, and Rail Road, inviting the outcasts of every city in the Union, . . . to seek . . . their subsistence from your bounty. . . . And so while your Banner, whose merciful insignia on the one side is Relief for the destitute sick, has been held up as a beacon of hope, it is painful to tell them to read the other side where want of funds has written Despair of further Relief."

Questions for Analysis
1. Identify Kempshall's complaints.
2. Explain Kempshall's point of view.

Questions for Comparison
1. Explain how historical situation shaped the arguments made in each of these documents.
2. Evaluate the extent of similarity between Carey's portrayal of poor women and families and that of Kempshall.
3. Evaluate the extent of difference between Carey's and Kempshall's approach to aiding poor women and families.

---

nativists Anti-immigrant Americans who launched public campaigns against foreigners in the 1840s. Nativism emerged as a response to increased immigration to the United States in the 1830s and 1840s, particularly the large influx of Catholic immigrants.

At the same time, economic competition intensified conflicts between immigrants and native-born Americans. By the 1840s Americans who opposed immigration took the name **nativists** and launched public political campaigns that blamed foreigners for poverty and crime. Samuel F. B. Morse, the inventor of the telegraph, was among the most popular anti-immigrant spokesmen. Irish Catholics were often targeted in attacks against immigrants. In May 1844 working-class nativists clashed with Irishmen in Philadelphia after shots were fired from a firehouse. A dozen nativists and one Irishman were killed the first day. The next night, nativists looted and burned Irish businesses and Catholic churches.

Many nativists blamed poverty among immigrants on their drinking habits. Others considered alcohol abuse, whether by native-born or immigrant Americans, the root cause not only of poverty but of many social evils.

REVIEW
What economic and social factors help explain the rise of nativism in the mid-1800s?

The Temperance Movement

Temperance advocates first organized officially in 1826 with the founding of the American Temperance Society. This all-male organization was led by clergy and businessmen but focused on alcohol abuse among working-class men. Religious revivals inspired the establishment of some 5,000 local chapters, and black and white men founded other temperance organizations as well. Over time, the temperance movement changed its goal from moderation to total abstinence, targeted middle-class and elite as well as working-class men, and welcomed women's support. Wives and mothers were expected to persuade male kin to stop drinking and sign a temperance pledge. Women founded dozens of temperance societies in the 1830s, which funded the circulation of didactic tales, woodcuts, and etchings about the dangers of "demon rum."

Some workingmen viewed temperance as a way to gain dignity and respect. For Protestants, in particular, embracing temperance distinguished them from Irish Catholic workers. A few working-class temperance advocates criticized liquor dealers, whom they claimed directed "the vilest, meanest, most earth-cursing and hell-filling business ever followed." More turned to self-improvement. In the 1840s small groups of laboring men formed Washingtonian societies — named in honor of the nation's founder — to help each other stop excessive drinking. Martha Washington societies appeared shortly thereafter, composed of the wives, mothers, and sisters of male alcoholics.

Despite the rapid growth of temperance organizations, appeals to morality failed to reduce alcohol consumption significantly. As a result, many temperance advocates turned to legal reform. In 1851 Maine was the first state to legally prohibit the sale of alcoholic beverages. By 1855 twelve more states had restricted the manufacture or sale of alcohol. Yet these stringent

▲ **Drunkard's Home, 1850** Temperance societies undertook a variety of activities to publicize the dangers of alcohol. This engraved illustration is from *The National Temperance Offering*, published by the Sons of Temperance, one of the oldest temperance organizations in the United States. **How does this image reinforce the arguments made by temperance advocates and moral reformers during the mid-1800s?**

TEACHING IDEA

Understanding Other Reform Movements

Assign students one of the two other significant reform movements from the Antebellum Era, either public education or prisons and asylums. In conducting their research, students must identify the main individuals (Horace Mann and Dorothea Dix, respectively) and actual reforms proposed by each movement. Most importantly, they will have to write at least a paragraph explaining how the efforts of their social reform movement impacted American society in the first half of the 1800s.

EXPLORING AP® THEMES

Politics and Power

Since this theme focuses on how different social and political groups have influenced society and government in the United States, have students research how the temperance movement went from engaging in moral persuasion to legal reform. Specifically, they should focus on Neal Dow and the Maine Law and those of the other states that restricted the manufacture or sale of alcohol. This issue can be revisited later when prohibition and the Eighteenth Amendment are covered in Period 7. After the class gets to share their findings, conclude the activity by asking students if it is a good idea to legislate morality and what implications it would have for the separation of church and state.

TEACHING IDEA

Class Discussion

Write the following questions on the board: What is the difference between temperance and prohibition? (Moderation vs. abstinence?) What groups supported which idea? (Religious leaders, business owners, or women?) What was their reasoning and who did they target? Then, in pairs, have students brainstorm answers and share out to the entire class.

measures inspired a backlash. Hostile to the imposition of middle-class Protestant standards on the population at large, Irish workers in Maine organized the Portland Rum Riot in 1855. It led to the Maine law's repeal the next year. Still, the diverse strategies used by temperance advocates gradually reduced, but did not eliminate, the consumption of beer, wine, and spirits across the United States.

REVIEW

- How did the efforts of temperance advocates compare to those of anti-poverty reformers of the mid-nineteenth century?

Utopian Communities

While most reformers reached out to the wider society to implement change, some activists established self-contained communities to serve as models for others. The architects of these **utopian societies**, most formed in the North and Midwest, gained inspiration from European intellectuals and reformers as well as American religious and republican ideals.

utopian societies Communities formed in the first half of the nineteenth century to embody alternative social and economic visions and to create models for society at large to follow.

In the 1820s Scottish and Welsh labor radicals such as Frances Wright, Robert Owen, and his son Robert Dale Owen established several utopian communities in the United States. They perceived the young republic as open to experiments in communal labor, gender equality, and (in Wright's case) racial justice. Their efforts ultimately failed, but they did arouse impassioned debate.

Then in 1841, former Unitarian minister George Ripley established a transcendentalist community at Brook Farm in Massachusetts. Four years later, Brook Farm was reorganized according to the principles of the French socialist Charles Fourier. Fourier believed that cooperation across classes was necessary to temper the conflicts inherent in capitalist society. He developed a plan for communities, called phalanxes, where residents chose jobs based on individual interest but were paid according to the contribution of each job to the community's well-being. Fourier also advocated equality for women. More than forty Fourierist phalanxes were founded in the northern United States during the 1840s.

AP® TIP Compare the goals and accomplishments of the temperance movement with those of the utopian communities in the mid-nineteenth century.

A more uniquely American experiment, the Oneida community, was established in central New York by John Humphrey Noyes in 1848. He and his followers believed that Christ's Second Coming had already occurred and embraced the communalism of the early Christian church. Noyes required members to relinquish their private property to the community and to embrace the notion of "complex marriage," in which women and men were free to have sexual intercourse with any consenting adult. He also introduced a form of birth control that sought to ensure women's freedom from constant childbearing and instituted communal child-rearing practices. Despite the public outrage provoked by Oneida's economic and sexual practices, the community recruited several hundred residents and thrived for more than three decades.

REVIEW

- How did mid-nineteenth-century utopian societies compare with more mainstream reform movements?

AP® WRITING HISTORICALLY — Responding to a Long-Essay Question

To answer the following Long-Essay Question, you will need to apply your knowledge of the historical developments covered in this module.

Evaluate the relative importance of different causes for American social reform movements in the period from 1800 to 1848.

TEACHING IDEA

Understanding Utopian Societies

For homework, have students create a one-page report on one of the main utopian societies from the Antebellum Era. Specifically, they can choose from Brook Farm, New Harmony, the Shakers, or Oneida. In addition to providing an overview and background information (i.e., which had socialist ideas, etc.), have students identify their respective founders. After students share their findings, conduct a class discussion about the worthiness of these social experiments and which had the greatest chance at success.

TRM Suggested Responses to Questions

TEACHING IDEA

AP® Writing Historically Workshop

This activity seeks to establish a greater understanding of how to incorporate contextualization into an essay. One of the characteristics of contextualization is how well students grasp a broader historical event or development. For this activity, consider posting four large pieces of butcher block or poster paper around the room with the following labels: immigration, industrialization, migration, and expansion. These are examples of broader historical processes in the context of the age of reform. Students' main task is to go to each poster and write supporting details of the broader historical process.

Part of contextualization is providing a couple of historical facts to buttress understanding of larger historical events. In this way, students are illustrating how well they know each broad event. Once all students have had the opportunity to write their answers, debrief as a class to ensure each answer is correct. Once you have done this, invite students to return to the poster they know best and select at least two historical facts written on the poster. Now they have a skeleton for writing contextualization for this long essay: a broad historical event with a couple of specific facts to support their assertion.

Step 1 **Break down the prompt.**

As always, this is the first step. Carefully read the prompt and make sure you understand what you are being asked to do. To successfully answer this question, not only will you will need to identify multiple social reform movements between 1800 and 1848, you also need to analyze what caused them. Be sure to also take note of how the task of the prompt is worded: a phrase like "Evaluate the relative importance of" is a clear signal that you need to make a judgment call when you write about this topic. In other words, how important were the causes of these social movements? As you likely recall from the writing you did for Period 3, thinking of causes in terms of a continuum is one helpful way to make sure that you are prepared to thoroughly answer the question.

Step 2 **List and categorize your historical knowledge.**

Start by writing down any relevant and specific pieces of historical evidence you remember (that is, "proper nouns"). Then, you can begin to gather your thoughts on various reform movements and their causes by using the following graphic organizer. Feel free to use another method if it fits better with your approach to writing. As you rate the importance of various causes, make sure that you have different levels of importance represented. You should also make sure that you have differentiated in some way between short- and long-term causes. While the blank graphic organizer provided here leaves space for two causes per movement, you can and should split those into even more rows if you can identify and analyze more causes than that.

Reform Movement	Short- and Long-Term Cause(s)	Relative Importance	Explanation of Relative Importance

(Continued)

TEACHING IDEA

Building Writing Skills

Remember that when students are writing a response to a question asking them to evaluate the "relative importance," they should rank the categories. Therefore, you may want to modify the box labeled "relative importance" in the graphic organizer by adding a numeric value to identify the relative importance (1–5 or 1–10). You may also want to add other reform movements, specifically public education and prisons/asylums. Students should also be given the College Board rubric to complement the outline on page 342 with the actual language like a thesis being "historically defensible" and providing a line of reasoning. Linkage statements for historical evidence (skill of supporting an argument) in the form of a concluding sentence would also be helpful. Lastly, have students attempt "historical complexity," for which there are multiple avenues they can take to try earning that point.

BUILDING AP® SKILLS

Claims and Evidence in Sources

Provide students with a copy of the article titled "National Expansion and Reform, 1815–1860" by Joyce Appleby. This secondary source from the Gilder Lehrman site discusses social reform movements (gilderlehrman.org). Have students read the article to identify the author's claim or argument, historical evidence, and reasoning used to support it.

TEACHING IDEA

AP® Central

Use the 2002 AP® U.S. History exam DBQ on antebellum reform movements and democratic ideals, which is available on the College Board's AP® U.S. History Past Exam Questions section under "2002: Free-Response Questions" (apcentral.collegeboard.org). To prepare for this topic, have students complete a chart. In the top row, list the following categories: movement, people, acts/laws, organizations/groups, and other related information. In the left column, the following movements should be listed: abolitionism, temperance, women's rights, public education, prisons/asylums, utopianism, and religion.

TRM Find **Handout 4.7 – Antebellum Reform Movements** in the Teacher's Resource Materials.

Step 3: Set the context and craft a thesis.

It is often helpful to work backward when writing an opening paragraph — although your thesis should be the last piece of your introduction, knowing where you're headed from the very beginning should make the task of contextualizing your argument easier to accomplish. Remember that your thesis should not only clearly identify multiple causes for the reform movements of the era but make at least three argumentative claims that briefly characterize the significance of each cause.

Once you have created your thesis, it's time to work backward to contextualize it. Remember, establishing the context for your historical argument is essentially setting the stage: how does the argument you're making connect to the larger picture of history? You should take your time here — it doesn't have to be a single sentence, and, in fact, most effective contextualization statements are two to four sentences long.

ACTIVITY

Use steps 1 through 3 to plan and write an essay in response to the essay prompt at the beginning of this box. Your introduction must include a multi-sentence contextualization statement that leads into your thesis. Remember to make three to four claims about causes of social movements in your thesis, and be sure that these claims evaluate the relative importance of each cause. Each of your body paragraphs should open with one of your thesis claims and include at least two pieces of evidence for that claim. Finally, be sure to explain *how* the evidence you've chosen to include in each body paragraph supports that particular claim — this is key to an effective historical argument.

You may use the following outline to guide your response:

I. Introductory paragraph
   A. Immediate/preceding contextualization statement
      1. Cite evidence of immediate/preceding context
      2. Explain influence of immediate/preceding context
   B. Thesis statement presenting three to four evaluative claims, situated along a continuum of relative importance, linking causes to effects

II. Claim 1 body paragraph
   A. Topic sentence presenting an evaluative claim of causation 1
   B. Supporting statement citing evidence of claim 1
   C. Cite additional evidence of claim 1
   D. Explain how evidence supports claim 1

III. Claim 2 body paragraph
   A. Topic sentence presenting an evaluative claim of causation 2
   B. Supporting statement citing evidence of claim 2
   C. Cite additional evidence of claim 2
   D. Explain how evidence supports claim 2

IV. Claim 3 body paragraph
   A. Topic sentence presenting an evaluative claim of causation 3
   B. Supporting statement citing evidence of claim 3
   C. Cite additional evidence of claim 3
   D. Explain how evidence supports claim 3

V. (Optional) Claim 4 body paragraph
   A. Topic sentence presenting an evaluative claim of causation 4
   B. Supporting statement citing evidence of claim 4
   C. Cite additional evidence of claim 4
   D. Explain how evidence supports claim 4

Module 4-8

Abolitionism and Sectionalism

TRM Suggested Responses to Questions

LEARNING TARGETS
By the end of this module, you should be able to:
- Explain the similarities and differences in the various efforts to limit or end slavery.
- Explain how abolitionism and other movements impacted the women's rights movement.

THEMATIC FOCUS
American and Regional Culture

Antislavery movements in the North steadily grew from the 1820s until the Civil War (1860–1865) as reformers split over banning the expansion of slavery into new territories or abolishing slavery throughout the United States. A women's rights movement also emerged, fueled in part by the backlash many women experienced from their participation in abolitionist organizations.

HISTORICAL REASONING FOCUS
Comparison

TASK ▶ As you read, consider the similarities and differences within the antislavery movements discussed in this module. Take special note of the points of comparison and overlap between the larger abolitionist movement and the mid-nineteenth-century movement for women's rights.

For a small percentage of Northerners, slavery was the ultimate injustice. While most Northerners considered it sufficient to rid their own region of human bondage, antislavery advocates argued that the North remained complicit in the institution. After all, enslaved people labored under brutal conditions to provide cotton for New England factories, sugar and molasses for northern tables, and profits for urban traders. Free black people were the earliest advocates of abolition, but their role in the movement generated conflict as more white people joined in the 1830s. The place of the church, of women, and of politics in antislavery efforts also stirred controversy. By the 1840s abolitionists disagreed over whether to focus on abolishing slavery in the South or simply preventing its extension into western territories. These debates often weakened individual organizations but expanded the range of antislavery associations and campaigns.

The Beginnings of the Antislavery Movement

In the 1820s African Americans and a few white Quakers led the fight to abolish slavery. They published pamphlets, lectured to small audiences, and helped enslaved people reach freedom when they fled from slaveholders. In 1829 David Walker wrote the militant antislavery statement, *Appeal . . . to the Colored Citizens of the World*. The free son of an enslaved father, Walker left his North Carolina home for Boston in the 1820s and became a writer for *Freedom's Journal*, the country's first newspaper published by African Americans. In his *Appeal*, Walker warned that enslaved people would claim their freedom by force if white people did not agree to emancipate them. Some northern black people feared Walker's radical *Appeal* would unleash a white backlash, while Quaker abolitionists like Benjamin Lundy, editor of the *Genius of Universal Emancipation*, admired Walker's courage but rejected his call for violence. Nonetheless the *Appeal* circulated widely among free and enslaved black people, with copies spreading from northern cities to Charleston, Savannah, New Orleans, and Norfolk.

TEACHING IDEA

Class Discussion

During the Antebellum Era, the antislavery movement evolved into various positions. Assign one of the following to each student and then let them meet in groups to discuss which approach was best and why: 1) preventing the extension/expansion of slavery; 2) immediate abolition of slavery; 3) providing compensation to the slaveholders of enslaved people to emancipate them; 4) achieve freedom through any means necessary, including the use of violence or armed force. Then, allow students the opportunity to share out and defend their position. Lastly, ask students if they think moral persuasion would be enough to abolish the "peculiar institution" of slavery or if political action would be needed.

BUILDING AP® SKILLS

Developments and Processes

One of the first antislavery organizations established in the United States was the American Colonization Society. Have students research this organization and explain how they proposed to solve the issue of slavery. Students should write a one-paragraph answer showing the organization's interest in creating a "Back to Africa" movement and the founding of Liberia. After everyone has submitted their work, conduct a brief discussion on how this was not a viable solution given the logistical challenges and the opposition they encountered on moral grounds.

The Beginnings of the Antislavery Movement

TRM Suggested Responses to Questions

TRM Module 4.8 AP® Analyzing Sources Handout 1

TEACHING IDEA

Incorporating Primary Sources

Provide students with excerpts from David Walker's *Appeal to the Colored Citizens of the World* and ask them to identify the evidence he cites for advocating for a more militant approach to bring slavery to an end, including the use of violence or armed force. The entire appeal can be found on the website for Documenting the American South (docsouth.unc.edu).

TEACHING IDEA

Understanding People Who Made a Difference

For homework, have students research William Lloyd Garrison and identify his main contributions to the abolition movement. Their answers should include his work with *The Liberator* newspaper and calls for the immediate emancipation of enslaved people without compensation. Students should also point out that he was the founder of the American Anti-Slavery Society in 1833. Discuss these findings with the entire class to ensure everyone has at least these fundamental understandings.

Period 4: 1800–1848

MODULE 4-8 Abolitionism and Sectionalism

AP® ANALYZING SOURCES

Source: David Walker, *Walker's Appeal to the Coloured Citizens of the World*, 1830

"Men of colour, who are also of sense, for you particularly is my APPEAL designed. Our more ignorant brethren are not able to penetrate its value. I call upon you therefore to cast your eyes upon the wretchedness of your brethren, and to do your utmost to enlighten them . . . Let the Lord see you doing what you can to rescue them and yourselves from degradation. Do any of you say that you and your family are free and happy, and what have you to do with the wretched slaves and other people? . . . Look into our freedom and happiness, and see of what kind they are composed!! They are of the very lowest kind—they are the very *dregs*!—they are the most servile and abject kind, that ever a people was in possession of! If any of you wish to know how FREE you are, let one of you start and go through the southern and western States of this country, and unless you travel as a slave to a white man (a servant is a *slave* to the man whom he serves) or have your free papers, (which if you are not careful they will get from you) if they do not take you up and put you in jail, and if you cannot give good evidence of your freedom, sell you into eternal slavery, I am not a living man: or any man of colour, immaterial who he is, or where he came from . . . the white Christians of America will serve him the same they will sink him into wretchedness and degradation for ever while he lives. And yet some of you have the hardihood to say that you are free and happy!"

Questions for Analysis
1. Identify Walker's immediate and larger audience.
2. Describe how Walker attempts to unite the concerns of free and enslaved black people in this excerpt.
3. Explain the impact of Walker's argument on the antislavery movement in the North.

American Anti-Slavery Society (AASS) Abolitionist society founded by William Lloyd Garrison in 1833 that became the most important northern abolitionist organization of the period.

underground railroad A series of routes from southern plantation areas to northern free states and Canada along which abolitionist supporters, known as conductors, provided hiding places and transportation for enslaved people fleeing slaveholders.

William Lloyd Garrison, a white Bostonian who worked on Lundy's newspaper, was inspired by Walker's radical stance. In 1831 he launched his own abolitionist newspaper, the *Liberator*. He urged white antislavery activists to embrace the goal of immediate emancipation without compensation to slaveholders, a position first advocated by the English Quaker Elizabeth Heyrick.

The *Liberator* demanded that white people take an absolute stand against slavery but use moral persuasion rather than armed force to halt its spread. With like-minded black and white activists in Boston, Philadelphia, and New York City, Garrison organized the **American Anti-Slavery Society (AASS)** in 1833. By the end of the decade, the AASS boasted branches in dozens of towns and cities across the North. Members supported lecturers and petition drives, criticized churches that refused to denounce slavery, and proclaimed the U.S. Constitution a proslavery document. Some Garrisonians also participated in the work of the **underground railroad**, a secret network of activists who assisted fugitives fleeing enslavement.

In 1835 Sarah Grimké and her sister, Angelina Grimké, joined the AASS and soon began lecturing for the organization. Daughters of a prominent South Carolina planter, they had moved to Philadelphia and converted to Quakerism. As white southerners, their denunciations of slavery carried particular weight. Yet as women, their public presence aroused fierce opposition. In 1837 Congregationalist ministers in Massachusetts decried their presence in front of "promiscuous" audiences of men and women, but 1,500 female millworkers still turned out to hear them at Lowell's city hall.

Maria Stewart, a free black widow in Boston, spoke out against slavery even earlier. In 1831 to 1832, she lectured to mixed-sex and interracial audiences, demanding that northern black people take more responsibility for ending slavery and fighting racial discrimination. In 1833 free black and white Quaker women formed an interracial organization, the Philadelphia Female Anti-Slavery Society, which advocated the boycott of cotton, sugar, and other goods produced using enslaved labor.

The abolitionist movement quickly expanded to the frontier, where debates over slave and free territory were especially intense. In 1836 Ohio claimed more antislavery groups than any other state, and Ohio women initiated a petition drive to abolish slavery in the District of

---

EXPLORING AP® THEMES

American and Regional Culture

Give students a blank map of the United States from the 1830s and ask them to note the three main regions (North, South, and West) and the largest groups of people within each one.

After students complete their maps, ask them to discuss how these different groups tried to shape government policies and the economy, especially when it came to the issue of slavery. This activity should allow students to see the role sectionalism was playing in American society at the time.

Columbia. The petition campaign, which spread across the North, inspired the first national meeting of women abolitionists in 1837. Other antislavery organizations, like the AASS, recruited male and female abolitionists, black and white. And still others remained all-white, all-black, and single-sex.

AP® ANALYZING SOURCES

Source: Elizabeth Emery and Mary P. Abbott, *Letter to* The Liberator, 1836

"The call of our female friends across the waters — the energetic appeal of those untiring sisters in the work of emancipation in Boston — above all, the sighs, the groans, the deathlike struggles of scourged sisters in the South — these have moved our hearts, our hands. We feel that woman has a place in this Godlike work, for woman's woes, and woman's wrongs, are borne to us on every breeze that flows from the South; woman has a place, for she forms a part in God's created intelligent instrumentality to reform the world. . . . We believe God gave woman a heart to feel — an eye to weep — a hand to work — a tongue to speak. Now let her use that tongue to speak on slavery. Is it not a curse — a heaven-daring abomination? Let her employ that hand, to labor for the slave. Does not her sister in bonds, labor night and day without reward? Let her heart grieve, and her eye fill with tears, in view of a female's body dishonored — a female's mind debased — a female's soul forever ruined! . . .

As Christian women, we will do a Christian woman's duty. . . .

Our preamble [from the Female Anti-Slavery Society in Andover, Massachusetts] gives our creed:

'We believe American Slavery is a sin against God — at war with the dictates of humanity, and subversive of the principles of freedom, because it regards rational beings as goods and chattel; robs them of compensation for their toil — denies to them the protection of law — disregards the relation of husband and wife, brother and sister, parent and child; shuts out from the intellect the light of knowledge; overwhelms hope in despair and ruins the soul — thus sinking to the level of brutes, more than one million of American females, who are created in God's image, a little lower than the angels', and consigns them over to degradation, physical, social, intellectual, and moral.'"

Questions for Analysis

1. Identify Emery and Abbott's intended audiences and their goals.
2. Describe how Emery and Abbott justify women's roles in the abolitionist movement.
3. Explain how Emery and Abbott's argument in this letter challenged prevailing beliefs about men's and women's proper spheres in the mid-nineteenth century.

TRM Suggested Responses to Questions

TRM Module 4.8 AP® Analyzing Sources Handout 2

REVIEW

- What roles did women play in the abolitionist movement in the 1830s, and what obstacles did they encounter?

Abolition Gains Ground and Enemies

AP® TIP
Analyze the causes of opposition to abolitionism in the North.

The growth of the abolitionist movement shocked many northerners, and in the late 1830s violence often erupted in response to antislavery agitation. Northern manufacturers and merchants were generally hostile, fearing abolitionists' effect on the profitable trade in cotton, sugar, cloth, and rum. And white workingmen feared increased competition for jobs. In the 1830s mobs routinely attacked antislavery meetings, lecturers, and presses. At the 1838 Antislavery Convention of American Women at Philadelphia's Pennsylvania Hall, mobs forced black and white women to flee and then burned the hall to the ground.

Massive antislavery petition campaigns in 1836 and 1837 generated opposition in and between the North and South. Thousands of abolitionists signed petitions to ban slavery in the District of Columbia, end the internal slave trade, and oppose the annexation of Texas. Some evangelical women considered

TEACHING IDEA

Understanding People Who Made a Difference

In pairs, have students research two black female abolitionists — Harriet Tubman and Sojourner Truth. They must identify their main contributions to the abolition movement. Their answers should include Tubman's work with the Underground Railroad and Truth's advocating not only against slavery but also for women's rights. Students should come across and read her famous poem: "Ain't I a woman?" which is readily available online. Discuss these findings with the entire class to ensure everyone has at least these fundamental understandings.

BUILDING AP® SKILLS

Comparison

Have students identify and describe why some people saw abolitionists in a positive light while others viewed them negatively as agitators. Then have them share out their answers, which may include:

- Positive: *slavery was morally wrong and abolitionists were fighting a worthy cause; religious beliefs made many think slavery was sinful.*

- Negative: *businessmen saw abolitionists as hurting the economy because the cotton trade needed the institution of slavery; some working-class people feared competition from free black laborers if slavery came to an end.*

EXPLORING AP® THEMES

American and National Identity

Although this theme is not specifically targeted in this period, it is still relevant to the material covered in this module. Specifically, have students focus on the definition of "citizenship" in the nation's founding documents and discuss whether African Americans (free or enslaved) should be included. Then have students research what abolitionists who were considered "radical," such as William Lloyd Garrison, believed about this issue. Students should discover that he advocated not only for emancipation but for African Americans to be turned into citizens as well.

TRM Suggested Responses to Questions

TRM Module 4.8 AP® Analyzing Sources Handout 3

TEACHING IDEA

Incorporating Primary/Secondary Sources

Provide students with excerpts from Frederick Douglass's abolitionist newspaper, *The North Star*, and ask them how his being an African American man and a former enslaved person provides a different perspective from white abolitionists like William Lloyd Garrison. The newspaper can be accessed by searching for "The North Star Vol. I No. 37" on the Smithsonian's transcription website (transcription.si.edu).

Period 4: 1800–1848

MODULE 4-8 Abolitionism and Sectionalism

◀ **Anti-abolitionist Poster, 1837** Opponents of abolitionism, fearful of social upheaval resulting from growing antislavery sentiment in the North, often resorted to violence against abolitionists. This 1837 poster encourages "Fellow Citizens" to protest an abolitionist meeting, albeit through ostensibly "peaceable means." **How does the language used in this image promote fear and anger toward abolitionists?**

such efforts part of their Christian duty, but most ministers (including Finney) condemned antislavery work as outside women's sphere. Most female evangelicals retreated in the face of clerical disapproval, but others continued their efforts alongside their non-evangelical sisters. Meanwhile southern politicians, incensed by antislavery petitions, persuaded Congress to pass the gag rule in 1836 (see Module 4-5).

But gag rules did not silence abolitionists. Indeed new groups of activists, especially enslaved people who had fled to reach freedom, offered potent personal tales of the horrors of bondage. The most famous fugitive abolitionist was Frederick Douglass, a Maryland-born enslaved man who in 1838 fled to New Bedford, Massachusetts. He met Garrison in 1841, joined the AASS, and four years later published his life story, *Narrative of the Life of Frederick Douglass, as Told by Himself*. Having revealed his identity as a formerly enslaved man, Douglass sailed for England, where he launched a successful two-year lecture tour. While he was abroad, British abolitionists purchased Douglass's freedom and Douglass returned to the United States a free man. In 1847 he decided to launch his own antislavery newspaper, the **North Star**, a decision that Garrison and other white AASS leaders opposed. Douglass moved to Rochester, where he had earlier found free black and white Quaker allies.

AP® ANALYZING SOURCES

Source: Frederick Douglass, *Narrative of the Life of Frederick Douglass, an American Slave, Written by Himself*, 1845

"Very soon after I went to live with Mr. and Mrs. Auld, she very kindly commenced to teach me the A, B, C. After I had learned this, she assisted me in learning to spell words of three or four letters. Just at this point of my progress, Mr. Auld found out what was going on, and at once forbade Mrs. Auld to instruct me further, telling her, among other things, that it was unlawful, as well as unsafe, to teach a slave to read. To use his own words, further, he said, . . . 'A nigger should know nothing but to obey his master—to do as he is told to do. Learning would spoil the best nigger in the world. Now,' said he, 'if you teach that nigger (speaking of myself) how to read, there would be no keeping him. It would forever unfit him to be a slave. He would at once become unmanageable, and of no value to his master. As to himself, it could do him no good, but a great deal of harm. It would make him discontented and unhappy.' . . . From that moment, I understood the pathway from slavery to freedom. . . . Though conscious of the difficulty of learning without a teacher, I set out with high hope, and a fixed purpose, at whatever cost of trouble, to learn how to read. The very decided manner with which he spoke, and strove to impress his wife with the evil consequences of giving me instruction, served to convince me that he was deeply sensible of the truths he was uttering. . . . In learning to read, I owe almost as much to the bitter opposition of my master, as to the kindly aid of my mistress."

Questions for Analysis

1. Identify what Douglass believed allowed white people to keep those they enslaved in bondage.
2. Explain how Douglass sought to prove that enslaved African Americans deserved freedom and equal rights.
3. Explain how Douglass's point of view shaped his account.

346

TEACHING IDEA

Sourcing and Situation

When analyzing sources, there are four things students can do that could be rewarded on the AP® exam — historical situation, intended audience, purpose, and/or point of view (a refresher of HIPP can be found on page 8). Since the activity on this page only calls for point of view, have students do the other sourcing or "extended analysis" for the Frederick Douglass document.

▲ **Differentiation**

In many cases, students only identify the sourcing or "extended analysis" of documents without adequately explaining their significance. To help these students, provide them with the historical situation, intended audience, and purpose of the document. Then, have them focus on explaining their significance by writing 1 or 2 sentences for each. For advanced learners, take this activity a step further by having them research and identify another source that could corroborate what Douglass says in this document. Have students explain their reasoning and justify their answers.

While eager to have formerly enslaved people tell their dramatic stories, many white abolitionists did not show vigorous support of African Americans who asserted an independent voice. Some abolitionists opposed slavery but still believed that black people were racially inferior; others supported racial equality but assumed that black abolitionists would defer to white leaders. Thus several affiliates of the AASS refused to accept black members. Ultimately, the independent efforts of Douglass and other black activists expanded the antislavery movement even as they made clear the limits of white abolitionist ideals.

Conflicts also arose over the responsibility of churches to challenge slavery. The major Protestant denominations included southern as well as northern churches. If mainstream churches — Presbyterians, Baptists, Methodists — refused communion to slaveholders, their southern branches would secede. Still, from the 1830s on, abolitionists pressured churches to take Christian obligations seriously and denounce human bondage. Individual congregations responded, but aside from the Society of Friends (Quakers), larger denominations failed to follow suit.

In response, abolitionists urged parishioners to break with churches that admitted slaveholders as members. Antislavery preachers pushed the issue, and some worshippers "came out" from mainstream churches to form antislavery congregations. White Wesleyan Methodists and Free Will Baptists joined African American Methodists and Baptists in insisting that their members oppose slavery. Although these churches remained small, they served as a living challenge to mainstream denominations.

REVIEW

- What challenges did abolitionists face during the 1830s and 1840s?
- What prejudices did African American abolitionists face from within the movement?

Abolitionism and Women's Rights

"come outer" movement
Protest movement whose members would frequently abstain from political office, activity, or voting to protest the government and other organizations' complicity in slavery.

AP® TIP
Analyze the influence of the abolitionist movement on the increasing demands for women's rights during the mid-1800s.

Declaration of Sentiments
Call for women's rights in marriage, family, religion, politics, and law issued at the 1848 Seneca Falls convention. It was signed by 100 of the 300 participants.

Women were increasingly active in the AASS and the **"come outer" movement**, but their growing participation aroused opposition even among abolitionists. By 1836 to 1837, female societies formed the backbone of many antislavery petition campaigns. More women also joined the lecture circuit, including Abby Kelley, a fiery orator who demanded that women be granted an equal role in the movement. But when Garrison and his supporters appointed Kelley to the AASS business committee in May 1839, angry debates erupted over the propriety of women participating "in closed meetings with men." Of the 1,000 abolitionists in attendance, some 300 walked out in protest. The dissidents, including many evangelical men, soon formed a new organization, the American and Foreign Anti-Slavery Society, which excluded women from public lecturing and office holding but encouraged them to support men's efforts.

Those who remained in the AASS then continued to expand the roles of women. In 1840 local chapters appointed a handful of female delegates, including Lucretia Mott of Philadelphia, to the World Anti-Slavery Convention in London. The majority of men at the meeting, however, rejected the female delegates' credentials. Women were then forced to watch the proceedings from a separate section of the hall, confirming for some that women could be effective in campaigns against slavery only if they gained more rights for themselves.

Finally, in July 1848 a small circle of women, including Lucretia Mott and a young American she met in London, Elizabeth Cady Stanton, organized the first convention focused explicitly on women's rights. Held in Stanton's hometown of Seneca Falls, New York, the convention attracted three hundred women and men. James Mott, husband of Lucretia, presided over the convention, and Frederick Douglass spoke, but women dominated the proceedings. One hundred participants signed the **Declaration of Sentiments**, which called for women's equality in everything from education and employment to legal rights and voting. Two weeks later, Post helped organize a second convention in Rochester, where participants took the radical action of electing a woman, Abigail Bush, to preside. Here, too, Douglass spoke alongside other black abolitionists and local working women.

TEACHING IDEA

Check for Understanding

Write the following on the board: "Abolitionists were NOT necessarily supporters of equality for African Americans." Evaluate the validity of this statement. Then, give students five minutes to reflect and jot down their take on this issue. Afterward, have students share out their position and ask them to support and develop it with historical evidence and reasoning. Possible answers include: *some abolitionists still believed that African Americans were racially inferior; others wanted to get rid of human bondage but did not want emancipated African Americans integrating into their societies.*

APPLY THE TIP

Ask students to work with a partner to answer the following question: How did the World Anti-Slavery Convention in London lead to the Seneca Falls Convention in New York? Once they have completed this task, ask them to join another pair and make groups of four to share their answers. To conclude, engage in a class discussion to ensure students understand how women being turned away from an abolitionist meeting impacted the women's rights movement. Clarify any misunderstandings.

TRM Suggested Responses to Questions

TRM Module 4.8 AP® Analyzing Sources Handout 4

TEACHING IDEA

Understanding People Who Made a Difference

In pairs, have students research two women's rights movement leaders — Lucretia Mott and Elizabeth Cady Stanton. Students must identify their main contributions to the women's rights movement. Their answers should include their work to organize the Seneca Falls Convention in 1848, the Declaration of Sentiments, and the fight for women's suffrage. Discuss these findings with the entire class to ensure everyone has at least these fundamental understandings.

AP® ANALYZING SOURCES

Source: Elizabeth Cady Stanton, *Declaration of Sentiments*, 1848

"We hold these truths to be self-evident: that all men and women are created equal; that they are endowed by their Creator with certain inalienable rights; that among these are life, liberty, and the pursuit of happiness. . . .

But when a long train of abuses and usurpations . . . reduce them under absolute despotism, it is their duty to throw off such government. . . .

The history of mankind is a history of repeated injuries and usurpations on the part of man toward woman, having in direct object the establishment of an absolute tyranny over her. . . .

He has never permitted her to exercise her inalienable right to the elective franchise.

He has compelled her to submit to laws, in the formation of which she had no voice. . . .

He has taken from her all right in property, even to the wages she earns.

He has made her . . . promise obedience to her husband, he becoming, to all intents and purposes, her master — the law giving him power to deprive her of her liberty, and to administer [punishment].

He has so framed the laws of divorce, as to what shall be the proper causes, and in case of separation, to whom the guardianship of the children shall be given . . . going upon the false supposition of the supremacy of man, and giving all power into his hands. . . .

He has monopolized nearly all the profitable employments, and from those she is permitted to follow, she receives but a scanty remuneration."

Questions for Analysis
1. Identify the main points of this excerpt from the *Declaration of Sentiments*.
2. Explain how women's experiences in the abolitionist movement and other social factors provide context for this document.

Questions for Comparison Thomas Jefferson, *Declaration of Independence*, 1776 (p. 179)
1. Evaluate the extent of similarity in the stated complaints listed in both documents.
2. Evaluate the extent of similarity between the context surrounding this document and the Declaration of Independence.

Although abolitionism provided much of the momentum for the women's rights movement, other movements also contributed. Strikes by seamstresses and mill workers in the 1830s and 1840s highlighted women's economic needs. Utopian communities experimented with gender equality, and temperance reformers focused attention on domestic violence and sought changes in divorce laws. A diverse coalition also advocated for married women's property rights in the mid-1840s. Women's rights were debated among New York's Seneca Indians as well. Like the Cherokee, Seneca women had lost traditional rights over land and tribal policy as their nation adopted Anglo-American ways. In the summer of 1848, the creation of a written constitution threatened to enshrine these losses in writing. The Seneca constitution did strip women of their dominant role in selecting chiefs but protected their right to vote on the sale of tribal lands. Earlier in 1848, revolutions had erupted against repressive regimes in France and elsewhere in Europe. Antislavery newspapers like the *North Star* covered developments in detail, including European women's demands for political and civil recognition. The meetings in Seneca Falls and Rochester drew on these ideas and influences even as they focused primarily on the rights of white American women.

REVIEW

How did the changes to the American Anti-Slavery Society during the 1840s differentiate it from earlier abolitionist organizations?

EXPLORING AP® THEMES

Politics and Power

Have students brainstorm about the issues confronting women at the time that led them to organize a women's rights movement. Then have students research the topic for specifics. Students should discover, among other possible answers, the need for: 1) *political rights (i.e., suffrage)*; 2) *protection from domestic violence and abuse (e.g., could not file for divorce)*; 3) *economic needs (e.g., paid lower wages)*. Lastly, help students make connections to the present day and the fight for equality in wages and the workplace.

The Rise of Antislavery Parties

Liberty Party Antislavery political party formed in 1840. The Liberty Party, along with the Free-Soil Party, helped place slavery at the center of national political debates.

AP® TIP
Evaluate the extent to which the abolitionist movement fostered shifts in political party platforms during the mid-1800s.

Free-Soil Party Party founded by political abolitionists in 1848 to expand the appeal of the Liberty Party by focusing less on the moral wrongs of slavery and more on the benefits of providing economic opportunities for northern white people in western territories.

As women's rights advocates demanded female suffrage, debates over the role of partisan politics in the antislavery campaign intensified. Keeping slavery out of western territories depended on the actions of Congress, as did abolishing slavery in the nation's capital and ending the internal slave trade. Moral arguments had seemingly done little to change minds in Congress or in the South. To force abolition onto the national political agenda, the **Liberty Party** was formed in 1840. Many Garrisonians were appalled at the idea of participating in national elections when the federal government supported slavery in numerous ways, from the three-fifths compromise to allowing slavery in newly acquired territories. Still, the Liberty Party gained significant support among abolitionists in New York, the Middle Atlantic states, and the Midwest.

The Whigs and Democrats generally avoided the antislavery issue to keep their southern and northern wings intact, but that strategy became more difficult once the Liberty Party entered campaigns. In 1840 the party won less than 1 percent of the popular vote but organized rallies that attracted large crowds. In 1844 the party more than doubled its votes, which was sufficient to deny Henry Clay a victory in New York State and thus ironically the election of slaveholder James K. Polk (see Module 5-1).

When President Polk led the United States into war with Mexico, interest in an antislavery political party surged. In 1848 the Liberty Party gained the support of antislavery Whigs, also called Conscience Whigs; northern Democrats who opposed the extension of slavery into the territories; and African American leaders like Frederick Douglass, who broke with Garrison on the utility of electoral politics. Seeing a political opportunity, more practically minded political abolitionists founded the **Free-Soil Party**, which quickly subsumed the Liberty Party. Free-Soilers focused less on the moral wrongs of slavery than on the benefits of keeping western territories free for northern white people seeking economic opportunity. The Free-Soil Party nominated former Democratic president Martin Van Buren in 1848 and won 10 percent of the popular vote. But once again, the result was to send a slaveholder to the White House — Zachary Taylor. Nonetheless, the Free-Soil Party had expanded beyond the Liberty Party, raising fears in the South and in the two major parties that the battle over slavery could no longer be contained.

REVIEW
- How did the Liberty Party and Free-Soil Party change American politics in the 1840s?

AP® WRITING HISTORICALLY: Responding to a Long-Essay Question

In this module, you learned about the rise of the American abolitionist movement during the 1820s, 1830s, and 1840s. Now, let's take a look at an essay prompt that asks you to draw on your knowledge from both this module and Module 4-7:

> Evaluate the extent of similarity between the abolitionist movement and other social movements during the period from 1820 to 1848.

Step 1 Break down the prompt.

Remember, anytime you are asked to write about the *extent* of something, you will need to not only craft claims about relevant historical developments but also make — and use evidence to defend — judgment calls about the importance of the developments you choose to include. This may seem like an uphill battle when you're faced with a prompt and a blank sheet of paper, but remembering two words can help: *how much*. You can use them to rephrase the prompt as a question: "*How much* similarity existed between the abolitionist movement and other social movements between 1820 and 1848?" While your answer to the prompt will not be as simple as "a little" or "a lot," asking yourself this question should help jumpstart your pre-writing.

Before moving to step 2, you may want to remind yourself that any prompt that mentions similarities without mentioning differences — or vice versa — still requires you to consider both. While comparative historical arguments typically assert that either similarity or difference is more

(Continued)

BUILDING AP® SKILLS

Comparison

Have students complete a Venn diagram that identifies some of the main similarities and differences between the Liberty Party (1840) and the Free-Soil Party (1848). Possible answers are included in italics.

- **Similarities:** *Both parties made abolition a political issue at the national level.*
- **Differences:** *While the Liberty Party opposed slavery on moral grounds, the Free-Soil Party focused on how slavery limited economic opportunities for whites; supporters (i.e., Free-Soilers had much broader appeal).*

Students may have to conduct some research to complete this activity. It would be a good idea for students to start by looking at the platforms of each respective political party.

TRM Suggested Responses to Questions

BUILDING AP® SKILLS

Contextualization

Since this is the final module in Period 4, it would be a good idea to help students transition to the next one — Period 5. Have students conduct a class discussion on what occurred in this final module that "sets the stage" or "lays a foundation" for a continuation of debates about westward expansion and the political issue of slavery. The elections of pro-expansionist and slaveholders James K. Polk (1844) and Zachary Taylor (1848) would ultimately put the United States on the road to the American Civil War. Specifically, ask students to write a timed 10-minute paragraph on contextualization. When they have completed their paragraphs, ask them to share their answers with a partner and note any use of different examples. Answers will vary.

TEACHING IDEA

Check for Understanding

Go back to the opening activity for the entire period — the timeline students created based on the Period 4 Review Chronology on page 353. Ask students to review the main political events and economic developments originally highlighted. Then, write a double-headed arrow on the board with a start date of 1800 and end date of 1848 and conduct a class discussion on which political and economic answers they think are the most important now that the entire period has been covered. Have them place one category on top and the other on the bottom of the arrow. Doing so will allow students to compare (and contrast) their original answers with those at the end. Since the period timeline starts in 1791 and ends in 1850, it would be perfectly acceptable for students to use examples that do not technically fall within the provided date range on the arrow.

TEACHING IDEA

AP® Central

Starting in August 2019, the College Board has provided teachers with an electronic platform where formative assessments may be conducted to monitor student progress and allow them to practice. For Unit 4, which covers the period from 1800 to 1848, students can practice with 35 Multiple-Choice Questions, 2 Short-Answer Questions (using primary and secondary sources), and 1 partial Long-Essay Question. Visit the AP® Central website to access and unlock these resources for your students (apcentral.collegeboard.org).

EXPLORING AP® THEMES

Migration and Settlement

Although this theme is not specifically targeted in this period, it is still relevant to the material covered in this module and as students move forward and discuss Manifest Destiny and the Mexican-American War. Specifically, have students think about how Americans moving into Mexican territory would transform the social and physical environments. For guidance, revisit the section on Texas to develop ideas about what is about to take place in what would become the American Southwest and the state of California. Students should identify that conflicts will emerge between those already inhabiting these lands and the arrival of American culture and institutions.

---

prominent — and the comparison prompts you come across in this course will certainly nudge you in one direction or the other — the most effective arguments establish that elements of both are present. As you likely recall from the comparative writing you did for Period 3, thinking of comparison in terms of a continuum can help you generate claims for a qualified argument that not only acknowledges similarities and differences but tackles their level of importance.

Step 2 List and categorize your historical knowledge.

As usual, start by writing down any specific and relevant historical information you can remember — in this case, about the abolitionist and other social movements of the mid-nineteenth century. You will likely notice some patterns emerge, and you can use these patterns to break your knowledge into different categories.

Some questions to ask yourself to generate ideas for categories include:

- Who supported each movement?
- What were the goals and motivations of their supporters?
- What tactics and strategies did each movement use?
- What was the overall level of success that each movement achieved in the time period?

You can also divide these larger categories into subtopics, too — for instance, by examining the similarities and/or differences of the movements' supporters by race, class, or region, or by comparing and contrasting the level of success these movements achieved as they attempted to sway public opinion and change the laws. Regardless of the method of organization you choose for your pre-writing, be sure to identify at least three areas of comparison. You should also make sure that both points of similarity and difference are represented. You may use the following blank graphic organizer, but you should also feel free to organize your pre-writing in whatever way works best for you.

Area of Comparison	Extent of Similarity/Difference	Explanation of the Similarity/Difference

Step 3 Set the context and craft a thesis.

Identify a large event or historical process that began immediately before or during the beginning of your essay's time period and use it to set the stage for your argument. One effective strategy to keep in mind when writing thesis statements for evaluative comparison essays is to start your thesis statement with a claim that lies on the other side of the continuum as your main argument. For instance, if your argument is mainly about similarity, you should start your thesis off with a claim about a small or moderate difference.

TEACHING IDEA

AP® Writing Historically Workshop

This activity seeks to use the model provided in step 2 for samples of student writing. Assign students to complete a long-essay response to the activity prior to class. Begin the activity by having students form groups of two or three. Have students select their best body paragraph to exchange with group members. Using the template provided in step 2, students will read and record in the appropriate boxes how well their group members answered the elements of the question. If students are able to fill in the graphic organizer completely, that means the writer achieved the basics of the response. On the other hand, if there are gaps on the graphic organizer then the writer will know something is missing. This is an efficient way for students to read multiple examples and provide basic feedback.

> **ACTIVITY**
>
> Use steps 1 through 3 to plan and write an essay in response to the essay prompt at the beginning of this box.
>
> You may use the following outline to guide your response:
>
> I. Introductory paragraph
>   A. Immediate/preceding contextualization statement
>   1. Cite evidence of immediate/preceding context
>   2. Explain influence of immediate/preceding context
>   B. Thesis statement presenting three to four evaluative claims of comparison that are situated along a continuum of relative importance
> II. Claim 1 body paragraph
>   A. Topic sentence presenting an evaluative claim of comparison 1
>   B. Supporting statement citing evidence of claim 1
>   C. Cite additional evidence of claim 1
>   D. Explain how evidence supports claim 1
> III. Claim 2 body paragraph
>   A. Topic sentence presenting an evaluative claim of comparison 2
>   B. Supporting statement citing evidence of claim 2
>   C. Cite additional evidence of claim 2
>   D. Explain how evidence supports claim 2
> IV. Claim 3 body paragraph
>   A. Topic sentence presenting an evaluative claim of comparison 3
>   B. Supporting statement citing evidence of claim 3
>   C. Cite additional evidence of claim 3
>   D. Explain how evidence supports claim 3
> V. (Optional) Claim 4 body paragraph
>   A. Topic sentence presenting an evaluative claim of comparison 4
>   B. Supporting statement citing evidence of claim 4
>   C. Cite additional evidence of claim 4
>   D. Explain how evidence supports claim 4

PERIOD 4 REVIEW 1800–1848

KEY CONCEPTS AND EVENTS

abolitionists, *326*
Adams-Onís Treaty, *279*
The Alamo, *312*
American Anti-Slavery Society (AASS), *344*
American System, *277*
American system of manufacturing, *266*
Amistad mutiny, *326*
Bank of the United States, *275*
Barbary States, *258*
Battle of Horseshoe Bend, *275*
Battle of New Orleans, *277*
boomtown, *332*
Cherokee Nation v. Georgia, *314*
"come outer" movement, *347*
Corps of Discovery, *259*
"corrupt bargain," *303*
cotton gin, *265*
cult of domesticity, *292*
Declaration of Sentiments, *347*
Democrats, *303*
deskilling, *294*
Embargo Act, *262*
Erie Canal, *278*
Free-Soil Party, *349*
Force Bill, *311*

gag rule, *313*
Haitian Revolution, *258*
Hartford Convention, *276*
Hudson River School, *336*
Indian Removal Act, *313*
judicial review, *261*
Judiciary Act, *261*
The *Liberator*, *344*
Liberty Party, *349*
Louisiana Purchase, *258*
Marbury v. Madison, *261*
market revolution, *287*
McCulloch v. Maryland, *261*
Missouri Compromise, *284*
Monroe Doctrine, *279*
multiplier effect, *265*
mutual aid societies, *290*
Nat Turner's rebellion, *326*
National Republicans, *303*
National Road, *264*
nativists, *338*
Non-Intercourse Act, *273*
North Star, *346*
nullification, *310*
Ordinance of Nullification, *310*
Panic of 1819, *281*

Panic of 1837, *295*
Petticoat Affair, *306*
planters, *262*
Romantic era, *331*
Second Bank of the United States, *281*
Second Great Awakening, *332*
Second Seminole War, *314*
separate spheres, *292*
spoils system, *307*
Tariff of 1816, *277*
Tariff of 1828, *303*
Tariff of Abominations, *309*
Tejanos, *312*
temperance, *290*
Trail of Tears, *316*
transcendentalism, *335*
Treaty of Ghent, *276*
Treaty of New Echota, *315*
underground railroad, *344*
unions, *295*
utopian societies, *340*
War of 1812, *274*
Whig Party, *317*
white supremacy, *328*
yeomen farmers, *327*

KEY PEOPLE

John Quincy Adams, *279*
Napoleon Bonaparte, *258*
John C. Calhoun, *303*
William Clark, *259*
Henry Clay, *277*
Thomas Cole, *336*
Frederick Douglass, *346*
Ralph Waldo Emerson, *335*
Charles Grandison Finney, *332*
Margaret Fuller, *336*
William Lloyd Garrison, *344*
Angelina Grimké, *344*
Sarah Grimké, *344*
William Henry Harrison, *273*
Sam Houston, *313*

Washington Irving, *331*
Andrew Jackson, *275*
Thomas Jefferson, *257*
Meriwether Lewis, *259*
Toussaint L'Ouverture, *258*
William Marbury, *261*
John Marshall, *261*
William Miller, *335*
James Monroe, *279*
Samuel F. B. Morse, *338*
James K. Polk, *349*
Sacagawea, *259*
Antonio López de Santa Anna, *312*
Winfield Scott, *315*
Samuel Slater, *265*

Joseph Smith, *334*
Elizabeth Cady Stanton, *347*
Zachary Taylor, *349*
Tecumseh, *273*
Tenskwatawa, *273*
Henry David Thoreau, *336*
Nat Turner, *325*
John Tyler, *317*
Martin Van Buren, *301*
David Walker, *343*
Mercy Otis Warren, *331*
Mason Weems, *331*
Eli Whitney, *265*
Jemima Wilkinson, *332*
Brigham Young, *335*

PERIOD 4 REVIEW 1800–1848

CHRONOLOGY

Date	Event
1791	Haitian Revolution
1793	Invention of cotton gin expands slavery
1798	Development of American system of manufacturing
1803	Louisiana Purchase
1804–06	Corps of Discovery expedition
1807	Embargo Act limits foreign trade
1812–14	War of 1812 ends with Treaty of Ghent in 1814
1814	Hartford Convention expresses Federalist dissent
1815	Battle of New Orleans
	Approval of National Road project
1819	Panic of 1819
	Adams-Onís Treaty
By 1820	Market economy well established
1820s	Emergence of Lowell mills and factory towns in New England countryside
1820s–30s	Second Great Awakening
1820	Missouri Compromise temporarily eases national tensions
1821	Federalists advocate for black and white male suffrage
	Mexico wins independence and claims Texas territory
1823	Monroe Doctrine established
1824	Election of President John Quincy Adams (Democratic-Republican) via "corrupt bargain"
By 1825	Elimination of voter qualifications for white males in most states
1825	Completion of Erie Canal
1827	Establishment of first workingmen's party
1828	Election of President Andrew Jackson (Democrat)
	Cherokee declare themselves an independent sovereign nation
1830s	Emergence of cultural norms emphasizing domesticity and separate spheres for women
	Abolitionist movement grows substantially
1830s–40s	Rapid spread of industrialization, immigration, urbanization, and nativism
	Wave of utopian communities established
1830s–50s	Massive forced migration of enslaved people to lower South
1830	Passage of Indian Removal Act
1831	Nat Turner's rebellion
	The Liberator started by William Lloyd Garrison
1832	South Carolina approves Ordinance of Nullification, resulting in the Force Bill
1833	Establishment of American Anti-Slavery Society (AASS)
1836	Texas applies for statehood
	Passage of gag rule
1836–37	Widespread antislavery campaigns
1837	Panic of 1837
	First national meeting of women abolitionists
1838–39	Forced removal of American Indians via the Trail of Tears
1839	Mutiny on the Amistad
By 1840s	Restrictions on black male voting rights in place nationwide
1844	First telegraph message sent
1845	Publication of Narrative of the Life of Frederick Douglass
1846	Brigham Young and followers settle near the Great Salt Lake
1847	North Star started by Frederick Douglass
1848	Free-Soil Party established
	Election of President Zachary Taylor (Whig)
	Seneca Falls convention
By 1850	One third of southerners are slaveholders

TRM Suggested Responses to Questions

Answers to Multiple-Choice Questions

1. c
2. b
3. c
4. a
5. c
6. b
7. d
8. c
9. c
10. a
11. b
12. a
13. c
14. a
15. c

AP® EXAM PRACTICE THROUGH 1848

Multiple-Choice Questions

Choose the correct answer for each question.

Questions 1–3 refer to the following excerpt.

Source: U.S. Supreme Court, *McCullouch v. Maryland*, 1819

"We admit, as all must admit, that the powers of the government are limited, and that its limits are not to be transcended. But we think the sound construction of the constitution must allow to the national legislature that discretion, with respect to the means by which the powers it confers are to be carried into execution, which will enable that body to perform the high duties assigned to it, in the manner most beneficial to the people. Let the end be legitimate, let it be within the scope of the constitution, and all means which are appropriate, which are plainly adapted to that end, which are not prohibited, but consist with the letter and spirit of the constitution, are constitutional. . . ."

1. The excerpt best serves as evidence of which of the following debates in the early republic?
   a. The extension of slavery into the territories
   b. Government support of industrialization
   c. Loose vs. strict interpretation of the Constitution
   d. Efforts to limit immigration from Europe

2. The ruling in the excerpt demonstrates which of the following tendencies of the Supreme Court in the period 1800 to 1830?
   a. Siding with business interests over labor
   b. Favoring national power over states' rights
   c. Upholding the sanctity of contracts
   d. Limiting the rights of enslaved people

3. Which of the following groups would have most likely supported the decision in the excerpt?
   a. Western farmers
   b. Jacksonian Democrats
   c. Former Federalists
   d. Owners of large southern plantations

Questions 4–5 refer to the following excerpt.

Source: Cherokee Women's Petition, 1831

"We believe the present plan of the General Government to effect our removal West of the Mississippi, and thus obtain our lands for the use of the State of Georgia, to be highly oppressive, cruel and unjust. And we sincerely hope there is no consideration which can induce our citizens to forsake the land of our fathers of which they have been in possession from time immemorial, and thus compel us, against our will, to undergo the toils and difficulties of removing with our helpless families hundreds of miles to unhealthy and unproductive country. We hope therefore the committee and Council will take into deep consideration our deplorable situation, and do everything in their power to avert such a state of things. And we trust by a prudent course their transactions with the General Government will enlist in our behalf the sympathies of the good people of the United States."

4. All of the following historical developments contributed to the concerns expressed in the petition EXCEPT
   a. the overcultivation of arable land in the Southeast.
   b. federal efforts to relocate American Indian settlements.
   c. the expansion of frontier settlements.
   d. attempts by American Indians to retain control of tribal lands and natural resources.

5. Which of the following groups would have been most likely to support the sentiments expressed in the petition?
   a. Southern plantation owners
   b. Frontier settlers
   c. Leaders of rival American Indian nations
   d. States' rights advocates

AP® Exam Practice: Through 1848

Period 4: 1800–1848

Questions 6–9 refer to the following excerpt.

Source: *The Force Bill*, 1833

"Be it enacted that whenever, by reason of unlawful obstructions, combinations, or assemblages of persons, it shall become impracticable . . . to execute the revenue laws, and collect the duties on imports in the ordinary way, in any collection district, . . . it shall and may be lawful for the President of the United States . . . to employ . . . land or naval forces, or militia of the United States, as may be deemed necessary for the purpose of preventing the removal of such vessel or cargo, and protecting the officers of the customs in retaining the custody thereof. . . . [T]he President shall be, and hereby is, authorized, promptly to employ such means to suppress the same, and to . . . cause the said laws or process to be duly executed. . . ."

6. The controversy generated by passage of the Force Bill reflected ongoing debates in the United States over
   a. the power of the presidency.
   b. federalism and states' rights.
   c. the legal use of military force.
   d. First Amendment rights of assembly and protest.

7. The provisions in the excerpt would have been most widely condemned by
   a. Massachusetts merchants.
   b. Pennsylvania small farmers.
   c. New York textile workers.
   d. South Carolina plantation owners.

8. Which of the following most directly resulted from the enactment of the Force Bill?
   a. An increase in federal tariff revenues
   b. An expansion of semisubsistence agriculture
   c. An increase in sectionalism
   d. An expansion of white male suffrage

9. The underlying principles in the excerpt are most consistent with those expressed in
   a. *Common Sense* (1776).
   b. the Northwest Ordinance (1787).
   c. the *Federalist Papers* (1787).
   d. Washington's Farewell Address (1796).

Questions 10–11 refer to the following map.

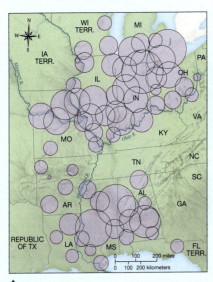

▲ Land Sold, 1830s

10. Which of the following factors most directly contributed to the activity depicted on the map?
    a. Overcultivation of land in the East
    b. American Indian resistance to expansion efforts
    c. Antislavery efforts in the North
    d. Rural migration to cities

11. The map most strongly supports which of the following arguments about the first half of the nineteenth century?
    a. Property qualifications for voting were a major incentive to land settlement north of the Ohio River.
    b. Federal efforts to control and relocate American Indian populations were largely successful.
    c. Plans such as Henry Clay's "American System" were of limited value in developing the nation's economy.
    d. The market revolution meant that slavery had a limited future west of the Mississippi River.

Period 4: 1800–1848

AP® Exam Practice: Through 1848

Questions 12–13 refer to the following excerpt.

Source: Ralph Waldo Emerson, "The Transcendentalist," 1842

"What is popularly called Transcendentalism among us, is Idealism; Idealism as it appears in 1842. As thinkers, mankind have ever divided into two sects, Materialists and Idealists; the first class founding on experience, the second on consciousness; the first class beginning to think from the data of the senses, the second class perceive that the senses are not final, and say, the senses give us representations of things, but what are the things themselves, they cannot tell. The materialist insists on facts, on history, on the force of circumstances, and the animal wants of man; the idealist on the power of Thought and of Will, on inspiration, on miracle, on individual culture."

12. Which of the following contributed to the rise of ideas reflected in the passage during the period 1830 to 1848?
    a. The influence of European Romanticism
    b. Shorter travel times resulting from new transportation systems
    c. The re-emergence of a two-party political system
    d. Increased immigration from Europe

13. The excerpt was written primarily to
    a. criticize immigration policies after 1800.
    b. respond to the creation of the two-party political system.
    c. challenge traditional beliefs about American society.
    d. address injustices to American Indians.

Questions 14–15 refer to the following lithograph.

The Drunkards Progress. From the First Glass to the Grave (1846) Text within image reads: STEP 1. A glass with a Friend. STEP 2. A glass to keep the cold out. STEP 3. A glass too much. STEP 4. Drunk and riotous. STEP 5. The summit attained / Jolly companions / A confirmed drunkard. STEP 6. Poverty and Disease. STEP 7. Forsaken by Friends. STEP 8. Desperation and crime. STEP 9. Death by suicide.

14. The most likely purpose of the artist in creating the image was to
    a. promote the efforts of temperance societies to change the behavior of individuals.
    b. advocate for political rights and gender equality throughout the United States.
    c. support the efforts of the nativist American Party to limit Irish immigration.
    d. advance the work of early labor unions seeking wage equality for working women.

15. Which of the following resulted from the conditions depicted in the image?
    a. Women were generally excluded from participating in social movements.
    b. Alcohol was prohibited by the U.S. Constitution.
    c. Americans engaged in voluntary organizations to reform society.
    d. Temperance surpassed abolition as the most controversial issue in the 1840s and 1850s.

Short-Answer Questions

Read each question carefully and write a short response. Use complete sentences.

1. Using the excerpts that follow, answer (a), (b), and (c).

    Source: Mary Hewitt, "Wage, Gender and the Artisan Tradition in Shoemaking 1780–1860," 1983

    "Sharing the bonds of womanhood both at work and in their domestic sphere, shoebinders in 1834 tried to organize themselves in terms of a female community of workers.... [But] ... the conditions under which many shoebinders labored — isolated from each other, employed by the shoe boss outside a group labor system and combining wage work with domestic responsibilities — discouraged collective activity. The tensions between their relationship to the artisan system and its equal rights ideology and their subordinate roles as females in the family were exposed by their arguments for a just wage for women. Neither the social relations of the artisan family nor the realities of working as a woman for the shoe boss encouraged [her] ... to identify with her working sister in the Lowell mills or conceive of herself as a worker capable of supporting herself who could unite with her peers to protest mistreatment."

    Source: Paul Johnson, *The Early American Republic, 1789–1829*, 2007

    "The brick mills and prim boarding houses ... occupied by sober, well-behaved farm girls ... produced a self-respecting sisterhood of independent, wage-earning women. Twice in the 1830s the women of Lowell went out on strike, proclaiming that they were not wage slaves but 'the daughters of freemen.' ... [M]any [former] Lowell women entered public life as reformers. Most of them married and became housewives but not on the same terms their mothers had known.... Thus the [male factory owners] kept their promise to produce cotton cloth profitably without creating a permanent working class. But they did not succeed in shuttling young women between rural and urban paternalism and back again. Wage labor, the ultimate degradation for agrarian-republican men, opened a road to independence for thousands of young women."

    a) Briefly explain ONE major difference between Johnson's and Hewitt's historical interpretations of how work affected women in the first half of the nineteenth century.
    b) Briefly explain how ONE specific historical event or development between 1800 and 1848 that is not explicitly mentioned in the excerpts could be used to support Johnson's argument.
    c) Briefly explain how ONE specific historical event or development between 1800 and 1848 that is not explicitly mentioned in the excerpts could be used to support Hewitt's argument.

Period 4: 1800–1848

2. Using the map that follows, answer (a), (b), and (c).

▲ **Map of American Indian Relocations, 1820s–1840s**

a) Briefly explain how ONE specific historical event or development contributed to the forced relocation of American Indians depicted in the map in the period 1820 to 1848.

b) Briefly explain ONE specific historical effect of the forced relocation of American Indians depicted in the map in the period 1820 to 1848.

c) Briefly explain ONE specific way American Indians resisted the forced relocations depicted in the map in the period 1820 to 1848.

3. Answer (a), (b), and (c).
a) Briefly describe ONE specific historical similarity between the first two-party system of Federalists and Democratic-Republicans from 1800 to 1820 and the second two-party system of Democrats and Whigs from 1833 to 1844.

b) Briefly describe ONE specific historical difference between the first two-party system of Federalists and Democratic-Republicans from 1800 to 1820 and the second two-party system of Democrats and Whigs from 1828 to 1840.

c) Briefly explain ONE specific historical reason for a difference between the first two-party system of Federalists and Democratic-Republicans from 1800 to 1820 and the second two-party system of Democrats and Whigs from 1828 to 1840.

4. Answer (a), (b), and (c).
a) Briefly describe ONE specific historical similarity between the First Great Awakening and the Second Great Awakening.

b) Briefly describe ONE specific historical difference between the First Great Awakening and the Second Great Awakening.

c) Briefly explain ONE specific historical impact of the Second Great Awakening on American society.

AP® Exam Practice: Through 1848

Period 4: 1800–1848

Document-Based Question

Question 1 is based on the accompanying documents. The documents have been edited for the purpose of this exercise. *Suggested reading period: 15 minutes. Suggested writing time: 45 minutes.*

1. Evaluate the extent of change in U.S. society that resulted from the activities of political parties from 1824 to 1840.

DOCUMENT 1

Source: John Marshall, Chief Justice of the U.S. Supreme Court as a delegate to the Virginia Convention to revise the state constitution, *Memorial of the Non-Freeholders of Virginia*, 1829

"Surely it were much to be desired that every citizen should be qualified for the proper exercise of all his rights and the due performance of all his duties. But the same qualifications that entitle him to assume the management of his private affairs and to claim all other privileges of citizenship equally entitle him, in the judgement of your memorialists, to be entrusted with this, the dearest of all privileges, the most important of all his concerns. . . .

Virtue, intelligence are not products of the soil. Attachments to property, often a sordid sentiment, is not to be confounded with the sacred flame of patriotism. The love of country, like that of parents and offspring, is engrafted in our nature. It exists in all climates, among all classes, under every possible form of government. Riches more often impair it than poverty."

DOCUMENT 2

Source: Margaret Bayard Smith, author and political commentator, *Letter to Jonathan Bayard Harrison Smith*, 1829

"But at the White House reception following the inauguration, what a scene did we witness!! The majesty of the people had disappeared, and instead a rabble, a mob . . . scrambling, fighting, romping. . . . The president after having literally been nearly pressed to death . . . escaped to his lodgings at Gadsby's. Cut glass and bone china to the amount of several thousand dollars hade been broken in the struggle to get refreshments. . . . Ladies fainted, men were seen with bloody noses. . . . Ladies and gentlemen only had been expected at this reception, not the people en masse. But it was the people's day, and the people's president. . . . The . . . rabble in the president's house brought to my mind descriptions I had read of the mobs in Tuileries and at Versailles."

DOCUMENT 3

Source: Alexis de Tocqueville, *Democracy in America*, 1831

"In the absence of great parties, the United States abound with lesser controversies; and public opinion is divided into a thousand minute shades of difference upon questions of very little moment. The pains which are taken to create parties are inconceivable, and at the present day it is no easy task. In the United States there is no religious animosity, because all religion is respected, and no sect is predominant; there is no jealousy of rank, because the people is everything, and none can contest its authority; lastly, there is no public indigence to supply the means of agitation, because the physical position of the country opens so wide a field to industry that man is able to accomplish the most surprising undertakings with his own native resources. Nevertheless, ambitious men are interested in the creation of parties, since it is difficult to eject a person from authority upon the mere ground that his place is coveted by others. The skill of the actors in the political world lies therefore in the art of creating parties. A political aspirant in the United States begins by discriminating his own interest, and by calculating upon those interests which may be collected around and amalgamated with it; he then contrives to discover some doctrine or some principle which may suit the purposes of this new association, and which he adopts in order to bring forward his party and to secure his popularity; just as the imprimatur of a King was in former days incorporated with the volume which it authorized, but to which it nowise belonged. When these preliminaries are terminated, the new party is ushered into the political world."

TRM Suggested Responses to Questions

Period 4: 1800–1848

AP® Exam Practice: Through 1848

DOCUMENT 4

Source: Andrew Jackson, *Veto Message to Congress on the National Bank,* 1832

"Equality of talents, of education, or of wealth can not be produced by human institutions. . . . [E]very man is equally entitled to protection by law; but when the laws undertake to add to these natural and just advantages artificial distinctions, to grant titles, gratuities, and exclusive privileges, to make the rich richer and the potent more powerful, the humble members of society-the farmers, mechanics, and laborers-who have neither the time nor the means of securing like favors to themselves, have a right to complain of the injustice of their Government. . . .

Nor is our Government to be maintained or our Union preserved by invasions of the rights and powers of the several States. In thus attempting to make our General Government strong we make it weak. Its true strength consists in leaving individuals and States as much as possible to themselves-in making itself felt, not in its power, but in its beneficence; not in its control, but in its protection; not in binding the States more closely to the center, but leaving each to move unobstructed in its proper orbit."

DOCUMENT 5

Source: Henry Clay, *Speech Against President Jackson on the Removal of the Deposits,* 1833

"The eyes and hopes of the American people are turned to Congress. They feel that they have been deceived and insulted; their confidence abused; their interests betrayed; and their liberties in danger. They see a rapid and alarming concentration of all power in one man's hands. They see that, by the exercise of the positive authority of the executive, and his negative power asserted over Congress, the will of one man alone prevails and governs the republic. The question is no longer what laws will Congress pass, but what will the executive not veto?"

DOCUMENT 6

Source: Fairfax Catlett, member of the Republic of Texas delegation to the United States, *Letter to Sam Houston, President of the Republic of Texas,* September 5, 1837

"The proposition for annexation was fairly made. . . . No means were left untried to secure a[n] . . . answer from the Executive. But it was all in vain. As might have been expected from a knowledge of Mr Van Buren's character. . . . He has mildly but decisively declined the proposition to treat upon the subject. It is the opinion of most of the members with whom I have conversed, that the question . . . will be forced up [in Congress] by the South some time next winter and will then produce a hurricane in that body more alarming than any which has ever rocked this Union to its centre. The Southern men with but few exceptions appear to regard the annexation of Texas as their last and forlorn hope. Should the measure fail and the Northern Abolitionists gain the ascendancy in Congress . . . it will be a question between the slave holding and non slave holding interests, (and there will be no middle ground upon which the two great parties can meet and compromise their differences). . . . With regard to Mr Van Buren's policy respecting the annexation of Texas I conceive it to be simply as follows[.] He would like to get Texas, but he is afraid of the consequences. . . . For by coming out as an open advocate of the measure, he would lose the North en masse . . . and dash his party into chaos. He would have to change his ground altogether and commence an entirely new system of operations. . . . The question is one of tremendous import, for it involves the destiny of North America for fifty years to come. . . . I doubt not that Mr Van Buren is fully alive to all the momentous bearings of the question upon the future welfare of the Union, and that he dreads the approach of the debate in Congress. . . . Yet it was not the less necessary that the proposition should be made. It has been made, declined, and it now rests with the Congress of the United States to determine whether Texas shall add another star to the cluster of the Union or—commence the conquest of the whole of Mexico. But the negotiation may be regarded as closed for the present."

DOCUMENT 7

Source: *Whig Campaign Ribbon*, 1840

Long-Essay Questions

Please choose one of the following three questions to answer. *Suggested writing time: 40 minutes.*

2. Evaluate the extent of change in the lives of middle-class women in the United States in the period 1800 to 1848.
3. Evaluate the extent of change in the lives of enslaved African Americans in the United States in the period 1800 to 1848.
4. Evaluate the extent of change in the lives of working-class men in the United States in the period 1800 to 1848.

PERIOD 5: 1844–1877

Expansion, Division, and Civil War

AP® Overview for Period 5

Even though the Civil War is the central historical event in the narrative of developments from 1844–1877, the United States did not knowingly drift toward disunion. Indeed, westward expansion, the belief in manifest destiny, the abolitionist movement, expansive territorial claims as a result of the Mexican War, and the increasingly sectional issue of enslavement came to define the turbulent 1840s. Much of the immediate context of the Civil War is rooted in the economic and social processes that crystallized sectionalism as Northerners came to define their identity in free labor amidst a growing capitalist nation dominated by fledgling industries. Conversely, Southerners clung to an agrarian and rigid hierarchical society. Reconstruction's complexity is in the debates and actions that represented the revolutionary changes wrought by the Civil War. However, students also need to understand how so-called Redeemers led a counterrevolution in the defeated southern states, reversed many civil rights gains for African Americans, and sought to rewrite the purposes of the Civil War. Students need to be aware of the breadth of perspectives on Reconstruction and both successes and setbacks of a government trying to come to grips with the institution of enslavement.

In addition to acquiring content knowledge of essential topics and historical developments, this period also cultivates the AP® historical thinking skills and reasoning processes necessary for students to succeed in the course and on the AP® exam. Pacing is crucial for this part of the curriculum and teachers should be aware of the import of not rushing through Reconstruction. Period 5 accounts for 10–17% of the AP® exam and can be the source of questions on the Short-Answer, Long-Essay, and Document-Based Questions.

Module 5-1: Manifest Destiny discusses the belief in manifest destiny and the attendant issues such as westward expansion. Manifest destiny was widely supported in theory; however, it came to represent more than a set of beliefs about America's so-called exceptionalism in the nineteenth century. As it were, this belief led to events such as the Mexican War, which would unleash a wave of abolitionist sentiment and further regionalism. The precipitous settlement in California would amplify the tensions over what to do with the new territory gained from the Mexican War and would further exacerbate tensions with American Indians. The thematic focus of geography and the environment and America in the world helps center students' focus on the effects of an expanding American nation.

Module 5-2: Compromise and Conflict takes a look at the lingering debates from the land expansion after the Mexican War, primarily related to the issue of slavery, which fostered increased tension over the future of slavery in the new territories. The sectional divide continued to fester as established political parties began to splinter and new parties such as the Free Soil party started. In an attempt to solve the sectional crisis, the Compromise of 1850 heightened tensions as much as it sought to find a middle road. Indeed, this omnibus bill carried with it a highly controversial Fugitive Slave Law that aggravated rather than assuaged sectional tension. The thematic focus on American and national identity, politics and power, and social structures synthesizes the prominent events of this module. Causation is central to both the historical thinking skill activities and the writing historically activity.

Module 5-3: From Sectional Crisis to Southern Secession focuses on the historical causes of the growing sectional crisis of the 1850s and the drift toward secession. Parallel to the acquisition of new territory was the growth in the abolitionist movement. The antislavery movement would extend its influence after the new Fugitive Slave Law of 1850 and the decisions within the Kansas-Nebraska Act. The fracturing of the second party system also influenced the antislavery movement as Republicans, although hardly abolitionists, refused to compromise on the extension of slavery into the unsettled territory from the Mexican War. The subjects of these intense sectional disagreements would come to a head in the *Dred Scott* case and subsequent Lincoln-Douglas debates. The thematic focus of politics and power and American and regional culture helps students understand how John Brown's raid crystallized southern fears. The election of 1860 serves as a turning point for students as the nation came to grapple with the constitutional and ideological effects of secession.

Module 5-4: Disunion and War explains the process of both Lower South and Upper South states seceding, which frames the ideological positions of secession. For some Confederate leaders, Lincoln's election was enough to act on the theory of secession, whereas leaders from the Upper South did not fully support secession until after the attack by Southerners on federal property, at Fort Sumter. After the Union dissolved and Civil War commenced, the Confederates experienced the high-water mark years of 1861 through early 1863, as they consistently controlled battles and the tide of war. The rationale and timing of Lincoln's Emancipation Proclamation are also integral to the narrative of this module and are buttressed with strong primary source selections. The war's effect on the home front, including draft riots, women's changing roles, and economic effects of the war, both northern and southern, are crucial elements for students to consider. The thematic focus of America in the world, along with the reasoning processes of comparison and continuity and change, will help students distill the tumultuous events of the beginning stages of the Civil War.

Module 5-5: Victory for the North illustrates how the tide of war turned beginning in 1863 with the Battles of Vicksburg and Gettysburg. President Lincoln's articulation of the continued prosecution of war and the decision to appoint Ulysses S. Grant to lead the Union Army became critical factors for furthering northern resolve to finish the war. The contributions of African Americans on the battlefield, in the workplace, and in helping the nation come to terms with what freedom meant are critical developments for students to evaluate. Generals Grant and Sherman, and their belief in total war, is an important topic for students to consider as they evaluate the end of the war and what the physical devastation of the South will do to southern attitudes after the war. President Lincoln's reelection in 1864, Union victories, African Americans, and Republicans all led the movement toward ratifying the Thirteenth Amendment, which would be one of the most important political consequences of the war. The thematic focus of American and national identity and America in the world frames students' inquiry in the global and regional effects of war. The reasoning processes of comparison and continuity and change allow students to study both the regional and national changes of the Civil War.

Module 5-6: Reconstruction Begins involves questions surrounding the consequences of war and which branch of government, legislative or executive, would facilitate the readmission of the former Confederate states. Moreover, fundamental questions surrounding the future of newly freedmen and southern planter aristocrats were all yet to be determined. The first wave of Reconstruction policies was the result of how northern Republicans interpreted the results of war, President Johnson's policies, and southern intransigence. Indeed, this revolutionary period was marked by the attempt to alter the meaning of freedom and citizenship for African Americans. African Americans were fully cognizant of what changes needed to be made for their freedom to be secured. Although the national government successfully passed the Fourteenth and Fifteenth Amendments, it was not without the obstinacy of southern leaders. The thematic focus of American and national identity and politics and power will certainly cause students to evaluate the circumstances surrounding what Reconstruction would mean.

Module 5-7: Reform and Resistance focuses on white southern resistance in concert with the thematic focus of politics and power, along with the reasoning process of causation. To be sure, Southerners did not accept many policies of Radical Republicans. While Southerners accepted the end of enslavement as a consequence of war, the movement to grant freedmen with political and civil rights was met with structural and personal resistance. The structural attempt by state and local governments to trap African Americans in an economic and social system was enslavement in all ways but the name. Many white Southerners expressed their antipathy toward African Americans by engaging in violent oppression. The processes explained in this module help students compare the rise of revolutionary measures explained in Module 5-6 with the anti-revolutionary reactions of white Southerners.

Module 5-8: Reconstruction Undone is characterized by a retreat of southern and northern commitment to Reconstruction policies that supported the rights of newly freedmen. As Reconstruction spanned into the late-1870s, many Americans simply did not support the extended work of the federal government in remaking the South. The Supreme Court also made decisions that granted states more control over Reconstruction policies, at the expense of freedmen. The formal ending of Reconstruction after the election of 1876 and the questions of legacies of Reconstruction allow students to examine the successes and setbacks of this revolutionary period in American history. The thematic focus of American and national identity appropriately requires students to think about how Reconstruction represents both a failure and a revolutionary era. The reasoning processes of comparison and continuity and change necessitate thoughtful reflection by students on how the Civil War and Reconstruction period came to define American history in the mid-nineteenth century.

Pacing Guide
Course Pacing for Period 5

Module #	Lesson Title	Instructional Period*	AP® Theme	AP® Topic	AP® Reasoning Process/Skill	Homework
5-1	N/A	N/A	Geography and the Environment America in the World	5.1 5.2 5.3	Causation / Historical Thinking Skills 1, 2, 3, 5	Reading and Source Analysis: 5-1
	Manifest Destiny	1	Geography and the Environment America in the World	5.1 5.2 5.3	Causation / Historical Thinking Skills 1, 2, 3, 5	Activity: AP® Writing Historically: Short-Answer Question Practice Reading and Source Analysis: 5-2
5-2	Review: AP® Writing Historically: Short-Answer Question Practice Compromise and Conflict	1	American and National Identity Politics and Power Social Structures	5.2 5.3 5.4 5.5	Comparison / Historical Thinking Skills 1, 2, 3, 5	Activity: AP® Writing Historically: Responding to a Long-Essay Question
	Workshop: AP® Writing Historically: Responding to a Long-Essay Question	1	American and National Identity Politics and Power Social Structures	5.5	Comparison / Historical Thinking Skills 1, 2, 3, 4, 5	Reading and Source Analysis: 5-3
5-3	From Sectional Crisis to Southern Secession	1	Politics and Power American and Regional Culture	5.5 5.6 5.7	Causation / Historical Thinking Skills 1, 2, 3, 5	Activity: AP® Writing Historically: Short-Answer Question Practice Reading and Source Analysis: 5-4
5-4	Review: AP® Writing Historically: Short-Answer Question Practice Disunion and War	1	America in the World	5.7 5.8 5.9	Comparison Continuity and Change / Historical Thinking Skills 1, 2, 3, 4, 5	Activity: AP® Writing Historically: Long-Essay Question Practice Reading and Source Analysis: 5-5
5-5	Review: AP® Writing Historically: Long-Essay Question Practice Victory for the North	1	American and National Identity America in the World	5.8 5.9	Comparison Continuity and Change / Historical Thinking Skills 1, 2, 3, 4, 5, 6	Activity: AP® Writing Historically: Short-Answer Question Practice Reading and Source Analysis: 5-6
5-6	Review: AP® Writing Historically: Short-Answer Question Practice Reconstruction Begins	1	American and National Identity Politics and Power	5.9 5.10	Causation / Historical Thinking Skills 1, 2, 3, 5	Activity: AP® Writing Historically: Using Context to Craft an Essay Conclusion
	Workshop: AP® Writing Historically: Using Context to Craft an Essay Conclusion	1	American and National Identity Politics and Power	5.10	Causation / Historical Thinking Skills 1, 2, 3, 5	Reading and Source Analysis: 5-7 Activity: AP® Writing Historically: Short-Answer Question Practice
5-7	Review: AP® Writing Historically: Short-Answer Question Practice Reform and Resistance	1	Politics and Power	5.10 5.11	Causation / Historical Thinking Skills 1, 2, 3, 5	Reading and Source Analysis: 5-8
5-8	Reconstruction Undone	1	American and National Identity	5.11	Comparison Continuity and Change / Historical Thinking Skills 1, 2, 3, 5	Activity: AP® Writing Historically: Responding to a Document-Based Question

(Continued)

Module #	Lesson Title	Instructional Period*	AP® Theme	AP® Topic	AP® Reasoning Process/Skill	Homework
	Workshop: AP® Writing Historically: Responding to a Document-Based Question	1	American and National Identity	5.11 5.12	Comparison Continuity and Change / Historical Thinking Skills 1, 2, 3, 4, 5, 6	Prepare for Assessment
Formative Assessment	AP® Exam Practice • 18 MCQs • 4 SAQs	0–1	All AP® U.S. History Course Themes	5.12 Personal Progress Check • 15 MCQs • 2 SAQs • 1 LEQ	All AP® History Reasoning Processes/Skills	
Summative Assessment	Unit 1 Test Bank • 55 MCQs • 4 SAQs • 1 DBQ • 4 LEQs	0–1	All AP® U.S. History Course Themes		All AP® History Reasoning Processes/Skills	

*Based on a standard 50-minute class period.

Period 5 Resources

The following resources can be found in the Resources section of the book's digital platform, by clicking on the link buttons in the Teacher's Edition e-book, or by opening the Teacher's Resource Materials.

- **TRM** Period 5 Overview Video
- **TRM** AP® Concepts and Skills Video
- **TRM** Period 5 Lecture Presentation Slides
- **TRM** Period 5 Workshop Rubrics
- **TRM** Period 5 Suggested Responses to Questions
- **TRM** Period 5 Guided Reading Worksheets

Module 5-1
- **TRM** Module 5.1 AP® Analyzing Sources Handout 1
- **TRM** Handout 5.1 – Treatment of American Indians in Eastern and Western Territories
- **TRM** Module 5.1 AP® Analyzing Sources Handout 2

Module 5-2
- **TRM** Module 5.2 AP® Analyzing Sources Handout 1
- **TRM** Handout 5.2 – KWL Chart
- **TRM** Module 5.2 AP® Analyzing Sources Handout 2
- **TRM** Module 5.2 AP® Analyzing Sources Handout 3

Module 5-3
- **TRM** Module 5.3 AP® Analyzing Sources Handout 1
- **TRM** Handout 5.3 – Missouri Compromise vs. Kansas-Nebraska Act
- **TRM** Module 5.3 AP® Analyzing Sources Handout 2
- **TRM** Module 5.3 AP® Analyzing Sources Handout 3

Module 5-4
- **TRM** Handout 5.4 – Early Civil War Strengths and Weaknesses
- **TRM** Module 5.4 AP® Analyzing Sources Handout 1
- **TRM** Module 5.4 AP® Analyzing Sources Handout 2
- **TRM** Module 5.4 AP® Analyzing Sources Handout 3

Module 5-5
- **TRM** Module 5.5 AP® Analyzing Sources Handout
- **TRM** Handout 5.5 – Regional Difficulties at the End of the Civil War

Module 5-6
- **TRM** Module 5.6 AP® Analyzing Sources Handout 1
- **TRM** Module 5.6 AP® Analyzing Sources Handout 2
- **TRM** Handout 5.6 – Comparing Reconstruction Plans
- **TRM** Module 5.6 AP® Analyzing Sources Handout 3
- **TRM** Module 5.6 AP® Analyzing Sources Handout 4

Module 5-7
- **TRM** Module 5.7 AP® Analyzing Sources Handout 1
- **TRM** Handout 5.7 – Reconstruction Era South
- **TRM** Module 5.7 AP® Analyzing Sources Handout 2
- **TRM** Module 5.7 AP® Analyzing Sources Handout 3

Module 5-8
- **TRM** Module 5.8 AP® Analyzing Sources Handout 1
- **TRM** Module 5.8 AP® Analyzing Sources Handout 2
- **TRM** Handout 5.9 – Regional Conditions at the End of Reconstruction

Period 5 Essential Activity

The events of the 1840s happened in the context of an expansionist attitude alongside further social and political reform movements that transformed the geography, demographics, and ethos of Americans. Even though the sectional divide, so evident throughout the 1850s, connected to several issues such as economic policy, western territory, and internal transportation developments, the issue of slavery consistently became the central topic. This activity seeks to move past analyzing the causes and course of the Civil War to examining the consequences of the Civil War during the Reconstruction period.

The main objective of this group activity is to have students examine Reconstruction from four perspectives. Arguably the most important point of view is from African Americans. Students will also have the opportunity to analyze the perspectives of Republicans, Democrats, and former Confederates. The goal is for students to account for the varied experiences and goals of the Reconstruction period.

After dividing students into groups of three or four, assign groups one of the four perspectives: African Americans, Republicans, Democrats, and former Confederates. Students will be evaluating how their assigned group encountered the revolutionary changes, overcame or were challenged by obstacles, and came to define the counterrevolution legacy of Reconstruction. Part of the difficulty with this activity is due to students having to explain their findings from the point of view of the group they represent. The goal is for students to see Reconstruction through the eyes of the various participants. Teachers can conduct this as a presentation after students answer the questions. Teachers could also have students conduct a gallery walk where they have the opportunity to read each other's responses.

Period 5 Alignment to the Fall 2019 AP® United States History Course Framework*

Relationship to the College Board Units

Period 5 in this book covers Topics 5.1–5.12 in Unit 5 of the College Board course framework. Students will be ready to take the Personal Progress Check for Unit 5 once they have completed this period.

Course Themes

Period 5 develops these course themes outlined in the course framework:

- **Geography and the Environment (GEO):** The pursuit of economic opportunity afforded by natural and mineral resources led to increased migration to the West. Debates over the expansion of slavery into western territories were ultimately settled by the Civil War, though questions about the status of formerly enslaved African Americans, Mexicans living in newly acquired territory, and American Indians remained.
- **America in the World (WOR):** The annexation of Texas, division of the Oregon Territory with Great Britain, and the Mexican War resulted in the acquisition of new territory as the United States extended its control of North America to the Pacific Ocean. Southern attempts to secure foreign assistance for the Confederacy were unsuccessful, and Union victory in the Civil War preserved the territorial integrity of the newly enlarged United States.
- **American and National Identity (NAT):** While the ideology of manifest destiny took hold across the nation in the 1840s and 1850s, competing views about the type of country the Unites States should become proved insurmountable by 1860. Both the Civil War and Reconstruction changed the way Americans viewed themselves, their government, and the nation.
- **American and Regional Cultures (ARC):** Regional differences, especially over issues related to slavery, increased tensions throughout the late 1840s and 1850s contributing to the Civil War. Concurrently, increased immigration to the United States, particularly from Ireland and Germany, led to a nativist backlash and the emergence of anti-immigration political efforts.
- **Social Structures (SOC):** Before the Civil War, many northerners (known as "Free-Soilers") viewed the westward expansion of slavery as a threat to their economic interests while abolitionists in the North worked to end slavery altogether. In the South, many white people believed that slavery was beneficial to white and black people, and after the Civil War, many white southerners resisted attempts to create a more equal society.
- **Politics and Power (POL):** Before the Civil War, debates over the expansion of slavery divided Americans and efforts at political compromise worsened the situation, leading to the demise of the Whig Party and emergence of the Republican Party. After the war, Reconstruction led to new debates about the role of the federal government and the ratification of three constitutional amendments while many white southerners used legal tactics and even violence to prevent African Americans from achieving equality.

Course Skills

Period 5 helps students to develop the following AP® Historical Thinking Skills identified in the course framework.

- **Skill 1: Developments and Processes** (Modules 5.1, 5.2, 5.3, 5.4, 5.5, 5.6, 5.7, 5.8)
- **Skill 2: Sourcing and Situation** (Modules 5.1, 5.2, 5.3, 5.4, 5.5, 5.6, 5.7, 5.8)
- **Skill 3: Claims and Evidence in Sources** (Modules 5.1, 5.2, 5.3, 5.4, 5.5, 5.6, 5.7, 5.8)
- **Skill 4: Contextualization** (Modules 5.2, 5.4, 5.5, 5.6, 5.8)

- **Skill 5: Making Connections** (Modules 5.1, 5.2, 5.3, 5.4, 5.5, 5.6, 5.7, 5.8)
- **Skill 6: Argumentation** (Modules 5.2, 5.4, 5.8)

Period 5 helps students to develop the following AP® History Reasoning Processes identified in the course framework.

- **Reasoning Process 1: Comparison** (Modules 5-2, 5-4, 5-5, 5-8)
- **Reasoning Process 2: Causation** (Modules 5-1, 5-3, 5-6, 5-7)
- **Reasoning Process 3: Continuity and Change** (Modules 5-4, 5-5, 5-8)

Learning Objectives and Historical Developments

Module	Topics	Learning Objectives	Historical Developments and Key Concepts
5-1	5.1, 5.2, 5.3	Unit 5: Learning Objective A Unit 5: Learning Objective B Unit 5: Learning Objective C	KC-5.1.I.A, KC-5.1.I.B, KC-5.1.I.C, KC-5.1.I.D, KC-5.1.I.C, KC-5.2.II.C
5-2	5.3, 5.4	Unit 5: Learning Objective C Unit 5: Learning Objective D	KC-5.1.I.C, KC-5.2.II.C, KC-5.1.I.E, KC-5.2.II.A, KC-5.2.II.B.i
5-3	5.5, 5.6, 5.7	Unit 5: Learning Objective E Unit 5: Learning Objective F Unit 5: Learning Objective G Unit 5: Learning Objective H	KC-5.1.II.A, KC-5.1.II.B, KC-5.2.I.A, KC-5.2.I.B, KC-5.2.I.C, KC-5.2.II.B.ii, KC-5.2.II.C, KC-5.2.II.D
5-4	5.8, 5.9	Unit 5: Learning Objective I Unit 5: Learning Objective J	KC;5.3.I.A, KC-5.3.I.B, KC-5.3.I,C, KC-5.3.I.D
5-5	5.8, 5.9	Unit 5: Learning Objective I Unit 5: Learning Objective J	KC;5.3.I.A, KC-5.3.I.B, KC-5.3.I,C, KC-5.3.I.D
5-6	5.10	Unit 5: Learning Objective K	KC-5.3.II.ii, KC-5.3.II.A, KC-5.3.II.B, KC-5.3.II.C
5-7	5.11	Unit 5: Learning Objective K Unit 5: Learning Objective L	KC-5.3.II.C, KC-5.3.II.D
5-8	5.11, 5.12	Unit 5: Learning Objective L Unit 5: Learning Objective M	KC-5.3.II.E

TRM A detailed alignment that can be sorted by Course Framework Unit, Topic, Learning Objective, Historical Development/Key Concept, or textbook period, is available in the Teacher's Resource Materials and via the book's online platform.

*Should changes be made to the Course Framework in the future, an updated alignment will be placed on our catalog page at bfwpub.com/fabric1e.

PERIOD 5 Expansion, Division, and Civil War

TEACHING IDEA

AP® Central

A great resource to help you teach this period is to read the information in the AP® U.S. History study guide for 1844–1877, available from the AP® United States History Classroom Resources section of AP® Central (apcentral.collegeboard.org).

PERIOD 5: 1844–1877

Expansion, Division, and Civil War

▲ **Knox Plantation, South Carolina, c. 1865** In this image, formerly enslaved African American women sit outside a cotton gin surrounded by raw cotton. Throughout the nineteenth century, Southern cotton supplied the factories of the northern states and England with the raw material necessary to make textile mills profitable. In this way, both enslaved African Americans and free white factory workers, southerners and northerners, and the rich and the poor on both sides of the Atlantic Ocean were all interwoven into the early industrial economy of textile production.

By the mid-nineteenth century, most Americans considered western expansion critical to revitalizing the economy. Southern planters, in turn, considered it necessary to slavery's success. While most white northerners were willing to leave slavery alone where it already existed, many hoped to keep it out of newly acquired territories.

The simultaneous growth of antislavery sentiment in the North and proslavery beliefs in the South fueled a series of political realignments in the decades before the Civil War. By 1860, debates over territorial expansion, regional economic interests, and demographic changes all revolved around the issue of slavery. It was the one abiding issue that consistently divided the nation along sectional lines.

And so, when the election of 1860 took place, many Americans — especially those who lived in slaveholding states — believed that the constitutionally elected president, Abraham Lincoln, was a threat to the rights guaranteed to American citizens in the Constitution. By Lincoln's inauguration in March of 1861, seven southern states had declared their independence from the United States.

Both North and South mobilized their economies and societies during the Civil War (1861–1865), and early on, the South achieved many victories despite its smaller population and largely agricultural economy. In 1862, President Abraham Lincoln issued the Emancipation Proclamation, thus shifting the north's goal from maintaining the Union to assuring freedom for enslaved African Americans in the American South. Ultimately, the North achieved victory through its military and economic advantages over the South.

The Thirteenth Amendment to the Constitution, which abolished slavery, proved to be both the most far-reaching and immediate result of the war. This sweeping reform was followed by the Fourteenth Amendment, which guaranteed that the federal government would protect civil rights, and the Fifteenth Amendment, which removed racial barriers to voting. Although these three amendments led to temporary political successes for formerly enslaved African Americans throughout the 1870s, northern support for Reconstruction — the remaking of the South with racial equality and economic justice — faltered as southern resistance to reforms, often in the form of violent attacks on African Americans and their northern and southern supporters, almost entirely reversed the progress that had been made in the first years after the war.

TEACHING IDEA

AP® Central

Make use of the College Board's resource America on the World Stage: Essays from the American Organization of Historians and AP®, available from the Classroom Resources section of AP® Central (apcentral.collegeboard.org). At this time, have students read and annotate the article "The Civil War, Emancipation, and Reconstruction on the World Stage." Whole-class discussion to follow.

PERIOD 5 PREVIEW

Module	AP® Thematic Focus
5-1: Manifest Destiny	**Geography and the Environment ▪ America in the World** The pursuit of economic opportunity afforded by natural and mineral resources led to increased migration to the West. After the Mexican-American War (1846–1848), the U.S. added western territory, spurring debates over whether to expand slavery. The aftermath of the war also raised questions about the status of American Indians and Mexicans already living in the newly acquired territory.
5-2: Compromise and Conflict	**American and National Identity ▪ Politics and Power ▪ Social Structures** The debates about the expansion of slavery in the aftermath of the Mexican-American War divided American political parties into northern and southern factions, which made compromise increasingly difficult. Because the northern industrial economy relied on free labor, many northerners (known as "Free-Soilers") saw the western expansion of slavery as a threat to their economic interests. Other northerners — abolitionists — worked to end slavery altogether using tactics such as publications, rallies, and an underground railroad system that helped enslaved African Americans escape to freedom. Many southerners who supported slavery claimed that it was both economically and socially beneficial to white and black people alike. Another popular proslavery argument held that the constitutional tradition of states' rights made any federal policy regarding slavery unconstitutional.
5-3: From Sectional Crisis to Southern Secession	**Politics and Power ▪ American and Regional Culture** Compromise over the expansion of slavery became increasingly difficult during the 1850s, and attempts such as the Compromise of 1850 and the *Dred Scott* case only worsened tensions. At the same time, increased immigration from both Europe and Asia led to the temporary rise of anti-immigrant parties throughout the North. These two factors contributed greatly to the breakdown of the Second Party System. Former Whigs and antislavery activists in the North formed the Republican Party, dedicated to ending the expansion of slavery. And, although Democrats held the White House from 1852 to 1860, the Democratic Party was split into northern and southern factions. The Democratic fracture helped Republican candidate Abraham Lincoln win the presidency in the election of 1860 without support from any southern states. By Lincoln's inauguration in March 1861, seven southern states had seceded from the Union, and the nation was divided into two.
5-4: Disunion and War	**America in the World** During the Civil War, the Union and the Confederacy increasingly depended upon commitment from their citizens, though both faced domestic opposition. At the onset of the war, the South won a number of battles.
5-5: Victory for the North	**American and National Identity ▪ America in the World** Over the course of the Civil War, Lincoln shifted from a strategy aimed at preserving the Union to one that promoted the emancipation of enslaved people. As Union troops invaded the South, this new strategy decimated the southern economy, which relied almost entirely upon slavery. It also led to the recruitment of black troops, and allowed Lincoln to reframe the war as a "new birth of freedom." These factors, along with the North's superior industrial production and larger population, ultimately led to victory for the Union.
5-6: Reconstruction Begins	**American and National Identity ▪ Politics and Power** Reconstruction inspired new debates about the role of the federal government. New amendments to the Constitution, including the Thirteenth Amendment, which abolished slavery, and the Fourteenth and Fifteenth Amendments, which granted African Americans citizenship, equal protection under the laws, and voting rights, provoked resistance in the South. These Republican efforts to ensure African American rights led to short-term successes, but this progress was eventually overturned as organized southern resistance met with fading northern interest. Despite many challenges, African Americans pursued new opportunities as free citizens, including education and land ownership, in the years following the Civil War.
5-7: Reform and Resistance	**Politics and Power** In spite of President Andrew Johnson's resistance, Republican efforts to ensure civil rights for freedpeople led to short-term successes, including the election of African Americans to local and federal offices. However, Southerners organized to resist these efforts, and diminishing investment by northern politicians allowed this resistance to gain power.
5-8: Reconstruction Undone	**American and National Identity** Because white landowners continued to control agricultural production in the South, most African Americans were unable to achieve economic independence, and many left for opportunities elsewhere. As white Southerners used both legal and criminal tactics to prevent African Americans from achieving equality, the federal government increasingly narrowed its protections for African Americans' rights. Reconstruction was essentially reversed by 1877, and its legacy left many civil rights issues unaddressed until the mid-twentieth century.

PERIOD 5 Expansion, Division, and Civil War

Module 5-1

Manifest Destiny

LEARNING TARGETS

By the end of this module, you should be able to:
- Explain how the appeal of manifest destiny encouraged western expansion and settlement.
- Explain the causes and effects of the Mexican-American War.

THEMATIC FOCUS

Geography and the Environment
America in the World

The pursuit of economic opportunity afforded by natural and mineral resources led to increased migration to the West. After the Mexican-American War (1846–1848), the U.S. added western territory, spurring debates over whether to expand slavery. The aftermath of the war also raised questions about the status of American Indians and Mexicans already living in the newly acquired territory.

HISTORICAL REASONING FOCUS

Causation

Remember that historians use causation as a way to analyze both the causes of events and their effects. One way to think of historical developments is to imagine them as links in a long chain of events — a particular event can be both an effect of earlier developments, whether immediate and distant, *and* a cause of events that have yet to unfold.

TASK ▶ As you read this module, consider not only particular causes and effects, but the ways in which multiple causes played a role in the settlement of the West and how that settlement affected local and national developments during the mid-nineteenth century.

During the 1830s and 1840s, national debates over slavery intensified. The most important battles now centered on western territories gained through victory in the war with Mexico. Before 1848, government-sponsored expeditions had opened up vast new lands for American pioneers seeking opportunity, and migrants moved west in growing numbers. Then, following the Mexican-American War and the discovery of gold in California, tens of thousands of men rushed to the Pacific coast seeking riches. But the West was already home to a diverse population that included American Indians, Mexicans, Mormons, and missionaries. The new settlers converged, and often clashed, with these groups.

Traveling the Overland Trails

In the 1830s, a growing number of migrants followed **overland trails** to the far West. The panic of 1837 further prompted families to head west. Thousands of U.S. migrants and European immigrants sought better economic prospects in Oregon, the Rocky Mountain region, and the eastern plains, while Mormons continued to settle in Salt Lake City. Some pioneers opened trading posts where American Indians exchanged goods with Anglo-American settlers or with merchants back east. Small settlements developed around these posts and near the expanding system of U.S. forts that dotted the region.

For many pioneers, the journey on the **Oregon Trail** began at St. Louis. From there, they traveled by wagon train across the Great Plains and the Rocky Mountains to the Pacific coast. By 1860 some 350,000 Americans had made the journey, claimed land from the Mississippi River to the Pacific, and transformed the United States into an expanding empire.

Because the journey west required funds for wagons and supplies, most pioneers were of middling status. The majority of pioneers made the three- to six-month journey with family members, to help share the labor. Men, mainly farmers, comprised some 60 percent of these

Oregon Trail The route west from the Missouri River to the Oregon Territory. By 1860, some 350,000 Americans had made the three- to six-month journey along the trail.

TRM Suggested Responses to Questions

TEACHING IDEA

Incorporating Videos

Show students the first 10 minutes of David Macaulay's "Mill Times" from PBS (available on YouTube). This informative video clip focuses mainly on life in the early mill towns of the upper Northeast and shows the process of spinning cloth. This is valuable to help students visualize the lives of those who worked in mills at this time.

TEACHING IDEA

Incorporating Videos

Assign students to watch Episode 4, "Division" from "America: The Story of Us," which is available online. Have students focus on the clip dealing with slavery in the South through the growth of industry within the North (00:06:23–00:16:03). The clip will help establish the economic divisions growing within the United States. Conduct a class discussion addressing the growth in slavery and how it compared and contrasted with growth in industry.

TEACHING IDEA

Incorporating Secondary Sources

For an overview of the West, students can read historian Richard White's essay, "Born Modern: An Overview of the West" to glean essential understandings and misconceptions. The essay can be found in Period 5 of the Gilder-Lehrman website (ap.gilderlehrman.org).

BUILDING AP® SKILLS

Causation

As students read Module 5-1 make use of the Cornell Note Taking System. First, have students compile a list of specific actions the government took to add territories to the U.S. After students have completed reading this module, have them add the effects of these actions in their notes. Students should be able to describe the short- and long-term impacts of these actions.

TEACHING IDEA

Incorporating Websites

Have students play the "Oregon Trail" game online (classicreload.com/oregon-trail). This entertaining game serves as a quick preview to the hardships faced by early settlers in their trek westward. Follow up the online game with a quick write, in which students address some of the difficult decisions and conditions settlers faced while migrating west.

Period 5: 1844–1877

MODULE 5-1 Manifest Destiny

TEACHING IDEA

Incorporating Primary Sources

Using the site Digital History, click on "eXplorations" under the category Active Learning and have students read the accounts in "Children and the Western Movement" (digitalhistory.uh.edu). After students have read through the passages, have them create a brief narrative on the lives of settlers as they headed west. Groups could create mini-posters highlighting terms, ideas, and facts that stand out to them. Have groups discuss their posters and reflections from the passages.

▲ **Differentiation**

Challenge your students to create pictures or slogans to summarize their impressions of the readings on their posters — the creativity forces students to summarize and process the information.

TRM Suggested Responses to Questions

TRM Module 5.1 AP® Analyzing Sources Handout 1

TEACHING IDEA

Check for Understanding

Have students research the dates when women received suffrage in each western territory and state. Follow up with a brief explanation for why women received the right to vote in western areas before women in the eastern parts of the U.S.

◀ **Emigrant Party Headed to California, 1850**
This hand-colored engraving of a wagon train heading through a mountain pass shows the presence of many family groups and the need for many adults and children to walk and carry goods for parts of the journey. **What obstacles faced by pioneers crossing the Rocky Mountains are reflected in this image?**

western migrants, but women and children traveled in significant numbers, often alongside relatives or neighbors from back east. Some courageous families headed west alone, but most traveled in wagon trains — from a few wagons to a few dozen — that provided support and security.

Traditional gender roles often broke down on the trail, and even conventional domestic tasks posed novel problems. Women had to cook unfamiliar food over open fires in all kinds of weather and with only a few pots and utensils. They washed laundry in rivers or streams and on the plains hauled water from great distances. Wood, too, was scarce on the plains, and women and children gathered buffalo dung (called "chips") for fuel. Men frequently had to gather food rather than hunt and fish, or they had to learn to catch strange (and sometimes dangerous) animals, such as jack rabbits and rattlesnakes. Few men were prepared for the dangerous work of floating wagons across rivers. Nor were many of them expert in shoeing horses or fixing wagon wheels, tasks that were performed by skilled artisans at home.

Expectations changed dramatically when men took ill or died. Then wives often drove the wagon, gathered or hunted for food, and learned to repair axles and other wagon parts. When large numbers of men were injured or ill, women might serve as scouts and guides or pick up guns to defend wagons under attack by American Indians or wild animals. Yet despite their growing burdens, pioneer women gained little power over decision making. Moreover, the addition of men's jobs to women's responsibilities was rarely reciprocated. Few men cooked, did laundry, or cared for children on the trail.

> "Don't let this letter dishearten anybody and never take no cutoffs and hurry along as fast as you can."
>
> Virginia Reed, fourteen-year-old survivor of the Donner Party, in a letter to her cousin after reaching California, 1847

AP® ANALYZING SOURCES

Source: Elizabeth Smith Geer, *Oregon Trail Diary*, 1847

"November 18.
It rains and snows. We start around the falls this morning with our wagons. We have five miles to go. I carry my babe and lead, or rather carry another, through snow, mud, and water almost to my knees. It is the worst road a team could possibly travel. I went ahead with my children and I was afraid to look behind me for fear of seeing the wagons overturn into the mud and water with everything in them. My children gave out with cold and fatigue and could not travel, and the boys had to unhitch the oxen and bring them and carry the children on to camp. I was so cold and numb that I could not tell by the feeling that I had any feet. We started this morning at sunrise and did not camp until after dark, and there was not one dry thread on one of us — not even on the babe. I had carried my babe and I was so fatigued that I could scarcely speak or step. When I got here I found my husband lying in Welch's wagon very sick. He had brought Mrs. Polk down the day before and was taken sick. We had to stay up all night for our wagons were left halfway back. I have not told half we suffered. I am not adequate to the task."

Questions for Analysis

1. Describe the conditions on the Oregon Trail, according to this diary entry.
2. Explain how this document reflects the way children both assisted and created problems for their parents on the Oregon Trail.
3. Explain how the weather affected travel on the Oregon Trail.
4. Explain how this document reveals the ways in which traditional gender roles could change during the journey.

TEACHING IDEA

Class Discussion

Have students discuss migration patterns within the United States from 1800 to 1844. Early colonies have started on the East Coast and slowly expanded "into" the continent. As students discuss various ways America has acquired land, make sure to point out that most acquisition came through forcibly removing people from their land. Have students trace the variety and pattern of migration from foreign lands.

In one area, however, relative equality reigned. Men and women were equally susceptible to disease, injury, and death during the journey. Accidents, gunshot wounds, drownings, broken bones, and infections affected people on every wagon train. Some groups were struck as well by deadly epidemics of measles or cholera. In addition, about 20 percent of women on the overland trail became pregnant, which posed even greater dangers than usual given the lack of medical services and sanitation. About the same percentage of women lost children or spouses on the trip west. Overall, about one in ten to fifteen migrants died on the western journey.

REVIEW

In what ways did traveling the overland trails both support and challenge traditional gender roles during the mid-nineteenth century?

The Politics of Expansion: Oregon and Texas

Despite the Whig victory in 1840, southern planters continued to hold considerable influence in Washington, D.C., because of the importance of cotton to the U.S. economy. In turn, southerners needed federal support to expand into more fertile areas. The presidential election of 1844 turned on this issue, with Democratic candidate James K. Polk demanding continued expansion into Oregon and Mexico. Once Polk was in office, his claims were contested not only by Britain and Mexico but also by the Comanche, whose territory spanned much of the southwest, including territory in the future states of Texas, New Mexico, Kansas, and Oklahoma. After the United States won vast Mexican territories in 1848, conflicts with American Indians and debates over slavery only intensified.

Southerners eager to expand the plantation economy were at the forefront of the push for territorial expansion. Yet expansion was not merely a southern strategy. Northerners demanded that the United States reject British claims to the Oregon Territory, and some northern politicians and businessmen advocated acquiring Hawaii and Samoa to benefit U.S. trade. In 1844 the Democratic Party built on these expansionist dreams to recapture the White House.

The Democrats nominated a Tennessee congressman and governor, James K. Polk. The Whigs, unwilling to nominate John Tyler for president, chose Kentucky senator Henry Clay. Polk declared himself in favor of the annexation of Texas. Clay, meanwhile, waffled on the issue. This proved his undoing when the **Liberty Party**, a small antislavery party founded in 1840, denounced annexation. Liberty Party candidate James G. Birney captured just enough votes in New York State to throw the state and the election to Polk.

In February 1845, a month before Polk took office, Congress passed a joint resolution annexing the Republic of Texas. That summer, John L. O'Sullivan's journal, the *Democratic Review*, captured the American mood by declaring that nothing must interfere with "the fulfillment of our manifest destiny to overspread the continent allotted by Providence." This vision of **manifest destiny** — of the nation's God-given right to expand its borders — defined Polk's presidency.

With the Texas question seemingly resolved, President Polk turned his attention to Oregon, which stretched from the forty-second parallel to latitude 54°40' and was jointly occupied by Great Britain and the United States. In 1842, three years before Polk took office, glowing reports of the mild climate and fertile soil around Puget Sound had inspired thousands of farmers and traders to flood into Oregon's Willamette Valley. Alarmed by this "Oregon fever," the British tried to confine Americans to areas south of the Columbia River. But U.S. settlers demanded access to the entire territory. President Polk encouraged migration into Oregon but was unwilling to risk war with Great Britain. Instead, diplomats negotiated a treaty in 1846 that extended the border with British Canada (the forty-ninth parallel) to the Pacific Ocean. Over the next two years, Congress admitted Iowa and Wisconsin to statehood, reassuring northern residents that expansion benefited all regions of the nation.

Some Americans hoped to gain even more territory by pushing Mexicans out of northern Mexico and California. Spanish missions and forts, built in the late eighteenth century, dotted the Pacific coast from San Diego to San Francisco. Mexico achieved independence from

Liberty Party Antislavery political party formed in 1840. The Liberty Party, along with the Free-Soil Party, helped place slavery at the center of national political debates.

manifest destiny Term coined by John L. O'Sullivan in 1845 to describe what he saw as the nation's God-given right to expand its borders. Throughout the nineteenth century, the concept of manifest destiny was used to justify U.S. expansion.

TEACHING IDEA

Incorporating Videos

Assign students to watch Episode 3, "Westward" from "America: The Story of Us," which is available online. Show the section on the Donner Party, which also discusses the impacts of disease, and the Mexican-American War (00:20:56–00:37:15). This clip will help students visualize the hardships along with the impacts of westward migration.

BUILDING AP® SKILLS

Contextualization

Have students look at John Gast's 1872 painting "American Progress" from the Library of Congress (loc.gov). Guide students to observe the action or movement within the piece. Students will recognize the angelic image in the center of the painting, but they should also pay attention to the four corners to establish the context of the painting. Notice the telegraph line that the angel is carrying in her hand and the images of "civilization" and settlement that are following behind her. Have students note the use of lightness and darkness to contrast from east to west. As a class, discuss the clear bias of the artist.

EXPLORING AP® THEMES

America in the World

When previewing and setting up the Civil War, ensure students do not overlook how the war was received within Europe and what role European countries played before and during the U.S. Civil War. Highlight the fact that most western European countries had outlawed slavery and slave trade upward of 50 years before the start of the U.S. Civil War.

BUILDING AP® SKILLS

Making Connections

Have students create a chart comparing and contrasting the conflicts between the settlers and the eastern American Indians in the seventeenth to eighteenth centuries. After students complete this first chart, have them create another to compare the treatment of eastern American Indians (combined periods) to that of western American Indians. Answers will vary, but the use of the American military to forcibly move American Indians is markedly harsher and more punitive in western territories.

TRM Find **Handout 5.1 – Treatment of American Indians in Eastern and Western Territories** in the Teacher's Resource Materials.

TEACHING IDEA

Incorporating Videos

Show the three-minute clip of "3 Minute Histories: The Mexican-American War," which highlights the Mexican-American War as a preview or follow-up to text coverage of this conflict (available on YouTube). Have students discuss the video after viewing.

Period 5: 1844–1877

MODULE 5-1 Manifest Destiny

Spain in 1821, and took control of this missionary and military network. Diseases carried by the Spanish and forced labor in their missions and forts had decimated some American Indian tribes in the region. As Mexican soldiers took control, some married into American Indian families, gaining land and social status and nurturing compound cultures. More often, however, diseases, guns, thefts of food and animals, sexual assault, and forced labor continued to devastate native peoples.

American Indians in the lands newly claimed by the U.S. government faced some of these same dangers. In addition, as the U.S. government forced eastern tribes to move west of the Mississippi, tensions increased among American Indian nations. When the Cherokee and other southeastern tribes were removed to Indian Territory, for example, they confronted tribes such as the Osage. Pushed into the Southwest, the Osage came into conflict with the Comanche, who had earlier fought the Apache for control of the southern plains. Other American Indian nations were pushed onto the northern plains from the Old Northwest. When tribes like the Mandan were decimated by smallpox in the 1830s, the Sioux came to dominate the region.

The flood of U.S. migrants into Texas and the southern plains transformed relations among American Indian nations as well as between American Indians and Mexico. In the face of Spanish and then Mexican claims on their lands, for example, the Comanche forged alliances with former foes like the Wichita and the Osage. The Comanche also developed commercial ties with tribes in Indian Territory and with both Mexican and Anglo-American traders. They thereby hoped to benefit from the imperial ambitions of the United States and Mexico while strengthening bonds among American Indians in the region.

Comanche expansion was especially problematic for Mexico. The young nation did not have sufficient resources to sustain the level of gift giving that Spanish authorities had used to maintain peace. As a result, Comanche warriors launched continual raids against Tejano settlements in Texas. But the Comanche also developed commercial relations with residents of New Mexico, who flaunted trade regulations promulgated in Mexico City. By 1846 Comanche trade and diplomatic relations with New Mexican settlements had seriously weakened the hold of Mexican authorities on their northern provinces.

REVIEW

- What caused migration to the West during the mid-nineteenth century?
- What effect did this migration west have on migrants?

Pursuing War with Mexico

At the same time, with Texas now a state, Mexico faced growing tensions with the United States. Conflicts centered on Texas's western border. Mexico insisted on the Nueces River as the boundary line, while Americans claimed all the land to the Rio Grande. In January 1846, Polk secretly sent emissary John Slidell to negotiate a border treaty with Mexico. But Polk also sent U.S. troops under General Zachary Taylor across the Nueces River. Mexican officials refused to see Slidell and instead sent their own troops across the Rio Grande. Meanwhile U.S. naval commanders prepared to seize San Francisco Bay from the Mexicans if war was declared. The Mexican government responded by sending more troops into the disputed Texas territory.

When fighting erupted near the Rio Grande in May 1846, Polk claimed that "American blood had been shed on American soil" and declared a state of war. Many Whigs in Congress opposed the declaration, arguing that the president had provoked the conflict. However, antiwar Whigs, like Representative Abraham Lincoln of Illinois, failed to convince the Democratic majority, and Congress voted to finance the **Mexican-American War**. Generals Zachary Taylor and Winfield Scott, who commanded U.S. forces, were themselves Whigs and later built political careers on their military successes. Although northern abolitionists protested the war, most Americans — North and South — considered westward expansion a boon.

Mexican-American War
1846–1848 war between the United States and Mexico. Ultimately, Mexico ceded approximately one million square miles to the United States, including the present-day states of California, Nevada, New Mexico, Arizona, Utah, and Texas, in the Treaty of Guadalupe Hidalgo. Debates over the status of slavery in these territories reignited the national debate about the expansion of slavery.

Pursuing War with Mexico

Period 5: 1844–1877

▲ MAP 5.1 **The Mexican-American War, 1846–1848** Although a dispute over territory between the Nueces River and the Rio Grande initiated the Mexican-American War, most of the fighting occurred between the Rio Grande and Mexico City. In addition, U.S. forces in California launched battles to claim independence for that region. **To what extent was expansion through war in 1846 a new policy for the United States?**

TEACHING IDEA

Geography Instruction

As students view Map 5.1 have them call out and identify the modern U.S. states that occupy the territory within Mexico before the Mexican-American War. Discuss the effects of the loss of this land on Mexico and how the land would benefit the U.S. Possible topics include the acquisition of farmland and plentiful mineral resources.

TEACHING IDEA

Incorporating Primary Sources

Have students read Persifor Smith's 1847 account, "The Mexican War," which is available from Digital History's website (digitalhistory.uh.edu). Have students work in small groups and create a poster that includes facts from the reading along with any bias they find. Have students assess the impact of this document and how it would have affected the public's opinion toward the war.

TRM Suggested Responses to Questions

TRM Module 5.1 AP® Analyzing Sources Handout 2

AP® ANALYZING SOURCES

Source: President James K. Polk, *War Message*, 1846

"The Mexican Government . . . , after a long-continued series of menaces, have at last invaded our territory, and shed the blood of our fellow-citizens on our own soil. . . .

. . . It became, therefore, of urgent necessity to provide for the defence of that portion of our country. Accordingly, on the 13th of January last, instructions were issued to the general in command of these troops to occupy the left bank of the Del Norte. This river which is the southwestern boundary of the state of Texas, is an exposed frontier. . . .

The movement of the troops to the Del Norte was made by the commanding general, under positive instructions to abstain from all aggressive acts toward Mexico or Mexican citizens, and to regard the relations between that republic and the United States as peaceful, unless she should declare war, or commit acts of hostility indicative of a state of war. . . .

(Continued)

361

Period 5: 1844–1877

MODULE 5-1 Manifest Destiny

The Mexican forces at Matamoras assumed a belligerent attitude, and, on the 12th of April, General Ampudia, then in command, notified General Taylor to break up his camp within twenty-four hours, and to retire beyond the Nueces river; and, in the event of his failure to comply with these demands, announced that arms, and arms alone, must decide the question. . . . A party of dragoons, of sixty-three men and officers, were on the same day despatched from the American camp up the Rio del Norte, on its left bank, to ascertain whether the Mexican troops had crossed or were preparing to cross the river, 'became engaged with a large body of these troops, and after a short affair, in which some sixteen were killed and wounded, appear to have been surrounded and compelled to surrender.'

The grievous wrongs perpetrated by Mexico upon our citizens throughout a long period of years remain unredressed; and solemn treaties, pledging her public faith for this redress, have been disregarded. A government either unable or unwilling to enforce the execution of such treaties, fails to perform one of its plainest duties."

Questions for Analysis

1. Identify the immediate cause that Polk provides for engaging in hostilities with Mexico.
2. Explain at least two distant causes of Polk's declaration of war.
3. Evaluate the extent to which Polk's declaration was caused by events beyond his control.

Source: Abraham Lincoln, *Spot Resolutions*, 1847

"*Resolved by the House of Representatives*, That the President of the United States be respectfully requested to inform this House—

1st. Whether the spot on which the blood of our citizens was shed, as in his messages declared, was or was not within the territory of Spain, at least after the treaty of 1819, until the Mexican revolution.

2d. Whether that spot is or is not within the territory which was wrested from Spain by the revolutionary Government of Mexico.

3d. Whether that spot is or is not within a settlement of people, which settlement has existed ever since long before the Texas revolution, and until its inhabitants fled before the approach of the United States army. . . .

5th. Whether the people of that settlement, or a majority of them, or any of them, have ever submitted themselves to the government or laws of Texas or the United States, by consent or compulsion, either by accepting office, or voting at elections, or paying tax, or serving on juries, or having process served upon them, or in any other way.

6th. Whether the people of that settlement did or did not flee from the approach of the United States army, leaving unprotected their homes and their growing crops, *before* the blood was shed, as in the messages stated; and whether the first blood so shed, was or was not shed within the enclosure of one of the people who had thus fled from it.

7th. Whether our *citizens*, whose blood was shed, as in his messages declared, were or were not, at that time, armed officers and soldiers, sent into that settlement by the military order of the President, through the Secretary of War."

Questions for Analysis

1. Identify the questions Lincoln poses in this excerpt.
2. Describe three causes that Lincoln implies are responsible for the conflict with Mexico.

Questions for Comparison

1. Explain how Lincoln's attitude toward the concept of America's "manifest destiny" compares to that of Polk.
2. Explain how the developments Lincoln implies caused the war with Mexico differ from those that Polk addresses in his War Message.

BUILDING AP® SKILLS

Claims and Evidence in Sources

Have students annotate Abraham Lincoln's *Spot Resolutions*. Ensure students find each question/claim raised in the resolution. Students should write a concise summary of Lincoln's resolution. Have students share their findings with classmates.

TEACHING IDEA

Class Discussion

For this activity, students should use the two documents along with their outside knowledge. Divide students into small groups, then split each group into two sides, one supporting the war and one opposing the war. Give students a short amount of time (about 15-20 minutes) to brainstorm and research evidence for their assigned position. Have students address their classmates and defend or oppose the United States' justifications in fighting the Mexican-American War. Students should address if the outcomes of the war justified it being waged.

Period 5: 1844–1877

"Hanging of the San Patricios," 1847 In 1846–1847 more than two hundred immigrants, most of them Irish Catholics who defected from U.S. army units, joined the Mexican army. They formed the *Batallón de San Patricios*, which fought fiercely in many battles. When dozens were captured after the Battle of Chapultepec, the soldiers were convicted of desertion. Samuel Chamberlain painted one of two mass hangings that followed. **In what way could religion and nativist sentiment have played a role in the creation and punishment of the Batallón de San Patricios?**

Once the war began, battles erupted in a variety of locations. In May 1846, U.S. troops defeated Mexican forces in Palo Alto and Resaca de la Palma. A month later, the U.S. army captured Sonoma, California with the aid of local settlers. John Frémont then led U.S. forces to Monterey, where the navy launched a successful attack and declared the California territory part of the United States. That fall, U.S. troops gained important victories at Monterrey, Mexico, just west of the Rio Grande, and Tampico, along the Gulf coast.

Despite major U.S. victories, Santa Anna, who reclaimed the presidency of Mexico during the war, refused to give up. In February 1847, his troops attacked U.S. forces at Buena Vista and nearly secured a victory. Polk then agreed to send General Winfield Scott to Veracruz with 14,000 soldiers. Capturing the port in March, Scott's army marched on to Mexico City. After a crushing defeat of Santa Anna at Cerro Gordo, the president-general was removed from power and the new Mexican government sought peace.

With victory ensured, U.S. officials faced a difficult decision: How much Mexican territory should they claim? The U.S. army in central Mexico faced continued guerrilla attacks. Meanwhile Whigs and some northern Democrats denounced the war as a southern conspiracy to expand slavery. In this context, Polk agreed to limit U.S. claims to the northern regions of Mexico. The president signed the **Treaty of Guadalupe Hidalgo** in February 1848, committing the United States to pay Mexico $15 million in return for control over Texas north and east of the Rio Grande plus California and the New Mexico territory.

Treaty of Guadalupe Hidalgo 1848 treaty ending the Mexican-American War. By the terms of the treaty, the United States acquired control over Texas north and east of the Rio Grande plus the New Mexico territory, which included present-day Arizona and New Mexico and parts of Utah, Nevada, and Colorado. The treaty also ceded Alta California, which had declared itself an independent republic during the war, to the United States.

REVIEW
How did the United States change as a result of the war with Mexico?

The Gold Rush

Despite the hazards, more and more Americans traveled overland to the Pacific coast, although only a few thousand Americans initially settled in California. Some were agents sent there by eastern merchants to purchase fine leather made from the hides of Spanish cattle. Several agents married into families of elite Mexican ranchers, known as **Californios**, and adopted their culture, even converting to Catholicism.

However, the Anglo-American presence in California changed dramatically after 1848 when gold was discovered at Sutter's Mill in northeastern California. Beginning in 1849, news of the discovery brought tens of thousands of settlers from the eastern United States, South America, Europe, and Asia. In the **California Gold Rush**, "forty-niners" raced to claim riches in California, and men vastly outnumbered women.

The rapid influx of gold seekers heightened tensions between newly arrived whites, local American Indians, and Californios. Forty-niners confiscated land owned by Californios, shattered the fragile ecosystem in the California mountains, and forced Mexican and American Indian men to labor for low wages or a promised share in uncertain profits. New conflicts erupted when migrants from Asia and South America joined the search for wealth. Forty-niners from the United States regularly stole from and assaulted these foreign-born competitors.

California Gold Rush The rapid influx of migrants into California after the discovery of gold in 1848. Migrants came from all over the world seeking riches.

BUILDING AP® SKILLS
Making Connections

After learning about the Mexican-American War and after viewing the image "Hanging of the San Patricios," have students think/pair/share other instances within U.S. history when the Catholic religion has been discussed and what the reaction to Catholics has tended toward during those instances. Students might mention Fundamental Orders, Maryland Act of Toleration, and William Penn's "Holy Experiment" as examples of limited acceptance of Catholicism within the U.S., but ultimately students will find few examples of true acceptance of Catholic beliefs and practices. What role (if any) did religion play in the U.S. government's response to Mexico in the Mexican-American War? How much freedom of religion was experienced during this time? Have students address these ideas as a class.

TEACHING IDEA
Connecting the Dots

Have students create a brief timeline covering the first American emigrants moving into the Mexican territory of Texas through the ending of the Mexican-American War (including the Gadsden Purchase). Students should practice their chronological thinking skills in the creation of this document. Post and discuss the importance of these events as needed with students for clarification.

EXPLORING AP® THEMES
Migration and Settlement

While the California Gold Rush was short-lived, it did cause a massive migration movement and created new settlements along the way from the East Coast to the West Coast. Introduce the concept of push/pull factors to students and have students work in pairs to create lists of conditions that either pushed or pulled people to the west. Have students compare and contrast an external immigration to the U.S., such as from Ireland, with an internal migration, such as the movement to California.

TEACHING IDEA
Incorporating Videos

Assign students to watch John Fritz's "The Start of the California Gold Rush (1849)" (available on YouTube). This eight-minute video covers the causes and effects of the short-lived California Gold Rush. Discuss with students the impacts of the rapid growth in population on the territory and highlight the Spanish and Mexican impacts upon the region's culture and heritage. Introduce the ideas of "boomtowns" at this time, as following modules will again address these towns.

TEACHING IDEA

Incorporating Primary Sources

Search the Digital History database and have students read William Swain's "Life in the California Gold Fields" and Norman Asing's "Chinese Immigrants in Gold Rush Era California" to have students gain further insight into life during the gold rush (digitalhistory.uh.edu). Have students annotate the texts and guide them to look especially for any bias in the two accounts. Have students discuss the impact of these accounts on the development of California.

BUILDING AP® SKILLS

Sourcing and Situation

Have students read Norman Asing's 1852 letter "To His Excellency Gov. Bigler, in Daily Alta California," which can be accessed through Digital History's database by searching for the author (digitalhistory.uh.edu). Have students complete a HIPP analysis for these documents and share their findings with a partner, or to the class as a whole, to demonstrate understanding of treatment of Chinese immigrants during this period (a refresher of HIPP can be found on page 8).

Period 5: 1844–1877

MODULE 5-1 Manifest Destiny

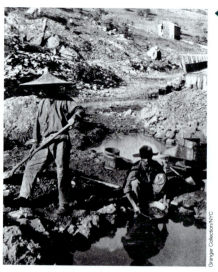

Gold Rush Miners, 1849 These prospectors were two of some 80,000 who traveled to California after gold was discovered. While many Chinese miners were run off their claims, these two men, dressed in a mix of Chinese and American attire, panned for gold with the tools of their trade — pickax, hoe, and pan. A shed in the background may have served as their home. **Based on this image, how would you characterize the forty-niners' interaction with their environment?**

The gold rush also led to the increased exploitation of women as thousands of male migrants demanded food, shelter, laundry, and medical care. While some California women earned a good living by renting rooms, cooking meals, washing clothes, or working as prostitutes, many faced exploitation and abuse. American Indian and Mexican women were especially vulnerable to sexual harassment and rape, while Chinese women were imported specifically to provide sexual services for male miners.

Chinese men were also victims of abuse by whites, who ran them off their claims. Yet some Chinese men used the skills traditionally assigned them in their homeland — cooking and washing clothes — to earn a far steadier income than prospecting for gold could provide. Other men also took advantage of the demand for goods and services. Levi Strauss, a German Jewish immigrant, moved from New York to San Francisco to open a dry-goods store in 1853. He soon made his fortune producing canvas and then denim pants that could withstand harsh weather and long wear.

REVIEW

- What effect did the Mexican-American War have on the Gold Rush?

A Crowded Land

While U.S. promoters of migration continued to depict the West as open territory, it was in fact the site of competing national ambitions in the late 1840s. Despite granting statehood to Texas in 1845 and winning the war against Mexico in 1848, the United States had to battle for control of the Great Plains with powerful American Indian nations, like the Sioux and Cheyenne.

Although attacks on wagon trains were rare, American Indians did threaten frontier settlements throughout the 1840s and 1850s. Settlers often retaliated, and U.S. army troops joined them in efforts to push American Indians back from areas newly claimed by whites. Yet in many parts of the West, American Indians were as powerful as whites, and they did not cede territory without a fight. The Reverend Marcus Whitman and his wife, Narcissa, became victims of their success in promoting western settlement when pioneers brought a deadly measles epidemic to the region, killing thousands of Cayuse and Nez Percé Indians. In 1847, convinced that whites brought disease but no useful medicine, a group of Cayuse Indians killed the Whitmans and ten other white settlers.

Yet violence against whites could not stop the flood of migrants into the Oregon Territory. Indeed, attacks by one American Indian tribe were often used to justify assaults on any American Indian tribe. Thus John Frémont and Kit Carson, whose party was attacked by Modoc Indians in Oregon in 1846, retaliated by destroying a Klamath Indian village and killing its inhabitants. The defeat of Mexico and the discovery of gold in California only intensified such conflicts.

Although American Indians and white Americans were the main players in many battles, American Indian nations also competed with each other. In the southern plains, drought and disease worsened those conflicts in the late 1840s and dramatically changed the balance of power there. In 1845 the southern plains were struck by a dry spell, which lasted on and off until the mid-1860s. In 1848, smallpox ravaged Comanche villages, and a virulent strain of cholera was introduced into the region the next year by forty-niners traveling to California.

TEACHING IDEA

Geography Instruction

Show students the "National atlas. Indian tribes, cultures & languages" map, which is available from the Library of Congress (loc.gov). Lead a brief class discussion asking students to discuss if any of the names are familiar to them in current times. Many of the names listed are commonly found within American communities and companies today. Ensure students see and note the variance among the different names and locations in which American Indians once thrived.

A Crowded Land

Period 5: 1844–1877

MAP 5.2 **Western Trails and American Indian Nations, c. 1850** As wagon trains and traders journeyed west in rapidly growing numbers during the 1830s and 1840s, the United States established forts along the most well-traveled routes. At the same time, American Indians claimed or were forced into new areas through the pressure of forced removals, white settlement, and the demands of hunting, trade, and agriculture. **What historical developments best explain the specific destinations for the wagon trains shown here?**

In the late 1840s, the Comanche nation was the largest American Indian group, with about twenty thousand members; by the mid-1850s, less than half that number remained.

Yet the collapse of the Comanche empire was not simply the result of outside forces. As the Comanche expanded their trade networks and incorporated smaller American Indian nations into their orbit, they overextended their reach. Most important, they allowed too many bison to be killed to meet the needs of their American Indian allies and the demand of Anglo-American and European traders. The Comanche also herded growing numbers of horses, which required expansive grazing lands and winter havens in the river valleys and forced the bison onto more marginal lands. Opening the Santa Fe Trail to commerce multiplied the problems by destroying vegetation and polluting springs, thereby diminishing resources in more of the region. The prolonged drought completed the depopulation of the bison on the southern plains. Without bison, the Comanche lost a trade item critical to sustaining their commercial and political control. As the Comanche empire collapsed, former American Indian allies sought to advance their own interests. These developments reignited American Indian wars on the southern plains as tens of thousands of pioneers poured through the region.

African Americans also participated in these western struggles. Many were held enslaved by southeastern tribes forced into Indian Territory, while others were freed and married Seminole or

EXPLORING AP® THEMES

Geography and the Environment

Have students do a quick write where they are given two minutes to address the effects of American settlers' interaction with their local environment compared to the Comanches' interactions with the same areas. Answers from students will vary, but keep the students focused on the text and the impact on the Comanche. Topic for further discussion: What impact did over-hunting and over-herding of livestock play in changing the ecosystems in the southern plains?

EXPLORING AP® THEMES

Geography and the Environment

This would be an ideal opportunity to highlight environmental impacts on human settlement and development. Have a brief discussion based on the reading of the effects of drought on the western plains. Make sure that students know the geographical climate zone and vegetation types for this region (i.e., small shrubs and grasses). Have the class discuss how the lack of water and limited quantity of trees would impact the lives of those living on the plains.

Period 5: 1844–1877

MODULE 5-1 Manifest Destiny

Cherokee spouses. The Creeks proved harsh slaveholders, prompting some enslaved people to escape north to free states or south to Mexican or Comanche territory. Yet as southern officers in the U.S. army moved to frontier outposts, they carried more enslaved people into the region. Many changed posts frequently, taking enslaved people into both slaveholding and free territories. Still, it was white planters who brought the greatest numbers of African Americans into Texas, Missouri, and Kansas, pushing the frontier of slavery ever westward. At the same time, some freedpeople joined the migration voluntarily in hopes of finding better economic opportunities and less overt racism in the West.

AP® TIP
Evaluate the role of slavery in the westward expansion during the 1800s.

REVIEW

- What groups competed for land and resources in the West?
- How did disease, drought, and violence shape this competition?

AP® WRITING HISTORICALLY — Short-Answer Question Practice

ACTIVITY

Read the following question carefully and write a short response. Use complete sentences.

Using the following image, answer (a), (b), and (c).

Source: Nathaniel Currier, *An available candidate. The one qualification for a Whig president*, 1848

a. Briefly describe ONE perspective about the Mexican-American War as expressed in this image.
b. Briefly explain ONE specific historical development or circumstance not mentioned in this document that contributed to this perspective.
c. Briefly explain ONE specific historical development in the American economy OR culture that led to the creation of this image.

TRM Suggested Responses to Questions

TEACHING IDEA

Check for Understanding

Remind students that for each question they can use *ACE* as a strategy (a refresher on *ACE* can be found on page 21). Too often students will only provide a few words or one sentence for each part of the SAQs on the AP® exam. Get your students in the habit of using the *ACE* strategy early during the year and use the size limitations imposed by the College Board to encourage students to be succinct in their answers. The College Board provides test booklets online for students and teachers to download and use for practice (apcentral.collegeboard.org). The single-sided exam sheet limits students to 23 standard width lines to complete their entire SAQ answer.

TEACHING IDEA

AP® Writing Historically Review

This question presupposes students' awareness of the political debates surrounding the Mexican-American War. Students should definitely be aware of these developments and the attendant political and military consequences. To ensure students are confident in responding to this question, consider the following activity. Organize students into groups of four and subdivide those groups into pairs. Assign one pair the Democrats and the other the Whigs. Ask each group to look through the module for evidence of the political debates surrounding the war. Students must develop at least three pieces of evidence to support how their assigned group perceived the war. Once students have completed this exercise, have them reestablish groups of four, share answers, and cross-reference the answers to the Short-Answer Question.

Module 5-2

Compromise and Conflict

LEARNING TARGETS
By the end of this module, you should be able to:
- Explain how regional attitudes shaped federal policy after the Mexican-American War.
- Explain the reasons for similarities and differences in regional attitudes about the role of the federal government.

THEMATIC FOCUS
American and National Identity
Politics and Power
Social Structures

The debates about the expansion of slavery in the aftermath of the Mexican-American War divided American political parties into northern and southern factions, which made compromise increasingly difficult. Because the northern industrial economy relied on free labor, many northerners (known as "Free-Soilers") saw the western expansion of slavery as a threat to their economic interests. Other northerners — abolitionists — worked to end slavery altogether using tactics such as publications, rallies, and an underground railroad system that helped enslaved African Americans escape to freedom. Many southerners who supported slavery claimed that it was both economically and socially beneficial to white and black people alike. Another popular proslavery argument held that the constitutional tradition of states' rights made any federal policy regarding slavery unconstitutional.

HISTORICAL REASONING FOCUS
Comparison

Comparison requires more than just a look at similarities and differences between two different places, societies, historical events, or processes. Sometimes, historians examine similarities and differences *within* the broader categories they are analyzing. The issue of slavery in both the northern and southern United States provides an opportunity for this kind of complex comparison.

TASK ▶ While reading this module, compare the reactions to the debate over slavery throughout the North and South in the aftermath of the Mexican-American War. Be sure to consider the extent to which this issue also produced divisions *within* each region.

TRM Suggested Responses to Questions

TEACHING IDEA
Incorporating Videos

Assign students to watch Episode 4, "Division" from "America: The Story of Us," which is readily available online. Show the segment in which the topic of sectionalism and the growth of cotton within the U.S. during its early development are discussed (00:00:00 – 00:08:45). Have students define the term "sectionalism" and give examples of how it has impacted the U.S. at this time.

BUILDING AP® SKILLS
Causation

As an introduction to this module have students brainstorm the specific social, political, and economic impacts of adding the newly gained territories that the U.S. claimed in Module 5-1.

While many Americans supported the idea of "manifest destiny" and the Mexican-American War, westward expansion caused conflict between native peoples and American settlers, as well as between Americans themselves. The issue of slavery proved especially divisive since the Treaty of Guadalupe Hidalgo left unclear the status of slavery in the territories gained in the war. The conflict over slavery spread from the plains of the West to the halls of Congress, and ultimately threatened to split both the Whigs and the Democrats. While Congress had established a compromise on the issue of Missouri in 1820 that lasted for thirty years, the Compromise of 1850, in the aftermath of the Mexican-American War, proved ultimately unsatisfying to all sides.

TEACHING IDEA

Check for Understanding

Have students make a list of all the presidential elections that have been controversial thus far by 1848. Answers will vary, but major elections — 1800, 1824, 1836, 1844, and 1848 — should be addressed. As students discuss some of the early elections and the controversies involved, highlight the fact that divisions and controversies have been a part of the U.S. political tradition from the nation's inception.

TEACHING IDEA

Class Discussion

Lead a classroom discussion asking students to identify examples of ways Americans encountered and worked through sectionalism from 1800–1848.

BUILDING AP® SKILLS

Making Connections

Have a brief check-in with students and discuss some of the important presidential elections covered so far in this course (e.g., the election of 1796 when the first political parties ran, the "Revolution of 1800" — a peaceful turnover of power to opposing party, the election of 1824 known as the "Corrupt Bargain," the election of 1828 that led to the "age of the common man," etc.). Then, have students discuss the effect of three political parties in 1848 and the continued impact into the 1850s. Students should begin to make the connection that there have been many elections that ended with seemingly odd results throughout U.S. history, as this trend will continue through the Modern Era.

Debates over Slavery Intensify

Wilmot Proviso 1846 proposal by Democratic congressman David Wilmot of Pennsylvania to outlaw slavery in all territory acquired from Mexico. The proposal was defeated, but the fight over its adoption foreshadowed the sectional conflicts of the 1850s.

AP® TIP
Compare the arguments made by the "Free-Soilers" to the arguments of groups such as the American Anti-Slavery Society.

Free-Soil Party Party founded by political abolitionists in 1848 to expand the appeal of the Liberty Party by focusing less on the moral wrongs of slavery and more on the benefits of providing economic opportunities for northern white people in western territories.

News of the U.S. victory in the Mexican-American War traveled quickly across the United States. In the South, planters imagined slavery spreading into the lands acquired from Mexico. Northerners, too, applauded the expansion of U.S. territory but focused on California as a center for agriculture and commerce. Still, the acquisition of new territory heightened sectional conflicts. Debates over slavery had erupted during the war, fueled by abolitionist outrage, and a few northern Democrats joined Whigs in denouncing "the power of SLAVERY" to "govern the country, its Constitutions and laws." In August 1846, Democratic congressman David Wilmot of Pennsylvania proposed outlawing slavery in all territory acquired from Mexico so that the South could not profit from the war. While the **Wilmot Proviso** passed in the House, southern and proslavery northern Democrats defeated it in the Senate. Nevertheless, Wilmot gave voice to a powerful northern anti-slavery bloc known as "Free-Soilers," who were less concerned with the plight of African-Americans, and more worried about the effect the spread of slavery to the West would have on the economic viability of small farmers and urban workers. Free-Soilism added to the debate and extended antipathy toward slavery through demographic groups like farmers and workers, who were not necessarily sympathetic to abolitionist moral arguments.

The presidential election of 1848 opened with the unresolved question of whether to allow slavery in the territories acquired from Mexico. With Polk declining to run for a second term, Democrats nominated Lewis Cass, a Michigan senator and ardent expansionist. Hoping to keep northern antislavery Democrats in the party, Cass argued that residents in each territory should decide whether to make the region free or slave. This strategy put the slavery question on hold but satisfied almost no one.

The Whigs, too, hoped to avoid the slavery issue for fear of losing southern votes. They nominated Mexican-American War hero General Zachary Taylor, a Louisiana slaveholder who had no declared position on slavery in the western territories. But they sought to reassure their northern wing by nominating Millard Fillmore of Buffalo, New York for vice president. As a member of Congress in the 1830s, Fillmore had opposed the annexation of Texas.

The Liberty Party, disappointed in the Whig ticket, decided to run its own candidate for president. Its leaders hoped to expand their support by reconstituting themselves as the **Free-Soil Party**. This party, following the arguments of David Wilmot's proviso in 1846, focused more on excluding enslaved people from western territories than on the moral injustice of slavery. The party nominated former president Martin Van Buren and appealed to small farmers and urban workers who hoped to benefit from western expansion.

Once again, the presence of a third party affected the outcome of the election. While Whigs and Democrats tried to avoid the slavery issue, Free-Soilers demanded attention to it. By focusing on the exclusion of slavery in western territories rather than its abolition, the party won more adherents in northern states. Indeed, Van Buren won enough northern Democrats so that Cass lost New York State and the 1848 election. Zachary Taylor and the Whigs won, but only by placing a southern slaveholder in the White House.

REVIEW

- What arguments did members of the Liberty Party make about the expansion of slavery?
- How do those arguments compare to the Free-Soil Party's perspective on expanding slavery?

California and the Compromise of 1850

In the winter of 1849, just before President Zachary Taylor's March inauguration, California applied for admission to the Union as a free state. Some California political leaders opposed slavery on principle. Others wanted to "save" the state for whites by outlawing slavery, discouraging free black migration, and restricting the rights of Mexican, American Indian, and Chinese residents. Yet the internal debates among Californians were not uppermost in the minds of politicians. Southerners were concerned about the impact of California's free-state status on the sectional balance in Congress, while northern Whigs were shocked when President Taylor suggested that slavery should be allowed anywhere in the West.

Other debates continued in Congress at the same time. Many northerners were horrified by the spectacle of slavery and slave trading in the nation's capital and argued that it damaged America's international reputation. Southerners, meanwhile, complained that the

California and the Compromise of 1850

The United States Senate, A.D. 1850 This print captures seventy-three-year-old Henry Clay presenting his Compromise of 1850 to colleagues in the Old Senate Chamber. An aged John C. Calhoun, seated to the left of the Speaker's chair, denounced the compromise, as did antislavery Whigs and Free-Soilers. Daniel Webster, sitting to the left of Clay, offered a passionate defense but failed to gain the compromise's passage. **What traditional regional interests do Clay, Calhoun, and Webster represent in this picture?**

Fugitive Slave Act of 1793 Act that ensured the right of slaveholders to capture enslaved people who had fled by mandating that local government seize and return them. However, the act was largely ignored by northerners.

Fugitive Slave Act of 1793 was being widely ignored in the North. A boundary dispute between Texas and New Mexico irritated western legislators, and Texas continued to claim that debts it accrued while an independent republic and during the Mexican-American War should be assumed by the federal government.

Senator Henry Clay of Kentucky, the Whig leader who had hammered out the Missouri Compromise in 1819 and 1820, again tried to resolve the many conflicts that stalled congressional action. He offered a compromise by which California would be admitted as a free state; the remaining land acquired from Mexico would be divided into two territories — New Mexico and Utah — and slavery there would be decided by popular sovereignty; the border dispute between New Mexico and Texas would be decided in favor of New Mexico, but the federal government would assume Texas's war debts; the slave trade (but not slavery) would be abolished in the District of Columbia; and a new and more effective fugitive slave law would be approved. Although Clay's compromise offered something to everyone, his colleagues did not immediately embrace it.

By March 1850, after months of passionate debate, the sides remained sharply divided, as did their most esteemed leaders. John C. Calhoun, a proslavery senator from South Carolina, refused to support any compromise that allowed Congress to decide the fate of slavery in the western territories. William H. Seward, an antislavery Whig senator from New York, proclaimed he could not support a compromise that forced northerners to help hunt down fugitives from slavery. While Daniel Webster, a Massachusetts Whig, urged fellow senators to support the compromise to preserve the Union, Congress adjourned with the fate of California undecided.

Before the Senate reconvened in September 1850, however, the political landscape changed in unexpected ways. Henry Clay retired the previous spring, leaving the Capitol with his last great legislative effort unfinished. On March 31, 1850, Calhoun died; his absence from the Senate made compromise more likely. Then in July, President Taylor died unexpectedly, and his vice president, Millard Fillmore, became president. Fillmore then appointed Webster as secretary of state, removing him from the Senate as well.

AP® ANALYZING SOURCES

Source: John C. Calhoun, *The Clay Compromise Measures*, 1850

"[H]ow can the Union be saved? To this I answer, there is but one way by which it can be, and that is, by adopting such measures as will satisfy the States belonging to the southern section that they can remain in the Union consistently with their honor and their safety. There is, again, only one way by which that can be effected, and that is, by removing the causes by which this belief has been produced. Do *that*, and discontent will cease, harmony and kind feelings between the sections be restored, and every apprehension of danger to the Union removed. The question then is, By what can this be done? . . . There is but one way by which it can with any certainty; and that is, by a full and final settlement, on the principle of justice, of all the questions at issue between the two sections. . . ."

(Continued)

TEACHING IDEA

Think/Pair/Share

Have students brainstorm with a partner the specific laws and actions taken by the U.S. government to either give or eliminate freedoms of enslaved people up until 1850. Answers will vary but might include the Three-Fifths Compromise, the Missouri Compromise, the Fugitive Slave Act, etc.

TEACHING IDEA

Geography Instruction

Have students research to find a map of the modern U.S. as well as the states' entry dates into the union from 1820 to 1860. In pairs, students should decide what the congressional balance of power was between slave/free states. Discuss with the class how the addition of territories after the Mexican-American War impacted the balance of power created by the Missouri Compromise.

TRM Suggested Responses to Questions

TRM Module 5.2 AP® Analyzing Sources Handout 1

BUILDING AP® SKILLS

Contextualization

Have students practice the skill of contextualization by writing succinctly yet specifically in tying the main event to the broader historical trends within the specific time. In three to four sentences maximum, have students separately describe the context in which the fugitive slave laws of 1793 and 1850 were created. Answers will vary, but have several students read their responses as examples of how to "set the stage" while describing the context surrounding these specific laws.

BUILDING AP® SKILLS

Sourcing and Situation

Have students do a HIPP review of Calhoun's speech (a refresher of HIPP can be found on page 8). Students should focus on the purpose of this document. Give students a brief amount of time to HIPP the document and then have a class discussion focusing on the background history between Henry Clay and John C. Calhoun. Remind students of how Calhoun was Andrew Jackson's first vice president, and touch upon the nullification crisis. Students should realize that past animosities between the two men had an impact on Calhoun's speech.

But can this be done? Yes, easily; not by the weaker party, for it can of itself do nothing—not even protect itself—but by the stronger. The North has only to will it to accomplish it—to do justice by conceding to the South an equal right in the acquired territory, and to do her duty by causing the stipulations relative to fugitive slaves to be faithfully fulfilled—to cease the agitation of the slave question, and to provide for the insertion of a provision in the Constitution, by an amendment, which will restore to the South in substance the power she possessed of protecting herself, before the equilibrium between the sections was destroyed by the action of this Government. There will be no difficulty in devising such a provision—one that will protect the South, and which at the same time will improve and strengthen the Government, instead of impairing and weakening it."

Questions for Analysis

1. Identify Calhoun's main argument.
2. Explain what Calhoun means by "equilibrium between the sections" in the second paragraph of this excerpt.
3. Evaluate the extent to which the return of fugitives from slavery to the South was the main reason for Calhoun's argument.

Compromise of 1850 Series of acts following California's application for admission as a free state. Meant to ease sectional tensions over slavery by providing something for all sides, the act ended up fueling more conflicts.

In fall 1850, with President Fillmore's support, a younger cohort of senators and representatives steered the **Compromise of 1850** through Congress, one clause at a time. This tactic allowed legislators to support only those parts of the compromise they found palatable. In the end, all the provisions passed, and Fillmore quickly signed the bills into law.

The Compromise of 1850, like the Missouri Compromise thirty years earlier, fended off a sectional crisis but signaled future problems. Would popular sovereignty prevail when later territories sought admission to the Union, and would northerners abide by a fugitive slave law that called on them to aid directly in the capture of fugitives from slavery?

REVIEW

What steps did legislators take in the 1840s and early 1850s to address the issue of the expansion of slavery?

The Fugitive Slave Act Inspires Northern Protest

Fugitive Slave Act of 1850 Act strengthening earlier fugitive slave laws, passed as part of the Compromise of 1850. The act provoked widespread anger in the North and intensified sectional tensions.

underground railroad A series of routes from southern plantation areas to northern free states and Canada along which abolitionist supporters, known as conductors, provided hiding places, transportation, and resources to enslaved people seeking freedom.

The fugitive slave laws of 1793 and 1824 mandated that all states aid in apprehending and returning fugitives from slavery to slaveholders. The **Fugitive Slave Act of 1850** was different in two important respects. First, it eliminated jury trials for alleged fugitives. Second, the law required individual citizens, not just state officials, to help return runaways. The act angered many northerners who believed that the federal government had gone too far in protecting the rights of slaveholders and thereby aroused sympathy for the abolitionist cause.

Before 1850, free black people led the effort to aid fugitives, including David Ruggles in New York City; William Still in Philadelphia; and, after his own successful escape, Frederick Douglass. Among their staunchest allies were white Quakers such as Amy and Isaac Post in Rochester, New York, Thomas Garrett in Chester County, Pennsylvania, and Levi and Catherine Coffin in Newport, Indiana. Political abolitionists, like wealthy reformer Gerrit Smith of Peterboro, New York, also aided the cause.

Following passage of the Fugitive Slave Act, the number of slaveholders and hired slave catchers pursuing fugitives increased dramatically. But so, too, did the number of northern abolitionists helping African Americans escape. Once enslaved people seeking freedom crossed into free territory, most contacted free African Americans or sought out Quaker, Baptist, or Methodist meetinghouses whose members might be sympathetic to their cause. They then began the journey along the **underground railroad**, from house to house or barn to barn, until they found

---

BUILDING AP® SKILLS

Making Connections

Have students create a Venn diagram for the Missouri Compromise and the Compromise of 1850. Students may struggle with finding similarities so a class discussion should help guide students through the process. Add a follow-up quick write, in which students are given four minutes to defend which compromise they feel was truly the fairest.

TEACHING IDEA

Incorporating Primary Sources

Have students read Benjamin Drew's 1850 account of his escape to freedom in Canada, which can be found on Digital History's website by searching for "Testimony of Canadian Fugitive" (digitalhistory.uh.edu). In small groups have students annotate the reading and then create a poster highlighting 5-10 facts or details that students found important. The personal account of Benjamin Drew is powerful and the primary source reading will help students grasp the human impacts of the Fugitive Slave Act.

TEACHING IDEA

Incorporating Websites

Have students visit the Harriet Tubman Historical Society's website and view the presentations dealing with the life and times of Harriet Tubman (harriet-tubman.org). The site has many useful features and contains lessons and video clips to help engage students. Before students visit the site it might be useful to gauge the students' understanding of what the Underground Railroad was (misconceptions by students who cite that the railroad was a subway system are seen on far too many AP® exams each year).

The Fugitive Slave Act Inspires Northern Protest

◀ **Anti-Fugitive Slave Law Convention, Cazenovia, New York, 1850** This rare daguerreotype captures abolitionists, outraged over the Fugitive Slave Law, at a massive protest meeting. Some 2,000 participants met in an apple orchard. Frederick Douglass sits at the left side of the table. The Edmondson sisters, in plaid shawls, stand behind him on either side of Gerrit Smith. The sisters were among fifty formerly enslaved people who attended the meeting. **What does this photograph reveal about the abolitionist movement?**

safe haven. A small number of fortunate enslaved people were led north by fugitives like Harriet Tubman, who returned south repeatedly to free dozens of family members and other enslaved men and women. Abolitionists purchased the freedom of a few others, including sisters Mary and Emily Edmondson who had been sold to slave traders after a failed escape attempt in 1848. Most fugitives followed disparate paths, depending on "conductors" to get them from one stop to the next. Despite its limits, the underground railroad was an important resource for fugitives seeking refuge in Canada or hoping to blend into free black communities stateside.

Free black people were endangered by the claim that enslaved people hid themselves in their midst. In Chester County, Pennsylvania, on the Maryland border, newspapers reported on at least a dozen free black people who were kidnapped or arrested as runaways in the first three months of 1851. The provisions of the Fugitive Slave Act encouraged such arrests and denied alleged fugitives basic legal protections. Accused runaways were denied a jury trial and defendants were not allowed to testify. Commissioners were paid $10 for each alleged fugitive they sent back to slavery in the South but only $5 for each they freed.

At the same time, a growing number of northerners challenged the federal government's right to enforce the law. Both black and white people organized protest meetings throughout the free states. At a meeting in Boston in 1851, William Lloyd Garrison denounced the law: "We execrate it, we spit upon it, we trample it under our feet." On July 5, 1852, Frederick Douglass asked a mixed-race audience, "What to the American slave, is your 4th of July? I answer, a day that reveals to him . . . the gross injustice and cruelty to which he is the constant victim." He then declared, "There is not a nation on the earth guilty of practices more shocking and bloody than are the people of these United States at this very hour."

Some abolitionists established vigilance committees to rescue fugitives who had been arrested. In Syracuse in October 1851, Jermaine Loguen, Samuel Ward, and the Reverend Samuel J. May led a well-organized crowd that broke into a Syracuse courthouse and rescued a fugitive known as Jerry. They successfully hid him from authorities before spiriting him to Canada.

Meanwhile Americans continued to debate the law's effects. John Frémont, one of the first two senators from California, helped defeat a federal bill that would have imposed harsher penalties on those who assisted runaways. And Congress felt growing pressure to calm the situation, including from foreign officials who were horrified by the violence required to sustain slavery in the United States. Black abolitionists denounced the Fugitive Slave Act across Canada, Ireland, and England, intensifying foreign concern over the law. Great Britain and France had abolished slavery in their West Indian colonies and could not support what they saw as extreme policies to keep the institution alive in the United States. Yet southern slaveholders refused to compromise further, as did northern abolitionists.

> " What to the American slave, is your 4th of July? I answer, a day that reveals to him . . . the gross injustice and cruelty to which he is the constant victim. . . . There is not a nation on the earth guilty of practices more shocking and bloody than are the people of these United States at this very hour. "
>
> —Frederick Douglass, 1852

TEACHING IDEA

Incorporating Websites

Have students do a quick exercise where they list any facts they know about the Underground Railroad. After students brainstorm, have them visit the PBS website, "The African Americans: Many Rivers to Cross" (pbs.org). On that vast and informative website, students should be sure to read Henry Louis Gates's article, "Who Really Ran the Underground Railroad?" As students read, encourage them to explore some of the other content cited and linked to his article. Have students complete a KWL chart (what do I Know, what do I Want to learn, and what did I Learn). Discuss student findings as a class.

TRM Find **Handout 5.2 – KWL Chart** in the Teacher's Resource Materials.

TEACHING IDEA

Incorporating Videos

The 2013 historical drama *12 Years a Slave* recreates portions of the 1853 memoir *Twelve Years a Slave* by Solomon Northup. This film depicting a man born free in New York state who was then sold into slavery would be a good avenue for students to see the harsh, inhumane realities of the institution of slavery.

▲ **Differentiation**

For students interested in learning more about this topic, assign excerpts from Northup's novel for discussion and possible comparison to the film.

BUILDING AP® SKILLS

Making Connections

Have students complete a five-minute timed writing exercise in which they make connections between the meaning of July 4th for enslaved Americans and Americans who already had their freedom. Students should share their writings with a small group or the class as a whole. Follow up with a class discussion on the meaning of the 4th of July for a variety of peoples within the United States.

EXPLORING AP® THEMES

America and the World

Help students understand that many European nations had already ended slavery within their own countries and colonies. The continued enslavement of peoples within the U.S. caused friction between the U.S. and many European nations, especially England, which had abolished slavery with the Slavery Abolition Act in 1833. Discuss what factors led to the United States' maintaining the institution for a longer period than the European countries.

TRM Suggested Responses to Questions

TRM Module 5.2 AP® Analyzing Sources Handout 2

TEACHING IDEA

Analyzing Art and Images

Have students view the abolitionist Theodore Parker's 1851 poster, "Caution, Colored People of Boston," which is readily available through an online search. Have students view the poster as they read William Nell's account. Follow up by having students list causes and effects of the Fugitive Slave Act. Ultimately, students should discover that the South desired the law to return their enslaved people. The South had also gained territories south of the 50°40′ line, which the North feared would upset the balance of political power in Congress. Abolitionists, free African Americans, and fugitives from slavery all had to openly defy this law through acts of civil disobedience to help enslaved people find freedom.

BUILDING AP® SKILLS

Sourcing and Situation

Have students do a quick HIPP review of President Fillmore's proclamation where the president calls on citizens to follow the law despite its unpopularity (a refresher on HIPP can be found on page 8). The president of the United States having to openly petition citizens in one area of the nation to specifically follow a law is unique in U.S. history. Ensure students understand the importance and impact of this presidential proclamation. Have students share their HIPP review with a partner or group.

AP® ANALYZING SOURCES

Source: William C. Nell, *Meeting of Colored Citizens of Boston*, 1850

"The Chairman [Lewis Hayden] announced, as a prominent feature in calling the present meeting—Congress having passed the infamous Fugitive Slave Bill—the adoption of ways and means for the protection of those in Boston liable to be seized by the prowling man-thief. He said that safety was to be obtained only by an united and persevering resistance of this ungodly, anti-republican law. . . .

The following resolutions were submitted, as a platform for vigilant action in the trial hour:—

Resolved, That the Fugitive Slave Bill, recently adopted by the United States Congress, puts in imminent jeopardy the lives and liberties of ourselves and our children; it deprives us of trial by jury, when seized by the infernal slave-catcher, and by high penalties forbids the assistance of those who would otherwise obey their heart-promptings in our behalf; in making it obligatory upon marshals to become bloodhounds in pursuit of human prey; leaving us no alternative . . . but to be prepared in the emergency for self-defense; therefore, assured that God has no attribute which can take sides with oppressors, we have counted the cost, and as we prefer *liberty* to *life*, we mutually pledge to defend ourselves and each other in resisting this God-defying and inhuman law, at any and every sacrifice, invoking Heaven's defense of the right.

Resolved, That . . . eternal vigilance is the price of liberty, and that they who would be free, themselves must strike the first blow."

Questions for Analysis

1. Identify the rights Nell asserts are violated by the Fugitive Slave Act.
2. Describe what Nell claims he is prepared to do to defend these rights.
3. Evaluate the extent to which Nell draws on the rhetoric of America's founding documents.

Source: President Millard Fillmore, *Proclamation 56 Calling on Citizens to Assist in the Recapture of a Fugitive Slave*, 1851

"Whereas information has been received that sundry lawless persons, principally persons of color, combined and confederated together for the purpose of opposing by force the execution of the laws of the United States, did, at Boston, in Massachusetts, on the 15th of this month, make a violent assault on the marshal or deputy marshals of the United States for the district of Massachusetts, in the court-house, and did overcome the said officers, and did by force rescue from their custody a person arrested as a fugitive slave, and then and there a prisoner lawfully [held] by the said marshal or deputy marshals of the United States, and other scandalous outrages did commit in violation of law:

Now, therefore, to the end that the authority of the laws may be maintained and those concerned in violating them brought to immediate and condign punishment, I have issued this my proclamation, calling on all well-disposed citizens to rally to the support of the laws of their country, and requiring and commanding all officers, civil and military, and all other persons, civil or military, who shall be found within the vicinity of this outrage, to be aiding and assisting by all means in their power in quelling this and other such combinations and assisting the marshal and his deputies in recapturing the above-mentioned prisoner; and I do especially direct that prosecutions be commenced against all persons who shall have made themselves aiders or abettors in or to this . . . offense."

Questions for Analysis

1. Identify the consequences President Fillmore proposes for disregarding the Fugitive Slave Act.
2. Describe how Fillmore views the Boston abolitionists who opposed the act.

BUILDING AP® SKILLS

Argumentation

After students read both passages, have them write one or two sentences that summarize the two authors' main arguments. Students should share their answers with the class or with a peer. Have a follow-up class discussion and address any clear bias within either of the documents and determine which author had the most valid argument. Students should practice finding an author's main argument within written texts, as this skill will help students to frame their arguments on written work within the AP® exam.

Questions for Comparison
1. Explain how those present at the meeting Nell describes would likely have responded to Fillmore's Proclamation.
2. Explain the ways in which conflicts over the Fugitive Slave Act in Boston reveal rising tensions across the nation during this time period.

REVIEW

Why did the Fugitive Slave Act of 1850 prompt protest from northerners?

Further Expansion under President Pierce

In the presidential election of 1852, the Whigs and the Democrats tried once again to appeal to voters across the North-South divide by running candidates who either skirted the slavery issue or voiced ambiguous views. The Democrats nominated Franklin Pierce of New Hampshire. A northern opponent of abolition, Pierce had served in Congress from 1833 to 1842 and in the U.S. army during the Mexican-American War. The Whigs rejected President Millard Fillmore, who had angered many by supporting popular sovereignty and vigorous enforcement of the Fugitive Slave Act. They turned instead to General Winfield Scott of Virginia. General Scott had never expressed any proslavery views and had served with distinction in the war against Mexico. The Whigs thus hoped to gain southern support while maintaining their northern base. The Free-Soil Party, too, hoped to expand its appeal by nominating John Hale, a New Hampshire Democrat.

Franklin Pierce's eventual victory left the Whigs and the Free-Soilers in disarray. Seeking a truly proslavery party, a third of southern Whigs threw their support to the Democrats in the election. Many Democrats who had supported Free-Soilers in 1848 were driven to vote for Pierce by their enthusiasm over the admission of California as a free state. But despite the Democratic triumph, that party also remained fragile. The nation now faced some of its gravest challenges under a president with limited political experience, no firm base of support, and a cabinet that included men of widely differing views. When confronted with difficult decisions, Pierce received contradictory advice and generally pursued his own expansionist vision.

Early in his administration, Pierce focused on expanding U.S. trade and extending the "civilizing" power of the nation to other parts of the world. Trade with China had declined in the 1840s, but the United States had begun commercial negotiations with Japan in 1846. These came to fruition in 1854, when U.S. emissary Commodore Matthew C. Perry, a renowned naval officer and founder of the Naval Engineer Corps, obtained the first formal trade agreement with Japan by coercion, threatening war if Japan would not accept its terms. Within four years, the United States had expanded commercial ties and enhanced diplomatic relations with Japan, in large part by supporting the island nation against its traditional enemies in China, Russia, and Europe.

Pierce had rejected Commodore Perry's offer to take military possession of Formosa and other territories near Japan, but he was willing to consider conquests in the Caribbean and Central America. For decades, U.S. politicians, particularly southerners, had looked to gain control of Cuba, Mexico, and Nicaragua. A **"Young America" movement** within the Democratic Party imagined manifest destiny reaching southward as well as westward. In hopes of stirring up rebellious Cubans against Spanish rule, some Democrats joined with private adventurers to send three unauthorized expeditions, known as **filibusters**, to invade Cuba. In 1854 the capture of one of the filibustering ships led to an international incident. Spanish officials confiscated the ship, and southern Democrats urged Pierce to seek an apology and redress from Spain. But many northern Democrats rejected any effort to obtain another slave state, and Pierce was forced to renounce the filibusters.

Other politicians still pressured Spain to sell Cuba to the United States. These included Pierce's secretary of state, William Marcy, and the U.S. ambassador to Great Britain, James Buchanan, as well as the ministers to France and Spain. In October 1854 these ministers met in Ostend, Belgium and sent a letter to Pierce urging the conquest of Cuba. When the **Ostend Manifesto** was leaked to the press, northerners were outraged. They viewed the episode as "a dirty plot" to gain more slave territory and

Ostend Manifesto 1854 letter from U.S. ambassadors and the secretary of state to President Franklin Pierce urging him to conquer Cuba. When it was leaked to the press, northerners voiced outrage at what they saw as a plot to expand slave territories.

TEACHING IDEA

Check for Understanding

Have students work in pairs to create a list of political parties encountered thus far in this course. Students could create a timeline or possibly a web graphic organizer showing the progression from the Democratic-Republicans/Federalists through to the Whig/Democrat/Republican/American political parties during the 1850s.

TEACHING IDEA

Connecting the Dots

Have a brief discussion of the United States' dealings with foreign nations. While the U.S. was involved with countries around the world from its inception, political power and respect were limited. Remind students of the importance of trade in established American foreign policy. While discussing these paragraphs highlight the idea of America as having "civilizing power." Ensure students make connections to the idea of manifest destiny both domestically and in foreign lands.

TEACHING IDEA

Check for Understanding

The important idea for students to understand from this section is that the Democratic Party was splitting between the northern and southern Democrats. Southern Democrats were pro-slavery and northern Democrats were divided over the issue of slavery. These divisions will lead to the creation of several new parties (Free-Soil, Liberty, American, Republican, Constitutional Union). The Know-Nothing Party was also gaining popularity on an anti-immigrant platform.

EXPLORING AP® THEMES

America in the World

It is important to highlight the fact that the United States has always been active in trade around the world, whether or not it was a major military power at the time. Ensure students understand that just as China in 1850 was not yet a manufacturing powerhouse, as it is today, nor was the United States. The Chief AP® Scorer Reports of the past several years (see 2014, 2016, 2018, 2019 reports on apcentral.collegeboard.org) have highlighted the fact the AP® students nationally do not link the growth across time in relation to American manufacturing.

TRM Suggested Responses to Questions

TRM Module 5.2 AP® Analyzing Sources Handout 3

EXPLORING AP® THEMES

America in the World

Ensure that students have not skimmed and missed the events listed on these pages linking American conquest of territories. Have students complete a think/pair/share activity in which they are asked to discuss how the United States was involved in foreign affairs from the 1820s through the 1850s. Answers will vary, and many students will focus on the issuing of the Monroe Doctrine, Mexican-American War, and territorial expansion, but U.S. involvement in trade globally should be addressed, as well as the growing involvement in Central America.

TRM Suggested Responses to Questions

Period 5: 1844–1877

MODULE 5-2 Compromise and Conflict

forced Pierce to give up plans to obtain Cuba. In 1855 a private adventurer named William Walker, who had organized four filibusters to Nicaragua, invaded that country and set himself up as ruler. He then invited southern planters to come to Nicaragua and establish plantations. Pierce and many Democrats endorsed his plan, but neighboring Hondurans forced Walker from power in 1857 and executed him three years later. Although Pierce's expansionist dreams failed, his efforts heightened sectional tensions.

AP® ANALYZING SOURCES

Source: *New York Daily Times*, "Commodore Perry at the Loo Choo Isles," 1853

"At last accounts Commodore Perry and Squadron had sailed from the Loo-Choo Islands, the southernmost group of the Japan Empire. Private letters from one of the officers of his Flag-ship give some interesting particulars not published in the Journals. Under date of July 1, this gentleman writes that: 'On the 6th of June we marched to Shudi, the capital of the Loo-Choo Islands, with all the officers, marines and sailors, with artillery, &c. It was a march of some three or four miles, over a magnificent paved road, through a rich and highly cultivated country. The clumps of trees and other ornamental embellishments of the way astonished us much less than our heavy cloth uniforms and accoutrements astonished the timid natives, who gathered along our road to gape at us with wonder and poorly concealed disquietude. They cannot tell what to make of this ambiguous demonstration. Poor devils! Their Japanese masters will find out one of these days. The object of this visit was to be received by the Regent of these Islands at his Royal Palace. The honor of the visit may have rebounded to his tawny Excellence, but it is certain the pleasure, such as it was, was all on our side. They are suspicious, and very ill at ease. Commodore Perry was carried in a sedan chair. The rest of us gave the natives a specimen of how Yankees . . . can march under a scorching sun on foot. If the Japanese give us a friendly reception, all will be smooth. If not, we will have a far more effective squadron here, one of these days, and teach them conformity to Christian manners. . . .

The land is inviting, and is, I think, destined to become a flourishing American colony.'"

Questions for Analysis

1. Describe the reception that Perry received in Japan, as reported in this excerpt.
2. Describe the ways in which the author of this document characterizes Japan in relation to the United States.
3. Explain how this document reveals the ways in which America's domestic economy shaped its trade relations with Asia during the mid-1800s.

REVIEW

In what ways were slavery and American expansionism linked during the 1840s and 1850s?

AP® WRITING HISTORICALLY — Responding to a Long-Essay Question

As you read in this module, the issue of slavery not only caused divisions between North and South, but also drove a wedge between northerners. While many remained indifferent to slavery after the Mexican-American War, and some actively supported its spread, a strong anti-slavery faction, the Free-Soilers, also arose. These northerners rejected slavery for reasons quite different from those of abolitionists, who were the longer-standing opponents to slavery in the North.

Consider the following Long-Essay Question, which asks you to reflect on what you have learned thus far in Period 5:

> Evaluate the extent to which different regional attitudes toward slavery affected federal policy during the period from 1848 to 1855.

TEACHING IDEA

Incorporating Websites

William Walker is an interesting figure in United States history. Have students write a one-page profile on William Walker. The Latin American Studies website has many articles with information regarding William Walker and the filibusters (latinamericanstudies.org). Students will discover that there was much U.S. involvement in Latin America during this period. By establishing this, students will find future content and connections easier to understand — specifically imperialism and the Roosevelt Corollary.

TEACHING IDEA

Check for Understanding

To ensure students are using a wide range of topics and information, have students brainstorm or think/pair/share together before writing. Have students work to compile a list of events that exemplify conflicting views on slavery per region. The process of working together encourages a wider range of answers.

Further Expansion under President Pierce

Period 5: 1844–1877

Step 1 **Break down the prompt.**
This prompt appears deceptively simple. However, after reading this module, you know that federal policy after the conclusion of the Mexican-American War in 1848 was a collection of compromises that, ultimately, no one in the North or South was entirely happy with. This means that you will have to frame your comparison carefully, making sure to address the divisions within the North.

Step 2 **List and categorize your historical knowledge.**
The next step is to brainstorm and pre-write your response. The following table will help you start your complex comparison. Notice that there are rows for three attitudes, and a column for you to note where this attitude was often found. There is also a column for you to explore reasons for each regional attitude. Filling out these columns will give you a good start for your complex comparison.

The last two columns of the table will help you deepen your historical argument. The column for "Effects on Federal Policy" asks you to connect each regional attitude to specific federal policies enacted between 1848 and 1855. For each regional factor, try to think of more than one resulting federal policy. Finally, the last column will help you put it all together to explain how each regional faction shaped federal policy during the era. The first row of the table has been modeled for you:

Attitude	Region	Reason for Attitude	Effects on Federal Policy	Why Effects Caused by Attitude?
Free-Soilers	Northern cities and West	Believed spread of slavery to the west hurt common workers and farmers	California admitted as a free state	Free-Soilers wanted to prevent slavery's spread to western territories like California.
			Popular sovereignty declared in New Mexico territory	Popular sovereignty allowed settlers to decide whether some territories would be open to slavery, allowing free-soil settlers some influence of a territory's future.
Abolitionists				
Slaveholders				

Step 3 **Set the context and write a thesis.**
Now you're ready to build your thesis statement. Using your pre-writing from step 2, write a thesis statement. Be sure to include three evaluative claims about the extent of regional influences on federal policy between 1848 and 1855. Then, decide whether you'd like to introduce your essay with immediate or preceding context. When you write your introductory paragraph, be sure to cite evidence of your contextualization statement and explain the influence of this context on your thesis statement.

ACTIVITY

Use steps 1-3 to plan and write an essay in response to the Long-Essay Question at the beginning of this box.
You may use the following outline to guide your response:
I. Introductory paragraph
   A. Immediate/preceding contextualization statement
      1. Cite evidence of immediate/preceding context
      2. Explain influence of immediate/preceding context
   B. Thesis statement presenting three to four evaluative claims of comparison that are situated along a continuum of relative importance
II. Claim 1 body paragraph
   A. Topic sentence presenting an evaluative claim of comparison 1
   B. Supporting statement citing evidence of claim 1
   C. Cite additional evidence of claim 1
   D. Explain how evidence supports claim 1

(Continued)

TEACHING IDEA

Think/Pair/Share

Have students develop a possible thesis and categories of argument before writing. Once students are finished writing, have them share their work with a partner or a small group. The collective group and surrounding discussion will ensure students create a stronger thesis and more cohesive arguments.

TEACHING IDEA

AP® Writing Historically Workshop

This question has two elements students need to unpack, define, and relate as they write their essay. Prior to having students write a response, consider the following activity. Because this question asks for both regional attitudes and federal policies relative to slavery, break the class into two large groups. One group will be tasked with developing answers that capture regional attitudes toward slavery. The other group will be tasked with developing answers using federal policies about slavery from 1848–1855. Using large butcher-block paper, groups will outline as many factual examples as they can brainstorm in five minutes. After groups have completed their brainstorm, have them visit the opposing group's brainstorm, recording as much information as they can in two minutes. Have students return to their original groups to form subgroups of two or three students. Next, have these smaller groups write a thesis statement using the information they have collected thus far. Finally, have groups post their thesis statements around the room so students can see the variance of the interpretations from the same evidence. The entire process takes less than 20 minutes and allows students to understand whether they are prepared to answer the prompt.

TEACHING IDEA

Skeleton Essay

Give students time to write their introduction paragraphs. Then, for each body paragraph, have them write a complete topic sentence and work to create bullet points listing all other supporting facts discussed within their paragraph. Have students share their outline with a partner for peer review.

▲ Differentiation

Have students work in pairs or small groups to create a skeleton outline of their possible essay on large butcher paper. After groups have created their outlines, compose a gallery walk by having groups post their introduction paragraphs and bullet point ideas from their body paragraphs. Have all groups rotate to each poster and view other groups' work. Groups can leave notes with ideas or suggestions for topics or points that need further support. When students return to their original poster they should have constructive feedback and ideas for areas to review/rework. From this point, each member of the class can then create their own essay based on their ideas and feedback from groups. Each essay should be different even though the entire class has been exposed to much of the same materials and ideas. This essay now becomes more focused on the process rather than the content and will allow teachers to appraise written skills.

III. Claim 2 body paragraph
   A. Topic sentence presenting an evaluative claim of comparison 2
   B. Supporting statement citing evidence of claim 2
   C. Cite additional evidence of claim 2
   D. Explain how evidence supports claim 2

IV. Claim 3 body paragraph
   A. Topic sentence presenting an evaluative claim of comparison 3
   B. Supporting statement citing evidence of claim 3
   C. Cite additional evidence of claim 3
   D. Explain how evidence supports claim 3

V. (Optional) Claim 4 body paragraph
   A. Topic sentence presenting an evaluative claim of comparison 4
   B. Supporting statement citing evidence of claim 4
   C. Cite additional evidence of claim 4
   D. Explain how evidence supports claim 4

Module 5-3

From Sectional Crisis to Southern Secession

LEARNING TARGETS

By the end of this module, you should be able to:

- Explain how immigration shaped American culture from 1844 to 1860.
- Explain how arguments over slavery caused tensions between regions in the United States from 1844 to 1860.
- Explain the effects of the election of President Abraham Lincoln in 1860.

THEMATIC FOCUS
Politics and Power
American and Regional Culture

Compromise over the expansion of slavery became increasingly difficult during the 1850s, and attempts such as the Compromise of 1850 and the *Dred Scott* case only worsened tensions. At the same time, increased immigration from both Europe and Asia led to the temporary rise of anti-immigrant parties throughout the North. These two factors contributed greatly to the breakdown of the Second Party System. Former Whigs and antislavery activists in the North formed the Republican Party, dedicated to ending the expansion of slavery. And, although Democrats held the White House from 1852 to 1860, the Democratic Party was split into northern and southern factions. The Democratic fracture helped Republican candidate Abraham Lincoln win the presidency in the election of 1860 without support from any southern states. By Lincoln's inauguration in March 1861, seven southern states had seceded from the Union, and the nation was divided into two.

HISTORICAL REASONING FOCUS
Causation

TASK ▶ While reading this module, consider the various reasons why developments in the 1850s continued to divide the country and how those divisions led to Lincoln's election in 1860 despite southern threats to secede from the Union. Also consider why efforts at compromise over the issue of the extension of slavery into territories failed despite the success of previous compromises.

The political crises of the early 1850s bred social turmoil, which in turn further pushed American politics from one crisis to the next. While the decade started out with hope for compromise, passion over the expansion of slavery, both for and against, caused upheaval from the streets of Boston to the plains of Kansas, the halls of Congress, and the Supreme Court. The weakness and fragmentation of the existing political parties gave rise to the Republican Party in 1854, which soon absorbed enough Free-Soilers, Whigs, and northern Democrats to become a major political force. The events that drove these cultural and political developments included the publication of *Uncle Tom's Cabin*, continued challenges to the Fugitive Slave Act, a battle over the admission of Kansas to the Union, and a Supreme Court ruling in the *Dred Scott* case.

MODULE 5-3 From Sectional Crisis to Southern Secession

Popularizing the Antislavery Movement

Uncle Tom's Cabin 1852 novel by Harriet Beecher Stowe. Meant to publicize the evils of slavery, the novel struck an emotional chord in the North and was an international best seller.

AP® TIP
Evaluate the degree to which abolitionists in the 1850s were influenced by earlier reform movements in U.S. history.

The Fugitive Slave Act forced northerners to reconsider their role in sustaining the institution of slavery. In 1852, just months before Franklin Pierce was elected president, their concerns were heightened by the publication of the novel *Uncle Tom's Cabin* by Harriet Beecher Stowe. Stowe's father, Lyman Beecher, and brother Henry were among the nation's leading evangelical clergy, and her sister Catharine had opposed Cherokee removal and promoted women's education. Stowe was inspired to write *Uncle Tom's Cabin* by passage of the Fugitive Slave Act in 1850. Published in both serial and book forms, the novel created a national sensation.

Uncle Tom's Cabin built on accounts by former enslaved people as well as tales gathered by abolitionist lecturers and writers, which gained growing attention in the North. The autobiographies of Frederick Douglass (1845), Josiah Henson (1849), and Henry Bibb (1849) set the stage for Stowe's novel. So, too, did the expansion of the antislavery press, which by the 1850s included dozens of newspapers. Antislavery poems and songs also circulated widely and were performed at abolitionist conventions and fund-raising fairs.

Still, nothing captured the public's attention as did *Uncle Tom's Cabin*. Read by millions in the United States and England and translated into French and German, the book reached a mass audience. Its sentimental portrait of saintly slaves and its vivid depiction of cruel masters and overseers offered white northerners a way to identify with enslaved black people. Although some African Americans expressed frustration that a white woman's fictional account gained far more readers than their factual narratives, most recognized the book's important contribution to the antislavery cause.

Yet the real-life stories of fugitives from slavery could often surpass their fictional counterparts for drama. In May 1854 abolitionists sought to free Anthony Burns from a Boston courthouse, where a slaveholder was attempting to reclaim him. They failed to secure his release, and Burns was soon marched to the docks to be shipped south. Twenty-two companies of state militia held back tens of thousands of angry Bostonians who lined the streets. A year later, supporters purchased Burns's freedom, but the incident raised anguished questions among local residents. In a city that was home to so many intellectual, religious, and antislavery leaders, Bostonians wondered how they had come so far in aiding and abetting slavery.

REVIEW

What factors increased the popularity of antislavery sentiment in the North?

The Kansas-Nebraska Act Stirs Dissent

transcontinental railroad A railroad linking the East and West Coasts of North America. Completed in 1869, the transcontinental railroad facilitated the flow of migrants and the development of economic connections between the West and the East.

Kansas-Nebraska Act 1854 act creating the territories of Kansas and Nebraska out of what was then American Indian land. The act stipulated that the issue of slavery would be settled by a popular referendum in each territory.

Kansas provided the first test of the effects of *Uncle Tom's Cabin* on northern sentiments toward slavery's expansion. As white Americans displaced American Indian nations from their homelands, diverse groups of American Indians settled in the northern half of the Louisiana Territory. This unorganized region had once been considered beyond the reach of white settlement, but Democratic senator Stephen Douglas of Illinois was eager to have a **transcontinental railroad** run through his home state. He needed the federal government to gain control of land along the route he proposed and thus argued for the establishment of a vast Nebraska Territory. But to support his plan, Douglas also needed to convince southern congressmen, who sought a route through their own region. According to the Missouri Compromise, states lying above the southern border of Missouri were automatically free. To gain southern support, Douglas sought to reopen the question of slavery in the territories.

In January 1854 Douglas introduced the **Kansas-Nebraska Act** to Congress. The act extinguished American Indians' long-held treaty rights in the region and repealed the Missouri Compromise. Two new territories — Kansas and Nebraska — would be carved out of the unorganized lands, and voters in each would determine whether to enter the nation as a slave or a free state (Map 5.3). The act spurred intense opposition from most Whigs and some northern Democrats who wanted to retain the Missouri Compromise line. Months of fierce debate followed, but the bill was ultimately voted into law.

Passage of the Kansas-Nebraska Act enraged many northerners who considered the dismantling of the Missouri Compromise a sign of the rising power of the South. They were infuriated that the South — or what some now called the "Slave Power" — had again benefited from northern politicians' willingness to compromise. Although few of these opponents considered the impact of

The Kansas-Nebraska Act Stirs Dissent

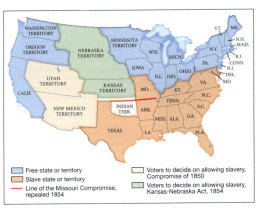

MAP 5.3 Kansas-Nebraska Territory
From 1820 on, Congress attempted to limit sectional conflict. But the Missouri Compromise (1820) and the Compromise of 1850 failed to resolve disagreements over slavery's expansion. **How did the Kansas-Nebraska Act attempt to ease tensions around the issues of slavery? To what extent did the act worsen these tensions?**

the law on American Indians, the act also shattered treaty provisions that had protected the Arapaho, Cheyenne, Ponco, Pawnee, and Sioux nations. These Plains Indians lost half the land they had held by treaty as thousands of settlers swarmed into the newly organized territories. In the fall of 1855, conflicts between white settlers and American Indians erupted across the Great Plains. The U.S. army then sent six hundred troops to retaliate against a Sioux village, killing eighty-five residents of Blue Water in the Nebraska Territory and triggering continued violence throughout the region.

As tensions escalated across the nation, Americans faced the 1854 congressional elections. The Democrats, increasingly viewed as supporting the priorities of slaveholders, lost badly in the North. But the Whig Party also proved weak, having failed to stop the Slave Power from extending its leverage over federal policies. A third party, the **American Party** (also known as the Know-Nothing Party), was founded in the early 1850s and attracted native-born workers and Protestant farmers who were drawn to its anti-immigrant and anti-Catholic message. They continued to seek limits on immigrants' political power and cultural influence. Responding to these political realignments, another new party, led by antislavery Whigs and Free-Soilers—the **Republican Party**—was founded in the spring of 1854. Among its early members was a Whig politician from Illinois, Abraham Lincoln.

Although established only months before the fall 1854 elections, the Republican Party gained significant support in the Midwest, particularly in state and local campaigns. Meanwhile the American Party gained control of the Massachusetts legislature and nearly captured New York. These victories marked the demise of the Whigs and the Second Party System. Unlike the Whig Party, however, with its national constituency, the Republican Party was rooted solely in the North. Like Free-Soilers, the Republicans argued that slavery should not be extended into new territories. But the Republicans also advocated a program of commercial and internal improvements to attract a broader base than earlier antislavery parties. The Republican Party attracted both ardent abolitionists and men whose main concern was keeping western territories open to free white men. This latter group was more than willing to accept slavery where it already existed.

The 1854 congressional elections increased sectional tensions by bringing representatives from a strictly northern party—the Republicans—into Congress. But the conflicts over slavery reached far beyond the nation's capital. After passage of the Kansas-Nebraska Act, advocates and opponents of slavery poured into Kansas in anticipation of a vote on whether the state would enter the Union slave or free.

As Kansas prepared to hold its referendum, settlers continued to arrive daily, making it difficult to determine who was eligible to vote. In 1855 southerners installed a proslavery government at Shawnee Mission, while abolitionists established a stronghold in Lawrence. Violence erupted when proslavery settlers invaded Lawrence, killing one resident, demolishing newspaper offices, and plundering shops and homes. Fearing that southern settlers in Kansas were better armed than antislavery northerners in the territory, eastern abolitionists raised funds to ship rifles to Kansas.

In 1856 longtime abolitionist John Brown carried his own rifles to Kansas. Four of his sons already lived in the territory. To retaliate for proslavery attacks on Lawrence, the Browns and two friends kidnapped five proslavery advocates from their homes along Pottawatomie Creek and hacked them to death. The so-called Pottawatomie Massacre infuriated southern settlers, who then drew up the Lecompton Constitution, which declared Kansas a slave state. President Pierce

American Party Also known as the Know-Nothing Party, a political party that arose in the Northeast during the 1840s. The party was anti-Catholic and anti-immigration. It also supported workers' rights against business owners, who were perceived to support immigration as a way to keep wages low.

Republican Party Party formed in 1854 that was committed to stopping the expansion of slavery and advocated economic development and internal improvements. Although their appeal was limited to the North, the Republicans quickly became a major political force.

TEACHING IDEA

Check for Understanding

For a quick spot check have students name the states where slavery was permitted. Next have students contrast these states with those that seceded. Students must understand that not all slaveholding states seceded from the Union.

BUILDING AP® SKILLS

Contextualization

The American Party, or Know-Nothings, was based in fear and anti-immigrant sentiments. Have students read Abraham Lincoln's 1855 statements regarding the American Party found on Digital History's website by searching for "Abraham Lincoln on the Know Nothing Party" (digitalhistory.uh.edu). After students read this brief discourse on the American Party, have them use HIPP to analyze the document (a refresher on HIPP can be found on page 8). Lincoln's purpose and perspective should be discussed within the class.

EXPLORING AP® THEMES

Politics and Power

Have students read the "Republican Party Platform of 1856," which is available through Teaching American History's website (teachingamericanhistory.org). Have students work in small groups and decide the top five statements or elements from the 1856 platform that had the greatest appeal to supporters. Have students explain why or how their supporters would be impacted by these platform ideas. Groups should brainstorm 3-4 possible reactions to the Republican platform. The class should discuss each group's insights and critique the overall impact of the 1856 Republican platform.

TEACHING IDEA

Incorporating Secondary Sources

Have students read the 2011 article, "John Brown: America's First Terrorist?" by Paul Finkelman found on the National Archives website (archives.gov). As students read, have them search for the thesis of the article. Students should produce a written response to the article stating whether they support the author's view or not. Student review can be an exit ticket or homework assignment, but their writing focus should be in finding support and claims or counterclaims of the author's thesis. Seeing how historians frame and support their theses will help students with their writing.

TEACHING IDEA

Incorporating Secondary Sources

Have students read the article, "Violence in Congress Before the Civil War: From Canings and Stabbings to Murder," by Becky Little, which can be found on the History Channel's website (history.com). Have students discuss their impressions of the events depicted in the article. The fact that the nation was divided and violence was brewing before the beginning of the Civil War is important to impart to students, as well as the fact that there were many violent actions within Congress, too.

TEACHING IDEA

Incorporating Websites

Have students search "Canefight! Preston Brooks and Charles Sumner," from U.S. History's website (ushistory.org). This site includes many links to newspaper editorials from this time. Students should select a sampling of editorials that support and repudiate the caning event. Have students select two to three editorials that support and two to three editorials that oppose the Sumner/Brooks incident. Next, students should assess the coverage within the newspapers and look for regional bias in the editorials. Discuss the role of bias within all of the accounts.

TRM Suggested Responses to Questions

TRM Module 5.3 AP® Analyzing Sources Handout 1

TEACHING IDEA

Class Discussion

The election of 1856 was not the first, nor the only, election in which a president was elected with an Electoral College win without receiving more than half of the popular vote. Have students research to find popular vote totals for presidents who won by the Electoral College. It is important for students to recognize that the Electoral College has played a role in deciding many important elections, including the elections of 1824, 1844, 1848, 1865, 1860, 1876, 1880, 1884, 1888, 1892, 1912, 1916, 1948, 1960, 1968, 1992, 1996, 2000, and 2016. After they've conducted their research, ask students to discuss the political implications for a president who received less than half of the popular vote.

▸ **John Doy and His Rescue Party, Kansas, 1859** John Doy and his son Charles were captured in Kansas in January 1859 while aiding thirteen enslaved people in an attempted escape. Taken to Missouri, Charles was set free, but his father was sentenced to five years in prison for abducting enslaved people. Abolitionist friends freed him, and the group (with John Doy seated) posed for this picture when they reached Lawrence. **What message does this photograph send to its intended audience(s)?**

Bleeding Kansas The Kansas Territory during a period of violent conflicts over the fate of slavery in the mid-1850s. This violence intensified the sectional division over slavery.

made his support of the proslavery government clear, but Congress remained divided. While Congress deliberated, armed battles continued. In the first six months of 1856, more than fifty settlers — on both sides of the conflict — were killed in what became known as **Bleeding Kansas**.

Fighting also broke out on the floor of Congress. Republican senator Charles Sumner of Massachusetts delivered an impassioned speech against the continued expansion of the Slave Power. He launched scathing attacks on planter politicians like South Carolina senator Andrew Butler. Butler's nephew, Preston Brooks, a Democratic member of the House of Representatives, rushed to defend his family's honor. He assaulted Sumner in the Senate chamber, beating him senseless with a cane. Sumner, who never fully recovered from his injuries, was considered a martyr in the North. Meanwhile Brooks was celebrated throughout South Carolina.

The presidential election of 1856 began amid an atmosphere poisoned by violence and recrimination. The Democratic Party nominated James Buchanan of Pennsylvania, a proslavery advocate. Western hero John C. Frémont headed the Republican Party ticket. The American Party, in its final presidential contest, selected former president Millard Fillmore as its candidate. The strength of nativism in politics was diminishing, however, and Fillmore won only the state of Maryland. Meanwhile Frémont attracted cheering throngs as he traveled across the nation. Large numbers of women turned out to see Jessie Frémont, the first presidential candidate's wife to play a significant role in a campaign. Frémont carried most of the North and the West. Buchanan captured the South along with Pennsylvania, Indiana, and Illinois. Although Buchanan won only 45.2 percent of the popular vote, he received a comfortable majority in the electoral college, securing his victory. The nation was becoming increasingly divided along sectional lines, and President Buchanan would do little to resolve these differences.

AP® ANALYZING SOURCES

Source: American (Know-Nothing) Party Platform, 1856

"*Resolved*, That the American democracy place their trust in the intelligence, the patriotism, and the discriminating justice of the American people. . . .

3. *Americans must rule America*; and to this end *native*-born citizens should be selected for all state, federal, and municipal offices of government employment, in preference to all others. *Nevertheless*,

BUILDING AP® SKILLS

Making Connections

Have students complete a Venn diagram for the Missouri Compromise and the Kansas-Nebraska Act. After students complete the diagram, have them summarize which document had the most balanced approach in creating a compromise between the two factions.

TRM Find **Handout 5.3 – Missouri Compromise vs. Kansas-Nebraska Act** in the Teacher's Resource Materials.

The Kansas-Nebraska Act Stirs Dissent

4. Persons born of American parents residing temporarily abroad, should be entitled to all the rights of native-born citizens. . . .

7. The recognition of the right of native-born and naturalized citizens of the United States, permanently residing in any territory thereof, to frame their constitution and laws, and to regulate their domestic and social affairs in their own mode, subject only to the provisions of the federal constitution, with the privilege of admission into the Union whenever they have the requisite population for one Representative in Congress: *Provided, always*, that none but those who are citizens of the United States under the constitution and laws thereof, and who have a fixed residence in any such territory, ought to participate in the formation of the constitution or in the enactment of laws for said territory or state. . . .

13. Opposition to the reckless and unwise policy of the present administration in the general management of our national affairs, and more especially as shown in removing 'Americans' (by designation) and conservatives in principle, from office, and placing foreigners and [abolitionists] in their places; as shown in a truckling subserviency to the stronger, and an insolent and cowardly bravado towards the weaker powers; as shown in reopening sectional agitation, by the repeal of the Missouri Compromise; as shown in granting to unnaturalized foreigners the right of suffrage in Kansas and Nebraska; as shown in its vacillating course on the Kansas and Nebraska question; as shown in the corruptions which pervade some of the departments of the government; as shown in disgracing meritorious naval officers through prejudice or caprice; and as shown in the blundering mismanagement of our foreign relations.

14. Therefore, to remedy existing evils and prevent the disastrous consequences otherwise resulting therefrom, we would build up the 'American Party' upon the principles hereinbefore stated."

Questions for Analysis

1. Identify an element of the American Party's platform that addresses the debate over slavery.
2. Describe the American Party's position on immigration in this excerpt.
3. Explain the contexts that shaped the American Party platform.

Source: *Republican Campaign Song*, 1856

"FREMONT AND VICTORY.

A Rallying Song—Tune of Marseilles Hymn[1]

Behold! the furious storm is rolling,
   Which border fiends, confederates, raise,
The dogs of war, let loose, are [howling],
   And lo! our infant cities blaze,
And shall we calmly view the ruin,
   While lawless force with giant stride,
Spreads desolation far and wide,
   In guiltless blood his hands imbruing?
     Arise, arise, ye brave!
       And let our war cry be,
   FREE SPEECH, FREE PRESS, FREE SOIL, FREE MEN,
    FRE-MONT AND LIBERTY! . . . .

(Continued)

TEACHING IDEA

Class Discussion

After students review the American (Know-Nothing) Party's platform, lead a class discussion on some of the major platform issues held by the party. Ensure that students understand the nativism within the platform. Discuss the reasons for nativism, its fears, and possible outcomes. Students may want to make the time-period jump to modern times and modern political parties — remind students that in framing any such connections, they must stay within the confines of historical events (i.e., the conditions in the 1850s are not the same conditions as in the 1880s, 1920s, nor modern times). Students must stay within a given time period in any discussion for questions on the AP® exam. AP® exam scorers often find that students make wild jumps between time periods, resulting in students not receiving credit due to students not addressing the actual question being asked. The College Board will ask questions with specific time frames. Create successful practices in your students with the constant reminder to stay within the time period discussed, as any answer outside of the specific question will not count toward their AP® exam score.

BUILDING AP® SKILLS

Making Connections

Have students compare and contrast the 1856 Republican platform (found in Module 5-2) with the American (Know-Nothing) Party platform. Students should share answers in small groups or with the whole class.

TEACHING IDEA

Incorporating Music

Campaign songs and jingles became popular in the 1820s with Andrew Jackson's "Old Hickory" slogans and jingles. By the 1850s campaign songs and rhetoric were commonplace. Have students search for popular songs from this time. Digital History's website has a wide assortment of music in the "Pre-Civil War" section (digitalhistory.uh.edu). Some students find it worthwhile even to sing or perform songs — don't overlook the chances to have a bit of fun within the AP® course framework.

EXPLORING AP® THEMES

Politics and Power

Have students write their own campaign songs or slogans by picking an election or event prior to the Civil War and incorporating the campaign ideas into song or slogan format. Students may enjoy running a political campaign for one of the political parties or personalities from this time period; having a class "mock election" where Fredrick Douglass, Susan B. Anthony, and Abraham Lincoln all face off can make for a dynamic class period. While the finished products will vary, the fun process of taking the complex issues from the time period and having students creatively connect with those ideas will build greater understanding.

Period 5: 1844–1877

MODULE 5-3 From Sectional Crisis to Southern Secession

> Hurrah, hurrah, from hill and valley;
> Hurrah from prairie wide and free!
> Around our glorious chieftain rally,
> For Kansas and for liberty!
> Let him who first her wilds exploring,
> Her virgin beauty gave to fame,
> Now save her from the curse and shame
> Which slavery o'er her soil is pouring.
> Our standard bearer then,
> The brave path finder be!
> FREE SPEECH, FREE PRESS, FREE SOIL, FREE MEN,
> FRE-MONT AND LIBERTY."
>
> [1]"La Marseillaise" was first written and popularized during the French Revolution and adopted by the French Republic as its national anthem in 1795. For Americans of the 1850s, the Marseillaise immediately called to mind the ideals of liberty and equality. The American national anthem, "The Star-Spangled Banner," was not adopted by the United States until the twentieth century.

Questions for Analysis

1. Identify the "furious storm" in the first line of the song.
2. Evaluate the extent to which this campaign song provides both a moral and a legal call to action.

Questions for Comparison

1. Identify the intended audiences for each document.
2. Explain how each document attempts to appeal to its intended audience.
3. Explain how the perspective towards slavery in the territories expressed in the American Party platform compares to that of the Republican campaign song.

REVIEW

- How did the violence in Kansas reflect and intensify growing sectional divisions in the U.S.?

The Dred Scott Decision

Dred Scott case 1857 Supreme Court case centered on the status of Dred Scott and his family. In its ruling, the Court denied the claim that black men had any rights and blocked Congress from excluding slavery from any territory.

Just two days after Buchanan's inauguration, the Supreme Court finally announced its decision in the *Dred Scott* case. Led by Chief Justice Roger Taney, a proslavery southerner, the majority ruled that an enslaved person was not a citizen and therefore could not sue in court. Indeed, Taney claimed that black men had no rights that a white man was bound to respect. The ruling annulled Scott's suit and meant that he and his wife remained enslaved. But the ruling went further. The *Dred Scott* decision declared that Congress had no constitutional authority to exclude slavery from any territory, thereby nullifying the Missouri Compromise and any future effort to restrict slavery's expansion. The ruling outraged many northerners, who were now convinced that a Slave Power conspiracy had taken hold of the federal government, including the judiciary.

In 1858, when Stephen Douglas faced reelection to the U.S. Senate, the Republican Party nominated Abraham Lincoln, a successful lawyer from Springfield, Illinois, to oppose him. The candidates participated in seven debates in which they explained their positions on slavery in the wake of the *Dred Scott* decision. Pointing to the landmark ruling, Lincoln asked Douglas how he could favor popular sovereignty, which allowed residents to keep slavery out of a territory, and yet support the *Dred Scott* decision, which protected slavery in all territories. Douglas claimed that if residents did not adopt local legislation to protect slaveholders' property, they could thereby exclude slavery for all practical purposes. At the same time, he accused Lincoln of advocating "negro equality," a position that went well beyond Lincoln's views. Lincoln did support economic opportunity for free black people, but not political or social equality. Still, the Republican candidate

---

TEACHING IDEA

Connecting the Dots

Throughout his life, Abraham Lincoln was willing to evolve in his viewpoints and beliefs. Have a brief discussion in regards to Lincoln's views toward black Americans, both enslaved and free, by directing students to the following well-known documents available online: The Joshua Speed letter (1855), House Divided (1858), Cooper Union (1860), First Inaugural Address (1861), Greeley Letter (1862), Conkling Letter (1863), Gettysburg Address (1863), Second Inaugural Address (1865). Students often view Lincoln as the "great emancipator," but fail to see how he changed in his views as time progressed from the early 1850s through the end of the Civil War.

The *Dred Scott* Decision

did declare that "this government cannot endure permanently half slave and half free. . . . It will become all one thing or all the other."

The **Lincoln-Douglas debates** attracted national attention, but the Illinois legislature selected the state's senator. Narrowly controlled by Democrats, it returned Douglas to Washington. Although the senator retained his seat, he was concerned by how far the Democratic Party had tilted toward the South. So when President Buchanan tried to push the Lecompton Constitution through Congress, legitimating the proslavery government in Kansas, Douglas opposed him. The two struggled over control of the party, with Douglas winning a symbolic victory in January 1861 when Kansas was admitted as a free state. By then, however, the Democratic Party had split into southern and northern wings, and the nation was on the verge of civil war.

Lincoln-Douglas debates
Series of debates between Abraham Lincoln and Stephen Douglas during the 1859 Illinois Senate race that mainly focused on the expansion of slavery.

AP® ANALYZING SOURCES

Source: Abraham Lincoln, *Speech at Edwardsville, Illinois*, 1858

"I have been requested to give a concise statement, as I understand it, of the difference between the Democratic and the Republican parties on the leading issues of this campaign. The question has just been put to me by a gentleman whom I do not know. I do not even know whether he is a friend of mine or a supporter of Judge Douglas in this contest; nor does that make any difference. His question is a pertinent one. . . .

The difference between the Republican and the Democratic parties on the leading issue of this contest, as I understand it, is, that the former consider slavery a moral, social and political wrong, while the latter *do not* consider it either a moral, social or political wrong; and the action of each, as respects the growth of the country and the expansion of our population, is squared to meet these views. . . . Every measure of the Democratic party of late years, bearing directly or indirectly on the slavery question, has corresponded with this notion of utter indifference whether slavery or freedom shall outrun in the race of empire across the Pacific—every measure, I say, up to the Dred Scott decision, where, it seems to me, the idea is boldly suggested that slavery is *better* than freedom. The Republican party, on the contrary, hold that this government was instituted to secure the blessings of freedom, and that slavery is an unqualified evil to the negro, to the white man, to the soil, and to the State. Regarding it an evil, they will not molest it in the States where it exists; they will not overlook the constitutional guards which our forefathers have placed around it; they will do nothing which can give proper offence to those who hold slaves by legal sanction; but they will use every constitutional method to prevent the evil from becoming larger and involving more negroes, more white men, more soil, and more States in its deplorable consequences. . . . All, or very nearly all, of Judge Douglas' arguments about "Popular Sovereignty," as he calls it, are logical if you admit that slavery is as good and as right as freedom; and not one of them is worth a rush if you deny it. This is the difference, as I understand it, between the Republican and the Democratic parties. . . ."

Questions for Analysis
1. Describe Lincoln's view of the Republican Party differences on the issue of slavery.
2. Explain how Lincoln appeals to his intended audience in this speech.

Questions for Comparison *Republican Campaign Song*, 1856 (p. 381)
1. Describe the similarities and differences between Lincoln's characterization of Republican Party goals and that of the campaign song.
2. Explain how specific historical developments account for the differences between Lincoln's argument and that of the campaign song.

REVIEW

- What historical developments led to the *Dred Scott* decision?
- How did the *Dred Scott* decision reflect and intensify growing sectional divisions within the U.S.?

TRM Suggested Responses to Questions

TRM Module 5.3 AP® Analyzing Sources Handout 2

BUILDING AP® SKILLS
Sourcing and Situation

Have students read Lincoln's 1858 "House Divided" speech (readily available online). Have students HIPP the speech, then follow up the activity with students writing a 4 to 6 sentence summary of the speech as well as Lincoln's view toward slavery and enslaved Americans (a refresher on HIPP can be found on page 8). Have students share their summaries with a partner, and ensure students are basing their summary on Lincoln's stated views. Follow up with a class discussion on Lincoln's stated views and hints toward future changes within these views.

TEACHING IDEA
Class Discussion

Have students read Lincoln's speech and discuss the main ideas found within this document. Challenge students to find Lincoln's personal views within the document. What does Lincoln say about slavery? Did he speak for the Republican Party or for himself? Answers will vary, but students will likely struggle to differentiate between Lincoln's political statements and personal beliefs.

TEACHING IDEA
Incorporating Videos

Have students watch the TED Talk video, "How One Piece of Legislation Divided a Nation," by Ben Labaree Jr. (available on YouTube). This six-minute video covers the Kansas-Nebraska Act through Bleeding Kansas. After the video, discuss the continued impact of the Kansas-Nebraska Act late into the 1850s as seen in the Lecompton Constitution.

Period 5: 1844–1877

MODULE 5-3 From Sectional Crisis to Southern Secession

From Crisis to Secession

John Brown's raid 1859 attack on the Federal arsenal at Harper's Ferry, Virginia, led by John Brown, who hoped to inspire a slave uprising and arm enslaved African Americans with the weapons taken from the arsenal. No uprising happened and Brown was captured and eventually executed for treason.

During the 1850s, a profusion of abolitionist lectures, conventions, and literature swelled antislavery sentiment in the North. Mainstream newspapers regularly covered rescues of fugitives, the *Dred Scott* case, and the bloody crisis in Kansas. Republican candidates in state and local elections also kept concerns about slavery's expansion and southern power alive. Nothing, however, riveted the nation's attention as much as **John Brown's raid** on the federal arsenal at Harpers Ferry, Virginia in 1859.

John Brown was committed not only to the abolition of slavery but also to complete equality between white and black people. A militant abolitionist and deeply religious man, Brown held views quite similar to those of David Walker, whose 1829 *Appeal* warned that enslaved people would eventually rise up and claim their freedom by force. Following the bloody battles in Kansas, Brown was convinced that direct action was the only answer. After the Pottawatomie killings, he went into hiding and reappeared back east, where he hoped to initiate an uprising to overthrow slavery.

Brown focused his efforts on the federal arsenal in Harpers Ferry, Virginia. With eighteen followers — five African Americans and thirteen whites, including three of his sons — Brown planned to capture the arsenal and distribute arms to enslaved people in the surrounding area. He hoped this action would ignite a rebellion that would destroy the plantation system. He tried to convince Frederick Douglass to join the venture, but Douglass considered it a foolhardy plan. However, Brown did manage to persuade a small circle of white abolitionists to bankroll the effort.

On the night of October 16, 1859, Brown and his men successfully kidnapped some leading townsmen and seized the arsenal. Local residents were stunned but managed to alert authorities, and state militia swarmed into Harpers Ferry. The next day, federal troops arrived, led by Colonel Robert E. Lee. With troops flooding into the town, Brown and his men were soon under siege, trapped in the arsenal. Fourteen rebels were killed, including two of Brown's sons. On October 18, Brown and three others were captured.

As word of the daring raid spread, Brown was hailed as a hero by many devoted abolitionists and depicted as a madman by southern planters. Southern whites were sure the raid was part of a widespread conspiracy led by power-hungry abolitionists. Federal authorities moved quickly to quell slaveholders' fears and end the episode. Brown rejected his lawyer's advice to plead insanity, and a local jury found him guilty of murder, criminal conspiracy, and treason. He was hanged on December 2, 1859.

John Brown's execution unleashed a massive outpouring of grief, anger, and uncertainty across the North. Abolitionists organized parades, demonstrations, bonfires, and tributes to the newest abolitionist martyr. Even many Quakers and other pacifists viewed John Brown as a hero for giving his life in the cause of emancipation. But most northern politicians and editors condemned the raid as a rash act that could only intensify sectional tensions.

Among southern whites, fear and panic greeted the raid on Harpers Ferry, and the execution of John Brown did little to quiet their outrage. By this time, southern intellectuals had developed a sophisticated proslavery argument that, to them, demonstrated the benefits of bondage for African Americans and its superiority to the northern system of wage labor. They argued that slaveholders provided care and guidance for African Americans from birth to death. Considering black people too childlike to fend for themselves, proslavery advocates saw no problem with the enslaved providing labor and obedience in return for their care. Such arguments failed to convince abolitionists, who highlighted the brutality, sexual abuse, and shattered families that marked the system of bondage. In this context, Americans on both sides of the sectional divide considered the 1860 presidential election critical to the nation's future.

Brown's hanging set the tone for the 1860 presidential campaign. The Republicans met in Chicago five months after Brown's execution and distanced themselves from the more radical wing of the abolitionist movement. The party platform condemned both John Brown and southern "Border Ruffians," who initiated the violence in Kansas. The platform accepted slavery where it already existed, but continued to advocate its exclusion from western territories. Finally, the platform insisted on the need for federally funded internal improvements and protective tariffs. The Republicans nominated Abraham Lincoln as their candidate for president. Recognizing the impossibility of gaining significant votes in the South, the party focused instead on winning large majorities in the Northeast and Midwest.

The Democrats met in Charleston, South Carolina. Although Stephen Douglas was the leading candidate, southern delegates were still angry with him over Kansas's admission as a free state. When Mississippi senator Jefferson Davis introduced a resolution to protect slavery in the territories, Douglas's northern supporters rejected it. President Buchanan also came out against Douglas, and the Democratic convention ended without choosing a candidate. Instead, various factions met

---

BUILDING AP® SKILLS

Making Connections

Students need to understand that slave revolts did occur within the American South prior to the Civil War although these were not well documented. Have students work in small groups to recall any uprisings or attempted uprisings studied thus far in the course. Answers will vary but might include: *The Stono Rebellion*, *Denmark Vesey*, *Nat Turner*, *United States v. The Amistad*, the *Creole Case*, etc.

TEACHING IDEA

Incorporating Videos

The Smithsonian Magazine's website has many great artifacts and images from John Brown's raid at Harpers Ferry (smithsonianmag.com). Have students watch the four-minute video entitled "The Raid on Harpers Ferry." This video explains the raid and following trial in a concise and informative presentation. After watching the video, students can search the site for additional details surrounding the raid and its aftermath.

TEACHING IDEA

Incorporating Music

The Civil War Era inspired the creation of many songs that depict the daily struggles along with divisive politics present for people during this period. The artist Pete Seeger has recreated many historical songs that are posted on YouTube. In class, play the song "John Brown's Body" and have students HIPP the song's lyrics (see page 8 for a refresher). Students will enjoy the wide range of songs posted by Pete Seeger — encourage students to listen to other songs and conclude where they fit within the time periods of U.S. history.

From Crisis to Secession

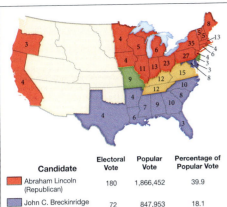

Candidate	Electoral Vote	Popular Vote	Percentage of Popular Vote
Abraham Lincoln (Republican)	180	1,866,452	39.9
John C. Breckinridge (Southern Democrat)	72	847,953	18.1
Stephen A. Douglas (Northern Democrat)	12	1,375,157	29.4
John Bell (Constitutional Union)	39	590,631	12.6

MAP 5.4 The Election of 1860 Four candidates vied for the presidency in 1860, and the voters split along clearly sectional lines. Although Stephen Douglas ran a vigorous campaign and gained votes in all regions of the country, he won a majority only in Missouri. Lincoln triumphed in the North and far West, and Breckinridge in most of the South. **What developments help explain why Stephen A. Douglas won so much of the popular vote but so few electoral votes?**

AP® TIP
Make sure you can explain how the issue of slavery divided the Democratic Party in 1860.

separately. A group of largely northern Democrats met in Baltimore and nominated Douglas. Southern Democrats selected John Breckinridge, the vice president, a slaveholder, and an advocate of annexing Cuba. The Constitutional Union Party, comprised mainly of former southern Whigs, advocated "no political principle other than the Constitution of the country, the union of the states, and the enforcement of the laws." Its members nominated Senator John Bell of Tennessee.

Although Lincoln won barely 40 percent of the popular vote, he carried a clear majority in the electoral college. With the admission of Minnesota and Oregon to the Union in 1858 and 1859, free states outnumbered slave states eighteen to fifteen, and Lincoln won all but one of them. Lincoln did not win a single southern electoral vote. However, since free states were more populous than slave states, they therefore controlled a large number of electoral votes. Douglas ran second to Lincoln in the popular vote, but Bell and Breckinridge captured more electoral votes than Douglas did because of their success in the South. Despite a deeply divided electorate, Lincoln became president.

Although many abolitionists were wary of the Republicans, who were willing to leave slavery alone where it existed, most were nonetheless relieved at Lincoln's victory and hoped he would become more sympathetic to their views once in office. Meanwhile, southern whites, especially those in the deep South, were furious that a Republican had won the White House without carrying a single southern state.

On December 20, 1860, six weeks after Lincoln's election, the legislature of South Carolina announced that because "a sectional party" had engineered "the election of a man to the high office of President of the United States whose opinions and purposes are hostile to slavery," the people of South Carolina dissolve their union with "the other states of North America." In early 1861, Mississippi, Florida, Alabama, Georgia, Louisiana, and Texas followed suit. Representatives from these states met on February 8 in Montgomery, Alabama, where they adopted a provisional constitution, elected Jefferson Davis as their president, and established the **Confederate States of America**, also known as the Confederacy.

Confederate States of America Name of the government that seceded from the Union after the election of President Lincoln in 1860.

AP® ANALYZING SOURCES

Source: Jefferson Davis, *Inaugural Address*, 1861

"[W]e have entered upon the career of independence, and it must be inflexibly pursued. Through many years of controversy, with our late associates, the Northern States, we have vainly endeavored to secure tranquillity, and to obtain respect for the rights to which we were entitled. As a necessity, not a choice, we have resorted to the remedy of separation; and henceforth, our energies must be directed to the conduct of our own affairs, and the perpetuity of the Confederacy which we have formed. If a just perception of mutual interest shall permit us, peaceably, to pursue our separate political career, my most earnest desire will have been fulfilled. But, if this be denied to us, and the integrity of our territory and jurisdiction be

(Continued)

BUILDING AP® SKILLS

Sourcing and Situation

Have students complete a HIPP analysis of Davis's speech (a refresher on HIPP can be found on page 8). As they work on this, they should list the reasons he gives for secession. Ask students to find specific examples of the events on their list taking place. Although this speech is laden with emotion, students need to be able to pinpoint the factual events listed by Davis. Students should share their findings in pairs. As a class make note of the emotional impact of the words and have students search for bias within the speech.

TEACHING IDEA

Incorporating Websites

Some historians believe that the Crittenden Compromise might have helped avoid the Civil War, if it had been passed. Have students review the modern U.S. Senate's view upon this historic legislation on their website (senate.gov). Find the "Crittenden Compromise" posted for the years 1851–1877 under Senate Stories. The write-up will spark classroom discussion about how the Civil War could have been avoided. Have students create a list of historical causes of the Civil War along with specific actions taken to help avoid or cause the war.

---

assailed, it will but remain for us, with firm resolve, to appeal to arms, and invoke the blessing of Providence on a just cause. . . .

Actuated solely by the desire to preserve our own rights and promote our own welfare, the separation of the Confederate States has been marked by no aggression upon others, and followed by no domestic convulsion. Our industrial pursuits have received no check—the cultivation of our fields has progressed as heretofore—and even should we be involved in war, there would be no considerable diminution in the production of the staples which have constituted our exports, and in which the commercial world has an interest scarcely less than our own. This common interest of the producer and consumer, can only be interrupted by exterior force, which should obstruct its transmission [of our staples] to foreign markets—a course of conduct which would be as unjust toward us as it would be detrimental to manufacturing and commercial interests abroad. Should reason guide the action of the Government from which we have separated, a policy so detrimental to the civilized world, the Northern States included, could not be dictated by even the strongest desire to inflict injury upon us; but if otherwise, a terrible responsibility will rest upon it, and the suffering of millions will bear testimony to the folly and wickedness of our aggressors. In the mean time, there will remain to us, besides the ordinary means before suggested, the well-known resources for retaliation upon the commerce of an enemy."

Questions for Analysis
1. Identify Davis's primary argument in this speech.
2. Describe how Davis characterizes the relationship between the Confederacy and the Union.
3. Explain the historical situation that contributed to Davis's claim that war will ultimately undermine the economies of the North and of "civilized" nations "abroad."

President Buchanan did nothing to stop the secession movement. His cabinet included three secessionists and two unionists, one of whom resigned in frustration over Buchanan's failure to act. But Washington, D.C. was filled with southern sympathizers, who urged caution on an already timid president. Although some northerners were shocked by the decision of South Carolina and its allies, many others supported their right to leave or believed they would return to the Union when they realized they could not survive economically on their own. Moreover, with Virginia, Maryland, and other Upper South slave states still part of the nation, the secession movement seemed unlikely to succeed.

In the midst of the crisis, Kentucky senator John Crittenden proposed a compromise that gained significant support. Indeed, Congress approved the first part of his plan, which called for a constitutional amendment to protect slavery from federal interference in any state where it already existed. But the second part of the **Crittenden Plan** failed to win Republican votes. It would have extended the Missouri Compromise line (latitude 36°30′) to the California border and barred slavery north of that line. South of that line, however, slavery would be protected, including in any territories "acquired hereafter." Fearing that passage would encourage southern planters to again seek territory in Cuba, Mexico, or Central America, Republicans in

Crittenden Plan A political compromise over slavery, which failed after seven southern states seceded from the Union in early 1861. It would have protected slavery from federal interference where it already existed and extended the Missouri Compromise line to California.

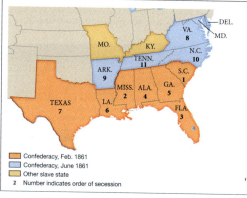

◀ **MAP 5.5 The Confederacy** Seven states in the Lower South seceded from the United States and formed the Confederate States of America in February 1861. While the original Confederacy was too limited in population and resources to defend itself against the U.S. government, its leaders hoped that other slave states would soon join them. **What factors best explain why these were the first states to secede from the Union?**

TEACHING IDEA

Check for Understanding

After students view Map 5.5, have them complete a quick two-minute writing exercise, in which they explain why the "Deep South" were the first southern states to secede, while the Upper South was reluctant to secede initially. Have students share their answers in small groups or as a class to gauge for understanding.

Congress rejected the proposal. Despite the hopes of the Buchanan administration, it was becoming apparent that compromise was impossible.

REVIEW

- Why did many southerners believe that the election of Abraham Lincoln was cause for secession?

AP® WRITING HISTORICALLY — Short-Answer Question Practice

ACTIVITY

Read the following question carefully and write a short response. Use complete sentences.

Using the following excerpts, answer (a), (b), and (c).

Source: Michael P. Johnson, *Toward a Patriarchal Republic: The Secession of Georgia*, 1977

"Secession was the ultimate test of the hegemony of slaveholders. Yet secession was necessary precisely because the hegemony of slaveholders was not secure. According to secessionists, . . . secession was necessary because of the internal divisions within the South [over] the degree to which the slaveholding minority could have its way in a government based ultimately on manhood suffrage. In particular, secessionists feared that many southerners would be receptive to Republican offers of patronage and would become the nucleus of a southern Republican party. . . .

In Georgia, secessionists translated that fear into a double revolution: a revolution for home rule—to eliminate the external threat; and a conservative revolution for those who ruled at home—to prevent the political realization of the internal threat. Men with conservative social and political ideas were instrumental not only in creating the small electoral margin that secessionists enjoyed in Georgia, but also in the definition and direction of the second revolution. The actions of the secession convention, including the new state constitution which they drafted, . . . represented an attempt to preserve the social status quo by reconciling the tension between the slaveholding minority and the enfranchised slaveless majority. . . .

Secession was [thus] driven by political conflict not only between the South and the North but also between the black belt and the upcountry, slaveholders and nonslaveholders, and those who feared democracy and those who valued it."

Source: J. Mills Thornton, *Politics and Power in a Slave Society: Alabama, 1800–1860*, 1978

"Antebellum Alabama was . . . obsessed with the idea of slavery. . . . [T]he fear of an imminent loss of freedom was a part of the inheritance which Alabama's citizens had received from their Revolutionary forebears. . . . [T]his tradition was lent considerable urgency by a daily familiarity with black slavery, . . . [B]ecause servility excluded one from [citizen]ship, . . . an Alabamian . . . [had] to prove his worth—his claim to possess the qualities of a free man—constantly, both to his fellows and to himself. . . . [S]lavery guaranteed, so it was believed, that very few white men would ever have to depend directly upon other white men for their sustenance. . . . [Thus,] the existence of slavery . . . came to seem an essential bulwark of freedom. . . .

[D]uring the 1850s, ... [Alabama's] Government at all levels became much more active; its expenditures increased enormously. . . . Control of the political mechanism began slipping from the hands of poorer citizens, as the influence of great planters . . . [increased in] significance. . . ."

(Continued)

TRM Suggested Responses to Questions

BUILDING AP® SKILLS

Making Connections

Have students complete a HIPP analysis for both Johnson's and Thornton's documents (see page 8 for a refresher). Once they have finished, students should complete a Venn diagram. The College Board often asks for students to address both similarities and differences on the AP® exam. When presented with two documents, students should be encouraged to practice this vital skill.

TEACHING IDEA

AP® Writing Historically Review

In the secondary source excerpts provided for Short-Answer Questions students can count on the fact that the interpretation will be visible. This might seem obvious, but too often students read the excerpts with the thought that each statement is of equal value. To encourage a discrete read, consider having groups of three or four students select three quotes from each excerpt that they think are illustrative of the overall interpretation. After they record the three quotes on poster paper, ask students to write a two or three sentence statement about what the argument is for each excerpt. This process will encourage a more thoughtful read of the excerpts and more accurate answers.

TEACHING IDEA

Check for Understanding

After students answer the three sections to the question at the end of Module 5-3, have students share their answers with a partner or class to gauge for understanding. Remember to seek out additional questions from the College Board's question bank in AP® Classroom (apcentral.collegeboard.org).

> [A]t this time, however, leadership within the [dominant] Democratic party . . . was passing to a second generation of politicians, less sensitive to the attitudes and apprehensions of the masses. . . . Only the villains offered by the southern rights advocates among them seemed capable of striking fire with the voters. . . . If Republicans controlled the federal government, [they argued], a southerner would be able to go to the territories only if he were willing to abandon a truly egalitarian, democratic world [rooted in slavery] for a hierarchical, elitist one, on the northern model. . . ."

a. Briefly describe ONE major difference between Johnson's and Thornton's historical interpretations of the reasons behind secession.
b. Briefly explain how ONE specific cause of secession from the period 1848–1860 that is not explicitly mentioned in the excerpts could be used to support Johnson's argument.
c. Briefly explain how ONE specific cause of secession from the period 1848–1860 that is not explicitly mentioned in the excerpts could be used to support Thornton's argument.

Module 5-4

Disunion and War

LEARNING TARGETS

By the end of this module, you should be able to:
- Explain the various factors that contributed to early southern success during the Civil War.
- Explain how Lincoln's leadership affected Northerners' views on slavery over the course of the war.
- Explain the contributions of American Indians, females, and African Americans to the Civil War.
- Explain how various groups' contributions to the war changed during the first two years of the conflict.

THEMATIC FOCUS
America in the World

During the Civil War, the Union and the Confederacy increasingly depended upon commitment from their citizens, though both faced domestic opposition. At the onset of the war, the South won a number of battles.

HISTORICAL REASONING FOCUS
Comparison
Continuity and Change

TASK ▶ As you read this module, consider the extent to which the strategies of both the Union and the Confederacy changed during the early years of the war.

When Abraham Lincoln took office, seven states in the Lower South had already formed the Confederate States of America, and more states threatened to secede. Lincoln had promised not to interfere with slavery where it existed, but many southern whites doubted such assurances. By seceding, southern slaveholders also proclaimed their unwillingness to become a permanent minority in the nation. Still, not all slave states were yet willing to cut their ties to the nation. Northerners, too, disagreed about the appropriate response to secession. Once fighting erupted, however, preparations for war became the primary focus in both the Union and the Confederacy.

The South Embraces Secession

Confederate president Jefferson Davis joined other planters in arguing that Lincoln's victory jeopardized the future of slavery and that secession was therefore a necessity. Advocates of secession contended that the federal government had failed to implement fully the Fugitive Slave Act and the *Dred Scott* decision. They were convinced that a Republican administration would do even less to support southern interests. White Southerners also feared that Republicans might inspire a massive uprising of enslaved people, and secession allowed whites to maintain control over the South's black population.

Still, when Lincoln was inaugurated, some legislators in the Upper South hoped a compromise could be reached, and the president hoped to bring the Confederates back into the Union without using military force. Most northern merchants, manufacturers, and bankers approved, wanting to maintain their economic ties to southern planters. Yet Lincoln also realized he must demonstrate Union strength to curtail further secessions. He focused on **Fort Sumter** in South Carolina's Charleston harbor, where a small Union garrison was running low on food and medicine. On April 8, 1861, Lincoln dispatched ships to the fort but promised to use force only if the Confederates blocked his peaceful effort to send supplies.

Fort Sumter Union fort that guarded the harbor in Charleston, South Carolina. The Confederacy's decision to fire on the fort and block resupply in April 1861 marked the beginning of the Civil War.

TRM Suggested Responses to Questions

TEACHING IDEA
AP® Central

Remember to consult the AP® U.S. History skills and themes found on the College Board website often (apcentral.collegeboard.org). In reviewing the themes and skills required for the AP® exam, note that there are few expectations of students having specific exposure to battles and general strategies within any wars. As such, it is advised not to over-teach this material. Students often have an interest in the Civil War and its major characters and specific events. In general, the causes and effects are the basic information needed for any war covered in this course. Look for the social and political trends within the war and continue to look toward lasting changes due to the Civil War.

BUILDING AP® SKILLS
Sourcing and Situation

Using Jefferson Davis's and Abraham Lincoln's inauguration addresses (both are readily available through an online search) have students use HIPP to analyze both documents (a refresher on HIPP can be found on page 8). Then have students complete a Venn diagram. Answers will vary, but students should be able to make many parallels between the two speeches. Have students look for the tone of each speech along with any bias they find. Class discussion should yield insight into student understanding of both speeches.

TEACHING IDEA
Incorporating Websites

Fort Sumter is an important site in the Civil War that students can visit virtually online. The National Parks Service has set up a website with informational videos, stories, and a virtual tour (nps.gov). Have students visit the site and then create a KWL chart (a refresher on KWL can be found on page 371). The four-minute informational video, "Fort Sumter," gives a solid background to the battle and its significance.

Period 5: 1844–1877

MODULE 5-4 Disunion and War

BUILDING AP® SKILLS

Making Connections

Remind students of the duties and powers within the Constitution given to the president as commander in chief during times of peace and times of war. Discuss some of the extra powers afforded to presidents during times of war as a preview to actions soon to be taken by President Lincoln.

EXPLORING AP® THEMES

Politics and Power

After students have reviewed the actions taken by President Lincoln at the beginning of the Civil War, have students list these actions and address if these would be allowable during non-war periods.

TEACHING IDEA

Check for Understanding

After students view the figure, "Economies of the North and South, 1860," have a brief discussion on what the chart illuminates prior to the start of the war. Charts give many students difficulties on the national AP® exam, so practice reviewing charts and graphs whenever possible within class and on assessments. Make sure that students know to emphasize trends from quantitative sources. Charts, graphs, and graphics can make great warmup or exit tickets as forms of practice.

> " Our new government is founded upon exactly the opposite idea [of racial equality]; its foundations are laid, its corner-stone rests, upon the great truth that the negro is not equal to the white man; that slavery subordination to the superior race is his natural and normal condition. This, our new government, is the first, in the history of the world, based upon this great physical, philosophical, and moral truth. "
>
> — Alexander Stephens, Vice President of the Confederacy, 1861

The Confederate government would now have to choose. It could attack the Union vessels and bear responsibility for starting a war or permit a "foreign power" to maintain a fort in its territory. President Davis and his advisers chose the aggressive course, demanding Fort Sumter's immediate and unconditional surrender. The commanding officer refused, and on April 12 Confederate guns opened fire. Two days later, Fort Sumter surrendered. On April 15, Lincoln called for 75,000 volunteers to put down the southern insurrection.

These hostilities led whites in the Upper South to reconsider secession. Some small farmers and landless whites were drawn to Republican promises of free labor and free soil and remained suspicious of the goals and power of secessionist planters. Yet the vast majority of southern whites, rich and poor, defined their liberty in relation to black bondage. They feared that Republicans would free enslaved people and introduce racial amalgamation, the mixing of white and black people, in the South.

Fearing more secessions, Lincoln used the powers of his office to keep the border states that allowed slavery — Maryland, Delaware, Missouri, and Kentucky — in the Union. He waived the right of habeas corpus (which protects citizens against arbitrary arrest and detention), jailed secessionists, arrested state legislators, and limited freedom of the press. However, four other slave states — North Carolina, Virginia, Tennessee, and Arkansas — seceded. Virginia, with its strategic location near the nation's capital, was by far the most significant. Richmond, which would soon become the capital of the Confederacy, was also home to the South's largest iron manufacturer, which could produce weapons and munitions.

While Northerners differed over how to respond when the first seven states seceded, the firing on Fort Sumter prompted most to line up behind Lincoln's call for war. Manufacturers and merchants, once intent on maintaining commercial links with the South, now rushed to support the president, while northern workers, including immigrants, responded to Lincoln's call for volunteers. They assumed that the Union, with its greater resources and manpower, could quickly set the nation right. New York editor Horace Greeley proclaimed, "Jeff Davis and Co. will be swingin' from the battlements at Washington at least by the 4th of July."

REVIEW

- How did northern public opinion about southern secession change after the firing on Fort Sumter?

Both Sides Prepare for War

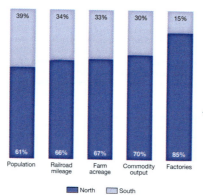

Population	Railroad mileage	Farm acreage	Commodity output	Factories
39%	34%	33%	30%	15%
61%	66%	67%	70%	85%

■ North   ■ South

At the onset of the war, the Union certainly held a decided advantage in resources and population. The Union states held more than 60 percent of the U.S. population, and the Confederate population included several million enslaved people who would not be armed for combat. The Union also far outstripped the Confederacy in manufacturing and even led the South in agricultural production. The North's many miles of railroad track ensured greater ease in moving troops and supplies. And the Union could launch far more ships to blockade southern ports.

◀ **Economies of the North and South, 1860** This figure provides graphic testimony to the enormous advantages in resources the North held on the eve of the Civil War. The North led the South in population, farm acreage, and railroad mileage as well as factories and commodity output. **Over four years of war, how might the differences in each area of this graph affect the ability of the Union and the Confederacy to pursue their objectives?**

Source: Data from Stanley Engerman, "The Economic Impact of the Civil War," in *The Reinterpretation of American Economic History*, ed. Robert W. Fogel and Stanley Engerman (New York: Harper and Row, 1971).

Yet Union forces were less prepared for war than the Confederates, who had been organizing troops and gathering munitions for months. To match their efforts, Winfield Scott, general in chief of the U.S. army, told Lincoln he would need at least 300,000 men committed to serve for two or three years. Scott believed that massing such huge numbers of soldiers would force the Confederacy to negotiate a peace. But fearing to unnerve Northerners, the president asked for only 75,000 volunteers for three months. Moreover, rather than forming a powerful national army led by seasoned officers, Lincoln left recruitment, organization, and training largely to the states. The result was disorganization and the appointment of officers based more on political connections than military expertise.

Confederate leaders also initially relied on state militia units and volunteers, but they prepared for a prolonged war from the start. Before the firing on Fort Sumter, President Davis signed up 100,000 volunteers for a year's service. The labor provided by enslaved people allowed a large proportion of white working-age men to volunteer for military service. And Southerners knew they were likely to be fighting mainly on home territory, where they had expert knowledge of the terrain. When the final four states joined the Confederacy, the southern army also gained important military leadership. It ultimately recruited 280 West Point graduates, including Robert E. Lee, Thomas "Stonewall" Jackson, James Longstreet, and others who had proved their mettle in the Mexican-American War.

The South's advantages were apparent in the first major battle of the war. And Confederate troops were also aided by information on Union plans sent by Rose Greenhow, a Washington, D.C. socialite who spied for the Confederacy during the war. When 30,000 Union troops marched on northern Virginia on July 21, 1861, Confederate forces were ready. At the **Battle of Bull Run** (or **Manassas**), later known as the First Battle of Bull Run, 22,000 Confederates repelled the Union attack. Civilians from Washington who traveled to the battle site to view the combat had to flee for their lives to escape Confederate artillery.

Despite Union defeats at Bull Run and then at Wilson's Creek, Missouri in August 1861, the Confederate army did not launch major strikes against Union forces. Meanwhile the Union navy began blockading the South's deepwater ports. By the time the armies settled into winter camps in 1861–1862, both sides had come to realize that the war was likely to be a long and costly struggle.

Battle of Bull Run (First Manassas) First major battle of the Civil War at which Confederate troops defeated Union forces in July 1861.

AP® TIP
Analyze how the First Battle of Bull Run shaped perceptions and expectations of the Civil War in both the North and the South.

▲ **Battle of Wilson's Creek** This colored lithograph depicts the First Iowa Regiment, led by General Nathaniel Lyon, charging Confederate forces at the Battle of Wilson's Creek, Missouri on August 10, 1861. The Confederates won the battle, and Lyon, on the ground here, became the first Union general to die in the war. The lithograph was created in 1893 based on a wartime sketch. **What does this image reveal about popular notions of war early in the conflict?**

BUILDING AP® SKILLS

Causation

Have students make a strengths and weaknesses chart for both the North and South as they entered the Civil War. Topics might include: *governmental stability*, *financial security*, *industry output*, *population (size and enslavement status)*, *foreign policy*, *public support*, *motivations*, *effectiveness of military leaders*, and *readiness to fight*.

TRM Find **Handout 5.4 – Pre-Civil War Strengths and Weaknesses** in the Teacher's Resource Materials.

TEACHING IDEA

Digging Deeper: Wilmer McLean

Relate the story of Wilmer McLean to students and his quote, "The war began in my front yard and ended in my front parlor." Discuss with students how this war impacted families and civilians on a scale like no other war in U.S. history. Wilmer McLean's life story can be found on the History Channel's website by searching for his name (history.com).

Period 5: 1844–1877

MODULE 5-4 Disunion and War

AP® ANALYZING SOURCES

Source: Robert Toombs, *Speech to the Georgia General Assembly*, 1860

"[T]he South at all times demanded nothing but equality in the common territories, equal enjoyment of them with their property, to that extended to Northern citizens and their property—nothing more.... In 1790 we had less than eight hundred thousand slaves. Under our mild and humane administration of the system they have increased above four millions. The country has expanded to meet this growing want, and Florida, Alabama, Mississippi, Louisiana, Texas, Arkansas, Kentucky, Tennessee, and Missouri have received this increasing tide of African labor; before the end of this century, at precisely the same rate of increase, the Africans among us in a subordinate condition will amount to eleven millions of persons. What shall be done with them? We must expand or perish.... The North understand it better—they have told us for twenty years that their object was to pen up slavery within its present limits—surround it with a border of free States, and like the scorpion surrounded with fire, they will make it sting itself to death."

Questions for Analysis
1. Identify Toombs's main argument in this speech.
2. Explain how Toombs supports his argument in this excerpt.
3. Evaluate the extent to which Toombs's claims in this speech represent a continuation of pre-Civil War pro-slavery arguments.

REVIEW

What advantages and disadvantages did each side have at the onset of the Civil War?

Military and Political Conflicts, 1861–1863

The Union and the Confederacy faced very different tasks in the war. The South had to defend its territory and force the federal government to halt military action. The North had a more complicated challenge. Initially, northern political leaders believed that secession was driven mainly by slaveholders and that high death rates and destruction of property would only alienate southern white people who favored reconciliation. But such a policy depended on early Union victories. With early defeats, it was clear the North would have to invade the South and isolate it from potential allies abroad. At the same time, most northern politicians believed that the nation could be reunited without abolishing slavery while abolitionists argued that only emancipation could resolve the problems that led to war. Meanwhile, enslaved African Americans immediately looked for ways to loosen their bonds.

The outbreak of war also intensified debates over abolition. Some 225,000 African Americans lived in the free states, and many offered their services in an effort to end slavery. African American leaders in Cleveland proclaimed, "Today, as in the times of '76, we are ready to go forth and do battle in the common cause of our country." But Secretary of War Simon Cameron had no intention of calling up black soldiers.

Northern optimism about a quick victory contributed to the rejection of African American volunteers. Union leaders feared that white men would not enlist if they had to serve alongside African Americans. In addition, Lincoln and his advisers were initially wary of letting a war to preserve the Union become a war against slavery, and they feared that any further threat to slavery might drive the four slave states that remained in the Union into the Confederacy. This political strategy, however, depended on quick and overwhelming victories; and with U.S. soldiers posted mainly on the western frontier and a third of officers joining the Confederacy, victories were few.

> "If I could save the Union without freeing *any* slave, I would do it; and if I could save it by freeing *all* the slaves, I would do it."
> —Abraham Lincoln, 1862

TRM Suggested Responses to Questions

TRM Module 5.4 AP® Analyzing Sources Handout 1

TEACHING IDEA

Incorporating Websites

African Americans have served, fought, and died in every American war dating back to the foundation of the country. Have students visit the Library of Congress website and search for "African-American Soldiers During the Civil War" (loc.gov). From this timeline page, students will find primary resources ranging from pictures to speeches and personal diaries. Have students work in small groups to create a visual representation of some of the information that they acquire from these resources. Each group will find a variety of resources and information to share. By summarizing and placing the information on a poster or other visual, students will have to create succinct summaries based on their major impressions. Have groups view each poster to gain a broader range of information.

TEACHING IDEA

Incorporating Websites

The National Archives has many collections of accounts from African American soldiers during the Civil War (archives.gov). Have students search for "Black Soldiers in the U.S. Military During the Civil War" and look through the many accompanying pages and resources. Students should create a KWL chart in regards to African American soldiers' experiences during the Civil War (a refresher of KWL can be found on page 371). Answers will vary but students should share their findings with the class by writing a summary of the motivations for African Americans to enlist and fight in the Civil War, and the conditions they experienced.

Nonetheless, a rush of volunteers allowed Union troops to push into Virginia while the Union navy captured crucial islands along the Confederate coast.

Wherever Union forces appeared in the South, enslaved people began considering freedom as a possibility. Enslaved people living near battle sites circulated information on Union troop movements. Then, as planters in Virginia began sending enslaved men to more distant plantations for fear of losing them, some managed to flee and headed to Union camps. Many slaveholders tracked fugitives behind Union lines and demanded their return. Some Union commanders denied enslaved people entrance or returned them to slaveholders. However, a few Union officers recognized these fugitives' value: They knew the local geography well, could dig trenches and provide other services, and drained the Confederate labor supply. At the Union outpost at Fort Monroe, Virginia in May 1861, General Benjamin Butler offered military protection to fugitives from slavery. He claimed them as **contraband** of war: property forfeited by the act of rebellion.

Lincoln endorsed Butler's policy because it allowed the Union to strike at the institution of slavery without proclaiming a general emancipation that might prompt border states where slavery remained legal to secede. Congress expanded Butler's policy in August 1861 by passing a **confiscation act**. It proclaimed that any enslaved people who were forced to work for the Confederate army would no longer be bound to slaveholders. Although it was far from a clear-cut declaration of freedom, the act spurred the hopes of northern abolitionists and many enslaved people in the South.

While Northerners continued to debate African Americans' role in the war effort, the Union army recruited a wide array of other ethnic and racial groups, including American Indians. Unlike black people, however, American Indians did not necessarily all support the Union. The Comanche negotiated with both Union and Confederate agents while raiding the Texas frontier for horses and cattle. The Confederacy gained significant support from slaveholding American Indians who had earlier been removed from the Southeast. The Cherokee split over the war as they had over removal. General Stand Watie led a pan-Indian force into battle for the Confederates. Initially John Ross joined the Confederates as well, but later he led a group of Cherokee into Union army ranks alongside the Osage, Delaware, Seneca, and other American Indian nations. Ely Parker, a Seneca sachem and engineer, became a lieutenant colonel in the Union army, serving with General Ulysses S. Grant.

Likewise, American Indians played crucial roles in a number of important early battles, particularly on the Confederate side. Cherokee and Seminole warriors fought valiantly with Confederates at the Battle of Pea Ridge in Tennessee in March 1862, but were defeated by a smaller but better supplied Union force. In late summer that same year, American Indians contributed to the Confederate efforts in major battles in Virginia and Maryland. The Confederate army recruited Mexican-American soldiers as well, hoping to gain control of the West's gold and silver mines. But a Union victory gained by a troop of Colorado miners at Glorieta Pass near Sante Fe, New Mexico ended that Confederate dream.

A series of Union military defeats in 1862 helped transform the attitudes of northern whites about slavery and about the place of African Americans in the war effort. That spring, Confederate general Stonewall Jackson won stunning victories against three Union armies in Virginia's Shenandoah Valley. That June and July, General Robert E. Lee fought a much better-equipped Union army under General George B. McClellan to a standstill in the Seven Days Battle near Richmond. Then in August, Lee, Jackson, and General James Longstreet joined together to defeat Union troops at the **Second Battle of Bull Run**.

As the war turned against the North, the North turned against slavery. In April 1862 Congress had approved a measure to abolish slavery in the District of Columbia, symbolizing a significant shift in Union sentiment. During that bloody summer, Congress passed a second confiscation act, declaring that the people held in slavery by anyone who supported the Confederacy should be "forever free of their servitude, and not again held as slaves." In July Congress also approved a militia act that allowed African Americans to serve in "any military or naval service for which they may be found competent."

Support for the 1862 militia act built on Union victories as well as defeats. In April 1862 a Union blockade led to the capture of New Orleans, while the **Battle of Shiloh** in Tennessee provided the army entrée to the Mississippi valley. There Union troops came face-to-face with slavery. Few of these soldiers were abolitionists, but many were shocked by what they saw, including instruments used to torture enslaved people. Southern black people also provided important intelligence to northern officers, making clear their value to the Union war effort.

---

contraband Term first used by Union general Benjamin Butler in May 1861 to describe enslaved people who had fled to Union lines to obtain freedom. By designating enslaved people as property forfeited by the act of rebellion, the Union was able to strike at slavery without proclaiming a general emancipation.

confiscation acts Laws passed by Congress during the Civil War that authorized the confiscation of Confederate property. Under the confiscation acts, any enslaved people who were forced to work for the Confederate army would no longer be bound to slaveholders.

AP® TIP
Be sure that you can explain how the outcomes of early Civil War battles affected northern attitudes toward slavery.

TEACHING IDEA

Digging Deeper: John Ross

The Civil War introduces many intriguing people to American history. Have students do a quick five-minute research online for John Ross. Students should find that Ross was instrumental in the fight against the removal of Cherokee American Indians during the Trail of Tears in the 1830s, then regains the national spotlight by fighting alongside Cherokee American Indians during the Civil War for both the Union and the Confederacy.

APPLY THE TIP

Have students define "contraband" as applied to enslaved people. Clarify that when Union officers labeled enslaved peoples as contraband, they were giving a different name to a continued form of enslavement and denying basic human rights to the former enslaved refugees.

Period 5: 1844–1877

MODULE 5-4 Disunion and War

EXPLORING AP® THEMES
Geography and the Environment

As students study Map 5.6, discuss the impact of centering the early Civil War battle locations around the coastline and within the northern region of the South. In reviewing the strategies of the North and South upon entering the war, how successful was the war by the end of 1862? Answers will vary, but the North needed to surround and invade the South, while the South planned on waiting out the North and hoping for foreign recognition.

EXPLORING AP® THEMES
Geography and the Environment

Have students review Map 5.6 and locate New Orleans and the battle site of Shiloh. Discuss the historical importance of New Orleans, including during the War of 1812 and the Louisiana Purchase. Ask students to list possible theories as to why this city has been so important to the development of the United States.

TEACHING IDEA
Incorporating Videos

The 1989 film *Glory* is based upon the hardships faced by the African American soldiers in the 54th Massachusetts Infantry Regiment. YouTube has many short highlight clips of this impactful movie. Search for the clips of the battle of Fort Wagner and the battle of Shiloh. Both scenes will encourage student discussion and highlight some of the brutal realities soldiers faced during the Civil War.

▲ **MAP 5.6 Early Civil War Battles, 1861–1862** In 1861 and 1862, the Confederate army stunned Union forces with a series of dramatic victories in Virginia and Missouri. However, the Union army won a crucial victory at Antietam (Sharpsburg); gained control of Confederate territory in Tennessee, Arkansas, and Mississippi; fended off Confederate efforts to gain New Mexico Territory; and established a successful naval blockade of Confederate ports. **What advantages did Union forces have during this period, even as they were losing battles?**

> "Visited during the day several plantations and saw enough of the horrors of slavery to make one an Abolitionist forever. On each plantation . . . [there] are] whips and other instruments of torture, for the benefit of those who had been guilty of loving liberty more than life."
>
> Rufus Kinsley, Union soldier, 1862

Whether in victory or defeat, rising death tolls increased support for African American enlistment. The bloodshed of the Battle of Shiloh, the deadliest battle in American history to that point, shocked both North and South. Earlier battles had resulted in a few hundred or perhaps a few thousand casualties; at Shiloh the toll was more than 23,000. As the war continued, such brutal battles became routine. The Union army would need every available man — white, black, and American Indian — to sustain its effort against the Confederates.

American Indian regiments had already proven themselves in battle, and African Americans soon followed suit. In October 1862 a group of black soldiers in the First Kansas Colored Volunteers repulsed Confederates at a battle in Missouri. In the South, white abolitionists serving as Union officers organized former enslaved men into units like the First South Carolina Volunteers in January 1863. A few months later, another black regiment — the Massachusetts Fifty-fourth — attracted recruits from across the North, including Frederick Douglass's three sons. For the next two years, tens of thousands of African American soldiers fought valiantly in dozens of battles.

REVIEW

- In what ways did white Americans' treatment of American Indians and African Americans change over the course of the Civil War?
- In what ways did this treatment remain the same?

Union Politicians and Emancipation

> "You will observe that I propose no crusade for abolition. [Emancipation] is to be presented strictly as a measure of military necessity."
>
> Charles Sumner, Massachusetts Senator, 1862

By the fall of 1862, African Americans and abolitionists had gained widespread support for emancipation as a necessary goal of the war. Lincoln and his cabinet realized that embracing abolition as a war aim would likely prevent international recognition of southern independence. Still, some Union politicians feared that emancipation might arouse deep animosity in the slaveholding border states and drive them from the Union.

From the Confederate perspective, international recognition was critical. Support from European nations might persuade the North to accept southern independence. More immediately, recognition would ensure markets for southern agriculture and access to manufactured goods and war materiel. Confederate officials were especially focused on Britain, the leading market for cotton and a leading producer of industrial products. President Davis considered sending Rose Greenhow to England to promote the Confederate cause.

Fearing that the British might capitulate to Confederate pressure, abolitionist lecturers toured Britain, reminding residents of their early leadership in the antislavery cause. The Union's formal

AP® ANALYZING SOURCES

Source: President Abraham Lincoln, *Letter to Horace Greeley*, 1862

"Executive Mansion, Washington,
August 22, 1862.
Hon. Horace Greeley—

Dear Sir:
I have just read yours of the 19th, addressed to myself through the New York *Tribune*....
As to the policy I 'seem to be pursuing,' as you say, I have not meant to leave any one in doubt.
I would save the Union. I would save it the shortest way under the Constitution. The sooner the National authority can be restored, the nearer the Union will be 'the Union as it was.' If there be those who would not save the Union unless they could at the same time *save* Slavery, I do not agree with them. If there be those who would not save the Union unless they could at the same time *destroy* Slavery, I do not agree with them. My paramount object in this struggle *is* to save the Union, and is *not* either to save or to destroy Slavery. If I could save the Union without freeing *any* slave, I would do it; and if I could save it by freeing *all* the slaves, I would do it; and if I could save it by freeing some and leaving others alone, I would also do that. What I do about Slavery, and the colored race, I do because I believe it helps to save the Union; and what I forbear, I forbear because I do *not* believe it would help to save the Union. I shall do *less* whenever I shall believe what I am doing hurts the cause, and I shall do *more* whenever I shall believe doing more will help the cause. I shall try to correct errors when shown to be errors; and I shall adopt new views so fast as they shall appear to be true views. I have here stated my purpose according to my view of *official* duty; and I intend no modification of my oft-expressed *personal* wish that all men, every-where, could be free.

Yours,
a. lincoln."

Questions for Analysis

1. Identify the relationship Lincoln sees between emancipation and saving the Union.
2. Explain what Lincoln means when he says, "If I could save the Union without freeing *any* slave, I would do it; and if I could save it by freeing *all* the slaves, I would do it."
3. Evaluate the extent to which Lincoln's position in this letter represents a change from his previous political positions.

BUILDING AP® SKILLS

Making Connections

The Emancipation Proclamation created many changes within the U.S. and abroad. Remind students that the Emancipation Proclamation is a diplomatic document in many ways. Have students read Christopher Teal's 2013 article "The Emancipation Proclamation and U.S. Foreign Policy" found on American Diplomacy's website (americandiplomacy.web.unc.edu). Have students complete a HIPP analysis of the document, then write a 3-5 sentence summary of the document (a refresher on HIPP can be found on page 8). Stress the significance of the document on England and its decision not to recognize and ultimately support the South during America's Civil War.

TRM Suggested Responses to Questions

TRM Module 5.4 AP® Analyzing Sources Handout 2

BUILDING AP® SKILLS

Claims and Evidence in Sources

After students have read "Letter to Horace Greeley," have students work in small groups to decide what Lincoln's objectives for the country were at the beginning of the Civil War. Have a class discussion highlighting Lincoln's views as president as opposed to his expressed personal outlook. Answers will vary, but note that Lincoln has not yet become the "great emancipator" and students need to recognize this change as it develops.

TEACHING IDEA

Digging Deeper: The Battle of Antietam

Have students briefly review the Battle of Antietam. The human cost of this battle is magnified by the fact that the North knew the South's plans by sheer luck. Copies of General Lee's orders for Antietam had been wrapped around cigars and were lost by Confederate General D.H. Hill only to be discovered by Union troops the following day. Information on this event can be found on the History Channel's website by searching for "Union troops discover Rebels' Antietam battle plan" (history.com).

BUILDING AP® SKILLS

Contextualization

Even though the Emancipation Proclamation is a powerful document, have students address some of its limitations. Why did Lincoln only free enslaved peoples in areas still in open rebellion and not within all of the United States? Encourage students to read further on this topic through the Khan Academy by searching for "Emancipation Proclamation" (khanacademy.org).

EXPLORING AP® THEMES

Politics and Power

A presidential proclamation is a powerful tool used by presidents. President Lincoln's Emancipation Proclamation likewise was a powerful tool for change. Have students read the Emancipation Proclamation, which can be found on the National Archives' website (archives.gov). In small groups ask students to annotate the document, looking for the justifications of its creation and what its intended purpose was. Have groups address what this document shows about the power of presidents during times of war and be able to articulate the actions outlined within the document.

▲ **President Lincoln Presenting the Emancipation Proclamation to His Cabinet** In this engraving, Lincoln reads the draft of his Emancipation Proclamation to his cabinet in September 1862. On the left are Secretary of War Edwin Stanton (seated) and Secretary of the Treasury Salmon P. Chase, the two strongest supporters of the proclamation. Postmaster General Montgomery Blair and Attorney General Edward Bates (seated), who opposed the plan, are on the right. **What point might the artist of this engraving have made by arranging its subjects in this way?**

Battle of Antietam September 1862 battle in Sharpsburg, Maryland. While it remains the bloodiest single day in U.S. military history, it gave Abraham Lincoln the victory he sought before announcing the Emancipation Proclamation.

Emancipation Proclamation January 1, 1863 proclamation that declared all enslaved people in areas still in rebellion "forever free." While stopping short of abolishing slavery outright, the Emancipation Proclamation was, nonetheless, seen by both black people and white abolitionists as a great victory.

commitment to emancipation would certainly increase British support for its position and prevent diplomatic recognition of the Confederacy. By the summer of 1862, Lincoln was convinced, but he wanted to wait for a military victory before making a formal announcement regarding emancipation.

Instead, the Union suffered a series of defeats that summer, and Lee marched his army into Union territory in Maryland. On September 17, Longstreet joined Lee in a fierce battle along Antietam Creek as Union troops brought the Confederate advance to a standstill near the town of Sharpsburg. Union forces suffered more than 12,000 casualties and the Confederates more than 10,000, the bloodiest single day of battle in U.S. history. Yet because Lee and his army were forced to retreat, Lincoln claimed the **Battle of Antietam** as a great victory. Five days later, the president announced his preliminary **Emancipation Proclamation** to the assembled cabinet, promising to free enslaved people in all states still in rebellion by January 1863.

On January 1, 1863, Lincoln signed the final edict, proclaiming that enslaved people in areas still in rebellion were "forever free" and inviting them to enlist in the Union army. Over the next two years, tens of thousands of enslaved men fled southern plantations and fought in the Union Army alongside equal numbers of free black men who volunteered to ensure the Confederacy's defeat. Still, the proclamation was a moderate document in many ways. Its provisions exempted from emancipation the 450,000 enslaved people in the loyal border states, as well as more than 300,000 enslaved people in Union-occupied areas of Tennessee, Louisiana, and Virginia. The proclamation also justified the abolition of southern slavery on military, not moral, grounds. Despite its limits, the Emancipation Proclamation inspired joyous celebrations among free black people and white abolitionists, who viewed it as the first step toward slavery's final eradication.

AP® ANALYZING SOURCES

Source: The *Charleston Mercury*, "President Lincoln and His Scheme of Emancipation," 1862

"[T]he Constitution of a country ought to be, in the relations of this world, as sacred as the Bible is in those of the next. Yet Abolitionism teaches a man that there is a higher law than the Constitution of the country, or the Bible itself. Hence, their [unethical] aggressions upon the slave institution of the South, in spite of the Constitution, and even the plain dictates of interest itself. Hence President LINCOLN['s] Proclamation for the abolition of slavery in the Confederate States, without a particle of constitutional authority. . . . The truth is, his Proclamation is declarative for emancipation to all the slaves of the South. That is what . . . [it] signifies, and that is what he means by it. President LINCOLN is not such a fool as not to know that the emancipation of all the slaves in the South, belonging to the citizens of the Confederate States, is also an emancipation of all the slaves belonging to the few traitors who affect allegiance to the United States. . . . The fellow is a rogue. He wishes to disguise the scope and atrocity of his unconstitutional and fiendish policy. . . . If he can deprive white men in the United States of their liberties, whenever he pleases, why can he not liberate black men?"

Questions for Analysis
1. Identify the author's intended audience.
2. Describe the evidence the author uses to support his position on the Emancipation Proclamation.
3. Evaluate the extent to which the author considers the Emancipation Proclamation a continuation of Lincoln's previous policies.

TRM Suggested Responses to Questions

TRM Module 5.4 AP® Analyzing Sources Handout 3

REVIEW

What events led to the Emancipation Proclamation?

The Front and the Homefront

Few soldiers entered the conflict knowing what to expect. A young private wrote that his idea of combat had been that the soldiers "would all be in line, all standing in a nice level field fighting, a number of ladies taking care of the wounded, etc., etc., but it isn't so." Improved weaponry turned battles into scenes of bloody carnage. The shift from smoothbore muskets to rifles, which had grooves that spun the bullet, made weapons far more effective at longer distances. The use of minié balls — small bullets with a deep cavity that expanded upon firing — increased fatalities as well. By 1863 Union army sharpshooters acquired new repeating rifles with metal cartridges. With more accurate rifles and deadlier bullets, the rival armies increasingly relied on heavy fortifications, elaborate trenches, and distant mortar and artillery fire when they could. Still, casualties continued to rise, especially since the trenches served as breeding grounds for disease.

The hardships and discomforts of war extended beyond combat itself. As General Lee complained before Antietam, many soldiers fought in ragged uniforms and without shoes. Rations, too, ran short. Food was dispensed sporadically and was often spoiled. Many Union troops survived primarily on an unleavened biscuit called hardtack as well as small amounts of meat and beans and enormous quantities of coffee. Their diet improved over the course of the war, however, as the Union supply system grew more efficient while Confederate troops subsisted increasingly on cornmeal and fatty meat. As early as 1862, Confederate soldiers began gathering food from the haversacks of Union dead.

For every soldier who died as a result of combat, three died of disease. Measles, dysentery, typhoid, and malaria killed thousands who drank contaminated water, ate tainted food, and were exposed to the elements. And infected soldiers on both sides carried yellow fever and malaria into

TEACHING IDEA

Incorporating Videos

Have students watch the History Channel's "America: The Story of Us, Episode 5 'Civil War'" clip (available on YouTube; 00:00:00–00:11:02). The discussion on the Minié ball and human body is particularly enlightening.

TEACHING IDEA

Incorporating Videos

Have students view the History Channel's "America: The Story of Us, Episode 5 'Civil War'" clip dealing with medicine during the Civil War (available on YouTube; 00:26:00–00:37:07). There are many pictures, descriptions, and video clips available online dealing with medicine during the Civil War and the grim conditions of those injured or sick. Once students have viewed these clips, ask them to research Clara Barton on the National Women's History Museum's website (womenhistory.org). As a fun and creative activity, have students create a resume for Clara Barton or any of the many women who served in the Civil War. Students should know 2-3 specific women and their accomplishments during the Civil War.

Period 5: 1844–1877

MODULE 5-4 Disunion and War

towns where they built fortifications. Prisoner-of-war camps, like Andersonville in Georgia, were especially deadly locales. Debilitating fevers in a camp near Danville, Virginia spread to the town, killing civilians as well as soldiers.

The sufferings of African American troops were particularly severe. The death rate from disease for black Union soldiers was nearly three times greater than that for white Union soldiers, reflecting their poorer health upon enlistment, the hard labor they performed, and the minimal medical care they received in the field. Southern black men who began their army careers in contraband camps fared even worse, with a camp near Nashville losing a quarter of its residents to death in just three months in 1864.

For all soldiers, medical assistance was primitive. Antibiotics did not exist, antiseptics were still unknown, and anesthetics were scarce. Union medical care improved with the U.S. Sanitary Commission, which was established by the federal government in June 1861 to promote and coordinate better medical treatment for soldiers. Nonetheless, a commentator accurately described most field hospitals as "dirty dens of butchery and horror," where amputations often occurred with whiskey as the only anesthetic.

As the horrors of war sank in, large numbers of soldiers deserted or refused to reenlist. With volunteers declining and deserters increasing, both the Confederate and the Union governments were forced to institute conscription laws to draft men into service.

As the war dragged on, the North's economic advantages became more apparent. Initially, the effects of the war on northern industry had been little short of disastrous. Raw cotton for textiles disappeared, southern planters stopped ordering shoes, and trade fell off precipitously. By 1863, however, the northern economy was in high gear and could provide more arms, food, shoes, and clothing to its troops as well as for those back home. As cotton production declined, woolen manufacturing doubled; and northern iron and coal production increased 25 to 30 percent during the war. Northern factories turned out weapons and ammunition while shipyards built the fleets that blockaded southern ports.

These economic improvements were linked to a vast expansion in the federal government's activities. War Department orders fueled the industrial surge. It also created the U.S. Military Railroads unit to construct tracks in newly occupied southern territories and granted large contracts to northern railroads to carry troops and supplies. With southern Democrats out of federal office, Congress also raised tariffs on imported goods to protect northern industries. In addition, the government hired thousands of "sewing women," who were contracted to make uniforms for Union soldiers. Other women joined the federal labor force as clerical workers to sustain the expanding bureaucracy and the enormous amounts of government-generated paperwork.

That paperwork multiplied exponentially when the federal government created a national currency and a national banking system. Before the Civil War, private banks (chartered by the states) issued their own banknotes, which were used in most economic transactions. During the war, Congress revolutionized this system, giving the federal government the power to create currency, issue federal charters to banks, and take on national debt. The government then flooded the nation with treasury bills, commonly called greenbacks. The federal budget mushroomed as well — from $63 million in 1860 to nearly $1.3 billion in 1865. By the end of the war, the federal bureaucracy had become the nation's largest single employer.

Northern manufacturers faced one daunting problem: a shortage of labor. Over half a million workers left their jobs to serve in the Union army, and others were hired by the expanding federal bureaucracy. Manufacturers dealt with the problem primarily by mechanizing more tasks and by hiring more women and children, native-born and immigrant. Combining the lower wages paid to these workers with production speedups, manufacturers improved their profits while advancing the Union cause.

In the South, industry and cities grew as well. Although Southerners had gone to war to protect an essentially rural lifestyle, the war encouraged the growth of cities and industry. The creation of a large governmental and military bureaucracy brought thousands of Southerners to the Confederate capital of Richmond. As the war expanded, refugees also flooded into Atlanta, Savannah, Columbia, and Mobile.

Industrialization also contributed to urban growth. With the South unable to buy industrial goods from the North and limited in its trade with Europe, military necessity spurred southern

---

> **AP® TIP**
> Evaluate the ways in which the Civil War promoted federal power and an industrial economy in the United States.

industrialization Massive shift from artisanal and homemade goods to factory mass production that occurred during the mid-nineteenth century.

BUILDING AP® SKILLS

Making Connections

The conditions in the Confederate prisoner of war camps are well documented and widely available online. The Library of Congress has many of the journals collected (loc.gov). Search for: "Samuel J. Gibson, a Union soldier who was incarcerated in the Confederate military prison in Andersonville, Georgia". Have students read entries from some of these journals and have them complete a quick write in which they summarize the accounts of soldiers within prison camps during this war.

TEACHING IDEA

Incorporating Videos

Show students the History Channel's "America: The Story of Us, Episode 5 'Civil War'" clip dealing with the North's use of technology (available on YouTube; 00:20:05–00:27:05). This will reinforce the vast industrial advantage the Northerners had during the Civil War. Have students create a strengths and weaknesses chart for both the North and South at this midway point of the war. Students will be able to compare this updated chart to the one they created on page 391. Answers will vary, but it should be clear that the few advantages the South had at the beginning of the war were dwindling and the North's advantages were becoming overwhelming.

BUILDING AP® SKILLS

Causation

The rise of industrialization impacted American manufacturing on a wholesale level. The video clip from PBS's "Mill Times" by David Macaulay illustrates this transformation (available on YouTube). Have students watch a clip, from the video for insight into the rise of industrialization (00:00:00–00:08:50). After watching the clip, have a brief discussion on the rise of industry in the U.S. and how it shaped employment in the North along with the changes it brought within the labor force.

industry. Clothing and shoe factories had "sprung up almost like magic" in Natchez and Jackson, Mississippi. The Tredegar Iron Works in Richmond expanded significantly as well, employing more than 2,500 men, black and white. More than 10,000 people labored in war industries in Selma, Alabama, where one factory produced cannons. With labor in short supply, widows and orphans, enslaved black people, and white men too old or injured to fight were recruited for industrial work in many cities.

Women of all classes contributed to the war effort, North and South. Thousands filled jobs in agriculture, industry, and the government that were traditionally held by men while others assisted the military effort more directly. Most Union and Confederate officials initially opposed women's direct engagement in the war. Yet it was women's voluntary organization of relief efforts that inspired the federal government to establish the U.S. Sanitary Commission. By 1862 tens of thousands of women volunteered funds and assistance through hundreds of local chapters across the North. They hosted fund-raising fairs, coordinated sewing and knitting circles, rolled bandages, and sent supplies to the front lines. With critical shortages of medical staff, some female nurses and doctors eventually gained acceptance in northern hospitals and field camps. Led by such memorable figures as Clara Barton, Mary Ann "Mother" Bickerdyke, and Dr. Mary Walker, northern women almost entirely replaced men as military nurses by the end of the war.

> **AP® TIP**
> Analyze the ways in which the Civil War affected women's roles within their families, in industries, and in politics.

In the South, too, much of the medical care was performed by women. But without government support, nursing was never recognized as a legitimate profession for women, and most nurses worked out of their own homes. As a result, a Confederate soldier's chances of dying from wounds or disease were greater than those of his Union counterpart. Southern women also worked tirelessly to supply soldiers with clothes, blankets, munitions, and food. But this work, too, was often performed locally and by individuals rather than as part of a coordinated Confederate effort.

Some Union and Confederate women played more unusual roles in the war. A few dozen women joined Rose Greenhow in gathering information for military and political leaders. One of the most effective spies on the Union side was the former fugitive Harriet Tubman, who gathered intelligence in South Carolina, including from many enslaved people, between 1862 and 1864. Even more women served as couriers, carrying messages across battle lines to alert officers of critical changes in military orders or in the opponent's position. In addition, at least four hundred women disguised themselves as men and fought as soldiers.

Union women also sought to influence wartime policies. Following the Emancipation Proclamation, Elizabeth Cady Stanton, Susan B. Anthony, and Lucy Stone founded the **Women's National Loyal League** and launched a massive petition drive to broaden Lincoln's policy. Collecting 260,000 signatures, two-thirds of them from women, the League demanded a congressional act "emancipating all persons of African descent" everywhere in the nation.

For soldiers and civilians seeking to survive the upheaval of war, political pronouncements rarely alleviated the dangers they faced. The war's extraordinary death tolls shocked Americans on both sides. On the home front, the prolonged conflict created labor shortages and severe inflation in both North and South. The war initially disrupted industrial and agricultural production as men were called to service, but the North recovered quickly by building on its prewar industrial base and technological know-how.

In the South, manufacturing increased, with enslaved laborers pressed into service as industrial workers, but this created shortages on plantations. The changed circumstances of the war required women to take on new responsibilities as well. Yet these dramatic transformations also inspired dissent and protest as rising death tolls and rising prices made the costs of war ever clearer.

In 1863 and 1864, frustration spread across the North and the South generally with increasing casualties, declining numbers of volunteers, and rising inflation. As the war dragged on, many white Northerners began to wonder whether defeating the Confederacy was worth the cost, and many white Southerners whether saving it was.

Dissent posed issues in some border states as well. From 1861 on, battles raged among residents in the border state of Missouri, with Confederate sympathizers refusing to accept living in a Union state. Pro-southern residents formed militias and staged guerrilla attacks on Union supporters. The militias, with the tacit support of Confederate officials, claimed thousands of lives during the war and forced the Union army to station troops in the area.

BUILDING AP® SKILLS

Causation

The economic impact of the Civil War affected the development of the U.S. for the coming century. Economic policy is a difficult topic for AP® U.S. History students nationally. The National Parks Service has an article that breaks the economic impacts of the Civil War into an accessible and reliable presentation (nps.gov). Search for Benjamin Arrington's "Industry and Economy during the Civil War." Have students read the article and create a list of positive and negative impacts of the Civil War on industry and the economy. Once students have compiled their lists, have students rank the top positive (and negative) impacts of the war on the economy.

▲ Differentiation

A creative way to have students organize causes and impacts is to have 5-10 students call out their personal top causes and impacts. As students call out new causes, have each of them write their own term on a sheet of paper. Once 5-10 different causes have been called out, have students stand in the front of the class and have the remaining students arrange the terms from most impactful on one side of the line to the least impactful at the other end of the line. As students are moved up or down within the line, make sure that some form of justification is given. The class discussion surrounding each event as it is moved up or down the line by importance is worthwhile for students to learn how to rank ideas.

TEACHING IDEA

Incorporating Websites

Ensure students remember the vital role women have played in every military conflict thus far in the AP® U.S. History course, be it on the frontline or in supporting roles, by reminding them of figures such as Molly Pitcher, Kate Barry, Deborah Sampson, Frances Clayton, etc. The American Civil War is a great way to highlight the ways women have contributed to shaping America. Have students search the Digital Public Library's website for "Women in the Civil War" (dp.la). Students will find a vast collection of journals and primary/secondary source materials, highlighting women and their roles within the Civil War. Once students have reviewed the sources have them present their findings to the class.

BUILDING AP® SKILLS

Sourcing and Situation

Have students read Elizabeth Cady Stanton's 1864 letter, "To the Women of the Republic" (readily found online by title search). Once students have read the document, ask them to complete a quick write review in which they provide the basic thesis of the letter and include 3-5 supporting facts or ideas from the document. Students should then share their summary with a partner and discuss the possible impacts of this document on women's suffrage.

TEACHING IDEA

Incorporating Videos

The New York Draft Riots of 1863 highlight the growing class conflict and brewing racial conflicts within New York City. Show students the video, "The New York City Draft Riots: US History Review" by Hip Hughes (available on YouTube). The video gives meaningful details and background of the riot and its impact. Have a class discussion following the video and highlight the role of civil disobedience and protests within U.S. history.

BUILDING AP® SKILLS

Making Connections

The Civil War was not the only war in America's history in which class conflict was exposed in military service and the draft. Introduce the slogan of "rich man's war, poor man's fight," as the slogan will come up in future wars and conflicts.

TEACHING IDEA

Incorporating Videos

The Draft Riots of 1863 were not limited to New York City; rather, violence broke out in many northern towns. Racial tensions were unleashed and the subsequent race riots led to lynching within New York. The History Guy's video, "New York City Draft Riots of 1863," highlights many of the moments from this tragic series of events (available on YouTube). Once students watch the video, have them complete a KWL chart (a refresher on KWL can be found on page 371).

Enrollment Act March 1863 Union draft law that provided for draftees to be selected by an impartial lottery. A loophole in the law allowing wealthy Americans to escape service by paying $300 or hiring a substitute created widespread resentment.

AP® TIP
Pay close attention to the impact of the Civil War on the growing relationship between the federal government and business interests during the nineteenth century.

MODULE 5-4 Disunion and War

New York City Draft Riots, July 1863 On July 13 the draft riots in New York City began with an attack on the Colored Orphan Asylum on Fifth Avenue. As the matron led 233 African American children to safety, mobs of white men and women looted the building and set it ablaze. This wood engraving appeared in illustrated weeklies from New York to London. **What were the main factors that caused these riots?**

By 1863, dissent broadened to include Northerners who earlier embraced the Union cause. Some white Northerners had always opposed emancipation, based on racial prejudice or fear that a flood of black migrants would increase competition for jobs. Then, just two months after the Emancipation Proclamation went into effect, a new law deepened concerns among many working-class Northerners. The **Enrollment Act**, passed by Congress in March 1863, established a draft system to ensure sufficient soldiers for the Union army. While draftees were to be selected by an impartial lottery, the law allowed a person with $300 to pay the government in place of serving or to hire another man as a substitute. Many workers deeply resented the draft's profound inequality.

Dissent turned to violence in July 1863 when the new law went into effect. Riots broke out in cities across the North. In New York City, where inflation caused tremendous suffering and a large immigrant population solidly supported the Democratic Party, implementation of the draft triggered four days of the worst rioting Americans had ever seen. Women and men — including many Irish and German immigrants — attacked Republican draft officials, wealthy businessmen, and the free black community. Between July 13 and 16, rioters lynched at least a dozen African Americans and looted and burned the city's Colored Orphan Asylum. The violence ended only when Union troops put down the riots by force. By then, more than one hundred New Yorkers, most of them black, lay dead.

By 1864 inflation also fueled protests in the North as it eroded the earnings of rural and urban residents. Women, children, and old men took over much of the field labor in the Midwest, trying to feed their families and the army while struggling to pay their bills. Factory workers, servants, and day laborers felt the pinch as well. With federal greenbacks flooding the market and military production a priority, the price of consumer goods climbed about 20 percent faster than wages. Although industrialists garnered huge profits, workers suffered. A group of Cincinnati seamstresses complained to President Lincoln in 1864 about employers "who fatten on their contracts by grinding immense profits out of the labor of their operatives." At the same

martial law A suspension of standard law in which the military takes over the normal operation of the government.

Copperheads Northern Democrats who did not support the Union war effort. Such Democrats enjoyed considerable support in eastern cities and parts of the Midwest.

time, employers persuaded some state legislatures to prohibit strikes in wartime. The federal government, too, supported business over labor. When workers at the Parrott arms factory in Cold Spring, New York struck for higher wages in 1864, the government declared **martial law** and arrested the strike leaders.

Northern Democrats saw the widening unrest as a political opportunity. Although some Democratic leaders supported the war effort, many others — whom opponents called **Copperheads**, after the poisonous snake — rallied behind Ohio politician Clement L. Vallandigham in opposing the war. Presenting themselves as the "peace party," these Democrats enjoyed considerable success in eastern cities where inflation was rampant and immigrant workers were caught between low wages and military service. The party was also strong in parts of the Midwest, like Missouri, where sympathy for the southern cause and antipathy to African Americans ran deep.

In the South, too, some whites expressed growing dissatisfaction with the war. Jefferson Davis signed a conscription act in April 1862, a year before Lincoln did so, inciting widespread opposition. Here, too, men could hire a substitute if they had enough money, and an October 1862 law exempted male slaveholders who kept twenty or more enslaved people from military service. Thus, large planters, many of whom served in the Confederate legislature, had effectively exempted themselves from fighting.

Small farmers were also hard hit by policies that allowed the Confederate army to take whatever supplies it needed. The army's forced acquisition of farm produce intensified food shortages that had been building since early in the war. Moreover, the lack of an extensive railroad or canal system in the South limited the distribution of what food was available.

Food shortages drove up prices on basic items like bread and corn, while the Union blockade and the focus on military needs dramatically increased prices on other consumer goods. As the Confederate government issued ever more treasury notes to finance the war, inflation soared 2,600 percent in less than three years. In spring 1863 food riots led by working-class women erupted in cities across the South, including the Confederate capital of Richmond.

Some state legislatures then tried to control food prices, but Richmond workers continued to voice their resentment. In fall 1863 a group proclaimed, "From the fact that he consumes all and produces nothing, we know that without [our] labor and production the man with money could not exist."

The devastation of the war added to all these grievances. Since most battles were fought in the Upper South or along the Confederacy's western frontier, small farmers in these regions saw their crops, animals, and fields devastated. A phrase that had seemed cynical in 1862 — "A rich man's war and a poor man's fight" — became the rallying cry of the southern peace movement in 1864. Secret peace societies flourished mainly among small farmers and in regions, like the western mountains, where plantation slavery did not develop. A secret organization centered in North Carolina provided Union forces with information on southern troop movements and encouraged desertion by Confederates. In mountainous areas, draft evaders and deserters formed guerrilla groups that attacked draft officials and actively impeded the war effort. Women joined these efforts, hiding deserters, raiding grain depots, and burning the property of Confederate officials.

When slaveholders led the South out of the Union in 1861, they had assumed the loyalty of yeomen farmers, the deference of southern ladies, and the privileges of the southern way of life. Far from preserving social harmony and social order, however, the war undermined ties between elite and poor Southerners, between planters and small farmers, and between women and men. Although most white Southerners still supported the Confederacy in 1864 and internal dissent alone did not lead to defeat, it did weaken the ties that bound soldiers to their posts in the final two years of the war.

> "All they want is to get you pumpt up and go to fight for their infernal negroes, and after you do their fighting you may kiss their hine parts for all they care."
>
> Alabama farmer, letter to his son, 1861

REVIEW

- How did social divisions fuel dissent and protest in the North and the South during the Civil War?

BUILDING AP® SKILLS

Making Connections

When Lincoln declared martial law, the scope and range of the order's impact was wide. Have students read "Proclamation by the President; Martial Law Declared in Kentucky. The Habeas Corpus Suspended. A Proclamation," published on July 6, 1864 in *The New York Times* (found by searching for the title in *The New York Times* archives). Ask students to read the proclamation and list out all of the limitations on civil liberties included within the document. Have students share their lists with a partner and discuss the lasting impacts of the power to implement such a proclamation for future presidents during any time of war.

TEACHING IDEA

Incorporating Websites

The Bread Riots were widespread and commonplace toward the end of the Civil War within the South. Have students visit the website History Is a Weapon and search for "Four Documents on Disaffection in the South During the Civil War" (historyisaweapon.com). Students should provide a 2-3 sentence summary of each document including important supporting facts. Once students complete their summaries, have students share their answers with a partner.

EXPLORING AP® THEMES

Politics and Power

Have a quick discussion with the class on the impacts of the public supporting a war or conflict and the results of a prolonged war on that support. Have students brainstorm possible impacts of the loss of public support for a war. Answers will vary and should draw upon other wars and conflicts within U.S. history thus far. Remind students that these arguments and issues were impacting support for the war in both the North and South. In the North during the election of 1864, Lincoln won reelection against a former U.S. general, McClellan, who was calling for an end to the war.

TRM Suggested Responses to Questions

TEACHING IDEA

Group Writing

Students need to practice their individual writing skills, but a group writing assignment can help reinforce weak skills and assist students to develop stronger skills and gain deeper insights. Have students brainstorm individually possible supporting evidence and details that relate to the essay topic provided. After students have individually brainstormed, have them work in pairs or small groups to collectively sort all of their evidence into three or four categories of reasons for the change in attitudes. Have groups work to create a possible thesis individually and then collectively. Once students have compiled groups of claims and have created a possible thesis, students should then write the essay individually. Follow up the next class meeting with a partner peer-reviewing the essays. The final essays should vary even though the students did brainstorm and work collectively; the difference in their approaches in writing is important for students to view. Students should conclude that even when given the same information and evidence there are many different ways to create an essay.

Period 5: 1844–1877

MODULE 5-4 Disunion and War

AP® WRITING HISTORICALLY Long-Essay Question Practice

ACTIVITY

Using information from Modules 5-3 and 5-4, answer the following prompt. *Suggested writing time: 40 minutes.*

Evaluate the extent to which northern attitudes on emancipation changed between 1850 and 1863.

You may use the following outline to structure your response.

I. Introductory paragraph
   A. Immediate/preceding contextualization statement
      1. Cite evidence of immediate/preceding context
      2. Explain influence of immediate/preceding context
   B. Thesis statement presenting three to four evaluative claims of continuity and change that are situated along a continuum of relative importance

II. Claim 1 body paragraph
   A. Topic sentence presenting an evaluative claim of continuity and change 1
   B. Supporting statement citing evidence of claim 1
   C. Cite additional evidence of claim 1
   D. Explain how evidence supports claim 1

III. Claim 2 body paragraph
   A. Topic sentence presenting an evaluative claim of continuity and change 2
   B. Supporting statement citing evidence of claim 2
   C. Cite additional evidence of claim 2
   D. Explain how evidence supports claim 2

IV. Claim 3 body paragraph
   A. Topic sentence presenting an evaluative claim of continuity and change 3
   B. Supporting statement citing evidence of claim 3
   C. Cite additional evidence of claim 3
   D. Explain how evidence supports claim 3

V. (Optional) Claim 4 body paragraph
   A. Topic sentence presenting an evaluative claim of continuity and change 4
   B. Supporting statement citing evidence of claim 4
   C. Cite additional evidence of claim 4
   D. Explain how evidence supports claim 4

TEACHING IDEA

AP® Writing Historically Review

This question centers on students' ability to categorize the many northern attitudes toward emancipation that existed before and during the Civil War. Consider starting the hour with a brief bell ringer activity designed to heighten their awareness of the elements of the question. Divide students into groups of three or four and have them develop at least three different "northern attitudes" toward slavery. Examples could include: hostile, ambivalent, actively supportive, contingent on military events, and politically motivated. The point is to make students aware of the intent of the question, which is about northern attitudes, and to ensure students know what that means.

Module 5-5

Victory for the North

LEARNING TARGETS

By the end of this module, you should be able to:
- Explain the factors that led to Northern victory over the Confederacy.
- Explain how the strategies and fighting changed over the course of the Civil War.

THEMATIC FOCUS

American and National Identity
America in the World

Over the course of the Civil War, Lincoln shifted from a strategy aimed at preserving the Union to one that promoted the emancipation of enslaved people. As Union troops invaded the South, this new strategy decimated the southern economy, which relied almost entirely upon slavery. It also led to the recruitment of black troops, and allowed Lincoln to reframe the war as a "new birth of freedom." These factors, along with the North's superior industrial production and larger population, ultimately led to victory for the Union.

HISTORICAL REASONING FOCUS

Comparison
Continuity and Change

When examining a period of rapid transformation like the Civil War, historians often characterize change (or lack of change) by comparing one era to another. In this module, which discusses the war's end, you will need to examine the extent of change in the conflict, both at home and on the battlefield, during this period.

TASK ▶ As you read this module, examine the extent of change in the conflict, both at home and on the battlefield, in the last years of the Civil War. Be sure to consider how the earliest tactics by both the North and South evolved in the last two years of the war.

In spring 1863, amid turmoil on the home front, General Robert E. Lee's army defeated a Union force twice its size at Chancellorsville, Virginia. The victory set the stage for a Confederate thrust into Pennsylvania, but Lee's decision to go on the offensive proved the Confederacy's undoing. In July 1863 the Union won two decisive military victories: at Gettysburg, Pennsylvania and Vicksburg, Mississippi. At the same time, the flood of African Americans, including former enslaved people, into the Union army transformed the very meaning of the war. By 1864, with the momentum favoring the Union, General Ulysses S. Grant implemented a strategy that forced the Confederacy to consider surrender.

Key Victories for the Union

In mid-1863 Confederate commanders believed the tide was turning in their favor. Following major victories in Virginia at Fredericksburg and Chancellorsville, General Lee launched an invasion of northern territory at the end of June. The demoralized Union army had maneuvered to protect Washington, D.C., and its new commander, General George A. Meade, was untested. He immediately faced a major engagement at the Battle of Gettysburg in Pennsylvania. If Confederates won a victory there, European countries might finally recognize the southern nation and force the North to accept peace.

TRM Suggested Responses to Questions

TEACHING IDEA

Incorporating Videos

The AP® exam does not focus on individual battles during wars; rather, it is important for students to know a few major turning points during any conflict. Crash Course is a great teaching and review series that covers many topics, including United States history. Have students watch "Battles of the Civil War: Crash Course US History #19" (available on YouTube). Follow up with a brief class discussion covering a few of the major battles covered and why they were turning points within the war.

TEACHING IDEA

Incorporating Websites

The three-day battle of Gettysburg is considered the "high water mark" for the South, who never again would be able to launch a major operation into the North. Have students visit the Civil War Trust's website and take a "virtual tour" of the battle of Gettysburg (virtual-tour.civilwar.org). As students tour the battlefield, have them look for two to three major skirmishes from each day and take notes on what they find. Once completed, students should conduct a KWL analysis. Have students share their answers in small groups to help gain insight and exposure to a variety of events from this battle.

Period 5: 1844–1877

MODULE 5-5 Victory for the North

EXPLORING AP® THEMES

Geography and the Environment

Lead students through a discussion about the physical geography of each of the battlefields depicted on this page. Have them address the following questions: How did geography and physical location impact the outcomes of the battles? How did the outcomes of each of these battles impact the war efforts of both the North and the South?

TEACHING IDEA

Incorporating Videos

The victory at Vicksburg was both a moral and strategic boost for the North. Have students watch the Smithsonian Channel's video, "Here's Why the Battle of Vicksburg Was So Important" (available on YouTube). Once the video is finished, have students complete a four-minute quick write to gauge their understanding of the battle's significance. Read three or four of the students' responses to the class, and have a discussion regarding the Battle of Vicksburg and its impacts based on student responses and class understanding.

▲ MAP 5.7 **Battles of Gettysburg and Vicksburg, 1863** The three-day Battle of Gettysburg and the six-week siege of Vicksburg led to critical victories for the Union. Together, these victories forced General Lee's troops back into Confederate territory and gave the Union control of the Mississippi River. Still, the war was far from over. Confederate troops controlled the southern heartland, and Northerners wearied of the ever-increasing casualties. **What was the military and political significance of northern victory in these two locations?**

Battle of Gettysburg July 1863 battle that helped turn the tide for the Union in the Civil War. The Union victory at Gettysburg, Pennsylvania, combined with a victory at Vicksburg, Mississippi the same month, eliminated the threat of European intervention in the war and positioned the Union to push farther into the South.

siege of Vicksburg After a prolonged siege, Union troops forced Confederate forces to surrender at Vicksburg, Mississippi, leading to Union control of the rich Mississippi River valley.

Neither Lee nor Meade set out to launch the **Battle of Gettysburg** in this small Pennsylvania town. But Lee was afraid of outrunning his supply lines, and Meade wanted to keep Confederates from gaining control of the roads that crossed at Gettysburg. So between July 1 and July 3, the opposing armies fought a desperate battle, with Union troops occupying the high ground and Confederate forces launching fierce assaults from below. Ultimately, Gettysburg proved a disaster for the South: More than 4,700 Confederates were killed, including a large number of officers; another 18,000 were wounded, captured, or missing. Although the Union suffered similar casualties, it had more men to lose, and it could claim victory.

As Lee retreated to Virginia, the South suffered another devastating defeat. Troops under General Grant had been pounding Vicksburg, Mississippi since May 1863. The **siege of Vicksburg** ended with the surrender of Confederate forces on July 4. This victory was even more important strategically than Gettysburg. Combined with a victory five days later at Port Hudson, Louisiana, the Union army controlled the entire Mississippi valley, the richest plantation region in the South. This series of victories also effectively cut Louisiana, Arkansas, and Texas off from the rest of the Confederacy, ensuring Union control of the West. In November 1863 Grant's troops achieved another major victory at Chattanooga, opening up much of the South's remaining territory

404

TEACHING IDEA

Incorporating Websites

Visit the American Battlefield Trust's website and search "10 Facts: The Vicksburg Campaign" (battlefields.org). Have students annotate the document as they read. Once students read the article, have them discuss with a partner the facts that they found interesting. Follow up with a short whole-class discussion to clarify any lingering questions students may have. Ask students to address why some historians have called the Battle of Vicksburg the turning point in the Civil War.

MODULE 5-5 Victory for the North

African Americans Contribute to Victory

to invasion. Thousands of enslaved people deserted their plantations, and many joined the Union war effort.

That same month, November 1863, President Lincoln spoke at the official dedication ceremony for the National Cemetery at Gettysburg, Pennsylvania. In his **Gettysburg Address**, Lincoln tied the war against slavery to the fulfillment of the nation's founding ideal "that all men are created equal." He insisted that the United States "shall have a new birth of freedom — and that government of the people, by the people, and for the people, shall not perish from the earth." Only in this way, he declared, could Americans ensure that the "honored dead" had not "died in vain."

As 1864 dawned, the Union had twice as many forces in the field as the Confederacy, whose soldiers were suffering from low morale, high mortality, and dwindling supplies. Although more difficult battles lay ahead, the war of attrition (in which the larger, better-supplied Union forces slowly wore down their Confederate opponents) had begun to pay dividends.

The changing Union fortunes increased support for Lincoln and his congressional allies. Union victories and the Emancipation Proclamation also convinced Great Britain not to recognize the Confederacy as an independent nation. And the heroics of African American soldiers, who engaged in direct and often brutal combat against southern troops, expanded support for emancipation. Republicans, who now fully embraced abolition as a war aim, were nearly assured the presidency and a congressional majority in the 1864 elections.

Northern Democrats still campaigned for peace and the readmission of Confederate states with slavery intact. They nominated George B. McClellan, the onetime Union commander, for president. McClellan attracted working-class and immigrant voters who traditionally supported the Democrats and bore the heaviest burdens of the war. But Democratic hopes for victory in November were crushed when Union general William Tecumseh Sherman captured Atlanta, Georgia just two months before the election. Lincoln and the Republicans won easily, giving the party a clear mandate to continue the war to its conclusion.

Gettysburg Address A speech given by President Lincoln to inaugurate the federal cemetery at Gettysburg, Pennsylvania in November 1863. In this speech, Lincoln expressed his belief that the war was a struggle for a "new birth of freedom."

AP® TIP
Analyze how Lincoln's victory in the election of 1864 affected the outcome of the Civil War.

REVIEW
What factors contributed to northern victories after 1863?

African Americans Contribute to Victory

Lincoln's election secured the eventual downfall of slavery. Yet the president and Congress did not eradicate human bondage on their own. From the fall of 1862 on, African Americans enlisted in the Union army and helped ensure that nothing short of universal emancipation would be the outcome of the war.

In the border states, which were exempt from the Emancipation Proclamation, enslaved men were adamant about enlisting since those who served in the Union army were granted their freedom. Because of this provision, slaveholders in these states did everything in their power to prevent enslaved people from joining the army. Despite these efforts, between 25 and 60 percent of military-age enslaved men in the four border states stole away and joined the Union army. By the end of the war, nearly 200,000 black men had served officially in the army and navy, and some 37,000 black men had given their lives for the Union.

Yet despite their courage and commitment, black soldiers felt the sting of racism. They were segregated in camps, given the most menial jobs, and often treated as inferiors by white soldiers and officers. Particularly galling was the Union policy of paying black soldiers less than whites. African American soldiers openly protested this discrimination even after a black sergeant who voiced his views was charged with mutiny and executed by firing squad in February 1864. The War Department finally equalized wages four months later.

One primary concern of African American soldiers was to liberate enslaved people as Union armies moved deeper into the South. At the same time, thousands of southern enslaved people

> "If we hadn't become sojers, all might have gone back as it was before. . . . But now tings can neber go back, because we have showed our energy and our courage and our naturally manhood."
>
> Private Thomas Long, former enslaved man serving with the First South Carolina Volunteers

---

BUILDING AP® SKILLS
Causation

Have students complete a quick write about the question: What impact did the victories at Vicksburg and Gettysburg have on northern resolve or purpose in fighting the war? Make sure students defend one or two pieces of historical evidence in their response.

APPLY THE TIP

The election of 1864 was one of the few wartime elections our country has ever seen. Lincoln faced George McClellan, whom Lincoln had fired as his top general during the Civil War. McClellan ran on a Democratic platform in which he openly called for ending the Civil War and letting the South secede. Sherman's capturing of Atlanta in September swayed public opinion back to supporting the war and helped ensure Lincoln's victory at the ballot. Have students read more about the election of 1864 at the American Battlefield Trust's website (battlefield.org). Have students create a list of the top issues in this election and the impacts of Lincoln's victory.

BUILDING AP® SKILLS
Making Connections

After students have read this far in the module, have a brief class discussion concerning the racism from the Union Army toward African Americans, both free and enslaved. Highlight the module passages that address this and discuss the possible impacts.

BUILDING AP® SKILLS
Sourcing and Situation

Have students read the Gettysburg Address (readily available through online title search). As they read the document, have them complete a HIPP analysis (a refresher on HIPP can be found on page 8).

▲ **Differentiation**

There are many dramatic readings of the Gettysburg Address that can be found online. Have students listen to the speech three times. The first time students listen to the speech, have them focus on vocabulary or phrases that they do not know, such as "Four score and seven years ago." The second time listening to the speech, have the class listen for major ideas covered in the speech. The third time have students listen for the major theme of the speech. After students have listened to the speech in this way, have them finally read the speech. By listening to the speech a few times, then reading the speech, students will be able to conduct a HIPP analysis with greater ease.

Period 5: 1844–1877

MODULE 5-5 Victory for the North

▲ **Portrait of a Black Union Soldier and Family, c. 1863–1865** Taken after African Americans were allowed to join the Union Army, this daguerreotype captures a Union soldier with his wife and two daughters. He was likely a member of one of the seven Union regiments raised in Maryland, where the picture was discovered. The dresses and hats worn by the wife and daughters suggest the family was free. **How could this image elicit sympathy for equal rights for African Americans among white Northerners?**

BUILDING AP® SKILLS

Claims and Evidence in Sources

Have students read some eyewitness accounts of the well-documented race relations during the Civil War. Digital History's website has several letters collected from both white and black Americans under the documents tab of the Civil War section of their site (digitalhistory.uh.edu). Have students read 3-4 of the letters and highlight 4-5 facts or statements that leave a lasting impression on the students. Students should share their insights with a small group or in a whole-class discussion. In particular, Samuel Shenk's letter, "A Union Soldier Describes His Attitudes Towards Race," is an expressive letter highlighting the racism present within the northern army.

EXPLORING AP® THEMES

American and National Identity

Music and art reflect the attitudes found within mass culture during any time period. Play some Civil War Era songs for the students, which can be found at Digital History's website (digitalhistory.uh.edu). As students listen to the songs, have them read along with the printed lyrics and highlight any sections that are particularly meaningful. Students should listen for the historical context of the lyrics and draw parallels to the events from the Civil War. Have students review songs in small groups to help students brainstorm together the meaning and context.

headed for Union lines. Even those forced to remain on plantations learned when Union troops were nearby and talked openly of emancipation. "Now they gradually threw off the mask," a freedperson remembered, "and were not afraid to let it be known that the 'freedom' in their songs meant freedom of the body in this world."

REVIEW

- What practical and idealistic reasons led African Americans to volunteer to fight for the Union?

The Final Battles of a Total War

In the spring of 1864, the war in the East entered its final stage. That March, Lincoln placed General Grant in charge of all Union forces. Grant embarked on a strategy of hard war, in which soldiers not only attacked military targets but also destroyed civilian crops, livestock, fields, and property to undermine morale and supply chains. Grant was also willing to accept huge casualties to achieve victory. Over the next year, he led his troops overland through western Virginia in an effort to take Richmond. Meanwhile, General Philip Sheridan devastated "The Breadbasket of the Confederacy" in Virginia's Shenandoah Valley, and General Sherman laid waste to the remnants of the plantation system in Georgia and the Carolinas.

Grant's troops headed toward Richmond, where Lee's army controlled strong defensive positions. The Confederates won a series of narrow, bloody victories, but Grant continued to push forward. Although Lee lost fewer men, they were losses he could not afford given the Confederacy's much smaller population. Combining high casualties with deserters, Lee's army was melting away with each engagement. Although soldiers and civilians — North and South — called Grant "the butcher" for his seeming lack of regard for human life, the Union general was undeterred.

The Final Battles of a Total War

AP® ANALYZING SOURCES

Source: Ulysses S. Grant, *The Personal Memoirs of Ulysses S. Grant*, 1885

"In my first interview with Mr. Lincoln alone he stated to me that he had never professed to be a military man or to know how campaigns should be conducted, and never wanted to interfere in them: but that procrastination on the part of commanders, and the pressure from the people at the North and Congress, *which was always with him*, forced him into issuing his series of 'Military Orders'—one, two, three, etc. He did not know but they were all wrong, and did know that some of them were. All he wanted or had ever wanted was some one who would take the responsibility and act, and call on him for all the assistance needed, pledging himself to use all the power of the government in rendering such assistance. Assuring him that I would do the best I could with the means at hand, and avoid as far as possible annoying him or the War Department, our first interview ended. . . .

My general plan now was to concentrate all the force possible against the Confederate armies in the field. There were but two such, as we have seen, east of the Mississippi River and facing north. The Army of Northern Virginia, General Robert E. Lee commanding, was on the south bank of the Rapidan, confronting the Army of the Potomac; the second, under General Joseph E. Johnston, was at Dalton, Georgia, opposed to Sherman, who was still at Chattanooga. Beside these main armies the Confederates had to guard the Shenandoah Valley, a great storehouse to feed their armies from, and their line of communications from Richmond to Tennessee. . . .

Little expeditions could not so well be sent out to destroy a bridge or tear up a few miles of railroad track, burn a storehouse, or inflict other little annoyances. Accordingly I arranged for a simultaneous movement all along the line. Sherman was to move from Chattanooga, Johnston's Army and Atlanta being his objective points."

Questions for Analysis
1. Identify Grant's new general plan for winning the war.
2. Describe how Grant characterizes Abraham Lincoln.
3. Evaluate the extent to which Grant's new general plan represented a change in Union tactics.

TRM Suggested Responses to Questions

TRM Module 5.5 AP® Analyzing Sources Handout

BUILDING AP® SKILLS

Sourcing and Situation

Have students create a HIPP review of the excerpt from *The Personal Memoirs of Ulysses S. Grant* and share their answer with a partner (a refresher on HIPP can be found on page 8). While partners are working together, have them address what role public pressure played in Lincoln's decision to appoint Grant as commanding general and for Lincoln to directly issue "military orders."

---

total war The strategy promoted by General Ulysses S. Grant in which Union forces destroyed civilian crops, livestock, fields, and property to undermine Confederate morale and supply chains.

Sherman's March to the Sea Total war tactics employed by General William Tecumseh Sherman to capture Atlanta and huge swaths of Georgia and the Carolinas, devastating this crucial region of the Confederacy in 1864.

In the fall of 1864, implementing **total war** tactics, Sheridan rendered the Shenandoah Valley a "barren waste." Called "the burning" by local residents, Sheridan's soldiers torched fields, barns, and homes and destroyed thousands of bushels of grain along with livestock, shops, and mills. His campaign demoralized civilians in the region and denied Confederate troops crucial supplies.

In the preceding months, Sherman had laid siege to Atlanta, but on September 2 his forces swept around the city and destroyed the roads and rails that connected it to the rest of the Confederacy. When General John B. Hood and his Confederate troops abandoned their posts, Sherman telegraphed Lincoln: "Atlanta is ours, and fairly won." That victory cut the South in two, but Sherman continued on. **Sherman's March to the Sea** introduced total war tactics to Southerners along the three-hundred-mile route from the Atlantic coast north through the Carolinas. His troops cut a path of destruction fifty to sixty miles wide. They confiscated or destroyed millions of pounds of cotton, corn, wheat, and other agricultural items; tore up thousands of miles of railroad tracks; and burned Columbia, the South Carolina capital. As Eleanor Cohen Seixas, whose family had earlier fled to Columbia for safety, recorded in her journal, "The fires raged fearfully all night" and the "vile Yankees took from us clothing, food, jewels, all our cows, horses, carriages, etc." Despite later claims that Sherman's men ravaged white women, instances of such behavior were rare, although Union soldiers did ransack homes and confiscate food and clothing.

Enslaved black people hoped that Sherman's arrival marked their emancipation. During his victorious march, nearly 18,000 enslaved men, women, and children fled ruined plantations and sought to join the victorious troops. To their dismay, soldiers refused to take them along. Union soldiers realized that they could not care for this vast number of people and carry out their military operations. Some Union soldiers went further, abusing African American men, raping black

TEACHING IDEA

Incorporating Videos

William T. Sherman played a critical role in the North's strategy of enacting total war on the South. Search for the History Channel's "Blood and Glory: The Civil War in Color: Sherman's March to Savannah" (available on YouTube). After students watch the four-minute video, discuss as a class the idea of total war as a strategy. Have students create a pros and cons list of reasons why the strategy should or should not be used. Have the class share their findings in a mini-debate.

TEACHING IDEA

Incorporating Secondary Sources

Search online for Robert Mitchell's article, "Sherman's March to the Sea." Have students read and annotate the article. Students should then complete a five-minute quick write in which they address whether or not Sherman's actions of total war were justified. While there is no clear answer to the question, encourage students to take a stance on Sherman's actions as either positively or negatively impacting the outcome of the war. For the AP® exam students will have to make a clear defense of their views on many complex topics — get students in the habit of defending their ideas and supporting their claims with facts rather than opinions.

TEACHING IDEA

Incorporating Videos

Have students watch the Charles H. Wright Museum's video, "Voices of the Civil War, Episode 36: 'Special Field Orders, No. 15'" (available on YouTube). Ask students to create a cause and effect list of Field Order Number 15. While such orders did not become the law of the land, they did have great impact. Have students evaluate the possible influence of the order if it had been enacted throughout the entire country after the war.

TEACHING IDEA

Incorporating Websites

Visit the Digital Public Library of America's website and utilize the Primary Resources Sets (dp.la). In particular, locate the Homestead Acts collection. Within this collection there are teaching ideas, maps, testimonies, activities, and discussion questions — all geared for introducing the Homestead Acts to students.

BUILDING AP® SKILLS

Continuity and Change

The assault on American Indians' lands and culture was not lessened during the Civil War. Have students read the 1863 account by George Bonga, "Conflict with Native Americans During the Civil War," which can be found on Digital History's website (digitalhistory.uh.edu). In addition, Digital History has several other accounts of the Sand Creek Massacre that are worthwhile for students to read. After students have read the account(s), have students assess the extent to which America changed or remained constant in its policies toward American Indians during the Civil War. Students can write an entire essay or simply complete a quick write. Ensure students understand that the American policy toward American Indians saw little to no change during the Civil War.

AP® TIP
Be sure you can explain how Field Order Number 15 affected freedpeople's ability to become economically independent.

women, or stealing their few possessions. Angry Confederates captured many black people who were turned away, killing some and reenslaving others.

These actions caused a scandal in Washington. In January 1865, Lincoln dispatched Secretary of War Edwin Stanton to Georgia to investigate the charges. At an extraordinary meeting in Savannah, Stanton and Sherman met with black ministers to hear their complaints and hopes. The ministers spoke movingly of the war lifting "the yoke of bondage." Freedpeople, they argued, "could reap the fruit of their own labor" and, if given land, "take care of ourselves, and assist the Government in maintaining our freedom." In response, Sherman issued **Field Order Number 15**, setting aside more than 400,000 acres of captured Confederate land to be divided into small plots for former enslaved people. The order proved highly controversial, but it offered black people some hope of significant change.

If many African Americans were disappointed by the actions of Union soldiers in the East, American Indians were even more devastated by developments in the West. Despite American Indian nations' substantial aid to Union armies, any hope of being rewarded for their efforts vanished by 1864. Tens of thousands of whites migrated west of the Mississippi during the Civil War, and congressional passage of the Homestead Act in 1864 increased the numbers. At the same time, the U.S. army grew exponentially during the war, using its increased power to assault western American Indian nations.

Attacks on American Indians were not an extension of total war policies, but rather a government-sanctioned effort to terrorize native communities. Beginning in 1862, Dakota Sioux went to war with the United States over broken treaties. After being defeated, four hundred warriors were arrested by military officials and thirty-eight executed. In 1863 California Volunteers slaughtered more than two hundred men, women, and children in a Shoshone-Bannock village in Idaho. Meanwhile thousands of white settlers had been flooding into Colorado after gold was discovered in 1858, forcing Cheyenne

▲
Richmond in Ruins, April 1865 This photograph shows the Richmond and Petersburg Railroad Depot following the capture of the Confederate capital by General Grant and his troops in April 1865. The black man sitting amid the devastation no doubt realized that Richmond's fall marked the defeat of the South. **How does this image reflect the ways that Union war tactics changed during the second half of the Civil War?**

The Final Battles of a Total War

Sand Creek Massacre
November 1864 massacre of nearly 200 Cheyenne and Arapaho Indians by the Third Colorado Cavalry of the U.S. army.

and Arapaho Indians off their land. In 1864 they were promised refuge at Sand Creek by officers at nearby Fort Lyon. Instead, Colonel John M. Chivington led his Third Colorado Cavalry in a rampage that left 125 to 160 American Indian men, women, and children dead. The **Sand Creek Massacre** ensured that white migrants traveling in the region would be subject to American Indian attacks for years to come. At the same time, in the Southwest, the Navajo were defeated by U.S. troops and their Ute allies and forced into a four-hundred-mile trek to a reservation in New Mexico.

U.S. army officers considered "winning the West" one way to restore national unity once the Civil War ended. For American Indian nations, the increased migration, expanded military presence, and sheer brutality they experienced in 1863 and 1864 boded ill for their future, whichever side won the Civil War.

As the defeat of the Confederacy loomed, the U.S. Congress finally considered abolishing slavery throughout the nation. With intense lobbying by abolitionists, petitioning by the Women's National Loyal League, the valiant efforts of Ohio Congressman James Ashley, and President Lincoln's lobbying of wavering senators, Congress passed the **Thirteenth Amendment** to the U.S. Constitution on January 31, 1865. It prohibited slavery and involuntary servitude anywhere in the United States. Some northern and western states had already enacted laws to ease racial inequities. Ohio, California, and Illinois repealed statutes barring African Americans from testifying in court and serving on juries. Then, in May 1865, Massachusetts passed the first comprehensive public-accommodations law in U.S. history, ensuring equal treatment in stores, schools, theaters, and other social spaces. Cities from San Francisco to Cincinnati and New York also desegregated their streetcars.

Thirteenth Amendment
Amendment to the Constitution abolishing slavery, passed in January 1865 and sent to the states for ratification.

Still hoping to stave off defeat, southern leaders also began rethinking their racial policies. The Confederate House passed a law to recruit enslaved men into the army in February 1865, but the Senate defeated the measure. It was too late to make a difference anyway.

In early April 1865, with Sherman heading toward Raleigh, North Carolina, Grant captured Petersburg, Virginia and then drove Lee and his forces out of Richmond. Seasoned African American troops led the final assault on the city and were among the first Union soldiers to enter the Confederate capital. On April 9, after a brief engagement at Appomattox Court House, Virginia, Lee surrendered to Grant. Within hours, Lee's troops began heading home. While sporadic fighting continued — Cherokee Stand Watie was the last Confederate general to surrender in June 1865 — the back of the Confederate army had been broken.

With Lee's surrender, many Northerners hoped that the reunited nation would be stronger and more just. Jubilation in the North was short lived, however. On April 14, Abraham Lincoln was shot at Ford's Theatre by a Confederate fanatic named John Wilkes Booth. The president died the next day, leading to great uncertainty about how peace and national unity would be achieved.

REVIEW

- What role did African Americans and American Indians play in the defeat of the Confederacy?
- How did white attitudes toward African Americans change in the final year of the war?

AP® WRITING HISTORICALLY — Short-Answer Question Practice

ACTIVITY

Read the following question carefully and write a short response. Use complete sentences.

Using the following excerpts, answer (a), (b), and (c).

> **Source:** Chandra Manning, *The Fight Against Slavery*, 2007
>
> "Enlisted Union soldiers came to the conclusion that winning the war would require the destruction of slavery partly because soldiers' personal observations of the South led many to decide that slavery blighted everything it touched. . . .
>
> Yet more influential than Union soldier's preexisting notions, or even their firsthand observations of the South, were their interactions with actual slaves, which led many to

(Continued)

PERIOD 5

TEACHING IDEA

Incorporating Primary Sources

Have the students read the entire Thirteenth Amendment, which can be found on the National Constitution Center's website (constitutioncenter.org). Once completed, discuss the impact of this new law and the nuance of the terms. Why was slavery left as an option if somebody was "duly convicted"? What dangers could that lead to?

TEACHING IDEA

Virtual Tour

Have students explore the Appomattox Court House on the National Park Service website (nps.gov). Ask students to complete a KWL chart looking for important facts that they find that relate to the surrender and conditions for ending of the Civil War (a refresher of KWL can be found on page 371). You want students to remember that the Civil War ended at Appomattox, but that reuniting the country was a difficult task after the war. Have students create a list of problems faced by the North, South, and West at the end of the war.

TRM Find **Handout 5.5 – Regional Difficulties at the End of the Civil War** in the Teacher's Resource Materials.

TRM Suggested Responses to Questions

TEACHING IDEA

AP® Writing Historically Review

These sources give examples of what motivated soldiers to prosecute the war. Think about providing categories of analysis to students so they can focus their energies on how the historians emphasize different historical evidence. For instance, if you give students the following categories, they will be better equipped to unpack the historians' interpretations: unionism, enslavement, and the U.S. Constitution. Now students can look for evidence of these categories to discover how and why the historians differ in their interpretations.

BUILDING AP® SKILLS

Sourcing and Situation

Have students conduct a HIPP analysis on both sources to help them gain insights as they address the accompanying questions (a refresher on HIPP can be found on page 8). During the AP® U.S. History exam, students will not have time to HIPP every document given to them. Prime students to practice looking for the HIPP information quickly; they do not need to write out an entire HIPP annotation in complete sentences for every document during their exam. Have them practice annotating the documents as they read so they can quickly find important information when it comes time to answering the questions.

TEACHING IDEA

AP® Central

Remember that a useful resource throughout this course is to check the College Board's test question database and personal progress checks (apcentral.collegeboard.org).

---

view slavery as a dehumanizing and evil institution that corroded the moral virtue necessary for a population to govern itself. . . .

Hostility to slavery did not necessarily mean support for racial equality. In fact, white Union soldiers strove mightily to keep the issues of slavery and black rights separate. . . .

[Still], contact with slaves and southern society convinced many Union troops that the immoral and blighting institution of slavery was antithetical to republican government, and that any republican government that tried to accommodate slavery was doomed to eventual failure. . . . [C]lear demands for the destruction of slavery plainly emerged among enlisted Union soldiers, especially those stationed in the slave states who were witnessing slavery with their own eyes for the first time. Even some border state Union soldiers joined the clamor, either because they had witnessed for years the violence that slavery could engender or out of shock and anger that slaveholders in their home states valued the peculiar institution over the Union. Slaves themselves did the most to force emancipation onto the Union agenda, . . . [primarily] by winning over enlisted Union soldiers, who, in the first year of the war, became the first major group after black Americans and abolitionists to call for an end to slavery. . . ."

Source: Gary Gallagher, *The Fight to Save the Union*, 2011

"The loyal American citizenry fought a war for the Union that also killed slavery. . . . Union always remained the paramount goal, a fact clearly expressed by Abraham Lincoln in speeches and other statements designed to garner the widest popular support for the war effort. . . . That hardpan of unionism held millions of Americans to the task of suppressing the slaveholders' rebellion, even as the human and material cost mushroomed. . . .

[The Union] represented a cherished legacy of the founding generation, a democratic republic with a constitution that guaranteed political liberty and afforded individuals a chance to better themselves economically. From the perspective of loyal Americans, their republic stood as the only hope for a democracy in [the] western world . . . [following] the failed European revolutions of the 1840s. Slaveholding aristocrats who established the Confederacy . . . posed a direct threat not only to the long-term success of the American republic but also to the broader future of democracy. . . .

Issues related to the institution of slavery precipitated secession and the outbreak of fighting, but the loyal citizenry initially gave little thought to emancipation in their quest to save the Union. By the early summer of 1862, long before black men donned blue uniforms in large numbers, victorious Union armies stood poised to win the war with slavery largely intact. . . . Eventually, most loyal citizens, though profoundly prejudiced by twenty-first century-standards and largely indifferent toward enslaved black people, embraced emancipation as a tool to punish slaveholders, weaken the Confederacy, and protect the Union from future internal strife."

a. Briefly describe ONE major difference between Manning's and Gallagher's historical interpretations of the motivations of Union soldiers in the Civil War.
b. Briefly explain how ONE historical event or development from the period 1861 to 1865 that is not explicitly mentioned in the excerpts could be used to support Manning's argument.
c. Briefly explain how ONE historical event or development from the period 1861 to 1865 that is not explicitly mentioned in the excerpts could be used to support Gallagher's argument.

Module 5-6

Reconstruction Begins

LEARNING TARGETS

By the end of this module, you should be able to:
- Explain the impact of emancipation on freedpeople.
- Explain the impact of northern efforts on assisting freedpeople during Reconstruction.
- Explain the effects of federal Reconstruction policies on society from 1865 to 1877.

THEMATIC FOCUS

American and National Identity
Politics and Power

Reconstruction inspired new debates about the role of the federal government. New amendments to the Constitution, including the Thirteenth Amendment, which abolished slavery, and the Fourteenth and Fifteenth Amendments, which granted African Americans citizenship, equal protection under the laws, and voting rights, provoked resistance in the South. These Republican efforts to ensure African American rights led to short-term successes, but this progress was eventually overturned as organized southern resistance met with fading northern interest. Despite many challenges, African Americans pursued new opportunities as free citizens, including education and land ownership, in the years following the Civil War.

HISTORICAL REASONING FOCUS

Causation

Reconstruction was the culmination of a long process of African American emancipation, but American politicians could not agree on how to approach rebuilding the nation in the aftermath of the Civil War. While leaders in Washington, D.C. debated various models of reconstruction, the expansion of suffrage to African Americans opened new debates about the rights of women and divided activists who sought justice for all Americans.

TASK ▶ As you read this module, consider the ways in which the many social changes in the immediate aftermath of the war were a product of multiple causes with roots in developments that began in the years before the war, as well as during the war itself. Be sure to also consider the causes and effects of various approaches to Reconstruction and the ways in which expanding the rights of African Americans led to further conflict about civil rights for other groups.

TRM Suggested Responses to Questions

BUILDING AP® SKILLS

Argumentation

While the Thirteenth Amendment ended slavery in the United States, the question of what should happen to former slaveholders will inevitably come up within class discussion. Let students discuss postwar America and have them debate what penalties could have been taken against former slaveholders as well as what actions should have been taken to help ensure the freedom of former enslaved people. While students' answers will vary, help keep class discussion framed in the historical fact that slavery had been legal prior to the war.

Even before the war came to a close, Reconstruction had begun on a small scale. During the Civil War, African Americans remaining in Union-occupied areas, such as the South Carolina Sea Islands, gained some experience with freedom. When Union troops arrived, most southern whites fled, but enslaved workers chose to stay on the land. Some farmed for themselves, but most worked for northern whites who moved south to demonstrate the profitability of free black labor. After the war, however, former plantation owners returned. Rather than work for these whites, freedpeople preferred to establish their own farms. If forced to hire themselves out, they insisted on negotiating the terms of their employment. Wives and mothers often refused to labor for whites at all in favor of caring for their own families. These conflicts reflected the priorities that would shape the actions of freedpeople across the South in the immediate aftermath of

---

EXPLORING AP® THEMES

American and National Identity

Have students brainstorm problems facing the North, South, and West after the Civil War ended. Have students discuss their list in small groups and also discuss who should oversee the rebuilding of the country — the president, Congress, or the individual states? In addition, have students discuss what assistance should have been provided to formerly enslaved people and what punishments enacted to former Confederate leaders. While you do not want to spend too much class time dwelling on history "what-ifs," having a brief understanding of the complex questions and conditions facing the country at the end of the Civil War is important in helping students frame the coming modules.

Period 5: 1844–1877

MODULE 5-6 Reconstruction Begins

the war. For freedom to be meaningful, it had to include economic independence, the power to make family decisions, and the right to control some community decisions.

On a national level, Presidents Abraham Lincoln and Andrew Johnson viewed Reconstruction as a process of national reconciliation. They sketched out terms by which the former Confederate states could reclaim their political representation in the nation without serious penalties. Congressional Republicans, however, had a more thoroughgoing reconstruction in mind. Like many African Americans, Republican congressional leaders expected the South to extend constitutional rights to the freedmen and to provide them with the political and economic resources to sustain their freedom. Over the next decade, these competing visions of Reconstruction played out in a tumultuous battle over the meaning of the South's defeat and the emancipation of black people.

African Americans Embrace Freedom

When U.S. troops arrived in Richmond, Virginia in April 1865, the city's enslaved population knew that freedom was, finally, theirs. Four days after Union troops arrived, 1,500 African Americans, including a large number of soldiers, packed First African Baptist, the largest of the city's black churches. During the singing of the hymn "Jesus My All to Heaven Is Gone," they raised their voices at the line "This is the way I long have sought." As news of the Confederacy's defeat spread, newly freed African Americans across the South experienced similar emotions. Many years later, Houston H. Holloway, a freedman from Georgia who had been sold three times before he was twenty years old, recalled the day of emancipation: "I felt like a bird out a cage. Amen. Amen, Amen. I could hardly ask to feel any better than I did that day."

For southern whites, however, the end of the war brought fear, humiliation, and uncertainty. From their perspective, the jubilation of former enslaved people poured salt in their wounds. In many areas, African Americans celebrated their freedom under the protection of Union soldiers. When the army moved out, freedpeople suffered deeply for their enthusiasm. White people beat, whipped, raped, and shot black people who they felt had been too joyous in their celebration or too helpful to the Yankee invaders. As one North Carolina freedman testified, the Yankees "tol' us we were free," but once the army left, the planters "would get cruel to the slaves if they acted like they were free."

Newly freed people also faced less visible dangers. During the 1860s, disease swept through the South and through the contraband camps that housed many freedpeople; widespread malnutrition and poor housing heightened the problem. A smallpox epidemic that spread south from Washington, D.C. killed more than sixty thousand freedpeople.

AP® TIP
Evaluate the extent to which the actions of the federal government and U.S. army during Reconstruction effectively protected the rights of African Americans in the South.

◀ **The Freedmen's Bureau**
In this image from the prominent northern magazine, *Harper's Weekly*, a Union soldier, representing the Freedman's Bureau, holds back an angry southern mob from attacking an equally outraged mob of freed African Americans. **In what ways do the hand gestures of the Union soldier represent the attitude of northern readers toward both former rebels and freedpeople?**

Library of Congress, LC-USZ62-105555

412

TEACHING IDEA

Check for Understanding

As students read this module, ensure they understand the connection between Abraham Lincoln's and Andrew Johnson's plans for Reconstruction. Both plans aimed to reconcile the tensions that divided the country and to quickly bring back the southern states into the Union.

APPLY THE TIP

As students read and interact with this module have them keep notes on the role of the northern army in the nations' Reconstruction efforts. As an assessment activity have students complete a quick write addressing how the presence of the North's military stationed within the South post-Civil War impacted the successes or failings of Reconstruction.

EXPLORING AP® THEMES

Social Structures

Have a brief discussion about the importance of land ownership for the newly freed African Americans. Make sure to touch upon how economic opportunities for a majority of people in the South was based around agriculture. Ownership of land equated power and gave a viable way to support families. Unfortunately, within a few years after the ending of the Civil War a majority of former enslaved peoples were still working on the same land on which they have been enslaved, and still living in the South in large numbers. There are many useful maps that show the changes or lack thereof in land ownership post-Civil War, which illustrates the continued prevalence of white land ownership within the South. Visit the website Mapping the Nation and show students a variety of land ownership maps from 1860 to 1880 (mappingthenation.com).

BUILDING AP® SKILLS

Contextualization

This image from *Harper's Weekly* is widely used by historians and clearly shows some of the struggles within the South following the war. Have the class discuss the image and address why the two groups were angry. What would happen when the Union soldiers were removed? Ensure students arrive at the context of this image and are able to explain the significance of the soldier.

African Americans Embrace Freedom

Despite the dangers, southern African Americans eagerly pursued emancipation. They moved; they married; they attended school; they demanded wages; they refused to work for whites; they gathered together their families; they created black churches and civic associations; they held political meetings. Sometimes, black women and men acted on their own, pooling their resources to advance their freedom. At other times, they received help from private organizations — particularly northern missionary and educational associations — staffed mostly by former abolitionists, free black people, and evangelical Christians.

Freedpeople also called on federal agencies for assistance and support. The most important of these agencies was the newly formed Bureau of Refugees, Freedmen, and Abandoned Lands, popularly known as the **Freedmen's Bureau**. Created by Congress in 1865 and signed into law by President Lincoln, the bureau provided formerly enslaved people with economic and legal resources. The Freedmen's Bureau also aided many in achieving one of their primary goals: obtaining land. A South Carolina freedman summed up the feeling of the newly emancipated. "Give us our own land and we take care of ourselves," he remarked. "But without land, the old masters can hire or starve us, as they please." During the last years of the war, the federal government had distributed to the freedpeople around 400,000 acres of abandoned land from the South Carolina Sea Islands to Florida. Immediately after hostilities ceased, the Freedmen's Bureau made available hundreds of thousands of additional acres to the men and women who had been recently emancipated.

Freedmen's Bureau Federal agency created in 1865 to provide freedpeople with economic and legal resources. The Freedmen's Bureau played an active role in shaping black life in the postwar South.

AP® ANALYZING SOURCES

Source: Henry Bram, *To the President of these United States*, 1865

"Edisto Island S.C. Oct 28th 1865. . . .

Here is where secession was born and Nurtured Here is where we have toiled nearly all Our lives as slaves and were treated like dumb Driven cattle, This is our home, we have made These lands what they are we were the only true and Loyal people that were found in posession of these Lands we have been always ready to strike for Liberty and humanity yea to fight if needs be To preserve this glorious union. Shall not we who Are freedman and have been always true to this Union have the same rights as are enjoyed by Others? Have we broken any Law of these United States? Have we forfeited our rights of property In Land? — If not then! are not our rights as A free people and good citizens of these United States To be considered before the rights of those who were Found in rebellion against this good and just Government. . . .

Why do the freedpeople believe their request justified?
Why do they think the former landowners do not deserve the land?

We have been encouraged by government to take up these lands in small tracts, receiving Certificates of the same — we have thus far Taken Sixteen thousand (16000) acres of Land here on This Island. We are ready to pay for this land When Government calls for it and now after What has been done will the good and just government take from us all this right and make us Subject to the will of those who have cheated and Oppressed us for many years God Forbid! We the freedmen of this Island and of the State of South Carolina — Do therefore petition to you as the President of these United States, that some provisions be made by which Every colored man can purchase land. and Hold it as his own. . . .

How does this show the importance of land-ownership to them?

In behalf of the Freedmen Committee
Henry Bram. Ishmael. Moultrie. yates. Sampson."

Questions for Analysis

1. Identify what Bram requests of the president of the United States.
2. Identify the reasons Bram gives to justify this request.
3. Explain how at least three historical causes provide context for Bram's request.
4. Evaluate the extent to which each of the three causes contributes to Bram's request.

TEACHING IDEA

Incorporating Websites

The Freedmen's Bureau did more than redistribute land in an attempt to help newly freed African Americans. The Bureau also tried to reunite families when possible. The Freedmen's Bureau records can be searched in an online database today (freedmensbureau.com). Have students research the three recorded categories — Murders and Outrages, Freedmen's Labor Records, and Marriage Records. Students should discuss their impressions and findings in small groups. Discuss how and why actual numbers reported to the Bureau are possibly biased.

BUILDING AP® SKILLS

Making Connections

Discuss with students the impacts of the slave codes passed in the 1830s, which made it illegal to teach enslaved people to read or write, and also excluded enslaved and often freed African Americans in the South from being able to obtain any legal documentation or political standing. Discuss the lasting impacts and legacy on formerly enslaved people who had been denied education en masse for hundreds of years.

The first priority for many newly freed people was to reunite families torn apart by slavery. Men and women traveled across the South to find family members. Well into the 1870s and 1880s, parents ran advertisements in newly established black newspapers, providing what information they knew about their children's whereabouts and asking for assistance in finding them. Milly Johnson wrote to the Freedmen's Bureau in March 1867, after failing to locate the five children she had lost under slavery. She finally located three of them, but any chance of discovering the whereabouts of the other two disappeared because the records of the slave trader who purchased them burned during the war. Despite such obstacles, thousands of formerly enslaved children were reunited with their parents in the 1870s.

Husbands and wives, or those who considered themselves as such despite the absence of legal marriage under slavery, also searched for each other. Those who lived on nearby plantations could now live together for the first time. Those whose spouse had been sold to distant plantations had a more difficult time. They wrote (or had letters written on their behalf) to relatives and friends who had been sold with their mate; sought assistance from government officials, churches, and even their former slaveholders; and traveled to areas where they thought their spouse might reside.

These searches were complicated by long years of separation and the lack of any legal standing for marriages of enslaved people. In 1866 Philip Grey, a Virginia freedman, located his wife, Willie Ann, and their daughter Maria, who had been sold away to Kentucky years before. Willie Ann was eager to reunite with her husband, but in the years since being sold, she had remarried and had three children. Her second husband had joined the Union army and was killed in battle. When Willie Ann wrote to Philip in April 1866, she explained her new circumstances, concluding: "If you love me you will love my children and you will have to promise me that you will provide for them all as well as if they were your own. . . . I know that I have lived with you and loved you then and love you still."

▲ **Winslow Homer, A Visit from the Old Mistress, 1876** Civil War correspondent and artist Winslow Homer visited Virginia in the mid-1870s and visually captured the tensions existing between freedpeople and former slaveholders. Here, a former mistress visits the home of three black women. Although the house is humble, one woman refuses to stand for the "old mistress" and the other two, one holding a free-born child, eye her warily. **To what extent does this painting portray a change from pre-Civil War society in the South?**

BUILDING AP® SKILLS

Claims and Evidence in Sources

During the Great Depression, part of the New Deal created the Federal Writers Project (FWP) as part of the Works Progress Administration (WPA), in which authors were tasked with collecting the stories of surviving African Americans who were born into slavery or shortly after the Civil War. The 1936–1938 project collected hundreds of accounts and took hundreds of pictures as evidence. The Library of Congress has digitalized the entire collection, and it can be found by searching for "Slave Narratives" on the Library of Congress website (loc.gov). Introduce the narratives and why they were created (future modules in this text will address the WPA and FWP). After students have viewed the collection, have them complete a five-minute quick write in which they share their impressions and insights gained by viewing the narratives. Have students share their reactions with the class.

Most black spouses who found each other sought to legalize their relationship. A superintendent for marriages for the Freedmen's Bureau in northern Virginia reported that he gave out seventy-nine marriage certificates on a single day in May 1866. In another case, four couples went right from the fields to a local schoolhouse, still dressed in their work clothes, where the parson married them.

Of course, some freedpeople hoped that freedom would allow them to leave unhappy relationships. Having never been married under the law, couples could simply separate and move on. Complications arose, however, if they had children. In Lake City, Florida in 1866, a Freedmen's Bureau agent asked his superiors for advice on how to deal with Madison Day and Maria Richards. They refused to legalize the relationship forced on them under slavery, but both sought custody of their three children. As with white couples in the mid-nineteenth century, the father was granted custody on the assumption that he had the best chance of providing for the children financially.

Seeking land and reuniting families were only two of the many ways that southern black people proclaimed their freedom. Learning to read and write was another. The desire to learn was all but universal. Enslaved people had been forbidden to read and write, and with emancipation they pursued what had been denied them. A newly liberated father in Mississippi proclaimed, "If I nebber does nothing more while I live, I shall give my children a chance to go to school, for I considers education [the] next best ting to liberty."

> **AP® TIP**
> Be sure you are able to explain the ways in which discrimination against African Americans following the Civil War illustrated continuity in U.S. history.

AP® ANALYZING SOURCES

Source: Colonel Eliphalet Whittlesey, *Report on the Freedmen's Bureau*, 1865

"All officers of the bureau are instructed—
- To aid the destitute, yet in such a way as not to encourage dependence.
- To protect freedmen from injustice.
- To assist freedmen in obtaining employment and fair wages for their labor.
- To encourage education, intellectual and moral. . . .

[W]e have in our camps at Roanoke Island and Newbern, many women and children, families of soldiers who have died in the service, and refugees from the interior during the war, for whom permanent provision must be made. . . . The reports prepared by Surgeon Hogan will show the condition of freedmen hospitals. In the early part of the summer much suffering and mortality occurred for want of medical attendance and supplies. This evil is now being remedied by the employment of surgeons by contract. . . .

Contrary to the fears and predictions of many, the great mass of colored people have remained quietly at work upon the plantations of their former masters during the entire summer. The crowds seen about the towns in the early part of the season had followed in the wake of the Union army, to escape from slavery. After hostilities ceased these refugees returned to their homes, so that but few vagrants can now be found. In truth, a much larger amount of vagrancy exists among the whites than among the blacks. It is the almost uniform report of officers of the bureau that freedmen are industrious.

The report is confirmed by the fact that out of a colored population of nearly 350,000 in the State, only about 5,000 are now receiving support from the government. Probably some others are receiving aid from kind-hearted men who have enjoyed the benefit of their services from childhood. To the general quiet and industry of this people there can be no doubt that the efforts of the bureau have contributed greatly."

Questions for Analysis
1. Identify the likely audience for Whittlesey's report.
2. Describe Whittlesey's perspective on both freedpeople and white Southerners.
3. Explain how Whittlesey measures the success of the Freedmen's Bureau.

EXPLORING AP® THEMES

Social Structures

Students might overlook the importance of the information presented in this section. Have a brief conversation with students and highlight the fact that in the 1800s, in cases of separations and divorces, the court system awarded custody of children to fathers due to the fact they could "support and provide for their children." Discuss why the courts tended to award custody to fathers from colonial times up until the heavy industrialization of the late 1880s. Have students brainstorm possible reasons for this shift, and follow the changes in families and parental roles in the coming modules.

TRM Suggested Responses to Questions

TRM Module 5.6 AP® Analyzing Sources Handout 2

TEACHING IDEA

Incorporating Websites

The Freedmen's Bureau helped newly freed African Americans along with poor whites through its establishment of a public school system within the South. Prior to the Civil War many of the southern states did not have any public school — only families with means could afford to send their children away to school. Students should examine the impact of Freedmen's Bureau schools on education within the South. Have students read Ronald E. Butchart's article, "Freedmen's Education during Reconstruction," on the New Georgia Encyclopedia's website (georgiaencyclopedia.org). After students review the main article and visit the related links, have them work in small groups and create an infographic that highlights some of their major findings, quotes, and facts. Students should be guided to focus on the role and impacts of the Freedmen's Bureau schools and the subsequent growth in education levels within the South.

BUILDING AP® SKILLS

Argumentation

After students read the report regarding the Freedmen's Bureau, have them identify the main argument and supporting facts within the account. Students should share their answers in pairs, then follow up with a class discussion. What was Whittlesey's main argument, and what bias did he show? Answers will vary, but highlight the clear bias as needed if students miss its presence, then challenge the students for its root causes and impacts.

BUILDING AP® SKILLS
Continuity and Change

Reconstruction had many failings and lasting successes, which students will need to be able to assess. Ask students to list and explain the ways that Reconstruction was successful and the ways it failed, along with what lasting impacts it had on the country. Instruct students to focus on the years 1865–1877 in creating their lists and explanations, as they may be tempted to jump to later time periods. Follow up with a class discussion of the students' findings. Have many students share their insights, as this will help the entire class build on their understanding. Remind students to stay within time periods while addressing specific questions for their College Board exams unless they are providing a brief amount of context.

TEACHING IDEA
Incorporating Websites

Have students visit the exhibition section of Digital History's website to explore the exhibit, "America's Reconstruction: People and Politics after the Civil War" (digitalhistory.uh.edu). Students can take advantage of the accompanying resources or simply take notes on their impressions of the exhibit. Exposing students to this evidence- and story-based exhibit will engage them and add a stronger framework to their understanding of the module and time period in general.

A variety of organizations opened schools for freedpeople during the 1860s and 1870s. By 1870 nearly a quarter million African Americans were attending one of the 4,300 schools established by the Freedmen's Bureau. Black and white churches and missionary societies sent hundreds of teachers, black and white, into the South to establish schools in former plantation areas. Their attitudes were often paternalistic and the schools were segregated, but the institutions they founded offered important educational resources for African Americans.

Parents worked hard to keep their children in school during the day. As children gained the rudiments of education, they passed on their knowledge to parents and older siblings whose jobs prevented them from attending school. In addition, many adult freedpeople also sought an education for themselves. In New Bern, North Carolina, where many black people labored until eight o'clock at night, a teacher reported that they then spent at least an hour "in earnest application to study."

Freedmen and freedwomen sought education for a variety of reasons. Some viewed it as a sign of liberation. Others knew that they must be able to read the labor contracts they signed if they were ever to challenge exploitation by whites. Some freedpeople were eager to correspond with relatives, others to read the Bible. Growing numbers hoped to participate in politics, particularly the public meetings organized by black people in cities across the South. When such gatherings set priorities for the future, the establishment of public schools was high on the list.

Despite the enthusiasm of African Americans and the efforts of the federal government and private agencies, schooling remained severely limited throughout the South. A shortage of teachers and of funding kept enrollments low among black and white people alike. The isolation of black farm families and the difficulties in eking out a living limited the resources available for education. By 1880, only about a quarter of African Americans were literate.

▲ **Freedmen's Bureau School, 1860s** This photograph of a one-room Freedmen's Bureau school in North Carolina in the late 1860s shows the large number and diverse ages of students who sought to obtain an education following emancipation. The teachers included white and black northern women sent by missionary and reform organizations as well as southern black women who had already received some education. **Why was education an important step toward ensuring rights for freedpeople?**

One of the constant concerns freedpeople expressed was the desire to read the Bible and interpret it for themselves. A few black congregations had existed under slavery, but most enslaved people had been forced to listen to white preachers who claimed that God created slavery.

From the moment of emancipation, freedpeople gathered at churches to celebrate community events. Black Methodist and Baptist congregations spread rapidly across the South following the Civil War. In these churches, African Americans were no longer forced to sit in the back benches or punished for moral infractions defined by white slaveholders. Now black people invested community resources in their own religious institutions where they filled the pews, hired the preachers, and selected boards of deacons and elders. Churches were the largest structures available to freedpeople in many communities and thus were used by a variety of community organizations. They often served as schools and hosted picnics, dances, weddings, funerals, festivals, and other events that brought black people together. Church leaders also often served as arbiters of community standards of morality.

In the early years of emancipation black churches also served as important sites for political organizing. Some black ministers worried that political concerns would overwhelm spiritual devotions. Others agreed with the Reverend Charles H. Pearce of Florida, who declared, "A man in this State cannot do his whole duty as a minister except he looks out for the political interests of his people." Whatever the views of ministers, black churches were among the few places where African Americans could express their political views free from white interference.

REVIEW

- How did freedpeople define freedom?
- What steps did freedpeople take to make freedom real for themselves and their children?

Lincoln and Johnson's Reconstruction Plans

In December 1863, President Lincoln issued the **Proclamation of Amnesty and Reconstruction**, which asked relatively little of the southern states. Lincoln declared that defeated states would have to accept the abolition of slavery, but then new governments could be formed when 10 percent of those eligible to vote in 1860 (which in practice meant white, but not black, southern men) swore an oath of allegiance to the United States. Lincoln's plan granted amnesty to all but the highest-ranking Confederate officials, and the restored voters in each state would elect members to a constitutional convention and representatives to take their seats in Congress. In the next year and a half, Arkansas, Louisiana, and Tennessee reestablished their governments under Lincoln's "Ten Percent Plan."

Republicans in Congress had other ideas. **Radical Republicans** argued that the Confederate states should be treated as "conquered provinces" subject to congressional supervision. In 1864 Congress passed the **Wade-Davis bill**, which established much higher barriers for readmission to the Union than did Lincoln's plan. For instance, the Wade-Davis bill substituted 50 percent of voters for the president's 10 percent requirement. Lincoln put a stop to this harsher proposal by using a pocket veto — refusing to sign it within ten days of Congress's adjournment.

Although Lincoln and congressional Republicans disagreed about many aspects of postwar policy, Lincoln was flexible, and his actions mirrored his desire both to heal the Union and to help southern black people. For example, the president supported the Thirteenth Amendment, abolishing slavery, which passed Congress in January 1865 and was sent to the states for ratification. In March 1865, Lincoln signed the law to create the Freedmen's Bureau. That same month, the president expressed his sincere wish for reconciliation between the North and the South. "With malice toward none, with charity for all," Lincoln declared in his second inaugural address, "let us strive on to finish the work . . . to bind up the nation's wounds." Lincoln would not, however, have the opportunity to implement his balanced approach to Reconstruction. When he was assassinated in April 1865, it fell to Vice President Andrew Johnson, a very different sort of politician, to lead the country through the process of reintegration.

The nation needed a president who could transmit northern desires to the South with clarity and conviction and ensure that they were carried out. Instead, the nation got a president who substituted his own aims for those of the North, refused to engage in meaningful

Radical Republicans
Republican politicians who actively supported abolition prior to the Civil War and sought tighter controls over the South in the aftermath of the war.

TEACHING IDEA

Secondary Sources

The role of the church as a social and political influence within African American communities pre- and post-Civil War is an important topic for students to understand. Many social and political movements will take their leaders from this religious institution. Have students read the brief introduction to the collection of writings found on Documenting the American South's website entitled "An Introduction to the Church in the Southern Black Community" (docsouth.unc.edu). After students read the article have a class mini-discussion on their findings and clear up any misunderstandings.

BUILDING AP® SKILLS

Continuity and Change

Have students create a graphic organizer comparing the Reconstruction plans of Lincoln, Johnson, and Congress. Students should share their diagrams with a partner and follow up with a class discussion to ensure students have found similarities and differences. Answers will vary, but students will find Lincoln and Johnson's plans tended to focus on quickly bringing the southern states back into the Union with limited additional provisions for protecting former enslaved people.

TRM Find **Handout 5.6 – Comparing Reconstruction Plans** in the Teacher's Resource Materials.

BUILDING AP® SKILLS

Comparison

Have students work in pairs to pre-write an essay in which they compare and contrast President Lincoln's plans for reconstruction and the Radical Republicans' plans. Answers will vary, but students should brainstorm their support and create an outline together. Students should complete the full essay individually. Have a follow-up discussion of how the nation could have looked if Lincoln had not been assassinated and his plan had been put into action.

EXPLORING AP® THEMES

Politics and Power

President Lincoln added Andrew Johnson as his vice president during his second term. The addition of Johnson was problematic for the nation and proves to be a major obstacle during Reconstruction. Have a brief discussion with students on Lincoln's reasons for adding Johnson as his vice president and some problems Johnson faced once he became president.

BUILDING AP® SKILLS

Continuity and Change

Highlight the continuity and change of the slave codes and then the black codes throughout the AP® U.S. History course thus far. Students should remember their origins back in colonial times, to the slave codes of the 1830s, up until the codes passed within the South during Reconstruction. Point out that many attempts were taken to outlaw such formal laws by Congress during Reconstruction, but southern society adapted the black codes into informal policies and cultural norms in order to avoid federal scrutiny.

---

compromise, and misled the South into believing that he could achieve restoration quickly. In the 1864 election, Lincoln chose Johnson, a pro-Union southern Democrat, as his running mate in a thinly veiled effort to attract border-state voters. The vice presidency was normally an inconsequential role, so it mattered little to Lincoln that Johnson was out of step with many Republican Party positions.

As president, however, Johnson's views took on profound importance. Born into rural poverty, Johnson had no sympathy for the southern aristocracy. Yet he had been a slaveholder, so his political opposition to slavery was not rooted in moral convictions. Instead, it sprang from the belief that slavery gave plantation owners inordinate power and wealth, which came at the expense of the majority of white Southerners, who were not slaveholders. Johnson saw emancipation as a means to "break down an odious and dangerous [planter] aristocracy," not to empower black people. Consequently, he was unconcerned with the fate of African Americans in the postwar South. Six months after taking office, President Johnson rescinded the wartime order to distribute confiscated land to freedpeople in the Sea Islands. He saw no reason to punish the Confederacy's leaders, because he believed that the end of slavery would doom the southern aristocracy. He hoped to bring the South back into the Union as quickly as possible and then let Southerners take care of their own affairs.

Johnson's views, combined with a lack of political savvy and skill, ensured his inability to work constructively with congressional Republicans, even the moderates who constituted the majority. Moderate Republicans shared the prevalent belief of their time that black people were inferior to white people, but they argued that the federal government needed to protect newly emancipated people. Senator Lyman Trumbull of Illinois, for example, warned that without national legislation, freedpeople would "be tyrannized over, abused, and virtually reenslaved." The moderates expected southern states, where 90 percent of African Americans lived, to extend basic civil rights to the freedpeople, including equal protection, due process of law, and the right to work and hold property.

Nearly all Republicans shared these positions, but the Radical wing of the party wanted to go further. Led by Senator Charles Sumner of Massachusetts and Congressman Thaddeus Stevens of Pennsylvania, this small but influential group advocated suffrage, or voting rights, for African American men as well as the redistribution of southern plantation lands to freedpeople. Stevens called on the federal government to provide freedpeople "a homestead of forty acres of land," which would give them some measure of autonomy. These efforts failed, and the Republican Party proved unable to pass a comprehensive land distribution program that enabled freedpeople to gain economic independence. Nonetheless, whatever disagreements between Radicals and moderates, all Republicans believed that Congress should have a strong voice in determining the fate of the former Confederate states. From May to December 1865, with Congress out of session, they waited to see what Johnson's restoration plan would produce, ready to assert themselves if his policies deviated too much from their own.

AP® TIP
Evaluate the extent of similarity in the views of Radical Republicans and southern freedpeople on Reconstruction.

◀ **Mourning at Stonewall Jackson's Gravesite, 1866** Many Northerners were concerned that the defeat of the Confederacy did not lessen white Southerners' devotion to the "Lost Cause" or the heroism of soldiers who fought to maintain a society based on the domination of African Americans. Women, who led the efforts to memorialize Confederate soldiers, are shown at the gravesite of General Stonewall Jackson in Lexington, Virginia. **What details in this picture support Northerners' fear of Southerners' devotion to the "Lost Cause"?**

TEACHING IDEA

Connecting the Dots

As students read about the "Lost Cause" of the Confederacy, discuss the modern debate over Confederate war memorials and statues. The discussion should be factually based, but highlight that many of the statues were built 50 to 60 years after the Civil War.

At first, it seemed as if Johnson would proceed as they hoped. He appointed provisional governors to convene new state constitutional conventions and urged these conventions to ratify the Thirteenth Amendment, abolishing slavery, and revoke the states' ordinances of secession. He also allowed the majority of white Southerners to obtain amnesty and a pardon by swearing their loyalty to the U.S. Constitution, but he required those who had held more than $20,000 of

AP® ANALYZING SOURCES

Source: *Mississippi Black Code*, 1865

"An Act to Confer Civil Rights on Freedmen, and for other Purposes. . . .

Section 2. All freedmen, free negroes and mulattoes may intermarry with each other, in the same manner and under the same regulations that are provided by law for white persons: Provided, that the clerk of probate shall keep separate records of the same.

Section 3. All freedmen, free negroes or mulattoes who do now and have heretofore lived and cohabited together as husband and wife shall be taken and held in law as legally married, and the issue shall be taken and held as legitimate for all purposes; and it shall not be lawful for any freedman, free negro or mulatto to intermarry with any white person; nor for any person to intermarry with any freedman, free negro or mulatto; and any person who shall so intermarry shall be deemed guilty of felony, and on conviction thereof shall be confined in the State penitentiary for life; and those shall be deemed freedmen, free negroes and mulattoes who are of pure negro blood, and those descended from a negro to the third generation, inclusive, though one ancestor in each generation may have been a white person.

Section 4. In addition to cases in which freedmen, free negroes and mulattoes are now by law competent witnesses, freedmen, free negroes or mulattoes shall be competent in civil cases, when a party or parties to the suit, either plaintiff or plaintiffs, defendant or defendants; also in cases where freedmen, free negroes and mulattoes is or are either plaintiff or plaintiffs, defendant or defendants. They shall also be competent witnesses in all criminal prosecutions where the crime charged is alleged to have been committed by a white person upon or against the person or property of a freedman, free negro or mulatto. . . .

An Act to Amend the Vagrant Laws of the State . . .

Section 2. All freedmen, free negroes and mulattoes in this State, over the age of eighteen years, found on the second Monday in January, 1866, or thereafter, with no lawful employment or business, or found unlawful[ly] assembling themselves together, either in the day or night time, and all white persons assembling themselves with freedmen, free negroes or mulattoes, or usually associating with freedmen, free negroes or mulattoes, on terms of equality, or living in adultery or fornication with a freed woman, freed negro or mulatto, shall be deemed vagrants, and on conviction thereof shall be fined in a sum not exceeding, in the case of a freedman, free negro or mulatto, fifty dollars, and a white man two hundred dollars, and imprisonment at the discretion of the court, the free negro not exceeding ten days, and the white man not exceeding six months. . . .

Section 6. The same duties and liabilities existing among white persons of this State shall attach to freedmen, free negroes or mulattoes, to support their indigent families and all colored paupers; and that in order to secure a support for such indigent freedmen, free negroes, or mulattoes, it shall be lawful, and is hereby made the duty of the county police of each county in this State, to levy a poll or capitation tax on each and every freedman, free negro, or mulatto, between the ages of eighteen and sixty years, not to exceed the sum of one dollar annually to each person so taxed, which tax, when collected, shall be paid into the county treasurer's hands, and constitute a fund to be called the Freedman's Pauper Fund, . . . for the maintenance of the poor of the freedmen, free negroes and mulattoes of this State."

Questions for Analysis

1. Identify the rights that are granted to freedpeople in this document.
2. Identify the rights that are reduced or restricted for freedpeople in this document.
3. Evaluate the extent to which black codes such as Mississippi's represent a continuity in the treatment of African Americans in the South.

TRM Suggested Responses to Questions

TRM Module 5.6 AP® Analyzing Sources Handout 3

BUILDING AP® SKILLS

Sourcing and Situation

Have students create a HIPP analysis for the *Mississippi Black Code* (a refresher on HIPP can be found on page 8). As students create their analysis, have them focus on the purpose and impacts of these black codes. Students should discuss their findings as a class or in small groups. Have students brainstorm any modern legacy of these codes.

BUILDING AP® SKILLS

Making Connections

As students review the actions taken by President Johnson and Congress, have them compile a list of Congress's actions and Johnson's reactions. Students should then write a final summary of the outcomes of the congressional and presidential battling plans for Reconstruction.

TEACHING IDEA

Incorporating Primary Sources

Have students read Sections 1 and 5 of the Fourteenth Amendment in pairs and list the provisions and protections outlined within the document. As a class, discuss the students' lists and the intended purpose of this document. Highlight areas where this amendment was not enforced or failed to provide intended protections.

---

taxable property — the members of the southern aristocracy — to petition him for a special pardon to restore their rights. Republicans expected him to be harsh in dealing with his former political foes. Instead, Johnson relished the reversal of roles that put members of the southern elite at his mercy. As the once prominent petitioners paraded before him, the president granted almost all of their requests for pardons.

By the time Congress convened in December 1865, Johnson was satisfied that the southern states had fulfilled his requirements for restoration. Moderate and Radical Republicans disagreed, seeing few signs of change or regret in the South. Mississippi, for example, rejected ratification of the Thirteenth Amendment. As a result of Johnson's liberal pardon policy, many former leaders of the Confederacy won election to state constitutional conventions and to Congress. Indeed, Georgians elected Confederate vice president Alexander H. Stephens to the U.S. Senate.

Far from providing freedpeople with basic civil rights, the southern states passed a variety of **black codes** intended to reduce African Americans to a condition as close to slavery as possible. Some laws prohibited black people from bearing arms; others outlawed intermarriage and excluded them from serving on juries. The codes also made it difficult for black people to leave plantations unless they proved they could support themselves. Laws like this were designed to ensure that white landowners had a supply of cheap black labor despite slavery's abolition.

Northerners viewed this situation with alarm. In their eyes, the postwar South looked very similar to the Old South, with a few cosmetic adjustments. If the black codes prevailed, one Republican proclaimed, "then I demand to know of what practical value is the amendment abolishing slavery?" Others wondered what their wartime sacrifices meant if the South admitted no mistakes, was led by the same people, and continued to oppress its black inhabitants.

black codes Racial laws passed by southern legislatures in the immediate aftermath of the Civil War that aimed to keep freedpeople in a condition as close to slavery as possible.

REVIEW

- What historical developments best explain President Lincoln's plans for Reconstruction?
- What was President Johnson's plan for Reconstruction, and how did his views compare to those of most Republican politicians?

Congressional Reconstruction and Resistance

Faced with growing opposition in the North, Johnson stubbornly held his ground. He insisted that the southern states had followed his plan and were entitled to resume their representation in Congress. Republicans objected, and in December 1865 they barred the admission of southern lawmakers. But Johnson refused to compromise. In January 1866, the president rejected a bill passed by Congress to extend the life of the Freedmen's Bureau for two years. A few months later, he vetoed the Civil Rights Act, which Congress had passed to protect freedpeople from the restrictions placed on them by the black codes. These bills represented a consensus among moderate and Radical Republicans on the federal government's responsibility toward formerly enslaved people.

Johnson justified his vetoes on both constitutional and personal grounds. He and other Democrats contended that so long as Congress refused to admit southern representatives, it could not legally pass laws affecting the South. The president also condemned the Freedmen's Bureau bill because it infringed on the right of states to handle internal affairs such as education and economic policies. Johnson's vetoes exposed his racism and his lifelong belief that the evil of slavery lay in the harm it did to poor white people, not to enslaved black people. Johnson argued that the bills he vetoed discriminated against whites, who would receive no benefits under them, and thus put whites at a disadvantage with black people who received government assistance. Johnson's private secretary reported in his diary, "The president has at times exhibited a morbid distress and feeling against the Negroes."

Johnson's actions united moderates and Radicals against him. In April 1866, Congress repassed both the Freedmen's Bureau extension and Civil Rights Act over the president's vetoes. In June, lawmakers adopted the **Fourteenth Amendment**, which incorporated many of the provisions of the Civil Rights Act, and submitted it to the states for ratification. Reflecting its confrontational dealings with the president, Congress wanted to ensure more permanent protection

Fourteenth Amendment Amendment to the Constitution defining citizenship and protecting individual civil and political rights from abridgment by the states. Adopted during Reconstruction, the Fourteenth Amendment overturned the *Dred Scott* decision.

Memphis Race Riot A skirmish between white policemen and black Union veterans on May 1, 1866 resulted in three days of rioting by white mobs that attacked the black community of Memphis, Tennessee. Before federal troops restored peace, numerous women had been raped, and forty-six African Americans and two whites had been killed. This illustration from Harper's Weekly depicts the carnage. **What does this image reveal about the resistance to Reconstruction in the South?**

> " The late riots in our city have satisfied all of one thing, that the *southern man* will not be ruled by the *negro*. "
>
> Editor, *Memphis Daily Avalanche*, 1866

for African Americans than simple legislation could provide. Lawmakers also wanted to act quickly, as the situation in the South seemed to be deteriorating rapidly. In May 1866, a race riot had broken out in Memphis, Tennessee. For a day and a half, white mobs, egged on by local police, went on a rampage, during which they terrorized black people and burned their homes and churches.

The Fourteenth Amendment defined citizenship to include African Americans, thereby nullifying the ruling in the *Dred Scott* case of 1857, which declared that black people were not citizens. It extended equal protection and due process of law to all persons, not only citizens. The amendment repudiated Confederate debts, which some state governments had refused to do, and it barred Confederate officeholders from holding elective office unless Congress removed this provision by a two-thirds vote. Although most Republicans were upset with Johnson's behavior, at this point they were not willing to embrace the Radical position entirely. Rather than granting the right to vote to black males at least twenty-one years of age, the Fourteenth Amendment gave the states the option of excluding black people and accepting a reduction in congressional representation if they did so.

Johnson remained inflexible. Instead of counseling the southern states to accept the Fourteenth Amendment, which would have sped up their readmission to the Union, he encouraged them to reject it. In the fall of 1866, Johnson decided to take his case directly to northern voters before the midterm congressional elections. Campaigning for candidates who shared his views, he embarked on a swing through the Midwest. Out of touch with northern opinion, Johnson attacked Republican lawmakers and engaged in shouting matches with audiences. On election day, Republicans increased their majorities in Congress and now controlled two-thirds of the seats, providing them with greater power to override presidential vetoes.

When the Fortieth Congress convened in 1867, Republican lawmakers charted a new course for **Reconstruction**. With moderates and Radicals united against the president, Congress intended to force the former Confederate states not only to protect the basic civil rights of African Americans but also to grant them the vote. Moderates now agreed with Radicals that unless black people had access to the ballot, they would not be able to sustain their freedom. Extending the

Reconstruction Period from 1865 to 1877, during which the eleven ex-Confederate states were subject to federal legislative and constitutional efforts to remake their societies as they were readmitted to the Union.

BUILDING AP® SKILLS

Claims and Evidence in Sources

The Memphis Race Riot of 1866 highlights the racial and economic tensions within southern society and across America as a whole following the Civil War. Have students read Mackenzie Lanum's article "Memphis Riot, 1866" found on BlackPast's website (blackpast.org). As students annotate the article, have them find the causes and outcomes of the race riots. In follow-up discussion highlight the economic tensions between immigrants, poor white people, and black people within the South.

BUILDING AP® SKILLS

Argumentation

Have students list the actions taken against former Confederate military and political leaders as found in this portion of the module. Have students research and create an infographic for the punitive measures taken toward major Confederate political or military leaders. Student answers will vary, but examples include: *Robert E. Lee's property became Arlington National Cemetery* and *Jefferson Davis's citizenship was revoked*. Have students share their findings as a class and discuss the impacts and limitations of these punishments.

TEACHING IDEA

Incorporating Videos

Assign students to watch Episode 22 "Reconstruction and 1876" from the Crash Course US History series (available on YouTube). Ask students to create a KWL chart and provide a summary of the overall effectiveness of Reconstruction (a refresher on KWL can be found on page 371). Student answers will vary, but students should understand that during the early days of Reconstruction there were marked improvements for the newly freed African Americans, but within a few years of the war's end, political divisions and corruption eroded and limited any further progress.

BUILDING AP® SKILLS

Claims and Evidence in Sources

Teaching American History's website has many Reconstruction documents and activities collected for students and teachers (teachingamericanhistory.org). Search for the document, "Reconstruction Acts," and have students compile a list of the provisions and explain if these were indeed accomplished.

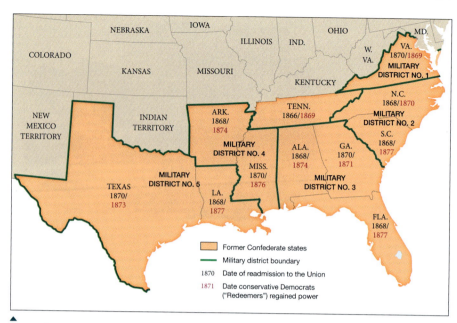

MAP 5.8 Reconstruction in the South In 1867 Congress enacted legislation dividing the former Confederate states into five military districts. All the states were readmitted to the Union by 1870, and white conservative Democrats (Redeemers) had replaced Republicans in most states by 1875. Only in Florida, Louisiana, and South Carolina did federal troops remain until 1877. **In what ways were these military districts a product of Radical Republican policy?**

Military Reconstruction Acts 1867 acts dividing Southern states into military districts and requiring those states to grant black male suffrage.

Tenure of Office Act Law passed by Congress in 1867 to prevent President Andrew Johnson from removing cabinet members sympathetic to the Republican Party's approach to congressional Reconstruction without Senate approval. Johnson was impeached, but not convicted, for violating the act.

suffrage to African Americans also aided the fortunes of the Republican Party in the South by adding significant numbers of new voters. By the end of March, Congress enacted three **Military Reconstruction Acts**. Together they divided ten southern states into five military districts, each under the supervision of a Union general. The male voters of each state, regardless of race, were to elect delegates to a constitutional convention; only former Confederate officials were disfranchised. The conventions were required to draft constitutions that guaranteed black suffrage and ratified the Fourteenth Amendment. Within a year, North Carolina, South Carolina, Florida, Alabama, Louisiana, and Arkansas had fulfilled these obligations and reentered the Union.

Having ensured congressional Reconstruction in the South, Republican lawmakers turned their attention to disciplining the president. Johnson continued to resist their policies and used his power as commander in chief to order generals in the military districts to soften the intent of congressional Reconstruction. In response, Congress passed the Command of the Army Act in 1867, which required the president to issue all orders to army commanders in the field through the General of the Army in Washington, D.C., Ulysses S. Grant. The Radicals knew they could count on Grant to carry out their policies. Even more threatening to presidential power, Congress passed the **Tenure of Office Act**, which prevented Johnson from firing cabinet officers sympathetic to congressional Reconstruction. This measure barred the chief executive from removing from office any appointee that the Senate had ratified previously without returning to the Senate for approval.

Convinced that the new law was unconstitutional and outraged at the effort to limit his power, the quick-tempered Johnson chose to confront the Radical Republicans directly rather than seek

TEACHING IDEA

Incorporating Videos

The impeachment of Andrew Johnson marks a dark milestone in U.S. history. Ensure students understand the process of impeachment and the cases in which presidents have been impeached. Remind students that there have been federal judges and other officials impeached and removed from office as well. Show students the six-minute CBS Sunday Morning video clip, "Andrew Johnson: The Impeached President" (aired February 18, 2018 and found by title search online or YouTube). After viewing the video, discuss the impacts of this impeachment on Congress's ability to control Reconstruction moving forward.

a way around a congressional showdown. In February 1868, Johnson fired Secretary of War Edwin Stanton, a Lincoln appointee and a Radical sympathizer, without Senate approval. In response, congressional Radicals prepared articles of impeachment.

In late February, the House voted 126 to 47 to impeach Johnson, the first president ever to be impeached, or charged with unlawful activity. The case then went to trial in the Senate, where the chief justice of the United States presided and a two-thirds vote was necessary for conviction and removal from office. After a six-week hearing, the Senate fell one vote short of convicting Johnson. Most crucial for Johnson's fate were the votes of seven moderate Republicans who refused to find the president guilty of violating his oath to uphold the Constitution. They were convinced that Johnson's actions were insufficient to merit the enormous step of removing a president from office. Although Johnson remained in office, Congress effectively ended his power to shape Reconstruction policy.

The Republicans had restrained Johnson, and in 1868 they won back the presidency. Ulysses S. Grant, the popular Civil War general, ran against Horatio Seymour, the Democratic governor of New York. Although an ally of the Radical Republicans, Grant called for reconciliation with the South. He easily defeated Seymour, winning nearly 53 percent of the popular vote and 73 percent of the electoral vote.

REVIEW

- What caused congressional resistance to President Johnson's Reconstruction plan?
- What priorities were reflected in congressional Reconstruction legislation?

The Struggle for Universal Suffrage

Fifteenth Amendment Amendment to the Constitution prohibiting the abridgment of a citizen's right to vote on the basis of "race, color, or previous condition of servitude." From the 1870s on, southern states devised numerous strategies for circumventing the Fifteenth Amendment.

American Equal Rights Association Group of black and white women and men formed in 1866 to promote gender and racial equality. The organization split in 1869 over support for the Fifteenth Amendment.

AP® TIP
Be sure you can explain how the debate over suffrage for African American men generated a broader debate about equality and American national identity.

In February 1869, Congress passed the **Fifteenth Amendment** to protect black male suffrage, which had initially been guaranteed by the Military Reconstruction Acts. A compromise between moderate and Radical Republicans, the amendment prohibited voting discrimination based on race, but it did not deny states the power to impose qualifications based on literacy, payment of taxes, moral character, or any other standard that did not directly relate to race. Subsequently, the wording of the amendment provided loopholes for white leaders to disfranchise African Americans. The amendment did, however, cover the entire nation, including the North, where states like Connecticut, Kansas, Michigan, New York, Ohio, and Wisconsin still excluded black people from voting.

The Fifteenth Amendment sparked serious conflicts not only within the South but also among old abolitionist allies. The American Anti-Slavery Society disbanded with emancipation, but many members believed that important work remained to be done to guarantee the rights of freedpeople. They formed the **American Equal Rights Association** immediately following the war, but members divided over the Fifteenth Amendment.

Some women's rights advocates, including Elizabeth Cady Stanton and Susan B. Anthony, had earlier objected to the Fourteenth Amendment because it inserted the word *male* into the Constitution for the first time when describing citizens. Although they had supported abolition before the war, Stanton and Anthony worried that postwar policies intended to enhance the rights of southern black men would further limit the rights of women. While most African American activists embraced the Fifteenth Amendment, a few voiced concern. At a meeting of the Equal Rights Association in 1867, Sojourner Truth noted, "There is quite a stir about colored men getting their rights, but not a word about colored women."

At the 1869 meeting of the Equal Rights Association, differences over the measure erupted into open conflict. Stanton and Anthony denounced suffrage for black men only, and Stanton now supported her position on racial grounds. She claimed that the "dregs of China, Germany, England, Ireland, and Africa" were degrading the U.S. polity and argued that white, educated women should certainly have the same rights as immigrant and African American men. Black and white supporters of the Fifteenth Amendment, including Frances Ellen Watkins Harper, Wendell Phillips, Abby Kelley, and Frederick Douglass, denounced Stanton's bigotry. Believing that southern black men urgently needed suffrage to protect their newly won freedom, they argued that ratification of the Fifteenth Amendment would speed progress toward the enfranchisement of women, black and white.

MODULE 5-6 Reconstruction Begins

Period 5: 1844–1877

> " I will cut off this right arm of mine before I will ever work or demand the ballot for the Negro and not the woman. "
>
> — Susan B. Anthony, 1866

This conflict led to the formation of competing organizations committed to women's suffrage. The **National Woman Suffrage Association**, established by Stanton and Anthony, allowed only women as members and opposed ratification of the Fifteenth Amendment. The American Woman Suffrage Association, which attracted the support of women and men, white and black, supported ratification. Less than a year later, in the spring of 1870, the Fifteenth Amendment was ratified and went into effect.

Since the amendment did not grant the vote to either white or black women, women suffragists attempted to use the Fourteenth Amendment to achieve their goal. In 1875 Virginia Minor, who had been denied the ballot in Missouri, argued that the right to vote was one of the "privileges and immunities" granted to all citizens under the Fourteenth Amendment. In *Minor v. Happersett*, the Supreme Court ruled against her, and most women continued to be denied national suffrage for decades thereafter.

AP® ANALYZING SOURCES

Source: Elizabeth Cady Stanton, *Speech to the Equal Rights Association*, 1869

"If the civilization of the age calls for an extension of the suffrage, surely the government of the most virtuous, education men and women would better represent the whole, and protect the interests of all than could the representation of either sex alone. But government gains no new element of strength in admitting all men to the ballot-box, for we have too much of the man-power already. We see this in every department of legislation, and it is a common remark, that unless some new virtue is infused into our public life the nation is doomed to destruction. Will the foreign element, the dregs of China, Germany, England, Ireland, and Africa supply this needed force, or the nobler types of American womanhood who have taught our presidents, senators, and congressmen the rudiments of all they know?"

Questions for Analysis

1. Identify Stanton's main objective in this excerpt.
2. Explain how historical situation shaped Stanton's statement.
3. Explain the intended political effect of Stanton's statement.

REVIEW

- To what extent did Reconstruction change the lives of African Americans in the South?

AP® WRITING HISTORICALLY — Using Context to Craft an Essay Conclusion

Although you have plenty of practice writing essays at this point in the school year, it is likely that as you have worked on honing your historical argument skills that you have not spent much time considering how best to wrap up your essays. A conclusion may sometimes seem like the least important portion of your essay — after all, you've just spent several paragraphs developing and defending a strong historical argument. However, a conclusion is more than just a final statement to finish your essay. It is also a place where you can once again express your knowledge of the context of your historical analysis.

As you may remember from Period 2, where you began to practice incorporating context into your introductory paragraphs, context shapes a given situation. An essay conclusion that includes meaningful context helps finish your argument by signaling to your reader the ways in which your topic shaped the future.

Let's think about how you might craft a conclusion to the following prompt:

> Evaluate the extent to which government policies regarding civil rights affected American society between 1860 and 1875.

TRM Suggested Responses to Questions

TRM Module 5.6 AP® Analyzing Sources Handout 4

TRM Suggested Responses to Questions

BUILDING AP® SKILLS

Claims and Evidence in Sources

Have students read the 1873 speech, "On Women's Right to Vote," by Susan B. Anthony to the House Committee on the Judiciary found on Digital History's website (digitalhistory.uh.edu). After students have read the document, have students cite reasons stated by the suffragists for women to obtain the right to vote. Discuss the possible reasons in the delay of women receiving the right to vote.

TEACHING IDEA

Incorporating Videos

Have students view Tom Army's video, "Minor-Happersett Decision 1875, A Battle for Women's Suffrage" (found on YouTube). After students view the 10-minute presentation discuss the debate of that court ruling.

Step 1 Break down the prompt.

Of course, we can't get to a conclusion without writing the essay first. So, we'll start where we always do: breaking down the prompt. Notice that it asks you to "evaluate the extent to which" government policies (plural) about civil rights affected American society. Remember, "extent" in these kinds of prompts is essentially code for "how much." To fully respond to this prompt, you will need to consider not just multiple government policies, but build a historical argument that takes a position on how much these policies changed American society.

Step 2 List and categorize your historical knowledge.

The next step is to pre-write. In this case, you may find it easiest to work backwards, in a sense. You can begin by considering the ways in which civil rights in American society changed between 1860 and 1875. Remember to consider changes in both the North and the South. Then, you can brainstorm a list of government policies between 1860 and 1875 that led to these changes. From there, you can choose which claims will make up your thesis and become topic sentences for your body paragraphs.

Step 3 Set the context, craft a thesis, and write the body of your essay.

Once you have completed your pre-writing to gather your thoughts and plan out the basic claims for your argument, you're ready to write your essay. Remember to begin with a contextualization statement that leads into a thesis that makes at least three claims. As you continue writing, make sure to begin each body paragraph with one of the claims from your thesis and use the best evidence you can think of to support that claim. Be sure to go beyond simply identifying evidence in support of your claims — you should always explain why that evidence is compelling. In other words, how does the evidence you chose relate to the claim you made?

Step 4 Craft your essay conclusion.

A good conclusion both reiterates your main claims and closes out with a statement that shows you understand the context of the topic. Generally, a good rule of thumb for concluding context is to take a "step forward" in the historical narrative by discussing the *immediate concluding context* or the *long-term concluding context* of your essay's topic. And, like your introduction, your context statement needs a citation of evidence and an explanation of how that evidence supports your concluding context statement. If this sounds familiar, that's because it uses a familiar approach: *ACE* (Answer, Cite, Explain).

You should keep in mind that when you take the AP® exam you will have the knowledge to make claims that extend past the time period in the prompt. For the purpose of this example, we've provided a model that includes historical developments you have not yet encountered in this textbook. You will learn more about these developments throughout the rest of the school year. For now, you should focus on how the examples provided can be used to build strong concluding context statements.

Let's start by exploring the immediate context following the time period in the prompt. You might build a strong set of concluding statements by creating a table like this one:

Answer stating immediate context	After 1875, the federal government increasingly turned away from issues of civil rights, and newly freed African Americans were left to the wrath of their infuriated former slaveholders.
Cite evidence of immediate context	Throughout the South, black codes and, later, restrictions on voting rights, marginalized African Americans and reduced them to second-class status, despite ratification of the Thirteenth, Fourteenth, and Fifteenth Amendments.
Explain influence of immediate context on essay topic	These restrictions on African American civil rights left Reconstruction with a mixed legacy, which lasted well into the twentieth century.

From these statements, you can craft a solid conclusion that describes the immediate concluding context for the prompt and restates your thesis:

> Between 1860 and 1875, the Emancipation Proclamation, the Thirteenth, Fourteenth, and Fifteenth Amendments, and Radical Republican policies reshaped the lives of all Americans, especially in the South, by granting more civil rights to the most downtrodden and rejuvenating the pursuit of suffrage for women **[restated thesis]**. Unfortunately, after 1875,

(Continued)

TEACHING IDEA

AP® Central

Students struggle to score full points on the written response portions of the national AP® exam. The College Board provides the grading rubrics to students and teachers via their website (apcentral.collegeboard .org). Make sure that students have been exposed to the scoring rubrics many times during the course of the school year. When students understand the grading standards and rubrics of the College Board, it will help ensure they are attempting to score maximum points.

TEACHING IDEA

AP® Writing Historically Workshop

This activity, to be used as a bell ringer, seeks to establish ways for students to think about historical context near the end or after the time period in a given question. Remind students that context, while preferred at the beginning of a response, can occur anywhere in the essay on the AP® exam. Moreover, context can be established before, during, or after the time period in a prompt. Offer students two choices: the 1870s and 1880–1900. In this way, you are giving students two time frames from which to brainstorm possible answers. Divide students into groups of four and have them develop an outline for how they would establish context using the two time periods. Remind students that contextualization has the following characteristics: one large historical development with two or three facts that substantiate students' understanding of the process they are writing about to illustrate contextualization.

---

the federal government increasingly turned away from issues of civil rights, and newly freed African Americans were left to the wrath of their infuriated former slaveholders **[immediate concluding context]**. Throughout the South, black codes and, later, restrictions on voting rights marginalized African Americans and reduced them to second-class status, despite the Thirteenth, Fourteenth, and Fifteenth Amendments **[evidence of context]**. These restrictions on African American civil rights left Reconstruction with a mixed legacy, which lasted well into the twentieth century **[explanation of context]**.

You can also apply this same strategy to long-term contexts. The following table explores some long-term concluding contexts you would be able to draw on to conclude an essay on the AP® exam:

Answer stating long-term context	While Reconstruction failed to secure civil rights for African Americans in the long term, the ideals of the Thirteenth, Fourteenth, and Fifteenth Amendments inspired later civil rights activists in the twentieth century.
Cite evidence of long-term context	Starting in the early twentieth century, and reaching high intensity during the 1950s and 1960s, African American civil rights activists protested and petitioned the federal government to live up to the promises made in the Reconstruction amendments.
Explain influence of long-term context on essay topic	Ultimately, almost one hundred years after the Civil War, the federal government once again took a hand in securing civil rights for African Americans, and sought to fulfill Lincoln's promise of a "new birth of freedom."

From this table, you can build a conclusion that incorporates long-term context for the prompt and connects to your thesis:

Between 1860 and 1875, the Emancipation Proclamation, Thirteenth, Fourteenth, and Fifteenth Amendments and Radical Republican policies reshaped the lives of all Americans, especially in the South, by granting more civil rights to the most downtrodden and rejuvenating the pursuit of suffrage for women, though many of these reforms proved short-lived after 1875 **[restated thesis]**. While Reconstruction failed to secure civil rights for African Americans in the long term, the ideals of the Thirteenth, Fourteenth, and Fifteenth Amendments inspired later civil rights activists in the twentieth century **[long-term concluding context]**. Starting in the early twentieth century, and reaching high intensity during the 1950s and 1960s, African American civil rights activists protested and petitioned the federal government to live up to the promises made in the Reconstruction amendments **[evidence of context]**. Ultimately, almost one hundred years after the Civil War, the federal government once again took a hand in securing civil rights for African Americans, and sought to fulfill Lincoln's promise of a "new birth of freedom" **[explanation of context]**.

ACTIVITY

Follow the steps provided in this box to craft a conclusion to the essay you wrote for the Writing Historically activity at the end of Module 5-2 (p. 374). Write two alternate conclusions: one that provides immediate context and one that provides long-term context. You may use the following outline to guide your writing:

VI. Conclusion
   A. Restated thesis
   B. Concluding context statement
   C. Evidence for concluding context statement
   D. Explanation of how evidence supports concluding context statement

Module 5-7

Reform and Resistance

LEARNING TARGETS
By the end of this module, you should be able to:
- Explain the causes of resistance to Reconstruction in the South and in the North.
- Explain the short-term successes of Reconstruction.

THEMATIC FOCUS
Politics and Power

In spite of President Andrew Johnson's resistance, Republican efforts to ensure civil rights for freedpeople led to short-term successes, including the election of African Americans to local and federal offices. However, Southerners organized to resist these efforts, and diminishing investment by northern politicians allowed this resistance to gain power.

HISTORICAL REASONING FOCUS
Causation

While Reconstruction promised to remake the South into a more just society, white Southerners mounted an aggressive resistance to Reconstruction-era policies. As a result, many of the reforms enacted between 1863 and 1877 were gradually undone.

TASK ▶ As you read this module, consider the many causes that led to the reversal of Reconstruction.

TRM Suggested Responses to Questions

BUILDING AP® SKILLS
Claims and Evidence in Sources

About 2,000 African American men held public office when Reconstruction ended in 1877. Recent publications have done much research into these men and the positions they held, as well as why power was taken away. Slate's website published excerpts from the historian Eric Foner's article, "South Carolina's Forgotten Black Political Revolution" (slate.com). Have students read the article and discuss their impressions in groups of three or four.

With President Johnson's power effectively curtailed, reconstruction of the South moved quickly. New state legislatures, ruled by a coalition of southern white and black people as well as white northern migrants, enacted political, economic, and social reforms that improved the overall quality of life in the South. Despite these changes, many black and white Southerners barely eked out a living under the planter-dominated sharecropping system. Moreover, the biracial Reconstruction governments lasted a relatively short time, as conservative whites used a variety of tactics, including terror and race baiting, to defeat their opponents at the polls.

Early Reconstruction in the South

During the first years of congressional Reconstruction, two groups of whites occupied the majority of elective offices in the South. A significant number of native-born Southerners joined Republicans in forging postwar constitutions and governments. Before the war, some had belonged to the Whig Party and opposed secession from the Union. Western sections of Alabama, Georgia, North Carolina, and Tennessee had demonstrated a fiercely independent strain, and many residents had remained loyal to the Union. Small merchants and farmers who detested large plantation owners also threw in their lot with the Republicans. Even a few ex-Confederates, such as General James A. Longstreet, decided that the South must change and allied with the Republicans. The majority of whites who continued to support the Democratic Party viewed these whites as traitors. They showed their distaste by calling them **scalawags**, an unflattering term meaning "scoundrels."

At the same time, Northerners came south to support Republican Reconstruction. They had varied reasons for making the journey, but most considered the South a new frontier to be conquered culturally, politically, and economically. Some — white and black — had served in the Union army during the war, liked what they saw of the region, and decided to settle there. Some of

scalawags Derogatory term for white Southerners who supported Reconstruction.

TEACHING IDEA
Building Vocabulary

Discuss the political effect terms such as "carpetbagger" and "scalawag" had on the Republicans in the South seeking to reconstruct state governments.

Period 5: 1844–1877

MODULE 5-7 Reform and Resistance

both races came to provide education and assist the freedpeople in adjusting to their new lives. As a relatively underdeveloped area, the South also beckoned fortune seekers and adventurers who saw opportunities to get rich. Southern Democrats denounced such northern interlopers, particularly whites, as **carpetbaggers**, suggesting that they invaded the region with all their possessions in a satchel, seeking to plunder it and then leave. While Northerners did seek economic opportunity, they were acting as Americans always had in settling new frontiers and pursuing dreams of success. In fact, much of the animosity directed toward them resulted primarily not from their mere presence, but from their efforts to ally with African Americans in reshaping the South.

carpetbaggers Derogatory term for white Northerners who moved to the South in the years following the Civil War. Many white Southerners believed such migrants were intent on exploiting their suffering.

Still, the primary targets of southern white hostility were African Americans who attempted to exercise their hard-won freedom. Black people constituted a majority of voters in five states — Alabama, Florida, South Carolina, Mississippi, and Louisiana — while in Georgia, North Carolina, Texas, and Virginia they fell short of a majority. They did not use their ballots to impose black rule on the South, as many white Southerners feared. Only in South Carolina did African Americans control the state legislature, and in no state did they manage to elect a governor. Nevertheless, for the first time in American history, black men won a wide variety of elected positions. More than six hundred black men served in state legislatures; another sixteen held seats in the U.S. House of Representatives; and two from Mississippi were chosen to serve in the U.S. Senate.

AP® ANALYZING SOURCES

Source: Thomas Nast, *This Is a White Man's Government*, 1874

About the source: The text at the bottom of the image reads, "We regard the Reconstruction Acts (so called) of Congress as usurpations, and unconstitutional, revolutionary, and void"– *Democratic platform*. The man in the center of the cartoon is wearing a belt with a buckle labeled "CSA," and holds a knife labeled "the lost cause." The man on the left is an Irish man, who holds a club labeled "a vote." The man on the right is wearing a button labeled "5 Avenue" and holding a wallet labeled "capital for votes." All three men have a foot on the back of an African American Union soldier, who is lying on the ground. In the background of the cartoon, a "colored orphan asylum" and a "southern school" are burning down, and African American children have been lynched nearby.

Questions for Analysis

1. Identify the demographic groups each of the four characters in the cartoon represents.
2. Identify Nast's intended audience.
3. Describe the main argument Nast makes in this cartoon.
4. Explain how social changes in the South caused the situation depicted in this image.

428

TEACHING IDEA

Analyzing Art and Images

Have students complete a HIPP analysis of this image. Students need to be able to source pictures, diagrams, and graphics in addition to print media. Have students get in the habit of quickly looking for the historical situation and purpose of any document regardless of the text's medium (a refresher on HIPP can be found on page 8).

TEACHING IDEA

Check for Understanding

Highlight the fact that initially after the Civil War, only one state had a majority of African American legislators, South Carolina. Few African American legislators were elected to national office from any state within the U.S. Only two states had minority governors elected during Reconstruction (Louisiana and California). Discuss the impact and implications of these voting results following the Civil War. Students need to make note of tracing voting trends of African Americans for further understanding in upcoming modules.

TRM Suggested Responses to Questions

TRM Module 5.7 AP® Analyzing Sources Handout 1

BUILDING AP® SKILLS

Continuity and Change

Remind students of the growing anti-immigrant sentiment within the country during this time period as well as the continued racism, anti-American-Indian, anti-Catholic, anti-Chinese, anti-Mexican, anti-Irish, and antisemitism trends, etc. In light of the growing discrimination, have students complete further analysis of Thomas Nast's image.

Freedpeople showed enthusiasm for politics in other ways, too. African Americans considered politics a community responsibility, and in addition to casting ballots, they held rallies and mass meetings to discuss issues and choose candidates. Although they could not vote, women attended these gatherings and helped influence their outcome. Covering a Republican convention in Richmond in October 1867, held in the First African Baptist Church, the *New York Times* reported that "the entire colored population of Richmond" attended. In addition, freedpeople formed mutual aid associations to promote education, economic advancement, and social welfare programs, all of which they saw as deeply intertwined with politics.

Southern black people also bolstered their freedom by building alliances with sympathetic whites. These interracial political coalitions produced considerable reform in the South. They created the first public school systems; provided funds for social services, such as poor relief and state hospitals; upgraded prisons; and rebuilt the South's transportation system. Moreover, the state constitutions that the Republicans wrote brought a greater measure of political democracy and equality to the South by extending suffrage to poor white men as well as black men. Some states allowed married women greater control over their property and liberalized the criminal justice system. In effect, these Reconstruction governments brought the South into the nineteenth century.

Obtaining political representation was one way in which African Americans defined freedom. Economic independence constituted a second. Without government-sponsored land redistribution, however, the options for southern black people remained limited. Lacking capital to purchase farms, most entered into various forms of tenant contracts with large landowners. **Sharecropping** proved the most common arrangement. Black and poor white people became sharecroppers for much the same reasons. They received tools and supplies from landowners and farmed their own plots of land on the plantation. In exchange, sharecroppers turned over a portion of their harvest to the owner and kept the rest for themselves.

The benefits of sharecropping proved less valuable to black farmers in practice than in theory. To tide them over during the growing season, croppers had to purchase household provisions on credit from a local merchant, who was often also their landlord. At the mercy of store owners who kept the books and charged high interest rates, tenants usually found themselves in considerable debt at the end of the year. To satisfy the debt, merchants devised a crop lien system in which tenants pledged a portion of their yearly crop to satisfy what they owed. Falling prices for agricultural crops in this period ensured that most indebted tenants did not receive sufficient return on their produce to get out of debt and thus remained bound to their landlords. For many African Americans, sharecropping turned into a form of virtual slavery.

The picture for black farmers was not all bleak, however. Through careful management and extremely hard work, black families planted gardens for household consumption and raised chickens for eggs and meat. Despite its pitfalls, sharecropping provided a limited measure of labor independence and allowed some black people to accumulate small amounts of cash. About 20 percent of black farmers managed to buy their own land, in spite of the grinding racism they faced.

Following the war's devastation, many of the South's white small farmers, known as yeomen, also fell into sharecropping. Meanwhile, many planters' sons abandoned farming and became lawyers, bankers, and merchants. Despite these changes, one thing remained the same: White elites ruled over black and poor white people, and they kept these two economically exploited groups from uniting by fanning the flames of racial prejudice.

Economic hardship and racial bigotry drove many black people to leave the South. In 1879 formerly enslaved people, known as **Exodusters**, pooled their resources to create land companies and purchase property in Kansas on which to settle. They encouraged an exodus of some 25,000 African Americans from the South. Kansas was ruled by the Republican Party and had been home to the great antislavery martyr John Brown. As one hopeful freedman from Louisiana wrote to the Kansas governor in 1879, "I am anxious to reach your state . . . because of the sacredness of her soil washed in the blood of humanitarians for the cause of black freedom." Poor-quality land and unpredictable weather often made farming on the Great Plains hard and unrewarding. Nevertheless, for many black migrants, the chance to own their own land and escape the oppression of the South was worth the hardships. In 1880 the census counted 40,000 black people living in Kansas.

sharecropping A system that emerged as the dominant mode of agricultural production in the South in the years after the Civil War. Under the sharecropping system, sharecroppers received tools and supplies from landowners in exchange for a share of the eventual harvest.

AP® TIP
Evaluate the degree to which conditions for African Americans under sharecropping reflected continuity with the pre-Civil War era.

Exodusters African Americans who migrated from the South to Kansas in 1879 seeking land, economic opportunity, and a better way of life.

TEACHING IDEA

Incorporating Videos
Have students visit the PBS website and watch the two-minute video, "Sharecropping as Slavery," as part of the 2012 *Slavery by Another Name* documentary (pbs.org). Have students write a five-minute position paper in which they defend or refute the practice of sharecropping and its impacts. Encourage students to take a stance and defend their position. Students must be able to effectively defend their positions on essays within the AP® exam and should practice this skill throughout the year.

APPLY THE TIP
Have students create a three-way Venn diagram for the living conditions and political power of landowners, poor whites, and poor African Americans in the South during the late Reconstruction Era. Have students share their Venn diagrams with partners and follow up with a class discussion.

TRM Find **Handout 5.7 – Reconstruction Era South** in the Teacher's Resource Materials.

EXPLORING AP® THEMES

American and Regional Culture
Have students visit the National Park Service website and search for "Exodusters – Homestead National Monument of America" (nps.gov). From this page students can view the Homestead monument and museum on a virtual tour along with being able to read primary and secondary source materials regarding Exodusters and the conditions they faced. After students visit the site, have them create an info brochure highlighting what drew the Exodusters to the West along with what they encountered once they settled.

TRM Suggested Responses to Questions

TRM Module 5.7 AP® Analyzing Sources Handout 2

TEACHING IDEA

Incorporating Videos

Have students watch the History Channel's "America: The Story of Us, Episode 6 'Heartland'" (available on YouTube; 0:00:00–00:13:00). As students watch the clip, have them take notes to highlight the conditions and hardships faced by Exodusters and other settlers as they headed westward. Discuss with students by asking: Why would people knowingly face such hardships?

Period 5: 1844–1877

MODULE 5-7 Reform and Resistance

AP® ANALYZING SOURCES

Source: *Sharecropper Contract*, 1882

"To every one applying to rent land upon shares, the following conditions must be read, and agreed to. To every 30 and 35 acres, I agree to furnish the team, plow, and farming implements, except cotton planters, and I do not agree to furnish a cart to every [share] cropper. The croppers are to have half of the cotton, corn, and fodder (and peas and pumpkins and potatoes if any are planted) if the following conditions are complied with, but—if not—they are to have only two-fifths (2/5). Croppers are to have no part or interest in the cotton seed raised from the crop planted and worked by them. No vine crops of any description, that is, no watermelons, muskmelons, . . . squashes or anything of that kind, except peas and pumpkins, and potatoes, are to be planted in the cotton or corn. All must work under my direction. All plantation work to be done by the croppers. My part of the crop to be housed by them, and the fodder and oats to be hauled and put in the house. All the cotton must be topped about 1st August. If any cropper fails from any cause to save all the fodder from his crop, I am to have enough fodder to make it equal to one-half of the whole if the whole amount of fodder had been saved.

For every mule or horse furnished by me there must be 1000 good sized rails . . . hauled, and the fence repaired as far as they will go, the fence to be torn down and put up from the bottom if I so direct. All croppers to haul rails and work on fence whenever I may order. Rails to be split when I may say. Each cropper to clean out every ditch in his crop, and where a ditch runs between two croppers, the cleaning out of that ditch is to be divided equally between them. Every ditch bank in the crop must be shrubbed down [perhaps to remove underbrush] and cleaned off before the crop is planted and must be cut down every time the land is worked with his hoe and when the crop is "laid by," the ditch banks must be left clean of bushes, weeds, and seeds. The cleaning out of all ditches must be done by the first of October. . . .

No cropper is to work off the plantation when there is any work to be done on the land he has rented, or when his work is needed by me or other croppers. . . .

Every cropper must feed or have fed, the team he works, Saturday nights, Sundays, and every morning before going to work, beginning to feed his team (morning, noon, and night every day in the week) on the day he rents and feeding it to including the 31st day of December. If any cropper shall from any cause fail to repair his fence as far as 1000 rails will go, or shall fail to clean out any part of his ditches, or shall fail to leave his ditch banks, any part of them, well shrubbed and clean when his crop is laid by, or shall fail to clean out stables, fill them up and haul straw in front of them whenever he is told, he shall have only two-fifths (2/5) of the cotton, corn, fodder, peas, and pumpkins made on the land he cultivates. . . .

The sale of every cropper's part of the cotton to be made by me when and where I choose to sell, and after deducting all they owe me and all sums that I may be responsible for on their accounts, to pay them their half of the net proceeds. . . ."

Questions for Analysis
1. Identify five details of a sharecropper's job description in this contract.
2. Explain the relationship this contract creates between the sharecropper and the landowner.
3. Explain the economic effects of this contract on the African Americans who signed it.

REVIEW
- What role did sharecropping play in reshaping the southern economy during Reconstruction?
- What role did African Americans play in remaking southern society during Reconstruction?

430

BUILDING AP® SKILLS

Contextualization

Have students read the *Sharecropper Contract* and explain the context in which it was written. Students should practice the skill of contextualization often during the year. Establish with students that their contextualization should be the background or setting of an event and that it should not be a mere mention or one simple sentence. Students should note that on both the DBQ and LEQ scoring rubrics one point is awarded for "contextualization." This should be 3 to 4 sentences with explanation of the historical setting or background in which an event took place.

White Resistance

AP® TIP
Analyze how amnesty for former Confederate soldiers affected the development of American politics, social structures, and national identity during Reconstruction.

AP® TIP
Be sure you can explain the role that terrorism played in white resistance to Reconstruction in the years following the Civil War.

Redeemers White, conservative Democrats who challenged and overthrew Republican rule in the South during Reconstruction.

Knights of the Ku Klux Klan (KKK) Organization formed in 1865 by General Nathan Bedford Forrest to enforce prewar racial norms. Members of the KKK used threats and violence to intimidate black people and white Republicans.

Force Acts Three acts passed by Congress in 1870 and 1871 in response to vigilante attacks on southern black people. The acts were designed to protect black political rights and end violence by the Ku Klux Klan and similar organizations.

Despite the Republican record of accomplishment during Reconstruction, white Southerners did not accept its legitimacy. They accused interracial governments of conducting a spending spree that raised taxes and encouraged corruption. Indeed, taxes did rise significantly, but mainly because legislatures funded much-needed educational and social services. Corruption on building projects and railroad construction was common during this time. Still, it is unfair to single out Reconstruction governments and especially black legislators as inherently depraved, as their Democratic opponents acted the same way when given the opportunity. Economic scandals were part of American life after the Civil War. As enormous business opportunities arose in the postwar years, many economic and political leaders made unlawful deals to enrich themselves. Furthermore, southern opponents of Reconstruction exaggerated its harshness. In contrast to revolutions and civil wars in other countries, only one rebel was executed for war crimes (the commandant of Andersonville Prison in Georgia); only one high-ranking official went to prison (Jefferson Davis); no official was forced into exile, though some fled voluntarily; and most rebels regained voting rights and the ability to hold office within seven years after the end of the rebellion.

Most important, these Reconstruction governments had only limited opportunities to transform the South. By the end of 1870, civilian rule had returned to all of the former Confederate states, and they had reentered the Union. Republican rule did not continue past 1870 in Virginia, North Carolina, and Tennessee and did not extend beyond 1871 in Georgia and 1873 in Texas. In 1874 Democrats deposed Republicans in Arkansas and Alabama; two years later, Democrats triumphed in Mississippi. In only three states — Louisiana, Florida, and South Carolina — did Reconstruction last until 1877.

The Democrats who replaced Republicans trumpeted their victories as bringing "redemption" to the South. Of course, these so-called **Redeemers** were referring to the white South. For black Republicans and their white allies, redemption meant defeat. Democratic victories came at the ballot boxes, but violence, intimidation, and fraud paved the way. In 1865 in Pulaski, Tennessee General Nathan Bedford Forrest organized Confederate veterans into a group called the **Knights of the Ku Klux Klan (KKK)**. Spreading throughout the South, its followers donned robes and masks to hide their identities and terrify their victims. Gun-wielding Ku Kluxers rode on horseback to the homes and churches of black and white Republicans to keep them from voting. When threats did not work, they beat and murdered their victims. In 1871, for example, 150 African Americans were killed in Jackson County in the Florida Panhandle. A black clergyman lamented, "That is where Satan has his seat." There and elsewhere, many of the individuals targeted had managed to buy property, gain political leadership, or in other ways defy white stereotypes of African American inferiority. Other white supremacist organizations joined the Klan in waging a reign of terror. During the 1875 election in Mississippi, which toppled the Republican government, armed terrorists killed hundreds of Republicans and scared many more away from the polls.

To combat the terror unleashed by the Klan and its allies, Congress passed three **Force Acts** in 1870 and 1871. These measures empowered the president to dispatch officials into the South to supervise elections and prevent voting interference. Directed specifically at the KKK, one law barred secret organizations from using force to violate equal protection of the laws. In 1872 Congress established a joint committee to probe Klan tactics, and its investigations produced thirteen volumes of gripping testimony about the horrors perpetrated by the Klan. Elias Hill, a freedman from South Carolina who had become a Baptist preacher and teacher, was one of those who appeared before Congress. Klansmen dragged Elias Hill out of his house and beat, whipped, and threatened to kill him. On the basis of such testimony, the federal government prosecuted some 3,000 Klansmen. Only 600 were convicted, however. As the Klan officially disbanded in the wake of federal prosecutions, other vigilante organizations arose to take its place.

BUILDING AP® SKILLS

Continuity and Change

After students have reviewed this module and studied sharecropping, have the class discuss if sharecropping type practices are present in other time periods in U.S. history. Student answers will vary but the ideas of continuity and change should be addressed. Students should highlight examples from U.S. history, such as *colonial taxes*, *indentured servants*, *slavery*, *predatory lending*, *high-interest loans*, *student debt*, etc.

TEACHING IDEA

Check for Understanding

Ensure students remember to *ACE* every question. While the skills seemingly are accessible, yearly AP® scores report that on the national AP® exam students' answers to free response questions often are not awarded points due to a lack of support within the answers. Remind students that the free response questions will be spread across the entirety of the AP® U.S. History framework — 1400s through Modern Era. Have students continue to practice addressing FRQ questions within each module (a refresher on *ACE* can be found on page 21).

TEACHING IDEA

Incorporating Videos

Have students watch the video, "What Ever Happened to Confederate President Jefferson Davis?" (available on YouTube). Conduct a brief discussion addressing if justice was truly served in the court trial against Jefferson Davis and if his imprisonment was warranted.

TRM Suggested Responses to Questions

TRM Module 5.7 AP® Analyzing Sources Handout 3

EXPLORING AP® THEMES
Politics and Power

The rise of the Ku Klux Klan and its impact during Reconstruction and beyond is well documented and accounts are readily available. Students taking the AP® U.S. History course need to know the basic origins and impacts of the group. Ensure students know the impact of the KKK on voting and the resulting loss of political power for southern African Americans. Have students visit the Khan Academy's website and search for "The First KKK" (khanacademy.org). Students should complete a quick write summarizing the causes and impacts of the KKK. Students should address the reasons why the group was founded and how the group was able to spread throughout the South and ultimately within the entire nation.

Period 5: 1844–1877

MODULE 5-7   Reform and Resistance

AP® ANALYZING SOURCES

Source: *Independent Monitor,* "A Prospective Scene in the 'City of Oaks,' 4th of March, 1869"

About the source: The text directly beneath this image reads, "Hang, curs, hang! ***** *Their* complexion is perfect gallows. Stand fast, good fate, to *their* hanging! ***** If they be not born to be hanged, our case is miserable."

Questions for Analysis
1. Identify the intended audience for this political cartoon.
2. Describe the message this image communicates to its intended audience.
3. Explain how the image portrays Northerners' relationship to the South.
4. Evaluate the extent to which Reconstruction efforts were undermined by Northerners.

REVIEW
- How did white Southerners fight back against Reconstruction?
- What role did terrorism play in this effort?

TEACHING IDEA

Incorporating Websites

Visit HarpWeek's website and search for the activity, "The Ku Klux Klan Hearings" (harpweek.com). Within the accompanying documents are eyewitness accounts of the KKK's actions taken during Reconstruction. There are several teaching simulations and activities, which might be meaningful to incorporate in class.

AP® WRITING HISTORICALLY — Short-Answer Question Practice

ACTIVITY

Read the following question carefully and write a short response. Use complete sentences.

Using the following excerpts, answer (a), (b), and (c).

Source: Eric Foner, *Reconstruction: America's Unfinished Revolution, 1863–1877*, 1998

"If blacks failed to achieve the economic independence envisioned in the aftermath of the Civil War, Reconstruction closed off even more oppressive alternatives than the Redeemers' New South. The post-Reconstruction labor system embodied neither a return to the closely supervised gang labor of the antebellum days, nor the complete dispossession and immobilization of the black labor force and coercive apprenticeship systems envisioned by white Southerners in 1865 and 1866. . . . As illustrated by the small but growing number of black landowners, businessmen, and professionals, the doors of economic opportunity that had opened could never be completely closed. Without Reconstruction, moreover, it is difficult to imagine the establishment of a framework of legal rights enshrined in the Constitution that, while flagrantly violated after 1877, created a vehicle for future federal intervention in Southern affairs. As a result of this unprecedented redefinition of the American body politic, the South's racial system remained regional rather than national, an outcome of great importance when economic opportunities at last opened in the North."

Source: Elliott West, "Reconstructing Race," *Western Historical Quarterly* 34, Spring 2003

"This Greater Reconstruction [of the whole nation] was even more morally ambiguous than the lesser one [in the South]. It included not one war but three—the Mexican War, Civil War, and War against Indian America—and while it saw the emancipation of one non-white people, it was equally concerned with dominating others. It included the Civil Rights Acts and the 13th, 14th, and 15th Amendments, but it began with U.S. soldiers clashing with a Mexican patrol on disputed terrain along the Rio Grande in 1846. . . . Always the Greater Reconstruction was as much about control as liberation, as much about unity and power as about equality. Indians were given roles they mostly didn't want, and freedmen were offered roles they mostly did, but both were being told that these were the roles they *would* play, like it or not. . . ."

a. Briefly describe ONE major difference between Foner and West's historical interpretations of Reconstruction.
b. Briefly explain how ONE historical event or development from the period 1865 to 1877 that is not explicitly mentioned in the excerpts could be used to support Foner's argument.
c. Briefly explain how ONE historical event or development from the period 1865 to 1877 that is not explicitly mentioned in the excerpts could be used to support West's argument.

TRM Suggested Responses to Questions

TEACHING IDEA

AP® Writing Historically Review

This activity attempts to give students a sense of the categories of analysis employed by each historian in a ten-minute bell ringer activity, which are Reconstruction, Greater Reconstruction, African Americans, American Indians, and Southerners. Students are to match each category to an excerpt and give a brief explanation for how each category is used by the historian. This activity can enliven students' sense of the categories historians choose to use and how those choices affect their interpretations.

TRM Suggested Responses to Questions

BUILDING AP® SKILLS

Claims and Evidence in Sources

The Force Acts have several names in the AP® U.S. History course, and students should know that the differing names are all in reference to the same laws. Other commonly used names include the First Ku Klux Klan Act, the Enforcement Acts, or the Civil Rights Acts of 1870 and 1871. Regardless of the name, the acts were important weapons given to the president to be able to enforce the Fourteenth Amendment throughout the United States. Have students read segments of the Force Acts and compile a list of some of the most important powers given to the president. The acts can be found within the Library of Congress website (loc.gov). Have students share their information with a small group to ensure students hear a wide range of the authorities given to the president within these acts.

Module 5-8

Reconstruction Undone

LEARNING TARGETS

By the end of this module, you should be able to:

- Explain the causes that led to the end of Reconstruction.
- Explain how and why Reconstruction affected both regional and national conceptions of American identity.
- Explain the impact of the Civil War on American values.

THEMATIC FOCUS

American and National Identity

Because white landowners continued to control agricultural production in the South, most African Americans were unable to achieve economic independence, and many left for opportunities elsewhere. As white Southerners used both legal and criminal tactics to prevent African Americans from achieving equality, the federal government increasingly narrowed its protections for African Americans' rights. Reconstruction was essentially reversed by 1877, and its legacy left many civil rights issues unaddressed until the mid-twentieth century.

HISTORICAL REASONING FOCUS

Comparison

Continuity and Change

By 1877, the nation had undergone enormous social change. However, many questions from before the Civil War remained unanswered: How could all Americans be guaranteed equal rights in practice? To what extent did economic inequality undermine political equality? What was the relationship of the federal government to the newly reconstructed states? How would national political parties negotiate the recent sectional divisions?

TASK ▶ As you read this module, consider the extent to which American society had changed by the end of Reconstruction, as well as the extent to which it remained the same.

The Retreat from Reconstruction

The violence, intimidation, and fraud perpetrated by Redeemers does not fully explain the unraveling of Reconstruction. By the early 1870s most white Northerners had come to believe that they had done more than enough for black Southerners, and it was time to focus on other issues. Growing economic problems intensified this feeling. Still reeling from the amount of blood shed during the war, white Americans, North and South, turned their attention toward burying and memorializing the Civil War dead. White America was once again united, if only in the shared belief that it was time to move on, consigning the issues of slavery and civil rights to history.

Most northern whites shared the racial prejudices of their counterparts in the South. Although they had supported protection of black civil rights and suffrage, they still believed that African Americans were inferior to whites and were horrified by the idea of social integration. They began to sympathize with southern whites' racist complaints that black people were not capable of governing honestly and effectively.

In 1872 a group calling themselves Liberal Republicans challenged the reelection of President Grant. Financial scandals had racked the Grant administration. This high-level corruption reflected other get-rich-quick schemes connected to economic speculation and development following the Civil War. Outraged by the rising level of immoral behavior in government and

TEACHING IDEA

Class Discussion

Have the class address the question, "To what extent did laws eliminate prejudice during Reconstruction?" Although there is no seemingly clear answer to the question, students should practice formulating an argument and defending their claims with facts and supporting details. The discussion will be enlightening during coming modules as students move forward within the course.

AP® TIP

Evaluate the degree to which the concerns expressed by Liberal Republicans in 1872 illustrated a shift in the Republican platform during Reconstruction.

business, Liberal Republicans nominated Horace Greeley, editor of the *New York Tribune*, to run against Grant. They linked government corruption to the expansion of federal power that accompanied Reconstruction and called for the removal of troops from the South and amnesty for all former Confederates. They also campaigned for civil service reform, which would base government employment on a merit system and abolish the "spoils system" — in which the party in power rewarded loyal supporters with political appointments — that had been introduced by Andrew Jackson in the 1820s.

The Democratic Party believed that Liberal Republicans offered the best chance to defeat Grant, and it endorsed Greeley. Despite the scandals that surrounded him, Grant remained popular. Moreover, the main body of Republicans "waved the bloody shirt," reminding northern voters that a ballot cast for the opposition tarnished the memory of brave Union soldiers killed during the war. The president won reelection with an even greater margin than he had four years earlier. Nevertheless, the attacks against Grant foreshadowed the Republican retreat on Reconstruction. Among the Democrats sniping at Grant was Andrew Johnson. Johnson had returned to Tennessee, and in 1874 the state legislature chose the former president to serve in the U.S. Senate. He continued to speak out against the presence of federal troops in the South until his death in 1875.

AP® ANALYZING SOURCES

Source: James Garfield, *Speech Delivered at Warren, Ohio*, 1872

"Democrats of the late Rebel States tell us they are for Greeley in spite of his doctrines of abolition and his financial theories because he is in favor or universal amnesty, and is their friend. For myself, I honor Mr. Greeley for his advocacy of universal amnesty, which I have several times voted for in the House of Representatives. But what would he do for the South were he the President? It is said that some of the Southern State governments have been badly and corruptly managed; and so they have. But how can the President interfere to remedy that evil? Congress, not the President, can remove political disabilities. . . . What change for the better do the people of the South expect from Mr. Greeley? It is the Ku-Klux law of which they complain? There has been no more vehement defender of that law in all the land than Mr. Greeley. I remember that when I, in the company of twenty-five other Republicans, successfully opposed the more extreme features of that bill as it was first introduced into the House, we were denounced by the editor of the Tribune, who declared that we had shorn the bill of its most valuable provisions. Do they expect him to aid in repealing the election law, which they call the bayonet law? Let them not forget that the editor of the Tribune complained that the law was confined to the Federal elections, and expressed the wish that it had been extended to State and local elections as well. Do they wish him to become champion of State rights, and to resist the supposed centralizing tendencies of the Republican party? Do they not know that he has been more nearly consistent in his advocacy and defence of that tendency, than in any other doctrine he has ever professed?

For this strange and unnatural combination between Republicans and Democrats it must result in one of the parties will be outrageously cheated, unless it be true that both have agreed to abandon all principles, all convictions, all aims and objects, except the simple one to win office, — to gain power."

Questions for Analysis

1. Identify why, according to Garfield, southern states supported Horace Greeley's campaign.
2. Describe why this support appears absurd to Garfield.
3. Evaluate the extent to which sectional divisions still shaped the national political parties in the election of 1872. Be sure to consider that Garfield represents the Republican Party in this speech.

EXPLORING AP® THEMES

Continuity and Change

Have students define the term "spoils system." The spoils system is closely associated with Andrew Jackson, but George Washington set the precedent when selecting his original four cabinet members during his first term. Reviewing the topic in this module will help in teaching the coming Gilded Age topics.

TRM Suggested Responses to Questions

TRM Module 5.8 AP® Analyzing Sources Handout 1

BUILDING AP® SKILLS

Sourcing and Situation

Show students the 1887 *Puck* cartoon of Republican Senator John Sherman "waving the bloody shirt," and James A. Wales's combined cartoon, "The 'Strong' Government 1869–1877 — The 'Weak' Government 1877–1881" (readily available online through title search). Have students complete a HIPP analysis for each of the three images (a refresher on HIPP can be found on page 8). These political cartoons reflect the growing disillusionment of the American public in the North and South toward the necessity of Reconstruction.

BUILDING AP® SKILLS

Claims and Evidence in Sources

Have students annotate the *Speech Delivered at Warren, Ohio* and find the thesis within the argument along with any bias. Discuss the impact and need to search for bias within any speech or primary source document. Have students share their findings in small groups or as a whole.

Period 5: 1844–1877

MODULE 5-8   Reconstruction Undone

EXPLORING AP® THEMES
Social Structures

Economic themes are present throughout the entire AP® U.S. History course description and framework, and as such, economic trends should be covered when possible. The Panic of 1873 is a complex and important topic for students to understand. Have students read the informative entry, "Panic of 1873," from Teaching History's website (teachinghistory.org). Students should take notes focusing on the reasons for the introduction of greenbacks and the importance of silver and gold backing the currency. The introduction of these concepts within this module will set the framework for future discussion of American banking and financial policy.

BUILDING AP® SKILLS
Causation

The Slaughterhouse Cases defined the Fourteenth Amendment for many years. Students should watch Hip Hughes's video, "The Slaughterhouse Cases: Interpreting the 14th Amendment" (available on YouTube). Have students write a summary of the cases and the lasting impacts. Then, students should share their answers with a partner when complete. Answers will vary.

Panic of 1873 Severe economic depression triggered by the collapse of the Northern Pacific Railroad.

AP® TIP
Analyze the role that economic upheaval played in the end of Reconstruction.

Civil Rights Act of 1875 Act extending "full and equal treatment" for all races in public accommodations, including jury service and public transportation. However, in 1883, the Supreme Court ruled the act was unconstitutional.

By the time Grant began his second term, Congress was already considering bills to restore officeholding rights to former Confederates who had not yet sworn allegiance to the Union. Black representatives, including Georgia congressman Jefferson Long, as well as some white lawmakers, remained opposed to such measures, but in 1872 Congress removed the penalties placed on former Confederates by the Fourteenth Amendment and permitted nearly all rebel leaders the right to vote and hold office. Two years later, for the first time since the start of the Civil War, the Democrats gained a majority in the House of Representatives and prepared to remove the remaining troops from the South.

Republican leaders also rethought their top priority, with economic concerns increasingly replacing racial considerations. The **Panic of 1873**, caused largely by the collapse of the Northern Pacific Railroad, triggered a severe economic depression lasting late into the decade. Tens of thousands of unemployed workers across the country worried more about finding jobs than they did about black civil rights. Businessmen, too, were plagued with widespread bankruptcy. When strikes erupted across the country in 1877, most notably the **Great Railway Strike**, in which more than half a million workers walked off the job, employers asked the U.S. government to remove troops from the South and dispatch them against strikers in the North and West.

While white Northerners sought ways to extricate themselves from Reconstruction, the Supreme Court weakened enforcement of the civil rights acts. In 1873 the **Slaughterhouse** cases defined the rights that African Americans were entitled to under the Fourteenth Amendment very narrowly. Reflecting the shift from moral to economic concerns, the justices interpreted the amendment as extending greater protection to corporations in conducting business than to black people. As a result, black people had to depend on southern state governments to protect their civil rights — the same state authorities that had deprived them of their rights in the first place. In *United States v. Cruikshank* (1876), the high court narrowed the Fourteenth Amendment further, ruling that it protected black people against abuses only by state officials and agencies, not by private groups such as the Ku Klux Klan. Seven years later, the Court struck down the **Civil Rights Act of 1875**, which had extended "full and equal treatment" in public accommodations for persons of all races.

REVIEW
Why did northern interest in Reconstruction fade during the 1870s?

The Presidential Compromise of 1876

The presidential election of 1876 set in motion events that officially brought Reconstruction to an end. The Republicans nominated the governor of Ohio, Rutherford B. Hayes, who was chosen partly because he was untainted by the corruption that plagued the Grant administration. The Democrats selected their own anticorruption crusader, Governor Samuel J. Tilden of New York.

The outcome of the election depended on twenty disputed electoral votes, nineteen from the South and one from Oregon. Tilden won 51 percent of the popular vote, but Reconstruction political battles in Florida, Louisiana, and South Carolina put the election up for grabs. In each of these states, the outgoing Republican administration certified Hayes as the winner, while the incoming Democratic regime declared for Tilden.

The Constitution assigns Congress the task of counting and certifying the electoral votes submitted by the states. Normally, this is a mere formality, but 1876 was different. Democrats controlled the House, Republicans controlled the Senate, and neither branch would budge on which votes to count. Hayes needed all twenty for victory; Tilden needed only one. To break the logjam, Congress created a fifteen-member Joint Electoral Commission, composed of seven Democrats, seven Republicans, and one independent. Ultimately, a majority voted to count all twenty votes for the Republican Hayes, making him president (Map 5.9).

TEACHING IDEA
Incorporating Videos

The election of 1876 was closely contested and the surrounding details of the compromise, which ultimately marked the official ending of Reconstruction, are important for students to understand. Have students watch Episode 23 "The Industrial Economy" from the Crash Course US History series or Hip Hughes's "The Election of 1876 Explained" (both videos available on YouTube). Have students complete a quick write as to why Reconstruction ended, then share their findings with a partner.

The Presidential Compromise of 1876

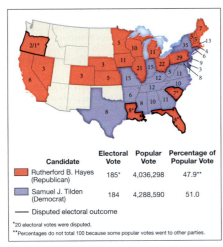

◀ **MAP 5.9 The Election of 1876**
The presidential election of 1876 got swept up in Reconstruction politics. Democrats defeated Republicans in Florida, Louisiana, and South Carolina, but both parties claimed the electoral votes for their candidates. A federal electoral commission set up to investigate the twenty disputed votes, including one from Oregon, awarded the votes and the election to the Republican, Rutherford B. Hayes. **How does this map reveal the extent to which sectionalism persisted in national politics after the end of the Civil War?**

compromise of 1877
Compromise between Republicans and southern Democrats that resulted in the election of Rutherford B. Hayes. Southern Democrats agreed to support Hayes in the disputed presidential election in exchange for his promise to end Reconstruction.

Still, Congress had to ratify this count, and disgruntled southern Democrats in the Senate threatened a filibuster — unlimited debate — to block certification of Hayes. With the March 4, 1877 date for the presidential inauguration creeping perilously close and no winner officially declared, behind-the-scenes negotiations finally settled the controversy. A series of meetings between Hayes supporters and southern Democrats led to a bargain. According to the agreement, Democrats would support Hayes in exchange for the president appointing a Southerner to his cabinet, withdrawing the last federal troops from the South, and endorsing construction of a transcontinental railroad through the South. This **compromise of 1877** averted a crisis over presidential succession, underscored increased southern Democratic influence within Congress, and marked the end of strong federal protections for African Americans in the South.

AP® ANALYZING SOURCES

Source: President Rutherford B. Hayes, *Inaugural Address*, 1877

"Many of the calamitous efforts of the tremendous revolution which has passed over the Southern States still remain. The immeasurable benefits which will surely follow, sooner or later, the hearty and generous acceptance of the legitimate results of that revolution have not yet been realized. Difficult and embarrassing questions meet us at the threshold of this subject. The people of those States are still impoverished, and the inestimable blessing of wise, honest, and peaceful local self-government is not fully enjoyed. Whatever difference of opinion may exist as to the cause of this condition of things, the fact is clear that in the progress of events the time has come when such government is the imperative necessity required by all the varied interests, public and private, of those States. But it must not be forgotten that only a local government which recognizes and maintains inviolate the rights of all is a true self-government.

With respect to the two distinct races whose peculiar relations to each other have brought upon us the deplorable complications and perplexities which exist in those States, it must be a government which guards the interests of both races carefully and equally. It must

(Continued)

EXPLORING AP® THEMES

Causation

Have the class discuss the reasons why Reconstruction ended. Within this class discussion focus students to the causes and impacts of the official ending of Reconstruction occurring in 1877. Remind students of the *Harper's Weekly* image from page 412 where a Union soldier was depicted separating angry white Southerners from black Southerners. Discuss the legacy of Reconstruction in the United States in regards to race relations, voting rights, anti-immigrant sentiments, etc.

TRM Suggested Responses to Questions

TRM Module 5.8 AP® Analyzing Sources Handout 2

TEACHING IDEA

Connecting the Dots

The impact of the Compromise of 1877 is an important concept for students to understand. Have students work in groups to list the causes and effects surrounding the Compromise of 1877. Groups should share their lists to conduct a jigsaw review (a refresher of the jigsaw model can be found on page 33). Students should then be split in pairs to create categories of analysis from their lists so they can write an essay dealing with causes and effects of the Compromise of 1877.

▲ Differentiation

For students who continue to struggle with writing essays, construct an essay for the class on butcher paper based solely on student responses and ideas. Have the students provide a sample thesis and categories to address. Lead the students through the process of writing an essay by using their facts and ideas presented directly from student call-outs. The teacher-created essay might be a simple outline or bulleting of major ideas provided by students, but demonstrating the process of creating an entire essay will help many students. After the class has created a group essay, reinforce the activity by having students create their own essay based on the same prompt.

be a government which submits loyally and heartily to the Constitution and the laws — the laws of the nation and the laws of the States themselves — accepting and obeying faithfully the whole Constitution as it is."

Questions for Analysis

1. Identify the main problems that, according to Hayes, the nation still faced in 1877.
2. Describe the solutions Hayes proposes to address these problems.
3. Evaluate the extent to which Hayes's solutions represent a continuation of previous Republican policies.

REVIEW

What common values and beliefs held by white Americans were reflected in the compromise of 1877?

The Legacies of Reconstruction

Reconstruction was, in many ways, profoundly limited. Notwithstanding the efforts of the Freedmen's Bureau, African Americans did not receive the landownership that would have provided them with economic independence and bolstered their freedom from the racist assaults of white Southerners. The civil and political rights that the federal government conferred did not withstand the efforts of former Confederates to deprive the freedpeople of equal rights, particularly the right to vote. The Republican Party shifted its priorities, and Democrats gained enough political power nationally to short-circuit federal intervention, even as numerous problems remained unresolved in the South. Northern support for racial equality did not run very deep, so white Northerners, who shared many of the prejudices of white Southerners, were happy to avoid further intervention in southern racial matters. Nor was there sufficient support to give women, white or black, the right to vote. Finally, federal courts, with growing concerns over economic rather than social issues, sanctioned Northerners' retreat by providing constitutional legitimacy for abandoning black Southerners and rejecting women's suffrage in court decisions that narrowed the interpretation of the Fourteenth and Fifteenth Amendments.

Despite all of this, Reconstruction did transform the country. As a result of Reconstruction, slavery was abolished and the legal basis for freedom was enshrined in the Constitution. Indeed, black people exercised a measure of political and economic freedom during Reconstruction that never entirely disappeared over the decades to come. In many areas, freedpeople, exemplified by Congressman Jefferson Franklin Long and many others, asserted what they never could have during slavery — control over their lives, their churches, their labor, their education, and their families. What they could not practice during their own time, their descendants would one day revive through the promises codified in the Fourteenth and Fifteenth Amendments.

African Americans transformed not only themselves; they transformed the nation. The Constitution became much more democratic and egalitarian through inclusion of the Reconstruction amendments. Reconstruction lawmakers took an important step toward making the United States the "more perfect union" that the nation's Founders had pledged to create. Reconstruction established a model for expanding the power of the federal government to resolve domestic crises that lay beyond the abilities of states and ordinary citizens. It remained a powerful legacy for elected officials who dared to invoke it. And Reconstruction transformed the South. It modernized state constitutions, expanded educational and social welfare systems, and unleashed the repressed potential for industrialization and economic development that the preservation of slavery had restrained. Ironically, Reconstruction did as much for white Southerners as it did for black Southerners in liberating them from the past.

REVIEW

To what extent was southern society changed by Reconstruction?

BUILDING AP® SKILLS

Comparison

Have students compare Reconstruction 1865–1868 to Reconstruction 1875–1877. Students should address the early successes within Reconstruction and trace the eventual failings and limiting of freedoms that preside during the end of Reconstruction. The major take-away for students must be analysis of Reconstruction in its entirety.

BUILDING AP® SKILLS

Making Connections

Students should create a chart in which they compare the conditions at the end of Reconstruction for the West, North, and South. Students should highlight political, economic, and social trends across these three regions. The conditions and outlook for all three regions will vary, but students should find commonalities in that all three regions are ready to expand economically and all three have bias toward minority groups — be it in terms of race, political power, or ethnic make-up. The resulting Venn diagram will be a meaningful segue into coming modules.

TRM Find **Handout 5.8 – Regional Conditions at the End of Reconstruction** in the Teacher's Resource Materials.

Period 5: 1844–1877

The Legacies of Reconstruction

AP® WRITING HISTORICALLY — Responding to a Document-Based Question

The following prompt requires you to draw on what you have learned about Reconstruction as well as seven accompanying documents.

> Evaluate the extent to which regional attitudes regarding civil rights changed between 1855 and 1877.

Step 1 Break down the prompt.

Be sure to note the topic of the prompt and the time range it specifies: 1855–1877. This span includes historical content from several modules in Period 5. The way the prompt is worded also provides important clues about what your response must do — as you will recall from your essay practice since Period 3, when you are asked to "evaluate the extent" of something, it means your essay needs to make an argument that tackles the importance of historical developments in relation to the topic of the prompt.

As with previous essays, in order to ACE this question, you should briefly create a list of information you already know about the prompt. Remember, it may be helpful to approach this prompt as if no documents were provided with it.

The following graphic organizer presents one way to approach organizing your historical knowledge prior to moving on to the documents. The first row has been partially completed for you as an example, but the "Explanation of Change" has been left blank — that's because only you can determine how important a given effect is within the context of your essay's argument. Your evaluation of this example may also depend on the other effects you decide to explore in this table.

Region	Evidence of Change/Continuity	Extent of Change/Continuity	Explanation of Change/Continuity
North	• New York Draft Riots and targeting of African Americans • Passage of 13th, 14th, 15th Amendments • Congress takes over Freedman's Bureau • Creation of Freedman's Bureau	• Lingering racism in north in places like New York City • Transformation of conflict from war for union to war for emancipation • Increasing attempt by Federal Government to protect Civil Rights for African Americans in the South	
South			

Remember, any prompt that asks you about the extent of change during a particular time period is also asking you to speak to continuity as well. As you pre-write, be sure that at least one of your claims addresses a continuity throughout the time period of 1855 to 1877.

Step 2 Read and annotate the documents.

As you read each of the seven documents that follow, remember to ask yourself the following questions:

- What is the document about? What historical situation does it describe or reference?
- Who was the intended audience for this document?
- What was the author's purpose in writing this document?
- What point of view does the author of this document express?
- How does this document relate back to the prompt?
- Does this document remind you of any other historical developments?

Finally, keep in mind how you can use each document to support the historical argument you are planning to make. How can these primary sources serve as evidence in your essay?

(Continued)

TRM Suggested Responses to Questions

TEACHING IDEA

AP® Writing Historically Workshop

Even though this question explicitly asks about change, implicitly it also provides students the opportunity to address the extent to which continuities occurred over regional attitudes toward civil rights. Before students write a response, consider this brief 10-minute activity, which seeks to make students aware of this historical phenomenon. Provide two categories on a butcher-block paper: continuities and changes. Have students sort each document to a category with a brief explanation about why they categorized each document to represent either a continuity or change. This way, students are aware of the many possible interpretations to this question.

BUILDING AP® SKILLS

Developments and Process

The periodization of this question is 1855–1877. Before students start to break down the elements of the question consider the following activity. Divide students into groups of three or four and ask for two or three categories of time they would use to illustrate their understanding of the question. For instance, groups could give the following: 1855–1861, 1861–1865, or 1865–1877. The first time period could be defined as the antebellum years of the U.S., the second time period as the Civil War, and the third as the traditional periodization of Reconstruction. Knowing this informs how they will illustrate change over time in their responses.

TEACHING IDEA

Organizing Evidence

Have students categorize each document to illustrate either a continuity or change in regional attitudes toward civil rights. Organizing the documents in advance of writing the DBQ is essential as it ensures students are focused on what the question is asking.

DOCUMENT 1

Source: Abraham Lincoln, *Speech at Edwardsville, Illinois*, 1858

"Our defense is in the preservation of the spirit which prizes liberty as the heritage of all men, in all lands, every where. Destroy this spirit, and you have planted the seeds of despotism around your own doors. Familiarize yourselves with the chains of bondage, and you are preparing your own limbs to wear them. Accustomed to trample on the rights of those around you, you have lost the genius of your own independence, and become the fit subjects of the first cunning tyrant who rises."

DOCUMENT 2

Source: *A Declaration of the Immediate Causes which Induce and Justify the Secession of the State of Mississippi from the Federal Union*, 1861

"Our position is thoroughly identified with the institution of slavery—the greatest material interest of the world. Its labor supplies the product which constitutes by far the largest and most important portions of commerce of the earth. These products are peculiar to the climate verging on the tropical regions, and by an imperious law of nature, none but the black race can bear exposure to the tropical sun. These products have become necessities of the world, and a blow at slavery is a blow at commerce and civilization. That blow has been long aimed at the institution, and was at the point of reaching its consummation. There was no choice left us but submission to the mandates of abolition, or a dissolution of the Union, whose principles had been subverted to work out our ruin."

DOCUMENT 3

Source: *New York Herald*, "What to Do with the Slaves When Emancipated," 1862

"What is to be done with the slaves when emancipated? It would not do to let them work or not, as they may think proper. If they were as willing to work as the white man there would be no slavery now in any Southern State. The proposed change would involve the necessity of transferring from the master to the State the superintendence of negro labor, and vagrant laws should be passed compelling negroes to work—laws which exist in many parts of Europe in reference to the white population, but infinitely more necessary for blacks, whose idea of paradise is to have nothing to do. The wages should be regulated by law, and be sufficient not only to procure food and clothing, but to enable the negro to lay up something for sickness and old age. On the whole, the negro would be worse off under this system than in servitude; but if the interests of the white men of the border slave States demand it the interests of the negro must be made subordinate, and the system which now gives him protection by law, and a provision for life, must be abolished. But of their own interests in the matter the citizens of the slave States alone are the proper judges, and the people of the free States have nothing whatever to do with the question."

DOCUMENT 4

Source: *Civil Rights Act*, 1866

"Be it enacted by the Senate and House of Representatives of the United States of America in Congress assembled, That all persons born in the United States and not subject to any foreign power, excluding Indians not taxed, are hereby declared to be citizens of the United States; and such citizens, of every race and color, without regard to any previous condition of slavery or involuntary servitude, except as a punishment for crime whereof the party shall have been duly convicted, shall have the same right, in every State and Territory in the United States, to make and enforce contracts, to sue, be parties, and give evidence, to inherit, purchase, lease, sell, hold, and convey real and personal property, and to full and equal benefit of all laws and proceedings for the security of person and property, as is enjoyed by white citizens, and shall be subject to like punishment, pains, and penalties, and to none other, any law, statute, ordinance, regulation, or custom, to the contrary notwithstanding."

DOCUMENT 5

Source: Elizabeth Cady Stanton and Susan B. Anthony, *Equal Rights Association: Stanton-Anthony Resolutions*, 1869

"Resolved, That the American Equal Rights Association, in loyalty to its comprehensive demands for the political equality of all American citizens, without distinction of race or sex, hails the extension of suffrage to any heretofore disfranchised, as a cheering part of the triumph of our whole idea.

Resolved, therefore, That we gratefully welcome the pending fifteenth amendment, prohibiting disfranchisement on account of race, and earnestly solicit the State Legislatures to pass it without delay.

Resolved, furthermore, That in view of this promised and speedy culmination of one-half of our demands, we are stimulated to redouble our energy to secure the further amendment guaranteeing the same sacred rights without limitation to sex.

Resolved, That until the constitution shall know neither black nor white, neither male nor female, but only the equal rights of all classes, we renew our solemn indictment against that instrument as defective, unworthy, and an oppressive charter for the self-government of a free people."

DOCUMENT 6

Source: Senator Hiram Revels (Mississippi), *On Readmission of Georgia to the Union*, 1870

"I maintain that the past record of my race is a true index of the feelings which today animate them. They bear toward their former masters no revengeful thoughts, no hatred, no animosities. They aim not to elevate themselves by sacrificing one single interest of their white fellow-citizens. They ask but the rights which are theirs by God's universal law, and which are the natural outgrowth, the logical sequence of the condition in which the legislative enactments of the nation have placed on them. They appeal to you and to me to see that they receive that protection which alone will enable them to pursue their daily avocations with success and enjoy the liberties of citizenship on the same footing with, their white neighbors and friends. I do not desire to simply defend my own race from unjust and unmerited charges, but I also desire to place upon record an express of my full and entire confidence in the integrity of purpose with which I believe the president, Congress, and the Republican party will meet these questions. . . not only to my own people, but to the whole South."

(Continued)

DOCUMENT 7

Source: Thomas Nast, *This Is a White Man's Government*, 1874

About the source: The text at the bottom of the image reads, "We regard the Reconstruction Acts (so called) of Congress as usurpations, and unconstitutional, revolutionary, and void" – *Democratic platform.* The man in the center of the cartoon is wearing a belt with a buckle labeled "CSA," and holds a knife labeled "the lost cause." The man on the left is an Irish man, who holds a club labeled "a vote." The man on the right is wearing a button labeled "5 Avenue" and holding a wallet labeled "capital for votes." All three men have a foot on the back of an African American Union soldier, who is lying on the ground. In the background of the cartoon, a "colored orphan asylum" and a "southern school" are burning down, and African American children have been lynched nearby.

ACTIVITY

Plan your response to the Document-Based Question at the beginning of this box by following the pre-writing steps provided. Then, write an argumentative essay that cites both outside evidence and evidence from the documents to answer the question.

Make sure to contextualize your argument in the opening paragraph before your thesis statement. Remember, your thesis should make three to four evaluative claims. Each of your body paragraphs should open with one of the claims in your thesis. Be sure to use at least six of the seven documents provided to support your claims throughout your essay, and to include evidence from your own historical knowledge as well. You should also remember to explain how all of the evidence you choose to include in each paragraph supports its central claim. Finally, craft a conclusion that includes a concluding context statement.

You may use the following outline to guide your response:

I. Introductory paragraph
   A. Immediate/preceding contextualization statement
      1. Cite evidence of immediate/preceding context
      2. Explain influence of immediate/preceding context
   B. Thesis statement presenting three to four evaluative claims that are situated along a continuum of relative importance.

II. Claim 1 body paragraph
   A. Topic sentence presenting evaluative claim of change or continuity 1
   B. Supporting statement citing evidence of claim 1 (from historical knowledge)
   C. Cite additional evidence of claim 1 (from a document)
   D. Cite additional evidence of claim 1 (from another document)
   E. Explain how evidence supports claim 1

III. Claim 2 body paragraph
   A. Topic sentence presenting evaluative claim of change or continuity 2
   B. Supporting statement citing evidence of claim 2 (from historical knowledge)
   C. Cite additional evidence of claim 2 (from a document)
   D. Cite additional evidence of claim 2 (from another document)
   E. Explain how evidence supports claim 2

IV. Claim 3 body paragraph
   A. Topic sentence presenting evaluative claim of change or continuity 3
   B. Supporting statement citing evidence of claim 3 (from historical knowledge)
   C. Cite additional evidence of claim 3 (from a document)
   D. Cite additional evidence of claim 3 (from another document)
   E. Explain how evidence supports claim 3

V. (Optional) Claim 4 body paragraph
   A. Topic sentence presenting evaluative claim of change or continuity 4
   B. Supporting statement citing evidence of claim 4 (from historical knowledge)
   C. Cite additional evidence of claim 4 (from a document)
   D. Cite additional evidence of claim 4 (from another document)
   E. Explain how evidence supports claim 4

VI. Conclusion
   A. Restated thesis
   B. Concluding context statement
   C. Evidence for concluding context statement
   D. Explanation of how evidence supports concluding context statement

PERIOD 5 REVIEW 1844–1877

KEY CONCEPTS AND EVENTS

American Equal Rights Association, *423*
American Party, *379*
Battle of Antietam, *396*
Battle of Bull Run (First Manassas), *391*
Battle of Gettysburg, *404*
Battle of Shiloh, *393*
black codes, *420*
Bleeding Kansas, *380*
California Gold Rush, *363*
Californios, *363*
carpetbaggers, *428*
Civil Rights Act of 1875, *436*
Compromise of 1850, *370*
compromise of 1877, *437*
Confederate States of America (Confederacy), *385*
confiscation acts, *393*
contraband, *393*
Copperheads, *401*
Crittenden Plan, *386*
Democratic Review, *359*
Dred Scott case, *382*
Emancipation Proclamation, *396*
Enrollment Act, *400*
Exodusters, *429*
Field Order Number 15, *408*
Fifteenth Amendment, *423*
filibuster, *374*
Force Acts, *433*
Fort Sumter, *389*
Fourteenth Amendment, *420*
Freedmen's Bureau, *412*
Free-Soil Party, *368*
Fugitive Slave Act of 1793, *369*
Fugitive Slave Act of 1850, *370*
Gettysburg Address, *405*
Great Railway Strike, *436*
industrialization, *398*
John Brown's raid, *384*
Kansas-Nebraska Act, *378*
Knights of the Ku Klux Klan (KKK), *432*
Liberty Party, *359*
Lincoln-Douglas debates, *383*
manifest destiny, *359*
martial law, *401*
Mexican-American War, *360*
Military Reconstruction Acts, *422*
National Woman Suffrage Association, *424*
overland trails, *357*
Oregon Trail, *357*
Ostend Manifesto, *374*
Panic of 1873, *436*
Proclamation of Amnesty and Reconstruction, *417*
Radical Republicans, *417*
Reconstruction, *421*
Redeemers, *432*
Republican Party, *379*
Sand Creek Massacre, *409*
Second Battle of Bull Run (Second Manassas), *393*
sharecropping, *429*
Sherman's March to the Sea, *407*
siege of Vicksburg, *404*
Slaughterhouse cases, *436*
Tenure of Office Act, *422*
Thirteenth Amendment, *409*
total war, *407*
transcontinental railroad, *378*
Treaty of Guadalupe Hidalgo, *363*
Uncle Tom's Cabin, *378*
United States v. Cruikshank, *436*
underground railroad, *370*
Wade-Davis bill, *417*
Wilmot Proviso, *368*
Women's National Loyal League, *399*
"Young America" movement, *374*

KEY PEOPLE

Susan B. Anthony, *399*
Clara Barton, *399*
John Wilkes Booth, *409*
John Brown, *379*
James Buchanan, *373*
Anthony Burns, *378*
John C. Calhoun, *369*
Henry Clay, *359*
John Crittenden, *386*
Jefferson Davis, *384*
Stephen Douglas, *378*
Frederick Douglass, *370*
Millard Fillmore, *368*
Nathan Bedford Forrest, *432*
John Frémont, *363*
William Lloyd Garrison, *371*
Ulysses S. Grant, *393*
Horace Greeley, *390*
John Hale, *373*
Rutherford B. Hayes, *436*
Stonewall Jackson, *391*
Andrew Johnson, *412*
Robert E. Lee, *384*
Abraham Lincoln, *360*
George A. Meade, *403*
George B. McClellan, *393*
John L. O'Sullivan, *359*
Franklin Pierce, *373*
James K. Polk, *359*
Dred Scott, *382*
Winfield Scott, *360*
William H. Seward, *369*
Horatio Seymour, *423*
Philip Sheridan, *406*
William Tecumseh Sherman, *405*
Edwin Stanton, *408*
Elizabeth Cady Stanton, *399*
Thaddeus Stevens, *418*
Lucy Stone, *399*
Harriet Beecher Stowe, *378*
Charles Sumner, *380*
Roger Taney, *382*
Zachary Taylor, *360*
Sojourner Truth, *423*
Harriet Tubman, *371*
Daniel Webster, *369*
David Wilmot, *368*

PERIOD 5 REVIEW 1844–1877

CHRONOLOGY

1830s	Economic opportunity leads to an increase in westward settlement
1837	Panic of 1837
1844	James K. Polk (Democrat) elected president
1846–48	Mexican-American War
1846	Wilmot Proviso proposed
1848	Treaty of Guadalupe Hidalgo signed
	Zachary Taylor (Whig) elected president
	California Gold Rush begins
1849	California applies for admission to the Union as a free state
1850	Compromise of 1850
1851	Mass protests over Fugitive Slave Act
1852	Franklin Pierce (Democrat) elected president
	Publication of *Uncle Tom's Cabin* by Harriet Beecher Stowe
1854	Ostend Manifesto leaked
	Republican Party established
	Kansas-Nebraska Act passed
1855	Pro-slavery government installed in Kansas
1856	Bleeding Kansas erupts
1858	Lincoln – Douglas debates
1859	John Brown's raid on Harpers Ferry
1860	Abraham Lincoln (Republican) elected president
	Crittenden plan proposed
1861	Confederate States of America established
	Attack on Fort Sumter
1861–62	U.S. Sanitary Commission established
	Series of Confederate victories
1862	Technological advances aid Union victory at Battles of Shiloh and Antietam
1863	Emancipation Proclamation takes effect
	Union victory at Gettysburg, followed by Gettysburg Address
	Lincoln's Proclamation of Amnesty and Reconstruction
1864	Launch of Ulysses S. Grant's "total war" campaign
	Sand Creek Massacre
By 1865	Federal government is nation's largest employer
1865–77	Reconstruction
	Carpetbaggers move south
1865	Sherman issues Field Order Number 15
	Lee surrenders to Grant at Appomattox
	Lincoln assassinated
	Thirteenth Amendment passed
	Republicans bar southern lawmakers from Congress
	Ku Klux Klan founded
1867	Start of Congressional Reconstruction
	Richmond Republican convention attracts African American voters
1868	Fourteenth Amendment passed
	Dred Scott verdict from 1857 nullified
	Congress votes to impeach Andrew Johnson
	Ulysses S. Grant (Republican) elected president
1869	Fifteenth Amendment passed
1870s	Violence toward African Americans widespread in the South
	Northern resentment toward aid to black Southerners grows
1870–71	Force Acts passed
1872	Grant's re-election challenged by Liberal Republicans
1873	Panic of 1873 triggers an economic depression
1873–77	Supreme Court restricts African American voting rights
1874	Andrew Johnson elected to Senate
	Restrictions on former Confederate leaders lifted
1877	Reconstruction ends
	Compromise of 1877
	Nationwide labor strikes
1879	Exodusters begin to move west

Suggested Responses to Questions

Answers to Multiple-Choice Questions

1. a
2. a
3. c
4. b
5. a
6. a
7. c
8. b
9. d
10. a
11. a
12. a
13. a
14. d

AP® EXAM PRACTICE THROUGH 1877

Multiple Choice Questions

Choose the correct answer for each question.

Questions 1–3 refer to the following excerpt.

> **Source:** United States Supreme Court, *Dred Scott v. Sandford*, March 1857
>
> "[I]t is the opinion of the court that the act of Congress which prohibited a citizen from holding and owning property of this kind in the territory of the United States north of the line therein mentioned is . . . void, and that neither Dred Scott himself nor any of his family were made free by being carried into this territory, even if they had been carried there by the owner with the intention of becoming a permanent resident."

1. The reasoning in the case is most similar to which prior Supreme Court precedent?
   a. The power to determine the meaning of the Constitution established in *Marbury v. Madison* (1803)
   b. The supremacy of federal legislation over state legislation established in *McCullough v. Maryland* (1819)
   c. The sanctity of contracts established in *Dartmouth College v. Woodward* (1819)
   d. The authority of federal government to regulate interstate commerce established in *Gibbons v. Ogden* (1824)

2. The Supreme Court ruling in *Dred Scott v. Sandford* most directly contradicted the provisions of the
   a. Missouri Compromise (1820).
   b. Compromise of 1850.
   c. Fugitive Slave Act (1850).
   d. Kansas-Nebraska Act (1854).

3. The Supreme Court's decision led to
   a. accelerating westward migration.
   b. increasing conflict with American Indian nations.
   c. deepening divisions between the North and South.
   d. strengthening the Second Party System.

4. Which of the following most directly changed the legal status of African Americans established by the Supreme Court's *Dred Scott v. Sandford* decision?
   a. Emancipation Proclamation (1862)
   b. Thirteenth Amendment (1865)
   c. Fourteenth Amendment (1868)
   d. Fifteenth Amendment (1870)

Questions 5–7 refer to the following excerpt.

> **Source:** *The Staunton Spectator*, "The Uses of Economy," Virginia, November 4, 1862
>
> "There is every reason to believe, from present appearances . . . that we shall be short of supplies for one army and people next year. . . . It behooves us therefore to observe the greatest frugality and economy in the use of what we have. It matters not that we have a plethora of money, or that there is an abundance elsewhere to supply our lack, when we are excluded from the markets of the world, and are compelled to rely upon what we have within ourselves. Money cannot produce one grain of corn, or increase by one pound, our quantity of meat. . . . Thousands of our gallant soldiers who were nursed in the lap of plenty, and brought up in the midst of affluence, have known what it is to go for days together without a meal. . . . The season, the condition of the country, the wants of those to whom we have referred, and the prospect before us, all call upon us, trumpet-tongued, to forego every species of luxury during the existence of this war."

5. This passage best serves as evidence of which of the following?
   a. The mobilization of economy and society to wage the Civil War
   b. The failure of the Confederacy to gain full diplomatic support from European powers
   c. The portrayal of the Civil War as a struggle to fulfill America's democratic ideals
   d. The failure of numerous attempts at compromise to reduce conflict

6. The issues brought up in the passage were primarily a result of which of the following?
   a. The southern economy's dependence on imports
   b. Improvements in Union leadership and strategy
   c. African Americans fleeing southern plantations
   d. Differing forms of government between the North and the South

AP® Exam Practice: Through 1877

Period 5: 1844–1877

7. This passage was most likely written in response to the
   a. considerable home front opposition faced by the Confederacy to waging the war.
   b. initiative and daring shown by the North early in the war.
   c. wartime destruction of the South's infrastructure.
   d. greater resources possessed by the North.

Questions 8–9 refer to the following excerpt.

Source: Abraham Lincoln, *Letter to Horace Greeley*, August 22, 1862

"[A]s to the policy I 'seem to be pursuing,' as you say, I have not meant to leave any one in doubt. I would save the Union. I would save it the shortest way under the Constitution. The sooner the National authority can be restored, the nearer the Union will be 'the Union as it was.' If there be those who would not save the Union unless they could at the same time *save* Slavery, I do not agree with them. If there be those who would not save the Union unless they could *destroy* Slavery, I do not agree with them. My paramount object in this struggle is to save the Union, and is not either to save or destroy Slavery. If I could save the Union without freeing *any* slave, I would do it; and if I could save it by freeing *all* the slaves, I would do it; and if I could save it by freeing some and leave others alone, I would also do that. . . . I have here stated my purpose according to my view of *official* duty; and I intend no modification of my oft-expressed *personal* wish that all men, every-where, could be free."

8. Which of the following events most directly contradicts Lincoln's views expressed in this passage?
   a. The enlistment of African Americans in the Union army
   b. The Copperhead Democrats' plan to negotiate a peace with the Confederacy
   c. The highly visible campaign of African American and white abolitionists against slavery
   d. The continued dominance of southern planters in the region after the war

9. Based upon the excerpt, Lincoln would most likely support
   a. the reinstatement of the Kansas-Nebraska Act.
   b. the Dred Scott decision.
   c. the settlement of freedpeople on former plantation lands.
   d. the Thirteenth Amendment.

Questions 10–11 refer to the following excerpt.

Source: *The Mississippi Black Code*, 1865

"Sec. 2 . . . All freedmen, free negroes and mulattoes in this State, over the age of eighteen years . . . with no lawful employment or business, or found unlawfully assembling themselves together, either in the day or night . . . shall be deemed vagrants . . . and shall be imprisoned at the discretion of the court. . . ." Sec. 2 . . . it shall not be lawful for any freedman, free negro or mulatto to intermarry with any white person . . . and any person who shall so intermarry, shall be deemed guilty of a felony, and upon conviction thereof shall be confined in the State penitentiary for life. . . . Sec. 1 . . . no freedman, free negro or mulatto, not in the military service of the United States government . . . shall keep or carry firearms of any kind, or any ammunition. . . . Sec. 5 . . . If any freedman, free negro or mulatto, convicted of any of the misdemeanors provided against in this act, shall fail or refuse . . . to pay the fine and costs imposed, such person shall be hired out by the sheriff or other officers . . . to any white person who will pay said fine and all costs, and take said convict. . . ."

10. The black codes emerged most directly from the context of which of the following?
    a. The compromise between the Virginia and New Jersey Plans during the Constitutional Convention
    b. Thomas Jefferson's reaction to the Alien and Sedition Acts
    c. The rise of democratic beliefs that influenced moral and social reforms
    d. The spread of the ideology of Social Darwinism

11. Which of the following groups of the period would have most directly opposed the creation of the black codes?
    a. Radical Republicans
    b. Labor activists
    c. The U.S. Supreme Court
    d. The Populist Party

Questions 12–14 refer to the following image.

Harper's Weekly Cover, 1874

12. The image is a response to which of the following developments in the United States?
    a. Republican efforts to reorder race relations in the defeated South
    b. The South's restriction of political opportunities and other leadership roles for freedpeople
    c. The abolitionist movement's willingness to use violence to achieve its goals
    d. The support for racial segregation in the *Plessy v. Ferguson* decision

13. An individual who agreed with the artist's perspective as portrayed in the cartoon would express the greatest support for
    a. placing limits on African American rights.
    b. maintaining full legal equality for African Americans.
    c. utilizing systems of patronage at all levels of government.
    d. a moral obligation of wealthy people to help the less fortunate in society.

14. The image most directly criticizes a growing trend in the North supporting policies in the South of political
    a. rights for Southern landholders.
    b. rights slipping away from African Americans.
    c. practice that is traditionally chaotic in the South.
    d. rights for African Americans.

AP® Exam Practice: Through 1877

Period 5: 1844–1877

Short-Answer Questions

Read each question carefully and write a short response. Use complete sentences.

1. Using the following excerpts, answer (a), (b), and (c).

   Source: Charles W. Ramsdell, "The Natural Limits of Slavery Expansion," *Mississippi Valley Historical Review*, 16 (September 1929): 157

   "It took more than twenty years of experimentation and adaptation with wind mills, dry-farming, and new drought-resisting feed crops for the cotton farmer to conquer the plains. There is little reason to believe that the conquest could have been effected earlier [than the 1880s]; there is even less basis for belief that the region would ever have been filled with plantations and slaves. . . . [I]t is likely that the institution of slavery would have declined toward extinction in the Old South before the cotton conquest of the plains could have been accomplished, even had there been no Civil War."

   Source: Stacey L. Smith, *Freedom's Frontier: California and the Struggle over Unfree Labor, Emancipation, and Reconstruction*, 2013

   "[Scholars have] done much to dispel the myth that the West was a landscape of liberty. . . . [They have] demonstrated how the region's vast geography and seemingly limitless opportunities restricted rather than enhanced workers' freedom. Reliant on employers and labor contractors to move them to and across the West's wide-open spaces, immigrant workers often became enmeshed in debt peonage and contract labor. . . . [Historians] have documented the journeys of slaves to the goldfields, California's systems of forced Indian labor, the lives of Chinese women bound in the sex trade, and the debates over imagined Chinese 'coolie' slavery on the Pacific coast. . . . [T]he idea that western environments, economies, or social structures were somehow incompatible with bound labor is gradually losing its force."

   a) Briefly describe ONE major difference between Ramsdell's and Smith's historical interpretations of the West in the nineteenth century.

   b) Briefly explain how ONE specific historical event or development from the period 1844 to 1861 that is not explicitly mentioned in the excerpts could be used to support Ramsdell's argument.

   c) Briefly explain how ONE specific historical event or development from the period 1844 to 1861 that is not explicitly mentioned in the excerpts could be used to support Smith's argument.

2. Using the following graph, answer (a), (b), and (c).

   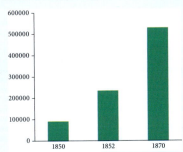

   California Population (Non-American Indians), 1850–1870

   a) Briefly explain ONE specific historical event or development that caused the change illustrated in the graph.

   b) Briefly explain ONE specific historical effect on national politics of the change illustrated in the graph.

   c) Briefly explain ONE specific historical effect within California of the change illustrated in the graph.

Period 5: 1844–1877

AP® Exam Practice: Through 1877

3. Answer (a), (b), and (c).
   a) Briefly describe ONE specific historical change in the political behavior of women in the period 1840 to 1877.
   b) Briefly explain ONE specific historical factor that led to the change you identified in (a).
   c) Briefly explain ONE specific historical result of the change you described in (a) on American politics.

4. Answer (a), (b), and (c).
   a) Briefly describe ONE specific historical difference in the economic lives of African Americans from the period before the Civil War to the period after.
   b) Briefly explain ONE specific historical similarity in the economic lives of African Americans from the period before the Civil War to the period after.
   c) Briefly explain ONE specific historical factor that caused the similarity you explained in (b).

Document-Based Question

Question 1 is based on the accompanying documents. The documents have been edited for the purpose of this exercise. *Suggested reading period: 15 minutes. Suggested writing time: 45 minutes.*

1. Evaluate the extent to which the Civil War altered the lives of Americans in the North and the South between 1861 and 1865.

DOCUMENT 1

Source: Thomas Drayton, a South Carolina plantation owner, *Letter to Percy Drayton, his brother and a Union naval officer*, April 17, 1861

"Dear Percy,
I have received yours of the 9th last, and as Mr. Lincoln has threatened to stop the mails from us to you after they pass the Confederate Boundary, it is probable this may be a long time in getting to you. . . .

You say I don't yet understand the position you have taken. I do fully—but certainly differ from you when you say that to side with us—would be 'battling for slavery against freedom'. . . .

We are fighting for home & liberty. Can the North say as much?—Good night. And don't say again, that in siding for us—you would be defending slavery and fighting for what is abhorrent to your feelings & conviction. On the contrary, in fighting on our side, you will be battling for law & order & against abstract fanatical ideas which will certainly bring about vastly greater evils upon our race, than could possibly result from the perpetuation of slavery among us. . . .

P.S. Don't imagine that I have meant anything personal in what I have written. . . . I could not help, while alone at this midnight hour, but write in sadness & anguish of heart at the perils which may so soon encompass the orphan children I may so shortly leave behind me. I have meant no unkindness to you. I could not wound one whom I love so well. Goodnight, and pray to God for our country!"

DOCUMENT 2

Source: Major-General Benjamin Butler, *Letter to Secretary of War Simon Cameron*, July 30, 1861

"But by the evacuation of Hampton, rendered necessary by the withdrawal of [Union] troops. . . . I have therefore now within the Peninsula, this side of Hampton Creek, 900 negroes, 300 of whom are able-bodied men, 30 of whom are men substantially past hard labor, 175 women, 225 children under the age of 10 years, 170 between 10 and 18 years, and many more coming in. The questions which this state of facts present are very embarrassing.

First—What shall be done with them? and, Second, What is their state and condition? . . . Is it forbidden to the troops to aid or harbor within their lines the negro children who are found therein, or is the soldier, when his march has destroyed their means of subsistence, to allow them to starve because he has driven off the rebel master? Now, shall the commander of regiment or battalion sit in judgment upon the question, whether any given black man has fled from his master, or his master fled from him? Indeed, how are the free born to be distinguished? . . .

In a loyal State I would put down a servile insurrection. In a state of rebellion I would confiscate that which was used to oppose my arms, and take all that property, which constituted the wealth of that State, and furnished the means by which the war is prosecuted, beside being the cause of the war; and if, in so doing, it should be objected that human beings were brought to the free enjoyment of life, liberty and the pursuit of happiness, such objections might not require much consideration."

445-e

TRM Suggested Responses to Questions

AP® Exam Practice

DOCUMENT 3

Source: Winslow Homer, "Our Women in the War," *Harper's Weekly*, September 6, 1862

About the source: The text at the top of the image, connected to the roots framing each scene, reads, "The influence of woman." The scene in the top center is labeled, "Soldier's shirts." The scene at bottom left is labeled, "The sister of charity," and the scene at bottom right is labeled, "Home tidings." The text centered below the image reads, "OUR WOMEN AND THE WAR."

Davis Museum at Wellesley College/Art Resource, NY

DOCUMENT 4

Source: *Enrollment Act*, March 3, 1863

"Be it enacted . . . that all able-bodied male citizens of the United States, and persons of foreign birth who shall have declared on oath their intention to become citizens under and in pursuance of the laws thereof, between the ages of twenty and forty-five years, except as hereinafter excepted, are hereby declared to constitute the national forces, and shall be liable to perform military duty in the service of the United States when called out by the President for that purpose. . . .

And, it be further enacted, That any person drafted and notified to appear as aforesaid, may, on or before the day fixed for his appearance, furnish an acceptable substitute to take his place in the draft; or he may pay to such person as the Secretary of War may authorize to receive it, such sum, not exceeding three hundred dollars, as the Secretary may authorize to receive it, such sum, not exceeding three hundred dollars, as the Secretary may determine, for the procuration of each substitute. . .and thereupon such person so furnishing the substitute, or paying the money, shall be discharged from further liability under that draft. . . ."

Period 5: 1844–1877　　　　　　　　　　　　　　　　　　　　　AP® Exam Practice: Through 1877

DOCUMENT 5　　**Source:** Hannah Johnson, *Letter to President Abraham Lincoln*, July 31, 1863

"My son went in the 54th regiment. I am a colored woman and my son was strong and able as any to fight for his country and the colored people have as much to fight for as any. My father was a Slave and escaped from Louisiana before I was born more than forty years ago. . . . I never went to school, but I know just as well as any what is right between man and man. Now I know it is right that a colored man should go and fight for his country, and so ought to a white man. I know that a colored man ought to run no greater risks than a white, his pay is no greater, his obligation to fight is the same. So why should not our enemies be compelled to treat him the same, Made to do it. . . .

You must put the rebels to work in State prisons to making shoes and things, if they sell our colored soldiers, till they let them all go. And give their wounded the same treatment. It would seem cruel, but there [is] no other way, and a just man must do hard things sometimes, that show him[self] to be a great man. . . .

Will you see that the colored men fighting now, are fairly treated. You ought to do this, and do it at once. Not let the thing run along; meet it quickly and manfully, and stop this, mean cowardly cruelty. We poor oppressed ones, appeal to you, and ask fair play."

DOCUMENT 6　　**Source:** *Prices and Real Wages During the Civil War*

Year	Union Prices	Union Real Wages	Confederate Prices	Confederate Real Wages (Adjusted for Inflation)
1860	100	100	100	100
1861	101	100	121	86
1862	113	93	388	35
1863	139	84	1,452	19
1864	176	77	3,992	11

DOCUMENT 7　　**Source:** *Black Codes of St. Landry's Parish, Louisiana*, 1865

"SECTION 2. . . . That every negro who shall be found absent from the residence of his employer after 10 o'clock at night, without a written permit from his employer, shall pay a fine of five dollars, or in default thereof, shall be compelled to work five days on the public road, or suffer corporeal punishments. . . .

SECTION 4. Be it further ordained, That every negro is required to be in the regular service of some white person, or former owner. . . .

SECTION 6. Be it further ordained, That no negro shall be permitted to preach, exhort, or otherwise declaim to congregations of colored people, without a special permission in writing from the president of the police jury. . . .

SECTION 7. Be it further ordained, That no negro who is not in the military service shall be allowed to carry fire-arms, or any kind of weapons, within the parish, without the special written permission of his employers, approved and endorsed by the nearest or most convenient chief of patrol."

AP® Exam Practice: Through 1877

Period 5: 1844–1877

Long-Essay Questions

Please choose one of the following three questions to answer. *Suggested writing time: 40 minutes.*

2. Evaluate the relative importance of different effects of western settlement on the United States economy in the years immediately before the end of the Civil War (1840–1865) and the years immediately after the Civil War (1865–1877).
3. Evaluate the extent to which Reconstruction fostered change in the lives of African Americans in the South from 1865 to 1877.
4. Evaluate the extent to which the Civil War and Reconstruction expanded the power of the federal government in the period from 1860 to 1877.

TRM Suggested Responses to Questions

PERIOD 6: 1865–1898
A Gilded Age

AP® Overview for Period 6

Period 6 of the AP® U.S. History curriculum framework is often referred to as the Gilded Age. For many, the label is apt due to the cacophony of subjects melded into one time period that can be studied through theme and chronology. The sudden and prodigious revolution in industry is often privileged during the Gilded Age, but students should recall that much of the land taken in the aftermath of the Civil War was taken from American Indians. This economic vitality happened in conjunction with the rise of immigration, urbanization, the rebuilding of the southern economy, and the labor movement. The rebuilding of the South led to a racialized economic system that discriminated against African Americans. While not unique to the Gilded Age, this era is also remembered for pervasive corruption among government officials and businesses. The Gilded Age also provides a bridge for students as they transition from the nineteenth to the twentieth century.

In addition to acquiring content knowledge of essential topics and historical developments, this period also cultivates the AP® historical thinking skills and reasoning processes necessary for students to succeed in the course and on the AP® exam. The modules in this period offer teachers and students a good fusion of theme and chronology. Period 6 accounts for 10–17% of the AP® exam and can be the source of questions on the Short-Answer, Long-Essay, and Document-Based Questions.

Module 6-1: Westward Expansion and American Indian Resistance focuses mainly on the AP® theme migration and settlement. This module discusses not only the settlement of the West but also covers government involvement in western expansion and the responses of American Indians that inhabited western lands. Much of the focus in this module is developing the reasoning process causation, and given the drive to settle the West and the subsequent American Indian resistance to western expansion, students should have ample opportunity to practice the skill. Above all, this module helps students see American Indians as active historical participants who resisted, compromised, and worked for the sovereignty of their respective tribes. The module ends by focusing on how the United States government responded and augmented their policies toward American Indians.

Module 6-2: Industry in the West also focuses heavily on the AP® theme migration and settlement, though this module focuses less on government intervention in American Indian affairs and more on economic opportunities that settlers could find in the West. Distinctive opportunities for primarily white settlers led to a variety of settlement patterns as miners, ranchers, railroad workers, and farmers each set out to realize these opportunities. The reasoning process of comparison and causation will help students draw contrasting reasons for settlement and lifestyles of settlers. The Homesteaders and prairie farmers who broke the plains in the nineteenth century adapted to and transformed the natural environment around them. Although primarily thought of as an east-to-west movement, Chinese immigrants offered the contrasting west-to-east migration pattern. Students have the opportunity to assess their understanding of these historical themes with a Short-Answer Question at the conclusion of this module.

Module 6-3: The New South depicts how the reasoning process of continuity and change supports inquiry on how the American and national identity changed as the southern region attempted to rebuild a fractured infrastructure after the Civil War. Southerners who advocated for a more industrialized, manufacturing-based economy promoted what they called the New South. This new vision also included a modern infrastructure on par with what northern states had built in the late nineteenth century. Although the southern region did improve its economic infrastructure, fundamentally it remained an agrarian region focused on racializing an economic and political system. The outcome of this concentration in the South became known as Jim Crow. Teachers should preview the pacing of this module as a very detailed activity about developing complexity in the Long-Essay Questions at the end of the module.

Module 6-4: America Industrializes is framed by the technological and business practice innovation of the late nineteenth century. The factors of industrialization also included the modernization of corporations as businesses produced manufactured goods that changed the demographics, wealth, and physical features of America. Leaders such as John D. Rockefeller and Andrew Carnegie are featured in this module, but students must not lose sight of understanding the larger historical processes that individual citizens helped initiate. The reasoning process of causation frames this module around understanding the many factors of industrialization. The thematic focus of work, exchange, and technology encourages students to make connections within and across time about business growth in America.

Module 6-5: Working People Organize highlights the demographic changes of the working population wrought by industrialization, which was one of many long-term consequences of a modern capitalist system in America. Indeed, as men, women, and some children propped up the wealth of business leaders, a hopeful effort to unionize and alter working conditions began. Even though labor united around the idea of workers' rights, the processes of unionization also revealed divisions about the categorizing of skilled and unskilled workers, and what specific rights were worth fighting for in the late nineteenth century. As this effort continued, a chasm in wealth and influence between labor and management grew ever wider throughout the Gilded Age. The reasoning process of continuity and change seeks to build students' understanding of the dynamics labor and management worked through during this time, which has natural connections to the thematic focus of work, exchange, and technology.

Module 6-6: A New Wave of Immigrants discusses how the influx of immigration at the turn of the twentieth century was distinctive because of the bicoastal nature of the movement. Also distinctive was the mass influx from diverse sources around the world. As these immigrant populations moved to urban centers they attempted to form enclaves within northern cities. This effort to carve out communities was at times met with extreme hostility, as nativists resisted immigrant populations by claiming citizenship was reserved for naturally born Americans. Even though nativists dominated the discussions around immigration, others sought ways to use immigrant populations for labor or politics. Throughout this module, students should be focused on the process of comparison as they encounter the many sources of migration patterns. Moreover, students should also incorporate the thematic focus of migration and settlement as they study the mass movement of people in the late nineteenth and early twentieth century.

Module 6-7: Becoming an Urban Nation has the thematic focus of migration and settlement, along with the reasoning process of continuity and change, which work in concert with the subject of this module: urban developments. The complex historical developments of industrialization, immigration, migration, and technological changes help explain how and when urbanization took place. The age of the city witnessed the vertical rise of new buildings aided by industrial and architectural innovations. While the cities housed tremendous positive developments, they also were home to dangerous living conditions in slums and political corruption from machine politics. Middle and upper class female reformers led much of the reform efforts aimed at the plight of cities. The disparate developments in urban centers helps prepare students for the writing analytically activity at the end of this module.

Module 6-8: Society and Culture in the Gilded Age focuses on how the Gilded Age changed previously held economic and political beliefs because of the immense amounts of wealth produced during the late nineteenth century. The changes wrought by the Gilded Age economy shaped significant developments in social and cultural norms, as well. Indeed, wealth, and the attendant issue of class, led to various leisure activities for the first time in American history. Sporting events, entertainment, music, and gender roles each accompanied the cultural fluctuations of the Gilded Age. Alongside these movements, women continued to define domesticity while embracing new consumer items. The thematic focus of social structures and the reasoning process of causation allow students to analyze the historical alterations caused by the Gilded Age. A detailed activity meant to have students explore how to write a Long-Essay Question with an argument focused on complexity is the final activity of this module.

Module 6-9: Gilded Age Ideologies highlights the diffuse ideologies of the Gilded Age. Most prominent among these beliefs was the laissez-faire mentality embraced by many of the nation's political and economic elite. Social Darwinism worked hand-in-glove with this belief, and those who propagated these values tended to be the beneficiaries of the capitalist system. Some coupled this belief system with Andrew Carnegie's "The Gospel of Wealth," in which the tycoon argued the wealthy were supposed to use their dynamic wealth to serve the betterment of their communities by embracing philanthropic work. Far from inactive through this process, laborers organized and challenged the capitalistic order. The belief in socialism paralleled the stratification of wealth in the Gilded Age. The reasoning process of causation and the thematic focus of social structures help students grapple with the various ideologies explained in this module.

Module 6-10: Politics and Protest ends Period 6 with a dynamic look at what many consider the most static part of the Gilded Age: political changes at a national level. True to the thematic focus of this module, politics and power, the political inefficiencies, inactive political leaders, and corrupt nature of politics frame students' understanding of the major political developments during the Gilded Age. To experience an economic maelstrom was to live in the new industrial-capitalist order of the late nineteenth century. Caught up in the cyclical nature of economic depressions such as the Panics of 1873 and 1893 were farmers whose allegiance was to the land, country, and independent identity they enjoyed for generations. This module focuses on politics and power in large measure due to the influence of the Populist movement. Farmers worked over time to organize and revolt against the established order. And while the Populist movement faded away as they merged with Democrats, their rhetoric lived on in the next century. The reasoning process of comparison fits the themes of this module and prepares students to evaluate a difficult subject.

Pacing Guide

Course Pacing for Period 6

Module #	Lesson Title	Instructional Period*	AP® Theme	AP® Topic	AP® Reasoning Process/Skill	Homework
6-1	N/A	N/A	Migration and Settlement	6.1 6.2	Causation / Historical Thinking Skills 1, 2, 3, 5	**Reading and Source Analysis:** 6-1 **Activity:** AP® Writing Historically: Short-Answer Question Practice, 6-1
	Review: AP® Writing Historically: Short-Answer Question Practice, 6-1 Westward Expansion and American Indian Resistance	1	Migration and Settlement	6.2 6.5	Causation / Historical Thinking Skills 1, 2, 3, 4, 5, 6	**Reading and Source Analysis:** 6-2 **Activity:** AP® Writing Historically: Short-Answer Question Practice, 6-2
6-2	**Review:** AP® Writing Historically: Short-Answer Question Practice, 6-2	1	Migration and Settlement	6.2	Comparison/Causation / Historical Thinking Skills 1, 2, 3, 4, 5, 6	**Reading and Source Analysis:** 6-3
6-3	The New South	1	American and National Identity	6.4 6.5	Continuity and Change / Historical Thinking Skills 1, 2, 3, 5	**Activity:** AP® Writing Historically: Putting It All Together: Developing Historical Complexity in an Essay, 6-3
	Workshop: AP® Writing Historically: Putting It All Together: Developing Historical Complexity in an Essay, 6-3	1	American and National Identity	6.4 6.5	Continuity and Change / Historical Thinking Skills 1, 2, 3, 4, 5	**Reading and Source Analysis:** 6-4 **Activity:** AP® Writing Historically: Short-Answer Question Practice, 6-4
6-4	**Review:** AP® Writing Historically: Short-Answer Question Practice, 6-4 America Industrializes	1	Work, Exchange, and Technology	6.5 6.6	Causation / Historical Thinking Skills 1, 2, 3, 4, 5, 6	**Reading and Source Analysis:** 6-5 **Activity:** AP® Writing Historically: Short-Answer Question Practice, 6-5
6-5	**Review:** AP® Writing Historically: Short-Answer Question Practice, 6-5 Working People Organize	1	Work, Exchange, and Technology	6.7	Continuity and Change / Historical Thinking Skills 1, 2, 3, 5, 6	**Reading and Source Analysis:** 6-6
6-6	A New Wave of Immigrants	1	Migration and Settlement	6.8 6.9	Comparison / Historical Thinking Skills 1, 2, 3, 5	**Activity:** AP® Writing Historically: Responding to a Long-Essay Question, 6-6
	Workshop: AP® Writing Historically: Responding to a Long-Essay Question, 6-6	1	Migration and Settlement	6.8 6.9	Comparison / Historical Thinking Skills 1, 2, 3, 4, 5, 6	**Reading and Source Analysis:** 6-7
6-7	Becoming an Urban Nation	1	Migration and Settlement	6.8 6.9	Continuity and Change / Historical Thinking Skills 1, 2, 3, 5	**Activity:** AP® Writing Historically: Document-Based Question Practice, 6-7
	Workshop: AP® Writing Historically: Document-Based Question Practice, 6-7	1	Migration and Settlement	6.8 6.9	Continuity and Change / Historical Thinking Skills 1, 2, 3, 4, 5, 6	**Reading and Source Analysis:** 6-8 **Activity:** AP® Writing Historically: Long-Essay Question Practice, 6-8

6-8	**Review:** AP® Writing Historically: Long-Essay Question Practice, 6-8 Society and Culture in the Gilded Age	1	Social Structures	6.10 6.11	Causation / Historical Thinking Skills 1, 2, 3, 4, 5	**Reading and Source Analysis:** 6-9 **Activity:** AP® Writing Historically: Short-Answer Question Practice, 6-9
6-9	**Review:** AP® Writing Historically: Short-Answer Question Practice, 6-9 Gilded Age Ideologies	1	Politics and Power Social Structures	6.11 6.12 6.13	Causation / Historical Thinking Skills 1, 2, 3, 4, 5, 6	**Reading and Source Analysis:** 6-10 **Activity:** AP® Writing Historically: Short-Answer Question Practice, 6-10
6-10	**Review:** AP® Writing Historically: Short-Answer Question Practice, 6-10 Politics and Protest	1	Politics and Power	6.12 6.13 6.14	Comparison / Historical Thinking Skills 1, 2, 3, 4, 5, 6	Prepare for Assessment
Formative Assessment	AP® Exam Practice • 18 MCQs • 4 SAQs	0-1	All AP® U.S. History Course Themes	6.14 Personal Progress Check • 15 MCQs • 2 SAQs • 1 LEQ	All AP® History Reasoning Processes/ Skills	
Summative Assessment	Unit 1 Test Bank • 55 MCQs • 4 SAQs • 1 DBQ • 4 LEQs	0-1	All AP® U.S. History Course Themes		All AP® History Reasoning Processes/ Skills	

*Based on a standard 50-minute class period.

Period 6 Resources

The following resources can be found in the Resources section of the book's digital platform, by clicking on the link buttons in the Teacher's Edition e-book, or by opening the Teacher's Resource Materials.

- **TRM** Period 6 Overview Video
- **TRM** AP® Concepts and Skills Video
- **TRM** Period 6 Lecture Presentation Slides
- **TRM** Period 6 Workshop Rubrics
- **TRM** Period 6 Suggested Responses to Questions
- **TRM** Period 6 Guided Reading Worksheets

Module 6-1

- **TRM** Handout 6.1 – Effects of Railroad Construction in the West
- **TRM** Module 6.1 AP® Analyzing Sources Handout 1
- **TRM** Module 6.1 AP® Analyzing Sources Handout 2

Module 6-2

- **TRM** Module 6.2 AP® Analyzing Sources Handout 1
- **TRM** Module 6.2 AP® Analyzing Sources Handout 2
- **TRM** Handout 6.2 – Comparing the Experiences of Californios and American Indians
- **TRM** Module 6.2 AP® Analyzing Sources Handout 3

Module 6-3

- **TRM** Module 6.3 AP® Analyzing Sources Handout
- **TRM** Handout 6.3 – GEM Worksheet

Module 6-4

- **TRM** Handout 6.4 – Causes and Effects of Industrialization
- **TRM** Module 6.4 AP® Analyzing Sources Handout 1
- **TRM** Module 6.4 AP® Analyzing Sources Handout 2

Module 6-5

- **TRM** Handout 6.5 – Causes and Effects of Labor Unionization
- **TRM** Module 6.5 AP® Analyzing Sources Handout 1
- **TRM** Module 6.5 AP® Analyzing Sources Handout 2
- **TRM** Module 6.5 AP® Analyzing Sources Handout 3
- **TRM** Handout 6.6 – Nineteenth-Century Labor Unions

Module 6-6

- **TRM** Handout 6.7 – Nineteenth-Century Immigration Push and Pull Factors
- **TRM** Module 6.6 AP® Analyzing Sources Handout 1
- **TRM** Handout 6.8 – Challenges Faced by Immigrants in the Nineteenth Century
- **TRM** Module 6.6 AP® Analyzing Sources Handout 2
- **TRM** Module 6.6 AP® Analyzing Sources Handout 3

Module 6-7

- **TRM** Handout 6.9 – Urban Population Growth, 1870–1890
- **TRM** Module 6.7 AP® Analyzing Sources Handout 1
- **TRM** Module 6.7 AP® Analyzing Sources Handout 2
- **TRM** Module 6.7 AP® Analyzing Sources Handout 3

Module 6-8

- **TRM** Handout 6.10 – Social Structures in the Gilded Age
- **TRM** Module 6.8 AP® Analyzing Sources Handout

Module 6-9

- **TRM** Handout 6.11 – Comparing the Gospel of Wealth and Social Darwinism
- **TRM** Module 6.9 AP® Analyzing Sources Handout

Module 6-10

- **TRM** Module 6.10 AP® Analyzing Sources Handout 1
- **TRM** Module 6.10 AP® Analyzing Sources Handout 2
- **TRM** Handout 6.12 – President Cleveland and the Depression of 1893
- **TRM** Module 6.10 AP® Analyzing Sources Handout 3

Period 6 Essential Activity

Charles Dudley Warner and Mark Twain described the Gilded Age as an era of extravagant wealth, but as discussed in this textbook, this wealth was superfluous and the veneer of gold masked an uglier truth about the historical developments of the era. The industrial wealth produced by the confluence of technological innovation, immigration, and urbanization was buttressed by an energetic government eager to assist business. This activity seeks to have students recognize the importance of these changes while also accounting for the underrepresented minorities who were integral to the wealth amassed during these years.

Beneficiaries	Underrepresented Minorities	Continuity or Change
Industrial Leaders, Political Leaders, Innovators, Business Leaders →	Immigrant Groups, African Americans, Women, American Indians →	?

Start by dividing students into groups of three or four. The first part of this activity asks students to choose one example from each of the first two categories and then narrow their selections from the broad categories to more specific examples. For instance, if students select industrial leaders and immigrant groups, they can distill their focus further to a specific industrial leader such as Andrew Carnegie and a specific immigrant group such as southeastern Europeans. The next task is to determine whether the relationship between the examples represents a continuity or change within the Gilded Age. It is important to emphasize the proper meshing of their selections so groups can decide whether a continuity or change occurred.

The final part to this activity is to tell students they must transfer their selections to a digital platform. Students should create three PowerPoint slides, with one picture on each slide, and then take three minutes to verbally defend their selections. Note that none of the slides should include words. Students must make their pictures and oral defense measure up to the selections they made. This can be a fun culminating activity for students as they finish Period 6.

Period 6 Alignment to the Fall 2019 AP® United States History Course Framework*

Relationship to the College Board Units

Period 6 in this book covers Topics 6.1–6.14 in Unit 6 of the College Board course framework. Students will be ready to take the Personal Progress Check for Unit 6 once they have completed this period.

Course Themes

Period 6 develops these course themes outlined in the course framework:

- **Migration and Settlement (MIG):** Transportation improvements and new economic opportunities drew settlers to the West resulting in conflict and the forced relocation of American Indians to reservations. International and internal migrants moved in large numbers to American cities changing urban life and politics.

- **American and National Identity (NAT):** Efforts to industrialize the South after the Civil War met with limited success as sharecropping and tenant farming continued to be the region's main economic activities. African Americans in the South were denied equal rights as the Supreme Court upheld Jim Crow laws permitting legal segregation while women's rights groups continued to fight for the right to vote.

- **Work, Exchange, and Technology (WXT):** Business entrepreneurs used technological inventions and new corporate and financial practices to create and consolidate large-scale corporations that dramatically increased the production of goods. In response to the growing power of large corporations, mechanization, and the loss of autonomy, workers created labor unions and used strikes to fight for better wages and working conditions.

- **Social Structures (SOC):** Industrialization and urbanization raised the standard of living for most Americans and provided new opportunities for leisure-time pursuits, which varied by social class and gender. While an emerging middle class led to an expansion of consumer culture, critics challenged the inequalities of industrial capitalism.
- **Politics and Power (POL):** Federal elections were closely contested after the end of Reconstruction as partisanship reached new heights even though it was an era of weak federal government. Farmers joined new movements for cooperative self-help and political action such as the Populist Party, while Democrats tightened their electoral hold on the South after the end of Reconstruction.

Course Skills

Period 6 helps students to develop the following AP® Historical Thinking Skills identified in the course framework.

- **Skill 1—Developments and Processes** (Modules 6-1, 6-2, 6-3, 6-4, 6-5, 6-6, 6-7, 6-8, 6-9, 6-10, 6-11, 6-12)
- **Skill 2—Sourcing and Situation** (Modules 6-1, 6-2, 6-3, 6-4, 6-5, 6-6, 6-7, 6-8, 6-9, 6-10, 6-11, 6-12)
- **Skill 3—Claims and Evidence in Sources** (Modules 6-1, 6-2, 6-3, 6-4, 6-5, 6-6, 6-7, 6-8, 6-9, 6-10, 6-11, 6-12)
- **Skill 4—Contextualization** (Modules 6-1, 6-3, 6-4, 6-6, 6-7, 6-8, 6-9, 6-10, 6-11, 6-12)
- **Skill 5—Making Connections** (Modules 6-1, 6-2, 6-3, 6-4, 6-5, 6-6, 6-7, 6-8, 6-10, 6-11, 6-12)
- **Skill 6—Argumentation** (Modules 6-1, 6-3, 6-4, 6-6, 6-7, 6-8, 6-10, 6-11, 6-12)

Period 6 helps students to develop the following AP® History Reasoning Processes identified in the course framework.

- **Reasoning Process 1: Comparison** (Modules 6-6, 6-10)
- **Reasoning Process 2: Causation** (Modules 6-1, 6-2, 6-4, 6-8, 6-9)
- **Reasoning Process 3: Continuity and Change** (Modules 6-3, 6-5, 6-6)

Learning Objectives and Historical Developments

Module	Topics	Learning Objectives	Historical Developments and Key Concepts
6-1	6.1, 6.2, 6.3	Unit 6: Learning Objective A Unit 6: Learning Objective B	KC-6.1.I.A, KC-6.2.II.A, KC-6.2.II.D, KC-6.2.II.E
6-2	6.1, 6.2, 6.3	Unit 6: Learning Objective B	KC-6.1.III.A, KC-6.2.II.B, KC-6.2.II.C
6-3	6.4	Unit 6: Learning Objective C	KC-6.1.II.D, KC-6.3.II.C
6-4	6.5, 6.6	Unit 6: Learning Objective D Unit 6: Learning Objective E	KC-6.1.I.B.i, KC-6.1.I, KC-6.1.B.ii, KC-6.1.I.D, KC-6.1.I.E.i
6-5	6.7, 6.11	Unit 6: Learning Objective E Unit 6: Learning Objective I	KC-6.1.I.C, KC-6.1.II.C, KC-6.1.II.B.i, KC-6.3.II.B.ii
6-6	6.8, 6.9	Unit 6: Learning Objective F Unit 6: Learning Objective G	KC-6.1.II.B.ii, KC-6.2.I.A, KC-6.2.I.C
6-7	6.8, 6.9, 6.13	Unit 6: Learning Objective F Unit 6: Learning Objective G Unit 6: Learning Objective K	KC-6.2.I.B, KC-6.3.III.B.i, KC-6.2.I.D
6-8	6.10	Unit 6: Learning Objective H	KC-6.2.I.E
6-9	6.9, 6.10, 6.11	Unit 6: Learning Objective G Unit 6: Learning Objective H Unit 6: Learning Objective I Unit 6: Learning Objective J	KC-6.3.I.A, KC-6.3.I.B, KC-6.3.I.C, KC-6.3.II.B.i, KC-6.1.II.A
6-10	6.12, 6.13, 6.14	Unit 6: Learning Objective B Unit 6: Learning Objective J Unit 6: Learning Objective K Unit 6: Learning Objective L	KC-6.1.III.B, KC-6.1.I.E.ii, KC-6.1.III.C, KC-6.3.II.A

TRM A detailed alignment that can be sorted by Course Framework Unit, Topic, Learning Objective, Historical Development/Key Concept, or textbook period, is available in the Teacher's Resource Materials and via the book's online platform.

*Should changes be made to the Course Framework in the future, an updated alignment will be placed on our catalog page at bfwpub.com/fabric1e.

TEACHING IDEA

AP® Central

A great resource to help you teach this period is the information in the AP® U.S. History study guide for 1865–1898, available from the AP® United States History Classroom Resources section of AP® Central (apcentral.collegeboard.org).

PERIOD 6: 1865–1898

A Gilded Age

▲ **Dakota Sioux Winter Count, 1911** Plains Indians used winter counts to record major events in a tribe's history in pictographs, each of which summarized a major event in a given year. This winter count records the history of the Yanktonai tribe between 1823 and 1911. According to the translations Linea Sundstrom provided for the Buechel Memorial Lakota Museum, some of the events portrayed here include: "1823 Pictograph of white attack on earthlodge," "1827 Starvation winter. The Santees ate two of their own people," "1853 They killed a lone Crow warrior who was on a suicide charge. This was on the Powder River," and "1890 Sitting Bull was killed; also Spotted Elk."

Mark Twain called the period from the end of the Civil War through the end of the nineteenth century "The Gilded Age," a nod to the process of gilding, which disguises something cheap by covering it with a thin layer of gold. Although Twain's term has stuck to the age, it is a satire that obscures more than it reveals. The generation after the Civil War experienced upheavals and hardships but also opportunities and prosperity.

Two broad changes — a second industrial revolution and millions of immigrants mostly from southern and eastern Europe — defined this age. As a result, many of America's towns and cities grew from ports of trade to centers of industrial production. The conditions in factories and the lives of the Americans who worked in them were often dire, and these production centers led to paradoxical results — increased wealth for most Americans as well as reform movements and worker protests. During this period, the American middle and upper classes continued building the consumer culture that began in the early nineteenth century. Yet, for many Americans these years accelerated — or simply changed the nature of — the oppression that they experienced before the Civil War. African Americans were relegated to second-class citizenship by the Jim Crow laws and sharecropping systems of the South; Mexican Americans struggled with growing Anglo settlements in the West; and women faced a cultural expectation of domesticity that allowed for some participation in reform efforts but denied them basic rights including suffrage.

During the Gilded Age, the West was integrated into the United States economy through the building of transcontinental railroads, the vast and varied migration of settlers, and the conquest and forced relocation of American Indians. Many Americans assumed that the diversity present in both in the West and in America's booming urban centers was temporary and that these people would merge into a "melting pot" of cultures based on the economic, social, and political structures of the predominantly white, northern European American majority. Yet, many immigrants, American Indians, and Mexican Americans resisted wholesale assimilation as they sought to define their own identity.

Politically, the nation was closely divided as government grappled with the destabilizing effects of industrialization. Americans argued over whether the government had an obligation to promote or control corporations for the sake of the common good. Workers and farmers sought relief through organizing and collective action, but labor unions and farmers' political efforts had limited success in the era. Throughout this period, reformers and civic leaders debated whether the people who were destabilized by the Industrial Revolution, including small businessmen and the working poor, could be better helped through government intervention or through private philanthropy.

TEACHING IDEA

AP® Central

Read the information on Urbanization in the Special Focus Materials available from the AP® United States History Classroom Resources section of AP® Central (apcentral.collegeboard.org).

PERIOD 6 PREVIEW

Module	AP® Thematic Focus
6-1: Westward Expansion and American Indian Resistance	**Migration and Settlement** Completion of the transcontinental railroad and the concurrent expansion of the U.S. railroad network facilitated the large-scale migration of white American settlers to the Great Plains and Far West. Military conquest and oft-broken treaties resulted in the forced relocation of American Indians onto reservations. American Indians struggled to maintain their cultural and tribal identities as reformers promoted a policy of assimilation.
6-2: Industry in the West	**Migration and Settlement** Despite numerous obstacles posed by difficult terrain, forbidding climate, and unfamiliar inhabitants of the land they sought to harness, internal and international migrants were attracted to the West by new economic opportunities in mining, lumber, ranching, and commercial farming. Pioneers and settlers used hard work and technological innovations to transform their environments.
6-3: The New South	**American and National Identity** Despite the expansion of the railroads and construction of textile mills, efforts to industrialize the South after the Civil War met with limited success as sharecropping and tenant farming continued to be the region's main economic activities. African Americans in the South were denied equal rights as the Supreme Court upheld the Jim Crow laws permitting legal segregation in its 1896 *Plessy v. Ferguson* ruling.
6-4: America Industrializes	**Work, Exchange, and Technology** Business entrepreneurs used technological inventions and new corporate and financial practices to create and consolidate large-scale corporations that dramatically increased the production of goods.
6-5: Working People Organize	**Work, Exchange, and Technology** In response to the growing power of large corporations, mechanization, and the loss of autonomy, workers created labor unions and used strikes to fight for better wages and working conditions. In most cases, states and the federal government favored business interests over workers in labor disputes, some of which became violent affairs.
6-6: A New Wave of Immigrants	**Migration and Settlement** During the late 1800s, immigration to the United States soared as so-called "new immigrants" from southern and eastern Europe came in increasingly large numbers alongside "old immigrants" from northern and western Europe. Most European immigrants settled in big cities along the East Coast or in the Midwest while immigrants from Asia settled in the West. The surge of immigration led to debates over assimilation, a nativist backlash, and passage of the first race-based federal immigration legislation, the Chinese Exclusion Act (1882).
6-7: Becoming an Urban Nation	**Migration and Settlement** American cities grew dramatically as hundreds of thousands of African Americans from the South and millions of Europeans came in search of economic opportunities. Urban newcomers clustered in ethnic neighborhoods as many cities struggled to cope with the challenges of rapid growth. In large cities, politics was dominated by corrupt political machines, which provided a measure of basic social services in exchange for votes.
6-8: Society and Culture in the Gilded Age	**Social Structures** Industrialization and urbanization raised the standard of living for most Americans and provided new opportunities for leisure-time pursuits, which varied by social class and gender. An emerging middle class led to an expansion of consumer culture.
6-9: Gilded Age Ideologies	**Politics and Power ▪ Social Structures** The ideologies of laissez-faire economics and Social Darwinism placed the burden of success or failure on the individual while restraining the federal government from intervention in the economy during the Gilded Age. Certain industrialists, notably Andrew Carnegie in his "Gospel of Wealth," promoted philanthropy as some academics called for a new social order.
6-10: Politics and Protest	**Politics and Power** Federal elections were closely contested during the two decades after Reconstruction as partisanship reached new heights, even though it was a time of weak federal government. Faced with falling food prices and overproduction, farmers joined new movements for cooperative self-help and political action, including the creation of the Populist Party. In the aftermath of the Depression of 1893, Republicans emerged as the majority party while Democrats tightened their control of the South and the Populist Party faded.

Module 6-1

Westward Expansion and American Indian Resistance

LEARNING TARGETS
By the end of this module, you should be able to:
- Explain the factors contributing to western settlement.
- Explain the effects of western settlement on American Indians living in those lands.
- Explain the various ways in which the United States sought to forcibly assimilate American Indians.
- Explain American Indian resistance to attempts to assimilate them into the United States.

THEMATIC FOCUS
Migration and Settlement

Completion of the transcontinental railroad and the concurrent expansion of the U.S. railroad network facilitated the large-scale migration of white American settlers to the Great Plains and Far West. Military conquest and oft-broken treaties resulted in the forced relocation of American Indians onto reservations. American Indians struggled to maintain their cultural and tribal identities as reformers promoted a policy of assimilation.

HISTORICAL REASONING FOCUS
Causation

TASK ▶ As you read this module, consider the historical linkages between the causes and effects of western settlement. Take note of how and why the federal government and private business interests promoted western settlement, the effects of western settlement on American Indians in the West, and the responses of American Indians to these changes.

TRM Suggested Responses to Questions

BUILDING AP® SKILLS
Causation

To address the learning targets and the historical reasoning focus, have students take notes to keep track of the causes of western settlement and the effects of western settlement on American Indians. Discuss the causes and effects at the conclusion of the module and allow students to compare answers.

BUILDING AP® SKILLS
Argumentation

Period 6 details the lives of those living in poverty in the late nineteenth century as well as the attempts to solve the issue of poverty. Contemporaries debated whether private philanthropy or government intervention would be better suited to help those living in poverty and those negatively impacted by industrialization. Ask the class to write a couple of sentences to answer the question: "Which route would be more successful in helping individuals who are living in poverty – government intervention or private philanthropy?" If time allows, discuss student answers.

Federal policy, foreign investment, and the expansion of the railroads were essential in transforming the West. Rugged and determined pioneers lured to the Great Plains by the appeal of cheap land and a fresh start found it less hospitable than earlier settlers who had forged their way beyond the Appalachians. American pioneers may have thought they were moving into a wilderness, but the West was home to large numbers of American Indians. Before pioneers and entrepreneurs could go west to pursue their economic dreams, the U.S. government would have to remove this obstacle to American expansion. Through treaties — most of which Americans broke — and war, white Americans conquered the American Indian tribes inhabiting the Great Plains and far West during the nineteenth century. After the native population was largely subdued, those who wanted to reform American Indian policy focused on carving up tribal lands and forcing American Indians to assimilate into white society.

The Great Plains

In the mid-nineteenth century, the western frontier lay in the **Great Plains**. Consisting of the wide expanse of land between the Rocky Mountains to the west and the Mississippi River to the east, the Great Plains is a semiarid region with an average yearly rainfall sufficient to sustain short grasslands but not many trees. Prospects for farmers, particularly in the drier western part of the region known as the High Plains, did not appear promising. In 1878 geologist John Wesley Powell issued a report that questioned whether the land beyond the easternmost portion of the Great Plains could support small farming. Lack of rainfall, he argued, would make it difficult or even impossible for homesteaders to support themselves on family farms of

EXPLORING AP® THEMES
Politics and Power

Period 6 focuses on the effects of industrialization, including the increased influence of corporations on American society and the government's attempts to balance out that power. Pose this question to the class, "How much control should the government have over the economy?" Allow students to discuss or write independently before discussing. If the discussion begins to stray away from the information in Period 6, ask: "Do people need protection from large corporations?" or "Should the government promote large corporations?" Once the discussion has concluded, remind students that this debate was only one of the changes that Americans had to navigate during the late nineteenth century.

Period 6: 1865–1898   MODULE 6-1 Westward Expansion and American Indian Resistance

160 acres. Instead, he recommended that for the plains to prove economically sustainable, settlers would have to work much larger stretches of land, around 2,560 acres (4 square miles). This would provide ample room to raise livestock under dry conditions.

Powell's words of caution did little to diminish Americans' conviction, dating back to Thomas Jefferson, that small farmers would populate the territories brought under U.S. jurisdiction and renew democratic values as they ventured forth. Charles Dana Wilber summed up the view of those who saw no barriers to the expansion of small farmers in the plains. Rejecting the idea that the Great Plains should remain a "perpetual desert," Wilber asserted that "in reality there is no desert anywhere except by man's permission or neglect." Along with millions of others, he had great faith in Americans' ability to turn the Great Plains into a place where Jefferson's republican vision could take root and prosper.

REVIEW

- What were the basic challenges facing prospective farmers on the Great Plains?
- Why were settlers undeterred by these challenges?

Federal Policy and Foreign Investment

Despite the popular association of the West with individual initiative and self-sufficiency, the federal government played a huge role in facilitating the settlement of the West. National lawmakers enacted legislation offering free or cheap land to settlers and to mining, lumber, and railroad companies. The U.S. government also provided subsidies for transporting mail and military supplies, recruited soldiers to subdue the American Indians who stood in the way of expansion, and appointed officials to govern the territories. Through these efforts, the government provided a necessary measure of safety and stability for new businesses to start up and grow as well as interconnected transportation and communication systems to supply workers and promote opportunities to develop new markets across North America.

Along with federal policy, foreign investment helped fuel development of the West. Lacking sufficient funds of its own, the United States turned to Europe to finance the sale of public bonds and private securities. European firms also invested in American mines, with the British leading the way. In 1872 an Englishman wrote that mines in

MAP 6.1 The American West, 1860–1900 Railroads played a key role in the expansion and settlement of the American West. The network of railroads running throughout the West opened the way for extensive migration from the East and for the development of a national market. None of this would have been possible without the land grants provided to the railroads by the U.S. government. **How does this map illustrate the roles of the federal government and private enterprise in opening the American West to settlement?**

450

TEACHING IDEA

Class Discussion

Divide the class into two groups, and further subdivide those two groups into quads. As a pre-writing exercise, task the first class-groupings with employing the "Twenty-Five-Word Drill" and the second class-groupings with employing the "Fifty-Word Drill" to address the following question: "Did the American government overstep its bounds by supporting westward expansion?" In addressing this prompt, students are required to write a response that is, depending upon the group to which they are assigned, no more than 25 or 50 words total (give or take). The product of the former exercise winds up as a concise statement of thesis, while the latter becomes more of an elaborate conclusive statement on the question. Upon completion of this exercise, reshuffle the quads so that a pair of persons from the first grouping are matched up with a pair of persons from the second grouping, and have them share and compare their products.

BUILDING AP® SKILLS

Making Connections

Use Map 6.1 to explain the connection that linked the involvement of the American government to the growth of the railroads. About what percentage of the railroads were possible due to government land grants? How did the expansion of the railroad connect to statehood? Possible answers include: *About 60–75% of the railroads were due to government land grants. As the railroads expanded west, people migrated as well. As populations increased, territories gained their statehood.*

Railroad Construction Crew Chinese and other immigrant groups were instrumental in the construction of the transcontinental railroad and other railway lines in the West. This photo shows Chinese workers building the Loma Prieta Lumber Company's railroad near Watsonville, California about 1885. In addition to transporting people, railroads were essential to the western lumber industry, which needed railways to transport timber from forest to sawmill. **How does this photograph reflect continuing racial hierarchies in the United States?**

transcontinental railroad
A railroad linking the East and West Coasts of North America. Completed in 1869, the transcontinental railroad facilitated the flow of migrants and the development of economic connections between the West and the East.

Nevada were "more British than American." The development of the western cattle range—the symbol of the American frontier and the heroic cowboy—was also funded by overseas financiers. At the height of the cattle boom in the 1880s, British firms supplied some $45 million to underwrite ranch operations. The largest share of money, however, that flowed from Europe to the United States came with the expansion of the railroads, the most important ingredient in opening the West.

The **transcontinental railroad** became the gateway to the West. In 1862 the Republican-led Congress appropriated vast areas of land that railroad companies could use to lay their tracks or sell to raise funds for construction. The Central Pacific Company built from west to east, starting in Sacramento, California. The construction project attracted thousands of Chinese railroad workers. From the opposite direction, the Union Pacific Company began laying track in Council Bluffs, Iowa, and hired primarily Irish workers. In May 1869, the Central Pacific and Union Pacific crews met at Promontory Point, Utah. Workmen from the two companies drove a golden spike to complete the connection. For many Americans recovering from four years of civil war and still embroiled in Reconstruction, the completion of the transcontinental railroad renewed their faith in the nation's ingenuity and destiny. A wagon train had once taken six to eight weeks to travel across the West. That trip could now be completed by rail in seven days. The railroad allowed both people and goods to move faster and in greater numbers than before. The West was now open not just to rugged pioneers but to anyone who could afford a railroad ticket.

The government-subsidized railroad construction boom also provided new opportunities for corruption. For example, Union Pacific promoters created a fake construction company called the

TEACHING IDEA

Analyzing Art and Images

Search the Digital Public Library of America online to find a photo of the Transcontinental Railroad "golden spike ceremony" in 1869 (dp.la). Analyze the photo with students. First discuss the historical context surrounding the construction of the Transcontinental Railroad. Then ask students, "Why was the event depicted in this photograph significant?"

TEACHING IDEA

Geography Instruction

Search PBS Learning Media for "Westward Expansion, 1860–1890" (pbslearningmedia .org). This interactive map will allow students to visualize the growth of the railroad system in the United States, as it shows a different map of the railroads for each decade between 1860 and 1890. Have students select the "Railroad Networks" filter and allow students to toggle through the different years on the timeline at the bottom of the map. You can also ask students to compare the location of the railroads with other features on the map, such as geologic features and locations of American Indian tribes of the West.

EXPLORING AP® THEMES

Migration and Settlement

Search the PBS Learning Media website for the video titled, "Transcontinental Railroad Recruits Chinese Laborers" (pbslearningmedia.org). This clip is taken from the American Experience series. While watching, have students answer the following questions:

- Why did railroad companies recruit immigrant labor?

- Describe early sentiments about Chinese immigrant laborers. How did perceptions change over time?

- List push and pull factors for Chinese immigration to the United States.

Period 6: 1865–1898   MODULE 6-1   Westward Expansion and American American Indian Resistance

Crédit Mobilier, which they used to funnel government bond and contract money into their own pockets. They also bribed congressmen to avoid investigation into their sordid dealings. Despite these efforts, in 1872 a congressional investigation exposed this corruption.

REVIEW

> Explain some of the positive and negative effects of railroad construction in the West.

American Indian Civilizations

AP® TIP
Make sure you can explain the impact of the Indian Removal Act on the development of the American west, especially in terms of conflicts associated with its expansion during the late 1800s.

The frontier was home to diverse peoples long before white and immigrant settlers appeared. The many native groups who inhabited the West spoke distinct languages, engaged in different economic activities, and competed with one another for power and resources. The descendants of Spanish conquistadors had also lived in the Southwest and California since the late sixteenth century, pushing the boundaries of the Spanish empire northward from Mexico. Indeed, Spaniards established the city of Santa Fe as the territorial capital of New Mexico years before the English landed at Jamestown, Virginia in 1607.

By the end of the Civil War, around 350,000 American Indians were living west of the Mississippi. They constituted the surviving remnants of the 1 million people who had occupied the land for thousands of years before Europeans set foot in America. Some of the tribes, such as the Cherokee, Creek, and Shawnee, had been forcibly removed from the East during Andrew Jackson's presidency in the 1830s.

Given the rich assortment of tribes, it is difficult to generalize about American Indian culture and society. The tribes each adapted in unique ways to the geography and climate of their home territories, spoke their own language, and had their own history and traditions. Some were hunters, others farmers; some nomadic, others sedentary, living in permanent dwellings. In New Mexico, for example, Apaches were expert horsemen and fierce warriors, while the Pueblo Indians built homes out of adobe and developed a flourishing system of agriculture. They also cultivated the land through methods of irrigation that foreshadowed modern practices. The Pawnees in the Great Plains periodically set fire to the land to improve game hunting and the growth of vegetation. American Indians on the southern plains gradually became enmeshed in the market economy for bison robes, which they sold to white American traders (Map 6.2).

AP® TIP
Analyze the ways that the experiences of native peoples in the Great Plains during the late 1800s illustrate continuity and change over time.

The lives of all native peoples were affected by the arrival of Europeans, but the consequences of cross-cultural contact varied considerably depending on the history and circumstances of each tribe. White people trampled on hunting grounds, polluted streams with acid run-off from mines, and introduced native peoples to liquor. They inflicted the greatest damage through diseases for which American Indians lacked the immunity that Europeans and white Americans had acquired. By 1870, smallpox had wiped out half the population of Plains Indians, and cholera, diphtheria, and measles caused serious but lesser harm. Nomadic tribes such as the Lakota Sioux were able to flee the contagion, while agrarian tribes such as the Mandan suffered extreme losses. As a result, the balance of power among Plains tribes shifted to the more mobile Sioux. American Indians were not pacifists, and they engaged in warfare with their enemies in disputes over hunting grounds, horses, and honor. However, the introduction of guns by European and American traders transformed American Indian warfare into a much more deadly affair than had existed previously. And by the mid-nineteenth century, some tribes had become so deeply engaged in the commercial fur trade with white settlers that they had depleted their own hunting grounds.

> "The White man knows how to make everything but he does not know how to distribute it."
>
> — Sitting Bull, Hunkpapa Lakota chieftain, 1885

American Indians had their own approach toward nature and the land they inhabited. While most tribes recognized the concept of private property in ownership of their horses, weapons, tools, and shelters, they did not accept private ownership of land, as white pioneers did. By contrast, they viewed the land as the common domain of their tribe, for use by all members. This communitarian outlook also reflected native attitudes toward the environment. American Indians considered human beings not as superior to the rest of nature's creations, but rather as part of an interconnected world of animals, plants, and natural elements. According to this view, all plants and animals were part of a larger spirit world, which flowed from the power of the sun, the sky, and the earth.

BUILDING AP® SKILLS

Causation

The construction of various railroads greatly impacted the American West. Have students identify the positive and negative effects of railroad construction during this period. Students can list specific effects as both positive and negative as long as they provide their reasoning for doing so.

TRM Find **Handout 6.1 – Effects of Railroad Construction in the West** in the Teacher's Resource Materials.

American Indian Civilizations

Period 6: 1865–1898

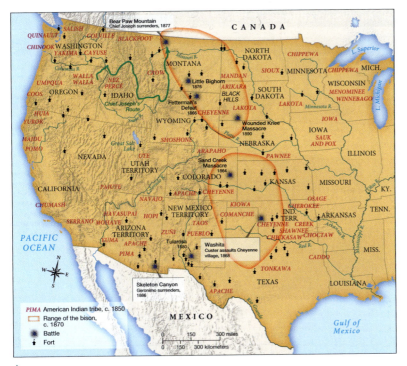

▲ **MAP 6.2 The American Indian Frontier, 1870** Western migration posed a threat to the dozens of American Indian tribes and the immense herds of bison in the region. The tribes had signed treaties with the U.S. government recognizing the right to live on their lands. The presence of U.S. forts did not protect the American Indians from settlers who invaded their territories. **What conclusions can you draw about the relationship between bison ranges, battles, and forts between white settlers and American Indians based on this map?**

Bison (commonly known as buffalo) played a central role in the religion and society of many tribes. By the mid-nineteenth century, approximately thirty million bison grazed on the Great Plains. Before acquiring guns, American Indians used a variety of means to hunt their prey, including bows and arrows and spears. Some rode their horses to chase bison and stampede them over cliffs. The meat from the buffalo provided food; its hide provided material to construct tepees and make blankets and clothes; bones were crafted into tools, knives, and weapons; dried bison dung served as an excellent source of fuel. It is therefore not surprising that the Plains Indians dressed up in colorful outfits, painted their bodies, and danced to the almighty power of the buffalo and the spiritual presence within it.

American Indian hunting societies, such as the Lakota Sioux and Apache, contained gender distinctions. The task of riding horses to hunt bison became men's work; women waited for the hunters to return and then prepared the buffalo hides. Nevertheless, women refused to think of their role as passive; they saw themselves as sharing in the work of providing food, shelter, and clothing for the members of their tribe. Similarly, the religious belief that the spiritual world touched every aspect of the material world gave women an opportunity to experience this transcendent power without the mediation of male leaders.

TEACHING IDEA

Check for Understanding

As a bell ringer or exit ticket, ask students, "To what extent did American Indians in the Great Plains rely on the buffalo?" Possible answers include: *American Indians relied on the buffalo for their meat, hides to construct tepees and clothing, and bones for the creation of tools.*

TEACHING IDEA

Check for Understanding

Compare and contrast gender roles of Great Plains American Indians. Possible answers include: *Men were buffalo hunters on horseback. Women prepared buffalo hides and provided food, clothing, and shelter. Both men and women had access to the spiritual world.*

Period 6: 1865–1898

MODULE 6-1 Westward Expansion and American Indian Resistance

AP® ANALYZING SOURCES

Source: Anonymous Shoshone artisan, *Buffalo Hunting*, c. 1875

About the source: This pictograph portrays a Shoshone man on a buffalo hunt. The drawing was made on a buffalo skin robe quilled by a tribal woman and worn by a hunter.

Questions for Analysis

1. Describe how this image reflects the role of the buffalo in the lives of American Indians on the Great Plains.
2. Explain the gender roles in Plains Indian societies that resulted from activities such as buffalo hunting.
3. Explain how this image reflects the impact of trade between American Indians and white settlers.

REVIEW

Characterize the relationship between the American Indian tribes on the Great Plains and in the West and the environments in which they lived.

Conflict Escalates in the West

Treaty of Fort Laramie 1851 treaty that sought to confine tribes on the northern plains to designated areas in an attempt to keep white settlers from encroaching on their land. In 1868, the second Treaty of Fort Laramie gave northern tribes control over the "Great Reservation" in parts of present-day Montana, Wyoming, North Dakota, and South Dakota.

The U.S. government started out by treating western American Indians as autonomous nations, thereby recognizing their stewardship over the land they occupied. In 1851 the **Treaty of Fort Laramie** confined tribes on the northern plains to designated areas in an attempt to keep white settlers from encroaching on their land. A treaty two years later applied these terms to tribes on the southern plains. American Indians generally kept their part of the agreement, but white miners racing to strike it rich did not. They roamed through American Indian hunting grounds in search of ore and faced little government enforcement of the existing treaties. In fact, the U.S. military made matters considerably worse. On November 29, 1864, a peaceful band of 700 Cheyennes and Arapahos under the leadership of Chief Black Kettle gathered at Sand Creek, Colorado, supposedly under guarantees of U.S. protection. Instead, Colonel John M. Chivington and his troops launched an attack, despite a white flag of surrender hoisted by the American Indians, and brutally killed some 270 American Indians, mainly women and children. A congressional investigation later determined that the victims "were mutilated in the most horrible manner." Although there was considerable public outcry over the incident, the government did nothing to increase enforcement of its treaty obligations. In almost all disputes between white settlers and American Indians, the government sided with the white settlers, regardless of the American Indians' legal rights. In 1867, the government once again

Sand Creek massacre November 29, 1864 massacre of 270 Cheyenne and Arapaho Indians — mostly women and children — by the United States Army. This led to the continuation of the Arapaho-Cheyenne war (1863–1865).

AP® TIP
Compare the experiences of native peoples on the Great Plains in the late 1800s to the experiences of native peoples in eastern North America during the 1600s and 1700s.

Battle of the Little Bighorn 1876 battle in the Montana Territory in which Lieutenant Colonel George Armstrong Custer and his troops were massacred by the Lakota Sioux.

buffalo soldiers African American cavalrymen who fought in the West against American Indians in the 1870s and 1880s.

> "We prefer to die in our own land under the tall cool pines. We will leave our bones with those of our people. It is better to die fighting than to starve."
>
> Victorio, Apache chief, 1877

signed treaties with tribes in the southern plains, with similarly devastating results. The **Treaty of Medicine Lodge** provided reservation lands for the Comanche, Kiowa-Apache, and Southern Arapaho to settle. Despite this agreement, white hunters soon invaded this territory and decimated the buffalo herds.

The dishonesty of the U.S. government was not without consequences. The **Sand Creek massacre** unleashed American Indian wars throughout the central plains, where the Lakota Sioux led the resistance from 1865 to 1868. After two years of fierce fighting, both sides signed a second Treaty of Fort Laramie, which gave northern tribes control over the "Great Reservation" set aside in parts of present-day Montana, Wyoming, North Dakota, and South Dakota. Another treaty placed the southern tribes in a reservation carved out of western Oklahoma.

One of the tribes that wound up in Oklahoma was the Nez Percé. Originally settled in the corner where Washington, Oregon, and Idaho meet, the tribe was forced to sign a treaty ceding most of its land to the United States and to relocate onto a southern reservation. In 1877 Chief Joseph led a small group of Nez Percé opposed to the treaty out of the Pacific Northwest, directing his people in a march of 1,400 miles over mountains into Montana and Wyoming as federal troops pursued them. Intending to flee to Canada and join up with Sitting Bull after the Battle of Little Bighorn, the Nez Percé were finally intercepted in the mountains of northern Montana, just thirty miles from the border. Subsequently, the government relocated these northwestern American Indians to the southwestern territory of Oklahoma. In 1879 Chief Joseph pleaded with lawmakers in Congress to return his people to their home and urged the U.S. government to live up to the original intent of the treaties. His words carried some weight, and the Nez Percé returned under armed escort to a reservation in Washington.

The treaties did not produce a lasting peace. Though most of the tribes relocated onto reservations, some refused. The Apache chief Victorio explained why he would not resettle his people on a reservation. "We prefer to die in our own land under the tall cool pines," he declared. "We will leave our bones with those of our people. It is better to die fighting than to starve." General William Tecumseh Sherman, commander of the military forces against the American Indians, ordered the army to wage a war of annihilation "against all hostile Indians till they are obliterated or beg for mercy." In November 1868, Lieutenant Colonel George Armstrong Custer took Sherman at his word and assaulted a Cheyenne village, killing more than one hundred inhabitants. Nearly a decade later, in 1876, American Indians, this time the Lakota Sioux, exacted revenge by killing Custer and all of his troops at the **Battle of the Little Bighorn** in Montana. Yet this proved to be the final victory for the Lakota nation, as the army mounted an extensive and fierce offensive against them that shattered their resistance.

Among the troops that battled the American Indians were African Americans. Known as **buffalo soldiers**, they represented a cross section of the postwar black population looking for new opportunities that were now available after their emancipation. Some black people enlisted to learn how to read and write; others sought to avoid unpleasant situations back home. Cooks, waiters, painters, bakers, and farmers signed up for a five-year stint in the army at $13 a month. A few gained more glory than money. In May 1880, Sergeant George Jordan of the Ninth Cavalry led troops under his command to fend off Apache raids in Tularosa, New Mexico, for which he was awarded the Congressional Medal of Honor.

By the late 1870s, American Indians had largely succumbed to U.S. military aggression. The tribes, as their many victories demonstrated, contained agile horsemen and skilled warriors, but the U.S. army was backed by the power of an increasingly industrial economy. Telegraph lines and railroads provided logistical advantages in the swift deployment of U.S. troops and the ability of the central command to communicate with field officers. Although American Indians had acquired firearms over the years, the army boasted an essentially unlimited supply of superior weapons. The diversity of American Indians and historic rivalries among tribes also made it difficult for them to unite against their common enemy. The federal government exploited these divisions by hiring American Indians to serve as army scouts against their traditional tribal foes.

The wholesale destruction of the bison was the final blow to American Indian independence. As railroads pushed their tracks beyond the Mississippi, they cleared bison from their path by sending in professional hunters with high-powered rifles to shoot the animals. At the

---

TEACHING IDEA

Project Idea

Create a timeline that includes the various treaties and conflicts that are highlighted in this module. Treaties could include the Treaty of Fort Laramie and the Treaty of Medicine Lodge. Conflicts could include the Sand Creek massacre, Wounded Knee massacre, and the Battle of Little Bighorn. Include the title, year, parties involved, and impact. Have students explain which event on the timeline had the largest impact.

BUILDING AP® SKILLS

Comparison

Ask students, "Was the experience of the Nez Perce and Chief Joseph more similar to, or more different from, the experience of other American Indian tribes during the nineteenth century? Explain."
Possible answers include: *The experiences of the Nez Perce and Chief Joseph were similar to other American Indian tribes because they were forcibly removed from their homeland. Or, the experiences of the Nez Perce and Chief Joseph were different from other American Indian tribes because the Nez Perce were escorted by the U.S. government back to a place near their homeland.*

TEACHING IDEA

Check for Understanding

As a bell ringer or exit ticket, have students list the reasons for the eventual loss of American Indian land to American settlers in the West. Ask them to determine which reason was the most impactful, and explain why. Possible answers include: *American Indians lost land due to the expansion of the railroad and telegraph lines, as the government set aside land grants for such expansion. American Indians also lost land due to mining enterprises, expanding western towns, cattle drive routes, and the western land rush.*

TEACHING IDEA

Analyzing Art and Images

Analyze the American Indian Drawing of Battle of Little Bighorn. Divide the image into four quadrants and have students describe what they see in each quadrant. This strategy will encourage students to focus on all parts of the image, including details, instead of simply glancing at the image as a whole. Then answer the corresponding question.

▲ Differentiation

Divide students into four groups and assign each group a quadrant to analyze. Then, regroup the students into new groups with at least one member representing each quadrant. Have the new groups jigsaw their answers to form a complete analysis of the image (a refresher of the jigsaw model can be found on page 33).

BUILDING AP® SKILLS

Sourcing and Situation

Analyze the American Indian Drawing of Battle of Little Bighorn. The source was created by an American Indian artist, Amos Bad Heart Buffalo. Who might have been the audience for this image? Why was this image created?

Period 6: 1865–1898

MODULE 6-1 Westward Expansion and American Indian Resistance

▲
American Indian Drawing of Battle of Little Bighorn This ink-on-paper drawing by Amos Bad Heart Buffalo (1869–1913) depicts the June 1876 Battle of Little Bighorn, also known as Custer's Last Stand. It portrays the retreat of Major Marcus Reno's forces. The painted warrior on the white horse who is shooting a soldier from his saddle is Crazy Horse, the Sioux chieftain. **What aspects of the drawing suggest it was created by an American Indian artist?**

same time, buffalo products such as shoes, coats, and hats became fashionable in the East. By the mid-1880s, hunters had killed more than thirteen million bison. As a result of the relentless move of white Americans westward and conspicuous consumption back east, bison herds were almost annihilated.

Faced with decimation of the bison, broken treaties, and their opponents' superior military technology, American Indians' capacity to wage war collapsed, and they had little choice but to settle on shrinking reservations that the government established for them. The absence of war, however, did not necessarily bring them security. In the late 1870s, gold discoveries in the Black Hills of North Dakota ignited another furious rush by miners onto lands supposedly guaranteed to the Lakota people. Rather than honoring its treaties, the U.S. government forced the tribes to relinquish still more land. General Custer's Seventh Cavalry was part of the military force trying to push American Indians out of this mining region, when it was annihilated at the Little Bighorn in 1876. Elsewhere, Congress opened up a portion of western Oklahoma to white homesteaders in 1889. Although this land had not been assigned to specific tribes relocated in Indian Territory, more than eighty thousand American Indians from various tribes lived there. This government-sanctioned **land rush** only added to the pressure from homesteaders and others to acquire more land at the expense of American Indians. A decade later, Congress officially ended American Indian control of Indian Territory.

REVIEW

- How and why did federal policy toward American Indians change between 1865 and 1880?
- What factors led to the defeat of American Indians on the Great Plains?

Reforming American Indian Policy

As reservations continued to shrink under expansionist assault and government policy, a movement arose to reform American Indian policy. Largely centered in the East, where few American Indians lived, reformers came to believe that the future well-being of American Indians lay not in sovereignty but in assimilation. In 1881 Helen Hunt Jackson published *A Century of Dishonor*, her exposé of the unjust treatment the American Indians had received. Roused by this depiction of the American Indians' plight, groups such as the Women's National Indian Association joined with ministers and philanthropists to advocate the transformation of native peoples into "full-fledged" Americans.

These well-intentioned reformers ultimately contributed to the oppression of American Indians by trying to eradicate their cultural heritage. Even most sympathetic reformers of the period offered an approach that supported assimilation as the only alternative to extinction. The influential Lewis Morgan, author of *Ancient Society* (1877), concluded that all cultures evolved through three stages: savagery, barbarism, and civilization. According to Morgan's theories, American Indians occupied the lower rungs and that by adopting white values they could become civilized. Thus, even those who thought they were helping American Indians rejected the legitimacy of their culture.

Reformers faced opposition from white Americans who doubted that American Indian assimilation was possible. For many white people, secure in their sense of their own superiority, the decline and eventual extinction of the American Indian peoples was an inevitable consequence of what they saw as American Indians' innate inferiority. For example, a Wyoming newspaper predicted: "The same inscrutable Arbiter that decreed the downfall of Rome has pronounced the doom of extinction upon the red men of America."

Reformers found their legislative spokesman in Senator Henry Dawes of Massachusetts. As legislative director of the Boston Indian Citizenship Association, Dawes shared Christian reformers' belief that becoming a true American would save both the American Indians and the soul of the nation. A Republican who had served in Congress since the Civil War, Dawes had the same condescending attitude toward American Indians as he had toward freedpeople. He believed that if both groups worked hard and practiced thrift and individual initiative in the spirit of seventeenth-century New England Puritans, they would succeed. The key for Dawes was private ownership of land.

Passed in 1887, the **Dawes Act** attempted to promote American Indian assimilation by encouraging the division of tribal lands into 160-acre homesteads. The act allocated one parcel to each family head. The government held the lands in trust for the American Indians for twenty-five years; at the end of this period, the American Indians would receive American citizenship. In return, they had to abandon their religious and cultural rites and practices, including storytelling and the use of medicine men. Whatever lands remained after this reallocation — and the amount was considerable — would be sold on the open market, and the profits from the sales would be placed in an educational fund for American Indians.

Unfortunately, like most of the policies it replaced, the Dawes Act proved detrimental to American Indians. Native families received inferior farmlands and inadequate tools to cultivate them, while speculators reaped profits from the sale of the "excess" American Indian lands. A little more than a decade after the Dawes Act went into effect, American Indians controlled 77 million acres of land, down sharply from the 155 million acres they held in 1881. Additional legislation in 1891 forced American Indian parents to send their children to boarding schools or else face arrest. At these educational institutions, American Indian children were given "American" names, had their long hair cut, and wore uniforms in place of their native dress. The program for boys provided manual and vocational training and the program for girls taught domestic skills, so that they could emulate the gender roles in middle-class American families. However, this schooling offered few skills of use in an economic world undergoing industrial transformation.

Ultimately, the federal government devised its policies based on flawed cultural assumptions. Even the most sensitive white administrators of American Indian affairs considered them a degraded race, in accordance with the scientific thinking of the time. At most, white people believed that American Indians could be lifted to a higher level of civilization, which in practice meant a withering away of their traditional culture and heritage.

AP® TIP

Make sure you can explain how conceptions of white supremacy shaped American Indian policies in the late nineteenth century.

Dawes Act 1887 act that ended federal recognition of tribal sovereignty and divided American Indian land into 160-acre parcels to be distributed to American Indian heads of household. The act dramatically reduced the amount of American Indian-controlled land and undermined American Indian social and cultural institutions.

APPLY THE TIP

As a bell ringer or exit ticket, ask students to describe how white superiority impacted American Indian policies in the late nineteenth century. Possible answers include: *Groups such as the Women's National Indian Association believed that they were helping American Indians by suggesting assimilation into a "civilized" white American culture. Religious reformers believed that their religion was the correct religion to follow, so they tried to convert American Indians. Other white Americans believed that American Indians should simply be removed, not assimilated, because of the belief of white American superiority. These Americans felt that American Indians could never truly be assimilated, so they were sent to remote reservations instead.*

TEACHING IDEA

Incorporating Primary Sources

Search the Stanford History Education Group's website to find the Reading Like a Historian lesson titled, "Carlisle Indian Industrial School" (sheg.stanford.edu). The lesson requires students to analyze sources in order to discover the purpose behind the creation of the Carlisle Indian Industrial School. Students will learn about assimilation efforts and their impact on American Indian children.

▲ Differentiation

The lesson about the Carlisle Indian Industrial School includes abridged documents, but the full documents are also available on the Stanford History Education Group's website. Use the appropriate documents for the level of your students.

TRM Suggested Responses to Questions

TRM Module 6.1 AP® Analyzing Sources Handout 2

BUILDING AP® SKILLS
Sourcing and Situation

Have students complete a HIPP analysis of *The School Days of an Indian Girl* written by Zitkala-Ša to better understand the historical context, intended audience, purpose, and point of view of the source (a refresher of HIPP can be found on page 8). Students can understand a source at a much deeper level if they can determine its origins. Then, assign students to answer the Questions for Analysis.

Period 6: 1865–1898

MODULE 6-1 Westward Expansion and American Indian Resistance

AP® ANALYZING SOURCES

Source: Zitkala-Ša, *The School Days of an Indian Girl*, 1921

"There were eight in our party of bronzed children who were going East with the missionaries [in 1884]. Among us were three young braves, two tall girls, and we three little ones, Judéwin, Thowin, and I. . . .

We were placed in a line of girls who were marching into the dining room. These were Indian girls, in stiff shoes and closely clinging dresses. The small girls wore sleeved aprons and shingled hair[1]. As I walked noiselessly in my soft moccasins, I felt like sinking to the floor, for my blanket had been stripped from my shoulders. I looked hard at the Indian girls, who seemed not to care that they were even more immodestly dressed than I, in their tightly fitting clothes. . . .

A small bell was tapped, and each of the pupils drew a chair from under the table. Supposing this act meant they were to be seated, I pulled out mine and at once slipped into it from one side. But when I turned my head, I saw that I was the only one seated, and all the rest at our table remained standing. Just as I began to rise, looking shyly around to see how chairs were to be used, a second bell was sounded. All were seated at last, and I had to crawl back into my chair again. I heard a man's voice at one end of the hall, and I looked around to see him. But all the others hung their heads over their plates. As I glanced at the long chain of tables, I caught the eyes of a paleface woman upon me. Immediately I dropped my eyes, wondering why I was so keenly watched by the strange woman. The man ceased his mutterings, and then a third bell was tapped. Every one picked up his knife and fork and began eating. I began crying instead, for by this time I was afraid to venture anything more.

But this eating by formula was not the hardest trial in that first day. Late in the morning, my friend Judéwin gave me a terrible warning. Judéwin knew a few words of English; and she had overheard the paleface woman talk about cutting our long, heavy hair. Our mothers had taught us that only unskilled warriors who were captured had their hair shingled by the enemy. Among our people, short hair was worn by mourners, and shingled hair by cowards!

We discussed our fate some moments, and when Judéwin said, "We have to submit, because they are strong," I rebelled.

"No, I will not submit! I will struggle first!" I answered. . . .

I remember being dragged out, though I resisted by kicking and scratching wildly. In spite of myself, I was carried downstairs and tied fast in a chair.

I cried aloud, shaking my head all the while until I felt the cold blades of the scissors against my neck, and heard them gnaw off one of my thick braids. Then I lost my spirit. Since the day I was taken from my mother I had suffered extreme indignities. People had stared at me. I had been tossed about in the air like a wooden puppet. And now my long hair was shingled like a coward's! In my anguish I moaned for my mother, but no one came to comfort me. Not a soul reasoned quietly with me, as my own mother used to do; for now I was only one of many little animals driven by a herder."

[1] A hair style cut short from the back of the head to expose the nape of the neck.

Questions for Analysis
1. Describe the methods used by the boarding school to forcibly assimilate American Indian students.
2. Explain how Zitkala-Ša's experience contrasts with the beliefs of nineteenth-century missionary reformers.
3. Evaluate the impact of American Indian boarding schools on the lives of their students and on tribal culture.

REVIEW
- How did the provisions of the Dawes Act affect American Indians?

American Indian Assimilation and Resistance

Not all American Indians conformed to the government's attempt at forced acculturation. Some refused to abandon their traditional social practices, and others rejected the white man's version of private property and civilization. Even on reservations, American Indians found ways to preserve aspects of their native traditions. Through close family ties, they communicated to sons and daughters their languages, histories, and cultural practices. Parents refused to grant full control of their children to white educators and often made sure that schools were located on or near reservations where they fit into the pattern of their lives. Yet, many others displayed more complicated approaches to survival in a world that continued to view American Indians with prejudice. Geronimo and Sitting Bull participated in pageants and Wild West shows but refused to disavow their heritage. Ohiyesa, a Lakota also known as Charles Eastman, went to boarding school, graduated from Dartmouth College, and earned a medical degree from Boston University. He supported passage of the Dawes Act and believed in the virtues of an American education. At the same time, he spoke out against government corruption and fraud perpetrated against American Indians. Reviewing his life in his later years, Ohiyesa (Eastman) reflected: "I am an Indian and while I have learned much from civilization . . . I have never lost my Indian sense of right and justice."

Disaster loomed for those who resisted assimilation and held on too tightly to the old ways. In 1888 the prophet Wovoka, a member of the Paiute tribe in western Nevada, had a vision that American Indians would one day regain control of the world and that white people would disappear. He believed that the Creator had provided him with a **Ghost Dance** that would make this happen. The dance spread to thousands of Lakota Sioux in the northern plains. Seeing the Ghost Dance as a sign of renewed American Indian resistance, the army attempted to put a stop to the revival. On December 29, 1890, the Seventh Cavalry chased three hundred ghost dancers to Wounded Knee Creek on the Pine Ridge Reservation in present-day South Dakota. In a confrontation with the Lakota leader Big Foot, a gunshot accidentally rang out during a struggle with one of his followers. The cavalry then turned the full force of their weaponry on the American Indians, killing 250 people, many of them women and children.

The message of the **Wounded Knee massacre** was clear for those who raised their voices against Americanization. As Black Elk, a spiritual leader of the Oglala Lakota tribe, asserted: "A people's dream died there. . . . There is no center any longer, and the sacred tree is dead." It may not have been the policy of the U.S. government to exterminate the Indians as a people, but it was certainly U.S. policy to destroy American Indian culture and society once and for all.

Ghost Dance Religious ritual performed by the Paiute Indians in the late nineteenth century. Following a vision he received in 1888, the prophet Wovoka believed that performing the Ghost Dance would cause white people to disappear and allow American Indians to regain control of their lands.

Wounded Knee massacre Massacre committed by U.S. military in South Dakota, December 29, 1890. The Plains Indians, on the edge of starvation, began the "Ghost Dance," which they believed would protect them from bullets and restore their old way of life. Following one of the dances, a rifle held by an American Indian misfired. In response, U.S. soldiers invaded the encampment, killing some 250 people.

REVIEW

- What methods did American Indians use to resist assimilation?
- Why and how did some American Indians adapt to dominant white culture?

AP® WRITING HISTORICALLY — Short-Answer Question Practice

ACTIVITY

Read the following question carefully and write a short response. Use complete sentences.

Answer (a), (b), and (c).

a. Briefly explain ONE specific historical cause of conflict between American Indians and white settlers in the period 1865 to 1900.
b. Briefly explain ONE specific response of the U.S. government to conflict between American Indians and white settlers in the period 1865 to 1900.
c. Briefly explain ONE specific way American Indians resisted or accommodated to their treatment by the U.S. government in the period 1865 to 1900.

BUILDING AP® SKILLS

Comparison

Divide the class into two groups. Have one group brainstorm the causes and effects of the Sand Creek massacre and have the second group do the same for the Wounded Knee massacre. Upon completion of the exercise, reshuffle the groups so that a pair of persons from the first grouping are matched with a pair of persons from the second grouping, and have them share and compare their findings.

TRM Suggested Responses to Questions

TEACHING IDEA

AP® Writing Historically Review

This causation question provides students with ample chronology to formulate a response. When students have longer time periods, they sometimes get confused about how to proceed to an answer. Therefore, start with the big picture historical topic such as the Gilded Age. Ask students to develop a list of three terms that relate to Gilded Age economic progress and are attendant to American Indians. For instance, one of the factors they might suggest would be transportation development. A good answer will name that cause and explain it with a more specific example such as the transcontinental railroad. Once students are aware of the context and related causes, they will be better able to answer the more discrete parts of this question in (b) and (c).

TEACHING IDEA

Check for Understanding

The SAQ asks students to distill much of the content from the module into three discrete chunks. Rather than trying to summarize large amounts of information, guide them to focus on one specific and historically significant cause of conflict between American Indians and white settlers in (a), one specific and historically significant action taken by the U.S. government in response to the conflict in (b), and one specific way that American Indians either resisted their treatment by the U.S. government or one specific way American Indians made accommodations to the way they were treated by the U.S. government in (c). Students can use the *ACE* strategy to answer each question by focusing on a single historical development in each part, citing an example or specific detail for that item, and explaining the connection or significance of the answer (a refresher of *ACE* can be found on page 21). Note the time periods for each part of the SAQ. Part (a) covers the first half of the module's time period, (b) stretches over the entire time period, and (c) focuses on the latter part of the time period.

TRM Suggested Responses to Questions

EXPLORING AP® THEMES

Migration and Settlement

Throughout the module, ask students to define the consequences of migration for both American Indians and white settlers. Remind students to include specific historical evidence to support their answer.

TEACHING IDEA

Class Discussion

Pose the following questions to students: "What obstacles did white Americans face while moving westward?" and "What obstacles did American Indians face in keeping their way of life?" Possible answers include: *White Americans expected to get rich quickly, but unlike hard work, riches were hard to come by. Many jobs, such as mining, were incredibly dangerous. Farmers faced extreme weather and failing crops, as well as the possibility of losing their land to a commercial ranch or farm. American Indians fought to preserve their way of life, but were removed from their homelands and were forced to assimilate into white American culture.*

Module 6-2

Industry in the West

LEARNING TARGETS

By the end of this module, you should be able to:
- Explain how industrialization shaped the economy of the West.
- Explain the effects of industrialization on the environment in the West.
- Explain the similarities and differences in the experiences of different peoples in the West.

THEMATIC FOCUS

Migration and Settlement

Despite numerous obstacles posed by difficult terrain, forbidding climate, and unfamiliar inhabitants of the land they sought to harness, internal and international migrants were attracted to the West by new economic opportunities in mining, lumber, ranching, and commercial farming. Pioneers and settlers used hard work and technological innovations to transform their environments.

HISTORICAL REASONING FOCUS

Comparison
Causation

TASK ▶ As you read this module, consider the motivations of westward migrants, the ways their lives were changed by moving west, how their actions and economic activities changed the West, and how the West was integrated into the larger economy of the United States. Take note of how specific groups of people had similar and different experiences in the West and how various pioneers — farmers, prospectors, and cowboys — eventually became wageworkers for larger corporations.

The West attracted a diverse group of settlers. Miners poured into Indian Territory in the Rocky Mountains in search of gold and silver. Despite visions of instant riches, the vast majority found only backbreaking work, danger, and frustration. Miners continued to face hardship and danger as industrial mining operations took over from individual prospectors. By 1900 the mining rush had peaked, and many of the boomtowns that had cropped up around the mining industry had emptied out. Closely related to mining, the lumber industry was less demographically diverse but also followed the pattern of eventual domination by big business.

Cattle ranching and farming in the West also increasingly became controlled by big business. Cowboys worked long hours in tough but boring conditions on the open range. Similarly, commercial farmers who headed west endured great hardships in trying to raise crops in an often inhospitable climate. Extreme weather and falling crop prices forced many ranchers and farmers out of business, and their lands and businesses were snatched up by larger, more consolidated commercial ranching and agricultural enterprises.

Mormon settlers trekked into Utah in search of religious freedom while Chinese immigrants fled war, starvation, and unemployment on their journey to the West Coast. Federal legislation targeted both groups by banning the Mormon practice of polygamy and excluding further Chinese immigration. Despite difficult conditions, western settlers of all types demonstrated grit and determination not only in surviving but in improving their lives.

The **Mining** and **Lumber Booms**

The discovery of gold in California in 1848 had set this mining frenzy in motion. Over the next thirty years, successive waves of gold and silver strikes in Colorado, Nevada, Washington, Idaho, Montana, and the Dakotas lured individual prospectors with shovels and wash pans. One of the biggest finds came with the **Comstock Lode** in the Sierra Nevada. All told, miners extracted around $350 million worth of silver from this source. One of those who came to try to share in the wealth was Samuel Clemens. Like most of his fellow miners, Clemens did not find his fortune in Nevada and soon turned his attention to writing, finally achieving success as the author called Mark Twain.

Like Twain, many of those who flocked to the Comstock Lode and other mining frontiers were men. Nearly half were foreign-born, many of them coming from Mexico or China. Using pans and shovels, prospectors could find only the ore that lay near the surface of the earth and water. Once these initial discoveries were played out, individual prospectors could not afford to buy the equipment needed to dig out the vast deposits of gold and silver buried deep in the earth. As a result, western mining became dominated by big businesses with the financial resources necessary to purchase industrial mining equipment.

When mining became an industry, prospectors became wageworkers. In Virginia City, Nevada, miners labored for $4 a day, an amount that barely covered the expenses of life in a mining boomtown. Moreover, the work was extremely dangerous. Mine shafts extended down more than a thousand feet, and working temperatures regularly exceeded 100 degrees Fahrenheit. Noxious fumes, fires, and floods of scalding water flowed through the shafts, and other threats killed or disabled thousands each year.

> **AP® TIP**
> Consider how the actions of the miners and the mine owners in the nineteenth-century West might reflect different sets of values in the development of American national identity.

Struggling with low pay and dangerous work, western miners sought to organize. In the mid-1860s, unions formed in the Comstock Lode areas of Virginia City and Gold Hill, Nevada. Although these unions had some success, they also provoked a violent backlash from mining companies determined to resist union demands. Companies hired private police forces to help break strikes. Such forces were often assisted by state militias deployed by elected officials with close ties to the companies. For example, in 1892 the governor of Idaho crushed an unruly strike by calling up the National Guard, a confrontation that resulted in the deaths of seven strikers. A year later, mine workers formed one of the most militant labor organizations in the nation, the Western Federation of Miners. Within a decade, it had attracted fifty thousand members, though membership did not extend to all ethnicities. The union excluded Chinese, Mexican, and American Indian workers from its ranks.

Hydraulic Mining Near French Corral, Nevada County, 1866 Hydraulic mining was a technique that used water from high pressure hoses to blast away rock and sediment in the search for deeper veins of gold. As individual miners exhausted surface deposits of gold, corporations brought in new and expensive equipment to continue the search. **How did the industrialization of mining affect the environment?**

TEACHING IDEA

Class Discussion

Draw a stick figure on the board/projector. Title the figure "Miners." Label the head and each limb with a different category: Motivations, Obstacles, Average Age, Sex, and Races. While students draw the same stick figure in their notes, work with students to fill in as much information on the stick figure as possible. This will allow students to understand who miners were. Once complete, ask students: "To what extent were miners successful in overcoming the obstacles that they faced?"

TEACHING IDEA

Analyzing Art and Images

Search the Digital Public Library of America for images of miners from the years 1865 to 1898 (dp.la). Post these images around the classroom along with a piece of paper large enough for students to write on. As a bell ringer, break students into groups so they are evenly spread out among the images. Have students use the provided paper to write down their observations and questions about the images. After about a minute, have students move to the next image.

Once students have seen all of the images, pose the following question to the class: "What was life like for miners during the late nineteenth century?" Encourage students to use specific historical evidence from the images to support their answers. Possible answers include: *Miners faced dangerous working conditions. Dust, heat, fires, floods, and dynamite were constant dangers. Most miners didn't strike it rich and were forced to work for large mining operations because mining equipment was too expensive for individuals to afford. Miners who attempted to improve working conditions faced resistance from mining companies.* To further the conversation, also ask the following questions:

- What information is missing from these photographs?

- How do these photographs compare to what we have read in the textbook?

TEACHING IDEA

Class Discussion

Draw a stick figure on the whiteboard. Title the figure "Women in the West." Label each limb with a different category: Occupations, Age, Motivations, and Obstacles. While students draw the same stick figure in their notes, work with students to fill in as much information on the stick figure as possible. Once complete, ask students: "Did women have more opportunities in the West or the East? Explain."

BUILDING AP® SKILLS

Continuity and Change

Challenge students to come up with as many specific pieces of historical evidence as they can to answer the following prompts:

- Explain how mining towns in the late nineteenth century changed.

- Explain how mining towns in the late nineteenth century stayed the same.

Possible answers include: *Mining towns boomed in populations and were abandoned shortly thereafter. Mining towns were inhabited by the same types of people, mostly young, single men and women. Over time, mining towns became increasingly divided among various ethnic groups, similar to the divisions in cities in the East.*

Discuss answers and in order to further the conversation, ask students, "Did mining towns in the late nineteenth century experience more change or continuity?"

Men worked the mines, but women flocked to the area as well. In Storey County, Nevada, the heart of the Comstock Lode, the 1875 census showed that women made up about half the population. Most employed women worked long hours as domestic laborers in boarding houses, hotels, and private homes. Prostitution, which was legal, accounted for the single largest segment of the female workforce. Most prostitutes were between the ages of nineteen and twenty-four, and they entered this occupation because few other well-paying jobs were available to them. The demand for their services remained high among the large population of unmarried men. Yet prostitutes faced constant danger, and many were victims of physical abuse, robbery, and murder.

As early as the 1880s, gold and silver discoveries had played out in the Comstock Lode. Boomtowns, which had sprung up almost overnight, now became ghost towns as gold and silver deposits dwindled. Even more substantial places like Virginia City, Nevada experienced a severe decline as the veins of ore ran out. One revealing sign of the city's plummeting fortunes was the drop in the number of prostitutes, which declined by more than half by 1880. The mining business then shifted from gold and silver to copper, lead, and zinc, centered in Montana and Idaho. As with the early prospectors in California and Nevada, these miners eventually became wageworkers for giant consolidated mining companies. By the end of the nineteenth century, the Amalgamated Copper Company and the American Smelting and Refining Company dominated the industry.

Mining towns that survived became only slightly less rowdy places, but they did settle into more complex patterns of urban living. At its height in the 1870s, Virginia City contained 25,000 residents and was among the largest cities west of the Mississippi River. It provided schools and churches and featured such cultural amenities as theaters and opera houses. Though the

▲ **Prostitution on the Frontier** Prostitution was one of the main sources of employment for women in frontier mining towns. A legal enterprise, it paid better than other work such as domestic service and teaching. In 1875 in the Comstock region of Nevada, 307 women plied their trade in brothels and saloons similar to the saloon shown here. **What economic and social factors led many younger women to work as prostitutes in mining towns?**

AP® TIP

Compare the impact of urban growth in the West to the issues of urbanization and industrialization in eastern cities.

population in mining towns remained predominantly young and male, the young men were increasingly likely to get married and raise families. Residents lived in neighborhoods divided by class and ethnicity. For example, in Butte, Montana, the west side of town became home to the middle and upper classes. Mine workers lived on the east side in homes subdivided into apartments and in boardinghouses. The Irish lived in one section; Finns, Swedes, Serbs, Croatians, and Slovenes in other sections. Each group formed its own social, fraternal, and religious organizations to relieve the harsh conditions of overcrowding, poor sanitation, and discrimination. Residents of the east side relied on one another for support and frowned on those who deviated from their code of solidarity. "They didn't try to outdo the other one," one neighborhood woman remarked. "If you did, you got into trouble. . . . If they thought you were a little richer than they were, they wouldn't associate with you." Although western mining towns retained distinctive qualities, in their social and ethnic divisions they came to resemble older cities east of the Mississippi River.

The mining industry created a huge demand for timber, as did the railroad lines that operated in the West. Initially small logging firms moved into the Northwest and California, cut down all the trees they could, sent them to nearby sawmills for processing, and moved on. By 1900, a few large firms came to dominate the industry and acquired vast tracts of forests. Frederick Weyerhaeuser purchased 900,000 acres of prime timberland in the Western Cascades of Oregon, largely bringing an end to the often chaotic competition of small firms that had characterized the industry in its early days. Increasingly, the western lumber industry became part of a global market that shipped products to Hawaii, South America, and Asia.

AP® TIP

Evaluate the impact of large corporations' consolidation on the establishment of industries related to different resources in the late nineteenth-century West.

Loggers and sawmill workers did not benefit from these changes. Exclusively male, large numbers of workers came from Scandinavia, and only a few were Asian or African American. Men died or lost limbs in cutting down the trees, transporting them on the rivers, or processing the wood in sawmills. As lumber camps and mill villages became urbanized, those who gained the most were the merchants and bankers who supplied the goods and capital.

REVIEW

- How did the mining and lumber industries shape the late-nineteenth century American economy?
- How did the lives of workers in those industries change over time?

The Life of a Cowboy

There is no greater symbol of the frontier West than the cowboy. As portrayed in novels and film, the cowboy hero was the essence of manhood, an independent figure who fought for justice and defended the honor and virtue of women. Never the aggressor, he fought to protect law-abiding residents of frontier communities.

This romantic image excited generations of American readers and, later, movie and television audiences. In reality, cowboys' lives were much more routine. Rather than working as independent adventurers, they increasingly operated in an industrial setting dominated by large cattle companies. Cowboys worked for paltry monthly wages, put in long days herding cattle, and spent part of the night guarding them on the open range. Their major task was to make the 1,500-mile **Long Drive** along the Chisholm Trail. Beginning in the late 1860s, cowboys moved cattle from ranches in Texas through Oklahoma to rail depots in Kansas towns such as Abilene and Dodge City; from there, cattle were shipped by train eastward to slaughterhouses in Chicago. Life along the trail was monotonous, and riders had to contend with bad weather, dangerous work, and disease.

Numbering around forty thousand and averaging twenty-four years of age, the cowboys who rode through the Great Plains from Texas to Kansas came from diverse backgrounds. The majority, about 66 percent, were white, predominantly southerners who had fought for the South during the Civil War. Most of the rest were divided evenly between Mexicans and African Americans, some of whom were formerly enslaved and others Union veterans of the Civil War.

APPLY THE TIP

Divide the class in half, then divide each half into pairs. The first set of pairs should work to brainstorm the impact of urban growth in the West. The second set of pairs should work to brainstorm the impact of urbanization in the East. Then, divide the class into groups of four so that each group contains a pair that worked on analyzing urban growth in the west and a pair that worked on analyzing urban growth in the east. Have students compare their findings in the Venn diagram. Possible answers include: *Both western and eastern urbanization led to the separation of ethnic groups and classes within the cities. Attempts were also made by social and religious organizations to relieve problems such as poor sanitation and overcrowding. Western cities were rowdier than eastern cities due to their rustic roots.*

APPLY THE TIP

Divide the class into two groups, and further subdivide those two groups into quads. As a pre-writing exercise, task the first class-groupings with employing the "Twenty-Five-Word Drill" and the second class-groupings with employing the "Fifty-Word Drill" to address the following prompt: "Evaluate the impact of large corporations' consolidation on the establishment of industries related to different resources in the late nineteenth-century West." In addressing this prompt, students are required to write a response that is, depending upon the group to which they are assigned, no more than 25 or 50 words total (give or take). The product of the former exercise winds up as a concise statement of thesis, while the latter becomes more of an elaborate conclusive statement on the question. Upon completion of this exercise, reshuffle the quads so that a pair of persons from the first grouping are matched up with a pair of persons from the second grouping, and have them share and compare their products.

TEACHING IDEA

Analyzing Art and Images

Search the Digital Public Library of America for images of cowboys from the years 1865 to 1898 (dp.la). Post these images around the classroom along with a piece of paper large enough for students to write on. As a bell ringer, break students into groups so they are evenly spread out among the images. Have students use the provided paper to write down their observations and questions about the images. After about a minute, have students move to the next image. Once students have seen all of the images, pose the following question to the class: "What was life like for cowboys during the late nineteenth century?" Encourage students to use specific historical evidence from the images to support their answers. Also ask the following questions:

- What information is missing from these photographs?
- How do these photographs compare to what we have read in the textbook?
- How do these photographs compare to the depictions of cowboys in television and movies?

TRM Suggested Responses to Questions

TRM Module 6.2 AP® Analyzing Sources Handout 1

TEACHING IDEA

Analyzing Art and Images

Divide the image titled "Buffalo Bill's Wild West and Congress of Rough Riders of the World, 1893" into four quadrants. Analyze the image with students one quadrant at a time, paying close attention to the details. What do students notice? After spending a few minutes noticing the details, ask students to answer the provided questions. This strategy helps students to slow down and notice all parts of an image before trying to determine its meaning.

▲ Differentiation

Divide students into four groups and assign each group a quadrant to analyze. Then, regroup the students into new groups with at least one member representing each quadrant. Have the new groups jigsaw their answers to form a complete analysis of the image (a refresher of the jigsaw model can be found on page 33).

Period 6: 1865–1898

MODULE 6-2 Industry in the West

AP® ANALYZING SOURCES

Cody's Wild West Show, 1893 (colour litho)/American School (19th century)/NEWBERRY LIBRARY/Newberry Library, Chicago, Illinois, USA/Bridgeman Images

Source: *Buffalo Bill's Wild West and Congress of Rough Riders of the World,* 1893

Questions for Analysis

1. Describe the portrayal of cowboys and American Indians in this poster.
2. Explain how the poster's portrayal of cowboys and American Indians reflected popular stereotypes.
3. Explain how changes in federal American Indian policy shaped the historical situation that made this portrayal of the West possible.

Source: George C. Duffield, *Driving Cattle from Texas to Iowa,* 1866

"12th
Hard Rain & Wind. Big stampede & here we are among the Indians with 150 head of Cattle gone. Hunted all day & the Rain pouring down with but poor success. Dark days are these to me. Nothing but Bread & Coffee. Hands all Growling & Swearing—everything wet & cold. [Steers] gone. Rode all day & gathered all but 35 mixed with 8 other Herds. Last Night 5000 Beeves stampeded at this place & a general mix up was the result. . . .

14th
Last night there was a terrible storm. Rain poured in torrents all night & up to 12 AM today. Our Beeves left us in the night but for once on the whole trip we found them all together near camp at day break. All the other droves as far as I can hear are scattered to the four winds. Our Other Herd was all gone. We are now 25 Miles from Ark River & it is Very High. We are water bound by two creeks & but Beef & Flour to eat, am not Homesick but Heart sick. . . .

16th
Last night was a dark Gloomey night but we made it all right. Today it is raining & we have crossed Honey creek & am informed that there is another creek 6 miles ahead swimming. Twelve o clock today it rained one Hour so hard that a creek close by rose 20 ft in the afternoon. All wet."

Questions for Analysis

1. Identify the most significant challenge Duffield faces in this diary excerpt.
2. Explain how Duffield's diary excerpt reveals the daily activities of cowboys during the cattle drive.

Questions for Comparison

1. Identify the intended audience for each document.
2. Explain how the intended audience for each document shapes its portrayal of cowboys.
3. Evaluate the extent to which Duffield's experience as a cowboy clashes with the depiction of cowboys in Buffalo Bill's poster.

Besides experiencing rugged life on the range, black and Mexican cowboys faced racial discrimination. Jim Perry, an African American who rode for the three-million-acre XIT Ranch in Texas for more than twenty years, complained: "If it weren't for my damned old black face I'd have been boss of one of these divisions long ago." Mexican *vaqueros*, or cowboys, earned one-third to one-half the wages of white counterparts, whereas black cowboys were usually paid on a par with white ones. Because the cattle kingdoms first flourished during Reconstruction, racial discrimination and segregation carried over into the Southwest. On one drive along the route to Kansas, a white boss insisted that a black cowboy eat and sleep separately from white men and shot at him when he refused to heed this order. Nevertheless, the proximity in which cowboys worked and the need for cooperation to overcome the pitfalls of the Long Drive made it difficult to enforce rigid racial divisions on the open range.

REVIEW

- How were the experiences of black and Mexican cowboys different from and similar to those of white cowboys?

The Rise of Commercial Ranching and Farming

Commercial ranches absorbed cowboys into their expanding operations. Spaniards had originally imported cattle into the Southwest, and by the late nineteenth century some five million Texas longhorn steers grazed in the area. Cattle that could be purchased in Texas for $3 to $7 fetched a price of $30 to $40 in Kansas. The extension of railroads across the West opened up a quickly growing market for beef in the East. The development of refrigerated railroad cars guaranteed that meat from slaughtered cattle could reach eastern consumers without spoiling. With money to be made, the cattle industry rose to meet the demand. Fewer than 40 ranchers owned more than 20 million acres of land. Easterners and Europeans joined the boom and invested money in giant ranches. By the mid-1880s, approximately 7.5 million head of cattle roamed the western ranges, and large cattle ranchers became rich. Cattle ranching had become fully integrated into the national commercial economy.

Then the bubble burst. Ranchers, often already raising more cattle than the market could handle, increasingly faced competition from cattle producers in Canada and Argentina. Prices spiraled downward. Another challenge came from homesteaders who moved into the plains and fenced in their farms with barbed wire, thereby reducing the size of the open range. Yet the greatest disaster occurred from 1885 to 1887. Two frigid winters, together with a scorching summer drought, destroyed 90 percent of the cattle on the northern plains of the Dakotas, Montana, Colorado, and Wyoming. Under these conditions, outside financial capital to support ranching diminished, and many of the great cattle barons went into bankruptcy. This economic collapse consolidated the remaining cattle industry into even fewer hands. The cowboy, never more than a hired hand, became a laborer for large corporations.

Like cowboys, farm families also endured hardships to make their living in the West. They struggled to raise crops in an often inhospitable climate in hopes that their yields would be sold for a profit. Falling crop prices, however, led to soaring debt and forced many farmers into bankruptcy and off their land, while others were fortunate enough to survive and make a living.

The federal government played a major role in opening up the Great Plains to farmers, who eventually clashed with cattlemen. The Republican Party of Abraham Lincoln had opposed the expansion of slavery in order to promote the virtues of free soil and free labor for white men and their families. During the Civil War, preoccupation with defeating the South did not stop the Republican-controlled Congress from passing the **Homestead Act**. As an incentive for western migration, the act established procedures for distributing 160-acre lots to western settlers, on condition that they develop and farm their land. What most would-be settlers did not know, however, was that lots of 160 acres were not viable in the harsh, dry climate of the Great Plains.

Reality did not deter pioneers and adventurers. In fact, weather conditions in the region temporarily fooled them. The decade after 1878 witnessed an exceptional amount of rainfall west of

AP® TIP
Analyze the role of the federal government in encouraging the settlement and industrial development of the West after the end of the Civil War.

Homestead Act 1862 act that established procedures for distributing 160-acre lots to western settlers, on condition that they develop and farm their land, as an incentive for western migration.

TRM Suggested Responses to Questions

TRM Module 6.2 AP® Analyzing Sources Handout 2

AP® ANALYZING SOURCES

Source: Ida Lindgren, Swedish homesteader, *Letter*, August 25, 1874

"[W]e have not had rain [on the Kansas Prairie] since the beginning of June, and then with the heat and often strong winds as well, you can imagine how everything has dried out. There has also been a general lamentation and fear for the coming year. We have gotten a fair amount of wheat, rye, and oats, for they are ready so early, but no one here will get corn or potatoes. We have a few summer potatoes, but many don't even have that, and we thought and hoped we would get a good crop of other potatoes, but will evidently get none. Instead of selling the oats and part of the rye as we had expected, we must now use them for the livestock, since there was no corn. We are glad we have the oats (for many don't have any and must feed wheat to the stock) and had hoped to have the corn leaves to add to the fodder. But then one fine day there came millions, trillions of grasshoppers in great clouds, hiding the sun, and coming down onto the fields, eating up *everything* that was still there, the leaves on the trees, peaches, grapes, cucumbers, onions, cabbage, everything, everything. Only the peach stones still hung on the trees, showing what had once been there.

They are not the kind of grasshoppers we see in Sweden but are large, grayish ones. Now most of them have moved southward, to devastate other areas since there was nothing more to consume here. Certainly it is sad and distressing and depressing for the body and soul to find that no matter how hard one drudges and works, one still has nothing, less than nothing."

Questions for Analysis
1. Identify the difficulties Lindgren's family encountered as homesteaders in Kansas.
2. Explain the reasons why immigrant families such Lindgren's settled on the Great Plains.

Questions for Comparison
George Duffield, *Driving Cattle from Texas to Iowa, 1866* (p. 464)
1. Identify each author's purpose for writing an account of daily life.
2. Explain the factors that account for the differences in each author's tone.
3. Evaluate the extent of similarity in the effect of the natural environment on homesteaders such as Ida Lindgren and on cowboys such as George Duffield.

---

the Mississippi. Though not precisely predictable, this cycle of abundance and drought had been going on for millennia. In addition, innovation and technology bolstered dreams of success. Farmers planted hardy strains of wheat imported from Russia that survived the fluctuations of dry and wet and hot and cold weather. Machines produced by industrial laborers in northeastern factories allowed western farmers to plow tough land and harvest its yield. Steel-tipped plows, threshers, combines, and harvesters expanded production greatly, and windmills and pumping equipment provided sources of power and access to scarce water. These improvements in mechanization led to a significant expansion in agricultural production, which helped to lower food prices for consumers.

The people who accepted the challenge of carving out a new life were a diverse lot. The Great Plains attracted a large number of immigrants from Europe, some two million by 1900. Minnesota and the Dakotas welcomed communities of settlers from Sweden and Norway. Nebraska housed a considerable population of Germans, Swedes, Danes, and Czechs. About one-third of the people who migrated to the northern plains came directly from a foreign country.

Railroads and land companies lured settlers to the plains with tales of the fabulous possibilities that awaited their arrival. The federal government had given railroads generous grants of public land on which to build their tracks as well as parcels surrounding the tracks that they could sell off to raise revenue for construction. Western railroads advertised in both the United States and Europe, proclaiming that migrants to the plains would find "the garden spot of the world."

EXPLORING AP® THEMES
Migration and Settlement

Have students read Chris Cillizza's article, "Watch the population center of the U.S. move westward, in 1 GIF" available on *The Washington Post*'s website (washingtonpost.com). Project the accompanying animated map of the Mean Center of Population for the United States, 1790 to 2010 for the whole class to see and ask students to determine what happened to the U.S. population over the period of time up to 1900 to cause these changes to happen. What specific historical evidence can explain this historical development?

BUILDING AP® SKILLS
Developments and Processes

As a bell ringer, ask students to describe the changes that the agricultural industry underwent during the late nineteenth century and their impacts. Possible answers include: *New technologies such as steel-tipped plows, threshers, combines, and harvesters expanded production. Water was made more available due to pumps and windmills. Farmers planted imported wheat, which was heartier and survived harsher weather. All of these changes led to increased production and cheaper food prices.*

Having enticed prospective settlers with exaggerated claims, railroads offered bargain rates to transport them to their new homes. Families and friends often journeyed together and rented an entire car on the train, known as "the immigrant car," in which they loaded their possessions, supplies, and even livestock. Often migrants came to the end of the rail line before reaching their destination. They completed the trip by wagon or stagecoach.

Commercial advertising alone did not account for the desire to journey westward. Settlers who had made the trip successfully wrote to relatives and neighbors back east and in the old country about the chance to start fresh. Linda Slaughter, the wife of an army doctor in the Dakotas, gushed: "The farms which have been opened in the vicinity of Bismarck have proven highly productive, the soil being kept moist by frequent rains. Vegetables of all kinds are grown with but little trouble."

Those who took the chance shared a faith in the future and a willingness to work hard and endure misfortune. They found their optimism and spirits sorely tested. Despite the company of family members and friends, settlers faced a lonely existence on the vast expanse of the plains. Homesteads were spread out, and a feeling of isolation became a routine part of daily life.

With few trees around, early settlers constructed sod houses. These structures let in little light but a good deal of moisture, keeping them gloomy and damp. A Nebraskan who lived in this type of house jokingly remarked: "There was running water in our sod house. It ran through the roof." Bugs, insects, and rodents, like the rain, often found their way inside to make living in such shelters even more uncomfortable.

If these dwellings were bleak, the climate posed even greater challenges. The plains did experience an unusual amount of rainfall in the late 1870s and early 1880s, but severe drought quickly followed. A plague of grasshoppers ravaged the northern plains in the late 1870s, destroying fruit trees and plants. Intense heat in the summer alternated with frigid temperatures in the winter. The Norwegian American writer O. E. Rolvaag, in *Giants in the Earth* (1927), described the extreme hardships that accompanied the fierce weather: "Blizzards from out of the northwest raged, swooped down and stirred up a greyish-white fury, impenetrable to human eyes. As soon as these monsters tired, storms from the northeast were sure to come, bringing more snow."

REVIEW

- How did the experiences of cowboys compare to those of miners and lumberjacks during the late nineteenth century?
- How did the federal government and private businesses facilitate western settlement during the late nineteenth century?

Homesteaders Farm the Great Plains

AP TIP
Compare the problems facing farmers in the American West to factory workers in the eastern U.S. during the late 1800s.

Surviving loneliness, drudgery, and bad weather still did not guarantee financial success for homesteaders. In fact, the economic realities of farming on the plains proved formidable. Despite the image of yeomen farmers — individuals engaged in subsistence farming with the aid of wives and children — most agriculture was geared to commercial transactions. Few farmers were independent or self-reliant. Farmers depended on barter and short-term credit. They borrowed from banks to purchase the additional land necessary to make agriculture economically feasible in the semiarid climate. They also needed loans to buy machinery to help increase production and to sustain their families while they waited for the harvest.

Instead of raising crops solely for their own use, farmers concentrated on the cash crops of corn and wheat. The price of these commodities depended on the vagaries of an international market that connected American farmers to growers and consumers throughout the world. When supply expanded and demand remained relatively stable during the 1880s and 1890s, prices fell. This **deflation** made it more difficult for farmers to pay back their loans, and banks moved to foreclose.

Under these challenging circumstances, almost half of the homesteaders in the Great Plains picked up and moved either to another farm or to a nearby city. Large operators bought up the

BUILDING AP SKILLS

Comparison

Draw a Venn diagram with three intersecting circles on the whiteboard. Label each circle with one of the following: Cowboys, Miners, and Lumberjacks. Ask students to provide information about each group to fill in the Venn diagram. Consider having students add information about average ages, races, obstacles, and motivations for moving to the West, which they have gathered in previous activities.

APPLY THE TIP

Assign half the class the role of a farmer living in the American West and assign the other half the role of a factory worker in the eastern U.S. Have each student write a letter as the roles describing the problems they are facing. Give 10–15 minutes to write. Once students have finished, ask them to swap letters with someone from the opposite role. Once pairs have read the letters, have them discuss the commonalities and differences.

TEACHING IDEA

Analyzing Art and Images

Find the "Great Plains Homesteaders" lesson on the Stanford History Education Group website (sheg.stanford.edu). This lesson can be used to analyze the photographs of Solomon Butcher, who documented the lives of homesteaders on the Great Plains. The lesson allows students to learn about life on the Great Plains, as well as discuss the extent to which the photographs are reliable.

APPLY THE TIP

After comparing the experiences of women in the West with women in the East, ask students, "Did women have more individual freedom in the West, or in the East?" Possible answers include: *Women had more freedom in the West because it was easier for a woman to obtain and hold land. Many of these western women owned dozens of acres, though they were single and descended from immigrants. Or, women in the East had more freedom because they had more job opportunities to choose from. Women in the West might have had access to land, but their lives were filled with more hardship than women in the East, who had access to more amenities and stable incomes.*

---

farms they left behind and ran them like big businesses. As had been the case in mining and ranching, western agriculture was increasingly commercialized and consolidated over the course of the second half of the nineteenth century.

The federal government unwittingly aided this process of commercialization and consolidation, to the benefit of large companies. The government sought to make bigger plots of land available in regions where small farming had proved impractical. The Desert Land Act (1877) offered 640 acres to settlers who would irrigate the land, but it brought small relief for farmers because the land was too dry. These properties soon fell out of the hands of homesteaders and into those of cattle ranchers. The Timber and Stone Act (1878) allowed homesteaders to buy 160 acres of forestland at $2.50 an acre. Lumber companies hired "dummy entrymen" to file claims and then quickly transferred the titles and added the parcels to their growing tracts of woodland.

The women of the family were responsible for making homesteads more bearable. Mothers and daughters were in charge of household duties, cooking the meals, canning fruits and vegetables, and washing and ironing clothing. Despite the drudgery of this work, women contributed significantly to the economic well-being of the family by occasionally taking in boarders and selling milk, butter, and eggs.

In addition, a surprisingly large number of single women staked out homestead claims by themselves. Some were young, unmarried women seeking, like their male counterparts, economic opportunity. Others were widows attempting to take care of their children after their husband's death. One such widow, Anne Furnberg, settled a homestead in the Dakota Territory in 1871. Born in Norway, she had lived with her husband and son in Minnesota. After her husband's death, the thirty-four-year-old Furnberg moved with her son near Fargo and eventually settled on eighty acres of land. She farmed, raised chickens and a cow, and sold butter and eggs in town. The majority of women who settled in the Dakotas were between the ages of twenty-one and twenty-five, had never been married, and were native-born children of immigrant parents. A sample of nine counties in the Dakotas shows that more than 4,400 women became landowners. Nora Pfundheler, a single woman, explained her motivation: "Well I was 21 and had no prospects of doing anything. The land was there, so I took it."

Once families settled in and towns began to develop, women, married and single, directed some of their energies to moral reform and extending democracy on the frontier. Because of loneliness and grueling work, some men turned to alcohol for relief. Law enforcement in newly established communities was often no match for the saloons that catered to a raucous and drunken crowd. In their roles as wives, mothers, and sisters, many women tried to remove the source of alcohol-induced violence that disrupted both family relationships and public decorum. In Kansas in the late 1870s, women flocked to the state's Woman's Christian Temperance Union, founded by Amanda M. Way. Although they did not yet have the vote, in 1880 these women vigorously campaigned for a constitutional amendment that banned the sale of liquor.

Temperance women also threw their weight behind the issue of women's suffrage. In 1884 Kansas women established the statewide Equal Suffrage Association, which delivered to the state legislature a petition with seven thousand signatures

> **AP® TIP**
> Compare the experiences of women on the western frontier in the late nineteenth century to those of women in the eastern United States during the first half of the nineteenth century.

Woman Homesteader in Kansas Ada McColl was among the thousands of homesteaders who moved west in the late nineteenth century. This 1893 photo shows her gathering buffalo chips (dry dung) to use for heating and cooking fuel, just as the American Indians had elsewhere on the Great Plains. **What hardships facing homesteaders are evident in this photograph?**

Kansas State Historical Society

in support of women's suffrage. Their attempt failed, but in 1887 women won the right to vote and run for office in all Kansas municipal elections. Julia Robinson, who campaigned for women's suffrage in Kansas, recalled the positive role that some men played: "My father had always said his family of girls had just as much right to help the government as if we were boys, and mother and he had always taught us to expect Woman Suffrage in our day." Kansas did not grant equal voting rights in state and national elections until 1912, but women obtained full suffrage before then in many western states starting with the Wyoming Territory in 1869.

REVIEW

- Why and how did commercial farming replace yeoman farming on the Great Plains?
- Why did the temperance and women's suffrage movements achieve early success in the West?

Mormons, Californios, and the Chinese Go West

Mormons Followers of Joseph Smith and Brigham Young who migrated to Utah to escape religious persecution; also known as the Church of Jesus Christ of Latter-Day Saints.

Mormons sought refuge in the West primarily for religious reasons. By 1870 the migration of Mormons (members of the Church of Jesus Christ of Latter-Day Saints) into the Utah Territory had attracted more than 85,000 settlers, most notably in Salt Lake City. Originally traveling to Utah under the leadership of Brigham Young in the late 1840s, Mormons had come under attack from opponents of their religion and the federal government for several reasons. Most important, Mormons believed in polygamy, the practice of having more than one wife at a time. Far from seeing the practice as immoral, Mormon doctrine held polygamy as a blessing that would guarantee both husbands and wives an exalted place in the afterlife. Non-Mormons denounced polygamy as a form of involuntary servitude. In reality, only a small minority of Mormon men had multiple wives, and most of these polygamists had only two wives.

Mormons also departed from the mainstream American belief in private property. The church considered farming a communal enterprise. To this end, church elders divided land among their followers, so that, as Brigham Young explained, "each person perform[ed] his several duties for the good of the whole more than for individual aggrandizement."

In the 1870s, the federal government took increased measures to control Mormon practices. In *Reynolds v. United States* (1879), the Supreme Court upheld the criminal conviction of a polygamist Mormon man. Previously in 1862 and 1874, Congress had banned plural marriages in the Utah Territory. Congress went further in 1882 by passing the Edmunds Act, which disfranchised men engaging in polygamy. In 1887 Congress aimed to slash the economic power of the church by limiting Mormon assets to $50,000 and seizing the rest for the federal Treasury. A few years later, under this considerable pressure, the Mormons officially abandoned polygamy. With the rejection of polygamy Congress accepted statehood for Utah in 1896.

Californios Spanish and Mexican residents of California. Before the nineteenth century, Californios made up California's economic and political elite. Their position, however, deteriorated after the conclusion of the Mexican-American War in 1848.

As with the nation's other frontiers, migrants to the West Coast did not find uninhabited territory. Besides American Indians, the largest group that lived in California consisted of Spaniards and Mexicans. Since the eighteenth century, these **Californios** had established themselves as farmers and ranchers. The 1848 Treaty of Guadalupe Hidalgo, which ended the Mexican-American War, supposedly guaranteed the property rights of Californios and granted them U.S. citizenship, but reality proved different. Mexican American miners had to pay a "foreign miners tax," and Californio landowners lost their holdings to squatters, settlers, and local officials. By the end of the nineteenth century, about two-thirds of all land originally owned by Spanish-speaking residents had fallen into the hands of Euro-American settlers. By this time, many of these once wealthy Californios had been forced into poverty and the low-wage labor force. The loss of land was matched by a diminished role in the region's government, as economic decline, ethnic bias, and the continuing influx of white migrants combined to greatly reduce the political influence of the Californio population.

Spaniards and Mexicans living in the Southwest met the same fate as the Californios. When Anglo cattle ranchers began forcing Mexican Americans off their land near Las Vegas, New Mexico, a rancher named Juan Jose Herrera assembled a band of masked night riders known as

EXPLORING AP® THEMES

Migration and Settlement

Search PBS Learning Media for "Map: Forced Migrations." This resource, part of PBS's American Experience, provides an overview of the various migrations that the Mormon people were forced to endure (pbslearningmedia.org). Six different migrations are described, each including the location, time period, "About This Place," "Mormon Developments," and "Why They Left." The last place is the only exception, in which the last heading says "Building a Community" instead of "Why They Left." This resource is great for providing a concise overview of the various places that Mormons settled, only to be removed again. Consider breaking students up into six groups to jigsaw the activity, assigning one migration to each group and having them note their conclusions (a refresher of the jigsaw model can be found on page 33). There is a map included, but you may want student groups to present information about their assigned migration to the class as well as put a pin on a map to visualize the location.

TEACHING IDEA

Incorporating Primary Sources

The Gilder Lehrman History Now feature provides students with a letter written by Samuel Russell describing some of the hazards he faced escorting pioneers to the settlement in Salt Lake City, Utah (available on gilderlehrman.org by searching for "On the emigrant trail, 1862"). Assign students in groups to read and break down the full transcript. Then have students answer the Questions for Discussion. Student products can then be shared out in a jigsaw fashion (a refresher of the jigsaw model can be found on page 33).

APPLY THE TIP

As a bell ringer or exit ticket, have each student come up with one piece of specific historical evidence that could describe the experiences of Californios and one piece of specific historical evidence that could describe the experiences of American Indians. List all evidence on a T-chart on the board/projector and discuss. Were the experiences of Californios and American Indians more similar, or different?

TRM Find **Handout 6.2 – Comparing the Experiences of Californios and American Indians** in the Teacher's Resource Materials.

TEACHING IDEA

Check for Understanding

Have students create a T-chart to list the push and pull factors for Chinese immigration to the United States. Possible push factors include: *the Opium Wars, poverty, family feuds, and peasant rebellion.* Possible pull factors include: *job opportunities and the gold rush.*

AP® TIP

Compare the experiences of Californios to those of native peoples in American history as settlers expanded westward in search of land during the mid- and late 1800s.

Las Gorras Blancas (The White Caps). According to fliers that they distributed promoting their grievances, the group sought "to protect the rights and interests of the people in general and especially those of the helpless classes." Enemies "of bulldozers and tyrants," they desired a "free ballot and fair court." In 1889 and 1890, as many as seven hundred White Caps burned Anglo fences, haystacks, barns, and homes. In the end, however, Spanish-speaking inhabitants could not prevent the growing number of white settlers from pouring onto their lands and isolating them politically, economically, and culturally.

California and the far West also attracted a large number of Chinese immigrants. Migration to California and the West Coast was part of a larger movement in the nineteenth century out of Asia that brought impoverished Chinese to Australia, Hawaii, Latin America, and the United States. The Chinese migrated for several reasons in the decades after 1840. Economic dislocation related to the British Opium Wars (1839–1842 and 1856–1860), along with bloody family feuds and a decade of peasant rebellion from 1854 to 1864, propelled migration. Faced with unemployment and starvation, the Chinese sought economic opportunity overseas.

Chinese immigrants were attracted first by the 1848 gold rush and then by jobs building the transcontinental railroad. By 1880 the Chinese population in the United States had grown to 200,000, most of whom lived in the West. San Francisco became the center of the transplanted Chinese population, which congregated in the city's Chinatown. Under the leadership of a handful of businessmen, Chinese residents found jobs, lodging, and meals, along with social, cultural, and recreational outlets. Most of those who came were young unmarried men who intended to earn enough money to return to China and start anew. The relatively few women who immigrated often worked as servants or prostitutes.

For many Chinese, the West proved unwelcoming. When California's economy slumped in the mid-1870s, many white people looked to the Chinese as scapegoats. White workingmen believed that Chinese laborers in the mines and railroads undercut their demands for higher wages. They contended that Chinese would work for less because they were racially inferior people who lived degraded lives. Anti-Chinese clubs mushroomed in California during the 1870s, and they soon became a substantial political force in the state. The Workingmen's Party advocated laws that

▲ **Rock Springs Massacre** This engraving depicts the Rock Springs massacre in Wyoming. On September 3, 1885, a mob of white coal miners killed at least 28 Chinese miners, injured 15, and burned 75 homes of Chinese residents. The violence came after years of anti-Chinese sentiment in the western United States. **What factors contributed to violence against the Chinese in the American West?**

Mormons, Californios, and the Chinese Go West

restricted Chinese labor, and it initiated boycotts of goods made by Chinese people. Vigilantes attacked Chinese people in the streets and set fire to factories that employed Asians. The Workingmen's Party and the Democratic Party joined forces in 1879 to craft a new state constitution that blatantly discriminated against Chinese residents. In many ways, these laws resembled the Jim Crow laws passed in the South that deprived African Americans of their freedom following Reconstruction (see Module 6-3).

Pressured by anti-Chinese sentiment on the West Coast, the U.S. government enacted drastic legislation to prevent any further influx of Chinese. The **Chinese Exclusion Act** of 1882 banned Chinese immigration into the United States, prohibited those Chinese already in the country from becoming naturalized American citizens, and set a precedent for a race-based immigration policy. The exclusion act, however, did not stop anti-Chinese assaults. In the mid-1880s, white mobs drove Chinese out of Eureka, California; Seattle and Tacoma, Washington; and Rock Springs, Wyoming. These attacks were often organized. In 1885, the Tacoma mayor and police led a mob that rounded up 700 Chinese residents and forced them to leave the city on a train bound for Portland.

Chinese Exclusion Act 1882 act that banned Chinese immigration into the United States and prohibited those Chinese already in the country from becoming naturalized American citizens.

AP® ANALYZING SOURCES

Source: Chinese Exclusion Act, 1882

"*Be it enacted by the Senate and House of Representatives of the United States of America in Congress assembled,* That from and after the expiration of ninety days next after the passage of this act, and until the expiration of ten years next after the passage of this act, the coming of Chinese laborers to the United States be . . . suspended; and during such suspension it shall not be lawful for any Chinese laborer to come, or having so come after the expiration of said ninety days to remain within the United States.

SEC. 2. That the master of any vessel who shall knowingly bring . . . any Chinese laborer, from any foreign port or place, shall be deemed guilty of a misdemeanor, and on conviction thereof shall be punished by a fine of not more than five hundred dollars for each and every such Chinese laborer so brought, and maybe also imprisoned for a term not exceeding one year. . . .

SEC. 9. That before any Chinese passengers are landed from any such line vessel, the collector, or his deputy, shall proceed to examine such passenger . . . and no passenger shall be allowed to land in the United States from such vessel in violation of law.

SEC. 10. That every vessel whose master shall knowingly violate any of the provisions of this act shall be deemed forfeited to the United States, and shall be liable to seizure and condemnation in any district of the United States into which such vessel may enter or in which she may be found. . . .

SEC. 12. That no Chinese person shall be permitted to enter the United States by land . . . And any Chinese person found unlawfully within the United States shall be caused to be removed therefrom to the country from whence he came . . ."

Questions for Analysis
1. Identify the main provisions of the Chinese Exclusion Act.
2. Describe the context of the passage of the Chinese Exclusion Act.
3. Explain why the Chinese Exclusion Act targeted vessel masters as well as Chinese immigrants.

REVIEW

- What factors contributed to the differences in the experiences of Mormons, Californios, and Chinese in the West?
- What experiences were common to all three groups?

TRM Suggested Responses to Questions

TRM Module 6.2 AP® Analyzing Sources Handout 3

BUILDING AP® SKILLS
Sourcing and Situation

Complete a HIPP analysis on the excerpt of the Chinese Exclusion Act (a refresher of HIPP can be found on page 8). Students should also be encouraged to draw from outside resources, where applicable. Students should practice this strategy often, as they are required to analyze sources on the AP® exam. Experience with the HIPP strategy will help students successfully use available sources to answer Multiple-Choice Questions, Short-Answer Questions, and the Document-Based Question.

BUILDING AP® SKILLS
Claims and Evidence in Sources

Use the Stanford History Education Group's lesson on Chinese Immigration and Exclusion to provide students with practice determining the claims and evidence within sources (sheg.stanford.edu). The lesson requires students to answer the prompt, "Why was Chinese immigration restricted in 1882?"

▲ **Differentiation**

The Stanford History Education Group provides abridged documents for their lesson on Chinese Immigration and Exclusion as well as the original, unabridged documents. Choose the documents that best fit the level of your students.

TRM Suggested Responses to Questions

TEACHING IDEA

Check for Understanding

Here is an SAQ with two very different historical interpretations on the meaning of the frontier in American history. The first excerpt is from Frederick Jackson Turner. Turner's frontier thesis became the prevailing historical understanding of the frontier during the first half of the twentieth century. In the 1980s, New West historians such as Patricia Limerick challenged both Turner's assumptions and conclusion. Since that time, historians have generally rejected Turner's thesis.

While the SAQ with secondary sources on the AP® U.S. History exam will probably not include an excerpt that directly references another excerpt, this set provides students with an excellent opportunity to think about the meaning and importance of the frontier in American history. Have students use the *ACE* strategy as they explain a significant difference between the interpretations in (a) and provide specific historical evidence to support each interpretation in (b) and (c) (a refresher of *ACE* can be found on page 21).

TEACHING IDEA

AP® Writing Historically Review

This question focuses on how historians have captured the meaning of the West over time. Because these excerpts are focused on defining the West, have students write down the descriptions each historian uses to describe the West. After they have done this, have students work in pairs to develop some categories of analysis. For instance, some might say that Turner describes it as a place of development whereas Limerick focuses more on the convergence of societies. Students can use these categories of analysis to answer part (a). For parts (b) and (c), the question does not give students a periodization; therefore, consider providing the years 1865–1898 for students to use. Before students write answers for (b) and (c), brainstorm why the years were selected. Understanding the chronology associated with the question allows students to develop more accurate answers.

Period 6: 1865–1898

MODULE 6-2 Industry in the West

AP® WRITING HISTORICALLY — Short-Answer Question Practice

ACTIVITY

Read the following question carefully and write a short response. Use complete sentences.

Using the following excerpts, answer (a), (b), and (c).

Source: Frederick Jackson Turner, *The Frontier in American History*, 1920

"[W]e have . . . a recurrence of the process of evolution in each western area reached in the process of expansion. Thus American development has exhibited not merely advance along a single line, but a return to primitive conditions on a continually advancing frontier line, and a new development for that area. American social development has been continually beginning over again on the frontier. This perennial rebirth, this fluidity of American life, this expansion westward with it new opportunities, its continuous touch with the simplicity of primitive society, furnish the forces dominating American character. . . . The frontier is the line of most rapid and effective Americanization. The wilderness masters the colonist. It finds him a European in dress, industries, tools, models of travel, and thought. It takes him from the railroad car and puts him in the birch canoe. It strips off the garments of civilization and arrays him in the hunting shirt and moccasin. . . . In short, at the frontier the environment is at first too strong for the man. . . . Little by little he transforms the wilderness, but the outcome is not the old Europe. . . . The fact is that here is a new product that is American. . . . Thus the advance of the frontier has meant a steady movement away from the influence of Europe, a steady growth of independence on American lines."

Source: Patricia Nelson Limerick, *The Legacy of Conquest: The Unbroken Path of the American West*, 1987

"Turner's frontier was a process, not a place. When 'civilization' had conquered 'savagery' at any one location, the process—and the historian's attention—moved on. In rethinking Western history, we gain the freedom to think of the West as a place—as many complicated environments occupied by natives who considered their homelands to be the center, not the edge. . . . Deemphasize the frontier and its supposed end, conceive of the West as a place and not a process, and Western American history has a new look. First, the American West was an important meeting ground, the point where Indian America, Latin America, Anglo-America, Afro-America, and Asia America intersected . . . Second, the working of conquest tied these diverse groups into the same story. Happily or not, minorities and majorities occupied a common ground. Conquest basically involved the drawing of lines on a map, the definition and allocation of ownership (personal, tribal, corporate, state, federal, and international), and the evolution of land from matter to property."

a. Briefly explain ONE major difference between Turner's and Limerick's interpretations of the frontier.
b. Briefly explain how ONE specific historical event or development from the period that is not explicitly mentioned in the excerpts could be used to support Turner's argument.
c. Briefly explain how ONE specific historical event or development from the period that is not explicitly mentioned in the excerpts could be used to support Limerick's argument.

Module 6-3

The New South

LEARNING TARGETS
By the end of this module, you should be able to:
- Explain the changes and continuities in the South's economy from the end of the Civil War to the end of the nineteenth century.
- Explain the changes and continuities in the lives of African Americans living in the South from the end of the Civil War to the end of the nineteenth century.

THEMATIC FOCUS
American and National Identity

Despite the expansion of the railroads and construction of textile mills, efforts to industrialize the South after the Civil War met with limited success as sharecropping and tenant farming continued to be the region's main economic activities. African Americans in the South were denied equal rights as the Supreme Court upheld the Jim Crow laws permitting legal segregation in its 1896 *Plessy v. Ferguson* ruling.

HISTORICAL REASONING FOCUS
Continuity and Change

TASK ▶ As you read this module, examine the amount and nature of change in the South's economy. Ask yourself why the South's industrial progress was limited during this era. Likewise, consider the changes and constants in the lives of African Americans and the reasons for changes and continuity.

TRM Suggested Responses to Questions

The industrial transformation of the United States economy continued in the decades after the end of the Civil War. In 1874, Henry Grady, the editor of the *Atlanta Constitution*, called for a "New South" with an economy based on textile mills, factories, and mining. Yet, efforts to industrialize the South met with uneven success.

For the majority of African Americans still living in the South, southern industrialization provided few benefits. Increased black migration to cities in the South yielded limited economic opportunities for most African Americans who relocated. In response to black aspirations for social and economic advancement, white politicians imposed a rigid system of racial segregation on the South. Although white people championed the cause of individual upward mobility, they restricted opportunities to achieve success to whites only.

Building a New South

New South Term popularized in the 1880s by newspaper editor Henry Grady, a proponent of the modernization of the southern economy in order for a "New South" to emerge.

Although the largely rural South lagged behind the North and the Midwest in manufacturing, industrial expansion did not bypass the region. Well aware of global economic trends and eager for the South to achieve its economic potential, southern business leaders and newspaper editors saw industrial development as the key to the creation of a **New South**. Attributing the Confederate defeat in the Civil War to the North's superior manufacturing output and railroad supply lines, New South proponents hoped to modernize their economy in a similar fashion. One of those boosters was Richard H. Edmonds, editor of the *Manufacturers' Record*. He extolled the virtues of the "real South" of the 1880s, characterized by "the music of progress — the whirr of the spindle, the buzz of the saw, the roar of the furnace, the throb of the locomotive." The South of Edmonds's vision would move beyond the regional separatism of the past and become fully integrated into the national economy.

EXPLORING AP® THEMES

American and National Identity

The post-Civil War era was a time of variation in American national identity, especially for African Americans. Even though slavery had become illegal, discrimination was still rampant in the Jim Crow South as well as elsewhere in the nation. African Americans had to try to reconcile this discrimination with their newfound freedom and decide how they were going to respond to such treatment. While reading the module, ask students to provide specific historical evidence to describe the continuities and changes in American national identity.

TEACHING IDEA

Connecting the Dots

Divide the class into two groups. Have students in one group individually describe the regional identity that existed in the South prior to the Civil War, and the other group individually describe the regional identity of the New South after the Civil War. Pair students up so each pair has one student from each original group. Ask students to write a thesis statement to answer the following question: "To what extent does the idea of the New South differ from that of the South prior to the Civil War?" Possible answers include: *Very few African Americans had the freedom to seek out new economic or political opportunities due to the consequences of the New South. Some proponents of the New South, such as Henry Grady, wanted to industrialize the South.* Or: *The New South was not very different. African Americans might have been freed, but opportunities were scarce and most available jobs consisted of menial labor. African Americans who had been imprisoned for minor offenses were also used as a labor force in a way that was reminiscent of the system of slavery. In addition, though the South was industrializing, the economy was still reliant on agriculture.*

Period 6: 1865–1898

MODULE 6-3 The New South

Railroads were the key to achieving such economic integration, so after the Civil War new railroad tracks were laid throughout the South. Not only did this expanded railroad system create direct connections between the North and the South, but it also facilitated the growth of the southern textile industry. Seeking to take advantage of plentiful cotton, cheap labor, and the improved transportation system, investors built textile mills throughout the South. Victims of falling prices and saddled with debt, sharecroppers and tenant farmers moved into mill towns in search of better employment. Mill owners preferred to hire girls and young women, who worked for low wages, to spin cotton and weave it on the looms. To do so, however, owners had to employ their entire family, for mothers and fathers would not let their daughters relocate without their supervision.

Agricultural refugees who flocked to cotton mills in the South also faced dangerous working conditions. Working twelve-hour days breathing the lint-filled air from the processed cotton posed health hazards. Textile workers also had to place their hands into heavy machinery to disentangle threads, making them extremely vulnerable to serious injury. Wages scarcely covered necessities, and on many occasions families did not know where their next meal was coming from. North Carolina textile worker J. W. Mehaffry complained that the mill owners "were slave drivers" who "work their employees, women, and children from 6 a.m. to 7 p.m. with a half hour for lunch." Mill workers' meals usually consisted of potatoes, cornbread, and dried beans cooked in fat. This diet, without dairy products and fresh meat, led to outbreaks of pellagra, a debilitating disease caused by niacin (vitamin B3) deficiency.

Whatever attraction the mills offered applied only to white people. The pattern of white supremacy emerging in the post-Reconstruction South kept African Americans out of all but the most menial jobs. Black people contributed greatly to the construction of railroads in the New South, but they did not do so as free men. Convicts, most of whom were African American, performed the exhausting work of laying tracks through hills and swamps. Southern states used the **convict lease** system, in which black people, usually imprisoned for minor offenses, were hired out to private companies to serve their time or pay off their fine. The convict lease system brought additional income to the state and supplied cheap labor to the railroads and planters, but it left African American convict laborers impoverished and virtually enslaved.

> **AP® TIP**
> Make sure you can explain how the development of industry in the New South in the late 1800s showed continuities with the development of industries in the North in the early 1800s.

convict lease The system used by southern governments to furnish mainly African American prison labor to plantation owners and industrialists and to raise revenue for the states. In practice, convict labor replaced slavery as the means of providing a forced labor supply.

AP® ANALYZING SOURCES

Source: Henry Grady, *The New South*, 1886

"What is the sum of our work? We have found out that in the general summary the free Negro counts more than he did as a slave. We have planted the schoolhouse on the hilltop and made it free to white and black. We have sowed towns and cities in the place of theories and put business above politics. We have challenged your spinners in Massachusetts and your iron-makers in Pennsylvania. We have learned that the $400,000,000 annually received from our cotton crop will make us rich, when the supplies that make it are home-raised. We have reduced the commercial rate of interest from twenty-four to six per cent, and are floating four per cent bonds. . . .

The old South rested everything on slavery and agriculture, unconscious that these could neither give nor maintain healthy growth. The new South presents a perfect democracy, the oligarchs leading in the popular movement—a social system compact and closely knitted, less splendid on the surface, but stronger at the core—a hundred farms for every plantation, fifty homes for every palace—and a diversified industry that meets the complex need of this complex age."

Questions for Analysis
1. Identify the main differences between the Old South and the New South, according to Grady.
2. Describe the point of view expressed by Grady in this excerpt.
3. Evaluate the impact of southern industrialization on working-class whites and on African Americans.

TRM Suggested Responses to Questions

TRM Module 6.3 AP® Analyzing Sources Handout

EXPLORING AP® THEMES

American and National Identity

As a bell ringer or exit ticket, have students answer the following prompt: "Describe the identity of the New South according to Henry Grady. According to Grady, to what extent has the identity of the South changed over time?" Possible answers include: *Grady argues that the New South is vastly different from the Old South. Specifically, he describes how the economy has changed from slavery and agriculture to a diversified industrial economy. Grady also describes how the lives of African Americans have changed greatly, as educational opportunities are more available than they were before slavery was abolished.*

BUILDING AP® SKILLS

Argumentation

Read the excerpt from Grady's speech, "The New South." Ask students, "To what extent does Grady's view of the New South relate to the reality of the South in the late nineteenth century? Provide specific historical evidence to support your answer." Possible answers include: *The Freedmen's Bureau increased the availability of education for freed African Americans, though opportunities for freed people were still scarce. The South was industrializing, but the economy was still mainly based on agriculture. Grady is accurate in reporting the growth of the southern economy, as this was a time of great economic growth for the entire United States.*

Building a New South

The South attracted a number of industries besides textile manufacturing. In the 1880s, James B. Duke established a cigarette manufacturing empire in Durham, North Carolina. Nearby tobacco fields provided the raw material that black workers prepared for white workers, who then rolled the cigarettes by machine. Acres of timber pines in the Carolinas, Florida, and Alabama sustained a lucrative lumber industry. Rich supplies of coal and iron in Alabama fostered the growth of the steel industry in Birmingham. (Map 6.3)

Plagued by poverty, sharecropping debt, and the added burden of racial oppression and violence in the post-Reconstruction period, rural black women and men migrated to southern cities. African American migrants found work as cooks, janitors, and domestic servants. Many found employment as manual laborers in manufacturing companies — including tobacco factories, which employed women and men; tanneries; and cottonseed oil firms — and as dockworkers. Although the overwhelming majority of black people worked as unskilled laborers for very low wages, others opened small businesses such as funeral parlors, barbershops, and construction companies or went into professions such as medicine, law, banking, and education that catered to residents of segregated black neighborhoods. Despite considerable individual accomplishments, by the turn of the twentieth century most black people in the urban South had few prospects for upward economic mobility.

Even with the frenzy of industrial activity and urban growth, the New South in many ways resembled the Old South. Southern entrepreneurs still depended on northern investors to supply

> **AP® TIP**
> Evaluate the extent of change in the lives of African Americans in the late nineteenth century.

MAP 6.3 The New South, 1900 Although the South remained largely agricultural by 1900, it had made great strides toward building industries in the region. This so-called New South boasted an extensive railway network that provided a national market for its raw materials and manufactured goods, including coal, iron, steel, and textiles. Still, the southern economy in 1900 depended primarily on raising cotton and tobacco. **How does this map illustrate both the limitations and successes of the New South?**

BUILDING AP® SKILLS

Making Connections

As a bell ringer, have students support the textbook's statement, "The New South in many ways resembled the Old South." Ask each student to write a piece of specific historical evidence that supports the statement on a sticky note. Put students into groups of four and have them organize their evidence into categories such as economy or social classes. Ask students for examples of their category names and write the category titles on the board. Consolidate the categories so there are only three or four. Explain that these categories can be used as the main topics for paragraphs in an essay. Next, have students bring their sticky notes to the board and stick them in the category in which they fit best. Discuss the evidence with the class and have each student write an introduction or concluding paragraph for the essay that you outlined as a class.

TEACHING IDEA

Connecting the Dots

After reading Henry Grady's sentiments in his speech to the New England Club, have students analyze Map 6.3. How does the map support Grady's ideas? How does the map refute Grady's ideas? Possible answers include: *There are areas showing regions of textile manufacturing. This supports Grady's argument that the New South has a new focus on manufacturing industries. The map refutes Grady's arguments because much of the South continued to focus on cotton- and tobacco-growing regions and only small portions were focused on textile manufacturing.*

much of the capital for investment. Investors were attracted by the low wages that prevailed in the South, but low wages also meant that southern workers remained poor and, in many cases, unable to buy the manufactured goods produced by industry. Efforts to diversify agriculture beyond tobacco and cotton were constrained by a sharecropping system based on small, inefficient plots. In fact, even though industrialization did make considerable headway in the South, the economy remained overwhelmingly agricultural. This suited many white southerners who wanted to hold on to the individualistic, agrarian values they associated with the Old South. Yoked to old ideologies and a system of forced labor, modernization in the South could go only so far.

REVIEW

How successful were late-nineteenth-century efforts to create a New South?

Black America and Jim Crow

AP® TIP
Make sure you understand and can explain how poll taxes and literacy tests were used to discriminate against African American voters.

Jim Crow Late nineteenth-century statutes that established legally defined racial segregation in the South. Jim Crow legislation helped ensure the social and economic disfranchisement of southern black people.

While wealthy, middle-class, and working-class white people experimented with new forms of social behavior, African Americans faced greater challenges to preserving their freedom and dignity. In the South, where the overwhelming majority of black people lived, post-Reconstruction southern governments adopted various techniques to keep black people from voting. To circumvent the Fifteenth Amendment, southern states devised suffrage qualifications that they claimed were racially neutral, and the Supreme Court ruled in their favor. They instituted the **poll tax**, a tax that each person had to pay in order to cast a ballot. Poll taxes fell hardest on the poor, a disproportionate number of whom were African American. Disfranchisement reached its peak in the 1890s, as white southern governments managed to deny the vote to most of the black electorate (Map 6.4). Literacy tests officially barred the uneducated of both races, but they were administered in a manner that discriminated against black people while allowing illiterate whites to satisfy the requirement. Many literacy tests contained a loophole called a "grandfather clause." Under this exception, men whose father or grandfather had voted in 1860 — a time when white men but not black men, most of whom were enslaved, could vote in the South — were excused from taking the test.

In the 1890s, white southerners also imposed legally sanctioned racial segregation on the region's black citizens. Commonly known as **Jim Crow** laws (named for a character in a minstrel show, where whites performed in blackface), these new statutes denied African Americans equal access to public facilities and ensured that black people lived apart from whites. In 1883, when the Supreme Court struck down the Civil Rights Act of 1875 (Module 5-6), it gave southern states the freedom to adopt measures confining black people to separate schools, public accommodations, seats on transportation, beds in hospitals, and sections of graveyards. In 1896 the Supreme Court sanctioned Jim Crow, constructing the constitutional rationale for legally keeping the races apart.

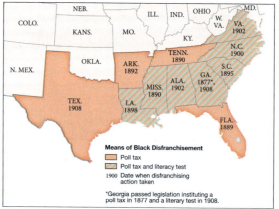

MAP 6.4 Black Disfranchisement in the South, 1889–1908 After Reconstruction, black voters posed a threat to the ruling Democrats by occasionally joining with third-party insurgents. To repel these challenges, Democratic Party leaders made racial appeals to divide poor whites and black people. Chiefly in the 1890s and early twentieth century, white leaders succeeded in disfranchising black voters (and some poor whites), mainly by adopting poll taxes and literacy requirements. **How does the process depicted by this map illustrate the challenges African Americans faced in their struggle for equality in the South?**

APPLY THE TIP

African Americans faced many obstacles while trying to exercise the right to vote. Prepare three large pieces of paper. Write one of the following terms on each piece of paper: poll tax, literacy test, and grandfather clause. Be sure to leave room for students to write on the paper. Post each piece of paper in a different spot in the room. Divide the class into three groups, assign each group to stand by one of the terms, and have each group write the definition of the term to which they were assigned on the paper. Ask one random student from each group to read the definition from the paper to the rest of the class. Next, give each student a sticky note. Ask students first to decide which of the three hurdles that African Americans faced while trying to vote had the greatest impact. They should write their reasoning and evidence for their decision on the sticky note. Next, have each student stand next to the paper that corresponds with their choice — poll tax, literacy test, or grandfather clause — and post their note on the piece of paper. Allow time for students to discuss their evidence and ask volunteers from each group to present their arguments to the class.

Black America and Jim Crow

Plessy v. Ferguson 1896 Supreme Court ruling that upheld the legality of Jim Crow legislation. The Court ruled that as long as states provided "equal but separate" facilities for white and black people, Jim Crow laws did not violate the equal protection clause of the Fourteenth Amendment.

In *Plessy v. Ferguson*, the high court ruled that a Louisiana law providing for "equal but separate" accommodations for "whites" and "coloreds" on railroad cars did not violate the equal protection clause of the Fourteenth Amendment. In its decision, the Court concluded that civil rights laws could not change racial destiny. "If one race be inferior to the other socially," the justices explained, "the Constitution of the United States cannot put them on the same plane." In practice, however, white southerners obeyed the "separate" part of the ruling but never provided equal services. If black people tried to overstep the bounds of Jim Crow in any way that whites found unacceptable, they risked their lives. Between 1884 and 1900, nearly 1,700 black people were lynched in the South. Victims were often subjected to brutal forms of torture before they were hanged or shot.

In everyday life, African Americans carried on as best they could. Segregation required African Americans to build their own businesses and churches; develop their own schools, staffed by black teachers; and form their own civic associations and fraternal organizations. Segregation, though harsh and unequal, did foster a sense of black community, promote a rising middle class, and create social networks that enhanced racial pride. Founded in 1898, the North Carolina Life Insurance Company, one of the leading black-owned and black-operated businesses, employed many African Americans in managerial and sales positions. Burial societies ensured that their members received a proper funeral when they died. As with whites, black men joined lodges such as the Colored Masons and the Colored Odd Fellows, while women participated in the YWCA and the National Association of Colored Women. A small percentage of southern black people resisted Jim Crow by migrating to the North, where black people still exercised the right to vote, more jobs were open to them, and segregation was less strictly enforced though racism against black people was still prevalent.

AP® TIP
Make sure you can explain the connection between the *Plessy v. Ferguson* decision and earlier racist policies and court decisions, as well as attitudes, in American history.

REVIEW
- What tactics did southern legislators use to discriminate against African Americans during the 1880s and 1890s?

AP® WRITING HISTORICALLY | Putting It All Together: Developing Historical Complexity in an Essay

By this point in the course, you have plenty of practice writing history essays. You know how to set context for your historical argument in either your introduction or conclusion, and how to craft a thesis that makes evaluative claims that take both sides of every historical reasoning process — cause and effect, continuity and change, and similarity and difference — into account. You have also learned how to support claims effectively with evidence drawn from your knowledge of historical developments and from your interpretation of multiple primary source documents. All of these skills are vital to crafting and developing an argument, and will serve you well not just on the AP® U.S. History exam, but in college as well.

Now, you're ready to add the last piece of the essay puzzle: developing complexity in your argument. While the skills you have learned in previous Periods — particularly making and supporting evaluative claims — lay much of the necessary groundwork for demonstrating a complex understanding of history, the strongest essays don't simply make and support historical claims in response to the topic of the prompt. Here, we'll walk you through three common strategies to deepen your historical analysis.

These approaches are abbreviated in one easy-to-remember acronym: *GEM*. You've probably heard the phrase, "diamond in the rough," before. It refers to something great that's a little rough around the edges, and it calls to mind the method by which precious stones are mined from the earth before being cut and smoothed for the final product. Likewise, each of the *GEM* tactics is designed to help you dig deeper into your analysis to uncover new insight to refine and polish your argument. So, what does *GEM* stand for?

- Generating nuance
- Explaining both sides
- Making connections that go beyond the prompt (either within or outside of the time period it specifies)

(Continued)

TEACHING IDEA

Incorporating Websites

The Oyez website is an extremely helpful resource for providing concise information on landmark Supreme Court cases (oyez.org). Search the Oyez website for the *Plessy v. Ferguson* case. Allow students to use the site to review the facts of the case, central question, involved justices, as well as the decision and opinion of the Court.

APPLY THE TIP

Review the outcome of the *Plessy v. Ferguson* case with the class. Divide students into groups. Assign each group a racist policy, court decision, or attitude, such as a poll tax or literacy test. Have each group explain how their assigned term connects to the *Plessy v. Ferguson* decision. Discuss as a class.

TRM Suggested Responses to Questions

TEACHING IDEA

AP® Writing Historically Workshop

Because this Long-Essay Question focuses on the development of complexity, think about using it with students who are ready to handle such an activity. Some students may not be ready for this question as they are still working on fundamental parts of writing an essay, such as creating a thesis. One way students can earn complexity is by illustrating a related historical phenomenon not explicitly asked for in the prompt. For instance, this question focuses students' attention on the South and West. While change did occur in those regions, change also occurred in the North. Have students comprise a list of economic changes in the North they could use to compare to the changes they illustrated in their essay. In this way, students are connecting changes across time and geographical area. This is a sophisticated approach to a Long-Essay Question. Students should think about making multiple comparisons as this will be evidence of a more intentional thought process.

TEACHING IDEA

Class Discussion

Break down the prompt as a class. Write the prompt on the board and ask students to point out important parts of the prompt. Circle the verb (evaluate). Underline the skill being assessed (the extent of change) and remind students that this means they should analyze both continuity and change. Put a box around the direct object, or what is changing or continuing (economies of the West and South). Put parentheses around the time period in question (1865 to 1898).

TEACHING IDEA

Building Vocabulary

Work with students to define the word "nuance." Merriam-Webster defines nuance as "a subtle distinction or variation" (merriam-webster.com). Be sure that students understand this term, as it is a major part of the GEM strategy.

Each of these strategies may appear difficult to carry out at first glance, but in reality they are simply ways to build on techniques you are already using when you write essays. Let's explore how you might pre-write for a more sophisticated response to the following prompt, which asks you to draw on what you have learned in Modules 6-1 to 6-3.

> Evaluate the extent of change in the economies of both the West and the South in the period 1865 to 1898.

Step 1 **Break down the prompt.**

As always, breaking down the prompt is the first thing you should do. This question in particular asks you to determine how much and, by extension, in what ways the economies of the West and South changed between 1865 and 1898.

It's important always to keep in mind that each of the three primary reasoning skills of the course is double-sided: a causation question is really about causes and effects, and a comparison question is asking for comparison and contrast. In this case, the phrase "extent of change" in the prompt refers to change *and* continuity.

Step 2 **List and categorize your historical knowledge, then use *GEM* to refine your historical argument.**

In brainstorming and preparing to write an essay focused on continuity and change, think about both economies, western and southern, as they were in 1865, at the end of the Civil War, and in 1898, at the end of the nineteenth century. Consider how each economy had changed over those decades. For each major change you identify, jot down as much evidence as you can to support your claims. Remember, thinking of relevant proper nouns is a great place to start.

Here is where *GEM* comes into the picture. Incorporating this approach into your pre-writing will ensure that you can bring complex and sophisticated analysis into your historical argument. Let's unpack this strategy and consider how we can generate nuance, explain both sides, and make connections at this stage in the process.

G: Generate nuance. You can use the pre-writing strategies you're already familiar with to demonstrate nuance in three ways. First, you can examine the relationship between multiple aspects of historical developments and weigh their significance. Think of this as taking one step beyond assessing the relative significance of a given development. For instance, if you plan to claim that one change in the West's economy was its integration into the larger economic system of the United States, then you could plan to discuss the relative impact of relationships between factors such as the extension of the railroads, the growth of population in the West, and the rise of commercial farming.

Second, you can draw on multiple perspectives to support the argument you are developing. For this prompt, your pre-writing might examine big picture factors such as the impact of geography, politics, or demographics on the economies of each region. For example, you could analyze how the natural resources and climate of the West fed the growth of an integrated, national economy. You can also look at more specific perspectives, such as the views of homesteaders versus American Indians toward land and economic development in the West.

Finally, you can qualify — that is, modify — your argument by considering evidence or perspectives that don't fully or obviously back up your position. For instance, you could plan to explain how the integration of the West into the national economy was slowed by droughts and harsh winters, which ended the Long Drive and forced hundreds of thousands of homesteaders to abandon their farms in the mid-1880s.

E: Explain both sides. This is a technique you already use to make evaluative claims in your writing. As you know from making evaluative claims, every historical reasoning process is like a coin with two sides, and just because the prompt only mentions one doesn't mean you're off the hook when it comes to the other. In this case, we'll need to look at continuities as well as changes. As you know, it's generally easier to focus most of your essay on the half of the skill mentioned in the prompt — changes to the West's and South's economies between 1865 and 1898. However, at least one paragraph ought to examine the implicit, or unspoken, side of the historical reasoning process of the prompt — in this case, continuities in the economies of the West and South. For instance, you could explain how both economies remained dependent on their respective geographies, as mining continued to play a vital role in the West while cotton cultivation remained a primary feature in the South. Ideally, you'll connect your explanation of both sides to nuanced analysis. Here, you might plan to mention how the workforces changed as wageworkers replaced independent miners in the West and sharecroppers replaced enslaved cotton farmers in the South.

M: Make connections that go beyond the prompt. These connections to historical events or developments add interest to your essay and help thread deeper insight into your historical argument. These connections need to be strong ones, not just passing references. Connections can be made across time periods by extending the argument chronologically, either forwards or backwards. For instance, if you plan to discuss the role of the federal government in promoting economic development in the West by subsidizing the transcontinental railroads, you can connect it to earlier federal efforts to promote transportation such as the American System in the Jacksonian era. On the exam, once you've learned all of the history, you can also take the argument forward in time, in this case to later efforts like the building of a national highway system after World War II, which you will learn about in Period 7. Connections can also be made within a time period to other regions or histories, but this is often more challenging than connecting your historical argument to other time periods because it often (but not always) involves bringing in knowledge you have gained through other courses, such as AP® World History. Making connections in this way is far from impossible, though. In this case, you could look at the relationship between American economic growth and the global economy or compare the economic motives and impacts of forcibly relocating American Indians onto reservations to the removal of indigenous peoples in other countries.

The following graphic organizer shows one way to incorporate the *GEM* strategy into your pre-writing. One column has been modeled for you. For each change or continuity you add to the chart, try to provide several pieces of evidence and at least one example of nuance. Also try to think of a connection or two you can make in your essay.

(Change)/ Continuity: Integration of the West's economy into the American economy	Change / Continuity:	Change / Continuity:	Change / Continuity:
Evidence: • Transcontinental railroads • Large-scale domestic and foreign investment in West's economy • Homesteaders farming cash crops instead of for subsistence	**Evidence:**	**Evidence:**	**Evidence:**
Nuance or Qualification of Claim: • Compare relative impact of domestic vs. foreign economic investment • Explain limitations of federal efforts to support West's economic growth (e.g., homesteaders needed more than 160 acres, Chinese Exclusion Act limited labor supply)	**Nuance or Qualification of Claim:**	**Nuance or Qualification of Claim:**	**Nuance or Qualification of Claim:**
Connection 1: Federal subsidies for transcontinental railroads promoted economic growth, as had federal and state efforts in the early 1800s (e.g., National Road, Erie Canal).		**Connection 2:**	

(Continued)

BUILDING AP® SKILLS

Comparison

The "E" in the GEM strategy, "Explain both sides," requires students to look not only at the changes in the western and southern economies but also at the continuities. One possible example of a continuity includes: *Even though the South was industrializing, the southern economy continued to rely on agricultural output. The textile industry relied heavily on southern cotton crops, so farmers continued to grow cotton.* To generate nuance and make connections, students could discuss the increasing use of sharecroppers as laborers that replaced the workforce primarily made up of enslaved persons. Connections could also be made between the system of sharecropping and the desire of many white southerners to maintain the status quo of white superiority in the South.

TEACHING IDEA

Connecting the Dots

Remind students that it is important to connect their essay responses to one of the AP® themes. For example, explain to students how this particular prompt could apply to the following themes: work, exchange, and technology or American and regional culture. As students discuss the extent of change in the economy, they can also focus on how these changes impacted the regional culture of the West and the South. References to the theme would be great additions to the "M" of the GEM strategy, which requires students to make connections that go beyond the prompt.

Period 6: 1865–1898

MODULE 6-3 The New South

Step 3 Set the context, craft a thesis, and write the introduction of your essay.

Now that you have constructed an outline for your essay that creates claims, lists evidence, and incorporates examples of complex reasoning, you can move on to setting the context and crafting your thesis in your opening paragraph. Even within the introduction approach you have been practicing since Period 3, you can begin to show that your essay will demonstrate a complex historical understanding by applying the *GEM* approach. Generate nuance by carefully articulating each claim and indicating the *extent* of change. Explain both sides by including at least one claim of continuity (the other half of the targeted historical reasoning process) in your thesis. Make connections by remembering to set the context and connect it to your argument. Once you have laid the foundation for a sophisticated response in your introduction, then it's just a matter of following through in the body paragraphs.

Step 4 Use both *ACE* and *GEM* to write the body of your essay.

The most straightforward way to write this essay is to devote one or two body paragraphs to each claim of change or continuity you stated in your thesis. Those claims become your topic sentences supported by the evidence, analysis, and reasoning you include from your pre-writing to support the claims. As you construct your paragraphs, keep the *ACE* (Answer, Cite, Explain) strategy in mind for each claim. The evidence you provide must connect to the claim in your paragraph's topic sentence, and you must explain how the evidence you've chosen to use supports your claim. Remembering *ACE* will keep you on track to fully support your argument throughout your essay.

Once you have explained how your evidence supports your claim, you can use *GEM* to deepen your analysis to demonstrate a complex understanding of the changes in the economies of the West and South. In addition to using examples from your pre-write, look for opportunities to close out each body paragraph by weaving the other two historical reasoning processes into your explanation of how the evidence you've chosen is relevant to each paragraph's central claim. For example, you could explain how the integration of the West into the American economy affected migration to and within the United States (causation). Or, you could examine the similarities and differences in the pace of industrialization in the West and South (comparison). You could even compare the impacts of technological innovation on working conditions in the West and South (complex comparison and causation). In all cases, try to be as precise with your wording as you can.

Step 5 Craft your essay conclusion.

The final step is to write a strong conclusion that not only summarizes but, ideally, extends your argument. Remember, you should fully restate your thesis — not word-for-word, but idea-for-idea. After all, it's one last chance to articulate a sound and complete answer to the prompt. As you learned in Module 5-6, your final paragraph is also a logical place to set an immediate concluding context by connecting your argument (in this case, about the economic changes in the West and the South) to a significant development shortly after the time period — such as progressive era reforms or the domestic impact of World War I, which you will be familiar with by the time you take the AP® exam.

Setting a context in your conclusion is also a final opportunity to demonstrate historical complexity by making a relevant and insightful connection between time periods (the "M" in *GEM*). You already know how to do this — it's simply a variation on the long-term concluding context you practiced at the end of Modules 5-6 and 5-9. The difference is that making a connection deals with longer periods of time, while contextualization situates your argument in events either in or near the time period. Finishing your essay by linking a part of your argument to a forward-looking context or making a connection to a later time period will once again demonstrate the sophistication that you have woven throughout your response.

ACTIVITY

Use the steps provided to write a full essay in response to the prompt at the beginning of this box. Be sure to incorporate multiple examples of historical complexity and sophistication in your essay by generating nuance in your response, explaining both sides of the targeted historical reasoning process, and making relevant and insightful connections within and across time periods (*GEM*). You may use the example claim in the graphic organizer in this box as well as the following outline to guide your response.

BUILDING AP® SKILLS

Making Connections

Utilize the accompanying handout to help students visualize the GEM process. The handout allows students to compile all steps of the process of developing historical complexity in essays: breaking down the prompt, brainstorming, generating nuance, explaining both sides, making connections, pre-contextualization, as well as writing the thesis.

TRM Find **Handout 6.3 – GEM Worksheet** in the Teacher's Resource Materials.

MODULE 6-3 The New South

I. Introductory paragraph
   A. Immediate/preceding contextualization statement
      1. Cite evidence of immediate/preceding context
      2. Explain influence of immediate/preceding context
   B. Thesis statement presenting three to four evaluative claims, situated along a continuum of relative extent of change, including at least one continuity
II. Claim 1 body paragraph: Change 1
   A. Topic sentence presenting an evaluative claim of claim 1
   B. Supporting statement citing evidence of claim 1
   C. Cite additional evidence of claim 1
   D. Explain how evidence supports claim 1
   E. Generate nuance by examining multiple variables, diverse perspectives, counter-evidence, or limitations of claim 1
III. Claim 2 body paragraph: Change 2
   A. Topic sentence presenting an evaluative claim of change 2
   B. Supporting statement citing evidence of claim 2
   C. Cite additional evidence of claim 2
   D. Explain how evidence supports claim 2
   E. Generate nuance by examining multiple variables, diverse perspectives, counter-evidence, or limitations of claim 2
IV. Claim 3 body paragraph: Continuity 1
   A. Topic sentence presenting an evaluative claim of continuity 1
   B. Supporting statement citing evidence of claim 3
   C. Cite additional evidence of claim 3
   D. Explain how evidence supports claim 3
   E. Generate nuance by examining multiple variables, diverse perspectives, counter-evidence, or limitations of claim 3
V. (Optional) Claim 4 body paragraph: Change 3 or Continuity 2
   A. Topic sentence presenting an evaluative claim 4
   B. Supporting statement citing evidence of claim 4
   C. Cite additional evidence of claim 4
   D. Explain how evidence supports claim 4
   E. Generate nuance by examining multiple variables, diverse perspectives, counter-evidence, or limitations of claim 4
VI. Conclusion
   A. Restate main claims
   B. Statement connecting historical argument to context immediately after the time range provided by the prompt OR statement connecting historical argument to a similar phenomenon and/or a long-term contextual trend in a later time period.
   C. Provide a piece of evidence for your context statement.
   D. Explain how your evidence supports your concluding context/connection in a later time period.

TEACHING IDEA

Check for Understanding

After students have written a response to the prompt in the AP® Writing Historically section, draw a continuum on the board/projector. Label one side "Nothing Changed" and the other side "Everything Changed." As a bell ringer or exit ticket, have students draw a dot on the continuum to illustrate the extent to which the economies of the West and the South changed from 1865 to 1898. Discuss with the class and remind students that there are multiple answers to many historical questions, including the Long-Essay Questions asked on the AP® exam. As long as relevant historical evidence is used to sufficiently argue a well-thought-out thesis, students can do well on the essay portion.

TRM Suggested Responses to Questions

BUILDING AP® SKILLS

Causation

While reading, have students write down the causes of industrialization as well as the impacts of industrialization on American businesses and the economy on the accompanying handout. This will allow students to keep track of details that help them understand the learning targets for this module.

TRM Find **Handout 6.4 – Causes and Effects of Industrialization** in the Teacher's Resource Materials.

Module 6-4

America Industrializes

LEARNING TARGETS

By the end of this module, you should be able to:
- Explain the factors that contributed to industrialization in the late 1800s.
- Explain the impact of industrialization on American businesses and the economy.
- Explain the impact of technological innovations on American businesses and the economy.

THEMATIC FOCUS

Work, Exchange, and Technology

Business entrepreneurs used technological inventions and new corporate and financial practices to create and consolidate large-scale corporations that dramatically increased the production of goods.

HISTORICAL REASONING FOCUS

Causation

TASK ▶ As you read, consider how railroads, technological inventions, and business practices led to the expansion of the United States economy. Weigh the positive and negative effects of these changes and the responses of the federal government to these changes.

Industrialization and big business reshaped the nation. Between 1870 and 1900, the United States grew into a global industrial power. Transcontinental railroads spurred this breathtaking transformation, linking regional markets into a national market and fueling increased international trade as well; at the same time, railroads themselves served as a massive new market for raw materials and new technologies. Innovations and new inventions promoted business consolidation and the growth of large corporations. Men like Andrew Carnegie became both the heroes and the villains of their age. They engaged in ruthless practices that would lead some to label the new industrialists **robber barons**, but they also created systems of industrial organization and corporate management that altered the economic landscape of the country and changed the place of the United States in the world.

robber barons A negative term applied to late nineteenth-century industrialists and capitalists who became very rich by dominating large industries.

The New Industrial Economy

The industrial revolution of the late nineteenth century originated in Europe. Great Britain was the world's first industrial power, but by the 1870s Germany had emerged as a major challenger for industrial dominance, increasing its steel production at a rapid rate and leading the way in the chemical and electrical industries. The dynamic economic growth and innovation stimulated by industrial competition quickly crossed the Atlantic.

Industrialization transformed the American economy. As industrialization took hold, the U.S. **gross domestic product**, the output of all goods and services produced annually, quadrupled — from $9 billion in 1860 to $37 billion in 1890. During this same period, the number of Americans employed by industry doubled. Moreover, the nature of industry itself changed, as small factories catering to local markets were displaced by large-scale firms producing for national and international markets. The midwestern cities of Chicago, Cincinnati, and St. Louis joined Boston, New York, and Philadelphia as centers of factory production, while the exploitation of the natural

---

TEACHING IDEA

Class Discussion

Display the definitions for "robber baron" and "captain of industry" (captain of industry is found on page 485).

- Robber baron: a negative term applied to late nineteenth-century industrialists and capitalists who became very rich by dominating large industries.
- Captain of industry: a positive term for the same industrialists and capitalists, emphasizing the good that they provided to the American economy.

Have students research one of the following men: Cornelius Vanderbilt, John D. Rockefeller, Andrew Carnegie, or J. P. Morgan. Then ask students to write a paragraph to explain whether they believe that the individual they read about should be considered a robber baron or captain of industry. Discuss student answers and arguments as a class. You could also choose to use modern-day millionaires or billionaires to connect history to the present.

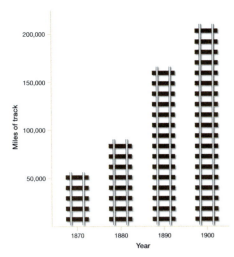

Expansion of the Railroad System, 1870–1900 The great expansion of the railroads in the late nineteenth century fueled the industrial revolution and the growth of big business. Connecting the nation from East Coast to West Coast, transcontinental railroads created a national market for natural resources and manufactured goods. The biggest surges in railroad construction occurred west of the Mississippi River and in the South. **What social and economic factors contributed to large-scale railroad expansion from 1870 to 1900?**

resources in the West took on an increasingly industrial character. Trains, telegraphs, and telephones connected the country in ways never before possible.

From 1870 to 1913, the United States experienced an extraordinary rate of growth in industrial output: In 1870 American industries turned out 23.3 percent of the world's manufacturing production; by 1913 this figure had jumped to 35.8 percent. In fact, U.S. output in 1913 almost equaled the combined total for Europe's three leading industrial powers: Germany, the United Kingdom, and France. By the end of the nineteenth century, the United States was surging ahead of northern Europe as the manufacturing center of the world.

At the heart of the American industrial transformation was the railroad. Large-scale business enterprises would not have developed without a national market for raw materials and finished products. A consolidated system of railroads crisscrossing the nation facilitated the creation of such a market. In addition, railroads were direct consumers of industrial products, stimulating the growth of a number of industries through their consumption of steel, wood, coal, glass, rubber, brass, and iron. Finally, railroads contributed to economic growth by increasing the speed and efficiency with which products and materials were transported.

Before railroads could create a national market, they had to overcome several critical problems. In 1877 railroad lines dotted the country in haphazard fashion. They primarily served local markets and remained unconnected at key points. This lack of coordination stemmed mainly from the fact that each railroad had its own track gauge (the width between the tracks), making shared track use impossible and long-distance travel extremely difficult.

The consolidation of railroads solved many of these problems. In 1886 railroad companies finally agreed to adopt a standard gauge. Railroads also standardized time zones, thus eliminating confusion in train schedules. During the 1870s, towns and cities each set their own time zone, a practice that created discrepancies among them. In 1882 the time in New York City and in Boston varied by 11 minutes and 45 seconds. The following year, railroads agreed to coordinate times and divided the country into four standard time zones. Most cities soon cooperated with the new system, but not until 1918 did the federal government legislate the standard time zones that the railroads had first adopted.

REVIEW

How did the expansion of railroads change life in the United States?

Innovations and Inventions

As important as railroads were, they were not the only engine of industrialization. American technological innovation created new industries, while expanding the efficiency and productivity of old ones. In 1866 a transatlantic telegraph cable connected the United States and Europe, allowing businessmen on both sides of the ocean to pursue profitable commercial ventures. New inventions also allowed business offices to run more smoothly: Typewriters were invented in 1868, carbon paper in 1872, adding machines in 1891, and mimeograph machines in 1892. As businesses grew, they needed more space for their operations. The construction of towering skyscrapers in the 1880s in cities such as Chicago and New York was made possible by two innovations: structural steel, which had the strength to support tall buildings, and elevators.

Alexander Graham Bell's telephone revolutionized communications. By 1880 fifty-five cities offered local service and catered to a total of 50,000 subscribers, most of them business customers. In 1885, Bell established the American Telephone and Telegraph Company (AT&T), and long-distance service connected New York, Boston, and Chicago. By 1900 around 1.5 million telephones were in operation.

Perhaps the greatest technological innovations that advanced industrial development in the late nineteenth century came in steel manufacturing. In 1859 Henry Bessemer, a British inventor, designed a furnace that burned the impurities out of melted iron and converted it into steel. The open-hearth process, devised by another Englishman, William Siemens, further improved the quality of steel by removing additional impurities from the iron. Railroads replaced iron rails with steel because it was lighter, stronger, and more durable than iron. Steel became the major building block of industry, furnishing girders and cables to construct manufacturing plants and office structures. As production became cheaper and more efficient, steel output soared from 13,000 tons in 1860 to 28 million tons in the first decade of the twentieth century.

Factory machinery needed constant lubrication, and the growing petroleum industry made this possible. A drilling technique devised in 1859 had tapped into pools of petroleum located deep below the earth's surface. In the post–Civil War era, new distilling techniques transformed petroleum into lubricating oil for factory machinery. This process of "cracking" crude oil also generated lucrative by-products for the home, such as kerosene and paraffin for heating and lighting and salve to soothe cuts and burns. After 1900, the development of the gasoline-powered, internal combustion engine for automobiles opened up an even richer market for the oil industry.

Railroads also benefited from innovations in technology. Improvements included air brakes and automatic coupling devices to attach train cars to each other. Elijah McCoy, a trained engineer and the son of freedpeople, was forced because of racial discrimination to work at menial railroad

▲ **Manufacturing of Steel Tubing, 1897** This engraving appeared in the December 18, 1897 issue of *Scientific American* and illustrates the manufacture of steel tubing pipes at the National Tube Works in McKeesport, Pennsylvania. With hot flames in the background, workers are welding rings on a 23-inch pipe. **What aspects of the image reveal the changes in industrial production during the late nineteenth century?**

BUILDING AP® SKILLS

Developments and Processes

Ask students to analyze the impact of the oil industry on manufacturers and on urban populations during the late nineteenth century. Possible answers include: *The oil industry grew greatly, providing jobs for many Americans. Oil was refined and the petroleum was used to lubricate factory machinery, which was used daily to produce consumer goods for Americans. Other oil by-products such as kerosene and paraffin were used for lighting and heating homes, making the lives of Americans more comfortable. This also led to increased danger of housefires. Upon the invention of the internal combustion engine, oil was used to power large machinery and vehicles that helped Americans complete jobs faster and move from place to place more quickly and easily.*

TEACHING IDEA

Check for Understanding

Divide the class into three or six groups, depending on class size. As a bell ringer or exit ticket, assign each group to one of the following topics: steel, the telephone, and the electric lightbulb. Have each group evaluate the extent to which their assigned topic impacted the lives of people of the late nineteenth century. Once each group has prepared a response, have them share with the class. If time allows, give opportunities for further class discussion or debate.

jobs shoveling coal and lubricating train parts every few miles to keep the gears from overheating. This experience encouraged him to invent and patent an automatic lubricating device to improve efficiency.

Early innovations resulted from the genius of individual inventors, but by the late nineteenth century technological progress was increasingly an organized, collaborative effort. Thomas Alva Edison and his team served as the model. In 1876 Edison set up a research laboratory in Menlo Park, New Jersey. Housed in a two-story, white frame building, Edison's "invention factory" was staffed by a team of inventors and craftsmen. In 1887 Edison opened another laboratory, ten times bigger than the one at Menlo Park, in nearby Orange, New Jersey. These facilities pioneered the research laboratories that would become a standard feature of American industrial development in the twentieth century.

Out of Edison's laboratories flowed inventions that revolutionized American business and culture. The phonograph and motion pictures changed the way people spent their leisure time. The electric light bulb illuminated people's homes and made them safer by eliminating the need for candles and gas lamps, which were fire hazards. It also brightened city streets, making them available for outdoor evening activities, and lit up factories so that they could operate all night long.

Like his contemporaries who were building America's huge industrial empires, Edison cashed in on his workers' inventions. He joined forces with the Wall Street banker J. P. Morgan to finance the Edison Electric Illuminating Company, which in 1882 provided lighting to customers in New York City. Goods produced by electric equipment jumped in value from $1.9 million in 1879 to $21.8 million in 1890. In 1892, Morgan helped Edison merge his companies with several competitors and reorganized them as the General Electric Corporation, which became the industry leader.

REVIEW

What was the relationship between technological innovation and industrialization during the late nineteenth century?

Industrial Consolidation

In the North, South, and West, nineteenth-century industrialists strove to minimize or eliminate competition. To gain competitive advantages and increase profits, industrial entrepreneurs concentrated on reducing production costs, charging lower prices, and outselling the competition. Successful firms could then acquire rival companies that could no longer afford to compete, creating an industrial empire in the process.

Building such industrial empires was not easy, however, and posed creative challenges for business ventures. Heavy investment in machinery resulted in very high fixed costs (or overhead) that did not change much over time. Because overhead costs remained stable, manufacturers could reduce the per-unit cost of production by increasing the output of a product — what economists call "economy of scale." Manufacturers thus aimed to raise the volume of production and find ways to cut variable costs — for labor and materials, for example. Through such savings, a factory owner could sell his product more cheaply than his competitors and gain a larger share of the market.

A major organizational technique for reducing costs and underselling the competition was **vertical integration**. "Captains of industry," as their admirers called them, did not just build a business; they created a system — a network of firms, each contributing to the final product. Men like Andrew Carnegie controlled the various phases of production from top to bottom (vertical), extracting the raw materials, transporting them to the factories, manufacturing the finished products, and shipping them to market. By using vertical integration, Carnegie eliminated middlemen and guaranteed regular and cheap access to supplies. He also lowered inventories and gained increased flexibility by shifting segments of the labor force to areas where they were most needed. His credo became "Watch the costs and the profits will take care of themselves."

Businessmen also employed another type of integration — **horizontal integration**. This approach focused on gaining greater control over the market by acquiring firms that sold the same products. John D. Rockefeller, the founder of the mammoth Standard Oil Company, specialized in this technique. In the mid-1870s, he brought a number of key oil refiners into an alliance with Standard Oil to control four-fifths of the industry. At the same time, the oil baron ruthlessly drove out of business or bought up marginal firms that could not afford to compete with him.

TEACHING IDEA

Incorporating Videos

Review the terms horizontal and vertical integration by having students watch Tom Richey's video, "Vertical vs. Horizontal Integration" (available on YouTube). In the video, Richey explains vertical integration by using the song "Head, Shoulders, Knees, and Toes" to describe how vertical integration combines different industries into one company. Richey explains horizontal integration by using the analogy of eating a large breakfast, lunch, dinner, and snacks. The belly would increase, and each "acquisition" of food is the same type of product, similar to the process of horizontal integration.

TRM Suggested Responses to Questions

TRM Module 6.4 AP® Analyzing Sources Handout 1

TEACHING IDEA

Additional Practice

Have students study the AP® Analyzing Sources section to help them answer this Short-Answer Question prompt:

a. Briefly explain ONE reason for the changes illustrated by the charts.

b. Briefly explain ONE reason for the continuities illustrated by the charts.

c. Evaluate the impact of ONE change or ONE continuity on American society.

Possible answers for each part of the Short-Answer Question prompt include:

a. *The workforce increased as a whole due to an increased population and immigration. Manufacturing grew faster than agriculture because there were many new industries and factories in the cities that needed laborers. Many people left the country to move to the city to find work.*

b. *Agriculture remained the largest industry in the nation because a growing population required an increased amount of food. Many people were also moving to the Great Plains specifically to start farms. The workforce of the mining industry did not increase much due to the dangerous nature of the work.*

c. *As the need for labor increased, cities grew. Overcrowding, poor sanitation, and poverty became prevalent issues in American cities as increased numbers of people, both native-born and immigrants, moved to the cities looking for work. Due to the continuing demand for food, agriculture remained an important American industry. People continued to move to the West, creating a uniquely "western" American culture. Westward expansion also led to increased conflict with American Indians in the Great Plains.*

Period 6: 1865–1898

MODULE 6-4 America Industrializes

AP® ANALYZING SOURCES

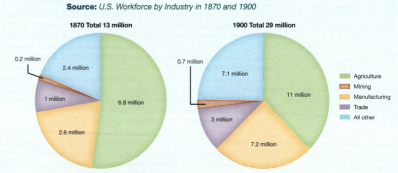

Source: U.S. Workforce by Industry in 1870 and 1900

Questions for Analysis

1. Identify the changes and continuities illustrated by these charts.
2. Explain the reasons for the changes illustrated by the charts.
3. Explain the reasons for the continuities illustrated by the charts.
4. Evaluate the impact of one change and one continuity on American society.

Horizontal integration was also a major feature in the telegraph industry. By 1861 Western Union had strung 76,000 miles of telegraph line throughout the nation. Founded in 1851, the company had thrived during the Civil War by obtaining most of the federal government's telegraph business. The firm had 12,600 offices housed in railroad depots throughout the country and strung its lines adjacent to the railroads. Seeing an opportunity to make money, Wall Street tycoon Jay Gould set out to acquire Western Union. In the mid-1870s, Gould, who had obtained control over the Union Pacific Railway, financed companies to compete with the giant telegraph outfit. Gould did not succeed until 1881, when he engineered a takeover of Western Union by combining it with his American Union Telegraph Company. Gould made a profit of $30 million on the deal. On February 15, the day after the agreement, the *New York Herald Tribune* reported: "The country finds itself this morning at the feet of a telegraphic monopoly," a business that controlled the market and destroyed competition.

Bankers played a huge role in engineering industrial consolidation. No one did it more skillfully than J. P. Morgan. In the 1850s, Morgan started his career working for a prominent American-owned banking firm in London, and in 1861 he created his own investment company in New York City. Morgan played the central role in channeling funds from Britain to support the construction of major American railroads. During the 1880s and 1890s, Morgan orchestrated the refinancing of several ailing railroads. To maintain control over these enterprises, the Wall Street financier created **interlocking directorates** by placing his allies on their boards of directors and selecting the companies' chief operating officers. Morgan then turned his talents for organization to the steel industry. In 1901 he was instrumental in merging Carnegie's company with several competitors in which he had a financial interest. Morgan's creation, United States Steel, became the world's largest industrial corporation, worth $1.4 billion. By the end of the first decade of the twentieth century, Morgan's investment house held more than 340 directorships in 112 corporations, amounting to more than $22 billion in assets, the equivalent of $525 billion in 2015, all at a time when there was no income tax.

REVIEW

How did vertical integration, horizontal integration, and the use of interlocking directorates promote industrial consolidation?

Period 6: 1865–1898

The Growth of Corporations

corporation A form of business ownership in which the liability of shareholders in a company is limited to their individual investments. The formation of corporations in the late nineteenth century greatly stimulated investment in industry.

trust Business monopolies formed in the late nineteenth and early twentieth centuries through mergers and consolidation that inhibited competition and controlled the market.

With economic consolidation came the expansion of corporations. Before the age of large-scale enterprise, the predominant form of business ownership was the partnership. Unlike a partnership, a **corporation** provided investors with "limited liability." This meant that if the corporation went bankrupt, shareholders could not lose more than they had invested. Limited liability encouraged investment by keeping the shareholders' investment in the corporation separate from their other assets. In addition, corporations provided "perpetual life." Partnerships dissolved on the death of a partner, whereas corporations continued to function despite the death of any single owner. This form of ownership brought stability and order to financing, building, and perpetuating what was otherwise a highly volatile and complex business endeavor.

Capitalists devised new corporate structures to gain greater control over their industries. Rockefeller's Standard Oil Company led the way by creating the **trust**, a monopoly formed by a small group of leading stockholders from several firms who manage the consolidated enterprise. To evade state laws against monopolies, Rockefeller created a petroleum trust. He combined other oil firms across the country with Standard Oil and placed their owners on a nine-member board of trustees that ran the company. Subsequently, Rockefeller fashioned another method of bringing rival businesses together. Through a **holding company**, he obtained stock in a number of other oil companies and held them under his control.

Between 1880 and 1905, more than three hundred mergers occurred in 80 percent of the nation's manufacturing firms. Great wealth became heavily concentrated in the hands of a relatively small number of businessmen. Around two thousand businesses, a tiny fraction of the total number, dominated 40 percent of the nation's economy.

In their drive to consolidate economic power and shield themselves from risk, corporate titans generally had the courts on their side. In *Santa Clara County v. Southern Pacific Railroad Company* (1886), the Supreme Court decided that under the Fourteenth Amendment, which originally dealt with the issue of federal protection of African Americans' civil rights, a corporation was considered a "person." In effect, this ruling gave corporations the same right of due process that the framers of the amendment had meant to give to freedpeople. In the 1890s, a majority of the Supreme Court embraced this interpretation. The right of due process shielded corporations from prohibitive government regulation of the workplace, including the passage of legislation reducing the number of hours in the workday.

EXPLORING AP® THEMES

Work, Exchange, and Technology

Spend time to make sure that students are able to differentiate between the following terms: corporation, trust, holding company, and monopoly. Discuss the similarities and differences and ask students to provide examples of modern-day businesses that can be classified as corporations or monopolies.

TRM Suggested Responses to Questions

TRM Module 6.4 AP® Analyzing Sources Handout 2

AP® ANALYZING SOURCES

"The Trust Giant's Point of View: What a Funny Little Government?" illustration from *The Verdict*, January 22, 1900 (colour litho)/Taylor, Horace (1881–1934)/NEW YORK HISTORICAL SOCIETY/© Collection of the New-York Historical Society, USA/Bridgeman Images

Source: Horace Taylor, *What a Funny Little Government*, 1900

About the source: The collar worn by the man in this cartoon is labeled, "ROCKEFELLER." He is holding the White House in the palm of his hand, and the U.S. Capitol building, labeled as "STANDARD OIL REFINERY," is pictured in the background. The dark building in the background, visible between Rockefeller's left hand and face, is labeled "TREASURY DEPT." Oil barrels fill the foreground.

Questions for Analysis

1. Identify the artist's perspective on the relationship between big business and government based on the major elements of this image.
2. Explain the historical developments that led to the situation depicted in the image.
3. Evaluate the effectiveness of the federal government's efforts to address the situation depicted in the image during the 1890s.

TEACHING IDEA

Making Connections

In order to make the actions of Rockefeller and Carnegie relatable to students, discuss the game Monopoly. If time and resources allow, bring in a few copies of the game and break students into groups to play for 20 minutes. Ask students how the goals of the game compare to what was occurring in American industry at this time. Then, have students read the article "Monopoly Was Designed to Teach the 99% About Income Inequality" by Mary Pilon, available from the Smithsonian Magazine's website about the origin and intention of the game (smithsonianmag.com). Whole-class discussion to follow.

Period 6: 1865–1898

MODULE 6-4 America Industrializes

Sherman Antitrust Act 1890 act outlawing monopolies that prevented free competition in interstate commerce.

Yet trusts did not go unopposed. In 1890 Congress passed the **Sherman Antitrust Act**, which outlawed monopolies that prevented free competition in interstate commerce. The bill passed easily with bipartisan support because it merely codified legal principles that already existed. Senator Sherman and his colleagues never intended to stifle large corporations, which through efficient business practices came to dominate the market. Rather, the lawmakers attempted to limit underhanded actions that destroyed competition. The judicial system further bailed out corporate leaders. In *United States v. E. C. Knight Company* (1895), a case against the "sugar trust," the Supreme Court rendered the Sherman Act virtually toothless by ruling that manufacturing was a local activity within a state and that, even if it was a monopoly, it was not subject to congressional regulation. This ruling left most trusts in the manufacturing sector beyond the jurisdiction of the Sherman Antitrust Act.

The introduction of managerial specialists, already present in European firms, proved the most critical innovation for integrating industry. With many operations controlled under one roof, large-scale businesses required a corps of experts to oversee and coordinate the various steps of production. As the expanding labor force worked to produce a rapidly rising volume of goods, efficiency experts sought to cut labor costs and make the production process operate more smoothly. Frederick W. Taylor, a Philadelphia engineer and businessman, developed the principles of **scientific management**. Based on his concept of reducing manual labor to its simplest components and eliminating independent action on the part of workers, managers introduced time-and-motion studies. Using a stopwatch, they calculated how to break down a job into simple tasks that could be performed in the least amount of time. From this perspective, workers were no different from the machines they operated. With production soaring, marketing and advertising managers were called upon to devise new techniques to gauge consumer interests and stimulate their demands.

scientific management Also known as Taylorism, a management style developed by Frederick W. Taylor that aimed to constantly improve the efficiency of employees by reducing manual labor to its simplest components — thus increasing productivity while decreasing cost.

Another vital factor in creating large-scale industry was the establishment of retail outlets that could sell the enormous volume of goods pouring out of factories. As consumer goods became less expensive, retail outlets sprang up to serve the growing market for household items. Customers could shop at department stores — such as Macy's in New York City, Filene's in Boston, Marshall Field's in Chicago, May's in Denver, Nordstrom's in Seattle, and Jacome's in Tucson — where they were waited on by a growing army of salesclerks. Or they could buy the cheaper items in Frank W. Woolworth's five and ten cent stores, which opened in towns and cities nationwide. Chain supermarkets — such as the Great Atlantic and Pacific Tea Company (A&P), founded in 1869 — sold fruits and vegetables packed in tin cans. They also sold foods from the meatpacking firms of Gustavus Swift and Philip Armour, which shipped them on refrigerated railroad cars. Mail-order catalogs allowed Americans in all parts

◀ **1899 Sears, Roebuck Catalog** The expansion of industrialization and completion of the transcontinental railroad created a national market for manufactured goods and led to the growth of consumer culture. The Chicago-based Sears, Roebuck used its mail-order catalog to attract customers throughout the United States and, as its cover suggests, the world. This colorful 1899 catalog offers the latest in carpets, furniture, china, fashion, and photographic equipment and supplies. **How does this image promote consumerism?**

488

TEACHING IDEA

Building Vocabulary

Discuss the term "scientific management." What was the purpose of scientific management? How is this principle present in our economy today? Possible answers include: *Scientific management was meant to make production faster and more efficient. Laborers only needed to learn one task and would perform that task repetitively. Modern-day assembly lines are an example. Each person on the assembly line has a role that they fulfill in order to assemble a product one part at a time. Machinery has also become an important part of this process over time.* Mention that scientific management utilized the idea of interchangeable parts, popularized by Eli Whitney in the eighteenth century. Each product is made of the same parts, so if one part breaks or is faulty, there are identical parts with which to replace it.

TEACHING IDEA

Analyzing Art and Images

The image of the 1899 Sears, Roebuck Catalog is incredibly detailed. Use the National Archives' Analyze a Poster worksheet to help students notice the details and determine their meaning. This can be found under Working with Primary Sources in the Educator Resources section of the website (archives.gov). The worksheet also requires students to use the image as historical evidence, which can be supplemental to the provided question, "How does the image reflect economic developments of the 1880s and 1890s?"

BUILDING AP® SKILLS

Causation

Ask students to determine how the demand for consumer goods led to changes in the production and distribution of goods. Possible answers include: *Many people worked long hours and did not have the time nor the resources to make their own goods or grow their own food, which led to an increase in the demand for finished consumer goods. The great increase in demand for consumer goods required companies to produce a greater number of goods with limited labor resources. This led to initiatives such as scientific management, where tasks were broken down and assigned to individuals who would specialize in the particular task, thereby increasing productivity. Retail outlets became a new, efficient way to distribute goods to the public. Consumers could visit a retail outlet and buy almost everything they needed. Catalogs were also a new way for consumers to buy goods and have them delivered to their homes. Instead of having to make everything at home or travel to multiple specialty stores to buy their goods, consumers could stop at one place or even do their shopping from home.*

of the country to buy consumer goods without leaving their home. The catalogs of Montgomery Ward (established in 1872) and Sears, Roebuck (founded in 1886) offered tens of thousands of items. Rural free delivery, instituted by the U.S. Post Office in 1891, made it even easier for farmers and others living in the countryside to obtain these catalogs and buy their merchandise without having to travel miles to the nearest post office. By the end of the nineteenth century, the industrial economy had left its mark on almost all aspects of life in almost every corner of America.

REVIEW

- What historical developments led to the growth of corporations?

AP® WRITING HISTORICALLY — Short-Answer Question Practice

ACTIVITY

Read the following question carefully and write a short response. Use complete sentences.

Using the following excerpts, answer (a), (b), and (c).

Source: Matthew Josephson, *The Robber Barons*, 1934

"But for the very reason that forces leading to combination were at work in the society, the general effect of the period [1877–1900] was one of strenuous contest for the market, of anarchic, individual appetite and money-lust, of ruinous competition conducted with more terrible instruments than before, out of which a few giant industrialists arose. . . .

With his measured spirit, with his organized might, [John D. Rockefeller] tested men and things. There were men and women of all sorts who passed under his implacable rod, and their tale . . . has contributed to the legend of the 'white devil' who came to rule over American industry.

A certain widow, a Mrs. [Fred M.] Backus of Cleveland, who had inherited an oil-refinery, had appealed to Mr. Rockefeller to preserve her, 'the mother of fatherless children.' And he had promised 'with tears in his eyes that he would stand by her.' But in the end he offered her only $79,000 for a property which had cost $200,000. The whole story of the defenseless widow and her orphans, the stern command, the confiscation of two-thirds of her property, when it came out made a deep stir and moved many hearts."

Source: Daniel Yergin, *The Prize: The Epic Quest for Oil, Money & Power*, 2012

"Rockefeller himself was not so troubled. He was, he thought, only operating in the spirit of capitalism. He even sought to enlist Protestant evangelists and Social Gospel clergy in defense of Standard Oil. Mostly he ignored the criticism; he remained confident and absolutely convinced that Standard Oil was an instrument for human betterment, replacing chaos and volatility with stability, making possible a major advance in society, and delivering the gift of the 'new light' to the world of darkness. It had provided the capital and organization and technology and had taken the big risks required to create and service a global market. 'Give the poor man his cheap light, gentlemen,' Rockefeller would tell his colleagues in the Executive Committee. As far as he was concerned, Standard Oil's success was a bold step into the future. 'The day of combination is here to stay,' Rockefeller said after he had stepped aside from active management of the company. 'Individualism has gone, never to return.' Standard Oil, he added, was one of the greatest, perhaps even the greatest, of 'upbuilders we ever had in this country.'"

a. Briefly explain ONE major difference between Josephson's and Yergin's interpretations of John D. Rockefeller's legacy.
b. Briefly explain how ONE specific historical event or development from the period that is not explicitly mentioned in the excerpts could be used to support Josephson's argument.
c. Briefly explain how ONE specific historical event or development from the period that is not explicitly mentioned in the excerpts could be used to support Yergin's argument.

TEACHING IDEA

AP® Writing Historically Review

The excerpts provide focus on John D. Rockefeller, but also speak to a larger historical development of the debate over whether to consider industrial leaders as captains of industry or robber barons. Have students define each of these terms and then make a list of three specific facts that relate to each label. This activity will prepare students to answer parts (b) and (c), which rely on factual knowledge. Students can focus on Rockefeller, but you can also encourage students to think about other examples they learned in Module 6-4.

TEACHING IDEA

Project Idea

Allow students to choose one of the following individuals: John D. Rockefeller, J. P. Morgan, Andrew Carnegie, Cornelius Vanderbilt, or Daniel Drew. Students will conduct research and create two posters. One poster will depict their individual as a hero, or captain of industry. The other poster will depict their individual as a villain, or robber baron. Students must include a thesis on each poster, three reasons supported by specific historical evidence, and a short conclusion.

Module 6-5

Working People Organize

LEARNING TARGETS

By the end of this module, you should be able to:

- Explain the continuities and changes in the lives of various groups of industrial workers.
- Explain how industrialization spurred the formation of labor unions and how the government responded to unionization.

THEMATIC FOCUS

Work, Exchange, and Technology

In response to the growing power of large corporations, mechanization, and the loss of autonomy, workers created labor unions and used strikes to fight for better wages and working conditions. In most cases, states and the federal government favored business interests over workers in labor disputes, some of which became violent affairs.

HISTORICAL REASONING FOCUS

Continuity and Change

TASK ▶ As you read this module, consider how the lives of workers changed as a result of technological inventions and the rise of large corporations. Examine how those changes led workers to create labor unions and evaluate the degree of success organized labor experienced during this time. Also consider how, how much, and why the role of government in the economy changed.

TRM Suggested Responses to Questions

BUILDING AP® SKILLS

Causation

To provide students practice with causation, assign students to determine the causes of unionization as well as the effects of unionization. The accompanying handout also requires students to create an argument to describe which cause and which effect had the greatest impact on American society, and why.

TRM Find **Handout 6.5 – Causes and Effects of Labor Unionization** in the Teacher's Resource Materials.

Just as industrialists had built powerful corporations to promote their economic interests, working men and women also saw the benefits of organizing to increase their political and economic leverage. Determined to secure decent wages and working conditions, workers joined labor unions, formed political parties, and engaged in a variety of collective actions, including strikes. However, workers' organizations were beset by internal conflicts over occupational status, race, ethnicity, and gender. They proved no match for the powerful alliance between corporations and the federal government that stood against them, and they failed to become a lasting national political force. Workers fared better in their own communities, where family, neighbors, and local businesses were more likely to come to their aid.

The Industrialization of Labor

The industrialization of the United States transformed the workplace, bringing together large numbers of laborers under difficult conditions. In 1870 few factories employed 500 or more workers. Thirty years later, more than 1,500 companies had workforces of this size. Just after the Civil War, manufacturing employed 5.3 million workers; thirty years later, the figure soared to more than 15.1 million. Most of these new industrial workers came from two main sources. First, farmers who could not make a decent living from the soil moved to nearby cities in search of factory jobs. Although mostly white, this group also included black people who sought to escape the oppressive conditions of sharecropping. Between 1870 and 1890, some 80,000 African Americans journeyed from the rural South to cities in the South and the North to search for employment. Second, the economic opportunities in America drew millions of immigrants from Europe over the course of the nineteenth century. Immigrant workers initially came from northern Europe. However, by the end of the nineteenth century, immigrants from southern and eastern European countries predominated.

BUILDING AP® SKILLS

Continuity and Change

Put students into groups to answer the following prompt: "Explain the continuities and changes in the lives of various groups of industrial workers." Assign each student group a different group of industrial workers, including women, immigrants, skilled workers, and children. Once all groups have provided sufficient evidence to answer the prompt, discuss the answers as a class.

Inside factories, unskilled workers, those with no particular skill or expertise, encountered a system undergoing critical changes, as small-scale manufacturing gave way to larger and more mechanized operations. Immigrants, who made up the bulk of unskilled laborers, had to adjust both to a new country and to unfamiliar, unpleasant, and often dangerous industrial work. A traveler from Hungary who visited a steel mill in Pittsburgh that employed many Hungarian immigrants compared the factories to prisons where "the heat is most insupportable, the flames most choking." Nor were any government benefits — such as workers' compensation or unemployment insurance — available to industrial laborers who were hurt in accidents or laid off from their jobs.

Skilled workers, who had particular training or abilities and were more difficult to replace, were not immune to the changes brought about by industrialization and the rise of large-scale businesses. In the early days of manufacturing, skilled laborers operated as independent craftsmen. They provided their own tools, worked at their own pace, and controlled their production output. This approach to work enhanced their sense of personal dignity, reflected their notion of themselves as free citizens, and distinguished them from the mass of unskilled laborers. Mechanization, however, undercut their autonomy by dictating both the nature and the speed of production through practices of scientific management. Instead of producing goods, skilled workers increasingly applied their craft to servicing machinery and keeping it running smoothly. While owners reaped the benefits of the mechanization and regimentation of the industrial workplace, many skilled workers saw such "improvements" as a threat to their freedom.

AP® ANALYZING SOURCES

Source: John Morrison, *Testimony of a Machinist before the Senate Committee on the Relations between Labor and Capital*, 1883

"**Question:** Is there any difference between the conditions under which machinery is made now and those which existed ten years ago?
Answer: A great deal of difference.

Question: State the differences as well as you can.
Answer: Well, the trade has been subdivided and those subdivisions have been again subdivided, so that a man never learns the machinist's trade now. Ten years ago he learned, not the whole of the trade, but a fair portion of it. Also, there is more machinery used in the business, which again makes machinery. The different branches of the trade are divided and subdivided so that one man may make just a particular part of a machine and may not know anything whatever about another part of the same machine. In that way machinery is produced a great deal cheaper than it used to be formerly, and in fact, through this system of work, 100 men are able to do now what it took 300 or 400 men to do fifteen years ago. By the use of machinery and the subdivision of the trade they so simplify the work that it is made a great deal easier and put together a great deal faster. There is no system of apprenticeship, I may say, in the business. You simply go in and learn whatever branch you are put at, and you stay at that unless you are changed to another. . . .

Question: Are the machinists here generally contented, or are they in a state of discontent and unrest?
Answer: There is mostly a general feeling of discontent, and you will find among the machinists the most radical workingmen, with the most revolutionary ideas. You will find that they don't so much give their thoughts simply to trade unions and other efforts of that kind, but they go far beyond that; they only look for relief through the ballot or through a revolution, a forcible revolution."

Questions for Analysis

1. Describe the changes in working conditions stated by Morrison.
2. Explain how the document reflects the longer-term positive and negative effects of trade subdivision for skilled workers.
3. Evaluate the extent to which the process of trade subdivision described in the excerpt represented a continuity in industrial working conditions.

BUILDING AP® SKILLS

Continuity and Change

As an exit card activity, have students describe how and why the American economy switched from a focus on skilled craftsmen to assembly lines. Possible answers include: *Assembly lines provided a more efficient way to produce goods by utilizing machinery and unskilled workers. Laborers did not need much training and specialized in a specific task. Doing away with extensive training saved money, and companies could pay unskilled laborers low wages. Assembly lines were also faster, as each person performed one task. This limited the time spent moving from one task to another. Skilled craftsmen were still important to the American economy, but they were not as necessary as they once were.*

TRM Suggested Responses to Questions

TRM Module 6.5 AP® Analyzing Sources Handout 1

BUILDING AP® SKILLS

Sourcing and Situation

Complete a HIPP analysis with the source written by John Morrison (a refresher of HIPP can be found on page 8). Provide some information from Module 6-5 to help describe the significance of the source. How do each of these components, such as Morrison's point of view and the intended audience, affect what Morrison says in his interview?

Still, most workers did not oppose the technology that increased their productivity and resulted in higher wages. Compared to their mid-nineteenth-century counterparts, industrial laborers now made up a larger share of the general population, earned more money, and worked fewer hours. During the 1870s and 1880s, the average industrial worker's real wages (actual buying power) increased by 20 percent. At the same time, the average workday declined from ten and a half hours to ten hours. From 1870 to 1890, the general price index dropped 30 percent, allowing consumers to benefit from lower prices.

Yet workers were far from content, and the lives of industrial workers remained extremely difficult. Although workers as a group saw improvements in wages and hours, they did not earn enough income to support their families adequately. Also, there were widespread disparities based on job status, race, ethnicity, sex, and region. Skilled workers earned more than unskilled workers. Whites were paid more than African Americans, who were mainly shut out of better jobs. Immigrants from northern Europe, who had settled in the United States before southern Europeans, tended to hold higher-paying skilled positions. And, southern factory workers, whether in textiles, steel, or armaments, earned less than their northern counterparts.

Between 1870 and 1900, the number of female wageworkers grew by 66 percent, accounting for about one-quarter of all nonfarm laborers. Women, an increasingly important component of the industrial workforce, earned, on average, only 25 percent of what men did. The majority of employed women, including those working in factories, were single and between the ages of sixteen and twenty-four. Overall, only 5 percent of married women worked outside the home, although 30 percent of African American wives were employed. Women workers were concentrated in several areas. White and black women continued to serve as maids and domestics. Others took over jobs that were once occupied by men. They became teachers, nurses, clerical workers, telephone operators, and department store salesclerks. Some women toiled in manufacturing jobs requiring fine eye-hand coordination, such as cigar rolling and work in the needle trades and textile industry.

Women also turned their homes into workplaces. In crowded apartments, they sewed furs onto garments, made straw hats, prepared artificial flowers, and fashioned jewelry. Earnings from piecework (work that pays at a set rate per unit) were even lower than factory wages, but they allowed married women with young children to contribute to the family income. When sufficient space was available, families rented rooms to boarders, and women provided meals and housekeeping for the lodgers. Some female workers found other ways to balance work with the needs and constraints of family life. To gain greater autonomy in their work, black laundresses began cleaning clothes in their own homes, rather than their white employers' homes, so that they could control their own work hours. In 1881 black washerwomen in Atlanta conducted a two-week strike to secure higher fees from white customers.

AP® TIP

Compare the experiences of women in the urban workforce in the late 1800s to the experience of women in the Lowell factory system during the early 1800s.

Manufacturing also employed many child workers. By 1900 about 10 percent of girls and 20 percent of boys between the ages of ten and fifteen worked, and at least 1.7 million children under the age of sixteen held jobs. Employers often exposed children to dangerous and unsanitary conditions. Most child workers toiled long, hard hours breathing in dust and fumes as they labored in textile mills, tobacco plants, print shops, and coal mines.

Breaker Boys at the North Ashland Colliery
Breaker boys used their bare hands to break coal into pieces, sort pieces by size, and remove impurities. The dirty and dangerous work often led to injury and disease, and was sometimes fatal. Public outrage, compulsory education requirements, technological innovations, and child labor laws eventually led to the discontinuance of the practice by the 1920s. **What does this photograph reveal about the working conditions of child laborers?**

The Industrialization of Labor

> "A family of workers can always live well, but the man with a family of small children to support, unless his wife works also, has a small chance of living properly."
>
> — Carroll D. Wright, Director of the Massachusetts Bureau of the Statistics of Labor, 1882

In Indiana, young boys worked the night shift in dark, windowless glass factories. Children under the age of ten, known as "breaker boys," climbed onto filthy coal heaps and picked out unprocessed material. Working up to twelve-hour days, these children received less than a dollar a day.

Women and children worked because the average male head of household could not support his family on his own pay, despite the increase in real wages. As Carroll D. Wright, director of the Massachusetts Bureau of the Statistics of Labor, reported in 1882, "A family of workers can always live well, but the man with a family of small children to support, unless his wife works also, has a small chance of living properly." For example, in 1883 in Joliet, Illinois, a railroad brakeman tried to support his wife and eight children on $360 a year. A state investigator described the way they lived: "Clothes ragged, children half dressed and dirty. They all sleep in one room regardless of sex. The house is devoid of furniture, and the entire concern is as wretched as could be imagined." Not all laborers lived in such squalor, but many wageworkers barely lived at subsistence level.

Many laborers put in more than 10 hours a day on the job even though the average number of working hours dropped during this era. In the steel industry, blast-furnace operators toiled 12 hours a day, 7 days a week. They received a day off every 2 weeks, but only if they worked a 24-hour shift. Given the long hours and backbreaking work, it is not surprising that accidents were a regular feature of industrial life. Each year tens of thousands were injured on the job, and thousands died as a result of mine cave-ins, train wrecks, explosions in industrial plants, and fires at textile mills and garment factories. Railroad employment was especially unsafe — accidents ended the careers of one in six workers.

Although wages and working hours improved slightly for some workers, employers kept the largest share of the increased profits that resulted from industrialization. In 1877 John D. Rockefeller collected dividends at the rate of at least $720 an hour, roughly double what his average employee earned in a year. Despite some success stories, prospects for upward mobility for most American workers remained limited. A manual worker might rise into the ranks of the semi-skilled but would not make it into the middle class. And to achieve even this small upward mobility required putting the entire family to work and engaging in rigorous economizing, what one historian called "ruthless underconsumption." Despite their best efforts, most Americans remained part of the working class.

AP® TIP

Make sure you can explain how the income gap between employers and employees in the late nineteenth century reflected both continuity and change in United States history.

AP® ANALYZING SOURCES

Source: Bernhard Gillam, "Hopelessly Bound to the Stake," *Puck* magazine, 1883

About the source: In this image, the heads at the ends of the logs on the fire include wealthy industrialists, a political machine boss, and the "monopoly press." The stake the man is tied to is labeled "MONOPOLY," and the belt that chains him to the stake is labeled "WORKMAN."

Questions for Analysis

1. Describe the intended audience for this image.
2. Explain how Gillam uses symbols to convey his main argument in this cartoon.
3. Explain the historical developments that led to the viewpoint expressed by the cartoonist.

TEACHING IDEA

Analyzing Art and Images

Ask students to compare Victor Gillam's cartoon, "Hopelessly Bound to the Stake" (1883) to the engraving printed in the 1897 issue of *Scientific American*, "Manufacturing of Steel Tubing" (found on page 484). Use the following to guide their comparisons:

- Compare the use and significance of fire in the two images.
- Explain the point of view expressed in each image toward industrialization.

EXPLORING AP® THEMES

Work, Exchange, and Technology

Focus on the Review question about experiences of women, children, and men in the workforce. Put students into groups of three. In each student group, assign one student to describe the experiences of women, one to describe the experiences of children, and one to describe the experiences of men. Have each group complete a three-part Venn diagram to compare and contrast the experiences of all three groups. Possible answers include: *All three faced dangerous working conditions, long work hours, and low wages, and all were hired for unskilled positions. Men were able to unionize more easily, as they were more accepted by a larger number of unions. Their wages were also the highest out of the three groups. Women were hired for a limited number of positions due to their sex. Children were hired to do jobs that required close quarters. Women and children were paid lower wages than men and found it more difficult to join labor unions.*

EXPLORING AP® THEMES

Work, Exchange, and Technology

As a bell ringer or exit ticket, ask students to determine how the growth of labor unions altered the involvement of the government in the American economy. Possible answers include: *Labor unions increased government involvement in the American economy. Unions called for legislation focused on safer working conditions, shorter work hours, and increased wages. Since this time period, legislation has been introduced to protect workers in all three of these aspects.*

Period 6: 1865–1898

MODULE 6-5 Working People Organize

REVIEW

- What effects did industrialization have on skilled versus unskilled workers?
- How were the experiences of women and children in the labor force similar to and different from the experiences of male workers?

Organizing Unions

unions Groups of workers seeking rights and benefits from their employers through their collective efforts.

Faced with improving but inadequate wages and with hazardous working conditions, industrial laborers sought to counter the concentrated power of corporate capitalists by joining forces. They attempted to organize **unions** — groups of workers seeking rights and benefits from their employers through their collective efforts. Union organizing was prompted by attitudes that were common among employers. Most employers were convinced that they and their employees shared identical interests, and they believed that they were morally and financially entitled to establish policies on their workers' behalf. They refused to engage in negotiations with labor unions (a process known as **collective bargaining**). Although owners appreciated the advantages of companies banding together to eliminate competition or to lobby for favorable regulations, similar collective efforts by workers struck them as unfair, even immoral. It was up to the men who supplied the money and the machines — rather than the workers — to determine what was a fair wage and what were satisfactory working conditions. In 1877 William H. Vanderbilt, the son of transportation tycoon Cornelius Vanderbilt, explained this way of thinking: "Our men feel that although I . . . may have my millions and they the rewards of their daily toil, still we are about equal in the end. If they suffer, I suffer, and if I suffer they cannot escape." Needless to say, many workers disagreed.

Industrialists expected their paternalistic values to reduce grievances among their workforce. They sponsored sports teams, set up social clubs, and offered cultural activities. The railroad magnate George Pullman built a model village to house his workers. In return, capitalists demanded unquestioned loyalty from their employees.

Yet a growing number of working people failed to see the relationship between employer and employee as mutually beneficial. Increasingly, they considered labor unions to be the best vehicle for communication and negotiation between workers and owners. Though not the first national workers' organization, the **Knights of Labor**, founded in 1869, initiated the most extensive and successful campaign after the Civil War to unite workers and challenge the power of corporate capitalists. "There is no mutuality of interests . . . [between] labor and capital," the Massachusetts chapter of the Knights proclaimed. "It is the iron heel of a soulless monopoly, crushing the manhood out of sovereign citizens." In fact, the essential premise of the Knights was that all workers shared common interests that were very different from those of owners.

The Knights did not enjoy immediate success and did not really begin to flourish until Terence V. Powderly became the head of the organization in 1879. Powderly advocated for an eight-hour workday, the abolition of child labor, and equal pay for women. Under his leadership, the Knights accepted African Americans, immigrants, and women as members, though they excluded Chinese immigrant workers, as did other labor unions. As a result, the Knights experienced a surge in membership from 9,000 in 1879 to nearly a million in 1885, about 10 percent of the industrial workforce.

Rapid growth proved to be a mixed blessing. As membership grew, Powderly and the national organization exercised less and less control over local chapters. In fact, local chapters often defied the central organization by engaging in strikes, a tactic Powderly had officially disavowed. Members of the Knights struck successfully against the Union Pacific Railroad and the Missouri Pacific Railroad in 1885. The following year, on May 1, 1886, local assemblies of the Knights joined a nationwide strike to press for an eight-hour workday. However, this strike was soon overshadowed by events in Chicago that would prove to be the undoing of the Knights.

For months before the general strike, the McCormick Harvester plant in Chicago had been at the center of an often violent conflict over wages and work conditions. On May 3, 1886, police killed two strikers in a clash between union members and strikebreakers who tried to cross the picket lines. In response, a group of anarchists led by the German-born activist August Spies called

Knights of Labor Founded in 1869, a labor federation that aimed to unite all workers in one national union and challenge the power of corporate capitalists.

> "Our men feel that although I . . . may have my millions and they the rewards of their daily toil, still we are about equal in the end. If they suffer, I suffer, and if I suffer they cannot escape."
>
> William H. Vanderbilt, son of transportation tycoon Cornelius Vanderbilt, 1877

TEACHING IDEA

Class Discussion

Put the following statement up on the board/projector: "Our men feel that although I [. . .] may have my millions and they the rewards of their daily toil, still we are about equal in the end. If they suffer, I suffer, and if I suffer they cannot escape." – Cornelius Vanderbilt. Have students compose a prewrite to evaluate the extent to which they agree with Vanderbilt's assertion. Once they have finished, conduct a mini-debate and ask whether the statement is true.

Organizing Unions

> "There is no mutuality of interests... [between] labor and capital. It is the iron heel of a soulless monopoly, crushing the manhood out of sovereign citizens."
>
> *The Labor Movement: The Problem of To-Day, 1887*

Haymarket riot 1866 rally in Haymarket Square that resulted in violence. In its aftermath, the union movement in the United States went into temporary decline.

American Federation of Labor (AFL) Trade union federation founded in 1886. Led by its first president, Samuel Gompers, the AFL sought to organize skilled workers into trade-specific unions.

for a rally in Haymarket Square to protest police violence. Consisting mainly of foreign-born radicals, such anarchists believed that government represented the interests of capitalists and stifled freedom for workers. Anarchists differed among themselves, but they generally advocated tearing down government authority, restoring personal freedom, and forming worker communes to replace capitalism. To achieve their goals, anarchists like Spies advocated the violent overthrow of government.

The Haymarket rally began at 8:30 in the evening of May 4 and attracted no more than 1,500 people, who listened to a series of speeches as rain fell. By 10:30 p.m., when the crowd had dwindled to some 300 people, 180 policemen decided to break it up. As police moved into the square, someone set off a bomb. The police fired back, and when the smoke cleared, seven policemen and four protesters lay dead. Most of the fatalities and injuries resulted from the police crossfire. A subsequent trial convicted eight anarchists of murder, though there was no evidence that any of them had planted the bomb or used weapons. Four of them, including Spies, were executed. Although Powderly and other union leaders denounced the anarchists and the bombing, the incident greatly tarnished the labor movement. Capitalists and their allies in the press attacked labor unionists as radicals prone to violence and denounced strikes as un-American. Following this incident, which came to be known as the **Haymarket riot**, the membership rolls of the Knights plunged to below 500,000. By the mid-1890s, the Knights had fewer than 20,000 members.

As the fortunes of the Knights of Labor faded, the **American Federation of Labor** (AFL) grew in prominence, offering an alternative vision of unionization. Instead of one giant industrial union that included all workers, skilled and unskilled, the AFL organized only skilled craftsmen—the labor elite—into trade unions. In 1886 Samuel Gompers became president of the AFL. Gompers considered trade unions "the business organizations of the wage earners to attend to the business of the wage earners" and favored the use of strikes. No social reformer, the AFL president concentrated on obtaining better wages and hours for workers so that they could share in the

▲ **Women in the Labor Movement, 1884** This wood engraving shows the wives of striking coal miners jeering at Pinkerton detectives as they escort strikebreakers into the mines in Buchtel, Ohio in 1884. It was common for the family and friends of strikers in local communities to rally support on their behalf. **How does this image illustrate a rejection of nineteenth-century gender roles?**

EXPLORING AP® THEMES

Work, Exchange, and Technology

Have students imagine that an employer, a labor union leader, a strikebreaker, and an anarchist went out to dinner together. Assign students to write a five-minute dialogue that illustrates how each of the four people would have reacted to the Haymarket riot. Within the dialogue, students should point out that the rally was made into a violent affair by anarchists. Even though the riot was denounced by union leaders, employers painted the labor unions as radicals who could not be bargained with. Strikebreakers were mostly people who needed to make a living, but were caught in the crossfire of this argument. If time allows, have some students volunteer to perform their dialogues in front of the class.

TEACHING IDEA

Analyzing Art and Images

Before analyzing the image *Women in the Labor Movement*, review what the values of industrialists were when industrialization began. Industrialists were paternalistic and believed that their workers would support their decisions. Industrialists mostly believed that by doing what was best for the industry, they were doing the best they could for their workers. Industrialists also provided social clubs and sports teams for their workers, expecting such things to ease the grievances leveled against capitalists by the workforce.

BUILDING AP® SKILLS

Developments and Processes

As a class, analyze the graph depicting union membership. Discuss the provided question with students and ask why the year 1886 was included in the graph specifically. Possible answers include: *Unions such as the Knights of Labor accepted workers of all races and ethnicities, as well as men and women. This led to a great surge in union membership. In addition, public awareness of workplace issues such as low wages and unsafe working conditions led to increased interest in improving working conditions. Unfortunately, large numbers of union members proved to be hard to control. The year 1886 was included because it was the year of the Haymarket riot. Violence at the riot resulted in a denunciation of the strategies of labor unions as anarchistic, even though the violent actions of anarchists were not sanctioned by labor union leaders. The American Federation of Labor took a different path, and labor union membership began to rise again after 1886.*

BUILDING AP® SKILLS

Comparison

Draw a Venn diagram on the board/projector. Label one circle "Knights of Labor" and the other "American Federation of Labor." Either as a bell ringer or exit ticket, ask students to write information on the board in order to compare the goals, membership, and leaders of the Knights of Labor with those of the American Federation of Labor.

Period 6: 1865–1898

MODULE 6-5 Working People Organize

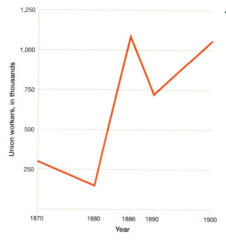

◀ **Union Membership, 1870–1900** Union membership fluctuated widely in the late nineteenth century. After reaching a low point in 1880, the number of union members rebounded. However, membership plummeted after 1886 only to soar again in the 1890s. **What developments account for the changes in union membership depicted on the graph between 1880 and 1900?**

Data from Richard B. Freeman, "Spurts in Union Growth: Defining Moments and Social Processes," working paper 6012, National Bureau of Economic Research, Cambridge, MA, 1997.

prosperity generated by industrial capitalism. By 1900 the AFL had around a million members. It achieved these numbers by recruiting the most independent, highest-paid, and least replaceable segment of the labor force — white male skilled workers. Unlike the Knights, the AFL had little or no place for women and African Americans in its ranks.

As impressive as the AFL's achievement was, the union movement as a whole experienced only limited success in the late nineteenth century. Only about one in fifteen industrial workers belonged to a union in 1900. Union membership was low for a variety of reasons. First, the political and economic power of corporations and the prospects of retaliation made the decision to sign up for union membership a risky venture. Second, the diversity of workers made organizing a difficult task. Foreign-born laborers came from many countries and were divided by language, religion, ethnicity, and history. Moreover, European immigrants quickly adopted native-born whites' racial prejudices against African Americans. Third, despite severe limitations in social mobility, American workers generally retained their faith in the benefits of the capitalist system. Finally, the government used its legal and military authority to side with employers and suppress militant workers.

Southern workers were the most resistant to union organizing. The agricultural background of mill workers left them with a heightened sense of individualism and isolation. In addition, their continued connection to family and friends in the countryside offered a potential escape route from industrial labor. Moreover, employers' willingness to use racial tensions to divide working-class black people and whites prevented them from joining together to further their common economic interests.

REVIEW

- What views did industrialists hold regarding organized labor?
- What were the primary differences between the Knights of Labor and the American Federation of Labor?

Labor Clashes Escalate

Homestead strike 1892 lockout strike by steelworkers at Andrew Carnegie's Homestead steel factory. The strike collapsed after a failed assassination attempt on Carnegie's plant manager, Henry Clay Frick.

Despite the difficulties of organizing workers, labor challenged some of the nation's largest industries in the late nineteenth century. Faced with owners' refusal to recognize or negotiate with unions, workers marshaled their greatest source of power: withholding their labor and going on strike. Employers in turn had powerful weapons at their command to break strikes. They could recruit strikebreakers and mobilize private and public security forces to protect their businesses. That workers went on strike against such odds testified to their desperation and courage (Map 6.5).

Labor mounted several highly publicized strikes in the 1890s in their efforts to combat industrial exploitation and secure better wages and working conditions. Perhaps the most famous was the 1892 **Homestead strike**. Steelworkers at Carnegie's Homestead, Pennsylvania factory near Pittsburgh played an active role in local politics and civic affairs. Residents generally believed that Andrew Carnegie's corporation paid decent wages that allowed them to support their families and buy their own homes. In 1892 craftsmen earned $180 a month, and they appeared to have

---

BUILDING AP® SKILLS

Causation

As an exit ticket, ask students, "How did employers react to the strategies of labor unions?" Possible answers include: *Employers hired strikebreakers to work in place of striking workers. Employers also employed security forces to protect their businesses and the strikebreakers. Sometimes the police were called to break up protests that were believed to be inciting violence.*

Labor Clashes Escalate

Period 6: 1865–1898

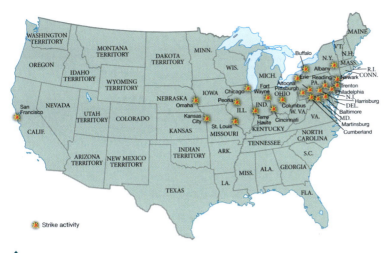

▲ **MAP 6.5 The Great Railroad Strike** This nationwide strike, precipitated by falling wages during the Depression of 1873, started in West Virginia and Pennsylvania and spread to Chicago, St. Louis, and San Francisco. The strike brought a halt to rail traffic as over 100,000 workers and another half a million sympathizers walked off their jobs. Violence broke out in Pittsburgh, resulting in more than twenty deaths. Federal troops were eventually dispatched to end the strike. Many workers quickly recognized the need to form unions to gain the power to stand up against employers and the government. **What factors account for the fact that most of the strike activity shown on this map is concentrated in a belt from the Mid-Atlantic to the Midwest?**

> **AP® TIP**
>
> Make sure you can explain both the immediate and distant causes of labor strikes and other conflicts between employers and workers in the late nineteenth century.

Carnegie's respect. Others, like John McLuckie, the twice elected mayor of Homestead and popular union boss, earned less than half that amount, and unskilled workers made even less.

In 1892, with steel prices falling, Carnegie decided to replace some of his skilled craftsmen with machinery, cut wages, save on labor costs, and bust McLuckie's union, the Amalgamated Association of Iron and Steel Workers. Knowing that his actions would provoke a strike and seeking to avoid the negative publicity that would result, Carnegie left the country and went to Scotland, leaving his plant manager, Henry Clay Frick, in charge.

Fiercely anti-union, Frick prepared for the strike by building a three-mile, fifteen-foot-high fence, capped with barbed wire and equipped with searchlights, around three sides of the Homestead factory. A hated symbol of the manager's hostility, the fence became known as "Fort Frick." Along the fourth side of the factory flowed the Monongahela River. Frick had no intention of negotiating seriously with the union on a new contract, and on July 1 he ordered a lockout. Only employees who rejected the union and accepted lower wages could return to work. The small town rallied around the workers, and the union members won a temporary victory. On July 6, barge-loads of armed **Pinkerton** detectives, hired by Frick to protect the plant, set sail toward the factory entrance alongside the Monongahela. From the shore, union men shot at the barges and set fire to a boat they pushed toward the Pinkertons. When the smoke cleared, the Pinkertons surrendered and hastily retreated onshore as women and men chased after them.

This triumph proved costly for the union. The battle left nine strikers and three Pinkerton detectives dead. Frick convinced the governor of Pennsylvania to send in state troops to protect the factory and the strikebreakers. Frick's efforts to end the strike spurred some radicals to action. Emma Goldman, an anarchist who advocated the violent overthrow of capitalism, declared that a blow against Frick would "strike terror in the enemy's ranks and make them realize that" America's

Pinkertons A company of private investigators and security guards sometimes used by corporations to break up strikes and labor disputes, most famously at the Homestead strike of 1892.

Period 6: 1865–1898

MODULE 6-5 Working People Organize

▲ **The Homestead Steel Strike, 1892** This lithograph depicts the battle between strikers at the Carnegie Steelworks in Homestead, Pennsylvania and Pinkerton detectives brought in to protect the mill and break the strike. The Pinkertons attempted to get to the plant by barge but were repelled by the strikers from the dock. The strike received international attention, and this illustration appeared in the British weekly newspaper *The Graphic* on July 30, 1892. **Why did each side resort to violence during the Homestead Steel Strike?**

working class "had its avengers." On July 23, Alexander Berkman, Goldman's partner, who had no connection with the union, entered Frick's office and shot the steel executive in the neck, leaving him wounded but alive. The resulting unfavorable publicity, together with the state's prosecution of the union, broke the strike. Subsequently, steel companies blacklisted the union leaders for life, and McLuckie fled Pennsylvania and wound up nearly penniless in Arizona.

Like Andrew Carnegie, George Pullman considered himself an enlightened employer, one who took good care of the men who worked in his luxury sleeping railcar factory outside Chicago. However, also like the steel titan, Pullman placed profits over personnel. In 1893 a severe economic depression prompted Pullman to cut wages without correspondingly reducing the rents that his employees paid for living in company houses. This dual blow to worker income and purchasing power led to a fierce strike the following year. The Pullman workers belonged to the American Railway Union, headed by Eugene V. Debs. After George Pullman refused to negotiate, the union voted to go on strike.

Pullman strike 1894 strike by workers against the Pullman railcar company. When the strike disrupted rail service nationwide, threatening mail delivery, President Grover Cleveland ordered federal troops to get the railroads moving again.

In the end, the **Pullman strike** was broken not by the Pullman company but by the federal government. President Grover Cleveland ordered federal troops to get the railroads operating, but the workers still refused to capitulate. Richard Olney, Cleveland's attorney general, then obtained an order from the federal courts to restrain Debs and other union leaders from continuing the strike. The government used the Sherman Antitrust Act (Module 6-4) to punish unions for conspiring to restrain trade, something it had rarely done with respect to large corporations. Refusing to comply, Debs and other union officials were charged with contempt, convicted under the Sherman Antitrust Act, and sent to jail. The strike collapsed.

AP® TIP
Be sure you can explain how and why the federal government responded to labor issues in the late nineteenth century.

Debs remained unrepentant. After serving his jail sentence, he became even more radical. In 1901 he helped establish the **Socialist Party of America**, appealing for working-class support by advocating the creation of a more just and humane economic system through the ballot box, not by violent revolution. Debs favored a nonviolent, democratic brand of socialism and managed to attract a base of supporters by articulating socialist doctrines in the language of cooperation and citizenship that many Americans shared. Debsian socialism appealed not only to industrial workers but also to dispossessed farmers and miners in the Southwest and Midwest.

BUILDING AP® SKILLS

Developments and Processes

As a bell ringer or exit ticket, ask students to provide specific historical evidence to answer the prompt, "How does the Pullman strike illustrate a change in government involvement in the economy?" Possible answers include: *The federal government became involved in the Pullman strike instead of staying out of the conflict as they had done before. Federal troops were sent in by President Grover Cleveland to get the railroads running again. Debs and other union leaders were arrested and convicted of restricting trade under the Sherman Anti-Trust Act.*

TEACHING IDEA

Incorporating Websites

Find the "Pullman Strike" lesson on the Stanford History Education Group's website (sheg.stanford.edu). This lesson requires students to analyze primary source sets. Students are asked to determine the point of view of each source, as one document in each primary source set supported the workers, and one document supported Pullman.

TEACHING IDEA

Incorporating Videos

Have students watch CNN Business' video "Labor Day's Violent Beginnings" (available on YouTube). This short video illustrates how Labor Day came to be, and how the Pullman strike essentially convinced the government to dedicate the first Monday of September as a national holiday, Labor Day. After watching the video, ask students to determine why Labor Day was established, as well as the other changes that came about due to the labor movement.

MODULE 6-5 Working People Organize

AP® ANALYZING SOURCES

Source: United States Supreme Court, *In re Debs*, 1895

"[W]e hold that the government of the United States is one having jurisdiction over every foot of soil within its territory, and acting directly upon each citizen; . . . that to it is committed power over interstate commerce and the transmission of the mail; . . . that in the exercise of those powers it is competent for the nation to remove all obstructions upon highways, natural or artificial, to the passage of interstate commerce or the carrying of the mail; . . . that the jurisdiction of courts to interfere in such matters by injunction is one recognized from ancient times and by indubitable authority; . . . that the complaint filed in this case clearly showed an existing obstruction of artificial highways for the passage of interstate commerce and the transmission of the mail - an obstruction not only temporarily existing, but threatening to continue; that under such complaint the Circuit Court had power to issue its process of injunction; that . . . the Circuit Court had authority to inquire whether its orders had been disobeyed, and when it found that they had been, then to proceed under section 725, Revised Statutes, which grants power 'to punish, by fine or imprisonment, . . . disobedience, . . . by any party . . . or other person, to any lawful writ, process, order, rule, decree or command . . . .'"

Questions for Analysis

1. Identify two federal powers cited by the Supreme Court to justify Debs's conviction.
2. Describe the Supreme Court's argument in this excerpt.
3. Explain the immediate and longer-term effects of the *Debs* decision on the labor movement.

AP® TIP

Analyze the ways that workers' organizations changed over the second half of the nineteenth century.

Industrial Workers of the World (IWW) Organization that grew out of the activities of the Western Federation of Miners in the 1890s and formed by Eugene V. Debs and other prominent labor leaders. Known as Wobblies, the IWW attempted to unite all skilled and unskilled workers in an effort to overthrow capitalism.

Western miners had a history of labor activism, and by the 1890s they were ready to listen to radical ideas. Shortly after the Homestead strike ended in 1892, silver miners in Coeur d'Alene, Idaho walked out after owners slashed their wages. Employers refused to recognize any union, obtained an injunction against the strike, imported strikebreakers to run the mines, and persuaded Idaho's governor to impose martial law. The work stoppage lasted four months, resulting in the arrest of six hundred strikers. Although the workers lost, the following year they succeeded in forming the Western Federation of Miners, which continued their fight.

The **Industrial Workers of the World** (IWW), which emerged largely through the efforts of the Western Federation of Miners, sought to raise wages, improve working conditions, and gain union recognition for the most exploited segments of American labor. The IWW, or "Wobblies" as they were popularly known, sought to unite all skilled and unskilled workers in an effort to overthrow capitalism. The Wobblies favored strikes and direct-action protests rather than collective bargaining or mediation. At their rallies and strikes, they often encountered government force and corporation-inspired mob violence. Nevertheless, the IWW had substantial appeal among lumberjacks in the Northwest, dockworkers in port cities, miners in the West, farmers in the Great Plains, and textile workers in the Northeast.

Even though industrialists usually had state and federal governments as well as the media on their side, workers continued to press for their rights. Workers used strikes as a last resort when business owners refused to negotiate or recognize their demands to organize themselves into unions. Although most late-nineteenth-century strikes failed, striking unionists nonetheless called for collective bargaining, higher wages, shorter hours, and improved working conditions — an agenda that unions and their political allies would build on in the future.

REVIEW

- How did the tactics used by management compare to those used by organized labor during the 1880s and 1890s?

TEACHING IDEA

Check for Understanding

There were many labor unions that originated during the mid- to late nineteenth century. To help students keep track of the various labor unions, assign a chart for students to describe the goals, leaders, and year of origin of each union. Students are also required to write a thesis and provide one piece of relevant historical evidence to argue which labor union was the most successful during this time period.

TRM Find **Handout 6.6 – Nineteenth Century Labor Unions** in the Teacher's Resource Materials.

MODULE 6-5 Working People Organize

TRM Suggested Responses to Questions

TEACHING IDEA

Analyzing Art and Images

Project the political cartoon, "The Tournament of To-Day — A Set-to Between Labor and Monopoly." Read about the source with students and point out each detail of the image that is referenced. Discuss the meaning of each label, such as "subsidized press," so students fully understand the terminology. You can also use the political cartoon analysis worksheet provided by the National Archives to help students slow down and try to understand every detail of the image before trying to determine its meaning as a whole (archives.gov).

▲ **Differentiation**

Provide additional help to students who struggle with reading political cartoons by allowing students to work in groups. Print out a colored copy of the political cartoon for each group. Allow the groups to circle important details and write questions in the margins of the paper. Circulate while students deconstruct the image to address any questions or misconceptions.

TEACHING IDEA

AP® Writing Historically Review

This question calls students' attention to their ability to construct an understanding through inference. To assist students along this path, consider the following activity. Using a few of the capitalized words in the cartoon such as "Monopoly," "Labor," "Strike," and "Legislature," have students connect one factual example of each term to the tone of the cartoon. For instance, some students might focus "Labor" on the Knights of Labor, and how they struggled for acceptance in the capitalist marketplace during the Gilded Age. Defining each of these terms with specific examples will cause students to think more about the historical examples that can be used to explain the cartoon.

Period 6: 1865–1898

AP® WRITING HISTORICALLY — Short-Answer Question Practice

ACTIVITY

Read the following question carefully and write a short response. Use complete sentences.

Using the following image, answer (a), (b), and (c).

Source: Friedrich Grätz, "The Tournament of To-Day — A Set-to Between Labor and Monopoly," *Puck* magazine, 1883

About the source: The text on the knight's shield reads "CORRUPTION OF LEGISLATURE," the plume in his helmet is labeled "ARROGANCE," the horse's armor is labeled "MONOPOLY," and the knight's lance is labeled "SUBSIDIZED PRESS." The banner in the far left reads, "RESERVED FOR CAPITALISTS." The man facing off against the knight is wearing a hat labeled "LABOR," holding a mallet labeled "STRIKE," and riding a mule labeled "POVERTY."

a. Briefly describe ONE perspective about economics expressed in the image.
b. Briefly explain ONE specific historical event or development that led to the perspective expressed in the image.
c. Briefly explain ONE specific historical argument that could be used to challenge the perspective expressed in the image.

Module 6-6

A New Wave of Immigrants

TRM Suggested Responses to Questions

LEARNING TARGETS

By the end of this module, you should be able to:

- Explain the factors that led to increased immigration to the United States.
- Explain the similarities and differences for why various groups migrated to the United States and the locations those groups generally settled in.
- Explain the debates caused by immigration to the United States.

THEMATIC FOCUS

Migration and Settlement

During the late 1800s, immigration to the United States soared as so-called "new immigrants" from southern and eastern Europe came in increasingly large numbers alongside "old immigrants" from northern and western Europe. Most European immigrants settled in big cities along the East Coast or in the Midwest while immigrants from Asia settled in the West. The surge of immigration led to debates over assimilation, a nativist backlash, and passage of the first race-based federal immigration legislation, the Chinese Exclusion Act (1882).

HISTORICAL REASONING FOCUS

Comparison

TASK ▶ As you read this module, remember that historical reasoning processes overlap. While you engage in the activity of comparison, you will need to examine causation (causes and effects). Think about both the push factors (reasons why immigrants would leave their homeland) and pull factors (reasons why immigrants would choose to come to the United States) for migration to the United States. Also consider how immigrants changed the demographics of urban cities and the West. Then, compare those causes and effects. Make sure also to compare the reactions toward various groups of immigrants.

A flood of immigrants entered the United States from 1880 to the outbreak of World War I in 1914. Unlike the majority of earlier immigrants, who had come from northern Europe, most of the more than 20 million people who arrived during this period came from southern and eastern Europe. A smaller number of immigrants came from Asia and Mexico. Most remained in cities, which grew as a result. Urban immigrants were welcomed by political bosses (see Module 6-7), who saw in them a chance to gain the allegiance of millions of new voters. At the same time, their coming upset many middle- and upper-class city dwellers who blamed these new arrivals for lowering the quality of urban life.

For more than three hundred years following the settlement of the North American colonies, the majority of white immigrants to America were northern European Protestants. Unlike European immigrants who came voluntarily, black people were brought forcibly from Africa, mainly by way of the West Indies and the Caribbean. Although African Americans originally followed their own religious practices, most eventually converted to Protestantism. By the end of the nineteenth century, however, a new pattern of immigration had emerged, one that included much greater ethnic and religious diversity. These new immigrants often encountered hostility from those whose ancestors had arrived generations earlier, and faced the difficult challenge of retaining their cultural identities while becoming assimilated as Americans.

TEACHING IDEA

Check for Understanding

There were many reasons for the increase of immigration during the nineteenth century. Help students practice recognizing the difference between push and pull factors by completing a T-chart in pairs.

TRM Find **Handout 6.7 – Nineteenth Century Immigration Push and Pull Factors** in the Teacher's Resource Materials.

Period 6: 1865–1898

MODULE 6-6 A New Wave of Immigrants

Immigrants Arrive from Many Lands

Immigration to the United States was part of a worldwide phenomenon. In addition to the United States, European immigrants also journeyed to other countries in the Western Hemisphere, Asia and India. Whereas most immigrants voluntarily left their homelands to find new job opportunities or to obtain land to start their own farms, some made the move bound by labor contracts that limited their movement during the terms of the agreement. Chinese, Mexican, and Italian workers made up a large portion of this group.

The late nineteenth century saw a shift in the country of origin of immigrants to the United States: Instead of coming from northern and western Europe, many now came from southern and eastern European countries, most notably Italy, Greece, Austria-Hungary, Poland, and Russia. Most of those settling on American shores after 1880 were Catholic or Jewish and hardly knew a word of English. They tended to be even poorer than immigrants who had arrived before them, coming mainly from rural areas and lacking suitable skills for a rapidly expanding industrial society. Even after relocating to a new land and a new society, such immigrants struggled to break patterns of poverty that were, in many cases, centuries in the making.

Immigrants came from other parts of the world as well. From 1860 to 1924, some 450,000 Mexicans migrated to the U.S. Southwest. Many traveled to El Paso, Texas, near the Mexican border, and from there hopped aboard one of three railroad lines to jobs on farms and in mines, mills, and construction. Cubans, Spaniards, and Bahamians traveled to the Florida cities of Key West and Tampa, where they established and worked in cigar factories.

Despite the 1882 Chinese Exclusion Act (Module 6-2), tens of thousands of Chinese attempted to immigrate, many claiming to be family members of those already in the country. Some first went to Canada or Mexico, but very few managed to cross over the border illegally. Although Congress excluded Chinese immigration after 1882, it did not close the door to migrants from Japan. Unlike the Chinese, the Japanese had not competed with white workers for jobs on railroad and other construction projects.

Immigrants came to the United States largely for economic, political, and religious reasons. Nearly all were poor and expected to find ways to make money in America. U.S. railroads and steamship companies advertised in Europe and recruited passengers by emphasizing economic opportunities in the United States. Early immigrants wrote to relatives back home extolling the virtues of what they had found, perhaps exaggerating their success.

AP® TIP
Compare the economic, political, and religious reasons for immigration in the late nineteenth century to those of earlier periods of American history.

AP® ANALYZING SOURCES

Victor Gillam/Judge, September 19, 1903/Wikimedia Commons

Source: F. Victor Gillam, "The Immigrant. Is He an Acquisition or a Detriment?" *Judge*, 1903

About the source: The signs in the cartoon read (from left to right): "HE IS A MENACE. – CITIZEN," "HE IS BRAWN AND MUSCLE FOR MY COUNTRY. – UNCLE SAM," "HE GIVES ME CHEAP LABOR. – CONTRACTOR," "HE CHEAPENS MY LABOR. [– WORKMAN]," "HE'S A PUZZLE TO ME. [– STATESMAN]," "HE BRINGS DISEASE. [– HEALTH OFFICER]," and "HE MAKES VOTES FOR ME. [– POLITICIAN]." The man in the center carries a box that reads, "ONE MILLION IMMIGRANTS CAME TO THE U.S. IN TWELVE MONTHS."

Questions for Analysis
1. Identify the arguments for and against immigration in this cartoon.
2. Describe one perspective about immigrants expressed in the cartoon.
3. Explain the causes of European immigration to the United States in the late 1800s.
4. Explain the context for the cartoon.

The importance of economic incentives in luring immigrants is underscored by the fact that millions returned to their home countries after they had earned sufficient money. Of the more than 10 million immigrants from 1875 to 1899, 3 million returned home. Immigrants facing religious or political persecution in their homeland were the least likely to return.

REVIEW

- In what ways was immigration from southern and eastern Europe in the late 1800s similar to immigration from northern and western Europe in the early 1800s?
- In what ways was it different?

Creating Immigrant Communities

In cities such as New York, Boston, and Chicago, immigrants occupied neighborhoods that took on the distinct ethnic characteristics of the groups that inhabited them. A cacophony of different languages echoed in the streets as new residents continued to communicate in their mother tongues. The neighborhoods of immigrant groups often were clustered together, so residents were as likely to learn phrases in their neighbors' languages as they were to learn English.

The formation of **ghettos** — neighborhoods dominated by a single ethnic, racial, or class group — eased immigrants' transition into American society. Living within these ethnic enclaves made it easier for immigrants to find housing, hear about jobs, buy food, and seek help from those with whom they felt most comfortable. Mutual aid societies sprang up to provide social welfare benefits, including insurance payments and funeral rites. Group members established social centers where immigrants could play cards or dominoes, chat and gossip over tea or coffee, host dances and benefits, or just relax among people who shared a common heritage. In San Francisco's Chinatown, the largest Chinese community in California, such organizations usually consisted of people who had come from the same towns in China. These groups performed a variety of services, including finding jobs for their members, resolving disputes, campaigning against anti-Chinese discrimination, and sponsoring parades and other cultural activities. One society member explained: "We are strangers in a strange country. We must have an organization to control our country fellows and develop our friendship." That same impulse to band together occurred in immigrant communities throughout the nation. The establishment of clubs and cultural centers in immigrant communities throughout the nation demonstrated the commitment of immigrant groups to enhance their communities.

AP® TIP
Compare the role of community and religion in the lives of new immigrants and the lives of African Americans in the late nineteenth century.

◀ **Polish Saloon in Chicago, 1903** The *Polska Scaya* was a saloon located in the heart of one of the Polish neighborhoods in Chicago. Saloons were a central institution of immigrant culture, where men spent a good deal of leisure time. They read newspapers written in their native languages, swapped information about job opportunities, enjoyed time away from overcrowded tenements, discussed politics, and fostered bonds of masculinity exclusive of women. However, the excessive drinking associated with saloons put a severe strain on family health and finances, especially when drunken husbands and fathers lost their tempers at home or squandered their wages on alcohol. **What does this photograph reveal about life in immigrant communities?**

TEACHING IDEA

Incorporating Websites

To deepen student understanding of the urban life in the 1900s, you may wish to incorporate the following in your class:

■ PBS' American Experience collection of photos of "Boston in the Early 1900s" compared with photos of Boston today. Available on PBS' website (pbs.org).

■ "21 pictures of New York City in the early 1900s" compiled by Sarah Jacobs. Available on Business Insider's website (businessinsider.com).

■ Friedman Fine Art's collection of "Historical Chicago Photographs" (chicago-photographs.com).

Besides family and civic associations, churches and synagogues provided religious and social activities for urban immigrants. Between 1865 and 1900, the number of Catholic churches nationwide more than tripled. Like mutual aid societies, churches offered food and clothing to those who were ill or unable to work and fielded sports teams to compete in recreational leagues. Immigrants altered the religious practices and rituals in their churches to meet their own needs and expectations, many times over the objections of their clergy. German Catholics challenged Vatican policy by insisting that each ethnic group have its own priests and parishes and various other ethnic groups and demanded that their parishes adopt religious icons that they had worshipped in the old country.

Religious worship also varied among Jews. German Jews had arrived in the United States in an earlier wave of immigration than their eastern European counterparts. By the late nineteenth century, they had embraced Reform Judaism and established a major cultural center in Cincinnati, Ohio with the founding of the Union of American Hebrew Congregations. This brand of Judaism relaxed strict standards of worship, including absolute fidelity to kosher dietary laws, and allowed prayers to be said in English. By contrast, eastern European Jews typically observed the traditional faith, maintained a kosher diet, and prayed in Hebrew.

With few immigrants literate in English, over a thousand new foreign-language newspapers came into existence to inform their readers of local, national, and international events. These newspapers helped sustain ethnic solidarity in the New World as well as maintain ties to the Old World. Newcomers could learn about social and cultural activities in their communities and keep abreast of news from their homeland.

Like other communities with poor, unskilled populations, immigrant neighborhoods bred crime. Young men joined gangs based on ethnic heritage and battled with those of other immigrant groups to protect their turf. Adults formed underworld organizations — some of them tied to international criminal syndicates, such as the Mafia — that trafficked in prostitution, gambling, robbery, and murder. Tongs (secret organizations) in New York City's and San Francisco's Chinatowns controlled the opium trade, gambling, and prostitution in their communities. New York City police and municipal court records from 1898 described the frequency "of forgery, violation of corporation ordinance, as disorderly persons (failure to support wife or family), both grades of larceny, and of the lighter grade of assault."

Crime was not the only social problem that plagued immigrant communities. Newspapers and court records reported husbands abandoning wives and children, engaging in drunken and disorderly conduct, or abusing their family. Boarders whom immigrant families took into their homes for economic reasons also posed problems. Cramped spaces created a lack of privacy, and male boarders sometimes attempted to assault the woman of the house while her husband and children were out to work or in school. Finally, generational conflicts within families began to develop as American-born children of immigrants questioned their parents' values. Thus the social organizations and mutual aid societies that immigrant groups established were

AP® TIP
Make sure you understand and can explain the effects of the challenges facing immigrant neighborhoods in the late 1800s.

◀ **Mulberry Street, New York City, c. 1900** This colorized photograph taken by Jacob Riis depicts a vibrant scene on Mulberry Street, in the heart of New York City's Little Italy. Street vendors can be seen selling fresh produce and other goods as pedestrians and horse-drawn carriages make their way. The population of New York City swelled from less than one million to over three million from 1870 to 1900, mostly due to European immigration. **What does the photograph reveal about life in New York City at the turn of the century?**

more than a simple expression of ethnic solidarity and pride. They were also a response to the very real problems that challenged the health and stability of immigrant communities.

REVIEW

- How did late-nineteenth-century immigrants adapt to life in America?
- What social problems did they face?

Hostility toward Recent Immigrants

On October 28, 1886, the United States held a gala celebration for the opening of the Statue of Liberty in New York Harbor, a short distance from Ellis Island. French sculptors Frédéric-Auguste Bartholdi and Alexandre-Gustave Eiffel had designed the monument to appear at the Centennial Exposition in Philadelphia in 1876. Ten years overdue, the statue arrived in June 1885, but funds were still needed to finish construction of a base on which the sculpture would stand. Ordinary people dipped into their pockets for spare change, contributing to a campaign that raised $100,000 so that Lady Liberty could finally hold her uplifted torch for all to see. In 1903 the inspiring words of Emma Lazarus, a Jewish poet, were inscribed on the pedestal welcoming new generations of immigrants.

> Give me your tired, your poor,
> Your huddled masses yearning to breathe free,
> The wretched refuse of your teeming shore,
> Send these, the homeless, tempest-tossed to me,
> I lift my lamp beside the golden door!

Despite the welcoming inscription on the Statue of Liberty, many Americans whose families had arrived before the 1880s considered the influx of immigrants from southern and eastern

AP® ANALYZING SOURCES

Source: Saum Song Bo, *A Chinese View of the Statue of Liberty*, 1885

"SIR: A paper was presented to me yesterday for inspection, and I found it to be specially drawn up for subscription among my countrymen toward the Pedestal Fund of the . . . Statue of Liberty. Seeing that the heading is an appeal to American citizens, to their love of country and liberty. . . . But the word liberty makes me think of the fact that this country is the land of liberty for men of all nations except the Chinese. I consider it as an insult to us Chinese to call on us to contribute toward building in this land a pedestal for a statue of Liberty. That statue represents Liberty holding a torch which lights the passage of those of all nations who come into this country. But are the Chinese allowed to come? As for the Chinese who are here, are they allowed to enjoy liberty as men of all other nationalities enjoy it? Are they allowed to go about everywhere free from the insults, abuse, assaults, wrongs and injuries from which men of other nationalities are free? . . .

[W]hether [the Chinese Exclusion Act] or the statue to Liberty will be the more lasting monument to tell future ages of the liberty and greatness of this country, will be known only to future generations.

Liberty, we Chinese do love and adore thee; but let not those who deny thee to us, make of thee a graven image[1] and invite us to bow down to it."

[1] An object of worship.

Questions for Analysis

1. Identify the reason Saum Song Bo wrote this letter.
2. Describe Saum Song Bo's complaint.
3. Explain the reasons why Saum Song Bo is skeptical of the promise of liberty for Chinese people in the United States.

(Continued)

TEACHING IDEA

Project Idea

Have students write a letter from the perspective of an immigrant to the United States to address the review questions. In the letter, students should describe the social problems that immigrants faced, such as language barriers, poverty, and crime, as well as the ways that immigrants adapted to life in America, such as living in communities with immigrants from similar cultures and being part of religious organizations.

TRM Suggested Responses to Questions

TRM Module 6.6 AP® Analyzing Sources Handout 2

BUILDING AP® SKILLS

Comparison

As a bell ringer or exit ticket, have students read the poem by Emma Lazarus and the letter written by Saum Song Bo. Would Saum Song Bo agree with the sentiments conveyed in the poem by Lazarus? Write a five-line response poem from Saum's perspective.

TEACHING IDEA

Incorporating Websites

Find "Explore It: The Statue of Liberty" on the PBS Learning Media website (pbslearningmedia.org). This interactive overview allows students to physically navigate the Statue of Liberty, learn fun facts, and watch a video to learn more about the statue. Have students discuss what they have learned in small groups.

Period 6: 1865–1898

MODULE 6-6 A New Wave of Immigrants

Source: United States Supreme Court, *Yick Wo v. Hopkins*, 1886

"[I]n 1880, San Francisco passed a fire-safety ordinance that all laundries operating in wooden buildings be licensed or the owners would risk criminal penalties. After the city government refused to grant licenses to nearly all Chinese laundries while approving those run by whites, Yick Wo, the owner of one rejected establishment, refused to close his business and was prosecuted. . . .

[P]etitioners have complied with every requisite, deemed by the law or by the public officers charged with its administration, necessary for the protection of neighboring property from fire, or as a precaution against injury to the public health. No reason whatever, except the will of the supervisors, is assigned why they should not be permitted to carry on, in the accustomed manner, their harmless and useful occupation, on which they depend for a livelihood. And while this consent of the supervisors is withheld from them and from two hundred others who have also petitioned, all of whom happen to be Chinese subjects, eighty others, not Chinese subjects, are permitted to carry on the same business under similar conditions. The fact of this discrimination is admitted. No reason for it is shown, and the conclusion cannot be resisted, that no reason for it exists except hostility to the race and nationality to which the petitioners belong, and which in the eye of the law is not justified. The discrimination is, therefore, illegal, and the public administration which enforces it is a denial of the equal protection of the laws and a violation of the Fourteenth Amendment of the Constitution. The imprisonment of the petitioners is, therefore, illegal, and they must be discharged."

Questions for Analysis

1. Identify the main issue in *Yick Wo v. Hopkins* and the Supreme Court's decision in that case.
2. Explain the reasoning behind the Supreme Court's decision in *Yick Wo v. Hopkins*.

Questions for Comparison

1. Explain how each document reflects a common context.
2. Evaluate the extent to which the *Yick Wo v. Hopkins* decision undermines Saum Song Bo's argument.

Europe, Mexico, the Caribbean, and Asia at best a necessary evil and at worst a menace. Industrialists counted on immigrants to provide cheap labor. Not surprisingly, existing industrial workers saw the newcomers as a threat to their economic livelihoods and believed that their arrival would result in greater competition for jobs and lower wages. Moreover, even though most immigrants came to America to find work and improve the lives of their families, a small portion antagonized and frightened capitalists and middle-class Americans with their radical calls for the reorganization of society and the overthrow of the government. Of course, the vast majority of immigrants were not radicals, but a large proportion of radicals were recent immigrants. During times of labor-management strife, this fact made it easier for businessmen and their spokesmen in the press to associate all immigrants with anti-American radicalism.

Anti-immigrant fears linked to ideas about race and ethnicity had a long history in the United States. In 1790 Congress passed a statute restricting citizenship to those deemed white. Among those excluded from citizenship were American Indians, who were regarded as savages, and African Americans, most of whom were enslaved at the time. In the 1857 *Dred Scott* case (Module 5-3) the Supreme Court ruled that even free black people were not citizens. From the very beginning of the United States, largely Protestant lawmakers debated whether Catholics and Jews qualified as whites. Although lawmakers ultimately included Catholics and Jews within their definition of "white," over the next two centuries Americans viewed racial categories as not simply matters of skin color. Ethnicity (nationality or culture of origin) and religion became absorbed into and intertwined with racial categories. A sociological study of Homestead, Pennsylvania, published in 1910, broke down the community along the following constructed racial lines: "Slav, English-speaking European, native white, and colored." Russian Jewish immigrants were often recorded as

---

BUILDING AP® SKILLS

Sourcing and Situation

In pairs, have students complete a HIPP analysis of both Saum Song Bo's letter and the decision of the U.S. Supreme Court in *Yick Wo v. Hopkins*, 1886 (a refresher on HIPP can be found on page 8). Once complete, have students answer the Questions for Comparison together.

TEACHING IDEA

Connecting the Dots

Throughout the module, have students create a timeline to help them visualize the progression of anti-immigrant fears in the United States. Include events like the 1790 statute declaring that only those deemed white were citizens and the 1857 *Dred Scott* case, among others.

EXPLORING AP® THEMES

Migration and Settlement

Ask students to put themselves in the shoes of a recent immigrant to the United States. Have students write a diary entry explaining their reactions to the connections made between radicals and immigrants, which fueled anti-immigrant fears. How do you feel about radicalism? Does anti-American radicalism truly reflect the sentiments of most immigrants? How does the anti-immigrant movement affect your ability to adapt to life in the United States?

"Hebrews" rather than as Russians, suggesting that Jewishness was seen by Christian America as a racial identity.

Natural scientists and social scientists gave credence to the idea that some races and ethnic groups were superior and others were inferior. Referring to Darwin's theory of evolution, biologists and anthropologists constructed measures of racial hierarchies, placing descendants of northern Europeans with lighter complexions — Anglo-Saxons, Teutonics, and Nordics — at the top of the evolutionary scale. Those with darker skin were deemed inferior "races," with black people and American Indians at the bottom. Scholars attempting to make disciplines such as history more "scientific" accepted these racial classifications. The prevailing sentiment of this era reflected demeaning images of many immigrant groups: Irish as drunkards, Mexicans and Cubans as lazy, Italians as criminals, Hungarians as ignorant peasants, Jews as cheap and greedy, and Chinese as drug addicts. These characteristics supposedly resulted from inherited biological traits, rather than from extreme poverty or other environmental conditions.

Newer immigrants, marked as racially inferior, became a convenient target of hostility. Skilled craftsmen born in the United States viewed largely unskilled workers from abroad who would work for low wages as a threat to their attempts to form unions and keep wages high. Middle-class city dwellers blamed urban problems on the rising tide of foreigners. In addition, Protestant purists felt threatened by Catholics and Jews and believed these "races" incapable or unworthy of assimilation into what they considered to be the superior white, Anglo-Saxon, and Protestant culture.

Nativism — the belief that foreigners pose a serious danger to one's native society and culture — arose as a reactionary response to immigration. Nativist sentiment, directed primarily at the large numbers of Irish and German immigrants in the 1840s and 1850s, fueled the rise of the short-lived American Party (Module 5-3). In 1887 Henry F. Bowers of Clinton, Iowa founded the American Protective Association. The group proposed restricting Catholic immigration, making English literacy a prerequisite to American citizenship, and prohibiting Catholics from teaching in public schools or holding public offices. New England elites, such as Massachusetts

AP® TIP
Evaluate the extent to which American attitudes toward race and ethnicity in the late nineteenth century represented a change from earlier eras.

nativism The belief that foreigners pose a serious danger to the nation's society and culture. Nativist sentiment rose in the United States as the size and diversity of the immigrant population grew.

AP® ANALYZING SOURCES

Source: *Secret Oath of the American Protective League*, 1893

"I do most solemnly promise and swear that I will always . . . use my utmost power to strike the shackles and chains of blind obedience to the Roman Catholic church from the hampered and bound consciences of a priest-ridden and church-oppressed people; . . . that I will use my influence to promote the interest of all Protestants everywhere in the world that I may be; that I will not employ a Roman Catholic in any capacity if I can procure the services of a Protestant.

I furthermore promise and swear that I will . . . do all in my power to retard and break down the power of the Pope, in this country or any other; . . . nor will I enter into any agreement with a Roman Catholic to strike or create a disturbance whereby the Catholic employees may undermine and substitute their Protestant co-workers. . . .

I furthermore promise and swear that I will not countenance the nomination, in any caucus or convention, of a Roman Catholic for any office in the gift of the American people, and that I will not vote for, or counsel others to vote for, any Roman Catholic, but will vote only for a Protestant, so far as may lie in my power. . . . that I will at all times endeavor to place the political positions of this government in the hands of Protestants, to the entire exclusion of the Roman Catholic church, of the members thereof, and the mandate of the Pope."

Questions for Analysis
1. Identify the main provisions of the American Protective League oath.
2. Describe the relationship between nativism and anti-Catholicism illustrated by this oath.
3. Explain the effects of the sentiments expressed in the oath on American society.

Period 6: 1865–1898

MODULE 6-6 A New Wave of Immigrants

senator Henry Cabot Lodge and writer John Fiske, argued that what they called "southern European, Semitic, and Slavic races" did not fit into the "community of race" that had founded the United States. In 1893 Lodge and fellow Harvard graduates established the Immigration Restriction League and lobbied for federal legislation that would exclude adult immigrants unable to read in their own language.

Proposals to restrict immigration, however, did nothing to deal with the millions of foreigners already in America. To preserve their status and power and increase the size of the native-born population, nativists embraced the idea of **eugenics** — a pseudoscience that advocated "biological engineering" — and supported the selective breeding of "desirable" races to counter the rapid population growth of "useless" races. Accordingly, eugenicists promoted the institutionalization of people deemed "unfit," sterilization of those considered mentally impaired, and the licensing and regulation of marriages to promote better breeding. In pushing for such measures, eugenicists believed that they were following the dictates of modern science and acting in a humane fashion to prevent those deemed unfit from causing further harm to themselves and to society.

Others took a less harsh approach. As had been the case with American Indians, reformers stressed the need for immigrants to assimilate into the dominant culture, embrace the values of individualism and self-help, adopt American styles of dress and grooming, and exhibit loyalty to the U.S. government. They encouraged immigrant children to attend public schools, where they would learn to speak English and adopt American cultural rituals by celebrating holidays such as Thanksgiving and Columbus Day and reciting the pledge of allegiance, introduced in 1892. Educators encouraged adult immigrants to attend night classes to learn English.

If immigrants were not completely assimilated, neither did they remain the same people who had lived on the farms and in the villages of Europe, Asia, Mexico, and the Caribbean. Some sought to become full-fledged Americans or at least see that their children did so. Writer Israel Zangwill, an English American Jew, furnished the enduring image of assimilation in his play *The Melting-Pot*. Zangwill portrayed people from distinct backgrounds entering the cauldron of American life, mixing together, and emerging as citizens identical to their native-born counterparts.

melting pot Popular metaphor for immigrant assimilation into American society. According to this ideal, all immigrants underwent a process of Americanization that produced a homogenous society.

However, the image of America as a **melting pot** worked better as an ideal than as a mirror of reality. Immigrants during this period never fully lost the social, cultural, religious, and political identities they had brought with them. Even if all immigrants had sought full assimilation, which they did not, the anti-immigrant sentiment of many native-born Americans reinforced their status as strangers and aliens. The same year that Zangwill's play was published, Alfred P. Schultz, a New York physician, provided a dim view of the prospects of assimilation in his book *Race or Mongrel*. Schultz dismissed the melting pot theory that public schools could convert the children of all "races" into Americans.

Thus most immigrants faced the dilemma of assimilating while holding on to their heritage. Sociologist and civil rights activist W. E. B. Du Bois summed up this predicament for one of the nation's earliest transported groups. In *The Souls of Black Folk*, Du Bois wrote that African Americans felt a "two-ness," an identity carved out of their African heritage together with their lives as enslaved and free people in America. This "double-consciousness . . . two souls, two thoughts, two unreconciled strivings" also applied to immigrants at the turn of the twentieth century. Immigrants who entered the country after 1880 were more like vegetable soup — an amalgam of distinct parts within a common broth — than a melting pot.

REVIEW

- What aspects of late nineteenth-century American life fostered hostility toward immigrants?
- In what ways was the United States a "melting pot" for immigrants? In what ways was it a "vegetable soup" for immigrants?

EXPLORING AP® THEMES

American and Regional Culture

Assign the following Short-Answer Question for homework:

a. What attempts were made to assimilate immigrants?

b. To what extent were immigrants assimilated?

c. How does the assimilation of immigrants compare to the assimilation of American Indians?

Possible answers include:

a. *Immigrants were forced to adopt American clothing, speak English, and celebrate American holidays.*

b. *Many immigrants began to adopt American customs, but treasured their own culture and language. Other immigrants sought to become as American as possible.*

c. *Both immigrants and American Indians were pressured into leaving behind their traditions in favor of American traditions. Loyalty to the United States was one aspect of assimilation that was pushed, as it was considered very important by many native-born Americans.*

TEACHING IDEA

Incorporating Videos

Find a video of Schoolhouse Rock's "The Great American Melting Pot" to show in class (available on YouTube). Before watching it, source the video with students by completing a HIPP analysis (a refresher on HIPP can be found on page 8). Watch the video and then ask students how the message in the video compares to the idea of the vegetable soup in the textbook.

AP® WRITING HISTORICALLY: Responding to a Long-Essay Question

Consider the following long-essay question, which asks you to reflect on what you have learned in this module as well as earlier modules in Period 6.

> Evaluate the extent of difference in the experiences of European and Asian immigrants to the United States in the period 1865 to 1900.

Step 1: Break down the prompt.

Notice that this prompt asks you to compare the experiences of two groups of immigrants, Europeans and Chinese, during the second half of the nineteenth century. While the prompt uses the term "extent of difference," evaluating the extent of difference is a reminder that you also need to evaluate the other, implicit half of the reasoning process, the extent of similarity. Being aware that you need to do both in your essay is the first step toward demonstrating historical complexity.

Step 2: List and categorize your historical knowledge, then use GEM to refine your historical argument.

Start your brainstorm by jotting down all the relevant historical information you can remember. Then begin to categorize that information under 3 or 4 topics, making sure that at least one topic represents a historical difference and at least one topic represents a historical similarity. Keep in mind both the ACE and GEM strategies as you build an outline for your response. Complete the following graphic organizer or one of your own making as you organize your thoughts to answer the prompt with a complex and well supported argument.

(Difference)/ Similarity	Difference / Similarity	Difference / Similarity	Difference / Similarity
Chinese immigrants faced more discrimination than European immigrants			
Evidence: • Chinese workers not allowed to join major labor unions • Anti-Chinese violence in western states • Chinese Exclusion Act	**Evidence:**	**Evidence:**	**Evidence:**
Nuance: • European immigrants faced discrimination and nativism, though to a lesser extent than Chinese immigrants • *Yick Wo v. Hopkins* ruling demonstrates that U.S. government did not always allow discrimination against the Chinese	**Nuance:**	**Nuance:**	**Nuance:**
Connection 1: Anti-Chinese sentiment was a continuation of nativist beliefs that emerged in response to the Irish and German immigration in the 1840s and 1850s.	**Connection 2:**		

Step 3: Set the context, craft a thesis, and write the introduction of your essay.

Immigration is a major topic in American history, so when thinking about setting the context you are going to want to think equally big. The phenomena of industrialization and urbanization are similarly large developments that could be used to provide context in the opening paragraph. For your thesis, remember to make 3 to 4 specific, evaluative claims, and to include at least one difference.

(Continued)

TRM Suggested Responses to Questions

TEACHING IDEA

AP® Writing Historically Workshop

This is a complex essay question that necessitates careful planning by students. For instance, students may want to consider how they define "experiences" in the prompt. As an example, some may focus their response on how immigrant populations were treated by Americans after they immigrated to the United States. Still others may focus their analysis on the experiences of immigrants as they settled into a new life in the United States. More complex answers will likely answer both the experiences of immigrant populations and the reactions to immigrant populations. Before students write, consider having them define these categories of analysis.

ACTIVITY

Follow the steps provided and use *ACE* (Answer, Cite, Explain) to structure your argument in a full essay that responds to the prompt at the beginning of the box. Be sure to also use *GEM* (Generate nuance, Explain both sides, Make relevant, insightful connections beyond the prompt, either within its time period or across multiple time periods) to incorporate multiple examples of historical complexity in your essay.

You may use the example claim in the graphic organizer in this box as well as the following outline to guide your response.

I. Introductory paragraph
   A. Immediate/preceding contextualization statement
      1. Cite evidence of immediate/preceding context
      2. Explain influence of immediate/preceding context
   B. Thesis statement presenting three to four evaluative claims, situated along a continuum of relative extent of change, including at least one continuity

II. Claim 1 body paragraph: Difference 1
   A. Topic sentence presenting an evaluative claim of claim 1
   B. Supporting statement citing evidence of claim 1
   C. Cite additional evidence of claim 1
   D. Explain how evidence supports claim 1
   E. Generate nuance by examining multiple variables, diverse perspectives, counter-evidence, or limitations of claim 1

III. Claim 2 body paragraph: Difference 2
   A. Topic sentence presenting an evaluative claim of change 2
   B. Supporting statement citing evidence of claim 2
   C. Cite additional evidence of claim 2
   D. Explain how evidence supports claim 2
   E. Generate nuance by examining multiple variables, diverse perspectives, counter-evidence, or limitations of claim 2

IV. Claim 3 body paragraph: Similarity 1
   A. Topic sentence presenting an evaluative claim of continuity 1
   B. Supporting statement citing evidence of claim 3
   C. Cite additional evidence of claim 3
   D. Explain how evidence supports claim 3
   E. Generate nuance by examining multiple variables, diverse perspectives, counter-evidence, or limitations of claim 3

V. (Optional) Claim 4 body paragraph: Difference 3 or Similarity 2
   A. Topic sentence presenting an evaluative claim 4
   B. Supporting statement citing evidence of claim 4
   C. Cite additional evidence of claim 4
   D. Explain how evidence supports claim 4
   E. Generate nuance by examining multiple variables, diverse perspectives, counter-evidence, or limitations of claim 4

VI. Conclusion
   A. Restate main claims
   B. Statement connecting historical argument to context immediately after the time range provided by the prompt OR statement connecting historical argument to a similar phenomenon and/or a long-term contextual trend in a later time period.
   C. Provide a piece of evidence for your context statement.
   D. Explain how your evidence supports your concluding context/connection in a later time period.

Module 6-7

Becoming an Urban Nation

LEARNING TARGETS

By the end of this module, you should be able to:
- Explain how the size, demographics, and nature of American cities changed.
- Explain how and why city politics changed.
- Explain how and why urban reformers attempted to improve living conditions in American cities.

THEMATIC FOCUS

Migration and Settlement

American cities grew dramatically as hundreds of thousands of African Americans from the South and millions of Europeans came in search of economic opportunities. Urban newcomers clustered in ethnic neighborhoods as many cities struggled to cope with the challenges of rapid growth. In large cities, politics was dominated by corrupt political machines, which provided a measure of basic social services in exchange for votes.

HISTORICAL REASONING FOCUS

Continuity and Change

TASK ▶ As you read this module, consider the various ways that American cities evolved over the second half of the nineteenth century. Think about the impacts of rural migration, white and black, as well as European immigration. Make sure to understand the linkage between the growth of urban political machines and immigration. Ask yourself how city life in 1900 compared to city life in 1860. What had stayed the same and what had changed?

In the half century after the Civil War, the population of the United States quadrupled, but the urban population soared sevenfold. In 1870 one in five Americans lived in cities with a population of 8,000 or more. By 1900 one in three resided in cities of this size. In 1870 only Philadelphia and New York had populations over half a million. Twenty years later, in addition to these two cities, Chicago's population exceeded 1 million; St. Louis, Boston, and Baltimore had more than 500,000 residents; and Cleveland, Buffalo, San Francisco, and Cincinnati boasted populations over 250,000. Urbanization was not confined to the Northeast and Midwest. Denver's population jumped from 4,700 in 1870 to more than 107,000 in 1890. During that same period, Los Angeles grew nearly fivefold, from 11,000 to 50,000, and Birmingham leaped from 3,000 to 26,000. This phenomenal urban growth also brought remarkable physical changes to the cities, as tall buildings reached toward the skies, electric lights brightened the nighttime hours, and water and gas pipes, sewers, and subways snaked below the ground.

Booming cities faced formidable and at times seemingly insurmountable problems in trying to absorb millions of immigrants. From a governmental standpoint, cities had limited authority over their own affairs. They were controlled by state legislatures and needed state approval to raise revenues and pass regulations. For the most part, there were no zoning laws to regulate housing construction. Private companies owned public utilities, and competition among them produced unnecessary duplication and waste. The government services that did exist operated on a segmented basis, with the emphasis on serving wealthier neighborhoods at the expense of the city at large. Missing was a vision of the city as a whole, working as a single unit.

TRM Suggested Responses to Questions

TEACHING IDEA

Connecting the Dots

Using the statistics listed here, specifically those about Los Angeles, Denver, and Birmingham, ask students to create a graph showing the growth of cities in the United States. Guide students as necessary. This graph can help students visualize just how much city populations grew between 1870 and 1890 and prepare them for the material covered in the module.

TRM Find **Handout 6.9 – Urban Population Growth, 1870–1890** in the Teacher's Resource Materials.

BUILDING AP® SKILLS

Continuity and Change

Have students draw a T-chart with "Continuities" on the left side and "Changes" on the right side. While reading this module, have students take notes on the T-chart. Anytime students encounter historical evidence that describes the size, demographics, or nature of the cities or city politics, they should determine if the evidence suggests a change or a continuity. For example, the population of Los Angeles quintupled between 1870 and 1890. This constitutes a change. Every time students add a change, have them also note the extent of the change. For the Los Angeles example, this is an extensive change. Once students have read the module and taken these notes, put students into pairs and have them compare their notes and discuss. Do they agree on the continuities and changes? Do they agree on the extent of continuity and change? Then, have students individually write a thesis to answer the prompt: "To what extent did cities change between the years 1865 and 1898?"

Period 6: 1865–1898

MODULE 6-7 Becoming an Urban Nation

The **New Industrial City**

frontier thesis The argument, made by historian Frederick Jackson Turner in the 1890s, that the closing of the western frontier endangered the existence of democracy because it removed the opportunity for the pioneer spirit that built America to regenerate.

Although cities have long been a part of the landscape, Americans have felt ambivalent about their presence. Many Americans have shared Thomas Jefferson's idea that democratic values were rooted in the soil of small, independent farms. In contrast to the natural environment of rural life, cities have been perceived as artificial creations in which corruption and contagion flourish. In the 1890s, the very identity of Americans seemed threatened as the U.S. Census Bureau declared the frontier closed, since a discernible frontier line no longer existed. Some agreed with the historian Frederick Jackson Turner, who argued in his "**frontier thesis**" that the closing of the western frontier endangered the existence of democracy because it removed the opportunity for the pioneer spirit that built America to regenerate. Rural Americans were especially uncomfortable with the country's increasingly urban life. When the small-town lawyer Clarence Darrow moved to Chicago in the 1880s he was horrified by the "solid, surging sea of human units, each intent upon hurrying by." Still, like Darrow, millions of people were drawn to the new opportunities cities offered.

Urban growth in America was part of a long-term worldwide phenomenon. Between 1820 and 1920, some 60 million people globally moved from rural to urban areas. Most of them migrated after the 1870s, and as noted earlier, millions journeyed from towns and villages in Europe to American cities. Yet the number of Europeans who migrated internally was greater than those who went overseas. As in the United States, Europeans moved from the countryside to urban areas in search of jobs. Many migrated to the city on a seasonal basis, seeking winter employment in cities and then returning to the countryside at harvest time.

Before the Civil War, commerce was the engine of growth for American cities. Ports like New York, Boston, New Orleans, and San Francisco became distribution centers for imported goods or items manufactured in small shops in the surrounding countryside. Cities in the interior of the country located on or near major bodies of water, such as Chicago, St. Louis, Cincinnati, and Detroit, served similar functions. As the extension of railroad transportation led to the development of large-scale industry, these cities and others became industrial centers as well.

Industrialization contributed to rapid urbanization in several ways. It drew those living on farms, who either could not earn a satisfactory living or were bored by the isolation of rural areas, into the city in search of better-paying jobs and excitement. One rural dweller in Massachusetts complained: "The lack of pleasant, public entertainments in this town has much to do with our young people feeling discontented with country life." In addition, while the mechanization of farming increased efficiency, it also reduced the demand for farm labor. In 1896 one person could plant, tend, and harvest as much wheat as it had taken eighteen farmworkers to do sixty years before.

Industrial technology and other advances also made cities more attractive and livable places. Electricity extended nighttime entertainment and powered streetcars to convey people around town. Improved water and sewage systems provided more sanitary conditions, especially given the demands of the rapidly expanding population. Structural steel and electric elevators made it possible to construct taller and taller buildings, which gave cities such as Chicago and New York their distinctive skylines. Scientists and physicians made significant progress in the fight against the spread of contagious diseases, which had become serious problems in crowded cities.

Many of the same causes of urbanization in the Northeast and Midwest applied to the far West. The development of the mining industry attracted business and labor to urban settlements. Cities grew up along railroad terminals, and railroads stimulated urban growth by bringing out settlers and creating markets. By 1900, the proportion of residents in western cities with a population of at least ten thousand was greater than in any other section of the country except the Northeast. More so than in the East, Asians and Hispanics inhabited western urban centers along with whites and African Americans. In 1899 Salt Lake City boasted the publication of two black newspapers as well as the president of the Western Negro Press Association. Western cities also took advantage of the latest technology, and in the 1880s and 1890s electric trolleys provided mass transit in Denver and San Francisco.

Although immigrants increasingly accounted for the influx into the cities across the nation, before 1890 the rise in urban population came mainly from Americans on the move. In addition to young men, young women left the farm to seek their fortune. The female protagonist of Theodore Dreiser's novel *Sister Carrie* (1900) abandons small-town Wisconsin for the lure of Chicago. In real life, mechanization created many "Sister Carries" by making farm women less valuable in the fields.

TEACHING IDEA

AP® Central

Make use of the College Board's resource America on the World Stage: Essays from the American Organization of Historians and AP®, available from the Classroom Resources section of AP® Central (apcentral.collegeboard.com). At this time, have students read and annotate the article "Driven to the City: Urbanization and Industrialization in the 19th Century." Whole-class discussion to follow.

TEACHING IDEA

Incorporating Videos

Assign students to watch Episode 25, "Growth, Cities, and Immigration," from the Crash Course US History series (available on YouTube). While watching, require students to take notes to support the learning target: "Explain how the size, demographics, and nature of American cities changed." After watching, have students discuss in small groups. Have each group share with the class two ways in which American cities changed. Possible answers include: *In 1880, 20% of Americans lived in cities and 12 cities had over 100,000 people. In 1900, 18 cities had over 100,000 people and 38% of Americans lived in cities. Immigration increased during this time period, and many immigrants settled in cities. Cities were diversified due to increased immigration. Nationalities were widely varied, and so was religion, as Jewish and Catholic immigrants moved in. Cities became more desirable due to the vast working opportunities available. Ethnic neighborhoods and tenements sprang up in cities. Subways and elevated railroads made transportation more efficient, but led to an increase in crime (pickpockets) and city segregation.*

EXPLORING AP® THEMES

Migration and Settlement

Put students into small groups. Require students to fill out a T-chart to organize the push and pull factors to explain the growing trend of populations moving from rural areas to urban areas. Possible push factors include: *extreme weather made farming difficult, the lack of available leisure pursuits in rural areas, and the demand for farm labor was decreasing due to new technology.* Possible pull factors include: *a more exciting night life, jobs in manufacturing, and cities were becoming cleaner and more comfortable places to live.*

BUILDING AP® SKILLS

Causation

Draw a T-chart on the board/projector. As a bell ringer or exit ticket, have each student think of either one cause or one effect of the growth of cities. Ask students for suggestions and compile the list on the T-chart. Causes could include job opportunities or increased immigration. Effects could include the invention of skyscrapers or the need to fight contagious diseases.

The possibility of purchasing mass-produced goods from mail-order houses such as Sears, Roebuck also left young women less essential as homemakers because they no longer had to sew their own clothes and could buy labor-saving appliances from catalogs.

REVIEW

- How did industrialization affect the growth of cities?
- How did industrialization affect the quality of life in cities?

Black Migration to Northern Cities

In 1890, although 90 percent of African Americans lived in the South, a growing number were moving to northern cities to seek employment and greater freedom. Boll weevil infestations during the 1890s decimated cotton production and forced sharecroppers and tenants off farms. At the same time, black people saw significant erosion of their political and civil rights in the last decade of the nineteenth century, which was reinforced by the Supreme Court's 1896 ruling in *Plessy v. Ferguson* (Module 6-3) upholding the doctrine of legal segregation. Most black citizens in the South were denied the right to vote and experienced rigid, legally sanctioned racial segregation in all aspects of public life. Between 1890 and 1914 approximately 485,000 African Americans left the South, with many headed to large cities such as New York, Chicago, and Philadelphia. An African American woman expressed her enthusiasm about the employment she found in Chicago, where she earned $3 a day working in a railroad yard. "The colored women like this work," she explained, because "we make more money . . . and we do not have to work as hard as at housework," which required working sixteen-hour days, six days a week.

Although many African Americans found they preferred their new lives to the ones they had led in the South, the North did not turn out to be the promised land of freedom. Black newcomers encountered discrimination in housing and employment. Residential segregation confined African Americans to racial ghettos. Black workers found it difficult to obtain skilled employment despite their qualifications, and women and men most often toiled as domestics, janitors, and part-time laborers.

Nevertheless, African Americans in northern cities built communities that preserved and reshaped their southern culture and offered a degree of insulation against the harshness of racial discrimination. A small black middle class appeared consisting of teachers, attorneys, and small business owners. In 1888 African Americans organized the Capital Savings Bank of Washington, D.C. Ten years later, two black real estate agents in New York City were worth more than $150,000 each, and one agent in Cleveland owned $100,000 in property. The rising black middle class provided leadership in the formation of mutual aid societies, lodges, and women's clubs. Newspapers such as the *Chicago Defender* and *Pittsburgh Courier* furnished local news to their subscribers and reported national and international events affecting people of color.

◀ **African American Family, 1900** Despite the rigid racial segregation and oppression that African Americans faced in the late nineteenth century, some black families found ways to achieve economic success and upward mobility. The father is a graduate of Hampton Institute, a historically black university founded after the Civil War to educate freedpeople. **What details in this photograph indicate the family's middle-class status?**

BUILDING AP® SKILLS

Argumentation

Divide the class into three groups, one group labelled "support," one group labelled "refute," and the third group labelled "modify." Then, present the class with the following prompt: "During the late nineteenth century, life for African Americans in the North was an improvement upon life in the South." Based upon the group students were placed in, assign them to come up with evidence that either supports, refutes, or modifies the prompt. At the conclusion of this step, recombine the class into groups of three, consisting of one supporter, one refuter, and one modifier. Have them share out and teach one another what they now know, and then as a group, have them craft a thesis statement together on the prompt, based upon their shared knowledge discussion.

▲ Differentiation

In order to obtain the maximal amount of contributions from students, the instructor could combine the room in such a way so that the strongest students work with those that are more challenged by the content, in either the paired phase, or the whole-group supporter/refuter phase. Furthermore, students of mixed ability levels could also be tasked with creating a skeletal outline of the LEQ response to the prompt, and then broken off into individuals for the purpose of writing a full response, based upon the collaborative work.

BUILDING AP® SKILLS

Making Connections

To connect African American migration during the Gilded Age to African American migration today, have students watch Vox's video, "Why African Americans left the south in droves – and what's bringing them back" (available on YouTube). This video focuses on African American migration to the North beginning in the late 1800s through the 1930s while explaining why migration occurred and the impacts that resulted. By watching, students should focus on the progression of African American migration since the late nineteenth century, allowing for a better understanding of the time period in connection with its impacts.

EXPLORING AP® THEMES

Migration and Settlement

Have students watch Carnegie Hall's "Migrations: The Great Migration" (available on YouTube). After watching, pair students up to discuss how the Great Migration led to new styles of music and African American expression. Possible answers include: *Upon migrating to the North, there were new opportunities for African Americans to branch out, share their work, and commercialize their music.*

EXPLORING AP® THEMES

Migration and Settlement

Present the Review question to students. Draw a T-chart on the board. Write "Opportunities" on one side and "Challenges" on the other. Ask students for historical evidence to include. Ask students if African Americans experienced more opportunities or challenges upon moving to the North. Possible opportunities include: *employment, freedom, rising middle class.* Possible challenges include: *employment discrimination, housing segregation, difficult work.*

BUILDING AP® SKILLS

Developments and Processes

Post images of modern cities around the classroom (available through Internet search). Use images that include subways, skyscrapers, elevators, bridges, electrical wires, and suburbs. As a bell ringer, split students up so there are a few students at each image. Ask students to list and describe technological developments and innovations that they see in the image that have origins in the late nineteenth century. Ask each group to answer the question, "How did the nineteenth century give rise to the city as we know it today?" by using evidence from their assigned photo.

As was the case in the South, the church was at the center of black life in northern cities. More than just religious institutions, churches furnished space for social activities and the dissemination of political information. By the first decade of the twentieth century, more than two dozen churches had sprung up in Chicago alone. Whether housed in newly constructed buildings or in storefronts, black churches provided worshippers freedom from white control. They also allowed members of the northern black middle class to demonstrate what they considered to be respectability and refinement. This meant discouraging enthusiastic displays of "old-time religion," which celebrated more exuberant forms of worship. As the Reverend W. A. Blackwell of Chicago's AME Zion Church declared, "Singing, shouting, and talking [were] the most useless ways of proving Christianity." This conflict over modes of religious expression reflected a larger process that was under way in black communities at the turn of the twentieth century. As black urban communities in the North grew and developed, tensions and divisions emerged within the increasingly diverse black community, as a variety of groups competed to shape and define black culture and identity.

REVIEW

What opportunities and challenges did African Americans from the South encounter as they migrated to northern cities?

Cities Expand Upward and Outward

As the urban population increased, cities expanded both up and out. Before 1860, the dominant form of brick and stone construction prevented buildings from rising more than four or five stories. However, as cities became much more populous, land values soared. Steep prices prompted architects to make the most of small, expensive plots of land by finding ways to build taller structures. Architects began using cast-iron columns instead of the thick, heavy walls of brick, resulting in buildings up to ten stories tall. The development of structural steel, which was stronger and more durable than iron, transformed construction with the creation of skyscrapers, which stretched some thirty stories into the air. With the invention of the electric elevator and the radiator, which replaced fireplaces with hot water circulated through pipes, even taller skyscrapers came to loom over downtown business districts in major cities.

Cities also expanded horizontally, as new transportation technology made it possible for residents to move around a much larger urban landscape. In the mid-nineteenth century in cities such as Boston and Philadelphia, pedestrians could still walk from one end of the city to the other within an hour. If residents preferred, they could pay a fare and hop on board a horse-drawn railcar. These vehicles moved slowly and left tons of horse manure in the streets. To avoid such problems, in 1873 San Francisco, followed by Seattle and Chicago, installed a system of cable-driven trolley cars. Still, these trolleys proved slow and unreliable at first.

Electricity provided the transportation breakthrough. In 1888 naval engineer Frank J. Sprague completed the first electric trolley line in Richmond, Virginia. Electric-powered streetcars traveled twice as fast as horse-drawn railcars without leaving a mess on the streets. Subways could run underground without asphyxiating passengers and workmen with a steam engine's smoke and soot. Boston opened the first subway in 1897, followed by New York City in 1904. By 1914, advances in transportation had converted walking cities into riding cities.

Bridges spanning large rivers and waterways also helped extend the boundaries of the inner city. In 1883 the Brooklyn Bridge opened, connecting Manhattan with the city of Brooklyn. Designed and engineered by John Augustus Roebling, the bridge had taken thirteen years to complete and cost twenty men their lives. It stretched more than a mile across the East River and was broad enough for a footpath, two double carriage lanes, and two railroad lines. During its first year in operation, more than 11 million people passed over the bridge; today, more than 51 million vehicles cross the bridge each year.

The electrification of public transportation and the construction of bridges made it feasible for some people to live considerable distances from their workplace. In the eighteenth and nineteenth centuries, middle- and upper-class merchants and professionals usually lived near their shops and offices in the heart of the city, surrounded by their employees. After 1880, the huge influx of immigration brought large numbers of impoverished workers to city centers. The resulting traffic congestion and overcrowded housing pushed wealthier residents to seek more open spaces in which to build houses. The new electric trolley lines allowed middle-class urbanites to move miles away from downtown areas. In 1850 the Boston metropolis spread in a radius of two to three miles around the city and had a population of 200,000. In 1900 suburban Boston ringed the city in a ten-mile radius, with a population of more than 1 million. Increasingly, cities divided into two parts: an inner commercial and industrial core housing the working class, and outer communities occupied by a wealthier class of white, older-stock Americans.

AP® ANALYZING SOURCES

Source: *Intersection of State Street and Madison Street, Chicago*, 1900

Questions for Analysis

1. Describe the scene in the photograph.
2. Explain the impact of technology on urban transportation between 1865 and 1900.
3. Evaluate the extent of change between 1865 and 1900 evident in the photograph.

REVIEW

How did steel and electricity each change life in American cities?

How the Other Half Lived

As the middle and upper classes fled the industrial urban center for the suburbs, the working poor moved in to replace them. They lived in old factories and homes and in shanties (small, crude shelters) and cellars. Because land values were higher in the city, rents were high and the poorest people could least afford them. To make ends meet, families crowded into existing apartments, sometimes taking in boarders to help pay the rent. This led to increased population density and overcrowding in the urban areas where immigrants lived. On New York's Lower East Side, the population density was the highest in the world. Such overcrowding fostered communicable diseases and frustration, giving the area the nicknames "typhus ward" and "suicide ward."

Overcrowding combined with extreme poverty turned immigrant neighborhoods into slums, which were characterized by substandard housing. Impoverished immigrants typically lived in run-down, multiple-family apartment buildings called **tenements** (legally defined as containing more than three families). First constructed in 1850, these early dwellings often featured window-less rooms and little or no plumbing and heating. In 1879 a New York law reformed the building codes to require minimal plumbing facilities and to stipulate that all bedrooms (but not all rooms) have a window. Constructed on narrow 25-by-100-foot lots, these five- and six-story buildings

tenements Multifamily apartment buildings that housed many poor urban dwellers at the turn of the twentieth century. Tenements were crowded, uncomfortable, and dangerous.

BUILDING AP® SKILLS

Sourcing and Situation

Find the lesson "Jacob Riis" – introduced on the following page – on the Stanford History Education Group website (sheg.stanford.edu). Put students into groups and give each group one image from the lesson. Have each group determine the historical context of the image first, and discuss their answers as a class. Next, have students analyze the image to draw conclusions about the living conditions in nineteenth-century cities. Do these images accurately portray the living experience of all who lived in the cities? Next, use the Guiding Questions from the lesson. These questions ask students to consider the source of the images and determine the biases of the photographer, Jacob Riis. Questioning the motives of a source is an important historical thinking skill to practice, as it can vastly change the meaning of a document or source.

Period 6: 1865–1898

MODULE 6-7 Becoming an Urban Nation

included four small apartments on a floor and had only two toilets off the hallway. Tenements stood right next to each other, with only an air shaft separating them. Although these reforms marked some improvement in living conditions, tenements still proved miserable places to live in — dark, damp, and foul smelling. In 1895 a federal government housing inspector observed that the air shafts provided "imperfect light and ventilation" and that "refuse matter or filth of one kind or another [was] very apt to accumulate at the bottom, giving rise to noxious odors." The air shafts also operated as a conduit for fires that moved swiftly from one tenement to another.

In fact, the density of late-nineteenth-century cities could turn individual fires into citywide disasters. The North Side of Chicago burned to the ground in 1871, and Boston and Baltimore suffered catastrophic fires as well. Such fires could, however, have long-term positive consequences. The great urban conflagrations encouraged construction of fireproof buildings made of brick and steel instead of wood. In addition, citizens organized fire watches and established municipal fire departments to replace volunteer companies. Fires also provided cities with a chance to rebuild. Chicago's skyscrapers and its system of urban parks were built on land cleared by fire.

In 1890 Jacob Riis, a Danish immigrant, newspaperman, and photographer, illustrated the brutal conditions endured by tenement families on New York's Lower East Side. "In the stifling July nights," he wrote in *How the Other Half Lives*, "when the big barracks are like fiery furnaces, their very walls giving out absorbed heat, men and women lie in restless, sweltering rows, panting for air and sleep." Under these circumstances, Riis lamented, an epidemic "is excessively fatal among the children of the poor, by reason of the practical impossibility of isolating the patient in a tenement." Despite their obvious problems, tenements soon spread to other cities such as Cleveland, Cincinnati, and Boston, and one block might have ten of these buildings, housing as many as four thousand people.

With all the misery they spawned as places to live, tenements also functioned as workplaces. Czech immigrants made cigars in their apartments from six in the morning until nine at night, seven days a week, for about 6 cents an hour. By putting an entire family to work, they could make $15 a week and pay their rent of $12 a month. Clothing contractors in particular saw these tenement **sweatshops** as a cheap way to produce their products. By jamming two or three sewing machines into an apartment and paying workers a fixed amount for each item they produced, contractors kept their costs down and avoided factory regulations.

Slums compounded the potential for disease, poor sanitation, fire, congestion, and crime. Living on poor diets, slum dwellers proved particularly vulnerable to epidemics. Cholera, yellow fever, and typhoid killed tens of thousands. Tuberculosis was even deadlier. An epidemic that began in a slum neighborhood could easily spread into more affluent areas of the city. Children

> " In the stifling July nights, when the big barracks are like fiery furnaces, their very walls giving out absorbed heat, men and women lie in restless, sweltering rows, panting for air and sleep. "
>
> Jacob Riis, *How the Other Half Lives*, 1890

AP® ANALYZING SOURCES

Source: Jacob Riis, "'Knee Pants' at forty-five cents a dozen — A Ludlow Street Sweater's Shop," *How the Other Half Lives*, 1890

Questions for Analysis
1. Describe the conditions depicted in this photograph.
2. Explain the factors that contributed to the conditions revealed in this photograph.
3. Explain how this photograph reveals Riis's point of view about working-class life in cities.

TEACHING IDEA

Analyzing Art and Images

Ask students to compare Jacob Riis's photograph, "'Knee Pants' at forty-five cents a dozen — A Ludlow Street Sweater's Shop" (1890) to the 1900 photograph "African American Family" (found on page 513). Use the following to guide their comparisons:

- Compare the intended audiences for each photograph.
- Contrast the view of home life portrayed in each photograph.

TRM Suggested Responses to Questions

TRM Module 6.7 AP® Analyzing Sources Handout 2

BUILDING AP® SKILLS

Sourcing and Situation

Students sometimes take primary sources at face value, so it is important for students to determine if there are biases or other situations surrounding the creation of a primary source. The Stanford Education History Group provides two "Beyond the Bubble" assessments using the photography of Jacob Riis (sheg.stanford.edu). Both assessments are excellent practice for students to consider the reliability of a primary source. In the resources it is pointed out that Riis paid some of the subjects in his photographs, which might impact the reliability of the source.

TEACHING IDEA

Incorporating Secondary Sources

In addition to analyzing the photo taken by Jacob Riis that is provided in the textbook, find the article titled "Jacob Riis, How the Other Half Lives, Knee-Pants at Forty-Five Cents a Dozen — A Ludlow Street Sweater's Shop," located on the Khan Academy website (khanacademy.org). This secondary source provides more background information on Jacob Riis as an author and photographer, as well as provides examples of his photographs. Divide the class into groups. Print the images in the article and give one image to each group of students. Have students use the same three questions provided in the AP® Analyzing Sources section to analyze other photos taken by Jacob Riis. What can we learn about the Gilded Age based on these images? Discuss as a class.

suffered the most. Almost one-quarter of the children born in American cities in 1890 did not live to celebrate their first birthdays.

Contributing to the outbreak of disease was faulty sewage disposal, a problem that vexed city leaders. Until the widespread adoption of the modern indoor flush toilet in the early twentieth century, people relied on outdoor toilets, with as many as eight hundred people using a single facility. All too often, cities dumped human waste into rivers that also supplied drinking water. In 1881 the exasperated mayor of Cleveland called the Cuyahoga River "an open sewer through the center of the city." At the same time, the great demand for water caused by the population explosion resulted in lower water pressure. Consequently, residents in the upper floors of tenements had to carry buckets of water from the lower floors. Until cities overcame their water and sanitation challenges, epidemics plagued urban dwellers.

Urban crowding created other problems as well. Traffic moved slowly through densely populated cities. Pedestrians and commuters had to navigate around throngs of people walking on sidewalks and streets, peddlers selling out of pushcarts, and piles of garbage cluttering the walkways. Streets remained in poor shape. In 1889 the majority of Cleveland's 440 miles of streets consisted of sand and gravel. Chicago did not fare much better. In 1890 many road surfaces were covered with wooden blocks, and three-quarters of the city's more than 2,000 miles of streets remained unpaved. Rainstorms quickly made matters worse by turning manure-filled streets into foul-smelling mud.

Poverty and overcrowding contributed to increased crime. The U.S. murder rate quadrupled between 1880 and 1900, at a time when the murder rates in most European cities were declining. In New York City, crime thrived in slums with the apt names of "Bandit's Roost" and "Hell's Kitchen," and groups of young hoodlums preyed on unsuspecting citizens. Poverty forced some of the poor to turn to theft or prostitution. One twenty-year-old prostitute, who supported her sickly mother and four brothers and sisters, lamented: "Let God Almighty judge who's to blame most, I that was driven, or them that drove me to the pass I'm in." Rising criminality led to the formation of urban police departments, though many law officers supplemented their incomes by collecting graft (illegal payments) for ignoring criminal activities.

REVIEW

What difficulties did poor urban residents face during the 1880s and 1890s?

Political Machines and City Bosses

political machine Urban political organizations that dominated many late-nineteenth-century cities. Machines provided needed services to the urban poor, but they also fostered corruption, crime, and inefficiency.

political boss The head of the local political machine. The boss worked to maintain authority by strengthening the machine and its loyalists.

City government in the late nineteenth century was fragmented. Mayors usually did not have much power, and decisions involving public policies such as housing, transportation, and municipal services often rested in the hands of private developers. Bringing some order out of this chaos, the **political machine** functioned to give cities the centralized authority and services that they otherwise lacked. At the head of the machine was the **political boss**. Although the boss held some public office, his real authority came from leadership of the machine. These organizations maintained a tight network of loyalists throughout city wards (districts), each of which contained designated representatives responsible for catering to the needs of their constituents. Whether Democratic or Republican, political machines did not care about philosophical issues; they were concerned primarily with staying in power.

The strength of political machines rested in large measure on immigrants. The organization provided a kind of public welfare when private charity could not cope satisfactorily with the growing needs of the poor. Machines doled out turkeys on holidays, furnished a load of coal for the winter, provided jobs in public construction, arranged for shelter and meals if tenement houses burned down, and intervened with the police and the courts when a constituent got into trouble. Bosses sponsored baseball clubs, held barbecues and picnics, and attended christenings, bar mitzvahs, weddings, and funerals. For enterprising members of immigrant groups — and this proved especially true for the Irish during this period — the machine offered upward mobility out of poverty as they rose through its ranks.

The poor were not the only group that benefited from connections to political machines. The machine and its functionaries helped businessmen maneuver through the maze of contradictory

TEACHING IDEA

Check for Understanding

Put students in pairs. Ask students to brainstorm a list of hardships that people living in the cities faced. Possible answers include: *City dwellers faced crowded living situations in tenements, sweatshops in tenements, poverty, poor sanitation, disease, crime, and fire.* Ask each pair to join with another pair to compile their lists. Ask for volunteers to share and as a class, compile a list on the board.

TEACHING IDEA

Incorporating Videos

Have students watch Steve Brodner's video, *An Introduction to Thomas Nast*, posted by the Norman Rockwell Museum (available on YouTube). The video briefly introduces Thomas Nast and discusses his legacy. Ask students to list details that describe Nast's impact on history.

TEACHING IDEA

Analyzing Art and Images

Review the terms "political machine" and "political boss" with your students before this activity. Search the Library of Congress for political cartoons drawn by Thomas Nast that depict political machines, such as Tammany Hall (loc.gov). Suggested images include: *Tammy Tiger Loose; Group of Vultures Waiting for the Storm to Blow Over; The City Treasury; The Elective System, Or, Master and Slave; The "Brains"; or Who Stole the People's Money? – Do Tell.* Split students into enough groups to give a different political cartoon to each group. Allow students to write on the political cartoons and circle details that stand out to them. Ask them to list details that they see, such as writing and symbols. After taking time to notice the details, allow students to determine the meaning of the cartoon. Project each cartoon for the entire class to see and have each group take turns to explain the meaning of their cartoon. As an exit ticket, ask students to answer the following questions: "How did Thomas Nast view political machines? Do you agree with his arguments? Include one specific piece of historical evidence to support your answer."

TEACHING IDEA

Building Vocabulary

To review the term "political machine," draw a pyramid on the board/projector. Segment the pyramid into four sections. Write the following terms in the pyramid from top to bottom: political boss, ward boss, local captain, and civilians. Ask students to describe how each group of people was interconnected, and what they could offer each other.

TRM Suggested Responses to Questions

TRM Module 6.7 AP® Analyzing Sources Handout 3

---

and overlapping codes regulating building and licenses that impeded their routine course of activities. In addition to assisting legitimate businessmen, the machine facilitated the underworld commerce of vice, prostitution, and gambling by acting as an arbiter to keep this trade within established boundaries — all for a cut of the illegal profits.

In return for these services, the machine received the votes of immigrants and money from businessmen. When challenged by reformers or other political rivals, the machine readily engaged in corrupt election practices to maintain its power. Mobilizing the "graveyard vote," bosses took names from tombstones to pad lists of registered voters. They also hired "repeaters" to vote more than once under phony names and did not hesitate from dumping whole ballot boxes into the river or using hired thugs to scare opponents from the polls.

Bosses enriched themselves through graft and corruption. They secured protection money from both legitimate and illegitimate business interests in return for their services. In the 1860s and 1870s, Boss Tweed, the head of **Tammany Hall**, New York City's political machine, swindled the city out of a fortune while supervising the construction of a lavish three-story courthouse in lower Manhattan. The original budget for the building was $250,000, but the city spent more than $13 million on the structure. The building remained unfinished in 1873, when Tweed was convicted on fraud charges and sent to jail. In later years, Tammany Hall's George Washington Plunkitt distinguished this kind of "dishonest graft" from the kind of "honest graft" that he practiced. If he received inside information about a future sale of city property, Plunkitt reasoned, why shouldn't he get a head start, buy it at a low price, and then sell it at a higher figure? As he delighted in saying, "I seen my opportunities and I took 'em."

The services of political machines came at a high cost. Corruption and graft led to higher taxes on middle-class residents. Moreover, the image of the political boss as a modern-day Robin Hood who stole from the rich and gave to the poor is greatly exaggerated. Much of the proceeds of machine activities went into the private coffers of machine bosses and other functionaries. Trafficking in vice might have run more smoothly under the coordination of the machine, but the safety and health of city residents hardly improved. Most important, although immigrants and

Tammany Hall New York City's political machine during the nineteenth century. It swindled the city out of a fortune while supervising the construction of a lavish three-story courthouse in lower Manhattan. The building remained unfinished in 1873, when Tweed was convicted on fraud charges and sent to jail.

> "I seen my opportunities and I took 'em."
>
> — George Washington Plunkitt, Tammany Hall boss, 1905

AP® ANALYZING SOURCES

Source: Jane Addams, *Why the Ward Boss Rules*, 1898

"The Alderman, therefore, bails out his constituents when they are arrested, or says a good word to the police justice when they appear before him for trial; uses his 'pull' with the magistrate when they are likely to be fined for a civil misdemeanor, or sees what he can do to 'fix up matters' with the State's attorney when the charge is really a serious one.

Because of simple friendliness, the Alderman is expected to pay rent for the hard-pressed tenant when no rent is forthcoming, to find jobs when work is hard to get, to procure and divide among his constituents all the places he can seize from the City Hall. The Alderman of the Nineteenth Ward at one time made the proud boast that he had two thousand six hundred people in his ward upon the public pay-roll. . . .

Indeed, what headway can the notion of civic purity, of honesty of administration, make against this big manifestation of human friendliness, this stalking survival of village kindness? The notions of the civic reformer are negative and impotent before it. . . .

The question does, of course, occur to many minds, Where does the money come from . . . Even when they are intelligent enough to complete the circle, and to see that the money comes, not from the pockets of the companies' agents, but from the street-car fares of people like themselves, it almost seems as if they would rather pay two cents more each time they ride than give up the consciousness that they have a big, warm-hearted friend at court who will stand by them in an emergency."

Questions for Analysis
1. Describe the methods used by aldermen to seek favor with voters, according to Addams.
2. Explain Addams's point of view toward party bosses and political machines.
3. Explain why voters supported machine politics despite obvious corruption.

the poor did benefit from an informal system of social welfare, the machine had no interest in resolving the underlying causes of their problems. As the dominant urban political party organization, the machine cared little about issues such as good housing, job safety, and sufficient wages. It remained for others to provide alternative approaches to relieving the plight of the urban poor.

REVIEW

- What tactics did political machines use to maintain control of city politics during the late nineteenth century?

Urban Reformers

Pendleton Civil Service Reform Act 1883 act that required federal jobs to be awarded on the basis of merit through competitive exams rather than through political connections.

The men and women who criticized the political bosses and machines—and the corruption and vice they fostered—usually came from the ranks of the upper middle class and the wealthy. Their solutions to the urban crisis typically centered around toppling the political machine and replacing it with a civil service that would allow government to function on the basis of merit rather than influence peddling and favoritism. Both locally and nationally, they pushed for civil service reform. In 1883 Congress responded to this demand by passing the **Pendleton Civil Service Reform Act**, which required federal jobs to be awarded on the basis of merit, as determined by competitive examinations, rather than through political connections. As for the immigrants who supported machine politics, these reformers preferred to deal with them from afar and expected that through proper education they might change their lifestyles and adopt American ways.

Another group of Americans from upper- and middle-class backgrounds put aside whatever prejudices they might have held about working-class immigrants and dealt directly with newcomers to try to solve various social problems. These reformers—mostly young people, and many of them women and college graduates—took up residence in **settlement houses** located in urban slums. Settlement houses offered a variety of services to community residents, including day care for children; cooking, sewing, and secretarial classes; neighborhood playgrounds; counseling sessions; and meeting rooms for labor unions. Settlement house organizers understood that immigrants gravitated to the political machine or congregated in the local tavern not because they were inherently immoral but because these institutions helped mitigate their suffering and, in some cases, offered concrete paths to advancement. Although settlement house workers wanted to Americanize immigrants, they also understood immigrants' need to hold on to remnants of their original culture. By 1900 approximately one hundred settlement houses had been established in major American cities.

Religiously inspired reform provided similar support for slum dwellers. Some Protestant ministers began to argue that immigrants' problems resulted not from chronic racial or ethnic failings but from their difficult environment. Some of them preached Christianity as a "social gospel," which included support for civil service reform, antimonopoly regulation, income tax legislation, factory inspection laws, and workers' right to strike.

social gospel Religious movement that advocated the application of Christian teachings to social and economic problems. The ideals of the social gospel inspired many progressive reformers.

Despite the efforts of **social gospel** advocates and the charitable organizations that arose to help relieve human misery, private attempts to combat the various urban ills, however well-meaning, proved insufficient. The problems were structural, not personal, and one group or even several operating together did not have the resources or power to make urban institutions more efficient, equitable, and humane. If reformers were to succeed in tackling the most significant social problems and make lasting changes in American society and politics, they would have to enlist state and federal governments.

REVIEW

- In what ways were federal and local reform efforts during the late nineteenth century similar, and in what ways did they differ?

TEACHING IDEA

Incorporating Primary Sources

Search the Digital Public Library of America for images of Hull House and Hiram House (dp.la). Allow time in class for students to view the images and describe the details and activities that they see. Ask students, "According to these images, what purpose did settlement houses serve?" and "To what extent did settlement houses impact nineteenth-century American society?"

TEACHING IDEA

Historical Vocabulary

Have students complete a Frayer model to define the term "social gospel." An overview of the Frayer model can be found in the Classroom Strategies section of adlit.org. While discussing the term, compare and contrast social gospel with the Gospel of Wealth. Did individuals such as Jane Addams (social gospel) and Andrew Carnegie (Gospel of Wealth) share the same goals?

TRM Suggested Responses to Questions

TEACHING IDEA

AP® Writing Historically Workshop

This activity is meant to be designed as a pre-writing strategy to be completed prior to attending class. One aspect of the DBQ students find challenging is reading through and selecting evidence in the fifteen-minute reading period allowed on exam day. Therefore, have students write down the historical claim made in each document about urban living conditions. With the exception of Document 5, these claims will be quotes of six-to-eight words that capture the overall message of the document. When students come to class, have groups of two form to exchange ideas. Then, ask students to connect their thesis to one of the documents they discussed in pairs. This allows them to have a quick pre-writing activity before they answer the entire question.

Period 6: 1865–1898

MODULE 6-7 Becoming an Urban Nation

AP® WRITING HISTORICALLY — Document-Based Question Practice

ACTIVITY

As you read the following Document-Based Question, reflect on what you have learned in Modules 6-3 through 6-7.

Evaluate the extent of change in the lives of urban residents in the United States in the period 1865 to 1900.

DOCUMENT 1

Source: Charles Loring Brace, *The Dangerous Classes of New York and Twenty Years Among Them*, 1872

"The source of juvenile crime and misery in New York, which is the most formidable, and, at the same time, one of the most difficult to remove, is the overcrowding of our population. The form of the city-site is such—the majority of the dwellings being crowded into a narrow island between two water-fronts—that space near the business-portion of the city becomes of great value. These districts are necessarily sought for by the laboring and mechanic classes, as they are near the places of employment. They are avoided by the wealthy on account of the population which has already occupied so much of them. The result is, that the poor must live in certain wards; and as space is costly, the landlords supply them with (comparatively) cheap dwellings, by building very high and large houses, in which great numbers of people rent only rooms, instead of dwellings. . . .

In the Seventeenth Ward, the Board of Health reports that in 1868, 4,120 houses contained 95,091 inhabitants, of whom 14,016 were children under five years. In the same report, the number of tenement-houses for the whole city is given at 18,582, with an estimate of one-half the whole population dwelling in them—say 500,000."

DOCUMENT 2

Source: James Bryce, *The American Commonwealth*, Vol. 1, 1888

"Now the Spoils System, with the party machinery which it keeps oiled and greased and always working at high pressure, is far more potent and pernicious in great cities than in country districts. For in great cities we find an ignorant multitude, largely composed of recent immigrants, untrained in self-government; we find a great proportion of the voters paying no direct taxes, and therefore feeling no interest in moderate taxation and economical administration; we find able citizens absorbed in their private businesses, cultivated citizens unusually sensitive to the vulgarities of practical politics, and both sets therefore specially unwilling to sacrifice their time and tastes and comfort in the struggle with sordid wire-pullers and noisy demagogues. In great cities the forces that attack and pervert democratic government are exceptionally numerous, the defensive forces that protect it exceptionally ill-placed for resistance."

DOCUMENT 3

Source: F. J. Kingsbury, "The Tendency of Men to Live in Cities," *Journal of Social Science*, No. 33, 1895

"We must remember too that cities as places of human habitation have vastly improved within half a century. About fifty years ago, neither New York nor Boston had public water, and very few of our cities had either water or gas . . .

A few years since, the great improvement of the lift, or elevator, added 10 percent, actually, and probably much more than that theoretically, to the possibilities of population on a given ground; and now within a very recent period three new factors have been suddenly developed which promise to exert a powerful influence on the problems of city and country life. These are the trolley, the bicycle, and the telephone. . . . it adds from five to fifteen miles to the radius of every large town, bringing all this additional area into new relations to business centers. Places five or ten miles apart and all the intervening distances are rendered accessible and communicable for all purposes of life as if they were in the next street."

DOCUMENT 4

Source: George Waring, New York City Commissioner of Street Cleaning, *Street-cleaning and the Disposal of a City's Wastes*, 1897

"Before 1895 the streets were almost universally in a filthy state. In wet weather they were covered with slime, and in dry weather the air was filled with dust. Artificial sprinkling in summer converted the dust into mud, and the drying winds changed the mud to powder. Rubbish of all kinds, garbage, and ashes lay neglected in the streets, and in the hot weather the city stank with the emanations of putrefying organic matter. It was not always possible to see the pavement, because of the dirt that covered it. . . . The sewer inlets were clogged with refuse; dirty paper was prevalent everywhere, and black rottenness was seen and smelt on every hand. . . .

New York is now thoroughly clean in every part . . .

The great, the almost inestimable, beneficial effect of the work of the department [of Street Cleaning of New York] is shown in the large reduction of the death-rate. . . . As compared with the average death-rate of 26.78 of 1882–94, that of 1895 was 23.10, that of 1896 was 21.52, and that of the first half of 1897 was 19.63."

DOCUMENT 5

Source: Geo. P. Hall & Son, *Curve at the Brooklyn Terminal, New York & Brooklyn Bridge*, 1898

Library of Congress, LC-USZ62-5414

(Continued)

DOCUMENT 6

Source: Royal Melendy, *The Saloon in Chicago*, 1900

"That same instinct in man which leads those of the more resourceful classes to form such clubs as the Union League Club, or the Marquette Club; which leads the college man into the fraternity, leads the laboring men into the clubs furnished them by the saloonkeeper.... That general atmosphere of freedom, that spirit of democracy, which men crave, is here realized; that men seek it and that the saloon tries to cultivate it is blazoned forth in such titles as 'The Freedom,' 'The Social,' 'The Club,' etc. Here men 'shake out their hearts together.' Intercourse quickens the thought, feeling, and action....

This is the workingman's school. He is both scholar and teacher. The problems of national welfare are solved here. Many as patriotic men as our country produces learn here their lessons in patriotism and brotherhood. Here the masses receive their lessons in civil government, learning less of our ideals, but more of the practical workings than the public schools teach. It is the most cosmopolitan institution in the most cosmopolitan of cities. One saloon advertises its cosmopolitanism by this title, 'Everybody's Exchange.' Men of all nationalities meet and mingle, and by the interchange of views and opinions their own are modified. Nothing short of travel could exert so broadening an influence upon these men. It does much to assimilate the heterogeneous crowds that are constantly pouring into our city from foreign shores. But here, too, they learn their lessons in corruption and vice. It is their school for good and evil."

DOCUMENT 7

Source: Theodore Dreiser, *Sister Carrie*, 1900

"At that time the department store was in its earliest form of successful operation, and there were not many. The first three in the United States, established about 1884, were in Chicago....

They were along the line of the most effective retail organisation, with hundreds of stores coordinated into one and laid out upon the most imposing and economic basis. They were handsome, bustling successful affairs, with a host of clerks and a swarm of patrons. Carrie passed along the busy aisles, much affected by the remarkable displays of trinkets, dress goods, stationery, and jewelry. Each separate counter was a show place of dazzling interest and attraction....

Not only did Carrie feel the drag of desire for all which was new and pleasing in apparel for women, but she noticed too, with a touch at the heart, the fine ladies who elbowed and ignored her, brushing past in utter disregard of her presence, themselves eagerly enlisted in the materials which the store contained.... A flame of envy lighted in her heart. She realised in a dim way how much the city held—wealth, fashion, ease—every adornment for women, and she longed for dress and beauty with a whole heart."

Use the content and writing strategies that you have learned in this unit to answer the prompt. Remember to Answer, Cite, and Explain (*ACE*) and to Generate nuance, Explain both sides, and Make connections (*GEM*) as you construct your response.

As you read each of the seven documents that accompany this prompt, remember to ask yourself the following questions:

- What is the document about? What historical situation does it describe or reference?
- Who was the intended audience for this document?
- What was the author's purpose in writing this document?
- What point of view does the author of this document express?
- How does this document relate back to the prompt?
- Does this document remind you of any other historical developments?

Keep in mind how you can use each document to support the historical argument you are planning to make. How can these primary sources serve as evidence in your essay?

You may use the following outline to guide your response.

I. Introductory paragraph
   A. Immediate/preceding contextualization statement
      1. Cite evidence of immediate/preceding context
      2. Explain influence of immediate/preceding context
   B. Thesis statement presenting three to four evaluative claims, situated along a continuum of relative extent of change, including at least one continuity

II. Claim 1 body paragraph:
   A. Topic sentence presenting an evaluative claim of claim 1
   B. Supporting statement citing evidence of claim 1
   C. Cite additional evidence of claim 1
   D. Explain how evidence supports claim 1
   E. Generate nuance by examining multiple variables, diverse perspectives, counter-evidence, or limitations of claim 1

III. Claim 2 body paragraph
   A. Topic sentence presenting an evaluative claim of change 2
   B. Supporting statement citing evidence of claim 2
   C. Cite additional evidence of claim 2
   D. Explain how evidence supports claim 2
   E. Generate nuance by examining multiple variables, diverse perspectives, counter-evidence, or limitations of claim 2

IV. Claim 3 body paragraph
   A. Topic sentence presenting an evaluative claim of continuity 1
   B. Supporting statement citing evidence of claim 3
   C. Cite additional evidence of claim 3
   D. Explain how evidence supports claim 3
   E. Generate nuance by examining multiple variables, diverse perspectives, counter-evidence, or limitations of claim 3

V. (Optional) Claim 4 body paragraph
   A. Topic sentence presenting an evaluative claim 4
   B. Supporting statement citing evidence of claim 4
   C. Cite additional evidence of claim 4
   D. Explain how evidence supports claim 4
   E. Generate nuance by examining multiple variables, diverse perspectives, counter-evidence, or limitations of claim 4

VI. Conclusion
   A. Restate main claims.
   B. Statement connecting historical argument to context immediately after the time range provided by the prompt *or* statement connecting historical argument to a similar phenomenon and/or a long-term contextual trend in a later time period.
   C. Provide a piece of evidence for your context statement.
   D. Explain how your evidence supports your concluding context/connection in a later time period.

TRM Suggested Responses to Questions

EXPLORING AP® THEMES
Social Structures

Throughout the module, have students take notes to keep track of the leisure-time pursuits, as well as categorize them by social class (i.e., wealthy, middle class, industrial workers) and gender. Create a key for students to easily decipher among the categories. For example, use an empty square to denote a wealthy male and a filled-in square to denote a wealthy female. An empty circle can denote a middle-class male and a filled-in circle can denote a middle-class female. Use a triangle (empty for male, filled-in for female) to depict the industrial working class. After students have read the module, ask students to review their notes and answer the following question: "Explain how social structure was impacted by industrialization."

TEACHING IDEA
Incorporating Videos

Have students watch PBS' American Experience's video, "Chapter 1 | The Gilded Age" (available on YouTube). The video provides an overview of the gap between the wealthiest Americans and the poorest Americans that expanded during the Gilded Age. After watching, allow students to talk to a partner to answer the prompt, "Which profile fit the United States during the Gilded Age best: 1) America was more like two nations, the poor and the wealthy, or 2) America was one nation where anyone could succeed?"

Module 6-8

Society and Culture in the Gilded Age

LEARNING TARGETS
By the end of this module, you should be able to:
- Explain how industrialization impacted the lifestyles of the wealthy, middle class, and industrial workers.
- Explain how industrialization led to changing gender roles for men and women.

THEMATIC FOCUS
Social Structures

Industrialization and urbanization raised the standard of living for most Americans and provided new opportunities for leisure-time pursuits, which varied by social class and gender. An emerging middle class led to an expansion of consumer culture.

HISTORICAL REASONING FOCUS
Causation

TASK ▶ As you read this module, consider how industrialization led to new forms of leisure-time activities and how it changed societal expectations for men and women. Make sure also to compare how the effects of economic changes reinforced social class divisions.

Gilded Age Term created by Mark Twain and Charles Dudley Warner to describe the late nineteenth century. It implies the golden appearance of the age was a shell covering corruption and materialism of the era's superrich under the surface.

Wealthy people in the late nineteenth century used their fortunes to support lavish lifestyles. For many of them, especially those with recent wealth, opulence rather than good taste was the standard of adornment. This tendency inspired writer Mark Twain and his collaborator Charles Dudley Warner to describe this era of wealth creation as the **Gilded Age**. Glittering on the outside, the enormous riches covered up the unbridled materialism and political rottenness that lay below the surface.

Twain and Warner had the very wealthy in mind when they coined the phrase, but others further down the social ladder found ways to participate in the culture of consumption. The rapidly expanding middle class enjoyed modest homes furnished with mass-produced consumer goods. Women played the central role in running the household, as most wives remained at home to raise children. Women and men often spent their free time attending meetings and other events sponsored by social, cultural, and political organizations. Despite the challenges industrial workers faced, a steady expansion of leisure time allowed for greater participation in sports, visiting dance halls, and other forms of cheap entertainment.

Wealthy and Middle-Class Leisure Pursuits

Industrialization and the rise of **corporate capitalism** led to the expansion of the wealthy upper class as well as the expansion of the middle class, and new lifestyles emerged. Urban elites lived lives of incredible material opulence. J. P. Morgan, William Vanderbilt, and John D. Rockefeller built lavish homes in New York City. High-rise apartment buildings also catered to the wealthy. Overlooking Central Park, the nine-story Dakota Apartments boasted fifty-eight suites, a banquet hall, and a wine cellar. Millionaire residents furnished their stately homes with an eclectic mix of priceless art objects and furniture in a jumble of diverse styles. The rich and famous established private social clubs, sent their children to exclusive prep schools and colleges, and worshipped in the most fashionable churches.

Second homes, usually for use in the summer, were no less expensively constructed and decorated. Besides residences in Manhattan and Newport, Rhode Island, the Vanderbilts constructed a "home away from home" in the mountains of Asheville, North Carolina. The Biltmore, as they named it, contained 250 rooms, 40 master bedrooms, and an indoor swimming pool.

The wealthy also built and frequented opera houses, concert halls, museums, and historical societies as testimonies to their taste and sophistication. For example, the Vanderbilts, Rockefellers, Goulds, and Morgans financed the completion of the Metropolitan Opera House in New York City in 1883. When the facility opened, a local newspaper commented about the well-heeled audience: "The Goulds and the Vanderbilts and people of that ilk perfumed the air with the odor of crisp greenbacks." Upper-class women often traveled abroad to visit the great European cities and ancient Mediterranean sites.

Industrialization and the rise of corporate capitalism also brought an array of white-collar workers in managerial, clerical, and technical positions. These workers formed a new, expanded middle class and joined the businesspeople, doctors, lawyers, teachers, and clergy who constituted the old middle class. More than three million white-collar workers were employed in 1910, nearly three times as many as in 1870.

Middle-class families decorated their residences with mass-produced furniture, musical instruments, family photographs, books, periodicals, and a variety of memorabilia collected in their leisure time. They could relax in their parlors and browse through mass-circulation magazines and popular newspapers. Or they could read some of the era's outpouring of fiction, including romances, dime novels, westerns, humor, and social realism, an art form that depicted working-class life.

> **AP® TIP**
> Analyze how media and popular culture affected the lifestyle of the various social classes in the late nineteenth century.

With more money and time on their hands, middle-class women and men were able to devote their efforts to charity. They joined a variety of social and professional organizations that were arising to deal with the problems accompanying industrialization. During the 1880s, charitable organizations such as the American Red Cross were established to provide disaster relief. In 1892 the General Federation of Women's Clubs was founded to improve women's educational and cultural lives. Four years later, the National Association of Colored Women organized to help relieve suffering among the black poor, defend black women, and promote the interests of the black race.

During these swiftly changing times, adults became increasingly concerned about the nation's youth and sought to create organizations that catered to young people. Formed in the 1840s in England and later expanded to the United States, the Young Men's Christian Association (YMCA) grew briskly during the 1880s as it erected buildings where young men could socialize, build moral character, and engage in healthy physical exercise. The Young Women's Christian Association (YWCA) provided similar opportunities for women. African Americans also participated in "Y" activities through the creation of racially separate branches.

REVIEW

- How did life change for the middle class during the Gilded Age?

Changing Gender Roles

Economic changes led to adjustments in lifestyles and gender roles during the industrial era. Middle-class wives generally remained at home, caring for the house and children, often with the aid of a servant. Whereas in the past farmers and artisans had worked from the home, now most men and women accepted as natural the separation of the workplace and the home caused by industrialization and urbanization. Although the birthrate and marriage rates among the middle class dropped during the late nineteenth century, wives were still expected to care for their husbands and family first to fulfill their feminine duties. Even though daughters increasingly attended colleges reserved for women, their families viewed education as a means of providing refinement rather than a career. One physician summed up the prevailing view that women could only use their brains "but little and in trivial matters" and should concentrate on serving as "the companion or ornamental appendage to man."

TEACHING IDEA

Analyzing Art and Images

First, search the Digital Public Library of America for "New York tenement" (dp.la). Choose 3–4 images to use in class. Next, show PMNC's video "Upstairs at the Biltmore House" (available on YouTube). This video provides a tour of the estate as well as background on the family and their lifestyle. Have students compare and contrast the living conditions of the poorest people in cities with the living conditions of one of the wealthiest families in the nation. Ask students to use the images as evidence to provide reasons for naming the time period the "Gilded Age."

EXPLORING AP® THEMES

Social Structures

The Gilded Age was characterized by a rise in the middle class, an increase in the wealthiest individuals in American society, as well as a great deal of poverty. Ask students to describe how each of these segments of society (industrial workers, the middle class, and the wealthy) were affected by industrialization. In addition, students should write a paragraph argument as to which group was affected the most.

TRM Find **Handout 6.10 – Social Structures in the Gilded Age** in the Teacher's Resource Materials.

Period 6: 1865–1898 — MODULE 6-8 Society and Culture in the Gilded Age

BUILDING AP® SKILLS
Continuity and Change

As a mini-project, allow students to choose one leisure pursuit from this module (bicycling, tennis, croquet, basketball, fraternal orders, baseball, boxing, dancing, amusement parks, theaters, music, etc.). Students will research the pastime and create a short presentation to inform the class about what it was like to take part in that particular pastime during the late nineteenth century. Ask students to compare the pastime in the nineteenth century to its counterpart today. To what extent has the pastime changed over time?

BUILDING AP® SKILLS
Making Connections

As a bell ringer or exit ticket, ask students, "To what extent did industrialization lead to a 'crisis of masculinity'? Provide specific historical evidence to support your answer." Possible answers include: *In working middle-class occupations, men lost some of their independence. Women were also working outside of the home, becoming more independent, as well as pushing for equal rights, which threatened men's control over society.*

◀ **Women Bicyclists** In the 1890s, with improvements in technology, middle-class women had both more leisure time and access to easy-to-ride bicycles. This photograph shows women at an early stage of the bicycle craze before changes in fashion allowed women to wear less-restrictive clothing that permitted exposed ankles and visible bloomers. In 1895, a Nebraska newspaper commented on the larger social implications of women bicyclists: The bicycle took "old-fashioned, slow-going notions of the gentler sex," and replaced them with "some new woman, mounted on her steed of steel." **How does this photograph illustrate both changing social norms for women and the limitations of those changes?**

Middle-class women threw themselves into the new consumer culture. Department stores, chain stores, ready-made clothes, and packaged goods, from Jell-O and Kellogg's Corn Flakes to cake mixes, competed for the money and loyalty of female consumers. Hairdressers, cosmetic companies, and department stores offered a growing and ever-changing assortment of styles. The expanding array of consumer goods did not, however, decrease women's domestic workload. They had more furniture to dust, fancier meals to prepare, changing fashions to keep up with, higher standards of cleanliness to maintain, and occasions to entertain guests. Yet the availability of mass-produced goods to assist the housewife in her chores made her role as consumer highly visible, while making her role as worker nearly invisible.

For the more socially and economically independent young women — those who attended college or beauty and secretarial schools — new worlds of leisure opened up. Bicycling, tennis, and croquet became popular sports for women in the late nineteenth century. So, too, did playing basketball, both in colleges and through industrial leagues. Indeed, women's colleges made sports a requirement, to offset the stress of intellectual life and produce a more well-rounded woman.

Middle-class men enjoyed new leisure pursuits, too. During the late nineteenth century 5.5 million men (of some 19 million adult men in the United States) joined fraternal orders, such as the Odd Fellows, Masons, Knights of Pythias, and Elks. These groups offered middle-class men a network of business contacts and gave them a chance to enjoy a communal, masculine social environment otherwise lacking in their lives.

In fact, historians have referred to a "crisis of masculinity" afflicting a segment of middle- and upper-class men in the late nineteenth and early twentieth centuries. Middle-class occupations whittled away the sense of autonomy that men had experienced in an earlier era when they worked for themselves. The emergence of corporate capitalism had swelled the ranks of the middle class with organization men, who held salaried jobs in managerial departments. At the same time, the expansion of corporations and big business stimulated a demand for clerical workers, female as well as male. This offered women many new opportunities to enter the job market. Along with this development, the push for women's rights, especially the right to vote, and women's increasing involvement in civic associations threatened to reduce absolute male control over the public sphere.

Responding to this gender crisis, middle-class men sought ways to exert their masculinity and keep from becoming frail and effeminate. Psychologists like G. Stanley Hall warned that unless men returned to a primitive state of manhood, they risked becoming spiritually paralyzed. To avoid this, went their advice, men should build up their bodies and engage in strenuous activities to improve their physical fitness.

TEACHING IDEA

As a bell ringer, have pairs of students describe how growing consumerism impacted the lives of women. Possible answers include: *More furniture meant more dusting. Women felt the need to keep up with ever-changing fashions. Women felt pressure to prepare fancy meals and put on lavish parties.*

Changing Gender Roles

Period 6: 1865–1898

AP® TIP
Evaluate the role that sports and other aspects of popular culture played in defining gender roles in the late nineteenth century.

Men turned to sports to cultivate their masculinity. Besides playing baseball and football, they could attend various sporting events. Baseball became the national pastime, and men could root for their home team and establish a community with the thousands of male spectators who filled up newly constructed ballparks. Baseball, a game played by elites in New York City in the 1840s, soon became a commercially popular sport. It spread across the country as baseball clubs in different cities competed with each other. The sport came into its own with the creation of the professional National League in 1876 and the introduction of the World Series in 1903 between the winners of the National League and the American League pennant races.

Boxing also became a popular spectator sport in the late nineteenth century. Bare-knuckle fighting — without the protection of gloves — epitomized the craze to display pure masculinity. A boxing match lasted until one of the fighters was knocked out, leaving both fighters bloody and battered.

AP® ANALYZING SOURCES

Source: *The Delineator*, a women's magazine, 1900

Questions for Analysis
1. Identify the primary activity in the image.
2. Describe the intended audience for this image.
3. Explain how the clothing worn by the woman reflects both economic and social changes of the late nineteenth century.
4. Evaluate the extent to which this image reflects gains for women in the public sphere during the late nineteenth century.

Source: Theodore Roosevelt, *Professionalism in Sports*, 1890

"It is hardly necessary at the present day to enter a plea for athletic exercise and manly outdoor sports. During the last twenty-five years there has been a wonderful growth of interest in and appreciation of healthy muscular amusements; and this growth can best be promoted by stimulating, within proper bounds, the spirit of rivalry on which all our games are based. The effect upon the physique of the sedentary classes, especially in the towns and cities, has already been very marked. . . . As a nation we have many tremendous problems to work out, and we need to bring every ounce of vital power possible to their solution. No people has ever yet done great and lasting work if its physical type was infirm and weak. Goodness and strength must go hand in hand if the Republic is to be preserved. The good man who is ready and able to strike a blow for the right, and to put down evil with the strong arm, is the citizen who deserves our most hearty respect. There is a certain tendency in

(Continued)

APPLY THE TIP

While discussing how popular culture defined gender roles, require students to compare emerging gender roles in the late nineteenth century with gender roles in an earlier period of time. You can either assign time periods (suggested time periods include the 1780s, 1830s, 1920s, 1940s, 1950s, 1960s) or allow students to choose which time period they would like to compare to.

TRM Suggested Responses to Questions

TRM Module 6.8 AP® Analyzing Sources Handout

BUILDING AP® SKILLS
Claims and Evidence in Sources

Put students into pairs. Have one student analyze the image of *The Delineator* and the other student analyze Theodore Roosevelt's "Professionalism in Sports." Separately, require the students to answer the Questions for Analysis for their respective sources. Once answered, allow students to discuss their answers and answer the Questions for Comparison together.

BUILDING AP® SKILLS
Sourcing and Situation

Have students practice describing historical context before analyzing *The Delineator* and Roosevelt's "Professionalism in Sports." Ask students to use concepts from the textbook to provide the background information necessary to understand the documents. Possible discussion topics include: *Leisure activities were becoming increasingly popular, as people had more time to devote to socializing. Women were experiencing more independence in leisure activities outside of the home, and men felt the need to stay active in order to protect their idea of masculinity from this social change.*

the civilization of our time to underestimate or overlook the need of the virile, masterful qualities of the heart and mind which have built up and alone can maintain and defend this very civilization. . . . There is no better way of counteracting this tendency than by encouraging bodily exercise, and especially the sports which develop such qualities as courage, resolution, and endurance."

Questions for Analysis

1. Describe Roosevelt's argument in this excerpt.
2. Describe Roosevelt's purpose in this excerpt.
3. Evaluate the extent to which changing middle class social norms contributed to the argument Roosevelt makes in this excerpt.

Questions for Comparison

1. Explain how Roosevelt's ideal of manhood compares with the ideal of womanhood depicted on the *Delineator* cover.
2. Explain how each source represents a reaction to changing social norms in the late 1800s.

During the late nineteenth century, middle-class women and men also had increased opportunities to engage in different forms of sociability and sexuality. Gay men and lesbians could find safe havens in New York City's Greenwich Village and Chicago's North Side for their own entertainment. Although treated by medical experts as sexual "inverts" who might be cured by an infusion of "normal" contact with members of the opposite gender, gays and lesbians began to emerge from the shadows of restrictive social norms around the turn of the twentieth century. "Boston marriages" constituted another form of relationship between women. The term apparently came from Henry James's book *The Bostonians* (1886), which described a female couple living together in a monogamous, long-term relationship. This association appealed to financially independent women who did not want to get married. Many of these relationships were sexual, but some were not. In either case, they offered women of a certain class an alternative to traditional, heterosexual marriage.

REVIEW

In what ways did gender roles change for both men and women during the late nineteenth century?

Working-Class Leisure in Industrial America

Despite the hardships industrial laborers faced in the late nineteenth century, workers carved out recreational spaces that they could control and that offered relief from their backbreaking toil. For many, Sunday became a day of rest that took on a secular flavor. Working-class leisure patterns varied by gender, race, and region. Women did not generally attend spectator sporting events, such as baseball and boxing matches, which catered to men. Nor did they find themselves comfortable in union halls and saloons, where men found solace in drink. Working-class wives preferred to gather to prepare for births, weddings, and funerals or to assist neighbors who had suffered some misfortune.

Once employed, working-class daughters found a greater measure of independence and free time by living in rooming houses on their own. Women's wages were only a small fraction of men's earnings, so workingwomen rarely made enough money to support a regular social life. Still, they found ways to enjoy their free time. Some single women went out in groups, hoping to meet men who would pay for drinks, food, or a vaudeville show. Others dated so that they knew they would be taken care of for the evening. Some of the men who "treated" on a date assumed a right to sexual favors in return, and some of these women then expected men to provide them with housing and

> **AP® TIP**
> Make sure you can explain the ways in which economic changes in the late nineteenth century both illustrated continuity and fostered change in social relationships.

TEACHING IDEA

Differing Views

Divide the class into three groups, one group labelled "support," one group labelled "refute," and a third group labelled "modify." Then, present the class with the following prompt: "Women experienced a great deal of freedom during the late nineteenth century." Based upon the group students were placed in, assign them to come up with evidence that either supports, refutes, or modifies the prompt. At the conclusion of this step, recombine the class into groups of three, consisting of one supporter, one refuter, and one modifier. Have them share out and teach one another what they now know, and then as a group, have them craft a thesis statement together on the prompt, based upon their shared knowledge discussion.

APPLY THE TIP

Pose the following question to students: "To what extent were social relationships impacted by economic changes in the late nineteenth century?" Allow students a few minutes to brainstorm before discussing in small groups. Require each group to write a thesis and provide two specific pieces of historical evidence to support their thesis. Have groups share their theses and evidence with the class.

gifts in exchange for an ongoing sexual relationship. Thus emotional and economic relationships became intertwined.

Around the turn of the twentieth century, dance halls flourished as one of the mainstays of working-class communities. Huge dance palaces were built in the entertainment districts of most large cities. They made their money by offering music with lengthy intermissions for the sale of drinks and refreshments. Women and men also attended nightclubs, some of which were racially integrated. In so-called red-light districts of the city, prostitutes earned money entertaining their clients with a variety of sexual pleasures.

Not all forms of leisure were strictly segregated along class lines. A number of forms of cheap entertainment appealed not only to working-class women and men but also to their middle-class counterparts. By the turn of the twentieth century, most large American cities featured amusement parks. Brooklyn's Coney Island stood out as the most spectacular of these sprawling playgrounds. In 1884, the world's first roller coaster was built at Coney Island, providing thrills to those brave enough to ride it. In Chicago at the 1893 World's Columbian Exposition, residents enjoyed the new Ferris wheel, which soared 250 feet in the air. Vaudeville houses — with their minstrel shows (white people in blackface) and comedians, singers, and dancers — brought howls of laughter to working-class audiences. Nickelodeons charged five cents to watch short films. Live theater generally attracted more wealthy patrons; however, the Yiddish theater, which flourished on New York's Lower East Side, and other immigrant-oriented stage productions appealed mainly to working-class audiences.

Itinerant musicians entertained audiences throughout the South. Lumber camps, which employed mainly African American men, offered a popular destination for these musicians. Each camp contained a "barrelhouse," also called a "honky tonk" or a "juke joint." Besides showcasing music, the barrelhouse also gave workers the opportunity to "shoot craps, dice, drink whiskey, dance, every modern devilment you can do," as one musician who played there recalled. From the Mississippi delta emerged a new form of music — the blues. W. C. Handy, "the father of the blues," discovered this music in his travels through the delta, where he observed southern black people performing songs of woe, accompanying themselves with anything that would make a "musical sound or rhythmical effect, anything from a harmonica to a washboard." Meanwhile in New Orleans, an amalgam of black musical forms evolved into jazz. Musicians such as "Jelly Roll" Morton experimented with a variety of sounds, putting together African and Caribbean rhythms with European music, mixing pianos with clarinets, trumpets, and drums. Blues and jazz spread throughout the South.

In mountain valley mill towns, southern whites preferred "old-time" music, but with a twist: they modified the lyrics of traditional ballads and folk songs, originally enjoyed by British settlers, to extol the exploits of outlaws and adventurers. Country music, which combined romantic ballads and folk tunes to the accompaniment of guitars, banjos, autoharps, dulcimers, and organs, emerged as a distinct brand of music by the twentieth century. As with African Americans, in the

◀ **Vaudeville, 1897** The popular comedy team of J. Sherrie Matthews and Harry Bulger performed in vaudeville shows throughout the country. This photo, taken in the San Francisco Bay area, shows Matthews playing the mandolin while Bulger dances. Notice the braid running down the front of Bulger's costume, apparently an attempt to ridicule the Chinese population in the area. In similar fashion, in minstrel shows, the predecessor of vaudeville, whites appeared in blackface to mock African Americans. **How did minstrel and vaudeville shows, such as the one in this image, reflect the social values of the era?**

TEACHING IDEA

Analyzing Art and Images

Compile images of the various leisure activities that are referenced in this module. These images can be found by searching the Library of Congress or the Digital Public Library of America online (loc.gov or dp.la). Post the images around the classroom along with a large piece of paper next to each image. Put students into groups so 3 or 4 students are looking at one image at a time. Give students time to look at the image and write the details that they noticed, what they think is happening in the image, as well as any questions that they may have on the piece of paper posted next to the image. After they have finished, prompt students to move to the next image. Repeat this process until all students have seen all of the images. Discuss as a class and ask students to explain how industrialization led to these new forms of leisure activities.

▲ Differentiation

Instead of posting the images by themselves, create questions that can help guide students through the process of analyzing each image. You might post these next to the images that students can reference as they navigate from image to image.

TEACHING IDEA

Incorporating Music

Play the music of W. C. Handy (*St. Louis Blues*, *Memphis Blues*, *Yellow Dog Blues*) and "Jelly Roll" Morton (*Jelly Roll Blues*, *King Porter Stomp*, *I Thought I Heard Buddy Bolden Say*) for the class (all available on YouTube). Discuss how new musical styles such as jazz and blues were heavily influenced by African and Caribbean rhythms mixed with European music and reflected the experiences of African Americans in the South.

late nineteenth century working-class and rural whites found new and exciting types of music to entertain them in their leisure. Religious music also appealed to both white and black audiences and drew crowds to evangelical revivals.

Mill workers also amused themselves by engaging in social, recreational, and religious activities. Women visited each other and exchanged confidences, gossip, advice on child rearing, and folk remedies. Men from various factories organized baseball teams that competed in leagues. Managers of a mill in Charlotte, North Carolina admitted that they "frequently hired men better known for their batting averages than their work records."

REVIEW

- How did working-class leisure activities compare to those of the middle and upper classes during the late nineteenth century?

AP® WRITING HISTORICALLY — Long-Essay Question Practice

ACTIVITY

To answer the following Long-Essay Question, use the *ACE* strategy (Answer, Cite, Explain) to write a full essay in response to the prompt at the beginning of this box. Be sure to also use *GEM* (generate nuance in your response, explain both sides of the targeted historical reasoning process, and make relevant and insightful connections within and across time periods) to incorporate multiple examples of historical complexity in your essay.

Evaluate the extent to which industrialization affected United States culture in the period from 1865 to 1898.

You may use the following outline to guide your response.

I. Introductory paragraph
   A. Immediate/preceding contextualization statement
      1. Cite evidence of immediate/preceding context
      2. Explain influence of immediate/preceding context
   B. Thesis statement presenting three to four evaluative claims, situated along a continuum of relative extent of change, including at least one continuity

II. Claim 1 body paragraph: Effect 1
   A. Topic sentence presenting an evaluative claim of claim 1
   B. Supporting statement citing evidence of claim 1
   C. Cite additional evidence of claim 1
   D. Explain how evidence supports claim 1
   E. Generate nuance by examining multiple variables, diverse perspectives, counter-evidence, or limitations of claim 1

III. Claim 2 body paragraph: Effect 2
   A. Topic sentence presenting an evaluative claim of change 2
   B. Supporting statement citing evidence of claim 2
   C. Cite additional evidence of claim 2
   D. Explain how evidence supports claim 2
   E. Generate nuance by examining multiple variables, diverse perspectives, counter-evidence, or limitations of claim 2

IV. Claim 3 body paragraph: Cause 1
   A. Topic sentence presenting an evaluative claim of continuity 1
   B. Supporting statement citing evidence of claim 3
   C. Cite additional evidence of claim 3
   D. Explain how evidence supports claim 3
   E. Generate nuance by examining multiple variables, diverse perspectives, counter-evidence, or limitations of claim 3

TEACHING IDEA

Check for Understanding

Have students work to identify and describe at least one form of entertainment for each of the following working-class groups: white men, white women, southern whites, and southern African Americans. Once students have finished, have them share their responses with a partner.

TRM Suggested Responses to Questions

TEACHING IDEA

AP® Writing Historically Review

This Long-Essay Question asks students to make historical connections between industry and culture. Therefore, consider the following activity as a pre-writing strategy. Have students create a T-chart with "Industry" and "Culture" as the main headings. Students should brainstorm all of the big historical ideas they can think of in 5–7 minutes. Think of this as the view from 15,000 feet in an airplane. Students are not getting too specific in their outline; instead, they are thinking of broad developments such as the the growth of corporations (industry) and the growth of immigration (culture). Students should then find two or three ways in which their historical development from the industry side of the chart affected the development from the culture side. Using the aforementioned example, students will notice how the growth of corporations incentivized further immigration due to economic opportunity. This can be a way of developing thesis categories.

V. (Optional) Claim 4 body paragraph: Effect 3 or Cause 2
   A. Topic sentence presenting an evaluative claim 4
   B. Supporting statement citing evidence of claim 4
   C. Cite additional evidence of claim 4
   D. Explain how evidence supports claim 4
   E. Generate nuance by examining multiple variables, diverse perspectives, counter-evidence, or limitations of claim 4

VI. Conclusion
   A. Restate main claims.
   B. Statement connecting historical argument to context immediately after the time range provided by the prompt *or* statement connecting historical argument to a similar phenomenon and/or a long-term contextual trend in a later time period.
   C. Provide a piece of evidence for your context statement.
   D. Explain how your evidence supports your concluding context/connection in a later time period.

TEACHING IDEA

Peer Review

After students have written an answer to the Long-Essay Question, have students complete a peer review. Ask students to focus specifically on reviewing each other's thesis statements, topic sentences, and conclusions, as well as how well their response answers the prompt. You may also wish to provide students with a rubric for AP® Long-Essay Questions available on the College Board website so they have practice with identifying responses that will earn full points on the AP® exam (apcentral.collegeboard.org).

TRM Suggested Responses to Questions

EXPLORING AP® THEMES
Social Structures

First, define "philanthropy." Merriam-Webster's dictionary defines the term as "an act or gift done or made for humanitarian purposes" (merriam-webster.com). Discuss Andrew Carnegie's view of the word "philanthropy" as well (found on page 533). Remind students that philanthropy is conducted by private citizens, not provided by the government. Pair students and ask each pair to come up with one example of philanthropy from any time period in U.S. history. Students might mention funding a soup kitchen, volunteering at a summer camp or nursing home, or donating money to hurricane relief organizations. Have students share some examples with the class. Finally, pose the following question to students: "In what ways could philanthropy change the structure of society?" Follow up with this question later in the module to gather examples from the Gilded Age, such as Andrew Carnegie donating money to build libraries. This philanthropic act could change the structure of society by providing all individuals with the means to access knowledge. Armed with knowledge, individuals can start to improve their lives.

Module 6-9

Gilded Age Ideologies

LEARNING TARGETS
By the end of this module, you should be able to:
- Explain the development of popular doctrines justifying the existing social and economic conditions in the late 1800s.
- Explain the development of critiques to the popular doctrines justifying the existing economic and social conditions in the late 1800s.

THEMATIC FOCUS
Politics and Power
Social Structures

The ideologies of laissez-faire economics and Social Darwinism placed the burden of success or failure on the individual while restraining the federal government from intervention in the economy during the Gilded Age. Certain industrialists, notably Andrew Carnegie in his "Gospel of Wealth," promoted philanthropy as some academics called for a new social order.

HISTORICAL REASONING FOCUS
Causation

TASK ▶ As you read this module, consider how proponents of the status quo used appeals to economic efficiency, individualism, and nature to justify growing economic inequality. Think about what factors caused the situation they sought to maintain and how those changes led to emerging critiques of their beliefs.

American industrialization developed as rapidly as it did in large part because it was reinforced by traditional ideas and values. The notion that hard work and diligence would result in success meant that individuals felt justified, even duty-bound, to strive to achieve upward mobility and accumulate wealth. Those who succeeded believed that they had done so because they were more talented, industrious, and resourceful than others. Thus prosperous businessmen regarded competition and the free market as essential to the health of an economic world they saw based on merit. Yet these same businessmen also created trusts that destroyed competition, and they depended on the government for resources and protection. This obvious contradiction, along with the profoundly unequal distribution of wealth that characterized the late-nineteenth-century economy, generated a good deal of criticism of business tycoons and their beliefs.

Doctrines of Success

laissez-faire French for "let things alone." Advocates of laissez-faire believed that the marketplace should be left to regulate itself, allowing individuals to pursue their own self-interest without any government restraint or interference.

Those at the top of the new industrial order justified their great wealth in a manner that most Americans could understand. The ideas of the Scottish economist Adam Smith, in *The Wealth of Nations* (1776), had gained popularity during the American Revolution. Advocating **laissez-faire** ("let things alone"), Smith contended that an "Invisible Hand," guided by natural law, guaranteed the greatest economic success if the government let individuals pursue their own self-interest unhindered by outside and artificial influences. In the late nineteenth century, businessmen and their conservative allies on the Supreme Court used Smith's doctrines to argue against restrictive government regulation. They equated their right to own and manage property with the personal liberty protected by the Fourteenth Amendment. Thus the Declaration of Independence, with its defense of "life, liberty, and the pursuit of happiness," and the Constitution, which enshrined citizens' political freedom, became instruments to guarantee unfettered economic opportunity and safeguard private property.

The view that success depended on individual initiative was reinforced in schools and churches. The McGuffey Readers, widely used to educate children, taught moral lessons of hard

---

BUILDING AP® SKILLS
Developments and Processes

Provide students with practice to describe historical developments by requiring them to create a timeline illustrating the development of popular doctrines justifying the existing social and economic conditions of the 1800s, as well as critiques to the popular doctrines that arose (such as Social Darwinism, the Gospel of Wealth, laissez-faire, and the social gospel). This will provide students not only with practice with explaining historical developments, but it will also cover the learning targets for this module.

Doctrines of Success

> "I say that you ought to get rich, and it is your duty to get rich, because to make money honestly is to preach the gospel."
>
> — Russell Conwell, "Acres of Diamonds" lecture, 1890

work, individual initiative, reliability, and thrift. The popular dime novels of Horatio Alger portrayed the story of young men who rose from "rags to riches" through a combination of "luck and pluck." Americans could also hear success stories in houses of worship. Russell Conwell, pastor of the Grace Baptist Church in Philadelphia, delivered a widely printed sermon entitled "Acres of Diamonds," which equated godliness with riches and argued that ordinary people had an obligation to strive for material wealth. "I say that you ought to get rich, and it is your duty to get rich," Conwell declared, "because to make money honestly is to preach the gospel."

If economic success was a matter of personal merit, it followed that economic failure was as well. The British philosopher Herbert Spencer proposed a theory of social evolution based on this premise in his book *Social Statics* (1851). Imagining a future utopia, Spencer wrote, "Man was not created with an instinct for his own degradation, but from the lower he has risen to the higher forms. Nor is there any conceivable end to his march to perfection." In his view, those at the top of the economic ladder were closer to perfection than were those at the bottom. Any effort to aid the unfortunate would only slow the march of progress for society as a whole. Spencer's book proved extremely popular, selling nearly 400,000 copies in the United States by 1900. Publication of Charles Darwin's landmark *On the Origin of Species* (1859) appeared to provide some scientific legitimacy for Spencer's view. The British naturalist argued that plants, animals, and humans progressed or declined because of their ability or inability to adapt favorably to the environment and transmit these characteristics to future generations. The connection between the two men's ideas led some people decades later to label Spencer's theory "**Social Darwinism**."

Social Darwinism The belief associated with the late nineteenth and early twentieth centuries and popularized by Herbert Spencer that drew upon some of the ideas of Charles Darwin. Stressing individual competition and the survival of the fittest, Social Darwinism was used to justify economic inequality, racism, imperialism, and hostility to federal government regulation.

Doctrines of success, such as Social Darwinism, gained favor because they helped Americans explain the rapid economic changes that were disrupting their lives. Although most ordinary people would not climb out of poverty to middle-class respectability, let alone affluence, they clung to ideas that promised hope. Theories such as Spencer's that linked success with progress provided a way for those who did not do well to understand their failure and blame themselves for their own inadequacies. At the same time, the notion that economic success derived from personal merit legitimated the fabulous wealth of those who did rise to the top.

Capitalists such as Carnegie found a way to soften both the message of extreme competition and its impact on the American public. Denying that the government should help the poor, they proclaimed that men of wealth had a duty to furnish some assistance. In his famous essay "**The Gospel of Wealth**" (1889), Carnegie argued that the rich should act as stewards of the wealth they earned. As trustees, they should administer their surplus income for the benefit of the community. Carnegie distinguished between charity (direct handouts to individuals), which he deplored, and philanthropy (building institutions that would raise educational and cultural standards), which he advocated. Carnegie was particularly generous in funding libraries (he provided the buildings but not the books) because they allowed people to gain knowledge through their own efforts.

"**The Gospel of Wealth**" 1889 essay by Andrew Carnegie in which he argued that the rich should act as guardians of the wealth they earned, using their surplus income for the benefit of the community.

Capitalists may have sung the praises of individualism and laissez-faire, but their actions contradicted their words. Successful industrialists in the late nineteenth century sought to destroy competition, not perpetuate it. Their efforts over the course of several decades produced giant corporations that measured the worth of individuals by calculating their value to the organization. As John D. Rockefeller, the master of consolidation, proclaimed, "The day of individual competition in large affairs is past and gone."

Nor did capitalists strictly oppose government involvement. Although industrialists did not want the federal government to take any action that *hindered* their economic efforts, they did favor the use of the government's power to *promote* their enterprises and to stimulate entrepreneurial energies. Thus manufacturers pushed for congressional passage of high tariffs to protect goods from foreign competition and to foster development of the national marketplace. Industrialists demanded that federal and state governments dispatch troops when labor strikes threatened their businesses. They persuaded Washington to provide land grants for railroad construction and to send the army to clear American Indians and bison from their tracks. They argued for state and federal courts to interpret constitutional and statutory law in a way that shielded property rights against attacks from workers. In large measure, capitalists succeeded not in spite of governmental support but because of it.

REVIEW

- What was the relationship between Social Darwinism and laissez-faire policies?

Period 6: 1865–1898

MODULE 6-9 Gilded Age Ideologies

Challenges to Laissez-Faire

Proponents of government restraint and unbridled individualism did not go unchallenged. Critics of laissez-faire created an alternative ideology for those who sought to organize workers and expand the role of government as ways of restricting capitalists' power over labor and ordinary citizens.

Lester Frank Ward attacked laissez-faire in his book *Dynamic Sociology* (1883). Ward did not disparage individualism but viewed the main function of society as "the organization of happiness." Contradicting Herbert Spencer, Ward maintained that societies progressed when government directly intervened to help citizens — even the unfortunate. Rejecting laissez-faire, he argued that what people "really need is more government in its primary sense, greater protection from" the aggressive greed of the "favored few."

Some academics supported Ward's ideas. Most notably, economist Richard T. Ely applied Christian ethics to his scholarly assessment of capital and labor. He condemned the railroads for dragging "their slimy length over our country, and every turn in their progress is marked by a progeny of evils." In his book *The Labor Movement* (1886), Ely suggested that the ultimate solution for social ills resulting from industrialization lay in "the union of capital and labor in the same hands, in grand, wide-reaching, co-operative enterprises."

Two popular writers, Henry George and Edward Bellamy, added to the critique of materialism and greed. In *Progress and Poverty* (1879), George lamented: "Amid the greatest accumulations of wealth, men die of starvation." He blamed the problem on rent, which he viewed as an unjustifiable payment on the increase in the value of land. His remedy was to have government confiscate rent earned on land by levying a single tax on landownership. Though he advocated government intervention, he did not envision an enduring role for the state once it had imposed the single tax. By contrast, Bellamy imagined a powerful central government. In his novel *Looking Backward, 2000–1887* (1888), Bellamy attacked industrialists who "maim and slaughter workers by thousands." In his view, the federal government should take over large-scale firms, administer them as workers' collectives, and redistribute wealth equally among all citizens.

Neither Bellamy, George, Ward, nor Ely endorsed the militant socialism of Karl Marx, a mid-nineteenth-century German philosopher who predicted that capitalism would be overthrown and replaced by a revolutionary movement of industrial workers that would control the means of economic production and establish an egalitarian society. Although his ideas gained popularity among European labor leaders, they were not widely accepted in the United States during this period. Most critics believed that the American political system could be reformed without resorting to the extreme solution of a socialist revolution. They favored a cooperative commonwealth of capital and labor, with the government acting as an umpire between the two.

> " Amid the greatest accumulations of wealth, men die of starvation. "
>
> Henry George, *Progress and Poverty*, 1879

AP® ANALYZING SOURCES

Source: Andrew Carnegie, *The Gospel of Wealth*, 1889

"In bestowing charity, the main consideration should be to help those who will help themselves; to provide part of the means by which those who desire to improve may do so; to give those who desire to rise the aids by which they may rise; to assist, but rarely or never to do all. Neither the individual nor the race is improved by almsgiving. Those worthy of assistance, except in rare cases, seldom require assistance. . . .

[T]he best means of benefiting the community is to place within its reach the ladders upon which the aspiring can rise — free libraries, parks, and means of recreation, by which men are helped in body and mind; works of art, certain to give pleasure and improve the public taste; and public institutions of various kinds, which will improve the general condition of the people; in this manner returning their surplus wealth to the mass of their fellows in the forms best calculated to do them lasting good.

Thus is the problem of rich and poor to be solved. The laws of accumulation will be left free, the laws of distribution free. Individualism will continue, but the millionaire will be but a trustee for the poor, intrusted for a season with a great part of the increased wealth of the community, but administering it for the community far better than it could or would have done for itself."

534

TRM Suggested Responses to Questions

TRM Module 6.9 AP® Analyzing Sources Handout

BUILDING AP® SKILLS

Claims and Evidence in Sources

Put students in pairs. Have one student read the excerpt from Andrew Carnegie's "Gospel of Wealth" and the other read the excerpt titled "A Workingman's Prayer." Require each student to answer the Questions for Analysis for their respective excerpt. Once complete, have students discuss and compare their excerpts and answer the Questions for Comparison together.

TEACHING IDEA

Incorporating Videos

Have students watch Learn Library's "Economic Growth in the Gilded Age – US Economic History 5" (available on YouTube). This video discusses the perspectives of economic historians concerning robber barons and captains of industry, and focuses on the involvement of the government in the economy. After watching, have students discuss in pairs the following scenario: "Imagine that you are a historian who supports the laissez-faire ideology. Would you be more likely to see nineteenth-century industrialists as robber barons, or captains of industry?" Students should explain that they would consider nineteenth-century industrialists to be captains of industry, as they are conducting business and competing with each other in a way that benefits society. Government intervention, according to a supporter of laissez-faire, would only hinder economic growth.

Questions for Analysis

1. Describe Carnegie's argument.
2. Explain how Carnegie's proposed solutions reflect his social-economic standing.
3. Evaluate the extent to which working conditions for laborers undermine Carnegie's argument.

Source: "A Workingman's Prayer," *The Coming Nation*, 1894

"Oh, Almighty Andrew Philanthropist Library Carnegie, who art in America when not in Europe spending the money of your slaves and serfs, thou art a good father to the people of Pittsburgh, Homestead and Beaver Falls. We bow before thee in humble obedience of slavery.... We have no desire but to serve thee. If you sayest black was white we believe you, and are willing, with the assistance of ... the Pinkerton's agency, to knock the stuffin[g] out of anyone who thinks different, or to shoot down and imprison serfs who dare say you have been unjust in reducing the wages of your slaves, who call themselves citizens of the land of the free and the home of the brave....

Oh, lord and master, we love thee because you and other great masters of slaves favor combines and trusts to enslave and make paupers of us all. We love thee though our children are clothed in rags. We love thee though our wives ... are so scantily dressed and look so shabby. But, oh master, thou hast given us one great enjoyment which man has never dreamed of before—a free church organ, so that we can take our shabby families to church to hear your great organ pour forth its melodious strains....

Oh, master, we thank thee for all the free gifts you have given the public at the expense of your slaves.... Oh, master, we need no protection, we need no liberty so long as we are under thy care. So we commend ourselves to thy mercy and forevermore sing thy praise."

Questions for Analysis

1. Describe the author's attitude toward wealthy industrialists.
2. Explain how specific effects of industrialization are portrayed in this excerpt.
3. Explain how the author's references to specific historical patterns and events contribute to the main argument of "A Workingman's Prayer."

Questions for Comparison

1. Explain how each document appeals to its particular audience.
2. Evaluate how effective "A Workingman's Prayer" is in rebutting Carnegie's argument.

REVIEW

- What were the main arguments against laissez-faire policies?

AP® WRITING HISTORICALLY — Short-Answer Question Practice

ACTIVITY

Read the following question carefully and write a short response. Use complete sentences.

Using the following image, answer (a), (b), and (c).

Source: Thomas Nast, "Uncle Sam," *The President's Message*, 1887

About the source: In this cartoon, Uncle Sam is shown holding a bowl labeled "Soap Fat." Using a pipe, he is blowing a bubble that reads, "GUARANTEEING EQUAL TAXATION." In the background, a bubble labeled "PROTECTION OF LABOR" floats above two bubbles — "FAIRNESS" and "JUSTICE," which have already burst. A pile of soap bars by Uncle Sam's feet read (clockwise) "MONOPOLY," "FAT," "TRUST," and "INFANT SOAP." The text beneath the illustration of Uncle Sam reads, "Uncle Sam, don't play with it —, be a Man. Monopolists' soap-bubbles soon burst."

(Continued)

BUILDING AP® SKILLS

Claims and Evidence in Sources

To dig deeper into the main arguments against laissez-faire policies, use excerpts from the books listed in this section (*Dynamic Sociology*, *The Labor Movement*, *Progress and Poverty*, and *Looking Backward*). Require students to provide direct quotes that argue against laissez-faire policies and write the meaning of each quote in their own words. You may also choose to make this activity into a jigsaw, where different students read excerpts from different books (a refresher of the jigsaw model can be found on page 33). Compile the quotes by posting them around the room. Give students time to walk from quote to quote. Then, engage in a "Four Corners" exercise, designating each corner of the room to a different book. Allow students to move to one of four labelled corners in the classroom based upon which arguments they believe to be the most compelling. Give the groups time to converse, and then engage in an inside-circle–outside-circle activity whereby each group advocates for its chosen argument to be the most compelling.

TRM Suggested Responses to Questions

Period 6: 1865–1898

MODULE 6-9 Gilded Age Ideologies

TEACHING IDEA

Check for Understanding

Before answering the Short-Answer Questions, require students to utilize their HIPP training to analyze the cartoon (a refresher on HIPP can be found on page 8). Remind students that Thomas Nast was the political cartoonist who popularized the current images of the Republican elephant and the Democratic donkey. Nast also created commentary on political machines, such as Tammany Hall.

▲ Differentiation

Instead of asking students simply to describe the historical context, intended audience, purpose, and point of view, consider providing some more questions that can guide students to the answers. For example, when asking about historical context, ask students to describe what time period the cartoon is from. What was life like during that time period? What issues were being confronted? Questions like these can help guide students in the correct direction.

Uncle Sam, don't play with it,—be a Man. Monopolists' soap-bubbles soon burst.

a. Briefly describe ONE perspective about government's role in society expressed in the image.
b. Briefly explain ONE specific historical event or development that led to the perspective expressed in the image.
c. Briefly explain ONE specific historical argument that could be used to support or challenge the perspective expressed in the image.

536

TEACHING IDEA

AP® Writing Historically Review

Political cartoons tend to be more challenging for students than other Short-Answer Questions. Therefore, consider using the following brief bell ringer activity. Have students select two words from the soap bars (for example, "monopoly" and "trust") and two words from the bubbles or the bubbles which have already burst (for example, "fairness" and "protection of labor"), and define the historical trend associated with each word. Put another way, if a student selects "monopoly" and "fairness," what takeaways can they describe? Now ask students to think about the cartoonist's perspective. Given the historical trends, what is the likely point of view being expressed? If students are struggling, consider emphasizing the language used in the caption.

MODULE 6-9 Gilded Age Ideologies

Module 6-10

Politics and Protest

LEARNING TARGETS

By the end of this module, you should be able to:

- Explain the similarities and differences between major political parties during the Gilded Age.
- Explain the causes of agrarian activism during the Gilded Age.
- Explain the impact of the Depression of 1893 on the economy and politics.

THEMATIC FOCUS

Politics and Power

Federal elections were closely contested during the two decades after Reconstruction as partisanship reached new heights, even though it was a time of weak federal government. Faced with falling food prices and overproduction, farmers joined new movements for cooperative self-help and political action, including the creation of the Populist Party. In the aftermath of the Depression of 1893, Republicans emerged as the majority party while Democrats tightened their control of the South and the Populist Party faded.

HISTORICAL REASONING FOCUS

Comparison

TASK ▶ As you read this module, use the lens of comparison to help you better understand the political parties and movements during the Gilded Age. Compare American politics before and after the Depression of 1893. Compare the farm-labor movements of the era — Grange, Farmers' Alliance, and Populists. In both cases, try to determine the reasons for the differences.

Politicians played an important role in the expanding industrial economy that provided new opportunities for the wealthy and the expanding middle class. For growing companies and corporations to succeed, they needed a favorable political climate that would support their interests. During this era, the office of the president was a weak and largely administrative post and legislators and judges were highly influenced and sometimes directly controlled by business leaders. For much of this period, the two national political parties battled to a standoff, which resulted in congressional gridlock with little accomplished. Yet spurred by fierce partisan competition, political participation grew among the electorate.

Farmers, like industrial workers, experienced severe economic hardships and a loss of political power in the face of rapid industrialization. The introduction of new machinery such as the combine harvester, introduced in 1878, led to substantial increases in the productivity of American farms. Soaring production, however, led to a decline in agricultural prices in the late nineteenth century, a trend that was accelerated by increased agricultural production around the world. Faced with an economic crisis caused by falling prices and escalating debt, farmers fought back, creating new organizations to champion their collective economic and political interests.

In early 1893, the bankruptcy of the Philadelphia and Reading Railroad set off a chain reaction that pushed one-quarter of American railroads into insolvency. As a result, on May 5, 1893, "Black Friday," the stock market collapsed in a panic, triggering the **depression of 1893**. Hundreds of banks failed, which hurt the businesspeople and farmers who relied on a steady flow of bank credit. The depression became the chief political issue of the mid-1890s and resulted in a realignment of power among the various national political parties.

depression of 1893 Severe economic downturn triggered by railroad and bank failures. The severity of the depression, combined with the failure of the federal government to offer an adequate response, led to the realignment of American politics.

TRM Suggested Responses to Questions

EXPLORING AP® THEMES

Politics and Power

Have students take notes to keep track of the causes and impacts of the Depression of 1893. Require that all impacts relate to political developments in order to provide information to fit the theme, politics and power. Students may point to the bankruptcy of the Philadelphia and Reading Railroad as a cause of the Depression of 1893. Some impacts that students might discuss include the rise of the Grangers, Farmers' Alliances, and the Populist Party.

BUILDING AP® SKILLS

Comparison

Draw a Venn diagram with three intersecting circles on the board. Label each circle with the following: Grangers, Farmers' Alliance, and Populists. Ask students for information to complete the Venn diagram. Once the Venn diagram is complete, ask students to describe why these three groups were different even though they had similar members.

Period 6: 1865–1898

Weak Presidencies and an Inefficient Congress

BUILDING AP® SKILLS

Argumentation

Divide the class into three groups, one group labelled "support," one group labelled "refute," and a third group labelled "modify." Then, present the class with the following prompt: "Great men became corporate leaders, not presidents." Based upon the group students were placed in, assign them to come up with evidence that either supports, refutes, or modifies the prompt. Allow students to use historical knowledge as well as current events to support their arguments. At the conclusion of this step, recombine the class into groups of three, consisting of one supporter, one refuter, and one modifier. Have them share out and teach one another what they now know, and then as a group, have them craft a thesis statement together on the prompt, based upon their shared knowledge discussion.

James Bryce, a British observer of American politics, devoted a chapter of his book *The American Commonwealth* (1888) to "why great men are not chosen presidents." He believed that the White House attracted mediocre occupants because the president functioned mainly as an executor. The stature of the office had shrunk following the impeachment of Andrew Johnson and the reassertion of congressional power during Reconstruction (Module 5-7). Presidents considered themselves mainly as the nation's top administrator. They did not see their roles as formulating policy or intervening on behalf of legislative objectives. With the office held in such low regard, great men became corporate leaders, not presidents.

Perhaps aware that they could expect little in the way of assistance or imagination from national leaders, voters refused to give either Democrats or Republicans solid support. No president in the two decades between Ulysses S. Grant and William McKinley won back-to-back elections or received a majority of the popular vote. The only two-time winner, the Democrat Grover Cleveland, lost his bid for reelection in 1888 before triumphing again in 1892.

Nevertheless, the presidency attracted accomplished individuals. Rutherford B. Hayes (1877–1881), James A. Garfield (1881), and Benjamin Harrison (1889–1893) all had served ably in the Union army as commanding officers during the Civil War and had prior political experience. The nation greatly mourned Garfield following his assassination in 1881 by Charles Guiteau, a disgruntled applicant for a job in the federal government. Upon Garfield's death, Chester A. Arthur (1881–1885) became president. He had served as a quartermaster general during the Civil War, had a reputation as being sympathetic to African American civil rights, and had run the New York City Customs House effectively. Grover Cleveland (1885–1889, 1893–1897) first served as mayor of Buffalo and then as governor of New York. All of these men, as even Bryce admitted, worked hard, possessed common sense, and were honest. However, they were uninspiring individuals who lacked qualities of leadership that would arouse others to action.

The most important factor in the weakened presidency was the structure of Congress, which prevented the president from providing vigorous leadership. Throughout most of this period, Congress remained narrowly divided. Majorities continually shifted from one party to the other. For all but two terms, Democrats controlled the House of Representatives, while Republicans held the majority in the Senate. Divided government meant that during his term in office no late-nineteenth-century president had a majority of his party in both houses of Congress. Turnover among congressmen in the House of Representatives, who were elected every two years, was quite high, and there was little power of incumbency. The Senate, however, provided more continuity and allowed senators, with six-year terms of office, to amass greater power than congressmen could.

For all the power that Congress wielded, it failed to govern effectively or efficiently. In the House, measures did not receive adequate attention on the floor because the Speaker did not have the power to control the flow of systematic debate. Committee chairmen held a tight rein over the introduction and consideration of legislation and competed with one another for influence in the chamber. Congressmen showed little decorum as they conducted business on the House floor and often chatted with each other or read the newspaper rather than listen to the speakers at the podium.

The Senate, though more manageable in size and more stable in membership (only one-third of its membership stood for reelection every two years), did not function much more smoothly. Senators valued their own judgments and business interests more than party unity. The position of majority leader, someone who could impose discipline on his colleagues and design a coherent legislative agenda, had not yet been created. Woodrow Wilson, the author of *Congressional Government* (1885) and a future president, concluded: "Our government is defective as it parcels out power and confuses responsibility." Under these circumstances, neither the president nor Congress governed efficiently.

> " Our government is defective as it parcels out power and confuses responsibility. "
>
> Woodrow Wilson, *Congressional Government*, 1885

REVIEW

- What did presidents during the 1880s and 1890s have in common?
- What factors contributed to congressional inefficiency?

The Business of Politics

> "A Congressman is a hog! You must take a stick and hit him on the snout!"
> — John Hay, American diplomat, 1869

Many lawmakers viewed politics as a business enterprise that would line their pockets with money. One cabinet officer grumbled, "A Congressman is a hog! You must take a stick and hit him on the snout!" Senators were elected by state legislatures, and these bodies were often controlled by well-funded corporations that generously spread their money around to gain influence. In both branches of Congress, party leaders handed out patronage to supporters regardless of their qualifications for the jobs, a practice known as the spoils system, which started during the Jacksonian era (Module 4-4). Modern-day standards of ethical conduct did not exist; nor did politicians see a conflict of interest in working closely with corporations. Indeed, there were no rules to prevent lawmakers from accepting payments from big business. Most congressmen received free passes from railroads and in turn voted on the companies' behalf. To be fair, most politicians such as Senator Sherman did not see a difference between furthering the legislative agenda of big corporations and promoting the nation's economic interests. Nevertheless, the public held politicians in very low esteem because they resented the influence of corporate money in politics.

The 1890 Congress stands out as an example of fiscal irresponsibility. Known as the **Billion Dollar Congress**, the same Republican legislative majority that passed the Sherman Anti-Trust Act adopted the highest tariff in U.S. history. Sponsored by Ohio congressman William McKinley, a close associate of the industrialist Mark Hanna, it lavishly protected manufacturing interests. Congress also spent enormous sums on special projects to enrich their constituents and themselves. Republicans spent so much money on extravagant enterprises that they wiped out the federal budget surplus.

Increasingly throughout the 1890s, many corporate leaders and their political allies joined together in favor of extending American influence and control over foreign markets and natural resources abroad, especially in Central America and the Pacific regions. They agreed that cyclical fluctuations in the domestic economy required overseas markets to assure high profits. To accomplish this would necessitate the building up of American military and commercial power.

Despite all the difficulties of the legislative process, political candidates eagerly pursued office and conducted extremely heated campaigns. The electorate considered politics a form of entertainment. Political parties did not stand for clearly stated issues or offer innovative solutions; instead, campaigns took on the qualities of carefully staged performances. Candidates crafted their oratory to arouse the passions and prejudices of their audiences, and their managers handed out buttons, badges, and ceramic and glass plates stamped with the candidates' faces and slogans. Partisanship helped fuel high political participation. During this period, voter turnout in presidential elections was much higher than at any time in the twentieth century. Region, as well as historical and cultural allegiances, replaced ideology as the key to party affiliation. The wrenching experience of the Civil War had cemented voting loyalties for many Americans. After Reconstruction, white southerners tended to vote Democratic; northerners and newly enfranchised southern black people generally voted Republican. However, geographic region alone did not shape political loyalties; a sizable contingent of Democratic voters remained in the North, and southern whites and black people periodically abandoned both the Democratic and Republican parties to vote for third parties.

Religion played an important role in shaping party loyalties during this period of intense partisanship. The Democratic Party tended to attract Protestants of certain sects, such as German Lutherans and Episcopalians, as well as Catholics. These faiths emphasized religious ritual and the acceptance of personal sin. They believed that the government should not interfere in matters of morality, which should remain the province of Christian supervision on earth and divine judgment in the hereafter. By contrast, other Protestant denominations, such as Baptists, Congregationalists, Methodists, and Presbyterians, highlighted the importance of individual will and believed that the law could be shaped to eradicate ignorance and vice. These Protestants were more likely to cast their ballots for Republicans, except in the South, where regional loyalty to the Democratic Party trumped religious affiliation.

Some people went to the polls because they fiercely disliked members of the opposition party. Northern white workers in New York City or Cincinnati, Ohio, for example, might vote against the Republican Party because they viewed it as the party of African Americans. Other voters cast their ballots against Democrats because they identified them as the party of Irish Catholics, intemperance, and secession.

AP® TIP

Compare the main characteristics of American politics in the late nineteenth century to those of the period prior to the Civil War.

TEACHING IDEA

Building Vocabulary

Draw a Frayer model on the board/projector. An overview of the Frayer model can be found in the Classroom Strategies section of adlit.org. Ask students to provide information to fill out the Frayer model while reviewing the term "spoils system." Have students review Andrew Jackson's use of the spoils system on page 307 to incorporate prior knowledge.

APPLY THE TIP

Require students to answer the following prompt: "To what extent did American politics change from the period prior to the Civil War to the late nineteenth century? Provide specific historical evidence to support your answer." Possible answers include: *The federal government became increasingly involved in the economy. As Americans moved westward, the federal government removed American Indians from their land and gave land grants to railroad companies as well as granted land to individuals who agreed to farm the land. The federal government also increased its involvement in labor disputes between employers and employees. Congress became increasingly fiscally irresponsible, especially considering that they wiped out the budget surplus in the 1890s. The way that federal employees secured their jobs also changed. The spoils system, which was common in the first half of the nineteenth century, was replaced by a merit-based system where employees had to pass a test in order to secure certain positions in the federal government. Election campaigns also became increasingly extravagant as they morphed into a form of entertainment instead of purely a means to elect new leaders. Over time, politics became more and more partisan as well.*

Period 6: 1865–1898

MODULE 6-10 Politics and Protest

Overall, the continuing strength of party loyalties produced equilibrium as voters cast their ballots primarily along strict party lines. The outcome of presidential elections depended on key "undecided" districts in several states in the Midwest and in New York and nearby states, which swung the balance of power in the electoral college.

REVIEW

- How were business interests able to maintain sway over Congress?
- What factors led to high voter turnout between 1876 and 1896?

Farmers Unite

From the end of the Civil War to the mid-1890s, increased production of wheat and cotton, two of the most important American crops, led to a precipitous drop in the price for these crops. Falling prices created a debt crisis for many farmers. Most American farmers were independent businessmen who borrowed money to pay for land, seed, and equipment. When their crops were harvested and sold, they repaid their debts with the proceeds. As prices fell, farmers increased production in an effort to cover their debts. This tactic led to a greater supply of farm produce in the marketplace and even lower prices. Unable to pay back loans, many farmers lost their property in foreclosures to the banks that held their mortgages and furnished them credit.

To make matters worse, farmers lived isolated lives. Spread out across vast acres of rural territory, farmers had few social and cultural diversions. As the farm economy declined, more and more of their children left the monotony of rural America behind and headed for cities in search of new opportunities and a better life.

Early efforts to organize farmers were motivated by a desire to counteract the isolation of rural life by creating new forms of social interaction and cultural engagement. In 1867, Oliver H. Kelly founded the Patrons of Husbandry to brighten the lonely existence of rural Americans through educational and social activities. Known as **Grangers** (from the French word for "granary"), the

Grangers Members of an organization founded in 1867 to meet the social and cultural needs of farmers. Grangers took an active role in the promotion of the economic and political interests of farmers.

▲ **Granger Movement, 1876** As the farmer's central placement in this lithograph implies, farmers were the heart of the Granger movement. The title is a variation on the movement's motto, "I Pay for All." A farmer with a plough and two horses stands at the center of the scene providing food for all, while other occupational types positioned around him echo a similar refrain based on their profession. **What argument does this poster make about farmers' role in the U.S. economy?**

TEACHING IDEA

Connecting the Dots

Compare the voter turnout in the late nineteenth century with the voter turnout today, available on the United States Elections Project website (electproject.org). Ask students why they believe voter turnout was so much higher during the nineteenth century. Will voter turnout continue to be low into the future? Why or why not? Keep discussions based in fact.

BUILDING AP® SKILLS

Argumentation

Pose the following question to students: "Did government intervention help farmers or businesses more? Provide specific historical evidence to support your answer." Depending on the time you have available, this prompt could become a class debate. Possible answers include: *Government intervention helped farmers more. Legislation such as the Homestead Act opened up new land for farmers to settle. The Sub-Treasury Plan also allowed farmers to trade their grain for government loans, using the grain as collateral. This allowed farmers to bypass the banks, who the farmers felt were taking advantage of them.* Or: *Government intervention helped businesses more. Government land grants to railroad companies helped ensure that businesses could ship raw materials and finished goods more efficiently and at cheaper prices. Congressmen who were gifted with railroad passes also voted for legislation to help railroad companies.*

BUILDING AP® SKILLS

Comparison

Draw a Venn diagram on the board. Label one circle "The Grange" and the other "Large Corporations." Ask students to provide information to answer the prompt: "Compare the goals and actions of the Grangers to those of large corporations in the late nineteenth century." While discussing the answers, fill in the Venn diagram on the board.

TEACHING IDEA

Analyzing Art and Images

Print a copy of the Granger Movement poster, "I Feed You All." You can find a printable copy on the Library of Congress website (loc.gov). Cut the image into eight pieces, one per section of the image, including the center. Either place the images around the room for students to navigate through like a gallery walk, or assign one part of the image each to eight different groups. Have students note the details and historical evidence that they see in the image. Bring the class together for a class discussion, show students the entire image as a whole, and answer the question, "What argument does this poster make about farmers' role in the U.S. economy?"

AP® TIP
Compare the goals and actions of the Grangers to those of large corporations in the late nineteenth century.

Interstate Commerce Commission (ICC) Regulatory commission created by the Interstate Commerce Act in 1887. The commission investigated interstate shipping, required railroads to make their rates public, and could bring lawsuits to force shippers to reduce "unreasonable" fares.

association grew rapidly in the early 1870s, especially in the Midwest and the South. Between 1872 and 1874, approximately fourteen thousand new Grange chapters were established.

Grangers also formed farm cooperatives to sell their crops at higher prices and pool their purchasing power to buy finished goods at wholesale prices. The Grangers' interest in promoting the collective economic interests of farmers led to their increasing involvement in politics. Rather than forming a separate political party, Grangers endorsed candidates who favored their cause. Perhaps their most important objective was the regulation of shipping and grain storage prices. In many areas, individual railroads had monopolies on both of these services and, as a result, were able to charge farmers higher-than-usual rates to store and ship their crops. By electing sympathetic state legislators, Grangers managed to obtain regulations that placed a ceiling on the prices railroads and grain elevators could charge. The Supreme Court temporarily upheld these victories in *Munn v. Illinois* (1877). In 1886, however, in *Wabash v. Illinois* the Supreme Court reversed itself and struck down these state regulatory laws as hindering the free flow of interstate commerce.

Another apparent victory for regulation came in 1887 when Congress passed the Interstate Commerce Act, establishing the **Interstate Commerce Commission** (ICC) to regulate railroads. Although big businessmen could not prevent occasional government regulation, they managed to render it largely ineffective. In time, railroad advocates came to dominate the ICC and enforced the law in favor of the railway lines rather than the shippers. Implementation of the Sherman Antitrust

AP® ANALYZING SOURCES

Source: Mary Elizabeth Lease, *Monopoly Is the Master*, 1890

"This is a nation of inconsistencies. The Puritans fleeing from oppression became oppressors. We fought England for our liberty and put chains on four million of black people. We wiped out slavery and our tariff laws and national banks began a system of white wage slavery worse than the first.

Wall Street owns the country. It is no longer a government of the people, by the people, and for the people, but a government of Wall Street, by Wall Street, and for Wall Street.

The great common people of this country are slaves, and monopoly is the master. The West and South are bound and prostrate before the manufacturing East.

Money rules, and our Vice-President is a London banker. Our laws are the output of a system which clothes rascals in robes and honesty in rags.

The [political] parties lie to us and the political speakers mislead us. . . . The politicians said we suffered from overproduction. Overproduction, when 10,000 little children, so statistics tell us, starve to death every year in the United States, and over 100,000 shop-girls in New York are forced to sell their virtue for the bread their [scanty] wages deny them. . . .

We want money, land and transportation. We want the abolition of the National Banks, and we want the power to make loans direct from the government. We want the foreclosure system wiped out. . . . We will stand by our homes and stay by our fireside by force if necessary, and we will not pay our debts to the loan-shark companies until the government pays its debts to us. The people are at bay; let the bloodhounds of money who dogged us thus far beware."

Questions for Analysis
1. Identify Lease's complaints in this speech.
2. Describe Lease's proposed remedies for those complaints.
3. Explain the economic context surrounding Lease's speech.
4. Evaluate the extent of similarity between the arguments Lease makes in this speech and the principles embraced by other labor movements of the late nineteenth century.

Questions for Comparison "A Workingman's Prayer," *The Coming Nation*, 1894 (p. 535)
1. Identify the intended audiences for Lease's speech and "A Workingman's Prayer."
2. Evaluate the extent of similarity between Lease's argument and that of "A Workingman's Prayer."

TRM Suggested Responses to Questions

TRM Module 6.10 AP® Analyzing Sources Handout 1

BUILDING AP® SKILLS
Argumentation

Read Mary Elizabeth Lease's "Monopoly Is the Master." Have students complete a HIPP analysis (a refresher of HIPP can be found on page 8). Students can read through prior pages of the textbook to find more details about Lease to determine her background and perspective. Next, have students find specific historical evidence in the textbook to both support Lease's argument as well as refute her argument. Possible answers include: *Political corruption and bribery could be evidence to support Lease's argument. The Sherman Anti-Trust Act could be evidence to refute her argument when she says, "monopoly is the master," as the Act's purpose was the breakup of monopolies.*

Period 6: 1865–1898

MODULE 6-10 Politics and Protest

Act also favored big business. From the standpoint of most late-nineteenth-century capitalists, national regulations often turned out to be more of a help than a hindrance.

By the late 1880s, the Grangers had abandoned electoral politics and once again devoted themselves strictly to social and cultural activities. A number of factors explain the Grangers' return to their original mission. First, prices began to rise for some crops, particularly corn, relieving the economic pressure on midwestern farmers. Second, the passage of regulatory legislation in a number of states convinced some Grangers that their political goals had been achieved. Finally, a lack of marketing and business experience led to the collapse of many agricultural collectives.

The withdrawal of the Grangers from politics did not, however, signal the end of efforts by farmers to form organizations to advance their economic interests. While farmers in the midwestern corn belt experienced some political success and an economic upturn, farmers farther west in the Great Plains and in the Lower South fell more deeply into debt, as the price of wheat and cotton on the international market continued to drop. In both of these regions, farmers organized **Farmers' Alliances**. In the 1880s, Milton George formed the Northwestern Farmers' Alliance. At the same time, Dr. Charles W. Macune organized the much larger Southern Farmers' Alliance. Southern black farmers, excluded from the Southern Farmers' Alliance, created a parallel Colored Farmers' Alliance. The Alliances formed a network of recruiters to sign up new members. No recruiter was more effective than Mary Elizabeth Lease, who excited farm audiences with her forceful and colorful rhetoric, delivering 160 speeches in the summer of 1890 alone. The Southern Farmers' Alliance advocated a sophisticated plan to solve the farmers' problem of mounting debt. Macune devised a proposal for a **subtreasury system**. Under this plan, the federal government would locate offices near warehouses in which farmers could store nonperishable commodities. In return, farmers would receive federal loans for 80 percent of the current market value of their produce. In theory, temporarily taking crops off the market would decrease supply and, assuming demand remained stable, lead to increased prices. Once prices rose, farmers would return to the warehouses, redeem their crops, sell them at the higher price, repay the government loan, and leave with a profit.

The first step toward creating a nationwide farmers' organization came in 1889, when the Northwestern and Southern Farmers' Alliances agreed to merge. Alliance leaders, including Lease, saw workers as fellow victims of industrialization, and they invited the Knights of Labor to join them. They also attempted to lower prevailing racial barriers by bringing the Colored Farmers' Alliance into the coalition. The following year, the National Farmers' Alliance and Industrial Union held its convention in Ocala, Florida. The group adopted resolutions endorsing the subtreasury system, as well as recommendations that would promote the economic welfare of farmers and extend political democracy to "the plain people." These proposals included tariff reduction, government ownership of banks and railroads, and political reforms to extend democracy, such as direct election of U.S. senators.

Finally, the Alliance pressed the government to increase the money supply by expanding the amount of silver coinage in circulation. In the Alliance's view, such a move would have two positive, and related, consequences. First, the resulting inflation would lead to higher prices for agricultural commodities, putting more money in farmers' pockets. Second, the real value of farmers' debts would decrease, since the debts were contracted in pre-inflation dollars and would be paid back with inflated currency. Naturally, the eastern bankers who supplied farmers with credit opposed such a policy. In fact, in 1873 Congress, under the leadership of Senator John Sherman, had halted the purchase of silver by the Treasury Department, a measure that helped reduce the money supply. Later, however, under the **Sherman Silver Purchase Act** (1890), the government resumed buying silver, but the act placed limits on its purchase and did not guarantee the creation of silver coinage by the Treasury. In the past, some members of the Alliance had favored expanding the money supply with greenbacks (paper money). However, to attract support from western silver miners, Alliance delegates emphasized the free and unlimited coinage of silver. Alliance supporters met with bitter disappointment, though, as neither the Republican nor the Democratic Party embraced their demands. Denied, farmers took an independent course and became more directly involved in national politics through the formation of the Populist Party.

Farmers' Alliances Regional organizations formed in the late nineteenth century to advance the interests of farmers. The most prominent of these organizations were the Northwestern Farmers' Alliance, the Southern Farmers' Alliance, and the Colored Farmers' Alliance.

TEACHING IDEA

Class Discussion

Put students in pairs. Require students to describe which system was more likely to solve the issue of mounting farmers' debt: the subtreasury system, or the expansion of the amount of silver coinage in circulation. One student should argue on behalf of the subtreasury system and the other on the expansion of silver coinage.

EXPLORING AP® THEMES

Politics and Power

Have each student write a response to the following question on a sheet of loose-leaf paper: "To what extent did the Farmers' Alliance have power in affecting domestic policy?" After each student has a response with evidence, have each student crumple up their paper and have a "snowball fight." After about 30 seconds of throwing the crumpled paper around the room, ask students to pick up one piece of paper. Go around the room and choose random volunteers to read the response on the paper. Discuss the responses briefly – did students agree, or were there a variety of opinions?

AP® ANALYZING SOURCES

A PARTY OF PATCHES.
Grand Balloon Ascension—Cincinnati, May 20th, 1891.

Source: Bernhard Gillam, "Party of Patches: Grand Balloon Ascension — Cincinnati, May 20th, 1891," *Judge*, 1891

About the source: The patches on the balloon in this image are labeled, "Anarchists," "Prohibition Party," "The People's Party: Cincinnati May 1891," "The Silver Party," "Communists," "Farmers' Alliance," "Old Greenback Party," "Socialists," "Old Granger Party," "Knights of Labor Party," and "Women's Rights." The man on the far left in the balloon basket is wearing a ribbon labeled, "Powderly," and the man second from the right is wearing a ribbon labeled "Simpson." The men are dropping papers out of the balloon, which read, "Free Coinage," "Government Control of R.Roads & Telegraphs," "Unlimited Greenbacks," and "Government Pawnshops." The balloon basket itself is labeled, "The Platform of Lunacy."

Questions for Analysis
1. Identify Gillam's main point in this cartoon.
2. Describe the details Gillam uses to illustrate his main point.
3. Explain how, and from whom, the changes proposed by the Populist Party might prompt the kind of response illustrated in this cartoon.

REVIEW
What goals and political proposals did the Grange and the Farmers' Alliance share?

Populists and Depression Politics

Populists The People's Party of America, formed in 1892. The Populists sought to appeal to both farmers and industrial workers.

> **AP® TIP**
> Evaluate the extent to which the demands of the Populist Party reflected changing views about laissez-faire philosophy and the role of government in the economy in the U.S.

In 1892 the National Farmers' Alliance moved into the electoral arena as a third political party. The People's Party of America, known as the **Populists**, held its first nominating convention in Omaha, Nebraska in 1892. In addition to incorporating the Alliance's Ocala planks into their platform, they adopted recommendations to broaden the party's appeal to industrial workers. Populists endorsed a graduated income tax, which would impose higher tax rates on higher income levels, the eight-hour workday, and immigration restriction, which stemmed from the unions' desire to keep unskilled workers from glutting the market and depressing wages. Reflecting the influence of women such as Mary Elizabeth Lease, the party endorsed women's suffrage. The party did not, however, offer specific proposals to prohibit racial discrimination or segregation. Rather, the party focused on remedies to relieve the economic plight of impoverished white and black farmers in general.

In 1892 the Populists nominated former Union Civil War general James B. Weaver for president. Although he came in third behind the Democratic victor, Grover Cleveland, and the Republican incumbent, Benjamin Harrison, he won over 1 million popular votes and 22 electoral votes.

At the state level, Populists performed even better. They elected 10 congressional representatives, 5 U.S. senators, 3 governors, and 1,500 state legislators. Two years later, the party made even greater strides by increasing its total vote by 42 percent and achieving its greatest strength in the South. This electoral momentum positioned the Populists to make an even stronger run in the next presidential election. The economic depression that began in 1893 and the political discontent it generated enhanced Populist chances for success.

543

Period 6: 1865–1898

MODULE 6-10 Politics and Protest

President Grover Cleveland's handling of the depression, accompanied by protest marches and labor strife, only made a bad situation worse. In the spring of 1894, Jacob Coxey, a Populist reformer from Ohio, led a march on Washington, D.C., demanding that Cleveland and Congress initiate a federal public works program to provide jobs for the unemployed. Though highly critical of the favored few who dominated the federal government, Coxey had faith that if "the people . . . come in a body like this, peaceably to discuss their grievances and demanding immediate relief, Congress . . . will heed them and do it quickly." After traveling for a month from Ohio, Coxey led a parade of some five hundred unemployed people into the nation's capital. Attracting thousands of spectators, **Coxey's army** attempted to mount their protest on the grounds of the Capitol building. In response, police broke up the demonstration and arrested Coxey for trespassing. Cleveland turned a deaf ear to Coxey's demands for federal relief and also disregarded protesters participating in nearly twenty other marches on Washington.

In the coming months, Cleveland's political stock plummeted further. He responded to the Pullman strike in the summer of 1894 (Module 6-5) by obtaining a federal court injunction against the strikers and dispatching federal troops to Illinois to enforce it. The president's action won him high praise from the railroads and conservative business interests, but it showed millions of American workers that the Cleveland administration did not have a solution for ending the suffering caused by the depression. "While the people should patriotically and cheerfully support their Government," the president declared, "its functions do not include the support of the people."

Coxey's army 1894 protest movement led by Jacob Coxey. Coxey and five hundred supporters marched from Ohio to Washington, D.C., to protest the lack of government response to the depression of 1893.

TEACHING IDEA

Check for Understanding

As a bell ringer or exit ticket, ask students to describe President Grover Cleveland's responses to the Depression of 1893, and the impacts of his decisions. Have students focus on the question, "To what extent was Cleveland successful in his handling of the Depression of 1893?"

TRM Find **Handout 6.12 – President Cleveland and the Depression of 1893** in the Teacher's Resource Materials.

TRM **Suggested Responses to Questions**

TRM **Module 6.10 AP® Analyzing Sources Handout 3**

BUILDING AP® SKILLS
Sourcing and Situation

As illustrated in this source, John Altgeld — the Governor of Illinois — is asking George Pullman — the owner of a business — to take action to help those who were suffering during the Depression of 1893. How does this development illustrate a departure from laissez-faire policies in favor of government intervention in the economy?

AP® ANALYZING SOURCES

Source: John Altgeld, Illinois Governor, *Letter to George Pullman*, August 21, 1894

"Sir:—I have examined the conditions at Pullman yesterday, visited even the kitchens and bedrooms of many of the people. Two representatives of your company were with me and we found the distress as great as it was represented. The men are hungry and the women and children are actually suffering. They have been living on charity for a number of months and it is exhausted. Men who had worked for your company for more than ten years had to apply to the relief society in two weeks after the work stopped.

I learn from your manager that last spring there were 3,260 people on the pay roll; yesterday there were 2,200 at work, but over 600 of these are new men, so that only about 1,600 of the old employees have been taken back, thus leaving over 1600 of the old employees who have not been taken back, a few hundred have left, the remainder have nearly all applied for work, but were told that they were not needed. These are utterly destitute. The relief committee on last Saturday gave out two pounds of oat meal and two pounds of corn meal to each family. But even the relief committee has exhausted its resources.

Something must be done at once. The case differs from instances of destitution found elsewhere . . . Four-fifths of those people are women and children. No matter what caused this distress, it must be met."

Questions for Analysis
1. Describe the conditions Altgeld refers to in this letter.
2. Explain the immediate and longer-term political and economic impacts of the conditions described in this letter.

Questions for Comparison
Mary Elizabeth Lease, *Monopoly Is the Master*, 1890 (p. 541)
1. Explain the context surrounding both Altgeld's letter and Lease's speech.
2. Evaluate the extent of similarity in the conditions faced by the industrial workers described in Altgeld's letter and the conditions faced by the farmers described in Lease's speech.

544

BUILDING AP® SKILLS
Sourcing and Situation

In addition to discussing the author, discuss the historical context and purpose of the excerpt by John Altgeld. What is happening at this point in time to make Altgeld write this letter? What are his motivations for trying to help those in poverty?

> "While the people should patriotically and cheerfully support their Government, its functions do not include the support of the people."
>
> President Grover Cleveland, Second Inaugural Address, 1893

Making matters worse, Cleveland convinced Congress to repeal the Sherman Silver Purchase Act. This angered western miners, who relied on strong silver prices, along with farmers in the South and Great Plains who were swamped by mounting debt. At the same time, the removal of silver as a backing for currency caused private investors to withdraw their gold deposits from the U.S. Treasury. To keep the government financially solvent, Cleveland worked out an agreement with a syndicate led by J. P. Morgan to help sell government bonds, a deal that netted the banker a huge profit. In the midst of economic suffering, this deal looked like a corrupt bargain between the government and the rich.

In 1894 Congress also passed the Wilson-Gorman Act, which raised tariffs on imported goods. Intended to protect American businesses by keeping the price of imported goods high, it also deprived foreigners of the necessary income with which to buy American exports. This drop in exports did not help economic recovery. The Wilson-Gorman Act did include a provision that the Populists and other reformers endorsed: a progressive income tax of 2 percent on all annual earnings over $4,000. No federal income tax existed at this time, so even this mild levy elicited cries of "socialism" from conservative critics, who challenged the tax in the courts. The next year the Supreme Court declared the income tax unconstitutional and denounced it as the opening wedge in "a war of the poor against the rich; a war constantly growing in intensity and bitterness."

With Cleveland's legislative program in shambles and his inability to solve the depression abundantly clear, the Democrats suffered a crushing blow at the polls. In the congressional elections of 1894, the party lost an astonishing 120 seats in the House. This defeat offered a preview of the political shakeup that loomed ahead.

REVIEW

- How did President Cleveland respond to the Depression of 1893?
- What similarities did the Populists and Farmers' Alliance share?

Political Realignment in the Election of 1896

The presidential election of 1896 marked a turning point in the political history of the nation. Democrats nominated William Jennings Bryan of Nebraska, a farmers' advocate who favored silver coinage. When he vowed that he would not see Republicans "crucify mankind on a cross of gold," the Populists endorsed him as well.

Republicans nominated William McKinley, the governor of Ohio and a supporter of the gold standard and high tariffs on manufactured and other goods. McKinley's campaign manager, Mark Hanna, an ally of Ohio senator John Sherman, raised an unprecedented amount of money, about $16 million, mainly from wealthy industrialists who feared that the free and unlimited coinage of silver would debase the U.S. currency. Hanna saturated the country with pamphlets, leaflets, and posters, many of them written in the native languages of immigrant groups. He also hired a platoon of speakers to fan out across the country denouncing Bryan's free silver cause as financial madness. By contrast, Bryan raised about $1 million.

The outcome of the election transformed the Republicans into the majority party in the United States. McKinley won 51 percent of the popular vote and 61 percent of the electoral vote. More important than this specific contest, however, was that the election proved critical in realigning the two parties. Voting patterns shifted with the 1896 election, giving Republicans the edge in party affiliation among the electorate not only in this contest but also in presidential elections over the next three decades.

What happened to produce this critical realignment in electoral power? The main ingredient was Republicans' success in fashioning a coalition that included both corporate capitalists and their workers. Many urban dwellers and industrial workers took out their anger on Cleveland's Democratic Party and Bryan as its standard-bearer for failing to end the depression. In addition, Bryan, who hailed from Nebraska and reflected small-town agricultural America and its values, could not win over the swelling numbers of urban immigrants who considered Bryan's world alien to their experience. Finally, fear that Bryan's free silver policy would lead to inflation, increasing

---

TEACHING IDEA

Incorporating Videos

As a class, watch Episode 26, "Gilded Age Politics," from the Crash Course US History series (available on YouTube). This video provides a review of political machines and their impact on the cities, the rise of the Grange, or Farmers' Alliance, and the Populist Party, as well as the election of 1896. While watching, have students take notes to keep track of the changes in political thought during the late nineteenth century. What political changes can be attributed to the Populist Party, and why were they necessary? Possible answers include: *graduated income tax, government ownership of railroads, and government control of currency. Changes were necessary due to political and industrial corruption.*

TEACHING IDEA

Check for Understanding

As a bell ringer or exit ticket, ask students to write a couple of sentences to answer the prompt: "To what extent did printing pamphlets and posters in the native languages of immigrant groups help the Republican nominee, William McKinley?"

TEACHING IDEA

Geography Instruction

Ask students to analyze Map 6.6 and determine how the map illustrates regional differences. What types of voters would have been located in the Northeast and Midwest, and why would they support the Republican candidate? What types of voters were located in the South and the West, and why would they support the Democratic candidate?

TEACHING IDEA

Incorporating Websites

Have students compare Map 6.6 to other elections throughout American history. A full timeline of Electoral College maps can be found at 270 to Win's website (270towin.com). As students navigate through maps of various elections, ask them to see if they can find other maps that are divided among regional lines, just like the election of 1896. Students will likely notice that for most elections between the years 1860 and 1908, there is a stark line between voters in the North and voters in the South. Have students discuss the following questions in groups: How do these maps compare? Do regional differences persist throughout American history, or do they change over time? What are the reasons for certain regional differences at different points in history? Be prepared to explain why some maps have states that are grayed out, or colored purple or green. Students might have questions about some of the first elections, as the main political parties were different than they are now. In addition, there are some years in which states did not participate, especially in the years surrounding the Civil War. Any states that are gray and do not have numbers are not part of the United States or are territories at the time of the particular election.

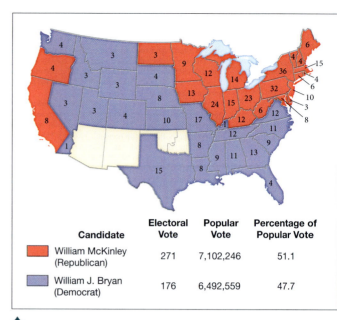

MAP 6.6 The Election of 1896 William McKinley's election in 1896 resulted in a realignment of political power in the United States that lasted until 1932. Republicans became the nation's majority party by forging a coalition of big business and urban industrial workers from the Northeast and Midwest. Democratic strength was confined to the South and to small towns and rural areas of the Great Plains and Rocky Mountain states. **Why did Republicans decisively win the electoral vote despite the fact that each party won a similar number of states?**

the costs of goods and services without a corresponding bump in factory wages, kept many urban workers from voting for him.

The election of 1896 broke the political stalemate of the preceding two decades. The core of Republican backing came from industrial cities of the Northeast and Midwest. Republicans won support from their traditional constituencies of Union veterans, businessmen, and African Americans and added to it the votes of a large number of urban wageworkers. The campaign persuaded voters that the Democratic Party represented the party of depression and that Republicans stood for prosperity and progress. They were soon able to take credit for ending the depression when, in 1897, gold discoveries in Alaska helped increase the money supply and foreign crop failures raised American farm prices. Democrats managed to hold on to the South as their solitary political base.

REVIEW

- What were the short- and long-term consequences of the election of 1896?

BUILDING AP® SKILLS

Causation

Visual note-taking can be a valuable tool, as visualization can help students better remember concepts. Have students draw a sketch of descending stairs in their notes that include at least four steps. Title the sketch "Decline of the Populists." In each step, ask students to find one reason for the fall of Populism. Examples may include disagreements over whether to emphasize free silver over the rest of its platform, the Northern Populists did not want to join with Democrats, the party lost the presidential election of 1896, industrial workers and farmers did not have enough in common to hold the party together, etc.

Decline of the Populists

The year 1896 also marked the end of the Populists as a national force, as the party was torn apart by internal divisions over policy and strategy. Populist leaders such as Tom Watson of Georgia did not want the Populist Party to emphasize free silver above the rest of its reform program. Northern Populists, who either had fought on the Union side during the Civil War or had close relatives who did, could not bring themselves to join the Democrats, the party of the old Confederacy. Nevertheless, the Populist Party officially backed Bryan, but to retain its identity, the party nominated Watson for vice president on its own ticket. After McKinley's victory, the Populist Party collapsed.

Losing the presidential election alone did not account for the disintegration of the Populists. Several problems plagued the third party. The nation's recovery from the depression removed one of the Populists' prime sources of electoral attraction. Despite appealing to industrial workers, the Populists were unable to capture their support. The free silver plank attracted silver miners in Idaho and Colorado, but the majority of workers failed to identify with a party composed mainly of farmers. As consumers of agricultural products, industrial laborers did not see any benefit in raising farm prices. Populists also failed to create a stable, biracial coalition of farmers. Most southern white Populists did not truly accept African Americans as equal partners, even though both groups had mutual economic interests.

To eliminate Populism's insurgent political threat, southern opponents found ways to disfranchise black and poor white voters. During the 1890s, southern states inserted into their constitutions voting requirements that virtually eliminated the black electorate and greatly diminished the white electorate. Seeking to circumvent the Fifteenth Amendment's prohibition against racial discrimination in the right to vote, conservative white lawmakers adopted regulations based on wealth and education because black people were disproportionately poor and had lower literacy rates. They instituted poll taxes, which imposed a fee for voting, and literacy tests, which asked questions designed to trip up black would-be voters. In 1898 the Supreme Court upheld the constitutionality of these voter qualifications in **Williams v. Mississippi**. Recognizing the power of white supremacy, the Populists surrendered to its appeals.

Tom Watson provides a case in point. He started out by encouraging racial unity but then switched to divisive politics. In 1896 the Populist vice presidential candidate called on citizens of both races to vote against the crushing power of corporations and railroads. By whipping up

Wilmington, North Carolina Massacre, 1898 In 1898, Populists in alliance with the Republican Party in Wilmington, N.C. elected a white mayor and a biracial city council. Two days after the election, on November 10, armed members of the defeated Democratic Party, the party of white supremacy, overthrew the new city government. A mob of around 2000 white men, some of whom are pictured here, set fire to the city's black newspaper building. White terrorists killed at least fifteen people and forced more than 2000 black people to flee the city permanently. **Why might men who committed violence willingly pose for a photograph? What does that suggest about the legal status of African Americans in the South?**

BUILDING AP® SKILLS
Developments and Processes

Third parties have historically struggled to win popular support. Many third parties end up joining with one of the two main political parties in the United States, the Democrats or the Republicans, in order to win elections or pass bills. This is what happened in the 1898 North Carolina election, when the Democrats faced a fusion party consisting of the Republicans and Populists joined together. The Stanford History Education Group has a lesson titled "1898 North Carolina Election" that gives students an opportunity to analyze primary sources in order to increase their understanding of the causes leading to the decline of the Populist Party (sheg.stanford.edu).

BUILDING AP® SKILLS
Making Connections

Discuss the image *Wilmington, North Carolina Massacre, 1898* with students. Refer students back to the excerpt written by Henry Grady on page 474. How does Grady's idea of the New South compare with this image and its caption?

TEACHING IDEA
Class Discussion

Ask students, "To what extent was the election of 1896 a turning point in American Politics?"

TEACHING IDEA

Connecting the Dots

Period 6 focuses on the following AP® themes: migration and settlement; American and national identity; social structures; politics and power; as well as work, exchange, and technology. Once students have read the entire period, put students into five groups. Assign each group one of the themes that are included in this period, and have each group create a list of as many concepts that fit into their assigned theme as possible. Then have each group summarize their assigned theme in two to three sentences, which they will share with the rest of the class.

TRM Suggested Responses to Questions

TEACHING IDEA

AP® Writing Historically Review

The following activity can be used to jump-start students' understanding of the claims made in these two sources. In the first excerpt, have students define the "agrarian myth" as well as what Hofstadter meant by "The Populists looked backward." This should help focus students' attention to the main elements of his argument. In the second excerpt, have students define the sentence, "On the contrary, the Populists…" Also have them define how Postel defends the assertion, "The Populists were just this kind of people." Starting students with two elements of each excerpt can help jump-start an understanding of how to differentiate between the historical arguments.

---

antagonism against black people, his Democratic opponents appealed to the racial pride of poor whites to keep them from defecting to the Populists. Embittered by the outcome of the 1896 election and learning from the tactics of his political foes, Watson embarked on a vicious campaign to exclude black people from voting. "What does civilization owe the Negro?" he bitterly asked. "Nothing! Nothing! NOTHING!!!" Only by disfranchising African Americans and maintaining white supremacy, Watson and other white reformers reasoned, would poor whites have the courage to vote against rich whites.

Nevertheless, even in defeat the Populists left an enduring legacy. Many of their political and economic reforms — direct election of senators, the graduated income tax, government regulation of business and banking, and a version of the subtreasury system (called the Commodity Credit Corporation, created in the 1930s) — became features of reform in the twentieth century. Perhaps their greatest contribution, however, came in showing farmers that their old individualist ways would not succeed in the modern industrial era. Rather than re-creating an independent political party, most farmers looked to organized interest groups, such as the Farm Bureau, to lobby on behalf of their interests.

REVIEW

- What were the major causes for the decline of the Populists?

AP® WRITING HISTORICALLY — Short-Answer Question Practice

ACTIVITY

Read the following question carefully and write a short response. Use complete sentences.

Using the following excerpts, answer (a), (b) and (c).

Source: Richard Hofstadter, *The Age of Reform: From Bryan to F.D.R.*, 1955

"As a businessman, the farmer was appropriately hardheaded; he tried to act upon a cold and realistic strategy of self-interest. As the head of the family, however, the farmer felt that . . . when he risked the farm he risked his home — that he was, in short, a single man running a personal enterprise in a world of impersonal forces. It was from this aspect of his situation — seen in the hazy glow of the agrarian myth — that his political leaders in the 1890s developed their rhetoric and some of their concepts of political action.

The utopia of the Populists was in the past, not the future. According to the agrarian myth, the health of the state was proportionate to the degree to which it was dominated by the agricultural class, and this assumption pointed to the superiority of an earlier age. The Populists looked backward with longing to the lost agrarian Eden, to the Republican America of the early years of the nineteenth century in which there were few millionaires, and as they saw it, no beggars when the laborer had excellent prospects and the farmer had abundance, when the statesman still responded to the mood of the people and there was no such thing as money power. What they meant — though they did not express themselves in such terms — was that they would like to restore the conditions prevailing before the development of industrialism and the commercialization of agriculture. . . . In Populist thought the farmer is not a speculating businessman, victimized by the risk economy of which he is a part, but rather a wounded yeoman preyed upon by those who are alien to the life of folkish virtue."

Source: Charles Postel, *The Populist Vision*, 2007

"The Populist world was too commercially and intellectually dynamic to resemble a traditional society in any meaningful sense of the term. This tells us something important about the nature of late nineteenth-century: the men and women of the Populist movement were modern people. The term *modern* does not mean 'good.' Nor is it a value judgment across the political spectrum from right to left. Moreover, to say that the Populists were modern does not imply that they were more modern than, say, their Republican or Democratic opponents. Nor does it imply that all rural people shared the Populists' modern sensibility. On the contrary, the Populists understood that the transformations they sought required the uprooting of ignorance, inertia, and force of habit. Populism formed a unique social movement that represented a distinctly modernizing impulse. . . .

Modernity also implied a particular kind of people with particular types of strivings . . . Modern men and women . . . 'look forward to future developments in their conditions of life and their relations with their fellow men.' The Populists were just this kind of people. They sought to improve their domestic economy and their national government. They sought renewal in local schoolhouses and federal credit systems. They sought to refashion associational ties with neighbors and commercial relations with the world. They sought new techniques, new acreage, and new avenues of spiritual expression."

a. Briefly explain ONE major difference between Hofstadter's and Postel's interpretations of the Populists.
b. Briefly explain how ONE specific historical event or development from the period that is not explicitly mentioned in the excerpts could be used to support Hofstadter's argument.
c. Briefly explain how ONE specific historical event or development from the period that is not explicitly mentioned in the excerpts could be used to support Postel's argument.

TEACHING IDEA

AP® Writing Historically Review

Review Hofstadter and Postel's sources. As a bell ringer or exit ticket, ask students to describe the extent to which the Populist Party tried to change the American political system, according to each author.

PERIOD 6 REVIEW 1865–1898

KEY CONCEPTS AND EVENTS

American Federation of Labor, *495*
Battle of the Little Bighorn, *455*
Billion Dollar Congress, *539*
buffalo soldiers, *455*
Californios, *469*
Chinese Exclusion Act, *471*
collective bargaining, *494*
Comstock Lode, *461*
convict lease, *474*
corporate capitalism, *524*
corporation, *487*
Coxey's army, *544*
Dawes Act, *457*
deflation, *467*
depression of 1893, *537*
eugenics, *508*
Farmers' Alliances, *542*
frontier thesis, *512*
ghettos, *503*
Ghost Dance, *459*
Gilded Age, *524*
"The Gospel of Wealth," *533*
Grangers, *540*
Great Plains, *449*
gross domestic product, *482*

Haymarket riot, *495*
holding company, *487*
Homestead Act, *465*
Homestead strike, *496*
horizontal integration, *485*
Industrial Workers of the World, *499*
interlocking directorates, *486*
Interstate Commerce Commission, *541*
Jim Crow, *476*
Knights of Labor, *494*
laissez-faire, *532*
land rush, *456*
Long Drive, *463*
melting pot, *508*
Mormons, *469*
nativism, *507*
New South, *473*
Pendleton Civil Service Reform Act, *519*
Pinkertons, *497*
Plessy v. Ferguson, *477*
political boss, *517*
political machine, *517*
poll tax, *476*
Populists, *543*

Pullman strike, *498*
robber barons, *482*
Sand Creek massacre, *455*
Santa Clara County v. Southern Pacific Railroad Company, *487*
scientific management, *488*
settlement houses, *519*
Sherman Antitrust Act, *488*
Sherman Silver Purchase Act, *542*
Social Darwinism, *533*
social gospel, *519*
Socialist Party of America, *498*
subtreasury system, *542*
sweatshops, *516*
Tammany Hall, *518*
tenements, *515*
transcontinental railroad, *451*
Treaty of Fort Laramie, *454*
Treaty of Medicine Lodge, *455*
trust, *487*
unions, *494*
United States v. E.C. Knight Company, *488*
vertical integration, *485*
Williams v. Mississippi, *547*
Wounded Knee massacre, *459*

KEY PEOPLE

Alexander Graham Bell, *484*
Henry Bessemer, *484*
William Jennings Bryan, *545*
Andrew Carnegie, *482*
Grover Cleveland, *498*
Jacob Coxey, *544*
George Armstrong Custer, *455*
Eugene V. Debs, *498*
W. E. B. Du Bois, *508*

Thomas Alva Edison, *485*
Geronimo, *459*
Samuel Gompers, *495*
Jay Gould, *486*
Henry Grady, *473*
Chief Joseph, *455*
William McKinley, *538*
J. P. Morgan, *485*
Terence V. Powderly, *494*

George Pullman, *494*
Jacob Riis, *516*
John D. Rockefeller, *485*
William Tecumseh Sherman, *455*
Sitting Bull, *455*
Frederick W. Taylor, *488*
Frederick Jackson Turner, *512*
Boss Tweed, *518*

PERIOD 6 REVIEW 1865–1898

CHRONOLOGY

1850s	Tenements begun to be built in cities
1851	Herbert Spencer proposes theory of social evolution in *Social Statistics*
1859	Invention of Bessemer converter
	Publication of Charles Darwin's landmark text *On the Origin of Species*
By 1861	Western Union ran 76,000 miles of telegraph line
1864	Sand Creek Massacre
1866	Transatlantic telegraph cable connects the United States and Europe
1867	Treaty of Medicine Lodge
1869	Central Pacific and Union Pacific Railroad crews meet in Utah
	Founding of the Knights of Labor
1870s	Gold discoveries in the Black Hills
1871	Chicago fire, in which the North Side of the city burned to the ground
1873	Congress halts purchase of silver by the Treasury Department, reducing the money supply
By 1874	Establishment of approximately 14,000 new Grange chapters
1874	Henry Grady calls for a "New South"
1875–99	10 million people immigrate to America
1876	Battle of the Little Bighorn
1877	Passage of the Desert Land Act
1879	Henry George critiques materialism and greed in *Progress and Poverty*
By 1880	Chinese population in America reaches 200,000
1880s	Height of cattle boom
	Development of new industry throughout the South
	Skyscrapers constructed thanks to invention of structural steel and elevators
	Establishment of numerous charitable organizations such as the American Red Cross
	Exodus of African Americans from the South begins
1881	Black washerwomen strike in Atlanta
1882	Chinese Exclusion Act of 1882
	Passage of the Edmunds Act
	Beginning of widespread electric lighting in New York City
	Homestead strike and collapse of steel prices
1883	The 1875 Civil Rights Act struck down by Supreme Court
	Construction is completed on the Brooklyn Bridge
	Passage of Pendleton Civil Service Reform Act
	Dynamic Sociology, by Lester Frank Ward, attacks laissez-faire policy
1885	Establishment of American Telephone and Telegraph Company (AT&T)
	Successful strike against the Union Pacific and Missouri Pacific Railroads
1886	Samuel Gompers becomes president of AFL
	Nationwide striking for eight-hour workday
	Opening of the Statue of Liberty
1887	Passage of the Dawes Act
	Establishment of the American Protective Association
1889	Publication of "The Gospel of Wealth," an essay by Andrew Carnegie
	Northwestern and Southern Farmers' Alliances merge
1890s	Jim Crow laws become prevalent in the South
	Frontier declared closed by U.S. Census Bureau
1890	Passage of the Sherman Antitrust Act
	Jacob Riis publishes how *How the Other Half Lives*
	Sherman Silver Purchase Act resumes government purchase of silver
1892	National Guard called upon to end striking in Idaho
	National Farmers' Alliance becomes a third political party, the Populists
1893	Establishment of the Immigration Restriction League
	Bankruptcy of the Philadelphia and Reading Railroads signals a nationwide economic depression
1894	Federal troops dispatched against Illinois strikers in Pullman strike
1896	*Plessy v. Ferguson* upholds Jim Crow segregation
	William McKinley wins presidential election
	Populist Party dissolves
1897	First subway opens, in Boston
By 1900	Peak of the mining rush
	200,000 miles of railroad track laid throughout the United States

Suggested Responses to Questions

Answers to Multiple-Choice Questions

1. b
2. a
3. c
4. a
5. d
6. a
7. c
8. b
9. d
10. a
11. b
12. a
13. b
14. b
15. a
16. b

AP® EXAM PRACTICE THROUGH 1898

Multiple Choice Questions

Choose the correct answer for each question.

Questions 1–3 refer to the following excerpt.

Source: Dawes Severalty Act, 1887

"[T]he President of the United States . . . is authorized . . . to allot the lands . . . [individually] to any Indian located thereon in quantities as follows: To each head of a family, one-quarter of a section; To each single person over eighteen years of age, one-eighth of a section; To each orphan child under eighteen years of age, one-eighth of a section; and To each other single person under eighteen years now living . . . one-sixteenth of a section. . . . [E]very [American Indian] to whom allotments have been made shall have the benefit of and be subject to the laws, both civil and criminal, of the State or Territory in which they may reside. . . ."

1. The policy toward American Indians expressed in the Dawes Severalty Act resulted from which of the following?
   a. American Indian society's treatment of women as equals
   b. Conflicts over landownership between white settlers and American Indians
   c. The development of unified alliances between American Indian tribes
   d. The growth of regional trade networks among American Indian tribes

2. The policy goals endorsed by the Dawes Severalty Act would have been most strongly supported by advocates of
   a. assimilation.
   b. the social gospel.
   c. nativism.
   d. agrarian cooperatives.

3. The growth of which of the following historical developments most threatened American Indians' way of life in the period 1850 to 1890?
   a. Telegraphs
   b. Sharecropping
   c. Railroads
   d. Newspapers

Questions 4–5 refer to the following excerpt.

Source: Philip Hubert, *The Business of a Factory*, 1897

"It is commonly admitted that while a man or woman who does some small thing in the manufacture of an article . . . may become marvelously expert, the operator runs the risk of becoming more or less of a machine . . . the minute division of labor that makes such wonders possible brutalizes the laborer, and . . . if the girl made the whole article instead of doing one operation out of fifty, she would gain in intelligence if not in expertness. From an economic, or rather an industrial point of view, however, manufacturing has to be carried on at present with the greatest subdivision possible. Fierce competition and a small margin of profit demand it."

4. The process described in the excerpt most directly led to controversies in the late nineteenth century over
   a. the wages and working conditions of workers.
   b. government intervention during economic downturns.
   c. government policies to create centers of commercial activity.
   d. urban neighborhoods segregated by ethnicity and class.

5. Which of the following would be most supportive of the ideas expressed in the excerpt?
   a. Utopians
   b. Advocates for the gospel of wealth
   c. Nativists
   d. The Knights of Labor

Period 6: 1865–1898

AP® Exam Practice: Through 1898

Questions 6–8 refer to the following map.

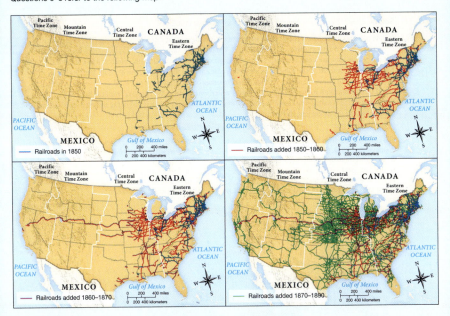

Expansion of the Railroad System, 1850–1890

6. Which of the following most directly contributed to the overall trend depicted in the maps?
   a. Technological innovations
   b. The rise of organized labor
   c. Improved standards of living
   d. Increased trade with Latin America

7. The trend depicted in the maps led to all of the following EXCEPT
   a. large numbers of migrants moving to the West.
   b. the rise of cattle ranching in Texas.
   c. an overall increase in consumer prices.
   d. the growth of cooperative organizations for farmers.

8. The federal government most directly contributed to the trend depicted in the maps by
   a. actively regulating the railroad industry.
   b. subsidizing railroad construction through land grants.
   c. passing federal income taxes to fund new railroads.
   d. taking direct ownership of the major railroad lines.

Period 6: 1865–1898

Questions 9–10 refer to the following excerpt.

Source: Essay by Yale Professor William Graham Sumner, 1880

"[T]he natural conditions of the struggle for existence produces inequalities between men. The struggle for existence is aimed against nature. It is from her . . . hand that we have to wrest the satisfactions for our needs, but our fellow-men are our competitors for the meager supply. Competition, therefore, is a law of nature. Nature is entirely neutral; she submits to him who most energetically and resolutely assails her. She grants her awards to the fittest, therefore, without regard to other considerations of any kind. . . . If we do not like it, and if we try to amend it, there is only one way in which we can do it. We can take from the better and give to the worse. . . . We shall thus lessen the inequalities. We shall favor the survival of the unfittest, and we shall accomplish this by destroying liberty."

9. The ideas expressed in the excerpt most directly led to controversies in the 1880s and 1890s over
   a. increasing numbers of international migrants.
   b. business efforts to secure international markets.
   c. wages and working conditions.
   d. the moral obligations of business leaders to improve society.

10. Which of the following ideologies express the greatest difference from the ideas expressed in the excerpt?
    a. Populism
    b. Social Darwinism
    c. Nativism
    d. Laissez-faire capitalism

Questions 11–12 refer to the following image.

▲
Thomas Nast, *Boss Tweed*, 1871

11. Which of the following would have most likely supported the arrangement of political power portrayed in the image?
    a. Sharecroppers in the South
    b. Recent immigrants
    c. College-educated women
    d. Utopians and socialists

12. The conditions depicted in the cartoon were most prevalent in which type of election race?
    a. City
    b. County
    c. State
    d. Federal

Questions 13–14 refer to the following excerpt.

Source: Theodore Roosevelt, "Professionalism in Sports," 1890

"It is hardly necessary at the present day to enter a plea for athletic exercise and manly out-door sports. . . . [T]his growth can best be promoted by stimulating, within proper bounds, the spirit of rivalry on which all our games are based. . . . As a nation we have many tremendous problems to work out, and we need to bring every ounce of vital power possible to the solution. No people has ever yet done great and lasting work if its physical type was infirm and weak. . . . In college — and in most of the schools which are preparatory for college — rowing, foot-ball, base-ball, running, jumping, sparring, and the like have assumed a constantly increasing prominence. Nor is this a matter for regret. . . . [A]thletic sports, if followed properly . . . are admirable for developing character, besides bestowing on the participants an invaluable fund of health and strength. . . ."

13. Roosevelt's remarks in the excerpt most directly reflected which of the following developments during the late nineteenth century?
    a. New cultural opportunities in urban areas
    b. Increasing amounts of leisure time for the middle and upper classes
    c. More numerous critics championing alternative visions for U.S. society
    d. The growing income gap between rich and poor

14. The professionalization of sports in the United States in the late nineteenth and early twentieth centuries most directly contributed to which of the following?
    a. Economic instability and political discontent among farmers
    b. Increasing urbanization of the United States
    c. Movements of women to seek greater equality with men
    d. Greater ethnic diversity in the industrial workforce

Questions 15–16 refer to the following excerpt.

Source: Speech by Mary Elizabeth Lease, political activist, 1890

"This is a nation of inconsistencies. . . . We fought England for our liberty and put chains on four million black people. We wiped out slavery and by our tariff laws and national banks began a system of white wage slavery worse than the first. Wall Street owns the country. It is no longer a government of the people, by the people, and for the people, but a government of Wall Street, by Wall Street, and for Wall Street. . . . Tariff is not the paramount question. The main question is the money question. . . . Kansas now suffers from two great robbers, the Santa Fe Railroad and the loan companies. The common people are robbed to enrich their masters. . . . We want money, land and transportation. We want the abolition of national banks, and we want the power to make loans from the government. We want the accursed foreclosure system wiped out."

15. A supporter of the ideas Lease expressed in the excerpt would most likely also have supported
    a. a stronger governmental role in regulating the American economic system.
    b. ideas such as the Gospel of Wealth.
    c. laissez-faire economic policies as pathways to growth in the long run.
    d. increased sharecropping and tenant farming.

16. The ideas expressed in the excerpt resulted most directly from
    a. public debates over assimilation.
    b. corporate consolidation in agricultural markets.
    c. battles between labor and management over wages and working conditions.
    d. the promotion of the idea of a "New South."

Period 6: 1865–1898

AP® Exam Practice: Through 1898

Short-Answer Questions

Read each question carefully and write a short response. Use complete sentences.

1. Using the following two excerpts, answer (a), (b), and (c).

   Source: Alfred D. Chandler Jr., *The Visible Hand: The Managerial Revolution in American Business*, 1977

   "The visible hand of management replaced the invisible hand of market forces. . . . [S]afe, regular, reliable movement of goods and passengers, as well as the continuing maintenance and repair of locomotives, rolling stock, and track, roadbed, stations, roundhouses, and other equipment, required . . . special skills and training which could only be commanded by a full-time salaried manager. . . . This career orientation and the specialized nature of tasks gave the railroad managers an increasingly professional outlook on their work."

   Source: Richard White, *Railroaded: The Transcontinentals and the Making of Modern America*, 2011

   "[Railroads] were not the harbingers of order, rationality, and effective large-scale organization. . . . Managers blamed their failures on accidents and contingent events, but they also used them to cover their mistakes and claim quite fortuitous results as the fruits of their planning. . . . [The railroad corporations] not only failed to institute the order they desired; they also just plain failed and repeatedly needed rescuing by the state and the courts. . . . The transcontinental railroads are sometimes fetishized as the ultimate manifestation of modern rationality, but, when seen from within, these astonishingly mismanaged railroads are the anteroom to mystery."

   a) Briefly explain ONE major difference between Chandler's and White's historical interpretations of corporate American railroads in the second half of the nineteenth century.
   b) Briefly explain how ONE specific historical event or development not directly mentioned in the excerpts could be used to support Chandler's argument.
   c) Briefly explain how ONE specific historical event or development not directly mentioned in the excerpts could be used to support White's argument.

2. Using the following political cartoon, answer (a), (b), and (c).

▲ **The Bosses of the Senate, 1893** The sign at the center top of the image reads, "This is the SENATE, of the MONOPOLISTS, by the MONOPOLISTS and FOR the MONOPOLISTS!" The labels on the men standing behind the senators read (from left to right, beginning with fourth from the left), "COAL," "TIN TRUST," "SUGAR TRUST," "IRON TRUST," "STANDARD OIL TRUST," "COPPER TRUST, and "STEEL BEEM TRUST." In the background, a man wearing a money bag labeled "NAIL TRUST" is walking through the "Entrance for MONOPOLISTS" door. In the background in the upper left quadrant of the image, the "PEOPLE'S ENTRANCE" door is barred shut, and has "CLOSED" sign running across it.

AP® Exam Practice: Through 1898

- a) Briefly explain ONE perspective about politics in the United States expressed by artist in the image.
- b) Briefly explain how ONE event or development led to the perspective expressed by the artist in the image.

3. Answer (a), (b), and (c).
   - a) Briefly explain ONE specific historical similarity in the interactions between the U.S. government and American Indians in the period 1825 to 1860 and in the period 1865 to 1898.
   - b) Briefly explain ONE specific historical difference in the interactions between the U.S. government and American Indians in the period 1825 to 1860 and in the period 1865 to 1898.

4. Answer (a), (b), and (c).
   - a) Briefly explain ONE specific historical similarity in the labor movement in the United States in the period 1820 to 1860 and in the period 1860 to 1898.
   - b) Briefly explain ONE specific historical difference in the labor movement in the United States in the period 1820 to 1860 and in the period 1860 to 1898.

- c) Briefly explain ONE specific effort to reform the conditions depicted by the artist in the image.

- c) Briefly explain ONE specific historical example of American Indian resistance to U.S. government policies in the period 1865 to 1898.

- c) Briefly explain ONE factor that accounts for the difference you indicated in (b).

Document-Based Question

Question 1 is based on the accompanying documents. The documents have been edited for the purpose of this exercise. *Suggested reading period: 15 minutes. Suggested writing time: 45 minutes.*

1. Evaluate the extent to which the settlement of the American West changed the lives of peoples in the region between 1865 and 1898.

DOCUMENT 1
Source: Comanche Chief Ten Bears, *Medicine Lodge Treaty Address*, October 1867

"I was born on the prairie where the wind blew free and there was nothing to break the light of the sun. I was born where there were no enclosures and where everything drew a free breath. I want to die there and not within walls. . . . When I was at Washington the Great Father told me that all the Comanche land was ours and that no one should hinder us in living upon it. So, why do you ask us to leave the rivers and the sun and the wind and live in houses? Do not ask us to give up the buffalo for the sheep. The young men have heard talk of this, and it has made them sad and angry. . . .

If the Texans had kept out of my country there might have been peace. But that which you now say we must live on is too small. The Texans have taken away the places where the grass grew the thickest and the timber was the best. Had we kept that we might have done the things you ask. But it is too late. The white man has the country which we loved, and we only wish to wander on the prairie until we die."

DOCUMENT 2
Source: *Acts of the Wyoming Territorial Legislature*, 1869 and 1870

"AN ACT to confer to women all the rights of citizenship.
   That every woman of the age of twenty-one years, residing in this territory, may, at every election . . . cast her vote. And her rights to the elective franchise, and to hold office, shall be the same under the election laws of the territory, as those electors.

AN ACT to protect married women in their separate property, and the enjoyment of their labor.
   That all the property, both real and personal, belonging to any married woman as her sole and separate property . . . shall, notwithstanding her marriage, be and remain . . . her sole and separate property, under her sole control, and be held, owned, possessed and enjoyed by her, the same as though she were [single] and unmarried, and shall not be subject to the disposal, control or interference of her husband."

TRM Suggested Responses to Questions

DOCUMENT 3

Source: *A Remonstrance from the Chinese in California to the Congress of the United States, c. 1870*

"When we were first favored with the invitations of your ship-captains to emigrate to California, and heard the [praises] which they published of the perfect and admirable character of your institutions, and were told of your exceeding respect and love toward the Chinese, we could hardly have calculated that we would now be the objects of your excessive hatred . . .

If . . . you grant us, as formerly, to mine and trade here, then it is our request that you will give instructions to your courts that they shall again receive Chinese testimony; that they shall cease their incessant discussions about expelling the Chinese; that they shall quit their frequent agitations as to raising the license fees; that they shall allow the Chinese peace in the pursuit of their proper employments; and that they shall effectually repress the acts of violence common among the mountains, so that robbers shall not upon one pretext or another injure and plunder us."

DOCUMENT 4

Source: *Advertisement of Railroad-Owned Land for Sale in Kansas, 1870s*

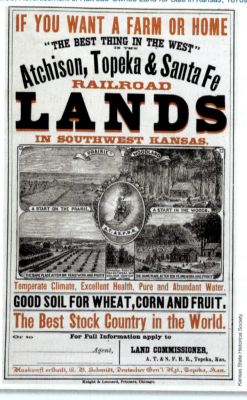

DOCUMENT 5

Source: Uriah Oblinger, a Nebraska Homesteader, *Letter to His Wife*, 1872

"I am confident that I can live when I have 160 [acres] of my own....

[T]he longer I stay here the better I like it, there are but very few old families here. They are mostly young families just starting in life the same as we are and I find them very generous indeed....

I think any one that is not able to own a farm in Indiana or any of the older states and make their living by farming are foolish for staying any longer than to just get enough to leave on.... It is going to be rough starting as I always told you but when started it will be ours.... Those that are here seem to be as happy as birds. They are all Homesteaders, yet there is not more than one in 25 that has a deed for their land yet."

DOCUMENT 6

Source: Interview of Nancy Guptil, a Black Migrant to Kansas, 1880

"Came from Middle Tennessee. Heard neighbors talking of Kansas two or three years. We received two or three circulars that told about Kansas . . . I find things here a heap better than I expected. We have forty acres. We came last May. We built our house in the fall. My husband finds enough work around here to support us. We had plenty of supplies to live on through the winter . . . People treats us better here than they did there because they is willing to pay us what we work for . . . I wouldn't go back for nothing . . . All my people are mighty well satisfied here."

DOCUMENT 7

Source: Joseph Nimmo Jr., "The American Cowboy," *Harper's New Monthly Magazine*, November 1886

"The Texas cowboys were frontiersmen, accustomed from their earliest childhood to the alarms and the struggles incident to forays of Indians of the most ferocious and warlike nature. The section of the State in which they lived was also for many years exposed to incursions of bandits from Mexico, who came with predatory intent upon the herds and the homes of the people of Texas.

The carrying of firearms and other deadly weapons was consequently a prevalent custom among them. And being scattered over vast areas, and beyond the efficient protection and restraints of civil law, they of necessity became a law unto themselves. It is not a strange thing that such an occupation and such environment should have developed a class of men whom persons accustomed to the usages of cultivated society would characterize as ruffians of the most pronounced type.

But among the better disposed of the Texas cowboys, who constitute, it is believed, much more than a majority of them, there were true and trusty men, in whom the dangers and fortunes of their lives developed generous and heroic traits of character. The same experiences, however, led the viciously inclined to give free vent to the worst passions. Upon slight provocation they would shoot down a fellow man with almost as little compunction as they fired upon the wild beasts."

Long-Essay Questions

Please choose one of the following three questions to answer. *Suggested writing time: 40 minutes.*

2. Evaluate the extent to which social reform movements changed society in the United States between 1865 and 1898.
3. Evaluate the extent to which urbanization changed politics in the United States between 1865 and 1898.
4. Evaluate the extent to which industrialization changed the economy of the United States between 1865 and 1898.

PERIOD 7: 1890–1945
New Imperialism and Global Conflicts

AP® Overview for Period 7

In many ways, Period 7 possesses the most expansive content of the AP® U.S. History course as the breadth of seminal moments in modern American history dot the historical landscape. The periodization forces students to comprehend the factors that transformed a fledgling modern America into a global superpower following World War II. Chief among the historical topics are economic changes and the varied responses of the government. From the panics of the nineteenth and early twentieth century to the duration of the Great Depression, students will examine economic phenomena throughout the modules. Cultural upheavals during progressivism and the 1920s also played a central role in helping to define the history of the early twentieth century. However, few themes in Period 7 are as important as America's changing role in the world. Imperialism and World War I present opportunities for students to reconcile the ideals of American foreign policy with the realities of an expanding economic footprint in global trade. More than any other topic, though, World War II and the attendant changes in American foreign policy and economic health mark perhaps the greatest turning point in America's role in the world.

The learning modules for Period 7 mark the beginning of students' exposure to more independent practice of historical reasoning and writing skills. Despite this movement, the book will continue to model ways for students to approach document analysis and historical writing associated with the AP® U.S. History course. Period 7 accounts for 10–17% of the material assessed on the AP® test. Period 7 can be the focus of a Short-Answer Question, Long-Essay Question, Document-Based Essay Question, and Multiple-Choice Questions. This important time period of the course should be carefully planned so students and teachers cover the requisite material with deliberate pacing.

Module 7-1: Progressivism and Social Reform focuses on the vibrant reform efforts of the late nineteenth and early twentieth century. Indeed, grassroots reform efforts such as those of muckrakers and female progressives in urban environments begin this thematic module. Extensive treatment of the unique issues minority populations fought against is a strength of this module as it details the many obstacles African Americans faced in a segregated and racially oppressive time period. Women reformers are central to both the political and moral reform crusades as suffrage, temperance, prohibition, and moral reform in urban areas frame the role women played. The thematic focus of work, exchange, and technology; politics and power; and social structures provide a solid conceptual framework for students to use the reasoning process of comparison to evaluate social reform.

Module 7-2: Progressive Political Reforms continues the analysis of progressivism from the solid foundation on reform movements covered in Module 7-1. Although focused on progressivism, this module focuses more on political and economic reform movements at the state and national level. Similar to progressivism on social issues, political reform covered disparate issues such as immigration and environmental protection, along with municipal and state reforms. Prominent presidents such as Theodore Roosevelt and Woodrow Wilson presented themselves as progressive reformers, though they varied in their goals and styles with which they fought for reform. The reasoning process of continuity and change allows students to see how progressivism continued and eventually lost momentum. The thematic focus of geography and the environment, politics and power, and social structures illustrates the breadth of political progressivism.

Module 7-3: The Awakening of Imperialism highlights how the settlement of the contiguous United States brought forth a call for new markets, expansion overseas, and a new focus on the development of the military to secure an economic foothold in the global marketplace. This new imperialist attitude, buttressed by racial, ethnic, and religious rationales about the self-perceived superiority of the American way of life, resulted in overseas expansion through force. The subsequent Spanish-American War and the Filipino insurrection represented the tension between extending and defending the ideals of democracy and the reality of becoming a colonial power. Students should see these developments as bridging the United States into the twentieth century because economic and military commitments would be continually debated in the years ahead. The thematic focus of America in the world, along with the reasoning process of comparison, frames the historical inquiry for this module.

Module 7-4: Foreign Policy and World War I has the thematic focus of politics and power and America in the world as well as the reasoning process of causation to focus students' attention on the reasons for and results of United States entry into World War I. Central to this development are the foreign policy ideals of President Woodrow Wilson. Both prior to and after World War I, President Wilson embraced defining American foreign policy through a moralistic tone with the goal of spreading democratic reforms around the world. More important than the battles and details of the war are the results of war and the subsequent peace process. Moreover, the changes to Americans sense of freedom and patriotism on the home front are also explored.

Module 7-5: The Effects of World War I at Home brings students through the end of the peace process of World War I to the turmoil of the post-war years on the home front. The political turmoil of the Harding administration was often overshadowed by widespread advancement in consumer goods and growth in innovative products such as the automobile. Despite the expanding economy, social turmoil through an influenza panic and the continued struggle against pervasive violence and racism toward African Americans continued to define a society in transition. African Americans continued to assert their agency from the war years as many chose to leave rural settings in the South for urban settings in the North and Midwest. This movement was part of a larger pattern of settlement in urban spaces among Americans in the 1920s. The thematic focus of work, exchange, and technology, along with migration and settlement and social structures help students see the breadth of issues post-war America faced. The reasoning process of causation prepares students to grapple with the reasons for these developments and their short-term outcomes.

Module 7-6: The Transitional 1920s was a complex decade when competing visions of America's values took center stage as the debate between modernity and fundamentalism defined cultural attitudes. Artists and writers of the Lost Generation were especially critical of how people embraced consumerism and an economy dominated by materialism. The ongoing changes within the African American civil rights movement is a major part of this module and students would be wise to recognize both battles over segregation and competing visions for society held by the various civil rights leaders. Students need to be able to define the diverse attitudes of fundamentalism and the attendant issues of radicalism, xenophobia, and violence. The thematic focus of American and regional culture and social structures are used in conjunction with the content to help prepare students to successfully complete the DBQ at the end of this module.

Module 7-7: Economic Instability and Depression is framed by the reasoning process of causation. Students should embrace what historians have known for years, which is that there is no singular cause of the Great Depression; instead, there are a variety of short-term and long-term causes, and it is that focus which fosters better historical inquiry of the Great Depression. The thematic focus of work, exchange, and technology; politics and power; and social structures frame the political ordeal of Herbert Hoover and help provide a structure for students to understand the effects the Depression had on minority populations. Moreover, Hoover's economic ethos is explored and the problems farmers encountered in the Dust Bowl are also central to the early years of the Depression.

Module 7-8: The New Deal continues exploring the ongoing political crisis of the Depression with a historical overview of President Franklin D. Roosevelt's New Deal. The themes of work, exchange, and technology and politics and power frame the historical continuities and changes students will encounter in this module. Students can study this as the rise of the New Deal, subsequent critiques, and response of the Second New Deal. Political critiques of Roosevelt's policies came from the conservative and liberal wings of the country. Though the New Deal caused a transformational political realignment, it still fell short of the widespread changes African Americans and other minority groups needed to effect real lasting alterations to the capitalist system. The module ends with a focus on the themes and legacies of one of the most controversial domestic programs in American history: The New Deal.

Module 7-9: America Enters World War II discusses how even though United States entry into World War II was caused by the Japanese attack on Pearl Harbor and Germany declaring war on the United States, the drift toward war was a result of complex, long-term processes rather than singular events. Teachers should emphasize the tension between groups such as America First who represented the isolationist perspective and leaders who were non-intervention internationalists. The latter embraced the idea of a United States foreign policy centered on a refusal to engage in conflict around the world, while also exercising diplomatic and economic agreements with nations. The prelude to U.S. entry in the war is also characterized by President Roosevelt's continuous attempts to alter foreign policy, once the war in Asia and Europe began. Causation is an intuitive reasoning process for this module, along with the thematic focus on politics and power and America in the world.

Module 7-10: Life on the Homefront mirrors the expectations of the AP® U.S. History course by focusing attention on the home front during monumental events such as World War II. Foreign policy shaped events at home and abroad. The drive to win the war created an atmosphere that privileged winning at all costs, even while violating the civil liberties of some Americans. The incongruent experiences of African Americans, Mexican Americans, Japanese Americans, and American Indians is also a significant part of this module. The aforementioned topics are framed through a thematic focus on work, exchange, and technology; politics and power; and social structures. Comparison is the historical reasoning process, which complements the varied experiences of citizens living on the home front during the war.

Module 7-11: Victory in World War II ends Period 7 with a focus on the reasons for Allied victory in World War II and the immediate implications for Americans. While some parts of the war, such as island-hopping, D-Day, and the development of atomic weapons are required information, most of the historical inquiry will be focused on the causes of victory and the short-term effects. Students are expected to understand how the two-front war affected the timing and results of battles. Another way students can glean the major concepts is to focus on turning-point battles and political decisions. The use of atomic weapons and the aftermath of the Holocaust provide students a way to comprehend some of the major decisions made toward the end of the war and the many ways in which the global community responded to humanitarian crises. The thematic focus of America in the world and causation reflect the content of Module 7-11 and help prepare students to create cogent interpretations about these events.

Pacing Guide
Course Pacing for Period 7

Module #	Lesson Title	Instructional Period*	AP® Theme	AP® Topic	AP® Reasoning Process/Skill	Homework
7-1	N/A	N/A	Work, Exchange, and Technology; Politics and Power; Social Structures	7.1, 7.2, 7.4	Comparison / Historical Thinking Skills 1, 2, 3, 5	**Reading and Source Analysis:** 7-1 **Activity:** AP® Writing Historically: Short-Answer Question Practice, 7-2
	Review: AP® Writing Historically: Short-Answer Question Practice, 7-1 Progressivism and Social Reform	1	Work, Exchange, and Technology; Politics and Power; Social Structures	7.2	Comparison / Historical Thinking Skills 1, 2, 3, 5	**Reading and Source Analysis:** 7-2
7-2	Progressive Political Reforms	1	Geography and the Environment; Politics and Power; Social Structures	7.3, 7.4	Continuity and Change / Historical Thinking Skills 1, 2, 3, 5	**Activity:** AP® Writing Historically: Document-Based Question Practice
	Workshop: AP® Writing Historically: Document-Based Question Practice, 7-2	1	Geography and the Environment; Politics and Power; Social Structures	7.4	Continuity and Change / Historical Thinking Skills 1, 2, 3, 4, 5	**Reading and Source Analysis:** 7-3
7-3	The Awakening of Imperialism	1	America in the World	7.2, 7.3, 7.5, 7.6	Comparison / Historical Thinking Skills 1, 2, 3, 5	**Activity:** AP® Writing Historically: Long-Essay Question Practice, 7-3
	Workshop: AP® Writing Historically: Long-Essay Question Practice, 7-3	1	America in the World	7.2, 7.5, 7.6	Continuity and Change / Historical Thinking Skills 1, 2, 3, 4, 5	**Reading and Source Analysis:** 7-4 **Activity:** AP® Writing Historically: Short-Answer Practice, 7-4
7-4	**Review:** AP® Writing Historically: Short-Answer Question Practice, 7-4 Foreign Policy and World War I	1	Politics and Power; America in the World	7.2, 7.5, 7.6	Causation / Historical Thinking Skills 1, 2, 3, 5, 6	**Reading and Source Analysis:** 7-5 **Activity:** AP® Writing Historically: Long-Essay Question Practice, 7-5
7-5	**Review:** AP® Writing Historically: Long-Essay Question Practice, 7-5 The Effects of World War I at Home	1	Work, Exchange, and Technology; Migration and Settlement; Social Structures	7.6	Causation / Historical Thinking Skills 1, 2, 3, 4, 5	**Reading and Source Analysis:** 7-6
7-6	The Transitional 1920s	1	American and Regional Culture; Social Structures	7.7, 7.8	Continuity and Change / Historical Thinking Skills 1, 2, 3, 5	**Activity:** AP® Writing Historically: Document-Based Question Practice, 7-6
	Workshop: AP® Writing Historically: Document-Based Question Practice, 7-6	1	American and Regional Culture; Social Structures	7.8	Continuity and Change / Historical Thinking Skills 1, 2, 3, 4, 5, 6	**Reading and Source Analysis:** 7-7 **Activity:** AP® Writing Historically: Long-Essay Question Practice, 7-7
7-7	**Review:** AP® Writing Historically: Long-Essay Question Practice, 7-7 Economic Instability and Depression	1	Work, Exchange, and Technology; Politics and Power; Social Structures	7.9, 7.10	Causation / Historical Thinking Skills 1, 2, 3, 4, 5, 6	**Reading and Source Analysis:** 7-8 **Activity:** AP® Writing Historically: Short-Answer Question Practice, 7-8
7-8	**Review:** AP® Writing Historically: Short-Answer Question Practice, 7-8 The New Deal	1	Work, Exchange, and Technology; Politics and Power	7.9, 7.10	Continuity and Change / Historical Thinking Skills 1, 2, 3, 4, 5, 6	**Reading and Source Analysis:** 7-9 **Activity:** AP® Writing Historically: Short-Answer Question Practice, 7-9

(Continued)

Module #	Lesson Title	Instructional Period*	AP® Theme	AP® Topic	AP® Reasoning Process/Skill	Homework
7-9	**Review:** AP® Writing Historically: Short-Answer Question Practice, 7-9 America Enters World War II	1	Politics and Power America in the World	7.11 7.12 7.13	Causation / Historical Thinking Skills 1, 2, 3, 4, 5	Reading and Source Analysis: 7-10 Activity: AP® Writing Historically: Long-Essay Question Practice, 7-10
7-10	**Review:** AP® Writing Historically: Long-Essay Question Practice, 7-10 Life on the Homefront	1	Work, Exchange, and Technology Politics and Power Social Structures	7.12 7.13 7.14	Comparison / Historical Thinking Skills 1, 2, 3, 4, 5	Reading and Source Analysis: 7-11 Activity: AP® Writing Historically: Short-Answer Question Practice, 7-11
7-11	**Review:** AP® Writing Historically: Short-Answer Question Practice, 7-11 Victory in World War II	1	America in the World	7.14 7.15	Causation / Historical Thinking Skills 1, 2, 3, 4, 5, 6	Prepare for Assessment
Formative Assessment	AP® Exam Practice • 18 MCQs • 4 SAQs	0-1	All AP® U.S. History Course Themes	7.15 Personal Progress Check • 15 MCQs • 2 SAQs • 1 LEQ	All AP® History Reasoning Processes/Skills	
Summative Assessment	Unit 1 Test Bank • 55 MCQs • 4 SAQs • 1 DBQ • 4 LEQs	0-1	All AP® U.S. History Course Themes		All AP® History Reasoning Processes/Skills	

*Based on a standard 50-minute class period.

Period 7 Resources

The following resources can be found in the Resources section of the book's digital platform, by clicking on the link buttons in the Teacher's Edition e-book, or by opening the Teacher's Resource Materials.

- TRM Period 7 Overview Video
- TRM AP® Concepts and Skills Video
- TRM Period 7 Lecture Presentation Slides
- TRM Period 7 Workshop Rubrics
- TRM Period 7 Suggested Responses to Questions
- TRM Period 7 Guided Reading Worksheets

Module 7-1

- TRM Module 7.1 AP® Analyzing Sources Handout 1
- TRM Module 7.1 AP® Analyzing Sources Handout 2
- TRM Module 7.1 AP® Analyzing Sources Handout 3
- TRM Module 7.1 AP® Analyzing Sources Handout 4
- TRM Module 7.1 AP® Analyzing Sources Handout 5
- TRM Handout 7.1 – Progressive Era Cross-Comparative Table
- TRM Module 7.1 AP® Analyzing Sources Handout 6

Module 7-2

- TRM Module 7.2 AP® Analyzing Sources Handout 1
- TRM Module 7.2 AP® Analyzing Sources Handout 2
- TRM Module 7.2 AP® Analyzing Sources Handout 3
- TRM Handout 7.2 – Dueling Dates, 1896 & 1912

Module 7-3

- TRM Module 7.3 AP® Analyzing Sources Handout 1
- TRM Module 7.3 AP® Analyzing Sources Handout 2
- TRM Module 7.3 AP® Analyzing Sources Handout 3
- TRM Module 7.3 AP® Analyzing Sources Handout 4
- TRM Module 7.3 AP® Analyzing Sources Handout 5
- TRM Handout 7.3 – Comparing Rooseveltian and Taftian Foreign Policy

Module 7-4

- TRM Handout 7.4 – Foreign Relations Between 1914 and 1917
- TRM Module 7.4 AP® Analyzing Sources Handout 1
- TRM Module 7.4 AP® Analyzing Sources Handout 2
- TRM Module 7.4 AP® Analyzing Sources Handout 3

Module 7-5

- TRM Module 7.5 AP® Analyzing Sources Handout 1
- TRM Module 7.5 AP® Analyzing Sources Handout 2
- TRM Handout 7.5 – Comparing the Gilded Age and the 1920s
- TRM Handout 7.6 – Modern Times: A Social Commentary

Module 7-6

- TRM Module 7.6 AP® Analyzing Sources Handout 1
- TRM Module 7.6 AP® Analyzing Sources Handout 2

- **TRM** Module 7.6 AP® Analyzing Sources Handout 3
- **TRM** Module 7.6 AP® Analyzing Sources Handout 4
- **TRM** Module 7.6 AP® Analyzing Sources Handout 5
- **TRM** Handout 7.7 – Comparing Nativist Fears of the 1840s and 1920s
- **TRM** Handout 7.8 – Charting Changes Within the Ku Klux Klan
- **TRM** Module 7.6 AP® Analyzing Sources Handout 6

Module 7-7
- **TRM** Module 7.7 AP® Analyzing Sources Handout 1
- **TRM** Module 7.7 AP® Analyzing Sources Handout 2
- **TRM** Module 7.7 AP® Analyzing Sources Handout 3

Module 7-8
- **TRM** Handout 7.9 – The New Deal and the "3-R's"
- **TRM** Module 7.8 AP® Analyzing Sources Handout 1
- **TRM** Module 7.8 AP® Analyzing Sources Handout 2
- **TRM** Module 7.8 AP® Analyzing Sources Handout 3
- **TRM** Module 7.8 AP® Analyzing Sources Handout 4
- **TRM** Module 7.8 AP® Analyzing Sources Handout 5

Module 7-9
- **TRM** Module 7.9 AP® Analyzing Sources Handout 1
- **TRM** Module 7.9 AP® Analyzing Sources Handout 2
- **TRM** Handout 7.10 – Comparing Prewar U.S. Foreign Policy: WWI vs. WWII
- **TRM** Module 7.9 AP® Analyzing Sources Handout 3

Module 7-10
- **TRM** Module 7.10 AP® Analyzing Sources Handout 1
- **TRM** Module 7.10 AP® Analyzing Sources Handout 2
- **TRM** Module 7.10 AP® Analyzing Sources Handout 3
- **TRM** Handout 7.11 – Comparing Racial Unrest, 1919 & 1943
- **TRM** Module 7.10 AP® Analyzing Sources Handout 4
- **TRM** Module 7.10 AP® Analyzing Sources Handout 5
- **TRM** Module 7.10 AP® Analyzing Sources Handout 6

Module 7-11
- **TRM** Handout 7.12 – European Theater and Pacific Theater Strategy and Operations
- **TRM** Module 7.11 AP® Analyzing Sources Handout

Period 7 Essential Activity

Cultural changes happen in myriad contexts; sometimes the most consequential augmentations occur during times of prosperity because innovation — technological or otherwise — causes new societal norms. Still other circumstances, such as economic panic, can so alter a society's sense of itself that previously held orthodoxies are reshaped. The time period between 1920 and 1941 illustrate each of these perspectives. The following activity seeks to have students recognize the validity of both perspectives while privileging one. Students begin the activity by defending the ways in which cultural changes were the most profound cause of change during the 1920s. After a thorough defense of the 1920s, students turn their attention to the 1930s to defend how economic malaise in this decade led to the most transformational cultural changes.

The final step is to construct a body paragraph that contains a claim, historical evidence, and a historical reasoning skill. This paragraph should be written on a piece of paper large enough for students to conduct a gallery walk at the conclusion of the activity. Remember, Period 7 possesses a breadth of historical content that prevents any single activity from being able to capture the entire time period. Therefore, a focus on a topic such as cultural changes can assess students' understanding of a wide range of history, while also allowing the opportunity to delve further into a more discrete topic.

Period 7 Alignment to the Fall 2019 AP® United States History Course Framework*

Relationship to the College Board Units

Period 7 in this book covers Topics 7.1–7.15 in Unit 7 of the College Board course framework. Students will be ready to take the Personal Progress Check for Unit 7 once they have completed this period.

Course Themes

Period 7 develops these course themes outlined in the course framework:

- **America in the World (WOR):** Starting in the 1890s, the United States asserted itself on the global stage, going to war with Spain in 1898 and extending its military and economic influence abroad, especially in the Western Hemisphere and the Pacific. After participation in World War I, the United States shunned collective security arrangements which many Americans feared might entangle the nation in an unwanted overseas conflict. Even as the United States drew closer to military involvement in the European conflict, the surprise attack on Pearl Harbor by Japan in 1941 brought the nation fully into World War II.

- **Social Structures (SOC):** Involvement in Progressive Era reform movements, securing the right to vote, and working in factories during World War I and World War II led to changes in women's roles in American society. African Americans continued to fight for greater equality with the creation of new civil rights organizations, movements promoting racial pride and self-sufficiency, and the "Double-V" campaign during World War II.

- **Politics and Power (POL):** Progressive reforms, legislation, and constitutional amendments shaped American politics in the years before and during World War I. After the laissez-faire policies of Republican administrations in the 1920s, federal responses to the Great Depression and World War II created a limited welfare state and permanently expanded the size and role of government in American society.

- **American and Regional Cultures (ARC):** Radio, movies, and national magazines contributed to the growth of a national culture, while new artistic and literary expressions emerged, including the Harlem Renaissance. Diverging cultural views led to debates over science, religion, immigration, and other controversial issues.
- **Migration and Settlement (MIG):** Immigration from Europe reached its height after World War I, contributing to a nativist backlash and passage of restrictive immigration legislation in the 1920s. Economic opportunities and wartime production needs drew migrants to America's cities, including a Great Migration of African Americans from the South.
- **Geography and the Environment (GEO):** The creation of national parks and early environmental legislation reflected a shift in views toward the environment and the use of natural resources. New technologies, especially the automobile, created long-lasting environmental impacts.
- **Work, Exchange, and Technology (WXT):** Mass production and new technological innovations changed how Americans worked and raised the standard of living. Wartime demand created new economic opportunities for African Americans and women in the workforce and spurred industrialization and the growth of organized labor.

Course Skills

Period 7 helps students to develop the following AP® Historical Thinking Skills identified in the course framework.

- **Skill 1—Developments and Processes** (Modules 7-1, 7-2, 7-3, 7-4, 7-5, 7-6, 7-7, 7-8, 7-9, 7-10, 7-11)
- **Skill 2—Sourcing and Situation** (Modules 7-1, 7-2, 7-3, 7-4, 7-5, 7-6, 7-7, 7-8, 7-9, 7-10, 7-11)
- **Skill 3—Claims and Evidence in Sources** (Modules 7-1, 7-2, 7-3, 7-4, 7-5, 7-6, 7-7, 7-8, 7-9, 7-10, 7-11)
- **Skill 4—Contextualization** (Modules 7-1, 7-2, 7-3, 7-5, 7-6, 7-7, 7-11)
- **Skill 5—Making Connections** (Modules 7-1, 7-2, 7-3, 7-4, 7-5, 7-6, 7-7, 7-8, 7-9, 7-10, 7-11)
- **Skill 6—Argumentation** (Modules 7-2, 7-3, 7-5, 7-6, 7-7, 7-11)

Period 7 helps students to develop the following AP® History Reasoning Processes identified in the course framework.

- **Reasoning Process 1: Comparison** (Modules 7-1, 7-3, 7-10)
- **Reasoning Process 2: Causation** (Modules 7-4, 7-5, 7-7, 7-9, 7-11)
- **Reasoning Process 3: Continuity and Change** (Modules 7-2, 7-3, 7-6, 7-8)

Learning Objectives and Historical Developments

Module	Topics	Learning Objectives	Historical Developments and Key Concepts
7-1	7.1, 7.4	Unit 7: Learning Objective A Unit 7: Learning Objective D	KC-7.1.II.A, KC-7.1.II.D
7-2	7.4	Unit 7: Learning Objective D Unit 7: Learning Objective E Unit 7: Learning Objective G	KC-7.1.II.B, KC-7.1.II.C, KC-7.2.II.A.i
7-3	7.2, 7.3	Unit 7: Learning Objective B Unit 7: Learning Objective C	KC-7.3.I.A, KC-7.3.I.B, KC-7.3.I.C
7-4	7.5	Unit 7: Learning Objective F	KC-7.3.II.A, KC-7.3.II.B, KC-7.3.II.C
7-5	7.6, 7.7, 7.8	Unit 7: Learning Objective G Unit 7: Learning Objective H	KC-7.2.I.C, KC-7.2.II.C, KC-7.1.I.A, KC-7.1.I.B, KC-7.1.I.C
7-6	7.8	Unit 7: Learning Objective G Unit 7: Learning Objective H Unit 7: Learning Objective I	KC-7.2.II.A.ii, KC-7.2.I.A, KC-7.2.I.B, KC-7.2.I.D, KC-7.2.II.D
7-7	7.9	Unit 7: Learning Objective J	KC-7.1.I, KC-7.1.I.C, KC-7.1.III
7-8	7.10	Unit 7: Learning Objective K	KC-7.1.III.A, KC-7.1.III.B, KC-7.1.III.C, KC-7.2.II.B.ii
7-9	7.11	Unit 7: Learning Objective B	KC-7.3.II.D, KC-7.3.II.E
7-10	7.12	Unit 7: Learning Objective L	KC-7.3.III.B, KC-7.3.III.C.i, KC-7.2.II.D
7-11	7.13, 7.14, 7.14	Unit 7: Learning Objective M Unit 7: Learning Objective N Unit 7: Learning Objective O	KC-7.3.III.A, KC-7.3.III.Cii, KC-7.3.III.D, KC-7.3.III.E

TRM A detailed alignment that can be sorted by Course Framework Unit, Topic, Learning Objective, Historical Development/Key Concept, or textbook period, is available in the Teacher's Resource Materials and via the book's online platform.

*Should changes be made to the Course Framework in the future, an updated alignment will be placed on our catalog page at bfwpub.com/fabric1e.

TEACHING IDEA

AP® Central

A great resource to help you teach this period is to read the information in the AP® U.S. History study guide for 1890–1945, available from the AP® United States History Classroom Resources section of AP® Central (apcentral.collegeboard.org).

PERIOD 7: 1890–1945

New Imperialism and Global Conflicts

Prohibition and Popular Opinion During the first decades of the twentieth century, the United States experimented with social reforms that pursued economic justice, greater democracy, gender equality in terms of suffrage, and the prohibition of alcohol. The Eighteenth Amendment, which prohibited the sale and production of alcoholic beverages in 1918, was unpopular — and, by the 1930s, it had become increasingly clear that the amendment was unenforceable. Peck and Peck, a New York clothing retailer founded in 1888, produced this patriotically themed handkerchief in 1933. It provides a window into what everyday people thought of the Eighteenth Amendment and how they expressed those opinions.

By the 1890s, the Second Industrial Revolution, the second period in U.S. history where industry and transportation transformed U.S. society and economy, had been in effect for nearly twenty-five years. Middle-class Americans reacted with some ambivalence to the rise of big business and urban political machines that seemingly undermined democracy. While many in the United States celebrated the economic changes of this period, others saw the rising inequality and corruption as threats to traditional American republicanism and free-market ideology. From these concerns arose an organized and activist reform movement, progressivism, that sought government regulation of elements of the economy and greater democracy in the political arena. Although laboring Americans continued to do often backbreaking and underpaid work, they also began to desire the consumable goods and leisure activities that were available to middle-class workers. Immigrants and their descendants, especially, began to imagine themselves as taking part in what came to be known as the "American Dream."

During the first decades of the twentieth century, consumption continued to rise, a middle class of consumers grew, and the national transportation infrastructure expanded. At the same time, many Americans protested against consumerism, persistent racism, and growing class divisions. These conflicts were temporarily eased by strict government controls on dissent and the United States' involvement in the First World War between 1917 and 1918.

By the 1920s and into the 1930s, challenges to the status quo came from diverse quarters — young Americans who inaugurated a so-called Jazz Age, African Americans who migrated to northern cities and initiated a cultural renaissance based primarily in Harlem in New York City, and young Latinos who struggled for social and cultural space in California. In the midst of this flux, the Great Depression shook the nation to its foundations and inaugurated the creation of a limited welfare state through Franklin Delano Roosevelt's New Deal.

The role played by the United States in world affairs also shifted substantially during this period. The era began with the proclaimed closing of the American frontier west of the Mississippi and ended as the United States stood as one of two superpowers able to exert global power. Between these two events, Americans debated the place of their overseas military ventures within the context of traditional American ideals. The tensions between Americans who held isolationist and those who held expansionist sentiments continued throughout the twentieth century, and both sides used the rights-based rhetoric of the American Revolution to justify their positions. This created a dynamic and high-stakes argument around American conceptions of liberty and equality.

TEACHING IDEA

Incorporating Websites

The Library of Congress has an excellent collection of primary documents, including audio recordings, titled "Born in Slavery: Slave Narratives from the Federal Writers' Project, 1936 to 1938" (loc.gov). As you go through this period, pull from this collection to supplement and enhance your instruction.

PERIOD 7 PREVIEW

Module	AP® Thematic Focus
7-1: Progressivism and Social Reform	**Work, Exchange, and Technology ▪ Politics and Power ▪ Social Structures** By the last decade of the nineteenth century, labor upheaval, government corruption, immigration, and rapid industrialization had transformed the lives of most Americans. In reaction to these great changes, many American pursued reform measures that they believed would relieve the problems raised by a quickly modernizing economy and society. To this end, some middle-class Americans increasingly imagined a society that promoted social reform through philanthropy and investigative journalism, while others turned to government to pass legislation to bring change.
7-2: Progressive Political Reforms	**Geography and the Environment ▪ Politics and Power ▪ Social Structures** By the late nineteenth and early twentieth centuries, progressive reform shaped local activism and government legislation throughout the United States. However, while the movement was framed as a set of new initiatives in changing times, it owed many of its ideals to former American reform movements and longstanding social structures.
7-3: The Awakening of Imperialism	**America in the World** Beginning in the second half of the nineteenth century, policy makers in the United States increasingly began to imagine the nation projecting its power outside of the continental United States. From Secretary of State Seward's acquisition of Alaska from Russia in 1867 to the domination of the Hawaiian economy in the 1880s, the United States pursued its interests overseas. Starting in the 1890s, American policy makers ramped up their efforts to compete with older imperial powers in Europe. This led to both conflict abroad and debate at home.

7-4: Foreign Policy and World War I	**Politics and Power ▪ America in the World** As the United States increasingly exercised its power beyond its borders, the major powers of Europe descended into conflict over regional borders and colonial holdings. Starting in summer 1914, the coalitions of Allied and Central Powers marched into warfare in what would be called the First World War. While the United States proclaimed its neutrality in the conflict, American policymakers and the public debated the proper response to the conflict until 1917, when the Senate declared war on Germany and the rest of the Central Powers. Soon after the declaration, President Woodrow Wilson claimed that the United States fought not for victory, but to "make the world safe for democracy." However, his broad vision for a remade postwar world inspired opposition at home, which ultimately left the legacy of the war a mixture of successes and failures for both the United States and the world.
7-5: The Effects of World War I at Home	**Work, Exchange, and Technology ▪ Migration and Settlement ▪ Social Structures** Though the nation was only involved in World War I during the war's last year, its effects reverberated through American society and economy during the 1920s and beyond. In addition, many of the economic and social changes after World War I owed their causes to other trends in the United States.
7-6: The Transitional 1920s	**American and Regional Culture ▪ Social Structures** During the 1920s, American culture and society appeared to be in a state of flux. Many women, African Americans, and middle-class youth experimented with new forms of self-identification and leisure. However, during this same period, conservative trends in American society revived reactionary organizations like the Ku Klux Klan and political ideologies like nativism. In this regard, culture and society in the United States during this period appeared to be growing increasingly modern, while at the same time seeking to restore perceived traditions from the past.
7-7: Economic Instability and Depression	**Work, Exchange, and Technology ▪ Politics and Power ▪ Social Structures** The seeming prosperity of the 1920s was built on credit, consumerism, and an ever-rising stock market. However, as in other eras in United States history, this economic boom was followed by an economic bust. The Great Depression of the 1930s shook many Americans' confidence in the ability of capitalism to maintain economic prosperity and led to financial strains that cut across American society.
7-8: The New Deal	**Work, Exchange, and Technology ▪ Politics and Power** Franklin Roosevelt, elected president in 1932, promised to counteract the effects of the Great Depression. Although Roosevelt's New Deal gave many Americans hope, critics saw it as wasteful and un-American.
7-9: America Enters World War II	**Politics and Power ▪ America in the World** While the United States experienced the trauma of the Great Depression and tried to counteract its effects with the New Deal, other industrialized nations suffered a similar economic collapse, but turned to other, less idealistic, solutions. In Europe, nations like Italy, Spain, and Germany adopted fascism, a hyper-nationalistic ideology that promoted racial superiority and a strong, centralized government. In Asia, Japan embraced militarism and tried to create a European-style empire of colonies under Japanese economic and political control. In the United States, citizens and policy makers debated a proper response to this aggressive turn.
7-10: Life on the Homefront	**Work, Exchange, and Technology ▪ Politics and Power ▪ Social Structures** During the Second World War, the United States marshalled the power of the economy and society behind the war effort. In this regard, the enhanced power of the federal government during the New Deal era laid the foundation for the war effort. While the domestic economy during the war offered opportunities for many Americans who had traditionally been left out of the industrial economy, not all of these opportunities were shared equally.
7-11: Victory in World War II	**America in the World** By 1942, the United States had entered its second world war in a generation. While during the First World War the U.S. fought primarily in Europe, by 1943 the United States was at war on two sides of the world, across the Atlantic and in the Pacific. Though the United States did not bear the brunt of the war (that bitter distinction fell to the people on whose soil the most devastating battles took place), the American effort proved essential to victory for the Allied forces. By the end of the war, it became clear that the United States had an enormous role in world affairs, and that the so-called isolationism of the 1920s and 1930s was no longer tenable.

Module 7-1

Progressivism and Social Reform

LEARNING TARGETS

By the end of this module, you should be able to:

- Explain how Progressive Era journalists critiqued political corruption, social injustice, and economic inequality.
- Explain how reformers, from the middle and upper classes, including many women, worked to effect social changes in cities and among immigrant populations.
- Explain how some progressives advocated expanding participation in government.
- Explain how progressives sought to regulate the economy and generate moral reform.

THEMATIC FOCUS

Work, Exchange, and Technology
Politics and Power
Social Structures

By the last decade of the nineteenth century, labor upheaval, government corruption, immigration, and rapid industrialization had transformed the lives of most Americans. In reaction to these great changes, many Americans pursued reform measures that they believed would relieve the problems raised by a quickly modernizing economy and society. To this end, some middle-class Americans increasingly imagined a society that promoted social reform through philanthropy and investigative journalism, while others turned to government to pass legislation to bring change.

HISTORICAL REASONING FOCUS

Comparison

TASK ▶ While reading this module, compare the varied problems facing the nation according to reform-minded Americans and the solutions they recommended.

TRM Suggested Responses to Questions

At the turn of the twentieth century, many Americans believed that the nation was in dire need of reform. Two decades of westward expansion, industrialization, urbanization, and skyrocketing immigration had transformed the country in unsettling ways. In the aftermath of the social and economic turmoil that accompanied the depression of the 1890s, many members of the middle and upper classes were convinced that unless they took corrective measures, the country would collapse under the weight of class conflict.

Reformers focused on the plight of urban immigrants, African Americans, and the underprivileged. They tried mainly to improve housing and working conditions for impoverished city dwellers. Their motives were not always purely altruistic. Unless living standards improved, many reformers reasoned, immigrants and racial minorities would contaminate the cities' middle-class inhabitants with communicable diseases, escalating crime, and threats to traditional cultural norms. These reformers also supported suffrage for women, whose votes, they believed, would help purify electoral politics and elect candidates committed to social and moral reform.

TEACHING IDEA

Incorporating Videos

Prior to introducing this module, assign students to watch Episode 27, "The Progressive Era," from the Crash Course US History series (available on YouTube). Use this 15-minute episode as a concise introduction for students of the initial major issues and events of Module 7-1 as part of preparation for either assessment or reinforcement.

BUILDING AP® SKILLS

Making Connections

This is a good point to re-engage students with earlier, similar examples of popular, political, and economic or class-based reform movements that they have covered thus far in the curriculum. Doing so gets students to think big in terms of overarching themes. By way of review with students, bring their attention back to earlier movements for change they have already encountered, such as in the Age of Jacksonian Democracy, and the antebellum reform movements around the time of the Second Great Awakening. It is useful to have students think of some of the themes of their course as moving up or down on a spiral staircase, as opposed to the "scaffolding" metaphor so often used by instructors, as certain ideas and concepts get periodically revisited within the American experience.

▲ Differentiation

Students could be tasked with creating a thematic timeline, whereby they utilize their textbooks to trace events over the course of the nineteenth century, but tied to a specific theme that the instructor assigns. Possible exemplar themes for assignment could include the rights of women, workplace reforms, education, economic regulation or oversight, race relations, political reform, etc.

Period 7: 1890–1945

The Roots of Progressivism

progressivism A movement that emerged during the late nineteenth century whose adherents were united by the belief that if people joined together and applied human intelligence to the task of improving the nation, progress was inevitable. Progressives advocated governmental intervention, yet sought change without radically altering capitalism or the democratic political system.

pragmatism Philosophy that holds that truth can be discovered only through experience and that the value of ideas should be measured by their practical consequences. Pragmatism had a significant influence on the progressives.

Progressives contended that old ways of governing and doing business did not address modern conditions. In one sense, supporters of **progressivism** inherited the legacy of the Populist movement of the 1890s. Progressives attacked laissez-faire capitalism, and by regulating monopolies they aimed to limit the power of corporate trusts. Like the Populists, progressives advocated instituting an income tax as well as a variety of initiatives designed to give citizens a greater say in government. However, progressives differed from Populists in fundamental ways. Perhaps most important, progressives were interested primarily in urban and industrial America, while the Populist movement had emerged in direct response to the problems that plagued rural America.

Progressives were heirs to the intellectual critics of the late nineteenth century who challenged laissez-faire and rejected Herbert Spencer's doctrine of the "survival of the fittest." **Pragmatism** greatly influenced progressives. Pragmatists contended that the meaning of truth did not reside in some absolute doctrine but could be discovered only through experience. Ideas had to be measured by their practical consequences. From these critics, progressives derived a skepticism toward rigid principles and instead relied on human experience to guide social action.

Reformers also drew inspiration from the religious ideals of the social gospel (see Module 6-7). In *Christianity and the Social Crisis* (1907), Walter Rauschenbusch urged Christians to embrace the teachings of Jesus on the ethical obligations for social justice and to put these teachings into action by working among the urban poor. Washington Gladden argued that unregulated private enterprise was "inequitable" and compared financial speculators to vampires "sucking the life-blood of our commerce." Progressive leaders combined the moral fervor of the social gospel with the rationalism of the gospel of scientific efficiency.

Pragmatism and the social gospel appealed to members of the new middle class. Before the Civil War, the middle class had consisted largely of ministers, lawyers, physicians, and small proprietors. The growth of large-scale businesses during the second half of the nineteenth century expanded the middle class, which now included men whose professions grew out of industrialization, such as engineering, corporate management, and social work. Progressivism drew many of its most devoted adherents from this new middle class.

AP® ANALYZING SOURCES

Source: Lincoln Steffens, *The Shame of the Cities*, 1904

"There is hardly an office from United States Senator down to Alderman in any part of the country to which the business man has not been elected; yet politics remains corrupt, government pretty bad....

The commercial spirit is the spirit of profit, not patriotism; of credit, not honor; of individual gain, not national prosperity; of trade and dickering, not principle. 'My business is sacred,' says the business man in his heart. 'Whatever prospers my business, is good; it must be. Whatever hinders it, is wrong; it must be. A bribe is bad, that is, it is a bad thing to take; but it is not so bad to give one, not if it is necessary to my business.'...

But there is hope, not alone despair, in the commercialism of our politics. If our political leaders are to be always a lot of political merchants, they will supply any demand we may create. All we have to do is to establish a steady demand for good government.... Why? Because if the honest voter cared no more for his party than the politician and the grafter, then the honest vote would govern, and that would be bad—for [corruption].... If we would vote in mass on the more promising ticket, or, if the two are equally bad, would throw out the party that is in, and wait till the next election and then throw out the other party that is in—then, I say, the commercial politician would feel a demand for good government and he would supply it."

Questions for Analysis

1. Identify the problem that Steffens believes lies at the heart of American politics.
2. Describe the solution Steffens proposes to address this problem.
3. Evaluate the extent to which Steffens's reform plan would represent a change in American politics.

Period 7: 1890–1945

muckrakers Investigative journalists during the late nineteenth and early twentieth centuries who specialized in exposing corruption, scandal, and vice. Muckrakers helped build public support for progressive causes.

AP® TIP
Analyze how the free press's investigation of both government and corporate corruption affected the events of the Progressive era.

The growing desire for reform at the turn of the century also received a boost from investigative journalists known as **muckrakers**. Popular magazines such as *McClure's* and *Collier's* sought to increase their readership by publishing exposés of corruption in government and the shady operations of big business. Filled with details uncovered through intensive research, these articles had a sensationalist appeal that both informed and aroused their mainly middle-class readers. In 1902 journalist Ida Tarbell lambasted the ruthless and dishonest business practices of the Rockefeller family's Standard Oil Company, the model of corporate greed. Lincoln Steffens wrote about machine bosses' shameful rule in many American cities. Ida B. Wells was born enslaved in Holly Springs, Mississippi and rose to become a teacher, writer, editor, and civil rights activist. She wrote scathing articles and pamphlets condemning the lynching of African Americans. Other muckrakers exposed fraudulent practices in insurance companies, child labor, drug abuse, and prostitution.

REVIEW
- What economic and social factors laid the foundations of progressivism?
- How did the Muckrakers help further progressive reforms?

Female Progressives and the Poor

Hull House The settlement house, based on Toynbee Hall in England, established by Jane Addams and Ellen Starr in Chicago in 1889. It served as a center for social reform and provided educational and social opportunities for working-class poor and immigrant women and their children.

AP® TIP
Evaluate the degree to which women's participation in the Progressive movement illustrated continuity with the idea of the "cult of domesticity" and women's reform movements from the 1800s.

segregation The purposeful separation of people into ethnic or racial groups. Segregation was often actively perpetuated and enforced through "black codes" and Jim Crow era legislation which persisted into the latter half of the twentieth-century.

National Association of Colored Women (NACW) Organization that became the largest federation of black local women's clubs in 1896. The group was designed to relieve suffering among poor black people, defend black women, and promote the interests of all black people.

Women played the leading role in efforts to improve the lives of the impoverished. Jane Addams had toured Europe after graduating from a women's college in Illinois. The Toynbee Hall settlement house (see Module 6-7) in London impressed her for its work in helping poor residents of the area. After returning home to Chicago in 1889, Addams and her friend Ellen Starr established **Hull House** as a center for social reform. Hull House inspired a generation of young women to work directly in immigrant communities. Many were college-educated, professionally trained women who were shut out of jobs in male-dominated professions. Staffed mainly by women, settlement houses became all-purpose urban support centers providing recreational facilities, social activities, and educational classes for neighborhood residents. Calling on women to take up **civic housekeeping**, Addams maintained that women could protect their individual households from the chaos of industrialization and urbanization only by attacking the sources of that chaos in the community at large.

Settlement houses and social workers occupied the front lines of humanitarian reform, but they found considerable support from women's clubs. Formed after the Civil War, these local groups provided middle-class women places to meet, share ideas, and work on common projects. By 1900 these clubs counted 160,000 members. Initially devoted to discussions of religion, culture, and science, club women began to help the needy and lobby for social justice legislation. "Since men are more or less closely absorbed in business," one club woman remarked about this civic awakening, "it has come to pass that the initiative in civic matters has devolved largely upon women." Starting out in towns and cities, club women carried their message to state and federal governments and campaigned for legislation that would establish social welfare programs for working women and their children.

In an age of strict racial **segregation**, African American women formed their own clubs. They sponsored day care centers, kindergartens, and work and home training projects. The activities of black club women, like those of white club women, reflected a class bias, and they tried to lift up poorer black people to ideals of middle-class womanhood. Yet in doing so, they challenged racist notions that black women and men were incapable of raising healthy and strong families. By 1916 the **National Association of Colored Women (NACW)**, whose motto was "lifting as we climb," boasted 1,000 clubs and 50,000 members.

White working-class women also organized, but because of employment discrimination there were few, if any, black female industrial workers to join them. Building on the settlement house movement and together with middle-class and wealthy women, working-class women founded the

TEACHING IDEA

Incorporating Primary Sources

The Stanford History Education Group includes a collection of numerous free online lessons in their Reading Like a Historian curriculum (sheg.stanford.edu). Included in the repository on this platform is a downloadable lesson focusing upon muckraking journalists and corporate America based upon both political cartoons of the period and Ida Tarbell's investigative work into The Standard Oil Company.

TEACHING IDEA

Incorporating Secondary Sources

Assign students to read Robyn Muncy, "The Ambiguous Legacies of Women's Progressivism," (available through online search). Require students to both identify Muncy's thesis and create a summative conclusive statement on their takeaways on her work. Have students share these out in small-group format, with students rotating among their peers.

APPLY THE TIP

Divide the class into two groups, and further subdivide those two groups into quads. As a pre-writing exercise, task the first class-groupings with employing the "Twenty-Five-Word Drill" and the second class-groupings with employing the "Fifty-Word Drill" to address the following prompt: "Evaluate the extent to which the participation of women in the Progressive movement (1890–1920) represented a continuity of the antebellum (1815–1860) idea of the cult of domesticity, elaborating upon what stayed the same and what became different with regards to women's roles and accomplishments during the two periods." In addressing this prompt, students are required to write a response that is, depending upon the group to which they are assigned, no more than 25 or 50 words total (give or take). The product of the former exercise winds up as a concise statement of thesis, while the latter becomes more of an elaborate conclusive statement on the question. Upon completion of this exercise, reshuffle the quads so that a pair of persons from the first grouping are matched up with a pair of persons from the second grouping, and have them share and compare their products.

TRM Suggested Responses to Questions

TRM Module 7.1 AP® Analyzing Sources Handout 2

EXPLORING AP® THEMES

Work, Exchange, and Technology

Assign students the primary source and interactive role-play simulation, "Protective Legislation for Women," located in the Labor and Working Class History portal of the Connecticut Department of Education (portal.ct.gov). This activity is built around the compelling question of who has the power to improve conditions in the workplace.

Period 7: 1890–1945

MODULE 7-1 Progressivism and Social Reform

AP® ANALYZING SOURCES

Source: United States Supreme Court, *Muller v. Oregon*, 1908

"That woman's physical structure and the performance of maternal functions place her at a disadvantage in the struggle for subsistence is obvious. This is especially true when the burdens of motherhood are upon her. Even when they are not, by abundant testimony of the medical fraternity continuance for a long time on her feet at work, repeating this from day to day, tends to injurious effects upon the body, and, as healthy mothers are essential to vigorous offspring, the physical well-being of woman becomes an object of public interest and care in order to preserve the strength and vigor of the race. . . .

Differentiated by these matters from the other sex, she is properly placed in a class by herself, and legislation designed for her protection may be sustained, even when like legislation is not necessary for men, and could not be sustained. It is impossible to close one's eyes to the fact that she still looks to her brother and depends upon him. Even though all restrictions on political, personal, and contractual rights were taken away, and she stood, so far as statutes are concerned, upon an absolutely equal plane with him, it would still be true that she is so constituted that she will rest upon and look to him for protection; that her physical structure and a proper discharge of her maternal functions—having in view not merely her own health, but the well-being of the race—justify legislation to protect her from the greed as well as the passion of man."

Questions for Analysis

1. Identify the main argument of this excerpt from the *Muller* decision.
2. Explain how this excerpt justifies this argument.
3. Evaluate the extent to which this justification represents continuity with previous conceptions of women's role in society.

Source: Louisa Dana Haring, "Unjust to Working Woman," *Woman's Tribune*, 1908

"Dear Madam:

The last number of your paper which you kindly sent me is just received, and I want to express appreciation of your editorial about the restriction of the working hours of women. It is the first sensible thing I have seen on the subject. If men want to curtail the hours of work for women, let them see to it that the rates per hour are raised, so as to afford compensation for loss of time. Who ever heard of limiting a working woman in a home (where she often does the rudest, heaviest sort of work) to eight hours of toil a day? If the government is interested in the welfare of women, one would think it would stop discriminating against them in civil service examinations and pay them as well as men when they do work for Uncle Sam!"

Questions for Analysis

1. Identify the argument Haring makes in her critique of the *Muller v. Oregon* decision.
2. Explain how Haring supports her argument for alternate reform.
3. Evaluate the extent to which Haring's opinion represents a continuity with conceptions of women's roles in American society.

Questions for Comparison

1. Explain how Haring's argument could be used to counter the *Muller v. Oregon* decision.
2. Evaluate the extent to which each document represents progressive ideals.

TEACHING IDEA

Differing Views

Assign students to read the pair of Analyzing Sources, *Muller v. Oregon* and "Unjust to Working Woman," and answer the accompanying questions for homework. The next day in class, have students share their responses in groups of 2 or 3. Then, have these groups synthesize these two documents with Lincoln Steffens's *Shame of the Cities* source from page 556, searching for continuities and contradictions between the three sources with regards to the AP® themes of work, exchange, and technology; politics and power; and/or social structures. Students can be tasked with addressing all three themes in their integration of the source documents, or they may be assigned a specific theme to contend with, depending upon the instructor's preferences.

Period 7: 1890–1945

AP® TIP

Analyze how progressive workplace reforms affected the arguments for women's equality during the late 1800s and early 1900s.

Muller v. Oregon 1908 Supreme Court ruling that upheld an Oregon law establishing a ten-hour workday for women.

National Women's Trade Union League (WTUL) in 1903. Recognizing that many women needed to earn an income to help support their families, the WTUL was dedicated to securing higher wages, an eight-hour day, and improved working conditions. Believing women to be physically weaker than men, most female reformers advocated special legislation to protect women in the workplace. They campaigned for state laws prescribing the maximum number of hours women could work, and they succeeded in 1908 when they won a landmark victory in the Supreme Court in *Muller v. Oregon*, which upheld an Oregon law establishing a ten-hour workday for women. These reformers also convinced lawmakers in forty states to establish pensions for mothers and widows. In 1912 their focus shifted to the federal government with the founding of the Children's Bureau in the Department of Commerce and Labor. Headed by Julia Lathrop, the bureau collected sociological data and devised a variety of publicly funded social welfare measures. In 1916 Congress enacted a law banning child labor under the age of fourteen (it was declared unconstitutional in 1918). In 1921 Congress passed the **Shepherd-Towner Act**, which allowed nurses to offer maternal and infant health care information to mothers.

Not all women believed in the idea of protective legislation for women. In 1898 Charlotte Perkins Gilman published *Women and Economics*, in which she argued against the notion that women were ideally suited for domesticity. She contended that women's reliance on men was unnatural: "We are the only animal species in which the female depends on the male for food." Emphasizing the need for economic independence, Gilman advocated the establishment of communal kitchens that would free women from household chores and allow them to compete on equal terms with men in the workplace. Emma Goldman, an anarchist critic of capitalism and middle-class sexual morality, also spoke out against the kind of marriage that made women "keep their mouths shut and their wombs open." These women considered themselves as **feminists** — women who aspire to reach their full potential and gain access to the same opportunities as men.

> "We are the only animal species in which the female depends on the male for food."
> — Charlotte Perkins Gilman, *Women and Economics*, 1898

feminist Someone who believes that women should have access to the same opportunities as men.

REVIEW

- In what ways did women progressives challenge traditional conceptions of women's roles in society?

Fighting for Women's Suffrage

National American Woman Suffrage Association A national organization created in 1890 that contributed to the passage of the Nineteenth Amendment in 1919, which guaranteed women's right to vote in the United States.

suffragists Supporters of voting rights for women. Campaigns for women's suffrage gained strength in the late nineteenth and early twentieth centuries and culminated in the ratification of the Nineteenth Amendment in 1920.

Until 1910, women did not have the right to vote, except in a handful of western states. Although the Fourteenth and Fifteenth Amendments extended citizenship to African Americans and protected the voting rights of black men, they left women, both white and black, ineligible to vote. Following Reconstruction, the two major organizations campaigning for women's suffrage at the state and national levels — Susan B. Anthony and Elizabeth Cady Stanton's National Woman Suffrage Association and Lucy Stone and Julia Ward Howe's American Woman Suffrage Association — failed to achieve major victories. In 1890 the two groups combined to form the **National American Woman Suffrage Association**, and by 1918 women could vote in fifteen states and the territory of Alaska.

Suffragists included a broad coalition of supporters and based their campaign on a variety of arguments. Reformers such as Jane Addams attributed corruption in politics to the absence of women's maternal influence. In this way, mainstream suffragists couched their arguments within traditional views of women as family nurturers and claimed that men should see women's vote as an expansion of traditional household duties into the public sphere. By contrast, suffragists such as Alice Paul rejected such arguments, asserting that women deserved the vote on the basis of their equality with men as citizens. She founded the **National Woman's Party** and in 1923 proposed that Congress adopt an Equal Rights Amendment to provide full legal equality to women.

TEACHING IDEA

Building Vocabulary

Point out to students that the terms "suffrage" and "the franchise" both refer to an individual's right to vote, and may be used interchangeably. It is also helpful for the instructor not only to use these words, together, early and often, but also to share with students explicitly through such modelling the importance for them as AP® students to be able to academically empower themselves by being able to employ these words fluently and seamlessly within their own historical conversations and written work. Instructors should emphasize that consciously doing so can help students demonstrate the appropriate use of historical information when they write free response questions.

TEACHING IDEA

Incorporating Videos

Have students view "The Colorado Experience: Suffrage," from Colorado Public Television (available on YouTube), which traces the steps that put the state on the path to be the first in the Union to legalize women's suffrage in 1893.

Period 7: 1890–1945

MODULE 7-1 Progressivism and Social Reform

TEACHING IDEA

Geography Instruction

Have students read Map 7.1 and point out to them that suffrage came to women in the western states first for two reasons. First, the territories, as territories, were anxious to become states as rapidly as possible, and increasing their eligible voter pools became one step to help expedite this process. Second, the class and gender hierarchy on the American frontier was historically not as established and rigid due to the pressing concerns and rigors of life in more undeveloped regions. As such, rigid gender distinctions were not a luxury that could be afforded in the more rudimentary and isolated cultural and living conditions of the West.

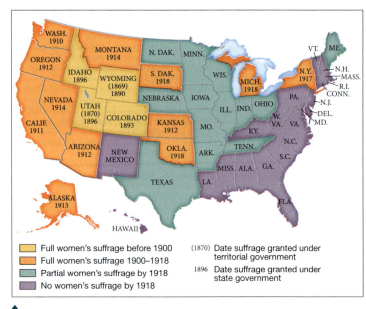

MAP 7.1 Women's Suffrage Western states and territories were the first to approve women's suffrage. Yet even as western states enfranchised women, most placed restrictions on or excluded African American, American Indian, Mexican American, and Asian American women. States granting partial suffrage allowed women to vote only in certain contests, such as municipal or school board, primary, or presidential elections. **How did popular views of women and minorities justify these restrictions?**

Both male and female opponents fought against women's suffrage. They believed that women were best suited by nature to devote themselves to their families and leave the world of politics to men. Suffrage critics insisted that extending the right to vote to women would destroy the home, lead to the moral degeneracy of children, and tear down the social fabric of the country.

Campaigns for women's suffrage did not apply to all women. White suffragists in the South often manipulated racial prejudice to support female enfranchisement. Outspoken white suffragists such as Rebecca Latimer Felton from Georgia, Belle Kearney from Mississippi, and Kate Gordon from Louisiana contended that as long as even a fraction of black men voted and the Fifteenth Amendment (see Module 5-6) continued to exist, allowing southern white women to vote would preserve white supremacy by offsetting black men's votes. These arguments also had a class component, since poll taxes disfranchised poor white people. Extending the vote to white women would benefit mainly those in the middle class who had enough family income to satisfy restrictive poll tax requirements.

Many middle-class women outside the South used similar reasoning, but they targeted newly arrived immigrants instead of African Americans. Many Protestant women and men viewed Catholics and Jews from southern and eastern Europe as racially inferior and spiritually dangerous. They blamed such immigrants for the ills of the cities in which they congregated, and some suffragists believed that the vote of middle-class Protestant women would help clean up the mess the immigrants created.

African American women challenged these racist arguments and mounted their own drive for universal female suffrage. They had an additional incentive to press for enfranchisement.

BUILDING AP® SKILLS

Argumentation

Assign students to read the Analyzing Sources piece, "Where Women Vote—Wyoming," and answer the accompanying questions individually (found on page 561). After doing so, place students into groups of three or four and present the students with the Long-Essay prompt, "Evaluate the extent to which granting women the right to vote reinforced or challenged traditional concepts of women's roles in society in the late nineteenth century." Have students engage in a thesis and contextualization-building exercise known as 4-1-1, whereby they must create an introductory paragraph consisting of four sentences of contextualization, one sentence for a thesis, and one sentence for a plan of attack in their paper (a refresher of the 4-1-1 model can be found on page 163).

▲ Differentiation

After the 4-1-1 exercise is complete, create new teacher-combined student groups in pairs whereby advanced students are paired with lower-level students for the purposes of preparing a skeletal outline of a full response based upon the prompt. In this next step, the paired students will create the complete first sentence of each body paragraph, and then list relevant specific evidence that could be used as support in that paragraph in bullet-point fashion. Upon completion of this task, have student pairs fold into quads to teach and share, and then from there into groups of eight to further teach and share. This will benefit students of all levels as they can both grow into the process, and then take on roles to share their knowledge with others who had different claims and evidence, ultimately concluding in a large-scale overall pre-writing product of thorough organization and factual detail.

Fighting for Women's Suffrage

Suffrage Campaign, 1913 During the Progressive Era, women mounted a determined campaign to gain suffrage from state and federal governments. They employed a variety of tactics, from persuasion through education to direct confrontation and getting arrested. On August 10, 1913, New York women suffragists took the opportunity to promote their cause at the New York Fair held in Yonkers, a suburb of New York City. Women won the right to vote in New York in 1917 and finally succeeded nationally with ratification of the Nineteenth Amendment in 1920. **What tactics did white women use to gain mainstream support for their suffrage?**

> **AP® TIP**
> Analyze the ways in which the woman's suffrage movement of the late 1800s and early 1900s reflected ongoing cultural, social, and political debates in the United States.

Nineteenth Amendment
Amendment to the Constitution granting women the right to vote, passed in 1919 and ratified into law in 1920.

As the target of white sexual predators during slavery and its aftermath, some black women saw the vote as a way to address this problem. "The ballot," Nannie Helen Burroughs, the founder of the NACW remarked, is the black woman's "weapon of moral defense." Although they did not gain much support from white suffragists, by 1916 African American women worked through the NACW and formed suffrage clubs throughout the nation.

The campaign for women's suffrage in the United States was part of an international movement. Victories in New Zealand (1893), Australia (1902), and Norway (1913) spurred on American suffragists. In the 1910s, radical American activists found inspiration in the militant tactics employed by some in the British suffrage movement. Activists such as Alice Paul conducted wide-ranging demonstrations in Washington, D.C., including chaining themselves to the gates of the White House. Although mainstream suffrage leaders denounced these new tactics, they gained much-needed publicity for the movement, which in turn aided the lobbying efforts of more moderate activists. In 1919 Congress passed the **Nineteenth Amendment**, granting women the vote. The following year, the amendment was ratified by the states.

AP® ANALYZING SOURCES

Source: National American Woman Suffrage Association, "Where Women Vote — Wyoming," *Woman Suffrage: History, Arguments, Results*, 1917

> "Despite the lack of effective organization, due to frontier conditions of life, the women have been able to exert considerable influence upon legislation. They have helped secure the following important measures:
> - Making gambling illegal.
> - Giving women absolute rights over their own property.
> - Making exactly equal inheritance by husband and wife, father and mother; giving the mother equal rights with the father over the children; limiting the hours of labor of women to ten a day.
> - Providing that men and women teachers shall receive equal pay for equal work.
> - Raising the age of protection of young girls to 18.
> - Providing penalties for child neglect, abuse or cruelty.
> - Forbidding the employment of children in certain industries.

(Continued)

TEACHING IDEA

Incorporating Videos

Assign students to watch the final 55 minutes of the HBO film, *Iron-Jawed Angels*, from 1:03:00 to its conclusion, at 1:57:30 (available on YouTube). This covers the advocating for the Nineteenth Amendment, divisions within the suffrage movement, activist strategies employed, and the general institutional resistance that the process for women's suffrage confronted.

APPLY THE TIP

Divide the class into thirds. For each third, assign them the task of addressing the AP® Tip question with regards to just one of the subcategories of the prompt: cultural, social, and political. Provide them with 15-20 minutes to do so. Then recombine the class when this phase is complete, reshuffle the class into groups of six, with each category represented by two individuals, and have students engage in a jigsaw process whereby each student shares with the new larger group what the student has learned and concluded (a refresher of the jigsaw model can be found on page 33). Follow this up with a thesis-building exercise that addresses the prompt of the AP® Tip.

TRM Suggested Responses to Questions

TRM Module 7.1 AP® Analyzing Sources Handout 3

TEACHING IDEA

Connecting the Dots

Engage the class in an activity of association by disassociation called "odd one out." Start by writing the following terms on the board/projector:
- Alice Paul
- Hull House
- Ida Tarbell
- *Muller v. Oregon*
- The Nineteenth Amendment

Then place students in small groups and ask them, "Which one is the odd one out and why? How do the remaining terms relate?" Give students approximately 7-10 minutes to complete this part, then share out student answers and discuss their conclusions and reasoning as a whole-class activity. There is no specific correct answer; the goal is to get students thinking in categorical habits of mind and defending their rationales.

TEACHING IDEA

Incorporating Secondary Sources

Assign students to read and annotate Lynda Dodd's monograph essay, "Sisterhood of Struggle: Leadership and Strategy in the Campaign for the Nineteenth Amendment" (available through online search). Whole-class discussion to follow.

Period 7: 1890–1945

MODULE 7-1 Progressivism and Social Reform

Making it unlawful to give or sell liquor or tobacco to children.
Establishing kindergartens and a State industrial school.
Providing for the care of dependent children and infirm, indigent or incompetent persons.
Making State pure food regulations conform with national law.
Providing for the initiative and referendum, the commission form of government, direct primaries, accounting of campaign expenses on the part of candidates for political offices, and the headless ballot.
Establishing pensions for mothers."

Questions for Analysis

1. Identify two reforms that represent continuity in conceptions of women and their role in society.
2. Identify two reforms that represent change in conceptions of women and their role in society.
3. Explain how the reforms that represent change are shaped by the historical situation of the early twentieth century.

REVIEW

In what ways did the pursuit of suffrage for women fit within the broader ideals of progressivism?

BUILDING AP® SKILLS

Comparison

Task students with completing a Venn diagram on the challenges and strategies of proponents of women's equality and that of the proponents of racial equality.

Progressivism and the Fight for Racial Equality

As with suffrage, social justice progressives faced huge barriers in the fight for racial equality. By 1900 white supremacists in the South had disfranchised most black voters and imposed a rigid system of segregation in education and all aspects of public life, which they enforced with violence. From 1884 to 1900, approximately 2,500 people were lynched, most of them southern African Americans. Antiblack violence also took the form of race riots that erupted in southern cities. Farther north, in Springfield, Illinois, a riot broke out in 1908 when the local sheriff tried to protect two black prisoners from a would-be lynch mob. This confrontation triggered two days of white violence against black people, some of whom fought back, leaving twenty-four businesses and forty homes destroyed and seven people (two black and five white) dead.

As the situation for African Americans deteriorated, black leaders responded in several ways. Booker T. Washington promoted an approach that his critics called accommodation but that he defended as practical. Born enslaved and emancipated at age nine, Washington attended Hampton Institute, run by sympathetic white people in his home state of Virginia. Such school officials believed that African Americans would first have to build up their character and accept the virtues of abstinence, thrift, and industriousness before seeking a more intellectual education. In 1881 Washington founded **Tuskegee Institute** in Alabama, which he modeled on Hampton. In 1895, he received an enthusiastic reception from white business and civic leaders in Atlanta for his message urging African Americans to remain in the South, accept racial segregation, concentrate on moral and economic development, and avoid politics. At the same time, he called on white leaders to protect black people from the growing violence directed at them.

White leaders in both the South and the North embraced Washington, and he became the most powerful African American of his generation. Although he discouraged public protests against segregation, he emphasized racial pride and solidarity among African Americans. Yet Washington was a complex figure who secretly financed and supported court challenges to electoral disfranchisement and other forms of racial discrimination.

Tuskegee Institute African American educational institute founded in 1881 by Booker T. Washington. Following Washington's philosophy, the institute focused on teaching industrious habits and practical job skills.

AP® ANALYZING SOURCES

Source: Booker T. Washington, *The Atlanta Exposition Address*, 1895

"The wisest among my race understand that the agitation of questions of social equality is the extremest folly, and that progress in the enjoyment of all the privileges that will come to us must be the result of severe and constant struggle rather than of artificial forcing. No race that has anything to contribute to the markets of the world is long in any degree ostracized. It is important and right that all privileges of the law be ours, but it is vastly more important that we be prepared for the exercise of those privileges. The opportunity to earn a dollar in a factory just now is worth infinitely more than the opportunity to spend a dollar in an opera house. . . .

I pledge that in your effort to work out the great and intricate problem which God has laid at the doors of the South, you shall have at all times the patient, sympathetic help of my race; only let this be constantly in mind that, while from representations in these buildings of the product of field, of forest, of mine, of factory, letters, and art, much good will come, yet far above and beyond material benefits will be that higher good, that, let us pray God, will come, in a blotting out of sectional differences and racial animosities and suspicions, in a determination to administer absolute justice, in a willing obedience among all classes to the mandates of law. This, coupled with our material prosperity, will bring into our beloved South a new heaven and a new earth."

Questions for Analysis

1. Identify what Washington believes will lead to civil rights for African Americans.
2. Explain what Washington means by the statement that the "opportunity to earn a dollar in a factory just now is worth infinitely more than the opportunity to spend a dollar in an opera house."
3. Evaluate the ways in which context shaped the pursuit of civil rights for African Americans in the decades following the end of Reconstruction.

Source: Ida B. Wells, "The Negro Problem from the Negro Point of View," *World Today*, 1904

"Industrial education for the Negro is Booker T. Washington's hobby. He believes that for the masses of the Negro race an elementary education of the brain and a continuation of the education of the hand is not only the best kind, but he knows it is the most popular with the white South. He knows also that the Negro is the butt of ridicule with the average white American, and that the aforesaid American enjoys nothing so much as a joke which portrays the Negro as illiterate and [shortsighted]; a petty thief or a happy-go-lucky inferior. . . .

Does this mean that the Negro objects to industrial education? By no means. It simply means that he knows by sad experience that industrial education will not stand him in place of political, civil and intellectual liberty, and he objects to being deprived of fundamental rights of American citizenship to the end that one school for industrial training shall flourish. To him it seems like selling a race's birthright for a mess of [thick soup]."

Questions for Analysis

1. Describe the type of civil rights reform Wells implies should be pursued in this excerpt.
2. Evaluate the extent to which Wells's argument represents a change in perceptions of African Americans' role in American society since the end of the Civil War.

Questions for Comparison

1. Identify Wells's primary critique of Washington.
2. Evaluate the extent to which both Wells's and Washington's arguments were products of their context.

TRM Suggested Responses to Questions

TRM Module 7.1 AP® Analyzing Sources Handout 4

BUILDING AP® SKILLS

Sourcing and Situation

Assign students to read both primary sources, *The Atlanta Exposition Address* and "The Negro Problem from the Negro Point of View," and answer the accompanying questions. Then, using the HIPP handout from Module 1-1, divide the class into four groups: one each for historical situation, intended audience, purpose, and point of view, and have each group complete the exercise for their assigned element (a refresher of HIPP and the HIPP handout can be found on page 8). Upon completion, recombine the groups with individuals from each element jigsaw-fashion and have students share and teach their findings (a refresher of the jigsaw model can be found on page 33).

TEACHING IDEA

Incorporating Secondary Sources

Assign students to read and annotate Martin Summers's "Manhood Rights in the Age of Jim Crow: Evaluating the 'End-of-Men' Claims in the Context of African American History" (available through online search). Ask students to both identify Summers's thesis and create a summative conclusive statement on their takeaways on his work. Have students share these out in small-group format, with students rotating among several of their peers.

EXPLORING AP® THEMES

American and National Identity

The Stanford History Education Group includes a collection of numerous free online lessons in their Reading Like a Historian curriculum (sheg.stanford.edu). Included in the repository on this platform is a downloadable lesson focusing upon an evaluation of whether Booker T. Washington or W. E. B. Dubois was the greater advocate for African Americans in the era of Jim Crow. Assign this activity to students and conclude it by having students create a thesis statement in small groups that addresses the question of who was the greater advocate for African American rights in this period. Have the student groups write their respective theses on butcher paper and post them around the room for a gallery walk exercise.

▲ Differentiation

Students could be asked to vote physically by moving to the thesis they believe is the strongest. Then for that evening, inform students that they will write a response to the question utilizing their preferred thesis as their line of departure on the next day in class. This will provide students who are challenged by writing assessments the time to engage in pre-writing preparation in a targeted manner, on a known prompt, and with a pre-constructed thesis to argue/defend.

> " The very frequent inquiry made after my lectures by interested friends is 'What can I do to help the cause?' The answer always is: 'Tell the world the facts.' "
>
> Ida B. Wells, *The Red Record: Tabulated Statistics and Alleged Causes of Lynching in the United States,* 1895

National Association for the Advancement of Colored People (NAACP) Organization founded by W. E. B. Du Bois, Ida B. Wells, Jane Addams, and others in 1909 to fight for racial equality. The NAACP strategy focused on fighting discrimination through the courts.

Washington's enormous power did not discourage opposing views among African Americans. Ida B. Wells, like Washington, had been born enslaved. In 1878 she took a job in Memphis as a teacher. Six years later, Wells sued the Chesapeake & Ohio Railroad for moving her from the first-class "Ladies Coach" to the segregated smoking car because she was black. She won her case in the lower court, but her victory was reversed by the Tennessee Supreme Court. Undeterred, she began writing for the newspaper *Free Speech*, and when her articles exposing injustices in the Memphis school system got her fired from teaching, she took up journalism full-time.

Unlike Washington, Wells believed that black leaders had to speak out vigorously against racial inequality and lynching. On March 9, 1892, three black men in Memphis were murdered by a white mob. The victims had operated a grocery store that became the target of hostility from white competitors. The black businessmen fought back and shot three armed attackers in self-defense. In support of their actions, Wells wrote, "When the white man . . . knows he runs as great a risk of biting the dust every time his Afro-American victim does, he will have greater respect for Afro-American life." Subsequently arrested for their armed resistance, the three men were snatched from jail and lynched.

In response to Wells's articles about the Memphis lynching, a white mob burned down her newspaper's building. She fled to Chicago, where she published a report refuting the myth that the rape of white women by black men was the leading cause of lynching. She concluded that racists used this brand of violence to ensure that African Americans would not challenge white supremacy. Wells waged her campaign throughout the North and in Europe. She also joined the drive for women's suffrage, which she hoped would give black women a chance to use their votes to help combat racial injustice.

W. E. B. Du Bois also rejected Washington's accommodating stance and urged black people to demand first-class citizenship. In contrast to Washington's and Wells's families, Du Bois's ancestors were free, and he grew up in Great Barrington, Massachusetts. He earned a Ph.D. in history from Harvard. Du Bois agreed with Washington about advocating self-help as a means for advancement, but he did not believe this effort would succeed without a proper education and equal voting rights. In *The Souls of Black Folk* (1903), Du Bois argued that African Americans needed a liberal arts education. Du Bois contended that a classical, humanistic education would produce a cadre of leaders, the "Talented Tenth," who would guide African Americans to the next stage of their development. Rather than forgoing immediate political rights, African American leaders should demand the universal right to vote. Only then, Du Bois contended, would African Americans gain equality, self-respect, and dignity as a race.

Du Bois was an intellectual who put his ideas into action. In 1905 he spearheaded the creation of the Niagara Movement, a group that first met on the Canadian side of Niagara Falls. The all-black organization demanded the vote and equal access to public facilities for African Americans. By 1909 internal squabbling and a shortage of funds had crippled the group. That same year, however, Du Bois became involved in the creation of an organization that would shape the fight for racial equality throughout the twentieth century: the **National Association for the Advancement of Colored People (NAACP)**. In addition to Du Bois, Ida B. Wells, and veterans of the Niagara Movement, white activists such as Jane Addams joined in forming the organization. Beginning in 1910, the NAACP initiated court cases challenging racially discriminatory voting practices and other forms of bias in housing and criminal justice. Its first victory came in 1915, when its lawyers convinced the Supreme Court to strike down the grandfather clause that discriminated against black voters (*Guinn v. United States*).

African Americans also pursued social justice initiatives outside the realm of politics. In the South, they remained committed to securing a quality education for their children after white people failed to live up to their responsibilities under *Plessy v. Ferguson* (see Module 6-3). Black schools remained inferior to white schools, and African Americans did not receive a fair return from their tax dollars; in fact, a large portion of their payments helped subsidize white schools.

Black women played a prominent role in promoting education. For example, in 1901 Charlotte Hawkins Brown set up the Palmer Memorial Institute outside of Greensboro, North Carolina. In these endeavors, black educators received financial assistance from northern philanthropists, white club women interested in moral uplift of the black race, and religious missionaries seeking converts in the South. By 1910 more than 1.5 million black children went to school in the South, most of them taught by the region's 28,560 black teachers. Thirty-four black colleges existed, and more than 2,000 African Americans held college degrees.

Like African Americans, American Indians struggled against injustice. American Indian muckrakers criticized government policies and anti-American Indian attitudes, but the magazines that exposed the evils of industrialization often ignored their plight. Instead, American Indian reformers turned to the *Quarterly Journal*, published by the Society of American Indians, to air their grievances. Carlos Montezuma was the most outspoken critic of American Indian policy. A Yavapai tribe member from Arizona, he called for the abolition of the Indian Office as an impediment to the welfare of American Indians. Arthur C. Parker, an anthropologist from the eastern tribe of the Seneca, challenged the notion that American Indians suffered mainly because of their own backwardness. In scathing articles, he condemned the United States for robbing American Indians of their cultural and economic independence. One American Indian who wrote for magazines with primarily white audiences, such as *Harper's Weekly*, was Zitkala-Ša, a Sioux woman whose essays exposed the practices of boarding schools designed to forcibly assimilate American Indians. Non-American Indian anthropologists such as Franz Boas and Ruth Benedict added their voices to those of American Indian journalists in attacking traditional views of them as inferior and uncivilized.

American Indian reformers, however, did not succeed in convincing state and federal governments to pass legislation to address their concerns. Nevertheless, activists did succeed in filing thirty-one complaints with the U.S. Court of Claims for monetary compensation for federal payments to which they were entitled but had not received. Like other exploited groups during the Progressive Era, American Indians created organizations, such as the Black Hills Treaty Council and others, to pressure the federal government and to publicize their demands.

> **AP® TIP**
> Analyze how American Indian leaders and scholars challenged U.S. government policies that negatively impacted American Indian lives and communities during this era.

REVIEW
- How did African Americans and American Indians work to bring about progressive reforms?
- How successful were these efforts?

Morality, Prohibition, and Social Control

In many cases, progressive initiatives crossed over from social reform to social control. Convinced that the "immorality" of the poor was the cause of social disorder, some reformers sought to impose middle-class standards of behavior and morality on the lower classes. As with other forms of progressivism, reformers interested in social control were driven by a variety of motives. However, regardless of their motives, efforts to prohibit alcohol, fight prostitution, and combat juvenile delinquency often involved attempts to repress and control the poor. So, too, did protective health measures such as birth control. Some social control progressives went even further in their efforts to impose their own morality, calling for restrictions on immigration, which they saw as a cultural threat.

Prohibition campaigns began long before the Civil War but scored few important successes until 1881, when Kansas became the first state whose constitution banned the consumption of alcohol. Women spearheaded the prohibition movement by forming the **Woman's Christian Temperance Union (WCTU)** in 1874 under the leadership of Frances Willard. Willard built the temperance movement around the need to protect the home. Husbands and fathers who drank excessively were also likely to abuse their wives and children and to drain the family finances. Prohibiting the consumption of alcohol would therefore help combat these evils. At the same time, the quality of family and public life would be improved if women received the right to vote and young children completed their education without having to go to work.

Woman's Christian Temperance Union (WCTU) Organization founded in 1874 to campaign for a ban on the sale and consumption of alcohol. In the late nineteenth century, under Frances Willard's leadership, the WCTU supported a broad social reform agenda.

Period 7: 1890–1945

MODULE 7-1 Progressivism and Social Reform

TRM Suggested Responses to Questions

TRM Module 7.1 AP® Analyzing Sources Handout 5

AP® ANALYZING SOURCES

Source: Frances Willard, *Address before the Second Biennial Convention of the World's Woman's Christian Temperance Union*, 1893

"The Temperance cause started out [almost] alone, but mighty forces have joined us in the long march. We are now in the midst of the Waterloo battle,[1] and in the providence of God the Temperance army will not have to fight that out all by itself. For Science has come up with its glittering contingent, political economy deploys its legions, the woman question brings an Amazonian[2] army upon the field, and the stout ranks of labor stretch away far as the eye can reach. As in the old Waterloo against Napoleon, so now against the Napoleon of the liquor traffic, no force is adequate except the 'allied forces'. . . .

It is quite likely that in the long, slow, and often weary march of these 20 years since the Crusade impulse came to us from heaven, we have not seen as much accomplished on the specific lines where we have wrought as we had hoped; but we must all remember how little it is possible for us to realize the outcome of our work. I do not know how it may be with other speakers and writers in the cause of temperance, woman, and labor, but for myself I seldom hear that anything has come of what I have tried to do. Yet now and then in ways most unexpected I have learnt of changes in the lives of individuals and even of communities, that have astounded me as results of my poor labors, and I conclude from this that if we were but to know all the good that is developed or conserved by our united and systematic efforts, we should indeed take heart of hope."

[1] The Battle of Waterloo (1815) was the final battle of the Napoleonic Wars, in which Napoleon was defeated by the English and Prussian armies.
[2] Amazons are mythical warrior women.

Questions for Analysis

1. Identify the changes that convinced Willard the temperance movement is gaining strength.
2. Explain the ways in which all the movements Willard identifies as now allied with temperance reflect progressive ideals.
3. Evaluate the ways in which context shaped the temperance movement during the late nineteenth century.

Eighteenth Amendment
1918 amendment to the Constitution banning the production and sale of alcoholic beverages. It was repealed in 1933 with the Twenty-First Amendment.

After Willard's death in 1898, the Anti-Saloon League (ASL) became the dominant force in the prohibition movement. Established in 1893, the league grew out of evangelical Protestantism. The group had particular appeal in the rural South, where Protestant fundamentalism flourished. Between 1906 and 1917, twenty-one states, mostly in the South and West, banned liquor sales. However, concern over alcohol was not confined to the South. Middle-class progressives in northern cities, who identified much of urban decay with the influx of immigrants, saw the tavern as a breeding ground for immoral activities. In 1913 the ASL convinced Congress to pass the Webb-Kenyon Act, which banned the transportation of alcoholic beverages into dry states. After the United States entered World War I in 1917, reformers argued that prohibition would help win the war by conserving grain used to make liquor and by saving soldiers from intoxication. The **Eighteenth Amendment**, ratified in 1919, made prohibition the law of the land until it was repealed in 1933.

Alarmed by the increased number of brothels and "streetwalkers" that accompanied the growth of cities, progressives sought to eliminate prostitution. Some framed the issue in terms of public health, linking prostitution to the spread of sexually transmitted diseases. Others presented it as an effort to protect female virtue. Such reformers were generally interested only in white women, who, unlike African American and Asian women in similar circumstances, were considered sexual innocents coerced into prostitution. Still others claimed that prostitutes themselves were to blame, seeing women who sold their sexual favors as inherently immoral.

TEACHING IDEA

Incorporating Videos

Assign students to watch a 15-minute excerpt, "The Time Is Now," of the PBS documentary, *Prohibition* (available on YouTube). After viewing the segment, the instructor should point out to students the ground-up grassroots nature of the prohibition movement, and students should be prepared to explain the strategies and tactics that led to its approval.

TEACHING IDEA

Understanding Political and Social Changes

It is important for the instructor to point out to students that the movements from temperance to prohibition were not some statist, top-down, big-government model of legislating morality at the national level. Instead, they were organic, grassroots, bottom-up movements that gradually rose in prominence over time, year by year, and convert by convert, culminating in national legislation to ban alcohol in 1919.

TEACHING IDEA

Incorporating Secondary Sources

Assign students to read and annotate "Alcoholic Dogs and Glory for All: The Anti-Saloon League and Public Relations, 1913," by Margot Opdycke Lamme, which is available on the Alcohol and Drugs History Society's website by searching for the author (historyofalcoholanddrugs.typepad.com). Whole-class discussion to follow in the next class meeting.

Morality, Prohibition, and Social Control

Period 7: 1890–1945

Year	Arrivals	Departures	Percentage of Departures to Arrivals
1900–1904	3,575,000	1,454,000	41%
1905–1909	5,533,000	2,653,000	48%
1910–1914	6,075,000	2,759,000	45%

Percentage of Immigrant Departures versus Arrivals, 1900–1914 The late nineteenth and early twentieth centuries saw one of the largest influxes of immigration in U.S. history. However, not all immigrants remained in the United States permanently. **What factors pulled immigrants to the U.S. during these years, and what factors might have compelled them to leave?**

Mann Act Also known as the White Slave Trade Act, the Mann Act was passed in 1910 and banned the transportation of women across state lines from immoral purposes. In practice, this legislation was used to enforce codes of racial segregation and standards of moral behavior that enforced traditional social roles for women.

Reformers offered two different approaches to the problem. Taking the moralistic solution, Representative James R. Mann of Chicago steered through Congress the White Slave Trade Act (known as the **Mann Act**) in 1910, banning the transportation of women across state lines for immoral purposes. By contrast, the American Social Hygiene Association, founded in 1914, subsidized scientific research into sexually transmitted diseases, funded investigations to gather more information, and drafted model ordinances for cities to curb prostitution. By 1915 every state had laws making sexual solicitation a crime.

Prosecutors used the Mann Act to enforce codes of traditional racial as well as sexual behavior. In 1910 Jack Johnson, an African American boxer, defeated the white heavyweight champion, Jim Jeffries. His victory upset some white men who were obsessed with preserving their racial dominance and masculine integrity. Johnson's relationships with white women further angered some white people, who eventually succeeded in bringing down the outspoken black champion by prosecuting him on morals charges in 1913.

Moral crusaders also sought to eliminate the use and sale of narcotics. By 1900 approximately 250,000 people in the United States were addicted to opium, morphine, or cocaine — far fewer, however, than those who abused alcohol. On the West Coast, immigration opponents associated opium smoking with the Chinese and tried to eliminate its use as part of their wider anti-Asian campaign. In alliance with the American Medical Association, reformers convinced Congress to pass the Harrison Narcotics Control Act of 1914, prohibiting the sale of narcotics except by a doctor's prescription.

Progressives also tried to combat juvenile delinquency. Led by women, these reformers lobbied for a juvenile court system that focused on rehabilitation rather than punishment for youthful offenders. Despite progressives' sincerity, many youthful offenders

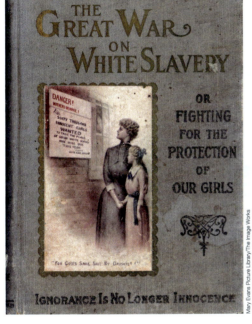

The Crusade against White Slavery Published by Clifford B. Roe and B. S. Steadwell in 1911, *The Great War on White Slavery* campaigned against prostitution and the criminals who lured impoverished young women into what they called "the human stockyards . . . for girls." As an assistant state's attorney in Chicago, Roe prosecuted more than 150 cases against sex traffickers. **How does this cover illustrate the kind of moral reform that progressives attempted to bring about?**

EXPLORING AP® THEMES

Politics and Power

The Ohio State University History Teaching Institute (hti.osu.edu) contains a collection of numerous free online lessons. Included in the repository on this platform is a downloadable lesson focusing upon progressive movements, the challenges they faced, and their influence on government policy through editorial cartoon analysis and online research. This specific lesson is available free online by searching for "Progressive Reforms." As a summative activity for Module 7-1, assign students to complete this lesson in its online format.

BUILDING AP® SKILLS

Sourcing and Situation

Assign students to study both the illustration on the book cover of *The Great War on White Slavery* and Margaret Sanger's first speech on page 568. Ask students to then determine what each source has in common and what is divergent, with regards to their respective visions for the roles and status of women in American society.

APPLY THE TIP

Assign students in small groups to complete a cross-comparative table for African Americans, immigrants, women, and the working class with regards to each group's goals, tactics, and achievements.

▲ Differentiation

This could be made into a jigsaw activity by pairs of students, placed together at the discretion of the instructor for the purposes of balancing each pair in terms of learning levels (a refresher of the jigsaw model can be found on page 33).

TRM Find **Handout 7.1 – Progressive Era Cross-Comparative Table** in the Teacher's Resource Materials.

TRM Suggested Responses to Questions

TRM Module 7.1 AP® Analyzing Sources Handout 6

BUILDING AP® SKILLS

Argumentation

Assign students, as a whole-class exercise, to create a single introductory paragraph including thesis and contextualization for the prompt. Once this is done, divide the class into three or four groups. Task each group with creating a single main body paragraph that addresses the thesis created by the class. Then, recombine the class into jigsaw groups, with one member from each of the body paragraph groups, and have each person contribute from their area of emphasis (a refresher of the jigsaw model can be found on page 33). In so doing, the class groups will ultimately create a set of "virtual essays."

Period 7: 1890–1945

MODULE 7-1 Progressivism and Social Reform

> **AP® TIP**
> Compare the goals, tactics, and achievements of reform efforts centered on immigrants, the working class, African Americans, and women during the Progressive era.

doubted their intentions. Young women often appeared before a magistrate because their parents did not like their choice of friends, their sexual conduct, or their frequenting dance halls and saloons. These activities, which violated middle-class social norms, had now become criminalized, even if in a less coercive and punitive manner than that applied to adults.

The health of women and families occupied reformers such as Margaret Sanger, the leading advocate of birth control. Working as a nurse mainly among poor immigrant women in New York City, she witnessed the damage that unrestrained childbearing produced on women's health. According to Sanger, contraception — the use of artificial means to prevent pregnancy — would save the lives of mothers by preventing unwanted childbearing and avoiding unsafe and illegal abortions, and would keep families from having large numbers of children they could not afford. Moreover, Sanger believed that if women were freed from the anxieties of becoming pregnant, they would experience more sexual enjoyment and make better companions for their spouses. Her arguments for birth control also had a connection to **eugenics**. Contraception, she believed, would raise the quality of the white race by reducing the chances of immigrant and minority women reproducing so-called unfit children.

eugenics The pseudoscience of producing genetic improvement in the human population through selective breeding. Supporters of eugenics often saw ethnic and racial minorities as genetically "undesirable" and inferior.

Sanger and her supporters encountered enormous opposition. It was illegal to sell contraceptive devices or furnish information about them. Nevertheless, in 1916 Sanger opened up the nation's first birth control clinic in an immigrant section of Brooklyn. The police quickly closed down the facility and arrested Sanger. Undeterred, she continued to agitate for her cause and push to change attitudes toward women's health and reproductive rights.

AP® ANALYZING SOURCES

Source: Margaret Sanger, *First Speech from a Debate On Birth Control*, 1920

> "On the one side we find those who do use means in controlling birth. What have they? They are the people who bring to birth few children. They are the people who have all the happiness, who have wealth and the leisure for culture and for mental and spiritual development. They are the people who rear their children to manhood and womanhood and who fill the universities and the colleges with their progeny. Nature has seemed to be very kind to that group of people. (*Laughter.*)
>
> On the other hand we have the group who have large families and who have for generations perpetuated large families, and I know from my work among these people that the great percentage of these people that are brought into the world in poverty and misery have been unwanted. I know that most of these people are just as desirous to have means to control birth as the women of wealth. I know she tries desperately to obtain that information, not for selfish purposes, but for her own benefit and for that of her children. In this group, what do we have? We have poverty, misery, disease, overcrowding, congestion, child labor, infant mortality, maternal mortality, all the evils which today are grouped in the crowd where there are large families of unwanted and undesired children."

Questions for Analysis

1. Identify the two types of families described by Sanger.
2. Describe the ways in which Sanger argues that children have affected these two types of families.
3. Evaluate the extent to which progressive ideas about social reform shaped Sanger's opinions.

REVIEW

• In what ways did progressives connect social and economic reform to moral reform?

AP® WRITING HISTORICALLY — Short-Answer Question Practice

ACTIVITY

Read the following question carefully and write a short response. Use complete sentences.

Using the excerpts that follow, answer (a), (b), and (c).

> **Source:** C. Vann Woodward, *Origins of the New South, 1877-1913*, 1971
>
> "Southern progressivism was essentially urban and middle class in nature, and the typical leader was a city professional man or businessman, rather than a farmer. Under the growing pressure of monopoly, the small businessmen and urban middle-class overcame their fear of reform and joined hands with the discontented farmers. They envisaged as a common enemy the plutocracy of the Northeast, together with its agents, banks, insurance companies, public utilities, oil companies, pipelines, and railroads. . . .
>
> The direct primary system of nominating party candidates was not invented in Wisconsin in 1903 . . . for by that time a majority of the Southern states were already practicing the system. . . . The joker in the Southern primaries was the fact that they were *white* primaries. Southern progressivism generally was progressivism for white men only. . . . The paradoxical combination of white supremacy and progressivism was not new to the region, but it never ceased to be a cause of puzzlement and confusion above the Potomac—and not a little, below. The paradox nevertheless had its counterpart in the North, where it was not uncommon for one man to champion both progressivism and imperialism. In such instances it was a matter of white supremacy over browns instead of blacks."

> **Source:** Glenda Elizabeth Gilmore, *Gender and Jim Crow: Women and the Politics of White Supremacy in North Carolina: 1896-1920*, 1996
>
> "From the debris of disfranchisement, black women discovered fresh approaches to serving their communities and crafted new tactics to dull the blade of white supremacy. . . . After disfranchisement . . . the political culture black women had created through thirty years of work in temperance organization, Republican Party aid societies, and churches furnished both an ideological basis and an organization structure from which black women could take on those tasks. After black men's banishment from politics, North Carolinas black women added a network of women's groups that crossed denominational—and later party—lines and took a multi-issue approach to civic action. In a nonpolitical guise, black women became the black community's diplomats to the white community. Black women might not be voters, but they could be clients, and in that role they could become spokespeople for and motivators of black citizens. They could claim a distinctly female moral authority and pretend to eschew any political motivation. The deep camouflage of their leadership style—their womanhood—helped them remain invisible as they worked toward political ends. At the same time, they could deliver not votes but hands and hearts through community organization: willing workers in city clean up campaigns, orderly children who complied with state educational requirements and hookworm-infested people eager for treatment at public health fairs. . . .
>
> As much as southern whites plotted to reserve progressivism for themselves, and as much as they schemed to alter the ill-fitting northern version accordingly, they failed. African American women embraced southern white progressivism, reshaped it, and sent back a new model that included black power brokers and grass roots activists. . . . Southern black women initiated every progressive reform that southern white women initiated, a feat they accomplished without financial resources, without the civic protection of their husbands, and without publicity."

a. Briefly describe ONE major difference between Woodward's and Gilmore's historical interpretations.
b. Briefly explain ONE specific piece of historical information not mentioned in the excerpts that could be used to support Woodward's argument.
c. Briefly explain ONE specific piece of historical information not mentioned in the excerpts that could be used to support Gilmore's argument.

TEACHING IDEA

AP® Writing Historically Review

The first question in the short-answer section of the AP® Test will have two secondary sources in opposition. At this point in the year, students should be familiar with this concept and more confident in their ability to answer these questions. To reaffirm this confidence, consider dividing the class into groups of two for an activity. Students will create a collaborative answer by first brainstorming on their own and then reconvening with their partner for parts (a), (b), and (c). In this way, a student has to work through each step individually, but has the benefit of checking each answer with their partner. After students have written their individual responses, create groups of four and have students select the best answer for parts (a), (b), and (c). They can cut those answers up and tape them to a separate sheet of paper to turn in.

TRM Suggested Responses to Questions

TRM Suggested Responses to Questions

Module 7-2

Progressive Political Reforms

LEARNING TARGETS

By the end of this module, you should be able to:

- Explain how progressives called for reliance on professional experts to make government more efficient.
- Explain how progressives debated immigration restrictions.
- Explain how progressive amendments to the Constitution supported progressive ideals.
- Explain how preservationists and conservationists supported the establishment of national parks, but disagreed over government intervention regarding overuse of natural resources.

THEMATIC FOCUS

Geography and the Environment
Politics and Power
Social Structures

By the late nineteenth and early twentieth centuries, progressive reform shaped local activism and government legislation throughout the United States. However, while the movement was framed as a set of new initiatives in changing times, it owed many of its ideals to former American reform movements and longstanding social structures.

HISTORICAL REASONING FOCUS

Continuity and Change

TASK ▶ As you read this module, consider the ways in which progressivism represented a change in American political, social, and economic practices, and the ways it represented a continuity with American reform in the past.

In an effort to diminish the power of corrupt urban political machines and unregulated corporations, progressives pushed for good government reforms, promoting initiatives they claimed would produce greater efficiency, openness, and accountability in government. Many of the progressives' proposed reforms appeared, at least on the surface, to give citizens more direct say in their government; however, a closer look reveals a more complicated picture.

Progressives advocated governmental intervention, yet they sought change without radically altering capitalism or the democratic political system. Not everyone endorsed progressives' goals, however. Conservatives continued to support individualism and the free market as a legitimate means to political and economic power, and radicals pressed for the socialist reorganization of the economy and the democratization of politics. Yet the public showed widespread support for progressivism by electing the reformers Theodore Roosevelt and Woodrow Wilson as presidents.

New Immigrants and New Challenges

The late nineteenth-century wave of immigration had changed the composition of the American population by the turn of the twentieth century. By 1910 one-third of the population was foreign-born or had at least one parent who came from abroad. These immigrants had come to the United States from primarily Europe, East Asia, Mexico, and Latin America. They tended to settle near their ports of entry in cities, where they usually joined people from their own country who had settled previously. The pattern of settlement varied widely among regions of the country (Map 7.2). Foreigners and their children made up more than three-quarters of the population of New York City, Detroit, Chicago, Milwaukee, Cleveland, Minneapolis, and San Francisco. Immigration, though not as extensive in the South as in the North, also altered the character of southern cities. About one-third of the population of Tampa, Miami, and New Orleans consisted of foreigners

EXPLORING AP® THEMES

American and National Identity

Assign students in groups to assume one of the following roles from this module's time period (1890–1920): an Italian immigrant, a Chinese immigrant, a native-born Anglo-Saxon white American, an American Indian enrolled in an American Indian boarding school. Have the students conduct online research to compile a sketch of what life was like for each of these individuals in turn-of-the-century America, specifically focusing upon the opportunities they sought and the challenges they faced. Have each group present their findings. Then, instruct each group to come up with one or two questions that they would like to ask of any of the other groups in the room. Give them time to ask these questions as a whole-class exercise, and allow questioned groups time to reply. This can then lead into a form of cross-examination and rebuttal, which the instructor can moderate. Lastly, assign each group the task of writing two paragraphs (5-8 sentences each), one in the character of their assigned role, and one as themselves in contemporary times, which addresses the following prompt: "Who or what, to your mind, is an American?"

New Immigrants and New Challenges

Period 7: 1890–1945

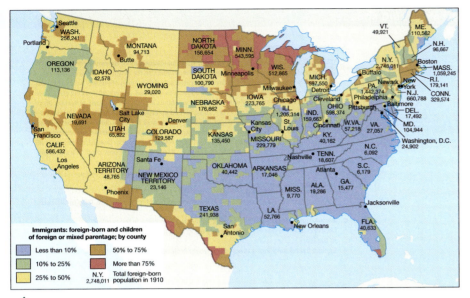

▲ MAP 7.2 **Immigrants in the U.S., 1910** By 1910, many immigrants had come to the United States from primarily Europe, East Asia, Mexico, and Latin America. They tended to settle near their ports of entry in cities, where they usually joined people from their own country who had settled previously. The pattern of settlement varied widely among regions of the country, as the map shows. **What common settlement patterns do you notice here? What explains these settlement patterns?**

BUILDING AP® SKILLS

Making Connections

After having students study Map 7.2 and read the text, engage in a whole-class discussion with students exploring the similarities and differences in the opportunities and challenges encountered by immigrants in contemporary times in comparison to those of the Progressive Era. Discussions should be based in fact.

and their immediate descendants. The borderland states of Texas, New Mexico, Arizona, and southern California contained similar percentages of immigrants, most of whom came from Mexico.

On the West Coast, the government established an immigration station at Angel Island in San Francisco Bay in 1910. In contrast to Ellis Island, Angel Island served mainly as a detention center where Chinese immigrants were imprisoned for months, even years, while they sought to prove their eligibility to enter the United States. Nevertheless, over the next thirty years, some 50,000 Chinese immigrants successfully passed through Angel Island. Some 260,000 Japanese immigrants also arrived in the United States during the first two decades of the twentieth century. Many of them settled on the West Coast, where they worked as farm laborers and gardeners and established businesses catering to a Japanese clientele. Although Japan was a major world power in the late nineteenth century and held American respect by defeating Russia in the Russo-Japanese War of 1904–1905, Japanese immigrants were still considered part of an inferior "yellow race" and encountered discrimination in their West Coast settlements.

Immigrants who left sweatshop apartments and went to work in factories during the early twentieth century continued to face exploitation regardless of the city they called home. For example, the Jewish and Italian clothing workers who toiled in the Triangle Shirtwaist Company, located in New York City's Greenwich Village, worked long hours for little pay. In 1911 a fire broke out on the eighth story of the factory and quickly spread to the ninth and tenth floors. The fire engines' ladders could not reach that high, and one of the exits on the ninth floor was locked to keep workers from stealing material. More than 140 people died in the **Triangle Shirtwaist fire**—some by jumping out the windows, but most by getting trapped behind the closed exit door. Following public outrage over the fire and through the efforts of reformers, New York City established a Bureau of Fire Protection, required safety devices in buildings, and prohibited smoking in factories. Furthermore, this tragedy spearheaded legislative efforts to improve working conditions in general, protect women workers, and abolish child labor.

Triangle Shirtwaist fire An infamous industrial fire at the Triangle Shirtwaist factory in New York City in 1911. Inadequate fire safety provisions led to the deaths of 146 workers, mostly young women and girls.

TEACHING IDEA

AP® Central

Have students read the essay, "Race and Citizenship," from the College Board series America on the World Stage: Essays from the American Organization of Historians and AP®, available in the Related Articles and Teaching Resources section of the Classroom Resources for AP® U.S. History on AP® Central (apcentral.collegeboard.org).

TEACHING IDEA

Incorporating Videos

Have students watch the HBO Documentary, "Triangle: Remembering the Fire," which was produced for the 100th anniversary of the industrial accident. The graphic 39-minute film covers the events leading up to the fire, the underlying institutional and social factors that allowed it to happen, and the political and social aftermath of the event. This video is available on YouTube by searching for the title.

TEACHING IDEA

Differing Views

Cornell University's Kheel Center houses a comprehensive online exhibit platform on the Triangle Shirtwaist Fire. Included in this site are several primary and secondary sources. Assign students to read and annotate a combination of primary and secondary source texts at the instructor's discretion in preparation for a whole-class discussion during the next class meeting (trianglefire.irl.cornell.edu).

▲ **Differentiation**

To account for varying ability and reading levels within a classroom, assign more advanced students to read the secondary sources and assign the primary source interview materials to students who are more challenged by the decoding of advanced secondary texts. Then, the next day in class, combine the students into groups where both source materials are represented, and allow them time to share out what they have annotated and concluded, and to take notes from one another's labors. This allows for all students to bring engaging historical analysis of value to the classroom, and provides a way to generate both contributions and confidence for learners that find the Advanced Placement course content more challenging.

TRM Suggested Responses to Questions

TRM Module 7.2 AP® Analyzing Sources Handout 1

TEACHING IDEA

Connecting the Dots

This is a good point to remind students, by way of review, of who benefited from the political machine model of local governance, and which factions stood to gain or lose due to its modification or reform. It is important to have students understand that the machine system, corrupt as it was, did offer legitimate services of value to immigrants in their urban neighborhoods.

AP® ANALYZING SOURCES

Source: "The Calamity," *New York Times*, 1911

"The building in which the fire occurred was unquestionably of fireproof construction. It stands to-day, intact, a blackened and awful monument to the nearly 150 persons who were alive and hopeful yesterday. The fire, discovered as a thin column of smoke, was an impassable wall of flames by the time the first alarm was sounded. Scores of working girls were hemmed in aisles formed by wooden sewing machines and filled with flimsy materials. More than fifty jumped from the windows, to be picked up either dead or fearfully injured. Many others were literally roasted to death. The Fire Department has been demanding the building of fire escapes on all sides of factory buildings. An expert lately advised the establishment of a fire drill in this particular building. Whether or not his advice was heeded, all or nearly all the human beings who were in it when the fire was discovered are now dead. It is a calamity to put the whole town in a sorrowful mood."

Questions for Analysis

1. Identify the factors that contributed to the high number of fatalities at the Triangle Shirtwaist factory, according to this article.
2. Identify the factors to prevent fire that were already in place in the building.
3. Describe how the owners of the factory addressed recommendations to prevent fatalities prior to the fire.
4. Explain the reforms that a progressive would likely recommend to prevent similar disasters.

REVIEW

- What challenges did immigrants face when coming to the United States during this period?

Municipal and State Reform

The expanding economy and rising immigration placed American cities at the forefront of government reform during the Progressive Era. Municipal governments had failed to keep up with the problems ushered in by accelerated urban growth, and political machines filled these needs by distributing city services—largely to immigrants—within a system bloated by corruption and graft (Module 6-7). Upper-middle-class businessmen and professionals fed up with wasteful and inefficient political machines sought to institute new forms of government that functioned more rationally and cost less.

The adoption of the commission form of government was a hallmark of urban reform. Commission governments replaced the old form of a mayor and city council with elected commissioners, each of whom ran a municipal department as if it were a business. By 1917 commissions had spread to more than four hundred cities throughout the country. Governments with a mayor and city council also began to appoint city managers, who functioned as chief operating officers, to foster businesslike efficiency. The head of the National Cash Register Company, who helped bring the city manager system to Dayton, Ohio, praised it for resembling "a great business enterprise whose stockholders are the people."

Reformers also adopted direct primaries so that voters could select candidates rather than allowing a handful of machine politicians to decide elections behind closed doors. To reverse the influence of immigrants clustered in ghettos who supported their own ethnic candidates and to topple the machines that catered to them, municipal reformers replaced district elections with citywide "at-large" elections. Ethnic enclaves lost not only their ward representatives but also a good deal of their influence because citywide election campaigns were expensive, shifting power to those who could afford to run. Working- and lower-class residents of cities still retained the right to vote, but their power was diluted.

In the South, where fewer immigrants lived, white supremacists employed these tactics to build on steps taken in the late nineteenth century to disfranchise African Americans. Southern

Municipal and State Reform · Period 7: 1890–1945

The Triangle Shirtwaist Company Fire, 1911 On March 25, 1911, fire erupted in the Triangle Shirtwaist factory in lower Manhattan. Most of the company's six hundred garment workers were immigrant women. The building had inadequate fire escapes and blocked exits, which resulted in the high death toll of 146 workers. This catastrophe aroused many New Yorkers to rally around factory reforms. In the aftermath of the fire, Rose Schneiderman, a Polish Jewish immigrant who had led a strike at the Triangle Shirtwaist Company in 1909, addressed a memorial gathering at the Metropolitan Opera House. **What factors surrounding this particular industrial disaster led to reform?**

lawmakers diminished whatever black political power remained by adopting at-large elections and commission governments. Throughout the South, direct primary contests (or "white primaries") were closed to black people.

If urban progressivism fell short of putting democratic ideals into practice, it did produce a number of mayors who carried out genuine reforms. Elected in 1901, Cleveland mayor Tom L. Johnson implemented measures to assess taxes more equitably, regulate utility companies, and reduce public transportation fares. Samuel "Golden Rule" Jones, who served as Toledo's mayor from 1897 to 1903, supported social justice measures by establishing an eight-hour workday for municipal employees, granting them paid vacations, and prohibiting child labor. Under Mayor Hazen Pingree, who served from 1889 to 1896, Detroit constructed additional schools and recreational facilities and put the unemployed to work on municipal projects during economic hard times.

Progressives also took action at the state level. Robert M. La Follette, Republican governor of Wisconsin from 1901 to 1906, led the way by initiating a range of reforms to improve the performance of state government and increase its accountability to constituents. During his tenure as governor, La Follette dismantled the statewide political machine by instituting direct party primaries, an expanded civil service, a law forbidding direct corporate contributions to political parties, a strengthened railroad regulatory commission, and a graduated income tax. In 1906 La Follette entered the U.S. Senate, where he battled for further reform.

Other states picked up and expanded La Follette's progressive agenda. In 1913 three-quarters of the states ratified the Seventeenth Amendment, which mandated that U.S. senators would be elected by popular vote instead of being chosen by state legislatures. This constituted another effort to remove the influence of money from politics.

AP® TIP
Evaluate the degree to which Progressive Era political reforms during the late 1800s and early 1900s reflected change in U.S. government and politics.

AP® TIP
Compare the goals and legislative achievements of La Follette in Wisconsin to earlier reforms supported by the Populists in the West.

REVIEW
- How did municipal reform during the Progressive Era shape the lives of city dwellers across America?

APPLY THE TIP
Assign students to complete a T-chart on the goals and accomplishments of La Follette and Progressives and the Populists in the West. Create these charts on poster paper, then place them around the room and allow students time for a gallery walk to compare their products.

BUILDING AP® SKILLS

Argumentation

Assign students to craft an introductory statement utilizing the "Fifty-Word Drill" model to address the question that concludes the caption of the photograph, "What factors surrounding this particular industrial disaster led to reform?" In addressing this prompt, students are required to write a response that is no more than 50 words total (give or take). Upon completion of this exercise, pair up students for the purposes of sharing their products for peer review and editing.

Period 7: 1890–1945

MODULE 7-2 Progressive Political Reforms

Conservation and Preservation of the Environment

conservationism Progressive Era political and social movement whose supporters worked for the preservation of America's wildlife and natural lands.

> **AP® TIP**
> Analyze how both large corporations and pervasive racism influenced Progressive Era reforms.

The penchant for efficiency that characterized good government progressivism also shaped progressive efforts to conserve natural resources. As chief forester in the Department of Agriculture, Gifford Pinchot emphasized the efficient use of resources and sought ways to reconcile the public interest with private profit motives. His approach often won support from large lumber companies, which had a long-term interest in sustainable forests. Large companies also saw **conservationism** as a way to drive their smaller competitors out of business, as large companies could better afford the additional costs associated with managing healthy forests.

This gospel of efficiency faced a stiff test in California. On April 18, 1906, a devastating earthquake in San Francisco set the city ablaze, causing about 1,500 deaths. San Francisco officials, coping with water and power shortages, asked the federal government to approve construction of a hydroelectric dam and reservoir in **Hetch Hetchy valley**, located in Yosemite National Park.

▲ **Theodore Roosevelt and John Muir, 1903** Taken in 1903, this photograph pictures President Theodore Roosevelt and his associates standing in front of the "Grizzly Giant," a towering sequoia tree over 200 feet in height in Yosemite National Park, California. Roosevelt is in the center, and standing to his front left is John Muir, the founder of the Sierra Club, who convinced Roosevelt to place Yosemite under federal control and establish it as a national park in 1906. **Why did conservation grow as a movement during the late 1800s and early 1900s in the United States?**

TEACHING IDEA

Incorporating Secondary Sources

Assign students to read and annotate John Freemuth's "The Progressive Movement and Conservation," available online from Boise State University's ScholarWorks (scholarworks.boisestate.edu). The next day in class, place students into quads and have them engage in a discussion on the monograph, while the instructor floats among and between the student groups.

BUILDING AP® SKILLS
Causation

Using the question in the photograph caption of Theodore Roosevelt and John Muir as a line of departure, have students create a cause-and-effect graphic that addresses the prompt. As part of this process, have them determine the relative importance of the causes they come up with, in rank order, including a rationale for their rank orders.

Conservation and Preservation of the Environment

Period 7: 1890–1945

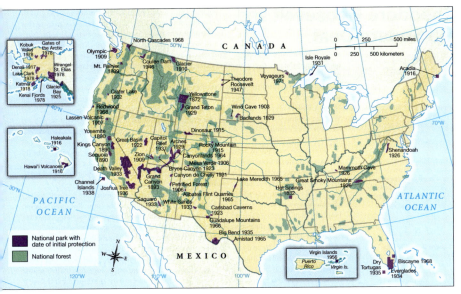

▲ **MAP 7.3 National Parks and Forests** In 1872, the federal government created the first national park at Yellowstone, which spread over portions of the future states of Wyoming, Montana, and Idaho. President Theodore Roosevelt added six sites — Crater Lake, Wind Cave, Petrified Forest, Lassen Volcanic, Mesa Verde, and Zion — to the park system. The construction of a dam and reservoir in Yosemite National Park's Hetch Hetchy valley divided reformers concerned with the environment such as Gifford Pinchot and John Muir during the Roosevelt administration. **How does this map reflect the conflicting goals of conservationists like Pinchot and preservationists like Muir?**

Pinchot supported the project because he saw it as the best use of the land for the greatest number of people. The famed naturalist John Muir strongly disagreed. He campaigned to save Hetch Hetchy from "ravaging commercialism" and warned against choosing economic gains over spiritual values. After a bruising seven-year battle, Pinchot (by this time a private citizen) triumphed. Still, this incursion into a national park helped spur the development of environmentalism as a political movement.

Besides the clash with preservationists, the Hetch Hetchy Dam project reveals another aspect of the progressive conservation movement. Like progressives who focused on urban and political issues, progressive conservationists had a racial bias. Conservationists such as Pinchot may have seen themselves as acting in the public interest, but their definition of "the public" did not include all Americans. In planning for the Hetch Hetchy Dam, progressives did not consult with the Mono Lake Paiutes who lived in Yosemite and who were most directly affected by the project. Conservation was meant to serve the interests of white San Franciscans and not those of the American Indian inhabitants of Yosemite.

REVIEW

In what ways did conservation during the Progressive Era benefit some groups at the expense of others?

BUILDING AP® SKILLS

Claims and Evidence in Sources

Assign students to read and annotate Jason Hanson's "The Hetch Hetchy Letters: If a Group of Intellectuals Argues in the Forest, and that Forest is Submerged Under Water, Does Their Argument Matter?" (available through Center West by online search of author and title). Require students to both identify Hanson's thesis and create a summative conclusive statement on their takeaways on his work. Have students share these out in small-group format, with students rotating among several of their peers.

TEACHING IDEA

Geography Instruction

Have students study Map 7.3, in conjunction with the text on pages 574–575, and then instruct them to discuss the prompt at the conclusion of the map caption. Then, assign them to write a letter to President Roosevelt advocating for a particular environmental course of action from the point of view of one of the following actors (assigned to students by the instructor):

- John Muir
- Gifford Pinchot
- The Paiutes
- A California lumber company
- A miner in Utah

Explain to students that they may use additional source material or information beyond their textbook if they so choose, in order to create their letter. The next day in class, combine the students into five groups, consisting of students that each adopted the same role. Allow them to confer, and then commence an inside-circle–outside-circle activity, centered around group responses to the following consideration: "Should the environmental movement of the early twentieth century have been increased or reduced in scale?"

Period 7: 1890–1945

MODULE 7-2 Progressive Political Reforms

Theodore Roosevelt and the Square Deal

The problems created by industrialization and the growth of big business were national in scope. Recognizing this fact, prominent progressives sought national leadership positions, and two of them, Presidents Theodore Roosevelt and Woodrow Wilson, instituted progressive reforms during their terms. In the process, they reinvigorated the presidency, an office that had declined in power and importance during the late nineteenth century.

Born into a moderately wealthy New York family, Theodore Roosevelt graduated from Harvard in 1880 and entered government service. In 1898, Roosevelt formed a regiment of soldiers — the "**Rough Riders**" — and fought in Cuba against Spanish forces during the Spanish-American War (see Module 7-3). That same year he was elected governor of New York. Elected as William McKinley's vice president in 1900, Roosevelt became president after McKinley's assassination a year later.

Roosevelt brought an activist style to the presidency. He considered his office a **bully pulpit** — a platform from which to promote his programs and from which he could rally public opinion. To this end, he used his energetic and extroverted personality to establish an unprecedented rapport with the American people.

For all his exuberance and energy, President Roosevelt pursued a moderate domestic course. Like his progressive colleagues, he opposed ideological extremism in any form. Roosevelt believed that as head of state he could serve as an impartial referee among competing factions and determine what was best for the public. To him, reform was the best defense against revolution.

As president, Roosevelt sought to provide economic and political stability, what he referred to as a "**Square Deal**." The coal strike that began in Pennsylvania in 1902 gave Roosevelt an opportunity to play the role of impartial mediator and defender of the public good. Miners had gone on strike for an eight-hour workday, a pay increase of 20 percent, and recognition of their union. Union representatives agreed to have the president create a panel to settle the dispute, but George F. Baer, president of the Reading Railroad, which also owned the mines, pledged that he would never agree to the workers' demands. Disturbed by what he considered the owners' "arrogant stupidity," Roosevelt threatened to dispatch federal troops to take over and run the mines. When the owners backed down, the president established a commission that hammered out a compromise, which raised wages and reduced working hours but did not recognize the union.

At the same time, Roosevelt tackled the problems caused by giant business trusts. In February 1902, the president instructed the Justice Department to sue the Northern Securities Company under the Sherman Antitrust Act (see Module 6-4). Financed by J. P. Morgan, Northern Securities held monopoly control of the northernmost transcontinental railway lines. In 1904 the Supreme Court ordered that the Northern Securities Company be dissolved, ruling that the firm had restricted competition. With this victory, Roosevelt affirmed the federal government's power to regulate business trusts that violated the public interest. Overall, Roosevelt initiated twenty-five suits under the Sherman Antitrust Act, including litigation against the tobacco and beef trusts and the Standard Oil Company, actions that earned him the title of "trustbuster."

Roosevelt distinguished between "good" trusts, which acted responsibly, and "bad" trusts, which abused their power. Railroads had earned an especially bad reputation with the public for charging higher rates to small shippers and those in remote regions while granting rebates to favored customers, such as Standard Oil. In 1903 Roosevelt helped persuade Congress to pass the **Elkins Act**, which outlawed railroad rebates. Three years later, the president increased the power of the Interstate Commerce Commission to set maximum railroad freight rates. Also in 1903 Roosevelt secured passage of legislation that established the **Department of Commerce and Labor**. Within this cabinet agency, the Bureau of Corporations gathered information about large companies in an effort to promote fair business practices.

Soaring in popularity, Roosevelt easily won reelection in 1904. During the next four years, the president applied antitrust laws even more vigorously than before. He steered through Congress various reforms concerning the railroads, such as the Hepburn Act (1906), which standardized shipping rates, and took a strong stand for conservation of public lands. Roosevelt charted a middle course between preservationists and conservationists. He reserved 150 million acres of timberland as part of the national forests, but he authorized the expenditure of more than $80 million in federal funds to construct dams, reservoirs, and canals largely in the West.

576

"Rough Riders" The nickname of Theodore Roosevelt's regiment of the 1st United States Volunteer Cavalry, which fought in Cuba during the Spanish-American War in 1898.

bully pulpit Term used by Theodore Roosevelt to describe the office of the presidency. Roosevelt believed that the president should use his office as a platform to promote his programs and rally public opinion.

"Square Deal" Theodore Roosevelt's plan to provide economic and political stability to the nation by guaranteeing the rights of everyday workers and protecting business interests.

AP® TIP
Compare President Roosevelt's response to the coal strike to responses earlier presidents gave to labor unrest such as the railroad strike of 1877 and Pullman strike of 1894.

Elkins Act 1903 act outlawing railroad rebates. The act was designed to protect smaller businesses and shippers who were paying higher rates than large favored customers, such as Standard Oil.

TEACHING IDEA

Incorporating Secondary Sources

The Miller Center at the University of Virginia has an extensive chronicle of Theodore Roosevelt as an individual, a politician, and a policymaker (millercenter.org). Assign students to read selected "Life in Depth Essays" and briefly discuss their findings in small groups with their peers the next day in class.

TEACHING IDEA

Check for Understanding

Pair students up and assign them to create a "cereal box" product for the Square Deal. This has the potential to engage students of multiple ability levels and is a more involved, tactile, and kinesthetic approach to learning. Templates and exemplars for creation of this type of product may be found at SampleTemplates' website by searching for "Cereal Box Book Reports" (sampletemplates.com).

TEACHING IDEA

Connecting the Dots

Place students into groups of four, and assign them to one of the following AP® themes: work, exchange, and technology; politics and power; social structures; or geography and the environment. With regards to their specific theme, task student groups with addressing the following question: "How or to what degree did the Progressive Movement change the relationship of the people to the state?" The next day, have student groups share their conclusions with the class, and the class can compile notes on the information.

Theodore Roosevelt and the Square Deal

AP® TIP
Identify and compare the various Progressive reforms that were influenced or instigated by muckrakers.

The Jungle 1906 muckraking novel by Upton Sinclair that portrayed the poor working and living conditions in the Chicago meatpacking district, as well as the unsanitary practices in the unregulated meat production industry, leading to a widespread call for government regulation of food safety.

Pure Food and Drug Act 1906 law to prevent the manufacturing, sale, and transportation of harmful "foods, drugs, medicines, and liquors."

Not all reform came from Roosevelt's initiative. Congress passed two notable consumer laws in 1906 that reflected the multiple and sometimes contradictory forces that shaped progressivism. That year, Upton Sinclair published *The Jungle*, a muckraking novel that portrayed the impoverished lives of immigrant workers in Packingtown (Chicago) and the deplorable working conditions they endured. Outraged readers responded to the vivid description of the shoddy and filthy ways the meatpacking industry slaughtered animals and prepared beef for sale. The largest and most efficient meatpacking firms had financial reasons to support reform as well. They were losing money because European importers refused to purchase tainted meat. Congress responded by passing the **Meat Inspection Act**, which benefited consumers and provided a way for large corporations to eliminate competition from smaller, marginal firms that could not afford to raise standards to meet the new federal meat-processing requirements.

In 1906 Congress also passed the **Pure Food and Drug Act**, which prohibited the sale of adulterated and fraudulently labeled food and drugs. The push for this law came from consumer groups, medical professionals, and government scientists. Dr. Harvey Wiley, a chemist in the Department of Agriculture, drove efforts for reform from within the government. He considered it part of his professional duty to eliminate harmful products.

Roosevelt initially gave African Americans reason to believe that they, too, would get a square deal. In October 1901, at the outset of his first term, Roosevelt invited Booker T. Washington to a dinner at the White House, outraging white supremacists in the South. Though Roosevelt dismissed this

AP® ANALYZING SOURCES

Source: Upton Sinclair, *The Jungle*, 1906

"A full hour before the party reached the city they had begun to note the perplexing changes in the atmosphere. It grew darker all the time, and upon the earth the grass seemed to grow less green. Every minute, as the train sped on, the colors of things became dingier; the fields were grown parched and yellow, the landscape hideous and bare. And along with the thickening smoke they began to notice another circumstance, a strange, pungent odor. . . . The new emigrants were still tasting it, lost in wonder, when suddenly the car came to a halt, and the door was flung open, and a voice shouted—'Stockyards!' . . .

[T]hey were left standing upon the corner, staring; down a side street there were two rows of brick houses, and between them a vista: half a dozen chimneys, tall as the tallest of buildings, touching the very sky—and leaping from them half a dozen columns of smoke, thick, oily, and black as night. . . . It was inexhaustible; one stared, waiting to see it stop, but still the great streams rolled out. They spread in vast clouds overhead, writhing, curling; then, uniting in one giant river, they streamed away down the sky, stretching a black pall as far as the eye could reach.

Then the party became aware of another strange thing. This, too, like the odor, was a thing elemental; it was a sound, a sound made up of ten thousand little sounds. You scarcely noticed it at first—it sunk into your consciousness, a vague disturbance, a trouble. It was like the murmuring of the bees in the spring, the whisperings of the forest; it suggested endless activity, the rumblings of a world in motion. It was only by an effort that one could realize that it was made by animals, that it was the distant lowing of ten thousand cattle, the distant grunting of ten thousand swine."

Questions for Analysis
1. Identify the reasons for the smoke and sounds that Sinclair describes.
2. Describe the effect of this factory on the environment, as portrayed by Sinclair.
3. Explain Sinclair's perspective on these effects.

Questions for Comparison Lincoln Steffens, *The Shame of the Cities*, 1904 (p. 556)
1. Explain how both Sinclair's and Steffens's accounts reflect progressive ideals.
2. Evaluate the extent of similarity between Sinclair's portrayal of the stockyards and Steffens's description of corrupt politics.

TRM Suggested Responses to Questions

TRM Module 7.2 AP® Analyzing Sources Handout 2

BUILDING AP® SKILLS
Sourcing and Situation

Assign students to compare the primary sources, "The Calamity" on page 572 and *The Jungle* on page 577. Ask students to then utilize their HIPP training to unpack each source, determining the commonalities and differences between the two sources in tone, form, and style, as well as explore the means employed by each author within their source in calling for reform in the United States (a refresher of HIPP can be found on page 8).

TEACHING IDEA

Connecting the Dots

Engage the class in an activity of association by disassociation called "Odd One Out." Write the following terms on the board/projector:

- Pure Food and Drug Act
- The Hetch Hetchy Dam controversy
- The Seventeenth Amendment
- The Triangle Shirtwaist Fire
- Elkins Act
- The city commission form of government

Then place students in small groups and ask them, "Which one is the odd one out and why? How do the remaining terms relate?" Give students approximately 7-10 minutes to complete this part, then share out student answers and discuss their conclusions and reasoning as a whole-class activity. There is no specific correct answer; the goal is to get students thinking in categorical habits of mind and defending their rationales.

Period 7: 1890–1945

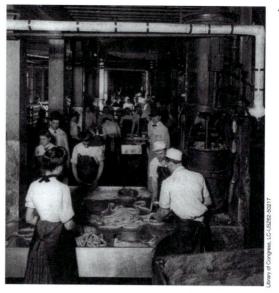

"The Jungle" Upton Sinclair's 1906 novel *The Jungle* exposed unsanitary conditions in the meatpacking industry and led to passage of the Meat Inspection Act. In this photo from around 1905, workers at the Swift company process sausages as they roll off machines at ten feet per second. **What aspects of this image reflect the issues highlighted in *The Jungle* and addressed by the Meat Inspection Act?**

criticism, he never invited another black guest. Also in his first term, Roosevelt supported the appointment of a few black Republicans to federal posts in the South.

Nevertheless, Roosevelt lacked a commitment to black equality and espoused the racist ideas of eugenics that were then in fashion. He deplored the declining birthrate of native-born white Americans compared with that of eastern and southern European newcomers and African Americans, whom he considered inferior stock. He argued that unless Anglo-Saxon women produced more children, white people would end up committing "race suicide." "If the women flinch from breeding," Roosevelt worried, "the . . . death of the race takes place even quicker."

Once he won reelection in 1904, Roosevelt had less political incentive to defy the white South. He stopped cooperating with southern black officeholders and maneuvered to build the Republican Party in the region with all-white support. One example illustrating his change in approach involved an incident that occurred in Brownsville, Texas, in 1906. White residents of the town charged that black soldiers stationed at Fort Brown shot and killed one man and wounded another. Roosevelt ordered that unless the alleged perpetrators stepped forward, the entire regiment would receive dishonorable discharges without a court-martial. Roosevelt never doubted the guilt of the black soldiers, and when no one admitted responsibility, he summarily dismissed 167 men from the military.

REVIEW

- What progressive reforms did Roosevelt undertake during his presidency?
- Who benefited most from these reforms?

The Retreat from Progressivism

When Roosevelt decided not to seek another term as president in 1908, choosing instead to back William Howard Taft as his successor, he thought he was leaving his reform legacy in capable hands. A Roosevelt loyalist, Taft easily defeated the Democratic candidate, William Jennings Bryan, who was running for the presidency for the third and final time.

Taft's presidency did not proceed as Roosevelt and his progressive followers had hoped. Taft did not have the charisma or energy of his predecessor and appeared to move in slow motion compared with Roosevelt. Taft proved a weak leader and frequently took stands opposite to those of progressives. After convening a special session of Congress in March 1909 to support lower tariffs, the president retreated in the face of conservative Republican opposition in the Senate. That year, when lawmakers passed the **Payne-Aldrich tariff**, which raised duties on imports, Taft signed it into law, thereby alienating key progressive legislators.

The situation deteriorated even further in the field of conservation. When Pinchot criticized Taft's secretary of the interior, Richard Ballinger, for returning restricted Alaskan coal mines to private mining companies in 1910, Taft fired Pinchot. Taft did not oppose conservation — he transferred more land from private to public control than did Roosevelt — but his dismissal of Pinchot angered conservationists.

Even more harmful to Taft's political fortunes, Roosevelt turned against his handpicked successor. After returning from overseas in 1910, Roosevelt became increasingly troubled by Taft's missteps. The loss of the House of Representatives to the Democrats in the 1910 elections highlighted the split among Republicans that had developed under Taft. A year later, relations between the ex-president and the incumbent further deteriorated when Roosevelt attacked Taft for filing antitrust litigation against U.S. Steel for a deal that the Roosevelt administration had approved in 1907. Ironically, Roosevelt, known as a trustbuster, believed that filing more lawsuits under the Sherman Antitrust Act yielded diminishing returns, whereas Taft, the conservative, initiated more antitrust litigation than did Roosevelt.

Convinced that only he could heal the party breach, Roosevelt announced his candidacy for the 1912 Republican presidential nomination. However, despite Roosevelt's widespread popularity among rank-and-file Republicans, Taft still controlled the party machinery and the majority of convention delegates. Losing to Taft on the first ballot, an embittered but optimistic Roosevelt formed a third party to sponsor his run for the presidency. Roosevelt excitedly told thousands of supporters gathered in Chicago that he felt "as strong as a BULL MOOSE," which became the nickname for Roosevelt's new **Progressive Party**.

Progressive Party Third party formed by Theodore Roosevelt in 1912 to facilitate his candidacy for president. Nicknamed the "Bull Moose Party," the Progressive Party split the Republican vote, allowing Democrat Woodrow Wilson to win the election. The party promoted an income tax, an eight-hour workday, unions, women's suffrage, and an end to child labor.

AP® ANALYZING SOURCES

Source: Woodrow Wilson, *The New Freedom: A Call For the Emancipation of the Generous Energies of a People*, 1913

"Gentlemen say, they have been saying for a long time, and, therefore, I assume that they believe, that trusts are inevitable. They don't say that big business is inevitable. They don't say merely that the elaboration of business upon a great co-operative scale is characteristic of our time and has come about by the natural operation of modern civilization. We would admit that. But they say that the particular kind of combinations that are now controlling our economic development came into existence naturally and were inevitable; and that, therefore, we have to accept them as unavoidable and administer our development through them....

I answer . . . that this attitude rests upon a confusion of thought. Big business is no doubt to a large extent necessary and natural. The development of business upon a great scale, upon a great scale of co-operation, is inevitable, and, let me add, is probably desirable. But that is a very different matter from the development of trusts, because the trusts have not grown. They have been artificially created; they have been put together, not by natural processes, but by the will, the deliberate planning will, of men who were more powerful than their neighbors in the business world, and who wished to make their power secure against competition."

Questions for Analysis
1. Identify the position Wilson takes regarding the rise of big business in the United States.
2. Describe what Wilson is unwilling to agree with when it comes to the rise of trusts.
3. Evaluate the extent to which Wilson's arguments were shaped by previous progressive reforms.

TEACHING IDEA

Understanding Political Changes

For homework, assign students to do their own general research on the ideas and philosophies of the New Nationalism and the New Freedom. The next day in class, place the students into groups of six. In each group, task three students with supporting the New Nationalism as the strongest pathway to deal with the challenges facing the nation in 1912, and task the other three students with refuting that claim, supporting the New Freedom instead. Instruct student triads then to share their reasoning with their opposite counterparts of their group of six, and then have the group of six record their arguments and assertions in a T-chart format.

TRM Suggested Responses to Questions

TRM Module 7.2 AP® Analyzing Sources Handout 3

BUILDING AP® SKILLS

Causation

A useful formative exercise to engage in with students at this point is a "How did we get here?" activity, whereby students in small groups are given a single event (e.g., Triangle Fire, Pure Food and Drug Act, Election of 1912, etc.) and have to explain its significance in the context of the Age of Progressivism. Then, student groups must migrate in the room and mingle with other student groups, to find which group's event or context led to their particular assigned event, and for which event or context their group's assigned event served as a catalyst. Students should write their thoughts in three or four sentences.

TEACHING IDEA

Incorporating Videos

To concisely provide a foundation for the policy prescriptions of the Progressive Era presidents, have the class watch the "History Channel — The Ultimate Guide to the Presidents 1899–1921" (available on YouTube). This 44-minute overview is a useful way to create context for Roosevelt, Wilson, and Taft, in an economy of time.

BUILDING AP® SKILLS

Comparison

Assign students in pairs to complete a "Dueling Dates" activity. For this activity, 1896 and 1912 are juxtaposed as a couplet of "Dueling Dates." Students will prove or justify that each of these dates constitutes a turning point in the history of the United States. They must give cause (involving evidence) for why each date could legitimately be called a turning point in American history. Then, choose one from each pair and defend the date as a better indication of a watershed year than the other.

TRM Find **Handout 7.2 – Dueling Dates, 1896 & 1912** in the Teacher's Resource Materials.

Period 7: 1890–1945

MODULE 7-2 Progressive Political Reforms

New Nationalism Agenda put forward by Theodore Roosevelt in his 1912 presidential campaign. Roosevelt called for increased regulation of large corporations, a more active role for the president, and the extension of social justice using the power of the federal government.

New Freedom Term used by Woodrow Wilson to describe his limited-government, progressive agenda. Wilson's New Freedom was offered as an alternative to Theodore Roosevelt's New Nationalism.

In accepting the nomination, Roosevelt articulated the philosophy of **New Nationalism**. He argued that the federal government should use its power to fight against the forces of special privilege and for social justice for the majority of Americans. To this end, the Progressive Party platform advocated income and inheritance taxes, an eight-hour workday, the abolition of child labor, workers' compensation, fewer restrictions on labor unions, and women's suffrage.

Roosevelt was not the only progressive candidate in the contest. The Democrats nominated Woodrow Wilson, the reform governor of New Jersey. As an alternative to Roosevelt's New Nationalism, Wilson offered his **New Freedom**. As a Democrat and a southerner (he was born in Virginia), Wilson had a more limited view of government than did Roosevelt. Wilson envisioned a society of small businesses, with the government's role confined to ensuring open competition among businesses and freedom for individuals to make the best use of their opportunities. Unlike Roosevelt's New Nationalism, Wilson's New Freedom did not embrace social reform and rejected federal action in support of women's suffrage and the elimination of child labor.

If voters considered either Roosevelt's or Wilson's brand of reform too mainstream, they could cast their ballots for Eugene V. Debs, the Socialist Party candidate who had been once imprisoned for his leadership in the Pullman strike. He favored overthrowing capitalism through peaceful, democratic methods and replacing it with government ownership of business and industry for the benefit of the working class.

The splintering of the Republican Party decided the outcome of the election. The final results gave Roosevelt 27 percent of the popular vote and Taft 23 percent. Together they had a majority, but because they were divided, Wilson became president, with 42 percent of the popular vote and 435 electoral votes. Finishing fourth, Debs did not win any electoral votes, but he garnered around a million popular votes (6 percent).

REVIEW

- In what ways did President Taft retreat from progressivism during his administration?
- In what ways did progressivism shape the election of 1912?

Woodrow Wilson and the New Freedom Agenda

AP® TIP
Analyze how the Roosevelt and Wilson administrations affected Americans' understanding of the role of the presidency and the federal government.

Sixteenth Amendment 1913 amendment providing a legal basis for a graduated income tax, which had been previously deemed unconstitutional.

Once in office, Wilson hurried to fulfill his New Freedom agenda. Even though he differed from Roosevelt about the scope of federal intervention, both men believed in a strong presidency. An admirer of the British parliamentary system, Wilson viewed the president as an active and strong leader whose job was to provide his party with a legislative program. The 1912 elections had given the Democrats control over Congress, and Wilson expected his party to support his New Freedom measures.

Tariff reduction came first. The **Underwood Act** of 1913 reduced import duties, a measure that appealed to southern and midwestern farmers who sought lower prices on the manufactured goods they bought that were subject to the tariff. The law also incorporated a reform that progressives had adopted from the Populists: the graduated income tax (tax rates that increase at higher levels of income). The ratification of the **Sixteenth Amendment** in 1913 provided the legal basis for the income tax after the Supreme Court had previously declared such a levy unconstitutional. The graduated income tax was meant to advance the cause of social justice by moderating income inequality. The need to recover revenues lost from lower tariffs provided an additional practical impetus for imposing the tax. Because the law exempted people earning less than $4,000 a year from paying the income tax, more than 90 percent of Americans owed no tax. Those with incomes exceeding this amount paid rates ranging from 1 percent to 6 percent on $500,000 or more.

Also in 1913, Wilson pressed Congress to consider banking reform. Farmers favored a system supervised by the government that afforded them an ample supply of credit at low interest rates.

TEACHING IDEA

Class Discussion

Divide the class into groups of 3 or 4 students and have each group address both of the following questions:

- To what extent did William Howard Taft retreat from Progressivism, and to what extent did he maintain it?

- To what extent was the election of 1912 a battle over different forms of Progressivism? Have the groups then write their conclusions on butcher paper and post them around the room for a gallery walk by students.

Woodrow Wilson and the New Freedom Agenda

▶ **Woodrow Wilson's New Freedom** Before Woodrow Wilson was elected president in 1912 he had been a college professor of political science and president of Princeton University. Having stepped out of the university's ivory tower into the White House, Wilson was prepared to "educate" his opponents about their economic and civic duties to the nation. **What connection does the artist of this political cartoon draw between Wilson's former occupation as a professor and his policies as president?**

Eastern bankers wanted reforms that would stabilize a system plagued by cyclical financial panics, the most recent in 1907, while keeping the banking system under the private control of bankers. The resulting compromise created the Federal Reserve System. The act established twelve regional banks. These banks lent cash reserves to member banks in their districts at a "rediscount rate," a rate that could be adjusted according to the fluctuating demand for credit. Federal Reserve notes became the foundation for a uniform currency. The Federal Reserve Board, appointed by the president and headquartered in Washington, D.C., supervised the system. Nevertheless, as with other progressive agencies, the experts selected to oversee the new banking system came from within the banking industry itself. Although farmers won a more rational and flexible credit supply, Wall Street bankers retained considerable power over the operation of the Federal Reserve System.

Next, President Wilson took two steps designed to help resolve the problem of economic concentration. First, in 1914 he persuaded Congress to create the Federal Trade Commission. The commission had the power to investigate corporate activities and prohibit "unfair" practices (which the law left undefined). Wilson's second measure directly attacked monopolies. Enacted in 1914, the **Clayton Antitrust Act** strengthened the Sherman Antitrust Act by banning certain corporate operations, such as price discrimination and overlapping membership on company boards, which undermined economic competition. The statute also exempted labor unions from prosecution under antitrust legislation, reversing the policy initiated by the federal government in the wake of the Pullman strike (see Module 6-5).

By the end of his second year in office, Wilson had achieved most of his New Freedom objectives. Political considerations, however, soon forced him to widen his progressive agenda and support measures he had previously rejected. With the Republican Party once again united after the electoral fiasco of 1912, Wilson, looking ahead to reelection in 1916, resumed the campaign for progressive legislation. Wilson appealed to Roosevelt's constituency by supporting New Nationalism social justice measures. In 1916 he signed into law the **Adamson Act**, which provided an eight-hour workday and overtime pay for railroad workers; the **Keating-Owen Act**, outlawing child labor in firms that engaged in interstate commerce; and the **Workmen's Compensation Act**, which provided insurance for federal employees in case of injury. In supporting programs that required greater intervention by the federal government, Wilson had placed political expediency ahead of his professed principles. He would later show a similar flexibility when he lent his support to a women's suffrage amendment, a cause he had long opposed.

Despite facing a challenge from a united Republican Party, Wilson won the 1916 election against former New York Governor Charles Evans Hughes with slightly less than 50 percent of the vote. Wilson's reelection owed little to support from African Americans. W. E. B. Du Bois, who backed Wilson in 1912 for pledging to "assist in advancing the interest of [the black] race," had become disillusioned with the president. Born in the South and with deep southern roots, Wilson surrounded himself with white appointees from the South. Despite black protests, Wilson held a screening in the White House of the film *Birth of a Nation*, which glorified the Ku Klux Klan and

Clayton Antitrust Act 1914 act that strengthened the Sherman Antitrust Act by banning certain corporate operations, such as price discrimination and overlapping membership on company boards, and by protecting labor unions. The Act was designed to encourage economic competition.

Adamson Act 1916 act establishing an eight-hour workday and overtime for workers in private industry — in this case, railroad workers.

Keating-Owen Act 1916 act preventing the interstate sale of goods made by children under the age of 14, among other protections for children. The Supreme Court ruled it unconstitutional in 1918.

Workmen's Compensation Act Regulation guaranteeing the rights of federal employees to receive financial compensation or pursue legal action for any injury occurring on the job.

TEACHING IDEA

Six Degrees of Separation

Have the students complete a "Six Degrees of Separation" activity. The prompt for this particular activity is as follows:

"From the passage of the Interstate Commerce Act (1887) to the passage of the Clayton Antitrust Act (1914)"

For the purpose of this exercise, students are given two events spanning time, but related by their theme. They must select four events in chronological order that link the first event in the series with the last. They will write the name of each selected event, and create an argument to support each of the events they selected. Explain to them that they must answer the question, "Why does it belong as a link in your chain of events?" for each link. Students must emphasize both cause and effect and/or demonstrate continuity or change over time in the linking. This can be done as either a formative assessment in class, or as a homework assignment involving student research of their textbooks, activities/lessons, lecture notes, and knowledge of the time period.

▲ Differentiation

The lesson may also be undertaken by students individually or in small groups, depending upon the situation and instructional context of the teacher and course. Additionally, a more advanced use of this exercise could have students be tasked in different groups to follow a specific theme from Period 7 through their activity. Assigned themes could include work, exchange, and technology; American and national identity; or politics and power.

TEACHING IDEA

Connecting the Dots

Divide the class into three groups. Assign each group two of the following six AP® themes: work, exchange, and technology; geography and the environment; migration and settlement; politics and power; American and regional culture; and social structures (for the present, disregard America in the world). Task each student group with creating a timeline for the Progressive Era of any events that are germane to their theme. As the groups complete their two theme timelines, have them either present them to the class and explain how the events they have tagged correspond to their assigned theme, or reshuffle the class into groups made up of members of the three original groups, and assign students to engage in sharing with their peers.

Period 7: 1890–1945

MODULE 7-2 Progressive Political Reforms

denigrated African Americans. Making the situation worse, Wilson introduced racial segregation into government offices and dining facilities in the nation's capital, and black people lost jobs in post offices and other federal agencies throughout the South. In Wilson's view, segregation and discrimination were in the "best interests" of African Americans.

Still, President Wilson achieved much of the progressive agenda — more, in fact, than he had intended to when he first came to office. By the beginning of his second term, the federal government had further extended regulation over the activities of corporations and banks. Big business and finance still wielded substantial power, but Wilson had steered the government on a course that also benefited ordinary citizens, including passage of social justice measures he had originally opposed.

REVIEW

- What reforms did the Wilson administration pursue?
- To what extent did these reforms reflect a progressive political agenda?

The Progressive Legacy

By the end of the Progressive Era, Americans had come to expect more from their government. They were more confident that their food and medicine were safe, that children would not have to sacrifice their health and education by going to work, that women laborers would not be exploited, and that political officials would be more responsive to their wishes. As a result of the efforts of environmentalists, the nation expanded its efforts both to conserve and to preserve its natural resources. These and other reforms accomplished what Theodore Roosevelt, Woodrow Wilson, and their fellow progressives wanted: to bring order out of chaos.

In challenging laissez-faire and championing governmental intervention, progressives sought to balance individualism with social justice and social control. Despite cloaking many of their political reforms in democratic garb, middle- and upper-class progressives generally were more interested in augmenting their ability to advance their own agenda than in expanding opportunities for political participation for all Americans. Confident that they spoke for the "interests of the people," progressives had little doubt that increasing their own political power would be good for the nation as a whole.

Racial boundaries shaped the progressive movement. American Indians campaigned and organized to get the federal government to repair its broken promises of justice. African Americans were active participants in progressivism, whether through extending educational opportunities, working in settlement houses, campaigning for women's suffrage, or establishing the NAACP. Nevertheless, racism was also a characteristic of progressivism. White southern reformers generally favored disfranchisement and segregation. Northern white people did not prove much more sympathetic. Immigrants also found themselves unwelcome targets of moral outrage as progressives forced these newcomers to conform to middle-class standards of social behavior. Campaigns for temperance, moral reform, and birth control all shared a desire to mold people deemed inferior into proper citizens, uncontaminated by chronic vice and corruption.

Progressivism was not monolithic and included a range of disparate and overlapping efforts to reorder political, social, moral, and physical environments. Except for the brief existence of the Progressive Party in 1912, reformers did not have a tightly knit organization or a fixed agenda. Leaders were more likely to come from the middle class, but support came from the rich as well as the poor, depending on the issue. Of course, many Americans did not embrace progressive principles, as conservative opponents continued to hold power and to fight against reform. Nevertheless, by 1917 a combination of voluntary changes and government intervention had cleared the way to regulate corporations, increase governmental efficiency, and promote social justice. Progressives succeeded in ameliorating conditions that might have produced violent revolution and more disorder. In time, they would bring their ideas to reordering international affairs.

AP® TIP
Evaluate the extent to which the Progressive Era maintained the continuity of existing economic, cultural, social, and political systems in the U.S.

REVIEW

- Who benefited most from progressive reforms?
- Who was left out and why?

TEACHING IDEA

Incorporating Videos

Assign students to watch Episode 29, "The Progressive Presidents," from the Crash Course US History series (available on YouTube). Use this 15-minute episode as a concise summative content review for students of the Roosevelt, Taft, and Wilson administrations as part of preparation for either summative assessment or reinforcement antecedent to moving forward into the next module.

APPLY THE TIP

To build upon the complexity of the AP® Tip at the top of this page, place students into four groups. First, assign each group one of the subtopics of the AP® Tip prompt: economic, cultural, social, or political systems. Have students compile information relative to an argument on this prompt only for their assigned subtopic. Then, recombine the class into quads with one member from each subset group represented. After each member student shares what their previous group had concluded about their respective assigned subtopic in jigsaw fashion, have these new quads craft a thesis statement utilizing the "Twenty-Five-Word Drill" process, or do so including a contextualization component along the lines of the more elaborate "Fifty-Word Drill" (a refresher of the jigsaw model can be found on page 33).

AP® WRITING HISTORICALLY — Document-Based Question Practice

ACTIVITY

The following question is based on the accompanying documents. The documents have been edited for the purpose of this exercise. *Suggested reading period: 15 minutes. Suggested writing time: 45 minutes.*

Evaluate the extent of change in the goals and strategies of reform movements that sought to improve the lives African Americans between 1895 and 1922.

DOCUMENT 1

Source: Booker T. Washington, *The Atlanta Exposition Address*, 1895

"The wisest among my race understand that the agitation of questions of social equality is the extremest folly, and that progress in the enjoyment of all the privileges that will come to us must be the result of severe and constant struggle rather than of artificial forcing. No race that has anything to contribute to the markets of the world is long in any degree ostracized. It is important and right that all privileges of the law be ours, but it is vastly more important that we be prepared for the exercise of those privileges. The opportunity to earn a dollar in a factory just now is worth infinitely more than the opportunity to spend a dollar in an opera house. . . .

I pledge that in your effort to work out the great and intricate problem which God has laid at the doors of the South, you shall have at all times the patient, sympathetic help of my race; only let this be constantly in mind that, while from representations in these buildings of the product of field, of forest, of mine, of factory, letters, and art, much good will come, yet far above and beyond material benefits will be that higher good, that, let us pray God, will come, in a blotting out of sectional differences and racial animosities and suspicions, in a determination to administer absolute justice, in a willing obedience among all classes to the mandates of law. This, coupled with our material prosperity, will bring into our beloved South a new heaven and a new earth."

DOCUMENT 2

Source: W. E. B. Du Bois, *The Talented Tenth*, 1903

"You misjudge us because you do not know us. From the very first it has been the educated and intelligent of the Negro people that have led and elevated the mass, and the sole obstacles that nullified and retarded their efforts were slavery and race prejudice; for what is slavery but the legalized survival of the unfit and the nullification of the work of natural internal leadership? Negro leadership therefore sought from the first to rid the race of this awful incubus that it might make way for natural selection and the survival of the fittest. In colonial days came Phillis Wheatley and Paul Cuffe striving against the bars of prejudice; and Benjamin Banneker, the almanac maker, voiced their longings. . . . Can the masses of the Negro people be in any possible way more quickly raised than by the effort and example of this aristocracy of talent and character? Was there ever a nation on God's fair earth civilized from the bottom upward? Never; it is, ever was and ever will be from the top downward that culture filters. The Talented Tenth rises and pulls all that are worth the saving up to their vantage ground. This is the history of human progress. . . ."

DOCUMENT 3

Source: Ida B. Wells, "The Negro Problem from the Negro Point of View," *World Today*, 1904

"Industrial education for the Negro is Booker T. Washington's hobby. He believes that for the masses of the Negro race an elementary education of the brain and a continuation of the education of the hand is not only the best kind, but he knows it is the most popular with the white South. He knows also that the Negro is the butt of ridicule with the average white American, and that the aforesaid American enjoys nothing so much as a joke which

(Continued)

TRM Suggested Responses to Questions

TEACHING IDEA

AP® Writing Historically Workshop

This DBQ asks students to consider two separate categories of analysis: goals and strategies. Before assigning this DBQ think about giving students the following homework assignment. Students will make two note cards, one labeled "goals" and the other "strategies." On the back of each note card, have students write down which documents belong to each category. In this way, they are considering the framework of the question before they sit down to write the response.

portrays the Negro as illiterate and [shortsighted]; a petty thief or a happy-go-lucky inferior. . . .

    Does this mean that the Negro objects to industrial education? By no means. It simply means that he knows by sad experience that industrial education will not stand him in place of political, civil and intellectual liberty, and he objects to being deprived of fundamental rights of American citizenship to the end that one school for industrial training shall flourish. To him it seems like selling a race's birthright for a mess of [thick soup]."

DOCUMENT 4

Source: Committee on the Negro "Call" for a National Conference, *Founding Document of the National Association for the Advancement of Colored People (NAACP)*, 1909

"If Mr. Lincoln could revisit this country in the flesh, he would be disheartened and discouraged. He would learn that on January 1st, 1909, Georgia had rounded out a new confederacy by disenfranchising the negro after the manner of all other Southern states. He would learn that the Supreme Court of the United States, supposedly a bulwark of American liberties, had dodged every opportunity to pass squarely upon this disfranchisement of millions, by laws avowedly discriminatory and openly enforced in such manner that the white men may vote and black men be without a vote in their government; he would discover, therefore, that taxation without representation is the lot of millions of wealth-producing American citizens, in whose hands rests the progress and welfare of an entire section of the country. . . . In many States . . . Lincoln would find justice enforced, if at all, by judges elected by one element in a community to pass upon the liberties and lives of another. He would see black men and women, for whose freedom a hundred thousand soldiers gave their lives, set apart in trains, in which they pay first-class fares for third-class service, in railway stations and in places of entertainment, while State after State declines to do its elementary duty in preparing the negro through education for the best exercise of citizenship."

DOCUMENT 5

Source: *The Crisis*, September 1912

"At the convention of the Progressive party Negroes from the South were denied seats. In Mississippi the delegates had been elected in a convention which was confined to white men. In most of the other Southern States Negroes were excluded. In the case of Florida both the White and colored delegations were excluded. South Carolina was not represented because only colored men offered to organize the party. A plank was laid before the convention affirming the right of the Negro to take part in government. This, after long debate, the platform committee refused to adopt. A few colored delegates sat for the Northern States and made a hard fight for justice. Three directors of the National Association for the Advancement of Colored People, Mr. J. E. Spingarn, Mr. Henry Moskowitz and Miss Jane Addams, worked strenuously, but without avail, to change the attitude of the convention.

    In the September election, Ohio will vote on two proposals touching the colored people. Proposal number 23 is to enfranchise women and to strike from the constitution the prohibition against voting by other persons than white men. Proposal number 24 does not enfranchise women, but does drop the word 'white.'

    The question of Negroes voting in Southern 'white' primaries continually comes to the fore. In Virginia, the new Byrd law apparently does not exclude the colored people from primary elections. In Texas the State attorney-general has landed down an opinion that Negroes may be prohibited from voting in such elections."

DOCUMENT 6

Source: *Congressional Anti-Lynching Bill*, 1918 (Defeated in the Senate in 1922)

"SEC. 3. That any State or municipal officer charged with the duty or who possesses the power or authority as such officer to protect the life of any person that may be put to death by any mob or riotous assemblage, or who has any such person in his charge as a prisoner, who fails, neglects, or refuses to make all reasonable efforts to prevent such person from being so put to death, or any State or municipal officer charged with the duty of apprehending or prosecuting any person participating in such mob or riotous assemblage who fails, neglects, or refuses to make all reasonable efforts to perform his duty in apprehending or prosecuting to final judgment under the laws of such State all persons so participating except such, if any, as are to have been held to answer for such participation in any district court of the United States, as herein provided, shall be guilty of a felony, and upon conviction thereof shall be punished by imprisonment not exceeding five years or by a fine of not exceeding $5,000, or by both such fine and imprisonment."

DOCUMENT 7

Source: NAACP, *The Shame of America* (a full-page advertisement in the *New York Times*), 1922

TRM Suggested Responses to Questions

Module 7-3

The Awakening of Imperialism

LEARNING TARGETS
By the end of this module, you should be able to:

- Explain how imperialists used economic opportunities, racial theories, competing European empires, and the so-called closing of the American frontier to justify expansion of American power around the globe.
- Explain how anti-imperialists used American traditions of self-determination, racial theories, and a tradition of isolationism to counter imperialist arguments.
- Explain how the arguments that supported the Spanish–American War led to acquisition of territories in the Caribbean and the Pacific, expanded involvement in Asia, and justified the suppression of an independence movement in the Philippines.

THEMATIC FOCUS
America in the World

Beginning in the second half of the nineteenth century, policy makers in the United States increasingly began to imagine the nation projecting its power outside of the continental United States. From Secretary of State Seward's acquisition of Alaska from Russia in 1867 to the domination of the Hawaiian economy in the 1880s, the United States pursued its interests overseas. Starting in the 1890s, American policy makers ramped up their efforts to compete with older imperial powers in Europe. This led to both conflict abroad and debate at home.

HISTORICAL REASONING FOCUS
Comparison

TASK ▶ While reading this module, consider the similarities and differences in attitudes about the nation's proper role in the world. What economic, political, and ideological factors accounted for the similarities and differences?

TEACHING IDEA

Incorporating Videos

Assign students to watch Episode 28, "American Imperialism," from the Crash Course US History series (available on YouTube). Use this 15-minute episode as a concise formative content introduction for students of the major issues and events of Module 7-3 as part of preparation for either assessment or reinforcement.

The United States became a modern imperial power relatively late. In the decades following the Civil War, the U.S. government concentrated most of its energies on settling the western territories, pushing American Indians aside, and extracting the region's resources. In many ways, westward expansion in the nineteenth century foreshadowed international expansion. The conquest of the American Indians reflected a broader imperialistic impulse within the country. Arguments based on racial superiority and the nation's duty to expand became justifications for expansion in North America and overseas. By the end of the nineteenth century, sweeping economic, cultural, and social changes led many in the United States to conclude that the time had come for the country to assert its power beyond its borders. This goal became particularly important as Americans came to believe that their internal frontier was rapidly closing through western expansion and settlement and they needed room for further development. In fact, the 1890 census of the nation's population announced that the frontier had disappeared. Based on this data, three years later the influential U.S. historian, Frederick Jackson Turner, argued that the ending of the frontier would require a "wider field" for the "exercise [of] American energy" and reinvigorating the nation's political, economic, and cultural strengths. Convinced of the argument for empire advanced by imperialists, U.S. officials led the nation in a burst of overseas expansion from 1898 to 1904, in which the United States acquired Guam, Hawaii, the Philippines, and Puerto Rico; established a protectorate in Cuba; and exercised force to build a canal through Panama. These gains paved the way for subsequent U.S. intervention in Haiti, the Dominican Republic, and Nicaragua.

BUILDING AP® SKILLS

Claims and Evidence in Sources

The Gilder Lehrman History Now feature provides students with a series of documents regarding imperialism and the Spanish-American War from several points of view (available on gilderlehrman.org by searching for "imperialism guided readings"). Assign students in groups to read and break down the fourteen documents (pre-reading on the part of the instructor is important here) to determine their historical context, intended audience, purpose, and point of view, in line with the HIPP format of document analysis (a refresher of HIPP can be found on page 8). Then have students answer the Questions for Discussion. Student products can then be shared out in a jigsaw fashion in order for students to evaluate and ascertain the nature of the arguments for and against expansion (a refresher of the jigsaw model can be found on page 33).

Cultural Justifications for Imperialism

The **Economics** of Expansion

The industrialization of the United States and the growth of corporate capitalism stimulated imperialist desires in the late nineteenth century. Throughout its early history, the United States had sought overseas markets for exports. However, the importance of exports to the U.S. economy increased dramatically in the second half of the nineteenth century, as industrialization gained momentum. In 1870 U.S. exports totaled $500 million. By 1910 the value of U.S. exports had increased threefold to $1.7 billion.

The bulk of U.S. exports went to the developed markets of Europe and Canada, which had the greatest purchasing power. Although the less economically advanced nations of Latin America and Asia did not have the same ability to buy U.S. products, businessmen still considered these regions — especially China, with its large population — as future markets for U.S. industries.

The desire to expand foreign markets remained a steady feature of U.S. business interests. The fear that the domestic market for manufactured goods was shrinking gave this expansionist hunger greater urgency. The fluctuating business cycle of boom and bust that characterized the economy in the 1870s and 1880s culminated in the depression of the 1890s. The social unrest that accompanied this depression worried business and political leaders about the stability of the country. The way to sustain prosperity and contain radicalism, many businessmen agreed, was to find foreign markets for U.S. goods. Senator William Frye of Maine argued, "We must have the market [of China] or we shall have revolution."

Similar commercial ambitions led many in the United States to covet Hawaii. U.S. missionaries first visited the Hawaiian Islands in 1820. As missionaries tried to convert native islanders to Christianity, U.S. businessmen sought to establish plantations on the islands, especially to grow sugarcane. In exchange for duty-free access to the U.S. sugar market, white Hawaiians signed an agreement in 1887 that granted the United States exclusive rights to a naval base at Pearl Harbor in Honolulu.

The growing influence of white sugar planters on the islands alarmed native Hawaiians. In 1891 Queen Liliuokalani, a strong nationalist leader who voiced the slogan "Hawaii for the Hawaiians," sought to increase the power of the indigenous peoples she governed, at the expense of the sugar growers. In 1893 white plantation owners, with the cooperation of the U.S. ambassador to Hawaii and 150 U.S. marines, overthrew the queen's government. Once in command of the government, they entered into a treaty of annexation with the United States. However, President Grover Cleveland opposed annexation and withdrew the treaty. Nevertheless, planters remained in power and waited for a suitable opportunity to seek annexation.

> **AP® TIP**
> Analyze the effects of laissez-faire capitalism on both the imperialism and the progressive politics of the late nineteenth and early twentieth centuries.

> "We must have the market [of China] or we shall have revolution."
> —Senator William Frye, 1894

REVIEW

- What historical trends led to American imperialism in the late nineteenth century?
- What role did economic developments play in prompting calls for a U.S. empire?

Cultural Justifications for Imperialism

Imperialists linked overseas expansion to practical, economic considerations, but race was also a key component in their arguments for empire. Many in the United States and western Europe declared themselves superior to nonwhite peoples of Latin America, Asia, and Africa. Buttressing their arguments with racist studies claiming to demonstrate scientifically the "racial" superiority of white Protestants, imperialists asserted a "natural right" of conquest and world domination.

Imperialists added an ethical dimension to this ideology by contending that "higher civilizations" had a duty to uplift inferior nations. In *Our Country* (1885), the Congregationalist minister Josiah Strong proclaimed the superiority of the Anglo-Saxon, or white northern European, race and the responsibility of the United States to spread the "blessings" of its Christian way of life throughout the world. Secular intellectuals, such as historian John Fiske, praised the English race for settling the United States and predicted that English society and culture would become "predominant" in the less civilized parts of the globe.

> **AP® TIP**
> Analyze the ways in which the ideology of white supremacy influenced the rise in support for imperialism during the late nineteenth century.

PERIOD 7

TEACHING IDEA

Building Vocabulary

As a study aid and teaching tool, train students to think of the root causes of imperialism in terms of a mnemonic device, such as the "Five D's" (Destiny, Defense, Dollars, Darwinism, and the Deity), or the "Six P's" (Patriotism, Profits, Piety, Politics, Paternalism, and Population). Walk students through the explanations of the roles each of these "D's" or "P's" played in contributing to expansion in a whole-class question–answer format.

TEACHING IDEA

Differing Views

Assign students to read Chapter 12, "The Empire and the People," from Howard Zinn's book, *A People's History of the United States*. Assign students to annotate the chapter in preparation for a whole-class discussion the next day. Upon completion of the roundtable, place students into pairs, and have them compare Zinn's presentation of imperialism to that of *Fabric of a Nation*.

TEACHING IDEA

Incorporating Primary Sources

Assign students to read and annotate pages 161–175 from Josiah Strong's *Our Country* (available in full on Google Books) and utilize their HIPP training to break down the source (a refresher of HIPP can be found on page 8). Then, have students read the excerpt of "The White Man's Burden" on page 588, answer the accompanying questions, and compare the two sources.

TRM Suggested Responses to Questions

TRM Module 7.3 AP® Analyzing Sources Handout 1

AP® ANALYZING SOURCES

Source: Rudyard Kipling, British author, "The White Man's Burden" (poem), 1899

"Take up the White Man's burden—
Send forth the best ye breed—
Go send your sons to exile
To serve your captives' need;
To wait in heavy harness
On fluttered folk and wild—
Your new-caught, sullen peoples,
Half devil and half child."

Questions for Analysis

1. Identify the "white man's burden" in this poem.
2. Describe the obligations the poem places on the "white man."
3. Explain the perceptions of colonized peoples portrayed in this poem.
4. Evaluate the extent to which the poem reflects previous conceptions of non-white peoples common in American history.

As in Hawaii, Christian missionaries served as foot soldiers for the advancing U.S. commercial empire. In fact, there was often a clear connection between religious and commercial interests. For example, industrialists John D. Rockefeller Jr. and Cyrus McCormick funded the efforts of young missionaries, many of them women, to spread Protestant Christianity throughout the world. In this way, it was no coincidence that China became a magnet for U.S. missionary activity. Many Americans hoped that, under missionary supervision, the Chinese would become consumers of both U.S. ideas and U.S. products.

Gender anxieties provided additional motivation for U.S. imperialism. In the late nineteenth century, with the Civil War long over, many in the United States worried that the rising generation of U.S. men lacked opportunities to test and strengthen their manhood. For example, in 1897 Mississippi congressman John Sharp Williams lamented the fading of "the dominant spirit which controlled in this Republic [from 1776 to 1865] . . . one of honor, glory, chivalry, and patriotism." Such gender anxieties were not limited to elites. The depression of the 1890s hit working-class men hard, causing them to question their self-worth as they lost the ability to support their families. By embracing imperialist ideals, they would regain their manly honor.

The growing presence of women as political activists in campaigns for suffrage and moral, humanitarian, and governmental reforms challenged traditional notions of male identity. Some men warned that dire consequences would result if women succeeded in feminizing politics. Many prominent imperialists believed that women's suffrage would undermine the nation's military security because women lacked the will to use physical force. Military historian Alfred Thayer Mahan asserted that giving the vote to women would destroy the "constant practice of the past ages by which to men are assigned the outdoor rough action of life and to women that indoor sphere which we call the family." For such men, calling U.S. men to action was often paired with a call for U.S. women to leave the public arena and return to the home.

Males in the United States could reassert their manhood by adopting a militant spirit. Known as **jingoists**, war enthusiasts such as Theodore Roosevelt saw war as necessary to the development of a generation of men who could meet the challenges of the modern age. "No greater danger could befall civilization than the disappearance of the warlike spirit (I dare say war) among civilized men," military historian Alfred Thayer Mahan asserted. "There are too many barbarians still in the world." Mahan and Roosevelt promoted naval power, and by 1900, the U.S. fleet contained seventeen battleships and six armored cruisers, making it the third most powerful navy in the world, up from twelfth place in 1880. Having built a powerful navy, the United States would soon find opportunities to use it.

> "No greater danger could befall civilization than the disappearance of the warlike spirit (I dare say war) among civilized men. There are too many barbarians still in the world."
>
> Alfred Thayer Mahan, military historian, 1890

jingoists Extremely patriotic supporters of the expansion and use of military power. Jingoists such as Theodore Roosevelt longed for a war in which they could demonstrate America's strength and prove their own masculinity.

588

BUILDING AP® SKILLS

Causation

Assign students in small groups to complete a chart on the causes of imperialism. Then, have them ascertain which cause they believe to be the most important, and provide an explanation as to why. Have student groups present their conclusions to the rest of the class.

The War with Spain

REVIEW

- How did American citizens and policy makers justify imperialism?
- In what ways were late nineteenth-century social norms used to justify imperialism?

Spanish–American War 1898 war in which the United States sided with Cuba in its ongoing war for independence from Spain because U.S. policymakers decided that Cuban independence was in the United States' economic and strategic interests. Cuba's eventual liberation from Spain, and the U.S. victory in the war, allowed the United States to gain control over a large portion of Spain's overseas empire, turning the United States into a major imperial power.

> "Our goal is not so much a mere political change as a good, sound, and just and equitable system."
>
> José Martí, Cuban revolutionary leader, 1892

The United States went to war with Spain over Cuba in 1898 not to defend itself from attack but because U.S. policymakers decided that Cuban independence from Spain was in the United States' economic and strategic interests. Victory over Spain, however, brought the United States much more than control over Cuba. In the peace negotiations following the war, the United States acquired a significant portion of Spain's overseas empire, turning the United States into a major imperial power. In the U.S., the war has traditionally been called the **Spanish–American War**, but this term fails to take into account the significant role played by the Cuban people and subsequently by the Filipinos who were also under Spanish rule.

The Cuban War for Independence began in 1895 around the concept of *Cubanidad* — pride of nation. José Martí envisioned that this war of national liberation from Spain would provide land to impoverished peasants and offer genuine racial equality for the large Afro-Cuban population that had been liberated from slavery less than a decade earlier, in 1886. "Our goal," the revolutionary leader declared in 1892, "is not so much a mere political change as a good, sound, and just and equitable system." Black Cubans flocked to the revolutionary cause and constituted a significant portion of the senior ranks in the rebel army.

The insurgents fought a brilliant guerrilla war. Facing some 200,000 Spanish troops, 50,000 rebels ground them down in a war of attrition. Within eighteen months, the rebellion had spread across the island and garnered the support of all segments of the Cuban population. The Spanish government's brutal attempts to crack down on the rebels only stiffened their resistance. By the end of 1897, the Spanish government recognized that the war was going poorly and offered the rebels a series of reforms that would give the island home rule within the empire but not independence. Sensing victory, the insurgents held out for total separation to realize their vision of **Cuba Libre**, an independent Cuba with social and racial equality.

The revolutionaries had every reason to feel confident as they wore down Spanish troops. First, they had help from the climate. One-quarter of Spanish soldiers had contracted yellow fever,

▲ **Cuban Revolutionary Soldiers** Under the command of General Maximo Gómez, these Cuban soldiers fought against Spanish forces in 1898. Gómez waged guerrilla warfare for Cuban independence from Spain before the United States entered the war. **To what extent did United States policy makers support Gómez's cause?**

TEACHING IDEA

Incorporating Videos

Show students selected excerpts of the PBS documentary, *Crucible of Empire: The Spanish-American War* (available on YouTube). Have students watch the following three chapters for a total of 43 minutes: "The Only Recourse," "The Cuba Story," and "Steps to War." Have students take brief notes on the film, and at the conclusion of the excerpts, divide the class up into three groups, each group focusing on one of the following AP® themes: America in the world, politics and power, or American and national identity. Task students with discussion based upon their assigned theme to create a general outline of how that theme connects with which aspects of the film excerpts they just viewed. Lastly, have each group present their findings to the class.

TEACHING IDEA

Connecting the Dots

The Stanford History Education Group includes a collection of numerous free online lessons (sheg.stanford.edu). Included in the repository on this platform is a downloadable lesson focusing upon the origins of the Spanish-American War as well as the explosion of the battleship USS *Maine*.

EXPLORING AP® THEMES

America in the World

Point out to students that the U.S. Navy ultimately concluded in 1974 that the USS *Maine* most likely was destroyed due to an internal explosion and not foul play. Viewed in that light, the Spanish-American War was begun due to incorrect assumptions. Discuss with students the similarities to the motivations for the United States to go to war in Iraq in 2003 on the basis of incorrect intelligence assessments that concluded that Iraq possessed weapons of mass destruction, which the ensuing war proved to be false.

TRM Suggested Responses to Questions

TRM Module 7.3 AP® Analyzing Sources Handout 2

---

malaria, and other tropical illnesses and remained confined to hospitals. Second, mounting a successful counterinsurgency would have required far more troops than Spain could spare. Its forces were spread too thin around the globe to keep the empire intact. Finally, antiwar sentiment was mounting in Spain, and on January 12, 1898, Spanish troops mutinied in Havana. Speaking for many, a former president of Spain asserted: "Spain is exhausted. She must withdraw her troops and recognize Cuban independence before it is too late."

With the Cuban insurgents on the verge of victory, President William McKinley came to favor military intervention as a way to increase U.S. control of postwar Cuba. By intervening before the Cubans won on their own, the United States staked its claim for determining the postwar relationship between the two countries and protecting its vital interests in the Caribbean, including the private property rights of U.S. landowners in Cuba.

The U.S. press, however, helped build support for U.S. intervention not by focusing on economic interests and geopolitics but by framing the war as a matter of U.S. honor. William Randolph Hearst's *New York Journal* competed with Joseph Pulitzer's *New York World* to see which could provide the most shocking coverage of Spanish atrocities. Known disparagingly as **yellow journalism**, these sensationalist newspaper accounts aroused jingoistic outrage against Spain.

On February 15, 1898, the battleship *Maine*, anchored in Havana harbor, exploded, killing 266 U.S. sailors. Newspapers in the United States blamed Spain. The *World* shouted the rallying cry "Remember the *Maine*! To hell with Spain!" Assistant Secretary of the Navy Theodore Roosevelt seconded this sentiment by denouncing the explosion as a Spanish "act of treachery." Why the

yellow journalism Sensationalist news accounts meant to provoke an emotional response in readers. Yellow journalism contributed to the growth of public support for American intervention in Cuba in 1898.

AP® ANALYZING SOURCES

Source: Assistant Secretary of State William Rufus Day, *Diplomatic Cable to Stewart L. Woodford (U.S. Minister to Spain)*, 1898

"[T]he President's desire is for peace. He cannot look upon the suffering and starvation in Cuba save with horror. The concentration of men, women, and children in the fortified towns, and permitting them to starve, is unbearable to a Christian nation geographically so close as ours to Cuba. All this has shocked and inflamed the American mind, as it has the civilized world, where its extent and character are known.

It was represented to him in November that the Blanco government would at once release the suffering and so modify the Weyler order as to permit those who were able to return to their homes and till the fields from which they had been driven. There has been no relief to the starving except such as the American people have supplied. . . .

There is no hope of peace through the Spanish arms. The Spanish government seems unable to conquer the insurgents. More than half of the island is under control of the insurgents. For more than three years our people have been patient and forbearing; we have patrolled our coast with zeal and at great expense, and have successfully prevented the landing of any armed force on the island. The war has disturbed the peace and tranquility of our people.

We do not want the island. The President has evidenced in every way his desire to preserve and continue friendly relations with Spain. He has kept every international obligation with fidelity. He wants an honorable peace. He has repeatedly urged the government of Spain to secure a peace. She still has the opportunity to do it, and the President appeals to her from every consideration of justice and humanity to do it. Will she? Peace is the desired end.

For your own guidance, the President suggests that if Spain . . . maintain the people until they can support themselves, and offer the Cubans full self-government . . . the President will gladly assist in its consummation. If Spain should invite the United States to mediate for peace and the insurgents would make like request, the President might undertake such office of friendship."

Questions for Analysis

1. Identify the conditions Spain was required to meet prior to U.S. involvement in Cuban affairs, according to this cable.
2. Explain why, according to Day, President McKinley avoided acting without Spanish involvement.
3. Explain the political and economic advantages that the United States stood to gain by its interference in the Cuban war for independence.

BUILDING AP® SKILLS

Argumentation

Task students with completing a "Fifty-Word Drill" exercise based upon the following prompt: "Evaluate the extent to which war between Spain and the United States could have been prevented by 1898." Do so in groups of 3 or 4. Then, have students share their products with their peers.

Spaniards would choose to blow up the *Maine* and provoke war with the United States while already losing to Cuba remained unanswered, but the incident was enough to turn U.S. opinion toward war.

On April 11, 1898, McKinley asked Congress to declare war against Spain. The declaration included an amendment proposed by Senator Henry M. Teller of Colorado declaring that Cuba "ought to be free and independent." Yet the document left enough room for U.S. maneuvering to satisfy the imperial ambitions of the McKinley administration. In endorsing independence, the war proclamation asserted the right of the United States to remain involved in Cuban affairs until it had achieved "pacification." On April 21, the United States officially went to war with Spain.

In going to war, McKinley embarked on an imperialistic course that had been building since the early 1890s. The president signaled the broader expansionist concerns behind the war when, shortly after it began, he successfully steered a Hawaiian annexation treaty through Congress. Businessmen joined imperialists in seizing the moment to create a commercial empire that would catch up to their European rivals.

It was fortunate for the United States that the Cuban insurgents had seriously weakened Spanish forces before the U.S. fighters arrived. The U.S. army lacked sufficient strength to conquer Cuba on its own, and McKinley had to mobilize some 200,000 National Guard troops and assorted volunteers. Theodore Roosevelt resigned from his post as assistant secretary of the navy and organized his own regiment, called "Rough Riders." U.S. forces faced several problems: They lacked battle experience; supplies were inadequate; their uniforms were not suited for the hot, humid climate of a Cuban summer; and the soldiers did not have immunity from tropical diseases.

African American soldiers, who made up about one-quarter of the troops, encountered additional difficulties. As more and more black troops arrived in southern ports for deployment to Cuba, they faced increasingly hostile crowds, angered at the presence of armed African American men in uniform. In Tampa, Florida, where troops gathered from all over the country to be transported to Cuba, racial tensions exploded on the afternoon of June 8. Intoxicated white soldiers from Ohio grabbed a two-year-old black boy from his mother and used him for target practice, shooting a bullet through his shirtsleeve. In retaliation, African American soldiers stormed into the streets and exchanged gunfire with white people, leaving three of them, along with twenty-seven black soldiers, wounded.

Despite military inexperience, logistical problems, and racial tensions, the United States quickly defeated the weakened Spanish military, and the war was over four months after it began. During this war, 460 U.S. soldiers died in combat, far fewer than the more than 5,000 who lost their lives to disease. The subsequent peace treaty ended Spanish rule in Cuba, ceded Puerto Rico and the Pacific island of Guam to the United States, and recognized U.S. occupation of the Philippines until the two countries could arrange a final settlement. As a result of the territorial gains in the war, U.S. foreign-policy strategists could now begin to construct an empire.

Although Congress had adopted the **Teller Amendment** in 1898 pledging Cuba's independence from Spain, President McKinley and his supporters insisted that Cuban self-rule would come only after pacification. Racial prejudice and cultural chauvinism blinded Americans to the contributions Cubans had made to defeat Spain. One U.S. officer reported to the *New York Times*: "The typical Cuban I encountered was a treacherous, lying, cowardly, thieving, worthless halfbreed mongrel, born of a mongrel spawn of [Spain], crossed upon the fetches of darkest Africa and aboriginal America." José Martí may have been fighting for racial equality, but the U.S. government certainly was not.

Because U.S. officials presumed that Cuba was unfit for immediate freedom, the island remained under U.S. military occupation until 1902. The highlight of Cuba's transition to self-rule came with the adoption of a governing document based on the U.S. Constitution. However, the Cuban constitution came with strings attached. In March 1901, Congress passed the **Platt Amendment**, introduced by Senator Orville Platt of Connecticut, which limited Cuban sovereignty. The amendment prohibited the Cuban government from signing treaties with other nations without U.S. consent, permitted the United States to intervene in Cuba to preserve independence and remove threats to economic stability, and leased Guantánamo Bay to the United States as a naval base. U.S. officials pressured Cuban leaders to incorporate the Platt Amendment into their constitution. When U.S. occupation ended in 1902, Cuba was not fully independent.

AP® TIP
Analyze how the Spanish–American War reflected existing cultural, racial, and social tensions in the United States.

Teller Amendment Amendment to the 1898 declaration of war against Spain stipulating that Cuba should be free and independent. The amendment was largely ignored in the aftermath of America's victory.

Platt Amendment 1901 act of Congress limiting Cuban sovereignty. American officials pressured Cuban leaders to incorporate the amendment into the Cuban constitution.

TEACHING IDEA

Incorporating Videos

Show students selected excerpts of the PBS documentary, *Crucible of Empire: The Spanish-American War* (available on YouTube). Have students watch the following three chapters for a total of 40 minutes: "They Are Our Redeemers," "To Cuba," and "The Liberator." Have students take brief notes on the film, focusing upon these three questions per chapter: 1) What is something I now know that I did not know before, 2) What is one question that I now have, and 3) What problems, challenges, or solutions does this film chapter bring up? Have students share their responses with one another.

BUILDING AP® SKILLS

Contextualization

It is important for students to understand that as a force for global projection of power, the United States military was in its infancy at this point. This is often a hard point for students to grasp, as in their own times, the notion that the United States can make its military presence felt anywhere on the planet is rather taken for granted. Point out to students that this was not always the case. In fact, the United States Army was stretched to its logistical and organizational capacity by this conflict, as it had been built around fighting the American Indian Wars for the last forty years leading up to war with Spain. Conducting an amphibious assault against an enemy coastline was not something it had any training or experience in whatsoever in 1898.

TEACHING IDEA

Differing Views

Assign students to read William Graham Sumner's anti-imperialist address, "The Conquest of the United States by Spain (1898)," available online at the Online Library of Liberty (oll.libertyfund.org). Have them annotate the piece, and then discuss its central points in comparison and contrast to the earlier excerpt from Josiah Strong, *Our Country*, from page 587 and Albert Beveridge, *The March of the Flag*, on page 592. Ask students to determine the commonalities and differences between all three sources, and share these out in small groups.

Period 7: 1890–1945

MODULE 7-3 The Awakening of Imperialism

TRM Suggested Responses to Questions

TRM Module 7.3 AP® Analyzing Sources Handout 3

TEACHING IDEA

Six Degrees of Separation

Have the students complete a "Six Degrees of Separation" activity. For the purpose of this exercise, students are given two events spanning time, but related by their theme. They must select four events in chronological order that link the first event in the series with the last. They will write the name of each selected event, and create an argument to support each of the events they selected. Explain to them that they must answer the question, "Why does it belong as a link in your chain of events?" for each link. Students must emphasize both cause and effect and/or demonstrate continuity or change over time in their linking. This can be done as either a formative assessment in class, or as a homework assignment involving student research of their textbooks, activities/lessons, lecture notes, and knowledge of the time period. The lesson may also be undertaken by students individually or in small groups. The prompt for this particular activity is as follows:

"From the Cuba Libre Movement to the Platt Amendment"

AP® ANALYZING SOURCES

Source: Albert Beveridge, *The March of the Flag*, 1898

"The Opposition tells us that we ought not to govern a people without their consent. I answer, the rule of liberty that all just government derives its authority from the consent of the governed, applies only to those who are capable of self-government. We govern the Indians without their consent, we govern our territories without their consent, we govern our children without their consent. How do they know [what] our government would be without their consent? . . .

They ask us how we shall govern these new possessions. I answer: Out of local conditions and the necessities of the case, methods of government will grow. If England can govern foreign lands, so can America. If Germany can govern foreign lands, so can America. If they can supervise protectorates, so can America. Why is it more difficult to administer Hawaii than New Mexico or California? Both had a savage and an alien population; both were more remote from the seat of government when they came under our dominion than the Philippines are today. . . .

The march of the flag! In 1789 the flag of the Republic waved over 4,000,000 souls in thirteen states, and their savage territory which stretched to the Mississippi, to Canada, to the Floridas. The timid minds of that day said that no new territory was needed, and, for the hour, they were right. But Jefferson, through whose intellect the centuries marched; Jefferson, who dreamed of Cuba as an American state; Jefferson, the first Imperialist of the Republic—Jefferson acquired that imperial territory which swept from the Mississippi to the mountains, from Texas to the British possessions, and the march of the flag began!

The infidels to the gospel of liberty raved, but the flag swept on! The title to that noble land out of which Oregon, Washington, Idaho, and Montana have been carved was uncertain; Jefferson, strict constructionist of constitutional power though he was, obeyed the Anglo-Saxon[1] impulse within him, whose watchword then and whose watchword throughout the world today is, 'Forward!': another empire was added to the Republic, and the march of the flag went on! . . .

The ocean does not separate us from lands of our duty and desire. . . . Steam joins us; electricity joins us—the very elements are in league with our destiny. Cuba not contiguous! Porto Rico not contiguous! Hawaii and the Philippines not contiguous! The oceans make them contiguous. And our navy will make them contiguous."

[1] Ancestors of the English people.

Questions for Analysis
1. Identify Beveridge's justification for imperialism.
2. Explain how Beveridge uses history to justify American imperialism.
3. Explain how Beveridge unites technology and the future of American power.

Questions for Comparison Rudyard Kipling, "The White Man's Burden," 1898 (p. 588)
1. Explain how these two documents were shaped by a common historical situation.
2. Evaluate the extent of similarity in the position each document takes on imperialism.

REVIEW

• What arguments did the United States use to justify war with Spain in 1898?

The Philippine War

Even before invading Cuba, the United States had won a significant battle against Spain on the other side of the world. At the outset of the war, the U.S. Pacific Fleet, under the command of Commodore George Dewey, attacked Spanish forces in their colony of the Philippines. Dewey defeated the Spanish flotilla in Manila Bay on May 1, 1898. Two and a half months later, U.S. troops followed up with an invasion of Manila, and Spanish forces promptly surrendered.

EXPLORING AP® THEMES

Politics and Power

Make sure to point out to students that the contrasts between the intentions of the Teller and Platt Amendments illustrate the two sides of the American mind when it came to expansion at the beginning of the twentieth century. The Teller Amendment of 1898 was more idealist in nature, stipulating that the United States had no territorial ambitions when it came to Cuba (past policies such as the Ostend Manifesto notwithstanding). The Platt Amendment of 1901, on the other hand, demonstrates a shift in American priorities; the United States may not desire to possess Cuba, but by 1902 it had no interest in seeing any other great power gain influence and sway in Cuba either. Explain to students that under the Platt Amendment, Cuba enjoyed the same sort of "freedoms" that they enjoy as adolescents living in their parents' homes — they are free to do absolutely whatever they want, as long as their parents say it is OK first. This analogy should be helpful to show students the limited nature of sovereignty that Cuba was going to face under the auspices of United States oversight with the Platt Amendment. Ask students to consider and discuss what might account for the difference or change between the two policy pronouncements.

The Philippine War

Period 7: 1890–1945

While pacifying Cuba, the U.S. government had to decide what to do with the Philippines. Imperialists viewed U.S. control of the islands as an important step forward in the quest for entry into the China market. The Philippines could serve as a naval station for the merchant marine and the navy to safeguard potential trade with the Asian mainland. Moreover, President McKinley believed that if the United States did not act, another European power would take Spain's place, something he thought would be "bad business and discreditable."

With this in mind, McKinley decided to annex the Philippines. As with Cuba, McKinley and most U.S. citizens believed that nonwhite Filipinos were not yet capable of self-government. Thus, McKinley set out "to educate the Filipinos, and uplift and Christianize them." As was often the case with imperialism, assumptions of racial and cultural superiority provided a handy justification for the pursuit of economic and strategic advantage.

The president's plans, however, ran into vigorous opposition. Anti-imperialists in Congress took a strong stand against annexing the Philippines. Their cause drew support from such prominent Americans as industrialist Andrew Carnegie, social reformer Jane Addams, writer Mark Twain, and labor organizer Samuel Gompers, all of whom joined the **Anti-Imperialist League**, founded in November 1898. Progressives like Addams who were committed to humanitarian reforms at home questioned whether the United States should exploit colonial people overseas. Some argued that the United States would violate its anticolonialist heritage by acquiring the islands. Union leaders feared that annexation would prompt the migration of cheap laborers into the country and undercut wages. Others worried about the financial costs of supporting military forces across the Pacific. Most anti-imperialists had racial reasons for rejecting the treaty. Like imperialists, they considered Asians to be inferior to Europeans. In fact, many anti-imperialists held an even dimmer view of the capabilities of people of color than did their opponents, rejecting the notion that Filipinos could be "civilized" under U.S. tutelage.

Despite this opposition, imperialists won out. Approval of the treaty annexing the Philippines in 1898 marked the beginning of problems for the United States. As in Cuba, rebellion had preceded U.S. occupation. At first, the rebels welcomed the Americans as liberators, but once it became clear that U.S. rule would simply replace Spanish rule, the mood changed. Led by Emilio Aguinaldo,

> **AP® TIP**
> Evaluate the extent to which U.S. actions in the Philippines after the Spanish–American War illustrated continuity with earlier eras.

Anti-Imperialist League An organization founded in 1898 to oppose annexation of the Philippines. Some feared the annexation would bring competition from cheap labor; others considered Filipinos racially inferior and the Philippines unsuitable as an American territory.

AP® ANALYZING SOURCES

Source: President William McKinley, *Remarks to a Methodist Delegation*, 1899

"When I next realized that the Philippines had dropped into our laps I confess I did not know what to do with them. . . . And one night late it came to me this way . . . 1) That we could not give them back to Spain—that would be cowardly and dishonorable; 2) that we could not turn them over to France and Germany—our commercial rivals in the Orient—that would be bad business and discreditable; 3) that we [could] not leave them to themselves—they are unfit for self-government—and they would soon have anarchy and misrule over there worse than Spain's wars; and 4) that there was nothing left for us to do but to take them all, and to educate the Filipinos, and uplift and civilize and Christianize them, and by God's grace do the very best we could by them, as our fellow-men for whom Christ also died."

Questions for Analysis
1. Describe McKinley's perspective on acquiring the Philippines.
2. Explain how the first three of McKinley's ideas about "how to deal with [the Philippines]" ultimately served U.S. interests.
3. Explain how McKinley's fourth idea about "how to deal with [the Philippines]" implies that the acquisition of these islands was for reasons other than imperialism.

Questions for Comparison Albert Beveridge, *The March of the Flag*, 1898 (p. 592)
1. Identify the similarities between the arguments of Beveridge and McKinley.
2. Identify the differences between the arguments of each.
3. Evaluate the relative appeal of each source to American policymakers during this period.

TEACHING IDEA

Differing Views

Assign students to one of four roles: Filipino insurgent, Christian missionary, U.S. Navy Commodore George Dewey, or member of the Anti-Imperialist League Andrew Carnegie. Task students with writing a letter to President McKinley advocating for his adoption of each of their preferred future courses of action with regards to the Philippines. The next day in class, place the students into groups of four, each one representing one of these individuals. Have them read their letters to one another, and have the other three students in the group create two questions that they would like to ask each group member. Allow students time to cross-examine one another. Lastly, have the groups share out with the class the nature of the conversations that took place in their group.

TRM Suggested Responses to Questions

TRM Module 7.3 AP® Analyzing Sources Handout 4

TEACHING IDEA

Class Discussion

As you begin this section, revisit an earlier idea from the course that has been a long-standing theme of the class: "Wars don't always solve old problems, sometimes they create new ones." Ask the students to discuss what this statement means and its ramifications in the context of their current module of study. Use the class conclusions then as a bridging exercise for connecting students back to earlier content such as the imperial struggles for control of North America in the mid-eighteenth century or the Civil War and Reconstruction.

TEACHING IDEA

Analyzing Art and Images

The Stanford History Education Group includes a collection of numerous free online lessons (sheg.stanford.edu). Included in the repository on this platform is a downloadable lesson focusing upon Philippine-American War political cartoons. Be sure to discuss with students the importance of them being able to interpret political cartoons. One of the key elements in interpretation, for instance, is that the relative size of objects or characters depicted in a political cartoon generally denotes the relative significance or importance of that object or character to the point the artist is trying to make. Another element to be on the lookout for is sarcasm or satire; that is, when the artist writes or shows something in their work, to point out that they actually believe the opposite of what is being depicted in the illustration. Impress upon students the certainty of the fact that such illustrations will appear on the national exam in Multiple Choice, SAQ, or DBQ formats, so practice in cartoon analysis/interpretation is no idle exercise.

insurgent forces fought back against the 70,000 troops sent by this latest colonial power. The rebels adopted guerrilla tactics and resorted to terrorist assaults against the U.S. army.

U.S. forces responded in kind, adopting harsh methods to suppress the uprising. General Jacob H. Smithy ordered his troops to "kill and burn, and the more you kill and burn, the better you will please me." Racist sentiments inflamed passions against the dark-skinned Filipino insurgents. One U.S. soldier wrote home saying that "he wanted to blow every nigger into nigger heaven." U.S. counterinsurgency efforts, which indiscriminately targeted combatants and civilians alike, alienated the native population. An estimated 200,000 Filipino civilians died between 1899 and 1902.

The country's taste for war and sacrifice quickly faded, as nearly 5,000 Americans died in the Philippine war, far more combat deaths than in Cuba. Dissenters turned imperialist arguments of manly U.S. honor upside down. Anti-imperialists claimed that the war had done nothing to affirm U.S. manhood; rather, they charged, the United States acted as a bully, taking the position of "a strong man" fighting against "a weak and puny child."

Despite growing casualties on the battlefield and antiwar sentiment at home, the conflict ended with a U.S. military victory. In March 1901, U.S. forces captured Aguinaldo and broke the back of the rebellion. Exhausted, the Filipino leader asked his comrades to lay down their arms. In July 1901, President McKinley appointed Judge William Howard Taft of Ohio as the first civilian governor to oversee the government of the Philippines. For the next forty-five years, except for a brief period of Japanese rule during World War II, the United States remained in control of the islands.

AP TIP

Be sure you can explain the reasons for conflict between Cubans and the American government after the Spanish–American War.

AP ANALYZING SOURCES

Source: Platform of the American Anti-Imperialist League, *The Commons*, 1899

"We hold that the policy known as imperialism is hostile to liberty and tends towards militarism, an evil from which it has been our glory to be free. We regret that it has become necessary in the land of Washington and Lincoln to reaffirm that all men, of whatever race or color, are entitled to life, liberty and the pursuit of happiness. We maintain that governments derive their just powers from the consent of the governed. We insist that the subjugation of any people is 'criminal aggression' and open disloyalty to the distinctive principles of our government.

We earnestly condemn the policy of the present national administration in the Philippines. It seeks to extinguish the spirit of 1776 in those islands. We deplore the sacrifice of our soldiers and sailors, whose bravery deserves admiration even in an unjust war. We denounce the slaughter of the Filipinos as a needless horror. We protest against the extension of American sovereignty by Spanish methods.

We demand the immediate cessation of the war against liberty, begun by Spain and continued by us. We urge that congress be promptly convened to announce to the Filipinos our purpose to concede to them the independence for which they have so long fought and which of right is theirs."

Questions for Analysis

1. Identify the rationale the Anti-Imperialist League provides for the U.S. to leave these smaller islands.
2. Evaluate the extent to which U.S. control over these protectorates during the late 1800s and early 1900s was similar to British control over the American colonies prior to the American Revolution.

Questions for Comparison Assistant Secretary of State William Rufus Day, *Diplomatic Cable to Stewart L. Woodford* (U.S. Minister to Spain), 1898 (p. 590)

1. Evaluate the extent to which this document critiques the arguments of the U.S. diplomatic cable to the Spanish ambassador in 1898.
2. Evaluate the extent to which the Anti-Imperialist League would support the message conveyed by the diplomatic cable and the war that then took place.

REVIEW

What were the main arguments against U.S. occupation of the Philippines?

BUILDING AP SKILLS

Comparison

Assemble the students in small groups, and engage them in a "Dueling Dates" exercise. Write "1896 vs. 1898" on the board. Instruct the student groups to provide evidence as to why each date could be considered to be a major turning point in American history, and then to make a case for which date represents the greater or more significant turning point. Have the groups then write their conclusions on butcher paper and post around the room for a gallery walk by students.

TRM Suggested Responses to Questions

TRM Module 7.3 AP Analyzing Sources Handout 5

TEACHING IDEA

Incorporating Videos

Show students selected excerpts of the PBS documentary, *Crucible of Empire: The Spanish-American War* (available on YouTube). Have students watch the final three chapters, approximately 31 minutes: "One Man, and All our Institutions," "The Philippine Disaster," and "Epilogue." At the conclusion, have students in small groups engage in a contextualization and thesis-building exercise along the lines of the 4-1-1 model of LEQ introduction, in response to the following question: "To what extent was war with Spain in the national interest?" (a refresher of the 4-1-1 model can be found on page 163). Follow up the 4-1-1 piece with a skeletal outline of an LEQ response, whereby students write the full first topic sentence of each body paragraph, and then, in bullet-point fashion, list the supporting evidence that would be located in each paragraph in support of the topic sentence.

▲ Differentiation

Upon completion of the thesis-building exercise, there are a number of directions you could lead your class depending on preference and student level. In the place of the skeletal outline, students could be tasked with writing a full essay based upon their thesis. Students could post their theses around the room, have a gallery walk, and vote on the strongest one. They could then be assigned to write a response to the prompt based upon that winning thesis, either for homework or in the next class. Students could be placed into groups to pre-write or outline a full essay based upon either their own theses or the class-selected one. Instructors should apply any and all of these strategies as the conditions of their own classroom context dictate.

Extending U.S. Imperialism, 1899–1913

> "Speak softly — carry a big stick — and you will go far. If you simply speak softly the other man will bully you. If you leave your stick at home you will find the other man did not. If you carry the stick only and forget to speak softly in nine cases out of ten, the other man will have a bigger stick."
>
> Theodore Roosevelt, 1900

The Spanish–American War turned the United States into an imperial nation. Once the war was over, and with its newly acquired empire in place, the United States sought to extend its influence, competing with its European rivals for even greater global power. President Theodore Roosevelt and his successors achieved imperialists' dreams of building a Central American canal and wielded U.S. military and financial might in the Caribbean with little restraint. At the same time, the United States took a more active role in Asian affairs.

After President McKinley was assassinated in 1901, Vice President Theodore Roosevelt succeeded him as president. A progressive reformer at home, Roosevelt believed that the national government must intervene in economic and social affairs to maintain stability and avoid class warfare. In similar fashion, he advocated using military power to protect U.S. commercial and strategic interests as well as to preserve international order. A Progressive Era interventionist, Roosevelt welcomed his nation's new role as an international policeman. "It is contemptible, for a nation, as for an individual," Roosevelt instructed Congress, "[to] proclaim its purposes, or to take positions which are ridiculous if unsupported by potential force, and then to refuse to provide this force."

To fulfill his international agenda, Roosevelt sought to demonstrate U.S. might and preserve order in the Caribbean and Central and South America. The building of the Panama Canal provides a case in point. Some considered a canal across Central America as vital because it would provide faster access to Asian markets by allowing ships to cross from the Atlantic to the Pacific without sailing around South America and improve the U.S. navy's ability to patrol two oceans effectively. The United States took a step toward realizing this goal in 1901, when it signed the **Hay-Pauncefote Treaty** with Britain, granting the United States the right to construct such a canal. After first considering Nicaragua, Roosevelt settled on Panama as the prime location. A French company had already begun construction at this site and had completed two-fifths of the operation; however, when it ran out of money, it sold its holdings to the United States.

Before the United States could resume building, it had to negotiate with the South American country of Colombia, which controlled Panama. Secretary of State John Hay and Colombian representatives reached an agreement highly favorable to the United States, which the Colombian government refused to ratify. When Colombia held out for a higher price, Roosevelt accused the Colombians of being "utterly incapable of keeping order" in Panama and declared that transit across Panama was vital to world commerce. In 1903 the president supported a pro-U.S. uprising by sending warships into the harbor of Panama City, an action that prevented the Colombians from quashing the insurrection. Roosevelt signed a treaty with the new government of Panama granting the United States the right to build the canal and exercise "power and authority" over it. In 1914, under U.S. control, the Panama Canal opened to sea traffic.

With the United States controlling Cuba, the Panama Canal, and Puerto Rico, President Roosevelt intended to deter any threats to U.S. power in the region. The economic instability of Central American and Caribbean nations provided Roosevelt with the opportunity to brandish what he called a **"big stick"** to keep these countries in check and prevent intervention by European powers also interested in the area. In 1904, when the government of the Dominican Republic was teetering on the edge of bankruptcy and threatened to default on $22 million in European loans, Roosevelt sprang into action. He announced U.S. opposition to any foreign intervention to reclaim debts, a position that echoed the principles of the Monroe Doctrine, which in 1823 proclaimed that the United States would not tolerate outside intervention in the Western Hemisphere. Moreover, Roosevelt added his own corollary to the Monroe Doctrine (see Module 4-2) by affirming the right of the United States to intervene in the internal affairs of any country in Latin America or the Caribbean that displayed "chronic wrong-doing" and could not preserve order and manage its own affairs. The **Roosevelt Corollary** proclaimed that the countries of Central America and the Caribbean had to behave according to U.S. wishes or face American military invasion. Accordingly, the president acknowledged that this region was part of the U.S. sphere of influence.

AP TIP
Evaluate the extent to which the actions the U.S. took to acquire the Panama Canal illustrated continuity with earlier American expansion.

"big stick" diplomacy
Aggressive foreign diplomacy backed by the threat of force. Its name comes from a proverb quoted by Theodore Roosevelt: "Speak softly and carry a big stick."

Roosevelt Corollary 1904 addition to the Monroe Doctrine that affirmed the right of the United States to intervene in the internal affairs of Caribbean and Latin American countries to preserve order and protect American interests.

REVIEW

What distinctions did United States policymakers make between American imperialism and European imperialism?

TEACHING IDEA

Connecting the Dots

Engage the class in an activity of association by disassociation called "Odd One Out." Start by writing the following terms on the board/projector:

- The Influence of Sea Power throughout History
- Roosevelt Corollary
- Yellow Journalism
- Teller Amendment
- The Anti-Imperialist League

Then place students in small groups and ask them, "Which one is the odd one out and why? How do the remaining terms relate?" Give students approximately 7–10 minutes to complete this part, then share out student answers and discuss their conclusions and reasoning as a whole-class activity. There is no specific correct answer; the goal is to get students thinking in categorical habits of mind and defending their rationales.

TEACHING IDEA

Building Vocabulary

Rather than simply having students blindly memorize "the Roosevelt Corollary" as a term, it is useful for students to understand the meaning of the latter word. Explain to students that a corollary is an addendum or attachment, as in "the Roosevelt Corollary to the Monroe Doctrine." This tends to generate more long-lasting understanding of the concept itself.

TEACHING IDEA

Analyzing Art and Images

Provide students with copies or project two political cartoons on the classroom projector: "The News Reaches Bogotá," and "The World's Constable" (both readily available through online search). Have students utilize their HIPP training to interpret the images (a refresher of HIPP can be found on page 8). Then, divide the class into two groups, and further subdivide those two groups into quads. As a pre-writing exercise, task the first class-groupings with employing the "Twenty-Five-Word Drill" and the second class-groupings with employing the "Fifty-Word Drill" to address the following prompt: "Evaluate the extent to which the expansion of the American sphere of influence in the Western Hemisphere was a positive development." In addressing this prompt, students are required to write a response that is, depending upon the group to which they are assigned, no more than 25 or 50 words total (give or take). The product of the former exercise winds up as a concise statement of thesis, while the latter becomes more of an elaborate conclusive statement on the question. Upon completion of this exercise, reshuffle the quads so that a pair of persons from the first grouping are matched up with a pair of persons from the second grouping, and have them share and compare their products.

TEACHING IDEA

AP® Central

Assign students in small groups to analyze the documents of the 1994 College Board AP® U.S. History DBQ on expansionism, which is available on the College Board's past exam questions resource "AP® United States History Document-Based Questions 1973–1999" (apcentral.collegeboard.org). Have students utilize their HIPP training (a refresher of HIPP can be found on page 8). This can be a useful penultimate warmup step toward the next teaching note.

TEACHING IDEA

AP® Central

As a summative assessment, assign students the 2018 College Board AP® U.S. History Operational DBQ question on the expanding role of the United States, which is available on the College Board's past exam questions resource for 2018: Free-Response Questions (apcentral.collegeboard.org).

▲ Differentiation

To assist students who struggle with the beginning processes of thesis and argument formation, it may be helpful to begin with the mandatory 15-minute reading period for students. However, instead of moving them from reading directly into writing, allow 6-8 minutes of small group student discussion to create introductory paragraphs along the lines of the 4-1-1 model (a refresher of the 4-1-1 model can be found on page 163). Once this is accomplished, return students to individual work, and have them write the full essay responses alone.

Opening the Door in China

Open Door policy 1899 policy in which Secretary of State John Hay informed the nations occupying China that the United States had the right of equal trade in China.

Roosevelt displayed U.S. power in other parts of the world. His major concern was protecting the **Open Door policy** in China that his predecessor McKinley had engineered to secure naval access to the Chinese market. By 1900 European powers had already dominated foreign access to Chinese markets, leaving scant room for newcomers. When the United States sent 2,500 troops to China in August 1900 to help quell a nationalist rebellion against foreign involvement known as the Boxer Rebellion, European competitors in return were compelled to allow the United States free trade access to China.

In 1904 the Russian invasion of the northern Chinese province of Manchuria prompted the Japanese to attack the Russian fleet. Roosevelt admired Japanese military prowess, but he worried that if Japan succeeded in driving the Russians out of the area, it would cause "a real shifting of equilibrium as far as the white races are concerned." To prevent that from happening, Roosevelt convened a peace conference in Portsmouth, New Hampshire, in 1905. Under the agreement reached at the conference, Japan received control over Korea and parts of Manchuria but pledged to support the United States' Open Door policy of equal (in effect, European and American) access to the Chinese market. In 1906 the president sent sixteen U.S. battleships on a trip around the globe in a show of force meant to demonstrate that the United States was serious about taking its place as a premier world power.

▲ **Boxer Rebellion** In 1900 the Society of Righteous and Harmonious Fists, a Chinese militaristic and secret society known as the Boxers, attacked foreign diplomatic offices in Beijing to expel outsiders. This illustration from Hunan province portrays the Boxers killing foreigners and burning Christian books. **What themes are emphasized in this image of the Boxer Rebellion?**

AP® TIP

Compare President Roosevelt's "Big Stick" diplomacy with President Taft's dollar diplomacy.

dollar diplomacy Term used by President Howard Taft to describe the economic focus of his foreign policy. Taft hoped to use economic policies and the control of foreign assets by American companies to influence Latin American nations.

When Roosevelt's secretary of war, William Howard Taft, became president (1909–1913), he continued his predecessor's foreign policy with slight modification. Proclaiming that he would rather substitute "dollars for bullets," Taft encouraged private bankers to invest money in the Caribbean and Central America, a policy known as **dollar diplomacy**. Yet Taft did not rely on financial influence alone. He dispatched more than 2,000 U.S. troops to the region to guarantee economic stability.

Taft's diplomacy also led to extensive intervention in Nicaragua. In 1909 U.S. fruit and mining companies in Nicaragua helped install a regime sympathetic to their interests. When a group of rebels threatened this pro-U.S. government, Taft invoked the Roosevelt Corollary and sent in U.S. marines to police the country and deter further uprisings. They remained there for another twenty-five years. Under this occupation, U.S. bankers took control of Nicaragua's customs houses and paid off debts owed to foreign investors, a move meant to prevent outside intervention in a nation that was now under U.S. "protection."

REVIEW

How did U.S. policies in Asia mirror U.S. policies in Latin America during the late nineteenth and early twentieth centuries?

AP® WRITING HISTORICALLY — Long-Essay Question Practice

ACTIVITY

Answer the following Long-Essay Question. *Suggested writing time: 40 minutes.*

Evaluate the extent of change in public attitudes about the United States' role in world affairs between 1890 and 1910.

APPLY THE TIP

Assign students in pairs to complete a chart comparing Big Stick and Dollar Diplomacy. One key point that students should discover is that at the end of the day, if monetary influence was not sufficient for the United States to achieve its regional aims in the Caribbean under the auspices of Dollar Diplomacy, the option to use military force was always considered to be present.

TRM Find **Handout 7.3 – Comparing Rooseveltian and Taftain Foreign Policy** in the Teacher's Resource Materials.

TRM **Suggested Responses to Questions**

TEACHING IDEA

AP® Writing Historically Workshop

For this Long-Essay Question, consider focusing on categories of analysis for a thesis statement and subsequent body paragraphs. The plural form of "attitudes" suggests there are a variety of views on America's changing role in the world. For homework, have students come up with two or three categories of analysis. During class, form groups of three or four students and ask the groups to select the best examples of categories of analysis that capture the element of the question related to "attitudes" of the role the U.S. had in world affairs during this time period. The goal of this task is for students to see there are multiple ways to answer a question.

TRM Suggested Responses to Questions

Module 7-4

Foreign Policy and World War I

LEARNING TARGETS

By the end of this module, you should be able to:

- Explain why the United States initially declared its neutrality in World War I and what factors ultimately led the United States into World War I in 1917.
- Explain how Woodrow Wilson's call for the preservation of democratic principles was used to justify U.S. entrance into World War I.
- Explain how United States support led to victory for the Allies in World War I.
- Explain why the U.S. Senate failed to ratify the Treaty of Versailles or join the League of Nations.

THEMATIC FOCUS

Politics and Power
America in the World

As the United States increasingly exercised its power beyond its borders, the major powers of Europe descended into conflict over regional borders and colonial holdings. Starting in summer 1914, the coalitions of Allied and Central Powers marched into warfare in what would be called the First World War. While the United States proclaimed its neutrality in the conflict, American policymakers and the public debated the proper response to the conflict until 1917, when the Senate declared war on the Germany and the rest of the Central Powers. Soon after the declaration, President Woodrow Wilson claimed that the United States fought not for victory, but to "make the world safe for democracy." However, his broad vision for a remade postwar world inspired opposition at home, which ultimately left the legacy of the war a mixture of successes and failures for both the United States and the world.

HISTORICAL REASONING FOCUS
Causation

TASK ▶ As you read this module, pay close attention to the causes of the First World War, the United States' part in this conflict, and the results of the war. Also consider the ways in which this war transformed the politics and national identity of Americans, while also fostering change in the United States' conception of its place in the world.

TEACHING IDEA

Incorporating Videos

Assign students to watch Episode 30, "America in World War I," from the Crash Course US History series (available on YouTube). Use this 15-minute episode as a concise formative content introduction for students of the initial major issues and events of Module 7-4 as part of preparation for either assessment or reinforcement.

When Woodrow Wilson became president in 1913, he pledged to open a new chapter in the United States' relations with Latin America and the rest of the world. Disdaining power politics and the use of force, Wilson vowed to place diplomacy and moral persuasion at the center of U.S. foreign policy. Diplomacy, however, proved less effective than he had hoped. Despite Wilson's stated commitment to the peaceful resolution of international issues, during his presidency the U.S. military intervened repeatedly in Latin America, and U.S. troops fought on European soil in the global conflict that contemporaries called the Great War.

Wilson and American Foreign Policy, 1912–1917

While he claimed a preference for moral diplomacy, Wilson preserved the U.S. sphere of influence in the Caribbean using much the same methods as had Roosevelt and Taft. To protect U.S. investments, the president sent marines to Haiti in 1915, to the Dominican Republic in 1916, and to Cuba in 1917. The most serious challenge to Wilson's diplomacy came in Mexico. The **Mexican Revolution** in 1911 spawned a civil war among various insurgent

EXPLORING AP® THEMES

America in the World

Assign students to read and annotate "Congress and Woodrow Wilson's Forays into Mexico," by Don Wolfensberger. This is the first event document posted on the Wilson Center website's article, "Congress and U.S. Military Interventions" (available by searching for the article at wilsoncenter.org). Whole-class discussion to follow the next day in class.

Wilson and American Foreign Policy, 1912–1917

Period 7: 1890–1945

factions. The resulting instability threatened U.S. interests in Mexico, particularly oil. When Mexicans refused to accept Wilson's demands to install leaders he considered "good men," Wilson withdrew diplomatic recognition from Mexico. In a disastrous attempt to influence Mexican politics, Wilson sent the U.S. navy to the port of Veracruz on April 22, 1914, leading to a bloody clash that killed 19 Americans and 126 Mexicans. The situation worsened after Wilson first supported and then turned against one of the rebel competitors for power in Mexico, General Francisco "Pancho" Villa. In response to this betrayal, Villa and 1,500 troops rode across the border and attacked the town of Columbus, New Mexico. In July 1916, Wilson ordered General John Pershing to send 10,000 army troops into Mexico in an attempt to capture Villa. The operation was a complete failure that only further angered Mexican leaders and confirmed their sense that Wilson had no respect for Mexican sovereignty.

At the same time as the situation in Mexico was deteriorating, a much more serious problem was developing in Europe. On June 28, 1914, a Serbian nationalist named Gavrilo Princip, intending to strike a blow against Austria-Hungary, assassinated the Austrian archduke Franz Ferdinand in Sarajevo, the capital of the province of Bosnia. This terrorist attack plunged Europe into what would become a world war. On August 4, 1914, the **Central Powers** — Germany, the Ottoman empire, and Austria-Hungary — officially declared war against the **Allies** — Great Britain, France, and Russia. (Italy joined the Allies in 1915.)

For the first three years of **World War I**, also known as the Great War, Wilson kept the United States neutral, though privately he supported the British. Nevertheless, the president urged Americans to remain "impartial in thought as well as action." Peace activists sought to keep Wilson to his word. In 1915 women reformers and suffragists such as Jane Addams and Carrie Chapman Catt organized the Women's Peace Party to keep the United States out of the war.

Central Powers Political allies during World War I consisting primarily of Austria-Hungary, Germany, and the Ottoman Empire.

Allies Political allies during World War I consisting primarily of Great Britain, France, and Russia. Italy joined in 1915 and the United States in 1917.

World War I Also known as the Great War, 1914–1918 war fought between the Central Powers and Allies. The United States entered the war in 1917.

▲ **MAP 7.4 European Alliances, 1914** Pre-war alliances helped precipitate World War I. The assassination of Archduke Ferdinand of Austria-Hungry by a Serbian revolutionary in Sarajevo set the countries in the Austro-Hungarian and German-led Central Alliance against the British-French-Russian Allied Powers on the map. **In what ways would the diverse American population pose a problem for the U.S. choosing a side in this conflict?**

TEACHING IDEA

Dueling Dates

Assemble the students in small groups, and provide them with these two dates: 1898 vs. 1914. Instruct the student groups to give cause (involving evidence) for why each date could legitimately be called a turning point in American history. Then, students should choose one from each pair and defend the date as a better indication of a watershed year than the other. Do emphasize that for the purposes of this exercise, they are to consider 1914 with regard to American history, and not world history. Lastly, have the class vote by movement, with students who picked 1898 congregating on one side of the room, and students that chose 1914 on the other. Have students pick out one person from across the room and meet up, to share their logic and reasoning for their respective choices.

APPLY THE TIP

Engage in "Four Corners" exercise. Label or designate each corner of the room as economic, political, social, and military, respectively. Allow students to study the prompt, and then move to one of four labeled corners in the classroom based upon which reasons they believe to be the most significant. Allow the groups time to converse, and then engage in an inside-circle–outside-circle activity whereby each group advocates for its chosen reason to be the most significant.

BUILDING AP® SKILLS
Comparison

Assign students in small groups to engage in a 4-1-1 contextualization and thesis-building exercise in response to the following prompt: "Which of the following played a greater role in shaping the United States' political and economic relations with European Great Powers between 1914 and 1917, ethnic ties or European geography?" (a refresher of the 4-1-1 model can be found on page 163). Once student groups have crafted their introductory paragraph, have them complete a T-chart of evidence that could be used to support each position.

TRM Find **Handout 7.4 – Foreign Relations Between 1914 and 1917** in the Teacher Resource Materials.

Period 7: 1890–1945

MODULE 7-4 Foreign Policy and World War I

Wilson faced two key problems in maintaining neutrality. First, the United States had closer and more important economic ties with the Allies than with the Central Powers, a disparity that would only grow as the war went on. The Allies purchased more than $750 million in U.S. goods in 1914, a figure that quadrupled over the next three years. By contrast, the Germans bought approximately $350 million worth of U.S. products in 1914; by 1917 the figure had shrunk to $30 million. Moreover, when the Allies did not have the funds to pay for U.S. goods, they sought loans from private bankers. Initially, the Wilson administration resisted such requests. In 1915, however, Wilson reversed course. Concerned that failure to keep up the prewar level of commerce with the Allies would hurt the country economically, the president authorized private loans. The gap in financial transactions with the rival war powers grew even wider; by 1917 U.S. bankers had loaned the Allies $2.2 billion, compared with just $27 million to Germany.

The second problem facing Wilson arose from Great Britain's and Germany's differing war strategies. As the superior naval power, Britain established a blockade of the North Sea to quarantine Germany and starve it into submission. The British navy violated international law by mining the waters to bottle up the German fleet and keep foreign ships from supplying Germany with food and medicines. Although Wilson protested this treatment, he did so weakly. He believed that the British could pay compensation for such violations of international law after the war.

Confronting a strangling blockade, Germany depended on the newly developed U-boat (*Unterseeboot*, or submarine) to counter the British navy. In February 1915, Germany declared a blockade of the British Isles and warned citizens of neutral nations to stay off British ships in the area. U-boats, which were lighter and sleeker than British battleships and merchant marine ships, relied on surprise. This strategy violated the rules of engagement under international maritime law, which required belligerent ships to allow civilians to leave passenger liners and cargo ships before firing. The British complicated the situation for the Germans by flying flags of neutral countries on merchant vessels and arming them with small "defensive" weapons. If U-boats played by the rules and surfaced before inspecting merchant ships, they risked being blown out of the water by disguised enemy guns.

Under these circumstances, U.S. neutrality could not last long. On May 15, 1915, catastrophe struck. Without surfacing and identifying itself, a German submarine off the Irish coast attacked the British luxury liner **Lusitania**, which had departed from New York City en route to England. Although the ship's stated objective was to provide passengers with transport, its cargo contained a large supply of ammunition for British weapons. The U-boat's torpedoes rapidly sank the ship, killing 1,198 people, including 128 Americans.

Outraged Americans called on the president to respond; some, including Theodore Roosevelt, advocated the immediate use of military force. Despite his pro-British sentiments, Wilson resisted going to war. Instead, he held the Germans in "strict accountability" for their action. Wilson demanded that Germany refrain from further attacks against passenger liners and offer a financial settlement to the *Lusitania*'s survivors. Unwilling to risk war with the United States, the Germans consented.

Wilson had only delayed the United States' entry into the war. By pursuing a policy of neutrality that treated the combatants unequally and by insisting that Americans had a right to travel on the ships of belligerent nations, the president diminished the chance that the United States would stay out of the war.

Throughout 1916, Wilson pursued two separate but interrelated policies that embodied the ambivalence that he and the U.S. people shared about the war. On the one hand, with Germany alternating between continued U-boat attacks and apologies, the president sought to build the country's military preparedness in the event of war. He signed into law the National Defense Act, which increased the size of the army, navy, and National Guard. On the other hand, Wilson stressed his desire to remain neutral and stay out of the war. With U.S. public opinion divided on the Great War, Wilson chose to run for reelection as a peace candidate. The Democrats adopted the slogan "He kept us out of war" and also emphasized the president's substantial record of progressive reform. Wilson won a narrow victory against Charles Evans Hughes, the former governor of New York, who wavered between advocating peace and criticizing Wilson for not sufficiently supporting the Allies.

AP® TIP
Evaluate the relative significance of the various reasons for increased U.S. involvement in World War I between 1914 and 1917.

Lusitania British passenger liner struck by German submarine torpedoes off the coast of Ireland on May 15, 1915. The U-boat's torpedoes sank the ship, killing 1,198 people, including 128 Americans.

AP® TIP
Analyze how the election of 1916 affected Woodrow Wilson's decisions about U.S. involvement in World War I prior to 1917.

REVIEW

- How did President Wilson justify both the United States' intervention in Mexico and its neutrality during the first three years of World War I?

TEACHING IDEA
Connecting the Dots

Point out to students that once the financial sector in the United States began to loan the Allies money, that almost automatically was going to lead to more American financial investment on the Allied side, in order to "cover their original bet," so to speak. A German victory would virtually assure that those loans would not have been repaid, so once the process began, the American financial sector had an increasing fiduciary stake over time in a war outcome more favorable to the Allied Powers than the Central Powers.

Making the World Safe for Democracy

As 1917 dawned, the war headed toward its third bloody year. Neither side wanted a negotiated peace because each counted on victory to gain sufficient territory and financial compensation to justify the great sacrifices in human lives and materiel caused by the conflict. Nevertheless, Wilson tried to persuade the belligerents to abandon the battlefield for the bargaining table. On January 22, 1917, he declared that the world needed a "peace without victory," one based on self-determination, freedom of the seas, respect for international law, and the end of hostile alliances. It was a generous vision from a nation that had made few sacrifices.

Germany quickly rejected Wilson's proposal. The United States had never been truly neutral, and Germany's increasingly desperate leaders saw no reason to believe that the situation would change. In 1915 and again in 1916, to prevent the United States from entering the war, Germany had pledged to refrain from using its U-boats against passenger and merchant ships. However, on February 1, 1917, the Germans chose to change course and resume unrestricted submarine warfare, calculating that they could defeat the Allies before the United States declared war and its

AP® ANALYZING SOURCES

Source: Woodrow Wilson, *Remarks to the Senate*, 1917

"On the eighteenth of December last I addressed [a] . . . note to the governments of the nations now at war requesting them to state, more definitely than they had yet been stated by either group of belligerents, the terms upon which they would deem it possible to make peace. I spoke on behalf of humanity and of the rights of all neutral nations like our own, many of whose most vital interests the war puts in constant jeopardy. The Central Powers united in a reply which stated merely that they were ready to meet their antagonists in conference to discuss terms of peace. The Entente Powers have replied much more definitely and have stated, in general terms, indeed, but with sufficient definiteness to imply details, the arrangements, guarantees, and acts of reparation which they deem to be the indispensable conditions of a satisfactory settlement. We are that much nearer a definite discussion of the peace which shall end the present war. We are that much nearer the discussion of the international concert which must thereafter hold the world at peace. In every discussion of the peace that must end this war it is taken for granted that that peace must be followed by some definite concert of power which will make it virtually impossible that any such catastrophe should ever overwhelm us again. Every lover of mankind, every sane and thoughtful man, must take that for granted. . . .

It is inconceivable that the people of the United States should play no part in that great enterprise. To take part in such a peace will be the opportunity for which they have sought to prepare themselves by the very principles and purposes of their polity . . . ever since the days when they set up a new nation in the high and honourable hope that it might in all that it was and did show mankind the way to liberty. . . .

No covenant of cooperative peace that does not include the peoples of the New World can suffice to keep the future safe against war. . . . The elements of that peace must be elements that engage the confidence and satisfy the principles of the American governments, elements consistent with their political faith and with the practical convictions which the peoples of America have once for all embraced and undertaken to defend."

Questions for Analysis

1. Identify what Wilson says is "inconceivable" about the war.
2. Explain how Wilson's reference to a "covenant of cooperative peace" revealed a shift in his approach to American foreign policy.
3. Evaluate the extent to which the position Wilson takes in this speech marked a change in American foreign policy.

BUILDING AP® SKILLS

Continuity and Change

Point out to students that protecting neutral prerogatives on the high seas is an American foreign policy objective of long standing. To prove this point, have students review earlier excerpts of their textbook relative to the causes for the United States' entry into the War of 1812, and compare those reasons to American entry into the First World War, with specific regards to the rights of neutral powers.

TRM Suggested Responses to Questions

TRM Module 7.4 AP® Analyzing Sources Handout 1

TEACHING IDEA

Check for Understanding

Divide the class in two, and assign groups to read one of two Jennifer Keene monographs each:

- "World War I," from the Gilder Lehrman Foundation's History Now website (gilderlehrman.org)
- "Why World War I Matters in American History," from The American Historian's website (tah.oah.org)

Divide the class into groups of four the next day, with two persons from each article assignment in the quad, and engage in miniature roundtable and peer-teaching discussion, with the instructor floating between all the groups.

TEACHING IDEA

Incorporating Primary Sources

The National Archives has an online interactive platform called DocsTeach, which includes a Unit of Instruction on the Zimmerman Telegram (available by search under Activities at docsteach.org). Assign students to access the lesson, and read and engage with the lessons and activities, either in pairs or individually.

BUILDING AP® SKILLS

Causation

Have students create a "Ladder of Escalation," in which each "rung" represents a German or British action, including the German or British rationale or motive for said action, and the next rung represents an American reaction to German or British action, complete with American motive or rationale. Start with the German and British blockades of one another as the bottom rung, and have the United States' Declaration of War in 1917 as the top rung.

▲ Differentiation

Arrange students in groups that are deliberately mixed by ability and have students discuss and craft a thesis paragraph using the Ladder of Escalation created that addresses the following question: "What steps could have been taken by either the Germans or the United States to prevent American involvement in the First World War?"

Period 7: 1890–1945

MODULE 7-4 Foreign Policy and World War I

Zimmermann telegram 1917 telegram in which Germany offered Mexico an alliance in the event that the United States entered World War I. The telegram's publication in American newspapers helped build public support for war.

AP® TIP
Be sure you can explain how issues in U.S.–Mexican relations throughout the nineteenth and early twentieth centuries set the stage for the offer Germany made in the Zimmermann telegram.

Selective Service Act 1917 act authorizing a nationwide draft.

troops could make a substantial difference. In response, Wilson used his executive power to arm merchant ships, bringing the United States one step closer to war.

The country moved even closer to war after the **Zimmermann telegram** became public. On February 24, the British turned over to Wilson an intercepted message from Arthur Zimmermann, the German foreign minister, to the Mexican government. The note revealed that Germany had offered Mexico an alliance in the event that the United States joined the Allies. If the Central Powers won, Mexico would receive the territory it had lost to the United States in the mid-nineteenth century — Texas, New Mexico, and Arizona. When U.S. newspapers broke the story several days later, it inflamed public opinion and provided the Wilson administration another reason to fear a German victory.

In late February and March, German U-boats sank several armed U.S. merchant ships, and on April 2, 1917, President Wilson asked Congress to declare war against Germany and the other Central Powers. After four days of vigorous debate led by opponents of the war — including Senator Robert M. La Follette of Wisconsin and the first female elected representative, Jeanette P. Rankin from Montana — Congress voted to approve the war resolution.

President Wilson had not reached his decision lightly. For three years, he resisted calls for war. In the end, however, Wilson decided that only by going to war would he be able to ensure that the United States played a role in shaping the peace. For the president, the security of the nation rested on respect for law, human rights, and extension of free governments. "The world must be made safe for democracy," he informed Congress in his war message, and he had concluded that the only way to guarantee this outcome was by helping to defeat Germany. This need became even more urgent when in November 1917 the **Russian Revolution** installed a Bolshevik (Communist) regime that negotiated a separate peace with the Central Powers.

It would take a while for Americans to make their presence felt in Europe. First, the United States needed a large army, which it created through the draft. The **Selective Service Act** of 1917 conscripted 3 million men by war's end. Mobilizing such a large force required substantial time, and the **American Expeditionary Forces (AEF)**, established in 1917 under General Pershing, did not make much of an impact until 1918. Before then, the U.S. navy made the greatest contribution. U.S. warships joined the British in escorting merchant vessels, combating German submarines, and laying mines in the North Sea. The United States also provided crucial funding and supplies to the Allies as their reserves became depleted.

The AEF finally began to make an impact in Europe in May 1918. From May through September, more than 1 million U.S. troops helped the Allies repel German offensives in northern France near the Belgian border. One momentous battle in the Argonne Forest lasted two months until the Allies broke through enemy lines and pushed toward Germany. Nearly 50,000 U.S. troops died in the fierce fighting, and another 230,000 were

◀ **Trench Warfare** Trench warfare was at the center of the fighting in World War I. This photograph snapped by Sergeant Leon H. Caverly on March 22, 1918 shows Red Cross workers in a trench caring for a wounded American soldier. **Why was American opinion generally against entering this conflict? What factors helped tip the balance toward war for U.S. policymakers?**

TEACHING IDEA

Incorporating Secondary Sources

Assign students to read and annotate Jennifer Keene's "Americans as Warriors: 'Doughboys' in Battle During the First World War" (available through online search from the Organization of American Historians). Instruct students in groups of three to then engage in free discussion on their impressions about the following inquiry: "What was the experience of fighting in the First World War?"

> "The world must be made safe for democracy."
>
> — Woodrow Wilson, war message to Congress, 1917

injured. Like their European counterparts, who suffered a staggering 8 to 10 million casualties, Americans experienced the horrors of war magnified by new technology. Dug into filthy trenches, soldiers dodged rapid machine-gun fire, heavy artillery explosions, and poison gas shells. In the end, however, the AEF succeeded in tipping the balance in favor of the Allies. On November 11, 1918, an exhausted Germany surrendered.

REVIEW

- Why did President Wilson find it so difficult to keep the United States out of World War I?

Fighting the War at Home

AP TIP
Analyze the effects of World War I on U.S. corporations and on workers.

Modern global warfare required full mobilization at home. In preparing to support the war effort, the country drew on recent experience. The progressives' passion for organization, expertise, efficiency, and moralistic control was harnessed to the effort of placing the economy on a wartime footing and rallying the American people behind the war. In the process, the government gained unprecedented control over American life. At the same time, the war effort also produced unforeseen economic and political opportunities.

Progressives had relied on government commissions to regulate business practices as well as health and safety standards, and in July 1917 the Wilson administration followed suit by establishing the **War Industries Board (WIB)** to supervise the purchase of military supplies and to gear up private enterprise to meet demand. However, the WIB was largely ineffective until March 1918, when the president found the right man to lead it. He chose Wall Street financier Bernard Baruch, who recruited staff from business enterprises that the board regulated. Baruch prodded businesses into compliance mainly by offering lucrative contracts rather than by coercion. Ultimately, the WIB created a government partnership with the corporate sector that would last beyond the war.

Labor also experienced significant gains through government regulation. Shortages of workers and an outbreak of strikes hampered the war effort. In April 1918 Wilson created the **National War Labor Board (NWLB)** to settle labor disputes. The agency consisted of representatives from unions, corporations, and the public. In exchange for obtaining a "no strike pledge" from organized labor, the NWLB supported an eight-hour workday with time-and-a-half pay for overtime, labor's right to collective bargaining, and equal pay for equal work by women.

The NWLB fell short of reaching this last goal, but the war employed more than a million women who had not held jobs before. As military and government services expanded, women found greater opportunities as telephone operators, nurses, and clerical workers. At the same time, the number of women employed as domestic servants declined. Women took over formerly male jobs driving streetcars, delivering ice, assembling airplane motors, operating drill presses, oiling railroad engines, and welding parts. Yet women's incomes continued to lag significantly behind those of men performing the same tasks.

Americans probably experienced the expanding scope of government intervention most directly through the efforts of three new agencies that regulated consumption and travel. Wilson appointed Herbert Hoover to head the **Food Administration**. Hoover sought to increase the military and civilian food supply mainly through voluntary conservation measures. He generated a massive publicity campaign urging Americans to adopt "wheatless Mondays," "meatless Tuesdays," and "porkless Thursdays and Saturdays." The government also mobilized schoolchildren to plant vegetable gardens to increase food production for the home front.

Consumers saved gas and oil under the prodding of the **Fuel Administration**. The agency encouraged fuel "holidays" along the line of Hoover's voluntary restrictions and created daylight savings time to conserve fuel by adding an extra hour of sunlight to the end of the workday. The Fuel Administration also offered higher prices to coal companies to increase productivity. Patterns

BUILDING AP® SKILLS

Causation

A useful review exercise to engage in with students at this point is a "How did we get here?" activity, whereby students in small groups are given a single event (e.g., Sinking of the *Lusitania*, Battle of the Argonne Forest, etc.) and have to explain its significance in the context of the American involvement in the First World War. Then, student groups must migrate in the room and mingle with other student groups, to find which group's event or context led to their particular assigned event, and which event or context their group's assigned event served as a catalyst for.

TEACHING IDEA

Connecting the Dots

Engage the class in an activity of association by disassociation called "Odd One Out." Write the following terms on the board/projector:

- National War Labor Board
- American Expeditionary Force
- Unrestricted Submarine Warfare
- Committee on Public Information
- Zimmerman Telegram

Then place students in small groups and ask them, "Which one is the odd one out and why? How do the remaining terms relate?" Give students approximately 7-10 minutes to complete this part, then share out student answers and discuss their conclusions and reasoning as a whole-class activity. There is no specific correct answer; the goal is to get students thinking in categorical habits of mind and defending their rationales.

EXPLORING AP® THEMES

Politics and Power

Have students compile and compare evidence from both the Civil War and the First World War in support of the following claim: "One constant of United States engagement in any major war has been an increase in the powers of the federal government."

TEACHING IDEA

Incorporating Videos

Have students view three short excerpts from the PBS documentary, *The Great War* (each available by searching for their respective titles at pbslearningmedia.org).

- "The Power of Popular Songs" (approximately 2 minutes, 40 seconds)
- "Targeting German Americans" (approximately 1 minute, 55 seconds)
- "Wartime Propaganda" (approximately 3 minutes, 12 seconds)

Have students discuss the differences between the three excerpts, accounting for how the content, context, and conditions in one excerpt could be the foundation for the next excerpt in sequence.

TEACHING IDEA

Incorporating Primary Sources

The Stanford History Education Group includes a collection of numerous free online lessons (sheg.stanford.edu). Included in the repository on this platform is a downloadable lesson focusing upon the motivations and consequences of the Sedition Act of 1917 through the investigation of primary sources.

---

of consumer travel changed under government regulation. The **Railroad Administration** acted more forcefully than most other agencies. Troop and supply shipments depended on the efficient operation of the railways. The administration controlled the railroads during the war, coordinating train schedules, overseeing terminals and regulating ticket prices, upgrading tracks, and raising workers' wages.

America's entry into the Great War did not immediately end the significant antiwar sentiment. Consequently, Wilson waged a campaign to rally support for his aims and to stimulate patriotic enthusiasm. To generate enthusiasm and ensure loyalty, the president appointed journalist George Creel to head the **Committee on Public Information (CPI)**, which focused on generating propaganda. Creel recruited a vast network of lecturers to speak throughout the country and spread patriotic messages. The committee coordinated rallies to sell bonds and raise money to fund the war. The CPI persuaded reporters to censor their war coverage, and most agreed in order to avoid government intervention. The agency helped produce films depicting the Allies as heroic saviors of humanity and the Central Powers as savage beasts. The CPI also distributed colorful and sometimes lurid posters emphasizing the depravity of the enemy and the nation's moral responsibility to defeat the Central Powers.

Propaganda did not prove sufficient, however, and many Americans remained deeply divided about the war. To suppress dissent, Congress passed the Espionage Act in 1917 and the Sedition Act a year later. Both limited freedom of speech by criminalizing certain forms of expression. The **Espionage Act** prohibited antiwar activities, including interfering with the draft. It also banned the mailing of publications advocating forcible interference with any laws. The **Sedition Act** punished individuals who expressed beliefs disloyal or abusive to the U.S. government, flag, or military uniform. Of the slightly more than two thousand prosecutions under these

Espionage Act 1917 act that prohibited antiwar activities, including opposing the military draft. It punished speech critical of the war as well as deliberate actions of sabotage and spying.

Sedition Act 1918 act added to the Espionage Act. It punished individuals for expressing opinions deemed hostile to the U.S. government, flag, or military.

▲ **World War I Posters** Many of the wartime posters were aimed at rallying women to provide help on the home front and mobilizing men to defend women by joining the military. The poster on the left was put out by the Food Administration and the one at the right, illustrated by Fred Spear for the Boston Committee of Public Safety, shows a mother and her infant drowning with the sinking of the *Lusitania* in 1915. **How does each image make a unique appeal for public support of America's entry to World War I?**

TEACHING IDEA

Analyzing Art and Images

Have students study the two posters at the bottom of the page and discuss the question at the end of the caption. Then, present them with additional period posters to study, in order to trace common themes in their messaging and content. Multiple options for presentation are available through the National Archives by navigating from Publications, to Posters and Facsimiles, and selecting World War I (archives.gov), or through the Library of Congress by searching their digital collections for World War I posters (loc.gov).

AP® TIP

Compare the purpose and effects of the Espionage and Sedition Acts of 1917 to the Alien and Sedition Acts of 1798.

laws, only a handful concerned charges of actual sabotage or espionage. Most defendants brought to trial were critics who merely spoke out against the war. In 1918, for telling a crowd that the military draft was a form of slavery, the Socialist Party's Eugene V. Debs was tried, convicted, and sentenced to ten years under the Espionage Act. (President Warren G. Harding pardoned Debs in 1921.) The Justice Department also went after the Industrial Workers of the World (IWW), which continued to initiate labor strikes during the war. The government broke into the offices of the IWW, ransacked the group's files for evidence of disloyalty, and arrested more than 130 members.

Government efforts to promote national unity and punish those who did not conform prompted local communities to enforce "one hundred percent Americanism." Civic groups banned the playing of German music and operas from concert halls, and schools prohibited teaching the German language. Foods with German origins were renamed — sauerkraut became "liberty cabbage," and hamburgers became "liberty sandwiches." Such sentiments were expressed in a more sinister fashion when mobs assaulted German Americans.

Prejudice toward German Americans was further inflamed by the formation of the **American Protective League (APL)**, a quasi-official association endorsed by the Justice Department. Consisting of 200,000 chapters throughout the country, the APL employed individuals to spy on German residents suspected of disloyal behavior. Most often, APL agents found little more than German immigrants who merely retained attachments to family and friends in their homeland. Gossip and rumor fueled many of the league's loyalty probes.

The repressive side of progressivism came to the fore in other ways as well. Anti-immigrant bias, shared by many reformers, flourished. The effort to conserve manpower and grain supplies bolstered the impulse to control standards of moral behavior, particularly those associated

APPLY THE TIP

Assign students to complete a Venn diagram on the purposes and effects of the Sedition Act of 1917, and the Sedition Acts of 1798. Then, assign students in groups to engage in a "Twenty-Five-Word Drill" thesis-building exercise addressing the prompt. Have students post their products around the room for peer review.

AP® ANALYZING SOURCES

Source: Eugene V. Debs, *Antiwar Speech in Canton, Ohio*, 1918

"I realize that, in speaking to you this afternoon, there are certain limitations placed upon the right of free speech. I must be exceedingly careful, prudent, as to what I say, and even more careful and prudent as to how I say it. I may not be able to say all I think; but I am not going to say anything that I do not think. I would rather a thousand times be a free soul in jail than to be a sycophant and coward in the streets. They . . . can not put the Socialist movement in jail. . . .

Socialism is a growing idea; an expanding philosophy. It is spreading over the entire face of the earth: It is as vain to resist it as it would be to arrest the sunrise on the morrow. . . . The little that I am, the little that I am hoping to be, I owe to the Socialist movement. . . .

When we unite and act together on the industrial field and when we vote together on election day we shall develop the supreme power of the one class that can and will bring permanent peace to the world. We shall then have the intelligence, the courage and the power for our great task. In due time industry will be organized on a cooperative basis. We shall conquer the public power. . . . We shall then have industrial democracy. We shall be a free nation whose government is of and by and for the people. . . .

In due time the hour will strike and this great cause triumphant — the greatest in history — will proclaim the emancipation of the working class and the brotherhood of all mankind."

Questions for Analysis

1. Describe Debs's vision when he says "When we unite and act together on the industrial field and when we vote together on election day we shall develop the supreme power of the one class that can and will bring permanent peace to the world."
2. Explain how the historical situation shaped Debs's message to his audience.
3. Evaluate the extent of similarity between Debs's argument in this speech and progressive reform policies.

TRM Suggested Responses to Questions

TRM Module 7.4 AP® Analyzing Sources Handout 2

TEACHING IDEA

Differing Views

Have students read Wilson's *Remarks to the Senate* on page 601 and Debs's *Antiwar Speech in Canton, Ohio* on page 605. Instruct students to contrast Wilson's sense of American identity with Debs's sense of American identity.

Period 7: 1890–1945

MODULE 7-4 Foreign Policy and World War I

with immigrants, such as drinking. This anti-immigrant prejudice in part explains the ratification of the Eighteenth Amendment in 1919, prohibiting the sale of all alcoholic beverages. Yet not all the moral indignation unleashed by the war resulted in restriction of freedom. After considerable wartime protest and lobbying, women suffragists succeeded in securing the right to vote.

President Wilson's goal "to make the world safe for democracy" appealed to oppressed minorities. They hoped the war would push the United States to live up to its rhetoric and extend freedom at home. Nearly 400,000 African Americans served in the war and more than 40,000 saw combat, but most were assigned to service units and worked in menial jobs. The army remained segregated, and few black officers commanded troops. Despite this discrimination, W. E. B. Du Bois echoed African Americans' hope that their patriotism would be rewarded at the war's end: "We of the colored race have no ordinary interest in the outcome."

The same held true for American Indians, more than ten thousand of whom participated in the war. Recruited from Arizona, Montana, and New York, they fought in the major battles in France and Belgium. Unlike African Americans, they did not fight in segregated units and saw action as scouts and combat soldiers. They gained recognition by communicating messages in their native languages to confuse the Germans listening in. Aware of the contradiction between their troubling treatment historically by the U.S. government and the nation's democratic war aims, they expected that their wartime patriotism would bring them a greater measure of justice. However, like African Americans, they would be disappointed.

REVIEW

- How did progressive policies and programs shape the United States' economy and society during World War I?

- How did U.S. policymakers attempt to generate and sustain public support for U.S. involvement in World War I?

Waging Peace after World War I

Fourteen Points The core principles President Woodrow Wilson saw as the basis for lasting peace, including freedom of the seas, open diplomacy, the establishment of the League of Nations, and the right to self-determination.

League of Nations The international organization proposed by Woodrow Wilson after the end of World War I to ensure world peace and security in the future through mutual agreement. The United States failed to join the league because Wilson and his opponents in Congress could not work out a compromise.

> " President Wilson and his Fourteen Points bore me. Even God Almighty has only ten! "
>
> Georges Clemenceau, President of France, 1918

In January 1918, ten months before the war ended, President Wilson presented Congress with his plan for peace. Wilson bundled his ideas in the **Fourteen Points**, principles that he hoped would prevent future wars. Based on his assessment of the causes of the Great War, Wilson envisioned a generous peace treaty that included freedom of the seas, open diplomacy and the abolition of secret treaties, free trade, self-determination for colonial subjects, and a reduction in military spending. More important than any specific measure, Wilson's proposal hinged on the creation of the **League of Nations**, a body of large and small nations that would guarantee peaceful resolution of disputes and back up decisions through collective action, including the use of military force as a last resort.

Following the armistice that ended the war on November 11, 1918, Wilson personally took his message to the Paris Peace Conference, the postwar meeting of the victorious Allied nations that would set the terms of the peace. The first sitting president to travel overseas, Wilson was greeted in Paris by joyous crowds.

For nearly six months, Wilson tried to convince reluctant Allied leaders to accept the central components of his plan. Having exhausted themselves financially and having suffered the loss of a generation of young men, the Allies intended to scoop up the spoils of victory and make the Central Powers pay dearly. The European Allies intended to hold on to their respective colonies regardless of Wilson's call for self-determination, and as a nation that depended on a strong navy, Britain refused to limit its options by discussing freedom of the seas. Perhaps Georges Clemenceau, France's president, best expressed his colleagues' skepticism about Wilson's idealistic vision: "President Wilson and his Fourteen Points bore me. Even God Almighty has only ten!"

During the conference, Wilson was forced to compromise on a number of his principles in order to retain the cornerstone of his diplomacy — the establishment of the League of Nations. He abandoned his hope for peace without bitterness by agreeing to a "war guilt" clause that levied huge economic reparations on Germany for starting the war. He was willing to sacrifice some of his ideals because the league took on even greater importance in the wake of the 1917 Communist revolution in Russia. The president believed that capitalism, as regulated and reformed during the Progressive Era, would raise

---

EXPLORING AP® THEMES

American and National Identity

Point out to students that a common thread that runs through minority participation in American wars has been the hope that demonstrations of patriotism and service on the part of minorities would earn them an increased place of legitimacy and equality in American society. Tie this together by walking students through examples of this from the Revolution, the Civil War, and World War I.

TEACHING IDEA

Differing Views

Assign half of the students to read and annotate "President Woodrow Wilson's Fourteen Points," available from The Avalon Project (avalon.law.yale.edu) and half of the students to read Henry Cabot Lodge's "Treaty of Peace with Germany, Reservations," available from the U.S. Capitol Visitor Center's website (visitthecapitol.gov).

In the next class meeting, have them briefly share their findings with their fellow students who were assigned the same source. Then, place students into groups of six, three per source, and have them assume the roles of both men and make their case as to why the Versailles Treaty represents a wise or unwise move in American foreign policy.

Treaty of Versailles 1919 treaty officially ending World War I.

living conditions throughout the world as it had done in the United States, would prevent the spread of **communism**, and would benefit U.S. commerce. Wilson needed the league to keep the peace so that war-ravaged and recovering nations had the opportunity to practice economic freedom and political democracy. In the end, the president won agreement for the establishment of his cherished League of Nations. The **Treaty of Versailles**, signed at the royal palace just outside Paris, authorized the league to combat aggression against any member nation through collective military action.

In July 1919, after enduring bruising battles in Paris, Wilson returned to Washington, D.C., only to face another wrenching struggle in the Senate over ratification of the Versailles treaty. The odds were stacked against Wilson from the start. The Republicans held a majority in the Senate, and Wilson needed the support of two-thirds of the Senate to secure ratification. Moreover, Henry Cabot Lodge, the Republican chairman of the Senate Foreign Relations Committee, opposed Article X of the League of Nations covenant, which sanctioned collective security arrangements against military aggression. Lodge argued that such an alliance compromised the United States' independence in conducting its own foreign relations. Lodge had at least thirty-nine senators behind him, more than enough to block ratification. Conceding the need to protect the country's national self-interest, the president agreed to modifications to the treaty so that the Monroe Doctrine and America's obligations in the Caribbean and Central America were kept intact. Lodge, however, was not satisfied and insisted on adding fourteen "reservations" limiting compliance with the treaty, including strong language affirming Congress's right to declare war before agreeing to a League of Nations military action.

> **AP® TIP**
> Evaluate the degree to which the debate between Woodrow Wilson and Henry Cabot Lodge reflected differences in interpretation regarding America's role in world and the powers of the three branches of U.S. government.

AP® ANALYZING SOURCES

Source: Woodrow Wilson, *Address at Pueblo, Colorado*, 1919

"[R]eflect, my fellow citizens, that the membership of [the League of Nations] is going to include all the great fighting nations of the world, as well as the weak ones. . . . And what do they unite for? They enter into a solemn promise to one another that they will never use their power against one another for aggression; that they never will impair the territorial integrity of a neighbor; that they never will interfere with the political independence of a neighbor; that they will abide by the principle that great populations are entitled to determine their own destiny and that they will not interfere with that destiny; and that no matter what differences arise amongst them they will never resort to war without first having done one or other of two things — either submitted the matter of controversy to arbitration, in which case they agree to abide by the result without question, or submitted it to the consideration of the council of the league of nations, laying before that council all the documents, all the facts, agreeing that the council can publish the documents and the facts to the whole world, agreeing that there shall be six months allowed for the mature consideration of those facts by the council, and agreeing that at the expiration of the six months, even if they are not then ready to accept the advice of the council with regard to the settlement of the dispute, they will still not go to war for another three months. In other words, they consent, no matter what happens, to submit every matter of difference between them to the judgment of mankind, and just so certainly as they do that, my fellow citizens, war will be in the far background, war will be pushed out of that foreground of terror in which it has kept the world for generation after generation, and men will know that there will be a calm time of deliberate counsel."

Questions for Analysis

1. Identify Wilson's main argument in this speech.
2. Describe the process nations would follow under this plan instead of declaring war.
3. Explain what Wilson states will give the league its authority.

TEACHING IDEA

Incorporating Secondary Sources

Assign students to read and annotate "Woodrow Wilson Wouldn't Yield," by Thomas A. Bailey (available through online search of author and title). Require students to both identify Bailey's thesis and create a summative conclusive statement on their takeaways on his work. Whole-class discussion to follow.

TRM Suggested Responses to Questions

TRM Module 7.4 AP® Analyzing Sources Handout 3

Wilson's stubbornness more than equaled Lodge's, and the president refused to compromise further over the League. Insisting that he was morally bound to honor the treaty he had negotiated in good faith, Wilson rejected additional changes. Making matters worse, Wilson faced resistance from sixteen lawmakers dubbed "irreconcilables," who opposed the league under any circumstances. Mainly Republicans from the Midwest and West, they voiced the traditional U.S. rejection of entangling alliances.

To break the logjam, the president attempted to rally public opinion behind him. In September 1919, he embarked on a nationwide speaking tour to carry his message directly to the American people. Over a three-week period, he traveled eight thousand miles by train, keeping a grueling schedule that exhausted him. After a stop in Pueblo, Colorado on September 25, Wilson collapsed and canceled the rest of his trip. On October 2, Wilson suffered a massive stroke that nearly killed him. The effects of the stroke, which left him partially paralyzed, emotionally unstable, and mentally impaired, dimmed any remaining hopes of compromise. The full extent of his illness was kept from the public, and his wife, Edith, ran the White House for the next eighteen months.

On November 19, 1919, the Senate rejected the amended treaty. The following year, Wilson had one final chance to obtain ratification, but still he refused to accept changes to the treaty despite members of his own party urging compromise. In March 1920, treaty ratification failed one last time, falling just seven votes short of the required two-thirds majority. Had Wilson shown the same willingness to compromise that he had in Paris, the outcome might have been different. In the end, however, the United States never signed the Treaty of Versailles or joined the League of Nations, weakening the league and diminishing the prospects for long-term peace.

REVIEW

- How did the League of Nations reflect progressive ideals?

BUILDING AP® SKILLS

Comparison

Assemble the students in small groups, and provide them with these two dates: 1917 vs. 1920. Instruct the student groups to give cause (involving evidence) for why each date could legitimately be called a turning point in American history. Then, choose one from each pair and defend the date as a better indication of a watershed year than the other. Upon conclusion, have the students in groups of 2-4 who picked the same year engage in a "Fifty-Word Drill" exercise to create a comprehensive introductory statement in defense of the choice they made.

TRM Suggested Responses to Questions

AP® WRITING HISTORICALLY — Short-Answer Question Practice

ACTIVITY

Read the following question carefully and write a short response. Use complete sentences.

Using the following excerpts, answer (a), (b), and (c).

Source: Arthur S. Link, *Woodrow Wilson and the Progressive Era, 1910–1917*, 1963

"In the final analysis, American policy was determined by the President and public opinion, which had a great, if unconscious, influence upon him. It was Wilson who decided to accept the British maritime system in the first instance, who set the American government against unrestricted use of the submarine, and who made the final decision for war instead of a continuance of armed neutrality. . . .

[I]f the German leaders had at any time desired a genuinely reasonable settlement and evidenced a willingness to help build a peaceful and orderly postwar world, they would have found a friend in the White House eager to join them in accomplishing these high goals.

The German decision to gamble on all-out victory or complete ruin...alone compelled Wilson to break diplomatic relations, to adopt a policy of armed neutrality, and finally to ask for a declaration of war—because American ships were being sunk and American citizens were being killed on the high seas, and because armed neutrality seemed no longer possible. Considerations of America's alleged economic stake in an Allied victory did not influence Wilson's thought during the critical weeks from February 1 to April 2, 1917. Nor did considerations of national interest, or of the great ideological issues at stake in the conflict."

BUILDING AP® SKILLS

Argumentation

Assign students in groups of three to craft a thesis statement in response to the review prompt. Then, task each student with writing one body paragraph in support of the thesis for homework. Then next day in class, have student groups engage in a jigsaw activity to "complete" the full paper, teaching and sharing their portion of the whole product with one another (a refresher of the jigsaw model can be found on page 33). Then, have each triad trade their overall product with another group, for the purposes of peer review and mock scoring. Instruct each group to explain and share their feedback in terms of why or how they scored the essay as they did.

Source: John Whiteclay Chambers II, *The Tyranny of Change: America in the Progressive Era, 1890–1920*, 2000

"Although the president emphasized German violation of neutral rights, neither American tradition nor law nor economic necessity required him to guarantee the right of Americans to travel on armed belligerent ships. Though he couched his policies in terms of international law and principle, Wilson was responsible for defining the growth of trade with Britain as a legitimate and profitable expression of neutral rights. He rejected definitions of other neutrals — Spain, the Netherlands, and the Scandinavian countries — that banned such passenger travel and embargoed guns and ammunition. In addition, he refused to consider the German and British blockades similarly or to hold Germany to a postwar accounting, as he did in the case of Britain. Thus by 1917 Wilson found himself constrained by the framework created by his earlier decisions about American rights. . . .

Wilson's policies reflected the traditional American belief that the ideals of America were the ideals of all humankind and that the other nations must conform to Americans prescriptions and ideals. . . . This global interventionism was new, but it drew on an attitude of superiority that had much earlier become a part of American culture. Germany had to be restrained because it had broken America's rules, disputed its ideals, threatened the rights and property of American citizens, and even challenged its security and hegemony through the proposed military alliance with Mexico."

a. Briefly describe ONE major difference between Link's and Chambers's historical interpretations of causes of U.S. entry into the First World War.
b. Briefly explain how ONE specific historical event or development during the period 1914 to 1917 that is not explicitly mentioned in the excerpts could be used to support Link's interpretation.
c. Briefly explain how ONE specific historical event or development during the period 1914 to 1917 that is not explicitly mentioned in the excerpts could be used to support Chambers's interpretation.

BUILDING AP® SKILLS

Argumentation

As a general strategy, the *ACE* method explained by the authors for LEQ purposes — "Answer the question, Cite your evidence, and Explain its meaning" — is also very useful for Short-Answer Questions (a refresher of *ACE* can be found on page 21). For each of the three tasks of an SAQ, use this model. In so doing, the three tasks of an SAQ are actually then addressed in nine discrete steps. If this method is followed, the depth of student responses to the three directed tasks of the SAQ should be such that it increases the likelihood of every SAQ point being earned with a comfortable margin.

TEACHING IDEA

AP® Writing Historically Review

Because the excerpts in this question focus on Woodrow Wilson, World War I, and the peace process, students can narrow their focus for parts (b) and (c) by completing the following activity. Prior to having students complete this question, consider having them brainstorm all the relevant historical examples of Woodrow Wilson's role in the peace process of World War I. After reading through the excerpts, allow students to use the list of knowledge to assist them in answering parts (b) and (c). This can serve as an excellent formative assignment because students will only develop answers they know and relate to the excerpts.

TRM Suggested Responses to Questions

Module 7-5

The Effects of World War I at Home

LEARNING TARGETS

By the end of this module, you should be able to:

- Explain the controversies resulting from restrictions on freedom of speech during World War I.
- Explain how the Red Scare and attacks on labor activism and immigrant culture were a reaction to the end of World War I.
- Explain how increased war production and labor during World War I led to migration to urban centers in search of economic opportunities.
- Explain why African Americans moved to the North and West during and after World War I, despite finding discrimination there.

THEMATIC FOCUS

Work, Exchange, and Technology
Migration and Settlement
Social Structures

Though the nation was only involved in World War I during the war's last year, its effects reverberated through America's society and economy during the 1920s and beyond. In addition, many of the economic and social changes after World War I owed their causes to other trends in the United States.

HISTORICAL REASONING FOCUS
Causation

TASK ▶ While reading this module about the economic and social changes after World War I, consider which of these changes were results of the war itself and which changes were caused by other historical trends or events.

The return of peace in 1918 brought with it problems that would persist into the 1920s. Government efforts to suppress opposition to U.S. involvement in World War I fostered an atmosphere of fear and repression that continued after the war. An influenza epidemic that killed hundreds of thousands of Americans and millions of people around the world heightened the climate of anxiety. Finally, the abrupt transition away from a wartime economy produced inflation, labor unrest, and escalating racial tensions.

Postwar Social Turmoil

Red Scare The fear of Communist-inspired radicalism in the wake of the Russian Revolution. The Red Scare culminated in the Palmer raids on suspected radicals.

The success of the Bolshevik Revolution in Russia in 1917 and the subsequent creation of the Union of Soviet Socialist Republics terrified officials of capitalist countries in western Europe and the United States. This fear intensified further in 1919 with the creation of the Comintern, an association of Communists who pledged to incite revolution in capitalist countries around the world. This sparked a panic over Communist-inspired radicalism known as the **Red Scare**, which set the stage for the suppression of dissent.

In this atmosphere of anxiety, on March 3, 1919, in *Schenck v. United States* the Supreme Court invoked the Espionage Act to uphold the conviction of Charles Schenck, the general secretary of the Socialist Party, for mailing thousands of leaflets opposing the military draft. Delivering the Court's unanimous opinion, Justice Oliver Wendell Holmes argued that during wartime Congress has the authority to prohibit individuals from using words that create "a clear and present danger" to the safety of the country. Although the trial record failed to show that Schenck's leaflets had convinced

---

TEACHING IDEA

Incorporating Videos

Assign students to watch Episode 32, "The Roaring 20's," from the Crash Course US History series (available on YouTube). Use this 13-minute episode as a concise formative content introduction for students of the initial major issues and events of Module 7-5 as part of preparation for either assessment or reinforcement.

BUILDING AP® SKILLS

Making Connections

As part of introducing the war's impact, it is important to stress with students that, in general, the experience of war historically breeds patriotism within the United States as a unifying force, which often accelerates into intolerance. Explain to students the historical notion that it is a short journey from "I love my country" to "I love my country so much, that if you do not love it as I do, you are not a good American." Explain to students that they have seen this before, for instance, in the backlash against the Federalists after the Hartford Convention and War of 1812, and will be seeing it again at various points in the curriculum in the twentieth and twenty-first centuries.

Postwar Social Turmoil

Period 7: 1890–1945

Abrams v. United States
1919 Supreme Court ruling limiting free speech by sustaining a guilty verdict of five anarchists who distributed leaflets denouncing U.S. military efforts to overthrow the Bolshevik regime.

any young men to resist conscription, the Court upheld his conviction under Holmes's doctrine. Later that year in **Abrams v. United States**, the Court further limited free speech by sustaining the guilty verdict of five anarchists who distributed leaflets denouncing U.S. military efforts to overthrow the Bolshevik regime.

Immediate postwar economic problems further increased the anxiety of American citizens, reinforcing the position of officials who sought to restore order by suppressing radicals. Industries were slow to convert their plants from military to civilian production, and consumer goods therefore remained in short supply. The war had brought jobs and higher wages on the home front, and consumers who had been restrained by wartime rationing were eager to spend their savings. With demand greatly exceeding supply, however, prices soared by 77 percent, frustrating consumers. At the same time, farmers, who had benefited from wartime conditions, faced falling crop prices as European nations resumed agricultural production and the federal government ended price supports.

> **AP® TIP**
> Evaluate the extent to which the U.S. government's actions during the Red Scare violated the rights of free speech and press established in the U.S. Constitution.

A series of widespread strikes launched by labor unions in 1919 contributed to the fear that the United States was under assault by sinister, radical forces. As skyrocketing inflation undercut wages and employers launched a new round of union-busting efforts, labor went on the offensive. In 1919 more than four million workers went on strike nationwide. In September, striking Boston policemen left the city unguarded, resulting in widespread looting and violence. Massachusetts governor Calvin Coolidge sent in the National Guard to break the strike and restore order.

Public officials and newspapers decried the violence, but they also greatly exaggerated the peril. Communists and socialists did support some union activities; however, few of the millions of workers who struck for higher wages and better working conditions had ties to extremists. The major prewar radical organization, the Industrial Workers of the World, never recovered from the government harassment that had crippled it during World War I. However, scattered acts of violence allowed government and business leaders to stir up anxieties about the Communist threat. On May 1, 1919, radicals sent more than thirty incendiary devices through the mail to prominent Americans, though authorities defused the bombs before they reached their targets. The following month, bombs exploded in eight cities, including one at the doorstep of the home of A. Mitchell Palmer, the attorney general of the United States.

> **AP® TIP**
> Compare Governor Coolidge's response to labor strife in 1919 with the responses of President Roosevelt in 1902 and President Hayes in 1877.

After the attack on his home, Palmer launched a government crusade to root out and prosecute Communists. Palmer traced the source of radicalism to recent immigrants, mainly those from

AP® ANALYZING SOURCES

Source: A. Mitchell Palmer, "The Case against the Reds," *Forum*, 1920

> "Like a prairie-fire, the blaze of revolution was sweeping over every American institution of law and order a year ago. It was eating its way into the homes of the American workman, its sharp tongues of revolutionary heat were licking the altars of the churches, leaping into the belfry of the school bell, crawling into the sacred corners of American homes, seeking to replace marriage vows with libertine laws, burning up the foundations of society.
>
> Robbery, not war, is the ideal of communism. This has been demonstrated in Russia, Germany, and in America. As a foe, the anarchist is fearless of his own life, for his creed is a fanaticism that admits no respect of any other creed. Obviously it is the creed of any criminal mind, which reasons always from motives impossible to clean thought. Crime is the degenerate factor in society."

Questions for Analysis

1. Identify the metaphor Palmer uses to describe revolution in this excerpt.
2. Explain how this metaphor supports Palmer's argument.
3. Explain how the comparison between communism and anarchism in this speech serves Palmer's purpose.
4. Evaluate the extent to which Palmer's argument in the second paragraph reflects progressive ideals.

APPLY THE TIP

Assign students, as a bell ringer or exit ticket, to compose an introductory statement to the prompt in the format of the "Twenty-Five-Word Drill." Share exemplars from the class products to enhance student learning.

▲ Differentiation

For students who struggle to begin their LEQs and DBQs, provide them with one of the stronger class exemplars with which to begin their papers, and then assign the whole class to write, either in class or for homework, a full response to the prompt. This can not only provide the students with a solid, clear, and evaluative introductory statement, it can allow them to develop the skill of using evidence on behalf of a clear beginning statement.

TRM Suggested Responses to Questions

TRM Module 7.5 AP® Analyzing Sources Handout 1

TEACHING IDEA

Incorporating Videos

Show students the excerpt video, "Influenza: Chapter 1," of the PBS documentary, *Influenza 1918* (pbs.org). Use this 10-minute excerpt as an introduction into studying the photograph. Ask students to determine what connections they see between disease and the anti-immigrant ethos of the early 1920s and their own times, with epidemics such as measles, Ebola, and swine flu.

Period 7: 1890–1945

MODULE 7-5 The Effects of World War I at Home

> " The fear in the hearts of people just withered them. They were afraid to go out, afraid to do anything. . . . It was a horror-stricken time. "
>
> Susanna Turner, volunteer at an emergency hospital during the influenza pandemic of 1918

▲
The Influenza Epidemic, Lawrence, Massachusetts, 1918 Nurses take care of patients suffering from the Spanish influenza epidemic in Lawrence, Massachusetts. This textile town had experienced an influx of immigrants from southern and eastern Europe around the turn of the twentieth century and was the scene of major union organizing and labor strife just before the epidemic struck. **How does the historical situation of the influenza outbreak help explain anti-immigrant sentiment during this era?**

Palmer raids Government roundup of some 6,000 suspected alien radicals in 1919–1920, ordered by Attorney General A. Mitchell Palmer and his assistant J. Edgar Hoover. The raids resulted in the deportation of 556 immigrants.

Bureau of Investigation Domestic investigative branch of the U.S. Department of Justice originally headed by J. Edgar Hoover. The organization was later renamed the Federal Bureau of Investigation (FBI).

influenza pandemic Worldwide flu pandemic, also known as the "Spanish Flu," following the end of World War I. It ultimately killed an estimated 50 million individuals, including approximately 675,000 Americans.

Russia and eastern and southern Europe. To track down suspected radicals, Palmer selected J. Edgar Hoover to head the General Intelligence Division in the Department of Justice. In November 1919, based on Hoover's research and undercover activities, government agents in twelve cities rounded up and arrested hundreds of foreigners, including the anarchist and feminist Emma Goldman. Goldman, and some 250 other people caught in the government dragnet, were soon deported to Russia. Over the next few months, the **Palmer raids** continued in more than thirty cities. Authorities seized approximately six thousand suspected radicals, took them to police stations, interrogated them without the benefit of legal counsel, and held them incommunicado without stipulating the charges against them. Of the thousands arrested, the government found reason to deport 556. The raids did not uncover any extensive plots to overthrow the U.S. government, nor did they lead to the arrest of the bombers.

Americans' initial support of the Palmer raids quickly faded in the face of civil liberty violations that accompanied the raids. In 1920 a group of pacifists, progressives, and constitutional lawyers formed the **American Civil Liberties Union (ACLU)** to monitor government abridgments of the Bill of Rights. Although the Palmer raids ended, the Red Scare extended throughout the 1920s. After J. Edgar Hoover became director of the **Bureau of Investigation** (later renamed the Federal Bureau of Investigation) in 1921, he continued spying and collecting information on suspected radicals and increasing his power over the next several decades.

Compounding Americans' anxieties, in late 1918, an **influenza pandemic** struck the United States. Part of a worldwide contagion, the disease infected nearly 20 percent of the U.S. population and killed more than 675,000 people. As the death toll mounted over the course of 1919, terror gripped the nation. Susanna Turner, a volunteer at an emergency hospital in Philadelphia, recalled: "The fear in the hearts of people just withered them. They were afraid to go out, afraid to do anything. . . . It was a horror-stricken time." A staggering 50 million people worldwide are estimated to have died from the flu before it subsided in 1920.

TEACHING IDEA

Connecting the Dots

The Stanford History Education Group includes a collection of numerous free online lessons (sheg.stanford.edu). Included in the repository on this platform is a downloadable document-based lesson focusing upon the Spanish Flu Pandemic of 1918.

Great Migration Population shift of more than 400,000 African Americans who left the South beginning in 1917–1918 and headed north and west to escape poverty and racial discrimination. During the 1920s another 800,000 black people left the South.

Racial strife also heightened postwar anxieties. Drawn by the promise of wartime industrial jobs, more than 400,000 African Americans left the South beginning in 1917 and 1918 and headed north, hoping to escape poverty, racial discrimination, and violence. (By 1930 another 800,000 black people had left the South.) This exodus became known as the **Great Migration**. During World War I, many black people found work in steel production, meatpacking, shipbuilding, and other heavy industries, but most were relegated to low-paying jobs. Still, as a carpenter earning $95 a month wrote from Chicago to a friend back in Hattiesburg, Mississippi: "I should have been here 20 years ago. I just begin to feel like a man." Most African American women remained employed as domestic workers, but more than 100,000 obtained manufacturing jobs.

For many African Americans, however, the North was not the "promised land" they expected. Instead, they encountered bitter opposition from white migrants from the South competing for employment and scarce housing. As black and white veterans returned from the war, racial hostilities exploded. In 1919 race riots erupted in twenty-five cities throughout the country, including one in Washington, D.C. The previous year, W. E. B. Du Bois of the NAACP had urged the black community to "close ranks" to fight Germany, but the racial violence against black people in 1919 embittered him. "By the God of Heaven," Du Bois wrote, "we are cowards and jackasses if now that that war is over, we do not marshal every ounce of our brain and brawn to fight a sterner, longer, more unbending battle against the forces of hell in our own land."

The worst of these disturbances occurred in Chicago. On a hot July day, a black youth swimming at a Lake Michigan beach inadvertently crossed over into an area of water customarily reserved for white people. In response, white bathers shouted at the swimmer to return to the black section of the beach and hurled stones at him. The black swimmer drowned, and word of the incident quickly spread through white and black neighborhoods in Chicago. For thirteen days, mobs of black and white people attacked each other, ransacked businesses, and torched homes. Over the course of the riots, at least 38 people (23 black and 15 white) died, 520 people (342 black and 178 white) were injured, and more than 1,000 black families were left homeless.

AP® TIP
Analyze the factors that encouraged African American migration during the early twentieth century, and evaluate the degree to which life changed for those who moved North.

> "By the God of Heaven, we are cowards and jackasses if now that that war is over, we do not marshal every ounce of our brain and brawn to fight a sterner, longer, more unbending battle against the forces of hell in our own land."
>
> W.E.B. Du Bois, 1919

REVIEW
- In what ways was the social turmoil after World War I a result of the war itself?
- To what extent did the Great Migration lead to greater freedom for African Americans in the United States after World War I?

Innovation and Consumerism

Despite the turbulence of the immediate postwar period and the persistence of underlying social and racial tensions, the 1920s were a time of vigorous economic growth and urbanization. Between 1922 and 1927, the economy grew by 7 percent a year. Unemployment rates remained low, as producers added new workers in an effort to keep up with increasing consumer demand. Aligning themselves with big business, government officials took an active role in stimulating industrial and economic growth. The average purchasing power of wage earners soared, although many Americans still did not share in this new abundance.

The general prosperity of the 1920s owed a great deal to backing by the federal government. Republicans controlled the presidency and Congress, and though they claimed to stand for principles of laissez-faire and opposed various economic and social reforms, they were willing to use governmental power to support large corporations and the wealthy. Senator Warren G. Harding of Ohio, who was elected president in 1920, declared that he and his party wanted "less government in business and more business in government." Harding's cabinet appointments reflected this goal. Treasury Secretary Andrew Mellon, a banker and an aluminum company titan, believed that the government should stimulate economic growth by reducing taxes on the rich, raising tariffs to protect manufacturers from foreign competition, and trimming the budget.

The Republican Congress enacted much of this agenda. During the Harding administration, tax rates for the wealthy, which had skyrocketed during World War I, plummeted from 66 percent to 20 percent. Mellon believed that those on the lower rungs of the economic ladder would prosper once businesspeople invested the extra money they received from tax breaks into expanding production. Supposedly, the wealth would trickle down through increased jobs and purchasing power.

AP® TIP
Evaluate the degree of similarity between government policies and political life during the 1920s with those of the Gilded Age.

TEACHING IDEA
Incorporating Websites
To deepen student understanding of the Great Migration, you may wish to incorporate the following in your class:

- "The Long-Lasting Legacy of the Great Migration" by Isabel Wilkerson. Available on the *Smithsonian Magazine*'s website (smithsonianmag.com).
- "It's Time to Stop Calling It 'The Great Migration'" by Brentin Mock. Available on CityLab's website (citylab.com).
- "The 'Great Migration' Was About Racial Terror, Not Jobs" by Brentin Mock. Available on CityLab's website (citylab.com).

TEACHING IDEA
Incorporating Secondary Sources
Assign students to read and annotate Joshua Rothman's "When Bigotry Paraded Through the Streets," about the rise and fall of the second Ku Klux Klan. This article is available on The Atlantic's website (theatlantic.com). Require students to both identify Rothman's thesis and create a summative conclusive statement on their takeaways. Have students share these out in small-group format, with students rotating among several of their peers.

APPLY THE TIP
Assign students to complete a chart comparing the governmental policies and political life of the 1920s and the Gilded Age. As part of this process, point out to students the cyclical nature of economic policy in the U.S. The Gilded Age was replaced by the Progressive Era, which in turn gave way to the laissez-faire 1920s, as the pendulum swung back and forth. Indicate to students that the next pendulum swing they will witness in the course will come in the 1930s.

TRM Find **Handout 7.5 – Comparing the Gilded Age and the 1920s** in the Teacher's Resource materials.

TEACHING IDEA
Incorporating Videos
To lay the groundwork for the pro-corporate policies of the presidential administrations of the 1920s, have the class watch an excerpt from "The Presidents 1913–1945 American History Channel" (available on YouTube). The Wilson to Roosevelt excerpt on Warren Harding and Calvin Coolidge is from 12:42 to 22:02. This 10-minute overview of their administrations is a useful way to create political and economic context for the remainder of the module to come.

TEACHING IDEA
Building Vocabulary
Explain to students that so-called "trickle-down" economics will also go by other names, such as supply-side economics, and in Period 9, "Reaganomics." It is important to impress upon students that this economic philosophy will be fundamental orthodoxy in the Republican Party for the remainder of the twentieth century.

BUILDING AP® SKILLS

Sourcing and Situation

Show students the first 19 minutes of Charlie Chaplin's *Modern Times* (available on YouTube). Have students watch the excerpt with the following handout in front of them. At the conclusion of the excerpt, have students in small groups compare their answers to the question and add to them. Lastly, assign them to write a thesis statement in response to the following prompt: "To what extent was modernism a positive development in the 1920s?"

TRM Find **Handout 7.6 – Modern Times: A Social Commentary** in the Teacher's Resource materials.

TEACHING IDEA

Incorporating Secondary Sources

Assign students to read and annotate Edward Grystar's "A Brief Essay on the 1909 and 1919 Steel Strikes in Lyndora" (available through online search). Whole-class discussion to follow in the next class meeting.

MODULE 7-5 The Effects of World War I at Home

At the same time, Republicans turned Progressive Era regulatory agencies such as the Federal Trade Commission and the Federal Reserve Board into boosters for major corporations and financial institutions by weakening enforcement.

Secretary of Commerce Herbert Hoover had an even greater impact than Mellon in cementing the government-business partnership during the 1920s. Hoover believed that the federal government had a role to play in the economy and in lessening economic suffering. Rejecting government control of business activities, however, he insisted on voluntary cooperation between the public and private sectors. Hoover favored the creation of trade associations in which businesses would collaborate to stabilize production levels, prices, and wages. In turn, the Commerce Department would provide helpful data and information to improve productivity and trade.

Hoover's vision fit into a larger Republican effort to weaken unions by promoting voluntary business-sponsored worker welfare initiatives. For example, under the **American Plan**, some firms established health insurance and pension plans for their workers. As early as 1914, Henry Ford provided his autoworkers over twenty-two years old "a share in the profits of the house" equal to a minimum wage of $5 a day, and he cut the workday from nine hours to eight. Already under pressure from such tactics, unions were further damaged by a series of Supreme Court rulings that restricted strikes and overturned hard-won victories such as child labor legislation and minimum wage laws. By 1929 union membership had dropped from approximately five million to three million, or about 10 percent of the industrial labor market.

Scandals during the presidency of Warren G. Harding diminished its luster but did not tarnish the shine of Republican economic policy. The **Teapot Dome scandal** grabbed the most headlines. In 1921 Interior Secretary Albert Fall collaborated with Navy Secretary Edwin Denby to transfer potential oil fields to the Interior Department. Fall then parceled out these properties to private

> **AP® TIP**
> Analyze how the U.S. government and business interests both undermined the power of labor unions in the 1920s.

Teapot Dome scandal Oil and land scandal that highlighted the close ties between big business and the federal government in the early 1920s.

▲ **Teapot Dome Scandal** Clifford K. Berryman, the political cartoonist for the Washington *Evening Star*, illustrates the Teapot Dome scandal, which damaged the Harding administration. Captioned "Juggernaut," this image shows Secretary of the Navy Edward Denby on the left and Secretary of the Interior Albert Fall on the right fleeing from charges of bribery and corruption that a Senate committee brought to light. **In what ways is this image a reflection of its historical situation?**

companies. As a result, Harry F. Sinclair's Mammoth Oil Company received a lease to develop the Teapot Dome section in Wyoming. In return for this handout, Sinclair delivered more than $300,000 to Fall. In the wake of congressional hearings, Fall and Sinclair were convicted on a number of criminal charges and sent to jail.

Harding's sudden death from a heart attack in August 1923 brought Vice President Calvin Coolidge to the presidency. Coolidge distanced himself from the scandals of his predecessor's administration but reaffirmed Harding's economic policies. "The chief business of the American people is business," President Coolidge remarked succinctly.

Despite the political scandals, the 1920s marked a period of economic expansion and general prosperity. National income rose from approximately $63 billion to $88 billion, and per capita income jumped from $641 to $847, an increase of 32 percent. The purchasing power of wage earners climbed approximately 20 percent.

This great spurt of economic growth in the 1920s resulted from the application of technological innovation and scientific management techniques to industrial production. Perhaps the greatest innovation came with the introduction of the assembly line. First used in the automobile industry before World War I, the assembly line moved the product to a worker who performed a specific task before sending it along to the next worker. This deceptively simple system, perfected by Henry Ford, saved enormous time and energy by emphasizing repetition, accuracy, and standardization. Streamlined production lowered costs, which, in turn, allowed Ford to lower prices.

Besides the automobile, the economy of the 1920s focused on the production of consumer-oriented goods previously considered luxuries. The electrification of urban homes created demand for a wealth of new labor-saving appliances. Refrigerators, washing machines, toasters, and vacuum cleaners appealed to middle-class housewives whose husbands could afford to purchase them. Wristwatches replaced bulkier pocket watches. Radios became the chief source of home entertainment.

Although such household items changed the lives of many Americans, no single product had as profound an effect on American life in the 1920s as the automobile. Auto sales soared in the 1920s from 1.5 million to 5 million, fueling the growth of related industries such as steel, rubber,

AP® ANALYZING SOURCES

Source: *Model T Fords Coming Off the Assembly Line,* 1900

About the source: Henry Ford perfected the mass production of low-cost, easy-to-repair automobiles in the early twentieth century and put them within the economic reach of many Americans. This photograph shows finished Model T cars being driven off the assembly line at the Ford Motor Company's plant in Highland Park, Michigan.

Questions for Analysis

1. Identify the elements of mass production seen in this image.
2. Explain the ways the Model T represented a turning point in American consumption.
3. Evaluate the extent to which the production of the Model T represented a continuity with previous technological innovation and labor practices.

TEACHING IDEA

Incorporating Secondary Sources

Assign students to read Chapter 8, "Fordism," from David Harvey's *The Condition of Postmodernity*. Require students to both identify Harvey's thesis and create a summative conclusive statement on their takeaways on his work. Have students share these out in small-group format, with students rotating among several of their peers.

TRM Suggested Responses to Questions

TRM Module 7.5 AP® Analyzing Sources Handout 2

EXPLORING AP® THEMES

Work, Exchange, and Technology

Divide the class in three. Assign one-third of the room the topic "Social," one-third "Political," and one-third "Economic." Then ask the three groups, from the perspective of their topic, to formulate an answer to the question, "What makes the 'Modern Era' of the 1920s 'modern'?" Allow them to discuss, and then place students into groups of six, with two persons from each topic represented. Have them share out jigsaw style (a refresher of the jigsaw model can be found on page 33). Then task these groups of six with crafting a response to the following question: "The most significant changes in the 1920s were _____, because…"

EXPLORING AP® THEMES

Social Structures

After students have read about Coolidge's most famous quotation, "The business of America is business," share with them this lesser-known, but equally revealing quotation from President Coolidge: "The man who builds a factory builds a temple; the man who works there, worships there." Ask students to discuss what these two quotations from the president of the United States say about the place of commerce and commercial men in the popular imagination and social structure of the time. Further ask them to discuss the policy and economic implications for the nation of such belief and philosophy.

BUILDING AP® SKILLS

Making Connections

As part of the discussion of "Modernism," it is helpful to point out to students that the 1920s is when the middle-class American home got the bathroom and kitchen as we know them today. Explain to students how they would recognize the components and trappings of the world around them in the 1920s, if they were placed in a time machine and sent back to that period. Although they may not know how to operate them, students would recognize automobiles, radios, refrigerators, and telephones for what they were. By contrast, if they were transported thirty years earlier, to the world of Morse code, the icebox, the outhouse, the washtub, the butcher shop, and transport by draft horses, they would not recognize the world around them, nor be able to function in it.

APPLY THE TIP

Assign students to address the prompt with a "Fifty-Word Drill" introductory statement exercise in small groups. In addressing this prompt, students are required to write a response that is 50 words total (give or take). Then, break them back up as individuals, and have them craft an LEQ response to the prompt, based upon their own group's created product.

◀ **Chevrolet Advertisement, 1920s** The 1920s boom in the production of automobiles posed a challenge for business marketers and advertisers. They had to convince consumers that items once considered as luxuries were now necessities that would improve their lives. **Describe the audience for this advertisement and the ways in which this audience was targeted.**

AP® TIP
Analyze the economic, social, cultural, and environmental impact of the automobile on the development of the United States.

petroleum, and glass. In 1929 Ford and his competitors at General Motors, Chevrolet, and Oldsmobile employed nearly 4 million workers, and around one in eight American workers toiled in factories connected to automobile production.

The automobile also changed day-to-day living patterns. Although most roads and highways consisted of dirt and contained rocks and ruts, enough were paved to extend the boundaries of suburbs farther from the city. By the end of the 1920s, around 17 percent of Americans lived in suburbia. Cars allowed families to travel to vacation destinations at greater distances from their homes. Even the roadside landscape changed, as gas stations, diners, and motels sprang up to serve motorists. Each year, vacation resorts on the east and west coasts of Florida attracted thousands of tourists who drove south to enjoy the state's beautiful beaches. Motorists also flocked to national parks in the Rocky Mountains and on the West Coast.

The automobile also provided new dating opportunities for young men and women. At the turn of the twentieth century, a young man courted a woman by going to her home and sitting with her on the sofa or out on the porch under the watchful eyes of her parents and family members. With the arrival of the automobile, couples could move from the couch in the parlor to the backseat of a car, away from adult supervision. Driving to a "lover's lane," the young couple could express their feelings with greater physicality than before.

Although Ford and his fellow manufacturers succeeded in lowering prices, they still had to convince Americans to spend their hard-earned money to purchase their products. Turning for help to the fledgling advertising industry, manufacturers nearly tripled their spending on advertising over the course of the 1920s. Firms pitched their products around price and quality, but they directed their efforts more than ever to the personal psychology of the consumer. Advertisers played on consumers' unexpressed fears, unfulfilled desires, hopes for success, and sexual fantasies. The producers of Listerine mouthwash transformed a product previously used to disinfect hospitals into one that fought the dreaded but made-up disease of halitosis (bad breath). Advertisers told people that they could measure success through consumption. Purchasing a General Electric all-steel refrigerator not only would preserve food longer but also would enhance the owners' reputation among their neighbors.

Although average wages and incomes rose during the 1920s, the majority of Americans did not have the disposable income to afford the bounty of new consumer goods. To resolve this problem, companies extended credit in dizzying amounts. By 1929 consumers purchased 60 percent of their cars and 80 percent of their radios and furniture on credit — mainly through the installment plan. "Buy now and pay later" became the motto of corporate America.

REVIEW

- How did American economic policy change during the 1920s?
- What factors contributed to the rise of the consumer economy during the 1920s?

TEACHING IDEA

Incorporating Secondary Sources

Assign students to read and annotate David Halberstam's article, "Citizen Ford" (available through online search of author and title). Whole-class discussion to follow.

Urban Growth and Perilous Prosperity

The growth of cities helped promote the spread of the consumer-oriented economy. Increasingly clustered in urban areas, people had more convenient access to department stores and chain stores. Advertisers targeted city residents because they were easier to reach. Although cities contained plenty of poor people who could not afford to buy items they considered luxuries, a large middle class of shoppers provided a growing market.

The census of 1920 reported that for the first time in U.S. history a majority of Americans lived in cities. In 1910 just over 54 percent of the nation lived in small towns and villages with fewer than 2,500 people. A decade later, only 49 percent inhabited these areas. The end of World War I brought a decline in demand for American agricultural goods, and about six million residents left their farms and villages and moved to cities. By 1930 the percentage of those living in rural America further dropped to 44 percent. The war had pushed large numbers of African Americans out of the rural South for jobs in the cities. Also, with war's end, immigration from southern and eastern Europe resumed.

The West grew faster than any other region of the country, and its cities boomed. From 1910 to 1930, the population of the United States increased by 33.5 percent; at the same time, the population of the West soared by nearly 59 percent. In northern California, the bay area cities of San Francisco, Oakland, and Berkeley nearly doubled in population. Seattle, Portland, Denver, and Salt Lake City also rose in prominence. After the war, western city leaders boasted of the business and employment opportunities and beautiful landscapes that awaited migrants to their urban communities.

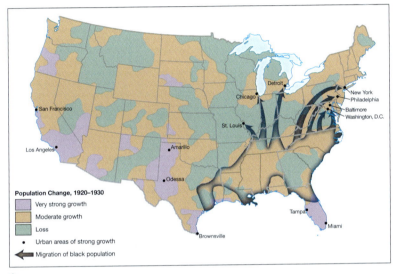

▲ **MAP 7.5 The Shift from Rural to Urban Population, 1920–1930** Throughout the late nineteenth and early twentieth centuries, the population of the nation had shifted from rural to urban areas. In the 1920s this migration continued, especially among African Americans in the South and Latinos in the Southwest and West. Many of these migrants from rural to urban landscapes actually stayed in the same region, particularly Latinos. **What historical trends fueled this migration?**

TEACHING IDEA

Building Vocabulary

Explain to students the concept of homogenization. One way to do this is to introduce a made-up word, by explaining to students that to homogenize is to "same-ify." For an example, discuss with students the names and locations of the major restaurants and retailers within their communities — the area commonly referred to as "the strip." After going down the road and naming the mass franchise operations that are there, pose this question: "How many places in America do you think are almost exactly like that?" This is a useful exercise to help students understand how the standardization of the world they live in, from the chain stores to the residential tract-housing subdivisions, got its start.

EXPLORING AP® THEMES

Migration and Settlement

Have students study the map and text on the page. Then review with them the primary economic and political concerns of the Populists of 1896. Point out that 1896 represented the high-water mark for the ability of agrarian America to mount a significant challenge to steer the course of the country. Explain how the demographic shifts of the 1920s represent the acceleration of a non-rural, non-Populist trend in the United States in terms of residency and social orientation, to the point today where only approximately 1-2% of Americans farm and feed the rest of the nation.

APPLY THE TIP

Explain to students the concept of an economic "bubble." Discuss with students the connections that are to be made through the recurring process of economic "correction" after trends such as the housing bubble and tech bubbles of the late nineteenth and early twentieth centuries, and show them how the stock market bubble of the 1920s was no different. To aid students in making connections over time, assign them to connect the income inequality of the 1920s to the business cycle.

TEACHING IDEA

Connecting the Dots

Engage the class in an activity of association by disassociation called "Odd One Out." Write the following terms on the board/projector:

- The Great Migration
- The homogenization of society
- The American Plan
- Assembly line production
- Buying stock on margin

Then place students in small groups and ask them, "Which one is the odd one out and why? How do the remaining terms relate?" Give students approximately 7-10 minutes to complete this part, then share out student answers and discuss their conclusions and reasoning as a whole-class activity. There is no specific correct answer; the goal is to get students thinking in categorical habits of mind and defending their rationales.

Los Angeles stood out for its growth, which skyrocketed from 319,000 residents in 1910 to over 1.2 million in 1930. The mild, sunny climate of southern California attracted midwesterners and northeasterners who were tired of rugged winters. Los Angeles was surrounded by beautiful mountains, and promoters enticed new residents to buy up real estate, which could be purchased cheaply and sold for a big profit. The city offered a dependable public transit system that connected Los Angeles and neighboring counties. During the 1920s, the motion picture industry settled here, and its movies delighted audiences throughout the nation. This urban boom boosted economic growth and, along with it, consumer spending.

Prosperity in the 1920s was real enough, but behind the impressive financial indicators flashed warnings that profound danger loomed ahead. Perhaps most important, the boom was accompanied by growing income inequality. A majority of workers lived below the poverty line, and farmers plunged deeper into hard times. Corporate profits increased much faster than wages, resulting in a disproportionate share of the wealth going to the rich. The combined income of the top 1 percent of families was greater than that of the 42 percent at the bottom; 66 percent lived below the income level necessary to maintain an adequate standard of living.

> **AP® TIP**
> Analyze the effects of growing income inequality on the American economy during the 1920s.

Income inequality was a critical problem because America's new mass-production economy depended on ever-increasing consumption, and higher income groups could consume only so much, no matter how much of the nation's wealth they controlled. While the expansion of consumer credit helped hide this fundamental weakness, the low wages earned by most Americans drove down demand over time. Cutbacks in demand forced manufacturers to reduce production, thereby reducing jobs and increasing unemployment, which in turn dragged down the demand for consumer goods even further. As a result, by 1926 the growth of automobile sales had begun to slow, as did new housing construction — signs of an economy heading for trouble.

At the same time, the wealthy few used their disproportionate wealth to speculate in the stock market and risky real estate ventures. To encourage investments, brokers promoted buying stocks on margin (credit) and required down payments of only a fraction of the market price. Without vigilant governmental oversight, banks and lending agencies extended credit without taking into account what would happen if a financial panic occurred and they were suddenly required to call in all of their loans. To make matters worse, the banking system operated on shaky financial grounds, combining savings facilities with speculative lending operations. With minimal interference from the Federal Trade Commission, businesspeople frequently managed firms in a reckless way that created a high level of interdependence among them. This interlocking system of corporate ownership and control meant that the collapse of one company could bring down many others, while also imperiling the banking houses that had generously financed them.

Rampant real estate speculation in Florida foreshadowed these dangers. In many cases, investors bought properties sight unseen, as speculators and unscrupulous agents worked under the assumption that land values in Florida would continue to increase forever. However, severe storms in 1926 and 1928 abruptly halted the rise in land values. Land prices spiraled downward, speculators defaulted on bank loans, and financial institutions tottered.

Throughout the 1920s, fortunes plummeted for farmers as well. Declining world demand following the end of World War I, together with increased productivity because of the mechanization of agriculture, drove down farm prices and income. Between 1925 and 1929, falling wheat and cotton prices cut farm income in half. The collapse of farm prices had the most devastating effects on tenants and sharecroppers, who were forced off their lands through mortgage foreclosures. Around three million displaced farmers migrated to cities.

Internationally, the United States encountered serious economic obstacles. World War I had destroyed European economies, leaving them ill equipped to repay the $11 billion they had borrowed from the United States. Much of the Allied recovery, and hence the ability to repay debts, depended on obtaining the reparations imposed on Germany at the conclusion of World War I. Germany, however, was in even worse shape than France and Britain and could not meet its obligations. Consequently, the U.S. government negotiated a deal by which the United States provided loans to Germany to pay its reparations and Britain and France reduced the size of Germany's payments. The result was a series of circular payments. American banks loaned money to Germany, which used the money to pay reparations to Britain and France, which in turn used Germany's reparations payments to repay debts owed to U.S. banks. What appeared a satisfactory

---

TEACHING IDEA

Incorporating Secondary Sources

Assign students to read and annotate "American 'Reparations' to Germany, 1919–1933," by Stephen Schuker (available through online search). Require students to both identify Schuker's thesis and create a summative conclusive statement on their takeaways on his work. Have students share these out in small-group format, with students rotating among several of their peers.

resolution at the time ultimately proved a calamity. In undertaking this revolving-door solution, U.S. bankers added to the cycle of spiraling credit and placed themselves at the mercy of unstable European economies. Compounding the problem, Republican administrations in the 1920s supported high tariffs on imports, reducing foreign manufacturers' revenues and therefore their nations' tax receipts, making it more difficult for these countries to pay off their debts.

REVIEW

- What factors account for the growth in urban areas during the 1920s?
- What were the main weaknesses of the U.S. economy during the 1920s?

AP® WRITING HISTORICALLY — Long-Essay Question Practice

ACTIVITY

Answer the following Long-Essay Question. *Suggested writing time: 40 minutes.*

Evaluate the extent to which the American consumer economy of the 1920s was a result of government policies enacted during World War I.

TRM Suggested Responses to Questions

EXPLORING AP® THEMES

Work, Exchange, and Technology

Assign students in small groups to contrast the economic and policy priorities of the Progressive Era with those of laissez-faire economic and policy priorities of the 1920s. This could be done in T-chart or Venn diagram format, or can be made into a Long-Essay Question prompt for students to write.

BUILDING AP® SKILLS

Argumentation

As a whole-class exercise, assign students to create a single introductory paragraph including thesis and contextualization for the prompt on this page. Once this is done, divide the class into three or four groups. Task each group with creating a single main body paragraph that addresses the thesis created by the class. Then, recombine the class into jigsawed groups, with one member from each of the body paragraph groups, and have each person contribute/share from their area of emphasis (a refresher of the jigsaw model can be found on page 33). In so doing, the class groups will ultimately create a set of "virtual essays."

TEACHING IDEA

AP® Writing Historically Review

The inherent challenge of this question is for students to connect the policies enacted during World War I to the economy of the 1920s. Consider having students make a T-Chart with economic policies during World War I on one side and economy of the 1920s on the other. The assignment rests on the fact that students have to match each side of the T-Chart. In other words, for every example they list, a corresponding factor must match. This will help students think through the historical connections of this question.

TRM Suggested Responses to Questions

Module 7-6

The Transitional 1920s

LEARNING TARGETS

By the end of this module, you should be able to:

- Explain how after World War I, nativist campaigns led to quotas that restricted immigration in the 1920s.
- Explain how the U.S. economy after World War I focused on the production of consumer goods, which contributed to changing living standards, greater mobility, and better communications.
- Explain how new forms of mass media spread national culture and greater awareness of regional cultures.
- Explain how urban areas offered opportunities for women, immigrants, and domestic migrants.
- Describe how migration generated new forms of art and literature that expressed ethnic and regional identities.
- Explain how and why Americans debated gender roles, modernism, science, religion, and issues related to race and immigration during the 1920s.

THEMATIC FOCUS

American and Regional Culture

Social Structures

During the 1920s, American culture and society appeared to be in a state of flux. Many women, African Americans, and middle-class youth experimented with new forms of self-identification and leisure. However, during this same period, conservative trends in American society revived reactionary organizations like the Ku Klux Klan and political ideologies like nativism. In this regard, culture and society in the United States during this period appeared to be growing increasingly modern, while at the same time seeking to restore perceived traditions from the past.

HISTORICAL REASONING FOCUS

Continuity and Change

TASK ▶ As you read this module, consider the extent to which social and cultural trends during the 1920s marked changes in the United States, and to what extent they represented long-standing trends in the nation's history.

TEACHING IDEA

Incorporating Videos

Before introducing the module, assign students to view excerpts of the PBS documentary "Against the Odds: Artists of the Harlem Renaissance" (available on YouTube). Preview the 54-minute film and utilize selected excerpts as a concise formative content introduction to the major aspects of the cultural, literary, and artistic blossoming of the Harlem Renaissance that figures prominently in Module 7-6 as part of preparation for either assessment or reinforcement.

While most of the nation ignored growing evidence of the fragility of American prosperity, the social and cultural consequences of consumerism in the 1920s received considerable attention, as new, distinctly modern cultural patterns emerged. Advertising and credit, two of the mainstays of modern capitalism, sought to bypass the time-honored virtues of saving and living within one's means. Conventional sexual standards came under assault from the growth of the film and automobile industries, which influenced clothing styles and dating practices. In addition to moral and social behavior, traditional racial assumptions came under attack. African American writers and artists condemned racism, drew on their rich racial legacies, and produced a cultural renaissance. Other black people, led by the Jamaican immigrant Marcus Garvey, rejected the integrationist strategy of the NAACP in favor of black nationalism. Attacks on traditional cultural and racial values did not go uncontested. During this era when technological innovations overturned traditional economic values, when modes of social behavior were in a state of flux, and when white supremacy came under assault, it is not surprising that many segments of the population resisted these changes. Rallying around ethnic and racial purity, Protestant fundamentalism, and family values, defenders of an older America attempted to roll back the tide of modernity. The enactment of prohibition was their greatest victory.

Culture Wars and Challenges to Social Conventions

Challenges to the virtues of thrift and sacrifice were accompanied by a transformation of the moral codes of late-nineteenth-century America, especially those relating to sex. The entertainment industry played a large role in promoting relaxed attitudes toward sexual relations to a mass audience throughout the nation. The motion picture business attracted women and men to movie palaces where they could see swashbuckling heroes and glamorous heroines.

Originally shown as short films for 5 cents in nickelodeons, movies appealed to a national audience. By the 1920s, films had expanded into feature-length pictures, Hollywood film studios had blossomed into major corporations, and movies were shown in ornate theaters in cities and towns across the country. The star system was born, and matinee idols influenced fashions and hairstyles. Female stars dressed as "flappers" and wooed audiences. Representing the liberated **new woman**, flappers wore short skirts, used ample makeup (formerly associated with prostitutes), smoked cigarettes in public, drank illegal alcoholic beverages, and gyrated to jazz tunes on the dance floor.

However, even as Americans enjoyed new entertainment opportunities most remained faithful to traditional values. By 1929 approximately 40 percent of households owned a radio. Shows such as *The General Motors Family* and *The Maxwell House Hour* blended product advertising with family entertainment. *Amos 'n' Andy* garnered large audiences by satirizing black working-class life, which, intentionally or not, reinforced racist stereotypes. In cities like New York and Chicago, immigrants could tune in to foreign-language radio programs aimed at non-English-speaking ethnic groups, which offered listeners an outlet for preserving their identity in the face of the increasing homogeneity fostered by the national consumer culture.

The most spirited challenge to both traditional values and the modern consumer culture came from a diverse group of intellectuals known as the **Lost Generation**. Author Gertrude Stein coined the term to describe the disillusionment that many of her fellow writers and artists felt after the ravages of World War I. Already concerned about the impact of mass culture and corporate capitalism on individualism and free

new woman 1920s term for the modern, sexually liberated woman. The new woman, popularized in movies and magazines, defied traditional morality.

Lost Generation Term coined by the writer Gertrude Stein to describe the writers and artists disillusioned with the consumer culture of the 1920s.

Hollywood Hollywood's silent movies provided audiences with graphic images of changing sexual values during the 1920s. Rudolph Valentino, pictured in this advertisement for *Blood and Sand* (1922), was the leading male heartthrob of the era. **How does this poster both uphold and challenge the gender norms of the early twentieth century?**

EXPLORING AP® THEMES

Social Structures

Point out to students that in terms of women's equality, most gender and feminist historians consider the 1920s to be more significant than the 1960s. A common generalization is that "women's liberation" began with the birth control pill in 1960. However, abandoning the corset, getting the right to vote, accessing the mobility of the automobile, and entering the workforce in large numbers were all accomplishments of the 1920s. In many ways, "the sixties" simply built on existing long-term trends that had their origins in this module.

TEACHING IDEA

Analyzing Art and Images

Task students with comparing the advertising image for *Blood and Sand* on this page with the advertising image for Chevrolet on page 616 from Module 7-5. Ask students to discuss what differences and similarities they find between the two images with regards to their messages on women's roles in society.

TRM Suggested Responses to Questions

TRM Module 7.6 AP® Analyzing Sources Handout 1

BUILDING AP® SKILLS

Argumentation

Divide the class into two groups, one group labeled "support," and the other group labeled "refute." Then, present the class with the following prompt: "The Lost Generation's criticisms of American life in the 1920s were overstated." Based upon the group students were placed in, assign them to come up with evidence that either supports or refutes the prompt. At the conclusion of this step, recombine the class into pairs, consisting of one supporter and one refuter. Have them share out and teach one another what they now know, and then as a pair, have them craft a thesis statement together on the prompt, based upon their shared knowledge discussion.

▲ Differentiation

In order to obtain the maximal amount of contributions from students, the instructor could combine the room in such a way so that the strongest students work with those that are more challenged by the content, in either the paired phase, or the whole-group supporter/refuter phase. Furthermore, students of mixed ability levels could also be tasked with creating a skeletal outline of the LEQ response to the prompt, and then split into individuals for the purpose of writing a full response, based upon the collaborative work.

Period 7: 1890–1945

MODULE 7-6 The Transitional 1920s

AP® ANALYZING SOURCES

Source: F. Scott Fitzgerald, *The Great Gatsby*, 1925

"Most of the big shore places were closed now and there were hardly any lights except the shadowy, moving glow of a ferryboat across the Sound. And as the moon rose higher the inessential houses began to melt away until gradually I became aware of the old island here that flowered once for Dutch sailors' eyes—a fresh, green breast of the new world. Its vanished trees, the trees that had made way for Gatsby's house, had once pandered in whispers to the last and greatest of all human dreams; for a transitory enchanted moment man must have held his breath in the presence of this continent, compelled into an aesthetic contemplation he neither understood nor desired, face to face for the last time in history with something commensurate to his capacity for wonder.

And as I sat there brooding on the old, unknown world, I thought of Gatsby's wonder when he first picked out the green light at the end of Daisy's dock. He had come a long way to this blue lawn, and his dream must have seemed so close that he could hardly fail to grasp it. He did not know that it was already behind him, somewhere back in that vast obscurity beyond the city, where the dark fields of the republic rolled on under the night.

Gatsby believed in the green light, the orgiastic future that year by year recedes before us. It eluded us then, but that's no matter—to-morrow we will run faster, stretch out our arms farther. . . . And one fine morning—

So we beat on, boats against the current, borne back ceaselessly into the past."

Questions for Analysis

1. Identify the role played by the Dutch sailors at the beginning of this passage.
2. Evaluate the extent to which the speaker sees his contemporaries' values as consistent with the goals of the Dutch sailors.
3. Evaluate the extent to which the final line critiques 1920s America.

AP® TIP
Compare the criticisms the Lost Generation made of American society to those the transcendentalists made during the early 1800s.

thought, they focused their talents on criticizing what they saw as the hypocrisy of old values and the conformity ushered in by the new. In the novel *This Side of Paradise* (1920), F. Scott Fitzgerald complained that his generation had "grown up to find all Gods dead, all wars fought, all faith in man shaken." In a series of novels, including *Main Street* (1920), *Babbitt* (1922), and *Elmer Gantry* (1927), Sinclair Lewis ridiculed the narrow-mindedness of small-town life, the empty materialism of businessmen, and the insincerity of evangelical preachers. Journalist Henry Louis (H. L.) Mencken picked up these subjects in the pages of his magazine, *The American Mercury*. From his vantage point in Baltimore, Maryland, he lampooned the beliefs and behavior of Middle America.

Scholars joined literary and social critics in challenging conventional ideas. Sigmund Freud, an Austrian psychoanalyst, shifted emphasis away from culture to individual consciousness. His disciples stressed the role of the unconscious mind and the power of the sex drive in shaping human behavior, beliefs that gained traction not only in university education but also in advertising appeals.

Scholars also discredited conventional wisdom about race. Challenging studies that purported to demonstrate the intellectual superiority of white people over African Americans, Columbia University anthropologist Franz Boas argued that any apparent intelligence gap between the races resulted from environmental factors and not heredity. His student Ruth Benedict further argued that the culture of so-called primitive tribes, such as the Pueblo Indians, produced a less stressful and more emotionally connected lifestyle than that of more advanced societies.

REVIEW

How did the economic and cultural changes that took place during the 1920s challenge early twentieth century American social norms?

TEACHING IDEA

Understanding Economic and Cultural Changes

Assign students to create a 4-1-1 contextualization/thesis introductory paragraph for the review prompt at the bottom of the page (a refresher of the 4-1-1 model can be found on page 163). Post these around the room for students to view in a gallery walk, followed by time for peer review and edit. Students can also be tasked with ranking which opening paragraphs they believe to be the top three in the room, and asked to give their rationale for their rankings.

The Harlem Renaissance and Black Nationalism

New Negro 1920s term for the second generation of African Americans born after emancipation and who stood up for their rights.

Harlem Renaissance The work of Harlem-based African American writers, artists, and musicians that flourished following World War I through the 1920s.

The greatest challenge to conventional notions about race came from African Americans. The influx of southern black migrants to the North during and after World War I created a black cultural renaissance, with New York City's Harlem and the South Side of Chicago leading the way. Gathered in Harlem — with a population of more than 120,000 African Americans in 1920 and growing every day — a group of black writers paid homage to the **New Negro**, the second generation born after emancipation. These New Negro intellectuals refused to accept white supremacy. They expressed pride in their race, sought to perpetuate black racial identity, and demanded full citizenship and participation in American society. Black writers and poets drew on themes from African American life and history for inspiration in their literary works.

The poets, novelists, and artists of the **Harlem Renaissance** captured the imagination of black and white people alike. Many of these artists increasingly rejected white standards of taste as well as staid middle-class black values. Writers Langston Hughes and Zora Neale Hurston in particular drew inspiration from the vernacular of African American folk life. In 1926 Hughes defiantly asserted: "We younger Negro artists who create now intend to express our dark-skinned selves without fear or shame. If white people are pleased, we are glad. If they are not, it doesn't matter."

Black music became a vibrant part of mainstream American popular culture in the 1920s. Musicians such as Ferdinand "Jelly Roll" Morton, Louis Armstrong, Edward "Duke" Ellington, and singer Bessie Smith developed and popularized two of America's most original forms of music — jazz and the blues. These unique compositions grew out of the everyday experiences of black life and expressed the thumping rhythms of work, pleasure, and pain. Such music did not remain confined to dance halls and clubs in black communities; it soon spread to white musicians

AP® ANALYZING SOURCES

Source: A. Philip Randolph and Chandler Owen, *The New Negro — What Is He?*, 1919

"In politics, the New Negro, unlike the Old Negro, cannot be lulled into a false sense of security with political spoils and patronage. . . . The New Negro demands political equality. He recognizes the necessity of selective as well as elective representation. He realizes that so long as the Negro votes for the Republican or Democratic party, he will have only the right and privilege to elect but not to select his representatives. And he who selects the representatives controls the representative. The New Negro stands for universal suffrage. . . .

Here, as a worker, he demands the full product of his toil. His immediate aim is more wages, shorter hours and better working conditions. As a consumer, he seeks to buy in the market, commodities at the lowest possible price.

The social aims of the New Negro are decidedly different from those of the Old Negro. Here he stands for absolute and unequivocal '*social equality*.' . . . He insists that a society which is based upon justice can only be a society composed of *social equals*. . . . He realizes that the acceptance of laws against intermarriage is tantamount to the acceptance of the stigma of inferiority. Besides, laws against intermarriage expose Negro women to sexual exploitation, and deprive their offspring, by white men, of the right to inherit the property of their father."

Questions for Analysis

1. Identify the aims and demands of the "New Negro," according to Randolph and Owen.
2. Explain how Randolph and Owen support their argument for addressing the aims of the "New Negro."
3. Evaluate the extent of continuity between Randolph and Owen's arguments and earlier efforts to obtain civil rights for African Americans.

BUILDING AP® SKILLS

Comparison

Present students with the following LEQ prompt: "Evaluate the extent to which the Lost Generation and the Harlem Renaissance were similar movements." Pair up the students, and assign half the pairs to address the respective similarities, and half of the pairs to address the respective differences. Once they have done so, merge the pairs into quads, made up of one similarity and one difference pair each, and have them jigsaw their information together, and then craft a "Fifty-Word Drill" introductory statement on the prompt (a refresher of the jigsaw model can be found on page 33).

TRM Suggested Responses to Questions

TRM Module 7.6 AP® Analyzing Sources Handout 2

TEACHING IDEA

Incorporating Primary Sources

The Library of Congress provides students with a series of documents regarding the Harlem Renaissance from several points of view (loc.gov). Visit the home page and navigate to Teachers, Classroom Materials, Primary Source Sets, and view the collection of The Harlem Renaissance. Assign students in groups to read and break down seven of twenty-one documents (these will be specifically assigned to groups by the instructor: prereading on the part of the instructor is important here) to determine their historical context, intended audience, purpose, and point of view, in line with the HIPP format of document analysis (a refresher of HIPP can be found on page 8). Then have students answer the Questions for Discussion. Student products can then be shared out in a jigsaw fashion so students can then evaluate and ascertain the cultural and social impact of the Harlem Renaissance (a refresher of the jigsaw model can be found on page 33).

EXPLORING AP® THEMES

Social Structures

Assign students to read the pair of Analyzing Sources on pages 623–624, and answer the accompanying questions for homework. The next day in class, have students share their responses in groups of two or three. Then, have these groups synthesize these two documents with the pair of documents on page 563, from Booker T. Washington and Ida Wells, searching for continuities and contradictions between the four sources with regards to the AP® themes of American and regional culture, American and national identity, and/or social structures. Students can be tasked with addressing all three themes in their integration of the source documents, or they may be assigned a specific theme to contend with, depending upon the instructor's preferences.

Period 7: 1890–1945

MODULE 7-6 The Transitional 1920s

and audiences for whom the hot beat of jazz rhythms meant emotional freedom and the expression of sexuality.

In addition to providing a fertile ground for African American intellectuals, Harlem became the headquarters of the most significant alternative black political vision of the 1920s. In 1916 the Jamaican-born Marcus Mosiah Garvey settled in Harlem and became the leading exponent

TRM Suggested Responses to Questions

TRM Module 7.6 AP® Analyzing Sources Handout 3

AP® ANALYZING SOURCES

Source: Zora Neale Hurston, *How It Feels to Be Colored Me*, 1928

"Someone is always at my elbow reminding me that I am the granddaughter of slaves. It fails to register depression with me. Slavery is sixty years in the past. The operation was successful and the patient is doing well, thank you. The terrible struggle that made me an American out of a potential slave said 'On the line!' The Reconstruction said 'Get set!'; and the generation before said 'Go!' I am off to a flying start and I must not halt in the stretch to look behind and weep. Slavery is the price I paid for civilization, and the choice was not with me. It is a bully adventure and worth all that I have paid through my ancestors for it. No one on earth ever had a greater chance for glory. The world to be won and nothing to be lost. It is thrilling to think—to know that for any act of mine, I shall get twice as much praise or twice as much blame. It is quite exciting to hold the center of the national stage, with the spectators not knowing whether to laugh or to weep.

The position of my white neighbor is much more difficult. No brown specter pulls up a chair beside me when I sit down to eat. No dark ghost thrusts its leg against mine in bed. The game of keeping what one has is never so exciting as the game of getting.

I do not always feel colored. Even now I often achieve the unconscious Zora of Eatonville before the Hegira[1]. I feel most colored when I am thrown against a sharp white background.

For instance at Barnard[2]. 'Beside the waters of the Hudson' I feel my race. Among the thousand white persons, I am a dark rock surged upon, and overswept, but through it all, I remain myself. When covered by the waters, I am; and the ebb but reveals me again.

Sometimes it is the other way around. A white person is set down in our midst, but the contrast is just as sharp for me. For instance, when I sit in the drafty basement that is The New World Cabaret with a white person, my color comes. We enter chatting about any little nothing that we have in common and are seated by the jazz waiters. In the abrupt way that jazz orchestras have, this one plunges into a number. It loses no time in circumlocutions[3], but gets right down to business. It constricts the thorax and splits the heart with its tempo and narcotic harmonies. This orchestra grows rambunctious, rears on its hind legs and attacks the tonal veil with primitive fury, rending it, clawing it until it breaks through to the jungle beyond. I follow those heathen—follow them exultingly. I dance wildly inside myself; I yell within, I whoop; I shake my assegai[4] above my head, I hurl it true to the mark *yeeeeoooww*! I am in the jungle and living in the jungle way. My face is painted red and yellow and my body is painted blue. My pulse is throbbing like a war drum. I want to slaughter something—give pain, give death to what, I do not know. But the piece ends. The men of the orchestra wipe their lips and rest their fingers. I creep back slowly to the veneer we call civilization with the last tone and find the white friend sitting motionless in his seat, smoking calmly."

[1] Exodus or migration, named for Muhammad's departure from Mecca to escape persecution.
[2] A college in New York City.
[3] Indirect and circuitous speech.
[4] A spear.

Questions for Analysis

1. Identify when Hurston feels "colored."
2. Explain what Hurston means by "colored me" and why that matters to her.
3. Evaluate the extent to which Hurston opposes assimilation into white American culture.

TEACHING IDEA

Incorporating Primary Sources

The Annenberg Learner's Essential Lens collection, "Place, Culture, and Representation: the Art and Politics of the Harlem Renaissance" contains several lessons and activities on the topic, which instructors may use at their own discretion as stand-alone or multiple scaffolded units of instruction (available by title search at learner.org). Sources included are both visual and textual in nature.

Universal Negro Improvement Association (UNIA) Organization founded by Marcus Garvey in 1914 to promote black self-help, pan-Africanism, and racial separatism.

of black nationalism. In 1914 Garvey had set up the **Universal Negro Improvement Association (UNIA)** in Jamaica, an organization through which he promoted racial separation and pride as well as economic self-help through black business ownership. Unlike the leaders of the NAACP, who sought equal access to American institutions and cooperation with white people, Garvey favored a "Back to Africa" movement that would ultimately repatriate many black Americans to their ancestral homelands on the African continent. His recently acquired Black Star Line steamship company planned to transport passengers between the United States, the West Indies, and Africa. Together with the indigenous black African majority, transplanted African Americans would help overthrow colonial rule and use their power to assist black people throughout the world.

In addition to offering a revival of black cultural heritage and providing an outlet for dreams of economic advancement, Garvey tapped into the racial discontent of African Americans for whom living in the United States had proved so difficult. He denounced what he saw as the accommodationist efforts of the NAACP and declared, "To be a Negro is no disgrace, but an honor, and we of the UNIA do not want to become white." Ironically, the UNIA and the Ku Klux Klan agreed on the necessity of racial segregation, though Garvey never accepted the premise that black people were inferior. Garvey's appeals to black manhood were accompanied by a celebration of black womanhood. He set up the Black Cross Nurses, and his wife, Amy Jacques Garvey, went beyond her husband's traditional notions of femininity to extol the accomplishments of black women in politics and culture. Garveyism became the first mass African American movement in U.S. history and was especially effective in recruiting working-class black people. UNIA branches were established in thirty-eight states throughout the North and South and attracted some 500,000 members.

Given his ideas and outspokenness, Garvey soon made powerful enemies. Du Bois and fellow members of the NAACP despised him. The black socialist labor leader A. Philip Randolph, who saw the UNIA program as just another form of exploitative capitalism, labeled Garvey an "unquestioned fool and ignoramus." Yet Garvey's downfall came from his own business practices. Convicted in 1925 of mail fraud related to his Black Star Line, Garvey served two years in federal prison until President Coolidge commuted his term and had the Jamaican citizen deported.

> **AP® TIP**
> Analyze how the Harlem Renaissance helped shaped twentieth-century African American identity and challenged racist stereotypes.

> " We younger Negro artists who create now intend to express our dark-skinned selves without fear or shame. If white people are pleased, we are glad. If they are not, it doesn't matter. "
>
> — Langston Hughes, "The Negro Artist and the Racial Mountain," 1926

◀ **Marcus Garvey** Dressed in military regalia, the Jamaican immigrant Marcus Garvey embodied the spirit of black nationalism after World War I. His Universal Negro Improvement Association, headquartered in Harlem, attracted a sizable following in the United States, the Caribbean, Central America, Canada, and Africa. Garvey advocated black political and economic independence. **To what extent were the aims of Garvey's civil rights movement similar to those of the NAACP?**

APPLY THE TIP

Assign students to compare and contrast Booker T. Washington's goals and priorities for racial progress with those of various leading figures of the Harlem Renaissance. This can be done in Venn diagram, T-Chart, or written response format.

TEACHING IDEA

Connecting the Dots

Columbia University's Mapping the African American Past Project has a multi-tiered lesson on Marcus Garvey and Garveyism, involving primary sources and role-play/simulation, which is usable in class on an individual or group basis, depending upon the instructor's preferences (map.columbia.edu). Visit the home page and navigate to Lesson Plans, Resistance, and Self-Determination, and view the resource of Marcus Garvey and the Rise of Black Nationalism.

BUILDING AP® SKILLS

Sourcing and Situation

Assign students to read Marcus Garvey's "Aims and Objects of Movement for Solution of the Negro Problem" (1924) available on Teaching American History's website (teachingamericanhistory.org). Have them annotate the piece, and create a summative conclusive statement on their takeaways on his work. Have students share these out in small-group format, with students rotating among several of their peers.

Period 7: 1890–1945

MODULE 7-6 The Transitional 1920s

AP® ANALYZING SOURCES

Source: Claude McKay, "If We Must Die" (poem), 1919

"If we must die, let it not be like hogs
Hunted and penned in an inglorious spot,
While round us bark the mad and hungry dogs,
Making their mock at our accursèd lot.
If we must die, O let us nobly die,
So that our precious blood may not be shed
In vain; then even the monsters we defy
Shall be constrained to honor us though dead!
O kinsmen! we must meet the common foe!
Though far outnumbered let us show us brave,
And for their thousand blows deal one death-blow!
What though before us lies the open grave?
Like men we'll face the murderous, cowardly pack,
Pressed to the wall, dying, but fighting back!"

Questions for Analysis

1. Identify the speaker's primary concern in this poem.
2. Describe the historical circumstances that raised this concern.
3. Explain how the solution the speaker proposes to address this concern reflects African-American social and cultural movements of the 1920s.

REVIEW

In what ways did the Harlem Renaissance challenge early twentieth century social and cultural norms?

Prohibition, Fundamentalism, and Modern American Life

AP® TIP
Analyze the ways in which prohibition was connected to early twentieth century Progressivism and conservatism.

After decades of efforts to combat the use of alcohol, in 1919 the Eighteenth Amendment, banning its manufacture and sale, was ratified. That same year Congress passed the Volstead Act, which set up the legal machinery to enforce the amendment. Supporters claimed that prohibition would promote family stability, improve morals, and prevent crime. They took aim at the ethnic culture of saloons associated with urban immigrants.

Enforcing this attempt to promote traditional values proved to be the problem. In rural areas "moonshiners" took grain and processed it into liquor. In big cities, clubs known as speakeasies offered illegal alcohol and the entertainment to keep their customers satisfied. Treasury Department agents roamed the country destroying stills and raiding speakeasies, but liquor continued to flow. Nevertheless, prohibition did reduce alcohol consumption, but crime flourished. Gangsters paid off police, bribed judges, and turned cities into battlegrounds between rival criminal gangs, reinforcing the notion among small-town and rural dwellers that urban life eroded American values. By the end of the decade, most Americans welcomed an end to prohibition.

Protestant fundamentalists also fought to uphold long-established values against modern-day incursions. Around 1910, two wealthy Los Angeles churchgoers had subsidized and distributed a series of booklets called *The Fundamentals*, informing readers that the Bible offered a true account of the genesis and development of humankind and the world and that its words had to be taken literally. After 1920, believers of this approach to interpreting the Bible became known as "fundamentalists." Their preachers spread the message of old-time religion through carnival-like

---

TRM Suggested Responses to Questions

TRM Module 7.6 AP® Analyzing Sources Handout 4

TEACHING IDEA

Incorporating Videos

Show the students an excerpt from the PBS documentary, *Prohibition*, "The Chicago Beer Wars" (available on YouTube). This video, approximately 13 minutes, details the rise of organized crime that came along with the prohibition of alcohol.

TEACHING IDEA

Class Discussion

Engage the class in a whole-class discussion premised around the following question: "To what extent should people be protected from themselves and their own choices, and what does this say about the power of the state?"

revivals, and ministers used the new medium of radio to broadcast their sermons. Fundamentalism's appeal was strongest in the Midwest and the South — the so-called Bible belt — where residents felt deeply threatened by the secular aspects of modern life that left their conventional religious teachings open to scepticism and scorn.

Nothing bothered fundamentalist Protestants as much as Charles Darwin's theory of evolution. In *On the Origin of Species* (1859), Darwin replaced the biblical story of creation with a scientific theory of the emergence and development of life that centered on evolution and natural selection. Fundamentalists rejected this explanation and repudiated the views of fellow Protestants who attempted to reconcile Darwinian evolution with God's Word by reading the Bible as a symbolic representation of what might have happened. To combat any other interpretation but the biblical one, in 1925 lawmakers in Arkansas, Florida, Mississippi, Oklahoma, and Tennessee made it illegal to teach in public schools and colleges "any theory that denies the story of the Divine Creation of man as taught in the Bible."

Shortly after the anti-evolution law passed, the town of Dayton, Tennessee decided to take advantage of it to attract new investment to the area. The townspeople recruited John Scopes, a general science high school teacher to defy the law by lecturing from a biology textbook that presented Darwin's theory. With help from the ACLU, which wanted to challenge the restrictive state statute on the grounds of free speech and academic freedom, Dayton turned an ordinary judicial hearing into the "trial of the century."

The resulting trial brought Dayton more fame, much of it negative, than the planners had bargained for. When court convened in July 1925, millions of people listened over the radio to the first trial ever broadcast. Reporters from all over the country descended on Dayton to keep their readers informed of the proceedings.

Clarence Darrow headed the defense team. A controversial criminal lawyer from Chicago, Darrow doubted the existence of God. On the other side, William Jennings Bryan, three-time Democratic candidate for president and secretary of state under Woodrow Wilson, assisted the prosecution. As a Protestant fundamentalist, Bryan believed that accepting scientific evolution would undermine the moral basis of politics and that communities should have the right to determine their children's school curriculum. A minister summed up what the fundamentalists considered to be at stake: "[Darwin's theory] breeds corruption, lust, immorality, greed, and such acts of criminal depravity as drug addiction, war, and atrocious acts of genocide."

The presiding judge, John T. Raulston, ruled that scientists could not take the stand to defend evolution because he considered their testimony "hearsay," given that they had not been present at the creation. The jury took only eight minutes to declare Scopes guilty, but his conviction was overturned by an appeals court on a technicality. Yet fundamentalists remained as certain as ever in their beliefs, and anti-evolution laws stayed in force until the 1970s. The trial had not "settled" anything. Rather, it served to highlight a cultural division over the place of religion in American society that persists to the present day.

TEACHING IDEA

Connecting the Dots

The Stanford History Education Group includes a collection of numerous free online lessons (sheg.stanford.edu). Included in the repository on this platform is a downloadable document-based lesson focusing upon the Scopes evolution trial.

TRM Suggested Responses to Questions

TRM Module 7.6 AP® Analyzing Sources Handout 5

AP® ANALYZING SOURCES

Source: Clarence Darrow and William Jennings Bryan, *Transcript from* The State of Tennessee v. John Thomas Scopes, 1925

"Q. [Mr. Darrow]. You have given considerable study to the Bible, haven't you, Mr. Bryan?
A. [Mr. Bryan]. Yes, sir, I have tried to.
Q. Then you have made a general study of it.
A. Yes, I have; I have studied the Bible for about fifty years, or sometime more than that. . . .
Q. You claim that everything in the Bible should be literally interpreted?
A. I believe everything in the Bible should be accepted as it is given there; some of the Bible is given illustratively. For instance: 'Ye are the salt of the earth.' I would not insist that man was actually salt, or that he had flesh of salt, but it is used in the sense of salt as saving God's people. . . .

(Continued)

TEACHING IDEA

AP® Central

Assign students to write a full response to the 1986 College Board U.S. History DBQ question, which is available on the College Board's past exam questions resource "AP® United States History Document-Based Questions 1973–1999" (apcentral.collegeboard.org). Note that this DBQ contains nine documents, so prior to distributing to students, the instructor may wish to remove two documents of their own choosing, in order to fully replicate the seven-document model of the current DBQ format.

Q. But when you read that Jonah swallowed the whale — or that the whale swallowed Jonah — excuse me please — how do you literally interpret that?
A. When I read that a big fish swallowed Jonah — it does not say whale.
Q. Doesn't it? Are you sure?
A. That is my recollection of it. A big fish, and I believe it, and I believe in a God who can make a whale and can make a man and can make both do what He pleases. . . .
Q. Now, you say, the big fish swallowed Jonah, and he there remained how long — three days — and then he spewed him upon the land. You believe that the big fish was made to swallow Jonah?
A. I am not prepared to say that; the Bible merely says it was done.
Q. You don't know whether it was the ordinary run of fish, or made for that purpose?
A. You may guess; you evolutionists guess. . . .
Q. You are not prepared to say whether that fish was made especially to swallow a man or not?
A. The Bible doesn't say, so I am not prepared to say. . . .
Q. But do you believe He made them — that He made such a fish and that it was big enough to swallow Jonah?
A. Yes sir. Let me add: One miracle is just as easy to believe as another. . . .
Q. Just as hard?
A. It is hard to believe for you, but easy for me. A miracle is a thing performed beyond what man can perform. When you get beyond what man can do, you get within the realm of miracles; and it is just as easy to believe the miracle of Jonah as any other miracle in the Bible."

Questions for Analysis

1. Identify Darrow's and Bryan's main arguments.
2. Describe how each supports his argument.
3. Explain how Darrow and Bryan represent different beliefs among Americans in the early twentieth century.

REVIEW

What factors contributed to the rise of fundamentalism in the 1910s and 1920s?

Immigration Restriction

Before the 1920s, anti-immigrant sentiment often reflected racial and religious bigotry, as reformers concentrated on preventing Catholics, Jews, and all non-Europeans from entering the United States. Social scientists validated these prejudices by categorizing darker-skinned immigrants as inferior races. The harshest treatment was reserved for Asians. In 1908 President Theodore Roosevelt entered into an executive agreement with Japan that reduced Japanese immigration to the United States. In 1913 the California legislature passed a statute barring Japanese immigrants from buying land, a law that twelve other states subsequently enacted.

In 1917 reformers succeeded in further restricting immigration. Congress passed legislation to ban people who could not read English or their native language from entering the country. The act also denied entry to other undesirables: "alcoholics," "feeble-minded persons," "epileptics," "people mentally or physically defective," "professional beggars," "anarchists," and "polygamists." In barring people considered unfit to enter the country, lawmakers intended to keep out those who could not support themselves and might become public wards of the state and, in the case of anarchists and polygamists, those who threatened the nation's political and religious values.

Prohibition reflected the surge in nativist (anti-immigrant) and racist thinking that in many ways revealed long-standing fears. In the past, temperance reform was aimed at immigrants. The end of World War I brought a new wave of Catholic and Jewish emigration from eastern and southern Europe, triggering religious prejudice among Protestants. Just as immigrants had been

AP® TIP

Compare the developments that spurred the rise in nativism during the early twentieth century with those that led to the formation of the American Party (also known as the Know-Nothing Party) during the 1840s.

APPLY THE TIP

Task students with completing a chart comparing the foundational reasons for the fears of immigrants in the 1840s and in the 1920s.

TRM Find **Handout 7.7 – Comparing Nativist Fears of the 1840s and 1920s** in the Teacher's Resource Materials.

Sacco and Vanzetti case 1920 case in which Nicola Sacco and Bartolomeo Vanzetti were convicted of robbery and murder. The trial centered on the defendants' foreign birth and political views, rather than the facts pertaining to their guilt or innocence.

linked to socialism and anarchism in the 1880s and 1890s, old-stock Americans associated these immigrants with immoral behavior and political radicalism and saw them as a threat to traditional U.S. culture and values. Moreover, as in the late nineteenth century, native-born workers saw immigrants as a source of cheap labor that threatened their jobs and wages.

The **Sacco and Vanzetti case** provides the most dramatic evidence of this nativism. In 1920 a botched robbery in South Braintree, Massachusetts resulted in the murder of two employees. Police charged Nicola Sacco and Bartolomeo Vanzetti with the crime. These two Italian immigrants shared radical political views as anarchists and World War I draft evaders. The subsequent trial revolved around their foreign birth and ideology more than the facts pertaining to their guilt or innocence. The presiding judge at the trial referred to the accused as "anarchistic bastards" and "damned dagos" (a derogatory term for "Italians"). Convicted and sentenced to death, Sacco and Vanzetti lost their appeals for a new trial. Criticism of the verdict came from all over the world. Workers in Mexico, Argentina, Uruguay, France, and Morocco organized vigils and held rallies in solidarity with the condemned men. Despite such support, the two men were executed in the electric chair in 1927.

The Sacco and Vanzetti case provides an extreme example of 1920s nativism, but the anti-immigrant views that contributed to the two men's conviction and execution were commonplace during the period and shared by Americans across the social spectrum. For example, Henry Ford saw immigrants as a threat to cherished traditions. Ford believed that immigrants were the cause of a decline in U.S. morality. He contended that aliens did not understand "the principles which have made our [native] civilization," and he blamed the influx of foreigners for society's "marked deterioration" during the 1920s. He stirred up anti-immigrant prejudices mainly by targeting Jews. Believing that an international Jewish conspiracy was attempting to subvert non-Jewish societies, Ford serialized in his company newspaper the so-called *Protocols of the Elders of Zion*, an antisemitic text concocted in czarist Russia to justify pogroms — ethnically and religiously motivated attacks — against Jews. Ford continued to publish it even after the document was proved a fake.

National Origins Act 1924 act establishing immigration quotas by national origin. It was intended to severely limit immigration from southern and eastern Europe as well as halt all immigration from East Asia.

Ford joined other nativists in supporting legislation to restrict immigration. In 1924 Congress passed the **National Origins Act**, a quota system on future immigration. The measure limited entry by any foreign group to 2 percent of the number of people of that nationality who resided in the United States in 1890. The statute's authors were interested primarily in curbing immigration from eastern and southern Europe. They chose 1890 as the benchmark for immigration because most newcomers from those two regions entered the United States after that year. Quotas established for northern Europe went unfilled, while those for southern and eastern Europe could not accommodate the vast number of people who sought admission. The law continued to bar East Asian immigration altogether. However, immigration from Mexico and elsewhere in the Western Hemisphere was exempted from the quotas of the Nation Origins Act because farmers in the Southwest needed Mexican laborers to tend their crops and pressured the government to excuse them from coverage. In a related measure, in 1924 Congress established the Border Patrol to control the flow of undocumented immigration from Mexico. Nevertheless, *legal* immigration to the United States from Mexico increased during the 1920s.

AP® TIP
Be sure to take note of the significance of the introduction of the idea of legal and illegal immigration during the 1920s.

With immigration of those considered "undesirable" severely if not completely curtailed, some nativist reformers shifted their attention to Americanization, which developed into one of the largest social and political movements in American history. Speaking about immigrants, educator E. P. Cubberly said, "Our task is to break up their groups and settlements, to assimilate and amalgamate these people as a part of our American race, to implant in their children the northern-European conception of righteousness, law and order, and popular government." Business corporations conducted Americanization and naturalization classes on factory floors. Schools, patriotic societies, fraternal organizations, women's groups, and labor unions launched citizenship classes.

In the Southwest and on the West Coast, white people aimed their Americanization efforts at the growing population of Mexican Americans. Subject to segregated education, Mexican Americans were expected to speak English in their classes. Anglo school administrators and teachers generally believed that Mexican Americans were suited only for farmwork and manual trades. For Mexican Americans, therefore, Americanization meant vocational training and preparation for low-status, low-wage jobs.

BUILDING AP® SKILLS

Claims and Evidence in Sources

Assign students to read and annotate one of two primary source materials on the Sacco and Vanzetti trial:

■ Frank Goodwyn's speech, "Sacco-Vanzetti and the Red Peril," available as an online resource by searching the Michigan State University Library's website (lib.msu.edu).

■ Felix Frankfurter's article from the March, 1927 issue of *The Atlantic Magazine*, "The Case of Sacco and Vanzetti" (theatlantic.com).

Divide the class into groups of four the next day, with two persons from each article assignment in the quad, and engage in miniature roundtable and peer teaching discussion, with the instructor floating between all the groups.

TEACHING IDEA

Incorporating Primary Sources

The Stanford History Education Group includes a collection of numerous free online lessons (sheg.stanford.edu). Included in the repository on this platform is a downloadable lesson focusing upon historical argument and Mexican immigration in the 1920s.

American Indians fared little better. During World War I, to save money the federal government had ceased appropriating funds for public health programs aimed at benefiting American Indians living on reservations. With the war over, the government failed to restore the funds. Throughout the 1920s, rates of tuberculosis, eye infections, and infant mortality spiked among the American Indian population. Boarding schools continued to promote menial service jobs for American Indian students. On the brighter side, in 1924, Congress passed the **Indian Citizenship Act** granting citizenship and the right to vote to all American Indians. Nevertheless, most remained outside the economic and political mainstream of American society with meager government help.

Chinese residents also continued to face discrimination and segregation. The Chinese Exclusion Act remained in operation, making it difficult for nurturing family life. By 1920, Chinese men outnumbered Chinese women by seven to one. Furthermore, immigration restrictions prohibited Chinese workingmen from bringing their wives into the country. The 1924 Immigration Act made matters worse by banning all Asian women from entering the country. That same year the Supreme Court upheld the segregation of Chinese children in public schools.

Chinese communities faced problems similar to those experienced by other ethnic groups. Tensions developed between those born in China and their American-born children over assimilation. One Chinese American who grew up in San Francisco noted, "There was endless discussion about what to do about the dilemma of being *caught in between*." Many Chinese parents prohibited their children from speaking English at home and sent them to Chinese-language schools after public school. Chinese American children found cultural preservation efforts an onerous burden as they increasingly partook in America's growing consumer culture.

Despite attempts at Americanization, ethnic groups did not dissolve into a melting pot and lose their cultural identities. First-generation Americans — the children of immigrants — learned English, enjoyed American popular culture, and dressed in fashions of the day. Yet in cities around the country where immigrants had settled, ethnic enclaves remained intact and preserved the religious practices and social customs of their residents.

REVIEW

- What was the connection between anti-immigrant sentiment and the defense of tradition during the 1920s?

The Resurrection of the Ku Klux Klan

Nativism received its most spectacular boost from the reemergence of the Ku Klux Klan in 1915. Originally an organization dedicated to terrorizing emancipated African Americans and their white Republican allies in the South during Reconstruction, the KKK branched out during the 1920s to the North, Midwest, and West. In addition to black people, the new Klan targeted Catholics and Jews, and immigrants, as well as anyone who was alleged to have violated community moral values or supported the teaching of evolutionary theory. The organization consisted of a cross section of native-born Protestants primarily from the middle and working classes who sought to reverse a perceived decline in their social and economic power. Revived by W. J. Simmons, a former Methodist minister, the new Klan celebrated its founding at Stone Mountain, Georgia, near Atlanta. There, Klansmen bowed to the twin symbols of their cause, the American flag and a burning cross that represented their fiery determination to stand up for their vision of Christian morality and against all those considered "un-American." People flocked to the new KKK, and by the mid-1920s, Klan membership totaled more than three million men and women. Not confined to rural areas, the revived Klan counted a significant following in cities such as Indianapolis, Detroit, Chicago, Denver, Portland, and Seattle. Many rural dwellers who had moved into cities with large numbers of black migrants and recent immigrants found solace in Klan vows to preserve "Native, white, Protestant supremacy."

The phenomenal growth of the KKK in the 1920s resulted from the desire to reestablish traditional values as well as sheer hostility toward black people and immigrants. In the face of challenges to conventional values, a changing sexual morality, and the flaunting of prohibition,

---

TEACHING IDEA

AP® Central

Assign students in small groups to analyze the 1973 College Board AP® U.S. History DBQ, which is available on the College Board's past exam questions resource "AP® United States History Document-Based Questions 1973–1999" (apcentral.collegeboard.org). Have students utilize their HIPP training (a refresher of HIPP can be found on page 8). Note that this DBQ consists of eleven documents, so it is not advisable to attempt to task students with writing a full response to the prompt, but creation of a thesis statement with contextualization is fully viable as a class activity.

TEACHING IDEA

Connecting the Dots

Engage the class in an activity of association by disassociation called "Odd One Out." Write the following terms on the board/projector:

- Indian Citizenship Act
- The Lost Generation
- United Negro Improvement Association (U.N.I.A.)
- The Scopes Trial
- Ku Klux Klan

Then place students in small groups and ask them, "Which one is the odd one out and why? How do the remaining terms relate?" Give students approximately 7-10 minutes to complete this part, then share out student answers and discuss their conclusions and reasoning as a whole-class activity. There is no specific correct answer; the goal is to get students thinking in categorical habits of mind and defending their rationales.

wives joined their husbands as devoted followers. Some Protestant women appreciated the Klan's message condemning abusive husbands and fathers and the group's affirmation of the status of white Protestant women as the embodiment of virtue. Nevertheless, the dominant principles of the resurgent KKK remained explicitly aggressive toward minority groups.

Like the original Klan, its successor employed terror tactics. Acting under cover of darkness and concealed in robes and hoods, Klansmen burned crosses to scare their victims, many of whom they beat, kidnapped, tortured, and murdered. To gain greater legitimacy and to appeal to a wider audience, the Klan also participated in electoral politics. The KKK succeeded in electing governors in Georgia and Oregon, a U.S. senator from Texas, numerous state legislators, and other officials in California, Indiana, Michigan, Ohio, and Oklahoma. Politicians routinely joined the Klan to advance their careers, whether they shared its views or not.

However, in 1925, the KKK's self-proclaimed role as guardians of morality was undermined by a scandal. David Curtiss Stephenson, who had been Grand Dragon of the Indiana KKK since 1923, was accused of kidnapping and raping Madge Oberholtzer, a representative of the Young People's Reading Circle, an office in the state's Department of Public Instruction that promoted literacy. Oberholtzer ultimately died of the wounds she received from Stephenson's assault on her. After Stephenson was convicted of second-degree murder in Oberholtzer's death, he hoped for a pardon from the governor of Indiana, Edward L. Jackson, who had expressed sympathy for the KKK. However, when no pardon was forthcoming from the governor, Stephenson began to provide the Indiana press with salacious details of bribes the KKK had offered to Indiana state officials, including Governor Jackson, which led to further arrests and convictions of both state officials and members of the KKK. Needless to say, these events made the Klan's claims to moral integrity suspect, and helped cause their declining membership through the late 1920s.

> **AP® TIP**
> Evaluate the extent of similarity between the goals, tactics, and political influence of the KKK during the 1920s with those of the KKK during Reconstruction.

AP® ANALYZING SOURCES

Source: Gerald W. Johnson, "The Ku Kluxer," *American Mercury*, 1924

"The Ku Klux Klan was swept beyond the racial boundaries of the Negro and flourishes now in the Middle West because it is a perfect expression of the American idea that the voice of the people is the voice of God. The belief that the average klansman is consciously affected by an appeal to his baser self is altogether erroneous. In the voice of the organizer he hears a clarion call to knightly and selfless service. It strikes him as in no wise strange that he should be so summoned; is he not, as an American citizen, of the nobility? Politics has been democratized. Social usage has been democratized. Religion has been most astoundingly democratized. Why, then, not democratize chivalry?

The klansman has already been made, in his own estimation, politically a monarch, socially a peer of the realm, spiritually a high priest. Now the Ku Klux Klan calls him to step up and for the trifling consideration of ten dollars he is made a Roland, a Lancelot, a knight-errant vowed to the succor of the oppressed, the destruction of ogres and magicians, the defense of the faith. Bursting with noble ideals and lofty aspirations, he accepts the nomination. The trouble is that this incantation doesn't work, as none of the others has worked, except in his imagination. King, aristocrat, high priest as he believes himself to be, he is neither royal, noble, nor holy. So, under his white robe and pointed hood he becomes not a Chevalier Bayard[1] but a thug."

[1] A French knight who lived during the late fifteenth and early sixteenth centuries. He was known for being virtuous and fearless.

Questions for Analysis
1. Describe how the article characterizes the Klansman in the first paragraph.
2. Describe how the article critiques this characterization in the second paragraph.
3. Explain how this article mocks the Ku Klux Klan.

(Continued)

APPLY THE TIP

Divide students into three groups, and provide all groups with a chart template. Further divide the thirds into pairs of students. Assign each pair, based upon their original third, one of the following topics for their chart of comparison between the Reconstruction KKK and the 1920s KKK: either "Goals," "Tactics," or "Political Influence." Assign pairs to complete their respective charts. Next, have the original one-third groupings re-convene to collaborate and share with regard to their specific material. Then, reshuffle the class into groups of three, with one member from each of the original thirds, and have the triads teach and share out their products.

TRM Find **Handout 7.8 – Charting Changes Within the Ku Klux Klan** in the Teacher's Resource Materials.

TRM **Suggested Responses to Questions**

TRM **Module 7.6 AP® Analyzing Sources Handout 6**

TEACHING IDEA

Making Connections

Have the students complete a "Six Degrees of Separation" activity. The prompt for this particular activity is as follows:

"From the Chinese Exclusion Act of 1882 to the National Origins Act of 1924."

For the purpose of this exercise, students are given two events spanning time, but related by their theme. They must select four events in chronological order that link the first event in the series with the last. They will write the name of each selected event, and create an argument to support each of the events they selected. Explain to them that they must answer the question, "Why does it belong as a link in your chain of events?" for each link. Students must emphasize both cause and effect and/or demonstrate continuity or change over time in the linking. This can be done as either a formative assessment in class, or a homework assignment involving student research of their textbooks, activities/lessons, lecture notes, and knowledge of the time period.

TEACHING IDEA

Differing Views

Assign students to read the pair of Analyzing Sources on pages 631–632, and answer the accompanying questions for homework. The next day in class, have students share their responses in groups of two or three. Then, have these groups synthesize these two documents with "If We Must Die" on page 626 and "How It Feels to Be Colored Me" on page 624, searching for continuities and contradictions between the four sources with regards to the AP® themes of American and national identity, politics and power, and/or social structures. Students can be tasked with addressing all three themes in their integration of the source documents, or they may be assigned a specific theme to contend with, depending upon the instructor's preferences.

TEACHING IDEA

Differing Views

Assign students to analyze the "Women of the Ku Klux Klan" source on this page in comparison with the pair of World War I posters on page 604, the *Muller v. Oregon* decision on page 558, and the "Suffrage Campaign" photograph on page 561. Task students with deconstructing all sources utilizing their HIPP training, and then comparing what the sources' messages are concerning the identities, abilities, and roles of women in American society (a refresher of HIPP can be found on page 8).

Source: *Women of the Ku Klux Klan*, 1927

"Objects and Purposes"

SECTION 1. The objects of this Order shall be to unite white female persons, native-born Gentile citizens of the United States of America, who owe no allegiance of any nature or degree to any foreign government, nation, institution, sect, ruler, person, or people; whose morals are good; whose reputations and vocations are respectable; whose habits are exemplary; who are of sound minds and 18 years or more of age, under a common oath into a Sisterhood of strict regulation, to cultivate and promote patriotism toward our Civil Government; to practice an honorable clannishness toward each other; to exemplify a practical benevolence; to shield the sanctity of the home and the chastity of womanhood; to maintain forever white supremacy; to teach and faithfully inculcate a high spiritual philosophy through an exalted ritualism, and by a practical devotion to conserve, protect, and maintain the distinctive institutions, rights, privileges, principles, traditions, and ideals of a pure Americanism."

Questions for Analysis

1. Identify the characteristics of a Ku Klux Klan member, according to this excerpt.
2. Describe the goals of the Ku Klux Klan, according to this excerpt.
3. Explain how this excerpt hides the racial violence at the core of the Klan's ideology.

Questions for Comparison

1. Identify the differences in how each document characterizes the Ku Klux Klan.
2. Explain the ways in which changes in American society during the 1920s shaped these differences.

REVIEW

How did nativism foster the reemergence of the Ku Klux Klan during the 1920s?

Politics and the Fading of Prosperity

AP® TIP
Analyze how racism and nativism shaped the outcome of the election of 1924.

The 1924 presidential election exposed serious fault lines within the Democratic Party. Since Reconstruction, Democrats had dominated the South, and Republicans ceased to compete for office in the region. Southern Democrats shared fundamentalist religious beliefs and support for prohibition that usually placed them at odds with big-city Democrats. The northern urban wing of the party also represented immigrants who rejected prohibition as contrary to their cultural practices. These distinctions, however, were not absolute — some rural dwellers opposed prohibition, and some urbanites supported temperance.

Delegates to the 1924 Democratic convention in New York City disagreed over a party platform and a presidential candidate. When northeastern urban delegates attempted to insert a plank condemning the Ku Klux Klan for its intolerance, they lost by a thin margin. The sizable number of convention delegates who either belonged to or had been backed by the Klan ensured the proposal's defeat.

The selection of the presidential ticket proved even more divisive. Urban Democrats favored New York governor Alfred E. Smith. Smith came from an Irish Catholic immigrant family, had grown up on New York City's Lower East Side, and was sponsored by the Tammany Hall machine. The epitome of everything that rural Democrats despised, Smith also denounced prohibition. After a fierce contest, the pride of New York City lost the nomination to John W. Davis, a West Virginia Protestant and a defender of prohibition. Left deeply divided going into the general election, Davis lost to Calvin Coolidge in a landslide (Map 7.6).

In 1928, however, when the Democrats met in Houston, Texas, the delicate cultural equilibrium within the Democratic Party had shifted in favor of the urban forces. With Stephenson and the Klan discredited and no longer a force in Democratic politics, the delegates nominated Al Smith as their presidential candidate.

Politics and the Fading of Prosperity

Period 7: 1890–1945

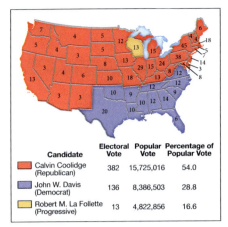

MAP 7.6 The Election of 1924 Republican Calvin Coolidge, who became president in August 1923 on the death of Warren Harding, continued Harding's policies of limited government regulation and corporate tax cuts. Coolidge easily defeated Democrat John Davis, whose strength was confined to the South. Running as the Progressive Party candidate, Senator Robert La Follette won 16 percent of the popular vote but carried only his home state of Wisconsin, with 13 electoral votes. **What do these election results reveal about public support for progressive reform in the 1920s?**

Candidate	Electoral Vote	Popular Vote	Percentage of Popular Vote
Calvin Coolidge (Republican)	382	15,725,016	54.0
John W. Davis (Democrat)	136	8,386,503	28.8
Robert M. La Follette (Progressive)	13	4,822,856	16.6

The Republicans selected Herbert Hoover, one of the most popular men in the United States. Affectionately called "the Great Humanitarian" for his European relief efforts after World War I, Hoover served as secretary of commerce during the Harding and Coolidge administrations. His name became synonymous with the Republican prosperity of the 1920s. In accepting his party's nomination for president in 1928, Hoover optimistically declared: "We in America today are nearer to the final triumph over poverty than ever before in the history of the land." A Protestant supporter of prohibition from a small town, Hoover was everything Smith was not.

The outcome of the election proved predictable. Hoover trounced Smith with 58 percent of the popular vote and more than 80 percent of the electoral vote. Despite the weakening economy, Smith lost usually reliable Democratic votes to religious and ethnic prejudices. The New Yorker prevailed only in Massachusetts, Rhode Island, and six southern states but failed to win his home state. A closer look at the election returns showed a significant party realignment under way. Smith succeeded in identifying the Democratic Party with urban, ethnic-minority voters and attracting them to the polls. Despite the landslide loss, he captured the twelve largest cities in the nation, all of which had gone Republican four years earlier. In another fifteen big cities, Smith did better than the Democrat ticket had done in the 1924 election. To break the Republicans' national dominance, the Democrats would need a candidate who appealed to both traditional and modern Americans. Smith's defeat, however, laid the foundation for future Democratic political success.

The Democrats and Republicans were not the only parties that attracted voters in the 1920s. Some voters continued to cast their ballot for the Socialist Party. Others took the opportunity to voice their disapproval of Republican policies by voting for the remaining progressive candidates. Progressives did manage to hold on to seats in Congress, and in 1921 they helped pass the Shepherd-Towner Act (see Module 7-1), which appropriated federal funds to establish maternal and child centers. Senator Thomas J. Walsh of Montana, a progressive Democrat, led the investigation into the Teapot Dome scandal. But their efforts to restrict the power of the Supreme Court, reduce tax cuts for the wealthy, nationalize railroads, and extend agricultural relief to farmers were rebuffed by conservative legislative majorities. In 1924 reformers nominated Senator Robert M. La Follette of Wisconsin to run for president on a revived Progressive Party ticket, but he came in a distant third. The Progressive Party collapsed soon after La Follette died in 1925.

Still, progressivism managed to stay alive on the local and state levels. Gifford Pinchot, a Roosevelt ally and a champion of conservation, twice won election as governor of Pennsylvania starting in 1922. Social workers continued their efforts to alleviate urban poverty and lobby for government assistance to the poor. Even at the national level, women in the Children's Bureau maintained the progressive legacy by supporting assistance to families and devising social welfare proposals. Progressivism did not disappear during the 1920s, but it did fight an uphill and often losing battle during an age of conservative political ascendancy. Its weakness contributed to the government's failure to check the worst corporate and financial practices, a failure that would play a role in the nation's economic collapse.

REVIEW

- How did divisions within the Democratic Party contribute to Republican victories in the 1920s?
- In what ways did progressive reforms continue to influence American politics during the 1920s?

TEACHING IDEA

Incorporating Videos

Show the students excerpts from the PBS documentary, *Prohibition*, Episode 3, approximately 39 minutes. This details the prohibition movement from its pinnacle to its ultimate repeal (pbs.org).

BUILDING AP® SKILLS

Sourcing and Situation

Assign students to read and annotate excerpts of Hiram Evans's speech, "The Klan's Fight for Americanism," available by title search on the Michigan State University Department of History's website (history.msu.edu). The next day, engage in a whole-class discussion, to include addressing the following questions:

- "Who is an American? Who should be?"
- "What, according to this piece, are the virtues of being not 'intellectualized'?"
- "How is the term 'Native American' used in his speech? Is there irony in this?"

Period 7: 1890–1945

MODULE 7-6 The Transitional 1920s

TRM Suggested Responses to Questions

TEACHING IDEA

AP® Writing Historically Workshop

This DBQ has the broad element of "change in American society" from which students need to develop categories of analysis. Have students bring in seven note cards and number them from 1 to 7, which correspond to the documents in the question. In groups of four, pass out envelopes with the following labels: race, consumerism, innovation, cultural tension. Have students select an envelope and then place the numbers they think are relevant to the category on the envelope. Encourage students to have structured debate or discussion among themselves as they make their decisions.

AP® WRITING HISTORICALLY — Document-Based Question Practice

ACTIVITY

The following question is based on the accompanying documents. The documents have been edited for the purpose of this exercise. *Suggested reading period: 15 minutes. Suggested writing time: 45 minutes.*

Evaluate the extent of change in American society during the 1920s.

DOCUMENT 1

Source: Marcus Garvey, *Address to the Second United Negro Improvement Association (UNIA) Convention*, 1921

"Just take your idea from the last bloody war, wherein a race was pitted against itself (for the whole white races united as one from a common origin), the members of which, on both sides, fought so tenaciously that they killed off each other in frightful, staggering numbers. If a race pitted against itself could fight so tenaciously to kill itself without mercy, can you imagine the fury, can you imagine the mercilessness, the terribleness of the war that will come when all the races of the world will be on the battlefield, engaged in deadly combat for the destruction or overthrow of the one or the other, when beneath it and as a cause of it lies prejudice and hatred? Truly, it will be an ocean of blood; that is all it will be. So that if I can sound a note of warning now that will echo and reverberate around the world and thus prevent such conflict, God help me to do it; for Africa, like Europe, like Asia, is preparing for the day."

DOCUMENT 2

Source: Sinclair Lewis, *Babbit*, 1922

"Just as he was an Elk, a Booster, a member of the Chamber of Commerce, just as the priests of the Presbyterian Church determined his every religious belief, and the senators who controlled the Republican Party decided in little smoky rooms in Washington what he should think about disarmament, tariff, and Germany, so did the large national advertisers fix the surface of his life, fix what he believed to be his individuality. These standard advertised wares—toothpastes, socks, tires, cameras, instantaneous hot-water-heaters—were his symbols and proofs of excellence; at first the signs, then the substitutes, for joy and passion and wisdom."

DOCUMENT 3

Source: *Blood and Sand* (film advertisement), 1922

DOCUMENT 4

Source: *Edythe Turnham and Her Knights of Syncopation*, Seattle, Washington, 1925

DOCUMENT 5

Source: Clarence Darrow and William Jennings Bryan, *Transcript from* The State of Tennessee v. John Thomas Scopes, 1925

"Q. [Mr. Darrow]. You have given considerable study to the Bible, haven't you, Mr. Bryan?
A. [Mr. Bryan]. Yes, sir, I have tried to.
Q. Then you have made a general study of it.
A. Yes, I have; I have studied the Bible for about fifty years, or sometime more than that, but, of course, I have studied it more as I have become older than when I was but a boy.
Q. You claim that everything in the Bible should be literally interpreted?
A. I believe everything in the Bible should be accepted as it is given there; some of the Bible is given illustratively. For instance: 'Ye are the salt of the earth.' I would not insist that man was actually salt, or that he had flesh of salt, but it is used in the sense of salt as saving God's people. . . .
Q. But when you read that Jonah swallowed the whale—or that the whale swallowed Jonah—excuse me please—how do you literally interpret that?
A. When I read that a big fish swallowed Jonah—it does not say whale.
Q. Doesn't it? Are you sure?
A. That is my recollection of it. A big fish, and I believe it, and I believe in a God who can make a whale and can make a man and can make both do what He pleases. . . .
Q. Now, you say, the big fish swallowed Jonah, and he there remained how long—three days—and then he spewed him upon the land. You believe that the big fish was made to swallow Jonah?
A. I am not prepared to say that; the Bible merely says it was done.
Q. You don't know whether it was the ordinary run of fish, or made for that purpose?
A. You may guess; you evolutionists guess.
Q. But when we do guess, we have a sense to guess right.
A. But do not do it often.
Q. You are not prepared to say whether that fish was made especially to swallow a man or not?
A. The Bible doesn't say, so I am not prepared to say. . . .
Q. But do you believe He made them—that He made such a fish and that it was big enough to swallow Jonah?
A. Yes sir. Let me add: One miracle is just as easy to believe as another. . . .
Q. Just as hard?
A. It is hard to believe for you, but easy for me. A miracle is a thing performed beyond what man can perform. When you get beyond what man can do, you get within the realm of miracles; and it is just as easy to believe the miracle of Jonah as any other miracle in the Bible.
Q. Perfectly easy to believe that Jonah swallowed the whale?

(Continued)

A. If the Bible said so; the Bible doesn't make as extreme statements as evolutionists do.
Q. That may be a question, Mr. Bryan, about some of those you have known?
A. The only thing is, you have a definition of fact that includes imagination.
Q. And you have a definition that excludes everything but imagination?
Gen. Stewart [attorney general]. I object to that as argumentative. . . .
Mr. Darrow. The Witness must not argue with me, either."

DOCUMENT 6

Source: *Women of the Ku Klux Klan*, 1927

"Objects and Purposes

SECTION 1. The objects of this Order shall be to unite white female persons, native-born Gentile citizens of the United States of America, who owe no allegiance of any nature or degree to any foreign government, nation, institution, sect, ruler, person, or people; whose morals are good; whose reputations and vocations are respectable; whose habits are exemplary; who are of sound minds and 18 years or more of age, under a common oath into a Sisterhood of strict regulation, to cultivate and promote patriotism toward our Civil Government; to practice an honorable clannishness toward each other; to exemplify a practical benevolence; to shield the sanctity of the home and the chastity of womanhood; to maintain forever white supremacy; to teach and faithfully inculcate a high spiritual philosophy through an exalted ritualism, and by a practical devotion to conserve, protect, and maintain the distinctive institutions, rights, privileges, principles, traditions, and ideals of a pure Americanism.

SEC. 2. To create and maintain an institution by which the present and succeeding generations shall commemorate the great sacrifice, chivalric service, and imperishable achievements of the Ku Klux Klan and the Women of the Reconstruction period of American History, to the end that justice and honor be done the sacred memory of those who wrought through our mystic society during that period, and that their valiant accomplishments be not lost to posterity; to perpetuate their faithful courage, noble spirit, peerless principles, and faultless ideals; to hold sacred and make effective their spiritual purpose in this and future generations, that they be rightly vindicated before the world by a revelation of the whole truth."

DOCUMENT 7

Source: *The Brox Sisters Listening to the Radio*, c. 1925

Module 7-7

Economic Instability and Depression

LEARNING TARGETS
By the end of this module, you should be able to:
- Explain how the United States continued to transition from a rural, agricultural economy to an urban, industrial economy.
- Explain why the Great Depression led to calls for a stronger financial regulatory system.

THEMATIC FOCUS
Work, Exchange, and Technology
Politics and Power
Social Structures

The seeming prosperity of the 1920s was built on credit, consumerism, and an ever-rising stock market. However, as in other eras in United States history, this economic boom was followed by an economic bust. The Great Depression of the 1930s shook many Americans' confidence in the ability of capitalism to maintain economic prosperity and led to financial strains that cut across American society.

HISTORICAL REASONING FOCUS
Causation

TASK ▶ While reading this section, consider the causes of the Great Depression, its effects, and attempts by local and federal officials to counteract those effects.

TRM Suggested Responses to Questions

Black Tuesday October 29, 1929, crash of the U.S. stock market. This event has historically marked the beginning of the Great Depression, though it was not the depression's root cause.

On October 29, 1929, a day that became known as **Black Tuesday**, stock market prices tumbled. Over the previous five years, the rising market, bolstered by optimistic buyers, earned huge profits for investors, and the value of stocks nearly doubled. In late October, panicked sellers sent stock prices into free fall. Although only 2.5 percent of Americans owned stock, the stock market collapse had an enormous impact on the economy and the rest of the world. Because so much of the stock boom depended on generous margin requirements (a down payment of only 5 to 10 percent), when investor-borrowers got caught short by falling prices, they could not repay the financial institutions that had extended them credit. Banks and lending agencies, with their interlocking management and overextension of credit, had difficulty withstanding the turmoil unleashed by the tumbling stock market.

Financial Crash

Great Depression Worldwide economic collapse caused by overproduction and financial speculation. It affected the United States from October of 1929 until the start of World War II in 1939.

The 1929 crash did not cause the decade-long **Great Depression** that followed. The seeds for the greatest economic catastrophe in U.S. history had been planted earlier. The causes stemmed from flaws in an economic system that produced a great disparity of wealth, inadequate consumption, overextension of credit both at home and abroad, and the government's unwillingness to relieve the plight of farmers. Republican administrations made matters worse by lowering taxes on the rich and raising tariffs to benefit manufacturers. The Federal Reserve Board worsened the situation by keeping interest rates high, thereby making it difficult for people to get loans and repay debts. The failure was not that of the United States alone; the depression affected capitalist nations throughout the world. The stock market collapse crushed the American public's

TEACHING IDEA

Incorporating Videos

Prior to introducing this module, assign students to view the first 30 minutes of the PBS documentary, *Landslide: A Portrait of President Herbert Hoover* (available on YouTube). This can also be used in conjunction with the note at the bottom of the page as a foundational activity.

BUILDING AP® SKILLS

Contextualization

Assign students to read and annotate Herbert Hoover's 1928 campaign speech, "Rugged Individualism," which is available on Digital History's website (digitalhistory.uh.edu). In a whole-class discussion the following day, pose the following question to students, among others: "Do the times make the person, or does the person make the times?"

Period 7: 1890–1945

MODULE 7-7 Economic Instability and Depression

confidence that the unfettered law of supply and demand and laissez-faire economics could ensure prosperity.

Herbert Hoover had the unenviable task of assuming the presidency in 1929 as the economy crumbled. Given his long history of public service, he seemed the right man for the job. Hoover, however, was unwilling to make a fundamental break with conventional economic approaches and proved unable to effectively communicate his genuine concern for the plight of the poor. Despite his sincere efforts, the depression deepened. As this happened, many Americans, made desperate by their economic plight and angered by the inadequate response of their government, took to the streets in protest.

National prosperity was at its apparent peak when the Republican Hoover entered the White House in March 1929. Hoover brought to the presidency a blend of traditional and progressive ideas. He believed that government and business should form voluntary partnerships to work toward common goals. Rejecting the principle of absolute laissez-faire, he nonetheless argued that the government should extend its influence lightly over the economy — to encourage and persuade sensible behavior, but not to impose itself on the private sector. In a notable exception, Hoover championed the 1929 **Agricultural Marketing Act**, a measure that aimed to raise prices for long-suffering farmers by having the government buy up farm surpluses.

The Great Depression sorely tested Hoover's beliefs. Having placed his faith more in cooperation rather than coercion, the president relied on voluntarism to get the nation through hard economic times. Hoover hoped that management and labor, through gentle persuasion, would hold steady on prices and wages. In the meantime, for those in dire need, the president turned to local communities and private charities. Hoover expected municipal and state governments to shoulder the burden of providing relief to the needy, just as they had during previous economic downturns.

Hoover's remedies failed to rally the country back to good economic health. Initially, businesspeople responded positively to the president's request to maintain the status quo, but when the economy did not bounce back, they lost confidence and defected. Nor did local governments and private agencies have the funds to provide relief to all those who needed it. With tax revenues in decline, some 1,300 municipalities across the country had gone bankrupt by 1933. Benevolent societies and religious groups could handle short-term misfortunes, but they could not cope with the ongoing disaster of mass unemployment.

As confidence in recovery fell and the economy sank deeper into depression, President Hoover shifted direction. He persuaded Congress to lower income tax rates and to allocate an unprecedented $423 million for federal public works projects.

Hoover's recovery efforts fell short, however. He retreated from initiating greater spending because he feared government deficits more than unemployment. With federal accounting sheets showing a rising deficit, Hoover reversed course in 1932 and joined with Congress in sharply raising income, estate, and corporate taxes on the wealthy. This effectively slowed down investment and new production, throwing millions more American workers out of jobs. The **Hawley-Smoot Act**, passed by Congress in 1930, made matters worse. In an effort to replenish revenues and protect American farmers and companies from foreign competition, the act increased tariffs on agricultural and industrial imports. However, other countries retaliated by lifting their import duties, which hurt American companies because it diminished demand for American exports.

In an exception to his aversion to spending, Hoover lobbied Congress to create the **Reconstruction Finance Corporation (RFC)** to supply loans to troubled banks, railroads, and insurance companies. By injecting federal dollars into these critical enterprises, the president and lawmakers expected to produce dividends that would trickle down from the top of the economic structure to the bottom. In 1932 Congress gave the RFC a budget of $1.5 billion to employ people in public works projects, a significant allocation for those individuals hardest hit by the depression.

This notable departure from Republican economic philosophy failed to reach its goal. The RFC spent its budget too cautiously, and its funds reached primarily those institutions that could best afford to repay the loans, ignoring the companies in the greatest difficulty. Wealth never trickled down. Although Hoover was not indifferent to the plight of others, he was incapable of breaking away from his ideological preconceptions. He refused to support expenditures for direct relief

BUILDING AP® SKILLS

Comparison

Assign students to compare the causes of the Panic of 1893 and the Great Depression of 1929. Task students with formulating their conclusions into a "Fifty-Word Drill" product, along with the first topic sentence of each body paragraph, to form a skeletal pre-write of a full LEQ prompt.

TEACHING IDEA

Understanding Economic Changes

Assign students in small groups to utilize their text and outside sources from online search to research the causes of the Great Depression. Have them then rank their causes in order of importance, along with rationales for their rank orders. Then have students present their listings and rationales to the class, and allow discussion time for each presentation.

TEACHING IDEA

Incorporating Videos

Assign students to watch Episode 33, "The Great Depression," from the Crash Course US History series (available on YouTube). Use this 14-minute episode as a concise formative content introduction for students to the initial major issues and events of Module 7-7 as part of preparation for either assessment or reinforcement.

AP® TIP
Evaluate the extent to which the Hoover administration's policies were successful in addressing both economic and cultural issues during the early years of the Great Depression.

Reconstruction Finance Corporation (RFC) Government corporation endorsed by Herbert Hoover and created by Congress. It provided federal support through loans to troubled banks, railroads, and insurance companies under the belief that the economic benefits would trickle down from the top of the economic structure to the bottom.

TEACHING IDEA

Check for Understanding

Make sure to point out to students that the characterization of Hoover as a "do-nothing" president in the face of the depression is inaccurate. The Reconstruction Finance Corporation represented a major insertion of the federal government into the economy. That being said, note that the RFC aided institutions such as banks and corporations; as a true believer in the power of the individual to shape his or her own destiny, Hoover could not bring himself to provide direct aid to American citizens, which he considered as something that would cripple them rather than help them in the long run. As a result, he was willing to, and did, pay the full political price for his principles.

(what today we call welfare) and hesitated to extend assistance for work relief because he believed that it would ruin individual initiative and character.

Hoover and the United States did not face the Great Depression alone; it was a worldwide calamity. By 1933 Germany, France, and Great Britain were all facing mass unemployment. In this climate of extreme social and economic unrest, authoritarian dictators came to power in a number of European countries, including Germany, Italy, Spain, and Portugal. Each claimed that his country's social and economic problems could be solved only by placing power in the hands of a single, all-powerful leader.

REVIEW

- How did Herbert Hoover attempt to combat the effects of the Great Depression?
- How successful were these attempts?

Hoovervilles and Dust Storms

The depression hit all areas of the United States hard. In large cities, families crowded into apartments with no gas or electricity and little food to put on the table. In Los Angeles, people cooked their meals over wood fires in backyards. In many cities, the homeless constructed makeshift housing consisting of cartons, old newspapers, and cloth — what journalists derisively dubbed Hoovervilles. Thousands of hungry citizens wound up living under bridges in Portland, Oregon; in wrecked autos in city dumps in Brooklyn, New York, and Stockton, California; and in abandoned coal furnaces in Pittsburgh.

Rural workers fared no better. Landlords in West Virginia and Kentucky evicted coal miners and their families from their homes in the dead of winter, forcing them to live in tents. Farmers in the Great Plains, who were already experiencing foreclosures, were little prepared for the even greater natural disaster that laid waste to their farms. In the early 1930s, dust storms swept through western Kansas, eastern Colorado, western Oklahoma, the Texas Panhandle, and eastern New Mexico, in an area that came to be known as the **Dust Bowl**, destroying crops and plant and animal life (Map 7.7). The storms resulted from both climatological and human causes. A series of droughts had destroyed crops and turned the earth into sand, which gusts of wind deposited on everything that lay in their path. Though they did not realize it at the time, plains farmers, by focusing on growing wheat for income, had neglected planting trees and grasses that would have kept the earth from eroding and turning into dust.

Dust Bowl Name for the southern plains of the United States during the Great Depression when the region experienced massive dust storms due to soil erosion caused by poor farming practices and drought.

AP® TIP
Be sure you can explain the effects of the Great Depression on both rural and urban areas during the 1930s.

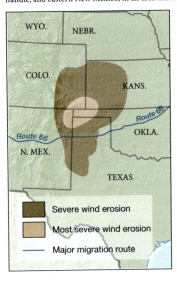

◀ **MAP 7.7 The Dust Bowl** Although "Okies" was the term used for the migrants escaping the Dust Bowl and heading to California, many of those who fled the terrible windstorms also journeyed from their homes in Kansas, Texas, and Colorado. **How was the Dust Bowl a product of human actions?**

TEACHING IDEA

Incorporating Videos

Assign students to watch excerpts from either the documentary *Stinging Dust & Forgotten Lives: The Dust Bowl* or PBS' *The Colorado Experience: The Dust Bowl* (both available on YouTube). Utilize either film as a segue into a class discussion of geography and the environment as an AP® History course theme.

APPLY THE TIP

Assign students to one of the following roles: a destitute farmer in western Kansas, or an unemployed factory worker in Chicago. Have them write a letter to the president, both explaining their plight, and indicating the nature of the assistance or supports that they would like to see implemented, to have their wants and needs met.

TRM Suggested Responses to Questions

TRM Module 7.7 AP® Analyzing Sources Handout 1

BUILDING AP® SKILLS

Comparison

Assemble the students in small groups, and provide them with these two dates: 1877 vs. 1929. Instruct the student groups to give cause (involving evidence) for why each date could legitimately be called a turning point in American history. Then, choose one from each pair and defend the date as a better indication of a watershed year than the other. Lastly, have the class vote by movement, with students who picked 1877 congregating on one side of the room, and students who chose 1929 on the other. Have students pick out one person from across the room and meet up, to share their logic and reasoning for their respective choices.

▲ **Differentiation**

Assign students to then complete either a "Twenty-Five-Word Drill" or "Fifty-Word Drill," dependent upon their fluency with the content and their respective skill level in the course.

Period 7: 1890–1945 MODULE 7-7 Economic Instability and Depression

AP® ANALYZING SOURCES

Source: Ann Marie Low, *Dust Bowl Diary*, 1934

"May 21, 1934, Monday
[S]aturday Dad, Bud, and I planted an acre of potatoes. There was so much dirt in the air I couldn't see Bud only a few feet in front of me. Even the air in the house was just a haze. In the evening the wind died down, and Cap came to take me to the movie. We joked about how hard it is to get cleaned up enough to go anywhere.

The newspapers report that on May 10 there was such a strong wind the experts in Chicago estimated 12,000,000 tons of Plains soil was dumped on that city. By the next day the sun was obscured in Washington, D.C., and ships 300 miles out at sea reported dust settling on their decks.

May 30, 1934, Wednesday
The mess was incredible! Dirt had blown into the house all week and lay inches deep on everything. Every towel and curtain was just black. There wasn't a clean dish or cooking utensil. There was no food. Oh, there were eggs and milk and one loaf left of the bread I baked the weekend before. . . .

Mama couldn't make bread until I carried water to wash the bread mixer. I couldn't churn until the churn was washed and scalded. We just couldn't do anything until something was washed first. Every room had to have dirt almost shoveled out of it before we could wash floors and furniture."

Questions for Analysis

1. Identify the ways in which the Dust Bowl disrupted the rhythms of farm life in this document.
2. Describe the different ways in which this disruption affected the men and women of this household.
3. Evaluate the extent to which this disruption was caused by environmental or economic factors.

As the storms continued through the 1930s, most residents — approximately 75 percent — remained on the plains. Millions, however, headed for California looking for relief from the plague of swirling dirt and hoping to find jobs in the state's fruit and vegetable fields. Although they came from several states besides Oklahoma, these migrants came to be known as "Okies," a derogatory term used by those who resented and looked down on the poverty-stricken newcomers to their communities. John Steinbeck's novel *The Grapes of Wrath* (1939) portrayed the plight of the fictional Joad family as storms and a bank foreclosure destroyed their Oklahoma farm and sent them on the road to California.

REVIEW

What factors contributed to the Dust Bowl?

Challenges for Minorities

Given the demographics of the workforce, the overwhelming majority of Americans who lost their jobs were white men; yet racial and ethnic minorities, including African Americans, Latinos, and Asian Americans, suffered disproportionate hardship. Racial discrimination had kept these groups from achieving economic and political equality, and the Great Depression added to their woes.

Traditionally the last hired and the first fired, black people occupied the lowest rungs on the industrial and agricultural ladders. "The depression brought everybody down a peg or two," the African American poet Langston Hughes wryly commented. "And the Negroes had but few pegs

---

TEACHING IDEA

Check for Understanding

PBS programming includes a collection of numerous free online lessons based upon the Ken Burns Documentary, *The Dust Bowl* (pbs.org/kenburns/dustbowl). Included in the repository on this platform are downloadable lessons focusing upon short film excerpts and primary source extracts, songs, statistical information, and personal interviews. Utilize any of these by navigating to the section For Educators.

AP® ANALYZING SOURCES

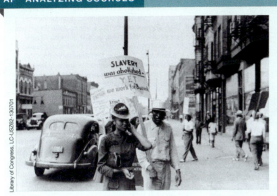

Source: John Vachon, *Picket Line*, Chicago, 1941.

About the source: This photograph shows African American protesters as they picket a realty company in Chicago in 1941. The sign in the foreground says, "SLAVERY was abolished — yet we work for $8 a week."

Questions for Analysis

1. Identify these demonstrators' concerns.
2. Explain the ways in which this protest is a product of the legacy of the migration of African Americans to cities during and after World War I.
3. Evaluate the extent to which African Americans had achieved the civil rights enjoyed by white Americans by the 1930s.

---

to fall." Despite the great migration to the North during and after World War I, three-quarters of the black population still lived in the South. Mainly sharecroppers and tenant farmers, black southerners were mired in debt that they could not repay as crop prices plunged to record lows during the 1920s. As white landowners struggled to save their farms by introducing machinery to cut labor costs, they forced black sharecroppers off the land and into even greater poverty. Nor was the situation better for black workers employed at the lowest-paying jobs as janitors, menial laborers, maids, and laundresses. On average, African Americans earned $200 a year, less than one-quarter of the average wage of white factory workers.

The economic misfortune that African Americans experienced was compounded by the fact that they lived in a society rigidly constructed to preserve white supremacy. The 25 percent of black people living in the North faced racial discrimination in employment, housing, and the criminal justice system, but at least they could express their opinions and desires by voting. By contrast, black southerners remained segregated and disfranchised by law. The depression also worsened racial tensions, as white and black people competed for the shrinking number of jobs. Lynching, which had declined during the 1920s, surged upward — in 1933 twenty-four black people lost their lives to this form of terrorism.

Events in Scottsboro, Alabama reflected the special misery African Americans faced during the Great Depression. Trouble erupted in 1931 when two young, unemployed white women, Ruby Bates and Victoria Price, snuck onto a freight train heading to Huntsville, Alabama. Before the train reached the Scottsboro depot, a fight broke out between black and white men on top of the freight car occupied by the two women. After the train pulled in to Scottsboro, the local sheriff arrested nine black youths between the ages of twelve and nineteen. Charges of assault quickly escalated into rape, when the women told authorities that the black men in custody had molested them on board the train.

Scottsboro Nine Nine African American youths convicted of raping two white women in Scottsboro, Alabama, in 1931. The Communist Party played a key role in defending the Scottsboro Nine and in bringing national and international attention to their case.

The defendants' court-appointed attorney was less than competent and had little time to prepare his clients' cases. It probably made no difference, as the all-white male jury swiftly convicted the accused and awarded the harshest of sentences; only the youngest defendant was not given the death penalty. The Supreme Court spared the lives of the **Scottsboro Nine** by overturning their guilty verdicts in 1932 on the grounds that the defendants did not have adequate legal representation and again in 1935 because black people had been systematically excluded from the jury pool. Although Ruby Bates had recanted her testimony and there was no physical evidence of rape, retrials in 1936 and 1937 produced the same guilty verdicts, but this time the defendants did not

---

TRM Suggested Responses to Questions

TRM Module 7.7 AP® Analyzing Sources Handout 2

BUILDING AP® SKILLS

Developments and Processes

Assign students the lesson, "Scottsboro Boys: A Trial Which Defined an Age" by Antonio Harrison, available by search from the Alabama Department of Archives & History (digital.archives.alabama.gov). This activity tasks students with primary source investigation and group-constructed newspapers that report on the "Scottsboro Boys" trial. Each newspaper will include each of the following five underlying elements of the trial: racism, antisemitism, communism, sectionalism, and classism. At the conclusion of the lesson, have students present their works to the class for reading and discussion.

TEACHING IDEA

Understanding Social Changes

For homework, assign students to explore the History Channel's online platform, "Last Hired, First Fired: How the Great Depression Affected African Americans" (history.com). The next day in class, divide the students into three groups, "social," "economic," and "political." Then ask the three groups, from the perspective of their topic, to formulate an answer to the question, "What was the degree of suffering experienced and opportunities for remedy available to African Americans during the Great Depression?" Allow them to discuss, and then place students into groups of six, with two persons from each topic represented. Have them share out jigsaw style, and then task these groups of six with crafting a response to the following prompt, utilizing the 4-1-1 model of contextualization and thesis construction (a refresher of the jigsaw model can be found on page 33 and a refresher of the 4-1-1 model can be found on page 163):

"The most significant obstacles encountered and opportunities faced by African Americans during this period were _____, because…"

BUILDING AP® SKILLS

Comparison

Assign students to visit the Library of Congress website and navigate to the Presentation and Activities on Immigration and the Mexican Experience (loc.gov). Then, the next day in class, utilizing their textbook and materials from the previous activity, ask students to compare the experiences of African Americans during the depression with those of Mexican Americans, in small group discussion format. Culminate this lesson by having students write a full response to the following Long-Essay Question prompt; "Evaluate the similarities and differences in the experiences of African Americans and Mexican Americans in surviving the Great Depression."

TEACHING IDEA

Analyzing Art and Images

Have students access the "Photos of the Great Depression's Forgotten Black Victims," online portfolio, by Savannah Cox (perform an Internet search on the title and photographer). The portfolio consists of 46 photographs, so previewing by the instructor is essential. Assign students to work in groups to compose a written analysis for any selected 6–8 photos, either for the whole class or by distributing the entirety of the portfolio among the class, depending upon instructor discretion. Groups should then present their analysis to the class.

◀ **Scottsboro Nine, 1933** Two years after their original conviction, the Scottsboro defendants discuss their new trial with their attorney Samuel Leibowitz in 1933 while still in prison. Flanked by two guards, they are from the left, Olen Montgomery, Clarence Norris, Willie Robertson, Andrew Wright, Ozie Powell, Eugene Williams, Charlie Weems, and Roy Wright. Haywood Patterson is seated next to Leibowitz. Known as the "Scottsboro Boys," at the time of their arrest they ranged in age from twelve to nineteen. **How does this photo reveal the impact of racism during the Great Depression?**

AP® TIP
Analyze the effects of systemic racism and discrimination on the African American community during the Great Depression.

receive the death penalty—a minor victory considering the charges. State prosecutors dismissed charges against four of the accused, all of whom had already spent six years in jail. Despite international protests against this racist injustice, the last of the remaining five did not leave jail until 1950.

Racism also worsened the impact of the Great Depression on Spanish-speaking Americans. Mexicans and Mexican Americans made up the largest segment of the Latino population living in the United States. Concentrated in the Southwest and California, they worked in a variety of low-wage factory jobs and as migrant laborers in fruit and vegetable fields. The depression reduced the Mexican-born population living in the United States in two ways. The federal government, in cooperation with state and local governments and private businesses, deported around one million Mexicans, a majority of whom were American citizens. Los Angeles officials organized more than a dozen deportation trains transporting thousands of Mexicans to the border. Many others returned to Mexico voluntarily when demand for labor in the United States dried up. By 1933 the number of repatriations had begun to decline. Fewer migrants came over the border after the depression began in 1929, thereby posing less of an economic threat. In addition, the Roosevelt administration adopted more humane policies, attempting not to break up families.

Those who remained endured growing hardships. Relief agencies refused to provide them with the same benefits as white people. Like African Americans, they encountered discrimination in public schools, in public accommodations, and at the ballot box. Conditions remained harshest for migrant workers toiling long hours for little pay and living in overcrowded and poorly constructed housing. In both fields and factories employers had little incentive to improve the situation because there were plenty of white migrant workers to fill their positions.

The transient nature of agricultural work and the vulnerability of Mexican laborers made it difficult for workers to organize, but Mexican American laborers engaged in dozens of strikes in California and Texas in the early 1930s. Most ended in defeat, but a few, such as a strike of pecan shellers in San Antonio, Texas, led by Luisa Moreno, won better working conditions and higher wages. Despite these hard-fought victories, the condition of Latinos remained precarious.

On the West Coast, Asian Americans also remained economically and politically marginalized. Japanese immigrants eked out livings as small farmers, grocers, and gardeners, despite California laws preventing them from owning land. Many of their college-educated U.S.-born children found few professional opportunities available to them, and they often returned to work in family businesses. The depression magnified the problem. Like other racial and ethnic minorities, the Japanese found it harder to find even the lowest-wage jobs now that unemployed white people were willing to take them. As a result, about one-fifth of Japanese immigrants returned to Japan during the 1930s.

TEACHING IDEA

Incorporating Secondary Sources

Assign students to read and annotate the academic monograph, "Women and Work: African-American Women in Depression-Era America," by Sarah Ward (available through online search). Whole-class discussion to follow.

Mexican Migrant Worker, 1937 This photograph by Dorothea Lange shows a Mexican field worker on the edge of a frozen pea field in the Imperial Valley, California. Demand for Mexican labor declined during the Great Depression as displaced farmers from the Dust Bowl moved west to take jobs formerly held by Mexicans. Government deportations further decreased the number of undocumented Mexican laborers in the United States. **In what ways did the Great Depression affect lower-income minority workers differently than middle-class white Americans?**

The Chinese suffered a similar fate. Although some 45 percent of Chinese Americans had been born in the United States and were citizens, people of Chinese ancestry remained isolated in ethnic communities along the West Coast. Discriminated against in schools and most occupations, many operated restaurants and laundries. During the depression, those Chinese who did not obtain assistance through governmental relief turned instead to their own community organizations and to extended families to help them through the hard times.

Filipino immigrants had arrived on the West Coast after the Philippines became a territory of the United States in 1901. Working as low-wage agricultural laborers, they were subject to the same kind of racial animosity as other dark-skinned minorities. Filipino farmworkers organized agricultural labor unions and conducted numerous strikes in California, but like their Mexican counterparts they were brutally repressed. In 1934 anti-Filipino hostility reached its height when Congress passed the **Tydings-McDuffie Act**. The measure accomplished two aims at once: The act granted independence to the Philippines, and it restricted Filipino immigration into the United States.

> **AP® TIP**
> Analyze the connection between trends in U.S. immigration policies and shifts in economic prosperity during the early twentieth century.

REVIEW

- Why did the Great Depression hit minorities in the United States especially hard?

Financial Strain and Organized Protest

With millions of men unemployed, women faced increased family responsibilities. Stay-at-home wives had to care for their children and provide emotional support for out-of-work husbands who had lost their role as the family breadwinner. Despite the loss of income, homemakers continued their daily routines of shopping, cooking, cleaning, and child rearing.

Disproportionate male unemployment led to an increase in the importance of women's income. The depression hit male-dominated industries like steel mills and automakers the hardest. As a result, men were more likely to lose their jobs than women. Although more women held on

TEACHING IDEA

Incorporating Videos

As this module nears its completion, this is a good point to assign students to view the last 30 minutes of the PBS documentary, *Landslide: A Portrait of President Herbert Hoover* (available on YouTube). This portion covers the consequences of the crash and its aftermath, culminating in Hoover's defeat in 1932.

TEACHING IDEA

Connecting the Dots

Engage the class in an activity of association by disassociation called "Odd One Out." Write the following terms on the board/projector:

- "Okies"
- Tydings-McDuffie Act
- Black Tuesday
- Reconstruction Finance Corporation
- Hoovervilles

Then place students in small groups and ask them, "Which one is the odd one out and why? How do the remaining terms relate?" Give students approximately 7-10 minutes to complete this part, then share out student answers and discuss their conclusions and reasoning as a whole-class activity. There is no specific correct answer; the goal is to get students thinking in categorical habits of mind and defending their rationales.

TRM Suggested Responses to Questions

TRM Module 7.7 AP® Analyzing Sources Handout 3

MODULE 7-7 Economic Instability and Depression

AP® TIP
Be sure you can explain how the Great Depression affected the opportunities for and attitudes toward women in the workforce.

to their jobs, their often meager wages had to go further because many now had to support unemployed fathers and husbands. During the 1930s, federal and local governments sought to increase male employment by passing laws to keep married women from holding civil service and teaching positions. Nonetheless, more and more married women entered the workplace, and by 1940 the proportion of women in the job force had grown by about 25 percent.

As had been the case in previous decades, a higher proportion of African American women than white women worked outside the home in the 1930s. By 1940 about 40 percent of African American women held jobs, compared to about 25 percent of white women. Racial discrimination played a key role in establishing this pattern. Black men faced higher unemployment rates than did their white counterparts, and what work was available was often limited to the lowest-paying jobs. As a result, black women faced greater pressure to supplement family incomes. Still, unemployment rates for black women reached as high as 50 percent during the 1930s.

Despite increased burdens, most American families remained intact and discovered ways to survive the economic crisis. They pared down household budgets, made do without telephones and new clothes, and held on to their automobiles for longer periods of time. What money they managed to save they often spent on movies. Comedies, gangster movies, fantasy tales, and uplifting films helped viewers forget their troubles, if only for a few hours. Radio remained the chief source of entertainment, and radio sales doubled in the 1930s as listeners tuned in to soap operas, comedy and adventure shows, news reports, and musical programs.

As the depression deepened, angry citizens found ways to express their discontent. Farmers had suffered economic hardship longer than any other group. Even before 1929, they had seen prices spiral downward, but in the early 1930s agricultural income plummeted 60 percent, and one-third of farmers lost their land. Some farmers decided that the time had come for drastic action. In the summer of 1932, Milo Reno, an Iowa farmer, created the Farm Holiday Association to organize farmers

AP® ANALYZING SOURCES

Source: Mrs. W. T. Gammel, *Letter to Governor Harvey Parnell*, 1931

"Governor Parnell:

I am writing to you because we haven't anything to eat.

You are putting out money to feed the people that are in need, I went this morning to get help and I was turned down. I don't know why, on this the Salvation Army captain's wife is mad at me, and she told the investigating committee something that then they would not help me, and we need help if any one ever did. My husband has not had any work since the 15th of Nov. [H]e was working for the state highway dept. and we have 7 children and no income at all and all there is in our house to eat just now is a little flour and we haven't had anything to eat but bread for several days. We are willing for our case to be investigated, but they won't ask anyone but the Salvation Army nor will they take my word, please help us some way. . . .

Mrs. W. T. Gammel"

Questions for Analysis
1. Identify Gammel's situation, as well as where she first turned for help.
2. Describe the reasons why she and her family have found themselves in the situation expressed in this letter.
3. Explain why Gammel was unsuccessful in her first attempt to get help.

Questions for Comparison Ann Marie Low, *Dust Bowl Diary*, 1934 (p. 640)
1. Identify the challenges faced by W. T. Gammel and Ann Marie Low.
2. Explain how these challenges differed, and what elements they shared in common.
3. Explain the common causes of these similarities and differences.
4. Evaluate the extent to which the differences are due to the fact that Ms. Low was a farmer and Mrs. Gammel was not.

TEACHING IDEA

Check for Understanding

Make sure to emphasize with students that for rural America, the Great Depression actually began with the end of World War I, rather than with the stock market crash. The weakness in this sector of the economy had been masked by the expansion of urban growth and industrial production during the 1920s. In fact, it is a fair stipulation to make that much of the urban and industrial growth was made possible by the extremely low prices for agricultural commodities that were omnipresent for the entire period prior to the Second World War.

Financial Strain and Organized Protest

AP® TIP

Compare the issues faced and solutions proposed by farmers' groups in the 1920s and 1930s to those of the Populists in the late 1800s.

to keep their produce from going to market and thereby raise prices. Strikers from the association blocked roads and kept reluctant farmers in line by smashing their truck windshields and headlights and slashing their tires. When law enforcement officials arrested fifty-five demonstrators in Council Bluffs, thousands of farmers marched on the jail and forced their release. Despite armed attempts to prevent foreclosures and the intentional destruction of vast quantities of farm produce, the Farm Holiday Association failed to achieve its goal of raising prices.

Disgruntled urban residents also resorted to protest. Although the Communist Party remained a tiny group of just over 10,000 members in 1932, it played a large role in organizing the dispossessed. In major cities such as New York, Communists set up unemployment councils and led marches and rallies demanding jobs and food. In Harlem, the party endorsed rent strikes by African American apartment residents against their landlords. Party members did not confine their activities to the urban Northeast. They also went south to defend the Scottsboro Nine and to organize industrial workers in the steel mills of Birmingham and sharecroppers in the surrounding rural areas of Alabama. On the West Coast, Communists unionized seamen and waterfront workers and led strikes. They also recruited writers, directors, and actors in Hollywood.

One of the most visible protests of the early 1930s centered on the Ford factory in Dearborn, Michigan. As the depression worsened after 1930, Henry Ford, who had initially pledged to keep employee wages steady, changed his mind and reduced wages. On March 7, 1932, spearheaded by Communists, three thousand autoworkers marched from Detroit to Ford's River Rouge plant in nearby Dearborn. When they reached the factory town, they faced policemen indiscriminately firing bullets and tear gas, which killed four demonstrators. The attack provoked great outrage. Around forty thousand mourners attended the funeral of the four protesters; sang the Communist anthem, the "Internationale"; and surrounded the caskets, which were draped in a red banner emblazoned with a picture of Bolshevik hero Vladimir Lenin.

Protests spread beyond Communist agitators. The federal government faced an uprising by some of the nation's most patriotic and loyal citizens—World War I veterans. Scheduled to receive a $1,000 bonus for their service, unemployed veterans could not wait until the payment date arrived in 1945. Instead, in the spring of 1932 a group of ex-soldiers from Portland, Oregon set off on a march on Washington, D.C. to demand immediate payment of the bonus by the federal government. By the time they reached the nation's capital, the ranks of this **Bonus Army** had swelled to around twenty thousand veterans. They camped in the Anacostia Flats section of the city, constructed ramshackle shelters, and in many cases moved their families in with them.

Bonus Army World War I veterans who marched on Washington, D.C. in 1932 to demand immediate payment of their service bonuses. President Hoover refused to negotiate and instructed the U.S. Army to clear the capital of protesters, leading to a violent clash.

Although many veterans returned home, the rest of the Bonus Army remained in place until late July. When President Hoover decided to clear the capital of the protesters, violence ensued. Rather than engaging in a measured and orderly removal, General Douglas MacArthur overstepped presidential orders and used excessive force to disperse the veterans and their families. The Third Cavalry, commanded by George S. Patton, torched tents and sent their residents fleeing from the city.

In this one-sided battle, the biggest loser was President Hoover. Through four years of the country's worst depression, Hoover had lost touch with the American people. His cheerful words of encouragement fell increasingly on deaf ears. As workers, farmers, and veterans stirred in protest, Hoover appeared aloof, standoffish, and insensitive.

REVIEW

- How did the Great Depression shape the lives of families in the United States during the 1930s?
- What were the results of organized protest during the Great Depression?

AP® WRITING HISTORICALLY — Long-Essay Question Practice

ACTIVITY

Answer the following Long-Essay Question. *Suggested writing time: 40 minutes.*

Evaluate the relative importance of different causes for the Hoover administration's ineffective response to the Great Depression.

TEACHING IDEA

Incorporating Secondary Sources

Assign class to read and annotate "Confrontation at Anacostia Flats: The Bonus Army of 1932," by Kendall D. Gott (available through online search). Require students to both identify Gott's thesis and create a summative conclusive statement on their takeaways on his work. Have students share these out in small-group format, with students rotating among several of their peers.

BUILDING AP® SKILLS

Sourcing and Situation

Assign students in small groups to read the primary source excerpts from "Bonus Army Research Documents" (available through online search). Utilizing their HIPP training, have students break down the documents for both authors' intent and reliability (a refresher of HIPP can be found on page 8). As a concluding exercise, present the student groups with the following question: "The Bonus March of 1932 — what really happened here?" Allow groups time to formulate an answer, and then have groups both present their conclusions and cross-examine other groups on their claims.

TRM Suggested Responses to Questions

TEACHING IDEA

AP® Writing Historically Review

While this question does not give students a period to consider in the answer, teachers can help students by providing a periodization such as 1920–1932. This gives students the ability to address how the prosperity of the 1920s affected President Hoover's attitude. Alternatively, you could ask the students what periodization they think makes sense, given the nature of the question. This type of discussion immediately gets students to think about the purpose of the question and the best way to answer it with an analytical approach.

TRM Suggested Responses to Questions

Module 7-8

The New Deal

LEARNING TARGETS

By the end of this module, you should be able to:
- Explain how government responded to the economic and social upheaval of the Great Depression by creating a limited welfare state.
- Explain how the New Deal tried to end the Great Depression by using government power to provide economic relief, recovery, and reform.
- Explain how movements from the left pushed Roosevelt toward greater efforts to permanently change the American economy.
- Explain how movements from the right sought to limit the New Deal's scope.
- Explain how the New Deal caused a long-term political realignment in which many ethnic groups and the working class moved toward the Democratic Party.

THEMATIC FOCUS

Work, Exchange, and Technology
Politics and Power

Franklin Roosevelt, elected president in 1932, promised to counteract the effects of the Great Depression. Although Roosevelt's New Deal gave many Americans hope, critics saw it as wasteful and un-American.

HISTOICAL REASONING FOCUS

Continuity and Change

TASK ▶ In this module, consider the extent to which the New Deal represented a change in the relationship between the federal government and citizens, and to what extent it represented a continuation of older trends.

The nation was ready for a change, and on election day 1932, with hard times showing no sign of letting up, Democratic presidential candidate Franklin Delano Roosevelt defeated Hoover easily. Roosevelt's sizable victory provided him with a mandate to take the country in a bold new direction. However, few Americans, including Roosevelt himself, knew exactly what the new president meant to do or what his pledge of a "new deal" would mean for the country.

Steps toward Relief

As a presidential candidate, Roosevelt presented no clear, coherent policy. He did not spell out how his plans for the country would differ from Hoover's, but he did refer broadly to providing a "new deal" and bringing to the White House "persistent experimentation." Roosevelt's appeal derived more from the genuine compassion he was able to convey than from the specificity of his promises. In this context his wife, Eleanor Roosevelt's, evident concern for people's suffering and her history of activism made Franklin Roosevelt even more attractive.

Instead of any fixed ideology, Roosevelt followed what one historian has called "pragmatic humanism." A seasoned politician who understood the need for flexibility, Roosevelt blended principle and practicality. "It is common sense," Roosevelt explained, "to take a method and try it.

TEACHING IDEA

Incorporating Videos

Assign students to watch Episode 34, "The New Deal," from the Crash Course US History series (available on YouTube). Use this 14-minute episode as a concise formative content introduction for students of the initial major issues and events of Module 7-8 as part of preparation for either assessment or reinforcement.

EXPLORING AP® THEMES

Politics and Power

It is important to point out to the class that there was no master plan for the New Deal. In contrast to the firmness of Hoover's philosophical belief in rugged individualism, which ultimately limited his flexibility under economic duress, FDR employed what may best be described as something of a scattershot approach in the New Deal. It was made up of programs that were designed and implemented in real time, and sometimes worked at cross-purposes to one another. A helpful analogy for students that may stay with them is the rather juvenile concept of throwing dirt clods at a wall. If there is some moisture in the center of the dirt clod, then it sticks to the wall; some New Deal programs "stuck," such as Social Security and the Fair Labor Standards Act (minimum wage). If the dirt clod is dry throughout, when it hits the wall it disintegrates into dust; some New Deal programs did the same, such as the Agricultural Adjustment Act and the National Industrial Recovery Act, both of which were declared unconstitutional by the Supreme Court.

Steps toward Relief

▲ **Franklin D. Roosevelt Campaigning in Kansas, 1932** New York governor Franklin Roosevelt promises a "new deal" to farmers in Topeka, Kansas as he campaigns for president in 1932 as the Democratic candidate. Photographers were careful not to show that Roosevelt was unable to use his legs, which were paralyzed after he contracted polio in 1921. Roosevelt forged a coalition of farmers and urban workers and easily defeated the incumbent Hoover. **Why would both farmers and urban workers find Roosevelt's message particularly compelling in 1932?**

If it fails, admit it frankly and try another. But above all, try something." More than any president before him, FDR, as he became known, created an expectation among Americans that the federal government would take concrete action to improve their lives. A Colorado woman expressed her appreciation to Eleanor Roosevelt: "Your husband is great. He seems lovable even tho' he is a 'politician.'" The policies supported by his administration would take twists and turns, but Roosevelt never lost the support of the majority of Americans.

Starting with his inaugural address, in which he declared that "the only thing we have to fear is fear itself," Roosevelt took on the task of rallying the American people and restoring their confidence in the future. Using the power of radio to communicate directly, Roosevelt delivered regular fireside chats in which he boosted morale and informed his audience of the steps the government was taking to help solve their problems. Not limited to rhetoric, Roosevelt's **New Deal** would provide relief, put millions of people to work, raise prices for farmers, extend conservation projects, revitalize America's financial system, and rescue capitalism.

President Roosevelt took swift action on entering office. In March 1933 he issued an executive order shutting down banks for several days to calm the panic that gripped many Americans in the wake of bank failures and the loss of their life's savings. Shortly after, Congress passed the administration's **Emergency Banking Act**, which subjected banks to Treasury Department inspection before they reopened, reorganized the banking system, and provided federal funds to bail out banks on the brink of closing. This assertion of federal power allowed solvent banks to reopen. Boosting confidence further, Congress passed the **Glass-Steagall Act** in June 1933. The measure created the **Federal Deposit Insurance Corporation (FDIC)**, insuring personal savings accounts up to $5,000, and detached commercial banks from investment banks to avoid risky speculation. The president also sought tighter supervision of the stock market. By June 1934

New Deal The policies and programs that Franklin Roosevelt initiated to combat the Great Depression. The New Deal represented a dramatic expansion of the role of government in American society.

Emergency Banking Act 1933 New Deal executive order that shut down banks for several days to calm widespread panic during the Great Depression.

Glass-Steagall Act 1933 New Deal legislation that allowed solvent banks to reopen and created the Federal Deposit Insurance Corporation (FDIC).

TEACHING IDEA

Incorporating Primary Sources

Assign students to read and annotate Franklin Roosevelt's First Inaugural Address, which can be found on The Avalon Project's website (avalon.law.yale.edu). The next day in small groups, have them apply HIPP training to the piece, as well as discuss the piece's meaning, intent, and significance in small groups, with students rotating between groups (a refresher of HIPP can be found on page 8).

TEACHING IDEA

AP® Central

Assign students in groups to break down the 1984 DBQ, which is available on the College Board's past exam questions resource "AP® United States History Document-Based Questions 1973–1999" (apcentral.collegeboard.org). Have students utilize their HIPP training (a refresher of HIPP can be found on page 8). This DBQ consists of eight documents, so it is not advisable to attempt to task students with writing a full response to the prompt without alteration, but creation of a thesis statement with contextualization is fully viable and acceptable as a class activity.

APPLY THE TIP

Assign one-half of the class, in groups of three, to compare the Hoover and Roosevelt administrations approaches to the depression, and one-half of the class to evaluate the similarity between Progressivism and the New Deal. When this is accomplished, reorganize the class into groups of six, with three from each original grouping. Have each triad alternate in presentations of their findings to the other triad in their group.

TEACHING IDEA

Building Vocabulary

Assign students to catalog the mission or goal of the major "Alphabet Soup" New Deal agencies. Specifically, students must determine which problem or problems each agency was established to confront or remedy. Then, utilizing the "3-R's" approach of the New Deal, ("Relief, Recovery, Reform"), task students with determining which category of the "R's" each studied agency falls into. This is useful for students in order to get them thinking in categorical habits of mind about the mass of agencies, which as proper-noun AP® terminology, are central to an understanding of the philosophy of the New Deal.

TRM Find **Handout 7.9 – The New Deal and the "3-R's"** in the Teacher's Resource Materials.

AP® TIP

Compare the efforts of the Roosevelt administration to address the Great Depression with those of the Hoover administration.

Twenty-first Amendment 1933 amendment repealing prohibition and the Eighteenth Amendment.

AP® TIP

Evaluate the degree of similarity between early twentieth-century progressive policies and the New Deal.

Agricultural Adjustment Act (AAA) 1933 New Deal act that raised prices for farm produce by paying farmers subsidies to reduce production. Large farmers reaped most of the benefits from the act. It was declared unconstitutional by the Supreme Court in 1936.

Roosevelt had signed into law measures setting up the **Securities and Exchange Commission (SEC)** to regulate the stock market and ensure that corporations gave investors accurate information about their portfolios.

The regulation of banks and the stock exchange did not mean that Roosevelt was antibusiness. He affirmed his belief in a balanced budget and sought to avoid a $1 billion deficit by cutting government workers' salaries and lowering veterans' pensions. Roosevelt also tried to keep the budget under control by ending prohibition, which would allow the government to tax alcohol sales and eliminate the cost of enforcement. The **Twenty-first Amendment**, ratified in 1933, ended the more than decade-long experiment with prohibition.

As important as these measures were, the Roosevelt administration had much more to accomplish before those hardest hit by the depression felt some relief. Roosevelt viewed the Great Depression as a crisis analogous to war and adapted many of the bureaus and commissions used during World War I to ensure productivity and mobilize popular support to fit the current economic emergency. Many former progressives lined up behind Roosevelt, including women reformers and social workers who had worked in government and private agencies during the 1920s. At his wife Eleanor's urging, Roosevelt appointed one of them, Frances Perkins, as the first woman to head a cabinet agency — the Department of Labor.

Rehabilitating agriculture and industry stood at the top of the New Deal's priority list. Farmers came first. In May 1933 Congress passed the **Agricultural Adjustment Act**, aimed at raising prices by reducing production. The Agricultural Adjustment Administration (AAA) paid farmers subsidies to produce less in the future, and for farmers who had already planted their crops and raised livestock, the agency paid them to plow under a portion of their harvest, slaughter hogs, and destroy dairy products. By 1935 the program succeeded in raising farm income by 50 percent. Large farmers remained the chief beneficiaries of the AAA because they could afford to cut back production. In doing so, especially in the South, they forced off the land sharecroppers who no longer had plots to farm. Even when sharecroppers managed to retain a parcel of their acreage, AAA subsidies went to the landowners, who did not always distribute the designated funds owed to the sharecroppers. Though poor white farmers felt the sting of this injustice, the system of white supremacy existing in the South guaranteed that black people suffered most.

The Roosevelt administration exhibited its boldest initiative in creating the **Tennessee Valley Authority (TVA)** in 1933 to bring low-cost electric power to rural areas and help redevelop the entire Tennessee River valley region through flood-control projects. In contrast to the AAA and other farm programs in which control stayed in private hands, the TVA owned and supervised the building and operation of public power plants. For farmers outside the Tennessee River valley, the Rural Electrification Administration helped them obtain cheap electric power starting in 1935, and for the first time tens of thousands of farmers experienced the modern conveniences that electricity brought (though most farmers would not get electric power until after World War II).

Roosevelt and Congress also acted to deal with the soil erosion problem behind the dust storms. In 1933 the Department of the Interior established a Soil Erosion Service, and two years later Congress created a permanent Soil Conservation Service in the Department of Agriculture. Although these measures would prove beneficial in the long run, they did nothing to prevent even more severe storms from rolling through the Dust Bowl in 1935 and 1936.

At the same time, Roosevelt concentrated on industrial recovery. In 1933 Congress passed the **National Industrial Recovery Act**, which established the **National Recovery Administration (NRA)**. This agency allowed business, labor, and the public (represented by government officials) to create codes to regulate production, prices, wages, hours, and collective bargaining. Designers of the NRA expected that if wages rose and prices remained stable, consumer purchasing power would climb, demand would grow, and businesses would put people back to work. For this plan to work, businesspeople needed to keep prices steady by absorbing some of the costs of higher wages. Businesses that joined the NRA displayed the symbol of the blue eagle to signal their patriotic participation.

However, the NRA did not function as planned, nor did it bring the desired recovery. Businesses did not exercise the necessary restraint to keep prices steady. Large manufacturers dominated the code-making committees, and because Roosevelt had suspended enforcement of the

Steps toward Relief

National Recovery Administration Eagles President Roosevelt initiated the National Recovery Administration in 1933 as the centerpiece of his New Deal to stimulate economic growth. The city of Miami Beach employed these women to attract conventioneers and vacationers to its hotels. They showed their support for the New Deal by sporting the NRA blue eagle insignia on their backs. **Which New Deal reforms would likely have appealed to these women?**

antitrust law, they could not resist taking collective action to force smaller firms out of business. The NRA legislation guaranteed labor the right to unionize, but the agency did not vigorously enforce collective bargaining. The government failed to intervene to redress the imbalance of power between labor and management because Roosevelt depended primarily on big business to generate economic improvement. Moreover, the NRA had created codes for too many businesses, and government officials could not properly oversee them all. In 1935 the Supreme Court delivered the final blow to the NRA by declaring it an unconstitutional delegation of legislative power to the president.

Economic recovery programs were important, but they took time to take effect, and many Americans needed immediate help. Thus relief efforts and direct job creation were critical parts of the New Deal. Created in the early months of Roosevelt's term, the Federal Emergency Relief Administration (FERA) provided cash grants to states to revive their bankrupt relief efforts. Roosevelt chose Harry Hopkins, the chief of New York's relief agency, to head the FERA and distribute its initial $500 million appropriation. On the job for two hours, Hopkins had already spent $5 million. He did not calculate whether a particular plan "would work out in the long run," because, as he remarked, "people don't eat in the long run — they eat every day."

Harold Ickes, secretary of the interior and director of the **Public Works Administration (PWA)**, oversaw efforts to rebuild the nation's infrastructure. Funding architects, engineers, and skilled workers, the PWA built the Grand Coulee, Boulder, and Bonneville dams in the West; the Triborough Bridge in New York City; 70 percent of all new schools constructed between 1933 and 1939; and a variety of municipal buildings, sewage plants, port facilities, and hospitals.

Yet neither the FERA nor the PWA provided enough relief to the millions who faced the winter of 1933–1934 without jobs or the money to heat their homes. In response, Hopkins persuaded Roosevelt to launch a temporary program to help needy Americans get through this difficult period. Both men favored "work relief" — giving people jobs rather than direct welfare payments whenever practical. The **Civil Works Administration (CWA)** lasted four months, but in that brief time it employed more than 4 million people on about 400,000 projects that built 500,000 miles of roads, 40,000 schools, 3,500 playgrounds, and 1,000 airports.

One of Roosevelt's most successful relief programs was the **Civilian Conservation Corps (CCC)**, created shortly after he entered the White House. The CCC recruited unmarried men between the ages of eighteen and twenty-five for a two-year stint, putting them to work planting forests; cleaning up beaches, rivers, and parks; and building bridges and dams. Participants received $1 per day, and the government sent $25 of the $30 in monthly wages directly to their families, helping make this the most popular of all New Deal programs. The CCC employed around 2.5 million men and lasted until 1942.

Public Works Administration (PWA) 1933 New Deal administration created to oversee the rebuilding of America's infrastructure, such as roads, schools, and libraries.

Civilian Conservation Corps (CCC) New Deal work program that hired young, unmarried men to work on conservation projects. It employed about 2.5 million men and lasted until 1942.

TEACHING IDEA

Class Discussion

Assign students to read and explore the background, details, and ruling in the *Schechter Poultry Corp. v. United States* "Sick Chicken" case available at the Georgia State University's encyclopedia of the U.S. Constitution (sites.gsu.edu/us-constipedia). After that is finished, engage the class in a discussion based upon the following prompt: "What is the appropriate level of involvement by the United States government in the economy, and to what degree should that involvement level be fluid, determined by economic conditions at any one time?" This conversation can be guided by the instructor beyond the Schechter decision into a discussion of the New Deal in general.

TEACHING IDEA

Building Vocabulary

This is an important place to introduce students to the concept and terminology of Keynesian economics. In previous modules, trickle-down or supply-side principles were introduced. The counter economic theory to that is Keynesian, name after John Maynard Keynes, which calls for counter-cyclical stimulation of the economy by the state in times of economic downturn or over-acceleration in order to maintain economic stability. Keynesian theories were born in the 1930s, and form the basis for one of the major economic schools of thought on what governmental economic policy should be.

TRM Suggested Responses to Questions

TRM Module 7.8 AP® Analyzing Sources Handout 1

BUILDING AP® SKILLS
Claims and Evidence in Sources

Divide the class up into small groups, and assign them to read and annotate differing selected portions of multiple historians' appraisals of the New Deal from the FDR Library, "FDR's First 100 Days: Did It Work?" (available through online search). Task each group with determining the main point of their selected historians for the New Deal, and then to present their historians' conclusions to their classmates, on a small-group rotating basis. Lastly, engage in a whole-class discussion on the wide range of conclusions, and have the students come up with and defend their own thesis on the effectiveness of the New Deal.

AP® ANALYZING SOURCES

Source: President Franklin Roosevelt, *Message to Congress on Making the Civilian Conservation Corps a Permanent Agency*, 1937

"On March 21, 1933, I addressed a message to the Congress in which I stated:

'I propose to create a civilian conservation corps to be used in simple work, not interfering with normal employment, and confining itself to forestry, the prevention of soil erosion, flood control and similar projects. I call your attention to the fact that this type of work is of definite, practical value, not only through the prevention of great present financial loss, but also as a means of creating future national wealth'. . . .

It is not necessary to go into detail regarding the accomplishments of the Corps. You are acquainted with the physical improvements that have taken place in our forests and parks as a result of the activities of the Corps and with the wealth that is being added to our natural resources for the benefit of future generations. More important than the material gain, however, is the improvement we find in the moral and physical well-being of our citizens who have been enrolled in the Corps and of their families who have been assisted by monthly allotments of pay. The functions of the Corps expire under authority of present law on June 30, 1937.

In my Budget Message to Congress on January 5 of this year I indicated that the Corps should be continued and recommended that legislation be enacted during the present session to establish the Corps as a permanent agency of the Government. Such continuance or establishment is desirable notwithstanding the great strides that have been made toward national recovery, as there is still need for providing useful and healthful employment for a large number of our youthful citizens.

I am convinced that there is ample useful work in the protection, restoration and development of our national resources, upon which the services of the Corps may be employed advantageously for an extended future period. It should be noted that this program will not in any respect reduce normal employment opportunities for our adult workers; in fact, the purchase of simple materials, of food and clothing and of other supplies required for the operations of the Corps tends to increase employment in industry.

I recommend, therefore, that provision be made for a permanent Corps of 300,000 youths (and war veterans), together with 10,000 Indians and 5,000 enrollees in our territories and insular possessions. It would appear, after a careful study of available information, that, with improved business conditions, these numbers represent the maximum expected enrollment. To go beyond this number at this time would open new and difficult classifications of enrollment, and the additional cost would seriously affect the financial position of the Treasury."

Questions for Analysis
1. Identify Roosevelt's reasons for making the Civilian Conservation Corps a permanent program.
2. Explain how the Civilian Conservation Corps compares with other jobs programs created during the New Deal.
3. Evaluate the extent to which Roosevelt's Civilian Conservation Corps represents continuity with previous government legislation regarding the environment.

REVIEW
- What steps did Roosevelt take to restore economic confidence early in his administration?
- Who were the primary targets of Roosevelt's relief measures? Who was overlooked?

BUILDING AP® SKILLS
Argumentation

Assign students to craft an introductory thesis statement addressing either one of the review questions at the bottom of the page. Then, task them with writing the first sentence of each main body paragraph, and listing the germane evidence that they would include in each main body paragraph, bullet-point style.

New Deal Critics

Despite the unprecedented efforts of the Roosevelt administration to spark recovery, provide relief, and encourage reform between 1933 and 1935, the country remained in depression, and unemployment still hovered around 20 percent. Roosevelt found himself under attack from both the left and the right. On the right, conservatives questioned New Deal spending and the growth of big government. On the left, the president's critics argued that he had not done enough to topple wealthy corporate leaders from power and relieve the plight of the downtrodden.

In 1934 officials of the Du Pont Corporation and General Motors formed the American Liberty League. From the point of view of the league's founders, the New Deal was little more than a vehicle for the spread of socialism and communism. The organization spent $1 million attacking what it considered to be Roosevelt's "dictatorial" policies and his assaults on free enterprise. The league, however, failed to attract support beyond a small group of northern industrialists, Wall Street bankers, and frustrated Democrats.

Corporate leaders also harnessed Christian ministers to promote their pro-capitalism, anti–New Deal message. The United States Chamber of Commerce and the National Association of Manufacturers allied with clergymen to challenge "creeping socialism." In 1935 the Reverend James W. Fifield founded Spiritual Mobilization and, from the pulpit of his wealthy First Congregational Church in Los Angeles, praised capitalism as a pillar of Christianity and attacked the "pagan statism" of the New Deal.

Roosevelt also faced criticism from the left. Communist Party membership reached its peak of around 75,000 in 1938, and though the party remained relatively small in numbers, it attracted intellectuals and artists whose voices could reach the larger public. Party members led unionizing drives in both the North and the South and displayed great talent and energy in organizing workers where resistance to unions was greatest. In the mid-1930s, the party followed the Soviet Union's antifascist foreign policy and joined with left-leaning, non-Communist groups, such as unions and civil rights organizations, to oppose the growing menace of fascism in Europe, particularly in Germany and Italy. By the end of the decade, however, the party had lost many members after the Soviet Union reversed its anti-Nazi foreign policy.

The greatest challenge to Roosevelt came from a trio of talented men who reflected diverse beliefs. Francis Townsend, a retired California physician, proposed a "Cure for Depressions." In 1934 he formed the **Old-Age Revolving Pensions Corporation**, whose title summed up the doctor's idea. Townsend would have the government give all Americans over the age of sixty a monthly pension of $200 if they retired and spent the entire stipend each month. Retirements would open up jobs for younger workers, and the income these workers received, along with the pension for the elderly, would pump ample funds into

Father Charles E. Coughlin Father Charles E. Coughlin spoke at Cleveland Stadium in 1936 on behalf of Ohio congressional candidates who had been endorsed by his National Union for Social Justice. Coughlin, a Catholic priest and a stern critic of President Roosevelt, advocated the nationalization of banks and other industries, protection of worker rights, and monetary reform. Coughlin also spread conspiracy theories that the Great Depression was caused by international Jewish bankers, who were working with President Roosevelt to destroy the United States. **Why would Coughlin's message be attractive to some Americans in the mid-1930s?**

BUILDING AP® SKILLS

Comparison

Assign students to read the sources and engage with selected specific activities (at the instructor's discretion) included in "Controversy and the New Deal," from the Historic New Orleans Collection (hnoc.org). In particular, assign students to complete the graphic organizer comparing the various critics of the New Deal and their political and economic positions. Allow students time to share and discuss their findings.

Period 7: 1890–1945

MODULE 7-8 The New Deal

the economy to promote recovery. The government would fund the Townsend plan with a 2 percent "transaction" or sales tax. By 1936 Townsend Clubs had attracted about 3.5 million members throughout the country, and one-fifth of all adults in the United States signed a petition endorsing the Townsend plan.

While Townsend appealed mainly to the elderly, Charles E. Coughlin, a priest from the Detroit area, attracted Catholics and a lower-middle-class following. Father Coughlin used his popular national radio broadcasts to talk about economic and political issues. Originally a Roosevelt supporter, by 1934 Coughlin had begun criticizing the New Deal for catering to greedy bankers. He spoke to millions of radio listeners about the evils of the Roosevelt administration, the godless Communists who had allegedly infested it, and international bankers — coded language referring to Jews — who supposedly manipulated it. As the decade wore on, his vocal antisemitism and his growing fondness for fascist dictatorships abroad overshadowed his economic justice message, and Catholic officials ordered him to stop broadcasting.

AP® ANALYZING SOURCES

Source: Huey Long, *Every Man a King*, 1934

"Now, we have organized a society, and we call it 'Share Our Wealth Society,' a society with the motto 'Every Man a King.'

Every man a king, so there would be no such thing as a man or woman who did not have the necessities of life, who would not be dependent upon the whims and caprices . . . of the financial barons for a living. . . .

We do not propose to divide it up equally. We do not propose a division of wealth, but we propose to limit poverty that we will allow to be inflicted upon any man's family. We will not say we are going to try to guarantee any equality, or $15,000 to a family. No; but we do say that one third of the average is low enough for any one family to hold, that there should be a guarantee of a family wealth of around $5,000; enough for a home, an automobile, a radio, and the ordinary conveniences, and the opportunity to educate their children; a fair share of the income of this land thereafter to that family so there will be no such thing as merely the select to have those things, and so there will be no such thing as a family living in poverty and distress.

We have to limit fortunes. Our present plan is that we will allow no one man to own more than $50,000,000. . . .

Another thing we propose is old-age pension of $30 a month for everyone that is 60 years old. Now, we do not give this pension to a man making $1,000 a year, and we do not give it to him if he has $10,000 in property, but outside of that we do.

We will limit hours of work. There is not any necessity of having overproduction. I think all you have got to do, ladies and gentlemen, is just limit the hours of work to such an extent as people will work only so long as it is necessary to produce enough for all of the people to have what they need. Why, ladies and gentlemen, let us say that all of these labor-saving devices reduce hours down to where you do not have to work but 4 hours a day; that is enough for these people, and then praise be the name of the Lord, if it gets that good. Let it be good and not a curse, and then we will have 5 hours a day and 5 days a week-, or even less than that, and we might give a man a whole month off during a year, or give him 2 months; and we might do what other countries have seen fit to do, and what I did in Louisiana, by having schools by which adults could go back and learn the things that have been discovered since they went to school."

Questions for Analysis
1. Identify three reforms proposed by Long.
2. Explain how these reforms draw on the ideas of the New Deal.
3. Evaluate the extent to which these ideas go beyond the reforms of the New Deal.

TRM Suggested Responses to Questions

TRM Module 7.8 AP® Analyzing Sources Handout 2

BUILDING AP® SKILLS

Comparison

Assign students to read the excerpt from Huey Long and answer the accompanying questions. Then, have them read excerpts from "The Omaha Platform: Launching the Populist Party" available from History Matters' website (historymatters.gmu.edu). Task students with comparing them for their relative policy denunciations. Lastly, have students engage in a "Fifty-Word Drill" exercise responding to the following prompt: "Evaluate the extent to which the Populists of the late nineteenth century and Huey Long in the 1930s shared the same political and economic beliefs."

TEACHING IDEA

Connecting the Dots

Point out to students that in times of economic or political crisis, people and societies that are affected by said crises often look for easy answers in a fast-changing world. This explains much historical scapegoating and identity politics that sweeps persons and groups up by their passions. This is a common theme seen in times of economic upheaval internationally, and the United States is not immune to this phenomenon. Explain to students how the same sorts of attitudes drove social policies such as nativism in the nineteenth century, as the economy, work, and population changed rapidly.

Huey Long of Louisiana posed the greatest political threat to Roosevelt. Unlike Townsend and Coughlin, Long had built and operated a successful political machine, first as governor and then as U.S. senator, taking on the special interests of oil and railroad corporations in his home state. Early on he had backed Roosevelt, but Long found the New Deal wanting. In 1934 Long established the **Share Our Wealth society**, promising to make "every man a king" by presenting families with a $5,000 homestead and a guaranteed annual income of $2,000. To accomplish this, Long proposed levying heavy income and inheritance taxes on the wealthy. Although the financial calculations behind his bold plan did not add up, Share Our Wealth clubs counted some seven million members. The swaggering senator departed from most of his segregationist southern colleagues by appealing to a coalition of disgruntled farmers, industrial workers, and African Americans. Before Long could help lead a third-party campaign for president, he was shot and killed in 1935.

AP® TIP
Analyze the effects that Dr. Frances Townsend, Father Charles Coughlin, and Senator Huey Long's criticism of the New Deal had on the policies enacted after 1934.

REVIEW
What criticisms did opponents of the New Deal raise?

The New Deal Moves to the Left

Facing criticism from within his own party about the pace and effectiveness of the New Deal, and with the 1936 election looming, Roosevelt moved to the left. He adopted harsher rhetoric against recalcitrant corporate leaders; beefed up economic and social programs for the unemployed, the elderly, and the infirm; and revived measures to redress the power imbalance between management and labor. In doing so, he fashioned a New Deal political coalition that would deliver a landslide victory in 1936 and allow the Democratic Party to dominate electoral politics for the next three decades.

Even though the New Deal had helped millions of people, millions of others still felt left out, as the popularity of Townsend, Coughlin, and Long indicated. "We the people voted for you," a Columbus, Ohio worker wrote the president in disgust, "but it is a different story now. You have faded out on the masses of hungry, idle people.... The very rich is the only one who has benefited from your new deal."

In 1935 the president seized the opportunity to win his way back into the hearts of impoverished "forgotten Americans." Although Roosevelt favored a balanced budget, political necessity forced him to embark on deficit spending to expand the New Deal. Federal government expenditures would now exceed tax revenues, but New Dealers argued that these outlays would stimulate job creation and economic growth, which ultimately would replenish government coffers. Based on the highly successful but short-lived Civil Works Administration, the **Works Progress Administration (WPA)** provided jobs for the unemployed with a far larger budget, starting out with $5 billion. To ensure that the money would be spent, Roosevelt appointed Harry Hopkins to head the agency. Although critics condemned the WPA for employing people on unproductive "make-work" jobs — a criticism not entirely unfounded — overall the WPA did a good deal of work. The agency constructed or repaired more than 100,000 public buildings, 600 airports, 500,000 miles of roads, and 100,000 bridges. The WPA employed about 8.5 million workers during its eight years of operation.

The WPA also helped artists, writers, and musicians. Under its auspices, the Federal Writers Project, the Federal Art Project, the Federal Music Project, and the Federal Theater Project encouraged the production of cultural works and helped bring them to communities and audiences throughout the country. Writers Richard Wright, Ralph Ellison, Clifford Odets, Saul Bellow, John Cheever, Margaret Walker, and many others nourished both their works and their stomachs while employed by the WPA. Some painters, such as Jacob Lawrence, worked in the "easel division"; others created elaborate murals on the walls of post offices and other government buildings. Historians and folklorists researched and prepared city and state guides and interviewed formerly enslaved African Americans whose narratives of the system of bondage would otherwise have been lost.

Works Progress Administration (WPA) New Deal agency established in 1935 to put unemployed Americans to work on public projects ranging from construction to the arts.

Period 7: 1890–1945

MODULE 7-8 The New Deal

New Deal Art The Works Progress Administration, established by the Roosevelt administration in 1935, put Americans to work amid the ongoing depression. The WPA's Federal Art Project employed artists such as Ingrid E. Edwards of Minnesota, whose painting *Communications* features a newspaper boy, a telephone operator, a radio announcer, and a railroad train. Many of these works adorned public buildings. **To what extent did the establishment of the CCC pave the way for that of the WPA? To what extent did the actions of WPA workers go beyond the relief measures offered by work for the CCC?**

> **AP® TIP**
> Be sure you can explain how the New Deal affected African Americans.

In addition to the WPA, the National Youth Administration (NYA) employed millions of young people. Their work ranged from clerical assignments and repairing automobiles to building tuberculosis isolation units and renovating schools. Heading the NYA in Texas, the young Lyndon B. Johnson worked hard to expand educational and construction projects to unemployed white and black people. The Division of Negro Affairs, headed by the Florida educator Mary McLeod Bethune and the only minority group subsection in the NYA, ensured that African American youths would benefit from the programs sponsored by the agency.

Despite their many successes, these relief programs had a number of limitations. The WPA paid participants relatively low wages. The $660 in annual income earned by the average worker fell short of the $1,200 that a family needed to survive. In addition, the WPA limited participation to one family member. In most cases, this meant the male head of the household. As a result, women made up only about 14 percent of WPA workers, and even in the peak year of 1938, the WPA hired only 60 percent of eligible women. With the exception of the program for artists, most women hired by the WPA worked in lower-paying jobs than men.

The elderly required immediate relief and insurance in a country that lagged behind the rest of the industrialized world in helping its aged workforce. In August 1935, the president rectified this shortcoming and signed into law the **Social Security Act**. The measure provided that at age sixty-five, eligible workers would receive retirement payments funded by payroll taxes on employees and employers. The law also extended beyond the elderly by providing unemployment insurance for those temporarily laid off from work and welfare payments for the disabled who were permanently out of a job as well as for destitute, dependent children of single parents.

The Social Security program had significant limitations. The act excluded farm, domestic, and laundry workers, who were among the neediest Americans and were disproportionately African American. The reasons for these exclusions were largely political. The president needed southern

Social Security Act Landmark 1935 act that created retirement pensions for most Americans, as well as unemployment insurance.

TEACHING IDEA

Incorporating Secondary Sources

Assign students to read and annotate "An Ambivalent Legacy: Black Americans and the Political Economy of the New Deal," by Paul Moreno, available in PDF format from the Independent Institute's website (independent.org). Conduct a whole-class discussion in the following class meeting.

TEACHING IDEA

Understanding Social and Political Changes

Assign students in groups of two or three to create T-charts illustrating the similarities and differences in how New Deal and Progressive Era programs treated minorities, children, the elderly, and women. Have students post their charts around the room, or write them on the board for use in discussion or comparison of their products.

BUILDING AP® SKILLS

Continuity and Change

Assign students to write an LEQ response in class addressing the following prompt: "To what extent did the programs and policies of the New Deal represent a continuation of Progressive Era reforms, and to what extent were they a departure?"

The New Deal Moves to the Left

Period 7: 1890–1945

AP® ANALYZING SOURCES

Source: Charles Fusco, Italian-American munitions worker, *Interview on the New Deal*, 1938

"[I]n the nine years of this depression even though I didn't feel it much because I always gave myself a push but think of the others who are weak—what about them? You know there shouldn't be a depression in this country. You know we have everything—even the most money but all you hear today is the same old baloney—the Democrats are in power and the Republicans won't let loose with the money. Well I say that the money men started this thing and I believe the government should make laws to force these capitalist[s] to bring back prosperity. They can do it if they wanted to. But all you hear nowadays is let's balance the budget. I don't believe this budget has been balanced since the [I]ndians were here so why the hell do it now. I don't mean that we should go overboard on everything and start spending money left and right because I am against [cheaters] and flukey jobs but let's get down to business and start manufacturing things and sell them to everybody who got the cash—and to those who haven't the cash give them enough credit and a job so that they can pay.

You know sometimes I wonder what way we are drifting—some of the laws that was passed in the last few years were very good for the people and I guess you know what happened. You take the N.R.A. I think that was very good—it gave everybody a chance except those who are misers and are never satisfied if they make 100 dollars a week. This other law the Social Security I believe is the best. The only fault I find is that a man has to reach the age of 65 before he can collect. Well how many do? They tell you nowadays that a person lives longer—well they used to before this depression but [expletive] today you worry your [expletive] head off on how to meet both ends and that makes your life much shorter. You see what I mean that this government wants to do something good for the people and does but [expletive] they put strings to it. Tell me how many reach the age of 65? Very few. Why [expletive] don't they give a person a break and say at 56 years old you should retire from work and enjoy life instead of waiting until he is almost dead they give him a few dollars a month. I think the whole shooting match is wrong. And unless we get the crooks and chislers out of Washington we'll remain the same."

Questions for Analysis

1. Identify the strengths and weaknesses of the New Deal, according to Fusco.
2. Describe how, according to Fusco, the government should extend the New Deal programs.
3. Evaluate the ways in which historical situation shaped Fusco's arguments in this interview.

Democrats to support this measure, and as a Mississippi newspaper observed: "The average Mississippian can't imagine himself chipping in to pay pensions for able bodied Negroes to sit around in idleness." The system of financing Social Security payments differed from traditional taxation. The payroll tax, which imposed the same fixed percentage on all incomes, was a regressive tax, one that fell hardest on those with lower incomes. Nor did Social Security take into account the unpaid labor of women who remained in the home to take care of their children. Social Security also did not provide benefits for widows or children who were not part of the labor force.

Even with its flaws, Social Security revolutionized the expectations of American workers. It created a compact between the federal government and its citizens, and workers insisted that their political leaders fulfill their moral responsibilities to keep the system going. President Roosevelt recognized that the tax formula might not be economically sound, but he had a higher political objective in mind. He believed that payroll taxes would give contributors the right to collect their benefits and that "with those taxes in there, no damn politician can ever scrap my social security program."

REVIEW

- Why and how did the New Deal shift to the left in 1934 and 1935?
- How did mid-1930s programs such as the WPA, Social Security, and the NYA differ from earlier New Deal programs?

TRM Suggested Responses to Questions

TRM Module 7.8 AP® Analyzing Sources Handout 3

BUILDING AP® SKILLS

Comparison

Assign students to read the excerpt from Charles Fusco and answer the accompanying questions. Then, have students compare the source to Huey Long's "Every Man a King" on page 652. Task students to employ their HIPP training to both sources (a refresher of HIPP can be found on page 8). Then have students answer the following three questions:

1. What do you think the two men would think of one another?
2. On what issues would they be in agreement or disagreement?
3. What are two questions that Charles Fusco would have for Long, and how do you believe Long would answer those questions?

Whole-class discussion to follow.

EXPLORING AP® THEMES

Work, Exchange, and Technology

The Stanford History Education Group includes a collection of numerous free online lessons (sheg.stanford.edu). Included in the repository on this platform is a downloadable lesson focusing upon an evaluation of labor conditions and the union movement in Paterson, New Jersey in 1933 (available by search). Assign this activity to students and conclude it by having students create a thesis statement in small groups, utilizing the "Twenty-Five-Word Drill," that addressed the extent of difficulty and hardship motivating workers to organize in the 1930s. Have the student groups write their respective theses on butcher paper and post them around the room for a gallery walk exercise.

Period 7: 1890–1945

MODULE 7-8 The New Deal

Organized Labor Strikes Back

National Labor Relations Act 1935 act (also known as the Wagner Act) that created the National Labor Relations Board (NLRB). The NLRB protected workers' right to organize labor unions without business owner interference.

In 1935 Congress passed the **National Labor Relations Act**, also known as the Wagner Act for its leading sponsor, Senator Robert F. Wagner Sr. of New York. The law created the **National Labor Relations Board (NLRB)**, which protected workers' right to organize labor unions without owner interference. During the 1930s, union membership rolls soared from fewer than 4 million workers to more than 10 million, including more than 800,000 women. At the outset of the depression, barely 6 percent of the labor force belonged to unions, compared with 33 percent in 1940.

Government efforts boosted this growth, but these spectacular gains were due primarily to workers' grassroots efforts set in motion by economic hard times. The number of striking workers during the first year of the Roosevelt administration soared from nearly 325,000 to more than 1.5 million. Organizers traveled the country to bring as many people as possible into the union movement. The most important development within the labor movement occurred in 1935, with the creation of the CIO. After the AFL, which consisted mainly of craft unions, rejected a proposal by John L. Lewis of the United Mine Workers to incorporate industrial workers under its umbrella, Lewis and representatives of seven other AFL unions defected and formed the CIO. Unlike the AFL, the new union sought to recruit a wide variety of workers without respect to race, gender, or region.

▲ **Women's Emergency Brigade, 1937** After the United Auto Workers initiated a sit-down strike against General Motors in Flint, Michigan for union recognition, better working conditions, and higher wages, a group of their women relatives, friends, and coworkers formed the Women's Emergency Brigade. In this February 1937 demonstration, they held the clubs that they had used to smash windows at the Chevrolet Plant occupied by the strikers. **To what extent did New Deal policies align with the goals of unions such as the United Auto Workers?**

TEACHING IDEA

Check for Understanding

Point out to students that concurrent with the beginnings of the New Deal was the rise of the Golden Age of Organized Labor, which will last until the early 1970s. This represents one of the most fundamental shifts in labor relations in American history, and will broaden access to the middle class for millions of working-class Americans over the course of the next four decades.

TEACHING IDEA

Incorporating Videos

Assign students to watch the first 42 minutes of the PBS documentary *Walter Reuther and the UAW* (available on YouTube). This excerpt deals with the establishment, challenges, and growth of the union and labor movement in general in the 1930s.

BUILDING AP® SKILLS

Comparison

Have students work in groups to develop two similarities in the results of labor protest during the 1930s and the results of labor protest in the aftermath of World War I. Students should be given five minutes to complete this activity.

AP® TIP
Compare the goals, tactics, and outcome of the United Auto Workers Strike in 1937 to those of the Pullman Strike in 1894.

In 1937 the CIO mounted a full-scale organizing campaign. More than 4.5 million workers participated in some 4,700 strikes. Unions found new ways to protest poor working conditions and arbitrary layoffs. Members of the United Auto Workers (UAW), a CIO affiliate, launched a **sit-down strike** against General Motors (GM) in Flint, Michigan to win union recognition, higher wages, and better working conditions. Strikers refused to work but remained in the plants, shutting them down from the inside. When the company sent in local police forces to evict the strikers on January 11, 1937, the barricaded workers bombarded the police with spare machine parts and anything that was not bolted down. The community rallied around the strikers, and wives and daughters called "union maids" formed the Women's Emergency Brigade, which supplied sit-downers with food and water and kept up their morale. Neither the state nor the federal government interfered with the work stoppage, and after six weeks GM acknowledged defeat and recognized the UAW.

Fair Labor Standards Act
1938 law that provided a minimum wage of 40 cents an hour and a forty-hour workweek for employees in businesses engaged in interstate commerce.

The following year, the New Deal added a final piece of legislation sought by organized labor. The **Fair Labor Standards Act** (1938) established minimum wages at 40 cents an hour and maximum working hours at forty per week. By the end of the decade "big labor," as the AFL and CIO unions were known, had become a significant force in American politics and a leading backer of the New Deal.

REVIEW
- How did the New Deal benefit the labor movement?

A Half Deal for Minorities

President Roosevelt made significant gestures on behalf of African Americans. He appointed Mary McLeod Bethune and Robert Weaver to staff New Deal agencies and gathered an informal "Black Cabinet" in the nation's capital to advise him on matters pertaining to race. The Roosevelt administration also established the Civil Liberties Unit (later renamed Civil Rights Section) in the Department of Justice, which investigated racial discrimination. Eleanor Roosevelt acted as a visible symbol of the White House's concern with the plight of African Americans. In 1939 Eleanor Roosevelt quit the Daughters of the American Revolution, a women's organization, when it refused to allow black singer Marian Anderson to hold a concert in Constitution Hall in Washington, D.C. Instead, the First Lady brought Anderson to sing on the steps of the Lincoln Memorial.

Perhaps the greatest measure of Franklin Roosevelt's impact on African Americans came when large numbers of black voters switched from the Republican to the Democratic Party in 1936, a pattern that has lasted to the present day. "Go turn Lincoln's picture to the wall," a black observer commented after the election. "That debt has been paid in full."

AP® TIP
Be sure you can explain how the New Deal affected American Indians.

Yet overall the New Deal did little to break down racial inequality. President Roosevelt believed that the plight of African Americans would improve, along with that of all downtrodden Americans, as New Deal measures restored economic health. Black leaders disagreed. They argued that the NRA's initials stood for "Negroes Ruined Again" because the agency displaced black workers and approved lower wages for them than for their white counterparts. The AAA dislodged black sharecroppers. New Deal programs such as the CCC and those for building public housing maintained existing patterns of segregation. Both the Social Security Act and the Fair Labor Standards Act omitted from coverage jobs that black Americans were most likely to hold. In fact, the New Deal's big labor/big government alliance left out non-unionized industrial and agricultural workers, many of whom were African American and lacked bargaining power.

This pattern of halfway reform persisted for other minorities. Since the 1890s, American Indians had lived in poverty, forced onto reservations where they were offered few economic opportunities and where white people carried out a relentless assault on their culture. By the early 1930s, American Indians earned an average income of less than $50 a year — compared with $800 for whites — and their unemployment rate was three times higher than that of white Americans. For the most part, they lived on lands that whites had given up on as unsuitable for

---

BUILDING AP® SKILLS

Argumentation

Assign students to craft an introductory response to the Review question, utilizing the 4-1-1 contextualization and thesis model of LEQ introduction. Task students to create this product in pairs. Allow approximately 6-8 minutes. When this is completed, return students to their desks and have them craft a full LEQ response to the prompt as individuals, using their 4-1-1 product as their own introduction.

EXPLORING AP® THEMES

Politics and Power

Discuss with students that the election of 1932 represents one of the major shifts in the voting behavior of the electorate. Divide the class into five groups, and task each group to compare this shift to one of the following elections: 1912, 1896, 1876, 1860, and 1828. Students should explore which key issues and conditions moved which key constituencies in each respective election cycle. Once the groups have finished, have students jigsaw their conclusions to compare all five years to 1932 (a refresher of the jigsaw model can be found on page 33).

TEACHING IDEA

AP® Central

Assign students to read and break down the 2003 College Board AP® U.S. History DBQ on FDR and the Great Depression, which is available on the College Board's past exam questions resource "AP® United States History 2003 Free-Response Questions" (apcentral.collegeboard.org). Have students utilize their HIPP training (a refresher of HIPP can be found on page 8). Students can then also be asked to create a thesis that addresses the prompt, and/or write a full DBQ response.

Period 7: 1890–1945

MODULE 7-8 The New Deal

TRM Suggested Responses to Questions

TRM Module 7.8 AP® Analyzing Sources Handout 4

AP® ANALYZING SOURCES

Source: John P. Davis, "A Black Inventory of the New Deal," *The Crisis*, 1935

"The Agricultural Adjustment Administration has used cruder methods in enforcing poverty on the Negro farm population. . . . The reduction of the acreage under cultivation through the government rental agreement rendered unnecessary large numbers of tenants and farm laborers. Although the contract with the government provided that the land owner should not reduce the number of his tenants, he did so. . . . Farm laborers are now jobless by the hundreds of thousands, the conservative government estimate of the decline in agricultural employment for the year 1934 alone being a quarter of a million. The larger portion of these are unskilled Negro agricultural workers—now without income and unable to secure work or relief.

But the unemployment and tenant evictions occasioned by the crop reductions policy of the A.A.A. is not all. For the tenants and sharecroppers who were retained on the plantations the government's agricultural program meant reduced income. Wholesale fraud on tenants in the payment of parity checks occurred. Tenants complaining to the Department of Agriculture in Washington have their letters referred back to the locality in which they live and trouble of serious nature often results. Even when this does not happen, the tenant fails to get his check. The remainder of the land he tills on shares with his landlord brings him only the most meagre necessities during the crop season varying from three to five months. The rest of the period for him and his family is one of 'root hog or die.'"

Questions for Analysis

1. Identify the policies of the Agricultural Adjustment Administration (AAA) described in this document.
2. Describe the troubles faced by African American tenant farmers as a result of these policies.
3. Evaluate the extent to which these troubles are also a continuation of the southern agricultural economy and race relations after the Civil War.

Indian Reorganization Act (IRA) 1934 act that ended the Dawes Act, authorized self-government for those living on reservations, extended tribal landholdings, and pledged to uphold native customs and language.

farming or mining. The policy of assimilation established by the Dawes Act of 1887 (see Module 6-1) had worsened the problem by depriving American Indians of their cultural identities as well as their economic livelihoods. In 1934 the federal government reversed its course. Spurred on by John Collier, the commissioner of Indian affairs, Congress passed the **Indian Reorganization Act (IRA)**, which terminated the Dawes Act, authorized self-government for those living on reservations, extended tribal landholdings, and pledged to uphold native customs and language.

Although the IRA brought economic and social improvements for American Indians, many problems remained. Despite his considerable efforts, Collier approached his role as commissioner of Indian affairs from the top down. One historian remarked that Collier had "the zeal of a crusader who knew better than the Indians what was good for them." Collier failed to appreciate the diversity of native tribes and administered laws that contradicted American Indian political and economic practices. For example, the IRA required the tribes to operate by majority rule, whereas many of them reached decisions through consensus, which respected the views of the minority. Although 174 tribes accepted the IRA, 78 tribes, including the Seneca, Crow, and Navajo, rejected it.

REVIEW

In what ways did the New Deal assist minorities in the United States? In what ways did it fall short?

BUILDING AP® SKILLS

Argumentation

Have students in small groups discuss their thoughts on the Review question for 5-7 minutes. Then, present students with the follow-up question: "Taken as a whole, did the good about the New Deal outweigh the bad?" Give them 7-10 minutes to mingle and migrate throughout the room, ultimately to end up on one side of the classroom or the other depending upon if they answer the question in the affirmative or the negative. Lastly, engage the class in an activity whereby the two factions in the room make and defend their case regarding the New Deal.

Decline of the New Deal

> **AP® TIP**
> Compare the reasons why each of the groups that were part of the New Deal coalition joined the Democratic Party after 1936.

court-packing plan 1937 proposal by Franklin Roosevelt to increase the size of the Supreme Court and reduce its opposition to New Deal legislation. Congress failed to pass the measure, and the scheme undermined Roosevelt's popular support.

Roosevelt's shift to the left paid political dividends, and in 1936 the president won reelection by a landslide. His sweeping victory proved to be one of the rare critical elections that signified a fundamental political realignment. Democrats replaced Republicans as the majority party in the United States, overturning thirty-six years of Republican rule. While Roosevelt had won convincingly in 1932, not until 1936 did the president put together a stable coalition that could sustain Democratic dominance for many years to come.

In 1936 Roosevelt trounced Alfred M. Landon, the Republican governor of Kansas, and Democrats increased their congressional majorities by staggering margins. The vote broke down along class lines. Roosevelt won the votes of 80 percent of union members, 81 percent of unskilled workers, and 84 percent of people on relief, compared with only 42 percent of high-income voters. Millions of new voters came out to the polls, and most of them supported Roosevelt's New Deal coalition of the poor, farmers, urban ethnic minorities, unionists, white southerners, and African Americans.

The euphoria of his triumph, however, proved short-lived. An overconfident Roosevelt soon reached beyond his electoral mandate and within two years found himself unable to extend the New Deal. In 1937 Roosevelt devised a **court-packing plan** to ensure support of New Deal legislation and asked Congress to increase the size of the Supreme Court. He justified this as a matter of reform, claiming that the present nine-member Court could not handle its workload. Roosevelt attributed a good deal of the problem to the advanced age of six of the nine justices, who were over seventy years old. Under his proposal, the president would make one new appointment for each judge over the age of seventy who did not retire so long as the bench did not exceed fifteen members. In reality, Roosevelt schemed to "pack" the Court with supporters to prevent it from declaring New Deal legislation such as Social Security and the Wagner Act unconstitutional.

The plan backfired. Conservatives charged Roosevelt with seeking to destroy the separation of powers enshrined in the Constitution among the executive, legislative, and judicial branches. In the end, the president failed to expand the Supreme Court, but he preserved his legislative accomplishments. In a series of rulings, the chastened Supreme Court approved Social Security, the Wagner Act, and other New Deal legislation. Nevertheless, the political fallout from the court-packing fight damaged the president and his plans for further legislative reform.

Roosevelt's court-packing plan alienated many southern Democratic members of Congress who previously had sided with the president. Traditionally suspicious of the power of the federal government, southern lawmakers worried that Roosevelt was going too far toward centralizing power in Washington at the expense of states' rights. Southern Democrats formed a coalition with conservative northern Republicans who shared their concerns about the expansion of federal power and excessive spending on social welfare programs. Their antipathy toward labor unions further bound them. Although they held a minority of seats in Congress, this conservative coalition could block unwanted legislation by using the filibuster in the Senate (unlimited debate that could be shut down only with a two-thirds vote). After 1938 these conservatives made sure that no further New Deal legislation passed.

Roosevelt also lost support for New Deal initiatives because of the recession of 1937, which FDR's policies had triggered. When federal spending soared after passage of the WPA and other relief measures adopted in 1935, the president lost his economic nerve for deficit spending. He called for reduced spending, which increased unemployment and slowed economic recovery. In addition, as the Social Security payroll tax took effect, it reduced the purchasing power of workers, thereby worsening the impact of reduced government spending. Making the situation worse, pension payments were not scheduled to begin for several years. This "recession within the depression" further eroded congressional support for the New Deal.

The country was still deep in depression in 1939. Unemployment was at 17 percent, with more than 11 million people out of work. Most of those who were poor at the start of the Great Depression remained poor. Recovery came mainly to those who were temporarily impoverished as a result of the economic crisis. The distribution of wealth remained skewed toward the top. In 1933 the richest 5 percent of the population controlled 31 percent of disposable income; in 1939 the latter figure stood at 26 percent.

Against this backdrop of persistent difficult economic times, the president's popularity began to fade. In the midterm elections of 1938, Roosevelt campaigned against Democratic conservatives in an attempt to reinvigorate his New Deal coalition. His efforts failed and upset many ordinary citizens who associated the tactic with that used by European dictators who had recently risen to power. As the decade came to a close, Roosevelt turned his attention away from the New Deal and increasingly toward a new war in Europe that threatened to engulf the entire world.

> **AP® TIP**
> Evaluate the degree to which the New Deal successfully addressed longstanding problems of overproduction, poor standards of living, and environmental crises facing farmers in the United States.

BUILDING AP® SKILLS

Comparison

Assign students to read and annotate Franklin Roosevelt's Second Inaugural Address, which can be found on The Avalon Project's website (avalon.law.yale.edu). The next day in small groups, have them compare this speech to FDR's First Inaugural Address (see note on page 647) and apply their HIPP training to the piece, as well as discuss similarities and differences of the two sources' meaning, intent, and significance in small groups, with students rotating between groups (a refresher of HIPP can be found on page 8).

TEACHING IDEA

Incorporating Secondary Sources

Assign students to read and annotate "Lessons from the Political Economy of the New Deal" by John Joseph Wallis (available through online search from the University of Maryland). Require students to both identify Wallis's thesis and create a summative conclusive statement on their takeaways on his work. Have students share these out in small-group format, with students rotating among several of their peers.

Period 7: 1890–1945

MODULE 7-8 The New Deal

TRM Suggested Responses to Questions

TRM Module 7.8 AP® Analyzing Sources Handout 5

TEACHING IDEA

Incorporating Primary Sources

The Library of Congress has a comprehensive New Deal Teaching Curriculum based upon primary source documents of textual, visual, and audio sources, complete with lessons (loc.gov). This can be found by navigating The New Deal under Primary Source Sets of the Classroom Materials. Assign students to explore this electronic platform, and assign selected interpretive lessons based upon instructor discretion.

TRM Suggested Responses to Questions

AP® ANALYZING SOURCES

Source: Clifford K. Berryman, *Old Reliable*, 1938

Questions for Analysis

1. Identify the Roosevelt administration policies that are critiqued in this cartoon.
2. Describe the arguments that support this critique of the New Deal.
3. Explain how this portrayal of Roosevelt is designed to undermine confidence in New Deal economic policy.

REVIEW

- Who benefited most from Roosevelt's New Deal reforms after 1934?
- How successful were these reforms in bringing about the end of the Great Depression?

AP® WRITING HISTORICALLY Short-Answer Question Practice

ACTIVITY

Read the following question carefully and write a short response. Use complete sentences.

Using the following excerpts, answer (a), (b), and (c).

Source: William E. Leuchtenburg, *Franklin D. Roosevelt and the New Deal, 1932–1940*, 1963

"Franklin Roosevelt re-created the modern Presidency. He took an office which had lost much of its prestige and power in the previous twelve years and gave it an importance which went well beyond what even Theodore Roosevelt and Woodrow Wilson had done. . . . Under Roosevelt, the White House became the focus of all government—the fountainhead of ideas, the initiator of action, the representative of the national interest.

"Despite this encroachment of government on traditional business prerogatives, the New Deal could advance impressive claims to being regarded as a 'savior of capitalism.' Roosevelt's sense of the land, of family, and of the community marked him as a man with deeply ingrained conservative traits. In the New Deal years, the government sought deliberately, in Roosevelt's words, 'to energize private enterprise.' The RFC financed business, housing agencies underwrote home financing, and public works spending aimed to revive the construction industry. . . . Yet such considerations should not obscure the more important point: that the New Deal, however conservative it was in some respects and however much it owed to the past, marked a radically new departure. . . . The New Deal achieved a more just society by recognizing groups which had been largely unrepresented—staple farmers, industrial workers, particular ethnic groups, and a new intellectual-administrative class. Yet this was still a halfway revolution; it swelled the ranks of the bourgeoisie but left many Americans—sharecroppers, slum dwellers, most Negroes—outside of the new equilibrium."

Source: Barton J. Bernstein, "The New Deal: The Conservative Achievements of Liberal Reform," *Towards a New Past: Dissenting Essays in American History*, 1969

"The liberal reforms of the New Deal did not transform the American system; they conserved and protected American corporate capitalism, occasionally by absorbing parts of threatening programs. There was no significant redistribution of power in American society, only limited recognition of other organized groups, seldom of unorganized peoples. Neither the bolder programs advanced by New Dealers nor the final legislation greatly extended the beneficence of government beyond the middle classes or draw upon the wealth of the few for the needs of the many. Designed to maintain the American system, liberal activity was directed toward essentially conservative goals. Experimentalism was most frequently limited to means; seldom did it extend to ends. Never questioning private enterprise, it operated within safe channels, far short of Marxism or even of [older] American radicalisms that offered structural critiques and structural solutions.

The New Deal was [not] . . . 'a half-way revolution,' as William Leuchtenburg concludes. Not only was the extension of representation to new groups less than full-fledged partnership, but the New Deal neglected many Americans—sharecroppers, tenant farmers, migratory workers and farm laborers, slum dwellers, unskilled workers, and unemployed Negroes. They were left outside the new order. . . . Yet by the power of rhetoric and through the appeals of political organization, the Roosevelt government managed to win or retain the allegiance of these people. Perhaps this is one of the crueler ironies of liberal politics, that the marginal men trapped in hopelessness were seduced by rhetoric, by the style and movement, of efforts seldom reaching beyond words."

a. Briefly describe ONE major difference between Leuchtenburg's and Bernstein's historical interpretations of the period 1933–1939.
b. Briefly explain how ONE specific historical event or development during the period 1933–1939 that is not explicitly mentioned in the excerpts could be used to support Leuchtenburg's interpretation.
c. Briefly explain how ONE specific historical event or development during the period 1933–1939 that is not explicitly mentioned in the excerpts could be used to support Bernstein's interpretation.

TEACHING IDEA

AP® Writing Historically Review

The excerpts provide students with two opposing interpretations, one of which focuses on the "half-way" revolution of the New Deal, while the other asserts the conservative nature of New Deal programs. Therefore, have students create two categories on butcher-block paper labeled "half-way" and "conservative." Students should find at least two or three quotes from each excerpt that correspond to the historical interpretations provided. This will help students have a more discrete reading of the excerpts.

TRM Suggested Responses to Questions

TEACHING IDEA

Differing Views

Divide the class into three groups, one group labeled "support," one group labeled "refute," and the third group labeled "modify." Then, present the class with the following prompt: "The United States' involvement in World War I was a colossal mistake." Based upon the group students were placed in, assign them to come up with evidence that either supports, refutes, or modifies the prompt. At the conclusion of this step, recombine the class into groups of three, consisting of one supporter, one refuter, and one modifier. Have them share out and teach one another what they now know, and then as a group, have them craft a thesis statement together on the prompt, based upon their shared knowledge discussion.

▲ Differentiation

In order to obtain the maximal amount of contributions from students, the instructor could combine the room in such a way so that the strongest students work with those that are more challenged by the content, in either the paired phase, or the whole-group supporter/refuter phase. Furthermore, students of mixed ability levels could also be tasked with creating a skeletal outline of the LEQ response to the prompt, and then broken off into individuals for the purpose of writing a full response, based upon the collaborative work.

Module 7-9

America Enters World War II

LEARNING TARGETS
By the end of this module, you should be able to:
- Explain why the Great Depression led many Americans to migrate to urban centers in search of economic opportunities.
- Explain how after World War I the United States pursued an "isolationist" foreign policy that used international investment, peace treaties, and occasional military intervention to promote U.S. interests.
- Explain why the rise of fascism and totalitarianism concerned many citizens in the United States.
- Explain why most Americans opposed military action against Nazi Germany and Japan until the attack on Pearl Harbor.

THEMATIC FOCUS
Politics and Power
America in the World

While the United States experienced the trauma of the Great Depression and tried to counteract its effects with the New Deal, other industrialized nations suffered a similar economic collapse, but turned to other, less idealistic, solutions. In Europe, nations like Italy, Spain, and Germany adopted fascism, a hyper-nationalistic ideology that promoted racial superiority and a strong, centralized government. In Asia, Japan embraced militarism and tried to create a European-style empire of colonies under Japanese economic and political control. In the United States, citizens and policy makers debated a proper response to this aggressive turn.

HISTORICAL REASONING FOCUS
Causation

TASK ▶ While you read this module, consider the effects of international crises on American citizens and policy makers and the debates these effects inspired.

The end of World War I did not bring peace and prosperity to Europe. The harsh peace terms imposed on the Central Powers in 1919 left the losers, especially Germany, deeply resentful. The war saddled both sides with a huge financial debt and produced economic instability, which contributed to the Great Depression. In the Far East, Japanese invasions of China and Southeast Asia threatened America's Open Door policy. The failure of the United States to join the League of Nations dramatically reduced the organization's ability to maintain peace and stability. German expansionism in Europe in the late 1930s moved President Roosevelt and the nation toward war, but it took the Japanese attack on Pearl Harbor to bring the United States into the global conflict.

The Road toward War

Kellogg-Briand Pact Arms control agreement that outlawed war as an instrument of national policy following World War I. The policy proved unenforceable.

Despite its failure to join the League of Nations, the United States did not withdraw from international affairs in the 1920s. It participated in arms control negotiations; signed the **Kellogg-Briand Pact**, which outlawed war as an instrument of national policy but proved unenforceable; and expanded its foreign investments in Central and Latin America, Asia, the Middle East, and western Europe. In 1933 a new possibility for trade emerged when the Roosevelt administration extended diplomatic recognition to the Soviet Union (USSR).

Overall, the country did not retreat from foreign affairs so much as it refused to enter into collective security agreements that would restrain its freedom of action. To the extent that

The Road toward War

isolationism Informal policy stemming from the belief that the United States should not become involved with the affairs of other nations. This mindset was especially popular following World War I.

American leaders practiced **isolationism**, they did so mainly in the political sense of rejecting internationalist organizations such as the League of Nations, institutions that might require military cooperation to implement their decisions.

The experience of World War I had reinforced this brand of political isolationism, which was reflected in an outpouring of antiwar sentiments in the late 1920s and early 1930s. Best-selling novels like Ernest Hemingway's *Farewell to Arms* (1929), Erich Maria Remarque's *All Quiet on the Western Front* (1929), and Dalton Trumbo's *Johnny Got His Gun* (1939) presented graphic depictions of the horror and futility of war. Beginning in 1934, Senate investigations chaired by Gerald Nye of North Dakota concluded that bankers and munitions makers — "merchants of death," as one contemporary writer labeled them — had conspired to push the United States into war in 1917. Nye's hearings appealed to popular antibusiness sentiment in Depression-era America.

Neutrality Acts Legislation passed between 1935 and 1937 to make it more difficult for the United States to become entangled in overseas conflicts. The Neutrality Acts reflected the strength of isolationist sentiment in 1930s America.

Following the **Nye Committee** hearings, Congress passed a series of **Neutrality Acts**, each designed to make it more difficult for the United States to become entangled in European armed hostilities. In 1935 Congress prohibited the sale of munitions to either warring side and authorized the president to warn Americans against traveling on passenger liners of belligerent nations. The following year, lawmakers added private loans to the ban, and in 1937 they required belligerents to pay cash for nonmilitary purchases and ship them on their own vessels — so-called cash-and-carry provisions.

AP® ANALYZING SOURCES

Source: *Kellogg-Briand Pact*, 1928

"Article I

The High Contracting Parties solemnly declare in the names of their respective peoples that they condemn recourse to war for the solution of international controversies, and renounce it, as an instrument of national policy in their relations with one another.

Article II

The High Contracting Parties agree that the settlement or solution of all disputes or conflicts of whatever nature or of whatever origin they may be, which may arise among them, shall never be sought except by [peaceful] means.

Article III

The present Treaty shall be ratified by the High Contracting Parties named in the Preamble in accordance with their respective constitutional requirements, and shall take effect as between them as soon as all their several instruments of ratification shall have been deposited at Washington.

This Treaty shall, when it has come into effect as prescribed in the preceding paragraph, remain open as long as may be necessary for adherence by all the other Powers of the world. Every instrument evidencing the adherence of a Power shall be deposited at Washington and the Treaty shall immediately upon such deposit become effective as; between the Power thus adhering and the other Powers parties hereto.

It shall be the duty of the Government of the United States to furnish each Government named in the Preamble and every Government subsequently adhering to this Treaty with a certified copy of the Treaty and of every instrument of ratification or adherence. It shall also be the duty of the Government of the United States telegraphically to notify such Governments immediately upon the deposit with it of each instrument of ratification or adherence.

IN FAITH WHEREOF the respective Plenipotentiaries have signed this Treaty in the French and English languages both texts having equal force, and hereunto affix their seals.

DONE at Paris, the twenty seventh day of August in the year one thousand nine hundred and twenty-eight."

Questions for Analysis

1. Identify three significant points made in the Kellogg-Briand Pact about international relations.
2. Explain how this pact was shaped by its historical situation.
3. Evaluate the extent to which the Kellogg-Briand Pact preserved American international power.

EXPLORING AP® THEMES

Politics and Power

Assign students in pairs to create a "cereal box" product for either the Kellogg-Briand Pact, or for the historical term, "Isolationism." This has the potential to engage students of multiple ability levels and is a more involved, tactile, and kinesthetic approach to accomplish the same task as the basic T-chart or Venn diagram for the two terms. Templates and exemplars for creation of this type of product may be found at SampleTemplates by searching for "Cereal Box Book Reports" (sampletemplates.com).

TRM Suggested Responses to Questions

TRM Module 7.9 AP® Analyzing Sources Handout 1

BUILDING AP® SKILLS

Making Connections

Point out to students the logical fallacies of the Kellogg-Briand Pact, specifically that if a nation declares war on another, the only way to stop them is to engage in warfare yourself, which defeats the entire point of the Pact. Explain to students that in many ways, the Pact's importance was more symbolic than legal; it was a manifestation of the degree to which the horrors of the First World War had "scared the Western Powers straight." Share with students that the Kellogg-Briand Pact of the 1920s, and the motivations that led to its creation, will presage all of the future appeasement of the 1930s.

EXPLORING AP® THEMES

America and the World

Point out to students that even though the United States was not a signatory, the longest-term consequences of the Munich Accord were that it would color and haunt the thinking of American policy advisers for the next eighty years. The giveaways of Munich, and their attendant role in leading to the Second World War, would be the prism through which essentially all major future international crises and negotiations would be viewed by the American foreign policy establishment, up to and including the present day.

Events in Europe, however, made U.S. neutrality ever more difficult to maintain. After rising to power as chancellor of Germany in 1933, Adolf Hitler revived Germany's economic and military strength despite the Great Depression. Hitler installed National Socialism (**Nazism**) at home and established the empire of the **Third Reich** abroad. The *Führer* (leader) whipped up patriotic fervor by scapegoating and persecuting Communists and Jews. To garner support for his actions, Hitler manipulated German feelings of humiliation for losing World War I and having been forced to sign the "war guilt" clause and pointed to the disastrous effects of the country's inflation-ridden economy. In 1936 Hitler sent troops to occupy the Rhineland between Germany and France in blatant violation of the Treaty of Versailles.

Hitler did not stop there. Citing the need for more space for the Germanic people to live, he pushed for German expansion into eastern Europe. In March 1938 he forced Austria to unite with Germany. In September of that year Hitler signed the **Munich Accord** with Great Britain and France, allowing Germany to annex the Sudetenland, the mainly German-speaking, western region of Czechoslovakia. Hitler still wanted more land and was convinced that his western European rivals would not stop him, so in March 1939 he sent German troops to invade and occupy the rest of Czechoslovakia. Hitler proved correct; Britain and France did nothing in response, a policy critics called **appeasement**.

appeasement The policy of England and France that allowed the Nazis to annex Czechoslovak territory in exchange for Hitler promising not to take further land—a pledge he soon violated.

Hitler's Italian ally, Benito Mussolini, joined him in war and conquest. In 1935 Italian troops invaded Ethiopia. The following year, both Germany and Italy intervened in the Spanish civil war, providing military support for General Francisco Franco in his effort to overthrow the democratically elected, socialist republic of Spain. While the United States and Great Britain remained on the sidelines, only the Soviet Union officially assisted the Loyalist defenders of the Spanish republic. In violation of American law, private citizens, many of whom were Communists, volunteered to serve on the side of the Spanish Loyalists and fought on the battlefield as the Abraham Lincoln Brigade. Other sympathetic Americans, such as J. Robert Oppenheimer, provided financial assistance for the anti-Franco government. Despite these efforts, Franco's forces seized control of Spain in early 1939, another victory for Hitler and Mussolini.

REVIEW

What major factors threatened the post–World War I order during the 1930s?

The Challenge to Isolationism

As Europe drifted toward war, public opinion polls revealed that most Americans wanted to stay out of any European conflict. The president, however, thought it likely that, to protect its own economic and political interests, the United States would eventually need to assist the Western democracies. Still, Roosevelt had to tread lightly in the face of the Neutrality Acts that Congress had passed between 1935 and 1937 and overwhelming public opposition to American involvement in Europe.

Germany's aggression in Europe eventually led to full-scale war. When Germany invaded Poland in September 1939, Britain and France declared war on Germany and Italy. Just before the invasion, the Soviet Union had signed a nonaggression agreement with Germany, which carved up Poland between the two nations and permitted the USSR to occupy the neighboring Baltic states of Latvia, Lithuania, and Estonia. Soviet leader Joseph Stalin had few illusions about Hitler's ultimate design on his own nation, but he concluded that by signing this pact he could secure his country's western borders and buy additional time. (In June 1941 the Germans broke the pact and invaded the Soviet Union.)

Roosevelt responded to the outbreak of war by reaffirming U.S. neutrality. Despite his sympathy for the **Allies** (primarily Great Britain and France), which most Americans had come to share, the president stated his hope that the United States could stay out of the war: "Let no man or woman thoughtlessly or falsely talk of America sending its armies to European fields."

> " Let no man or woman thoughtlessly or falsely talk of America sending its armies to European fields. "
> — Franklin D. Roosevelt, 1939

With the United States on the sidelines, German forces marched toward victory. By the spring of 1940, German armies had launched a *Blitzkrieg* (lightning war) across Europe, defeating and occupying Denmark, Norway, the Netherlands, Belgium, and Luxembourg. With German victories mounting, committed opponents of American involvement in foreign wars organized the **America First Committee**. America First tapped into the feeling of isolationism and concern among a diverse group of Americans who did not want to get dragged into another foreign war.

America First Committee Isolationist organization founded by Senator Gerald Nye in 1940 to keep the United States out of World War II.

BUILDING AP® SKILLS

Sourcing and Situation

Assign students to read a series of speeches by Charles Lindbergh on behalf of the America First Committee (charleslindbergh.com/americanfirst). Task students with applying the HIPP training to each speech they are assigned, and be prepared to deliver a summary of Lindbergh's central points in each assigned speech to their classmates in small groups (a refresher of HIPP can be found on page 8).

The Challenge to Isolationism

Period 7: 1890–1945

America First Committee Rally, 1941 Organized in 1940, the America First Committee campaigned against U.S. entry into World War II. One of its leaders, the popular aviator Charles Lindbergh, addressed a rally of 3,000 people in Ft. Wayne, Indiana on October 5, 1941. The isolationist group blamed eastern bankers, British sympathizers, and Jewish leaders for promoting war fever. The committee dissolved soon after this 1941 rally and the Japanese attack on Pearl Harbor. **How did these arguments echo those made by conservative critics of FDR's New Deal?**

The greatest challenge to isolationism occurred in June 1940 when France fell to the German onslaught and Nazi troops marched into Paris. Britain now stood virtually alone, and its position seemed tenuous. The British had barely succeeded in evacuating their forces from France by sea when the German *Luftwaffe* (air force) began a bombing campaign on London and other targets in the Battle of Britain.

The surrender of France and the Battle of Britain drastically changed Americans' attitude toward entering the war. Before Germany invaded France, 82 percent of Americans thought that the United States should not aid the Allies. After France's defeat, in a complete turnaround, some 80 percent of Americans favored assisting Great Britain in some way. However, four out of five Americans polled still opposed immediate entry into the war. As a result, the politically astute Roosevelt portrayed all U.S. assistance to Britain as a way to prevent American military intervention by allowing Great Britain to defeat the Germans on its own.

Nevertheless, the Roosevelt administration found acceptable ways of helping Britain. On September 2, 1940, the president sent fifty obsolete destroyers to the British in return for leases on British naval bases in Newfoundland, Bermuda, and the British West Indies. Two weeks later, on September 16, Roosevelt persuaded Congress to pass the **Selective Training and Service Act of 1940**, the first peacetime military draft in U.S. history, which quickly registered more than 16 million men.

This political maneuvering came as Roosevelt campaigned for an unprecedented third term in 1940. He defeated the Republican Wendell Willkie, a Wall Street lawyer who shared Roosevelt's anti-isolationist views. However, both candidates accommodated voters' desire to stay out of the European war, and Roosevelt went so far as to promise American parents: "Your boys are not going to be sent into any foreign war."

AP® TIP
Analyze how the Roosevelt administration helped shape public opinion to increasingly support the Allies in World War II.

Selective Training and Service Act of 1940
Legislation requiring men between the ages of 18 and 35 to register for the draft, later expanded to age 45. It was the first peacetime draft in U.S. history.

TEACHING IDEA

Incorporating Secondary Sources

Assign one-half of students to read and annotate "America's Undeclared Naval War" by James Marino, available at the Fleet Reserve Association's website (frabr245.org), and one-half of students to read "American Isolationism, 1939–1941" by Justus Doenecke, available by search on the Mises Institute's website (mises.org). The next day in class, have students discuss both pieces in two separate groups. When this has concluded, place students into groups of six, with three from each article, and task them with sharing their information and conclusions from their respective annotations and roundtables.

BUILDING AP® SKILLS

Argumentation

Assign students to craft a full LEQ response to the following prompt: "Evaluate the extent to which American neutrality measures came one war too late."

▲ Differentiation

Place students in small groups, and have students construct a thesis statement with contextualization in response to the prompt along the lines of the 4-1-1 model (a refresher of the 4-1-1 model can be found on page 163). Then, inform students that they will write an LEQ on this prompt the next day in class, and they will be required to begin with the 4-1-1 introduction that they just created. This will allow students who struggle with beginning a long-essay response to take a premade introduction and prepare to address and evidence it the following day in class.

Period 7: 1890–1945

MODULE 7-9 America Enters World War II

Lend-Lease Act March 1941 law permitting the United States to lend or lease military equipment and other commodities to Great Britain and its allies. Its passage marked the end of American neutrality before the U.S. entered World War II.

Roosevelt's campaign promises did not halt the march toward war. Roosevelt succeeded in pushing Congress to pass the **Lend-Lease Act** in March 1941. With Britain running out of money and its shipping devastated by German submarines, this measure circumvented the cash-and-carry provisions of the Neutrality Acts. The United States would lend or lease equipment, but no one expected the recipients to return the used weapons and other commodities. To protect British ships carrying American supplies, the president extended naval and air patrols in the North Atlantic. In response, German submarines began sinking U.S. ships. By May 1941, Germany and the United States were engaged in an undeclared naval war.

AP® ANALYZING SOURCES

Source: Charles Lindbergh, *Who Are the War Agitators?*, September, 1941

"National polls showed that when England and France declared war on Germany, in 1939, less than 10 percent of our population favored a similar course for America. But there were various groups of people, here and abroad, whose interests and beliefs necessitated the involvement of the United States in the war. I shall point out some of these groups tonight, and outline their methods of procedure. In doing this, I must speak with the utmost frankness, for in order to counteract their efforts, we must know exactly who they are.

The three most important groups who have been pressing this country toward war are the British, the Jewish and the Roosevelt administration.

Behind these groups, but of lesser importance, are a number of capitalists, Anglophiles, and intellectuals who believe that the future of mankind depends upon the domination of the British empire. Add to these the Communistic groups who were opposed to intervention until a few weeks ago, and I believe I have named the major war agitators in this country.

I am speaking here only of war agitators, not of those sincere but misguided men and women who, confused by misinformation and frightened by propaganda, follow the lead of the war agitators.

As I have said, these war agitators comprise only a small minority of our people; but they control a tremendous influence. Against the determination of the American people to stay out of war, they have marshaled the power of their propaganda, their money, their patronage."

Questions for Analysis
1. Identify the perpetrators of war according to Lindbergh.
2. Describe, according to Lindbergh, the rationale behind these perpetrators' actions.
3. Evaluate the extent of similarity between the ideas expressed by Lindbergh and the ideas expressed by supporters and members of the KKK in the 1920s.

REVIEW
- How did many Americans justify isolationism during the late 1930s?
- What factors undermined isolationist sentiments?

The United States Enters the War

Financially, militarily, and ideologically, the United States had aligned itself with Britain, and Roosevelt expected that the nation would soon be formally at war. As Germany and Italy successfully expanded their empires, they endangered U.S. economic interests and democratic values. President Roosevelt believed that American security abroad was threatened by the German Nazis and Italian Fascists. After passage of the Lend-Lease Act, American and British military planners agreed that

---

TRM Suggested Responses to Questions

TRM Module 7.9 AP® Analyzing Sources Handout 2

BUILDING AP® SKILLS
Developments and Processes

Assign students in groups of four to compare U.S. foreign policy before World War I to U.S. foreign policy before World War II, in order to document the similarities and differences. This can be done with a chart to begin. Next, have students construct a "Fifty-Word Drill" introductory paragraph addressing this comparison.

TRM Find **Handout 7.10 – Comparing Prewar U.S. Foreign Policy: WWI vs. WWII** in the Teacher's Resource Materials.

TEACHING IDEA
Incorporating Videos

Assign students to watch The United States War Department film, "Why We Fight, Episode 7: War Comes to America" (available on YouTube). Inform students that this film series was required viewing for all persons inducted into the United States Armed Forces during World War II. Have them apply their HIPP training to the film, and determine its key themes and thesis (a refresher of HIPP can be found on page 8).

TEACHING IDEA
Connecting the Dots

Engage the class in an activity of association by disassociation called "Odd One Out." Write the following terms on the board/projector:
- Destroyers for Bases Deal
- Appeasement
- "Merchants of Death"
- America First Committee
- Selective Service Act

Then place students in small groups and ask them, "Which one is the odd one out and why?" How do the remaining terms relate?" Give students approximately 7-10 minutes to complete this part, then share out student answers and discuss their conclusions and reasoning as a whole-class activity. There is no specific correct answer; the goal is to get students thinking in categorical habits of mind and defending their rationales.

The United States Enters the War

Roosevelt, Churchill, and the Atlantic Charter, 1941 U.S. President Franklin D. Roosevelt and British Prime Minister Winston Churchill converse aboard the battleship *Prince of Wales* off the coast of Newfoundland on August 10, 1941. The five-day secret meeting produced the Atlantic Charter, a declaration that shaped the Anglo-American alliance of World War II. **What common interests did the United States and Great Britain have in this conflict?**

defeating Germany would become the top priority if the United States entered the war. In August 1941, Roosevelt and British prime minister Winston Churchill met in Newfoundland, where they signed the **Atlantic Charter**, a lofty statement of war aims that included principles of freedom of the seas, self-determination, free trade, and "freedom from fear and want" — ideals that laid the groundwork for the establishment of a postwar United Nations. At the same meeting, Roosevelt promised Churchill that the United States would protect British convoys in the North Atlantic as far as Iceland while the nation waited for a confrontation with Germany that would rally the American public in support of war. The president got what he wanted. After several attacks on American ships by German submarines in September and October, the president persuaded Congress to repeal the neutrality legislation of the 1930s and allow American ships to sail across the Atlantic to supply Great Britain. By December, the nation was close to open war with Germany.

The event that finally prompted the United States to enter the war, however, occurred not in the Atlantic but in the Pacific Ocean. For nearly a decade, U.S. relations with Japan had deteriorated over the issue of China's independence and maintaining the Open Door to Chinese markets. The United States did little to challenge the Japanese invasion and occupation of Manchuria in 1931, but after Japanese armed forces moved farther into China in 1937, the United States supplied arms to China.

Relations worsened in 1940 when the Japanese government signed the **Tripartite Pact** with Germany and Italy, which created a mutual defense agreement among the three. That same year, Japanese troops invaded northern Indochina, and Roosevelt responded by

AP® TIP
Evaluate the extent of similarity between the ideas expressed in the Atlantic Charter and those expressed in President Wilson's Fourteen Points.

Tripartite Pact 1940 mutual defense agreement between Japan, Germany, and Italy.

APPLY THE TIP

Assign students to read and annotate either the Atlantic Charter or Wilson's Fourteen Points, both available at The Avalon Project's website (avalon.law.yale.edu). Then, the next day in class, place students into groups of eight, with four students per assigned document, and instruct them to try to make the case for their assigned document containing stronger ideas.

TEACHING IDEA

Incorporating Secondary Sources

Assign students to read and annotate "The Myth of American Isolationism," by Bear F. Braumoeller (available through online search), with whole-class discussion to follow in the next class meeting.

embargoing sales of products that Japan needed for war. This embargo did not deter the Japanese; in July they occupied the remainder of Indochina to gain access to the region's natural resources. The Roosevelt administration retaliated by freezing Japanese assets and cutting off all trade with Japan.

On the quiet Sunday morning of December 7, 1941, Japan attacked the U.S. Pacific Fleet stationed at Pearl Harbor in Honolulu, Hawaii. This surprise air and naval assault killed more than 2,400 Americans and seriously damaged ships and aircraft. The **attack on Pearl Harbor** abruptly ended isolationism and rallied the American public behind President Roosevelt, who pronounced December 7 "a date which will live in infamy." The next day, Congress overwhelmingly voted to go to war with Japan, and on December 11 Germany and Italy, upholding the Tripartite Pact, declared war on the United States in response. In little more than a year after his reelection pledge to keep the country out of war, Roosevelt sent American men to fight overseas. Still, an overwhelming majority of Americans now considered entry into the war as necessary to preserve freedom and democracy against assaults from fascist and militaristic nations.

attack on Pearl Harbor
December 7, 1941 Japanese attack on the U.S. Pacific Fleet stationed at Pearl Harbor in Honolulu, Hawaii. This surprise air and naval assault killed more than 2,400 Americans, seriously damaged ships and aircraft, and abruptly ended isolationism by prompting U.S. entry into World War II.

AP® ANALYZING SOURCES

Source: Monica Sone, *Memories of the Pearl Harbor Attack on December 7, 1941*, 1953

"On a peaceful Sunday morning, December 7, 1941, Henry, Sumi, and I were at choir rehearsal singing ourselves hoarse in preparation for the annual Christmas recital of Handel's 'Messiah.' Suddenly Chuck Mizuno, a young University of Washington student, burst into the chapel, gasping as if he had sprinted all the way up the stairs. . . .

'Listen, everybody!' he shouted. 'Japan just bombed Pearl Harbor . . . in Hawaii. It's war!'

The terrible words hit like a blockbuster, paralyzing us. Then we smiled feebly at each other, hoping this was one of Chuck's practical jokes. Miss Hara, our music director, rapped her baton impatiently on the music stand and chided him, 'Now Chuck, fun's fun, but we have work to do. Please take your place. You're already half an hour late.'

But Chuck strode vehemently back to the door. 'I mean it, folks, honest! I just heard the news over my car radio. Reporters are talking a blue streak. Come on down and hear it for yourselves.' . . .

I felt as if a fist had smashed my pleasant little existence, breaking it into jigsaw puzzle pieces. An old wound opened up again, and I found myself shrinking inwardly from my Japanese blood, the blood of an enemy. I knew instinctively that the fact that I was an American by birthright was not going to help me escape the consequences of this unhappy war.

One girl mumbled over and over again, 'It can't be, God, it can't be!' Someone else was saying, 'What a spot to be in! Do you think we'll be considered Japanese or Americans?'

A boy replied quietly, 'We'll be Japs, same as always. But our parents are enemy aliens now, you know.'

A shocked silence followed."

Questions for Analysis
1. Identify the students' reaction to the attack on Pearl Harbor.
2. Describe the dilemma it creates for the author of this document.
3. Explain why some of the people in this document fear "We'll be Japs, same as always. . . ."

REVIEW

- What events in Europe and the Pacific ultimately brought the United States into World War II?

TRM Suggested Responses to Questions

TRM Module 7.9 AP® Analyzing Sources Handout 3

TEACHING IDEA

Six Degrees of Separation

Have the students complete a "Six Degrees of Separation" activity. For the purpose of this exercise, students are given two events spanning time, but related by theme. They must select four events in chronological order that link the first event in the series with the last. They will write the name of each selected event, and create an argument to support each of the events they selected. Explain to them that they must answer the question, "Why does it belong as a link in your chain of events?" for each link. Students must emphasize both cause and effect and/or demonstrate continuity or change over time in their linking. This can be done as either a formative assessment in class, or as a homework assignment involving student research of their textbooks, activities/lessons, lecture notes, and knowledge of the time period. The lesson may also be undertaken by students individually or in small groups. The prompt for this particular activity is as follows:

"From the Treaty of Versailles to the attack on Pearl Harbor"

BUILDING AP® SKILLS

Argumentation

In preparation for writing a full LEQ response to the review prompt, assign students to craft a comprehensive statement of introduction utilizing the "Fifty-Word Drill" method. Allow students to share their products, and then engage in responding to the prompt as individuals.

TEACHING IDEA

Incorporating Videos

As a concluding activity in this module, while simultaneously setting the stage for Module 7-10, assign students to watch Episode 36, "World War II Part 2," from the Crash Course US History series (available on YouTube). Use this 14-minute episode as an introductory bridge both explaining and making the point of the concurrence of the international affairs that thoroughly involved the United States with the simultaneous domestic transformations and upheaval brought about by the conflict.

AP® WRITING HISTORICALLY — Short-Answer Question Practice

ACTIVITY

Read the following question carefully and write a short response. Use complete sentences.

Using the following image, answer (a), (b), and (c).

Source: Winsor McCay, *Let Sam Do It*, 1931

a. Briefly describe ONE perspective expressed by the artist about the role of the United States during the international conflicts of the 1930s.
b. Briefly explain how ONE event or development led to the historical situation depicted in the image.
c. Briefly explain ONE specific outcome of debates during the 1930s about the role of the United States during these crises.

TRM Suggested Responses to Questions

BUILDING AP® SKILLS

Argumentation

As a general strategy, the *ACE* method explained by the authors for LEQ purposes — "Answer the question, Cite your evidence, and Explain its meaning" — is also very useful for Short-Answer Questions (a refresher of *ACE* can be found on page 21). For each of the three tasks of an SAQ, use this model. In so doing, the three tasks of an SAQ are actually then addressed in nine discrete steps. If this method is followed, the depth of student responses to the three directed tasks of the SAQ should be such that it increases the likelihood of every SAQ point being earned with a comfortable margin.

TEACHING IDEA

AP® Writing Historically Review

Consider having students analyze the words found in the cartoon prior to answering the question. For instance, have students analyze the League of Nations, Japan and China, and U.S. Foreign Policy (Uncle Sam) all in the historical context of the 1930s. Completing this activity before answering the question allows students time to consider the historical situation this cartoon was created in, which will help them make a connection to the author's point of view.

TRM Suggested Responses to Questions

Module 7-10

Life on the Homefront

LEARNING TARGETS

By the end of this module, you should be able to:

- Explain why war production and labor during World War II further drew many Americans to migrate to American cities.
- Explain how mass mobilization helped end the Great Depression.
- Explain how the country's strong industrial base helped the Allies win World War II.
- Explain how women and minorities took advantage of opportunities caused by World War II.
- Explain how reactions to World War II challenged civil liberties.
- Explain why migration to the United States from the rest of the Western Hemisphere increased during World War II.

THEMATIC FOCUS

Work, Exchange, and Technology
Politics and Power
Social Structures

During the Second World War, the United States marshalled the power of the economy and society behind the war effort. In this regard, the enhanced power of the federal government during the New Deal era laid the foundation for the war effort. While the domestic economy during the war offered opportunities for many Americans who had traditionally been left out of the industrial economy, not all of these opportunities were shared equally.

HISTORICAL REASONING FOCUS

Comparison

TASK ▶ In this section, compare the ways economic and social changes during World War II shaped the lives of different groups in American society.

The global conflict had profound effects on the American home front. World War II ended the Great Depression, restored economic prosperity, and increased labor union membership. At the same time, it smoothed the way for a closer relationship between government and private defense contractors, later referred to as the military-industrial complex. The war extended U.S. influence in the world and offered new economic opportunities at home. Despite fierce and bloody military battles throughout the world, Americans kept up morale by rallying around family and community.

Managing the Home-Front Economy

To mobilize for war, President Roosevelt increased federal spending to unprecedented levels. Federal government employment during the war expanded to an all-time high of 3.8 million workers, setting the foundation for a large, permanent Washington bureaucracy. War orders fueled economic growth, productivity, and employment. The gross domestic product increased from the equivalent of nearly $900 billion in 1939 (in 1990 prices) to nearly $1.5 trillion (in 1990 prices) at the end of the war, union membership rose from around 9 million to nearly 15 million, and unemployment dropped from 8 million to less than 1 million. The armed forces helped reduce unemployment significantly by enlisting 12 million men and women, 7 million of whom had been unemployed.

TEACHING IDEA

Incorporating Videos

Prior to introducing this module, assign students to view Episode 2 of the *America Goes to War* documentary series, "Praise the Lord and Pass the Ammunition" (available on YouTube). Use this 26-minute episode as a concise formative content introduction for students of the initial major issues and events of Module 7-10 as part of preparation for either assessment or reinforcement.

TEACHING IDEA

Connecting the Dots

As the instructor introduces the scope and nature of the American economic turnaround that came with the United States' entry into the Second World War, it is important to connect back to the previous module and point out that the New Deal did not end the Great Depression. Instead, it was World War II that definitively concluded the long economic downturn. That being said, point out that the reason that American involvement in the war terminated the depression was due to Keynesian economics (see Module 7-9) on a massive scale that dwarfed the domestic expenditures of the New Deal. In a purely economic sense then, it could be argued that the American commitment to total war from 1941 to 1945 represented the ultimate jobs and economic stimulus program.

Prosperity was not limited to any one region. The industrial areas of the Northeast and Midwest once again boomed, as automobile factories converted to building tanks and other military vehicles, oil refineries processed gasoline to fuel them, steel and rubber companies manufactured parts to construct these vehicles and the weapons they carried, and textile and shoe plants furnished uniforms and boots for soldiers to wear. As farmers provided food for the nation and its allies, farm production soared. The economy diversified geographically. Fifteen million Americans — 11 percent of the entire population — migrated between 1941 and 1945. The war transformed the agricultural South into a budding industrial region. The federal government poured more than $4 billion in contracts into the South to operate military camps, contract with textile factories to clothe the military, and use its ports to build and launch warships. The availability of jobs in southern cities attracted sharecroppers and tenant farmers, black and white, away from the countryside and promoted urbanization while reducing the region's dependency on the plantation economy.

No region was changed more by the war than the West. The West Coast prospered because it was the gateway to the Pacific war. The federal government established aircraft plants and shipbuilding yards in California, Oregon, and Washington, resulting in extraordinary population growth in Los Angeles, San Diego, San Francisco, Portland, and Seattle. The West's population grew three times as fast as the rest of the nation's. Los Angeles led the way in attracting defense contracts, as its balmy climate proved ideal for test-flying the aircraft that rolled off its assembly lines.

Following the attack on Pearl Harbor, Congress passed the **War Powers Act**, which authorized the president to reorganize federal agencies any way he thought necessary to win the war. In 1942 the president established the **War Production Board** to oversee the economy. The agency enticed business corporations to meet ever-increasing government orders by negotiating lucrative contracts that helped underwrite their costs, lower their taxes, and guarantee large profits. The government also suspended antitrust enforcement, giving private companies great leeway in running their enterprises. Much of the antibusiness hostility generated by the Great Depression evaporated as the Roosevelt administration recruited business executives to supervise government agencies. Indeed, the close relationship between the federal government and business that emerged during the war produced the **military-industrial complex**, which would have a vast influence on the future development of the economy.

In the first three years of the war, the United States increased military production by some 800 percent. American factories accounted for more than half of worldwide manufacturing output. By 1945 the United States had produced 86,000 tanks, nearly 300,000 airplanes, 15 million rifles and machine guns, and 6,500 ships.

Financing this enormous enterprise took considerable effort. The federal government spent more than $320 billion, ten times the cost of World War I. To pay for the war, the federal government sold $100 billion in bonds, only about half of what was needed. The rest came from increased income tax rates, which for the first time affected low- and middle-income workers, who had paid

> **AP® TIP**
> Compare the effects of World War I and World War II on the power of the federal government.

War Powers Act 1942 act passed after the attack on Pearl Harbor. It authorized the president to reorganize federal agencies any way he thought necessary to win the war.

military-industrial complex The government-business alliance related to the military and national defense that developed out of World War II and greatly influenced future development of the U.S. economy.

Tuskegee Airmen Twenty black pilots, among those known as the Tuskegee airmen, line up for a photograph, which they signed. The Army Air Corps created two segregated units of African American airmen, the 442nd Bombardment Group and the 99th Pursuit Squadron. The latter flew combat missions in Europe. The success of the Tuskegee airmen contributed to the postwar desegregation of the armed forces. **How might the motivations of the Tuskegee airmen differ from other U.S. military pilots in World War II?**

Courtesy National Park Service, Museum Management Program and Tuskegee Airmen National Historic Site, TUAI 31.

APPLY THE TIP

Revisit the concept from the First World War that American involvement in major conflicts has always expanded federal power, without exception. Assign students in small groups to identify and explain the growth in said powers. Each group is tasked with doing so for one of three conflicts: the Civil War, the First World War, or the Second World War. When this phase is concluded, recombine student groups for peer teaching of what they have discovered. Lastly, place the original groups back together and have them list or write up their conclusions on butcher paper/poster paper, and allow students time to conduct a gallery walk and take notes on the class findings.

BUILDING AP® SKILLS

Continuity and Change

Point out to students that FDR famously said that "Dr. New Deal has been replaced by Dr. Win-the-War." To further make this point, assign students to take specific New Deal programs and the problems they addressed, and connect them to specific wartime programs that succeeded them and addressed those same problems.

TEACHING IDEA

Incorporating Websites

The National Gallery of Art has a powerful exhibition of photographs titled "Gordon Parks: The New Tide, Early Work 1940–1950" (npa.gov). Have students look through the collection for photographs of the airmen, among others, to enhance their understanding.

TEACHING IDEA

Incorporating Secondary Sources

Assign students to read and annotate "Resource Mobilization for World War II: the U.S.A., U.K., U.S.S.R., and Germany, 1938–1945," by Mark Harrison (available through online search). Require students to both identify Harrison's thesis and create a summative conclusive statement on their takeaways on his work. Have students share these out in small-group format, with students rotating among several of their peers.

Period 7: 1890–1945

MODULE 7-10 Life on the Homefront

APPLY THE TIP

Place students into three groups. Assign one group the topic "Social," one group the topic "Political," and one group the topic "Economic." Then ask the three groups, from the perspective of their topic, to evaluate the extent of continuity in African American experiences in the four conflicts of the prompt. Allow them to discuss, and then place students into groups of six, with two persons from each topic represented. Have them share out jigsaw style, and then task these groups of six with crafting an introductory response to the overall prompt (a refresher of the jigsaw model can be found on page 33). Have students share these responses on the board and vote upon which one they believe to be the strongest.

TRM Suggested Responses to Questions

TRM Module 7.10 AP® Analyzing Sources Handout 1

AP® TIP

Evaluate the extent of continuity in the experiences of African Americans in World War II, World War I, the Spanish-American War, and the Civil War.

Tuskegee airmen African American airmen who overcame prejudice during World War II. They earned fame escorting U.S. bomber aircraft in Europe and North Africa.

little or no tax before. At the same time, the tax rate for the wealthy was boosted to 94 percent. In addition to paying higher taxes, American consumers shouldered the burden of shortages and high prices.

Building up the armed forces was the final ingredient in the mobilization for war. In 1940 about 250,000 soldiers were serving in the U.S. military. By 1945 American forces had grown to more than 12 million men and women through voluntary enlistments and a draft of men between the ages of eighteen and forty-five. The military reflected the diversity of the U.S. population. The sons of immigrants fought alongside the sons of older-stock Americans. Although the military tried to exclude homosexuals, many managed to join the fighting forces. Some 700,000 African Americans served in the armed forces, but civilian and military officials confined them to segregated units in the army, assigned them to menial work in the navy, and excluded them from the U.S. Marine Corps. The Army Air Corps created a segregated fighting unit trained at Tuskegee Institute in Alabama, and these **Tuskegee airmen**, like their counterparts among the ground forces, distinguished themselves in battle.

Women could not fight in combat, but 140,000 joined the **Women's Army Corps (WACs)**, and 100,000 joined the navy's **Women Accepted for Voluntary Emergency Service (WAVES)**. In these and other service branches, women contributed mainly as nurses and performed transportation and clerical duties. Women also played an important but secretive role in bolstering Allied

AP® ANALYZING SOURCES

Source: Carl Murphy, *An Open Letter Home*, 1943

"[I], a commissioned officer of the United States Army, am denied the rights and privileges of an officer. I am excluded by members of my own rank and station in the Army. I am denied the privilege to use the Officer's Club. Although members of my race are used as waiters and general help around the club, I am denied the privilege of using it. It has been a source of embarrassment for a Negro soldier working there to ask me if I am denied the privilege of the club. I ask you, gentlemen, what would you say or do if a soldier, who respected you as an officer of the Army, knew that you, an officer sworn to uphold and defend the principles of this democracy, were being denied the very thing you are and asking them to lay down their life for. How can we demand the respect of men under our command when we are not respected by members of our own rank.

Gentlemen, I have seen men come from States of the South where my race is persecuted beyond belief. I have seen them come cowed. I have seen them come with no self respect. I have seen them come eager in the belief of what their state did to them, their government would not uphold. I have heard them upon entering the Army say, that an Army post is under Federal regulations and that they would not be subjected to injustices of State rule. Yet these men have been let down by the very government they swore to uphold. They see their government inflict upon them and a large number of the white race a segregation neither one desires.

They see a great Federal government built on the principle of 'Liberty and justice for all' being swayed by sectional customs and traditions that were defeated in a war seventy-five years ago. . . .

These type of conditions seriously injure the morale of the Negro soldier and tend to give him an air of indifference that he is sure to carry with him to civilian life. I have heard it expressed openly, hundreds of times by Negro soldiers that they would just as soon give their life fighting the injustices inflicted upon him right here in the United States than to fight to correct the injustices of other people they know nothing about on foreign soil. This state of mind has been brought about by the reluctance of the federal government to uphold firmly the rights of all men."

Questions for Analysis
1. Identify the three injustices that Murphy describes in this document.
2. Describe what Murphy expects of the federal government, according to this letter.
3. Evaluate the extent to which Murphy's appeal is based on recent historical trends.

EXPLORING AP® THEMES

Social Structures

Point out to students that the institution of the draft, coupled with mass voluntary enlistments, allowed for a sort of large scale cross-cutting social class mixing and integration brought about by the military experience that was and is unique in American social relations. The sheer numbers involved and the relative clarity of the nature of the struggle meant that the class and education-based deferments of the Vietnam era were not nearly as prominent in the 1940s as they became in the 1960s.

Managing the Home-Front Economy

Period 7: 1890–1945

> **AP® TIP**
> Be sure you can explain how attitudes toward women in the military and the workforce changed during World War II.

military efforts. The navy and army recruited thousands of women college students and small-town school teachers to Washington, D.C., where they worked on deciphering German and Japanese diplomatic and military codes. These young, unmarried women worked very long, tedious hours during the week as well as on weekends, and succeeded in providing the U.S. military with secret information of enemy planning. In this way, they joined the efforts already begun by British female codebreakers operating at Bletchley Park, England.

The government relied on corporate executives to manage wartime economic conversion, but without the sacrifice and dedication of American workers, their efforts would have failed. The demands for wartime production combined with the departure of millions of American workers to the military created a labor shortage that gave unions increased leverage. By 1945 the membership rolls of organized labor had grown from 9 million to nearly 14 million. In 1942 the Roosevelt administration established the National War Labor Board (see Module 7-4), which regulated wages, hours, and working conditions and authorized the government to take over plants that refused to abide by its decisions. Unions at first refrained from striking, but later in the war organized strikes to protest the disparity between workers' wages and corporate profits. In 1943 Congress responded by passing the Smith-Connally Act, which prohibited walkouts in defense

AP® ANALYZING SOURCES

Source: President Franklin Roosevelt, *State of the Union Address*, 1944

"Let us remember the lessons of 1918. In the summer of that year the tide turned in favor of the Allies. But this government did not relax, nor did the American people. In fact, our national effort was stepped up. In August 1918, the draft age limits were broadened from twenty-one to thirty-one, all the way to eighteen to forty-five. The president called for 'force to the utmost,' and his call was heeded. And in November, only three months later, Germany surrendered.

That is the way to fight and win a war—all out—and not with half an eye on the battle-fronts abroad and the other eye and a half on personal, selfish, or political interests here at home.

Therefore, in order to concentrate all of our energies, all of our resources on winning this war, and to maintain a fair and stable economy at home, I recommend that the Congress adopt:

First, a realistic and simplified tax law—which will tax all unreasonable profits, both individual and corporate, and reduce the ultimate cost of the war to our sons and our daughters. The tax bill now under consideration by the Congress does not begin to meet this test.

Secondly, a continuation of the law for the renegotiation of war contracts—which will prevent exorbitant profits and assure fair prices to the government. For two long years I have pleaded with the Congress to take undue profits out of war.

Third, a cost of food law—which will enable the government to place a reasonable floor under the prices the farmer may expect for his production; and to place a ceiling on the prices a consumer will have to pay for the necessary food he buys. This should apply, as I have intimated, to necessities only and this will require public funds to carry it out. It will cost in appropriations about 1 percent of the present annual cost of the war. . . .

And [finally], a national service law—which, for the duration of the war, will prevent strikes, and, with certain appropriate exceptions, will make available for war production or for any other essential services every able-bodied adult in this whole nation."

Questions for Analysis

1. Identify Roosevelt's reasons for taking these steps to ensure a stable economy.
2. Explain how the war allowed Roosevelt to impose greater controls over the free market.
3. Evaluate the ways in which Roosevelt's requests to Congress were a product of historical situation.

TRM Suggested Responses to Questions

TRM Module 7.10 AP® Analyzing Sources Handout 2

BUILDING AP® SKILLS

Sourcing and Situation

Utilizing their HIPP training, assign students to compare the 1944 State of the Union Address on this page to FDR's first inaugural speech in 1933, which can be found on The Avalon Project's website (avalon.law.yale.edu). Have students discuss the similarities and differences in how the president reacted to two very different national emergencies (a refresher of HIPP can be found on page 8).

TEACHING IDEA

Understanding Political Changes

It is important for students to understand that during times of war, the United States allows for governmental economic oversight and national economic control in ways and extent that would never be accepted in peacetime. The examples of the National War Labor Board and Office of Price Administration are instructive here. Point out to students that they are examples of what is called "War Socialism," whereby the state directs the economy in a command model, which is antithetical to the principles of free market capitalism that Americans generally embrace. A useful contrast is to point out the political, legal, and constitutional pushback generated by the National Industrial Recovery Act and the Agricultural Adjustment Act just a half-dozen years earlier, compared to the relative lack of national political resistance to highly similar statist measures (and more) that were enacted during the war.

Period 7: 1890–1945

MODULE 7-10 Life on the Homefront

industries and set a thirty-day "cooling-off" period before unions could go out on strike. As in World War I, the government set up an agency, the **Office of War Information**, to promote patriotism and urge Americans to contribute to the war effort any way they could.

REVIEW

- How did the wartime economy of World War II compare to that of World War I?

New Opportunities for Women

World War II opened up new opportunities for women in the paid workforce. Between 1940 and the peak of wartime employment in 1944, the number of employed women rose by more than 50 percent, to 6 million. Given severe labor shortages caused by increased production and the exodus of male workers into the armed forces, for the first time in U.S. history married working women outnumbered single working women. At the start of the war, about half of women employees held poorly paid clerical, sales, and service jobs. Women in manufacturing labored mainly in low-wage textile and clothing factories. During the war, however, the overall number of women in manufacturing grew by 141 percent; in industries producing directly for war purposes, the figure jumped by 463 percent. By contrast, the number of women in domestic service dropped by 20 percent. As women moved into defense-related jobs, their incomes also improved.

As impressive as these figures are, they do not tell the whole story. First, although married women entered the job market in record numbers, most of these workers were older and without young children. Women over the age of thirty-five accounted for 60 percent of those entering the workforce. The government did little to encourage young mothers to work, and few efforts were made to provide assistance for child care for those who did. In contrast to this situation, in Great Britain child care programs were widely available. Second, openings for women in manufacturing jobs did not guarantee equality. Women received lower wages for labor comparable to the work that men performed, and women did not have the same chances for advancement. Typical union benefits, such as seniority, hurt women, who were generally the most recent hires. In fact, some contracts stipulated that women's tenure in jobs previously held by men would last only for the duration of the war.

Gender stereotypes continued to dominate the workforce and society in general. Magazine covers with the image of "Rosie the Riveter," a woman with her sleeves rolled up and her biceps bulging, became a symbol for the recruitment of women, but reality proved different. Women who took war jobs were viewed not so much as war workers but as women temporarily occupying "men's jobs" during the emergency. As the war drew to a close, public relations campaigns shifted gears and encouraged the same women they had recently recruited to prepare to return home. This included nearly all of the brilliant women codebreakers secretly at work in Washington, D.C. who were ordered to go back home.

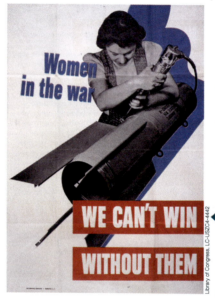

Women Workers during the War During the war, women worked in industrial jobs in unprecedented numbers. Corporations and the federal government actively recruited women through posters and advertisements and promised women that factory work was something that would benefit them, their families, and their nation. As the Allies neared victory, however, the message changed, and women were urged to prepare to return to the home to open up jobs for returning soldiers. **To what extent was this a change in the roles women played in previous American conflicts?**

TEACHING IDEA
Incorporating Videos

Assign students to view Episode 4 of the *America Goes to War* documentary series, "A String of Pearls (available on YouTube). This 26-minute excerpt covers the role of American women in the Second World War.

BUILDING AP® SKILLS
Comparison

Task the students with comparing the posters on pages 674 and 675 to the pair of World War I posters on page 604 from Module 7-4. Ask students to explore any similarities and differences in both the messages of the respective posters, as well as what they say about society's views of womanhood and women in their times.

TEACHING IDEA
Incorporating Primary Sources

"Beyond Rosie the Riveter: Women's Contributions during World War II," a History Now lesson from the Gilder Lehrman Institute of American History, provides students with the opportunity to evaluate numerous different primary sources in both research- and project-based formats, to build a comprehensive understanding of the ways that women contributed to victory in World War II, and how those contributions represented significant political, social, and economic changes (gilderlehrman.org). Assign various portions and activities at the instructor's discretion to enhance student learning of this topic.

EXPLORING AP® THEMES
Work, Exchange, and Technology

The National Women's History Museum contains several oral history accounts of women's experiences in the workforce during World War II in the online platform, "Rosie the Riveter Oral Histories," found in the Digital Classroom Resources (womenshistory.org). Assign students to listen to and analyze several of these accounts. Then assign them to answer the following LEQ prompt: "Evaluate the extent to which women were impacted by their labor experiences during the Second World War."

AP® ANALYZING SOURCES

Source: Office of War Information, *Rosie the Riveter*, 1943

Questions for Analysis

1. Identify the features of the advertisement — both the imagery and in the text — that were meant to appeal to viewers.
2. Describe the ways in which these features were intended to appeal to viewers.
3. Explain the ways in which this image both upholds and challenges traditional images of American women.

REVIEW

- What opportunities were available to women during World War II?
- To what extent were these opportunities different from those available to women during previous wars?

Fighting for Equality at Home

The war also had a significant impact on race relations. The fight to defeat Nazism, a doctrine based on racial prejudice and white supremacy, offered African Americans a chance to press for equal opportunity at home. By contrast, Japanese Americans experienced intensified discrimination and oppression as wartime anti-Japanese hysteria led to the internment of Japanese Americans, an erosion of their civil rights. They were freed toward the end of the war, but their incarceration left scars. Finally, Mexican Americans and American Indians benefited from wartime jobs and military service but continued to experience ethnic prejudice.

In 1941 A. Philip Randolph, the head of the Brotherhood of Sleeping Car Porters, applied his labor union experience to the struggle for civil rights. He announced that he planned to lead a 100,000-person march on Washington, D.C. in June 1941 to protest racial discrimination in government and war-related employment as well as segregation in the military. Although Randolph believed in an interracial alliance of working people, he insisted that the march should be all-black to show that African Americans could lead their own movement. Inching the country toward war, but not yet engaged militarily, President Roosevelt wanted to avoid any embarrassment the proposed march would bring to the forces supporting democracy and freedom. With his wife, Eleanor, serving as go-between, Roosevelt agreed to meet with Randolph and worked out a compromise. Randolph called off the march, and in return, on June 25, 1941, the president issued Executive Order 8802, creating the Fair Employment Practice Committee (FEPC). Roosevelt refused to order the desegregation of the military, but he set up a committee to investigate inequality in the armed forces. Although the FEPC helped African Americans gain a greater share of jobs in key industries than they had before, the effect was limited because the agency did not have enforcement power.

The march on Washington movement was emblematic of rising civil rights activity. Black leaders proclaimed their own "two-front war" with the symbol of the **Double V** to represent victory against racist enemies both abroad and at home. The National Association for the Advancement of Colored People continued its policy of fighting racial discrimination in the courts. In 1944

AP® TIP
Evaluate the extent to which Franklin Roosevelt successfully used executive power to address issues of inequality in the United States.

Double V The slogan African Americans used during World War II to state their twin aims to fight for victory over fascism abroad and victory over racism at home.

MODULE 7-10 Life on the Homefront

TEACHING IDEA

Incorporating Videos

Assign students to watch Episode 9, "Mood Indigo: Blacks and Whites," from the documentary series, *America Goes to War* (available on YouTube). This 26-minute excerpt covers the role of African Americans during the Second World War both at home and overseas, and the prejudices, challenges, and opportunities they experienced.

BUILDING AP® SKILLS

Comparison

Assign students to compare the causes, content, and consequences of the 1919 race riots in Chicago with the causes, content, and consequences of the 1943 Zoot Suit Riots in Los Angeles — evaluating and explaining which factors were different and which factors remained similar. Have students complete a graphic organizer or T-chart to this effect, as well as create a thesis that addresses the prompt.

TRM Find **Handout 7.11 – Comparing Racial Unrest, 1919 & 1943** in the Teacher's Resource Materials.

AP® TIP
Analyze how African Americans and Mexican Americans took action to address racial inequality in the U.S. during World War II.

the organization won a significant victory in a case from Texas, *Smith v. Allwright*, which outlawed all-white Democratic primary elections in the traditionally one-party South. As a result of the decision, the percentage of African Americans registered to vote in the South doubled between 1944 and 1948. In 1942 early civil rights activists also founded the interracial **Congress of Racial Equality (CORE)** in Chicago. CORE protested directly against racial inequality in public accommodations. Its members organized "sit-ins" at restaurants and bowling alleys that refused to serve African Americans. Students at Howard University in Washington, D.C. used the same tactics, with some success, to protest racial exclusion from restaurants and cafeterias in the nation's capital. Although these demonstrations did not get the national attention that postwar protests would, they constituted the prelude to the civil rights movement.

Population shifts on the home front during World War II worsened racial tensions, resulting in violence. As jobs opened up throughout the country at military installations and defense plants, hundreds of thousands of African Americans moved from the rural South to the urban South, the North, and the West. Cities could not handle this rapid influx of people and failed to provide sufficient housing to accommodate those who migrated in search of employment. Competition between white and black workers for scarce housing spilled over into tensions in crowded transportation and recreational facilities. In 1943 the stress caused by close wartime contact between the races exploded in more than 240 riots. The most serious one occurred in Detroit, where federal troops had to restore order after white and black people fought with each other following a dispute at a popular amusement park that killed thirty-four people.

Immigration from Mexico increased significantly during the war. To address labor shortages in the Southwest and on the Pacific coast and departing from the deportation policies of the 1930s, in 1942 the United States negotiated an agreement with Mexico for contract laborers (*braceros*) to enter the country for a limited time to work as farm laborers and in factories. *Braceros* had little or no control over their living spaces or working conditions. Not surprisingly, they conducted numerous strikes for higher wages in the agricultural fields of the Southwest and Northwest. Most U.S. residents of Mexican ancestry were, however, American citizens. Like other Americans, they settled into jobs to help fight the war, while more than 300,000 Mexican Americans served in the armed forces.

The war heightened Mexican Americans' consciousness of their civil rights. As one Mexican American World War II veteran recalled: "We were Americans, not 'spics' or 'greasers.' Because when you fight for your country in a World War, against an alien philosophy, fascism, you are an American and proud to be in America." In southern California, newspaper publisher Ignacio Lutero Lopez campaigned against segregation in movie theaters, swimming pools, and other public accommodations. He organized boycotts against businesses that discriminated against or excluded Mexican Americans. Wartime organizing led to the creation of the Unity Leagues, a coalition of Mexican American business owners, college students, civic leaders, and GIs that pressed for racial equality.

In Texas, Mexican Americans joined the **League of United Latin American Citizens (LULAC)**, a largely middle-class group that challenged racial discrimination and segregation in public accommodations. Members of the organization emphasized the use of negotiations to redress their grievances, but when they ran into opposition, they resorted to economic boycotts and litigation. The war encouraged LULAC to expand its operations throughout the Southwest.

◀ **Navajo Code Talkers, 1943** Private First Class Preston Toledo and Private First Class Frank Toledo, cousins and Navajo Indians, attached to a Marine Artillery Regiment in the South Pacific, relay orders over a field radio in their native language on July 7, 1943. These "code talkers" were among the more than 400 bilingual Navajo soldiers deployed to transmit secret communications in their complex tribal language. **What interests could American Indians have had in the results of World War II?**

EXPLORING AP® THEMES

Social Structures

Assign students to read and annotate an excerpt of the National Park Service Theme Study, "World War II and the American Home Front" (nps.gov). Assign specifically pages 104–123 of "Part Four: African Americans and Other Minorities on the Home Front," by Harvard Sitkoff. Whole-class discussion to follow the next day in class, addressing the following prompt: "What opportunities and challenges existed within the American social order for African Americans from 1939 to 1945?"

Mexican American citizens encountered hostility from recently transplanted white people and longtime residents. Tensions were greatest in Los Angeles. A small group of Mexican American teenagers joined gangs and identified themselves by wearing zoot suits — colorful, long, loose-fitting jackets with padded shoulders and baggy pants tapered at the bottom. Not all zoot-suiters were gang members, but many outside their communities failed to make this distinction and found the zoot-suiters' dress and swagger provocative. On the night of June 4, 1943, squads of sailors stationed in Long Beach invaded Mexican American neighborhoods in East Los Angeles and indiscriminately attacked both zoot-suiters and those not dressed in this garb, setting off four days of violence. Mexican American youths tried to fight back. The **zoot suit riots** ended as civilian and military authorities restored order. In response, the Los Angeles city council banned the wearing of zoot suits in public.

zoot suit riots Series of riots in 1943 in Los Angeles, California, sparked by white hostility toward Mexican American teenagers who dressed in zoot suits — suits with long jackets with padded shoulders and baggy pants tapered at the bottom.

Some twenty-five thousand American Indians served in the military during the war. Although the Iroquois nation challenged the right of the United States to draft American Indians, in 1942 it separately declared war against the Axis powers. The armed forces used Navajo soldiers in the Pacific theater to confuse the Japanese by sending coded messages in their tribal language. In addition to those serving the military, another forty thousand American Indians worked in defense-related industries. Their migration off of reservations opened up new opportunities and fostered increased pride in the part they played in winning the war. Nevertheless, for most American Indians the war did not improve their living conditions or remove hostility to their tribal identities.

AP® ANALYZING SOURCES

Source: Lawrence E. Davies, "Zoot Suits Become Issue on Coast," *New York Times*, 1943

"LOS ANGELES, June 12 — The zoot suit with the reat pleat [or reet pleat], the drape shape and the stuff cuff has been the object of much amusement and considerable derision from Harlem to the Pacific during the last two or three years. Psychiatrists may have their own ideas about it, but, according to the reasoning of many newcomers to the armed services, especially hundreds of young sailors in this area, the zoot suit has become the symbol these last ten days of a fester on the body politic which should be removed by Navy vigilantes, if police will not or cannot do the job.

Adventurers of the Navy boys in trying to accomplish their purpose have been watched with such interest in all quarters — bringing cheers from some and causing concern to others — that newspapers were snatched up eagerly on downtown street corners the other day when newsboys handling late afternoon and morning 'bulldog' editions shouted:

'No more zoot suits!' . . .

[R]ear Admiral David W. Bagley, commandant of the Eleventh Naval District . . . plac[ed] this city under 'temporarily restricted liberty for naval personnel.' This means that only in special cases could sailors be at large in the city.

This greatly reduced, if it failed to stop altogether, clashes between small bands of zoot-suit wearers, chiefly of Mexican descent, and groups of Navy seamen out to retaliate for attacks on lone sailors or their girls by the pork-pie-hatted hoodlums."

Questions for Analysis

1. Identify why the men who wore zoot suits were considered a threat.
2. Describe the grievances expressed by both sides in this conflict.
3. Explain how the conflict described in this article reflected other racial and ethnic tensions in the United States during the Second World War.

REVIEW

- How did activists further the cause of civil rights at home during World War II?
- What effects did World War II have on the lives of Mexican Americans and American Indians?

The Ordeal of Japanese Americans

World War II marked a significant crossroads for the protection of civil liberties. In general, the federal government did not repress civil liberties as harshly as it had during World War I, primarily because opposition to World War II was not nearly as great. The chief potential for radical dissent came from the Communist Party, but after the Germans attacked the Soviet Union in June 1941, Communists and their sympathizers rallied behind the war effort and did whatever they could to stifle any protest that threatened the goal of defeating Germany. On the other side of the political spectrum, after the attack on Pearl Harbor conservative isolationists in the America First Movement quickly threw their support behind the war.

Of the three ethnic groups associated with the Axis enemy — Japanese, Germans, and Italians — Japanese Americans received by far the worst treatment from the civilian population and state and federal officials. Germans had experienced animosity and repression on the home front during World War I but, like Italian immigrants, had generally assimilated into the wider population. In addition, German Americans and Italian Americans had spread out across the country, while Japanese Americans remained concentrated in distinct geographical pockets along the West Coast. Although German Americans and Italian Americans experienced prejudice, they had come to be considered racially white, unlike Japanese Americans. Nevertheless, the government arrested about 1,500 Italians considered "enemy aliens" and placed around 250 of them in internment camps. It also arrested more than 11,000 Germans, some of them American citizens, who were considered a danger.

internment The relocation of persons seen as a threat to national security to isolated camps during World War II. Nearly all people of Japanese descent living on the West Coast were forced to sell or abandon their possessions and relocate to internment camps during the war.

The **internment**, or forced relocation and detainment, of Italians and Germans in the United States paled in comparison with that of the Japanese. On March 21, 1942, President Roosevelt issued **Executive Order 9066** authorizing military commanders on the West Coast to take any measures necessary to promote national security. Nearly all people of Japanese descent lived along the West Coast. Government officials relocated all of those living there — citizens and noncitizens alike — to camps in Arizona, Arkansas, California, Colorado, Idaho, Texas, Utah, and Wyoming. In Hawaii, the site of the Japanese attack on Pearl Harbor, the Japanese population, nearly one-third of the territory's population, was too large to transfer and instead lived under martial law. The few thousand Japanese Americans living elsewhere in the continental United States remained in their homes.

On May 9, 1942, the military ordered the Korematsu family to report to Tanforan Racetrack in San Mateo, from which they would be transported to internment camps throughout the West.

AP® ANALYZING SOURCES

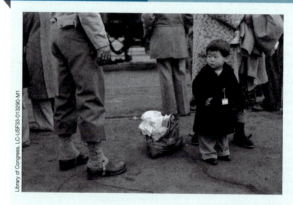

Source: Russell Lee, *Japanese American Child on the Way to Internment*, 1942

Questions for Analysis

1. Identify three details that reveal this photograph is taken of the process of interning Japanese Americans during World War II.
2. Explain how the framing of this photograph creates sympathy for the child.
3. Evaluate the extent to which Japanese internment was a continuation of the treatment of Asian Americans in the United States.

TEACHING IDEA

Six Degrees of Separation

Assign students to study the photo *Japanese American Child on the Way to Internment*, and answer the accompanying questions. Then engage them in a "Six Degrees of Separation" exercise. For the purpose of this exercise, students are given two events spanning time, but related by their theme. They must select four events in chronological order that link the first event in the series with the last. They will write the name of each selected event, and create an argument to support each of the events they selected. Explain to them that they must answer the question, "Why does it belong as a link in your chain of events?" for each link. Students must emphasize both cause and effect and/or demonstrate continuity or change over time in their linking. This can be done as either a formative assessment in class, or as a homework assignment involving student research of their textbooks, activities/lessons, lecture notes, and knowledge of the time period. The lesson may also be undertaken by students individually or in small groups. The prompt for this particular activity is as follows:

"From the Chinese Exclusion Act of 1882 to Executive Order 9066 in 1942"

TRM Suggested Responses to Questions

TRM Module 7.10 AP® Analyzing Sources Handout 5

The Ordeal of Japanese Americans

Although the rest of his family complied with the order, Fred refused. Three weeks later, he was arrested and then transferred to the Topaz internment camp in south-central Utah. Found guilty of violating the original evacuation order, Korematsu received a sentence of five years of probation. It did not matter that Fred Korematsu had been born in the United States, had a white girlfriend of Italian heritage, and counted white people among his best friends. His parents had come from Japan, and for much of the American public, his racial heritage meant that he was not a true American. As one American general put it early in the war, "A Jap's a Jap. It makes no difference whether he is an American citizen or not." Along with more than 100,000 people of Japanese descent, two-thirds of whom were American citizens, Korematsu spent most of the war in an internment camp. Unlike Nazi concentration camps, these facilities did not work inmates to death or execute them. Yet Japanese Americans lost their freedom and protection under the Bill of Rights and the Fourteenth Amendment. Despite scant evidence that Japanese Americans were disloyal or harbored spies or saboteurs, U.S. officials chose to believe that as a group they threatened national security. The government established a system that questioned German American and Italian Americans on an individual basis if their loyalty came under suspicion. By contrast, U.S. officials identified all Japanese Americans and Japanese resident aliens with the nation that had attacked Pearl Harbor and incarcerated them. In this respect, the United States was not unique. Following the United States' lead, Canada interned its Japanese population, more than 75 percent of whom held Canadian citizenship.

For their part, Japanese Americans made the best they could out of this situation. They had been forced to dispose of their homes, possessions, and businesses quickly, either selling or renting them at very low prices or simply abandoning them. They left their neighborhoods with only the possessions they could carry. They lived in wooden barracks divided into one-room apartments and shared communal toilets, showers, laundries, and dining facilities. The camps provided schools, recreational activities, and opportunities for religious worship, except for Shintoism, the official religion of Japan. Some internees attempted to farm, but the arid land on which the camps were located made this nearly impossible. Inmates who worked at jobs within the camp earned monthly wages of $12 to $19, far less than they would have received outside the camps.

Japanese Americans responded to their internment in a variety of ways. Many formed community groups, and some expressed their reactions to the emotional upheaval by writing of their experiences or displaying their feelings through artwork. Contradicting beliefs that their ancestry made them disloyal or not real Americans, some 18,000 men joined the army, and many fought gallantly in some of the war's fiercest battles on the European front with the 442nd Regiment, one of the most heavily decorated units in the military. Nisei soldiers were among the first, along with African American troops, to liberate Jews from German concentration camps. Others, like Fred Korematsu, remained in the camps and challenged the legality of President Roosevelt's executive order, which had allowed military officials to exclude Japanese Americans from certain areas and evacuate them from their homes. However, the Supreme Court ruled against him and others. Finally, in December 1944, shortly after he won election to his fourth term as president, Roosevelt rescinded Executive Order 9066.

In contrast to the treatment of Japanese Americans, the status of Chinese Americans improved markedly during the war. With China under Japanese occupation, Congress repealed the Chinese Exclusion Act in 1943, making the Chinese the first Asians who could become naturalized citizens. Chinese American men also fought in integrated military units like their Filipino peers. For the first time, the war opened up jobs to Chinese American men and women outside their ethnic economy.

Despite the violation of the civil liberties of Japanese American citizens, the majority did not become embittered against the United States. Rather, most of the internees returned to their communities after the war and resumed their lives, still intent on pursuing the American dream from which they had been so harshly excluded; however, some 8,000 Japanese Americans renounced their U.S. citizenship and repatriated to Japan in 1945. In the name of national security, the government had established the precedent of incarcerating groups deemed "suspect." It took four decades for the U.S. government to admit its mistake and apologize, and in 1988 Congress awarded reparations of $20,000 to each of the 60,000 living internees.

BUILDING AP® SKILLS

Comparison

Task students in small groups with the prompt, "To what extent was the German-American experience during the First World War similar to the Japanese-American experience during the Second World War, and to what extent were the experiences of the two groups different?" Instruct them to create a 4-1-1 model of contextualization and thesis construction to address this prompt, as well as a skeletal pre-write outline, with each body paragraph's topic sentence fully complete, and followed by relevant specific evidence to support it in bullet-point fashion (a refresher of the 4-1-1 model can be found on page 163).

TEACHING IDEA

Incorporating Primary Sources

Assign students in small groups or as individuals the lesson, "Japanese-American Internment in World War II," from the University of Maryland, Baltimore County website (umbc.edu). This lesson consists of primary source textual and visual analysis, and student interpretation. Utilize components of this lesson package at the instructor's discretion.

TEACHING IDEA

Connecting the Dots

Engage the class in an activity of association by disassociation called "Odd One Out." Start by writing the following terms on the board/projector:

- The Double-V Campaign
- Zoot Suit Riots
- Women's Army Corps (WACs)
- Executive Order 9066
- War Production Board

Then place students in small groups and ask them, "Which one is the odd one out and why? How do the remaining terms relate?" Give students approximately 7–10 minutes to complete this part, then share out student answers and discuss their conclusions and reasoning as a whole-class activity. There is no specific correct answer; the goal is to get students thinking in categorical habits of mind and defending their rationales.

TRM Suggested Responses to Questions

TRM Module 7.10 AP® Analyzing Sources Handout 6

BUILDING AP® SKILLS
Sourcing and Situation

Assign students to read *Internment Diary* and answer the accompanying questions. Then, task students with connecting or synthesizing the source to the photograph, *Japanese American Child on the Way to Internment*. Ask students to discuss the following question: "Is it essential for something to be true, or is it enough if people think it is true, and why?"

EXPLORING AP® THEMES
Social Structures

Assign students in triads to notate and analyze a series of Dr. Seuss wartime cartoons compiled by Natasha Karunaratne in her article, "Understanding Dr. Seuss' Depictions of the 'Other' in His Political Cartoons," available on Re-imagining Migration's website (reimaginingmigration.org).

Have students answer the Reflection Questions that accompany the illustrations, and then discuss the concepts of racism and stereotype and the degree of influence those forces played in American National Security policy decisions on the West Coast and in U.S. Armed Forces-occupied territories from 1942 to 1945.

TRM Suggested Responses to Questions

Period 7: 1890–1945

MODULE 7-10 Life on the Homefront

AP® ANALYZING SOURCES

Source: Charles Kikuchi, *Internment Diary*, 1942

"There was a terrific rainstorm last night and we have had to wade through the 'slush alleys' again. Everyone sinks up to the ankles in mud. Some trucks came in today with lumber to build new barracks, but the earth was so soft that the truck sank over the hubs and they had a hell of a time pulling it out. The Army certainly is rushing things. About half of the Japanese have already been evacuated from the restricted areas in this state. Manzanar, Santa Anita, and Tanforan will be the three biggest centers. Now that [San Francisco] has been almost cleared the American Legion, the Native Sons of the Golden West, and the California Joint Immigration Committee are filing charges that the Nisei[1] should be disfranchised because we have obtained citizenship under false pretenses and that "we are loyal subjects of Japan" and therefore never should have been allowed to obtain citizenship. This sort of thing will gain momentum and we are not in a very advantageous position to combat it. I get fearful sometimes because this sort of hysteria will gain momentum.

The [San Francisco] Registrar has made a statement that we will be sent absentee ballots to which Mr. James Fisk of the Joint Immigration Committee protests greatly. Tomorrow I am going to carry a petition around to protest against their protests. I think that they are stabbing us in the back and that there should be a separate concentration camp for these so-called Americans. They are a lot more dangerous than the Japanese in the U.S. ever will or have been."

[1] Children born in America to Japanese parents.

Questions for Analysis
1. Describe the ways in which internees were denied their rights as Americans in Kikuchi's account.
2. Explain the arguments for the denial of these rights.
3. Explain the implicit counterarguments Kikuchi makes in this account.

Questions for Comparison
Monica Sone, *Memories of the Pearl Harbor Attack on December 7, 1941*, 1953 (p. 668)
1. Describe how Kikuchi's diary entry compares to Monica Sone's memories of the attack on Pearl Harbor.
2. Explain the historical situation that shaped both of these sources.
3. Evaluate the extent of similarity in what these two documents reveal about the challenges faced by Japanese Americans during World War II.

REVIEW
- Why were Japanese Americans singled out as a particular threat to national security during World War II?

AP® WRITING HISTORICALLY — Long-Essay Question Practice
ACTIVITY
Answer the following Long-Essay Question. **Suggested writing time: 40 minutes.**

Evaluate the extent of similarity between the social and cultural changes that took place during the 1920s and those that occurred during World War II.

TEACHING IDEA

AP® Writing Historically Review

Prior to answering this Long-Essay Question, consider having students complete the following activity. Have students create a graphic organizer that delineates the elements of the question: social and cultural changes of the 1920s and social and cultural changes of World War II. Provide students with the opportunity to brainstorm with two other students all of the historical information they can think of for each time period. After they have finished brainstorming, give students an additional five minutes to locate both similarities and differences in their list of historical information. This will allow students to account for all of the elements of the question before they respond in writing.

Module 7-11

Victory in World War II

LEARNING TARGETS

By the end of this module, you should be able to:

- Explain how U.S. citizens framed World War II as a fight for freedom and democracy against fascism.
- Explain how revelations about Japanese wartime atrocities, Nazi concentration camps, and the Holocaust supported U.S. citizens' perceptions of America's role in the war.
- Describe how the United States and the Allies achieved military victory through cooperation, scientific advances, the contributions of servicemen and women, and military campaigns such as "island-hopping" and the D Day invasion.
- Explain why the use of atomic bombs brought the end of the war in the Pacific and generated debates about using these weapons.
- Explain how the results of World War II allowed the United States to become the most powerful nation on Earth.

THEMATIC FOCUS

America in the World

By 1942, the United States had entered its second world war in a generation. While during the First World War the U.S. fought primarily in Europe, by 1943 the United States was at war on two sides of the world, across the Atlantic and in the Pacific. Though the United States did not bear the brunt of the war (that bitter distinction fell to the people on whose soil the most devastating battles took place), the American effort proved essential to victory for the Allied forces. By the end of the war, it became clear that the United States had an enormous role in world affairs, and that the so-called isolationism of the 1920s and 1930s was no longer tenable.

HISTORICAL REASONING FOCUS

Causation

TASK ▶ While you read this section, consider the reasons for Allied victory in general, and American success in particular, in the Second World War. Also, consider the effects of this victory on the United States both domestically and internationally.

TRM Suggested Responses to Questions

World War II pitted the "Grand Alliance" of Great Britain, the Soviet Union, the French government in exile, and the United States against the Axis powers of Germany, Japan, and Italy. From the outset, the United States deployed military forces to contain Japanese aggression, but its most immediate concern was to defeat Germany. Before battles in Europe, Asia, and four other continents concluded, more than 60 million people perished, including 405,000 Americans. Six million Jewish civilians died in the Holocaust, the Nazi regime's genocidal effort to eradicate Europe's Jewish population. Millions of other civilians — Slavic peoples, Romani, Jehovah's Witnesses, homosexuals, the disabled, and Communists — also were systematically murdered by the Nazis. The Soviet Union experienced the greatest losses — nearly 27 million soldiers and civilians, more than two-fifths of all those killed.

TEACHING IDEA

Incorporating Videos

Assign students to watch Episode 35, "World War II Part 1," from the Crash Course US History series (available on YouTube). Use this 13-minute episode as a concise formative content introduction for students to more of the major issues and events of Module 7-11 as part of preparation for either assessment or reinforcement.

BUILDING AP® SKILLS

Developments and Processes

Discuss with students the role that conflict in general plays in history, as opposed to the role that conflict plays upon the national AP® exam. It is very important that instructors point out to students that when it comes to warfare, the actual test will focus on "causes and consequences" to a far greater degree than "bullets and bombs." In other words, the technology, weaponry, and actual combat itself is not a central focus of the AP® curriculum and exam, not unlike historical study within academia (the subfield of military history being an obvious exception). As such, students should be prepared to explore the Second World War in this manner, with the long-term developments and processes that both led to the war, and were brought about by the war, being central to their study. This should be emphasized by the instructor upon starting the study of any war in American history that the course content and curriculum cover.

Global War Erupts

United against Hitler, the Grand Alliance divided over how quickly to mount a counterattack directly on Germany. The Soviet Union, which bore the brunt of the fighting in trying to repel the German army's invasion, demanded the opening of a **second front** through France and into Germany to take the pressure off its forces. The British wanted to fight first in northern Africa and southern Europe, in part to remove Axis forces from territory that endangered their economic interests in the Mediterranean and the Middle East and in part to buy time to rebuild their depleted fighting strength. President Roosevelt understood the Soviet position, but worried about losing public support early in the war if the United States experienced heavy casualties. He approved his military advisers' plans for an invasion of France from England in 1943, but in the meantime he agreed with Churchill to fight the Germans and Italians on the periphery of Europe.

From a military standpoint, this circuitous approach proved successful. In October 1942 British forces in North Africa overpowered the Germans at El Alamein, pushing them out of Egypt and removing their threat to the Suez Canal. The following month, British and American troops landed in Algeria and Morocco. After some early defeats, the combined strength of British and American ground, air, and naval forces drove the Germans out of Africa in May 1943.

These military victories failed to relieve political tensions among the Allies. Although the Soviets had managed to stop the German offensive against Stalingrad, the deepest penetration of enemy troops into their country, Stalin expected the second front to begin as promised in the

▲ **MAP 7.8 World War II in Europe, 1941–1945** By late 1941, the Axis powers had brought most of Europe and the Mediterranean region under their control. But between 1942 and 1945, the Allied powers drove them back. Critical victories at Leningrad and Stalingrad, in North Africa, and on the beaches of Normandy forced the retreat, and then the defeat, of the Axis powers. **What does this map reveal about the relationship between the conflict in Europe and the countries of Africa and Asia?**

TEACHING IDEA

Incorporating Secondary Sources

Assign students to read and annotate "Allied Strategy in World War II: The Churchill Era, 1942–1943," by De Lamar Jensen (available through online search). Whole-class discussion to follow.

TEACHING IDEA

Differing Views

The National World War II Museum website contains a vast array of lessons, sources, and activities for both teachers and students (ww2classroom.org). Assign students the role-play simulation scenario lesson, "The War in Europe: Evaluating Historic Decisions," in which students will evaluate real-life decisions from the war, propose a course of action as the actual leaders had to do, and then justify their responses, comparing them to what actually happened.

spring of 1943. He was bitterly disappointed when Roosevelt postponed the cross–English Channel invasion of France until 1944. To Stalin, it appeared as if his allies were looking to gain a double triumph by letting the Communists and Nazis beat each other into submission.

Instead of opening a second front in France, British, American, and Canadian troops invaded Italy from its southern tip in July 1943. Their initial victories quickly led to the removal of Mussolini and his retreat to northern Italy, where he lived under German protection (Map 7.8). Not until June 4, 1944 did the Allies occupy Rome in central Italy and force the Germans to retreat.

To overcome Stalin's dissatisfaction with the postponement of opening the second front, President Roosevelt issued orders to give the Soviets unlimited access to Lend-Lease supplies to sustain their war efforts and to care for their citizens. In November 1943, Roosevelt, Churchill, and Stalin met in Tehran, Iran. Roosevelt and Stalin seemed to get along well. Stalin agreed to deploy troops against Japan after the war in Europe ended, and Roosevelt agreed to open the second front within six months. Churchill joined Roosevelt and Stalin in supporting the creation of an international organization to ensure postwar peace.

This time the Americans and British kept their word, and the Allies finally embarked on the second-front invasion. On June 6, 1944 — called **D Day** — more than 1.5 million American, British, and Canadian troops crossed the English Channel in 4,000 boats and landed on the beaches of Normandy, France. Despite deadly machine-gun fire from German troops placed on higher ground, the Allied forces managed to establish a beachhead. The bravery and discipline of the troops, along with their superior numbers, overcame the Germans and opened the way for the Allies to liberate Paris in August 1944. By the end of the year, the Allies had regained control of the rest of France and most of Belgium.

Amid these Allied victories, Roosevelt won a fourth term against Republican challenger Thomas E. Dewey, governor of New York. He dumped from the campaign ticket his vice president, Henry A. Wallace, a liberal on economic and racial issues, and replaced him with Senator Harry S. Truman of Missouri, who was more acceptable to southern voters. Despite his declining health, Roosevelt won easily.

D Day June 6, 1944 invasion of German-occupied France by Allied forces. The D Day landings opened up a second front in Europe and marked a major turning point in World War II.

AP® TIP
Compare the military cooperation in the D-Day invasion with the "island hopping" strategy in the Pacific theater of World War II.

REVIEW
- Why did the Soviet Union want the Allies to open a second front early in the war?
- Why did the Allies wait until later in the conflict to do so?

War in the Pacific

With the Soviet Union bearing the brunt of the fighting in eastern Europe, the United States shouldered the burden of fighting Japan. U.S. military commanders began a two-pronged counterattack in the Pacific in 1942. General Douglas MacArthur, whose troops had escaped from the Philippines as Japanese forces overran the islands in May 1942, planned to regroup in Australia, head north through New Guinea, and return to the Philippines. At the same time, Admiral Chester Nimitz directed the U.S. Pacific Fleet from Hawaii toward Japanese-occupied islands in the western Pacific. If all went well, MacArthur's ground troops and Nimitz's naval forces would combine with General Curtis LeMay's air forces to overwhelm Japan. This strategy was known as "**island-hopping**." Accordingly, American and allied forces would leapfrog over heavily fortified Japanese positions and concentrate their resources on lightly defended Japanese islands that would provide bases capable of sustaining the campaign to attack the nation of Japan.

All went according to plan in 1942. Shortly after the Philippines fell to the Japanese, the Allies won a major victory in May in the Battle of the Coral Sea, off the northwest coast of Australia. The following month, the U.S. navy achieved an even greater victory when it defeated the Japanese in the **Battle of Midway Island**, northwest of Hawaii. In August, the fighting moved to the Solomon Islands, east of New Guinea, where U.S. forces waged fierce battles at Guadalcanal Island. After six months of heavy casualties on both sides, the Americans finally dislodged

island-hopping This strategy, employed in the Pacific by the U.S. in World War II, directed American and Allied forces to avoid heavily fortified Japanese islands and concentrate on less heavily defended islands in preparation for a combined air, land, and sea invasion of Japan.

BUILDING AP® SKILLS
Comparison

Assign students to read and complete the National Archives' DocsTeach online lesson, "The Night Before D-Day," which compares General Eisenhower's Order of the Day message to Allied troops on the eve of the invasion with the message he had written as a precautionary measure announcing the invasion's failure (docsteach.org).

APPLY THE TIP

As military ventures, the European Normandy Invasion and the Pacific Island-hopping campaign shared some core similarities and numerous differences. Assign students in pairs or triads to complete a graphic organizer that codifies these differences and similarities.

TRM Find **Handout 7.12 – European Theater and Pacific Theater Strategy and Operations** in the Teacher's Resource Materials.

TEACHING IDEA
Incorporating Videos

Assign students to view the History Channel's program *World War II in HD*, Episode 8, "Glory and Guts" (available on YouTube). This 44-minute program chronicles the European and Pacific campaigns in late 1944 and 1945, including the Battle of the Bulge and assault at Iwo Jima.

Period 7: 1890–1945

MODULE 7-11 Victory in World War II

▲ **MAP 7.9 World War II in the Pacific, 1941–1945** After bombing Pearl Harbor on December 7, 1941, Japan captured the Philippines and seized control of Asian colonies from the British, French, and Dutch and then occupied eastern China. The Allied powers, led by U.S. forces, eventually defeated Japan by winning a series of hard-fought victories on Central Pacific islands and by the atomic bombing of Hiroshima and Nagasaki. **How did "island hopping" contribute to U.S. victory in the Pacific?**

the Japanese. By late 1944, American, Australian, and New Zealand troops had put the Japanese on the defensive.

In 1945 the United States mounted its final offensive against Japan. In preparation for an invasion of the Japanese home islands, American marines won important battles on **Iwo Jima** and **Okinawa**, two strategic islands off the coast of Japan. The fighting proved costly — on Iwo Jima alone, the Japanese fought and died nearly to the last man while killing 6,000 Americans and wounding 20,000 others. At the same time, the U.S. Army Air Corps conducted firebomb raids over Tokyo and other major cities, killing some 330,000 Japanese civilians. These attacks were conducted by newly developed B-29 bombers, which could fly more than 3,000 miles and could be dispatched from Pacific island bases captured by the U.S. military. The purpose of this strategic bombing was to destroy Japan's economic capability to sustain the war rather than to destroy their

684

BUILDING AP® SKILLS

Sourcing and Situation

The Library of Congress contains numerous oral histories in its "Experiencing War: Stories from the Veterans History Project" (loc.gov/vets/stories/wwiilist.html). Randomly assign students to access three different persons and their interview excerpts from the site, and summarize their experience. Then, assign students in groups of three to share out the results of their research. Lastly, task each student in the group to ask their peers one question, then their peers ask a question of them, and finally, the original questioner poses one remaining question back. Have students record both their questions and responses.

TEACHING IDEA

Connecting the Dots

The National Endowment for the Humanities' EDSITEment online platform contains several useful lessons for student enrichment and study of the Second World War within the online curriculum unit, "The United States in World War II: 'The Proper Application of Overwhelming Force'" (edsitement.neh.gov). In this instance, assign students to explore and complete Lesson 1, "Turning the Tide in the Pacific, 1941–1943," which focuses upon the initial overall strategies pursued by the Japanese and the Allies in Asia and the Pacific.

military forces. At the same time, the navy blockaded Japan, further crippling its economy and reducing its supplies of food, medicine, and raw materials (Map 7.9). Still, the Japanese government refused to surrender and indicated its determination to resist by launching *kamikaze* attacks (suicidal airplane crashes) on American warships and airplanes.

REVIEW

What was the United States' strategy in the Pacific theater of World War II?

Ending the War

In the European theater, the Germans had launched one last offensive in mid-December 1944. Mobilizing troops from remaining outposts in Belgium, they attacked Allied forces in the **Battle of the Bulge**. After an initial German drive into enemy lines, by late January 1945 American and British fighting men had recovered and sent the Germans retreating across the Rhine River and back into Germany. The Allies then prepared to push into the German heartland. With victory in sight in both Europe and the Pacific, the Allies addressed problems of postwar relations. In February 1945 Roosevelt and Churchill met with Stalin in the resort city of Yalta in the Ukraine. There they clashed over the question of the postwar government of Poland and whether to recognize the claim of the Polish government in exile in London, which the United States and Great Britain supported, or that of the pro-Soviet government, which had spent the war in the USSR. The loosely worded **Yalta Agreement**, which resulted from the conference, called for the establishment of permanent governments in Poland and the rest of eastern Europe through free elections.

Despite this controversy, the Allies left Yalta united over other issues. They renewed their commitment to establishing the United Nations, and the Soviets reaffirmed their intention to join the war against Japan three months after Germany's surrender. The Allies also reached a tentative agreement on postwar Germany. The United States, Great Britain, the Soviet Union, and France would divide the country into four zones, each occupied by one of the powers. They would further subdivide Berlin into four sectors because the capital city fell within the Soviet occupation area. As with the accord over Poland, the agreement concerning Germany created tension after the war.

The Yalta Conference concluded just as the final assault against Germany got under way. Pushing from the west, American general Dwight D. Eisenhower stopped at the Elbe River, where he had agreed to meet up with Red Army troops who were charging from the east to Berlin. After an intense assault by the Soviets, the German capital of Berlin fell, and on April 25 Russian and American forces linked up in Torgau on the Elbe River. They achieved this triumph two weeks after Franklin Roosevelt died at the age of sixty-three from a cerebral hemorrhage. On April 30, 1945, with Berlin shattered, Hitler committed suicide in his bunker. A few days earlier, Italian anti-fascist partisans had captured and executed Mussolini in northern Italy. On May 2, German troops surrendered in Italy, and on May 7 the remnants of the German government formally surrendered. The war in Europe ended the next day.

With the war over in Europe, the United States made its final push against Japan. Since 1942, J. Robert Oppenheimer and his team of scientists and engineers had labored feverishly to construct an atomic bomb. Few people knew about the top-secret **Manhattan Project**, and Congress appropriated $2 billion without knowing its true purpose.

Vice President Harry S. Truman did not learn about the details of the Manhattan Project until Roosevelt's death on April 12, and in July he found out about the first atomic test while en route to a conference in Potsdam, Germany with Stalin and Churchill. He ordered the State Department to issue a vaguely worded ultimatum to the Japanese demanding their immediate surrender or else face annihilation. When Japan indicated that it would surrender if the United States allowed the country to retain its emperor, Hirohito, the Truman administration refused and demanded unconditional surrender. As a further blow to Japan, Stalin was ready to send the Soviet military to attack Japanese troops in Manchuria on August 8, which would seriously weaken Japan's ability to hold out.

Yalta Agreement Agreement negotiated at the 1945 Yalta Conference by Roosevelt, Churchill, and Stalin about the fate of postwar Eastern Europe. The Yalta Agreement did little to ease growing tensions between the Soviet Union and its Western Allies.

AP® TIP
Evaluate the role of the Yalta Agreement in ensuring post–World War II cooperation and conflict in Europe.

Manhattan Project Code name for the secret program to develop an atomic bomb. The project was launched in 1942 and directed by the United States with the assistance of Great Britain and Canada.

TEACHING IDEA

Incorporating Videos

Assign students to view the History Channel's program *World War II in HD*, Episode 9, "The Edge of the Abyss" (available on YouTube). This 43-minute excerpted piece covers the conclusion of conflict in Europe and the death of Franklin Roosevelt.

APPLY THE TIP

Assign students to compare the agreements, achievements, and limitations of the Yalta Conference to those of the Potsdam Conference in small groups. Then, pose one of the following questions to each group:

- To what extent did the end of WWII see Germany reduced to a state just as bad as it had after WWI?
- To what extent was the Allied Powers' alliance formed out of convenience, not out of a genuine respect for each other?
- To what extent was FDR's death a turning point in post-war agreements?
- To what extent was the Soviet Union to blame for the beginning of the Cold War?

When the process of addressing each of these prompts is complete, assign students to present their findings to the whole class, still subdivided by groups. Task each group with creating one question to ask the presenting group. Allow the presenting group time to respond, and ask a counter-question, if applicable.

TEACHING IDEA

Differing Views

The Stanford History Education Group includes a collection of numerous free online lessons (sheg.stanford.edu). Included in the repository on this platform is a downloadable lesson focusing upon the merits of the decision to drop the atomic bomb from both Japanese and American points of view. Modify at the instructor's discretion, to include an LEQ prompt, "To what extent was the use of atomic weapons to end the Second World War morally justifiable?"

▲ Differentiation

Assign half the students in the class to complete the NY Regents Examination preparation question on the decision to drop the atomic bombs, which is a document-based reasoning exercise with follow-up questions for each source, leading into an overall question upon the morality of the decision. This exercise is more structured and scaffolded in terms of document analysis skills, and may be helpful for students who struggle with primary source interpretation. The exercise is available online at the Morningside Center's website by searching for "atomic bomb" (morningsidecenter.org). At the conclusion of the lessons, group together students from each lesson activity and have them share their interpretations and conclusions.

Period 7: 1890–1945

MODULE 7-11 Victory in World War II

TEACHING IDEA

AP® Central

Assign students to break down the 1988 College Board AP® U.S. History DBQ on the atomic bomb, which is available on the College Board's past exam questions resource "AP® United States History Document-Based Questions 1973–1999" (apcentral.collegeboard.org). Task students in pairs with utilizing their HIPP training to analyze the documents (a refresher of HIPP can be found on page 8). Culminate the activity by having students construct an introductory contextualization and thesis along the lines of the 4-1-1 format (a refresher of the 4-1-1 model can be found on page 163). Have students write these on butcher paper or the board, and have them review one another's work in a gallery walk.

TEACHING IDEA

Incorporating Videos

Assign students to view an abridged 60-minute version of the PBS documentary, *Victory in the Pacific*, which makes the claim that the fanaticism of Japanese resistance in conventional combat proved to be instrumental in moving along the decision of the United States to deploy atomic weapons to conclude the war (available on YouTube).

TRM Suggested Responses to Questions

TRM Module 7.11 AP® Analyzing Sources Handout

The Aftermath of Hiroshima The dropping of the atomic bomb on Hiroshima devastated most of the city and killed 70,000–80,000 people in the blast and immediate aftermath. **In what ways was the use of this weapon a change in the way the United States waged war?**

On August 6 the *Enola Gay*, an American B-29 bomber, dropped an atomic bomb on **Hiroshima**. The weapon immediately killed as many as 80,000 civilians, and tens of thousands later died slowly from radiation poisoning. Three days later, on August 9, Japan still had not surrendered, and the Army Air Corps dropped another atomic bomb on **Nagasaki**, killing more than 100,000 civilians. Five days later, on August 14, Japan announced that it would surrender; the formal surrender was completed on September 2.

At the time, and for many years afterward, very few Americans questioned the decision to drop atomic bombs on Japan. Truman believed that had Roosevelt been alive, he would have authorized use of the bombs. Newly on the job, Truman hesitated to reverse a decision already reached by his predecessor. He reasoned that his action would save American lives because the U.S. military would not have to launch a costly invasion of Japan's home islands. He also felt justified in giving the order because he sought retaliation for the surprise attack on Pearl Harbor and for Japanese atrocities against American soldiers, especially in the Philippines.

AP® ANALYZING SOURCES

Source: Father Johannes Siemes, *Eyewitness Account of the Hiroshima Bombing*, 1945

"More than thirty hours had gone by until the first official rescue party had appeared on the scene. We find both children and take them out of the park: six-year old girl who was uninjured, and a twelve-year old girl who had been burned about the head, hands, and legs, and who had lain for thirty hours without care in the park. The left side of her face and the left

TEACHING IDEA

Connecting the Dots

The National Endowment for the Humanities' EDSITEment online platform contains several useful lessons for student enrichment and study of the Second World War within the online curriculum unit, "The United States in World War II: 'The Proper Application of Overwhelming Force'" (edsitement.neh.gov). In this instance, assign students to explore and complete Lesson 4, "Victory in the Pacific, 1943–1945," which focuses upon the initial overall strategies pursued by the Japanese and the Allies in Asia and the Pacific.

eye were completely covered with blood and pus, so that we thought that she had lost the eye. When the wound was later washed, we noted that the eye was intact and that the lids had just become stuck together. On the way home, we took another group of three refugees with us. The first wanted to know, however, of what nationality we were. They, too, feared that we might be Americans who had parachuted in. When we arrived in Nagatsuka,[1] it had just become dark. . . .

Thousands of wounded who died later could doubtless have been rescued had they received proper treatment and care, but rescue work in a catastrophe of this magnitude had not been envisioned; since the whole city had been knocked out at a blow, everything which had been prepared for emergency work was lost, and no preparation had been made for rescue work in the outlying districts. Many of the wounded also died because they had been weakened by under-nourishment and consequently lacked in strength to recover. Those who had their normal strength and who received good care slowly healed the burns which had been occasioned by the bomb. There were also cases, however, whose prognosis seemed good who died suddenly. There were also some who had only small external wounds who died within a week or later, after an inflammation of the pharynx and oral cavity had taken place. . . .

Up to this time small incised wounds had healed normally, but thereafter the wounds which were still unhealed became worse and are to date (in September) still incompletely healed. The attending physician diagnosed it as leucopenia.[2] There thus seems to be some truth in the statement that the radiation had some effect on the blood. . . . It was noised about that the ruins of the city emitted deadly rays and that workers who went there to aid in the clearing died, and that the central district would be uninhabitable for some time to come."

[1] A Jesuit monastery in Hiroshima.
[2] A decrease in white blood cells.

Questions for Analysis

1. Identify the immediate and long-term results of the bombing of Hiroshima detailed in this account.
2. Describe some of the effects of the bombing of Hiroshima, as detailed in this account.
3. Evaluate the extent to which the bombing of Hiroshima represented a change in the United States' approach to international warfare.

REVIEW

- How did President Truman justify dropping atomic bombs on Hiroshima and Nagasaki?

Evidence of the Holocaust

Holocaust The Nazi regime's genocidal effort to eradicate Europe's Jewish population during World War II, which resulted in the death of 6 million Jews and millions of other "undesirables" — Slavs, Poles, Gypsies, homosexuals, the physically and mentally disabled, and Communists.

The end of the war revealed the full extent and horror of the **Holocaust** — Germany's calculated and methodical slaughter of certain religious, ethnic, and political groups. As Allied troops liberated Germany and Poland, they saw for themselves the brutality of the Nazi concentration camps that Hitler had set up to execute or work to death 6 million Jews and millions of other "undesirables" — Slavs, Poles, Gypsies, homosexuals, the physically and mentally disabled, and Communists. At Buchenwald and Dachau in Germany and at Auschwitz in Poland, the Allies encountered the skeletal remains of inmates tossed into mass graves, dead from starvation, illness, and executions. Crematoria on the premises contained the ashes of inmates first poisoned and then incinerated. Troops also freed the "living dead," those still alive but seriously ill and undernourished.

These horrific discoveries shocked the public, but evidence of what was happening had appeared early in the war. Journalists like Varian Fry had outlined the Nazi atrocities against the Jews several years before. "Letters, reports, tables all fit together. They add up to the most appalling picture of mass murder in all human history," Fry wrote in the *New Republic* magazine in 1942.

TEACHING IDEA

Incorporating Videos

Assign students to view PBS *Frontline* documentary, *The Memory of the Camps*, which is the Allied Military unfinished 58-minute official historical record for what was found at German death camps (available on YouTube). Be advised that graphic images are included.

EXPLORING AP® THEMES

America and the World

Assign students to read selected documents from "FDR and the Holocaust" (available through online search by the FDR Presidential Library & Museum). Instructor discretion will be needed to assign the documents proportionally to various student groups. Have students utilize their HIPP training to analyze the documents, and then for their specific assigned documents, create a "Twenty-Five-Word Drill" product that addresses the following prompt: "To what extent was the United States responsible for not accelerating the end of the Holocaust?" (a refresher of HIPP can be found on page 8).

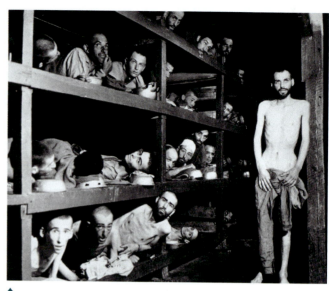

Holocaust Survivors When American troops of the 80th Army Division liberated the Buchenwald concentration camp in Germany, they found these emaciated victims of the Holocaust. Elie Wiesel (seventh from the left on the middle bunk next to the vertical post) went on to become an internationally famous writer who wrote about his wartime experiences and won the Nobel Peace Prize. **In what ways might this image reinforce the American public's perceptions about the war?**

The Roosevelt administration did little in response, despite receiving evidence of the Nazi death camps beginning in 1942. It chose not to send planes to bomb the concentration camps or the railroad lines leading to them, deeming it too risky militarily and too dangerous for the inmates. "The War Department," its assistant Secretary John J. McCloy wrote the director of the War Refugee Board in defending this decision, "is of the opinion that the suggested air operation is impracticable. It could be executed only by the diversion of considerable air support essential to the success of our forces now engaged in decisive operations and would in any case be of such very doubtful efficacy that it would not amount to a practical project." In a less defensible decision, the Roosevelt administration refused to relax immigration laws to allow Jews and other persecuted minorities to take refuge in the United States, and only 21,000 managed to find asylum. The State Department, which could have modified these policies, was staffed with antisemitic officials, and though President Roosevelt expressed sympathy for the plight of Hitler's victims, he believed that winning the war as quickly as possible was the best way to help them.

Nevertheless, even when it had been possible to rescue Jews, the United States balked. In 1939 a German liner, the SS *St. Louis*, embarked from Hamburg with 937 Jewish refugees aboard and set sail for Cuba. Blocked from entry by the Cuban government, the ship sailed for the coast of Florida, hoping to gain permission to enter the United States. However, the United States refused, maintaining that the passengers did not have the proper documents required under the Immigration Act of 1924. The ship then headed back to Europe, where the

TEACHING IDEA

Incorporating Secondary Sources

Assign students to read and annotate "America and the Holocaust," by William J. Vanden Heuvel (available by online search of author and title). Whole-class discussion to follow.

> **AP® TIP**
> Be sure you can explain how antisemitism and nativism influenced the U.S. immigration policies enacted and enforced during World War II.

United Kingdom, Belgium, the Netherlands, and France took in the passengers. Unfortunately, in 1940, when the Nazis invaded Belgium, the Netherlands, and France and sent their Jewish residents to concentration camps, an estimated 254 of the *St. Louis* passengers died along with countless others.

Although not nearly to the same extent as in the Holocaust, the Japanese committed numerous war atrocities. Around 50,000 U.S. soldiers and civilians became prisoners of war and about half of them were forced to work as enslaved laborers. From June 1942 to October 1943, the Japanese constructed a 300-mile railroad between Burma (Myanmar) and Thailand using 60,000 Allied prisoners of war and 200,000 Asian conscripts. Working under inhumane conditions, approximately 13,000 Allied workers and 80,000 Asian laborers died before the railway was completed. About 40 percent of American POWs died in Japanese captivity (in contrast only 1 percent died in Nazi camps). One reason why POWs were treated so poorly was because the Japanese believed that surrender was a cowardly act and those who did so were beneath contempt. Far more than the Americans and their allies, Chinese civilians and native residents of such countries as Burma and the Dutch East Indies (Indonesia) were brutalized and killed by the Japanese occupying forces.

REVIEW
- Why did U.S. policymakers fail to provide assistance to European Jews during World War II?

The Impact of World War II

Franklin Roosevelt initially charted a course of neutrality before the United States entered World War II. Yet Roosevelt believed that the rise of European dictatorships and their expansionist pursuits throughout the world threatened American national security. He saw signs of trouble early, but responding to antiwar sentiment from lawmakers and the American public, Roosevelt waited for a blatant enemy attack before declaring war. The Japanese attack on Pearl Harbor in 1941 provided that justification.

On the domestic front, World War II accomplished what Franklin Roosevelt's New Deal could not. Prosperity and nearly full employment returned only after the nation's factories began supplying the Allies and the United States joined in the fight against the Axis powers. Mobilization for war also furthered the tremendous growth and centralization of power in the federal government that had begun under the New Deal. Washington, D.C. became the chief source of authority to which Americans looked for solutions to problems concerning economic security and financial development. The federal government showed that it would use its authority to expand equal rights for African Americans. The war swung national power against racial discrimination, and various civil rights victories during the war served as precursors to the civil rights movement of subsequent decades. The war also heightened Mexican Americans' consciousness of oppression and led them to organize for civil rights. However, in neither case, nor that of American Indians, did the war erase white prejudice.

At the same time, the federal government did not hesitate to trample on the civil liberties of Japanese Americans. The president succumbed to wartime antagonism against Japanese immigrants and their children. With China a wartime ally, Chinese Americans escaped a similar fate. Yet like white and black Americans, the Nisei displayed their patriotism by distinguishing themselves as soldiers on the battlefields of Europe.

The war brought women into the workforce as never before, providing a measure of independence and distancing them from their traditional roles as wives and mothers. Nevertheless, the government and private employers made it clear that they expected most female workers to give up their jobs to returning servicemen and to become homemakers once the war ended.

Finally, the war thrust the United States onto the world stage as one of the world's two major superpowers alongside the Soviet Union. This position posed new challenges. In sole possession of the atomic bomb, the most powerful weapon on the planet, and fortified by a robust economy, the

Period 7: 1890–1945

MODULE 7-11 Victory in World War II

AP® TIP
Evaluate the extent to which World War II brought change to the status of women, African Americans, and the working class.

United States filled the international power vacuum created by the weakening and eventual collapse of the European colonial empires. The fragile alliance that had held together the United States and the Soviet Union shattered soon after the end of World War II. The Atomic Age, which J. Robert Oppenheimer helped usher in with a powerful weapon of mass destruction, and the government oppression that Fred Korematsu endured in the name of national security did not disappear. Rather, they expanded in new directions and shaped the lives of all Americans for decades to come.

REVIEW

- How did World War II affect American policies at home and overseas?

AP® WRITING HISTORICALLY — Short-Answer Question Practice

ACTIVITY

Read the following question carefully and write a short response. Use complete sentences.

Using the following excerpts, answer (a), (b), and (c).

Source: David S. Wyman, *The Abandonment of the Jews: America and the Holocaust, 1941–1945*, 1984

"America's response to the Holocaust was the result of action and inaction on the part of many people. In the forefront was Franklin D. Roosevelt, whose steps to aid Europe's Jews were very limited. If he had wanted to, he could have aroused substantial public backing for a vital rescue effort by speaking out on the issue. If nothing else, a few forceful statements by the President would have brought the extermination news out of obscurity and into the headlines. But he had little to say about the problem and gave no priority to rescue at all. . . .

[E]ven when interested in rescue action, Roosevelt was unwilling to run a political risk for it, as his response to the free-ports plan showed. The [War Refugee Board's] original rescue strategy depended on America's setting an example to other nations by offering to open several temporary havens. The President, by agreeing to only one American camp, signaled that little was expected of any country. A more extensive free-ports program would have strained relations with Congress. It might also have cost votes, and 1944 was an election year. . . .

[I]t appears that Roosevelt's overall response to the Holocaust was deeply affected by political expediency. Most Jews supported him unwaveringly, so an active rescue policy offered little political advantage. A pro-Jewish stance, however, could lose votes. American Jewry's great loyalty to the President thus weakened the leverage it might have exerted on him to save European Jews."

Source: Richard Breitman and Allan J. Lichtman, *FDR and the Jews*, 2013

"For most of his presidency Roosevelt did little to aid the imperiled Jews of Germany and Europe. He put other policy priorities well ahead of saving Jews and deferred to fears of an anti-Semitic backlash at home. He worried that measures to assist European Jews might endanger his political coalition at home and then a wartime alliance abroad. . . . When he engaged Jewish issues, he maneuvered, often behind the scenes. When he hesitated, other American officials with far less sympathy for Jews set or carried out policies.

Still, at times, Roosevelt acted decisively to rescue Jews, often withstanding contrary pressures from the American public, Congress, and his own State Department. . . . He was a far better president for Jews than any of his political adversaries would have been. Roosevelt defied most Republican opponents and some isolationist Democrats to lead political and military opposition to Nazi Germany's plans for expansion and world domination. . . ."

APPLY THE TIP

Place students into three groups. Assign one group the topic "women," one group the topic "African Americans," and one group the topic "the working class." Then ask the three groups, from the perspective of their topic, to evaluate the extent to which the war brought change. Allow them to discuss, and then place students into groups of six, with two persons from each topic represented. Have them share out their perspectives and then task these groups of six with crafting an introductory response to the overall prompt. Have students share these responses on the board for peer review.

TRM Suggested Responses to Questions

BUILDING AP® SKILLS
Argumentation

As a general strategy, the *ACE* method explained by the authors for LEQ purposes — "Answer the question, Cite your evidence, and Explain its meaning" — is also very useful for Short-Answer Questions (a refresher of *ACE* can be found on page 21). For each of the three tasks of an SAQ, use this model. In so doing, the three tasks of an SAQ are actually then addressed in nine discrete steps. If this method is followed, the depth of student responses to the three directed tasks of the SAQ should be such that it increases the likelihood of every SAQ point being earned with a comfortable margin.

BUILDING AP® SKILLS
Causation

A useful review exercise to engage in with students at this point is a "How did we get here?" activity, whereby students in small groups are given a single event (e.g., Battle of Midway, Yalta Agreement, etc.) and have to explain its significance in the context of the American involvement in the Second World War. Then, student groups must migrate in the room and mingle with other student groups, to find which group's event or context led to their particular assigned event, and which event or context their group's assigned event served as a catalyst for.

> [T]he story of FDR and the Jews is ultimately a tragic one that transcends the achievements and failures of one leader. Even if FDR had been more willing to override domestic opposition and twist arms abroad, he could not have stopped the Nazi mass murder of some six million Jews. For Hitler and his followers, the annihilation of the Jews was not a diversion from the war effort, but integral to its purpose. For America and Britain, the rescue of Jews, even if practical, was ultimately subordinate to the overriding priorities of total war and unconditional surrender of the enemy."

a. Briefly describe ONE major similarity between Wyman's and Breitman and Lichtman's historical interpretations of American policy toward European Jews between 1933 and 1945.
b. Briefly describe ONE major difference between Wyman's and Breitman and Lichtman's historical interpretations of American policy toward European Jews between 1933 and 1945.
c. Briefly explain how ONE specific historical event or development during the period 1933–1945 that is not explicitly mentioned in the excerpts could be used to support Breitman and Lichtman's interpretation.

TEACHING IDEA

AP® Writing Historically Review

While both historians agree that President Roosevelt did not act swiftly enough to help Jewish people in Europe during World War II, they disagree on the extent to which Roosevelt assisted Jews overall during his presidency. While these Short-Answer Questions are designed to have students decipher the differences in interpretations, remind them that sometimes historians agree on the basic premise but disagree on subsequent details. In order to further this perspective, have students acknowledge how Roosevelt fell short in helping Jewish people during World War II. Next, have students think of at least one way in which President Roosevelt was criticized for helping Jewish people too much during the New Deal. This activity can be an explicit part of sections (a) and (c) of this question.

PERIOD 7 REVIEW 1890–1945

KEY CONCEPTS AND EVENTS

Abrams v. United States, 611
Adamson Act, 581
Agricultural Adjustment Act (AAA), 648
Agricultural Marketing Act, 638
Allies (WWI), 599
America First Committee, 664
American Civil Liberties Union (ACLU), 612
American Expeditionary Forces (AEF), 602
American Plan, 614
American Protective League (APL), 605
Anti-Imperialist League, 593
appeasement, 664
Atlantic Charter, 667
attack on Pearl Harbor, 668
Battle of the Bulge, 685
Battle of Iwo Jima, 684
Battle of Midway Island, 683
Battle of Okinawa, 684
"big stick" diplomacy, 595
Black Tuesday, 637
bombing of Hiroshima and Nagasaki, 686
Bonus Army, 645
bully pulpit, 576
Bureau of Investigation, 612
Central Powers, 599
civic housekeeping, 557
Civil Works Administration (CWA), 649
Civilian Conservation Corps (CCC), 649
Clayton Antitrust Act, 581
Committee on Public Information (CPI), 604
communism, 607
Congress of Racial Equality (CORE), 676
conservationism, 574
court-packing plan, 659
Cuba Libre, 589
D Day, 683
Department of Commerce and Labor, 576
dollar diplomacy, 597

Double V, 675
Dust Bowl, 639
Eighteenth Amendment, 566
Elkins Act, 576
Emergency Banking Act, 647
Espionage Act, 604
Eugenics, 568
Executive Order 9066, 678
Fair Labor Standards Act, 657
Federal Deposit Insurance Corporation (FDIC), 647
feminist, 559
Food Administration, 603
Fourteen Points, 606
Fuel Administration, 603
Glass-Steagall Act, 647
Great Depression, 637
Great Migration, 613
Harlem Renaissance, 623
Hawley-Smoot Act, 638
Hay-Pauncefote Treaty, 595
Hetch Hetchy valley, 574
Holocaust, 687
Hull House, 557
Indian Citizenship Act, 630
Indian Reorganization Act (IRA), 658
influenza pandemic, 612
internment, 678
island-hopping, 683
isolationism, 663
jingoists, 588
The Jungle, 577
Keating-Owen Act, 581
Kellogg-Briand Pact, 662
League of Nations, 606
League of United Latin American Citizens (LULAC), 676
Lend-Lease Act, 666
Lost Generation, 621
Lusitania, 600
Manhattan Project, 685
Mann Act, 567
Meat Inspection Act, 577
Mexican Revolution, 598

military-industrial complex, 671
muckrakers, 557
Muller v. Oregon, 559
Munich Accord, 664
National American Woman Suffrage Association, 559
National Association for the Advancement of Colored People (NAACP), 564
National Association of Colored Women (NACW), 557
National Industrial Recovery Act, 648
National Labor Relations Act, 656
National Labor Relations Board (NLRB), 656
National Origins Act, 629
National Recovery Administration (NRA), 648
National War Labor Board (NWLB), 603
National Woman's Party, 559
Nazism, 664
Neutrality Acts, 663
New Deal, 647
New Freedom, 580
New Nationalism, 580
New Negro, 623
new woman, 621
Nineteenth Amendment, 561
Nye Committee, 663
Office of War Information, 674
Old-Age Revolving Pensions Corporation, 651
Open Door policy, 596
Palmer raids, 612
Payne-Aldrich tariff, 579
Platt Amendment, 591
pragmatism, 556
Progressive Party, 579
Progressivism, 556
Public Works Administration (PWA), 649
Pure Food and Drug Act, 577
Railroad Administration, 604
Reconstruction Finance Corporation, 638
Red Scare, 610

(Continued)

PERIOD 7 REVIEW 1890–1945

Roosevelt Corollary, 595
"Rough Riders", 576
Russian Revolution, 602
Sacco and Vanzetti case, 629
Schenck v. United States, 610
Scottsboro Nine, 641
second front, 682
Securities and Exchange Commission (SEC), 648
Sedition Act, 604
segregation, 557
Selective Service Act, 602
Selective Training and Service Act of 1940, 665
Share Our Wealth society, 653
Shepherd-Towner Act, 559
sit-down strike, 657
Sixteenth Amendment, 580
Social Security Act, 654
Spanish–American War, 589
"Square Deal", 576
suffragists, 559
Teapot Dome scandal, 614
Teller Amendment, 591
Tennessee Valley Authority (TVA), 648
Third Reich, 664
Treaty of Versailles, 607
Triangle Shirtwaist fire, 571
Tripartite Pact, 667
Tuskegee airmen, 672
Tuskegee Institute, 562
Twenty-first Amendment, 648
Tydings-McDuffie Act, 643
Underwood Act, 580
Universal Negro Improvement Association (UNIA), 625
War Industries Board (WIB), 603
War Powers Act (1942), 671
War Production Board, 671
Women Accepted for Voluntary Emergency Service (WAVES), 672
Women's Army Corps (WACs), 672
Woman's Christian Temperance Union (WCTU), 565
Workmen's Compensation Act, 581
Works Progress Administration (WPA), 653
World War I, 599
Yalta Agreement, 685
yellow journalism, 590
Zimmermann telegram, 602
zoot suit riots, 677

KEY PEOPLE

Jane Addams, 557
Emilio Aguinaldo, 593
Susan B. Anthony, 559
Louis Armstrong, 623
Ruth Benedict, 565
Franz Boas, 565
William Jennings Bryan, 578
Carrie Chapman Catt, 599
Winston Churchill, 667
Calvin Coolidge, 615
Charles E. Coughlin, 652
George Creel, 604
Clarence Darrow, 627
Eugene V. Debs, 580
W. E. B. Du Bois, 564
Dwight D. Eisenhower, 685
Edward "Duke" Ellington, 623
Henry Ford, 614
Marcus Garvey, 620
Charlotte Perkins Gilman, 559
Emma Goldman, 559
Warren G. Harding, 605
William Randolph Hearst, 590
Oliver Wendell Holmes, 610
Herbert Hoover, 603
J. Edgar Hoover, 612
Harry Hopkins, 649
Julia Ward Howe, 559
Langston Hughes, 623
Zora Neale Hurston, 623
Robert M. La Follette, 573
Curtis LeMay, 683
John L. Lewis, 656
Queen Liliuokalani, 587
Henry Cabot Lodge, 607
Huey Long, 653
Douglas MacArthur, 645
Alfred Thayer Mahan, 588
José Martí, 589
William McKinley, 576
Andrew Mellon, 613
Carlos Montezuma, 565
Ferdinand "Jelly Roll" Morton, 623
John Muir, 575
Chester Nimitz, 683
J. Robert Oppenheimer, 664
A. Mitchell Palmer, 611
Arthur C. Parker, 565
George S. Patton, 645
Alice Paul, 559
Frances Perkins, 648
Gifford Pinchot, 574
Joseph Pulitzer, 590
A. Philip Randolph, 625
Eleanor Roosevelt, 646
Franklin Delano Roosevelt, 646
Theodore Roosevelt, 570
Nicola Sacco, 629
Margaret Sanger, 568
Upton Sinclair, 577
Bessie Smith, 623
Elizabeth Cady Stanton, 559
Lincoln Steffens, 557
Lucy Stone, 559
Josiah Strong, 587
William Howard Taft, 578
Ida Tarbell, 557
Francis Townsend, 651
Harry S. Truman, 683
Bartolomeo Vanzetti, 629
Francisco "Pancho" Villa, 599
Booker T. Washington, 562
Ida B. Wells, 557
Frances Willard, 565
Zitkala-Ša, 565

PERIOD 7 REVIEW 1890–1945

CHRONOLOGY

1890	Creation of National American Woman Suffrage Association
1890s	Beginning of pragmatism
1893–97	Depression of 1893
1893	White plantation owners overthrow Hawaiian government
1898	Spanish-American War
	Foundation of the Anti-Imperialist League
1901	President McKinley assassinated
	Roosevelt launches "Square Deal" and becomes "bully pulpit" president
1902	Ida Tarbell exposes Standard Oil Company corruption
1903	Creation of National Women's Trade Union League to improve workplace conditions
	Department of Labor and Commerce established to promote fair business practices
1904	Lincoln Steffens publishes *The Shame of the Cities*
	Announcement of Roosevelt Corollary extends the U.S. sphere of influence
1906	Pure Food and Drug Act passed
	Meat Inspection Act passed
	Hepburn Act passed
1907	Publication of *Christianity and the Social Crisis* inspires Social Gospel movement
1909	Taft becomes president, operating under policy of dollar diplomacy
	Foundation of National Association for the Advancement of Colored People
1911	Triangle Shirtwaist Company factory fire inspires government regulation
1912	Presidential election of Woodrow Wilson on New Freedom platform
1913	Sixteenth Amendment introduces a graduated income tax
	Seventeenth Amendment establishes the election of senators by popular vote
	Federal Reserve System created
1914	Serbian nationalist Gavrilo Princip assassinates Austrian archduke Franz Ferdinand
	Central Powers declare war against Allied Powers
	Marcus Garvey establishes Universal Negro Improvement Association (UNIA)
	Panama Canal opens
	Federal Trade Commission created
	Clayton Antitrust Act passed
1915	Sinking of passenger liner *Lusitania* by German U-Boat
1916	Adamson Act establishes eight-hour workday for railroad workers
	Keating-Owen Act outlaws child labor in firms engaged in interstate commerce
1917–1945	Beginning of the Great Migration of African Americans from the South to the North, culminating during World War II, but continuing to a lesser extent through the 1960s
1917	Germany resumes unrestricted submarine warfare
	Publication of Zimmerman Telegram turns public opinion towards war
	Wilson asks Congress for declaration of war against Central Powers
	Russian Revolution establishes Bolshevik regime
	Reformers succeed in series of immigration restrictions to ban "undesirables"
1918	End of World War I following armistice
	Influenza epidemic
	Massive labor union strikes cause instability
	Keating-Owen Act repealed
1919–1920	Series of Supreme Court cases limiting free speech
1919	Treaty of Versailles establishes League of Nations
	Red Scare escalates in U.S.
	Race riots explode across the nation
	Eighteenth Amendment prohibits the sale and consumption of alcohol
	U.S. deports hundreds of immigrants and radicals
by 1920	More Americans live in urban than rural areas for the first time in American history
1920s	KKK targets African Americans, Catholics, Jews, and anyone considered to be immoral
1920	Foundation of the American Civil Liberties Union (ACLU)
	Sacco and Vanzetti found guilty of murder
	Passage of Nineteenth Amendment grants women the right to vote
1921	Teapot Dome Scandal

PERIOD 7 REVIEW 1890–1945

1924	Congress passes the Indian Citizenship Act and the National Origins Act
1925	Lawmakers in five states make teaching evolution in public schools and colleges illegal
1928	Presidential election of Herbert Hoover
1929	Ford factories employ more than 4 million workers
	Stock market crashes on Black Tuesday
	Hoover signs Agricultural Marketing Act
1930	Congress passes Hawley-Smoot Act, worsening the Great Depression
1932	Reconstruction Finance Corporation supplies loans to troubled banks, as well as to railroad and insurance companies
	Bonus Army marches on Washington, D.C.
	Presidential election of Franklin Roosevelt
by 1933	Economic depression is worldwide
1933–45	The Holocaust
1933	Adolf Hitler becomes Chancellor of Germany
	Creation of the Tennessee Valley Authority (TVA) and Agricultural Adjustment Act
	Passage of National Recovery Act and the Glass-Steagall Act
1934	American Liberty League launches in opposition to New Deal policies
1935	Creation of Works Progress Administration (WPA)
	Passage of the Social Security Act
	Italy invades Ethiopia
	The Supreme Court rules the National Recovery Administration unconstitutional
1936	Hitler sends troops to occupy the Rhineland
1937	Roosevelt unsuccessfully attempts Supreme Court packing plan
1938	Munich Accord allows Germany to annex the Sudetenland
	Minimum wage established by Fair Labor Standards Act
1939	Hitler unchallenged sends troops to occupy the rest of Czechoslovakia
	Germany invades Poland
1940	Germany occupies Paris
1941	Germany and the United States engaged in an undeclared naval war
	Creation of Fair Employment Practice Committee
	Japanese attack Pearl Harbor, prompting a U.S. declaration of war
	Passage of War Powers Act
1942	Roosevelt establishes War Production Board and creates Japanese internment camps
1944	Wartime employment reaches peak
	Launch of operation D Day leading to liberation of Paris in August
1945	Roosevelt, Churchill, and Stalin make Yalta Agreement
	Roosevelt dies suddenly and Harry S. Truman becomes president
	Germany surrenders following Hitler's suicide
	U.S. drops atomic bombs on Hiroshima and Nagasaki
	Japan surrenders, marking the end of World War II

TRM Suggested Responses to Questions

Answers to Multiple-Choice Questions

1. c
2. d
3. a
4. a
5. d
6. d
7. a
8. d
9. b
10. a
11. b
12. b
13. a
14. c
15. b
16. d
17. a
18. a

AP® EXAM PRACTICE THROUGH 1945

Multiple Choice Questions

Choose the correct answer for each question.

Questions 1–3 refer to the following excerpt.

Source: Upton Sinclair, *The Jungle*, 1906

"There were those who made the tins for the canned meat; and their hands, too, were a maze of cuts, and each cut represented a chance for blood poisoning. Some worked at the stamping machines, and it was very seldom that one could work long there at the pace that was set, and not give out and forget himself and have a part of his hand chopped off.... [A]nd as for the other men, who worked in tank rooms full of steam, and in some of which there were open vats near the level of the floor, their peculiar trouble was that they fell into the vats; and when they were fished out, there was never enough of them left to be worth exhibiting, — sometimes they would be overlooked for days, till all but the bones of them had gone out to the world as Durham's Pure Beef Lard!"

1. The conditions described in the passage resulted most directly from
   a. reliance on unskilled labor in meatpacking industry.
   b. mechanization leading to lower meat prices.
   c. an unregulated business environment emphasizing profits.
   d. labor unions prioritizing pay raises over workplace safety.

2. During which earlier time period did American factory workers most commonly face comparably dangerous working conditions as those described in the excerpt?
   a. 1650 to 1700
   b. 1700 to 1750
   c. 1750 to 1800
   d. 1800 to 1850

3. The publication of muckraking accounts such as *The Jungle* most directly contributed to which of the following changes?
   a. Expanded governmental oversight of businesses
   b. Increased use of automation in factories
   c. Consolidation of large corporations into trusts
   d. Outsourcing of factories to lower wage countries

Questions 4–6 refer to the following excerpt.

Source: Woodrow Wilson, *Address to Congress*, January 8, 1918

"It will be our wish that the processes of peace, when they are begun, shall be absolutely open and that they shall involve and permit henceforth no secret understandings of any kind. The day of conquest and aggrandizement has gone by; so is the day of secret covenants entered into in the interest of particular governments and likely at some unlooked-for moment to upset the peace of the world.... We entered this war because violations of right had occurred which touched us to the quick and made the life of our own people impossible unless they were corrected and the world secure once for all against their recurrence. What we demand in this war, therefore, is nothing peculiar to ourselves. It is that the world be made fit and safe to live in.... All the peoples of the world are in effect partners in this interest and for our own part we see very clearly that unless justice be done to others it will not be done to us."

AP® Exam Practice: Through 1945

Period 7: 1890–1945

4. Which of the following issues of the period was Wilson most likely concerned with in the excerpt?
   a. The defense of humanitarian and democratic principles
   b. The pursuit of a unilateral American foreign policy
   c. The rise of fascism and totalitarianism
   d. The economic opportunities presented by imperialism

5. Based on the excerpt, which of the following would Wilson most likely NOT have supported?
   a. The Washington Naval Conference
   b. The Selective Service Act
   c. The Kellogg-Briand Pact
   d. Unrestricted submarine warfare

6. In the decades following Wilson's speech, significant divisions emerged within the United States over all of the following issues EXCEPT the
   a. ratification of the Treaty of Versailles.
   b. aggression of Nazi Germany.
   c. foreign policy tradition of noninvolvement in European affairs.
   d. appropriate national response to the Japanese attack on Pearl Harbor.

Questions 7–8 refer to the following photograph.

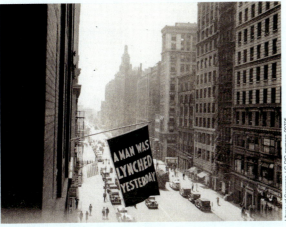

▲ c. 1920, New York City

7. Which of the following developments most directly resulted from the context captured in the image?
   a. Increased migration of African Americans to northern cities
   b. Passage of federal anti-lynching legislation
   c. Growth of militant civil rights movements for black power
   d. Emergence of new groups promoting political violence

8. The African American community resisted segregation and discrimination in the first half of the twentieth century in all of the following ways EXCEPT by
   a. launching a series of legal challenges.
   b. developing new forms of art and literature.
   c. demanding financial reparations.
   d. appealing for greater equality in the military.

Period 7: 1890–1945

AP® Exam Practice: Through 1945

Questions 9–11 refer to the following excerpt.

Source: Huey Long, United States Senator, *Every Man a King*, 1934

"We have to limit fortunes.... It may be necessary, in working out of the plans, that no man's fortune would be more than $10,000,000 or $15,000,000. But be that as it may, it will still be more than any one man, or any one man and his children and their children, will be able to spend in their lifetimes; and it is not necessary or reasonable to have wealth piled up beyond that point where we cannot prevent poverty among the masses.... Those are the things we propose to do. 'Every Man a King.' Every man to eat when there is something to eat; all to wear something when there is something to wear. That makes us all a sovereign. You cannot solve these things through these various and sundry alphabetical codes.... You know what the trouble is.... Now my friends, we have got to hit the root with the ax. Centralized power in the hands of a few, with centralized credit in the hands of a few, is the trouble."

9. Huey Long's ideas expressed in the excerpt participate in the 1930s trend in the United States of increasing
   a. conservative attempts to limit the scope of the economic change.
   b. populist-style political movements seeking change in the United States economic system.
   c. calls for totalitarianism to solve economic crises.
   d. state and local efforts aimed at ending the Great Depression.

10. In highlighting "these various and sundry alphabetical codes," Long referred most directly to
    a. New Deal programs.
    b. United States espionage against Japan.
    c. efforts for industrial efficiency emphasized by Progressive reformers.
    d. union movements pushing for more extensive economic change.

11. The ideas of Huey Long, as expressed in the excerpt, had most in common with the ideas of
    a. Social Darwinists in the 1880s.
    b. critics of the status quo in the 1890s.
    c. government reformers after 1900.
    d. industrialists in the 1920s.

Questions 12–13 refer to the following excerpt.

Source: *The Agricultural Adjustment Act*, 1933

"Sec. 2. It is hereby declared to be the policy of Congress — 1) To establish and maintain such balance between the production and consumption of agricultural commodities ... as will reestablish prices to farmers at a level that will give agricultural commodities a purchasing power with respect to articles that farmers buy, equivalent to the purchasing power of agricultural commodities in the base period. The base period in the case of all commodities ... shall be the prewar period.... 2) To approach such equality of purchasing power by gradual correction of the present inequalities therein at as rapid a rate as is deemed feasible in view of the current consumptive demand in domestic and foreign markets."

12. The challenges faced by the agricultural sector of the economy in the 1930s were driven primarily by
    a. federal deregulation of agricultural markets.
    b. improvements in mechanization increasing productivity.
    c. changes in regional cultures.
    d. patterns of mass migration.

13. The legislation in the excerpt emerged most directly from the context of
    a. Franklin Roosevelt's attempts to stimulate the economy.
    b. debates over the best means to maintain traditional cultural values.
    c. movement of the majority of the United States population to urban centers.
    d. the expansion of popular participation in government.

AP® Exam Practice: Through 1945

Period 7: 1890–1945

Questions 14–16 are based on the following excerpt.

Source: Burton K. Wheeler, Senator from Montana (Democrat), *Speech on the Lend-Lease Act*, January 12, 1941

"The lend-lease policy, translated into legislative form, stunned a Congress and a nation wholly sympathetic to the cause of Great Britain. . . . It warranted my worst fears for the future of America, and it definitely stamps the President as war-minded. The lend-lease program is the New Deal's Triple-A policy; it will plow under every fourth American boy. . . . Approval of this legislation means war, open and complete warfare. I, therefore, ask the American people before they supinely accept it, Was the last World War worthwhile?"

14. Wheeler based his appeal most directly upon the precedent of
    a. Woodrow Wilson's efforts to preserve humanitarian principles through the League of Nations.
    b. bipartisan political enthusiasm for interventionism.
    c. popular support for isolationism after World War I.
    d. the United States' tradition of anti-imperialism.

15. Wheeler's views expressed in the excerpt best reflect the United States citizens'
    a. commitment to resist totalitarianism.
    b. preference for a unilateral foreign policy.
    c. popular view of World War II as a fight for democracy.
    d. opposition to genocide.

16. The ideas expressed by Wheeler in the excerpt are most similar to the ideas of
    a. Democratic-Republicans during the War of 1812.
    b. supporters of manifest destiny in the 1840s.
    c. Republicans during the Civil War.
    d. anti-imperialists in the 1890s.

Questions 17–18 refer to the following excerpt.

Source: Merlo J. Pusey, "The Revolution at Home," *South Atlantic Quarterly*, Volume 42, pp. 207–219.

"We have built an enormous portion of our vast war plant within close range of big industries where expert management and skilled labor were at hand. Baltimore, Indianapolis, Buffalo, Hartford, St. Louis, Detroit, Los Angeles, Portland, Seattle, and numerous other cities find their manufacturing plants expanding at a rate that seemed impossible in peacetime. . . . The meaning of these social and economic upheavals is plain. . . . The consequences will be far reaching. For in this . . . there is no chance to maintain the status quo. If strategy and geography do not thrust a community into the maelstrom of war activity, its resources will be drained into other areas where they can better serve the national interest. So the whole pattern of our economic and social life is undergoing kaleidoscopic changes, without so much as a bomb being dropped on our shores."

17. Which of the following most directly resulted from the changes described in the excerpt?
    a. New economic opportunities for African Americans and women
    b. The establishment of increased barriers to immigration
    c. A reversal of the World War I Great Migration
    d. The emergence of new forms of mass media

18. Pusey's observations in the excerpt most directly reflect which of the following developments?
    a. The end of the Great Depression
    b. Challenges to civil liberties at home
    c. A decline in public confidence in government's ability to solve economic problems
    d. An increase in laissez-faire policies that promoted economic growth

TRM Suggested Responses to Questions

Period 7: 1890–1945

AP® Exam Practice: Through 1945

Short-Answer Questions

Read each question carefully and write a short response. Use complete sentences.

1. Using the following two excerpts, answer (a), (b), and (c).

   Source: Elisabeth Israels Perry, "Men Are from the Gilded Age, Women Are from the Progressive Era," 2002

   " 'When was the Progressive Era exactly?' my students ask. Roughly during the first two decades of the twentieth century, I tell them. . . . Some historians still use 1900 as a starting date, although more recently 1890 has become popular. . . . From the perspective of women progressives, however, these boundaries need to be much more fluid. . . . The women who founded social settlements in the 1880s, along with the temperance and suffrage campaigners, comprise a group of American citizens active in conceptualizing progressive reform long before the presumed dawn of progressivism."

   Source: Rebecca Edwards, *New Spirits: Americans in the "Gilded Age," 1865–1905*, 2015

   "Millions of freedmen, immigrants, students, workers, artists, intellectuals, and reformers believed that post–Civil War America offered a chance to start anew. . . . Many Americans worked energetically between 1865 and 1900 to purify politics, restrict the power of big business, and fight injustice. Those decades witnessed the first march on Washington, the first federal welfare programs, the first elections in which women and black men voted for president, and the first national park in the world. At the same time, problems that plagued the so-called Gilded Age continued and even intensified during the so-called Progressive Era."

   a) Briefly explain ONE major difference between Perry's and Edwards's historical interpretations of the late nineteenth and early twentieth centuries.

   b) Briefly explain how ONE specific historical event or development not directly mentioned in the excerpts could be used to support Perry's argument.

   c) Briefly explain how ONE specific historical event or development not directly mentioned in the excerpts could be used to support Edwards's argument.

2. Using the following map, answer (a), (b), and (c).

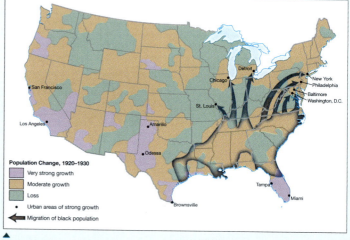

Population Change, 1920–1930

AP® Exam Practice: Through 1945

Period 7: 1890–1945

a) Briefly explain ONE specific historical event or development that caused a population trend illustrated in the map.
b) Briefly explain ANOTHER specific historical event or development that caused a population trend illustrated in the map.
c) Briefly explain ONE significant historical result of the population trend you explained in (a) OR (b).

3. Answer (a), (b), and (c).
   a) Briefly explain ONE specific historical similarity between the causes of the Great Depression (1929–1939) and the causes of an earlier economic recession or depression in the United States.
   b) Briefly explain ONE specific historical difference in the causes of the Great Depression (1929–1939) from the causes of an earlier economic recession or depression in the United States.
   c) Briefly explain how ONE specific historical event or development demonstrates a change in the United States caused by the Great Depression (1929–1939).

4. Answer (a), (b), and (c).
   a) Briefly explain ONE specific historical similarity between U.S. military participation in World War I and World War II.
   b) Briefly explain ONE specific historical difference between U.S. military participation in World War I and World War II.
   c) Briefly explain ONE specific historical effect of U.S. military participation in World War I or World War II on American society.

Document-Based Question

Question 1 is based on the accompanying documents. The documents have been edited for the purpose of this exercise. *Suggested reading period: 15 minutes. Suggested writing time: 45 minutes.*

1. Evaluate the extent of continuity in the experiences of women in the United States from 1890 to 1945.

DOCUMENT 1   Source: *Ladies' Home Journal,* January 1890

"Reforms in women's apparel are again being discussed, and public interest is once more awakened on this oft-mooted question. That some of the present style of dress adopted by American women are, to some extent, physically injurious and inconsistent with good taste, can scarcely be denied. But the radical reforms suggested, as, for example the substitution of the trousers for the petticoat, and similar departures from modern customs, are not destined to bring about the looked-for result . . . to advise a young woman to dress herself with any such serious departure from the prevailing fashion of her day and class is to ask her to incur a penalty that will invariably follow such an innovation.

'God has implanted in the minds of all, but especially in the female breast, the love of beauty. . . . It is a duty which every woman owes to herself, to her family, and to her society to dress tastefully, and as well as her means shall allow. It is woman's instinct to admire pretty dresses, and it is right that she should. . . .

In this matter of women's dress, then, when we sum it all up, the fact is plain that, as the love of dress in inherent in all true women, it would be as unwise as it would be useless to strive against it by any radical suggestiveness of reform."

TRM Suggested Responses to Questions

DOCUMENT 2

Source: Rose Schneiderman, labor activist, *Speech Delivered at a Memorial Meeting at the Metropolitan Opera House in New York City*, April 2, 1911

"I would be a traitor to those poor burned bodies if I were to come here to ask good fellowship. We have tried you good people of the public — and we have found you wanting.

The old Inquisition had its rack and its thumb screws and its instruments of torture with iron teeth. We know what these things are today: the iron teeth are our necessities, the thumbscrews are the high-powered and swift machinery close to which we must work, and the rack is here in the firetrap structures that will destroy us the minute they catch fire.

This is not the first time girls have been burned alive in this city. Every week I learn of the untimely death of one of my sister workers. Every year thousands of us are maimed. The life of men and women is so cheap and property is so sacred! There are so many of us for one job, it matters little if 140-odd are burned to death. . . .

Public officials have only words of warning for us — warning that we must be intensely orderly and must be intensely peaceable, and they have [prison] just back of all their warnings. The strong hand of the law beats us back when we rise — back into conditions that make life unbearable.

I can't talk fellowship to you who are gathered here. Too much blood has been spilled. I know from experience it is up to the working people to save themselves. And the only way is through a strong working-class movement."

DOCUMENT 3

Source: Miss N. H. Burroughs, "Black Women and Reform," *The Crisis*, August 1915

"I was asked by a Southern white woman who is an enthusiastic worker for 'votes for (white) women,' 'What can the Negro woman do with the ballot?' I asked her, 'What can she do without it?' When the ballot is put into the hands of the American woman the world is going to get a correct estimate of the Negro woman. She is a tower of strength of which poets have never sung, orators have never spoken, and scholars have never written. . . .

[T]he Negro woman, therefore, needs the ballot to get back, by the wise *use* of it, what the Negro man has lost by *misuse* of it. A fact worthy of note is that in every reform in which the Negro woman has taken part, during the last fifty years, she has been as aggressive, progressive, and dependable as those who inspired the reform or led it. The world has yet to learn that the Negro woman is quite superior in bearing moral responsibility. A comparison with the men of her race, in moral issues, is odious. She carries the burdens of the Church, and of the school and bears a great deal more than her economic share in the home.

The ballot, wisely used, will bring to her the respect and protection that she needs. It is her weapon of moral defence. Under present conditions, when she appears in court in defence of her virtue, she is looked upon with amused contempt. She needs the ballot to reckon with men who place no value upon her virtue, and to mould healthy public sentiment in favor of her own protection."

DOCUMENT 4

Source: Margaret Sanger, *Woman and the New Race*, 1920

"The basic freedom of the world is woman's freedom. A free race cannot be born of slave mothers. A woman enchained cannot choose but give a measure of that bondage to her sons and daughters. No woman can call herself free who does not own and control her body. No woman can call herself free until she can choose consciously whether she will or will not be a mother. . . .

Woman must have her freedom; the fundamental freedom of choosing whether or not she shall be a mother and how many children she will have. Regardless of what man's attitude may be, that problem is hers; and before it can be his, it is hers alone.

She goes through the vale of death alone, each time a babe is born. As it is the right neither of man nor the state to coerce her into this ordeal, so it is her right to decide whether she will endure it. That right to decide imposes upon her the duty of clearing the way to knowledge by which she may make and carry out the decision.

Birth control is woman's problem. The quicker she accepts it as hers and hers alone, the quicker will society respect motherhood. The quicker, too, will the world be made a fit place for her children to live."

DOCUMENT 5

Source: Advertisement, *Good Housekeeping Magazine*, November 1924

Her habit of measuring time in terms of dollars gives the woman in business keen insight into the true value of a Ford closed car for her personal use.

This car enables her to conserve minutes, to expedite her affairs, to widen the scope of her activities. Its low first cost, long life and inexpensive operation and upkeep convince her that it is a sound investment value.

And it is such a pleasant car to drive that it transforms the business call which might be an interruption into an enjoyable episode of her busy day.

TUDOR SEDAN, $590   FORDOR SEDAN, $685   COUPE, $525   (All prices f. o. b. Detroit)

Ford CLOSED CARS

DOCUMENT 6 Source: Norman Cousins, "Will Women Lose Their Jobs?" *Current History*, 1939

"There are approximately 10,000,000 people out of work in the United States today. There are also 10,000,000 or more women, married and single, who are job-holders. Simply fire the women, who shouldn't be working anyway, and hire the men. Presto! No Unemployment. No relief rolls. No depression.

This is the general idea behind the greatest assault on women's rights in two decades. . . . Of such concern is this trend that it has been called the greatest single issue to affect women since their victorious fight for suffrage. . . .

Fundamentally, the unemployment of men is not caused by women who hold jobs but by the infirmities of the economic structure itself. Nor is the depression an affliction visited exclusively upon the male; the woman must bear her part in the burden, as more than 2,000,000 unemployed women can attest. . . .

But even outside the economic sphere, arguments against the working wife reveal weakness. There is much talk about the mother's place in the home, very little about the fact that the home has changed. Housekeeping for the average family is no longer a full-time job. . . .

This change is reflected not only in employment of married women but in the growth of social and church work, and the spread of adult education, of culture and entertainment groups."

DOCUMENT 7 Source: *A Woman at Work on a "Vengeance" Dive Bomber, Tennessee*, 1943

AP® Exam Practice: Through 1945

Long-Essay Questions

Please choose one of the following three questions to answer. *Suggested writing time: 40 minutes.*

2. Evaluate the extent of difference in the priorities and goals of United States foreign policy in the years immediately before United States involvement in the First World War (1904–1917) and the priorities and goals of United States foreign policy in the years immediately after United States involvement in the First World War (1918–1930).

3. Evaluate the extent of difference in the effects of federal policies on African Americans in the Progressive Era (1890–1920) to the effects of federal policies on African Americans in the New Deal Era (1933–1941).

4. Evaluate the extent of difference in the effects of federal policies on women in the Progressive Era (1890–1920) to the effects of federal policies on women in the New Deal Era (1933–1941).

TRM Suggested Responses to Questions

PERIOD 8: 1945–1980
Cold War America

AP® Overview for Period 8

Period 8 of the AP® U.S. History course is defined by an obvious dynamism of content, themes, and questions for students to engage in as they near the end of the required curriculum. The events that make up this period in the course outline necessitate careful thought and planning as teachers matriculate their way through the events of this period. The results and aftermath of World War II created more questions than answers for the United States. The geopolitical changes attendant to the Cold War not only altered U.S. foreign policy but also amplified the tenor surrounding the civil rights movement. Gains made by civil rights advocates inspired a number of subsequent movements for a more democratic society. And amidst all this change, the demographics of the United States underwent yet another transformation. Period 8 in many ways is about Americans challenging the established orthodoxy. From individual rights, to the push to protect the environment, to the fight to save democratic institutions while government obfuscation was rampant, this period invites students to engage in historical inquiry over a bevy of topics.

The learning modules for Period 8 are in keeping with the design of this book, which is to say by this point in the year students should be more independent in their practice of historical reasoning processes. Yet, even though students are supposed to be more independent, the book still models ways teachers can scaffold the writing process, analyses of primary and secondary sources, and the writing components of the AP® U.S. History exam. Period 8 accounts for 10–17% of the material assessed on the AP® exam. Period 8 can be the focus of a Short-Answer Question, Long-Essay Question, Document-Based Question, and Multiple-Choice Questions. Not only is this a time period that demands an intensive study, in many ways, it invites intensive historical queries.

Module 8-1: The Early Cold War, 1945–1953 is an intensive analysis of the beginning stages of the Cold War, the evolution of containment, and how the Korean War changed U.S. foreign policy. Aside from explaining the big events of the origins of the Cold War, this module helps students conceptualize how policies changed over time in response to both global events and a new view of the world put forward by U.S. leaders. America in the world is the thematic focus of this module, which helps students frame their understanding through a historical theme. The historical reasoning process of continuity and change works well due to the subtle changes in U.S. foreign policy and the continuous effort to contain communism throughout this time period. Teachers should continue to expose students to different interpretations, which will help students perform on the Short-Answer Question at the end of the module.

Module 8-2: The Second Red Scare depicts the tenor of the Red Scare, which created fissures in Americans' sense of their identity, political unity, and societal ideas about what means were acceptable to combat communism. This chronological module illustrates change over time as well as asks students to work through the various examples of how the Red Scare intensified over time. The historical reasoning process of causation couples well with the thematic focus on American and national identity because many of the events from the Red Scare can be studied as causes of a changing American identity. This module's focus on primary sources prepares students well for the Short-Answer Question that uses a primary source as the stimulus for the question.

Module 8-3: Peacetime Transition and Boom Years continues to look at events in the immediate aftermath of World War II, from 1945 through the 1950s. This module focuses on the economic surge and subsequent migration patterns that transformed where and how citizens lived. Evident among many economic themes is the structural divide that existed among races in suburban and urban environments. Rather than chronological, this module focuses on overarching themes of work, exchange, and technology in concert with migration and settlement. The historical reasoning focus of causation should assist students as they grapple with the causes and consequences of economic growth in the 1950s. The thematic focus will also help students formulate a plan for the Long-Essay Question at the end of this module.

Module 8-4: Cultural Shifts in 1950s America highlights a decade rife with conflict, conformity, and cultural changes brought on by new mass media inventions and a popular culture that appealed to the sensibilities of the youth. Although conformity among middle-class Americans was prevalent, the 1950s also witnessed a restless new wave of music and an intellectual class who criticized mass consumerism and conformity. The historical reasoning process of continuity and change works well with the thematic focus of American and regional culture because the 1950s highlight the tension between those who wanted to maintain the status quo and those who yearned for change. The Long-Essay Question at the end of this module allows students to draw from this and earlier modules.

Module 8-5: Civil Rights in an Era of Conformity combines a chronological study of African American civil rights and a chronological study of other racial minorities' fight for civil rights. The focus on how grassroots activism persisted in the midst of conformity is an important takeaway for students. Moreover, students need to see the ongoing struggle for civil rights as an active process and not as a movement with a finite ending. The thematic focuses of social structures and politics and power match the double-pronged approach of civil rights advocates to effect societal change through the political process. The historical reasoning process of causation can help students distill the reasons why large historical processes changed over time. The AP® Writing Historically assignment at the end draws on students' ability to understand different interpretations to a dynamic movement.

Module 8-6: The Cold War Expands at Home and Abroad, 1953–1961 is a balanced approach to how the expansion of the Cold War affected foreign policy during the presidencies of Dwight D. Eisenhower and John F. Kennedy as well as how these events changed the lives of everyday Americans. In many ways a symbiotic relationship developed between Cold War policies and reactions on the home front. The thematic focuses on America in the world and politics and power mirror the goals of this module as students need to start thinking about how those themes can interlock at moments in history. The historical reasoning process of comparison allows students to compare policy, reactions to global events, and effectiveness of each president. Comparing perspectives prepares students to grapple with the Short-Answer Question at the end of this module.

Module 8-7: The Vietnam War is a chronological look at U.S. entry, escalation, and failure to contain communism in Vietnam. Initially couched in the larger context of Cold War policy aimed at stemming the tide of communism in Asia, the war in Vietnam morphed into an American quagmire. The war had devastating effects on U.S. society as the country splintered along racial, socioeconomic, and political lines. The historical reasoning focus of this module is causation, which should aid students as they ponder the extent to which both internal and external factors drove decisions in Vietnam. The thematic focus for the Vietnam War is America in the world, which asks students to also understand the geopolitical aspects of this conflict.

Module 8-8: The Fight for Civil Rights, 1961–1979 is a concise narrative both chronological and thematic. Teachers should be aware of the timing of instruction as this module includes a DBQ over African American civil rights. The civil rights struggle of the 1960s contained both continuities and changes from earlier movements of African Americans in the 1940s and 1950s. Students should not only be aware of these continuities and changes but also should look to compare the two periods, as this is the historical reasoning focus for this module. Politics and power and social structures, although separate themes, can be used in tandem to help students see the broad developments and processes of the civil rights movement in this era.

Module 8-9: Liberalism and Its Challengers, 1960–1973 contains a breadth of liberal movements, which varied greatly, as well as conservative responses to the liberal tide of the 1960s. Students need to remember that liberalism had many iterations and liberal groups were no monolith as they often feuded with one another over domestic and foreign policy. From grassroots groups to the federal government, liberalism marked much of the 1960s and 1970s until conservative groups began to change the political tenor of the nation. Continuity and change is the historical reasoning focus, which allows students to see how liberalism changed and stayed the same throughout this period. Because this module contains so many disparate movements, the thematic focus extends to include three different themes.

Module 8-10: American Politics in Transition, 1968–1980 focuses on the major economic and political changes that followed the liberal wave of the 1960s. Much of the story of the 1970s revolves around the economic and political malaise in the context of the Vietnam War, Watergate, and an energy crisis. This module also examines how the Cold War changed as the United States endured domestic crises as well as how the focus of foreign policy shifted toward the Middle East. The thematic focus of politics and power matches the historical reasoning focus well because students should be continuously examining the causes of political changes. This module contains a DBQ as the AP® Writing Historically assignment, which should test how well students have synthesized the information.

Module 8-11: The Persistence of Liberalism and the Rise of the New Right examines the continued aspirations of liberalism represented by the women's movement and the push for environmental reform. The other half of the module introduces how grassroots conservatism, mainly focused on economic and moral reform movements, engendered support among many middle-class Americans who were ready to move away from liberal ideas. The historical reasoning focus of causation helps students trace the reasons for the emergence of conservatism. The thematic focuses of geography and the environment, along with American and regional culture, help students see how varied movements occurred simultaneously.

Pacing Guide

Course Pacing for Period 8

Module #	Lesson Title	Instructional Period*	AP® Theme	AP® Topic	AP® Reasoning Process/Skill	Homework
8-1	N/A	N/A	America in the World	8.1 8.2	Continuity and Change / Historical Thinking Skills 1, 2, 3, 5	**Reading and Source Analysis:** 8-1 **Activity:** AP® Writing Historically: Short-Answer Question Practice, 8-1
	Review: AP® Writing Historically: Short-Answer Question Practice, 8-1 The Early Cold War	1	America in the World	8.2 8.3 8.7	Continuity and Change / Historical Thinking Skills 1, 2, 3, 4, 5	**Reading and Source Analysis:** 8-2 **Activity:** AP® Writing Historically: Short-Answer Question Practice, 8-2

(Continued)

Module #	Lesson Title	Instructional Period*	AP® Theme	AP® Topic	AP® Reasoning Process/Skill	Homework
8-2	**Review:** AP® Writing Historically: Short-Answer Question Practice, 8-2 The Second Red Scare	1	American and National Identity	8.2 8.3 8.7	Causation / Historical Thinking Skills 1, 2, 3, 4, 5	**Reading and Source Analysis:** 8-3 **Activity:** AP® Writing Historically: Long-Essay Question Practice, 8-3
8-3	**Review:** AP® Writing Historically: Long-Essay Question Practice, 8-3 Peacetime Transition and the Boom Years	1	Work, Exchange, and Technology Migration and Settlement	8.4 8.5 8.7	Causation / Historical Thinking Skills 1, 2, 3, 4, 5, 6	**Reading and Source Analysis:** 8-4 **Activity:** AP® Writing Historically: Long-Essay Question Practice, 8-4
8-4	**Review:** AP® Writing Historically: Long-Essay Question Practice, 8-4 Cultural Shifts in 1950s America	1	American and Regional Culture	8.4 8.5	Continuity and Change / Historical Thinking Skills 1, 2, 3, 4, 5, 6	**Reading and Source Analysis:** 8-5 **Activity:** AP® Writing Historically: Short-Answer Question Practice, 8-5
8-5	**Review:** AP® Writing Historically: Short-Answer Question Practice, 8-5 Civil Rights in an Era of Conformity	1	Social Structures Politics and Power	8.6	Causation / Historical Thinking Skills 1, 2, 3, 4, 5, 6	**Reading and Source Analysis:** 8-6 **Activity:** AP® Writing Historically: Short-Answer Question Practice, 8-6
8-6	**Review:** AP® Writing Historically: Short-Answer Question Practice, 8-6 The Cold War Expands at Home and Abroad	1	America in the World Politics and Power	8.2 8.3 8.7	Comparison / Historical Thinking Skills 1, 2, 3, 4, 5	**Reading and Source Analysis:** 8-7 **Activity:** AP® Writing Historically: Short-Answer Question Practice, 8-7
8-7	**Review:** AP® Writing Historically: Short-Answer Question Practice, 8-7 The Vietnam War	1	America in the World	8.7 8.8	Causation / Historical Thinking Skills 1, 2, 3, 4, 5	**Reading and Source Analysis:** 8-8
8-8	The Fight for Civil Rights	1	Politics and Power Social Structures	8.10 8.11	Comparison / Historical Thinking Skills 1, 2, 3, 5	**Activity:** AP® Writing Historically: Document-Based Question Practice, 8-8
	Workshop: AP® Writing Historically: Document-Based Question Practice, 8-8	1	Politics and Power Social Structures	8.10 8.11	Comparison / Historical Thinking Skills 1, 2, 3, 4, 5	**Reading and Source Analysis:** 8-9 **Activity:** AP® Writing Historically: Long-Essay Question Practice, 8-9
8-9	**Review:** AP® Writing Historically: Long-Essay Question Practice, 8-9 Liberalism and Its Challengers	1	Migration and Settlement Politics and Power American and Regional Culture	8.9 8.11 8.12 8.14	Continuity and Change / Historical Thinking Skills 1, 2, 3, 4, 5, 6	**Reading and Source Analysis:** 8-10
8-10	American Politics in Transition	1	Politics and Power	8.14	Causation / Historical Thinking Skills 1, 2, 3, 5	**Activity:** AP® Writing Historically: Document-Based Question Practice, 8-10
	Workshop: AP® Writing Historically: Document-Based Question Practice, 8-10	1	Politics and Power	8.2 8.14	Causation / Historical Thinking Skills 1, 2, 3, 5	**Reading and Source Analysis:** 8-11 **Activity:** AP® Writing Historically: Short-Answer Question Practice, 8-11
8-11	**Review:** AP® Writing Historically: Short-Answer Question Practice, 8-11 The Persistence of Liberalism and the Rise of the New Right	1	Geography and the Environment American and Regional Culture	8.13 8.14	Causation / Historical Thinking Skills 1, 2, 3, 4, 5	Prepare for Assessment

(Continued)

Module #	Lesson Title	Instructional Period*	AP® Theme	AP® Topic	AP® Reasoning Process/Skill	Homework
Formative Assessment	AP® Exam Practice • 18 MCQs • 4 SAQs	0–1	All AP® U.S. History Course Themes	8.15 Personal Progress Check • 15 MCQs • 2 SAQs • 1 LEQ	All AP® History Reasoning Processes / Skills	
Summative Assessment	Unit 1 Test Bank • 55 MCQs • 4 SAQs • 1 DBQ • 4 LEQs	0–1	All AP® U.S. History Course Themes		All AP® History Reasoning Processes / Skills	

*Based on a standard 50-minute class period.

Period 8 Resources

The following resources can be found in the Resources section of the book's digital platform, by clicking on the link buttons in the Teacher's Edition e-book, or by opening the Teacher's Resource Materials.

- **TRM** Period 8 Overview Video
- **TRM** AP® Concepts and Skills Video
- **TRM** Period 8 Lecture Presentation Slides
- **TRM** Period 8 Workshop Rubrics
- **TRM** Period 8 Suggested Responses to Questions
- **TRM** Period 8 Guided Reading Worksheets

Module 8-1
- **TRM** Map 8A – The World
- **TRM** Module 8.1 AP® Analyzing Sources Handout 1
- **TRM** Module 8.1 AP® Analyzing Sources Handout 2
- **TRM** Handout 8.1 – Understanding American Commitment to Containment

Module 8-2
- **TRM** Module 8.2 AP® Analyzing Sources Handout 1
- **TRM** Handout 8.2 – Comparing the First and Second Red Scare
- **TRM** Module 8.2 AP® Analyzing Sources Handout 2

Module 8-3
- **TRM** Module 8.3 AP® Analyzing Sources Handout 1
- **TRM** Handout 8.3 – Effects of Consumerism
- **TRM** Module 8.3 AP® Analyzing Sources Handout 2

Module 8-4
- **TRM** Module 8.4 AP® Analyzing Sources Handout 1
- **TRM** Module 8.4 AP® Analyzing Sources Handout 2
- **TRM** Handout 8.4 – Women and Contextualization

Module 8-5
- **TRM** Module 8.5 AP® Analyzing Sources Handout 1
- **TRM** Module 8.5 AP® Analyzing Sources Handout 2
- **TRM** Handout 8.5 – Comparing Civil Rights Activists
- **TRM** Module 8.5 AP® Analyzing Sources Handout 3

Module 8-6
- **TRM** Handout 8.6 – Comparing the Truman Doctrine and the Eisenhower Doctrine
- **TRM** Module 8.6 AP® Analyzing Sources Handout 1
- **TRM** Module 8.6 AP® Analyzing Sources Handout 2

Module 8-7
- **TRM** Map 8B – Europe, Asia, and Africa
- **TRM** Module 8.7 AP® Analyzing Sources Handout 1
- **TRM** Module 8.7 AP® Analyzing Sources Handout 2

Module 8-8
- **TRM** Handout 8.7 – Comparing Civil Rights Movements, 1940s–1970s
- **TRM** Module 8.8 AP® Analyzing Sources Handout 1
- **TRM** Module 8.8 AP® Analyzing Sources Handout 2

Module 8-9

- **TRM** Handout 8.8 – Categories of the Great Society
- **TRM** Module 8.9 AP® Analyzing Sources Handout 1
- **TRM** Module 8.9 AP® Analyzing Sources Handout 2

Module 8-10

- **TRM** Module 8.10 AP® Analyzing Sources Handout 1
- **TRM** Module 8.10 AP® Analyzing Sources Handout 2
- **TRM** Handout 8.9 – Foreign Policy Decisions of the 1970s

Module 8-11

- **TRM** Module 8.11 AP® Analyzing Sources Handout 1
- **TRM** Module 8.11 AP® Analyzing Sources Handout 2
- **TRM** Handout 8.10 – New Right and State Politics

Period 8 Essential Activity

The end of World War II through the malaise of the 1970s is a time of profound changes evidenced by the advent of the thermonuclear age, a continuous Cold War which altered American foreign policy, a dramatic alteration in the rights of African Americans, political party realignments, and migration patterns that transformed the demographics of the United States. The following activity is meant to enliven students' historical sensibilities of these changes and a score of many others. Moreover, this activity seeks to offer students choices to deepen their understanding of one aspect of the post-war period while exposing them to a breadth of other examples. Have students consider this list of post-war period changes:

Migration Patterns | Rise of Conservatism | Rise of Liberalism | Cold War | Women's Movement | African American Civil Rights

If students have other specific categories, be open to those possibilities too. The activity has four overarching goals. The first task is for students to illustrate how their selected event inspired transformational change across a portion, or all of, this period. The next task will be for students to address the causes of these changes. The third task is for students to address any seminal, or turning point moments that help illustrate the first two points. And the final task is for students to explain the extent to which their selected event also fostered continuity.

The actual product students will produce will depend on your flexibility as a teacher. Sometimes we inspire student ownership of an assignment when we remain open to a number of possible products. The final product could be produced on a graphic organizer, a short documentary, a podcast, a large tri-fold project board, or a written response to the stated goals.

Regardless, at this point in the year, teachers should be ready to turn students loose so they can create a meaningful product over a pivotal topic in American history.

Period 8 Alignment to the Fall 2019 AP® United States History Course Framework*

Relationship to the College Board Units

Period 8 in this book covers Topics 8.1–8.15 in Unit 8 of the College Board course framework. Students will be ready to take the Personal Progress Check for Unit 8 once they have completed this period.

Course Themes

Period 8 develops these course themes outlined in the course framework:

- **America in the World (WOR):** In the aftermath of World War II, fundamental differences between the United States and the Soviet Union over ideology and the fate of Europe led to the ending of the wartime alliance and the beginning of the Cold War. The United States pursued a policy of containment to limit the expansion of communism, resulting in the formation of NATO, an arms race, and U.S. participation in direct and indirect conflicts including the Korean War and Vietnam War.

- **American and National Identity (NAT):** Cold War fears of conflict with the Soviet Union abroad and domestic communist spying led to the Second Red Scare as Americans debated the balance between civil liberties and security.

- **Work, Exchange, and Technology (WXT):** After World War II, the United States economy experienced a remarkable period of growth, significantly expanding the ranks of the middle class and noticeably lessening income inequality. However, increased global competition posed challenges to American manufacturers, leading to deindustrialization and long-term structural changes to the U.S. economy.

- **Migration and Settlement (MIG):** Fueled by the baby boom, federal subsidies, and the application of mass production techniques to home construction, millions of Americans, especially young families, moved to the suburbs. Immigrants from Latin America and Asia came to the United States in increasing numbers as the 1965 Immigration and Naturalization Act abolished national origin quotas while favoring skilled labor and family reunification.

- **American and Regional Cultures (ARC):** In the 1950s and early 1960s, the rise of television reinforced traditional values, especially toward women, even as a distinctly teenage culture began to form with the emergence of rock 'n' roll music and Hollywood movies aimed at teenagers' sense of rebellion. Protests against the Vietnam War, the civil rights movements for African Americans and other groups, and the emergence of a counterculture movement led to social conflicts and a revival of conservatism.

- **Geography and the Environment (GEO):** An environmentalist movement emerged in the 1960s and 1970s resulting in the first Earth Day, establishment of the Environmental Protection Agency, and passage of environmental legislation regulating air and water pollution and protecting endangered species.

- **Social Structures (SOC):** After World War II, a reinvigorated civil rights movement emphasizing nonviolent actions such as marches and sit-ins scored major victories with the *Brown* decision, the Civil Rights Act of 1964, and the Voting Rights Act of 1965. In the mid-1960s and 1970s, the African American civil rights movement splintered as some leaders encouraged violence or separation in response to the lack of economic improvement and persistence of racism and discrimination, while other groups such as women, Hispanics, American Indians, and homosexuals also launched movements for greater rights.

- **Politics and Power (PCE):** After World War II, a Cold War liberal consensus prevailed as both Democratic and Republican presidents vowed to take a tough stance against communist threats overseas and within the United States. Public confidence in the federal government declined in the late 1960s and 1970s as the Vietnam War, Watergate scandal, and debates over Warren Court rulings and Great Society legislation divided Americans.

Course Skills

Period 8 helps students to develop the following AP* Historical Thinking Skills identified in the course framework.

- **Skill 1—Developments and Processes** (Modules 8-1, 8-2, 8-3, 8-4, 8-5, 8-6, 8-7, 8-8, 8-9, 8-10, 8-11)
- **Skill 2—Sourcing and Situation** (Modules 8-1, 8-2, 8-3, 8-4, 8-5, 8-6, 8-7, 8-8, 8-9, 8-10, 8-11)
- **Skill 3—Claims and Evidence in Sources** (Modules 8-1, 8-2, 8-3, 8-4, 8-5, 8-6, 8-7, 8-8, 8-9, 8-10, 8-11)
- **Skill 4—Contextualization** (Modules 8-1, 8-2, 8-3, 8-4, 8-5, 8-6, 8-7, 8-8, 8-9, 8-11)
- **Skill 5—Making Connections** (Modules 8-1, 8-2, 8-3, 8-4, 8-5, 8-6, 8-7, 8-8, 8-9, 8-10, 8-11)
- **Skill 6—Argumentation** (Modules 8-3, 8-4, 8-5, 8-9)

Period 8 helps students to develop the following AP* History Reasoning Processes identified in the course framework.

- **Reasoning Process 1: Comparison** (Modules 8-6, 8-8)
- **Reasoning Process 2: Causation** (Modules 8-2, 8-3, 8-5, 8-7, 8-10, 8-11)
- **Reasoning Process 3: Continuity and Change** (Modules 8-1, 8-4, 8-9)

Learning Objectives and Historical Developments

Module	Topics	Learning Objectives	Historical Developments and Key Concepts
8-1	8.1, 8.2	Unit 8: Learning Objective A Unit 8: Learning Objective B	KC-8.1.I.A, KC-8.1.I.B.i, KC-8.1.I.C
8-2	8.3	Unit 8: Learning Objective C	KC-8.1.II.A
8-3	8.4	Unit 8: Learning Objective D Unit 8: Learning Objective E	KC-8.3.I.A, KC-8.3.I.B
8-4	8.5	Unit 8: Learning Objective F	KC-8.3.II.A
8-5	8.6	Unit 8: Learning Objective G	KC-8.2.I, KC-8.2.I.B.i
8-6	8.2, 8.7	Unit 8: Learning Objective B Unit 8: Learning Objective H	KC-8.1.I.A, KC-8.1.I.B.i, KC-8.1.I.C, KC-8.1.I.E, KC-8.1.II.C.i, KC-8.1.I.D.i
8-7	8.8	Unit 8: Learning Objective I	KC-8.1.I.B.ii, KC-8.1.D.ii, KC-8.1.II.C.ii
8-8	8.10	Unit 8: Learning Objective L Unit 8: Learning Objective M	KC-8.2.1.A, KC-8.2.I.C, KC-8.2.I.B.ii, KC-8.2.III.B.ii
8-9	8.9, 8.11, 8.12, 8.14	Unit 8: Learning Objective J Unit 8: Learning Objective K Unit 8: Learning Objective L Unit 8: Learning Objective N	KC-8.2.II.C, KC-8.2.III.A, KC-8.2.III.B.i, KC-8.3.I.C, KC-8.2.II.B, KC-8.2.II.A, KC-8.3.II.B.i, KC-8.1.II.B, KC-8.2.III.D, KC-8.3.II.B.ii, KC-8.2.III.C
8-10	8.2, 8.14	Unit 8: Learning Objective B Unit 8: Learning Objective J	KC-8.1.I.A, KC-8.1.I.B.i, KC-8.1.I,C, KC-8.2.III.E
8-11	8.13, 8.14, 8.15	Unit 8: Learning Objective J Unit 8: Learning Objective O Unit 8: Learning Objective P Unit 8: Learning Objective Q	KC-8.1.II.D, KC-8.2.II.D, KC-8.2.III.F, KC-8.3.II.C

TRM A detailed alignment that can be sorted by Course Framework Unit, Topic, Learning Objective, Historical Development/Key Concept, or textbook period, is available in the Teacher's Resource Materials and via the book's online platform.

*Should changes be made to the Course Framework in the future, an updated alignment will be placed on our catalog page at bfwpub.com/fabric1e.

TEACHING IDEA

AP® Central

A great resource to help you teach this period is to read the information in the AP® U.S. History study guide for 1945–1980, available from the AP® United States History Classroom Resources section of AP® Central (apcentral.collegeboard.org).

PERIOD 8: 1945–1980

Cold War America

▲ **Hard Hat Riot, May 8, 1970** Four days after the shooting of four students at Kent State University during an antiwar protest, approximately 1,000 antiwar protesters gathered in New York City to denounce the killings. Approximately 250 construction workers, under the direction of the state AFL-CIO, attacked the protesters in what became known as the "Hard Hat Riot." Many of the counter protesters carried American flags.

The postwar period promised to be expansive for American interests and ideals. Once the United States, the Soviet Union, and the other Allied Powers defeated the Axis Powers of Europe and Asia, they set in motion an international order that was grounded in the new United Nations and in statutes that protected universal human rights. However, in the final days of the Second World War, the United States and the USSR established the parameters of a global conflict that lasted for nearly fifty years.

The Cold War was waged between people living in two fundamentally different political and economic systems and reflected a precarious balance between the two world powers left standing in the aftermath of 1945. The destructive capabilities of modern warfare, especially after the invention of nuclear weaponry, made direct conflict between these two "superpowers" unthinkable for most leaders. Instead, in Europe, Asia, and the Caribbean, a series of **"proxy wars"** on the fringes of each nation's sphere of influence broke out regularly throughout this period. These proxy wars inspired an ongoing culture of preparedness and anxiety domestically, including debates about the power of the federal government over individuals in an age of constant fear of war.

By the early 1960s, protests against the Vietnam War (a proxy war within the Cold War) and the civil rights movement dominated newspaper headlines in the United States and inspired movements for gender and sexual equality and for African American, Latin American, and Native American rights. These movements especially influenced millions of young Americans who were coming of age in high schools and colleges. By the end of the decade, the assassinations of Martin Luther King Jr., Malcolm X, and Robert F. Kennedy and riots in the poor and predominantly African American neighborhoods of large American cities ignited widespread calls for reform.

These revolutionary sentiments produced a countermovement of self-proclaimed conservatives like Ronald Reagan and Phyllis Schlafly who took inspiration from the presidential candidacy of Barry Goldwater in 1964 and looked back to an unspecified time when American society was at peace and the American economy was in a state of prosperity. For many Americans, the first decades after the Second World War represented a time when all that had gone smoothly before seemed suddenly to have become jagged and out of alignment. Already anxious from the Cold War and the ongoing threat of global nuclear destruction, many Americans felt further threatened by new value systems that challenged old conventions, by the emergence of new interest groups that demanded recognition and respect, and by the arrival of new immigrants from locations outside of Europe. These sentiments provided the seeds of a revitalized conservatism in the 1970s and 1980s, breaking through on the federal level with the election of Ronald Reagan as president in 1980.

TEACHING IDEA

AP® Central

Have students read the essay, "Cold War and Global Hegemony, 1945–1991," from the College Board series America on the World Stage: Essays from the American Organization of Historians and AP®, available in the Related Articles and Teaching Resources section of the Classroom Resources for AP® U.S. History on AP® Central (apcentral.collegeboard.org).

PERIOD 8 PREVIEW

Module	AP® Thematic Focus
8-1: The Early Cold War, 1945–1953	**America in the World** In the aftermath of World War II, fundamental differences between the United States and the Soviet Union over ideology and the fate of Europe led to the ending of the wartime alliance and the beginning of the Cold War. The United States pursued a policy of containment to limit the expansion of communism and committed itself to preserving the security of Western Europe through the investment of billions of dollars, joining a permanent military alliance, and greatly increased military spending. President Truman sent U.S. troops, under the authority of a United Nations resolution, to fight in the Korean War against the invasion by Communist North Korea, ultimately resulting in a military stalemate.
8-2: The Second Red Scare	**American and National Identity** As the Cold War solidified and Europe was divided by an iron curtain, Americans faced the threat of devastating war with a nuclear-armed Soviet Union seemingly bent on worldwide Communist domination. Efforts to uncover potential domestic Communist activity took on new urgency as a Communist revolution in China, the Korean War, and the capture of spies stealing atomic secrets led to a growing climate of fear known as the Second Red Scare. Investigations by the House Un-American Activities Committee, Federal Employee Loyalty review boards, and Senator Joseph McCarthy failed to uncover significant Communist spying but did result in renewed debates over the balance between civil liberties and public safety.
8-3: Peacetime Transition and the Boom Years	**Work, Exchange, and Technology ■ Migration and Settlement** After an initial postwar transition, during which Congress curtailed labor union rights, the United States economy experienced a remarkable period of growth significantly expanding the ranks of the middle class and noticeably lessening income inequality. The application of mass production techniques to home construction and federal subsidies for mortgages led to a sharp increase in home ownership as millions of Americans, especially young families resulting from the postwar baby boom, moved to newly built suburbs.

Module	AP® Thematic Focus
8-4: Cultural Shifts in 1950s America	**American and Regional Culture** The rise of television reinforced traditional values, especially toward women, by generally depicting white, middle-class families in wholesome situations. At the same time a distinctly teenage culture began to form with the emergence of rock 'n' roll music and Hollywood movies aimed at teenagers' sense of rebellion. Church attendance soared to record heights as millions of Americans sought personal connections in a changing world and comfort from the threat of nuclear annihilation. Despite mainstream expectations of conformity, writers and intellectuals challenged the cultural homogeneity of postwar American society.
8-5: Civil Rights in an Era of Conformity	**Politics and Power ▪ Social Structures** After fighting for a double victory in World War II against fascism abroad and racism at home, African American veterans returned to a country in which they faced discrimination in the North and legal segregation in the South. In response, civil rights groups initiated lawsuits, boycotts, and sit-ins resulting in the Supreme Court overturning school segregation in *Brown v. Board of Education*, the desegregation of Montgomery's buses, and the integration of lunch counters in the South. White segregationists resisted civil rights by blocking passage of civil rights legislation, using threats and intimidation, and sometimes through violence and terror.
8-6: The Cold War Expands at Home and Abroad, 1953–1961	**Politics and Power ▪ America in the World** President Eisenhower oversaw a shift in U.S. military spending as his administration emphasized the production of nuclear weapons over conventional forces. After the development of the hydrogen bomb in the early 1950s, an arms race ensued with the Soviet Union and a policy of deterrence based on mutually assured destruction took hold. Domestically, Eisenhower increased federal spending on highways to speed mobilization of U.S. military forces in wartime, and education funding to counter Soviet advances in rocket technology. In 1960, Kennedy defeated Nixon in a close election in which both candidates promised to take a hard line against communism. Two years later the Cuban Missile Crisis brought the U.S. and USSR to the brink of war before it was peacefully resolved. To prevent Communist gains in Latin America, Asia, and Africa the U.S. often supported repressive regimes, and sometimes engineered CIA supported coups to install friendlier governments.
8-7: The Vietnam War	**America in the World** Despite the thousands of U.S. military advisors sent to South Vietnam by the Eisenhower and Kennedy administrations after the defeat of the French in 1954, the anti-Communist regime continued to struggle against a determined Communist insurgency. In 1964, President Lyndon Johnson, capitalizing on a controversial naval attack, escalated the conflict into a full-scale war, drafting hundreds of thousands of U.S. soldiers into the fight. Four years later, as public opinion on the war soured, Nixon was elected on a promise of "peace with honor." Even as U.S. forces were drawn down, Nixon expanded the conflict into neighboring countries in an unsuccessful effort to secure better terms at the peace negotiations. Elsewhere, the Nixon administration had more success as it opened relations with China and signed the first nuclear arms treaty with the Soviet Union. Yet, the withdrawal of U.S. military forces from South Vietnam in 1973 led to its defeat two years later.
8-8: The Fight for Civil Rights, 1961–1979	**Politics and Power ▪ Social Structures** As the 1960s began, civil rights leaders looked to build upon their postwar successes through continued nonviolent protests, voter registration drives, and political pressure. After the widely seen images from Birmingham and the March on Washington, Kennedy supported and Johnson eventually succeeded in pushing through Congress momentous civil rights legislation including the Civil Rights Act of 1964, the Voting Rights Act, and the Twenty-fourth Amendment. Yet, new voices such as Malcom X and the Black Panther Party, emphasizing black power, challenged the approach of King and others as young urban African Americans in the North and West expressed their frustration with the lack of meaningful change for them by participating in urban uprisings. As the focus of the civil rights movement shifted toward racial integration and equal opportunity outside the South, policies such as forced busing and affirmative action generated controversy and were eventually limited by court rulings.
8-9: Liberalism and Its Challengers, 1960–1973	**Migration and Settlement ▪ Politics and Power ▪ American and Regional Culture** Promising to create a Great Society, Johnson's legislative successes rivaled the New Deal with reforms aimed at civil rights, immigration, poverty, education, health care, and environmental protection. Together with rulings by the Warren Court expanding civil liberties, the 1960s represented the height of a liberal consensus in American politics. Yet, protests against the Vietnam War stimulated the growth of a New Left movement, which rejected the Cold War emphasis on containment and conformity. Liberation movements also emerged for women, Hispanics, American Indians, and homosexuals while a small but noticeable counterculture movement took root among disaffected youths in select cities. Many middle-class and working-class Americans disapproved of the cultural changes taking place, setting the stage for a revival of conservatism.
8-10: American Politics in Transition, 1968–1980	**Politics and Power** Having won the presidency in 1968 amid the turmoil of antiwar protests, high profile assassinations, urban riots, and political demonstrations, Nixon's victory and reelection signaled a rightward shift in American politics. However, the Watergate scandal temporarily reversed this trend and led to Carter's election in 1976. Rising prices, unemployment, and overseas competition disrupted American economic growth as workers, businesses, and politicians struggled to adapt to the new conditions. After a period of détente, relations with the Soviet Union deteriorated because of its invasion of Afghanistan in 1979.
8-11: The Persistence of Liberalism and the Rise of the New Right	**Geography and the Environment ▪ American and Regional Culture** In the 1970s Americans witnessed a continuation of the cultural changes and rights movements from the previous decade. Environmentalists won new protections for air and water quality as well as endangered species while the Supreme Court ruled in favor of abortion rights for women. Yet, a growing conservative movement opposed to the expansion of government, high taxes, and social changes mobilized to block ratification of the Equal Rights Amendment and launched a grassroots taxpayer revolt. A newly formed Christian Right joined the New Right as a potent counterweight to liberal activism of the era.

Module 8-1

The Early Cold War, 1945–1953

LEARNING TARGETS

By the end of this module, you should be able to:

- Explain why the alliance between the U.S. and USSR quickly dissolved after World War II.
- Explain how developments in Europe led the U.S. to adopt a strategy of containment.
- Explain how the U.S. used economic assistance and collective security in its postwar foreign policy.
- Explain how the Korean War affected U.S. Cold War strategy and presidential power.

THEMATIC FOCUS
America in the World

In the aftermath of World War II, fundamental differences between the United States and the Soviet Union over ideology and the fate of Europe led to the ending of the wartime alliance and the beginning of the Cold War. The United States pursued a policy of containment to limit the expansion of communism and committed itself to preserving the security of Western Europe through the investment of billions of dollars, joining a permanent military alliance, and greatly increased military spending. President Truman sent U.S. troops, under the authority of a United Nations resolution, to fight in the Korean War against the invasion by Communist North Korea, ultimately resulting in a military stalemate.

HISTORICAL REASONING FOCUS
Continuity and Change

TASK ▶ As you read this module, consider how United States foreign policy changed in the period after World War II. Ask yourself, what accounts for the changes, whether the changes were inevitable, and how the changes affected American politics.

TRM Suggested Responses to Questions

BUILDING AP® SKILLS
Continuity and Change

Often, students have an easier time substantiating claims about changes in historical developments than they do substantiating claims about continuities. At this point in the year students should be able to delineate reasons for changes and continuities. To help build out this skill, consider the following assignment. Provide students with three historical developments or events and ask if the beginning stages of the Cold War represent a change or continuity from the examples. You could use examples such as the Potsdam Conference, the Communist system under Joseph Stalin, and the Yalta Conference.

The wartime partnership between the United States and the Soviet Union (USSR) was an alliance of necessity. Putting aside ideological differences and a history of mutual distrust, the two nations joined forces to combat Nazi aggression. As long as the Nazi threat existed, the alliance held, but as the war ended and attention turned to the postwar world, the allies became adversaries. The two nations did not engage directly in war, but they entered into a prolonged struggle for political, economic, and military dominance known as the Cold War.

After 1947 the Cold War intensified. Both sides increased military spending and took measures to enhance their military presence around the world. Fueled by growing distrust, the Soviet Union and the United States engaged in inflammatory rhetoric that added to the danger the conflict posed to world peace. In 1950 the United States, in cooperation with the United Nations, sent troops to South Korea to turn back an invasion from the Communist North. President Truman took advantage of Cold War hostilities to expand presidential power through increased military spending and the creation of a vast national intelligence network.

TEACHING IDEA

Incorporating Videos

Even though this module focuses on the reasoning process of continuity and change, it is good practice for students to be aware of the context of the period they are studying. Therefore, consider using parts of a lecture on Period 8 by historian John Lewis Gaddis on the Gilder Lehrman site for AP® U.S. History teachers (ap.gilderlehrman.org). In the lecture, Gaddis describes how historians come to understand causation, and the bulk of the video is about the direct causes of the Cold War.

The Early Cold War, 1945–1953

Period 8: 1945–1980

MODULE 8-1 The Early Cold War, 1945–1953

Mutual Misunderstandings

Cold War The political, economic, and military conflict, short of direct war on the battlefield, between the United States and the Soviet Union between 1945 and 1991.

> " Unless Russia is faced with an iron fist and strong language another war is in the making. "
>
> —President Harry Truman, 1945

AP® TIP
Analyze how new atomic weapons affected the relationship between the U.S. and the USSR.

containment Belief that the Soviet Union desired the spread of communism throughout the world. To prevent this spread U.S. diplomat George Kennan advocated a strict policy of containing communism where it already existed and preventing its spread.

The roots of the **Cold War** stretched back several decades. After the Bolshevik Revolution of 1917, the United States refused to grant diplomatic recognition to the Soviet Union and sent troops to Russia to support anti-Bolshevik forces seeking to overturn the revolution, an effort that failed. At the same time, the American government, fearing Communist efforts to overthrow capitalist governments, sought to wipe out communism in the United States by deporting immigrant radicals during the Red Scare (see Module 7-5). The United States continued to deny diplomatic recognition to the USSR until 1933, when President Roosevelt reversed this policy. Nevertheless, relations between the two countries remained uneasy.

World War II brought a thaw in tensions. President Roosevelt went a long way toward defusing Joseph Stalin's concerns at the Yalta Conference in 1945. The Soviet leader viewed the Eastern European countries that the USSR had liberated from the Germans, especially Poland, as a buffer to protect his nation from future attacks by Germany. Roosevelt understood Stalin's reasoning and recognized political realities: The Soviet military already occupied Eastern Europe, a state of affairs that increased Stalin's bargaining position. Still, the president attempted to balance Soviet influence by insisting that the Yalta Agreement include a guarantee of free elections in Eastern Europe.

By contrast, Roosevelt's successor, Harry S. Truman, took a much less nuanced approach to U.S.-Soviet relations. Stalin's ruthless purges within the Soviet Union in the 1930s and 1940s convinced Truman that the Soviet dictator was paranoid and extremely dangerous. He believed that the Soviets threatened "a barbarian invasion of Europe," and he intended to deter it. In his first meeting with Soviet foreign minister Vyacheslav Molotov in April 1945, Truman rebuked the Russians for failing to support free elections in Poland. Molotov, recoiling from the sharp tone of Truman's remarks, replied: "I have never been talked to like that in my life."

Despite this rough start, Truman did not immediately abandon the idea of cooperation with the Soviet Union. At the **Potsdam Conference** in Germany in July 1945, Truman and Stalin agreed on several issues. The two leaders reaffirmed the concept of free elections in Eastern Europe; Soviet troop withdrawal from the oil fields of northern Iran, which bordered the USSR; and the partition of Germany (and Berlin itself) into four Allied occupation zones.

Within six months of the war's end, however, relations between the two countries soured. The United States was the only nation in the world with the atomic bomb and boasted the only economy reinvigorated by the war. As a result, the Truman administration believed that it held the upper hand against the Soviets. With this in mind, the State Department offered the Soviets a $6 billion loan, which the country needed to help rebuild its war-ravaged economy. But when the Soviets undermined free elections in Poland in 1946 and established a compliant government, the United States withdrew the offer. Soviet troops also remained in northern Iran, closing off the oil fields to potential capitalist enterprises. The failure to reach agreement over international control of atomic energy proved the last straw. The United States wanted to make sure it would keep its atomic weapons, while the Soviets wanted the United States to destroy its nuclear arsenal. Clearly, the former World War II allies did not trust each other.

Truman had significantly underestimated the strength of the Soviet position. The Soviets were well on their way toward building their own atomic bomb, negating the Americans' nuclear advantage. The Soviets could also ignore the enticement of U.S. economic aid by taking resources from East Germany and mobilizing the Russian people to rebuild their country's industry and military. Indeed, on February 9, 1946, Stalin delivered a tough speech to rally Russians to make sacrifices to enhance national security. By asserting that communism was "a better form of organization than any non-Soviet social system," he implied, according to George Kennan, that capitalist nations could not coexist with communism and that future wars were unavoidable unless communism triumphed over capitalism.

Whether or not Stalin meant this speech as an unofficial declaration of a third world war, U.S. leaders interpreted it this way. A few days after Stalin spoke, Kennan sent an 8,000-word telegram from the U.S. Embassy in Moscow to Washington, blaming the Soviets for stirring up international tensions and confirming that Stalin could not be trusted. Kennan warned that Stalin was committed to expanding communism throughout the world and advised President Harry S. Truman to adopt a policy of **containment**. In Kennan's view, all Soviet efforts at expansion should be met

---

TEACHING IDEA

Geography Instruction

Using a blank map of the world, have students color-code areas of interest and conflict in the years 1945–1953. Consider having students use different colors in various areas and countries to indicate the severity of conflict. For example, red, orange, and yellow could be used to distinguish severity. The main idea is to have students recognize and distinguish between conflicts in the early years of the Cold War.

TRM Map 8A – The World

TEACHING IDEA

Incorporating Websites

PBS produced a documentary called *Secrets, Lies, and Atomic Spies* detailing the code-breaking Venona Project. This video is housed on local PBS sites, or more information can be found on the PBS International site under Programs A-Z (pbsinternational.org). This video is a wonderful accompaniment to discussions about the use of the atomic weapon and the subsequent debates over its use.

TEACHING IDEA

Incorporating Secondary Sources

Teachers looking to read more about this topic can consult Robert Dallek's book, *The Lost Peace: Leadership in a Time of Horror and Hope, 1945–1953*. Dallek details how events, leaders, and circumstances led to a failed effort at securing long-term peace in the aftermath of World War II and is a useful resource for teachers looking to expand their understanding of the time period to share with students.

BUILDING AP® SKILLS

Claims and Evidence in Sources

Any conversation in class discussing the policy of containment should begin with an analysis of George Kennan's "Long Telegram" in 1946. Teaching American History's website provides the primary source and helpful tools such as podcast and video to assist with instructing the document (teachingamericanhistory.org). Students should be especially aware of the many arguments Kennan asserts about the nature of the conflict with the Soviets and what the American government should do in response to the Communist threat.

with firm resistance. At the same time, the United States should take an active role in rebuilding the economies of war-torn Western European countries, thereby reducing the appeal of communism to their populations. Kennan's concept of containment would become the basis for President Truman's Cold War foreign policy. The following month, on March 15, former British Prime Minister Winston Churchill gave a speech in Truman's home state of Missouri. Declaring that "an **iron curtain** has descended across the Continent" of Europe, Churchill observed that "there is nothing [the Russians] admire so much as strength, and there is nothing for which they have less respect than for . . . military weakness." This comment reaffirmed Truman's sentiments expressed the previous year: "Unless Russia is faced with an iron fist and strong language another war is in the making." The message was clear: Unyielding resistance to the Soviet Union was the only way to avoid another world war.

iron curtain Term coined by Churchill that described the ideological and political divide between the Communist Soviet Union and the non-Communist western world.

Not all Americans agreed with this view. Led by Roosevelt's former vice president Henry Wallace, who served as Truman's secretary of commerce, critics voiced concern about taking a "hard line" against the Soviet Union. Stalin was pursuing a policy of expansion, they agreed, but for limited reasons. Wallace claimed that the Soviets merely wanted to protect their borders by surrounding themselves with friendly countries, just as the United States had done by establishing spheres of influence in the Caribbean. Except for Poland and Romania, Stalin initially accepted an array of governments in Eastern Europe, allowing free elections in Czechoslovakia, Hungary, and, to a lesser extent, Bulgaria. Only as Cold War tensions escalated did the Soviets tighten control over all of Eastern Europe. Critics such as Wallace considered this outcome the result of a self-fulfilling prophecy; by misinterpreting Soviet motives, the Truman administration pushed Stalin to counter the American hard line with a hard line of his own.

AP® ANALYZING SOURCES

Source: Henry Wallace, *The Way to Peace*, 1946

" 'Getting tough' never bought anything real and lasting—whether for schoolyard bullies or businessmen or world powers. The tougher we get, the tougher the Russians will get. . . .

We must not let our Russian policy be guided or influenced by those inside or outside the United States who want war with Russia. This does not mean appeasement. . . .

The real peace treaty we now need is between the United States and Russia. On our part, we should recognize that we have no more business in the political affairs of Eastern Europe than Russia has in the political affairs of Latin America, Western Europe, and the United States. We may not like what Russia does in Eastern Europe. Her type of land reform, industrial expropriation, and suppression of basic liberties offends the great majority of the people of the United States. But whether we like it or not the Russians will try to socialize their sphere of influence just as we try to democratize our sphere of influence. . . .

Russia must be convinced that we are not planning for war against her and we must be certain that Russia is not carrying on territorial expansion or world domination through native communists faithfully following every twist and turn in the Moscow party line. But in this competition, we must insist on an open door for trade throughout the world. There will always be an ideological conflict—but that is no reason why diplomats cannot work out a basis for both systems to live safely in the world side by side."

Questions for Analysis

1. Identify the goals Wallace hopes to achieve.
2. Describe Wallace's perspective on "sphere[s] of influence."
3. Explain both the immediate and broader context for Wallace's argument in this speech.
4. Evaluate the extent to which Wallace's argument is consistent with American foreign policy in the period 1900 to 1940.

EXPLORING AP® THEMES

Work, Exchange, and Technology

A vital question for students to continually ask themselves as they move through the study of the Cold War is the extent to which the economy was affected by developments in foreign policy. The competition of the Cold War drove the United States to expand its technological reach as research and development in the sciences led to transformational new products. At this point in the module, you can simply ask students to develop answers to the following prompts:

- Identify ONE specific way in which the Cold War transformed the American economy from 1945 to 1953.

- Identify ANOTHER specific way in which the Cold War transformed the American economy from 1945 to 1953.

TEACHING IDEA

Building Vocabulary

As students explore the early events in the Cold War, they will come across phrases such as "hard line" or "iron fist" that are used to describe policy positions. Have students use the phrase "hard line" for the following activity. Their goal is to define what it meant to be a hard line advocate from both an American and Soviet perspective. Have students use at least one historical development in their response.

An example might look something such as this: *At times, President Truman used a hard line to defend U.S. interests in Europe. For example, his advocacy of the development of a hydrogen weapon was seen by many as a hard line answer to the development of an atomic weapon by the Soviet Union in 1949.* This activity invites students to distinguish between policies, which leads to a more nuanced understanding.

TRM Suggested Responses to Questions

TRM Module 8.1 AP® Analyzing Sources Handout 1

BUILDING AP® SKILLS

Sourcing and Situation

Before reading the source by Henry Wallace, have students develop the historical situation of the document through an analysis of the source. Remind students to look at the source, see if they recognize the author (they should in this case as Henry Wallace is referenced in the last paragraph on this page), and examine the title and date. A simple way to accomplish this is to have students write down 2 or 3 major historical developments around the time period of the document. As an example in this document, students might come up with answers such as the end of World War II, the formation of the UN, or the division of Germany. Regardless, students will be better equipped to read the document after they consider the historical situation.

Period 8: 1945–1980

MODULE 8-1 The Early Cold War, 1945–1953

Thus, after World War II, the United States came to believe that the Soviet Union desired world revolution to spread communism, a doctrine hostile to free market individualism. At the same time, the Soviet Union viewed the United States as seeking to make the world safe for capitalism, thereby reducing Soviet chances to obtain economic resources and rebuild its war-shattered economy. Each nation tended to see the other's actions in the most negative light possible and to see global developments as a zero-sum game, one in which every victory for one side was necessarily a defeat for the other.

REVIEW

How and why did the U.S. and USSR interpret relations with each other prior to 1947 in dramatically different ways?

The Truman Doctrine, the Marshall Plan, and Economic Containment

By 1947 U.S.-Soviet relations had reached a new low. International arms control had proved futile, the United States had gone to the United Nations to pressure the Soviets to withdraw from Iran, and the rhetoric from both sides had become warlike. From the American vantage point, Soviet actions to expand communism in Eastern Europe appeared to threaten democracies in Western Europe. By contrast, the Soviets viewed the United States as seeking to extend economic control over nations close to their borders and to weaken communism in the Soviet Union.

Events in Greece allowed Truman to take the offensive and apply Kennan's policy of containment. To maintain access to the Middle East and its Asian colonies, the United Kingdom considered it vitally important to keep Greece within its sphere of influence. In 1946 a civil war broke out in Greece between the right-wing monarchy and a coalition of insurgents consisting of members of the wartime anti-Nazi resistance, Communists, and non-Communist opponents of the repressive government. Exhausted by the war and in desperate financial shape, the British turned to the United States for help.

The Truman administration believed that the presence of Communists among the Greek rebels meant that Moscow was behind the insurgency. In fact, Stalin was not aiding the revolutionaries; the assistance came from the Communist leader of Yugoslavia, Josip Broz (known then as Marshall Tito), who acted independently of the Soviets and would soon break with them. Following Kennan's lead in advocating containment, Truman incorrectly believed that all Communists around the world were ultimately controlled by the Kremlin.

While Truman was convinced that the United States had to intervene in Greece to contain the spread of communism, he still had to convince the Republican-controlled Congress and the American people to go along. To overcome potential opposition to its plans, the Truman administration exaggerated the danger of Communist influence in Greece. Truman sent Undersecretary of State Dean Acheson to testify before a congressional committee that "like apples in a barrel infected by one rotten one, the corruption of Greece would infect Iran and all to the east." The administration's presentation of the issues to the American public was even more dramatic. On March 12, 1947, Truman gave a speech to a joint session of Congress that was broadcast over national radio to millions of listeners. He interpreted the civil war in Greece as a titanic struggle between freedom and **totalitarianism** that threatened the free world. "I believe," the president declared, "that it must be the policy of the United States to support free peoples who are resisting attempted subjugation by armed minorities or by outside pressures." Truman's rhetoric stretched the truth on many counts—the armed minorities to which the president referred had fought Nazi totalitarianism; the Soviets did not supply the insurgents; and the right-wing monarchy, propped up by the military, was hardly democratic. Nevertheless, Truman achieved his goal of frightening both lawmakers and the public, and Congress appropriated $400 million in military aid to fortify the existing governments of Greece and neighboring Turkey.

The **Truman Doctrine**, which pledged to protect democratic countries and contain the expansion of communism, was the cornerstone of American foreign policy throughout the Cold

> **AP® TIP**
> Be sure you can explain how containment affected relations between the U.S. and the USSR in the years following World War II.

Truman Doctrine U.S. pledge to contain the expansion of communism around the world. Based on the idea of containment, the Truman Doctrine was the cornerstone of American foreign policy throughout the Cold War.

BUILDING AP® SKILLS
Contextualization

This module is situated well for students to work on the reasoning process of contextualization. As students contemplate the factors that led to a Cold War between the United States and the Soviet Union, consider the following activity to work on contextualizing the time period they are studying. Have students select a major historical development such as the political or economic systems of the United States and the Soviet Union. Next, have students develop at least two facts that substantiate why either the economic or political system was an essential factor in the context of the start of the Cold War.

APPLY THE TIP

This AP® Tip is especially useful for students as they consider the contours of the foreign policy of containment. Start by providing a timeline for students to consider such as 1945–1950. Next, give students some historical examples such as Kennan's Long Telegram, Berlin Airlift, Potsdam Conference, Marshall Plan, and Truman Doctrine. Have students select at least two of the terms and explain how those examples illustrate the ways in which containment altered relations between the United States and the Soviet Union.

EXPLORING AP® THEMES
Geography and the Environment

After students analyze excerpts of the Truman Doctrine, provide for them a map of Greece and Turkey that highlights the location of the Dardanelles straits. Using the geographical location of the Dardanelles, ask students to write an explanation as to the geopolitical importance of Greece and Turkey in the Cold War.

TEACHING IDEA
Building Vocabulary

To develop an awareness of the differences in political systems following World War II, ask students to define totalitarianism in the following manner. First, ask students to write out a base definition of the term. Next, ask students to cite a specific example from the reading. The final step is for students to relate the term back to the origins of the Cold War.

Period 8: 1945–1980

AP® TIP
Evaluate the degree to which the Truman Doctrine marked a change in traditional U.S. foreign policy.

War. The United States committed itself to shoring up governments, whether democratic or dictatorial, as long as they were avowedly anti-Communist. Americans believed that the rest of the world's nations wanted to be like the United States and therefore would not willingly accept communism, which they thought could be imposed only from the outside by the Soviet Union and never reasonably chosen from within.

Although Truman misread Soviet intentions with respect to Greece, Stalin's regime had given him cause for worry. Soviet actions that imposed communism in Poland, along with the USSR's refusal to withdraw troops from the Baltic states of Latvia, Lithuania, and Estonia, reinforced the president's concerns about Soviet expansionism and convinced many in the U.S. government that Stalin had no intention of abiding by his wartime agreements. Difficulties in negotiating with the Soviets about international control of atomic energy further worried American foreign-policy makers about Russian designs for obtaining the atomic bomb.

George Kennan's version of containment called for economic and political aid to check Communist expansion. In this context, to prevent Communist inroads and offer humanitarian assistance to Europeans facing homelessness and starvation, the Truman administration offered economic assistance to the war-torn continent. In doing so, the United States also hoped to guarantee increased trade with Europe. In a June 1947 speech that drew heavily on Kennan's ideas, Secretary of State George Marshall sketched out a plan to provide financial assistance to Europe. Although he invited any country, including the Soviet Union, that experienced "hunger, poverty, desperation, and chaos" to apply for aid, Marshall did not expect Stalin to ask for assistance. To do so would require the Soviets to supply information to the United States concerning the internal operations of their economy and to admit to the failure of communism.

Marshall Plan Post World War II European economic aid package developed by Secretary of State George Marshall. The plan helped rebuild Western Europe and served American political and economic interests in the process.

Following up Marshall's speech, Truman asked Congress in December 1947 to authorize $17 billion for European recovery. With conservative-minded Republicans still in control of Congress, the president's spending request faced steep opposition. The Soviet Union inadvertently came to Truman's political rescue. Stalin interpreted the proposed **Marshall Plan** of economic assistance as a hostile attempt by the United States to gain influence in Eastern Europe. To prevent this possibility, in late February 1948 the Soviets extinguished the remaining democracy in Eastern Europe by engineering a Communist coup in Czechoslovakia. Congressional lawmakers viewed this action as further proof of Soviet aggression. In April 1948, they approved the Marshall Plan, providing $13 billion in economic assistance to sixteen European countries over the next five years.

REVIEW
How did the Truman Doctrine and the Marshall Plan each support the policy of containment?

Military Containment

The New Deal and World War II had increased the power of the president and his ability to manage economic and military crises. The Cold War further strengthened the presidency and shifted the balance of governmental power to the executive branch, creating what has been called the **imperial presidency**.

As the Cold War heated up, Congress granted the president enormous authority over foreign affairs and internal security. The National Security Act, passed in 1947, created the Department of Defense as a cabinet agency (replacing the Department of War), consolidated control of the various military services under its authority, and established the Joint Chiefs of Staff, composed of the heads of the army, navy, air force, and marines. To advise the president on military and foreign affairs, the act set up the **National Security Council**, a group presided over by the national security adviser and consisting of the secretaries of state, defense, the army, the navy, and the air force and any others the president might appoint.

AP® TIP
Analyze how changes in American federal bureaucracy affected the power of the executive branch.

In addition to this panel, the National Security Act established the **Central Intelligence Agency (CIA)** as part of the executive branch. The CIA was given the responsibility of coordinating intelligence gathering and conducting espionage abroad to counter Soviet spying operations. Another new intelligence agency, the National Security Agency, created in 1949, monitored overseas communications through the latest technological devices. Together, these agencies

---

TEACHING IDEA
Analyzing Art and Images

Use the Library of Congress exhibition, "Herblock's History – Political Cartoons from the Crash to the Millennium" (loc.gov). Have students select the cartoon from January 26, 1949, titled "It's the same thing without mechanical problems." This cartoon by Herblock can be a useful source to engage students in a cartoon analysis. You can ask questions such as: Who is pictured in the cartoon? What is the tone of the cartoon's caption? Why did the Soviet Union turn down the invitation to accept Marshall Plan money? How did Western Europeans respond to Marshall Plan money? Why are the persons in the cartoon given different qualities of clothes? Questions such as these invite students to interpret both the document and the historical situation of the document.

BUILDING AP® SKILLS
Claims and Evidence in Sources

"The Marshall Plan Speech" at Harvard University by George C. Marshall in June of 1947 is a clear example of the effort by the United States to contain communism in Europe. This speech is available by search on The George C. Marshall Foundation website (marshallfoundation.org). Students should concentrate their efforts on finding Marshall's claim about the condition of Europe and the necessary response by the United States. To further distill students' focus, have them find 3–4 excerpts that demonstrate parts of Marshall's argument.

APPLY THE TIP

The imperial presidency is a crucial topic for students to understand from Period 8. To begin the process of having students analyze this historical development, consider the following activity. As a result of the National Security Act of 1947, the executive branch of government grew in scope and power.

For instance, the National Security Agency, Central Intelligence Agency, Joint Chiefs of Staff, and the National Security Council were all formed. Have students write a 2 or 3 sentence answer to how the idea of an imperial presidency was shaped by the experiences of the early Cold War years.

Period 8: 1945–1980

MODULE 8-1 The Early Cold War, 1945–1953

▲ **The Berlin Airlift** This group of West Berliners anxiously waits as an American C-47 cargo plane prepares to land at Tempelhof Airfield to deliver food in July 1948. The Soviets had blockaded ground transportation to the Allied sector of West Berlin, prompting President Truman to airlift supplies. At the height of the Berlin airlift, planes landed every 45 seconds bringing desperately needed supplies for the two and a half million residents of West Berlin. **What does the scene in the photograph reveal about the conditions in West Berlin in 1948?**

enhanced the president's ability to conduct foreign affairs with little congressional oversight and out of public view.

By 1948 the Truman administration had decided that an economically healthy Germany, with its great industrial potential, provided the key to a prosperous Europe and consequently a depression-proof United States. Rebuilding postwar Germany would also fortify the eastern boundary of Europe against Soviet expansion. In mid-1948 the United States, the United Kingdom, and France consolidated their occupation zones, created the Federal Republic of Germany (West Germany), and initiated economic reforms to stimulate a speedy recovery. The Soviet Union saw a strong Germany as a threat to its national security and responded by closing the access roads from the border of West Germany to Berlin, located in the Soviet zone of East Germany, which effectively cut off the city from the West.

The Soviet blockade of West Berlin turned the Cold War even colder. Without food, fuel, and other provisions from the United States and its allies in West Germany, West Berliners could not survive. In an effort to break the blockade, Truman ordered a massive airlift, during which American and British planes transported more than 2.5 million tons of supplies to West Berlin. After nearly a year of these flights, the **Berlin airlift** ended in the spring of 1949 when the Russians lifted the blockade.

Meanwhile, in November 1948 Truman won election for a second term. He drew opposition from critics on his left and right for his handling of the Cold War, challenging both his aggressiveness toward the Soviets and his increased spending for containment. Nevertheless, most Americans stood behind his anti-Communist foreign policy as the Cold War continued.

The two superpowers sustained the conflict when each fashioned military alliances to keep the other at bay. In April 1949, prompted in part by the Berlin crisis, the United States joined eleven European countries in the **North Atlantic Treaty Organization (NATO)**. A peacetime military alliance, NATO established a collective security pact in which an attack on one member was viewed as an attack on all (Map 8.1). In 1949 the Russians followed suit by organizing the Council for Mutual Economic Assistance to help their satellite nations rebuild and six years later by

Berlin airlift The mass-scale transport of food and supplies to West Berlin by U.S. and British government air forces during the Soviet blockade of Berlin from 1948 to 1949.

North Atlantic Treaty Organization (NATO) Cold War military alliance intended to enhance the collective security of the United States and Western Europe.

BUILDING AP® SKILLS

Causation

In many ways, 1949 was a turning point year in early Cold War history. From 1945 to 1949, the United States and Soviet Union slowly, but consistently, expressed a distrust of one another. Have students write a thesis statement with at least three categories of analysis while weighing the significance of their interpretation to the following prompt: Evaluate the factors of the beginning of the Cold War between the United States and the Soviet Union from 1945 to 1949.

TEACHING IDEA

Building Vocabulary

Have students define the meaning of humanitarian aid. After they have successfully defined the term, have them explain the effectiveness of using humanitarian aid as a strategy to contain communism. Students should use at least two examples to substantiate their claim.

TEACHING IDEA

Check for Understanding

The actions of the United States in the aftermath of World War I and World War II are vastly different. In this activity students have four tasks. Students' first task is to define collective security. Next, have students develop an answer to how the United States responded to the efforts to have collective security after World War I through the League of Nations. Then have students select at least two ways in which the United States embraced collective security after World War II. Finally, have students explain at least one reason for the difference in views of collective security.

Military Containment

▲ **MAP 8.1 The Cold War in Europe, 1945–1955** In 1946, the four major victorious wartime allies divided Germany and Berlin into distinct sectors, leading to increasing conflict. Between 1949 and 1955, the descent of what Winston Churchill called the "iron curtain" of communism and the creation of rival security pacts headed by the United States and the Soviet Union hardened these postwar divisions into the Cold War. **What short-term effects of World War II does this map reveal?**

Warsaw Pact Russian military alliance with seven satellite nations in response to the U.S. Marshall Plan and establishment of NATO.

AP® TIP
Be sure you can explain how NSC-68 affected U.S. military and foreign policy after 1950.

NSC-68 April 1950 National Security Council document that advocated the intensification of the policy of containment both at home and abroad.

creating the **Warsaw Pact** military alliance, the respective counterparts in Eastern Europe to the Marshall Plan and NATO.

Amid the growing militarization of the Cold War, 1949 brought two new shocks to the United States and its allies. First, in September the Russians successfully tested an atomic bomb. Second, Communist forces within China led by Mao Zedong and Zhou Enlai succeeded in overthrowing the U.S.-backed nationalist government of Jiang Jieshi (Chiang Kai-shek) and creating the People's Republic of China. These two events convinced many in the United States that the threat posed by communism was escalating rapidly.

In response, the National Security Council met to reevaluate U.S. strategy in fighting the Cold War. In April 1950 the NSC recommended to Truman that the United States intensify its containment policy both abroad and at home. The document it handed over to the president, entitled **NSC-68**, spelled out the need for action in ominous language. "The Soviet Union, unlike previous aspirants to hegemony," NSC-68 warned, "is animated by a new fanatic faith, antithetical to our own, and seeks to impose its absolute authority over the rest of the world. It is in this context that this Republic and its citizens . . . stand in their deepest peril." NSC-68 proposed that the United States develop an even more powerful nuclear weapon, the hydrogen bomb; increase military spending; and continue to negotiate NATO-style alliances around the globe. Departing from the original guidelines for the CIA, the president's advisers proposed that the United States engage in "covert means" to stir up support for "unrest and revolt in selected strategic [Soviet] satellite countries." At home, they added, the government should prepare Americans for the Communist danger by enhancing internal security and civil defense programs.

TEACHING IDEA

Connecting the Dots

1949 is a turning point in Cold War history. Have students identify and explain which events from 1949 are turning points. Remember, a turning point in history is something so significant that you can measure historical significance before and after the development in question.

BUILDING AP® SKILLS

Argumentation

This activity connects well with the previous note. After students have identified and explained the reasons why 1949 is a turning point, have them write a thesis to the following question: Evaluate the extent of change in United States foreign policy as a result of the following events from 1949: formation of NATO, detonation of the Soviets' first atomic weapon, and Chinese Communists winning the battle for political power in China.

TEACHING IDEA

Connecting the Dots

Organize the class into groups of 3 or 4 students. Have students extract all quotes from the paragraph from this page covering the details of NSC-68 on a piece of butcher-block paper. Next, have students select what they consider to be the top two ideas from the excerpts. Finally, have students write a 1 or 2 sentence response answering why NSC-68 was a fundamental shift in United States foreign policy in the Cold War. After groups are done writing their responses, have them write their answers on the same butcher-block paper. You can wrap up this exercise by having students do a gallery walk, where they roam the room to see the answers other groups developed.

▲ Differentiation

For students who are already showing mastery of the ways in which the Cold War changed American foreign policy, consider the following activity. Have students define the differences between a political and military alliance. Next, ask students to link examples from after World War I and after World War II. Students should notice that the United States was reticent to agree to any military alliances after World War I, but were very prepared to do so following World War II. The end assignment is for students to create a mini argument explaining the reasons for this change. Students get three presentation slides, with one picture per slide. After they have created their slide show, students get three minutes to deliver their arguments.

Period 8: 1945–1980

MODULE 8-1 The Early Cold War, 1945–1953

Truman agreed with many of the principles behind NSC-68 but worried about the cost of funding it. The problem remained a political one. Though the Democrats once again controlled both houses of Congress, there was little sentiment to raise taxes and slash the economic programs established during the New Deal. However, circumstances abruptly changed when, in June 1950, shortly after the president received the NSC report, Communist North Korea invaded U.S.-backed South Korea. In response to this attack, Truman took the opportunity to put into practice key recommendations of NSC-68.

REVIEW

- How did passage of the National Security Act in 1947 and NSC-68 change American foreign policy?

The Korean War

AP® TIP
Evaluate the degree to which America's entry into the Korean War marked a dramatic change in U.S. foreign policy.

Korea emerged from World War II divided between U.S. and Soviet spheres of influence. Above the 38th parallel, the Communist leader Kim Il Sung ruled North Korea with support from the Soviet Union. Below that latitude, the anti-Communist leader Syngman Rhee governed South Korea. The United States supported Rhee, but in January 1950 Secretary of State Dean Acheson commented that he did not regard South Korea as part of the vital Asian "defense perimeter" protected by the United States against Communist aggression. Truman had already removed remaining American troops from the country the previous year. On June 25, 1950, an emboldened Kim Il Sung sent military forces to invade South Korea, seeking to unite the country under his leadership.

Following the invasion Korea took on new importance to American policymakers. If South Korea fell, the president believed, Communist leaders would be "emboldened to override nations closer to our own shores." Thus the Truman Doctrine was now applied to Asia as it had previously been applied to Europe. This time, however, American financial aid would not be enough. It would take the U.S. military to contain the Communist threat.

Truman did not seek a declaration of war from Congress. Instead, he chose a multinational course of action. With the Soviet Union boycotting the United Nations over its refusal to admit the Communist People's Republic of China, on June 27, 1950, the United States obtained authorization from the UN Security Council to send a peacekeeping force to Korea. Fifteen other countries joined UN forces, but the United States supplied the bulk of the troops, as well as their commanding officer, General Douglas MacArthur. In reality, MacArthur reported to the president, not the United Nations.

Before MacArthur could mobilize his forces, the North Koreans had penetrated most of South Korea, except for the port of Pusan on the southwest coast of the peninsula. In a daring counterattack, on September 15, 1950, MacArthur dispatched land and sea forces to capture Inchon, northwest of Pusan on the

MAP 8.2 The Korean War, 1950–1953 Considered a "police action" by the United Nations, the Korean War cost the lives of nearly 37,000 U.S. troops. Approximately 1 million Koreans were killed, wounded, or missing. Each side pushed deep into enemy territory, but neither could achieve victory. When hostilities ceased in 1953, a demilitarized zone near the original boundary line separated North and South Korea. **What do the dotted lines and the final armistice line on this map reveal about the successes and failures of each side in the Korean War?**

APPLY THE TIP

The Korean War is an essential topic for students to understand how the policy of containment and collective security work on a global stage. It is also useful to draw contrasts from previous war policies such as World War II. Consider having students define both unconditional surrender and containment. Next, have students explain the degree to which these policies were effective in World War II and Korea. To close the activity ask students to write a 1 or 2 sentence explanation detailing how the policies during the Korean War marked a significant change in U.S. foreign policy.

TEACHING IDEA

Incorporating Videos

Too often the details of the Korean War get lost among the many other transformational events in the mid-twentieth century. Humanizing history can make the event more understandable and can also help students see the big picture to the import of the Korean War. Consider watching parts of the PBS American Experience Season 29 Episode 4, "The Battle of Chosin" (pbs.org). This documentary not only details the men who fought in the Chosin Reservoir but also uses that event to detail the larger picture of the Korean War.

TEACHING IDEA

Incorporating Secondary Sources

Consider assigning students historian Allan R. Millett's essay, "The Korean War," which is available on the Gilder Lehrman site for AP® U.S. History teachers (ap.gilderlehrman.org). This piece gives a broad view of the war that will serve as a foundation for more in-depth understanding.

The Korean War

> **AP® TIP**
> Compare the United Nations' role in the Korean War to that of the League of Nations in European affairs in the years leading up to World War II.

opposite coast, to cut off North Korean supply lines. Joined by UN forces pushing out of Pusan, MacArthur's Eighth Army troops chased the enemy northward back over the 38th parallel.

Now Truman had to make a key decision. MacArthur wanted to invade North Korea, defeat the Communists, and unify the country. Instead of sticking to his original goal of containing Communist aggression against South Korea, Truman succumbed to the lure of liberating all of Korea from the Communists. MacArthur received permission to proceed, and on October 9 his forces crossed into North Korea. Within three weeks, UN troops marched through the country until they reached the Yalu River, which bordered China. With the U.S. military massed along their southern perimeter, the Chinese warned that they would send troops to repel the invaders if the Americans crossed the Yalu. Both General MacArthur and Secretary of State Acheson, guided by CIA intelligence, discounted this threat. The intelligence, however, was faulty. Truman approved MacArthur's plan to cross the Yalu, and on November 27, 1950, China sent more than 300,000 troops south into North Korea. Within two months, Communist troops regained control of North Korea, allowing them once again to invade South Korea. On January 4, 1951, the South Korean capital of Seoul fell to Chinese and North Korean troops.

By the spring of 1951, the war had degenerated into a stalemate. UN forces succeeded in recapturing Seoul and repelling the Communists north of the 38th parallel. This time, with the American public anxious to end the war and with the presence of the Chinese promising an endless, bloody predicament, the president sought to replace combat with diplomacy. The American objective would be containment, not Korean unification.

Truman's change of heart infuriated General MacArthur, who was willing to risk an all-out war with China and to use nuclear weapons to win. After MacArthur spoke out publicly against Truman's policy by remarking, "There is no substitute for victory," the president removed him from command on April 11, 1951. However, even with the change in strategy and leadership, the war dragged on for two more years, until July 1953, when a final armistice agreement was reached. By that time, the Korean War had cost the United States close to 37,000 lives and $54 billion.

The **Korean War** boosted the imperial presidency by allowing the president to bypass Congress and the Constitution to initiate wars in the name of "police actions." The war permitted Truman to expand his powers as commander in chief and augmented the strength of the national

Korean War Conflict fought between the northern Communist, Democratic People's Republic of Korea and the United Nations-backed southern Republic of Korea from 1950 to 1953.

AP® ANALYZING SOURCES

Source: John N. Wheeler, *Letter Home from Korean War*, 1950

"Can't say as I blame you, Dad, for your opinions of Mr. Truman and his administration. However, you must remember that his opinions as well as his actions represent the vast majority of the 'Soft-bellied Americans' who, for the life of them, couldn't see giving up a few of the needless luxuries of life to support a military machine big enough to protect the peace and liberty that they take for granted. Only those who have visited foreign countries can realize what they mean. It would be a good lesson to the Americans if they had to fight a war on their own soil, and had to lie for a short time under the sadistic rule of this band of perverted sadists who call themselves communists. They claim that they want to help the 'worker'—all they want to do is to help themselves. Mass murder, rape, torture, and starvation is the rule and not the exception with them. They have proved it here as well as everywhere else. I could see nothing more fitting for a young man to do then [sic] to devote his entire life to killing everyone of them."

Questions for Analysis
1. Describe Wheeler's point of view toward those critical of American involvement in the Korean War.
2. Explain the historical developments that provide context for Wheeler's assertion that Truman and his administration were part of the "vast majority of 'Soft-bellied Americans.'"
3. Evaluate the extent to which Wheeler's perspective is influenced by his experience in combat during the Korean War.

TEACHING IDEA

Incorporating Primary Sources

Prior to reading the letter by John N. Wheeler, ask students to demonstrate an understanding of the early commitment to containment expressed by many Americans. Students can use any events between 1945 and 1950 to explain why this commitment existed, but they must show a link between three events.

TRM Find **Handout 8.1 – Understanding American Commitment to Containment** in the Teacher's Resource Materials.

TRM Suggested Responses to Questions

TRM Module 8.1 AP® Analyzing Sources Handout 2

BUILDING AP® SKILLS

Continuity and Change

The following activity is meant to gauge where students are in their understanding of the fact that as much as the Cold War caused changes in United States foreign policy, it also fostered significant continuities. Therefore, provide students with the events of World War II and the Korean War and ask them to develop three examples of events that illustrate changes in U.S. foreign policy and three events that illustrate continuities in U.S. foreign policy.

Period 8: 1945–1980

MODULE 8-1 The Early Cold War, 1945–1953

security state over which he presided. As a result of the Korean conflict, the military draft became a regular feature of American life for young men over the next two decades. The expanded peacetime military was active around the globe, operating bases in Europe, Asia, and the Middle East. During the war, the military budget rose from $13.5 billion to $50 billion, strengthening the connection between economic growth and permanent mobilization to fight the Cold War. The war also permitted President Truman to reshape foreign policy along the lines sketched in NSC-68, including the extension of U.S. influence in Southeast Asia. Consequently, he authorized economic aid to support the French against Communist revolutionaries in Vietnam.

Yet the power of the imperial presidency did not go unchecked. Congress deferred to Truman on key issues of military policy, but on one important occasion the Supreme Court stepped in to restrain him. The central issue grew out of a labor dispute in the steel industry. In 1952 the United Steel Workers of America threatened to go on strike for higher wages, which would have had a serious impact on war production as well as the economy in general. On May 2, after the steel companies refused the union's demands, Truman announced the government seizure and operation of the steel mills to keep them running. He argued that as president he had the "inherent right" to take over the steel plants.

The steel companies objected and brought the matter before the Supreme Court. On June 2, 1952, the Court ruled against Truman. It held that the president did not have the intrinsic authority to seize private property, even during wartime. For the time being, the Supreme Court affirmed some limitations on the unbridled use of presidential power even during periods of war.

> **AP® TIP**
> Be sure you can explain the relationship between the policy of containment, NSC-68, and the Korean War.

> **AP® TIP**
> Analyze the role of the legislative and judicial branches in limiting the growth of the imperial presidency.

REVIEW

- How did the Korean War fit within the broader context of America's Cold War strategy?
- How did the Korean War expand the powers of the presidency?

AP® WRITING HISTORICALLY — Short-Answer Question Practice

ACTIVITY

Read the following question carefully and write a short response. Use complete sentences.

Using the following excerpts, answer (a), (b), and (c).

Source: William Appleman Williams, *The Tragedy of American Diplomacy*, 1959

"The leaders who succeeded [Franklin] Roosevelt understood neither the dilemma nor the need to alter their outlook. A handful of them thought briefly of stabilizing relations with the Soviet Union on the basis of economic and political agreements, but even that tiny minority saw the future in terms of continued open-door expansion[1]. The great majority rapidly embarked upon a program to force the Soviet Union to accept America's traditional conception of itself and the world. This decision represented the final stage in the transformation of the policy of the open door from a utopian idea into an ideology, from an intellectual outlook for changing the world into one concerned with preserving it in the traditional mold.

American leaders had internalized, and had come to *believe*, the theory and the morality of open-door expansion. Hence they seldom thought it necessary to explain or defend the approach. Instead, they *assumed* the premises and concerned themselves with exercising their apparent freedom to deal with the necessities defined by such an outlook. As far as American leaders were concerned, the philosophy and practice of open-door expansion had become, in both its missionary and economic aspects, *the* view of the world. Those who did not recognize and accept that fact were not only wrong, but they were incapable of thinking correctly."

[1] Access to overseas markets.

EXPLORING AP® THEMES

Politics and Power

As much as the Cold War was an ideological battle between the United States and the Soviet Union over governmental systems, it also caused fissures in the American political environment. Consider asking students to develop explanations for at least three events that caused intense political disagreements between Republicans and Democrats during President Truman's time in office.

BUILDING AP® SKILLS

Argumentation

Consider the following activity as a way to bring this module to a close and as a way to check students' understanding of the developments at the beginning of the Cold War. Provide for students the following thesis: Although the Cold War's causes can be traced to the ideological differences in governmental systems of communism and democracy, by far the most significant reason for the start of the Cold War was the battle over how to rebuild Europe in the first decade after the Second World War. In this thesis there are two categories established: ideological differences and rebuilding of Europe. Ask students to select one of these categories and write a body paragraph building an argument to substantiate that part of the thesis.

TRM Suggested Responses to Questions

TEACHING IDEA

Incorporating Secondary Sources

Sometimes it can be difficult to unpack the argument of a historian. This could be due to specific phrases or words used in the excerpt. Therefore, have students highlight the last sentence of the first paragraph and first sentence of the second paragraph. Ask students to identity words or phrases they do not know. Examples could be utopian idea, ideology, open door expansion, etc. Next, spend time with students defining both the words and meaning of the phrases used by Williams. After you do this, students will be better equipped to read the excerpt. The same can be done for the Gaddis excerpt on the following page.

Source: John Lewis Gaddis, *The United States and the Origins of the Cold War*, 1972

"Moscow's position would not have seemed so alarming to American officials . . . had it not been for the Soviet Union's continued commitment to an ideology dedicated to the overthrow of capitalism throughout the world. Hopes that the United States might cooperate successfully with the USSR after the war had been based on the belief, encouraged by Stalin himself, that the Kremlin had given up its former goal of exporting Communism. . . . It seems likely that Washington policy makers mistook Stalin's determination to ensure Russian security through spheres of influence for a renewed effort to spread communism outside the borders of the Soviet Union . . . But [Stalin] failed to make the limited nature of his objectives clear.

Revisionists are correct in emphasizing the importance of internal constraints, but they have defined them too narrowly: by focusing so heavily on economics, they neglect the profound impact of the domestic political system on the conduct of American foreign policy. . . . The delay in opening the second front, nonrecognition of Moscow's sphere of influence in Eastern Europe, and the decision to retain control of the atomic bomb can all be explained far more plausibly by citing the Administration's need to maintain popular support for its policies rather than by dwelling upon requirement of the economic order . . . , Stalin's paranoia, together with the bureaucracy of institutionalized suspicion with which he surrounded himself, made the situation much worse."

a. Briefly explain ONE major difference between Williams's and Gaddis's interpretations of the origins of the Cold War.
b. Briefly explain how ONE specific historical event or development from the period that is not explicitly mentioned in the excerpts could be used to support Williams's argument.
c. Briefly explain how ONE specific historical event or development that is not explicitly mentioned in the excerpts could be used to support Gaddis's argument.

TEACHING IDEA

AP® Writing Historically Review

The Short-Answer Questions that provide two secondary sources in opposition typically cover major events in U.S. history such as the origins of the Cold War. Most of the time, parts (b) and (c) ask students to defend one of the historical arguments with evidence not mentioned in the excerpt. When students are in a timed writing setting, they will often read too quickly. To help students develop a process of slowing down in these situations, have students highlight all of the historical evidence they can find in the two excerpts. In this way, students are identifying the historical evidence they are not allowed to use. Next, have students form groups of 3 or 4 students and have them compare answers. After they compare answers, have students brainstorm what historical evidence they could use to answer parts (b) and (c).

TRM Suggested Responses to Questions

Module 8-2

The Second Red Scare

LEARNING TARGETS

By the end of this module, you should be able to:
- Explain why the Second Red Scare emerged in the late 1940s.
- Explain the measures taken by the government and private organizations in response to the Second Red Scare.
- Explain how Senator McCarthy amplified the Second Red Scare and used it for political purposes.
- Explain how individual Americans responded to the climate of fear during the Second Red Scare.

THEMATIC FOCUS
American and National Identity

As the Cold War solidified and Europe was divided by an iron curtain, Americans faced the threat of devastating war with a nuclear-armed Soviet Union seemingly bent on worldwide Communist domination. Efforts to uncover potential domestic Communist activity took on new urgency as a Communist revolution in China, the Korean War, and the capture of spies stealing atomic secrets led to a growing climate of fear known as the Second Red Scare. Investigations by the House Un-American Activities Committee, Federal Employee Loyalty review boards, and Senator Joseph McCarthy failed to uncover significant Communist spying but did result in renewed debates over the balance between civil liberties and public safety.

HISTORICAL REASONING FOCUS
Causation

TASK ▶ As you read this module, consider how events in Europe and Asia as well as revelations of spying in the United States led to creation of a climate of fear resulting in the Second Red Scare. Ask yourself how the actions of Congress and the Truman administration contributed to those fears, and examine the impact of those actions on American society.

The Korean War heightened fear of the threat of Communist infiltration in American society. In one striking example, the presiding judge in an espionage trial for two American citizens, Julius and Ethel Rosenberg, sentenced them to death in 1951 because he believed their actions "caused . . . the Communist aggression in Korea, with the resultant casualties exceeding 50,000." For most of Truman's second administration, fear of Communist subversion within the United States consumed domestic politics. Increasing evidence of Soviet espionage fueled this anti-Communist obsession. Yet in an atmosphere of fear, lawmakers and judges blurred the distinction between actual Soviet spies and political radicals who were merely attracted to Communist beliefs. In the process, these officials sometimes trampled on individual constitutional freedoms.

Loyalty and the Second Red Scare

The postwar fear of communism echoed earlier anti-Communist sentiments. The government had initiated the Palmer raids during the First Red Scare following World War I, which led to the deportation of hundreds of immigrants suspected of holding Communist, socialist, or anarchist views (see Module 7-5). In 1938 conservative congressional opponents of

TEACHING IDEA

Check for Understanding

There is no singular cause of the Red Scare; instead, many events, both domestic and foreign, contributed to the hysteria of the fear of communism. You can give the following activity to students at the beginning of the module and they can develop answers as they read. Use a chart to help students explain how European foreign affairs, Asian foreign affairs, espionage, and government politics all contributed to the Second Red Scare.

EXPLORING AP® THEMES

American and National Identity

The thematic focus of this module is American and national identity, which should provide a good challenge for students to consider ways in which the Second Red Scare challenged and supported Americans' sense of collective identity. To help facilitate an intellectually balanced conversation in class, consider asking students to develop at least two reasons why Americans supported the efforts of the anti-Communists during the Second Red Scare. Put another way, what was attractive about groups such as HUAC? Next, ask students to provide at least two reasons why Americans opposed the efforts of anti-Communist groups during the Second Red Scare.

Period 8: 1945–1980

Loyalty and the Second Red Scare

House Un-American Activities Committee (HUAC) U.S. House of Representatives committee established in 1938 to investigate domestic communism. After World War II, HUAC conducted highly publicized investigations of Communist influence in government and the entertainment industry.

Second Red Scare Fear of Communist influence infiltrating the United States and threatening national security in the 1940s and 1950s. Such fears resulted in the creation of government-controlled programs and entities such as the House Un-American Activities Committee and the Federal Employee Loyalty Program.

Federal Employee Loyalty Program Program established by President Truman in 1947 to investigate federal employees suspected of disloyalty and Communist ties.

the New Deal established the **House Un-American Activities Committee (HUAC)** to investigate domestic communism, which they tied to the Roosevelt administration. Much of anticommunism, however, was bipartisan. In 1940 Roosevelt signed into law the **Smith Act**, which prohibited teaching or advocating the "duty, necessity, desirability, or propriety of overthrowing or destroying any government in the United States by force or violence" or belonging to any group with that aim. At the same time, President Roosevelt secretly authorized the FBI to monitor and wiretap individuals suspected of violating the act.

The Cold War produced the **Second Red Scare**. Unlike the First Red Scare following World War I, which was based on a general fear of foreign radicalism, including communism, the Second Red Scare was directly caused by a fear that Communist influence was infiltrating the United States and threatening its national security. Just two weeks after his speech announcing the Truman Doctrine in March 1947, the president signed an executive order creating the **Federal Employee Loyalty Program**. Under this program, a board investigated the approximately two and a half million federal employees to see if "reasonable grounds [existed] to suspect disloyalty." Soviet espionage was, in fact, a cause for legitimate concern. Spies operated in both Canada and the United States during and after World War II, and they had infiltrated the Manhattan Project.

The loyalty board, however, did not focus on espionage. Rather, it concentrated its attention on individuals who espoused dissenting views on a variety of issues. It failed to uncover a single verifiable case of espionage or find any actual Communists in public service. Yet the board dismissed hundreds of government employees for their political beliefs and personal behavior. Some employees were fired because they were homosexuals and considered susceptible to blackmail by foreign agents. (Heterosexual men and women who were having extramarital affairs were not treated in the same manner.) The accused rarely faced their accusers and at times did not learn the nature of the charges against them. As loyalty boards spread to state and municipal governments, labor unions, and the private sector Americans from all walks of life were questioned, required to sign loyalty oaths, and sometimes fired for suspected disloyalty.

BUILDING AP® SKILLS

Claims and Evidence in Sources

The Library of Congress has an excellent selection of political cartoons by Herbert Block (Herblock), and one that students might want to use is about the activities of HUAC. The cartoon, published in October of 1947, can be found by searching for "It's okay – we're hunting communists" (loc.gov). Divide the class into groups of 3 or 4 students, then have each group analyze the document and write a one-sentence explanation of the claim of the author about HUAC's activities.

TRM Suggested Responses to Questions

TRM Module 8.2 AP® Analyzing Sources Handout 1

TEACHING IDEA

Check for Understanding

Developing ways in which students can make connections across time is an essential ingredient for any successful AP® U.S. History program. Consider asking students to complete a Venn diagram that compares and contrasts the First Red Scare from the Second Red Scare.

TRM Find **Handout 8.2 – Comparing the First and Second Red Scare** in the Teacher's Resource Materials.

AP® ANALYZING SOURCES

Source: Motion Picture Association of America, *Press Release*, December 3, 1947

"Members of the Association of Motion Picture Producers deplore the action of the 10 Hollywood men who have been cited for contempt by the House of Representatives. We do not desire to prejudge their legal rights, but their actions have been a disservice to their employers and have impaired their usefulness to the industry.

We will forthwith discharge or suspend without compensation those in our employ, and we will not reemploy any of the 10 until such time as he is acquitted or has purged himself of contempt and declares under oath that he is not a Communist.

On the broader issue of alleged subversive and disloyal elements in Hollywood, our members are likewise prepared to take positive action.

We will not knowingly employ a Communist or a member of any party or group which advocates the overthrow of the government of the United States by force or by any illegal or unconstitutional methods. . . .

Nothing subversive or un-American has appeared on the screen, nor can any number of Hollywood investigations obscure the patriotic services of the 30,000 loyal Americans employed in invaluable aid to war and peace."

Questions for Analysis

1. Identify the intended audience and purpose for the press release.
2. Describe the rationale given in the press release for blacklisting the Hollywood 10.
3. Explain how the Motion Picture Association of America could take "positive action" during the Second Red Scare.

TEACHING IDEA

Building Vocabulary

This document contains words and sentences that some students might find confusing such as deplore, forthwith, acquitted, and purged. Before students read the document, consider taking the time to define each of these words to ensure an accurate read.

BUILDING AP® SKILLS

Comparison

During the time before and after World War II both Republicans and Democrats opposed communism at home and abroad. In this activity students will be creating an answer that compares by illustrating similarities. Consider asking students to develop at least two specific examples of Republicans and Democrats opposing communism.

Period 8: 1945–1980

MODULE 8-2 The Second Red Scare

Congress also investigated communism in the private sector, especially in industries that shaped public opinion. In 1947 HUAC broadened the anti-Red probe from Washington to Hollywood. Convinced that the film industry had come under Communist influence and threatened to poison the minds of millions of moviegoers, HUAC conducted hearings that attracted much publicity. HUAC cited for contempt ten witnesses, among them directors and screenwriters, for refusing to answer questions about their political beliefs and associations. These and subsequent hearings assumed the form of a ritual. The committee already had information from the FBI about the witnesses; HUAC really wanted the accused to confess their Communist sympathy publicly and to show remorse by naming their associates. Those who did not comply were considered "unfriendly" witnesses and were put on an industry blacklist that deprived them of employment.

HUAC grabbed even bigger headlines in 1948. With Republicans in charge of the committee, they launched a probe of Alger Hiss, a former State Department official in the Roosevelt

TEACHING IDEA

Incorporating Secondary Sources

The Gilder Lehrman site for AP® U.S. History teachers has a number of compelling historical essays that are fairly short reads for students (ap.gilderlehrman.org). Consider using an essay by historian Wendy Wall, "Anti-Communism in the 1950s" to support their understanding of the time. This essay can be found on the Period 8 page.

TRM Suggested Responses to Questions

TRM Module 8.2 AP® Analyzing Sources Handout 2

TEACHING IDEA

Digging Deeper: Paul Robeson

The *Smithsonian Magazine* has an excellent essay by Gilbert King called "What Paul Robeson Said," which provides students with some background and contextual information on Paul Robeson's life (smithsonianmag.com). While it is not always possible to provide background essays for historical figures that students study, there are some people, such as Robeson, that students will likely find compelling.

AP® ANALYZING SOURCES

Source: Paul Robeson, *Statement on the Un-American Activities Committee*, 1949

"Quite clearly America faces a crisis in race relations. The Un-American Activities Committee moves now to transform the Government's cold war policy against the Negro people into a hot war. Its action incites the Ku Klux Klan, that openly terrorist organization, to reign of mob violence against my people in Florida and elsewhere. This Committee attempts to divide the Negro people from one another in order to prevent us from winning jobs, security and justice under the banner of peace.

The loyalty of the Negro people is not a subject for debate. I challenge the loyalty of the Un-American Activities Committee. This committee maintains an ominous silence in the face of the lynchings . . . and the violence and unpunished murders of scores of Negro veterans by white supremacists since V-J Day. . . . Every pro-war fascist-minded group in the country regards the Committee's silence as license to proceed against my people, unchecked by Government authorities and unchallenged by the courts.

Our fight for peace in America is a fight for human dignity, and an end to ghetto life. It is the fight for constitutional liberties, the civil and human rights of every American. This struggle is the decisive struggle with which my people are today concerned. This fight is of vital concern to all progressive Americans, white as well as Negro. . . .

It is not the Soviet Union that threatens the life, liberty and the property and citizenship rights of Negro Americans. The threat comes from within. To destroy this threat our people need the aid of every honest American, Communist and non-Communist alike. Those who menace our lives proceed unchallenged by the Un-American Activities Committee."

Questions for Analysis
1. Identify the real threats to African Americans, according to Robeson.
2. Describe Robeson's point of view toward the House Un-American Activities Committee.
3. Explain why Robeson does not view communism as a threat to African Americans.

Questions for Comparison Motion Picture Association of America, *Press Release*, December 3, 1947 (p. 711)
1. Explain how each excerpt reflects the context of the Second Red Scare.
2. Evaluate the extent of similarity in the patriotic appeals made in each excerpt.
3. Evaluate the extent to which each excerpt represents a continuity with historical developments and prevailing social norms during the First Red Scare (1919–1920).

BUILDING AP® SKILLS

Sourcing and Situation

By this point in the year students should be familiar with the concept of sourcing a document before reading it. You can provide a quick formative assessment of this by asking students to individually recall 2–3 events prior to 1949 that would amplify the importance of a testimony of a famous African American actor before HUAC.

administration who had accompanied the president to the Yalta Conference. The hearings resulted from charges brought by former Soviet spy Whittaker Chambers that Hiss had passed him classified documents. Hiss denied the allegations, and President Truman dismissed them as a distraction. In fact, Democrats viewed the charges as a politically motivated attempt by Republicans to characterize the Roosevelt and Truman administrations as having been riddled with Communists.

Following Truman's victory in the 1948 presidential election, first-term Republican congressman Richard M. Nixon kept the Hiss affair alive. A member of HUAC, Nixon went to Chambers's farm and discovered a cache of State Department documents that Chambers had stored for safekeeping. Armed with this evidence, Nixon reopened the case. While the statute of limitations for espionage from the 1930s had expired, the federal government had enough evidence to prosecute Hiss for perjury—lying under oath about passing documents to Chambers. One trial produced a hung jury, but a second convicted Hiss; he was sentenced to five years in prison.

Hiss's downfall tarnished the Democrats, as Republicans charged them with being "soft on communism." It did not matter that Truman was a cold warrior who had advanced the doctrine of containment to stop Soviet expansionism or that he had instituted the federal loyalty program to remove any Communists from government. In fact, in 1949 Truman tried to demonstrate his cold warrior credentials by authorizing the Justice Department to prosecute twelve high-ranking officials of the Communist Party for violating the Smith Act. In the 1951 decision in *Dennis v. United States*, the Supreme Court upheld the conviction of the Communist leaders on the grounds that they posed a "clear and present danger" to the United States by advocating the violent overthrow of the government. Despite lacking evidence of an immediate danger of a Communist uprising, the justices decided that "the gravity of the [Communist] evil" was enough to warrant conviction.

When the Russians successfully tested an atomic bomb in 1949, many believed that they must have received assistance from Communist spies, and anyone accused of helping them obtain this weapon fell under suspicion. The following year, the Truman administration prosecuted Julius and Ethel Rosenberg in a sensational court case for passing atomic secrets to the Soviets. Unlike the *Dennis* case, which involved political beliefs, the Rosenbergs were charged with espionage. The outbreak of the Korean War, within weeks of their arrests, heightened fears of communism throughout the country. After a lengthy trial in 1951, the Rosenbergs were convicted and received the death penalty. Julius and Ethel Rosenberg became the first spies executed in American history during peacetime.

By 1950 the anti-Communist crusade included Democrats and Republicans, liberals and conservatives. Liberals had the most to lose because conservatives could easily brand them as ideologically tainted. In his successful campaign to become a U.S. senator from California in 1950, Richard Nixon had accused his opponent, the liberal Democrat Helen Douglas, of being "pink down to her underwear," not quite a Red but close enough. Liberal civil rights and civil liberties groups as well as labor unions were particularly vulnerable to such charges and rushed to rid their organizations of suspected Communists. Such efforts did nothing, however, to slow down conservative attacks. In 1950 Republicans supported legislation proposed by Senator Pat McCarran, a conservative Democrat from Nevada, which required Communist organizations to register with the federal government, established detention camps to incarcerate radicals during national emergencies, and denied passports to American citizens suspected of Communist affiliations. The severity of the **McCarran Internal Security Act** proved too much for President Truman, and he vetoed it. Reflecting the bipartisan consensus on the issue, the Democratic-controlled Congress overrode the veto.

> **AP® TIP**
> Compare the decision made in *Dennis v. United States* to the outcome of *Schenck v. United States* in 1919 (Module 7-5).

> **AP® TIP**
> Analyze the ways in which the second Red Scare affected the development and division of political parties in the United States.

REVIEW

• How did President Truman and Congress respond to the fears of Communist influence in American society?

EXPLORING AP® THEMES

Politics and Power

To help students examine the political aspects of the Cold War and to help further their ability to make historical interpretations, consider the following assignment: Provide students with two explanations as to why Republicans used anti-communism with great effectiveness in the 1950s. One could be the results of the 1932–1948 presidential elections and the other could be the real threats Americans faced by the Communists such as espionage. Next, have students select one reason and explain why Republicans responded to the politics of the Cold War in the manner in which they did.

APPLY THE TIP

The Second Red Scare intensified partisan politics throughout the Cold War. To help students understand how and why fighting communism became a partisan issue, consider having students develop a 3–4 sentence explanation about the causes of this development. In their response students should use at least two specific examples. Examples might include: *HUAC, Korean War, presidential elections,* and *McCarthyism.*

▲ Differentiation

Consider putting students into groups of 4, having each student write about one of the causes of this partisan issue. Then, give groups time to discuss which two of these causes they feel had the most contribution to this development.

Period 8: 1945–1980

MODULE 8-2 The Second Red Scare

McCarthyism

Joseph McCarthy, the junior Republican senator from Wisconsin, did not create the phenomenon of postwar anticommunism, which was already in full swing from 1947 to 1950, but he served as its most public and feared voice from 1950 until 1954. Although McCarthy bullied people, exaggerated his military service, drank too much, and did not pull his punches in making speeches, his anti-Communist tirades fit into mainstream Cold War politics for a time. Aware of the power of the Communists-in-government issue, and with the support of many fellow Republicans such as Ohio Senator Robert A. Taft, McCarthy gave a speech in February 1950 in Wheeling, West Virginia. Waving sheets of paper in his hand, the senator announced that he had "the names of 205 men known to the Secretary of State as being members of the Communist Party and who nevertheless are still working and shaping the policy of the State Department." As he campaigned for Republican congressional candidates across the country, he kept changing the number of alleged Communists in the government. When Senator Millard Tydings of Maryland, a Democrat who headed the Senate Foreign Relations Committee, launched an investigation of McCarthy's charges, he concluded that the allegations were irresponsible and unfounded.

This finding did not stop McCarthy; if anything, it emboldened him to go further. He accused Tydings of being "soft on communism" and campaigned against his reelection in 1952. Tydings's defeat in the election scared off many critics from openly confronting McCarthy. McCarthy won reelection to the Senate the same year and became chair of the Permanent Investigations Subcommittee on Government Operations. Senator McCarthy used his position to harass current and former government officials and employees who, he claimed, collaborated with the Communist conspiracy. Not only did he make false accusations and smear witnesses with anti-Communist allegations, but he also dispatched two aides to travel to Europe and purge what they considered disreputable books from the shelves of overseas libraries sponsored by the State Department.

McCarthy stood out among anti-Communists not for his beliefs but for his tactics. **McCarthyism** became synonymous with anticommunism as well as with manipulating the truth. McCarthy publicly hurled charges so astounding, especially coming from a U.S. senator, that people thought there must be something to them. By the time the accusations could be discredited, the damage was already done. The senator bullied and badgered witnesses, called them names, and if necessary furnished phony documents and doctored photographs linking them to known Communists.

In 1954 McCarthy finally went too far. After one of his aides was drafted and the army refused to give him a special commission, McCarthy accused the army of harboring Communists. To sort out these charges and to see whether the army had acted appropriately, McCarthy's own Senate subcommittee conducted an investigation, with the Wisconsin senator stepping down as chair. For two months, the relatively new medium of television broadcast live the army-McCarthy hearings, during which the cameras showed many viewers for the first time how reckless McCarthy had become. As his public approval declined, the Senate decided that it could no longer tolerate McCarthy's outrageous behavior. The famous television journalist Edward R. Murrow ran an unflattering documentary on McCarthy on his evening program on CBS, which further cast doubt on the senator's character and honesty. In December 1954 the Senate voted to censure McCarthy for conduct unbecoming a senator, having violated senatorial etiquette by insulting colleagues who criticized him. McCarthy retained his seat on the subcommittee, but he never again wielded substantial power. In 1957 he died from acute hepatitis, a disease related to alcoholism.

AP® TIP
Evaluate the extent to which McCarthyism challenged American political identity and threatened American values.

McCarthyism Term used to describe the harassment and persecution of suspected political radicals. Senator Joseph McCarthy was one of many prominent government figures who helped incite anti-Communist hysteria in the early 1950s.

AP® TIP
Be sure you can explain how the American press addressed the danger of McCarthyism.

◀ **Army-McCarthy Hearings** Wisconsin Republican Senator Joseph McCarthy gestures in front of a map depicting alleged Communist Party organization in the United States. The army-McCarthy hearings in 1954 were carried live on television and watched by millions of Americans. McCarthy's bullying tactics and unsubstantiated allegations against U.S. army personnel ultimately led to his political downfall. **How does the map in this photograph reinforce McCarthy's allegations of Communist influence in the United States?**

McCarthyism

The anti-Communist consensus did not end with the execution of the Rosenbergs in 1953 or the censure of Joseph McCarthy in 1954. Even J. Robert Oppenheimer, "the father of the atomic bomb," came under scrutiny. In 1954 the Atomic Energy Commission revoked Oppenheimer's security clearance for suspected, though unproven, Communist affiliations. That same year, Congress passed the Communist Control Act, which required "Communist infiltrated" groups to register with the federal government. Federal, state, and municipal governments required employees to take a loyalty oath affirming their allegiance to the United States and disavowing support for any organization that advocated the overthrow of the government. In addition, the blacklist continued in Hollywood throughout the rest of the decade. After the Supreme Court declared racial segregation in public schools unconstitutional in 1954, a number of southern states, including Florida and Louisiana, set up committees to investigate Communist influence in the civil rights movement. In a case concerning civil liberties, the Supreme Court upheld HUAC's authority to investigate communism and to require witnesses who came before it to answer questions about their affiliations. Yet the Court did put a stop to the anti-Communist momentum. In 1957 the high court dealt a severe blow to enforcement of the Smith Act by ruling in *Yates v. United States* that the Justice Department could not prosecute someone for merely advocating an abstract doctrine favoring the violent overthrow of the government. In response, Congress tried, but failed, to limit the Supreme Court's jurisdiction in cases of this sort.

REVIEW

How did McCarthy's tactics fuel the Second Red Scare? In what ways were McCarthy's actions shaped by the Cold War?

AP® WRITING HISTORICALLY — Short-Answer Question Practice

ACTIVITY

Read the following question carefully and write a short response. Use complete sentences.

Using the following image, answer (a), (b), and (c).

Source: Herblock, "Fire," *The Washington Post,* June 1949

a. Briefly describe ONE historical perspective expressed in the image.
b. Briefly explain how ONE event or development in the period 1940 to 1955 led to the historical situation depicted in the image.
c. Briefly explain ONE specific outcome of the historical situation in the period 1940 to 1955 depicted in the image.

EXPLORING AP® THEMES

Politics and Power

Divide students into groups of 3 or 4 students for the following activity. Provide students with the following three historical developments: New Deal, civil rights, and Hollywood 10. Next, ask groups to explain why Republicans attempted to link these to communism. After students have provided explanations, have the groups rank the political effectiveness of trying to link these developments to communism. When students are finished, have the class conduct a gallery walk where each group examines the results of other groups over the same historical examples. The goal is to both see the varying results and discuss why each group arrived at their respective ranking.

TRM Suggested Responses to Questions

BUILDING AP® SKILLS

Sourcing and Situation

Prior to having students answer the questions that accompany the Herblock cartoon, ask them the following questions:

1. What are two specific anti-Communist activities that took place between 1945 and 1950?
2. What does hysteria mean?

Simple, but these questions force students to think through the language employed by Herblock and the historical situation in which it was created.

TEACHING IDEA

AP® Writing Historically Review

This activity can serve as a great review of both how to answer a question and what constitutes a fully developed answer. Have students form groups of eight and have each member answer each part of the question individually. Next, have students pair up with someone in their group. Their task is to identify which response is the better one. After this is determined, have the four remaining students in each group pair up and identify the best response. Repeat this step with the final two students in the group until the best answer is determined. If you have a class of twenty-four, in this drill you would narrow the responses down to the best three answers in the class and those would be the exemplars to go over with the whole class. You can manipulate these group numbers to reflect your class size.

TRM Suggested Responses to Questions

TEACHING IDEA

Building Vocabulary

At the beginning of this module have students define the historical meaning of the word migration. Be sure students consider time period, ethnicity, race, and class in their definitions. Once they have a working definition, have students theorize at least three reasons why some people moved to the suburbs following the Second World War. This simple exercise can get students in the right frame of mind as they begin studying the affluence of the post-war years.

TEACHING IDEA

Incorporating Videos

Teachers can find excellent resources on Gilder Lehrman's AP® U.S. History site (ap.gilderlehrman.org). Period 8 includes a lecture from historian James Patterson about the post-war economy called "Grand Expectations: The United States 1945–1974." This is an informative video, which provides useful details about the economy before and after the Second World War. For teachers looking to learn more about the economic dynamism of this period, this video is a great starting point.

TEACHING IDEA

Incorporating Primary Sources

The Gilder Lehrman' History Now feature provides students with an instructional film for teenagers in 1950, *A Date with Your Family*, released by Encyclopedia Britannica Films. Assign students to watch the ten-minute film, which provides a great visual for the nuclear family ideal, and read the background information before answering the questions for discussion in groups.

Module 8-3

Peacetime Transition and the Boom Years

LEARNING TARGETS

By the end of this module, you should be able to:

- Explain the political and economic challenges facing the United States as it transitioned from World War II to peacetime.
- Explain the factors that contributed to the economic growth of the 1950s.
- Explain the causes and effects of the post-World War II baby boom.
- Explain the reasons why Americans moved to suburbs and to the Sun Belt after World War II.

THEMATIC FOCUS

Work, Exchange, and Technology
Migration and Settlement

After an initial postwar transition, during which Congress curtailed labor union rights, the United States economy experienced a remarkable period of growth significantly expanding the ranks of the middle class and noticeably lessening income inequality. The application of mass production techniques to home construction and federal subsidies for mortgages led to a sharp increase in home ownership as millions of Americans, especially young families resulting from the postwar baby boom, moved to newly built suburbs.

HISTORICAL REASONING FOCUS
Causation

TASK ▶ As you read this module, consider the sustained economic growth in the United States between 1945 and 1960. Ask yourself, what caused this economic boom and how did it affect American families and where they lived. Think about the impact of technological and scientific innovations in American society.

Though the nation struggled with economic and social challenges immediately after the Second World War, by 1950 Americans had more disposable income than they had enjoyed in decades. While President Truman struggled to hold together the New Deal coalition, consumers responded enthusiastically to the wide range of products that advertisers promised would improve their lives. The search for the good life propelled middle-class families from cities to the suburbs. At the same time, a postwar baby boom added millions of children to the population and created a market to supply them with goods from infancy and childhood to adolescence.

Economic and Political Challenges, 1945–1948

Before Americans could work their way toward prosperity, they faced considerable challenges. Immediately after the war, consumers experienced shortages and high prices, businesses complained about tight regulations, and labor unions sought higher wages and a greater voice in companies' decision making. The return to peace also occasioned debates about whether married women should continue to work outside the home.

By mid-1946, nine million American soldiers had returned to a changed world. The war had exerted pressures on traditional family life as millions of women had left home to work jobs that

TEACHING IDEA

Building Vocabulary

The decade of the 1950s is often associated with the societal emphasis on the value of the nuclear family. Really, everything in pop culture revolved around this ideal. Knowing the definition of this ideal is critical as students begin Module 8-3; therefore, have students work on defining nuclear family and the reasons why people valued this idea after World War II.

▲ **Differentiation**

If students are struggling with the idea of a nuclear family, have them compare television sitcoms across eras to emphasize the skill of comparison. For example, you could have students compare the makeup of a nuclear family in the sitcom *Father Knows Best* with *Modern Family*. What similarities and differences exist and what does that say about the time period in which they were filmed?

Economic and Political Challenges, 1945–1948

Period 8: 1945–1980

> "While we alarm ourselves with talk of . . . atom bombs, we are complacently watching the disintegration of our family life."
>
> —William C. Menninger, 1948

Servicemen's Readjustment Act (GI Bill) 1944 act that offered educational opportunities and financial aid to veterans as they readjusted to civilian life. Known as the GI Bill, the law helped millions of veterans build new lives after the war.

Dixiecrats Southern Democrats who created a segregationist political party in 1948 as a response to federal extensions of civil rights. Dixiecrats advocated for a state's right to legislate segregation. The Dixiecrat Party ran Strom Thurmond in an unsuccessful bid for the presidency in 1948 against Truman.

AP® TIP
Be sure you can explain the relationship between the Taft-Hartley Act and previous anti-union policies.

men had vacated. Most of the 150,000 women who served in the military received their discharge, and like their male counterparts they hoped to obtain employment. Many other women who had tasted the benefits of wartime employment also wanted to keep working and were reluctant to give up their positions to men.

The war disrupted other aspects of family life as well. During the war, husbands and wives had spent long periods apart, resulting in marital tensions and an increased divorce rate. The relaxation of parental authority during the war led to a rise in juvenile delinquency, which added to the anxieties of adults. In 1948 the noted psychiatrist William C. Menninger observed, "While we alarm ourselves with talk of . . . atom bombs, we are complacently watching the disintegration of our family life." Some observers worried that the very existence of the traditional American family was in jeopardy.

Even before the war ended, the U.S. government took some steps to meet postwar economic challenges. In 1944, for example, Congress passed the **Servicemen's Readjustment Act**, commonly known as the GI Bill, which offered veterans educational opportunities and financial aid as they adjusted to civilian life. Nevertheless, veterans, like other Americans, faced shortages in the supply of housing and consumer goods and high prices for available commodities.

President Harry Truman ran into serious difficulty handling these and other problems. In the years immediately following the war, real incomes fell, undermined by inflation and reduced overtime hours. As corporate profits rose, workers in the steel, automobile, and fuel industries struck for higher wages and a greater voice in company policies. Truman responded harshly. Labor had been one of Franklin Roosevelt's strongest allies, but his successor put that relationship in jeopardy. In 1946 the federal government took over railroads and threatened to draft workers into the military until they stopped striking. Truman took a tough stance, but in the end union workers received a pay raise, though it did little to relieve inflation.

Political developments forced Truman to change course with the labor unions. In the 1946 midterm elections, Republicans won control of Congress. Stung by this defeat, Truman sought to repair the damage his anti-union policies had done to the Democratic Party coalition. In 1947 Congress passed the **Taft-Hartley Act**, which hampered the ability of unions to organize and limited their power to strike if larger national interests were seen to be at stake. Seeking to regain labor's support, Truman vetoed the measure. Congress, however, overrode the president's veto, and the Taft-Hartley Act became law.

Truman's handling of domestic and foreign affairs brought out several challengers for the 1948 election. Much of the opposition came from his own party. From the left, former Democratic vice president Henry Wallace ran on the Progressive Party ticket, backed by disgruntled liberals who opposed Truman's hardline Cold War policies. From the right, Democratic governor Strom Thurmond of South Carolina campaigned mainly on preserving racial segregation in the South and headed up the States' Rights Party, known as the **Dixiecrats**. Both Wallace and Thurmond threatened to take Democratic votes from the president. However, Truman's strongest challenge came from the popular Republican governor of New York, Thomas E. Dewey. Indeed, political pundits and public opinion polls predicted that Truman would lose the 1948 presidential election.

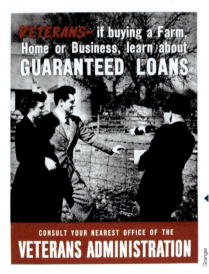

◀ **The GI Bill of Rights** The GI Bill provided a variety of benefits for World War II veterans. Not only did it pay for veterans to get a high school, vocational, or college degree, it also offered low-cost home mortgages and low-interest loans for business and farm ventures. The government distributed this 1945 lithograph to make GIs aware of some of these benefits. **How did the GI Bill help veterans adjust to life after World War II and set the stage for future economic growth in the United States?**

BUILDING AP® SKILLS

Argumentation

During President Truman's time in office, he battled unions, Southerners, and extreme anti-Communist Republicans. Each of these historical developments created political problems for him as he ran for president in 1948. Have students account for the reasons why each of these issues created political problems for him, but also have students choose the one issue they feel caused him the most political damage. Learning how to recognize the validity of some evidence, while privileging other evidence is a critical component of developing an argument. This could be done to close class on an exit card. Give students a guide of 3–4 sentences and give them about ten minutes to complete the exercise.

EXPLORING AP® THEMES

Politics and Power

The book will give students a clear narrative for the dynamics of the election of 1948; however, it may be helpful for students to compare election cycles from 1944 and 1948. Have students look through 270 to Win's website to see a visual of the changes wrought by Truman's stance on civil rights (270towin.com).

TEACHING IDEA

Connecting the Dots

Even though this time period is known as the age when the nuclear family was held in high esteem, it also was a time of great upheaval. From 1941 to 1948, the Second World War caused tremendous changes in family dynamics and marriages. Have students select one historical reason for this development and then have them create a presentation with one picture and one sentence that captures their explanation.

TRM Suggested Responses to Questions

TRM Module 8.3 AP® Analyzing Sources Handout 1

BUILDING AP® SKILLS

Sourcing and Situation

Continue to stress to students the importance of sourcing primary sources before they read them. For instance, have students brainstorm at least two foreign policy events from 1945 to 1947 that would have influenced someone supporting the attempt to weaken unions. Knowing this allows the student to understand the historical situation of this document and allows for a better analysis.

TEACHING IDEA

Incorporating Secondary Sources

Have students go to the Gilder Lehrman AP® U.S. History site to read "The Fifties" by Alan Brinkley in Period 8 (ap.gilderlehrman.org). This essay covers some of the main topics students have been reading about such as the Cold War, Affluent Society, and Fifties Society. This essay can be a nice review for students as they near the end of the module.

AP® ANALYZING SOURCES

Source: Representative Homer D. Angell, *Speech Supporting the Taft-Hartley Bill*, April 1947

"1. The right to join with his fellow workers to select as their bargaining agent the union that they want not the union that is forced upon them.

2. The right to get a job without joining any union.

3. The right to vote by secret ballot in a fair in free election. On whether his employer and they union can make him join the union to keep his job.

4. The right to require the union that is his bargaining agent to represent him without discriminating against him in anyway or for any reason even if he's not a member of the union. . . .

15. The right to settle his own grievances with his employer.

16. The right without fear of reprisal to support any candidate for public office that he chooses and to decide for himself whether or not his money will be spent for political purposes."

Questions for Analysis
1. Identify the labor issues addressed in the excerpt.
2. Describe the context surrounding the passage of the Taft-Hartley Bill.
3. Explain why Angell frames his argument in terms of workers' "rights."
4. Explain why organized labor opposed the "rights" supported by Angell.

AP® TIP
Be sure you can explain how arguments over civil rights divided the Democratic Party during the election of 1948.

Truman confounded expectations by winning the presidency. Truman traveled across the country, delivering dozens of fiery "give 'em hell, Harry" speeches and railing against a "do-nothing" Republican Congress. His victory resulted from his vigorous campaign style and the complacency of his Republican opponent, who placed too much faith in opinion polls. In addition, Wallace and Thurmond failed to draw significant votes away from Truman, demonstrating the continuing power of the New Deal coalition. Truman succeeded in holding together the coalition of labor, minorities, farmers, and liberals and winning enough votes in the South to come out ahead. Truman's electoral victory showed that most voters in 1948 favored a strong anti-Communist policy abroad and supported a brand of reform capitalism at home that encouraged economic growth rather than a redistribution of wealth to lift Americans into the middle class.

REVIEW
- How did Truman respond to the economic challenges after World War II?
- How was Truman able to win reelection in 1948 despite facing a popular Republican challenger and challengers from within his own party?

The Boom Years

While the United States faced political challenges, the economy flourished in the decade and a half after the Second World War. Between 1945 and 1960 the gross domestic product (GDP) more than doubled while per capita income (total income divided by the population) grew 35 percent. During this fifteen-year period, the average real income (actual purchasing power) for American workers increased by as much as it had during the fifty years preceding World War II. Equally striking, 60 percent of Americans achieved middle-class status, and the number of salaried office workers rose 61 percent. Factory workers also experienced gains. Union membership leaped to the highest level in U.S. history, reaching nearly 17 million.

The affluence of the 1950s was much more equally distributed than the prosperity of the 1920s had been. As the middle class grew, the top 5 percent of wealthy families dropped in the percentage

The Boom Years

Period 8: 1945–1980

◀ **Economic Growth, 1945–1965** As industries shifted from war equipment to consumer goods, productivity remained high. More Americans entered the middle class in the two decades following World War II, while rising union membership ensured higher incomes for the working class. As a result, the purchasing power of most Americans increased in the immediate postwar period. **What factors promoted the growth of the middle class in the 1950s?**

> **AP® TIP**
> Analyze the relationship between consumerism and economic prosperity during the post-war era.

of total income they earned from 21.3 percent to 19 percent. Though poverty remained a persistent problem, the rate of poverty decreased, falling from 34 percent in 1947 to 22.1 percent in 1960. A college education served as a critical marker of middle-class status. Traditionally, colleges and universities had been accessible only to the upper class. That began to change between 1940 and 1960 as the number of high school students who entered college more than doubled, due in part to the GI Bill's college benefits for veterans.

The market for consumer goods skyrocketed. TV sets became a household staple in the 1950s, and by 1960, 87 percent of Americans owned a television. Americans also continued to purchase automobiles—75 percent owned a car. With gas supplies plentiful and the price per gallon less than 30 cents, automakers concentrated on size, power, and style to compete for buyers. With more cars on the road, motel chains such as Holiday Inn sprang up along the highways. Fast-food establishments proliferated to feed motorists and their families.

During the postwar years, with traditional gender roles largely reinstated as wartime factories shifted to peacetime production and laid off many female workers, and with the economy booming, nuclear families began to grow. In 1955 Illinois governor Adlai Stevenson told the women graduates at Smith College that they could do their part to maintain a free society as wives and mothers. Educated women had an important role to play in maintaining a household that boosted their husband's morale. The mothers of these female college graduates had suffered through the Great Depression, when keeping the birthrate low was one way to assist the family. That was about to change.

Between 1946 and 1964, a **baby boom** occurred in the United States as the population dramatically increased. Economic prosperity made it easier to support large families, women's early age at marriage contributed to high fertility, and improved health care led to the survival of more children. In the 1940s and 1950s on average, men married for the first time at the age of just under twenty-three, and 49 percent of women married by nineteen. Couples produced children at such an astonishing pace that in the 1950s, the growth rate in the U.S. population approached that of India.

Marriage and parenthood reflected a culture spurred by the Cold War. Public officials and the media urged young men

baby boom Sharp population increase between 1946 and 1964 as a result of the end of World War II, increased economic prosperity, improvements in healthcare, and a trend toward marriage at younger age.

◀ **Children Receiving the Polio Vaccine, 1954** These children participated in a successful trial of the polio vaccine created by Dr. Jonas Salk in 1954. Before introduction of the polio vaccine, polio crippled 15,000 Americans yearly and infected three times as many. Within a decade, fewer than 1,000 Americans contracted the disease and less than 100 were paralyzed from it. In 1979, polio was deemed officially eradicated in the United States. **What does this image suggest about public confidence in science and medicine?**

TEACHING IDEA

Incorporating Primary Sources

When students encounter data-driven documents they need to consider the historical trends revealed by the document. For instance, rather than citing specific data from particular years in this document, students should note trends across decades. Divide students into groups of 3 or 4. Have each group write a one-sentence explanation of a historical trend from the graph on Economic Growth. Answers should vary, which will be useful as you explain the many options presented by historical data.

EXPLORING AP® THEMES

Social Structures

Gender expectations and definitions were a significant part of consumer society in the 1950s. Have students select three historical developments, events, or processes to explain how and why women were expected to embrace a role marked by domesticity and consumerism.

TEACHING IDEA

Incorporating Videos

In 2013, PBS aired a documentary titled *Makers: Women Who Make America*, which explored women's history from the end of World War II to present. The first fifteen minutes of Episode 1 are particularly well-suited for this module as the post-war feminine ideal is explored. Have students watch the clip from Makers' website (makers.com/documentaries). This clip can be useful to begin a discussion in class on this topic.

BUILDING AP® SKILLS

Causation

Causation has two ends to the historical reasoning process — cause and effect. To show the interdependence of gender roles, suburbs, baby boom, and consumerism, consider assigning students a graphic organizer that illustrates how the embrace of consumerism caused an embrace of gender roles, suburbs, and baby boom.

TRM Find **Handout 8.3 – Effects of Consumerism** in the Teacher's Resource Materials.

and women to build nuclear families in which the father held a paying job and the mother stayed at home and raised her growing family. Doing so would, they implied, strengthen the moral fiber of the United States in its battle against Soviet communism.

Parents could also look forward to their children surviving diseases that had resulted in many childhood deaths in the past. In the 1950s, children received vaccinations against diphtheria, whooping cough, and tuberculosis before they entered school. The most serious illness affecting young children remained the crippling disease of polio, or infantile paralysis. On April 12, 1955, news bulletins interrupted scheduled television programs to announce that Dr. Jonas Salk had developed a successful injectable vaccine against the disease. As one writer recalled, "citizens rushed to ring church bells and fire sirens, shouted, clapped, sang, and made every kind of joyous noise they could." By the mid-1960s polio was no longer a public health menace in the United States.

REVIEW

- Why did a baby boom occur in the years after World War II?
- How was family life shaped by the context of the Cold War?

Changes in Living Patterns

With larger families and larger family incomes came an increased demand for better housing. The economic and demographic booms encouraged migration out of the cities so that growing families could have their own homes, greater space, and a healthier environment. To meet this demand, the federal government provided Americans opportunities to purchase their own homes. The **Federal Housing Administration**, created in the 1930s, provided long-term mortgages to qualified buyers at low interest rates. After the war, the Veterans Administration offered even lower mortgage rates and did not require substantial down payments for ex-GIs. The federal government also cooperated by building highways that allowed drivers to commute to and from the suburbs. By 1960 nearly 60 million people, one-third of the nation's population, lived in suburbs.

William Levitt, a thirty-eight-year-old veteran from Long Island, New York, devised the formula for attracting home buyers to the suburbs. In 1948, Levitt remarked: "No man who owns his own house and lot can be a Communist. He has too much to do." After World War II, Levitt, his father, and his brother saw opportunity in the housing crunch and pioneered the idea of adapting Henry Ford's mass-production principles to the housing industry. To build his subdivision of **Levittown** in Hempstead, Long Island, twenty miles from Manhattan, he bulldozed 4,000 acres of potato fields and brought in trucks that dumped piles of building materials at exact intervals of sixty feet. Specialized crews then moved from pile to pile, each performing their assigned job. In July 1948, Levitt's workers constructed 180 houses a week, or 36 a day, in two shifts. Mass-production methods kept prices low, and Levitt quickly sold his initial 17,000 houses and soon built other subdivisions in Pennsylvania and New Jersey. With Levitt leading the way, the production of new single-family homes nearly doubled from 937,000 in 1946 to 1.7 million in 1950.

Although millions of Americans took advantage of opportunities to move to the suburbs, Levitt closed his subdivisions to African Americans. He was supported by the Federal Housing Authority, which guaranteed financing for sales of housing in all-white communities. Many whites moved out of the cities to distance themselves from the growing number of southern black people who migrated north during World War II and the influx of Puerto Ricans who came to the United States after the war, and they did not welcome these minorities to their new communities. Many communities in the North adopted restrictive covenants, which prohibited resale of homes to black people and members of other minority groups, including Hispanics, Jews, and Asian Americans. Although the Supreme Court outlawed restrictive covenants in *Shelley v. Kraemer* (1948), housing discrimination remained prevalent in urban and suburban neighborhoods. Real estate brokers steered minority buyers away from white communities, and banks refused to lend money to black purchasers who sought to move into white locales, an illegal policy called redlining.

Nevertheless, a few African Americans succeeded in cracking suburban racial barriers, but at great risk. In August 1957, a black couple, William Myers, an electrical engineer, and his wife Daisy, managed to buy a new $12,500 ranch-style house in Levittown, Pennsylvania. However,

Levittown Suburban subdivision built in Long Island, New York in the 1950s in response to the postwar housing shortage. Subsequent Levittowns were built in Pennsylvania and New Jersey.

> "No man who owns his own house and lot can be a Communist. He has too much to do."
> —William Levitt, 1948

AP® TIP
Evaluate the extent to which the culture of the 1950s illustrated continuity in race relations within the United States.

AP® ANALYZING SOURCES

Source: *Restrictive Housing Covenant in King County, Washington, April 1929*

"3. No chickens or fowl, or animals, except individual household pets, shall at any time be kept or maintained upon said property.

4. No person or persons of Asiatic, African or Negro blood, lineage or extraction shall be permitted to occupy a portion of said property, or any building thereupon; except domestic servant or servants may be actually and in good faith employed by white occupants of such premises.

5. No house or part thereof, or other structure, shall be constructed or maintained upon said premises nearer to the front street margin than the line described upon the plat as 'building limit.'

Upon the violation of any of the foregoing restrictions . . . the entire estate in the herein described property shall revert to the grantor herein, its successors or assigns."

Questions for Analysis

1. Identify the groups barred from owning or living in this house and the consequences for violating the agreement.
2. Describe how the covenant deals with racial exclusions as compared to other restrictions in the excerpt.
3. Explain why the covenant provides an exception for domestic servants.
4. Evaluate the impact of restrictive covenants on housing policy and homeowner demographics post–World War II.

---

once the couple moved in they faced two weeks of intimidation and assaults from mobs of disapproving white community residents. When local police refused to protect them, the governor dispatched state troopers to keep them safe. Although they succeeded in remaining in Levittown, having proclaimed "We're here to stay," their experience underscored the racially discriminatory housing practices that existed in the North.

The baby boom and mass-produced, cheap housing led to sustained growth. No sections of the nation expanded faster than the West and the South. Attracted by the warmer climate and jobs in the defense, petroleum, and chemical industries, many Americans moved to California, Texas, and Florida. The advent of air conditioning made it feasible for these new residents to live and work in hotter parts of the country. California's population increased the most, adding nearly six million new residents between 1940 and 1960, including a large influx of Asians and Latinos. In 1957, in a sign of the times, New York City lost two of its baseball teams, the New York Giants and the Brooklyn Dodgers, to San Francisco and Los Angeles. This migration to the **Sun Belt**, as the southern and western states would be called, transformed the political and social landscapes of the nation.

Sun Belt The southern and western part of the United States to which millions of Americans moved after World War II. Migrants were drawn by the region's climate and jobs in the defense, petroleum, and chemical industries.

REVIEW

- What factors led to the creation of the new suburbs?
- How did the new suburbs change American society?

AP® WRITING HISTORICALLY — Long-Essay Question Practice

ACTIVITY

Answer the following Long-Essay Question with a complete essay. *Suggested writing time: 40 minutes.*

Evaluate the relative importance of different causes for economic growth in the United States between 1945 and 1960.

TRM Suggested Responses to Questions

TRM Module 8.3 AP® Analyzing Sources Handout 2

TEACHING IDEA

Incorporating Primary Sources

Divide students into groups of 3 or 4. Before students read the *Restrictive Housing Covenant*, have students define the meaning of these covenants. Next, have students define personal racism and structural racism. To close the short activity, have students explain how restrictive covenants were examples of structural racism.

TEACHING IDEA

Incorporating Videos

California Newsreel has a special documentary on race in America, titled *Race: The Power of Illusion*. There is an especially useful part titled "The House We Live In," which explores the role of race as the suburbs developed in the 1950s and 1960s. This part of the documentary is a powerful look at the dynamics of wealth, race, and suburbia and is available to rent online (newsreel.org).

TRM Suggested Responses to Questions

TEACHING IDEA

AP® Writing Historically Review

The following activity helps prepare students to draft a plan for the essay, while paying special attention to not "double-dipping" in context and historical evidence. On the AP® U.S. History rubrics, students have to illustrate both an understanding of broader processes and discrete historical evidence to marshal through their essay. Remind students they are not allowed to "double-dip" evidence from contextualization to evidence in the essay. Put another way, whatever evidence is used in contextualization may not be used in the rest of the essay. To help students prepare for the essay and to avoid this pitfall, have students work in groups to identify what evidence they will use in their essay for contextualization and what evidence will be used as historical evidence for their body paragraphs. This can be a quick five- to ten-minute bell ringer activity.

TRM Suggested Responses to Questions

BUILDING AP® SKILLS
Continuity and Change

This module concentrates on the historical reasoning process of continuity and change in the cultural shifts America experienced in the 1950s. There are several historical topics you can provide students with to help them envision why these changes and continuities took place. Conformity, consumerism, and the Cold War are useful topics to have students think about at the beginning of the module. At the end of the module, have students select a topic and explain continuities in cultural patterns. Also, have students select a different topic and explain the changes in cultural patterns. The goal is to get students thinking about this from the beginning of the module.

Module 8-4

Cultural Shifts in 1950s America

LEARNING TARGETS
By the end of this module, you should be able to:
- Explain how 1950s popular culture reflected the expanding consumer-oriented economy.
- Explain how television, movies, and music shaped American culture in the 1950s.
- Explain the factors that led to a revival of religious sentiment.
- Explain how mainstream culture reinforced traditional views of women.
- Explain how teenagers, Beats, and other groups challenged accepted cultural norms.

THEMATIC FOCUS
American and Regional Culture

The rise of television reinforced traditional values, especially toward women, by generally depicting white, middle-class families in wholesome situations. At the same time a distinctly teenage culture began to form with the emergence of rock 'n' roll music and Hollywood movies aimed at teenagers' sense of rebellion. Church attendance soared to record heights as millions of Americans sought personal connections in a changing world and comfort from the threat of nuclear annihilation. Despite mainstream expectations of conformity, writers and intellectuals challenged the cultural homogeneity of postwar American society.

HISTORICAL REASONING FOCUS
Continuity and Change

TASK ▶ As you read this module, consider the changes and continuities in American society during the 1950s. Ask yourself how popular culture reflected both changes and continuities in the lives of Americans in the 1950s. Think about the reasons why some groups challenged accepted cultural values.

In the 1950s, new forms of popular culture developed as the United States confronted difficult political, diplomatic, and social issues. Amid this turmoil, television played a large role in shaping people's lives, reflecting their desire for success and depicting the era as a time of innocence. The rise of teenage culture as a powerful economic force also influenced this portrayal of the 1950s. Teenage tastes and consumption patterns reinforced the impression of a simpler and more carefree time. Religion painted a similar picture, as attendance at houses of worship rose. Still, the decade held a more complex social reality. Women did not always act the suburban parts that television and society assigned them, and cultural rebels—writers, actors, and musicians—emerged to challenge mainstream values.

The Rise of Television and a New Teenage Culture

Few postwar developments had a greater impact on American society and politics than the advent of television. The three major television networks—the Columbia Broadcasting System (CBS), the National Broadcasting Company (NBC), and the American Broadcasting Company (ABC)—offered programs nationwide that appealed to mainstream tastes while occasionally challenging the public with serious drama, music, and documentaries. During the 1950s, television networks began to feature presidential campaign coverage, from the national nominating conventions to election-day vote tallies, and political advertisements began to fill the airwaves.

Period 8: 1945–1980

AP® TIP

Compare the social, cultural, political, and economic effects of television in the 1950s to those of the radio in the 1920s.

If many Americans recall the 1950s as a time of innocence, they have in mind television programs aimed at children, such as *Howdy Doody*, *Superman*, *Hopalong Cassidy*, *The Cisco Kid*, and *The Lone Ranger*, which showcased a simple world of moral absolutes. In the course of a half hour, these shows pitted good versus evil; honesty and decency inevitably triumphed.

In similar fashion, adults enjoyed evening television shows that depicted old-fashioned families entertaining themselves, mediating quarrels peacefully, and relying on the wisdom of parents. In *The Adventures of Ozzie and Harriet*, the Nelsons raised two clean-cut sons. In *Father Knows Best*, the Andersons—a father and mother and their three children—lived a tranquil life in the suburbs, and the father solved whatever dilemmas arose. The same held true for the Cleaver family on *Leave It to Beaver*. Television portrayed working-class families in grittier fashion on shows such as *The Life of Riley*, whose lead character worked at a factory, and *The Honeymooners*, whose male protagonists were a bus driver and a sewer worker. Nevertheless, like their middle-class counterparts, these families stayed together and worked out their problems despite their more challenging financial circumstances.

By contrast, African American families received little attention on television. Black female actors usually appeared as maids, and the one show that featured an all-black cast, *The Amos 'n' Andy Show*, highlighted the racial stereotypes of the period. American Indians faced similar difficulties. Few appeared on television, and those who did served mainly as targets for "heroic" cowboys defending the West from "savage" American Indians. One exception was Tonto, the Lone Ranger's sidekick. Played by Jay Silverheels, a Canadian Mohawk, he challenged the image of the hostile American Indian by showing his loyalty to his white partner and his commitment to the code of "civilized" justice.

If parents expected young people to behave like Ozzie and Harriet Nelson's sons, the popular culture industry provided teenagers with alternative role models. In *Rebel Without a Cause* (1955), actor James Dean portrayed a seventeen-year-old filled with anguish about his life. A sensitive but misunderstood young man, he muses that he wants "just one day when I wasn't all confused . . .

▲ *Rebel Without a Cause*, 1955 James Dean starred in the movie *Rebel Without a Cause*, playing Jim Stark, a troubled teenager struggling with his middle-class life in post–World War II Los Angeles. The movie explored the conflict between parents and teenagers, what we call today "the generation gap." Dean's outfit of leather jacket and blue jeans and his anguished demeanor both reflected and shaped teenage culture. **What elements from the movie poster reflect the notion of teenage angst and rebellion?**

APPLY THE TIP

The development of mass media is a concept that allows students to see broad historical effects throughout the 1950s. Have students select two of the following categories: cultural, economic, and political. Next, have students explain specific ways mass media affected historical developments of their selected categories.

TEACHING IDEA

Incorporating Secondary Sources

Examining the television sitcoms of the 1950s can be an effective peek into the idealized lifestyle of 1950s suburbia. David Halberstam examines the ideal and reality of the television shows and their respective starts in Chapter 34 of his book, *The Fifties*. A quick read and one that provides useful analysis can be a good idea for teachers and students alike interested in learning more about this topic. Halberstam analyzes the context and substance of *Leave It to Beaver*, *The Adventures of Ozzie and Harriet*, and *Father Knows Best*.

TEACHING IDEA

Analyzing Art and Images

Sometimes a picture or piece of art will resonate with students more quickly than a written argument. Therefore, have students look up one picture of a movie or television show that represented how conformity was challenged in the 1950s and another picture representing the embrace of conformity. Students should accompany their selections with 1 or 2 sentence explanations. Students can look up films of James Dean, Marlon Brando, or Elvis Presley to get started with the search. Encourage students also to use examples in this module to help them brainstorm.

BUILDING AP® SKILLS

Contextualization

Social history is an ideal time to work on contextualization because it connects to so many other topics. For instance, mass media is a topic students could use to contextualize the essay question at the end of this module. Ask students to think about at least two specific factual references that would help substantiate the idea that mass media influenced the economic and technological changes in 1950s society.

Period 8: 1945–1980 MODULE 8-4 Cultural Shifts in 1950s America

[when] I wasn't ashamed of everything . . . [when] I felt I belonged some place." *The Wild One* (1954), which starred Marlon Brando, also popularized youthful angst. The leather-outfitted leader of a motorcycle gang, Brando rides into a small town, hoping to shake it up. When asked by a local resident, "What are you rebelling against?" he coolly replies, "Whaddya got?" Real gangs did exist on the streets of New York and other major cities. Composed of working-class youth from various ethnic and racial backgrounds, these gangs were highly organized, controlled their neighborhood turfs, and engaged in "rumbles" (fights) with intruders. A romanticized version of these battles appeared on Broadway with the production of *West Side Story* (1957), which pitted a white gang against a Puerto Rican gang in a musical rendering of *Romeo and Juliet*.

Hollywood rarely portrayed women as rebels, but instead as mothers, understanding girlfriends, and dutiful wives. If they sought a career, like many of the women played by actor Doris Day, they pursued it only as long as necessary to meet the right man. Yet the film industry did offer a more tantalizing woman, a sexual being who displayed her attributes to seduce and outwit men. Marilyn Monroe in *The Seven Year Itch* (1955) and Elizabeth Taylor in *Cat on a Hot Tin Roof* (1958) revealed that women also had a powerful libido, though in the end they became domesticated or paid a terrible price.

In 1941 *Popular Science* magazine coined the term *teenager*, and by the middle of the next decade members of this age group viewed themselves not as prospective adults but as a distinct group with its own identity, patterns of behavior, and tastes. Postwar prosperity provided teenagers with money to support their own choices and styles. In 1959 *Life* magazine found that teenagers had $10 billion at their disposal, "a billion more than the total sales of GM [General Motors]."

Teenagers owned 10 million record players, more than 1 million TV sets, and 13 million cameras. They spent 16 percent of their disposable income on entertainment, particularly the purchase of rock 'n' roll records. The comic book industry also attracted a huge audience among teenagers by selling inexpensive, illustrated, and easy-to-read pulp fiction geared toward romance and action adventure.

> **AP® TIP**
> Evaluate the degree to which attitudes toward and portrayals of women illustrated continuity in the 1950s.

AP® ANALYZING SOURCES

Source: Senate Subcommittee to Investigate Juvenile Delinquency, *Interim Report on Comic Books and Juvenile Delinquence*, 1955

"[O]ver a period of several months the subcommittee has received a vast amount of mail from parents expressing concern regarding the possible deleterious effect upon their children of certain of the media of mass communication. . . .

[I]t was the consensus that the need existed for a thorough, objective investigation to determine whether, as has been alleged, certain types of mass communication media are to be reckoned with as contributing to the country's alarming rise in juvenile delinquency. These include: 'crime and horror' comic books and other types of printed matter; the radio, television, and motion pictures. . . .

Delinquency is the product of many related causal factors. But it can scarcely be questioned that the impact of these media does constitute a significant factor in the total problem. . . .

One of the most significant changes of the past quarter century has been the wide diffusion of the printed word, particularly in certain periodicals, plus the phenomenal growth of radio and television audiences.

The child today in the process of growing up is constantly exposed to sights and sounds of a kind and quality undreamed of in previous generations. As these sights and sounds can be a powerful force for good, so too can they be a powerful counterpoise working evil."

Questions for Analysis
1. Identify the purpose for the committee's report.
2. Describe the concerns expressed in the report.
3. Explain how the report reflects cultural changes in the 1950s.
4. Evaluate the extent of similarity between the concerns outlined by the report and concerns commonly expressed about young people in the 1920s.

APPLY THE TIP

Not only did women play an integral role in the cultural attitudes in the 1950s, they also had ideals imposed upon them. For instance, the Cold War and consumerism shaped how women were viewed in the 1950s. Divide students into groups of four and have each group select either Cold War or consumerism. Next, have students explain one way in which their selected historical development shaped continuities in the expectations Americans had for women in the 1950s.

TRM Suggested Responses to Questions

TRM Module 8.4 AP® Analyzing Sources Handout 1

BUILDING AP® SKILLS
Sourcing and Situation

This source is about the ways in which centers of authority felt threatened by the new communication mediums of the 1950s. Before students start reading the document, have them develop at least two examples for ways mass media challenged authority between 1920 and 1949. To help students brainstorm possibilities, encourage them to brainstorm around significant historical processes and developments: for instance, during the so-called "Roaring Twenties," the Great Depression, and World War II.

EXPLORING AP® THEMES
Work, Exchange, and Technology

Perceptive students will notice the implicit ways in which technological innovation led to generational schisms in 1950s society. Have students select one mass media form of communication or entertainment and explain the ways in which this led to generational conflict. In order for students to think about the many ways in which this happened, have students share their answers with at least three other students. This can be done as a bell ringer activity prior to a lesson involving the source on juvenile delinquency.

Public high schools reinforced teenage identity. Following World War II, high school attendance exploded. In 1930, 50 percent of working-class children attended high school; thirty years later, the figure had jumped to 90 percent. The percentage of black youths attending high school also grew, doubling from 1940 to 1960. For the first time, many white middle-class teenagers saw the fashions and heard the language of working-class youths close up and both emulated and feared what they encountered.

More than anything else, rock 'n' roll music set teenagers apart from their elders. The pop singers of the 1940s and early 1950s—such as Frank Sinatra, Perry Como, Rosemary Clooney, and Patti Page, who had appealed to both adolescents and parents—lost much of their teenage audience after 1954 to rock 'n' roll, with its heavy downbeat and lyrics evoking teenage passion and sexuality. Black artists such as Chuck Berry, Little Richard, and Antoine "Fats" Domino popularized the sound of classic, up-tempo rock.

Although black people pioneered the sound, the music entered the mainstream largely through white artists who added rural flavor to rhythm and blues. Born in Tupelo, Mississippi, and living in Memphis, Tennessee, Elvis Presley adapted the fashion and sensuality of black performers to his own style. Elvis's snarling singing and pelvic gyrations excited young people, both black and white, while upsetting their parents. In an era when matters of sex remained private or were not discussed at all and when African Americans were still treated as second-class citizens, a white man singing "black" music and shaking his body to its frenetic tempo caused alarm. When Elvis sang on the popular *Ed Sullivan Show* in 1956, cameras were allowed to show him only from the waist up to uphold standards of decency.

REVIEW

- How did television shape — and in what ways was it shaped by — American culture in the 1950s?

- What factors drove the development of American teenage culture during the 1950s?

TEACHING IDEA

Connecting the Dots

If your school saves historical yearbooks, think about the following activity as a way of teaching local history. Have students select multiple years across the 1950s: 1951, 1955, and 1959, for example. Next, have students select one of their own yearbooks from high school. Their goal is to compare the clubs, activities, demographics, etc. from the 1950s to present. Their goal is to explain what changed and what stayed the same in their community.

TEACHING IDEA

Incorporating Music

Rock 'n' roll music, as it came to be known in the 1950s, began with black musicians and many famous white musicians in the 1960s such as The Beatles, covered the music of black artists. For students who have a firm grasp on the material, think about having them explore the music of the black artists mentioned in the book and more. Consider having students develop a three-song playlist that illustrates the popularity of black artists in the 1950s.

TEACHING IDEA

Class Discussion

At the conclusion of this section, lead a class discussion by asking students to consider the following:

- To what extent did television shows in the 1950s reflect American culture and to what extent did they shape American culture?

- How did the portrayal of men and women in movies differ from their portrayal on television in the 1950s?

- Describe the evolution of teenage culture in the 1950s.

Social Changes of the 1950s

AP® TIP

Analyze the ways in which the experiences of women in World War I, the 1920s, and World War II influenced their responses to continued restrictions during the 1950s.

Throughout the 1950s, movies, women's magazines, mainstream newspapers, and medical and psychological experts informed women that only by embracing domesticity could they achieve personal fulfillment. Dr. Benjamin Spock's best-selling *Common Sense Book of Baby and Child Care* (1946) advised mothers that their children would reach their full potential only if wives stayed at home and watched over their offspring. In another best seller, *Modern Women: The Lost Sex* (1947), Ferdinand Lundberg and Marynia Farnham called the independent woman "a contradiction in terms." A 1951 study of corporate executives found that most businessmen viewed the ideal wife as one who devoted herself to her husband's career. College newspapers described female undergraduates who were not engaged by their senior year as distraught. Certainly many women professed to find domestic lives fulfilling, but not all women were so content. Many experienced anxiety and depression. Far from satisfied, these women suffered from what the social critic Betty Friedan would later call "a problem that has no name," a malady that derived not from any personal failing but from the unrewarding roles women were expected to play.

Not all women fit the stereotype. Although most married women with families did not work during the 1950s, the proportion of working wives doubled from 15 percent in 1940 to 30 percent in 1960, with the greatest increase coming among women over the age of thirty-five. Married women were more likely to work if they were African American or came from working-class immigrant families. Moreover, women's magazines offered readers a more complex message than domesticity. Alongside articles about and advertisements directed at stay-at-home mothers, these periodicals profiled career women, such as Maine senator Margaret Chase Smith, the African American educator Mary McLeod Bethune, and sports figures such as the golf and tennis great Babe (Mildred) Didrikson Zaharias. At the same time, working women played significant roles in labor unions, where they fought to reduce disparities between men's and women's income and provide a wage for housewives, recognizing the importance of their unpaid work to maintaining families. Many other women joined clubs and organizations like the Young Women's Christian

BUILDING AP® SKILLS

Argumentation

As students are exploring social changes, particularly those changes experienced by women, consider the following activity. Divide the class into groups of 3 or 4 and give each group one of the following historical events/developments: Great Depression, World War II, and consumerism. Next, have students defend the validity of their event/development as having the most significant impact on women in the period between 1929 and 1959.

TRM Suggested Responses to Questions

TRM Module 8.4 AP® Analyzing Sources Handout 2

EXPLORING AP® THEMES
Social Structures

Before students read the excerpt from *The Feminine Mystique*, consider having them complete the following exercise, which can be used as an intro to the document analysis. No historical events happen in a vacuum, and the women's rights movement is no exception. Have students provide at least two historical reasons why the civil rights movement influenced the women's rights movement. Next, have them write 2 or 3 sentences explaining their reasoning.

▲ **Differentiation**

If students are struggling to provide evidence, have students work in pairs to first create a Venn diagram that compares the civil rights movement to the women's rights movement. This should help students to see the influences.

TEACHING IDEA
Analyzing Art and Images

Have students read the Go Retro article, "Mother's Little Helper: Vintage Drug Ads Aimed at Women" (goretro.com). How do these ads relate to Betty Friedman's *The Feminine Mystique*?

TEACHING IDEA
Connecting the Dots

As students have studied the post-war culture in America, they have no doubt encountered material that has explained what the feminine ideal was to many Americans. For instance, have students think about the implications for women to live in a culture that embraces consumerism and conformity in the context of the growth of suburbs. To review that historical concept and to assess students' understanding of the excerpt by Friedan, consider incorporating the following activity in your post-read discussion of this document. Have groups of students develop three characteristics that defined the feminine ideal. Next, have students compare the ideal they described with the Friedan excerpt. Students should find multiple ways Friedan challenges the characteristics of the feminine ideal.

AP® ANALYZING SOURCES

Source: Betty Friedan, *The Feminine Mystique*, 1963

"The suburban housewife—she was the dream image of the young American women and the envy, it was said, of women all over the world. The American housewife—freed by science and labor-saving appliances from the drudgery, the dangers of childbirth, and the illnesses of her grandmother. She was healthy, beautiful, educated, concerned only about her husband, her children, her home. She had found true feminine fulfillment. . . .

In the fifteen years after World War II, this mystique of feminine fulfillment became the cherished and self-perpetuating core of contemporary American culture. Millions of women lived their lives in the image of those pretty pictures of the American suburban housewife, kissing their husbands goodbye in front of the picture window, depositing their stationwagonsful of children at school, and smiling as they ran the new electric waxer over the spotless kitchen floor. . . .

If a woman had a problem in the 1950's and 1960's, she knew that something must be wrong with her marriage, or with herself. Other women were satisfied with their lives, she thought. What kind of woman did not feel this mysterious fulfillment waxing the kitchen floor? She was so ashamed to admit her dissatisfaction that she never knew how many other women shared it. . . ."

Questions for Analysis
1. Identify the reasons suburban housewives should be content, according to the excerpt.
2. Describe the 1950s ideal of womanhood expressed in the excerpt.
3. Explain why, according to Friedan, many women experienced depression and anxiety during the 1950s.
4. Evaluate how social, cultural, and economic developments in the 1950s shaped the ideals of womanhood described in the excerpt.

> "The people in the suburbs want to feel psychologically secure, adjusted, at home in their environment. Being religious and joining a church is . . . a fundamental way of 'adjusting' and 'belonging.'"
>
> — Will Herberg, "Protestant-Catholic-Jew: An Essay in American Religious Sociology," 1955

Association (YWCA), where they engaged in charitable and public service activities. Some participated in political organizations, such as Henry Wallace's Progressive Party, and peace groups, such as the Women's International League for Peace and Freedom, to campaign against the violence caused by racial discrimination at home and Cold War rivalries abroad.

Along with marriage and the family, religion experienced a revival in the postwar United States. The arms race between the United States and the Soviet Union heightened the dangers of international conflict for ordinary citizens as the possibility of nuclear annihilation loomed like a shadow over everyday life. Social and economic changes that accompanied the Cold War intensified personal anxiety. Churchgoing underscored the contrast between the United States, a religious nation, and the "godless" communism of the Soviet Union. The link between religion and Americanism prompted Congress in 1954 to add "under God" to the pledge of allegiance and to make "In God We Trust" the national motto in 1956.

Americans worshipped in growing numbers. Between 1940 and 1950, church and synagogue membership rose by 78 percent, and more than 95 percent of the population professed a belief in God. Yet religious affiliation appeared to reflect a greater emphasis on togetherness than on specific doctrinal beliefs. It offered a way to overcome isolation and embrace community in an increasingly alienating world. "The people in the suburbs want to feel psychologically secure, adjusted, at home in their environment," theologian Will Herberg explained. "Being religious and joining a church is . . . a fundamental way of 'adjusting' and 'belonging.'"

Television spread religiosity into millions of homes. The Catholic bishop Fulton J. Sheen spoke to a weekly television audience of ten million and alternated his message of "a life worth living" with attacks on atheistic Communists. The Methodist minister Norman Vincent Peale, also a popular TV figure, combined traditional religious faith with self-help remedies prescribed in his best-selling book *The Power of Positive Thinking* (1952). The Reverend Billy Graham, from Charlotte, North Carolina, preached about the unhappiness caused by personal sin at huge outdoor crusades in baseball parks and large arenas, which were broadcast on television. Americans derived

BUILDING AP® SKILLS
Contextualization

After students have read all of Module 8-4 and the Friedan excerpt, consider giving students the opportunity to explore issues connected to race and class to help teach contextualization. Provide students with the following categories:

- African American women
- Latina women

Next, have students explain how race and class affect the feminine ideal and/or the extent to which the excerpt from Friedan would resonate with these groups of women.

TRM Find **Handout 8.4 – Women and Contextualization** in the Teacher's Resource Materials.

Women in the Home and in the Workplace In the 1950s married women were encouraged to stay at home. Modern appliances like this refrigerator (left) supposedly made housework less difficult, but wives had to spend a great deal of time keeping it fully stocked and attending to other household chores. With all the new devices at their disposal, wives were expected to keep the home neat and spotless, while caring for their children. But not all married women stayed at home and tended the family. Margaret Chase Smith (right) was an influential Republican senator from Maine who took on Senator Joseph McCarthy in Congress and challenged his harsh anti-Communist methods. Here she is engaged in serious deliberations with Democratic majority leader Lyndon B. Johnson at a Senate hearing in 1957. **How did these images send mixed signals to American women during the 1950s?**

Beats A small group of young poets, writers, intellectuals, musicians, and artists who challenged mainstream American politics and culture in the 1950s.

AP® TIP
Be sure you can explain how the Beats challenged the culture and politics of the 1950s.

a variety of meanings from their religious experiences, but many embraced Americanism as their national religion. A good American, one magazine proclaimed, could not be "un-religious."

As many Americans migrated to the suburbs, spent money on leisure and entertainment, and cultivated religion, a small group of young poets, writers, intellectuals, musicians, and artists attacked mainstream politics and culture. Known as **Beats** (derived from "beaten down"), they offered stinging critiques of what they considered the sterility and conformity of white middle-class society. In 1956 Allen Ginsberg began his epic poem *Howl* (1956) with the line "I saw the best minds of my generation destroyed by madness, starving hysterical naked." In his novel *On the Road* (1957), Jack Kerouac praised the individual who pursued authentic experiences and mind-expanding consciousness through drugs, sexual experimentation, and living in the moment. At a time when whiteness was not just a skin color but a standard of beauty and virtue, the Beats and authors such as Norman Mailer looked to African Americans as cultural icons, embracing the spontaneity and coolness they attributed to inner-city black people. The Beats formed their own artistic enclaves in New York City's Greenwich Village and San Francisco's North Beach and Haight-Ashbury districts.

The Beat writers frequently read their poems and prose to the rhythms of jazz, reflecting both their affinity with African American culture and the innovative explorations taking place in music. From the big bands of the 1930s and 1940s, postwar jazz musicians formed smaller trios, quartets, and quintets and experimented with sounds more suitable for serious listening than for dancing. The bebop rhythms of trumpeter Dizzy Gillespie and alto saxophonist Charlie Parker revolutionized jazz, as did trumpeter Miles Davis and tenor saxophonist John Coltrane, who experimented with more complex and textured forms of this music and took it to new heights. Like rock 'n' roll musicians, these black artists broke down racial barriers as their music attracted white audiences.

Homosexuals also attempted to live nonconformist lifestyles, albeit secretly. According to studies by researcher Dr. Alfred Kinsey of Indiana University, homosexuals made up approximately 10 percent of the adult population. Despite growing gay and lesbian communities during World War II, homosexuality remained taboo and states outlawed gay and lesbian sexual relations. In 1951, politically radical gay men formed the country's first gay rights organization, the Mattachine Society, which was followed three years later by the founding of the country's first lesbian civil rights organization, the Daughters of Bilitis. Because of police harassment and public

Period 8: 1945–1980

MODULE 8-4 Cultural Shifts in 1950s America

The Beat Generation The literary rebels of the Beat Generation questioned the dominant values of the 1950s. They attacked materialism and conventional sexual morality. They explored Eastern religions as an alternative to Christianity and Judaism, and experimented with psychedelic drugs to reach a higher consciousness. This photograph captures the rebels-to-be as they attended Columbia University in the mid-1940s. From left to right are Hal Chase, Jack Kerouac, Allen Ginsberg, and William S. Burroughs. **What characteristics of the Beat movement are evident in the photograph?**

> "I saw the best minds of my generation destroyed by madness, starving hysterical naked..."
>
> Allen Ginsberg, "Howl," 1956

prejudice, most homosexuals refused to reveal their sexual orientation, which made sense practically but reduced their ability to counter anti-homosexual discrimination.

Dr. Kinsey also shattered myths about conformity among heterosexuals. In two landmark publications examining sexual behavior, he revealed that 85 percent of men and 50 percent of the women he interviewed had had sexual intercourse before marriage, and 25 percent of women had had extramarital affairs. Kinsey's findings were supported by other data. Between 1940 and 1960, the frequency of out-of-wedlock births among all women rose from 7.1 newborns to 21.6 newborns per thousand women of childbearing age. The sexual experiences that Kinsey documented reflected what many Americans practiced but did not talk about. The brewing sexual revolution went public in 1953 with the publication of *Playboy* magazine, founded by Hugh Hefner. Through a combination of serious articles and photographs of nude women, the controversial magazine provided its chiefly male readers with a guide to pursuing sexual pleasure and a sophisticated lifestyle.

Many writers denounced the conformity and shallowness they found in suburban America. Novelist Sloan Wilson wrote about the alienating experience of suburban life in *The Man in the Gray Flannel Suit* (1955). In J. D. Salinger's novel *Catcher in the Rye* (1951), the young protagonist, Holden Caulfield, mocks the phoniness of the adult world while ending up in a mental institution. Journalists and scholars joined in the criticism. Such critics often overstated the conformity that characterized the suburbs by minimizing the ethnic, religious, and political diversity of their residents. Yet they tapped into a growing feeling, especially among a new generation of young people, of the dangers of a mass culture based on standardization, compliance, and bureaucratization.

REVIEW

- In what ways did American culture offer examples for women that differed from traditional notions of suburban domesticity in the 1950s?
- How did nonconformists challenge American society in the 1950s?

AP® WRITING HISTORICALLY — Long-Essay Question Practice

ACTIVITY

Answer the following Long-Essay Question with a complete essay. *Suggested writing time: 40 minutes.*

Evaluate the extent to which economic growth and technological innovations fostered cultural change in the United States in the period 1945 to 1960.

TEACHING IDEA

Connecting the Dots

Art and sex challenged accepted norms that influenced the ubiquitous nature of conformity in the 1950s. Consider the following activity as a way to develop interpretation and argumentation skills. Have students select either art or sex as a category of analysis. Once they have made their selection, ask students to develop a 5–7 sentence interpretation as to why their category caused greater societal upheaval in the 1950s. They should use evidence provided from the textbook and incorporate the analytical writing skills they have been working on all year to produce a sound response. You can involve the entire class if you want to by having students select the top two from each category to be posted in the room.

TRM Suggested Responses to Questions

BUILDING AP® SKILLS

Continuity and Change

Even though this essay question centers on the skill of change, more developed responses may include what continuities were fostered by economic growth and technological change. To have students be more aware of this prior to writing the essay, consider asking students to outline at least one significant continuity from either economic growth or technological change. The goal is to first make the students aware of the continuity and then encourage them to incorporate it in their analysis.

TEACHING IDEA

AP® Writing Historically Review

To further students' ability to decode a question, provide the following clues to students on the white board: Topic 1, Topic 2, Subtopic 1, and Time Period. Have students identify which parts of the question match the clues. Key – Topic 1: economic growth, Topic 2: technological innovations, Subtopic 1: cultural change, Time Period: 1945–1960 (post-World War II through the 1950s). This is a crucial step for students as this determines the extent to which they have addressed the thesis category and argument development.

Module 8-5

Civil Rights in an Era of Conformity

LEARNING TARGETS
By the end of this module, you should be able to:
- Explain how the NAACP and CORE sought to advance African American civil rights in the 1940s and 1950s.
- Explain the impact of Brown v. Board of Education, the Montgomery bus boycott, and the sit-in movement on the struggle for civil rights.
- Explain how white segregationists resisted civil rights advancements.
- Explain how Mexican Americans, Chinese Americans, and Japanese Americans strived for civil rights in the 1950s.

THEMATIC FOCUS
Politics and Power
Social Structures

After fighting for a double victory in World War II against fascism abroad and racism at home, African American veterans returned to a country in which they faced discrimination in the North and legal segregation in the South. In response, civil rights groups initiated lawsuits, boycotts, and sit-ins resulting in the Supreme Court overturning school segregation in *Brown v. Board of Education*, the desegregation of Montgomery's buses, and the integration of lunch counters in the South. White segregationists resisted civil rights by blocking passage of civil rights legislation, using threats and intimidation, and sometimes through violence and terror.

HISTORICAL REASONING FOCUS
Causation

TASK ▶ As you read this module, analyze the factors that led to the early successes of the civil rights movement in the 1950s. Consider the relative importance of grass roots activism versus governmental intervention. Make sure to think about not only the effects of the civil rights movement on the lives of African Americans but also the reactions to the movement by various white Americans and the ways the movement influenced the pursuit of civil rights by other ethnic groups in the 1950s.

TRM Suggested Responses to Questions

African Americans wanted what most other Americans desired after World War II — the opportunity to make a decent living, buy a nice home, raise a healthy family, and get the best education for their children. Yet black people faced much greater obstacles in obtaining these dreams than white people did, particularly in the Jim Crow South. Determined to eliminate racial injustices, black Americans mounted a campaign against white supremacy in the decades after World War II. African Americans increasingly viewed their struggle as part of an international freedom movement of black people in Africa and other nonwhites in the Middle East and Asia to obtain their freedom from Western colonial rulers. Embracing similar hopes, Asian Americans and Latinos pursued their own struggles for equality.

The Rise of the Southern Civil Rights Movement

With the war against Nazi racism over, African Americans continued their fight for full citizenship rights in the United States. During World War II, black people waged successful campaigns to pressure the federal government to tackle discrimination and organizations such as the Congress of Racial Equality (CORE) and the NAACP attacked racial injustice (see Module 7-1). African American veterans returned home to the South

TEACHING IDEA

Check for Understanding

Students should be aware of the context of the civil rights movement of the 1950s as they begin Module 8-5. Therefore, consider providing an example from their prior learning, such as the Double V campaign of World War II, and have students evaluate the degree to which civil rights advocates were successful prior to the 1950s. This activity can be a great bell ringer activity to get students ready to start this module. Simply provide the example, in this case Double V campaign, and ask students to cite at least one piece of historical evidence to substantiate their interpretation. Answers will vary, but students should use 2 to 3 sentences in their responses.

BUILDING AP® SKILLS

Developments and Processes

Civil rights activism had its origins in grassroots reformers who marched, boycotted, and organized in an effort to change structural racism. Fundamentally, these activists were looking to cause changes in law and gradually governments at all levels took action. Familiarizing students with the difference between grassroots activism and government intervention will help students sort historical examples as they encounter them in the reading. What follows is a word-sort activity. Provide students with two categories: grassroots activism and government intervention. Next, give them the following list of words to sort.

- Voter registration drives
- Supreme Court cases
- Executive Orders
- Non-violent marches
- Student groups (Student Non-Violent Coordinating Committee)
- Federal legislation
- Church leadership (Southern Christian Leadership Conference)

Students do not have to know each group to successfully complete this activity. Instead, they should think about the characteristics of grassroots activism and government intervention, based on prior learning, and apply it to this group of words.

MODULE 8-5 Civil Rights in an Era of Conformity

BUILDING AP® SKILLS

Continuity and Change

Using the time period 1941–1952, have students brainstorm the continuities and changes to racist policies against African Americans in the following categories: military, athletics, and education. Once students determine whether or not the category represents a continuity or a change, have them write a one-sentence answer for each with historical evidence.

APPLY THE TIP

One of the ways in which African Americans protested was by using the Fourteenth and Fifteenth Amendments, originally passed during the Reconstruction Era. As students consider how World War II affected their struggle to gain civil rights, consider extracting parts of the Fourteenth and Fifteenth Amendments to narrow their focus. For instance, you can ask students to determine the extent to which World War II affected African Americans' access to equal protection under the law, rights of citizenship, and access to voting. In this way, students are taught to be discrete with historical evidence in their response.

TEACHING IDEA

Digging Deeper: Thurgood Marshall

Thurgood Marshall was a transformational African American civil rights leader throughout the post-war period. The Thurgood Marshall website is devoted to gaining a greater understanding of who he was and how he helped advance civil rights (thurgoodmarshall.com). Consider assigning groups of students different aspects of his life so the class gains a biographical sketch. You could assign the following categories to groups of 4 or 5 students: childhood, academic history, NAACP, Supreme Court, and legacy. Each group creates a presentation highlighting various aspects of his life. The goal is to allow students to see how one civil rights leader rose to prominence in an era filled with racism.

U.S. Racial Integration of the Military in Korea, 1950 In 1948, President Truman issued an executive order to desegregate the armed forces. During the Korean War African American soldiers served in integrated combat units. On the top left of this November 20, 1950 photo, Sergeant First Class Major Cleveland, the African American squad leader of this racially integrated unit fighting with the Second Infantry Division, points out a Communist-led North Korean position to his machine gun crew. **In what ways would a desegregated military help the United States in fighting the Cold War?**

AP® TIP
Analyze how African Americans' service in the military during World War II affected their struggle to gain civil rights after it ended.

determined to build on these victories, especially by extending the right to vote. Yet African Americans found that most whites resisted demands for racial equality.

In 1946 violence surfaced as the most visible evidence of many white people's determination to preserve the traditional racial order. A race riot erupted in Columbia, Tennessee, in which black people were killed and black businesses were torched. In South Carolina, Isaac Woodard, a black veteran still in uniform and on his way home on a bus, got into an argument with the white bus driver. When the local sheriff arrived, he pounded Woodard's face with a club, permanently blinding the ex-GI. In Mississippi, Senator Theodore Bilbo, running for reelection in the Democratic primary, told white audiences that they could keep black people from voting "by seeing them the night before" the election. Groups such as the NAACP and the National Association of Colored Women demanded that the president take action to combat this reign of terror.

In December 1946, President Truman responded by issuing an executive order creating the President's Committee on Civil Rights. While the committee conducted its investigation, in April 1947, Jackie Robinson became the first black baseball player to enter the major leagues. This accomplishment proved to be a sign of changes to come.

After extensive deliberations, the committee, which consisted of both black and white people, as well as northerners and southerners, issued its report, **To Secure These Rights,** on October 29, 1947. Placing the problem of "civil rights shortcomings" within the context of the Cold War, the report argued that racial inequality and unrest could only aid the Soviets in their global anti-American propaganda efforts. "The United States is not so strong," the committee asserted, "the final triumph of the democratic ideal not so inevitable that we can ignore what the world thinks of us or our record." A far-reaching document, the report called for racial desegregation in the military, interstate transportation, and education, as well as extension of the right to vote. The following year, under pressure from African American activists, the president signed an executive order to desegregate the armed forces.

REVIEW

What factors shaped the struggle for African American civil rights during the late 1940s?

School Segregation and the Montgomery Bus Boycott

Led by the NAACP, African Americans also launched a prolonged legal assault on school segregation. First the association filed lawsuits against states that excluded black people from publicly funded law schools and universities. After victories in Missouri and Maryland, the group's chief lawyer, Thurgood Marshall, convinced the Supreme Court in 1950 to disband the separate law school that Texas had established for black people and admit them to the University of Texas Law School. At the same time, the Court eliminated separate facilities for black students at the University of Oklahoma graduate school and ruled against segregation in interstate rail transportation.

TEACHING IDEA

Class Discussion

To help students understand how the issues of separate and unequal are still present in the American school system, consider using Keith Meatto's article, "*Still Separate, Still Unequal: Teaching about School Segregation and Educational Inequality*" available on the *New York Times* website (nytimes.com).

TEACHING IDEA

Incorporating Websites

One of the central pieces of evidence the NAACP used in the argument to desegregate the school systems in America was the results of Kenneth and Mamie Brown's "Doll Test." The article, "The Significance of 'The Doll Test,'" from the NAACP website offers students and teachers alike excellent resources on the purposes, results, and influence of the "Doll Test" in *Brown v. Board of Education* (naacpldf.org).

School Segregation and the Montgomery Bus Boycott

AP® ANALYZING SOURCES

Source: North Carolina State Legislature, *Jim Crow Public Transportation Laws in Effect in 1954*

"Section 94: Separate but equal station and travel accommodations shall be provided, including steamboats. Separate cars shall be maintained or separate compartments shall be used under the supervision of the State utilities commission. Exempted from this provision are sleeping cars, express trains through the State, servants and prisoners.

Section 95: Exemptions to the act may be granted in a few cases of small trains operating in out of the way places.

Section 96: In emergencies, a car may be apportioned by the conductor (that is, different races may occupy the car without a partition as long as races are seated separately in the car).

Section 97: Company violation of this act will result in fines of $100 for each day of violation.

Section 98: In one-car trains and similar conveyances, the utilities commission will decide on a solution to the usual provision of maintaining jim-crow toilets. . . .

Section 101: No passenger may enter any part of the train if the conductor has told him not to. To do so, constitutes a misdemeanor for which a fine of $10 may be imposed.

Section 103: A passenger may be ejected for lack of payment or for violating the above provisions. . . .

Section 135: (The following three provisions are for streetcar and interurban trolleys only.) This provision reads the same as No. 94 above plus the fact that these vehicles are to be apportioned by the conductor in accordance with the usual amount of traffic of either race.

Section 136: Whites must take seats from the front and colored from the rear. If a passenger is told to move in order to maintain this pattern of seating, he must do it or face a misdemeanor charge for which he may be fined $50 or 30 days. Company officials have police powers to carry out the provisions of this act.

Section 137: These companies will not be liable for mistakes in seating."

Questions for Analysis
1. Identify the consequences stated in the excerpt for violations of these laws.
2. Describe how the laws in this excerpt maintained segregation in public transportation.
3. Explain why banning segregation in interstate transportation would not necessarily undo these laws.
4. Evaluate the extent to which these laws were consistent with the doctrine of "separate but equal" in the 1898 *Plessy v. Ferguson* ruling.

Before African Americans could attend college, they had to obtain a first-class education in public schools. All-black schools typically lacked the resources provided to white schools, and the NAACP understood that southern officials would never live up to the "separate but equal doctrine" asserted in *Plessy v. Ferguson* (1896). African Americans sought to integrate schools not only because they wanted the freedom to have their children attend their local public schools, but because they also believed that integration offered the best and quickest way to secure quality education.

On May 17, 1954, in **Brown v. Board of Education of Topeka, Kansas**, the Supreme Court overturned *Plessy*. In a unanimous decision read by Chief Justice Earl Warren, the Court concluded that "in the field of public education the doctrine of 'separate but equal' has no place. Separate educational facilities are inherently unequal." This ruling undercut the legal foundation for segregation and officially placed the law on the side of those who sought racial equality. Nevertheless, the ruling did not end the controversy; in fact, it led to more battles over segregation. In 1955 the Court issued a follow-up opinion calling for implementation with "all deliberate speed." But it left enforcement of *Brown* to federal district courts in the South, which consisted mainly of white

Brown v. Board of Education of Topeka, Kansas Landmark 1954 Supreme Court case that overturned the "separate but equal" principle established by *Plessy v. Ferguson* and applied to public schools. Few schools in the South were racially desegregated for more than a decade.

Period 8: 1945–1980

TRM Suggested Responses to Questions

TRM Module 8.5 AP® Analyzing Sources Handout 1

TEACHING IDEA

Building Vocabulary

Before students read and analyze this primary source, have them reflect on information they already learned. Consider this brief bell ringer activity as a way to develop historical context for the reading of this source. Have students define the meaning of Jim Crow using at least three of the following terms/phrases: Separate but equal, *Plessy v. Ferguson*, "Redeemer" governments, "Home Rule," and structural racism. The goal is for students to root their understanding of the context of this document prior to reading and answering the accompanying questions.

TEACHING IDEA

Connecting the Dots

Legislation can present students with some unique challenges. For instance, legislation is sometimes filled with vernacular students are less accustomed to reading. This can often result in confusion or misunderstandings about the purpose of the text. To ensure students are aware of the takeaways to this document, consider having students select two sections from the document and then have them rewrite the section in their own words with a connection to Jim Crow.

▲ **Differentiation**

Working in groups allows for a faster transition as the class shares responses. Consider pairing students of different ability level. The key here is to reword the language of the section without losing the meaning and to connect the explanation to Jim Crow.

TEACHING IDEA

Connecting the Dots

Provide students with the following pieces of historical evidence: Twenty-fourth Amendment, Civil Rights Act of 1957, *Brown v. Board of Education*, President Eisenhower's response to the Little Rock Nine. Have students rank and explain the effectiveness of these actions, each of which was intended to support the expansion of civil rights. The goal is for students to recognize both the expansiveness and limitations of early civil rights gains.

BUILDING AP® SKILLS

Claims and Evidence in Sources

Most students will understand the connection between Jim Crow, *Plessy v. Ferguson*, and segregation. However, most students are not as familiar with the language of the majority decision. In particular, what might surprise students the most is that the court denied the case was about race. Consider the following excerpt from the majority decision in *Plessy v. Ferguson*: "We consider the underlying fallacy of the plaintiff's argument to consist in the assumption that the enforced separation of the races stamps the colored race with a badge of inferiority. If this be so, it is not by reason of anything found in the act, but solely because the colored race chooses to put that construction on it."

To turn this into an activity at the beginning of the class period, think about waiting until after students have already read this part of the textbook, then provide them with the quote at the beginning of the next class period. Finally, working in groups, have students reflect and develop a response, which explains how the court could deny the role of race in a decision that legalized Jim Crow laws.

TEACHING IDEA

Check for Understanding

The Montgomery Bus Boycott was a strategic move on the part of civil rights activists. Some students may not be struck by the importance of using the busing system to take a stand for civil rights. Ask students to define how the busing system in Montgomery presented civil rights leaders with a strategic opportunity to change social and economic structures in the city. They must use at least one piece of evidence for both social and economic changes.

EXPLORING AP® THEMES

Social Structures

At the very beginning of the module students were asked to make word associations with grassroots organizers. At this point in the module, it may benefit students to work on a historical explanation for grassroots activists. Consider having groups of 3 or 4 students develop a definition, with historical evidence, of grassroots activism. After each group shares responses, have a discussion about the importance of this idea when studying the civil rights movement.

TEACHING IDEA

Incorporating Videos

In 2014, *Frontline* — an investigative documentary series by PBS — focused on the sixtieth anniversary of *Brown v. Board of Education* and how schools are still racially divided. The episode "Separate and Unequal" is available on the PBS website through title search (pbs.org). This documentary can elicit powerful conversations about the long-term effects of structural racism.

TEACHING IDEA

Digging Deeper: Claudette Colvin

Help students understand that there were several instances of quiet protests at this time by having them read Margot Adler's article, "Before Rosa Parks, There Was Claudette Colvin" or listen to the accompanying 6-minute recording, both available on NPR's website (npr.org).

MODULE 8-5 Civil Rights in an Era of Conformity

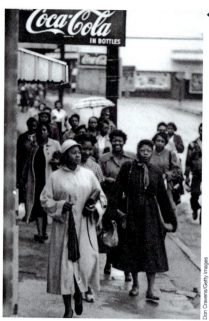

◀ **Montgomery Bus Boycott, 1956** Two months after African American residents of Montgomery, Alabama began their boycott of the city buses to protest segregation and mistreatment, the black community kept up its boycott despite violence and intimidation. Black women had made up the majority of bus riders, and this photograph, taken on February 1, 1956, shows many of them walking to work or to stores for shopping. **What does this photograph reveal about the goals of and participants in the civil rights movement in the mid-1950s?**

Montgomery bus boycott Thirteen-month bus boycott that began with the arrest of Rosa Parks for refusing to give up her seat to a white man. The successful protest catapulted Martin Luther King, Jr., a local pastor, into national prominence as a civil rights leader.

Southern Christian Leadership Conference (SCLC) Organization founded in 1957 by Martin Luther King Jr. and other black ministers to encourage nonviolent protests against racial segregation and disfranchisement in the South.

southerners who espoused segregationist views. As a result, southern officials emphasized "deliberate" rather than "speed" and slowed the implementation of the *Brown* decision.

The *Brown* decision encouraged African Americans to protest against other forms of racial discrimination. In 1955 in Montgomery, Alabama, the Women's Political Council, a group of middle-class and professional black women, petitioned the city commission to improve bus service for black passengers. Among other things, they wanted black people not to have to give up their seats to white passengers who boarded the bus after black passengers did. Their requests went unheeded until December 1, 1955, when Rosa Parks, a black seamstress and an NAACP activist, refused to give up her seat to a white man. Parks's arrest rallied civic, labor, and religious groups and sparked a bus boycott that involved nearly the entire black community. Instead of riding buses, black commuters walked to work or joined car pools. White officials refused to capitulate and fought back by arresting leaders of the Montgomery Improvement Association, the organization that coordinated the protest. Other whites hurled insults at black people and engaged in violence. After more than a year of conflict, the Supreme Court ruled in favor of the complete desegregation of Montgomery's buses.

Out of this landmark struggle, Martin Luther King Jr. emerged as the civil rights movement's most charismatic leader. His personal courage and power of oratory could inspire nearly all segments of the African American community. Twenty-six years old at the time of Parks's arrest, King was the pastor of the prestigious Dexter Avenue Baptist Church. Though familiar with the nonviolent methods of the Indian revolutionary Mohandas Gandhi and the civil disobedience of the nineteenth-century writer Henry David Thoreau, King mainly drew his inspiration and commitment to these principles from the black church and secular leaders such as A. Philip Randolph and Bayard Rustin. King understood how to convey the goals of the civil rights movement to sympathetic white Americans, but his vision and passion grew out of black communities. At the outset of the **Montgomery bus boycott**, King noted proudly of the boycott: "When the history books are written in future generations, the historians will have to pause and say 'There lived a great people — a Black people — who injected new meaning and dignity into the veins of civilization.'"

The Montgomery bus boycott made King a national civil rights leader, but it did not guarantee him further success. In 1957 King and a like-minded group of southern black ministers formed the **Southern Christian Leadership Conference (SCLC)** to spread nonviolent protest throughout the region, but except in a few cities, such as Tallahassee, Florida, additional bus boycotts did not take hold.

REVIEW

- In what ways did the Brown ruling change racial segregation in the South, and in what ways did it fall short?
- How did bus boycotts show both the strength and limitations of the civil rights movement during the 1950s?

Combatting White Resistance to Desegregation

Little Rock Nine Nine students who, in 1957, became the first African Americans to attend Central High School in Little Rock, Arkansas. Federal troops were required to overcome the resistance of white officials and the violence of white protesters.

> "When the history books are written in future generations, the historians will have to pause and say 'There lived a great people — a Black people — who injected new meaning and dignity into the veins of civilization.'"
>
> Martin Luther King Jr., 1955

Segregationists responded forcefully to halt black efforts to eliminate Jim Crow. In 1956, 101 southern congressmen issued a manifesto denouncing the 1954 *Brown* opinion and pledging to resist it through "lawful means." Other southerners went beyond the law. In 1957 a federal court approved a plan submitted by the Little Rock, Arkansas school board to integrate Central High School. However, the state's governor, Orval Faubus, obstructed the court ruling by sending the state National Guard to keep out nine black students chosen to attend Central High. Faced with blatant state resistance to federal authority, President Eisenhower placed the National Guard under federal control and sent in the 101st Airborne Division to restore order after a mob blocked the students from entering the school. These black pioneers, who became known as the **Little Rock Nine**, attended classes for the year under the protection of the National Guard but still encountered considerable harassment from white students. In defiance of the high court, other school districts, such as Prince Edward County, Virginia, chose to close their public schools rather than desegregate. By the end of the decade, public schools in the South remained mostly segregated.

The white South used other forms of violence and intimidation to preserve segregation. The third incarnation of the Ku Klux Klan (KKK) appeared after World War II to strike back at growing African American challenges to white supremacy. This terrorist group threatened, injured, and killed black people they considered "uppity." Following the *Brown* decision, segregationists also formed the **White Citizens' Council (WCC)**. The WCC drew members largely from businessmen and professionals. Rather than condoning violence, the WCC generally intimidated black people by threatening to fire them from jobs or denying them credit from banks. In Alabama, WCC members launched a campaign against radio stations playing the kind of rock 'n' roll music that Alan Freed popularized in New York City because they believed that it fostered close interracial contact.

AP® ANALYZING SOURCES

Source: *The Southern Manifesto*, 1956

"We regard the decision of the Supreme Court in the school cases as a clear abuse of judicial power. It climaxes a trend in the Federal Judiciary undertaking to legislate, in derogation of the authority of Congress, and to encroach upon the reserved rights of the states and the people. . . .

This unwarranted exercise of power by the Court, contrary to the Constitution, is creating chaos and confusion in the States principally affected. It is destroying the amicable relations between the white and Negro races that have been created through ninety years of patient effort by the good people of both races. It has planted hatred and suspicion where there has been heretofore friendship and understanding.

Without regard to the consent of the governed, outside agitators are threatening immediate and revolutionary changes in our public-school systems. If done, this is certain to destroy the system of public education in some of the States. . . .

We pledge ourselves to use all lawful means to bring about a reversal of this decision which is contrary to the Constitution and to prevent the use of force in its implementation."

Questions for Analysis

1. Identify the main argument in the *Southern Manifesto*.
2. Describe the tactics used to resist desegregation in the South that would have been supported by the signers of the *Southern Manifesto*.
3. Evaluate the extent of similarity in the rhetoric used to defend segregation in the *Southern Manifesto* and that used to defend slavery before the Civil War.

TEACHING IDEA

Incorporating Videos

Available in many schools as well as online, the classic PBS documentary, *Eyes on the Prize*, while older, is still a great resource for small video clips on civil rights moments from the 1950s through the 1960s. The segment on the Little Rock Nine is found in Episode 2, "Fighting Back: 1957–1962," between 8:00 and 29:00. The documentary is available on Vimeo through title search (vimeo.com). With original footage and interviews, this is a resource still worth using in class.

TRM Suggested Responses to Questions

TRM Module 8.5 AP® Analyzing Sources Handout 2

BUILDING AP® SKILLS

Sourcing and Situation

The Southern Manifesto articulated a vision of how white southerners were going to respond to continued civil rights activism. Prior to reading this document, consider having students brainstorm the major civil rights victories between 1950 and 1956. Next, ask students which civil rights victories most bothered white southerners. You can end this activity by asking students what implications they can imagine would stem from this document. This simple brainstorming activity is a good way to approach a pre-read strategy for primary source analysis.

TEACHING IDEA

Building Vocabulary

Civil rights activists were battling not only personal racism of individuals in the United States but also structural racism embedded in law. Students should understand the distinction between someone's personal racist views and a structural racist system. Working in groups of 2 or 3, have students define each of these terms. This can be used as a bell ringer activity to the section on white resistance.

BUILDING AP® SKILLS

Claims in Sources and Evidence

One of the tropes of southern white leaders was the notion that race relations prior to the civil rights movement were acceptable between white leaders and African Americans. This assertion was often directed at northern civil rights leaders. Have students highlight the document for claims that fit this description. Examples: "destroying the amicable relations between the white and Negro races," "planted hatred and suspicion where there has been heretofore friendship," and "outside agitators."

TEACHING IDEA

Incorporating Videos

The Emmett Till story is a haunting illustration of the consequences of individual acts of violence in a society imbued with racism. The PBS series *American Experience* produced a documentary titled *The Murder of Emmett Till*, and having students watch parts or all of this film humanizes a tragedy of the civil rights era. If your school does not own a copy, it can be watched online at PBS's American Experience website (pbs.org/wgbh/americanexperience).

TEACHING IDEA

Incorporating Websites

Carolyn Bryant, the white woman who accused Emmett Till, admitted years later that her accusation was false. Share excerpts from Sheila Weller's article, "How Author Timothy Tyson Found the Woman at the Center of the Emmett Till Case" from Vanity Fair's website with students to gain fuller understanding of the tragedy (vanityfair.com).

TEACHING IDEA

Building Vocabulary

As students use Map 8.3 detailing the areas where lunch counter sit-ins occurred, consider having a conversation about the trends in the geography of the protest. For instance, students should notice that many of the sit-ins occurred in Virginia and North Carolina, states some historians refer to as "Upper South." Ask students why the sit-ins most often occurred in these states, as opposed to Mississippi or Alabama.

The Desegregation of Central High School, 1957 In 1957 nine black teenagers attempted to desegregate Central High School in Little Rock, Arkansas, pursuant to a federal court order. This photograph captures fifteen-year-old Elizabeth Eckford, one of the Little Rock Nine, surrounded by an angry white crowd on the first day of school. The photo also shows an enraged white student, Hazel Bryan, shouting at her to go home. Neither Eckford nor the other black students managed to attend school that day, but they entered Central High after President Eisenhower sent in federal troops to protect them. **What role did students play in the battle to desegregate schools?**

The WCC and the KKK created a racial climate in the deep South that encouraged whites to believe they could get away with murder to defend white supremacy. In the summer of 1955, Emmett Till, a fourteen-year-old from Chicago who was visiting his great-uncle in Mississippi, was kidnapped and brutally beaten to death because he allegedly flirted with a white woman in a country store. Till's mother insisted on an open casket funeral. The horrifying photographs of his badly mutilated body shocked African Americans across the country and brought widespread attention to the injustice of white

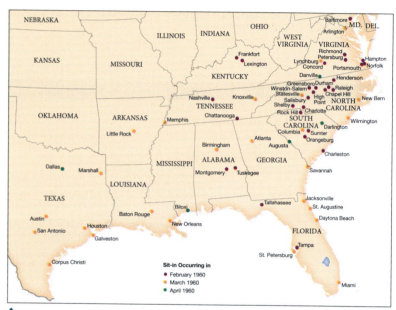

▲ **MAP 8.3 Lunch Counter Sit-Ins, February–April 1960** After starting slowly in the late 1950s, lunch counter sit-ins exploded in 1960 following a sit-in by college students in Greensboro, North Carolina. Within three months, sit-ins erupted in fifty-eight cities across the South. The participation of high school and college students revitalized the civil rights movement and led to the formation of the Student Nonviolent Coordinating Committee in April 1960. **How did the sit-in movement differ from prominent civil rights protests in the 1950s?**

supremacist violence. Although the two accused killers were quickly brought to trial, an all-white jury acquitted them. The following year, the acquitted killers admitted their guilt in a paid magazine interview, knowing they could not be tried again because of legal protections against double jeopardy. In 2007, Till's accuser confessed that she had lied under oath about Till's behavior toward her.

With boycotts petering out and white violence rising, African Americans, especially high school and college students, developed new techniques to confront discrimination, including sit-ins, in which protesters seat themselves in a strategic spot and refuse to move until their demands are met or they are forcibly evicted. These mass protests did not really get off the ground until February 1960, when four students at North Carolina A&T University in Greensboro initiated sit-ins at the whites-only lunch counters in Woolworth and Kress department stores. Their demonstrations sparked similar efforts throughout the Southeast, leading to fifty-eight sit-ins within three months.

A few months after the sit-ins began, a number of participants formed the **Student Nonviolent Coordinating Committee (SNCC)**. The organization's young members sought not only to challenge racial segregation in the South but also to create interracial communities based on economic equality and political democracy. This generation of black and white sit-in veterans came of age in

Student Nonviolent Coordinating Committee (SNCC) Civil rights organization that grew out of the sit-ins of 1960. The organization focused on taking direct action and political organizing to achieve its goals.

AP® ANALYZING SOURCES

Source: Ella Baker, "Bigger Than a Hamburger," *Southern Patriot*, June 1960

"The Student Leadership Conference[1] made it crystal clear that current sit-ins and other demonstrations are concerned with something much bigger than a hamburger or even a giant-sized Coke.

Whatever may be the difference in approach to their goal, the Negro and white students, North and South, are seeking to rid America of the scourge of racial segregation and discrimination—not only at lunch counters, but in every aspect of life.

In reports, casual conversations, discussion groups, and speeches, the sense and the spirit of the following statement that appeared in the initial newsletter of the students at Barber-Scotia College, Concord, N.C., were re-echoed time and again: 'We want the world to know that we no longer accept the inferior position of second-class citizenship. We are willing to go to jail, be ridiculed, spat upon, and even suffer physical violence to obtain First Class Citizenship.'

By and large, this feeling that they have a destined date with freedom, was not limited to a drive for personal freedom, or even freedom for the Negro in the South. Repeatedly it was emphasized that the movement was concerned with the moral implications of racial discrimination for the 'whole world' and the 'Human Race.' This universality of approach was linked with a perceptive recognition that 'it is important to keep the movement democratic and to avoid struggles for personal leadership.'

It was further evident that desire for supportive cooperation from adult leaders and the adult community was also tempered by apprehension that adults might try to 'capture' the student movement. The students showed willingness to be met on the basis of equality, but were intolerant of anything that smacked of manipulation or domination."

[1] A meeting of students sponsored by the Southern Christian Leadership Conference.

Questions for Analysis
1. Identify the main goal of the Student Leadership Conference, according to Baker.
2. Describe the similarities and differences in tactics discussed in the excerpt.
3. Explain why Baker believes the movement is "bigger than a hamburger."

Questions for Comparison *The Southern Manifesto*, 1956 (p. 733)
1. Explain how the context surrounding each document informs the central argument it makes.
2. Explain how Baker defines "rights" differently than the signers of *The Southern Manifesto*.
3. Evaluate the extent to which the new generation of civil rights activists challenged both southern segregationists and older civil rights advocates.

TRM Suggested Responses to Questions

TRM Module 8.5 AP® Analyzing Sources Handout 3

BUILDING AP® SKILLS

Sourcing and Situation

Prior to having students read the document by Ella Baker, ask students to brainstorm the ways students were involved in grassroots activism prior to 1960. Consider providing students with one sticky note each. On the sticky note they should write their answer and as everyone finishes, have students place the answers on the front board of class. Next, the teacher can gather and categorize the responses and discuss the results. The goal is for students to see the many ways in which students were involved in civil rights activism.

BUILDING AP® SKILLS

Comparison

Both SNCC and SCLC were committed to a strategy of non-violence as they fought for civil rights. While the groups have some important similarities, they also possess a few distinctive differences. Consider having students complete a Venn diagram about SNCC and SCLC.

TRM Find **Handout 8.5 – Comparing Civil Rights Activists** in the Teacher's Resource Handout.

BUILDING AP® SKILLS

Claims and Evidence in Sources

Have students look for a specific excerpt from the document that illustrates a claim about generational divide in the civil rights movement. One of the reasons Ella Baker wanted students to develop their own organization stemmed from her fear that adults were not giving students the autonomy they needed to be successful. After students locate an excerpt, consider having them write a 1 or 2 sentence explanation about Baker's claim.

the 1950s at a time when Cold War democratic rhetoric and the Supreme Court's *Brown* decision raised their expectations for racial equality. Yet these young activists often saw their hopes dashed by southern segregationist resistance, including the murder of Emmett Till, which both horrified and helped mobilize them to fight for black equality.

REVIEW

- What tactics did white supremacists use to resist social change in the South?
- What accounts for the similarities and differences between the Student Nonviolent Coordinating Committee (SNCC) and the Southern Christian Leadership Conference (SCLC)?

The Civil Rights Movement and Minority Struggles in the West

World War II also sparked a continuation of the migration of African Americans to the West, part of the **Great Migration** (see Module 7-5), and part of the larger population movement to the Sun Belt. From 1940 to 1960, the black population in the region jumped from 4.9 to 5.4 percent of the total population and numbered more than 1.2 million. Encountering various forms of racial discrimination, African Americans waged boycotts and sit-ins of businesses that refused black people equal service in Lawrence, Kansas and Albuquerque, New Mexico. Perhaps the most significant protest occurred in Oklahoma City. In August 1958, the teenagers of the NAACP Youth Council and their adult adviser, Clara M. Luper, led sit-ins to desegregate lunch counters in downtown stores. Having succeeded in integrating a dozen facilities, the movement waged a six-year struggle to end discrimination in public accommodations throughout the city.

Like African Americans, other groups in the postwar West struggled for equality. For Mexican Americans World War II inspired such efforts. In southern California, Unity Leagues formed to protest segregation, and they often joined with African American groups in seeking equality. In 1947, the League of United Latin American Citizens (LULAC) won a case in federal court in *Mendez v. Westminster* prohibiting separate public schools for Mexican-American students. Spurred on by such efforts, Mexican Americans in 1949 succeeded in electing Edward Roybal to the Los Angeles City Council, the first American of Mexican descent to serve on that body since 1888. In Texas LULAC succeeded through litigation and boycotts in desegregating movie theaters, swimming pools, restaurants, and other public accommodations. LULAC also brought an end to discrimination in jury selection. Once Jackie Robinson integrated baseball in 1947, he opened the way for Afro-Hispanic ballplayers. Two years later, Orestes "Minnie" Miñoso, an Afro-Cuban, made it to the major leagues and the Cleveland Indians.

World War II had advanced civil rights for the Chinese. In 1943 Congress repealed the exclusion law and followed up by passing the War Brides Act in 1945, which resulted in the admission of 6,000 Chinese women to the United States. However, the fall of China to the Communists in 1949 and the beginning of the Korean War the next year posed new challenges to Chinese communities on the West Coast. Although organizations such as the Six Companies of San Francisco denounced Communist China and pledged their loyalty to the United States, Cold War witch-hunts targeted the Chinese. With the Chinese Communists fighting against the United States in Korea, some regarded Chinese people in America with suspicion. "People would look at you in the street and think," one Chinese woman recalled, "'Well you're one of the enemy.'" The federal government established a "Confession Program" by which Chinese people illegally in the country would be allowed to stay if they came forward, acknowledged their loyalty to the United States, and provided information about friends and relatives. Some 10,000 Chinese in San Francisco participated in this program.

Despite these hardships, the Chinese made great economic strides. Chinatowns shrank in population as their upwardly mobile residents moved to the suburbs. By 1959 Chinese Americans had a median family income of $6,207, compared with $5,660 for all Americans.

EXPLORING AP® THEMES

Migration and Settlement

The Great Migration of African Americans in the early-to-mid twentieth century is a crucial part of the civil rights movement. Consider extending students' analysis of this topic by assigning Chapter 4, "The Passage to the North," of Ira Berlin's book, *The Making of African America: The Four Great Migrations*. This critical accounting of the Great Migration can help students make connections across the twentieth century. Ask students to describe the cultural, political, economic, and social effects of this migration pattern.

TEACHING IDEA

Incorporating Primary Sources

Langston Hughes published a poem titled "Long View Negro: Emancipation 1865," and it is in many ways a reflection of what many civil rights activists felt about the progress of the movement by the mid-1960s. This poem can be found on The Poetry Foundation's website (poetryfoundation.org). Reading and discussing this poem can be a great bell ringer activity for students as they learn about the development of civil rights activism. The poem is short and compares emancipation in 1865 to the reality of civil rights in 1965.

BUILDING AP® SKILLS

Comparison

As students begin to read about civil rights among other minority groups, consider assigning them a comparative analysis of Latinos with African Americans. In this exercise, students will be looking for similarities only. Broad categories of society, politics, and economics allow students to look for more discrete examples of similarities.

During the late 1940s and 1950s, Japanese Americans attempted to rebuild their lives following their wartime evacuation and internment. Overall, they did remarkably well. Although many returned to the West Coast and found their neighborhoods occupied by other ethnic groups and their businesses in other hands, they took whatever jobs they could find and stressed education for their children. The **McCarran-Walter Immigration Act** of 1952 made it possible for Japanese non-citizens to become U.S. citizens, though it maintained a race-based system of immigration and discriminatory quotas. In addition, California repealed its Alien Land Law of 1913, which prohibited noncitizen Japanese from purchasing land. In 1955 about 40,000 Japanese Americans lived in Los Angeles, a figure slightly higher than the city's prewar population. Like other Americans, they began moving their families to suburbs such as Gardena, a half-hour ride from downtown Los Angeles. Still, the federal government neither apologized for its wartime treatment of the Japanese nor awarded them financial compensation for their losses; this would happen three decades later.

REVIEW

- What similarities did the strategies employed by Mexican Americans, Chinese Americans, and Japanese Americans to gain civil rights share?

- How did these strategies draw on those used by African American civil rights activists?

AP® WRITING HISTORICALLY — Short-Answer Question Practice

ACTIVITY

Read the following question carefully and write a short response. Use complete sentences.

Using the following excerpts, answer (a), (b), and (c).

Source: Jacquelyn Dowd Hall, "The Long Civil Rights Movement and the Political Uses of the Past," *Journal of American History*, 2005

> "Another force also rose from the caldron of the Great Depression and crested in the 1940s: a powerful social movement sparked by the alchemy of laborites, civil rights activists, progressive New Dealers, and black and white radicals, some of whom were associated with the Communist party. . . . [T]he movement's commitment to building coalitions, the expansiveness of its social democratic vision, and the importance of its black radical and laborite leadership. A national movement with a vital southern wing, civil rights unionism was not just a precursor of the modern civil rights movement. It was its decisive first phase.
>
> The link between race and class lay at the heart of the movement's political imagination. . . . [C]ivil rights unionists sought to combine protection from discrimination with universalistic social welfare policies and individual rights with labor rights. For them, workplace democracy, union wages, and fair and full employment went hand in hand with open, affordable housing, political enfranchisement, educational equity, and an enhanced safety net, including health care for all. . . . Extending the New Deal and reforming the South were two sides of the same coin. . . . To challenge the southern Democrats' congressional stranglehold, the movement had to enfranchise black and white southern workers and bring them into the house of labor, thus creating a constituency on which the region's emerging pro-civil rights, pro-labor politicians could rely."

(Continued)

TRM Suggested Responses to Questions

EXPLORING AP® THEMES

American and National Identity

One of the challenges students face when studying the civil rights movement is coming to terms with how we remember the movement and what legacy is attributed to the movement. Historian Jacquelyn Dowd Hall addresses this concept in a short video on Gilder Lehrman's AP® U.S. History site (ap.gilderlehrman.org). Go to Period 8 to find the video. Prior to watching the video you can give students an open-ended question that acts as a precursor to the purpose of the video. Consider using the time to focus on an AP® theme such as American Identity. Think about using questions such as:

- How did the American identity on race change as a result of the civil rights movement?

- How was the civil rights movement of the 1950s a turning point in Americans' sense of their collective identity?

These questions and the video can be a nice way to bring the module to a close.

TEACHING IDEA

Building Vocabulary

Sometimes historians will use words that students are less familiar with or have never encountered before. Understanding vocabulary in short excerpts is essential to unpacking what the historian is arguing. In this excerpt, consider writing caldron, alchemy, universalistic social welfare, and enfranchise on the board at the beginning of the class period. See if any students are able to define the words. If none are able, divide students into groups of four and have a student be responsible for looking up and defining each word or phrase. Next, each group member shares with their group so that full understanding is achieved.

BUILDING AP® SKILLS

Claims and Evidence in Sources

Similar to Hall's excerpt on page 737, it is important for students to understand phrases and words in a passage so they are better able to unpack the argument. Consider selecting the following phrases and ask groups of 3 or 4 students to define what their meaning is in their own language: "genuine economic democracy," "institutional structures," and "state-supported white supremacy." Being able to define these phrases correctly is paramount to understanding the argument.

TEACHING IDEA

AP® Writing Historically Review

The Short-Answer Questions that provide two secondary sources in opposition typically cover major events in U.S. history such as the origins of the civil rights movement. Sometimes the historians' interpretations vary greatly, other times there are subtleties that separate the excerpts. To distill students' focus, have them write a one-sentence explanation for each paragraph in each excerpt. Next, have them explain each excerpt in one sentence, without using too much of the language found in the excerpt. Students need to remember they are explaining the differences between the excerpts, as opposed to giving a synopsis of each interpretation using the same words already provided by the historians. This is a crucial distinction to make with students.

Source: Steven F. Lawson, "Long Origins of the Short Civil Rights Movement, 1954–1968," in *Freedom Rights: New Perspectives on the Civil Rights Movement,* 2011

"There was a genuine movement for social change in the South during the New Deal era, but it took on a different shape from the civil rights movement that followed in the next two decades. Civil rights unions . . . performed the work of extending civil rights and laid the groundwork for what followed, but this remained distinct from the civil rights movement. . . . Class mattered more than race, and critics targeted capitalism as the source of black oppression. . . . [O]nly through a restructuring of corporate capitalism would genuine economic democracy emerge and white supremacy collapse. Although African American progressives actively participated in unions . . . , the leadership and membership of these organizations in in the South consisted mainly of whites. . . . These activists were courageous, visionary, and essential, but they composed only a tiny fraction of the southern population. Their influence should be neither ignored nor exaggerated. . . .

[B]y the time of the *Brown* decision and [Emmett] Till's murder, African Americans possessed the institutional structures necessary to mobilize to close the gap between their expectations of change and the brutal reality of white supremacy. At the national level the NAACP led the way, followed by the SCLC, CORE, and SNCC. Indeed, after *Brown,* state-led efforts to destroy the NAACP, considered the most radical of black organizations by southern white authorities, spurred the creation of new protest organizations locally and throughout the South. Black churches, civic associations, and informal community networks added organizational muscle to the demands for racial equality during the 1950s and 1960s. Without these structures . . . , the yearning for civil rights would not have grown into a movement, and people would not have taken action against the power of state-supported white supremacy."

a. Briefly explain ONE major difference between Hall's and Lawson's interpretations of the origins of the civil rights movement.
b. Briefly explain how ONE specific historical event or development from the period that is not explicitly mentioned in the excerpts could be used to support Hall's argument.
c. Briefly explain how ONE specific historical event or development that is not explicitly mentioned in the excerpts could be used to support Lawson's argument.

Module 8-6

The Cold War Expands at Home and Abroad, 1953–1961

LEARNING TARGETS

By the end of this module, you should be able to:
- Explain how the Eisenhower administration pursued a policy of containment abroad and Modern Republicanism at home.
- Explain why President Eisenhower warned against the emergence of a military-industrial complex in his farewell address.
- Explain how Eisenhower administration policies affected American Indians and Mexican immigrants.
- Explain how foreign policy challenges during the Kennedy administration intensified the Cold War.

THEMATIC FOCUS

**Politics and Power
America in the World**

President Eisenhower oversaw a shift in U.S. military spending as his administration emphasized the production of nuclear weapons over conventional forces. After the development of the hydrogen bomb in the early 1950s, an arms race ensued with the Soviet Union and a policy of deterrence based on mutually assured destruction took hold. Domestically, Eisenhower increased federal spending on highways to speed mobilization of U.S. military forces in wartime, and education funding to counter Soviet advances in rocket technology. In 1960, Kennedy defeated Nixon in a close election in which both candidates promised to take a hard line against communism. Two years later the Cuban Missile Crisis brought the U.S. and USSR to the brink of war before it was peacefully resolved. To prevent Communist gains in Latin America, Asia, and Africa the U.S. often supported repressive regimes, and sometimes engineered CIA supported coups to install friendlier governments.

HISTORICAL REASONING FOCUS

Comparison

TASK ▶ As you read this module, consider the Cold War developments in the 1950s and early 1960s. Compare the responses of Truman (see Module 8-1), Eisenhower, and Kennedy. Analyze how American politics and society were impacted by Cold War events during each presidential administration.

With the end of the Korean War in 1953, the United States and the Soviet Union each spent huge sums of money and manpower building up their arsenal of nuclear weapons and military forces. They did not engage directly on the battlefield, but they attempted to spread their influence around the world while protecting their spheres of influence closer to their borders. The growing presence of nuclear weapons hung over diplomatic crises wherever they emerged, occasionally prompting the leaders of the two most powerful nations to seek an accommodation.

Despite the existence of civil rights protesters, rock 'n' roll upstarts, intellectual dissenters, and sexual revolutionaries, the 1950s seemed to many a tranquil, even dull period. This impression owes a great deal to the leadership of President Dwight D. Eisenhower. Serving two terms from 1953 to 1961, Eisenhower, or "Ike" as he was affectionately called, convinced the majority

---

TRM Suggested Responses to Questions

BUILDING AP® SKILLS

Comparison

Consider assigning students a comparison chart that asks them to compare and contrast the unique policies of Presidents Truman, Eisenhower, and Kennedy. Each president has one aspect of their foreign policy — containment, brinkmanship, and flexible response — and the task for each student is to find similarities and differences among the policies of these presidents as they work their way through Module 8-6. While not all-encompassing, the goal is to make students aware of comparison throughout the module.

TEACHING IDEA

Geography Instruction

Give students blank world maps from Module 8-1 and ask them to color-code at least two spheres of influence for the Soviets and Americans. The goal is for students to imagine what areas of the world both super powers were most interested in during the period from 1945 to 1963.

EXPLORING AP® THEMES

America in the World

Consider giving students the following prompt: Provide three specific historical examples about how the United States and its role in the world changed from 1945 to 1959. Examples will include, but not be limited to, answers such as the leader of the UN, leader of NATO, believer in a permanent military establishment in Europe and Asia, and leading economic power.

BUILDING AP® SKILLS

Claims and Evidence in Sources

President Eisenhower's farewell address, often referred to as the military-industrial complex speech, is required reading of students. Therefore, use the excerpt on page 743 for a condensed version and ask students to identify Eisenhower's claim about how U.S. foreign policy changed as a result of World War II.

TEACHING IDEA

Building Vocabulary

Under President Eisenhower, the United States talked about a dramatic change in foreign policy called the "New Look" strategy. To evaluate the extent to which this actually evolved into a significant change, provide students with the following comparison activity. Give students two categories of analysis. One category will be labeled "continuity with President Truman's containment strategy," while the other will be labeled "change from President Truman's containment strategy." Students have to list as many examples as they can for both categories. The goal is to develop students' awareness of the continuities and changes to American foreign policy under President Eisenhower.

TEACHING IDEA

Incorporating Videos

Eugene Jarecki's documentary, *Why We Fight*, is an excellent resource for teachers looking to explain the changes to American foreign policy under President Eisenhower. The film uses the military-industrial complex speech as a vehicle of analysis. Of particular note is how well the film details the immediate buildup in the armaments industry following World War II and what effects it had on the home front.

Period 8: 1945–1980

MODULE 8-6 The Cold War Expands at Home and Abroad, 1953–1961

of Americans that their country was in good hands regardless of political turbulence at home and heated international conflicts abroad.

By 1960, however, the nation was ready for a new generation of leadership. In a close election, John F. Kennedy defeated Eisenhower's vice president, Richard Nixon, becoming the youngest person ever elected to the White House. In office, Kennedy faced a series of Cold War challenges in Cuba, Vietnam, and Berlin that threatened to draw the United States into conflict overseas.

Nuclear Weapons and Containment

In foreign affairs, President Dwight D. Eisenhower perpetuated Truman's containment doctrine while at the same time espousing the contradictory principle of "rolling back" communism in Eastern Europe. However, when Hungarians rose up against their Soviet-backed regime in 1956, the U.S. government did little in response. Rather than pushing back communism, the Eisenhower administration expanded the doctrine of containment around the world by entering into treaties to establish regional defense pacts.

Eisenhower's commitment to fiscal discipline had a profound effect on his foreign policy. The president worried that the alliance among government, defense contractors, and research universities — which he dubbed "the military-industrial complex" — would bankrupt the economy and undermine individual freedom. With this in mind, he implemented the **New Look** strategy, which placed a higher priority on building a nuclear arsenal and delivery system than on the more expensive task of maintaining and deploying armed forces on the ground throughout the world. Nuclear missiles launched from the air by U.S. air force bombers or fired from submarines would give the United States, as Secretary of Defense Charles Wilson asserted, "a bigger bang for the buck." With the nation now armed with nuclear weapons, the Eisenhower administration threatened "massive retaliation" in the event of Communist aggression.

The New Look may have saved money and slowed the rate of defense spending, but it had serious flaws. First, it placed a premium on "brinksmanship," taking Communist enemies to the precipice of nuclear destruction, risking the death of millions, and hoping the other side would back down. Second, massive retaliation did not work for small-scale conflicts. For instance, in the event of a confrontation in Berlin, would the United States launch nuclear missiles toward Germany and expose its European allies in West Germany and France to nuclear contamination? Third, the buildup of nuclear warheads provoked an arms race by encouraging the Soviet Union to do the same. Peace depended on the superpowers terrifying each other with the threat of nuclear annihilation — that is, if one country attacked the other, retaliation was guaranteed to result in shared obliteration. This strategy was known as **mutually assured destruction**, and its acronym — MAD — summed up its nightmarish qualities. As each nuclear power increased its capacity to destroy the other many times over, the potential for mistakes and errors in judgment increased, threatening a nuclear holocaust that would leave little to rebuild.

National security concerns occupied a good deal of the president's time. Fearing that a Soviet nuclear attack could wipe out nearly a third of the population before

mutually assured destruction (MAD) Defense strategy built around the threat of a massive nuclear retaliatory strike. Adoption of the doctrine of mutually assured destruction contributed to the escalation of the nuclear arms race during the Cold War.

◀ **Bomb Shelter, 1954** The successful test of an atomic bomb by the Soviets in 1949 followed by the Korean War prompted many Americans to begin preparing for a possible nuclear attack. This Houston, Texas family, including their dog, pose in their bomb shelter stocked with food, first aid supplies, weapons, and ammunition. **What does this photograph suggest about the values and anxieties of middle-class American families in the 1950s?**

John Dominis/Getty Images

the United States could retaliate, the Eisenhower administration stepped up civil defense efforts. Schoolchildren took part in "duck and cover" drills, in which teachers shouted "take cover" and students hid under their desks. In the meantime, both the United States and the Soviet Union began producing intercontinental ballistic missiles armed with nuclear warheads. They also stepped up aboveground tests of nuclear weapons, which contaminated the atmosphere with dangerous radioactive particles.

Despite doomsday rhetoric of massive retaliation, Eisenhower generally relied more on diplomacy than on military action. Stalin's death in 1953 and his eventual replacement by Nikita Khrushchev in 1955 permitted a relaxation of tensions between the two superpowers. In July 1955 Eisenhower and Khrushchev, together with British and French leaders, gathered in Geneva to discuss arms control. Nothing concrete came out of this summit, but Eisenhower and Khrushchev did ease tensions between the two nations. In a speech to Communist officials two years later, Khrushchev denounced the excesses of Stalin's totalitarian rule and reinforced hopes for a new era of peaceful coexistence between the Cold War antagonists. In 1958, Vice President Richard Nixon visited the Soviet Union, the first top elected official to do so since the onset of the Cold War, as a sign of warming relations between the two nations. Nixon and Khrushchev attended a U.S. exhibition in Moscow on July 24, 1959, where the two leaders debated the relative merits of capitalism and communism, while looking at an American kitchen that displayed the latest household appliances. This so-called **Kitchen Debate** did not dissuade Khrushchev from making a twelve-day visit to the United States later that year. Yet peaceful coexistence remained precarious. Just as President Eisenhower was about to begin his own tour of the Soviet Union in 1960, the Soviets shot down an American U-2 spy plane flying over their country. Eisenhower canceled his trip, and tensions resumed.

REVIEW

In what ways did Eisenhower's foreign policy toward the USSR differ from Truman's approach?

Interventions in the Middle East, Latin America, and Africa

While relations between the Soviet Union and the United States thawed and then cooled during the Eisenhower era, the Cold War advanced into new regions. The efforts of Iranian, Guatemalan, and Cuban leaders to seize control of their countries' resources mirrored the surge of nationalism that swept through former European colonies in the 1950s. Following World War II, revolutionary nationalists in the Middle East, Africa, and Southeast Asia toppled colonial governments and wielded the power of their newly liberated regimes to take charge of their own development. Postwar decolonization and the rise of militant nationalism collided with U.S. Cold War policy, as these non-white nations remained neutral. At the **Bandung Conference** in Indonesia in 1955, twenty-nine Asian and African nations, many of them recently liberated, condemned continued colonization, particularly control in North Africa by France, a close U.S. ally, and asserted their intention to remain non-aligned with either side in the Cold War. The U.S. government took a dim view of the Bandung Conference and refused to send representatives. Especially worrisome to the U.S., the Communist Chinese government made serious overtures to form closer relations with these nations. The United States frequently took a heavy handed approach when it suspected newly decolonized nations were edging to the side of the Soviets. In a manner first suggested in NSC-68, the Eisenhower administration deployed the CIA to help topple governments considered pro-Communist as well as to promote U.S. economic interests. For example, after Prime Minister Mohammed Mossadegh of Iran nationalized foreign oil corporations in 1953, the CIA engineered a successful coup that ousted his government and installed the pro-American shah Mohammad Reza Pahlavi in his place. Mossadegh was not a Communist, but by overthrowing him American oil companies obtained 40 percent of Iran's oil revenue.

In 1954 the economics of fruit and shipping replaced oil as the catalyst for U.S. intervention into a developing nation within its own sphere of influence. The elected socialist regime of Jacobo Arbenz Guzmán in Guatemala had seized 225,000 acres of land held by the United Fruit

TEACHING IDEA

Incorporating Videos

Throughout the 1950s the Civil Defense Agency produced public service announcements about the dangers of nuclear war and what Americans should do in the event of one. Perhaps the most famous of these was the "Bert the Turtle" video. Examples of this ten-minute video are available on YouTube through title search.

TEACHING IDEA

Incorporating Videos

During the so-called "Kitchen Debate," Vice President Nixon focused much of his energy on comparing technological and consumer goods. Consider showing students footage of portions of this debate in class. Multiple examples can be easily found by searching "Kitchen Debate" on YouTube. Have students take notes on the ways in which Vice President Nixon uses technological and consumer goods to verbally spar with Nikita Khrushchev.

EXPLORING AP® THEMES

America in the World

Many students will likely be very unfamiliar with the details of the Bandung Conference; however, most students will remember well topics such as imperialism, colonialism, and nationalism. Knowing these themes will allow students to better understand key takeaways to this example of Cold War foreign policy. Consider asking students to reconcile the claim that the United States was for political freedom around the world and yet chose not to send representatives. This is a good activity to have students form groups to develop answers. After groups have developed answers, consider having each group share out so students can hear a wide array of responses.

TEACHING IDEA

Check for Understanding

The CIA changed dramatically under President Eisenhower because he actively used them in missions meant to change the political structure of countries throughout the world. Three in particular — Cuba, Guatemala, and Iran — are useful examples of how Eisenhower used the CIA in Cold War foreign policy. Consider dividing students into groups of three and assign each student Cuba, Guatemala, or Iran. Their goal is to explain how the CIA was used in these countries and the extent of its effectiveness.

TEACHING IDEA

Connecting the Dots

Nationalism is a concept students are already familiar with from earlier modules. Consider having students explain the revolutions in Cuba and Egypt in two steps. In the first step, students explain the revolutions from the perspective of increased nationalism within those countries. In the second step, students explain the perspective of American policymakers and their view of the nationalist leaders from Cuba and Egypt.

BUILDING AP® SKILLS

Comparison

Both the Truman Doctrine of containment and the Eisenhower Doctrine of containment are required information for students. Both of these speeches are available in full form at the Avalon Project (avalon.law.yale.edu). Therefore, consider having students compare and contrast the purposes and effectiveness of these policies. Students need to develop at least two differences and one similarity in the purposes and effectiveness of these policies.

TRM Find **Handout 8.6 – Comparing the Truman Doctrine and the Eisenhower Doctrine** in the Teacher's Resource Materials.

Company, a powerful American company in which Secretary of State John Foster Dulles and his brother, CIA director Allen Dulles, held stock. According to the Dulles brothers, the land's seizure by the Guatemalan government posed a threat to the nearby Panama Canal. Eisenhower allowed the CIA to hatch a plot that resulted in a coup d'état, or government overthrow, that installed a right-wing military regime in Guatemala, which safeguarded both the Panama Canal and the United Fruit Company.

The success of the CIA's covert efforts in Guatemala prompted the Eisenhower administration to plan a similar action in Cuba, ninety miles off the coast of Florida. In 1959 Fidel Castro led an uprising and came to power in Cuba after overthrowing the American-backed dictator Fulgencio Batista. A Cuban nationalist in the tradition of José Martí, Castro sought to regain full control over his country's economic resources, including those owned by U.S. corporations. He appropriated $1 billion worth of American property and signed a trade agreement with the Soviet Union. To consolidate his political rule, Castro jailed opponents and installed a Communist regime. In 1960 President Eisenhower authorized the CIA to design a clandestine operation to overthrow the Castro government, but he left office before the invasion could occur.

The United States and the Soviet Union each tried to gain influence over emerging nations. Many newly independent countries tried to practice neutrality in foreign affairs, accepting aid from both of the Cold War protagonists. Nonetheless, they were often drawn into East-West conflicts. Such was the case in Egypt, which achieved independence from Great Britain in 1952. Two years later, under General Gamal Abdel Nasser, the country sought to modernize its economy by building the hydroelectric Aswan Dam on the Nile River. Nasser welcomed financial backing from the United States and the Soviet Union, but the Eisenhower administration refused to contribute so long as the Egyptians accepted Soviet assistance. In 1956 Nasser, falling short of funds, sent troops to take over the Suez Canal, the waterway run by Great Britain and through which the bulk of Western Europe's oil was shipped. He intended to pay for the dam by collecting tolls from canal users. In retaliation, Britain and France, the two European powers most affected by the seizure, invaded Egypt on October 29, 1956. Locked in a struggle with Egypt and other Arab nations since its creation in 1948, Israel joined in the attack. The invading forces — all U.S. allies — had not warned the Eisenhower administration of their plans. Coming at the same time as the Soviet crackdown against the Hungarian revolution, the British-French-Israeli assault placed the United States in the difficult position of condemning the Soviets for intervening in Hungary while its anti-Communist partners waged war in Suez. Instead, Eisenhower cooperated with the United Nations to negotiate a cease-fire and engineer a pullout of the invading forces in Egypt. Ultimately, the Soviets proved the winners in this Cold War skirmish. The Suez invasion revived memories of European imperialism and fueled anti-Western sentiments and pan-Arab nationalism (a sense of unity among Arabs across national boundaries), which worked to the Soviets' advantage.

The Eisenhower administration soon moved to counter growing Soviet power in the region. In 1957, to throttle increasing Communist influence in the Middle East, Congress approved the **Eisenhower Doctrine**, which gave the president a free hand to use U.S. military forces in the Middle East "against overt armed aggression from any nation controlled by International Communism." In actuality, the Eisenhower administration proved more concerned with protecting access to oil fields from hostile Arab nationalist leaders than with any Communist incursion. In 1958, when an anti-American, non-Communist regime came to power in Iraq, the president sent 14,000 marines to neighboring Lebanon to prevent a similar outcome there.

Just before Eisenhower left office in January 1961, his administration intervened in a civil war in the newly independent Congo. This former colony of Belgium held valuable mineral resources, which Belgium and the United States coveted. After the Congo's first prime minister, Patrice Lumumba, stated his intentions to remain neutral in the Cold War, President Eisenhower and CIA director Allen Dulles declared him unreliable in the conflict with the Soviet Union. With the support of Belgian military troops and encouragement from the United States, the resource-rich province of Katanga seceded from the Congo in 1960. After the Congolese military, under the leadership of Joseph Mobuto, overthrew Lumumba's government, the CIA launched an operation that culminated in the execution of Lumumba on January 17, 1961. Several years later, Mobuto became president of the country, changed its name to Zaire, and allied with the West.

Eisenhower Doctrine A doctrine guiding U.S. intervention in the Middle East. In 1957 Congress granted President Dwight Eisenhower the power to send military forces into the Middle East to combat Communist aggression. Eisenhower sent U.S. marines into Lebanon in 1958 under this doctrine.

AP® ANALYZING SOURCES

Source: President Dwight D. Eisenhower, *Farewell Address*, 1961

"Our military organization today bears little relation to that known by any of my predecessors in peacetime, or indeed by the fighting men of World War II or Korea.

Until the latest of our world conflicts, the United States had no armaments industry. American makers of plowshares could, with time and as required, make swords as well.

But now we can no longer risk emergency improvisation of national defense; we have been compelled to create a permanent armaments industry of vast proportions.

Added to this, three and a half million men and women are directly engaged in the defense establishment.

We annually spend on military security more than the net income of all United States Corporations.

This conjunction of an immense military establishment and a large arms industry is new in the American experience.

The total influence — economic, political, even spiritual — is felt in every city, every State house, every office of the Federal government. . . .

In the councils of government, we must guard against the acquisition of unwarranted influence, whether sought or unsought, by the military-industrial complex.

The potential for the disastrous rise of misplaced power exists and will persist.

We must never let the weight of this combination endanger our liberties or democratic processes.

We should take nothing for granted.

Only an alert and knowledgeable citizenry can compel the proper meshing of the huge industrial and military machinery of defense with our peaceful methods and goals, so that security and liberty may prosper together."

Questions for Analysis

1. Identify the main concern Eisenhower expresses in the excerpt.
2. Describe the change in the American military establishment after World War II reflected in this excerpt.
3. Explain the context for Eisenhower's address and the concerns he expresses in it.
4. Evaluate the extent to which the Eisenhower administration's foreign policy contributed to the development of the American military-industrial complex.

TRM Suggested Responses to Questions

TRM Module 8.6 AP® Analyzing Sources Handout 1

BUILDING AP® SKILLS

Claims and Evidence in Sources

Consider having students focus on finding the most important takeaways to the *Farewell Address* by President Eisenhower. Two takeaways students should have are both his support of and warning about what he called a "permanent armaments industry of vast proportions." This is the essence of the speech. President Eisenhower was certainly concerned with the expansive growth of this industry, yet he recognized the need for such a development. Remind students that the nuance of this position is one of the reasons this is such an important document. Have students develop 1 or 2 sentence explanations for both positions.

▲ **Differentiation**

If students are struggling to explain both positions, divide students into groups of four. Have two students from the group work to explain the position of supporting the growth of the industry and have the other two students work to explain the position of concern. Once students have their responses, have each pair share their result with the other.

REVIEW

How did the Cold War shape the United States' foreign policy toward Latin American, African, and Middle Eastern nations during the mid-twentieth century?

Modern Republicanism and the Election of 1960

Modern Republicanism The political approach of President Dwight Eisenhower that tried to fit traditional Republican Party ideals of individualism and fiscal restraint within the broad framework of the New Deal.

President Eisenhower, a World War II hero, radiated strength and trust, qualities the American people found very attractive as they rebuilt their lives and established families in the 1950s. In November 1952, Eisenhower coasted to victory over the Democratic candidate Adlai Stevenson, winning 55 percent of the popular vote and 83 percent of the electoral vote. The Republicans managed to win slim majorities in the Senate and the House, but within two years the Democrats regained control of Congress.

Eisenhower adopted what one of his speechwriters called **Modern Republicanism**, which tried to fit the traditional Republican Party ideals of individualism and fiscal restraint within the broad framework of Franklin Roosevelt's New Deal. As Eisenhower wrote to his brother, "Should any political party attempt to abolish social security, unemployment insurance, and eliminate labor laws and farm programs, you would not hear of that party again in our political history." With

EXPLORING AP® THEMES

Politics and Power

The changing nature of the Republican Party in the aftermath of the New Deal and World War II is essential to understanding the political success Republicans enjoyed during the Eisenhower years. Have students compare the economic beliefs of Eisenhower's Republican Party to the beliefs of the Republican Party in the 1930s in a Venn diagram.

BUILDING AP® SKILLS

Making Connections

Often, more nuanced approaches from students on AP® Free Response Questions centered on foreign policy include brief analyses on the extent to which foreign policy influenced domestic policy. Consider providing students with the following examples from Module 8-6: National Interstate and Defense Highway Act, National Defense Education Act, and the development of NASA. Next, have students develop a 2 or 3 sentence explanation about how these domestic policies were affected by foreign policy.

APPLY THE TIP

Consider having students draw historical parallels about American Indians from the 1880s to the 1950s. For many students, it may be helpful to have this comparison revolve around a concept such as "relocation." Relocation of American Indians had many iterations, but for this analysis have students compare the Dawes Act with the relocation by the BIA in the 1950s.

National Interstate and Defense Highway Act 1956 act that provided funds for construction of 42,500 miles of roads throughout the United States.

Sputnik First artificial satellite, launched in 1957 by the Soviet Union.

> " Should any political party attempt to abolish social security, unemployment insurance, and eliminate labor laws and farm programs, you would not hear of that party again in our political history. "
>
> — President Dwight Eisenhower, 1954

AP® TIP
Be sure you can explain how the Eisenhower administration's policies toward American Indians reflected continuity in American history.

Democrats in control of Congress after 1954, Republicans agreed to raise Social Security benefits and to include coverage for some ten million additional workers. Congress and the president retained another New Deal mainstay, the minimum wage, and increased it from 75 cents to $1 an hour. Departing from traditional Republican criticism of big government, the Eisenhower administration added the Department of Health, Education, and Welfare to the cabinet in 1953. In 1956 the Eisenhower administration sponsored the **National Interstate and Defense Highway Act**, which provided funds for the construction of 42,500 miles of roads throughout the country, boosting both suburbanization and national defense. In addition, in 1958 Eisenhower signed into law the **National Defense Education Act**, which provided funding for instruction in science, math, and foreign languages and graduate fellowships and loans for college students. He portrayed the new law as a way to catch up with the Soviets, who the previous year had successfully launched the first artificial satellite, called *Sputnik*, into outer space.

For six of Eisenhower's eight years in office, the president had to work with Democratic majorities in Congress. Overall, he managed to forge bipartisan support for his proposals. Nowhere was this more significant than with civil rights legislation. Under his administration's leadership, Republicans joined with Democrats, led by Senate Majority Leader Lyndon B. Johnson, to pass the first pieces of civil rights legislation since Reconstruction. In 1957 and 1960, Eisenhower signed into law two bills that extended the authority of the federal government to file court challenges against southern election officials who blocked African Americans from registering to vote. However, southern Democratic senators thwarted Congress from passing even stronger voting measures or acts that would have enforced school desegregation.

Eisenhower administration policy, however, did not work to the benefit of American Indians. The federal government reversed many of the reforms instituted during the New Deal. In the 1950s the **Bureau of Indian Affairs (BIA)** adopted the policy of termination and relocation of American Indian tribes. Those tribes deemed to have achieved the most "progress," such as the Flatheads of Montana, the Klamaths of Oregon, and the Hoopas of northern California, were treated as ordinary American citizens, which resulted in termination of their federal benefits and transfer of their tribal lands to state and local governments. The National Congress of American Indians fought unsuccessfully against this program.

The government also relocated American Indians to urban areas. Between 1952 and 1960, the BIA encouraged more than 30,000 American Indians to move from their reservations to cities. The American Indian population of Los Angeles grew to 25,000, including members of the Navajo, Sioux, and Cherokee nations. Although thousands of American Indians took advantage of the relocation program, many had difficulty adjusting to urban life and fell into poverty.

The Eisenhower administration also repatriated undocumented Mexican laborers. The *bracero* program instituted in 1942 (see Module 7-10) had not eliminated illegal immigration from Mexico into the United States as large agricultural growers sought more cheap labor. Although some who came legally through the program stayed beyond the period allowed, far more Mexicans simply crossed the border illegally, seeking work. Mexico complained about these illegal immigrants because it needed a larger supply of agricultural workers, and American labor groups protested that illegal immigrants took jobs away from Americans. In 1954, Eisenhower's Immigration and Naturalization Service rounded up undocumented Mexicans, mainly in Texas and California, and returned them to Mexico. Those deported often suffered harsh conditions, and seven deportees drowned after they jumped ship. "**Operation Wetback**," as the program was dubbed using a derogatory term for Mexicans, forced an estimated 250,000 to 1.3 million Mexicans to leave the United States.

After winning a second term in 1956, Eisenhower clashed with the Democratic majority in Congress over spending. He vetoed bills that increased expenditures for public housing, public works projects, and urban renewal in an attempt to keep the budget balanced. Yet under Eisenhower the country overcame two recessions, the middle class grew in size, and inflation remained low. However, for forty million Americans poverty, not prosperity, remained the reality.

Even after serving two terms in office, Eisenhower remained popular. However, he could not run for a third term, barred by the Twenty-second Amendment (1951), and Vice President Richard M. Nixon ran as the Republican candidate for president in 1960. Unlike Eisenhower, Nixon was not universally liked or respected. His reputation for unsavory political combat drew the scorn of Democrats, especially liberals. Moreover, Nixon had to fend off charges that Republicans, as embodied in the seventy-year-old Eisenhower, were out-of-date and out of new ideas.

1960 Presidential Debate Watching A family watches Democratic nominee John F. Kennedy during a televised presidential debate against Republican nominee Richard M. Nixon. The 1960 presidential election featured the first televised debates and were watched by tens of millions of Americans. **How does this image show the ways in which TV and radio had a similar effect on politics? How does it show the ways in which they had a different effect?**

Running as the Democratic candidate for president in 1960, Senator John F. Kennedy of Massachusetts promised to instill renewed "vigor" in the White House and get the country moving again. Yet Kennedy did not differ much from his Republican rival on domestic and foreign policy issues. While Kennedy employed a rhetoric of high-minded change, he had not compiled a distinguished or courageous record in the Senate. Moreover, his family's fortune had paved the way for his political career, and he had earned a well-justified reputation in Washington as a playboy and womanizer.

The outcome of the 1960 election turned on several factors. The country was experiencing a slight economic recession, reviving memories in older voters of the Great Depression, which had begun with the Republican Herbert Hoover in power. In addition, presidential candidates faced off on television for the first time, participating in four televised debates. TV emphasized visual style and presentation. In the first debate, with Nixon having just recovered from a stay in the hospital and looking haggard, Kennedy convinced a majority of viewers that he possessed the presidential bearing for the job. Nixon performed better in the next three debates, but the damage had been done. Still, Kennedy had to overcome considerable religious prejudice to win the election. No Catholic had ever won the presidency, and the prejudices of Protestants, especially in the South, threatened to divert critical votes from Kennedy's Democratic base. While many southern Democrats did support Nixon, Kennedy balanced out these defections by gaining votes from the nation's Catholics, especially in northern states rich in electoral votes.

Race also exerted a critical influence. Nixon and Kennedy had similar records on civil rights, and if anything, Nixon's was slightly stronger. However, on October 19, 1960, when Atlanta police arrested Martin Luther King Jr. for participating in a restaurant sit-in, Kennedy sprang to his defense, whereas Nixon kept his distance. Kennedy telephoned the civil rights leader's wife to offer his sympathy and used his influence to get King released from jail. As a result, King's father, a Protestant minister who had intended to vote against the Catholic Kennedy, now endorsed the Democrat. In addition to the elder King, Kennedy won back for Democrats 7 percent of black voters who had supported Eisenhower in 1956. Kennedy triumphed by a margin of less than 1 percent of the popular vote, underscoring the importance of the African American electorate.

> **AP® TIP**
> Analyze how both television and changing population demographics influenced the victory of John F. Kennedy in the election of 1960.

REVIEW

- How did Eisenhower attempt to redefine Republicanism, and to what extent was he successful?
- What factors contributed to Kennedy's narrow victory in the 1960 presidential election?

Kennedy, the Cold War, and Cuba

The Kennedy administration showed great interest in fighting the Cold War abroad. The president believed that reform capitalism, which worked well in the United States, should become a global model. Communism, like fascism before it, posed a fundamental threat to American interests and to other countries' ability to copy the economic miracle of the United States. The faith of liberals in U.S. ingenuity, willpower, technological superiority, and moral righteousness encouraged them to reshape the "free world" in America's image.

APPLY THE TIP

The 1960 debate is a prime opportunity for students to see how television affected the political developments of the presidential election. Consider comparing clips of the first 1960 presidential debate with still pictures of the two candidates on stage. Ask students to what extent they see the narrative about Nixon's appearance to be true based on photographs. Next, show them clips of the debate, which can be located on YouTube, and ask students how Vice President Nixon's appearance matches the narrative provided by their textbook. A number of clips exist online; therefore, select a video of five to ten minutes in length such as clips that show the closing statements of each candidate.

BUILDING AP® SKILLS

Claims and Evidence in Sources

President Kennedy's 1961 inaugural address contains many phrases that students can analyze to understand how the new president proposed to change American foreign and domestic policy. Have students highlight at least two examples of references to foreign policy and two references to domestic policy. Next, ask students the extent to which these claims represented a shift in American political thought.

Period 8: 1945–1980

MODULE 8-6 The Cold War Expands at Home and Abroad, 1953–1961

Bay of Pigs invasion Unsuccessful 1961 attempt under the Kennedy administration to overthrow the Castro regime in Cuba.

> **AP® TIP**
> Analyze the ways in which the Cuban Missile Crisis and the construction of the Berlin Wall affected the Kennedy administration's policies.

Berlin Wall Physical and ideological barrier between East and West Berlin which existed from 1961 until 1989. The wall was designed to prevent Soviet controlled East Berliners from fleeing to the West.

President Kennedy's first Cold War battle took place in Cuba. Before his election, Kennedy learned of a secret CIA plan, devised by the Eisenhower administration, to topple Fidel Castro from power. After becoming president, Kennedy approved the scheme that Eisenhower had set in motion.

The operation ended disastrously. On April 17, 1961, the invasion force of between 1,400 and 1,500 Cuban exiles, trained by the CIA, landed by boat on Cuba's southwest coast, launching the **Bay of Pigs invasion**. Kennedy refused to provide backup military forces for fear of revealing the U.S. role in the attack. Castro's troops defeated the insurgents in three days. CIA planners had underestimated Cuban popular support for Castro, falsely believing that the invasion would inspire a national uprising against the Communist regime. The Kennedy administration had blundered into a bitter foreign policy defeat.

Two months later, Kennedy met Soviet leader Nikita Khrushchev at a summit meeting in Vienna. Khrushchev took advantage of the president's embarrassing defeat in Cuba to press his own demands. After the confrontational summit meeting between the superpowers, Kennedy persuaded Congress to increase the defense budget, dispatch additional troops to Europe, and bolster civil defense. In August, the Soviets responded by constructing the **Berlin Wall**, making it more difficult for refugees fleeing poverty and oppression in East Berlin to escape to West Berlin.

Despite the Bay of Pigs disaster, the United States continued its efforts to topple the Castro regime. Such attempts were unsuccessful. In response, Castro invited the Soviet Union to install short- and intermediate-range nuclear missiles in Cuba to protect the country against any U.S. incursion. After their discovery by American U-2 spy planes, Kennedy went on national television on October 22, 1962 to inform the American people that the Soviets had placed missiles in Cuba. The Kennedy administration decided to blockade Cuba to prevent Soviet ships from supplying the deadly warheads that would make the missiles fully operational. If Soviet ships defied the blockade, the president would order air

AP® ANALYZING SOURCES

Source: President John F. Kennedy, *Address before the American Society of Newspaper Editors*, April 20, 1961

> "The message of Cuba, of Laos, of the rising din of Communist voices in Asia and Latin America—these messages are all the same. The complacent, the self-indulgent, the soft societies are about to be swept away with the debris of history. Only the strong, only the industrious, only the determined, only the courageous, only the visionary who determine the real nature of our struggle can possibly survive.
>
> No greater task faces this country or this administration. No other challenge is more deserving of our every effort and energy. Too long we have fixed our eyes on traditional military needs, on armies prepared to cross borders, on missiles poised for flight. Now it should be clear that this is no longer enough—that our security may be lost piece by piece, country by country, without the bringing of a single missile or the crossing of a single border.
>
> We intend to profit from this lesson. We intend to reexamine and reorient our forces of all kinds—our tactics and our institutions here in this community. We intend to intensify our efforts for a struggle in many ways more difficult than war, where disappointment will often accompany us.
>
> For I am convinced that we in this country and in the free world possess the necessary resource, and the skill, and the added strength that comes from a belief in the freedom of man. And I am equally convinced that history will record the fact that this bitter struggle reached its climax in the late 1950's and the early 1960's. Let me then make clear as the President of the United States that I am determined upon our system's survival and success, regardless of the cost and regardless of the peril!"

Questions for Analysis
1. Identify the "lesson" Kennedy shares in his speech.
2. Describe the immediate context for Kennedy's speech.
3. Explain why Kennedy claims the "struggle" is "in many ways more difficult than war."
4. Evaluate the validity of Kennedy's claim that "this bitter struggle reached its climax in the late 1950's and early 1960's."

TEACHING IDEA

Building Vocabulary

Studying President Kennedy's policy of "flexible response" allows students to study the continuities and changes to American foreign policy during the Cold War. In this bell ringer activity, have students look up the meaning of flexible response. Next, give students the option of either selecting the Bay of Pigs invasion, the Berlin Wall, or the Cuban Missile Crisis. Have students explain flexible response by using their selected event. To end the activity, have students explain whether this was a continuity or a change in American foreign policy.

TRM Suggested Responses to Questions

TRM Module 8.6 AP® Analyzing Sources Handout 2

BUILDING AP® SKILLS

Claims and Evidence in Sources

Before students answer the accompanying questions, have them read the primary document with two highlighter colors. One highlighter will be for students to highlight any excerpts that illustrate ideological differences with Communist nations in politics. The other highlighter will be for highlighting any excerpts that address ideological differences with Communist nations in economics.

BUILDING AP® SKILLS

Contextualization

The award-winning 2003 documentary *Fog of War*, by Errol Morris, is an excellent resource for students to draw large historical connections about the Cuban Missile Crisis. The film highlights lessons learned by Robert McNamara, who was Secretary of Defense at the time of the Cuban Missile Crisis. You can show the excerpts about the Cuban Missile Crisis in less than 10 minutes. The clip is titled "Cuban Missile Crisis" in the film.

strikes and an invasion to destroy the missiles and overthrow Castro. Ordinary Americans nervously contemplated the very real possibility of nuclear destruction as Soviet ships sailed toward the blockade.

On the brink of nuclear war, both sides chose compromise. Khrushchev agreed to remove the missiles, and Kennedy pledged not to invade Cuba and secretly promised to dismantle U.S. missile sites in Turkey aimed at the Soviet Union. The world breathed a sigh of relief, and Kennedy and Khrushchev, having stepped back from the edge of nuclear holocaust, worked to ease tensions further. In 1963 they signed a Partial Nuclear Test Ban Treaty — which prohibited atmospheric but not underground testing — and installed an electronic "hot line" to ensure swift communications between Washington and Moscow.

Kennedy sought to balance his hardline, anti-Communist policies with new outreach efforts to inspire developing nations to follow a democratic path. The Peace Corps program sent thousands of volunteers to teach and advise developing nations, and Kennedy's Alliance for Progress supplied economic aid to emerging democracies in Latin America.

REVIEW

- How did Kennedy's Cold War policies almost lead the U.S. to open conflict in Cuba during the early 1960s?

AP® WRITING HISTORICALLY — Short-Answer Question Practice

ACTIVITY

Read the following question carefully and write a short response. Use complete sentences.

Using the following image, answer (a), (b), and (c).

Source: Edward Valtman, "This hurts me more than it hurts you!" *Hartford Times*, October 1962

About the source: This cartoon depicts Cuban President Fidel Castro (left) and Soviet Premier Nikita Khrushchev (right).

a. Briefly describe ONE perspective expressed by the artist about the Cold War.
b. Briefly explain how ONE development led to the historical situation shown in the image.
c. Briefly explain ONE specific outcome of Cold War era debates about United States foreign policy.

TEACHING IDEA

Incorporating Primary Sources

For students who are already developing a good understanding of the foreign policy changes in the 1950s and early 1960s, consider the following activity. President Kennedy's June 10, 1963 speech at American University, nicknamed the Peace Speech, is a good document to introduce students to at the conclusion of this module. The speech is, in many ways, a call for détente with the Soviet Union. President Kennedy specifically discussed a new view toward nuclear power. Have students read the speech to find specific parts that represent a change from his tone in the inaugural address of 1961. The speech can be found on the JFK Presidential Library website (jfklibrary.org).

TRM Suggested Responses to Questions

BUILDING AP® SKILLS

Sourcing and Situation

Prior to answering the Short-Answer Question, have students brainstorm the following: What events between Nikita Khrushchev and Fidel Castro in 1962 is this cartoon specifically addressing? How do you know that to be true? This contextual information allows students to approach the question with prior knowledge about the historical event(s) in question.

TEACHING IDEA

AP® Writing Historically Review

The following is a group activity meant to sharpen responses from a political cartoon. Organize students into groups of three. Next, assign each student one part of the question — (a), (b), or (c) — and have each student write an answer. After all students in a group are finished, have them pass their response to one of their group members. The goal of the recipient is to edit the response of their group member. Go through one more rotation of edits until each member of the group has edited the two parts they did not answer. The final step is for students to discuss the edits and write a group response for parts (a), (b), and (c). Have students turn in their group answer.

TRM Suggested Responses to Questions

EXPLORING AP® THEMES
America in the World

The Vietnam War can be used to illustrate how the Cold War affected America's role throughout the world. Consider giving students three areas of conflict during the Cold War years: Europe, Asia, and Latin America. Have students select one of the areas and then form subgroups of 3 or 4 students. Once the subgroups are formed, have students write a 2–3 sentence response detailing U.S. involvement in the region during the Cold War. Next, have groups meet and share answers. The goal of this activity is to get students thinking about the themes that will be present in this module.

Module 8-7

The Vietnam War

LEARNING TARGETS
By the end of this module, you should be able to:
- Explain the origins of America's involvement in Vietnam in the 1950s and early 1960s.
- Explain how Johnson escalated the conflict in Vietnam into a war, the strategies used by Johnson and Nixon during the war, and why the U.S. was unable to win the war.
- Explain how U.S. military involvement in the Vietnam War led to a decline in public trust in the federal government.
- Explain the successes and failures of Nixon's approach to foreign policy.

THEMATIC FOCUS
America in the World

Despite the thousands of U.S. military advisors sent to South Vietnam by the Eisenhower and Kennedy administrations after the defeat of the French in 1954, the anti-Communist regime continued to struggle against a determined Communist insurgency. In 1964, President Lyndon Johnson, capitalizing on a controversial naval attack, escalated the conflict into a full-scale war, drafting hundreds of thousands of U.S. soldiers into the fight. Four years later, as public opinion on the war soured, Nixon was elected on a promise of "peace with honor." Even as U.S. forces were drawn down, Nixon expanded the conflict into neighboring countries in an unsuccessful effort to secure better terms at the peace negotiations. Elsewhere, the Nixon administration had more success as it opened relations with China and signed the first nuclear arms treaty with the Soviet Union. Yet, the withdrawal of U.S. military forces from South Vietnam in 1973 led to its defeat two years later.

HISTORICAL REASONING FOCUS
Causation

TASK ▶ As you read this module, consider the short- and long-term causes of the Vietnam War and the impact of the war on American society. Be sure to weigh the relative importance of foreign policy concerns (e.g., containment) and domestic political concerns (e.g., not appearing soft on communism). Assess the reasons why America lost the Vietnam War and the effectiveness of Nixon's foreign policy.

W hile substantial progress was made on civil rights and liberal reforms at home, the Eisenhower, Kennedy, and Johnson administrations enjoyed far less success in fighting communism abroad. Following the overthrow of French colonial rule in Vietnam in 1954, the Cold War spread to Southeast Asia, where the United States applied the doctrine of containment. Believing that the situation in Vietnam posed a threat to the whole of Southeast Asia and American credibility abroad, the United States deployed hundreds of thousands of troops to fight the spread of Communist rule to South Vietnam in what was, instead, a civil war.

Early Intervention in Vietnam, 1954–1963

One offshoot of the Korean War was increased U.S. intervention in Vietnam, resulting in profound, long-term consequences. By the 1950s, Vietnamese revolutionaries (the Vietminh) had been fighting for independence from the French for decades. They were led by Ho Chi Minh, a revolutionary who had studied Communist doctrine in the Soviet Union but was not controlled by the Soviets. In fact, he modeled his 1945 Vietnamese Declaration of Independence on that of

TEACHING IDEA
Geography Instruction

Students need to be familiar with the geography of Asia and Southeast Asia. Consider passing out a plain map of these areas and have students color-code the following countries: Russia, China, North Korea, South Korea, Japan, Vietnam, Laos, and Cambodia. Next, have students explain the domino theory on a separate piece of paper. This bell ringer activity is meant to familiarize students with the geography so they can visualize the geographical location of the nations mentioned in this module. A reproducible version of this map is available in the Teacher's Resource Materials.

TRM Map 8B – Europe, Asia, and Africa

the United States. Despite sizable U.S. economic assistance for the French military effort, in 1954 the Vietminh defeated the French at the Battle of Dien Bien Phu. With the backing of the United States, the Soviet Union, and China, both sides agreed to divide Vietnam at the seventeenth parallel and hold free elections to unite the country in 1956.

President Dwight Eisenhower, who had brought the Korean War to a close in 1953, believed that if Vietnam fell to the Communists, the rest of Southeast Asia and Japan would "go over very quickly" like "a row of dominoes," threatening American strategic power in the Far East as well as free access to Asian markets. Convinced that Ho Chi Minh and his followers would win free elections, in 1955 the Eisenhower administration supported the anti-French, anti-Communist Ngo Dinh Diem to lead South Vietnam and then backed his regime's refusal to hold national elections in 1956. The anti-Communist fears of the United States had trumped its democratic promises. With the country now permanently divided, Eisenhower funneled economic aid to Diem to undertake needed land reforms that would strengthen his government and weaken the appeal of Ho Chi Minh. The president also dispatched hundreds of military advisers to support the South Vietnamese government. However, Diem used most of the money to consolidate his power rather than implement reforms, which only widened opposition to his regime from Communists and non-Communists alike. This prompted Ho Chi Minh in 1959 to support the creation in the South of the National Liberation Front, or **Vietcong**, to wage a military insurgency against Diem. By the end of the decade, the Eisenhower administration faced a major diplomatic problem with no clear plan for its resolution.

Like Eisenhower, President Kennedy believed in the **Domino Theory**, that if Communists toppled one regime in Asia, one country after another would fall like dominoes to the Communists. Kennedy, a World War II veteran, also believed that aggressive nations that attacked weaker ones threatened world peace unless they were challenged.

Kennedy's containment efforts in Vietnam ran into difficulty because the United States did not control the situation on the ground. By 1961 Diem had spent more than $1 billion of American aid on building up military and personal security forces to suppress political opposition rather than implement the land reform that he had promised. That year, Kennedy sent additional U.S. military special forces to train the South Vietnamese military in counterinsurgency. But the situation deteriorated in 1963 when the Catholic Diem prohibited the country's Buddhist majority from holding religious celebrations. In protest, Buddhist monks committed suicide by setting themselves on fire, a grisly display captured on television news programs in the United States. With political opposition mounting against Diem and with the war going poorly, the Kennedy administration endorsed a military coup to replace the Diem government with one more capable of fighting Communists. On November 1, 1963, the coup leaders removed Diem from office, assassinating him and key members of his regime within days, and installed a military government.

Diem's death, however, did little to improve the worsening war against the Communists. The Vietcong had more support in the rural countryside than did the South Vietnamese government. The rebels promised land reform and recruited local peasants opposed to the corruption and ruthlessness of the Diem regime. The Kennedy administration committed itself to supporting Diem's successor, but by late November 1963 Kennedy seemed torn between sending more American troops and finding a way to negotiate a peace.

Vietcong The popular name for the National Liberation Front (NFL) in South Vietnam, which was formed in 1959. The Vietcong waged a military insurgency against the U.S.-backed president, Ngo Dinh Diem, and received support from Ho Chi Minh, the leader of North Vietnam.

Domino Theory Prevalent belief during the Cold War maintaining that if one country fell under the influence of communism, other surrounding countries would soon similarly fall under the influence of communism, like a row of falling dominoes.

AP® TIP
Compare the policies and actions of the Eisenhower and Kennedy administrations in responding to conflicts in Vietnam in the 1950s and 1960s.

REVIEW
- Why did the Eisenhower administration become involved in Vietnam, and why were its efforts unsuccessful?
- How did the Kennedy administration's involvement in Vietnam compare to that of Eisenhower?

Johnson Escalates the War in Vietnam

When Lyndon Johnson took office after Kennedy's assassination on November 22, 1963, there were 16,000 American military advisers in Vietnam. Although Johnson privately harbored reservations about fighting in Vietnam, he feared appearing soft on communism and was concerned that a demonstration of weakness would jeopardize congressional support for his domestic plans. Although Johnson eventually concluded that more U.S. forces had to be sent to Vietnam, he waited for the right moment to rally Congress and the American public behind an escalation of the war.

BUILDING AP® SKILLS

Comparison

This activity is meant to have students compare and contrast a very specific element of Cold War foreign policy. Instead of just comparing the Korean War and the Vietnam War, direct students' attention to comparing the process by which the U.S. supported non-Communist leaders in South Korea and South Vietnam. Why did the American government choose the particular leaders, even though those leaders had questionable leadership skills?

TEACHING IDEA

Analyzing Art and Images

The Buddhist monks' collective protests against the Diem regime garnered attention in the United States and around the globe. A simple Google search will yield a number of (often graphic) pictures that capture the stoic violence. The photos will inspire questions and should lead to a thought-provoking discussion of the protests and the reactions people in the United States had to these events.

TEACHING IDEA

Building Vocabulary

Students need to be aware of the different groups of people in Vietnam discussed in this module. Therefore, provide students with the following list: Vietminh, Vietcong, South Vietnamese, and North Vietnamese. Have students work in groups to define who they were and what their political beliefs were during the Vietnam War.

TEACHING IDEA

Incorporating Videos

The award-winning 2003 documentary *Fog of War*, by Errol Morris, is an excellent resource for students to draw large historical connections about the Vietnam War. The film highlights lessons learned by Robert McNamara, who was Secretary of Defense at the time of the escalation of the Vietnam War. You can show the excerpts about the Gulf of Tonkin incident in less than 10 minutes. The clip is titled "Gulf of Tonkin" in the documentary.

TRM Suggested Responses to Questions

TRM Module 8.7 AP® Analyzing Sources Handout 1

BUILDING AP® SKILLS

Source Claims and Evidence

That the Gulf of Tonkin incident was lacking credible information and was clouded in uncertainty are historical facts. However, the Johnson administration pursued the subsequent Gulf of Tonkin Resolution immediately. Take an excerpt such as, "Whereas these attackers are part of deliberate and systematic campaign of aggression," and ask students to reconcile the confusion of events with the certainty of language in the excerpt. Why would the government knowingly use incomplete knowledge?

TEACHING IDEA

Connecting the Dots

General William Westmoreland was the general in charge during the escalation phase from 1964 to 1968. His adopted strategy was a "war of attrition" that would simply outlast the force of the Communist regime in North Vietnam. Have students hypothesize why this strategy was supported by the civilian leaders in government in the U.S. This can be a great bell ringer activity or an exit card strategy.

Period 8: 1945–1980

MODULE 8-7 The Vietnam War

AP® ANALYZING SOURCES

Source: *Gulf of Tonkin Resolution*, 1964

"To promote the maintenance of international peace and security in southeast Asia.
   Whereas naval units of the Communist regime in Vietnam, in violation of the principles of the Charter of the United Nations and of international law, have deliberately and repeatedly attacked United Stated naval vessels lawfully present in international waters, and have thereby created a serious threat to international peace; and
   Whereas these attackers are part of deliberate and systematic campaign of aggression that the Communist regime in North Vietnam has been waging against its neighbors and the nations joined with them in the collective defense of their freedom; and
   Whereas the United States is assisting the peoples of southeast Asia to protest their freedom and has no territorial, military or political ambitions in that area, but desires only that these people should be left in peace to work out their destinies in their own way: Now, therefore be it
   Resolved by the Senate and House of Representatives of the United States of America in Congress assembled, That the Congress approves and supports the determination of the President, as Commander in Chief, to take all necessary measures to repel any armed attack against the forces of the United States and to prevent further aggression."

Questions for Analysis

1. Identify the goal of the Gulf of Tonkin Resolution.
2. Describe the reasons for the Gulf of Tonkin Resolution expressed in this excerpt.
3. Explain how the Gulf of Tonkin Resolution would allow the President to expand the conflict in Vietnam into a war.
4. Evaluate the extent to which U.S. military involvement in the Vietnam War represents a continuation of U.S. Cold War policy in the late 1940s and 1950s.

Gulf of Tonkin Resolution 1964 congressional resolution giving President Johnson wide discretion in the use of U.S. forces in Vietnam. The resolution followed reported attacks by North Vietnamese gunboats on two American destroyers.

escalation Johnson administration policy of continuously increasing the numbers of ground troops in Vietnam and bombing campaigns.

Vietnam War Conflict between the Communist nationalist government in North Vietnam backed by the Soviet Union and China, against the United Nations and U.S. backed South Vietnam government. The war is seen as part of a series of proxy wars as a result of Cold War tensions between the U.S. and Soviet Union between 1954 to 1975.

That moment came in August 1964. On August 2, North Vietnamese gunboats attacked a U.S. Navy destroyer sixty miles off the North Vietnamese coast in the Gulf of Tonkin in response to South Vietnamese naval raids along the coast. Two days later, another U.S. destroyer reported coming under torpedo attack, but because of stormy weather the second ship was not certain that it had been fired on. Despite the considerable uncertainty about what actually happened and the lack of damage, Johnson seized the opportunity to urge Congress to authorize military action. On August 7, 1964 Congress passed the **Gulf of Tonkin Resolution**, which provided the president with unlimited power to make military decisions regarding Vietnam.

After winning election in 1964, President Johnson stepped up U.S. military action. In March 1965, with North Vietnamese forces flooding into the South, the president initiated a massive bombing campaign called Operation Rolling Thunder. For more than three years, American planes dropped a million tons of bombs on North Vietnam, more than the total amount the United States used in World War II. Despite this massive firepower, the operation proved ineffective. A largely agricultural country, North Vietnam did not have the type of industrial targets best suited for air attacks. It stored its vital military resources underground and was able to reconstruct rudimentary bridges and roads to maintain the flow of troops into the South within hours after U.S. bombers had pounded them.

Responding to the need to protect American air bases and the persistent ineffectiveness of the South Vietnamese military, Johnson deployed ever-increasing numbers of ground troops to Vietnam, a continuation of the U.S. policy of **escalation** that transformed the conflict into the **Vietnam War**. Troop levels rose from 16,000 in 1963, to 380,000 in 1966, 485,000 in 1967, and 536,000 in 1968. The U.S. military also deployed napalm bombs, which spewed burning jellied gasoline, and Agent Orange, a chemical that defoliated the Vietnamese countryside and produced long-term adverse health effects for those who came in contact with it, including American soldiers. These attacks added to the resentment of South Vietnamese peasants and helped the Vietcong gain new recruits.

The United States confronted a challenging guerrilla war in Vietnam. The Vietcong often fought at night and blended in during the day as ordinary residents of cities and villages. They did

---

EXPLORING AP® THEMES

America in the World

Have students read a selection from Tim O'Brien's book, *The Things They Carried*, to get a sense of what happens to American citizens who are asked to fight for their nation in an ideological war such as Vietnam. What does it say about America's role in the world? How did citizens react? What circumstances does O'Brien describe that policymakers do not think through when fighting ideological wars? There are short sections such as the chapter titled "Friends" that can leave a lasting impact and lead to great discussion among students.

BUILDING AP® SKILLS

Causation

Consider having students construct a chart, which explains the varied strategies and tactics employed by the United States in the conflict in Vietnam. Some strategies and tactics to consider: massive bombing campaigns, escalation, napalm, "winning hearts and minds," and the use of air power. Have students write out reasons for why the U.S. used these strategies and what level of success the strategy/tactic had from 1964 to 1968. If the strategy was unsuccessful, ask students why the U.S. persisted in the war in Vietnam.

Period 8: 1945–1980

Johnson Escalates the War in Vietnam

AP® ANALYZING SOURCES

Source: Philip Caputo, *A Rumor of War*, 1977

"On March 8, 1965, as a young infantry officer, I landed at Danang with a battalion of the 9th Marine Expeditionary Brigade, the first U.S. combat unit sent to Indochina. . . .

For Americans who did not come of age in the early sixties, it may be hard to grasp what those years were like — the pride and overpowering self-assurance that prevailed. Most of the thirty-five hundred men in our brigade, born during or immediately after World War II, were shaped by that era, the age of Kennedy's Camelot. We went overseas full of illusions, for which the intoxicating atmosphere of those years was as much to blame as our youth.

War is always attractive to young men who know nothing about it, but we had also been seduced into uniform by Kennedy's challenge to 'ask what you can do for your country' and by the missionary idealism he had awakened in us. America seemed omnipotent then: the country could still claim it had never lost a war, and we believed we were ordained to play cop to the Communists' robber and spread our own political faith around the world. Like the French soldiers of the late eighteenth century, we saw ourselves as the champions of 'a cause that was destined to triumph.' So, when we marched into the rice paddies on that damp March afternoon, we carried, along with our packs and rifles, the implicit convictions that the Viet Cong would be quickly beaten and that we were doing something altogether noble and good. We kept the packs and rifles; the convictions, we lost.

The discovery that the men we had scorned as peasant guerrillas were, in fact, a lethal, determined enemy and the casualty lists that lengthened each week with nothing to show for the blood being spilled broke our early confidence. By autumn, what had begun as an adventurous expedition had turned into an exhausting, indecisive war of attrition in which we fought for no cause other than our own survival."

Questions for Analysis
1. Identify the reasons for Caputo's initial confidence as a soldier in Vietnam.
2. Describe the change in Caputo's perspective during the Vietnam War.
3. Explain how "peasant guerrillas" were able to outlast the U.S. military in Vietnam.
4. Evaluate the extent to which Caputo's account rejects the idea of American exceptionalism.

My Lai massacre March 16, 1968 unprovoked U.S. massacre of nearly 500 of the elderly, women, and children in the South Vietnam area of My Lai during the Vietnam War.

not provide a visible target, and they recruited women and men of all ages, making it difficult for U.S. ground forces to distinguish friend from foe. Although U.S. military commanders realized the necessity of "winning hearts and minds" in Vietnam, in the end, the U.S. military effort alienated the population it was designed to safeguard.

On the ground, frustration grew as many conscripted American soldiers realized that war was not winnable and that public support for it was flagging back home. Frustrated by rising casualties from an enemy they could not see, in March 1968 an American platoon killed several hundred unarmed Vietnamese civilians in an event that came to be known as the **My Lai massacre**. Although dozens of U.S. military personnel participated in the massacre and

◄ **American and South Vietnamese Forces Assault Viet Cong camp, 1965** South Vietnamese soldiers move toward a Viet Cong camp near the Cambodian border as U.S. Army helicopters provide covering fire and reconnaissance. **How does this photograph illustrate both the advantages possessed by the U.S. military in Vietnam as well as the challenges it faced?**

TRM Suggested Responses to Questions

TRM Module 8.7 AP® Analyzing Sources Handout 2

BUILDING AP® SKILLS

Causation

Before reading the document from Philip Caputo, consider having students work on a causation bell ringer. Ask students to respond to the following question: Most of the soldiers who fought in Vietnam had fathers who fought in World War II. In what ways would the experiences of their fathers shape their perceptions about the rationale to fight in Vietnam?

TEACHING IDEA

Building Vocabulary

Be sure to let students know that the term for "winning hearts and minds" is known as "pacification."

TEACHING IDEA

Incorporating Videos

The My Lai massacre was a moment during the Vietnam War that caused Americans to pause and rethink what the realities of the conflict were. More than a cover-up, it was a dispute among servicemen about what the conduct of war includes. The PBS *American Experience* documentary, *My Lai*, is an excellent resource to use because it teaches the context of the massacre and uses interviews with men who took part in the massacre.

TEACHING IDEA

Incorporating Videos

Filmmaker Ken Burns's epic documentary, *The Vietnam War*, can be used to supplement the perspectives of both American and Vietnamese soldiers. Throughout the documentary, all sides of this conflict are explored through interviews with veterans. This can be a powerful way to hook students' interest in this transformational historical event. In particular, Episode 4, "Resolve," examines the experiences of soldiers. Available on Netflix and the PBS website (pbs.org).

Period 8: 1945–1980

MODULE 8-7 The Vietnam War

BUILDING AP® SKILLS
Argumentation

The historical thinking skill of argumentation involves making discrete decisions about what interpretation makes sense, given the historical evidence available. Try using an argumentative essay question such as the following: To what extent was 1968 a turning point in U.S. foreign policy in the Vietnam War? There should be a variety of responses, so this activity works well when students are able to share answers and hold a class discussion after sharing.

EXPLORING AP® THEMES
America in the World

The historian George Herring has an accessible essay on the My Lai massacre and the Vietnam War located on Gilder Lehrman's AP® U.S. History site (ap.gilderlehrman.org). Select Period 8 to find the article. Students will find it approachable, engaging, and informative. To condense their focus, ask students what the thesis of the essay is and have students write two or three sentences explaining Herring's thesis.

TEACHING IDEA
Building Vocabulary

The historical phrase of "credibility gap" is often used during and after the Vietnam War era. Consider spending time with students teaching them this concept, connecting this concept to the war and the decisions the federal government made during the war. This is a crucial concept to understand and can provide students with further historical evidence to use when writing about the Vietnam War.

MAP 8.4 The Vietnam War, 1968 The United States wielded vastly more military personnel and weaponry than the Vietcong and North Vietnamese but faced a formidable challenge in fighting a guerrilla war in a foreign country. Massive American bombing failed to defeat the North Vietnamese or stop their troop movements and supply lines along the Ho Chi Minh Trail. The 1968 Tet Offensive demonstrated the shortcomings in the U.S. strategy. **What does this map reveal about the scope of the Tet Offensive?**

Tet Offensive January 31, 1968 offensive mounted by Vietcong and North Vietnamese forces against population centers in South Vietnam. The offensive was turned back, but its ferocity shocked many Americans and increased public opposition to the war.

subsequent coverup attempt, only one soldier was ever convicted of a crime.

The My Lai carnage came in the aftermath of the **Tet Offensive**. On January 31, 1968, the Buddhist New Year of Tet, some 67,000 Communist forces mounted a surprise offensive throughout South Vietnam that targeted major population centers and even included a dramatic attack on the U.S. Embassy in Saigon (Map 8.4). U.S. forces finally repelled the Tet Offensive, but the battle proved psychologically costly to the United States. Following it, the most revered television news anchor of the era, Walter Cronkite of CBS, turned against the war and expressed the doubts of a growing number of viewers when he announced: "To say that we are mired in stalemate seems the only reasonable, yet unsatisfactory conclusion." His report heralded a growing change in public sentiment against the war demonstrating the impact of the Tet Offensive in the United States.

Tet marked the beginning of the end of the war's escalation. On March 31, 1968, President Johnson ordered a halt to the bombing campaign and called for peace negotiations. He also stunned the nation by announcing that he would not seek reelection. By the time Johnson left the White House in January 1969, peace negotiations had stalled and some 36,000 Americans had died in combat, along with 52,000 South Vietnamese troops. The escalation of the war had exacted another high price as well: It created a crisis of public confidence in government and turned many ordinary Americans into dissenters against the political establishment.

REVIEW

- How did the Johnson administration transform the conflict in Vietnam into the Vietnam War?
- Why were Johnson's policies in Vietnam unsuccessful?

Nixon and the Failure of Vietnamization

After Richard Nixon won the 1968 presidential election, Vietnam plagued him as it had his Democratic predecessor. In 1968, Nixon won the presidential election in part by promising "an honorable end to the war in Vietnam." Despite hinting during the campaign that he had a secret plan to end the war, Nixon's approach to Vietnam turned out to look much the same as Johnson's. Henry Kissinger, who served first as national security adviser and then as

TEACHING IDEA
Connecting the Dots

For students who are already grasping the major concepts associated with this module, consider the following activity. Ask students to delineate the Republican and Democratic presidents involved in the Vietnam War. Next, have students explain their various policy decisions about the conflict and then have them answer the fundamental question for the activity: To what extent did political pressures at home shape foreign policy decisions in Vietnam?

Nixon and the Failure of Vietnamization

> "To say that we are mired in stalemate seems the only reasonable, yet unsatisfactory conclusion."
>
> Walter Cronkite, CBS news anchor, 1968

AP® TIP

Evaluate whether the policy of Vietnamization was a dramatic change from the policies the Eisenhower, Kennedy, and Johnson administrations pursued in Vietnam.

secretary of state, continued peace talks with the North Vietnamese, which had been initiated by Johnson. Over the next four years, Nixon and Kissinger devised a strategy that removed U.S. ground forces and turned over greater responsibility for the fighting to the South Vietnamese army, a process called **Vietnamization**.

Vietnamization did not mean an end to U.S. military involvement in the region, however. In fact, Nixon widened the conflict before ultimately bringing it to an end. In 1969, at the same time that American troop levels were being drawn down, the president ordered secret bombing raids in Cambodia, a neutral country adjacent to South Vietnam that contained enemy forces and parts of the Ho Chi Minh Trail. Meant to pressure the North Vietnamese into accepting U.S. peace terms, the bombing accomplished little. In April 1970 Nixon ordered an invasion of eastern Cambodia to destroy enemy bases, which destabilized the country and eventually brought to power the Communist organization Khmer Rouge, which later slaughtered two million Cambodians. In 1971 the United States sponsored the South Vietnamese invasion of Laos, a neighboring country that harbored North Vietnamese troops and supply lines, which again yielded no battlefield gains. Finally, in December 1972, shortly before Christmas, the United States carried out a massive eleven-day bombing campaign of targets in North Vietnam meant to force the North Vietnamese government to come to a peace accord.

The intense bombing of North Vietnam did end formal U.S. involvement in the war. An agreement signed on January 27, 1973 stipulated that the United States would remove all American troops, the North Vietnamese would return captured U.S. soldiers, and North and South Vietnam would strive for peaceful national unification. Crucially, the agreement did not require the withdrawal of North Vietnamese troops from South Vietnam. Despite this agreement, peace had clearly not been achieved. The war in Vietnam continued, now without the participation of the U.S. military, and in April 1975 North Vietnamese and Vietcong forces captured Saigon, resulting in a Communist victory. In the end, the Vietnam War extracted a terrible cost. Some 58,000 American soldiers, 215,000 South Vietnamese soldiers, 1 million North Vietnamese and Vietcong soldiers, and an estimated 4 million South and North Vietnamese civilians were killed in the conflict.

▲ **The Fall of Saigon, 1975**   On April 29, 1975, the day before Communist troops took control of Saigon, crowds of South Vietnamese, many of whom had supported the United States, scramble to climb the wall of the U.S. Embassy. They were making a desperate attempt to get to evacuation helicopters, but with space limited on available aircraft, many of these people were left behind. **What does the photograph suggest about conditions in South Vietnam right before the Communist victory?**

APPLY THE TIP

Rather than focusing on all three presidents (Eisenhower, Kennedy, and Johnson), divide students into groups of three. Next, assign each student either Eisenhower, Kennedy, or Johnson, and then have students answer the AP® Tip question by focusing their comparison of Vietnamization with one other president. After each member is finished, have students share their responses.

BUILDING AP® SKILLS

Argumentation

Although this style of question will not necessarily be seen on the AP® exam, it does provide students with the opportunity to work on making historical arguments. Provide students with the following prompt: The failures during the Vietnam War can be attributed to misguided presidential policies, which were more concerned about Cold War politics, than realities on the ground in Vietnam. Support, modify, or refute this statement with historical evidence.

TEACHING IDEA

Connecting the Dots

The following activity focuses on the skill of change over time. At the beginning of the class period, provide students with the following controversies from the Vietnam War: Tet Offensive, My Lai massacre, Pentagon Papers. Have students select one as the most egregious controversy and have them explain their response in 2 or 3 sentences. Students with different answers will form groups and share their responses. Be sure to emphasize the fact that each event is a viable option.

Period 8: 1945–1980

MODULE 8-7 The Vietnam War

The Nixon administration's war efforts generated great controversy at home. The invasion of Cambodia in April 1970 touched off widespread campus demonstrations. At Kent State University in Ohio, four student protesters were shot and killed on May 4, 1970 by the National Guard in an incident that became known as the **Kent State Massacre**. Large crowds of antiwar demonstrators descended on Washington in 1969 and 1971, though the president refused to heed their message. Nevertheless, a majority of the American public, not just radicals, had turned against the war. By 1972 more than 70 percent of those polled believed that the Vietnam War was a mistake. Growing numbers of Vietnam veterans also spoke out against the war. Contributing to this disillusionment, in 1971 the *New York Times* and the *Washington Post* published a classified report known as the **Pentagon Papers**. This document confirmed that the Kennedy and Johnson administrations had misled the public about the origins and nature of the Vietnam War. Congress reflected growing disapproval for the war by repealing the Gulf of Tonkin Resolution in 1970 after the Cambodian invasion. In 1973 Congress passed the **War Powers Act**, which required the president to consult with Congress within forty-eight hours of deploying military forces and to obtain a declaration of war from Congress if troops remained on foreign soil beyond sixty days. Although Nixon oversaw the winding down of American military involvement in Vietnam, his handling of the Vietnam War remained controversial throughout his time in office.

War Powers Act 1973 act that required the president to consult with Congress within forty-eight hours of deploying military forces and to obtain a declaration of war from Congress if troops remained on foreign soil beyond sixty days.

REVIEW

- How did Nixon change American tactics in Vietnam?
- Why was Nixon's approach also unsuccessful?

AP® WRITING HISTORICALLY   Short-Answer Question Practice

ACTIVITY

Read the following question carefully and write a short response. Use complete sentences.

Answer (a), (b), and (c).

a. Briefly explain ONE specific historical factor that contributed to United States involvement in the Vietnam War.
b. Briefly explain ONE specific historical factor that contributed to the failure of the United States to win the Vietnam War.
c. Briefly explain ONE specific historical effect of United States involvement in the Vietnam War on American society.

TRM Suggested Responses to Questions

TEACHING IDEA

Group SAQ

Have the class form into groups of 3 or 4 students. Next, have each student respond to the Short-Answer Question. After students are finished, have them select the best answer for parts (a), (b), and (c). They will then form a new "group answer" using the best response for (a), (b), and (c). If you want to make this interactive, have students write their group answer on butcher-block paper and then conduct a gallery walk where students travel the room to see the different responses.

TEACHING IDEA

AP® Writing Historically Review

Of the eight themes associated with the AP® U.S. History course, at least three are directly relevant to the purposes of the question. American and national identity, politics and power, and America in the world could be used to help students brainstorm possible answers. Think about writing these themes on the white board and ask students to select which one can be applied to parts (a), (b), and (c). Next, have students brainstorm discrete historical evidence to answer each question.

Module 8-8

The Fight for Civil Rights, 1961–1979

LEARNING TARGETS

By the end of this module, you should be able to:

- Explain the tactics and strategies used by Martin Luther King Jr. and leading civil rights organizations in the early and mid-1960s.
- Explain the legislative and legal accomplishments of the civil rights movement in the 1960s and early 1970s and the effects of those accomplishments on American society.
- Explain the factors that led to the rise of the black power movement and its impact on the larger civil rights movement.
- Explain why the use of forced busing and affirmative action to further racial integration was controversial.

THEMATIC FOCUS

Politics and Power
Social Structures

As the 1960s began, civil rights leaders looked to build upon their postwar successes through continued nonviolent protests, voter registration drives, and political pressure. After the widely seen images from Birmingham and the March on Washington, Kennedy supported and Johnson eventually succeeded in pushing through Congress momentous civil rights legislation including the Civil Rights Act of 1964, the Voting Rights Act, and the Twenty-fourth Amendment. Yet, new voices such as Malcom X and the Black Panther Party, emphasizing black power, challenged the approach of King and others as young urban African Americans in the North and West expressed their frustration with the lack of meaningful change for them by participating in urban uprisings. As the focus of the civil rights movement shifted toward racial integration and equal opportunity outside the South, policies such as forced busing and affirmative action generated controversy and were eventually limited by court rulings.

HISTORICAL REASONING FOCUS

Comparison

TASK ▶ As you read this module, compare the goals, strategies, and support of the civil rights movement in the late 1940s and 1950s (see Module 8-5) with the 1960s and 1970s. Consider the reasons for the similarities and differences between the movement in each time period. Think about the how the civil rights movement both changed and remained the same between 1945 to 1970.

TRM Suggested Responses to Questions

EXPLORING AP® THEMES

Social Structures

Think about opening this module of study by having students define structural racism. Next, provide three categories of analysis: public facilities, voting, and lynching. Ask students to explain the continuities in structural racism for one of the given categories from 1940 to 1960. This activity works well as a bell ringer activity to begin the class period and can be the source of historical inquiry to begin this module.

At home, the most critical issue facing the nation in the early 1960s was the intensification of the civil rights movement. As a candidate, Kennedy had promised vigorous action on civil rights, but as president he did little to follow through on his promises. With southern Democrats occupying key positions in Congress and threatening to block any civil rights proposals, Kennedy sought to appease this critical component of his political base. Following Kennedy's death in 1963, President Johnson succeeded in breaking the legislative logjam and signed into law three major pieces of civil rights legislation. He did so under considerable pressure from the civil rights movement. At the height of their triumphs, however, many civil rights activists became increasingly skeptical of nonviolence and integration and turned to the racial nationalism and self-determination of black power.

BUILDING AP® SKILLS

Comparison

The purpose of this activity is to have students leverage prior knowledge and compare it to new knowledge at the end of this module. Start by handing out the comparison chart located in the Teacher's Resource Materials. The chart has two columns for the decades of the 1940s/1950s and the 1960s/1970s. It also has three rows for the goals, strategies, and organizations of civil rights activists. The purpose of this exercise is to draw on prior knowledge and complete the 1940s/1950s half of the chart at the beginning of the module and complete the 1960s/1970s half of the chart at the end of the module.

TRM Find **Handout 8.7 – Comparing Civil Rights Movements, 1940s–1970s** in the Teacher's Resource Materials.

The Fight for Civil Rights, 1961–1979

Period 8: 1945–1980

MODULE 8-8 The Fight for Civil Rights, 1961–1979

Freedom Rides

Freedom Rides Integrated bus rides through the South organized by CORE in 1961 to test compliance with Supreme Court rulings on segregation.

> **AP® TIP**
> Evaluate the extent to which the federal government's actions in response to racist violence in the 1960s represent continuity over time. Consider the 1920s–1950s, the late nineteenth century, and the Reconstruction era.

The Congress of Racial Equality took the offensive on May 4, 1961. Similar to Bayard Rustin's efforts in the 1940s, CORE mounted racially integrated **Freedom Rides** to test whether facilities in the South were complying with the 1960 Supreme Court ruling that outlawed segregated bus and train stations serving passengers who were traveling interstate. CORE alerted the Justice Department and the FBI of its plans, but the riders received no protection when Ku Klux Klan–dominated mobs in Anniston and Birmingham, Alabama attacked two of its buses, seriously wounding several activists.

After safety concerns forced CORE to forgo the rest of the trip, members of the Student Nonviolent Coordinating Committee (SNCC) rushed to Birmingham to continue the bus rides. The Kennedy administration urged them to reconsider, but Diane Nash, an SNCC founder, explained that although the group realized the peril of resuming the journey, "we can't let them stop us with violence. If we do, the movement is dead." When the replenished busload of riders reached Montgomery on May 20, they were brutally assaulted by a mob. Dr. Martin Luther King Jr. subsequently held a rally in a Montgomery church, where white mobs threatened the lives of King and the Freedom Riders inside the building. Faced with the prospect of serious bloodshed, the Kennedy administration dispatched federal marshals to the scene and persuaded the governor to call out the Alabama National Guard to ensure the safety of everyone in the church.

The president and his brother, Attorney General Robert F. Kennedy, worked out a compromise to let the rides continue with minimal violence, and with minimal publicity. The Cold War worked in favor of the protesters. With the Soviet Union publicizing the violence against Freedom Riders in the South, the Kennedy administration attempted to preserve America's image abroad by persuading the Interstate Commerce Commission to issue an order prohibiting segregated transportation facilities. Still, southern whites resisted. When Freedom Riders encountered opposition in Albany, Georgia in the fall of 1961, SNCC workers remained in Albany and helped local leaders organize residents against segregation and other forms of racial discrimination. But even with the assistance of Dr. King and the Southern Christian Leadership Conference (SCLC), the Albany movement stalled.

REVIEW

- How did Freedom Riders confront continued segregation in the South?
- How successful were they in challenging systematic racial discrimination?

Kennedy Supports Civil Rights

> **AP® TIP**
> Evaluate the extent to which nonviolent resistance to racism, segregation, and discrimination was ultimately successful.

Despite the setback in Albany, the civil rights movement kept up pressure on other fronts. In September 1962 Mississippi governor Ross Barnett tried to block the registration of James Meredith as an undergraduate at the University of Mississippi. Barnett's obstruction led to a riot on campus, and President Kennedy dispatched army troops and federalized the Mississippi National Guard to restore order, but not before two bystanders were killed.

The following year, King and the SCLC joined the Reverend Fred Shuttlesworth's movement in Birmingham, Alabama in its battle against discrimination, segregation, and police brutality. With the white supremacist Eugene "Bull" Connor in charge of law enforcement, civil rights protesters, including children from age six to sixteen, encountered violent resistance, vicious police dogs, and high-powered water hoses. Connor ordered mass arrests, including Dr. King's, prompting the minister to write his famous "Letter from Birmingham Jail," in which he justified the use of nonviolent direct action. Seeking to defuse the crisis, President Kennedy sent an emissary in early May 1963 to negotiate a peaceful solution that granted concessions to black residents of Birmingham and ended the demonstrations.

Angered by the events in Birmingham and King's imprisonment, Kennedy finally embraced the nation's duty to guarantee equal rights regardless of race. On June 11, 1963, shortly after negotiating the Birmingham agreement, Kennedy delivered a nationally televised address. He acknowledged that the country faced a "moral crisis" heightened by the events in Birmingham,

---

> **TEACHING IDEA**
>
> **Incorporating Videos**
>
> Think about incorporating some of the PBS *American Experience* documentary, *Freedom Riders*, to supplement the narrative in this module (available on YouTube). A recent production, this film recounts the events of the Freedom Rides and includes interviews and footage students will find intriguing. Of particular interest are sections from the events in Birmingham, Alabama through the end of the Freedom Rides in Jackson, Mississippi.

> **TEACHING IDEA**
>
> **Analyzing Art and Images**
>
> The images from the Freedom Rides are powerful tools to use during instruction. Think about having students make a digital collage of images from the Freedom Rides. Well-balanced collages will illustrate change over time, and focusing on events in Alabama and Mississippi will illustrate those well. After students have made their collages, have students either print their images or display them on an overhead. The goal of this assignment is for students to create a historical narrative of events with powerful images.

> **BUILDING AP® SKILLS**
>
> **Causation**
>
> The Freedom Rides ended between May 24 and May 28, 1961 in Jackson, Mississippi because of a deal between the governor of Mississippi, Ross Barnett, and the Kennedy administration. In an exchange for no violence brought upon the Freedom Riders, the Kennedy administration agreed to allow the authorities in Mississippi to arrest the riders. Ask students in what ways the Cold War could have caused this decision by President Kennedy. Also ask students in what ways the complicated relationship between state and federal governments affected this deal.

> **APPLY THE TIP**
>
> Have students use the Montgomery Bus Boycott, Little Rock Nine, and Freedom Riders to examine the effectiveness of nonviolent protest. Students should analyze the effectiveness by evaluating the extent of change after the protest.

> **TEACHING IDEA**
>
> **Analyzing Art and Images**
>
> Consider assigning this activity to students who are demonstrating mastery of the content thus far in Module 8-8. The goal of this activity is to capture the story of the marches in Birmingham in 1963. Students can use one photo, write two sentences, and explain their interpretation to the class in no more than three minutes. Think of it as a 1-2-3 exercise. Students have choice, the opportunity to practice argumentation, and the chance to share their results with their peers.

Kennedy Supports Civil Rights

Period 8: 1945–1980

AP® ANALYZING SOURCES

Source: Martin Luther King Jr., *Letter from Birmingham Jail*, April 1963

"We know through painful experience that freedom is never voluntarily given by the oppressor; it must be demanded by the oppressed. Frankly, I have never yet engaged in a direct-action movement that was 'well timed' according to the timetable of those who have not suffered unduly from the disease of segregation. For years now I have heard the word 'wait.' It rings in the ear of every Negro with a piercing familiarity. This 'wait' has almost always meant 'never.' . . . But when you have seen vicious mobs lynch your mothers and fathers at will and drown your sisters and brothers at whim; when you have seen hate-filled policemen curse, kick, brutalize, and even kill your black brothers and sisters with impunity; when you see the vast majority of your twenty million Negro brothers smothering in an airtight cage of poverty in the midst of an affluent society; when you have to concoct an answer for a five-year-old son asking in agonizing pathos, 'Daddy, why do white people treat colored people so mean?'; . . . when you are humiliated day in and day out by nagging signs reading 'white' and 'colored'; . . . when you are forever fighting a degenerating sense of 'nobodyness'—then you will understand why we find it difficult to wait. . . .

I must confess that over the last few years I have been gravely disappointed with the white moderate. I have almost reached the regrettable conclusion that the Negro's great stumbling block in the stride toward freedom is not the White Citizens Councillor or the Ku Klux Klanner but the white moderate who is more devoted to order than to justice; who prefers a negative peace which is the absence of tension to a positive peace which is the presence of justice; who constantly says, 'I agree with you in the goal you seek, but I can't agree with your methods of direct action'; who paternalistically feels that he can set the timetable for another man's freedom; who lives by the myth of time; and who constantly advises the Negro to wait until a 'more convenient season.' Shallow understanding from people of good will is more frustrating than absolute misunderstanding from people of ill will."

Questions for Analysis

1. Identify the immediate context for King's letter.
2. Describe King's disappointment with sympathetic white moderates.
3. Explain how King appeals to readers in his letter.
4. Explain why King is unwilling to "wait" until a "more convenient season" for civil rights.

and he noted the difficulty of preaching "freedom around the world" while "this is a land of the free except for Negroes." He proposed congressional legislation to end segregation in public accommodations, increase federal power to promote school desegregation, and broaden the right to vote.

Events on the day Kennedy delivered his powerful speech reinforced the need for swift action. Earlier that morning, Alabama governor George C. Wallace stood in front of the administration building at the University of Alabama to block the entrance of two black undergraduates. To uphold the federal court decree ordering their admission, Kennedy deployed federal marshals and the Alabama National Guard, and Wallace, having dramatized his point, stepped aside. However, victory soon turned into tragedy. That evening Medgar Evers, the head of the NAACP in Mississippi, was shot and killed in the driveway of his home by the white supremacist Byron de la Beckwith. (Following two trials that resulted in hung juries, de la Beckwith remained free until 1994, when he was retried and convicted for Evers's murder.)

Nonetheless, Congress was still unwilling to act. To increase pressure on lawmakers, civil rights organizations held the **March on Washington for Jobs and Freedom** on August 28, 1963, carrying out an idea first proposed by A. Philip Randolph in 1941 (see Module 7-10). With Randolph as honorary chair, his associate Bayard Rustin directed the proceedings as 250,000 black and white peaceful protesters rallied in front of the Lincoln Memorial. Two speakers in particular caught the attention of the crowd. John Lewis, the chairman of SNCC, expressed the frustration of militant black people with both the Kennedy administration and Congress. "The revolution is

---

TRM Suggested Responses to Questions

TRM Module 8.8 AP® Analyzing Sources Handout 1

BUILDING AP® SKILLS

Source and Situation

This activity is meant as a pre-read strategy for students to work on the skill of sourcing a document. Dr. King addressed his letter in the following manner, "My Dear Fellow Clergymen." The goal of this short activity is for students to source the intended audience. Rather than simply identifying the audience, consider asking students to explain why Dr. King would choose clergymen as his audience for this letter. To extend the activity, ask students to find a phrase in the document that corroborates their explanation.

TEACHING IDEA

Class Discussion

The goal of this class discussion is for students to consider what the differences are between political and moral issues and where, despite the inherent differences, political and moral issues intersect. To start the discussion ask students to identify a political issue from the post-World War II era as well as a moral issue from the same era. Ask students why they chose different topics for each category. What distinguishes a political and moral issue? Next, provide the following quote from President Kennedy's 1963 television address on race: "We are confronted primarily with a moral issue. It is as old as the scriptures and is as clear as the American Constitution." What specific events or developments would cause him to meld the political nature of civil rights with morality?

BUILDING AP® SKILLS

Comparison

The following activity builds out greater detail about the speeches of June 11, 1963 by President Kennedy and Governor Wallace. The goal is for students to read the excerpts and compare the purpose and audience of each document. In this way, your students are working on the skill of comparison and sourcing primary documents.

- Find Kennedy's "Radio and Television Report to the American People on Civil Rights, June 11, 1963" from the John F. Kennedy Presidential Library and Museum website (jfklibrary.org). Students can either listen to the speech or read the transcript.

- Find Wallace's "School House Door Speech" from the Alabama Department of Archives and History website (archives.alabama.gov).

▲ Differentiation

Divide the class into pairs. Have one student from each pair read President Kennedy's speech and have the other student listen to the audio recording. Ask students to discuss what they took away from their respective mediums. Then, have students switch. This can help students understand how speeches can convey meaning beyond the words of the text. Once the pairs have also read Governor Wallace's speech, have them discuss how an audience member who heard the speech might have been impacted differently.

TEACHING IDEA

Incorporating Secondary Sources

Consider using the *New York Times* article, "King's Forgotten Manifesto," by historian David W. Blight and Allison Scharfstein about Dr. Martin Luther King's request for a second emancipation proclamation to be issued by the Kennedy administration. While never announced, the request is a striking example of what Dr. King thought was necessary to move civil rights forward.

BUILDING AP® SKILLS

Claims and Evidence in Sources

Dr. King's "I Have a Dream" speech is traditionally studied with particular attention to the end of the speech. However, consider focusing on the beginning of the speech where Dr. King uses the metaphor of a promissory note to explain what guarantees African Americans have for freedom. After they read the excerpt, ask students to identify Dr. King's central claim and why he would use the metaphor of a check. The speech is available from the National Archives' website (archives.gov).

EXPLORING AP® THEMES

Politics and Power

In this activity, students compare and contrast the meaning and rights of the Fourteenth Amendment with the Civil Rights Act of 1964. Using information gleaned from the reading of the textbook, ask students to identify and explain how these acts are related to the themes of politics and power as well as American and national identity. Put another way, how does Americans' sense of their identity cross currents with political movements? And what are historical examples of why it took a century for Americans to return to the promises of the Fourteenth Amendment and attempt to defeat this type of structural racism?

Period 8: 1945–1980

MODULE 8-8 The Fight for Civil Rights, 1961–1979

◀ **Women and the March on Washington for Jobs and Freedom, 1963** Although black women played central roles in grassroots organizing within the civil rights movement, they received far less attention on the national stage than did male leaders, such as Martin Luther King Jr. and A. Philip Randolph. At the historic 1963 March on Washington, women, black and white, turned out in large numbers, as this photograph shows, but they were not chosen to give any of the major speeches or march at the front of the line with the leading men. **What does this photograph reveal about the marchers?**

Wally McNamee/Getty Images

at hand. . . . We will not wait for the President, nor the Justice Department, nor Congress," Lewis asserted. "But we will take matters into our own hands." In a more conciliatory tone, King delivered an impassioned speech expressing his hope for racial reconciliation: "I have a dream today that my four little children will one day live in a nation where they will not be judged by the color of their skin but by the content of their character." Still, King issued a stern warning to "those who hope that the Negro needed to blow off steam and will now be content. . . . There will be neither rest nor tranquility in America until the Negro is granted his citizenship rights." Weeks later, the Ku Klux Klan dynamited Birmingham's Sixteenth Street Baptist Church, a freedom movement staging ground. The blast killed four young girls attending services on Sunday, September 15, 1963. After the assassination of President Kennedy in November, it was up to Vice President Lyndon Johnson to step into the breach.

REVIEW

- What efforts to advance civil rights were made in 1963?
- What responses did those efforts receive?

Freedom Summer and Voting Rights

Civil Rights Act of 1964 Wide-ranging civil rights act that, among other things, prohibited discrimination in public accommodations and employment and increased federal enforcement of school desegregation.

Freedom Summer 1964 civil rights project in Mississippi launched by SNCC, CORE, the SCLC, and the NAACP. Some eight hundred volunteers, mainly white college students, worked on voter registration drives and in freedom schools to improve education for rural black youngsters.

Following Kennedy's death, President Johnson took charge of the pending civil rights legislation. Capitalizing on public sympathy over Kennedy's assassination and his own backroom deal-making skills honed as the former Senate Majority Leader, Johnson marshalled a bipartisan coalition to pass the **Civil Rights Act of 1964**. The law prohibited discrimination in public accommodations, increased federal enforcement of school desegregation and the right to vote, and created the Community Relations Service, a federal agency authorized to help resolve racial conflicts. The act also contained a final measure to combat employment discrimination on the basis of race and sex.

Yet even as President Johnson signed the Civil Rights Act into law on July 2, black freedom forces launched a new offensive to secure the right to vote in the South. The 1964 act contained a voting rights provision but did little to address the main problems of the discriminatory use of literacy tests and poll taxes and the biased administration of registration procedures that kept the majority of southern black people from registering. Beatings, killings, acts of arson, and arrests became a routine response to voting rights efforts. Although the Justice Department filed lawsuits against uncooperative voter registrars and police officers, the government refused to send in federal personnel or instruct the FBI to safeguard vulnerable civil rights workers.

To focus national attention on this problem, SNCC, CORE, the NAACP, and the SCLC launched the **Freedom Summer** project in Mississippi. They assigned eight hundred volunteers from around the nation, mainly white college students, to work on voter registration drives and in "freedom schools" to improve education for rural black youngsters. White supremacists fought back against what they perceived as an enemy invasion. In the summer of 1964, the Ku Klux Klan, sometimes in collusion with local law enforcement officials, killed three civil rights workers and attacked over thirty black churches. These tragedies focused national attention and energized civil rights workers who continued to encounter white violence and harassment throughout Freedom Summer.

758

MODULE 8-8 The Fight for Civil Rights, 1961–1979

AP® ANALYZING SOURCES

Source: *Prospectus for the Mississippi Freedom Summer,* 1964

"[A] program is planned for this summer which will involve the massive participation of Americans dedicated to the elimination of racial oppression. Scores of college students, law students, medical students, teachers, professors, ministers, technicians, folk artists, and lawyers from all over the country have already volunteered to work in Mississippi this summer—and hundreds more are being recruited. . . .

Mississippi at this juncture in the movement has received too little attention—that is, attention to what the state's attitude really is. . . . Either the civil rights struggle has to continue, as it has for the past few years, with small projects in selected communities with no real progress on any fronts, or [there must be a] task force of such a size as to force either the state and the municipal governments to change their social and legal structures, or the Federal Government to intervene on behalf of the constitutional rights of its citizens.

Since 1964 is an election year, the clear-cut issue of voting rights should be brought out in the open. Many SNCC and CORE workers in Mississippi hold the view that Negroes will never vote in large numbers until Federal marshals intervene. . . . [M]any Americans must be made to realize that the voting rights they so often take for granted involve considerable risk for Negroes in the South. . . . Major victories in Mississippi, recognized as the stronghold of racial intolerance in the South, would speed immeasurably the breaking down of legal and social discrimination in both North and South. . . ."

Questions for Analysis

1. Identify the goals expressed in the prospectus.
2. Describe the context surrounding the Mississippi Freedom Summer.
3. Explain the rationale for the Mississippi Freedom Summer expressed in this excerpt.
4. Explain the relationship between grassroots protests such as the Mississippi Freedom Summer and federal legislation such as the Civil Rights Act of 1964.

AP® TIP
Be sure you can explain the role African American women played in the struggle for civil rights throughout U.S. history.

One outcome of the Freedom Summer project was the creation of the **Mississippi Freedom Democratic Party (MFDP)**. Because the regular state Democratic Party excluded black people, the civil rights coalition formed an alternative Democratic Party open to everyone. In August 1964 the mostly black MFDP sent a delegation to the Democratic National Convention, meeting in Atlantic City, New Jersey, to challenge the seating of the all-white delegation from Mississippi. One MFDP delegate, Fannie Lou Hamer, who had lost her job for her voter registration activities, offered passionate testimony that was broadcast on television. Johnson then hammered out a compromise that gave the MFDP two at-large seats, seated members of the regular delegation who took a loyalty oath, and prohibited racial discrimination in the future by any state Democratic Party. While both sides rejected the deal, four years later an integrated delegation, which included Hamer, represented Mississippi at the Democratic National Convention in Chicago.

Freedom Summer highlighted the problem of disfranchisement, but it took further demonstrations in Selma, Alabama to resolve it. After state troopers shot and killed a black voting rights demonstrator in February 1965, Dr. King called for a march from Selma to the capital, Montgomery, to petition Governor Wallace to end the violence and allow black people to vote. On Sunday, March 7, as black and white marchers left Selma, the sheriff's forces sprayed them with tear gas, beat them, and sent them running for their lives. A few days later, a white pastor who had joined the protesters was killed by a group of white thugs. On March 21, following another failed attempt to march to Montgomery, King finally led protesters on the fifty-mile hike to the state capital, where they arrived safely four days later. Still, after the march, the Ku Klux Klan murdered a white female marcher from Michigan.

Events in Selma prompted President Johnson to take action. On March 15 he addressed a joint session of Congress and told lawmakers and a nationally televised audience that the black "cause

---

TRM Suggested Responses to Questions

TRM Module 8.8 AP® Analyzing Sources Handout 2

BUILDING AP® SKILLS

Claims and Evidence in Sources

Mississippi was notoriously slow to move on questions of racial justice. Ask students to look for claims in the source that help explain why focus was put on Mississippi in the summer of 1964. Put another way, given all students know about events in states such as Alabama, why focus on Mississippi?

EXPLORING AP® THEMES

Politics and Power

This activity is meant for students to explore the role state and federal governments played in the civil rights movement, as well as the struggle for power over decisions made regarding civil rights. Using the time period 1957–1964, have students select the three most important examples and explain how they illustrate a battle between the federal and state governments.

TEACHING IDEA

Connecting the Dots

Even though the focus of this module is on how civil rights leaders pursued continued reforms, students need to recall the resistance of white Americans during this era. Think about having students compare and contrast how white southerners, northerners, and westerners resisted civil rights. They should think about personal and structural racism in their answer. If you are looking to make this a group activity, simply divide up the class into three groups and then subdivide if necessary to form groups of 3 or 4 students. Each group is given a region and their job is to become experts in that area. After students finish, they compare answers with other groups.

TEACHING IDEA

Incorporating Secondary Sources

Consider assigning the Period 8 essay on Gilder Lehrman's AP® U.S. History site by historian Clarence Taylor, "Civil Rights Leadership and the 1964 Civil Rights Act" (ap.gilderlehrman.org). This condensed essay is accessible and provides students with further historical analysis concerning the importance, context, and takeaways about this pivotal piece of civil rights legislation.

TEACHING IDEA

Connecting the Dots

Using the voter registration data on this page, have students work on the skill of describing trends from documents that provide quantitative information. Too often, students pinpoint specifics from a source without giving a historical trend. Therefore, have students cite and explain two specific reasons for the changes in voting patterns in the chart.

TEACHING IDEA

Incorporating Primary Sources

The more varied voices students can read and hear about the civil rights movement, the more well-rounded their understandings will be about the different views black Americans had throughout the 1960s. One voice of particular note is James Baldwin. Consider having students read the 1963 "A Talk to Teachers" speech (available through online search from Saint Paul Public Schools). Ask students to describe Baldwin's claims about the civil rights movement and its meaning.

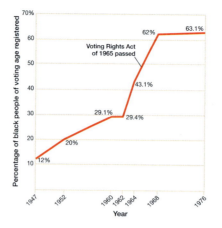

Black Voter Registration in the South, 1947–1976 After World War II, the percentage of black adults registered to vote in the South slowly but steadily increased, largely as a result of grassroots voting drives. Despite the Kennedy administration's support for voter registration drives, a majority of southern black people remained prohibited from voting in 1964. The passage of the 1965 Voting Rights Act removed barriers such as literacy tests and poll taxes, strengthened the federal government's enforcement powers, and enabled more than 60 percent of southern black people to vote by the late 1960s. **What historical developments contributed to the steeper rise in black voter registration during the Johnson administration (1963–1968) than in the years before and after his presidency?**

Voting Rights Act 1965 act that eliminated many of the obstacles to African American voting in the South and resulted in dramatic increases in black participation in the electoral process.

AP® TIP
Analyze the impact of federal protections for voting rights during the twentieth century.

must be our cause too" and "we shall overcome." On August 6, 1965, the president signed the **Voting Rights Act**, which banned the use of literacy tests for voter registration, authorized a federal lawsuit against the poll tax (which succeeded in 1966), empowered federal officials to register disfranchised voters, and required seven southern states to submit any voting changes to Washington, D.C. before they went into effect. With strong federal enforcement of the law, by 1968 a majority of black southerners and nearly two-thirds of black Mississippians could vote.

However, these civil rights victories had exacted a huge toll on the movement. SNCC and CORE had come to distrust Presidents Kennedy and Johnson for failing to provide protection for voter registration workers. Furthermore, Johnson's attempt to broker a compromise at the 1964 Atlantic City Convention convinced MFDP supporters that the liberal president had sold them out. The once united movement showed signs of cracking.

REVIEW

- In what ways did the Johnson administration support the civil rights movement in 1964 and 1965?
- In what ways did the Johnson administration fail to support the civil rights movement in 1964 and 1965?

From Civil Rights to Black Power

Increasingly after 1964, SNCC and CORE began exploring new ways of seeking freedom through strategies of black self-determination and self-defense. They were greatly influenced by Malcolm X. Born Malcolm Little, he had engaged in a life of crime, which landed him in prison. Inside jail, he converted to the Nation of Islam, a religious sect based partly on Muslim teachings and partly on the belief that white people were devils (not a doctrine associated with orthodox Islam). After his release from jail, Malcolm rejected his "slave name" and substituted the letter X to symbolize his unknown African forebears. Minister Malcolm helped convert thousands of disciples in black ghettos by denouncing whites and encouraging black people to embrace their African heritage and beauty as a people. Favoring self-defense over nonviolence, he criticized civil rights leaders for failing to protect their communities. After 1963, Malcolm X broke away from the Nation of Islam, visited the Middle East and Africa, and accepted the teachings of traditional Islam. He moderated his anti-white rhetoric but remained committed to black self-determination. He had already influenced the growing number of disillusioned young black activists when, in 1965, members of the Nation of Islam murdered him, apparently in revenge for challenging the organization.

Black militants, echoing Malcolm X's ideas, challenged racial liberalism. They renounced the principles of integration and nonviolence in favor of black power and self-defense. Instead of welcoming whites within their organizations, black radicals believed that African Americans had to assert their independence from white America. In 1966 SNCC expelled white members and created an all-black organization. Stokely Carmichael, SNCC's chairman, proclaimed "black power" as the central goal of the freedom struggle and linked the cause of African American freedom to revolutionary conflicts in Cuba, Africa, and Vietnam.

Black power emerged against a backdrop of riots in black ghettos, which erupted across the nation starting in the mid-1960s: in Harlem and Rochester, New York, in 1964; in Los Angeles in 1965; and in Cleveland, Chicago, Detroit, Newark, and Tampa in the following two years. While the civil rights movement had lifted the hopes of African Americans throughout the country by dismantling segregation in public facilities and impediments to voting, urban black people, many in the North and West, faced problems of high unemployment, broken-down housing, and police mistreatment that civil rights legislation had done nothing to correct. Many whites perceived the ghetto uprisings solely as an exercise in criminal behavior, while many black people viewed the violence as an expression of political discontent—as rebellions, not riots. The Kerner Commission, appointed by President Johnson to assess urban disorders, concluded in 1968 that white racism remained at the heart of the problem: "Our nation is moving toward two societies, one black, one white—separate and unequal."

New groups emerged to take up the cause of black power. In 1966 Huey P. Newton and Bobby Seale, college students in Oakland, California, formed the **Black Panther Party**. Dressed in black leather, sporting black berets, and carrying guns, the Black Panthers appealed mainly to black men. They did not, however, rely on armed confrontation and bravado alone. The Black Panthers established day care centers and health facilities, often run by women, which gained the admiration of many in their communities. Much of this good work was overshadowed by violent confrontations with the police, which led to the deaths of Black Panthers in shootouts and the imprisonment of key party officials. By the early 1970s, government crackdowns on the Black Panthers had destabilized the organization and reduced its influence.

The assassination of Martin Luther King Jr. in 1968 furthered black disillusionment. King was shot and killed by James Earl Ray in Memphis, where he was supporting demonstrations by striking sanitation workers while preparing to launch a Poor People's Campaign to fight for economic justice for poor people, both black and white. In the wake of his murder, riots erupted in hundreds of cities throughout the country. Little noticed amid the fiery turbulence, President Johnson signed into law the 1968 Fair Housing Act, the final piece of civil rights legislation of his term.

Black Panther Party Organization founded in 1966 by Huey P. Newton and Bobby Seale to advance the black power movement in black communities.

AP® TIP
Evaluate the degree to which the legislation passed in the 1960s addressed the political and economic legacies of racial discrimination in the United States.

REVIEW
Why did elements of the civil rights movement embrace black power during the mid-1960s?

Racial Struggles Continue

The civil rights struggle did not end with the 1960s. The civil rights coalition of organizations that banded together in the 1960s had disintegrated, but the National Association for the Advancement of Colored People (NAACP) remained active, as did local organizations in communities nationwide. Following passage of the 1965 Voting Rights Act, electoral politics became the new form of activism. By 1992 there were more than 7,500 black elected officials in the United States. Many of them had participated in the civil rights movement and subsequently worked to gain for their constituents the economic benefits that integration and **affirmative action** had not yet achieved. During this time, the number of Latino American and Asian American elected officials also increased.

The issue of **school busing** highlighted the persistence of racial discrimination. In the fifteen years following the landmark 1954 decision in *Brown v. Board of Education of Topeka, Kansas*, few schools had been integrated. Starting in 1969, the U.S. Supreme Court ruled that genuine racial integration of the public schools must no longer be delayed. In 1971 the Court went even further in *Swann v. Charlotte-Mecklenburg Board of Education* by requiring school districts to bus pupils to achieve integration. Cities such as Charlotte, North Carolina; Lexington, Kentucky; and Tampa, Florida, embraced the ruling and carefully planned for it to succeed.

However, the decision was more controversial in other municipalities around the nation and it exposed racism as a national problem. In many northern communities racially discriminatory housing policies created segregated neighborhoods and, thus, segregated schools. When white parents in the

affirmative action Programs meant to overcome historical patterns of discrimination against minorities and women in education and employment. By establishing guidelines for hiring and college admissions, the government sought to advance equal opportunities for minorities and women.

school busing Mandatory nationwide initiative to integrate schools, begun in 1971 to comply with the 1954 Supreme Court decision *Brown v. Board*. The practice of school busing continued in the U.S. well into the 1990s. Also known as "busing" or "desegregation busing."

TEACHING IDEA

Incorporating Videos

The PBS documentary series *Eyes on the Prize* is still a useful teaching resource due to the interviews and original footage used to describe the events of the civil rights movement. Two episodes in particular are well-suited for use in this part of the module: "Two Societies" and "Power." These episodes address both the Black Panther Party as well as the riots in Detroit and Chicago. Many of the usable clips are within seven-to-ten minutes. You should preview and decide which clips will provide the most salient points for students to ponder.

BUILDING AP® SKILLS

Comparison

Prior to using this bell ringer activity, write de jure (by law) and de facto (by custom) segregation on the front board. Next, have students define these terms with historical evidence. After students have working definitions for these terms, focus students' attention on the northern reaction to forced busing. Ask students to explain how and why many northerners had a violent reaction to integration. This can be a useful way to begin a conversation about issues of civil rights which plagued northern communities.

Period 8: 1945–1980

MODULE 8-8 The Fight for Civil Rights, 1961–1979

◀ **Boston Anti-busing March, 1975** Boston City Council member Louise Day Hicks (in center) arrives to address a large demonstration in South Boston's Columbus Park to protest federal court-ordered busing of black students to all-white neighborhood schools. Joining her were some men dressed in Revolutionary War era outfits. In 1976, Hicks was elected as the first woman president of the City Council. **What do the costumes and American flags shown in this photograph suggest about the arguments of school busing opponents?**

whites were fleeing the cities and moving to the suburbs where few black people lived.

Detroit suburbs objected to busing their children to inner-city, predominantly black schools, the Supreme Court in 1974 departed from the *Swann* case and prohibited busing across distinct school district boundaries. This ruling created a serious problem for integration efforts because many

As the conflict over school integration intensified, violence broke out in communities throughout the country. In Boston, Massachusetts, busing opponents led by Louise Day Hicks tapped into the racial and class resentments of the largely white working-class population of South Boston, which was paired with the black community of Roxbury for busing, leaving mainly middle- and upper-class white communities unaffected. In the fall of 1974, battles broke out inside and outside the schools. Despite the violence, schools stayed open, and for the next three decades Boston remained under court order to continue busing.

From 1970 to 1977, with the acceleration of affirmative action programs, the number of African Americans attending college doubled, constituting nearly 10 percent of the student body, a few percentage points lower than the proportion of black people in the national population. Though African Americans still earned lower incomes than the average white family, black family income as a percentage of white family income had grown from 55.1 percent in 1965 to 61.5 percent ten years later. African Americans, however, still had a long way to go to catch up with whites. The situation was even worse for those who did not reach middle-class status: About 30 percent of African Americans slid deeper into poverty during the decade.

Along with busing, affirmative action generated fierce controversy, as the case of Alan Bakke showed. Bakke, a white male in his thirties, was twice denied admission to the medical program at the University of California at Davis in the early 1970s. Bakke sued the university after learning it awarded sixteen of its one hundred spots to minorities, as part of its affirmative action policy to recruit a more racially and ethnically diverse student body. In court, he contended that the policy violated his constitutional rights of equal protection under the Fourteenth Amendment and amounted to "reverse discrimination." He provided evidence that he had higher qualifications than some of the minority students accepted into the medical school. "I realize that the rationale for these quotas is that they attempt to atone for past racial discrimination," Bakke stated. "But insisting on a new racial bias in favor of minorities is not a just situation." In 1978, in *Regents of the University of California v. Bakke*, the U.S. Supreme Court struck down the use of strict racial quotas in college admissions but allowed for the continued consideration of race as one of many factors.

Despite the persistence of economic inequality, many whites believed that affirmative action placed them at a disadvantage with black people in the educational and economic marketplaces. In particular, many white men condemned policies that they thought recruited black people at their expense. Polls showed that although most white people favored equal treatment of African Americans, they disapproved of affirmative action as a form of "reverse discrimination." Over the next three decades affirmative action opponents succeeded in narrowing the use of racial consideration in employment and education.

AP® TIP
Analyze how the Supreme Court both supported and limited the implementation of civil rights legislation.

❝ We know through painful experience that freedom is never voluntarily given by the oppressor; it must be demanded by the oppressed. ❞
— Martin Luther King Jr., "Letter from Birmingham Jail," 1963

AP® TIP
Analyze the role that the Supreme Court played in combatting state-sanctioned discrimination during the 1950s and 60s.

REVIEW

• Why were affirmative action and school busing so controversial during the 1960s and 1970s?

TEACHING IDEA

Building Vocabulary

In the 1970s and beyond, white Americans, concerned with programs such as affirmative action, became increasingly critical of civil rights. Many claimed "reverse discrimination" and fought to slow down affirmative action. Have students define affirmative action and explain at least two reasons why some white Americans believed in this theory. Make sure that discussions are grounded in facts.

EXPLORING AP® THEMES

Politics and Power

This activity is one intended for students to reflect on Module 8-8 and make a historical interpretation. The central question to this activity is: Which branch of government was the most active proponent of civil rights during the 1960s and 1970s? Provide students with the following options: legislative, executive, or judicial. Students make an interpretation and write a 2–4 sentence explanation.

AP® WRITING HISTORICALLY — Document-Based Question Practice

ACTIVITY

The following question is based on the accompanying documents. The documents have been edited for the purpose of this exercise. *Suggested reading period: 15 minutes. Suggested writing time: 45 minutes.*

Evaluate the extent of change within the movement for African American civil rights in the period 1945 to 1970.

DOCUMENT 1

Source: *Brown v. Board of Education of Topeka,* 1954

"Segregation of white and colored children in public schools has a detrimental effect upon the colored children. The impact is greater when it has the sanction of the law, for the policy of separating the races is usually interpreted as denoting the inferiority of the negro group. A sense of inferiority affects the motivation of a child to learn. Segregation with the sanction of law, therefore, has a tendency to [slow] the educational and mental development of negro children and to deprive them of some of the benefits they would receive in a racial[ly] integrated school system.

Whatever may have been the extent of psychological knowledge at the time of *Plessy v. Ferguson,* this finding is amply supported by modern authority. Any language in *Plessy v. Ferguson* contrary to this finding is rejected.

We conclude that, in the field of public education, the doctrine of 'separate but equal' has no place. Separate educational facilities are inherently unequal...."

DOCUMENT 2

Source: Martin Luther King Jr., *Speech at Holt Street Baptist Church,* December 5, 1955

"My FRIENDS, we are certainly very happy to see each of you out this evening. We are here this evening for serious business. We are here in a general sense because first and foremost we are American citizens and we are determined to apply our citizenship to the fullness of its meaning. We are here also because of our love for democracy, because of our deep-seated belief that democracy transformed from thin paper to thick action is the greatest form of government on earth.

But we are here in a specific sense, because of the bus situation in Montgomery. We are here because we are determined to get the situation corrected. This situation is not at all new. The problem has existed over endless years. For many years now Negroes in Montgomery and so many other areas have been inflicted with the paralysis of crippling fears on buses in our community. On so many occasions, Negroes have been intimidated and humiliated and impressed-oppressed-because of the sheer fact that they were Negroes....

And you know, my friends, there comes a time when people get tired of being trampled over by the iron feet of oppression. There comes a time, my friends, when people get tired of being plunged across the abyss of humiliation, where they experience the bleakness of nagging despair....

We are here, we are here this evening because we're tired now. And I want to say that we are not here advocating violence. We have never done that. I want it to be known throughout Montgomery and throughout this nation that we are Christian people. We believe in the Christian religion. We believe in the teachings of Jesus. The only weapon that we have in our hands this evening is the weapon of protest. That's all."

(Continued)

TRM Suggested Responses to Questions

BUILDING AP® SKILLS

Contextualization

Prior to having students answer the DBQ, consider having them work on the reasoning process of contextualization. For students who need assistance in starting their contextualization statements, provide a few developments that fit the criteria of broader processes that relate to the question. For example, World War II, the Cold War, and the Great Migration all are relevant historical influences to this question.

BUILDING AP® SKILLS

Argumentation

For students who are struggling to develop a thesis for this question, consider having them do the following pre-write strategy. After students read through and annotate all seven documents, have them organize the documents into groups of analysis. Next, have students develop thesis categories based on their grouping. This can get students started in the process of developing a thesis.

TEACHING IDEA

Incorporating Primary Sources

By this point in the year students know the process of analyzing primary sources. Now is the time of year when students need to focus on continuing to sharpen these skills in a timed setting. Consider having students underline or highlight the section of the document they will be incorporating in their response before they begin writing. On the test, students have 15 minutes to plan for responses for the DBQ. Of this 15 minutes, it is reasonable to think that students will spend around 10 minutes reading and analyzing documents.

TEACHING IDEA

AP® Writing Historically Workshop

One of the more fundamental decisions students will make when answering a Document-Based Question is how they choose to organize the documents. This workshop activity is meant to teach students how to broaden their view of organizing historical evidence. Organize students into groups of 4 or 5 and provide each group with the documents from the DBQ cut into single sheets of paper, for a total of seven pieces of paper. Next, have groups read and discuss the documents. Following that conversation, have groups arrange the documents into categories of analysis. Students will organize the documents and write the label of their category on a blank piece of paper above the documents. The final product will be to have the documents with labels in separate piles on a desk. Next, students visit the product of the other groups to see how many different ways the documents can be organized.

Period 8: 1945–1980 MODULE 8-8 The Fight for Civil Rights, 1961–1979

TEACHING IDEA

Incorporating Primary Sources

Remind students that non-textual documents are an opportunity to illustrate their ability to infer information. Document 3 gives students the opportunity to make inferences about the historical context from which this document comes. Encourage students to source this document by evaluating the historical situation.

BUILDING AP® SKILLS

Continuity and Change

This question centers on students' ability to demonstrate the extent of change in the civil rights movement. Students should look for two qualities from the documents: those that demonstrate a dramatic change from the mainstream civil rights movement and those that may demonstrate continuity. Not only will this allow students to organize the documents better, it will also lead to a more nuanced interpretation.

DOCUMENT 3 **Source:** *Sit-in at a Woolworth's Lunch Counter*, Jackson, Mississippi, May 28, 1963

The Granger Collection, New York

DOCUMENT 4 **Source:** Malcom X, *Speech to Mississippi Youth*, December, 1964

"I myself would go for nonviolence if it was consistent, if everybody was going to be nonviolent all the time. I'd say, okay, let's get with it, we'll all be nonviolent. But I don't go along with any kind of nonviolence unless everybody's going to be nonviolent. If they make the Ku Klux Klan nonviolent, I'll be nonviolent. If they make the White Citizens Council nonviolent, I'll be nonviolent. But as long as you've got somebody else not being nonviolent, I don't want anybody coming to me talking any nonviolent talk. I don't think it is fair to tell our people to be nonviolent unless someone is out there making the Klan and the Citizens Council and these other groups also be nonviolent."

DOCUMENT 5 **Source:** Huey Newton and Bobby Seale, *Black Panther Party Platform and Program*, October 1966

"1. We want freedom. We want power to determine the destiny of our Black community. . . .
2. We want full employment for our people.
   We believe that the federal government is responsible and obligated to give every man employment or a guaranteed income. . . .
3. We want an end to the robbery by the white man of our Black community. . . .
4. We want decent housing, fit for shelter of human beings. . . .
5. We want education for our people that exposes the true nature of this decadent American society. We want education that teaches us our true history and our role in the present-day society. . . ."

6. We want all Black men to be exempt from military service. We believe that all black men should not be forced to fight in the military service to defend a racist government that does not protect us. . . .
7. We want an immediate end to POLICE BRUTALITY and MURDER of Black people. . . . The Second Amendment to the Constitution of the United States gives a right to bear arms. We therefore believe that all black people should arm themselves for self-defense.
8. We want freedom for all Black men held in federal, state, county, and city prisons and jails. . . .
9. We want all Black people when brought to trial to be tried in court by a jury of their peer group or people from their Black communities . . .
10. We want land, bread, housing, education, clothing, justice and peace. . . ."

DOCUMENT 6

Source: *Chicago Student Non-Violent Coordinating Committee Leaflet, 1967*

"The black man in America is in a perpetual state of slavery no matter what the white man's propaganda tells us. . . .

We must not get hung-up in the bag of having one great leader who we depend upon to make decisions. This makes the Movement too vulnerable to those forces the white man uses to keep us enslaved, such as the draft, murder, prison or character assassination. . . .

We have got to begin to say and understand with complete assuredness what black is. Black in an inner pride that the white man's language hampers us from expressing. Black is being a complete fanatic, who white society considers insane. We have to learn that black is so much better than belonging to the white race . . .

. . . We believe that we belong to the 90 percent majority of the people on earth that the white man oppresses and that we should not beg the white man for anything. We want what belongs to us as human beings and we intend to get it through BLACK POWER."

DOCUMENT 7

Source: *Kerner Commission Report, 1968*

"This is our basic conclusion: Our nation is moving toward two societies, one black, one white—separate and unequal.

Reaction to last summer's [urban riots] has quickened the movement and deepened the division. Discrimination and segregation have long permeated much of American life; they now threaten the future of every American. . . .

Segregation and poverty have created in the racial ghetto a destructive environment totally unknown to most white Americans.

What white Americans have never fully understood—but what the Negro can never forget—is that white society is deeply implicated in the ghetto. White institutions created it, white institutions maintain, and white society condones it. . . .

Our recommendations embrace three basic principles:

To mount programs on a scale equal to the dimension of the problems;

To aim these programs for high impact in the immediate future in order to close the gap between promise and performance;

To undertake new initiatives and experiments that can change the system of failure and frustration that now dominates the ghetto and weakens our society.

These programs will require unprecedented levels of funding and performance, but they neither probe deeper nor demand more than the problems which called them forth. There can be no higher priority for national action and no higher claim on the nation's conscience. . . ."

TEACHING IDEA

Check for Understanding

Students need to be well versed in the timing of planning the DBQ in the allotted 15 minute reading period. Consider having students practice this by having them complete their outline in 15 minutes and then, if necessary, backtrack through the Teaching Ideas and Building AP® Skills notes from pages 763–765.

TRM Suggested Responses to Questions

Module 8-9

Liberalism and Its Challengers, 1960–1973

LEARNING TARGETS
By the end of this module, you should be able to:
- Explain how Johnson's Great Society attempted to end poverty, expand civil rights, and remedy other social problems.
- Explain the factors that contributed to the rise of the New Left, free speech, and counterculture movements and their impacts on American society.
- Explain how Warren Court rulings expanded civil liberties and why a backlash emerged to those rulings from conservatives.
- Explain how women, American Indians, Chicanos, and gays fought for civil rights in the 1960s.
- Explain how the roots of a new conservatism took hold amidst the height of liberalism in the 1960s.

THEMATIC FOCUS
Migration and Settlement
Politics and Power
American and Regional Culture

Promising to create a Great Society, Johnson's legislative successes rivaled the New Deal with reforms aimed at civil rights, immigration, poverty, education, health care, and environmental protection. Together with rulings by the Warren Court expanding civil liberties, the 1960s represented the height of a liberal consensus in American politics. Yet, protests against the Vietnam War stimulated the growth of a New Left movement, which rejected the Cold War emphasis on containment and conformity. Liberation movements also emerged for women, Hispanics, American Indians, and homosexuals while a small but noticeable counterculture movement took root among disaffected youths in select cities. Many middle-class and working-class Americans disapproved of the cultural changes taking place, setting the stage for a revival of conservatism.

HISTORICAL REASONING FOCUS
Continuity and Change

TASK ▶ As you read this module, consider the ways and the extent to which American politics and society changed as a result of the Great Society, Vietnam War, Warren Court rulings, and rights movements by various groups. Make sure to take into account the growth of a new conservatism as you weigh the extent of change.

TEACHING IDEA

Building Vocabulary

While students may be familiar with the term liberalism, this activity is meant to calibrate their understanding to the specific historical context of the 1960s and early 1970s. Consider dividing students into groups of 2 or 3 and allow them to select one of the following categories: civil rights, women's movement, and Vietnam War. Have students define liberalism using their selected category, which should help narrow their focus.

Hoping to build on the legacy of the New Deal, liberals sought to increase the role of the federal government in the economy, education, and health care. Most liberals supported a staunchly anti-Communist foreign policy, differing with Republicans more over means than over ends. Indeed, when Democrats recaptured the White House in 1960, Presidents Kennedy and Johnson seized opportunities in Cuba and Southeast Asia to vigorously challenge the expansion of Soviet influence.

President Johnson's liberal accomplishments reached beyond civil rights to include an ambitious expansion of social welfare policies, the Great Society. At the heart of Johnson's agenda was a war on poverty, which included expanding health care coverage and educational opportunities for the young, old, and sick. While Johnson pressed ahead in the legislative arena, Chief Justice Earl Warren's Supreme Court issued rulings that extended social justice to minorities and the economically oppressed and favored those who believed in a firm separation of church and state, free speech, and a right to privacy.

EXPLORING AP® THEMES

Politics and Power

Traditionally, political history centers analysis on elections, party platforms, and perhaps big historical personalities. However, political history should also include how grassroots-level organizations changed the goals, makeup, and landscape of politics in a given era. Lisa McGirr's groundbreaking study of the rise of the New Right in her book, *Suburban Warriors: The Origins of the New American Right*, is an excellent source to use to broaden students' views of political changes in this period. Chapters 1 and 2, in particular, provide the context for the changes in the Republican Party in Orange County, California, which would later help explain the national changes.

Even at its peak in the 1960s, liberalism faced major challenges from both the left and the right. Young activists became impatient with what they saw as the slow pace of social progress and were increasingly distressed by the escalation of the Vietnam War. At the same time, the right was disturbed by the failure of the United States to win the war as well as by the liberal reforms they believed diminished individual initiative and benefited racial minorities at the expense of the white middle class. Conservatives depicted the left as unpatriotic and out of step with mainstream American values. By 1969 liberalism was in retreat, and Richard Nixon, a political conservative, had captured the White House.

Federal Efforts toward Social Reform, 1960–1968

With victory in World War II and the revival of economic prosperity, liberal thinkers regained confidence in capitalism. Many saw the postwar American free-enterprise system as different from the old-style capitalism that had existed before Franklin Roosevelt's New Deal. In their view, this new "reform capitalism," or democratic capitalism, created abundance for all and not just for the elites. Rather than pushing for the redistribution of wealth, liberals now called on the government to help create conditions conducive to economic growth and increased productivity. The liberal economist John Kenneth Galbraith thus argued in *The Affluent Society* (1958) that increased public investments in education, research, and development were the key to American prosperity and progress.

These ideas guided the thinking of Democratic politicians such as Senator John F. Kennedy of Massachusetts. Elected president in 1960, the forty-three-year-old Kennedy brought good looks, charm, a beautiful wife, and young children to the White House. Kennedy pledged a **New Frontier** to battle "tyranny, poverty, disease, and war," but lacking strong majorities in Congress, he contented himself with making small gains on the New Deal's foundation. Congress expanded unemployment benefits, increased the minimum wage, extended Social Security benefits, and raised appropriations for public housing, but Kennedy's caution disappointed many liberals. Tragically, Kennedy was assassinated on November 22, 1963 by Lee Harvey Oswald as Kennedy and his wife rode in an open motorcade in Dallas, Texas during an early campaign event. Days later, Oswald was shot to death by nightclub owner Jack Ruby. The assassination shocked the nation. Millions of grieving Americans watched the elaborate televised funeral modeled after President Lincoln's funeral proceedings. In death, Kennedy achieved immense popularity, yet his legislative agenda remained unfulfilled.

For newly inaugurated President Lyndon Johnson, a product of modest upbringing in rural Texas, urban and rural poverty were issues that required action. Awareness of social and economic inequality had increased with the publication of *The Other America* (1962) in which socialist author Michael Harrington exposed the invisibility of the poor in America. In an address at the University of Michigan on May 22, 1964, President Johnson sketched out his dream for the **Great Society**, one that "rests on abundance and liberty for all. It demands an end to poverty and racial injustice, to which we are totally committed in our time. But that is just the beginning."

Besides poverty and race, he outlined three broad areas in need of reform: education, the environment, and cities. Toward this end, the Elementary and Secondary School Act (1965) was the most far-reaching federal law ever passed. It provided federal funds directly to public schools to improve their quality. The Model Cities program (1966) set up the Department of Housing and Urban Affairs, which coordinated efforts at urban planning and rebuilding neighborhoods in decaying cities. The Department of Transportation sought to ensure a fast, safe, and convenient transportation system. In addition, the president pushed Congress to pass hundreds of environmental protection laws, including those dealing with air and water pollution, waste disposal, the use of natural resources, and the preservation of wildlife and wilderness areas. Still, it was the War on Poverty that garnered the most attention.

The opening battle of the War on Poverty came with passage of the Economic Opportunity Act of 1964. Through this measure, Johnson wanted to offer the poor "a hand up, not a handout." Among its major components, the law provided job training, food stamps, rent supplements, redevelopment of depressed rural areas, remedial education (later to include the preschool program Head Start), a domestic Peace Corps called Volunteers in Service to America (VISTA), and a

Great Society President Lyndon Johnson's vision of social, economic, and cultural progress in the United States. The size and scope of Johnson's Great Society programs were rivaled only by Roosevelt's New Deal.

TEACHING IDEA

Building Vocabulary

While students may be familiar with the term conservatism, this activity is meant to calibrate their understanding to the specific historical context of the 1960s and early 1970s. Consider dividing students into groups of 2 or 3 and allow them to select one of the following categories: civil rights, women's movement, and Vietnam War. Have students define conservatism using their selected category, which should help narrow their focus.

BUILDING AP® SKILLS

Claims and Evidence in Sources

This activity builds off the explanation about the Great Society speech provided in the text. Consider conducting a close read of the speech, which is available from the American Rhetoric website (americanrhetoric.com). Pay close attention to the words "imagination," "initiative," and "indignation," which appear in the fifth paragraph of the transcript. Students can use the excerpt of the fifth and sixth paragraphs to hypothesize what President Johnson meant by these three words, especially indignation.

TEACHING IDEA

Incorporating Secondary Sources

Consider using excerpts from historian Julian Zelizer's book, *The Fierce Urgency of Now: Lyndon Johnson, Congress, and the Battle for the Great Society,* which is an accessible text for students. Chapter 6, "The Fabulous Eighty-Ninth Congress," is a particularly useful section because it delineates the unique nature of the Congressional representation that enabled this type of liberal agenda to be passed.

EXPLORING AP® THEMES

Politics and Power

The Great Society was an expansive reform effort that encompassed political, economic, and social goals of new left liberals. Much like the New Deal, the Great Society can overwhelm students with the amount of programs and legislation. Therefore, consider providing students with an organizational chart that condenses students' focus to the major categories of the Great Society: poverty, race, education, environment, and urban reform.

TRM Find **Handout 8.8 – Categories of The Great Society** in the Teacher's Resource Materials.

TRM Suggested Responses to Questions

TRM Module 8.9 AP® Analyzing Sources Handout 1

BUILDING AP® SKILLS

Sourcing and Situation

When students read about and study issues related to poverty, the economics of the inquiry can become mired in abstract generalizations. Therefore, consider using the following activity to root students in the practice of sourcing this primary source with more specific historical developments. Provide students with the categories of rural, urban, and suburban to analyze issues related to wealth and poverty that Harrington addresses in the excerpt. When students evaluate the claims by Harrington, have them couch their explanations in one or more of the categories.

TEACHING IDEA

Incorporating Websites

The 1964 presidential election was a turning point election because of the results in southern states and the overwhelming victory experienced by President Johnson, despite the defection by southern states to the Republican Party. Consider using the electoral map of the 1964 election from the 270 to Win website (270towin.com). Have students evaluate the reasons why so many southern states left the Democratic Party and switched to the Republican Party.

Period 8: 1945–1980

MODULE 8-9 Liberalism and Its Challengers, 1960–1973

AP® ANALYZING SOURCES

Source: Michael Harrington, *The Other America*, 1962

"There is a familiar America. It is celebrated in speeches and advertised on television and in the magazines. It has the highest mass standard of living the world has ever known.

In the 1950s this America worried about itself, yet even its anxieties were products of abundance. The title of a brilliant book was widely misinterpreted, and the familiar America began to call itself 'the affluent society. . . .'

While this discussion was carried on, there existed another America. In it dwelt somewhere between 40,000,000 and 50,000,000 citizens of this land. They were poor. They still are. . . .

The millions who are poor in the United States tend to become increasingly invisible. Here is a great mass of people, yet it takes an effort of the intellect and will even to see them. . . .

Now the American city has been transformed. The poor still inhabit the miserable housing in the central area, but they are increasingly isolated from contact with, or sight of, anybody else. Middle-class women coming in from Suburbia on a rare trip may catch the merest glimpse of other America on the way to an evening at the theater, but the children are segregated in suburban schools. The business or professional man may drive along the fringes of slums in a car or bus, but it is not an important experience to him. The failure, the unskilled, the disabled, the aged, and the minorities are right there, across the tracks, where they have always been. But hardly anyone else is.

In short, the very development of the American city has removed poverty from the living, emotional experience of millions upon millions of middle-class Americans. . . .

That the poor are invisible is one of the most important things about them. They are not simply neglected and forgotten as in the old rhetoric of reform; what is much worse, they are not seen."

Questions for Analysis

1. Identify the fundamental contradiction Harrington highlights in the excerpt.
2. Describe how the poor have become invisible to the middle class, according to Harrington.
3. Explain why Harrington argues that poverty is worse than it used to be.
4. Evaluate the extent of similarity between Harrington's argument and the arguments of progressives about urban poverty at the turn of the twentieth century.

Community Action Program that empowered the poor to shape policies affecting their own communities. Between 1965 and 1968, expenditures targeted for the poor doubled, from $6 billion to $12 billion. The antipoverty program helped reduce the proportion of poor people from 20 percent in 1963 to 13 percent five years later, and it helped reduce the rate of black poverty from 40 percent to 20 percent during this same period.

Johnson intended to fight the War on Poverty through the engine of economic growth, which would create new jobs for the unemployed without redistributing wealth. With this in mind, he persuaded Congress to enact significant tax cuts. Johnson's tax cut, which applied across the board, stimulated the economy and sent the gross national product soaring from $591 billion in 1963 to $977 billion by the end of the decade. Despite the gains made, many liberals believed that Johnson's spending on the War on Poverty did not go far enough. Whatever the shortcomings, Johnson campaigned on his antipoverty and civil rights record in his bid to recapture the White House in 1964. His Republican opponent, Senator Barry Goldwater of Arizona, personified the conservative right wing of the Republican Party. The Arizona senator condemned big government, supported states' rights, and accused liberals of not waging the Cold War forcefully enough. His aggressive conservatism appealed to his grassroots base in small-town America, especially in southern California, the Southwest, and the South. His tough rhetoric, however, scared off moderate Republicans, resulting on election day in a landslide for Johnson as well as considerable Democratic majorities in Congress.

> **AP® TIP**
> Be sure you can explain the differences between the Democratic and Republican Parties' platforms during the late 1960s.

TEACHING IDEA

Incorporating Videos

One of the most iconic moments in presidential election history is the infamous 1964 "Daisy Girl" television advertisement (available on YouTube). Show the short advertisement as a way to highlight the manner in which the Johnson administration tried to portray Barry Goldwater. Ask students: What is most effective about the advertisement?

Flush with victory, Johnson pushed Congress to move quickly. Working together, they achieved remarkable results. To cite only a few examples, the Eighty-ninth Congress (1965–1967) subsidized health care for the elderly and the poor by creating Medicare and Medicaid, expanded voting rights for African Americans in the South, raised the minimum wage, and created national endowments for the fine arts and the humanities. The 1965 Immigration Act repealed discriminatory national origins quotas established in 1924, resulting in a shift of immigration from Europe to Asia and Central and South America.

The Warren Court reflected this high tide of liberalism. The Court affirmed the constitutionality of the Voting Rights Act. In 1967, the justices overturned state laws prohibiting interracial marriages. A year later, fourteen years after the *Brown* decision, they ruled that school districts in the South could no longer maintain racially exclusive schools and must desegregate immediately. In a series of cases, the Warren Court ensured fairer legislative representation for both black and white people by removing the disproportionate power that rural districts had held over urban districts.

The Supreme Court's most controversial rulings dealt with the criminal justice system, religion, and private sexual practices. Strengthening the rights of criminal defendants, the justices ruled in *Gideon v. Wainwright* (1963) that states had to provide poor people accused of felonies with an attorney, and in *Miranda v. Arizona* (1966) they ordered the police to advise suspects of their constitutional rights.

The Warren Court also moved into new, controversial territory concerning school prayer, contraception, and pornography. In 1962 the Court outlawed a nondenominational Christian prayer recited in New York State schools as a violation of the separation of church and state guaranteed by the First Amendment. Three years later, in *Griswold v. Connecticut*, the justices struck down a state law that banned the sale of contraceptives because such laws, they contended, infringed on an individual's right to privacy. In a 1966 case the justices ruled that states could not prohibit what they deemed pornographic material unless it was "utterly without redeeming social value," a standard that opened the door for the dissemination of sexually explicit books, magazines, and films. These verdicts unleashed a firestorm of criticism, especially from religious groups that accused the Warren Court of undermining traditional values of faith and decency.

REVIEW

- How did Johnson's Great Society attempt to address issues of poverty, race, education, health care, and the environment?
- Why were the Warren Court rulings controversial?

The New Left and the Counterculture

The civil rights movement had inspired many young people to activism. Combining ideals of freedom, equality, and community with direct-action protest, civil rights activists offered a model for those seeking to address a variety of problems, including the threat of nuclear devastation, the loss of individual autonomy in a corporate society, racism, poverty, sexism, and environmental degradation. The formation of SNCC in 1960 illuminated the possibilities for personal and social transformation and offered a movement culture founded on democracy.

Tom Hayden helped apply the ideals of SNCC to predominantly white college campuses. After spending the summer of 1961 registering voters in Mississippi and Georgia, the University of Michigan graduate student returned to campus eager to recruit like-minded students who questioned America's commitment to democracy.

Students for a Democratic Society (SDS) Student activist organization formed in the early 1960s that advocated the formation of a "New Left" that would overturn the social and political status quo.

Hayden became an influential leader of the **Students for a Democratic Society (SDS)**, which advocated the formation of a "New Left." They considered the "Old Left," which revolved around communism and socialism, as autocratic and no longer relevant. "We are people of this generation," SDS proclaimed, "bred in at least modest comfort, housed now in universities, looking uncomfortably to the world we inherit." In its **Port Huron Statement** (1962), SDS condemned mainstream liberal politics, Cold War foreign policy, racism, and research-oriented universities

---

TEACHING IDEA

Connecting the Dots

The Emergency Quota Act of 1921 and the National Origins Act of 1924 were passed in the context of heightened xenophobia following World War I. These quotas lasted until the Immigration Act of 1965. To highlight the dramatic shifts that took place as a result of the 1965 law, provide students with the following information. The 1921 law used the 1910 census to establish a quota, which was set at 3% of an ethnic group from the 1910 census. The goal was to increase northern and western European immigration while limiting eastern and southern European immigration. However, many nativists were not satisfied with the results. In 1924 the law changed to use the 1890 census and drop the percentage to 2%, while also completely excluding Asiatic immigration. Ask students what factors existed between 1924 and 1965 that would have prevented change from happening sooner. Consider asking them about how this change has affected immigration to America today.

BUILDING AP® SKILLS

Argumentation

Students are required to know how Warren Court decisions extended civil rights throughout the 1960s. Under the direction of Chief Justice Earl Warren, the court earned the reputation of being a liberal court. To work on the skill of argumentation, have students select one of the Warren Court decisions from the textbook and explain the extent to which it represents a more liberal approach by the Supreme Court.

Period 8: 1945–1980

MODULE 8-9 Liberalism and Its Challengers, 1960–1973

APPLY THE TIP

For this AP® Tip, students need to concentrate on explaining continuities among liberal groups from earlier time periods to the New Left liberals of the 1960s. It might be useful to help students narrow their focus. Consider providing them with another group such as the Old Left from the 1930s, who were also critical of government policies.

EXPLORING AP® THEMES

American and Regional Culture

Liberal student groups on the left went beyond protesting the Vietnam War by broadening their movement to include critiques of the social and economic system propagated by leaders in government. Students for a Democratic Society (SDS) delineated their goals in the Port Huron Statement in 1962. Consider using Teaching American History's website to search for the document (teachingamericanhistory.org). Ask students to highlight sections of the document where critiques move beyond military matters to include social and political topics. The fact that this document predates escalation in Vietnam helps students understand how the New Left criticized many parts of government throughout the 1960s.

AP® TIP
Analyze the ways in which the New Left illustrated continuity with earlier groups critical of the federal government's actions and policies.

Free Speech Movement (FSM) Movement protesting policies instituted by the University of California at Berkeley that restricted free speech. In 1964 students at Berkeley conducted sit-ins and held rallies against these policies.

that cared little for their undergraduates. It called for the adoption of "participatory democracy," which would return power to the people. In an ironic twist, the framers of the manifesto picked up the rhetoric of the moderate Republican president, Dwight Eisenhower, in condemning the military-industrial complex (see Module 8-6). "Not only is ours the first generation to live with the possibility of world-wide cataclysm," the statement declared, "it is the first to experience the actual social preparation for cataclysm, the general militarization of American society." The attack on the military-industrial complex and the unrestrained power of the executive branch to conduct foreign and military policy would become a staple of New Left protest. The New Left, however, never consisted of one central organization; after all, many protesters challenged the very idea of centralized authority. In fact, SDS did not initiate the New Left's most dramatic early protest. In 1964 the University of California at Berkeley banned political activities just outside the main campus entrance in response to CORE protests against racial bias in local hiring. When CORE defied the prohibition, campus police arrested its leader, prompting a massive student uprising. Student activists then formed the **Free Speech Movement (FSM)**, which held rallies in front of the administration building, culminating in a nonviolent, civil rights–style sit-in. When California governor Edmund "Pat" Brown dispatched state and county police to evict the demonstrators, students and faculty joined in protest and forced the university administration to yield to FSM's demands for amnesty and reform. By the end of the decade, hundreds of demonstrations had erupted on campuses throughout the nation.

The Vietnam War accelerated student radicalism, and college campuses provided a strategic setting for antiwar activities. Like most Americans in the mid-1960s, undergraduates had only a dim awareness of U.S. activity in Vietnam. Yet all college men were eligible for the draft once they graduated and lost their student deferment. As more troops were sent to Vietnam, student concern intensified.

Protests escalated in 1966 when President Johnson authorized an additional 250,000-troop buildup in Vietnam. With induction into the military a looming possibility, student protesters launched a variety of campaigns and demonstrations. Others resisted the draft by fleeing to Canada, and still others engaged in various forms of civil disobedience. Most college students, however, were not activists — between 1965 and 1968, only 20 percent of college students attended demonstrations. Nevertheless, the activist minority received extensive media attention and helped raise awareness about the difficulty of waging the Vietnam War abroad and maintaining domestic tranquility at home.

By the end of 1967, as the number of troops in Vietnam approached half a million, protests increased. Antiwar sentiment had spread to faculty, artists, writers, businesspeople, and elected officials. In April Martin Luther King Jr. delivered a powerful antiwar address at Riverside Church in New York City. "The world now demands," King declared, "that we admit that we have been wrong from the beginning of our adventure in Vietnam, that we have been detrimental to the life of the Vietnamese people." As protests spread and the government clamped down on dissenters, some activists

The Berkeley Free Speech Movement Mario Savio, a student leader at the University of California at Berkeley and a Freedom Summer volunteer, stands among demonstrators sitting in at Sproul Hall on December 3, 1964, to protest university curbs on free speech. A day earlier, Savio had declared: "There's a time when the operation of the machine becomes so odious . . . you've got to put your bodies upon the gears . . . and you've got to make it stop." **To what extent were the free speech sit-ins in universities similar to the sit-ins to desegregate public facilities in the South?**

AP Photo/Robert Houston

TEACHING IDEA

Building Vocabulary

Now that students have worked on developing more nuanced understandings of the terms liberal and conservative, consider a brief bell ringer activity to check for understanding. Ask students to explain at least two pieces of historical evidence for how college-aged students represented both liberal and conservative views of government.

counterculture Young cultural rebels of the 1960s who rejected conventional moral and sexual values and used drugs to reach a higher consciousness.

substituted armed struggle for nonviolence. SDS split into factions, with the most prominent of them, the Weathermen, going underground and adopting violent tactics.

The New Left's challenge to liberal politics attracted many students, and the **counterculture's** rejection of conventional middle-class values of work, sexual restraint, and rationality captivated even more. Cultural rebels emphasized living in the present, seeking immediate gratification, expressing authentic feelings, and reaching a higher consciousness through mind-altering drugs. Despite differences in approach, both the New Left and the counterculture expressed concerns about modern technology, bureaucratization, and the possibility of nuclear annihilation and sought new means of creating political, social, and personal liberation.

Rock 'n' roll became the soundtrack of the counterculture. In 1964 Bob Dylan's song "The Times They Are A-Changin'" became an anthem for youth rebellion. That same year, the Beatles, a British quartet influenced by 1950s black and white rock 'n' rollers, toured the United States and revolutionized popular music. Originally singing melodic compositions of teenage love and angst, the Beatles embraced the counterculture and began writing songs about alienation and politics, flavoring them with the drug-inspired sounds of psychedelic music. Although most of the songs that reached the top ten on the record charts did not undermine traditional values, the music of groups like the Beatles, the Rolling Stones, the Who, the Grateful Dead, Jefferson Airplane, and the Doors spread counterculture messages.

The counterculture viewed the elimination of sexual restrictions as essential for transforming personal and social behavior. The 1960s generation did not invent sexual freedom, but it did a great deal to shatter time-honored moral codes of monogamy, fidelity, and moderation. Casual sex, extramarital affairs, and public nudity all gradually became more acceptable, and the broader culture reflected these changes. The Broadway production of the musical *Hair* showed frontal nudity, the movie industry adopted ratings of "X" and "R" that made films with nudity and profane language available to a wider audience, and new television comedy shows featured sketches with risqué content.

AP® TIP
Evaluate the degree to which American attitudes toward women's independence changed during the 1960s.

With sexual conduct in flux, society had difficulty maintaining the double standard of behavior that privileged men over women. In particular, the availability of birth control pills for women, introduced in 1960, made sexual freedom more possible. Although sexual liberation still carried more risks for women than for men, increased openness in discussing sexuality allowed many women to gain greater control over their bodies and their relationships.

The antiwar movement and counterculture influenced popular culture in many ways. Rock musicians such as Bruce Springsteen, Jackson Browne, and Billy Joel sang of loss, loneliness, urban decay, and adventure. The film *M*A*S*H* (1970), though dealing with the Korean War, was a thinly veiled satire of the horrors of the Vietnam War, and in the late 1970s filmmakers began producing movies specifically about Vietnam and the toll the war took on ordinary Americans who served there. The television sitcom *All in the Family* gave American viewers the character of Archie Bunker, an opinionated, white, blue-collar worker, in a comedy that dramatized the contemporary political and cultural wars as conservative Archie taunted his liberal son-in-law with politically incorrect remarks about minorities, feminists, and liberals.

REVIEW

- What factors led to student protests in the 1960s?
- In what ways did the counterculture affect broader American culture in the 1960s and 1970s?

Liberation Movements

The varieties of political protest and cultural dissent emboldened other oppressed groups to emancipate themselves. Latinos, American Indians, and gay Americans all launched liberation movements.

Despite passage of the Nineteenth Amendment in 1920, which gave women the right to vote, women did not have equal access to employment, wages, or education or control over reproduction. Nor did they have sufficient political power to remove these obstacles to full equality. Yet by 1960 nearly 40 percent of all women held jobs, and women made up 35 percent of college enrollments. The social movements of the 1960s — civil rights, the New Left, and the counterculture — attracted

---

BUILDING AP® SKILLS

Comparison

As students study the liberal movements of the 1960s and 1970s it is important that they distinguish among the several groups. For instance, consider having students conduct a comparison of the New Left and counterculture. Have students be especially attuned with the political and social goals, beliefs, and demographics.

APPLY THE TIP

There are a lot of different categories students could focus on in this particular tip. However, consider providing a more specific approach by having students compare the emergence and reaction to birth control in the 1920s with the 1960s (information on birth control in the 1920s can be found in Module 7-1). This category will give students an idea of how to answer the degree to which American attitudes toward women's independence changed during the 1960s.

TEACHING IDEA

Connecting the Dots

While it is true that the American Indian, women, Latino, as well as gay and lesbian movements were influenced by the civil rights movement of African Americans, they were also inspired by other aspects of cultural trends of the 1960s and 1970s. Consider having students select one of the following movements: American Indian, women, Latino, or gay and lesbian. Next, have students connect an aspect of cultural changes that influenced this group, other than the African American civil rights movement.

large numbers of women. Groups like SNCC empowered female staff in community-organizing projects, and women also played central roles in antiwar efforts, leading many to demand their own movement for liberation.

The women's liberation movement also built on efforts of the federal government to address gender discrimination. In 1961 President Kennedy appointed the **Commission on the Status of Women**. The commission's report, *American Women*, issued in 1963, reaffirmed the primary role of women in raising the family but cataloged the inequities women faced in the workplace. In 1963 Congress passed the Equal Pay Act, which required employers to give men and women equal pay for equal work. The following year, the 1964 Civil Rights Act opened up further opportunities when it prohibited sexual bias in employment and created the Equal Employment Opportunity Commission (EEOC).

In 1963 Betty Friedan published a landmark book, *The Feminine Mystique*, which questioned society's prescribed gender roles and raised the consciousness of mostly college-educated women. In *The Feminine Mystique*, she described the post-college isolation and alienation experienced by her female friends who got married and stayed home to care for their children (see Module 8-4). However, not all women saw themselves reflected in Friedan's book. Many working-class women and those from African American and other minority families had not had the opportunity to attend college or stay home with their children, and younger college women had not yet experienced the burdens of domestic isolation.

Nevertheless, in October 1966, Betty Friedan and like-minded women formed the **National Organization for Women (NOW)**. With Friedan as president, NOW dedicated itself to moving society toward "true equality for all women in America, and toward a fully equal partnership of the sexes." NOW called on the EEOC to enforce women's employment rights more vigorously and favored passage of an **Equal Rights Amendment (ERA)**, paid maternity leave for working women, the establishment of child care centers, and reproductive rights. Although NOW advocated job training programs and assistance for impoverished women, it attracted a mainly middle-class white membership. Some black people were among its charter members, but most African American women chose to concentrate first on eliminating racial barriers that affected black women and men alike. Some union women also continued to oppose the ERA, and advocates opposed to abortion wanted to steer clear of NOW's support for reproductive rights.

Young women, black and white, had also faced discrimination, sometimes in unexpected places. Even within the civil rights movement women were not always treated equally, often being assigned clerical duties. Men held a higher status within the antiwar movement because women were not eligible for the draft. As a result of these experiences, radical women formed their own, mainly local organizations. They created "consciousness-raising" groups that allowed them to share their experiences of oppression in the family, the workplace, the university, and movement organizations.

These women's liberationists went beyond NOW's emphasis on legal equality and attacked male domination, or patriarchy, as a crucial source of women's subordination. They criticized the nuclear family and cultural values that glorified women as the object of male sexual desires, and they protested creatively against discrimination. In 1968 radical feminists picketed the popular Miss America contest in Atlantic City, New Jersey, and set up a "Freedom Trash Can" into which they threw undergarments and cosmetics. Radical groups such as the Redstockings condemned all men as oppressors and formed separate female collectives to affirm their identities as women. In contrast, other feminists attempted to build the broadest possible coalition. In 1972 Gloria Steinem, a founder of NOW, established *Ms.* magazine in hope of attracting readers from across the feminist political spectrum. The magazine featured women's art and poetry alongside articles on sisterhood, child rearing, and abortion.

In 1973 feminists won a major battle in the Supreme Court over a woman's right to control reproduction. In *Roe v. Wade*, the high court ruled that states could not prevent a woman from obtaining an abortion in the first three months of pregnancy but could impose some limits in the next two trimesters. In furthering the constitutional right of privacy for women, the justices classified abortion as a private medical issue between a patient and her doctor. This decision marked a victory for a woman's right to choose to terminate her pregnancy, but it also stirred up a fierce reaction from women and men who considered abortion to be the murder of an unborn child.

National Organization for Women (NOW) Feminist organization formed in 1966 by Betty Friedan, Gloria Steinem, and other like-minded activists.

Equal Rights Amendment (ERA) A proposed amendment mandating the "equality of rights under law . . . by the United States or any State on the basis of sex." Not enough states had ratified the amendment by 1982, when the ratification period expired, so it was not adopted.

Roe v. Wade The 1973 Supreme Court decision that affirmed a woman's constitutional right to abortion.

BUILDING AP® SKILLS

Comparison

As with any reform movement, the women's reform movement of the 1960s was divided into different ideological wings. For instance, the National Organization for Women (NOW) had a mainstream reputation while the Redstockings had a more radical one. Consider having students compare and contrast the rhetoric of the National Organization for Women Statement of Purpose from 1966 with the Redstockings Manifesto of 1969. The NOW Statement of Purpose can be found by searching on NOW's website (now.org). The Redstockings Manifesto can be found on Teaching Tolerance's website (tolerance.org).

EXPLORING AP® THEMES

Social Structures

The definitions for what men and women thought of what it meant to be truly feminine in the 1950s and 1960s changed dramatically. Have students write a paragraph explanation of how the feminine ideal changed in the 1950s and 1960s due to issues of class, race, and gender.

TEACHING IDEA

Incorporating Videos

The PBS documentary, *Makers: Women Who Make America*, is an excellent resource to examine the changes of the women's movement in the 1960s and 1970s (makers.com/documentaries). Episode 2 in particular explains the many viewpoints of different women's organizations and also explains the conservative backlash.

TEACHING IDEA

Incorporating Primary Sources

Women advocating for political power was not a one-sided movement of liberal feminists. For example, Phyllis Schlafly provided a powerful conservative voice representing the backlash to the women's movement by conservatives. Consider using Schlafly as an example for how Republican women responded to the feminist movement by having students read "STOP ERA Letter from Phyllis Schlafly" from the National Archives (docsteach.org).

Liberation Movements

AP® TIP

Analyze the impact of *Roe v. Wade* on women's rights and on political party divisions in the United States.

Latinas joined the feminist movement, often forming their own organizations, but they, like black women, also joined men in struggles for racial equality and advancement. During the 1960s, the size of the Spanish-speaking population in the United States tripled from three million to nine million. Hispanic Americans were a diverse group who hailed from many countries and backgrounds. In the 1950s, Cesar Chavez had emerged as the leader of oppressed Mexican farmworkers in California. In seeking the right to organize a union and gain higher wages and better working conditions, Chavez shared King's nonviolent principles. In 1962 Chavez and Dolores Huerta formed the National Farm Workers Association, and in 1965 the union called a strike against California grape growers, one that attracted national support and finally succeeded after five years.

Younger Mexican Americans, especially those in cities such as Los Angeles and other western *barrios* (ghettos), supported Chavez's economic goals but challenged older political leaders who sought cultural assimilation. Borrowing from the Black Panthers, Mexican Americans formed the Brown Berets, a self-defense organization. In 1969 some 1,500 activists gathered in Denver and declared themselves *Chicanos*, a term that expressed their cultural pride and identity. Chicanos created a new political party, **La Raza Unida (The United Race)**, to promote their interests, and

La Raza Unida (The United Race) A Chicano political party, formed in 1969, that advocated job opportunities for Chicanos, bilingual education, and Chicano cultural studies programs in universities.

AP® ANALYZING SOURCES

Source: Dolores Huerta, *Statement before U.S. Senate Subcommittee on Migratory Labor*, 1969

"Mr. Chairman and members of the committee, we are again glad to be here and present our long, sad story of trying to organize the farmworkers. . . .

The horrible state in which farmworkers find themselves, faced with such extreme poverty and discrimination, has taught us that the only way we can change our situation is by organization of a union. . . .

As you know, UFWOC[1] has undertaken an international boycott of all California-Arizona table grapes in order to gain union recognition for striking farmworkers. We did not take up the burden of the boycott willingly. It is expensive. It is a hardship on the farmworkers' families who have left the small valley towns to travel across the country to boycott grapes.

But, because of the table grape growers' refusal to bargain with their workers, the boycott is our major weapon and I might say a nonviolent weapon, and our last line of defense against the growers who use foreign labor to break our strikes.

It is only through the pressure of the boycott that UFWOC has won contracts with major California wine grape growers. At this point, the major obstacles to our efforts to organize farmworkers are obstacles to our boycott.

Our boycott has been met with well-organized and well-financed opposition by the growers and their sympathizers. Most recently, several major California grape growers joined with other agribusiness interests and members of the John Birch Society to form an employer-dominated "union" the Agricultural Workers Freedom To Work Association (AWFWA), for the sole purpose of destroying UFWOC. . . .

In spite of this type of antiunion activity, our boycott of California-Arizona table grapes has been successful. It is being successful for the simple reason that millions of Americans are supporting the grape workers strike by not buying table grapes. . . ."

[1]United Farm Workers Organizing Committee.

Questions for Analysis

1. Identify the tactics used by each side in the labor dispute that Huerta refers to in this statement.
2. Describe the challenges and successes of the farmworkers, according to Dolores Huerta.
3. Evaluate the extent of similarity between the UFWOC protest and other civil rights movement protests.
4. Evaluate the extent to which Huerta's activism reflects the influence of the feminist movement and the influence of the Chicano movement.

TRM Suggested Responses to Questions

TRM Module 8.9 AP® Analyzing Sources Handout 2

BUILDING AP® SKILLS

Sourcing and Situation

To work on establishing the historical situation of this document, consider having students select either one women's rights gain or one civil rights gain in order to provide a broader context of the Latino movement. The goal is to select the example that provides the most directly related concept. In this way, students are not only comparing social movements but also working on developing document analysis skills.

EXPLORING AP® THEMES

Social Structures

As students are reading about the Latino movement of the 1960s, consider an activity that focuses on social structures while also working on argumentation. Provide students with two options: counterculture and civil rights movement. Ask students to select the category they feel most influenced the development of the Latino movement.

▲ **Differentiation**

As a challenge, have students who chose counterculture stand on one side of the room and students who chose the civil rights movement stand on the other side of the room. If the division is more-or-less equal, consider pairing students up so that one person in each pair represents each option. Have students defend their decision to their partner. If the division is not equal, allow groups to formulate an argument and debate their chosen option.

Period 8: 1945–1980

MODULE 8-9 Liberalism and Its Challengers, 1960–1973

TEACHING IDEA

Incorporating Videos

Consider assigning students part of a lecture by historian Michael Kazin from Gilder Lehrman's AP® U.S. History website (ap.gilderlehrman.org). Students can go to Period 8 and find the video "Religion vs. Spirituality in 1960s America." The lecture is broad in scope and engaging. Students may find this a helpful resource as the module comes to a close.

> **AP® TIP**
> Analyze how the civil rights movement of the 1950s and 60s influenced movements for the rights of other groups in the United States.

American Indian Movement (AIM) An American Indian group, formed in 1968, that promoted "red power" and condemned the United States for its continued mistreatment of American Indians.

Stonewall riots 1969 uprising after New York City police raided The Stonewall Inn, a gathering place for gay men, and tried to arrest patrons. This uprising helped inspire the gay liberation movement of the 1970s.

the party and its allies sponsored demonstrations to fight for jobs, bilingual education, and the creation of Chicano studies programs in colleges. Chicano and other Spanish-language communities also took advantage of the protections of the Voting Rights Act, which in 1975 was amended to include sections of the country — from New York to California to Florida and Texas — where Hispanic literacy in English and voter registration were low.

In similar fashion, Puerto Ricans organized the Young Lords Party (YLP). Originating in Chicago in 1969, the group soon spread to New York City. Like the Black Panthers, the organization established inner-city breakfast programs and medical clinics. The YLP supported bilingual education in public schools, condemned U.S. imperialism, favored independence for Puerto Rico, and supported women's reproductive rights.

American Indians also joined the upsurge of activism and self-determination. By 1970 some 800,000 people identified themselves as American Indians, many of whom lived in poverty on reservations. They suffered from inadequate housing, high alcoholism rates, low life expectancy, staggering unemployment, and lack of education. Conscious of their heritage as the first Americans, they determined to halt their deterioration by asserting "red power" and pride and established the **American Indian Movement (AIM)** in 1968. The following year, American Indians occupied the abandoned prison island of Alcatraz in San Francisco Bay, where they remained until 1971. Among their demands, they offered to buy the island for $24 in beads and cloth — a reference to the purchase of Manhattan Island in 1626 — and turn it into an American Indian educational and cultural center. In 1972 AIM occupied the headquarters of the Federal Bureau of Indian Affairs in Washington, D.C. AIM demonstrators also seized the village of Wounded Knee, South Dakota, the scene of the 1890 massacre of Sioux residents by the U.S. Army, to dramatize the impoverished living conditions on reservations. They held out for more than seventy days with eleven hostages until a shootout with the FBI ended the confrontation, killing one protester and wounding another.

The results of the red power movement proved mixed. Demonstrations focused media attention on the plight of American Indians but did little to halt their downward spiral. Nevertheless, courts became more sensitive to American Indian claims and protected mineral and fishing rights on reservations.

Asian American college students on the West Coast formed their own liberation struggle. At the University of California, Berkeley and San Francisco State University, they participated in demonstrations against the Vietnam War and racism. In 1968 Asian American students at San Francisco State joined the Third World Liberation Front and, along with the Black Student Union, went on strike for five months, succeeding in the establishment of programs in Asian American and Black studies.

The children of newly arrived Chinese immigrants faced different problems, doing poorly in public schools that taught exclusively in English. Established in 1969, the Chinese for Affirmative Action filed a lawsuit against San Francisco school officials for discriminating against students with limited English-language skills. In *Lau v. Nichols* (1974), the Supreme Court upheld the group's claim, accelerating opportunities for bilingual education.

During this period many Japanese American high school and college students learned for the first time about their parents and grandparents' internment during World War II. Like other activists, they expressed pride in their ethnic heritage and joined in efforts to publicize the injustices that earlier generations had endured. The activism of this third generation of Japanese helped convince the moderate Japanese American Citizens League in 1970 to endorse reparations for the internees, the first step in an ultimately successful two-decade effort.

Unlike African Americans, Chicanos, American Indians, and Asian Americans, homosexuals were not distinguished by the color of their skin. Estimated at 10 percent of the population, gays and lesbians remained largely invisible to the rest of society. In the 1950s, gay men and women created their own political and cultural organizations and frequented bars and taverns outside mainstream commercial culture, but most lesbians and gay men hid their identities. It was not until 1969 that they took a major step toward asserting their collective grievances in a very visible fashion. Police regularly cracked down on gay bars like the Stonewall Tavern in New York City's Greenwich Village. But on June 27, 1969, gay patrons battled back. The *Village Voice* called the **Stonewall riots** "a kind of liberation, as the gay brigade emerged from the bars, back rooms, and bedrooms of the Village and became street people." In the manner of black power, the New Left, and radical feminists, homosexuals organized the Gay Liberation Front, voiced pride in being gay, and demanded equality of opportunity regardless of sexual orientation.

As with other oppressed groups, gays achieved victories slowly and unevenly. In the decades following the 1960s, gay men and lesbians faced discrimination in employment, could not marry or receive domestic benefits, and were subject to violence for public displays of affection.

REVIEW

- How did the women's movement evolve in the 1960s and early 1970s?
- What did the Chicano, Asian American, and gay rights movements have in common? How were they different?

The Revival of Conservatism

These diverse social movements did a great deal to change the political and cultural landscapes of the United States, but they did not go unchallenged. Many Americans worried about black militancy, opposed liberalism, and were even more dismayed by the radical offshoots they spawned. Conservatives soon attracted support from many Americans who did not see change as progress. Many believed that the political leadership of the nation did not speak for them about what constituted a great society.

The brand of conservatism that emerged in the 1960s united libertarian support for a laissez-faire political economy with opposition to social welfare policies and moralistic concerns for defeating communism and defending what they saw as religious devotion, moral decency, and family values. Unlike earlier conservatives, the new generation believed that the United States had to escalate the struggle against the evil of godless communism anywhere it posed a threat in the world, but they opposed internationalism as represented in the United Nations.

Conservative religious activists who built grassroots organizations to combat liberalism joined forces with political and intellectual conservatives such as William F. Buckley, the founder of the *National Review*, an influential journal of conservative ideas. The Reverend Billy Joe Hargis's Christian Crusade and Dr. Frederick Charles Schwartz's Christian Anti-Communist Crusade, both formed in the early 1950s, promoted conspiracy theories about how the eastern liberal establishment intended to sell the country out to the Communists by supporting the United Nations, foreign aid, Social Security, and civil rights. The John Birch Society packaged these ideas in periodicals and radio broadcasts throughout the country and urged readers and listeners to remain vigilant to attacks against their freedom.

In the late 1950s and early 1960s, the conservative revival grew, mostly unnoticed, at the grassroots level in the suburbs of southern California and the Southwest. Bolstered by the postwar economic boom that centered around military research and development, these towns in the Sun Belt attracted college-educated engineers, technicians, managers, and other professionals from the Midwest (or Rust Belt) seeking new economic opportunities. These migrants brought with them Republican loyalties as well as traditional conservative political and moral values. Women played a large part in conservative causes, especially in protesting against public school curricula that they perceived as un-Christian and un-American. Young housewives built an extensive network of conservative study groups.

In addition, the conservative revival, like the New Left, found fertile recruiting ground on college campuses. In October 1960 some ninety young conservatives met at William Buckley's estate in Sharon, Connecticut to draw up a manifesto of their beliefs. "In this time of moral and political crisis," the framers of the Sharon Statement declared, "the foremost among the transcendent values is the individual's use of his God-given free will, whence derives his right to be free from the restrictions of arbitrary force." Based on this essential principle, the manifesto affirmed the conservative doctrines of states' rights, the free market, and anticommunism. Participants at the conference formed the **Young Americans for Freedom (YAF)**, which six months later boasted 27,000 members. In 1962 the YAF filled Madison Square Garden to listen to a speech by the politician who most excited them: Republican senator Barry M. Goldwater of Arizona.

Goldwater's book *The Conscience of a Conservative* (1960) attacked New Deal liberalism and advocated abolishing Social Security; dismantling the Tennessee Valley Authority, the government-owned public power utility; and eliminating the progressive income tax. His firm belief in states' rights put him on record against the ruling in *Brown v. Board of Education* and prompted

TEACHING IDEA

Incorporating Secondary Sources

An excellent resource on the disparate groups that came to form the resurgence of conservatism, historian Darren Dochuk's book *From Bible Belt to Sunbelt: Plain-Folk Religion, Grassroots Politics, and the Rise of Evangelical Conservatism* highlights the reasons for the emergence of a strong conservative movement in the late 1960s. In particular, Chapter 12, "Moral Majority," traces the roots of the power the Sunbelt offered and the role of Nixon's "Silent Majority" in the emerging conservative movement.

BUILDING AP® SKILLS

Causation

The rise of conservatism had many roots, but chief among those were the role religion and anticommunism played. To evaluate this phenomenon, have students select either anticommunism or religion and write a 2 to 3 sentence explanation about its significance as a cause of conservatism.

TEACHING IDEA

Connecting the Dots

The Young Americans for Freedom (YAF) was an important group for young conservatives looking to counter groups such as Students for a Democratic Society (SDS) and Free Speech Movement (FSM). Have students look up the Sharon Statement, which encapsulates the beliefs of YAF and contrast that with groups of the New Left. What does this say about the youth of America in the 1960s?

him to vote against the Civil Rights Act of 1964, positions that won him increasing support from conservative white southerners. However, Goldwater's advocacy of small government did not prevent him from supporting increased military spending to halt the spread of communism. The senator may have anticipated growing concerns about government excess, but his defeat in a landslide to Lyndon Johnson in the 1964 presidential election indicated that most voters perceived Goldwater's brand of conservatism as too extreme.

The election of 1964 also brought George C. Wallace onto the national stage as a leading architect of the conservative revival. As Democratic governor of Alabama, the segregationist Wallace had supported states' rights and opposed federal intervention to reshape social and political affairs. Wallace began to attract white northerners fed up with rising black militancy, forced busing to promote school integration, and open housing laws to desegregate their neighborhoods. Running in the Democratic presidential primaries in 1964, the Alabama governor garnered 34 percent of the votes in Wisconsin, 30 percent in Indiana, and 43 percent in Maryland.

More so than Goldwater, Wallace united a populist message against the political establishment with concern for white working-class Americans. Wallace voters identified with the governor as an "outsider." Many of them also backed Wallace for attacking privileged college students who, he claimed, mocked patriotism, violated sexual taboos, and looked down on hardworking, churchgoing, law-abiding Americans. How could "all those rich kids — from the fancy suburbs," one father wondered, "[avoid the draft] when my son has to go over there and maybe get his head shot off?" Each in his own way, George Wallace and Barry Goldwater waged political campaigns against liberals for undermining the economic freedom of middle- and working-class whites and coddling what they considered "racial extremists" and "countercultural barbarians."

> **AP® TIP**
> Evaluate the extent to which the Great Society was successful in addressing educational, environmental, and economic issues.

REVIEW

- What factors contributed to the revival of conservatism in the 1960s?
- How successful were prominent conservative politicians in promoting their ideas during the early 1960s?

AP® WRITING HISTORICALLY — Long-Essay Question Practice

ACTIVITY

Answer the following Long-Essay Question with a complete essay. *Suggested writing time: 40 minutes.*

Evaluate the extent to which different rights movements fostered change in American society in the 1960s.

TEACHING IDEA

Building Vocabulary

From the beginning to the end of this module students have been examining the differences between liberals and conservatives. Consider having students do one more analysis of this concept. You can provide three categories of analysis: foreign policy, civil rights, and counterculture. Have students select either conservative or liberal and define the views of their selected groups using all three of the categories. After students are finished, consider a gallery walk where students get to peruse the room to look at each other's responses.

TRM Suggested Responses to Questions

TEACHING IDEA

Connecting the Dots

If students are struggling to answer the Long-Essay Question, consider providing categories of analysis such as foreign policy, civil rights, counterculture, and women. For students who are excelling, consider having them formulate an essay response that addresses both continuities and changes as that will lead to a more nuanced response.

TEACHING IDEA

AP® Writing Historically Review

This activity is meant to work on helping students write complex historical analyses, which is one point on the AP® U.S. History rubrics. Bear in mind, this activity is not meant to show students a guaranteed way to earn the complexity point; instead, the activity seeks to demonstrate one way to conceptualize writing a nuanced historical interpretation to a question. The first item for students to consider is how they can illustrate both change and continuity for this question. Provide each student with two yellow sticky notes and ask students to identify a continuity and change that could be used to answer this question.

Have students make a class collection of continuities and changes by clustering the sticky notes in two locations, one for each category. Next, have students conduct a gallery walk and record the best two continuities and best change. While it is not necessary to be imbalanced in their approach, it does show complexity for a student to demonstrate both continuity and change, while concentrating more on the former when the question asks about change. The final step is to write the essay. This activity at least provides a road map for students to follow as they consider ways to illustrate complexity.

Module 8-10

American Politics in Transition, 1968–1980

LEARNING TARGETS

By the end of this module, you should be able to:

- Explain how Nixon shaped conservatism and won reelection in 1972.
- Explain the Watergate scandal and how it led to Nixon's resignation.
- Explain the causes of stagflation and deindustrialization and how the federal government responded to the economic challenges of the 1970s.
- Explain the foreign policy approaches of Nixon and Carter and the successes and failures of their policies.

THEMATIC FOCUS

Politics and Power

Having won the presidency in 1968 amid the turmoil of antiwar protests, high profile assassinations, urban riots, and political demonstrations, Nixon's victory and reelection signaled a rightward shift in American politics. However, the Watergate scandal temporarily reversed this trend and led to Carter's election in 1976. Rising prices, unemployment, and overseas competition disrupted American economic growth as workers, businesses, and politicians struggled to adapt to the new conditions. After a period of détente, relations with the Soviet Union deteriorated because of its invasion of Afghanistan in 1979.

HISTORICAL REASONING FOCUS

Causation

TASK ▶ As you read this module, consider the causes and effects of the political and economic changes in the 1970s. Ask yourself how developments during the decade shook public confidence in the government.

TRM Suggested Responses to Questions

PERIOD 8

In winning the presidency in 1968, Richard Nixon paid close attention to international affairs. Having pledged to end the war in Vietnam, it took him another four years to do so. Nixon was a fierce anti-Communist, but he considered himself a realist in foreign affairs. He was concerned more with a stable world order than with promoting American ideals. Nixon and Secretary of State Henry Kissinger worked to establish closer relations with both the People's Republic of China and the Soviet Union. While the Soviet Union and China competed for influence in Asia, Nixon exploited this conflict to keep these nuclear powers divided. His administration succeeded in bringing a thaw in Cold War relations, but he was less successful in navigating Arab-Israeli hostilities in the Middle East, a misstep that caused pain for consumers of gasoline and oil at home.

Nixon won the presidency in 1968 by forging a conservative coalition behind him and blaming liberals for the radical excesses of the 1960s. Nixon won reelection in 1972, but his victory was short-lived. In an effort to ensure electoral success, the Nixon administration engaged in illegal activities that subsequently came to light and forced the president to resign.

Though deeply disillusioned by Vietnam and the Watergate scandal, most Americans hoped that, with these disasters behind them, better times lay ahead. This was not to be. During the administration of the Democratic president Jimmy Carter, the economy worsened as oil-producing nations in the Persian Gulf and Latin America raised the price of petroleum. Carter's efforts to revive the economy and rally the country behind energy conservation were ineffective. In foreign policy President Carter sought to negotiate with the Soviets over arms reduction while at the same time challenging them to do more to protect human rights. In practice, Carter found

TEACHING IDEA

Check for Understanding

Richard Nixon's election in 1968 represented a shift in tone and political goals of the United States. Two campaign themes in particular, "Peace with Honor" and "Silent Majority," resonated with many Americans. Consider this activity for a bell ringer or exit card activity. Have students write one-sentence answers that explain how each campaign theme resonated with some Americans.

BUILDING AP® SKILLS

Causation

To bridge the gap between Module 8-9 and 8-10, consider having students start this module by reflecting on the historical developments of the 1960s. Provide three categories of analysis for students to distill their focus. For instance, consider foreign policy, counterculture, and generational changes as categories of analysis. Divide students into groups of 3 to 4 and assign them one of the categories. Students create a timeline of three events that explains how their category was a cause of social change in the 1960s.

Period 8: 1945–1980

MODULE 8-10 American Politics in Transition, 1968–1980

this balancing act difficult to sustain, and despite his desire to find ways to cooperate with the Soviets, relations between the superpowers deteriorated over the course of his term in office. Despite successful diplomatic efforts in the Middle East, trouble in the Persian Gulf added to the Carter administration's woes.

The Election of 1968

The year 1968 was a turbulent one. In January, the Vietcong launched the Tet Offensive in South Vietnam demonstrating that the war was far from over despite official prior pronouncements to the contrary. In February, police shot indiscriminately into a crowd gathered for civil rights protests at South Carolina State University in Orangeburg, killing three students. In March, student protests at Columbia University led to a violent confrontation with the New York City police. On April 4, the murder of Martin Luther King Jr. sparked an outburst of rioting by black people in more than one hundred cities throughout the country. The assassination of the likely Democratic presidential nominee, Robert Kennedy, in June further heightened the mood of despair. Adding to the unrest, demonstrators gathered in Chicago in August at the Democratic National Convention to press for an antiwar plank in the party platform. Thousands of protesters were beaten and arrested by Chicago police officers. Many

AP® ANALYZING SOURCES

Source: Richard M. Nixon, *Address Accepting the Presidential Nomination at the Republican National Convention*, August 8, 1968

"[T]o those who say that law and order is the code word for racism, there and here is a reply:

Our goal is justice for every American. If we are to have respect for law in America, we must have laws that deserve respect.

Just as we cannot have progress without order, we cannot have order without progress, and so, as we commit to order tonight, let us commit to progress.

And this brings me to the clearest choice among the great issues of this campaign.

For the past five years we have been deluged by government programs for the unemployed; programs for the cities; programs for the poor. And we have reaped from these programs an ugly harvest of frustration, violence and failure across the land.

And now our opponents will be offering more of the same—more billions for government jobs, government housing, government welfare.

I say it is time to quit pouring billions of dollars into programs that have failed in the United States of America. . . .

But for those who are able to help themselves—what we need are not more millions on welfare rolls—but more millions on payrolls in the United States of America.

Instead of government jobs, and government housing, and government welfare, let government use its tax and credit policies to enlist in this battle the greatest engine of progress ever developed in the history of man—American private enterprise.

Let us enlist in this great cause the millions of Americans in volunteer organizations who will bring a dedication to this task that no amount of money could ever buy. . . .

Black Americans, no more than white Americans, they do not want more government programs which perpetuate dependency.

They don't want to be a colony in a nation.

They want the pride, and the self-respect, and the dignity that can only come if they have an equal chance to own their own homes, to own their own businesses, to be managers and executives as well as workers, to have a piece of the action in the exciting ventures of private enterprise."

Questions for Analysis
1. Identify Nixon's response to accusations that his platform is racist.
2. Describe the contrast Nixon makes between his party platform and Democratic proposals.
3. Evaluate the extent to which Nixon's speech reflects conservative ideology.

EXPLORING AP® THEMES

Politics and Power

The 1968 presidential election was influenced by domestic and Cold War events in Vietnam. Have students focus on the domestic events that influenced the resurgence of the Republican Party. Put another way, what was happening in the United States from 1964 to 1968 that prompted voters to turn to the Republicans?

TRM Suggested Responses to Questions

TRM Module 8.10 AP® Analyzing Sources Handout 1

BUILDING AP® SKILLS

Claims and Sources in Evidence

In this speech Richard Nixon uses some iteration of government program at least ten times. Have students focus on Nixon's use of government programs to describe what Nixon's claim is in this excerpt. Why would some Americans be receptive to this argument in 1968?

BUILDING AP® SKILLS

Sourcing and Situation

Although Richard Nixon never mentions the Great Society explicitly by name, he is clearly trying to draw a contrast in vision that espoused a move away from the Great Society. Have students highlight at least three sections that illustrate this point.

Americans watched in horror as television networks broadcast the bloody clashes, but a majority of viewers sided with the police rather than the protesters.

Similar protests occurred around the world. In early 1968, university students outside Paris protested educational policies and what they perceived as their second-class status. When students at the Sorbonne in Paris joined them in the streets, police attacked them viciously. In June, French president Charles de Gaulle sent in tanks to break up widespread student demonstrations and concurrent labor strikes but also instituted political and economic reforms. Protests also erupted during the spring in Prague, Czechoslovakia, where President Alexander Dubček vowed to reform the Communist regime by initiating "socialism with a human face." In August the Soviet Union sent its military into Prague to crush the reforms, bringing this brief experiment in freedom remembered as the "Prague Spring" to a violent end. During the same year, student-led demonstrations erupted in Yugoslavia, Poland, West Germany, Italy, Spain, Japan, and Mexico.

It was against this backdrop of global unrest that Richard Nixon ran for president against the Democratic nominee Hubert H. Humphrey and the independent candidate, George C. Wallace, the segregationist governor of Alabama and a popular archconservative. To outflank Wallace on the right, Nixon declared himself the "law and order" candidate, a phrase that became a code for reining in black militancy. To win southern supporters, he pledged to ease up on enforcing federal civil rights legislation and oppose forced busing to achieve racial integration in schools. He criticized antiwar protesters and promised to end the Vietnam War with honor. Seeking to portray the Democrats as the party of social and cultural radicalism, Nixon geared his campaign message to the "silent majority" of voters — what one political analyst characterized as "the unyoung, the unpoor, and unblack." This conservative message appealed to many Americans who were fed up with domestic uprisings and war abroad.

Although Nixon won 301 electoral votes, 110 more than Humphrey, none of the three candidates received a majority of the popular vote. Yet Nixon and Wallace together garnered about 57 percent of the popular vote, a dramatic shift to the right compared with Lyndon Johnson's landslide victory just four years earlier. The New Left had given way to an assortment of old and new conservatives, overwhelmingly white, who were determined to contain, if not roll back, the Great Society.

REVIEW

- What factors contributed to Nixon's election in 1968?
- Why were the electoral results of 1968 so different than the results of 1964?

Pragmatic Conservatism

AP TIP
Analyze how the federal government's role in addressing environmental concerns changed during the 1970s.

On the domestic front, Nixon had pledged during his 1968 campaign to "reverse the flow of power and resources from the states and communities to Washington." He kept his promise by dismantling Great Society social programs, cutting funds for the War on Poverty, and eliminating the Office of Economic Opportunity. In 1972 the president adopted a program of revenue sharing, which transferred federal tax revenues to the states to use as they wished. Hoping to rein in the liberal Warren Court, Nixon nominated conservative justices to the Supreme Court.

However, in several areas Nixon departed from conservatives who favored limited government. In 1970 he persuaded Congress to pass the Environmental Protection Act, which strengthened federal oversight of environmental programs throughout the country. In 1972 the federal government increased its responsibility for protecting the health and safety of American workers through the creation of the Occupational Safety and Health Administration (OSHA). The Consumer Products Safety Commission was established to provide added safety for the buying public. In addition, the president signed a law banning cigarette advertising on radio and television because of the link between smoking and cancer.

Nixon also applied a pragmatic approach to racial issues. In general, he supported "benign neglect" concerning the issue of race and rejected new legislative attempts to use busing to promote school desegregation. In this way, Nixon courted southern conservatives in an attempt to deter George Wallace from mounting another third-party challenge in 1972. Still, Nixon moved back to

EXPLORING AP® THEMES

America in the World

To help students understand the broader processes associated with the late 1960s, consider using the theme of America in the World in an activity focused on contextualization. Have students select two global events from the textbook and have them relate the events back to the theme of societal change around the world. This advances students' understanding of how social change in America related to societal changes around the world.

TEACHING IDEA

Building Vocabulary

To ensure student comprehension of the "Silent Majority," have students define the demographics of this group. Nixon appealed to the Silent Majority out of political expedience, and it is crucial for students to understand the demographics because it will allow them to trace Nixon's domestic policies.

TEACHING IDEA

Incorporating Videos

The PBS documentary, *Earth Days*, focuses on the post-World War II environmental movement (available on YouTube). President Nixon is of particular note, because of the focus the documentary places on his role in the environmental movement of the late 1960s and early 1970s. The second half of the documentary focuses attention on the role of the federal government during Nixon's presidency.

APPLY THE TIP

The federal government went through dramatic changes in policy as it took an increasingly important lead in addressing environmental issues. Have students select three events, developments, or pieces of legislation to illustrate the degree to which the federal government changed in using its authority to address environmental issues.

the political center with efforts that furthered civil rights. Expanding affirmative action programs begun under the Johnson administration, he adopted plans that required construction companies and unions to recruit minority workers according to their percentage in the local labor force. His support of affirmative action was part of a broader approach to encourage "black capitalism," a concept designed to convince African Americans to seek opportunity within the free-enterprise system rather than through government handouts. Moreover, in 1970 Nixon signed the extension of the 1965 Voting Rights Act, thereby renewing the law that had provided suffrage to the majority of African Americans in the South. The law also lowered the voting age from twenty-one to eighteen for national elections. Support for the measure reflected the impact of the Vietnam War: If young men could fight at eighteen, then they should be able to vote at eighteen. In 1971 the **Twenty-sixth Amendment** was ratified to lower the voting age for state and local elections as well.

The Nixon administration also veered away from the traditional Republican free market philosophy by resorting to wage and price controls to curb rising inflation brought on, for the most part, by increased military spending during the Vietnam War. In 1971 the president by executive order declared a ninety-day freeze on wages and prices, placed a temporary 10 percent surtax on imports, and let the value of the dollar drop on the international market, leading to increased U.S. exports. Taken together, these measures stabilized consumer prices, reduced unemployment, and boosted the gross national product. Although these proved to be only short-term gains, they improved Nixon's prospects for reelection.

REVIEW

- What conservative policies did the Nixon administration implement?
- In what areas did Nixon diverge from conservative ideas?

The Cold War Thaws

détente An easing of tense relations with the Soviet Union during the Cold War.

Strategic Arms Limitation Treaty (SALT I) 1972 agreement between the United States and Soviet Union to curtail nuclear arms production during the Cold War. The pact froze for five years the number of antiballistic missiles (ABMs), intercontinental ballistic missiles (ICBMs), and submarine-based missiles that each nation could deploy.

Nixon and Kissinger's greatest triumph came in easing tensions with the country's Cold War adversaries, a policy known as **détente**. In part to gain leverage against North Vietnam during the peace negotiations and exploit fissures between the USSR and China, Kissinger engaged in secret maneuvering to prepare the way for Nixon to visit mainland China in 1972. After blocking the People's Republic of China's admission to the United Nations for twenty-two years, the United States announced that it would no longer oppose China's entry to the world organization. This cautious renewal of relations with China opened up possibilities of mutually beneficial trade between the two countries.

The closer relations between China and the United States worried the USSR. Although both were Communist nations, the Soviet Union and China had pursued their own ideological and national interests. To check growing Chinese influence with the United States, Soviet premier Leonid Brezhnev invited President Nixon to Moscow in May 1972, the first time an American president had visited the Soviet Union since the end of World War II. The main topic of discussion concerned arms control, and with the Soviet Union eager to make a deal in the aftermath of Nixon's trip to China, the two sides worked out the historic **Strategic Arms Limitation Treaty (SALT I)**, the first treaty to curtail nuclear arms production during the Cold War. The pact froze the number of intercontinental ballistic missiles and submarine-based missiles for five years and restricted the number of antiballistic missiles that each nation could deploy.

Nixon and Kissinger pursued a *realpolitik* foreign policy, which prioritized American economic and strategic interests over fostering democracy or human rights. In Chile, the United States overthrew the democratically elected socialist president Salvador Allende after he nationalized U.S. properties, resulting in nearly two decades of dictatorial rule in that country. Under Nixon's leadership, the United States also supported repressive regimes in Nicaragua, South Africa, the Philippines, and Iran.

Nixon's diplomatic initiatives, however, failed to resolve festering problems in the Middle East. Since its victory in the Six-Day War of 1967, Israel had occupied territory once controlled by Egypt and Syria as well as the former Palestinian capital of Jerusalem. On October 6, 1973, during the start of the Jewish High Holidays of Yom Kippur, Egyptian and Syrian troops, fortified with Soviet

Period 8: 1945–1980

arms, launched a surprise attack on Israel. An Israeli counterattack, reinforced by a shipment of $2 billion of American weapons, repelled Arab forces, and the Israeli military stood ready to destroy the Egyptian army. To avoid a complete breakdown in the balance of power, the United States and the Soviet Union agreed to broker a cease-fire that left the situation the same as before the war.

U.S. involvement in the struggle between Israel and its Arab enemies exacerbated economic troubles at home. In October 1973, during the midst of the Yom Kippur War, the **Organization of Petroleum Exporting Countries (OPEC)** imposed an oil embargo on the United States as punishment for its support of Israel. As a result of the embargo, the price of oil skyrocketed. The effect of high oil prices rippled through the economy, leading to increased inflation and unemployment. The crisis lasted until May 1974, when OPEC lifted its embargo following six months of diplomacy by Kissinger.

REVIEW

- What were the main accomplishments and failures of President Nixon's foreign policy?

The Nixon Landslide and Watergate Scandal, 1972–1974

> **AP® TIP**
> Compare the effects of the division in the Democratic Party in the election of 1972 to those of the division in the Republican Party in the election of 1912.

By appealing to voters across the political spectrum, Nixon won a monumental victory in 1972. The president invigorated the "silent majority" by demonizing his opponents and encouraging Vice President Spiro Agnew to aggressively pursue his strategy of polarization. Agnew called protesters "kooks" and "social misfits" and attacked the media and Nixon critics with heated rhetoric. As Nixon had hoped, George Wallace ran in the Democratic primaries. Wallace won impressive victories in the North as well as the South, but his campaign ended after an assassination attempt left him paralyzed. With Wallace out of the race, the Democrats helped Nixon look more centrist by nominating George McGovern, a liberal antiwar senator from South Dakota.

Winning in a landslide, Nixon captured more than 60 percent of the popular vote and nearly all of the electoral votes. Nonetheless Democrats retained control of Congress. However, Nixon would have little time to savor his victory, for within the next two years his conduct in the campaign would come back to destroy his presidency.

In the early hours of June 17, 1972, five men broke into Democratic Party headquarters in the Watergate apartment complex in Washington, D.C. What appeared initially as a routine robbery turned into the most infamous political scandal of the twentieth century. It was eventually revealed that the break-in had been authorized by the Committee for the Re-Election of the President in an attempt to steal documents from the Democrats.

President Nixon may not have known in advance the details of the break-in, but he did authorize a cover-up of his administration's involvement. Nixon ordered his chief of staff, H. R. Haldeman, to get the CIA and FBI to back off from a thorough investigation of the incident. To silence the burglars at their trials, the president promised them $400,000 and hinted at a presidential pardon after their conviction.

> **AP® TIP**
> Be sure you can explain the ways in which the Watergate scandal endangered the American political system.

Nixon embarked on the cover-up to protect himself from revelations of his administration's other illegal activities. Several of the Watergate burglars belonged to a secret band of operatives known as "the plumbers," which had been formed in 1971 and authorized by the president to find and plug up unwelcome information leaks from government officials. On their first secret operation, the plumbers broke into the office of military analyst Daniel Ellsberg's psychiatrist to look for embarrassing personal information with which to discredit Ellsberg, who had leaked the *Pentagon Papers* (see Module 8-7). The president had other unsavory matters to hide. In an effort to contain leaks about the administration's secret bombing of Cambodia in 1969, the White House had illegally wiretapped its own officials and members of the press.

Watergate Scandal and cover-up that forced the resignation of Richard Nixon in 1974. The scandal revolved around a break-in at Democratic Party headquarters in 1972 and subsequent efforts to conceal the administration's involvement in the break-in.

Watergate did not become a major scandal until after the election. The trial judge forced one of the burglars to reveal the men's backers. This revelation led two *Washington Post* reporters, Bob Woodward and Carl Bernstein, to investigate the link between the administration and the plumbers. With the help of Mark Felt, a top FBI official whose identity long remained secret and whom the reporters called "Deep Throat," Woodward and Bernstein succeeded in exposing the

---

BUILDING AP® SKILLS

Causation

The 1970s saw a precipitous decline in relations with many countries from the Middle East. Remind students that these developments occurred as a result of many policy decisions made in the post–World War II context of the Cold War. Working on the skill of causation can assist this effort. For instance, consider asking students how U.S. decisions in Iran in 1953 and the immediate support for the development of Israel right after World War II were catalysts for anti-American sentiment in the Middle East.

BUILDING AP® SKILLS

Claims and Evidence in Sources

As students study the events surrounding Watergate, the so-called "smoking gun" tape is of particular use. Have students visit President Nixon's Presidential Library website and locate the "smoking gun" transcript (nixonlibrary.gov). This document made it clear that President Nixon was a central character in the effort to cover up the Watergate scandal. Ask students to find one or two statements made by the president, which would implicate him in the cover-up.

APPLY THE TIP

One way you can make this tip more focused is to provide students with a way to explain the way in which Watergate endangered the U.S. political system. For instance, provide the historical phrase "credibility gap," which they should be familiar with from their studies of the Vietnam Era. Next, ask them to explain how and why the Watergate scandal amplified the credibility gap.

Period 8: 1945–1980

MODULE 8-10 American Politics in Transition, 1968–1980

true nature of the crime. The Senate created a special committee in February 1973 to investigate the scandal. White House counsel John Dean, whom Nixon had fired, testified about discussing the cover-up with the president and his closest advisers. His testimony proved accurate after the committee learned that Nixon had secretly taped all Oval Office conversations. When the president refused to release the tapes to a special prosecutor, the Supreme Court ruled against him.

With Nixon's cover-up revealed, and impeachment and conviction likely, Nixon resigned on August 9, 1974. The scandal took a great toll on the administration: Attorney General John Mitchell and Nixon's closest advisers, H. R. Haldeman and John Ehrlichman, resigned, and twenty-five government officials went to jail. Watergate also damaged the office of the president, leaving Americans wary and distrustful.

Vice President Gerald Ford served out Nixon's remaining term. The Republican representative from Michigan had replaced Vice President Spiro Agnew after Agnew resigned in 1973 following charges that he had taken illegal kickbacks while governor of Maryland. Ford chose Nelson A. Rockefeller, the moderate Republican governor of New York, as his vice president; thus, neither man had been elected to the office he now held. President Ford's most controversial and defining act took place shortly after he entered the White House. Explaining to the country that he wanted to quickly end the "national nightmare" stemming from Watergate, Ford pardoned Nixon for any criminal offenses he might have committed as president. Rather than healing the nation's wounds, this preemptive pardon polarized Americans and cost Ford considerable political capital. Ford also wrestled with a troubled economy as Americans once again experienced rising prices and high unemployment.

REVIEW

- How did the Watergate scandal lead to Nixon's resignation?

Jimmy Carter and the Limits of Affluence

Despite his political shortcomings, Gerald Ford received the Republican presidential nomination in 1976 and ran against James Earl (Jimmy) Carter, a little-known former governor of Georgia, who used his "outsider" status to his advantage. Shaping his campaign with Watergate in mind, Carter stressed personal character over economic issues. As a moderate, post-segregationist governor of Georgia, Carter won the support of the family of Martin Luther King Jr. and other black leaders. Carter needed all the help he could get and eked out a narrow victory.

The greatest challenge Carter faced once in office was a faltering economy. America's consumer-oriented economy depended on cheap energy, a substantial portion of which came from sources outside the United States. By the 1970s, four-fifths of the world's oil supply came from Saudi Arabia, Iran, Iraq, and Kuwait, all members of the Arab-dominated Organization of Petroleum Exporting Countries (OPEC). The organization had been formed in 1960 by these Persian Gulf countries together with Venezuela, and it used its control of petroleum supplies to set world prices. In 1973, during the Nixon administration, OPEC imposed an oil embargo on the United States as punishment for its support of Israel during the Yom Kippur War with Egypt and Syria. The price of oil skyrocketed as a result. By the time Carter became president, the cost of a

◀ **Gas Shortages, 1973** A gas station owner in Perkasie, Pennsylvania lets his customers know he is out of gas. OPEC's 1973 oil embargo during the Yom Kippur War caused gas shortages and soaring prices in the United States. Motorists scrambling to find available supplies at gas stations created long lines. **How does this image reflect the ways in which the Arab Oil Embargo affected American society?**

TEACHING IDEA

Incorporating Primary Sources

Have students visit the Period 8 section of the Gilder Lehrman AP® U.S. History website so they can use a primary source titled "President Ford's statement on pardoning Richard Nixon, 1974" (ap.gilderlehrman.org). Have students read the document and cite two specific reasons why President Ford pardoned President Nixon.

EXPLORING AP® THEMES

American and National Identity

The 1970s is often described as a decade of economic, political, and social malaise. Have students first look up the word "malaise" so they know what it means and why it was used. Next, have students explain why a sense of malaise hung over Americans throughout the 1970s. Also ask students how this malaise affected Americans' sense of identity.

BUILDING AP® SKILLS

Causation

Although the United States was experiencing a number of economic issues at home such as a gas shortage, American industries were also facing new competition from political allies such as West Germany and Japan. Have students explain how and why economic competition from those two nations worsened the economic malaise of the 1970s.

Jimmy Carter and the Limits of Affluence

barrel of oil had jumped to around $30. American drivers who had paid 30 cents a gallon for gas in 1970 paid more than four times that amount ten years later.

Energy concerns helped reshape American industry. With energy prices rising, American manufacturers sought ways to reduce costs by moving their factories to nations that offered cheaper labor and lower energy costs. This outsourcing of American manufacturing had two significant consequences. First, it weakened the American labor movement, particularly in heavy industry. In the 1970s, union membership dropped from 28 to 23 percent of the workforce and continued to decline over the next decade. Second, this process of **deindustrialization** accelerated a significant population shift that had begun during World War II from the old industrial areas of the Northeast and the Midwest (the Rust Belt) to the South and the Southwest (the Sun Belt), where cheaper costs and lower wages were enormously attractive to businesses (Map 8.5). Only 14 percent of southern workers were unionized in a region with a long history of opposition to labor organizing. Consequently, Sun Belt cities such as Houston, Atlanta, Phoenix, and San Diego flourished, while steel and auto towns in Ohio, Michigan, and Pennsylvania decayed.

These monumental shifts in the American economy produced widespread pain. Higher gasoline prices affected all businesses that relied on energy, leading to serious inflation. To maintain their standard of living in the face of rising inflation and stagnant wages, many Americans went into debt, using a new innovation, the credit card, to borrow collectively more than $300 billion. The American economy had gone through inflationary spirals before, but they were usually accompanied by high employment, with wages helping to drive up prices. In the 1970s, however, rising prices were accompanied by growing unemployment, a situation that economists called "**stagflation**." Traditionally, remedies to control inflation increased unemployment, yet most unemployment cures also spurred inflation. With both occurring at the same time, economists were confounded, and many Americans felt they had lost control over their economy.

President Carter tried his best to find a solution. To reduce dependency on foreign oil, in 1977 Carter devised a plan for energy self-sufficiency, which he called the "moral equivalent of war."

deindustrialization Decline of industrial activity in a specific town, region, or nation. In the U.S. it led to significant drops in union membership and population shifts across the country as people moved in search of new types of economic opportunity.

stagflation Period of economic instability in the 1970s as the rising cost of living occurred in conjunction with an increase in unemployment.

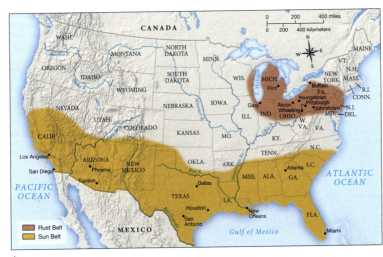

▲ **MAP 8.5 The Sun and Rust Belts** Dramatic economic and demographic shifts during the 1970s led to industrial development and population growth in the "Sun Belt" in the South and Southwest at the expense of the "Rust Belt" in the Northeast and Midwest. As manufacturers sought cheap, non-unionized labor, they moved factories to the South or overseas while defense industries and agribusiness fueled growth from Texas to California. **How did the migration of Americans to the Sun Belt impact American society?**

EXPLORING AP® THEMES
Migration and Settlement

There are many different types of migration patterns such as external immigration, migration across a neighboring border with a return to the country of origin, and internal migrations. Using Map 8.5 have students explain two reasons for the internal migration away from the so-called Rust Belt toward the so-called Sun Belt. This can be an easy bell ringer to use at the beginning of the class period.

BUILDING AP® SKILLS
Causation

Although the internal migration pattern from the Midwest to the South during the 1970s and 1980s was in many ways caused by economic trends of the 1970s, the effects were both economic and political. Consider having students focus on the political ramifications of this migration pattern. Students should focus on at least two specific effects in explaining their answer.

Critics called the proposal weak and gave it a mocking acronym, "MEOW". A more substantial accomplishment came on August 4, 1977, when Carter signed into law the creation of the Department of Energy, with responsibilities covering research, development, and conservation of energy. In 1978, he backed the **National Energy Act**, which set gas emission standards for automobiles and provided incentives for installing alternate energy systems, such as solar and wind power, in homes and public buildings. He also supported congressional legislation to spend $14 billion for public sector jobs as well as to cut taxes by $34 billion, which reduced unemployment but only temporarily.

In many other respects Carter embraced conservative principles. Believing in fiscal restraint, he rejected liberal proposals for national health insurance and more expansive employment programs. Instead, he signed into law bills deregulating the airline, banking, trucking, and railroad industries, measures that appealed to conservative proponents of free market economics.

> **AP® TIP**
> Analyze how the oil embargo and the American economic crisis of the 1970s affected U.S. environmental policies.

REVIEW

- What economic and foreign policy challenges did the Carter administration face, and how were those challenges related?
- In what ways did President Carter support a conservative agenda?

The Perils of Détente

In the area of foreign policy Carter departed from Nixon. Whereas Nixon was a realist who considered the U.S. role in world affairs as an exercise in power politics, Carter was an idealist who made human rights a cornerstone of his foreign policy. Unlike previous presidents who had supported dictatorial governments as long as they were anti-Communist, Carter intended to hold such regimes to a higher moral standard. Thus the Carter administration cut off military and economic aid to repressive regimes in Argentina, Uruguay, and Ethiopia. Still, Carter was not entirely consistent in his application of moral standards to diplomacy. Important U.S. allies around the world such as the Philippines, South Korea, and South Africa were hardly models of democracy, but national security concerns kept the president from severing ties with them.

One way that Carter tried to set an example of responsible moral leadership was by signing an agreement to return control of the Panama Canal Zone to Panama at the end of 1999. The treaty that President Theodore Roosevelt negotiated in 1903 gave the United States control over this ten-mile piece of Panamanian land forever. Panamanians resented this affront to their sovereignty, and Carter considered the occupation a vestige of colonialism.

The president's pursuit of détente, or the easing of tensions, with the Soviet Union was less successful. In 1978 the Carter administration extended full diplomatic recognition to China. After the fall of China to the Communists in 1949, the United States had supported Taiwan, an island off the coast of

Afghan Mujahideen, January 1980 On December 25, 1979, Soviet troops invaded Afghanistan to suppress *mujahideen* guerrillas who were trying to overthrow the nation's secular, pro-Soviet regime. These rebel forces were among the guerrillas who defeated the Soviets after a decade of warfare and eventually established an Islamic theocracy. **What parallels can be drawn from the photograph between the experience of the Soviet military in Afghanistan and the experience of the U.S. military in Vietnam?**

AP® ANALYZING SOURCES

Source: Warren Christopher, Deputy Secretary of State, *Presidential Review Memorandum on Human Rights*, May 20, 1977

"The over-all objective of our human rights policy is to encourage the respect that governments accord to human rights. . . .

First, the right to be free from governmental violations of the integrity of the person: such violations include torture; cruel, inhuman or degrading treatment and punishment; arbitrary arrest or imprisonment; denial of fair public trial; and invasion of the home ('the first group').

Second, economic and social rights: the right to be free from government action or inaction which either obstructs an individual's efforts to fulfill his vital needs for food, shelter, health care and education or fails adequately to support the individual in meeting basic needs ('the second group').

Third, the right to enjoy civil and political liberties: freedom of thought, of religion, of assembly, of speech, of the press; freedom of movement both within and outside one's own country; freedom to take part in government ('the third group'). . . .

In countries where the first group of rights is denied or threatened, the protection of those rights has obvious priority, since human life and fundamental human dignity is threatened. In countries where the first group of rights is generally observed, but political and civil rights are abridged or non-existent, our policy should emphasize the promotion of those rights. Promotion of economic rights is, for the US, primarily a matter of cooperation with and contribution to bilateral and multilateral foreign assistance efforts. We should do our share."

Questions for Analysis

1. Identify both the immediate and the broader intended audiences for Christopher's memo.
2. Explain the basic challenges in implementing the human rights-centric approach to foreign policy recommended in the excerpt.
3. Evaluate the extent of similarity between the foreign policy framework expressed in the excerpt and the *realpolitik* approach of Nixon and Kissinger.
4. Evaluate the extent to which the foreign policy recommended in the excerpt represents a continuation of U.S. foreign policy after World War II.

TRM Suggested Responses to Questions

TRM Module 8.10 AP® Analyzing Sources Handout 2

BUILDING AP® SKILLS

Sourcing and Situation

This activity is designed for students to complete after they read the primary source by Warren Christopher. Ask students to identify one Cold War foreign policy that contradicts the belief in human rights. Encourage students to be as specific as possible, as this will make for a better historical analysis.

EXPLORING AP® THEMES

America in the World

This activity is meant to get students thinking about historical connections within a discrete time period. The belief in human rights espoused by the Carter administration was seen as contradictory in countries such as Iran. Have students predict why Iranians, in particular, would charge the United States as being contradictory in its belief in human rights. Ask students how this affected the view of the United States around the world, in the context of the Cold War.

SALT II 1979 strategic arms limitation treaty agreed on by President Jimmy Carter and Soviet leader Leonid Brezhnev. After the Soviet Union invaded Afghanistan, Carter persuaded the Senate not to ratify the treaty.

AP® TIP
Be sure you can explain why President Carter's Afghanistan policies were supported by conservatives in the United States.

China, as an outpost of democracy against mainland China. In abandoning Taiwan by recognizing China, Carter sought to drive a greater wedge between China and the Soviet Union. Nevertheless, Carter did not give up on cooperation with the Soviets. In June 1979 Carter and Soviet leader Leonid Brezhnev signed **SALT II**, a new strategic arms limitation treaty. Six months later, however, the Soviet Union invaded Afghanistan to bolster its pro-Communist Afghan regime. President Carter viewed this action as a violation of international law and a threat to Middle East oil supplies, and he therefore persuaded the Senate to drop consideration of SALT II. In addition, Carter obtained from Congress a 5 percent increase in military spending, reduced grain sales to the USSR, and led a boycott of the 1980 Olympic Games in Moscow.

Of perhaps the greatest long-term importance was President Carter's decision to authorize the CIA to provide covert military and economic assistance to Afghan rebels resisting the Soviet invasion. Chief among these groups were the *mujahideen*, or warriors who wage jihad. Although portrayed as freedom fighters, these Islamic fundamentalists (including a group known as the Taliban) did not support democracy in the Western sense. After a decade of warfare, the Soviets were defeated leading to the eventual establishment of an Islamic theocracy. Among the mujahideen who received assistance from the United States was Osama bin Laden, a Saudi Arabian Islamic fundamentalist, who later planned the 9/11 attacks against the United States.

In ordering these CIA operations, Carter ignored recent revelations about questionable intelligence practices. Responding to presidential excesses stemming from the Vietnam War and the Watergate scandal, the Senate had held hearings in 1975 into clandestine CIA and FBI activities at home and abroad. Led by Frank Church of Idaho, the Senate Select Committee to Study

Governmental Operations with Respect to Intelligence Activities (known as the Church Committee) issued reports revealing that both intelligence agencies had illegally spied on Americans and that the CIA had fomented revolution abroad, contrary to the provisions of its charter. Despite the Church Committee's findings, Carter revived some of these murky practices to combat the Soviets in Afghanistan.

REVIEW

- How did the Carter administration's foreign policy differ from that of Nixon?
- In what ways was it similar?

Challenges in the Middle East

Camp David accords 1978 peace accord between Israel and Egypt facilitated by the mediation of President Jimmy Carter.

Before President Carter attempted to restrain the Soviet Union in Afghanistan, he did have some notable diplomatic successes. Five years after the 1973 Yom Kippur War, with relations between Israel and its Arab neighbors in a deadlock, Carter invited the leaders of Israel and Egypt to the United States. Following two weeks of discussions in September 1978 at the presidential retreat at Camp David, Maryland, Israeli prime minister Menachem Begin and Egyptian president Anwar Sadat reached an agreement on a "framework for peace." For the first time in its history, Egypt would extend diplomatic recognition to Israel in exchange for Israel's agreement to return the Sinai Peninsula to Egypt, which Israel had captured and occupied since 1967. Carter facilitated Sadat's acceptance of the **Camp David accords** by promising to extend foreign aid to Egypt. The treaty, however, left unresolved controversial issues between Israelis and Arabs concerning the establishment of a Palestinian state and control of Jerusalem.

Whatever success Carter had in promoting peace in the Middle East suffered a serious setback in the Persian Gulf nation of Iran. In 1953 the CIA had helped overthrow Iran's democratically elected president, replacing him with a monarch and staunch ally, Mohammad Reza Pahlavi, the shah of Iran. For more than two decades, the shah ruled Iran with U.S. support, seeking to construct a modern, secular state allied with the United States. In doing so, he used repressive measures against Islamic fundamentalists, deploying his secret police to imprison, torture, and exile dissenters. In 1979 revolutionary forces headed by Ayatollah Ruholla Khomeini, an Islamic fundamentalist exiled by the shah, overthrew his government. Khomeini intended to end the growing secularism in Iran and reshape the nation according to strict Islamic law.

When the deposed shah needed treatment for terminal cancer, President Carter invited him to the United States for medical assistance as a humanitarian gesture, despite warnings from the Khomeini government that it would consider this invitation a hostile action. On November 4, 1979, the ayatollah ordered fundamentalist Muslim students to seize the U.S. Embassy in Tehran and hold its fifty-two occupants hostage until the United States returned the shah to Iran to stand trial. President Carter retaliated by freezing all Iranian assets in American banks, breaking off diplomatic relations, and imposing a trade embargo. In response, Khomeini denounced the United States as "the Great Satan." As the impasse dragged on and with the presidential election of 1980 fast approaching, Carter became desperate. After a failed U.S. rescue attempt that left one Iranian civilian and eight American soldiers dead, Khomeini's guards separated the hostages, making any more rescue efforts impossible. Carter suffered a bruising defeat at the polls in November, the revolution under Khomeini seized on its victory to consolidate power and support, and Iran and the United States would become long-term enemies, deeply complicating geopolitics in the oil-rich Middle East. Further humiliating Carter personally, Khomeini released the hostages on January 20, 1981, the inauguration day of Carter's successor, Ronald Reagan.

REVIEW

- To what extent was the Carter administration's foreign policy toward the Middle East a success?

TEACHING IDEA

Connecting the Dots

The goal of this activity is to have a retrospective look at the foreign policy decisions made by presidents in the 1970s and to illustrate the continuities and changes throughout the decade. Presidents Nixon, Ford, and Carter each had a commitment to combating communism, but varied greatly in their approaches. This worksheet seeks to make those differences more obvious to students.

TRM Find **Handout 8.9 – Foreign Policy Decisions of the 1970s** in the Teacher's Resource Materials.

TEACHING IDEA

Incorporating Secondary Sources

The United States and Iran have a complicated history in the context of the Cold War. For teachers looking to extend lessons on the Iranian hostage crisis, or looking for a supplemental resource that helps explain how the United States viewed Iran throughout the Cold War, consider the essay, "Iran and the United States in the Cold War," by Malcolm Byrne. This essay provides students with a wide-view look at relations between these two nations during the Cold War and is available at Gilder Lehrman's AP® U.S. History site on the Period 8 page (ap.gilderlehrman.org).

AP® WRITING HISTORICALLY — Document-Based Question Practice

ACTIVITY

The following question is based on the accompanying documents. The documents have been edited for the purpose of this exercise. *Suggested reading period: 15 minutes.* *Suggested writing time: 45 minutes.*

Evaluate the relative importance of different causes for the decline in public confidence and trust in the government during the 1970s.

DOCUMENT 1

Source: "Vietnam: The Public's Need to Know," *The Washington Post*, June 17, 1971

"There are a number of things to be said about the McNamara [Pentagon] Papers. . . .

[T]he story that unfolds is not new in its essence—the calculated misleading of the public, the purposeful manipulation of public opinion, the stunning discrepancies between public pronouncements and private plans—we had bits and pieces of all that before. But not in such incredibly damning form, not with such irrefutable documentation. That is what brings you up breathless: the plain command to the Secretaries of Defense and State and the head of CIA from McGeorge Bundy, in the President's name, to carry out decisions to expand and deepen our involvement in the war as rapidly as possible, while making every effort to project a very gradual evolution, with no change in policy; the careful concealment of clandestine intervention in Laos and North as well as South Vietnam in early 1964; the clear 'consensus' of at least the main body of presidential advisers in September 1964 in favor of bombing the North even while President Johnson was publicly promising in campaign speeches not to 'go North,' not to send American boys to fight wars Asian boys ought to fight for themselves."

DOCUMENT 2

Source: Anonymous, *Letter to Florida Governor Reubin Askew*, 1972

"Dear Governor Askew,

I am a Jr. High student and will be bussed to a Sr. High, 55 blocks away in the fall, as I will be in 10th grade. I would like to say that I think the Supreme Court and School Boards are very, very wrong!

In Civics, we are studying democracy and would like to quote two statements from the book; *What You Need to Know About Democracy and Why.*

'___ for democracy serves no man except as it serves every man.' P. 186

'Democracy's great strength derives from a basic precept: the individual is more important [than] the system under which he lives.' P. 184

If the individual *is* more important, then **why** do children . . . have to be bussed!! Especially forcibly!!

This country is going from a democracy to a communism! While those men in the Supreme Court are sitting there, smoking cigars, and okaying this and that for bussing, there are children of all ages being bussed from here to who knows where? It just isn't fair. They complain about how they want equal education. Well, if they would quit spending all that money on busses and all the **junk** and put the money into the schools that need it, then we'd have equal education.

All the men of the Supreme Court should put themselves and their children, instead of putting them into private schools, in our place they wouldn't like it either! Getting up at 5:30 A.M., leaving 6:30 A.M., walking 12 or 13 blocks for a bus, etc. Especially when 8 or 9 more blocks, there is a perfectly good Senior High or any school for each age. . . .

Many friends, parents, and kids hold my views, so JUST THINK ABOUT IT. . . .

[signature redacted] 15 years old"

(Continued)

TEACHING IDEA

Categorizing Documents

While students do not have to categorize the documents to formulate a thesis, this strategy can help students organize the documents. Consider reminding students, especially if they are struggling with thesis statements, to look over the documents to develop a thesis statement.

TEACHING IDEA

Connecting the Dots

Students are responsible for incorporating one piece of outside evidence as a part of their analysis. Often there are "gaps" in the documents. Put another way, major concepts, people, years, and events are left out of the documents so students can develop quality evidence to use in their response. Consider reminding students of this and also point out that all of President Ford and most of President Carter's time in office are not included in the documents. This may trigger some brainstorming that will lead to informative evidence in their responses.

Period 8: 1945–1980

MODULE 8-10 American Politics in Transition, 1968–1980

DOCUMENT 3

Source: *Confidence and Concern: Citizens View American Government,* 1973

"In the Fall of 1973, for the first time since the 1968 assassinations of Martin Luther King and Robert Kennedy, a majority of the American people (by 53-37 percent) felt 'there is something deeply wrong in America' today, that these are no ordinary times of crisis....

By 45-35 percent, the public tends to believe that the quality of life in the country has deteriorated....

As a young medical engineer in Del Ray, Florida, put it: 'I feel I have a permanent hand in my pocket, picking my money out every couple of hours. That isn't comfortable.' A retired man in Sarasota added: 'I thought I had worked all my life to retire comfortably. Now inflation is out of control, and I feel poor all the time.'

Still another public complaint about the quality of life is that crime has not been checked. As a 44-year old processing working in Texarkana, Texas, put it: 'We get a lot of talk about law and order and nobody seems to do much or care much if we actually have it. That makes the quality of life worse, as far as I'm concerned.' Others talked about drug abuse, Watergate, loss of confidence in government, erosion of moral standards, shortages of food and gasoline, unrest, and high taxes."

DOCUMENT 4

Source: *Articles of Impeachment Adopted by the House of Representatives Committee on the Judiciary,* July 27, 1974

"Article I

In his conduct of the office of President of the United States, Richard M. Nixon, in violation of his constitutional oath . . . has prevented, obstructed, and impeded the administration of justice, in that:

On June 17, 1972, and prior thereto, agents of the Committee for the Re-election of the President committed unlawful entry of the headquarters of the Democratic National Committee in Washington, District of Columbia, for the purpose of securing political intelligence. Subsequent thereto, Richard M. Nixon, using the powers of his high office, engaged personally and through his close subordinates and agents, in a course of conduct or plan designed to delay, impede, and obstruct the investigation of such illegal entry; to cover up, conceal and protect those responsible; and to conceal the existence and scope of other unlawful covert activities. . . .

Article II

Using the powers of the office of President of the United States, Richard M. Nixon . . . has repeatedly engaged in conduct violating the constitutional rights of citizens, impairing the due and proper administration of justice and the conduct of lawful inquiries, or contravening the laws governing agencies of the executive branch and the purposed of these agencies. . . .

Article III

In his conduct of the office of President of the United States, Richard M. Nixon . . . has failed without lawful cause or excuse to produce papers and things as directed by duly authorized subpoenas . . . and willfully disobeyed such subpoenas. . . . In refusing to produce these papers and things Richard M. Nixon, substituting his judgment as to what materials were necessary for the inquiry, interposed the powers of the Presidency against the lawful subpoenas of the House of Representatives, thereby assuming to himself functions and judgments necessary to the exercise of the sole power of impeachment vested by the Constitution in the House of Representatives.

In all of this, Richard M. Nixon has acted in a manner contrary to his trust as President and subversive of constitutional government, to the great prejudice of the cause of law and justice, and to the manifest injury of the people of the United States.

Wherefore, Richard M. Nixon, by such conduct, warrants impeachment and trial, and removal from office."

MODULE 8-10 American Politics in Transition, 1968–1980

TEACHING IDEA

Analyzing Art and Images

Documents that illustrate quantitative data call for students to demonstrate an understanding of the trends shown in the document. Rather than pinpointing specific data points, remind students of the need to read the document holistically so they can identify and explain trends.

DOCUMENT 7

Source: *United States Unemployment Rate and Inflation Rate (the "Misery Index"), 1970–1980*

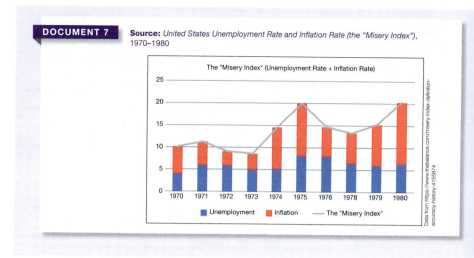

Data from https://www.thebalance.com/misery-index-definition-accuracy-history-4155874

DOCUMENT 5

Source: President Carter, *Address to the Nation on Energy and National Goals* (also known as "The Malaise Speech"), July 15, 1979

"[I] want to talk to you right now about a fundamental threat to American democracy. . . .

The threat is nearly invisible in ordinary ways. It is a crisis of confidence. It is a crisis that strikes at the very heart and soul and spirit of our national will. We can see this crisis in the growing doubt about the meaning of our own lives and in the loss of a unity of purpose for our Nation.

The erosion of our confidence in the future is threatening to destroy the social and the political fabric of America. . . .

In a nation that was proud of hard work, strong families, close-knit communities, and our faith in God, too many of us now tend to worship self-indulgence and consumption. Human identity is no longer defined by what one does, but by what one owns. But we've discovered that owning things and consuming things does not satisfy our longing for meaning. We've learned that piling up material goods cannot fill the emptiness of lives which have no confidence or purpose.

The symptoms of this crisis of the American spirit are all around us. For the first time in the history of our country a majority of our people believe that the next 5 years will be worse than the past 5 years. Two-thirds of our people do not even vote. The productivity of American workers is actually dropping, and the willingness of Americans to save for the future has fallen below that of all other people in the Western world.

As you know, there is a growing disrespect for government and for churches and for schools, the news media, and other institutions. This is not a message of happiness or reassurance, but it is the truth and it is a warning."

DOCUMENT 6

Source: *U.S. Embassy Workers Being Held Hostage in Tehran, Iran*, November 4, 1979

(Continued)

TEACHING IDEA

Weighing Evidence

Students need to be continually aware of the fact that historical evidence is not weighed equally. When students develop their interpretations to this question, they should consider what evidence or documents allow them to demonstrate a historical development that made either public confidence or trust erode more or at a faster rate. The ability to do this signals an understanding in how to pivot during an argument, which is the mark of a better response.

BUILDING AP® SKILLS

Sourcing and Situation

Non-textual documents such as the photograph in Document 6 provide students with an opportunity to work on sourcing. Additionally, non-textual documents can often be sourced with an analysis of the historical situation in which the document was produced. Encourage students to use the historical situation to illustrate their ability to source non-textual documents.

Module 8-11

The Persistence of Liberalism and the Rise of the New Right

TRM Suggested Responses to Questions

LEARNING TARGETS

By the end of this module, you should be able to:

- Explain the rise of the New Right and how it differed from Nixon's pragmatic conservatism.
- Explain the successes and failures of the women's rights movement in the 1970s.
- Explain the growth of the environmental movement and its impact on American society.
- Explain the factors that led to the rise of the Christian Right and impact of the Christian Right on American politics and society in the 1970s.

THEMATIC FOCUS

Geography and the Environment
American and Regional Culture

In the 1970s Americans witnessed a continuation of the cultural changes and rights movements from the previous decade. Environmentalists won new protections for air and water quality as well as endangered species while the Supreme Court ruled in favor of abortion rights for women. Yet, a growing conservative movement opposed to the expansion of government, high taxes, and social changes mobilized to block ratification of the Equal Rights Amendment and launched a grassroots taxpayer revolt. A newly formed Christian Right joined the New Right as a potent counterweight to liberal activism of the era.

HISTORICAL REASONING FOCUS

Causation

TASK ▶ As you read this module, consider the factors that led to the growth of a new conservatism in the 1970s. Think about the impact of growing conservatism on the environmental movement and women's movement.

Despite the growing conservatism, political activism did not die out in the 1970s. Many of the changes sought by liberals and radicals during the 1960s had entered the political and cultural mainstreams in the 1970s. The counterculture, with its long hairstyles and colorful clothes, also entered the mainstream, and rock continued to dominate popular music. Some Americans experimented with recreational drugs, and the remaining sexual taboos of the 1960s fell. Many parents became resigned to seeing their daughters and sons living with boyfriends or girlfriends before getting married. And many of those same parents engaged in extramarital affairs or divorced their spouses. The divorce rate increased by 116 percent in the decade after 1965; in 1979 the rate peaked at 23 divorces per 1,000 married couples.

As the 1970s progressed, the backlash against affirmative action and the ERA confirmed that liberal reformers were losing ground to conservatives. By the end of the decade, liberalism had become identified with special interests and elitism. At the same time, the pragmatic conservatism of Richard Nixon was being displaced by a harder edged brand of conservatism called the New Right. The New Right was founded on the budding conservatism of the 1960s as represented in the Sharon Statement and the presidential candidacy of Barry Goldwater (see Module 8-9). In the 1970s it expanded for a variety of reasons: the revolt against higher taxes, the backlash against the growth of the federal government, the disillusionment of former liberal intellectuals, and the growth of the Christian Right.

EXPLORING AP® THEMES

Politics and Power

Consider having students read part or all of Chapter 6 of Lisa McGirr's *Suburban Warriors: The Origins of the New American Right*. The chapter titled "New Social Issues and Resurgent Evangelicalism" traces issues from the late 1960s and explores how those social issues were used by Republicans and Ronald Reagan in 1980. This can help students establish a historical context for the rise of the New Right.

BUILDING AP® SKILLS

Comparison

Have students compare the Republican Party of the 1950s — led by Dwight Eisenhower — with the Republican Party vision of the late 1960s and early 1970s — led by the vision of Barry Goldwater. Encourage them to focus their comparison on economic and social issues, as those will draw strong contrasts.

Period 8: 1945–1980

MODULE 8-11 The Persistence of Liberalism and the Rise of the New Right

The Women's Movement

AP® TIP
Evaluate the degree to which efforts to resist the passage of the ERA reflected continuity with the values of the nineteenth-century concept of the cult of domesticity.

In the 1970s the women's movement gained strength, but it also attracted powerful opponents. The 1973 Supreme Court victory for abortion rights in *Roe v. Wade* did not end the controversy over the legality of abortion. In 1976 Congress responded to abortion opponents by passing legislation prohibiting the use of federal funds for impoverished women seeking to terminate their pregnancies.

Feminists engaged in other debates in this decade, often clashing with more conservative women. The National Organization for Women (NOW) and its allies succeeded in getting thirty-five states out of a necessary thirty-eight to ratify the Equal Rights Amendment (ERA), which prevented the abridgment of "equality of rights under law . . . by the United States or any State on the basis of sex" (see Module 8-9). In response, other women activists formed their own movement to block ratification. Phyllis Schlafly, a conservative activist, founded the Stop ERA organization to prevent the creation of a "unisex society." Despite the inroads made by feminists, traditional notions of femininity appealed to many women and to male-dominated legislatures. The remaining states refused to ratify the ERA, thus killing the amendment in 1982, when the ratification period expired.

Beyond the failure to ratify the Equal Rights Amendment, the women's movement experienced other successes and challenges. In 1972 Congress passed the Educational Amendments Act. Title IX of this law prohibited colleges and universities that received federal funds from discriminating on the basis of sex, leading to substantial advances in women's athletics. Many more women sought and received relief against job discrimination through the Equal Employment Opportunity Commission. NOW membership continued to grow, and the number of battered women's shelters and rape crisis centers multiplied in towns and cities across the country. Women saw their ranks increase on college campuses, in both undergraduate and professional schools. Women also began entering politics in greater numbers, especially at the local and state levels. At the same time, women of color sought to broaden the definition of feminism to include struggles against race and class oppression as well as sex discrimination. In 1974 a group of black feminists, led by author Barbara Smith, organized the Combahee River Collective and proclaimed: "We . . . often find it difficult to separate race from class from sex oppression because in our lives they are most often experienced simultaneously." Chicana and other Latina feminists also sought to extend women's liberation beyond the confines of the white middle class. In 1987 feminist poet and writer Gloria Anzaldúa wrote: "Though I'll defend my race and culture when they are attacked by non-mexicanos . . . I abhor some of my culture's ways, how it cripples its women . . . our strengths used against us, lowly [women] bearing humility with dignity."

> "Though I'll defend my race and culture when they are attacked by non-mexicanos . . . I abhor some of my culture's ways, how it cripples its women . . . our strengths used against us, lowly [women] bearing humility with dignity."
>
> Gloria Anzaldúa, 1987

AP® ANALYZING SOURCES

Source: Gloria Steinem, *Testimony before the Senate Judiciary Committee Hearing on the Equal Rights Amendment*, May 6, 1970

"During 12 years of working for a living, I have experienced much of the legal and social discrimination reserved for women in this country. I have been refused service in public restaurants, ordered out of public gathering places, and turned away from apartment rentals; all for the clearly stated, sole reason that I am a woman. And all without the legal remedies available to blacks and other minorities. I have been excluded from professional groups, writing assignments on so-called 'unfeminine' subjects such as politics, full participation in the Democratic Party, jury duty, and even from such small male privileges as discounts on airline fares. Most important to me, I have been denied a society in which women are encouraged, or even allowed to think of themselves as first-class citizens and responsible human beings. . . .

The truth is that all our problems stem from the same sex based myths. . . . Like racial myths, they have been reflected in our laws. Let me list a few.

That woman are biologically inferior to men. In fact, an equally good case can be made for the reverse. Women live longer than men, even when the men are not subject to business pressures. Women survived Nazi concentration camps better . . . and are so much more durable at every stage of life that nature must conceive 20 to 50 percent more males in order to keep the balance going. . . .

Another myth, that children must have full-time mothers. American mothers spend more time with their homes and children than those of any other society we know about. In the

---

APPLY THE TIP

Condense the focus of this tip further by providing students with a chronology to focus on as they consider continuities and changes. The periodization of Period 8, 1945–1980, is a common and useful way to explore the issue of the women's movement because it starts students in a post-World War II context and moves them through the liberalism of the 1970s.

TEACHING IDEA

Incorporating Videos

The PBS documentary *Makers: Women Who Make America* is an excellent resource for women's history from 1945 to the present (makers.com/documentaries). Episodes 2 and 3 are useful to this module because of the focus on the Equal Rights Amendment and the rise of conservatism through the 1980s. Teachers can consult these episodes for powerful 10-minute clips to be used as bell ringers or supplements to lessons.

TRM Suggested Responses to Questions

TRM Module 8.11 AP® Analyzing Sources Handout 1

TEACHING IDEA

Building Vocabulary

Phyllis Schlafly led a conservative backlash to the progressive views espoused by feminists in the 1960s and 1970s. Schlafly had an MA in Political Science from Harvard, ran for Congress twice, and considered herself a staunch conservative. When she led the group Stop ERA, the word "stop" was often used as an acronym by Schlafly's group to mean the following: Stop Taking Our Privileges. Provide this information for students and ask them to delineate a list of so-called privileges Schlafly's group was referring to in this campaign. This activity can serve as a great bell ringer or exit card.

BUILDING AP® SKILLS

Claims and Evidence in Sources

Steinem claims that women do not have the same protections against discrimination as many racial and ethnic groups. Have students locate where this claim is made and then consider asking students to explain Steinem's purpose in making this claim. Why would she feel this would be a powerful argument to make before Congress?

past, joint families, servants, a prevalent system in which grandparents raised the children, or family field work in the agrarian systems—all these factors contributed more to child care than the labor-saving devices of which we are so proud.

The truth is that most American children seem to be suffering from too much mother, and too little father. Part of the program of Women's Liberation is a return of fathers to their children. If laws permit women equal work and pay opportunities, men will then be relieved of their role as sole breadwinner. Fewer ulcers, fewer hours of meaningless work, equal responsibility for his own children . . . Women's Liberation is Men's Liberation too."

Questions for Analysis
1. Identify Gloria Steinem's main argument and the reasons she uses to support her argument.
2. Describe the benefits of women's liberation for men according to Steinem.
3. Explain the strategies Steinem uses to support her argument.

Source: *The Phyllis Schlafly Report* 5, no. 7, February 1972

"Of all the classes of people who ever lived, the American woman is the most privileged. We have the most rights and rewards, and the fewest duties. . . .

1. We have the immense good fortune to live in a civilization which respects the family as the basic unit of society. This respect is part and parcel of our laws and our customs. It is based on the fact of life—which no legislation or agitation can erase—that women have babies and men don't.

If you don't like this fundamental difference, you will have to take up your complaint with God because He created us this way. The fact that women, not men, have babies is not the fault of selfish and domineering men, or of the establishment, or of any clique of conspirators who want to oppress women. It's simply the way God made us. . . .

2. [W]e are the beneficiaries of a tradition of special respect for women which dates from the Christian Age of Chivalry. The honor and respect paid to Mary, the Mother of Christ, resulted in all women, in effect, being put on a pedestal. . . .

3. [T]he great American free enterprise system has produced remarkable inventors who have lifted the backbreaking 'women's work' from our shoulders. . . .

Thus, household duties have been reduced to only a few hours a day, leaving the American woman with plenty of time to moonlight. She can take a full or part-time paying job, or she can indulge to her heart's content in a tremendous selection of interesting educational or cultural or homemaking activities. . . .

The 'women's lib' movement is *not* an honest effort to secure better jobs for women who want or need to work outside the home. This is just the superficial sweet-talk to win broad support for a radical 'movement.' Women's lib is a total assault on the role of the American woman as wife and mother, and on the family as the basic unit of society."

Questions for Analysis
1. Identify Phyllis Schlafly's main argument and the reasons she uses to support her argument.
2. Describe how Schlafly dismisses the women's liberation movement.
3. Explain the strategies Schlafly uses to support her argument.

Questions for Comparison
1. Explain how each author appeals to tradition to support her argument.
2. Evaluate the extent to which each excerpt reflects 1970s politics and society.

REVIEW
- What were the major successes and failures of the women's movement during the 1970s?

TEACHING IDEA

AP® Central

Assign students the College Board's AP® U.S. History Practice DBQ from 2016, devoted to the women's movement from 1940 to 1975. This is available on the College Board's website under Past Exam Questions (apcentral.collegeboard.org). Teachers can consult this question as an assignment or activity in class. These released questions can often be used for document analysis, grouping documents, or writing body paragraphs.

BUILDING AP® SKILLS

Claims and Evidence in Sources

Both documents use the word liberation or lib multiple times. Have students identify where each speaker uses the term. Next, ask students to explain the tone and purpose of each reference.

TEACHING IDEA

Incorporating Primary Sources

The primary sources by Gloria Steinem and Phyllis Schlafly give diverging views of women's rights. Have students select one or two excerpts from the Steinem document that conservatives would have considered radical. Next, have students select one or two phrases from the Schlafly document that feminists would have considered retrogressive.

Period 8: 1945–1980

MODULE 8-11 The Persistence of Liberalism and the Rise of the New Right

Environmentalism

Another outgrowth of 1960s liberal activism that flourished in the 1970s was the effort to clean up and preserve the environment. The publication of Rachel Carson's *Silent Spring* in 1962 had renewed awareness of what Progressive Era reformers called conservation. Carson expanded the concept of conservation to include ecology, which addressed the relationships of human beings and other organisms to their environments. By exploring these connections, she offered a revealing look at the devastating effects of pesticides on birds and fish, as well as on the human food chain and water supply.

This new environmental movement not only focused on open spaces and national parks but also sought to publicize urban environmental problems. By 1970, 53 percent of Americans considered air and water pollution to be one of the top issues facing the country, up from only 17 percent five years earlier. Responding to this shift in public opinion, in 1971 President Nixon established the **Environmental Protection Agency** (EPA) and signed the Clean Air Act, which regulated auto emissions.

Not everyone embraced environmentalism. As the EPA toughened emission standards, automobile manufacturers complained that the regulations forced them to raise prices and hurt an industry that was already feeling the threat of foreign competition, especially from Japan. Workers were also affected, as declining sales forced companies to lay off employees. Similarly, passage of the Endangered Species Act of 1973 pitted timber companies in the Northwest against environmentalists. The new law prevented the federal government from funding any projects that threatened the habitat of animals at risk of extinction.

Several disasters heightened public demands for stronger government oversight of the environment. In 1978 women living near Love Canal outside Niagara Falls, New York, complained about unusually high rates of illnesses and birth defects in their community. Investigations revealed that

> "Nature has introduced great variety into the landscape, but man has displayed a passion for simplifying it. Thus he undoes the built-in checks and balances by which nature holds the species within bounds."
>
> —Rachel Carson, *Silent Spring*, 1963

AP® ANALYZING SOURCES

Source: Michael McCloskey, *Ecotactics: The Sierra Club Handbook for Environmental Activists*, 1970

"A few years ago, our friends in law school laughed at us because we wanted to 'change the world.' Young activists in the Fifties, of course, represented the silent majority. Their laughing peers believed the lessons of the Thirties and Forties had already exposed the delusion of Grand Causes.

But with the causes of the Sixties—civil rights, anti-poverty and peace—activism became a less lonely avocation. Suddenly, students discovered they could make a difference—and they did, producing some profound changes in public policy. Now, as the Seventies begin, we face a crisis that affects everyone in ways some of the earlier crises never did. The ecology of Earth's life-support system is disintegrating.

A revolution is truly needed—in our values, outlook and economic organization. For the crisis of our environment stems from a legacy of economic and technical premises which have been pursed in the absence of ecological knowledge. That other revolution, the industrial one that is turning sour, needs to be replaced by a revolution of new attitudes toward growth, goods, space and living things."

Questions for Analysis
1. Identify the intended audience for this excerpt.
2. Describe the point of view on technology and industrialization that McCloskey expresses in this excerpt.
3. Explain the relationship between the activism of the 1960s and the environmental movement of the 1970s.
4. Evaluate the extent to which environmental activism of the 1970s represented a continuity with the conservation movement of the Progressive Era.

TEACHING IDEA

Incorporating Videos

The PBS documentary *Earth Days* is an engaging history of the environmental movement from 1945 to the present (available on YouTube). Much of the film focuses on how the movement evolved from the 1960s through the 1970s. Earth Day, overpopulation, and government responses are all significant parts of the film.

TRM Suggested Responses to Questions

TRM Module 8.11 AP® Analyzing Sources Handout 2

EXPLORING AP® THEMES

Geography and the Environment

Teachers should consider using primary sources directly related to environmentalism. Steven Stoll's primary source reader, *U.S. Environmentalism since 1945: A Brief History with Documents*, is an excellent resource for teachers to use as they help students explore environmental history. Beyond the value of the documents, it also provides a brief overview of environmental history, which can be useful as teachers make their way through the AP® curriculum. Major voices in the environmental movement such as Garrett Hardin, Paul Ehrlich, Rachel Carson, Barry Commoner, and Denis Hayes are included.

TEACHING IDEA

Incorporating Videos

If you are looking for an introductory video for a lesson on environmentalism in the 1970s, consider using a video from Gilder Lehrman's AP® U.S. History site (ap.gilderlehrman.org). Go to Period 8 and look for "Earth Day 1970 and the Teach-In That Made the Green Generation" by Adam Rowe. The video illustrates the context and underpinnings that led to the movement, and shows how the movement inspired a generation. A short clip of under 5 minutes, this can be used to introduce a lesson or to close a lesson.

New Forms of Conservatism

Three Mile Island Nuclear Power Plant, 1979 On March 28, 1979, the Three Mile Island nuclear power plant, outside Harrisburg, Pennsylvania, started leaking radioactive steam that contaminated the surrounding area. The governor called for a voluntary evacuation within a twenty-mile distance. The cooling tower of the nuclear plant stands behind an abandoned playground, where children had been playing only days earlier. **What does this photograph suggest about the potential consequences of a nuclear meltdown at Three Mile Island?**

their housing development had been constructed on top of a toxic waste dump. This discovery spawned grassroots efforts to clean up this area as well as other contaminated communities. In 1980 President Carter and Congress responded by passing the **Comprehensive Environmental Response, Compensation, and Liability Act** (known as the EPA's Superfund) to clean up sites contaminated with hazardous substances. Further inquiries showed that the presence of such poisonous waste dumps disproportionately affected minorities and the poor. Critics called the placement of these waste locations near African American and other minority communities "environmental racism" and launched a movement for environmental justice.

The most dangerous threat came in March 1979 at the Three Mile Island nuclear power plant near Harrisburg, Pennsylvania. A broken valve at the plant leaked coolant and threatened the meltdown of the reactor's nuclear core. As officials quickly evacuated residents from the surrounding area, employees at the plant narrowly averted catastrophe by fixing the problem before an explosion occurred. Grassroots activists protested and raised public awareness against the construction of additional nuclear power facilities.

REVIEW

How did environmental disasters help shape the environmentalist movement of the 1970s?

New Forms of Conservatism

New Right The conservative coalition of old and new conservatives, as well as disaffected Democrats.

neoconservatives Disillusioned liberals who condemned the Great Society programs they had originally supported. Neoconservatives were particularly concerned about affirmative action programs, the domination of campus discourse by New Left radicals, and left-wing criticism of the use of American military and economic might to advance U.S. interests overseas.

In the 1970s, working- and middle-class white resentment centered on big government spending and higher taxes. During the 1970s, taxation claimed 30 percent of the gross domestic product while the wealthiest Americans were taxed at a 70 percent marginal tax rate. Although Americans still paid far less in taxes than their counterparts in Western Europe, Americans objected to raising state and federal taxes. Leading the tax revolt was the Sun Belt state of California. In a 1978 referendum, California voters passed Proposition 13, a measure that reduced property taxes and placed strict limits on the ability of local governments to raise them in the future. In the wake of Proposition 13, a dozen states enacted similar measures.

Economic conservatives also set their sights on reducing the federal income tax. They supported cutting personal and corporate taxes by a third in the belief that reducing taxes would encourage new investment and job creation. "Supply-side" economists argued that lowering tax rates would actually boost tax receipts: With lower taxes, companies and investors would have more capital to invest, leading to expanded job growth; with increased employment, more people would be paying taxes. At the same time, supply-side conservatives called for reduced government spending, especially in the social service sector, to ensure balanced budgets and to eliminate what they saw as unnecessary spending on domestic programs.

The **New Right** also benefited by the defection of disillusioned liberals. Labeled **neoconservatives**, intellectuals such as Irving Kristol, Norman Podhoretz, and Nathan Glazer reversed course and condemned the Great Society programs that they had originally supported. They believed that

MODULE 8-11 The Persistence of Liberalism and the Rise of the New Right

Tax Revolt in California, 1978 California residents gather in support of Proposition 13, a state constitutional amendment that proposed a cap on property tax rates. The amendment also required a two-thirds vote by any local or state government to increase taxes in the future. The initiative passed overwhelmingly by a state-wide vote on June 6, 1978. **What do the signs held by anti-tax protestors in the photograph reveal about the reasons many Californians supported Proposition 13?**

AP® TIP
Compare the political platform of the New Right to that of the New Left (Module 8-9).

Christian Right A coalition of evangelical Christians and Catholics that supported traditional values, laissez-faire economics, and an uncompromising anti-communist foreign policy. They joined forces with political conservatives.

federal policies, such as affirmative action, had aggravated rather than improved the problems government planners intended to solve. They considered the New Left's opposition to the Vietnam War and its disapproval of foreign intervention a threat to national security.

Perhaps the greatest spark igniting the New Right came from religious and social conservatives, mainly evangelical Christians and Catholics. Evangelicals considered themselves to have been "born again" — having experienced Jesus Christ's saving presence inside of them. By the end of the 1970s, evangelical Christians numbered around 50 million, about a quarter of the population. As evangelicals became politically active, a **Christian Right** emerged that opposed abortion, gay rights, and sex education; criticized Supreme Court rulings banning prayer in the public schools; rejected Charles Darwin's theory of evolution in favor of divine creationism; supported the traditional role of women as mothers and homemakers; and backed a hardline, anti-Communist stand against the Soviet Union. Certainly not all evangelical Christians, such as President Carter, held all of these beliefs. Still, conservative Christians believed that the liberals and radicals of the 1960s had spread the secular creed of individual rights and personal fulfillment at the expense of established Christian values.

Social conservatives worried that the traditional nuclear family was in danger, as households consisting of married couples with children declined from 30 percent in the 1970s to 23 percent thirty years later, and the divorce rate soared. The number of unmarried couples living together doubled over the last quarter of the twentieth century. In 1970, 26.4 percent of infants were born to single mothers; by 1990 the rate had risen to 43.8. This increase was part of a trend in developed countries worldwide. Moreover, social conservatives united in fierce opposition to abortion, which the Supreme Court legalized in *Roe v. Wade* (see Module 8-9). They argued that an unborn fetus is a person and therefore has a right to life protected by the Constitution.

One direct impetus pushing conservative evangelicals into politics came when the Internal Revenue Service (IRS) removed tax-exempt status from a fundamentalist Christian college. Bob Jones University in South Carolina defended racial segregation on biblical grounds, but under pressure from the federal government began admitting some African American students in the mid-1970s. However, the school continued practicing discrimination by prohibiting interracial dating. In 1976, when the IRS revoked the university's tax exempt status, conservative Christians charged that the federal government was interfering with religious freedom. This sparked a grassroots political campaign to rally Christian evangelicals around a host of grievances.

Since the 1950s, Billy Graham, a charismatic Southern Baptist evangelist from North Carolina, had used television to conduct nationwide crusades. Television became an even greater instrument in the hands of New Right Christian preachers in the 1970s and 1980s. The Reverend Pat Robertson of Virginia founded the Christian Broadcasting Network, and ministers such as Jerry Falwell used the airwaves to great effect. What distinguished Falwell and Robertson from earlier evangelists like Graham was their fusion of religion and electoral politics. In 1979 Falwell founded the Moral Majority, an organization that backed political candidates who supported a "family values" social agenda. Within two years of its creation, the Moral Majority counted four million members who were eager to organize in support of New Right politicians. The New Right also lined up advocacy groups such as the American Enterprise Institute and the Heritage Foundation to generate and promote conservative ideals. The alliance of economic, intellectual, and religious conservatives offered a formidable challenge to liberalism.

REVIEW

What factors contributed to the rise of each of the new forms of conservatism?

New Forms of Conservatism

AP® WRITING HISTORICALLY — Short-Answer Question Practice

ACTIVITY

Read the following question carefully and write a short response. Use complete sentences.

Using the following excerpts, answer (a), (b), and (c).

Source: Dan T. Carter, *From George Wallace to Newt Gingrich: Race in the Conservative Counterrevolution, 1963–1994*, 1996

"Historians of the American left have made much of the way in which the civil rights movement influenced the social movements of the 1960s and 1970s, inspiring, for example, the women's rights movement and the politics of sexual liberation. But the movement's counterrevolutionary effects are equally important. In the three decades following the emergence of George Wallace, the rhetoric of racial politics evolved: from the issues of public accommodations to school desegregation, busing, housing, quotas, and struggles over job discrimination, and proposals for economic affirmative action. . . .

Economic and social conservatives — particularly those who have been lifelong opponents of racial bigotry — have bridled at the attempt to link what neoconservatives have called the 'new majoritarianism' of the 1980s with the politics of race. Nevertheless, I think it is fair to say that even though the streams of racial and economic conservatism have sometimes flowed in separate channels, they ultimately joined in the political coalition that reshaped American politics from the 1970s through the mid-1990s. . . . [George] Wallace's sensitivity to being "looked down on" and his identity as a beleaguered white southerner strengthened his appeal to white ethnic minorities and working class Americans."

Source: Daniel Williams, *God's Own Party: The Making of the Christian Right*, 2010

"During . . . the late 1960s, conservative Protestants succeeded not only in making alliances with Republican politicians, but in changing the agenda of the party. This time, they focused more on the culture wars than the Cold War. Conservative Protestants who mobilized against feminism, abortion, pornography, and gay rights acquired control of the Republican Party, partly because of their long-standing alliances with Republican politicians, but perhaps more important because of the united front that they presented, and because of demographic and political shifts that favored evangelicals. . . . The sexual revolution, sex education, race riots, the counterculture, increases in drug use, and the beginning of the feminist movement convinced them that the nation had lost its Christian identity and that the family was under attack.

The end of the civil rights movement facilitated the formation of the Christian political coalition, because it enabled fundamentalists and evangelicals who had disagreed over racial integration to come together. After the passage of federal civil rights legislation and the end of nationally publicized civil rights marches, fundamentalists such as Jerry Falwell accepted the reality of racial integration and began forging political alliances with mainstream Republicans who would have been embarrassed by their segregationist rhetoric only a few years earlier. At the same time, moderate evangelicals who had once cautiously supported the civil rights movement reacted in horror to the race riots and began taking more conservative stances on civil rights. Both fundamentalists and evangelicals embraced Richard Nixon's call for 'law and order.'"

a. Briefly explain ONE major difference between Carter's and Williams's interpretations of the rise of the New Right.
b. Briefly explain how ONE specific historical event or development from the period that is not explicitly mentioned in the excerpts could be used to support Carter's argument.
c. Briefly explain how ONE specific historical event or development that is not explicitly mentioned in the excerpts could be used to support Williams's argument.

TRM Suggested Responses to Questions

TEACHING IDEA

Building Vocabulary

Consider dividing students into groups of 3 to 4 for this brief bell ringer activity. After forming groups and prior to reading these sources, have students look up and define the words fundamentalist and evangelical. After they have defined the words, check for understanding by providing students with the correct definitions. Knowing these words is crucial to understanding the point Daniel Williams is making.

▲ Differentiation

For students who already have a clear understanding of the differences between fundamentalist and evangelical, ask them to look up examples from the 1920s to draw a comparison with how fundamentalists and evangelicals affected political debates in the 1920s such as evolution or prohibition.

TEACHING IDEA

AP® Writing Historically Review

The Short-Answer Questions that provide two secondary sources in opposition typically cover major events in U.S. history such as the rise of conservatism in the late twentieth century. Sometimes the titles of secondary works provide useful insights into the subtopic being addressed in the excerpt. Being cognizant of this can help students determine the different interpretations as well as develop historical evidence to use in parts (b) and (c). To help students along in this process, write the following on the white board: Topic of Interpretation, Subtopic from Carter, and Subtopic from Williams. Students are narrowing their focus to the topic of the prompt and subtopics from the historians. Their answers will look similar to the following — Topic of Interpretation: conservatism; Subtopic from Carter: racial politics; Subtopic from Williams: Christian Coalition/Moral Majority. Knowing this in advance of the read can help students develop better responses.

PERIOD 8 REVIEW 1945–1980

KEY CONCEPTS AND EVENTS

affirmative action, 761
American Indian Movement (AIM), 774
baby boom, 719
Bandung Conference, 741
Bay of Pigs invasion, 746
Beats, 727
Berlin airlift, 704
Berlin Wall, 746
Black Panther Party, 761
Brown v. Board of Education of Topeka, Kansas, 731
Bureau of Indian Affairs (BIA), 744
Camp David accords, 786
Central Intelligence Agency (CIA), 703
Christian Right, 796
Civil Rights Act of 1964, 758
Cold War, 700
Commission on the Status of Women, 772
Comprehensive Environmental Response, Compensation, and Liability Act, 795
containment, 700
counterculture, 771
deindustrialization, 783
Dennis v. United States, 713
détente, 780
Dixiecrats, 717
Domino Theory, 749
Eisenhower Doctrine, 742
Environmental Protection Agency (EPA), 794
Equal Rights Amendment (ERA), 772
escalation, 750
Federal Employee Loyalty Program, 711
Federal Housing Administration, 720
Freedom Rides, 756
Freedom Summer, 758
Free Speech Movement (FSM), 770
Great Migration, 736
Great Society, 767

Gulf of Tonkin Resolution, 750
House Un-American Activities Committee (HUAC), 711
imperial presidency, 703
iron curtain, 701
Kent State massacre, 753
Kitchen Debate, 741
Korean War, 707
La Raza Unida (The United Race), 773
Levittown, 720
Little Rock Nine, 733
March on Washington for Jobs and Freedom, 757
Marshall Plan, 703
McCarran Internal Security Act, 713
McCarran-Walter Immigration Act, 737
McCarthyism, 714
Mississippi Freedom Democratic Party (MFDP), 759
Modern Republicanism, 743
Montgomery bus boycott, 732
mujahideen, 785
mutually assured destruction (MAD), 740
My Lai massacre, 751
National Defense Education Act, 744
National Energy Act, 784
National Interstate and Defense Highway Act, 744
National Organization for Women (NOW), 772
National Security Council (NSC), 703
neoconservatives, 795
New Frontier, 767
New Look, 740
New Right, 795
North Atlantic Treaty Organization (NATO), 704
NSC-68, 705
Operation Wetback, 744
Organization of Petroleum Exporting Countries (OPEC), 781

Pentagon Papers, 754
Port Huron Statement, 769
Potsdam Conference, 700
realpolitik, 780
Roe v. Wade, 772
SALT II, 785
school busing, 761
Second Red Scare, 711
Servicemen's Readjustment Act (GI Bill), 717
Smith Act, 711
Southern Christian Leadership Conference (SCLC), 732
Sputnik, 744
stagflation, 783
Stonewall riots, 774
Strategic Arms Limitation Treaty (SALT I), 780
Student Nonviolent Coordinating Committee (SNCC), 735
Students for a Democratic Society (SDS), 769
Sun Belt, 721
Taft-Hartley Act, 717
Tet Offensive, 752
To Secure These Rights, 730
totalitarianism, 702
Truman Doctrine, 702
Twenty-sixth Amendment, 780
Vietcong, 749
Vietnamization, 753
Vietnam War, 750
Voting Rights Act, 760
War Powers Act, 754
Warsaw Pact, 705
Watergate, 781
White Citizens' Council (WCC), 733
Yates v. United States, 715
Young Americans for Freedom (YAF), 775

PERIOD 8 REVIEW 1945–1980

KEY PEOPLE

- Chuck Berry, *725*
- Marlon Brando, *724*
- Leonid Brezhnev, *780*
- William F. Buckley, *775*
- Stokely Carmichael, *761*
- Jimmy Carter, *777*
- Fidel Castro, *742*
- Whittaker Chambers, *713*
- Cesar Chavez, *773*
- Frank Church, *785*
- Winston Churchill, *701*
- John Coltrane, *727*
- Eugene "Bull" Connor, *756*
- Miles Davis, *727*
- James Dean, *723*
- John Dean, *782*
- Ngo Dinh Diem, *749*
- Bob Dylan, *771*
- Dwight D. Eisenhower, *739*
- Medgar Evers, *757*
- Jerry Falwell, *796*
- Gerald Ford, *782*
- Betty Friedan, *725*
- Dizzy Gillespie, *727*
- Allen Ginsberg, *727*
- Barry Goldwater, *768*
- Billy Graham, *726*
- Fannie Lou Hamer, *759*
- Tom Hayden, *769*
- Alger Hiss, *712*
- Dolores Huerta, *773*
- Hubert H. Humphrey, *779*
- Lyndon B. Johnson, *744*
- George Kennan, *700*
- John F. Kennedy, *740*
- Robert F. Kennedy, *756*
- Jack Kerouac, *727*
- Ayatollah Ruholla Khomeini, *786*
- Nikita Khrushchev, *741*
- Martin Luther King Jr., *732*
- Dr. Alfred Kinsey, *727*
- Henry Kissinger, *752*
- William Levitt, *720*
- John Lewis, *757*
- Douglas Macarthur, *706*
- Norman Mailer, *727*
- George Marshall, *703*
- Thurgood Marshall, *730*
- Joseph McCarthy, *714*
- George McGovern, *781*
- James Meredith, *756*
- Ho Chi Minh, *748*
- John Mitchell, *782*
- Marilyn Monroe, *724*
- Huey P. Newton, *761*
- Richard M. Nixon, *713*
- Rosa Parks, *732*
- Norman Vincent Peale, *726*
- Elvis Presley, *725*
- A. Philip Randolph, *732*
- Ronald Reagan, *786*
- Pat Robertson, *796*
- Jackie Robinson, *730*
- Ethel Rosenberg, *710*
- Julius Rosenberg, *710*
- Edward Roybal, *736*
- Bayard Rustin, *732*
- Dr. Jonas Salk, *720*
- Phyllis Schlafly, *792*
- Bobby Seale, *761*
- Frank Sinatra, *725*
- Barbara Smith, *792*
- Dr. Benjamin Spock, *725*
- Joseph Stalin, *700*
- Gloria Steinem, *772*
- Emmett Till, *734*
- Harry S. Truman, *700*
- George C. Wallace, *757*
- Henry Wallace, *701*
- Earl Warren, *731*
- Bob Woodward, *781*
- Malcolm X, *760*
- Mao Zedong, *705*

PERIOD 8 REVIEW 1945–1980

CHRONOLOGY

1940	Smith Act bars supporting overthrow of U.S. government
1941	Term *teenager* coined
1944	GI Bill subsidizes education, mortgages, healthcare for veterans
1945	Yalta Conference
1946	Churchill delivers "iron curtain" speech
1947	U.S. provides military aid to Greece and Turkey
	Marshall Plan proposed
	Taft-Hartley Act limits power of labor unions
	Truman creates Federal Employee Loyalty Program
	HUAC holds hearings on Communist influence in Hollywood
	Mendez v. Westminster prohibits separate schools for Mexican Americans
1948	Creation of West Germany; Berlin Airlift begins
	Creation of Levittown
	Truman wins re-election
	President Truman orders desegregation of U.S. military
1949	Formation of NATO alliance
	Russia tests its first atomic bomb
1950	Korean War begins
	McCarran Internal Security Act passed over Truman's veto
	NSC-68 urges more aggressive U.S. posture toward USSR
1951	*Dennis v. United States* labels Communist leaders as dangerous
1952	McCarran-Walter Immigration Act allows Japanese non-citizens to become citizens
	Eisenhower wins election on Modern Republicanism platform
1953	Korean War ends with an armistice agreement
	Rosenbergs executed for sharing atomic bomb secrets with USSR
1954	Army-McCarthy hearings
	Senate censures McCarthy
	"Under God" added to the pledge of allegiance
	Brown v. Board of Education Supreme Court decision overturns Jim-Crow era "separate but equal" doctrine
	Mass deportation of undocumented Mexican immigrants in "Operation Wetback"
	Overthrow of French colonial rule in Vietnam
1955	Introduction of polio vaccine
	James Dean stars in *Rebel Without a Cause*
	Arrest of Rosa Parks and start of Montgomery bus boycott
1956	Elvis Presley appears on the *Ed Sullivan Show*
	Publication of Allen Ginsberg's poem "Howl"
	"In God We Trust" becomes the official motto of the United States
	Eisenhower wins second term
	National Interstate and Defense Highway Act passed
	Supported by the U.S., Ngo Dinh Diem rejects national elections in Vietnam
1957	*Yates v. United States* severely weakens Smith Act
	Crisis of integration of Central High School in Little Rock, Arkansas
	Formation of the Southern Christian Leadership Conference (SCLC)
	Eisenhower Doctrine approved by Congress
	Soviets launch *Sputnik* satellite into space
1958	Vice President Richard Nixon visits the Soviet Union
1959	Nixon and Krushchev engage in "Kitchen Debate"
	Fidel Castro leads uprising in Cuba
By 1960	One third of Americans live in suburbs
	90 percent of teens attending high school
1960	Sit-in at Woolworth's lunch counter in Greensboro, NC
	Formation of the Student Nonviolent Coordinating Committee (SNCC)
	American U-2 spy plane shot down by Soviet Union
	Birth control pills made available to American public
	Barry Goldwater's *The Conscience of a Conservative* published
	John F. Kennedy wins close presidential election
1961	Bay of Pigs invasion fails to create popular uprising against Castro
	Freedom Rides to integrate transportation facilities in South
1962	Soviets construct Berlin Wall
	Cuban Missile Crisis brings U.S. and USSR to brink of war
	Port Huron Statement by Students for a Democratic Society
	Silent Spring by Rachael Carson increases awareness of environmental concerns
1963	Partial Nuclear Test Ban Treaty signed
	Publication of *The Feminine Mystique* by Betty Friedan

PERIOD 8 REVIEW 1945–1980

- Kennedy endorses coup to replace Diem in Vietnam
- Civil rights protests in Birmingham
- March on Washington for Jobs and Freedom
- KKK bombing of Sixteenth Street Baptist Church
- Assassination of President Kennedy

1964
- Gulf of Tonkin Resolution grants president control of Vietnam conflict
- Johnson launches Great Society program and War on Poverty
- Civil Rights Act prohibits discrimination in public accommodations, education, and employment
- Economic Opportunity Act establishes War on Poverty agencies: Head Start, VISTA, Job Corps, and Community Action Program
- Freedom Summer voter registration drive in South
- Johnson wins reelection in a landslide

1965
- President Johnson launches Operation Rolling Thunder, a massive bombing campaign
- Civil Rights March from Selma to Montgomery
- Assassination of Malcolm X
- Elementary and Secondary Education Act provides federal funding for elementary and secondary schools
- Medical Care Act provides Medicare health insurance for citizens sixty-five years and older and Medicaid health benefits for the poor
- Voting Rights Act bans literacy tests for voting, authorizes federal registrars to be sent into seven southern states, and monitors voting changes in these states
- Immigration and Nationality Act abolishes quotas on immigration that reduced immigration from non-Western and southern and eastern European nations
- Water Quality Act establishes and enforces federal water quality standards
- Air Quality Act establishes and enforces air pollution standards for motor vehicles
- National Arts and Humanities Act establishes the National Endowment of the Humanities and National Endowment of the Arts to support the work of scholars, writers, artists, and musicians

1966
- Formation of Black Panther Party
- National Organization of Women (NOW) founded
- Model Cities Act approves funding for the rehabilitation of inner cities
- Anti-war protests escalate

1968
- Tet Offensive
- My Lai Massacre
- American Indian Movement (AIM) established
- Assassination of Martin Luther King Jr.
- Fair Housing Act signed into law
- Assassination of Robert F. Kennedy
- Richard Nixon wins presidential election

1969
- Stonewall riots signal emergence of gay liberation movement
- Chicanos form *La Raza Unida* political party

1970
- U.S. Invasion of Cambodia
- Kent State Massacre
- Environmental Protection Act passed

1971
- Publication of the *Pentagon Papers* further undermines public support for Vietnam War
- Supreme Court mandates forced busing to achieve integration in *Swann* case
- Twenty-sixth Amendment lowers voting age to eighteen
- Environmental Protection Agency established
- Clean Air Act passed

1972
- SALT I Treaty limits nuclear arsenals and ushers in détente
- Nixon wins re-election
- Title IX greatly expands women's collegiate athletics

1973
- War Powers Act limits presidential power to wage war without congressional approval
- *Roe v. Wade* affirms women's constitutional right to abortion
- Watergate investigations begin
- Vice President Spiro Agnew resigns
- OPEC oil embargo
- Endangered Species Act signed into law

1974
- President Nixon resigns over Watergate scandal
- President Ford pardons Nixon

1975
- Fall of Saigon to North Vietnam

1976
- Jimmy Carter wins presidential election

1978
- *Bakke* case ruling limits use of affirmative action in college admissions
- Camp David accords bring peace between Egypt and Israel
- Proposition 13 passed by California voters, launching nationwide taxpayer protests

1979
- Iranian hostage crisis begins
- Three Mile Island nuclear reactor meltdown
- Jerry Falwell founds the Moral Majority

1980
- U.S. boycotts Moscow Olympics
- Reagan wins presidential election

1981
- Iranian hostages released on Reagan's inauguration day

1982
- Ratification of Equal Rights Amendment (ERA) defeated

TRM Suggested Responses to Questions

Answers to Multiple-Choice Questions

1. d
2. c
3. b
4. c
5. d
6. a
7. a
8. a
9. a
10. a
11. a
12. a
13. c
14. a
15. a

AP® EXAM PRACTICE THROUGH 1980

Multiple Choice Questions

Choose the correct answer for each question.

Questions 1–4 refer to the following excerpt.

> **Source:** George Kennan, United States diplomat in Moscow, "Long Telegram" to the Secretary of State, February 1946
>
> "I am convinced that there would be far less hysterical anti-Sovietism in our country today if the realities of this situation were better understood by our people. There is nothing as dangerous or as terrifying as the unknown. . . . World communism is like a malignant parasite which feeds only on diseased tissue. This is the point at which domestic and foreign policies meet. Every courageous and incisive measure to solve the internal problems of our own society . . . is a diplomatic victory over Moscow. . . . Many foreign peoples, in Europe at least, are tired and frightened by experiences of the past, and are less interested in abstract freedom than in security. They are seeking guidance rather than responsibilities. We should be better able than Russians to give them this. And unless we do, the Russians certainly will."

1. The arguments expressed in the excerpt are best understood in the context of the
   a. U.S. military involvement in the Korean and Vietnam wars.
   b. fluctuation between confrontation and coexistence with the Soviet Union.
   c. emergence of nationalist movements across the globe after World War II.
   d. end of the wartime alliance between the United States and the Soviet Union.

2. The "hysteria" mentioned by Kennan in the excerpt refers most directly to
   a. widespread public protests against the draft.
   b. growing scientific concern about the environmental dangers of a nuclear war.
   c. a domestic search for communists working in the government or mass media.
   d. legislation restricting free speech and limiting criticism of U.S. foreign policy.

3. Kennan's arguments expressed in the excerpt most directly supported a foreign policy of
   a. détente.
   b. containment.
   c. isolationism.
   d. imperialism.

4. The most direct result of Kennan's ideas expressed in the excerpt was the
   a. establishment of the United Nations.
   b. spread of Cold War competition to Latin America.
   c. creation of the North Atlantic Treaty Organization.
   d. growth of a large military-industrial complex in the United States.

Questions 5–7 refer to the following excerpt.

> **Source:** "Homeowners Guide: Some Information for Residents of Levittown to Help Them Enjoy Their Homes," Levittown, Pennsylvania, 1957
>
> "In order that you may enjoy your house, and derive the utmost pleasure from it, we have undertaken to prepare this handbook so that you may better understand our position and your responsibilities. . . .
>
>   No single feature contributes so much to the charm and beauty of the individual home and locality as well-kept lawns. Stabilization of values, yes, increase in values, will most often be found in those neighborhoods where lawns show as green carpets, and trees and shrubbery join to impart the sense of residential elegance. Where lawns and landscape material are neglected the neighborhood soon amasses a sub-standard or blighted appearance and is naturally shunned by the public. Your investment in your garden is large at the beginning, but will grow larger and larger as the years go by. For while furniture, houses, and most material things tend to depreciate with the years, your lawn, trees, and shrubs become more valuable both esthetically and monetarily."

5. The excerpt best serves as evidence of which of the following developments in United States society after World War II?
   a. Increasing numbers of immigrants seeking access to economic opportunities
   b. The rapid growth of evangelical Christian churches and organizations
   c. The introduction of greater informality into U.S. culture
   d. The migration of the middle class to the suburbs

6. The sentiments expressed in the excerpt were most likely intended to
   a. promote an increasingly homogenous culture in the postwar years.
   b. challenge the Sunbelt as a significant political and economic force.
   c. inspire critiques of conformity by artists and intellectuals.
   d. advocate a link between homeownership and social mobility.

7. In the period 1945 to 1960, communities such as Levittown grew most directly as a result of
   a. the baby boom.
   b. the growing power of political machine organizations.
   c. changes in sexual norms.
   d. passage of new immigration laws.

Questions 8–10 refer to the following excerpt.

Source: "Anti-Little Rock Intervention," editorial by Karr Shannon, *Arkansas Democrat,* March 10, 1958

"Little Rock's Central High School is still under military occupation. The troops are still there—on the campus, in the building.

The troops are still there, despite the fact that their presence is resented by the big majority of the students, the parents, and the people in general throughout the South.

The troops continue to stand guard during school hours, despite the fact that there is no law or precedent—Federal or State—that permits them to do so.

There is not even an order, or so much as a sanction, from the U.S. Supreme Court that makes its own 'laws' on mixing of races in the public schools. . . .

Education, or attempted education, under the scrutiny of armed troops in un-American, un-Godly. . . .

How much longer will Congress sit idly by and let such brazen violation of American principle and law continue on and on and on?"

8. In making mention of "'laws' on mixing of the races," the author refers most directly to the Supreme Court's
   a. *Brown v. Board of Education* case.
   b. *Dred Scott v. Sanford* case.
   c. *Plessy v. Ferguson* case.
   d. rulings against New Deal programs.

9. The ideas expressed by Shannon in the excerpt show the greatest similarity to
   a. antebellum advocates of states' rights.
   b. proponents of Reconstruction in the 1860s and 1870s.
   c. supporters of desegregation of the United States armed forces in the 1940s.
   d. those calling for a Great Society in the 1960s.

10. Support for Shannon's ideas would most likely have been greatest in
    a. newly politicized conservative organizations.
    b. movements for Hispanic rights.
    c. groups organizing for gay and lesbian rights.
    d. increasingly activist environmental organizations.

Questions 11–13 refer to the following excerpt.

Source: "No More Miss America," press release for 1968 Pageant Protest

"On September 7th in Atlantic City, the Annual Miss America Pageant will again crown 'your ideal.' . . . We will protest the image of Miss America, an image that oppresses women in every area in which it purports to represent us. There will be: Picket Lines; Guerrilla Theater; Leafleting; Lobbying Visits to the contestants urging our sisters to reject the Pageant Farce and join us; a huge Freedom Trash Can (into which we will throw bras, girdles, curlers, false eyelashes, wigs, and representative issues of *Cosmopolitan, Ladies' Home Journal, Family Circle,* etc. . . . we will also announce a Boycott of all those commercial products related to the Pageant, and the day will end with a Women's Liberation rally at midnight when Miss America is crowned on live television."

11. The sentiments expressed in the excerpt most directly resulted from
    a. court decisions expanding individual rights.
    b. the rise of a youth counterculture.
    c. declining public trust in the government.
    d. the rise of a mass media.

12. Which of the following developments resulted from women's activism as described in the excerpt?
    a. A conservative backlash against the challenge to traditional values
    b. Passage of the Equal Rights Amendment
    c. Advances by women in the leadership of major corporations
    d. The election of women to the Senate and the House of Representatives

13. Which rights movement most directly influenced the tactics and goals of the women's rights movement?
    a. American Indian
    b. Chicano/Latino
    c. African American
    d. Gay and Lesbian

Questions 14–15 refer to the following excerpt.

Source: Daniel Bell, *The Coming of Post-Industrial Society: A Venture in Social Forecasting,* 1973

"In the place of the farmer came the industrial worker, and for the last hundred years or so the vicissitudes[1] of the industrial worker — his claims to dignity and status, his demand for a rising share of industrial returns, his desire for a voice in the conditions which affected his work and conditions of employment — have marked the struggles of the century. . . .

Yet if one takes the industrial worker as the instrument of the future . . . then this vision is warped. For the paradoxical fact is that as one goes along the trajectory of industrialization — the increasing replacement of men with machines — one comes logically to the erosion of the industrial worker himself. . . . Instead of the industrial worker, we see the dominance of the professional and technical class in the labor force. . . A post-industrial society is based upon services. Hence, it is a game between persons. What counts is not raw muscle power, or energy, but information. The central person is the professional, for he is equipped . . . to provide the kinds of skill which are increasingly demanded in a post-industrial society."

[1] Changes in fortune.

14. The ideas expressed in the excerpt most likely emerged from concerns about
    a. deindustrialization of the Upper Midwest and Northeast.
    b. mass migration of Americans to the Sunbelt.
    c. new movements to protect natural resources.
    d. loss of public confidence in government's ability to solve problems.

15. A historian could best support Bell's argument from the excerpt using statistics from the 1970s about
    a. industrial union members in each year as a percentage of the total workforce.
    b. census data tracking migration patterns of the U.S. population.
    c. changes in the real cost of living.
    d. fluctuations in the international trade deficit.

AP® Exam Practice: Through 1980

Period 8: 1945–1980

Short-Answer Questions

Read each question carefully and write a short response. Use complete sentences.

1. Using the following two excerpts, answer (a), (b), and (c).

   Source: Barbara Ransby, *Ella Baker and the Black Freedom Movement*, 2003

   "The conflict between [Martin Luther King Jr. and Ella Baker] reveals more fundamental conflicts between black politics and African American culture over the meanings of American democracy and the pathways toward social change.... Baker described [King] as a pampered member of Atlanta's black elite ... a member of a coddled 'silver spoon brigade.' ... In Baker's eyes, King did not identify closely enough with the people he sought to lead. He did not situate himself among them but remained above them.... Baker and King ... translated religious faith into their political identities in profoundly different ways. Above all, they defined the confluence of their roles as individuals and their roles as participants in a mass movement for social change quite distinctly. Baker was a militant egalitarian, and King was a sophisticated southern Baptist preacher."

   Source: Thomas F. Jackson, *From Civil Rights to Human Rights: Martin Luther King, Jr., and the Struggle for Economic Justice*, 2013

   "By 1965, King's radical voice rang more clearly when he confessed that his dream had turned into a 'nightmare.' The dream shattered when whites murdered voting rights workers in Alabama, when police battled blacks in Los Angeles, when he met jobless and 'hopeless' blacks on desperate Chicago streets, and when he saw hunger and poverty in rural Mississippi and Appalachia. But King picked up the shards of his shattered dreams and reassembled them into more radical visions of emancipation for all poor people.... Dreams of decent jobs, affordable integrated housing, and adequate family incomes remained central to King's public ministry until his death."

   a) Briefly explain ONE major difference between Ransby's and Jackson's historical interpretations of the civil rights movement.

   b) Briefly explain how ONE specific historical event or development that is not explicitly mentioned in the excerpts could be used to support Ransby's argument.

   c) Briefly explain how ONE specific historical event or development that is not explicitly mentioned in the excerpts could be used to support Jackson's argument.

2. Using the following three maps, answer (a), (b), and (c).

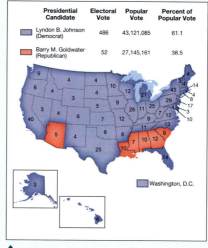
▲ 1964 Presidential Election Map

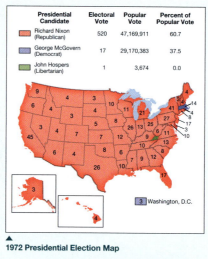
▲ 1968 Presidential Election Map

▲ 1972 Presidential Election Map

a) Briefly explain ONE specific historical event or development that accounts for the change depicted in the maps.

b) Briefly explain ANOTHER specific historical event or development that accounts for the change depicted in the maps.

c) Briefly explain ONE specific historical effect of the change depicted in the maps.

AP® Exam Practice: Through 1980

Period 8: 1945–1980

3. Answer (a), (b), and (c).
   a) Briefly describe ONE specific historical difference between President Franklin Roosevelt's New Deal (1933–1940) and President Lyndon Johnson's Great Society (1964–1968).
   b) Briefly describe ONE specific historical similarity between President Franklin Roosevelt's New Deal (1933–1940) and President Lyndon Johnson's Great Society (1964–1968).
   c) Briefly explain ONE specific historical effect of President Lyndon Johnson's Great Society (1964–1968) on United States society.

4. Answer (a), (b), and (c).
   a) Briefly explain ONE specific cause of suburban growth in the United States after World War II.
   b) Briefly explain ANOTHER specific cause of suburban growth in the United States after World War II.
   c) Briefly explain ONE specific effect of suburban growth in the United States after World War I

Document-Based Question

Question 1 is based on the accompanying documents. The documents have been edited for the purpose of this exercise. *Suggested reading period: 15 minutes. Suggested writing time: 45 minutes.*

1. Evaluate the extent of difference between United States foreign policy in the period 1945 to 1963 and United States foreign policy in the period 1964 to 1980.

DOCUMENT 1

Source: Secretary of State George Marshall, *Speech at Harvard University*, June 5, 1947.

"I need not tell you gentlemen that the world situation is very serious. That must be apparent to all intelligent people. I think one difficulty is that the problem is one of such enormous complexity that the very mass of facts presented to the public by press and radio make it exceedingly difficult for the man in the street to reach a clear appraisement of the situation. Furthermore, the people of this country are distant from the troubled areas of the earth and it is hard for them to comprehend the plight and consequent reaction of the long-suffering peoples, and the effect of those reactions on their governments in connection with our efforts to promote peace in the world. . . .

Aside from the demoralizing effect on the world at large and the possibilities of disturbances arising as a result of the desperation of the people concerned, the consequences to the economy of the United States should be apparent to all. It is logical that the United States should do whatever it is able to do to assist in the return of normal economic health in the world, without which there can be no political stability and no assured peace. Our policy is directed not against any country or doctrine but against hunger, poverty, desperation, and chaos. Its purpose should be the revival of working economy in the world so as to permit the emergence of political and social conditions in which free institutions can exist."

TRM Suggested Responses to Questions

DOCUMENT 2 **Source:** General Douglas MacArthur, Farewell Address to Congress, April 19, 1951.

"The Communist threat is a global one. Its successful advance in one sector threatens the destruction of every other sector.

You can not appease or otherwise surrender to communism in Asia without simultaneously undermining our efforts to halt its advance in Europe. . . .

But once war is forced upon us, there is no other alternative than to apply every available means to bring it to a swift end. . . . War's very object is victory, not prolonged indecision. In war there is no substitute for victory. There are some who, for varying reasons, would appease Red China. They are blind to history's clear lesson, for history teaches with unmistakable emphasis that appeasement but begets new and bloodier war. It points to no single instance where this end has justified that means, where appeasement has led to more than a sham peace. Like blackmail, it lays the basis for new and successively greater demands until, as in blackmail, violence becomes the only other alternative."

DOCUMENT 3 **Source:** President John F. Kennedy, Televised Address to the American Public, October 22, 1962.

"For many years, both the Soviet Union and the United States . . . have deployed strategic nuclear weapons with great care, never upsetting the precarious status quo which insured that these weapons would not be used in the absence of some vital challenge. Our own strategic missiles have never been transferred to the territory of any other nation under a cloak of secrecy and deception; and our history—unlike that of the Soviets since the end of World War II—demonstrates that we have no desire to dominate or conquer any other nation or impose our system upon its people. Nevertheless, American citizens have become adjusted to living daily on the bull's-eye of Soviet missiles located inside the U.S.S.R. or in submarines. . . .

We are prepared to discuss new proposals for the removal of tensions on both sides, including the possibilities of a genuinely independent Cuba, free to determine its own destiny. We have no wish to war with the Soviet Union—for we are a peaceful people who desire to live in peace with all other peoples.

But it is difficult to settle or even discuss these problems in an atmosphere of intimidation. That is why this latest Soviet threat—or any other threat which is made either independently or in response to our actions this week—must and will be met with determination. Any hostile move anywhere in the world against the safety and freedom of peoples to whom we are committed, including in particular the brave people of West Berlin, will be met by whatever action is needed."

DOCUMENT 4 **Source:** Harold Bryant, a Vietnam soldier recalling his tour of duty in August 1965.

"When I came to Vietnam, I thought we were helping another country to develop a nation. About three or four months later I found out that wasn't the case. . . .

I thought we had got into the beginning of a war. But I found out that we were just in another phase of their civil wars.

And we weren't gaining any ground. We would fight for a hill all day, spend two days or two nights there, and then abandon the hill. Then maybe two, three months later, we would have to come back and retake the same piece of territory. . . .

And they had a habit of exaggerating a body count. If we killed 7, by the time it would get back to base camp, it would have gotten to 28. Then by the time it got down to [General William] Westmoreland's office in Saigon, it done went up to 54. And by the time it left from Saigon going to Washington, it had went up to about 125. To prove we were really out there doing our jobs, doing, really, more than what we were doing."

DOCUMENT 5

Source: President Richard Nixon, State of the Union Address to Congress, January 30, 1974.

"Tonight, for the first time in 12 years, a President of the United States can report to the Congress on the state of a Union at peace with every nation of the world. . . .

In the coming year, however, increased expenditures will be needed. They will be needed to assure the continued readiness of our military forces, to preserve present force levels in the face of rising costs, and to give us the military strength we must have if our security is to be maintained and if our initiatives for peace are to succeed.

The question is not whether we can afford to maintain the necessary strength of our defense, the question is whether we can afford not to maintain it, and the answer to that question is no. We must never allow America to become the second strongest nation in the world.

I do not say this with any sense of belligerence, because I recognize the fact that is recognized around the world. America's military strength has always been maintained to keep the peace, never to break it. It has always been used to defend freedom, never to destroy it. The world's peace, as well as our own, depends on our remaining as strong as we need to be as long as we need to be.

In this year 1974, we will be negotiating with the Soviet Union to place further limits on strategic nuclear arms. Together with our allies, we will be negotiating with the nations of the Warsaw Pact on mutual and balanced reduction of forces in Europe. And we will continue our efforts to promote peaceful economic development in Latin America, in Africa, in Asia."

DOCUMENT 6

Source: President Carter, Inauguration Day Remarks, January 20, 1977

"I have chosen the occasion of my inauguration as President to speak not only to my own countrymen—which is traditional—but also to you, citizens of the world who did not participate in our election but who will nevertheless be affected by my decisions.

I also believe that as friends you are entitled to know how the power and influence of the United States will be exercised by its new Government.

I want to assure you that the relations of the United States with the other countries and peoples of the world will be guided during my own administration by our desire to shape a world order that is more responsive to human aspirations. The United States will meet its obligation to help create a stable, just, and peaceful world order.

We will not seek to dominate nor dictate to others. As we Americans have concluded one chapter in our Nation's history and are beginning to work on another, we have, I believe, acquired a more mature perspective on the problems of the world. It is a perspective which recognizes the fact that we alone do not have all the answers to the world's problems. . . .

As friends, you can depend on the United States to be in the forefront of the search for world peace. You can depend on the United States to remain steadfast in its commitment to human freedom and liberty. And you can also depend on the United States to be sensitive to your own concerns and aspirations, to welcome your advice, to do its utmost to resolve international differences in a spirit of cooperation.

The problems of the world will not be easily resolved. Yet the well-being of each and every one of us—indeed our mutual survival—depends on their resolution. As President of the United States I can assure you that we intend to do our part. I ask you to join us in a common effort based on mutual trust and mutual respect."

Period 8: 1945–1980

AP® Exam Practice: Through 1980

DOCUMENT 7   **Source:** *U.S. Global Defense Treaties, 1945-1980*

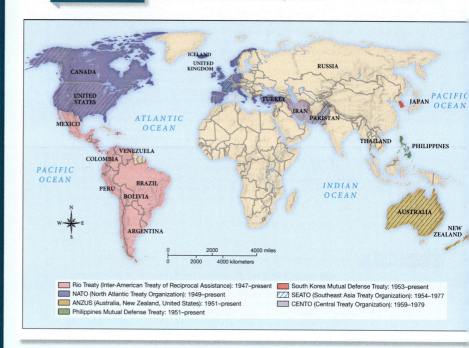

- Rio Treaty (Inter-American Treaty of Reciprocal Assistance): 1947–present
- NATO (North Atlantic Treaty Organization): 1949–present
- ANZUS (Australia, New Zealand, United States): 1951–present
- Philippines Mutual Defense Treaty: 1951–present
- South Korea Mutual Defense Treaty: 1953–present
- SEATO (Southeast Asia Treaty Organization): 1954–1977
- CENTO (Central Treaty Organization): 1959–1979

AP® Exam Practice: Through 1980

Period 8: 1945–1980

Long-Essay Questions

Please choose one of the following three questions to answer. *Suggested writing time: 40 minutes.*

2. Evaluate the extent of change in United States society resulting from the women's rights movement in the period 1945 to 1980.
3. Evaluate the extent of change in United States society resulting from international and internal migrations in the period 1945 to 1980.
4. Evaluate the extent of change in United States society resulting from technological innovations in the period 1945 to 1980.

TRM Suggested Responses to Questions

PERIOD 9: 1980–The Present
Challenges in a Globalized World

AP® Overview for Period 9

After the divisiveness of the war in Vietnam, Watergate, and the economic malaise of the 1970s, Americans turned to a new political ideology as conservatism made a resurgence under the leadership of Ronald Reagan. Conservatism shaped foreign policy views and domestic political priorities throughout the 1980s as the "Reagan Revolution" took hold. The end of the Cold War and its immediate aftermath highlight the focus of the first two modules along with the culture wars of the 1980s and 1990s. The downfall of the Soviet Union and the subsequent globalization of the economy characterize the transition to the New World Order of the late twentieth century. Conflicts throughout the Middle East, including the turning point of the events of September 11, 2001, frame the foreign policy of the rest of Period 9. Continued globalization, along with the technological revolution, frame the economic and political changes at the beginning of the twenty-first century.

AP® themes covered in Period 9 include politics and power; America in the world; work, exchange, and technology; as well as migration and settlement. The historical developments from Period 9 make up 4–6% of the content on the AP® Exam and will appear in the Multiple-Choice portion and can also be included as parts of Short-Answer and Long-Essay Questions. The Document-Based Question will not address this time period.

Module 9-1: The Triumph of Conservatism discusses how Ronald Reagan's election would fundamentally alter the political, economic, and social makeup of the United States during his presidency and well after he left office. The conservative movement forced a realignment of the two major political parties, and the Republicans used this to pass legislation that would change how capitalism worked in America. Most notably, the anti-tax and deregulation ethos of conservatives would change not only the economic circumstances of the wealthy but also those living on the economic margins of the country. For as much as Reaganomics benefitted the wealthy, it also amplified poverty in urban centers. President Reagan's foreign policy embraced confrontation with the USSR, which he referred to as the "Evil Empire." The policy decisions throughout the 1980s affected the ways in which the Cold War would end. Moreover, the Middle East would continue to evolve and become the epicenter of American foreign policy after Reagan left office.

Module 9-2: The End of the Cold War focuses on foreign policy framed by America in the world and causation. After Ronald Reagan left office, the conservative movement he helped usher in continued under President George H. W. Bush. Indeed, while Bush argued for a "kinder and gentler" conservative approach in domestic policies, his foreign policy decisions would continue Reagan's focus of ending the Cold War. While American decisions certainly affected the downfall of communism, the internal politics in the Soviet Union and places such as East Germany also expedited the end of the Cold War. This module focuses on the global changes as a result of the formal breakup of the Soviet Union and the internal disputes in East Germany and China. Globalization and the increasing tensions in the Middle East are significant parts of the aftermath of the Cold War as America wrestled with the implications of being the sole super power in the world. A practice Short-Answer Question bookends the module and focuses on broad connections to the Cold War.

Module 9-3: Toward the Twenty-First Century is perhaps the most complex module in Period 9 due to the global focus of issues related to the themes work, exchange, and technology and migration and settlement. Causation is the historical reasoning process employed to focus students' analyses of these events. The culture wars of issues such as health care and gun ownership frame the social and political effects of the Clinton presidency. Additionally, the economic vision of President Clinton, as a result of globalization, is detailed as organizations committed to free trade provide a structure for students to evaluate the global economy. Concomitant to the end of the Cold War and the subsequent globalization of the economy, the technological revolution affected the American economy as well as how global citizens communicated and conducted business. The final section of this module examines the demographic changes in the late twentieth and early twenty-first century as migration within America and immigration from Asia and Latin America continued to shape and reshape the population of the United States. The Short-Answer Question at the end of the module gives students the opportunity to illustrate their understanding of global changes during the early twenty-first century.

Module 9-4: The Global War on Terror and Political Conflict at Home helps students evaluate the many changes the United States experienced in the twenty-first century through the thematic focus on work, exchange, and technology; politics and power; and America in the world, along with the historical reasoning skill of causation. The presidency of George W. Bush and the effects of September 11 are forefront in this module and provide a framework from which to analyze the subsequent policy decisions of the Bush administration. In particular, the war in Iraq seemed to affect not only foreign policy but also economic decisions due to the war's high cost. The events surrounding the Great Recession foster an understanding of how to bridge the presidencies of George W. Bush and Barack Obama. Not only was the election of President Barack Obama a turning point, it also meant a distinctive change in domestic policy goals as health care became the main topic of debate. President Obama's policy focus, along with the backlash from conservatives, set the stage for students to understand the women's movement and the election of Donald Trump. The Short-Answer Question at the end of the module focuses on broad issues related to the period 1980–present.

Pacing Guide
Course Pacing for Period 9

Module #	Lesson Title	Instructional Period*	AP® Theme	AP® Topic	AP® Reasoning Process/Skill	Homework
9-1	N/A	N/A	Politics and Power	9.1 9.2	Continuity and Change / Historical Thinking Skills 1, 2, 3, 5	**Reading and Source Analysis:** 9-1 **Activity:** AP® Writing Historically: Long-Essay Question Practice, 9-1
	Review: AP® Writing Historically: Long-Essay Question Practice, 9-1 The Triumph of Conservatism	1	Politics and Power	9.2 9.3	Continuity and Change / Historical Thinking Skills 1, 2, 3, 4, 5, 6	**Reading and Source Analysis:** 9-2 **Activity:** AP® Writing Historically: Short-Answer Question Practice, 9-2
9-2	**Review:** AP® Writing Historically: Short-Answer Question Practice, 9-2 The End of the Cold War	1	America in the World	9.2 9.3	Causation / Historical Thinking Skills 1, 2, 3, 4, 5	**Reading and Source Analysis:** 9-3 **Activity:** AP® Writing Historically: Short-Answer Question Practice, 9-3
9-3	**Review:** AP® Writing Historically: Short-Answer Question Practice, 9-3 Toward the Twenty-First Century	1	Work, Exchange, and Technology Migration and Settlement	9.4 9.5	Causation / Historical Thinking Skills 1, 2, 3, 5	**Reading and Source Analysis:** 9-4 **Activity:** AP® Writing Historically: Short-Answer Question Practice, 9-4
9-4	**Review:** AP® Writing Historically: Short-Answer Question Practice, 9-4 The Global War on Terror and Political Conflict at Home	1	Work, Exchange, and Technology Politics and Power America in the World	9.4 9.5 9.6	Causation / Historical Thinking Skills 1, 2, 3, 4, 5, 6	Prepare for Assessment
Formative Assessment	AP® Exam Practice • 18 MCQs • 4 SAQs	0–1	All AP® U.S. History Course Themes	9.7 Personal Progress Check • 15 MCQs • 2 SAQs • 1 LEQ	All AP® History Reasoning Processes / Skills	
Summative Assessment	Unit 1 Test Bank • 55 MCQs • 4 SAQs • 1 DBQ • 4 LEQs	0–1	All AP® U.S. History Course Themes		All AP® History Reasoning Processes / Skills	

*Based on a standard 50-minute class period.

PERIOD 9 Challenges in a Globalized World

Period 9 Resources

The following resources can be found in the Resources section of the book's digital platform, by clicking on the link buttons in the Teacher's Edition e-book, or by opening the Teacher's Resource Materials.

- **TRM** Period 9 Overview Video
- **TRM** AP® Concepts and Skills Video
- **TRM** Period 9 Lecture Presentation Slides
- **TRM** Period 9 Workshop Rubrics
- **TRM** Period 9 Suggested Responses to Questions
- **TRM** Period 9 Guided Reading Worksheets

Module 9-1

- **TRM** Handout 9.1 – Liberal Policies and Conservative Arguments
- **TRM** Module 9.1 AP® Analyzing Sources Handout 1
- **TRM** Handout 9.2 – Presidential Economic Policies throughout the Twentieth Century
- **TRM** Module 9.1 AP® Analyzing Sources Handout 2
- **TRM** Module 9.1 AP® Analyzing Sources Handout 3
- **TRM** Module 9.1 AP® Analyzing Sources Handout 4
- **TRM** Module 9.1 AP® Analyzing Sources Handout 5
- **TRM** Handout 9.3 – Assessing President Reagan's Policies

Module 9-2

- **TRM** Module 9.2 AP® Analyzing Sources Handout
- **TRM** Handout 9.4 – Collapse of the Soviet Union
- **TRM** Handout 9.5 – Effects of Globalization

Module 9-3

- **TRM** Module 9.3 AP® Analyzing Sources Handout 1
- **TRM** Handout 9.6 – Technological Innovation
- **TRM** Module 9.3 AP® Analyzing Sources Handout 2

Module 9-4

- **TRM** Module 9.4 AP® Analyzing Sources Handout 1
- **TRM** Module 9.4 AP® Analyzing Sources Handout 2
- **TRM** Handout 9.7 – Domestic Policies of George W. Bush and George H. W. Bush
- **TRM** Module 9.4 AP® Analyzing Sources Handout 3
- **TRM** Handout 9.8 – The Impact of Crises During George W. Bush's Presidency
- **TRM** Module 9.4 AP® Analyzing Sources Handout 4
- **TRM** Handout 9.9 – Comparing the Great Recession to the Great Depression
- **TRM** Module 9.4 AP® Analyzing Sources Handout 5
- **TRM** Module 9.4 AP® Analyzing Sources Handout 6
- **TRM** Module 9.4 AP® Analyzing Sources Handout 7
- **TRM** Module 9.4 AP® Analyzing Sources Handout 8

Period 9 Essential Activity

The period from 1980 to present is marked by domestic and foreign policy developments that are turning points in history. The end of the Cold War and the events of September 11, 2001 are each significant turning points in both United States and world history. Likewise, the economic transformations caused by globalization and technological revolutions altered the United States economically and socially. The following activity seeks to provide students with choice as they examine turning points in history.

Provide students with two foreign policy and two domestic policy events such as the following:

- Foreign Policy: End of the Cold War and 9/11
- Domestic Policy: Globalization and Technological Revolution

Have students select one foreign policy and one domestic policy. Their task is to examine how and why the foreign policy and domestic policy events they selected represent the most important turning points in the modern era.

The activity has three essential tasks. First, students must illustrate the context of the event by writing a 3 or 4 sentence explanation of the broader processes that influenced their selected topic. Next, students need to account for the historical changes ushered in by the event. Finally, students need to account for the continuities after the event in question. Students should write multiple sentences for the final two tasks because they are evaluating a broad topic with many possible answers. Encourage students to think about the broader implications to the historical events selected.

Period 9 Alignment to the Fall 2019 AP® United States History Course Framework*

Relationship to the College Board Units

Period 9 in this book covers Topics 9.1–9.7 in Unit 9 of the College Board course framework. Students will be ready to take the Personal Progress Check for Unit 9 once they have completed this period.

Course Themes

Period 9 develops these course themes outlined in the course framework:

- **Politics and Power (PCE):** The election of Ronald Reagan in 1980 marked a new conservative era in American politics with a resurgence of support for free-market economics, traditional social values, and a reduced role for the federal government. In the early twenty-first century, new challenges and opportunities arose as the United States responded to the September 11, 2001 terrorist attacks and elected its first African American president, Barack Obama, in 2008.
- **America in the World (WOR):** With the end of the Cold War, the United States increasingly faced the twin prospects of peace with its former rivals and greater instability in new regions as U.S. policymakers struggled to redefine the nation's place as the sole superpower, while also debating the role of the United States in this new era.
- **Work, Exchange, and Technology (WXT):** Fundamental economic changes reshaped the American economy as the United States transitioned from a reliance on manufacturing and industry to a service- and knowledge-based economy. The percentage of unionized workers continued to decline as globalization and new technologies disrupted various industries.
- **Migration and Settlement (MIG):** Increased immigration from Latin America and Asia expanded the U.S. labor force, changed American culture, and generated political debates. Sunbelt migration and suburbanization continued to shape where Americans lived in the late twentieth- and early twenty-first centuries.

Course Skills

Period 9 helps students to develop the following AP® Historical Thinking Skills identified in the course framework.

- **Skill 1—Developments and Processes** (Modules 9-1, 9-2, 9-3, 9-4)
- **Skill 2—Sourcing and Situation** (Modules 9-1, 9-2, 9-3, 9-4)
- **Skill 3—Claims and Evidence in Sources** (Modules 9-1, 9-2, 9-3, 9-4)
- **Skill 4—Contextualization** (Modules 9-1, 9-2, 9-3, 9-4)
- **Skill 5—Making Connections** (Modules 9-1, 9-2, 9-3, 9-4)
- **Skill 6—Argumentation** (Modules 9-1, 9-4)

Period 9 helps students to develop the following AP® History Reasoning Processes identified in the course framework.

- **Reasoning Process 2: Causation** (Modules 9-2, 9-3, 9-4)
- **Reasoning Process 3: Continuity and Change** (Module 9-1)

Learning Objectives and Historical Developments

Module	Topics	Learning Objectives	Historical Developments and Key Concepts
9-1	9.1, 9.2, 9.3, 9.5	Unit 9: Learning Objective: A Unit 9: Learning Objective: B Unit 9: Learning Objective: C Unit 9: Learning Objective: E	KC-9.1.I.A, KC-9.1.I.B, KC-9.1.I.C, KC-9.1.I, KC-9.II.C, KC-9.3.I.A, KC-9.3.I.B, KC-9.2.II.A, KC-9.2.II.B
9-2	9.3, 9.4	Unit 9: Learning Objective: C Unit 9: Learning Objective: D	KC-9.3.I.B, KC-9.3.I.C, KC-9.2.I.A, KC-9.2.I.C
9-3	9.4, 9.5	Unit 9: Learning Objective D Unit 9: Learning Objective E	KC-9.2.I.B, KC-9.2.II.B
9-4	9.4, 9.5, 9.6, 9.7	Unit 9: Learning Objective D Unit 9: Learning Objective E Unit 9: Learning Objective F Unit 9: Learning Objective G	KC-9.2.I.D, KC-9.2.II.B, KC-9.3.II.A, KC-9.3.II.B, KC-9.3.II.C, KC-9.3.II.D

TRM A detailed alignment that can be sorted by Course Framework Unit, Topic, Learning Objective, Historical Development/Key Concept, or textbook period, is available in the Teacher's Resource Materials and via the book's online platform.

*Should changes be made to the Course Framework in the future, an updated alignment will be placed on our catalog page at bfwpub.com/fabric1e.

TEACHING IDEA

AP® Central

A great resource to help you teach this period is to read the information in the AP® U.S. History study guide for 1980–present, available from the AP® United States History Classroom Resources section of AP® Central (apcentral.collegeboard.org).

PERIOD 9: 1980–THE PRESENT

Challenges in a Globalized World

AIDS Quilt in Washington, DC, 1987 The AIDS Quilt began in 1987 as a project in San Francisco to memorialize those who had died from the effects of Acquired Immune Deficiency Syndrome (AIDS), with one three-by-six foot panel for each person who had died of the disease. In this image, the AIDS Quilt is on display in Washington, DC in 1987, when it comprised almost 2,000 panels and covered a space larger than a football field. Since then, the AIDS Quilt has grown to comprise almost 50,000 panels.

For many Americans, after the 1960s and 1970s society seemed jagged and out of alignment. Already anxious from the Cold War and the ongoing threat of global nuclear destruction, many in the United States felt further threatened by new value systems that challenged old conventions, by the emergence of new interest groups that demanded recognition and respect, and by the arrival of new immigrants from locations outside of Europe. The instability of American society and culture initiated a political backlash that claimed to represent traditional American values and interests. This conservative movement grew in intensity throughout the 1970s and came to fruition with the election of Ronald Reagan as president in 1980.

In hindsight, some Americans called the election of Ronald Reagan in 1980 the beginning of the "Reagan revolution." Although there is debate over the meaning of this phrase, most historians agree that Reagan's election represented a shift in American political rhetoric and policy. It seemed that the liberal project that began with Franklin D. Roosevelt and reached its high tide with the Great Society programs of Lyndon B. Johnson had come to an end.

Reagan's election represented the political maturity of two divergent social movements that began in the early 1960s — the New Right and the New Left. In these two ideologies, free-market economics and "traditional" moral beliefs collided with civil rights activism, identity politics, and environmentalism. This shift in sensibilities, especially regarding a government and society overseen by experts, bound both the New Right and the New Left to each other while raising tensions between the two throughout this period.

Despite these tensions, the United States entered the twenty-first century in the midst of economic prosperity and peace. Drawing lessons from the collapse of the Soviet Union, the United States celebrated the Cold War policies that supported containment and encouraged capitalism around the world to bring an end to what Ronald Reagan called an "evil empire."

In the aftermath of the terrorist attacks of September 11, 2001 the nation seemed to overcome these debates and reinvigorate the ideals that united the nation. But that unified front proved short-lived. The Bush administration's response to the attacks, the administration's attempts to overhaul key New Deal legislation, and lingering anger over the contested presidential election of 2000 deepened the ideological divide and signaled the dawn of a new era of bitter political partisanship and cultural conflict.

While the election of Barack Obama in 2008 promised progress in the nation's historical struggle for racial justice, a long recession triggered by a mortgage crisis, ongoing anxiety over terrorism and immigration, a rougher political discourse fueled by the rise of social media, and the close election of 2016 caused many Americans to face the new century with apprehension.

PERIOD 9 PREVIEW

Module	AP® Thematic Focus
9-1: The Triumph of Conservatism	**Politics and Power** During the 1980s, diverse groups debated the role of government in social, political, and economic policy as well as the rights of citizens. Likewise, these debates shaped the economy of the United States. Ronald Reagan's free-market ideology drove these debates and fostered a resurgence of support for free-market economics, the deregulation of the economy, and a renewed confrontation with the Soviet Union.
9-2: The End of the Cold War	**America in the World** With the end of the Cold War, the United States increasingly faced the twin prospects of peace with its former rivals and greater instability in new regions. In the years after Reagan's presidency, U.S. policymakers struggled to redefine the nation's place as the sole superpower, while also debating the role of the United States in this new era.
9-3: Toward the Twenty-First Century	**Work, Exchange, and Technology ▪ Migration and Settlement** Starting in the 1990s, the United States underwent profound economic, technological, and social changes. Americans elected the first president born after World War II, Bill Clinton, who was also the first president in nearly fifty years who did not have to fight the Cold War. Throughout the decade, Americans continued to debate the legacy of the 1960s, while at the same time, they embraced new digital technologies that opened the economy to new markets. High levels of domestic consumption of foreign-made goods transformed the U.S. economy from a focus on manufacturing to a focus on service.
9-4: The Global War on Terror and Political Conflict at Home	**Work, Exchange, and Technology ▪ Politics and Power ▪ America in the World** At the dawn of the twenty-first century, the United States stood at the center of a global economy that stretched across the planet, from production centers in Asia, through regions of high consumption in Western Europe and the United States. But these economic changes, generally called "globalization," also caused unemployment among manufacturing workers in North America and Western Europe while at the same time benefiting consumers with lower prices. Also in the twenty-first century, Americans could no longer convince themselves that war and environmental degradation were worries for people far away as terrorist attacks by non-state groups, both domestic and international, shook American society and the effects of climate change became increasingly apparent throughout the world.

TEACHING IDEA

Teaching Current Historical Content

A significant part of historical inquiry is the effort to evaluate how primary sources affect our understanding of the past. While historians use the work of secondary sources and their own interpretations to inform their evaluations, they are beholden to the historical evidence. Historians evaluate, interpret, and inform our understanding of the past. When polarizing topics are studied, historians offer unique training to help students understand developments instead of simply reacting to historical events. Rather than impulsive emotional reactions, historians offer intellectual interpretations rooted in appropriate context and scholarship. In our current historical context, we need to be especially aware of this reality. We are in the classroom to teach our students how to analyze documents, write cogent interpretations, and discuss a variety of perspectives on topics, including controversial or partisan issues. We are there to train them in ways to think, not what to think. As you reflect on the issues in Period 9, think about how you can empower students to be empathetic and critical consumers of information.

Module 9-1

The Triumph of Conservatism

LEARNING TARGETS

By the end of this module, you should be able to:

- Explain why Ronald Reagan's victory in the presidential election of 1980 allowed conservatives to enact tax cuts and continue the deregulation of many industries.
- Explain conservative arguments against liberal policies for fighting poverty and stimulating economic growth.
- Explain conservative arguments for traditional social values.
- Explain how Reagan raised tensions with the Soviet Union.

THEMATIC FOCUS
Politics and Power

During the 1980s, diverse groups debated the role of government in social, political, and economic policy as well as the rights of citizens. Likewise, these debates shaped the economy of the United States. Ronald Reagan's free-market ideology drove these debates and fostered a resurgence of support for free-market economics, the deregulation of the economy, and a renewed confrontation with the Soviet Union.

HISTORICAL REASONING FOCUS
Continuity and Change

TASK ▶ While reading this section, consider the ways in which Reagan's economic policies fostered a change in the U.S. economy and the extent to which it represented a continuation of older historical trends.

TRM Suggested Responses to Questions

EXPLORING AP® THEMES
Politics and Power

Ronald Reagan held conservative ideas and supported free enterprise and small government. Review the term "free enterprise" (limited government involvement in the economy; demand determines supply and prices) and "small government" (limited government involvement in both economic and social issues). Using prior knowledge, explain why Reagan did not approve of Lyndon B. Johnson's Great Society programs. Students should recall that Johnson's Great Society increased the reach of the federal government by providing programs such as Medicare and Medicaid, which use taxpayer money to provide health care to individuals, and the Housing and Urban Development Act, which provided federal funding for urban renewal and increased access to mortgages for those living in poverty. Reagan would have been opposed to the Great Society, as the government took an active role in the economy and society, and Reagan would have believed that the federal government was overstepping and abusing its power. The textbook also includes that Reagan believed that the Great Society programs threatened private property and individual liberty. Then, have students analyze Reagan's degree of success in opposing liberal policies.

Reagan and Reaganomics

The election of former California governor Ronald Reagan as president in 1980 reflected the spectacular growth in political power of the New Right. Reagan pushed the conservative economic agenda of lower taxes and business deregulation alongside the New Right's concern for traditional religious and family values. His presidency installed conservatism as the dominant political ideology for the remainder of the twentieth century.

Ronald Reagan's presidential victory in 1980 consolidated the growing New Right coalition and reshaped American politics for a generation to come. The former movie actor had transformed himself from a New Deal Democrat into a conservative Republican politician when he ran for governor of California in 1966. As governor, he implemented conservative ideas of free enterprise and small government and denounced Johnson's Great Society for threatening private property and individual liberty. His support for conservative economic and social issues carried him to the presidency.

Reagan easily beat Jimmy Carter and John Anderson, a moderate Republican who ran as an independent candidate (Map 9.1). The high unemployment and inflation of the late 1970s worked in Reagan's favor. Reagan appealed to a coalition of conservative Republicans and Democrats, promising to cut taxes and reduce spending, to relax federal supervision over civil rights programs, and to end what was left of expensive Great Society measures and affirmative action. The 1980 and subsequent presidential elections demonstrated the rising political, economic, and social influence of the American South and West, especially as these regions continued their rapid population

---

EXPLORING AP® THEMES
Politics and Power

While reading this module, have students take notes to address the learning target, "Explain conservative arguments against liberal policies for fighting poverty and stimulating economic growth."

TRM Find **Handout 9.1 — Liberal Policies and Conservative Arguments** in the Teacher's Resource Materials.

Reagan and Reaganomics

Period 9: 1980–The Present

Ronald Reagan Campaigns for President, 1980 During his 1980 campaign, Reagan expressed the main principle of antigovernment conservatism: "Government is like a baby, [a digestive tract] with a big appetite at one end and no sense of responsibility at the other." **What events preceding Reagan's election help explain why this statement appealed to many Americans?**

growth by drawing migrants from other areas of the nation. Finally, Reagan energized members of the religious right, who flocked to the polls to support Reagan's platform, which included voluntary prayer in the public schools, defeat of the Equal Rights Amendment, and a constitutional amendment to outlaw abortion. In fact, the religious right attracted its strongest supporters from the growing population of the South and West.

In his inaugural address, Reagan underscored his conservative approach to government. It's "not my intention to do away with government," the president declared. "It is rather to make it work — work with us, not over us; to stand by our side, not ride on our back. Government can and must provide opportunity, not smother it; foster productivity, not stifle it." With this in mind, his first priority was stimulating the stagnant economy. The president's strategy, known as **Reaganomics**, reflected the ideas of both conservative Republicans and **supply-side** economists, who argued that tax cuts and industry deregulation would raise incomes and lower unemployment, thereby promoting economic growth. According to supply-side economics, deregulation of

Reaganomics Ronald Reagan's economic policies based on the theories of supply-side economists and centered on tax cuts and cuts to domestic programs.

AP® ANALYZING SOURCES

Source: Reginald Stuart, "Michigan Requests Federal Loan to Bolster Unemployment Fund," *New York Times*, 1980

"The state of Michigan, its economy shaken by the prolonged slump in the nation's automobile industry, has asked the Federal Government for a $260 million loan so it can continue paying unemployment benefits over the next three months, the Michigan Employment Security Commission disclosed today.

Gov. William G. Milliken requested the funds from the Department of Labor, stating that a rising load of unemployment claims and the repayment of earlier Federal loans would 'exhaust' Michigan's unemployment compensation trust fund, although no specific time was given. By law, according to the employment commission, such requests must cover a three-month period, and Michigan's request will carry the fund from Feb. 1 through April 30, it said. . . .

Michigan's unemployment rate rose to 8.5 percent in December from 7.9 percent in November, and the state employment commission estimated that 369,000 of its residents were out of work last month. Some 250,000 residents were drawing unemployment benefits last month, the commission reported, including 88,000 people who signed up in the week end[ing] Dec. 27. . . ."

Questions for Analysis

1. Identify the dilemma Michigan faces, according to this excerpt.
2. Describe the economic circumstances that have brought the state to this dilemma.
3. Evaluate the extent to which the economic circumstances reported in this excerpt represent a change in the twentieth-century American economy.

TEACHING IDEA

Analyzing Art and Images

As a bell ringer, have students look at the image and read through the caption, "Ronald Reagan Campaigns for President, 1980." In pairs, students should discuss the provided question as well as write down a list of previous events that would explain why many Americans would agree with Reagan's statement comparing government to a baby. Ask volunteers to share their answers with the class. Next, tell student pairs to meet up with another pair to make a group of 4. Allow students to debate whether or not they agree with Reagan's statement.

TRM Suggested Responses to Questions

TRM Module 9.1 AP® Analyzing Sources Handout 1

TEACHING IDEA

Differing Views

Have students watch the video, "Ronald Reagan 1980 Campaign Ad" (available on YouTube). Ask students to consider the following questions: What is the message of the ad? What about this ad would appeal to voters? How would the opposition respond to this ad?

▲ Differentiation

Have students work in groups to create a script for an opposition ad. If time allows, have students film their ads and show them to the class, or perform them live. Students should take notes on any recurring points in the class ads and follow up with a whole-class discussion.

TEACHING IDEA

Incorporating Videos

Have students watch the History Channel's video, "Here's Why Reaganomics Is so Controversial" (available on YouTube). The video covers the main idea behind Reaganomics in a visual way. While watching, have students take notes to keep track of the pros and cons of trickle-down (or supply-side) economics. *Pros include that if corporate taxes are cut, corporations can increase production, hire more people, and pay higher wages to employees. Employees then use their increased cash flow to buy goods, spurring the economy. Cons include that cutting taxes for corporations does not always benefit the lower classes and can make the wealthy even wealthier.*

BUILDING AP® SKILLS

Argumentation

Utilize the lesson "Reaganomics" on the Stanford History Education Group's website (sheg.stanford.edu). This lesson is a structured academic controversy, where students are given a point of view that they must argue. In this case, students are paired up and one student argues that Reaganomics policies were good for the United States, while the other student argues that Reaganomics policies were not good for the United States. Documents are provided for students to gather evidence, and the discussion is structured so students take turns supporting the perspective that they were assigned. After the discussion, students are given the opportunity to argue their personal point of view in a writing assignment.

BUILDING AP® SKILLS

Contextualization

Popular culture such as television shows and movies reflected the economic trends of the 1980s. Put students into groups of 3 and assign each student one of the following: *Dallas*, *Dynasty*, and *Wall Street*. Require each student to individually research their assigned topic. Once each student has an understanding of what the show or movie was about, each group of 3 should discuss the following: What were the themes of the show or movie? How does the show or movie reflect the historical context in which it was created? Students should make connections between the plots and themes, the rising wealth of the United States during the 1980s, and corporate growth.

APPLY THE TIP

Have students compare the economic policies of the Reagan administration with those of the 1920s, the New Deal, and the Great Society.

TRM Find **Handout 9.2 — Presidential Economic Policies throughout the Twentieth Century** in the Teacher's Resource Materials.

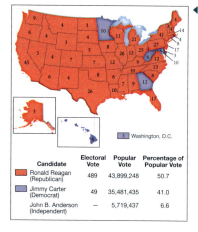

▶ **MAP 9.1 The Election of 1980** Ronald Reagan won 50.7 percent of the popular vote in the 1980 election, but his margin of victory over Jimmy Carter was much greater in the electoral vote. Reagan won the votes of the South and many discontented Democrats in the urban North. A third-party candidate, John Anderson of Illinois, won 6.6 percent of the popular vote, demonstrating significant disapproval with both major parties. **What does this map reveal about Americans' reaction to the cultural and social trends of the 1960s and 1970s?**

> " [I]n this present crisis, government is not the solution to our problem; government is the problem. "
>
> Ronald Reagan, Inaugural Address, 1981

AP® TIP
Compare the economic policies of the Reagan administration to those of the presidential administrations of the 1920s, the New Deal, and the Great Society.

industry and low taxes on corporations would fuel economic expansion for businesses, which would ultimately lead to more jobs and higher wages. Reagan subscribed to the idea of trickle-down economics in which the gains reaped at the top of a strong economy would trickle down to the benefit of those below, thus reducing the need for large government social programs. During his campaign Reagan stated that "in this present crisis, government is not the solution to our problem; government is the problem." After election, he followed this up by asking Congress for a huge income tax cut of 30 percent over three years, a reduction in spending for domestic programs of more than $40 billion, and new monetary policies to lower rising rates for loans.

The president did not operate in isolation from the rest of the world. He learned a great deal from Margaret Thatcher, the British prime minister who took office two years before Reagan. Thatcher combated inflation by slashing welfare programs, selling publicly owned companies, and reducing the budgets of health and education programs. An advocate of supply-side economics, Thatcher reduced income taxes on the wealthy by more than 50 percent to encourage new investment. West Germany also moved toward the right under Chancellor Helmut Kohl, who reined in welfare spending. In the 1980s Reaganomics and Thatcherism dominated the United States and the two most powerful nations of Western Europe.

In March 1981 Reagan survived a nearly fatal assassin's bullet. More popular than ever after his recovery, the president persuaded the Democratic House and the Republican Senate to pass his economic measures in slightly modified form in the **Economic Recovery Tax Act**. These cuts in taxes and spending did not produce the immediate results Reagan sought — unemployment rose to 9.6 percent in 1983 from 7.1 percent in 1980. However, the government's tight money policies, as engineered by the Federal Reserve Board, reduced inflation from 14 percent in 1980 to 4 percent in 1984. By 1984 the unemployment rate had fallen to 7.5 percent, while the gross national product grew by a healthy 4.3 percent, an indication that the recession of the previous two years had ended.

The poor and the lower middle class saw fewer of the benefits of Reaganomics than others. The president reduced spending for food stamps, school lunches, Aid to Families with Dependent Children (welfare), and Medicaid, while maintaining programs that middle-class voters relied on, such as Medicare and Social Security. The savings that came from reduced social spending went into increased military appropriations. Together with lower taxes, these expenditures benefited large corporations that received government military contracts and favorable tax write-offs.

As a result of Reagan's economic policies, financial institutions and the stock market earned huge profits. The Reagan administration relaxed antitrust regulations, encouraging corporate mergers to a degree unseen since the Great Depression. Fueled by falling interest rates, the stock market created wealth for many investors. The number of millionaires doubled during the 1980s, as the top 1 percent of families gained control of 42 percent of the nation's wealth and 60 percent of corporate stock. Reflecting this phenomenal accumulation of riches, television produced nighttime soap operas depicting the lives of oil barons (such as *Dallas* and *Dynasty*), whose characters lived glamorous lives filled with intrigue and extravagance.

EXPLORING AP® THEMES

Social Structures

Put students into groups of 3. Pose the following questions: Who was more greatly impacted by Reaganomics: the poor, the middle class, or the wealthy? Were these impacts beneficial or detrimental? Ask one student to argue that the poor were impacted more greatly, one to argue that the middle class was impacted more greatly, and the last that the wealthy were impacted more greatly. Require students to provide specific historical evidence. Possible answers include: *The poor were impacted more greatly because Reagan cut spending for food stamps, school lunches, Medicaid, and welfare. These impacted the poor negatively. Or, the middle class was impacted more greatly. Reagan's administration relied on middle-class voters, so programs such as Medicare and Social Security were protected. This impact was mainly positive, though some in the lower middle class suffered due to cuts to school lunches and Medicaid. Or, the wealthy were impacted more greatly due to the relaxation of antitrust legislation and the increasing stock prices that greatly increased their wealth. Impacts to the wealthy were mostly positive.*

Reagan and Reaganomics

AP® TIP
Analyze the effects that Reaganomics had on America's society and economy during the 1980s.

air traffic controllers strike
1981 strike by air traffic controllers for better working conditions and pay. President Reagan responded by firing employees who did not return to work within 48 hours.

At the same time that a small number of Americans grew wealthier, the gap between the rich and the poor widened. Contrary to the promises of Reaganomics, the wealth did not trickle down. During the 1980s, the nation's share of poor people rose from 11.7 percent to 13.5 percent, representing 33 million Americans. The number of homeless people grew to as many as 400,000 during the 1980s. The middle class also diminished from a high of 53 percent of families in the early 1970s to 49 percent in 1985.

The Reagan administration also challenged labor unions. During the **air traffic controllers strike** in 1981, the president fired the strikers who refused to return to work, and in their place he hired new controllers. Reagan's anti-union actions both reflected and encouraged a decline in union membership throughout the 1980s, with union membership falling to 16 percent, its lowest level since the New Deal. Without union protection, wages failed to keep up with inflation, further increasing the gap between rich and poor.

Reagan continued the business deregulation initiated under Carter. Federal agencies concerned with environmental protection, consumer product reliability, and occupational safety saw their key functions shifted to the states, which made them less effective. Reagan also extended banking deregulation, which encouraged savings and loan institutions (S&Ls) to make risky loans to real estate ventures. When real estate prices began to tumble, savings and loan associations faced collapse and Congress appropriated over $100 billion to rescue them.

Reagan's landslide reelection over Democratic candidate Walter Mondale in 1984 sealed the national political transition from liberalism to conservatism. Voters responded overwhelmingly to the improving economy, Reagan's defense of traditional social values, and his boundless optimism about America's future. Despite the landslide, the election was notable for the nomination of Representative Geraldine Ferraro of New York as Mondale's Democratic running mate, the first woman to run on a major party ticket for national office.

Reagan's second term did not produce changes as significant as did his first term. Democrats still controlled the House and in 1986 recaptured the Senate. The Reagan administration focused on foreign affairs and the continued Cold War with the Soviet Union, thus escalating defense spending. Most of the Reagan economic revolution continued as before, but with serious consequences. With lower tax revenue, supply-side economics failed to fund the increase in military spending: The federal deficit grew, and by 1989 the nation had a $2.8 trillion debt.

AP® TIP
Be sure you can explain how Reaganomics and increased military spending affected the U.S. federal deficit.

AP® ANALYZING SOURCES

Source: Presidential Campaign for Ronald Reagan, *Morning in America* (televised commercial), 1984

> "It's morning again in America. Today more men and women will go to work than ever before in our country's history. With interest rates at about half the record highs of 1980, nearly 2,000 families today will buy new homes, more than at any time in the past four years. This afternoon 6,500 young men and women will be married, and with inflation at less than half of what it was just four years ago, they can look forward with confidence to the future.
>
> It's morning again in America, and under the leadership of President Reagan, our country is prouder and stronger and better. Why would we ever want to return to where we were less than four short years ago?"

Questions for Analysis
1. Identify the statistics that this political advertisement uses to support its main argument.
2. Describe the argument this political advertisement makes.
3. Explain how the advertisement uses the image of "morning" to convey a message to viewers.
4. Explain how the context surrounding this advertisement shaped its argument.

TRM Suggested Responses to Questions

TRM Module 9.1 AP® Analyzing Sources Handout 2

TEACHING IDEA

Incorporating Videos

Have students watch the Reagan Foundation's video, "Morning in America" (available on YouTube). This video was the 1984 re-election campaign ad for Ronald Reagan. Once they have finished watching, have students answer the Questions for Analysis in pairs. Discuss their answers as a class. As an exit ticket, ask students to answer the prompt: "How true is the argument presented in the video, 'Prouder, Stronger, Better'?"

APPLY THE TIP

As a bell ringer, give each student a sticky note. Ask students to individually write one way in which the federal deficit was impacted by Reagan's policies. Put students into groups of 4 and have each student share their response with their group and compile answers. Each group should choose one volunteer to come up to the board and post the notes that were written by their group (leaving out any repeated responses). Discuss the responses as a class and ask students what conclusions could be drawn from the evidence provided. Students should recognize that even though federal spending was decreased in some areas, such as Medicaid and school lunches, the money was diverted to other priorities, such as funding the military, which eventually led to an actual increase in the federal deficit.

The president further reshaped the future through his nominations to the U.S. Supreme Court. Starting with the choice of Sandra Day O'Connor, the Court's first female justice, in 1981, Reagan's appointments moved the Court in a more conservative direction. The elevation of Associate Justice William Rehnquist to chief justice in 1986 reinforced this trend, which would have significant consequences for decades to come.

REVIEW

To what extent did Reaganomics represent a change in federal economic policy in the U.S. since the 1950s?

Social Conservatism

Throughout his two terms, President Reagan's policies aligned with the New Right's social agenda. Conservatives blamed political liberalism for what they saw as a decline in family values. Their solution was a renewed focus on conservative Christian principles. In addition to trying to remove evolution and sex education from the classroom and bring in prayer, the New Right stepped up its opposition to abortion and imposed limits on reproductive rights. The Reagan administration required family planning agencies seeking federal funding to notify parents of children under age eighteen before dispensing birth control, ceased financial aid to international organizations supporting abortion, and provided funds to promote sexual abstinence. Despite these efforts, conservatives could not convince the Supreme Court to overturn *Roe v. Wade*. However, they did see the Equal Rights Amendment go down to defeat in 1982 when it failed to get the required two-thirds approval from the states.

Social conservatives also felt threatened by more tolerant views of homosexuality. The gay rights movement, which began in the 1960s, strengthened during the 1970s as thousands of gay men and lesbians made known their sexual orientation, fought discrimination, and expressed pride in their sexual identity. Then, in the early 1980s, physicians traced an outbreak of a deadly illness among gay men to a virus that attacked the immune system (human immunodeficiency virus, or HIV), making it vulnerable to infections that were usually fatal. This disease, called **acquired immune deficiency syndrome (AIDS)**, was transmitted through bodily fluids during sexual intercourse, through blood transfusions, and by intravenous drug use. Scientists could not explain why the disease initially showed up among gay men in the United States; however, some members of the religious right believed that AIDS was a plague visited on sexual deviants by an angry God. As the epidemic spread beyond the gay community, gay rights organizers and their heterosexual allies raised research money and public awareness. By the early 1990s, medical advances had begun to extend the lives of AIDS patients and manage the disease.

acquired immune deficiency syndrome (AIDS) Immune disorder that reached epidemic proportions in the United States in the 1980s, especially among gay men and drug users.

◀ **ACT UP Protest, 1988** Amid the AIDS epidemic in the gay community, the militant group AIDS Coalition to Unleash Power (ACT UP) campaigned for better funding of programs to fight the disease. This photo shows ACT UP protesters blocking the entrance to the headquarters of the Food and Drug Administration (FDA) in Rockville, Maryland on Oct. 11, 1988. **What reforms do these activitsts seek?**

Increased immigration also troubled social conservatives as another reflection of the general societal breakdown. The number of immigrants to the United States rose dramatically in the 1970s and 1980s following the relaxation of foreign quota restrictions after 1965. During these decades, immigrants came mainly from Mexico, Central America, the Caribbean, and eastern and southern Asia and tended to settle in California, Florida, Texas, New York, and New Jersey. Like those who came nearly a century before, most sought economic opportunity, political freedom, and escape from wars. By 1990 one-third of Los Angeles's and New York City's populations were foreign-born, figures similar to the high numbers of European immigrants at the turn of the twentieth century.

As happened during previous immigration waves, many Americans whose ancestors had immigrated to the United States generations earlier expressed hostility toward the new immigrants. Some members in the New Right provoked traditional fears that immigrants took away jobs and depressed wages, and questioned whether these culturally diverse people could assimilate into American society, while other conservatives argued that immigration was a hallmark of American history and provided a dedicated and inexpensive workforce for the economy. In 1986 the Reagan administration departed from many of his conservative anti-immigrant supporters and, with bipartisan congressional support, fashioned a compromise that extended amnesty to undocumented aliens residing in the United States for a specified period and allowed them to acquire legal status. At the same time, the **Immigration Reform and Control Act** penalized employers who hired new undocumented workers. The measure allowed Reagan and the Republicans to appeal to Latino voters in the Sun Belt states while convincing the New Right that the administration intended to halt further undocumented immigration.

AP TIP
Evaluate the extent to which the Reagan administration's immigration policies reflected a change from previous eras.

Immigration Reform and Control Act 1986 act extending amnesty to undocumented immigrants in the United States for a specified period intended to give them time to obtain legal status. The law also penalized employers who hired undocumented workers.

REVIEW

- What were the primary social concerns of the New Right?
- How were these concerns a reaction to cultural changes dating from the 1960s?

Reagan and the Cold War, 1981–1988

> "I've called for whatever it takes to be so strong that no other nation will dare violate the peace."
>
> Ronald Reagan, 1980

AP TIP
Compare the effects of military spending and SDI under President Reagan with those of NSC-68 in the 1940s.

Strategic Defense Initiative (SDI) Policy first announced by Ronald Reagan in 1983 proposing a missile defense system that would use satellite lasers to protect the United States from military attack by shooting down enemy missiles. The initiative was never completed.

As Ronald Reagan entered the White House determined to pose a direct challenge to liberalism, so too did he intend to confront the Soviets. Reagan and Secretary of State George Shultz believed that détente would become feasible only after the United States achieved military supremacy over the Soviet Union. Reagan also took strong measures to fight communism around the globe, from Central America to the Middle East. Yet military superiority alone would not defeat the Soviet Union. A shift of leadership within the USSR, as well as a worldwide protest movement for nuclear disarmament, helped bring an end to the Cold War and prepare the way for the dissolution of the Soviet empire.

In running for president in 1980, Reagan wrapped his anti-Communist message in the rhetoric of peace. "I've called for whatever it takes to be so strong that no other nation will dare violate the peace," he told the Veterans of Foreign Wars Convention on August 18, 1980. Once in the White House, Reagan left no doubt about his anti-Communist stance. He called the Soviet Union "the evil empire," regarding it as "the focus of evil in the modern world." The president planned to confront that evil with both words and deeds, backing up his rhetoric with a massive military buildup.

In a show of moral and economic might, Reagan proposed the largest military budget in American history. The defense budget grew by about 7 percent per year, increasing from $157 billion in 1981 to around $282 billion in 1988.

The president also sought to develop new weapons to be deployed in outer space. He proposed the **Strategic Defense Initiative (SDI)**, which in theory would use sky-based lasers to shoot down enemy missiles. Critics dubbed this program "Star Wars." The SDI was never carried out, though the government spent $17 billion on research.

TRM Suggested Responses to Questions

TRM Module 9.1 AP® Analyzing Sources Handout 3

TEACHING IDEA

Incorporating Videos

Have students watch the Educational Video Group's "President Ronald Reagan 'Tear Down This Wall' Speech at Berlin Wall" (available on YouTube). Require students to answer the Questions for Analysis individually. After answering the questions, students should pair up to share and discuss their responses. Discuss as a class or collect student responses to check for understanding.

TEACHING IDEA

Differing Views

Ask students to imagine that they lived during the Reagan administration. To address the Review question (How did Reagan administration policies affect the relationship between the U.S. and the USSR?), assign students to write a letter to the president either praising or admonishing the president for his policies based on the impact of those policies on the relationship between the two nations. Students' letters will mostly be critical of the president's policies, as the relationship deteriorated between the U.S. and USSR based on the actions of both nations during this time period.

AP® ANALYZING SOURCES

Source: Ronald Reagan, *Tear Down This Wall* (speech at the Berlin Wall), 1987

"[W]e hear much from Moscow about a new policy of reform and openness. Some political prisoners have been released. Certain foreign news broadcasts are no longer being jammed. Some economic enterprises have been permitted to operate with greater freedom from state control. Are these the beginnings of profound changes in the Soviet state? Or are they token gestures, intended to raise false hopes in the West, or to strengthen the Soviet system without changing it? We welcome change and openness; for we believe that freedom and security go together, that the advance of human liberty can only strengthen the cause of world peace.

There is one sign the Soviets can make that would be unmistakable, that would advance dramatically the cause of freedom and peace. General Secretary Gorbachev, if you seek peace, if you seek prosperity for the Soviet Union and Eastern Europe, if you seek liberalization: Come here to this gate! Mr. Gorbachev, open this gate! Mr. Gorbachev, tear down this wall!"

Questions for Analysis

1. Identify the signs of a change in Soviet policy that Reagan notes in this speech.
2. Identify what conditions Reagan believes must be met to be convinced these changes are permanent.
3. Describe the significance of the "wall" that Reagan refers to.
4. Evaluate the extent to which this speech reflects a shift in American attitudes toward the Cold War and the Soviets.

Strategic Arms Reduction Talks (START) Negotiations between the Reagan administration and the Soviet Union that began in 1982 under the principle of "zero option," which called for the USSR to dismantle all its intermediate-range missiles. The Soviets ultimately rejected these terms, believing they promoted the idea of American nuclear superiority.

Reagan was unyielding in his initial dealings with the Soviet Union, and negotiations between the superpowers moved slowly and unevenly. The Reagan administration's initial "zero option" proposal called for the Soviets to dismantle all of their intermediate-range missiles in exchange for the United States agreeing to refrain from deploying any new medium-range missiles. The administration presented this option merely for show, expecting the Soviets to reject it. However, in 1982, after the Soviets accepted the principle of "zero option," Reagan sent negotiators to begin **Strategic Arms Reduction Talks (START)**. Influenced by antinuclear protests in Europe, which had a great impact on European governments, the Americans proposed shelving the deployment of 572 Pershing II and cruise missiles in Europe in return for the Soviets' dismantling of Eastern European–based intermediate-range ballistic missiles that were targeted at Western Europe. The Soviets viewed this offer as perpetuating American nuclear superiority and rejected it.

Relations between the two superpowers deteriorated in September 1983 when a Soviet fighter jet shot down a South Korean passenger airliner, killing 269 people. In reaction, the United States sent additional missiles to bases in West Germany, Great Britain, and Italy; in response, the Soviets abandoned the disarmament talks and replenished their nuclear arsenal in Czechoslovakia and East Germany. More symbolically, the Soviets boycotted the 1984 Olympic Games in Los Angeles, in retaliation for the U.S. boycott of the Olympics in Moscow four years earlier. As the two adversaries swung from peace talks to threats of nuclear confrontation, one European journalist observed: "The second Cold War has begun."

REVIEW

• How did Reagan administration policies affect the relationship between the U.S. and the USSR?

TEACHING IDEA

Incorporating Videos

Have students watch NBC News' "The 1980 Moscow Olympics Boycott | Flashback" and "Soviet Union Pulls Out of 1984 Olympics BBC NEWS" (both available on YouTube). Discuss the videos and ask the class, "How do these boycotts reflect the relationship between the U.S. and the USSR during this time period?"

Human Rights and the Fight against Communism

The Reagan administration extended its firm Cold War position throughout the world. The president saw threats of Soviet intervention in Central America and the Middle East, and he aimed to contain them. During the 1980s, the United States continued its economic isolation of Cuba via the trade embargo, and it sought to prevent other Communist or leftist governments from emerging in Central America and the Caribbean.

In the late 1970s Nicaraguan revolutionaries, known as the National Liberation Front or **Sandinistas**, overthrew the tyrannical government of General Anastasio Somoza, a brutal dictator. President Jimmy Carter, who had originally supported Somoza's overthrow, halted all aid to Nicaragua in 1980 after the Sandinistas began nationalizing foreign companies and drawing closer to Cuba. Under Reagan, Secretary of State Shultz suggested a U.S. invasion of Nicaragua, reflecting the administration's belief that the revolution in Nicaragua had been sponsored by Moscow. Instead Reagan adopted a more indirect approach. In 1982 he authorized the CIA to train approximately two thousand guerrilla forces outside the country, known as **Contras** (Counterrevolutionaries), to overthrow the Sandinista government. The group consisted of pro-Somoza reactionaries as well as anti-Marxist democrats who blew up bridges and oil dumps, burned crops, and killed civilians. In 1982 Congress, unwilling to support such actions, passed the **Boland Amendment**, which prohibited direct aid to the Contras. In the face of congressional opposition, Reagan and his advisers came up with a plan that would secretly fund the efforts of the Contras. The CIA and the National Security Council (NSC) raised money from anti-Communist leaders abroad and wealthy conservatives at home. This effort, called "Project Democracy," raised millions of dollars and by 1985 the number of Contra troops had swelled from 10,000 to 20,000. In violation of federal law, CIA director William Casey also authorized his agency to continue training the Contras in assassination techniques and other methods of subversion.

Elsewhere in Central America, the Reagan administration supported a government in El Salvador that, in an effort to put down an insurgency, sanctioned military death squads and killed forty thousand people during the 1980s. In reaction, the Reagan administration maintained that Communist regimes in Nicaragua and Cuba were behind the Salvadoran insurgents. The United States sent more than $5 billion in aid to El Salvador and trained its military leaders to combat guerrilla forces.

While many Americans supported Reagan's strong anti-Communist stance, others opposed to the president's policy mobilized protests. Marches, rallies, and teach-ins were organized in cities and college campuses nationwide. Civil wars in Central America also drove many people to flee their dangerous, poverty-stricken countries and seek asylum in the United States. Between 1984 and 1990, 45,000 Salvadorans and 9,500 Guatemalans applied for asylum in the United States, but because the United States supported the established governments in those two nations, nearly all requests for refugee status were denied. Approximately five hundred American churches and synagogues established a sanctuary movement to provide safe haven for those fleeing Central American civil wars. Other Americans, especially in California and Texas, began to view the influx of refugees from Central America with alarm. This immigration, both legal and illegal, meant an increase in medical and educational costs for state and local communities, which some taxpayers considered a burden.

In addition to providing financial support for pro-American governments in Central America, on October 25, 1983, the United States sent 7,000 marines to invade the Caribbean island of Grenada. After a coup toppled the leftist government of Maurice Bishop, who had received Cuban and Soviet aid, the United States stepped in, ostensibly to protect American medical school students in Grenada from political instability following the coup. A pro-American government was installed. The **invasion of Grenada** boosted Reagan's popularity.

Reagan's firm stance against communism extended around the world, and his administration supported repressive governments in the Middle East, Asia, Latin America, and Africa. Reagan's ambassador to the United Nations, Jeane Kirkpatrick, explained this foreign policy strategy as

---

Contras Nicaraguan counterrevolutionaries, trained by the United States CIA, who fought to overthrow the new Sandinista government in Nicaragua during the 1980s.

AP® TIP
Analyze how Reagan's support of the Contras affected perceptions of American actions in Latin American countries during the 1980s.

Boland Amendment 1982 act of Congress prohibiting direct aid to the Nicaraguan Contra forces.

AP® TIP
Be sure you can explain how U.S. policies in Latin American nations during the 1980s affected immigration to the U.S. during this decade.

invasion of Grenada A U.S. invasion that installed a pro-American government after a 1983 coup toppled the Caribbean island's leftist, Soviet-supported government.

APPLY THE TIP

Both AP® Tips on this page focus on the relationship between the U.S. and other nations (or immigrants from other nations). After responding to each AP® Tip, have students write an article for a national newspaper either supporting or opposing the foreign policies of the Reagan administration.

Period 9: 1980–The Present

MODULE 9-1 The Triumph of Conservatism

Antiapartheid Protest, Cornell University In 1986 students on college campuses such as Cornell protested apartheid in South Africa. They constructed shantytowns to highlight the poverty of nonwhite South Africans. Their immediate goal was to persuade their universities to remove their investments in companies that did business in South Africa. **Explain how these protest movements drew inspiration from the protest movements in the 1960s and 1970s.**

BUILDING AP® SKILLS
Making Connections

Put students into groups of 4. Assign one of the following topics to an individual student in the group: Greensboro sit-ins, Berkeley free speech protests, Kent State Vietnam War protests, and the Student Nonviolent Coordinating Committee. Allow time for students to conduct research into their topic as well as take a few notes to sum up the goal of the protest or group as well as who the participants were. Next, students will share what they have learned with the other students in their group. Finally, each group should discuss the prompt: Explain how the Apartheid protest at Cornell University drew inspiration from the protest movements in the 1960s and 1970s. Possible answers include: *University students continued to take an interest in human rights. Many protest movements throughout history have been initiated by young students who want to see a change in the world. These examples illustrate this trend.*

apartheid Legal and institutionalized system of discrimination and segregation based on race in South Africa from 1948 until 1994.

Comprehensive Anti-Apartheid Act 1986 act prohibiting new trade and investment in South Africa because of apartheid. President Reagan vetoed the act but Congress overrode his veto.

one that distinguished between non-Communist "authoritarian" nations, which were acceptable, and Communist "totalitarian" regimes, which were not. The South African government was an example of an acceptable authoritarianism, even though it practiced **apartheid** (white supremacy and racial separation). The fact that the South African Communist Party had joined the fight against apartheid led the Reagan administration to support the white-minority, anti-Communist government. In response, some protesters across the United States and the world spoke out against South Africa's government and campaigned for divestment of public and corporate funds from South African companies. After years of pressure from the divestment movement on college campuses and elsewhere, in 1986 Congress passed the **Comprehensive Anti-Apartheid Act**, which prohibited new trade and investment in South Africa. President Reagan vetoed it, but Congress overrode the president's veto.

REVIEW

How did anticommunism shape Reagan's international policy?

TEACHING IDEA
Differing Views

Ask students to consider whether the Reagan administration's emphasis on anticommunism was the correct choice for the administration to make. Require each student to write a five-minute dialogue between President Reagan and a student from Cornell University who took part in the anti-apartheid protest. How would each side feel about Reagan making anticommunism a priority? Students will express that Reagan likely believed that communism was so evil that it had to be eradicated at any cost, but the Cornell University student would insist that other evils exist, such as segregation, that require prioritization.

Fighting International Terrorism

terrorism The use of violence to inspire fear in service of achieving a political goal.

Palestine Liberation Organization (PLO) Organization founded in 1964 with the goal of achieving independence from Israel, through armed force if necessary. For many years the PLO was considered a terrorist organization by the U.S.

Two days before the Grenada invasion in 1983, the U.S. military suffered a grievous blow halfway around the world. In the tiny country of Lebanon, wedged between Syrian occupation on its northern border and the Palestine Liberation Organization's fight against Israel to the south, a civil war raged between Christians and Muslims. Reagan believed that stability in the region was in America's national interest. With this in mind, in 1982 the Reagan administration sent 800 marines, as part of a multilateral force that included French and Italian troops, to keep the peace. On October 23, 1983, a suicide bomber drove a truck into a marine barracks, killing 241 soldiers. Reagan withdrew the remaining troops.

The removal of troops did not end threats to Americans in the Middle East. **Terrorism**, the attempt by non-state actors to foster political change by spreading fear through violence, had become an ever-present danger, especially since the Iranian hostage crisis in 1979–1980. In 1985, 17 American citizens were killed in terrorist assaults, and 154 were injured. In June 1985, Shi'ite Muslim extremists hijacked a TWA airliner in Athens with 39 Americans on board and flew it to Beirut. That same year, commandos of the **Palestine Liberation Organization (PLO)** hijacked the Italian ocean liner *Achille Lauro*, which was cruising from Egypt to Israel. One of the 450 passengers, the wheelchair-bound, elderly Jewish American Leon Klinghoffer, was murdered and thrown overboard. After three days, Egyptian authorities negotiated an end to the terrorist hijacking.

In response to the 1985 PLO cruise ship attack, the Reagan administration retaliated against the North African country of Libya. Its military leader, Muammar al-Qaddafi, supported the Palestinian cause and provided sanctuary for terrorists. The Reagan administration had placed a trade embargo on Libya, and Secretary of State Shultz remarked: "We have to put Qaddafi in a box and close the lid." In 1986, after the bombing of a nightclub in West Berlin killed two American

TEACHING IDEA
Class Discussion

As a class discussion, have students evaluate the extent to which U.S. interventions in Latin America represented a change in international policy from earlier in the twentieth century.

Fighting International Terrorism

Period 9: 1980–The Present

▲ **MAP 9.2 The United States in the Middle East, 1978–1991** The United States has historically needed access to the rich oil reserves of the Middle East. From the 1970s to the 1990s, both Democratic and Republican administrations were committed to the security of Israel, supportive of Afghan rebels fighting Soviet invaders, and opposed to the rising power of Islamic regimes. **According to this map, which Middle Eastern nations stood the greatest chance of affecting U.S. policy through control of oil distribution?**

TEACHING IDEA

Project Idea

Have students create a timeline from 1978–1991 to illustrate the conflicts and U.S. foreign policy in the Middle East. Use the events shown on Map 9.2 to complete the timeline.

TEACHING IDEA

Incorporating Videos

Have students watch the History Channel's "What Was the Iran-Contra Affair?" (available on YouTube). While watching, ask students to take notes on the following:

1. Describe Reagan's involvement in Nicaragua.
2. What was the Boland Amendment?
3. How was the nation of Iran involved in the affair?
4. How did the public react to the affair?

Whole-class discussion to follow.

AP® TIP
Analyze how the growing threat of terrorism affected the development of U.S. foreign policy during the 1980s.

servicemen and injured 230, the Reagan administration held Qaddafi responsible. In late April the United States retaliated by sending planes to bomb the Libyan capital of Tripoli. Following the bombing, Qaddafi took a much lower profile against the United States. Reagan had demonstrated his nation's military might despite the retreat from Lebanon (Map 9.2).

In the meantime, the situation in Lebanon remained critical as the strife caused by civil war led to the seizing of American hostages. By mid-1984, seven Americans in Lebanon had been kidnapped by Shi'ite Muslims financed by Iran. Since 1980, Iran, a Shi'ite nation, had been engaged in a protracted war with Iraq, which was ruled by military leader Saddam Hussein and his Sunni Muslim party, the chief rival to the Shi'ites. With relations between the United States and Iran having deteriorated in the aftermath of the 1979 coup, the Reagan administration backed Iraq in this war. The fate of the hostages in Lebanon, however, motivated Reagan to make a deal with Iran. In late 1985 Reagan's national security adviser, Robert McFarlane, negotiated secretly with an Iranian intermediary for the United States to sell antitank missiles to Iran in exchange for the Shi'ite government using its influence to induce the Muslim kidnappers to release the hostages.

Had the matter ended there, the secret deal might never have come to light. However, NSC aide Lieutenant Colonel Oliver North developed a plan to transfer the proceeds from the arms-for-hostages deal to fund the Contras in Nicaragua and circumvent the Boland Amendment, which prohibited direct aid to the rebels.

Iran-Contra affair Reagan administration scandal involving the funneling of funds from an illegal arms-for-hostages deal with Iran to the Nicaraguan Contras in the mid-1980s.

In 1986 information about the **Iran-Contra affair** came to light. In the summer of 1987, televised Senate hearings exposed much of the tangled, covert dealings with Iran. In 1988 a special federal prosecutor indicted NSC adviser Vice Admiral John Poindexter (who had replaced McFarlane), North, and several others on charges ranging from perjury to conspiracy to obstruction of justice. Reagan took responsibility for the transfer of funds to the Contras, but he managed to weather the political crisis. His successor, George H. W. Bush, ultimately pardoned many of those involved in the scandal.

Period 9: 1980–The Present

MODULE 9-1 The Triumph of Conservatism

TRM Suggested Responses to Questions

TRM Module 9.1 AP® Analyzing Sources Handout 4

BUILDING AP® SKILLS

Sourcing and Situation

Have students complete a HIPP analysis on Reagan's Address to the Nation (a refresher on HIPP can be found on page 8). What historical developments are occurring that would motivate Reagan to make this speech? For the intended audience, to whom is Reagan speaking? Try to elicit a more specific response than "American citizens" from students. Reagan could be speaking to those who would criticize his actions in order to stem the opposition. He might also have been speaking to his supporters in a plea to keep their support. Depending on the intended audience, the purpose might vary, but students can agree that Reagan wanted to de-escalate the situation and diminish his involvement in the affair. For point of view, students should discuss who Reagan was and what his beliefs were surrounding the Iran-Contra affair.

AP® ANALYZING SOURCES

Source: Ronald Reagan, *Address to the Nation on the Iran Arms Contra Aid Controversy*, 1987

"First, let me say I take full responsibility for my own actions and for those of my administration. As angry as I may be about activities undertaken without my knowledge, I am still accountable for those activities. As disappointed as I may be in some who served me, I'm still the one who must answer to the American people for this behavior. And as personally distasteful as I find secret bank accounts and diverted funds—well, as the Navy would say, this happened on my watch.

Let's start with the part that is the most controversial. A few months ago I told the American people I did not trade arms for hostages. My heart and my best intentions still tell me that's true, but the facts and the evidence tell me it is not. As the Tower board reported, what began as a strategic opening to Iran deteriorated, in its implementation, into trading arms for hostages. This runs counter to my own beliefs, to administration policy, and to the original strategy we had in mind. There are reasons why it happened, but no excuses. It was a mistake. . . .

Now, another major aspect of the Board's findings regards the transfer of funds to the Nicaraguan contras. The Tower board wasn't able to find out what happened to this money, so the facts here will be left to the continuing investigations of the court-appointed Independent Counsel and the two congressional investigating committees. I'm confident the truth will come out about this matter, as well. As I told the Tower board, I didn't know about any diversion of funds to the contras. But as President, I cannot escape responsibility. . . .

Now, what should happen when you make a mistake is this: You take your knocks, you learn your lessons, and then you move on. That's the healthiest way to deal with a problem. This in no way diminishes the importance of the other continuing investigations, but the business of our country and our people must proceed. I've gotten this message from Republicans and Democrats in Congress, from allies around the world, and—if we're reading the signals right—even from the Soviets. And of course, I've heard the message from you, the American people. You know, by the time you reach my age, you've made plenty of mistakes. And if you've lived your life properly—so, you learn. You put things in perspective. You pull your energies together. You change. You go forward."

Questions for Analysis

1. Identify the actions that Reagan refers to in this excerpt.
2. Explain the ways in which Reagan takes responsibility for these actions.
3. Evaluate the extent to which these actions represent a continuation of American Cold War policy.

REVIEW

How did terrorism affect the Reagan administration's policy in the Middle East?

The Nuclear Freeze Movement

Rising protests against nuclear weapons in the United States and Europe in the early 1980s revealed a public increasingly anxious about the possibility of nuclear confrontation with the Soviet Union. At the end of the Carter administration, the United States had promised NATO that it would station new missiles in England, Italy, West Germany, and Belgium. Coupled with his firm stance against the Soviet Union, Reagan's decision to implement this policy sparked protests. One such protest came in 1981 when peace activists set up camp at Greenham Common in England outside of one of the military bases prepared to house the arriving missiles, one of twenty such camps in England. The peace camp at Greenham Common, where protesters sang, danced, and performed skits to affirm women's solidarity for peace, became the model for the Women's Encampment for a Future of Peace and Justice at Seneca Falls, where activists staged demonstrations.

TEACHING IDEA

Incorporating Primary Sources

Have students read Bob Drogin's article, "Nuclear Freeze Movement, With Eye on '86 Elections, Renewing Its Fight for Peace," available from the *Los Angeles Times* (latimes.com). Ask students to describe the struggles that the Nuclear Freeze Movement faced, as well as their successes, according to the article. Possible answers include: *The movement seemed to be fading, but they were able to raise money in order to help politicians who supported the movement to win elections in 1984.*

The Nuclear Freeze Movement

Women's Peace Encampment Vigil On October 24, 1983, protesters from the Women's Encampment for a Future of Peace and Justice held a candlelight vigil outside the Seneca Army Depot in Romulus, New York. Originally organized by feminist women, the protests also drew men. Together they campaigned to shut down the base, which was used as a munitions storage and disposal facility. In 1995 the military closed the depot. **In what ways did the Women's Encampment for a Future of Peace and Justice show both continuity and change from the American antiwar movement from the 1960s and 1970s?**

These activities were part of a larger **nuclear freeze movement** that began in 1980. Its proponents called for a "mutual freeze on the testing, production, and deployment of nuclear weapons and of missiles and aircraft designed primarily to deliver nuclear weapons." Grassroots activists also held town meetings throughout the United States to mobilize ordinary citizens to speak out against nuclear proliferation. In 1982 some 750,000 people rallied in New York City's Central Park to support a nuclear freeze resolution presented at the United Nations. Despite opposition from the United States and its NATO allies, measures favoring the freeze passed in the UN General Assembly. In the 1982 elections, peace groups placed nonbinding, nuclear freeze referenda on local ballots, which passed with wide majorities. The nuclear freeze movement's momentum carried over to Congress, where the House of Representatives narrowly rejected an "immediate freeze" by only two votes.

Demonstrations in the United States and in Europe influenced Reagan. According to a 1982 public opinion poll, 57 percent of Americans favored an immediate nuclear freeze. Reagan acknowledged that he was more inclined to reconsider deploying missiles abroad because European leaders felt pressure from protesters in their home countries. However, the freeze movement inside and outside the United States contributed to a favorable climate in which the president and Soviet leaders could negotiate a genuine plan for nuclear disarmament by the end of the decade.

Ronald Reagan won reelection in 1984 by a landslide. Following his enormous victory, the president softened his stance and became more amenable to negotiating with the USSR. It took a president with impeccable credentials in fighting communism, like Nixon's détente with China in the 1970s, to reduce Cold War conflicts. Reagan espoused conservative principles during his presidency, but he refused to let rigid dogma interfere with more pragmatic considerations to foster peace. By the time President Reagan left office, little remained of the Cold War.

In the mid-1980s, powerful changes were sweeping through the Soviet Union, which also helped bring the Cold War to a close. In September 1985, Mikhail Gorbachev became general secretary of the Communist Party and head of the Soviet Union. Gorbachev introduced a program of economic and political reform. Through *glasnost* (openness) and *perestroika* (restructuring), the Soviet leader hoped to reduce massive state control over the declining economy and to extend democratic elections and freedom of speech and freedom of the press. Gorbachev understood that the success of his reforms depended on reducing Cold War tensions with the United States and slowing the arms escalation that was bankrupting the Soviet economy. Gorbachev's *glasnost* brought the popular American musical performer Billy Joel to the Soviet Union in August 1987, staging the first rock concert in the country.

The changes that Gorbachev brought to the internal affairs of the Soviet Union carried over to the international arena. From 1986 to 1988, the Soviet leader negotiated in person with the American president, something that had not happened during Reagan's first term. In 1986 at a summit in Reykjavik, Iceland, the two leaders agreed to cut the number of strategic nuclear missiles in half. In 1987 the two sides negotiated an **Intermediate Nuclear Forces Treaty**, which provided for the destruction of existing intermediate-range missiles and on-site inspections to ensure compliance. The height of détente came in December 1987, when Gorbachev traveled to the United States to take part in the treaty-signing ceremony. Reagan no longer referred to the USSR as "the evil empire," and Gorbachev impressed Americans with his personal charm and by demonstrating the media savvy associated with American politicians.

nuclear freeze movement 1980s protests calling for an end to the testing, production, and deployment of missiles and aircraft designed primarily to deliver nuclear weapons.

glasnost Policy of political "openness" initiated by Soviet leader Mikhail Gorbachev in the 1980s. Under *glasnost*, the Soviet Union extended democratic elections, freedom of speech, and freedom of the press.

perestroika Policy of economic "restructuring" initiated by Soviet leader Mikhail Gorbachev. Gorbachev hoped that by reducing state control he could revive the Soviet economy.

Intermediate Nuclear Forces Treaty 1987 treaty between the U.S. and the Soviet Union that required the destruction of existing intermediate-range missiles and mandated on-site inspections to ensure both countries continued to adhere to the treaty terms.

BUILDING AP® SKILLS
Continuity and Change

In pairs, have students draw a T-chart in their notes with "Continuities" on the left and "Changes" on the right. Ask students to compare the Nuclear Freeze Movement with the anti-war movements in the 1960s and 1970s. Possible answers include: *There were peaceful movements in both time periods, though anti-war movements tended to become violent. Anti-war movements also broke the law when it came to draft-dodging and burning draft cards.*

EXPLORING AP® THEMES
Politics and Power

Assign students to watch Episode 43, "The Reagan Revolution," from the Crash Course US History series (available on YouTube). This video does an excellent job of summing up Reagan's two terms in office. While watching, have students take notes to address the following prompt: To what extent did Ronald Reagan's approach to foreign policy change from his first term to his second term? Possible answers include: *The largest change was how Reagan approached the Cold War. In his first term, Reagan increased military spending, pushed for the Strategic Defense Initiative, and convinced European nations to station missiles within their borders. In his second term, Reagan took a different approach and was more willing to work with the Soviet Union (mostly Gorbachev) to de-escalate the Cold War and negotiate terms that both nations could be happy with.*

TRM Suggested Responses to Questions

TRM Module 9.1 AP® Analyzing Sources Handout 5

BUILDING AP® SKILLS

Continuity and Change

Draw a continuum on the board. Label the left side "Nothing Changed" and the right side "Everything Changed." Have students individually review Reagan's economic policy as described in Module 9-1 and respond to the prompt: "To what extent did Reagan's economic policy foster a change in the U.S. economy?" Give each student a sticky note on which they will write historical evidence to support their answer. Next, have all students put their sticky note on a point along the continuum on the board. The point they choose should correspond to the extent to which Reagan's economic policies represented a change. Next, collect evidence and fill in a T-chart on the board (label the left "Continuities" and the right "Changes"). Once the class has provided all of the evidence they can think of, instruct students to individually write a thesis statement to respond to the prompt. To conclude, have students pair up and exchange their thesis statements with their partners. Students should peer-review the thesis statements.

TRM Suggested Responses to Questions

TEACHING IDEA

Check for Understanding

During his terms as president, Ronald Reagan faced issues with the American economy, the AIDS epidemic, as well as the Cold War. After reading Module 9-1, have students assess Reagan's policies for homework.

TRM Find **Handout 9.3 — Assessing President Reagan's Policies** in the Teacher's Resource Materials.

The following year, Reagan flew to the Soviet Union and hugged Gorbachev at the tomb of the founder of the USSR, Vladimir Lenin. He later told reporters, "They've changed," referring to the once and not-so-distant "evil empire." Citizens of the two adversarial nations breathed a collective sigh of relief; at long last, the icy terrain of the Cold War appeared to be melting.

AP® ANALYZING SOURCES

Source: Ronald Reagan, *Address at the University of Virginia*, 1988

"But now the question: How do we keep the world moving toward the idea of popular government? Well, today I offer three thoughts—reflections and warnings at the same time—on how the Soviet-American relationship can continue to improve and how the cause of peace and freedom can be served.

First, the Soviet-American relationship: Once marked by sterility and confrontation, this relationship is now characterized by dialog—realistic, candid dialog—serious diplomatic progress, and the sights and sounds of summitry. All of this is heady, inspiring. And yet my first reflection for you today is: All of it is still in doubt. And the only way to make it last and grow and become permanent is to remember we're not there yet.

Serious problems, fundamental differences remain. Our system is one of checks and balances. Theirs, for all its reforms, remains a one-party authoritarian system that institutionalizes the concentration of power. Our foreign relations embrace this expanding world of democracy that I've described. Theirs can be known by the company they keep: Cuba, Nicaragua, Ethiopia, Libya, Vietnam, North Korea. Yes, we welcome Mr. Gorbachev's recent announcement of a troop reduction, but let us remember that the Soviet preponderance in military power in Europe remains. . . .

So, we must keep our heads, and that means keeping our skepticism. We must realize that what has brought us here has not been easy, not for ourselves nor for all of those who have sacrificed and contributed to the cause of freedom in the postwar era.

So, this means in our treaty negotiations, as I've said: Trust, but verify. I'm not a linguist, but I learned to say that much in Russian and have used it in frequent meetings with Mr. Gorbachev: 'Dovorey no provorey.' It means keeping our military strong. It means remembering no treaty is better than a bad treaty. It means remembering the accords of Moscow and Washington summits followed many years of standing firm on our principles and our interests, and those of our allies."

Questions for Analysis
1. Identify the events that have led to a thawing of the Cold War, according to Reagan.
2. Identify the reasons for Reagan's continued skepticism.
3. Evaluate the extent to which the approach to communism Reagan takes in this speech represents a change in U.S. Cold War policy.

REVIEW

- What factors led the Cold War to thaw during the late 1980s?

AP® WRITING HISTORICALLY — Long-Essay Question Practice

ACTIVITY

Answer the following Long-Essay Question. *Suggested writing time: 40 minutes.*

Evaluate the extent of change in U.S. foreign policy during the presidency of Ronald Reagan (1981–1989).

TEACHING IDEA

AP® Writing Historically Review

If students are struggling to formulate categories of analysis, try the following activity. Ronald Reagan was known as a strong anti-communist throughout his presidency, as evidenced by the buildup of the U.S. military and his willingness to confront communist nations. Yet President Reagan also believed in a foreign policy known as "Peace through Strength." Have students explain whether the ideas of being strong on communism and "Peace through Strength" complement or contradict one another. In this way, students will need to analyze whether or not there was change in American foreign policy during President Reagan's time in office. Completing this activity will allow students to understand how to approach writing a historically defensible interpretation to the prompt.

Module 9-2

The End of the Cold War

LEARNING TARGETS
By the end of this module, you should be able to:

- Explain how elevated military spending on the part of the United States, economic stagnation in the Soviet Union, and protests in Eastern Europe contributed to the end of the Cold War.
- Explain how the end of the Cold War fostered new diplomatic decisions and debates about the role of the United States in the world.
- Explain how President George H. W. Bush tried to transform conservative ideology into "kinder" and "gentler" policies.

THEMATIC FOCUS
America in the World

With the end of the Cold War, the United States increasingly faced the twin prospects of peace with its former rivals and greater instability in new regions. In the years after Reagan's presidency, U.S. policymakers struggled to redefine the nation's place as the sole superpower, while also debating the role of the United States in this new era.

HISTORICAL REASONING FOCUS
Causation

TASK ▶ While reading this module, analyze the causes of changes in the international order.

After Reagan left office, his two-term vice president, George H. W. Bush, generally carried on his conservative legacy at home and abroad. While sharing most of Reagan's views, Bush called for a "kinder, gentler nation" in dealing with social justice and the environment. When Bush became president in 1989, he also encountered a very different Soviet Union from the one Ronald Reagan had faced a decade earlier. The USSR was undergoing an internal revolution, which allowed Bush and the United States to take on a new role in a world that was no longer divided between capitalist and Communist nations and their allies. Globalization became the hallmark of the post–Cold War era, replacing previously opposed economic and political systems, with mixed consequences. Following the collapse of the old world order, local and regional conflicts long held in check by the Cold War broke out along religious, racial, and ethnic lines.

"Kinder and Gentler" Conservatism

In his 1988 presidential campaign against Michael Dukakis, the Democratic governor of Massachusetts, Bush defended conservative principles when he promised, "Read my lips: No new taxes." The Republican candidate attacked Dukakis for his liberal positions and accused him of being soft on crime. Bush also affirmed his own opposition to abortion and support for gun rights and the death penalty.

However, once in office Bush had to deal with several economic challenges. Reagan's economic programs and military spending had left the nation with a mounting federal budget deficit, which slowed economic growth, resulting in another recession in 1990. Unemployment rose from 5.3 percent when Bush took office in 1989 to 7.5 percent by 1992, and state and local governments

TEACHING IDEA

Differing Views

George H. W. Bush ran his campaign on the promise that he would not establish any new taxes. Later in his presidency, he was forced to go back on that promise. Discuss his decision with the class. Have students take on the perspective of President Bush as well as the perspective of a Reagan conservative by writing a "tweet" (280 characters or less) that sums up their point of view and their reasoning. This character restriction will force students to be concise in their answers, summing up the most important information in their response.

EXPLORING AP® THEMES

Geography and the Environment

Watch NBC News' "The Exxon Valdez Oil Spill | Flashback" (available on YouTube). This video provides clips of news coverage of the oil spill and provides visuals for students to see the impact of the spill. Discuss the aftermath of the oil spill with students. How did President Bush respond to the oil spill? *President Bush signed the Clean Air Act in 1990, which reduced emissions.* How might conservative business owners have reacted to President Bush's response? *The Act reduced emissions from cars and power plants, which would mean that some businesses would have to change their practices, which can be costly. Conservative business owners would have opposed the Act, but would have been happy that President Bush didn't push further for limits on carbon dioxide emissions.*

Period 9: 1980–The Present

MODULE 9-2 The End of the Cold War

◀ **Anita Hill Testifies Against the Supreme Court Nomination of Clarence Thomas, 1991** Anita F. Hill is sworn-in to testify before the Senate Judiciary Committee on the confirmation of Clarence Thomas to the U.S. Supreme Court by chairman Joseph Biden, a Democrat from Delaware, on October 11, 1991. Hill claimed Thomas had sexually harassed her when she had worked for him in the early 1980s. There were no women serving on the Judiciary Committee at that time. **To what extent did the process and outcome of Hill's testimony reflect a change in American politics?**

Americans with Disabilities Act (ADA) 1990 act extending legal protections and accessibility mandates for Americans with physical and mental handicaps.

Clean Air Act 1990 act that set new standards to reduce car and power plant emissions.

had difficulty paying for the educational, health, and social services that the Reagan and Bush administrations had transferred to them. In 1990, to improve economic conditions, he supported a deficit reduction package that included more than $130 billion in new taxes, which angered many Americans who had voted for him. He also departed from some conservatives when he signed the **Americans with Disabilities Act (ADA)** in 1990, extending a range of protections to some 40 million Americans with physical and mental handicaps. The act provided protections against discrimination similar to those in the landmark Civil Rights Act of 1964, and required employers and municipalities to provide accommodations so as to offer disabled Americans equal opportunity under the law.

Bush had a mixed record on the environment. In 1989 the oil tanker *Exxon Valdez* struck a reef off the coast of Alaska, dumping nearly 11 million gallons of oil into Prince William Sound. This disaster created pressure for stricter environmental legislation. Thus, in 1990 the president signed the **Clean Air Act**, which reduced emissions from automobiles and power plants. However, in 1992 Bush opposed international efforts to limit carbon dioxide emissions, greenhouse gases that contribute to climate change.

In 1991, Bush nominated Clarence Thomas to fill the Supreme Court vacancy left by Justice Thurgood Marshall, the first African American justice. Thomas belonged to a rising group of conservative African Americans who shared Republican views supporting private enterprise and the free market system and opposing affirmative action. He had previously served as chief of the Equal Employment Opportunity Commission (EEOC) under President Reagan. He also opposed abortion and welfare. During the course of Thomas's Senate confirmation hearing, Anita Hill, Thomas's assistant at the EEOC, testified before the Senate Judiciary Committee and a nationally televised audience that Thomas had made unwanted sexual advances to her on and off the job, which she quit in 1983. Hill's charges of sexual harassment did not stop his confirmation to the Supreme Court. Nevertheless, membership in women's political associations — such as Emily's List, founded in 1984, and the Fund for a Feminist Majority, founded in 1987 — soared following Hill's testimony. In the 1992 midterm elections, more women were elected to the House of Representatives than in any previous election, and the number of women in the Senate tripled. While this unprecedented "Year of the Woman" was a product of many long-term cultural and social trends, Anita Hill's testimony placed women's struggle for equal rights at the forefront of public consciousness at a key moment in American history.

> **AP® TIP**
> Analyze how the Anita Hill hearings affected the feminist movement and the political landscape of the United States.

REVIEW

- How did President George H. W. Bush's domestic policies differ from the economic and social policies of the Reagan administration?

818

APPLY THE TIP

Discussions about topics such as sexual harassment can become heated, so before discussing the Anita Hill hearings, establish ground rules for discussion with your students. Talk with your class about the importance of using facts to support their responses during class discussions as well as directing their responses to the topic at hand and not at the opinions of fellow students. As an attention-getter for this activity, watch PBS NewsHour's "Supreme Court Moments in History: Clarence Thomas and Anita Hill" (available on YouTube). In small groups, have students discuss the prompt: "To what extent were the feminist movement and the political landscape of the United States impacted by the hearing?" Possible answers include: *The popularity increased for women's political associations such as Emily's List and Fund for a Feminist Majority. The number of women in the Senate tripled. More women were elected to the House of Representatives than in any previous election.* Ask student volunteers to share their answers with the class. Depending on the class's ability to remain objective, you may choose to connect the hearings with more recent events that have gained national notoriety.

The Breakup of the Soviet Union

Solidarity Polish trade union movement led by Lech Walesa. During the 1980s, Solidarity played a central role in ending Communist rule in Poland.

Bush's first year in office coincided with upheavals in the Soviet-controlled Communist bloc, with Poland leading the way. In 1980 Polish dockworker Lech Walesa had organized **Solidarity**, a trade union movement that conducted a series of popular strikes that forced the Communist government to recognize the group. Solidarity had ten million members and attracted various opponents of the Communist regime, including working-class democrats, Catholics, and nationalists who favored breaking ties with the Soviet Union. In 1981 Soviet leaders, disturbed by Solidarity's growing strength, forced the Polish government to crack down on the organization, arrest Walesa, and ban Solidarity. However, in 1989 Walesa and Solidarity were still active and seized on the changes ushered in by Mikhail Gorbachev's *glasnost* in the USSR to press their demands for democracy in Poland. This time, the Soviets refused to intervene, and Poland conducted its first free elections since the beginning of the Cold War, electing Lech Walesa as president of the country. In July 1989, Gorbachev further broke from the past and announced that the Soviet Union would respect the national sovereignty of all the nations in the Warsaw Pact, which the Soviet Union had controlled since the late 1940s.

Gorbachev's proclamation spurred the end of communism throughout Eastern Europe. Within the next year, Soviet-sponsored regimes fell peacefully in Hungary and Czechoslovakia, replaced by elected governments. Bulgaria held free elections, which brought reformers to power. Only in Romania did Communist rulers put up a fight. There, it took a violent popular uprising to topple the brutal dictator Nicolae Ceaușescu. The Baltic states of Latvia, Lithuania, and Estonia, which the Soviets had incorporated into the USSR at the outset of World War II, also regained their independence, sparking the political breakup of the Soviet Union itself.

Perhaps the most striking symbolism in the dismantling of the Soviet empire came in Germany, a country that had been divided between East and West states since 1945. With Communist governments collapsing around them, East Germans demonstrated against the regime of Erich Honecker. With no Soviet help forthcoming, Honecker decided to open the border between East and West

AP® ANALYZING SOURCES

Source: Francis Fukuyama, *The End of History?*, 1989

"In watching the flow of events over the past decade or so, it is hard to avoid the feeling that something very fundamental has happened in world history. The past year has seen a flood of articles commemorating the end of the Cold War, and the fact that "peace" seems to be breaking out in many regions of the world. Most of these analyses lack any larger conceptual framework for distinguishing between what is essential and what is contingent or accidental in world history, and are predictably superficial. If Mr. Gorbachev were ousted from the Kremlin or a new Ayatollah proclaimed the millennium for a desolate Middle Eastern capital, these same commentators would scramble to announce the rebirth of a new era of conflict. . . .

What we may be witnessing . . . [is] not just the end of the Cold War, or the passing of a particular period of post-war history, but the end of history as such: that is, the end point of mankind's ideological evolution and the universalization of Western liberal democracy as the final form of human government. This is not to say that there will no longer be events to fill the pages of *Foreign Affairs*'s yearly summaries of international relations, for the victory of liberalism has occurred primarily in the realm of ideas or consciousness and is as yet incomplete in the real or material world. But there are powerful reasons for believing that it is the ideal that will govern the material world in the long run."

Questions for Analysis

1. Identify the signs of change Fukuyama perceives in the world.
2. Explain the significance of these changes, according to Fukuyama.
3. Evaluate the extent to which the changes Fukuyama names were brought about by the policies of the United States.

BUILDING AP® SKILLS

Causation

To illustrate the breakup of the Soviet Union in a visual way, have students draw a chain of events in their notes. This chain should look like a row of boxes connected by arrows connecting one event to the next. The chain will not be a timeline but will depict the events that led to the breakup of the Soviet Union in chronological order. Students should include events such as: *the establishment of Solidarity, Poland conducts free elections, Gorbachev respects the national sovereignty of nations in the Warsaw Pact, Hungary and Czechoslovakia elect governments, etc.* In addition to each description added to the chain of events, students should include a small doodle, such as a ballot box or stick figures voting. Adding visuals to notes can help with information retention.

TRM Suggested Responses to Questions

TRM Module 9.2 AP® Analyzing Sources Handout

BUILDING AP® SKILLS

Claims and Evidence in Sources

In this activity, students will answer the Questions for Analysis using Fukuyama's source. Have each student individually identify one sign of change that Fukuyama perceives in the world, according to the primary source provided, and write the change down on a piece of paper. Have all students crumple up their paper. For thirty seconds, allow students to have a "snowball fight" with the crumpled up paper. After thirty seconds, each student should pick up a snowball and open it up. They should then complete the second Question for Analysis and explain the significance of the change, according to Fukuyama. Students will again crumple up the paper and have another thirty-second snowball fight. After thirty seconds, each student should pick up a piece of paper, read the responses on it individually, and answer the last Question for Analysis: To what extent did U.S. policies bring about this change (that is written on their paper)? Have one more snowball fight and call on random students to read the responses on their paper. Students should feel comfortable sharing, as the answers on the paper likely belong to other students in the class.

TEACHING IDEA

Incorporating Videos

Have students watch ABC News' "Nov. 10, 1989: Celebration at the Berlin Wall" (available on YouTube). Allow students to discuss in pairs: How did East Berliners and West Berliners react to the destruction of the wall? How does the destruction of the Berlin Wall symbolize the decline of the Soviet Union as a whole? Possible answers include: *East and West Berliners were elated. There are celebrations as people knew that the Berlin Wall was going to be destroyed. The destruction of the Berlin Wall was symbolic of the Soviet Union breaking apart and allowing for more freedom; in this case, more freedom of movement.*

BUILDING AP® SKILLS

Argumentation

Put students into pairs. Have one student support Gorbachev and his actions during the late 1980s and early 1990s. Have the other student oppose Gorbachev and his actions during the same time period. Allow time for students to answer the prompt: Evaluate the extent to which Gorbachev shaped Cold War events in Europe. Possible answers include: *Gorbachev's actions led to positive impacts, as he opened the Soviet Union to the rest of the world via his glasnost and perestroika policies. This benefited the nation and its people.* Or: *Gorbachev's actions led to negative impacts. His decision to end the Soviet-Afghan War left Afghanistan greatly unstable. Instead of staying to stabilize the nation, Gorbachev left the people of Afghanistan to fend for themselves.*

Period 9: 1980–The Present

MODULE 9-2 The End of the Cold War

Germany. On November 9, 1989, East and West Germans flocked to the Berlin Wall and jubilantly joined workers in knocking down the concrete barricade that divided the city. A year later, East and West Germany merged under the democratic, capitalist Federal Republic of Germany.

Gorbachev also brought an end to the costly nine-year Soviet-Afghan War. When the Soviets withdrew their last troops on February 15, 1989, they left Afghanistan in shambles. One million Afghans had perished, and another 5 million fled the country for Pakistan and Iran, resulting in the political destabilization of Afghanistan. Following a civil war, the **Taliban**, a group of Sunni Muslim fundamentalists, came to power in the mid-1990s and established a theocratic regime that, among other things, strictly regulated what women could wear in public and denied them educational and professional opportunities. The Taliban also provided sanctuary for many of the mujahideen rebels who had fought against the Soviets, including Osama bin Laden, who would use the country as a base for his **al-Qaeda** organization to promote terrorism against the United States.

Meanwhile, the Soviet Union disintegrated. Free elections were held in 1990, which ironically threatened Gorbachev's own power by bringing non-Communists to local and national political offices. Although an advocate of economic reform and political openness, Gorbachev remained a Communist and was committed to preserving the USSR. Challenges to Gorbachev came from both ends of the political spectrum. Boris Yeltsin, his former protégé, led the non-Communist forces that wanted Gorbachev to move more quickly in adopting capitalism; on the other side, hard-line generals in the Soviet army disapproved of Gorbachev's reforms and his cooperation with the United States. On August 18, 1991, a group of hard-core conspirators staged a coup against Gorbachev, placed him under house arrest, and surrounded the parliament building with troops. Yeltsin, the president of the Russian Republic, rallied fellow legislators and Muscovites against the plotters and brought the uprising to a peaceful end. Several months later, in early December, Yeltsin and the leaders of the independent republics of Belarus and Ukraine formed the

Taliban Group of Sunni Muslim fundamentalists that ruled Afghanistan in the mid-1990s. The Taliban established a strict theocracy and became the base of al-Qaeda, a Sunni Muslim terrorist organization.

al-Qaeda Terrorist organization led by Osama Bin Laden, created in 1988. Al-Qaeda is a loosely organized radical religious fundamentalist organization, which opposes westernization and orchestrated the September 11, 2001 attacks on the United States.

▲ **MAP 9.3 The Fall of Communism in Eastern Europe and the Soviet Union, 1989–1991** The collapse of Communist regimes in Eastern Europe was due in part to political and economic reforms initiated by Soviet premier Mikhail Gorbachev, including agreements with the United States to reduce nuclear arms. These changes inspired demands for free elections that were supported by popular uprisings, first in Poland and then in other former Soviet satellites. **What does this map reveal about the reasons why the uprisings happened in nations like Poland and East Germany?**

820

TEACHING IDEA

Geography Instruction

Analyze Map 9.3 with students. Ask students to identify why various events are denoted in boxes on the map. *Each box lists events that were impactful in the decline of the Soviet Union.* Discuss the provided question: What does this map reveal about the reasons why the uprisings happened in nations like Poland and East Germany? *Students should recognize that these nations were farther to the west than other nations, therefore they were influenced more by western nations and also were located farther from the center of the Soviet government. Other nations that were closer to the Soviet Union would have had a harder time breaking away, being surrounded by other Soviet satellites.*

Commonwealth of Independent States (CIS), consisting of the Russian Federation and eleven of fifteen former Soviet states. Shortly after, the CIS removed the hammer and sickle, the symbol of communism, from its flag.

Under these circumstances, on December 25, 1991, Gorbachev resigned. The next day, the Soviet legislative body passed a resolution dissolving the USSR. With the Soviet Union dismantled, Yeltsin, as head of the Russian Federation and the CIS, expanded the democratic and free market reforms initiated by Gorbachev (Map 9.3).

Before Gorbachev left office, he completed one last agreement with the United States to curb nuclear arms. In mid-1991, just before conspirators staged their abortive coup, Gorbachev met with President Bush, who had traveled to Moscow to sign a strategic arms reduction treaty. Under this pact, each side agreed to reduce its bombers and missiles by one-third and to trim its conventional military forces. This accord led to a second strategic arms reduction treaty (START II), signed in 1993. Gorbachev's successor, Boris Yeltsin, met with Bush in January 1993, and the two agreed to destroy their countries' stockpile of multiple-warhead intercontinental missiles within a decade.

REVIEW

What factors led to the collapse of the Soviet Union?

Globalization and the New World Order

globalization The extension of economic, political, and cultural relationships among nations, through commerce, migration, and communication.

With the end of the Cold War, cooperation replaced economic and political rivalry between capitalist and Communist nations in a new era of **globalization** — the extension of economic, political, and cultural interconnections among nations, through commerce, migration, and communication. In 1976 the major industrialized democracies had formed the Group of Seven (G7). Consisting of the United States, the United Kingdom, France, West Germany, Italy, Japan, and Canada, the G7 nations met annually to discuss common problems related to issues of global concern, such as trade, health, energy, the environment, and economic and social development. After the fall of communism, Russia joined the organization, which became known as G8. This group of countries represented only 14 percent of the globe's population but produced 60 percent of the world's economic output.

Globalization was accompanied by the extraordinary growth of multinational (or transnational) corporations — companies that operate production facilities or deliver services in more than one country. Between 1970 and 2000, the number of such firms soared from 7,000 to well over 60,000. By 2000 the 500 largest corporations in the world generated more than $11 trillion in revenues, owned more than $33 trillion in assets, and employed 35.5 million people. American companies left their cultural and social imprint on the rest of the world. **Walmart** greeted shoppers in more than 1,200 stores outside the United States, and **McDonald's** changed global eating habits with its more than 1,000 fast-food restaurants worldwide. As American firms penetrated other countries with their products, foreign companies changed the economic landscape of the United States. For instance, by the twenty-first century Japanese automobiles, led by **Toyota** and **Honda**, captured a major share of the American market, surpassing Ford and General Motors, once the hallmark of the country's superior manufacturing and salesmanship.

Globalization also affected popular culture and media. In the 1990s reality shows, many of which originated in Europe, became a staple of American television. At the same time, American programs were shown as reruns all over the world. As cable channels proliferated, American viewers of Hispanic or Asian origin could watch programs in their native languages. The **Cable News Network (CNN)**, the **British Broadcasting Corporation (BBC)**, and **Al Jazeera**, an Arabic-language television channel, competed for viewers with specially designed international broadcasts.

Globalization had some negative consequences as well. Organized labor in particular suffered a severe blow. By 2004 union membership in the United States had dropped to 12.5 percent of the industrial workforce. Fewer and fewer consumer goods bore the label

---

BUILDING AP® SKILLS

Causation

In order to address the Review question, have students use the following handout to list a factor and its impact, as well as argue which factor had the greatest impact on the Soviet Union's collapse.

TRM Find **Handout 9.4 — Collapse of the Soviet Union** in the Teacher's Resource Materials.

EXPLORING AP® THEMES

America in the World

To explore the increasing trend toward globalization in more detail, divide students into groups of 4. Assign each student in the group a different topic: The Group of Seven (G7/G8), Walmart and McDonald's, Toyota and Honda, or BBC and Al Jazeera. Each student should conduct individual research to determine how their topic contributed to globalization. Possible answers include: *G7 met every year to discuss issues of international concern. Walmart and McDonald's spread consumerism and fast food to other nations. Toyota and Honda broke into the U.S. market, outselling Ford and General Motors. The BBC and Al Jazeera provided international news stories.* Students will share their research with their group members and discuss in order to determine which of the four topics had the greatest impact on increasing globalization.

Period 9: 1980–The Present

MODULE 9-2 The End of the Cold War

BUILDING AP® SKILLS

Making Connections

Put students in groups of 4. Split up the reading on this page so each student reads only one paragraph, starting with the paragraph that begins, "Globalization had some negative consequences as well." Have students individually read their assigned paragraph and write a concise summary of the paragraph. After reading, each student will share their summary with the group and the group will discuss: Which effect of globalization had the largest negative impact? Students should then read all of the content on the page.

APPLY THE TIP

Have students work in groups of 3 to explain both the positive and negative effects of globalization on international relations, the living standards of workers, and the environment.

TRM Find **Handout 9.5 — Effects of Globalization** in the Teacher's Resource Materials.

AP® TIP
Be sure you can explain both the positive and negative effects of globalization — especially on relations between the U.S. and other nations, the living standards of workers, and on the environment.

greenhouse gases Gases that absorb energy from the sun and other radiant sources, which warm the Earth.

global warming Also known as climate change, the long-term rise in the temperature of the atmosphere and oceans that threatens life on earth.

Kyoto Protocol 1998 agreement amongst many nations to curtail greenhouse gas emissions and thus curb global warming. The U.S. Senate refused to ratify it.

◀ **Globalization, 1980s** Following the efforts of Presidents Nixon, Ford, and Carter to normalize relations with Communist China, companies established commercial enterprises there, including American fast food chain restaurants. Here a Chinese soldier, standing beside a replica of Colonel Sanders, picks up his order at the bike ride-up window of a Kentucky Fried Chicken restaurant. **Why would American corporations be interested in investing in Communist China during the 1980s and 1990s?**

"Made in America," as multinational companies shifted manufacturing jobs to low-wage workers in developing countries. Many of these foreign workers earned more than the prevailing wages in their countries, but by Western standards their pay was extremely low. There were few or no regulations governing working conditions or the use of child labor, and many foreign factories resembled the sweatshops of early-twentieth-century America. Not surprisingly, workers in the United States could not compete in this market. Furthermore, China, which by 2007 had become a prime source for American manufacturing, failed to regulate the quality of its products closely. Chinese-made toys, including the popular Thomas the Train, showed up in U.S. stores with excessive lead paint and had to be returned before endangering millions of children.

Perhaps the biggest downside to globalization was the danger it posed to the world's environment. As poorer nations sought to take advantage of the West's appetite for low-cost consumer goods, they industrialized rapidly, with little concern for the excessive pollution that accompanied their efforts. The desire for wood products and the expansion of large-scale farming eliminated one-third of Brazil's rain forests. The health of indigenous people suffered wherever globalization-related manufacturing appeared. In Taiwan and China, chemical byproducts of factories and farms turned rivers into polluted sources of drinking water and killed the rivers' fish and plants.

The older industrialized nations added their share to the environmental damage. Besides using nuclear power, Americans consumed electricity and gas produced overwhelmingly from coal and petroleum. The burning of fossil fuels by cars and factories released **greenhouse gases**, raising the temperature of the atmosphere and the oceans and contributing to the phenomenon known as **global warming** or **climate change**. Most scientists believe that global warming has led to the melting of the polar ice caps and threatens human and animal survival on the planet. However, after the industrialized nations of the world signed the **Kyoto Protocol** in 1998 to curtail greenhouse-gas emissions, the U.S. Senate refused to ratify it. Critics of the agreement maintained that it did not address the newly emerging industrial countries that polluted heavily and thus was unfair to the United States.

Globalization also highlighted health problems such as the AIDS epidemic. By the outset of the twenty-first century, approximately 33.2 million people worldwide suffered from the disease, though the number of new cases diagnosed annually had dropped to 2.5 million from more than 5 million a few years earlier. Africa remained the continent with the largest number of AIDS patients and the center of the epidemic. Increased education and the development of more effective pharmaceuticals to treat the illness reduced cases and prolonged the lives of those affected by the disease. Though treatments were more widely available in prosperous countries like the United States, agencies such as the United Nations and the World Health Organization, together with nongovernmental groups such as Partners in Health, were instrumental in offering relief in developing countries.

REVIEW

• How did globalization affect living standards throughout the world during the 1980s and early 1990s?

TEACHING IDEA

Incorporating Websites

Assign the Stanford History Education Group's lesson on the Kyoto Protocol (sheg.stanford.edu). The lesson covers the central question, "Why didn't the U.S. ratify the Kyoto Protocol?" Students are required to read a couple of primary sources, write a hypothesis to answer the question, read two additional primary sources, and revise their hypothesis if necessary. This lesson reminds students that it is important to have as much information as possible before coming to a conclusion.

Managing Conflict after the Cold War

The end of the Cold War left the United States as the only remaining superpower. After the breakup of the Soviet Union, the question remained how the United States would use its strength to preserve world order and maintain peace.

Events in China showed the limitations of American military might. In May 1989 university students in Beijing and other major cities in China held large-scale protests to demand political and economic reforms in the country. Some 200,000 demonstrators consisting of students, intellectuals, and workers gathered in the capital city's huge **Tiananmen Square**, where they constructed a papier-mâché figure resembling the Statue of Liberty and sang songs borrowed from the African American civil rights movement. Deng Xiaoping, Mao Zedong's successor, cracked down on the demonstrations by declaring martial law and dispatching the army to disperse the protesters. Peaceful activists were mowed down by machine guns and stampeded by tanks. In response, President Bush issued a temporary ban on sales of weapons and nonmilitary items to China. When outrage over the Tiananmen Square massacre subsided, normal trade relations resumed.

Flexing military muscle in Panama, however, was more feasible for the Bush administration than doing so in China. During the 1980s, the United States had developed a precarious relationship with Panamanian general Manuel Noriega. Although Noriega channeled aid to the Contras with the approval and support of the CIA, he worsened relations with the Reagan administration by maintaining close ties with Cuba. Noriega also cooperated with the U.S. Drug Enforcement Agency in halting shipments of cocaine from Latin America headed for the United States at the same time that he helped Latin American drug kingpins launder their profits. In 1988 two Florida grand juries had indicted the Panamanian leader on charges of drug smuggling and bribery. As a result, the Reagan administration cut off aid to Panama and the U.S. Senate passed a resolution asking Noriega to resign. Not only did Noriega refuse to step down, but he also nullified the results of the 1989 presidential election in Panama and declared himself the nation's "maximum leader."

After the United States tried unsuccessfully to bring about an internal coup against Noriega, in 1989 the Panamanian leader proclaimed a "state of war" between the United States and his country. On December 28, 1989, President Bush launched **Operation Just Cause**, sending some 27,000 marines to invade Panama. The Bush administration justified the invasion as necessary to protect the Panama Canal and the lives of American citizens, as well as to halt the drug traffic promoted by Noriega. In reality, the main purpose of the mission was to overthrow and capture the Panamanian dictator. In Operation Just Cause, the United States easily defeated a much weaker enemy. The U.S. government installed a new regime, and the marines captured Noriega and sent him back to Florida to stand trial on the drug charges. In 1992 he was found guilty and sent to prison.

The Bush administration deployed much more military force in Iraq. Maintaining a steady flow of oil from the Persian Gulf was vital to U.S. strategic interests. During the prolonged Iraq-Iran War in the 1980s, the Reagan administration had taken steps to ensure that neither side emerged too powerful. Though the administration had orchestrated the arms-for-hostages deal with Iran, it had also courted the Iraqi dictator Saddam Hussein. U.S. support for Hussein ended in 1990, after Iraq sent 100,000 troops to invade the small oil-producing nation of Kuwait, on the southern border of Iraq.

President Bush responded by warning the Iraqis that their invasion "will not stand." Hussein needed to revitalize the Iraqi economy, which was devastated after a decade of war with Iran. Bush feared that the Iraqi dictator would also attempt to overrun Kuwait's neighbor Saudi Arabia, an American ally, thereby giving Iraq control of half of the world's oil supply. Bush was also concerned that an emboldened Saddam Hussein would then upset the delicate balance of power in the Middle East and pose a threat to Israel by supporting the Palestinians. The Iraqis were rumored to be quickly developing nuclear weapons, which Hussein could use against Israel.

Rather than act unilaterally, President Bush organized a multilateral coalition against Iraqi aggression. Secretary of State James Baker persuaded the United Nations to adopt a resolution calling for Iraqi withdrawal from Kuwait and imposing economic sanctions. Thirty-eight nations, including the Arab countries of Egypt, Saudi Arabia, Syria, and Kuwait, contributed 160,000 troops, roughly 24 percent of the 700,000 allied forces that were deployed in Saudi Arabia in preparation for an invasion if Iraq did not comply.

With military forces stationed in Saudi Arabia, Bush gave Hussein a deadline of January 15, 1991 to withdraw from Kuwait or else risk attack. However, the president faced serious opposition at

Tiananmen Square Location of 1989 protests by Chinese university students who wanted political and economic reforms. China's leader, Deng Xiaoping, dispatched the military to break up the protests, killing thousands.

Operation Just Cause The U.S. invasion of Panama in 1989, after Manuel Noriega rejected the results of a democratic election and claimed he was the "maximum leader" of Panama.

TEACHING IDEA

Incorporating Videos

Assign students to watch Episode 44, "George HW Bush and the End of the Cold War," from the Crash Course US History series (available on YouTube). While watching, students should take notes about President Bush's military efforts. Why were these conflicts, as described by John Green, messier than they had been in the past? Possible answers include: *The Cold War was over, and conflicts were messier because there wasn't a black and white delineation between Soviet-backed and U.S.-backed nations.* Also, ask students to describe how a downturn in the economy led to Bush's declining popularity. Possible answers include: *Interest rates remained high and people lost jobs. Bush was not prepared to handle the economic downturn and, as a wealthy man, appeared out of touch with the American public. Bush also promised that there would be no new taxes and, due to the economic downturn, had to go back on that promise.*

EXPLORING AP® THEMES

America in the World

Put students into groups of 3. In this activity, students will analyze the conflicts in China, Panama, and Iraq, and assess President Bush's responses to the conflicts. After each individual student researches their topic (or reads and summarizes the information in the textbook concerning their topic), students will share the information that they found. While discussing, students should compare and contrast the three conflicts. Were Bush's responses similar, or different? How extreme were his responses? How do these conflicts reflect a continuation of American intervention in other areas of the world?

TEACHING IDEA

Project Idea

For this project, students will take on the role of a newspaper reporter. They can either write a newspaper article or create an audio or video newscast to cover the events leading up to, surrounding, and following Operation Desert Storm. As news reporters, students should remain unbiased and purely factual in their reporting.

▲ Differentiation

Students can work in groups of 3 on this project. Groups can split up the parts of the story so one student covers the events leading up to Desert Storm, one student covers the operation itself, and the third student focuses on the impact of Desert Storm. Allowing students to choose their project medium (written, audio, or video) can also allow students to choose a format that they are familiar with.

BUILDING AP® SKILLS

Argumentation

Have students support the following statement: "The Civil Rights Movement had a lasting impact on Americans. For example, the protests surrounding the Gulf War were inspired by civil rights protests." Students could use the image on this page as evidence, as the protestors reference Martin Luther King, Jr. in their protest signs. In addition, the protest was peaceful, which was a key characteristic of King's protests.

Operation Desert Storm Code name of the 1991 allied air and ground military offensive that pushed Iraqi forces out of Kuwait.

home against waging a war. Demonstrations occurred throughout the nation, and most Americans supported the continued implementation of economic sanctions, which were already causing serious hardships for the Iraqi people. In the face of widespread opposition, the president requested congressional authorization for military operations against Iraq. After long debate, Congress narrowly approved Bush's request.

Saddam Hussein let the deadline pass. On January 16, **Operation Desert Storm** began when the United States launched air attacks on Baghdad and other key targets in Iraq. After a month of bombing, Hussein still refused to capitulate, so a ground offensive was launched on February 24, 1991. More than 500,000 allied troops moved into Kuwait and easily drove Iraqi forces out of that nation; they then moved into southern Iraq. Although Hussein had confidently promised that the U.S.-led military assault would encounter the "mother of all battles," the vastly outmatched Iraqi army, worn out from its ten-year war with Iran, was quickly defeated. Desperate for help, Hussein ordered the firing of Scud missiles on Israel to provoke it into war, which he hoped would drive a wedge between the United States and its Arab allies. Despite sustaining some casualties, Israel refrained from retaliation. The ground war ended within one hundred hours, and Iraq surrendered. An estimated 100,000 Iraqis died; by contrast, 136 Americans perished.

With the war over quickly, President Bush resisted pressure to march to Baghdad and overthrow Saddam Hussein. Bush's stated goal had been to liberate Kuwait; he did not wish to fight a war in the heart of Iraq. The administration believed that such an expedition would involve house-to-house, urban guerrilla warfare. Marching on Baghdad would also entail battling against Hussein's elite Republican Guard, not the weaker conscripts who had put up little resistance in Kuwait. Bush's Arab allies opposed expanding the war, and the president did not want to risk losing their support. Finally, getting rid of Hussein might make matters worse by leaving Iran and its Muslim fundamentalist rulers the dominant power in the region.

Operation Desert Storm succeeded because of its limited military objectives. President Bush and his advisers understood that the United States had triumphed because it had pieced together a genuine coalition of nations, including Arab ones, to coordinate diplomatic and military action. Military leaders had a clear and defined mission — the liberation of Kuwait — as well as adequate troops and supplies. When they carried out their purpose, the war was over. However, American withdrawal later allowed Saddam Hussein to slaughter thousands of Iraqi rebels, including Kurds and Shi'ites, to whom Bush had promised support. In effect, the Bush administration had applied the Cold War policy of limited containment in dealing with Hussein.

This successful U.S. military intervention in the Middle East provided President Bush an opportunity to address other explosive issues in the region. Following the end of the Iraq war, Bush set in motion the peace process that brought the Israelis and Palestinians together to sign a 1993 agreement providing for eventual Palestinian self-government in the Gaza Strip and the West Bank. In doing so, the United States for the first time officially recognized Yasser Arafat, the head of the PLO, whom both the Israelis and the Americans had previously labeled a terrorist.

In several areas of the globe, the move toward democracy that had begun in the late 1980s proceeded peacefully into the 1990s. The oppressive, racist system of apartheid fell in South Africa, and antiapartheid activist Nelson Mandela was released after

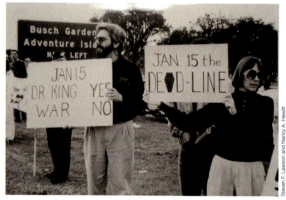

◀ **Gulf War Protests, 1991** The United States gave Iraq a January 15, 1991 deadline to withdraw from Kuwait or face military force. Protesters at the University of South Florida in Tampa favored continued diplomatic efforts. They carry signs that refer to the January 15 deadline, which also is the birthday of Martin Luther King Jr., a critic of U.S. militarism. **How does the choice to use Martin Luther King Jr.'s birthday as a date for Gulf War protests show continuity with social movements and conflicts of the 1960s?**

twenty-seven years in prison to become president of the country in 1994. In 1990 Chilean dictator Augusto Pinochet stepped down as president of Chile and ceded control to a democratically elected candidate. That same year, the pro-Communist Sandinista government lost at the polls in Nicaragua, and in 1992 the ruling regime in El Salvador signed a peace accord with the rebels.

Despite his successes abroad, Bush's popularity plunged at home. After the president dispatched American troops and defeated Iraqi military forces in Kuwait in 1991, his approval rating stood at a whopping 89 percent. In sharp contrast, Bush's poll numbers plummeted to 34 percent in 1992. This precipitous decline resulted mainly from the fact that the economy continued to sag.

Bush ran for reelection against Governor William Jefferson (Bill) Clinton of Arkansas. Learning from the mistakes of Michael Dukakis as well as the successes of Reagan, Clinton ran as a centrist Democrat who promised to reduce the federal deficit by raising taxes on the wealthy and who supported conservative social policies such as the death penalty, tough measures against crime, and welfare reform. Though he did pledge to extend health care and opposed discrimination against homosexuals, Clinton relied on his mainstream southern Democratic credentials to deflect any claims that he was a liberal. Bush also faced a challenge from the independent candidate Ross Perot, a wealthy self-made businessman from Texas, whose campaign against rising government deficits won 19 percent of the popular vote, mostly at Bush's expense. In turn, Clinton defeated the incumbent by a two-to-one electoral margin.

> **AP® TIP**
> Be sure you can explain how the conservatism of the 1980s affected the election of 1992.

REVIEW

- How did Bush's efforts to manage international conflict after the end of the Cold War affect his popularity at home?

AP® WRITING HISTORICALLY   Short-Answer Question Practice

ACTIVITY

Read the following question carefully and write a short response. Use complete sentences.

Using the following image, answer (a), (b), and (c).

Source: Jeff Hook, *If at first...*, 1990

About the source: Saddam Hussein is pictured on the left, and Adolf Hitler is pictured on the right.

a. Briefly describe ONE perspective about the United States' role in the world after the Cold War that is expressed in this image.
b. Briefly explain ONE specific U.S. action or policy in the period 1900–1945 that led to the historical situation depicted in the image.
c. Briefly explain ONE specific U.S. action or policy in the period 1945–1990 that led to debates over the United States' role in world affairs.

TRM Suggested Responses to Questions

EXPLORING AP® THEMES
Work, Exchange, and Technology

Have students search national news websites or local newspapers to find news articles that cover the increase of employment in the service sector or the decrease in employment in the manufacturing industry in the United States. Search keywords such as "service sector employment 1990s." Available news websites vary by region and paid school subscriptions. Ask students to write a one-paragraph summary to describe the main points of the article that they chose. Students should then share their summary with a small group of students and discuss the prompt: "Explain why service sector employment increased and manufacturing decreased, which led to a decline in union membership, during the 1990s." This will allow students to focus on one of the learning targets.

EXPLORING AP® THEMES
Work, Exchange, and Technology

As an extension activity to the previous note, consider allowing students to find current articles that cover the growth or decline of employment in the service sector and manufacturing industries. Discuss these articles with students: Have the trends that began in the 1990s — the service sector growth and the decline of employment in manufacturing — continued? In what ways? Students will find that the trend has continued over time, though there has been a small push to increase employment in American manufacturing industries recently instead of outsourcing jobs overseas.

Module 9-3

Toward the Twenty-First Century

LEARNING TARGETS
By the end of this module, you should be able to:
- Explain how debates regarding free-trade, government programs, and the financial system shaped domestic policies during the closing years of the twentieth century.
- Explain how debates over immigration policy, diversity, and gender roles shaped political discourse.
- Explain how digital communications enabled increased economic opportunities on a global scale.
- Explain how computers, mobile technology, and the Internet shaped daily life in the United States.
- Explain why service sector employment increased and manufacturing decreased, which led to a decline in union membership, during the 1990s.

THEMATIC FOCUS
Work, Exchange, and Technology
Migration and Settlement

Starting in the 1990s, the United States underwent profound economic, technological, and social changes. Americans elected the first president born after World War II, Bill Clinton, who was also the first president in nearly fifty years who did not have to fight the Cold War. Throughout the decade, Americans continued to debate the legacy of the 1960s, while at the same time, they embraced new digital technologies that opened the economy to new markets. High levels of domestic consumption of foreign-made goods transformed the U.S. economy from a focus on manufacturing to a focus on service.

HISTORICAL REASONING FOCUS
Causation

TASK ▶ As you read this module, consider the causes of the cultural and economic changes in the United States during the 1990s.

The 1990s marked a period of great optimism, economic growth, and technological advancement in the United States. President Bill Clinton, the first president born after 1945, promised a youthful optimism in the aftermath of the Cold War. His wife, Hillary Rodham Clinton, was influenced by the ideals of 1960s feminism and aimed to be politically and socially active in the role of First Lady. The nation also underwent a technological revolution. Computers allowed both small and large businesses to reach new markets and transform the workplace. Digital technology also altered the way individuals worked, purchased goods and services, communicated, and spent their leisure time. As the Internet connected Americans to the rest of the world, corporate leaders embraced globalization as the key to economic prosperity. They put together business mergers so that their companies could operate more powerfully in the international market. Government officials generally supported their efforts by reducing regulations on business and financial practices. Globalization not only thrust American business enterprises outward but also brought a new population of immigrants to the United States.

BUILDING AP® SKILLS
Developments and Processes

Put students into groups of 3. Assign each individual student in each group one of the following topics: immigration policy, diversity, and gender roles. Require students to determine how debates over their individual topics shaped political discourse at this time. Have students discuss within their groups so all students have an understanding of each topic.

Clinton's Domestic and Economic Policy

AP® TIP

Evaluate the degree to which Clinton administration policies marked a dramatic change from the policies of conservatism in the 1980s.

Family and Medical Leave Act 1993 act protecting individuals' right to take up to twelve weeks of unpaid leave for medical reasons or parenthood without risk of losing their jobs.

Brady Handgun Violence Prevention Act 1993 act establishing a five-day waiting period and background check for gun buyers.

Bill Clinton served five terms as Democratic governor of his home state of Arkansas. As governor, Clinton supported equal opportunity, improved education, and economic development. After defeating President George H. W. Bush in 1992, Clinton entered the White House as the first Democrat to serve as president since Jimmy Carter.

In 1993, Clinton sought to reverse Reagan-Bush policies. He persuaded Congress to raise taxes on wealthy individuals and corporations, while his administration reduced defense spending following the end of the Cold War. Taken together, these measures stimulated an economic growth of 4 percent annually, established over 22 million jobs, lowered the national debt, and created a budget surplus. Clinton further departed from his Republican predecessors by signing executive orders expanding federal assistance for legal abortion. Clinton also approved the 1993 **Family and Medical Leave Act**, which allowed parents to take up to twelve weeks of unpaid leave to care for newborn children without risk of losing their jobs.

The president had less success opening the military to gays and lesbians, though many already served secretly. His policy of "don't ask, don't tell" permitted homosexuals to serve in the armed forces so long as they kept their sexual orientation a secret, a compromise that failed to end discrimination. The Clinton administration's most stinging defeat came when Congress did not pass universal medical coverage, a proposal guided by his wife, Hillary Clinton.

Clinton tried to appeal to voters across the political spectrum on other issues. He signed a tough anticrime law that funded the recruitment of an additional 100,000 police officers to patrol city streets, while supporting gun control legislation. Although the prison population had been on the rise before the 1990s, Clinton's anticrime bill accelerated the rate of incarceration. Critics of the bill believed it had a disproportionately negative effect on African Americans and Latinos. Despite opposition from the **National Rifle Association**, in 1993 Clinton signed the **Brady Handgun Violence Prevention Act** (popularly known as the Brady Bill), which imposed

AP® ANALYZING SOURCES

Source: President Bill Clinton, *Address to Congress on Health Care Reform*, 1993

"Every one of us knows someone who's worked hard and played by the rules and still been hurt by this system that just doesn't work for too many people. . . . We have to preserve and strengthen what is right with the health care system, but we have got to fix what is wrong with it.

Now, we all know what's right. We're blessed with the best health care professionals on Earth, the finest health care institutions, the best medical research, the most sophisticated technology. My mother is a nurse. I grew up around hospitals. Doctors and nurses were the first professional people I ever knew or learned to look up to. They are what is right with this health care system. But we also know that we can no longer afford to continue to ignore what is wrong.

Millions of Americans are just a pink slip[1] away from losing their health insurance and one serious illness away from losing all their savings. Millions more are locked into the jobs they have now just because they or someone in their family has once been sick and they have what is called a preexisting condition. And on any given day, over 37 million Americans, most of them working people and their little children, have no health insurance at all. . . ."

[1] Notification of losing a job.

Questions for Analysis

1. Identify the main strength and the main weakness of the U.S. health care system, according to Clinton.
2. Describe what Clinton broadly proposes as a solution to the health care system's weakness.
3. Evaluate the extent to which Clinton's argument in this excerpt represents a continuation of progressive ideals from the early twentieth century.

APPLY THE TIP

Put students into groups of 5. Assign the following domestic and economic policies of President Clinton to individual students: taxes, defense spending, federal assistance for legal abortion, Family and Medical Leave Act, and "don't ask, don't tell." Students should individually research their topic and prepare to share a description of the topic and how much it marks a change from conservatism with their group. After discussion, have students answer the prompt: "To what extent did the Clinton administration's policies mark a change from the policies of conservatism in the 1980s?" Students will recognize that each topic marked a great change from conservatism, though the Family and Medical Leave Act stressed women's rights as well as family values, an issue important to conservatives.

TRM Suggested Responses to Questions

TRM Module 9.3 AP® Analyzing Sources Handout 1

TEACHING IDEA

Incorporating Videos

Consider showing the Netflix documentary *13th* (netflix.com). This critically acclaimed film analyzes the U.S. prison boom and the disproportionate ways that African Americans were negatively affected, which illustrate the structural racism attendant to the effort of the government in the 1980s and 1990s to be tough on crime.

BUILDING AP® SKILLS

Sourcing and Situation

It's important to understand the motivations of a person before and while reading a source. Before reading Bill Clinton's Address to Congress on Health Care Reform, discuss the point of view with students. Students should recognize that in this document, Bill Clinton, a Democrat, is speaking to Congress about a controversial issue: health care. Because the president is speaking to Congress, Clinton is likely trying to persuade Congress to pass legislation concerning health care. Ask a student volunteer to read the first paragraph. Discuss the purpose of Clinton's address. Students should say that Clinton's goal was to improve the health care system. Ask another student volunteer to read the next paragraph. Discuss Clinton's point of view: What about Clinton's background makes him interested in health care reform? Students will point out that Clinton's mother was a nurse and Clinton "grew up around hospitals." Ask a new volunteer to read the last paragraph and allow time for students to answer the Questions for Analysis.

Period 9: 1980–The Present

MODULE 9-3 Toward the Twenty-First Century

Federal Assault Weapons Ban 1994 ban prohibiting the manufacturing and use of semi-automatic firearms in the United States. The law was allowed to expire in 2004.

AP® TIP
Analyze the ways in which America's role in world affairs changed during the 1990s.

North American Free Trade Agreement (NAFTA) Free trade agreement approved in 1993 by the United States, Canada, and Mexico.

Contract with America A document that called for reduced welfare spending, lower taxes, term limits for lawmakers, and a constitutional amendment for a balanced budget. In preparation for the 1994 midterm congressional elections, Republicans, led by Representative Newt Gingrich, drew up this proposal.

Personal Responsibility and Work Opportunity Reconciliation Act 1996 act reforming the welfare system in the United States. The law required adults on the welfare rolls to find work within two years or lose their welfare benefits.

Defense of Marriage Act (DOMA) 1996 act denying married same-sex couples the federal benefits granted to heterosexual married couples. DOMA was ruled unconstitutional in 2013.

a five-day waiting period to check the background of gun buyers and, in 1994, a **Federal Assault Weapons Ban**, which prohibited the production and use of semi-automatic weapons by civilians.

To further expand the nation's economy, Clinton embraced the economic regional cooperation of Europe. In 1993 western European nations formed the **European Union (EU)**, which encouraged free trade and investment among member nations. In 1999 the EU introduced a common currency, the euro, which twenty-three nations have now adopted. Clinton encouraged the formation of similar economic partnerships in North America. In 1993, together with the governments of Mexico and Canada, the U.S. Congress ratified the **North American Free Trade Agreement (NAFTA)**. The agreement removed tariffs and other obstacles to commerce and investment among the three countries to encourage trade. NAFTA produced noteworthy gains: Between 1994 and 2004, trade among NAFTA nations increased by nearly 130 percent. Although Mexico saw a significant drop in poverty rates and a rise in real income, NAFTA harmed workers in the United States to a certain extent. From 1994 to 2007, net manufacturing jobs dropped by 3,654,000 as U.S. companies outsourced their production to Mexico, taking advantage of its low wage and benefits structure. However, many more manufacturing jobs were lost to automation.

Clinton also actively promoted globalization through the **World Trade Organization (WTO)**. Created in 1995, the WTO consists of more than 150 nations and seeks "to ensure that trade flows as smoothly, predictably, and freely as possible." The policies of the WTO generally benefited wealthier nations, such as the United States. From 1978 to 2000, the value of U.S. exports and imports jumped from 17 percent to 25 percent of the gross domestic product.

Despite his free-trade economic policies, conservatives were fiercely opposed to Clinton on several fronts, including the effort to reform health care. Many conservatives also opposed Clinton's liberal positions on issues such as feminism, abortion, affirmative action, and secularism. Opponents called attention to his and his wife's pre-presidential dealings in a controversial real estate development project known as **Whitewater**, which prompted the appointment in 1994 of a special prosecutor to investigate allegations of misconduct.

Facing conservative criticism, the president and the Democratic Party fared poorly in the 1994 congressional elections, losing control of both houses of Congress for the first time since 1952. Republicans, led by House Minority Leader Newt Gingrich of Georgia, championed the **Contract with America**. This document embraced conservative principles, including a constitutional amendment for a balanced budget, reduced welfare spending, lower taxes, and term limits for lawmakers. The election also underscored the increasing electoral influence of white evangelical Christians, who voted in large numbers for Republican candidates.

In the wake of this defeat, Clinton shifted rightward and championed welfare reform. In 1996 he signed the **Personal Responsibility and Work Opportunity Reconciliation Act**. It replaced the Aid to Families with Dependent Children provision of the Social Security law, the basis for welfare in the United States since the New Deal, with a new measure that required adult welfare recipients to find work within two years or lose the benefits provided to families earning less than $7,700 annually. The law also placed a lifetime limit of five years on these federal benefits. Also in 1996, the president approved the **Defense of Marriage Act (DOMA)**, which denied married same-sex couples the federal benefits granted to heterosexual married couples, including Social Security survivor's benefits.

In adopting such positions as welfare reform, Clinton angered many of his liberal supporters but ensured his reelection in 1996. Running against Republican senator Robert Dole of Kansas and the independent candidate Ross Perot, Clinton captured 49 percent of the popular vote and 379 electoral votes. Dole received 41 percent of the vote, and Perot came in a distant third.

During his two terms in office, Clinton faced numerous foreign policy challenges, though these challenges did not result from customary military aggression by one nation against another; rather, the greatest threats came from the implosion of national governments into factionalism and genocide, as well as the dangers posed by Islamic extremists. For example, Clinton faced a long-simmering conflict in the former Communist nation of Yugoslavia. In 1989 Yugoslavia splintered when the predominantly Roman Catholic states of Slovenia and Croatia declared their independence from the largely Russian Orthodox Serbian population in Yugoslavia. In 1992 the mainly Muslim territory of Bosnia-Herzegovina also broke away, despite protests by its substantial Serbian population. As a result, a civil war erupted between Serb and Croatian minorities and the Muslim-dominated

---

TEACHING IDEA

Differing Views

To help students understand the arguments surrounding the ratification of NAFTA, utilize the Stanford History Education Group's lesson titled "NAFTA" (sheg.stanford.edu). The lesson provides a background on the North American Free Trade Agreement as well as three primary sources written by Bill Clinton, Ralph Nader, and Pat Buchanan. Students are required to answer a final prompt that asks students to describe the arguments against NAFTA that Nader and Buchanan presented, as well as how President Clinton addressed those concerns in the words that he spoke at the signing of the legislation.

▲ Differentiation

The Stanford History Education Group's lesson plans offer differentiated documents. Depending on the ability of your students, you may choose to use the edited documents that include vocabulary tips, or you can use the original documents for more advanced readers.

EXPLORING AP® THEMES

America in the World

Put students into groups of 3. Assign each student a topic: European Union (EU), North American Free Trade Agreement (NAFTA), and the World Trade Organization (WTO). Have each student conduct research on their topic and share a short description of their topic with their group. As a group, students will discuss how each of these three topics illustrates a trend toward globalization and international cooperation.

ethnic cleansing Ridding an area of a particular ethnic minority to achieve ethnic uniformity. In the civil war between Serbs and Croatians in Bosnia from 1992 to 1995, the Serbian military attempted to eliminate the Croatian population through murder, rape, and expulsion.

AP® TIP
Compare the Clinton administration's foreign policy with that of George H. W. Bush's administration.

Bosnian government. Supported by Slobodan Milošević, the leader of the neighboring province of Serbia, Bosnian Serbs wrested control of large parts of the region and slaughtered tens of thousands of Muslims through what they euphemistically called **ethnic cleansing**. In 1995 Clinton sponsored NATO bombing raids against the Serbs, dispatched 20,000 American troops as part of a multilateral peacekeeping force, and brokered a peace agreement. In 1999 renewed conflict erupted when Milošević's Serbian government attacked the province of Kosovo to eliminate its Albanian Muslim residents. Clinton and NATO initiated air strikes against the Serbs and placed troops on the ground, actions that preserved Kosovo's independence. Clinton also began to expand NATO into Eastern Europe during his presidency, eventually incorporating the Baltic states and nations like Poland and Hungary into the alliance.

The United States faced an even graver danger from Islamic extremists intent on waging a religious struggle (jihad) against their perceived enemies and establishing a transnational Muslim government, or caliphate. The United States' close relationship with Israel placed it high on the list of terrorist targets, along with pro-American Muslim governments in Egypt, Pakistan, and Indonesia. In 1993 Islamic militants orchestrated the bombing of the World Trade Center's underground garage, killing six people and injuring more than one thousand. Five years later, terrorists blew up American embassies in Kenya and Tanzania, killing hundreds and injuring thousands of local workers and residents. In retaliation, Clinton ordered air strikes against terrorist bases in Sudan and Afghanistan. However, the danger persisted. In 2000 al-Qaeda terrorists blew a gaping hole in the side of the USS *Cole*, a U.S. destroyer anchored in Yemen, killing seventeen American sailors.

AP® TIP
Compare the Whitewater scandal of the Clinton administration to the Watergate scandal of the Nixon administration (Period 8).

During his second term, President Clinton faced a severe domestic challenge to his presidency that led to him being only the second impeached president in American history. Starting in 1995, Clinton had engaged in sexual relations with Monica Lewinsky, a twenty-two-year-old White House intern. Clinton denied these charges under oath and before a national television audience, but when Lewinsky testified about the details of their sexual encounters, the president recanted his earlier statements. After an independent prosecutor concluded that Clinton had committed perjury and obstructed justice, the House voted to impeach the president on December 19, 1998. However, on February 12, 1999, the Senate failed to muster the necessary two-thirds vote to convict Clinton on the impeachment charges.

Clinton's second term also saw economic prosperity. In 1998, the unemployment rate fell to 4.3 percent, the lowest level since the early 1970s. The rate of home ownership reached a record-setting 66 percent. As the "misery index" — a compilation of unemployment and inflation — fell, the gross domestic product grew by more than $250 billion. In 1999 the stock market's Dow Jones average reached a historic high of 10,000 points. That same year the president signed into law a measure that freed banks to merge commercial, investment, and insurance services, prohibited since 1933 under the Glass-Steagall Act, allowing them to undertake profitable but sometimes risky ventures. The Clinton administration boasted that its economic policies had succeeded in canceling the budget deficit, yielding a surplus for the fiscal year 2000. This boom, however, did not affect everyone equally. African Americans and Latinos lagged behind whites economically, and the gap between rich and poor widened as the wealthiest 13,000 American families earned as much income as the poorest 20 million.

REVIEW
- How did policies enacted during Clinton's administration reflect both Democratic and Republican policies from earlier in the twentieth century?

The Computer Revolution

During the 1990s, computers began to revolutionize the lives of average Americans. The first working computers were developed for military purposes during World War II and the Cold War and were enormous in size and cost. Engineers began to reduce the size and cost of computers with the creation of transistors. Invented in the late 1940s, these small electronic devices came into widespread use in running computers during the 1960s. The design of integrated circuits in the 1970s led to the production of microcomputers in which a silicon chip the size

APPLY THE TIP

Put students into groups of four. Require two students in each group to describe Clinton's foreign policy, and the other two to describe George H. W. Bush's foreign policy. After students have completed this first part, have the groups of four discuss and compile a Venn diagram to compare and contrast the foreign policy of the two presidents.

APPLY THE TIP

Put students into pairs. Have one student write down everything that they can remember about the Watergate scandal and the other write down everything they know about the Whitewater scandal. Encourage students to conduct online research, though only allow a maximum of ten minutes to complete this first part of the activity. Require students to include information that covers the 5 W's (who, what, where, when, why) and how. After students have a list of information written, tell the pair to complete a Venn diagram that compares and contrasts the two scandals.

Period 9: 1980–The Present

MODULE 9-3 Toward the Twenty-First Century

AP® TIP
Analyze the effects of new computer technology on America's economy, workers, and culture during the 1990s.

Internet Interconnected computer communication network, which started as a military communication system in the 1970s.

World Wide Web Established in 1991, as a way to access the Internet and connect documents and other resources to one another through hyperlinks.

of a nail head did the work once performed by huge computers. Bill Gates, the founder of **Microsoft**, was not the only one to recognize the potential market of microcomputers for home and business use. Steve Jobs, like Gates a college dropout, founded **Apple Computer Company** with Stephen Wozniak in 1976, turned it into a publicly traded corporation, and became a multimillionaire.

Microchips and digital technology found a market beyond home and office computers. Over the last two decades of the twentieth century, computers came to operate everything from standard appliances such as televisions and telephones, to new electronic devices such as CD players, fax machines, and cell phones. Computers controlled traffic lights on the streets and air traffic in the skies. They also changed the leisure patterns of youth: Many young people preferred to play video games indoors than to engage in outdoor activities. Consumers purchased goods online, and, later, companies such as **eBay** and **Amazon** sold merchandise through the Internet without any retail stores.

The **Internet** — an open, global series of interconnected computer networks that transmit data, information, electronic mail, and other services — grew out of military research in the 1970s, when the Department of Defense constructed a system of computer servers connected to one another throughout the United States. The main objective of this network was to preserve military communications in the event of a Soviet nuclear attack. At the end of the Cold War, the Internet was repurposed for nonmilitary use, linking government, academic, business, and organizational systems. In 1991 the **World Wide Web** came into existence as a way to access the Internet and connect documents and other resources to one another through hyperlinks. By 2019 about 90 percent of people in the United States used the Internet, up from 50 percent in 2000. Internet use worldwide leapt by more than 800 percent between 2000 and 2017, from nearly 361 million people to nearly 4 billion.

The incredible growth of the computer industry led to increased business consolidation, making it possible for large firms to keep control of their far-flung operations by communicating instantly within the United States and throughout the world. The federal government aided the merger process by relaxing financial regulation. Media companies took the greatest advantage of this situation. For example, in 1990 the giant Warner Communications merged with Time Life to create an entertainment empire that included a film studio (Warner Brothers), a television cable network (Home Box Office), a music company (Atlantic Records), a baseball team (the Atlanta Braves), and several magazines (*Time*, *Sports Illustrated*, and *People*).

Other mergers mirrored the trend in the media: The estimated number of business mergers rose from 1,529 in 1991 to 4,500 in 1998. The market value of these transactions in 1998 was approximately $2 trillion, compared with $600 billion for 1989, the previous peak year for consolidation. Corporate consolidation also brought corporate wrongdoing, as some chief executives abused their power by expanding their companies too quickly and making risky financial deals, which put workers and stockholders in jeopardy.

REVIEW

• How did technological innovation during the 1990s change the U.S. economy and culture?

The Changing American Population

AP® TIP
Compare the social, economic, and political effects of immigration to the U.S. during the late twentieth century with the effects of immigration during the late nineteenth century and early twentieth century.

As the technological revolution transformed the U.S. economy and society, an influx of immigrants began to alter the composition of the American population. Since passage of the Immigration Act of 1965, which repealed discriminatory national origins quotas established in 1924, the country had experienced a wave of immigration comparable to that at the turn of the twentieth century. As the population of the United States grew from 202 million to 300 million between 1970 and 2006, immigrants accounted for some 28 million of the increase. They came to the United States for much the same reasons as those arriving earlier: to seek economic opportunity and to find political and religious freedom.

Most newcomers in the 1980s and 1990s arrived from Latin America and South and East Asia. Relatively few Europeans (approximately 2 million) moved to the United States, though their numbers increased after the collapse of the Soviet empire in the early 1990s. Poverty and political unrest pushed migrants out of Mexico, Central America, and the Caribbean. At the beginning of the twenty-first century, Latinos (35 million) had surpassed African Americans (34 million)

BUILDING AP® SKILLS

Making Connections

Ask students to compare online shopping (eBay and Amazon) to catalog shopping (Sears in the late nineteenth century). How did each of these innovations impact the American economy and culture? Possible answers include: *Both online shopping and catalog shopping opened up markets to new consumers who do not live near the stores at which they want to shop. In addition, both led to a boost in the shipping industry and a boost in consumerism. On the other hand, catalogs were sent out by established businesses, but anyone can make an account on eBay and sell their goods. In this way, consumers have become sellers as well.*

EXPLORING AP® THEMES

Work, Exchange, and Technology

In order to guide students to answer the review questions, require students to describe how computers, online shopping, and the Internet as a whole changed the U.S. economy and culture.

TRM Find **Handout 9.6 — Technological Innovation** in the Teacher's Resource Materials.

APPLY THE TIP

Draw a Venn diagram with three intersecting circles on the board. Require students to draw the same diagram in their notes. Label the three sections with Late 20th Century, Late 19th Century, and Early 20th Century. Ask students to compare the social, economic, and political effects of immigration to the U.S. during each of these time periods. Possible answers include: *For all three time periods, American citizens pushed back against increased immigration. Immigrants in the late nineteenth century were mostly from western Europe and China until the Chinese Exclusion Act was passed. In the early twentieth century, immigration from eastern Europe increased and immigrants from Asian nations were barred from entry into the United States. Because of the Immigration and Nationality Act in the late twentieth century, immigration quotas were abolished. As a result, Asian immigration increased and immigrants from Latin America increased until they became the nation's largest minority group.*

The Changing American Population

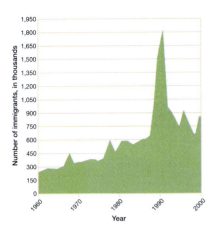

Immigration to the United States rose dramatically in the 1970s and 1980s, peaking in the early 1990s. Between 1970 and 2000, nearly 21 million immigrants arrived in the United States, mainly from Mexico, Central America, the Caribbean, and eastern Asia. **How do these immigration trends compare to those during the late 1800s and early 1900s?**

as the nation's largest minority group. However, with the arrival of Caribbean and African immigrants, black America was also becoming more diverse.

In addition to the 16 million immigrants who came from south of the U.S. border, another 9 million headed eastward from Asia, including Chinese, South Koreans, and Filipinos, together with refugees from Vietnam and Cambodia. By 2010 an estimated 3.18 million Indians from South Asia lived in the United States, most arriving after the 1960s. Indian Americans became the third-largest Asian American group behind Chinese and Filipinos. Another 1 to 2 million people came from predominantly Islamic nations such as Pakistan, Lebanon, Iraq, and Iran.

California displayed this change most vividly. Latinos and Asians had long settled there, and by 2016, 27 percent of the state's population was foreign-born. The majority of Californians consisted of Latinos, Asian Americans, and African Americans, with whites in the minority. In addition to California, immigrants also flocked to the Southwest and to northeastern and midwestern cities like New York City, Jersey City, Chicago, and Detroit. However, now they also fanned out across the Southeast, adding to the growing populations of Atlanta, Raleigh-Durham, Charlotte, Columbia, and Memphis and providing these cities with an unprecedented ethnic mixture. Like immigrants before them, they created their own businesses, spoke their own languages, and retained their own religious and cultural practices.

AP® ANALYZING SOURCES

Source: Jennifer Medina, "New Suburban Dream Born of Asia and Southern California," *New York Times*, 2013

"SAN MARINO, Calif.—Beneath the palm trees that line Huntington Drive, named for the railroad magnate who founded this Southern California city, hang signs to honor families who have helped sponsor the centennial celebration here this year. There are names like Dryden, Crowley and Telleen, families that have lived here for generations. But there are newer names as well: Sun, Koo and Shi.

A generation ago, whites made up roughly two-thirds of the population in this rarefied Los Angeles suburb, where most of the homes are worth well over $1 million. But Asians now make up over half of the population in San Marino, which has long attracted some of the region's wealthiest families and was once home to the John Birch Society's Western headquarters.

The transformation illustrates a drastic shift in California immigration trends over the last decade, one that can easily be seen all over the area: more than twice as many immigrants to the nation's most populous state now come from Asia than from Latin America.

And the change here is just one example of the ways immigration is remaking America, with the political, economic and cultural ramifications playing out in a variety of ways. The number of Latinos has more than doubled in many Southern states, including Alabama, Georgia and North Carolina, creating new tensions. Asian populations are booming in New Jersey, and Latino immigrants are reviving small towns in the Midwest.

Much of the current immigration debate in Congress has focused on Hispanics, and California has for decades been viewed as the focal point of that migration. But in cities

(Continued)

TEACHING IDEA

Incorporating Websites

Show students the interactive immigration map from the Metrocosm article, "Here's Everyone Who's Immigrated to the U.S. Since 1820" (available through online search). Have students jot down notes to describe the patterns they see. Where were immigrants coming from during various time periods? Use the late nineteenth century, early twentieth century, and late twentieth century as reference points. How did immigration to the United States change over time? See the note on page 830 for possible answers about the origins of immigrants during these time periods.

TRM Suggested Responses to Questions

TRM Module 9.3 AP® Analyzing Sources Handout 2

TEACHING IDEA

Incorporating Websites

To help students understand the struggles that immigrants faced upon arriving in the United States, utilize the interactive "Immigrant Experience" from Experience Magazine (expmag.com/immigrant-experience). This website allows students to put themselves into an immigrant's perspective. Students can compare the experience of immigrants across many time periods between 1848 and 2003.

TEACHING IDEA

Connecting the Dots

Ask student volunteers to read through Jennifer Medina's article one paragraph at a time (starting on page 831). After each paragraph, have students write the main idea of the paragraph on their paper. Ask volunteers to share their main points with the class. This will help remind students that slowing down to determine the main point is an important aspect of close reading of a source. This strategy forces students to avoid skimming and ensures a deeper understanding. After reading through the entire article, give students time to answer the Questions for Analysis. Encourage students to try to answer the questions by only using the main points that they wrote down instead of the whole article. This will help students realize if their main points sufficiently sum up the paragraph, or if they need to try rewriting their main points.

TRM Suggested Responses to Questions

TEACHING IDEA

AP® Writing Historically Review

Have students look up the historical theme of Work, Exchange, and Technology in Topic 9.4 of the AP® U.S. History course framework, available from AP® Central (apcentral.collegeboard.org). Have students highlight major concepts that connect to the American manufacturing economy. They will likely identify factors such as technological innovation and worldwide economic opportunities. Students are to select the most relevant example from the topic page and then detail an actual historical example. For instance, if students select technological innovation, they might identify computers, which would be relevant to business' ability to further automate production, thereby illustrating the trend in the line graph. Students should use the topic pages to help identify specific historical examples.

---

in the San Gabriel Valley—as well as in Orange County and in Silicon Valley in Northern California—Asian immigrants have become a dominant cultural force in places that were once largely white or Hispanic.

'We are really looking at a different era here,' said Hans Johnson, a demographer at the Public Policy Institute of California who has studied census data. 'There are astounding changes in working-class towns and old, established, wealthy cities. It is not confined to one place.'

Asians have become a majority in more than half a dozen cities in the San Gabriel Valley in the last decade, creating a region of Asian-dominated suburbs that stretches for nearly 30 miles east of Los Angeles. In the shopping centers, Chinese-language characters are on nearly every storefront, visible from the freeways that cut through the area. . . ."

Questions for Analysis

1. Identify the demographic changes Medina notes in this excerpt.
2. Explain how these demographic changes have transformed the regions Medina describes.
3. Evaluate the extent to which the demographic changes Medina describes represent a change in the history of immigration to the United States.

REVIEW

What accounts for the changing demographics of immigrants to the United States during the 1990s?

AP® WRITING HISTORICALLY — Short-Answer Question Practice

ACTIVITY

Read the following question carefully and write a short response. Use complete sentences.

Using the following image, answer (a), (b), and (c).

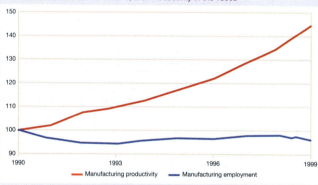

Source: St. Louis Federal Reserve, *U.S. Productivity in the 1990s*

a. Briefly explain how ONE specific historical factor contributed to the change depicted on the graph.
b. Briefly explain ONE specific historical effect that resulted from the change depicted on the graph.
c. Briefly explain ANOTHER specific historical effect that resulted from the change depicted on the graph.

Module 9-4

The Global War on Terror and Political Conflict at Home

LEARNING TARGETS

By the end of this module, you should be able to:

- Explain how in the twenty-first century the effects of free-trade agreements, the scope of the social safety net, and growth of the U.S. financial system continued to shape policy debates.
- Explain how issues such as immigration, social diversity, gender roles, and family structure continued to shape cultural and political debates.
- Explain why economic inequality grew in the early twenty-first century.
- Explain why the United States became involved in conflicts in Afghanistan and Iraq.
- Explain how increased security measures after the September 11 attacks raised debates about civil liberties at home and abroad.
- Explain how concerns about climate change have affected the foreign and domestic policies pursued by the United States in the twenty-first century.

THEMATIC FOCUS

Work, Exchange, and Technology
Politics and Power
America in the World

At the dawn of the twenty-first century, the United States stood at the center of a global economy that stretched across the planet, from production centers in Asia, through regions of high consumption in Western Europe and the United States. But these economic changes, generally called "globalization," also caused unemployment among manufacturing workers in North America and Western Europe while at the same time benefitting consumers with lower prices. Also in the twenty-first century, Americans could no longer convince themselves that war and environmental degradation were worries for people far away as terrorist attacks by non-state groups, both domestic and international, shook American society and the effects of climate change became increasingly apparent throughout the world.

HISTORICAL REASONING FOCUS

Causation

TASK ▶ While reading this module, consider the causes of the economic and social changes experienced by Americans during the first two decades of the twenty-first century, and determine the effects of those changes.

TRM Suggested Responses to Questions

At the beginning of the twenty-first century, the United States found itself the sole superpower, with peace at home and what appeared to be a future of free markets and international peace abroad.

President George W. Bush began his presidency with a call for "compassionate conservativism," including faith-based policy initiatives to temper the rougher elements of modern free-market capitalism. However, eight months into his presidency, the terrorist attacks on September 11, 2001 occurred, and the Bush administration was faced with its first major challenge. By 2003, policymakers had established new forms of surveillance to prevent future attacks, and had entered into conflicts in Afghanistan and Iraq in an attempt to wage a global war on terrorism.

The new century also experienced an economic shock and long recession brought about by changes in the American economy. Barack Obama, the nation's first African-American president, faced two terms with economic challenges, lingering overseas conflicts in the Middle East, and strong resistance from conservatives. Obama nevertheless saw the Great Recession end during his presidency, and he expanded access to healthcare. However, prosperity returned unevenly.

In 2016, Republican nominee Donald Trump won the presidential election against Hillary Clinton, the Democratic nominee, in a close race.

BUILDING AP® SKILLS

Argumentation

Ask students to determine: Has globalization made us more connected, or more detached? Consider the involvement of the United States in overseas conflicts such as conflicts in the Middle East, the impact of the Internet on the economy and society, as well as increased globalization of business and the outsourcing of jobs, including manufacturing work. This exercise will give students more practice with the term "globalization" and an increased understanding of the concept.

TEACHING IDEA

Class Discussion

To address the learning target, "Explain how increased security measures after the September 11th attacks raised debates about civil liberties at home and abroad," first discuss the attacks themselves. Next, divide the class into three groups. Within the groups, put students into pairs. Have one student from each pair in Group One research the Patriot Act and find reasons to support its passage. Have the other student from each pair in Group One research the Patriot Act and find reasons to oppose its passage. This way, each pair has one student supporting the policy and one student opposing the policy. Split up Group Two in the same way, asking one student in each pair to support increased airport security and the other to oppose it. Group Three will be split up so one student in each pair will support the use of Guantanamo Bay as a detention center for suspected terrorists, while the other student will oppose it. For Group Three, ask students to steer clear of debates about the use of torture, as it can be agreed that torture is unethical; instead, focus on the incarceration of suspects without the guarantee of a trial. After students have researched, allow students to discuss within their pairs. You could also structure the discussion in a way so students are searching for advantages and disadvantages of each policy, especially if you prefer a tamer discussion instead of a debate.

Bush and Compassionate Conservatism

In 2000 the Democratic candidate, Vice President Al Gore, ran against George W. Bush, the Republican governor of Texas and son of the forty-first president. Gore ran on the coattails of the Clinton prosperity while Bush campaigned as a "compassionate conservative." Also in the race was Ralph Nader, an anti-corporate activist who ran under the banner of the Green Party, a party formed in 1991 to support grassroots democracy, environmentalism, social justice, and gender equality.

AP® ANALYZING SOURCES

Source: George W. Bush, *Presidential Nomination Acceptance Speech*, 2000

"Tonight, in this hall, we resolve to be . . . not the party of repose, but the party of reform. We will write, not footnotes, but chapters in the American story. . . .

We will strengthen Social Security and Medicare for the greatest generation, and for generations to come. Medicare does more than meet the needs of our elderly, it reflects the values of our society. We will set it on firm financial ground, and make prescription drugs available and affordable for every senior who needs them. . . .

Now is the time for Republicans and Democrats to end the politics of fear and save Social Security, together.

For younger workers, we will give you the option — your choice — to put a part of your payroll taxes into sound, responsible investments. This will mean a higher return on your money, and, over 30 or 40 years, a nest egg to help your retirement, or pass on to your children. When this money is in your name, in your account, it's not just a program, it's your property.

Now is the time to give American workers security and independence that no politician can ever take away.

On education, too many American children are segregated into schools without standards, shuffled from grade-to-grade because of their age, regardless of their knowledge. This is discrimination, pure and simple — the soft bigotry of low expectations. And our nation should treat it like other forms of discrimination. . . . We should end it.

One size does not fit all when it comes to educating our children, so local people should control local schools.

And those who spend your tax dollars must be held accountable. When a school district receives federal funds to teach poor children, we expect them to learn. And if they don't, parents should get the money to make a different choice. . . .

I will use this moment of opportunity to bring common sense and fairness to the tax code. And I will act on principle. . . .

On principle, no one in America should have to pay more than a third of their income to the federal government. So we will reduce tax rates for everyone, in every bracket.

On principle, those in the greatest need should receive the greatest help. So we will lower the bottom rate from 15% to 10% and double the child [tax] credit. . . .

Big government is not the answer.

But the alternative to bureaucracy is not indifference. It is to put conservative values and conservative ideas into the thick of the fight for justice and opportunity.

This is what I mean by compassionate conservatism. And on this ground we will lead our nation."

Questions for Analysis

1. Identify three reforms George W. Bush proposes in this speech.
2. Describe the ways in which these reforms, according to Bush, will improve American society and boost the economy.
3. Evaluate the extent to which these reforms are similar to those of the Progressive Era (1900–1920).

EXPLORING AP® THEMES

Politics and Power

Put students into groups of 3. Have each group read through George W. Bush's entire *Presidential Nomination Acceptance Speech*. To address the Questions for Analysis, assign one of the three reforms mentioned to each student in the group: Social Security and Medicare, education, and tax reform. Students should "describe the ways in which the reform, according to Bush, will improve American society and boost the economy." Next, have students create a Venn diagram to compile their responses for question three: "Evaluate the extent to which these reforms are similar to those of the Progressive Era (1900–1920)."

TRM Suggested Responses to Questions

TRM Module 9.4 AP® Analyzing Sources Handout 1

TEACHING IDEA

Incorporating Videos

Have students watch the History Channel's "How the U.S. Supreme Court Decided the Presidential Election of 2000" (available on YouTube). The video covers the election of 2000 and explains why Florida was so important to the election. The video also addresses the Supreme Court ruling in *Bush v. Gore* (2000). After watching, have students write three sentences to summarize the controversy surrounding the election as well as the results.

Nader's candidacy drew votes away from Gore, who won a narrow plurality of the popular vote (48.4 percent, compared with 47.8 percent for Bush and 2.7 percent for Nader). However, Bush won a slim majority of the electoral votes: 271 to 267. The key state in this Republican victory was Florida, where George W. Bush's brother, Jeb Bush, was governor, and where Bush outpolled Gore by fewer than 500 popular votes. When litigation over the recount reached the U.S. Supreme Court in December 2000, the Court, which included conservative justices appointed by Ronald Reagan and George H. W. Bush, proclaimed Bush the winner.

While Republicans still controlled the House, the Democrats had gained a one-vote majority in the Senate. President Bush promoted the agenda of the evangelical Christian wing of the Republican Party and spoke out against gay marriage, abortion, and federal support for stem cell research, a scientific procedure that used discarded embryos to research cures for diseases. Bush created a special office in the White House to coordinate **faith-based initiatives**, providing religious institutions with federal funds for social service activities without violating the First Amendment's separation of church and state.

These initiatives reflected a change in American religious life at the turn of the twenty-first century, when a growing number of churchgoers were joining megachurches. These Protestant congregations each contained 2,000 or more worshippers. Between 1970 and 2005, the number

faith-based initiatives White House initiative under George W. Bush that created a special office to provide religious institutions with federal funds for social services.

AP® ANALYZING SOURCES

Source: *Sanctuary Building of the First Baptist Church in Dallas, Texas, 2014*

About the source: This photograph shows the modernist sanctuary building that is part of the First Baptist Church, a megachurch with nearly 10,000 members located in Dallas, Texas. The former building that housed this church, originally built in the 1890s, can be seen in the reflection of the windows beside the doors.

Questions for Analysis
1. Explain the ways in which this building conveys details specific to American religious life during the twenty-first century.
2. Explain how this photograph reveals continuity with earlier American religious traditions.
3. Evaluate the extent to which the growth of megachurches during the twenty-first century reflects changes in American society.

TEACHING IDEA

Check for Understanding

In the Electoral College system, a presidential candidate must win 270 electoral votes to win the election. Third parties have historically been able to win electoral votes, but sometimes third parties act as more of an election "spoiler" than intended. For example, in the election of 2000, Republican George W. Bush ran against the Democrat Al Gore. Ralph Nader, a candidate running for the Green Party, was a third-party candidate in the election. Because Nader appealed to those on the left side of the political spectrum, some of the more liberal Americans voted for Nader instead of Gore. Gore won the popular vote with a plurality but lost the election to George W. Bush by a close margin of electoral votes. This "spoiler effect" is an unintended consequence of third parties.

of megachurches jumped from 50 to more than 1,300, with California, Texas, and Florida taking the lead. The establishment of massive churches was part of a worldwide movement, with South Korea home to the largest congregation. Joel Osteen—the evangelical pastor of Lakewood Church in Houston, Texas, the largest megachurch in the United States—drew average weekly audiences of 43,000 people, with sermons available in English and Spanish.

During his presidency, Bush also pursued policies that appealed to economic conservatives. In 2001, Bush signed the Economic Growth and Tax Relief Reconciliation Act, and in 2003, he signed the Jobs and Growth Tax Relief Reconciliation Act. Both of these acts provided tax cuts to most Americans. However, critics of these policies believed that causing growing deficits without substantially reducing government spending would ultimately hinder economic growth and worsen income inequality.

At the same time, Bush showed the compassionate side of his conservatism. His cabinet appointments reflected racial, ethnic, and gender diversity. They included African Americans Colin Powell, secretary of state, and national security adviser Condoleezza Rice, who later succeeded Powell as secretary of state. Bush's compassionate conservatism also included educational reform, under the program **No Child Left Behind (NCLB)**, which sought to raise national standards and education opportunity, especially for those attending school in underprivileged areas. In addition, in 2003 Bush signed into law the **Medicare Prescription Drug, Improvement, and Modernization Act**, which aimed to lower the cost of prescription drugs to some 40 million senior citizens enrolled in Medicare.

No Child Left Behind (NCLB) 2001 legislation that aimed to raise national standards in education in underprivileged areas.

Medicare Prescription Drug, Improvement, and Modernization Act Also known as the Medicare Modernization Act, a 2003 act that dramatically expanded Medicare benefits and reduced costs associated with prescriptions.

REVIEW

In what ways did George W. Bush's version of "compassionate conservativism" differ from his father's domestic policies, and in what ways did it show continuity with them?

International and Domestic Challenges

President Bush ultimately spent little of his presidency focusing on domestic issues, however. Events originating abroad vaulted him into the role of wartime president. In foreign affairs, Bush relied heavily on Vice President Richard (Dick) Cheney, Secretary of Defense Donald Rumsfeld, and Condoleezza Rice. The president's closest advisers sought to reshape critical parts of the post–Cold War world through preemptive force, most notably in the Persian Gulf.

Less than a year into the Bush presidency, the United States experienced the worst terrorist attack in its history. The terrorist organization responsible for the attack was al-Qaeda, which began in the late 1980s as one of many groups who fought the Soviet Union's occupation of Afghanistan. However, starting in the 1990s, the group's leader, Osama bin Laden, increasingly aimed the organization's efforts against the United States because of its support for Israel and its occupation of bases in Saudi Arabia in the aftermath of the first Gulf War. On September 11, 2001, nineteen al-Qaeda terrorists hijacked four American planes from airports in Boston, Washington, D.C., and Newark, New Jersey. Two groups of these terrorists hijacked two planes departing from Boston and crashed them into the Twin Towers at the World Trade Center in New York City. A third group of terrorists hijacked and crashed a third plane into the Pentagon in Washington, D.C. While passengers on the fourth plane attempted to halt the attack by charging the cockpit, the terrorists in control of the plane crashed it in the Pennsylvania countryside. After the Twin Towers burned for over two hours, both collapsed, killing civilians and rescue workers inside. All told, almost 3,000 Americans died in the 9/11 attacks.

After the attacks on the World Trade Center and the Pentagon, Bush launched a **Global War on Terror (GWOT)** that led to protracted and costly conflicts in Afghanistan and Iraq and debates over civil liberties at home. First, the president dispatched U.S. troops to Afghanistan, whose Taliban leaders refused to turn over Osama bin Laden and other terrorists operating training centers in the country. A combination of anti-Taliban warlords and U.S. military forces toppled the Taliban regime and installed a pro-American government; however, the elusive bin Laden escaped into a remote area of Pakistan.

On the home front, the war on terror prompted passage of the **Patriot Act** in October 2001. The measure eased restrictions on domestic and foreign intelligence gathering and expanded the authority of law enforcement and immigration officials in detaining and deporting immigrants

AP® TIP
Evaluate the extent to which the Global War on Terror marked a shift in American foreign policy.

Global War on Terror (GWOT) Military campaign launched by the George W. Bush administration after the September 11, 2001 attacks. The campaign led to long and costly conflicts in Afghanistan and Iraq.

Patriot Act 2001 law passed in response to the September 11 terror attacks. The law eased restrictions on domestic and foreign intelligence gathering and expanded governmental power to deport immigrants suspected of terrorism.

BUILDING AP® SKILLS

Comparison

Assign students to compare and contrast George W. Bush's "compassionate conservatism" with George H. W. Bush's "kinder and gentler conservatism" to help them answer the review question.

TRM Find **Handout 9.7 — Domestic Policies of George W. Bush and George H. W. Bush** in the Teacher's Resource Materials.

EXPLORING AP® THEMES

Politics and Power

To increase understanding of the Patriot Act, use the lesson plan titled "Security, Liberty, and the USA PATRIOT ACT" on the Bill of Rights Institute website (billofrightsinstitute.org). This lesson requires students to evaluate which civil liberties might be threatened by the Patriot Act and asks students if the Act provides a balance between security and liberty.

BUILDING AP® SKILLS

Comparison

Show a video of President Franklin D. Roosevelt's "Day of Infamy" Speech and George W. Bush's "Address to the Nation" following the September 11th attacks (both speeches are available separately on YouTube). There are different length videos of each, so you can either show the entire speech or just a clip, depending on the time that you have available. Before watching, ask students to draw a Venn diagram in their notes. Source each video by discussing the historical context and point of view and write the sourcing information in the Venn diagram. While watching, ask students to use the diagram to record the main points of the speech as well as the tone of the speakers. After watching, discuss the intended audience of each speech as well as the purpose.

▲ Differentiation

While watching the videos, turn on the closed captioning or provide a transcript of the speeches to your students. This will help them follow along with the words in a visual form as well as in audio form. Students will also be able to reread portions that they may not have understood, or possibly missed while writing down information.

International and Domestic Challenges

Period 9: 1980–The Present

AP® TIP
Compare the Global War on Terror's impact on civil liberties with the effects of other conflicts, including the Civil War, World War I, and World War II.

Department of Homeland Security A cabinet-level agency created in 2002 that is responsible for developing a national strategy against terrorist threats.

AP® TIP
Evaluate the extent to which the Bush Doctrine represented a continuation of American foreign policy.

Bush Doctrine President George W. Bush's proposal to engage in preemptive war against tyrannical governments that were perceived as a threat to U.S. national security, even if the danger was not immediate.

axis of evil Term coined by president George W. Bush in 2002. Bush claimed Iraq, Iran, and North Korea were a part of an "axis of evil" due to their support of terrorist organizations and pursuit of chemical, biological, and nuclear weapons.

suspected of terrorism-related acts. The act gave law enforcement agencies nearly unlimited authority to wiretap telephones, retrieve e-mail messages, and search the medical, financial, and library borrowing records of individuals, including U.S. citizens, suspected of involvement in terrorism overseas or at home. The computer age had provided terrorist networks like al-Qaeda with the means to communicate quickly across national borders through electronic mail and cell phones and to raise money and launder it into safe bank accounts online. Computer technology also gave U.S. intelligence agencies ways to monitor these communications and transactions. Despite some criticism of the provisions of the Patriot Act as harsh, in 2006 Congress renewed the act with only minor changes.

As part of the effort to monitor terrorist threats to America, in 2002 Congress created a cabinet-level superagency, the **Department of Homeland Security**, responsible for developing a national strategy against further terrorist threats. In 2004 Congress created the Office of the Director of National Intelligence to coordinate the work of security agencies more effectively.

Amid rising anti-Muslim sentiments in the weeks and months following September 11, some people committed acts of violence against mosques, Arab American community centers and businesses, and individual Muslims and people they thought were Muslims.

President Bush and his advisers sought to expand the war on terror beyond defeating the Taliban in Afghanistan. They envisioned a larger plan to reshape the politics of the Middle East and Persian Gulf regions along pro-American lines. By replacing authoritarian regimes with democratic governments in places like Iraq and Afghanistan, the Bush administration envisioned a domino effect that would lead to the toppling of reactionary leaders throughout the region. Political stability and pro-western governments in these regions would also ensure that they continued to export enough natural resources, such as oil, to meet consumer demand in the United States and its European allies. In crafting this strategy, the Bush administration departed from the post–World War II policy of containing enemies short of going to war. Instead, the **Bush Doctrine** proposed undertaking preemptive war against despotic governments deemed a threat to U.S. national security, even if that danger was not imminent.

Embracing this doctrine, President Bush declared in January 2002 that Iraq was part of an "**axis of evil**," along with Iran and North Korea. The Bush administration considered Saddam Hussein, the Iraqi dictator, a sponsor of terrorism and sought to remove him from power. The administration believed this would also open a path to overthrowing the radical Islamic government of neighboring Iran.

AP® ANALYZING SOURCES

Source: Office of the President, *Proposal to Create the Department of Homeland Security*, 2002

"The President proposes to create a new Department of Homeland Security, the most significant transformation of the U.S. government in over a half-century by largely . . . realigning the current confusing patchwork of government activities into a single department whose primary mission is to protect our homeland. The creation of a Department of Homeland Security is one more key step in the President's national strategy for homeland security.

Immediately after last fall's attack, the President took decisive steps to protect America—from hardening cockpits and stockpiling vaccines to tightening our borders. The President used his maximum legal authority to establish the White House Office of Homeland Security and the Homeland Security Council to ensure that our federal response and protection efforts were coordinated and effective. The President also directed Homeland Security Advisor Tom Ridge to study the federal government as a whole to determine if the current structure allows us to meet the threats of today while anticipating the unknown threats of tomorrow. After careful study of the current structure—coupled with the experience gained since September 11 and new information we have learned about our enemies while

(Continued)

BUILDING AP® SKILLS

Argumentation

After students learn about the Patriot Act, use the lesson plan titled "2015: Debating the USA PATRIOT Act" on the Newseum website (newseumed.org). This lesson asks students to consider how Congress should act when weighing security and privacy.

TRM Suggested Responses to Questions

TRM Module 9.4 AP® Analyzing Sources Handout 3

BUILDING AP® SKILLS

Sourcing and Situation

The *Proposal to Create the Department of Homeland Security* is a great document to use to review historical context. Students should recognize that, due to the attacks on September 11, 2001 and the growing threat of terrorism, the Bush administration felt it was necessary to create a new executive department.

fighting a war—the President concluded that our nation needs a more unified homeland security structure. In designing the new Department, the Administration considered a number of homeland security organizational proposals that have emerged from outside studies, commissions, and Members of Congress."

Questions for Analysis

1. Describe the changes the creation of the Department of Homeland Security is meant to bring.
2. Explain how this document reveals the rationale for founding the Department of Homeland Security.
3. Evaluate the extent to which the creation of the Department of Homeland Security represents a continuity in American policies during international conflict throughout the twentieth century.

Source: President George W. Bush, *News Conference on Iraq*, 2003

"This has been an important week on two fronts on our war against terror. First, thanks to the hard work of American and Pakistani officials, we captured the mastermind of the September the 11th attacks against our nation. Khalid Sheikh Mohammed conceived and planned the hijackings and directed the actions of the hijackers. We believe his capture will further disrupt the terror network and their planning for additional attacks.

Second, we have arrived at an important moment in confronting the threat posed to our nation and to peace by Saddam Hussein and his weapons of terror. In New York tomorrow, the United Nations Security Council will receive an update from the chief weapons inspector. The world needs him to answer a single question: Has the Iraqi regime fully and unconditionally disarmed, as required by Resolution 1441, or has it not? . . .

Iraqi operatives continue to hide biological and chemical agents to avoid detection by inspectors. In some cases, these materials have been moved to different locations every 12 to 24 hours, or placed in vehicles that are in residential neighborhoods. . . .

These are not the actions of a regime that is disarming. These are the actions of a regime engaged in a willful charade. These are the actions of a regime that systematically and deliberately is defying the world. If the Iraqi regime were disarming, we would know it, because we would see it. Iraq's weapons would be presented to inspectors, and the world would witness their destruction. Instead, with the world demanding disarmament, and more than 200,000 troops positioned near his country, Saddam Hussein's response is to produce a few weapons for show, while he hides the rest and builds even more."

Questions for Analysis

1. Identify the ways in which Saddam Hussein's actions raised suspicions about his willingness to disarm.
2. Explain how President Bush drew connections between the September 11, 2001 attacks and Saddam Hussein's actions.
3. Explain how this document illustrates the Bush Doctrine.
4. Evaluate the extent of continuity in American foreign policy regarding Iraq during the presidencies of George H. W. Bush (1989–1993) and George W. Bush (2001–2009).

Questions for Comparison

1. Explain the immediate effects of the conflict with Iraq and the creation of the Department of Homeland Security on American domestic and international policy.
2. Evaluate the extent to which President Bush's news conference remarks reflect the same goals that led to the creation of the Department of Homeland Security.

BUILDING AP® SKILLS

Comparison

Put students into pairs. Have half of the groups in the class read the *Proposal to Create the Department of Homeland Security* and have the other half read Bush's *News Conference on Iraq*. After reading, each group should answer the Questions for Analysis. Once the questions are answered, have each pair group up with one other pair that read the opposite document. Have students discuss what they have read as well as their responses to the questions. Then, as a group of 4, students should answer the Questions for Comparison. Allow time for discussion and debate, as the answers for the last portion could vary based on the interpretation of the student.

TEACHING IDEA

Incorporating Websites

Visit the Department of Homeland Security's website (dhs.gov). In the menu at the top of the page, navigate to "Topics." Give students time to go through each of the topics to determine the current roles of the Department of Homeland Security. Ask students to compare the current responsibilities with the original intent of the Department (review the *Proposal to Create the Department of Homeland Security* to determine the original purpose). To what extent have the responsibilities of the Department changed over time? Do new responsibilities still reflect the original goals of the Department?

Operation Iraqi Freedom 2003–2011 military conflict that began when the U.S. and its allies launched an invasion of Iraq in an effort to overthrow its dictatorship.

By late 2002, Congress and a majority of the American people were convinced that Iraq presented an immediate danger to the security of the United States. This was due in part to the misconception that Saddam Hussein was connected to the 9/11 al-Qaeda terrorists. The administration also believed that Iraq was well advanced in building and stockpiling "weapons of mass destruction," despite evidence to the contrary. In March 2003, after a congressional vote of approval, U.S. military aircraft unleashed bombing attacks on Baghdad. In the 1991 Gulf War, the first President Bush had responded to the Iraqi invasion of Kuwait by leading a broad coalition of nations, including Arab countries. In 2003 the United States led a smaller alliance of nations, with only Great Britain supplying significant combat troops to **Operation Iraqi Freedom**. Within weeks Hussein went into hiding, and he was captured several months later.

Although it at first appeared to many that the military conflict would be short-lived, the war dragged on, despite the presence of 130,000 U.S. and 30,000 British troops. More American soldiers — over 4,000 — died after the invasion than had died during it. The perception of the United States as an occupying power destabilized Iraq, leading to a civil war between the country's Shi'ite Muslim majority, which had been persecuted under Saddam Hussein, and its Sunni minority, which Hussein represented. In the northern part of the nation, the Kurdish majority, another group brutalized by Hussein, also battled Sunnis. Moreover, al-Qaeda forces, which previously had been absent from the country, joined the fray.

Guantánamo The site of a U.S. military base in Cuba, where the George W. Bush administration imprisoned suspected al-Qaeda members without due process of law. Despite campaigning on promises to end this policy, the Obama administration failed to close the Guantánamo Bay prison, and it continues to operate today.

At the same time, the Bush administration instituted the policy of incarcerating suspected al-Qaeda rebels in the U.S. military base in **Guantánamo**, Cuba, without due process of the law. The facility housed more than six hundred men classified as "enemy combatants," who were subject to extreme interrogation.

Amid a protracted war in Iraq, President Bush won reelection in 2004 by promising to stay the course and deter further terrorism. Although the Democratic presidential candidate, Senator John Kerry of Massachusetts, criticized Bush's handling of Iraq, Bush emerged victorious with a majority of the popular vote (50.7 percent) and 286 electoral votes.

Hurricane Katrina Storm that hit the Gulf coast states of Louisiana, Mississippi, and Alabama in 2005. The hurricane caused massive flooding in New Orleans after levees broke, resulting in approximately 1,800 deaths.

During his second term, President Bush's approval rating suffered. Several issues — sectarian violence in Iraq, mounting death tolls, and the failures of the U.S.-supported Iraqi government — turned the majority of Americans against the war. Little changed, however, as American troops remained in Iraq and Afghanistan. With turmoil also continuing in the Persian Gulf, the threat of nuclear proliferation grew. Iraq did not have nuclear weapons, but Iran sought to develop nuclear capabilities. Iranian leaders claimed that they wanted nuclear technology for peaceful purposes, but the Bush administration believed that Iran's real purpose was to build nuclear devices to attack Israel and establish its supremacy in the region. Likewise, in Asia, North Korea began to refine its nuclear capabilities in hopes of maintaining its Communist dictatorship.

AP® TIP
Analyze how George W. Bush responded to both foreign and domestic crises during his presidency.

President Bush also faced domestic challenges during his second term. On August 29, 2005, **Hurricane Katrina** slammed into the Gulf coast states of Louisiana and Mississippi. This powerful storm devastated New Orleans, a city with a population of nearly 500,000, a majority of whom were African American. The flood surge caused poorly maintained levees to break, flooding large areas of the city and trapping 50,000 residents.

In the days after the storm hit, chaos reigned in New Orleans. Evacuees were housed in the Superdome football stadium and a municipal auditorium without adequate food, water, and sanitary facilities. The flooding killed at least 1,800 residents of the Gulf coast, New Orleans's population dropped by around 130,000 residents, and critics blamed state and local officials, as well as the federal government, for a slower response to the crisis than they believed necessary.

REVIEW

- How did the September 11, 2001 attacks shape George W. Bush's foreign and domestic policy?
- What domestic challenges did Bush face between 2001 and 2005?

TEACHING IDEA

Incorporating Videos

Have students watch Episode 43, "Terrorism, War, and Bush," from the Crash Course US History Series (available on YouTube). Ask students to take notes during the video to review George W. Bush's domestic and foreign policy. After watching, put students in pairs and have them discuss the policies and conduct research (if needed) to determine if the policies are still impacting the decisions of the federal government and American citizens.

APPLY THE TIP

Assign the following handout activity help students explain how both foreign and domestic crises affected George W. Bush's presidency. Issues covered include the War on Terror and Hurricane Katrina.

TRM Find **Handout 9.8 — The Impact of Crises During George W. Bush's Presidency** in the Teacher's Resource Materials.

The Great Recession

In 2008, the last year of his presidency, President Bush faced his greatest domestic challenge. The boom times of the previous decade came to a sudden halt. The stock market's Dow Jones Industrial Average, which had hit a high of 14,000, fell 6,000 points, the steepest percentage drop since 1931. Americans who had invested their money in the stock market lost trillions of dollars. The gross domestic product fell by about 6 percent, a loss too great for the economy to absorb quickly. Millions of Americans lost their jobs as consumer spending decreased, and many forfeited their homes when they could no longer afford to pay their mortgages. Unemployment jumped from 4.9 percent in January 2008 to 7.6 percent a year later. Confronted by this spiraling disaster, President Bush approved a $700 billion bailout plan to rescue the nation's largest banks and brokerage houses.

> **AP® TIP**
> Compare the causes and effects of the Great Recession of 2008 with those of the Great Depression of the 1930s.

Great Recession The severe economic decline in the United States and throughout the world that began in 2008, leading to bank failures, high unemployment, home foreclosures, and large federal deficits.

The causes of the **Great Recession** were many and had developed over a long period. Since the Reagan presidency, the federal government had relaxed regulation of the financial industry, including repeal of the Glass-Steagall Act (see Module 7-3) during the Clinton administration. Also, the Federal Reserve Bank encouraged excessive borrowing by keeping interest rates very low and relaxed its oversight of Wall Street practices that placed ordinary investors' money at risk. Investment banks developed elaborate computer models that produced new and risky kinds of financial instruments, which went unregulated and whose complex nature few people understood. Insurance companies such as American International Group (AIG) marketed so-called credit default swaps as protection for risky securities, worsening the financial crisis. Consumers also shared some of the blame. Many took advantage of risky but easily accessible mortgage policies that appealed to borrowers with low incomes or poor credit ratings. When the housing market collapsed, many homeowners ended up owing banks and mortgage companies much more than their homes were worth and wound up in foreclosure.

The economy might have experienced a less severe downturn if there had been greater economic equality to bolster consumer spending. But this was not the case. Wealth remained concentrated in relatively few hands. In 2007 the top 1 percent of households owned 34.6 percent of all privately held wealth, and the next 19 percent held 50.5 percent. The other 80 percent of Americans owned only 15 percent of the wealth, and the gap between rich and poor continued to widen. This level of wealth inequality made it extremely difficult to support an economy that required ever-expanding purchasing power and produced steadily rising personal debt.

With the interdependence of economies through globalization, the Great Recession spread rapidly throughout the world. Great Britain's banking system teetered on the edge of collapse. Other nations in the European Union (EU), most notably Greece and Spain, verged on bankruptcy and had to be rescued by stronger EU nations. In providing financial assistance to its member states, the EU required countries such as Greece to slash spending for government services and to lower minimum wages. Even in China, where the economy had boomed as a result of globalization, businesses shut down and unemployment rose as global consumer demand for its products declined.

◀ **Wealth Inequality (Capital Income), 2011** The decline of American manufacturing and the expansion of the low-wage service sector, combined with the rise of high-tech industries and unregulated investment banking, led to growing disparities of wealth in the early twenty-first century. Disparities existed even within the top 20th percentile, as the top 1 percent controlled more than half of all capital income in 2011. Compare the top 20 percent and the bottom 20 percent of Americans with respect to capital income. **How does the distribution of wealth in the graph compare to the distribution of wealth in America in the late 1800s?**

REVIEW

- What economic changes after 1988 contributed to the Great Recession?
- What were the global effects of the Great Recession?

Obama and Domestic Politics

Analyze how Barack Obama's victory in the election of 2008 reflected changes in American society and politics.

Patient Protection and Affordable Care Act ("Obamacare") Passed in 2010, this law expanded health insurance to millions of Americans previously uncovered through a variety of measures including extending Medicaid, setting up health-insurance exchanges, allowing children to remain under their parents' coverage until the age of twenty-six, and preventing insurance companies from excluding coverage based on pre-existing conditions.

Development, Relief, and Education for Alien Minors (DREAM) Act Legislation proposed in 2001 to provide the children of undocumented immigrants in the U.S. the opportunity to gain legal residency status. The proposed legislation failed to pass Congress.

In the midst of the Great Recession, the United States held the 2008 presidential election. The Republican candidate, John McCain, was a Vietnam War hero and a senator from Arizona. His Democratic opponent from Illinois, Barack Obama, had served a mere four years in the Senate. For their vice-presidential running mates, McCain chose Sarah Palin, the first-term governor of Alaska, and Obama selected Joseph Biden, the senior senator from Delaware.

In the end, Obama connected with voters throughout America by speaking about his background as an interracial child, the son of an immigrant from Kenya and the grandson of a World War II veteran from Kansas. As important, the former community organizer succeeded in building a nationwide, grassroots political movement through digital technology. He raised an enormous amount of campaign money from ordinary donors through the Internet and used Web sites and text messaging to mobilize his supporters. Obama's victory was also aided by the fact that many Americans blamed the Bush administration for the recession, and Obama's campaign platform offered hope for economic recovery. Obama captured 53 percent of the popular vote, obtaining a majority of votes from African Americans, Latinos, women, and the young, who turned out in record numbers, and 365 electoral votes. The Democrats also won majorities in the House and Senate.

President Obama achieved notable victories during his first term in office. He continued the Bush administration's bailout of collapsing banks and investment firms and expanded it to include American automobile companies, which within three years bounced back, became profitable again, and began paying back the government for the bailout. In 2009 the president supported passage of an economic stimulus plan that provided federal funds to state and local governments to create jobs and keep their employees, including teachers, on the public payroll. More controversially, President Obama pushed Congress to pass the **Patient Protection and Affordable Care Act** ("Obamacare") in 2010, a reform measure mandating that all Americans had to obtain health insurance or face a tax penalty, that no one could be denied coverage for a preexisting condition, and that insurance companies extend coverage for dependents up to age twenty-six. Obama also signed into law the repeal of President Clinton's "don't ask, don't tell" policy, which discriminated against gays in the military.

President Obama also took action to address the divisive issue of immigration. Congress had failed to pass the **Development, Relief, and Education for Alien Minors (DREAM) Act**, first introduced in 2001, which would have provided an opportunity for undocumented minors in the United States to gain legal residency status. To protect these so-called "Dreamers," in 2012, the president instituted the

◀ **A Political Cartoonist's View of the Presidential Election of Barack Obama, 2008** Published by politico.com on November 6, 2008, two days after the election of Barack Obama, this cartoon drawn by Matt Wuerker captures the joyous response of many Americans, black and white, to the victory of the first African American president. **Why does the cartoonist include the Lincoln Memorial and the Capitol building in the image? How does he convey his attitude toward the election of Barack Obama in this cartoon?**

APPLY THE TIP

Ask students to describe how Barack Obama's campaign in 2008 "reflected changes in American society and politics." Discuss how the Internet has impacted political campaigns as well as how social media has provided a new platform for political discourse. Has the ease of access to information made us more knowledgeable about issues? Ask students also to determine the influence of targeted advertisements on the Internet (advertisements that target certain viewers based on their past Internet activity) and how to know whether the information that is posted on social media or elsewhere on the Internet is trustworthy.

BUILDING AP® SKILLS

Developments and Processes

Have students compare the use of the radio, television, and the Internet in providing a new platform for political campaigns and the spread of information about politics. Consider using the following examples: Franklin D. Roosevelt's "Fireside Chats" in the 1930s, the Kennedy v. Nixon debates in the election of 1960 that appeared on television, and the use of the Internet in recent electoral campaigns. How did each of these innovations impact the dissemination of information? Specifically in comparing the Kennedy v. Nixon debates and the use of grassroots digital campaign techniques of the election of 2008, how did these innovations impact the outcome of the elections?

BUILDING AP® SKILLS

Developments and Processes

Put students in groups of 5. As students read through this page, ask them to describe how each of the following policies reflected a change in American society and politics. Assign one of the following policies to each individual student in the group: the economic stimulus plan; the Patient Protection and Affordable Care Act; the repeal of the "don't ask, don't tell" policy; the Development, Relief, and Education for Alien Minors (DREAM) Act; and the Deferred Action for Childhood Arrivals (DACA) policy. Allow time for discussion in small groups and discuss as a class if more clarification is needed.

Period 9: 1980–The Present

MODULE 9-4 The Global War on Terror and Political Conflict at Home

TRM Suggested Responses to Questions

TRM Module 9.4 AP® Analyzing Sources Handout 4

BUILDING AP® SKILLS
Comparison

Draw a Venn diagram with three intersecting circles on the board. Have students draw the same diagram in their notes. Title the diagram "Social Safety" and label the sections of the diagram with the following titles: Obama Administration, Lyndon B. Johnson's Great Society, and Roosevelt's New Deal. Work as a class to fill in the circles. Possible answers include: *All three pushed for more government intervention in society in order to protect the American public. Obama and Johnson both pushed through health care reform in the form of the Affordable Care Act and Medicare and Medicaid. Roosevelt focused more on helping Americans economically, though Social Security did help those with disabilities. Obama and Roosevelt faced the Great Recession and the Great Depression, respectively. Both had to try to help the American people survive financial hardship.*

AP® ANALYZING SOURCES

Source: President Barack Obama, *Address to Congress on Health Care*, 2009

"I am not the first President to take up this cause, but I am determined to be the last. It has now been nearly a century since Theodore Roosevelt first called for health care reform. And ever since, nearly every President and Congress, whether Democrat or Republican, has attempted to meet this challenge in some way. . . .

Our collective failure to meet this challenge—year after year, decade after decade—has led us to the breaking point. Everyone understands the extraordinary hardships that are placed on the uninsured, who live every day just one accident or illness away from bankruptcy. . . .

But the problem that plagues the health care system is not just a problem for the uninsured. Those who do have insurance have never had less security and stability than they do today. More and more Americans worry that if you move, lose your job, or change your job, you'll lose your health insurance too. More and more Americans pay their premiums, only to discover that their insurance company has dropped their coverage when they get sick, or won't pay the full cost of care. It happens every day. . . .

Then there's the problem of rising cost. We spend one and a half times more per person on health care than any other country, but we aren't any healthier for it. This is one of the reasons that insurance premiums have gone up three times faster than wages. It's why so many employers—especially small businesses—are forcing their employees to pay more for insurance, or are dropping their coverage entirely. It's why so many aspiring entrepreneurs cannot afford to open a business in the first place, and why American businesses that compete internationally—like our automakers—are at a huge disadvantage. And it's why those of us with health insurance are also paying a hidden and growing tax for those without it—about $1,000 per year that pays for somebody else's emergency room and charitable care.

Finally, our health care system is placing an unsustainable burden on taxpayers. When health care costs grow at the rate they have, it puts greater pressure on programs like Medicare and Medicaid. If we do nothing to slow these skyrocketing costs, we will eventually be spending more on Medicare and Medicaid than every other government program combined. Put simply, our health care problem is our deficit problem. Nothing else even comes close. Nothing else."

Questions for Analysis

1. Identify three problems that Obama sees in the American health care system.
2. Describe how these problems affect middle class Americans, according to Obama.
3. Explain how Obama connects health care reform to progressive reforms from the early twentieth century.
4. Evaluate the extent of similarity between Obama's health care reform efforts and previous expansions of the social safety net during Roosevelt's New Deal (1930s) and Johnson's Great Society (1960s).

Deferred Action for Childhood Arrivals (DACA) This policy, initiated under the administration of Barack Obama in 2012, allows undocumented immigrant children to receive a two-year extension of their residency in the U.S. along with eligibility for work permits.

Deferred Action for Childhood Arrivals (DACA) policy, which allows children who have entered the country illegally to receive a renewable two-year extension of their residence in the U.S. along with eligibility for work permits.

Despite many policy accomplishments, President Obama encountered vigorous political opposition. Most Republican lawmakers did not support his economic stimulus and health

TEACHING IDEA

Digging Deeper: The Tea Party

Have students read "Tea Party Supporters: Who They Are and What They Believe" by Brian Montopoli from CBS News' website (cbsnews.com). This article provides statistics that describe the demographics as well as the beliefs of the Tea Party movement. Information about the polling methods is also included at the bottom of the article. Then have students read "The Tea Party Movement, Its Economic Platform, and History" by Kimberly Amadeo from The Balance website (thebalance.com). The Balance article includes fewer statistics and provides a background on the origins and beliefs of the Tea Party movement. These resources will help students gain a deeper understanding of the Tea Party movement as a whole.

▲ Differentiation

As a more challenging extension to this activity, split the class into groups. Have groups read a different part of Montopoli's article and then create graphs to show the statistics in a visual way. Post the graphs around the room and conduct a gallery walk.

Tea Party movement A loose coalition of conservatives and libertarians that formed around 2008. The Tea Party advocated small government, low taxes, and reduced federal deficits.

> **AP® TIP**
>
> Analyze how the rise of both the Tea Party and the Occupy Wall Street movements reflected changes in the American political system in the early twenty-first century.

Occupy Wall Street movement A loose coalition of progressive and radical forces that emerged in 2011 in New York City and around the country to protest what they perceived to be corporate greed and federal policies that benefit the very wealthy.

Obergefell v. Hodges 2015 U.S. Supreme Court decision legalizing same-sex marriage throughout the nation.

Black Lives Matter Social protest movement that formed after a civilian shot and killed Trayvon Martin, an unarmed African American youth, in 2012. Organized by protesters around the social media hashtag #blacklivesmatter, the movement advocated a policy agenda that mainly focused on criminal justice and police reforms.

care reform bills. A group of conservatives and libertarians formed the **Tea Party movement**, which organized protests against what they perceived as an effort to expand federal control over the economy and diminish individual liberty with the health care act. The rise of the Tea Party reflected growing partisanship within the country. In the 2010 midterm elections, Republicans regained a majority in the House while the Democratic majority in the Senate narrowed.

Obama also encountered political difficulties from the left. Although the president's policies saved the financial system from collapse, at the end of 2011 unemployment remained higher than 8 percent (a drop from its high of 10.2 percent). In 2011 protesters in cities around the nation launched the **Occupy Wall Street movement**, which attacked what they perceived as corporate greed, economic inequality, and government ineffectiveness. Many in the movement were inspired to act by declining tax revenues that they saw as responsible for state budget deficits and cuts in spending on education, social services, and infrastructure while young people faced high unemployment and crushing student loan debts.

With unemployment remaining high, economic growth moving at a slow pace, and a number of European nations unable to pay mounting debts, the economy loomed as the top issue in the 2012 presidential election. The Republican nominee, Mitt Romney, the former governor of Massachusetts, appealed to conservative voters by advocating for a reduction in the role of the federal government in the healthcare market and for a general reduction in federal spending coupled with a reduction of income tax rates. Despite the slower-than-expected economic recovery, Barack Obama won reelection by holding together his coalition of African American, Latino, female, young, and lower-income voters.

During President Obama's second term, the economy showed greater improvement. The unemployment rate dropped to 4.9 percent in February 2016, the lowest figure in eight years. From 2010 to 2014, the gross domestic product grew steadily by an average of more than 2 percent, and the strengthening economy cut the budget deficit significantly. However, as the economy recovered from recession, real wages declined and income and wealth inequality widened. The top 1 percent gained about 95 percent of the income growth since 2009, and the top 10 percent held its highest share of income since World War I. One reason for this widening gap was that since 2000 the U.S. lost 5 million good-paying manufacturing jobs and many of the jobs created by the recovery were low-wage service positions, whereas the wealthiest Americans benefited from the soaring stock market and rising capital gains. At the same time, union membership continued its long-term decline, thereby eliminating a major avenue for workers to increase their wages.

In two other areas, equality in marriage and the environment, the Obama administration made major policy changes in its second term. Initially Obama had supported civil unions rather than same-sex marriage, but in 2012 he changed his position in support of same-sex marriage. The following year, the Supreme Court overturned the 1996 Defense of Marriage Act, thereby extending recognition of same-sex marriage. In 2015, in *Obergefell v. Hodges* the Court legalized same-sex marriage nationwide. With respect to the environment, the Obama administration sought to address climate change by encouraging fuel efficiency and clean energy production and by extending protection of significant cultural and natural landmarks.

Obama's second term also saw renewed calls by activists for criminal justice and policing reforms to address racism in the United States. The movement that came to be known as **Black Lives Matter** formed in the wake of the fatal shooting of Trayvon Martin, an unarmed African American teenager, by a civilian in 2012. This event, in addition to a series of high-profile incidents of police brutality against African Americans in 2014 and 2015, spurred the growth of the Black Lives Matter movement. Technology helped spread its message through **Twitter** and social networking. As a result of federal investigations, in 2015 the Justice Department found a pattern of systemic racism and excessive use of force in the Ferguson, Missouri and Cleveland, Ohio police departments and negotiated settlements that instituted reforms.

APPLY THE TIP

To help students better understand the Occupy Wall Street movement, utilize the New York Times lesson "Who Are the 99%? Ways to Teach About Occupy Wall Street" by Sarah Kavanagh, Holly Epstein Ojalvo, and Katherine Schulten from the New York Times' Learning Network (learning.blogs.nytimes.com). This lesson provides a background on the movement as well as a variety of activities to apply student learning, such as investigating the history of the protests, determining the future impact of the movement, comparing the movement to other similar movements in American history, and many more activities.

TEACHING IDEA

Incorporating Videos

Have students watch "A History of the Black Lives Matter Movement" from Bloomberg (available on YouTube). There are disturbing images in the video, so be sure to determine if the video is appropriate to show to your class. Topics covered include the motivations for the Black Lives Matter movement, as well as information about Trayvon Martin and Michael Brown. After watching, ask students to describe how the Black Lives Matter movement reflects early movements, such as the civil rights movement.

TEACHING IDEA

Incorporating Websites

To help students gain a background of the Black Lives Matter movement, utilize the lesson titled "Black Lives Matter: From Hashtag to Movement" on the Anti-Defamation League's website (adl.org). The ADL's "mission is to protect the Jewish people and to secure justice and fair treatment for all," but the lesson plan is not biased and uses unbiased sources. Students will be able to explore the background and motivations of the Black Lives Matter movement.

TRM Suggested Responses to Questions

TRM Module 9.4 AP® Analyzing Sources Handout 5

APPLY THE TIP

In pairs, have students draw a Venn diagram to compare the foreign policy challenges that Obama and George W. Bush faced. Allow students to complete the diagram in pairs. Possible answers include: *Both Obama and Bush faced conflict in the Middle East. Bush began the search for Osama bin Laden, and U.S. Special Forces killed him during the Obama administration. During Bush's presidency, the War on Terror resulted in an increasing number of American troops being sent to Middle Eastern nations. While Obama was president, the number of American forces in Iraq was decreasing, but more troops were sent to Afghanistan. New issues that Obama faced were the rise of ISIS and the Syrian civil war, which led to many Syrian refugees seeking asylum.* Once finished, students should individually write a thesis statement to answer the following prompt: To what extent were the foreign policy challenges faced by Barack Obama and George W. Bush similar?

Period 9: 1980–The Present

MODULE 9-4 The Global War on Terror and Political Conflict at Home

AP® ANALYZING SOURCES

Source: Frederick C. Harris, *The Price of the Ticket: Barack Obama and the Rise and Decline of Black Politics*, 2012

"[W]ith the election of Barack Obama as the forty-fourth president of the United States, one could easily draw the conclusion that black America reached the pinnacle of political empowerment—a journey that has taken blacks from one of the most marginalized groups in American history (alongside Native Americans) to a key constituency that helps to elect a man of African descent to lead the nation. . . . Far from black America gaining greater influence in American politics, Obama's ascendancy to the White House actually signals a decline of a politics aimed at challenging racial inequality head on. . . .

In the age of Obama . . . the majority of black voters have struck a bargain with Obama. In exchange for the president's silence on community-focused interests, black voters are content with a governing philosophy that helps 'all people' and a politics centered on preserving the symbol of a black president and family in the White House. . . . Indeed, the symbol of a black president is not a trivial matter. Yet, the grand bargain granting black pride in exchange for silence on race-specific issues and the marginalization of targeted policies by the Obama administration have left much to be desired. . . .

[T]his one-dimensional approach to policymaking will not catch all the social ills facing black communities. . . . For black America—and its leaders—the dispiriting silence to this reality is the price paid for the election of the nation's first black president."

Questions for Analysis

1. Identify the "grand bargain" that Harris claims African-American voters struck with Obama.
2. Describe the shortcomings of this "grand bargain," according to Harris.
3. Evaluate the extent to which the election of Barack Obama marked a change in American race relations.

REVIEW

What major domestic challenges did Obama face during his presidency?

Obama and the World

AP® TIP
Evaluate the degree to which the foreign policy challenges of Obama's administration reflected continuity with those of George W. Bush's administration.

Arab Spring Political movement in the Middle East in 2011, which led to the toppling of pro-Western but despotic governments in Egypt, Tunisia, and Yemen. Armed rebels overthrew Libyan dictator Muammar al-Qaddafi. The movement was spurred on by the aid of technology such as cell phones and the utility of social media networks to spread their messages.

Throughout Obama's two terms, his administration faced serious tests of its international leadership. In 2008 the president had appointed Hillary Clinton, the former First Lady and a senator from New York, as his secretary of state. The U.S. military increased combat troop withdrawals from Iraq and turned over security for the country to the newly elected Iraqi government. At the same time, the Obama administration stepped up the war in Afghanistan by increasing U.S. troop levels, which led to a rise in casualties. Then, in 2011, Obama achieved a dramatic success when U.S. special forces killed Osama bin Laden in his hideout in Pakistan. By 2016, with John Kerry now his secretary of state, the president had withdrawn most combat soldiers from Afghanistan. Yet Iraq remained unstable in the absence of a strong American military presence, and the outcome of the war against the Taliban in Afghanistan remained uncertain. Despite bin Laden's death, radical jihadists continued to pose a serious danger.

Other international challenges continued as well. From 2006 to 2013, a hostile North Korea tested a series of nuclear weapons. During this period, instability in other parts of Asia, the Middle East, and the Persian Gulf also heightened U.S. security concerns and underscored the difficulties of achieving lasting peace in these regions (Map 9.4). In 2011, in a period known as the **Arab Spring**, great changes swept across the Middle East, as young people, armed mainly with cell phones and connected through social media networks, toppled pro-Western but despotic governments in Egypt and Tunisia and convinced the leader of Yemen to step down. In Libya armed rebels succeeded in overthrowing the anti-American dictator Muammar al-Qaddafi.

TEACHING IDEA

Incorporating Videos

Have students watch the History Channel's "Here's How the Arab Spring Started and How It Affected the World" (available on YouTube). Have students answer the following questions while watching the video:

1. What caused the Arab Spring? (Discuss political leaders and the spark of the movement.) *President Zine el Abidine ben Ali of Tunisia, an authoritarian leader, was corrupt. A man named Mohamed Bouazizi, a vegetable vendor, was harassed by the police and his complaint ignored by the government.* *He set himself on fire in front of a government office and became a martyr for the movement.*

2. What issue did the movement address? *The movement addressed political corruption and unemployment.*

3. How did the movement spread so far so quickly? *The use of cell phones and social media to spread information increased the reach of the movement.*

4. What were the short-term and long-term results of the uprising in Tunisia? *Short-term: The president fled and the Tunisian uprising inspired other movements in the region. Long-term: Uprisings in Egypt, Yemen, and Libya were also successful in removing their corrupt governments. Working-class people did not benefit from each revolt. Extremist groups such as ISIS gained prominence. The Syrian civil war has led to a massive refugee crisis.*

MODULE 9-4 The Global War on Terror and Political Conflict at Home

Obama and the World

MAP 9.4 The Middle East, 2000–2017 Since 2000 the Middle East has been marked by both terrorism and democratic uprisings. After 9/11 the United States tried to transform Iraq and Afghanistan by military might, which led to prolonged wars. Yet popular rebellions in 2011, led by young people and fueled by new technology, created hope that change was possible. However, by 2016 the military had regained power in Egypt, and Libya had descended into civil war. Syria remained involved in a brutal civil war. The terrorist, military organization ISIS captured sections of Syria as well as territory in Iraq, but in 2017 they were driven out of most of this territory by Syrian government, Russian, and American-backed military forces. *What similarities do all the countries where these uprisings took place share?*

BUILDING AP® SKILLS

Making Connections

Analyze Map 9.4 as a class. What similarities do all the countries share where these uprisings took place? Possible answers include: *The countries are located in the Middle East and northern Africa. Most are oil-rich countries that are or were led by authoritarian regimes.* Put students into groups of 5. Assign one of the following nations to each student in the group: Tunisia, Egypt, Yemen, Libya, and Syria. Have students conduct individual research to learn about the causes, goals, and outcomes of the recent revolutions in their assigned nation. Students will then share among their group and look for further similarities. Are there still conflicts or wars occurring in the nations studied? Have the goals of the movements been realized? To what extent was the United States involved in the conflicts?

TEACHING IDEA

Incorporating Videos

Show students "The rise of ISIS, explained in 6 minutes" from Vox (available on YouTube). Before watching, review the terms Sunni and Shi'a with students. Have students answer the following questions in their notes while watching the video:

- What factors led to the rise of ISIS?
- What was the main goal of ISIS?
- What led to the decline of ISIS?

Then, put students into groups of 3 or 4 to compare answers. Have each group submit their responses.

Islamic State of Iraq and Syria (ISIS) Jihadist terrorist group originally founded in 1999, which gained strength from the sectarian violence that followed the 2003 U.S. invasion of Iraq. The group captured territory in Iraq and Syria and claimed responsibility for terrorist attacks in Paris, San Bernardino, California, and Lebanon.

However, many of these changes in the Middle East did not last. The military returned to power in Egypt, and civil war consumed Libya and Syria. Even more dangerous was the rise of a new militant terrorist organization in the region known as the **Islamic State of Iraq and Syria (ISIS)**, an offshoot of al-Qaeda that grew out of the sectarian violence following the overthrow of Saddam Hussein in Iraq. ISIS took over parts of Syria and Iraq, prompting the United States and some Arab nations to launch air strikes against its forces.

The ongoing Syrian civil war had profound effects on the rest of the world. Starting in 2010, millions of Syrians fled their homes, and tens of thousands sought refuge in Western Europe and the United States. This movement of refugees, which is greater than at any time since World War II, overwhelmed those European countries to which they first came — Greece, Hungary, and the Czech Republic. Hungary constructed fences to stop the flow of migrants, while the EU split over how to manage the crisis. In 2015 President Obama pledged to accept 10,000 additional Syrian refugees into the United States during 2016, but that number paled in comparison to the numbers who needed safe havens. Meanwhile, the humanitarian crisis of providing food, shelter, and medical attention to the refugees remained largely unresolved.

> "Change will not come if we wait for some other person or if we wait for some other time. We are the ones we've been waiting for. We are the change that we seek."
>
> — Barack Obama, 2008

From the outset of his first term in 2009, President Obama fought the war against terror by stepping up the use of remote-controlled armed drones (unmanned, aerial vehicles) against al-Qaeda and ISIS leaders in Pakistan, Afghanistan, Yemen, and Somalia. Although some top terrorist leaders were killed, drone attacks also resulted in significant civilian deaths. At home, antiterrorist surveillance provoked growing controversy. Under the Patriot Act, the National Security Agency (NSA) began collecting and storing phone records of U.S. citizens. The NSA did not listen to the calls, but it drew on this bulk data to track suspected terrorists. The existence of this operation came to light in 2013, when Edward Snowden, an intelligence analyst contracted by the

---

TEACHING IDEA

Project Idea

Have students watch *Vanity Fair*'s "Edward Snowden—Patriot or Traitor?" (available on YouTube). To give students an opportunity to describe both sides in the debate surrounding Edward Snowden, assign the following project: Students must create a poster that is split in two. On one side, they will create a monument to Edward Snowden that illustrates the ways in which he can be described as a patriot. The monument should have an inscription with detailed information. On the other side, students will create a wanted poster that illustrates the ways in which Snowden can be described as a traitor. The wanted poster should also include detailed information. Encourage students to conduct additional research to learn more about each side of the debate.

TRM Suggested Responses to Questions

TRM Module 9.4 AP® Analyzing Sources Handout 6

TEACHING IDEA

Incorporating Secondary Sources

Read "U.S.-Cuba Relations" by Claire Felter, Danielle Renwick, and Rocio Cara Labrador on the Council on Foreign Relations website (cfr.org). This secondary source covers a history of U.S.-Cuba relations, as well as the Cuban thaw during the Obama administration and President Trump's responses to the thaw. Ask students to determine the extent to which U.S.-Cuba relations have changed since the 1950s.

AP® ANALYZING SOURCES

Source: President Barack Obama, *Remarks by the President on the Middle East and North Africa*, 2011

"[F]or six months, we have witnessed an extraordinary change taking place in the Middle East and North Africa. Square by square, town by town, country by country, the people have risen up to demand their basic human rights. Two leaders have stepped aside. More may follow. And though these countries may be a great distance from our shores, we know that our own future is bound to this region by the forces of economics and security, by history and by faith. . . .

[A]lready, we've done much to shift our foreign policy following a decade defined by two costly conflicts. After years of war in Iraq, we've removed 100,000 American troops and ended our combat mission there. In Afghanistan, we've broken the Taliban's momentum, and this July we will begin to bring our troops home and continue a transition to Afghan lead. And after years of war against al-Qaeda and its affiliates, we have dealt al-Qaeda a huge blow by killing its leader, Osama bin Laden. . . .

The story of this revolution, and the ones that followed, should not have come as a surprise. The nations of the Middle East and North Africa won their independence long ago, but in too many places their people did not. In too many countries, power has been concentrated in the hands of a few. . . .

In the face of these challenges, too many leaders in the region tried to direct their people's grievances elsewhere. The West was blamed as the source of all ills, a half century after the end of colonialism. Antagonism toward Israel became the only acceptable outlet for political expression. Divisions of tribe, ethnicity, and religious sect were manipulated as a means of holding on to power, or taking it away from somebody else.

But the events of the past six months show us that strategies of repression and strategies of diversion will not work anymore. Satellite television and the Internet provide a window into the wider world—a world of astonishing progress in places like India and Indonesia and Brazil. Cell phones and social networks allow young people to connect and organize like never before. And so a new generation has emerged. And their voices tell us that change cannot be denied."

Questions for Analysis

1. Identify the causes of the "extraordinary change" taking place in the Middle East, according to Obama.
2. Describe how U.S. policy in the Middle East has shifted, according to Obama.
3. Evaluate the extent of similarity in how technology has been used in protests between the United States and the Middle East during the twenty-first century.

NSA, leaked the information to the *Guardian* newspaper before seeking refuge abroad. In doing so, he believed he ensured public scrutiny of the balance between national security and individual privacy, while Snowden's critics claimed that he undermined national security and endangered Americans in an age of terrorist threats.

On other foreign issues, President Obama departed from previous foreign policy. In 2014 he set in motion the normalization of diplomatic relations with Cuba and, the following year, along with several other world powers, negotiated an agreement with Iran on restricting its nuclear program. In contrast, relations with Russia deteriorated. In 2014 Russia, led by Vladimir Putin, annexed its former territory of the Crimea and in 2015 provided military support for pro-Russian separatists in Ukraine. In response the United States and the EU imposed economic sanctions on Russia but declined to take military action. Later in 2015 Russia sent military forces to Syria to support the government of the dictator Bashar al-Assad, a long-time ally, and fight his opponents, both ISIS and rebels backed by the United States.

The United States faced global economic and environmental challenges as well. As China flourished economically, American workers lost jobs, and the Chinese amassed a nearly

TEACHING IDEA

Incorporating Secondary Sources

Assign students to read "Patient Diplomacy and a Reluctance to Act: Obama's Mark on Foreign Policy" by Scott Horsley from NPR's website (npr.org). This article reviews foreign policy decisions made during the Obama administration as well as focuses on the reactions of President Obama's supporters and opposition to his foreign policy decisions. Ask students to draw a T-chart in their notes to keep track of reasons to support and reasons to oppose President Obama's foreign policy decisions.

AP® ANALYZING SOURCES

Source: Edward Snowden, *Interview* for The Guardian, July 18, 2014

"We constantly hear the phrase 'national security' but when the state begins . . . broadly intercepting the communications, seizing the communications by themselves, without any warrant, without any suspicion, without any judicial involvement, without any demonstration of probable cause, are they really protecting national security or are they protecting state security?

What I came to feel . . . is that a regime that is described as a national security agency has stopped representing the public interest and has instead begun to protect and promote state security interests. And the idea of western democracy as having state security bureaus, just that term, that phrase itself, 'state security bureau,' is kind of chilling. . . .

Generally, it's not the people at the working level you need to worry about. It's the senior officials, it's the policymakers who are shielded from accountability, who are shielded from oversight and who are allowed to make decisions that affect all of our lives without any public input, any public debate, or any electoral consequences because their decisions and the consequences of the decisions are never known.

Because of the advance of technology, storage becomes cheaper and cheaper year after year and when our ability to store data outpaces the expense of creating that data, we end up with things that are no longer held for short-term periods, they're held for long-term periods and then they're held for a longer term period. At the NSA for example, we store data for five years on individuals. And that's before getting a waiver to extend that even further."

Questions for Analysis

1. Identify the aspects of public surveillance that Snowden believes have increasingly "shielded [policymakers] from accountability."
2. Explain how technology fueled these surveillance measures.
3. Evaluate the extent to which the consequences of the surveillance measures Snowden describes represent a change from the U.S. government's interpretation of Americans' right to privacy and due process during the twentieth century.

$200 billion trade surplus with the United States. In addition, the growth of manufacturing and the market economy in China resulted in the rising consumption of oil and gasoline. The increase in carbon emissions in China and other parts of Asia contributed to the problem of climate change. According to climate scientists, emissions of greenhouse gases into the atmosphere in the twentieth and twenty-first centuries resulted in an increase in global temperatures, causing a cascade of side effects. As temperatures climb they cause the melting of glaciers, a rise in the sea level and ocean temperature, extreme fluctuations of weather with severely damaging storms, and famines. Disruptions in industrial and agricultural production caused by storms and the subsequent expense of rebuilding have had a negative impact on the U.S. and world economies. Recognizing the increasing dangers of climate change, in December 2015 the United States joined 194 nations, including China and India, in signing the **Paris Climate Agreement** to reduce greenhouse gas emissions produced from fossil fuels.

In the context of international debates over terrorism, refugees, and climate change, controversies continued in the United States over immigration. However the issue is resolved, by the end of the twenty-first century the population of the United States will look much different than it did at the beginning. In 2012 the U.S. Census Bureau reported that nonwhite babies made up the majority of births for the first time. If the current trends in immigration and birthrates continue, the percentage of Latinos and Asian Americans in the nation will increase, while that of white and black people will decline. In addition, the racial and ethnic composition of the population has been transformed through intermarriage. In 2010 the Census Bureau disclosed that one of seven new marriages, or 14.6 percent, was interracial or interethnic. In 1961, when

Paris Climate Agreement
Worldwide agreement by the U.S. and 194 other nations in 2015 to dramatically reduce greenhouse gas emissions produced from fossil fuels. In 2017, President Donald Trump retracted the U.S. commitment to the agreement.

TRM Suggested Responses to Questions

TRM Module 9.4 AP® Analyzing Sources Handout 7

EXPLORING AP® THEMES
Work, Exchange, and Technology

Have students read "Law Enforcement Officials Try to Warn Facebook off Its Encryption Plans" by Colin Dwyer from NPR's website (npr.org). Ask students to support and refute Facebook's use of messaging encryption. What are the reactions of law enforcement to Facebook's plan? Why might people support the plan to encrypt messages?

TEACHING IDEA
Building Vocabulary

In order to discuss the language around climate change, consider assigning *The Guardian*'s article, "Why *The Guardian* is changing the language it uses about the environment" (theguardian.com).

EXPLORING AP® THEMES
America in the World

Read "So What Exactly Is in the Paris Climate Accord?" by Camila Domonoske from NPR's website (npr.org). Ask students to answer the following question: What are the reasons for, and the goals of, the Paris Climate Accord? Possible answers include: *The climate is changing and the Earth has already warmed by 1 degree Celsius. The goals of the Accord are to slow the warming of the planet and eventually reach net-zero emissions of greenhouse gases.* The United States has since pulled out of the Paris Climate Accord. If there is time, watch BBC News' "Trump pulls US out of Paris climate deal" to determine why President Trump removed the U.S. from the agreement (available on YouTube).

TEACHING IDEA
Incorporating Videos

Have students watch Episode 47, "Obamanation," from Crash Course's US History series (available on YouTube). While watching, require students to answer the following questions:

- What impact did NINJA loans have on the financial crisis?
- How did the financial crisis in the United States impact the world?
- What were the goals of the Obama administration?
- Describe President Obama's domestic and foreign policies.

After concluding the video, have students discuss their responses as a class.

Barack Obama was born, the figure for interracial marriages was less than 0.1 percent. Thus, in an increasingly globalized nation, debates over immigration, race, and citizenship have taken new forms and significance.

REVIEW

To what extent did the Obama administration's foreign policies differ from those of the George W. Bush administration?

The 2016 Election

AP® TIP
Evaluate the extent to which President Donald Trump's campaign platform illustrated change from conservative politics of the twentieth and early twenty-first centuries.

As Barack Obama's second term drew to a close in 2016, Americans elected Donald Trump to succeed him. A New York City real estate tycoon and the host of the reality television show *The Apprentice*, Trump was a political outsider who had never held political office before running for the presidency.

After waging hard-fought primaries, Donald Trump and President Obama's former secretary of state, Hillary Clinton, faced each other in the general election. Running as an antiestablishment candidate, Trump adopted the slogan "Make America Great Again." Trump embraced populist opposition to immigration by promising to build a wall along the Mexican border and opposed free-trade agreements that he claimed shipped jobs overseas. He criticized international military alliances such as NATO, a major component of U.S. foreign policy since World War II, by claiming that not all alliance members contribute their fair share.

Trump's campaign strategy of questioning international alliances was also evident in Western Europe. Most notably, in June 2016, voters in the United Kingdom approved a referendum, which was given the nickname *Brexit* (British exit), to withdraw from the European Union. Trump's position aligned with the sentiment in the United Kingdom (particularly in England) which opposed trade agreements, open borders, and military alliances.

Clinton ran on a progressive platform that focused on addressing growing wealth inequality. Her platform included proposals for campaign finance reform, affordable college education, and a path to citizenship for undocumented immigrants.

Both campaigns attacked their opponent's fitness for office. Clinton attacked Trump's demeanor, in particular his alleged efforts to encourage the Russian government to intervene in the election and his behavior toward women. Trump attacked Clinton's service as secretary of state and her use of a private e-mail server to conduct State Department business. Trump charged that Clinton had transmitted classified material, posing a threat to national security, and that she had erased the classified e-mails to cover this up. The FBI investigated and reported that although Clinton had acted unwisely, she was not guilty of a crime. After the election, two congressional committees and a special prosecutor appointed by the Justice Department, Robert Mueller, looked into Russian hacking and possible collusion between members of the Trump campaign and Kremlin-sponsored operatives seeking to damage Hillary Clinton's campaign. While the Mueller Report found that the "Russian government interfered in the 2016 presidential election in sweeping and systemic fashion," it determined no criminal conspiracy existed between the Russian efforts and the Trump campaign.

Until election day, many pollsters were confident that Clinton would become the first woman president, though some polling organizations considered the race too close to predict. Although Clinton won the popular vote by nearly 3 million ballots, she lost in the Electoral College, 304–227. Trump captured six states that Obama had won in 2012. With the exception of Florida, those swing states from the Upper Midwest and mid-Atlantic were among the areas slowest to rebound from the Great Recession and were still grappling with the economic changes brought on by globalization.

The reasons for Trump's victory were varied, and there has been much debate about who is the typical Trump supporter and whether a Trump coalition even exists. He ran a populist, anti-establishment, anti-politician campaign, which appealed to an electorate fed up with politics-as-usual, corruption, and gridlock in Washington, D.C. His agenda resonated especially with older white men, residents of small towns and rural areas, workers who had lost their jobs to automation and globalization, and those who had not completed a college education. Yet a supposed "working-class rebellion" does not tell the whole story — the median household income of Trump voters was higher than the median household income of Clinton voters.

APPLY THE TIP

Ask students to answer the AP® Tip prompt in pairs. This AP® Tip provides students with an opportunity to find more examples of continuities, as Trump's campaign differed from former conservative campaigns. Possible answers include: *Trump utilized social media, such as Twitter, to share information about his campaign as well as drum up support. This was a departure from prior campaign strategies. On the other hand, Trump's mottos of "America First" and "Make America Great Again" are reminiscent of prior conservative campaigns that preferred isolationism and wanted to focus more on American manufacturing and domestic issues rather than on issues abroad.*

TEACHING IDEA

Incorporating Videos

Have students watch PBS News Hour's "All of the Mueller report's major findings in less than 30 minutes" (pbs.org/newshour). As a class, discuss the impact that the investigation into President Trump had on his presidency.

TEACHING IDEA

Incorporating Websites

Use the 2016 Election Map from the website 270 to Win that shows the outcome of that year's Electoral College votes (270towin.com). Give students time to navigate the page and to answer the following questions:

- Who won the electoral vote? By how many votes?
- Who won the popular vote? By how many votes?
- What are faithless electors? What was their impact on the 2016 election?
- How does the election of 2016 reflect changes from prior elections in history?

And there are other contradictions to consider in assessing President Trump's victory. Trump earned a majority of the vote from white women (53 percent), although Clinton won a majority of women's votes due to her overwhelming support among African American women. Trump succeeded by bringing out enough alienated Democratic and independent voters willing to take a chance on him, while retaining most traditional Republican voters.

Working-class and middle-class economic anxieties and grievances certainly played a role in Trump's victory, but exit polls showed that those who ranked the economy as the most important issue voted for Clinton. Instead, for many white voters, attitudes toward minorities and immigrants determined whom they supported in the election.

REVIEW

What major factors shaped the outcome of the 2016 presidential election?

The Trump Presidency

> "I have joined the political arena so that the powerful can no longer beat up on people that cannot defend themselves. Nobody knows the system better than me, which is why I alone can fix it."
>
> — Donald Trump, Republican National Convention, 2016

U.S. Immigration and Customs Enforcement (ICE) A branch of the Department of Homeland Security created in 2003, which oversees the investigations of criminal actions by illegal immigrants in the United States.

Iran Nuclear Agreement Compliance agreement in 2015 between Iran and the United Nations Security Council, which reduced nuclear facilities in Iran in exchange for a lift on economic sanctions by partner nations. In 2017 President Trump decertified the agreement.

Once in the White House, President Trump's relationship with the mainstream American media remained complicated. While he sometimes praised conservative outlets such as Fox News, Trump regularly criticized other mainstream media outlets, claiming they promoted "fake news." Trump also regularly used Twitter to bypass the filter of conventional media and directly communicate his thoughts with the American public.

President Trump had mixed success in achieving his legislative agenda. Congress narrowly rejected his signature campaign promise to repeal and replace the Patient Protection and Affordable Care Act (Obamacare). Yet the Tax Cuts and Jobs Act of 2017, which included major changes to the tax code, successfully passed. This act reduced tax rates for businesses and individuals while limiting some deductions and exemptions.

As is typical of the modern presidency, Trump used executive orders to advance his policy agenda. He put into effect a ban on immigrants from countries he deemed to be state sponsors of terrorism, which were primarily Muslim nations. He revoked the Deferred Action for Childhood Arrivals (DACA) executive order issued by President Obama, which had allowed those who had been brought to the country as children by their undocumented immigrant parents, known as "Dreamers," to remain indefinitely. His administration also revoked the provisional residency permits of more than 200,000 immigrants from El Salvador, Haiti, and Honduras who had fled to the U.S. following natural disasters in their countries. The children subsequently born into these families are U.S. citizens, and the deportation of one or both of their parents would separate their families. During his second year in office, **U.S. Immigration and Customs Enforcement (ICE)** also began to separate the children of undocumented immigrants from their parents at the U.S. border, provoking an outcry from both sides of the political spectrum. In 2018, a federal judge in California ordered the reunification of separated families and an end to forced separation.

President Trump appointed cabinet secretaries and heads of regulatory agencies who favored limited governance and privatization of public services. Deregulation efforts, such as challenging California's authority to limit auto emissions and overturning "net neutrality" rules mandating Internet providers treat all traffic equally, may make it easier for businesses to operate but result in fewer regulations protecting the environment and consumers.

President Trump was successful in winning confirmation of his appointments of Neil Gorsuch and Brett Kavanaugh, both conservatives, to the Supreme Court. Kavanaugh's confirmation proved especially controversial when a psychology professor, Dr. Christine Blasey Ford, accused Kavanaugh of sexually assaulting her at a party both attended when in high school. Kavanaugh strongly denied the charges and was eventually confirmed to the Supreme Court.

President Trump also achieved some of his foreign policy goals. He withdrew the U.S. from the Paris Climate Agreement, rolled back Obama-initiated trade and travel relations with Cuba, and decertified the **Iran Nuclear Agreement**. Trump met with North Korean dictator Kim Jong-un in a bid to reduce nuclear weapons on the Korean peninsula, despite earlier verbal clashes between the two leaders. Yet the relationship between China (now the world's biggest economy)

TEACHING IDEA

Connecting the Dots

Evaluate the extent to which Donald Trump's supporters connected his candidacy to the economic recession.

BUILDING AP® SKILLS

Making Connections

Before discussing Christine Blasey Ford's testimony and Brett Kavanagh's nomination as a U.S. Supreme Court Justice, determine if your class can handle the responsibility of conducting an unbiased discussion about the events surrounding the nomination. Discussions about sexual assault can be disturbing for some students, so be aware of your students before discussing this topic. Compare the situations surrounding the nominations of Clarence Thomas and Brett Kavanagh to the U.S. Supreme Court. Remind students to focus on the situations and the resulting movements as a whole instead of debating whether or not the Supreme Court nominees were guilty of sexual assault. What parallels can be drawn between the two situations? What was the result of each hearing? *Students will make connections between the two nominations concerning the allegations of sexual assault against the Supreme Court nominees. In each situation, the nominee was confirmed and became a Supreme Court Justice. A wider movement supporting the women also grew, as well as a push for women's rights as a whole.*

and the United States has been strained during the Trump administration, as the U.S. has levied tariffs on Chinese goods and China has retaliated with duties on American products. Underlying the tensions are disagreements over equitable access to markets, protection of intellectual property, economic competition, and disagreements over human rights.

AP ANALYZING SOURCES

Source: Sam Schlinkert, "Facebook Is Invading Your Phone," *Daily Beast*, 2013

"It's a phone! It's an app! It's . . . just an app.

The long-awaited Facebook phone has finally arrived, making its debut Thursday afternoon to a crowd of tech journalists sitting at the social network's headquarters at 1 Hacker Way in Menlo Park, California.

'Today we're finally gonna talk about that Facebook phone,' Facebook founder Mark Zuckerberg said as he strode on the stage to muted laughter, clutching an oversized microphone, citing the moniker that for years has followed Facebook's gradual prioritization of mobile.

Would it be hardware designed by Zuck? Would it just be a Facebook button?

We know now the 'Facebook Phone' moniker is a misnomer. It's just a collection of apps called 'Home'—and it can live on any Android device.

'Today our phones are designed around apps, not people,' the hoodie-wearing Zuckerberg proclaimed. Rather than an app-centric phone, he asked, what would it feel like if our phones were designed around people?

Facebook Home will be deeply integrated, with your friends' photos, faces, and messages displayed front and center, on what Zuckerberg calls 'a great social phone.'

There is Cover Feed, which brings your lock screen to life. There are Chat Heads, a new way of messaging with friends and family. And there's App Launcher, which keeps you close lest your mind were to wander to an app outside of Facebook's environment.

Cover Feed transforms your phone's lock screen by making it a rotating gallery of ever-present Facebook photos on which you can 'like' and leave comments.

With Chat Heads, SMS and Facebook messages display on top of any app you're already using, with your friends coming up as circular profile pictures (thus the name Chat Heads).

And then there's the App Launcher, which contains all of the apps on your phone—in the demo this pointedly included Google Maps, Tumblr, DropBox, and other potential competitors. In a sense it's a replacement for your home screen, so you never leave Home.

The software will be available for download beginning April 12 on a variety of Android phones. In a few months, you can get it for tablets as well.

Underscoring the company's commitment to being mobile first, with Wall Street investors anxiously looking on, Zuckerberg proclaimed, 'We think this is the best version of Facebook there is.'

He later added, 'At one level, this is just the next mobile version of Facebook. At a deeper level this will start to be a change to the relationship with how we use these computing devices.'

In other words, Zuck wants to make his relationship with your phone 'Facebook official.' The question is, will you hit accept?"

Questions for Analysis

1. Describe how Facebook became integrated into mobile devices.
2. Evaluate the extent to which the innovations described in this document represent a change in communications in the United States.

Questions for Comparison
Edward Snowden, *Interview for* The Guardian, July 18, 2014 (p. 847)

1. Evaluate the extent to which the integration of Facebook into mobile technology represents the kind of technological innovation Snowden criticizes in his interview.
2. Evaluate the extent to which early twenty-first century innovations led to the changes in technology identified by both Snowden and Schlinkert's article.

TRM Suggested Responses to Questions

TRM Module 9.4 AP® Analyzing Sources Handout 8

TEACHING IDEA

Class Discussion

Ask students to individually provide at least one piece of specific historical evidence to answer the following question: In what ways, and to what extent, did President Trump erase President Obama's legacy? Possible answers include: *Trump and Republicans in Congress attempted to repeal the Affordable Care Act, but were ultimately unsuccessful. Trump withdrew the United States from the Paris Climate Accord, negotiated during the Obama administration. Trump rolled back trade and travel relations with Cuba that were established during the Obama administration. Trump also decertified the Iran Nuclear Deal, also negotiated by the Obama administration.* Have each student ball up their paper and have a thirty-second "snowball fight." After thirty seconds, have each student pick up a piece of paper. Ask volunteers to provide the evidence that is written on the paper that they picked up, and write this evidence on the board. Next, ask students: Were Trump's attempts to erase Obama's legacy more similar to, or different from, other presidential actions? Possible answers include: *Trump's attempts are similar to other administrations, as each time an opposition political party wins the White House (such as Trump, a Republican, replacing Obama, a Democrat), they try to change policies to match their own political beliefs. Or, Trump's attempts go farther than other presidents in history, as he tried to erase policies that Obama put in place without having an alternative, as is the case with attempting to repeal the Affordable Care Act.*

BUILDING AP® SKILLS

Sourcing and Situation

Assign students in groups to read and break down Sam Schlinkert's article to determine its Historical situation, Intended audience, Purpose, and Point of view, in line with the HIPP format of document analysis (a refresher of HIPP can be found on page 8). Then have students answer the Questions for Analysis.

A Century of Anxiety and Hope

REVIEW

What domestic and foreign policies did the Trump administration pursue, and what were the results of those efforts?

Since 1993 Americans have faced new forms of globalization, new technologies, and new modes of warfare. The computer revolution begun by Bill Gates and others helped change the way Americans gather information, communicate ideas, purchase goods, and conduct business. It has also shaped national and international conflicts. The September 11, 2001 attacks on the World Trade Center and the Pentagon demonstrated that terrorists could use technology to organize and wreak havoc on the most powerful nation in the world. Barack Obama's 2008 presidential campaign, protesters demonstrating against various Middle East dictatorships, and the leaders of the Tea Party and Occupy Wall Street movements also used technology to promote their causes. On the other hand, in the interest of combating terrorism, the U.S. government has used this technology to monitor the activities of citizens it considers a threat to national security, thereby raising concerns about civil liberties.

The Bush administration responded to the 9/11 terrorist attacks by fighting wars in Iraq and Afghanistan. President Obama ended the Iraq war and steadily withdrew troops from Afghanistan, but neither administration was able to build stable governments in these countries. The rise of ISIS, which grew out of sectarian violence in Iraq, posed an even greater danger than did al-Qaeda to stability in the Middle East and the spread of terrorism throughout the world. At the same time, the United States and its allies faced a militarily revitalized Russia seeking to extend its influence in Ukraine and Syria, once again heightening the prospect of confrontation between the world's major nuclear powers.

Beginning with the attack by two students on Columbine High School in Colorado in 1999, the United States experienced a growing trend in mass shootings. While there is no single definition of a mass shooting, the murder of thirty-two students and faculty members at Virginia Polytechnic Institute and State University in 2007; twenty children and six adults at Sandy Hook Elementary School in Newton, Connecticut on December 14, 2012; nine African American worshipers by a white supremacist at the Emanuel African Methodist Episcopal Church in Charleston, South Carolina on June 17, 2015; and fifty patrons at the Pulse nightclub in Orlando, Florida on June 12, 2016 led many Americans to believe that they had entered an era in which mass violence seemed to be an everyday occurrence broadcast by the media.

On October 1, 2017, outdoor concert attendees in Las Vegas, Nevada were victims of the deadliest mass shooting in American history to date. Fifty-nine people were murdered when a gunman used a high-powered, long range rifle to shoot into the crowd from the thirty-ninth floor of a nearby hotel. The following year, on February 14, 2018, a gunman murdered seventeen people at Marjory Stoneman Douglas High School in Parkland, Florida. In the aftermath of the Parkland attack, national protests calling for background checks and gun control measures, led largely by the students of Marjory Stoneman Douglas High School, inspired Florida legislators to raise the minimum age for

Women's March on Washington, D.C., 2017 About 500,000 demonstrators gather in the nation's capital on January 21, 2017, a day after President Trump's inauguration, to attend the Women's March on Washington. Marchers supported a wide range of goals, including gender equality, racial equality, worker rights, immigration reform, health care expansion, and environmental protection. **What does this photograph reveal about American politics at the beginning of Trump's presidency?**

EXPLORING AP® THEMES

Work, Exchange, and Technology

Ask students to individually write down an answer to the Review question on a blank sticky note: Provide one example to explain how new technology affected American society and politics during the Trump presidency. After each student has written down an answer, have them stick their sticky notes on the board. Work with the class to organize the evidence on the sticky notes into categories such as the Internet, social media, mobile devices, etc. These could serve as main topics if students were to write an essay to address the Review question.

TEACHING IDEA

Incorporating Videos

Have students watch the *Wall Street Journal*'s "Women's March: Massive Protests Across U.S., World" (available on YouTube). The video shows the scale of women's marches and protests that occurred in the hours and days after Trump's inauguration as president of the United States. Use this video as well as the image showing the Women's March on Washington, D.C. to discuss the provided question: What does this photograph [and the videos] reveal about American politics at the beginning of Trump's presidency? Possible answers include: *American politics was becoming increasingly divided. Women continued to push for their voices to be heard.*

Period 9: 1980–The Present

MODULE 9-4 The Global War on Terror and Political Conflict at Home

BUILDING AP® SKILLS
Causation

Ask the class to brainstorm Trump's domestic and foreign policies. Write a list on the board as students provide specific evidence to cover topics such as immigration, the climate, and the economy, among others. After writing the brainstormed list on the board, put students into pairs to account for the reactions (both support and opposition) to his policies.

TRM Suggested Responses to Questions

gun ownership and institute background checks before purchasing. The legislation also allowed for the arming of properly trained teachers. However, gun legislation remained a controversial topic in the closing years of the century's second decade.

Along with the computer revolution, globalization has encouraged vast economic transformations throughout the world. Presidents as politically different as Bill Clinton and George W. Bush supported deregulation, free trade, and other policies that fostered corporate mergers and allowed businesses to reach beyond U.S. borders for cheap labor, raw materials, and new markets. While the 1990s witnessed the fruits of the new global economy, in 2008 the dangers of financial speculation and intertwined national economies became strikingly clear with the onset of the Great Recession. This economic collapse has underscored the inequalities of wealth that continue to widen, aggravated by racial, ethnic, and gender disparities.

The Obama administration succeeded in ending the worst features of the recession and extended health care coverage to some of the country's most vulnerable citizens. Yet Obama faced increased political opposition from both legislative houses that made other aspects of his political agenda difficult to achieve.

The election of Donald Trump to the presidency in 2016 demonstrated that many Americans felt that career politicians did not prioritize the issues they faced and that the economic recovery begun in the Obama era was uneven. Trump waged a populist political campaign that appealed to voters who wanted to see a break from politics as usual, drawing on his experience as a businessman as evidence he would be able to strike deals in the American people's best interests. Trump's election also reflected an increased political polarization in America's electorate that remains sharper than at any time since the turbulent 1960s and is exacerbated by social media.

Social media also provided a place to come together for causes, however. Originated by Tarana Burke, an African American social activist, and promoted by the actress Alyssa Milano, the **#MeToo movement** linked tens of millions of women on Twitter and Facebook. Many of them shared their stories of rape, sexual harassment, and sexual assault. The movement gained momentum after allegations by more than 80 women against movie mogul Harvey Weinstein led to his removal from his film company, and ultimately to his arrest. As a result, by the end of 2018, numerous women had come forward with complaints of sexual misconduct by media, entertainment, and sports celebrities, corporate executives, and politicians of both parties, leading in many cases to the swift firing or resignation of these men. The #MeToo movement changed the national conversation on sexual misconduct.

Throughout its history, the United States has shown great strength in finding solutions to its problems. The nation has incorporated diverse populations into its midst, redefined old cultural identities and created new ones, expanded civil rights and civil liberties, extended economic opportunities, and joined other nations to fight military aggression and address other international concerns. As the twenty-first century continues to progress, the United States will continue to draw on these strengths to maintain its global leadership and unique legacy in an ever-changing world.

#MeToo movement The social movement linking tens of millions of women through social media networks in opposition to sexual harassment and abuse.

AP® WRITING HISTORICALLY — Short-Answer Question Practice

ACTIVITY

Read the following question carefully and write a short response. Use complete sentences.

Using the following excerpts, answer (a), (b), and (c).

Source: John D'Emilio and Estelle Freedman, *Intimate Matters: A History of Sexuality in America*, 1998

"Although the political activity of the New Right and the threat of AIDS seemed to [predict] a [reduction] in the behavior of many Americans, as the 1980s drew to a close it was not at all clear what the future would bring. Certainly the outcome of current controversies about sex would have to build upon the complicated set of sexual meanings that had evolved over generations. For instance, in seeking a restoration of sexuality

(Continued)

852

BUILDING AP® SKILLS
Claims and Evidence in Sources

Put students into pairs. Have one student in each pair read the excerpt from *Intimate Matters: A History of Sexuality in America*, and the other student read the excerpt from *The Silent Majority: Suburban Politics in the Sunbelt South* (on page 853). Require students to individually determine the author's "historical interpretations of changes in American society since the 1980s." Each student should also find evidence to support the author's argument for the document that they were assigned.

to marriage, replete with reproductive consequences, advocates of the new chastity had to contend with the permeation of the erotic throughout American culture, the expansive and varied roles available to American women, and a contraceptive technology that sustained the nonprocreative meanings of sexual behavior. A new sexual system that harkened back to a vanished world could not simply be wished into existence. . . ."

Source: Matthew D. Lassiter, *The Silent Majority: Suburban Politics in the Sunbelt South*, 2006

"The United States became a definitively suburban nation during the final decades of the twentieth century, with the regional convergence of metropolitan trends and the reconfiguration of national politics around programs to protect the consumer privileges of affluent white neighborhoods and policies to reproduce the postindustrial economy of the corporate Sunbelt. Since the rediscovery of Middle America during the Nixon era, the suburban orientation of the bipartisan battle for the political center has remained persistently unreceptive to civil rights initiatives designed to address the structural disadvantages facing central cities and impoverished communities. Despite the ritual declarations that the federal courts would not permit public opposition to influence the enforcement of constitutional principles, the historical fate of collective integration remedies for educational and residential segregation demonstrated the responsiveness of the judicial and policymaking branches to the grassroots protests of affluent suburban families. The color-blind and class-driven discourse popularized in the Sunbelt South helped create a suburban blueprint that ultimately resonated from the 'conservative' subdivisions of southern California to the 'liberal' townships of New England: a bipartisan political language of private property values, individual taxpayer rights, children's educational privileges, family residential security, and white racial innocence."

a. Briefly describe ONE major difference between Lassiter's and D'Emilio and Freedman's historical interpretations of changes in American society since the 1980s.
b. Briefly explain how ONE historical event or development from the period 1980 to the present that is not explicitly mentioned in the excerpts could be used to support Lassiter's argument.
c. Briefly explain how ONE historical event or development from the periods 1980 to the present that is not explicitly mentioned in the excerpts could be used to support D'Emilio and Freedman's argument.

TEACHING IDEA

AP® Writing Historically Review

This activity is meant to be used as a bell ringer before students respond to the Short-Answer Question. In groups, have students outline the cultural debates surrounding gender roles and diversity in the twenty-first century. They can discuss interest groups, regionalism, political parties, generational conflicts, etc. Their goal is to account for the current debate in society before they read the secondary sources. In doing so, they will provide a historical context for the debates of the twentieth century addressed in the excerpts.

EXPLORING AP® THEMES

America in the World

In small groups, give students time to debate the question: To what extent did globalization increase the impact of the Great Recession? Possible answers include: *The Great Recession was made worse by the bursting of the housing bubble in the United States. Due to this development, the GDP of the U.S. dropped by about 6%, which negatively impacted international trade. Eventually, the recession in the United States reverberated throughout the world due to the globalization of trade.*

PERIOD 9 REVIEW 1980–THE PRESENT

KEY CONCEPTS AND EVENTS

acquired immune deficiency syndrome (AIDS), 808
air traffic controllers strike, 807
Al Jazeera, 821
Amazon, 830
Americans with Disabilities Act (ADA), 818
apartheid, 812
Apple Computer Company, 830
Arab Spring, 844
axis of evil, 837
Black Lives Matter, 843
Boland Amendment, 811
Brady Handgun Violence Prevention Act, 827
British Broadcasting Corporation (BBC), 821
Bush Doctrine, 837
Cable News Network (CNN), 821
Clean Air Act, 818
climate change, 822
Comprehensive Anti-Apartheid Act, 812
Contract with America, 828
Contras, 811
Defense of Marriage Act (DOMA), 828
Deferred Action for Childhood Arrivals (DACA), 842
Department of Homeland Security, 837
Development, Relief, and Education for Alien Minors (DREAM) Act, 841
eBay, 830

Economic Recovery Tax Act, 806
ethnic cleansing, 829
European Union (EU), 828
faith-based initiatives, 835
Family and Medical Leave Act, 827
Federal Assault Weapons Ban, 828
glasnost, 815
globalization, 821
Global War on Terror (GWOT), 836
Great Recession, 840
greenhouse gases, 822
Guantánamo, 839
Honda, 821
Hurricane Katrina, 839
Immigration Reform and Control Act, 809
Intermediate Nuclear Forces Treaty, 815
Internet, 830
invasion of Grenada, 811
Iran-Contra affair, 813
Iran Nuclear Agreement, 849
Islamic State of Iraq and Syria (ISIS), 845
Kyoto Protocol, 822
McDonald's, 821
Medicare Prescription Drug, Improvement, and Modernization Act, 836
#MeToo movement, 852
Microsoft, 830
National Rifle Association, 827
No Child Left Behind (NCLB), 836
North American Free Trade Agreement (NAFTA), 828
nuclear freeze movement, 815
Obergefell v. Hodges, 843

Occupy Wall Street movement, 843
Operation Desert Storm, 824
Operation Iraqi Freedom, 839
Operation Just Cause, 823
Palestine Liberation Organization (PLO), 812
Paris Climate Agreement, 847
Patient Protection and Affordable Care Act ("Obamacare"), 841
Patriot Act, 836
perestroika, 815
Personal Responsibility and Work Opportunity Reconciliation Act, 828
al-Qaeda, 820
Reaganomics, 805
Sandinistas, 811
Solidarity, 819
Strategic Arms Reduction Talks (START), 810
Strategic Defense Initiative (SDI), 809
supply-side economics, 805
Taliban, 820
Tea Party movement, 843
terrorism, 812
Tiananmen Square, 823
Toyota, 821
Twitter, 843
U.S. Immigration and Customs Enforcement (ICE), 849
Walmart, 821
Whitewater, 828
World Trade Organization (WTO), 828
World Wide Web, 830

KEY PEOPLE

Yasser Arafat, 824
Bashar al-Assad, 846
George H. W. Bush, 813
George W. Bush, 833
Dick Cheney, 836
Bill Clinton, 825
Hillary Clinton, 827

Geraldine Ferraro, 807
Christine Blasey Ford, 849
Bill Gates, 830
Mikhail Gorbachev, 815
Neil Gorsuch, 849
Anita Hill, 818
Saddam Hussein, 813

Steve Jobs, 830
Kim Jong-un, 849
Brett Kavanaugh, 849
Osama bin Laden, 820
Monica Lewinsky, 829
Nelson Mandela, 824
Trayvon Martin, 843

(Continued)

PERIOD 9 REVIEW 1980–THE PRESENT

Slobodan Milošević, *829*
Robert Mueller, *848*
Manuel Noriega, *823*
Barack Obama, *833*
Sandra Day O'Connor, *808*
Ross Perot, *825*
Colin Powell, *836*

Vladimir Putin, *846*
Muammar al-Qaddafi, *812*
Ronald Reagan, *804*
William Rehnquist, *808*
Condoleezza Rice, *836*
Donald Rumsfeld, *836*
Edward Snowden, *845*

Clarence Thomas, *818*
Donald Trump, *833*
Lech Walesa, *819*
Stephen Wozniak, *830*
Deng Xiaoping, *823*
Boris Yeltsin, *820*

CHRONOLOGY

Date	Event
1980s	AIDS epidemic spreads
	Rise of the nuclear freeze movement
1980s–1990s	Immigration surges from Mexico, Central America, the Caribbean, and South and East Asia
1980	Ronald Reagan (Republican) wins presidential election on conservative, anti-Communist platform
1981	Assassination attempt on Reagan
	Passage of the Economic Recovery Tax Act
	Air traffic controllers strike
1982	Strategic Arms Reduction Talks with Soviet Union
	Boland Amendment passed
	Ratification period expires for Equal Rights Amendment
1983	U.S. invasion of Grenada
	USSR shoots down a South Korean passenger airliner
1984	President Reagan wins re-election
1986	Passage of Immigration Reform and Control Act
1987	Senate hearings on Iran-Contra affair
	Intermediate Nuclear Forces Treaty signed
1988	George H. W. Bush (Republican) wins presidential election
1989	Tiananmen Square protests
	Fall of the Berlin Wall
1990	Americans with Disabilities Act passed
	Clean Air Act passed
	Passage of the Omnibus Budget Reconciliation Act
1991	Operation Desert Storm begins; U.S. pushes Iraq out of Kuwait
	Further strategic arms reduction talks with Soviet Union
	World Wide Web created
	Collapse of the Soviet Union
1992	Bill Clinton (Democrat) wins presidential election
1993	Second strategic arms reduction treaty (START II) signed
	North American Free Trade Agreement ratified
1994	Whitewater investigation
	Contract with America announced
c. 1995	Taliban comes to power in Afghanistan
1995	Creation of World Trade Organization
1996	Clinton wins re-election
	Personal Responsibility and Work Opportunity Reconciliation Act passed
	Defense of Marriage act passed
1998	U.S. refuses to ratify Kyoto Protocol to reduce greenhouse emissions
	U.S. House of Representatives votes to impeach Clinton
1999	Stock market reaches historic high
	U.S. Senate votes against Clinton's impeachment
2000	Supreme Court rules in favor of George W. Bush in contested presidential election
2001	September 11 attacks on World Trade Center and Pentagon
	Bush launches Global War on Terror
	U.S. troops invade Afghanistan
	Patriot Act passed
2002	Department of Homeland Security created
2003–2011	War in Iraq
2005	Hurricane Katrina
2008	Great Recession begins
	Barack Obama (Democrat) wins presidential election
c. 2009	Tea Party movement formed
2010	Patient Protection and Affordable Care Act ("Obamacare") passed

PERIOD 9 REVIEW 1980–THE PRESENT

- **2011** — Arab Spring protests
- Occupy Wall Street movement formed
- **2012** — Obama wins re-election
- Deferred Action for Childhood Arrivals (DACA) policy enacted
- **c. 2013** — Black Lives Matter movement formed
- **2015** — Supreme Court legalizes same-sex marriage nationwide
- **2016** — Donald Trump (Republican) wins presidential election
- **2019** — Special Prosecutor Robert Mueller submits report on Russian interference in the 2016 election

AP® EXAM PRACTICE THROUGH THE PRESENT

Multiple Choice Questions

Choose the correct answer for each question.

Questions 1–2 refer to the following excerpt.

> **Source:** Speech by President Ronald Reagan, March 20, 1981
>
> "We're not cutting the budget simply for the sake of sounder financial management. This is only the first step toward returning power to the States and communities, only a first step toward reordering the relationship between citizen and government. We can make government again responsive to the people not only by cutting its size and scope and thereby ensuring that its legitimate functions are performed efficiently and justly.
>
> Because ours is a consistent philosophy of government, we can be very clear: We do not have a social agenda, separate economic agenda, and a separate foreign agenda. We have one agenda. Just as surely as we seek to put our financial house in order and rebuild our nation's defenses, so too we seek to protect the unborn, to end the manipulation of schoolchildren by utopian planners, and permit the acknowledgment of a Supreme Being in our classrooms just as we allow such acknowledgments in other public institutions."

1. Based upon the excerpt, Reagan would most likely support
   a. cutbacks in military programs.
   b. reductions in spending on social welfare programs.
   c. a universal health care system.
   d. a greater role of government in protecting natural resources.

2. Reagan's ideas expressed in the excerpt found the greatest support among
   a. union organizations and laborers.
   b. the youth counterculture.
   c. Protestant evangelical Christians.
   d. feminists and gay activists.

Questions 3–4 refer to the following excerpt.

> **Source:** Editorial from *The New York Times*, April 2, 1989
>
> "The we-they world that emerged after 1945 is giving way to the more traditional struggles of great powers. That contest is more manageable. It permits serious negotiations. It creates new possibilities — for cooperation in combating terrorism, the spread of chemical weapons and common threats to the environment, and for shaping a less violent world.
>
> True, Europe remains torn in two; but the place where four decades of hostility began is mending and changing in complicated patterns. True, two enormous military machines still face each other around the world; but both sides are searching for ways to reduce the burdens and risks. Values continue to clash, but less profoundly as Soviet citizens start to partake in freedom. . . .
>
> The Bush Administration seems less attentive to these issues and more preoccupied with Mr. Gorbachev's seizing headlines worldwide. It would do better to think of him as part of the solution, not the problem. . . .
>
> Hints dribble out about senior [Bush Administration] officials worrying that Mr. Reagan was too friendly with Mr. Gorbachev and too eager for arms-control. That's self-defeating talk. . . . It would be unfortunate if the Bush team worried too much about their right flank and tried to prove that it can out-tough Mr. Reagan. That would drain them of the imagination and boldness necessary to go beyond the cold war."

TRM Suggested Responses to Questions

Answers to Multiple-Choice Questions

1. b
2. c
3. a
4. a
5. c
6. a
7. d
8. c
9. a
10. c
11. d

3. The excerpt from the *New York Times* editorial placed the greatest responsibility for ending the Cold War on
   a. President Reagan's military escalations.
   b. the risks posed by the global war on terrorism.
   c. long-term success of the policy of containment.
   d. the power of the United States' unilateral foreign policy.

4. The trends described in the *New York Times* editorial contributed most directly to
   a. intensifying debates over the appropriate use of American power in the world.
   b. a greater emphasis in American foreign policy on imperialist territorial ambitions.
   c. increased calls for international isolationism in U.S. public opinion.
   d. new awareness of the dangers of permanent foreign alliances.

Questions 5–8 refer to the following excerpt.

> **Source:** Republican Party Contract with America, 1994
>
> "[W]ithin the first 100 days of the 104th Congress, we shall bring to the House Floor the following bills . . .
>
> 1. THE FISCAL RESPONSIBILITY ACT: A balanced budget/ tax limitation amendment and a legislative line-item veto to restore fiscal responsibility to an out-of-control Congress, requiring them to live under the same budget constraints as families and businesses.
> 2. THE TAKING BACK OUR STREETS ACT: An anti-crime package including stronger truth-in-sentencing, 'good faith' exclusionary rule exemptions, effective death penalty provisions, and cuts in social spending from this summer's 'crime' bill to fund prison construction and additional law enforcement to keep people secure in their neighborhoods and kids safe in their schools.
> 3. THE PERSONAL RESPONSIBILITY ACT: Discourage illegitimacy and teen pregnancy by prohibiting welfare to minor mothers and denying increased [Aid to Families with Dependent Children] for additional children while on welfare, cut spending for welfare programs, and enact a tough two-years-and-out provision with work requirements to promote individual responsibility. . . .
> 6. THE NATIONAL SECURITY RESTORATION ACT: No U.S. troops under U.N. command and restoration of the essential parts of our national security funding to strengthen our national defense and maintain our credibility around the world. . . .
> 8. THE JOB CREATION AND WAGE ENHANCEMENT ACT: Small business incentives, capital gains cut and indexation, neutral cost recovery, risk assessment/cost-benefit analysis, strengthening the Regulatory Flexibility Act and unfunded mandate reform to create jobs and raise worker wages."

5. The excerpt from the Republican Party resulted most directly from
   a. the end of the Cold War.
   b. demographic shifts in the United States.
   c. the rise of new conservative political movements.
   d. the rapid nature of economic globalization.

6. The policies proposed in the excerpt from the "Contract with America" are best understood in the context of growing concerns about
   a. the decay of traditional United States moral values.
   b. the effects of growing international migration from Latin America and Asia.
   c. lessening the political influence of union organizations.
   d. international free-trade agreements.

7. The proposals in the excerpt best represent a continuation of the policies of which previous presidential administration?
   a. Woodrow Wilson
   b. Franklin Roosevelt
   c. Lyndon Johnson
   d. Ronald Reagan

8. Advocates for legislation enacting the "Contract with America" were LEAST likely to endorse which of the following policy goals?
   a. Promoting economic growth
   b. Reducing the social safety net
   c. Expanding civil liberties
   d. Deregulating businesses

AP® Exam Practice: Through the Present

Period 9: 1980–The Present

Questions 9–11 refer to the following graph.

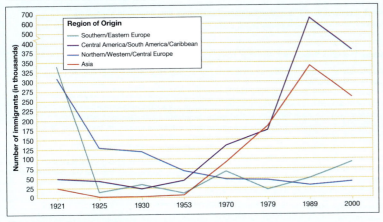

Immigration to America, 1921–2000

9. The pattern depicted in the graph between 1921 and 1953 most directly resulted from
   a. federal laws strictly limiting the number of immigrants.
   b. nativist violence toward undocumented immigrants.
   c. efforts to deport immigrants to their countries of origin.
   d. increased security along the Mexican and Canadian borders.

10. The majority of immigrants who arrived in the U.S. between 1970 and 2000 settled
    a. throughout the small towns of rural America.
    b. in the Northeast and Midwest.
    c. in the South and West.
    d. along the borders with Canada and Mexico.

11. The pattern depicted in the graph between 1979 and 2000 directly contributed to all of the following EXCEPT
    a. providing a vital source of labor for the American economy.
    b. ongoing political debates over U.S. immigration policy.
    c. fears of cultural changes diminishing traditional values.
    d. declining economic productivity from a surplus of unskilled immigrant labor.

TRM Suggested Responses to Questions

Period 9: 1980–The Present

AP® Exam Practice: Through the Present

Short-Answer Questions

Read each question carefully and write a short response. Use complete sentences.

1. Using the following two excerpts, answer (a), (b), and (c).

   Source: Thomas J. Sugrue, *Not Even Past: Barack Obama and the Burden of Race*, 2010

   "[Barack Obama] situating himself in a current of civil rights history that emphasized its radical currents would be political suicide.
      "But there was something deeper than simple political instrumentality at work. During his journey through the polarized racial world of late twentieth-century America, Obama discovered his calling . . . to overcome the acrimonious history of racial polarization—whether it be black power or the culture wars . . . to act on the understanding that such polarization was anathema to national unity. . . . By the time that Obama was inaugurated president, he had recast himself as an agent of national unification, one who could finally bring to fruition the few lingering, unmet promises of the civil rights movement. . . . From the cacophony[1] of the recent past, from its messiness and tumult, Obama extracts a powerful, reassuring message of progress . . . both true and mythological at the same time. Thus Barack Obama's own quest for identity and the distinctive history of the black freedom struggle, of urban politics, of civil rights and black power, became the American story. What Obama called 'my story' became 'our story.'"

   [1]A loud and confusing set of noises.

   Source: Michael Eric Dyson, *The Black Presidency: Barack Obama and the Politics of Race in America*, 2016

   "It is understandable that Obama prefers being seen as the black *president* rather than the *black* president. But his refusal to address race except when he has no choice—a kind of racial procrastination—leaves him little control of the conversation. When he is boxed into a racial corner, often as a result of black social unrest sparked by claims of police brutality, Obama has been mostly uninspiring: he has warned (black) citizens to obey the law and affirmed the status quo. Yet Obama energetically peppers his words to blacks with talk of responsibility in one public scolding after another. When Obama upbraids black folks while barely mentioning the flaws of white America, he leaves the impression that race is the concern solely of black people, and that blackness is full of pathology."

   a) Briefly explain ONE major difference between Sugrue's and Dyson's historical interpretations of the Obama presidency.
   b) Briefly explain how ONE specific historical event or development from the period 2000 to the present that is not explicitly mentioned in the excerpts could be used to support Sugrue's interpretation.
   c) Briefly explain how ONE specific historical event or development from the period 2000 to the present that is not explicitly mentioned in the excerpts could be used to support Dyson's interpretation.

AP® Exam Practice: Through the Present

Period 9: 1980–The Present

2. Using the following image, answer (a), (b), and (c).

a) Briefly explain ONE historical perspective about the changes from the 1950s to the early 2000s expressed in the cartoon.
b) Briefly explain how ONE specific event or development led to a historical change suggested by the cartoon.
c) Briefly explain ONE specific result of a historical change suggested by the cartoon in the period 2000 to the present.

3. Answer (a), (b), and (c).
a) Briefly explain why ONE of the following developments led to the most significant changes in United States society after 1980.
  - religious fundamentalism among Christians
  - economic policies of deregulation
  - taxation and budgetary policies
b) Briefly explain how ONE specific historical event or development supports your argument in (a).
c) Briefly explain why ONE of the other options less significantly changed United States society after 1980.

4. Answer (a), (b), and (c).
a) Briefly explain ONE specific historical similarity between immigration to the U.S. in the period 1880 to 1920 and in the period 1980 to the present.
b) Briefly explain ONE specific historical difference between immigration to the U.S. in the period 1880 to 1920 and in the period 1980 to the present.
c) Briefly explain ONE specific historical effect of immigration to the U.S. in the period 1980 to the present.

Period 9: 1980–The Present

AP® Exam Practice: Through the Present

Document-Based Question

Question 1 is based on the accompanying documents. The documents have been edited for the purpose of this exercise. *Suggested reading period: 15 minutes. Suggested writing time: 45 minutes.*

1. Evaluate the extent to which technological innovations have changed the American economy since 1980.

DOCUMENT 1

Source: Andrew Pollack, "Rising Trend of the Computer Age: Employees Who Work at Home," *The New York Times,* March 12, 1981

"Louise Priester used to key-punch insurance claims into a computer in the office of Blue Cross–Blue Shield of South Carolina. Now she does the same thing from a bedroom in her house in Columbia, S.C., using a terminal connected to the office's computer by telephone.

Like Mrs. Priester, a small but growing number of workers are doing office work at home on small computers or terminals with typewriter keyboards. Corporations encourage the practice, to save commuting time for their employees and to recruit some workers, such as mothers of small children, who might not be able to hold conventional jobs.

Working at home gives employees more flexibility in scheduling other activities. 'I can get up when I want to and work when I want to,' said Mrs. Priester, adding that she can now take better care of her elderly mother.

Companies and workers say the new system can transform relationships between co-workers, between employees and employers and between workers and their families.

What we're really talking about is returning production to the home, which is where it was before the Industrial Revolution."

DOCUMENT 2

Source: *Ford Assembly Line,* 1980

DOCUMENT 3

Source: Martin Feldstein, *American Economic Policy in the 1980s*, 1995

"The decade of the 1980s was a time of fundamental changes in American economic policy. These changes were influenced by the economic conditions that prevailed as the decade began, by the style and political philosophy of President Ronald Reagan, and by the new intellectual climate among economists and policy officials. . . . Ronald Reagan's election in 1980 . . . provided a president who was committed to achieving low inflation, to lowering tax rates, and to shrinking the role of the government in the economy."

DOCUMENT 4

Source: Peter F. Drucker, "Beyond the Information Revolution," *The Atlantic*, October 1999

"The truly revolutionary impact of the Information Revolution is just beginning to be felt. . . . It is something that practically no one foresaw or, indeed, even talked about ten or fifteen years ago: e-commerce—that is, the explosive emergence of the Internet as a major, perhaps eventually the major, worldwide distribution channel for goods, for services, and, surprisingly, for managerial and professional jobs. This is profoundly changing economies, markets, and industry structures; products and services and their flow; consumer segmentation, consumer values, and consumer behavior; jobs and labor markets. . . .

E-commerce is to the Information Revolution what the railroad was to the Industrial Revolution—a totally new, totally unprecedented, totally unexpected development. And like the railroad 170 years ago, e-commerce is creating a new and distinct boom, rapidly changing the economy, society, and politics. . . .

In the new mental geography created by the railroad, humanity mastered distance. In the mental geography of e-commerce, distance has been eliminated. There is only one economy and only one market."

DOCUMENT 5

Source: Bureau of Labor Statistics, U.S. Department of Labor, *Projection of Fastest Growing Jobs, 2000–2010*, November 2001

Period 9: 1980–The Present

DOCUMENT 6

Source: Leroy McClelland Sr., a steelworker, *Interview with Bill Barry*, 2006

"Mr. McClelland: [W]ith technology being advanced and computers and what have you, we've had operations that would never ever operate unless you had a person there. Now, that's not necessary. In fact, it can have a crew—it used to be six people on a mill reduced to three. Why? Computer, and then it advances further on down the road for technology. When that happened, too, you've got to understand that the idea of the union was to protect jobs, create jobs, not eliminate jobs. Well, I had the unfortunate experience of being the zone committeeman at the time when a lot of this technology was starting to really grow.

Mr. Barry: When was this?

Mr. McClelland: Well, it really started in 1975, from '75 on, '80, '90s, biggest part being in the '80s really, the advanced technology. But when these other things started to take place, guys and gals sort of looked at this change coming down, felt hey, that's a God send, not realizing that when that takes place you ain't going to be there to see it because your job is going to be gone.... I mean reality is technology is the future and competitiveness is strong. If you can't deal with competitiveness, if you don't have tons per hour and manpower per hour was the way it was, and that's what had to happen....

Mr. Barry: These were people who were eligible to retire and the technology in effect drove them out?

Mr. McClelland: Yes, absolutely it did. And change is tough for anybody."

DOCUMENT 7

Source: Robin Harding, "Technology Shakes Up U.S. Economy," *Financial Times*, March 26, 2014

"New technologies are transforming the structure of the US economy but creating only modest numbers of jobs, according to the biggest official survey of businesses, conducted only once every five years....

It highlights concerns that recent innovations in information technology tend to raise productivity by replacing existing workers, rather than creating new products that demand more labour to produce....

In manufacturing, the story is of a productivity boom that allowed a solid increase in sales, coupled with falling employment and payrolls. Manufacturing sales rose 8 per cent between 2007 and 2012 to reach $5.8 trillion.

However, the industry shed 2.1 million jobs—employment falling to 11.3 million—and its payroll dropped $20 billion to $593 billion.

The relatively greater drop in jobs than payrolls highlights how remaining jobs in the sector are becoming more skilled. Annual payroll per employee in the manufacturing sector rose from $45,818 in 2007 to $52,686 in 2012.

That is among the highest of any big industry, but highlights how manufacturing increasingly employs skilled engineers to tend complex equipment, rather than being a source of well-paid jobs for less-skilled workers."

Long-Essay Questions

Please choose one of the following three questions to answer. *Suggested writing time: 40 minutes.*

2. Evaluate the extent to which demographic shifts changed politics in the United States from 1980 to 2000.
3. Evaluate the extent to which demographic shifts changed culture in the United States from 1980 to 2000.
4. Evaluate the extent to which the end of the Cold War changed U.S. foreign policy from 1980 to 2010.

TRM Suggested Responses to Questions

AP® United States History Practice Exam

Exam Overview

Section	Question Type	Number of Questions	Timing	% of Total Exam Score
Section I	Part A: Multiple-Choice Questions	55 questions	55 minutes	40%
	Part B: Short-Answer Questions	3 questions	40 minutes	20%
Section II	Part A: Document-Based Question	1 question	60 minutes	25%
	Part B: Long-Essay Question	1 question	40 minutes	15%

SECTION I

Part A: Multiple-Choice Questions

55 minutes

DIRECTIONS: Choose the correct answer for each question.

Questions 1–3 refer to the following excerpt.

> "The extremely heterogeneous population confronted Pennsylvania with a unique set of problems that could have impeded the creation of a stable society. Nevertheless, despite the inevitable tensions, exacerbated by waves of new immigration, wars, and religious conflict, colonial Pennsylvanians managed to develop new ideals of pluralism and tolerance on which they built their province.... William Penn ... set forth a new, ideological basis for pluralism and tolerance that transformed the tentative pattern of relative harmony and toleration into one of official policy.
>
> ... [H]e drafted a series of constitutions that guaranteed religious freedom and promoted his colony not only in the British Isles but on the Continent as well."
>
> Sally Schwartz, *"A Mixed Multitude": The Struggle for Toleration in Colonial Pennsylvania*, 1987

1. Which of the following later developments can best be used to support Schwartz's argument regarding colonial culture in Pennsylvania?
   a. A strong abolitionist movement developed in Pennsylvania in the eighteenth and nineteenth centuries.
   b. Relations with American Indians deteriorated over time as colonists demanded more land.
   c. Pennsylvania's nineteenth-century leaders rejected the development of a strong national government.
   d. African Americans resisted enslavement in overt ways by forming open revolts against slaveholders.

2. Which of the following best explains the context in which Pennsylvania's culture in the colonial era developed?
   a. Leaders' insistence on tolerance in accordance with religious policy in England
   b. The colony's strong emphasis on economic goods as Pennsylvania was founded as a corporate colony
   c. The Anglicization of diverse migrants to Pennsylvania
   d. The Quaker founders' established policies favoring tolerance and individual freedom of conscience

---

TRM Suggested Responses to Questions

Answers to Multiple-Choice Questions

1. a
2. d
3. d
4. c
5. b
6. c
7. a
8. b
9. d
10. b
11. b
12. a
13. a
14. a
15. b
16. d
17. c
18. b
19. c
20. b
21. b
22. d
23. a
24. a
25. c

26. b
27. a
28. d
29. a
30. b
31. b
32. c
33. d
34. a
35. c
36. d
37. c
38. c
39. c
40. c
41. b
42. a
43. b
44. c
45. d
46. b
47. a
48. b
49. c
50. c
51. c
52. b
53. a
54. a
55. c

3. In the seventeenth century, Pennsylvania merchants engaged in the transatlantic trade most extensively by
   a. exporting tobacco from Pennsylvania to England.
   b. importing enslaved Africans to Pennsylvania.
   c. exporting staple crop rice from Pennsylvania to the Caribbean.
   d. importing goods manufactured in England.

Questions 4–6 refer to the following image.

▲ Segregated Waiting Room, Union Station, Jacksonville, Florida, 1921

4. This image illustrates which of the following trends in African Americans' experience in the period 1917–1945?
   a. The expansion of civil rights and suffrage that accompanied new opportunities for African Americans in the North
   b. The restrictions placed on African American voting rights in the North and the South
   c. The expansion of job opportunities in the North because of wartime labor shortages
   d. The tendency of African Americans to abandon Northern industrial jobs in favor of agricultural opportunities in the South

5. The process depicted in this image can best be understood as a contributing factor to the development of which of the following?
   a. Progressive Era
   b. Harlem Renaissance
   c. Romantic movement
   d. Reconstruction

6. Which of the following was likely the most important contributing factor in the decisions made by the individuals pictured in this image?
   a. Support for civil rights of African Americans in the North
   b. Passage of laws that disenfranchised African Americans in the South
   c. Inability of most African Americans to escape the system of sharecropping
   d. Propaganda created by northern political machines to attract voters

Questions 7–9 refer to the following excerpt.

> The Prime Immunity in Mans State, is that he is most properly the Subject of the Law of Nature. He is the Favourite Animal on Earth; in that this Part of Gods Image . . . God has provided a Rule for Men in all their Actions; obliging each one to the performance of that which is Right, not only as to Justice, but likewise as to all other Moral Vertues, which is nothing but the Dictate of Right Reason founded in the Soul of Man. . . .
>
> The Second Great Immunity of Man is an Original Liberty [ingrained] upon his Rational Nature. He that intrudes upon this Liberty, Violates the Law of Nature. . . .
>
> The Third Capital Immunity belonging to Mans Nature, is an equality amongst Men; Which is not to be denied by the Law of Nature, till Man has Resigned himself with all his Rights for the sake of a Civil State; and then his Personal Liberty and Equality is to be cherished, and preserved to the highest degree."
>
> John Wise, *A Vindication of the Government of New England Churches*, 1717

7. This excerpt could be best used as evidence to support an argument that
   a. Enlightenment ideals spread through transatlantic print culture influenced colonial political ideology.
   b. American Indian political systems such as the Iroquois League shaped colonial ideas about government.
   c. British North American colonies developed an original political philosophy.
   d. Parliament failed in efforts to control American political developments.

8. The ideas expressed in this excerpt most directly support a belief in
   a. the importance of religion in government.
   b. the rights of subjects.
   c. a rigid social hierarchy.
   d. royal authority.

9. The ideas expressed by John Wise in this excerpt share the greatest continuity with later ideas expressed in
   a. the Declaration of Sentiments.
   b. the U.S. Constitution.
   c. Thomas Paine's *Common Sense*.
   d. the Declaration of Independence.

Questions 10–13 refer to the following image.

"The Bloody Massacre," Paul Revere, 1770

10. The events portrayed in this image resulted most directly from
    a. a declaration of independence by colonial Americans.
    b. British attempts to assert royal authority over the North American colonies.
    c. the organization of the Sons of Liberty to promote a unified North American colonial government.
    d. the growing rivalry between England and France for control of North America

11. The point of view expressed in this image best represents the ideology of
    a. colonial governors.
    b. Patriots.
    c. British soldiers.
    d. the Great Awakening.

12. Which of the following most directly led to the events represented in this image?
    a. British enforcement of mercantilist policies in the colonies
    b. Disagreements among Protestant evangelicals
    c. George Washington's appointment as general of the Continental army
    d. British royal decrees that formally recognized American Indian lands west of the Appalachians

13. The image could best be used as evidence to support an argument that colonial leaders
    a. incorporated popular movements into calls for changes in British policy.
    b. used the free press to secure European allies to support colonial independence.
    c. placed political freedom and liberty above economic interests.
    d. demanded independence from British colonial rule as early as 1770.

Questions 14–16 refer to the following excerpt.

"The President assumes, what no one doubts, that the late rebel States have lost their constitutional relations to the Union, and are incapable of representation in Congress, except by permission of the Government. It matters but little, with this admission, whether you call them States out of the Union, and now conquered territories, or assert that because the Constitution forbids them to do what they did do, that they are therefore only dead as to all national and political action, and will remain so until the Government shall breathe into them the breath of life anew and permit them to occupy their former position. In other words, that they are not out of the Union, but are only dead carcasses lying within the Union. In either case, it is very plain that it requires the action of Congress to enable them to form a State government and send representatives to Congress. Nobody, I believe, pretends that with their old constitutions and frames of government they can be permitted to claim their old rights under the Constitution. . . . Dead men cannot raise themselves. Dead States cannot restore their existence 'as it was.' Whose especial duty is it to do it? In whom does the Constitution place the power? Not in the judicial branch of Government, for it only adjudicates and does not prescribe laws. Not in the Executive, for he only executes and cannot make laws. Not in the Commander-in-Chief of the armies, for he can only hold them under military rule until the sovereign legislative power of the conqueror shall give them law."

Thaddeus Stevens, Speech to Congress, December 18, 1865

14. Which of the following best explains the context in which Thaddeus Stevens delivered this speech?
    a. The debates over Reconstruction that immediately followed the end of the Civil War
    b. Political resistance to radical Republican use of military districts in Reconstruction
    c. Debate over passage of the Thirteenth Amendment in Congress
    d. The challenge presented by the passage in southern states of Black Codes after the Civil War

15. Thaddeus Stevens's arguments regarding which branch of the federal government holds power over the status of lands and admission of states shows the greatest similarity to the debates surrounding the
    a. Kansas-Nebraska Act.
    b. *Dred Scott* decision.
    c. Missouri Compromise.
    d. Louisiana Purchase.

16. The most important cause of the northern victory in the Civil War was
    a. the superiority of northern military leadership.
    b. aid from European allies for the Union.
    c. the advantageous geographical features of Union states.
    d. its greater resources.

Questions 17–19 are based on the following image.

◀ King Andrew the First, 1833

The text above the cartoon reads, "BORN TO COMMAND." The text to the right of the cartoon reads, "HAD I BEEN CONSULTED." The text beneath the cartoon reads, "KING ANDREW THE FIRST." The text to the left of the cartoon reads, "OF VETO MEMORY." "King Andrew" is shown holding a scroll that says "veto" on it, and he is standing on the U.S. Constitution and a document labeled, "Internal Improvements, U.S. Bank."

17. This cartoon most directly reflects the political views of the
    a. Federalist Party.
    b. Democratic Party.
    c. Whig Party.
    d. Republican Party.

18. At the time of its publication in 1833, this cartoon criticized political developments in the federal government that increased the
    a. role of Congress in promoting national economic growth.
    b. power of the president.
    c. power of the Supreme Court in enforcing judicial decisions.
    d. role of the people in electing federal politicians.

19. All of the following developments during the 1820s and 1830s reveal similar political party divisions as those reflected in this cartoon EXCEPT
    a. federal investment in roads, canals, and railroads.
    b. the gag rule passed in Congress to avoid confrontations over slavery.
    c. resistance to Indian removal by federal politicians.
    d. refusal to recharter the national bank.

Questions 20–23 refer to the following excerpt.

"Most of the men was gone, and . . . most of the women was in my bracket, five or six years younger or older. I was twenty-four. There was a black girl that hired in with me. I went to work the next day, sixty cents an hour. . . . I could see where they made a difference in placing you in certain jobs. They had fifteen or twenty departments, but all the Negroes went to Department 17 because there was nothing but shooting and bucking rivets. . . . Some weeks I brought home twenty-six dollars . . . then it gradually went up to thirty dollars. . . . Whatever you make you're supposed to save some. I was also getting that fifty dollars a month from my husband and that was just saved right away. I was planning on buying a home and a car. . . . My husband came back [from the war, and] . . . looked for a job in the cleaning and pressing place. . . . But what we both weren't thinking about was that they [North American] have better benefits because they did have an insurance plan and a union to back you up. Later he did come to work there, in 1951 or 1952. . . . [After I left to have a baby] North American called me back [and] was I a happy soul! . . . It made me live better. It really did. We always say that Lincoln took the bale off of the Negroes. I think there is a statue up there in Washington, D.C., where he's lifting something off the Negro. Well, my sister always said — that's why you can't interview her because she's so radical — 'Hitler was the one that got us out of the white folks' kitchen.'"

Fanny Christina (Tina) Hill, "War Work: Social and Racial Mobility,"
from *Rosie the Riveter Revisited*, by Sherna B. Gluck, 1987

20. Fanny Hill's experiences working in World War II differed most from those of women working in World War I in that
    a. during World War I industries hired almost exclusively white workers.
    b. when World War I ended most female workers left the industrial workforce.
    c. the World War II factory jobs were concentrated in the Sunbelt.
    d. women working during World War II refused to join labor unions.

21. The story told by Fanny Hill in this excerpt could be used to support all of the following arguments EXCEPT
    a. employers hired women to produce weapons during World War II.
    b. women experienced more respect for their work in World War II than in World War I.
    c. World War II led to improvements in working conditions.
    d. labor unions advocated on behalf of women workers during World War I.

22. Fanny Hill's sister's comments can best be understood as resulting most directly from
    a. international concerns leading to the founding of the United Nations.
    b. political and cultural expressions of domestic anticommunism.
    c. increasingly confrontational African American civil rights movement.
    d. foreign policies aiming at containment.

23. The experiences Fanny Hill discusses in this excerpt illustrate which of the following post-World War II developments?
    a. Suburbanization
    b. The civil rights movement
    c. The rise of conservatism
    d. The creation of a more educated populace

Questions 24–26 refer to the following excerpt.

"The question whether or no there shall be slavery in the new territories . . . is a question between the grand body of white workingmen, the millions of mechanics, farmers, and operatives of our country, with their interests on the one side — and the interests of the few thousand rich, 'polished,' and aristocratic owners of slaves at the South, on the other side. Experience has proved . . . that a stalwart mass of respectable workingmen, cannot exist, much less flourish, in a thorough slave State. Let any one think for a moment what a different appearance New York, Pennsylvania, or Ohio, would present — how much less sturdy independence and family happiness there would be — were slaves the workmen there, instead of each man as a general thing being his own workman. . . .

Slavery is a good thing enough . . . to the rich — the one out of thousands; but it is destructive to the dignity and independence of all who work, and to labor itself. . . . All practice and theory . . . are strongly arrayed in favor of limiting slavery to where it already exists."

Walt Whitman, "American Workingmen, versus Slavery," Editorial, September 1, 1847

24. Which of the following developments led most directly to this editorial by Walt Whitman?
    a. The U.S.-Mexico War
    b. Conflicts with Britain over Oregon
    c. The discovery of gold in California
    d. The underground railroad

25. The ideas expressed by Whitman in the second paragraph share the most continuity to the later political platform of the
    a. Progressive Party.
    b. Reconstruction-era Democratic Party.
    c. antebellum era Republican Party.
    d. Populist Party.

26. The ideas expressed by Walt Whitman in this excerpt show the most similarity to
    a. the Cult of Domesticity.
    b. free soil ideology.
    c. the Supreme Court decisions of the Marshall Court.
    d. abolitionist ideology.

Questions 27–30 refer to the following map.

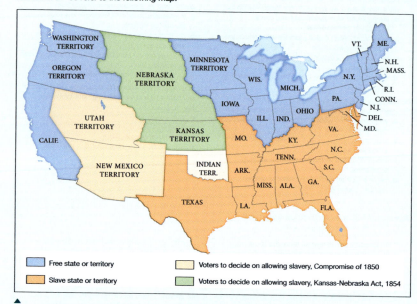

The Compromise of 1850 and the Kansas–Nebraska Act of 1854

27. In reference to territorial agreements shown in this map, which of the following was the most important concession made to southern congressmen in exchange for the agreement regarding California?
    a. The passage of a new Fugitive Slave Law
    b. The establishment of popular sovereignty in the Kansas Territory
    c. The repeal of the Missouri Compromise
    d. The federal government investment in a transcontinental railroad

28. This map illustrates a trend after the U.S.-Mexico War in the direction of
    a. maintaining the same number of free states and slave states in the Senate.
    b. expansion of women's rights to vote granted by western states.
    c. more extensive efforts to assimilate and incorporate American Indians.
    d. allowing local autonomy in decisions over slavery.

29. The Kansas-Nebraska Act changed federal policy most significantly by
    a. eliminating the 36°30′ division in territory gained in the Louisiana Purchase.
    b. introducing measures reducing American Indian tribal lands.
    c. promoting the establishment of Homestead Act settlements by farmers.
    d. opening western lands to migrations of African American farmers such as the Exodusters.

30. Agreements made in the Kansas-Nebraska Act and the Compromise of 1850 show the greatest continuity with the
    a. Three-Fifths Compromise.
    b. Missouri Compromise.
    c. Treaty of Guadalupe Hidalgo.
    d. Tariff of 1833.

Questions 31–33 refer to the following excerpt.

"It was upon these gentle lambs, imbued by the Creator with all the qualities we have mentioned, that from the very first day they clapped eyes on them the Spanish fell like ravening wolves upon the fold, or like tigers and savage lions who have not eaten meat for days. The pattern established at the outset has remained unchanged to this day, and the Spaniards still do nothing save tear the natives to shreds, murder them and inflict upon them untold misery, suffering and distress, tormenting, harrying and persecuting them mercilessly.... When the Spanish first journeyed there, the indigenous population of the island of Hispaniola stood at some three million; today only two hundred survive. The island of Cuba, which extends for a distance almost as great as that separating Valladolid from Rome, is now to all intents and purposes uninhabited; and two other large, beautiful and fertile islands, Puerto Rico and Jamaica, have been similarly devastated. Not a living soul remains today on any of the islands of the Bahamas.... On the mainland, we know for sure that our fellow-countrymen have, through their cruelty and wickedness, depopulated and laid waste an area which once boasted more than ten kingdoms, each of them larger in area than the whole of the Iberian Peninsula.... At a conservative estimate, the despotic and diabolical behaviour of the Christians has, over the last forty years, led to the unjust and totally unwarranted deaths of more than twelve million souls, women and children among them, and there are grounds for believing my own estimate of more than fifteen million to be nearer the mark."

Bartolomé de las Casas, *A Short Account of the Destruction of the Indies*, 1542

31. This excerpt is best understood in the context of
    a. exile of de las Casas from the Spanish colonies.
    b. debates in Spain over the treatment of Native Americans.
    c. establishment of the Atlantic slave trade with Africa.
    d. abolition of slavery in all Spanish colonies.

32. The most direct effect of the ideas expressed by de las Casas in the excerpt was
    a. the Columbian Exchange.
    b. European competition for lands in the Americas.
    c. debates over Spanish imperial policies.
    d. King Philip's War.

33. This excerpt from de las Casas could best be used as evidence to support an argument that the Spanish
    a. justified their treatment of American Indians as self-defense.
    b. allied with American Indians to create a mestizo society.
    c. creoles held preferred status in the Spanish caste system.
    d. used native labor in the *encomienda* system, regardless of the cost.

Questions 34–36 refer to the following image.

▶ James A. Wales, "Where both platforms agree — no vote — no use to either party," *Puck*, July 1880

The plank facing the viewer is labeled "REPUBLICAN PLANK." The plank facing away from the viewer is labeled "DEMOCRATIC PLANK."

34. Which of the following most directly led to the situation that preceded the 1870s conflict portrayed in this cartoon?
   a. Job opportunities created by rapid expansion of railroads
   b. Victory of the United States in the U.S.-Mexico War
   c. Limitations on Mexican immigration established by nativist quotas
   d. Increasing acceptance of Irish immigrants into the Democratic Party

35. This cartoon could best be used as evidence to support which of the following conclusions about the late nineteenth century?
   a. Republicans expressed a partisan support for Chinese immigration in opposition to the Democratic Party.
   b. Labor unions consistently opposed Chinese immigration.
   c. Nativist ideology grew in strength.
   d. Most Progressive-era reformers advocated for protections of Chinese American interests.

36. Which of the following best summarizes the trend in federal government immigration policy from the late nineteenth century through 1930?
   a. Immigration restrictions focused on the Chinese while allowing Europeans open immigration.
   b. Immigration restrictions against the Chinese were viewed as failed policies and reversed by the early twentieth century.
   c. Immigration restrictions lost the bipartisan support of Congress as business leaders advocated for more cheap labor.
   d. Immigration restrictions began with the Chinese and expanded to limit other groups, including Europeans.

Questions 37–39 refer to the following excerpt.

"Municipal health officials and city inspectors did make some advances against disease, especially through the improvement of the urban environment. They banned pigs from city streets, regulated notoriously unhealthy dairies inside city limits, and stepped up oversight of street cleaning and garbage removal. . . . [T]he Ladies Health Protective Association . . . shared a concern for the vile odors emanating from a manure handler along the East River . . . [and] the entire slaughter-house district near . . . the tenements fouled by sickening smells and backed-up sewage. . . . [T]he association contacted business owners directly with their complaints, and . . . organized demonstrations at the offending locations, inviting the press to witness their lay inspections. . . . The women also gained considerable publicity when they brought their complaints to the Board of Health."

David Stradling, *The Nature of New York: An Environmental History of the Empire State*, 2010

37. The sentiments expressed in this excerpt most directly support which of the following reform movements?
   a. Social Darwinism
   b. Social Gospel
   c. Progressivism
   d. Gospel of Wealth

38. The developments described by Stradling most directly reflect the context of
   a. an increasing role of the federal government in protection of the environment through propaganda campaigns.
   b. an expanding role of state governments ensuring public health through legislation.
   c. both lessening and modification of gender roles defined by domesticity.
   d. stable support for *laissez-faire* economic policies.

39. The actions of women described in this excerpt are most similar to the role of women reformers active during
   a. the First Great Awakening.
   b. the American Revolution.
   c. the Second Great Awakening.
   d. Reconstruction.

Questions 40–42 refer to the following image.

◀ John Sloan, "In Memoriam — The Real Triangle," 1911

40. The point of view expressed in this cartoon is most directly critical of the ideology of
   a. the Social Gospel.
   b. the Gospel of Wealth.
   c. *laissez faire*.
   d. late nineteenth-century domesticity.

41. People sharing the ideas supported in this cartoon also most likely supported
   a. the application of Social Darwinist philosophy to explain poverty.
   b. the passage of labor reforms and the expansion of worker unions.
   c. the creation of federal regulations to protect the natural environment.
   d. continuing federal government policies denying legal sanction to labor unions.

42. Images and political cartoons like this one were most effectively used to sway public opinion to support
   a. local ordinances to protect workers in the workplace.
   b. federal legislation to limit working hours.
   c. state laws to limit the power of railroads.
   d. expansion of suffrage rights to women.

Questions 43–45 refer to the following excerpt.

"In March, 1933, I appealed to the Congress of the United States and to the people of the United States in a new effort to restore power to those to whom it rightfully belonged. The response to that appeal resulted in the writing of a new chapter in the history of popular government. You, the members of the Legislative branch, and I, the Executive, contended for and established a new relationship between Government and people. What were the terms of that new relationship? They were an appeal from the clamor of many private and selfish interests, yes, an appeal from the clamor of partisan interest, to the ideal of the public interest. Government became the representative and the trustee of the public interest. Our aim was to build upon essentially democratic institutions, seeking all the while the adjustment of burdens, the help of the needy, the protection of the weak, the liberation of the exploited and the genuine protection of the people's property. . . . To be sure, in so doing, we have invited battle. We have earned the hatred of entrenched greed."

Franklin Roosevelt, "Annual Message to Congress," 1936

43. In this excerpt, Roosevelt most directly contradicts the ideology of
    a. liberalism.
    b. *laissez faire*.
    c. the Social Gospel.
    d. prohibition.

44. The ideas expressed by Roosevelt in this excerpt contributed most directly to a trend leading to
    a. a return to a nineteenth-century conception of federal government power.
    b. limitations on the powers of the federal government in favor of states' rights.
    c. a renewal of federal activism building on Progressive-era policies.
    d. a return to ideas about government common among elected officeholders during the Gilded Age of the late nineteenth century.

45. Which of the following individuals would most likely have supported Franklin Roosevelt's argument regarding use of federal power in this excerpt?
    a. Ronald Reagan
    b. Phyllis Schlafly
    c. Andrew Jackson
    d. Jane Addams

Questions 46–47 refer to the following excerpt.

"Within the context of cultural unrest and the attack on tradition made by women like [Betty] Friedan, the catalyst for a profounder criticism and a mass mobilization of American women proved to be the young female participants in the social movements of the 1960s. These daughters of the middle class had received mixed, paradoxical messages about what it meant to grow up to be women in America. On the one hand, the cultural ideal . . . informed them that their only true happiness lay in the twin roles of wife and mother. At the same time they could observe the reality that housewifery was distinctly unsatisfactory for millions of suburban women. . . . Such contradictions left young, educated women in the 1960s dry tinder for the spark of revolt. . . ."

Sara Evans, *Personal Politics: The Roots of Women's Liberation in the Civil Rights Movement and the New Left*, 1979

46. Which of the following best represents the "social movements of the 1960s" in which women's experiences led to greater activism?
    a. The movement for a Great Society
    b. African American civil rights movement
    c. The environmental movement
    d. The antinuclear movement

47. Women's activism experienced the greatest success in the 1960s and 1970s from
    a. policies requiring equal pay.
    b. passage of a constitutional amendment for equal rights.
    c. elimination of the cultural double standard in sexual norms.
    d. overcoming social expectations of domesticity.

Questions 48–50 refer to the following excerpt.

> "I want you to know that this administration is motivated by a political philosophy that sees the greatness of America in you, her people, and in your families, churches, neighborhoods, communities — the institutions that foster and nourish values like concern for others and respect for the rule of law under God.
>
> Now, I don't have to tell you that this puts us in opposition to, or at least out of step with, a prevailing attitude of many who have turned to a modern-day secularism, discarding the tried and time-tested values upon which our very civilization is based. No matter how well intentioned, their value system is radically different from that of most Americans. And while they proclaim that they're freeing us from superstitions of the past, they've taken upon themselves the job of superintending us by government rule and regulation. Sometimes their voices are louder than ours, but they are not yet a majority. . . .
>
> Freedom prospers when religion is vibrant and the rule of law under God is acknowledged. When our Founding Fathers passed the First Amendment, they sought to protect churches from government interference. They never intended to construct a wall of hostility between government and the concept of religious belief itself. Last year, I sent the Congress a constitutional amendment to restore prayer to public schools. . . ."
>
> Ronald Reagan, "The Rule of Law Under God," Speech to National Association of American Evangelicals, 1983

48. The ideas expressed by Reagan in this excerpt most directly appeal to a late twentieth-century trend toward
    a. increasing environmental regulation.
    b. politically active Christian evangelical churches and organizations.
    c. free-trade agreements.
    d. increased rights for women.

49. Reagan's ideas expressed in this excerpt led most directly to policies
    a. increasing military spending.
    b. deregulating major industries.
    c. that sought to end legalized abortion.
    d. decreasing taxes.

50. In the 1980s Reagan and the national Republican Party built a political coalition based on all of the following demographic groups EXCEPT
    a. suburbanites.
    b. former Democrats in the South.
    c. college graduates in urban areas.
    d. wealthy white Protestants.

Questions 51–53 refer to the following excerpt.

> "His [Alexander Hamilton's] plans . . . were not only a catalyst for sectional confrontation. They seemed an excellent confirmation of persistent Antifederalist suspicions of an engulfing federal power. . . . Coming in conjunction with the high style of the new government, the antipopulistic pronouncements of some of its supporters, and measures such as an excise tax and a professional army, the Hamiltonian program might as well have been designed to awaken specific expectations about the course and nature of governmental decay that were never very far beneath the surface of revolutionary minds."
>
> Lance Banning, *The Jeffersonian Persuasion: Evolution of a Party Ideology*, 1978

51. Which of the following developments best supports Banning's argument in this excerpt?
    a. Fear of rebellion as seen in the Stono Rebellion
    b. Failure of state government control as seen in Shays's Rebellion
    c. Anger at federal tax policy expressed in the Whiskey Rebellion
    d. Dissatisfaction with trade policy established by Pinckney's Treaty

52. The most immediate cause for the formulation of Hamilton's financial plans was the
    a. threat of war with France and Great Britain created by the Napoleonic Wars.
    b. crisis over issues of debt generated by the American Revolution.
    c. establishment of the first cabinet during Washington's administration.
    d. ratification debates that led to a loss of trust in the federal government.

53. Which of the following is the best example of the type of "sectional confrontation" referred to by Banning in this excerpt?
    a. The state of Virginia's resistance to the assumption of state debts
    b. The state of Massachusetts's opposition to establishment of a federal navy
    c. State competitions over land claims in the trans-Appalachian West
    d. Refusal of city leaders in New York and Philadelphia to support creation of a national bank

Questions 54–55 refer to the following figure.

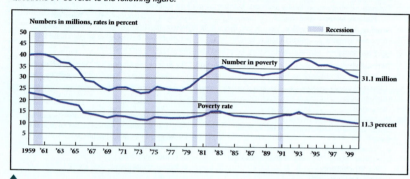

Number of Poor and Poverty Rate in America, 1959–2000

54. The information from this graph would likely be utilized by liberals to argue that
    a. Great Society programs dramatically reduced poverty in the U.S.
    b. U.S. involvement in the Vietnam War undermined the accomplishments of the Johnson administration.
    c. federal aid to those in poverty did not drastically alter living conditions in urban areas.
    d. the early accomplishments of the Great Society were reversed by use of block grants to states.

55. Which of the following presidential policies was inspired by the level of poverty in the U.S. in the period 1959–1961?
    a. New Frontier
    b. Affirmative Action
    c. War on Poverty
    d. Reaganomics

SECTION I

Part B: Short-Answer Questions

40 minutes

DIRECTIONS: Answer all parts of every question using complete sentences.

> "[T]he guarantor state . . . under the New Deal was . . . a vigorous and dynamic force in the society, energizing and . . . supplanting private enterprise when the general welfare required it. . . . When social and economic problems . . . were ignored or shirked by private enterprise, then the federal government undertook to do the job. [If] private enterprise failed to provide adequate and sufficient housing for a minimum standard of welfare for the people, then the government would build houses. . . . Few areas of American life were beyond the touch of the experimenting fingers of the New Deal. . . . The New Deal Revolution has become so much a part of the American Way that no political party which aspires to high office dares now to repudiate it."
>
> Carl N. Degler, *Out of Our Past: The Forces That Shaped Modern America*, 1959

> "The critique of modern capitalism that had been so important in the early 1930s . . . was largely gone. . . . In its place was a set of liberal ideas essentially reconciled to the existing structure of the economy and committed to using the state to compensate for capitalism's inevitable flaws. . . . When liberals spoke now of government's responsibility to protect the health of the industrial world, they defined that responsibility less as a commitment to restructure the economy than as an effort to stabilize it and help it to grow. They were no longer much concerned about controlling or punishing 'plutocrats' and 'economic royalists,' an impulse central to New Deal rhetoric in the mid-1930s. Instead, they spoke of their commitment to providing a healthy environment in which the corporate world could flourish and in which the economy could sustain 'full employment.' "
>
> Alan Brinkley, *The End of Reform: New Deal Liberalism in Recession and War*, 1995

1. Using the two excerpts, answer (a), (b), and (c).
   a. Briefly describe ONE major difference between Degler's and Brinkley's historical interpretations of the New Deal.
   b. Briefly explain how ONE specific historical event or development during Franklin Roosevelt's presidency (1933–1945) that is not explicitly mentioned in the excerpts could be used to support Degler's argument.
   c. Briefly explain how ONE specific historical event or development during Franklin Roosevelt's presidency (1933–1945) that is not explicitly mentioned in the excerpts could be used to support Brinkley's argument.

AP® United States History Practice Exam

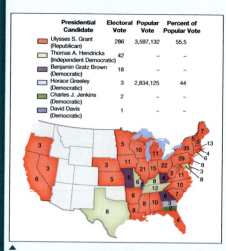

The Presidential Election of 1872

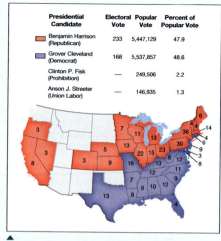

The Presidential Election of 1888

2. Using the two maps, answer (a), (b), and (c).
   a. Briefly explain how ONE specific historical event or development in the South led to a change in election patterns depicted on the maps.
   b. Briefly explain ONE specific historical change to southern society that resulted from a change in electoral patterns depicted on the maps.
   c. Briefly explain ONE specific change to the role of the federal government in the South resulting from a change in electoral patterns depicted on the maps.

DIRECTIONS: Choose EITHER Question 3 OR Question 4.

3. a. Briefly explain ONE specific historical difference between the Missouri Compromise (1820) and the Compromise of 1850.
   b. Briefly explain ONE specific historical similarity between the Missouri Compromise (1820) and the Compromise of 1850.
   c. Briefly explain ONE specific historical event or development resulting from either the Missouri Compromise (1820) OR the Compromise of 1850.

4. a. Briefly describe ONE specific historical similarity in the movement for African American civil rights between the period 1860 to 1880 and 1950 to 1970.
   b. Briefly describe ONE specific historical difference in the movement for African American civil rights between the period 1860 to 1880 and 1950 to 1970.
   c. Briefly explain ONE specific historical event or development that resulted from the movement for African American civil rights during the period 1950 to 1970.

SECTION II

Part A: Document-Based Question

60 minutes

DIRECTIONS: Question 1 is based on the accompanying documents. The documents have been edited for the purpose of this exercise. Write an essay using the seven documents below.

1. Evaluate the extent of difference between the impact of United States involvement in World War I (1914–1919) and the impact of United States involvement in World War II (1939–1945) on American society.

DOCUMENT 1   **Source:** *Factory workers applying camouflage to military armaments, c. 1917*

Library of Congress/Getty Images

DOCUMENT 2 **Source:** *Interview with Rubie Bond,* an African-American recollecting her experiences as a ten-year old in 1917, recorded in 1976

"I'm wondering why your family decided to leave Mississippi. How was that decision made and why was it made?

Well, the North offered better opportunities for blacks. . . . I've heard that recruiters were often in danger in Mississippi if they came down to get workers for northern companies.

Do you recall him ever expressing any fear about this job that he was doing?

Yes. I know that many of the blacks would leave the farms at night and walk for miles. Many of them caught the train to come North . . . Usually they would leave with just the clothes on their backs. Maybe the day before they would be in the field working and the plantation owner wouldn't even know that they planned to go and the next day he would go and the little shanty would be empty. . . .

Now, as a young girl, did you agree with this decision to move North? Did you think it was a good idea?

Yes. I think I did. Because even as a child I think I was pretty sensitive to a lot of the inequalities that existed between blacks and whites, and I know that after we came here my mother and dad used to tell me that if I went back to Mississippi, they would hang me to the first tree. . . ."

DOCUMENT 3 **Source:** George Creel, *How We Advertised America,* 1920

"The printed word, the spoken word, the motion picture, the telegraph, the cable, the wireless, the poster, the sign-board—all these were used in our campaign to make our own people and all other peoples understand the causes that compelled America to take arms. All that was fine and ardent in the civilian population came at our call until more than one hundred and fifty thousand men and women were devoting highly specialized abilities to the work of the Committee [on Public Information], as faithful and devoted in their service as though they wore the khaki. . . .

What we had to have was no mere surface unity, but a passionate belief in the justice of America's cause that should weld the people of the United States into one white-hot mass instinct with fraternity, devotion, courage, and deathless determination. The war-will, the will-to-win, of a democracy depends upon the degree to which each one of all the people of that democracy can concentrate and consecrate body and soul and spirit in the supreme effort of service and sacrifice. What had to be driven home was that all business was the nation's business, and every task a common task for a single purpose."

DOCUMENT 4 **Source:** General Dewitt, *Final Report; Japanese Evacuation of the West Coast,* 1942

"The security of the Pacific Coast continues to require the exclusion of Japanese from the area now prohibited to them and will so continue as long as that military necessity exists. . . . More than 115,000 persons of Japanese ancestry resided along the coast and were significantly concentrated near many highly sensitive installations essential to the war effort. Intelligence services records reflected the existence of hundreds of Japanese organizations in California, Washington, Oregon and Arizona which, prior to December 7, 1941, were actively engaged in advancing Japanese war aims. These records also disclosed that thousands of American-born Japanese had gone to Japan to receive their education and indoctrination there and had become rabidly pro-Japanese and then had returned to the United States. Emperor-worshipping ceremonies were commonly held and millions of dollars had flowed into the Japanese imperial war chest from the contributions freely made by Japanese here. The continued presence of a large, unassimilated, tightly knit and racial group, bound to an enemy nation by strong ties of race, culture, custom and religion along a frontier vulnerable to attack constituted a menace which had to be dealt with."

DOCUMENT 5 Source: Office of Price Administration, *How to Shop with War Ration Book Two*, 1943

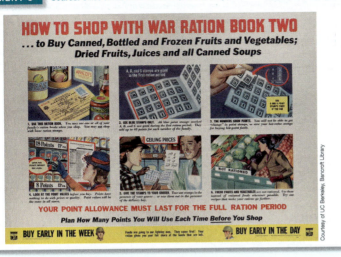

DOCUMENT 6 Source: Merlo J. Pusey, "Revolution at Home," *South Atlantic Quarterly 42*, July 1943

"Taken as a unit, the West is feeling the stimulus of war industry more keenly than either the North or the South. In 1940 the West had only 10.5 per cent of the country's population. But more than 13 per cent of the government's war-plant fund is being spent there, chiefly for permanent assets. . . . The Golden State [California] as a whole is getting more than $390,000,000 in Federal money for war plants. That gives it a sizable lead on the great industrial state of New York, and puts it far ahead of all New England in the wartime expansion of industrial capacity.

In the Northwest, Seattle is the hub of an amazing workshop for war. Grand Coulee and Bonneville dams are doing for the Northwest what Boulder Dam has done for Southern California and Nevada. . . . War has thus thrown into double-quick pace the industrial revolution that was already under way in the West. . . .

Nevada has acquired new government-financed plants costing the equivalent of nearly $600 for every resident. The agricultural Dakotas have no new war plants. In each case the consequences will be far-reaching. For in this nationwide mobilization there is no chance to maintain the status quo. If strategy and geography do not thrust a community into the maelstrom of war activity, its resources will be drained into other areas where they can better serve the national interest. So the whole pattern of our economic and social life is undergoing kaleidoscopic changes, without so much as a bomb being dropped on our shores."

DOCUMENT 7

Source: Bernhard J. Stern, "The Challenge of Advancing Technology," *The ANNALS of the American Academy of Political and Social Science*, 1945

"Even before the announcement of the unlocking of atomic energy, it could be said that advances in technology during the years of the war had been far greater than during many preceding decades. . . .

With the development of prefabricated houses, transport and passenger planes and helicopters, quick-frozen, dehydrated, and other processed and packaged foods, improved gasoline, and new and improved types of power for industrial production, for transportation, for illumination, and for easing household burdens, cities can be freer to develop functionally in terms of the harmonious living of their populations. Advances in public health and in medicine have made possible precipitous declines in death and morbidity rates, so that healthy city populations can enjoy the leisure which shorter working hours make available to them. Illiteracy and ignorance, long anachronisms in industrial societies, can more easily be liquidated through advances in human psychology and in educational processes.

The tools are ready. Will we be thwarted in their use?"

SECTION II

Part B: Long-Essay Questions

40 minutes

DIRECTIONS: Choose one of the following three questions to answer.

2. Evaluate the extent to which the ideology of "republican motherhood" fostered changes in definitions of citizenship in the United States between 1789 and 1820.
3. Evaluate the extent to which the nineteenth-century women's rights movement fostered changes in definitions of citizenship in the United States between 1820 and 1877.
4. Evaluate the extent to which the Progressive Era suffrage movement fostered changes in definitions of citizenship in the United States between 1890 and 1940.

Glossary/Glosario

English	Español
A	
abolitionists Members of the movement seeking to end the system of slavery.	**abolicionistas** Partidarios del movimiento que busca poner fin al sistema de esclavitud.
Abrams v. United States 1919 Supreme Court ruling limiting free speech by sustaining a guilty verdict of five anarchists who distributed leaflets denouncing U.S. military efforts to overthrow the Bolshevik regime.	***Abrams vs. Estados Unidos*** Resolución de la Corte Suprema de 1919 que limitó la libertad de expresión al declarar culpables a cinco anarquistas que distribuyeron panfletos que denunciaban las campañas militares del gobierno estadounidense para derrocar el régimen bolchevique.
acquired immune deficiency syndrome (AIDS) Immune disorder that reached epidemic proportions in the United States in the 1980s, especially among gay men and drug users.	**síndrome de inmunodeficiencia adquirida (SIDA)** Trastorno inmunológico que alcanzó proporciones epidémicas durante la década de 1980 en Estados Unidos sobre todo entre hombres homosexuales y consumidores de drogas.
Act of Religious Toleration 1649 act passed by the Maryland Assembly granting religious freedom to all Christians.	**Ley de tolerancia religiosa** Ley aprobada por la Asamblea de Maryland en 1649 que concedía libertad de culto a todos los cristianos.
Adams-Onís Treaty Treaty negotiated by John Quincy Adams and signed in 1819 by which Spain ceded all of its lands east of the Mississippi River to the United States.	**Tratado de Adams-Onís** Tratado firmado en 1819 y negociado por John Quincy Adams a través del cual España cedió a los Estados Unidos todas las tierras al este del río Misisipi.
Adamson Act 1916 act establishing an eight-hour workday and overtime for workers in private industry — in this case, railroad workers.	**Ley Adamson** Ley aprobada en 1916 que establece una jornada laboral de ocho horas y compensación por horas extraordinarias para los trabajadores de la industria privada. En este caso, trabajadores ferroviarios.
affirmative action Programs meant to overcome historical patterns of discrimination against minorities and women in education and employment. By establishing guidelines for hiring and college admissions, the government sought to advance equal opportunities for minorities and women.	**Acción afirmativa** Programas destinados a reducir los patrones históricos de discriminación contra las minorías y las mujeres en la educación y el empleo. A través del establecimiento de normas para la contratación y admisión a universidades, el gobierno buscó promover la igualdad de oportunidades para las minorías y las mujeres.
Agricultural Adjustment Act (AAA) 1933 New Deal act that raised prices for farm produce by paying farmers subsidies to reduce production. Large farmers reaped most of the benefits from the act. It was declared unconstitutional by the Supreme Court in 1936.	**Ley de ajuste agrícola (AAA, por sus siglas en inglés)** Ley federal del *New Deal* de 1933 que elevó los precios de los productos agrícolas a través del pago de subsidios a los agricultores para reducir la producción. Los grandes agricultores fueron los más beneficiados por esta ley. Fue declarada inconstitucional por la Corte Suprema en 1936.
Agricultural Marketing Act 1929 act aimed at raising prices for goods created by farmers to alleviate their financial suffering.	**Ley de comercialización agrícola** Ley promulgada en 1929 que buscó elevar los precios de los bienes agrícolas para mitigar los problemas financieros de los agricultores.
air traffic controllers strike 1981 strike by air traffic controllers for better working conditions and pay. President Reagan responded by firing employees who did not return to work within 48 hours.	**Huelga de controladores aéreos** En 1981, los controladores de tráfico aéreo declararon una huelga buscando mejoras en sus condiciones de trabajo y remuneración. En respuesta, el presidente Reagan respondió despidiendo a los trabajadores que no volvieran a trabajar en 48 horas.
Al Jazeera Arabic-language television channel, specifically designed for international broadcasts. Al Jazeera was established in 1996 and rose in prominence after its live coverage of the war in Afghanistan.	**Al Jazeera** Canal de televisión en lengua árabe diseñado específicamente para transmisiones internacionales. Al Jazeera fue fundada en 1996 y cobró importancia por su cobertura en directo de la guerra de Afganistán.
al-Qaeda Terrorist organization led by Osama Bin Laden, created in 1988. Al-Qaeda is a loosely organized radical religious fundamentalist organization, which opposes westernization and orchestrated the September 11, 2001 attacks on the United States.	**al-Qaeda** Organización terrorista fundada en 1988 por Osama bin Laden y basada en redes de militantes. Este movimiento fundamentalista radical antioccidental organizó los ataques del 11 de septiembre de 2001 contra los Estados Unidos.

Glossary/Glosario

Alamo Texas fort captured by General Santa Anna on March 6, 1836, from rebel defenders. Sensationalist accounts of the siege of the Alamo increased popular support in the United States for Texas independence.	**El Álamo** Fortaleza en Texas tomada por defensores rebeldes y capturada por el general Santa Anna del Ejército Mexicano el 6 de marzo de 1836. Las narraciones sensacionalistas sobre el asedio de El Álamo aumentaron el apoyo popular en Estados Unidos al movimiento de independencia de Texas.
Albany Plan of Union 1754 plan put together by Benjamin Franklin to create a more centralized colonial government that would establish policies regarding defense, trade, and territorial expansion, as well as aim to facilitate better relations between colonists and American Indians. The plan was never implemented.	**Plan Albany de la Unión** Plan elaborado por Benjamin Franklin en 1754 para crear un gobierno colonial más centralizado que estableciera políticas de defensa, comercio y expansión territorial y facilitara mejores relaciones entre colonos y nativos americanos. El plan nunca fue implementado.
Alien and Sedition Acts 1798 security acts passed by the Federalist-controlled Congress. The Alien Act allowed the president to imprison or deport noncitizens; the Sedition Act placed significant restrictions on political speech.	**Leyes de extranjería y sedición** Leyes de seguridad aprobadas en 1798 por el congreso controlado por federalistas. La Ley de extranjería permitía al presidente encarcelar o deportar a no-ciudadanos; la Ley de sedición impuso importantes restricciones a la expresión política.
Allies (World War I) Political allies during World War I consisting primarily of Great Britain, France, and Russia. Italy joined in 1915 and the United States in 1917.	**Los aliados (Primera Guerra Mundial)** Alianza política entre Gran Bretaña, Francia y Rusia durante la Primera Guerra Mundial. Italia se unió en 1915 y Estados Unidos en 1917.
almshouse A charitable public institution where the homeless, hungry, or aged could stay or receive goods or services. Almshouses, also known as poorhouses, were typically run by local governments and peaked in the second half of the nineteenth century. After the passage of the Social Security Act in 1935 they fell out of favor.	**hospicio** Institución pública de caridad donde las personas sin hogar, hambrientas o de edad avanzada podían permanecer o recibir bienes o servicios. Los hospicios o casas de beneficencia eran administradas por los gobiernos locales y alcanzaron su punto máximo en la segunda mitad del siglo XIX. Estas instituciones cayeron en desuso después de la aprobación de la Ley de seguridad social en 1935.
Amazon Online retail company established in 1994.	**Amazon** Empresa de comercio por internet fundada en 1994.
America First Committee Isolationist organization founded by Senator Gerald Nye in 1940 to keep the United States out of World War II.	**Comité America First** Aislacionista organización fundada por el senador Gerald Nye en 1940 para mantener a los Estados Unidos fuera de la Segunda Guerra Mundial.
American Anti-Slavery Society (AASS) Abolitionist society founded by William Lloyd Garrison in 1833 that became the most important northern abolitionist organization of the period.	**Sociedad antiesclavista estadounidense (AASS, por sus siglas en inglés)** Sociedad abolicionista fundada por William Lloyd Garrison en 1833 que se convertiría en la organización antiesclavista más importante de la época en el norte.
American Civil Liberties Union (ACLU) Founded as the National Civil Liberties Bureau in 1917, the ACLU (renamed in 1920) defends civil liberties through civil litigation. The ACLU was the first such organization to defend civil liberties for all individuals, rather than specific groups.	**Unión estadounidense por las libertades civiles (ACLU, por sus siglas en inglés)** Esta asociación, fundada en 1917 bajo el nombre de Oficina nacional de libertades civiles y que cambió de nombre a ACLU en 1920, se dedica a defender las libertades civiles a través de litigios. La ACLU fue la primera organización de este tipo en defender las libertades civiles de todos los individuos, en lugar de enfocarse en grupos específicos.
American Equal Rights Association Group of black and white women and men formed in 1866 to promote gender and racial equality. The organization split in 1869 over support for the Fifteenth Amendment.	**American Equal Rights Association** Grupo multirracial de hombres y mujeres formado en 1866 para promover la igualdad racial y de género. La organización se dividió en 1869 por diferencias con respecto a la decimoquinta enmienda.
American Expeditionary Forces (AEF) Established in 1917 after the United States entered World War I. These army troops served in Europe under the command of General John J. Pershing.	**Fuerzas expedicionarias americanas (AEF, por sus siglas en inglés)** Establecidas en 1917 después de que los Estados Unidos entraran en la Primera Guerra Mundial. Estas tropas del ejército sirvieron en Europa bajo el mando del general John J. Pershing.
American Federation of Labor (AFL) Trade union federation founded in 1886. Led by its first president, Samuel Gompers, the AFL sought to organize skilled workers into trade-specific unions.	**Federación estadounidense del trabajo (AFL, por sus siglas en inglés)** Federación de sindicatos fundada en 1886. Dirigida por Samuel Gompers, su primer presidente, la AFL buscó organizar a los trabajadores calificados en sindicatos sectoriales.
American Indian Movement (AIM) An American Indian group, formed in 1968, that promoted "red power" and condemned the United States for its continued mistreatment of American Indians.	**Movimiento indio estadounidense (AIM, por sus siglas en inglés)** Grupo de nativos americanos formado en 1968, que impulsó el "poder rojo" y denunció al gobierno estadounidense por su continuo maltrato a los nativos americanos.
American Party Also known as the Know-Nothing Party, a political party that arose in the Northeast, during the 1840s. The party was anti-Catholic and anti-immigration. It also supported workers' rights against business owners, who were perceived to support immigration as a way to keep wages low.	**Partido Estadounidense** También conocido como el Partido *Know-Nothing* (saber nada), este partido político surgió en el noreste durante la década de 1840. Además de ser anticatólico y antiinmigración, el partido apoyaba los derechos de los trabajadores en contra de los dueños de negocios, por considerar que éstos últimos estaban a favor de la migración para mantener bajos los salarios.

Glossary/Glosario

American Plan Voluntary program initiated by businesses in the early twentieth century to protect worker welfare. The American Plan was meant to undermine the appeal of labor unions.	**Plan estadounidense** Programa voluntario iniciado por varias empresas a principios del siglo XX para proteger el bienestar de los trabajadores. El Plan estadounidense buscaba socavar el atractivo de los sindicatos.
American Protective League (APL) An organization of private citizens that cooperated with the Justice Department and the Bureau of Investigation during World War I to spy on German residents suspected of disloyal behavior.	**Liga protectora estadounidense (APL, por sus siglas en inglés)** Organización de ciudadanos privados que cooperó con el Departamento de justicia y la Oficina de investigación durante la Primera Guerra Mundial para espiar a residentes alemanes sospechosos de conducta desleal.
American System Plan proposed by Henry Clay to promote the U.S. economy by combining federally funded internal improvements to aid farmers with federal tariffs to protect U.S. manufacturing and a national bank to oversee economic development; not to be confused with the American system of manufacturing (see Module 4-1).	**Sistema americano** Plan propuesto por Henry Clay para impulsar la economía estadounidense a través del financiamiento federal de infraestructura para el comercio agrícola, aranceles federales para proteger la manufactura estadounidense y un banco nacional para supervisar el desarrollo económico. No debe confundirse con el Sistema americano de manufactura (véase Módulo 4-1).
American system of manufacturing Production system focused on water-powered machinery, division of labor, and the use of interchangeable parts. The introduction of the American system in the early nineteenth century greatly increased the productivity of American manufacturing.	**Sistema americano de manufactura** Sistema de producción centrado en la maquinaria hidráulica, la división del trabajo y el uso de piezas intercambiables. La introducción del sistema americano a principios del siglo XIX aumentó considerablemente la productividad de la industria manufacturera estadounidense.
Americans with Disabilities Act (ADA) 1990 act extending legal protections and accessibility mandates for Americans with physical and mental handicaps.	**Ley para estadounidenses con discapacidades (ADA, por sus siglas en inglés)** Ley promulgada en 1990 que amplia las protecciones legales y los mandatos de accesibilidad para los estadounidenses con discapacidades físicas y mentales.
***Amistad* Mutiny** 1839 slave rebellion on the *Amistad*, a slave ship headed for Cuba. The mutineers were captured two months later, and their ship was towed to Connecticut, a slave state. There, the mutineers sued for their freedom, and in 1841 the U.S. Supreme Court declared them to be free because it was illegal to import enslaved people from Africa to America.	**Motín de *La Amistad*** Rebelión de personas esclavizadas de 1839 en el barco de esclavos *La Amistad* que se dirigía a Cuba. Las personas esclavizadas fueron capturadas dos meses después y su barco fue remolcado a Connecticut, un estado esclavista. Allí, los amotinados presentaron una demanda exigiendo su libertad y en 1841 la Corte Suprema los declaró libres porque era ilegal importar personas esclavizadas de África.
Anglicization Adoption of or becoming English in character and tradition. In colonial America, this took the form of English legal and social traditions dominating colonial institutions by the eighteenth century.	**anglicanización** Adopción de la cultura y tradiciones británicas. Durante la época colonial, este proceso llevó a que las tradiciones legales y sociales británicas dominaran las instituciones coloniales para el siglo XVIII.
Anglo-Powhatan Wars Series of conflicts in the 1620s between the Powhatan Confederacy and English settlers in Virginia and Maryland.	**Guerras Anglo-Powhatan** Series de conflictos en la década de 1620 entre la Confederación Powhatan y un grupo de colonos ingleses en Virginia y Maryland.
Anti-Imperialist League An organization founded in 1898 to oppose annexation of the Philippines. Some feared the annexation would bring competition from cheap labor; others considered Filipinos racially inferior and the Philippines unsuitable as an American territory.	**Liga antiimperialista** Organización fundada en 1898 para oponerse a la anexión de Filipinas. Algunos temían que la anexión llevaría a mayor competencia de mano de obra barata; otros consideraban que los filipinos eran racialmente inferiores y las Filipinas no eran aptas para ser territorio estadounidense.
Antifederalists Opponents of ratification of the Constitution. They were generally from more rural and less wealthy backgrounds than the Federalists.	**antifederalistas** Opositores a la ratificación de la Constitución. Por lo general, los antifederalistas provenían de contextos más rurales y menos adinerados que los federalistas.
apartheid Legal and institutionalized system of discrimination and segregation based on race in South Africa from 1948 until 1994.	**apartheid** Sistema legal e institucionalizado de discriminación y segregación racial en Sudáfrica que estuvo en vigor desde 1948 hasta 1994.
appeasement The policy of England and France that allowed the Nazis to annex Czechoslovak territory in exchange for Hitler promising not to take further land — a pledge he soon violated.	**apaciguamiento** Política de Inglaterra y Francia que permitió a los nazis anexionar territorio checoslovaco a cambio de que Hitler prometiera no tomar más tierras –promesa que pronto rompería.
Apple Computer Company Electronics company founded in 1976 known for its iconic apple logo and iPhone.	**Apple Computer Company** Empresa de productos electrónicos fundada en 1976, conocida por el iPhone y su emblemático logotipo de la manzana.
Arab Spring Political movement in the Middle East in 2011, which led to the toppling of pro-Western but despotic governments in Egypt, Tunisia, and Yemen. Armed rebels overthrew Lybian dictator Muammar al-Qaddafi. The movement was spurred on by the aid of technology such as cell phones and the utility of social media networks to spread their messages.	**Primavera árabe** Movimiento político del Medio Oriente en 2011 que condujo al derrocamiento pacífico de gobiernos pro Occidentales pero despóticos en Egipto, Túnez y Yemen. Grupos de rebeldes armados derrocaron al dictador libio Muamar el Gadafi. El movimiento fue impulsado por el uso de tecnología, los teléfonos celulares y las redes sociales para difundir sus mensajes.

Glossary/Glosario

aristocratic Members of the highest class of society, typically nobility who inherited their ranks and titles.	**aristócratas** Miembros de la clase más alta de la sociedad, usualmente nobles que heredaron sus rangos y títulos.
Articles of Confederation Plan for national government proposed by the Continental Congress of 1777 and ratified in March 1781. The Articles of Confederation gave the national government limited powers, reflecting widespread fear of centralized authority, and were replaced by the Constitution in 1789.	**Artículos de la Confederación** Plan para un gobierno nacional propuesto por el Congreso Continental de 1777 y ratificado en marzo de 1781. Los Artículos de la Confederación otorgaron al gobierno nacional poderes limitados, reflejando el temor generalizado a la autoridad centralizada, y fueron reemplazados por la Constitución en 1789.
astrolabe A tool invented by Greek astronomers and sailors for navigation or astrological problems.	**astrolabio** Instrumento inventado por astrónomos y marineros griegos para la navegación o resolución de problemas astrológicos.
Atlantic Charter August 1941 agreement between Franklin Roosevelt and Winston Churchill that outlined potential war aims and cemented the relationship between the United States and Britain.	**Carta del Atlántico** Acuerdo firmado en agosto de 1941 entre Franklin Roosevelt y Winston Churchill que esbozaba los posibles objetivos de guerra y cimentaba la relación entre Estados Unidos y Gran Bretaña.
Atlantic World The interactions between the peoples from the lands bordering the Atlantic Ocean — Africa, the Americas, and Western Europe — beginning in the late fifteenth century.	**mundo atlántico** Las interacciones entre los pueblos de las tierras que limitan con el Océano Atlántico, es decir, África, América y Europa Occidental, a partir de finales del siglo XV.
attack on Pearl Harbor December 7, 1941 Japanese attack on the U.S. Pacific Fleet stationed at Pearl Harbor in Honolulu, Hawaii. This surprise air and naval assault killed more than 2,400 Americans, seriously damaged ships and aircraft, and abruptly ended isolationism by prompting U.S. entry into World War II.	**ataque a Pearl Harbor** Ataque japonés realizado el 7 de diciembre de 1941 contra la Flota del Pacífico de Estados Unidos apostada en Pearl Harbor en Honolulu, Hawái. Este sorpresivo ataque aéreo y naval mató a más de 2,400 estadounidenses, causó severos daños a barcos y aviones, y terminó abruptamente con el aislacionismo al provocar la entrada de Estados Unidos a la Segunda Guerra Mundial.
axis of evil Term coined by president George W. Bush in 2002. Bush claimed Iraq, Iran, and North Korea were a part of an "axis of evil" due to their support of terrorist organizations and pursuit of chemical, biological, and nuclear weapons.	**eje del mal** Término acuñado por el presidente George W. Bush en 2002. Bush afirmó que Irak, Irán y Corea del Norte eran parte de un "eje del mal" por su apoyo a organizaciones terroristas y búsqueda de armas químicas, biológicas y nucleares.
Aztec Spanish term for the Mexica, an indigenous people who built an empire in present-day Mexico in the centuries before the arrival of the Spaniards.	**azteca** El término español para designar a los mexicas, pueblo indígena que construyó un imperio en el territorio actual de México durante los siglos anteriores a la llegada de los españoles.
B	
baby boom Sharp population increase between 1946 and 1964 as a result of the end of World War II, increased economic prosperity, improvements in healthcare, and a trend toward marriage at younger age.	**explosión de natalidad** Notable incremento de la población entre 1946 y 1964 como resultado del final de la Segunda Guerra Mundial, la prosperidad económica, los avances en la salud y una tendencia a casarse a una edad más temprana.
Bacon's Rebellion 1676 uprising in Virginia led by Nathaniel Bacon. Bacon and his followers, many of whom were former servants, were upset by the Virginia governor's unwillingness to send troops to intervene in conflicts between settlers and American Indians and by the lack of representation of western settlers in the House of Burgesses.	**Rebelión de Bacon** Levantamiento armado en Virginia en 1676 liderado por Nathaniel Bacon. Bacon y sus seguidores, muchos de los cuales eran exsirvientes, estaban molestos por la falta de voluntad del gobernador de Virginia para enviar tropas a intervenir en conflictos entre colonos y nativos americanos y por la falta de representación de los colonos occidentales en la Cámara de los Burgueses.
Bandung Conference A conference of twenty-nine Asian and African nations held in Indonesia in 1955, which declared their neutrality in the Cold War struggle between the United States and the Soviet Union and condemned colonialism.	**Conferencia de Bandung** Reunión de veintinueve estados asiáticos y africanos celebrada en Indonesia en 1955, en la que las naciones asistentes declararon su neutralidad en la Guerra Fría entre Estados Unidos y la Unión Soviética y condenaron el colonialismo.
Bank of the United States National bank established in 1791. The bank was responsible for holding large portions of federal funds and distributing loans and currency.	**Banco de los Estados Unidos** Banco nacional establecido en 1791. Esta institución era responsable de la tenencia de grandes porciones de fondos federales y de la distribución de préstamos y dinero circulante.
Barbary States Series of states in North Africa that used state-sanctioned piracy to gain wealth from other weaker nations in the Atlantic world. The pirates would frequently seize American ships and hold the sailors for ransom in the eighteenth and early nineteenth centuries.	**estados de Berbería** Estados de África del norte que utilizaron la piratería autorizada por el Estado para obtener riqueza de otras naciones más débiles del mundo atlántico. Los piratas solían apoderarse de barcos estadounidenses y retener a los marineros para pedir rescate durante los siglos XVIII y principios del XIX.
Battle of Antietam September 1862 battle in Sharpsburg, Maryland. While it remains the bloodiest single day in U.S. military history, it gave Abraham Lincoln the victory he sought before announcing the Emancipation Proclamation.	**Batalla de Antietam** Conflicto ocurrido en Sharpsburg, Maryland, en septiembre de 1862. Aunque sigue siendo el día más sangriento de la historia militar de Estados Unidos, esta batalla le dio a Abraham Lincoln la victoria que buscaba para anunciar su Proclamación de Emancipación.

English	Español
Battle of the Bulge Last German offensive launched in mid-December of 1944, which resulted in a German retreat across the Rhine River back into Germany.	**Batalla de las Ardenas** Última ofensiva alemana lanzada a mediados de diciembre de 1944, que resultó en una derrota para las tropas alemanas, quienes cruzaron el río Rin en retirada hacia el territorio alemán.
Battle of Bull Run (First Manassas) First major battle of the Civil War at which Confederate troops defeated Union forces in July 1861.	**Batalla de Bull Run (Primera Batalla de Manassas)** Primer gran combate de la Guerra Civil en el que las tropas confederadas derrotaron al ejército de la Unión en julio de 1861.
Battle of Bunker Hill 1775 American Revolution battle in which British troops narrowly defeated patriot militias, emboldening patriot forces.	**Batalla de Bunker Hill** Batalla de 1775 durante la Revolución Estadounidense, en la que las tropas británicas derrotaron por un estrecho margen a las milicias revolucionarias, revitalizando el esfuerzo independentista.
Battle of Fallen Timbers Battle at which U.S. General Anthony Wayne won a major victory over a multi-tribe coalition of American Indians in the Northwest Territory in 1794.	**Batalla de los Árboles Caídos** Batalla en la que el general estadounidense Anthony Wayne ganó una importante victoria sobre una coalición de tribus de nativos americanos en el Territorio del Noroeste en 1794.
Battle of Gettysburg July 1863 battle that helped turn the tide for the Union in the Civil War. The Union victory at Gettysburg, Pennsylvania, combined with a victory at Vicksburg, Mississippi the same month, eliminated the threat of European intervention in the war and positioned the Union to push farther into the South.	**Batalla de Gettysburg** Batalla librada en julio de 1863 que ayudó a cambiar el rumbo de la Unión en la Guerra Civil. La victoria de la Unión en Gettysburg, Pensilvania, combinada con una victoria en Vicksburg, Misisipi, el mismo mes, eliminó la amenaza de la intervención europea en la guerra y posicionó a la Unión para presionar más hacia el Sur.
Battle of Horseshoe Bend In 1814, Tennessee militia led by Andrew Jackson fought alongside Cherokee warriors to defeat Creek forces allied with Britain during the War of 1812.	**Batalla de Horseshoe Bend** En 1814, la milicia de Tennessee liderada por Andrew Jackson luchó junto a los guerreros Cherokee para derrotar a las fuerzas de nativos creek aliados con Gran Bretaña durante la Guerra de 1812.
Battle of Iwo Jima March 1945 battle in which the U.S. captured Iwo Jima, a heavily fortified Japanese island.	**Batalla de Iwo Jima** Batalla librada en marzo de 1945 en la que Estados Unidos capturó Iwo Jima, una isla japonesa muy fortificada.
Battle of the Little Bighorn 1876 battle in the Montana Territory in which Lieutenant Colonel George Armstrong Custer and his troops were massacred by the Lakota Sioux.	**Batalla de Little Bighorn** Tuvo lugar en el territorio de Montana en 1876. El teniente coronel George Armstrong Custer y sus tropas fueron masacrados por fuerzas sioux lakota.
Battle of Midway Island First engagement between Japanese and U.S. Navy six months after the Japanese attack on Pearl Harbor in June of 1942. The battle resulted in a U.S. victory.	**Batalla de Midway Island** Primer conflicto entre la armada japonesa y la estadounidense, seis meses después del ataque japonés a Pearl Harbor en junio de 1942. La batalla resultó en una victoria de Estados Unidos.
Battle of New Orleans January 8, 1815 battle during the War of 1812, resulting in an American victory. The Treaty of Ghent, which had technically ended the war, had been signed two weeks prior to the battle, but forces on neither side knew the war had ended.	**Batalla de Nueva Orleans** Librada el 8 de enero de 1815 entre Estados Unidos y Gran Bretaña, durante la Guerra de 1812. Resultó en una victoria para Estados Unidos. El Tratado de Gante, que técnicamente había puesto fin a la guerra, se había firmado dos semanas antes de la batalla, pero ninguno de los ejércitos presentes en la batalla sabían que la guerra había terminado.
Battle of Okinawa The last major battle and amphibious assault in the Pacific theater of World War II. It was one of the costliest battles of the war for the U.S., resulting in 6,000 American casualties.	**Batalla de Okinawa** La última gran batalla y el mayor asalto anfibio en el teatro del Pacífico de la Segunda Guerra Mundial. Fue una de las batallas más costosas de la guerra para Estados Unidos, con 6,000 bajas estadounidenses.
Battle of Saratoga Key American Revolution battle fought at Saratoga, New York. The patriot victory there in October 1777 provided hope that the colonists could triumph and increased the chances that the French would formally join the patriot side.	**Batalla de Saratoga** Batalla de la Revolución Estadounidense en Saratoga, Nueva York. La victoria patriota en octubre de 1777 infundió esperanzas de que los colonos pudieran triunfar y aumentó las posibilidades de que los franceses se aliaran formalmente al lado de los patriotas.
Battle of Shiloh April 1862 battle in Tennessee that provided the Union entrance to the Mississippi valley. Shiloh was the bloodiest battle in American history to that point.	**Batalla de Shiloh** Batalla librada en abril de 1862 en Tennessee en la que la Unión entró al valle de Misisipi. Shiloh fue la batalla más sangrienta de la historia de Estados Unidos hasta ese momento.
Battle of Yorktown Decisive battle in which the surrender of British forces on October 19, 1781, at Yorktown, Virginia, effectively sealed the patriot victory in the American Revolution.	**Batalla de Yorktown** Batalla decisiva en la que las fuerzas británicas se rindieron el 19 de octubre de 1781 en Yorktown, Virginia, con lo cual se afianzó definitivamente la victoria patriota en la Revolución Estadounidense.
Bay of Pigs invasion Unsuccessful 1961 attempt under the Kennedy administration to overthrow the Castro regime in Cuba.	**invasión de Bahía de Cochinos** Intento fallido bajo el gobierno de Kennedy, en 1961, de derrocar el régimen de Castro en Cuba.

Glossary/Glosario

English	Español
Beats A small group of young poets, writers, intellectuals, musicians, and artists who challenged mainstream American politics and culture in the 1950s.	**Beats** Pequeño grupo de jóvenes poetas, escritores, intelectuales, músicos y artistas que desafiaron la política y la cultura estadounidense en la década de 1950.
Berlin airlift The mass-scale transport of food and supplies to West Berlin by U.S. and British government air forces during the Soviet blockade of Berlin from 1948 to 1949.	**puente aéreo de Berlín** Transporte masivo de alimentos y suministros a Berlín Occidental por parte de las fuerzas aéreas de los gobiernos de Estados Unidos y Gran Bretaña durante el bloqueo soviético de Berlín de 1948 a 1949.
Berlin Wall Physical and ideological barrier between East and West Berlin which existed from 1961 until 1989. The wall was designed to prevent Soviet controlled East Berliners from fleeing to the West.	**Muro de Berlín** Barrera física e ideológica entre Berlín Oriental y Berlín Occidental que estuvo en pie entre 1961 y 1989. El muro fue diseñado para impedir que los habitantes de la ciudad de Berlín Oriental, controlada por los soviéticos, huyeran al Occidente.
"big stick" diplomacy Aggressive foreign diplomacy backed by the threat of force. Its name comes from a proverb quoted by Theodore Roosevelt: "Speak softly and carry a big stick."	**diplomacia del "gran garrote"** Práctica agresiva de diplomacia exterior respaldada por la amenaza de la fuerza. Su nombre proviene de un proverbio citado por Theodore Roosevelt: "Habla suavemente y lleva un gran garrote".
Bill of Rights The first ten amendments to the Constitution. These ten amendments helped reassure Americans who feared that the federal government established under the Constitution would infringe on the rights of individuals and states.	**Carta de Derechos** Las primeras diez enmiendas a la Constitución. Estas diez enmiendas ayudaron a tranquilizar a los estadounidenses que temían que el gobierno federal establecido por la Constitución violaría los derechos de los individuos y los Estados.
Billion Dollar Congress The Republican-controlled Congress of 1890 that spent huge sums of money to promote business and other interests.	**Congreso de los mil millones de dólares** El Congreso de 1890, controlado por republicanos, que gastó enormes sumas de dinero para impulsar negocios y otros intereses.
black codes Racial laws passed by southern legislatures in the immediate aftermath of the Civil War that aimed to keep freedpeople in a condition as close to slavery as possible.	**Códigos negros** Leyes raciales aprobadas por las legislaturas del sur inmediatamente después de la Guerra Civil con el objetivo de mantener a las personas liberadas en condiciones lo más cercanas posible a la esclavitud.
Black Lives Matter Social protest movement that formed after a civilian shot and killed Trayvon Martin, an unarmed African American youth, in 2012. Organized by protestors around the social media hashtag #blacklivesmatter, the movement advocated a policy agenda that mainly focused on criminal justice and police reforms.	**Black Lives Matter (Las vidas negras importan)** Movimiento de protesta social que se formó después de que un civil armado disparara y matara a Trayvon Martin, un joven afroamericano desarmado, en 2012. El movimiento, organizado por manifestantes en torno al *hashtag #blacklivesmatter* en redes sociales, abogó por una agenda política que se centrara principalmente en la justicia penal y las reformas policiales.
Black Panther Party Organization founded in 1966 by Huey P. Newton and Bobby Seale to advance the black power movement in black communities.	**Partido Pantera Negra** Organización fundada en 1966 por Huey P. Newton y Bobby Seale para promover el movimiento *black power* (poder negro) en las comunidades negras.
Black Tuesday October 29, 1929 crash of the U.S. stock market. This event has historically marked the beginning of the Great Depression, though it was not the depression's root cause.	**Martes negro** El 29 de octubre de 1929, día del desplome del mercado de valores de los EE.UU. Este evento marca el comienzo de la Gran Depresión, aunque no fue su causa principal.
Bleeding Kansas The Kansas Territory during a period of violent conflicts over the fate of slavery in the mid-1859s. This violence intensified the sectional division over slavery.	**Sangrado de Kansas** Período de conflictos violentos en torno a la legalidad de la esclavitud en el Territorio de Kansas a mediados de 1859. Esta violencia intensificó la división sectorial al respecto de la esclavitud.
Boland Amendment 1982 act of Congress prohibiting direct aid to the Nicaraguan Contra forces.	**Enmienda Boland** Ley del Congreso de 1982 que prohibió la ayuda directa a las fuerzas de la Contra nicaragüense.
bombing of Hiroshima and Nagasaki Atomic bombs dropped by the U.S. on the Japanese cities of Hiroshima on August 6, 1945 and Nagasaki on August 9. The Hiroshima bomb immediately killed 70,000–80,000 civilians. The Nagasaki explosion immediately killed 100,000 civilians. Many survivors of these bombings later developed health issues due to the radiation exposure. Five days after the second bomb was dropped, Japan announced its surrender.	**bombardeo de Hiroshima y Nagasaki** Bombas atómicas lanzadas en 1945 por Estados Unidos sobre las ciudades japonesas de Hiroshima el 6 de agosto y Nagasaki el 9 de agosto de ese año. La bomba de Hiroshima mató inmediatamente a 70,000–80,000 civiles. La explosión de Nagasaki causó la muerte inmediata de 100,000 civiles. Muchos sobrevivientes de estos bombardeos posteriormente desarrollaron problemas de salud debido a la exposición a la radiación. Cinco días después del lanzamiento de la segunda bomba, Japón anunció su rendición.
Bonus Army World War I veterans who marched on Washington, D.C. in 1932 to demand immediate payment of their service bonuses. President Hoover refused to negotiate and instructed the U.S. Army to clear the capital of protestors, leading to a violent clash.	**Bonus Army** Grupo de veteranos de la Primera Guerra Mundial que marcharon a Washington, D.C. en 1932 para exigir el pago inmediato de sus bonos de servicio. El presidente Hoover se negó a negociar y llamó al ejército para que despejara la capital de manifestantes, lo que condujo a un enfrentamiento violento.

Glossary/Glosario

boomtown Areas that rapidly developed following the swift arrival of capital, typically from mining enterprises or the railroad, in the west.

boomtown (ciudad próspera) Comunidades que pasaron por un rápido crecimiento y desarrollo económico después de la llegada del capital minero o del ferrocarril al oeste.

Boston Massacre 1770 clash between colonial protesters and British soldiers in Boston that led to the death of five colonists. The bloody conflict was used to promote the patriot cause.

Masacre de Boston Choque ocurrido en 1770 entre manifestantes coloniales y soldados británicos en Boston que provocó la muerte de cinco colonos. El sangriento conflicto se utilizó para promover la causa patriota.

Boston Tea Party Rally against British tax policy organized by the Sons of Liberty on December 16, 1773, consisting of about fifty men disguised as American Indians who boarded British ships and dumped about forty-five tons of tea into the Boston Harbor.

Motín del Té Protesta contra la política fiscal británica organizada por los Hijos de la Libertad el 16 de diciembre de 1773. Cincuenta hombres disfrazados de nativos americanos abordaron barcos británicos y vertieron cuarenta y cinco toneladas de té en las aguas del puerto de Boston.

Brady Handgun Violence Prevention Act 1993 act establishing a five-day waiting period and background check for gun buyers.

Ley Brady de prevención de la violencia con armas de fuego Ley aprobada en 1993 que estableció un período de espera de cinco días y una verificación de antecedentes para los compradores de armas de fuego.

British Broadcasting Corporation (BBC) Public service broadcasting company established under a British Royal Charter in 1922 as the British Broadcasting Company.

British Broadcasting Corporation (BBC) Servicio público de radio y televisión del Reino Unido, establecido en 1922 bajo el mandato de una Carta Real Británica como la British Broadcasting Company.

Brown v. Board of Education of Topeka, Kansas Landmark 1954 Supreme Court case that overturned the "separate but equal" principle established by *Plessy v. Ferguson* and applied to public schools. Few schools in the South were racially desegregated for more than a decade.

Brown vs. Consejo de educación de Topeka, Kansas Caso histórico de la Corte Suprema en 1954 que revocó el principio de "separados pero iguales" establecido por *Plessy vs. Ferguson* y aplicado a las escuelas públicas. Durante más de una década hubo pocas escuelas en el Sur que pasaron por el proceso de integración racial.

buffalo soldiers African American cavalrymen who fought in the West against American Indians in the 1870s and 1880s.

soldados búfalo Miembros afroamericanos del Regimiento de Caballería que lucharon en el oeste contra los nativos americanos en las décadas de 1870 y 1880.

bully pulpit Term used by Theodore Roosevelt to describe the office of the presidency. Roosevelt believed that the president should use his office as a platform to promote his programs and rally public opinion.

púlpito intimidatorio Término usado por Theodore Roosevelt para describir el cargo presidencial. Roosevelt creía que el presidente debía usar su cargo como plataforma para promover sus programas y movilizar la opinión pública.

Bureau of Indian Affairs (BIA) Established in 1824, the BIA is responsible for management of American Indian lands and implementation of federal policy towards American Indian nations.

Oficina de asuntos de los nativos americanos (BIA, por sus siglas en inglés) Establecida en 1824, la BIA es responsable de la gestión de las tierras de los nativos americanos y de la aplicación de políticas federales que conciernen a los pueblos nativos.

Bureau of Investigation Domestic investigative branch of the U.S. Department of Justice originally headed by J. Edgar Hoover. The organization was later renamed the Federal Bureau of Investigation (FBI).

Oficina de investigación Rama de investigación nacional del Departamento de Justicia de los Estados Unidos dirigida inicialmente por J. Edgar Hoover. Más tarde, la organización cambió de nombre a Oficina Federal de Investigaciones (FBI, por sus siglas en inglés).

Bush Doctrine President George W. Bush's proposal to engage in preemptive war against tyrannical governments that were perceived as a threat to U.S. national security, even if the danger was not immediate.

doctrina Bush Propuesta del presidente George W. Bush de participar en una guerra preventiva contra gobiernos tiránicos que eran percibidos como una amenaza a la seguridad nacional de Estados Unidos, incluso si el peligro no era inmediato.

C

Cable News Network (CNN) An American news company established in 1980 by Ted Turner, which broadcasts news 24 hours a day.

Cable News Network (CNN) Empresa de noticias estadounidense, establecida en 1980 por Ted Turner, que transmite noticias las 24 horas del día.

Cahokia Pre-Columbian mound building society along the Mississippi river with trade networks from the Great Lakes to the Gulf of Mexico.

Cahokia Sociedad precolombina constructora de montículos que se asentó a lo largo del río Misisipi, y cuyas redes comerciales se extendieron desde los Grandes Lagos hasta el Golfo de México.

California Gold Rush The rapid influx of migrants into California after the discovery of gold in 1848. Migrants came from all over the world seeking riches.

Fiebre del oro de California La rápida afluencia de inmigrantes a California tras el descubrimiento de yacimientos de oro en 1848. Los migrantes venían de todas partes del mundo en busca de riquezas.

Glossary/Glosario

Californios Spanish and Mexican residents of California. Before the nineteenth century, Californios made up California's economic and political elite. Their position, however, deteriorated after the conclusion of the Mexican-American War in 1848.	**californios** Residentes españoles y mexicanos en California. Antes del siglo XIX, los californios constituían la élite económica y política de California. Sin embargo, su posición acomodada cayó en decadencia después del fin de la guerra entre México y Estados Unidos en 1848.
Calvinism Developed in Switzerland by John Calvin, a version of Protestantism in which civil magistrates and reformed ministers ruled over a Christian society.	**calvinismo** Versión del protestantismo desarrollada en Suiza por Juan Calvino, en la que magistrados civiles y ministros reformados gobernaban sobre una sociedad cristiana.
Camp David accords 1978 peace accord between Israel and Egypt facilitated by the mediation of President Jimmy Carter.	**acuerdos de Camp David** Acuerdo de paz entre Israel y Egipto firmado en 1978 y facilitado por la mediación del presidente Jimmy Carter.
capitalism An economic system based on private ownership of property and the open exchange of goods between property holders.	**capitalismo** Sistema económico basado en la propiedad privada y el libre intercambio de bienes entre los propietarios.
caravel A small and swift sailing ship invented by the Portuguese during the fifteenth century.	**carabela** Velero pequeño y veloz inventado por los portugueses en el siglo XV.
carpetbaggers Derogatory term for white Northerners who moved to the South in the years following the Civil War. Many white Southerners believed such migrants were intent on exploiting their suffering.	**carpetbaggers (oportunistas)** Término peyorativo para los norteños blancos que se mudaron al sur en los años posteriores a la Guerra Civil. Muchos sureños blancos creían que esos migrantes tenían la intención de explotar su sufrimiento.
cash crop A crop produced for profit rather than for subsistence.	**cultivo comercial** Cultivo producido con fines de lucro y no de subsistencia.
Central Intelligence Agency (CIA) Intelligence organization established by the 1947 National Security Act. The CIA is part of the executive branch and is responsible for gathering and conducting espionage in foreign nations. Originally created to counter Soviet spying operations.	**Agencia central de inteligencia (CIA, por sus siglas en inglés)** Organización de inteligencia establecida por la Ley de seguridad nacional de 1947. La CIA es parte del poder ejecutivo y es responsable de reunir y llevar a cabo operaciones de espionaje en naciones extranjeras. Fue creada originalmente para contrarrestar el espionaje soviético.
Central Powers Political allies during World War I consisting primarily of Austria-Hungary, Germany, and the Ottoman Empire.	**Potencias centrales** Coalición de aliados políticos durante la Primera Guerra Mundial, formada principalmente por Austria-Hungría, Alemania y el Imperio Otomano.
Cherokee Nation v. Georgia 1831 Supreme Court ruling that denied the Cherokee claim to be a separate independent nation, ruling that all American Indian nations were "domestic dependent nations" rather than fully sovereign governments.	***Nación Cherokee vs. Georgia*** Sentencia de la Corte Suprema de 1831 que negó que los cherokees fueran una nación independiente y separada, y dictaminó que todas las naciones nativas americanas eran "naciones dependientes domésticas" en lugar de gobiernos plenamente soberanos.
Chinese Exclusion Act 1882 act that banned Chinese immigration into the United States and prohibited those Chinese already in the country from becoming naturalized American citizens.	**Ley de exclusión de chinos** Ley de 1882 que prohibió la inmigración de chinos a Estados Unidos y prohibió que los chinos que ya se encontraban en el país se convirtieran en ciudadanos estadounidenses naturalizados.
Chinook North American Indians who lived in present-day Washington and Oregon, who built extensive plank houses, lived in extended kinship groups, and were known for their extensive trade networks.	**Chinook** Grupo de nativos americanos que vivían en el actual territorio de Washington y Oregón, que construyeron extensas casas de tablones, vivían en tribus de parentesco extendido y eran conocidos por sus extensas redes comerciales.
Christian Right A coalition of evangelical Christians and Catholics that supported traditional values, laissez-faire economics, and an uncompromising anti-communist foreign policy. They joined forces with political conservatives.	**Derecha cristiana** Coalición de cristianos evangélicos y católicos que apoyan los valores tradicionales, la economía *laissez-faire* y una política exterior firmemente anticomunista. Unieron fuerzas con los conservadores políticos.
Chumash Indians who lived along and navigated the Pacific, who used ocean-going canoes called *tomol* to hunt fish and whale.	**Chumash** Pueblo nativo que vivía en las costas del Pacífico y utilizaba canoas oceánicas llamadas *tomol* para cazar peces y ballenas.
Church of England National church established by King Henry VIII after he split with the Catholic Church in 1534.	**Iglesia de Inglaterra** Iglesia nacional establecida por el rey Enrique VIII después de su separación de la iglesia católica en 1534.
civic housekeeping Idea promoted by Jane Addams for urban reform using women's traditional skills as domestic managers; caregivers for children, the elderly, and the needy; and community builders.	**quehacer cívico** Idea promovida por Jane Addams para una reforma urbana que hiciera uso de las habilidades tradicionales de las mujeres como administradoras domésticas; cuidadoras de niños, ancianos y necesitados; y constructoras de comunidades.
Civil Rights Act of 1875 Act extending "full and equal treatment" for all races in public accommodations, including jury service and public transportation. However, in 1883, the Supreme Court ruled the act was unconstitutional.	**Ley de derechos civiles de 1875** Ley que extiende el "trato pleno e igualitario" para todas las razas en establecimientos públicos, incluyendo el servicio de jurado y el transporte público. Sin embargo, en 1883 la Corte Suprema dictaminó que la ley era inconstitucional.

Glossary/Glosario

Civil Rights Act of 1964 Wide-ranging civil rights act that, among other things, prohibited discrimination in public accommodations and employment and increased federal enforcement of school desegregation.

Ley de derechos civiles de 1964 Ley de derechos civiles de amplio alcance que, entre otras cosas, prohibía la discriminación en establecimientos públicos y en el empleo, y aumentaba el control federal sobre la desegregación escolar.

Civil Works Administration (CWA) 1933 New Deal program which only lasted four months but employed more than 4 million people on 400,000 projects, such as building schools, roads, playgrounds, and airports.

Administración de obras civiles (CWA, por sus siglas en inglés) Organización creada en el marco del *New Deal* en 1933, que sólo duró cuatro meses pero empleó a más de 4 millones de personas en 400,000 proyectos como la construcción de escuelas, carreteras, zonas de juegos infantiles y aeropuertos.

Civilian Conservation Corps (CCC) New Deal work program that hired young, unmarried men to work on conservation projects. It employed about 2.5 million men and lasted until 1942.

Cuerpo civil de conservación (CCC) Programa de trabajo del *New Deal* en el que se contrató a hombres jóvenes y solteros para trabajar en proyectos de conservación. Empleó a unos 2,5 millones de hombres y estuvo activo hasta 1942.

Clayton Antitrust Act 1914 act that strengthened the Sherman Antitrust Act by banning certain corporate operations, such as price discrimination and overlapping membership on company boards, and by protecting labor unions. The Act was designed to encourage economic competition.

Ley Clayton antimonopolio Ley aprobada en 1914 que reforzó la Ley antimonopolio Sherman al prohibir ciertas operaciones corporativas, como la discriminación de precios y la duplicación de miembros en los consejos de administración de las empresas. También ofreció protecciones a los sindicatos. Esta ley fue concebida para fomentar la competencia económica.

Clean Air Act 1990 act that set new standards to reduce car and power plant emissions.

Ley de aire limpio Ley de 1990 que estableció nuevas normas para reducir emisiones de automóviles y plantas de energía.

Coercive Acts 1774 acts of Parliament passed in response to the Boston Tea Party. The acts closed the port of Boston until residents paid for the damaged property and moved Massachusetts court cases against royal officials back to England in a bid to weaken colonial authority.

Leyes coactivas Leyes emitidas en 1774 por el Parlamento Británico en respuesta al Motín del té. Las leyes cerraron el puerto de Boston hasta que los residentes pagaran por la propiedad dañada y trasladaron los casos de la corte de Massachusetts contra funcionarios reales de vuelta a Inglaterra en un intento por debilitar la autoridad colonial.

Cold War The political, economic, and military conflict, short of direct war on the battlefield, between the United States and the Soviet Union between 1945 and 1991.

Guerra Fría Conflicto político, económico y militar entre los Estados Unidos y la Unión Soviética entre 1945 y 1991 que abarcó todos los aspectos posibles excepto la guerra directa en el campo de batalla.

collective bargaining The process of negotiation between labor unions and employers.

negociación colectiva Proceso de negociación entre sindicatos y empleadores.

colonization The process of settling and controlling an already inhabited area for the economic benefit of the settlers, or colonizers.

colonización Proceso de asentamiento y control de un área ya habitada para el beneficio económico de los colonos o colonizadores.

Columbian Exchange The biological exchange between the Americas and the rest of the world between 1492 and the end of the sixteenth century. Although its initial impact was strongest in the Americas and Europe, it was soon felt globally.

Intercambio colombino Intercambio de productos agrícolas entre las Américas y el resto del mundo entre 1492 y finales del siglo XVI. Aunque su impacto inicial fue mayor en América y Europa, sus efectos pronto se sintieron a nivel mundial.

"come outer" movement Protest movement whose members would frequently abstain from political office, activity, or voting to protest the government and other organizations' complicity in slavery.

movimiento come-outer Movimiento de protesta cuyos miembros frecuentemente se abstenían de ocupar cargos políticos, realizar actividades o votar, como protesta contra la complicidad del gobierno y de otras organizaciones en la esclavitud.

Commission on the Status of Women Commission appointed by President Kennedy in 1961. The commission's 1963 report, *American Women*, highlighted employment discrimination against women and recommended legislation requiring equal pay for equal work regardless of sex.

Comisión de la condición jurídica y social de la mujer Comisión establecida por el presidente Kennedy en 1961. El informe de 1963 de la Comisión *American Women* destacaba la discriminación contra las mujeres en el empleo y recomendaba promulgar una legislación que exigiera la igualdad de remuneración por el mismo trabajo, independientemente del sexo.

committee of correspondence Type of committee first established in Massachusetts to circulate concerns and reports of protest and other events to leaders in other colonies in the aftermath of the Sugar Act.

Comité de correspondencia Tipo de comité establecido por primera vez en Massachusetts para hacer circular preocupaciones e informes de protestas y otros eventos a los líderes de otras colonias después de la Ley del azúcar.

Committee on Public Information (CPI) Committee established in 1917 to create propaganda and promote censorship to generate enthusiasm for World War I and stifle antiwar dissent.

Comité de información pública (CPI, por sus siglas en inglés) Comité establecido en 1917 para crear propaganda y promover la censura con el fin de generar entusiasmo por la Primera Guerra Mundial y sofocar la disidencia contra la guerra.

common law Law established from custom and the standards set by previous judicial rulings.

derecho anglosajón Sistema legal establecido a partir de la costumbre y de las normas establecidas por sentencias judiciales anteriores.

communism An economic theory and revolutionary ideology that imagines the overthrow of capitalism by the working class and the creation of an egalitarian society where the means of production are controlled by the state.	**comunismo** Teoría económica e ideología revolucionaria que imagina el derrocamiento del capitalismo por la clase obrera y la creación de una sociedad igualitaria donde los medios de producción son controlados por el Estado.
Comprehensive Anti-Apartheid Act 1986 act prohibiting new trade and investment in South Africa because of apartheid. President Reagan vetoed the act but Congress overrode his veto.	**Ley general contra el apartheid** Ley de 1986 que prohíbe el comercio y la inversión en Sudáfrica a causa del apartheid. El presidente Reagan vetó la ley, pero el Congreso anuló su veto.
Compromise of 1850 Series of acts following California's application for admission as a free state. Meant to ease sectional tensions over slavery by providing something for all sides, the act ended up fueling more conflicts.	**Compromiso de 1850** Conjunto de leyes aprobadas después de la solicitud de admisión de California a la Unión como estado libre. Estas leyes, que buscaban llegar a acuerdos intermedios para aliviar tensiones seccionales sobre la esclavitud, terminaron alimentando más conflictos.
compromise of 1877 Compromise between Republicans and southern Democrats that resulted in the election of Rutherford B. Hayes. Southern Democrats agreed to support Hayes in the disputed presidential election in exchange for his promise to end Reconstruction.	**compromiso de 1877** Acuerdo entre republicanos y demócratas del sur que resultó en la elección de Rutherford B. Hayes. Los demócratas sureños acordaron apoyar a Hayes en las disputadas elecciones presidenciales a cambio de que su régimen pusiera fin a la Reconstrucción.
Comstock Lode Massive silver deposit discovered in the Sierra Nevada in the late 1850s.	**Veta Comstock** Inmenso depósito de plata descubierto en Sierra Nevada a finales de la década de 1850.
Confederate States of America Name of the government that seceded from the Union after the election of President Lincoln in 1860.	**Estados Confederados de América** Nombre del gobierno que se separó de la Unión después de la elección del presidente Lincoln en 1860.
confiscation acts Laws passed by Congress during the Civil War that authorized the confiscation of Confederate property. Under the confiscation acts, any enslaved people who were forced to work for the Confederate army would no longer be bound to slaveholders.	**leyes de confiscación** Leyes aprobadas por el Congreso durante la Guerra Civil que autorizaron la confiscación de bienes confederados. En virtud de las leyes de confiscación, las personas esclavizadas que fueran obligadas a trabajar para el ejército confederado ya no estarían vinculadas a los dueños de esclavos.
Congress of Racial Equality (CORE) An interracial organization founded in 1942 that directly protested against racial inequality in public accommodations.	**Congreso para la igualdad racial (CORE, por sus siglas en inglés)** Organización interracial fundada en 1942 que protestó directamente contra la desigualdad racial en establecimientos públicos.
conquistadors Also known as *encomenderos*, Spanish soldiers who were central to the conquest of the civilizations of the Americas. Once conquest was complete, conquistadors often extracted wealth from the people and lands they came to rule.	**conquistadores** Soldados españoles, también conocidos como encomenderos, que fueron fundamentales en la conquista de las civilizaciones de las Américas. Una vez que se logró la conquista, los conquistadores extrajeron riquezas de los pueblos y de las tierras que llegaron a gobernar.
conservationism Progressive Era political and social movement whose supporters worked for the preservation of America's wildlife and natural lands.	**conservacionismo** Movimiento político y social de la Era Progresista cuyos partidarios lucharon por la preservación de la vida silvestre y las tierras naturales de Estados Unidos.
Constitutional Convention Meeting to draft the United States Constitution in Philadelphia from May to September of 1787. This document established the framework for a strong federal government with executive, legislative, and judicial branches.	**Convención constitucional** Reunión en Filadelfia para redactar la Constitución de los Estados Unidos, que tuvo lugar entre mayo y septiembre de 1787. Este documento estableció el marco para un gobierno federal sólido con poderes ejecutivo, legislativo y judicial.
consumer revolution A process through which status in the colonies became more closely linked to financial success and a refined lifestyle rather than birth and family pedigree during the seventeenth and eighteenth centuries. The consumer revolution was spurred by industrialization and increased global trade.	**revolución del consumidor** Proceso mediante el cual la jerarquía social en las colonias se vinculó más estrechamente con el éxito financiero y un estilo de vida refinado que con el linaje familiar durante los siglos XVII y XVIII. La revolución del consumidor fue impulsada por la industrialización y el aumento del comercio mundial.
containment Belief that the Soviet Union desired the spread of communism throughout the world. To prevent this spread U.S. diplomat George Kennan advocated a strict policy of containing communism where it already existed and preventing its spread.	**contención** Creencia de que la Unión Soviética deseaba que el comunismo se extendiera por todo el mundo. Para evitar esta propagación, el diplomático estadounidense George Kennan abogó por una política estricta de contener el comunismo donde ya existía e impedir su proliferación.
Continental Army Army created by the Second Continental Congress after the battles of Lexington and Concord began the American Revolution in 1775.	**Ejército continental** Ejército creado por el Segundo Congreso Continental después de que las batallas de Lexington y Concord dieran inicio a la Revolución Estadounidense en 1775.
Continental Congress Congress convened in Philadelphia in 1774 in response to the Coercive Acts. The delegates hoped to reestablish the freedoms colonists had previously enjoyed.	**Congreso continental** Asamblea de delegados de las colonias en Filadelfia en 1774, formada en respuesta a las Leyes coactivas. Los delegados buscaban restablecer las libertades de las que los colonizadores habían gozado anteriormente.

contraband Term first used by Union general Benjamin Butler in May 1861 to describe enslaved people who had fled to Union lines to obtain freedom. By designating enslaved people as property forfeited by the act of rebellion, the Union was able to strike at slavery without proclaiming a general emancipation.

Contract with America A document that called for reduced welfare spending, lower taxes, term limits for lawmakers, and a constitutional amendment for a balanced budget. In preparation for the 1994 midterm congressional elections, Republicans, led by Representative Newt Gingrich, drew up this proposal.

Contras Nicaraguan counterrevolutionaries, trained by the United States CIA, who fought to overthrow the new Sandinista government in Nicaragua during the 1980s.

convict lease The system used by southern governments to furnish mainly African American prison labor to plantation owners and industrialists and to raise revenue for the states. In practice, convict labor replaced slavery as the means of providing a forced labor supply.

Copperheads Northern Democrats who did not support the Union war effort. Such Democrats enjoyed considerable support in eastern cities and parts of the Midwest.

corporate capitalism An industrialized, market economy that is dominated by large corporations.

corporation A form of business ownership in which the liability of shareholders in a company is limited to their individual investments. The formation of corporations in the late nineteenth century greatly stimulated investment in industry.

Corps of Discovery Expedition organized by the U.S. government to explore the Louisiana Territory. Led by Meriwether Lewis and William Clark and aided by American Indian interpreters like Sacagawea, the expedition set out in May 1804 and journeyed to the Pacific coast and back by 1806.

"corrupt bargain" Agreement between Henry Clay and John Quincy Adams in the 1824 presidential election that Clay would withdraw from the race in exchange for an appointment in Adams's cabinet.

cotton gin Machine invented by Eli Whitney in 1793 to deseed short-staple cotton. The cotton gin dramatically reduced the time and labor involved in deseeding, facilitating the expansion of cotton production in the South and West.

counterculture Young cultural rebels of the 1960s who rejected conventional moral and sexual values and used drugs to reach a higher consciousness.

court-packing plan 1937 proposal by Franklin Roosevelt to increase the size of the Supreme Court and reduce its opposition to New Deal legislation. Congress failed to pass the measure, and the scheme undermined Roosevelt's popular support.

Covenant Chain The alliance formed between Iroquois leaders and colonists during a meeting Albany in 1677 in hopes of salvaging their fur trade and preventing future conflict.

Coxey's army 1894 protest movement led by Jacob Coxey. Coxey and five hundred supporters marched from Ohio to Washington, D.C., to protest the lack of government response to the depression of 1893.

contrabando Término utilizado por primera vez por el general de la Unión Benjamin Butler en mayo de 1861 para describir a las personas esclavizadas que habían huido a las líneas de la Unión para obtener la libertad. Al designar a las personas esclavizadas como bienes confiscados por el acto de rebelión, la Unión pudo atacar la esclavitud sin proclamar una emancipación general.

Contrato con Estados Unidos Documento que exigía la reducción de los gastos de asistencia social, la disminución de impuestos, límites de mandato para los legisladores y una enmienda constitucional para garantizar un presupuesto equilibrado. Esta propuesta fue elaborada por los republicanos, encabezados por el diputado Newt Gingrich, en preparación para las elecciones legislativas de 1994.

Contras Nicaragüenses contrarrevolucionarios entrenados por la CIA, que lucharon para derrocar al nuevo gobierno sandinista en Nicaragua durante la década de 1980.

arrendamiento de convictos Sistema utilizado por los gobiernos del sur para proporcionar mano de obra de convictos principalmente afroamericanos a los propietarios de plantaciones y fábricas, y para recaudar ingresos para los estados. En la práctica, el trabajo de los convictos reemplazó a la esclavitud como suministro de trabajo forzado.

Copperheads (cabezas de cobre) Demócratas del norte que estaban en contra de la guerra civil. Estos demócratas contaban con un apoyo considerable en las ciudades del este y en partes del oeste central.

capitalismo corporativo Economía industrializada y de mercado dominada por las grandes corporaciones.

corporación Forma de propiedad empresarial en la que la responsabilidad de los accionistas de una compañía se limita a sus inversiones individuales. La formación de corporaciones a finales del siglo XIX estimuló enormemente la inversión en la industria.

Cuerpo de descubrimiento Expedición organizada por el gobierno de los Estados Unidos para explorar el Territorio de Luisiana. Liderada por Meriwether Lewis y William Clark y con la ayuda de intérpretes nativos americanos como Sacagawea, la expedición partió en mayo de 1804, viajó a la costa del Pacífico y regresó en 1806.

acuerdo corrupto Arreglo establecido entre Henry Clay y John Quincy Adams durante la elección presidencial de 1824, según el cual Clay se retiraría de la carrera a cambio de formar parte del gabinete de Adams.

desmotadora de algodón Máquina inventada por Eli Whitney en 1793 para quitar las semillas del algodón. La desmotadora de algodón redujo considerablemente el tiempo y la mano de obra necesaria para procesar el algodón, facilitando la expansión de la producción de algodón en el Sur y el Oeste.

contracultura Jóvenes rebeldes de los años 60 que rechazaron las convenciones culturales, morales y sexuales de la época y consumieron drogas para alcanzar un estado superior de conciencia.

court-packing plan (plan de recomposición de la corte) Propuesta de Franklin Roosevelt en 1937 para aumentar el tamaño de la Corte Suprema y reducir su oposición a la legislación del *New Deal*. El Congreso no aprobó la medida, pero la maniobra fallida socavó el apoyo popular que tenía Roosevelt.

Cadena de la amistad Alianza formada entre los líderes iroqueses y los colonos durante una reunión en Albany en 1677 con la esperanza de salvaguardar el comercio de pieles y prevenir futuros conflictos.

ejército de Coxey Movimiento de protesta de 1894 liderado por Jacob Coxey. Coxey y quinientos partidarios marcharon de Ohio a Washington, D.C., para protestar por la falta de respuesta del gobierno a la depresión de 1893.

Glossary/Glosario

Crittenden Plan A political compromise over slavery, which failed after seven southern states seceded from the Union in early 1861. It would have protected slavery from federal interference where it already existed and extended the Missouri Compromise line to California.	**Plan Crittenden** Acuerdo político sobre la esclavitud que fracasó cuando siete estados del sur se separaron de la Unión a principios de 1861. El acuerdo habría protegido la esclavitud de la interferencia federal donde ya existía, y habría también extendido la Línea del Compromiso de Missouri hasta California.
Cuba Libre Vision of Cuban independence developed by José Martí, who hoped that Cuban independence would bring with it greater social and racial equality.	**Cuba Libre** Visión de la independencia de Cuba desarrollada por José Martí, quien esperaba que la independencia de Cuba trajera consigo una mayor igualdad social y racial.
cult of domesticity New ideals of womanhood that emerged alongside the middle class in the 1830s and 1840s that called for women to be confined to the domestic sphere and devote themselves to the care of children, the home, and hard-working husbands.	**culto a la domesticidad** Nuevos ideales de feminidad que surgieron junto a la clase media en las décadas de 1830 y 1840 y que exigían que la mujer se limitara a la esfera doméstica y se dedicara al cuidado de los hijos, el hogar y los maridos trabajadores.
Currency Act 1764 act of Parliament preventing colonial assemblies from printing paper money or bills of credit, curtailing the ability of local colonial economies to expand.	**Ley de moneda** Ley del Parlamento emitida en 1764 que prohibía a las asambleas coloniales imprimir papel moneda o certificados de crédito, lo que limitó la capacidad de expansión de las economías coloniales locales.

D

D Day June 6, 1944 invasion of German-occupied France by Allied forces. The D Day landings opened up a second front in Europe and marked a major turning point in World War II.	**Día D** El 6 de junio de 1944, invasión del territorio francés bajo ocupación alemana por las fuerzas aliadas. Los desembarcos del Día D abrieron un segundo frente en Europa y marcaron un punto de inflexión en la Segunda Guerra Mundial.
Daughters of Liberty Group of female patriots who sought to challenge the imposition of new taxes on the colonists through economic boycotts and the homespun movement.	**Hijas de la libertad** Grupo de mujeres patriotas que buscaron desafiar la imposición de nuevos impuestos a los colonos a través de boicots económicos y la producción de ropa casera.
Dawes Act 1887 act that ended federal recognition of tribal sovereignty and divided American Indian land into 160-acre parcels to be distributed to American Indian heads of household. The act dramatically reduced the amount of American Indian-controlled land and undermined American Indian social and cultural institutions.	**Ley Dawes** Ley de 1887 que puso fin al reconocimiento federal de la soberanía tribal y dividió las tierras de los nativos americanos en parcelas de 160 acres para ser distribuidas a los jefes de familia de los nativos americanos. La ley redujo drásticamente la cantidad de tierras controladas por los nativos americanos y socavó las instituciones sociales y culturales de los pueblos nativos.
Declaration of Independence Document declaring the independence of the colonies from Great Britain. Drafted by Thomas Jefferson and then debated and revised by the Continental Congress, the Declaration was made public on July 4, 1776.	**Declaración de Independencia** Documento que declara la independencia de las trece colonias de Gran Bretaña. La Declaración fue redactada por Thomas Jefferson, debatida y revisada por el Congreso Continental, y publicada el 4 de julio de 1776.
Declaration of Sentiments Call for women's rights in marriage, family, religion, politics, and law issued at the 1848 Seneca Falls convention. It was signed by 100 of the 300 participants.	**Declaración de sentimientos** Llamado a los derechos de la mujer en el matrimonio, la familia, la religión, la política y la ley, emitido en la convención de Séneca Falls de 1848. Fue firmada por 100 de los 300 participantes.
Declaratory Act 1766 act announcing Parliament's authority to pass any law "to bind the colonies and peoples of North America" closer to Britain.	**Ley declaratoria** Ley de 1766 que anuncia la autoridad del Parlamento para aprobar cualquier ley que "someta a las colonias y los pueblos de América del Norte" a la voluntad de Gran Bretaña.
Defense of Marriage Act (DOMA) 1996 act denying married same-sex couples the federal benefits granted to heterosexual married couples. DOMA was ruled unconstitutional in 2013.	**Ley de defensa del matrimonio (DOMA, por sus siglas en inglés)** Ley promulgada en 1996 que niega a las parejas casadas del mismo sexo los beneficios federales otorgados a las parejas casadas heterosexuales. La DOMA fue declarada inconstitucional en 2013.
Deferred Action for Childhood Arrivals (DACA) This policy, initiated under the administration of Barack Obama in 2012, allows undocumented immigrant children to receive a two-year extension of their residency in the U.S. along with eligibility for work permits.	**Acción diferida para los llegados en la infancia (DACA, por sus siglas en inglés)** Esta política, iniciada durante el gobierno de Barack Obama en 2012, permite a los niños inmigrantes indocumentados recibir una extensión de dos años de su residencia en los Estados Unidos y les otorga elegibilidad para permisos de trabajo.
deflation A fall in prices caused by supply exceeding demand.	**deflación** Caída de los precios provocada por una oferta superior a la demanda.
deindustrialization Decline of industrial activity in a specific town, region, or nation. In the U.S. it led to significant drops in union membership and population shifts across the country as people moved in search of new types of economic opportunity.	**desindustrialización** Disminución de la actividad industrial en una ciudad, región o nación específica. En los Estados Unidos, este proceso condujo a caídas significativas en la membresía sindical y a cambios en la población en todo el país a medida que la gente se movía en busca de nuevos tipos de oportunidades económicas.

Glossary/Glosario

Democratic Review Magazine founded by Democrat John O'Sullivan in 1837. The magazine acted as a prominent mouthpiece for the Young America Movement and the Democratic Party and Jacksonian Democracy. The magazine is largely credited with coining the term "manifest destiny" in 1845.	**Democratic Review** Revista fundada por el demócrata John O'Sullivan en 1837. La revista actuó como portavoz prominente del movimiento América Joven y del Partido Demócrata y la Democracia Jacksoniana. A esta revista se le atribuye en gran medida el haber acuñado el término "destino manifiesto" en 1845.
Democractic-Republicans Political party that emerged out of opposition to Federalist policies in the 1790s. The Democratic-Republicans chose Thomas Jefferson as their presidential candidate in 1796, 1800, and 1804.	**Demócratas-Republicanos** Partido político que surgió de la oposición a las políticas federalistas en la década de 1790. Los demócratas-republicanos eligieron a Thomas Jefferson como su candidato presidencial en 1796, 1800 y 1804.
Democrats and National Republicans Two parties that resulted from the split of the Democratic-Republicans in the early 1820s. Andrew Jackson emerged as the leader of the Democrats, while figures like Henry Clay and John Quincy Adams emerged as leaders of the National Republicans.	**Demócratas y Republicanos Nacionales** Dos partidos que resultaron de la división de los Demócratas-Republicanos a principios de la década de 1820. Andrew Jackson surgió como el líder de los Demócratas, mientras que figuras como Henry Clay y John Quincy Adams surgieron como líderes de los Republicanos Nacionales.
Dennis v. United States 1951 Supreme Court decision upholding the conviction of Communist leaders on the grounds they posed a "clear and present danger," despite the absence of any evidence of an immediate uprising or plot.	**Dennis vs. Estados Unidos** Decisión de la Corte Suprema en 1951 que sostuvo la condena de líderes comunistas por el hecho de que representaban un "peligro claro y presente," a pesar de la ausencia de pruebas de un levantamiento o conspiración inmediata.
Department of Commerce and Labor Government agency created in 1906 to gather information about large companies in an effort to promote fair business practices.	**Departamento de comercio y trabajo** Agencia gubernamental creada en 1906 para recopilar información sobre grandes empresas en un esfuerzo por promover prácticas comerciales justas.
Department of Homeland Security A cabinet-level agency created in 2002 that is responsible for developing a national strategy against terrorist threats.	**Departamento de seguridad nacional** Agencia a nivel ministerial creada en 2002, responsable de desarrollar una estrategia nacional contra las amenazas terroristas.
depression of 1893 Severe economic downturn triggered by railroad and bank failures. The severity of the depression, combined with the failure of the federal government to offer an adequate response, led to the realignment of American politics.	**depresión de 1893** Fuerte recesión económica provocada por la quiebra de ferrocarriles y bancos. La gravedad de la depresión, combinada con la incapacidad del gobierno federal para ofrecer una respuesta adecuada, llevó a un reajuste de la política estadounidense.
deskilling The replacement of skilled labor with unskilled labor and machines.	**descalificación** El reemplazo de mano de obra calificada por mano de obra no calificada y máquinas.
détente An easing of tense relations with the Soviet Union during the Cold War. This process moved unevenly through the 1970s and early 1980s but accelerated when the Soviet leader Mikhail Gorbachev came to power in the mid-1980s.	**détente** Reducción de las tensas relaciones con la Unión Soviética durante la Guerra Fría. Este proceso se desarrolló de manera desigual durante los años setenta y principios de los ochenta, pero se aceleró cuando el líder soviético Mijaíl Gorbachov llegó al poder a mediados de los ochenta.
Development, Relief, and Education for Alien Minors (DREAM) Act Legislation proposed in 2001 to provide the children of undocumented immigrants in the U.S. the opportunity to gain legal residency status. The proposed legislation failed to pass Congress.	**Ley de fomento para el progreso, alivio y educación para menores extranjeros (DREAM, por sus siglas en inglés)** Legislación propuesta en 2001 para proporcionar a los hijos de inmigrantes indocumentados en los Estados Unidos la oportunidad de obtener la residencia legal. La legislación propuesta no fue aprobada por el Congreso.
Dixiecrats Southern Democrats who created a segregationist political party in 1948 as a response to federal extensions of civil rights. Dixiecrats advocated for a state's right to legislate segregation. The Dixiecrat Party ran Strom Thurmond in an unsuccessful bid for the presidency in 1948 against Truman.	**Dixiecrats** Partido político segregacionista fundado en 1948 por demócratas sureños como respuesta a las extensiones federales de los derechos civiles. Los *dixiecrats* abogaron por el derecho de cada estado a legislar la segregación. El Partido Dixiecrat llevó a Strom Thurmond a una carrera infructuosa por la presidencia en 1948 contra Truman.
dollar diplomacy Term used by President Howard Taft to describe the economic focus of his foreign policy. Taft hoped to use economic policies and the control of foreign assets by American companies to influence Latin American nations.	**diplomacia del dólar** Término utilizado por el presidente Howard Taft para describir el enfoque económico de su política exterior. Taft esperaba utilizar políticas económicas y el control de activos extranjeros por parte de empresas estadounidenses para ejercer influencia sobre países latinoamericanos.
Dominion of New England The consolidation of Northeastern colonies by King James II in 1686 to establish greater control over them, resulting in the banning of town meetings, new taxes, and other unpopular policies. The Dominion was dissolved during the Glorious Revolution.	**Dominio de Nueva Inglaterra** Consolidación de las colonias del noreste por el rey Jacobo II en 1686 con el fin de establecer un mayor control sobre ellas, resultando en la prohibición de asambleas municipales, la creación de nuevos impuestos y otras políticas impopulares. El Dominio fue disuelto durante la Revolución Gloriosa.
Domino Theory Prevalent belief during the Cold War maintaining that if one country fell under the influence of communism, other surrounding countries would soon similarly fall under the influence of communism, like a row of falling dominoes.	**Teoría dominó** Creencia predominante durante la Guerra Fría que sostenía que si un país caía bajo la influencia del comunismo, llevaría a que otros países circundantes también cayeran bajo su influencia, generando un efecto dominó.

Glossary/Glosario

Double V The slogan African Americans used during World War II to state their twin aims to fight for victory over fascism abroad and victory over racism at home.

Doble V Eslogan utilizado por combatientes afroamericanos durante la Segunda Guerra Mundial para afirmar su objetivo dual de luchar por la victoria sobre el fascismo en el extranjero y la victoria sobre el racismo dentro del país.

Dred Scott case 1857 Supreme Court case centered on the status of Dred Scott and his family. In its ruling, the Court denied the claim that black men had any rights and blocked Congress from excluding slavery from any territory.

caso Dred Scott Caso de la Corte Suprema de 1857 centrado en la situación de Dred Scott y su familia. En su fallo, la Corte negó la afirmación de que los hombres afroamericanos tenían derechos y bloqueó la capacidad del Congreso para prohibir la esclavitud en cualquier territorio.

Dunmore's Proclamation 1775 proclamation issued by the British commander Lord Dunmore that offered freedom to all enslaved African Americans who joined the British army. The proclamation heightened concerns among some patriots about the consequences of independence.

Proclamación de Dunmore Proclamación emitida en 1775 por el comandante británico Lord Dunmore que ofrecía la libertad a todas las personas esclavizadas que se unieran al ejército británico. La proclamación aumentó la preocupación de algunos patriotas por las consecuencias de la Independencia.

Dust Bowl Name for the southern plains of the United States during the Great Depression when the region experienced massive dust storms due to soil erosion caused by poor farming practices and drought.

Dust Bowl (Cuenco de polvo) Nombre que se le dio a las llanuras del sur de los Estados Unidos durante la Gran Depresión, cuando la región experimentó fuertes tormentas de polvo debido a la erosión del suelo causada por las malas prácticas agrícolas y la sequía.

E

eBay Online auction site established in 1995.

eBay Sitio de subastas en línea establecido en 1995.

Economic Recovery Tax Act Act signed into law by President Ronald Reagan in 1981 that slashed income and estate taxes, especially on those in the highest income brackets.

Ley de impuestos para la recuperación económica Ley firmada por el presidente Ronald Reagan en 1981 que redujo drásticamente los impuestos sobre la renta y sobre el patrimonio, especialmente para las personas de ingresos más altos.

effigy A roughly made image or model of a person, typically created in order to be destroyed in an act of protest.

efigie Una imagen o representación de una persona, generalmente creada para ser destruida en un acto de protesta.

Eighteenth Amendment 1918 amendment to the Constitution banning the production and sale of alcoholic beverages. It was repealed in 1933 with the Twenty-First Amendment.

Decimoctava enmienda Enmienda a la Constitución propuesta en diciembre de 1917 y aprobada en 1919, que prohíbe la producción y venta de bebidas alcohólicas.

Eisenhower Doctrine A doctrine guiding U.S. intervention in the Middle East. In 1957 Congress granted President Dwight Eisenhower the power to send military forces into the Middle East to combat Communist aggression. Eisenhower sent U.S. marines into Lebanon in 1958 under this doctrine.

Doctrina Eisenhower Doctrina que guió la intervención de Estados Unidos en el Medio Oriente. En 1957 el Congreso concedió al presidente Dwight Eisenhower el poder de enviar fuerzas militares al Medio Oriente para combatir la agresión comunista. Bajo esta doctrina, Eisenhower envió marines estadounidenses a Líbano en 1958.

electoral college A group comprised of electors who vote in the formal election of the president and vice president after the general election votes are tallied. The electoral college was a compromise between determining the president via a direct popular vote or via congressional vote.

colegio electoral Grupo formado por electores que votan en la elección formal del presidente y vicepresidente después de las elecciones generales. Los colegios electorales constituyen un punto medio entre la elección del presidente a través del voto popular directo y el voto del Congreso.

Elkins Act 1903 act outlawing railroad rebates. The act was designed to protect smaller businesses and shippers who were paying higher rates than large favored customers, such as Standard Oil.

Ley Elkins Ley de 1903 que prohíbe los reembolsos a los ferrocarriles. La ley fue diseñada para proteger a empresas pequeñas y transportistas que estaban pagando tarifas más altas que los grandes clientes como Standard Oil.

Emancipation Proclamation January 1, 1863 proclamation that declared all enslaved people in areas still in rebellion "forever free." While stopping short of abolishing slavery outright, the Emancipation Proclamation was, nonetheless, seen by both black people and white abolitionists as a great victory.

Proclamación de emancipación Proclama emitida el 1 de enero de 1863 que declaraba "libres para siempre" a todas las personas esclavizadas en zonas aún en rebelión. Aunque no llegó a abolir la esclavitud, la Proclamación de emancipación fue vista tanto por los afroamericanos como por los abolicionistas blancos como una gran victoria.

embargo A ban on trade with a particular country.

embargo Prohibición del comercio con un país en particular.

Embargo Act 1807 act that prohibited American ships from leaving their home ports until Britain and France repealed restrictions on U.S. trade. The act had a devastating impact on American commerce.

Ley de embargo Ley de 1807 que prohibía a los barcos estadounidenses abandonar sus puertos de origen hasta que Gran Bretaña y Francia derogaron las restricciones al comercio de Estados Unidos. La ley tuvo un impacto devastador sobre el comercio estadounidense.

Emergency Banking Act 1933 New Deal executive order that shut down banks for several days to calm widespread panic during the Great Depression.

Ley de emergencia bancaria Orden ejecutiva del *New Deal* de 1933 que decretó el cierre de los bancos durante varios días para calmar el pánico generalizado durante la Gran Depresión.

Glossary/Glosario

enclosure movements The privatized use of common land for personal or financial gain by noblemen, who evicted commoners who relied on the land for subsistence. This led to increased social conflict, famine, inflation, and immigration to North America.	**cercamiento** La privatización de tierras comunes para beneficio personal o financiero de los nobles, quienes desalojaron a los plebeyos que dependían de esas tierras para su subsistencia. Esto condujo a un aumento de los conflictos sociales, el hambre, la inflación y la migración a América del Norte.
encomienda System first established by Christopher Columbus by which Spanish leaders in the Americas received land and the labor of all American Indians residing on it. For American Indians, the encomienda system amounted to enslavement.	***encomienda*** Sistema establecido por Cristóbal Colón por el cual los líderes españoles de las Américas recibían tierras y la mano de obra de todos los nativos americanos que residían en ellas. Para los nativos americanos, el sistema de encomienda equivalía a la esclavitud.
English Civil War (1642–1651) Series of civil wars fought to determine who should control England's government.	**Guerra Civil Inglesa** (1642–1651) Serie de guerras civiles libradas para determinar quién debía controlar el gobierno de Inglaterra.
Enlightenment European cultural movement spanning the late seventeenth century to the end of the eighteenth century emphasizing rational and scientific thinking over traditional religion and superstition.	**Ilustración** Movimiento cultural europeo que duró desde finales del siglo XVII hasta finales del siglo XVIII y exaltó el pensamiento racional y científico por encima de la religión tradicional y la superstición.
Enrollment Act March 1863 Union draft law that provided for draftees to be selected by an impartial lottery. A loophole in the law allowing wealthy Americans to escape service by paying $300 or hiring a substitute created widespread resentment.	**Ley de reclutamiento** Proyecto de ley de la Unión de marzo de 1863 que disponía que los reclutas fueran seleccionados por una lotería imparcial. Una laguna en la ley que permitía a los estadounidenses ricos escapar del servicio militar si pagaban $300 o contrataban a un sustituto generó resentimiento generalizado entre la población.
Environmental Protection Agency (EPA) Federal agency established by Richard Nixon in 1971 to regulate activities that resulted in pollution or other environmental degradation.	**Agencia de protección ambiental (EPA, por sus siglas en inglés)** Agencia federal establecida por Richard Nixon en 1971 para regular actividades que generan contaminación o degradación ambiental.
Equal Rights Amendment (ERA) A proposed amendment that prevented the abridgment of "equality of rights under law . . . by the United States or any State on the basis of sex." Not enough states had ratified the amendment by 1982, when the ratification period expired, so it was not adopted.	**Enmienda de igualdad de derechos (ERA, por sus siglas en inglés)** Enmienda propuesta que impide la negación de la "igualdad de derechos bajo la ley... por parte de los Estados Unidos o de cualquier estado por motivos de sexo". En 1982, cuando expiró el plazo de ratificación, la enmienda no había sido ratificada por un número suficiente de estados, por lo que no fue adoptada.
Erie Canal Canal built in the early 1820s that made water transport from the Great Lakes to New York City possible. The success of the Erie Canal inspired many similar projects and ensured New York City's place as the premier international port in the United States, fueling industrial development throughout the Northeast.	**Canal de Erie** Canal construido a principios de la década de 1820 que hizo posible el transporte por agua desde los Grandes Lagos hasta la ciudad de Nueva York. El éxito del Canal de Erie inspiró la realización de muchos proyectos similares y aseguró el papel protagónico de la ciudad de Nueva York como el principal puerto internacional de los Estados Unidos, impulsando el desarrollo industrial en todo el noreste.
escalation Johnson administration policy of continuously increasing the numbers of ground troops in Vietnam and bombing campaigns.	**Escalada bélica** Política de la administración de Johnson de aumentar continuamente el número de tropas y de campañas de bombardeo en Vietnam.
Espionage Act 1917 act that prohibited antiwar activities, including opposing the military draft. It punished speech critical of the war as well as deliberate actions of sabotage and spying.	**Ley de espionaje** Ley de 1917 que prohibió las actividades antibélicas, incluida la oposición al servicio militar. Castigó la expresión en contra de la guerra y las acciones deliberadas de sabotaje y espionaje.
ethnic cleansing Ridding an area of a particular ethnic minority to achieve ethnic uniformity. In the civil war between Serbs and Croatians in Bosnia from 1992 to 1995, the Serbian military attempted to eliminate the Croatian population through murder, rape, and expulsion.	**limpieza étnica** Proceso de eliminación de una minoría étnica en particular de una región para lograr la uniformidad étnica. En la guerra civil entre serbios y croatas en Bosnia entre 1992 y 1995, los militares serbios intentaron eliminar a la población croata mediante asesinatos, violaciones y desplazamientos forzados.
eugenics The pseudoscience of producing genetic improvements in the human population through selective breeding. Proponents of eugenics often saw ethnic and racial minorities as genetically "undesirable" and inferior.	**eugenesia** Pseudociencia que busca producir mejoras genéticas en la población humana a través de la reproducción selectiva. Los partidarios de la eugenesia generalmente consideraban a las minorías étnicas y raciales como genéticamente "indeseables" e inferiores.
European Union (EU) Founded in 1993, a coalition of European nations that engage in free trade and investment with member nations. The EU introduced a common currency, the euro, in 1999.	**Unión Europea (UE)** Coalición fundada en 1993 de naciones europeas que participan en el libre comercio y la inversión con los demás países miembros. La UE introdujo una moneda común, el euro, en 1999.
Executive Order 9066 1942 executive order issued by President Franklin Roosevelt requiring all people of Japanese descent living on the West Coast to be relocated to internment camps.	**Orden ejecutiva 9066** Orden ejecutiva emitida en 1942 por el presidente Franklin Roosevelt en la que se decretó que todas las personas de ascendencia japonesa que residieran en la Costa Oeste serían reubicadas a campos de internamiento.
Exodusters African Americans who migrated from the South to Kansas in 1879 seeking land, economic opportunity, and a better way of life.	**Exodusters** Afroamericanos que emigraron del Sur a Kansas en 1879 en busca de tierra, oportunidades económicas y una mejor forma de vida.

F

Fair Labor Standards Act 1938 law that provided a minimum wage of 40 cents an hour and a forty-hour workweek for employees in businesses engaged in interstate commerce.	**Ley de normas laborales justas** Ley aprobada en 1938 que establecía un salario mínimo de 40 centavos por hora y una semana laboral de cuarenta horas para los empleados de empresas dedicadas al comercio interestatal.
faith-based initiatives White House initiative under George W. Bush that created a special office to provide religious institutions with federal funds for social services.	**iniciativas basadas en la fe** Durante el gobierno de George W. Bush, la Casa Blanca creó una oficina especial para proporcionar fondos federales a instituciones religiosas para servicios sociales.
Family and Medical Leave Act 1993 act protecting individuals' right to take up to twelve weeks of unpaid leave for medical reasons or parenthood without risk of losing their jobs.	**Ley de ausencia familiar y médica** Ley de 1993 que protege el derecho a tomar hasta doce semanas de ausencia del trabajo sin goce de sueldo por razones médicas o familiares sin riesgo de perder el empleo.
Farmers' Alliances Regional organizations formed in the late nineteenth century to advance the interests of farmers. The most prominent of these organizations were the Northwestern Farmers' Alliance, the Southern Farmers' Alliance, and the Colored Farmers' Alliance.	**alianzas de agricultores** Organizaciones regionales formadas a finales del siglo XIX para promover los intereses de los agricultores. Las más importantes fueron la Alianza de agricultores del noroeste, la Alianza de agricultores del sur y la Alianza de agricultores de color.
Federal Assault Weapons Ban 1994 ban prohibiting the manufacturing and use of semi-automatic firearms in the United States. The law was allowed to expire in 2004.	**Prohibición federal de armas de asalto** Ley aprobada en 1994 que prohibía la fabricación y el uso de armas de fuego semiautomáticas en los Estados Unidos. Se permitió que la ley expirara en 2004.
Federal Deposit Insurance Corporation (FDIC) Federal agency created under the New Deal in 1933. It insured bank deposits up to $5,000, a figure that would substantially rise over the years.	**Corporación federal de seguro de depósitos (FDIC, por sus siglas en inglés)** Agencia federal creada bajo el *New Deal* en 1933. En el momento de su creación, la agencia aseguró depósitos bancarios de hasta $5,000. Esta cifra aumentaría sustancialmente con el paso de los años.
Federal Employee Loyalty Program Program established by President Truman in 1947 to investigate federal employees suspected of disloyalty and Communist ties.	**Programa federal de fidelización de empleados** Programa establecido por el presidente Truman en 1947 para investigar a los empleados federales sospechosos de deslealtad y lazos comunistas.
Federal Housing Administration Agency created in 1934 by the Franklin Roosevelt Administration to devise housing construction standards and provide long-term mortgages to qualified buyers at low interest rates.	**Administración federal de vivienda (FHA, por sus siglas en inglés)** Agencia creada en 1934 por el gobierno de Franklin Roosevelt para diseñar estándares de construcción de viviendas y proporcionar hipotecas a largo plazo y a bajas tasas de interés a compradores calificados.
The Federalist Papers 85 essays by Federalists Alexander Hamilton, James Madison, and John Jay. Published in newspapers throughout the U.S., *The Federalist Papers* promoted the ratification of the Constitution.	*El Federalista* Colección de 85 ensayos escritos por los federalistas Alexander Hamilton, James Madison y John Jay. Publicados en periódicos de todo Estados Unidos, los ensayos de *El Federalista* promovieron la ratificación de la Constitución.
Federalists Supporters of ratification of the Constitution, many of whom came from urban and commercial backgrounds.	**Federalistas** Partidarios de la ratificación de la Constitución, muchos de los cuales provenían de contextos urbanos y comerciales.
feminist Someone who believes that women should have access to the same opportunities as men.	**feminista** Persona que cree que las mujeres deben tener acceso a las mismas oportunidades que los hombres.
feudalism A social and economic system organized by a hierarchy of hereditary classes. Lower social orders owed loyalty to the social classes above them and, in return, received protection or land.	**feudalismo** Sistema social y económico organizado en una jerarquía de clases hereditarias. Las órdenes sociales inferiores debían lealtad a las clases sociales por encima de ellas y, a cambio, recibían protección o tierras.
Field Order Number 15 Order issued by General William Sherman in January 1865 setting aside more than 400,000 acres of Confederate land to be divided into plots for freedpeople. Sherman's order came in response to pressure from African American leaders.	**Orden de campo número 15** Orden emitida por el general William Sherman en enero de 1865, que ordenaba que se apartaran más de 400,000 acres de tierra confederada para ser divididos en parcelas para familias de personas anteriormente esclavizadas. Esta orden de Sherman fue emitida en respuesta a la presión ejercida por parte de líderes afroamericanos.
Fifteenth Amendment Amendment to the Constitution prohibiting the abridgment of a citizen's right to vote on the basis of "race, color, or previous condition of servitude." From the 1870s on, southern states devised numerous strategies for circumventing the Fifteenth Amendment.	**Decimoquinta enmienda** Enmienda a la Constitución que prohíbe al gobierno negar el derecho de un ciudadano a votar por motivo de su "raza, color o condición anterior de servidumbre." A partir de la década de 1870, los estados del sur idearon numerosas estrategias para eludir la decimoquinta enmienda.

Glossary/Glosario

filibuster Unauthorized military expeditions launched by U.S. adventurers to gain control of Cuba, Nicaragua, and other Spanish territories in the 1850s.

filibustero Expediciones militares no autorizadas lanzadas por aventureros estadounidenses para tomar el control de Cuba, Nicaragua y otros territorios españoles en la década de 1850.

Food Administration New government agency created during World War I to regulate food production and consumption. Its head, Herbert Hoover, sought to increase the military and civilian food supply through a massive public campaign of voluntary conservation measures such as family gardens and "meatless Mondays."

Administración de alimentos Agencia gubernamental creada durante la Primera Guerra Mundial para regular la producción y el consumo de alimentos. Su líder, Herbert Hoover, intentó aumentar el suministro de alimentos a militares y civiles a través de una campaña pública masiva de medidas voluntarias de conservación tales como huertos familiares y "lunes sin carne".

Force Acts Three acts passed by Congress in 1870 and 1871 in response to vigilante attacks on southern black people. The acts were designed to protect black political rights and end violence by the Ku Klux Klan and similar organizations.

Leyes de cumplimiento Tres leyes aprobadas por el Congreso en 1870 y 1871 en respuesta a los ataques extrajudiciales contra afroamericanos en el sur. Estas leyes fueron diseñadas para proteger los derechos políticos de los afroamericanos y poner fin a la violencia del Ku Klux Klan y organizaciones similares.

Force Bill 1833 bill passed by Congress in response to South Carolina's Ordinance of Nullification. It gave the president the authority to use military force to enforce national laws.

Proyecto de ley de fuerza Propuesta de ley de 1833 aprobada por el Congreso en respuesta a la Ordenanza de nulidad de Carolina del Sur. Le dio al presidente la autoridad de usar la fuerza militar para imponer el cumplimiento de las leyes nacionales.

Fort Sumter Union fort that guarded the harbor in Charleston, South Carolina. The Confederacy's decision to fire on the fort and block resupply in April 1861 marked the beginning of the Civil War.

Fuerte Sumter Fortaleza de la Unión que protegía el puerto de Charleston, en Carolina del Sur. La decisión de la Confederación de disparar contra la fortaleza y bloquear el abastecimiento en abril de 1861 marcó el inicio de la Guerra Civil.

Fourteen Points The core principles President Woodrow Wilson saw as the basis for lasting peace, including freedom of the seas, open diplomacy, the establishment of the League of Nations, and the right to self-determination.

Catorce puntos Principios básicos que el presidente Woodrow Wilson propuso como base para una paz duradera, entre los cuales se encuentran la libertad de navegación, la diplomacia abierta, el establecimiento de la Sociedad de las Naciones y el derecho a la autodeterminación.

Fourteenth Amendment Amendment to the Constitution defining citizenship and protecting individual civil and political rights from abridgment by the states. Adopted during Reconstruction, the Fourteenth Amendment overturned the *Dred Scott* decision.

Decimocuarta enmienda Enmienda a la Constitución que define la ciudadanía y protege los derechos civiles y políticos de los individuos contra restricciones por parte de los estados. Adoptada durante la Reconstrucción, la decimocuarta enmienda anuló la decisión de *Dred Scott*.

Franciscan Member of a Catholic religious order founded by St. Francis of Assisi in the thirteenth century.

franciscano Miembro de una orden religiosa católica fundada por San Francisco de Asís en el siglo XIII.

Free Speech Movement (FSM) Movement protesting policies instituted by the University of California at Berkeley that restricted free speech. In 1964 students at Berkeley conducted sit-ins and held rallies against these policies.

Movimiento por la libertad de expresión (FSM, por sus siglas en inglés) Protesta estudiantil contra las políticas instituidas por la Universidad de California en Berkeley que restringían la libertad de expresión. En 1964, los estudiantes de Berkeley llevaron a cabo sentadas y concentraciones contra estas políticas.

Free-Soil Party Party founded by political abolitionists in 1848 to expand the appeal of the Liberty Party by focusing less on the moral wrongs of slavery and more on the benefits of providing economic opportunities for northern white people in western territories.

Partido del Suelo Libre Partido fundado por abolicionistas en 1848 para ampliar el atractivo del Partido de la libertad centrándose menos en los problemas morales de la esclavitud y más en los beneficios de proporcionar oportunidades económicas a los blancos del norte en los territorios occidentales.

Freedmen's Bureau Federal agency created in 1865 to provide freedpeople with economic and legal resources. The Freedmen's Bureau played an active role in shaping black life in the postwar South.

Buró de los libertos Agencia federal creada en 1865 para proporcionar recursos económicos y legales a las personas liberadas. El Buró de los libertos desempeñó un papel activo en la configuración de la vida de los afroamericanos en el Sur de la posguerra.

Freedom Rides Integrated bus rides through the South organized by CORE in 1961 to test compliance with Supreme Court rulings on segregation.

Viajes de la libertad Viajes en autobús por el Sur organizados por CORE en 1961 para comprobar el cumplimiento de las sentencias de la Corte Suprema con respecto de la segregación.

Freedom Summer 1964 civil rights project in Mississippi launched by SNCC, CORE, the SCLC, and the NAACP. Some eight hundred volunteers, mainly white college students, worked on voter registration drives and in freedom schools to improve education for rural black youngsters.

Verano de la libertad Proyecto de derechos civiles llevado a cabo en 1964 en Misisipi y organizado por SNCC, CORE, el SCLC y la NAACP. Unos ochocientos voluntarios, en su mayoría estudiantes universitarios blancos, trabajaron en campañas de inscripción de votantes y en escuelas de libertad para mejorar la educación de los jóvenes afroamericanos en zonas rurales.

Glossary/Glosario

The French Revolution A revolution between 1789 and 1799 in which French people, inspired by the ideals of the American Declaration of Independence, overthrew King Louis XVI (r. 1774–1792). The resulting uprising disrupted French agriculture among other aspects of life, increasing demand for American wheat, while the efforts of French revolutionaries to institute an egalitarian republic gained support from many Americans. However, in late 1792, as French revolutionary leaders began executing thousands of their opponents in the Reign of Terror and declared war against Prussia, Austria, and finally Great Britain, merchants worried about the impact on trade. In response, President Washington proclaimed U.S. neutrality in April 1793, prohibiting Americans from providing support or war materials to any belligerent nations.

Revolución Francesa Conflicto ocurrido entre 1789 y 1799 en el que el pueblo francés, inspirado por los ideales de la Declaración de Independencia de los Estados Unidos, derrocó al rey Luis XVI (r. 1774–1792). El levantamiento afectó la agricultura francesa, entre muchos otros aspectos de la vida en la región, aumentando la demanda de trigo estadounidense, mientras que los esfuerzos de los revolucionarios franceses por instituir una república igualitaria recibieron el apoyo de muchos estadounidenses. Sin embargo, a finales de 1792, cuando los líderes revolucionarios franceses comenzaron a ejecutar a miles de sus oponentes durante el Reino del Terror y se declararon en guerra contra Prusia, Austria y, finalmente, Gran Bretaña, los comerciantes comenzaron a preocuparse por el posible impacto en el comercio. En respuesta, el presidente Washington proclamó la neutralidad de Estados Unidos en abril de 1793, prohibiendo a los estadounidenses proporcionar apoyo o materiales de guerra a cualquier nación beligerante.

frontier thesis The argument, made by historian Frederick Jackson Turner in the 1890s, that the closing of the western frontier endangered the existence of democracy because it removed the opportunity for the pioneer spirit that built America to regenerate.

Tesis de la frontera Argumento planteado por el historiador Frederick Jackson Turner en la década de 1890, según el cual el cierre de la frontera occidental ponía en peligro la existencia de la democracia, porque eliminaba la oportunidad de que se regenerara el espíritu pionero con el que se construyó Estados Unidos.

Fuel Administration Government agency created during World War I to manage the production and distribution of fuel such as coal and oil.

Administración de combustible Agencia gubernamental creada durante la Primera Guerra Mundial para gestionar la producción y distribución de combustibles como el carbón y el petróleo.

Fugitive Slave Act of 1793 Act that ensured the right of slaveholders to capture enslaved people who had fled by mandating that local government seize and return them. However, the act was largely ignored by northerners.

Ley de esclavos fugitivos de 1793 Ley que garantizó el derecho de los dueños de esclavos a capturar a las personas esclavizadas que hubieran huido. La ley ordenaba a los gobiernos locales que incautaran y devolvieran a los fugitivos. Sin embargo, la ley fue prácticamente ignorada por los norteños.

Fugitive Slave Act of 1850 Act strengthening earlier fugitive slave laws, passed as part of the Compromise of 1850. The act provoked widespread anger in the North and intensified sectional tensions.

Ley de esclavos fugitivos de 1850 Ley que fortaleció las leyes anteriores de fugitivos de la esclavitud, aprobada como parte del Compromiso de 1850. Esta ley provocó indignación generalizada en el Norte e intensificó las tensiones seccionales.

G

gag rule Rule passed by the House of Representatives in 1836 to postpone action on all antislavery petitions without hearing them read in an attempt to stifle debate over slavery. It was renewed annually until it was rescinded in 1844.

regla mordaza Regla aprobada por la Cámara de Representantes en 1836 para posponer cualquier acción con respecto a la esclavitud, prohibiendo la lectura en voz alta de todas las peticiones en contra de la esclavitud, en un intento por sofocar el debate. Fue renovada anualmente hasta que fue rescindida en 1844.

gang labor A particularly harsh labor system that forced enslaved Africans and African Americans to work at a continuous pace throughout the day.

trabajo en cuadrilla Sistema de trabajo particularmente brutal que obligó a los africanos y afroamericanos esclavizados a trabajar a un ritmo continuo durante todo el día.

Gettysburg Address A speech given by President Lincoln to inaugurate the federal cemetery at Gettysburg, Pennsylvania in November 1863. In this speech, Lincoln expressed his belief that the war was a struggle for a "new birth of freedom."

Discurso de Gettysburg Discurso del presidente Lincoln pronunciado para inaugurar el cementerio federal de Gettysburg, Pensilvania, en noviembre de 1863. En este discurso, Lincoln expresó su creencia de que la guerra era una lucha por un "nuevo nacimiento de la libertad".

ghettos Neighborhoods dominated by a single ethnic, racial, or class group.

guetos Vecindarios dominados por un solo grupo étnico, racial o de clase.

Ghost Dance Religious ritual performed by the Paiute Indians in the late nineteenth century. Following a vision he received in 1888, the prophet Wovoka believed that performing the Ghost Dance would cause white people to disappear and allow American Indians to regain control of their lands.

Danza de los Espíritus Ritual religioso realizado por los nativos Paiute a finales del siglo XIX. Después de recibir una visión en 1888, el profeta Wovoka creía que realizar la Danza de los espíritus haría desaparecer a los blancos y permitiría a los nativos americanos recuperar el control de sus tierras.

Gilded Age Term created by Mark Twain and Charles Dudley Warner to describe the late nineteenth century. It implies the golden appearance of the age was a shell covering corruption and materialism of the era's superrich under the surface.

Edad de oro Término acuñado por Mark Twain y Charles Dudley Warner para describir a los Estados Unidos de fines del siglo XIX. Implica que la apariencia dorada de la época era una capa superficial que cubría la corrupción y el materialismo de la clase adinerada.

glasnost Policy of political "openness" initiated by Soviet leader Mikhail Gorbachev in the 1980s. Under *glasnost*, the Soviet Union extended democratic elections, freedom of speech, and freedom of the press.

glasnost Política de "apertura" iniciada por el líder soviético Mijaíl Gorbachov en los años ochenta. Bajo la *glasnost*, la Unión Soviética implementó elecciones democráticas y eliminó restricciones a la libertad de expresión y de prensa.

Glossary/Glosario

English	Spanish
Glass-Steagall Act 1933 New Deal legislation that allowed solvent banks to reopen and created the Federal Deposit Insurance Corporation (FDIC).	**Ley Glass-Steagall** Legislación del *New Deal* de 1933, que permitió que los bancos solventes volvieran a abrir y creó la Corporación federal de seguro de depósitos (FDIC, por sus siglas en inglés).
Global War on Terror (GWOT) Military campaign launched by the George W. Bush administration after the September 11, 2001 attacks. The campaign led to long and costly conflicts in Afghanistan and Iraq.	**Guerra contra el terrorismo (GWOT, por sus siglas en inglés)** Campaña militar lanzada por el gobierno de George W. Bush tras los atentados del 11 de septiembre de 2001. La campaña condujo a conflictos largos y costosos en Afganistán e Irak.
global warming Also known as climate change, the long-term rise in the temperature of the atmosphere and oceans that threatens life on earth.	**calentamiento global** También conocido como cambio climático, se refiere al aumento a largo plazo de la temperatura de la atmósfera y los océanos; amenaza la vida en la Tierra.
globalization The extension of economic, political, and cultural relationships among nations, through commerce, migration, and communication.	**globalización** Extensión de las relaciones económicas, políticas y culturales entre las naciones a través del comercio, la migración y la comunicación.
Glorious Revolution 1688 rebellion that forced James II from the English throne and replaced him with William and Mary. The Glorious Revolution led to greater political and commercial autonomy for the British colonies.	**Revolución Gloriosa** Rebelión de 1688 que derrocó a Jacobo II del trono de Inglaterra y lo reemplazó con Guillermo y María de Orange. La Revolución Gloriosa condujo a una mayor autonomía política y comercial de las colonias británicas.
"The Gospel of Wealth" 1889 essay by Andrew Carnegie in which he argued that the rich should act as guardians of the wealth they earned, using their surplus income for the benefit of the community.	**El evangelio de la riqueza** Ensayo escrito por Andrew Carnegie en 1889 en el que argumentaba que los ricos debían actuar como guardianes de la riqueza que ganaran, utilizando sus excedentes de ingresos para el beneficio de la comunidad.
Grangers Members of an organization founded in 1867 to meet the social and cultural needs of farmers. Grangers took an active role in the promotion of the economic and political interests of farmers.	**Grangers** Miembros de una organización fundada en 1867 para atender las necesidades sociales y culturales de los agricultores. Los miembros del movimiento *granger* asumieron un papel activo en la promoción de los intereses económicos y políticos de los agricultores.
Great Awakening Series of religious revivals in colonial America that began in 1720 and lasted to about 1750.	**Gran Despertar** Serie de movimientos de revitalización religiosa en la América colonial que comenzó en 1720 y duró hasta alrededor de 1750.
Great Depression Worldwide economic collapse caused by overproduction and financial speculation. It affected the United States from October of 1929 until the start of World War II in 1939.	**Gran Depresión** Colapso económico global causado por la sobreproducción y la especulación financiera. Afectó a Estados Unidos desde octubre de 1929 hasta el comienzo de la Segunda Guerra Mundial en 1939.
Great Migration Population shift of more than 400,000 African Americans who left the South beginning in 1917–1918 and headed north and west to escape poverty and racial discrimination. During the 1920s another 800,000 black people left the South.	**Gran Migración** Desplazamiento poblacional de más de 400,000 afroamericanos que abandonaron el Sur a partir de 1917–1918 y se dirigieron hacia el norte y el oeste para escapar de la pobreza y la discriminación racial. Durante la década de 1920, otros 800,000 afroamericanos abandonaron el Sur.
Great Plains Semiarid territory in central North America.	**Grandes Llanuras** Territorio semiárido al centro de América del Norte.
Great Railway Strike Series of nationwide railway worker strikes in 1877 following the collapse of several railroads and wage cuts at others. In response to these strikes, U.S. troops were removed from the South and sent north and west to contain the strikes.	**Gran huelga del ferrocarril** Serie de huelgas de trabajadores ferroviarios a nivel nacional en 1877 después del colapso de algunos ferrocarriles y de los recortes salariales en otros. En respuesta a estas huelgas, las tropas estadounidenses fueron retiradas del sur y enviadas al norte y al oeste para contener las huelgas.
Great Recession The severe economic decline in the United States and throughout the world that began in 2008, leading to bank failures, high unemployment, home foreclosures, and large federal deficits.	**Gran Recesión** El fuerte declive económico en los Estados Unidos y en todo el mundo que comenzó en 2008, llevando a quiebras bancarias, alto desempleo, ejecuciones hipotecarias y grandes déficits federales.
Great Society President Lyndon Johnson's vision of social, economic, and cultural progress in the United States.	**Gran Sociedad** Serie de propuestas del presidente Lyndon Johnson para el progreso social, económico y cultural en los Estados Unidos.
greenhouse gases Gases that absorb energy from the sun and other radiant sources, which warm the Earth.	**gases de efecto invernadero** Gases que absorben la energía del sol y otras fuentes radiantes, y que provocan el calentamiento de la Tierra.
gross domestic product The yearly output of all of a nation's goods and services.	**producto interno bruto** La producción anual de todos los bienes y servicios de una nación.
Guantánamo The site of a U.S. military base in Cuba, where the George W. Bush administration imprisoned suspected al-Qaeda members without due process of law. Despite campaigning on promises to end this policy, the Obama administration failed to close the Guantánamo Bay prison, and it continues to operate today.	**Guantánamo** Ubicación de una base militar estadounidense en Cuba donde el gobierno de George W. Bush encarceló a presuntos miembros de Al Qaeda sin el debido proceso legal. A pesar de las promesas de poner fin a esta política, el gobierno de Obama no logró cerrar la prisión de la Bahía de Guantánamo y continuó operando.

Glossary/Glosario

guerilla Nontraditional military tactics typically employed against a larger, better supplied force.	**guerrilla** Tácticas militares no tradicionales que suelen ser empleadas contra ejércitos más grandes y mejor abastecidos.
Gulf of Tonkin Resolution 1964 congressional resolution giving President Johnson wide discretion in the use of U.S. forces in Vietnam. The resolution followed reported attacks by North Vietnamese gunboats on two American destroyers.	**Resolución del Golfo de Tonkin** Ley emitida por el Congreso en 1964 que otorga al presidente Johnson amplia discreción en el uso de fuerzas estadounidenses en Vietnam. La resolución se dictó en respuesta a los ataques reportados por lanchas cañoneras norvietnamitas contra dos destructores estadounidenses.

H

Haitian Revolution Revolt against French rule by free and enslaved black people in the 1790s on the island of Saint Domingue. It led to the establishment of the Republic of Haiti, the first independent black-led nation in the Americas, in 1803.	**Revolución Haitiana** Revuelta contra el dominio francés por parte de negros libres y esclavizados en la isla de Saint Domingue en la década de 1790. Esto llevó a la fundación de la República de Haití en 1803, la primera nación independiente liderada por negros en las Américas.
Harlem Renaissance The work of Harlem-based African American writers, artists, and musicians that flourished following World War I through the 1920s.	**Renacimiento de Harlem** Movimiento de escritores, artistas y músicos afroamericanos basados en Harlem que floreció después de la Primera Guerra Mundial, en la década de 1920.
Hartford Convention 1814 convention of Federalists opposed to the War of 1812. Delegates to the convention considered a number of constitutional amendments, as well as the possibility of secession.	**Convención de Hartford** Reunión en 1814 de Federalistas opuestos a la Guerra de 1812. Los delegados discutieron una serie de enmiendas constitucionales, así como la posibilidad de secesión.
Hawley-Smoot Act 1930 act designed to increase tariffs on agricultural and industrial imports in order to aid struggling farmers. However, the act caused retaliatory tariffs by other countries, which broadly hurt American business.	**Ley Hawley-Smoot** Ley de 1930 que aumentó los aranceles sobre las importaciones agrícolas e industriales con el fin de ayudar a los agricultores afectados por la Gran Depresión. Sin embargo, la ley causó aranceles de represalia por parte de otros países, lo cual perjudicó ampliamente a la industria estadounidense.
Hay-Pauncefote Treaty 1901 treaty between the United States and Great Britain granting the United States the right to construct the Panama Canal.	**Tratado Hay-Pauncefote** Tratado firmado en 1901 entre Estados Unidos y Gran Bretaña, que otorga a los Estados Unidos el derecho a construir el Canal de Panamá.
Haymarket riot 1866 rally in Haymarket Square that resulted in violence. In its aftermath, the union movement in the United States went into temporary decline.	**Revuelta de Haymarket** Disturbio de 1866 en Haymarket Square, Chicago, que terminó de forma violenta. Después de este evento, el movimiento sindical en los Estados Unidos entró en un declive temporal.
headright system Created in Virginia in 1618, it rewarded those who imported indentured laborers and settlers with fifty acres of land.	**sistema headright** Creado en Virginia en 1618, recompensó con cincuenta acres de tierra a quienes importaban trabajadores y colonos.
Hetch Hetchy valley Site of controversial dam built to supply San Francisco with water and power in the aftermath of the 1906 earthquake. The dam was built over the objections of preservationists such as John Muir.	**Valle Hetch Hetchy** Sitio de la controversial presa construida para abastecer a San Francisco de agua y electricidad tras el terremoto de 1906. La presa se construyó pese a las objeciones de conservacionistas como John Muir.
Hohokam North American Indian groups who lived in present-day Arizona around 500 C.E.	**hohokam** Cultura de nativos norteamericanos que vivieron en el territorio actual de Arizona alrededor del 500 d.C.
holding company A company that controls one or more companies by owning their stock.	**sociedad gestora (holding)** Sociedad comercial que controla o administra las acciones de otras empresas.
Holocaust The Nazi regime's genocidal effort to eradicate Europe's Jewish population during World War II, which resulted in the death of 6 million Jews and millions of other "undesirables" — Slavs, Poles, Gypsies, homosexuals, the physically and mentally disabled, and Communists.	**Holocausto** Esfuerzo genocida del régimen nazi para erradicar a la población judía de Europa durante la Segunda Guerra Mundial, que resultó en la muerte de 6 millones de judíos y millones de "indeseables": eslavos, polacos, gitanos, homosexuales, comunistas y discapacitados físicos y mentales.
Homestead Act 1862 act that established procedures for distributing 160-acre lots to western settlers, on condition that they develop and farm their land, as an incentive for western migration.	**Ley de asentamientos rurales** Ley de 1862 que establece procedimientos para la distribución de lotes de 160 acres a los colonos del oeste, con la condición de que desarrollaran y cultivaran sus tierras, como incentivo para la migración al oeste.
Homestead strike 1892 lockout strike by steelworkers at Andrew Carnegie's Homestead steel factory. The strike collapsed after a failed assassination attempt on Carnegie's plant manager, Henry Clay Frick.	**Huelga de Homestead** Huelga de cierre patronal realizada en 1892 por los trabajadores de la fábrica de acero de Homestead, de Andrew Carnegie. La huelga colapsó después de un intento fallido de asesinato contra el gerente de la planta de Carnegie, Henry Clay Frick.
Honda Japanese automobile company, which originated in 1937 as a parts supplier for Toyota. In 1946 they began manufacturing motorcycles, in 1963 they produced their first four wheeled vehicle, and in 1995 the company again branched out to produce jet aircrafts.	**Honda** Compañía japonesa de automóviles fundada en 1937 como proveedor de piezas para Toyota. En 1946 comenzaron a fabricar motocicletas, en 1963 fabricaron su primer vehículo de cuatro ruedas y en 1995 la empresa volvió a diversificarse para producir aviones de reacción.

Hopewell Indian people who established a thriving culture near the Mississippi River in the early centuries C.E.	**Hopewell** Pueblo indígena que estableció una próspera cultura cerca del río Misisipi en los primeros siglos de nuestra era.
horizontal integration The ownership of as many firms as possible in a given industry by a single owner. John D. Rockefeller pursued a strategy of horizontal integration when he bought up rival oil refineries.	**integración horizontal** La adquisición de tantas empresas como sea posible en un sector determinado por un único propietario. John D. Rockefeller siguió una estrategia de integración horizontal al comprar refinerías de petróleo rivales.
horticulture A form of agriculture in which people work small plots of land with simple tools.	**horticultura** Forma de agricultura en la que se trabajan pequeñas parcelas de tierra con herramientas sencillas.
House of Burgesses Local governing body in Virginia established by the English crown in 1619.	**Cámara de los burgueses** Órgano de gobierno local en Virginia establecido por la corona inglesa en 1619.
House Un-American Activities Committee (HUAC) U.S. House of Representatives Committee established in 1938 to investigate domestic communism. After World War II, HUAC conducted highly publicized investigations of Communist influence in government and the entertainment industry.	**Comité de actividades antiestadounidenses (HUAC, por sus siglas en inglés)** Comité de la Cámara de Representantes de Estados Unidos establecido en 1938 para investigar el comunismo doméstico. Después de la Segunda Guerra Mundial, la HUAC llevó a cabo investigaciones muy publicitadas sobre la influencia comunista en el gobierno y la industria del entretenimiento.
household mode of production A system of exchange, managed largely through barter, that allowed individual households to function even as they became more specialized in what they produced. Whatever cash was obtained could be used to buy imported goods.	**modo de producción doméstico** Sistema de intercambio basado en el trueque que permitía a los hogares funcionar incluso cuando se especializaban en lo que producían. El dinero en efectivo que se obtuviera podía utilizarse para comprar mercancías importadas.
Hudson River School A mid-nineteenth century American artistic movement in which artists painted romanticized landscapes, primarily from New York's Catskill and Adirondack Mountains.	**Escuela del río Hudson** Movimiento artístico estadounidense de mediados del siglo XIX en el que los artistas pintaban paisajes románticos, especialmente de las montañas Catskill y Adirondack en Nueva York.
Huguenots French Protestants who fought for religious liberties and were heavily persecuted during the sixteenth and seventeenth centuries in the predominantly Catholic nation of France.	**Hugonotes** Protestantes franceses que lucharon por la libertad de culto y fueron fuertemente perseguidos durante los siglos XVI y XVII en la nación predominantemente católica de Francia.
Hull House The settlement house, based on Toynbee Hall in England, established by Jane Addams and Ellen Starr in Chicago in 1889. It served as a center of social reform and provided educational and social opportunities for working-class poor and immigrant women and their children.	**Hull House** Casa de asentamiento inspirada en Toynbee Hall, en Inglaterra, que fue establecida por Jane Addams y Ellen Starr en Chicago en 1889. Sirvió como un centro de reforma social y proporcionó oportunidades educativas y sociales para las mujeres pobres e inmigrantes de la clase trabajadora y sus hijos.
Hurricane Katrina Storm that hit the Gulf coast states of Louisiana, Mississippi, and Alabama in 2005. The hurricane caused massive flooding in New Orleans after levees broke, resulting in approximately 1,800 deaths.	**Huracán Katrina** Tormenta que azotó los estados de la costa del Golfo, Luisiana, Misisipi y Alabama en 2005. El huracán provocó que colapsaran los diques, lo cual produjo inundaciones masivas en Nueva Orleans, que ocasionaron unas 1,800 muertes.

I

Immigration and Customs Enforcement Agency (ICE) A branch of the Department of Homeland Security created in 2003, which oversees the investigations of criminal actions by illegal immigrants in the United States.	**Servicio de inmigración y control de aduanas (ICE, por sus siglas en inglés)** Agencia del Departamento de seguridad nacional creada en 2003 para supervisar las investigaciones de actividades delictivas de los inmigrantes ilegales en los Estados Unidos.
Immigration Reform and Control Act Law signed by President Ronald Reagan in 1986, which extended amnesty to undocumented immigrants in the United States for a specified period and allowed them to obtain legal status. At the same time, the law penalized employers who hired undocumented workers.	**Ley de reforma y control de la inmigración** Ley firmada por el presidente Ronald Reagan en 1986 que extendió una amnistía a los inmigrantes indocumentados en los Estados Unidos por un período específico y les permitió legalizar su estancia. Al mismo tiempo, esta ley penaliza a los empleadores que contratan a trabajadores indocumentados.
imperial presidency Term used to describe the growth of presidential powers during the Cold War, particularly with respect to war-making powers and the conduct of national security.	**presidencia imperial** Término utilizado para describir el crecimiento de los poderes presidenciales durante la Guerra Fría, particularmente en cuanto a poderes bélicos y seguridad nacional.
imperialism A policy of expanding the border and increasing the global power of a nation, typically via military force.	**imperialismo** Política de expansión fronteriza e incremento del poder global de una nación, generalmente a través de la fuerza militar.
impressment The forced enlistment of civilians into the army or navy. The impressment of residents of colonial seaports into the British navy was a major source of complaint in the eighteenth century.	**leva** El alistamiento obligatorio de civiles en el ejército o la marina. El reclutamiento forzado de los residentes de los puertos marítimos coloniales en la marina británica fue una de las principales fuentes de quejas durante el siglo XVIII.

Glossary/Glosario

Incas Andean people who built an empire in the centuries before the arrival of the Spaniards amid the fertile land of the Andes Mountains along the Pacific coast. Reaching the height of their power in the fifteenth century, the Incas controlled some sixteen million people.	**Incas** Cultura andina que construyó un imperio en los siglos anteriores a la llegada de los españoles en medio de la fértil tierra de la Cordillera de los Andes a lo largo de la costa del Pacífico. Los Incas, que alcanzaron la cima de su poder en el siglo XV, llegaron a controlar a unos 16 millones de personas.
indentured servitude Servants contracted to work for a set period of time without pay. Many early migrants to the English colonies indentured themselves in exchange for the price of passage to North America.	**trabajo no abonado** Empleados contratados para trabajar sin remuneración durante un periodo de tiempo determinado. Muchos de los primeros inmigrantes a las colonias inglesas trabajaron en esta modalidad a cambio del precio del pasaje a América del Norte.
Indian Citizenship Act 1924 act extending citizenship and the right to vote to all American Indians.	**Ley de ciudadanía de nativos americanos** Ley de 1924 que extiende la ciudadanía y el derecho al voto a todos los nativos americanos.
Indian Removal Act 1830 act, supported by President Andrew Jackson, by which American Indian peoples in the East were forced to exchange their lands for territory west of the Mississippi River.	**Ley de traslado forzoso de nativos americanos** Ley aprobada en 1830 y apoyada por el presidente Andrew Jackson, por la cual se obligaba a los pueblos nativos de Estados Unidos en el este a intercambiar sus tierras por territorios al oeste del río Misisipi.
Indian Reorganization Act (IRA) 1934 act that ended the Dawes Act, authorized self-government for those living on reservations, extended tribal landholdings, and pledged to uphold native customs and language.	**Ley de reorganización de nativos (IRA, por sus siglas en inglés)** Ley de 1934 que puso fin a la Ley Dawes, autorizó el autogobierno de los nativos que vivían en las reservas, amplió la propiedad de las tierras tribales y se comprometió a respetar las costumbres y el idioma de los nativos americanos.
Indian Trade and Intercourse Act 1790 act to regulate and maintain fair trade between American Indian and white settlers. The act was widely ignored, and relations between the two groups continued to worsen.	**Ley de comercio y relaciones de los nativos americanos** Ley de 1790 que reguló y preservó el comercio justo entre los nativos americanos y los colonos blancos. Esta ley fue ampliamente ignorada y las relaciones entre los dos grupos continuaron deteriorándose.
indulgences Payments to the Catholic Church as penance in exchange for the forgiveness of sins.	**indulgencias** Pagos a la Iglesia Católica como penitencia a cambio del perdón de los pecados.
Industrial Workers of the World (IWW) Organization that grew out of the activities of the Western Federation of Miners in the 1890s and formed by Eugene V. Debs and other prominent labor leaders. Known as Wobblies, the IWW attempted to unite all skilled and unskilled workers in an effort to overthrow capitalism.	**Trabajadores industriales del mundo (IWW, por sus siglas en inglés)** Organización surgida de las actividades de la Federación occidental de mineros en la década de 1890 y fundada por Eugene V. Debs y otros destacados líderes sindicales. Conocidos como los *wobblies*, la IWW intentó unir a todos los trabajadores calificados y no calificados en un esfuerzo por derrocar al capitalismo.
industrialization Massive shift from artisanal and homemade goods to factory mass production that occurred during the mid-nineteenth century.	**industrialización** El cambio radical de la producción artesanal y casera a la producción en masa en las fábricas que tuvo lugar a mediados del siglo XIX.
inflation Market-wide increase in prices, leading to the devaluation of currency.	**inflación** Aumento de los precios en todo el mercado, que lleva a la devaluación de la moneda.
influenza pandemic Worldwide flu pandemic, also known as the "Spanish Flu," following the end of World War I. The pandemic ultimately killed an estimated 50 million individuals, approximately 675,000 of whom were Americans.	**pandemia de gripe** Epidemia también conocida como "gripe española" que azotó a nivel global tras el final de la Primera Guerra Mundial. La pandemia acabó con la vida de unos 50 millones de personas, de las cuales aproximadamente 675,000 eran estadounidenses.
Inquisition A religious judicial institution designed to find and eliminate beliefs that did not align with official Catholic practices. The Spanish Inquisition was first established in 1478.	**Inquisición** Institución judicial religiosa diseñada para buscar y eliminar creencias que no se alineaban con las prácticas católicas oficiales. La Inquisición española se estableció por primera vez en 1478.
interlocking directorates The practice of placing allies on boards of directors of multiple competing firms or companies to maintain control over several companies or industries.	**juntas directivas interconectadas** La práctica de poner aliados en las juntas directivas de múltiples empresas competidoras para mantener el control sobre varias corporaciones o industrias.
Intermediate Nuclear Forces Treaty 1987 treaty between the U.S. and the Soviet Union that required the destruction of existing intermediate-range missiles and mandated on-site inspections to ensure both countries continued to adhere to the treaty terms.	**Tratado sobre fuerzas nucleares de rango intermedio** Tratado firmado en 1987 entre los Estados Unidos y la Unión Soviética que requería la destrucción de los misiles existentes de alcance intermedio e imponía inspecciones *in situ* para confirmar que ambos países siguieran acatando los términos del tratado.
Internet Interconnected computer communication network, which started as a military communication system in the 1970s.	**Internet** Red de comunicaciones informáticas que comenzó como un sistema de comunicación militar en la década de 1970.
internment The relocation of persons seen as a threat to national security to isolated camps during World War II. Nearly all people of Japanese descent living on the West Coast were forced to sell or abandon their possessions and relocate to internment camps during the war.	**internamiento** Reubicación de personas consideradas como una amenaza para la seguridad nacional en campos aislados durante la Segunda Guerra Mundial. Casi todas las personas de ascendencia japonesa que vivían en la costa oeste se vieron obligadas a vender o abandonar sus posesiones y trasladarse a campos de internamiento durante la guerra.

Glossary/Glosario

Interstate Commerce Commission (ICC) Regulatory commission created by the Interstate Commerce Act in 1887. The commission investigated interstate shipping, required railroads to make their rates public, and could bring lawsuits to force shippers to reduce "unreasonable" fares.	**Comisión de comercio interestatal (ICC, por sus siglas en inglés)** Comisión reguladora creada por la Ley de comercio interestatal de 1887. La comisión investigó el transporte marítimo interestatal, exigió a los ferrocarriles que hicieran públicas sus tarifas y estaba autorizada para interponer demandas judiciales para obligar a los transportistas a reducir las tarifas "irrazonables".
Intolerable Acts The name by which the colonial patriots referred to the Coercive Acts and the Quebec Act.	**Leyes intolerables** Nombre con el que los patriotas coloniales se refirieron a las Leyes coactivas y a la Ley de Quebec.
invasion of Grenada A U.S. invasion that installed a pro-American government after a 1983 coup toppled the Caribbean island's leftist, Soviet-supported government.	**invasión de Granada** Invasión estadounidense que instauró un gobierno pro estadounidense después de que un golpe de estado en 1983 derrocara al gobierno izquierdista de la isla caribeña respaldado por los soviéticos.
Iran Nuclear Agreement Compliance agreement in 2015 between Iran and the United Nations Security Council, which reduced nuclear facilities in Iran in exchange for a lift on economic sanctions by partner nations. In 2017 President Trump decertified the agreement.	**Acuerdo nuclear con Irán** Acuerdo firmado en 2015 entre Irán y el Consejo de Seguridad de las Naciones Unidas, que redujo las instalaciones nucleares en Irán a cambio del levantamiento de las sanciones económicas por parte de los países socios. En 2017, el presidente Trump descertificó el acuerdo.
Iran-Contra affair Reagan administration scandal involving the funneling of funds from an illegal arms-for-hostages deal with Iran to the Nicaraguan Contras in the mid-1980s.	**Escándalo Irán-Contras** Escándalo del gobierno de Reagan que involucraba un acuerdo ilegal de venta de armas a Irán a cambio de rehenes y la canalización de los fondos obtenidos por este medio para financiar a los Contras nicaragüenses a mediados de la década de 1980.
iron curtain Term coined by Churchill that described the ideological and political divide between the Communist Soviet Union and the non-Communist western world.	**cortina de hierro** Término acuñado por Churchill que describe la división ideológica y política entre la Unión Soviética comunista y el mundo Occidental no comunista.
Iroquois Confederacy A group of allied American Indian nations that included the Mohawk, Oneida, Onondaga, Cayuga, Seneca, and later the Tuscarora. The Confederacy was largely dissolved by the final decade of the 1700s.	**Confederación Iroquesa** Alianza de naciones nativas americanas que incluía a los Mohawk, Oneida, Onondaga, Cayuga, Seneca y, más tarde, a los Tuscarora. La Confederación se disolvió casi por completo en la última década del siglo XVIII.
Islamic State of Iraq and Syria (ISIS) Jihadist terrorist group originally founded in 1999, which gained strength from the sectarian violence that followed the 2003 U.S. invasion of Iraq. The group captured territory in Iraq and Syria and claimed responsibility for terrorist attacks in Paris, San Bernardino, California, and Lebanon.	**Estado islámico de Irak y Siria (ISIS, por sus siglas en inglés)** Grupo terrorista yihadista fundado originalmente en 1999, que se fortaleció con la violencia sectaria que surgió de la invasión estadounidense de Irak en 2003. El grupo capturó territorio en Irak y Siria y se declaró responsable de los ataques terroristas en París, San Bernardino, en California, y Líbano.
island-hopping This strategy, employed in the Pacific by the U.S. in World War II, directed American and Allied forces to avoid heavily fortified Japanese islands and concentrate on less heavily defended islands in preparation for a combined air, land, and sea invasion of Japan.	**salto de rana** Esta estrategia, empleada en el Pacífico por los Estados Unidos durante la Segunda Guerra Mundial, consistía en que las fuerzas estadounidenses y aliadas evitaran las islas japonesas fuertemente fortificadas y se concentraran en las islas menos defendidas en preparación para una invasión a Japón por aire, tierra y mar.
isolationism Informal policy stemming from the belief that the United States should not become involved with the affairs of other nations. This mindset was especially popular following World War I.	**aislacionismo** Política informal derivada de la creencia de que Estados Unidos no debe involucrarse en los asuntos de otras naciones. Esta mentalidad fue especialmente popular después de la Primera Guerra Mundial.

J

Jamestown The first successful English colony in North America. Settled in 1607, Jamestown was founded by soldiers and adventurers under the leadership of Captain John Smith.	**Jamestown** La primera colonia inglesa permanente en Norteamérica. Establecida en 1607, Jamestown fue fundada por soldados y aventureros bajo el liderazgo del Capitán John Smith.
Jay Treaty 1796 treaty that required British forces to withdraw from U.S. soil, required American repayment of debts to British firms, and limited U.S. trade with the British West Indies.	**Tratado de Jay** Tratado firmado en 1796 que requería que las fuerzas británicas se retiraran del suelo estadounidense, exigía el pago de las deudas de Estados Unidos a las empresas británicas y limitaba el comercio de Estados Unidos con las Indias Occidentales británicas.
Jim Crow Late nineteenth-century statutes that established legally defined racial segregation in the South. Jim Crow legislation helped ensure the social and economic disfranchisement of southern black people.	**Jim Crow** Leyes de finales del siglo XIX que establecieron la segregación racial en el Sur. La legislación de Jim Crow tenía como objetivo el desamparo social y económico de los afroamericanos en el sur.
jingoists Extremely patriotic supporters of the expansion and use of military power. Jingoists such as Theodore Roosevelt longed for a war in which they could demonstrate America's strength and prove their own masculinity.	**jingoístas** Nacionalistas extremadamente patrióticos, partidarios de la expansión y el uso de la fuerza militar. Los jingoístas como Theodore Roosevelt anhelaban una guerra en la que pudieran demostrar la fuerza de Estados Unidos y su propia masculinidad.

Glossary/Glosario

English	Español
John Brown's raid 1859 attack on the Federal arsenal at Harper's Ferry, Virginia, led by John Brown, who hoped to inspire a slave uprising and arm enslaved African Americans with the weapons taken from the arsenal. No uprising happened and Brown was captured and eventually executed for treason.	**Asalto de John Brown** Ataque dirigido por John Brown en 1859 contra el arsenal federal en Harper's Ferry, Virginia. Brown esperaba inspirar un levantamiento de personas esclavizadas y armar a los afroamericanos esclavizados con las armas tomadas del arsenal. No hubo levantamiento alguno y Brown fue capturado y finalmente ejecutado por traición.
joint-stock companies Companies in which large numbers of investors own stock. They were able to quickly raise large amounts of risk and reward equally among investors.	**sociedades anónimas** Sociedades en las que un gran número de inversionistas poseen acciones. Fueron capaces de recaudar rápidamente grandes cantidades de capital de riesgo y de recompensar por igual a los inversionistas.
judicial review The Supreme Court's ability to rule on cases at both the federal and state level.	**revisión judicial** La capacidad de la Corte Suprema para dictaminar casos tanto federales como estatales.
Judiciary Act Act passed in 1801 by the Federalist-controlled Congress to expand the federal court system by creating sixteen circuit (regional) courts, with new judges appointed for each, just before Democratic-Republicans took control of the presidency and Congress.	**Ley Judicial** Ley aprobada en 1801 por el Congreso controlado por federalistas para expandir el sistema judicial federal mediante la creación de dieciséis tribunales de circuito (regionales), con nuevos jueces designados para cada uno, justo antes de que los demócratas-republicanos tomaran el control de la presidencia y el Congreso.
The Jungle 1906 muckraking novel by Upton Sinclair that portrayed the poor working and living conditions in the Chicago meat-packing district, as well as the unsanitary practices in the unregulated meat production industry, leading to a widespread call for government regulation of food safety.	***La Jungla*** Novela escrita por Upton Sinclair en 1906 que retrataba las pésimas condiciones laborales y de vida en el distrito de procesamiento de carne de Chicago, así como las prácticas insalubres en una industria cárnica poco regulada, lo que llevó a un clamor generalizado para que el gobierno estableciera normas de manipulación de alimentos.

K

English	Español
Kansas-Nebraska Act 1854 act creating the territories of Kansas and Nebraska out of what was then American Indian land. The act stipulated that the issue of slavery would be settled by a popular referendum in each territory.	**Ley de Kansas-Nebraska** Ley de 1854 que creó los territorios de Kansas y Nebraska a partir de lo que entonces eran territorios de los nativos americanos. La ley estipulaba que la cuestión de la esclavitud se resolvería mediante un referéndum popular en cada territorio.
Keating-Owen Act 1916 act preventing the interstate sale of goods made by children under the age of 14, among other protections for children. The Supreme Court ruled it unconstitutional in 1918.	**Ley Keating-Owen** Ley de 1916 que prohíbe la venta interestatal de productos fabricados por niños menores de 14 años, e introdujo otras protecciones para los niños. La Corte Suprema la declaró inconstitucional en 1918.
Kellogg-Briand Pact Arms control agreement that outlawed war as an instrument of national policy following World War I. The policy proved unenforceable.	**Pacto Kellogg-Briand** Acuerdo de control armamentista que prohibió el uso de la guerra como instrumento de política nacional después de la Primera Guerra Mundial. Esta política resultó inaplicable.
Kent State massacre The killing of four students and wounding of nine others by the National Guard during a 1970 Kent State campus protest about the U.S. invasion of Cambodia as part of the Vietnam War. The incident sparked further anti-war sentiment and massive protests.	**masacre de la Universidad Estatal de Kent** Suceso en el que cuatro estudiantes fueron asesinados y nueve fueron heridos por la Guardia Nacional durante una protesta en el campus de la Universidad de Kent en 1970 en contra de la invasión estadounidense de Camboya como parte de la guerra de Vietnam. El incidente provocó una mayor oposición contra la guerra y protestas masivas.
King George's War 1739–1748 war between France, Spain, and England fought in North America.	**Guerra del rey Jorge** Conflicto entre Francia, España e Inglaterra que se libró en Norteamérica entre 1739 y 1748.
King William's War 1689–1697 war that began as a conflict over competing French and English interests on the European continent but soon spread to the American frontier. Both sides pulled American Indian allies into the war.	**Guerra del rey Guillermo** Conflicto ocurrido entre 1689 y 1697 que comenzó como una disputa entre los intereses de Francia e Inglaterra en el continente europeo, pero que pronto se extendió a la frontera con Estados Unidos. Ambos bandos trajeron a sus aliados nativos americanos a la guerra.
Kitchen Debate July 24, 1959 impromptu debate during the Cold War at the American National Exhibition in Moscow in front of a display of an American kitchen between Nixon and the Soviet Union's First Secretary Nikita Khrushchev about the merits of capitalism and communism.	**Debate de cocina** Debate improvisado entre Nixon y el Primer Secretario de la Unión Soviética, Nikita Jrushchov, sobre los méritos del capitalismo y el comunismo durante la Guerra Fría, el 24 de julio de 1959, en la Exposición Nacional Norteamericana en Moscú frente a una exhibición de una cocina estadounidense.
Knights of the Ku Klux Klan (KKK) Organization formed in 1865 by General Nathan Bedford Forrest to enforce prewar racial norms. Members of the KKK used threats and violence to intimidate black people and white Republicans.	**Caballeros del Ku Klux Klan (KKK)** Organización fundada en 1865 por el general Nathan Bedford Forrest para imponer por mano propia las normas raciales de la preguerra. Los miembros del KKK utilizaron amenazas y violencia para intimidar a los afroamericanos y a los republicanos blancos.

Glossary/Glosario

Knights of Labor Founded in 1869, a labor federation that aimed to unite workers in one national union and challenge the power of corporate capitalists.	**Caballeros del Trabajo** Federación de trabajadores fundada en 1869 que tenía como objetivo unir a los trabajadores en un sindicato nacional y desafiar el poder de los capitalistas corporativos.
Korean War Conflict fought between the northern Communist, Democratic People's Republic of Korea and the United Nations-backed southern Republic of Korea between 1950 to 1953.	**Guerra de Corea** Conflicto entre el norte comunista, la República Popular Democrática de Corea, y la República de Corea del sur, respaldada por las Naciones Unidas, entre 1950 y 1953.
Kyoto Protocol 1998 agreement amongst many nations to curtail greenhouse gas emissions and thus curb global warming. The U.S. Senate refused to ratify it.	**Protocolo de Kyoto** Acuerdo firmado en 1998 entre muchas naciones para reducir las emisiones de gases de efecto invernadero y así frenar el calentamiento global. El senado de los Estados Unidos se negó a ratificarlo.

L

La Raza Unida (The United Race) A Chicano political party, formed in 1969, that advocated job opportunities for Chicanos, bilingual education, and Chicano cultural studies programs in universities.	**La Raza Unida** Partido político chicano formado en 1969 que propugnó por oportunidades de trabajo para los chicanos, educación bilingüe y programas de estudios culturales chicanos en las universidades.
laissez-faire French for "let things alone." Advocates of laissez-faire believed that the marketplace should be left to regulate itself, allowing individuals to pursue their own self-interest without any government restraint or interference.	**laissez-faire** Expresión en francés que significa "dejar hacer". Los defensores del laissez-faire creen que el mercado debe dejarse solo para que se regule a sí mismo, permitiendo que los individuos busquen sus propios intereses sin ninguna restricción o interferencia del gobierno.
land rush 1889 government-sanctioned race to acquire land in formerly American Indian territory in Oklahoma.	**carrera de la tierra** Ocupación autorizada por el gobierno estadounidense en 1889 para adquirir tierras en el territorio nativo americano de Oklahoma.
League of Nations The international organization proposed by Woodrow Wilson after the end of World War I to ensure world peace and security in the future through mutual agreement. The United States failed to join the league because Wilson and his opponents in Congress could not work out a compromise.	**Sociedad de las Naciones** Organización internacional propuesta por Woodrow Wilson después del final de la Primera Guerra Mundial para garantizar la paz y la seguridad mundial en el futuro mediante un acuerdo mutuo. Estados Unidos no pudo unirse a la liga porque Wilson y sus opositores en el Congreso no lograron llegar a un acuerdo.
League of United Latin American Citizens (LULAC) Mexican American group consisting of largely middle-class members that challenged racial discrimination and segregation in public accommodations, engaging in economic boycotts and litigation.	**Liga de ciudadanos latinoamericanos unidos (LULAC, por sus siglas en inglés)** Grupo activista mexicano-americano compuesto en su mayoría por miembros de clase media que desafiaron la discriminación racial y la segregación en los alojamientos públicos a través de su participación en litigios y boicots económicos.
Leisler's Rebellion Class revolt by urban artisans and landless renters led by Merchant Jacob Leisler in 1689 New York over new taxes and centralized rule.	**Rebelión de Leisler** Levantamiento de artesanos urbanos e inquilinos sin tierra liderados por el comerciante Jacob Leisler en Nueva York en 1689 en contra de los nuevos impuestos y el gobierno centralizado.
Levittown Suburban subdivision built in Long Island, New York in the 1950s in response to the postwar housing shortage. Subsequent Levittowns were built in Pennsylvania and New Jersey.	**Levittown** Subdivisión suburbana construida en Long Island, Nueva York, en la década de 1950 en respuesta a la escasez de viviendas de posguerra. Posteriormente se construyeron Levittowns en Pensilvania y Nueva Jersey.
libel A false written statement designed to damage the reputation of its subject.	**difamación** Declaración falsa por escrito con la intención de dañar la reputación de otra persona.
The Liberator Radical abolitionist newspaper launched by William Lloyd Garrison in 1831. Through *The Liberator*, Garrison called for immediate, uncompensated emancipation of enslaved people.	***The Liberator*** Revista radical publicada por William Lloyd Garrison en 1831. A través de *The Liberator*, Garrison exigió la emancipación inmediata y sin compensación de las personas esclavizadas.
Liberty Party Antislavery political party formed in 1840. The Liberty Party, along with the Free-Soil Party, helped place slavery at the center of national political debates.	**Partido de la libertad** Partido político antiesclavista fundado en 1840. El Partido de la libertad, junto con el Partido del Suelo libre, ayudó a colocar la esclavitud al centro de los debates políticos nacionales.
Lincoln-Douglas debates Series of debates between Abraham Lincoln and Stephen Douglas during the 1859 Illinois Senate race that mainly focused on the expansion of slavery.	**debates Lincoln-Douglas** Serie de debates entre Abraham Lincoln y Stephen Douglas en 1859, durante la carrera por el senado de Illinois, que se centró principalmente en la expansión de la esclavitud.
Little Rock Nine Nine students who, in 1957, became the first African Americans to attend Central High School in Little Rock, Arkansas. Federal troops were required to overcome the resistance of white officials and the violence of white protesters.	**Little Rock Nine (Los nueve de Little Rock)** Nueve estudiantes afroamericanos de Little Rock que, en 1957, se convirtieron en los primeros estudiantes afroamericanos en asistir a la Escuela Secundaria Central en Little Rock, Arkansas. Se requirió la presencia de tropas federales para sobreponerse a la resistencia de los oficiales blancos y para proteger a los estudiantes ante la reacción violenta de los manifestantes.

Glossary/Glosario

Long Drive Cattle drive from the grazing lands of Texas to rail depots in Kansas. Once in Kansas, the cattle were shipped eastward to slaughterhouses in Chicago.	**Long Drive** Transporte de ganado desde las tierras de pastoreo de Texas hasta los depósitos de ferrocarril en Kansas. Una vez en Kansas, el ganado era enviado hacia el este, a los mataderos de Chicago.
Lost Generation Term coined by the writer Gertrude Stein to describe the writers and artists disillusioned with the consumer culture of the 1920s.	**Generación Perdida** Término acuñado por la escritora Gertrude Stein para describir a los escritores y artistas desilusionados con la cultura de consumo de la década de 1920.
Louisiana Purchase U.S. government's 1803 purchase from France of the vast territory stretching from the Mississippi River to the Rocky Mountains and from New Orleans to present-day Montana, doubling the size of the nation.	**Compra de Luisiana** En 1803, el gobierno de Estados Unidos compró a Francia el vasto territorio que se extiende desde el río Misisipi hasta las Montañas Rocosas y desde Nueva Orleans hasta la actual Montana, duplicando el tamaño de la nación.
loyalists Colonial supporters of the British during the American Revolution.	**lealista** Partidarios de los británicos durante la Revolución Estadounidense.
Lusitania British passenger liner struck by German submarine torpedoes off the coast of Ireland on May 15, 1915. The U-boat's torpedoes sank the ship, killing 1,198 people, including 128 Americans.	*Lusitania* Transatlántico de pasajeros británico que fue atacado por torpedos submarinos alemanes frente a las costas de Irlanda el 15 de mayo de 1915. Los torpedos del submarino hundieron el barco, matando a 1,198 personas, entre ellas 128 estadounidenses.
M	
Mandan North American Plains Indians who lived in semi-permanent dwellings, farmed, and traded with other native groups on the plains. Mandan society began to decline around 1250 C.E.	**Mandan** Pueblo de las llanuras de América del Norte que vivía en viviendas semipermanentes, y cultivaba y comerciaba con otros pueblos nativos de las llanuras. La sociedad mandan comenzó a declinar alrededor del año 1,250 d.C.
Manhattan Project Code name for the secret program to develop an atomic bomb. The project was launched in 1942 and directed by the United States with the assistance of Great Britain and Canada.	**Proyecto Manhattan** Nombre clave del programa secreto para desarrollar la bomba atómica. El proyecto fue lanzado en 1942 y dirigido por los Estados Unidos con la ayuda de Gran Bretaña y Canadá.
manifest destiny Term coined by John L. O'Sullivan in 1845 to describe what he saw as the nation's God-given right to expand its borders. Throughout the nineteenth century, the concept of manifest destiny was used to justify U.S. expansion.	**destino manifiesto** Término acuñado por John L. O'Sullivan en 1845 para describir lo que vio como el derecho otorgado por Dios a la nación para expandir sus fronteras. A lo largo del siglo XIX, el concepto de destino manifiesto se utilizó para justificar la expansión de EE. UU.
Mann Act Also known as the White Slave Trade Act, the Mann Act was passed in 1910 and banned the transportation of women across state lines for immoral purposes. In practice, this legislation was used to enforce codes of racial segregation and standards of moral behavior that enforced traditional social roles for women.	**Ley Mann** También conocida como la Ley de comercio de esclavos blancos, la Ley Mann fue aprobada en 1910 y prohibió el transporte de mujeres entre las fronteras estatales con fines inmorales. En la práctica, esta legislación se utilizó para imponer los códigos de segregación racial y estándares de comportamiento moral que implicaban los roles sociales tradicionales de la mujer.
Marbury v. Madison 1803 Supreme Court decision that established the authority of the Supreme Court to rule on the constitutionality of federal laws.	*Marbury vs. Madison* Decisión de la Corte Suprema de 1803 que estableció la autoridad de la Corte Suprema para regir sobre la constitucionalidad de las leyes federales.
March on Washington for Jobs and Freedom August 28, 1963 rally by civil rights organizations in Washington, D.C. that brought increased national attention to the movement.	**Marcha en Washington por el empleo y la libertad** Manifestación realizada el 28 de agosto de 1963 en Washington, D.C., por organizaciones de derechos civiles y que puso de relieve el movimiento a nivel nacional.
mariners A term for sailors.	**marineros** Término usado para miembros de una tripulación naval.
market revolution Innovations in agriculture, industry, communication, and transportation in the early 1800s that fueled increased efficiency and productivity and linked northern industry with western farms and southern plantations.	**revolución del mercado** Innovación en la agricultura, industria, comunicación y transporte a principios de 1800 que impulsó una mayor eficiencia y productividad y vinculó la industria del norte con las granjas del oeste y las plantaciones del sur.
Marshall Plan Post World War II European economic aid package developed by Secretary of State George Marshall. The plan helped rebuild Western Europe and served American political and economic interests in the process.	**Plan Marshall** Paquete europeo de ayuda económica posterior a la Segunda Guerra Mundial desarrollado por el secretario de estado George Marshall. El plan ayudó a reconstruir Europa Occidental y sirvió al interés político y económico estadounidense en el proceso.
martial law A suspension of standard law in which the military takes over the normal operation of the government.	**ley marcial** Una suspensión de la ley estándar en la que los militares toman control sobre el funcionamiento normal del gobierno.
Maya People who established large cities on the Yucatán peninsula with strong irrigation and agricultural techniques. The Maya civilization was strongest between 300 and 800 C.E.	**Mayas** Pueblo que estableció grandes ciudades en la península de Yucatán con importantes técnicas agrícolas y de riego. La civilización maya tuvo su apogeo entre 300 y 800 e. c.

Mayflower Compact Written agreement created by the Pilgrims upon their arrival in Plymouth. It was the first written constitution adopted in North America.	**Pacto del Mayflower** Acuerdo por escrito creado por los peregrinos a su llegada a Plymouth. Fue la primera constitución escrita adoptada en América del Norte.
McCarran Internal Security Act 1950 Republican-supported legislation proposed by Senator Pat McCarran, which required Communist organizations to register with the federal government, established detention camps for radicals, and denied passports to American citizens who had communist affiliations. Truman vetoed the bill, but Congress overrode his veto making the act law.	**Ley de seguridad interna McCarran** Legislación de 1950 apoyada por republicanos y propuesta por el senador Pat McCarran, que requería que las organizaciones comunistas se registraran con el gobierno federal. Asimismo, le ley estableció campos de detención para radicales y negó el pasaporte a ciudadanos estadounidenses que tenían afiliaciones comunistas. Truman vetó la propuesta de ley, pero el Congreso anuló su veto haciéndola una ley.
McCarran-Walter Immigration Act 1952 legislation that made it possible for Japanese non-citizens to become U.S. citizens. However, the act still maintained a race-based system of discriminatory national-origin quotas.	**Ley de inmigración McCarran-Walter** Legislación de 1952 que hizo posible que los no-ciudadanos japoneses se convirtieran en ciudadanos estadounidenses. Sin embargo, la ley aún mantuvo un sistema discriminatorio racial de cuotas de origen nacional.
McCarthyism Term used to describe the harassment and persecution of suspected political radicals. Senator Joseph McCarthy was one of many prominent government figures who helped incite anti-Communist hysteria in the early 1950s.	**Macartismo (o Mccarthismo)** Término utilizado para describir el acoso y la persecución de presuntos radicales políticos. El senador Joseph McCarthy fue una de las muchas figuras prominentes del gobierno que ayudaron a incitar el furor anticomunista a principios de la década de 1950.
McCulloch v. Maryland 1819 Supreme Court decision that reinforced the federal government's ability to employ an expansive understanding of the implied powers clause of the Constitution.	**McCulloch vs. Maryland** Decisión de 1819 de la Corte Suprema para reforzar la capacidad del gobierno federal de emplear una comprensión expansiva de la cláusula de poderes implícitos de la Constitución.
McDonald's American fast food company founded in 1940. In 1953 the company developed their golden arches logo and began to dramatically expand as a franchise business.	**McDonald's** Compañía estadounidense de comida rápida (*fast-food*), fundada en 1940. En 1953, la compañía desarrolló su logotipo de arcos dorados y comenzó a expandirse drásticamente como un negocio de franquicias.
Me Too movement The social movement linking tens of millions of women through social media networks in opposition to sexual harassment and abuse.	**movimiento *Me Too* (yo también)** Movimiento social que vinculó a millones de mujeres a través de las redes sociales en contra del acoso sexual y el abuso.
Meat Inspection Act Regulatory standards passed by Congress in the early twentieth century, raising meatpacking standards to larger federal requirements. The act inadvertently hurt smaller businesses that could not afford new equipment to meet the new standards.	**Ley de inspección de la carne** Normas regulatorias aprobadas por el Congreso a principios del siglo XX para establecer estándares de empaquetado de carne. La ley perjudicó inadvertidamente a pequeñas empresas que no tenían acceso al equipo necesario para cumplir con los nuevos estándares.
Medicare Prescription Drug, Improvement, and Modernization Act Also known as the Medicare Modernization Act, a 2003 act that dramatically expanded Medicare benefits and reduced costs associated with prescriptions.	**Ley de mejoramiento y modernización de las recetas médicas de Medicare** También conocida como la Ley de modernización de Medicare, una ley de 2003 que amplió drásticamente los beneficios de Medicare y redujo los costos asociados con recetas médicas.
melting pot Popular metaphor for immigrant assimilation into American society. According to this ideal, all immigrants underwent a process of Americanization that produced a homogenous society.	**crisol** Metáfora popular que responde a la asimilación de inmigrantes en la sociedad estadounidense. Según este ideal, todos los inmigrantes se sometieron a un proceso de americanización que produjo una sociedad homogénea.
mercantilism Economic system centered on maintaining a favorable balance of trade for the home country, with more gold and silver flowing into that country than flowed out. Seventeenth- and eighteenth-century British colonial policy was heavily shaped by mercantilism.	**mercantilismo** Sistema económico enfocado en mantener un balance comercial favorable para el país de origen, con más oro y plata entrando al país que saliendo de él. La política colonial británica de los siglos XVII y XVIII fue fuertemente moldeada por el mercantilismo.
Metacom's War 1675–1676 conflict between New England settlers and the region's American Indians. The settlers were the eventual victors, but fighting was fierce and casualties on both sides were high.	**Guerra de Metacome (o guerra del rey Felipe)** Conflicto de 1675–1676 entre los colonos de Nueva Inglaterra y los nativos americanos de la región. Finalmente, la victoria fue de los colonos, pero la lucha fue feroz y las pérdidas en ambos lados fueron altas.
Methodism A form of Protestantism based on Pietist ideas, founded by Englishman John Wesley.	**Metodismo** Una forma de protestantismo basada en ideas pietistas, fundada por el inglés John Wesley.
Mexican Revolution 1911 revolution in Mexico, which led to nearly a decade of bloodshed and civil war.	**Revolución Mexicana** Revolución de 1911 en México, que condujo a casi una década de guerra civil sangrienta.

Glossary/Glosario

English	Spanish
Mexican-American War 1846–1848 war between the United States and Mexico. Ultimately, Mexico ceded approximately one million square miles to the United States, including the present-day states of California, Nevada, New Mexico, Arizona, Utah and Texas, in the Treaty of Guadalupe Hidalgo. Debates over the status of slavery in these territories reignited the national debate about the expansion of slavery.	**Guerra Mexicana-Americana** Guerra de 1846–1848 entre Estados Unidos y México. Finalmente, México le cedió aproximadamente un millón de millas cuadradas a Estados Unidos, incluidos los actuales estados de California, Nevada, Nuevo México, Arizona, Utah y Texas, en el Tratado de Guadalupe Hidalgo. Los debates sobre el estado de la esclavitud en estos territorios reavivaron el debate nacional sobre la expansión de la esclavitud.
Microsoft Computer software company established by Bill Gates and Paul Allen in 1975.	**Microsoft** Empresa de *software* de computación fundada por Bill Gates y Paul Allen en 1975.
Middle Passage The brutal voyage of slave ships laden with human cargo from Africa to the Americas. It was the middle segment in a triangular journey that began in Europe, went first to Africa, then to the Americas, and finally back to Europe.	**Pasaje del medio** El brutal viaje que realizaban los barcos de esclavos transportando seres humanos desde África a las Américas. Era el segmento intermedio del viaje triangular que iniciaba en Europa con dirección hacia África, luego a las Américas y de regreso a Europa.
Military Reconstruction Acts 1867 acts dividing Southern states into military districts and requiring those states to grant black male suffrage.	**Leyes de reconstrucción militar** Leyes de 1867 que dividían los estados del sur en distritos militares y requerían que aquellos estados otorgaran el sufragio a los hombres afroamericanos.
military-industrial complex The government-business alliance related to the military and national defense that developed out of World War II and greatly influenced future development of the U.S. economy.	**complejo militar-industrial** La alianza entre gobierno y empresas relacionada con los militares y la defensa nacional que se desarrolló a partir de la Segunda Guerra Mundial y que en gran medida influenció el futuro desarrollo de la economía de EE.UU.
Minutemen Militia groups trained to prepare quickly for local defense in case of British attack.	**Minutemen** Grupos de milicias entrenadas para prepararse rápidamente para la defensa local en caso de un ataque británico.
mission system System established by the Spanish in 1573 in which missionaries, rather than soldiers, directed all new settlements in the Americas.	**sistema de misiones** Sistema establecido por los españoles en 1573 en el cual los misioneros, en lugar de los soldados, dirigían todos los nuevos asentamientos en las Américas.
missionaries People who travel to foreign lands with the goal of converting those they meet and interact with to a new religion.	**misioneros** Personas que viajan a tierras foráneas con la finalidad de convertir a aquellos que conocen y con quien interactúan a una nueva religión.
Mississippi Freedom Democratic Party (MFDP) Political party formed in 1964 to challenge the all-white state Democratic Party for seats at the 1964 Democratic presidential convention and run candidates for public office. Although unsuccessful in 1964, MFDP efforts led to subsequent reform of the Democratic Party and the seating of an interracial convention delegation from Mississippi in 1968.	**Partido Democrático de Libertad de Misisipi (MFDP, por sus siglas en inglés)** Partido político fundado en 1964 para desafiar al Partido Demócrata estatal totalmente blanco, por asientos en la convención presidencial demócrata de 1964 y postular candidatos a cargos públicos. Aunque no tuvo éxito en 1964, los esfuerzos del MFDP condujeron a la posterior reforma del Partido Demócrata y permitieron sentar una delegación en la convención interracial de Misisipi en 1968.
Mississippians Term for people who lived between 800 B.C.E to the arrival of Europeans in North America during the seventeenth century. The Mississippian culture spread across the Great Plains, primarily along rivers, and largely consisted of intensive agriculture of corn, beans, and squash and included societies such as Cahokia.	**Misisipiense** Término para las personas que vivieron entre el año 800 a. e. c. y la llegada de los europeos a América del Norte durante el siglo XVII. La cultura de Misisipi se extendió por las Grandes Llanuras, principalmente a lo largo de los ríos, y consistió en gran parte en una agricultura intensiva de maíz, frijoles y calabazas; incluyó a sociedades como la Cahokia.
Missouri Compromise 1820 act that allowed Missouri to enter the Union as a slave state and Maine to enter as a free state and established the southern border of Missouri as the boundary between slave and free states throughout the Louisiana Territory.	**Compromiso de Missouri** Ley de 1820 que permitió a Missouri ingresar a la Unión como un estado esclavo y a Maine como un estado libre; también estableció la frontera sur de Missouri como límite entre los estados libres y los esclavistas en todo el territorio de Luisiana.
Modern Republicanism The political approach of President Dwight Eisenhower that tried to fit traditional Republican Party ideals of individualism and fiscal restraint within the broad framework of the New Deal.	**republicanismo moderno** El enfoque político con el que el presidente Dwight Eisenhower trató de forzar los ideales tradicionales de individualismo y restricción fiscal del Partido Republicano, dentro del amplio marco del *New Deal*.
Monroe Doctrine Assertion by President James Monroe in 1823 that the Western Hemisphere was part of the U.S. sphere of influence. Although the United States lacked the power to back up this claim, it signaled an intention to challenge Europeans for authority in the Americas.	**Doctrina Monroe** Afirmación del presidente James Monroe en 1823 de que el hemisferio occidental era parte de la esfera de influencia de Estados Unidos. Aunque Estados Unidos carecía del poder para respaldar esta afirmación, la doctrina pretendía desalentar el interés de los europeos por las Américas.
Montgomery bus boycott Thirteen-month bus boycott that began with the arrest of Rosa Parks for refusing to give up her seat to a white man. The successful protest catapulted Martin Luther King, Jr., a local pastor, into national prominence as a civil rights leader.	**boicot de autobuses de Montgomery** Boicot de autobuses durante trece meses, que comenzó con el arresto de Rosa Parks por negarse a ceder su asiento a un hombre blanco. La exitosa protesta lanzó a Martin Luther King, Jr., un pastor local, a la fama nacional como líder de derechos civiles.

Glossary/Glosario

Mormons Followers of Joseph Smith and Brigham Young who migrated to Utah to escape religious persecution; also known as the Church of Jesus Christ of Latter-Day Saints.

Mormones Seguidores de Joseph Smith y Brigham Young que emigraron a Utah para escapar de la persecución religiosa; también conocida como la Iglesia de Jesucristo de los Santos de los Últimos Días.

muckrakers Investigative journalists during the late nineteenth and early twentieth centuries who specialized in exposing corruption, scandal, and vice. Muckrakers helped build public support for progressive causes.

muckrakers Periodistas de investigación de finales del siglo XIX y principios del XX que se especializaron en exponer la corrupción, el escándalo y el vicio. Los *muckrakers* ayudaron a generar apoyo público para causas progresistas.

mujahideen Religiously inspired Afghan rebels who resisted the Soviet invasion of Afghanistan in 1979.

muyahid Afganos rebeldes inspirados por la religión para resistir la invasión soviética en Afganistán en 1979.

Muller v. Oregon 1908 Supreme Court ruling that upheld an Oregon law establishing a ten-hour workday for women.

Muller vs. Oregón Resolución de la Corte Suprema de 1908 que confirmó una ley de Oregón que establecía una jornada laboral de diez horas para las mujeres.

multiplier effect The diverse changes spurred by a single invention, including other inventions it spawns and the broader economic, social, and political transformations it fuels.

efecto multiplicador Los diversos cambios impulsados por un solo invento, incluyendo otros inventos derivados del mismo y las transformaciones económicas, sociales y políticas alcanzadas.

Munich Accord 1938 agreement between Germany, Great Britain, and France, which allowed Germany to annex the Sudetenland, a western region of Czechoslovakia, in an agreement Germany would not acquire any more land afterwards. However, the following year German troops occupied the rest of Czechoslovakia.

Acuerdo de Múnich Acuerdo de 1938 entre Alemania, Gran Bretaña y Francia, que permitió a Alemania anexarse a los Sudetes, una región occidental de Checoslovaquia, en un pacto según el cual Alemania no tomaría más tierras después. Sin embargo, al año siguiente las tropas alemanas ocuparon el resto de Checoslovaquia.

mutual aid societies Voluntary associations that provide a variety of economic and social benefits to their members.

sociedades de ayuda mutua Asociaciones voluntarias que brindan una variedad de beneficios económicos y sociales a sus miembros.

mutually assured destruction (MAD) Defense strategy built around the threat of a massive nuclear retaliatory strike. Adoption of the doctrine of mutually assured destruction contributed to the escalation of the nuclear arms race during the Cold War.

destrucción mutua asegurada (MAD, por sus siglas en inglés) Estrategia de defensa construida alrededor de la amenaza de un ataque nuclear masivo de represalia. La adopción de esta doctrina contribuyó al incremento de la carrera armamentista nuclear en la Guerra Fría.

My Lai massacre March 16, 1968 unprovoked U.S. massacre of nearly 500 of the elderly, women, and children in the South Vietnam area of My Lai during the Vietnam War.

masacre de My Lai Matanza no provocada de casi 500 mujeres, ancianos y niños en manos de soldados de EE. UU. el 16 de marzo de 1968, durante la guerra de Vietnam.

N

Nat Turner's rebellion 1831 slave uprising in Virginia led by Nat Turner. Turner's rebellion generated panic among white southerners, leading to tighter control of African Americans by white southerners, leading to the passage of stricter slave codes in southern states.

rebelión de Nat Turner Levantamiento de personas esclavizadas en Virginia de 1831 dirigido por Nat Turner. La rebelión de Turner generó pánico entre los sureños blancos, resultando en un control más severo sobre los afroamericanos, así como un código más estricto de esclavos en los estados del sur.

National American Woman Suffrage Association A national organization created in 1890 when the American Woman Suffrage Association and the National Woman Suffrage Association combined. The group contributed to the passage of the Nineteenth Amendment in 1919, which guaranteed women's right to vote in the United States.

Asociación nacional americana por el sufragio de la mujer Una organización nacional creada en 1890 cuando la Asociación americana de sufragio de la mujer y la Asociación nacional de sufragio de la mujer se combinaron. El grupo contribuyó a la aprobación de la decimonovena enmienda en 1919, que garantizaba el derecho de las mujeres a votar en Estados Unidos.

National Association for the Advancement of Colored People (NAACP) Organization founded by W. E. B. Du Bois, Ida B. Wells, Jane Addams, and others in 1909 to fight for racial equality. The NAACP strategy focused on fighting discrimination through the courts.

Asociación nacional para el progreso de las personas de color (NAACP, por sus siglas en inglés) Organización fundada por W. E. B. Du Bois, Ida B. Wells, Jane Addams y otros en 1909 para luchar por la igualdad racial. La estrategia de la NAACP se centró en combatir la discriminación desde los tribunales.

National Association of Colored Women (NACW) Organization that became the largest federation of black local women's clubs in 1896. The group was designed to relieve suffering among poor black people, defend black women, and promote the interests of all black people.

Asociación nacional de mujeres de color (NACW, por sus siglas en inglés) Organización que se convirtió en la federación más grande de clubes locales de mujeres afroamericanas en 1896. El grupo fue diseñado para aliviar el sufrimiento entre los afroamericanos pobres, defender a las mujeres afroamericanas y promover los intereses de todos los afroamericanos.

National Defense Education Act 1958 Cold War era act in response to the Soviet launch of *Sputnik*, which provided aid for instruction in science, math, and foreign language, and grants and fellowships for college students.

Ley de educación de defensa nacional Ley de 1958 de la Guerra Fría en respuesta al lanzamiento soviético del *Sputnik*, que proporcionó apoyo para la enseñanza en ciencias, matemáticas e idiomas extranjeros, y subvenciones y becas para estudiantes universitarios.

Glossary/Glosario

National Energy Act Legislation signed into law by President Jimmy Carter in 1978, which set gas emissions standards for automobiles and provided incentives for installing alternative energy systems, such as wind and solar power.	**Ley nacional de energía** Legislación promulgada por el presidente Jimmy Carter en 1978, que estableció los estándares de emisiones de gas para automóviles y proporcionó incentivos para la instalación de sistemas de energía alternativa, como la eólica y solar.
National Industrial Recovery Act 1933 New Deal legislation establishing the National Recovery Administration to work with businesses and the public to regulate prices, wages, and production.	**Ley de recuperación de la industria nacional** Legislación de 1933 del *New Deal* que establece la Administración nacional de recuperación para trabajar de la mano con las empresas y el público, para regular los precios, los salarios y la producción.
National Interstate and Defense Highway Act 1956 act that provided funds for construction of 42,500 miles of roads throughout the United States.	**Ley nacional de autopistas interestatales y de defensa** Ley de 1956 que proporcionó fondos para la construcción de 42,500 millas de carreteras en todo Estados Unidos.
National Labor Relations Act 1935 act (also known as the Wagner Act) that created the National Labor Relations Board (NLRB). The NLRB protected workers' right to organize labor unions without business owner interference.	**Ley nacional de relaciones laborales** Ley de 1935 (también conocida como la Ley Wagner) que creó la Junta nacional de relaciones laborales (NLRB, por sus siglas en inglés). La NLRB protegía el derecho de los trabajadores a organizar sindicatos sin la interferencia del dueño del negocio.
National Labor Relations Board (NLRB) Organization created by the National Labor Relations Act in 1935. The NLRB protected workers' right to organize labor unions without business owner interference.	**Junta nacional de relaciones laborales (NLRB, por sus siglas en inglés)** Organización creada por la Ley nacional de relaciones laborales en 1935. La NLRB protegió el derecho de los trabajadores a organizar sindicatos sin la interferencia del dueño del negocio.
National Organization for Women (NOW) Feminist organization formed in 1966 by Betty Friedan, Gloria Steinem, and other like-minded activists.	**Organización nacional de las mujeres (NOW, por sus siglas en inglés)** Organización feminista formada en 1966 por Betty Friedan, Gloria Steinem y otras activistas con ideas afines.
National Origins Act 1924 act establishing immigration quotas by national origin. It was intended to severely limit immigration from southern and eastern Europe as well as halt all immigration from East Asia.	**Ley de origen nacional (o Ley de inmigración de 1924)** Ley de 1924 que establece cuotas de inmigración por origen nacional. La ley tenía la intención de limitar severamente la inmigración desde el sur y el este de Europa, así como prohibir toda inmigración desde el este de Asia.
National Recovery Administration (NRA) New Deal agency established in 1933 to create codes to regulate production, prices, wages, hours, and collective bargaining. The NRA failed to produce the intended results and was eventually ruled unconstitutional.	**Administración nacional de recuperación (NRA, por sus siglas en inglés)** Esta agencia propia del *New Deal* se estableció en 1933 para crear códigos de regulación de producción, precios, horas salariales y negociación colectiva. La NRA no logró producir los resultados previstos y finalmente fue declarada inconstitucional.
National Rifle Association Pro-gun rights organization founded in 1871.	**Asociación nacional del rifle** Organización que promueve el derecho a poseer armas; fundada en 1871.
National Road Road constructed using federal funds that ran from western Maryland through southwestern Pennsylvania to Wheeling, West Virginia; also called the Cumberland Road. Completed in 1818, it was part of a larger push to improve the nation's infrastructure.	**Carretera Nacional** Carretera construida con fondos federales que corría desde el oeste de Maryland hasta el suroeste de Pensilvania hasta Wheeling, Virginia Occidental. También conocida como Cumberland Road, se terminó en 1818 y fue parte de un esfuerzo mayor para mejorar la infraestructura de la nación.
National Security Council (NSC) Council created by the 1947 National Security Act to advise the president on military and foreign affairs. The NSC consists of the national security adviser and the secretaries of state, defense, the army, the navy, and the air force.	**Consejo de seguridad nacional (NSC, por sus siglas en inglés)** Consejo creado por la Ley de seguridad nacional de 1947 para asesorar al presidente sobre asuntos militares y exteriores. El NSC está formado por el asesor de seguridad nacional y los secretarios de estado, defensa, ejército, marina y fuerza aérea.
National War Labor Board (NWLB) Government agency created in 1918 to settle labor disputes. The NWLB consisted of representatives from unions, corporations, and the public.	**Consejo nacional del trabajo de guerra (también conocida como Junta laboral de guerra o NWLB, por sus siglas en inglés)** Agencia gubernamental creada en 1918 para resolver disputas laborales. El NWLB se conformaba por representantes de sindicatos, corporaciones y el público.
National Woman Suffrage Association In the aftermath of the Civil War, the National Woman Suffrage Association sought voting rights for women.	**Asociación nacional de sufragio de la mujer** A raíz de la Guerra Civil, la Asociación nacional de sufragio de la mujer buscó los derechos de voto de las mujeres.
National Woman's Party Political organization created in 1916, headed by Alice Paul and Lucy Burns. The group promoted more militant tactics than the National American Woman Suffrage Association. They picketed the White House, promoted hunger strikes, and engaged in mass protests in their campaign for women's suffrage as well as an unsuccessful push for the passage of the Equal Rights Amendment of 1923.	**Partido Nacional de la Mujer** Organización política creada en 1916, encabezada por Alice Paul y Lucy Burns. El grupo promovió tácticas más militantes que la Asociación nacional de sufragio de la mujer. Protestaron en contra de la Casa Blanca, promovieron las huelgas de hambre y se involucraron en protestas masivas en su campaña por el sufragio de las mujeres, así como en un intento fallido por la aprobación de la enmienda de igualdad de derechos de 1923.

Glossary/Glosario

nativism The belief that foreigners pose a serious danger to the nation's society and culture. Nativist sentiment rose in the United States as the size and diversity of the immigrant population grew.	**nativismo** La creencia de que los extranjeros representan un grave peligro para la sociedad y la cultura de la nación. El sentimiento nativista aumentó en Estados Unidos a medida que creció el tamaño y la diversidad de la población inmigrante.
nativists Anti-immigrant Americans who launched public campaigns against foreigners in the 1840s. Nativism emerged as a response to increased immigration to the United States in the 1830s and 1840s, particularly the large influx of Catholic immigrants.	**nativistas** Estadounidenses antiinmigrantes que lanzaron campañas públicas contra extranjeros en la década de 1840. El nativismo surgió como respuesta al aumento de inmigrantes a Estados Unidos en las décadas de 1830 y 1840, particularmente tras el gran influjo de inmigrantes católicos.
naturalization The process by which a noncitizen becomes a citizen of a nation.	**naturalización** El proceso por el cual un no ciudadano se convierte en ciudadano de una nación.
Naturalization Act 1798 act passed by the Federalist-controlled Congress that raised the residency requirement for citizenship from five to fourteen years to delay the naturalization of immigrants who largely voted Democratic-Republican.	**Ley de naturalización** Ley de 1798 aprobada por el Congreso controlado por federalistas, que aumentó el requisito de residencia para ciudadanía de cinco a catorce años, para así retrasar la naturalización de los inmigrantes que en gran medida votaron por los demócratas-republicanos.
Navigation Acts Acts passed by Parliament in the 1650s and 1660s that prohibited smuggling, established guidelines for legal commerce, and set duties on trade items.	**Leyes de navegación** Leyes aprobadas por el Parlamento en las décadas de 1650 y 1660 que prohibieron el contrabando, establecieron pautas para el comercio legal y aranceles sobre los artículos comerciales.
Nazism Ideology of the German fascist party, the National Socialists, which included virulent antisemitism, militarism, and autocratic state restriction of civil liberties. Adolf Hitler was the sole leader of the Nazi Party when this ideology ruled Germany from 1933 to 1945. Nazism was the primary cause of World War II in Europe, and the Nazis organized and carried out the Holocaust during the war.	**Nazismo** Ideología del partido fascista alemán nacionalsocialista, que incluía el antisemitismo virulento, el militarismo y la restricción autocrática de las libertades civiles por parte del estado. Adolf Hitler fue el único líder del Partido Nazi cuando esta ideología gobernó Alemania entre 1933 hasta 1945. El nazismo fue la causa principal de la Segunda Guerra Mundial en Europa, y los nazis organizaron y llevaron a cabo el Holocausto durante la guerra.
neoconservatives Disillusioned liberals who condemned the Great Society programs they had originally supported. Neoconservatives were particularly concerned about affirmative action programs, the domination of campus discourse by New Left radicals, and left-wing criticism of the use of American military and economic might to advance U.S. interests overseas.	**neoconservadores** Liberales desilusionados que condenaron los programas de la Gran Sociedad a los que originalmente habían apoyado. Los neoconservadores estaban particularmente preocupados por los programas de acción afirmativa, el control del discurso de campus en manos de los radicales de la Nueva Izquierda y las críticas de izquierda al uso del poderío militar y económico de Estados Unidos para promover los intereses estadounidenses en el extranjero.
Neutrality Acts Legislation passed between 1935 and 1937 to make it more difficult for the United States to become entangled in overseas conflicts. The Neutrality Acts reflected the strength of isolationist sentiment in 1930s America.	**Actos de neutralidad** Legislación que se aprobó entre 1935 y 1937 para evitar que Estados Unidos se inmiscuyera en conflictos extranjeros. Las leyes de neutralidad reflejaban la fuerza del sentimiento aislacionista en Estados Unidos durante los años treinta.
Neutrality Proclamation 1793 proclamation declaring U.S. neutrality in any conflicts between other nations, including France and Great Britain. Britain largely ignored U.S. neutrality and seized American merchant vessels heading for France.	**Proclamación de neutralidad** Proclamación de 1793 que declaró la neutralidad de los EE. UU. en cualquier conflicto entre otras naciones, incluyendo Francia y Gran Bretaña. Gran Bretaña ignoró en gran medida la neutralidad de EE. UU. y se apoderó de buques mercantes estadounidenses que se dirigían a Francia.
New Deal The policies and programs that Franklin Roosevelt initiated to combat the Great Depression. The New Deal represented a dramatic expansion of the role of government in American society.	**New Deal** Las políticas y programas que Franklin Roosevelt inició para combatir la Gran Depresión. El *New Deal* representó una expansión dramática del papel del gobierno en la sociedad estadounidense.
New Freedom Term used by Woodrow Wilson to describe his limited-government, progressive agenda. Wilson's New Freedom was offered as an alternative to Theodore Roosevelt's New Nationalism.	**Nueva Libertad** Término utilizado por Woodrow Wilson para describir su agenda progresista y de gobierno limitado. La nueva libertad de Wilson se planteó como una alternativa al nuevo nacionalismo de Theodore Roosevelt.
New Frontier President John F. Kennedy's domestic agenda. Kennedy promised to battle "tyranny, poverty, disease, and war," but, lacking strong majorities in Congress, he achieved relatively modest results.	**Nueva Frontera** La agenda doméstica del presidente John F. Kennedy. Kennedy prometió luchar contra la "tiranía, la pobreza, la enfermedad y la guerra", pero sus resultados fueron relativamente modestos dad su falta de apoyo en el Congreso.
New Jersey Plan A proposal to the 1787 Constitutional Convention that highlighted the needs of small states by creating one legislative house in the federal government and granting each state equal representation in it.	**Plan de Nueva Jersey** Una propuesta a la Convención Constitucional de 1787 que destacaba las necesidades de los estados pequeños por medio de la creación de una asamblea legislativa en el gobierno federal y el otorgamiento de una representación igualitaria a cada estado.

Glossary/Glosario

New Light clergy Colonial clergy who called for religious revivals and emphasized the emotional aspects of spiritual commitment. The New Lights were leaders in the Great Awakening.	**clero de la Nueva Luz** Clero colonial que representó un llamado de renacimiento religioso y enfatizó los aspectos emocionales del compromiso espiritual. La Nueva Luz fueron líderes del Gran Despertar.
New Look The foreign policy strategy implemented by President Dwight Eisenhower that emphasized the development and deployment of nuclear weapons in an effort to cut military spending.	**Nueva Mirada** La estrategia de política exterior implementada por el presidente Dwight Eisenhower que enfatizó el desarrollo y despliegue de armas nucleares como un esfuerzo para reducir el gasto militar.
New Nationalism Agenda put forward by Theodore Roosevelt in his 1912 presidential campaign. Roosevelt called for increased regulation of large corporations, a more active role for the president, and the extension of social justice using the power of the federal government.	**Nuevo Nacionalismo** Agenda presentada por Theodore Roosevelt en su campaña presidencial de 1912. Roosevelt exigió una mayor regulación de las grandes corporaciones, un rol más activo para el presidente y la extensión de justicia social a través del poder del gobierno federal.
New Negro 1920s term for the second generation of African Americans born after emancipation and who stood up for their rights.	**Nuevo Negro** Término de los años veinte para referirse a la segunda generación de afroamericanos nacidos después de la emancipación y que lucharon por sus derechos.
New Right The conservative coalition of old and new conservatives, as well as disaffected Democrats.	**Nuevo Derecho** La coalición conservadora de antiguos y nuevos conservadores, así como de demócratas descontentos.
New South Term popularized in the 1880s by newspaper editor Henry Grady, a proponent of the modernization of the southern economy in order for a "New South" to emerge.	**Nuevo Sur** Término popularizado en la década de 1880 por el editor de periódico Henry Grady, un defensor de la modernización de la economía sureña para que pudiese surgir un "nuevo Sur".
new woman 1920s term for the modern, sexually liberated woman. The new woman, popularized in movies and magazines, defied traditional morality.	**nueva mujer** Término de los años veinte para la mujer moderna, sexualmente liberada. La nueva mujer, popularizada en películas y revistas, desafiaba la moralidad tradicional.
Nineteenth Amendment Amendment to the Constitution granting women the right to vote, passed in 1919, and ratified into law in 1920.	**Decimonovena enmienda** Enmienda a la Constitución que otorga a las mujeres el derecho al voto, aprobada en 1919 y ratificada como ley en 1920.
No Child Left Behind (NCLB) 2001 legislation that aimed to raise national standards in education in underprivileged areas.	**Que ningún niño se quede atrás (NCLB, por sus siglas en inglés)** Legislación de 2001 que buscaba elevar estándares nacionales educativos en zonas desfavorecidas.
Non-Intercourse Act Act passed by Congress in 1809 allowing Americans to trade with every nation except France and Britain. The act failed to stop the seizure of American ships or improve the economy.	**Ley de no-relaciones** Ley aprobada por el Congreso en 1809 que permitía a los estadounidenses comerciar con todas las naciones, excepto Francia y Gran Bretaña. La ley no logró detener la captura de barcos estadounidenses ni mejorar la economía.
North American Free Trade Agreement (NAFTA) Free trade agreement approved in 1993 by the United States, Canada, and Mexico.	**Tratado de libre de comercio (TLC o NAFTA, por sus siglas en inglés)** Tratado de libre comercio aprobado en 1993 por Estados Unidos, Canadá y México.
North Atlantic Treaty Organization (NATO) Cold War military alliance intended to enhance the collective security of the United States and Western Europe.	**Organización del Tratado del Atlántico Norte (OTAN o NATO, por sus siglas en inglés)** Alianza militar de la Guerra Fría destinada a mejorar la seguridad colectiva de Estados Unidos y Europa Occidental.
The *North Star* Abolitionist newspaper started by fugitive from slavery and antislavery activist Frederick Douglass in 1847.	***North Star*** Periódico abolicionista iniciado por Frederick Douglass, un fugitivo de la esclavitud y activista, en 1847.
Northwest Ordinances 1785 act of the confederation congress that provided for the survey, sale, and eventual division into states of the Northwest Territory. A 1787 act then clarified the process by which territories could become states.	**Ordenanzas del noroeste** Ley de 1785 del congreso confederado que definía la situación, venta y eventual división en estados del Territorio del Noroeste. Una ley de 1787 luego aclaró el proceso por el cual los territorios podrían convertirse en estados.
NSC-68 April 1950 National Security Council document that advocated the intensification of the policy of containment both at home and abroad.	**NSC-68** Documento del Consejo nacional de seguridad de abril de 1950, que abogó por la intensificación de la política de contención tanto en el país como en el extranjero.
nuclear freeze movement 1980s protests calling for an end to the testing, production, and deployment of missiles and aircraft designed primarily to deliver nuclear weapons.	**movimiento por la congelación nuclear** Protestas de la década de 1980 que buscaban el fin de las pruebas, la producción y el despliegue de misiles y aviones diseñados principalmente para distribuir armas nucleares.
nullification The doctrine that individual states have the right to declare federal laws unconstitutional and, therefore, void within their borders. South Carolina attempted to invoke the doctrine of nullification in response to the tariff of 1832.	**anulación** La doctrina en que los estados individualmente tienen derecho a declarar las leyes federales inconstitucionales y, por lo tanto, nulas dentro de sus fronteras. Carolina del Sur intentó aplicar la doctrina de anulación en respuesta a la tarifa de 1832.

Glossary/Glosario

Nye Committee Committee chaired in 1934 by Republican senator Gerald Nye to investigate the actions of munitions manufacturers to ensure they were not pushing the country towards a second great war for financial profit. The Nye Committee blamed weapons manufacturers, arms dealers, and bankers who loaned funds to the Allied Powers for the outbreak of World War I.

Comité de Nye Comité presidido en 1934 por el senador republicano Gerald Nye para investigar las acciones de los fabricantes de municiones para asegurarse de que no empujaran al país hacia una segunda gran guerra para obtener ganancias financieras. El Comité Nye culpó a los fabricantes y traficantes de armas y banqueros que prestaron fondos a las potencias aliadas por el estallido de la Primera Guerra Mundial.

O

Obergefell v. Hodges The 2015 U.S. Supreme Court decision legalizing same-sex marriage throughout the nation.

Obergefell vs. Hodges Decisión de la Corte Suprema en 2015 de legalizar el matrimonio para personas del mismo sexo en toda la nación.

Occupy Wall Street movement A loose coalition of progressive and radical forces that emerged in 2011 in New York City and around the country to protest what they perceived to be corporate greed and federal policies that benefit the very wealthy.

movimiento Occupy Wall Street (La toma de Wall Street) Una coalición de fuerzas progresistas y radicales que surgieron en 2011 en la ciudad de Nueva York y en todo el país para protestar contra la avaricia corporativa y las políticas federales que benefician a los ya muy ricos.

Office of War Information Government office set up during World War II to promote patriotism and urge Americans to contribute to the war effort any way they could.

Oficina de información de guerra Oficina gubernamental instalada durante la Segunda Guerra Mundial para promover el patriotismo e incitar a los estadounidenses a contribuir al esfuerzo de la guerra de cualquier manera que pudieran.

Old Light clergy Colonial clergy from established churches who supported the religious status quo in the early eighteenth century.

clero de la Vieja Luz Clero colonial de iglesias establecidas que apoyaban el *statu quo* a principios del siglo XVIII.

Old-Age Revolving Pensions Corporation A pension plan also known as the Townsend Plan, developed by Francis Townsend. It advocated for a $200 per month pension for every citizen over the age of 60 in the United States.

Corporación de pensiones rotativas de la vieja edad Un plan de pensiones, también conocido como el Plan Townsend, desarrollado por Francis Townsend. Abogaba por una pensión de 200 dólares por mes para cada ciudadano mayor de 60 años en Estados Unidos.

Open Door policy 1899 policy in which Secretary of State John Hay informed the nations occupying China that the United States had the right of equal trade in China.

política de puertas abiertas Política de 1899 en la cual el secretario de estado John Hay informó a las naciones que estaban ocupando a China que Estados Unidos tenía el derecho de comercio igualitario con China.

Operation Desert Storm Code name of the 1991 allied air and ground military offensive that pushed Iraqi forces out of Kuwait.

Operación tormenta del desierto Nombre en clave de la ofensiva militar aliada terrestre y aérea de 1991 que expulsó a las fuerzas iraquíes de Kuwait.

Operation Iraqi Freedom 2003–2011 military conflict that began when the U.S. and its allies launched an invasion of Iraq in an effort to overthrow its dictatorship.

Operación libertad iraquí Conflicto militar entre 2003 y 2011 que comenzó cuando Estados Unidos y sus aliados lanzaron una invasión a Iraq en un esfuerzo por derrocar a su dictadura.

Operation Just Cause The U.S. invasion of Panama in 1989, after Manuel Noriega rejected the results of a democratic election and claimed he was the "maximum leader" of Panama.

Operación causa justa La invasión estadounidense en Panamá de 1989, después de que Manuel Noriega rechazó los resultados de una elección democrática y afirmó que él era el "máximo líder" de Panamá.

Operation Wetback Forced deportation of 250,000 to 1.3 million undocumented Mexican immigrants during the Eisenhower administration.

Operación espalda mojada Deportación forzada de 250,000 a 1.3 millones de inmigrantes mexicanos indocumentados durante la administración Eisenhower.

Ordinance of Nullification 1832 law passed by South Carolina proclaiming several congressional tariff acts null and void within the state and threatening secession if the federal government attempted to enforce the tariffs.

Ordenanza de anulación Ley de 1832 aprobada por Carolina del Sur que proclamaba varios actos arancelarios del Congreso nulos e inválidos dentro del estado y amenazaba con la secesión si el gobierno federal intentaba ejecutar los aranceles.

Oregon Trail The route west from the Missouri River to the Oregon Territory. By 1860, some 350,000 Americans had made the three- to six-month journey along the trail.

La senda de Oregón La ruta al oeste desde el río Missouri hasta el territorio de Oregón. Para el año 1860, unos 350,000 estadounidenses ya habían realizado el viaje (de tres a seis meses) a lo largo de la senda.

Organization of Petroleum Exporting Countries (OPEC) Organization formed by oil-producing countries to control the price and supply of oil on the global market.

Organización de países exportadores de petróleo (OPEP) Organización formada por países productores de petróleo para controlar el precio y el suministro de petróleo en el mercado global.

original sin Christian belief that all humans are born into sin because of the biblical sin of Adam eating the forbidden fruit from the tree of knowledge in the Garden of Eden.

pecado original Creencia cristiana de que todos los humanos nacen pecadores a causa del pecado bíblico de Adán de haber comido el fruto prohibido del árbol del conocimiento en el Jardín del Edén.

Glossary/Glosario

Ostend Manifesto 1854 letter from U.S. ambassadors and the secretary of state to President Franklin Pierce urging him to conquer Cuba. When it was leaked to the press, northerners voiced outrage at what they saw as a plot to expand slave territories.	**Manifiesto de Ostend** Carta de 1854 de los senadores de EE. UU. y del secretario de estado al presidente Franklin Pierce urgiéndolo a conquistar Cuba. Cuando se filtró a la prensa, los norteños expresaron su indignación ante lo que vieron como un complot para expandir los territorios de esclavos.
overland trails Nineteenth-century wagon and stagecoach routes that began in Missouri and headed westward, carrying settlers and goods to present-day California and Oregon.	**rutas terrestres** Rutas de vagones y carretas del siglo XIX que comenzaban en Missouri en dirección oeste, llevando colonos y mercancías a los actuales estados de California y Oregón.

P

Palestine Liberation Organization (PLO) Organization founded in 1964 with the goal of achieving independence from Israel, through armed force if necessary. For many years the PLO was considered a terrorist organization by the U.S.	**Organización para la liberación de palestina (OLP)** Organización fundada en 1964 con el objetivo de independizarse de Israel, a través de la fuerza armada si es necesario. Durante muchos años, la OLP fue considerada una organización terrorista por los Estados Unidos.
Palmer raids Government roundup of some 6,000 suspected alien radicals in 1919–1920, ordered by Attorney General A. Mitchell Palmer and his assistant J. Edgar Hoover. The raids resulted in the deportation of 556 immigrants.	**redadas de Palmer** Arresto gubernamental de unos 6,000 extranjeros radicales sospechosos entre 1919 y 1920, ordenado por el fiscal general A. Mitchell Palmer y su asistente J. Edgar Hoover. Las redadas resultaron en la deportación de 556 inmigrantes.
Panic of 1819 The nation's first severe recession. It lasted four years and resulted from irresponsible banking practices and the declining demand abroad for American goods, including cotton.	**Pánico de 1819** La primera recesión severa del país. Duró cuatro años y fue resultado de prácticas bancarias irresponsables y la disminución de la demanda en el extranjero de bienes estadounidenses, incluido el algodón.
Panic of 1837 Severe economic recession that began shortly after Martin Van Buren's presidential inauguration. The Panic of 1837 started in the South and was rooted in the changing fortunes of American cotton in Great Britain.	**Pánico de 1837** Recesión económica severa que comenzó poco después de la toma de posesión presidencial de Martin Van Buren. El Pánico de 1837 comenzó en el sur y se debió a los altibajos del algodón estadounidense en Gran Bretaña.
Panic of 1873 Severe economic depression triggered by the collapse of the Northern Pacific Railroad.	**Pánico de 1873** Depresión económica severa provocada por el colapso del ferrocarril del Pacífico norte.
Paris Climate Agreement Worldwide agreement by the U.S. and 194 other nations in 2015 to dramatically reduce greenhouse gas emissions produced from fossil fuels. In 2017 President Donald Trump retracted U.S. commitment to the agreement.	**Acuerdo climático de París** Acuerdo mundial entre EE. UU. y otras 194 naciones en 2015 para reducir drásticamente las emisiones de gases de efecto invernadero producidas por los combustibles fósiles. En 2017, presidente Donald Trump se retractó del compromiso de EE. UU. con el acuerdo.
Patient Protection and Affordable Care Act ("Obamacare") Passed in 2010, this law expanded health insurance to millions of Americans previously uncovered through a variety of measures including extending Medicaid, setting up of health-insurance exchanges, allowing children to remain under their parents' coverage until the age of twenty-six, and preventing insurance companies from excluding coverage based on pre-existing conditions.	**Ley de protección al paciente y cuidado de salud asequible ("Obamacare")** Aprobada en 2010, esta ley amplió el seguro de salud a millones de estadounidenses previamente sin seguro a través de una variedad de medidas; por ejemplo, la extensión de Medicaid, la creación de intercambios de seguro de salud, permitiendo que los hijos permanezcan bajo la cobertura de los padres hasta la edad de veintiséis años y evitando que las compañías de seguros excluyan la cobertura a personas con condiciones preexistentes.
patriarchal family Model of the family in which fathers have absolute authority over wives, children, and servants. Most colonial Americans accepted the patriarchal model of the family, at least as an ideal.	**familia patriarcal** Modelo de la familia en la cual los padres tienen autoridad absoluta sobre esposas, hijos y sirvientes. La mayoría de los estadounidenses coloniales aceptaron el modelo patriarcal de la familia, al menos como un ideal.
Patriot Act 2001 law passed in response to the September 11 terror attacks. The law eased restrictions on domestic and foreign intelligence gathering and expanded governmental power to deport immigrants suspected of terrorism.	**Ley patriótica** Ley de 2001 aprobada como respuesta a los ataques terroristas del 11 de septiembre. La ley suavizó las restricciones sobre la recopilación de inteligencia nacional y extranjera y expandió el poder gubernamental para deportar inmigrantes.
patriots American colonists who favored the movement for independence during the 1770s.	**patriotas** Colonos estadounidenses que favorecieron el movimiento por la independencia durante la década de 1770.
Payne-Aldrich tariff 1909 legislation increasing the amount of duties paid on imports.	**tarifa Payne-Aldrich** Legislación de 1909 que aumentó la cantidad de aranceles pagados sobre las importaciones.
Peace of Paris 1763 peace treaty ending the Seven Years' War (French and Indian War). Under its terms, Britain gained control of North America east of the Mississippi River and of present-day Canada.	**Tratado de paz de París** Tratado de paz de 1763 que puso fin a la Guerra de los Siete Años (Guerra de Francia e India). Bajo sus términos, Gran Bretaña tomó control de Norte América al este del Río Misisipi y de la actual Canadá.
Pendleton Civil Service Reform Act 1883 act that required federal jobs to be awarded on the basis of merit through competitive exams rather than through political connections.	**Ley de reforma del servicio civil de Pendleton** Ley de 1883 que requería la adjudicación de empleos federales basado en el mérito obtenido en exámenes competitivos en lugar de a través de conexiones políticas.

Pentagon Papers Classified report on U.S. involvement in Vietnam leaked to the press in 1971. The report confirmed that the Kennedy and Johnson administrations had misled the public about the origins and nature of the Vietnam War.

Pequot War 1636–1637 conflict between New England settlers, their Narragansett allies, and the Pequots. The English saw the Pequots as both a threat and an obstacle to further English expansion.

perestroika Policy of economic "restructuring" initiated by Soviet leader Mikhail Gorbachev. Gorbachev hoped that by reducing state control he could revive the Soviet economy.

Personal Responsibility and Work Opportunity Reconciliation Act 1996 act reforming the welfare system in the United States. The law required adults on the welfare rolls to find work within two years or lose their welfare benefits.

Petticoat Affair 1829 political conflict over Andrew Jackson's appointment of John Eaton as secretary of war. Eaton was married to a woman of allegedly questionable character, and the wives of many prominent Washington politicians organized a campaign to snub her.

Pietists German Protestants who criticized the power of established churches and urged individuals to follow their hearts rather than their heads in spiritual matters. Pietism had a profound influence on the leaders of the Great Awakening.

Pilgrims Also known as Separatists, a group of English religious dissenters who established a settlement at Plymouth, Massachusetts, in 1620. Unlike more mainstream Protestants, the Pilgrims aimed to cut all connections with the Church of England.

Pinckney Treaty 1796 treaty that defined the boundary between U.S. and Spanish territory in the South and opened the Mississippi River and New Orleans to U.S. shipping.

Pinkertons A company of private investigators and security guards sometimes used by corporations to break up strikes and labor disputes, most famously at the Homestead strike of 1892.

planters White southern slaveholders who owned the largest plantations and forged a distinct culture and economy around the institution of slavery.

Platt Amendment 1901 act of Congress limiting Cuban sovereignty. American officials pressured Cuban leaders to incorporate the amendment into the Cuban constitution.

Plessy v. Ferguson 1896 Supreme Court ruling that upheld the legality of Jim Crow legislation. The Court ruled that as long as states provided "equal but separate" facilities for white and black people, Jim Crow laws did not violate the equal protection clause of the Fourteenth Amendment.

political boss The head of the local political machine. The boss worked to maintain authority by strengthening the machine and its loyalists.

political machine Urban political organizations that dominated many late-nineteenth-century cities. Machines provided needed services to the urban poor, but they also fostered corruption, crime, and inefficiency.

Papeles del Pentágono El informe clasificado sobre la participación de Estados Unidos en Vietnam que se filtró a la prensa en 1971. El informe confirmó que las administraciones de Kennedy y Johnson habían engañado al público sobre los orígenes y la naturaleza de la Guerra de Vietnam.

Guerra Pequot Conflicto de 1636–1637 entre los colonos de Nueva Inglaterra, sus aliados de Narragansett, y los pequots. Los ingleses vieron a los pequots como una amenaza y un obstáculo para una mayor expansión inglesa.

perestroika Política de "restructuración" económica iniciada por el líder soviético Mijaíl Gorbachov. Gorbachov esperaba que al reducir el control estatal pudiera revivir la economía soviética.

Ley de reconciliación de la responsabilidad personal y la oportunidad de trabajo Ley de 1996 que reformó el sistema de bienestar social en Estados Unidos. La ley requería que los adultos en las listas de asistencia social encontraran trabajo dentro de dos años o perderían sus beneficios de asistencia social.

asunto de enaguas (*Petticoat Affair*) Conflicto político de 1829 sobre el nombramiento de John Eaton como secretario de guerra de Andrew Jackson. Eaton estaba casado con una mujer de carácter supuestamente cuestionable, y las esposas de muchos políticos prominentes de Washington organizaron una campaña para desairarla.

Pietistas Protestantes alemanes que criticaban el poder de las iglesias establecidas e incitaban a las personas a seguir sus corazones en lugar de sus cabezas en asuntos espirituales. El pietismo tuvo una profunda influencia en los líderes del Gran Despertar.

Peregrinos También conocidos como separatistas, fueron un grupo de disidentes religiosos ingleses que establecieron un asentamiento en Plymouth, Massachusetts, en 1620. A diferencia de los protestantes más convencionales, los peregrinos tenían como objetivo cortar todas las conexiones con la Iglesia de Inglaterra.

Tratado de Pickney Tratado de 1796 que definió el límite entre Estados Unidos y el territorio español al sur y abrió el río Misisipi y Nuevo Orleans para embarcaciones estadounidenses.

Pinkertons Una compañía de investigadores privados y guardias de seguridad a veces utilizados por corporaciones para disolver huelgas y disputas laborales, principalmente conocidos por la huelga Homestead de 1892.

plantador Esclavistas blancos del sur que poseían las plantaciones más grandes y forjaron una cultura y una economía distintas en torno a la institución de la esclavitud.

Enmienda de Platt Ley del Congreso de 1901 que limita la soberanía cubana. Los funcionarios estadounidenses presionaron a los líderes cubanos para que incorporaran la enmienda en la constitución cubana.

Plessy vs. Ferguson Resolución de la Corte Suprema de 1896 que confirmó la legalidad de la legislación de Jim Crow. El Tribunal dictaminó que mientras los estados proporcionaran instalaciones "igualitarias pero separadas" para las personas blancas y los afroamericanos, las leyes de Jim Crow no violaban la cláusula de igual protección de la decimocuarta enmienda.

jefe político El director de la máquina política local. El jefe trabajaba para mantener la autoridad fortaleciendo la máquina y sus partidarios leales.

maquinaria política Organizaciones políticas urbanas que dominaban muchas ciudades a finales del siglo XIX. Las maquinarias políticas proporcionaban servicios que necesitaban los pobres en las zonas urbanas, pero también fomentaron la corrupción, el crimen y la ineficiencia.

political sovereignty The freedom to self-govern.	**soberanía política** La libertad de autogobernarse.
poll tax Tax that required each person to pay a fee in order to cast a ballot in elections. The taxes were designed to disenfranchise the poor and minority voters who could often not afford to pay.	**Impuesto al sufragio** Impuesto que requería que cada persona pagara una cuota para poder votar en las elecciones. Este impuesto fue diseñado para evitar que los votantes pobres y minoritarios votaran, pues a menudo no podían pagar.
Populists The People's Party of America, formed in 1892. The populists sought to appeal to both farmers and industrial workers.	**Populistas** El Partido Popular de Estados Unidos, formado en 1892. Los populistas intentaron atraer tanto a agricultores como obreros industriales.
Port Huron Statement Students for a Democratic Society manifesto written in 1962 that condemned liberal politics, Cold War foreign policy, racism, and research-oriented universities. It called for the adoption of "participatory democracy."	**Declaración de Port Huron** Estudiantes a favor de un manifiesto para una sociedad demócrata escrito en 1962, que condenó la política liberal, la política exterior de la Guerra Fría, el racismo y las universidades centradas en la investigación. Pidió la adopción de la democracia participativa.
Potsdam Conference Meeting in July of 1945 in Germany, between Truman and Stalin. The two leaders agreed to free elections in Eastern Europe, Soviet withdrawal from Northern Iran, and creation of four Allied occupation zones in Germany.	**Conferencia de Potsdam** Reunión en julio de 1945 entre Truman y Stalin. Los dos líderes acordaron elecciones libres en Europa del Este, así como la retirada soviética del norte de Irán y la creación de cuatro zonas de ocupación aliadas en Alemania.
Powhatan Confederacy Large and powerful confederation of Algonquian-speaking American Indians in Virginia. The Jamestown settlers had a complicated and often combative relationship with the leaders of the Powhatan Confederacy.	**Confederación de Powhatan** Confederación grande y poderosa de nativos americanos de habla algonquina en Virginia. Los colonos de Jamestown tenían una relación complicada con los líderes de la Confederación de Powhatan que a menudo resultaba en combate.
pragmatism Philosophy that holds that truth can be discovered only through experience and that the value of ideas should be measured by their practical consequences. Pragmatism had a significant influence on the progressives.	**pragmatismo** Filosofía que sostiene la noción de que la verdad sólo puede descubrirse a través de la experiencia y que el valor de las ideas debe medirse por sus consecuencias prácticas. El pragmatismo tuvo una influencia significativa en los progresistas.
predestination Religious belief that God has pre-determined who is worthy of salvation, and thus it could not be earned through good works or penance.	**predestinación** Creencia religiosa de que Dios ha predeterminado quién es digno de la salvación y, por lo tanto, ésta no podría ganarse con buenas obras o penitencia.
Privy Council A powerful group of advisors appointed to provide guidance to the British monarch.	**Consejo privado** Un poderoso grupo de asesores designados para brindar orientación al monarca británico.
Proclamation of Amnesty and Reconstruction 1863 proclamation that established the basic parameters of President Abraham Lincoln's approach to Reconstruction. Lincoln's plan would have readmitted the South to the Union on relatively lenient terms.	**Proclamación de amnistía y reconstrucción** Proclamación de 1863 que estableció los parámetros básicos del enfoque del presidente Abraham Lincoln para la Reconstrucción. El plan de Lincoln readmitió el Sur a la Unión en términos relativamente indulgentes.
Proclamation Line of 1763 Act of Parliament that restricted colonial settlement west of the Appalachian Mountains. The Proclamation Line sparked protests from rich and poor colonists alike.	**Línea de proclamación de 1763** Ley del Parlamento que restringió el asentamiento colonial al oeste de los Montes Apalaches. La Línea de proclamación provocó protestas de colonos ricos y pobres por igual.
Progressive Party Third party formed by Theodore Roosevelt in 1912 to facilitate his candidacy for president. Nicknamed the "Bull Moose Party," the Progressive Party split the Republican vote, allowing Democrat Woodrow Wilson to win the election. The party promoted an income tax, an eight-hour workday, unions, women's suffrage, and an end to child labor.	**Partido Progresista** Tercer partido formado por Theodore Roosevelt en 1912 para facilitar su candidatura a la presidencia. Apodado el "*Bull Moose Party*" (Partido del Alce Macho), el Partido Progresista dividió el voto republicano, permitiendo al demócrata Woodrow Wilson ganar la elección. El partido promovió un impuesto sobre la renta, una jornada laboral de ocho horas, sindicatos, sufragio femenino y el fin del trabajo infantil.
progressivism A movement that emerged during the late nineteenth century whose adherents were united by the belief that if people joined together and applied human intelligence to the task of improving the nation, progress was inevitable. Progressives advocated governmental intervention, yet sought change without radically altering capitalism or the democratic political system.	**progresismo** Un movimiento que surgió a fines del siglo XIX, cuyos seguidores estaban unidos por la creencia de que si las personas se unían y aplicaban la inteligencia humana a la tarea de mejorar la nación, el progreso sería inevitable. Los progresistas abogaron por la intervención gubernamental, pero buscaban el cambio sin alterar radicalmente el capitalismo o el sistema político democrático.
Protestant Reformation Widespread break from the Roman Catholic Church due to its perceived abuses of power throughout the sixteenth century. It spurred the creation of many Protestant religions and was a source of conflict throughout Europe and North America during the seventeenth century.	**Reforma Protestante** División de la iglesia católica romana debido a sus supuestos abusos de poder a lo largo del siglo XVI. Incitó la creación de muchas religiones protestantes y fue una fuente de conflicto en toda Europa y América del Norte durante el siglo XVII.
proxy wars Armed conflicts between nations that are prompted or sanctioned by other nations that do not officially participate in the conflicts.	**guerras subsidiarias (o guerras proxy)** Conflictos armados entre naciones, que son impulsados o sancionados por otras naciones que no participan oficialmente en los conflictos.

Public Works Administration (PWA) 1933 New Deal administration created to oversee the rebuilding of America's infrastructure, such as roads, schools, and libraries.	**Administración de obras públicas (PWA, por sus siglas en inglés)** Administración de 1933 creada por el *New Deal* para supervisar la reconstrucción de la infraestructura de Estados Unidos, como carreteras, escuelas y bibliotecas.
Pueblo American Indian peoples who lived in present-day New Mexico and Arizona and built permanent multi-story adobe dwellings.	**Pueblo** Nativos americanos que vivían en el actual Nuevo México y Arizona, y que construyeron viviendas permanentes de adobe de varios pisos.
Pueblo revolt 1680 uprising of Pueblo Indians against Spanish forces in New Mexico that led to the Spaniards' temporary retreat from the area. The uprising was sparked by mistreatment and the suppression of Pueblo culture and religion.	**rebelión del Pueblo** Levantamiento de 1680 de nativos pueblo en contra de las fuerzas españolas en Nuevo México que condujo a la retirada temporal de los españoles de la zona. El levantamiento se desató por el maltrato y la supresión de la cultura y la religión pueblo.
Pullman strike 1894 strike by workers against the Pullman railcar company. When the strike disrupted rail service nationwide, threatening mail delivery, President Grover Cleveland ordered federal troops to get the railroads moving again.	**huelga Pullman** Huelga de trabajadores en 1894 contra la compañía de vagones Pullman. Cuando la huelga interrumpió el servicio de ferrocarril en todo el país, amenazando la entrega del correo, el presidente Grover Cleveland ordenó a las tropas federales que volvieran a mover los ferrocarriles.
Pure Food and Drug Act 1906 law to prevent the manufacturing, sale, and transportation of harmful "foods, drugs, medicines, and liquors."	**Ley de pureza de alimentos y medicamentos** Ley de 1906 para prohibir la fabricación, venta y transporte de "alimentos, fármacos, medicamentos y licores" dañinos.
Puritans Radical English Protestants who hoped to reform the Church of England. The first Puritan settlers in the Americas arrived in Massachusetts in 1630.	**Puritanos** Protestantes radicales ingleses que esperaban reformar la iglesia anglicana. Los primeros puritanos de las Américas llegaron y se asentaron en Massachusetts en 1630.
Puritan migration The mass migration of Puritans from Europe to New England during the 1620s and 1630s.	**migración Puritana** Migración masiva de puritanos europeos a Nueva Inglaterra entre las décadas de 1620 y 1630.

Q

Quartering Act 1765 act ensuring British troops would remain stationed in the colonies after the end of the Seven Years' War.	**Ley de acuartelamiento** Ley de 1765 que aseguraba que las tropas británicas permanecerían estacionadas en las colonias al terminar la Guerra de los Siete Años.
Quebec Act 1774 act of Parliament extending the boundary of Quebec to areas of the Ohio River valley that American colonists wanted to settle. This act also set up a colonial government without a local representative assembly in Quebec.	**Ley de Quebec** Ley del Parlamento de 1774 que extendió el límite de Quebec hasta las áreas del valle del río Ohio en donde los colonos estadounidenses querían establecerse. Esta ley también estableció un gobierno colonial sin una asamblea representativa local en Quebec.
Queen Anne's War 1702–1713 war over control of Spain and its colonies; also known as the War of the Spanish Succession. Although the Treaty of Utrecht that ended the war in 1713 was intended to bring peace by establishing a balance of power, imperial conflict continued to escalate.	**Guerra de la Reina Ana** Guerra de 1702–1713 por el control de España y sus colonias; también conocida como la Guerra de Sucesión Española. Aunque el Tratado de Utrecht que terminó la guerra en 1713 tenía la intención de traer la paz mediante el establecimiento de un poder equilibrado, el conflicto imperial continuó escalando.

R

Radical Republicans Republican politicians who actively supported abolition prior to the Civil War and sought tighter controls over the South in the aftermath of the war.	**republicanos radicales** Políticos republicanos que apoyaron activamente la abolición previa a la Guerra Civil y buscaron controles más estrictos sobre el Sur después de la guerra.
Railroad Administration World War I era government agency tasked with coordinating train schedules, regulating ticket prices, upgrading tracks, and raising workers' wages. The Railroad Administration acted more forcefully than most other agencies because of military reliance on the efficiency of railroads.	**Administración de ferrocarriles** Agencia gubernamental de la Primera Guerra Mundial encargada de coordinar los horarios de los trenes, regular los precios de los boletos, mejorar las vías y aumentar los salarios de los trabajadores. La Administración de ferrocarriles actuó con más fuerza que la mayoría de las otras agencias debido a que los militares dependían de que los ferrocarriles fueran eficientes.
ratified Formally adopted or approved.	**ratificado** Formalmente aprobado o adoptado.
Reaganomics Ronald Reagan's economic policies based on the theories of supply-side economists and centered on tax cuts and cuts to domestic programs.	**Reaganomía** Las políticas económicas de Ronald Reagan basadas en las teorías de economistas centrados en la oferta y en los cortes de impuestos y programas domésticos.
realpolitik Foreign policy based on practical economic and strategic needs of the U.S. rather than any ideological or human rights goals.	*realpolitik* Política exterior basada en las necesidades prácticas económicas y estratégicas de los EE. UU. en lugar de cualquier objetivo ideológico o de derechos humanos.

Reconstruction Period from 1865 to 1877, during which the eleven ex-Confederate states were subject to federal legislative and constitutional efforts to remake their societies as they were readmitted to the Union.	**Reconstrucción** Período entre 1865 y 1877 en el cual los once estados ex confederados fueron sujetos a esfuerzos legislativos y constitucionales federales para rehacer sus sociedades cuando fueron readmitidos en la Unión.
Reconstruction Finance Corporation (RFC) Government corporation endorsed by Herbert Hoover and created by Congress. It provided federal support through loans to troubled banks, railroads, and insurance companies under the belief that the economic benefits would trickle down from the top of the economic structure to the bottom.	**Corporación financiera de reconstrucción (RFC, por sus siglas en inglés)** Corporación gubernamental respaldada por Herbert Hoover y creada por el Congreso. Brindó apoyo federal con préstamos a bancos, ferrocarriles y compañías de seguros con problemas, bajo la creencia de que los beneficios económicos llegarían de arriba a abajo en la estructura económica.
Red Scare The fear of Communist-inspired radicalism in the wake of the Russian Revolution. The Red Scare culminated in the Palmer raids on suspected radicals.	**temor rojo** El miedo al radicalismo comunista inspirado a raíz de la Revolución Rusa. El temor rojo culminó con las incursiones de Palmer contra presuntos radicales.
Redeemers White, conservative Democrats who challenged and overthrew Republican rule in the South during Reconstruction.	**Redentores** Demócratas blancos, conservadores que desafiaron y derrocaron al gobierno republicano en el Sur durante la Reconstrucción.
redemptioners Immigrants who borrowed money from shipping agents to cover the costs of transport to America, loans that were repaid, or "redeemed," by colonial employers. Redemptioners worked for their "redeemers" for a set number of years.	**redentorista** Inmigrantes que tomaban dinero prestado de los agentes de envío para cubrir los costos de transporte a Estados Unidos, préstamos estos que eran pagados o "redimidos" por los empleadores coloniales. Los redentoristas trabajaban para sus "redentores" durante un número determinado de años.
Renaissance The cultural and intellectual flowering that began in fifteenth-century Italy and then spread north throughout the late fifteenth and sixteenth centuries. During this time, European rulers pushed for greater political unification of their states.	**El Renacimiento** El florecimiento cultural e intelectual que comenzó en Italia en el siglo XV y luego se extendió hacia el norte a finales del siglo XV y XVI. Durante esta época, los gobernantes europeos se esforzaron por una mayor unificación política de sus estados.
republican motherhood Concept proposed by some American political leaders in the 1790s, which supported women's education so that they could in turn instruct their sons in principles of republican government.	**maternidad republicana** Concepto propuesto por algunos líderes políticos estadounidenses en la década de 1790, que apoyaba la educación de las mujeres para que a su vez pudieran instruir a sus hijos en los principios del gobierno republicano.
Republican Party Party formed in 1854 that was committed to stopping the expansion of slavery and advocated economic development and internal improvements. Although their appeal was limited to the North, the Republicans quickly became a major political force.	**Partido Republicano** Partido formado en 1854 que se comprometió a detener la expansión de la esclavitud y abogó por el desarrollo económico y las mejoras internas. Aunque su atractivo se limitó al Norte, los republicanos se convirtieron rápidamente en una importante fuerza política.
requerimiento A legal document issued by the Spanish crown in 1513 to justify the Spanish conquest of territory in the Americas.	***requerimiento*** Un documento legal emitido por la corona española en 1513 para justificar la conquista española de territorios en las Américas.
robber barons A negative term applied to late nineteenth-century industrialists and capitalists who became very rich by dominating large industries.	**barón ladrón** Un término despectivo aplicado a industrialistas y capitalistas de finales del siglo XIX que se enriquecieron mucho por dominar industrias grandes.
Roe v. Wade The 1973 Supreme Court decision that affirmed a woman's constitutional right to abortion.	***Roe vs. Wade*** Decisión de la Corte Suprema de 1973 que afirmaba el derecho constitucional de la mujer de abortar.
Romantic era Early nineteenth-century artistic and intellectual movement that reflected a belief in human perfectibility and challenged Enlightenment ideas of rationality by insisting on the importance of human passion, the mysteries of nature, and the virtues of common folk.	**era Romántica** Movimiento artístico e intelectual de principios del siglo XIX que reflejaba una creencia en la perfección humana y desafiaba las ideas racionales de la Ilustración al insistir en la importancia de la pasión humana, los misterios de la naturaleza y las virtudes de la gente común.
Roosevelt Corollary 1904 addition to the Monroe Doctrine that affirmed the right of the United States to intervene in the internal affairs of Caribbean and Latin American countries to preserve order and protect American interests.	**Corolario Roosevelt** Adición de 1904 a la Doctrina de Monroe que reafirmaba el derecho de Estados Unidos a intervenir en los asuntos internos de países del Caribe y Latinoamérica para mantener el orden y proteger los intereses estadounidenses.
"Rough Riders" The nickname of Theodore Roosevelt's regiment of the 1st United States Volunteer Cavalry, which fought in Cuba during the Spanish-American War in 1898.	**Jinetes Rudos (*Rough Riders*)** El apodo del regimiento de Theodore Roosevelt, de la Primera Caballería Voluntaria de Estados Unidos, que luchó en Cuba durante la Guerra Hispano-estadounidense en 1898.
Russian Revolution Also known as the Bolshevik Revolution, named for the working class radicals called Bolsheviks, the Russian Revolution was led by Vladimir Lenin against the Tsarist government of Nicholas II. After the revolution, the Bolsheviks created the Soviet Union, a communist state.	**Revolución Rusa** También conocida como la Revolución Bolchevique, llamada así por los radicales de la clase trabajadora llamados bolcheviques, la Revolución Rusa fue dirigida por Vladimir Lenin contra el gobierno zarista de Nicolás II. Después de la revolución, los bolcheviques crearon la Unión Soviética, un Estado comunista.

S

Sacco and Vanzetti case 1920 case in which Nicola Sacco and Bartolomeo Vanzetti were convicted of robbery and murder. The trial centered on the defendants' foreign birth and political views, rather than the facts pertaining to their guilt or innocence.

caso de Sacco y Vanzetti Caso de 1920 en el cual Nicola Sacco y Bartolomeo Vanzetti fueron condenados por robo y asesinato. El juicio se centró en el nacimiento extranjero de los acusados y sus opiniones políticas, en lugar de los hechos relacionados con su culpabilidad o inocencia.

SALT II 1979 strategic arms limitation treaty agreed on by President Jimmy Carter and Soviet leader Leonid Brezhnev. After the Soviet Union invaded Afghanistan, Carter persuaded the Senate not to ratify the treaty.

SALT II Acuerdo estratégico de limitación de armas aprobado por Jimmy Carter y el líder soviético Leonid Brezhnev. Después de que la Unión Soviética invadió Afganistán, Carter persuadió al Senado para que no ratificara el tratado.

salutary neglect British colonial policy from around 1700 to 1760 that relaxed supervision of internal colonial affairs as long as the North American colonies produced sufficient raw materials and revenue. Also known as benign neglect.

negligencia conveniente Política colonial británica de alrededor de 1700 y 1760 que disminuyó la supervisión de asuntos coloniales internos siempre y cuando las colonias de América del Norte produjeran suficientes materias primas e ingresos. También conocida como negligencia benigna.

Sand Creek Massacre November 1864 massacre of 270 Cheyenne and Arapaho Indians by the Third Colorado Cavalry of the U.S. army.

Masacre de Sand Creek Masacre en noviembre de 1864 de 270 nativos cheyenne y arapaho a manos de la Tercera Caballería de Colorado del ejército estadounidense.

Sandinistas Also known as the National Liberation Front, Nicaraguan revolutionaries of the 1970s who overthrew the dictator Anastasio Somoza with the support of the USSR. As a result, the U.S. supported the overthrow of the Sandinista government.

Sandinistas También conocidos como el Frente Nacional de Liberación, estos revolucionarios nicaragüenses de la década de 1970 derrocaron al dictador Anastasio Somoza con el apoyo de la URSS. Como resultado, EE.UU apoyó el derrocamiento del gobierno sandinista.

Santa Clara County v. Southern Pacific Railroad Company 1886 Supreme Court decision that determined a corporation was considered a "person" under the Fourteenth Amendment. This ruling gave corporations the same right of due process that the framers of the amendment had meant to give to freedpeople, thus shielding corporations from government regulation of the workplace.

El Condado de Santa Clara vs. la Compañía de Ferrocarriles del Pacífico Decisión de 1886 de la Corte Suprema que determinó que una corporación se consideraba "persona" según la decimocuarta enmienda. Esta resolución otorgó a las corporaciones el mismo derecho al debido proceso que los redactores de la enmienda habían querido otorgar a las personas libres, protegiendo así a las corporaciones de la regulación gubernamental del lugar de trabajo.

scalawags Derogatory term for white Southerners who supported Reconstruction.

scalawags (malvados) Término despectivo para los Sureños que apoyaban la Reconstrucción.

Schenck v. United States 1919 Supreme Court ruling upholding the conviction of the Socialist Party general secretary Charles Schenck under the Espionage Act for disseminating anti-conscription pamphlets. Justice Oliver Wendell Holmes argued that during wartime Congress has the authority to prohibit individuals from using words that create "a clear and present danger."

Schenck vs. Estados Unidos Fallo de 1919 de la Corte Suprema que defendía la condena del secretario general del Partido Socialista, Charles Scheck, bajo la Ley de espionaje por difundir panfletos en contra del reclutamiento. El juez Oliver Wendell Holmes argumentó que en tiempos de guerra, el Congreso tiene la autoridad de prohibir a las personas usar palabras que ocasionen "un peligro claro y presente."

school busing Mandatory nationwide initiative to integrate schools, begun in 1971 to comply with the 1954 Supreme Court decision *Brown v. Board*. The practice of school busing continued in the U.S. well into the 1990s. Also known as "busing" or "desegregation busing."

transporte escolar Iniciativa nacional obligatoria para integrar escuelas. Se inició en 1971 para cumplir con la decisión *Brown vs. Board* de la Corte Suprema de 1954. La práctica del transporte escolar continuó en EE. UU. hasta bien entrada la década de 1990. También conocido como "busing" o "transporte de integración."

scientific management Also known as Taylorism, a management style developed by Frederick W. Taylor that aimed to constantly improve the efficiency of employees by reducing manual labor to its simplest components — thus increasing productivity while decreasing cost.

gestión científica También conocida como taylorismo, un estilo de gestión desarrollado por Frederick W. Taylor que tenía como objetivo mejorar constantemente la eficiencia de los empleados reduciendo el trabajo manual a sus componentes más simples, aumentando así la productividad y disminuyendo los costos.

Scottsboro Nine Nine African American youths convicted of raping two white women in Scottsboro, Alabama, in 1931. The Communist Party played a key role in defending the Scottsboro Nine and in bringing national and international attention to their case.

Los chicos de Scottsborro (*Scottsborro Nine*) Nueve jóvenes afroamericanos condenados por violar a dos mujeres blancas en Scottsborro, Alabama, en 1931. El Partido Comunista desempeñó un papel clave en la defensa de Los chicos de Scottsborro y en llamar la atención nacional e internacional hacia este caso.

Second Bank of the United States Bank established in 1816 that distributed national currency and regulated state banks after the First Bank of the United States' charter expired. It ceased operation in 1836.

Segundo Banco de los Estados Unidos Banco establecido en 1816 que distribuyó la moneda nacional y reguló los bancos estatales después de que expiró el estatuto del Primer Banco de los Estados Unidos. Dejó de funcionar en 1836.

Glossary/Glosario

English	Español
Second Battle of Bull Run (Second Manassas) This battle took place from April 28–30, 1862, and resulted in a Union defeat, which led President Lincoln to relieve General Pope of command and replace him with George B. McClellan.	**Segunda Batalla de Bull Run (o Segunda Batalla de Manassas)** Esta batalla tuvo lugar del 28 al 30 de abril de 1862 y resultó en una derrota de la Unión, lo que llevó al presidente Lincoln a destituir al general John Pope y reemplazarlo con George B. McClellan.
Second Continental Congress Assembly of colonial representatives that served as a national government during the American Revolution. Despite limited formal powers, the Continental Congress coordinated the war effort and conducted negotiations with outside powers.	**Segundo Congreso Continental** Asamblea de representantes coloniales que sirvió como gobierno nacional durante la Revolución Estadounidense. A pesar de los poderes formales limitados, el Congreso Continental coordinó los esfuerzos bélicos y condujo negociaciones con poderes extranjeros.
second front The desire expressed in 1942 by Joseph Stalin for an immediate invasion by U.S., British, and Canadian forces of German-occupied France to take pressure off the Soviet forces fighting the Germans on the eastern front. The attack in Western Europe did not begin until 1944, a fact Stalin resented.	**segundo frente** El deseo expresado en 1942 por Joseph Stalin de una invasión inmediata por parte de las fuerzas estadounidenses, británicas y canadienses a Francia, ocupada por los alemanes, para quitarle presión a las fuerzas soviéticas que luchaban contra los alemanes en el frente oriental. El ataque en Europa Occidental no comenzó hasta 1944, un hecho que Stalin resintió.
Second Great Awakening Evangelical revival movement that began in the South in the early nineteenth century and then spread to the North. The social and economic changes of the first half of the nineteenth century were a major spur to religious revivals, which in turn spurred social reform movements.	**Segundo Gran Despertar** Movimiento de renacimiento evangélico que comenzó en el sur a principios del siglo XIX y luego se extendió al norte. Los cambios sociales y económicos de la primera mitad del siglo XIX fueron un gran incentivo para los renacimientos religiosos, lo que a su vez estimularon movimientos de reforma social.
Second Red Scare Fear of Communist influence infiltrating the United States and threatening national security in the 1940s and 1950s. Such fears resulted in the creation of government-controlled programs and entities such as the House Un-American Activities Committee and the Federal Employee Loyalty Program.	**Segundo Temor Rojo** Miedo a que la influencia Comunista se infiltrara en Estados Unidos y amenazara la seguridad nacional en las décadas de 1940 y 1950. Tales temores resultaron en la creación de programas y entidades controladas por el gobierno, como el Comité de actividades antiestadounidenses y el Programa de fidelización de empleados federales.
Second Seminole War 1835–1842 war between the Seminoles, including enslaved African Americans who had escaped captivity and had joined the tribe, and the U.S. government over whether the Seminoles would be forced to leave Florida and settle west of the Mississippi River. Despite substantial investments of men, money, and resources, it took seven years for the United States to achieve victory.	**Segunda Guerra Semínola** Guerra de 1835–1842 entre los seminolas (incluidos afroamericanos esclavizados que habían escapado del cautiverio y se habían unido a la tribu), y el gobierno de EE. UU. por la decisión de obligar a los seminolas a abandonar Florida y establecerse al oeste del río Misisipi. A pesar de la considerable inversión de hombres, dinero y recursos, a los Estados Unidos les tomó siete años lograr la victoria.
Securities and Exchange Commission (SEC) 1934 New Deal commission designed to regulate the stock market and ensure that corporations gave investors accurate information about their investments.	**Comisión de bolsa y valores (SEC, por sus siglas en inglés)** Comisión del *New Deal* de 1934 diseñada para regular el mercado de valores y garantizar que las corporaciones brinden a los inversionistas información precisa sobre sus inversiones.
Sedition Act 1918 act added to the Espionage Act. It punished individuals for expressing opinions deemed hostile to the U.S. government, flag, or military.	**Ley de sedición** Ley de 1918 agregada a la Ley de espionaje. Castigaba a individuos por expresar opiniones consideradas hostiles al gobierno, la bandera o el ejército de EE. UU.
seditious Behavior or language aimed at starting a rebellion against a government.	**sedicioso** Comportamiento o lenguaje dirigido a iniciar una rebelión contra un gobierno.
segregation The purposeful separation of people into ethnic or racial groups. Segregation was often actively perpetuated and enforced through "black codes" and Jim Crow era legislation which persisted into the latter half of the twentieth century.	**segregación** La separación intencional de personas en grupos étnicos o raciales. La segregación a menudo se perpetuaba activamente y se hacía cumplir mediante "códigos negros" y la legislación de la era de Jim Crow que persistió hasta la segunda mitad del siglo XX.
Selective Service Act 1917 act authorizing a nationwide draft.	**Ley de servicio selectivo** Ley de 1917 que autorizaba un reclutamiento a nivel nacional.
Selective Training and Service Act of 1940 Legislation requiring men between the ages of 18 and 35 to register for the draft, later expanded to age 45. It was the first peacetime draft in U.S. history.	**Ley de servicio y formación selectiva de 1940** Legislación que obligaba a los hombres entre las edades de 18 y 35 a registrarse para reclutamiento. Luego se extendió hasta los 45 años. Fue el primer reclutamiento en tiempo de paz en Estados Unidos.
separate spheres Widespread social belief that emerged in the late 1700s and early 1800s that men and women had separate roles and should occupy separate places in society. According to this belief, men should occupy the social public sphere and work, while women belonged in the domestic private sphere, caring for their family and household.	**esferas separadas** Creencia social generalizada que surgió a finales de 1700 y principios de 1800 de que los hombres y las mujeres tenían roles separados y debían ocupar lugares separados en la sociedad. Según esta creencia, los hombres deberían ocupar la esfera pública social y el trabajo, mientras que las mujeres pertenecían a la esfera doméstica privada, cuidando del hogar y la familia.

Glossary/Glosario

Servicemen's Readjustment Act (GI Bill) 1944 act that offered educational opportunities and financial aid to veterans as they readjusted to civilian life. Known as the GI Bill, the law helped millions of veterans build new lives after the war.	**Ley de readaptación militar (GI Bill)** Ley de 1944 que ofreció oportunidades educativas y ayuda financiera a los veteranos mientras se adaptaban a la vida civil. Conocida como la *GI Bill*, la ley ayudó a millones de veteranos a construir nuevas vidas después de la guerra.
settlement houses Community centers established by urban reformers in the late nineteenth century. Settlement house organizers resided in the institutions they created and were often female, middle-class, and college educated.	**casas de asentamiento** Centros comunitarios establecidos por reformadores urbanos a finales del siglo XIX. Las organizadoras de las casas de asentamiento residían en las instituciones que crearon y a menudo eran mujeres de clase media y con educación universitaria.
Seven Years' War (French and Indian War) 1754–1763 global conflict between European nations, primarily Britain and France, that began in North America in 1754, erupted in Europe in 1756, and ended in 1763. France ultimately ceded all of its North American territories to England and Spain, but the enormous cost of the war also damaged the British economy.	**Guerra de los Siete Años (Guerra franco-india)** Conflicto global en 1754–1763 entre naciones europeas, principalmente Gran Bretaña y Francia, que inició en Estados Unidos en 1754, estalló en Europa en 1756 y terminó en 1763. Francia finalmente cedió todo su territorio norteamericano a Inglaterra y España, pero el enorme costo de la guerra también dañó la economía británica.
Share Our Wealth Society Economic plan created by Huey Long in 1934. Long believed the New Deal did not go far enough and advocated for a nationwide standard of living through wealth sharing.	**Sociedad Compartamos Nuestra Riqueza (Share Our Wealth)** Plan económico creado por Huey Long en 1934. Long creía que el *New Deal* no llegó lo suficientemente lejos. Así que abogó por un mejor estándar de vida a nivel nacional por medio del reparto de la riqueza.
sharecropping A system that emerged as the dominant mode of agricultural production in the South in the years after the Civil War. Under the sharecropping system, sharecroppers received tools and supplies from landowners in exchange for a share of the eventual harvest.	**aparcería** Un sistema que surgió como el modo dominante de producción agrícola en el Sur en los años posteriores a la Guerra Civil. Bajo el sistema de aparcería, los aparceros recibían herramientas y suministros de los propietarios a cambio de una parte de la cosecha final.
Shays's Rebellion 1786 rebellion by western Massachusetts farmers caused primarily by economic hardships in the aftermath of the American Revolution.	**La rebelión de Shays** Rebelión de 1786 por parte de los agricultores del oeste de Massachusetts, causada principalmente por dificultades económicas a raíz de la Revolución Estadounidense.
Shepherd-Towner Act Legislation passed in 1921 that allowed nurses to offer material and infant health care information to mothers.	**Ley Shepherd-Towner** Legislación aprobada en 1921 que permitía a las enfermeras ofrecer a las madres material e información sobre la salud y el cuidado infantil.
Sherman Antitrust Act 1890 act outlawing monopolies that prevented free competition in interstate commerce.	**Ley Sherman antimonopolio** Ley de 1890 que prohibió los monopolios que impedían la libre competencia del comercio interestatal.
Sherman Silver Purchase Act 1890 act that increased the amount of silver the U.S. government was required to purchase to back production of federal dollars. The goal of this annual silver purchase was to raise inflation, and thereby raise the prices farmers were paid for their crops.	**Ley Sherman de compra de plata** Ley de 1890 que aumentó la cantidad de plata que el gobierno de los Estados Unidos debía comprar para respaldar la producción de dólares federales. El objetivo de esta compra anual de plata era aumentar la inflación y, por lo tanto, aumentar los precios que se les pagaban a los agricultores por sus cultivos.
Sherman's March to the Sea Total war tactics employed by General William Tecumseh Sherman to capture Atlanta and huge swaths of Georgia and the Carolinas, devastating this crucial region of the Confederacy in 1864.	**Marcha de Sherman hacia el mar** Tácticas totales de guerra aplicadas por el general William Tecumseh Sherman para capturar Atlanta y grandes franjas de Georgia y las Carolinas, devastando esta región crucial de la Confederación en 1864.
siege of Vicksburg After a prolonged siege, Union troops forced Confederate forces to surrender at Vicksburg, Mississippi, leading to Union control of the rich Mississippi River valley.	**asedio de Vicksburg** Después de un asedio prolongado, las tropas de la Unión obligaron a las fuerzas confederadas a rendirse en Vicksburg, Misisipi, lo que condujo al control del rico valle del río Misisipi por parte de la Unión.
sit-down strike A strike in which workers occupy their place of employment. In 1937 the United Auto Workers conducted sit-down strikes in Flint, Michigan against General Motors to gain union recognition, higher wages, and better working conditions. The union won its demands.	**huelga sentada** Una huelga en la que los trabajadores ocupan el mismo lugar en el que trabajan. En 1937, United Auto Workers realizó huelgas sentadas en Flint, Michigan, contra General Motors para obtener reconocimiento sindical, salarios más altos y mejores condiciones de trabajo. El sindicato alcanzó sus objetivos.
Sixteenth Amendment 1913 amendment providing a legal basis for a graduated income tax, which had been previously deemed unconstitutional.	**Decimosexta enmienda** Enmienda de 1913 que proporcionó una base legal para el impuesto sobre la renta gradual, que anteriormente se había considerado inconstitucional.
***Slaughterhouse* cases** 1873 Supreme Court decision that was one of the first tests of the Fourteenth Amendment when it decided that, although the Fourteenth Amendment guaranteed federal protection for black people, that protection did not extend to civil or property rights, which were to be determined by the states.	**casos de *Slaughterhouse* (matadero)** Decisión de la Corte Suprema, una de las primeras que pusieron a prueba la decimocuarta enmienda, en la que se declaraba que a pesar de que la decimocuarta enmienda garantizaba la protección federal de los afroamericanos, dicha protección no se extendía a los derechos civiles o de propiedad, que serían determinados por el estado.

Glossary/Glosario

slave code Laws restricting enslaved peoples' rights, largely due to slaveholders' fears of rebellion.	**código negro** Leyes que restringían los derechos de las personas esclavizadas, principalmente por el miedo a la rebelión que sentían los dueños de las personas esclavizadas.
slave laws A series of laws that defined slavery as a distinct status based on racial identity and which passed that status on through future generations.	**leyes de esclavos** Una serie de leyes que definían la esclavitud como un estatus distinto basado en la identidad racial y que transmitían ese estatus a futuras generaciones.
Smith Act Law signed by Franklin Roosevelt in 1940, which prohibited teaching or advocating for the destruction of the United States government.	**Ley de Smith** Ley firmada por Franklin Roosevelt en 1940 que prohibía enseñar o abogar por la destrucción del gobierno de los Estados Unidos.
Social Darwinism The belief associated with the late nineteenth and early twentieth centuries and popularized by Herbert Spencer that drew upon some of the ideas of Charles Darwin. Stressing individual competition and the survival of the fittest, Social Darwinism was used to justify economic inequality, racism, imperialism, and hostility to federal government regulation.	**Darwinismo Social** Creencia de fines del siglo XIX y principios del XX y popularizada por Herbert Spencer relacionada con algunas de las ideas de Charles Darwin. Haciendo hincapié en la competencia individual y la supervivencia del más apto, el darwinismo social se utilizó para justificar la desigualdad económica, el racismo, el imperialismo y la hostilidad a la regulación del gobierno federal.
social gospel Religious movement that advocated the application of Christian teachings to social and economic problems. The ideals of the social gospel inspired many progressive reformers.	**evangelio social** Movimiento religioso que abogó por la aplicación de las enseñanzas cristianas a los problemas sociales y económicos. Los ideales del evangelio social inspiraron a muchos reformadores progresistas.
Social Security Act Landmark 1935 act that created retirement pensions for most Americans, as well as unemployment insurance.	**Ley de seguridad social** Ley histórica de 1935 que creó las pensiones de jubilación para la mayoría de los estadounidenses, así como el seguro de desempleo.
Socialist Party of America A political party established in 1901 by Eugene V. Debs. It advocated for labor interests and economic reforms, as well as for public ownership of business through democratic processes.	**Partido Socialista de Estados Unidos** Un partido político establecido en 1901 por Eugene V. Debs. Abogó por los intereses laborales y las reformas económicas, así como por la propiedad pública de las empresas a través de procesos democráticos.
Solidarity Polish trade union movement led by Lech Walesa. During the 1980s, Solidarity played a central role in ending Communist rule in Poland.	**Solidaridad** Movimiento sindical polaco dirigido por Lech Walesa. Durante la década de 1980, Solidaridad desempeñó un papel central en el fin del gobierno comunista de Polonia.
Sons of Liberty Boston organization of colonial men first formed to protest the Stamp Act. The Sons of Liberty spread to other colonies and played an important role in the unrest leading to the American Revolution.	**Hijos de la Libertad** Organización bostoniana de hombres coloniales formada para protestar la Ley del sello. Los Hijos de la Libertad se extendieron a otras colonias y jugaron un papel importante en los disturbios que condujeron a la Revolución Estadounidense.
Southern Christian Leadership Conference (SCLC) Organization founded in 1957 by Martin Luther King Jr. and other black ministers to encourage nonviolent protests against racial segregation and disfranchisement in the South.	**Conferencia sur de liderazgo cristiano (SCLC, por sus siglas en inglés)** Organización fundada en 1957 por Martin Luther King Jr. y otros ministros afroamericanos para alentar las protestas no violentas contra la segregación racial y la privación de derechos en el Sur.
Spanish caste system A system developed by the Spanish in the sixteenth century that defined the status of diverse populations based on a racial hierarchy that privileged Europeans.	**sistema de castas colonial** Un sistema desarrollado por los españoles en el siglo XVI que definió el estatus de diversas poblaciones basado en una jerarquía racial que privilegiaba a los europeos.
Spanish–American War 1898 war in which the United States sided with Cuba in its ongoing war for independence from Spain because U.S. policymakers decided that Cuban independence was in the United States' economic and strategic interests. Cuba's eventual liberation from Spain, and the U.S. victory in the war, allowed the United States to gain control over a large portion of Spain's overseas empire, turning the United States into a major imperial power.	**Guerra Hispano-Estadounidense** Guerra de 1898 en la cual Estados Unidos apoyó a Cuba para que esta pudiera independizarse de España. Los políticos estadounidenses decidieron que la independencia cubana estaba entre los intereses económicos y estratégicos de Estados Unidos. La eventual liberación de Cuba y la victoria de Estados Unidos en la guerra, le permitió a EE. UU. obtener el control de una gran parte del imperio de ultramar de España, convirtiendo a Estados Unidos en una gran potencia imperial.
speculators People who invest in business ventures in order to make a profit.	**especuladores** Personas que invierten en negocios para obtener ganancias.
spoils system Patronage system introduced by Andrew Jackson in which federal offices were awarded on the basis of political loyalty. The system remained in place until the late nineteenth century.	**spoils system (clientelismo)** Sistema de patrocinio introducido por Andrew Jackson en el que se otorgaban oficinas federales en base a la lealtad política. El sistema permaneció en uso hasta finales del siglo XIX.
Sputnik First artificial satellite, launched in 1957 by the Soviet Union.	***Sputnik*** Primer satélite artificial lanzado en 1957 por la Unión Soviética.

Glossary/Glosario

"Square Deal" Theodore Roosevelt's plan to provide economic and political stability to the nation by guaranteeing the rights of everyday workers and protecting business interests.	**"Square Deal" (Acuerdo justo y honesto)** El plan de Theodore Roosevelt para proporcionar estabilidad económica y política a la nación garantizando los derechos de los trabajadores comunes y protegiendo los intereses comerciales.
stagflation Period of economic instability in the 1970s as the rising cost of living occurred in conjunction with an increase in unemployment.	**estanflación** Período de inestabilidad económica en la década de 1970, debido a que el aumento del costo de la vida se produjo junto con un aumento del desempleo.
Stamp Act 1765 act of Parliament that imposed a duty on all transactions involving paper items. The Stamp Act prompted widespread, coordinated protests and was eventually repealed.	**Ley del sello** Ley del parlamento de 1765 que impuso una tarifa a todas las transacciones que involucran artículos en papel. La Ley del sello provocó protestas generalizadas y coordinadas, y finalmente fue derogada.
Stamp Act Congress An assembly of twenty-seven delegates from nine colonies that met in New York City in October 1765 and petitioned Parliament to repeal the Stamp Act.	**Congreso de la ley del sello** Una asamblea de veintisiete delegados de nueve colonias que se reunieron en la ciudad de Nueva York en octubre de 1765 para solicitar que el Parlamento derogara la Ley del sello.
staple crops Crops that are frequently planted and eaten, and therefore a central part of one's diet.	**cultivos básicos** Cultivos que se plantan y comen con frecuencia y, por lo tanto, son una parte central de la dieta.
Statute of Religious Freedom 1786 Virginia Assembly statute that ensured the separation of church and state and largely guaranteed freedom of religion. Many other states followed Virginia's lead.	**Estatuto por la libertad de religión** Estatuto de la Asamblea de Virginia de 1786 que garantizaba la separación de la iglesia y el estado y, en gran medida, garantizaba la libertad de religión. Muchos otros estados siguieron el ejemplo de Virginia.
Stonewall riots 1969 uprising after New York City police raided the Stonewall Inn, a gathering place for gay men, and tried to arrest patrons. The uprising helped inspire the gay liberation movement of the 1970s.	**disturbios de Stonewall** La violencia de 1969 entre homosexuales y la policía de Estados Unidos tras la redada policiaca del Stonewall Inn, un bar de homosexuales en Greenwich Village, cuyos clientes lucharon contra la policía en respuesta al hostigamiento. Este suceso ayudó a impulsar el movimiento de liberación homosexual.
Stono Rebellion 1739 uprising by enslaved Africans and African Americans in South Carolina. In its aftermath, white fear of slave revolts intensified.	**Rebelión de Stono** Levantamiento de 1739 de africanos y afroamericanos esclavizados en Carolina del Sur. Como consecuencia, el miedo blanco a las revueltas de personas esclavizadas se intensificó.
Strategic Arms Limitation Treaty (SALT I) 1972 agreement between the United States and Soviet Union to curtail nuclear arms production during the Cold War. The pact froze for five years the number of antiballistic missiles (ABMs), intercontinental ballistic missiles (ICBMs), and submarine-based missiles that each nation could deploy.	**SALT I (Tratado sobre la limitación de armas estratégicas)** Acuerdo de 1972 entre Estados Unidos y la Unión Soviética para reducir la producción de armas nucleares durante la Guerra Fría. El pacto congeló durante cinco años la cantidad de misiles antibalísticos (ABM, por sus siglas en inglés), misiles balísticos intercontinentales (ICBM, por sus siglas en inglés) y misiles lanzados por submarinos que cada nación podría desplegar.
Strategic Arms Reduction Talks (START) Negotiations between the Reagan administration and the Soviet Union that began in 1982 under the principle of "zero option," which called for the USSR to dismantle all its intermediate-range missiles. The Soviets ultimately rejected these terms, believing they promoted the idea of American nuclear superiority.	**START (Conversaciones sobre la limitación de armas estratégicas)** Negociaciones entre el gobierno de Reagan y la Unión Soviética que comenzaron en 1982 bajo el principio de "opción cero", que exigía que la URSS desmantelara todos sus misiles de alcance intermedio. Los soviéticos finalmente rechazaron estos términos, pues les parecía que promovían la idea de que los Estados Unidos era superior desde un punto de vista nuclear.
Strategic Defense Initiative (SDI) Policy first announced by Ronald Reagan in 1983 proposing a missile defense system that would use satellite lasers to protect the United States from military attack by shooting down enemy missiles. The initiative was never completed.	**Iniciativa de defensa estratégica (SDI, por sus siglas en inglés)** Política anunciada por primera vez por Ronald Reagan en 1983, que proponía un sistema de defensa antimisiles que usaría láseres satelitales para proteger a Estados Unidos de un ataque militar al derribar misiles enemigos. La iniciativa nunca se completó.
Student Nonviolent Coordinating Committee (SNCC) Civil rights organization that grew out of the sit-ins of 1960. The organization focused on taking direct action and political organizing to achieve its goals.	**Comité coordinador estudiantil no violento (SNCC, por sus siglas en inglés)** Organización de derechos civiles que surgió de las huelgas sentadas de 1960. La organización se centró en tomar medidas directas y organizarse de manera política para lograr sus objetivos.
Students for a Democratic Society (SDS) Student activist organization formed in the early 1960s that advocated the formation of a "New Left" that would overturn the social and political status quo.	**Estudiantes por una sociedad democrática (SDS, por sus siglas en inglés)** Organización activista de estudiantes formada a principios de los años sesenta que abogaba por la formación de una "nueva izquierda" que derrocaría el *status quo* social y político.
subsistence farmers Farmers who grow crops for their own needs rather than for profit.	**agricultores de subsistencia** Agricultores que cultivan para sus propias necesidades y no para obtener ganancias.

Glossary/Glosario

subtreasury system A proposal by the Farmers' Alliances in the 1880s for the federal government to extend loans to farmers and store their crops in warehouses until prices rose and they could buy back and sell their crops to repay their debts.	**sistema de subtesoro** Una propuesta de las alianzas de agricultores en la década de 1880 para que el gobierno federal otorgara préstamos a los agricultores y guardara sus cultivos en almacenes hasta que los precios subieran y pudieran volver a comprar y vender sus cultivos para pagar sus deudas.
suffragists Supporters of voting rights for women. Campaigns for women's suffrage gained strength in the late nineteenth and early twentieth centuries and culminated in the ratification of the Nineteenth Amendment in 1920.	**sufragistas** Partidarios del derecho al voto de las mujeres. Las campañas para el sufragio femenino se fortalecieron a fines del siglo XIX y principios del XX y culminaron con la ratificación de la decimonovena enmienda en 1920.
Sugar Act 1764 act of Parliament imposing an import tax on sugar, coffee, wines, and other luxury items. It sparked colonial protests that would escalate over time as new revenue measures were enacted.	**Ley del azúcar** Ley del parlamento de 1764 que imponía un impuesto a la importación de azúcar, café, vinos y otros artículos de lujo. Provocó protestas coloniales que se intensificarían con el tiempo a medida que se promulgaban nuevas medidas de ingresos.
Sun Belt The southern and western part of the United States to which millions of Americans moved after World War II. Migrants were drawn by the region's climate and jobs in the defense, petroleum, and chemical industries.	**Cinturón del Sol** La zona del sur y del oeste de Estados Unidos. Después de la Segunda Guerra Mundial, millones de estadounidenses se mudaron al Cinturón del Sol, atraídos por el clima de la región y la oferta laboral en las industrias de defensa, petróleo y química.
supply-side economics Economic theory that tax cuts and industry deregulation raise wages and lower unemployment, thereby promoting economic growth.	**economía de oferta** Teoría económica que plantea que los recortes de impuestos y la desregulación de la industria aumentan los salarios y reducen el desempleo, promoviendo así el crecimiento económico.
sweatshops Small factories or shops in which workers toiled under poor conditions. Business owners, particularly in the garment industry, turned tenement apartments into sweatshops.	**maquiladoras** Pequeñas fábricas o tiendas en las que los trabajadores operan en malas condiciones. Los dueños de negocios –particularmente en la industria de la ropa– convirtieron edificios de departamentos en maquiladoras.

T

Taft-Hartley Act 1947 law that curtailed unions' ability to organize. It prevented unions from barring employment to non-union members and authorized the federal government to halt a strike for eighty days if it interfered with the national interest.	**Ley de Taft-Hartley** Ley de 1947 que restringió la capacidad de los sindicatos para organizarse. Impidió que los sindicatos limitaran el empleo a trabajadores no sindicalizados y autorizó al gobierno federal a detener una huelga durante ochenta días si esta contravenía el interés nacional.
Taliban Group of Sunni Muslim fundamentalists that ruled Afghanistan in the mid-1990s. The Taliban established a strict theocracy and became the base of al-Qaeda, a Sunni Muslim terrorist organization.	**Talibán** Grupo de fundamentalistas musulmanes sunitas que gobernaron Afganistán a mediados de la década de 1990. Los talibanes establecieron una estricta teocracia y se convirtieron en la base de al-Qaeda, una organización terrorista musulmana sunita.
Tammany Hall New York City's political machine during the nineteenth century. It swindled the city out of a fortune while supervising the construction of a lavish three-story courthouse in lower Manhattan. The building remained unfinished in 1873, when Tweed was convicted on fraud charges and sent to jail.	**Tammany Hall** La maquinaria política de la ciudad de Nueva York durante el siglo XIX. Estafó a la ciudad por una fortuna mientras supervisaba la construcción de un lujoso palacio de justicia de tres pisos en el bajo Manhattan. El edificio permaneció sin terminar en 1873, cuando Tweed fue condenado por cargos de fraude y enviado a la cárcel.
Tariff of 1816 Protective tariff designed to increase the cost of imported manufactured goods in order to improve domestic sales.	**Arancel de 1816** Arancel de protección diseñado para aumentar el costo de los productos manufacturados importados con el fin de mejorar las ventas nacionales.
Tariff of 1828 Tariff that extended duties to include raw materials such as wool, hemp, and molasses. It was passed despite strong opposition from southeastern states.	**Arancel de 1828** Arancel que extendió las tarifas sobre materias primas como la lana, el cáñamo y la melaza. Fue aprobado a pesar de la fuerte oposición de los estados del sureste.
Tariff of Abominations White southerners' name for the 1828 tariff act that benefited northern manufacturers and merchants at the expense of agriculture, especially southern plantations.	**Arancel de abominaciones** Nombre que pusieron los sureños blancos a la ley arancelaria de 1828 que benefició a los fabricantes y comerciantes del norte a expensas de la agricultura, especialmente las plantaciones del sur.
Tea Act 1773 act of Parliament, also known as the tea tax, that aimed to reduce the financial debts of Britain and the British East India Company by providing the company with a tea monopoly in the British American colonies. This resulted in colonial protests.	**Ley del té** Ley del parlamento de 1773, también conocida como Impuesto del té, que buscaba reducir las deudas financieras de Gran Bretaña y de la Compañía Británica de las Indias Orientales al proporcionar a la compañía un monopolio de té en las colonias británicas estadounidenses. Esto dio lugar a protestas coloniales.
Tea Party movement A loose coalition of conservatives and libertarians that formed around 2008. The Tea Party advocated small government, low taxes, and reduced federal deficits.	**Movimiento del Partido del Té** Una coalición de fuerzas conservadoras libertarias que surgió alrededor de 2008. En general, el Partido del Té abogó por un gobierno pequeño, impuestos bajos y déficits federales reducidos.

Teapot Dome scandal Oil and land scandal that highlighted the close ties between big business and the federal government in the early 1920s.

Tejanos Mexican residents of Texas. Although some Tejano elites allied themselves with American settlers, most American settlers were resistant to adopting Tejano culture.

Teller Amendment Amendment to the 1898 declaration of war against Spain stipulating that Cuba should be free and independent. The amendment was largely ignored in the aftermath of America's victory.

tenements Multifamily apartment buildings that housed many poor urban dwellers at the turn of the twentieth century. Tenements were crowded, uncomfortable, and dangerous.

Tennessee Valley Authority (TVA) New Deal agency that brought low-cost electricity to rural Americans and redeveloped the Tennessee River valley through flood-control projects. The agency built, owned, and supervised a number of power plants and dams.

Tenochtitlán Capital city of the Aztec Empire.

Tenure of Office Act Law passed by Congress in 1867 to prevent President Andrew Johnson from removing cabinet members sympathetic to the Republican Party's approach to congressional Reconstruction without Senate approval. Johnson was impeached, but not convicted, for violating the act.

terrorism The use of violence to inspire fear in service of achieving a political goal.

Tet Offensive January 31, 1968 offensive mounted by Vietcong and North Vietnamese forces against population centers in South Vietnam. The offensive was turned back, but its ferocity shocked many Americans and increased public opposition to the war.

theologians People who study religious beliefs or theology.

Third Reich Adolf Hitler's name for the Nazi regime in Germany (1933–1945). Accordingly, the First Reich was the Holy Roman Empire (800–1806), and the Second Reich was the German Empire (1871–1918).

three-fifths compromise Compromise between northern and southern delegates to the 1787 Constitutional Convention to count enslaved persons as three-fifths of a free person in deciding the proportion of representation in the House of Representatives and taxation by the federal government.

Tiananmen Square Location of 1989 protests by Chinese university students who wanted political and economic reforms. China's leader, Deng Xiaoping, dispatched the military to break up the protests, killing thousands.

To Secure These Rights Report issued by President Harry Truman's Committee on Civil Rights in 1947 that advocated extending racial equality. Among its recommendations was the desegregation of the military, which Truman instituted by executive order in 1948.

total war The strategy promoted by General Ulysses S. Grant in which Union forces destroyed civilian crops, livestock, fields, and property to undermine Confederate morale and supply chains.

totalitarianism Type of government that puts the state first, with all other parts of life designed to support and sustain the government first and foremost.

Glossary/Glosario

Townshend Acts 1767 acts of Parliament that instituted an import tax on a range of items including glass, lead, paint, paper, and tea. They prompted a boycott of British goods and contributed to violence between British soldiers and colonists.	**Leyes de Townshend** Leyes del parlamento de 1767 que instituyeron un impuesto a la importación de una variedad de artículos, incluyendo vidrio, plomo, pintura, papel y té. Esto provocó un boicot a los productos británicos y contribuyó a la violencia entre los soldados británicos y los colonos.
Toyota Japanese automobile company established in 1937. Toyota is the world's leader in hybrid-electric vehicles such as the Prius.	**Toyota** Compañía automotriz japonesa establecida en 1937. Toyota es el líder mundial en vehículos híbridos eléctricos, como el Prius.
Trail of Tears The forced march of some 15,000 Cherokees from Georgia to areas west of the Mississippi River that were designated as Indian Territory, beginning in 1831. Inadequate planning, food, water, sanitation, and medicine led to the deaths of thousands of Cherokees.	**Sendero de lágrimas** La marcha forzada de unos 15,000 cherokees de Georgia hasta el oeste del río Misisipi a áreas que se designaron como territorio nativo a partir de 1831. La planificación inadecuada, la falta de alimentación, agua, higiene y medicina, provocaron la muerte de miles de cherokees.
transcendentalism Movement founded by Ralph Waldo Emerson in the 1830s that proposed that individuals look inside themselves and to nature for spiritual and moral guidance rather than to formal religion. Transcendentalism attracted a number of important American writers and artists to its vision.	**trascendentalismo** Movimiento fundado por Ralph Waldo Emerson en la década de 1830 que propuso que las personas buscaran orientación espiritual y moral en su interior y en la naturaleza en lugar de en la religión formal. El trascendentalismo atrajo a varios escritores y artistas estadounidenses importantes.
transcontinental railroad A railroad linking the East and West Coasts of North America. Completed in 1869, the transcontinental railroad facilitated the flow of migrants and the development of economic connections between the West and the East.	**ferrocarril transcontinental** Un ferrocarril que unió las costas este y oeste de América del Norte. Terminado en 1869, el ferrocarril transcontinental facilitó el flujo de migrantes y el desarrollo de conexiones económicas entre este y oeste.
Treaty of Fort Laramie 1851 treaty that sought to confine tribes on the northern plains to designated areas in an attempt to keep white settlers from encroaching on their land. In 1868, the second Treaty of Fort Laramie gave northern tribes control over the "Great Reservation" in parts of present-day Montana, Wyoming, North Dakota, and South Dakota.	**Tratado de Fort Laramie** Tratado de 1851 que buscaba confinar tribus de las llanuras del norte a áreas designadas con el fin de evitar que los colonos blancos invadieran sus tierras. En 1868, el segundo Tratado de Fort Laramie otorgó a las tribus del norte el control sobre la "Gran Reserva" en partes de las actuales Montana, Wyoming, Dakota del Norte y Dakota del Sur.
Treaty of Ghent Accord signed in December 1814 that ended the War of 1812 and returned to U.S. and Britain the lands each controlled before the war.	**Tratado de Ghent** Acuerdo firmado en diciembre de 1814 que finalizó la Guerra de 1812 y devolvió a EE. UU. y a Gran Bretaña las tierras que controlaban antes de la guerra.
Treaty of Greenville 1795 treaty signed following the Battle of Fallen Timbers. The treaty forced American Indians in the Northwest Territory to cede vast tracts of land to the U.S.	**Tratado de Greenville** Tratado de 1795 firmado tras la Batalla de los Árboles Caídos. El tratado obligó a los nativos americanos del territorio del noroeste a ceder grandes extensiones de tierra a EE. UU.
Treaty of Guadalupe Hidalgo 1848 treaty ending the Mexican-American War. By the terms of the treaty, the United States acquired control over Texas north and east of the Rio Grande plus the New Mexico territory, which included present-day Arizona and New Mexico and parts of Utah, Nevada, and Colorado. The treaty also ceded Alta California, which had declared itself an independent republic during the war, to the United States.	**Tratado de Guadalupe Hidalgo** Tratado de 1848 que finalizó la Guerra mexicana-estadounidense. Bajo los términos del tratado, Estados Unidos adquirió control sobre Texas, al norte y este del río Bravo, más el territorio de Nuevo México, que incluía las actuales Arizona y Nuevo México, y partes de Utah, Nevada y Colorado. El tratado también cedió Alta California, que se había autoproclamado una república independiente de Estados Unidos durante la guerra.
Treaty of Medicine Lodge 1867 treaty that provided reservation lands for the Comanche, Kiowa-Apache, and Southern Arapaho to settle. Despite this agreement, white hunters soon invaded this territory and decimated the buffalo herd.	**Tratado de Medicine Lodge** Tratado de 1867 que proporcionó tierras de reserva para que se establecieran los comanches, los apaches-kiowa y arapahos del sur. A pesar de este acuerdo, los cazadores blancos pronto invadieron este territorio y diezmaron a los búfalos.
Treaty of New Echota 1836 treaty in which a group of Cherokee men agreed to exchange their land in the Southeast for money and land in Indian Territory. Despite the fact that the treaty was obtained without tribal sanction, it was approved by the U.S. Congress.	**Tratado de Nueva Echota** Tratado de 1836 en el cual un grupo de hombres cherokee aceptaron intercambiar sus tierras al sureste por dinero y tierras en el territorio nativo. A pesar de que el tratado se obtuvo sin sanción tribal, se aprobó por el congreso de EE. UU.
Treaty (Peace) of Paris 1783 treaty that formally ended the American Revolution.	**Tratado (de paz) de París** Tratado de 1783 que formalmente finalizó la Revolución Estadounidense.
Treaty of Utrecht 1713 Treaty that ended Queen Anne's War. It aimed to achieve peace by balancing the interests of European powers and their colonial possessions.	**Tratado de Utrech** Tratado de 1713 que finalizó la Guerra de la reina Ana. Su objetivo fue lograr la paz equilibrando los intereses de las potencias europeas y sus posesiones coloniales.
Treaty of Versailles 1919 treaty officially ending World War I.	**Tratado de Versalles** Tratado de 1919 que oficialmente finalizó la Primera Guerra Mundial.
Triangle Shirtwaist fire An infamous industrial fire at the Triangle Shirtwaist factory in New York City in 1911. Inadequate fire safety provisions led to the deaths of 146 workers, mostly young women and girls.	**incendio de Triangle Shirtwaist** Un infame incendio industrial en la fábrica de Triangle Shirtwaist en la ciudad de Nueva York en 1911. Las disposiciones de seguridad contra incendios eran inadecuadas y provocaron la muerte de 146 trabajadores, en su mayoría mujeres y niñas.

tribute The exchange of goods or services in return for protection, frequently used as a method of control or exploitation in colonies and territories.	**tributo** El intercambio de bienes o servicios a cambio de protección, a menudo usado como método de control de explotación en colonias y territorios.
Tripartite Pact 1940 mutual defense agreement between Japan, Germany, and Italy.	**Pacto tripartito** Acuerdo de defensa en 1940 mutua entre Japón, Alemania e Italia.
Truman Doctrine U.S. pledge to contain the expansion of communism around the world. Based on the idea of containment, the Truman Doctrine was the cornerstone of American foreign policy throughout the Cold War.	**Doctrina Truman** El compromiso de Estados Unidos por contener la expansión del comunismo alrededor del mundo. Fundamentada en la idea de la contención, la Doctrina Truman fue la piedra angular de la política exterior estadounidense durante la Guerra Fría.
trust Business monopolies formed in the late nineteenth and early twentieth centuries through mergers and consolidation that inhibited competition and controlled the market.	**fideicomiso** Monopolios comerciales que se formaron a fines del siglo XIX y principios del XX a través de fusiones y consolidaciones que inhibieron la competencia y controlaron el mercado.
Tuscarora War War launched by Tuscarora Indians from 1711 to 1715 against European settlers in North Carolina and their allies from the Yamasee, Catawba, and Cherokee nations. The Tuscaroras lost their lands when they signed the peace treaty and many then joined the Iroquois Confederacy to the north.	**Guerra tuscarora** Guerra iniciada por los nativos tuscarora entre 1711 y 1715 en contra de los colonos europeos en Carolina del Norte y sus aliados de las naciones yamasee, catawaba y cherokee. Los tuscaroras perdieron sus tierras cuando firmaron el tratado de paz y muchos de ellos se unieron a la Confederación iroquesa en el Norte.
Tuskegee airmen African American airmen who overcame prejudice during World War II. They earned fame escorting U.S. bomber aircraft in Europe and North Africa.	**Aviadores de Tuskgee** Aviadores afroamericanos que superaron los prejuicios durante la Segunda Guerra Mundial. Ganaron fama escoltando aviones bombarderos estadounidenses en Europa y el norte de África.
Tuskegee Institute African American educational institute founded in 1881 by Booker T. Washington. Following Washington's philosophy, the institute focused on teaching industrious habits and practical job skills.	**Instituto Tuskgee** Instituto educacional afroamericano fundado en 1881 por Booker T. Washington. Partiendo de su filosofía, el instituto se centró en la enseñanza de hábitos laboriosos y habilidades prácticas de trabajo.
Twenty-first Amendment 1933 amendment repealing prohibition and the Eighteenth Amendment.	**Vigésima primera enmienda** Enmienda de 1933 que derogó la Ley seca (o prohibición) y la decimoctava enmienda.
Twenty-sixth Amendment 1971 amendment lowering the voting age to eighteen in federal, state, and local elections.	**Vigésima sexta enmienda** Enmienda de 1971 que redujo la edad para votar en elecciones federales, estatales y locales, a dieciocho años.
Twitter Interactive social media site launched in 2006 that allows users to make short posts called tweets to their platform.	**Twitter** Sitio interactivo de redes sociales lanzado en 2006 que permite a los usuarios hacer publicaciones cortas llamadas *tweets* en su plataforma.
Tydings-McDuffie Act 1934 act granting independence to the Philippines and restricting Filipino immigration into the United States.	**Ley de Tydings-McDuffie** Ley de 1934 que garantizó la independencia de las Filipinas y restringió la inmigración filipina a Estados Unidos.
tyranny An unfair or oppressive form of rule.	**tiranía** Una forma de gobierno injusta u opresiva.

U

English	Spanish
Uncle Tom's Cabin 1852 novel by Harriet Beecher Stowe. Meant to publicize the evils of slavery, the novel struck an emotional chord in the North and was an international best seller.	*La Cabaña del Tío Tom* Novela de 1852 de Harriet Beecher Stow. Escrita con la intención de dar a conocer lo maligno de la esclavitud, la novela tocó una fibra emotiva en el norte y fue un éxito internacional de ventas.
underground railroad A series of routes from southern plantation areas to northern free states and Canada along which abolitionist supporters, known as conductors, provided hiding places, transportation, and resources to enslaved people seeking freedom.	**ferrocarril subterráneo** Una serie de rutas desde las áreas de plantaciones del sur hasta los estados libres del norte y Canadá, a lo largo de las cuales los partidarios abolicionistas, conocidos como conductores, proporcionaban escondites, transporte y recursos a las personas esclavizadas que buscaban la libertad.
Underwood Act 1913 act reducing import duties. The Underwood Act appealed to farmers and southerners who sought lower prices on manufactured goods.	**Ley de Underwood** Ley de 1913 que redujo los aranceles de importación. La Ley Underwood fue un llamado a los agricultores y sureños que buscaban precios más bajos en productos manufacturados.
unions Groups of workers seeking rights and benefits from their employers through their collective efforts.	**sindicatos** Grupos de trabajadores que buscaban derechos y beneficios de sus jefes a través de sus esfuerzos colectivos.
United States v. Cruikshank 1876 Supreme Court ruling that further defined and limited the federal powers under the Fourteenth Amendment after the 1873 *Slaughterhouse* ruling, which protected black people against abuses only by state officials and agencies but exempted private groups, such as the Ku Klux Klan.	*Estados Unidos vs. Cruikshank* Resolución de la Corte Suprema de 1876 que definió y limitó aún más los poderes federales en virtud de la decimocuarta enmienda después de la resolución de *Slaughterhouse* en 1873, que protegió a los afroamericanos del abuso sólo por parte de funcionarios y agencias estatales, pero exentó a grupos privados, como el Ku Klux Klan.

Glossary/Glosario

United States v. E. C. Knight Company 1895 Supreme Court ruling that manufacturing was a local activity within a state and that, even if it was a monopoly, it was not subject to congressional regulation. This ruling rendered the Sherman Antitrust Act virtually powerless, as it left most trusts in the manufacturing sector, thus beyond the act's jurisdiction.	**Estados Unidos vs. E. C. Knight Company** Resolución de 1895 de la Corte Suprema que dictaminó que la manufactura era una actividad local dentro de un estado y que, aunque fuera un monopolio, no estaba sujeto a la regulación del Congreso. Esta decisión dejó a la Ley Sherman antimonopolio prácticamente impotente, ya que dejó a la mayoría de los fideicomisos del sector manufacturero más allá de la jurisdicción de la ley.
Universal Negro Improvement Association (UNIA) Organization founded by Marcus Garvey in 1914 to promote black self-help, pan-Africanism, and racial separatism.	**Asociación universal para la mejora del hombre negro (UNIA, por sus siglas en inglés)** Organización fundada por Marcus Garvey en 1914 para promover la autoayuda entre los afroamericanos, el panafricanismo y el separatismo racial.
Ute North American nomadic hunter-gatherers who lived and hunted in the Great Basin region into southwest Colorado and Utah. They lived in small kindship bands and kept limited possessions.	**Ute** Cazadores-recolectores nómadas norteamericanos que vivían y cazaban en la región de la Gran Cuenca en el suroeste de Colorado y Utah. Vivían entre pequeñas bandas de gentes y tenían posesiones limitadas.
utopian societies Communities formed in the first half of the nineteenth century to embody alternative social and economic visions and to create models for society at large to follow.	**sociedades utópicas** Comunidades formadas en la primera mitad del siglo XIX para encarnar visiones sociales y económicas alternativas y así crear modelos para la sociedad.
V	
vertical integration The control of all elements in a supply chain by a single firm. For example, Andrew Carnegie, a vertically integrated steel producer, sought to own suppliers of all the raw materials used in steel production.	**integración vertical** El control de todos los elementos en una cadena de suministro por una sola empresa. Por ejemplo, Andrew Carnegie, un productor de acero integrado verticalmente, buscaba tener proveedores de todas las materias primas utilizadas en la producción de acero.
veto The right to block a decision made by a governing body.	**veto** El derecho a bloquear una decisión tomada por un órgano rector.
Vietcong The popular name for the National Liberation Front (NFL) in South Vietnam, which was formed in 1959. The Vietcong waged a military insurgency against the U.S.-backed president, Ngo Dinh Diem, and received support from Ho Chi Minh, the leader of North Vietnam.	**Vietcong** El nombre popular para el Frente de Liberación Nacional (NFL, por sus siglas en inglés) en Vietnam del Sur, formado en 1959. El Vietcong condujo una insurgencia militar contra el presidente Ngo Dinh Diem, respaldado por Estados Unidos, y recibió el apoyo de Ho Chi Minh, el líder de Vietnam del Norte.
Vietnam War Conflict between the Communist nationalist government in North Vietnam backed by the Soviet Union and China, against the United Nations and U.S. backed South Vietnam government. The war is seen as part of a series of proxy wars as a result of Cold War tensions between the U.S. and Soviet Union between 1954 to 1975.	**Guerra de Vietnam** Conflicto entre el gobierno nacionalista comunista de Vietnam del Norte respaldado por la Unión Soviética y China, contra las Naciones Unidas y el gobierno de Vietnam del Sur respaldado por Estados Unidos. La guerra es considerada como parte de una serie de guerras subsidiarias (guerras *proxy*), resultado de las tensiones de la Guerra Fría entre Estados Unidos y la Unión Soviética entre 1954 y 1975.
Vietnamization President Richard Nixon's strategy of turning over greater responsibility for the fighting of the Vietnam War to the South Vietnamese army.	**vietnamización** La estrategia el presidente Richard Nixon de entregar una mayor responsabilidad por la lucha en la Guerra de Vietnam al ejército de Vietnam del Sur.
Virginia and Kentucky Resolutions Resolutions passed by legislatures in Virginia and Kentucky that declared the Alien and Sedition Acts (1798) "void and of no force" in their states.	**Resoluciones de Virginia y Kentucky** Resoluciones aprobadas por las legislaturas de Virginia y Kentucky, que declararon las Leyes de extranjería y sedición (1798) "nulas y sin fuerza" en sus estados.
Virginia Plan Plan put forth at the beginning of the 1787 Constitutional Convention that introduced the ideas of a strong central government, a bicameral legislature, and a system of representation based on population.	**Plan de Virginia** Plan presentado a principios de la Convención Constitucional de 1787 que introdujo ideas de un gobierno central fuerte, una legislatura bicameral y un sistema de representación basado en la población.
Virginia Resolves Five resolutions passed in 1765 by the Virginia House of Burgesses to denounce taxation without representation.	**Resoluciones de Virginia** Cinco resoluciones aprobadas en 1765 por la Cámara de Burgueses de Virginia para denunciar los impuestos sin representación.
virtual representation British claim that direct representation of colonists was unnecessary because Parliament virtually represented the interests of the colonies.	**representación virtual** La afirmación británica de que la representación directa de los colonos era innecesaria ya que el Parlamento prácticamente representaba los intereses de las colonias.
Voting Rights Act 1965 act that eliminated many of the obstacles to African American voting in the South and resulted in dramatic increases in black participation in the electoral process.	**Ley de derechos de votación** Ley de 1965 que eliminó muchos de los obstáculos para la votación de los afroamericanos en el Sur y dio como resultado un aumento dramático en la participación de los afroamericanos en el proceso electoral.

Vox Populi A group of American colonists dedicated to repealing the Stamp Act. The Vox Populi took its name from the Latin phrase, which means "voice of the people."	**Vox Populi** Un grupo de colonos estadounidenses dedicados a derogar la Ley del sello. El Vox Populi tomó su nombre de la frase latina que significa "voz del pueblo."

W

Wade-Davis bill 1864 bill that created higher barriers for the Confederate states to be readmitted to the Union and granted freedmen the right to vote. President Lincoln vetoed the bill.	**Propuesta de ley Wade-Davis** Propuesta de ley de 1864 que creó más obstáculos para que los estados confederados fueran readmitidos en la Unión y otorgó a los hombres liberados el derecho a votar. El presidente Lincoln vetó la propuesta.
Walking Purchase 1737 treaty that allowed Pennsylvania to expand its boundaries at the expense of the Delaware Indians. The treaty, likely a forgery, allowed the British to add territory that could be walked off in a day and a half.	**Compra de Walking** Tratado de 1737 que permitió a Pensilvania expandir su territorio a expensas de los nativos americanos de Delaware. El tratado, probablemente una falsificación, permitía a los británicos anexar un territorio que se pudiera recorrer en un día y medio.
Walmart American company founded by Sam Walton in 1962. Walmart is the United States' largest revenue-making company in the country.	**Walmart** Compañía estadounidense fundada por Sam Walton en 1962. Walmart es la empresa que genera más ingresos en Estados Unidos.
War of 1812 1812–1815 war between the United States and Great Britain. The war was one consequence of ongoing conflict between Great Britain and France, as each nation sought to forcibly restrict the United States' trade with the other.	**Guerra de 1812** Guerra de 1812–1815 entre Estados Unidos y Gran Bretaña. La guerra fue consecuencia del continuo conflicto entre Gran Bretaña y Francia, ya que cada nación trató de restringir por la fuerza el comercio de Estados Unidos con el otro.
War Industries Board (WIB) Government commission created in 1917 to supervise the purchase of military supplies and oversee the conversion of the economy to meet wartime demands. The WIB embodied a government-business partnership that lasted beyond World War I.	**Comisión de industrias de guerra (WIB, por sus siglas en inglés)** Comisión gubernamental creada en 1917 para supervisar la compra de suministros militares y la conversión de la economía para satisfacer las demandas en tiempos de guerra. La WIB encarnó una asociación gobierno-empresa que llegó más allá de la Primera Guerra Mundial.
War Powers Act 1942 act passed after the attack on Pearl Harbor. It authorized the president to reorganize federal agencies any way he thought necessary to win the war.	**Ley de poderes de guerra de 1942** Aprobada después del ataque en Pearl Harbor. Autorizó al presidente a reorganizar las agencias federales de cualquier forma que considerara necesaria para ganar la guerra.
War Powers Act 1973 act that required the president to consult with Congress within forty-eight hours of deploying military forces and to obtain a declaration of war from Congress if troops remained on foreign soil beyond sixty days.	**Ley de poderes de guerra de 1973** Requería que el presidente consultara con el Congreso dentro de las cuarenta y ocho horas posteriores al despliegue de las fuerzas militares y obtuviera una declaración de guerra de parte del Congreso, si las tropas permanecían en territorio extranjero por más de sesenta días.
War Production Board Board established in 1942 to oversee the economy during World War II. It was part of a larger effort to convert American industry to the production of war materials.	**Junta de producción de guerra** Junta establecida en 1942 para supervisar la economía durante la Segunda Guerra Mundial. Buscaba que la industria estadounidense produjera más suministros de guerra.
Warsaw Pact Russian military alliance with seven satellite nations in response to the U.S. Marshall Plan and establishment of NATO.	**Pacto de Varsovia** Alianza militar rusa con siete países satélites en respuesta al Plan Marshall de Estados Unidos y al establecimiento de la OTAN.
Watergate Scandal and cover-up that forced the resignation of Richard Nixon in 1974. The scandal revolved around a break-in at Democratic Party headquarters in 1972 and subsequent efforts to conceal the administration's involvement in the break-in.	**Watergate** Escándalo y encubrimiento que forzó la renuncia de Richard Nixon en 1974. El escándalo giró en torno a un robo en la sede del Partido Demócrata en 1972 y los esfuerzos posteriores para ocultar la participación de la administración en dicho robo.
Whig Party Political party formed in the 1830s to challenge the power of the Democratic Party. The Whigs attempted to forge a diverse coalition from around the country by promoting commercial interests and moral reforms.	**Partido Whig** Partido político formado en la década de 1830 para desafiar el poder del Partido Demócrata. Los *whigs* intentaron forjar una coalición diversa de todo el país promoviendo intereses comerciales y reformas morales.
Whiskey Rebellion Uprising by western Pennsylvania farmers who led protests against the excise tax on whiskey in the early 1790s.	**Rebelión del whisky** Levantamiento de agricultores del oeste de Pensilvania que lideraron protestas contra el impuesto específico sobre el whisky a principios de la década de 1790.
White Citizens' Council (WCC) Organization created in protest following the *Brown v. Board* decision. The WCC consisted primarily of businessmen and professionals who intimidated black members of the community by threatening their jobs, denied bank loans to African Americans, and rejected rock 'n' roll music.	**Consejo de ciudadanos blancos (WWC, por sus siglas en inglés)** Organización creada en protesta tras la decisión de *Brown vs Board*. El WWC consistió principalmente en hombres de negocios y profesionales que intimidaban a miembros afroamericanos de la comunidad amenazando sus trabajos, negándoles préstamos bancarios y rechazando la música rocanrol.
white supremacy An ideology promoted by southern planters and intellectuals that maintained that all white people, regardless of class or education, were superior to all black people.	**supremacía blanca** Una ideología promovida por intelectuales y plantadores sureños según la cual todos los blancos, independientemente de su clase o educación, eran superiores a todos los afroamericanos.

Glossary/Glosario

English	Spanish
Whitewater A real estate scandal involving investments made by the Clintons while Bill Clinton was governor of Arkansas. A special prosecutor was appointed in 1994 to investigate allegations of criminal misconduct.	**Whitewater** Un escándalo de bienes raíces que involucró inversiones realizadas por los Clinton mientras Bill Clinton era gobernador de Arkansas. En 1994 se designó un fiscal especial para investigar las denuncias de conducta delictiva.
Williams v. Mississippi 1898 Supreme Court ruling that upheld Jim Crow voter qualifications, such as poll taxes and literacy tests, which disenfranchised African Americans.	***Williams vs. Mississippi*** Resolución de la Corte Suprema de 1898, que confirmó los requerimientos de los votantes que había establecido Jim Crow, como impuestos a las encuestas y a las pruebas de alfabetización, lo que privó a los afroamericanos de derechos.
Wilmot Proviso 1846 proposal by Democratic congressman David Wilmot of Pennsylvania to outlaw slavery in all territory acquired from Mexico. The proposal was defeated, but the fight over its adoption foreshadowed the sectional conflicts of the 1850s.	**Condición de Wilmot** Propuesta de 1846 del congresista demócrata David Wilmot para prohibir la esclavitud en todo el territorio adquirido de México. La propuesta fue rechazada, pero la lucha por su adopción presagió los conflictos seccionales de la década de 1850.
Woman's Christian Temperance Union (WCTU) Organization founded in 1874 to campaign for a ban on the sale and consumption of alcohol. In the late nineteenth century, under Frances Willard's leadership, the WCTU supported a broad social reform agenda.	**Unión cristiana de mujeres por la templanza (WCTU, por sus siglas en inglés)** Organización fundada en 1874 para hacer campaña a favor de la prohibición de la venta y el consumo de alcohol. A fines del siglo XIX, bajo el liderazgo de Frances Willard, la WCTU apoyó una amplia agenda de reformas sociales.
Women Accepted for Voluntary Emergency Service (WAVES) The navy volunteer organization for women during World War II, ultimately disbanded in 1972.	**Mujeres aceptadas para el servicio voluntario de emergencia (WAVES, por sus siglas en inglés)** La organización de voluntariado naval para mujeres durante la Segunda Guerra Mundial, finalmente se disolvió en 1972.
Women's Army Corps (WACs) The army volunteer organization for women during World War II.	**Cuerpo de mujeres del ejército (WACs, por sus siglas en inglés)** La organización de voluntariado del ejército para mujeres durante la Segunda Guerra Mundial.
Women's National Loyal League Organization founded by abolitionist women during the Civil War to press Lincoln and Congress to enact universal emancipation.	**Liga nacional de mujeres leales** Organización fundada por mujeres abolicionistas durante la Guerra Civil para presionar a Lincoln y al Congreso de promulgar la emancipación universal.
Workmen's Compensation Act Regulation guaranteeing the rights of federal employees to receive financial compensation or pursue legal action for any injury occurring on the job.	**Ley de compensación al trabajador** Reglamento que garantizaba el derecho de los empleados federales a recibir compensación financiera o emprender acciones legales por cualquier lesión que ocurriera en el trabajo.
Works Progress Administration (WPA) New Deal agency established in 1935 to put unemployed Americans to work on public projects ranging from construction to the arts.	**Administración del progreso laboral (WPA, por sus siglas en inglés)** Agencia del *New Deal* establecida en 1935 para dar trabajo a estadounidenses desempleados en proyectos públicos que iban desde construcción hasta las artes.
World Trade Organization (WTO) Organization created in 1995 to promote free trade between its 150 member nations.	**Organización Mundial del Comercio** Organización creada en 1995 para promover el libre comercio entre los 150 países miembros.
World War I Also known as the Great War, 1914–1918 war fought between the Central Powers and Allies. The United States entered the war in 1917.	**Primera Guerra Mundial** También conocida como la Gran Guerra. Duró de 1914 a 1918 y participaron los Poderes Centrales y los Aliados. Estados Unidos entró a la guerra en 1917.
World Wide Web Established in 1991, as a way to access the Internet and connect documents and other resources to one another through hyperlinks.	**World Wide Web** Establecida en 1991 como una forma de acceder al Internet y conectar documentos y otros recursos entre sí a través de hipervínculos.
Wounded Knee massacre Massacre committed by U.S. military in South Dakota, December 29, 1890. The Plains Indians, on the edge of starvation, began the "Ghost Dance," which they believed would protect them from bullets and restore their old way of life. Following one of the dances, a rifle held by an American Indian misfired. In response, U.S. soldiers invaded the encampment, killing some 250 people.	**masacre de Wounded Knee** Masacre cometida por el ejército estadounidense en Dakota del Sur, el 29 de diciembre de 1890. Los nativos americanos de las llanuras, al borde de inanición, comenzaron la "danza fantasma," que según sus creencias los protegería de las balas y restablecería su antigua forma de vida. Después de uno de los bailes, un rifle en manos de un nativo americano falló. En respuesta, los soldados estadounidenses invadieron el campamento y mataron a unas 250 personas.

X

English	Spanish
XYZ Affair 1798 incident in which French agents demanded bribes before meeting with American diplomatic representatives.	**Caso XYZ** Incidente del año 1798 en el que agentes franceses exigieron sobornos para reunirse con los representantes diplomáticos de Estados Unidos.

Y

Yalta Agreement Agreement negotiated at the 1945 Yalta Conference by Roosevelt, Churchill, and Stalin about the fate of postwar Eastern Europe. The Yalta Agreement did little to ease growing tensions between the Soviet Union and its Western Allies.

Yamasee War A pan-American Indian war from 1715 to 1717 led by the Yamasee who intended, but failed, to oust the British from South Carolina.

Yates v. United States 1957 Supreme Court ruling establishing that the Justice Department could not prosecute someone for merely advocating an abstract doctrine favoring the violent overthrow of the government. The ruling was seen as a severe blow to the enforcement of the 1940 Smith Act.

yellow journalism Sensationalist news accounts meant to provoke an emotional response in readers. Yellow journalism contributed to the growth of public support for American intervention in Cuba in 1898.

yeoman farmers Southern independent landowners who were not slaveholders. Although yeomen farmers had connections to the South's plantation economy, many realized that their interests were not always identical to those of the planter elite.

"Young America" movement Mid-nineteenth century political movement that supported nationalism, manifest destiny, and expansionism.

Young Americans for Freedom (YAF) A group of young conservatives from college campuses formed in 1960 in Sharon, Connecticut. The group favored free market principles, states' rights, and anticommunism.

Z

Zimmermann telegram 1917 telegram in which Germany offered Mexico an alliance in the event that the United States entered World War I. The telegram's publication in American newspapers helped build public support for war.

zoot suit riots Series of riots in 1943 in Los Angeles, California, sparked by white hostility toward Mexican American teenagers who dressed in zoot suits — suits with long jackets with padded shoulders and baggy pants tapered at the bottom.

Credits

Module 1-3
Nzinga Mvemba, "Appeal to the King of Portugal," from *The African Past*, ed. Basil Davidson. Copyright ©1964 by Basil Davidson. Reproduced with permission of Curtis Brown Group Ltd, London on behalf of The Beneficiaries of the Estate of Basil Davidson.

Period 1 AP® Exam Practice
Nancy Qian and Nathan Nunn, "The Columbian Exchange." Copyright American Economic Association; Reproduced with permission of the Journal of Economic Perspectives. Reproduced with permission of Nancy Qian and Nathan Nunn.

Module 7-8
John P. Davis, "A Black Inventory of the New Deal." The publisher wishes to thank Crisis Publishing Co., Inc., the publisher of the magazine of the National Association for the Advancement of Colored People, for the use of this material first published in the May 1935 issue of *Crisis Magazine*.

Module 7-10
Lawrence E. Davies, "Zoot Suits Become Issue on Coast," *New York Times*, June 13, 1943, E10. ©1943 The New York Times. All rights reserved. Used by permission and protected by the copyright laws of the United States. The printing, copying, redistribution, or retransmission of this content without express written permission is prohibited.

Module 7-11
Father Johannes Siemes, "Hiroshima, August 6, 1945," *Bulletin of the Atomic Scientists 1*, no. 11 (1946): 5-6. Reproduced with permission of Taylor & Francis Ltd.

Period 7 AP® Exam Practice
Merlo J. Pusey, "The Revolution at Home," *South Atlantic Quarterly*, Volume 42, pp. 207–219. Copyright 1943, Duke University Press. All rights reserved. Republished by permission of the copyright holder, Duke University Press, www.dukepress.edu.

Norman Cousins, "Will Women Lose Their Jobs?" Reprinted with permission from *Current History Magazine* 51:1, September 1939. ©2017 Current History, Inc.

Module 8-1
Henry Wallace, "The Way to Peace," in *The Annals of America* (Chicago: Encyclopedia Britannica, 1968), 16:372-73.

Module 8-3
Restrictive Housing Covenant, King County, Washington. Seattle Civil Rights & Labor History Project. Nothing on this site may be reproduced without the written permission of the director or project coordinator of the Seattle Civil Rights and Labor History Project.

Module 8-5
Jacquelyn Dowd Hall, "The Long Civil Rights Movement and the Political Uses of the Past." Reproduced with permission of Oxford University Press — Journals. *Journal of American History*, 91, (March 2005), 1245-46. Permission Conveyed through Copyright Clearance Center, Inc.

Module 8-8
Martin Luther King Jr., *Letter from Birmingham* Jail. Reprinted by arrangement with The Heirs to the Estate of Martin Luther King Jr., c/o Writers House as agent for the proprietor New York, NY. ©1955 Dr. Martin Luther King Jr., © renewed 1991 Coretta Scott King.

Martin Luther King Jr., Speech at Holt Street Baptist Church. Reprinted by arrangement with The Heirs to the Estate of Martin Luther King Jr., c/o Writers House as agent for the proprietor New York, NY. ©1963 Dr. Martin Luther King Jr., © renewed 1991 Coretta Scott King.

Period 8 AP® Exam Practice
"Anti-Little Rock Intervention," by Karr Shannon in *Arkansas Democrat* (March 10, 1958). Reproduced with permission. "No More Miss America" press release for 1968 Pageant Protest. Excerpted with permission from *Sisterhood Is Powerful*, Robin Morgan, 1970 (Random House, NY). Reproduced with permission of Robin Morgan.

Module 9-1
Reginald Stuart, "Michigan Requests Federal Loan to Bolster Unemployment Fund," *New York Times*, July 17, 1980. ©1980 The New York Times. All rights reserved. Used by permission and protected by the copyright laws of the United States. The printing, copying, redistribution, or retransmission of this content without express written permission is prohibited.

Module 9-2
Jennifer Medina, "New Suburban Dream Born of Asia and Southern California," *New York Times*, April 29, 2013. ©2013 The New York Times. All rights reserved. Used by permission and protected by the copyright laws of the United States. The printing, copying, redistribution, or retransmission of this content without express written permission is prohibited.

Module 9-4
Alan Rusbridger and Ewen MacAskill, "Edward Snowden Interview," *Guardian*, July 18, 2014. Copyright Guardian News & Media Ltd 2019.

Sam Schlinkert, "Facebook Is Invading Your Phone," *The Daily Beast*, 2013. Reproduced with permission of The Daily Beast.

Index

Page numbers followed by *(i)* indicate illustrations, *(f)* indicate figures, *(s)* indicate sources, *(m)* indicate maps, *(t)* indicate tables.

A

Abandonment of the Jews, The (Wyman), 690*(s)*
Abbott, Mary, 345*(s)*
Abolitionism, 224, 313, 327–328, 343–351
   antislavery parties and, 349
   beginnings of, 343–345
   Civil War, 355, 392
   Fugitive Slave Act and, 368–369
   growth of, 344–345
   Harpers Ferry raid and, 384–385
   literature in, 378
   Quakers in, 219, 224
   Republican Party and, 379, 384–387
   universal suffrage and, 423–424
   in Virginia, 326, 327
   women in, 326
   women's rights and, 347–348
Abolitionists, 326
Abortion
   birth control and, 568
   Bush, George H. W., on, 817
   Bush, George W., on, 835
   the Christian Right on, 796
   the New Right and, 808
   Roe v. Wade and, 772, 792
Abraham Lincoln Brigade, 664
Abrams v. United States, 611
Abstinence, temperance and, 339–340
Accommodation, 562
"Account of the Boston Tea Party," 169*(s)*
Account of the Stono Rebellion, 1739 (Cato), 111–112*(s)*
ACE (answer, cite, explain), 21–23
Acheson, Dean, 702, 706
Achille Lauro (ship), 812
Acoma massacre, 49
Acoma people, 36
Acquired immune deficiency syndrome (AIDS), 808, 822
Act of Religious Toleration (1649), 61–62
ACT UP (AIDS Coalition to Unleash Power), 808*(i)*
Active reading, 6–7
Adams, Abigail, 218–219
Adams, John
   Declaration of Independence and, 178
   judges appointed by, 261
   navy under, 275
   in peace term negotiations, 191
   as president, 242–245
   speech to Congress, 247*(s)*
   as vice president, 210, 230
Adams, John Quincy, 279, 303–304, 305, 309, 326
Adams, Samuel, 162, 164*(i)*
   Boston Massacre and, 167
   on the Townshend Act, 165

Adams-Onis Treaty, 279
Adams-Onis Treaty line, 263*(m)*
Addams, Jane, 518*(s)*, 557, 559, 564, 593, 599
Adding machines, 483
Address Accepting the Presidential Nomination at the Republican National Convention (Nixon), 778*(s)*
Address and Reasons of Dissent of the Minority of the Convention of Pennsylvania to Their Constituents, 213*(s)*
Address at Pueblo, Colorado (Wilson), 607*(s)*
Address at the University of Virginia (Reagan), 816*(s)*
Address before the American Society of Newspaper Editors (Kennedy), 746*(s)*
Address before the Second Biennial Convention of the World's Woman's Christian Temperance Union (Willard), 566*(s)*
Address of the Workingmen's Party of Charlestown, Massachusetts, 298*(s)*
Address to Congress on Health Care (Obama), 842*(s)*
Address to Congress on Health Care Reform (Clinton), 827*(s)*
Address to Governor William Henry Harrison (Tecumseh), 274*(s)*
Address to the Nation on Energy and National Goals (Carter), 789*(s)*
Address to the Nation on the Iran Arms Contra Aid Controversy (Reagan), 814*(s)*
Address to the Second United Negro Improvement Association Convention (Garvey), 634*(s)*
Address to the Southern States (Calhoun), 310*(s)*
Adventures of Ozzie and Harriet, The (TV show), 723
Advertising
   effect of on social conventions, 621
   in the twenties, 616, 616*(i)*
Advocate of Moral Reform, The, 336
Affirmative action, 761–762
   controversy over, 796
   Nixon and, 780
   reverse discrimination and, 762
Affluent Society, The (Galbraith), 767
Afghanistan
   mujahideen assisted in, 784*(i)*, 785–786, 813*(m)*
   Obama on, 844
   Soviet withdrawal from, 820
   war on terrorism in, 836
AFL. *See* American Federation of Labor (AFL)
Afonso I, King of the Kongo, 27
Africa
   AIDS in, 822
   Back to Africa movement, 625

   in Columbian Exchange, 24, 25, 26*(m)*
   Gold Coast, 18
   immigrants from, 1990s to twenty-first century, 831, 831*(f)*
   portrayals of, 28
   Portuguese trade with, 17, 19*(m)*
   resettlement of black people in, 225
   slave trade, 27–29
   trade with, 98
   transatlantic trade with, 41
   World War II in, 682
African Americans. *See also* Civil rights movement; Free black people
   after the Civil War, 408
   in the American Revolution, 147, 176–177, 180, 180*(i)*, 183
   Beat culture and, 727
   black nationalism and, 625
   buffalo soldiers, 455
   citizenship of, 421, 506
   in the Civil War, 392, 393, 394, 405–406, 406*(i)*, 408
   Civil War death rates of, 398
   in Civil War draft riots, 400, 400*(i)*
   cowboys, 463, 465
   cultural divisions and, 287
   depictions of the early republic, 225
   economic opportunities for, 429
   education of, 224–225, 415–417, 562–564
   in the election of 1960, 745, 745*(i)*
   employment of women, 492
   excluded from Social Security, 655
   Exodusters, 429
   Freedmen's Bureau and, 438
   freedom of religion and, 417
   in the Great Depression, 640–643
   great migration of, 613, 736
   Harlem Renaissance and, 623–625, 623*(s)*
   housing segregation and, 720–721, 721*(s)*
   identity of, 508
   as indentured servants, 61
   Irish immigrants in conflict with, 290
   as itinerant musicians, 529
   Jazz Age, 553
   Jim Crow and, 471, 476–477
   lynchings of, 477, 557, 562
   migration north by, 490
   minstrel shows and, 290
   on Missouri slavery, 283
   the New Deal and, 654, 655, 658, 659*(s)*
   police shootings of, 843
   political participation of, 428–429
   Populists and, 547–548

African Americans (Continued)
  post-Revolution struggle of for rights, 217, 219
  poverty and, 557
  progressivism and, 555, 557, 562–565, 581–582
  religion and, 134, 219, 325, 501, 514
  resettlement of in Africa, 225
  in rock 'n' roll, 725
  in the Second Great Awakening, 332
  Seminoles and, 314
  sharecropping and, 429, 430(s)
  in social reform movements, 336
  in the Spanish-American War, 591
  Square Deal and, 577–578
  in teenage culture, 725
  on television, 723
  in unions, 496
  in urbanization, 290, 512
  violence against, 302, 431–432, 433(s), 477, 613
  voting rights for, 301–302, 423–424
  in western cities, 512
  in western migration, 365–366, 736
  in Wilmington (North Carolina) massacre, 547(i)
  Wilson supported by, 581
  women, in the workforce, 725, 727
  women, rights and roles of, 219–220
  women's clubs, 557
  women's suffrage and, 559, 560–561, 560(m)
  in World War I, 606
  in World War II, 672, 675–676
African Methodist Episcopal Church, 224, 302, 514
Agent Orange, 750
Age of Homespun, The (Bushnell), 299(s)
Age of Reform, The (Hofstadter), 548(s)
Agnew, Spiro, 781, 782
Agricultural Adjustment Act (1933), 648
Agricultural Marketing Act (1929), 638
Agriculture. *See also* Tobacco
  after the Revolution, 197
  after World War I, 617, 620
  braceros in, 676
  in the Civil War, 401, 407
  colonial era, 80, 86–87, 94
  Columbian Exchange in, 25
  commercial, in the West, 465–467
  cotton production and, 265–266, 267–270
  debt in, 202–203, 281–282, 540, 542
  Dust Bowl and, 639–640, 639(m)
  English enclosure movements and, 55
  European, 17
  family labor in, 131
  farmer organization and, 540–542
  farmers and westward migration, 263
  French Revolution and, 238
  GI Bill and, 717, 717(i)
  Granger movement in, 540–541, 540(i)
  in the Great Depression, 638, 642–643
  on the Great Plains, 449–450, 467–469
  horticulture as, 4–5
  Incan, 8
  industrialization and, 473
  the market revolution and, 287

  Mexican Americans in, 744, 773
  migrant laborers in, 642–643
  the New Deal and, 648
  in the New South, 474, 475
  in the North *vs.* South, 390(f)
  organized protests in, 642, 643
  plantation, 321–322
  political crises from indebted farmers in, 202–203
  population growth and, 262
  Populist Party and, 548(s)
  Populists and, 547
  in Portugal and Spain, 18
  production levels in, 540
  sharecropping, 427, 429, 430(s)
  Shays's Rebellion and, 202–203
  slavery and Caribbean, 33
  slavery and southern, 109–110
  in the South, 327
  Tariff of Abominations and, 309–310
  technology in, 265–266, 465, 537
  technology in, urbanization and, 512–513
  transportation improvements and, 287
  unions in, 499
  Whiskey Rebellion and, 239–240
  in World War II, 671
  yeomen farmers, 327
Aguinaldo, Emilio, 593
AIDS (acquired immune deficiency syndrome), 808, 822
AIDS Coalition to Unleash Power (ACT UP), 808(i)
AIDS Quilt, 802(i)
Aid to Families with Dependent Children, 806, 828
Air controllers strike, 807
Alabama
  black majority in, 428
  cotton production in, 321(m)
  desegregation blocked in, 756, 767–768
  Freedom Rides in, 756
  Freedom Summer in, 759–760
  lumber industry in, 475
  readmitted to the Union, 417, 422
  Scottsboro Nine, 641–642, 642(i)
  secession of, 385, 387(s)
  statehood of, 277
  steel industry in, 475
Alamo, 312
Alaska
  coal mining in, 579
  Exxon Valdez oil spill, 818
  gold discoveries in, 546
  women's suffrage in, 559
Albany (Georgia), 756
Albany Plan of Union, 150
Albuquerque (New Mexico), 736
Alcatraz occupation, 774
Alcoholism, immigrants and, 503. *See also* Temperance movement
Alger, Horatio, 533
Algeria, in World War II, 682
Algonquian Indians, 93
  Dutch conflict with, 47
Alien Act (1798), 243–244
Alien and Sedition Acts (1798), 243, 244(s), 248
Al Jazeera, 822

Allen, Richard, 224
Allende, Salvador, 780
Alliance for Progress, 747
Allies (World War I), 599, 599(m)
Allies (World War II), 664, 682(m), 697
All Quiet on the Western Front (Remarque), 663
Almshouses, 136
Alta California, 280
Amalgamated Copper Company, 462
Amazon, 830
AME Zion Church, 514
America First Committee, 664–665, 665(i)
America First Movement, 678
American Academy of Arts and Sciences, 220
American and Foreign Anti-Slavery Society, 347
American Anti-Slavery Society (AASS), 344, 347, 423
American Broadcasting System (ABS), 722
American Civil Liberties Union (ACLU), 612, 627
American Commonwealth, The (Bryce), 520(s), 538
American Dictionary of the English Language (Webster), 330
American Dream, 553
American Duties Act (England, 1764), 161
American Enterprise Institute, 796
American Equal Rights Association, 423, 440–441(s)
American Expeditionary Forces (AEF), 602–603
American Federation of Labor (AFL), 495–496, 656
American Indian Movement (AIM), 774
American Indians, 4–16, 12(m). *See also specific people by name*
  American Indian Wars, 155–156, 155(m)
  Americanization of, 630
  in the American Revolution, 147, 180–181, 181(i), 191, 192
  assimilation of, 456, 457, 459, 657–658
  bison and, 365, 453, 453(m)
  British conflicts with, 155–156, 155(m)
  Central and South American, 7–10
  citizenship of, 506, 630
  civilizations of, 452–454, 453(m)
  in the Civil War, 393, 394, 408–409
  colonial expansion and conflict with, 41, 60, 60(i), 93–94, 118–128
  Columbian Exchange with, 3, 25–27
  conflicts in New England, 76, 78, 119–120
  conservationism and, 575
  Continental Congress and, 198–199
  conversion of to Catholicism, 36, 41
  cotton cultivation by, 268–269
  defeat of, 456
  depictions of in the early republic, 221–222
  education of, 222, 457, 458(s)
  under Eisenhower, 744
  English colonies and, 56–57
  enslavement and torture of, 120
  epidemics among, 74, 360, 452
  European rivalries and, 120–122
  expansion and conflict with, 46(m), 47, 63–65, 147, 198, 237
  federal policy on, 457–458
  French trade and conflict with, 44–45
  frontier conflicts with, 155–156, 155(m)

I-2

gold rush and, 363–364
Great Awakening and, 134
how to subjugate, 60–61
imperialism toward, 586
under Jackson, 313–316
Kansas-Nebraska Act and, 378–379
land cessions by, 263(m)
land treaties with, 197, 201(s)
liberation movement of, 774
measles and, 364
narratives of captivity by, 124–125(s)
the New Deal and, 657–658, 744
Northwest Ordinance on, 201
pan-Indian alliances among, 273–274
in Pennsylvania, 93–94, 93(m)
petition to free a slave, 124(s)
praying towns and, 119
progressivism and, 565, 582
relocated from reservations, 744
removal of, 313–316, 315(m)
resistance to European encroachment, 78, 118–120
resistance to western settlement, 452–459
in Seven Years' War, 149–155
slavery of, 30, 34–36, 34(i), 49–50, 365–366
Spanish trade with, 30
on television, 723
terrorization of, 408–409
tobacco cultivation and, 58–59
trade with, 41
Treaty of Greenville, 228(s)
voting rights of, 301
western settlement and, 364–365, 365(m), 449
westward migration and, 262–265, 263(m)
women, rights and roles of, 220
in World War I, 606
in World War II, 675, 676–677, 676(i)
American Indian Wars (1754–1763), 155–156, 155(m)
American International Group (AIG), 840
American League of Baseball, 527
American Liberty League, 651–652
American Mercury, The (magazine), 622
American Party, 379, 380, 380–381(s)
American (or Know-Nothing) Party Platform, 380–381(s)
American Philosophical Society, 220
American Plan, 614
American Protective Association, 507
American Protective League (APL), 507(s), 604(i)
American Railway Union, 498
American Red Cross, 525, 602(i)
American Revolution (1775–1783), 147, 173–206
choosing sides in, 180–184
critical years in, 185–186
debt after, 147, 198, 202–203, 232–233, 237
Declaration of Independence in, 178–179
economic challenges after, 198
eruption of armed conflict, 174–178
fighting in, 185–186, 190(m)
financing, 198–199
France in, 186, 188–191
governing during, 195–197
international conflicts preceding, 149–159
legacies of, 217–229
neutral parties in, 182
in the North, 185–187, 190(m)
slavery question in, 222–223

southern fighting in, 191–192, 192(m)
victory in, 191–193
western fighting in, 191–192, 192(m)
women in, 174, 179, 180, 182, 183, 186–188
American Smelting and Refining Company, 462
American Social Hygiene Association, 567
American Society of Newspaper Editors, 746(s)
American Spelling Book (Webster), 330, 331(i)
Americans with Disabilities Act (1990), 818
American System, 277
American system of manufacturing, 266
American Telephone and Telegraph Company (AT&T), 484
American Temperance Society, 339–340
American Union Telegraph Company, 486
American Whig Review, 298(s)
American Woman Suffrage Association, 559, 561–562(s)
American Women, 772
Americanization, 629–630
Amish, neutrality of in the American Revolution, 182
Amistad mutiny, 326
Amos 'n' Andy (radio show), 621
Amos 'n' Andy Show, The (TV show), 723
Amusement parks, 529
Anarchists, 494–495
deportation of, 612
in the Homestead strike, 497–498
Ancient Society (Morgan), 457
Anderson, Alexander, 273(i)
Anderson, John, 804, 806(m)
Anderson, Marion, 657
Andersonville prison, 431
Angel Island, 571
Angell, Homer D., 718(s)
Anglicanism, 71, 196
Anglicization, 74–75
Anglo-Powhatan Wars, 118
Anglo-Saxons, 587
Annotation of sources, 9–10
Anthony, Susan B., 399, 423, 440–441(s), 559
Anthropology, on American Indians, 565, 622
Anti-authoritarianism, 177
Antietam, Battle of (1862), 394(m), 396, 398
Antifederalists, 209, 214(s)
"Anti-Fugitive Slave Law Convention, Cazenovia, New York," 371(i)
Anti-immigrant fears, 504–508, 605, 606
Anti-imperialism, 593, 594(s)
Anti-Imperialist League, 593, 594(s)
Anti-Muslim sentiments, 837
Anti-Saloon League, 566
Antisemitism, 290
Coughlin and, 652
in the State Department during World War II, 688
in the twenties, 629
Antislavery Convention of American Women, 345
Anti-Slavery Societies, 345–346
Anzaldúa, Gloria, 792
Apache Indians, 360. *See also* Geronimo
civilization of, 452
raids against Pueblo people, 49, 50
reservation land for, 455
Apartheid, 812, 812(i), 824–825
Appeal . . . to the Colored Citizens of the World (Walker), 343, 344(s), 384

Appeal to the Wealthy of the Land (Carey), 337–338(s)
Appeasement, 664
Apple Computer Company, 830
Appomattox Court House, 409
Apprentice, The (TV show), 848
Arab Spring, 844
Arafat, Yasser, 824
Arapaho Indians
Kansas-Nebraska Act and, 379
Sand Creek massacre, 409, 454–455
Arawak people, 25
Argentina, repressive regime in, 784
Argonne, Battle of the (1918), 602–603
Argument at the New York State Ratification Convention (Williams), 214(s)
Aristocratic, 26
Aristocrats, English colonization and, 55
Arizona, internment camps in, 678
Arkansas
internment camps in, 678
readmitted to the Union, 417, 422
secession of, 390
Arkwright, Richard, 265
Armour, Philip, 488
Armstrong, Louis, 623
Army Air Corps, 672(i), 673
Army-McCarthy hearings, 714, 714(i)
Arthur, Chester A., 538
Articles of Confederation, 196–197, 197(s), 198, 199(m), 202, 207–208
Arts, 221–222. *See also* Literature
Harlem Renaissance and, 623–625, 623(s)
nineteenth century, 335–336, 335(i)
in the twenties, 621–624
Works Progress Administration and, 653, 654(i)
Asheville (North Carolina), 525
Ashley, James, 409
Asian Americans. *See also* Chinese Americans; Japanese Americans
after World War II, 721
civil rights movement and, 736–737
in the Great Depression, 642–643
liberation movement of, 774
quota system on, 628
Asians, early migration to the Americas, 3, 4, 5(m)
Askew, Reubin, 787(s)
Al-Assad, Bashar, 846
Assembly line, 615
Assessment of the Causes of King Philip's War (Randolph), 126(s)
Assimilation
Americanization in the twenties and, 629–630
of immigrants, 501, 508, 831
of American Indians, 457, 459, 565, 657–658
melting pot metaphor for, 508
Astrolabe, 18
Aswan Dam, 742
Atlanta (Georgia), 398, 830
Civil War capture of, 405, 407
Atlanta Braves, 830
Atlanta Constitution (newspaper), 473
Atlanta Exposition Address, The (Washington), 563(s), 583(s)
Atlantic Charter, 667, 667(i)

Index

Atlantic Monthly, 175(s)
Atlantic Records, 830
Atlantic slave trade, 101, 107–109
Atlantic World, 24, 28
Atlatl, 11
Atomic Age, 690
Atomic Energy Commission, 715
Atomic weapons. *See* Nuclear weapons
Attucks, Crispus, 167
Auschwitz, 687
Australia
   women's suffrage in, 561
   in World War II, 683, 684
Austria
   in Seven Year's War, 152
   unification of with Germany, 664
Austria-Hungary, in World War I, 599
Authoritarianism, 639
   totalitarianism *vs.*, 811–812
   World War II, 664, 685, 689
Automobiles
   after World War II, 719
   bailouts of manufacturers, 841
   emission standards for, 784
   factories in World War II, 671
   influence of on American life, 615–616
   internal combustion engine and, 484
   multinational corporations and, 822
   production and consumption of, 615–616, 615(i), 616(i)
   sales decline in the twenties, 618
   sexual norms and, 620
Awashonks, 124–125(s)
Axis, World War I, 678, 682(m)
Axis, World War II, 697
Axis of evil, 837–839
Azariah Caverly Family, The (Davis), 297(i)
Aztecs, 3, 7, 20(m), 25, 25(i), 31–33, 32(i)
   art, 9(i), 10

B

B-29 bombers, 684
Babbitt (Lewis), 622, 634(s)
Baby boom, 719
Bache, Benjamin Franklin, 247
Back to Africa movement, 625
Bacon, Nathaniel, 64–65
Bacon's Rebellion, 63–65, 135
Bad Heart Buffalo, Amos, 456(i)
Baer, George F., 576
Bahamas, immigrants from, 502
Baker, Ella, 735(s)
Baker, James, 823
Bakke, Allan, 762
Balkans, 828–829
Ball, Joseph, 114(s)
Ballard, Martha, 267
Ballinger, Richard, 579
Baltimore
   fire in, 516
   population of, 511
   transportation revolution in, 289
Bandung Conference, 741
Bank of the United States, 232–233, 275
   Jackson and, 310–311
   Second, 261, 281, 318
Banks and banking
   African Americans in, 513
   bailouts of, 841
   Black Tuesday and, 637
   deregulation of under Clinton, 829
   deregulation of under Reagan, 807
   Farmers' Alliance on, 542
   in the Great Depression, 647–648
   in industrial consolidation, 486
   under Jackson, 310–311
   Panic of 1819, 281–282
   redlining by, 720–721
   regulation of, 647–648
   in the twenties, 618–619, 620
   Wilson's reforms of, 580–581
Banneker, Benjamin, 234, 234(s)
Baptist churches
   abolitionism and, 347
   black, 412
   enslaved people in, 325
   rejection of class and racial distinctions by, 176–177
   Second Great Awakening and, 332
Barbados, 84, 84(m), 85, 87(m)
   slave laws in, 85
   slave markets, 108
Barbary pirates, 198, 258
Barbary States, 257
Barnes, Christine, 182(s)
Barnett, Ross, 756
Barrelhouses, 529
Bartholdi, Frédéric-Auguste, 505
Barton, Clara, 399
Bartram, William, 220
Baseball, 527, 528, 730, 736
Batallón de San Patricios, 363(i)
Bates, Edward, 396(i)
Bates, Ruby, 641–642
Batista, Fulgencio, 742
Battle of Britain, 665
Battle of the Little Bighorn (1876), 455, 456(i)
Bayard Smith, Margaret, 306
Bay of Pigs, Cuba, 745–746, 747(s)
Beans, 4–5, 10
Beatles, 771
Beats, 727, 728(i)
Becoming America (Butler), 159(s)
Beecher, Catharine, 378
Beecher, Henry, 378
Beecher, Lyman, 333–334(s), 378
Beef trust, 576
Begin, Menachem, 786
Belarus, 820–821
Belgium, in World War II, 664
Bell, Alexander Graham, 484
Bell, John, 385, 385(m)
Bellamy, Edward, 534
Bellow, Saul, 653
Benedict, Ruth, 565, 622
Benezet, Anthony, 224
Benign neglect, 160
Berkeley (California), 617
   Asian American and Black studies at, 774
   New Left in, 769–770
Berkeley, William, 63–64, 65
Berkman, Alexander, 498
Berlin airlift, 704, 704(i)
Berlin Wall, 747, 810(s), 820
Bernstein, Barton J., 661(s)
Bernstein, Carl, 781–782
Berry, Chuck, 725
Berryman, Clifford K., 614(i), 660(i)
Bessemer, Henry, 484
Bethune, Mary McLeod, 654, 725
Bett, Mum, 222
Beveridge, Albert, 592(s)
Bibb, Henry, 378
Bickerdyke, Mary Ann "Mother," 399
Bicycles, 526(i)
Biddle, Nicholas, 310
Biden, Joseph, 818(i), 841
"Bigger Than a Hamburger" (Baker), 735(s)
Big labor, 657
"Big stick" diplomacy, 595
Bilbo, Theodore, 730
Bilingual education, 774
Billion Dollar Congress, 539
Bill of Rights, 208–209, 210, 230, 231, 231–232(s)
   the Alien and Sedition Acts and, 243–244
   Japanese American internment and, 678
   Red Scare abridgment of, 610–611
Biltmore, 525
Bin Laden, Osama, 785, 820, 836, 844
Birch, William Russell, 235(i)
Birmingham (Alabama), 475, 645
   Freedom Rides in, 756
   Kennedy's intervention in, 756–758
   population of, 511
Birney, James G., 359
Birth control, 568. *See also* Contraception
Birth of a Nation (film), 581–582
Birthrate
   baby boom, 719
   Europe, 17
Bison, 365
   role of for American Indians, 453, 453(m)
   slaughter of, 455–456
   white hunters in decimating, 455
"Black Cabinet," 657
Black capitalism, 780
Black codes, 419(s), 420
Black Cross Nurses, 625
Black Elk, 459
Black Friday (1893), 537
Black Hawk, 314
Black Hills Treaty Council, 565
"Black Inventory of the New Deal" (Davis), 658(s)
Black Kettle, 454
Black Legend, 34(i)
Black Lives Matter movement, 843
Black nationalism, 620, 625
Black Panther Party, 761, 764–765(s)
Black power, 760–761
Black Star Line, 625
Black Student Union, 774
Black Tuesday, 637
Blacklisting, 712
Blackwell, W. A., 514
Blair, Montgomery, 396(i)
Blanc, Honoré, 266
Bleeding Kansas, 379–380, 380(i), 384

Bletchley Park, England, 673
Blitzkrieg, 664
Blood and Sand (film), 621(i), 634(s)
Bloomers, 526(i)
Blues, 529, 623–624
Boas, Franz, 565, 622
Bob Jones University, 796
Boland Amendments (1982, 1984), 811, 813
Bolivia, 25
Boll weevils, 513
Bolsheviks, 602, 610, 700
Bonaparte, Napoleon, 258–259, 275
Bonneville Dam, 649
Bonus Army, 645
Book of Mormon, The, 334
Boom and bust cycles, 587
Boomtowns, 332, 460
Boone, Daniel, 180
Booth, John Wilkes, 409
Border Patrol, 629
Bosnia-Herzegovina, 828–829
Bosses, political, 517–519, 557, 572
Boston, 74, 102(i)
   Davenport's sermons in, 134
   desegregation in, 762, 762(i)
   fire in, 516
   fugitives from slavery in, 378
   immigrant communities in, 503
   impressment riots in, 152
   industry in, 482
   Meeting of Colored Citizens of, 372(s)
   police strike in, 611
   population of, 511
   school busing in, 762, 762(i)
   suburbs around, 516
   time zone in, 483
Boston Almshouse, 102
Boston Committee of Public Safety, 604(i)
Bostonians, The (James), 528
Boston Indian Citizenship Association, 457
Boston marriages, 528
Boston Massacre, 167, 167–168(s), 168
Boston School Committee, 762
Boston Tea Party, 168–169, 169(s), 221
Boulder Dam, 649
Bow and arrow, 11
Bowdoin, James, 202–203
Bowers, Henry F., 507
Boxer uprising (1900), 596, 596(i)
Boxing, 527, 567
Brace, Charles Loring, 520(s)
Braceros, 676, 744
Braddock, Edward, 151–152
Bradford, William, 72
Brady Handgun Violence Prevention Act (1993), 827–828
Bram, Henry, 413(s)
Brant, Joseph, 180
Brazil, 39
   rain forest destruction in, 822
   sugar production in, 25
Bread riots, 135
Breaker boys, 492(i), 493
Breckinridge, John, 385, 385(m)
Breen, T. H., 103(s)
Breitman, Richard, 690–691(s)

Brexit, 848
Brezhnev, Leonid, 780, 781, 785
Bridges, 514
Brief Account of the Destruction of the Indies, A (Las Casas), 35
Brinksmanship, 740
Britain, Battle of, 665
British Broadcasting Corporation (BBC), 822
Broadening the Franchise (Keyssar), 307–308(s)
Brodhead, Daniel, 226(s)
Brook Farm, 340
Brooklyn (New York), Hooverville in, 639
Brooklyn Bridge, 514, 522(s)
Brooklyn Dodgers, 721
Brooks, Preston, 380
Brotherhood of Sleeping Car Porters, 675
Brown Berets, 773
Brown, Charlotte Hawkins, 564
Brown, Edmund "Pat," 770
Brown, John, 379–380, 384
   Exodusters and, 429
Brown, Moses, 265
Brown v. Board of Education of Topeka, Kansas, 731–732, 733(s), 763(s)
   Goldwater on, 775–776
   school busing and, 761, 762(i)
Brownsville (Texas), 578
Broz, Josip, 702
Bryan, Hazel, 734(i)
Bryan, William Jennings, 545–546, 546(m), 578
   Populists and, 547
   in the Scopes trial, 627, 627–628(s), 635–636(s)
Bryce, James, 520(s), 538
Buchanan, James, 374, 380, 385, 386
Buchenwald concentration camp, 687, 688(i)
Buchtel (Ohio), 495(i)
Buckley, William F., 775
Buffalo. *See* Bison
Buffalo Bill's Wild West and Congress of Rough Riders of the World, 464(s)
Buffalo (New York), population of, 511
Buffalo soldiers, 455
Bulgaria, fall of the Soviet regime in, 819
Bulger, Harry, 529(i)
Bull Moose Party, 579
Bull Run, First Battle of (1861), 391, 394(m)
Bull Run, Second Battle of (1862), 393
Bully pulpit, 576
Bunker Hill, Battle of (1775), 175, 176(i), 190(m), 202
Bureau of Corporations, 576
Bureau of Indian Affairs (BIA), 744, 774
Bureau of Investigation, 612
Bureau of Refugees, Freedmen, and Abandoned Lands. *See* Freedmen's Bureau
Burgoyne, John, 186, 190(m)
Burke, Tarana, 852
Burns, Anthony, 378
Burr, Aaron, 241, 245–246, 270(s)
Burroughs, Nannie Helen, 561
Burroughs, William S., 728(i)
Bus boycott, Montgomery, 732, 732(i)
Bush, Abigail, 347
Bush Doctrine, 837
Bush, George H. W., 817–819
   arms reduction treaty of, 821

   in the election of 1992, 825
   Iran-Contra affair and, 813
   Noriega and, 823
   Operation Desert Storm and, 823–824, 839
Bush, George W., 833–840
   9/11 attacks and, 836
   the Great Recession and, 840
   on Iraq, 838(s)
   Iraq War and, 837–839
   presidential nomination acceptance speech, 834(s)
   second term of, 839–840
Bushman, Richard, 103
Bushnell, Horace, 299(i)
Business. *See also* Industrialization
   computer revolution in, 829–830
   consolidation in, 830
   management in, 488
   women in, after the Revolution, 219
Butler, Andrew, 380
Butler, Benjamin, 393
Butler, Jon, 159(s)
Butte (Montana), 462–463

C

Cable News Network (CNN), 822
Cabot, Francis, 266–267
Cacao, 25
Caddo Indians, 46(m), 51, 120
Cahokia people, 13, 39
Calhoun, John C., 303, 310, 328(s), 369, 369–370(s), 369(i)
California
   after World War II, 721
   agricultural worker strikes in, 642, 643, 773
   anti-Chinese assaults in, 471
   Asian Americans in the Great Depression, 642–643
   Chinese immigrants in, 471
   civil rights movement in, 736–737
   Compromise of 1850 and, 368–370
   expansion into, 359–360
   gold rush in, 357, 363–364, 364(i), 461
   growth of in the twenties, 617–618, 617(m)
   Hetch Hetchy valley in, 574–575
   immigrants in, 503, 831
   internment camps in, 678
   Ku Klux Klan in, 631
   lumber industry in, 463
   Okies in, 640
   refugees in, 811
   statehood of, 363
   tax revolt in, 795, 796(i)
   wagon trains to, 358(i)
   in World War II, 671
California Trail, 365(m)
Californios, 469–470
Calvert, Cecilius, 61
Calvin, John, 71, 74
Calvinism, 46
Cambodia
   immigrants from, 1990s to twenty-first century, 831, 831(f)
   invasion of, 753
Cameron, Simon, 392
Camp David accords, 786
Camp followers, 182, 187

Index

Canada
　British control over, 153, 153(m)
　colonial expansion in, 41
　Embargo Act and, 262
　exports to, 587
　fugitives from slavery in, 371
　in the Group of Seven (G7), 821
　Japanese American internment in, 679
　NAFTA and, 828
　Oregon and, 359
　Seven Years' War and, 153(m)
　War of 1812 and, 275
Canals, 278–279, 287, 289
Cane Ridge (Kentucky), camp meeting at, 332
Cape of Good Hope, 18, 19(m)
Cape Verde Islands, 21
Capitalism, 26
　black, 780
　communism on, 700, 702
　Haymarket incident and, 494–495
　laissez-faire, 532–533
　the New Deal and, 651
　progressivism and, 556
　reform, after World War II, 718, 745
　Russian Revolution and, 606–607
　social gospel and, 556
　socialism and, 498
　Wilson on, 606–607
Capitol, U.S., 234–235, 235(i)
Captains of industry, 485
Caputo, Philip, 751(s)
Caravels, 18
Carbon paper, 483
Carey, Matthew, 337–338(s)
Caribbean
　immigrants from, 1960–2000, 809
　immigrants from, 1990s to twenty-first century, 830–831, 831(f)
　imperialism in, 586
　Roosevelt Corollary on, 595
　slavery in, 33
　Spanish exploration of, 3
　Wilson and, 598
Carmichael, Stokely, 761
Carnegie, Andrew, 482, 485
　Homestead strike and, 496–497, 498(i)
　Morgan and, 485
　on philanthropy, 533, 534(s)
　on the Philippines, 593
Carolinas
　labor in, 87–88
　slavery in, 110
Carpetbaggers, 428
Carson, Kit, 364
Carson, Rachel, 794
Carter, Dan T., 797(s)
Carter, Jimmy, 777–778, 782–785
　the Christian Right and, 796
　economic policies and, 782–784, 789(s)
　in the election of 1980, 804, 806(m)
　foreign policy under, 784–786
　"Malaise Speech," 789(s)
　Nicaragua and, 811
Carteret, George, 91
"Case against the Reds, The" (Palmer), 611(s)
Casey, William, 811
Cash-and-carry provisions, 666

Cash crops, 58, 467
Cass, Lewis, 368
Caste system, 33–34
Castro, Fidel, 742, 746–747, 747(s)
Catawba people, 120
Catcher in the Rye (Salinger), 728
Catherine of Aragon, 71
Catholics
　American Indians and, 41
　blamed for fallen women, 337
　costs of colonization and, 34–36
　cultural divisions and, 287
　immigrants, 330, 502, 628–629
　immigrants as white or not, 506
　immigration restrictions against, 506
　Irish immigrants, 289
　Ku Klux Klan on, 630
　in Maryland, 61–62
　mission system and, 50(i)
　nativists on, 338
　the New Right and, 796
　prejudice against, 290
　as president, 745
　Protestant Reformation and, 70–71
　revolutionary era, 196
　Spanish conquest and, 33
　Spanish reconquest and, 18, 20
　in the twenties, 628–629
Catlin, George, 336
Cato, George, 111–112(s)
Cat on a Hot Tin Roof (film), 724
Catt, Carrie Chapman, 599
Cattle ranches, 463–467, 464(s)
　commercial, 465–467
　foreign investment in, 451, 465
Causation, 17, 24, 54, 130, 185, 257, 272, 287, 309, 319, 330, 357, 411
　connecting distant causes to immediate causes, 65–66
　evaluating, 157–158
　identifying, 149
　showing in short-answer question responses, 28–29
　using in historical arguments, 47–49
Cavelier, René-Robert, 45
Caverly, Leon H., 602(i)
Cayuse Indians, 364
Cazenovia (New York), 371(i)
Ceausescu, Nicolae, 819
Cell phones, 830
Census, U.S.
　of 1850, 292(s)
　of 1920, 617
　of 2010, 847
Centennial Exposition (1876), 505
Central America, anticommunist interventions in, 811
Central Intelligence Agency (CIA), 703–704
　Bay of Pigs and, 745–746
　intervention in Afghanistan, 785–786
　intervention in Chile, 780
　intervention in Nicaragua, 811
　interventions in the Middle East, Latin America, and Africa, 741–742
　Senate hearing on clandestine activities by, 785–786

　Watergate scandal and, 781–782
Central Pacific Company, 451
Central Powers, 599–609, 599(m)
A Century of Dishonor (Jackson), 457
Chamberlain, Samuel, 363(i)
Chambers, John Whiteclay II, 609(s)
Chambers, Whittaker, 713
Champlain, Samuel de, 44
Chancellorsville, Battle of (1863), 403
Change, 30
Channing, William Ellery, 334
Charitable organizations, 295–296, 337
　Gilded Age, 525
　in the Great Depression, 638
Charity, philanthropy vs., 533
Charles I (King of England), 61–62, 77
Charles I (King of Spain), 35
Charles II (King of England), 62, 65, 77, 85, 90, 93, 100, 109
Charles V (Holy Roman Emperor), 35
Charleston (South Carolina), 86, 101(i), 280
　American Revolution in, 191, 192(m)
　nullification and, 318(i)
　slave trade in, 86, 322(i)
　tea boycott in, 168
Charleston Mercury, 397(s)
Chase, Hal, 728(i)
Chase, Salmon P., 396(i)
Chattanooga, Battle of (1863), 404
Chavez, Cesar, 773
Cheever, John, 653
Cheney, Richard, 836
Cherokee Nation v. Georgia, 314
Cherokee people, 120
　in the American Revolution, 181
　civilization of, 452
　in the Civil War, 393, 409
　land conflicts with, 202
　Sand Creek massacre of, 454–455
　in Seven Years' War, 151
　Trail of Tears, 313–316, 316(i)
　in War of 1812, 275
　women's rights among, 348
Chesapeake Indians, 61–62, 61(m)
Chesapeake & Ohio Railroad, 564
Chesapeake region
　rice cultivation in, 109, 110
　slavery in, 109, 110
Chevrolet, 616, 616(i)
Cheyenne Indians, 364
　Custer and, 455
　Kansas-Nebraska Act and, 379
　Sand Creek Massacre, 408–409
Chicago
　African American population of, 513
　fire in, 516
　gays and lesbians in, 528
　ghetto riots in, 761
　the great migration to, 613
　Haymarket Square, 494–495
　immigrants in, 503, 831
　industry in, 482
　Intersection of State Street and Madison Street, Chicago (photograph), 515(s)
　Irish immigrants in, 289

I-6

Ku Klux Klan in, 630
Polish immigrants in, 503(i)
race riots of 1919 in, 613
railroad strike in, 497(m)
settlement houses in, 557
skyscrapers in, 484
slaughterhouses in, 463
streets in, 517
trolleys in, 515
World's Columbian Exposition, 529
Chicago Defender (newspaper), 513
Chicago Student Non-Violent Coordinating Committee Leaflet, 765(s)
Chicanos, 773–774
Chickasaw Indians, 202
Child labor, 254(s), 492–493, 516
of enslaved people, 323
globalization and, 822
muckrakers on, 557
outlawed, 580
progressivism on, 559, 571
in the twenties, 614
unions on, 494
Children
baby boom, 719
colonial era, 131
digital technology and, 830
of enslaved people, 322
of formerly enslaved people, 414, 415
labor of, 492–493
in western migration, 358–359, 358(s)
Children's Bureau, 559, 633
Chile, Pinochet in, 825
China
Boxer uprising in, 596, 596(i)
climate change and, 846–847
colonial-era trade, 98
communist revolution in, 705
environmental damage in, 822
globalization and, 822
immigrants from, 1990s to twenty-first century, 831, 831(f)
Japanese invasion of Manchuria, 667
manufacturing in, regulation of, 822
missionaries in, 588
Nixon and, 777, 780
Open Door policy in, 596–597, 662
Opium Wars in, 470
spice trade with, 17
Tiananmen Square massacre, 823
trade with, 98, 238, 238(i), 280, 373–374, 587
China, People's Republic of, 705
Korean War and, 706–709
Nixon and, 777, 780
overtures of in the Middle East, Latin America, and Africa, 741
in the United Nations, 706
Vietnam and, 749
Chinatowns, 503, 736
Chinese Americans
affirmative action and, 774
civil rights movement and, 736
in the Great Depression, 643
in the twenties, 630
in World War II, 679
Chinese Exclusion Act (1882), 471, 471(s), 502, 630
repealed, 679, 736
Chinese for Affirmative Action, 774
Chinese immigrants
California gold rush and, 364, 364(i)
equal protection for, 506(s)
labor contracts with, 502
legislation against, 471, 502
opium and, 567
in railroad building, 451(i)
restrictions on, 460
Rock Springs massacre of, 470(i), 471
in the twenties, 630
in unions, 494
vaudeville on, 529(i)
in the West, 470–471
Chinese View of the Statue of Liberty, A (Song Bo), 505(s)
Chinook people, 11
Chisholm Trail, 463
Chivington, John M., 409
Chocolate, 25
Choctaw Indians, 45, 202
in Seven Years' War, 151
Cholera, 359, 452, 516
Christian Anti-Communist Crusade, 775
Christian Crusade, 775
Christian Right, 791, 796
Christianity
Boxer uprising and, 596, 596(i)
conversion of native peoples to, 34–36, 34(i)
costs of colonization and, 34–36
the New Right and, 795–796, 797(s)
Second Great Awakening, 332–334
slavery justified in, 28, 326
social gospel in, 519, 556
Spanish exploration and, 18
Christianity and the Social Crisis (Rauschenbusch), 556
Christopher, Warren, 785(s)
Chumash Indians, 11
Church, Benjamin, 124–125(s)
Church, Frank, 785–787
Church of England, 60, 76
Protestant Reformation and, 70–71
Puritans and, 74, 75–76
Church of Jesus Christ of Latter-Day Saints. *See* Mormons
Churchill, Winston, 667, 667(i), 682, 683
on the iron curtain, 701, 705(m)
Yalta Agreement and, 685
Cigarette manufacturing, 475
Cincinnati (Ohio), 262
growth of, 281, 288
industry in, 482
population of, 511
racial violence in, 302
seamstresses in, 400–401
CIO. *See* Congress of Industrial Organizations (CIO)
Cisco Kid, The (TV show), 723
Citizenship
of African Americans, 421
of American Indians, 506, 630
of Californios, 469
immigrants and, 504, 506, 507
of Japanese Americans, 679, 737
voting rights and, 559

City bosses, 517–519
City managers, 572
City upon a Hill, 73
Civic housekeeping, 557
Civil disobedience, 732
Civil Disobedience (Thoreau), 336
Civilian Conservation Corps (CCC), 649, 650(s), 657
Civil Liberties Unit, 657
Civil rights
in the 1960s, 755–765
Bill of Rights on, 208–209, 210, 231, 231–232(s)
conservatism on, 775
of freedpeople, 412
legislation in the 1950s and 1960s, 744
Mexican Americans, 676
in Reconstruction, 414
Red Scare abridgment of, 610–611
in state constitutions, 196
war on terrorism and, 836–837, 845–846
in World War II, 675–677, 678–680, 690
Civil Rights Act (1866), 420, 436, 441(s)
Civil Rights Act (1875), 76, 436
Civil Rights Act (1964), 758, 772, 776
Civil rights movement, 690, 697, 729–738
beginning of, 737–738(s)
black power and, 760–761
Freedom Rides in, 756
Freedom Summer in, 758–760
Kennedy's support of, 756–758
Kennedy vs. Nixon in, 745
Mexican American, 676
Montgomery bus boycott in, 732, 732(i)
origins of, 675–677
rise of the southern, 729–735, 730(i)
school busing and, 761–762, 762(i)
school segregation and, 730, 731–732, 733, 734(i)
sit-ins in, 734(m), 735, 735(s), 764(s)
suspected Communist influence in, 715
voting rights and, 758
in the West, 736–737
white resistance to desegregation and, 733–735, 733(s), 734(i)
women in, 771–773
Civil Rights Section, 657
Civil service, 519, 644
Civil War, 355, 391–410
African Americans and American Indians in, 392, 393, 394, 405–406
American Indians living west of the Mississippi after, 452
brutality of, 394, 397–398, 407(s), 408–409
dissent and protests in, 399–401, 400(i)
early battles in, 391–394, 394(m)
end of, 409
final battles of, 406–409
freedom after, 411–417
key Union victories in, 403–405, 404(m)
life and death on the battlefield in, 397–398
northern economic expansion in, 398–399
preparations for, 390–392
Reconstruction after, 411–433
secession of the South and, 385–386(s), 385–387, 386(m), 389–390
telegraphs in, 486
transformations from, 398–401
victory in, 403–410

I-7

Index

Civil War (Continued)
  as war against slavery, 395
  why Union soldiers fought in, 408–409(s)
  women in, 398, 399
  women spies in, 391
Civil Works Administration (CWA), 649, 654
Clark, William, 259–260, 259(s), 260(m)
Class revolts, 91
Clay, Henry, 277, 283, 303, 309, 311, 349, 359, 369, 369(i)
Clay Compromise Measures, The (Calhoun), 369–370(s)
Clayton Antitrust Act (1914), 581
Clean Air Act (1971), 794
Clean Air Act (1990), 818
"Clear and present danger" doctrine, 610, 713
Clemenceau, Georges, 606
Clemens, Samuel, 461, 524
Clerical workers, 492, 526
Clermont (steamboat), 264(i), 265
Cleveland, Grover, 538
  depression of 1893 and, 544–545
  in election of 1892, 543
  Hawaii annexation and, 587
Cleveland (Ohio)
  Black Lives Matter in, 843
  ghetto riots in, 761
  population of, 511
  progressivism in, 573
  sewage disposal in, 517
  streets in, 517
Cleveland Indians, 736
Cliff dwellings, 10, 11(i)
Climate change, 822, 847
  fifteenth-century, 17
  settling of the Americas and, 5(m)
Clinton, Bill, 825, 827
  domestic and economic policy of, 827–829
  global challenges facing, 828–829
  on health care, 827, 827(s)
  impeachment of, 829
  reelection of, 828
Clinton, Henry, 222
Clinton, Hillary Rodham, 826, 827
  in the 2016 election, 848–849
  as secretary of state, 844
Clooney, Rosemary, 725
Cloth industry
  global trade in, 98
  Navigation Acts and, 101
  in South Carolina, 88
  technology in, 265–266
Clothing factories
  in tenements, 516
  in World War II, 670, 671
Coal mining, 493, 576
  child labor in, 492(i), 493
Codebreakers, 673
Codex Mendoza, 2(i)
Cody, William F. "Buffalo Bill," 464(s)
Coercive Acts (England, 1774), 169–170, 174
Coeur d'Alene (Idaho), 499
Coffeehouses, 99, 177
Coffin, Catherine, 370
Coffin, Levi, 370
Cold Spring (New York), 401

Cold War, 705(m), 803
  anticommunism and, 748–749
  civil rights movement and, 736, 756
  conflict management after, 823–825
  containment policy in, 700–701
  early, 699–709
  end of the, 809–821
  espionage in, 711
  expansion of, 739–747
  fall of the Soviet Union and, 819–821, 820(m)
  fighting communism at home in, 710–715
  hardening of positions in, 703
  human rights and, 811–812
  the Internet and, 830
  Kennedy and, 756–757
  Korean War in, 706–709
  McCarthyism in, 714–715
  Middle East, Latin America, and Africa interventions in, 741–743
  military containment in, 703–706
  mutual misunderstandings in, 700–702
  Nixon and, 778, 780–781
  nuclear de-escalation and, 815–816
  nuclear freeze movement and, 814–816, 815(i)
  origins of, 699–702
  Red Scare in, 710–715
  space race in, 744
  the Truman Doctrine in, 702–703
  Vietnam and, 748–754
  Wallace on, 701(s), 702
Cole, Nathan, 138(s)
Cole, Thomas, 223(s), 335(i), 336
Collective bargaining, 494
Colleges and universities
  after World War II, 717, 719
  colonial era, 119
  desegregation of, 730
Collet, John, 140(s)
Collier, John, 658
Collier's (magazine), 557
Colombia, Panama Canal and, 595
Colonial America, 40–145
  American Indian alliances and conflict in, 78
  American Indian resistance in, 49–50, 118–120
  Atlantic economy in, 98–106
  consumer cultures in, 101–103
  cost of Seven Year's War in, 152–154
  costs and benefits of empire in, 100–102
  daily life in, 66–69
  economic competition in, 94–95
  ethnicity and racial diversity in, 109–110
  European wars and, 77–78
  expansion and conflict in, 93–95, 93(m)
  grievances against the British, 160–161, 162–165
  identities in, 159(s), 173
  imperial conflicts and, 149–159
  international conflicts and, 149–159
  labor in, 86–88, 94
  political awakenings in, 135–136, 147
  religion in, 61–62, 68, 70–76, 78–82, 131–133
  resistance to Britain in, 159–172
  rural conditions, 94
  sex ratios in, 67, 110
  southern frontier conflicts, 122–123
  trade and, 98–102, 99(m)
  unity in, 161–165
  westward expansion of, 155

Colonies, 40–97
  expansion and conflict in, 94–95
  New England, 70–82
  West Indies, 83–86, 83(i), 87(m)
Colonization, defined, 45
Colorado
  American Indians displaced in, 408–409
  cattle ranching in, 465
  internment camps in, 678
  Populists and, 547
Colored Farmers' Alliance, 542
Colored Masons, 477
Colored Odd Fellows, 477
Colored Orphan Asylum, 400, 400(i)
Coltrane, John, 727
Columbia (Tennessee), race riot in, 730
Columbia Broadcasting System (CBS), 722
Columbian Exchange, 3, 21, 24–29, 25(i), 26(m), 33, 39
  English economy and, 54–55
  Puritans and, 74
Columbus, Christopher, 19–21, 20(m), 30, 31
Comanche people, 260(m), 360, 364–365
  in the Civil War, 393
  civilization of, 452
  claims contested by, 359
  epidemics among, 359, 364
  Texas recognized by, 313
Combahee River Collective, 792
Come outer movement, 347
Comic books, 724, 724(s)
Coming Nation, The, 535(s)
Comintern, 610
Command of the Army Act (1867), 422
Commission governments, 572–573
Commission on the Status of Women, 772
Committee for the Re-Election of the President, 781
Committee on Public Information (CPI), 604
Committees of correspondence, 161, 168, 169–170, 174
Committees of safety, 169
Commodity Credit Corporation, 548
"Commodore Perry at the Loo Choo Isles" (*New York Daily Times*), 374(s)
Common law, 74–75
Common Sense (Paine), 177, 177(s), 212(s)
Common Sense Book of Baby and Child Care (Spock), 725
Commonwealth of Independent States, 820–821
Communication
  industrialization and, 484
  newspapers in, 290–291
  telephone, 484
Communications (Edwards), 654(i)
Communism
  in Cambodia, 753
  capitalism vs., 700, 702
  in China, 705
  Chinese Americans and, 736
  conservativism in the 1960s and, 775
  Eisenhower Doctrine on, 742
  fall of the Soviet Union and, 819–821, 820(m)
  fear of in the twenties, 610–611
  human rights and the fight against, 811–812
  Kennedy and, 745–747
  Levitt on housing and, 720

McCarthyism and, 714–715
Reagan on, 809–810
Red Scare and, 610–612, 612(s), 710–715
religious revival in the 1950s and, 727
Russian Revolution and, 602, 606–607
in Vietnam, 748–754
Communist Control Act (1954), 715
Communist Party
in the Great Depression, 645
on the New Deal, 651
Smith Act violations by, 713
in World War II, 678
Community Action Program, 768
Community Relations Service, 758
Como, Perry, 725
Companionate marriage, 267
Comparison, 14, 43, 195, 272, 287, 367, 389
in historical arguments, 47–49
thesis statements based on, 51–53
Compassionate conservatism, 834
Comprehensive Anti-Apartheid Act (1986), 812
Comprehensive Environmental Response, Compensation, and Liability Act (1980), 795
Compromise of 1850, 368–370, 379(m)
Compromise of 1877, 436–437
Computers, 829–831, 851–852
Comstock Lode, 461, 462
Concentration camps, 678–679, 687–689, 688(i), 690–691(s)
Concerning the Just Causes of the War against the Indians (Sepúlveda), 35
Concord, Battle of, 175
Coney Island, 529
Confederate States of America, 385–386(s), 385–389, 386(m)
amnesty for officials from, 412, 417, 435(s)
conflict and dissent in, 401
devotion to the "Lost Cause" in, 418(i)
end of the war and, 409
Confession Program, 736
Confidence and Concern, 788(s)
Confiscation acts, 393
Conflicts of interest, 539
Conglomerates, 830
Congo, civil war in, 742
Congress
in Federal Hall, 231(i)
gag rule of 1836, 313
industrialization and, 539–540
inefficiency of, 539
the New Deal and, 659
police actions and, 707–708
war powers and, 753–754
Congress of Industrial Organizations (CIO), 656–657
Congress of Racial Equality (CORE), 676, 729
Freedom Rides, 756
Freedom Summer and, 758–760
Free Speech Movement and, 770
Congressional Anti-Lynching Bill, 585(s)
Congressional Government (Wilson), 538
Connecticut, 75
Constitution ratified by, 210, 211(t)
royal charter of, 77
Connor, Eugene "Bull," 756
Conquistadors, 3, 20(m), 30–33, 452
wealth of, 25

Conscience of a Conservative, The (Goldwater), 775
Conscience Whigs, 349
Consciousness-raising groups, 772
Conservation. *See also* Environment
energy, 782–784
Conservatism, 697
Bush, George H. W., and, 817–819
Bush, George W., and, 834–836
Carter and, 782–784
Christian, 796
on the Clintons, 828
compassionate, 834
"kinder and gentler," 817–818
Modern Republicanism and, 743–744
neoconservatives in, 796
new forms of, 795–796
Nixon and, 778–779
persistence of liberalism and, 791–797
pragmatic, 779–780
Reaganomics and, 804–808
revival of in the 1960s, 775–776
social, 808–809
tax revolt and, 795, 796(i)
Tea Party movement, 843
triumph of in 1980–1992, 804–816
Trump and, 848–851
Conservative coalition, 659
Constitution, 227(s). *See also individual amendments to*
amendments to, 231, 231–232(s)
Bill of Rights in, 208–209, 231, 231–232(s)
Constitutional Convention and, 207–209
debates over, 212–216(s)
imperial presidency and, 707–708
implied powers clause in, 261
laissez-faire and, 532
ratification of, 146(i), 209–211, 211(t)
Reconstruction amendments, 438
slavery abolished in, 409
Supreme Court's authority in interpreting, 261
Constitutional Convention (1787), 207–209
Constitutional Union Party, 385, 385(m)
Constructive engagement, 812
Consumer culture, 447, 553
colonial, 101–102
emergence of the middle class and, 291–293, 291(i)
in the Gilded Age, 524–525, 527(s)
industrialization and, 488(i)
teenage culture and, 724
in the twenties, 613–616
Consumer Products Safety Commission, 779
Consumer revolution, 101–102
Consumer safety, 577, 578(i), 779
Containment policy, 700–701, 748
Bush Doctrine on, 837
economic, 703
military containment, 703–706
nuclear weapons in, 740–741
Operation Desert Storm and, 824
Context, 8–10, 90, 173
establishing in an essay introduction, 184
presenting in a historical argument, 95–97
Continental Army, 188–189
back pay of, 147, 198
building, 176–177

camp followers, 182, 187
established, 174
Hamilton in, 202
Lafayette in, 188(i)
military takeover threatened by, 198
mutiny in, 198
Shays in, 202
shortages in, 183
smallpox in, 176, 186
victories of, 186, 191–193
Continental Congress, 174, 178, 189–190
American Indian affairs and, 198–199
Articles of Confederation and, 196–197, 197(s)
Continental Army and, 174, 189, 198
Declaration of Independence and, 178–179
land claims and, 198–200
peace offer rejected by, 185
return of to Philadelphia, 186
Second, 175, 199
Continuity, 30, 389
Contraband, 393
Contraception, 568, 769, 808
Contract with America, 828
Contras, 811, 813, 814(s)
Convict lease system, 474
Conwell, Russell, 533
Coolidge, Calvin, 611, 615
in the election of 1924, 632–633, 633(m)
Garvey deported by, 625
Copper mining, 462
Copperheads, 401
Corbin, Margaret, 187
Corbin, Richard, 115(s)
Corn, 4–5, 13
Cornplanter, 200, 200(i)
Cornstalk, 180
Cornwallis, Charles, 191
Corporations
consolidation in, 830
growth of, 487–489, 487(s), 488(i)
laissez-faire and, 533
multinational, 821–822
profits of in the twenties, 618
support of in the twenties, 613–614
working conditions in, 491
Corps of Discovery, 259–260, 260(m)
Corrupt bargain, 303
Cortés, Hernán, 20(m), 31–33, 31(i)
Cosby, William, 135–136
Cotton
boll weevil infestations, 513
Civil War and, 398
expansion of, 281, 321, 321(m)
manufacturing, 254(s), 265–266
Navigation Acts on, 100–101
in the New South, 475(m)
Panic of 1837 and, 295–296
production levels of, 322, 540
slavery and, 267–270, 319
technology and expanded production of, 267–270, 268(t)
Cotton gin, 265–266, 267–268, 268(i), 319, 354(i)
Cotton, John, 75–76
Coughlin, Charles E., 651(i), 652, 653
Council Bluffs (Iowa), 644–645
Council for Mutual Economic Assistance, 704–705

Counterculture, 771, 791
Country music, 529
Court-packing plan, 659
Covenant Chain, 120
Cowboys, 451, 460, 463–465
Coxey, Jacob, 544
Coxey's army, 544
Craft work, decline of, 294–295
Crater Lake, 573
Crawford, William, 303
Crazy Horse, 456(i)
Creationism, 626–627, 635–636(s), 796
Credit
  effect of on social conventions, 621
  in the twenties, 616, 618, 619
Crédit Mobilier, 451–452
Creek people, 275, 275(m)
  civilization of, 452
  land conflicts with, 202
  in Seven Years' War, 151
Creel, George, 604
Crime
  in cities, 517
  in immigrant neighborhoods, 503–504
  nativists on, 338
Crimea, annexation of, 846
Criminal justice system
  African Americans in, 409
  Black Lives Matter and, 843
  Fugitive Slave Act on, 370
  juvenile, 567–568
  Warren court on, 769
Criollos, 34
Crisis (magazine), 584(s), 658(s)
Crisis of masculinity, 526–527, 588
Crittenden, John, 386–387
Crittenden plan, 386–387
Croatia, 828–829
Cromwell, Oliver, 62, 77, 100
Cronkite, Walter, 752
Cross Keys, Battle of (1862), 394(m)
"Cross of gold" speech (Bryan), 545
Crow Indians, Indian Reorganization Act and, 658
Cuba, 328
  Bay of Pigs, 745–746
  CIA intervention in, 742
  filibusters to, 374
  immigrants from, 502
  independence from Spain, 589–592, 589(i)
  normalization of diplomatic relations with, 846
  pacification of, 593
  U.S. intervention in, 589–592, 598
  War for Independence in, 589–592, 589(i)
Cuba Libre, 589
Cuban missile crisis, 745–746, 747(s)
Cubanidad, 589
Cubberly, E. P., 629
Cultivator, The (magazine), 298(s)
Cult of domesticity, 291–293
Culture
  of the 1950s, 722–725
  African American, 324–325, 513–514
  assimilation and, 508
  Gilded Age, 524–528
  globalization and, 821–822

  as justification for imperialism, 587–588, 595
  national, building, 330–331
  popular, in the 1970s, 791, 792
Cumberland Road, 264, 277
"Cure for Depressions" (Townsend), 651
Currency
  after the Revolution, 217
  in the Civil War, 398
  in the Revolution, 189–190
  silver backing of, 542, 545
Currency Act (England, 1764), 161, 162
Currier, Nathaniel, 366(i)
Curry, James, 323
Custer, George Armstrong, 455, 456(i)
Cuzco, 8
Czechoslovakia
  Communist coup in, 703
  fall of the Soviet regime in, 819
  German annexation of, 664
  Prague Spring in, 779
Czech Republic, 846

D

D Day (1944), 683
Dachau, 687
Da Gama, Vasco, 18
Daily Beast, 850(s)
Dakota Apartments (New York City), 524
Dakota Indians, 45, 446(i)
Dakota Territory, 467
Dance halls, 529
Dangerous Classes of New York and Twenty Years Among Them (Brace), 52(s)
Darragh, Lydia, 187
Darrow, Clarence, 512, 627, 627–628(s), 635–636(s)
Darwin, Charles, 533, 626, 627–628(s), 796
Daughters of Bilitis, 727
Daughters of Liberty, 162
Davenport, George, 264(t)
Davenport, James, 134
Davies, Lawrence E., 677(s)
Davis, Jefferson, 384–385
  Britain and, 395
  conscription act by, 401
  imprisonment of, 431
  inaugural address of, 385–386(s)
  secession of the South and, 391
Davis, John P., 658(s)
Davis, John W., 632, 633, 633(m)
Davis, Joseph, 297(i)
Davis, Miles, 727
Dawes Act (1887), 457, 658
Dawes, Henry, 457
Day, Doris, 724
Day, Madison, 415
Day, Rufus, 590(s)
Dayton (Ohio), 572
Dayton (Tennessee), 627
De Bry, Theodor, 34(i)
De Gaulle, Charles, 779
De Kalb, Johann Baron, 188
De Sahagún, Bernardino, 25(i)
De Tocqueville, Alexis, 306(s)
Dean, James, 723–724, 723(i)

Dean, John, 782
Dearborn (Michigan), Ford factory strike, 645
Death penalty, 817, 825
Debs, Eugene V., 498
  antiwar speech, 605(s)
  conviction of under the Espionage Act, 605
  in election of 1912, 580
Debt
  after the Revolution, 198, 217–218
  under Clinton, 829
  of farmers after the Revolution, 202–203
  of farmers in the nineteenth century, 540, 542
  in the Great Depression, 638
  Hamilton's agenda on, 232–233
  under Obama, 843
  under Reagan, 807
Declaration against Governor William Berkeley (Bacon), 64–65(s)
Declaration of Independence, 178–179, 179(s), 180(i), 193, 217, 532
  French Revolution influenced by, 238
  signers of in the Constitutional Convention, 207
Declaration of Sentiments, 347, 348(s)
Declaratory Act (England, 1766), 164, 165
Decolonization, 741
Deep Throat, 781–782
Deerskin Cloak (Powhatan), 56(i)
Defense of Marriage Act (1996), 828, 843
Deferred Action for Childhood Arrivals (DACA), 841–842
Deflation, 467
Deforestation, 13
Deindustrialization, 783
Delacroix, Eugène, 331
Delaware, 78, 93, 210, 211(t)
Delaware Indians, 93–94, 93(m), 95
  in the Civil War, 393
  in Seven Years' War, 150–151
Delineator, The (magazine), 527(s)
D'Emilio, John, 852–853(s)
Democratic National Convention
  of 1964, 759
  of 1968, 778–779
Democratic Party, 303, 378
  abolitionism and, 349
  African Americans in, 658, 659(s)
  after the Civil War, 438
  anti-Chinese movement in, 471
  black disfranchisement and, 476(m)
  Civil War and, 405
  congressional majority by, 538
  Copperheads, 401
  election of 1828 and, 305
  election of 1840 and, 317–318
  election of 1852 and, 373
  election of 1860, 384–385, 385(m)
  election of 1896, 545–546, 546(m)
  election of 1912, 580
  Greeley endorsed by, 435
  Hiss affair and, 712–713
  Jackson and, 309–310
  on Kansas-Nebraska Act, 379
  on Mexican-American War, 363
  Mississippi Freedom, 759
  the New Deal and, 651, 659

I-10

Redeemers, 431
  on slavery, 367, 380
  Truman and, 717–718
  in the twenties, 632–633
  in Wilmington (North Carolina) massacre, 547(i)
  workingmen's interests and, 295
Democratic-Republicans, 147, 241–246, 246(m), 255
  in election of 1828, 304
  expansion of federal powers by, 261–262, 277–278
  federal power limited by, 258
  national identity and, 257
  presidents from, 300
  Second Bank of the United States and, 261
  War of 1812 and, 274–275
Democratic Review, 359
Demographics. *See also* Census, U.S.
  baby boom, 719
  late twentieth to twenty-first century, 830–831, 831(f)
  nineteenth century, 290
  Sun and Rust Belt, 783(m)
  twenty-first century, 847–848
  of western migration, 358
Denby, Edward, 614, 614(i)
Deng, Xiaoping, 823
Denmark, in World War II, 664
Dennis v. United States, 713
Denver
  growth of in the twenties, 617
  Ku Klux Klan in, 630
  population of, 511
Department of Agriculture, 648
Department of Commerce and Labor, 576
Department of Energy, 784
Department of Health, Education, and Welfare, 744
Department of Homeland Security, 837
Department of Housing and Urban Affairs, 767
Department of the Interior, 648
Department of Transportation, 767
Department stores, 488, 492
Deportation
  of radicals in the Red Scare, 612, 710
  of undocumented Mexicans, 744
Depression of 1893, 537, 544–545
Deregulation
  under Carter, 784
  under Clinton, 829
  the Great Recession and, 840
  under Reagan, 805–806, 807
Desegregation, 787(s)
  backlash against, 761–762
  Kennedy and, 756–758
  for Mexican Americans, 736
  of public transportation, 409
  Supreme Court on, 730, 732
  white resistance to, 731–732, 733–735, 734(i)
Desert Land Act (1877), 468
Deskilling of labor, 294–295
Détente, 780, 784–786, 809
Detroit
  captured in War of 1812, 275
  ghetto riots in, 761
  immigrants in, 831

Ku Klux Klan in, 630
  progressivism in, 573
  race riots in, 676
Development, Relief, and Education for Alien Minors (DREAM) Act, 841
Dew, Thomas, 326, 328
Dewey, George, 593
Dewey, Thomas E., 683, 717–718
Dial, The, 336
Diary Entry (Trent), 156(s)
Dias, Bartolomeu, 18
Dickinson, John, 164, 165, 175
Didier, E., 282(i)
Dien Bien Phu, 748–749
Dien Bien Phu, Battle of (1954), 748
Diet
  of factory workers, 493
  during World War I, 603
Digital technology, 830–831
Diphtheria, 452, 720
Diplomatic Cable to Stewart L. Woodford (Day), 590(s)
Diseases
  in California, 360
  child mortality and, 131
  in the Civil War, 397–398
  Columbian Exchange in, 3, 44
  impact of on American Indians, 452
  Pilgrims and, 118
  tenements and, 516–517
  urban crowding and, 516
  vaccinations against, 720
  western settlement and, 359, 364–365
Dissent, suppression of, 610–613
District of Columbia
  Compromise of 1850 on, 368–370
  slavery in, 344–345, 369
Diversity. *See also* Immigrants
  Americanization efforts and, 629–630
  colonial era, 110
  in New York, 92
  nineteenth century, 287, 290
  in the twenty-first century, 830–831
  in the West, 469–471
  in western cities, 12
Division of labor, 491(s)
Division of Negro Affairs, 654
Divorce
  in the 1970s, 791
  abolitionism and, 348
  colonial era, 131
  legalization of, 218
  in the Oneida community, 340
Dixiecrats, 717
Dole, Robert, 828
Dollar diplomacy, 597
Domestic labor
  in the 1950s, 725, 726(s)
  cult of domesticity and, 291–292
  women in, 492, 674
  as women's purpose, 719
Domestic production, 266–267, 299(s)
Domestic violence, 504
Dominican Republic, 586, 595, 598
Domino, Antoine "Fats," 725
Domino Theory, 749
Dominion of New England, 77

"Don't ask, don't tell" policy, 827, 841
The Doors, 771
Double standard, 771
Double V, 675
Douglas, Helen Gahagan, 713
Douglas, Stephen, 378–379, 382, 383
  in the election of 1860, 384–385, 385(m)
  Harpers Ferry raid and, 384
Douglass, Frederick, 345, 345(s), 347, 371, 371(i), 394
  autobiography of, 378
  on the Fifteenth Amendment, 423
  on the Fugitive Slave Act, 370
  on voting rights, 423
Doy, Charles, 380(i)
Doy, John, 380(i)
Draft, military
  of American Indians, 676
  Civil War, 400, 400(i)
  Korean War, 708
  Vietnam War, 770
  World War I, 602
  World War II, 665, 676–677
Draft cards, 770
Dreamers, 841–842, 849
Dred Scott decision, 377, 382–383, 389, 421
Dreiser, Theodore, 512, 523(s)
Driving Cattle from Texas to Iowa (Duffield), 464(s)
Drones, 845
Drug abuse
  Beats on, 727
  counterculture and, 771
  muckrakers on, 557
  progressivism on, 567
Drunkard's Home, 339(i)
Dubček, Alexander, 779
Du Bois, W. E. B., 508, 564, 581, 583(s), 606, 613
  on Garvey, 625
"Duck and cover" drills, 741
Due process
  for corporations, 487
  Guantánamo prisoners and, 839
Duffield, George C., 464(s)
Dukakis, Michael, 817, 825
Duke, James B., 475
Dulles, Allen, 742
Dulles, John Foster, 742
Dunmore, Lord, 176, 179, 222
Dunmore's Proclamation, 176–177, 179
Dust Bowl, 639–640, 639(m)
Dust Bowl Diary (Low), 640(s)
Dylan, Bob, 771
Dynamic Sociology (Ward), 534

E

East India Company, 168–169
East Indies, 25
Eastern Europe
  as buffer between Germany and the USSR, 700, 701
  fall of Communism in, 820–821, 820(m)
  the Marshall Plan in, 703
Eastman, Charles, 459
Easton, John, 125(s)
Eaton, John, 306–307

Index

Eckford, Elizabeth, 734(i)
Economic depressions
  of 1893, 537
  after the Revolution, 217–218
  after World War I, 611
  Black Tuesday and, 637
  the Great Depression, 637–660
  imperialism and, 587
  Panic of 1837, 294, 295–296
  Panic of 1873, 436
Economic Opportunity Act (1964), 767
Economic policy
  American System, 277
  of Carter, 782–784
  of Clinton, Bill, 827–829
  under Hamilton, 232–233
Economic Recovery Tax Act (1982), 806
Economics and Politics of Charleston's Nullification Crisis, The (Pease and Pease), 318(i)
Economy, industrial, 482–483
Economy of scale, 485
Ecotactics (McCloskey), 794(s)
Ed Sullivan Show (TV show), 725
Edison Electric Illuminating Company, 485
Edison, Thomas Alva, 485
Edisto Island (South Carolina), 413(s)
Edmonds, Richard H., 473
Edmondson, Emily, 371, 371(i)
Edmondson, Mary, 371, 371(i)
Edmunds Act (1882), 469
Edmunds-Tucker Act (1887), 469
Education. *See also* Colleges and universities
  for African Americans, 326, 415–417, 562–564
  of American Indians, 457, 458(s), 565
  in arts and sciences, 220–221
  bilingual, 774
  Cold War and, 744
  desegregation of, 730, 731–732, 733, 734(i)
  in the early republic, 220–221, 222, 330–331, 331(i)
  emergence of the middle class and, 291
  of enslaved people, 323
  for free black people, 220
  GI Bill and, 717, 717(i)
  Gilded Age, 526
  Great Society programs in, 767
  of Mexican Americans, 736
  national identity and, 330
  New Deal school construction and, 649
  segregation in, 477
  in the South, 320, 327
  teenage culture and, 725
  for women, 219–220
  women teachers in, 492
Educational Amendments Act (1972), 792
Edwards, Ingrid E., 654(i)
Edwards, Jonathan, 133, 139(s)
Egypt
  Arab Spring in, 844
  Camp David accords, 786
  Cold War conflict over, 742
  Six-Day War, 780–781
  uprisings in, 845(m)
  in World War II, 682
Ehrlichman, John, 782
Eiffel, Alexandre-Gustave, 505
Eighteenth Amendment, 552(i), 566–567, 606, 626

Eisenhower Doctrine, 742
Eisenhower, Dwight D.
  black voter registration and, 760(i)
  containment under, 730–740, 749
  domestic politics under, 743–744
  farewell address, 743(s)
  interventions in the Middle East, Latin America, and Africa, 741–742
  on the military-industrial complex, 740, 770
  Modern Republicanism and, 743–744
  reelection of, 744
  Vietnam and, 749
  in World War II, 685–686
El Alamein, Battle of (1942), 682
Elections
  of 1796, 241–242, 242(m)
  of 1800, 245–246, 246(m)
  of 1816, 279
  of 1824, 303, 304(i)
  of 1828, 303, 304–305, 304(i)
  of 1840, 317–318, 359
  of 1844, 349, 359
  of 1848, 368
  of 1852, 373
  of 1856, 380
  of 1860, 384–385, 385(m)
  of 1876, 435–437, 437(m)
  of 1892, 543
  of 1894, 545
  of 1896, 545–546, 546(m)
  of 1912, 580
  of 1916, 581, 600
  of 1924, 632, 633(m)
  of 1928, 632–633
  of 1944, 683
  of 1948, 713, 717–718
  of 1960, 740, 743–745, 745(i)
  of 1964, 768, 774–775
  of 1968, 752, 778–779
  of 1972, 777, 779
  of 1976, 782
  of 1980, 804–805, 806(m)
  of 1984, 807
  of 1988, 817
  of 1992, 825, 827
  of 1996, 828
  of 2000, 834–835
  of 2004, 839
  of 2008, 841, 841(i)
  of 2012, 841
  of 2016, 848–849
  Farmers' Alliance on, 542
  progressive reforms of, 572–573
  television coverage of, 722
Electoral college, 208
  determination of electors to, 245
  political parties and, 245
Electric trolleys, 512
Electricity
  consumer goods in the twenties and, 616
  lighting and, 485, 512, 514–515
  rural electrification, 648
  urbanization and, 514–515
Elementary and Secondary School Act (1965), 767
Elevators, 514
"Eleventh Pillar of the Great National Dome," 215(i)

Eliot, John, 119
Elizabeth I (Queen of England), 71
Elkins Act (1903), 576
Ellicott, Andrew, 234
Ellington, Edward "Duke," 623
Ellis Island, 505, 571
Ellison, Ralph, 653
Ellsberg, Daniel, 781
Elmer Gantry (Lewis), 622
Elmina Castle, 18
El Paso (Texas), 502
El Salvador, 811
Ely, Richard T., 534
Emancipation, 411
  African American embrace of, 411–417
  education and, 415–417
  family reunification and, 414–415
  freedom of religion and, 417
  in Pennsylvania, 227–228(s)
  universal suffrage and, 423–424
Emancipation Proclamation (1863), 355, 395–397, 395(s), 396, 396(i), 397(s)
  exemptions from, 405
  women's support of, 399
Emanuel African Methodist Episcopal Church shooting, 851
Embargo Act (1807), 262, 267, 273(i)
Emergency Banking Act (1933), 647
Emerson, Ralph Waldo, 335–336
Emery, Elizabeth, 345(s)
"Emigrant Party Headed to California," 358(i)
Emily's List, 818
Enclosure movements, 55
Encomienda, 25, 30, 36, 39, 41
  in New Mexico, 49
  wealth from, 33
Endangered Species Act (1973), 794
The End of History?, 819(s)
Enemy combatants, 839
Energy crisis, 782–783
Energy use, 783–784
England. *See also* American Revolution (1775–1783); Great Britain; United Kingdom
  after the Revolution, 217
  civil war in, 61–62, 74, 75
  colonial expansion and conflict, 41, 58–60
  colonial government by, 77–78
  colonial policies of, 147, 160–165
  colonial resistance against, 160–172
  colonial trade, 100–102
  colonies of, 41, 46(m), 54–69, 61(m), 67(m), 83–86
  convicts transported by, 55, 59, 62
  economic causes of colonization by, 54–55
  emergence of slavery and, 62–63
  expansion and conflict with, 43
  Glorious Revolution in, 77, 78, 90
  impressment by, 135, 152–153, 152(s)
  King William's War, 120–121
  mercantilism in, 100–102
  Middle Colonies, 90–97
  New Amsterdam taken by, 47
  New England colonies, 70–82
  Oregon and, 359
  Panic of 1837 and, 317
  Protestant Reformation in, 70, 71
  Puritan view of, 73

Queen Anne's War and, 121
restoration in, 90
Seven Years' War, 149–155, 153(m)
slave trade, 65, 101, 107–109, 327–328
Spanish Armada and, 44, 46, 71
trade and, 41, 98–99
War of 1812, 274–276
wars with France, 120–121
West Indies colonies, 83–86, 83(i), 87(m)
English Civil War, 61–62, 74, 75
English language
bilingual education and, 774
citizenship and, 507
immigration restrictions based on, 628
Enlightenment, 41, 131–133, 193
American Revolution and, 177
Romanticism and, 331
Enola Gay, 686
Enrollment Act (1863), 400, 400(i)
Entrepreneurs, nineteenth century, 289–290
Enumerated articles, 100–101
Environment
climate change and, 822, 847, 849
the Dust Bowl and, 639–640, 639(m)
Exxon Valdez oil spill and, 818
globalization and, 822
under Johnson, 767
Obama on, 847
progressivism on, 555, 574–575
Trump on, 849
Environmental Protection Act (1970), 779
Environmental Protection Agency (EPA), 794
Environmental racism, 795
Environmentalism, 582
in the 1970s, 794–795, 795(i)
Taft and, 579
Epidemics, 39, 516–517
AIDS, 808, 822
Columbian Exchange and, 25
influenza, 610, 612, 612(i)
Episcopal Church, 333
Equal Employment Opportunity Commission (EEOC), 772, 792, 818
Equal Pay Act (1963), 772
Equal protection, 506(s)
Equal Rights Amendment, 559, 772, 792, 792–793(s)
defeated, 805, 808
Ericson, David F., 318(i)
Erie Canal, 278, 288, 288(i)
Erik the Red, 19
Erikson, Leif, 19
Escalation, 750
Espionage Act (1917), 604–605, 610
Essay on Female Education (Rush), 218
Estonia, 664, 703, 819
Ethiopia, repressive regime in, 784
Ethnic cleansing, 829
Eugenics, 508, 568, 578
Eureka (California), 471
Europe
antinuclear protests in, 810
exploration of the Americas, 17–23, 19(m), 20(m)
exports to, 587
gold from the Americas, 25–26
long-distance trade networks, 3

the Marshall Plan in, 703
refugees in, 845
road toward World War II in, 662–664
European Union (EU), 828
Brexit, 848
the Great Recession and, 840
refugees in, 845
Evangelicalism, 269, 327
abolitionism and, 345–346, 347
the New Right and, 796
prohibition and, 566
Second Great Awakening and, 332–334
Evans, Oliver, 264
Evening Star (newspaper), 614(i)
Evers, Medgar, 758
Every Man a King (Long), 652(s)
Evidence, citing to support claims, 22
Evils of Intemperance, The (Beecher), 333–334(s)
Evolution, 635–636(s), 796
fundamentalism on, 626–628
racism and, 508
social, 533
Excise taxes, on whiskey, 239–240
Executive Mansion, 234, 235
Executive Order 9066, 678
Exodusters, 429
Expansionism, 553
Exxon Valdez oil spill, 818
Eyewitness Account of the Hiroshima Bombing (Siemes), 686–687(s)

F

"Facebook Is Invading Your Phone" (Schlinkert), 850(s)
Factionalism, 210
Factory towns, 287–288
Fair Employment Practice Committee (FEPC), 675
Fair Housing Act (1968), 761
Fair Labor Standards Act (1938), 657
Fairholt, Frederick W., 68(i)
Faith-based initiatives, 835
Fake news, 849
Fall, Albert, 614
Fallen Timbers, Battle of, 240, 273
Falwell, Jerry, 796
Families
African American, 414–415, 414(i), 513(i)
after World War II, 716–717, 719–720
in the American Revolution, 186–187
Census data on, 292(s)
colonial era, 75, 79–80, 101–103
in domestic production, 267
enslaved, 268–269, 322
Gilded Age, 526–527
in the Great Depression, 643–644
immigrant, generational conflict in, 504
middle-class, 291–293
patriarchal, 74, 75, 130, 131
piecework and, 492
reunified after slavery, 414–415
on television, 723
women's status and, 79–80
working, 131
Family and Medical Leave Act (1993), 827
Family values
in the 1960s, 776

the Christian Right and, 796
Reagan and, 808–809
women's rights and, 827
Farewell to Arms (Hemingway), 663
Farm Bureau, 548
Farm foreclosures, 644–645
Farm Holiday Association, 644–645
Farmers. *See* Agriculture
Farmers' Alliances, 542
Farnham, Marynia, 725
Fascism, 651
Fast food, 719, 821, 822(i)
Father Knows Best (TV show), 723
Faubus, Orval, 733
FDR and the Jews (Breitman and Lichtman), 690–691(s)
Federal Art Project, 654(i)
Federal Bureau of Indian Affairs, 774
Federal Bureau of Investigation (FBI)
on Clinton, Hillary, 848
Freedom Rides and, 756
Freedom Summer and, 758
House Un-American Activities Committee and, 711
in the Red Scare, 612
Senate hearing on clandestine activities by, 785–786
Watergate scandal and, 781–782
Federal Deposit Insurance Corporation (FDIC), 647
Federal Emergency Relief Administration (FERA), 649
Federal Employee Loyalty Program, 711
Federal Hall, 231(i)
Federal Housing Administration, 720
Federal Housing Authority, 720
"Federal Pillars, The," 214–215(s)
Federal Reserve Board, 581
in the 1980s, 806
Great Depression and, 637
the Great Recession and, 840
in the twenties, 614
Federal Reserve System, 581
Federal Trade Commission, 581, 614, 618
Federalist Argument at the New York State Convention (Hamilton), 209–210(s), 214
Federalist Papers, The (Madison, Jay, and Hamilton), 210, 213(s)
Federalists, 147, 209, 237, 255
decline of, 303
in election of 1800, 245–246, 246(m)
in the first party system, 241–245
Supreme Court and, 261
War of 1812 and, 276
Whiskey Rebellion and, 239–240
Felt, Mark, 781–782
Felton, Rebecca Latimer, 560
Female Association for the Relief of Women and Children in Reduced Circumstances, 295
Feminine Mystique, The (Friedan), 726(s)
Feminism
in the 1970s, 792, 792–793(s)
progressivism and, 559
women's liberation and, 771–773
Femme covert, 75, 79
Ferdinand II of Aragon, 18, 19–20, 31, 33
Ferguson (Missouri), 843

I-13

Index

Ferraro, Geraldine, 807
Ferris wheel, 529
Fertility rates, colonial era, 110
Feudalism, 26, 62
Field Order Number 15, 408
Fifield, James W., 651
Fifteenth Amendment, 355, 423–424, 438
    Jim Crow laws and, 471, 477
    poll taxes and, 547
    women's suffrage and, 559
Fight Against Slavery, The (Manning), 409–410(s)
Fight to Save the Union, The (Gallagher), 410(s)
Filibusters, 374
Filipino immigrants, 643, 679
Fillmore, Millard, 368, 369, 370, 372(s), 373, 380
Film industry
    in the 1950s, 723–724, 723(i)
    Communists in, 645
    computers and, 830
    counterculture and, 771
    in the Great Depression, 644
    House Un-American Activities Committee and, 712–713
    sexual values and, 621, 621(i)
    in the twenties, 621, 621(i)
Finney, Charles Grandison, 332, 332–333(s), 346
"Fire" (Herblock), 715(s)
Fire departments, 516, 571
Fires, 516
Fireside chats, 647
First African Baptist Church, Richmond (Virginia), 412
First South Carolina Volunteers, 394
First Speech from a Debate On Birth Control (Sanger), 568(s)
Fiske, John, 508, 587
Fitzgerald, F. Scott, 622, 622(s)
Flappers, 621
Flathead Indians, 744
Flint (Michigan), GM strike in, 656–657, 656(i)
Flood-control projects, 648
Florida
    in the 2000 election, 835
    after World War II, 721
    black majority in, 428
    ceded to England, 154
    civil rights movement investigation in, 715
    immigrants in, 502
    Ku Klux Klan in, 431
    lumber industry in, 475
    readmitted to the Union, 422
    real estate speculation in, 618
    secession of, 385
    Seminole wars in, 279, 314
    Spanish exploration of, 36
Foner, Eric, 433(s)
Food Administration, 603, 604(i)
For Secession (Toombs), 392(s)
Force Act (1807), 262
Force Acts (1970, 1871), 431–432
Force Bill (1833), 311, 318(i)
Ford, 822
Ford, Christine Blasey, 849
Ford, Gerald, 782
Ford, Henry, 614, 615, 629, 645
Ford River Rouge plant, 645

Foreign policy
    under Bush, George W., 836–839
    under Carter, 784–786
    under Clinton, 828–829
    under Eisenhower, 739–740, 741–742
    under Roosevelt, Theodore, 595–597
    under Taft, 597
    under Truman, 710
    the Truman Doctrine in, 702–703
    under Wilson, 598–603
Forgotten Americans, 653
Forrest, Nathan Bedford, 431
Fort Brown, 578
Fort Crown Point, 153
Fort Dearborn, 275
Fort Donelson, Battle of (1862), 394(m)
Fort Duquesne, 150, 151, 153
Fort Frontenac, 153
Fort Henry, Battle of (1862), 394(m)
Fort Lyon, 409
Fort Mackinac, 275
Fort Monroe, 393
Fort Mose, 112
Fort Orange, 47
Fort Pitt, 153, 155
Forts, 357
Fort Stanwix, 190(m), 200–201
Fort Sumter, 389, 391, 394(m)
Fort Ticonderoga, 153, 175, 186, 190(m)
Fort Wayne (Indiana), 665(i)
Forty-niners, 363–364
Forum (magazine), 612(s)
Fossil fuels, 822
Fourier, Charles, 340
Fourierist phalanxes, 340
Fourteen Points (Wilson), 606–607
Fourteenth Amendment, 355, 420–421, 422, 438
    corporate personhood and, 487
    Japanese American internment and, 678
    property rights as personal liberty in, 532
    ratification of, 422
    reverse discrimination and, 762
    same-sex marriage and, 843
    United States v. Cruikshank and, 436
    women excluded from voting in, 423, 424
    women's suffrage and, 423, 424
Fox people, 314
Frame of Government, 92
Frame of the Government of the Province of Pennsylvania, The (Penn), 93(s)
France
    American Indian alliances with, 150–151
    American Revolution and, 186, 188–191
    appeasement by, 664
    Bandung Conference and, 741
    colonial expansion and conflict, 41
    colonies of, 44–45, 46(m)
    Embargo Act and, 262
    English wars with, 54
    European wars with, 120–121
    expansion and conflict with, 43
    exploration by, 44–45, 46(m)
    fall of to Germany, 665
    the Great Depression in, 639
    in the Group of Seven (G7), 821
    Haitian Revolution and, 258
    industrialization in, 483

King William's War, 120–121
Louisiana Purchase from, 258–259
mercantilism in, 100
in Paris Peace Conference, 606–607
protests in 1968, 779
seizures of U.S. ships by, 243
Seven Years' War, 149–155, 153(m)
slavery abolished in, 371
Vietnam and, 748–749
in World War I, 599, 602–603
in World War II, 665, 682, 683, 685
World War II declared by, 664
XYZ affair, 243
Franciscans, 36
Franco, Francisco, 664
Franklin, Benjamin, 94, 131, 132(s)
    Albany Plan of Union by, 150
    Declaration of Independence and, 178
    as envoy to Paris, 186, 188
    first political cartoon by, 151(s)
    "Join or Die" (Franklin), 151(s)
    Paine and, 177
    in peace term negotiations, 191
    on Whitefield, 138–139(s)
Franklin D. Roosevelt and the New Deal (Leuchtenberg), 660–661(s)
Franz Ferdinand, assassination of, 599
Fraternal organizations, 477, 526
Freake, Elizabeth, 79(i)
Freake, John, 79(i)
Freake, Mary, 79(i)
Free black people
    abuse of in Sherman's March to the Sea, 408
    church governance and, 224
    citizenship of, 506
    in development of Washington, D.C., 234
    education for, 415–417
    emigration of to Africa, 225
    on the Fugitive Slave Act, 370–371
    migration of from the South, 224
    political participation by, 428–429
    in southern cities, 320–321
Free silver, 545–546
Free Speech (newspaper), 564
Free Speech Movement (FSM), 770, 770(i)
Free trade agreements, 828
Free Will Baptists, 347
Freed, Alan, 733
Freedman, Estelle, 852–853(s)
Freedmen's Bureau, 412(i), 414, 438
    creation of, 413, 417
    extended, 420
    Johnson on, 420
    marriage certificates from, 415
    schools, 416, 416(i)
Freedom of religion
    for African Americans, 417
    the New Right and, 796
Freedom of speech
    French Revolution and, 238
    limits on in the Red Scare, 610–611
Freedom Rides, 756
Freedom Schools, 758–760
Freedom's Journal, 343
Freedom Summer, 758–760, 759(s)
Freedom Trash Can, 772
Free-enterprise system, 718, 745

I-14

Free-Soil Party, 349, 368, 377
  election of 1852 and, 373
Frémont, Jessie, 380
Frémont, John C., 361(m), 363, 364, 371, 380, 381–382(s)
  in election of 1856, 380
French and Indian War, 122, 147, 149–155
French Revolution (1789–1799), 238–239, 248
Freneau, Philip, 221–222
Freud, Sigmund, 622
Frick, Henry Clay, 497
Friedan, Betty, 725, 726(s), 772
From George Wallace to Newt Gingrich (Carter), 797(s)
Frontier. *See also* West
  after the Revolution, 197, 198, 202, 237, 255
  American Indian resistance to settlement along, 452–459
  as American symbol, 472(s), 512
  antislavery parties and, 349
  closing of the, 553, 586
  conflicts with American Indians along, 118–123, 198–201, 237, 240–241
  mining towns, 462–463, 462(i)
  the myth of the, 512
  official closing of, 586
  Whiskey Rebellion and, 239–240, 239(i)
  women homesteaders in, 468–469, 468(i)
Frontier in American History, The (Turner), 472(s)
Frontier thesis, 512
Front Royal, Battle of (1862), 394(m)
Fry, Varian, 687
Frye, William, 587
Fuel Administration, 603–604
Fugitive Slave Act (1850), 369–371
  Fillmore on, 378
  opposition to, 368–369, 370–372, 377
  the South on, 389
  Uncle Tom's Cabin and, 378
Fugitives from slavery
  in abolitionism, 347, 349
  in the Civil War, 393
  claimed as contraband of war, 393
  Constitutional Convention on, 208
  in New Bedford, 290
  stories of, 378
  underground railroad and, 344
Fukuyama, Francis, 819(s)
Fuller, Margaret, 336
Fulton, Robert, 264–265, 264(i)
Fundamentalism, 626–628, 635–636(s). *See also* Evangelicalism
Fundamentals, The, 626
Fund for a Feminist Majority, 818
Fur trade
  Covenant Chain and, 120
  Dutch, 46–47
  French, 45, 121
Furnberg, Anne, 468
Fusco, Charles, 655(s)

G

Gabriel (enslaved man), 258, 269, 270(s)
Gaddis, John Lewis, 709(s)
Gadsden, Christopher, 163
Gag rule (1836), 313

Galbraith, John Kenneth, 767
Gallagher, Gary, 410(s)
Gallatin, Albert, 264
Gambling, 504
Gammel, Mrs. W. T., 644(s)
Gandhi, Mohandas, 732
Gang labor, 110, 323
Gangs
  in the 1950s, 724
  immigrants in, 504
  nineteenth century, 290
Garfield, James A., 435(s), 538
Garrison, William Lloyd, 344, 346, 371
Garvey, Amy Jacques, 625
Garvey, Marcus, 620, 624–625, 625(i), 634(s)
Gary (Indiana), steel strike in, 708
Gas emission standards, 784
Gates, Bill, 830, 851
Gay Liberation Front, 774
Gay liberation movement, 774–775
Gays. *See* Homosexuals
Gaza Strip, 824
Geer, Elizabeth Smith, 358(s)
Geer, Joseph, 358(s)
Gender and Jim Crow (Gilmore), 569(s)
Gender discrimination
  in employment, 557–559, 558(s)
  Muller v. Oregon and, 558(s), 559
  women's liberation and, 771–773
Gender roles
  in the 1970s, 792
  after World War II, 716–717
  among American Indians, 453
  colonial, 66–67, 131
  imperialism and, 588
  industrialization and, 525–528
  progressivism on, 559
  in western migration, 358–359
  women's liberation and, 771–773
  in World War II, 674
General Electric Corporation, 485
General Federation of Women's Clubs, 525
General Intelligence Division, 612
General Motors, 616, 657, 822
General Motors Family, The (radio show), 621
General Trades Union, 295
Generation gap, 723–724, 723(i)
Genêt, Edmond, 239
Genius of Universal Emancipation, 343
Genocide
  in the Balkans, 828–829
  the Holocaust, 681, 687–689, 688(i), 690–691(s)
George, Henry, 534
George, Milton, 542
George II (King of England), 122
George III (King of England), 154, 161, 163, 179, 180(i), 191
George Whitefield (anonymous), 140(s)
George Whitefield Preaching at a Revival (Collet), 140(s)
Georgia, 83
  American Indian removal and, 313–314
  American Revolution in, 191
  black voters in, 428
  charter of, 78

Constitution ratified by, 210, 211(t)
Ku Klux Klan in, 630, 631
readmission of, 441(s)
secession of, 385, 387(s), 392(s)
German immigrants, 94, 95
  in the 1820s, 289
  in Civil War draft riots, 400, 400(i)
  colonial era, 41, 67–68, 93
  as farmers, 467
  suspicion of in World War I, 605
  in World War II, 678
Germany
  after World War I, 618–619
  Berlin Wall in, 746
  deal with Mexico, 602
  expansionism of, 664
  the Great Depression in, 639
  in the Group of Seven (G7), 821
  Hitler's rise in, 664
  Holocaust in, 687–689, 688(i), 690–691(s)
  industrialization in, 482, 483
  occupation zones in, 704, 705(m)
  in Paris Peace Conference, 606–608
  Pietists, 133
  rebuilding after World War II, 704, 704(i)
  reparations by, 606–607, 618–619
  reunification of, 819–820
  in Seven Year's War, 152
  Tripartite Pact of, 667–668
  welfare spending in, 806
  in World War I, 599–609
  in World War II, 664–668, 678, 682–683, 685
Geronimo, 459
Gettysburg, Battle of (1863), 403–404, 404(m)
Gettysburg Address (Lincoln), 405
Ghettos, 503, 761
Ghost Dance, 459
GI Bill (1944), 717, 717(i)
Giants in the Earth (Rolvaag), 467
Gideon v. Wainwright, 769
Gilded Age, 446–447
  ideologies, 532–536
  politics and protests, 537–549
  society and culture in, 524–531
Gillam, Bernhard, 493(s), 543(s)
Gillam, F. Victor, 502(s)
Gillespie, Dizzy, 727
Gilman, Charlotte Perkins, 559
Gilmore, Glenda Elizabeth, 569(s)
Gingrich, Newt, 828
Ginsberg, Allen, 727, 728(i)
Gladden, Washington, 556
Glasnost, 815, 819
Glass-Steagall Act (1933), 647, 829, 840
Glazer, Nathan, 795
Global warming, 822
Global War on Terror (GWOT), 836–839
Globalization, 802–852
  Atlantic economy and, 98–106
  Clinton, Bill, on, 827
  colonialism and, 41
  Columbus and, 21
  the Great Recession and, 840
  new world order and, 821–822
Glorious Revolution, 77, 78, 87, 90, 91
Godey's Lady's Book, 291(i)
God's Own Party (Williams), 797(s)

Index

Gold
  in Alaska, 546
  Aztec, 32
  in the Black Hills, 456
  in Indian Territory, 461
  Spanish exploration for, 25–26
Gold rush, in California, 357, 363–364, 364(i)
Gold standard, 545
Goldman, Emma, 497–498, 559, 612
Goldwater, Barry M., 697, 768, 775–776, 791
Gómez, Maximo, 589(i)
Gompers, Samuel, 495–496, 593
Gorbachev, Mikhail, 815–816, 819–821
Gordon, Kate, 560
Gore, Al, 834–835
Las Gorras Blancas (The White Caps), 469–470
Gorsuch, Neil, 849
Gospel of Wealth, The (Carnegie), 533, 534(s)
Gould, Jay, 486
Government
  during the American Revolution, 195–197
  colonial era, 72–75, 78
  by commission, 603
  laissez-faire and, 533
  Locke on, 77
  organizing the federal, 209–210
  progressivism on, 572–585
  promotion of the economy by in the twenties, 613–616
  reframing after the Revolution, 207–216
  during World War I, 603–606
Grady, Henry, 473, 474(s)
Graft, 517, 518, 519
Graham, Billy, 727, 796
Grand Alliance, 681
Grand Coulee Dam, 649
Grandfather clauses, 476, 476(m), 564
Grangers, 540–541, 540(i)
Grant, Ulysses S., 393
  Civil War policies of, 404, 406–408
  end of the war and, 408–409
  memoirs of, 407(s)
  as president, 423
  in Reconstruction, 422
  reelection of, 436, 538
  scandals surrounding, 434–435
  Vicksburg and, 404, 404(m)
Grapes of Wrath, The (Steinbeck), 640
Graphic organizers, 37–38
Grateful Dead, 771
Grätz, Friedrich, 500(s)
Great Atlantic and Pacific Tea Company (A&P), 488
Great Awakening, 41, 130, 131–145
  communication and, 162
  Second, 332–334
Great Britain. *See also* England; United Kingdom
  appeasement by, 664
  Civil War and, 395
  frontier conflicts with, 240–241
  the Great Depression in, 639
  the Great Recession and, 840
  imperialism of, 588(s)
  industrialization in, 265
  investment in development of the West, 450–451, 486
  Jay Treaty with, 239
  nuclear freeze movement in, 814

  in Paris Peace Conference, 606–608
  slavery abolished in, 371
  Suez Canal and, 742
  Thatcherism in, 806
  U.S. sovereignty undermined by, 202
  war debt to, 241
  Whiskey Rebellion and, 239–240
  women's suffrage in, 561
  in World War I, 599, 600
  in World War II, 665, 682–683, 685
  World War II declared by, 664
Great Depression, 553, 637–660
  causes of, 637–638
  dust storms in, 639–640, 639(m)
  election of 1960 influenced by, 745
  ended by World War II, 670
  families in, 643–644
  farm foreclosures in, 644–645
  Hoover's response to, 638–639
  Hoovervilles in, 639–640
  minorities during, 640–643
  New Deal and, 646–661
  organized protest in, 645
  worldwide effects of, 639
Great Dying, 25
Great Gatsby, The (Fitzgerald), 622(s)
Great Lakes, the market revolution and, 289
Great migration, 613, 736
Great Plains, 364–365, 365(m), 449–450
  American Indians of, 11, 452–454, 453(m)
  Dust Bowl in, 639–640, 639(m)
  farming on the, 465–467
Great Railway Strike, 436
Great Recession, 840, 841, 852
Great Society programs, 767–768, 779, 803
  Reagan on, 804
Great War on White Slavery, The (Roe and Steadwell), 567(s)
Greece
  civil war in, 702
  the Great Recession in, 840
  refugees in, 845
Greeley, Horace, 336, 390, 395(s), 435, 435(s)
Green Party, 834
Greenbacks, 398, 542
Greene, Catherine, 265
Greenham Common, England, 814
Greenhouse gases, 818, 822, 847
Greenhow, Rose O'Neal, 391, 395, 399
Greensboro (North Carolina), sit-ins in, 734
Greenwich Village, 528, 571, 727, 774
Grenada, 811
Grenville, George, 161, 162
Grey, Philip, 414
Grey, Willie Ann, 414
Grimké, Angelina, 344
Grimké, Sarah, 344
Griswold, Roger, 243(i)
Griswold v. Connecticut, 769
Gross domestic product
  industrialization and, 482
  in World War II, 670
Gross national product (GNP), 718
Group of Seven (G7), 821
Guadalcanal Island, 683, 684(m)
Guam, 591

Guantánamo Bay
  incarcerations at, 839
  naval base at, 591
Guardian (newspaper), 845–846, 847(s)
Guatemala, 811
Guatemala, CIA covert action in, 741–742
Guerrilla warfare, 152, 175, 751
Guinn v. United States, 564
Guiteau, Charles, 538
Gulf of Tonkin Resolution (1964), 750, 750(s)
Gulf War, 823–824, 824(i), 839
Gun rights
  Brady Bill and, 827–828
  Bush, George H. W., on, 817
Gun trade, 28
Gun violence, 851–852
Gunpowder, 18
Guns
  American Indian conflicts and trade in, 120
  manufacturing of, 266
Guzmán, Jacobo Arbenz, 741–742

H

Hair (musical), 771
Haiti, U.S. intervention in, 586, 598
Haitian Revolution (1791–1799), 258, 269, 325
Haldeman, H. R., 782
Hale, John, 373
Hall, Basil, 297(i)
Hall, G. Stanley, 526
Hall, Jacquelyn Dowd, 737(s)
Hamer, Fannie Lou, 759
Hamilton, Alexander, 147, 202, 233(s), 245–246
  Adams' presidency and, 242
  in Annapolis convention, 202
  duties on imports recommended by, 198
  Federalist Papers by, 210
  foreign trade and, 232–233, 237–238
  on governmental structure, 202
  as secretary of the treasury, 230, 232–233
  on Shays's Rebellion, 203
  on war debt, 218
  Whiskey Rebellion and, 240
Hamilton, Andrew, 136
Hammond, Catherine, 320
Hammond, James Henry, 320
Hampton Institute, 513(i), 562
Handy, W. E., 529
"Hanging of the San Patricios" (Chamberlain), 363(i)
Hanna, Marcus Alonzo, 539, 545
Hard Hat Riot, 696(i)
Hard war strategy, 406–408
Harding, Warren G., 605, 613–614, 633(m)
Hargis, Billy Joe, 775
Haring, Louisa Dana, 558(s)
Harlem Renaissance, 623–625, 623(s)
Harper, Frances Ellen Watkins, 423
Harpers Ferry (Virginia), raid on, 379, 384
Harper's Weekly, 412(i)
Harrington, Michael, 767, 768(s)
Harris, Frederick C., 844(s)
Harrison, Benjamin, 538, 543
Harrison Narcotics Control Act (1914), 567
Harrison, William Henry, 273–274, 274(s), 317–318
Hartford Convention, 276
Hartford Times (newspaper), 747(s)

I-16

Harvard College, 119, 220
Hawaii, 280
  annexation of, 586, 587, 591
  martial law in, 678
Hawley-Smoot Act (1930), 638
Hawthorne, Nathaniel, 337
Hay, John, 595
Hayden, Tom, 769–770
Hayes, Rutherford B., 436–437, 437–438(s), 437(m), 538
Haymarket Square, 494–495
Hayne, Robert, 310
Hay-Pauncefote Treaty (1901), 595
Headright system, 58
Head Start, 767
Health care
  for American Indians, 630
  in the Civil War, 397–398
  Clinton, Bill, on, 827, 827(s)
  of enslaved people, 325
  globalization and, 822
  Medicare and, 769
  Obama on, 841
  Trump on, 849
  women in, 398, 399, 492
Health insurance
  American Plan on, 614
  Carter on, 784
  Obama on, 841
Hearst, William Randolph, 590
Hefner, Hugh, 728
Hemingway, Ernest, 663
Henry IV (King of France), 54
Henry the Navigator, 18
Henry, Patrick, 162, 163(s), 212(s), 232
Henry VIII (King of England), 71
Henson, Josiah, 378
Hepburn Act (1906), 576
Herberg, Will, 727
Herblock, 715(s)
Heritage Foundation, 796
Hernán Cortés Assisted by the Tlaxcalan People of Mexico, 32(i)
Herrera, Juan Jose, 469–470
Hessian mercenaries, 186
Hetch Hetchy valley, 574–575
Heyrick, Elizabeth, 344
Hicks, Louise Day, 762, 762(i)
Higher education, after World War II, 717, 719
Highways, after World War II, 720, 744
Hill, Anita, 818, 818(i)
Hill, David, 181(i)
Hill, Elias, 431
Hirohito, 685
Hiroshima, atomic bomb dropped on, 685–686, 686(i)
Hispaniola, 20, 20(m), 25
Hiss, Alger, 712–713
Historical Reasoning
  causation and, 17, 24, 43, 54, 83, 130, 149, 185, 257, 272, 287, 309, 319, 330, 357, 411, 427
  comparison and, 43, 195, 272, 287, 367, 389
  contextualization and, 90, 173
  continuity and change in, 30, 70, 160, 207, 319, 389
History of the Revolution (Warren), 331

Hitler, Adolf, 664, 665, 685, 825(s)
HIV (human immunodeficiency virus), 808
Ho Chi Minh, 748–749
Ho Chi Minh Trail, 752(m), 753
Hoban, James, 235
Hofstadter, Richard, 548(s)
Hohokam people, 10
Holding companies, 487
Holiday Inn, 719
Holloway, Houston H., 412
Hollywood, 621(i), 645
Holmes, Oliver Wendell, 610
Holocaust, 681, 687–689, 688(i), 690–691(s)
Home Box Office, 830
Homelessness, in the Great Depression, 639–640
Homer, Winslow, 414(i)
Homes for Virtuous and Friendless Females, 336
Homestead (Pennsylvania), 496–497, 498(i)
Homestead Act (1862), 465
Homestead Act (1864), 407
Homestead strike, 496–497, 498(i)
Homosexuals
  in the 1950s, 727–728
  "don't ask, don't tell" policy on, 827, 841
  gay liberation movement and, 774–775
  Gilded Age, 528
  in the Holocaust, 681, 687
  marriage for, 828, 835, 843
  in the military, 827, 841
  Red Scare and, 711
  social conservatism and, 808
  in World War II, 672
Honda, 822
Honecker, Erich, 819–820
Honeymooners, The (TV show), 723
Hongs at Canton, 238(i)
Honky tonks, 529
Hook, Jeff, 825(s)
Hoopas, 744
Hoover, Herbert, 603, 633, 745
  Bonus Army and, 645
  response to the Great Depression, 638–639
  unions weakened by, 614
Hoover, J. Edgar, 612
Hoovervilles, 638–639
Hopalong Cassidy (TV show), 723
Hopelessly Bound to the Stake (Gillam), 493(s)
Hopkins, Harry, 649, 653
Horizontal integration, 485
Horseshoe Bend, Battle of, 275
Horticulture, 4–5
  in Mexico, 4–5
Horton, James Oliver, 308
Horton, Lois E., 308
House of Burgesses, 59, 62, 63, 112–113(s)
House of Representatives
  Constitutional Convention on, 207–208
  first woman elected to, 602
  turnover in, 538
House Un-American Activities Committee (HUAC), 711–713, 711(s), 715
Household mode of production, 80
Housework, in the 1950s, 725, 726(s), 727
Housing
  after World War II, 720–721, 721(s)
  in black ghettos, 761

GI Bill and, 717, 717(i)
Gilded Age, 524–525
  public, in the 1960s, 767
  sales decline in the twenties, 618
  segregation in, 513, 676, 720–721
  segregation in, school busing and, 761–762, 762(i)
  settlement houses, 519
  in tenements, 515–517
  in World War II, 676
  zoning and, 511
Houston, Sam, 313
Houston (Texas), 740(i)
How It Feels to Be Colored Me (Hurston), 624(s)
How the Other Half Lives (Riis), 516
Howard University, 676
Howdy Doody (TV show), 723
Howe, Julia Ward, 559
Howe, William, 175, 185–186
Howl (Ginsberg), 727
Hudson River School, 335(i), 336
Huerta, Dolores, 773, 773(s)
Hughes, Charles Evans, 581, 600
Hughes, Langston, 623, 640–641
Huguenots, 44
Hull House, 557
Hull, John, 57(i)
Human immunodeficiency virus (HIV), 808
Human rights, 697
  Carter on, 784, 785(s)
  under Reagan, 811–812
Humanism, pragmatic, 646
Humanitarian reforms, 555, 557
Humphrey, Hubert, 779
Hungary
  anti-Soviet revolution in, 740
  fall of the Soviet regime in, 819
  refugees in, 845
Hunkpapa Lakota, 452
Hunters and gatherers, 5, 11, 12
  in Seven Years' War, 150–151
Huron people, 155
Hurricane Katrina, 839
Hurston, Zora Neale, 623, 624(s)
Hussein, Saddam, 813, 823–824, 825(s), 845
  as sponsor of terrorism, 837–839
Hutchinson, Anne, 75–76, 135
Hutchinson, William, 75
Hydrogen bomb, 705

I

Ickes, Harold, 649
Idaho
  miner riot in, 461
  mining in, 462
  Populists and, 547
  silver miner strike in, 499
Identity
  colonial America, 41, 159(s)
  gay, 774–775
  Harlem Renaissance and, 623–624
  literature and culture in, 220–221
  national, development of, 330–331
  national, dilemmas of, 218–222
  the new capital and, 233–234
  in the South, 319
  teenage, in the 1950s, 725

Index

If at first . . . (Hook), 825(s)
"If We Must Die" (McKay), 626(s)
Illinois, statehood of, 277
"The Immigrant. Is He an Acquisition or a Detriment," 502(s)
Immigrants
    after World War I, 617
    Americanization of, 629–630
    American Party on, 379
    anarchists, 494–495
    arrivals of 1960–2000, 809
    assimilation of, 447, 501, 508
    bilingual education and, 774
    blamed for fallen women, 337
    California gold rush and, 363–364, 364(i)
    in Civil War draft riots, 400, 400(i)
    colonial era, 41, 94
    colonial era expansion and conflict among, 94–95
    communities of, 503–505
    Democratic Party and, 633
    departures *vs.* arrivals of, 503
    dreamers, 841–842
    early twentieth century, 501–509
    economic incentives for, 503
    in the election of 1896, 545
    as farmers on the Great Plains, 466–467
    fear of communism and, 610–611
    generational conflicts among, 504
    hostility toward recent, 504–508
    industrialization and, 294–295, 491
    late nineteenth century, 501–510
    late twentieth to twenty-first century, 830–831, 831(f)
    the lure of urban life and, 289–290
    in mining, 461
    narcotic use and, 567
    nativism and, 338, 507–508, 628–630
    numbers of in the nineteenth century, 289–290, 289(i)
    political bosses and, 517
    political cartoons on, 502(s)
    Populists on, 543
    progressivism and, 555, 557–559, 566–567, 567(t), 582
    quota system on, 639, 769
    radicalism and, 506
    radio shows for, 621
    return to home countries by, 503
    social conservatives against, 809
    in social reform movements, 337, 338
    in southern cities, 321
    suburb development and, 514–515
    Trump on, 848, 849
    twenties attitudes toward, 628–630
    in the twenty-first century, 847–848
    undocumented, under Reagan, 809
    in the union movement, 494–495
    urban crowding and, 515–516
    urbanization and, 289, 290–291
    in the West, 467, 469–471
    women's suffrage and, 560–561
Immigration Act (1924), 688
Immigration Act (1965), 830
Immigration and Nationality Act (1965), 769
Immigration and Naturalization Service, 744
Immigration Reform and Control Act (1986), 809
Immigration Restriction League, 508

Impeachment, 788(s), 829
Imperialism, 84, 586–597. *See also* Colonies
    anti-imperialism *vs.*, 593, 594(s)
    awakening of, 586–597
    colonial era, 84
    cultural justifications for, 587–588
    economics of, 587
    extension of, 595–597
    under Monroe, 279–280
    Philippine war and, 592–594
    under Roosevelt, 595–597
    Suez invasion and, 742
    war with Spain and, 589–592
    Wilson and, 598–603
    World War I and, 598–609
Imperial presidency, 703, 708
Implied powers clause, 261
Import duties, 161
Impressment, 135, 273
    in Seven Years' War, 152–153, 152(s)
Impressment by the British (anonymous), 152(s)
Incarceration rates, 827
Incas, 3, 7–8, 20(m), 25, 33
Incidents in the Life of a Slave Girl (Jacobs), 269(s)
Income. *See also* Wealth
    after World War II, 718–719, 719(f)
    Chinese American, 736
    inequality, in the twenties, 618
    racial differences in, 762, 795
    in the twenties, 615, 616
    of women in World War II, 674
Income inequality
    colonial era, 67
    Gilded Age, 447, 532–533
    Middle Colonies, 91–92, 92(i)
Income tax
    graduated, 580
    in the Great Depression, 638
    progressivism on, 556, 580
    Wilson-Gorman Act on, 545
Indentured servitude, 41, 55
    in colonial America, 55, 57, 64(i)
    conflict with American Indians and, 62, 63–64
    English, 41
    in Jamestown, 57
    land ownership and, 94
    in Maryland, 64(i)
    Puritans and, 74
    in tobacco cultivation, 58–59, 61, 62, 63
    West Indies, 84
    women in, 66–67
India
    immigrants from, 1990s to twenty-first century, 831, 831(f)
    in Paris Climate Agreement, 847
    Seven Years' War in, 153(m), 154
    spice trade with, 17
    trade with, 98
"Indian Burying Ground" (Freneau), 221–222
Indian Citizenship Act (1924), 630
Indian Converts (Mayhew and Prince), 119(s)
Indian Ocean, 17, 18, 19(m)
Indian Removal Act (1830), 313–314, 313–314(s), 315(m)
Indian Reorganization Act (IRA), 658
Indian Territory, 456

Indian Trade and Intercourse Act (1790), 240
Indiana
    Ku Klux Klan in, 630, 631
    statehood of, 277
Indianapolis, 630
Indigenous people, globalization and, 822
Indigo, 88, 98, 100–101, 109, 110
Indios, 34
Individualism
    in early republic arts, 220–221
    laissez-faire and, 532–533
    Lost Generation on, 621–622
    Modern Republicanism and, 743–744
    progressivism and, 556
Indulgences, 71
Industrialization, 254(i), 482–500
    cities and, 512–513
    Civil War, 398–399
    consolidation in, 485–486
    corporations in, 487–488, 487(s), 488(i)
    the decline of craft work and, 294–295
    energy crisis and, 783–784, 783(m)
    environmentalism and, 555
    factories in World War II, 671
    factory towns and, 293–294
    gender roles and, 525–528
    Gilded Age, 447
    immigrants and, 289
    imperialism and, 587
    innovations and inventions in, 483–485
    labor movements and, 490–499
    laissez-faire and, 532–533
    leisure and, 528–530
    the market revolution and, 287–295
    mechanization in, 294–295, 491(s)
    mid-nineteenth century, 293–294
    national politics and, 538–539
    North *vs.* South, 390–391
    Panic of 1837 and, 295–296
    politics and, 538–540
    railroads and, 483(f)
    in the South, 354(i), 398–399, 474–476, 475(m)
    technology and, 264–266
    in the twenties, 615–616, 637–638
    wealth from, 493
    women in, 293–294
    workday length and, 294
    worker conditions in, 492–493
    in World War II, 670–671
Industrial revolution, 447
    second, 553
Industrial Workers of the World (IWW), 499, 605
Inflation
    in the 1970s, 780, 783, 790(s)
    after World War I, 611
    under Clinton, 829
    English colonization and, 54–55
Influential Woman Converts, An (Finney), 332–333(s)
Influenza epidemic of 1918, 610, 612, 612(i)
Information flows, 99
Infrastructure
    after World War II, 720–721
    under Jackson, 309
    road and turnpikes, 263–264
    Works Progress Administration and, 653
Inglis, Charles, 177, 178(s)

Inheritance taxes, 580
In re Debs, 499(s)
Instructions given by Richard Corbin, Esq., to his agent for the management of his plantations, 115(s)
Instructions on Managing Enslaved Workers (Ball), 114(s)
Integration, economic, 474
Interchangeable parts, 266
Interest groups, 548
Interim Report on Comic Books and Juvenile Delinquence, 724(s)
Interlocking directorates, 486
Intermediate Nuclear Forces Treaty, 815
Internal combustion engine, 484
Internal Revenue Service (IRS), 796
Internet, 830
Internment camps, Japanese American, 678–680, 737
reparations for, 774
Internment Diary (Kikuchi), 680(s)
Interracial political coalitions, 429
Interstate commerce, Annapolis conference on, 202
Interstate Commerce Act (1887), 542
Interstate Commerce Commission (ICC), 542, 576
Intimate Matters (D'Emilio and Freedman), 852–853(s)
Intolerable Acts (England, 1774), 169–170, 173
"Invisible Hand," 532
Iowa, statehood of, 359
Iran
  in axis of evil, 837–839
  Cold War intervention in, 741
  hostage crisis, 781, 789(s), 813
  Islamic revolution in, 781
  nuclear program in, 846
  Reagan's backing of, 813
  repressive regime supported in, 780
Iran-Contra affair, 813, 814(s)
Iran Nuclear Agreement, 849
Iraq
  in axis of evil, 837–839
  Operation Desert Storm in, 823–824
  Reagan and, 813
Iraq War (2003–), 837–839
  under Obama, 844
  weapons in, 838(s)
Irish immigrants
  in the 1820s, 289
  in Civil War draft riots, 400, 400(i)
  colonial era, 41, 67–68
  conflict of with African Americans, 290
  as indentured servants, 61
  in mining towns, 463
  nativists on, 338
  in New York City, 262
  political bosses and, 517
  in textile mills, 295
Iron curtain, 701, 705(m)
Iroquois Confederacy, 47, 119–120
  in the American Revolution, 180–181
  British alliance with, 150–151
Iroquois people, 12, 14, 93
  fur trade, 121
  King William's War, 121
  land treaties with, 200

Walking Purchase with, 95
in World War II, 676
Irrigation, 5, 468
  Aztec, 7
  Incan, 8
Irving, Washington, 331
Isabella of Castile, 18, 19–20, 31, 33
ISIS, 845, 845(m)
Islam
  enslaved people and, 325
  long-distance trade and, 18
  Spanish reconquest and, 18, 20
Islamic extremism
  Obama on, 844
  terrorism and, 820, 829
Islamic State of Iraq and Syria (ISIS), 845, 845(m)
Island-hopping, 683
Isolationism, 553
  after Pearl Harbor, 678
  Germany's challenges to, 664–666
  before World War II, 663, 664–666
Israel
  Camp David accords, 786
  Gaza Strip and West Bank and, 824
  in the Gulf War, 824
  Six-Day War, 708–781
  U.S. policies on, 813(m)
Italian immigrants
  labor contracts with, 502
  New Deal and, 655(s)
  in World War II, 678
Italy
  city-states and trade in, 17–18, 20
  the Great Depression in, 639
  in the Group of Seven (G7), 821
  long-distance trade by, 3
  road to World War II in, 664
  Spanish conquest of, 33
  Tripartite Pact of, 667–668
  war declared on, 664
  in World War I, 599
  in World War II, 664, 666
Itinerant preachers, 133–134
Iwo Jima, Battle of (1945), 684–685

J

Jackson, Andrew, 275, 275(m), 276(i), 277, 279, 303, 304–307, 452
  American Indian removal and, 313–316
  Second Bank and, 310
  tariffs and, 309–311
  Texas and, 313
Jackson, Helen Hunt, 457
Jackson (Mississippi), 399, 764(s)
Jackson, Rachel, 305, 306
Jackson, Thomas "Stonewall," 391, 393, 418(i)
Jacobs, Harriet, 269(s)
Jamaica, slave markets in, 108
James, Henry, 528
James I (King of England), 56, 59, 60, 77
James II (King of England), 77, 90, 91
Jamestown colony, 41, 54, 56–57, 57(i), 58
  Bacon's Rebellion and, 64
  native attack on, 59(i)
Japan

atomic bombs dropped on, 685–686, 686–687(s)
in the Group of Seven (G7), 821
Pearl Harbor attack by, 662, 668, 668(s)
Russian invasion of Manchuria and, 596
trade with, 373
Tripartite Pact of, 667–668
war atrocities by, 689
in World War II, 683–684, 684(m), 685–687, 689
Japanese American Citizens League, 774
Japanese Americans
  civil rights movement and, 737
  in the Great Depression, 642
  internment of, 675, 678–680, 737, 774
  reparations to internees, 774
  in World War II, 668(s)
Japanese immigrants, 502, 571, 628
Jay, John, 241
  in England, 239
  Federalist Papers by, 210
  in peace term negotiations, 191
Jay Treaty (1794), 239, 241
Jazz, 529, 623–624, 727
Jazz Age, 553
Jefferson Airplane, 771
Jefferson, Thomas, 147, 277
  agrarian vision of, 237–238, 450
  on the Alien and Sedition Acts, 244
  American system of manufacturing and, 266
  on Bank of the United States, 232
  on capital location, 233
  challenges facing, 257–258
  Declaration of Independence and, 178–179, 179(s)
  in election of 1800, 245–246
  Embargo Act and, 262
  on Haitian Revolution, 270(s)
  on Hamilton's policies, 232, 237–238
  inaugural address of, 249, 330
  Louisiana Purchase and, 257, 258–260
  on the Neutrality Proclamation, 239
  reelection of, 260
  as secretary of state, 230
  as vice president, 242
  on Whiskey Rebellion, 240
  White House under, 235
Jeffries, Jim, 567
Jehovah's Witnesses, 681
Jennings, Peter, 275
Jennings, Samuel, 219(s), 220
Jesuits, 45
Jews
  colonial era, 92, 196
  crimes committed by, 504
  generational conflicts among, 504
  Holocaust of, 681, 687–689, 688(i), 690–691(s)
  immigrants, 330, 501, 502, 628–629
  immigrants as white or not, 506–507
  international conspiracy of, 629
  Ku Klux Klan on, 630
  prejudice against, 290
  in Spain, 18
  in the twenties, 628–629
Jieshi, Jiang, 705

I-19

Index

Jihad, 844
Jim Crow, 447
    laws, 471, 476–477, 547, 729–730, 731(s)
    minstrel show character, 289
    white resistance to dismantling, 733–735
Jingoists, 588, 590
Jobs, Steve, 830
John Birch Society, 775
Johnny Got His Gun (Trumbo), 663
Johnson, Andrew, 414, 417
    congressional resistance to, 420–423
    impeachment of, 423, 538
    Reconstruction under, 412, 417–420
    in the state legislature, 435
Johnson, E. A. J., 106(s)
Johnson, Gerald W., 631(s)
Johnson, Guy, 180, 181(i)
Johnson, Jack, 567
Johnson, Lyndon B., 654, 727(i)
    black voter registration and, 760(i)
    in civil rights legislation, 744
    civil rights movement and, 755, 756, 758–760
    Freedom Summer killings and, 759–760
    Great Society programs, 767–768
    Kerner Commission and, 761
    Pentagon Papers on, 753
    reelection of, 768, 776, 779
    Vietnam War and, 749–752, 752(m), 770–771
Johnson, Michael P., 387(s)
Johnson, Milly, 414
Johnson, Tom L., 573
Johnston, Joseph E., 407(s)
"Join or Die" (Franklin), 151(s)
Joint Chiefs of Staff, 703
Joint Electoral Commission, 436
Joint-stock companies, 56
Jones, Samuel "Golden Rule," 573
Jordan, George, 455
Joseph, Chief, 455
Josephson, Matthew, 489(s)
Journalism
    muckrakers in, 556(s), 557, 564
    yellow, 590
Judge (magazine), 502(i), 543(s)
Judicial review, 261
Judicial system
    Constitutional Convention on, 207–208
    in the early republic, 230–231
    influence of business on, 539
    Puritan, 74–75
Judiciary Act (1789), 230
Judiciary Act (1801), 261
Juke joints, 529
Jungle, The (Sinclair), 577, 577(s)
Justice Department, 230
Juvenile delinquency, 567–568
    after World War II, 717
    senate investigation of, 724(s)

K

Kamikaze, 685
Kansas, 377
    Bleeding Kansas, 379–380, 380(i)
    the Dust Bowl in, 649(m)
    Exodusters in, 429
    homesteaders in, 466(s)
    prohibition in, 565
    temperance movements in, 468–469
    women homesteaders in, 468(i)
Kansas-Nebraska Act (1854), 378–380, 379(m)
Kant, Immanuel, 131, 331
Karonghyontye, 181(i)
Kavanaugh, Brett, 849
Kearney, Belle, 560
Keating-Owen Act (1916), 581
Kelley, Abby, 347, 423
Kellogg-Briand Pact, 662, 663(s)
Kelly, Oliver H., 541
Kempshall, Emily G., 338(s)
Kennan, George, 700–701, 703
Kennedy, John F., 740, 744–745, 745(i)
    assassination of, 758, 767
    black voter registration and, 760(i)
    civil rights movement and, 755–758
    Cold War and, 745–747
    Commission on the Status of Women, 772
    Cuba and, 745–747, 746(s), 747(s)
    New Frontier pledge of, 767
    Pentagon Papers on, 753
    Vietnam interventions by, 748–749
Kennedy, Robert, 756, 778
    assassination of, 697, 788(s)
Kent State University, 753
Kentucky, statehood of, 263
Kentucky Resolution, 244–245(s), 249
Kergorlay, Louis de, 306(s)
Kerner, Otto, 761
Kerner Commission, 761, 765(s)
Kerosene, 485
Kerouac, Jack, 727, 728(i)
Kerry, John, 844
Keyssar, Alexander, 307–308
Khmer Rouge, 753
Khomeini, Ayatollah Ruholla, 786
Khrushchev, Nikita, 741, 746–747
Kikuchi, Charles, 680(s)
Kim Il Sung, 706
Kim Jon-un, 849
King, Boston, 226–227(s)
King, Martin Luther, Jr., 73, 745
    antiwar address by, 770
    assassination of, 697, 761, 778, 788(s)
    birthday of, 824(i)
    Carter supported by, 782
    in the civil rights movement, 758(i)
    Freedom Riders and, 756
    Letter from Birmingham Jail, 756, 757(s)
    in march to Montgomery, 759
    Speech at Holt Street Baptist Church, 763(s)
King, Rufus, 270(s), 279, 282–283(s)
King George's War (1744–1748), 40(i), 122, 135, 147, 150
King Philip's War, 126(s)
King William's War, 78, 120, 122, 135, 147, 150
King's College, 220
Kingsbury, F. J., 520–521(s)
Kinsey, Alfred, 727, 728
Kinship systems, 12
Kiowa Indians, 452
Kipling, Rudyard, 588(s)
Kirkpatrick, Jeane, 811–812
Kissinger, Henry, 752–753, 777, 780
Kitchen Cabinet, 307
Kitchen Debate, 741
KKK. *See* Ku Klux Klan
Klamath Indians, 364, 744
Klinghoffer, Leon, 812
"Knee Pants' at forty-five cents a dozen" (Riis), 516(s)
Knights of Labor, 494, 542
Knights of Syncopation, 635(s)
Know-Nothing Party. *See* American Party
Knox, Henry, 230
Kohl, Helmut, 806
Korea
    demilitarized zone in, 706(m)
    immigrants from, 1990s to twenty-first century, 831, 831(f)
    Japanese control over, 596
Korean War, 706–709, 706(m), 710
    imperial presidency and, 707–708
    racial integration in, 730(i)
Korematsu, Fred, 678–679, 690
Krimmel, John Lewis, 301(i)
Kristol, Irving, 795
"Ku Kluxer, The" (Johnson), 631(s)
Ku Klux Klan, 430–431, 432(s), 436
    Birmingham church bombing by, 758
    in *Birth of a Nation*, 581–582
    civil rights movement and, 733–735
    Democratic convention of 1924 on, 632
    Freedom Rides and, 756
    Freedom Summer and, 758–760
    resurrection of in the twenties, 630–632, 631–632(s)
    women in, 635–636(s)
Kuwait, Iraqi invasion of, 823–824, 824(i)
Kyoto Protocol (1998), 822

L

La Follette, Robert M., 573, 602, 633, 633(m)
Labor. *See also* Slave trade
    bound, 28
    during the Civil War, 400–401
    colonial America, 62–67, 68(i), 79, 86–88, 94
    colonialism and, 3
    coping with economic distress by, 101–102
    decline of craft work and, 294–295
    deskilling of, 94
    emergence of the middle class and, 291–293
    in Europe, 25
    in families, 131
    immigrants as competition for, 629
    indentured, 41, 55, 57
    industrialization and, 293–294, 490–499
    shortages of in the Civil War, 399
    socialism and, 534
    in spinning mills, 266–267
    transient, 102
    West Indies, 84
    women's, 79–80, 291–292, 293–294, 526
    during World War I, 603
Labor Movement, The (Ely), 534
Labor movements
    in the 1960s and 1970s, 773
    after World War I, 611–612
    after World War II, 717

Civil War, 400–401
  depression of 1893 and, 544
  energy crisis and, 783
  globalization and, 822
  in the Great Depression, 643, 648–649
  industrialization and, 490–499
  in mining, 461
  New Deal and, 648–649, 656–657
  Reagan and, 807
  Solidarity, 819
  Truman and, 708
  women in, 495(i)
  in World War II, 673–674
Labor unions. *See* Unions
Ladies Association of Philadelphia, 187
"Lady's Adieu to her TEA-TABLE, A"
  (anonymous), 166(s)
Lafayette, Marquis de, 188, 188(i), 191
Laissez-faire, 532–533
  in the 1960s, 775
  challenges to, 534–535
  the Great Depression and, 627–638
  progressivism on, 556
  in the twenties, 613–614
Lake City (Florida), 415
Lakewood Church, 836
Lakota Sioux, 452, 455, 456(i)
Lancaster Turnpike, 263
Land claims
  American Indians and, 197, 198–201, 201(s), 456
  of freedpeople, 411, 412, 413, 413(s)
  Northwest Ordinance on, 201
  sharecropping and, 429
  as solution to economic depression, 201–202
  in the West, 277, 450–451
  westward migration and, 262–265
Landon, Alfred M., 659
Land ownership
  colonial era, 67, 86–88
  England, 55
  Puritans and, 74
  tobacco cultivation and, 58–59
  Virginia Company and, 70–71
Land rush, 456
Landscape, changes to from urbanization, 288–289
Lange, Dorothea, 643(i)
Las Casas, Bartolomé de, 35–36
Lassen Volcanic, 575(m)
Lassiter, Matthew D., 853(s)
Las Vegas (New Mexico), 469–470
Lathrop, Julia, 559
Latin America, emerging democracies supported in, 747
Latinos/Latinas
  in feminism, 773
  in the Great Depression, 642
  influx of after World War II, 721
  liberation movement of, 773–774
Latrobe, Benjamin, 235
Latvia, 664, 703, 819
Lau v. Nichols, 774
Lawrence, Jacob, 653
Lawrence (Kansas), 379, 736
Lawrence (Massachusetts), 612(i)
Lawson, Steven F., 738(s)
Lazarus, Emma, 505

Lead mining, 462
League of Nations, 606–608, 607(s), 662
League of United Latin American Citizens (LULAC), 676, 736
Lease, Mary Elizabeth, 541(s), 542, 543
Leave It to Beaver (TV show), 723
Lebanon, 813
Lecompton Constitution, 379, 383
Lee, Jeremiah, 164(i)
Lee, Richard Henry, 178
Lee, Robert E., 384, 391, 396
  at Antietam, 396
  in Battle of Chancellorsville, 403
  on the condition of his soldiers, 398
  end of the war and, 409
  Gettysburg, Vicksburg, and, 403–404, 404(m)
Lee, Russell, 678(s)
Legacy of Conquest, The (Limerick), 472(s)
Legal system, Puritan, 74–75
"Legend of Sleepy Hollow, The" (Irving), 331
Legislative branch. *See also* House of Representatives; Senate
  big business and, 538–539
  Constitutional Convention on, 207–208
Leibowitz, Samuel, 642(i)
Leisler, Jacob, 91, 135
Leisler's Rebellion, 91, 135
Leisure
  automobiles and, 616
  Gilded Age, 524–525, 526–530, 527–528(s)
  the middle class and, 294
  nineteenth century, 289
  working-class, 528–530
LeMay, Curtis, 683
Lenape Indians, 47
Lend-Lease-Act (1941), 666
L'Enfant, Pierre Charles, 235
Lenin, Vladimir, 645
Leningrad, Battle of, 682(m)
Lenni-Lenape Indians, 93
Lesbians. *See* Homosexuals
"Let Sam Do It" (McCay), 669(s)
Letter from a Gentleman of the City of New York to Another, 91(s)
Letter from Birmingham Jail (King), 756, 757(s)
Letter on Jamestown Settlement (Rolfe), 58(s)
Letter to Aaron Burr (Sansay), 270(s)
Letter to Don Luis Valdés (King Philip IV of Spain), 49–50(s)
Letter to Florida Governor Reubin Askew (anonymous), 787(i)
Letter to General George Washington (Brodhead), 226(s)
Letter to George Pullman (Altgeld), 544(s)
Letter to Governor Harvey Parnell (Gammel), 644(s)
Letter Home from Korean War (Wheeler), 707(s)
Letter to Horace Greeley, 395(s)
Letter to John III, King of Portugal (Nzinga), 27
Letter to The Liberator (Emery and Abbott), 345(s)
Letter to Louis de Kergorlay (Tocqueville), 307(s)
Letter to Queen Anne (Oliver), 121(s)
Letter to the Rochester Female Charitable Society (Kempshall), 338(s)
Letter to Rufus King (Jefferson), 270(s)

Letter to Thomas Jefferson (Banneker), 234(s)
Leuchtenberg, William E., 660–661(s)
Levitt, William, 720
Levittown, Long Island, 720–721
Lewinsky, Monica, 829
Lewis, John, 758
Lewis, John L., 656
Lewis, Meriwether, 259–260
Lewis, Sinclair, 622, 634(s)
Lexington, Battle of, 174–175
LGBTQ. *See* Homosexuals
Libel laws, colonial, 136
Liberalism, 766–776. *See also* New Deal
  civil rights movement and, 755–765
  conservatism's revival and, 775–776
  counterculture and, 771
  environmentalism and, 794–795, 795(i)
  federal efforts toward social reform and, 767–769
  liberation movements and, 771–773
  New Frontier in, 767
  New Left and counterculture in, 769–771
  persistence of in the 1970s, 791–797
  politics of, 766–767
  Warren court and, 769
Liberal Republicans, 434–436
Liberation movements, 771–773
Liberator (newspaper), 344, 345(s)
Liberty Displaying the Arts and Sciences (Jennings), 220, 221(i)
Liberty Party, 349, 359, 368
Library Company of Philadelphia, 221(s)
Libya, 812–813, 845(m)
Lichtman, Allan J., 690–691(s)
Life (magazine), 724
Life of Riley, The (TV show), 723
Life of Washington (Weems), 331
Light bulbs, 485
Ligon, Richard, 84(m)
Liliuokalani (Queen of Hawaii), 587
Limerick, Patricia Nelson, 472(s)
Limited liability, 487
Limits of Democratic Expansion, The (Horton and Horton), 308(s)
Lincoln, Abraham, 379, 389, 395(s)
  on abuse of freed African Americans, 408
  assassination of, 409
  debates with Douglas, 383
  in the election of 1860, 384–385, 385(m)
  on emancipation, 395(s), 396
  Emancipation Proclamation, 355
  Freedmen's Bureau created by, 413, 417
  Gettysburg Address by, 405
  Grant and, 406
  inaugural address of, 417
  Johnson as vice president of, 412
  Meade appointed by, 403
  on Mexican-American War, 360
  Obama's election and, 841(i)
  Reconstruction plan of, 412, 417–423
  reelection of, 405
  seamstresses' complaint to, 400–401
  secession and, 389–390
  speech at Edwardsville (Illinois), 383(s), 440(s)
  Spot Resolutions, 362(s)
  Thirteenth Amendment and, 409

Index

Lincoln, Benjamin, 203(s)
Lindbergh, Charles, 665(i), 666(s)
Lindgren, Ida, 466(s)
Link, Arthur S., 608(s)
Listerine, 616
Literacy tests, voting and, 476, 476(m), 547, 758
Literature
    in the 1950s, 726, 728
    American, 330–331, 331(i)
    Beat, 726, 728(i)
    in the early republic, 220
    Harlem Renaissance, 623, 623(s), 624(s), 626(s)
    on slavery, 378
    in the twenties, 621–622
Lithuania, 664, 703, 819
Little Bighorn, Battle of the (1876), 455, 456, 456(i)
Little Rock (Arkansas), desegregation in, 733, 734(i)
Little Rock Nine, 733, 734(i)
Little Turtle, 240
Livingston, Robert, 178
Living wage, 493
Locke, John, 77, 131, 132, 179
Locomotives, 484–485
Lodge, Henry Cabot, 508, 607–608
Logan, James, 95
Loguen, Jermaine, 371
London Merchants' Petition to Repeal the Stamp Act, 165(s)
Lone Ranger, The (TV show), 723
"Long Civil Rights Movement, The" (Hall), 737(s)
Long Drive, 463
Long, Huey Pierce, 652(s), 653
Long, Jefferson Franklin, 436, 438
Long, Thomas, 405
"Long Origins of the Short Civil Rights Movement" (Lawson), 738(s)
Longstreet, James, 391, 396, 427
Looking Backward, 2000–1887 (Bellamy), 534
Loom and Spindle or Life among the Early Mill Girls (Robinson), 294(s)
Lopez, Ignacio Lutero, 676
Los Angeles
    American Indian population in, 744
    Brooklyn Dodgers moved to, 721
    foreign born population of, 809
    ghetto riots in, 761
    in the Great Depression, 642
    growth of in the twenties, 617(m), 618
    population of, 511
    in World War II, 671
    zoot suit riots, 677
Lost Generation, 621–622
Louisiana
    black majority in, 428
    ceded to Spain, 154
    civil rights movement investigation in, 715
    cotton production in, 321(m)
    Hurricane Katrina, 839
    Long in, 652(s), 653
    readmitted to the Union, 417, 422
    secession of, 385
Louisiana Purchase, 257, 258–260, 262
Louisiana Territory, 257, 260(m)
    Lewis and Clark expedition and, 259–260, 260(m)

Louis XIV (King of France), 45, 100, 120
Louis XVI (King of France), 238
L'Ouverture, Toussaint, 258, 302
Love Canal (New York), 795
Low, Ann Marie, 640(s)
Lowell, James Russell, 334
Lowell (Massachusetts), 293–295
Loyalists, 182, 183(m), 217
Lumber industry, 450, 463
    environmentalism and, 794
    itinerant musicians in, 529
    land claims by, 468
    in the South, 475
    unions in, 499
Lumumba, Patrice, 742
Lunch counter sit-ins, 734(m), 735–736, 735(s), 764(s)
Lundberg, Ferdinand, 725
Lundy, Benjamin, 343
Luper, Clara M., 736
Lusitania, 600, 604(i)
Luther, Martin, 71
Luxembourg, in World War II, 664
Lynchings, 432(s), 477, 557, 562, 564, 585(s)
    congressional bill on, 585(s)
Lyon, Matthew, 243(i), 391, 391(i)

M

MacArthur, Douglas, 645, 683, 706–707
Mackintosh, Ebenezer, 163, 174
Macune, Charles W., 542
Madison, Dolley, 275–276
Madison, James, 147, 202
    on the Alien and Sedition Acts, 244
    amendments submitted by, 231, 231–232(s)
    in Annapolis convention, 202
    on Bank of the United States, 233
    economic policies of, 277–278
    Federalist Papers by, 210, 213(s)
    on governmental structure, 202
    on Hamilton's policies, 233, 237–238
    judge appointments and, 261
    as president, 272–274
    War of 1812, 274–276
    on Whiskey Rebellion, 240
Mafia, 504
Mahan, Alfred Thayer, 588
Mailer, Norman, 727
Main Street (Lewis), 622
Maine, 75
    alcohol sales prohibited in, 339–340
    in Massachusetts colony, 78
Maine, sinking of the, 590–591
Maize, 4–5, 10, 25, 39
"Malaise Speech, The" (Carter), 789(s)
Malaria, 590
Malcolm X, 760, 764(s)
    assassination of, 697
Male domination, 772
Malintzin, 31–33, 31(i)
Mammoth Oil Company, 615
Man in the Gray Flannel Suit, The (Wilson), 728
Management, corporate, 488
Manassas, Battle of (1861), 391
Manchuria, Japanese invasion of, 667

Mandan people, 11, 39
    epidemics among, 452
Mandela, Nelson, 824–825
Manhattan Project, 685–686
Manifest destiny, 359, 367
Mann, James R., 567
Mann Act (1910), 567
The manner how to bring the Indians into subjugation (Martin), 60–61(s)
Manning, Chandra, 409–410(s)
Manufacturers' Record, 473
Manufacturing, 254(i), 262
    after World War II, 718, 719(f)
    American system of, 266
    assembly line in, 615
    child workers in, 492–493
    Civil War, 398–399, 401
    domestic, 266–267
    loss of jobs in, 843
    technology in, 264–266
    women in, 674
Manumission, 326
Mao Zedong, 705
Marbury v. Madison, 261
Marbury, William, 261
March of the Flag, The (Beveridge), 592(s)
March on Washington for Jobs and Freedom (1963), 758(i), 758
March to the Sea, 407–408
Marcy, William, 374
Mariners, 18
Market revolution, 255, 287–295
    consumer culture and, 488(i)
    railroads and, 482–483
    women in, 291–292
Marketplace of the Revolution, The (Breen), 103(s)
Marks of a True Conversion (Whitefield), 137–138(s)
Marmaduke Multiply's Merry Method of Making Minor Mathematics, 331(i)
Marriage. *See also* Divorce
    after World War II, 719–720
    colonial era, 45, 66–67, 79–80
    companionate, 267
    "complex," in the Oneida community, 340
    cult of domesticity and, 291–293
    of enslaved people, 324(i), 414–415
    of freed people, 414–415
    Gilded Age, 526–527
    interracial, 769, 848
    polygamy and, 334, 469
    progressivism on, 559
    same-sex, 828, 835, 843
Marshall, George, 703
Marshall, John, 261
Marshall Plan, 703
Marshall, Thurgood, 730, 818
Martha Washington societies, 339
Martí, José, 589, 591, 742
Martin, Trayvon, 843
Martineau, Harriet, 298(s)
Marx, Karl, 534
Mary II (Queen of England), 77, 78
Maryland, 61–62
    Constitution ratified by, 211(t)
    slavery in, 110
Masculinity, crisis of, 526–527

Mass media
  globalization and, 822
  mergers in, 830
  in the twenties, 621–622, 621(i)
Mass shootings, 851–852
Mass transit, 12, 290–291, 514–515
Massachusetts
  arts and science in, 220
  charter of, 78
  committee of correspondence, 161
  Constitution ratified by, 210, 211(t)
  education for all children in, 220
  Fifty-fourth Colored Infantry, 394
  influenza epidemic of 1918 in, 612(i)
  land claims by, 200
  Pilgrims in, 70–75
  public-accommodations law in, 409
  Puritan migration to, 72–75
  Shays's Rebellion in, 202–203
  witchcraft trials in, 79
Massachusetts Bay Company, 73–74
Massachusetts Centinel, 213–214(s)
Massachusetts Gazette, 166(s), 169(s)
Massachusetts Indians, 72–73, 74
Massasoit, 72–73
Matrilineal kinship systems, 12
Matroon, Ebenezer, 235
Mattachine Society, 727
Matthewes, Peter Bassnett, 223(s)
Matthews, J. Sherrie, 529(i)
Maxwell House Hour, The (radio show), 621
May, Samuel J., 371
Maya, 7, 25, 31
Mayflower, 71
Mayflower Compact, 72, 72(s)
Mayhew, Experience, 119(s)
McCain, John, 841
McCarran, Pat, 713
McCarran-Walter Immigration Act (1952), 737
McCarthy, Joseph Raymond, 714–715, 714(i), 727(i)
McCarthyism, 714–715
McCay, Winsor, 669(s)
McClellan, George B., 393, 405
McCloy, John J., 688
McClure's (magazine), 557
McCormick, Cyrus, 588
McCoy, Elijah, 484
McCulloch v. Maryland, 261
McDonald's, 821
McFarlane, Robert, 813
McGovern, George, 781
McGuffey Readers, 532–533
McKay, Claude, 626(s)
McKeesport (Pennsylvania), 484(i)
McKinley, William, 538, 539
  Cuba under, 591
  in election of 1896, 545–546, 546(m)
  Hawaii annexation by, 591
  on intervention in Cuba, 590–591
  Open Door policy of, 596–597
  on the Philippines, 593(s)
  Philippine war and, 592–594, 595
  Populists and, 546
  Roosevelt as vice president of, 576
McLuckie, John, 497
Meade, George A., 403–404

Measles, 359, 364, 452
Meat Inspection Act, 577, 578(i)
Meatpacking industry, 488, 577, 578(i)
Mechanization, 491(s)
Medicaid, 769, 806
Medical education, 221
Medicare, 769, 806
Medicare Prescription Drug, Improvement, and Modernization Act (2003), 836
Medina, Jennifer, 831–832(s)
Mediterranean world, 18–20, 26
Meeting of Colored Citizens of Boston (Nell), 372(s)
Megachurches, 835–836, 835(s)
Mehaffry, J. W., 474
Mellish, Thomas, 101(i)
Mellon, Andrew, 613
Melting pot, 447, 508
Melting-Pot, The (Zangwill), 508
Memoirs of Boston King (King), 226–227(s)
Memories of the Pearl Harbor Attack (Sone), 668(s)
"Memory of a British Officer Stationed at Lexington and Concord," 175(s)
Memphis (Tennessee), 831
  lynching in, 564
  race riot in, 421, 421(i)
Mencken, Henry Louis (H. L.), 622
Mendez v. Westminster, 736
Menlo Park (New Jersey), 485
Menninger, William C., 717
Mennonites, 182
Mercantilism, 100–102
Meredith, James, 756
Merian, Mattaeus, 59(i)
Mergers and acquisitions, 830
Mesa Verde, 11(i), 575(m)
Message to Massachusetts Provincial Congress (Oneida Leaders), 181(s)
Mestizos, 34
Metacom, 120
Metacom's War, 119–120, 124(s)
Methodism, 133
  abolitionism and, 347
  black churches, 417
  enslaved people and, 325
  Second Great Awakening and, 333
MeToo movement, 852
Metropolitan Opera House, 525, 573(i)
Mexica. *See* Aztecs
Mexican Americans, 447
  Americanization of, 629
  Californios in the West, 469–470
  civil rights movement of, 736
  cowboys, 463
  under Eisenhower, 744
  in the Great Depression, 642
  migrant workers, 642–643, 643(i)
  women's suffrage and, 560(i)
  in World War II, 675, 676
Mexican-American War, 357, 360–363, 361(m), 367, 391, 469
Mexican immigrants
  1990s to twenty-first century, 830–831, 831(f)
  arrivals of 1960–2000, 809
  labor contracts with, 502
  quota system on, 629
  in World War II, 676

Mexican revolution (1911), 598–599
Mexico
  California and, 359–360
  horticulture in, 4–5
  illegal immigration from, in the 1950s and 1960s, 744
  Missouri Compromise and, 284(m)
  NAFTA and, 828
  Pike expedition in, 260
  silver mining in, 25
  slavery banned in, 328
  Spanish exploration of, 36
  U.S. expansion into, 280
  World War I and, 602
Miami Beach, 648(i)
Miami people, 240
  in Seven Years' War, 150–151
Michigan, 289, 631
"Michigan Requests Federal Loan to Bolster Unemployment Fund" (Stuart), 805(s)
Microchips, 829–830
Microsoft, 830
Middle Atlantic region, education in, 220
Middle class
  African Americans in, 513, 513(i)
  the counterculture on, 771
  emergence of the, 291–293
  growth of after World War II, 718–719, 719(f)
  industrialization and, 493, 524
  leisure pursuits of, 524–525, 529
  under Reagan, 807
  progressivism and, 556
  second industrial revolution and, 553
  in the South, 327
  temperance and, 333
Middle Colonies, 90–97
  New York and New Jersey, 91–92, 92(i)
  Pennsylvania, 92–95
Middle East
  Arab Spring in, 844
  Carter and, 786
  Reagan and, 811, 812–813, 813(m)
  Six-Day War, 780–781
  terrorism and democratic uprisings in, 845(m)
Middle Passage, 108–109, 108(i)
Midway Island, Battle of (1942), 683, 684(m)
Midwest
  immigrants in, 289
  industrialization in, 473, 482
Migrant workers, 642–643, 643(i)
Milano, Alyssa, 852
Military-industrial complex, 670, 700, 740, 743(s)
Military Reconstruction Acts (1867), 422
Militias, 63, 110
  in American Revolution, 174–175
  Civil War, 399
Miller, William, 334, 335
Millerites, 334, 335
Milošević, Slobodan, 829
Mimeograph machines, 483
Minié balls, 397
Minimum wage laws
  in the 1950s, 744
  in the 1960s, 767
  New Deal, 657
  in the twenties, 614

I-23

Index

Mining
  Californios in, 469
  child labor in, 492–493, 492(i)
  Incan, 8
  in the New South, 475(m)
  pollution from, 452
  strikes, 495(i), 499
  urbanization and, 512
  in the West, 450, 461–463
Minnesota, 385, 466
Minor v. Happersett, 424
Minor, Virginia, 424
Miñoso, Orestes "Minnie," 736
Minstrel shows, 289, 529, 529(i)
Minutemen, 173–175
Miranda v. Arizona, 769
Misery index, 790(s), 829
Miss America pageant protests, 772
Mission system, 36, 39, 49–50, 359–360
Missionaries
  to American Indians, 222, 313
  Boxer uprising and, 596(i)
  in exploration of the Americas, 18
  on gender roles, 220
  in Hawaii, 587
  in imperialism, 588
  Jesuit, 45
  praying towns and, 119
  Pueblo Revolt and, 50
  in schools for freedpeople, 416
Mississippi
  black code in, 419(s)
  black majority in, 428
  civil rights movement in, 730
  cotton production in, 321(m)
  desegregation resistance in, 756
  Freedom Summer in, 758–760
  Ku Klux Klan in, 431
  secession of, 385, 440(s)
  statehood of, 277
Mississippi Freedom Democratic Party (MFDP), 759
Mississippi River, 265
  French trade on, 45
Mississippian cultures, 3, 13, 13(i), 25, 39
Missouri, 357, 399
Missouri Compromise, 282–284, 284(m), 378, 379(m), 382
  Crittenden plan and, 386–387
Missouri Pacific Railroad, 494
Mitchell, John, 782
Mixtec art, 9(i), 10
Mizuno, Chuck, 668(s)
Mobile (Alabama), 398
Mobuto, Joseph, 742
Model Cities Act (1965), 767
Model of Christian Charity, A (Winthrop), 73(s)
Modern Republicanism, 743–744
Modern Women: The Lost Sex (Lundberg and Farnham), 725
Modernism, fundamentalism vs., 626–628
Modoc Indians, 363
Mohawk Indians, 47, 121
  in the American Revolution, 180–181, 181(i)
Molotov, Vyacheslav, 700
Mondale, Walter, 807

Money supply
  Farmers' Alliance on, 542
  Panic of 1819 and, 281–282
Monitor vs. Merrimack (1862), 394(m)
Monopolies
  political power and, 487(s)
  railroad, farmers and, 541
  Sherman Antitrust Act and, 487(s), 488
  telegraph, 486
  trusts and, 487–488
Monopoly Is the Master (Lease), 541(s)
Monroe Doctrine, 279, 279–280(s), 595, 607
Monroe, James, 207, 258, 279–280
Monroe, Marilyn, 724
Montana
  American Indian reservations in, 455
  cattle ranching in, 465
  mining in, 462–463
Montesquieu, Baron de, 132
Montezuma, 31–33, 31(i)
Montezuma, Carlos, 565
Montgomery (Alabama)
  bus boycott, 732, 732(i)
  Freedom Rides in, 756
Montgomery Improvement Association, 732
Montgomery, Olen, 642(i)
Montgomery Ward, 489
Montreal, 120, 176, 190(m)
Moonshiners, 626
Moral Majority, 796
Moral suasion, 336
Moral uplift, 562, 565
Morality
  baby boom and, 719
  progressivism and, 565–568
  wealth and, 532–533
Moravians, 182
More, Thomas, 55
Moreno, Luisa, 642, 742
Morgan, John Pierpont, 485, 486, 524, 545, 576
Morgan, Lewis, 457
Morgan, Nancy Hart, 187
Mormon Trail, 365(m)
Mormons, 334–335, 357, 460, 469
Morning in America (ad), 807(s)
Morocco, in World War II, 682
Morris, Lewis, 135–136
Morrisites, 135–136
Morrison, John, 491(s)
Morse, Samuel F. B., 338
Mortgages
  after World War II, 720
  GI Bill and, 717, 717(i)
  the Great Recession and, 803, 840
  racial discrimination in, 720–721
  under Reagan, 807
  savings and loan collapse and, 807
Morton, "Jelly Roll," 529, 623
Mossadegh, Mohammed, 741
Motel chains, 719
Motion Picture Association of American, 711(s)
Mott, James, 347
Mott, Lucretia, 347
Ms. (magazine), 772
Muckrakers, 556(s), 557, 564
  on meatpacking, 577, 578(i)
Mueller, Robert, 848

Muir, John, 574(i), 575
Mujahideen, 784–785, 784(i), 813(m), 820
Mulattos, 34
Mulberry Street (New York City), 504(i)
Muller v. Oregon, 558(s), 559
Multinational corporations, 821–822
Multiplier effect, 265
Munich Accord, 664
Municipal reforms, 572–573
Munn v. Illinois, 541
Murphy, Carl, 672(s)
Murray, John, 218(i)
Murray, Judith Sargent, 218(i), 219, 219(s)
Murrow, Edward R., 714
Music
  in the 1950s, 727
  the blues, 529
  counterculture and, 771
  itinerant musicians, 529
  rock 'n' roll, 725
  in teenage culture, 725
  in the twenties, 623–624
Mussolini, Benito, 664, 685
Mutual aid societies, 290, 295, 302, 336, 412
  African American, 513
  immigrant, 503–504
Mutually assured destruction (MAD), 740
Myers, Daisy, 720–721
Myers, William, 720–721
My Lai massacre (1968), 751–752

N

Nader, Ralph, 834–835
Nagasaki, atomic bomb dropped on, 686
Nahaton, William, 124(s)
Nahuatl, 31
Naldi, Nita, 621(i)
Napalm, 750
Napoleonic Wars, 273, 281
Narragansett Indians, 75
Narrative of Captivity (Rowlandson), 126–127(s)
Narrative of the Life of Frederick Douglass (Douglass), 346(s)
Nash, Diane, 756
Nasser, Gamal Abdel, 742
Nast, Thomas, 428(s), 442(s), 535–536(s)
Natchez (Mississippi), 399
Nation of Islam, 760
National Association for the Advancement of Colored People (NAACP)
  black nationalism and, 625
  civil rights movement and, 676, 729, 730
  Evers in, 758
  founding of, 564, 584(s)
  Freedom Summer and, 758–760
  integrationist strategy of, 620
  on lynching, 585(s)
  sit-ins by, 734(m), 735, 735(s)
National Association of Colored Women (NACW), 477, 525, 557, 561, 730
National Association of Manufacturers, 651
National Broadcasting Company (NBC), 722
National Cash Register Company, 572
National Congress of American Indians, 744
National Defense Act (1916), 600
National Defense Education Act (1958), 744

I-24

National Energy Act (1978), 784
National Farm Workers Association, 773
National Industrial Recovery Act (1933), 648
National Interstate and Defense Highway Act (1956), 744
National Labor Relations Act (1935), 656
National Labor Relations Board, 656
National League of Baseball, 527
National Liberation Front (Vietcong), 748–750
National Organization for Women (NOW), 772, 792
National Origins Act (1924), 629
National parks and forests, 575(m), 576, 794
National Recovery Administration (NRA), 648–649, 648(i)
National Republicans, 303, 305
National Review (journal), 775
National Rifle Association, 827–828
National Road, 264
National Security Act (1947), 703
National Security Agency, 703–704, 845
National Security Council (NSC), 703, 705–706, 811
National Socialism, 664
  Holocaust under, 681, 687–689, 688(i), 690–691(s)
National Temperance Offering, The, 339(i)
National Trades Union, 295
National Tube Works, 484(i)
National Union for Social Justice, 651(i)
National War Labor Board (NWLB), 603, 673
National Woman's Party, 559
National Woman Suffrage Association, 424
National Women's Trade Union League (WTUL), 559
National Youth Administration, 654
Native Americans. *See* American Indians
Native Attack on Jamestown (Merian), 59(i)
Nativism, 338, 507–508
  Ku Klux Klan resurrection and, 630–632, 631–632(s)
  in the twenties, 628–630
  twenty-first century, 831
Nativists, 338, 380
Nat Turner's rebellion, 325–326
Natural law, 132
Natural resources, conservation and preservation of, 574–575
Naturalization Act (1798), 243
"Nature" (Emerson), 335
Nauvoo (Illinois), 334
Navajo people
  civilization of, 452
  code talkers in World War II, 676–677, 676(i)
  forced onto reservation, 409
  Indian Reorganization Act and, 658
  raids against Pueblo people, 49
Navigation Acts (England, 1660), 100–101, 161
Navigational instruments, 18
Nazism. *See* National Socialism
Nebraska
  bicycles in, 526(i)
  immigrant farmers in, 466
  sod houses in, 467
Nebraska Territory, 378–380
Necklace with Gold Frog Ornaments, 9(i), 10

"Negro Problem from the Negro Point of View, The" (Wells), 563(s), 583–584(s)
Nell, William C., 372(s)
Neoconservatives, 795–796
Neolin, 155
Netherlands
  colonies of, 46–47
  expansion and conflict with, 43
  Middle Colonies and, 90
  Protestant Reformation and, 71
  shipbuilding and trade in, 26
  Spanish control of, 33
  sugar industry, 84
  in World War II, 664
Neutrality Acts, 663, 666
Neutrality Proclamation (1793), 238–239
Nevada, 461, 462
Nevis, 84
New Amsterdam, 47
  English control of, 91
New Bedford (Massachusetts), 290
New Bern (North Carolina), 416
New Deal, 553, 646–661
  after World War II, 716, 718
  communism and, 711
  critics of, 651–653, 651(i)
  decline of the, 659
  direct assistance and relief in, 649, 653
  effectiveness of, 660–661(s)
  minorities and, 657–658, 744
  moves to the left in, 653–655
  New Frontier and, 767
  organized labor and, 656–657
  philosophy behind, 646–647
  Social Security in, 654–655
  steps toward recovery in, 646–649
  "The New Deal: The Conservative Achievements of Liberal Reform" (Bernstein), 661(s)
New England
  agricultural land in, 79
  bread riots, 135
  colonization of, 71–75
  compared with English society, 77–78
  divorce in, 131
  education in, 220
  factories in, 288
  Metacom's War, 119–120, 124(s)
  religious challenges in, 75–76
  settlement of, 70–75
  Seven Years' War in, 152
  textile mills in, 293–294
  transient workers in, 102
  wars in, 76, 78
  workday length in, 295
New England Courant, 94
New Freedom, 580–582, 581(i)
The New Freedom (Wilson), 579(s)
New Frontier, 767
New Guinea, in World War II, 683
New Hampshire
  Constitution ratified by, 210, 211(t)
  farmers' march in, 202
New Jersey, 78
  colonial era, 91–92, 92(i)
  constitution of, 196
  Constitution ratified by, 210, 211(t)
  free black people in, 224

  Revolution battles in, 185
  suburbs in, 720
New Jersey Plan, 208
New Jersey Pro-Jackson Convention, 305–306(s)
New Left, 769–771, 796, 803
New Light clergy, 133–134, 133(m), 135, 162
New Look strategy, 740
New Mexico
  Compromise of 1850 on, 368–370
  immigrants in, 502
  Spanish exploration of, 36, 49–50
  statehood of, 363
New Nationalism, 580
New Negro, 623
"The New Negro—What Is He?" (Randolph and Owen), 623(s)
New Orleans
  Battle of, 276(i), 277
  Civil War capture of, 393
  closed by Spain, 198
  as commercial center, 262
  Hurricane Katrina, 839
  jazz in, 529
New Republic (magazine), 687
New Right, 791, 795–796, 797(s), 803
  Reagan and, 804–805
  social conservatism and, 808–809
New South, 473–481, 475(m)
New South, The (Grady), 474
"New Suburban Dream Born of Asia and Southern California" (Medina), 831–832(s)
New woman, 621
New York
  black people in colonial, 92
  canals in, 278, 288–289
  class rebellions, 135
  colonial era, 91–92, 92(i)
  Constitution debates in, 214(s)
  Constitution ratified by, 210–211, 211(t)
  ghetto riots in, 761
  Love Canal in, 795
  population of, 288
  revivals in, 332
  Women's Peace Encampment in, 815(i)
  young residents in, 290
New York City
  African American population of, 513
  American Revolution in, 185, 190(m)
  auction in, 282(i)
  baseball teams lost by, 721
  Beats in, 727
  charter of, 135
  crime in, 517
  Democratic convention of 1924 in, 632
  draft riots in, 400, 400(i)
  electric lighting in, 485
  Federal Hall in, 231(i)
  foreign born population of, 809
  free black people in, 224
  gays and lesbians in, 528, 774
  Gilded Age in, 524–525
  Harlem Renaissance, 623–625
  immigrant communities in, 503, 571
  immigrants in, 503, 831
  impressment riots in, 152
  industry in, 482
  labor activism in, 295

I-25

Index

New York City (Continued)
  Mulberry Street, 504(i)
  nuclear freeze movement in, 815
  political machine in, 518
  population density in, 515–516
  population of, 262, 511
  public transportation in, 290–291
  sanitation in, 522(s)
  skyscrapers in, 484
  slave revolts in, 111
  on slavery, 208
  Society of Pewterers banner, 146(i)
  Stonewall riots, 774
  tenant revolts, 135
  tenements, 515–517
  time zone in, 483
  tongs in, 504
  women's suffrage movement in, 561(i)
New York Daily Times, 373–374(s)
New York Giants, 721
New York Herald (newspaper), 440(s)
New York Herald Tribune (newspaper), 486
New York Journal (newspaper), 590
New York Times, 429, 572(s), 591, 677(s), 753, 805(s), 831–832(s)
New York Tribune, 336, 435
New York World (newspaper), 590
New Zealand
  women's suffrage in, 561
  in World War II, 683, 684
Newark (New Jersey), ghetto riots in, 761
Newburgh (New York), army officers encamped at, 198
Newell, Ellen, 106(s)
Newfoundland, 44
Newport (Rhode Island), 525
Newport African Union Society, 225
News Conference on Iraq (Bush), 838(s)
News wives, 64
Newspapers, 290–291
  abolitionist, 344, 346, 348, 378
  African American, 513
  for immigrants, 504
  on the Red Scare, 611
  yellow journalism in, 590
Newton, Huey P., 761, 764–765(s)
Nez Percé Indians, 364, 455
Ngo Dinh Diem, 749
Niagara Movement, 564
Nicaragua
  filibusters to, 374
  repressive regime supported in, 780
  Sandinistas, 811, 825
  U.S. intervention in, 586, 597
Nickelodeons, 529
Nightclubs, 529
Nimitz, Chester, 683
9/11 attacks, 836, 851
Nineteenth Amendment, 561, 561(i), 771
Nixon, Richard M., 740, 777
  address accepting the presidential nomination, 778(s)
  Cold War and, 780–781
  in the election of 1960, 744–745, 745(i)
  in the election of 1968, 752, 778–779
  in the election of 1972, 779
  foreign policy under, 784

Hiss affair and, 713
  impeachment articles, 788(s)
  Kitchen Debate, 741
  Middle East crisis and, 780–781
  pragmatic conservatism of, 779–780, 795
  reelection of, 778
  reputation of, 744
  "Speech Accepting the Republican Nomination for President," 778(s)
  Vietnamization and, 752–754
  Watergate scandal, 781–782
  wiretapping by, 781–782
No Child Left Behind (NCLB), 836
Noble Order of the Knights of Labor, 494
Non-Intercourse Act (1809), 273
Nonviolence, 732, 760
Nonviolent direct action, 756
Noriega, Manuel, 824
Normandy, D Day at, 682(m), 683
Norris, Clarence, 642(i)
Norse exploration and settlements, 19
North American Free Trade Agreement (NAFTA), 828
North Atlantic Treaty Organization (NATO), 704–705, 815, 829
North Carolina, 78
  black voters in, 428
  cigarette manufacturing in, 485
  colony of, 62–63
  Constitution ratified by, 211, 211(t)
  Freedmen's Bureau schools, 416(i)
  land ownership in, 67
  lumber industry in, 475
  readmitted to the Union, 422
  secession of, 390
  sit-ins in, 734(m), 735, 735(s)
  Tuscarora War, 120
North Carolina Life Insurance Company, 477
North Dakota
  American Indian reservations in, 455
  cattle ranching in, 465
  gold in, 456
North, Frederick, Lord, 189
North Korea, 706–709
  in axis of evil, 839
  nuclear weapons testing in, 844
North, Oliver, 813
North Star (newspaper), 346, 348
Northern Pacific Railroad, 436
Northern Securities Company, 576
Northup, Solomon, 322, 323–324(s)
Northwest Ordinances, 201, 201(s), 227(s)
Northwest Territory, 201–202, 272
  frontier conflicts and, 240–241
  slavery in, 208
Northwestern Farmers' Alliance, 542
Norway
  women's suffrage in, 561
  in World War II, 664
Note taking, 6–7
Nova Scotia, freedpeople in, 224
Noyes, John Humphrey, 340
NSC-68, 705, 741
Nuclear arms race, 740–741
  Cuban missile crisis and, 745–746, 747(s)
  de-escalation of, 815–816
  North Korea and, 844

  under Reagan, 809–810
  SALT I Treaty on, 780
  SALT II Treaty on, 784
Nuclear freeze movement, 814–816, 815(i)
Nuclear power, 795, 795(i)
Nuclear weapons
  bomb shelters and, 740(i)
  Cold War and, 697
  Cuban missile crisis and, 745–746, 747
  in Iran, 839, 846
  New Left on, 771
  nuclear freeze movement and, 814–816, 815(i)
  in origins of the Cold War, 701
  the Rosenbergs and, 710, 713
  strategic arms reduction treaty on, 821
  in World War II, 685–687, 686–687(s), 686(i)
Nullification, 310, 311, 318(i)
Nullification Crisis, American Republicanism, and the Force Bill Debate (Ericson), 318(s)
Nye Committee, 663
Nye, Gerald, 663
Nzinga, Mvemba A, 27

O

Oakland (California), 617
Obama, Barack, 803, 841–848, 852
  African Americans' expectation of, 844(s)
  domestic policies of, 841–844
  election of, 841
  foreign policy of, 844–847
  on health care, 842(s)
  on the middle East and North Africa, 846(s)
  Syrian refugees and, 845
  war on terrorism and, 844–846
Obamacare, 841, 849
Obergefell v. Hodges, 843
Occupational Safety and Health Administration (OSHA), 779
Occupy Wall Street movement, 843
O'Connor, Sandra Day, 808
Odd Fellows, 477
Odets, Clifford, 653
Office of Economic Opportunity, 779
Office of the Director of National Intelligence, 837
Office of War Information, 674, 675(s)
Ohio
  abolitionism in, 344–345
  Ku Klux Klan in, 631
  the market revolution and, 290
  statehood of, 263
Ohio River valley, land conflicts in, 93–94, 199–200, 240–241
Ohiyesa, 459
Oil embargo, 781
Ojibwe, 45
Okies, 640
Okinawa, Battle of (1945), 684–685
Oklahoma
  American Indian reservations in, 455
  Ku Klux Klan in, 631
Old-Age Revolving Pensions Corporation, 651–652
Old Light clergy, 133, 134, 142
"Old Reliable" (Berryman), 660(i)

I-26

Oldsmobile, 616
Oliver, Andrew, 162–164
Oliver, Thomas, 121(s)
Olney, Richard, 498
Olympic Games, 784, 810
"On Being Brought from Africa to America" (Wheatley), 183(s)
On George Whitefield Coming to Connecticut (Cole), 138(s)
On George Whitefield, the Great Revivalist (Franklin), 138–139(s)
"On the Equality of the Sexes" (Murray), 219(s)
On the Origin of Species (Darwin), 533
On the Road (Kerouac), 727
Oñate, Juan de, 36
Oneida community (New York), 340
Oneida Indians, 121, 181, 181(s)
Opechancanough, 59(i), 60, 60(i)
Open Door policy, 596–597, 662, 667
Open-hearth process of steel manufacturing, 484
Open Letter Home, An (Murphy), 672(s)
Operation Desert Storm, 823–824
Operation Just Cause, 823
Operation Rolling Thunder (1965), 750
Operation Wetback, 744
Opium, 567
Opium trade, 504
Opium Wars (1839–1942, 1856–1860), 470
Oppenheimer, J. Robert, 664, 685, 690
   suspected of Communist affiliations, 715
Ordinance of Nullification, 310, 311
Oregon
   expansion into, 359
   Ku Klux Klan in, 630, 631
   lumber industry in, 463
   in World War II, 671
Oregon Territory, 358(s), 359
   statehood of, 385
Oregon Trail, 357, 358(s), 359, 365(m)
Oregon Trail Diary (Geer), 358(s)
Organization of Petroleum Exporting Countries (OPEC), 781, 782–783
Organized crime, in prohibition, 626
Original sin, 132
Origins of the New South (Woodward), 569(s)
Osage Indians, 360, 393
Osceola, 314
Osteen, Joel, 836
Ostend Manifesto, 374
O'Sullivan, John L., 359
Oswald, Lee Harvey, 767
Other America, The (Harrington), 767, 768(s)
Ottawa Indians, 155
Ottoman empire, 26, 599
Our Country (Strong), 587
Overland trails, 357–359
Overseers of the Poor, 102
Owen, Chandler, 623(s)
Owen, Robert, 340
Owen, Robert Dale, 340

P

Pacifists, 182
Page, Patti, 725
Pahlavi, Mohammad Reza, 741, 786
Paine, Thomas, 177, 177(s), 188, 212(s)

Paiute Indians, 575
Pakenham, Edward, 276(i)
Palestine
   Camp David accords on, 786
   Gaza Strip and West Bank and, 824
   terrorism and, 812
Palestine Liberation Organization (PLO), 812, 824
Palin, Sarah, 841
Palmer, A. Mitchell, 611(s), 611–612
Palmer Memorial Institute, 564
Palmer raids, 612
Pamphlets, 177, 177–178(s)
Panama, Noriega and, 824
Panama Canal, 586, 595, 742, 784
Pan-Arab nationalism, 742
Panic of 1819, 281–282, 300, 301
Panic of 1837, 294, 295–296, 357
Panic of 1873, 436
Paraffin, 484
Paris Climate Agreement (2015), 847, 849
Paris Peace Conference (1918), 606–608
Parker, Arthur C., 565
Parker, Charlie, 727
Parker, Ely, 393
Parks, Rosa, 732
Parnell, Harvey, 644(s)
Parrott arms factory, 401
Partial Nuclear Test Ban Treaty (1963), 747
Partners in Health, 822
Partnerships, corporations compared with, 487
"Party of Patches" (Gillam), 543(s)
Patient Protection and Affordable Care Act (2010), 841, 849
Patriarchal family, 74, 75, 130, 131
Patriarchy, 772
Patriot Act (2001), 836–837, 845
Patriots, 173–174, 183(m)
Patronage, 539
Patrons of Husbandry, 540, 540(i)
Patterson, Haywood, 642(i)
Patterson, William, 208
Patton, George S., 645
Paul, Alice, 559, 561
Pawnee Indians
   civilization of, 452
   Kansas-Nebraska Act and, 379
Payne-Aldrich tariff (1909), 579
Pea Ridge, Battle of (1862), 393, 394(m)
Peace Corps, 747, 767
Peace movements, 727
Peace of Paris, 154, 155, 156, 191–192
Peace societies, 401
Peale, Charles Willson, 150(i), 220
Peale, Norman Vincent, 727
Pearce, Charles H., 417
Pearl Harbor
   atomic bombs as retaliation for, 686
   Japanese attack on, 662, 668(s), 678
   naval base at, 587
Pease, Jane H., 318(i)
Pease, William H., 318(i)
Peck and Peck, 552(i)
Pendleton Civil Service Reform Act (1883), 519
Peninsulares, 34
Penn, William, 92–93, 94–95
Pennsylvania, 78, 92–95, 93(m)
   abolition of slavery in, 227–228(s)

   constitution of, 195
   Constitution ratified by, 210, 211(t)
   emancipation of enslaved people in, 224
   expansion and conflict in, 93(m), 94–95
   German immigrants to, 93
   redemptioners in, 94
   road development in, 263
   steel manufacturing in, 484(i)
   suburbs in, 720–721
   Three Mile Island, 795, 795(i)
   Whiskey Rebellion in, 239–240, 239(i)
Pennsylvania Act for the Gradual Abolition of Slavery, 227–228(s)
Pennsylvania Gazette, 94, 151(s)
Pennsylvania Magazine, 177
Pension plans
   Townsend on, 651–652
   in the twenties, 614
Pentagon attack, 836, 851
Pentagon Papers, 753, 781, 787(s)
People's Party of America. *See* Populist Party
Pequot Indians, 76, 119
Pequot War, 76, 117, 119
Perestroika, 815
Perkins, Frances, 648
Permanent Investigation Subcommittee of the Committee on Government Operations, 714
Perot, Ross, 825, 828
Perry, Jim, 465
Perry, Matthew C., 373–374
Perry, Oliver, 275
Pershing, John, 599, 602
Personal Memoirs of Ulysses S. Grant (Grant), 407(s)
Personal Responsibility and Work Opportunity Reconciliation Act (1996), 828
Peter, Hugh, 76
Petition for Renewal of Patent on Cotton Gin (Whitney), 265–266(s)
Petition of Enslaved African Americans to the Massachusetts Legislature, 223(s), 226(s)
Petition to Free an Indian Slave (Nahaton), 124(s)
Petition to the South Carolina Senate (Cole, Matthewes, Webb), 223(s)
Petrified Forest, 575(s)
Petroleum industry
   Carter presidency and, 782–784
   cracking in, 484
   horizontal integration in, 487
   Iran intervention and, 741
   Mexican revolution and, 599
   the Middle East and, 813(m)
   oil embargo of 1973 and, 781, 782(i)
   OPEC control of, 782–783
   Operation Desert Storm and, 823, 824
   trusts in, 487
Petticoat Affair, 306–307, 310
Pfundheler, Nora, 468
Phalanxes, Fourierist, 340
Philadelphia
   African American churches in, 333
   African American population of, 513
   African Americans in, 290
   American Philosophical Society in, 220
   American Revolution in, 186, 190, 190(m)
   capital moved from, 233
   capital moved to, 231(i), 232

Index

Philadelphia (Continued)
  charitable organizations in, 295
  election day in, 301(i)
  free black people in, 224
  industry in, 482
  influenza epidemic in, 612
  population of, 288, 511
  population of, nineteenth century, 262
  racial violence in, 302
  transportation revolution in, 289
  yellow fever in, 237, 240
  young residents in, 290
Philadelphia and Reading Railroad bankruptcy, 537
Philadelphia Female Anti-Slavery Society, 344
Philanthropy
  Carnegie in, 533
  Progressive Era, 564–565
Philip II (King of Spain), 33, 46, 71
Philip IV (King of Spain), 49–50
Philippines
  annexation of, 485, 593
  immigrants from, 1990s to twenty-first century, 831, 831(f)
  independence of, 643
  McKinley on, 594
  occupation of, 593
  rebellion of, 593–594
  repressive regime supported in, 780
  war for, 592–594
  in World War II, 683, 684(m)
Phillips, Wendell, 423
Phyllis Schlafly Report, The, 793(s)
Picket Line (Vachon), 641(s)
Pictographs, 442(s)
Piecework, 492
Pierce, Franklin, 373–374, 378, 379–380
Pietists, 133
Pike, Zebulon, 260, 260(m)
Pilgrims, 71, 72–75
Pinchot, Gifford, 574
  fired by Taft, 579
Pinckney, Charles Cotesworth, 245
Pinckney, Thomas, 241
Pinckney Treaty (1796), 241, 241(s)
Pingree, Hazen, 573
Pinkerton detectives, 495(i), 497, 498(i)
Pinochet, Augusto, 825
Pirates, Barbary, 198, 258
Pittsburgh
  Hoovervilles in, 639
  railroad strike in, 497(m)
Pittsburgh Courier (newspaper), 513
Pizarro, Francisco, 20(m), 33, 39
Plan of Union, 150
Plane hijacking, 812
Plantation economy, 63–65, 66–67, 355
  slave revolts and, 325–326
  South Carolina, 85–88
  unification against abolitionism in, 327–328
  yeomen farmers and, 327
Plantation slavery, 320
  domestic production in, 267
  Harpers Ferry raid and, 384
Platt, Orville, 591
Platt Amendment, 591
Playboy (magazine), 728

Pledge of allegiance, 727
Plessy v. Ferguson, 477, 563, 731
Plunkitt, George Washington, 518
Plymouth colony, 72–74
Pocahontas, 57, 58, 59(i)
Podhoretz, Norman, 795
Poindexter, John, 813
Poland
  communism imposed in, 703
  free elections in, 701
  German invasion of, 664
  Solidarity in, 819
  as USSR buffer, 700
Police actions, 707–708
Police departments, 517, 611
Polio
  Roosevelt and, 647(i)
  vaccine for, 719(i), 720
Polish immigrants, 503(i)
Political campaigns, television coverage of, 722
Political cartoons
  on the Alien and Sedition Acts, 243(i)
  of an exciseman, 239(i)
  on the Cuban missile crisis, 747(s)
  on the election of Obama, 841(i)
  on the Embargo Act, 273(i)
  first American, 151(s)
  on government and monopolies, 487(s)
  "Join or Die" (Franklin), 151(s)
  on labor movements, 500(s)
  on the League of Nations, 669(s)
  on monopolies, 536(s)
  on the New Deal, 660(i)
  on Reconstruction, 428(s)
  on the Red Scare, 715(s)
  on Saddam Hussein, 825(s)
  on Teapot Dome, 614(i)
  on Wilson's New Freedom, 581(i)
Political machines, 517–519
  muckrakers on, 557
  progressivism on, 572
Political parties, 147. *See also specific parties*
  antislavery, 349
  in the election of 1796, 242–243
  in the election of 1800, 245–246
  first party system, 241–245
  second party system, 300–308
  in the twenties, 632–633
  workingmen's, 295
Political sovereignty, 160
Politico.com, 841(i)
Politics
  big business and, 487(s), 539
  colonial era, 41, 135–136
  farmer organizations and, 540–542
  industrialization and, 538–539
  in the twenties, 632–633
  urbanization and, 517–519
Politics and Power in a Slave Society (Thornton), 387–388(s)
Polk, James K., 349, 359, 360, 360–362(s), 368
Poll taxes, 476, 476(m), 547, 560, 758
Polska Scaya, 503(i)
Polygamy, 334, 460, 469
Ponco Indians, 379
Pontiac, 155

Poor Richard's Almanack, 131, 132(s)
Popé, 50
Popular Science (magazine), 724
Population growth
  after World War II, 719
  colonial era, 67–68, 94
  in the early republic, 262–265, 277
  immigrants in, 830–831, 831(f)
  in the North *vs.* South, 390(f)
  in the twenties, 617–618, 617(m)
  "undesirable" races and, 506–507
  unemployment and, 102
  Union *vs.* Confederate, 390
  urban, 287
  in World War II, 671
Populism, 548–549(s)
  in the 1964 election, 776
  progressivism and, 556
Populist Party, 543, 543(s)
  decline of, 547–548
Populist Vision, The (Postel), 549(s)
Pornography, 769
Port Hudson, Battle of (1863), 404
Port Huron Statement, 769–770
Portland (Maine), Rum Riot, 340
Portland (Oregon)
  Hooverville in, 639
  Ku Klux Klan in, 630
  in World War II, 671
Portsmouth (New Hampshire), Peace conference (1905), 596
Portugal
  American exploration by, 17–23, 19(m)
  the Great Depression in, 639
  long-distance trade by, 3
  in Seven Year's War, 152
  Spanish conquest of, 33
Post, Amy, 292(s), 334, 347, 370
Post, Isaac, 292(s), 370
Post Office, U.S., 489
Postel, Charles, 549(s)
Potatoes, 25
Potawatomi Indians, 155
Potosí, 33
Potsdam Conference (1945), 700
Pottawatomie Massacre, 379–380, 384
Poverty
  of American Indians, 657–658
  in cities, 515–517
  decline in after World War II, 718–719
  before the Great Depression, 638
  in the Great Depression, 639, 659
  Great Society programs on, 767–768
  laissez-faire and, 534
  morality and, 337–338
  NAFTA and, 828
  New Frontier on, 767
  progressivism and, 557–559
  race and, 795
  under Reagan, 806–807
  reform movements on, 337–338
  in the twenties, 618, 637
Powderly, Terence V., 494, 495
Powell, Colin, 836
Powell, John Wesley, 449–450
Powell, Ozie, 642(i)
Power looms, 266–267

Power of Positive Thinking, The (Peale), 727
Powhatan, 56–57, 58
Powhatan Confederacy, 56–57, 58
Pragmatic conservatism, 779–780
Pragmatic humanism, 646
Pragmatism, 556
Prague Spring, 779
Praying towns, 119
Predestination, 71, 74
Presbyterian Church
    abolitionism and, 347
    Second Great Awakening and, 332
"President Lincoln and His Scheme of Emancipation" (*Charleston Mercury*), 397(s)
President's Committee on Civil Rights, 730
Presidential Review Memorandum on Human Rights (Christopher), 785(s)
Presidents. *See also specific by name*
    Constitutional Convention on election of, 208
    election of 1824, 303, 304(i)
    election of 1828, 303, 304–305, 304(i)
    election of 1840, 317–318
    election of 1896, 545–546, 546(m)
    election of 1924, 632
    election of 1928, 632–633
    industrialization and, 538
    progressivism under, 576–578
Presley, Elvis, 725
Preston, Thomas, 167
Price of the Ticket, The (Harris), 844(s)
Price, Victoria, 641–642
Prince, Thomas, 119(s)
Prince of Wales, 667(i)
Printing
    American Revolution, 177, 177–178(s)
    in colonial resistance to Britain, 162
    the Enlightenment and, 131–132
Privy Council, 60
Prize, The (Yergin), 489(s)
Proceedings of the Anti-Jackson Convention in Richmond, 305(s)
Proclamation 56 Calling on Citizens to Assist in the Recapture of a Fugitive Slave (Fillmore), 372(s)
Proclamation Line of 1763, 155(m), 156
Proclamation of 1763, 147
Proclamation of Amnesty and Reconciliation (1863), 417
Progress, success linked with, 533
Progress and Poverty (George), 534
Progressive Party, 579–580, 582
    in the election of 1948, 718
    in the twenties, 633, 633(m)
    women in, 727
Progressivism, 553, 555–585
    African Americans and, 562–565
    American Indians and, 565
    birth control and, 568
    conservation and, 794
    drug abuse and, 567
    environmentalism and, 574–575, 794
    government and, 572–585
    in the Great Depression, 648
    immigrants and, 570–572
    immigration restriction and, 628
    imperialism and, 586, 593
    juvenile delinquency and, 567–568
    legacy of, 582
    morality and social control in, 565–568
    muckrakers in, 557
    municipal and state reforms in, 572–573
    origins of, 555
    political reform and, 570–585
    poverty and, 557–559
    presidential, 576–578
    prohibition and, 565–567
    prostitution and, 566, 567(i)
    retreat from, 578–580
    roots of, 556–557
    social justice reform and, 557–559
    Square Deal and, 576–578
    Taft and, 578–579
    in the twenties, 633
    Wilson and, 608–609(s)
    women in, 557–559, 558(s)
    on women's suffrage, 557, 559–561, 560(m), 561(i)
    World War I and, 605–606
Prohibition, 552(i), 565–567, 606, 626
    Democrats and, 632
    ended, 648
Project Democracy, 811
Propaganda
    World War I, 604, 604(i)
    World War II, 674
Property rights
    American Indians and, 198–200
    of Californios, 469–470
    colonial era, 74–75, 78, 135–136, 174
    corporations and, 533
    of freedpeople, 413
    Mormons on, 469
    as personal liberty, 532
    squatters after the Revolution and, 200
    voting rights connected to, 301
    of women, 218, 219
Prophet Town, 273–274
Proposal to Create the Department of Homeland Security, 837–838 (s)
Proposition 13, 795, 796(i)
Prospective Scene in the 'City of Oaks,' A, 432(s)
Prospectus for the Mississippi Freedom Summer, 759(s)
Prostitution
    Chinese immigrants and, 470
    on the frontier, 462, 462(i)
    muckrakers on, 557
    progressivism and, 566, 567(i)
    in red-light districts, 529
    social reform movements against, 337–338
    tongs in, 504
Protestant Reformation, 70–71
Protestantism, 71. *See also individual denominations*
    American Indian removal and, 315
    immigrants and, 290
    prohibition and, 566
    racial inferiority and, 506–507
    Second Great Awakening in, 332–334
    temperance and, 339
Protocols of the Elders of Zion, 629
Providential Detection, The (anonymous), 242(s), 248(s)

Proxy wars, 697
Prussia, 152
Psychoanalysis, 622
Public assistance. *See also* Social welfare
    colonial era, 102
    industrialization and, 295–296
Public health
    progressivism and, 566–567
    sanitation and, 512, 517
Public transportation, 290, 512, 514–515
    Freedom Rides and, 756
    Montgomery bus boycott of, 732, 732(i)
    segregation in, 730–731, 732
Public utilities, 517
Public Works Administration (PWA), 649
Public works projects, 638
Publishing, 99
Pueblo "Cliff Palace" at Mesa Verde, Colorado, 11(i)
Pueblo people, 10, 11(i), 14, 25, 39, 452
    anthropologists on, 622
    civilization of, 452
    rebellion by, 36, 49–50
    Villasur expedition ambush by, 45(i)
Pueblo revolt, 50
Puerto Ricans, 724, 774
Puerto Rico, annexation of, 586, 591
Pulaski, Casimir Count, 188
Pulitzer, Joseph, 590
Pullman, George, 498
Pullman strike, 498, 544
Pulse nightclub shooting, 851
Pure Food and Drug Act (1906), 577
Puritan Migration, 74
Puritans, 775
    American Indians and, 118, 119
    dissenters, 75–76
    Hutchinson and, 75–76
    religious anxieties and, 78–80
    wars with, 78–81
    worldview of, 73–74
Putin, Vladimir, 846
"Putting the 'Political' Back in Political Economy" (Newell), 106(s)

Q

Al-Qaddafi, Muammar, 812–813, 844
Al-Qaeda, 820
    9/11 attacks by, 836
Quakers, 196, 330
    in abolitionism, 219, 327, 334, 343–344
    on the Fugitive Slave Act, 370
    growth of, 330
    Harpers Ferry raid and, 384
    Library Company of, 221(s)
    Pennsylvania as refuge for, 93–94
    Seneca reservations and, 316
Quartering Act (England, 1765), 161, 169
Quarterly Journal, 565
Quebec, 44
    Battle of, 176, 190(m)
    in Seven Years' War, 153
Quebec Act (England, 1774), 169
Queen Anne's War, 121, 122, 135, 147, 150
Queen's College, 220
Quinto real (royal fifth), 33

R

Race and ethnicity. *See also specific groups by name*
  and Americanization in the twenties, 629–630
  anthropology on, 622
  anti-immigrant fears and, 504–508
  Baptist churches on, 176–177
  in colonial America, 41, 67(m), 109–110
  in the Great Depression, 640–643
  justifications for imperialism and, 587–588, 588(s)
  labor unions and, 295
  liberation movements and, 773–774
  in the Philippines, 594
  slavery based on, 28
  Spanish caste system, 33–34
  stereotypes about, 506–507
  "superior" *vs.* "inferior," 507
  in the twenties, 620
  "whiteness" of immigrants and, 506–507
  white supremacy and, 319, 328
  World War I and, 605, 606
Race or Mongrel (Schultz), 508
Racism. *See also* Civil rights movement
  anticrime legislation and, 827
  against Chinese, 505–506(s)
  the Christian Right and, 796
  in the Great Depression, 640–643
  Great Society programs on, 767–768
  in housing, 720–721, 721(s)
  immigrants and, 496
  immigration restriction and, 628
  industrialization and, 474
  New Deal and, 657–658
  in the New South, 474
  Populism and, 547–548
  progressivism and, 555, 562–565, 566, 567
  in railroads, 484–485
  reverse, 762
  in the twenties, 613, 620
  twenty-first century, 831
  urbanization and, 513
  Wilson on, 581–582
  women's suffrage and, 557, 559, 560–561
Radiators, 514
Radical Republicans, 417, 420, 422–423
Radicalism
  black power and, 760–761
  detention camps for, 713
  in feminism, 772
  immigrants and, 506
  Red Scare and, 610–611, 612
Radicalism of the American Revolution, The (Wood), 159(s)
Radio, 621, 636(s), 644
"Rags to riches" stories, 533
Railroad Administration, 604
Railroads, 289
  bison slaughter by, 455–456
  British investment in, 450–451, 486
  in the Civil War, 398
  commercial ranching and, 465, 466–467
  depression of 1893 and, 537
  freight rate regulations, 576
  government takeover of, 717

Grangers and, 541
industrialization and, 482–483, 483(f), 484
Kansas-Nebraska Act and, 378–379
land grants to, 466
locomotives, 484
in the New South, 474, 475(m)
in the North *vs.* South, 390, 390(f)
political influence of, 539
progressive reforms of, 576
Pullman strike, 498, 544
segregation in, 477
in settlement of the West, 450, 450(m), 451–452
in the South, 320
standardization of, 483, 484
steel rails in, 484
strikes against, 494, 497(m), 498, 544
telegraph and, 476
transcontinental, 436, 447
troop deployment against the American Indians and, 455
urbanization and, 512
U.S. advertised by, 502
in westward migration, 466–467
worker safety in, 493
Rain forests, 822
Randolph, A. Philip, 623(s), 625, 675, 732, 758
  in the civil rights movement, 758(i)
Randolph, Edmund, 230
Randolph, Edward, 126(s)
Rankin, Jeanette P., 602
Rape. *See* Sexual violence
Ratification, 195
Raulston, John T., 627
Rauschenbusch, Walter, 556
Ray, James Earl, 761
La Raza Unida (The United Race), 773–774
Reading
  active, 6–7
  in source analysis, 9
Reading Railroad, 576
Reagan, Ronald, 697, 803
  Address at the University of Virginia, 816(s)
  anti-Soviet rhetoric of, 809–810
  Contras and, 811
  election of, 804–805, 805(i), 806(m)
  Iran-Contra affair, 813, 814(s)
  Iran hostage release and, 786
  Noriega and, 824
  nuclear de-escalation under, 815–816
  nuclear freeze movement and, 814–816, 815(i)
  reelection of, 807, 815
  social conservatism and, 808–809
  Tear Down This Wall speech, 810(s)
  terrorism fighting under, 812–813
Reaganomics, 805–807
Real estate speculation, 618
Reality shows, 822
Realpolitik, 780
Rebel Without a Cause (film), 723–724, 723(i)
"Reconstructing Race" (West), 433(s)
Reconstruction, 355, 411, 417–423, 426–433
  black political participation and economic opportunity in, 428–429
  compromise of 1877 and, 436–437
  congressional, 420–423, 538
  congressional retreat from, 434
  early, in the South, 427–430

economic scandals in, 431
Grant and, 423
judicial retreat from, 436
legacies of, 438
Lincoln and Johnson's plan for, 417–423
Lincoln's plans for reunification and, 412
military districts in, 422, 422(m)
presidential, 417–418
unraveling of, 434–436
white resistance to, 431–432
Reconstruction: America's Unfinished Revolution (Foner), 433(s)
Reconstruction Finance Corporation (RFC), 638–639
Red-light districts, 529
Red power movement, 774
Red Scare, 610–612, 611(s), 700
  second, 710–715
Redeemers, 431, 434
Redemptioners, 94
Redlining, 720–721
Redstockings, 772
Reed, Esther De Berdt, 187(s)
Refinement of America, The (Bushman), 103(s)
Reform capitalism, 718, 745
Reform movements
  humanitarian, 555, 557–559
  mid-nineteenth-century, 336–340
  Progressive Era, 555–585
  temperance movement, 339–340, 339(i)
  urban, 519
  working conditions, 516
Refrigerators, 616, 727(i)
Refugees, 811, 845
Regents of the University of California v. Bakke, 762
Regional economies, 280–281
Rehnquist, William, 808
Reign of Terror (France), 238–239
Relation of the Indian War, A (Easton), 125(s)
Religion. *See also individual religions*
  in the 1950s, 727
  abolitionism and, 347
  anxieties over, 78–80
  Beat Generation, 727(i)
  colonial era, 41, 61–62, 68, 70–76, 130–143, 162
  dissension in, 134–136
  in the early republic, 217
  emergence of the middle class and, 291
  enslaved people and, 269
  on homosexuality, 808
  immigrants and, 290–291, 501
  in imperialism, 587–588
  liberalism opposed by, 775
  megachurches, 835–836, 835(s)
  modernism *vs.* fundamentalism, 626–628
  music in, 530
  the New Deal and, 651, 651(i)
  the New Right and, 796
  Pilgrims, 72–73
  Protestant Reformation, 70–71
  revolutionary era, 196
  Second Great Awakening, 330, 332–334
  separation of church and state, 196
  witchcraft and, 79
Religious toleration, 196
  colonial era, 61–62, 92–93, 134–136
  in Maryland, 61–62

Remarks by the President on the Middle East and North Africa (Obama), 846(s)
Remarks Occasioned by the Late Conduct of Mr. Washington (Bache), 247(s)
Remarks to a Methodist Delegation (McKinley), 593(s)
Remarks to the Senate (Wilson), 601(s)
Remarque, Erich Maria, 663
Renaissance, 17
Reno, Marcus, 456(i)
Reno, Milo, 644–645
Rent strikes, 645
Report on the Freedmen's Bureau (Whittlesey), 415(i)
Report on the Subject of Manufactures (Hamilton), 233, 233(s)
Representation
   slavery and, 208
   three-fifths compromise, 208
   virtual, 162
Republican Campaign Song, 381–382(s)
Republican motherhood, 218
Republican National Convention of 1968, 778(s)
Republican Party
   African Americans switching from, 657
   after the Civil War, 438
   congressional majority by, 538
   conservatism's revival in the 1960s and, 775–776
   Contract with America, 828
   Eisenhower and, 743–744
   in the election of 1856, 380
   in the election of 1860, 384–387, 385(i)
   in the election of 1896, 545–546, 546(m)
   in the election of 1912, 580
   in the election of 1928, 632–633
   founding of, 379
   Frémont and, 371, 380, 380–381(s), 381(s)
   Lincoln and, 382–383
   Modern Republicanism and, 743–744
   Obama and, 842–843
   Reconstruction under, 412, 417–423, 427
   retreat from Reconstruction by, 434–436
   rise of, 379
   Tea Party movement in, 843
   Trump and, 848–851
   in the twenties, 632–633
   in Wilmington (North Carolina) massacre, 547(i)
Republican societies, 239–240
Requerimiento, 31, 39
Restrictive (housing) covenants, 720–721, 721(s)
Retail outlets, 488
Retirement
   New Deal and, 651–652
   Social Security and, 654–655
Revels, Hiram, 441(s)
Revere, Paul, 168, 174
Reverse discrimination, 762
Revivals, religious
   in the 1950s, 727
   Great Awakening, 130–143
   music in, 530
   Second Great Awakening, 332–334, 333–334(s)
   temperance movement and, 339–340

Revolutionary era, 146–253
Reykjavik, Iceland, summit in, 815
Reynolds v. United States, 469
Rhee, Syngman, 706
Rhineland, German occupation of the, 664
Rhode Island, 75, 76
   Constitution ratified by, 211, 211(t)
   religious toleration in, 75
   royal charter of, 77
Rice, 85–86
Rice, Condoleezza, 836
Rice, slavery and, 109–110
Rice, Thomas, 290
Richards, Maria, 415
Richmond (Virginia)
   capture of, 408(i), 409
   as Confederate capital, 398
   emancipation in, 412
Riis, Jacob, 504(i), 516, 516(s)
"Rip Van Winkle" (Irving), 331
Ripley, George, 340
Roads, 263–264
   after World War II, 720
   automobiles and improvement of, 616
   in cities, 517
   Incan, 8
   transportation revolution and improvement in, 278(m), 279
Robber barons, 482, 489(s)
Robber Barons, The (Josephson), 489(s)
Robertson, Pat, 796
Robertson, Willie, 642(i)
Robeson, Paul, 712(s)
Robinson, Harriet, 293, 294(s)
Robinson, Jackie, 730, 736
Robinson, Julia, 469
Rochambeau, Comte de, 191
Rochester (New York)
   growth of, 288
   revivals in, 332
Rock Island (Illinois), 264(t)
Rock 'n' roll, 725
   counterculture and, 771
Rock Springs massacre, 470(i), 471
Rockefeller, John D., 485, 487, 487(s), 489(s), 493, 533
   income of, 493
   lavish home of, 524
Rockefeller, John D. Jr., 588
Rockefeller, Nelson A., 782
Rockville (Maryland), 808(i)
Roe, Clifford B., 567(i)
Roe v. Wade, 772, 792, 808
Roebling, Emily, 514
Roebling, John Augustus, 514
Roebling, Washington, 514
Rolfe, John, 58
Rolling Stones, 771
Rolvaag, O. E., 467
Romani, in the Holocaust, 681, 687
Romania, fall of the Soviet regime in, 819
Romanticism, 331
Romney, Mitt, 843
Romulus (New York), 815(i)
Rooming houses, 528
Roosevelt Corollary, 595, 597

Roosevelt, Eleanor, 646
   African Americans and, 657
   as go-between with Randolph, 675
   Perkins and, 648
Roosevelt, Franklin, 553, 647(i)
   Atlantic Charter and, 667, 667(i)
   Black Cabinet of, 657
   on Civilian Conservation Corps, 650(s)
   civil rights movement and, 675–676
   confidence instilled by, 647
   court-packing plan of, 659
   critics of, 651–653
   death of, 685
   election of, 646
   on entry into World War II, 664
   fireside chats of, 647
   the Holocaust and, 688–689, 690–691(s)
   House Un-American Activities Committee and, 711
   Japanese American internment under, 678–679
   labor and, 717
   New Deal of, 646–661
   on Pearl Harbor, 668
   polio of, 647(i)
   reelection of, 659, 665, 683
   on the second front, 682
   State of the Union Address, 673(s)
   wartime economy under, 670–674
   Yalta Agreement and, 685, 700
Roosevelt, James, 647(i)
Roosevelt, Theodore
   Big Stick diplomacy of, 595
   conservation and, 574(i)
   in Cuba, 591
   in election of 1912, 580
   foreign policy of, 595–597
   Japanese immigration restricted by, 628
   on the *Maine*, 590
   national parks created by, 575(m)
   Open Door policy and, 596–597
   progressivism and, 570
   on sports, 527–528(s)
   Square Deal of, 576–578
   Taft and, 579
   on war and manhood, 588
   on World War I, 600
Rosenberg, Ethel, 710, 713, 715
Rosenberg, Julius, 710, 713, 715
Rosie the Riveter, 674, 675(s)
Ross, Betsy, 182
Ross, John, 313, 314, 393
Rough Riders, 576, 591
Rowlandson, Mary, 126–127(s)
Rowson, Susanna, 331
Royal African Company, 65, 107, 109(s), 110
Royal Navy (England)
   Embargo Act and, 261–262
   impressment by, 135, 152–153, 152(s), 273
   U.S. neutrality ignored by, 238–239
Ruby, Jack, 767
Ruggles, David, 370
Rum, 75, 85(i), 99
Rum Riot (1855), 340
Rumor of War, A (Caputo), 751(s)
Rumsfeld, Donald, 836
Rural Electrification Administration, 648

Index

Rural free delivery (RFD), 489
Rural life
   colonial era, 79–80
   family labor in, 131
   in the Great Depression, 639–640, 642–643
   in the twenties, 617, 617(m)
   urbanization vs, 512–513, 617, 617(m)
Russia. *See also* Union of Soviet Socialist Republics (USSR)
   Bolshevik Revolution in, 610–611, 700
   election interference by, 848
   expansionism of, 846
   in the Group of Seven (G7), 821
   Manchuria invaded by, 596
   serfs in, 328
   in Seven Year's War, 152
   in World War I, 599
Russian Federation, 821
Russian Revolution, 602, 606–607
Russo-Japanese War (1904–1905), 571
Rust Belt, 783(m)
Rustin, Bayard, 732
   in March on Washington for Jobs and Freedom, 758

S

Sacagawea, 259–260, 262
Sacco, Nicola, 629
Sacco and Vanzetti case, 629
Sadat, Anwar, 786
Saigon, fall of, 753, 753(i)
Sakonnet Indians, 124–125(s)
Salem witchcraft trials, 79, 135
Salinger, J. D., 728
Salk, Jonas, 719(i), 720
Saloons, 468, 522(s)
SALT II, 784
Salt Lake City, 469
   diversity in, 512
   growth of in the twenties, 617
Salutary neglect, 160
Same-sex marriage, 828, 835, 843
Samoa, 280
Sampson, Deborah, 188
Sanctuary Building of the First Baptist Church in Dallas, Texas, 835(s)
San Diego, in World War II, 671
San Esteban del Rey Mission, 50(i)
San Francisco
   Beats in, 727
   growth of in the twenties, 617, 617(m)
   Hetch Hetchy damn and, 574–575
   immigrants in, 504
   New York Giants moved to, 721
   population of, 511
   railroad strike in, 497(m)
   tongs in, 504
   trolleys in, 514
   in World War II, 671
San Patricios, 363(i)
San Salvador, 20, 20(m)
Sand Creek Massacre, 409, 454–455
Sandinistas, 811, 825
Sandy Hook Elementary School shooting, 851
Sanger, Margaret, 568, 568(s)
Sansay, Leonora, 270(s)

Santa Anna, Antonio Lopez de, 312–313, 363
Santa Clara County v. Southern Pacific Railroad Company, 487
Santa Fe (New Mexico), 36
   as territorial capital, 452
Santa Fe Trail, 277, 280, 365, 365(m)
Santees, 442(s)
Saratoga, Battle of (1777), 186, 188, 190(m)
Sauk people, 314
Savannah (Georgia), 191, 280, 398
Savings and loan institutions, 807
Savio, Mario, 770(i)
Scacki, Francisco, 276(i)
Scalawags, 427
Scandinavian immigrants
   in the 1820s, 289
   as farmers, 466
   in the lumber industry, 463
   in mining towns, 463
Scarlet Letter, The (Hawthorne), 337
Schenck, Charles, 610–611
Schenck v. United States, 610–611
Schlafly, Phyllis, 697, 792, 793(s)
Schlinkert, Sam, 850(s)
Schneiderman, Rose, 573(i)
School busing, 761–762, 762(i), 787(s)
School Days of an Indian Girl, The (Zitkala-Ša), 458(s)
School prayer, 769
School shootings, 851–852
Schultz, Alfred P., 508
Schwartz, Frederick Charles, 775
Scientific American (magazine), 484(i)
Scientific management, 488
Scopes, John, 626–627, 627–628(s), 635–636(s)
Scots-Irish immigrants, 94, 95
   colonial era, 67–68, 93
   Whiskey Rebellion and, 240
Scott, Dred, 382–383, 383(s), 389
Scott, Winfield, 315–316, 360, 363, 373, 391
Scottish immigrants
   in the Carolinas, 87
   colonial era, 41
Scottsboro Nine, 641–642, 642(i)
Seale, Bobby, 761, 764–765(s)
Sears, Roebuck and Co., 488(i), 489
Seattle
   anti-Chinese assaults in, 471
   growth of in the twenties, 617
   Ku Klux Klan in, 630
   trolleys in, 514
   in World War II, 671
Second Bank of the United States, 261, 281, 310–311
Second Continental Congress, 175
Second front, World War II, 682
Second Great Awakening, 332–334
Second Red Scare, 710–715
Second Seminole War, 314
Second Treatise on Civil Government (Locke), 77–78(s)
Sectional crises, 377–388
   antislavery sentiment and, 378
   Bleeding Kansas and, 379–380
   Compromise of 1850 and, 368–370
   Dred Scott decision and, 377, 382–383
   John Brown's raid and, 384
   Kansas-Nebraska Act and, 378–380, 379(m)

secession of the South and, 385–386(s), 385–387, 386(m)
Securities and Exchange Commission (SEC), 648
Sedition Act (1798), 243–244, 244(s), 248
Sedition Act (1918), 604–605
Seditious, 136
Segregation
   black nationalism and, 625
   cowboys and, 465
   declared unconstitutional, 715
   in education, 564
   in government offices, 582
   Jim Crow laws, 471, 476–477
   of Latinos, 643, 676
   in the military, 606, 672, 675, 730(i)
   progressivism on, 562–564, 563(s)
   in public transportation, 409
   in suburbs, 720–721
   urbanization and, 513
   Wilson on, 581
   in World War I, 606
   in World War II, 672, 675
Seixas, Eleanor Cohen, 407
Selected Statutes Passed (Virginia House of Burgesses), 63(s), 113–114(s)
Selective Service Act (1917), 602
Selective Service Act (1940), 665
Selma (Alabama), 399, 759–760
Seminole Indians, 279, 393
Senate
   Constitutional Convention on, 207–208
   continuity in, 538
   election by popular vote for, 573
Senate Foreign Relations Committee, 714
Senate Select Committee to Study Governmental Operations with Respect to Intelligence Activities, 785–786
Senate Subcommittee to Investigate Juvenile Delinquency, 724(s)
Seneca Falls, Women's Encampment for a Future of Peace and Justice, 814
Seneca Falls convention, 347–348
Seneca Indians, 316
   in the Civil War, 393
   Indian Reorganization Act and, 658
   land treaties with, 200, 200(i)
   on women's rights, 348
Sentiments of an American Woman, The (Reed), 187(s)
Separate but equal, 477, 564, 730
Separate spheres, 292–293
Separation of church and state, 196, 835
Separatists. *See* Pilgrims
Sepúlveda, Juan Ginés de, 35–36
Serpent Mount, 13(i)
Servants
   Chinese immigrants as, 470
   colonial era, 80
   domestic labor by, 267
   women employed as, 290, 492
Servicemen's Readjustment Act (1944), 717, 717(i)
Settlement houses, 519, 557
Seven Days Battle (1862), 393
Seven Year Itch, The (film), 724
Seven Years' War, 122, 147, 149–155, 153(m), 161
   North America before and after, 154(m)

Seventeenth Amendment, 573
Seventh-Day Adventist Church, 335
Sewage systems, 512
Seward, William H., 369
Sewing women, 398
Sexual coercion, 131
Sexual harassment, 818
Sexual violence
    against enslaved people, 321, 322
    MeToo movement and, 852
    myth of black men raping white women, 326, 564
    Scottsboro Nine and, 641–642, 642(i)
    women's suffrage and, 561
Sexuality, 852–853(s). See also Homosexuals
    in 1950s movies, 724
    in the 1970s, 791, 792
    changing norms of in the twenties, 616, 621–622, 621(i)
    the Christian Right on, 796
    colonial era, 131
    counterculture on, 771
    double standard on, 771
    Kinsey on, 728
Seymour, Horatio, 423
Shakers, 182
Shame of America, The (ad), 585(s)
Shame of the Cities, The (Steffens), 556(s)
Share Our Wealth society, 652(s), 653
Sharecropping, 427, 429, 430(s), 447
    agreements on, 430(s)
    Communist Party and, 645
    in the Great Depression, 641
    industrialization and, 474
    New Deal and, 657
    urbanization and, 513
    in World War II, 671
Sharon Statement, 775, 791
Shawnee Indians, 93–94, 93(m), 273–274, 274(s)
    civilization of, 452
    land treaties with, 200
    in Seven Years' War, 150–151
Shawnee Mission (Kansas), 379
Shays, Daniel, 202–203, 203(s)
Shays's Rebellion (1787), 202–203, 239
Shelley v. Kraemer, 720
Shepherd-Towner Act (1921), 559, 633
Sheridan, Philip, 406–407
Sherman Antitrust Act (1890), 487(s), 488
    big business favored in implementation of, 541–542
    Roosevelt's Square Deal and, 576
Sherman, John, 487, 488, 539
    Hanna and, 545
    money supply under, 542
Sherman, Roger, 178
Sherman Silver Purchase Act (1890), 542, 545
Sherman, William Tecumseh, 405, 406–408, 455
Shiloh, Battle of (1862), 393–394, 394(m)
Short-Answer Question prompts, 15–16
Shoshone people, 262
Shultz, George, 809
    on the Iran-Contra affair, 813
    on Nicaragua, 811
    on Qaddafi, 812
Shuttlesworth, Fred, 756
Siemens, William, 484
Siemes, Johannes, 686–687(s)

Sierra Club, 574(i), 794(s)
Sierra Leone, 224
Silent Majority, The (Lassiter), 853(s)
Silent Spring (Carson), 794
Silver, 25, 33
    currency backed by, 545
Silver mining, 462
Silverheels, Jay, 723
Simmons, W. J., 630
Sinatra, Frank, 725
Sinclair, Upton, 577, 577(s), 578(i)
Sinners in the Hands of an Angry God (Edwards), 139(s)
Sioux Indians, 93, 446(i)
    Battle of the Little Bighorn, 455, 456(i)
    Kansas-Nebraska Act and, 379
    war of over broken treaties, 408–409
    Wounded Knee massacre of, 459, 774
Sister Carrie (Dreiser), 512, 522(s)
Sit-down strikes, at General Motors, 546(i), 657
Sit-ins, 676, 734(m), 735, 735(s), 745, 764(s)
    at Berkeley, 770, 770(i)
Sitting Bull, 442(s), 455, 459
Six Companies of San Francisco, 736
Six-Day War (1967), 780–781
Sixteenth Amendment, 580
Sketchbook (Irving), 331
Skilled workers, 491(s), 492
Skyscrapers, 484, 512, 514
Slater, Samuel, 265, 266
Slaughter, Linda, 467
Slaughterhouse cases, 436
Slave code, 62, 63
    Barbados, 85
    South Carolina, 85–86
Slave laws, 109–110
Slave revolts, 111–112, 111–112(s), 269, 302, 302(i), 319, 325–326
    in Haiti, 258, 269
Slave trade, 3, 39, 65, 101, 107–109
    ads, 322(s)
    African, 107–109
    Atlantic, 101, 107–109
    in Atlantic economy, 98, 99(m)
    banning of, 321
    Constitutional Convention on, 208
    England in, 107
    human cost of, 107–109
    international, banning of, 326
    markets in, 322
    Middle Passage in, 108–109
    in New York City, 92
    numbers in, 108(i)
    plan of a slave ship, 108(i)
    South Carolina, 86
Slavery, 255, 319. See also Abolitionism
    abolished, 409, 417
    African resistance against, 111–112
    after the Revolution, 201–202, 222–225
    of American Indians, 49–50, 120
    American Revolution and, 196
    building of Washington, D.C. and, 233–234
    Civil War as war on, 392
    in colonial America, 41, 59
    Compromise of 1850 and, 368–370
    Constitutional Convention on, 208
    cotton and, 267–270, 321–322, 321(m)

    Crittenden plan on, 386–387
    in domestic labor, 267
    Dred Scott case on, 377, 382–383
    Dunmore's Proclamation and, 176–177
    Emancipation Proclamation and, 395–397, 395(s), 396, 397(s)
    emergence of, 62–63
    expansion of after the American Revolution, 147
    expansion of in the West, 349
    expansion of with cotton production, 268–270, 268(t), 321–322, 321(m)
    family reunification after, 414–415
    Fugitive Slave Act on, 368–372, 371(i)
    history of, 27–28
    Kansas-Nebraska Act on, 378–380, 379(m)
    marriage under, 414–415
    Missouri Compromise on, 282–284
    in New York, 92
    non-slaveholders on, 327
    Northwest Ordinance on, 201–202
    petition to free an Indian slave, 124(s)
    race and, 28
    religion and, 269
    resistance to, 111–112, 325–326
    rise of in the South, 107–117
    South Carolina, 85–87
    southern economy fueled by, 322–323, 355
    tobacco and, 65–66, 68(i)
    weddings in, 324(i)
    western expansion and, 377, 382–383
    western settlement and, 367–372
    West Indies, 84–86, 85(i)
Slavery a Positive Good (Calhoun), 328(s)
Slidell, John, 360
Slovenia, 828–829
Slums, 517, 519
Smallpox, 25, 25(i), 33, 364, 412
    American Indians and, 72, 452
    in the American Revolution, 176
    in Continental Army, 186
    freedpeople killed by, 412
    Massachusetts Indians and, 74
    Plymouth and, 72
    Puritans and, 74
Smith Act (1940), 711, 713, 715
Smith, Adam, 237, 532
Smith, Alfred E., 632, 633
Smith, Barbara, 792
Smith, Bessie, 623
Smith College, 719
Smith-Connally Act (1943), 673–674
Smith, Gerrit, 370, 371(i)
Smith, John, 56–57, 60(i)
Smith, Joseph, 334
Smith, Margaret Chase, 725, 727(i)
Smith v. Allwright, 676
Smithy, Jacob H., 594
Smuggling, 161
Snowden, Edward, 845, 847(s)
Social activism
    Gilded Age, 447
    mid-nineteenth-century, 336–340, 349
    against poverty, 337–338
    temperance movement, 339–340, 339(i)
Social Darwinism, 533, 556
Social evolution, 533

Social gospel, 519, 556
Social media, 845–846
    Trump's use of, 849
Social Security, 654–655
    in the 1960s, 767
    conservative opposition to, 775
    payroll tax for, 659
    raised in 1954, 744
    under Reagan, 806
    welfare and, 828
Social Security Act (1935), 654–655, 657, 659
Social Statics (Spencer), 533
Social structure
    colonial era, 62–65, 66–67, 91, 130, 131–132, 135–136
    consumer revolution and, 101–102
    emergence of the middle class and, 291–293
    Gilded Age, 524–530
    laissez-faire and, 533
    in mining towns, 462–463
    nineteenth century, 290
    reform movements, 336–340
    technology and transformation of, 829–830
    in the twenties, 610–613, 617–618
Social welfare. *See also* New Deal
    in the 1960s, 775–776
    under Bush, George H. W., 817–818
    under Clinton, 828
    immigrants and, 831
    political machines and, 517–519
    poverty and, 557–559
    progressivism and, 557–559, 633
    under Reagan, 806, 807
Social workers, 557
Socialism, 534
    Bellamy on, 534
    Debs on, 605(s)
    income tax as, 545
    the New Deal as, 651–653
    in Spain, 664
    unions and, 498
Socialist Party of America, 498, 580, 633
Society in America (Martineau), 298(s)
Society of American Indians, 565
Society of Friends. *See* Quakers
Society of Pewterers, 146(i)
Sod houses, 467
Soil Conservation Service, 648
Soil Erosion Service, 648
Solar power, 784
Solidarity, 819
"Some Evidence of Mercantilism in Massachusetts Bay" (Johnson), 106(s)
Somoza, Anastasio, 811
Sone, Monica, 668(s)
Song Bo, Saum, 505(s)
Sons of Liberty, 162–163, 167, 168–169, 174
Sons of Temperance, 339(i)
Sorbonne protests, 779
Souls of Black Folk, The (Du Bois), 508, 564
Sources
    analyzing, 8–10, 32(i)
    secondary, 103–106
South. *See also* Civil War
    African American migration from, 513
    after World War II, 721

American Revolution in, 191–192, 192(m)
civil rights movement in, 729–736
Civil War legacy in, 409, 411–412
colonial era, 41
cotton and slavery in, 267–270
devotion to the "Lost Cause" in, 418(i)
education in, 220
food shortages in, 401
the great migration from, 613
immigrants in, 830, 831
industrialization in, 473–475, 475(m)
itinerant preachers in, 134
Jim Crow laws, 471, 476–477
New, 473–480, 475(m)
non-slaveholders in, 327
plantation society in, 320
political, economic, and social influence of, 804–805
Populist Party in, 547
Reconstruction in, 427–430
resistance to desegregation in, 733–735, 734(i)
resistance to Reconstruction in, 431–432
rise of slavery in, 107–117
secession of, 385–386(s), 385–387, 386(m)
slavery in after the Revolution, 201–202
small farmers vs. planters in, 262
unification against abolition in, 327–328
union movement in, 496
urban life in, 320–321
voter registration in, 676
South Africa
    apartheid in, 812, 812(i), 824–825
    repressive regime supported in, 780
South Carolina, 78, 85–88, 87(m)
    black majority in, 428
    civil rights movement in, 730
    Constitution ratified by, 210, 211(t)
    daily life in eighteenth-century, 86–88
    Edisto Island, 413(s)
    emancipation of enslaved people in, 224
    Fort Sumter, 389–390
    indigo in, 101
    lumber industry in, 475
    nullification and, 310
    racial violence in, 302, 302(i)
    readmitted to the Union, 422
    Sea Islands, 413, 418
    secession of, 385
    Sherman's March to the Sea through, 407–408
    slave code, 85–86(s)
    slavery in, 85–87, 354(i)
    Stono rebellion, 111–112
    Tuscarora War, 120
South Carolina Exposition and Protest (Calhoun), 310
South Carolina State University, 778
South Dakota, 455, 465
South Korea, 706–709
    passenger airliner of shot down, 810
Southern Christian Leadership Conference (SCLC), 732, 756, 758–760
Southern Democrats, 659
Southern Farmers' Alliance, 542
Southern Manifesto, The, 733(s)
Southern Patriot, 735(s)

Soviet-Afghan War (1980–1989), 820
Soviet missile crisis, Cuba, 745–746, 747(s)
Soviet Union. *See* Union of Soviet Socialist Republics (USSR)
Space exploration, 744
Space race, 744
Spain
    Adams-Onís Treaty with, 279
    American exploration by, 17–23, 20(m)
    American Indian civilizations and, 452
    American Indian land complaints to, 200
    in American Revolution, 188
    Armada of, 44, 46, 71
    California and, 359–360
    Californios and, 469–470
    civil war in, 664
    colonial rule by, 33–34
    colonial society of, 30–38
    colonies of, 46(m), 49–51
    Cuba and, 374
    Cuban War for Independence from, 589–592, 589(i)
    decline of global empire, 36
    English colonies and, 41
    English conflicts with, 122
    expansion and conflict with, 43
    French rivalry with, 44
    frontier conflicts with, 241
    fugitives from slavery and, 112
    gold from the Americas and, 25–26, 30
    the Great Depression in, 639
    the Great Recession in, 840
    immigrants from, 502
    imperialist wars with, 589–592
    New Orleans closed by, 198
    Philippine war with, 592
    Protestant Reformation and, 71
    Pueblo Revolt and, 49–50
    reconquest of, 18
    in Seven Year's War, 152
    slavery in, 328
    torture and enslavement by, 34–36, 34(i)
    tribute to, 2(i), 33, 36
    U.S. sovereignty undermined by, 202
    U.S. war with, 589–592
    War of the Spanish Succession, 121
    Whiskey Rebellion and, 239
Spanish-American War (1898–1899), 589–592
Spanish Armada, 44
Spanish caste system, 33–34
Spanish Loyalists, 664
Spanish Trail, 365(m)
Speaker of the House, 538
Spear, Fred, 604(s)
Special interests, liberalism and, 795–796
Speculation, 99
Speculators, 156
Speech at Holt Street Baptist Church (King), 763(s)
Speech Delivered at Warren, Ohio (Garfield), 435(s)
Speech Supporting the Taft-Hartley Bill (Angell), 718(s)
Speech to Congress on the Admission of Missouri to the United States (Walker), 283(s)
Speech to Congress on the Admission of Missouri to the United States (King), 282–283(s)
Speech to the Equal Rights Association (Stanton), 424(s)

Speech to the Georgia General Assembly (Toombs), 392(s)
Speech to Mississippi Youth (Malcolm X), 764(s)
Spencer, Herbert, 533, 534, 556
Spice trade, 17
Spies, August, 494–495
Spinning machines, 265
Spiritual Mobilization, 651
Spock, Benjamin, 725
Spoils system, 307, 435
Sports
   baseball, 527, 530, 730, 736
   crisis of masculinity and, 526–527, 527–528(s)
   desegregation of, 730, 736
   leisure and, 530
   women in, 526(i)
   working-class leisure and, 528
Spot Resolutions (Lincoln), 362(s)
Spotted Elk, 442(s)
Springfield (Illinois), riot of 1908, 562
Sputnik, 744
Square Deal, 576–578
Squash, 10
SS *St. Louis*, 688
St. Christopher, 84
St. Louis
   industry in, 482
   Irish immigrants in, 289
   population of, 511
   railroad strike in, 497(m)
Stagflation, 783
Stalin, Joseph, 682–683
   Greek civil war and, 702
   Khrushchev on, 740
   on the Marshall Plan, 703
   nonaggression agreement with Hitler, 664
   purges by, 700
   Truman and, 700, 701
   Yalta Agreement and, 685, 700
Stalingrad, Battle of, 682(m)
Stamp Act (England, 1765), 162–165, 163(s), 165(s)
Stamp Act Congress, 163, 174, 231(i)
Standard Oil Company, 485, 487(s)
   antitrust action against, 576
   muckrakers on, 557
Standard Oil Trust, 487
Standish, Myles, 72–73, 118
Stanton, Edwin, 396(i), 408, 423
Stanton, Elizabeth Cady, 347, 348(s), 399, 423, 424(s), 440–441(s), 559
Staple crops, 25
Starr, Ellen, 557
State Department, 230
Statement on the Un-American Activities Committee (Robeson), 712(s)
Staten Island (New York), 843
States
   constitutionality of laws by, 261
   Constitution on powers of, 208, 255
   constitutions of, 195–196
   currency laws of after the Revolution, 218
   land claims of, 198–201
   Northwest Ordinance on, 201–202
   nullification by, 310
   progressive reforms in, 572–573
   Revolutionary war debts of, 232–233

States' Rights Party, 717
Statue of Liberty, 505
Statute of Religious Freedom, 196
Steadwell, 567(i)
Steam engines, 264–265
Steel industry, 484(i)
   in Birmingham, 475
   consolidation in, 486
   Homestead strike, 496–497
   skyscrapers and, 484
   strikes in, 708
   technological innovations in, 484
Steffens, Lincoln, 556(s), 557
Stein, Gertrude, 621
Steinbeck, John, 640
Steinem, Gloria, 772, 792–793(s)
Stem cell research, 835
Stephens, Alexander H., 420
Stephenson, David Curtis, 631, 632
Stereotypes, 507
   gender, in World War II, 674
   slavery and, 28, 326
Stevens, Thaddeus, 418
Stevenson, Adlai, 719, 743
Stewart, Maria, 344
Still, William, 370
Stock market
   Black Tuesday, 637
   SEC regulation of, 648
   speculation in the twenties, 618
Stockton (California), 639
Stone, Lucy, 399, 559
Stone Mountain (Georgia), 630
Stonewall riots (1969), 774
Stono rebellion, 111–112, 135
Stop ERA, 792
Story, Joseph, 306
Stowe, Harriet Beecher, 377, 378
Strategic Arms Limitation Treaty (SALT I), 780
Strategic Arms Limitation Treaty (SALT II), 784
Strategic Arms Reduction Talks (START), 810
Strategic Defense Initiative (SDI), 809
Strauss, Levi, 364
Streetcars, 290, 514
Strong, Josiah, 587
Structural steel, 403–484, 512
Stuart, Reginald, 805(s)
Student Nonviolent Coordinating Committee (SNCC), 734(m), 735, 735(s)
   black power and, 760
   Freedom Rides and, 756
   Freedom Summer and, 758–760
Students for a Democratic Society (SDS), 769–770
Subsistence farmers, 87
Subtreasury system, 542, 548
Suburbs, 514–515, 720–721
Success, doctrines of, 532–533
Sudetenland, German annexation of, 664
Suez Canal, 682, 742
Sugar, 25
   in Brazil, 39
   Embargo Act and, 261–262
   Hawaii annexation and, 587
   Navigation Acts on, 100–101
   West Indies, 84–86, 85(i)
Sugar Act (England, 1764), 147, 161, 162

Sugar trust, 488
Sullivan, John, 200
Sumner, Charles, 380, 396, 418
Sumter, Thomas, 191
Sunbelt, 853(s)
Sun Belt, 721, 775, 783(m)
Sundstrom, Linea, 442(s)
Superfund, 795
Superman (TV show), 723
Supermarkets, 488
Supply-side economics, 795, 805–807
Supreme Court, 261
   on the 2000 election, 835
   on anti-Communism, 715
   antitrust cases, 576
   Bush, George H. W. nominations to, 818
   on Chinese rights, 506(s)
   on citizenship of freedpeople, 506
   Constitutional Convention on, 207–208
   on contraception, 769
   court-packing plan on, 659
   on desegregation, 730, 731
   on equal but separate, 477
   established, 230–231
   on gay marriage, 843
   on grandfather clauses, 564
   on income tax, 545
   on Japanese American internment, 679
   on Jim Crow, 476–477
   laissez-faire and, 533
   on the National Recovery Administration, 649
   on New Deal legislation, 659
   Nixon nominations to, 779
   Reagan nominees to, 808
   in the Red Scare, 610–611
   on school desegregation, 731
   on school segregation, 715
   on the Scottsboro Nine, 641
   on steel plants seizure, 708
   Trump appointments to, 849
   on unions, 499
   unions damaged by, 614
   on voter qualifications, 547
   under Warren, 766, 769
   on working conditions for women, 558(s), 559
   Yates v. United States, 715
Supreme Court cases
   Abrams v. United States, 611
   Brown v. Board of Education of Topeka, Kansas, 731–732, 733(s), 761, 763(s)
   Cherokee Nation v. Georgia, 314
   Dennis v. United States, 713
   Dred Scott, 377, 382–383, 389, 421
   Gideon v. Wainwright, 769
   Griswold v. Connecticut, 769
   Guinn v. United States, 564
   Lau v. Nichols, 774
   Marbury v. Madison, 261
   McCloskey, Michael, 794(s)
   McCulloch v. Maryland, 261
   Minor v. Happersett, 424
   Miranda v. Arizona, 769
   Muller v. Oregon, 558(s), 559
   Munn v. Illinois, 541
   Obergefell v. Hodges, 843
   Plessy v. Ferguson, 477, 564, 731
   In re Debs, 499

Index

Supreme Court cases (Continued)
   Regents of the University of California v. Bakke, 762
   Reynolds v. United States, 469
   Roe v. Wade, 772, 792, 808
   Santa Clara County v. Southern Pacific Railroad Company, 487
   Schenck v. United States, 610–611
   Shelley v. Kraemer, 720
   Slaughterhouse cases, 436
   Smith v. Allwright, 676
   Swann v. Charlotte-Mecklenburg Board of Education, 761, 762
   United States v. Cruikshank, 436
   United States v. E.C. Knight Company, 488
   Wabash v. Illinois, 541
   Williams v. Mississippi, 547
   Worcester v. Georgia, 314
   Yick Wo v. Hopkins, 506(s)
Survival of the fittest, 533, 556
Susquehannock people, 60(i), 63–64
Sutter's Mill, 363
Swann v. Charlotte-Mecklenburg Board of Education, 761, 762
Sweatshops, 516, 516(i), 822
Sweden, in Seven Year's War, 152
Swift company, 577(i)
Swift, Gustavus, 488
Syria
   civil war in, 845, 845(m)
   Russian intervention in, 846
   Six-Day War, 780–781

T

Tacoma (Washington), anti-Chinese assaults in, 471
Taft-Hartley Act (1947), 717
Taft, Robert A., 714
Taft, William Howard, 578–579, 595, 597
Taino people, 25
Taiwan, environmental damage in, 822
Talented Tenth, 564, 583(s)
Taliban, 784, 820, 836, 844
Tallahassee (Florida), bus boycott in, 732
Tallmadge, James, Jr., 282
Tammany Hall, 518, 633
Tammend, 221
Tampa (Florida)
   black troops attacked in, 591
   ghetto riots in, 761
   Gulf War protests in, 824(i)
Taney, Roger, 382
Tanforan Racetrack, 678–679, 680(s)
Tarbell, Ida, 557
Tariff of 1816, 277
Tariff of 1828, 303–304
Tariff of 1833, 311
Tariff of Abominations, 309–310
Tariffs
   Billion Dollar Congress and, 539
   Farmers' Alliance on, 542
   under Hamilton, 233
   imperialism and, 587
   under Jackson, 309–311
   Payne-Aldrich, 579
   in the twenties, 613, 620
   Wilson-Gorman Act on, 545
   Wilson on, 580

Tarleton, Banastre, 191
Taxes
   Bush, George H. W., on, 817, 818
   under Bush, George W., 836
   in the Great Depression, 638
   under Johnson, Lyndon, 768
   political machines and, 518
   Populists on, 543
   revolt against in the 1970s, 795, 796(i)
   Social Security and, 654–655
   in the twenties, 614
Taylor, Elizabeth, 724
Taylor, Frederick W., 488
Taylor, Horace, 487(s)
Taylor, Zachary, 349, 360, 362(s), 368, 369
Tea Act (England, 1773), 168
Tea Party movement, 843
Teapot Dome scandal, 614–615, 614(i), 633
Tear Down This Wall (Reagan), 810(s)
Technology
   globalization and, 829–830
   industrialization and innovation in, 483–485
   twenties consumer goods production and, 615–616, 616(i)
   urbanization and, 512–513
Tecumseh, 273–274, 274(s), 275
Teenage culture, 723–725
   movies and, 723–724, 723(i)
Tehran, U.S. Embassy hostages in, 786, 789(s), 813
Tejanos, 312, 360
Tejas Indians, 51
Telegraph, 483, 486
Telephone
   cell phones, 830
   invention of, 484
   women operators for, 492
Television, 719
   the Christian Right and, 796
   Nixon-Kennedy debate on, 745, 745(i)
   reality shows, 822
   the rise of, 722–723
Teller, Henry M., 591
Teller Amendment (1898), 591
Temperance movement, 290, 333, 333–334(s), 339–340, 339(i)
   on the frontier, 468–469
   prohibition and, 565–567, 606, 626
   Second Great Awakening and, 333–334
Ten Percent Plan, 417
Tenant revolts, 135
"Tendency of Men to Live in Cities" (Kingsbury), 520–521(s)
Tenements, 515–517
Tennessee
   Battle of Shiloh, 393–394
   secession of, 390
   statehood of, 263
Tennessee Valley Authority (TVA), 648
Tenochtitlán, 7, 32–33, 32(i), 39
Tenskwatawa, 273, 274, 317
Terrorism, 851
   9/11 attacks, 836
   al-Qaeda in, 820, 836
   Obama in the war against, 844–846
   Reagan and, 812–813

Testimony before the Senate Judiciary Committee Hearing on the Equal Rights Amendment (Steinem), 792–793(s)
Testimony of a Machinist before the Senate Committee on the Relations between Labor and Capital (Morrison), 491(s)
Tet Offensive, 752, 752(m), 778
Texas
   after World War II, 721
   agricultural worker strikes in, 642
   annexation of, 359–360
   battle for, 311–313
   black voters in, 428
   Compromise of 1850 on, 368–370
   Declaration of Independence, 312(s)
   the Dust Bowl in, 639(m)
   immigrants in, 502
   internment camps in, 678
   Mexican immigrants in, 502
   Missouri Compromise and, 284(m)
   refugees in, 811
   Spanish claims to, 71
   statehood of, 360
Textile manufacturing, 254(i), 295, 354(i)
   child labor in, 492
   Civil War and, 398
   in the New South, 474, 475(m)
   in the South, 398
   unions in, 499
   women workers in, 287–288
   working conditions in, 492–493
   in World War II, 670, 671
Thatcher, Margaret, 806
Thatcherism, 806
Thayendanegea, 180–181
Theater, 290, 529
Theologians, 71
Thesis statements, 80–82
   based on comparison, 51–53
Thinking Historically
   active reading for, 6–7
   analyzing sources, 8–10
   applying comparison, 14
   connecting distant causes to immediate causes, 65–66
   evaluating causes, 157–158
   note taking and, 6–7
   using comparison and causation in historical arguments, 47–49
Third World Liberation Front, 774
Thirteenth Amendment, 355, 409, 417, 419–420
This Is a White Man's Government (Nast), 428(s), 442(s)
This Side of Paradise (Fitzgerald), 622
Thomas, Clarence, 818, 818(i)
Thomas the Train, 822
Thoreau, Henry David, 336, 732
Thornton, J. Mills, 387(s)
Thornton, William, 235
Three-fifths compromise, 208, 227(s), 328
Three Mile Island nuclear power plant, 795, 795(i)
Thurmond, Strom, 717, 718
Tiananmen Square massacre (1989), 824
Tilden, Samuel J., 436, 437(m)
Till, Emmett, 734–735, 736
Timber and Stone Act (1878), 468
Timbuktu, 27

Time-and-motion studies, 488
Time Life, 830
Time zones, 483
Tippecanoe, Battle of, 317
Title IX, 792
Tito, Marshall, 702
Tlaxcalan, 31, 32(i)
To Secure These Rights, 730
To the President of these United States (Bram), 413(s)
Tobacco, 54, 58–60, 61–62, 65–66
   antitrust action against, 576
   child labor in, 492
   cigarette manufacturing, 475
   income inequality and, 67
   Navigation Acts on, 100–101
   in the New South, 475(m)
   slavery and, 65–66, 68(i), 109
   West Indies, 84
Toledo, Frank, 676(i)
Toledo (Ohio), 573
Toledo, Preston, 676(i)
Tomatoes, 25
Tongs, 504
Toombs, Robert, 392(s)
Topeka (Kansas), 647(i)
Topic sentences, 68–69
Totalitarianism, authoritarianism vs., 702, 811–812
Total war, 407–409
Tournament of To-Day—A Set-to Between Labor and Monopoly (Grätz), 500(s)
Toward a Patriarchal Republic: The Secession of Georgia (Johnson), 387(s)
Townsend, Francis, 651–652, 653
Townsend Clubs, 651–652
Townshend, Charles, 165
Townshend Acts (England, 1767), 165, 168
Toynbee Hall, 557
Toyota, 822
Trade
   with Africa, 27–28
   after the Revolution, 217–218
   agricultural, 5
   Atlantic economy in, 98–106, 99(m)
   Billion Dollar Congress and, 539
   city growth and, 512
   colonial America, 85–86, 99–102
   consumer culture and, 101–103
   efforts to regulate after the Revolution, 197, 198
   expansion of U.S., 373–374
   foreign, 1792–1796, 232–233
   globalization of, 98–99, 830
   imperialism and, 587
   infrastructure development and, 263–264
   international, 539
   Mediterranean world, 18–19, 19(m)
   mercantilism and, 100–102
   Puritans in, 118
   Seven Years' War and, 155
Trading posts, 264(t), 357
Tragedy of American Diplomacy, The (Williams), 708(s)
Trail of Tears, 313–316, 316(i)
Transatlantic world, 41
Transcendentalism, 335–336, 340

Transcontinental railroad, 436, 452
Transnational corporations, 821–822
Transportation
   in cities, 290
   industrialization and, 484(f)
   nineteenth century revolution in, 278–279, 278(m), 287–288
   regulation of during World War I, 603–604
   urbanization and, 288, 514–515
   in the West, 450–452, 450(m)
Travels (Bartram), 220
Travels in North America (Hall), 297(s)
Treasury bills, 398
Treasury Department, 230, 626
Treaty of Aix-la-Chapelle, 40(i)
Treaty of Alliance between the United States and France, 1778, 189(s)
Treaty of Fort Laramie, 454–455
Treaty of Fort Stanwix, 200–201
Treaty of Ghent, 276
Treaty of Greenville, 228(s), 240, 263(m)
Treaty of Guadalupe Hidalgo, 363, 367, 469
Treaty of Medicine Lodge, 455
Treaty of Paris, 191–192, 193(s), 217
Treaty of Utrecht, 121, 122(s)
Treaty of Versailles, 607–608, 664
Tredegar Iron Works, 399
Trench warfare, 602(i), 603
Trent, William, 156(s)
Trenton, Battle of (1777), 186
Triangle Shirtwaist Company fire, 571, 572(s), 573(i)
Triborough Bridge, 649
Trickle-down economics, 614
   Hoover and, 638
   Reaganomics, 805–807
Tripartite Pact, 667–668
Tripoli
   bombing of, 813
   capture of, 258
Trolley cars, 514
True interest of America impartially stated, The (Inglis), 178(s)
Truman Doctrine, 702–703, 710
   Korean War and, 706–709
Truman, Harry S.
   atomic bombs dropped by, 685–686
   Berlin airlift and, 704, 704(i)
   civil rights movement and, 730
   containment policy of, 700–701, 749
   the imperial presidency and, 707–708
   Korean War and, 706–709
   labor and, 717
   the Marshall Plan and, 703
   New Deal coalition of, 716
   NSC-68 and, 705–706
   reelection of, 704, 718
   steel plants seized by, 708
   the Truman Doctrine and, 702–703
   U.S.-Soviet relations under, 700–701
   as vice president, 683
Trumbo, Dalton, 663
Trumbull, Lyman, 418
Trump, Donald, 848–851, 852
   election of, 848–849

Trusts, 487–488, 532
   Clayton Antitrust Act on, 580
   muckrakers on, 557
   Roosevelt and, 576
   Taft on, 579
   World War II and, 671
Truth, Sojourner, 423
Tuberculosis, 516, 720
Tubman, Harriet, 371, 399
Tunisia, 844
Turkey, U.S. military bases in, 702, 747
Turner, Frederick Jackson, 472(s), 512, 586
Turner, Nat, 325–326
Turner, Susanna, 612
Turnham, Edythe, 635(s)
Tuscarora War, 120
Tuskegee airmen, 671(i), 672
Tuskegee Institute, 562
Twain, Mark, 447, 461, 524, 593
Tweed, William Marcy, 518
Twelve Years a Slave (Northup), 323–324(s)
Twenties (1920s), 613–636
   challenges to social conventions in, 621–622
   consumer culture in, 613–616
   culture wars in, 626–627
   economic warning signs in, 618–619
   the financial crash in, 637–639
   government promotion of the economy in, 613–616
   innovation and consumerism in, 613–616
   politics in, 632–633
   progressivism in, 633, 633(m)
   racial violence in, 613
   the Red Scare in, 610–612
   social turmoil in, 610–613
   urbanization in, 617–618, 617(m)
Twenty-first Amendment, 648
Twenty-sixth Amendment, 780
Twitter, 843
Two Treatises of Government (Locke), 77
Tydings, Millard, 714
Tydings-McDuffie Act (1934), 643
Tyler, John, 317, 318, 359
Typewriters, 483
Typhus, 516
Tyranny, 163, 210
Tyranny of Change, The (Chambers), 609(s)

U

U-boats, 600, 601, 666
Ukraine, 821, 846
"Uncle Sam" (Nast), 535–536(s)
Uncle Tom's Cabin (Stowe), 377, 378
Underground railroad, 344, 370–371
Underwood Act (1913), 580
Unemployment
   in the 1970s, 783, 784, 790(s)
   under Bush, George H. W., 817–818
   under Clinton, 829
   colonial era, 94
   Coxey's army and, 544
   in the Great Depression, 640, 643–644
   nineteenth century, 282(i)
   under Obama, 843
   under Reagan, 806

Unemployment (Continued)
    in the twenties, 618
    in World War II, 670
Unemployment benefits, 767
Union maids, 657
Union of Soviet Socialist Republics (USSR), 777
    Afghanistan and, 784–785, 784(i)
    atomic bomb tested by, 706
    Bay of Pigs and, 745–747
    Berlin wall and, 704
    breakup of the, 819–821, 820(m)
    Cold War with, 700–721
    creation of and the Red Scare, 610
    détente with, 784–786
    Egypt and, 742
    as "the evil empire," 809
    iron curtain and, 701, 705(m)
    Nixon and, 777, 780
    nonaggression agreement of with Germany, 664
    nuclear de-escalation and, 815–816
    nuclear freeze movement and, 814–816, 815(i)
    Prague Spring and, 779
    rebuilding after World War II, 701
    Six-Day War and, 780–781
    Sputnik launched by, 744
    U-2 spy plane shot down over, 741
    U.S. diplomatic recognition of, 662, 700
    U.S. racism publicized by, 756
    in World War II, 678, 681, 682, 685, 700
Union Pacific Railroad, 451, 486, 494
Unions, 295
    after World War I, 611
    after World War II, 717, 719(f)
    clashes with owners and, 496–499, 497(m)
    definition of, 494
    globalization and, 822
    mining, 461
    New Deal and, 656–657
    organization of, 494–496
    Pullman strike, 498, 544
    under Reagan, 807
    Roosevelt's Square Deal and, 576
    strikes by, 494–495
    weakened in the twenties, 614
    women in, 495(f)
    during World War I, 603
    in World War II, 670, 673–674
Unitarians, 330
United Auto Workers, 557
United Fruit Company, 741–742
United Kingdom. *See also* England; Great Britain
    Brexit, 848
    in the Group of Seven (G7), 821
    industrialization in, 483
United Mine Workers, 656
United Nations, 812, 822
    conservative opposition to, 775
    on human rights, 697
    on Iraqi invasion of Kuwait, 823
    in the Korean War, 706–707, 706(m)
    Soviet boycott of, 706
    Suez Canal crisis and, 742
United Negro Improvement Association (UNIA), 634(s)
United States and the Origins of the Cold War, The (Gaddis), 709(s)

United States Chamber of Commerce, 651
United States Steel, 486, 579
United States v. Cruikshank, 436
United States v. E.C. Knight Company, 488
United Steel Workers of America, 708
Unity Leagues, 676, 736
Universal Negro Improvement Association, 625
University of California, 762, 769–770
University of Michigan, 767
University of Oklahoma, 730
University of Pennsylvania, 221
University of Texas Law School, 730
"Unjust to Working Woman" (Haring), 558(s)
Unskilled workers, 491(s)
Upward mobility, 513, 513(i), 532, 533
    for African Americans, 513, 513(i)
    industrialization and, 493
Urbanization, 511–523. *See also* Suburbs
    Civil War, 398–399
    colonial politics and, 135–136
    commerce and, 511
    disorder in, 290–291
    electric lighting and, 485
    industrialization and, 475
    the lure of urban life and, 289–290
    the market revolution and, 287–288
    nineteenth century, 262, 279, 287–291
    politics and, 517–519
    Portugal, 18
    poverty in, 515–517
    progressive reforms and, 572–573
    progressivism and, 570
    reformers and, 519
    rural migration and, 540
    in the South, 320–321, 398–399, 475
    Spain, 18
    technology in, 514–515
    in the twenties, 617–618, 617(m)
    upward and outward expansion of, 514–515
    wealth and, 135
    in World War II, 671
    worldwide, 512
Uruguay, repressive regime in, 784
U.S. Military Railroads, 398
U.S. Navy, 588
    in World War I, 602
    in World War II, 683–685, 684(m)
U.S. Sanitary Commission, 398
U.S. Senate Subcommittee on Migratory Labor, 773(s)
USSR. *See* Union of Soviet Socialist Republics (USSR)
U.S. Steel, 579
U.S. Treasury, gold deposits withdrawn from, 545
Utah
    American Indians in, 12
    Compromise of 1850 on, 358–370
    internment camps in, 678
    Mormon migration to, 334–335, 357, 469
    statehood of, 469
    women's suffrage in, 469
Ute people, 12
Utopianism
    Bellamy on, 534
    societies for, 340

Utopia; or, the Best State of a Commonwealth (More), 55(s)
Utrecht, Treaty of, 121, 122(s)

V

Vachon, John, 641(s)
Valdés, Don Luis, 49–50
Valentino, Rudolph, 621(i), 634(s)
Valladolid, 35–36
Vallandigham, Clement L., 401
Valley Forge, 186, 188, 188(i)
Valtman, Edward, 747(s)
Van Buren, Martin, 301, 303, 317, 349, 368
Van de Passe, Simon, 59(i)
Vanderbilt, Cornelius, 494
Vanderbilt, William, 494, 525
Vanzetti, Bartolomeo, 629
Vaqueros, 465
Vaudeville, 528, 529, 529(i)
Velásquez, Diego de, 31
Vermont, slavery abolished in, 196, 222
Vertical integration, 485
Vesey, Denmark, 302, 302(i), 325
Veterans Administration, 720
Veto, 59
Vicksburg, Battle of (1862), 394(m), 404
Vicksburg, siege of (1863), 404, 404(m)
Victorio, 455
Video games, 830
Vietcong, 748–750, 752(m)
Vietminh, 748–749
Vietnam
    early intervention in, 748–749
    immigrants from, 1990s to twenty-first century, 831, 831(f)
"Vietnam: The Public's Need to Know," 787(s)
Vietnam War (1961–1969), 697, 748–754, 752(m), 767
    antiwar protests against, 753, 770–771
    escalation in, 750
    fall of Saigon in, 73, 753(i)
    My Lai massacre in, 751–752
    neoconservatives on, 796
Vietnamization, 752–754
View of the Round-Top in the Catskills Mountains (Cole), 335(i)
Vigilance committees, 371
Villa, Francisco "Pancho," 599
Village Voice, 774
Villasur expedition, 45(i)
Vinland, 19
Virginia
    Bacon's Rebellion, 63–65
    black voters in, 428
    colonies in, 56–60
    constitution of, 196
    Constitution ratified by, 210–211, 211(t)
    House of Burgesses, 59, 63
    land claims by, 200
    land ownership in, 67
    map of, 60(i)
    Resolves on the Stamp Act, 162, 163(s), 212(s)
    secession of, 390
    slave laws in, 62–63
    slave rebellions in, 258, 269, 270(s), 325–326

slavery in, 109–110
tobacco in, 58–60
Virginia and Kentucky Resolutions, 244
Virginia City (Nevada), 461, 462
Virginia Company, 56–57, 58–59, 60, 70–71
Virginia Declaration of Rights, 178, 209
Virginia Plan, 207–208
Virginia Resolves, 162, 163(s), 212(s)
Virtual representation, 162
A Visit from the Old Mistress (Homer), 414(i)
Visit with Awashonks, Sachem of the Sakonnet, A (Church), 124–125(s)
Volstead Act (1919), 626
Voltaire, 131, 132
Voluntarism, in the Great Depression, 638
Volunteers in Service to America (VISTA), 767–768
Von Steuben, Friedrich, 188
Voter registration
  of African Americans in the South, 760(i)
  civil rights movement and, 676
  legislation on blocking, 744
Voting fraud
  political machines and, 518
Voting rights
  for African Americans, 419
  colonial era, 78, 196
  Constitution on, 208
  early state constitutions on, 195–196
  expansion of, 295, 300–301, 307–308
  of free black people after the Revolution, 220
  Freedom Summer and, 758–760
  Jim Crow laws and, 471, 476–477, 476(m)
  poll taxes and, 547
  for poor white men, 429
  progressivism on, 570
  struggle for universal, 423–424
  for women, 218–219, 347–348, 423–424, 438, 468–469, 557, 559–561, 560(m), 561(i)
Voting Rights Act (1965), 760, 760(i)
  Chicanos and, 774
  electoral politics after, 761
  extension of, 780
Vox Populi, 162
Voyages of Samuel de Champlain: 1567–1635 (Champlain), 44(s)

W

Wabash v. Illinois, 541
Wade-Davis Bill (1864), 417
Wagner Act (1935), 656, 659
Wagner, Robert F., Sr., 656
Wagon trains, 357–358, 358(i), 358(s), 451
Wahunsonacock. *See* **Powhatan**
Walden (Thoreau), 36
Walesa, Lech, 819
Walker, David, 343, 344(s), 384
Walker, Freeman, 283(s)
Walker, Margaret, 653
Walker, Mary E., 399
Walker, Quock, 222
Walker, William, 374
Walking Purchase, 95
Wall Street (film), 806

Wallace, George C., 757–758, 776
  in the election of 1968, 779
  in the election of 1972, 779
  the New Right and, 797(s)
  Nixon and, 779
Wallace, Henry A., 683, 701(s), 702, 717, 718, 727
Walmart, 81
Walsh, Thomas J., 633
Waltham (Massachusetts), 293
Wampanoag people, 72–73, 74, 118
  Metacom's War, 119–120, 124–126(s)
  narrative of captivity by, 126–127(s)
War, as test of masculinity, 588
War Brides Act (1945), 736
War Department, 230, 398, 405, 408
War Industries Board (WIB), 603
War Message (Polk), 361–362(s)
War of 1812, 235(i), 272, 274–276, 275(m)
War of Austrian Succession (1744–1748), 40(i), 122
War of the Spanish Succession, 121
War on Poverty, 767–768, 779
War Powers Act (1942), 671
War Powers Act (1973), 754
War Production Board, 671
Ward, Lester Frank, 534
Ward, Samuel, 371
Waring, George, 521(s)
Warner, Charles Dudley, 524
Warner Communications, 830
Warren, Earl, 731, 766, 769
Warren, Mercy Otis, 210
Warsaw Pact, 705, 819
Washington (state)
  anti-Chinese assaults in, 471
  in World War II, 671
Washington, Booker T., 562, 583(s)
  Atlanta Exposition address, 563(s)
  invited to the White House, 577–578
  Wells on, 563(s), 583–584(s)
Washington, D.C.
  100,000-person march on, 675–676
  Battle of, 394(m)
  Bonus Army in, 645
  building of, 233–236, 235(i)
  Coxey's army in, 544
  March on Washington for Jobs and Freedom, 758
  race riots of 1919 in, 613
  smallpox epidemic in, 412
  in War of 1812, 275–276
  Women's March on, 851(i)
Washington, George, 147
  Adams and, 242
  in American Revolution, 175–176, 185–186, 188(i), 191
  on Articles of Confederation, 202
  on Bank of the United States, 232
  biographies of, 331
  on capital location, 233
  Farewell Address of, 241, 247(s)
  French Revolution and, 238–239
  on frontier rebellions, 203
  inauguration of, 231(i)
  land surveyed by, 200
  militant officers confronted by, 198
  on political parties, 241

portraits of, 220
  as president, 211, 230, 232–233
  in Seven Years' War, 150, 150(i), 151–152
  spies for, 187
  western lands purchased by, 156
  Wheatley poems sent to, 183
  Whiskey Rebellion and, 240
Washington Post, 715(s), 753, 787(s)
Washingtonian societies, 339
Watergate scandal, 777, 781–782
Watie, Stand, 409
Watson, Tom, 547–548
Way, Amanda M., 468
Wayne, Anthony, 240, 273
Way to Peace, The (Wallace), 701(s)
Wealth
  colonial consumer culture and, 101–103
  colonial era, 135, 136
  early nineteenth century, 267
  Gilded Age, 524–525
  the Great Recession and, 840
  industrialization and, 486, 493
  laissez-faire and, 532–533
  New Frontier on, 767
  philanthropy and, 533
  redistribution of, 718–719
Wealth inequality, 135, 487, 493
  under Bush, George W., 836
  under Clinton, 829
  in the Great Depression, 659
  under Obama, 841(f), 843
  under Reaganomics, 806–807
  in the twenties, 618
  in the twenty-first century, 841(f)
Wealth of Nations, The (Smith), 532
Weathermen, 771
Weaver, James B., 543
Webb-Kenyon Act (1913), 566
Webb, Matthew, 223(s)
Webster, Daniel, 309, 310, 311, 318, 369, 369(i)
Webster, Noah, 220, 330, 331(i)
Weems, Charlie, 642(i)
Weems, Mason, 331
Welfare. *See* Social welfare
Wells, Ida B., 557, 563(s), 564, 583–584(s)
Wesley, John, 133
West, 449–472, 450(m)
  after World War II, 731
  American Indian resistance to expansion in, 452–459
  American Revolution in, 191–192, 192(m)
  cattle industry and commercial farming in, 463–465
  civil rights movement in, 736–737
  commercial farming in, 465–467
  cowboys in, 463–465, 464(s), 465
  diversity in, 469–471
  federal American Indian policy and, 457–458
  federal policy and foreign investment in, 450–452
  the Great Plains in, 449–450
  growth of in the twenties, 617–618, 617(m)
  lumber in, 463
  mining in, 461–463
  the myth of the, 445–450
  opening the, 450–452

Index

West (Continued)
  political, economic, and social influence of, 805–806
  urbanization in, 512
  in World War II, 671
West Bank, 824
West, Benjamin, 181(i)
West, Elliott, 433(s)
West Indies
  English and Spanish conflict over, 122
  English colonies, 83–86
  Seven Years' War in, 153(m), 154
  slave rebellions in, 258
  slavery abolished in, 371
  slavery in, 109
  South Carolina and, 85–88
  U.S. trade with, 238–239
West Side Story (film), 724
Western Federation of Miners, 461, 499
Western Negro Press Association, 512
Western settlement, 262–265, 357–368. *See also* Frontier
  Compromise of 1850 and, 368–370
  expansionism and, 373–374
  the gold rush and, 363–364, 364(i)
  overland trails and, 357–359
  slavery and, 367–372
Western Union, 486
Weyerhaeuser, Frederick, 463
What a Funny Little Government (political cartoon), 487(s)
"What to Do with the Slaves when Emancipated," 440(s)
Wheat, 540
Wheatley, Phillis, 183, 183(s)
Wheeler, John N., 707(s)
Wheeling (West Virginia), McCarthy speech in, 714
"Where Women Vote — Wyoming" (National American Woman Suffrage Association), 561–562(s)
Whigs, 255, 317–318, 377
  abolitionism and, 349
  Compromise of 1850 and, 368–370
  election of 1840 and, 317–318
  election of 1852 and, 373
  on Kansas-Nebraska Act, 379
  on Mexican-American War, 360, 363
  on slavery, 367–368, 378
  workingmen's interests and, 295
Whiskey Rebellion (1794), 239–240, 240(s)
White Citizens' Council (WCC), 733–734, 773
"White Man's Burden, The" (Kipling), 588(s)
White primaries, 573, 676
White Slave Trade Act (1910), 567, 567(i)
White supremacy, 319, 328, 474, 475. *See also* Ku Klux Klan
  black nationalism and, 625
  civil rights movement against, 729–736
  gender and, 569(s)
  in the Great Depression, 640–641
  Populists and, 547–548
  progressivism and, 560, 562, 567
  in South Africa, 812, 812(i)
  in the twenties, 630–632

  in Wilmington (North Carolina) massacre, 547(i)
  women's suffrage and, 560
Whitefield, George, 133–134, 133(m), 137–139(s), 140(s)
Whiteness
  cultural justification for imperialism and, 587–588
  in World War II, 678
Whitman, Marcus, 364
Whitman, Narcissa, 364
Whitney, Eli, 265–266
Whittlesey, Eliphalet, 415(i)
The Who, 771
Who Are the War Agitators? (Lindbergh), 666(s)
Whooping cough, 720
Why the Ward Boss Rules (Addams), 518(s)
Wiesel, Elie, 688(i)
Wilbur, Charles Dana, 450
Wild One, The (film), 724
Wild West shows, 459, 464(s)
Wiley, Harvey, 577
Wilkinson, Jemima, 332
Willard, Frances, 565, 566(s)
William and Mary, College of, 220, 326
William of Orange, 77, 78
Williams, Daniel, 797(s)
Williams, Eugene, 642(i)
Williams, John, 214(s)
Williams, John Sharp, 588
Williams, Roger, 75, 76, 135
Williams v. Mississippi, 547
Williams, William Appleman, 708(s)
Willkie, Wendell, 665
Wilmington (North Carolina) massacre, 547(i)
Wilmot, David, 368
Wilmot Proviso, 368
Wilson, Charles, 740
Wilson, Edith, 608
Wilson-Gorman Act (1894), 545
Wilson, Sloan, 728
Wilson, Woodrow, 538, 579(s)
  diplomacy and, 598–600
  in election of 1912, 580
  foreign policy of, 598–603
  Fourteen Points by, 606–607
  on League of Nations, 607(s)
  New Freedom agenda of, 579(s), 580–582, 581(i)
  progressivism and, 570
  reelection of, 600
  stroke suffered by, 608
  World War I and, 599–604
Wilson's Creek, Battle of (1861), 391, 391(i), 394(m)
Winchester, Battle of (1862), 394(m)
Wind Cave, 575(m)
Wind power, 784
Winter counts, 442(s)
Winthrop, John, 73
Wisconsin
  progressivism in, 573
  statehood of, 359
Witchcraft, 79

Witness Testimony in the Trial of the British Soldiers of the Nineteenth Regiment of Foot, 167–168(s)
Wobblies, 499
Woman in the Nineteenth Century (Fuller), 36
Woman's Christian Temperance Union, 468, 565–566, 566(s)
Women. *See also* Feminism
  in the 1950s, 725–727, 727(i)
  in abolitionism, 326, 343, 347–348
  after the Revolution, 218–220
  after World War II, 716–717
  in American Indian hunting, 453
  authors, 331
  the baby boom and, 719–720
  in bread riots, 135
  California gold rush and, 364
  Chinese immigrants, 470
  in the civil rights movement, 758(i)
  in the Civil War, 398, 399, 409
  in colonial America, 59, 66–67
  colonial era, 44, 74–75, 79–80, 131
  in companionate marriage, 267
  cult of domesticity and, 291–293
  divorce and, 131
  in domestic production, 267
  double standard and, 771
  education of, 220
  in the election of 1840, 318
  employment of in the nineteenth century, 290, 492
  equality for, gender difference and, 558(s), 559
  equal pay for, 494, 528
  excluded from Social Security, 655
  in factories, 492
  factory workers, 293–294
  gender roles and, 131
  in the Gilded Age, 447, 525–526, 527(s)
  in the Great Depression, 643–644
  as homesteaders, 468–469, 468(i)
  imperialism and, 588
  in the Ku Klux Klan, 631, 632(i), 632(s)
  in labor movements, 495(i)
  labor unions and, 295
  MeToo movement, 852
  in mining towns, 462, 462(i)
  in movies of the 1950s, 724
  in New Deal programs, 654
  political participation by, 300, 301(i)
  poverty and, 337–338
  in progressivism, 557–559, 558(s)
  Quakers, 345
  in religion, 325
  in religious renewal, 332
  republican motherhood and, 219
  in the Revolution, 174, 179, 180, 182–183, 186–188
  in social reform movements, 336–337
  as spies, 391, 399
  Stevenson on purpose for, 719
  temperance movement and, 339
  in the Townshend Act boycott, 166
  in the twenties, 621
  in unions, 495
  unions and, 494
  in urbanization, 512–513

in western migration, 358–359
Whigs and, 318
workday length for, 558(s), 559
in the workforce, 725–726
working outside the home, 643–644
in World War I, 603, 604(i)
in World War II, 672–673, 674, 674(i), 689–690
Women Accepted for Voluntary Emergency Service (WOMEN), 672
Women and Economics (Gilman), 559
Women of the Ku Klux Klan, 632(s), 636(s)
Women's Army Corps, 672
Women's clubs, 557
Women's Emergency Brigade, 656(i), 657
Women's Encampment for a Future of Peace and Justice, 814, 815(i)
Women's International League for Peace and Freedom, 726
Women's liberation movement, 771–773
Women's March on Washington (2017), 851(i)
Women's movement, 792
Women's National Indian Association, 457
Women's National Loyal League, 399, 409
Women's Peace Party, 599
Women's Political Council, 732
Women's rights
  abolitionism and, 347–348
  Clinton, Bill on, 827
  crisis of masculinity and, 526–527
  Stanton and Anthony resolutions on, 440–441(s)
  women pioneers and, 468–469
Women's suffrage, 218–219, 347–348, 771
  emancipation and, 423–424, 438
  frontier women on, 468–469
  male identity and, 588
  Populists on, 543
  progressivism on, 557, 559–561, 560(m), 561(i)
  Stanton and Anthony resolutions on, 440–441(s)
  World War I and, 606
Wood, Gordon, 159(s)
Woodford, Stewart L., 590(s)
Woodrow Wilson and the Progressive Era (Link), 608(s)
Woodward, Bob, 781–782
Woodward, C. Vann, 569(s)
Woolworth, Frank W., 488
Worcester v. Georgia, 314
Wordsworth, William, 331
Workday length, 294, 295
  corporate personhood and, 487
  industrialization and, 493
  unions and, 494
  during World War I, 603
Workhouses, 102, 337
Working class, leisure and, 528–530
Working conditions
  after World War II, 717
  globalization and, 822
  industrialization and, 492–493
  OSHA and, 779
  progressivism on, 557–559, 558(s)

unions and, 495
  for women, 557–559, 558(s), 559
"Workingman's Prayer," 535(s)
Workingmen's Party, 471
Works Progress Administration (WPA), 653, 654(i)
World Anti-Slavery Convention, 347
World Health Organization, 822
World's Columbian Exposition (1893), 529
World Series, 527
World Trade Center attack, 836, 851
World Trade Organization (WTO), 828
World War I (1914–1918), 553, 599–609, 602(i)
  alliances, 599, 599(m)
  Bonus Army, 645
  casualties in, 603
  debts after, 618–619
  effects of at home, 610–619
  fighting of at home, 603–606
  government commissions during, 603
  harsh peace terms after, 662
  isolationism after, 663, 664–666
  making the world safe for democracy, 601–603
  peace plan after, 606–608
  U-boats in, 600
  U.S. entry into, 601–603
  U.S. neutrality in, 598–600
  winning hearts and minds in, 603–605
World War II (1933–1945), 662–691
  casualties in, 681
  challenges to isolationism in, 664–666
  crisis in Europe leading to, 664
  economic boom after, 717–718
  ending, 685–687
  in Europe, 681–683
  global war in, 682–687, 682(m)
  Great Depression ended by, 670
  the Holocaust in, 687–689, 688(i), 690–691(s)
  the home-front economy in, 670–674
  impact of, 689–690
  Japanese American internment in, 678–680, 678(s)
  the Marshall Plan after, 703
  mobilization for, 671
  in the Pacific, 683–685, 684(m)
  paying for, 671–672
  peacetime challenges after, 716–718
  race relations and, 675–677
  the road toward, 662–664
  U.S. entry into, 666–669
  U.S. neutrality in, 665
  war declared in, 664, 668
  wartime economy in, 670–675
  women in, 672–673, 674, 674(i), 675(i), 689–690
World Wide Web, 830
Wounded Knee massacre (1890), 459, 774
Wovoka, 459
Wright, Andrew, 642(i)
Wright, Carroll D., 493
Wright, Frances, 340
Wright, Richard, 653

Wright, Roy, 642(i)
Writing Historically
  ACE for, 21–23
  breaking down Short-Answer Question prompts, 15–16
  crafting a thesis statement based on comparison, 51–53
  crafting a thesis statement based on continuity and change, 80–82
  Document-Based Question practice, 520–523, 583–585, 763–765, 787–790
  establishing context in an essay introduction, 184
  evaluating causation in a document-based essay, 246–250
  evaluating continuity and change in a document-based essay, 210–216
  evaluating continuity and change in an essay, 170–172
  evaluating effects in an essay, 193–194
  a full essay, 88–89
  Long-Essay Question practice, 402, 530–531, 619, 645, 680, 721, 776
  making evaluative comparisons in a document-based essay, 225–229
  making evaluative comparisons in an essay, 203–206
  presenting context in a historical argument, 95–97
  putting it all together, 477–481
  responding to a Document-Based Question, 112–117, 136–143, 296–298, 439–443
  responding to a Document-Based Question with five primary sources, 123–129
  responding to Long-Essay Questions, 284–286, 340–342, 349–351, 374–376, 509–510
  responding to Short-Answer Questions, 37–38
  responding to Short-Answer Questions with secondary sources, 103–106
  Short-Answer Question practice, 159, 271, 307–308, 318, 329, 366, 409–410, 433, 472, 489, 500, 536, 548–549, 569, 608–609, 660–661, 669, 737–738, 797(s), 825(s), 832(s), 852–853
  Short-Answer Question responses, 21–23
  topic sentences for an essay, 68–69
  using categories to respond to Short-Answer Questions, 28–29
  using context to craft essay conclusions, 424–426
Wuerker, Matt, 841(i)
Wyman, David S., 690(s)
Wyoming
  American Indian reservations in, 455
  cattle ranching in, 465
  internment camps in, 678
  Rock Springs massacre, 470, 470(i)
  Teapot Dome scandal and, 614–615
  women's suffrage in, 469

X

XIT Ranch, 465
XYZ affair, 243

Y

Yale College, 220
Yalta Agreement, 685
Yalta Conference, 713
Yamasee people, 120
Yamasee War, 120
Yanktonai tribe, 442(s)
Yates v. United States, 715
Yellow Bird, 156(s)
Yellow fever, 237, 240, 516
   in Cuban War for Independence, 589–590
Yellow journalism, 590
Yellowstone National Park, 575(m)
Yeltsin, Boris, 820–821
Yemen, 844
Yeomen farmers, 327, 401
Yergin, Daniel, 489(s)

Yick Wo v. Hopkins, 506(s)
Yiddish theater, 529
Yom Kippur War (1967), 781
York (enslaved man), 259
Yorktown, Battle of (1781), 191
Yosemite National Park, 574(i), 575
Young, Brigham, 334–335, 469
"Young America" movement, 374
Young Americans for Freedom (YAF), 775
Young Lords Party (YLP), 774
Young Men's Christian Association (YMCA), 525
Young Women's Christian Association (YWCA), 477, 525, 725, 726
Youth culture, 723–725
   movies and, 723–724, 723(i)
Yugoslavia, breakup of, 828–829

Z

Zaharias, Babe "Mildred" Didrikson, 725
Zaire, 742
Zangwill, Israel, 508
Zenger, John Peter, 136
Zero option proposal, 810
Zhou Enlai, 705
Zimmermann, Arthur, 602
Zimmermann telegram, 602
Zinc mining, 462
Zion National Park, 575(m)
Zitkala-Ša, 458(s), 565
Zoning laws, 511
Zoot suit riots, 677
Zoot suits, 677
"Zoot Suits Become Issue on Coast" (Davies), 677(s)